PICTORIAL BIBLICAL ENCYCLOPEDIA

A VISUAL GUIDE TO THE OLD AND NEW TESTAMENTS

Edited by
GAALYAHU CORNFELD, ASSISTED BY BIBLE SCHOLARS, HISTORIANS AND ARCHAEOLOGISTS

1964
THE MACMILLAN COMPANY, NEW YORK
COLLIER-MACMILLAN, LTD., LONDON

Tel Aviv
First Printing

THE MACMILLAN COMPANY, NEW YORK
Collier-Macmillan, Canada, Ltd., Galt, Ontario
Divisions of the Crowell-Collier Publishing Company

PRINTED IN ISRAEL
Peli-P.E.C. Printing Works Ltd, Ramat Gan

ACKNOWLEDGMENTS

Prof. D.N. Freedman read the entire manuscript of the Encyclopedia and made valuable observations and suggestions, many of which were adopted and have been incorporated into the text.

Prof. Ch. Rabin, Dr. H. Tadmor, Dr. R. Giveon and many other scholars have given inestimable help and advice to the editor in the selection of the material available, in focussing attention on the salient points and in checking the accuracy of the facts and views presented.

Contributions were made by Ch. Rabin, R. Giveon, J. Licht; J. Naveh, M. Weinfeld; A. Negev; A. Hurwitz; E. Stern; S. Ahitub; J. O'Dell; I. Ef'al; D. Bahat; M. Eilat; J. Meshorer; U. Rappoport; Z. Shoer; G. Dagan; P. Dagan; S. Lerner; J. Gefen; A. Tweig; M. Yeshayahu; G. Cornfeld; S. Neufeld; V. Mindlin. The editor acknowledges his deep indebtedness to these contributors, who represent a cross-section of the younger school of biblical scholarship and archaeology in Israel.

In the preparation of this Encyclopedia extensive use was made of the major works of leading contemporary scholars in the field of biblical studies, history and archaeology. Their views, referred to in the body of the work, have guided the editor and contributors throughout all the stages of the project.

INTRODUCTION

Material: This Encyclopedia is an attempt at a concise and authoritative account of the results of biblical research since World War I, presented in terms of "readable scholarship". The material incorporates the most up-to-date findings on the major concerns and central themes of the Old and New Testaments, the inter-testamental period, the literature uncovered in the Judean wilderness (Dead Sea Scrolls) and the many wider areas of Near Eastern studies. Its aim is to put into perspective the progress that has been made in all these fields up to the moment of publication (1964).

In nearly every article the text is amplified and illustrated by the inclusion of the most relevant and often the latest available photographic material bearing on the history, customs and background of biblical and Near Eastern life from the 3rd millenium BCE to the 2nd century CE.

To do justice to this vast subject could easily call for a small library of volumes. In its attempt at a synthesis of essential material, this Encyclopedia is selective. It is designed to provide the busy reader with everything that is important in an evaluation of the Bible in its setting within the ancient world.

Presentation: *Asterisks*(*) in the text indicate where a subject, referred to in one article, is treated in more detail under a separate heading. All references to subjects, names, places, etc. mentioned in the articles are indicated in the comprehensive Index at the end of the book, where the figures in italics indicate the major entry and ordinary figures show the general range of references.

There are no captions to the illustrations. Every picture is numbered and its explanation is integrated into the text, where the reader is referred to the illustration by its number in bold figures (**1–814**). He is thus able to see, in correlation with the text, the essential historical developments of Hebrew life.

The Text: Modern biblical research is focussed upon Israel, its literature and civilization, the development of its religious ideas and on the world out of which these arose. This Encyclopedia benefits from the insights which have emerged from scholarly studies. Detailed analysis and elaborate documentation, however, were felt to be out of place in a work intended for the general reader as much as for the scholar. The edifice of biblical thought is here considered as a whole, with the emphasis on a historical, rather than specifically theological approach.

Many of the articles are small monographs in themselves. The survey of Ancient Cities, for instance, includes the most recent material from the excavations of Arad, Ashdod, Caesarea, Jerusalem and Shechem. The religion, culture and civilization of Canaan are fully investigated. There are major articles on Assyria, Babylonia, Early Christianity, the Dead Sea Scrolls, Egypt, the institutions of the Family, Feasts and Festivals, the processes and institutions of government and authority, the history of Israel from the days of Abraham to the last days of Bar-Kochba, Hellenism under its various aspects, Inscriptions, Nabateans, Samaritans, Persia and Israel, Rome and the Jews, shipping, trade, and the history and practice of warfare. Articles describe daily life in antiquity from birth to burial in terms of handicrafts, arts, tools, dress, weapons, building, animals and plants, and developments in contemporary civilization in writing, poetry, prophecy and philosophy (wisdom). The majority of the articles reflect an extensive revision of older theories, the reconstructions suggested by new evidence, and the general widening of biblical horizons which have taken place in recent years.

The Pictures: The illustrations to the articles include scores of new pictures hitherto (up to 1964) unpublished in this type of literature, selected by the general editor from Israeli and foreign archaeological institutes, private collections and the extensive archives which he has amassed from the museums of the world. They show, more vividly than any description, scenes from history and monuments, the details of everyday life, the practice of a variety of faiths, the ways of peace and the incidents of war.

The Maps: New maps have been specially prepared using data on biblical geography provided by the most recent scholarly researches in Israel. These maps have not previously appeared in any publication; they are based on a new approach and distinctive technique, which have made it possible to correct the faults in conception and execution which mar many current atlases.

EXPLANATIONS

The brief quotations from the Bible are taken from the Revised Standard Version, the National Council of Churches of Christ in the U.S.A. having kindly given permission for the use of this text.

When the letter "a" or "b" is added to the verse number in a biblical reference, it signifies the first or second half of the verse (e.g. Gn. 2:4a).

Abbreviations:

Books of the Bible:

Gn.	Genesis
Ex.	Exodus
Lv.	Leviticus
Nu.	Numbers
Dt.	Deuteronomy
Jos.	Joshua
Jud.	Judges
Rt.	Ruth
I Sam.	I Samuel
II Sam.	II Samuel
I K.	I Kings
II K.	II Kings
I Ch.	I Chronicles
II Ch.	II Chronicles
Ezr.	Ezra
Neh.	Nehemiah
Est.	Esther
Job	Job
Ps.	Psalms
Pr.	Proverbs.
Eccl.	Ecclesiastes
Song	Song of Solomon
Is.	Isaiah
Jer.	Jeremiah
Lam.	Lamentations
Ezkl.	Ezekiel
Dan.	Daniel
Hos.	Hosea
Jl.	Joel
Am.	Amos
Ob.	Obadiah
Jnh.	Jonah
Mic.	Micah
Nhm.	Nahum
Hab.	Habakkuk
Zeph.	Zephaniah
Hag.	Haggai
Zech.	Zechariah
Mal.	Malachi

New Testament:

Mt.	Matthew
Mk.	Mark
Lk.	Luke
Jn.	John
Ac.	Acts
Ro.	Romans
I Co.	I Corinthians
II Co.	II Corinthians
Gal.	Galatians
Eph.	Ephesians
Ph.	Philippians
Col.	Colossians
I Th.	I Thessalonians
II Th.	II Thessalonians
I Ti.	I Timothy
II Ti.	II Timothy
Tit.	Titus
Phil.	Philemon
Heb.	Hebrews
Jam.	James
I Pet.	I Peter
II Pet.	II Peter
I Jn.	I John
II Jn.	II John
III Jn.	III John
Jude	Jude
Rev.	Revelation

Books of the Apocrypha:	Ecclus.	Ecclesiasticus (Ben Sira)
	I Mac.	I Maccabees
	II Mac.	II Maccabes

Others: ANET "Ancient Near Eastern Texts Relating to the O.T." (ed. J.B. Pritchard)

c.	century	BCE	Before Common Era (B.C.)
ca	circa	CE	Common Era (A.D.)
illus.	illustration	cf.	compare

Transliteration and Vocalization of Hebrew and Semitic words:

Consonants:

Aleph — ' a slight breath at the beginning or in the middle of a word, as in *'ashām*.

Ayin — ' a guttural breath at the beginning or in the middle of a word, as in *ba'al*.

Heth — "ḥ" an initial letter as in *ḥerem*, pronounced like the "ch" in the Scottish "*loch*".

Taw — is shown as "t" as in "*torah*" or frequently as "th" as in *Thothmes, Hamath*.

Samekh and Sin are both shown as "s".

Shin — is shown as "š" as in š l š (*shalosh*).

Kaph — is shown as "k" or "kh" as in m l k (*melekh*).

Qoph — (a guttural k) is shown as "q" as in *Qumran*.

Tsaddhe or Saddhe (Ts or Tz) is shown as "ṣ" as in *ṣemed* (*Tzemed*).

Vowels:

a — the Hebrew aleph, short "a" as in the English *and.*

â or ā, a long "a" as in the English *father*, or the Hebrew *askārah, shālîsh.*

o — (short) as in English *dog*, or in Hebrew *ethrog*.

ô — (long) as in English *atone*, or in Hebrew, *adôn, armôn.*

i — (short) as in English *him*, or Hebrew *millah.*

î — (long, as in the French il), the English *keep* or Hebrew *abîr* (abeer) or *saddîn* (saddeen).

e — (short) as in *bed* or, Hebrew, *eben.*

ê — (long) as in *bear* or *cake* or, in Hebrew, *bêth.*

u — (short) as in *bull* or, in Hebrew, *zug* (zoog).

û — (longer) as in *boon* or, Hebrew, *menûhah.*

Vocalization:

Where Hebrew or Semitic words appear in the main text of this book, consonants are usually fully vocalized, e.g. bāmah. However, in the transliteration of original inscriptions from monuments, seals, etc. only consonants are reproduced (vowel letters were not generally used at the time, or were indicated in only certain cases, leaving the vocalization to the Hebrew reader's own sense of what was appropriate), i.e. the consonantal š m š represents shemesh or shamash; 'bd is pronounced 'ebed; lmlk, lamelekh (see article on Alphabet and Writing).

A

AARON. — Aaron's life and career have been preserved in some of the oldest traditions of Exodus*, closely linked with the life story of his brother Moses*. On the other hand, Aaron's priestly functions and character are to be found in the later traditions in the book of Exodus and the rest of the Pentateuch which reflect the traditions concerning the establishment and organization of the Aaronid priesthood.

In the oldest traditions of the Pentateuch, those defined by the schools of literary criticism as the J and JE sources (see Biblical Criticism*), Aaron begins as a rather hazy figure. His character acquires a much clearer definition later on but it remains impossible to make a clear distinction between the earlier and the later sources or to be dogmatic about the precise order in which the texts should follow one another.

Aaron in the Earlier Traditions: Exodus 4:14–15 refers to Aaron as "the Levite", but this is in the sense of a member of the tribe of Levi, not necessarily as an active priest. He was the brother of Moses and acted as Moses' spokesman before the people (4:30–31) and before Pharaoh (7:1, passim), to demand the Hebrews' release. Aaron took part in the miracles or "signs" which demonstrated the superiority of the Israelite god over those of the Egyptians (7:8–12; for an evaluation of these miracles, see Moses*). When God sent the ten plagues against Egypt it was Aaron who stretched out his rod to turn the Nile water to blood (7:19–20) and stir up the plagues of frogs (8:5–6) and gnats (8:16–17). He was also summoned each time to avert the plagues (8:8, passim). At the battle of Rephidim he stood at Moses' side and helped to support his uplifted hands to ensure victory over the Amalekites (Ex. 17:8–13). At the meeting with Jethro (Ex. 18:12) and again at Sinai (Ex. 19:24; 24:1, 9) Aaron was Moses' companion and aide. These early sources (the E and J strands) present Aaron as having a prominent role as the leading elder of Israel. Not once, however, do these earlier traditions present him as a priest or an ancestor of priests. On the contrary, Aaron opposes Moses on religious questions, leading a revolt with his sister Miriam (Nu. 12) and even making the Golden Calf (Ex. 32, see below).

There is very little definite information about Aaron's and Moses' Levitic ancestry. Indeed, the names of his family which are mentioned have a distinctly Egyptian sound: Phinehas, Putiel, and Hofni. However, he was the first to meet Moses when he returned from his Exile and his divine encounter at Mount Horeb. Aaron was the first of the Levites to adopt the new faith and his claim to leadership alongside Moses appears to have been fully accepted by all the Israelites. The point is, though, that it was secular leadership. The oldest traditions of the Exodus* had nothing to say about a division of authority between the two brothers, giving Aaron the position of a specifically religious leader.

The Early Traditions of the Sanctuaries: These ancient J and E traditions belong to the early period of Israel's history before the centralization of religion around the Jerusalem Temple*, in the days when a variety of sanctuaries existed at different places in the country (see Sanctuaries*; High Places*) and laymen as well as Levites might officiate at the altars as priests (Ex. 23:19). These sources reflect the ancient popular background and bear little relation to the ceremonial at the central sanctuaries established much later on after Israel's establishment in Canaan (see Judges*; Samuel*). As a whole, this body of tradition (J and E) accurately reflects historical facts and conditions. To this extent it differs fundamentally from the idealistic and utopian accounts of the P (priestly) traditions.

The priestly writers (see Biblical Criticism*) assumed that a tabernacle (see Tabernacle*, Ark and Cherubim) of the dimensions and magnificence of a full-scale Temple, was erected immediately after the theophany on Sinai, the functions and activities of the priests being laid down at the same time. In fact however, the functions and organization of the priesthood, as defined in the Priestly sources, belong to the very much later period when a physical House of the Lord in Jerusalem was a familiar image (see Priests and Levites*).

Although the early sources refer to Aaron as an officiating priest and as the foremost of the priests, quite obviously he could hardly have fulfilled such a function under the conditions prevailing during the bondage in Egypt, nor in the wilderness when the Israelites had no real sanctuaries. Even the description of him as "the Levite" in Ex. 4:14 probably reflects no more than the general feeling that his office was more appropriate to a member of the Levi clan. In later thought the terms "Levite" and "priest" were to become practically synonymous and this is a case of the association being imposed on the older tradition at a later date.

The Golden Calf: One of the early (probably JE) traditions of Exodus 32 records that because Moses "delayed to come down from" Mount Sinai, the people despaired of seeing him again and demanded that Aaron make them gods to worship. Under pressure, Aaron acquiesced. He had the men collect their womenfolk's gold jewellery and from it made them a molten calf "fashioning it with a graving tool" (Ex. 32:1–4). An altar was built before it and burnt sacrifices offered, Aaron presumably officiating.

The narrative about the Golden Calf is no longer in its original simple form. It is notable, however, that Aaron proclaimed a "festival to the Lord" to be held in front of the Golden Calf. This seems to have some connection with the story in I K. 12:26–30 about Jeroboam making the Golden Calves, for he uses exactly the same phrase that is given to Aaron in Exodus: "Behold your gods, O Israel, who brought you up out of the land of Egypt."

There is a theory that the original ancient tradition concerning Aaron's priesthood was that he was the founder of a popular cult which combined Yahwistic and other non-Mosaic elements and might have extended to the "apostasy" of the golden calf, as part of a syncretist form of worship (see Idol Worship in Israel*). Alternatively,

Aaron may have been forced to take part in the pagan worship as the only means of maintaining his supremacy among the people.

When Moses returned from the mountain. the narrative, which seems to belong to a different tradition, emphasizes his anger and the vengeance he took on the people (32:19–29). Calling on the Levites to aid him in re-asserting his authority, Moses sent them through the camp to "slay every man his brother and every man his companion and every man his neighbour" (Ex. 32:27), by which action the Levites "ordained themselves for the service of the Lord" (32:29).

Many scholars believe that the story of the Golden Calf and its sequel contain the echoes of tensions which developed between the House of Aaron and the tribe of Levi. In this incident Aaron is shown leading the people to their sin of the golden calf — an act which called for the most forceful reprisals by Moses and the Levites.

Additional evidence of opposition to Aaron's supreme position comes from the story of the rebellion of the non-priestly Levites, led by Korah (Nu. 16), who rose against Moses and Aaron demanding the priesthood for themselves. On this occasion, Aaron faced the rebels at Moses' side and, when the leaders had been destroyed (16:25–35) and their supporters punished by a plague, Aaron and his censer stopped the plague from spreading further among the people (16:40–50). The incident is rounded off by the account of the miraculous flowering of Aaron's rod as a sign that the Lord had chosen him above all his fellows (17:1–11) – which seems to be a good example of hindsight in the traditions.

Aaron's Revolt Against Moses: Aaron himself is recorded as challenging Moses' authority in Nu. 12. He and his sister Miriam complained about Moses' marriage to a Cushite woman, although the real basis of their protest seems to have been their resentment of Moses' unique position as the mouthpiece of God. They too, they argued, had received divine revelation, "Has the Lord indeed spoken only through Moses? Has he not spoken through us also?" (Nu. 12:2). Their insolence was answered by God in the form of a pillar of cloud proclaiming his complete confidence in Moses who "is entrusted with all my house." (12:7). Punishment was limited to Miriam who was smitten with leprosy and excluded from the camp for seven days, but was pardoned when Aaron interceded with Moses. The fact that the Israelites halted their march for the time Miriam was in disgrace suggests that her "sin" may possibly have involved more than herself and Aaron.

Aaron as High Priest and Priestly Ancestor: In contrast to the secular leader of the earliest traditions, the Aaron of the Priestly traditions is quite a different character. A picture is built up of Aaron "the Levite", i.e. an officiating priest, Moses' religious vice-regent and the first High Priest of Israel. From him all lawful priests must be descended, other members of the tribe of Levi acting as their servants (Ex. chs. 28, 29 and 39; Lv. 8–15; Nu. 17–18). Throughout the "priestly" regulations for the tabernacle and religious organization (see Exodus, Book of*), the phrase "Aaron and his sons" is used to mean the priesthood in general.

This new picture marked the triumph of the trend towards centralization and specialization within the religious organization. There was no room in the single central sanctuary for more than one Levite family to officiate as priests and the line thus distinguished was the "house of Aaron". They cannot have reached this position without encountering opposition, which is probably echoed in the unfavourable stories of the Golden Calf (Ex. 32) and the rebellion of Aaron and Miriam (Nu. 12). Many scholars consider that the story of the calf and its sequel provides the basis for the consecration of the Levites to the service of the Lord (Ex. 32:29) for on this occasion they proved their unquestioning loyalty to God and obtained recognition of their position.

The "P" source is unique in regarding the priesthood as the sole prerogative of Aaron's house, and this uncompromising attitude marks it is an unhistorical source. The source records that after Aaron's two eldest sons, Nadab and Abihu, were slain by God as a punishment for offering a burnt sacrifice in an unorthodox manner, the two younger sons, Eleazar and Ithamar became the forebears of all the priestly families of Israel. Sixteen priestly generations were traced back to Eleazar and eight to Ithamar (I Ch. 24). Eleazar succeeded Aaron on his father's death (Dt. 10:6; Nu. 20:28). Traditionally he became the ancestor of Zadok, the first High Priest of Jerusalem from whom all future High Priests claimed descent down to the time of Antiochus Epiphanes (see Hasmoneans*; Priests and Levites*). The house of Eli, which was installed at the tribal shrine of Shiloh claimed their descent from Ithamar. This element represents the only certain historical context in the annals of the house of Aaron. Before the central sanctuary was established in Jerusalem, the house of Eli and the central sanctuary they served, had outstripped all the other sanctuaries (Bethel, Dan, Hebron, Gilgal etc.) and their priests, although this does not mean that they were the one and only sacerdotal family in Israel.

In post-Exilic times (Ezr. 2:61–63) the claims of the house of Aaron to undisputed tenure of the priestly office were fully recognized. Levites and priests who could not claim a proper genealogy were excluded from service at the altar and limited to subsidiary duties (for a further discussion of priests* and Levites, see article).

Development of the Picture of Aaron: The way Aaron and his role are presented can best be understood in terms of the long story of the priesthood, first of all in the sanctuaries, then in Jerusalem (see Priests and Levites*; Tabernacle*; Temple*).

The contradictory accounts of Aaron's role in the Exodus reflect the struggle between different groups of priests, but it is not possible to trace this development in detail. Accordingly a variety of hypotheses have been put forward. The most moderate and widely accepted theory is that the priests who returned from Babylon at the time of Ezra* (see Restoration*) and who were probably descendants of Zadok (David's High Priest, apparently a Levite with no special pedigree), had somehow to amalgamate with a non-Zadokite group claiming descent from Aaron, who had stayed on in Palestine during the Exile. These priests were the family of Abiathar and they laid claim to the levitical genealogy of the house of Eli which, they maintained, had been chosen as priests while the Israelites were still in Egypt (I Sam. 2:27–28). In the course of time, as Aaron became acknowledged the first High Priest of Israel, they also claimed descent from him. During the long period of a number of sanctuaries, there was no great urgency in the disputes between the rival priestly families but when all worship and priestly privileges were centred in the Jerusalem Temple — particularly after Josiah's reform (see Israel and Judah*, Part IV) — the struggle for recognition became much more acute.

Eventually, after the Exile, an agreement was reached by which the two leading families shared the priesthood on an equal footing as "Sons of Aaron". The post-Exilic Chronicler provided them with the necessary titles to this office in his genealogies of Levi and Aaron (I Ch. 6:3–15) and the priestly organization which was ascribed to David (I Ch. 24:1–6), in which it is clearly stated that all Aaron's sons were priests, Zadok being a descendant of Eleazar (or Phinehas) and Abiathar being descended from Ithamar (see Priests and Levites*).

The question of Aaron's historicity is further considered together with that of Moses in the article on Moses*.

Aaron died in the 39th year of the Israelites' wanderings, on the eve of the Conquest*. Nu. 20:24–29 records his death on the top of Mount Hor, on the borders of Edom.

ABRAHAM (see Patriarchs*)

ACTS OF THE APOSTLES. — *Outline. I. Authorship; Date; Sources; Purpose; Legal Position of the Christians. II. Organization; Contents. III. Paul's Journeys: The First Journey; The Apostolic Council of Jerusalem; The Second Journey; The Third Journey; Ephesus; Paul's Arrest; Journey to Rome; Paul in Rome.*

Although this particular volume of the New Testament is generally referred to as "The Acts of the Apostles" or, more simply, "The Acts", the nomenclature is misleading. Peter and Paul are the only two apostles whose words and deeds are described at length. Actually, the author of Acts relates the growth and development of the primitive church, from its early centre in Jerusalem to its propagation, under the influence of Paul*, among the Gentiles.

I. AUTHORSHIP: Since the second century the tradition has been that the author of the Acts was identical with the author of the Third Gospel, i. e. Luke* (see Synoptic Gospels*). This traditional view has never been seriously challenged and most scholars of our day tend to subscribe to it.

Acts begins with a prologue which is addressed to a certain Theophilus. The Third Gospel is likewise addressed to Theophilus. The author of Acts also speaks (1:1) of his "first volume", presumably the Gospel of Luke. Whereas the "first volume" purported to relate all that Jesus had done and taught until he ascended into heaven, the second book (Ac.) continues with the story of the early Church after the ascension of Christ. The literary style and vocabulary of the two volumes also show such marked similarities that there can be little doubt that they are the work of the same author.

One of the most telling arguments for the Lukan authorship of Acts is the so-called "we-sections" (Ac. 16:10–17; 20:5–15; 21:1–18; 27:1–28:16) in which the author speaks in the first person plural, all of which occur in the narratives of Paul's missionary journeys. That a certain Luke was among the companions of Paul is borne out by Col. 4:14; Phil. 24 and II Tim. 4:11. Though Paul had other companions, the evidence seems to confirm Luke as the author of Acts.

Date: Various dates are ascribed to the book of Acts. Those who tend to date it somewhat later (90–100 CE) argue that Luke was familiar with and made use of the works of the Jewish historian, Flavius Josephus. However, this argument is not convincing since Luke's dependence on Josephus has never been proved conclusively. There is no reason to assume that the events and occurrences known and recorded by Josephus should not have been equally well known to Luke. Quite conceivably they made use of common sources.

A much earlier date is suggested by those who believe that Acts was written before the martyrdom of Paul (ca. 64 CE), on the grounds that this tragedy is not recorded by the author. This is not conclusive either. Luke may have had a special reason for omitting this event (see below, Purpose). It might have been difficult to explain to the Gentile world why this great leader of the early Church was sentenced to death by the Roman authorities, particularly as Luke was trying to portray Christianity as a "legitimate" religion of the Roman Empire. However, this is a weak argument by itself. Apologists were never at a loss to explain how great catastrophes were nevertheless part of the scheme of God. Martyrdom certainly never presented any problems.

The majority of scholars have tended to place Acts after the Third Gospel for the obvious reason that Acts refers to a "first volume", i.e. Luke. The dating of Luke's Gospel (see Synoptic Gospels*) hinges in turn on the dating of Mark which must have antedated the Gospel of Luke. Those who accept a date of 60–70 for Mark, put Luke at 70–80 CE and, allowing for a few years' interval between Luke and Acts, date Acts between 80–90 CE.

Scholars who accept a date before 64 CE for Acts naturally assign appropriately earlier dates to Luke and Mark (see Synoptic Gospels*).

Sources: It is difficult to ascertain exactly what sources were at the author's disposal for the book of Acts. If Luke was indeed the author, then he was in a uniquely favourable position to collect first and second-hand information, and had a wealth of material at hand. As one of Paul's companions, he would have heard of or actually experienced many of the events in the life of that apostle. Philip, one of the Seven chosen by the Jerusalem community to aid the Twelve Apostles (Ac. 6:5–6; 21:8) was a personal friend and through him Luke would have had easy access to material pertaining to the early Church at Jerusalem. Moreover Luke would have had ample time and opportunity to collect material during the two years (Ac. 24:27) he spent in Palestine while Paul was being held at Caesarea (cf. Ac. 21:17; 27:1 ff).

It is apparent from Col. 4:10, 14 that Luke also came into contact with Mark, whose Gospel he probably used in writing his own (see Synoptic Gospels*). Very probably he also learned additional information from Mark himself which was not included in the second Gospel. Several passages (including Ac. 11:19–26; 13:1–3, and perhaps also 11:27–30) which deal with the church at Antioch may stem from the early traditions of that church.

It used to be supposed that, like most of the historians of his day, Luke freely attributed speeches to the leading characters of his work which, far from being authentic, were entirely invented by the author. Thus the speeches of Peter (particularly 2:14–41 and 3:12–26), Stephen (7:1–53), and Paul (13:16–41; 17:22–31; 20:18–35; 22:1–21; 24:10–21; 26:2–29) were all thought to have been composed by Luke. However, while the speeches may well have been edited and embellished by Luke, the literary stylist, there is good reason for believing that many of them are essentially the original versions. The speeches of Peter and Stephen, for example, reveal a more primitive, less sophisticated theology than those of Paul. Luke may even have had a written source for the earlier material. There is also a quite different approach in Paul's speeches, depending on his audience, whether Jews (as in 13:16–41) or Gentiles (17:22–31). As Paul's companion, Luke would either have heard these speeches for himself or would have been able to learn their broad outline from the apostle direct. When he had such ready access to the original sources, it seems very far-fetched to suppose that Luke invented the speeches.

Purpose: In the first four verses of his Gospel, Luke very aptly states his purpose in writing both the Gospel and the Acts of the Apostles as well. His intention was to record the life and teachings of Jesus Christ and to trace the subsequent development of His church. Luke, however, was more than a historian. He was a zealous and willing participant in the historical drama he described. Acts, accordingly, may be not so much a history of the early Church as a defence of Christianity. Luke was the apologist par excellence for the early Christian Church.

By the time he wrote Acts, great changes had taken place within the Church. Christianity had broken out of its Jewish shell, so to speak, and this metamorphosis had been accompanied by a friction so serious as to threaten the very fabric of the early Church (cf. Gal. 2:1–17). Many scholars consider that Luke was inclined to gloss over this near schism and to play down the fundamental differences between the "Jewish" and "Gentile" groups within the Church (Ac. 15:7–21), although with the limited historical records available, it is difficult to make any definite assessment.

Luke shows Peter and Paul as apparently in perfect accord with one another, although from other sources it would appear that they were very far from being of one mind. Luke also manages to preserve the precarious balance between the leaders of the two factions by the skilful arrangement of his book (see Organization) so that neither appears inferior to the other

In his Gospel, as well as in Acts, Luke was writing consciously for a Gentile public. In the great majority of incidents it was the Jews who stirred up trouble for the Christians; the Gentile authorities were quick to protect the law-abiding apostles.

Legal Position of the Christians: Luke attempts to show that Christianity was the legitimate off-shoot of Judaism and that therefore it was one of the religions which could claim official "toleration" within the Roman Empire (see Christianity, Early*, II; Paul*). Christian believers were not a subversive element, he maintained; such charges were the malicious lies spread by the apostles' enemies (Ac. 17:7–8). One school of thought finds in this attitude the reason why Luke ended his account of Paul's missionary activities without recording the apostle's martyrdom. It would have been impossible to blame his death on the Jews, for Paul had appealed to Roman justice and it was the Romans who sentenced him to death. This being the case, there were only two possible explanations for his death. Either Christianity was a subversive teaching or there had been a miscarriage of Roman justice. Both explanations would be equally offensive to a Gentile reader.

Against this opinion, however, there is another school which holds that Acts was written before the death of Paul (ca. 64 CE). These scholars maintain that as a good historian, Luke would certainly have recorded Paul's martyrdom had it taken place before he wrote Acts. The argument that Luke deliberately avoided mentioning it is vitiated, they consider, by the fact that he also makes no mention of the death of James, who was martyred by the Jews, not the Romans. Accordingly, Luke could not have written as he did in the 80's. It was only possible up to 64 when Nero revealed the true nature of Roman justice. Luke, after all, does not suppress or deny in his Gospel that the Romans were legally responsible for the death of Jesus.

Luke makes another strong point in favour of "Gentile" Christianity in the blessing of the Holy Spirit which is imparted to Gentile as well as Jew, thus showing that there is no fundamental difference between Jewish and Gentile Christians.

One of the major problems facing Luke was how to explain why Jesus, the long awaited Messiah of the Jews, was rejected by his own people. According to Luke, the Early Christian Church was the true "Israel" because she accepted Jesus as the Messiah; the Jews who rejected him were heretics who had deliberately turned their backs on Divine salvation and had thus forfeited their calling as the Chosen People. Thus Luke could show his readers that the Church which by that time was spreading rapidly among the Gentiles of the Roman Empire was the true representative of the God of Israel, the sole Creator and Ruler of the Universe.

II. ORGANIZATION: Luke's skilful literary arrangement of his material serves both to strengthen and emphasize his message (see: Purpose). The first chapter relates the ascension of Jesus and his charge to his disciples. Then Luke describes the visitation of the Holy Ghost upon the apostles at Pentecost and the ensuing development of the Early Church. Finally, the conversion of Paul is recounted and then the events of his three missionary journeys which firmly established Christianity among the Gentiles. Thus, in the book of Acts, we can distinguish three phases in the development of the Early Church: 1. Jesus and his immediate disciples; 2. the "Jewish" Christian Church at Jerusalem; and 3. the establishment and growth of Christianity among the Gentiles.

The dividing line in the book of Acts is undoubtedly Luke's account (in ch. 15) of the Apostolic Council of Jerusalem. Here Gentile Christianity is officially approved as is Paul's calling to minister to the Gentiles. The first part of Acts leads up to this Council; the second part describes its consequences as Paul continues his work in Asia Minor, Greece, and finally Rome.

In the first chapters of Ac. Peter is the dominant personality. He is the leader of the "Jewish" Christian community. By far the larger part of the book, however, is devoted to Paul and his work among the Gentiles. Yet Peter is not made to seem inferior to Paul. According to Luke, it was Peter himself who made the first Gentile conversion (Ac. 9) and at the Apostolic Council, Peter defended (15:7–11) the right of the Gentiles to be converted without first submitting to the Jewish rite of circumcision, although at the Council (see below) it was James who played the leading and decisive role.

Luke strikes a balance between the deeds of Peter and Paul, the parallels between them being too obvious to have occurred unintentionally. Among others, there are the healing of the lame (3:1–11 and 14:8–10); the raising of the dead (9:36–43 as against 20:9–12), the miraculous escapes from prison (5:17–25 and 12:3–10 compared to 16:23–34) and the magical power of healing (5:15 and 19:11–12). Thus Luke sought to heal old wounds within the Christian community and present a solid and united front to the outside world.

Contents: After the introduction (1:1–5) addressed to Theophilus, chapter 1 recounts Jesus' charge to his disciples (1:6–8) and his ascension into heaven (1:9–11) on a cloud (reminiscent of the "Son of man" in Dan. 7:13). The remainder of the chapter (1:12–26) gives an account of the actions of the disciples before the first Pentecost and their choice of Matthias to take the place of the traitor Judas among the Twelve.

Thereafter the book can be divided into three major sections:

a. *Acts* 2:1–8:3 records the history of the church in Jerusalem, in which Peter is the main character. The section begins with the narrative of Pentecost and the coming of the Holy Spirit (2:1–13) and reports Peter's first sermon (2:14–41) delivered to the "men of Israel". After this (2:42–47) the life of the early Jewish-Christians in Jerusalem is described. It is interesting to compare their community with its communal sharing of goods and common meal with the sectarian community of Qumran (see Dead Sea Scrolls*). 3:1–11 relates Peter's healing of the lame beggar and his sermon (12–26) to the astonished crowd which gathered round the healed man. 4:1–22 reports the first opposition to the young church and the arrest and hearing of Peter and John, while 21–31 records their release and the rejoicing among the Christians. 32-37 is a further description of their communal life and sharing of property. Ch. 5:1–11 continues this theme with the story of Ananias and his wife Sapphira who sold some property and kept some of the proceeds for themselves, swearing that they were presenting the whole to the Apostles for the common fund. Because they thus lied to God they were struck dead.

5:12–16 tells of miraculous healings by Peter and the apostles and 17–25 recounts their arrest, imprisonment and subsequent delivery from prison by an angel. In 26–42 the apostles are brought before the High Court (Sanhedrin, see Authority and Government*) of the Jews, but are released after the Pharisee* Gamaliel has pleaded for tolerance and forebearance.

6:1–7 describes how seven disciples were chosen to help the apostles, in response to a demand from the Hellenist Jews (see Jewish Christians*; Hellenism in the Diaspora*). One of the seven was Stephen, whose works and arrest are the subject of 6:8–15. 7:1–53 contains Stephen's speech before the council (see Jewish Christians*) and 54–60 tells of his stoning and death. 8:1–3 records the persecution of the early Christian community and the part played in it by Saul (Paul*).

b. *The second section, Ac.* 8:4–12:25, traces the gradual transition from an almost exclusively "Jewish" Christianity* (see article) to a faith that included and welcomed "the Gentiles". The rest of Ch. 8 deals with Philip, describing his work in Samaria, his encounter with the magician, Simon Magus (4–25) and Philip's conversion of the Ethiopian eunuch (26–40).

9:1–22 contains the first of three narratives in Acts (the others are 22:3–21 and 26:9–20) which tell the story of Saul's conversion on the road to Damascus (see Paul*). There follows (23–31) the account of Paul's first visit to Jerusalem and the misgivings with which he was received by the Jewish-Christians whom he had earlier persecuted. He was taken in by Barnabas (9:27) who later became his companion on his first missionary journey. Paul stayed in Jerusalem until his disputes with the Hellenists (Greek-speaking Jews) aroused such animosity that he had to flee back to his native town of Tarsus (9:29–30). 9:32–43 is devoted to Peter's missionary efforts in the towns of Lydda and Joppa.

Ch. 10 contains the first major statement of the Christian church as something not exclusively "Jewish". Peter has a divinely inspired vision (9–16) in which he sees all the animals and birds and reptiles of the earth and is commanded to slaughter and eat them. He refuses on the grounds that they are unclean according to Jewish Law (see Impurity*) but a voice reprimands him and tells him that he should not call "common" (i. e. unclean) that which God has cleansed. Peter is then summoned to the house of an Italian Centurion, Cornelius (17–33), who is converted to Christianity with all his household (34–46) and baptized (47–48). Peter was criticized by the "circumcision party" within the Church for eating with the "uncircumcized", and defended his action, finally persuading them that "to the Gentiles also God has granted repentance unto life" (11:1–18). The chapter continues with a description of the spread of Christianity to Antioch and the establishment of a Christian community there (11:19–26). It ends with the famine in Jerusalem and the aid sent from Antioch through Paul and Barnabas (27–30).

Persecution of the Jerusalem church by Herod Agrippas (king of Judea from 41–44 CE) is the theme of ch. 12. The apostle James, the brother of John, was executed (12:2) and Peter thrown into prison, whence he was rescued by an angel (12:3–11) and went into hiding. Peter's escape so enraged Herod that he ordered the execution of the guards of his prison (12:19). Vs. 20–23 relate the death of Herod and the closing verses (24–25) record the spread of the "Word of God" and the return of Saul and Barnabas from Jerusalem (accompanied by John Mark).

c. *The third section*, Ch. 13 to the end of the book is mainly concerned with the activities of the apostle Paul* and his missionary journeys which helped to establish

1

Christianity throughout the Roman empire. The section can be sub-divided into 1. the first missionary journey (chs. 13–14); 2. the Council of Jerusalem (15:1–34); 3. the second missionary journey (15:36–18:22); 4. the third missionary journey (18:23–21:3); 5. Paul's return to Jerusalem (21:6–17) and his arrest (21:18–23:35); 6. his imprisonment in Caesarea (chs. 24–26); and 7. his journey to Rome (27-28).

III. PAUL'S JOURNEYS: The journeys of Paul have been greatly elucidated by researches in Asia Minor and Syria (see Paul*). Major sites have been the subject of much attention by archaeologists.

The First Journey begins (13:1–3) with Paul and Barnabas being sent out as missionaries by the church at Antioch. Their first stop was at Cyprus (13:4–12), Barnabas' homeland (Ac. 4:36). (The appearance of the people may be judged from this 3rd c. CE Cypriote tombstone panel **(1)** showing a banquet scene. It is surmounted by a recumbent lion.) The apostles then went on (13:13–15) to Perga, whose imposing ruins **(2)** can be seen today, then to Pisidian Antioch in Asia Minor (not to be confused with Antioch in Syria, see map **(4)**. There Paul's sermon in the synagogue is recorded (13:16–43), and also the Jews' rejection of his teaching and their expulsion of the apostles from the city (44–52). Paul and Barnabas continued to Iconium (modern Konya) but again were forced to flee (14:1–7). They went on to Lystra where Paul healed a lame man which made the people acclaim the apostles as gods (Zeus and Hermes; 8–18). However, opposition gathered once more and Paul was stoned (19–20). The apostles went on to Derbe and then homeward to Antioch (14:21–28). On their way they passed Attalia on the coast, where the huge amphitheatre of Aspendus has been preserved **(3)**. See map **(4)**.

The Apostolic Council of Jerusalem described in 15:1–34 (see Paul*) is one of the most significant milestones of the early Church. It also occupies an important place in the literary structure of Acts. In the preceding chs. the stage had been set for the inclusion of Gentile Christianity. The basic problem involved was whether a Gentile could become a Christian without first becoming a Jew. Certain conservative groups within the early Church insisted that Gentile converts be circumcized and adhere to the laws pertaining to ritual cleanliness (see Jewish Christians*). At the Council of Jerusalem, "Gentile" Christianity was formally approved, however, and the remainder of Acts deals with Paul's efforts to bring Gentiles into the Christian Church.

The "circumcision party" demanded that Gentiles be circumcized and Paul and Barnabas went up to Jerusalem to put the question to the Church leaders (15:1–5). A council was convened at which Peter spoke in defence of

2

3

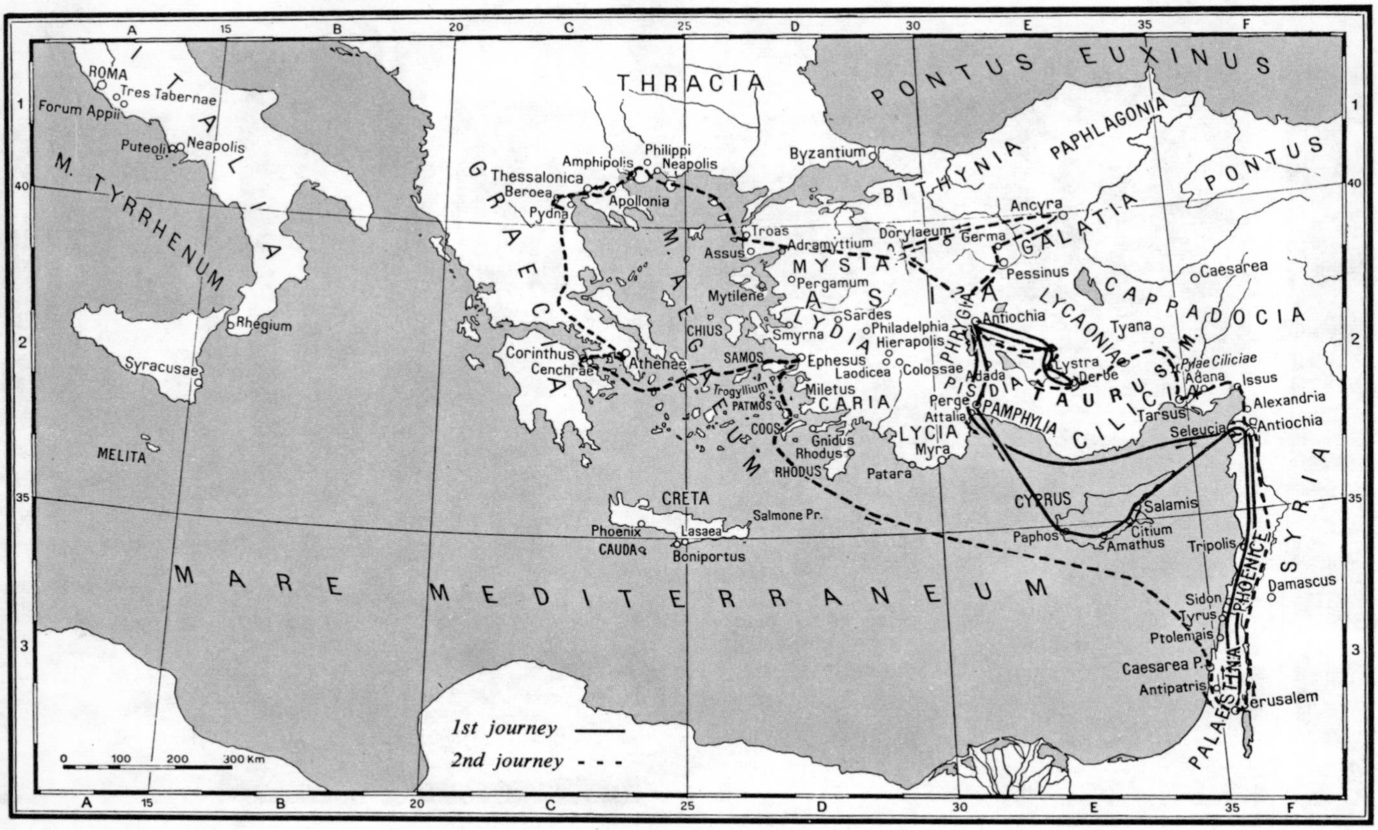

4

the Gentiles and Paul and Barnabas reported their successes. The issue was settled when James proposed a compromise by which the "Gentile" Christians would be acceptable if they refrained from idolatry, fornication and from things "strangled" and from "blood". The last two requests reflect the strict Jewish prohibition against eating blood. James' judgment prevailed and the compromise was accepted, letters being sent to the various communities to inform them of this decision (15:6–29). The announcement was received at Antioch with joy and Judas and Silas, who had been sent by the council to carry the news to Antioch with Paul and Barnabas, returned peacefully to Jerusalem.

The account of this council recorded in Acts is considerably modified by comparison with Paul's report in Gal. 2:1–17. However, one should bear in mind the differences in time and attitude between the writing of Acts and the Epistle to the Galatians. Luke's work, intended as an apology for the early Church, was written some time after the council and long after the dispute had been settled. It was in Luke's interest to portray the church as an indivisible and united body including both Jew and Gentile (see above, Purpose). Paul, on the other hand, was deeply involved in the argument and was writing shortly after the council to a church threatened with disruption by Judaizing elements who were challenging his authority (see Paul*; Epistle to the Galatians*).

In Luke's account, Peter is credited with a favourable attitude towards Gentile Christianity whereas in Galatians 2:11–21, Paul writes that he criticized him severely for his intolerant opposition to the Gentiles. As an apologist for the Church, Luke seems to have been attempting to gloss over a serious rift in the early Christian community by portraying Peter and Paul as having been in complete agreement.

The Second Journey (15:35–18:22). In Antioch, Paul and Barnabas decided to pay a return visit to the churches established during their first journey (15:35–36) but disagreed over whether John Mark should accompany them. When Paul refused to take Mark with them, the two apostles separated, Barnabas going with Mark and Paul taking Silas with him (37–40).

Paul's route lay first through Syria and Cilicia (see map **(4)** and then westwards through the towns of Derbe and Lystra (15:41–16:1) where he was joined by another disciple, Timothy. Timothy was the son of a Jewish mother and a Greek father and Paul had him circumcized "because of the Jews" (16:2–3). Paul was a Jew and adhered to Jewish law, although he did not believe that Gentile converts need do so. However, according to Jewish law, Timothy — the son of a Jewess — was a Jew and as such had to be circumcized so as not to offend the Jewish communities which Paul hoped to win over. In general it seems clear that none of the Apostles adopted an inflexible position on the question. Luke was probably right in his portrayal of the situation.

Paul and his companions continued through Mysia, by-passing Bithynia, to Troas (ancient Troy; 16:7–8) where Paul had a vision of a man beckoning him further west to Macedonia (Greece, 16:9). The next verse (16:10) begins one of the "we-sections" (see above, Authorship) which records a sea journey to Philippi where they meet and convert the Jewess, Lydia (11–15). Paul healed a slave girl possessed of a "spirit", thereby arousing the anger of her masters who had found her a profitable source of income. At their instigation, the Philippians had Paul and his companion beaten and cast into prison (16:16–24). During the night, there was an earthquake which flung wide the prison doors and broke the prisoners' fetters. The jailer was afraid his prisoners had escaped, but Paul reassured and then converted him (16:25–34). In the morning, the city magistrates tried to release Paul and Silas surreptitiously, but Paul insisted on a public apology for the maltreatment he — a Roman citizen — had suffered (35–37). Only when the magistrates came and apologized in person did Paul and Silas agree to leave Philippi (39–40).

They went on to Thessalonica where Paul preached in the local synagogue but although some of the Jews accepted his message, others tried to lay hands on the apostle (17:1–5). Not finding him, they dragged Jason, one of the local converts, before the authorities on the charge of sheltering men who had been teaching a subversive doctrine (6–8). Jason was released after giving a pledge to the magistrates as surety of his future good behaviour (9) but Paul and Silas were hurried by night to the nearby city of Beroea. There, Paul's message was well received until hostile Jews from Thessalonica again began stirring up trouble and forced Paul to flee to Athens (10–15).

In Athens, Paul argued with Stoic and Epicurean philosophers who finally brought him to the Areopagus, the central council of Athens, for him to present his case (16–21). Paul had noticed an altar dedicated to "an unknown god" and this he made the text for his sermon (22–31). This was well received until he spoke of the resurrection which was greeted with derision and, even though a few people had been converted (32–34), Paul left, first to Corinth, then Ephesus, then to Jerusalem and back to Antioch.

The Third Journey (18:23–20:3). This journey was begun with visits to the Christian communities of Galatia and Phrygia (18:23). The narrative is then broken off for the account (18:24–28; cf. I Cor. 3:5–6; 16:12) of a Jew from Alexandria named Apollos who, well-versed in the scriptures, interpreted them in a Christian sense although he "knew only the baptism of John" (see Jewish Christians*). Instructed in the "true way" by Aquila and Priscilla — Paul's friends in Corinth — Apollos became a powerful force in converting the Jews of Ephesus and Corinth. While Apollos was in Corinth, Paul met a group of disciples of John the Baptist* in Ephesus. After Paul had explained the significance of John as the fore-runner of Jesus, they agreed to be baptized once more, this time in the name of Jesus (19:1–7).

Paul remained in Ephesus for about two years (19:8–20). The ancient town was situated some 45 miles south of modern Izmir and, at that time, was the prosperous capital of the Roman province in Asia Minor, with a population of over 300,000. Paul began as always by preaching in the synagogue but when the Jews rejected him he turned to the Gentiles and his fame spread throughout the area. So much so, that some local Jewish exorcists attempted to exorcize an evil spirit in the name of "the Jesus whom Paul preaches", but they were not very successful (13–17). Paul eventually decided to go to Jerusalem via Macedonia and Achaia and he sent Timothy and Erastus ahead of him into Macedonia (21–22). See map (**4a**).

4a

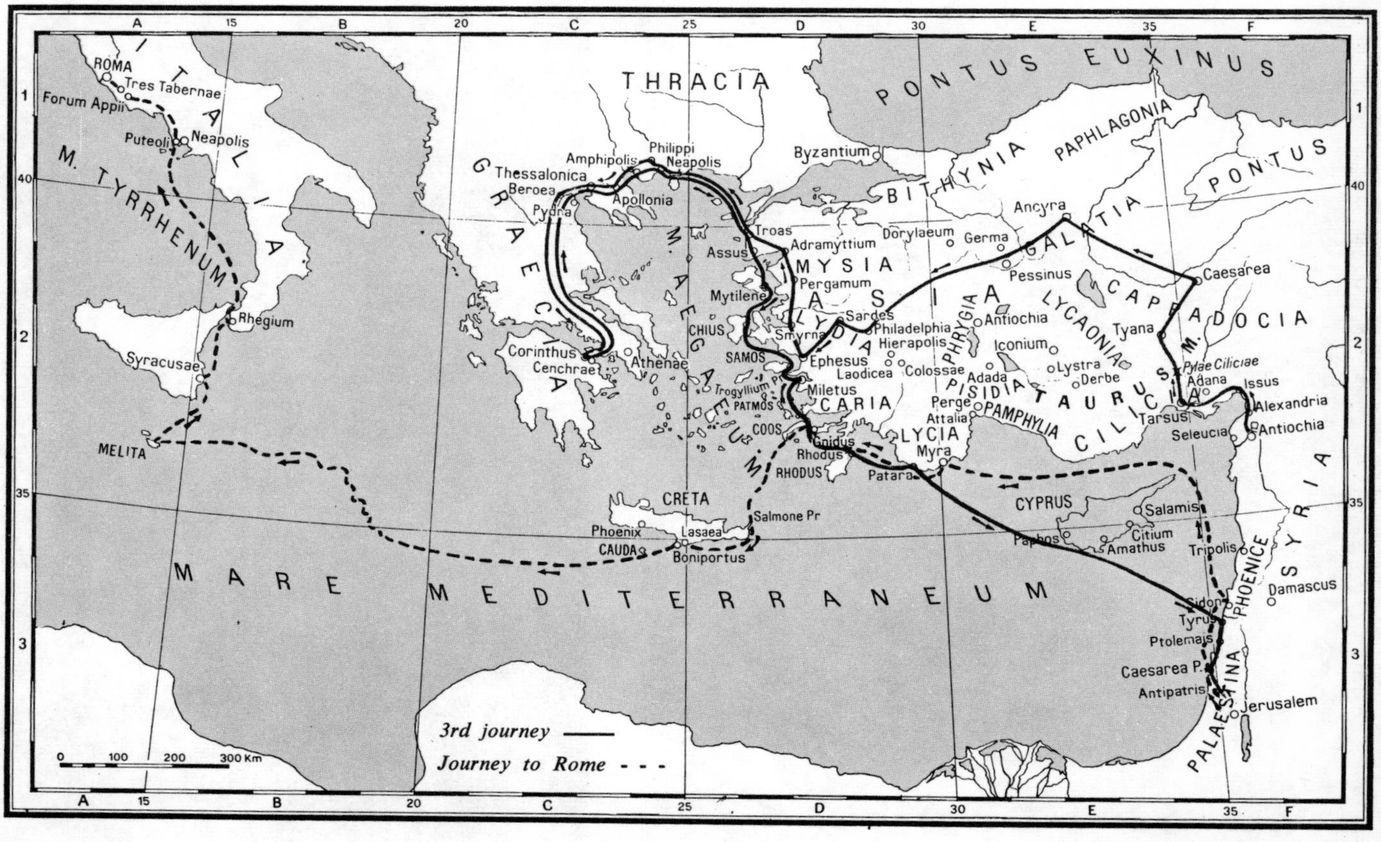

5

Ephesus: The temple of Diana of the Ephesians (the Roman Artemis) at Ephesus, supported by a hundred columns, was one of the wonders of the ancient world. Statues (**6**) of the multibreasted goddess, whose worship was combined with oriental fertility-rites, have been found there. Ephesus attracted pilgrims from far and wide who made a profitable market for the cult objects made by the silversmiths (**5**). One of these, named Demetrius, persuaded his fellow-workers that Paul and his teaching were endangering their livelihood by drawing people away

6

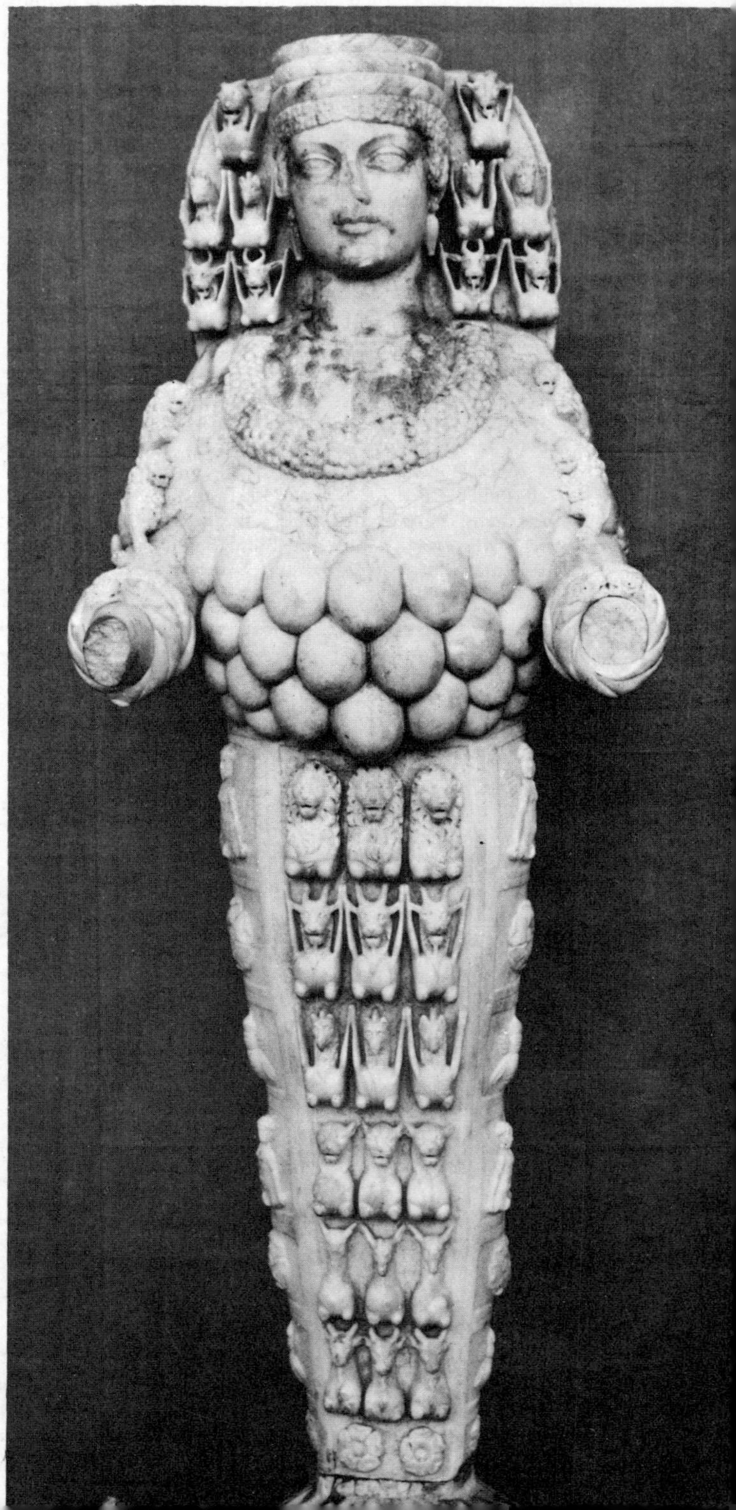

Amphitheatre

from worshipping the goddess. A mob gathered and two of Paul's companions, Gaius and Aristarchus, were seized and dragged before the Assembly in the theatre (**7**). (The theatre was connected to the harbour by the Arkadiane, a wide, marble-paved street lined with a colonnade, with shops and store-rooms behind it **8**). The assembly was in some

8

disorder but at last the town clerk managed to quiet and then disperse the crowd by threatening them with proceedings for taking part in mob violence (19:23–41). Luke appears to take the affair much less seriously than Paul himself (I Cor. 15:32; II Cor. 1:8), or perhaps he was trying to show Roman justice in a more favourable light. An inscription of "Demetrius son of Menophilus" may refer to Paul's opponent there (19:24). "Asiarch" as applied to Ephesian officials is correctly used by Luke, according to contemporary inscriptions.

As planned, Paul departed for Macedonia, then went on to Greece (20:1–2). From there he began the long journey home through Philippi in Macedonia then by sea to Troas (20:3–6) where he restored to life the young man Eutychus, killed in a fall from a window while Paul was preaching (20:7–12).

From Troas, Paul and his companions sailed south along the western coast of Asia Minor to Miletus near modern Aydin (13–16). In Miletus, Paul sent for the elders of the church of Ephesus to take leave of them (17–38), then he sailed on via Rhodes and Patara to Tyre (21:1–6), ending there his third missionary journey.

The return to Jerusalem: From Tyre, Paul and his companions took ship south to Ptolemais (Acre) and from there went on to Caesarea where they stayed with Philip the evangelist. Although warned by the prophet Agabus that imprisonment awaited him there, Paul continued to Jerusalem, to be well received by the Christian community (21:7–17).

Paul's Arrest: Paul reported on his experiences to James and the elders of the Jerusalem church (21:18–19) and they warned him about rumours which had been spread that he had been teaching the Jews of the diaspora (see Hellenism and the Jews of the Diaspora*) to forsake the Law (20–21). To prove his continued adherence to Jewish Law, Paul went to the Temple with four Jewish Christians who had taken a Nazirite vow, to arrange for an offering. He was recognized by Jews from Asia who stirred up the crowd against him, charging him with bringing a Gentile into the Temple, an act which was strictly forbidden (27–29). Paul was seized by the mob and dragged out of the Temple but before he had been seriously hurt, Roman soldiers came to his rescue and took him into custody. The captain of the guard took Paul for the Egyptian leader of a band of Sicarii assassins (see Rome and the Jews*) and was quite surprised when Paul spoke to him in Greek asking his permission to address the crowd. Hearing that Paul was a Jew from Tarsus, the Roman allowed him to speak to the people (30–40). At first, Paul spoke of his persecution of the Christians and his subsequent conversion to their faith (22:1–20) and the crowd listened to him in silence, but when he turned to his mission to the Gentiles (21) there was such an uproar that the soldiers hurried him away (22–24). Being a Roman citizen, Paul was spared the scourging ordered by the Roman tribune (25–29). Instead, the next day, he was brought before the Sanhedrin (22:30–23:5). Knowing the Council included both Pharisees* and Sadducees*, Paul pleaded that he was a Pharisee and had been brought to trial for preaching the resurrection of the dead — a major source of disagreement between the two parties. The two factions began to argue among themselves, becoming so violent that Paul was again taken into protective custody by the Roman soldiers (6–10).

A plot among some forty Jews to kill Paul was overheard by his nephew and reported to the Roman captain (23:12–22), who ordered Paul to be taken to Caesarea by night by an armed guard and with elaborate precautions (23–30; see Ancient Cities*: Caesarea, for illustrations of the town).

Paul was held in Caesarea until the high priest and some elders arrived to lay their case against him before the Roman governor, Felix. In spite of their pleadings, Felix refused to announce any decision. He kept Paul in custody for two years until a new governor, Porcius Festus, was appointed for Judea (24:1–27). The elders appealed to the new governor to have Paul sent to Jerusalem for trial but Paul, well aware of the hostility to him in that city, insisted on his prerogative as a Roman citizen to appeal to Caesar and obtained Festus' agreement (25:1–12).

A little later, the Jewish king Agrippa II visited Festus at Caesarea and the Roman asked his advice concerning Paul. Paul's speech in his own defence before the king was so convincing that Agrippa is recorded as saying that he could have been freed had he not appealed to Caesar (25:13–26:32).

The Journey to Rome: (chs. 27–28). Accompanied by Luke, Paul set sail from Caesarea under the guard of a centurion, going first to Sidon (27:1–3), then north along the Syrian coast and westwards to Myra in Asia Minor (see map 4a). There the prisoners were transferred to another ship on its way from Alexandria to Rome. In this they slowly made their way along the coast of Crete (4–8). It was now well into winter and sailing was hazardous. Although Paul warned the sailors of the dangers involved, the ship's master insisted on going on (9–13) and the ship was soon caught in a tempest and driven helpless before a north-east wind (14–20). Paul prophesied that although the ship was doomed no one would be lost (21–26) and, as he had predicted, the vessel was finally wrecked on the coast of Malta (Melita), without loss of life (27–44).

The company stayed in Malta for three months, during which time Paul made a great impression on the population. First he was bitten by a viper without suffering any harm, then he healed the sick father of one of the island's leading men. At the end of the winter they took passage on another ship which brought them to Puteoli, a port near Naples and from there they went on foot to Rome (28:1–16).

Paul in Rome: In Rome, Paul summoned the leaders of the Jewish community and explained the Christian message to them. He told them that salvation would be sent to the Gentiles, because the Jews had rejected God's plan. The Jewish leaders went away, divided about whether or not this new teaching should be accepted (28:17–28).

Paul remained for two years in Rome, preaching the kingdom of God (30–31) and on this note of triumph the book of Acts ends. No mention is made of Paul's death. The "good news" of Christ, which had begun in a small corner of the Empire, had now reached the Eternal City. (For further discussion, see articles on Luke*; Paul*.)

(See also illust. under Epistles*, Pauline).

AEGEAN CIVILIZATION AND ITS IMPACT ON PALESTINE. — East Mediterranean Civilization: The term "Aegean civilization" generally refers to a whole group of different cultures of the Eastern Mediterranean belonging to a continuous civilization which flourished in the 2nd mill. BCE, alongside those of Mesopotamia, Egypt and the Western Semitic spheres. These were the cultures of the Greek mainland and islands, usually divided into four main groups named after their principal centres, i.e. the cultures of a) Crete (Minoan culture); b) the islands of the Cyclades; c) the Peleponese (Mycenaean culture) and d) Thessaly or the Greek mainland. Each of these had its own particular characteristics and, as a consequence, its own specific chronology. At the same time, all four shared many common features.

Through trade, migration and, later on, armed invasion, there was a constant exchange of cultural influences between the Aegean and the Egyptian and Asiatic mainlands — including northern Canaan. The most significant of the Aegean influences on Canaan came from the Minoan and Mycenaean spheres, apparently by way of Cyprus. There was also a large reciprocal import from Canaan to the Aegean centres during this millenium.

Cretan Cultures: The earliest of the Aegean cultures was the Cretan "Middle Minoan", dated by reference to Egyptian chronology to around 2000–1700 BCE. The people who brought it to Crete appear to have come from the Near East, and F. H. Stubbing has connected their arrival with disturbances in Syria and Egypt in the Middle Bronze Age which led to the Hyksos* conquest of Lower Egypt. A dim recollection of these origins was preserved in the myth of Europa who was carried from Syria to Crete where she became the mother of Minos.

Middle Minoan culture developed into Late Minoan around the time the Hyksos were expelled from Egypt (1570 BCE). The transition was marked by the arrival of foreign rulers of Crete, e.g. Danaus, who came from Egypt, or Kadmus of Syria, whom Greek legend credits with the invention of writing (see Alphabet and Writing*). This is the period of the legendary heroes of Greek myth.

About 1400 BCE, Knossos, the capital of Crete, was completely destroyed and cultural leadership shifted to the Mycenaean mainland culture.

Throughout the whole period, the cultures of the Aegean were prominent among the variety of influences to which Middle Bronze Age Canaan was subjected. The great development in Aegean civilization led to a corresponding expansion of sea trade. Goods imported from Crete and later the Greek mainland have been found throughout Syria, Palestine and Egypt. After the 20th c. BCE, goods sent in exchange appear in Crete and Cyprus. Between 1600–1400 BCE, the Cretan share in this trade dwindled, but after the fall of Knossos, Mycenaean trade eastwards expanded considerably, continuing until the beginning of the 12th c. BCE. Mycenaean III culture declined with the fall of Troy (1183 BCE, see below) and the appearance of the Sea Peoples.

The Sea Peoples: One important group of these "Peoples of the Sea" were the Philistines* (see article) who settled in Palestine shortly after 1190 BCE. Their pottery was very close in style and decoration to the pottery of the Mycenaean III culture. Such pottery has been recovered in substantial quantities from Tel abu-Hawam (on the Bay of Acre), Alalakh in Syria and Ugarit* in Northern Canaan, up to the time they were destroyed by the Sea Peoples around 1180 BCE. Up to the 11th c. BCE trade between Syria and the Aegean appears to have been mainly in the hands of the Sea Peoples.

Crete: Excavations were begun in Crete in 1898 CE by P. Evans and D. Mackenzie. They continued for 25 years, notably in the palace of Phaistos in Knossos and in the row of tombs at Aya Tryada. An American expedition also dug for eight years at Gurnia, Vasiliki and other places.

These excavations revealed a highly developed civilization which flourished from the 3rd mill. BCE and reached its peak in the middle of the 2nd mill. BCE. It was dated mainly in terms of Egyptian chronology, on the basis of Egyptian vessels found in Crete or Cretan pottery found in Egypt. For the earlier years there are only a few parallel vessels, but from the first half of the 2nd mill. BCE, as a result of the close contacts which existed between the two centres of civilization, ample evidence was available for working out a parallel chronology.

Mycenaean Culture: After the fall of Knossos, Crete was taken over by the Achaeans. These were a people who, coming originally from the northern Balkans, had established a number of kingdoms in the Greek mainland, adopting and adapting the civilization of their predecessors. As from the 14th c. BCE this new development, with its centre in Mycenae in the Peleponese, became the dominant culture in the region. While it may never have reached quite the heights achieved by the Late Minoan in the 15th c. BCE, the Achaean and Mycenaean culture developed to a very high level. It came to an end with the fall of Troy, about 1183 BCE.

Early Greeks: It is now thought that this was not so much an achievement of the Achaeans as the result of incursions by Dorian Greeks who were also responsible for the violent destruction of many other sites in the Peleponese. The Dorians were a people who invaded from the north, putting an end to the supremacy of the Mycenaeans and their civilization, and replacing it with what was to become known as "Helladic" or "Greek" culture, art and architecture. The decline of Mycenaean culture brought to an end the contacts which had existed during almost the whole of the 2nd mill. BCE between Canaan and the two leading cultures of the Aegean.

The distinctive features of all the Aegean civilizations appear especially in their architecture, pottery and writing.

Cretan Architecture: The remains of many large palaces have been discovered in Crete and the Peleponese, all built to the same design: Around a central courtyard, with proportions always in the ratio of 2:3, are reception, administrative, store and living rooms and workshops, all connected by long narrow corridors, intersected by enclosed yards and with light provided by windows in the ceilings. In addition, there are magnificent staircases and many large halls, supported by rows of undecorated columns. The outside walls were covered with orthostats (carved stone slabs) while the inside walls had a single row of orthostats with plaster above it, decorated with coloured

9

stucco in the early buildings. Later on, the walls were given painted frescoes showing realistic pictures of the sea, marine life and vegetation and impressionist scenes of man's daily life, religion, agriculture, athletics, feasting and fighting. One such example is the painting (9) on the throne of King Minos in Knossos. Towards the end of the period, a much greater use was made of carved stone.

Cretan towns lie very close together and — in contrast to the cities of the Peloponese — they were not fortified. This suggests that a powerful central ruler controlled the whole island and the seas around its coasts. It has also emerged from the results of excavations that until their destruction by the Achaeans, none of the towns of Crete had been destroyed except by earthquakes, further indication of a strong single authority. Some unique vaulted tombs were discovered and also some built with conical ceilings. This is a style which originated in Crete but has also been found in Cyprus, in Ugarit (**10**) on the Syrian coast and Mycenae (**11**), and perhaps also in the early excavations of Megiddo made by Schumacher.

Pottery: Mycenaean (Peleponese) pottery was of a very high quality, decorated with motifs taken from the plant and animal worlds, especially those of the sea. Space between the main motifs on a vessel would be filled with designs of the seashore, corals, sea shells, snails and octopii. The designs on the early pottery, the kind exported extensively to Palestine, are naturalistic in style and make use of many colours. Later on, the motifs became much more stylized and were generally executed in black on white. This is the pottery known as the "Palace Style" which dates from the 15th–14th c. BCE (stage B of later Mycenaean). During this period, the earlier styles disappeared and new motifs made their appearance, the best known being the winged bird pluming its feathers (**13, 17**). Small porcelain figurines of women with bare breasts and wearing long skirts (**14**) have been discovered from this period. Presumably they represented priestesses or goddesses. Some of them hold snakes or incense burners decorated with many handles and snakes.

10

11

14

Writing: Three different types of writing developed among the peoples of Crete and the mainland of Greece. The earliest of these is a hieroglyphic writing which has not yet been deciphered. The others, (**15**) "Linear A" and "Linear B" puzzled scholars for years. At last, the latest, "Linear B", dating from the late Mycenaean period III (like the pottery described above) was deciphered by M. Ventriss and was found to be in early Greek. Linear A writing dates from the middle Mycenaean period II.

Aegean Civilization and Palestine: Palestine felt the Aegean's influence most noticeably during its period of decline, i. e. after the destruction of Knossos and the replacement of Minoan civilization by Mycenaean (Late Bronze). During this period, many new coastal settlements and ports were apparently established in Palestine, for instance at Tel abu-Huwam (a trading city of the late Bronze Age onward), Athlit, Dor and others (see Shipping and Navigation*). Through them, trading connections were established with the Aegean, especially Crete and Cyprus, whose products became increasingly familiar in Palestine. All over Syria and Canaan — from Qatna and Ugarit in the north as far south as the Negeb of Palestine — huge quantities of Mycenaean vases have been found. These once contained the perfumes and cosmetics imported from the Aegean during the century and a half around 1375 to 1225 BCE. In return, Canaan exported purple garments, ivory plaques for decorating furniture, gold ornaments, grain, myrrh and balsam.

Cyprus and Palestine: Many scholars are inclined to doubt whether there was any direct contact with the Peleponese or Crete, believing that Mycenaean goods came to Palestine via Cyprus, along with that country's own produce. In this view, many of the discoveries now labelled "Mycenaean ware" may in fact have been made in Cyprus. The problem of differentiation has often bedevilled archaeologists. Nevertheless, the different products can be distinguished and the labels serve a useful purpose.

Aegean and Cypriot Ware in Palestine: Most probably the Aegean pottery found in Palestine came both from Mycenae and from Cyprus. Cypriot pottery was imported in large quantities as early as the beginning of the Late Bronze Age (approx. 1550–1400 BCE) and continued throughout the middle of that period. The Cypriots of this age made good pottery, using a high quality clay and an efficient firing system which gave their glazed vessels a metallic pitch. The vessels are usually made on a ring-like base, hence their name, "base ring ware". There was little variation in form (as shown in this reconstructed Cypriot tomb of the early Iron Age (**16**), all their pottery shapes belonging to five or six main types which are found over and over again (see Pottery*).

The Mycenaean vessels which first appeared in Palestine around 1400 BCE (middle Late Bronze Age) are very fine, made of viscous loam, with a lustrous chrome glaze, and usually decorated with horizontal lines of reddish-brown. Only one example of an earlier vessel, of late Minoan style has been found. This was a cup made in Mycenae in the 15th c. BCE, found in Lachish. All other pottery of this type belongs to the late Mycenaean III period, dating to the 14th–13th c. BCE. It is generally agreed by the scholars

13

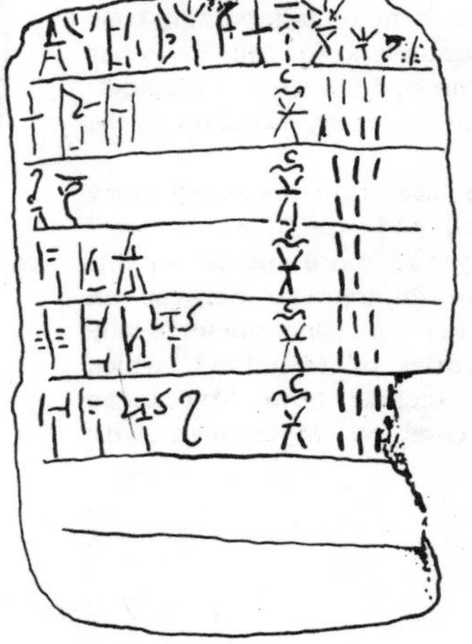

15

15

16

that after 1230 BCE no more Mycenaean pottery was imported into Palestine. Local potters attempted to imitate the style, but without much success. The results are vastly inferior both in material and decoration.

Mycenaean pottery has been excavated from strata belonging to the second half of the late Bronze Age in, amongst other places, Hazor*, Beth-Shean*, Megiddo*, Ta'anach, Shechem*, Jerusalem*, Gezer, Beth-Shemesh*, Lachish*, Tel-beit-Mirsim, Jericho*, Rabbat-Ammon and Medaba in Transjordan, and all along the coast from Tel abu-Hawam to Ashdod*, Ashkelon*, and Tel-Ajjul (south of Gaza).

A number of Mycenaean sacred vessels were also unearthed from Megiddo and Beth-Shean, including bronze jugs for incense decorated with four rings and various reliefs; other bronze jugs in the form of pillars; ring-base pottery libation vessels and containers for oil or other liquids. In addition to these, the tombs discovered at Megiddo by Schumacher are also thought by many scholars to be of Mycenaean origin.

Aegean influence can also be seen from the many ivory miniatures which were imported and which, again, local craftsmen tried to imitate. They had more success in this field for it is often difficult to differentiate between an actual imported Mycenaean ivory and one made locally to Mycenaean designs. The ivories of Megiddo*, which date from the 13th–12th cs., include both Mycenaean originals and pieces which combine Mycenaean with Canaanite forms.

17

18

Again, the same influence can be seen in seals*. Cylinder seals imported from Cyprus and distinguished by their individual motifs and by the quality of their workmanship, have been discovered in many places along the coastal plain, especially at Tel abu-Hawam, and Tel Ajjul.

In the military sphere, contacts with the Aegean had a pronounced effect on Palestine's native methods of warfare. New techniques were adopted such as, for instance, digging secret tunnels to ensure adequate water supplies in case of siege (see Water Supply*). New weapons were also introduced. A number of Egyptian reliefs depicting their wars in Palestine, from the time of Ramses II (1290–1224 BCE) and perhaps even earlier, suggest that the Egyptian army included units mobilized from among various Aegean tribes. At first these were mainly the Sardana (see Philistines*). These units were equipped with metal helmets, cuirasses and, notably, long, straight, double-edged swords (see Arms and Weapons*), all improvements on the locally made and used equipment of the other Near Eastern armies. None of these has so far been discovered in excavations in Palestine but it seems reasonable that by their very superiority they must have influenced the style and manufacture of weapons in Palestine. Votive figurines **(18)** found in the sanctuary of Aya Irini (late Iron Age) represent martial figures and illustrate Cypriot costume, chariots and workmanship in clay.

Aegean influences in Palestine were continued by the "Sea Peoples" and Philistines, whose civilization came directly from the same roots (see Philistines*; Philistine Civilization and Israel*). Trade between Syria and the Aegean appears to have been mainly in their hands up to the 11th c. BCE. The long era of Phoenician trade began later, in the 10th c. BCE (see Phoenicia*).

AGRICULTURE AND ANIMAL HUSBANDRY —

Outline: I. The Land and its Crops: Field Crops; Ploughing and Harvesting; Sowing; Vineyards; Fruit Trees; Olives; The Cycle of Seasons. Poultry Breeding. II. Animal Husbandry: Cattle; Goats; Sheep; Asses; Mules; Camels; Horses. III. Pre-Exilic Land Tenure: Royal Domains; Freehold and Family Property; Irrigation. IV. Post-Exilic Agriculture: Loans to Peasants; the Zenon Papyri; Hasmonean Period; Roman Period; Progress of Land Tenure and Ownership; The Sabbatical Year.

Throughout the biblical period, the main occupation and major source of livelihood of the people of Palestine was agriculture. This gave it a central place in biblical literature. Not only are agricultural activities described in many stories, but similes and metaphors based on agriculture are widely used, even by the most "urban" prophet, Isaiah.

I. THE LAND AND ITS CROPS: The Bible praises the fertility of the "promised land". The widespread remains of ancient settlements which have been found even in regions which are uninhabited today, demonstrate that agriculture

19

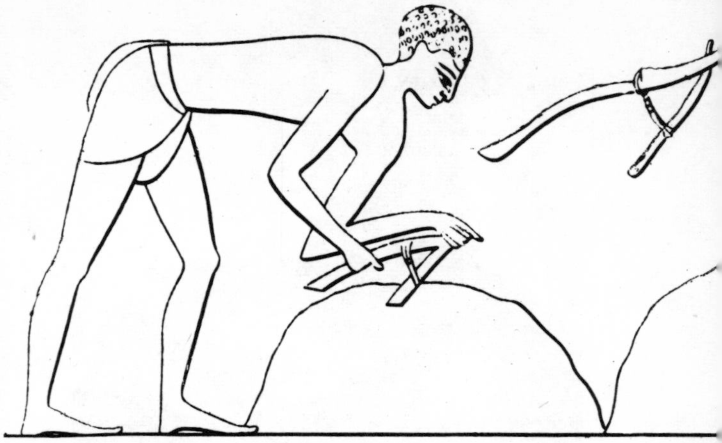

21

was intensive throughout the country and that the land could support large numbers of people. In view of the barrenness of the country under Arab and Turkish rule, a variety of theories were put forward to explain the contrast. Claims that climatic conditions have changed fundamentally in the last two or three thousand years have proved to be unfounded. Modern Jewish settlement of the land has proved that it can support a large population given proper care and husbandry.

Field Crops: The principal crops were grain, wine and olive oil (Dt. 7:13; Hos. 2:8).

Grain, i.e. *wheat* (triticum monocoecum), *barley* (hordeum sativum) and *spelt* (triticum dicoecum), has been found in the ruins of even the earliest settlements, going back to prehistoric times, while mortars (**19**) were found at El-Wad cave. Many authorities agree that grain was first cultivated by people living at the foot of Mount Carmel in the Mesolithic (in Palestine, Natufian) Age (8th millenium BCE) or perhaps even earlier. Vestiges of village life and grain production have also been found in the Lake Huleh region of the northern Jordan Valley dating from the 7th mill. BCE. With other 7th mill. farming villages found at Jarmo in Northern Mesopotamia and at Hacilar in Asia Minor, these are considered the earliest indications of cultivation that have so far been found in the Near East. Although the oldest town yet discovered, Jericho* (see article) goes back to the 8th millenium, this was a walled town, depending on trade, probably in salt and bitumen and revealing no traces of special agricultural developments although, obviously, there must have been regular food production to support its population. In Egypt, no village life has yet been found earlier than the late 5th mill. BCE.

Grain silos have been found in the underground dwelling caves of prehistoric man of the Chalcolithic Age (4th millenium) near Beersheba (Tel abu Matar). The silos, bell shaped and with a capacity of 40–55 litres were found both in the living chambers and the connecting galleries. From the later Bronze and Iron Ages, silos dug into the floors of houses for the storage of grain from one year to the next and larger granaries serving a communal or administrative purpose become a commonplace of excavations. Of these, the best preserved and largest is the stone lined silo at Megiddo, from the time of Jeroboam II (8th c. BCE), or the granary excavated at Gezer (**20**).

Ploughing and Harvesting: The earliest fields were worked with hoes. In the Stone Age these were made of a sharpened flint attached to a wooden stick (**21**). Wooden implements, digging sticks, etc. were used earlier, in the opinion of some scholars, but the remains of this "wood age" which may have come before the Stone Age, have disappeared from the wet soil of Israel. Presumably, stone implements were used along

20

22

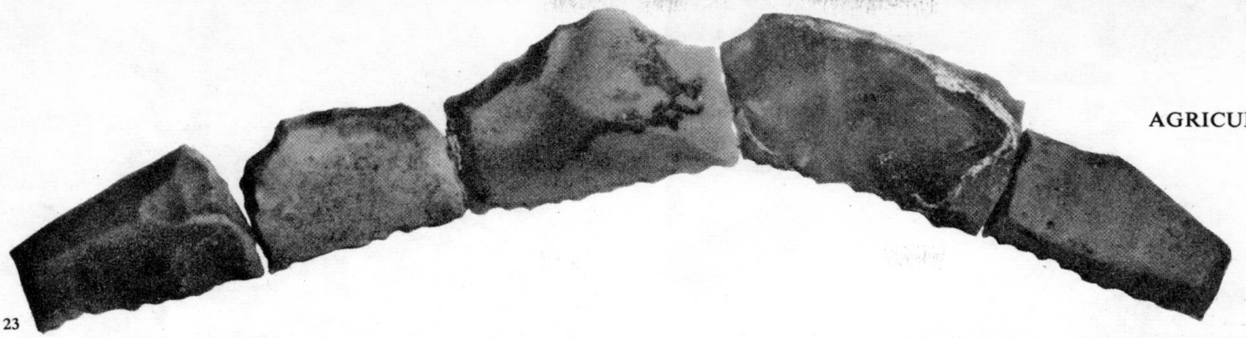

23

with wood from the earliest times, as shown by hand-axes used by men who lived in caves several millenia before the Mesolithic and Neolithic ages (**22**). The substitution of bronze for stone in the third millenium meant an improvement in implements. Bronze hoes bearing the name of the priest were uncovered at Ugarit. These were probably used in ceremonies meant to ensure the fertility of the soil, for bronze was in use much earlier than Ugarit.

The biggest step forward came with the introduction of the plough. Ploughs were made — as they still are today in primitive communities — of a piece of wood, later tipped with metal, drawn by one or two oxen. At the beginning of the Israelite period (early Iron Age), copper or bronze was used but, by the 11th century (Late Iron Age), iron had been introduced. At first (I Sam 13:20), manufacture and repair of iron implements was monopolized by the Philistines*, who may have introduced the use of iron into Israel. From the Neolithic to the late Bronze Age, flint sickles (**23**) were used in harvesting. About 1100–1000 BCE iron began to be used for all types of tools and weapons (see Philistines*) and iron sickles displaced the flint ones. By the time of the divided monarchy, it is clear from the number of iron agricultural tools that have been found that the metal was readily available to everyone. Even so, a plough of this type could only scratch the surface to a depth of 7–10 cms. It could not turn the soil into a furrow (see illus. under Crafts: Ploughs).

Sowing: The basic grain crops were wheat and barley. The wheat was of a very poor variety compared to modern strains. Rye was unknown apparently. By the time of the monarchy, other seeds such as spelt and flax were also sown. Sowing was done by scattering the seed by hand. The land was then ploughed again to cover it, branches being dragged behind the plough to smooth the ground over the seed, (Is. 28:24–5; Job 39:10). It might take weeks of laborious work for the Israelite to sow a small field.

Vineyards: Economically, vineyards came second in importance to fields, but they needed a great deal more care and evoked a strong attachment in their owners — as witness the story of Naboth's vineyard. A vineyard was a precious possession. It called for much hard work — it had to be weeded and fenced and a stone watch tower erected to guard it against animals and marauders — and then many years of waiting were needed before it came to fruition.

The grain harvest was a festive season, as we learn from the Book of Ruth, but the grape gathering was even more important for the peasant.

Vines were grown sometimes as bushes or small trees; in other cases, fig trees might be used to support the vines. From this came the phrase "every man under his own vine and under his fig tree" (1 K. 4:25) as a symbol of an ideal of social well-being.

The "Song of the Vineyard" (Isaiah **5**) is a moving parable of the care demanded by a vineyard, which gives a vivid description of the agricultural operations involved. It is typical of Isaiah that he used such a parable to plead for justice for the small man and the peasant, "Woe to those who join . . . field to field" (5:8).

Nothing remains of these ancient vineyards. The little heaps of stone which cover many slopes in the Negeb were once taken for vestiges of vineyards or grapevine hills, but this is now known to have been a mistake. They were used to divert rain water from hill slopes to terraced "wadis" or cisterns. What do remain are the grape-presses although the ones known are from post-Exilic times.

Grape Presses: When the grapes were ripe, they were gathered and dumped, one or two baskets at a time, into a small vat whose floor sloped down towards a small basin. The grapes were trampled by foot to extract the juice, as pictured in this Egyptian tomb painting (ca. 2300 BCE) showing men treading out grapes to the accompaniment of music (**24**). Some of the grape presses found in the Judean lowlands (the Shephelah), may also have been used to extract olive oil by a similar method. Wine presses cut in solid rock (**25**) abound in Judah and Samaria. Some are single square vats for treading out the grapes. Others had three sections, one where the grapes were trodden, one for refining and one for storing the juice. One of the oldest known is the 7th c. wine press at Gibeon with dipping basin and stone trough, left, and openings to four vats, right (**25a, b**).

Fruit Trees: Figs (*ficus carica*): Figs were a staple of the country's diet, being, with dates, one of the ancient Near East's main sources of sugar.

An alternate variety was the *sycamore fig*, grown mainly in southern Palestine. Amos (7:14) was "a dresser of sycamore trees", meaning that he punctured the green fig while still on the tree, to ensure the softening of the fruit, after which it rapidly ripened and became edible. One of the officials of David's government was responsible for his olive and sycamore fig plantations (I Ch. 27:28).

Fig syrup, like that of carobs, was used for sweetening, while dried and pressed figs were a convenient preserve, easy to transport and acceptable as gifts. Abigail gave David

24

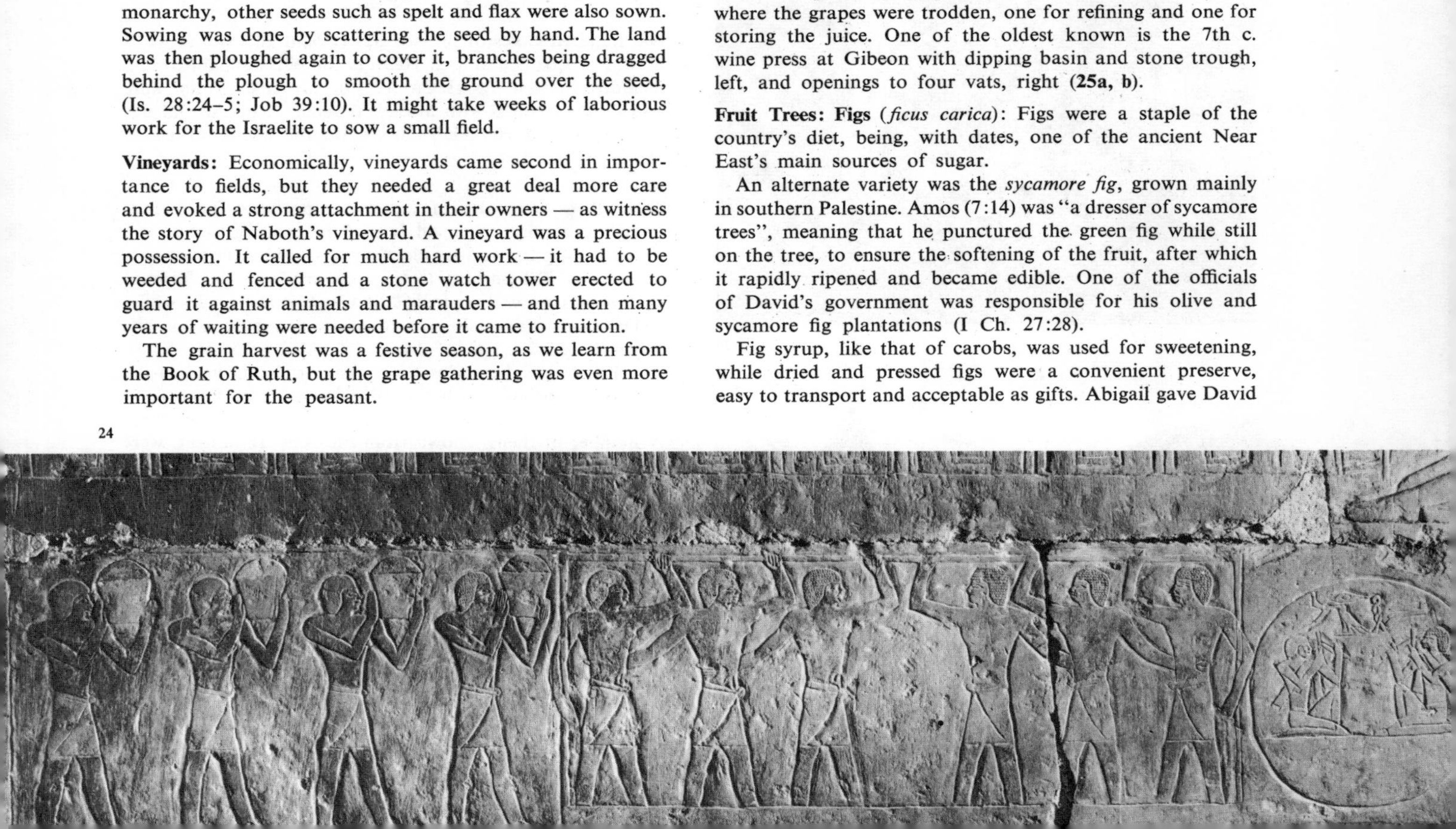

25 a

25 b

26

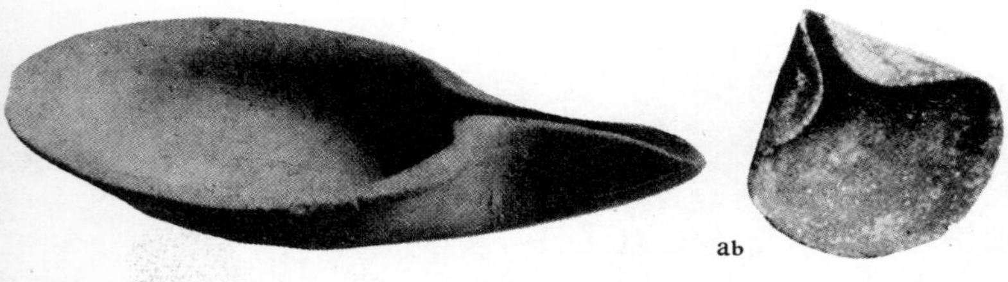

ab

two hundred cakes of pressed figs (I Sam 28:18) and when he was proclaimed king at Hebron, the gifts brought to him included pressed figs (I Ch. 12:40). Moreover, they were apparently credited with medicinal value. A poultice of figs was applied to Hezekiah's boils, on the advice of Isaiah (38:21; II K. 20:7).

Olive Trees were also of supreme importance for biblical Israel's economy. Olive oil is used in cooking, for lamps, for cosmetic purposes, as a cleaning agent and in the treatment of wounds. Oil burning lamps were made in the form of shallow saucers with a pinched lip which held a wick **26**ab

There are many allusions to olives and olive oil in the Bible, (Ex. 27:20; I K. 17:14; Is. 1:6; Mic. 6:15; Mt. 25:3). The Feast of Tabernacles which was originally held in the fall was associated with the olive harvest (see Festivals*). Many place-names were connected with olive growing. A number of them, known from the New Testament, were near Jerusalem: Bethzetha (the "House of the Olive"), the mount of Olives, and Gethsemane, in Hebrew, Gath-shemen — oil press (Mk. 14:32).

To extract the oil, the ripe olives were put into the vat and then either trodden or pounded with a stone or pestle — the oil thus produced was the finer "beaten oil". The pulp left behind was then placed under heavy weights to squeeze out the rest of the oil. Commercial oil presses had large vats which would be filled with olives and heavily weighted. Presses like this dating from the 10th to 6th centuries BCE, were found at Debir and Beth-Shemesh (see Crafts*); a press at Gezer is shown above; vats below (**27a, b**). Part of the payment Solomon made to Hiram, King of Tyre, for cedar wood and carpenters supplied for the building of the Temple was in olive oil, in lots of 20,000 quat.

Other fruit trees were the *date palm*, *pistachio*, *apricot*, *mulberry* and *pomegranate* (Punicum granatum).

The Cycle of Seasons: Because of the fundamental importance of agriculture, the year was divided and festivals timed in relation to the farmer and his needs. Even where festivals later acquired a religious and national significance, they retain traces of their original function as the festive seasons of an agricultural community. The biblical civil calendar* (see article) gave the months numbers, counting from the first (fall) month to the twelfth (cf. Jos. 4:19; I K. 12:32 ff). This system originated with the Israelites and replaced the Canaanite nomenclature. The peasants, whether Canaanite or Hebrew, listed the months according to the tasks to be performed in the different periods of the agricultural year. This is illustrated by a stone tablet from Gezer (**28**) assumed to be part of a 10th century BCE schoolboy's exercise. It is not an official calendar. In seven lines, it lists the months and seasons as:

1: 2 *months Olive Harvest* (Sept/Oct or Oct/Nov), first the picking of the olives then the pressing for oil.

2: 2 *months Sowing:* The next two months (Nov./Dec or Dec/Jan) come, in Israel, after the first winter rains and, as a rule, after the ploughing, done at the end of October and early November. This was the grain-sowing season.

3: 2 *months Late Planting:* January to March was the time for sowing millet, sesame, lentils, chick peas, melons, cucumbers and so on.

4: 1 *month Hoeing:* This was especially the period for cutting the flax. This was done with a hoe as the plants must be cut close to the ground so that the full length of the stalk can be used, when dried and treated, (see Clothing*) to make thread and cloth.

5: 1 *month Grain Harvest:* Barley is harvested in April in the south and in May in the north. Wheat and spelt come later in May/June. The grain was cut by a sickle, made before the 10th cent. BCE from flint chips set in a haft made of wood or bone. Later, a small curved wooden blade was affixed to a wooden handle. The grain was separated from the straw and husks by spreading the cut plants on a specially prepared threshing floor outside the village and then driving oxen round and round,over it, pulling a threshing sledge (**29**) which might be flat or on small rollers (Is.

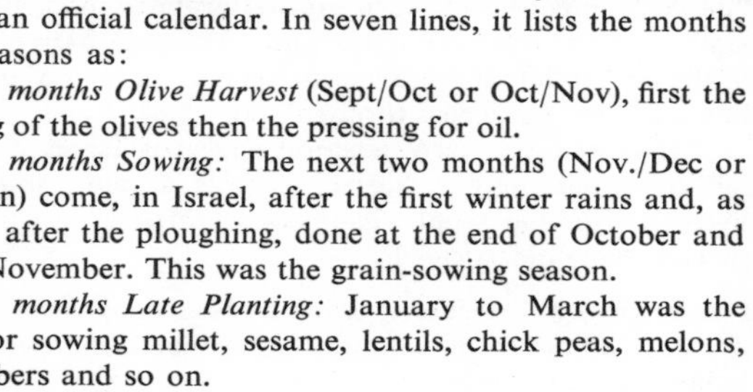

29

27 a

29 b

28

THE SHEAVES ARE SPREAD OUT ON A THRESHING-FLOOR AND DONKEYS, KEPT MOVING IN A CIRCLE BY FREQUENT BLOWS FROM STICKS, TREAD OUT THE GRAIN. AT THE LEFT THE STALKS ARE COLLECTED WITH A PITCH-FORK INTO A HUGE STACK.

WINNOWING IS DONE BY LIFTING THE GRAIN HIGH IN THE AIR IN A PAIR OF WINNOWING SCOOPS HELD EDGE TO EDGE WHICH WHEN SEPARATED ALLOW THE GRAIN TO FALL WHILE THE CHAFF IS CARRIED ASIDE BY THE WIND. A PILE IS SWEPT TOGETHER BY A GIRL WITH A BROOM IN EACH HAND.

THRESHING

FROM A WALL-RELIEF IN THE TOMB OF RAEMKAÏ FROM SAKKARA, NOW IN THE METROPOLITAN MUSEUM OF ART. DYN. V (ABOUT 2750-2625 B.C.)

WINNOWING

FROM A WALL-RELIEF IN THE TOMB OF PAHERI AT EL KAB. DYN. XVIII (ABOUT 1500 B.C.)

30

28:27–8). The grain was then winnowed and sieved, see Egyptian painting (**30**) and finally stored in large jars. Rooms full of such jars are not uncommon in excavations.

6: 1 *month Festivals:* Seven weeks from the beginning of the grain harvest (Dt. 16:9) or at about the time it was completed, a pilgrimage was made to the sanctuary bearing an offering of "first fruits" for the festival of Pentecost (Shavuoth; see Festivals*). In later usage, the Hebrew terms for "early harvest" or "first fruits" have acquired the wider meaning of "choice" fruits or produce.

7: 2 *months Vine Tending:* During the hot summer months of June/July or July/August, after the grain harvest, vines were pruned and the vineyards weeded and cleaned in preparation for the grape harvest.

8: 1 *month Summer Fruits:* The last month of the agricultural calendar (August/Sept.) was devoted to harvesting summer fruit, especially grapes, figs and pomegranates.

The names of the months gradually changed to the Babylonian terms, which were probably adopted for official use either in the 8th century BCE when both Israel and Judah were under Assyrian control, or when Judah became a vassal of Babylonia in the late 6th century. After the Exile they came into general use and have been preserved in Hebrew ever since. According to the oldest liturgical calendars, (Ex. 23:14–17; 34:18–23), the first month, Nisan, during which the feast of Unleavened Bread was celebrated, began in the spring, approximately March-April in modern terms. An autumnal year was introduced in Hellenistic times and was gradually adopted by the Jews, the year beginning either end Elul or Tishri (September-October) at the Feast of Ingathering (see Calendar*; Festivals*).

Poultry breeding: The earliest evidence of chicken farming came from a seal (**31**) showing a cock found in Tel-el-Nasbeh (ancient Mizpeh) and dating from about 600 BCE.

31

II. ANIMAL HUSBANDRY: — Sheep breeding was one of the Hebrews' earliest occupations and it continued to be an important activity. The most rational way of exploiting the poorer soils of the hilly parts of the country, especially around Jerusalem and to the south, was for sheep and cattle raising. The Hebrew word "midbar", usually translated as "desert", in fact means such grazing grounds, poor pasture-land unfit for intensive agriculture. The real barren desert of the far south had other names, such as "a land of drought in a land that none pass through" (Jer. 2:6).

Throughout the early pastoral stages of Israelite life in biblical times, animal husbandry was a main source of livelihood for the people. Animals of different varieties and species were domesticated.

Cattle: (*Baqar* in Hebrew) is the biblical designation for all domestic animals belonging to the bovinae sub-group of the hollow-horned family. The origins of cattle in Israel are rather obscure, though it is thought that the wild ox (bos primigenius) was the first beast to be so called. Pre-historic engravings found on rocks at Kilwah in Transjordan depict a gigantic specimen of the bovine family, but no conclusion can be drawn from this engraving as to the animal's domesticity. Domestication of animals began in several parts of Asia and Europe at about the same time, although it is not certain exactly where or when. Forms, including horns and bones, of ancient cattle found in the Jericho and Gezer excavations are of various domestic animals. R.A.S. Macalister pointed out at the beginning of this century that while the species or breed of cattle found in Israel varies from one stratum of excavation to the other, all are of the short-horned variety, including the oxen bones unearthed at Megiddo*. Mosaics and paintings found in Israel, dating from the Roman and Byzantine periods, show zebu-like cattle, which are unlike the cattle unearthed in the earlier excavations. In the later drawings and paintings of the same period, zebu-like and short-horned cattle appear in the same herd.

The zebu cattle were common in Mesopotamia and Egypt in very early times and were later brought to Asia Minor and Syria. The types of cattle prevalent there underwent some changes, i.e. the short-horned and zebu-like cattle replaced the long-horns that had been common, as in this late Phoenician mosaic (**32**).

In biblical times there were great numbers of cattle in Israel, and in both the semi-nomadic and settled stages of society the extent of a man's wealth was measured by the number of heads he owned. The stalled ox was a symbol of luxury (Pr. 15:17).

It is obvious from drawings, engravings (**33**), bas-reliefs (**34**) and inscriptions found in the ancient Near Eastern countries that cattle were plentiful and used for sacrificial rites as well as for ploughing, threshing and transport. The Bible refers several times to the farming uses of cattle (Is. 30:24; Job 1:14; Dt. 25:4; Hos. 10:11; Nu. 7:3; I Sam. 6:7; I Ch. 12:40). Oxen were harnessed to a yoke for ploughing (I K. 19:19; Nu. 19:2; I Sam. 6:7) and urged on by a goad (Jud. 3:31) or a spur (I Sam. 13:21). Cattle used for such farming work and for transport were kept in stables or stalls, while the others, who were in the majority, were left to graze in pastures. The best grazing areas in Israel were in Bashan, which was famed for its high quality cows (Ezk. 39:18; Ps. 22:12). The Sharon and other valleys in the country also contained many rich grazing fields. The importance of cattle to the economy of the country led King David* to apoint special commissioners of cattle in those areas (I Ch. 27:29).

Milking cattle were not widespread in Israel, and the few dairy products mentioned in the Old Testament, such as milk and butter (sour-milk was presumably meant by "butter" in the Old Testament) came from sheep and goats (see below; Dt. 32:14; I Sam. 17:18; II Sam. 17:29). In Egypt and Mesopotamia milking cattle were more common. Beef, however, was regarded as a delicacy in Israel and was served at royal banquets or when important guests were entertained (Gn. 18:7; I K. 4:23). Cattle dung was used as fuel, but was not well regarded (Ezk. 4:15).

Goats: The wild goat of Persia (capra aegagius), which was apparently the progenitor of the domestic goat, was also common in the Aegean Islands, Asia Minor, Syria, Mesopotamia, Afghanistan and northwestern India. There are numerous species of goats differing from each other in build and length of hair, ears and horns. Unlike other cattle, the goat can exist in extremely arid areas. In ancient times, it was the only source of meat for the semi-nomads, and was raised by the Patriarchs (Gn. 15:9 passim). Kid meat was regarded as an excellent food (Gn. 27:9) although adult goats were not considered very highly. They were more important as suppliers of hair for tent and garment cloth, carpets and harnessing for horses and camels, while their skins were used for leather flasks for water, wine and oil.

Milk Products: Goats' milk was drunk, churned into butter or soured into clabbered milk. Known as "leben" in Arabic, this was made from both goats' and sheep's milk by adding a little to fresh milk to make it ferment. Shaken violently

33

34

in a goatskin bag, it became semi-solid and, with the water squeezed out, yielded a soft cheese (see Arab scene (**35**).

Sheep: Most of the eleven species of wild sheep which are known originated in Asia, but the domestic sheep has been familiar in Palestine and Syria for so long that its original home is uncertain. Probably it derives from some of the west Asian varieties of wild sheep. Israel's sheep are of the fat tail variety, in which the tail may reach a weight of 10 or 11 pounds. As this was considered a delicacy — the fat of the tail is still regarded as the choice portion in the East — the whole tail was burned when a sheep was sacrificed (Ex. 29:22; Lv. 3:9; 7:3; 8:25; 9:19).

The best time for shearing sheep is in the spring, after the last heavy rains, when the nights are no longer cold and cannot harm the shorn ewes, or affect their milk yield. In biblical times a second shearing might sometimes take place in the summer, but this was very rare. The shearing was a day of festivity and rejoicing. The sheep-farmer would invite his relatives and friends to come and watch the shepherds and shearers and when the shearing was over, would provide entertainment and a sumptuous feast for them all.

The Sheep in Biblical Metaphor: There are hundreds of references to sheep, sheepfolds and shepherds in the Bible. From the Patriarchs of Genesis, to the shepherds grazing their flocks below Bethlehem, the sheep was enough a part of daily life for almost every family to have its pet sheep as a plaything for the children, even drinking from their cup (II Sam. 12:3). A fruitful flock was a sign of economic prosperity (Ps. 144: 13) and also something demanding constant care and watchfulness. The shepherd of a hundred sheep would yet rejoice over one lost lamb that was returned (Mt. 18:12–13). This is literally illustrated by a Syrian statuette of a shepherd carrying a lamb (**38**) made almost two millenia before.

Above all, the purity and meekness of sheep and their loyalty to their shepherd provided a natural image for the New Testament writers who thought of Jesus as the "Lamb of God" and saw his death on the cross as a parallel to the slaughter of the innocent lamb brought to the altar in expiation of the people's sins (Rev. 5:6–8; I Co. 5:7; Jn. 1:29; see Sacrifice*, Jewish Christians*).

The relationship of a shepherd to his sheep also inspired the prophets (e.g. Ezk. 34) or the psalmist (e.g. Psalm 23, "The Lord is my Shepherd, I shall not want", or Psalm 78:52–53). Jesus used the same symbol for his parable of the Good Shepherd (Jn. 10:1–18) and the parable of Mt. 12:11–12.

Asses: The ass belongs to the same family as the horse and developed mainly in warm areas like Arabia and North Africa, the biblical domestic ass being a descendant of the African wild ass. Apparently asses were domesticated in the fourth millenium BCE. Discoveries in Egypt reflect its wide-spread use there as a beast of burden as early as the pre-dynastic age. The kings of Mesopotamia owned caravans of asses as early as the 3rd mill. BCE and they are mentioned again during the reign of Hammurabi (18th cent. BCE). Evidence for the use of asses in the 19th and 18th centuries BCE has also been found in Cappodocia of Asia Minor and from the records of Mari. The first caravans in the Near East were probably of asses, as illustrated in the 19th century BCE painting of the caravan of Beni-Hasan (see Clothing*). Inscriptions in the Temple of No-Amon in Egypt speak of asses sent from Canaan to Egypt as tribute in the 15th century BCE, while Mesopotamian sources of the period refer to the ass as being used in farming and for transport. In Patriarchal times, before camels came into general use, the ass was the Hebrews' most important means of transport (see below).

The Bible frequently mentions asses as valuable possessions. Even its manner of feeding is noted (Gn. 42:27; Jud. 19:19). An abundance of asses was a sign of riches (Gn. 12:16; 30: 43). Asses were used to carry loads (Gn. 45:23; II Sam. 16:1; Neh. 13:15) and for women to ride (Jos. 15:18; I Sam. 25:20). However, for a man to ride an ass was considered a sign of modesty (Zec. 9:9). For earthly kings, such a conveyance was a humiliation. After the conquest of Megiddo, Thutmosis III sent off the rulers of the defeated countries on asses — instead of in their chariots. Kings and knights rode on mules (David) or in chariots pulled by horses. The messianic king, however, would ride on a beast of peace. This is

35

38

the basis for the legendary description of Jesus' entry into Jerusalem riding on an ass's colt (Lk. 19:30 ff; Mk. 11:4 ff).

The Law* of Moses forbids harnessing an ass and an ox to the same plough (Dt. 22:10), although both animals were used in farming. Other specific laws, such as resting the ass on the Sabbath day; returning a lost ass to its owner; or helping the owner of an ass which had fallen under the weight of its burden, all bear witness to the important place which this animal occupied in the Israelite economy. King David* appointed a special overseer of asses (I Ch. 27:30).

The exiles returning from Babylonia brought with them thousands of asses (Ezr. 2:67; Neh. 7:69). To some extent the ass was used in war (II K. 7:7), perhaps to draw war chariots (Is. 21:7). It is known that in the 8th century BCE, an Assyrian military unit included two asses among other draft animals.

Mules: ("pered" in Hebrew) are the offspring of the big he-ass and a mare. They are very strong and hardy pack animals and although forbidden by Mosaic Law (Lv. 19:19), were used early in the Monarchy (II Sam. 13:29). David even rode on one (I K. 1:33) and they became quite common afterwards. Importing mules was an important item in trade, Ezekiel (27:14) referring to obtaining them from Togarmah (north of Assyria). They were known in Egypt as well as Assyria. According to Ezra (2:66) the returning Israelites brought 245 mules with them from Babylon.

Camels: There are two varieties of camel, the single hump (c. dromedarius), common in the west and south of Asia and in North Africa, and the double hump (c. bactrianus) found mainly in central Asia. The camel's unique physical qualities enable it to survive the severe conditions of the desert. It can feed on the hard, thorny desert plants, can store food and water for several days in its stomach and nourish itself on the fat and water accumulated in its hump. The thick layer of padding on its paws makes it possible for the camel to plod along the hot shifting sand of the desert routes and on the paths in the rocky regions. These abilities together with its swaying walk have earned the camel the title of "ship of the desert". (See single-humped baby camel **39** .

The Bible contains numerous references to the uses of the camel (Gn. 12:16; 24:10; 31:17; 32:7, 15) but few to its habits and manner of living. According to Old Testament tradition, camels were commonly used by the ancient Hebrews from the days of Abraham (Gn. 12:16; 24:10; 31:7, 15). Several scholars have advanced evidence that the general use of the camel began during the last quarter of the second millenium BCE. However, more recent research (J.P. Free) warrants the view that the references to camels as early as Patriarchal times are not necessarily anachronistic.

The single hump camel which was one of the first animals to be utilized by man, was known at the end of the Mesolithic (Middle Stone) age. Carvings of two single hump domesticated camels were found in Kilwah, southeast of Transjordan, dating from that early period. In eastern Turkestan bones of a domesticated bactrian camel from the Chalcolithic age were discovered. Later archaeological materials seem, in the opinion of some scholars, to prove the large scale domestication of the camel at the end of the 2nd millenium BCE. There are no references to camel caravans in any source before the 12th–11th centuries BCE and other scholars consider that camels came into use for transport shortly before or after that date. In Mesopotamia, carvings from the time of Tiglat-Pileser I (ca 1100 BCE) and Shalmaneser III (9th c. BCE) were found (**40**). These show Bactrian camels being presented as gifts to the Assyrian

39

40

kings. The inscription of Shalmaneser III, in which he boasts of his victory in the Battle of Qarqar (853 BCE) refers to Gindibu the Arabian who commanded a battalion of one-thousand camel(s) (riders?). The camel was an important means of transportation for both domestic and military purposes (I Sam. 30:17; Is. 21:7). The camel was also a vital factor in the development of the caravan trade-routes, as it is able to cover some 60 to 90 miles per day and carry a load of 450 to 500 pounds (Gn. 37:25; I K. 10:2; I Ch. 12: 40). A straw cushion was placed on its hump to make riding more comfortable (Gn. 31:34), particularly for the women and families the beast transported (Gn. 24:61; 31:17). The camel was also used for ploughing, its wool for weaving and its dung for manure. It is possible that in the Patriarchal* period the milk of the she-camel was drunk, indicated by the fact that Jacob sent milking she-camels, together with their calves, as a present to Esau (Gn. 32:15). This is doubted, however, by scholars who consider the camel an anachronism in these days. In the time of David*, there were many camels in Israel and Obil the Ishmaelite was appointed their overseer (I Ch. 27:30).

Assyrian records of the beginning of the first millenium BCE contain the first references to the oases in the Syrian and Arabian deserts, e.g. Emah, Dumah and Dedan. Apparently these were important centres for international caravan trade. The Bible records that Israel's neighbours, notably the nomadic elements among them, were rich in camel herds (Gn. 37:25; Ju. 6:5; 8:21, 26; I Sam. 15:3; 27:9; I K. 10:2; II K. 8:9; I Ch. 5:21; II Ch. 9:1; 14:14; Jer. 49:29). The exiles returning from Babylon brought considerable numbers of camels with them and without question they must have been used for transport (Neh. 7:69). The camel is not mentioned often in the New Testament. John the Baptist wore an outer garment of camel hair (Mt. 3:4; Mk. 1:6) and Jesus refers to the camel in one or two pithy sayings (Mt. 19:24; 23:24).

Horses: The horse developed in the wide grazing lands of the steppes of Asia and Europe and seems to have reached Canaan from southwestern Asia. It appears to have been the last of the draft and transport animals to be domesticated. This took place around the same time in western Europe, southwestern Asia and Mongolia. The horse is mentioned in Akkadian documents of the end of the 3rd millenium BCE where it is called the "mountain ass" or "foreign ass". It is referred to as "an ass of the west" in a fable of the time of Hammurabi (1750 BCE). This coincides with the early period of the Hyksos who introduced the horse into Egypt for military purposes, particularly drawing war chariots. The Bible states that horses originated in Egypt and that the kings of Aram and the Hittites purchased their horses there (I K. 10:28–29). However such an origin has not been verified by archaeology. It seems more likely that the horses were first brought to Egypt from the north. The passage in I K. 10 suggests that horses seem to have come from Cilicia (Asia Minor), while chariots came from Egypt. The passage is quite difficult but the implication is that Solomon acted as middleman, getting the chariots from Egypt and the horses from Kue (Cilicia). This Egyptian horse dates from ca. 1415 (**41**).

Mounted cavalry first appeared in the Near East around 1000 BCE, although it had previously been used by northern

41

42

peoples in the Black Sea region. Warriors on horse-back are shown on the bas-relief of Tel Halaf (**42**) at the beginning of the 9th cent. BCE, and some cavalry were introduced into the Assyrian army at about the same time.

Dt. (17:16) expressly forbids the king of Israel to increase greatly the number of his horses "nor cause the people to return to Egypt to the end that he should multiply his horses" (see Deuteronomy*, Date). This suggests that Egypt was the main source of supply for the horses used in Palestine.

Under the governorship of Joseph*, horses and cattle were accepted in Egypt in exchange for bread. During the Exodus*, the Egyptians pursued the Israelites with chariots and horses (Ex. 14: 9). When the Israelites arrived in Canaan, they found that the Canaanites already had horses and war chariots (Jos. 11:4). The Bible and Egyptian and Assyrian inscriptions frequently mention horses, mainly in connection with war. The Bible refers to horsemen and those who drive

43

a horse or a chariot (Is. 28:28; Ezk. 27:14; Joel 2:4; II Sam. 1:6). The mare is used as a symbol of beauty in the Song of Songs (1:9). The term *'abîr* (a mighty one) is synonymous with a swift war horse (Jud. 5:22; Jer. 8:16; 47:3; 50:11), while *reḥesh* refers to a riding or chariot horse (I K. 4:28; Mic. 1:13; Est. 6:8, 10).

In the time of David*, the Arameans and Canaanites had large numbers of chariots and war horses. But the Israelites still made no use of them. David is reported to have destroyed the animals and it was Absalom, apparently, who was the first to have a chariot and horses (II Sam. 15: 1). Solomon, who had 1400 chariots and 12,000 horsemen (I K. 10:26) built many stables in chariot towns, and developed an extensive international trade in horses and chariots (see above). In the archaeological excavations at Megiddo*, stables large enough to accommodate 450 horses were unearthed. They belonged to the kings of Israel (see Megiddo*), the present ones, apparently, to Ahab, but it is certain that Solomon had stables there as well. Ahab's interest in horses appears from the story of the drought which occurred during his reign and his concern to find grass to save them (I K. 18:5).

Although horses were used almost exclusively for military purposes — hardly at all in farming — the Israelites had no cavalry. In stories of the monarchical period, the term "parashîm" which is often translated "horsemen" or cavalry", meant either chariot teams or the men who rode in chariots, like those shown in this Assyrian engraving (**43**). Even much later, during the time of the Maccabees, the Jews could field only infantry against the Syrians, at least in their first encounters. Herod, however, had 6,000 cavalry in his army, besides 30,000 infantrymen.

III. PRE-EXILIC LAND TENURE: There were many different types of agricultural property in the country. After the Conquest of Cannan, where land had been held on a feudal system (see Cities*, Canaanite) the Hebrews introduced a new social order and a new system of land tenure. The area allotted to a tribe was divided into large estates and allocated by lot to heads of families or clans, (Nu. 33:54; 34:13; 26:54; Jos. 13–21). Inheritance went first to sons, then daughters if there were no sons, then other next of kin if there were no children (Nu. 27:6–11). Land could not pass from one tribe to another (Nu. 36:1–13).

Before the monarchy, the tribal areas were not clearly defined and the amount of land included in them fluctuated. Under the monarchy, the boundaries became more firmly fixed.

The story of David records that Nabal, Abigail's unfortunate husband (I Sam 25) had great possessions in Carmel (of Judah) plus 3,000 sheep and 1,000 goats. The story of Ruth pictures Boaz as a wealthy farmer, although on a smaller scale.

In theory, landed property was held by inalienable right by the tribe, the clan or the family. It was not subject to the will of the king. Nor does anything in the biblical code suggest different treatment for the average landowner or one who served in the king's army. In practice, there are one or two indirect indications that the "Gibborim" (heroes) who went to war were granted extensive privileges denied to those who did not.

The kings themselves were great landowners and much interested in agriculture. Saul, for instance, received the call to rule while ploughing with his oxen, (I Sam 11:5) while II Chronicles (26:10 ff) records of King Uzziah that "he built towers in the wilderness, and hewed out many cisterns, for he had large herds, both in the Shephelah and in the plain, and he had farmers and vinedressers in the hills and in the fertile lands, for he loved the soil." This 15th c. Egyptian painting shows a landowner receiving his produce (**44**).

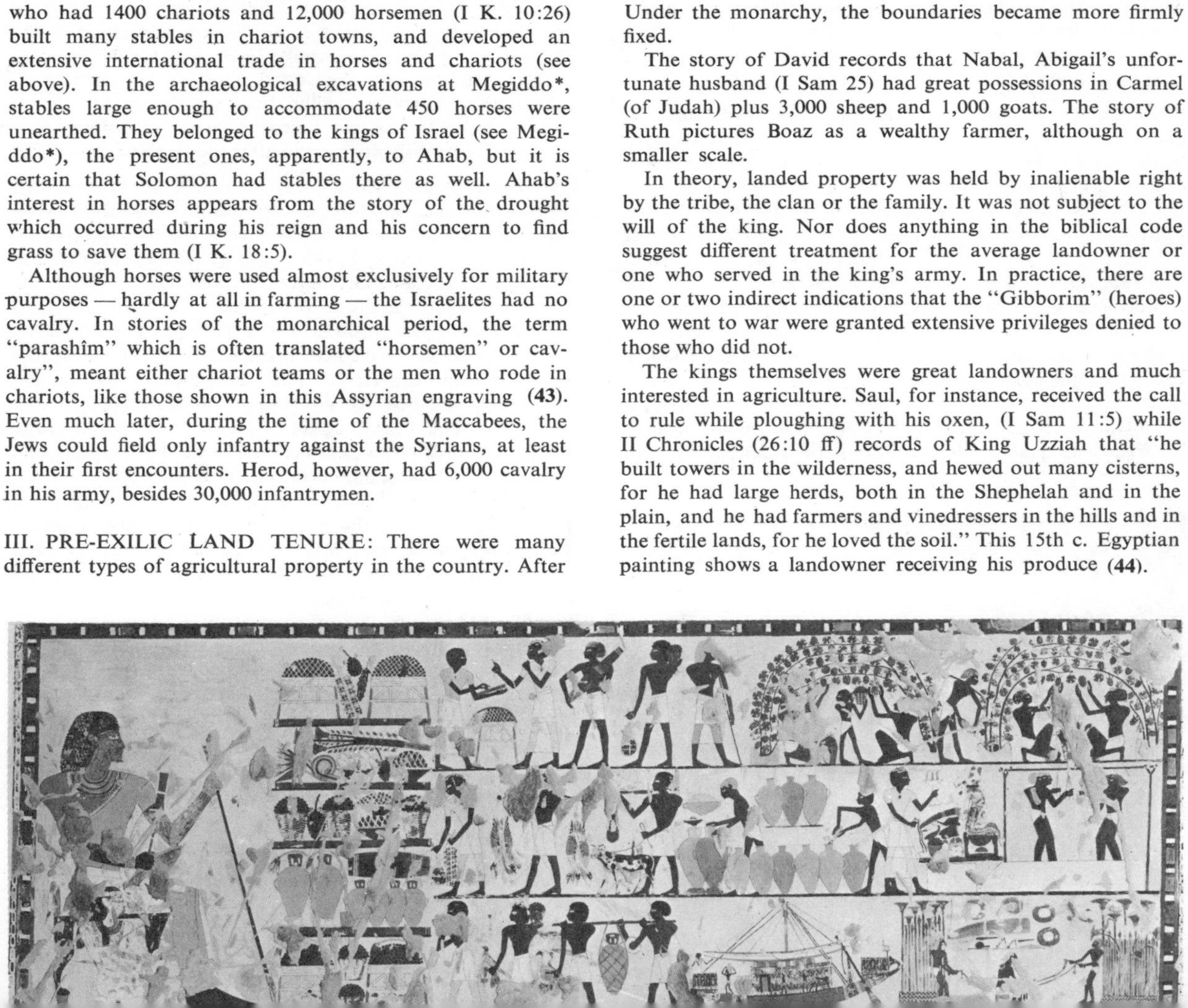

44

Royal Domains were worked by peasants who were obliged to give part of their labour to the king. A letter recently discovered in an Israelite settlement on the coast near Jabneh from the time of Josiah provides an interesting commentary on their position. One of the workers complained to the governor of the fort where the letter was found, that the foreman had taken his coat as a punishment for negligence (**45**; see Inscriptions*).

Freehold and Family Property: The only very large holdings, worked by slaves or tenant-farmers holding on lease, were in the Negeb and Transjordania. There were only a few of these. Most of the Israelite settlements were in the hilly regions and, for practical purposes, had to be divided into small estates. Thus the bulk of the land was farmed in small and middle-size holdings.

During the monarchy, the system of tenant farming under which the farmer paid a proportion (usually half) of the produce as rent to the landowner who furnished stock and seed became more prevalent. Amos (5:11) condemns the rich for taking tribute from the corn of the poor.

Side by side with the tenant-farmers, a free land-owning peasantry continued to exist. Family holdings, however, were threatened by the parcellization of land which resulted from the law of inheritance (a holding had to be divided among a man's children or next of kin, see above). It did not pass on intact from one generation to the next. The holdings that resulted were often too small to support a man and his family. Richer landowners and moneylenders took advantage of the difficulties of the poor and of the widow (who had no rights of inheritance in land) and orphan to buy up freeholds. This trend is condemned repeatedly by the prophets, especially Isaiah, Jeremiah and Amos (see below: The progress of land tenure and ownership; and article on Property, Land and its Conveyance*).

Irrigation: In biblical times irrigation was hardly used in agriculture, the agriculturalist depending on what wells he could dig for his cattle and what rain fell for his fields. Unlike Egypt and Babylon, where administration and political life were greatly influenced by the necessity for central control of the water supply, in Palestine the direct influence of the government on agriculture was very limited. The rain on which the economy depended was beyond the competence of any human agency, although prayers for rain and the many stories involving miraculous showers are evidence of its central importance in the life of the country and its people (see Water Supply*).

IV. POST-EXILIC AGRICULTURE: The major change in organization after the restoration of a Jewish state in Palestine was the prevalence of small and medium holdings. The great estates of the royal house were a thing of the past although the later kings, especially Herod, continued to own large tracts of land.

Agriculture remained the mainstay of the country — in spite of persecutions, civil wars and political unrest. Throughout the Hasmonean and Herodian eras, the majority of the population were occupied in agriculture and agricultural produce formed the bulk of the country's exports.

Loans to Peasants: The only kind of loan which Mosaic Law allowed to a fellow-Israelite was without interest (Ex. 22:25; Lv. 25:35–8), although one might lend at interest to a foreigner (Dt. 23:20). Economic developments and the example of Israel's neighbours where lending at interest was accepted, led to frequent violation of the Mosaic rule. Usury is one of the sins for which Jerusalem was condemned by Ezekiel (22:12).

The position was just as bad after the Exile, according to the Book of Nehemiah, our best source for the Persian period. He records several years of drought which reduced farmers to selling their land — or even their children — to repay debts they had incurred. Interest rates on loans at this period reached 25%, although under the Ptolemies (311–200 BCE) interest was limited to 12%. Rabbinical* sources make it clear that the Jerusalem temple, which acted as the country's treasury, also lent money at interest. From the parable in Matthew 25:27 (Luke 19:23) it appears that the practice continued and was recognized during New Testament times.

To safeguard the well-being of the mass of the people, Nehemiah insisted on lower rates of interest and forced wealthy creditors to remit some debts and even to return lands wrested from their debtors (Neh. 5:1–12). Nehemiah's agrarian reform laid the foundations of an agricultural community in which smallholdings predominated. Nevertheless, large estates continued to exist, according to J. Klausner, especially during and after the Hasmonean period.

The Zenon Papyri: Zenon was an official of Ptolemy II's finance minister, Apollonius, who lived in the middle of the third century BCE (286–259 BCE). An archive of letters and records, discovered in Fayum, Egypt, make up the "Zenon Papyri", an invaluable source of information about the many aspects of the life of that period.

In 259 BCE Zenon paid a visit to Palestine and 30 papyri relating to the visit have been preserved. While the Ptolemies ruled Palestine (up to 200 BCE), trade was a government monopoly, handled by government officials, not private merchants. The Papyri speak of Palestine's exports: grain, olives and olive oil, wine, meat and fish, but they give no details of land-ownership, taxation or other factors.

In general, the available evidence for the Hellenistic period suggests that the population had greatly increased and become more varied following the fusion of western and native elements. New crops, better equipment and more efficient methods had been introduced. The rapid hellenization of the towns and their prosperity also acted as a powerful impetus to agricultural production, although this did not materially improve the conditions under which the poor farmers lived. (See statuette of a peasant in Hellenistic times (**46**). In fact these conditions deteriorated under the Herodians and Romans (see Romans and Jews.*)

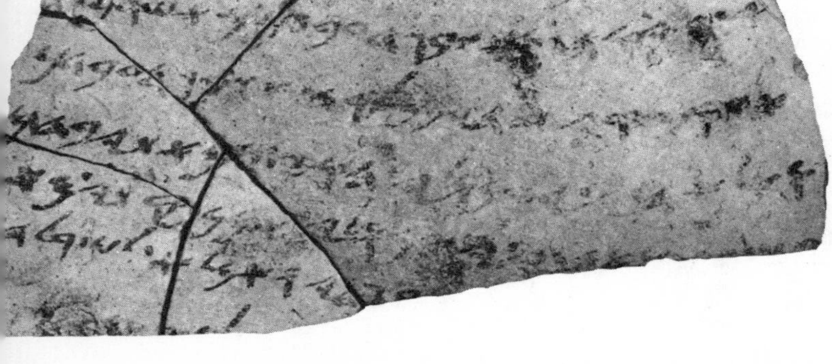

45

Hasmonean Period: Even before the conquests of the later Maccabean and Hasmonean* leaders, Jews had settled in Transjordan and Galilee, as well as Judea. Ample evidence for this comes from the accounts in the Books of Maccabees of reprisals against the Jews by local gentile populations.

Once the Hasmoneans had established their rule in Edom, Transjordan, Galilee and the coastal plain, Jewish settlements expanded and multiplied, the acquisition of agricultural holdings increasing especially as a result of the conquests of Alexander Jannaeus (see Hasmoneans*). The population continued to be occupied principally with agriculture. Even when Hasmonean conquests in the coastal plain made it possible for the Jews to engage in maritime trade, commerce remained second in importance to agriculture and rural population the major section of the country's inhabitants.

Nothing is known of the taxation* of the Hasmoneans, although the Jerusalem Talmud records that the traditional tithe was levied in the time of John Hyrcanus but that the proceeds were not applied exclusively to the services and upkeep of the Temple. Tithes were imposed on agricultural produce and there was, naturally, a good deal of evasion, which John Hyrcanus tried to prevent.

Roman Period: The most reliable of a variety of sources for the Roman period is Flavius Josephus*, although there is also ample evidence in Talmudic literature.

Josephus gives a full description of Galilee showing that it was densely populated and intensively cultivated, producing as in earlier years, olives, olive oil, figs and other fruit, fish from the Sea of Galilee and dairy produce. Olive oil from the Holy Land was in great demand in the diaspora, for the Jews were forbidden to use oil made by gentiles. Oil was accordingly exported in large quantities to the Jewish centres of Syria, Egypt, Babylonia and even further afield (see Hellenism in the Diaspora*). This frieze of the Synagogue at Chorazin (**47**) shows grapes being trodden.

Another source, the Natural History of Pliny the Elder (XIV, II, 44) records that Judea was noted for the quality of its figs (000). Josephus adds that fruit trees of all kinds flourished there while there was also extensive pasture land. Jericho* and Ein Gedi* were famous for exotic and valuable products like camphor, myrrh, and dates. The balsam of Jericho and Ein Gedi (see articles) was widely used for medicinal purposes. It is not surprising that Cleopatra demanded the Jericho district as a gift from Antony.

47

46

Cattle and sheep raising continued to be of importance, especially in the Sharon Plain, Moab and the Hebron district of southern Judea.

In the caves of Murabba'at (see Bar Kochba*), some very interesting food remains of the 2nd century CE were found. Uncalcified ears of corn and grains of wheat and barley belonged to the varieties enumerated above (see Field Crops). In addition, samples were found there, for the first time, of the "missing link" between the wild wheat (triticum dicoccoides) and the hard wheat (triticum durum) cultivated in Palestine and Syria for the last few centuries CE.

The Progress of Land tenure and ownership: In addition to land-owners and working farmers, tenant-farmers, lease-holders and labourers were also known. Rabbinical* and Pharisaic legal and literary traditions refer to a variety of systems of rent-holding and, in New Testament times, the parable of Matthew 21:33–41 is evidence for the prevalence of tenant-farming. The earliest documentary evidence, dated 133 CE, was found in the caves of Murabba'at in the form of letters (leases) from Bar-Kochba* to his tenants.

One system was the pre-Exilic pattern of tenant-farming, under which the tenant paid half his produce to the landowner.

Other tenants leased their land for a year, paying a cash rental and keeping the harvest as their own property. In addition there were the landless labourers who might be hired for wages for an agreed period which could be as little as a week but not more than seven years. Usually, the term of service was three years. The least privileged were the daily-wage labourers who were hired for seasonal work, harvesting, fruit-picking and so forth. In addition, slaves could be put to work in the fields although this was only possible for very rich owners. Most slaves were used in domestic work and not in agriculture. After the destruction of the Temple, the whole countryside became the domain of the state and land was leased from the government, or men worked as agricultural labourers on the state-owned plantations.

The Sabbatical Year (Before and after the Exile): The alienation of family lands and the extension of borrowing at interest (see above, Loans to farmers), resulted in a growing number of paupers (see Amos*) and the enslavement of defaulting debtors or their families. Pre-Exilic and post-Exilic religious legislation attempted to remedy these evils by enforcing the provision for a Sabbatical year and a Jubilee year, which had been included in the Covenant Code, and in Leviticus 25.

These Mosaic laws had laid it down that fields, vineyards and olive groves must be left to lie fallow every seventh year ("sh^{e}mittah" in Hebrew, meaning years of release, or remission), during which time their produce was reserved for the poor, (Ex. 23:10–12; Dt. 15:1–18). For the farmer this meant a further division of the overall cycle of his working life, beyond the yearly cycle of seasons (see above).

Dt. (15:1 and 12–18) extended this provision to apply to Israelite slaves and debtors. Israelite slaves must be freed after six years and debts remitted after seven (Ex. 21:2–6, see Law*). Leviticus 25 provides that the land's sabbatical rest must take place every seventh year according to a cycle reckoned from the Hebrews' entry into the Promised Land. God thereby pledged his promise (Lv. 25:21–22) that the sixth year would produce enough for the peasants to live through the seventh year of fallow and until the harvest of the following year. The same seven year cycle governed the freeing of slaves and remission of debts (see also Jubilee year*).

Many scholars argue that apart from the legislative texts in the Pentateuch and occasional references in Isaiah (37:30; or II Ch. 36:21), there is very little actual evidence in the Bible for the institution of the Sabbatical year. R. de Vaux maintains that it was an ancient institution, although it is doubtful how faithfully it was observed by the Israelites. All the evidence for its observance comes from later times and periods of national and religious fervour.

After the return from Exile, for instance, Nehemiah* exacted a promise from the people to keep the "sh^{e}mittah" (10:31), although the existing situation demanded an immediate solution, and could not wait upon the seven year cycle.

The institution was certainly maintained under the Hasmoneans. There is clear proof in the statement (I Mac. 6:49, 53) that in 163–162 BCE, the Jews lacked provisions "for it was a sabbatical year granted to the land." (See also Jubilee* ; Law*).

This remained true in Herodian days, while the scrolls of Bar Kochba* from the caves of Murabba'at demonstrate that the land was again granted its septennial rest. The contracts for land found in Murabba'at dated February 132 CE, the beginning of a seven-year period, all apply up to the next Sabbatical year, when they would have to be renewed.

ALPHABET AND WRITING. — *Outline: I. Development of Writing: Consonantal Writing; Egyptian Hieroglyphic Writing; Cuneiform; Common Features; Origins of Writing. II. Scripts: Palaeo-Sinaitic and Proto-Canaanite Inscriptions; North-Western Semitic Writing; Early Hebrew Inscriptions; Texts; Aramean Script; Dead Sea Scrolls; Southern Semitic Writing; Vowels. III. The Alphabet: Ugarit Alphabetic Tablet; Order of the Alphabet; Names of Letters; Later Developments. IV. Writing Materials: Implements; Papyrus.*

I. DEVELOPMENT OF WRITING: There is a Greek legend that writing was invented by a man called Kadmus. In the past many attempts were made to find a connection between this name and the Semitic word, "Kedem", meaning "east". This idea has recently found support in the results of the most modern research, from which it appears that the invention of the alphabet can be traced to the Phoenician-Palestinian area around 1500 BCE, its transfer to Greece taking place some five hundred years later (see Phoenicia*).

Consonantal Writing: In contrast to all earlier attempts made by man to find a system of writing down words, the Canaanite (Phoenician) alphabet was the first to base itself on the consonantal principle. This followed from the Canaanite language in which the words are all derived from roots made up of a few consonants. The meaning is changed and varied by a different vocalization of the consonants. In writing, only the consonants would be reproduced, the vocalization (and therefore the exact meaning) being left to the reader's own sense of what was appropriate. A script without vowel signs was in danger of being misunderstood, for example "zārak" = he sprinkled, might be read "zôrak" = it was sprinkled. To take a parallel example from English, the consonants "bd" might be b(a)d, b(e)d, b(i)d, b(u)d, (a)b(i)d(e). "Strng" might be str(o)ng, st(i)rr(i)ng or str(i)ng. This may seem a very imprecise method of recording language but, in fact, it represented quite an advance on earlier attempts, based on picture writing: hieroglyphs and cuneiform, even though earlier forms of syllabic writing could be much more precise. The ambiguity of the Canaanite and Hebrew use of the consonantal alphabet was lessened by the use of the symbols for certain weak sounds to indicate the long vowels, e.g. h for â; w for ô, û; y for ê, î. Not for more than a millenium were signs for the short vowels derived and placed under or over the consonants (see Bible Canon and Text*).

Egyptian Hieroglyphic Writing: Egyptian writing began with drawing pictures of objects — a house or courtyard 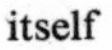, a mouth 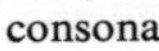 and many others. In the end, about 750 signs were established which at first meant only the object actually pictured. Later on, the same signs were used to represent actions accomplished through or suggested by the objects, e.g. the sail  also meant wind, the bull 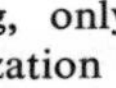, strength, the knife 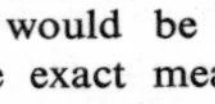, cutting and so on.

This allowed for a much wider range of meanings but, even so, many notions, especially the more abstract, remained inexpressible.

Cuneiform: At about the same time as the Egyptians were tracing their familiar pictograms on papyrus and stone, the Sumerians took the same basic idea of picture writing, adapted it to the soft clay tablets on which they first wrote and developed the stylized geometric shapes typical of cuneiform writing.

Common Features: Simplification becomes possible with the transition from the ideogram to the syllable, i.e. when the picture of an object becomes merely the symbol of the sound of the word and can thus be joined to other symbols to form another single word made up of a number of syllables. This process took place in both Egypt and Mesopotamia, possibly in terms of the picture coming to represent merely the first syllable of the name of the object, finally merely the initial letter. For instance the word for house was "beth" and the sign concerned ⊏⊐ came to represent first the syllable "be" and ultimately the letter 𐤁 = b.

Until the 2nd millenium BCE, the signs used, especially when transposed from an earlier language to a newer, different one, could always mean any of a number of related concepts or objects. No wonder reading was as much an art among the ancients as writing. By 1500 BCE the alphabet was in use in Syria-Palestine. Essentially it had been created by taking certain Egyptian (and possibly Byblos) hieroglyphic signs, giving them the Semitic names for the thing they represented, and using them in an unconventional manner to represent the sounds of the different language: e.g. the Egyptian ⊂⊃ mouth, with a letter value of "ra" became in Hebrew "peh" = mouth, with the value of the letter "p" (see below).

The different forms of the alphabet and scripts in the ancient Near East are shown in these tables **(48, 49)**.

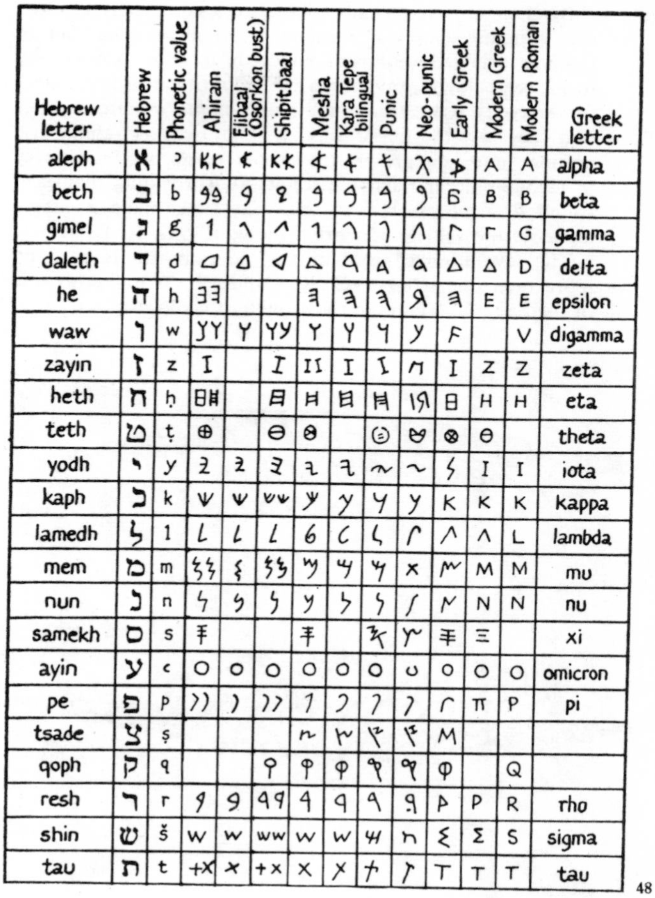

Hebrew letter
Hebrew
Phonetic value
Ahiram
Elibaal (Osorkon bust)
Shipitbaal
Mesha
Kara Tepe bilingual
Punic
Neo-punic
Early Greek
Modern Greek
Modern Roman
Greek letter
aleph א ʾ alpha
beth ב b beta
gimel ג g gamma
daleth ד d delta
he ה h epsilon
waw ו w digamma
zayin ז z zeta
heth ח ḥ eta
teth ט ṭ theta
yodh י y iota
kaph כ k kappa
lamedh ל l lambda
mem מ m mu
nun נ n nu
samekh ס s xi
ayin ע ʿ omicron
pe פ p pi
tsade צ ṣ
qoph ק q
resh ר r rho
shin ש š sigma
tau ת t tau

48

49

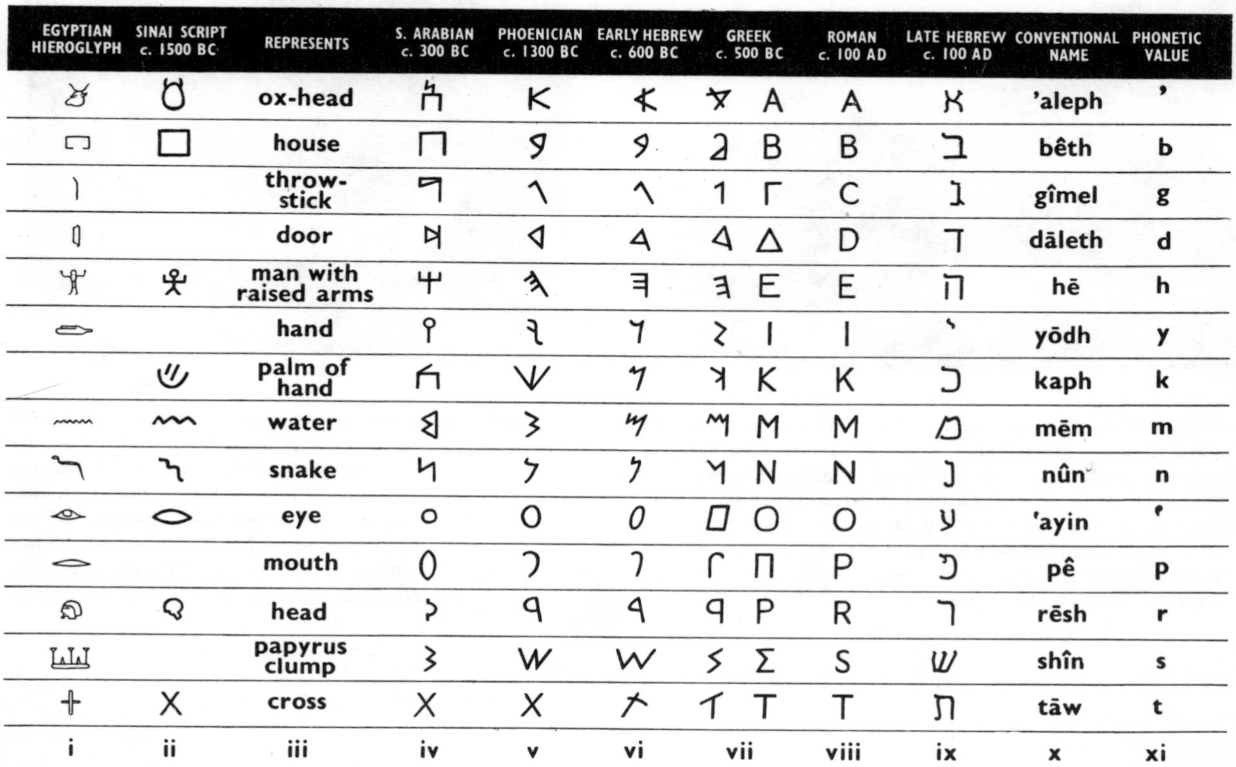

EGYPTIAN HIEROGLYPH
SINAI SCRIPT c. 1500 BC
REPRESENTS
S. ARABIAN c. 300 BC
PHOENICIAN c. 1300 BC
EARLY HEBREW c. 600 BC
GREEK c. 500 BC
ROMAN c. 100 AD
LATE HEBREW c. 100 AD
CONVENTIONAL NAME
PHONETIC VALUE
ox-head 'aleph '
house bêth b
throw-stick gîmel g
door dāleth d
man with raised arms hē h
hand yōdh y
palm of hand kaph k
water mēm m
snake nûn n
eye 'ayin ʿ
mouth pê p
head rēsh r
papyrus clump shîn s
cross tāw t
i
ii
iii
iv
v
vi
vii
viii
ix
x
xi

By changing over from a picture to a completely abstract sign meaning simply a consonantal sound, the number of symbols was reduced from hundreds to thirty (eventually to 22, see below), providing a far more practical instrument for everyday use. "It was the merit of the western Semites that they saw the importance of this discovery (alphabetic writing) and, discarding the whole cumbrous machinery of ideographic and syllabic scripts and providing that each sound was represented by only one sign, made a simple alphabet the vehicle of written thought." (G. R. Driver)

The revolution effected by this development is cited by more than one scholar (G. R. Childe, L. Woolley) as one of the essential factors in the growth of civilization.

51

50

53

52

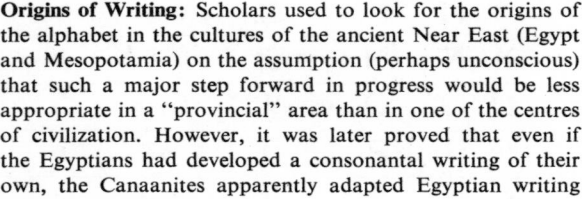

Origins of Writing: Scholars used to look for the origins of the alphabet in the cultures of the ancient Near East (Egypt and Mesopotamia) on the assumption (perhaps unconscious) that such a major step forward in progress would be less appropriate in a "provincial" area than in one of the centres of civilization. However, it was later proved that even if the Egyptians had developed a consonantal writing of their own, the Canaanites apparently adapted Egyptian writing to alphabetic purposes and thus may still take credit for establishing the system which reduced the number of letters to a minimum. Even though Egyptian pictographic writing may have influenced the form of some of the Canaanite characters, this does not affect the main question of the development of their use as an alphabet. Some resemblance and influence is hardly surprising in view of the close contacts between Egypt and Syria/Palestine during and before the

2nd millenium BCE (see Ugarit*; Phoenicia*), and in view of the enormous number of graphic signs used by the Egyptians.

II. SCRIPTS: **Palaeo-Sinaitic and Proto-Canaanite Inscriptions:** The oldest known alphabetic inscriptions come from Palestine and the Sinai peninsula and have been dated to the 2nd millenium BCE. A number of potsherds (ostraca) and javelin and arrow heads **(50)** bearing inscriptions have been found in the south of Palestine (Beth-Shemesh; Gezer **51**; See photo), near Bethlehem and elsewhere. Although these are badly broken and, partly for this reason, have not yet been deciphered, the signs on them make it clear that they represent one of the earliest stages of the Canaanite alphabet. In the opinion of J. T. Milik and F. M. Cross, the javelin heads were written in a South Canaanite dialect of the 11th century BCE and represent the vital link between Proto-alphabetic inscriptions (variously designated as Sinaitic, early Canaanite or Proto-Phoenician script) and the earliest true Phoenician inscriptions of the 10th century BCE. Another early Canaanite inscription was found on a Lachish bowl of the 13th c. BCE **(53)**.

In the turquoise mines of Serabit-el-Khadem in the Sinai peninsula, other inscriptions were found, since called, for convenience, "Palaeo-Sinaitic" inscriptions **(52)**. Theyic are words scratched on the rock face, apparently by Semit slaves working in the mines. The words which have so far been deciphered include the name of the Canaanite goddess "Ba'alat" written in signs which are remarkably close to the Canaanite letters "B'lt" (see Inscriptions). Hints like this suggest that all these inscriptions belong to different phases of the development of the Canaanite alphabet which first appeared in Phoenicia around 1000 BCE. It is still very difficult to put them into any sequence or to fit them into a general history of the alphabet, but they do suggest some such development as indicated in the chart **(54)** published by J. T. Milik and F. M. Cross.

North-Western Semitic Writing: After 1000 BCE it becomes easier to trace the course of development. Much more written material is available, including long and continuous texts which have been successfully deciphered (whereas the inscriptions of the 2nd millenium are still a largely unsolved problem). The later material is particularly rich in north-western Semitic texts, the best known of the Canaanite material being the ancient Byblos (Gebal) inscriptions which represent a key phase in the development of the alphabet during the early first millenium BCE. For this, the most important is the royal inscription on the sarcophagus of Ahiram, king of Byblos (**55**, below), written around 1000 BCE and now in the Louvre museum. Other inscriptions found in Byblos were in pseudo-hieroglyphic script **(56)**, and this has given rise to considerable scholarly confusion.

In fact there is as yet no final agreement among scholars as to the exact spot or even approximate date in which to place the origins of alphabetic signs. It is agreed that they began somewhere on the shores of the Eastern Mediterranean, but whether the 15th century BCE Ugarit alphabet, the rather later Byblos writing or the Palaeo-Sinaitic script of Serabit el-Khadem represent the first words ever written in the letters of an alphabet, is still disputed. Nor can it be stated with certainty whether alphabetic writing developed directly

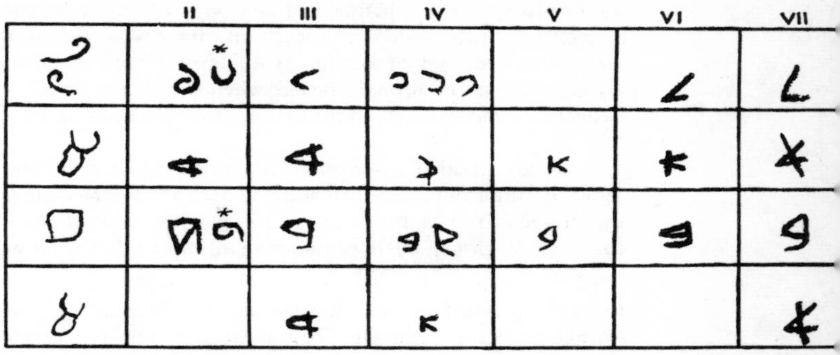

Proto-Canaanite and Phoenician Scripts from the Fifteenth to beginning of the Ninth Century, B. C.

I. Proto-Canaanite Texts from Sinai (fifteenth century, B. C.).
II. The Lachish Ewer and Bowl (first column), and (with asterisk) the Goetze Seal (thirteenth century, B. C.).
III. The Aijalon Seal (twelfth century, B. C.).
IV. The El-Ḫaḍr Arrowheads (twelfth century, B. C.).
V. The Ruweiseh Arrowhead (eleventh century, B. C.).
VI. The Byblian Spatula (late eleventh century, B. C.).
VII. The Nora Inscription (late tenth or early ninth century B. C.).

54

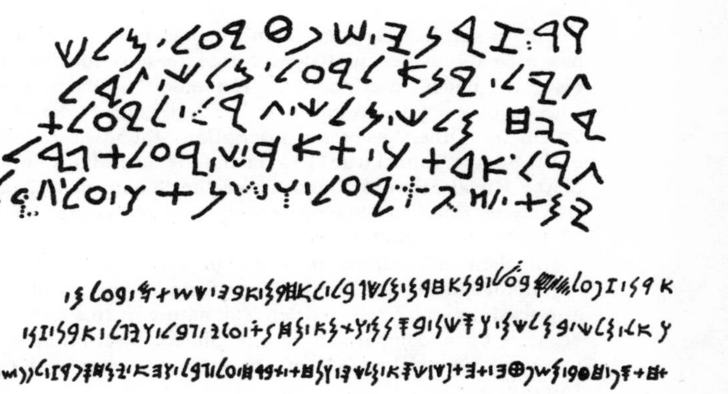

55

56

out of ideograms or whether mankind found some short cut to spelling out the sounds of speech into their basic elements and using inscribed or written symbols to represent them. Agreement may be brought nearer when it becomes possible to decipher and understand the earliest inscriptions completely.

In Moab, another inscription in a north-western Semitic script, dating from about 850 BCE (see Moab*, Mesha Stone) was found. From a historical and linguistic point of view this is of much greater importance than many other inscriptions.

Early Hebrew Inscriptions: It is not known where the Hebrew learned to write. The Old Testament has nothing to say either about the origins of writing or when the Hebrews' ancestors began to write. Writing is not mentioned in the stories of the Patriarchs, although quite early on people were able to write, for instance Gideon (Jud. 8:14), or Jezebel (I K. 21:8–11) who wrote the elders of Jezreel a letter which they — at least some of them — could read. There is no evidence that either Gideon or Jezebel used cuneiform, as did the Canaanite rulers who wrote the Amarna* letters or other diplomatic correspondence in the 14th century BCE. The origins of Hebrew writing must be sought elsewhere (see below).

Only a surprisingly small number of Hebrew inscriptions has been discovered in Palestine (the reasons for this are discussed under Inscriptions*). The oldest of them is the 10th century BCE Gezer calendar (see Agriculture*, Seasonal Calendar). Others were the inscriptions found at the end of the Siloam Tunnel (ca. 710 BCE) and the funeral inscription of the Royal Steward found above the Siloam valley, tentatively ascribed to "Shebna who is over the house" of Is. 22:15–16 (see Inscriptions*).

All these are carved in stone in early "lapidary" or "monumental" style. The lapidary form of the script was also used on seals* (see article). The nature of this style can be seen by a comparison of the Siloam inscription with the royal jar handles (**57**) of the 8th–6th century BCE (see Inscriptions*).

The sort of cursive or current hand which Israelite writers of the 11th or 10th c. BCE may have used in texts can be seen in the inscribed arrow heads mentioned above (see Part II, Scripts) and other smaller writings which are generally dated to around 1000 BCE (see Inscriptions*) although the date is disputed by Y. Yadin and some other scholars.

Texts: The earliest body of texts known is made up of 75 ostraca from Samaria assigned to the reign of Jeroboam II (ca. 760 BCE) or earlier. The script changed very little between then and the end of the monarchy (ca. 590–586 BCE) when the Lachish ostraca (see Lachish*) or a similar ostracon from Matzad Hashabyahu (see Inscriptions*) were penned. These were scratched "in common characters" (Is. 8:1), quite unlike the carved stone inscriptions from Gezer or Siloam. The letters of the Hebrew current hand used in the Lachish ostraca are shown here (**58**). Like other Semitic languages, Hebrew reads from right to left and the letters are printed in that order.

Aramean Script: The elegant "calligraphic" hand which rounds the contours of the letters and joins them together to look as though the word were written with one stroke of

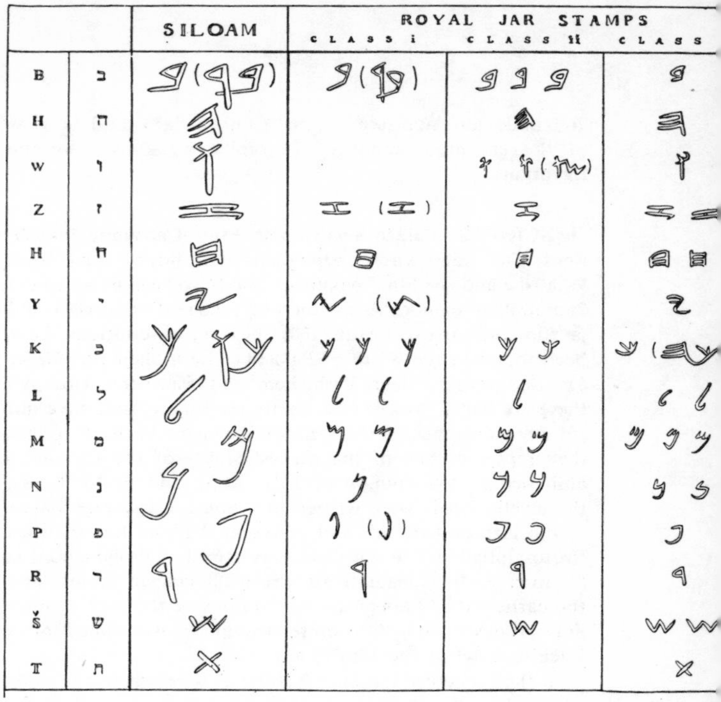
SILOAM
ROYAL JAR STAMPS
CLASS I
CLASS II
CLASS
B ב
H ה
W ו
Z ז
Ḥ ח
Y י
K כ
L ל
M מ
N נ
P פ
R ר
Š ש
T ת

57

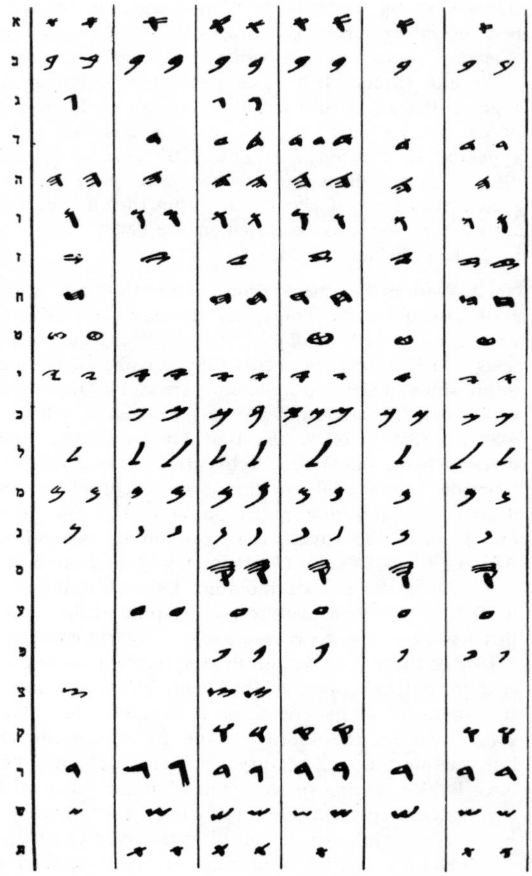

58

59

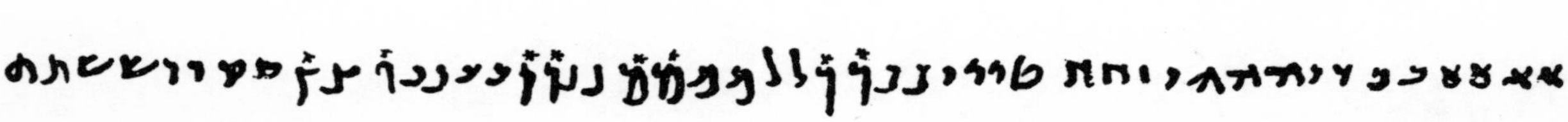

the pen makes its first appearance in Aramaic. The ancient Israelites had used the old Canaanite (or Palaeo-Hebrew) script but after the return of the exiles from Babylon, the "calligraphic" system took its place. This was the period during which the imperial-Aramaic language spread through the whole Near East as the lingua franca of government and administration in the different countries joined for a time in the Persian Empire. The Jews who spoke Aramaic in Elephantine in Egypt in the 5th c. BCE wrote it on papyrus. The Syrian and Arabic scripts in turn developed from this source, their words being written as groups of letters joined together. The so-called "Assyrian" or square Hebrew in which the books of the Bible were written also derived from this source, becoming in turn the prototype for the modern Hebrew alphabet. The archaic Canaanite (Hebrew) script has been preserved only among the Samaritans* and on Maccabean coins (see Inscriptions*) and on those of the First and Second Revolts against Rome. In all other spheres the old writing was completely displaced. Ascribing the change to Ezra*, however, may merely reflect a pious desire to give the novelty the authority of his venerated name. Equally, of course, Ezra may indeed have been responsible for the use of the new script in the copying of biblical manuscripts. The allusion in Mt. 5:18 to the "iota" (the Hebrew "yod") is only intelligible in reference to the new square script which was presumably in general use by the 1st c. CE.

Dead Sea Scrolls: Some of the scrolls discovered at Qumran were found to be written in the older style. In the opinion of many scholars, the Palaeo-Hebrew script which was dominant in pre-Exilic Israel for some four centuries "was taken up anew in the era of nationalistic revival of the 2nd c. BCE to judge from its use as a monumental script by the Hasmoneans on their coinage (see Coins*), as well as its resurgence as a Biblical hand. It is in the Hasmonean era that the Samaritan Pentateuchal text (see Samaritans*) separates from the main stream of Jewish tradition, preserving in its special hand the Palaeo-Hebrew tradition. This new development is reflected in the series of the manuscripts of Qumran, as well as in the coinage of the First and Second Jewish Revolts (see Rome and the Jews*), and in the earliest Samaritan epigraphs . . . one can best explain these characteristics . . . by assuming that . . . the old script was preserved alive in some narrow circle, presumably by a coterie of erudite scribes, as a Biblical book hand." (F. M. Cross)

Between the Hasmonean period (150–30 BCE) and the Herodian age (30 BCE – 70 CE), formal writing developed the squarer, more angular style seen in its earliest form in the Nash papyrus **(59)** which dates to 150 BCE. After 70 CE, cursive script was no longer a literary vehicle but had become an extremely complex way of writing — as can be seen from the Bar Kochba* letters found in the wilderness of Judea.

Southern Semitic Writing: A number of inscriptions — many of them very short — have been discovered in Southern Arabia, written in a southern Semitic script **(60)** (which should not be confused with the present Arabic alphabet **(61)** which is a derivation from the Aramaic). Notably, this alphabet contains 29 consonants which is more, not only than north-western Semitic (22), but also than classic Arabic (28). This development appears to be typical of proto-Semitic

60

61

scripts. The earliest example is the text of the Balu'a stele in Moab* (see article and illustration) ca. 1200–1100 BCE, where the affinity to Sinaitic can still be seen, although divergent forms were already developing.

The southern Arabian script travelled to Ethiopia and developed there. The manner in which consonants were to be vocalized was indicated by variations in the shape of the letters.

Vowels: Centuries earlier, the Greeks overcame the lack of graphic representation of vowels by using for this purpose the guttural letters of Semitic languages which are not needed in Greek (Greek being a language without gutturals). Thus the Canaanite (Phoenician) consonant "aleph" ᚲ became the sign for the Greek vowel "A" as in art; the Canaanite "ayin" o — a consonant which has no equivalent in Greek— became "o" as in "dog". The Greeks are thus considered to have created the first true alphabet in which both consonants and vowels could be represented by distinct signs. The Phoenicians (see above) had used only consonants and no vowels, although as early as the 9th c. BCE, Aramaic and Moabite also had vowel letters.

The graphic forms of the letters of north-western and southern Semitic contain a number of differences which have suggested that both derived individually from a proto-Semitic script, rather than developing one from the other. There are also differences between them in the order of the alphabet. It is not clear just what is the relationship in this respect between southern-Arabian and Ethiopian, nor between them and the north-western Semitic branch. However, the antiquity of the northern Semitic alphabet order appears to have been confirmed by recent discoveries of material going back to the 15th c. BCE.

III. THE ALPHABET: **Ugarit Alphabetic Tablet:** A small tablet unearthed in Ugarit in 1949 (see Ugarit*, Alphabetic Writing), proved to be a sample-alphabet, giving the letters of the north-west Semitic alphabet (plus some additional ones) in the same order as in Hebrew and Aramaic, but with the letters replaced by cuneiform equivalents. Thus the simplicity of the existing Canaanite alphabet was combined with the Mesopotamian system of writing on clay with a hard stylus and the consonantal alphabet was transcribed into cuneiform writing. Because it was used for both Semitic languages (i.e. Accadian) and non-Semitic (e.g. Hurrian), it contained 32 signs, representing consonants: the Canaanite alphabet of 27 signs (the 22 Hebrew letters plus five additional ones not found in Hebrew) with another five consonants and, in addition, three forms of the alef which could be "a" "i" or "u" depending on the vowels used with it. Rendered into modern Hebrew, (reading from right to left), the list runs as shown in the Table; **(65)**.

When the Greeks took over the Phoenician alphabet around 800 BCE they also added a number of new letters of Hellenic origin to represent the different sounds of their language.

The five letters inserted in the Canaanite alphabet represent the sounds H̱ ṢẒṮ Ḡ, which are known to have belonged to the Bronze Age stock of northwest Semitic phonemes. Their reappearance in the Ugarit tablet proves that the linear Canaanite alphabet of the 15th c. BCE still possessed these five sounds. The tablet is also conclusive evidence that the familiar Hebrew, Aramaic and Greek order of the letters of the alphabet must go back to at least the same time, if not earlier.

Order of the Alphabet: In fact, it appears that apart from one or two variations inherent in the idiom of Ugarit, the discovery of the tablet merely confirmed the order of the alphabet as it was known from much later, i.e. younger sources such as the Jewish-Aramaic tradition and the Greek order of the alphabet. For instance, certain chapters of the Bible are arranged in an acrostic order (the first letters of each verse forming a complete alphabet; Lam. 1–4; Pr. 31:10–35; Ps. 9, 10, 24, 25, 111, 112, 119, 145). This order is also known from an 8th c. BCE carved inscription of the first five letters discovered at Lachish **(62)**. These had been scribbled, presumably by a schoolboy, on the steps of the palace and represent the first known evidence of the Hebrew language being learned systematically.

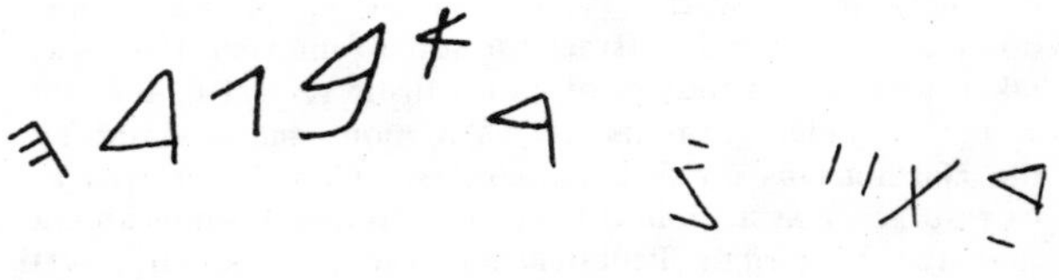

62

Names of Letters: The modern Hebrew alphabet, which probably corresponds in part, although not altogether, to the names of early Hebrew letters, runs as follows: 'aleph, beth, gimel, daleth, he, waw, zayin, heth, teth, yod, kaph, lamed, mem, nun, samekh, ayin, pe, sade, qoph, resh, shin, taw. The phonetic value of each letter is that of the first letter of its name, a device known as the "acrophonic principle". Thus the value of the letter beth is b; of gimel, g (hard as in good) and of daleth, d, etc.

Modern Hebrew took over the ancient names of the letters of the alphabet which had been preserved in the Talmud in Syriac and Greek, although variations between the names

63

ORIGINAL PICTOGRAPH c. 3500 BC	SIMPLIFIED CHARACTER c. 3000 BC	ARCHAIC SUMERIAN c. 2800 BC	OLD BABYLONIAN c. 1800 BC	ASSYRIAN c. 800 BC	NEO-BABYLONIAN c. 600 BC	IDEOGRAPHIC AND SYLLABIC TRANSLITERATION	MEANING
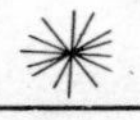						DINGIR an, ìl	**god heaven**
						UTU ud etc	**sun day light**

suggest that the Greek and Jewish traditions first drew on Phoenician and Canaanite sources for the names of the alphabet with some variations later. For instance, the letter 𐤓 is "resh" in Hebrew from the Aramaic word for "head" (resh). The Greeks took the Canaanite sign for "rosh" (also "head") but dropped the "sh" so that in Greek it became "rho" ῥῶ.

The acrophonic principle offers the most plausible explanation for the origin of the names of letters as, by this means, most of them can be traced back to the names of the objects originally represented by the form of the letter. The objects were deliberately chosen so that the first letter of each one would be different from all the others and was thus suitable to provide one of the consonants out of which all words could be formed.

The process of evolution can be traced from its beginnings somewhere in Syria-Palestine, through pictographs to Phoenician letters and right up to modern Hebrew in some of the varying forms of the alphabet (see table above).

Clearly, the forms of letters known today have come a long way from their primary origins. Later schematization and stylization however does not demolish the argument. The modern Hebrew letter מ ("mem") for instance began as the symbol for water ("maym" in Hebrew), but from its beginnings an evolutionary process took place as shown here: **(64)**

64

An additional change was produced by the switch from vertical to horizontal writing. As letters came to be written across the page instead of up and down it, the position of many of them was shifted ninety degrees. This can be seen in the case of "mem" above. If it was natural to write the letter "mem" horizontally when the next letter came above it, it was equally convenient to write the same thing vertically when the next letter was to come at the side.

A similar process of simplification of letters from pictograms can be seen in the Accadian cuneiform "star" letters **(63)**, meaning god and heaven, as shown in this table **(63)**. (Accadian and Ugaritic — see the alphabetic tablet above — are the only Semitic languages written in cuneiform and not in alphabetic writing.)

It seems impossible to reconstruct the original figure on which some of the letters were based. To explain this, there is a theory that the answer lies in a combination of letters. For instance, scholars explain the Hebrew "tet" ⊗ as a combination of the Canaanite "ayin" o with taw ×, which produced the Canaanite ⊗ subsequently reduced to ⊗. Probably it is more important to remember that the deciphering of other inscriptions is very likely to reveal additional transition stages in the development of letters and thus add to present knowledge of their origins.

Later Developments: From Greek, the letters of the alphabet passed to the Latins (probably through the Etruscans) and from them they were transmitted to Europe to become the vehicle of expression for all modern western cultures. Their names remain, fundamentally, those the Semites used and did not progress beyond the Greek, as shown in this table (000). See also: Use of Writing in Biblical Times (under Inscriptions*); Texts, Bible Canon and Text*.

IV. WRITING MATERIALS: The materials commonly used in antiquity for recording messages, plans, surveys or accounts in Babylonia, Assyria and related lands were clay tablets **(66)**. Throughout the Near East, inscriptions were cut on stone, monumental texts on a prepared stele or cliff face, and testimonia or public edicts on stone slabs or tablets (see Inscriptions*; Moab*: Mesha Stone). Softer or uneven surfaces would be covered with a plaster coating to provide a surface on which to write legibly — an Egyptian custom also recommended (Dt. 27:2–3) for the Israelites' altar stones. The Ten Commandments (Ex. 32:16; 34:28 ff; Dt. 4:13) and Joshua's proclamation (Jos. 8:32) would have been incised on a stone tablet in this way.

For receipts, short letters and other more transient purposes, pieces of pottery (ostraca), wood, bark or other materials found to hand were used in biblical times (see Inscriptions* for a fuller discussion of the use of these materials in Palestine). The word "gillayon" (Is. 8:1) is believed to have referred to hard sheets or the blank surfaces of wooden, clay or leather tablets engraved or scratched with a stylus **(66a)**.

66

66 a

אַ ב ג ח' ד ה ו ז ח ט י כ ש' ל מ ש² נ ט ס' ע פ צ ק ר ת' ע' ת א אֶ ס²

65

[s 'u 'i] t [g] ŧ r q ṣ p ' s [z] n đ m l [š] k y ṭ ḥ z w h d [ḫ] g b 'a

Writing boards of wood or ivory were recessed to hold an inlaid wax surface. The earliest (705 BCE) so far found (at Nimrud in Assyria*) contains 6000 lines. The same type frequently appears in representations of scribes (**70**). Similar writing boards, the forerunners of the school slate, were also widely used in Greek and Roman times (cf. Lk. 1:63).

The writing boards, tablets or scrolls were inscribed in any number of columns of any length, as desired. The column was called a "delet" (door; Jer. 36:23). In Old and New Testament times, a "book" was usually a roll or scroll (megillah) of leather (parchment), or papyrus. The text would be written on the inside and, if necessary, continued "outside" on the back (cf. Ezk. 2:10). The Hebrew word "sefer" (book) means any written document. It could be applied to either a roll or a scroll, such as these columns from a modern handwritten Torah (**67**).

The Bible never refers explicitly to the use of leather or papyrus, but the materials used by later Hebrew scribes probably differed very little from those used at all periods by the Egyptians and pictured in many of their drawings. Jer. 36:4 and Ezk. 2:9–10 both refer to the writing of scrolls, while other literary evidence suggests that leather (parchment) was widely used in ancient Israel and neighbouring countries. Parchment was made from the skins of young lambs or goats. Ex. 26:14 refers to the preparation of leather, implying that the art was known at least early in the 1st mill. BCE.

Implements: The scribes wrote in ink "and I wrote them with ink in the book" (Jer. 36:18). The "pen of the scribes" (Jer. 8:8) which was used for writing on ostraca, papyrus or other smooth surfaces, was a reed (**69**), split or cut into a stiff brush. In Graeco-Roman times the reeds were sharpened to a point and split like a quill pen, the "kalamos" of the New Testament world. Even today Hebrew scrolls of the Law are written in ink on parchment with reed pens. The pens (**68, 68a**) were kept in cases or palettes with hollows for the cakes of ink, ". . . who had the writing case at his side" (Ezk. 9:3), illustrated in the Aramaic stele of Bar Rekub (**70**). A good example of writer's equipment came from Qumran (**71**) — two ink wells, one of bronze and one of earthenware — just as the Dead Sea Scrolls are probably some of the most familiar examples of ancient Hebrew writings.

הבאים אחריהם בים לא נשאר בהם עד אחד ובני ישראל הלכו
ביבשה בתוך הים והמים להם חמה מימינם ומשמאלם ויושע
יהוה ביום ההוא את ישראל מיד מצרים וירא ישראל את מצרים
מת על שפת הים וירא ישראל את היד הגדלה אשר עשה יהוה
במצרים וייראו העם את יהוה ויאמינו ביהוה ובמשה עבדו

אז ישיר משה ובני ישראל את השירה הזאת ליהוה ויאמרו
לאמר אשירה ליהוה כי גאה גאה סוס
ורכבו רמה בים עזי וזמרת יה ויהי לי
לישועה זה אלי ואנוהו אלהי
אבי וארממנהו יהוה איש מלחמה יהוה
שמו מרכבת פרעה וחילו ירה בים ומבחר
שלשיו טבעו בים סוף תהמת יכסימו ירדו במצולת כמו
אבן ימינך יהוה נאדרי בכח ימינך
יהוה תרעץ אויב וברב גאונך תהרס
קמיך תשלח חרנך יאכלמו כקש וברוח
אפיך נערמו מים נצבו כמו נד
נזלים קפאו תהמת בלב ים אמר
אויב ארדף אשיג אחלק שלל תמלאמו
נפשי אריק חרבי תורישמו ידי נשפת
ברוחך כסמו ים צללו כעופרת במים
אדירים מי כמכה באלם יהוה מי
כמכה נאדר בקדש נורא תהלת עשה
פלא נטית ימינך תבלעמו ארץ נחית
בחסדך עם זו גאלת נהלת בעזך אל נוה
קדשך שמעו עמים ירגזון חיל
אחז ישבי פלשת אז נבהלו אלופי
אדום אילי מואב יאחזמו רעד נמגו
כל ישבי כנען תפל עליהם אימתה
ופחד בגדל זרועך ידמו כאבן עד
יעבר עמך יהוה עד יעבר עם זו
קנית תבאמו ותטעמו בהר נחלתך מכון
לשבתך פעלת יהוה מקדש אדני כוננו
ידיך יהוה ימלך לעלם ועד כי
בא סוס פרעה ברכבו ובפרשיו בים וישב יהוה עלהם את מי
הים ובני ישראל הלכו ביבשה בתוך הים

ותקח מרים הנביאה אחות אהרן את התף בידה ותצאן כל הנשים
אחריה בתפים ובמחלת ותען להם מרים שירו ליהוה כי גאה גאה
סוס ורכבו רמה בים ויסע משה את ישראל מים סוף
ויצאו אל מדבר שור וילכו שלשת ימים במדבר ולא מצאו מים
ויבאו מרתה ולא יכלו לשתת מים ממרה כי מרים הם על כן קרא שמה מרה

67

68

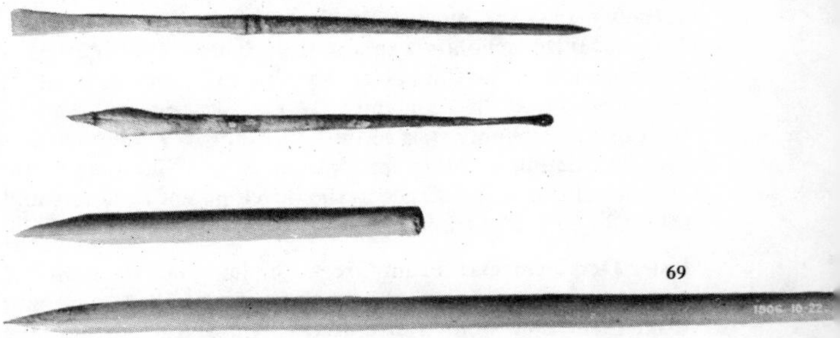

69

70

The ink used on parchment was usually made from soot or charcoal mixed with oil or gum. A metallic ink substance was used for ostraca or papyrus. The ink of the Lachish ostraca was a mixture of carbon and iron (or copperas). Stone, metal, clay or ivory were of course inscribed with metal chisels and styluses or engraving tools, (see Seals*; Crafts: Tools and Implements*).

Papyrus: Made from the reeds that grew in abundance in the marshes of the delta of the Nile, or, in Phoenicia, in the Lake Hulah swamp and along the Jordan, papyrus was the first paper ever used. This example of Egyptian writing and drawing (**72**) is on papyrus (extracts from the prescribed ritual relating to the transmigrations of the human soul).

The papyrus was made by cutting the pith of the reed stalk into thin strips which were then laid close together in two layers, one above the other crossways. Pressed, dried and smoothed it formed a thin sheet, more durable than the best modern paper (a word which is derived from its ancient prototype). Later on, papyrus sheets were imported into Palestine either direct from Phoenicia* or through Byblos from Egypt. There is archaeological evidence for the use of papyrus in the kingdom of Judah. This comes mainly from seal impressions which bear on their backs the marks of the papyrus to which they were originally attached. The papyrus has perished, but these traces remain.

68 a

71

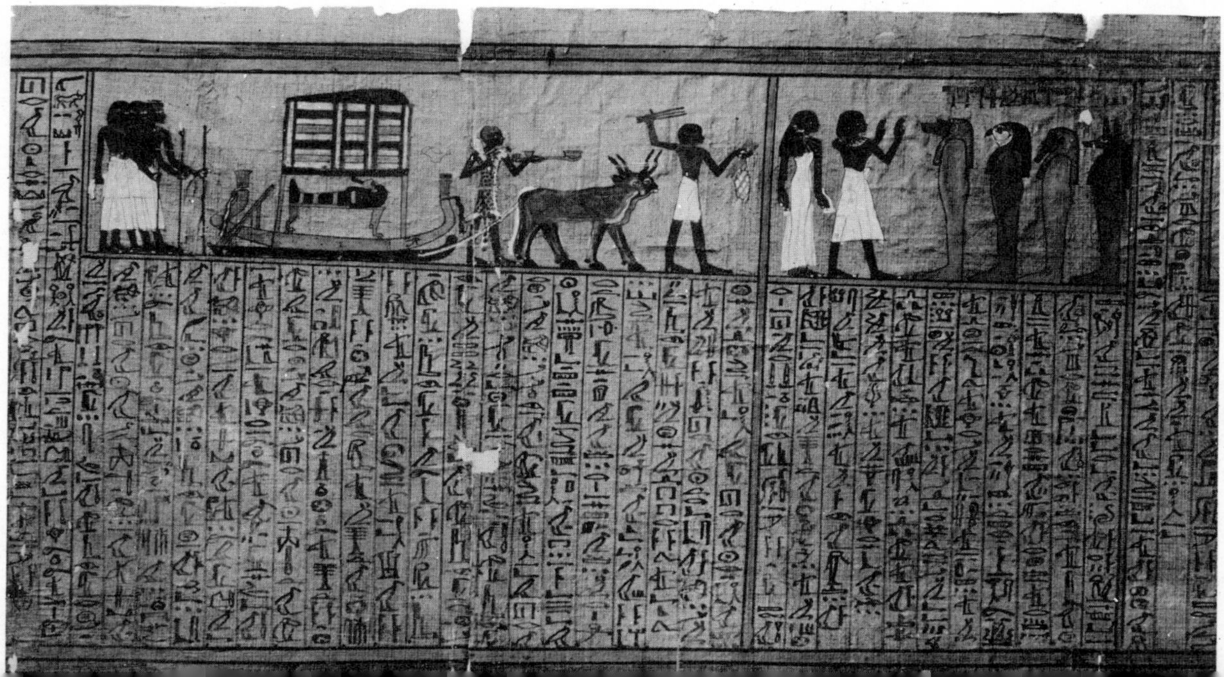

72

In post-Exilic times papyrus became relatively common, as witness this letter (**73**) sent from Elephantine in Egypt to Judea in the 5th c. BCE. Papyrus copies of Deuteronomy in Greek, dating from the 2nd c. BCE have also been found. The best known papyri which have survived from post-biblical times are the Dead Sea Scrolls and the papyri from the time of Bar-Kochba* discovered in the caves of the wilderness of Judea. A few similar ones have also been found in other places in Palestine dating between the 2nd c. BCE and 2nd CE (see Inscriptions*).

WRITING (See Alphabet and Writing)

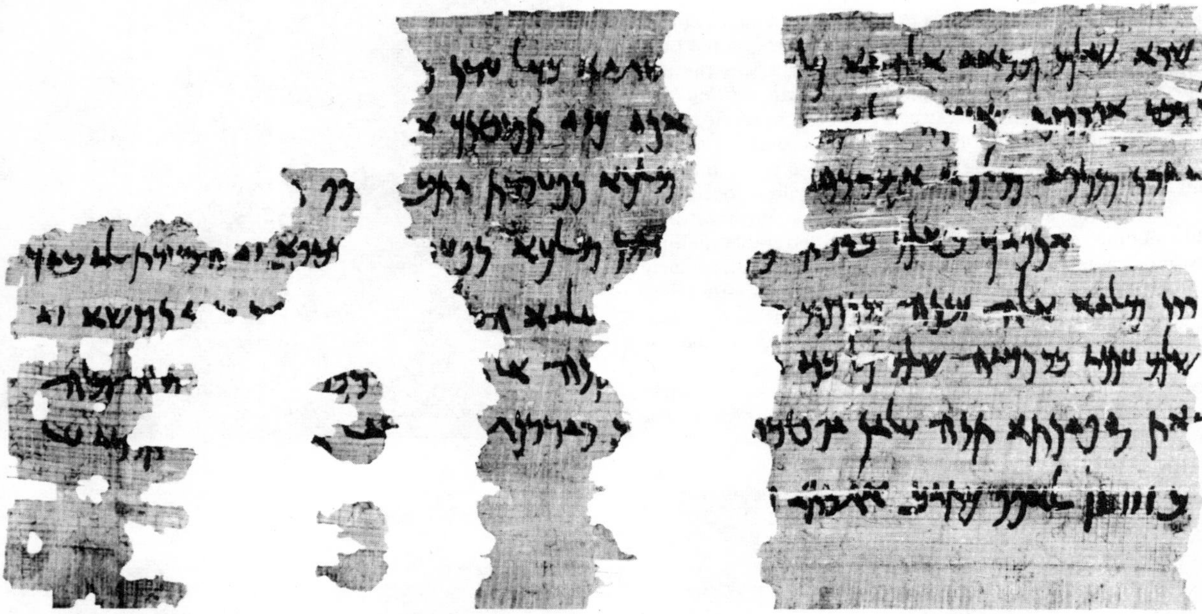

73

AMARNA LETTERS, TEL EL. — The Tel el Amarna letters are a series of clay tablets, dating from approx. 1400 to 1350 BCE, written in cuneiform in the Akkadian* language, the *lingua franca* of the day. Discovered in the palace of Pharaoh Akhenaton at the site of Tel el Amarna, they are a series of letters sent to the Pharaoh from his vassals in Phoenicia, Syria and Canaan, like this one written to him by the king of Byblos* (**75**).

Historical Background: The Egyptian empire's holdings in Asia (see Egypt*) were captured under Thotmes III between 1490 and 1435 BCE. However, the Egyptians were not strongly established and were vulnerable to attacks from the rising power of the Hittites*. From 1375 to 1340 BCE, the Hittite leader Shuppiluliuma instigated a series of revolts in the Amorite* city-kingdoms of northern Syria aimed at undermining Egypt's expansion in Asia and destroying her alliances with Western Asiatic princes. The Amorite example was quickly followed by the Canaanite cities. Wandering bands of warriors, who camped on the outskirts of the rebellious cities, took advantage of the break-up of the Egyptian Asiatic empire and may even have started some of the trouble. These were the Habiru*, peoples of uncertain origin — not a single ethnic group but mixed communities like the group from which sprang the Hebrews of Patriarchal days (see Patriarchs*). The Amarna tablets include letters from Canaanite rulers with Hurrian* and Indo-European names, reflecting the continued presence and importance of non-Semitic elements who had settled in the area during the centuries following the Hyksos'* occupation of Palestine, corresponding roughly to the period of the Patriarchs (see Egypt*).

Dissolution of Egypt's Empire in Asia: Pharaoh Akhenaton could send no help to his beleaguered vassals. He was fully occupied with internal religious reform and struggles with the Egyptian priesthood. Egyptian control of Palestine lapsed and was not reestablished until 1320–1290 BCE, the reigns of Seti I and Ramses II. The Hittites made full use of their

74

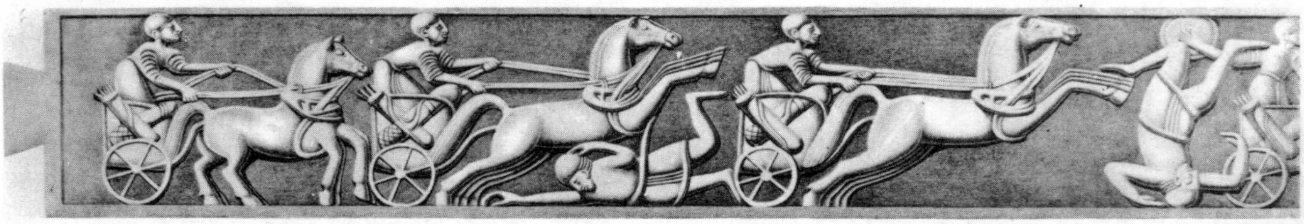

75

opportunity in the interim, extending their power over Syria and Northern Canaan, although they did not advance south of Galilee.

Canaanite and Habiru Upheaval: Many of the Amarna letters were written by the vassal King Rib-adda of the Phoenician* city of Byblos*(**75**). He was under constant pressure from the Amorite kings, who were advancing on Byblos, led by one Abdi-Ashirta. Rib-adda also notes complaints about the Habiru*, normally called "outlaws" by their enemies. In his letters, he makes many references to a high Egyptian officer, Yanhamu, who was apparently in charge of affairs in Palestine. This is the gist of another letter to Yanhamu from Ba'lu, a south Palestinian king. The court received letters from other Canaanite princes as well. Prince Abdi-Heba of Jerusalem, for example, writes about an attack by the Prince of Gezer* and a Habiru chieftain on a northern district: "They rushed troops of Gezer, troops of Gath and troops of Qeilah; they took the land of Rubutta (north), the land of the king went over to the Habiru people." (Letter 290:8–13.) The letter equates rebellion with "going over to the Habiru". A battle scene is reproduced on an ivory plaque from Megiddo (**74** ; late 14th c. BCE).

Labayu of Shechem: One of the letters, from King Biridiya of Megiddo, accuses King Labayu of Shechem who controlled much of the central hills north of Jerusalem, of helping the Habiru to attack Megiddo and of giving them Shechem. This was a cardinal sin, for all the established princes were expected to unite against the Habiru "outlaws". Biridiya later captured Labayu and imprisoned him in Acre. Payment of a ransom secured his freedom but some time afterwards he was killed, leaving his sons to continue collaboration with the Habiru in fomenting revolt against the Egyptian authority among the neighbouring city-states.

Peoples and Conditions in the Amarna Age: The Amarna letters contain a wealth of political, historical, geographical and social information which makes them an excellent source of knowledge of the peoples and conditions of the Late Bronze Age — 15th and 14th centuries BCE.

From the letters it appears that loyal local princes were, in fact, merely Egyptian puppets. They could not withstand their rebellious "hupshu" (serfs). Letter 118:22–23 states: "Truly at the rebelling of the hupshu, the Habiru seize the city." Apparently the Habiru were eager to join the winning side whenever victory seemed possible. They had no place in organized society and they were prepared to sell their loyalty to whoever made the best offer. The Amorites who fought Rib-adda of Byblos welcomed malcontents like the Habiru and tried to win them over. Biblical parallels can be found from the 13th and 12th centuries BCE, for example the "outlaws" (the Bible uses the word in a pejorative sense) who joined Abimelech and Jephthah (Jud.* 9, 11:3). G. E. Mendenhall has suggested that "Habiru" was used during the Amarna Age as a contemptuous term for any enemies.

The Royal Domain and Forced Labour: The Egyptian system of governmental control and taxation during the period is clearly brought out in the Amarna letters. A hierarchy of officials in charge of each vassal state was responsible for obtaining tribute for the Egyptian treasury as well as overseeing the corvée (forced labour) in the government-owned fields. Each local prince or king was obliged to pay his share of the *mazza* (Hebrew *mas* or tax) and had to supply either grain from his own fields or men for the forced labour contingents. An example of how the system worked is found in a letter sent by King Biridiya of Megiddo*, who was responsible for the royal Egyptian domain established in Megiddo by Thotmes III. Biridiya writes that he will not be able to supply the stipulated quota of grain unless the Egyptians send military reinforcements. The local vassals were also expected to send expensive gifts of precious stones, ivory, copper, slaves, concubines or, in general, "caravans" to the Egyptian court as illustrated by this wall painting (**76**; 13th c. BCE).

76

The Habiru and the Conquest*: The similarity of the Habiru of the Amarna age to the "outlaws" mentioned above has provoked considerable scholarly discussion of possible historical connections between the Amarna correspondence and the biblical narratives. Whether or not any of the Patriarchal stories coincide with this period remains an open question. The Amarna letters relate to social and political conditions in Canaan at least a century before the Exodus* and Conquest* (according to the most recent scholarly consensus), while the biblical Hebrews were still in Egypt. In addition the kingdoms east of the Jordan, which the Israelites encountered during their journey to the Promised Land, were not established entities before the 13th century BCE. Excavation of the cities which according to biblical tradition were conquered by the Israelites under Joshua (Bethel*, Debir, Eglon, Lachish*, Hazor*), has produced evidence for a series of devastating military attacks launched during the period from 1250 to 1200 BCE, which fits the Bible stories but also puts them much later than the Amarna letters. Similarly, the Hebrews and the Habiru are also separated in time and place, although there are substantial indications of a more general, indirect relationship.

AMOS. — *Outline: Date and Historical Background; Personality and Social Background; Contents and Unity of the Book; Amos' Style; His Message; His Attitude to the Popular Cult; At Bethel; Amos and the New Prophecy; Amos and Hosea.*

Amos appears in the Canon of the Old Testament as the third of the Minor Prophets, although, chronologically, he was the earliest of them. He prophesied during the reigns of Jeroboam II of Israel — an important figure in Amos' prophecies — and Uzziah of Judah, who ruled at almost the same time (Amos 1:1). Amos is the first of the prophets whose oracles have been recorded more or less as delivered, although he himself did not compose or write down his book. He came before Isaiah, whose vision of dedication took place "In the year that King Uzziah died" (Is. 6:1).

Date and Historical Background: Amos announces (1:1) that he began prophesying "in the days of Uzziah the king . . . two years before the earthquake". As it is not known exactly when the earthquake took place, this does not establish a precise date for the beginning of Amos' mission. Instead, scholars have attempted to define the period of Amos' activity by reference to the historical background reflected in his prophecies.

Jeroboam II and Uzziah ruled during the first half of the 8th c. BCE, a period of prosperity and greatness for both their kingdoms. Following the defeat of Aram-Damascus by Adadnirari III of Assyria in 805 BCE, Jehoash, Jeroboam's father, retrieved for Israel cities which Damascus had taken from her in previous years (II K. 10:32; 13:25). Between them, the kings of Israel and Judah controlled an area more or less the same as the empire which Solomon had ruled, along with the main trade routes to the Red Sea and Arabian ports (see map, Israel and Judah*, II; Trade*; Ships*). After the death of Adadnirari III (782 BCE), a series of weak kings in Assyria left the Palestinian kingdoms free from external threats.

Amos' oracles reflect this period of internal development and commercial expansion. A class of wealthy landowners and merchants grew richer and, simultaneously, more oppressive towards the small peasants and poorer people. Rich men found means of dispossessing the poorer farmers and turning them out of the lands that had been their fathers'. Social equality became a thing of the past and many of Israel's most hallowed traditions were destroyed by the unthinking drive for wealth of those who, as Amos complains, "trample upon the needy and bring the poor of the land to an end . . . (and) buy the needy for a pair of sandals" (8:4–6). A new social structure developed, increasingly dependent upon the Court, and moving further and further away from the concept of obligation as well as privilege that had been a conspicuous feature of the Covenant Law (see Law*; Agriculture*).

In spite of social strain in some quarters, the general atmosphere of the country was one of affluence and security and this feeling is also reflected in Amos' oracles — evidence in the view of many scholars that he lived and prophesied before Tiglat-Pileser came to the Assyrian throne in 745 BCE and began his westward expansion, a few years after the end of Jeroboam's brilliant reign (748 BCE). Amos' prophecies of disaster all hinged on theological and ethical considerations — without reference to contemporary international politics. Amos foretold that the corruption of the ruling classes would lead to disaster, but he gave no indication of the direction from which that disaster would come. He even appears to have visualized the "Day of Yahweh" as a combination of earthquake (2:14–15), war and exile (7:11; passim), in contrast to contemporary popular beliefs that that "Day" would see God's intervention in the world to fulfill his promises to the Hebrews.

Personality and Social Background: Of Amos himself we know almost nothing apart from his experience at Bethel (see below). He was a shepherd (or small sheep farmer) and "dresser of sycamore trees" (perhaps figs or mulberries) in Tekoa, on the borders of the Judean wilderness (1:1; 7:14). A peasant and a worker himself, living far from the busy life of the cities, he looked at society from the point of view of the lower classes and vividly records the realities of social life. His rural background is apparent in all his prophecy. He likens God to a roaring lion (3:4, 8) in the forest or wilderness and speaks of the "mourning" pastures and withered mountain tops (1:2). The wealthy ladies of Samaria he calls "cows of Bashan" and he envisages the remnant of Israel as the legs or piece of an ear of a sheep rescued from the mouth of a lion (3:12). His metaphors are also strongly reminiscent of country life. These were the standard literary clichés of his age and may not be a valid clue to Amos' personality. Certainly they give no indication of his spiritual experience and his concern for social righteousness. Nor should it be assumed from his rural background that Amos was ignorant or uneducated. His utterances are all phrased in a polished Hebrew. Nothing is known about how his call to prophecy came to him, beyond his own express denial that he had been a member of the prophetic guilds (see below). His book also makes it clear that he was familiar with city life and its temptations to corruption. He condemns urban luxury (6:4–7), extortion and immorality (2:4–8) and the superficial attitude to religion that sees all obligations discharged by a pilgrimage and a few sacrifices without reference to righteousness or morality (4:4–5; see Contents, below).

Although Amos was born in Tekoa, in Judah, most of the prophecies recorded in his name were uttered in the northern Kingdom of Israel, although he also spoke about Judah. Various theories have been put forward to account for this, for instance that his birthplace was another Tekoa in Israel, or that he settled in Judah after being expelled from Israel. None of these theories carry much weight in the face of the general evidence of the book itself. For Amos, the people of Judah and Israel were one people. He prophesied in Israel simply because, at the time, this was the richer and more important of the two kingdoms. Wherever he uttered his prophecies — whether in Bethel at the northern king's sanctuary (7:13) or in its capital, Samaria, Amos spoke to the whole of "Zion", sure of God's care for all "His people".

Contents and Unity of the Book: Like all the books of prophecy, Amos is not a single whole, but a series of oracles, made orally, remembered, transmitted and later written down. Nevertheless, most of the book is straightforward in plan and the few literary or textual problems it raises are mainly the oracle in ch. 6 and the prologue (see below).

The book opens with an introduction (1:1–2:16) which surveys the countries surrounding Israel and condemns their characteristic crimes. Then he compares Israel's own evil-doing to her neighbours' transgressions (especially their social injustices) and predicts a similar punishment. This is followed (chs. 3, 4 and 5–6) by three separate addresses, not originally connected, first extolling the grace of God, then bemoaning the sins of Israel and her refusal to take heed of earlier warnings. He predicts the punishment that shall be executed on the "Day of Yahweh" when God will raise up against Israel a nation who "shall oppress you from the entrance of Hamath to the Brook of the Arabah", namely from the north to the south (6:14).

This is followed (7–9:8) by five visions of judgment and punishment: the vision of locusts (7:1–3); drought (7:4–6); the plumb-line (7:7–9); the basket of summer fruits (8:1–3) and the destruction of Israelites (9:1–4). A brief insertion (7:10–17) describes a lively exchange between Amos and the priest of Bethel. Finally comes the epilogue (9:8b–15) which is in striking contrast to the tone of the rest of the book, for it speaks of the eventual restoration of Israel and the prosperity which "the remnant" will enjoy.

Thus, side by side with Amos' condemnation of the crimes of Israel's neighbours, comes his censure of Israel for its social injustice and of Judah for rejecting "the law of the Lord and have not kept his statutes, but their lies have led them astray, after which their fathers walked" (2:4). At one time, scholars doubted whether the section was justly attributed to Amos, and they also believed that the oracle about Edom (1:11–12) must have been composed during or just after the destruction of the state. However, as Edom and Judah hated each other cordially ever after David's conquest of Edom, there seems no reason why Amos should not have included it in his catalogue of evildoers. The background to many of the oracles is not clear enough for them to be completely interpreted today. However, it appears to some scholars that the text of 6:2, which refers to the destruction of Calneh, Hamath and Gath, is a later addition. Calneh is assumed by some to be the city in Assyria; Hamath in Syria was destroyed by Assyria late in the 8th c. BCE, Gath in 711 BCE. This is all much too late for Amos and was presumably inserted by the later Judean editors under the influence of Isaiah 19 (which refers to the conquests of Tiglat-Pileser III between 740 and 732 BCE). Another later insertion, according to another school of thought, is the reference to the rebuilding of "the booth of David that is fallen", referring, apparently, to the dynasty of David. This prophecy in their opinion can only have been composed after the fall of the Judean kingdom, probably towards the end of the Babylonian Exile, or at least at the end of the Davidic dynasty (580 BCE).

It is probably going too far, however, to try to deny Amos authorship of the whole of the epilogue simply because it is in a different mood from the earlier doom-laden prophecies. Disaster was not the whole of Amos' message. Like the other prophets, he saw calamities as a means of purging Israel of her wrong-doing and bringing her back to God and an eventual joyful future.

Amos' Style: Apart from the use of metaphor drawn from the country life he knew, Amos' whole poetic style is simple and direct, very much as might be expected of one who lived close to nature. His main concessions to rhetoric are the repeated "for three transgressions and for four. . ." (1:3, 6, 9, 11, 13; 2:1, 4, 6; passim) and the use of the imperative, "Hear this word . . .". The passage 3:3–8 is also in the form of a series of rhetorical questions.

His Message: Amos' most outstanding feature is his concern with social behaviour and ethics. He cries out against the oppression of the poor by the wealthy and powerful (2:6–7; 3:10; 4:1; 5:11), against dishonest merchants (8:4–6), against those who divert justice by bribery (5:7, 10–12) and against the idleness and luxury of the wealthy (6:4–7). Alongside the decline of social morality, religion too had become corrupt, the shrines being centres of sin (4:4), prostitution and intemperance (2:7–8). In retribution, Amos proclaims, the rich and their property shall be destroyed (3:11, 15; 4:3; 5:11, 16; 7:11) and the shrines cut down (3:14; 5:5; 7:9, passim).

Amos' view of God was as the Lord of nature, creator of the world and of man (5:8; 9:5–6). Typically, he refers to God not as "the God of Israel" but as "Lord (or God) of Hosts" (3:13; 4:13; 5:14, 17), who brought Israel out of Egypt. It was also God who brought the Philistines from Caphtor and the Syrians from Kir (9:7). At present, Amos does not believe that Israel stands any higher in God's regard than the Ethiopians (9:7). The difference is that Israel's election as God's "Chosen People" means that Israel will not be totally destroyed because of its sins. A remnant will be saved to enjoy the promise of the Covenant (9:11–15) after sinners have been wiped out (9:8–10). These views do not belong exclusively to the post-Exilic period. They are entirely in keeping with the whole of Amos' theology and the tone of his prophecy.

Amos' Attitude to the Popular Cult: The passage 5:21–25 reads like a total rejection of the popular cult, its sacrifices and ritual. In the light of all his teaching it seems that Amos was not rejecting the formal cult as such, but the idea that ritual was the main element in the worship of God. He rejected a cult that was practiced side by side with prostitution and drunkenness (2:7–8; 4:4) and without regard to true righteousness or repentance. Instead of burnt offerings and songs, God, he taught, demands justice in everyday dealings and a righteous life.

Amos at Bethel: The narrative about Amos and Amaziah, the priest of Bethel, official sanctuary of the northern Kingdom (7:10–17), has been made the basis for a number of theories about Amos' position in Israel and the relationship of his ministry to Bethel. Taking Amos for one of the professional "Sons of the Prophets" (see Elijah*; Elisha*), stirring up revolution as such prophets had often done before (e. g. II K. 9:1 ff.), Amaziah ordered him to leave Bethel and Israel and flee to Judah (7:12–13). Amos indignantly denied the charge. He declared that he was "no prophet nor a prophet's son" (7:14), but a herdsman and dresser of sycamore trees. He did not belong to the ranks of the ecstatic or professional prophets attached to courts and rulers (I K. 22:6 ff) and subservient to them. However, he certainly regarded himself as a prophet in the most ancient sense of someone, like Moses, called by God to serve: "and the Lord took me from following the flock and the Lord said to me, 'Go prophesy to my people Israel" (7:15). From his words it seems that there had been legitimate prophets before him. In fact, there may have been something like a continuous line going all the way back to Moses (Dt. 34:10). In earlier times, the Israelites drew no absolute distinctions between prophet, diviner, poet or charismatic leader. Amos came with a call to repentance and a return to the true God. This was the classic prophetic message, the true voice of divine inspiration.

Bethel is mentioned frequently in the various oracles — generally unfavourably — and the description of his clash with the official priesthood there is clear evidence that Amos did indeed prophesy at the northern shrine. Whether he prophesied there only, however, is not so clear. Amos would have expressed his condemnation of Bethel in any case, both for itself, and as representing all the other polluted shrines. Secondly, as a Judean, Amos may well have regarded the Temple of Jerusalem as the only genuine seat of Yahweh (1:2). Whether or not this encounter with Amaziah actually ended Amos' ministry at Bethel or in Israel is not certain.

Amos and the New Prophecy: Before Amos, the prophecies of his predecessors (Elijah, Elisha, Samuel or Nathan) were recorded only as part of the general history of their time. These earlier prophets combined more than one function or gift. Some scholars today consider that they can be classified as either interpreters of signs or ecstatics. Ecstatic prophecy was of particularly wide-spread importance in the days of Samuel and the early monarchy. It was during this period that the prophetic groups known as the "Sons of the Prophets" (see Elisha*) appeared and this may indicate a search for a more suitable vehicle for promoting ecstatic prophecy.

Unlike Amos, the earlier prophets were prepared to foretell the immediate future like the magicians and diviners of contemporary courts and Elisha, at least, used the stimulation of music to inspire his prophecy (II K. 3:15). It is possible that this and other obviously ecstatic practices were learned from the Canaanites out of deference to their culture.

Amos and Hosea*: These two prophets were contemporaries and prophesied at almost the same time. The general historical background to their words was thus the same. Both were active in Israel in the days of Jeroboam II. Like Amos, Hosea also stresses the social corruption, extortion and deceit of the age and the decadence of the popular cult (Hos. 4:12–14). He also quarrels with the sanctuaries, especially Bethel which he calls Beth Aven (house of sin; Hos. 4:15; 10:5, etc.). While it is doubtful whether Amos thought of Bethel as actually a pagan shrine, Hosea certainly did (Hos. 8:6). He probably prophesied a few years later than Amos.

In spite of the many similarities between them, it used to be thought that they were the antitheses of each other, Hosea being regarded as the prophet of love and mercy and Amos as a wrathful prophet of doom. In fact, the distinction is superficial and is essentially one of emphasis. Both prophets proclaimed a "Day of Yahweh" on which Israel's sins would be punished. Though Hosea's descriptions of judgment and his denunciations are as strong, if not stronger, than anything Amos says, he expresses the hope that Israel will repent in time, and will return, as a bride, to her Lord. Then, after accounts have been settled, a reformed Israel will live in full enjoyment of God's love and grace. For Amos, on the other hand, the "Day of Yahweh" is a day of "darkness not light" and while, at the end, he holds out hopes of mercy for the "remnant of Israel", his main concern is with the sinners and the terrible punishment that will be meted out to them. However, he does teach that Israel, alone among the nations, can hope for salvation, provided they repent in time (5:14–15).

ANCIENT CITIES, EXCAVATED SITES, BIBLICAL ARCHAEOLOGY AND ARCHAEOLOGICAL SEQUENCE. — *Followed by descriptions of ancient cities in Palestine, in alphabetic order.*

Reference is made throughout this book to the ancient towns of Palestine, many of which have been excavated and have provided material evidence for different periods and aspects of biblical history. The artifacts and other traces of past civilizations which have been unearthed are a major source of information about cultural developments within the country over periods stretching from the 7th mill. BCE to the 1st c. CE. Today, as a result of these discoveries, archaeology and biblical studies have gained a vast amount of knowledge which was not available a century, or even thirty years ago. Many people — including certain popular writers on the subject — assume that the chief value of biblical archaeology is to confirm the historical statements in the Bible. In fact, archaeology rarely proves a biblical statement true in the sense that it exactly reproduces its image. What it has done — and continues to do — is to illuminate the historical, cultural and religious background of the biblical narratives and, in addition, to provide factual evidence which can help in assessing the significance of the stories themselves.

This archaeological evidence can be grouped under various headings, as follows:

a. **The Patriarchal Period,** i.e. the culture and organization of Palestine's towns and society in the first half of the 2nd mill. BCE, the Middle Bronze Age. Excavation of towns such as Jericho*, Lachish*, Tel Beit Mirsim, Gezer*,

Hazor* and Shechem* has built up a fairly good picture of this period, described in the articles on these and other towns in question, and on Cities, Canaanite*; Canaan* Gods and Idols; Agriculture*, Crafts*, Arms*, War*, etc (cf. Index).

b. **Conquest and Settlement:** While archaeological discovery has illuminated the background to the Israelites' emergence in Canaan, it has also raised as many problems as it solved. Excavation of the key sites related to the biblical narrative, (Jericho*, Bethel and Ai*, Lachish*, Ashdod*, etc.) has revealed a vast amount of chronological data but has signally failed to provide any conclusive evidence about the actual date of the Exodus and the events that followed it. What has been made clear is that in fact the process of establishment in the Promised Land was far more complex than the Old Testament texts would suggest, (see Conquest*; Joshua*; Books of Joshua and Judges*). It is also very apparent that there was no major break in the pattern of cultures until after 1200 BCE. Thus it seems that what probably happened was both a sweeping invasion and a slow process of infiltration and the gradual assertion of Israelite supremacy over the Canaanites, possibly completed around 1000 BCE with the emergence of the first Israelite kingdom (see Judges*; Saul*; Samuel*).

c. **The Monarchy:** Evidence for the culture and daily life of the Israelites during this historical period has been amply illustrated from the excavation of both the larger cities and many smaller sites, (described in the articles following this introduction).

Every excavation has produced examples of the tools*, weapons*, musical instruments (see Music*), ritual implements (see Sacrifice*), household goods and foods in daily use by the people; while potteries, oil and dyeing workshops and major discoveries like those of the copper mines of the Arabah and Solomon's smelting plant at Ezion Geber have strikingly illustrated economic life, in this case in Solomon's kingdom.

Together with the ruins of the cities unearthed, remains like these have done much to amplify the biblical narratives. The biblical account of the foundation of Samaria during the reign of Omri, for instance, was confirmed by the pottery found on the site — none of which can be dated earlier than the Middle Iron Age, around 900 BCE. The manner in which the stones of city walls were cut can also testify to cultural developments. The walls of Ahab's Samaria* were found to have been cut in a style similar to the Phoenician tombs at Achzib or the buildings of Ugarit* — sure evidence of foreign cultural influence.

Excavations have also shed light on contemporary attitudes to Israel's religion. The frequent discovery of Ashtoreth (Astarte) figurines (see Canaan, Gods and Idols*; Idol Worship in Israel*), from the period of the Monarchy are a vivid demonstration of just how real was the threat of a spread of the idolatrous practices against which the prophets thundered.

In addition, many of the biblical statements or references which have puzzled scholars for generations have also been satisfactorily explained by archaeological discoveries. Ahab's "ivory house" for instance (I K. 22:39), was found from excavation to have been almost exactly that. Fragments of ivory carvings found in Samaria had apparently once adorned a palace — or its furniture — decorated with ivory tablets or plaques, as illustrated by the fragments (**176**) whence the name 'ivory house'. Similarly, two of the water* installations specifically mentioned in the Bible have been identified: the Pool of Samaria (I K. 22:38) and the Siloam Tunnel (II K. 20:20).

d. **Post-Exilic Palestine:** The culture and organisation of life during Hasmonean*, Hellenistic* and Roman* times (5th c. BCE to 2nd c. CE) has been extensively documented by the excavation of such sites as Maresha*, Gezer*, Gerasa, Herod's Samaria*, Caesarea* and Jerusalem*.

Written Sources: In general, one of the richest sources of information about the background and history of Israel is provided by the written material found by excavations, enumerated in a number of articles (Amarna Letters*, Assyria*, Babylonia*, Egypt*, Israel and Judah, kingdoms of*, Moab*, Hellenism* and Rome and the Jews*). Seals* and Inscriptions* on monuments and ostraca are obviously a valuable indication for dating ancient sites and their contents.

Discoveries of ancient written materials have often had a revolutionary effect on knowledge and theories about particular periods or subjects. The Dead Sea Scrolls*, to take a recent outstanding example, have made a very substantial contribution to knowledge of Jewish religion in the days of the Second Temple*; the origins of Christianity and the history of the books of the Old Testament.

Material Remains: Written sources are extensively supplemented by the material remains of vanished ages, represented in the illustrations throughout this book. The most important remains are architectural — the buildings and associated installations of Canaanite*, Israelite*, Philistine*, Phoenician* and Hellenistic* Cities. The installations include things like kilns and ovens (see Pottery*, Food*, Crafts: Tools and Implements*), cisterns (see Water Supply*), vats and pits for the storage of food and so on.

Movable objects include weapons*, jewellery (see Clothing*), utensils and tools* and, above all, pottery (see below).

Topographical Information: Archaeological data have often served to correct misconceptions about the identification of certain places based only on similarities of name. Thus it has been shown that the present day Khirbet Burj' as-Sur is not the site of Beth Zur, although it preserves the name. The true site of the ancient town and its Hasmonean* system of walls (**77**) is at Khirbet el-Tubeiqa nearby

Topographical research has also contributed to general biblical history. For example, evidence has been found to confirm the biblical narratives by showing that during the period of the Patriarchs* (Middle Bronze Age), most of the people of Palestine lived in the plains and valleys, leaving the tree-covered hills as sparsely-populated pastures. In the same way, the study of the ruins of Transjordania confirmed the impression given by the story in Gn. 14 that the "Kings' Highway" (see Roads*) was an important line of communication as early as the 18th c. BCE. On the other hand, dating the Exodus* has been, if anything, further confused by the results of archaeology.

Archaeological Sequence or Chronology: The chronology of developments within a single site or a whole culture can

77

often be established with a surprising degree of accuracy by means of a careful study of commonplace objects. The most valuable are the objects and pieces of pottery* found in great quantities in every excavation in Palestine. Pottery is one of the best indications of links with the cultures of adjacent peoples and regions. More important, the evolution of the potter's craft and the various styles employed by different peoples and at different times is now so well known that it is possible to date a piece of pottery to within a relatively very short period (sometimes as little as 50 years).

The relation of archaeological periods to Bible history, as generally accepted by archaeologists is shown on the following brief table:

CHRONOLOGICAL TABLE

Archaeological Period	*Date*	*Historical Parallel*
Chalcolithic	4000–3100 BCE	Proto-urban period (see e.g. Beersheba* Jericho*, Beth-Shean*, Beth-Yerach).
Early Bronze	3000–2000 BCE	Before Patriarchal* period.
Middle Bronze I	2000–1750 BCE	
Middle Bronze II	1750–1550 BCE	Patriarchal period. Hyksos era.
Late Bronze	1550–1230 BCE	Egyptian domination of Canaan; Exodus*; Conquest*
Iron I	1230–900 BCE	Israelite Setttlement* in Canaan; Judges*; United Kingdom.
Iron II	930–586 BCE	Kingdoms of Judah and Israel*.
Iron III (Persian period)	586–332 BCE	Babylonian* rule in Palestine: Exile*; Restoration* and Persian* Rule.
Hellenistic	332–63 BCE	Hellenistic* kingdoms; Maccabean revolt; Hasmonean* dynasty.
Roman (to Hadrian's rule)	63 BCE–136 CE	Herodian* dynasty; First Jewish-Roman War*; Fall of Jerusalem*; Destruction of the Second Temple*; Second Jewish-Roman War (Bar-Kochba*).

Ancient Cities: The variety of disciplines that make up the science of biblical archaeology take the discoveries of excavations and from them extract every piece of information bearing upon the Bible — directly or indirectly. Brief surveys of the results so far obtained can be found in the following articles on the sites in question. These include not only major excavations but also less important ones where discoveries were made which were significant for certain biblical periods or institutions (see map **78**). The articles on cities in ancient Israel are arranged under the name of the site in alphabetical order. The cities of the Philistines* and Phoenicians*, Nabatean* sites such as Petra or Hellenistic cities* like Gerasa (Jerash), are included in the articles under those headings.

Data on Israelite daily life and various phases of her cultural development from the Middle Bronze Age to Graeco-Roman times appear in articles under more general headings and may be found via the Index.

ANCIENT CITIES OF PALESTINE

ARAD. — The Canaanite City of the Time of Moses: Arad is mentioned in Numbers 21:1–3 as the royal stronghold of a Canaanite king. During the early phase of the Conquest*, this king was initially successful in rallying other cities of southern Canaan against the Hebrews who were trying to invade the country from the south. He defeated the Hebrews at the neighbouring town of Hormah (situated apparently at Tel-M'shash, some 18 kms. to the southwest of the Arad of the Conquest). Arad was later captured by Joshua (Jos. 12:14) with the defeat of the southern league of Canaanite kings, and it became part of the tribal portion of Judah. The Kenites*, kinsmen of Judah, settled the region. This town of Arad is now identified with Tel-Melhata, lying close to Tel-M'shash (and not Tel-Arad as explained below).

Two Towns with the Same Name: In the borderland between the Negeb and the southern hills of Judah, some 25 kms. south of Hebron*, lies an ancient mound (tel) called Tel-Arad by the natives. In past years, archaeologists commonly identified it with the Canaanite city of the Late Bronze Age. However, recent research has questioned whether the Arabs of the locality had preserved the name from ancient times, and whether this was identical with the biblical site (see below). Exploration of the locality failed to uncover pottery belonging to the time of Moses and Joshua (Late Bronze Age, 14th–13th c. BCE). The site of Tel-Arad can therefore not be regarded as the town of the Canaanite king who fought the invading Hebrews, and the biblical city of Arad has to be sought further afield.

The existence of towns named Arad in two places is explained, however, by an extra-biblical source. The famous list of the Egyptian, Shoshenk (ca. 945 BCE) on the Bubastite Gate at Karnak mentions Arad among the towns he claims to have conquered in southern Palestine (see Israel and Judah*, Part II). It speaks of Arad "of the house of Yeruham" next to Arad "the great". It would appear that two towns by that name existed in Shoshenk's time, i.e. shortly after the death of King Solomon*, one of them bearing the name of the Judahite-Kenite clan (Jeruham) well known in the region (see Kenites*). Excavations conducted in Tel-Arad in 1962–63 CE by J. Aharoni (described below) have shown

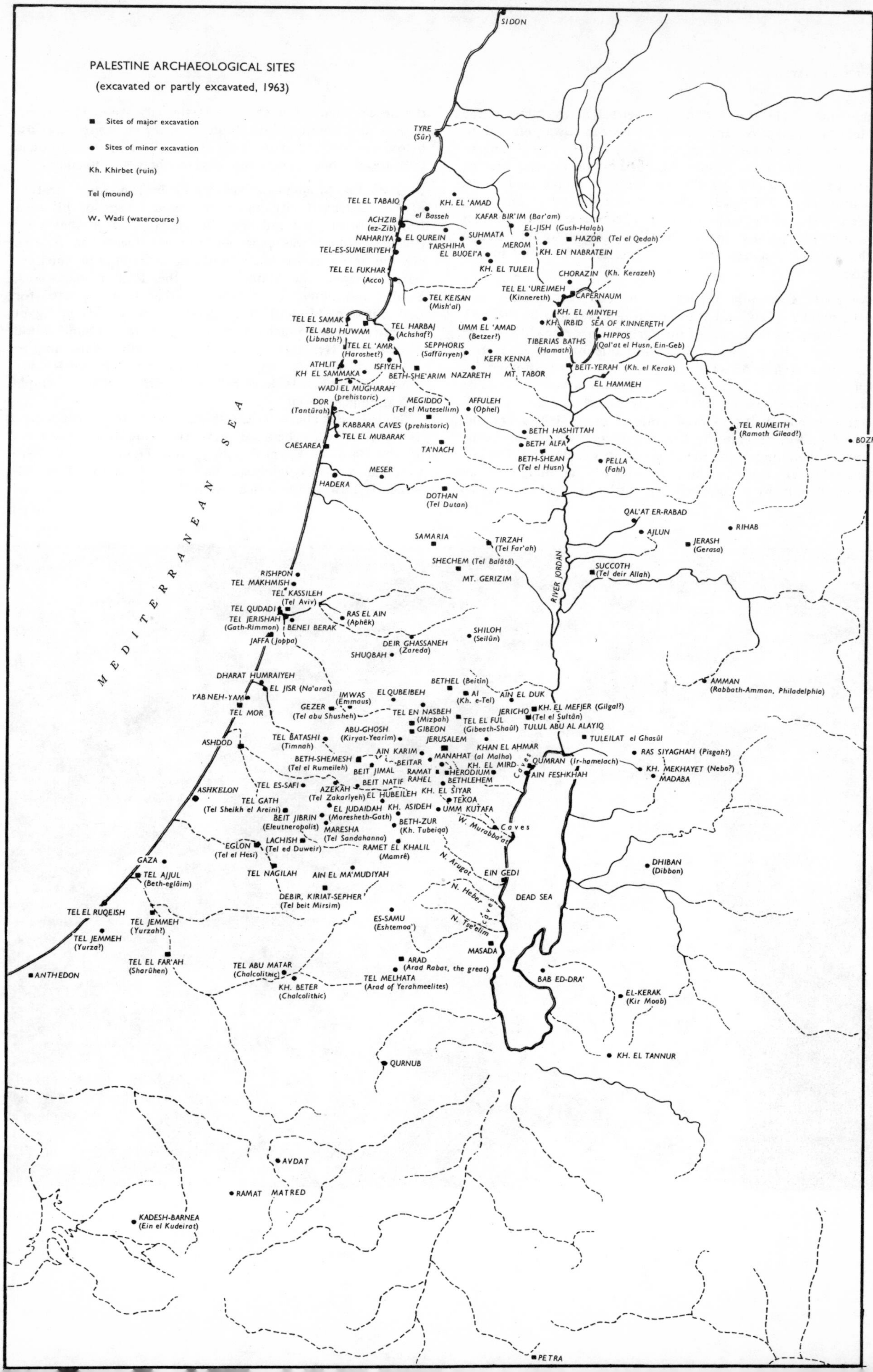
PALESTINE ARCHAEOLOGICAL SITES
(excavated or partly excavated, 1963)
Sites of major excavation
Sites of minor excavation
Kh. Khirbet (ruin)
Tel (mound)
W. Wadi (watercourse)
MEDITERRANEAN SEA
SIDON
TYRE (Sûr)
TEL EL TABAIQ
KH. EL 'AMAD
el Basseh
KAFAR BIR'IM (Bar'am)
ACHZIB (ez-Zib)
NAHARIYA
EL QUREIN
SUHMATA
EL-JISH (Gush-Halab)
HAZOR (Tel el Qedah)
TEL-ES-SUMEIRIYEH
TARSHIHA
EL BUQEI'A
MEROM
KH. EN NABRATEIN
KH. EL TULEIL
TEL EL FUKHAR (Acco)
CHORAZIN (Kh. Kerazeh)
TEL EL 'UREIMEH (Kinnereth)
CAPERNAUM
TEL KEISAN (Mish'al)
KH. EL MINYEH
KH. IRBID
SEA OF KINNERETH
TEL EL SAMAK
TEL ABU HUWAM (Libnath?)
TEL HARBAJ (Achshaf?)
UMM EL 'AMAD (Betzer?)
TIBERIAS BATHS (Hamath)
HIPPOS (Qal'at el Husn, Ein-Geb)
TEL EL 'AMR (Haroshet?)
SEPPHORIS (Saffûriyeh)
KEFR KENNA
ATHLIT
ISFIYEH
BEIT-YERAH (Kh. el Kerak)
KH EL SAMMAKA
BETH-SHE'ARIM
NAZARETH
MT. TABOR
EL HAMMEH
WADI EL MUGHARAH (prehistoric)
DOR (Tantûrah)
MEGIDDO (Tel el Mutesellim)
AFFULEH (Ophel)
KABBARA CAVES (prehistoric)
TEL EL MUBARAK
BETH HASHITTAH
TEL RUMEITH (Ramoth Gilead?)
BOZRAH
CAESAREA
TA'NACH
BETH ALFA
BETH-SHEAN (Tel el Husn)
PELLA (Fahl)
MESER
HADERA
DOTHAN (Tel Dutan)
QAL'AT ER-RABAD
AJLUN
RIHAB
SAMARIA
TIRZAH (Tel Far'ah)
JERASH (Gerasa)
SHECHEM (Tel Balâta)
MT. GERIZIM
RIVER JORDAN
SUCCOTH (Tel deir Allah)
RISHPON
TEL MAKHMISH
TEL KASSILEH (Tel Aviv)
TEL QUDADI
TEL JERISHAH (Gath-Rimmon)
RAS EL AIN (Aphêk)
BENEI BERAK
JAFFA (Joppa)
SHILOH (Seilûn)
DEIR GHASSANEH (Zareda)
SHUQBAH
DHARAT HUMRAIYEH
EL JISR (Na'arat)
BETHEL (Beitin)
AMMAN (Rabbath-Ammon, Philadelphia)
YABNEH-YAM
IMWAS (Emmaus)
EL QUBEIBEH
AI (Kh. e-Tel)
AIN EL DUK
GEZER (Tel abu Shusheh)
TEL EN NASBEH (Mizpah)
JERICHO
KH. EL MEFJER (Gilgal?)
(Tel el Sultân)
TEL MOR
TEL EL FUL (Gibeath-Shaûl)
TULUL ABU AL ALAYIQ
ABU-GHOSH (Kiryat-Yearim)
GIBEON
TULEILAT el Ghasûl
ASHDOD
TEL BATASHI (Timnah)
JERUSALEM
KHAN EL AHMAR
RAS SIYAGHAH (Pisgah?)
BETH-SHEMESH (Tel el Rumeileh)
AIN KARIM
BEITAR
MANAHAT (al Malha)
QUMRAN (Ir-hamelach)
KH. MEKHAYET (Nebo?)
BEIT JIMAL
RAMAT RAHEL
KH. EL MIRD
HERODIUM
AIN FESHKHAH
MADABA
Caves
TEL ES-SAFI
BEIT NATIF
BETHLEHEM
ASHKELON
AZEKAH (Tel Zakariyeh)
EL HUBEILEH
KH. EL SIYAR
TEL GATH (Tel Sheikh el Areini)
TEKOA
EL JUDAIDAH (Moresheth-Gath)
KH. ASIDEH
UMM KUTAFA
BEIT JIBRIN (Eleutheropolis)
BETH-ZUR (Kh. Tubeiqa)
W. Murabba'at
MARESHA (Tel Sandahanna)
LACHISH (Tel ed Duweir)
EGLON (Tel el Hesi)
RAMET EL KHALIL (Mamrê)
GAZA
N. Arugot
DHIBAN (Dibbon)
TEL AJJUL (Beth-eglâim)
TEL NAGILAH
AIN EL MA'MUDIYAH
EIN GEDI
DEBIR, KIRIAT-SEPHER (Tel beit Mirsim)
N. Heber
DEAD SEA
TEL EL RUQEISH
TEL JEMMEH (Yurzah?)
ES-SAMU (Eshtemoa')
N. Tse'elim
TEL JEMMEH (Yurza?)
MASADA
ARAD (Arad Rabat, the great)
TEL EL FAR'AH (Sharûhen)
TEL ABU MATAR (Chalcolithic)
BAB ED-DRA'
ANTHEDON
TEL MELHATA (Arad of Yerahmeelites)
KH. BETER (Chalcolithic)
EL-KERAK (Kir Moab)
QURNUB
KH. EL TANNUR
AVDAT
RAMAT MATRED
KADESH-BARNEA (Ein el Kudeirat)
PETRA

that one of the towns had been settled at the time of the Hebrew monarchy, and seems to be the town referred to as Arad "the great". The Arad occupied by the "King of Arad" in the Late Bronze Age had to be located nearby, and the nearest possible site was Tel-Melhata (about 14 kms. southwest of Tel-Arad). The apparent difficulty caused by the transfer of the name of the city from one site to another is not infrequently encountered by archaeologists, though the distance between the two is greater than usual in this case.

An Early Canaanite Walled Town: The early anonymous settlement of Tel-Arad ("the great"), excavated in 1962–63, dates from the beginning of the Early Bronze Age (3000–2700; **79**). This early city was quite remarkable for its size, covering 25 acres. A line of walls a kilometre long surrounded the city and included three circular towers (see War*). The city was destroyed about 3000 BCE by desert nomads and left uninhabited. Well-preserved grain, almost 5000 years old, was found in stone mortars in one of the houses, apparently ready for milling at the time the city was destroyed. The city lies relatively close to the surface of the ground, its ruins covered only by a thin layer of dust blown over them by the desert winds. On the left is the city wall. The broad houses, 3–7 metres wide, built of unhewn stones are just below the surface. This Early Bronze II clay model house (**80**) found there, gives the key to their architecture.

Bitumen for Mummies: Excavations in this early stratum of the destroyed city have uncovered lumps of bitumen brought from the Dead Sea. The theory that, at that early period, bitumen was exported from the Dead Sea via this city for the purpose of mummification cannot be substantiated, despite the statement of the Roman historians, Strabo and Pliny, that bitumen of that type was used for that purpose. Modern investigation of mummies in Egypt has proven that no such bitumen was used for mummification prior to the Hellenistic period (from 332 BCE). According to A. Lucas, bitumen was never used until Graeco-Roman times, although it is described in modern books as a staple embalming material.

Some jars of characteristic shape, known to archaeologists as "Abydos" ware because they were found in large numbers at this famous Egyptian site (First Dynasty) and were thought to have originated there, have been found at Tel-Arad. It now seems more likely that certain products, oil

79

80

and perfumes for example, were brought to Egypt from Palestine and these jars of Tel-Arad were made in Palestine, possibly in this ancient city.

The Israelite Period of Settlement in Arad: After the destruction of the Early Bronze city, the site remained unoccupied for a very long time. It was settled at the time of Solomon (10th c. BCE), long after the Conquest*. Only a limited part of the ancient site was occupied again and the new town served mainly as a royal stronghold, with a fortress at its centre. S. Aharoni identifies it with the fortified town Shoshenk captured, called "Arad the great", though no explanation has yet been offered for this designation. Five fortresses, one on top of the other, were built at different stages (and in different strata) of Israelite history (from the 10th to the 6th c. BCE). The people living in this small fortress town, which guarded the important trading route from Hebron to Elath and Edom, were also active in various peacetime crafts and occupations. One of the rooms brought to light was a veritable kitchen-workshop for the preparation of cosmetics.

Israelite Inscriptions: The importance of Israelite Arad in peacetime as a developed urban centre for traders and as a manufacturing town explains the large number of inscriptions found there: weight-stones with simple inscriptions (see Weights and Measures*), and a number of ostraca (ink inscriptions on pottery) with data of a commercial nature, accounts, etc. Some of the ostraca are of a military and political nature, suggesting Arad's administrative importance as well. A number of the inscriptions apparently belong to the period of the First Temple, while others, in Aramaic, date to a later time, from the 4th c. BCE onwards. They promise to shed light on the commerce of the period of the Second Temple.

An Israelite Sanctuary and Holy of Holies of the 10th–9th c. BCE, without precedent in biblical discoveries, has been unearthed in Arad (**81**). Steps of unhewn stone led up to

81

82

the debîr from the "hekhāl" (see Temple*). At the front of the d^e^bîr stood two altars, with traces of calcinated bones still visible in the centre. In the background are two matzebôth or stele, with another to the right of the altar.

The uncovering of a sanctuary in this house (**81**) at Tel-Arad gives evidence of the religious life there in the days of the Judean monarchy. For the first time during a century of exacavation in Palestine, an altar was found with the charred bones of the sacrificial animal still *in situ* on the altar (**81**) (9th or 8th c. BCE). The sanctuary of Arad has provided important material for the study of Israelite religious architecture. Another find at Tel-Arad also belongs to the religious-magical sphere of the life of its people: some fragments of a pottery bowl of the 9th c. BCE showed when joined together, that the name "Arad" was engraved on it six times in ancient Hebrew (**82**). Several of the names are written in reverse order. It has been assumed that it was engraved once more on the missing part of the bowl and together the holy number, seven, would emerge. The invocations repeating the name of the city seven times could have had a magical intent. (This bowl, in the opinion of the discoverers, is additional evidence for identifying the tel with Israelite Arad.) The later fortifications of Tel-Arad date from the Hellenistic and Roman periods. The last fortifications built by the Romans as part of their defences around the country lasted until the Byzantine age.

The Arad of the Time of Joshua: It may be assumed that excavations at Tel-Melhata will reveal something of the past of the Arad of Late Canaanite times, at the time of the Conquest*. Surface examinations at Tel-Melhata have indicated mainly post-Exilic and Roman occupation levels. Meanwhile, the finds at Tel-Arad proper, from its earliest layers dating to the beginning of human history and the building of cities, and especially from its Israelite strata, show that it could be compared for its size, importance and riches to Hazor* of Canaanite times in Galilee.

83

ASHDOD. — Ashdod was the principal city of the Philistine pentapolis, established on the coastal plain early in the 11th c. BCE. Its name is preserved in the Arab village of Isdud, situated on the tel itself. Excavation of the site was initiated by a joint American-Israeli expedition in 1962 and preliminary results can serve to supplement previous knowledge of the city derived from the Bible and other documents.

One of the most striking results of the first archaeological season was the discovery that Tel Ashdod is one of the largest Iron Age cities, by Palestinian standards, with an area of over one hundred acres, or 400 dunams. (The area of Megiddo* is some 17 acres or 70 dunams.) The site comprises the upper and lower city: The upper city covers about 70 dunams, about the same as Megiddo* or Hazor*. The lower city, also walled, is much larger, covering several hundred dunams. Other cities probably had such lower towns as well, but they have never been investigated carefully, or they have not survived.

Excavation was concentrated on the southwestern part of the tel, where four areas were opened up. This is an aerial view of areas A, B (**84**). The earliest period of occupation was the Canaanite, to which brick houses, grain pits and ovens may be assigned. Imported pottery found in the three levels of Canaanite settlement bears witness to trade relations

85

84

86

with the Aegean Islands* and Cyprus. Such is this Cypriot juglet (**83**). Ornaments on pottery sherds (**85**), mainly of swan-like birds, suggest Aegean influence.

A tablet recently discovered in Ugarit* mentions the import of purple cloth from Ashdod, good indication of the importance of Ashdod's position on the international highway — the "Way of the Sea" (Via Maris).

Israelite Period: The biblical story of the capture of the Ark (I Sam. 4) mentions Ashdod as the city to which the victorious Philistines* first took it. There they installed it as a trophy of war in the temple of their god, Dagon (I Sam. 5). This temple, which may well have been destroyed and rebuilt many times, was apparently still in existence in the Hellenistic period, until reputedly destroyed by Jonathan the Hasmonean* (I Mac. 10:84).

Ample evidence of Philistine occupation was found with the excavation of a Philistine fortress in area A, whose strong brick wall is seen (**86**), and the discovery of a rubbish pit containing a rich and varied assortment of Philistine pottery. The same pottery was also found intruding in other parts of the tel (see Philistines*).

Under the Monarchy: In the period of the divided monarchy, Amos* foretold the destruction of Ashdod and its palaces. His prophecy was fulfilled, most probably in the first half of the 8th c. BCE, by King Uzziah of Judah who is said (II Ch. 26:6) to have breached the walls of Ashdod. The destruction may also be attributed to Sargon II in 712 BCE (see Assyrians*). However, the city quickly recovered. The new city which rose on the site is provisionally attributed by the excavators to a later date in the 8th c. BCE. In this

87

level, both male and female clay figurines were found, possibly representing the local deities. There were also libation bowls to which zoomorphic images mostly of domestic anaimals were attached. Other objects and installations uncovered were mainly of a cultic nature.

Under the Assyrians: Direct evidence of the capture and destruction of the city in 712 BCE, following an anti-Assyrian rebellion, is provided by fragments of the stele of Sargon found in the excavation in 1963, thus offering direct confirmation and vivid illustration of the biblical and Assyrian accounts. The story is also told in the inscriptions of Sargon found at Khorsabad. Apparently, Azuri, king of Ashdod, withheld tribute from Sargon and spread dissension among his neighbours. For this he was deposed, presumably by Assyrian officers, and his brother Ahimiti made ruler in his place. This move was opposed by the people of Ashdod who overthrew their new ruler and replaced him by a certain Iamani (who, to Sargon, was a usurper). Iamani followed Azuri's anti-Assyrian policy, perhaps with Egyptian backing. In response, Sargon sent an army against Philistia. Ashdod is listed among the cities captured by the Assyrians. Iamani fled to Nubia by way of Egypt but he was turned over to the Assyrians by the local authorities. In accordance with Assyrian policy, Ashdod's population was carried into captivity and new settlers were brought to the city from other parts of the empire. In 711 BCE it was made the centre of an Assyrian province under an imperial governor (Is. 20–1). Later on it reappears, ruled by local kings who are mentioned as paying tribute to the Assyrian emperors, Sennacherib and Esarhaddon.

The level corresponding to the last years of the Kingdom of Judah contained numerous ash pits which appear to be connected with the pottery making industry; at least six pottery kilns have been found with pottery inside. Two pottery kilns are shown here **(87)**. Towards the end of the 7th c. BCE, the city was destroyed, either, it is thought, by Psametik (Psammetichus) I, the king of Egypt, who is reported by Herodotus to have besieged Ashdod for 29 years before capturing it, or by Josiah, king of Judah, who enlarged the borders of his country to the west and south.

Under Persian Rule: In the time of Nebuchadrezzar, Ashdod was a small vassal kingdom of Babylonia and it became the capital of a semi-autonomous province while the Persians ruled Palestine. Nehemiah* speaks with bitterness and scorn of the Jews who had married Ashdodite women and the corrupt dialect which they and the children of these mixed marriages spoke (Neh. 13:23–24). Evidence of this is an ostracon of the 5th c. BCE, presumably in this dialect which is actually Hebrew or Aramaic.

Graeco-Roman Period: The earliest level reached on the summit of the tel by the 1962 excavations was the city of the Hellenistic period. Large stone buildings and other objects uncovered bear witness to a busy and prosperous community. This is a stone altar of incense **(88)** of the period. A red terra-sigilata bowl **(89)** is scratched with an inscription ZH whose meaning is not clear. Ashdod is called Azotus in Hellenistic documents. Its destruction by the Hasmoneans was recorded under this name. Nearly a century later (63 BCE) Pompey took the district away from the Jews, but it was returned to Herod in 30 BCE and became an important Jewish centre in Roman times.

The top two levels, containing the rich Herodian and Roman cities have been largely destroyed through erosion and cultivation, although remains of impressive building survive. In later Roman and Byzantine times, Ashdod declined in importance, its place being taken by the neighbouring port city of Azotus Paralius (ancient Ashdod Yam; see Ashkelon*; Philistines*).

88

89

91

ASHKELON (ASCALON): — The biblical town stood on a mound by the edge of the sea, within the wide half-circle of walls, aqueducts and forts which surrounded the much later Crusader port, shown in this view (**91**). Like Gaza to the south and Ashdod* to the north, which have also retained their ancient names, Ashkelon lay on the Way of the Sea (Via Maris), the coastal route linking Egypt* and Western Asia.

Egyptian Connection: Excavations in 1920–21 uncovered Hellenistic and Roman buildings just below the ground and through a succession of layers, went down to the pre-Philistine fortress and beaten earth ramparts (terre pisée) which resemble defence works found in other parts of the country and attributed to the Hyksos* period.

Ashkelon was in contact with Egypt from a very early period. Egyptian alabaster ware was uncovered in the Late Bronze Age layers (II-V) of the town, together with Cypro-Phoenician and Mycenaean pottery (see Aegean Civilization and Palestine*). The first mention of the town occurs in the Egyptian execration tablets of the 19th c. BCE (see Egypt*). During the 13th c. BCE the town revolted against Egypt on several occasions. A siege and capture of the fortress of Ashkelon during the time of Ramses II (1300 BCE) is portrayed (**92**) in the temple of Ammon at Karnak. Bearded Canaanites stand on the tower with arms outstretched, as a sign of submission to the Egyptians; a man at the right holds a flaming incense burner; defenders at the left let down a woman and a child; in the middle an Egyptian is hacking at a door with an axe. The Israel Stele refers at a later date to the capture of Ashkelon by Mernephtach at the beginning of his reign (1229 BCE). A more or less contemporary ivory tablet of Megiddo bears the inscription "The Great Prince of Ashkelon, Karkar."

Philistine Ashkelon: At the end of the 13th c. BCE, Ashkelon was captured by the Philistines* and became one of their five major cities, retaining its independence almost throughout the Israelite kingdom.

Traces of burned objects in the first of the Iron Age layers (VI-VII Philistine period) suggest that the city may have been destroyed by fire at the beginning of the Iron Age

92

Brick buildings with stone foundations have been uncovered from this Philistine period, together with a variety of vessels and implements which came to be known as "Philistine" (i.e. locally manufactured) pottery in the tradition of the early Hellenic settlement in Asia Minor

In the Days of Judges: The Philistines controlled the whole southern Mediterranean coast throughout the period of Judges*. In Jos. 13:3, one of the five Philistine lords was the "seren" of Ashkelon. The town is mentioned in the Samson saga (Jud. 14:19) and in the episode of the wanderings of the ark (I Sam. 6:17).

In the Days of the Monarchy: During the monarchy, it is referred to as one of the principal kingdoms of the Philistines (II Sam. 1:20). Assyrian sources of the same period refer to the kingdom of Ashkelon as covering wide areas in the southern Shephelah, extending northwards along the coast as far as Joppa (present Tel-Aviv). However, during the 8th c. BCE, under constant pressure from the Assyrians, Ashkelon declined and in 734 BCE it fell victim to Assyrian expansion. At the turn of the century it joined king Hezekiah of Judah in the alliance against Assyria, but the rebellion was broken and Ashkelon fell to Sennacherib in 700 BCE.

Under Assyria and Babylonia: It served as an Assyrian base during the campaigns of Esarhaddon and Ashurbanipal against Egypt. When Assyrian ascendancy was replaced by new Near Eastern powers, the town continued to be used by the armies of the rival Egyptian and Babylonian empires (end of 7th and beginning of 6th c. BCE). The fate of Ashkelon in this situation is echoed in prophetic visions of the time (Zep. 2:4; Jer. 25:20; 47:5, 7; Zec. 9:5). It is assumed that Judea also laid claim to Ashkelon and its region (Zep. 2:7).

When Nebuchadrezzar of Babylonia was campaigning in Palestine, Ashkelon, like Judea, looked to Egypt for help. Their hopes were disappointed, and instead, many of its inhabitants were exiled to Babylonia. Court documents found in Babylon refer to the sons of the king of Ashkelon and various other notables as exiles. In the excavations at Nof (Egypt), an Aramaic letter was found written by an anonymous ruler appealing for Egyptian help against the Babylonian army, and referring to the king of Ashkelon.

Persian Rule: A little later, at the beginning of the period of Persian ascendancy (5th c. BCE) Ashkelon became an important trading centre for the Tyrians (Phoenicians). This made it one of the leading cities of the Persian province at the extreme south of the lands "beyond the River", i.e. the part of the Persian empire west of the Euphrates.

Graeco-Roman Times: In Hellenistic times, Ashkelon was a leading Tyrian city with a mixed population, including a substantial Jewish community which endured for the first few centuries CE. The Hellenistic, pagan population worshipped Ashtoreth (Aphrodite) under the names Atargatis or Kerketo. These qᵉdeshôth or temple prostitutes reflect the cult (**93**). Their local Ba'al was Herakles.

In spite of repeated attacks during the wars of the Hasmoneans, Ashkelon maintained its independence and, in 104 BCE, it was granted autonomous status by the Seleucids (see Hasmoneans*), with the right to mint its own currency and follow a calendar of its own. The town became famous for its beauty and as the residence of Greek philosophers and grammarians. Herod was born in Ashkelon and although it never came under his rule, he adorned the town with imposing buildings. This is borne out by a collection of Graeco-Roman relics (**94**) brought over from the vast ruins. The goddess of victory, Niki, is seen holding a palm-branch, standing on the world, supported by Atlas (3rd. c. CE).

The town maintained its eminent position during the Roman and Byzantine periods and its prosperity continued under the first Arab invaders. At the time of the Crusades, Ashkelon and its district, including Ashdod, formed the "Seigneurie d'Ascalon". Later on, it declined and, in 1270 CE, Ashkelon was completely destroyed by Sultan Bebars.

93

94

95

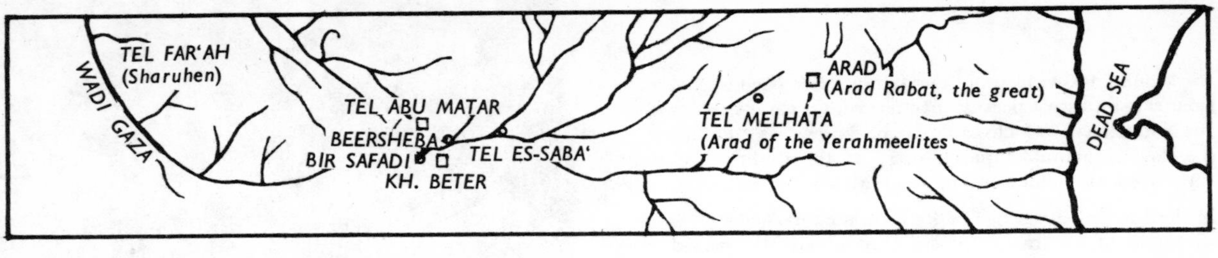

BEERSHEBA. — Midway between the Mediterranean and the southern end of the Dead Sea, on the main caravan route from Egypt to the Negeb, Hebron, Jerusalem and Transjordan, stood the ancient city of Beersheba. The modern town is built on a different site to the west of the original city, (see map **95**).

Foundation and Name: Tradition ascribes both the founding of the city and its name to Abraham*. According to Gn. 21:25–32, there was a dispute with Abimelech about some wells which Abraham had dug and, to settle their difference, the two men made a covenant, "Sheba" over the well, "be'er".

Another tradition has it that the name means "Seven" (sheba) "wells" (be'er), the number dug by Abraham and Isaac. The many wells in the town seem to bear out this interpretation. The two different traditions regarding the origin of the town's name have somehow been combined and in any case, both emphasize the connection with Abraham. He planted a tamarisk tree at a nearby high-place* (Gn. 21:33) and called it El-Olam, a name very reminiscent of the Canaanite divinity later superseded by Yahweh, (see Patriarchs: Religion*; Canaan: Gods and Idols*). This is probably the sanctuary to which Amos referred (8:14) as "the way of Beersheba", at which God was believed to have appeared to Isaac to confirm the promise made to Abraham. Jacob also sacrificed there to the God of his fathers.

Veneration: The ancient Israelites venerated Beersheba because of its association with the Patriarchal Epics, and the nearby high-place remained an important sanctuary for the Israelites for many generations. In the period of the monarchy pilgrimages were still made there, although unorthodox or idolatrous practices made the shrine an object of suspicion and hostility to the prophets, (Am. 5:5; 8:14).

History: At the time of the Settlement. Beersheba was included in the territory allotted to the tribe of Simeon. The significance of the site is reflected in the phrase, "from Dan to Beersheba", meaning from end to end of Palestine. Beersheba was the southernmost religious, administrative and judicial centre for the country, as well as being the centre for the peoples of the northern Negeb. In view of its importance, Beersheba was certainly well fortified and must have been surrounded by a wall. The site of the ancient town must, therefore, be sought in a tel or mound. It cannot, as has been suggested, be identified with Bir-es-Saba, the site of a Roman fortress and a modern Arab settlement. Today it is generally agreed that the original Beersheba was at the place now known as Tel-es-Saba, three miles to the east of the present Arab town. The site has not yet been excavated, although a quantity of pottery dating from the Early and Middle Iron Ages has been found on the surface.

Beersheba was resettled by Jews after the Restoration* (Neh. 11:27, 30). Following the destruction of the Second Temple in 70 CE, the Romans fortified the place and stationed a garrison there as a frontier post against the Nabateans*, whose main towns lay to the south, east and west of Beersheba.

Bir-Abu-Matar: A site a mile to the south-east of modern Beersheba was excavated by M.J. Perrot in 1954. It consists of a mound of wind-blown dust covered by alluvial loam in which peoples of the Chalcolithic Age (4th mill. BCE) had cut themselves subterranean dwellings (**96**). Some of these dwellings even penetrated the underlying rock to various depths. Their culture was apparently linked to that of Teleilat-Ghassul, a little way north-east of the Dead Sea, and other pre-historic sites of Palestine such as Hadera on the coast or Affuleh in the Plain of Jezreel. Abu-Matar does not appear to have any connection with historic Beersheba, as by the 2nd mill. BCE its culture had long been forgotten.

96

BETHEL AND AI. — In Israelite times, Bethel was an important religious, economic and military centre. Twelve miles north of Jerusalem, it stood in the heart of the central highlands at the crossing of the main north-south road with the east-west route from Jericho to the Mediterranean Sea.

Early Biblical Period: With the exception of Jerusalem, Bethel is mentioned more often in the Bible than any other town. The association of its "High Place"* with the pre-history of the Hebrews in the Patriarchal epics is the oldest and best-attested in the traditions. Abraham is said to have erected an altar there (Gn. 12:8). It was also the site of Jacob's vision (Gn. 28:11–22) and he also built an altar. The name of the place was changed from the Canaanite Luz (meaning "place of refuge") to Beth-El, (the House of God, Gn. 28:19). Because of its connections with the Patriarchs, Bethel acquired the highest religious importance for later generations of Israelites. Its site has been identified as the modern village of Beitin. (The change in pronunciation dates from Arab times and is found elsewhere in Palestine, e.g. Jezreel became Ser'in).

Although similar tales of patriarchal exploits often combined with the mystic appeal of "high places" elsewhere to produce popular rites strongly reminiscent of Canaanite cults, the sanctuary at Bethel remained specifically Israelite even after the Conquest*, with a special significance for the Northern tribes. During the period of Judges*, Bethel was one of the places where the Tabernacle and the Ark were housed, (Jud. 20:26–27) and also the oracles, Urim and Thummin. The Israelites used to go to Bethel to pray, fast and offer sacrifices, (Jud. 20:18, 26–27).

Excavation of the site in 1934 by W. F. Albright and again in 1954 by an expedition led by J. L. Kelso showed that the site had been occupied from the middle Bronze period (see **97**). A temple of the middle Canaanite period (15th c. BCE) contained an altar bearing marks which were proved by modern methods to be blood-stains. In the late Canaanite period just before the Israelite Conquest, a strong and rich city flourished on the site. This was destroyed by fire in the early 13th c. BCE. When occupation began again, a much smaller and poorer city was built to a different plan and belonging to a quite different culture. It was also built on a slightly different site.

The Monarchy: When Solomon built the Temple in Jerusalem as the principals hrine for the whole united kingdom, Bethel's importance as a place of pilgrimage dwindled, to be revived however following the division of the kingdom. Bethel stood on the new border, just inside Israel and Jeroboam established it as the religious centre for the northern kingdom, erecting his shrine of the golden calves there. This shrine was heartily condemned by the later prophets Amos* and Hosea*, who objected to the form of worship practiced there, (see Idol Worship in Israel*) and the challenge to Jerusalem which the existence of the shrine represented.

Against this, neither the prophets Elijah* and Elisha*, nor the reforming king Jehu ever condemned the Bethel sanctuary in the same way as they did Canaanite shrines. This suggests that although idolatrous, the Bethel cult conformed to early Israelite customs. The shrine survived the dissolution of the Northern Kingdom (721 BCE), but was destroyed a

97

hundred years later in the course of Josiah's reforming attack against all the "high places" (II K. 23:15).

Graeco-Roman period: The Babylonian army completely destroyed Bethel in 587 BCE, just before the destruction of Jerusalem, but the town was resettled during the Persian period (5th c. BCE) and continued to exist in the Hellenistic and Maccabean eras. It surrendered to Rome in 70 CE and was reoccupied in later Roman and Byzantine times. The Byzantines discovered the ancient Bronze Age city and made use of it as the major stone quarry for their defence system. The re-use of the ancient stones continued throughout the period of Arab domination, after the 7th c. CE. The modern village of Bethel (Beitin) contains a mosque built over a Byzantine church with a massive tower (Burj Beitin) whose heavy stones suggest the presence of a mediaeval monastery beside the church.

'AI: The site of 'Ai is 2 miles away from Bethel and W. F. Albright concluded that occupation of the two sites must have been complementary, for apparently 'Ai and Bethel were only rarely occupied at the same time. The site where Abraham pitched his tent (Gn. 12:8; 13:3) was apparently 'Ai and this became a Canaanite royal city, reputedly destroyed by Joshua (Jos. chs. 7, 8). However, when 'Ai was excavated (by Mme J. Marquet-Krause in 1933–35) the results appeared to contradict the story in Joshua (see Joshua and Judges*, Conquest*).

Tombs found on the site suggest that 'Ai was already occupied in the proto-Urban phase. The main line of the Early Bronze Age fortifications could be traced. The ramparts included a huge tower on the walls and enclosed a large

98 a

98 b

building (**98a, b**) which might be a palace or a temple, showing, top, the main hall of the palace; the bases of three columns which supported the roof are still visible; below: reconstruction of the west side of the palace, 3rd mil. BCE. Among the ruins is a sanctuary with three rooms in succession, possibly with the same functions as the plan of Solomon's Temple*; and a small area of houses. This site was abandoned at the end of the Early Bronze Age and was not occupied again until well into the Iron Age. This is in complete contradiction to the story in Joshua and it has been suggested that one reason for this discrepancy may be that a confusion arose between the history of 'Ai and that of the nearby town of Bethel.

BETHLEHEM. — Birthplace of King David* and Jesus* and once an important military post, Bethlehem stands 770 metres above sea level, nine kilometres south of Jerusalem. In ancient times, Bethlehem belonged to the territory of the tribe of Judah. The city is first mentioned in one of the Tel el Amarna* letters (No. 290) which shows that it was settled in the Late Bronze Age. Its name at this time is to be interpreted as Beth-ilu-Lachama (House of the goddess Lachama) which suggests that it was dedicated to the goddess.

David's Birthplace: Bethlehem is famous as the birthplace of King David and the site of his anointing as the future ruler (I Sam 16: 1 ff). The town became the symbol of the Davidic dynasty and the focal point of the mystique of messianism since, according to a biblical tradition based on Micah 5:2, ff, the Messiah will be a descendant of the House of David. The town is also the setting for the Book of Ruth*. According to the Gospels of Matthew and Luke, Bethlehem was the birthplace of Jesus*; and is thus holy in Christian eyes (the problem of Jesus' birthplace is discussed under Jesus*). At the time he was born, Bethlehem was a modest village, probably not exceeding 1000 people.

Strategic Importance: Bethlehem's strategic importance was based on its key position on the Jerusalem-Hebron-Egypt caravan route, where it "stood guard" over northern Judea. Before David's time, the town was protected from attack from the north by a Philistine garrison. It is mentioned later as a part of the line of fortifications built by the Judean kings to guard Jerusalem from the south and southeast. By the time of the Talmud and the writings of the Christian fathers, Eusebius and Hieronymus, it seems that Bethlehem had lost its strategic importance. It is described as bordering on the north of the "Darom", the large southern district of Judea. Few references to Jewish inhabitants are found until New Testament times.

Archaeological Discoveries: The Church of the Nativity (**100**) was built in Bethlehem by the first Christian Roman Emperor, Constantine, and his mother Helena in 330 CE. Fragmentary remains of a sumptuous mosaic pavement discovered beneath the modern floor of the church led Pere Vincent to believe that the Emperor Theodosius replaced the stone floor of the original basilica by this mosaic floor in the 4th c. CE. It was reconstructed by Justinian after the 5th c. CE. He raised the floor level and paved the building with stone. This was done again by the Crusaders in the 11th c. Though few, if any, relics remain from the time of Jesus, the church offers a unique religious experience to Christian pilgrims seen in the foreground of a view of the town (**99**).

99

100

Because of the difficulty of digging at a holy site in an urban centre, none of the Israelite or Christian places in Bethlehem has been excavated. While this has inhibited investigation of the Old Testament period, several important finds dating from pre-historic times, as well as the geologic Tertiary era, have been made nearby. These include discoveries of species of elephant, hippopotamus, rhinoceros, tortoise and a diminutive horse.

BETH-SHEAN. — Standing where the eastern end of the Valley of Jezreel runs into the Jordan Valley, the imposing mound (Tel el Husn) of the ancient fortified town still dominates the plain of Beth-Shean. The modern town that bears the same name lies some distance to the south.

Biblical Record: The Bible records that Beth-Shean was one of many Canaanite towns that, for generations, resisted the Israelite invaders, a fact borne out by excavations. The town was held by the Philistines during their war with Saul* and the bodies of Saul and Jonathan were strung up on its gates after their defeat on nearby Mount Gilboa.

It was in the territory allotted to the tribe of Manasseh but there is no proof that the Manassites ever controlled the town. David's* victories made it part of the kingdom. In Solomon's* time it belonged, like Megiddo, to the 5th administrative district (see Government and Authority*). When the kingdom was divided, Beth-Shean was one of the principal towns of Israel* under Baasha and Omri.

A Storehouse of Archaeology: Though biblical references are sparse, excavation and extra-biblical documents have given Beth-Shean considerable importance. An archaeological expedition of the University of Pennsylvania in 1921–23 CE found 18 strata (layers of occupation) below the surface. Since the earliest Chalcolithic inhabitants dug roughly-roofed pits out of the rock at the bottom of the mound, about 3,500 BCE, the site was continuously occupied for some 5 millennia up to Arab times. The first settlement parallels the first strata of Megiddo*. It was followed by structures belonging to the Proto-Urban period of the Early Bronze Age (3100 or 3000 BCE).

The five lowest strata, up to the 13th, cover more than a thousand years of the Early Bronze Age until the middle of the 3rd mill. BCE. Up to the first half of the Middle Bronze Age, Beth-Shean reflects an almost pre-historic period in Palestinian history. Stratum 10, belonging to the second phase of the Middle Bronze Age, represents the historic Hyksos period*, although there is little evidence of it at Beth-Shean.

Egyptian Rule: The 9th stratum, on the other hand, was extremely rich in finds. During the centuries of Egyptian occupation of Canaan (beginning mid 2nd mill. BCE), Beth-Shean was an important administrative and military centre, and its importance continued for several centuries, while Egypt maintained its control over the north-eastern entrance into Palestine. Evidence of this was first found in the 9th stratum where the excavators found a whole area of temples, all typically Egyptian, as were those of the next (8th) stratum (end 14th c. BCE). The oldest of these was dated about 1350 BCE, at the beginning of the Rameside period. The next three and a half centuries (up to about

101

1000 BCE) covering strata 9 to 6, were some of the most critical in Beth-Shean's history. Egyptian temples, inscriptions and other evidence all bear witness to the impact of Egyptian rule.

The most important object found in the temple of stratum 8 (end 14th c.), is a relief carved in basalt **(101)** showing a fight between a dog and a lion. This probably had some mythological and religious significance and is notable because it shows a greater affinity with Mesopotamian than with Egyptian art. The other objects, inscriptions and scarabs found in this level are of Egyptian origin or Hittite patterns, testifying to the penetration of Hittite culture in the 13th c.

Egyptian influences and contributions were tempered by native Canaanite culture. A stele of Mekal, God of Beth-Shean, in the Egyptian style proves the presence of Egyptians, but the divinities they worshipped there were Canaanite, as we learn from a later local temple of Ramses III dedicated to 'Anat. The extent to which native ways held their own in the face of Egyptian penetration and influence bears witness to the vitality of Canaanite culture.

A good many of the pottery fragments, pots, incense burners etc. found in layers of the Late Bronze Age, were decorated with a snake motif. Serpent worship was one of the foundations of the Beth-Shean cult. The town's name came from the serpent god, Shehan.

Organization of Egyptian Rule: The 8th Stratum (Late Bronze) contained the stele of Seti I **(102)** which records the war he waged in the first year of his reign (1320 BCE). He reports attacks on the garrison at Beth-Shean which involved the nearby Canaanite cities of Hamath, Pella and Rehob. One stele lists victories in various places, giving careful topographical details, thus making it one of the most valuable extra-biblical sources of information about the town. It vividly demonstrates Beth-Shean's long and close connection with Egypt, confirmed by the large quantities of Egyptian material found there. In other Canaanite towns, a local ruler was appointed by the Egyptians. He was independent in everyday matters although tribute had to be paid to the Egyptians, and they had ultimate military control. In Beth-Shean, however, Egyptian rule was direct and absolute. A large garrison was stationed there and a variety of officials governed the town under the Pharaoh's direct control.

Another stele of Seti I also found in Beth-Shean refers, most intriguingly, to unrest stirred up by the Hapiru (Habiru*), who may perhaps have been forerunners of a wave of Hebrew invaders (see Conquest*).

A Philistine Garrison? Anthropoid coffins **(103)** and spear butts like those of the Philistines, found in Beth-Shean, have suggested that there may have been a Philistine garrison there under Egyptian rule. Alternatively, they may have belonged to a group of "Sea People" of Aegean* and Anatolian origin, not identical with but related to the

102

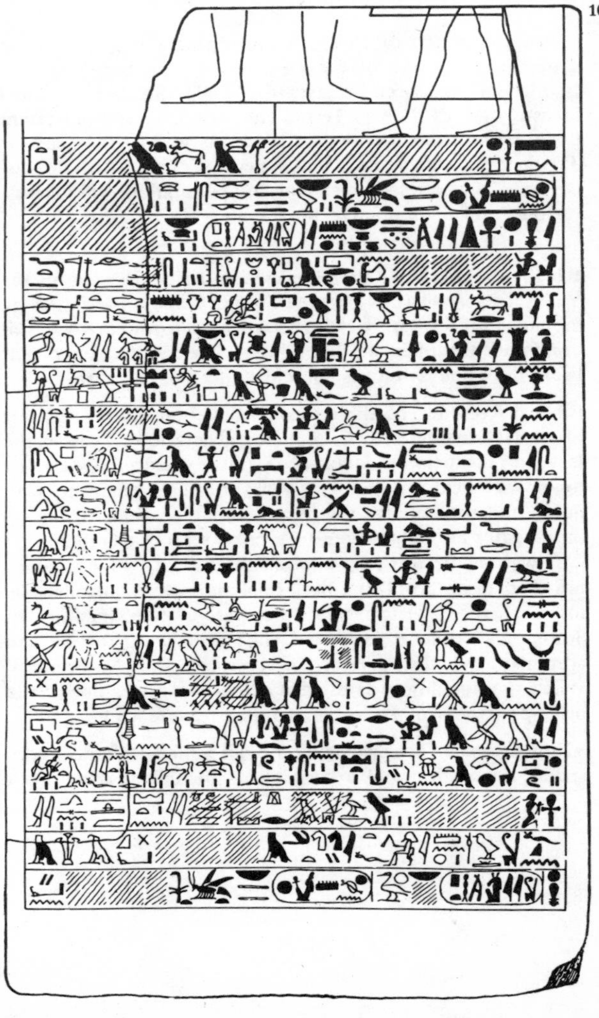

Philistines, known as the Tjeker or Sakkala (see Philistines*), who settled on the northern coast of Palestine and were employed as Egyptian mercenaries. These people may have joined forces with the Philistines in the south at the time of Saul's wars. As a result of David's decisive victory over the Philistines in the Beth-Shean Valley, they were driven out of that area permanently.

In fact, this phase of the Iron Age marks the gradual disappearance of the Philistine ware and pottery from Beth-Shean and Megiddo — where it was also found earlier.

The Canaanite Temples: In *Strata* 7–6 of the late Bronze Age, besides a statue of Ramses II and inscriptions of Ramses II and III and their successors, there was evidence of the rebuilding of two Canaanite temples. Stratum 7 also contained remains of the 13th c. BCE, contemporary with the Israelite conquest*. Among these were a round granary pit and an administrative building.

Stratum 5, dated around 1200–1000 BCE, is a typical Iron Age settlement. Its walls were built of stones worked in the same fashion as the buildings of Samaria and Megiddo, which belong to the same period. By this time, as explained above, Beth-Shean was no longer under Egyptian domination but was held for some 75 years by the Philistines or their allies, the Tjeker, until David conquered the town in 1000 BCE.

Israelite Times: Stratum 5 contained two Canaanite temples which may have been in existence at the time of the Battle of Mt. Gilboa (see Saul*). Since the biblical record refers to a temple of Dagon and a temple of Ashtaroth (see Canaan: Gods and Idols*), they may equally well have been built after the town was taken over by the Israelites for the first time. The pottery and cultic ware found in the temples were also used in the Israelite period in connection with fertility rites (see Canaan: Cult*). This is true of the small house shrine models **(104)**, many of them decorated with snakes and doves, and also of incense stands like those found at Megiddo*. This evidence provides an interesting commentary on the cosmopolitan cult permitted by Solomon, but violently condemned by later prophets. As noted under Seals*, Egyptian scarabs with their magical attributes continued to be used for centuries after they first made their appearance.

Stratum 4, belonging to the period of the Israelite monarchy was found to be in a very poor state of preservation. Very little is known of the history of Beth-Shean after the division of the two Hebrew kingdoms. Archaeology has not filled the blank which exists between the 8th and 4th cs. BCE. The town was settled by non-Jews after the restoration of Judea and rebuilt by Hellenists following Alexander's conquest.

Scythopolis, the Graeco-Roman Settlement: *Stratum* 3 contained the remains of the Greek temple of Dionysus and the theatre to the south of the ancient mound, the latter being used for religious purposes.

The new Hellenistic town, called Scythopolis, extended far to the west of the ancient mound. As Megiddo declined in local importance, Scythopolis developed as its rival. Beth-Shean was conquered by the Hasmonean*, Hyrcanus. When Pompey annexed Palestine to the Roman Empire, the town's independence was restored as a Greek "polis", one of the ten cities forming the Hellenistic Decapolis. Its Hebrew name was preserved only in Jewish annals (I Mac. 5:42).

103

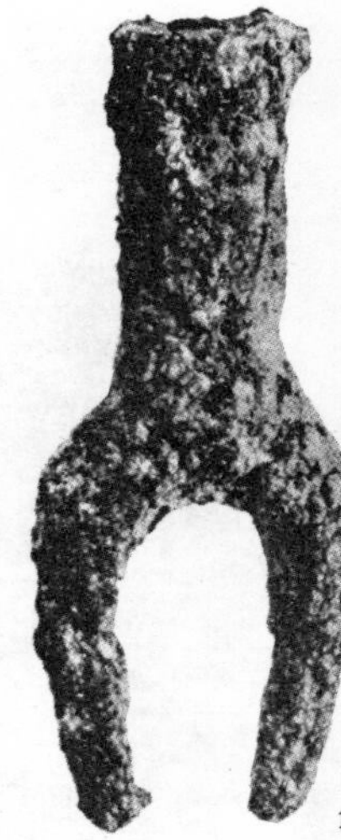

103 a

104

105

A Roman theatre (**105**), in a good state of preservation, was excavated in 1961 CE and the remains of a hippodrome are clearly visible nearby. The stage of the theatre is seen (**106**) with the ancient Canaanite-Israelite tel in the background.

Strata 2–1 belong to the Byzantine period. A sumptuous synagogue dating from the early 6th c. CE, containing cult objects and a beautiful mosaic floor was unearthed in 1962. The pavement bore an inscription giving the names of the craftsmen who made it — the same as those who made the mosaic floor in the Beth-Alpha synagogue, one of the most famous in Palestine. A 6th c. CE monastery, also with a beautiful mosaic floor, was uncovered near the synagogue*.

The first and highest stratum belongs to the 7th c. early Arab occupation of Palestine. In the course of excavation, the top five strata were removed, leaving the late Bronze Age Canaanite and earlier strata at the top of the mound. Hundreds of objects, tombs and other remains related to all these periods were found in the valley around the town.

106

BETH-SHEMESH. — The town stood in the foothills of Judah, close to the main road joining Jerusalem and the maritime plain. It has been identified with Tel-el-Rumeileh, which stands near a group of ruins, preserving the ancient name of the place as Ein Shams.

In the Old Testament, names which include the word "Beth" usually mean the site of the sanctuary of a major divinity. Beth-Shemesh (sun, in Hebrew) is thought to have been associated with Canaanite sun-worship which is known to have been prevalent in this area (see also Hazor*). A place named But-Shemesh, mentioned in the Egyptian Execration texts of the 19th c. BCE, seems to refer to this city.

Israelite Times: Called 'Ir Shemesh (Jos. 19:41) or, in some manuscripts, 'Ein Shemesh, the town was included in the Dan territory, although according to Jud. 1:33 the Danites were unable to dispossess the town's Amorite inhabitants. (This passage refers to a town under the name of "Har Cheres" but this is usually assumed to mean Beth-Shemesh.) Later on, when the Danites abandoned their territory in southern Palestine and trekked northwards, the town came into the hands of the tribe of Judah (Jos. 15:7: see Judges*), and at some time it became a priestly town of the Benjaminites.

It is not clear, however, at what point the Israelites occupied Beth-Shemesh. By the time of the restoration of the Ark by the Philistines (I Sam. 6:12–21), the town already belonged to the Israelites and later it was included in the second administrative district of Solomon's kingdom (I K. 4:9). It was at Beth-Shemesh that Jehoash, king of Israel, fought Amaziah, King of Judah (II K. 14:11–13), while in the time of Ahaz, the town was captured by the Philistines (II Ch. 28:18). Beth-Shemesh is mentioned in the Talmud (Jerus. Megillah 81:81) as a small town and Eusebius (One 54, lines 11–13) places it about nine miles from Eleutheropolis (Beth Gobrin) on the way to Nicopolis (Emmaus).

Archaeological Evidence: The site has been excavated twice. The first expedition, led by Duncan Mackenzie of the Palestine Exploration Fund in 1911–12 cleared the ruins of a Byzantine monastery which had stood on the site and carefully marked the walls and gate of the town. A large number of graves from various periods, found outside the walls, were also examined. Mackenzie was able to distinguish four layers of settlement: 1. the Canaanite town; 2. the town of the period of Judges, from which a quantity of Philistine pottery* was recovered; 3. a town which had existed under the monarchy and at the time of Sennacherib (701 BCE); 4. a small, poor town of the post-Exilic period.

Between 1928–1933 CE, a second more extensive excavation was carried out by G. E. Wright and Elihu Grant. By the time of this second investigation, the science and techniques of archaeology had advanced very considerably and the later expedition was able to make a much more exhaustive examination of the site. This revealed six strata of settlement: The lowest (VI) dated from the end of the third mill. BCE. There was then a break until a new settlement (V) was established during the Middle Bronze Age (ca. 1750–1550 BCE). Ruins of a solid wall, a gate and a substantial structure in the centre of the town were uncovered from this period. In addition, numerous burial caves containing ceramic articles were discovered both inside and outside the city boundaries.

Stratum IV, dating from the Late Bronze Age (1550–1200 BCE), was of a very prosperous town which yielded evidence of a metal industry, pottery, oil and wine manufacture and much imported pottery from Mycenae and Cyprus. During the period, Beth-Shemesh was under Egyptian rule, as indicated by porphyry vessels imported from that country (as well as from other places) and by a number of inscriptions bearing the names of Pharaohs. Two of these were particularly important. One was written in a Late Bronze script which varies slightly from the usual Ugaritic alphabet on an earthenware object shaped like a hatchet head. The other was in proto-Canaanite characters on some indeterminate pottery object (see Inscriptions*; Alphabet*). Stratum III, belonging to the period of Judges, revealed large quantities of Philistine ceramic pottery materials, and also showed that it had been destroyed by fire — perhaps by the Israelites. The major value of the excavators' work was in the information it provided about early Israelite occupation of the town between the 12th and 9th cs. BCE.

Stratum II, the Monarchy town, was subdivided into three separate periods. In the first two (10th–6th cs. BCE), the ancient Bronze Age wall had still been in use, although repaired where necessary — first by David as a protection against Philistine attacks; then by later kings. One whole section of the wall had been rebuilt in the style of the Monarchy period. From the excavations it was possible to reconstruct the plan of the city, thus gaining valuable information about life in a representative Israelite town of the Iron Age (See Cities, Israelite*; Crafts*). During the last period of stratum II, Beth-Shemesh was an unwalled town.

The ruins of a big granary were found in the Israelite town, as well as evidence of oil and wine presses. A number of burial caves containing funerary vessels and objects were also discovered. Among the smaller objects were seals* bearing Hebrew names and statuettes of Ashtoreth (see Idol-worship in Israel*).

Post-Exilic and Roman Times: The tel was abandoned after the destruction of the first Temple; there is no evidence of any settlement during the Persian, Hellenistic or Roman periods. The town returned to life only in the Byzantine age when a big monastery was erected there. In the Arab period, a number of small private residences were built near this monastery, forming a village known as Ein Shams. In the course of time, however, this too was abandoned.

CAESAREA (Jewish and Roman Times). — The forerunner of Herod's Caesarea was a flourishing port built by the Phoenicians in the 4th c. BCE (early Hellenistic period) midway between Joppa (Jaffa) and Acco (Acre). Beyond its name — Straton's Tower, from Strato, the Greek form of the Phoenician name 'Abd Ashtart — very little is known of the history of the earlier town. One relic is a fragment of a 3rd c. BCE incense stand (**107**). In addition, excavation of the Jewish quarter of the town (carried out during 1962) revealed a heap of fragments of Aegean and Greek pottery, possibly thrown into a pile when the area was cleared later for Herod's enormous building schemes. A corner of a Hellenistic house, apparently abandoned at the beginning

107

of the 1st c. BCE, was also uncovered. The nearby remains of a massive wall built in the sea also appear to be part of the mole of Straton's Tower. Towards the end of the 2nd c. BCE, Straton's Tower was united by Zoilus, tyrant of Dor, with the nearby port of Dor, into a single political unit. He then sold them both for 400 talents of gold to Alexander Jannaeus' expanding kingdom (see Hasmoneans*).

Herod's Caesarea: The Roman conquest of the Hasmonean state (64 BCE) cut off the coast from Judea and annexed it to Syria. The area of Straton's Tower was returned to Herod by Caesar Augustus after his victory at Actium and Herod set about transforming it into an imposing Graeco-Roman city with a wide safe harbour, according to Josephus, larger than Piraeus. He named it Caesarea in honour of the emperor and later the town was also known as Caesarea Sebaste, Caesarea Palestina and Caesarea Maritima. Its port was named Limen Sebastos after the emperor (Augustus = Sebaste; see Herod*).

Work on the town and port lasted for 12 years (22 to 10 BCE). When completed, the port had a breakwater running 600 metres out to sea and a huge mole where ships could anchor within the protection of the sea walls. Herod used the port on his frequent voyages. According to Josephus, reinforced "vaulted chambers" connected with the mole were used as storehouses. Remains of "vaulted chambers" **(108)** were discovered by the recent excavations underneath the Crusaders' cathedral, a short distance from the sea, (see diagram **(109)**. They contained storage jars which, in the opinion of A. Negev, supported their identification as early Roman warehouses.

Massive towers flanked the entrance to the port and, for the convenience of sailors and passengers a promenade surrounded the whole port area. On a raised plot, visible from a great distance out to sea, stood a temple of Augustus, containing two colossal statues, one of the emperor, the other symbolizing the city of Rome. Josephus records that there were six other gigantic statues at the entrance to the port. The base of one of these, embedded in the sea bottom, was seen by members of the E. A. Link underwater expedition carried out in 1960.

108

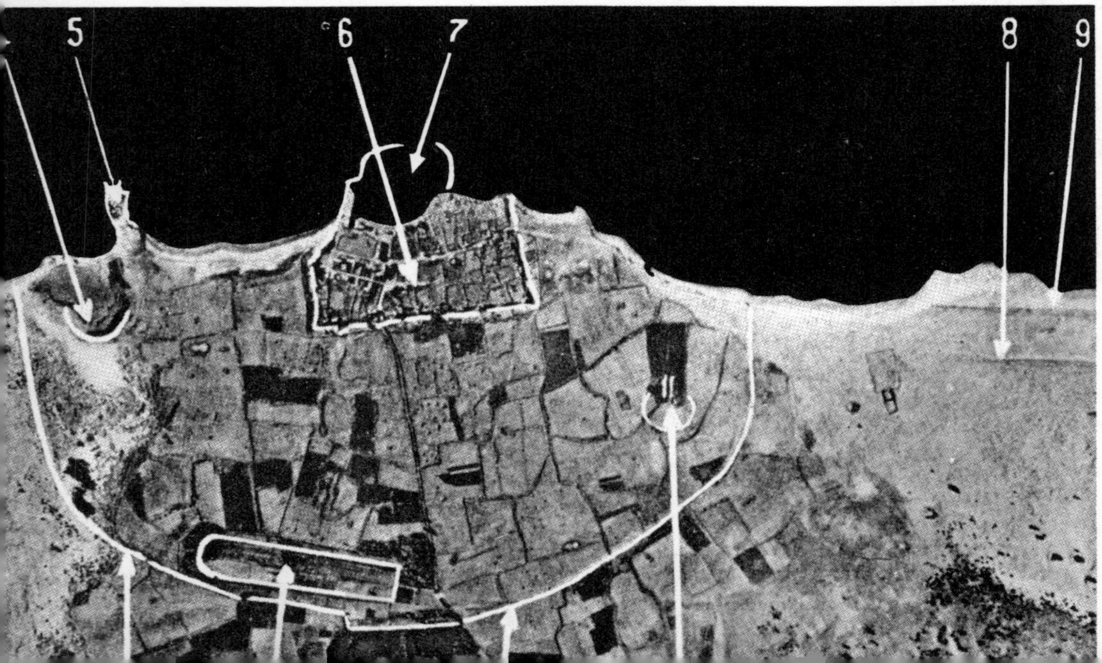

109

1. ancient Roman wall;
2. ancient hippodrome;
3. amphitheatre;
4. theatre (see opp. page);
5. ruins of pier;
6. the Crusaders' town, walled;
7. ancient circular harbour and breakwaters;
8. the low Roman aqueduct;
9. the high aqueduct (see **112**).

110

The town contained an amphitheatre, a theatre, a court of justice and other magnificent structures, while outside the city walls, a hippodrome was erected. The streets of the city all converged on the port and, to keep the city clean, a drainage system was constructed with underground channels running out to sea (according to Josephus' description: Ant. 15:9, 6). His account has been confirmed by excavation. Traces of the channels were discovered in areas close to the shore and under the Crusaders' walled town which was built on top of the Roman ruins. The city walls enclosing a semi-circular area, stretched out about a mile along the shore. The building of the original aqueduct is also attributed to Herod's days (see below).

In 1958 the Italian excavation mission organized by the Milan Academy of Letters and Sciences, uncovered Herod's theatre (**111**). Part of the original "cavea" with its stone seats, plus the "orchestra" in the middle were cleared, to show that the theatre had been constructed on Hellenistic lines. The cavea and orchestra were rebuilt during the 2nd–3rd cs. CE on the latest Roman patterns, but materials

111

112

used in the earlier structure were employed again. Thus an inscription mentioning Pontius Pilate (**110**) was found embedded in the later theatre.

Herod's successor, Archelaus, was eventually banished by the Romans and a Roman Procurator (governor) installed (see Rome and the Jews*). Caesarea thereafter became the seat of the Roman administration, all the procurators including Pontius Pilate taking up their residence in the city.

Jews and Romans in Caesarea: In fact, from its very foundation, the Jews always constituted a minority of the city's population. They formed a substantial and wealthy community but never succeeded in establishing good relations with the dominant Greek-Syrian inhabitants. Tension between the two groups grew during the first decades of the 1st c. CE until, at the end of the term of office of the procurator Felix (52–60 CE), it flared into open clashes. Under Gessius Florus (66 CE), open warfare broke out and most of the 20,000 Jews living in the town were massacred. The riots in Caesarea were one of the immediate causes of the great Roman-Jewish war which culminated in the destruction of Jerusalem and the Temple in 70 CE (see Rome and Jews*).

The first commander of the Roman army sent to crush the revolt, Vespasian, used Caesarea as his base and, in 69 CE, he was acclaimed emperor by his legions there. In recognition, he made the city a Roman colony, exempted it from taxation and, shortly after, established it as the capital of Roman Palestine, renaming it Colonia Prima Flavia Augusta Caesarensis, a title which appears on this inscription (**113**). After the destruction of Jerusalem, Titus withdrew to Caesarea, taking with him the spoils of the Temple and thousands of captives. On October 4, 70 CE, a great Roman festival was held to celebrate his victory and in the "games" held in Caesarea's amphitheatre, 2500 Jewish prisoners were said to have perished in combat with wild beasts.

The Aqueducts: Contrary to opinions held until recently, archaeological evidence, according to A. Negev, places the erection of the western high level aqueduct in Herod's time, and not in the early 2nd c. CE. The 2nd, 6th and 10th Roman legions effected major repairs to an existing structure at the time of the Bar Kochba* war, and Jewish prisoners were put to work on it. It brought running water to the city from the springs of the lower Carmel range, some ten miles away. Another lower aqueduct was built east of the high one in Roman times, possibly the beginning of the 1st c. CE; both of these were repaired at the end of the 4th c. CE and again under Justinian in the 6th c., continuing in use until the 10th or 11th cs. CE (see illust. **112**).

Period of Expansion: The 2nd and 3rd cs. CE saw a big expansion of Caesarea. A new Jewish community took part in the city's general growth and during the later Roman period it expanded very considerably. Synagogues and schools were built and many prominent scholars set up their academies in the city (see Rabbis*). The ruins of a synagogue (**114**) dating from the 3rd c. CE have been found in Caesarea by M. Avi-Yonah, although "houses of prayer" certainly existed there as early as the time of Herod Agrippa and Paul (one of these may have been meant by the reference in Ac. 18:22). This column capital, decorated with a menorah (**115**) dates from the 5th–6th c. CE, i.e. to the Byzantine city which expanded far beyond the limits of

113

115

114

the Jewish-Roman town of the 1st and 2nd cs. CE. The recent excavations have been able to trace the line of these later outside walls, as shown in the diagram (**109**).

The extent of the expansion is illustrated by this stepped street of the 5th or 6th c. CE. Two headless statues (**116**), apparently belonging to Hadrian's time, were brought there in Byzantine days. The one on the left is in white marble, the other (right) in red porphyry. Statues and columns flank a triple doorway to a palatial structure which has not yet been satisfactorily identified.

Christian Caesarea: Side by side with the Jewish community, a substantial Samaritan settlement grew up in Caesarea in the early centuries CE. Together with them there was an important Christian community as a result of the early spread of the movement to Caesarea. The founder of the

116

early Jewish-Christian* church in Caesarea was probably Philip (Ac. 8:40), and Cornelius was baptized there by Peter (Ac. 10). Paul passed through the city after his first visit to Jerusalem (Ac. 9:30) and was later imprisoned there for two years under Felix (Ac. 23:22–35). When the Herodian Jewish king Agrippa II and his sister Berenice visited the city (Ac. 25:6, 23–27; 26:1–32) a new Procurator, Porcius Festus brought Paul to trial before them. Later, Paul left for Rome from the port.

From the end of the 2nd c. CE until about 451 CE. Caesarea was the residence of the metropolitan bishop of Palestine. Beginning in 195 CE, several church councils were held there. The great scholar and Church Father, Origen (183–253 CE) taught there about the middle of the 3rd c. CE and founded the famous library of Caesarea. Another bishop was Eusebius (313–340 CE), author of the first history of the Church and the Onomasticon. Procopius, the historian of the emperor Justinian, was a native of Caesarea.

Byzantine Caesarea has yielded a number of mosaic floors dating from the 4th to the beginning of the 7th c. CE. Some of them come from big, ornate civil buildings, others from churches. One of these includes a quotation from the New Testament: "Would you have no fear of him who is in authority? Then do what is good." (Rom. 13:3). A small 6th c. CE statue shows Christ carrying a lamb (**117**).

Caesarea surrendered to the Arabs in 639 CE and was captured from them by the Crusaders in 1101 CE. However, the history of these later phases lies beyond the scope of this article.

117

'EIN GEDI. — 'Ein Gedi was situated in both ancient and modern times around an oasis on the western shore of the Dead Sea.

In the Canaanite period, an "Amorite" settlement existed there, called Hatzetzon-Tamar (Gn. 14:7; cf. II Ch. 20:2). This name continued to be used, side by side with the Hebrew name, 'Ein Gedi, until the reign of Jehoshaphat, king of Judah (II Ch. 20:2), when the Ammonites, Moabites and Maonites gathered there to prepare their attack on the Judahite king. After this, the old name appears to have dropped out of use. Later literature only refers to 'Ein Gedi.

During the period of the First Temple, 'Ein Gedi belonged to the territory of Judah. David took refuge there (I Sam. 24:1–2) when he fled from Saul.

Balsam, Spices and Fruits: Because of its plentiful supply of water and its tropical climate, palm trees and rare spices could be grown there. As early as the reign of Solomon, 'Ein Gedi was one of the richest centres in Palestine for the production of spices and perfumes. The Song of Songs (1:14) speaks of the "clusters of henna blossoms in the vineyards of Eingedi." Balsam trees also grew there.

There is an ancient tradition, referred to by Flavius Josephus*, that balsam saplings were among the presents brought to Solomon by the Queen of Sheba. Apparently the cultivation of balsam was begun by the king.

Balsam was a valuable material for the Babylonians too. The account of the Jews being carried into exile (Jer. 52:16) states that some of the poorest people of the land were left behind to act as "vine-dressers". A tradition in the Talmud (Sabbath 26:1) interprets this: "Vine-dressers, according to Rabbi Joseph, were the gatherers of balsam at 'Ein Gedi." The town is known to have been destroyed by the Babylonians at the same time as the Temple in Jerusalem, but apparently the balsam groves were left unharmed.

In the Persian period, 'Ein Gedi was part of the Satrapy of Judea — a fact illuminated by a seal, inscribed "Y^ehud" which was found when the site was excavated (see below). By the time of the Second Temple (Roman period), 'Ein Gedi was once again a prosperous Jewish centre where, according to Josephus, "beautiful palm-trees and balsam trees grow in plenty." (Ant. Bk. 9:1, 2)

During the first war against Rome*, the Zealots captured 'Ein Gedi and destroyed the town. Pliny the Elder, writing at the end of the war, relates that they tried to destroy the balsam trees, an action which the Romans strenuously resisted. The town itself did not escape. Pliny describes 'Ein Gedi "as second only to Jerusalem (J. T. Milik suggests that he meant to say Jericho) in the fertility of the country and its groves of palm-trees, but now, like it, reduced to ashes."

Balsam trees (see the leaves and tree of "commiphora opobalsamum" **118**) were included in the war booty which Titus carried to Rome and, after the war, most of the balsam groves of 'Ein Gedi became the jealously guarded property of the Roman authorities. In Tannaitic and Talmudic literature, a clear distinction was made between "Balsam of Caesar's House" and "Balsam of Rabbi's House" to draw the attention of observant Jews to the source and help them avoid the former on grounds of ritual impurity*.

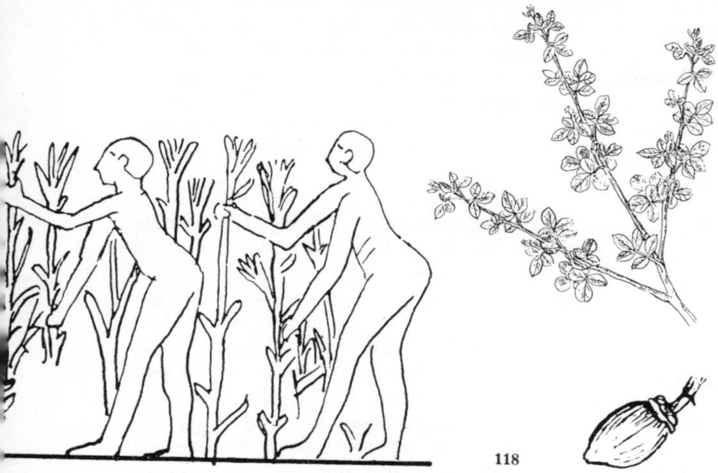

118

The town appears to have recovered quickly from the disasters of the first War with Rome*, for 'Ein-Gedi's inhabitants took an active part in the second revolt of Bar-Kochba*. Letters sent to the town's leaders by "Simon Bar-Kosba, Prince of Israel", were preserved by them at the end of the revolt, when they escaped the destruction of the town only to meet death in the caves of the surrounding wilderness.

The town revived during the late Roman and Byzantine period. At the end of the 4th c. CE, Eusebius described 'Ein Gedi as a "large village of Jews", where the cultivation of balsam still flourished. It came to an end, however, when the groves, their Jewish cultivators and their homes were destroyed by Arab conquerors (7th c. CE). After that, it remained deserted until modern times.

The Evidence of Archaeology: Ancient 'Ein Gedi (Tel Juran) was excavated in 1961–62 by an expedition led by Prof. B. Mazar. Five layers of settlement were found. The earliest stratum (V) covers the period from Josiah and his successors to 'Ein Gedi's destruction by the Babylonians (630–580 BCE). Stratum IV represents the city of the Persian period (5th–4th cs. BCE); stratum III that of the Hellenistic city (3rd–2nd cs. BCE) and stratum II the city from the Hasmoneans, notably Alexander Jannaeus, up to 40 CE. The Hellenistic fortifications of the city were pulled down by Alexander and replaced by a wall 2 metres thick with a watch-tower on the western wall, guarding the approaches to the town from that direction. This city was replaced by the Roman-Byzantine city (stratum I) which lasted from the 1st c. BCE to the 6th c. CE.

The Balsam Industry: Stratum V — the period of the First Temple — showed many traces of a prosperous settlement. The town covered the whole tel, protected by a sloping wall and a moat. The houses and their courtyards were used for the preparation of the balsam. Underneath the ruins a wide range of items connected with the industry were found; potsherds of large cooking pots for boiling, jars and smaller containers; utensils and tools of stone, wood and metal; and scales and weights bearing the seal of the Israelite royal house. Hebrew seals were also found, with the names of individuals, like "Tabshalem", "Uriahu ben Azariahu", etc. In Tabshalem's house a covered jar was also found, containing the silver ingots used instead of money at that time (see Coins*).

Stratum IV revealed a considerable number of plastered pools which had also apparently been connected with the balsam industry. The Roman-Byzantine city (Stratum I) yielded little of interest, apart from a few buildings and terraced agricultural land. The Jewish settlement which apparently flourished up to the defeat of Bar-Kochba* can only have existed from the end of the first war with Rome.

So far, nothing has been found of the Canaanite settlement, nor of an Israelite settlement before the 7th c. BCE. Quite possibly they were built on a different site. In compensation for this disappointment, a sanctuary of the Chalcolithic Age (**119**) (dating from the 4th mill. BCE) in an excellent state of preservation, has been uncovered on the slope near the high spring of 'Ein Gedi. A main entrance, left, led to an altar (**120**) in the court. In the course of excavations conducted in the nearby caves of Nahal-Mishmar in 1961 some 430 small objects, mostly made of bronze, were disclosed, wrapped in a straw mat. P. Bar-Adon who found them believes that they belonged originally to the Chalcolithic sanctuary of 'Ein Gedi or possibly originated from another holy site in the Negeb.

119

120

121

GEZER (Tel Jezer). — Occupied continuously from the Chalcolithic Age (4th mill. BCE) to Roman and Byzantine times, Gezer was one of the most important sites of Judah. It stood at a cross-roads between the empires of Assyria and Egypt, where the foothills of the Judean highlands bordered the Philistine plain.

The site of Tel Jezer was first discovered by the French archaeologist Clermont-Ganneau, in 1878 CE. It was excavated for the Palestine Exploration Fund by the Englishman, R. A. S. Macalister, in 1902–03 and additional excavations were made at the western end of the tel by A. Rowe in 1934. The great advances made in archaeology since then have recently made possible the interpretation of many of the early finds.

Proto-Urban Settlement: The earliest layers belonged to an unfortified settlement, which included tombs containing traces of burnt bodies — a custom which has not yet been explained satisfactorily. The settlers of this age apparently arrived from the north and east. Their pottery has affinities with that found in the Jericho tombs of the same period.

The Bronze Age Cities: The town of the Early Bronze layers (3rd mill. BCE) had expanded and was fortified by a stone wall buttressed by battered earth. During the Middle and Late Bronze Ages (20th–14th cs. BCE), the walls of Gezer were rebuilt in stone, 4 metres (13 ft.) thick, fortified by square towers and with a massive gate at the southern end of the town. The gate had three entrances, one inside the other, further protected by two towers in front. Rowe found part of an additional fortified structure from the Middle Bronze Age, as well as caves, tombs and cisterns.

122

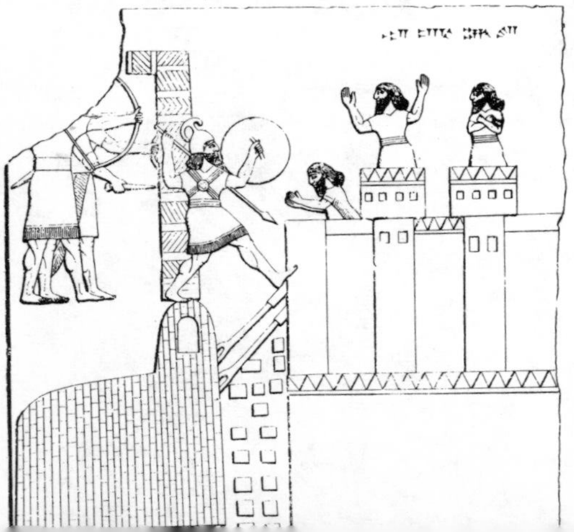

Egyptian Presence: The Middle Bronze layer also yielded a variety of objects imported from Egypt. Archaeological evidence for connections with Egypt is supported by the first written mention of Gezer which comes from Egyptian inscriptions dating from the New Kingdom (15th c. BCE). The town was destroyed during the campaign of Thothmes III in the same century and he proudly recorded his victory (see Egypt*).

The Evidence of the Amarna Letters: Eleven of the letters discovered in Tel el Amarna* (14th and 13th cs. BCE; see article) referred to Gezer and mentioned the names of three of its rulers. These names suggest a Semitic origin for the kings, and presumably their people. Gezer was one of the most important fortified centres in Palestine, and its king, Milkili, attempted to gain control over territory to the north, leading him to fight the king of Jerusalem. The Amarna* letters record the constant struggles of the rulers of Gezer with other petty city-kings and against the Egyptians. A tablet was also found in the remains of Gezer itself, containing a letter written to the king by the Egyptian official stationed in a nearby town, demanding the payment of seven bulls. Enraged, Milkili turned against Egypt, even going so far as to rob the Egyptian caravans passing through the town on their way north and east (see Roads*) and for his attempted rebellion, he was deposed.

The town of this period (Late Bronze and Early Iron Ages) possessed a water supply which included a tunnel 67 metres long, bringing water from a spring outside the city gate into the town (see Water Supply*). At the northern end of the tel, an alignment of stone menhirs between 1.5 and 3 metres (10 feet) in height, set up from the 21st c. BCE onwards, were found, seven of them still standing (**121**). These were probably a series of tombstones of important personages, perhaps the kings of Gezer. Pottery imported from Mycenae and Cyprus, abundant in the neighbouring Philistine region, was also discovered in Gezer.

Gezer During and After the Conquest: Gezer is mentioned in the Bible quite frequently during the early stages of the Conquest. After Joshua had defeated the southern Canaanite alliance, Horam, king of Gezer, came to their help (Jos. 10:33; 12:12) and was defeated. It appears from other passages that the town was not occupied by the Israelites, nor did the excavations show any sign that the town had been destroyed in the 14th or 13th c. BCE. Throughout the period of the Conquest* and Settlement, Gezer appears to have remained a Canaanite city-state, forming the western end of the chain of autonomous Canaanite cities which separated the southern and central Israelite tribes. Biblical tradition claims that Gezer paid tribute to the conquering Israelites (Jos. 16:10; Jud. 1:29)

Apart from its conquest by Joshua, Gezer was also claimed as a conquest by Pharaoh Mernephtach who included in his "Israel Stele" (1219 BCE, see Exodus*, Egypt*, Conquest*) the phrase, "Canaan was looted, Ashkelon was conquered, Gezer was seized." Apparently, the Egyptian recovered the coastal cities conquered by the Israelites to prevent a hostile people gaining control of the Via Maris, one of the Egyptian empire's vital lines of communication.

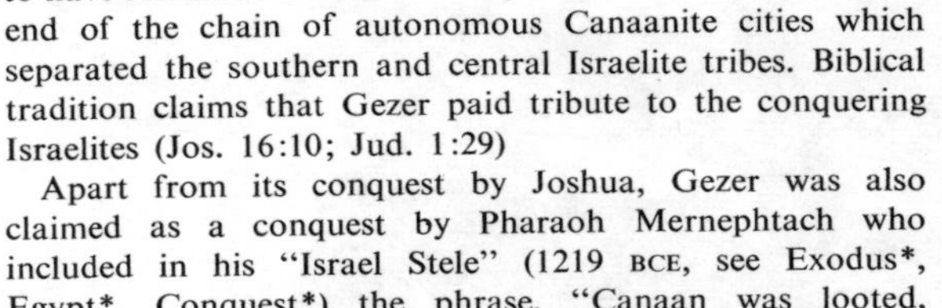

123

The Philistines in Gezer: When the Philistines invaded in the 12th c. BCE, it appears that they conquered Gezer and used it as a base of operations from which they set out to conquer Ephraim, (see Philistines*). David routed them "from Geba (Gibeon) to Gezer" (II Sam. 5:25; I Ch. 14:16) and even after he had established his kingdom, he still had to fight "the Philistines at Gezer" (I Ch. 20:4). Thereafter the fate of the town remains obscure until the latter part of Solomon's reign. It was destroyed and burnt by the Egyptians who, according to the Bible, slaughtered its Canaanite inhabitants. Gezer was excavated before archaeological techniques had developed sufficiently to disentangle the superimposed remains of successive periods and thus find proof of the city's destruction.

Gezer in Solomon's Empire: The Bible also records that Gezer was annexed to Solomon's kingdom as part of the dowry brought to him by his marriage to the daughter of Pharaoh Shoshenk (Shishak), (I K. 9:15–16).

Solomon rebuilt Gezer (10th c. BCE) and fortified it. The city gate of this period, unearthed by Macalister, had four successive entrances, and is practically identical with the gates of Megiddo and Hazor. Solomon apparently built all three fortifications to the same plan. From this period comes the "Gezer Tablet" (described under Agriculture*, The Seasons) which is a clay tablet written in a Canaanite dialect very much like Biblical Hebrew, inscribed with a list of the agricultural seasons of the year.

According to B. Mazar, administrative division of the country during the early monarchy included Gezer in the 2nd district of Ephraim (I K. 4:8). There are two references to it as a Levite town in the territory of Ephraim (Jos. 21:21; I Ch. 6:67).

The Divided Monarchy: The Old Testament hardly refers to Gezer again after the end of Solomon's reign. It is mentioned in the stele of Shishak, king of Egypt*, as one of the towns he conquered during his campaign in Palestine shortly before or after the death of Solomon, in the 5th year of the reign of Rehoboam (see Israel and Judah*, Part III). B. Mazar believes that the Egyptians occupied Gezer for a time and then destroyed it. The excavations proved that soon after the campaign the town was abandoned and left to a few poor settlers. On the basis of evidence of excavation, K. Kenyon believes that there was only slight occupation of Gezer between 960 and 500 BCE.

In the town of this period (before and during the Assyrian invasion) several coins and weights were found stamped "lmlk" ("belonging to the king"; see Weights and Measures*). A drawing (**122**) on a relief from Nimrud of the time of Tiglat-Pileser III (first half 8th c. BCE), shows the town of "Gazru" (possibly Gezer) under attack by a battering ram, while from the walls the defenders make gestures of surrender.

After the collapse of the Kingdom of Israel, Gezer was repeopled with Assyrians and peoples of other nationalities, according to the usual Assyrian practice, as well as a few surviving Israelites. Evidence for this comes from two Mesopotamian tablets inscribed in cuneiform and dated to 651 and 649 BCE which carry lists of names in Assyrian and Aramaic.

124
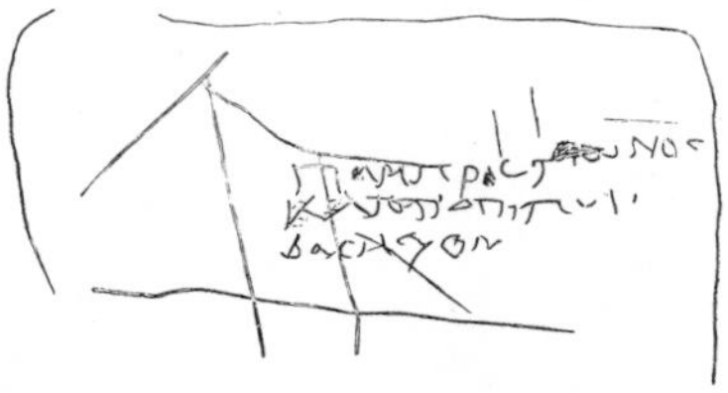

125

The Persian Period: Under Persian rule, Gezer again developed into an important centre, being in a key position on the frontier between the sub-satrapies of Ashdod and Judea (cf. I Mac. 14:34). Typical jar handles of this period. stamped with the words "Yhud" (the Aramaic term for the Persian satrapy of Judea) and "yršlm" (Jerusalem) were found in Gezer (see Inscriptions*: Period of the Second Temple).

Hellenistic and Maccabaean Period: Gezer is mentioned frequently in connection with the wars of the Hasmoneans*. At the beginning of the Maccabaean revolt, it served as a refuge for the Seleucid forces after their defeats in the hills of Judah and Ephraim (for the first defeats of the Syrians under Gorgias, see I Mac. 4:1–15; for the defeat of Nicanor, see I Mac. 7:43–45). The Syrian general, Bacchides, fortified Gezer in 160 BCE (I Mac. 9:52) and it remained a Syrian stronghold until, after a long siege, it was finally stormed and captured by Simon the Hasmonean in 142 BCE. The conquest of Gezer and Jaffa marked the beginning of an independent Hasmonean political policy (see Hasmoneans*). Simon banished all Gentile inhabitants, settled the town with Jews and fortified it strongly (I Mac. 13:43–48). That this policy had less than whole-hearted support from the inhabitants is suggested by a graffito (**124**) found in the former governor's palace. A forced worker, possibly a dispossessed hellenized native, had scratched on a stone he placed in the wall, "May fire consume Simon's palace, says Pampras".

The ruins of a fortress (**125**) of this period uncovered by the excavations, are probably those of the Hasmonean's fort. The inscriptions "Tehum Gezer" (boundary of Gezer) found engraved on rocks in the surrounding fields helped to identify the site of the ancient city (**123**).

The Hasmonean period marked the peak of Gezer's importance. It became one of the key strongholds of the Hasmoneans and the headquarters of Simon's son, John (Hyrcanus), while he was commander-in-chief of his father's forces (I Mac. 13:53). Hyrcanus was there when Simon and his two eldest sons were assassinated in a plot against the whole dynasty. Forewarned, he was able to defend himself against his assailants and go on to Jerusalem to be crowned one of the Jews' great kings (I Mac. 16:19–22).

The Roman Period: This was a time of increasing difficulty for the inhabitants and Gezer's prosperity declined. It was taken by Lucius Aeneas on the orders of Vespasian during the first Rebellion against Rome. The bulk of the population was killed, the rest sold into slavery. From that time until the Crusaders came, the ruins of the once mighty city of Gezer lay abandoned and almost forgotten.

126

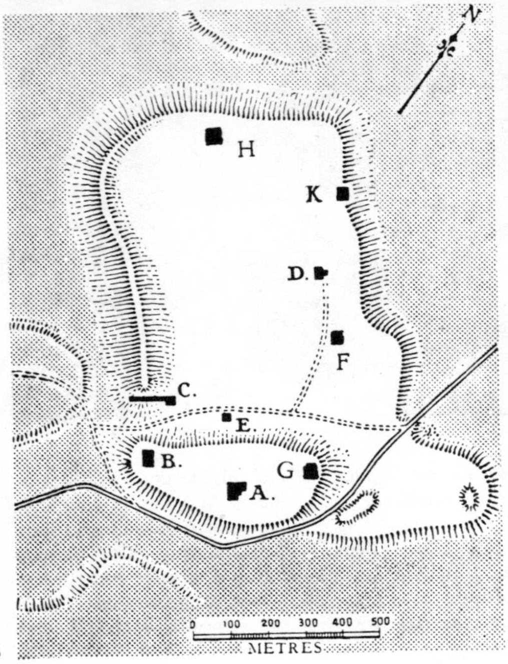

HAZOR. — One of the largest and most important of the fortified cities of Canaan, Hazor is situated in the upper Jordan Valley, between Lake Huleh and the Sea of Galilee. Its name comes from the word "hazer", meaning an enclosed area protected by embankments or artificial fortifications (ramparts).

Written Records: Hazor is mentioned in some of the earliest records. Its name appears in the Egyptian execration texts (19th c. BCE; see Egypt*), and in Akkadian inscriptions among the Mari* documents of the 18th c. BCE, in one of which Hazor's king, Ibn Addu, is mentioned. The Mari archives show that during this period, Hazor was an important centre, forming part of the political and economic network of the Amorite-Mesopotamian states, and with extensive trade contacts with Mari.

Hazor is listed by Thothmes III and Amenhotep II (15th c. BCE), by Seti I (end of 14th c. BCE) and by Ramses III (12th c. BCE). It is mentioned in the Tel el Amarna* letters (14th c. BCE) and in Papyrus Anastasi I (13th c. BCE, time of Ramses II).

127

Leading the Canaanite Kingdoms: The Old Testament ascribes eminence to Hazor, "for Hazor was formerly the head of all those kingdoms" (Jos. 11:10). It was at the head of the northern Canaanite coalition opposing the invading Israelite tribes. Its king, Jabin, led the fight against Joshua by the waters of Merom. After the Canaanite defeat, Hazor — alone among the cities of the area — was destroyed by fire. (For details, see Conquest*, Part II, Conquest and Settlement in the North; Judges*).

Whether the "King of Hazor" of the period of the Conquest ruled over as mighty a kingdom as had been known in the 18th c. BCE seems doubtful. It has been suggested that the statement that Hazor "formerly was the head of all those kingdoms" did not refer to the actual situation at the time of Joshua, but to the city of the earlier, Middle Bronze Age. The position given to Hazor in resisting the Israelites probably represents the last stage in the greatness of a once mighty kingdom, when the king of Hazor had indeed been King of Canaan.

Once Israelite domination was acknowledged, Hazor was included in the territory of the Naphtali tribe* (Jos. 19:36). Later, it was rebuilt and fortified by Solomon (I K. 9:15). Some authorities think that Hazor was captured by the Arameans during the campaign of Ben Hadad I (see Israel and Judah* and compare I K. 15:20; II Ch. 16:4). Finally, it was destroyed by Tiglat-Pileser in 732 BCE during the Assyrian invasion of Palestine (II K. 15:29); Hazor's existence as a city came to an end, but the citadel contined to be used down to the Hellenistic period.

Later sources (1 Mac. 11:67) refer to the Valley of Hazor as the scene of the battle between Jonathan, the Hasmonean* prince, and Demetrius II, but make no mention of a town. Josephus* described its position (Ant. Bk. 5, 5:1) as "above lake Semechonitis".

Archaeological History of Hazor: Hazor was identified with Tel Waqas south-west of the Huleh Lake by J. Garstang in 1926.

The size and importance of the town suggested by the written records were amply confirmed by the extensive and methodical excavations of Tel Waqas carried out between 1955–1958 by the James A. de Rothschild Expedition at Hazor. The tel forms a rectangle 700 × 1000 metres (about 183 acres), making it by far the largest site to be excavated in Palestine. To deal with this huge area, the main site was divided into nine excavation areas, marked A—K, plus one or two smaller subsidiary sections. The site consists of two principal divisions; the tel proper, or the upper town on the south-west corner of the area (marked A B G, **126**), and a huge fortified plateau to the north (areas C F H K).

Discoveries: Altogether, 21 superimposed layers of human settlement, representing 25 centuries of occupation, were uncovered.

The lowest strata (21–19) contained pottery from the Early Bronze Age III (2700–2400 BCE), but no traces of buildings. Stratum 18 revealed potsherds from the Middle Bronze Age I (2100–1900 BCE), corresponding to the period when Hazor is mentioned in the Egyptian execration texts (see Egypt*; Inscriptions*). During all these periods, people lived only in the restricted area of the tel proper, which continued to be occupied until Hellenistic times.

Founding of the Lower City: Strata 17–16 of the Middle Bronze Age II (18th–16th cs. BCE) belong to the period during which the town reached the peak of its prosperity and importance (see above, Written Records). It was at this time that the lower town was built, protected by impressive fortifications. These were formed by a deep ditch surmounted by a high bank **(127)** protecting the western approaches. This arrangement is characteristic of Hyksos fortifications and its use here is evidence of Hazor's importance to their empire.

The city's gate, one of the most formidable found in Palestine, was uncovered on the north side (K) together with part of a thick wall. The defence system remained in use with slight changes right through the Bronze Age and lasted perhaps into the beginning of the 13th c. BCE.

Stratum 15 (15th c. BCE) revealed a large sanctuary in area H. It was built on the plan used throughout the Bronze Age, with three halls opening one into the other, as shown in this illustration **(129)**. This lion carved on a basalt orthostat, was found nearby **(128)**.

Strata 14 and 13 were both of the Canaanite period (1400–1200 BCE). The earlier layer appears to have been of a rich and prosperous city. Rubble from this city was used as the foundation upon which the more modest city of stratum 13 was erected. In area C, where the remains of the last 13th c. Canaanite city were discovered, a small sanctuary from this period was found built into the earthen ramparts. A description of the two temples and the cult furniture found there, is given under Canaan: Gods and Idols, Cult*. A network of stone tunnels and a large stone altar were uncovered in section F.

128

Occupation of the lower plateau ceased some time in the 13th c., perhaps when Hazor was captured by the Israelites. After this, the inhabited area was confined to the upper town.

Israelite Settlement: Strata 12 and 11 (12th–11th cs. BCE) are the remains of a temporary and unimportant Israelite occupation similar to early Israelite settlements elsewhere. Prosperity returned to Hazor during Solomon's reign (stratum 10, 963–930 BCE) when the city was again fortified. A solid wall was built around the upper town and a fort erected in the Acropolis (the western part of the tel). The Solomonic city gate **(130)** containing six rooms built on either side of an internal passage was also uncovered.

129

130

It is similar to the gates found in contemporary layers at Megiddo* and Gezer*. In the picture, the background shows the double wall (with cross walls making casemates) leading to the gate. A pillared building of King Ahab's time is shown in (**131**).

This town (stratum 9) continued almost unchanged throughout the 10th and early part of the 9th c. BCE. Stratum 8 is attributed to the period of Ahab (9th c. BCE). The town was extended eastward and surrounded by a new wall, built in the best style of the time. No gate for this wall has yet been uncovered, although in section A a big store-house was found, with two columns of stone in front of it. The fortress of the town was uncovered in section B, the western elevated part of the tel. Slightly altered, the fortifications continued to be used in stratum 7 (second half of the 9th c. BCE), stratum 6 (end of the 9th and beginning of the 8th c. BCE) and stratum 5 (8th c. until 732 BCE). In 732, during the reign of Pekah ben Remaliahu, the upper town was destroyed by Tiglat-Pileser III, the Assyrian conqueror (see Israel and Judah* part IV).

This was the last Israelite town. However, small forts built on the higher eastern part of the tel (section B) existed during the Assyrian period (strata 4 and 3) and the Persian stratum (2), and continued in use until the Hellenistic period (stratum 1). The site was finally abandoned about 150 BCE.

131

HEBRON. — The foundation of this important and ancient city of Palestine is mentioned in the Old Testament in a unique manner: "And Hebron was built seven years before Zoan of Egypt" (Nu. 13:22). The date of the foundation of Zoan (Tanis-Avaris), which served as the capital of the Hyksos, can be calculated from extra-biblical sources as ca. 1720 BCE (see Exodus*: The 400 Year Stele). It may therefore be assumed that Hebron was built at the beginning of the Middle Bronze (Canaanite) Age II, which coincides with the Hyksos period. This estimate is also borne out by the frequent mention of Hebron in the Patriarchal* Epics (Gn. 13:18; 35:27, and elsewhere), as the Patriarchal period also coincides with that of the Hyksos.

Canaanite Period: Indications of Canaanite occupation of Hebron occur several times in the Old Testament. One such tradition is the account of Abraham's purchase of the Field of Machpelah in Hebron from Ephron the Hittite (Gn. 23:17–20). The Cave of Machpelah (see below) in the field later became the burial-place of Abraham, Sarah, Isaac, Rebecca, Jacob and Leah.

The Old Testament also notes that Arba, father of the Anak clan, lived in Hebron and that the whole family was destroyed by Joshua* when he conquered the Judean mountains (Jos. 11:21–22). Kiryat Arba, the other name of Hebron, is thought to be derived from the name of the father of the Anakites. Talmudic tradition, however, attributes the name to the four patriarchal couples who were buried at Hebron, while modern research leans towards the view that "Arba" refers to the four separate quarters that make up Hebron (see below). One of the quarters, Mamre, is mentioned in the Old Testament (Gn. 13:18; 35:27).

During the Conquest*, King Hoham of Hebron joined the Southern Canaanite coalition led by Adoni-Zedek, King of Jerusalem. The coalition was defeated by Joshua at Gibeon, and Hebron was later awarded to Caleb ben Jephuneh (Jos. 10:3; 15:13; Jud. 1:20). In I Ch. 2:43, the names of four clans claiming descent from Caleb, "father" of Hebron, are mentioned. Prof. B. Mazar favours the view that each of these clans lived in one of the quarters of Kiryat Arba.

During the Monarchy: Hebron reached its zenith in the early part of David's* reign, serving as his capital for the first seven and a half years of his rule over Judea (II Sam. 2:1–4). Subsequently, Jerusalem was made the capital of the united kingdom. Hebron was also the site of David's anointing as King of all Israel (II Sam. 5:1–3). In deference to the tombs of the Patriarchs within its boundaries, Hebron continued to be regarded as a political and religious centre throughout the period of the monarchy. It became a Levitical city, i. e. a city for priests and Levites, as well as a haven of refuge (see Priests*).

It was at Hebron that Joab killed Abner ben-Ner, and Absalom raised the banner of revolt against his father (II Sam. 15:7–10). Rehoboam* fortified Hebron, as well as many other places in the Judean mountains (II Ch. 11:10). It also served as an important administrative centre in the later period of the monarchy, as can be gathered from the seals* bearing the inscription "lmlk hbrn" = (to the king of Hebron) found stamped on jars in many sites in Judah (see Seals*).

Post-Exilic and Roman Period: Jews settled in Hebron after their return from the Babylonian Exile* (Neh. 11:25). In the early period of the Second Temple, the Edomites occupied the southern part of Judea, including Hebron. The Hasmoneans* later wrested it from them, destroyed it, and burned down its walls (Ant. Bk. 12, 8:6). Herod* erected many buildings in Hebron, including an imposing structure over the Cave of Machpelah with an outer wall modelled on that of the Temple Mount **(150)**. It was made of huge blocks of stone, characteristic of the best Herodian masonry. Herod also erected other buildings in the Mamre quarter.

Though Hebron's position in the Great War with Rome was insignificant, it continued to be revered because of the Patriarchal Tombs (Josephus, War of the Jews, Bk. 4, 9:7). It was occupied in 68 CE by Shimon Bar Giora, leader of the Zealots, and later razed by the Romans (War of the Jews, Bk. 4, 9:9).

Scant Archaeological Evidence: The present site of Hebron is on four hills: Al Muhawer, Nimrah, Jabal al Ja'barah, and Jabal ar-Rumaidah. As yet no systematic excavations of the town have been carried out; there is no unanimity as to the location of Hebron and its quarters in Old Testament times. Nevertheless, there is a strong presumption, based on a number of potsherds from the Iron Age, that the town first stood on Jabal ar-Rumaidah. Among the sites uncovered on that hill was one of a tomb containing pottery dating from the Middle Bronze Age (ca. 1700 BCE), which seems to fit in with the literary materials bearing on the age of Hebron.

The Cave of Machpelah: According to tradition, the site of the Cave is at Haram el-Khalil in the eastern part of modern Hebron. The Cave, which is sacred to Moslems, is surrounded by an enclosure or "Haram" measuring sixty by thirty-three metres, and a building whose foundations date to the time of Herod. After the Arab conquest, the Cave of Machpelah was covered by a synagogue. Following the Crusades, the Arabs banned the entry of non-Moslems. Those few who have entered report the presence of a blocked cave under the sealed enclosure.

Mamre and Abraham's Tent: The place where Abraham pitched his tent (Gn. 13:18; 18:1) is near Hebron. Apparently the location has been shifted a number of times because of its association with an ancient oak tree. During Herod's reign and for a long time thereafter, one such tree existed north of Hebron at Ramat-el-Khalil. The site of the tent at Mamre was probably fixed during this period, as Herod built a rectangular enclosure of magnificent masonry there at the same time that he erected the "Haram". The site was rebuilt as a pagan centre with a great market-place during the Hadrianic era. It was chiefly remembered by Jews as the place where, after the Bar Kochba War*, thousands of their co-religionists were sold into slavery for less than the price of cattle.

A prominent church and monastery were later built in Hebron and the site became a centre of pilgrimage for Christians. The Arabic name of Hebron, "al-Khalil", meaning "the friend of God", is a significant indication of the reverence in which Abraham's name is held by Moslems. Abraham is revered as the original founder of the three great religious traditions: Judaism, Christianity, Islam.

JERICHO. — *Outline: Pre-biblical Jericho: The Evidence of Archaeology; The Oldest Town in the World; The Jericho Clay Figures and the Myth of Creation; Prehistoric Trade of Jericho; The Walls of Jericho; The Riddle of Jericho's Fall; Evidence of Jericho's People; Biblical Jericho; Post-Exilic Jericho; Herodian and Roman Times; New Testament Times; A Neighbour of Qumran.*

In the south of the Jordan Valley, about 10 km. (6.5 miles) north-west of the Dead Sea, an oasis fed by a number of sweet-water springs marks the site of Jericho, the earliest town so far known in the world. Dating back to about 9000 BCE, it was first built a millenium or two before the appearance of farming villages in Egypt, Mesopotamia and Syria or in the upper Jordan Valley and elsewhere in Palestine during the 7th and 6th mill. BCE (see Agriculture*). Ranking as the oldest fortified town yet known in Palestine with a record of about 5 millennia before Joshua's Conquest, Jericho's long period of existence before biblical times is of especial interest.

Pre-biblical Jericho: The Evidence of Archaeology: A series of excavations showed that the site of Jericho had moved at different periods. The Canaanite and Old Testament town stood near the rich springs of Tel el-Sultan (Elisha's spring), some 4.5 miles west of the Jordan, while the Hellenistic-Roman town had shifted to Talul Abu-Alaiq, further west at the point where the canyon of Wadi el-Kelt opens out into the plain of Jericho. The later Jericho of Byzantine-Arab times stood at a third site, Arîha (modern Jericho), some 2 km. south-east of Tel el-Sultan.

A number of expeditions have excavated Tel el-Sultan seeking, among other things, scientific evidence for the story of the Israelites' conquest of Jericho. The first work there was done by the Palestine Exploration Fund in 1873 but it was not until the expedition led by John Garstang in 1930–31 that a coherent chronology began to emerge. Garstang found four walled towns, the first, Town A, dating from the Early Bronze Age (first centuries, 3rd mill. BCE); Town B dated from the Early Bronze Ages II and III (second half, 3rd mill. BCE); Town C dated from the late Middle Bronze Age (1750–1550 BCE) and Town D dated from the Late Bronze Age, mainly the 15th and early 14th cs. BCE. He also found traces of a fifth, later town which he attributed to the period of the monarchy, but which had no wall. In the north-eastern part of the tel, Garstang dug a deep ditch which revealed seventeen layers of settlement, dating from the pre-pottery Neolithic Age (7th mill. BCE, the lowest stratum, resting on virgin soil) to the Early Bronze Age.

The Oldest Town in the World: Garstang's work was extended and, in places, corrected by the expedition led by Dr. Kathleen Kenyon of the Institute of Archaeology of the University of London in 1952–57. By deepening Garstang's ditch and digging another in the western part of the tel, it was possible to reach natural rock in two different places. (This showed that Garstang had mistaken a continuation of the water-course for virgin rock.) The "carbon 14" method of dating could not be applied to the very lowest strata but the material which could be tested gave a date between the years 6250–5850 BCE. This led K. Kenyon to the conclusion that the lowest strata could be dated from the 9th–8th mill. BCE (Mesolithic Age), i. e. that habitation had begun around 8000 BCE or earlier. Although pottery was unknown at the time, the first inhabitants were sufficiently well organized to plan and erect a walled city with an effective defence system. Since there is no evidence for fortified towns elsewhere before the late 4th mill BCE, this established Jericho as the oldest fortified town so far known in the world as shown by the great stone tower of the pre-pottery Neolithic defences **(132)**.

132

Continuously inhabited by different groups of people, the first town developed into a town of the pre-pottery Neolithic period (ca. 7000 BCE). No less than 11 building stages were distinguished from this period, 22 plastered floors to buildings being found in one place, one on top of the other. The record of Jericho, in Dr. Kenyon's words, "provides evidence of the process for which archaeologists have long been looking, of the transition from man as a hunter to man as a member of a settled community." This **(134)** is a house of the pre-pottery Neolithic B period.

It is not yet clear whether there was a gap in occupation before the arrival of the Neolithic people (to whom pottery was known) or, after them, before the proto-Urban groups established themselves in Jericho.

The Jericho Clay Figures and the Myth of Creation: Although the earliest inhabitants of pre-pottery Jericho did not make clay vessels, they did produce life-size human figures and images of faces modelled in clay. Dr. Kenyon discovered about ten such heads, modelled over a skull, as shown in this illustration **(133)**. Parts of limbs modelled in clay over a framework of reeds or canes which formed a kind of skeleton were also found. In the opinion of Ruth Amiran, the significance of these discoveries lies in their very close conceptual relationship to the much later Creation Epics of Babylonia and Israel. Man in each case was formed of clay, in the Genesis story of the creation of Eve, around Adam's rib. The Babylonian Gilgamesh Epic tells how the hero Enkiddu was "built" of clay and the Hebrew story of Eve uses the same word for "build". The pre-pottery Neolithic B clay figures from Jericho appear to be a material expression of this same theme of later eastern mythologies (see Genesis*; Creation). "There seems to be an intrinsic affinity between Near Eastern myths, according to which man was created from clay, and the clay figures and plastered skulls discovered in Jericho." (Ruth Amiran)

Prehistoric Trade of Jericho: The pre-pottery people who built the enormous stone walls of Jericho around the 8th mill. BCE had very little knowledge of other urban arts. They lived in temporary structures and left no evidence behind them of any great agricultural or economic advance which could explain the growth of the town. The only thing which can explain the existence and expansion of the town, in the opinion of E. Anati, is trade; trade in the salt, bitumen and possibly sulphur in which the Dead Sea was rich and which were all essential products in the ancient Near East. Salt was a necessity of life and, as the evidence shows, also very important for religious ceremonies and sacrifices as early as the Early Bronze Age (4th mill. BCE; compare Job 6:6; Nu. 18:19 and Mk. 9:49). Some of the oldest trade routes of the Near East began with the traffic in salt; the Jericho people may have been the earliest to develop this trade from the Dead Sea. Bitumen was needed for fastening sickles and other flint tools to their handles, for boat-building (see Flood*) and as a necessary raw material. Sulphur was in demand for medicines and fire-lighters. All three materials are perishable, so few traces of them have survived in the town, although evidence of trade has been found. This remains the most logical explanation for Jericho's early development.

The Walls of Jericho: After a gap in occupation which followed the Neolithic period, Jericho was continuously occupied all through the Early Bronze Age. The town was walled throughout this period (3100–2100 BCE), although in the course of a thousand years the wall was destroyed and rebuilt 17 times. Defences were obviously a major concern of Jericho's inhabitants, for the town was very vulnerable to attack from the east. The walls were made of unbaked mud bricks and stood 16–17 metres high. This made a substantial barrier to attackers but it needed constant care to prevent water erosion and to repair the effects of the earthquakes which appear to have occurred on an average of some four times per century (see western part of the tel with stone revetment wall at the bottom, **135**).

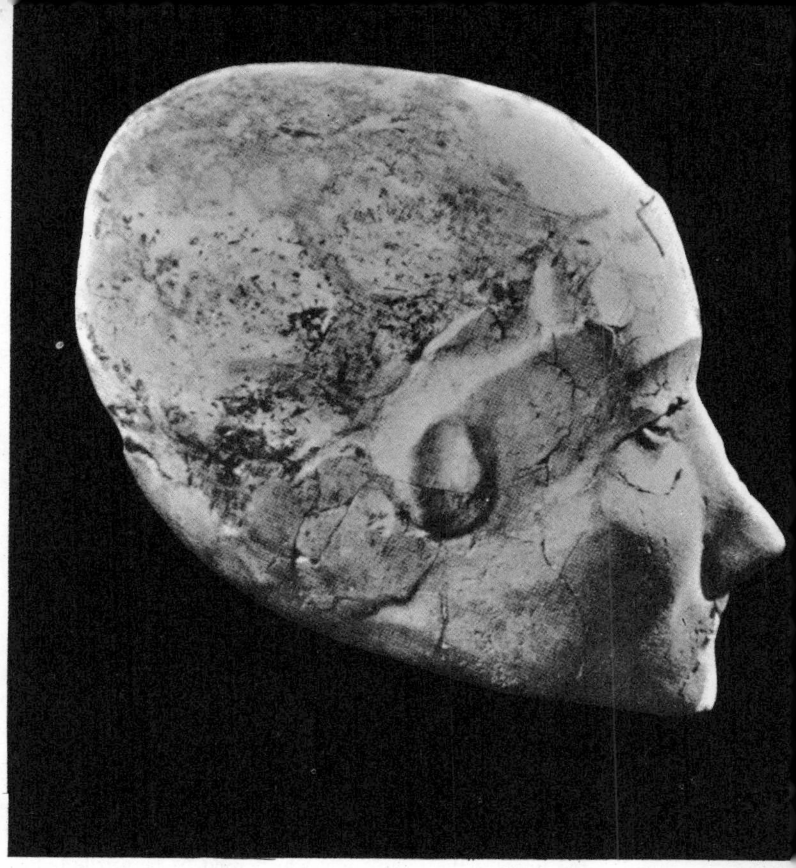

During the Middle Bronze Age A (2100–1900 BCE) while semi-nomadic elements lived in Palestine and intensive building activities were going on elsewhere in the country, Jericho was an open town. In the course of Middle Bronze Age B the town was fortified by a smooth earthwork and later this was replaced by smooth stone walls. These walls and the whole town were apparently destroyed when the town was occupied by the Egyptians in 1580 BCE. For a century and a half the site lay abandoned but around 1400

134

135

BCE a new town was built and it was this stratum (Late Bronze Age) which was presumably the town Joshua captured. Unfortunately, the last expedition led by Dr. Kenyon showed that almost all traces of it had been eroded and had served as a quarry for stone and earth for later building. The expedition was even able to demonstrate that one of the lines of the town walls which used to be attributed to this period had actually belonged to the Early Bronze Age. In fact, apart from a few potsherds of the Mycenaean period, and a number of scarabs inscribed with the names of different Pharaohs, the only traces of the Late Bronze Age town were a few fragments of houses (**136**), probably dating from the 14th c. BCE. This town was abandoned about 1325 BCE and left unoccupied for some 400 years, during which time erosion obliterated almost every trace of it.

The Riddle of Jericho's Fall: This situation has left undecided the question of the date of Joshua's conquest, a problem which has exercised the minds of eminent archaeologists such as W. F. Albright, J. Garstang, B. Mazar and many others. The 400 years of desertion seem to fit in with the biblical account of Joshua's curse of Jericho and its abandonment for a similar period, but Joshua's conquest must have taken place at least a century later than 1325 (see Exodus*). Dr. Kenyon suggests that the biblical record may have compressed events which took place over a comparatively long period into a chronological sequence which it is difficult to confirm today in view of the limited archaeological evidence available, (see Conquest*). The dramatic capture of Jericho as recorded in the Book of Joshua was probably written down many years later, on the basis of popular recollections of a memorable event. The exact relation between the abandonment of Jericho in the 14th c. and the Israelite conquest of the Promised Land remains uncertain.

Evidence of Jericho's People: Outside the walls of the Early Bronze Age town, numerous mass graves were uncovered which yielded important evidence of the vessels and tools used at that time. During the Middle Bronze Age A, tombs were uncovered for the first time, of single burials (see Burial*) and held few vessels and tools.

The following town (Middle Bronze Age B) revealed a large structure in the eastern part of the tel, which the excavators labelled "The Palace". Nearby were storehouses containing numerous bottles and jars filled with carbonized grains. Outside the town, many tombs were uncovered and were found to contain not only a large variety of vessels and tools but also wooden objects — tables, chairs, bowls etc. — which, thanks to the dry climate, had been preserved in excellent condition.

Biblical Jericho: In the late Bronze Age (14th c. BCE), Jericho stood to the west of a ford used by all travellers crossing that section of the Jordan. It plays an important role in the biblical narrative of Israelite penetration of the country from the East. The book of Joshua (2–6) records that the Israelites camped before the town, which was surrounded by a high wall with houses built into it. The story of how Joshua's spies were hidden in such a house is well known (Jos. 2) as is the tradition that the walls sealing the town fell on the seventh day of the Israelite attack, at the sound of the trumpets. After its capture, the town was destroyed and its inhabitants slaughtered, with the sole exception of Rahab the harlot, who had harboured the spies, and her family. Finally, Joshua laid a curse on anyone who should attempt to rebuild Jericho. The available archaeological evidence (see above), has not so far made it possible to solve the riddle which the biblical narrative represents.

In the distribution of the land among the tribes, Jericho was assigned to Benjamin (Jos. 18:21); but it was lost when the king of Moab captured it with the help of the Ammonites and the Amalekites (Jud. 3:13). The area was apparently inhabited during David's reign, (II Sam 10:5) but during the reign of Ahab, Hiel Beth Ha'eli brought down Joshua's

136

curse on his head by "rebuilding" Jericho, (presumably fortifying the town, I K. 16:34).

An extensive structure, called the "Greek house" by its German excavators, was discovered from the 10th century BCE town of the period of Judges. In fact it is a typical Israelite building of the time, built in four sections. Over its ruins buildings had been erected during the late monarchy and these may conceivably represent the town built by Hiel Beth Ha'eli.

Jericho was a meeting place for the prophets. Both Elijah and Elisha stayed there. Elijah was taken up to heaven nearby, (II K. 2:4–11) and Elisha purified its water (II K. 2:19–22). The Judean prisoners released by the Israelites after their defeat of King Ahaz were returned to Jericho (II Ch. 28:15), while in the Plain of Jericho, Zedekiah, the last king of Judah, was captured as he was fleeing from the conquering Babylonians (Jer. 39:5). Jericho was destroyed by the Babylonians in 587 BCE and its inhabitants deported with the Jews from the rest of the country.

In the list of the exiles who returned from Babylon, Nehemiah (7:36) records 345 "sons of Jericho" who re-settled in their native town. Some of them took part in the reconstruction of Jerusalem (Neh. 3:2).

Post-Exilic Jericho: During the Persian period, Jericho was ruled by the Satraps, a fact attested by the discovery of seals* of the period inscribed "Yhud" (the name of the Persian province of Judea). In 352–351 BCE, the town was destroyed by King Artaxerxes III (Ochus) of Persia as a reprisal for a rebellion by the Jericho Jews. Later on, the town and its surrounding territory were taken over by the Nabateans*.

The site at Tel el Sultan was abandoned during this (the Hellenistic) period and the settled population moved west to Talul Abu-Alaiq. This site was excavated in 1950–51 by J. L. Kelso and J. B. Pritchard. They found the ruins of a Hellenistic fortress, attributed either to Bacchides or Simon the Hasmonean. It is known that during the Maccabaean revolt, Jericho was fortified by the Seleucid general Bacchides (I Mac. 9:50; see Hasmoneans*) and Simon the last of the five Hasmonean brothers was killed just outside the town (I Mac. 16:14–15). John Hyrcanus (see Hasmoneans*) took over the town and he and his successors built palaces there and two small forts, Taurus and Thrax. Later (ca. 63 BCE), these were destroyed by the Roman general, Pompey (see Rome and the Jews*).

Herodian and Roman times: During the Roman period, Jericho's reputation stood high as a centre for the cultivation of balsam and other perfumes, (see Ein Gedi*). When Cleopatra was intriguing to take control of Judea and Arabia, Mark Antony compromised by awarding her the palm (**137**) and balsam groves of Jericho. Herod perforce agreed, but he leased the plantations from her and "farmed" out the rent to his advantage, (i. e. acquired the right to collect the Queen's royal revenues).

Following the deaths of Antony and Cleopatra, Augustus restored Jericho to Herod. Josephus records that Herod enriched the town with a number of public buildings, including a hippodrome, and an amphitheatre, together with a winter palace for himself and villas for the Jewish upper class in the new town west of ancient Jericho. He also built a new wall with two towers around the town, one tower

137

named Kypros after his mother and one named Phasael for his brother. When Herod died, his palace was burned down, but his son, Archelaus, rebuilt it and improved its palm plantations.

New Testament Times: Jesus was familiar with all the district. The scene of the Temptation may have been in the desolate mountains above the town and the place of his baptism by John* was not far away. He made the road leading to Jericho the scene of his parable of the Good Samaritan (Lk. 10:30). The road he took on his last visit to Jerusalem led Jesus to Jericho where he stayed at the house of Zacchaeus, a rich publican (tax collector, Lk. 19:1–9), and restored the sight of the blind beggar, (18:35–43 and parallels).

Jericho, in Jesus' time, was a thriving, prosperous city, the centre of development of the Romanized Jericho Valley. It contained a small wealthy middle class and a great number of poor people who lived in hopes of better things to come.

The town was destroyed by Vespasian during the first Jewish-Roman war, although later on a garrison was stationed there. Hadrian rebuilt Jericho and it continued in existence throughout the Byzantine period.

A Neighbour of Qumran: Jericho was the nearest town to Qumran (see Dead Sea Scrolls*) and anyone going there to or from Jerusalem passed through Roman Jericho. A path some 8 miles long wound along the Judean foothills to the sectaries' home. Probably the skins on which the Scrolls were written were brought from Jericho, although the sectaries would need to be assured that they were ritually pure. The stores for the Essene community were probably also brought from the town.

Biblical manuscripts were found in various places near Jericho, from the Roman period up to the 8th c. CE. Additional research may reveal further data on the links between New Testament Jericho and Qumran.

138

139

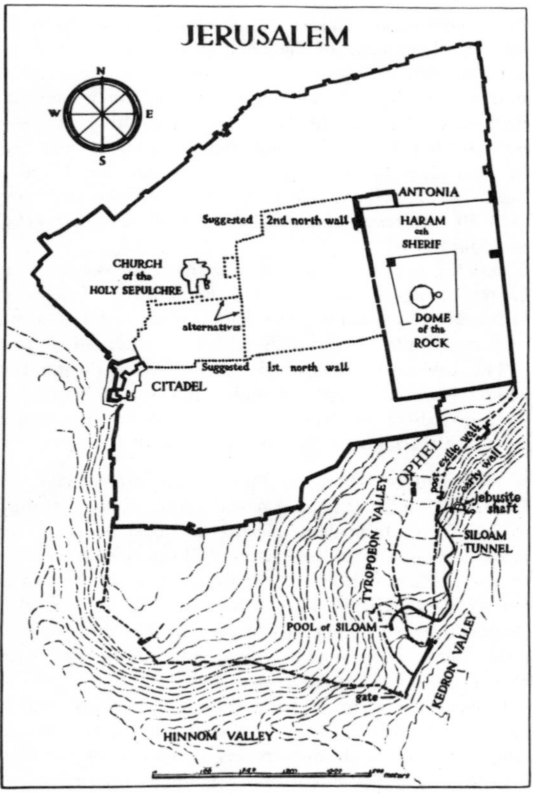

JERUSALEM: The principal city of Palestine was built on two unequal ridges running south from an eastward spur of the central mountain range, seen in this aerial view of Jerusalem (**138**). Compare with map (**139**).

The northern section of the oldest city lies underneath the present walled "Old City". This is surrounded by a mediaeval Turkish wall which still stands (shown as the dark crenellated line on the map, **139**) and is often used as a convenient point of reference for comparison with the biblical walls. Two ridges run south from the Old City: the western ridge on which stand monuments and parts of the town (marked 1, 3, 3A, **138**) and the eastern ridge (marked 4A and 6, **138**). Between the two ran the Tyropeon Vale, which was much deeper in early antiquity but was later filled in by an accumulation of debris 56 ft. (18m.) high. The Vale runs north through the centre of the Old City and originally it formed a clear line of demarcation between the eastern and western parts of the town. To the east of the Old City runs the Kidron Valley (marked 4B) with the region known as Ophel (marked 4A) lying on its western slopes. On the west, the city is bounded by the Valley of Hinnom (marked 1A). This curves round eastwards to form the southern boundary, meeting the Kidron valley at almost the same point as the Tyropeon. This apex of the three valleys lies approximately 700 yards (630 metres) from the walls of the Old City.

Archaeology of Jerusalem: Innumerable expeditions have tried to tackle the problems of the archaeology of Jerusalem over the past century, beginning with the Palestine Exploration Fund in 1864–7 and ending (for the present) with the investigation of Ophel by K. Kenyon and R. de Vaux in

141

1961–63. However, in a site which has been lived in continuously for some five thousand years and is still occupied, excavation is extremely difficult and most of the results so far published have been inconclusive.

In the areas to the south and north, outside the walls of the present Old City, successive phases of occupation have made earlier remains very fragmentary. The most recent excavations of 1961–63 were able to discover many new facts and to correct a number of assumptions which had been suggested by earlier excavations, before criteria for exact dating and interpretation had been developed.

pre-Israelite Ophel: Ophel lay above the Giḥon spring (or Virgin's Fountain, whose entrance is shown here **140**), the only perennial spring close to the walls of the city. Because of its proximity to water, the site of Ophel to the south of the present walled city, guarded by the two valleys on either side, was always strongly fortified. The only gap in its defences came on the neck joining it to the upper spur of the Old City (just above the point marked "early wall" on the map **139**). The earliest pottery found in Ophel came from rock-cut tombs dating from the Proto-Urban period. This is the time (late 4th mill. BCE) when newcomers were laying the foundations for the growth of the Early Bronze Age towns of Palestine. During the 3rd and 2nd mill. BCE the site developed into a town. Its name, apparently "Jšlmm" first occurs in the Egyptian Execration texts (see Egypt*) dating around 1900 BCE (it is known as "'ršlm" in the 15th c. Amarna Letters*). The 1961 CE excavations found the first traces of the unmortared stone wall (**141, 2**) dating ca. 1800 BCE, which girded the slopes of Ophel in the Middle Bronze Age.

140

For a thousand years from that time until the 7th c. BCE, a wall stood on this line, thus marking the limits of the Jebusite town and of the City of David (see below).

(The heaps of stone lying on either side and below the wall were thrown up by the excavations. The Spring of Giḥon is underneath the lower building in the centre of the pictures (**141, 142**).

Jerusalem was a powerful stronghold of the Canaanite clan of the Jebusites in the Late Bronze Age. It is as a Jebusite town that it makes its first appearance in the Bible, which notes its long defiance of Israelite attacks. One of the outstanding results of the 1961–62 excavations (published by K. Kenyon) has been to disprove earlier identification of the remains of fortifications on the crest of Ophel above this 18th c. BCE wall as a Davidic tower and Jebusite ramp or bastion. The ruins of the tower (**143**) have now been shown to be the remains of a 2nd c. BCE Maccabean fortification and the so-called "Jebusite" ramp (**144**) to have covered houses of Jerusalem destroyed by the Babylonians in 586 BCE. Further work will be needed to determine what other remains there are of the Jebusite period.

It appears that this old city was the capital of a Canaanite city-state, presumably the same "Šalem" that was ruled by Melchi-zedek, who honoured Abraham (Gn. 14:18–19). A tradition recorded in Ezk. 16:3 suggests that it had a mixed population and one theory ascribes its foundation to the Hyksos rule, which left behind elements of Hittite and Hurrite habitation in Palestine. The Amarna letters* (14th c. BCE) include one (**145**) written when the ruler of Jerusalem, Abdi-Hiba, was threatened by the Habiru* invaders and appealed to his Egyptian overlord for help.

Capture of the Jebusite Stronghold: The first capture of the Jebusite city before the 10th c. BCE is recorded in two contradictory accounts in Joshua* and Judges*. According to the theoretical, ideal allocation of Canaan in Jos. 18:28, the city was assigned to Benjamin (see Tribes*), but Jud. 1:8 claims that it was captured by Judah immediately after Joshua's death. The king of Jerusalem, Adoni-Zedek, was defeated but it seems that his city remained an independent enclave between the tribal areas of Benjamin north of Jerusalem and Judah to the south. Or, according to some, it may have been captured and then regained its independence. The biblical record (Jud. 1:21; 19:11) is explicit that the city remained a Jebusite stronghold and it appears to have retained its independence for some two centuries after Joshua, eventually with Philistine* help, until it was captured by David around 1000–995 BCE. Its importance is apparent from the fact that only after it had been captured for Israel could the northern tribes, which occupied the central mountain range, and the tribe of Judah, which occupied its southern part, unite into a single nation (see map **385**), and the great period of Israel's history begin. Its strength is suggested by the strategy which finally reduced the town, (see David*). Joab entered the city through an underground water shaft to take the defenders in the rear, (see illus. in Water Supply*).

The City of David*: The city which David took covered only the small area of Ophel, but he fortified it and, according to Canaanite custom, took it as his own "royal city", "his" by right of conquest. It was neutral ground between the northern and southern tribes and around it they could unite as equals. It became the capital of the new state David was bent on creating, and he gave it a special religious significance by making it the permanent home of the Ark (II Sam. 6). The key point of the city's defences was the "Millo" probably a tower, perhaps built on a solid packed stone platform. So far, excavations have not definitely identified the "Millo" although a massive substructure of the 10th c. BCE at the top of the sloping wall of the city (**141**) may indicate the foundations for such a tower. However, this is not certain. After David's death, Solomon is also credited with having built "the Millo and the wall of Jerusalem" (I K. 9:15), possibly the northern section of the eastern ridge which ends in Ophel.

Solomon's greatest building achievements were his own palace and the Temple* (I K. 6-7; see David and Solomon*) both of them constructed on a lavish scale, with the elegant stonework and sophisticated decoration of the best Phoenician craftsmen of the day. Their highly developed workmanship can be illustrated by excavations at Samaria* and Hazor*. While a few fragments underneath the post-Exilic Herodian Temple* have been claimed as relics of Solomon's temple there are no indisputable traces on the top of Ophel, which is covered today by the site of the present Dome of the Rock (see Temple* and bottom illustration **142**).

It is assumed that Solomon's Temple lay outside the narrow confines of the City of David, apparently a few hundred yards to the north. If it was enclosed in the city wall, then this must first have been extended to encircle the summit of the hill (see map **139**). It is also assumed that there is a continuity of tradition between Solomon's Temple and the post-Exilic ones of Zerubbabel and Herod.

145

144

143

142

146

Ophel in Iron Age Times: So far as the city on the slopes of Ophel is concerned, a series of sub-structures with elaborate retaining rib-walls was built along the eastern ridge. Iron Age houses were later built on platforms which lay close to the earliest Late Bronze platforms (**146**). Other platforms, in this exiguous area, date from the earliest period of the Monarchy and extend well down the eastern slope. In the series of disasters that befell Jerusalem during the next 7 centuries, the buildings erected on the platforms slowly disappeared, one after the other, down the slope — a vivid illustration of the chequered history of the city.

Under the later kings, the city spread beyond the limits of Solomon's capital on to the western ridge (II K. 14:13; 22:14). In the 8th c. BCE the walls crossed the Tyropeon Valley and from the pottery discovered on the western hill, it is clear that this was occupied by the 7th c. "Tyropeon" is derived from Tyre. Phoenician traders of that city maintained their quarters in the valley. K. Kenyon believes that from the 7th c. to Hellenistic times, Jerusalem and its walls had two salients to the south, following the contours of the two ridges. In fact at the end of the last century, fragments of a wall and a rock scarp were found on the west and east sides of the western ridge.

The Second Wall: On the other side of the city, the north wall ran from the Citadel at the head of the Valley of Hinnom along a line just south of the present David Street, meeting the wall of the Temple enclosure at a point about two fifths of its presumed contemporary length, as shown on this map (**139**). Thus the Temple area would have formed a prominent salient in the line of the city boundary. Fragments found along this line probably belonged to this (first) north wall.

During the troubled period of the Judean kingdom, when the city was under repeated attack, there were innumerable rebuildings and strengthenings of the walls. The city was plundered by the Egyptian Shoshenk ca. 915 BCE; its walls were breached by Joash king of Israel in 785 and the city was also attacked by the king of Aram* (see Israel and Judah* II, III, IV, V). However, it is impossible to identify the traces of these rebuildings amongst the complex mass of rough walls unearthed on the sides of Ophel. One of the few remaining pieces of evidence about important engineering works is the water conduit built by King Hezekiah in 700 BCE and named after him. This carried the waters of the Giḥon spring away from the pool of Siloam into a "lower pool" inside the walls. Apparently it was built in preparation for the Assyrian siege (it is described and illustrated under Water Supply* and Inscriptions*). King Uzziah had also strengthened the city walls, adding towers and "war engines". In addition to the tunnel, Hezekiah again repaired the walls and added "another wall without" (II Ch. 32:5) perhaps to enclose the "mishneh" (second quarter or suburb) of the expanded town. This outside wall is usually identified with the Second (northern) wall (see below).

Post-Exilic Times: Jerusalem fell to the Babylonians in 586 BCE. The city was destroyed, the Temple and the royal palace razed and the population deported. Fifty years later (538 BCE) Cyrus allowed some of the exiles to return to rebuild the Temple. They built a modest structure in which worship could be resumed and Jerusalem became the capital of the Persian province of Yehud, with a considerable degree of internal autonomy (see Restoration*; Seals* and Inscriptions*). Its walls were not rebuilt, however, until the governorship of Nehemiah* (ca 445–433 BCE). His rebuilding followed the lines of the walls which had been destroyed in 586. The people were encouraged to resettle there and, ruled by their priests, they and their city prospered materially well into the Hellenistic period. One factor contributing to this prosperity was the growth of the Jewish diaspora which regarded Jerusalem as its spiritual centre and sent large sums of money to the people (see Hellenism and the Diaspora*).

The Hasmonean Era: The spread of the hellenizing movement — and the opposition to it — had very far-reaching effects on Jerusalem. The hellenizers established a parallel Greek "polis" on the western ridge of the city (see Hasmoneans*), but the struggle between them and the mass of the people intensified. It reached a climax in 168 BCE when Antiochus, the Jews' Syrian overlord, sacked Jerusalem and massacred many of its inhabitants. Then he established a fortress, the "Akra of the Syrians" in the north which dominated the town and the Temple for the next 30 years. Many scholars identify the site of the Akra with the site of the Birta (i. e. Baris, Greek for castle) on which the Antonia tower was built later (see below). The Hasmonean princes captured Jerusalem and at the end of the Maccabean wars, it became the capital of their new kingdom. A century later however (63 BCE), struggles for power between a later generation of Hasmoneans brought the intervention of the Romans and Jerusalem was besieged and captured by Pompey. He had the city walls destroyed but he respected the Temple and it survived unharmed. Julius Caesar allowed the city walls to be rebuilt (47 BCE) and granted the Hasmonean dynasty considerable powers. However, their continuing quarrels paved the way for Herod* the Idumean and in 40 BCE he captured Jerusalem and ruled Judea as a Roman vassal for the next 36 years (until 4 BCE). During his reign, he instituted a vast building program including the rebuilding of the Temple* (for details, see Herod*).

For the first time, archaeologists have reliable evidence by which to date the fortifications of the last 2 cs. BCE. The continued expansion of the city eastwards is apparent from the 2nd c. BCE tower built on the site of the ancient Jebusite City of David. Similarly evidence for the city's growth north and west came from the excavations carried out by C. N. Johns in 1934–48 at the site of the Citadel, (in the centre of the west side of the present walled city, see map **139**). He found a line of wall curling around towards the east-west line, with three towers on it. Three different styles of building could be distinguished. The first could be dated no earlier than the early Hellenistic or Hasmonean city. The second belonged to the time of Alexander Jannaeus and the third was found in the Phasael tower (**147** left, middle ground) built by Herod*. The base of this tower which still survives to a quite considerable height has been popularly dubbed the "Tower of David". Some of its stones measure 9m × 4 × 2m (**148**). According to Josephus*, it was built as one of the three towers of Herod's new palace in the far corner of the north-west quarter of Jerusalem.

A massively built town gateway was found by an earlier excavation conducted by J. W. Crowfoot and G. M. Fitzgerald in 1927 on the western side of Ophel. Following the line of this southern course of Maccabean fortifications, the 1961 excavations of the eastern side of the eastern ridge confirmed that work on the defences had been carried out there early in the Maccabean period. Thus this whole area (bottom, right map **139**), which earlier excavations had ascribed to the period of David, can now be dated with certainty (according to K. Kenyon) to ca. 150 BCE.

Herodian Glories: The Herodian period rivals the Solomonic for external glories conferred upon Jerusalem. This time, the architecture was Graeco-Roman in style and buildings such as arcades of shops, a theatre and an amphitheatre all helped to "westernize" (i. e. "hellenize") the town. Unfortunately, the sites of these new buildings are un-

148

147

151

known. Herod's reign was a period of great commercial expansion in the cities of Palestine and Jerusalem shared in this. The resident population had grown considerably and it was swelled to enormous proportions at the three great Jewish festivals* by the huge influx of pilgrims coming from all over the Diaspora. Josephus records that Herod set so many masons and other craftsmen to work on his building projects, that at his death 18,000 or more were left unemployed (Ant. 20, 1:7). As an emergency relief measure, Agrippas II put them to work paving the streets with marble slabs. Herod did not extend the actual length of the walls, but he strengthened the city's defences by building the great Antonia (**149**) fortress, perhaps on the site of the Akra, and the three great towers, Phasael (see above), Hippicus and Mariamme, beneath the present Citadel next to his palace.

Then he embarked on his most grandiose project, the rebuilding of the Temple. On this 10,000 artisans were employed, besides specially trained priests who completed the sanctuary (for full description, see Temple*; Herod*). The huge Temple esplanade involved massive new terraced walls on the eastern and southern sides — one corner stone standing there weighs 100 tons. A tiny part of the outer wall stands still today, the "Wailing Wall (**150**), where pious Jews gather and there mourn the Temple's destruction according to an ancient custom. Additional portions of his foundation walls are also visible beneath the Haram el-Sherif or Moslem sanctuary shown in the picture (**151**), on the left. The lower section of Jerusalem, centre, stands over the Tyropeon Vale: the hill on the right is the western section, the "higher town".

After Herod's death and the deposition of his successor Archelaus, Jerusalem was ruled, like the rest of Palestine, by Roman Procurators (see Rome and the Jews*). Between 40–44 CE, Jerusalem enjoyed a brief golden age of renewed economic prosperity and relative peace, during the reign of Herod's grandson, Agrippa II. The city had expanded so much that he built a new wall to enclose the new northern quarter of Bezetha and other sections to the north of the second wall. It used to be assumed that this wall followed the line of the present north wall (marked as the darkest line on the map) but this assumption has been questioned as a result of recent research. In 1925–27, the remains of an exceedingly massive wall in the Herodian style were traced by E. L. Sukenik and L. A. Meyer for a distance of about 800 yards, some 450 yards to the north of the present wall which seems to fit the extension in Agrippa's time, although there is no archaeological evidence to prove this. The completion of the line of this wall can be conjectured from the contours of the ground and the foundations uncovered (**152**). The tower of Psephinus stood somewhere in the NW corner on high ground (somewhere "opposite" Herod's tower Hippicus, according to Josephus, Ant. V, 4, 3). Originally it formed an octagon of great height.

Agrippa's wall may also possibly have been left unfinished to meet Agrippa's fears that the Romans might suspect him of over-ambitious plans. The 1961 excavations also revealed that he had built a wall right across the Tyropeon Valley joining the eastern and western ridges.

The period of rule by the Procurators that followed Agrippa's death is one of the darkest in the whole history of Judea. It culminated in the revolt and war against Rome (67–73 CE) which ended in the devastation of almost the whole country. The final attack, siege and capture of Jerusalem by Titus in 70 CE are vividly described by Josephus* (and see article on Rome and the Jews*). At the end Jerusalem lay in ruins, and the Temple had been reduced to a heap of charred rubble.

Position of the 1st c. Walls and the Holy Sepulchre: Josephus describes three successive walls which Titus had to breach before he could reach the Temple, (the sanctuary was also, of course, strongly fortified; see Rome and the Jews*). The course of the first wall is now generally agreed as shown

152

149

150

on the map, but the line of the second wall (the one built at the time of Hezekiah or perhaps Menasseh, (see above) is still hotly disputed and it is this wall (the one before Agrippa built his) which would have been the city wall at the time of the Crucifixion (30 CE). Josephus' description is ambiguous but it appears that its east end joined the Antonia Tower at the N–W corner of the Temple enclosure (see map **139**). Josephus states that its western end was at the Gate Gennath (Garden) on the First Wall, but the position of this gate is unknown. There is a theory that this arch (**152a**) formed the top of Gate Gennath, indicating that older levels lie below, but this is purely hypothetical. L. H. Vincent places it just east of the Citadel, while J. Simons believed it to be about a third of the distance from the Citadel to the wall of the Temple enclosure. On the basis of these two identifications, three major theories of the line of the second wall have been worked out.

Vincent's own theory, which is the one most generally accepted, takes a line near the Citadel and follows a course which includes a pronounced indentation around the knoll of rock in a valley that cuts into the western ridge, (just by the church of the Holy Sepulchre) which he believes to be Calvary (Golgotha).

Simon's theory places the Gate Gennath further east on the line of the first Wall and takes the second wall south from that point to the east of the Church of the Holy Sepulchre. (Both lines are shown on the map **139**).

The third theory, (Clark and Norris), starts at the same point as the third, but curves around without the indentation.

The first two hypotheses place the Church of the Holy Sepulchre outside the walls of the time of the Crucifixion, thus confirming the authenticity of the site. The third theory denies all authenticity to the site and relegates it to a mere tradition of the time of Constantine, (whose pious mother Helena claimed that the site had been revealed to her in a vision), some three centuries after the Crucifixion. In this view, the Crucifixion and tomb of Christ (Golgotha) would be situated at Gordon's Calvary, a knoll outside the present wall (**153, 153a**). All three thories depend on the discovery of isolated fragments of wall and the application of military theories about the probable strategic value of different lines. Widely differing opinions on both counts have been expressed. The only conclusive proof would be extensive excavation over the whole area and this is virtually excluded in an area which is both densely populated and extraordinarily sacred. On the basis of the archaeological evidence which exists today no final conclusion as to the course of any of the north walls of biblical Jerusalem is possible.

Jerusalem after the 2nd c. CE: After the destruction of Jerusalem in 70 CE, its western quarter was garrisoned by the Roman Tenth Legion Fretensis and few Jews stayed in it. For a time the city was liberated by the revolt of Bar Kochba* (132–135 CE, see article), but when that last attempt at independence was crushed, Hadrian destroyed ancient Jerusalem. The city was completely razed and a new city Aelia Capitolina built over its ruins, Jews being forbidden to approach it on pain of death. This covered roughly the area of the present walled Old City east and north of this wall (**147**). The original building of the Damascus Gate may possibly belong to this period. The colummed

152 a

153

153 a

154

street running south from the Gate, which is shown on the 5th c. CE Madeba mosaic map of Aelia (**154**) may also have originated at this time.

Jerusalem prospered during the Byzantine period, for with the Christianization of the Roman Empire (4th c. CE), Jerusalem became a holy city for all the rapidly increasing number of adherents to the new religion. The Church of the Holy Sepulchre was first built in 335 CE after Queen Helena had made her pilgrimage to Jerusalem.

Jerusalem fell to the caliph Omar in 638. The Dome of the Rock, the great Moslem sanctuary set up by the Ummayad Caliph Abdel Malik in 661 CE in the Temple esplanade (see Temple*) is one of the supreme examples of early Arab art and architecture (**151**).

LACHISH. — Identified with Tel el-Duweir, Lachish was the major fortified city of Palestine all through the history of Israel. From the Conquest* to the Restoration*, Lachish takes a prominent place in the Bible story and also appears in other sources — mainly Assyrian — as an important Judean city. Strategically situated in the Shephela in the foothills of the Judean range, Lachish was the largest of the chain of fortresses guarding the approach to the mountains. Its acropolis covered 18 acres.

Excavations: The Wellcome-Marston expedition directed by J. Starkey began excavations in 1932. These were continued for six seasons until 1938, when the murder of Starkey forced their abandonment. Up to that time only Israelite levels had been uncovered. Evidence for earlier periods remains scanty.

Prehistoric Lachish: The first settlement of Lachish began in caves to the north-west of the tel in the Chalcolithic period (around 3500 BCE). During the period of urbanization in Palestine some 1,500 years later the settlers moved up to the top of the tel and the former cave dwellings were used for burials.

Patriarchal and Canaanite Age: Lachish was first fortified during the age of the Patriarchs. The approach to its walled summit was protected by a steep white plastered glacis, with a wide fosse (ditch) at the foot. Such a defence system suggests the presence of the Hyksos, who controlled Egypt and Palestine from the 18th to the middle of the 16th century BCE, when they were expelled and replaced by the Egyptians. The Egyptians discarded the old defences. The fosse was filled in, and in its place a small temple was built. Between 1480 and 1260 BCE, the temple was twice rebuilt and enlarged. The richness of its contents and its position outside the city wall bear witness to the prosperity and security of the period.

The Canaanite Temple: Dr. K. Kenyon described the 15th c. BCE Canaanite temple of Lachish (**155**) and its sacrificial altar: "The temple was simple in plan, consisting of an oblong sanctuary with two attached rooms, only one of which was entered from the sanctuary. It is notable that there was no inner room or Holy of Holies, such as was required by the Hebrew religion and has been found in much earlier Semitic sanctuaries. The roof had been supported on columns, probably of wood, of which the bases were found in position on the central axis. The entrance was screened by a wall which prevented a view into the sanctuary from the outside. The shrine consisted of a low bench, one foot high, from the front of which three rectangular blocks

155

projected. It is suggested that the cult objects stood on the bench and that the projecting blocks served as altars. The existence of three projections suggest that a trinity of deities was worshipped. On the central axis in front of the shrine were two jars sunk in the floor, which may have been receptacles into which libations were poured, while against one end of the bench was found a great pile of vessels, abandoned when the temple was rebuilt, which presumably served as containers of liquid and solid offerings. Outside the temple was found a number of pits used for the disposal of vessels which had served a similar purpose. There was also a long bench along one wall, which, on the analogy of the more numerous benches found in the later structure, may also have served for the deposit of offerings." The remains suggest that the deities worshipped in this temple and its successors were Resheph, the Canaanite-Syrian god of war and storm, and possibly the goddess Elath.

The first mention of Lachish in documents comes during this (Late Bronze) period. In the 14th century BCE El Amarna* letters, there is a statement by the King of Jerusalem that the people of Lachish made common cause with the Habiru* and killed their king. This has been confirmed by a tablet found in nearby Tel-el-Hesi.

Lachish Conquered by the Israelites?: The third and last temple appears to have been violently destroyed. Because of an Egyptian hieratic (cursive) inscription found on a bowl, dated by the excavators to around 1200 BCE and referring to the 4th year of the Pharaoh's reign, some scholars think the temple may have been destroyed during a raid by the Egyptian Pharaoh Mernephtach, whose fourth year was 1220 BCE. Mernephtach's great "victory" stele recording his victory over "Israel" (see Conquest*) dates from the 5th year of his reign, which could be a year after the capture of Lachish.

Other scholars credit Joshua with the destruction of Lachish, accepting as accurate the detailed description of its conquest given in the book of Joshua (10:1–5, 31–33). Having defeated a Canaanite coalition army, Joshua hanged its leaders and assigned the town to the tribe of Judah.

Lachish in the Kingdom of Judah: After being deserted for a time, Lachish took its place as one of the foremost fortified cities of the separate Kingdom of Judah. Level V, the first

156

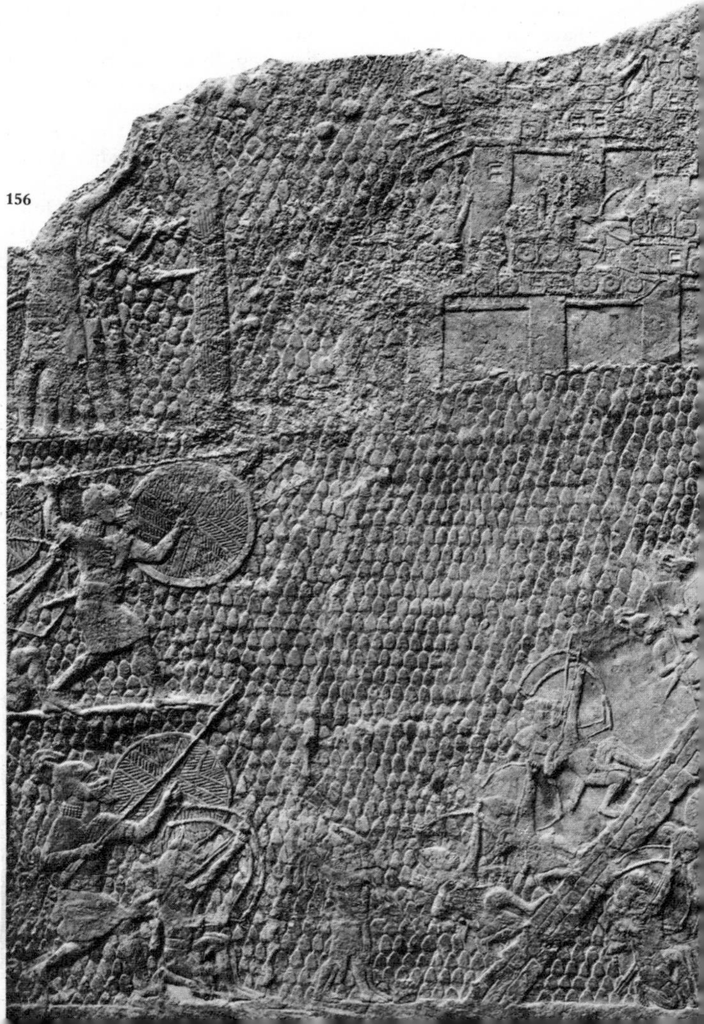

157

Israelite city, had been surrounded by a brick wall which enclosed a large palace built on a platform 32 metres square, made of stones packed with earth. This may be an example of a millo (filling) like the one which David constructed in Jerusalem. Lachish was probably fortified along with other Judean cities by Rehoboam, the first Judean king (II Ch. 11:9) around the time of Pharaoh Shishak's Palestinian campaign in 925 BCE. Lachish was spared on that occasion and her importance may have increased as a result of the destruction of two of her neighbours, Debir (Tel Beit Mirsim) and Beth-Shemesh, at that time.

During the 9th century BCE, a second brick wall on a stone foundation was added, and the palace was rebuilt. This expansion was probably part of the building programs of the kings, Asa and Jehoshaphat, recorded in the Bible (II Ch. 14:6–7; 17:12). The double-walled city stood until Sennacherib's Palestine campaign nearly two centuries later.

Sennacherib at Lachish: The Assyrian siege and capture of the town, and its sequel, is one of the most vividly documented of all ancient engagements. The whole story was pictured in detail on a large wall relief (**156–7**) in Sennacherib's palace

158

in Nineveh. It also serves as a good illustration of the city's importance at the time as a Judean military base. Sennacherib had set out (in 701 BCE) to crush an anti-Assyrian coalition formed among Syria, Palestine and Egypt, led by the Judean king, Hezekiah. The Egyptians were defeated at Elteke. Sennacherib then took Ashkelon and Joppa and laid siege to Lachish (II K. 18:14).

The relief shows Assyrian soldiers in formation: spearmen carrying round shields and wearing helmets with bronze crests (one was found at Lachish); pairs of bowmen and slingers with stones in their hands. Lachish was defended by a double wall constructed on the principle of salients and recesses (pictured in the relief and confirmed by excavation). After a "bombardment" by slings and arrows Assyrian sappers attacked the walls under cover of "siege-engines" **(157)** pushed up the slope on wooden legs. From behind towers and shields, the defenders hurled stones and brands on to the siege-engines, which were kept soaked with water as a defensive measure. After the battle, the city's surrender is shown **(158)**, with the townspeople, wearing long robes, leaving the city carrying their possessions. Nearby hang three impaled bodies **(157)**.

Away from the battle, Sennacherib is pictured seated on his throne **(159)** in front of his tent and chariot. He welcomes his victorious soldiers while captive Judeans prostrate themselves before him. The inscription above his head reads: "Sennacherib, King of the World, King of Assyria, sat upon a throne and passed in review the booty (taken) from Lachish." The area's hilly nature is indicated by the continuous scale pattern; fruit trees and vines are also shown. While Sennacherib was encamped at Lachish, he received the tribute from Hezekiah (II K. 18:14–16) which saved Jerusalem and with it all Judah from total destruction.

Apart from the burnt debris found in the corresponding level (III), other evidence of the conquest of Lachish included a large pit which contained a jumbled mass of more than 1,500 bodies. Starkey interpreted this as the debris raked up in the city after the war. Three trepanned skulls found among them are interesting evidence for early medical practice. An unfinished well, 144 feet deep, which had probably been intended as a water supply for the besieged city but had had to be abandoned was also found.

Judean Lachish under Nebuchadrezzar: During the following (7th) century, a new stone wall and a gate were built, with guardrooms in the gatehouse between the walls. In one of these rooms, the Lachish letters were found.

The beginning of the 6th cent. BCE, Judah's darkest hour, saw Lachish attacked twice: first (in 598–597 BCE) by Nebuchadrezzar, who invaded Judea in response to an attempted rebellion against Babylonian domination by Jehoiakim and in reprisal exiled the cream of Judean

159

citizenry to Babylon. The second attack is attributed to the final Babylonian conquest of 586 BCE, when Lachish was apparently the last city to fall before Jerusalem. This is reported by the Bible (Jer. 34:7) and confirmed by the Lachish letters (see Israel and Judah*, Part V; Inscriptions*: Ostraca; Jeremiah*).

The Lachish Letters (Ostraca): The Lachish letters, the outstanding discovery of the last Israelite level (II), consist of 21 inscribed potsherds, mostly letters, but including various lists and business records. Now in the British Museum, only about a third of them could be deciphered. They were published by H. Torczyner (Tur-Sinai). W. F. Albright has commented on their significance: "Since they form the only known corpus of documents in classical Hebrew prose, they have unusual philological significance, quite aside from the light they shed on the time of Jeremiah." They all appear to have been addressed to Yoash, the commander of the fortress at Lachish, by Hoshaiah, commander of an unidentified outpost not far from the town. He is mentioned by name once only, but a certain continuity in theme suggests that he sent all the letters.

The letters can be dated to the last days of Zedekiah just before the final conquest, by Letter IV (Inscrip.*) in which Hoshaiah writes: "And let (my lord) know that we are watching for the signals of Lachish, according to the indications which my lord hath given, for we cannot see Azekah." Apparently Azekah had already fallen and Lachish and Jerusalem faced the enemy alone. This is the position described by Jeremiah (34:7) when Nebuchadrezzar fought against "all the cities of Judah that were left, Lachish and Azekah; for these were the only fortified cities of Judah that remained." With its destruction by the Babylonians, the main period of occupation of Lachish came to an end.

A Supplement to Jeremiah: Other sections of the letters have also been interpreted against the background of the Book of Jeremiah and seem to supplement its information. The letters indicate a conflict between the king and an unnamed prophet. Jeremiah is accused of "weakening the hands of the people", presumably by preaching against the Egyptian anti-Babylon alliance, then official policy in Jerusalem. The book of Jeremiah records that because of this attitude, he and the prophet Tuviah were officially persecuted. A Lachish letter deals with the same situation in relation to "a prophet" who is not named. It has been suggested that this may have been the same Tuviah. Alternatively, three different parallel cases (Jeremiah, Tuviah and the prophet of the Lachish letters) may reflect a whole party jointly opposing official policy and being punished for it.

Persian Period: The last level of Lachish belongs to the period of resettlement of Judah after the Persian conquest, during the time of Nehemiah (11:30), about the middle of the 5th century BCE. An administrative centre was built on the acropolis, with a large building serving apparently as the governor's residence. A small temple, dedicated to the sun and facing east was also found. This remained in use until the site was finally abandoned in the 2nd c. BCE. Settlers during the Roman period made their homes at Duweir, south of the tel.

MEGIDDO. — *Outline: Excavation; History; Megiddo's Temples; Egyptian Execration Texts; Megiddo's Golden Age; The Amarna Period; Canaanite Art Treasures; Megiddo's Water Supply; Israel at Megiddo; Megiddo in the Israelite Kingdom; In Assyrian Times.*

Megiddo guarded the pass of Wadi Arah, which formed a great defensive barrier across the ancient route connecting Egypt and Mesopotamia — Africa and Asia. It had an age-long importance as a strategic, military, commercial and cultural centre between the countries of the Mediterranean and the lands that lay north and east.

Excavation: The site, 13 acres in area, was dug before the first world war by a German expedition led by Schumacher and afterwards by the Oriental Institute of the University of Chicago (1925–39). At first, the American expedition worked on the Iron Age levels over the whole surface of the tel. Later, efforts were concentrated on three limited areas: "AA", in the northern quarter, where the town gates had been, together with the palace of the Canaanite kings nearby; "BB", the "temenos" or sacred area, the only portion to be cleared right down to bedrock; and "CC" on the south side which was abandoned after a time (**160**). The three areas are shown in the model reconstruction (**161**). The top layers are Israelite; the lower, right, are Canaanite.

History: Twenty layers of continuous occupation were discovered, the earliest being a settlement of the Neolithic period (which ended around 4000 BCE). This was continued in a Chalcolithic village (end of the 4th millenium BCE) which contained an interesting temple, 4 metres by 12, with an altar facing east (and the plain of Jezreel) and a doorway opposite it in one of the long sides.

The next three layers (Strata XVIII to XVI) revealed early Bronze Age towns, dated by the excavators between 2500 and 1950 BCE, in pre-Patriarchal times. A large altar for burnt offerings which had formed part of a "bamah" or high place (see Canaan*, High Places*), was discovered in Stratum XVII. The inhabitants of the succeeding city (Stratum XVI) continued to make use of the bamah, altering it, however, in certain respects.

Megiddo's Temples: Megiddo XV belongs to the beginning of the Middle Bronze Age (around the 19th century BCE). The round altar of the "high place" was preserved, probably out of respect for the ancestral cult. It continued to be used on certain occasions. However, these cities contained three new temples. Two temples were erected first, side by side. Then a third was erected, at a slight angle to the other two and over the ruined wall of one of them. This is the best preserved. It consists of two rooms, an altar room and a porch, one behind the other, lying north and south. The altar is a rough square, about 2.50 metres on each side. It is made of uncut stone reminiscent of the biblical prescription in Ex. 20:25, although unlike Israelite altars, four steps lead up to the top of it. The remains of the temples are shown (**162**) with the round "bamah" at the left. See also diagram (**163**).

Next to this altar and in the same room, stood a much smaller altar, showing that more than one deity was worshipped in this temple, or that the smaller altar was consecrated to the consort of the principal deity. In front of the altars were the bases of two columns, both well

161

162

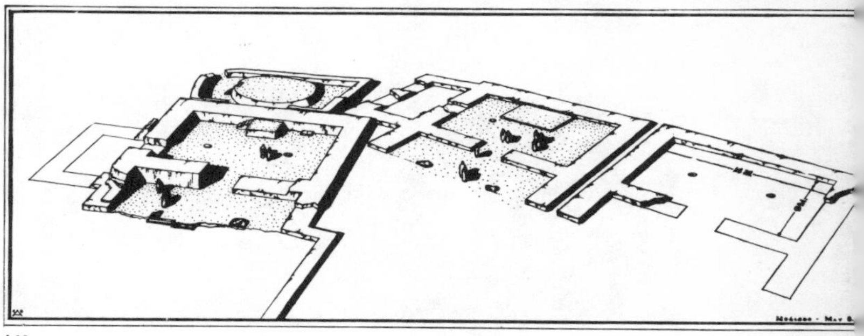

163

carved, which suggest that there was a second storey to the temple. The porch, which was probably uncovered, was reached by a central door. At the outer edge were the bases of two more columns. Probably these had no architectural function but, like Jachin and Boaz in Solomon's temple, served as symbols of the god and his power. East of the altar room was a side room and there may have been other rooms in the second storey.

The very thick walls of the temple suggest that, like the Temple of Jerusalem, this one could also serve as a fortress in times of emergency.

Egyptian Execration Texts: There are traces of Egyptian occupation in this and other levels at Megiddo. The best evidence for Egyptian involvement in Canaan is provided by the so-called execration texts of Sesostris III (1887–1850 BCE) and other Egyptian kings. These are hieratic (cursive) inscriptions naming the leaders of different cities or certain groups of people, found on clay pots or statuettes **(403)** which had been deliberately broken as part of a magic ritual intended to bring about the destruction of the enemies named. For a period when other sources for the history of the land of Canaan are very scarce, these texts have significant value.

The most revealing feature of the later level XIII city (Middle Bronze) was found in the area around the town gateway, where a part of the town wall, the gateway and steps leading up to it were uncovered.

Megiddo's Golden Age: The cities which follow, XII to X, belong to the latter part of the Middle Bronze Age (18th–15th centuries BCE, corresponding to the Patriarchal* period) when the Hyksos ruled Egypt and Canaan. They represent a Golden Age for Megiddo, not again equalled until the time of Solomon.

There was considerable dislocation of life in Palestine in the period immediately following the Hyksos domination (1720–1570 BCE). Conditions continued disturbed until more intensive Egyptian control was established under Thutmosis III (see Egypt*). In the "Annals" which he had inscribed on the walls of the temple of Ammon at Karnak, he describes the decisive battle at Megiddo in 1479 BCE. The Egyptians faced a strong coalition of Canaanite princes under the leadership of the Canaanite king of Kadesh-on-Orontes. Their forces were drawn up in the Jezreel Valley awaiting an Egyptian onslaught from the south. Instead, Pharaoh took a direct route through a valley near Megiddo which he calls the valley of the Kenites* — an interesting reference to this group very far north of their traditional homeland. (There may be an echo of this group in the story of Deborah, where the commander of the Canaanite forces, Sisera, was killed by Jael, wife of Heber "the Kenite"; see Judges*; Kenites*).

164

The Canaanites, on this earlier occasion, abandoned their chariots and fled before the Egyptian army into the walled city of Megiddo. Victory might have been immediate had not the Egyptian soldiers stopped to plunder. Instead of a lightning campaign, the king had to organize a siege which lasted for months. In the end, the town fell and was destroyed. In the Karnak inscription the Pharaoh gloatingly includes a long list of booty of different kinds, a good indication of the commercial and military importance of the city at that time. It is hardly surprising to read that "his Majesty appointed princes anew . . . now the fields were made into plots and assigned to inspectors of the palace . . . in order to reap their harvest". The valley of Jezreel very likely remained a royal domain during much of early biblical history as a result of these administrative measures of Thutmosis (Thothmes) III.

Having destroyed the resistance of the Canaanite coalition, Thutmosis went on to the Euphrates, thus fixing the borders of the Egyptian empire in western Asia.

Megiddo itself was rebuilt (Stratum VIII) on much the same lines as the earlier city IX, and became a key-point of Egyptian rule, although it was not garrisoned by the Egyptians as was nearby Beth-Shean*. Its well-made gateway **(164)** is still visible while, in the old temple-district, a new temple was erected, very simple in plan but with extremely thick, strong walls. This temple is of special interest for its evidence about the religion of the Canaanites*. It consisted of one main hall, with a shallow niche in the back wall that presumably housed the cult-object. There is nothing resembling a "Holy of Holies" and worshippers were apparently admitted directly into the presence of the deity. Two small rooms on either side of the entrance may have served as priests' rooms or storerooms. This temple was similar to one built in Shechem* at the same time. Among the pottery found in this layer there is much imported ware from the Aegean* area, indicating that during this period Mycenaean culture made a great impact on Canaan.

The Amarna Period: Among the Tel el Amarna* letters (which date to the first half of the 14th c. BCE) are some written by Biridiya, king of Megiddo. These provide a vivid picture of life in the Canaanite city at a time when it was threatened on all sides, and near-anarchy prevailed in the whole land (see Amarna letters*). These circumstances help to explain the hoard of treasure **(166,7)** found under the floor of the royal palace in Stratum VIII.

Canaanite Art Treasures: The hoard of gold, precious stones, ivory and cosmetic jars of a familiar Egyptian type also included personal ornaments (beads, gold headbands)

165

suggesting that it was all the property of one of the ladies of the court. The whole collection is of immense value for the history of the art and culture of Canaan on the eve of the Hebrew conquest.

The next stratum, Megiddo VII, disclosed the base of a statue of Ramses VI (about 1148–1142 BCE) which is the latest dating for this stratum. The treasure house of the royal palace of this city was found to contain a large number of ivory objects, discarded by the invaders who overwhelmed Megiddo in the mid-12th c. BCE. Outstanding among these is an ivory plaque, the "Celebration of Victory" **(165)**. This shows a Canaanite king twice, once sitting on his throne at a feast; once leading prisoners who are naked but for their headresses, which are similar to the ones used in Egyptian representations of the Beduins called Shosu. In an Egyptian letter (Papyrus Anastasi I, of the time of Ramses II) there is a reference to the Wadi Ara near Megiddo which is "dangerous because of Beduins (Shosu) hidden under the bushes." The plaque may celebrate a successful raid against them.

166

167

168

Megiddo's Water Supply: Stratum VII also contained a water system **(168)** consisting of a 30 metre shaft, connected to a tunnel about 60 metres long which led to a spring. This considerable feat of engineering was designed to provide an emergency supply of water — there are richer springs nearer the town — and was constructed on a plan used in Mycenaean towns (see Water Supply*).

Israel at Megiddo: The late Bronze Age Megiddo VII was totally destroyed, a 2–6 foot thick layer of ashes separating it from the next town which made no use of earlier foundations. This destruction may have been the work of the Philistines. There is nothing in the biblical record to suggest that it was the work of the Israelites. For some time Megiddo lay a deserted heap of ruins, a name, hardly remembered. It was apparently no longer a fortified Canaanite town in the days of Deborah (see Judges* 5:19, Song of Deborah).

Eventually another, modest town was built on the site (Stratum VI), its inhabitants following a way of life much like that of their predecessors. Megiddo remained outside the Israelite commonwealth during the period of the tribal league, possibly because it was under Philistine control during much of the time. Typically Philistine pottery was found in this level, although there is no way to be sure whether this reflects Philistine occupation or merely trade with them. Biblical and archaeological evidence indicates the presence of Philistine garrisons in Beth-Shean and Afulah (Ophel) at the time.

This occupation level at Megiddo seems to have lasted until it too was destroyed in about 1000 BCE and the area left unoccupied once more. There is no evidence that this was due to Israelite activity, although the Israelites may have taken over control of the territory during the period of its abandonment.

Megiddo in the Israelite Kingdom: Although it is nowhere recorded in the Bible, the incorporation of Megiddo into the Israelite kingdom must have taken place during the period of David's expansion northwards. Israelite influence however, does not seem to have made itself strongly felt in the town (Megiddo V, 10th c. BCE). The inhabitants continued their same way of life and a number of Canaanite cult objects were recovered (see Canaan: Gods and Idols*, Cult).

Afterwards, Megiddo became one of the "Store cities that Solomon had, and cities of his chariots and cities for his horsemen" (I K. 9:19). Under Solomon's administrative reform, Megiddo was made the capital of the important 5th district. When stables **(170)**, see also reconstruction **(172)** and mangers **(171)**, for 450 horses were found at this level, they were naturally identified with the biblical reference to Solomon. Later research has suggested that they may, in fact, belong to the time of Ahab (see Israel and Judah*). His interest in chariotry is confirmed by the Bible (e.g. I K. 18:5) and the Assyrian account of the battle of Qarqar (853 BCE) credits him with 2000 chariots, the largest single grouping at the disposal of the anti-Assyrian alliance. The city's monumental gate **(160, 164)** similar to those at Gezer* and Hazor* confirm the Bible statement that Solomon and his successors employed Phoenician builders.

In spite of its casemate walls, formidable six-roomed city gate and northern fort, Solomon's (10th c. BCE) city was destroyed, at least in part, by Pharaoh Shoshenk I (950–929 BCE) as part of his unsuccessful drive to re-establish Egyptian suzereinty in western Asia. A fragment of a stela bearing his name, found at Megiddo **(169)**, bears out his claim in the Karnak list, to have conquered Megiddo (see Egypt*).

The outstanding feature of the city that rose after this (Stratum IV) is a solid city wall of the "offset and inset" type, partly built on top of the remains of the casemate wall (see Cities, Israelite*: Fortifications). The acropolis of Megiddo, at left and in the background of the site, **(164)** like Ahab's Samaria* and, perhaps Jerusalem* and Lachish*, was occupied by a complex of government buildings which dominated the town. The earlier German expedition found the famous seal of Shema, servant of King Jeroboam I, with the lion, which belongs to this period (see Seals*).

During the revolt of Jehu against Ahab, Ahaziah, king of Judah, was killed in Megiddo. The destruction of this

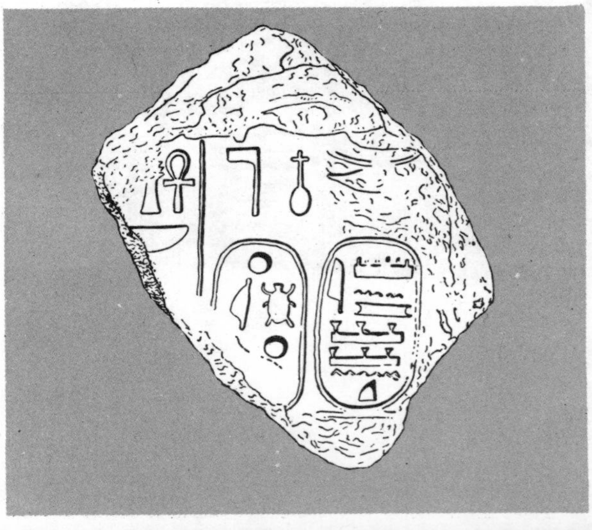

169

170

city (Megiddo IV A) was probably the work of King Hazael of Damascus.

Megiddo III was a modest city, built after King Jehoash of Israel recovered the cities lost by his father. It remained an important centre, a large brick-lined grain silo (see Agric.*) indicates that the peasants of the Jezreel Valley were expected to pay regular taxes to the city governor.

In Assyrian Times: The conquests of Tiglat-Pileser III included Megiddo (734 BCE). A new city (Stratum II) became the capital of the Assyrian administrative region of Megiddo, from which they ruled Galilee. While the Assyrians were attacked by the Medes and Babylonians prior to their collapse in 612 BCE, Josiah, king of Judah, seized what seemed to be an opportunity to recover the northern area. Whether or not he actually fortified Megiddo, he chose it as the spot at which to oppose the Egyptian army which Pharaoh Neco took through Palestine on his way to help the Assyrians recoup their losses. Josiah fell in the battle (609 BCE; see Israel and Judah*, V). Again the site lay deserted until some time after 450 BCE (the Persian period). In the days of Ezra and Nehemiah, a modest village grew up there.

Following Alexander the Great's conquests, Palestine became part of his empire and new settlers from Syria and Macedonia came to Megiddo. As elsewhere, the top of the mound of the old city was too small for extensive development and a new city was founded a few miles away, at the site of the present Arab village Lajjun (so-called from the Roman Legion who built their walled camp there). The history of Megiddo had come to an end. But its name remained a powerful symbol. In Christian eschatology*, the hill of Megiddo (Har-Megiddo in Hebrew) seemed a fitting place for the last battle on earth. The kings of the earth "will be gathered to the battle of that great day . . . into a place called in the Hebrew tongue Armageddon." (Revelation 16:14, 16).

171

172

SAMARIA. — According to biblical tradition, the city of Samaria was founded by King Omri (1 K. 16:24). It was the capital city of the Northern Kingdom of Israel from 880 to 721 BCE. The name applied also to the province of central Palestine from Persian times. The Bible explains the original name of the city by derivation from Shemer, the former owner of the hill. Traces of sporadic occupation during the proto-Urban period have been discovered in the hill. There were also remains of Canaanite occupation so it appears that, as in many other cases, the Israelite city of Samaria was actually built on top of the earlier Canaanite stronghold.

In contrast to the continued efforts to establish legitimate ownership of the Cave of Machpelah in another early story, or the unsuccessful attempt by Ahab the son of Omri to achieve legal possession of the vineyard of Naboth, the story of the purchase from Shemer served to legitimatize possession of the site of Samaria as the personal property and royal residence of the king.

Lying beside a main north-south route through Palestine, Samaria was well placed to foster commerce and peaceful cultural exchanges among the ten tribes of the Northern Kingdom. Eleven kilometres north-west of the modern town of Nablus (Shechem*), geographically in the centre of Palestine, the hill of Samaria dominates the countryside around it although it was more open to attack in war time than Jerusalem. It was first conquered by Israel's northern enemies the Arameans*, and later by the Assyrians.

History: Very little is known about the rule of Omri in the city. The few brief phrases with which the Bible dismisses his reign are quite out of proportion to his actual achievements. His son, Ahab, receives a much more detailed treatment. The prophet Elijah's denunciations of the spread of Canaanite culture and religion under the influence of his Phoenician wife reflect a vivid picture of the urban leisure in Samaria and its court.

Omri's dynasty was ended by the revolution of Jehu. Samaria remained the focal centre of northern Israel under a succession of kings, one of the most famous being Jeroboam II. His death in 748 BCE brought to an end a period of prosperity for Samaria and the Northern Kingdom (see Israel and Judah*, IV). Israel was then threatened by Assyrian expansion. When Tiglat-Pileser attacked Israel and Judah, Israel was defeated, losing the districts of Megiddo, Dor and Gilead. Her king, Hoshea, ruled Samaria as a vassal of Assyria until the death of Tiglat-Pileser aroused hopes of independence. With Egyptian support, Hoshea stopped payment of tribute. This brought swift retribution from the new Assyrian ruler, Shalmaneser V. Hoshea was taken prisoner and the whole of Israel, with the sole exception of Samaria, fell into Assyrian hands. The city was able to hold out for two years against the besieging forces of Shalmaneser, ample testimony to the strength of its defences and the determination of its citizens. Finally, in 721 BCE, it fell, bringing the kingdom of Israel to an end (II K. 17). The Assyrians followed their usual policy in conquered Israel. The local inhabitants were deported and their place taken by foreigners. The new, mixed population of Samaria were ancestors of the Samaritan* sect of Judaism. Their way of life represented a combination of older Israelite patterns and the customs of the newcomers, producing a highly syncretistic form of Yahwism.

Samaria was rebuilt as the administrative centre of a province called Samerina. Under Persian rule (6th to 4th centuries BCE) it remained a provincial capital. In fact Samaria took control of the whole area. It had long since eclipsed ancient Shechem as a political and religious centre of central and northern Israel. Shechem, destroyed in the 8th century BCE, then resettled, was used by the Israelite kings for the collection of taxes in kind.

When the Jews returned from Babylon, the Samaritans whose centre was in Shechem offered their help to the builders of Jerusalem. Its rejection and subsequent clashes gave rise to a deep and lasting antagonism between the Samaritans and the people of Judea, the "Jews" (see Samaritans*).

During the lifetime of Nehemiah* (beginning of the second half of the 5th century BCE), the governor of the province of Samaria was a man named Sanballat. On Nehemiah's evidence (2:19; 4:7), he was the most prominent individual west of the Jordan, and one who harassed Judea (see Restoration*). New Aramaic papyri have been found which come from Samaria and belong to the 4th century BCE. They mention Sanballat's name and family. During the latter part of the 4th century BCE, the Samaritans rebuilt Samaria as their metropolis (see below: Persian Period).

Samaria was captured by Alexander the Great in 332 BCE. Many of the Samaritans, it is said, were deported to Shechem while Samaria was resettled by Syrian and Macedonian mercenaries. The two cities continued to flourish, Shechem, which had made a vigorous recovery, as the Samaritan centre, and Samaria as a pagan, Hellenistic colony.

173

174

Samaria was captured and destroyed by the Hasmonean* John Hyrcanus, in 107 BCE, twenty years after he had destroyed Shechem. The Hasmoneans* forcibly imposed Judaism on the Samaritans so that aside from one or two older traditions, they have practically nothing in common with the Samaritans of earlier times. They were essentially Jews in belief, but not belonging to the major groups (see Samaritans*). In the Roman period, the town was rebuilt by Gabinius, Pompey's successor, but its greatest glory came with the reign of Herod the Great*. Between 30 and 20 BCE, he built a new wall around the city and constructed a temple in honour of Augustus, a forum **(178)**, a basilica and an aqueduct. Herod renamed the town in honour of his patron, Caesar Augustus, Sebastia (Greek for "Augustus") and this has remained the name of the Arab village, Sebastiyeh, which stands on the site to this day.

In New Testament times, Samaria and the Samaritans played an important role. In contrast to official Jewish religious attitudes, the early Christians were willing to accept the Samaritans as equals, while they offered the Christians their first field of missionary activity.

The Evidence of Archaeology: Samaria was continuously occupied for fifteen centuries from the 9th century BCE to the Byzantine period. From its long history, rich discoveries have been made of architectural, artistic and scriptural significance.

It was excavated, first in 1908–1910 CE, then again between 1931 and 1935 by Harvard University, the Palestine Exploration Fund and the Hebrew University. These excavations recovered evidence of the whole history of occupation.

The site covered 25 acres, which included a large acropolis surrounded by a casemate wall (see Cities, Israelite*: Fortifications). Within it was a royal palace built in the Assyrian manner. Three major stages in Samaria's history are illustrated by the following pictures:

a. **The Omri-Ahab Period** (880–850 BCE) The simple walls **(173)** that surrounded Omri's city could be traced on the summit of the hill and a walled basin from the period recalls the "pool" in which Ahab's chariot was washed after his death. Ahab built much more extensively than his predecessors. Nearly all the walls of his palace **(174)** are casemate walls. Later kings built their palaces within the precincts of the earlier ones. Pilaster capitals of the Israelite entrance wall (restored) of a Proto-Ionic type **(175)**, are evidence of their sophistication.

Two of the most important finds of all the excavations were made in this area. The first were the ivories of

175

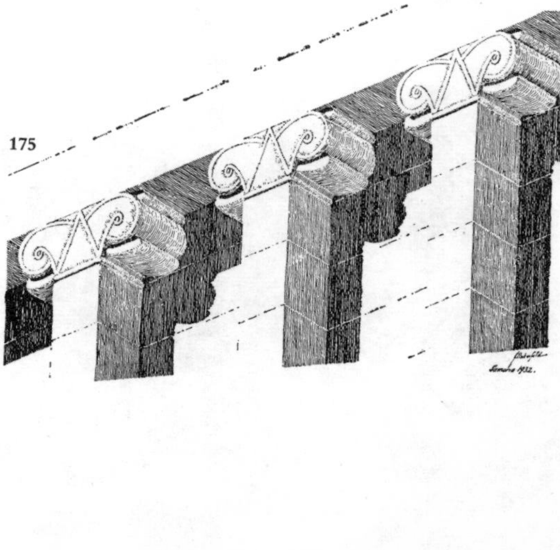

176

177

178

Samaria (**176**). They may be assigned to the end of the 8th c. BCE, though the dating is uncertain. The pieces of ivory inlay found in Samaria show that there was a house whose walls and furnishings were lavishly decorated with ivory carvings. They brilliantly illuminate the reference to the "house of ivory" which Ahab is said to have built (I K. 22:39).

These ivories are of great significance for a history of art in ancient Israel. They show a strong connection with the art of Phoenicia and, through this, Egyptian culture, evoking the world of leisure and culture of that period, at least as it appeared in the palaces of kings.

b. **Samaria at Its Zenith** (810–745 BCE). The other outstanding discoveries were the Ostraca of Samaria (see Inscriptions*) whose dating is also disputed. They appear to date from the time of Menachem, king of Israel (747–737 BCE), but an alternative opinion puts them in the time of Jeroboam II (789–748 BCE). They are a collection of broken sherds, bearing short inscriptions which are capable of various interpretations. Y. Yadin sees in them the accounts of royal officials who accepted deliveries of oil and wine for the royal store rooms. On this understanding, ostracon 18 (Insc.*), for instance, would read: "In the tenth year. From Hazeroth. Belonging to Gaddiyahu. A jar of fine oil."

c. **Persian Period** (6th–4th c. BCE). New evidence relating to life in Samaria during the last days of Persian rule was brought to light in 1963 when P. W. Lapp discovered a hoard of papyri in the caves of Wadi Daliyeh in the Jordan valley, east of Samaria. Dating to between ca 375–335 BCE, the papyri were deciphered by F. M. Cross and were found to be the records of transactions concerning real estate, loans, broken contracts including divorce (see Family*), and the sale, transfer and manumission of slaves*. At the time, Samaria was governed by successive members of the house of Sanballat, the last of the line being Sanballat III, a descendant of Sanballat I (ca. 445 BCE) who had been "pḥt šmrn" (governor of Samaria) when Nehemiah came to Jerusalem (see above).

d. The Graeco-Roman City. Magnificent fortifications were discovered from the Hellenistic period, outstanding among them being a round tower, well built and preserved.

The Roman city, richly endowed by Herod, has left impressive remains of colonnaded streets **(178)**, shops, theatre **(177)** and temples. Of Herod's temple, dedicated to Augustus, nothing remains but the monumental flight of steps **(179)**. In early Christian times, churches were erected in honour of John the Baptist*, who was reputed to have been buried in Samaria.

During the Byzantine era (6th century CE), Samaria lost its former importance and in the Arab period, the once great city shrank to the dimensions of a minor village in the midst of the ruins of the ancient cities.

179

SHECHEM. — An important Canaanite and Israelite city at the eastern end of the pass between Mt. Gerizim and Mt. Ebal in central Palestine, Shechem controlled the major route through Jerusalem between Egypt and Phoenicia and Syria. It was the centre of the tribal federation and in the early days of the monarchy ranked second only to Jerusalem.

Early History: Shechem's earliest inhabitants were semi-nomads who gathered around the spring of Tel Balata in the Chalcolithic Age (5th mill. BCE). In the 19th c. BCE Egyptian "Execration Texts" (inscriptions on clay figurines, see Egypt*), Shechem appears as "škmm". Another reference of about the same period appears on a stele of the time of Sesostris III (1848–1843 BCE), whose general had to make war against the people of Shechem. The city is listed as an enemy of Egypt and apparently it formed a centre of opposition to Egyptian rule. However, there are no clear traces of any of the buildings of the Shechem of these early days (20th–18th cs. BCE). The first real building activity which has been discovered at Shechem so far dates from the Middle Bronze Age II (ca. 1800 BCE). By far the most important and best documented period, however, is that of its successor, the Hyksos city.

Patriarchal Age (Middle and Late Bronze): In the Bible, Shechem appears first during the Patriarchal period and in recent years scholars have made considerable progress in establishing a relationship between biblical traditions and the archaeological evidence amassed over the past fifty years.

According to Gn. 12:1–7, Abraham made his first contact with the Canaanites at Shechem. "The Lord appeared" to him there and he built an altar. From the stories of the later Patriarchs* (Gn. 33:18–34:31; 48:22 ff, passim), it appears that from the 18th to the 14th cs. BCE, Shechem was a centre of Canaanite religious and political life. This period included the years of Hyksos domination over Egypt and central Canaan (1720–1550 BCE) during which Shechem was one of their vital centres, on a level with the other fortified cities built by the Hyksos, such as Jericho* and Hazor*.

Shechem figures in many of the patriarchal traditions, but the picture which emerges from the different references is far from homogeneous. For instance in Gn. 33:18–20 or 37:12–14, the Hebrews enjoy peaceful relations with the inhabitants of Shechem, whereas in Gn. 34 (cf., 48:22; 49:5–7), the Hebrew tribes of Simeon and Levi (see Tribes*) are shown in violent conflict with the people of Shechem. Possibly this was after the Hyksos occupation, although before Simeon became identified with Judah in the south, and before the Levites became a priestly tribe (see Priests and Levites*).

This early and obscure phase of pre-Conquest settlement by the Hebrews in Canaan may be an echo of the activities of the Habiru* marauders who, according to the Amarna* letters, threatened all the central area of Palestine. Lab'ayu, the writer of some of the letters and ruler of a Canaanite kingdom in the hill country of central Palestine, appears to have played a leading role in the intrigues undermining Egyptian control of Canaan in the 14th c. BCE.

The Evidence of Archaeology: Excavation of Tel-Balata, the biblical Shechem, was begun under German auspices between 1913–14 and continued by the Drew-McCormick Archaeological Expedition between 1956–62. Another season is planned for 1964. Four main periods of building have been distinguished: Middle Bronze Age; Late Bronze Age; Israelite Monarchy (Iron Age); Samaritan and Hellenistic period.

Middle Bronze Age: Recent excavations unearthed a great processional way leading from the lower fortified city of the Hyksos to a Middle Bronze Age Temple (marked V on the plan of the excavated area **180**) which stood on a site which dominated the whole city. The temple is the largest Canaanite shrine so far discovered in Palestine. It was built in the later Hyksos period (ca 1650–1550 BCE, or Middle Bronze II C).

The evidence indicates that after the early Hyksos period (Middle Bronze II B phase, or ca. 1720–1650) Shechem was destroyed (around 1650) and that there was then a complete break in architectural traditions before the building

180

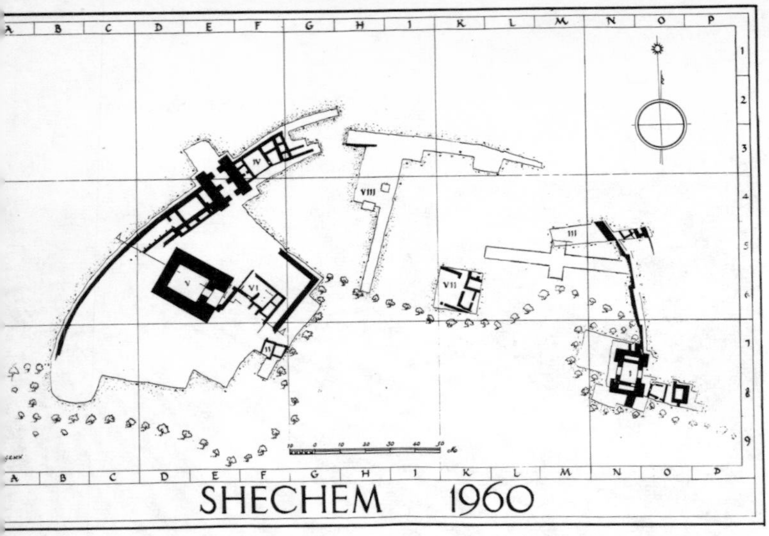

of the Temple and the other major structures, the palace and the East Gate (see below).

The Temple was built as a rectangle 69 ft. × 85 ft. with walls 17 ft. thick. It may have been designed to serve as a fortress as well as a place of worship. The illustration **(181)**, taken from the north, shows (A) the large stones of the first retaining outer wall; (B) the later Hyksos wall and (C) the north-west corner of the Temple. It contained a massive earthen altar of sacrifices flanked by a pair of high "matzebot" or Canaanite sacred pillars, set in stone sockets (see Canaan, Gods and Idols*: Cult). Originally the altar platform must have been visible from any point in the city.

The Palace: To the right of the L-shaped wall (marked VI on the plan **180** and shown in the centre and left background of the illustration **181**) was the palace area. In the Middle Bronze Age this area was separated from the rest of the city by a massive stone wall (the L-shaped wall). Inside this fortified area, a space was left between the outer wall and the wall of the palace to make room for a drain and a cobbled street (nine superimposed layers of cobblestones were found there). The illustration **(182)** shows the archaeologists' trenches and the nine rooms of the palace excavated in 1960. Three bordering on the street were workshops, one provided with two clay ovens, a kneading block and a stone-lined pit for the storage of grain.

Under the floor of the palace, a tomb was found containing the remains of a small child who had been buried in a stone jar **(183)**, wearing a bead necklace and surrounded by funeral offerings in delicate pottery vessels. Many of the objects found here offer additional evidence of the influence of contemporary Egypt (Hyksos) on Canaan.

The East Gate: The most striking feature of the city's defence system in the Middle Bronze II C period was the East Gate (photographed here **184**, looking east). The steps in the foreground lead up to a roadway, with the guard towers of the gate on either side of the entry (see Cities, Israelite*: Fortifications). It bears all the marks of repeated destruction between the Hyksos period (Middle Bronze Age) and the time of Abimelech (see below). This is apparently the gate mentioned in the story of Ga'al (Jud. 9:34–41).

Late Bronze Age: After 1570 BCE, when the Egyptians of the 18th dynasty reconquered Palestine, the importance of Shechem declined. The Late Bronze inhabitants were content to rebuild the city, making use of the structures of their predecessors wherever they could. The temple was rebuilt on the site, the original forecourt being retained, its surface raised two feet. The new building did not have the massive walls of its predecessor and it was placed at a slightly different angle, oriented (like the later Jerusalem Temple) towards the rising sun. This re-orientation may have been connected with Canaanite sun worship and its ritual. The most significant new feature was the erection of a huge "matzebah" in a stone socket directly in front of the entrance to the Temple. In addition to the new pillar, a new stone altar was built on the site of the earlier earthen structure.

The Centre of the Tribal Federation: There is no mention of any conquest of Shechem by the invading Israelites

181

under Joshua (13th c. BCE), but immediately after the Conquest*, Shechem appears as the rallying point for the tribal confederation and as the scene of Joshua's covenant renewal ceremony (Jos. 24). The apparently peaceful transition of Shechem from Canaanite city-state to Israelite tribal centre has been interpreted as indicating that it was already in friendly hands when the Israelites entered central Palestine. Shechem has no place in the lists of Joshua's conquests, nor is there any archaeological evidence of destruction such as was found at Hazor*, Lachish*, Bethel* and other towns to mark the change-over from Canaanite to Israelite control (see Conquest*, Exodus*).

The question of how Shechem became an Israelite city remains. Many scholars assume that the peaceful transition reflected in the Jacob narratives eventually led to early Hebrew infiltration of the city during the Late Bronze Age and that the occupation of Shechem was achieved without recourse to arms. Thus Hebrew elements were established alongside the Canaanites before the final phase of the Conquest. Alternatively, the invading (or infiltrating) Israelites may have linked up with a group of Habiru who had occupied the city since Patriarchal times.

The House of Ba'al berith: The Late Bronze temple (see above) is tentatively identified with the "House of Ba'al b^e^rîth" (temple of the Lord of the Covenant) of Jud. 9:4, which Abimelech destroyed after his conquest of the lower city (Jud. 9; see Judges*). The floors of the Middle Bronze and Late Bronze temple were found to be covered with debris, which may represent Abimelech's destruction of the city and the Canaanite high place. At that time, Shechem was still a mixed Hebrew and Canaanite city, probably acting as a centre of Canaanite influence — which might also be an explanation of Abimelech's abortive attempt to establish himself there as a king. (He was the son of a Hebrew father and a Canaanite mother). The "pillar at Shechem" beside which he was proclaimed king may possibly have been the stone matzebah which dominated the high place.

182

183

184

185

A Levitical City: In later times, Shechem acquired the status of a Levitical city of refuge (Jos. 20:7) and played an important role in Israel's religion and early political organization. It seems likely that it was in fact much more important than the biblical record suggests. However, the later centralization of the cult and the Davidic dynasty in Jerusalem meant a natural tendency in the Judahite traditions of the Old Testament to play down Shechem and its importance in Israel.

Shechem under the Monarchy: On the eve of the schism between the kingdoms of Israel and Judah, Rehoboam met "all Israel" at Shechem to receive the crown (I K. 12:1 ff; see Israel and Judah*). Once the kingdoms had split, late in the 10th c. BCE, Jeroboam, the first king of Israel, made Shechem his capital and fortified the city (I K. 12:25). He moved the capital later to Penuel from where it was moved again, first to Tirzah, then to Samaria*.

Israelite houses uncovered in Shechem (marked VII on the plan **180**) belonged to the 9th and 8th cs. BCE. They measured approximately 30 × 40 ft, with a large central room, surrounded by a narrow corridor on three sides, with small chambers opening off it (see Cities, Israelite*). Near the houses two beautiful seals were found (see description under Seals*). Next to the large houses were the remains of ancient slums, a combination which suggests both prosperity and poverty side by side.

During this period the Israelites began to make use of the site of the ancient Canaanite temple. The stone foundations of an Israelite granary (belonging to Iron Age II) were found above the north-west corner of the ancient temple. These foundations were not built directly over the Temple remains. The site had been covered by an earth refill, with a thick layer of plaster all over it, and the foundations rested on this. The granary contained pits and silos. Shechem was probably the centre of an administrative district and this may have been a government warehouse (see Government and Authority*: Monarchy).

The Israelite city came to a violent end with its destruction by Shalmaneser V in 724 BCE. The floors of the latest Israelite houses are covered with fragments of storage jars which had once stood on the roofs. Recent excavations have shown that Shechem was again attacked and destroyed at a later stage, for a layer of ashes and scorched pottery has been found, with sling stones and an iron arrowhead lying among the ruins. J. A. Callaway considers that this could have been the work of king Josiah of Judah (see Israel and Judah*, IV), who occupied the province of Samaria in 621 BCE for the purpose of extending his control over the west and north of Palestine (the old kingdom of Israel), and imposing his religious reform on the remnant of the Israelites. From Jeremiah 41:4–5, it appears that pious Jews from Shechem were still making pilgrimages to Jerusalem after the fall of the northern kingdom.

Samaritan Occupation: After the late 8th c. BCE, life in Shechem declined very considerably until revived by Samaritan settlers (see article). The fresh data on social institutions in Persian Palestine (6th–4th cs. BCE) provided by the discovery of Samarian papyri, coins and other objects in 1963, is discussed in the article on Samaria*: Persian Period. The most significant fact which has emerged from recent archaeological research in Shechem is that the town was reborn in the 4th c. as a large powerfully defended city. An imposing system of fortifications was constructed along the lines of the ancient Hyksos city walls.

This new settlement followed the massacre of the citizens of Samaria by Alexander the Great's conquering Macedonians (ca 332 BCE, see Samaria*). The survivors were driven out of Samaria and came to Shechem, near to the Samaritan holy mountain, Gerizim, where they reestablished themselves. Their settlement took place in four successive stages, with new buildings erected mainly on top of the ruins of the Israelite town. One Samaritan home can be seen in the right background of the illustration (**185**) which shows the carefully prepared thresholds and door frame. In the 3rd c. BCE (see Hasmoneans*) the Seleucids won control of the country from its Ptolemaic overlords, destroying Shechem in the process. One of the inhabitants who fled before them was a Samaritan, named Simonides to judge by this Greek inscription on a potsherd (**186**), who left behind a cache of Ptolemaic coins* (see article).

Violence continued to mark the latter part of Shechem's history. In 128 BCE, the Hasmonean*, John Hyrcanus again destroyed the city and it lay abandoned until Roman times. The Romans built a settlement called "Neapolis" nearby, which is now the Arab town of Nablus, where a small colony of Samaritans lives to this day (see article on Samaritans*).

186

ANGELS. — *Outline: As a Messenger; Origin of the Belief in Angels; The Heavenly Host; Development of the Concept of Angels; The Angel of Yahweh; Angel of Yahweh in the Heavenly Court; Angels in Prophetic Vision; Angelology in Post-Exilic Writings; Angels in Apocryphal Literature; Angels in the Dead Sea Scrolls; New Testament Period; Angels in Rabbinic Literature; Jesus and the Angels; The Angel of Death.*

The Hebrew term *mal'akh* (angel) is etymologically derived from the verb *lakh* (to "carry a message" or "perform a mission" in Ugaritic, Arabic and Ethiopian).

As a Messenger: Functionally, an angel is an agent of another person as in Gn. 32:6, Judges 9:31, II Kings 6:32, or a messenger of God, as in Haggai 1:13, Isaiah 63:9; 45:12; Malachi 3:1. As a superhuman messenger of God, he may be called the "Angel of God" (see below). In the Old Testament, the word "angel" is both generic and functional, and is applied to the bearer of a message without distinguishing between human or superhuman beings. The former, however, determines the angel as a simple messenger while the latter may imply a wider function. While angels invariably appear in the Bible in human form and are frequently confused with men, the emphasis is always on their function and not on their being. In time, "angel" took on the exclusive meaning of a superhuman being serving God. The Septuagint frequently uses *aggelos* = *angelos* (a messenger), rendered *angelus* in Latin, the root of "angel" in English and other Western languages.

Origin of the Belief in Angels: Most modern scholars agree that the origin of the generic term "angel" is the pantheon or council of gods of pagan semitic mythology, such as the gods or divine beings who served as angels (messengers) in the Ugaritic texts. Scholars disagree, however, in attempts to relate the belief in angels to specific stages in the development of Israel's religion, although it is certain that its origin is pre-biblical. The study of Ugaritic literature has aided the evaluation of the origin of this tradition. In Canaanite mythology, El inhabited a remote and inaccessible region which he left only at some dramatic moment, such as the death of Ba'al. Generally the superior divinity, be it El or Yam, god of the sea, did not move about. When a divinity wished to communicate with another one, he delegated *ml'km* (Canaanite equivalent of the Hebrew *mal'akhim*). The Patriarchs* may have found the idea of the messenger of the supreme god among the Canaanites who worshipped El Elyon, like Melchizedeck, King of Salem. Although some elements of the Canaanite religion of El, the supreme god, found their way into the biblical tradition, it selected only what was of higher value to attribute to Abraham's personal god (see Patriarchs*). It is quite likely that this selectivity was based on a distinction between God and His Angel and on a desire to protect the transcendence of God, as the Bible saw Him (see below).

The basic common element in all the data is the angel's role of messenger, divine and human in ancient society, Israelite and pagan. Such were the *angulu*, *sukallu* or *kal* of the Assyro-Babylonians, which according to A. Deimel, were the terms used for the servants of god. The Assyro-Babylonians also believed in good and bad demons, *shedu* and *lamassu*. In the poems of Ugarit, the god of the sea sent messages to El, the head of the Canaanite pantheon and the gods surrounding him. The goddess Asherah is also given servants, Kadeh and Amrar, who accompany her on her journeys.

The members of the heavenly court who were not gods or semi-gods could also be designated generically and functionally as "servants" (as in the court of a king) who shone in their master's glory. This notion of servants of god might have expanded if it had existed in a milieu not already haunted by a variety of gods and semi-gods. In paganism, with its multiplicity of gods, this was impossible. Instead, the notion of angel-servants fluctuated sharply between the divinity and its servants. Pagan origin did not impede the gradual development of the biblical concept of God's angels performing missions in a genuine human relationship that eventually replaced belief in God's direct revelation to man. This concept was both awesome and filled with the danger of anthropomorphic representation. While not identical, Yahweh and His angel became so closely related functionally, that the word of one was the word of the other. If not a visible manifestation of the deity, the Angel at least came to represent the embodiment of His word and authority. Although biblical tradition emphasizes the belief in the supernatural contact between God and his faithful servants, and in a personal God who talks directly to man and guides his actions, Canaanite influence is also found.

The Heavenly Host: In addition to angels, the Old Testament refers to other supernatural beings such as Cherubim, Seraphim, the "heavenly host", the "holy ones", etc., which have no human form but are winged creatures who are referred to as the Keepers of Eden (Gn. 3:24; Ezk. 28:11–19). Isaiah 6, Ezekiel 10 and Psalms describe them as winged beings who mainly serve as the chariot upon which God's glory appears. They form an independent entity in Israel's religious symbolism and therefore are not directly associated with the concept of angels as God's messengers. They people the heavens, as members of the heavenly council — followers and worshippers of God the great king, glorifying and exalting Him (Ps. 103, 148). Several biblical passages refer to some of them as beings who act somewhat independently, without carrying out the divine will. Their origin lies in older pagan sources.

Generally speaking, "heavenly host" is the biblical term that corresponds to the pagan pantheon or the council of gods, and therefore includes the angels. This concept is excluded from the understanding of "mal'akhim" as primarily groups of heavenly beings with whom men come into contact because they serve to deliver messages from God to man.

Development of the Concept of Angels: Instances of the divine presence addressing chosen individuals, as opposed to revelation via angels, are more common in the earlier biblical narratives, (e. g. the Book of Judges), becoming less frequent in the later books, according to S. Licht. It is likely that when the holy character and unique nature of Yahweh began to be accepted, the belief that He personally appeared among man necessarily became more and more untenable. Yahweh receded further from man while His angel appeared in His stead; there are angels in Zechariah* and in Daniel* (see below). The transcendental conception triumphs in the end.

It is possible to distinguish two attidudes *vis a vis* the form in which the generic term "angel" is used in the Bible. One, based on reluctance to describe God in anthropomorphic terms or to describe the physical aspects of His revelation to man, delegates the manifestation of His word and the embodiment of His authority to His messenger. The other attitude denies the angel-messenger such prominence, and when called for by the narrative, pictures the divine presence in terms of action.

The Angel of Yahweh: The "Angel of Yahweh", also called the Angel of God, occupies a special position. He is considered a great angel, not merely one among the angels, and may, in a sense, be regarded as the guardian angel of the nation of Israel, i.e. Michael in later tradition. He appears as Israel's representative in important crises, such as the sacrifice of Isaac (Gn. 22:11, 15 ff); the dramatic developments of Exodus (3:2; 14:19; 23:23); Numbers (22:22); Judges (6:11); II Kings (1:3) and Zech. (1:9). His manifestations vary in these theophanies and on other occasions. Although he did not actually reveal his presence, the acts are described as the revelation of the divine will, through divine manifestations and visual or auditory theophanies, such as with Abraham (Gn. 22:11ff.) and with Jacob in his dream (Gn. 32).

Angels were not always recognized by mortals in their human guise; they appeared and disappeared miraculously, as in the days of Judges* (Gideon, Jud. 6:11–23) and in David's story (II Sam. 24:16 ff.). They sometimes performed a permanent function, "the angel who redeems me from all evil" (Gn. 48:16), or carried out a practical mission, such as preceding the Israelites in the Exodus, or smiting Sennacherib's army (II K. 19:35). Although their superhuman character may have inspired awe, as in Isaiah's vision (6) and Ezekiel (1), this attitude did not extend to individual angels.

The distinction between the terms "Yahweh" and "Angel of Yahweh" is clearly maintained. Note, for example, the debate between Moses and Yahweh as to whether Yahweh Himself or His Angel would lead the Israelites from Egypt (Ex. 32:34; 33:2). The Bible states that God "in his glory" will not appear among the people (Ex. 33:22). This denial was apparently intended as a punishment, although it was eventually revoked due to Moses' pleading. This must have been a moment of tremendous anxiety for Moses, as according to pre-Exilic biblical tradition, the Angel was not sufficient to lead Israel to Canaan. While he could serve as a substitute or surrogate for Yahweh, the Angel was a being quite distinct from Yahweh, although serving as His personal, special messenger, and having prerogatives beyond those of the ordinary angels. Significantly, he was specifically the bearer of the name of Yahweh. In Near-Eastern thought, as in pagan literature, one god could be identified with the "name" of another.

Whatever the theological difficulties involved in the bewildering alternation of Yahweh and His Angel in the stories of the Pentateuch, the pictorial situation is relatively clear. The Angel is a distinct person, like all other angels, but since he is the primary agent of God in relation to man and the world, and his function is so nearly that of Yahweh Himself, the biblical authors often thought in terms of the Angel of Yahweh as executing or commanding things. Nevertheless, the understanding could only have been that the Angel could not act independently of Yahweh, as authority and direction came only from God Himself.

Angel of Yahweh in the Heavenly Court: The Angel of Yahweh often carried out the function of mediator, intercessor or advocate for mankind before the heavenly court of God. The Bible presents impressive scenes of judgment (I K. 22:19–24; Zech. 3; Job 16:19;) in which the Angel speaks for man in a confrontation with Satan or another adversary who acts as the prosecuting attorney or accuser of man (see Job*). G. E. Mendenhall has noted that the Angel as a witness in the heavenly court is a concept that existed in ancient Canaanite mythology. The courtroom scene now associated with the "Last Judgment" is a familiar feature of Near Eastern religions, and relates to the final disposition of human cases before the deity, determining their fate in the netherworld. Although God sits as judge, the Bible makes it clear that His sympathies are with man.

Angels in Prophetic Vision: The development of classical (written) prophecy gave rise to the concept of the prophets as God's spokesmen in lieu of angels, i. e. human as against divine angel — the function being the same. In later stages, and particularly post-Exilic prophecy, angels are no longer described as visible manifestations, but as visions of the prophets. In the visions of Ezekiel (8–11) and Zechariah (1–5) angels appear as mediums of divine revelation for the purpose of inspiring the performance of certain symbolic acts. During a vision the prophet may carry out the act, but speak little. The visions of post-Exilic prophecy were not as clear as the direct and simple revelations of angels to the earlier prophets, but required elucidation, evidence of a growing distinction between God and man.

Angelology in Post-Exilic Writings: The tendency towards a growing transcendence of the deity and his removal from direct contact with man (a feature of pre-Exilic Israelite theology, see Revelation*), together with a desire to represent the resplendent glory of the heavenly retinue of legions and armies of angels as a symbol of God's power, is further demonstrated by the introduction of a well-defined angelology, in which the more powerful angels and archangels attained specialized functions and names. Emphasis was placed on the variation of angels and on the specialisation of angelic nature and functions, as well as on poetic colouration.

There was always place for angels in biblical religion from the beginning onwards but it was relatively restrained in the classical pre-Exilic period. The rich efflorescence of angelology in post-Exilic times corresponds to a decline in prophetic tradition and the emergence of apocalyptic* (see article).

Angels in Apocryphal Literature: Angelic intercession between God and man emerged when a special notion, partly under foreign influence, began to develop. This established angelic ability to convey human prayers to God, to serve as mediators between man and the transcendental deity. The progressive exaltation of God brought with it a number of significant theological consequences. Men gave more and more thought to God's hidden ways and the wondrous manner in which He directed the universe. God's picture was no longer that of a simple and familiar deity who was close to man. Man's concept of the world grew more complex and far more transcendental. There was a reaction against speaking of God in anthropomorphic terms, resulting in an increasing stress on the role of the angels as intermediaries. Although they intervened, the angels did not receive man's prayers, which continued to be directed to God.

In principle, all angels were the personification of a particular divine will, act or function. The mediating function is vividly portrayed by the heavenly messenger to Daniel (10:1–9) and is most clearly expressed in Tobit 12:12, where the angel Gabriel is quoted. Emphasis on angels as both messengers and mediators was stressed in apocalyptic* literature and repeated in the New Testament* (Rev. 1:20; 8:3), establishing the belief that nations and churches have their own angels. The doctrine of the national guardian angel mentioned in Daniel, is also found in II Maccabees 15:23, "Judas asked the Lord to send a good angel before us to sow fear and fright among the enemy." The origin of this tale appears to be in Exodus, where Yahweh, after Moses' pleading, promised to send His angel before the Israelites. It was to the Angel of Yahweh that the Hebrews attributed their victory over Canaan.

The names of angels, which were sometimes listed in groups of seven or four, increased during the early Hellenistic* period. In the apocalyptic literature of Enoch*, the angels reveal the mysteries of heaven: the fallen angels (see Magic*) and the beneficent archangels such as Gabriel, Michael, Uriel and Raphael who were permanently close to God, who interceded before Him for humanity and who were instrumental in punishing sinners (Enoch 1). The differentiation between the categories of angels gradually disappeared later. The heavenly hosts are described in Enoch 61 as arranged in divisions, but without system. It is possible that the matter of God's power in relation to the greater and lesser processes of nature hastened the differentiation of function. Natural phenomena such as clouds and hail were presided over by angels, and occasionally the stars also appeared as angels. Despite this angelic participation in human affairs, there is no trace at any time of any cult of angels such as existed in Mesopotamia, although the possibility is hinted at in both the Old and New Testaments. In the latter, Paul rebukes angel worship at Colossae, which became more widespread in later centuries (Col. 2:18). His disparaging references to principalities, powers, dominions, thrones, etc. have to do with the speculations about various ranks of angels.

Angels in the Dead Sea Scrolls: That the sectaries of the Dead Sea were deeply interested in angels is apparent from all their writings (see Dead Sea Scrolls*), and in Josephus' description of the Essenes (War. II, 142). According to him, their vision of the new age was one in which they would live eternally in the presence of the "holy ones", the angels of God, and even in the very presence of the Holy God.

New Testament Period: This ideal is typical of the New Testament attitude towards eternal life. Although the angelology of the New Testament is very complex, it has been rendered more comprehensible by the Dead Sea Scrolls' discussion of angels, and the light they have shed on early Christianity* and the Judaism of that period. In the elaborate angelology and dualism of Qumran, their Old Testament origins have been blurred and transmuted partly under Iranian influence. The two angels of the heavenly court (see above) become the two opposing principles of "Light" (truth) and "Darkness" (error). This dualism of the heavenly spirits survived to some extent in Johannine writings. Although the figure of Paraclete or advocate (Jn. 14:17; 15:26; 16:7, 13) is a reflection of the Qumran "Spirit of Truth", its origin is in the heavenly court of Yahweh of the Old Testament. In John, the Paraclete bears witness to Christ and to the future. His belief in the Day of Judgment and the New Creation is accompanied by a belief in an eternal life to be shared with the angels in heaven in a manner similar to that expressed in Luke 20:36.

Angels in Rabbinic Literature: By and large, the Jews did not preserve the type of literature that could give evidence of the doctrine of angels during the days of the Second Temple. Although many of the extravagances of the current pseudepigraphic and apocalyptic literature on angels were set aside by the rabbis*, some special trends have found their way into the New Testament, Midrashic and Talmudic aggadah, and ancient mystic literature. In the rabbinic period, the Hebrew word *mal'akh* referred only to a superhuman angel, distinct from a human messenger (*shaliah* in Hebrew).

Jesus and the Angels: It is assumed that in Jesus' era it was generally believed that angels acted as God's ambassadors and were endowed with superhuman powers, and at other times acted as simple messengers. The sections in Matthew* and Luke* that are devoted to the birth and infancy of Jesus*, stress the prominent role of angels and visions as a means by which God made His will known to His servants, such as the angel's announcement of Mary's conception of Jesus. God was also said to have consulted His household of angels on every subject. There was a popular idea that a special angel was assigned to each person, which is what Jesus refers to in Mt. 18:10.

Righteous men were accorded angelic rank and could rise even higher in the Resurrection* or in Revelation*. In Christianity, Jesus is substituted for the angels as the intermediary between God and man, as it is either he or the Holy Spirit who speaks directly to man. The Epistle of the Hebrews (Ch. 1–2) whose point of departure is the Old Testament doctrine of angels, lays special emphasis upon the fact that the angels are created and that they are subordinate to Christ. The law was thought to have been given through the agency of angels (He. 2:12; Ac. 7:53; Gal. 3:19), which was one of the reasons advanced by Paul and the author of Hebrews* for the superiority of the revelation through Jesus.

The Angel of Death: All angels developed from a particular functional expression of the deity. The Angel of Death, the divine messenger charged with the duty of taking the soul from the body, developed functionally into a relatively independent entity with a distinct awesome character, as described in the Apocalypse of John. In the Old Testament, he is one of the host of "destroying angels", and is personified in several Psalms and other poems in a manner that must be based on the representation of the Canaanite God, Mot, the god of death and the underworld, as his name clearly shows (see Canaan: Gods and Idols*). The Angel of Death is simply the Hebrew version of this Canaanite deity, whose imagery has been adapted from the rich poetic literature of Canaanite mythology, which is why death is treated in such personal terms.

In rabbinic literature, death and the Angel of Death were also associated with demons, such as Satan, Samael, the prince of demons, the tempter, the accuser, etc., since death is normally experienced by man as a negative and destructive occurrence. (See also Tabernacle and Ark*: Cherubim.)

APOCALYPSE. — *Outline: The Passing of Prophecy; The Form of Apocalypse; The Significance of Apocalypse; Apocalypse and the Dead Sea Scrolls. I. Apocalyptic Literature: Daniel; Enoch; Testaments of the Twelve Patriarchs; Second Baruch; Fourth Ezra; The Assumption of Moses and the Testament of Moses; The Syriac Apocalypse of Baruch; Third Baruch; II. Apocalypse in the New Testament: Revelation; Conclusion.*

Apocalyptic teaching is, in essence, an attempt to find a mystical interpretation of the meaning of history and God's ultimate purpose for mankind.

God's control over history and his determination to create a people worthy of him are classical themes of the Old Testament. Using a picturesque, figurative language, full of visions, "appearances" and "revelations" of secrets beyond the bounds of normal human knowledge, the apocalyptists tried to analyse this purpose and to explain the mysteries of God and nature. It seemed to them that the "end" of the world and of all history was imminent and that the "present" world was already living through its "last days". Out of these ideas they developed a new theology of history known as "eschatology*", a complex of ideas about the "last things" of the "end of the world" and the Day of Judgment.

The Passing of Prophecy: Centuries earlier, in times of equal adversity, the great classical prophets had appeared, to preach of God's judgment on his people, and to offer a solution in terms of a human return to the Commandments. Later, thinkers and men of God pored over these prophetic writings searching for the divine message that would answer their own problems. They became, in the words of N. Friedlander and J. Klausner, the "popular prophets" of a later age. The ancient prophets had spoken of a "golden age" in a world transformed but still earthy. The "popular prophets" who studied and wrote apocalyptic literature believed that something more radical was needed. The Kingdom could only come through a cataclysmic ending to the mortal world and all its history.

The Form of Apocalypse: Apocalyptic works (like the Pseudepigrapha) are often written in the form of testimony attributed to the heroes of the Bible, or descriptions of their visions and life histories.

The Significance of Apocalypse: The apocalyptists wrote in Hebrew or Aramaic in Palestine, or in Greek in Alexandria and North Africa. At the time, the tiny country of the Jews, their customs and their traditions were under continual fire from neighbouring peoples and powerful surrounding empires. Apocalyptic preoccupation with the "last things" of the world is always closely related to the grim realities of contemporary life. There are frequent references to historical events and to the tribulations of rule by Hasmonean*, Herodian* and Roman.

A bitter reality continued and seemed unending. The conditions under which they lived seemed to make nonsense of the Jews' age-old belief in God's concern with the world and his chosen people*. To preserve their faith, they shifted the emphasis from this world to the "next", when the Day of Judgment would see justice done, punishment meted out and the righteous rewarded.

The present wicked world would be replaced by a tranquil kingdom in which men would live at peace with each other and, together, would enjoy the fruits of God's beneficence. This "world to come" was something very real to them and their descriptions of it endowed it with historical features. It was a realistic programme they offered — not, in their own eyes, an other-worldly doctrine. The apocalyptists looked forward to a cataclysmic upheaval which they believed was inevitable and close at hand. In preparation for it, they issued their call to mankind to repent — and quickly.

The important point, of course, was when this day of reckoning would actually come. To discover this, "calculators of the end" pondered and debated an endless series of computations based on the assumption that the history of the world had been immutably fixed at the time of the creation. Everything that had happened and was to happen since then had been foreseen by God, who was able, if he chose, to reveal his secrets to selected humans.

Nevertheless, like the classical prophets, there were also apocalyptists who did not fix the exact time of the end, only emphasized that it was imminent and would come when least expected, like a thief in the night.

Apocalypse and Dead Sea Scrolls: Although to modern eyes, apocalyptic may seem no more than the wild imaginings of visionaries and dreamers, the finding of original sectarian works at Qumran very similar to previously known apocalypses, imposes the conclusion that all this literature arose directly out of the actual life of the time. It is essentially escapist literature, but of a kind which encouraged a fanatical devotion to the Jews' faith and way of life. It produced numerous martyrs and a stubborn resistance to all attempts to change traditional ways. Its subject matter included ancient traditions, history and law as well as mysticism and religion. The movement had its origins in a broadly based popular culture, tinged with Babylonian and Greek influences but mainly rooted in eschatology* (the vision of the last days).

After the national and spiritual revival of the Maccabean period, such a movement can be traced first to the Hassidim* but, principally, to the development of a range of nonconformist trends within Judaism, best demonstrated by the Dead Sea Scrolls*.

The theology of the New Testament and gnostic writings was to be strongly influenced by Jewish apocalyptic writings and many scholars have attributed this to attempts by the early Church to find support for their Jewish-Christian theology. Whether or not this is the case, the Church's interest in these writings partly explains the paradox that they were preserved outside the main stream of Hebrew literature, only to reappear by chance in their original garb among the Dead Sea Scrolls.

Fragments of these works found in Qumran, together with the many similarities between them and the Scrolls all point to a close association and common background in the middle of the 2nd c. BCE. At the same time, it is now recognised that apocalyptic thought had quite a considerable influence on both the mystical and eschatological aspects of talmudic literature, in spite of its being generally scorned in later rabbinic circles.

I. APOCALYPTIC LITERATURE. — **Daniel:** The earliest and outstanding example is the biblical book of Daniel* (see article) containing most of the elements of later apocalyptic literature which all follows similar lines.

The first section of the book (chs. 1–6) is made up of various legendary narratives about Daniel as an interpreter of dreams during the Babylonian exile, related in the third person. This is not specifically apocalyptic, although chapter 2 blends an apocalyptic vision (in the form of dream and dream interpretation) with a typical martyr story. This is to be compared with a similar vision in chapter 7, which also deals with the sequence of empires and their eagerly awaited termination. The apocalyptic section makes up chs. 7–12, written in the first person and consisting of a series of visions which refer obliquely to the persecutions of Antiochus Epiphanes, and his downfall.

While all the stories in Daniel are not in themselves apocalyptic, they provide the setting in which apocalyptic developed one very important aspect: its function as martyr literature. Visions of a triumphant "End" gave the martyrs a reason and the courage to remain steadfast in the face of persecution.

Enoch: This book, the largest of the apocalypses, is made up of a number of heterogeneous writings, attributed to different authors. The book was never universally accepted as inspired, although Jude quotes it as Scriptures and apparently regarded it as authoritative, and some churches included it in their Bibles. However, in general, the New Testament ignored it. It is not listed in the authoritative canons of the church, was dropped at a fairly early date, and was only preserved in the Ethiopian church. The Ethiopic version of the book has 108 chapters forming five sections, dating from different periods:

i. Enoch's journey through the earth, the underworld (Sheol) and the heavens, (chs. 1–36), is built around a still older fragment, the "Apocalypse of Noah" (chs. 6–11) which dates from the 3rd or even the 4th century BCE and tells that Noah lived at the time of the fallen angels, who fathered the "nephilim" (agents of evil) from the daughters of men. With Azazel (a figure of Satan), the fallen angels taught mankind crafts and skills, but only as a temptation to evil. The rest of the section deals with the lot of the wicked and the righteous, with Enoch's journeys during which he learns the secrets of the cosmic mysteries, and with the names of the archangels (see Angels*) and their functions. For all this, the authors drew heavily on concepts belonging to the mythology of Israel's neighbours.

ii. The "Similitudes" (or Parables) of Enoch (chs. 37–71) are among the best examples of apocalyptic literature. They tell of the coming of the heavenly deliverer in the form of a pre-existent divine Messiah, the Son of Man, and of the establishment of the Kingdom of God in a new heaven and new earth. So far, it appears that this section was unknown in Qumran, and it may represent a later development.

iii. The Book of the Heavens (chs. 72–82) is a work of astrology belonging to the 3rd or 2nd century BCE. It shows Noah wandering through the heavens, guided by angels. He sees the Garden of Eden and Gehenna, thus discovering the secrets of the universe and of the last days, and learns the reward that awaits the righteous in the hereafter. This book also draws on obsolete myths from Israel's neighbours, especially Babylon and Persia. The ancient art of astrology* flourished right through post-Exilic days. The astronomical speculations in this book suggest a link with Jubilees (see Apocrypha*) and the literature of Qumran.

iv. Chapters 83–90 are a series of dreams and visions which make up an allegory of the whole history of the world, mankind and Israel, seen as a prelude to the coming of the Messiah, whose birth makes the climax of the whole work. Part of this and the following section (chapters 84–95), refer especially to the fate of the wicked and the social struggle on earth, painting a picture of acute class hatred between rich and poor.

v. The last section (Chs. 91–108) is an Apocalypse of Weeks, the coming of the Temporary Kingdom and the resurrection of the righteous. These may be considered together, although they come from different sources. While not directly related to the birth of Christianity, these sections are the richest in background material for the study of the New Testament.

Fragments of the lost Aramaic originals of this book, long known only in translation, were recovered in Qumran. They corresponded to parts of all the above sections, with the total exception of section ii. This has suggested that parts of the book originated in the early 2nd century BCE, (i.e. pre-Qumran). The fourth section seems to have been composed after the death of Judas Maccabeus (160 BCE). He is the latest historical figure mentioned. There is still a question about the language of the original. The fragments found in Qumran were all in Aramaic. Although these could have been translations from a Hebrew original, the weight of evidence so far available seems to suggest that the book was first composed in Aramaic.

Testaments of the Twelve Patriarchs: Similar in many ways to the Book of Jubilees (see Apocrypha*), the book was apparently written during the prosperous reign of John Hyrcanus (end 2nd cent. BCE), and reflects the orthodoxy of the Hassidim*. It is made up of a legendary history and system of laws for each of the twelve patriarchs, followed by a summing up of the moral to be drawn from their conduct. These offer remarkable anticipations of New Testament thought, e.g: the Testament of Gad's plea for forgiveness, "Love ye one another from the heart; and if a man sin against thee, speak peaceably unto him . ." (Test. Gad 6:3 ff)

The book speaks of a Messiah stemming from both Judah and Levi, which would provide for a Hasmonean deliverer (the Hasmoneans were of the house of Levi), or may have referred to two Messiahs as expected by the sectaries of Qumran and the authors of Jubilees.

Second Baruch is a pseudepigraphical Palestinian work of the 3rd c. BCE, whose author took the name of Baruch ben Neriyah, Jeremiah's secretary. Strongly nationalistic, the book is set against the background of the fall of Jerusalem. A faithful remnant carried on services amidst the ruins of the Temple. On the evidence of this book, exiles in Babylon sent them vessels from the Temple that had been carried away as loot, plus the means to perform sacrifices (1:6–14). The end of the book, attributed to another author, closes with a promise of return and future glories for Israel at a time when evildoers will be punished and the Messiah will appear.

Fourth Ezra: Also written after the destruction of the Temple, in Hebrew, then translated first, into Greek, thence into Syriac, Ethiopian and Latin, it has much in common with Second Baruch.

The heart of the book, written (ca. 90 CE), in the period of despair that followed the Roman victory, is found in chapters 3–13, the rest being later Christian additions. The book tries to offer the Jews some consolation for their tragic defeat.

"Ezra" bemoans Israel's sad fate in a series of visions interpreted for him by angels. In one vision, Zion is represented by a woman mourning over her son. In another, the heathens vanish, evil is brought to an end and Israel is established on the Final Day by the advent of the Messiah. Commanded by the angel, Ezra hides for forty days and dictates God's words to five scribes. He completes 94 books, 24 of which are revealed as the Bible and 70 reserved for those expert in esoteric lore.

The Assumption of Moses and the Testament of Moses: These books, also dating from the Roman domination of Judea during the 1st century CE, are of Pharisaic origin. They protest against the growing tendency to mix political unrest with messianic hopes, although they do not deny belief in the coming of the kingdom. Significantly, some of the book's political and religious ideals come close to the views of Jesus, while new materials in which Moses also plays a central part have been found in Qumran.

The Syriac Apocalypse of Baruch: This is not the same as the apocryphal Book of Baruch, but another, written mostly after the destruction of the Temple. Contemporary with the New Testament, it reflects a similar spirit and shows many interesting parallels with Christian concepts. In its idea of sin, it echoes Paul and its concept of a future age of incorruptibility, following the days of corruption, is also reminiscent of the New Testament.

Third Baruch: Also referred to as the Greek Apocalypse of Baruch because it was composed in that language, it is dated about 100 CE. It elaborates the idea of the seven heavens, describing the movement of some of the heavenly bodies and attendant angels, and their intervention in human destiny.

II. APOCALYPSE IN THE NEW TESTAMENT. — **Revelation:** There is considerable difference of opinion about the dating of Revelation. Many scholars now incline to believe that it was composed around the time of the fall of Jerusalem (ca. 68–69 CE), while others hold to the older theory that places the book within the later years of Domitian (ca. 95 CE), a time of intense Christian persecution. (There is a mediating view which regards the nucleus as coming from the earlier period, while the existing setting and framework were provided by an editor or later author in the 90's.) In any case, its author (or authors) appear to have lived for a time in Palestine and then to have been exiled to the Roman penal settlement of Patmos.

The pretext for Christian persecution by the Romans was their refusal to join in officially imposed worship of the emperor as divine. The series of visions which make up the book clearly refer to these tribulations of the young church at the hands of "the Beast" (Rome). Using some material from Daniel and other apocalypses, as well as much from Old Testament prophecy, the book is an answer to the cry, "How long, O Master . . . dost thou not . . . avenge our blood?" (Rev. 6:10). The answer is that the very intensity of the struggle is a guarantee that the end is near, when God will finally triumph over the spiritual powers of darkness and establish his kingdom in the "New Jerusalem", where the saints will dwell forever. A fundamental distinction between this and other apocalypses is that the author of Revelation foretells, not the coming of a Messiah, but the return of a Messiah who has already triumphed over sin and death himself, and whose kingdom will see the final victory over "the Beast", Satan and, ultimately, death. Whatever agony the Christian churches might be called upon to face, they were assured that the day was close at hand when, "God himself will be with them; he will wipe away every tear from their eyes, and death shall be no more, neither shall there be mourning nor crying nor pain any more, for the former things have passed away." (Rev. 21:3–4)

Conclusion: The body of inter-testamental literature reveals a Judaism in the process of change and growth, very much alive to changing circumstances, with an unalterable belief in God and a firm adherence to the Mosaic tradition. The Jews of this period remained convinced, not only of the truth of the prophetic message, but of its immediate and imminent relevance for Israel and the world.

The variety of parties and sects which appeared at this time may be bewildering, but they are further evidence of the vigour and originality of the Jewish spirit of the age. Although schools of philosophy and wisdom and historians in the biblical or new Hellenic traditions also flourished, apocalyptic literature appears as the most distinctive product of this period of Judaism. In short, the centuries represented by the literature discussed here (and under Apocrypha*) were a rich creative period for Judaism as it explored its own traditions and confronted the pagan world of its day (see Apocrypha and Pseudepigrapha*).

APOCRYPHA AND PSEUDEPIGRAPHA. —

Outline: Apocrypha; Pseudepigrapha; General Characteristics; I. Stories and Homilies: a. Judith, b. Tobiah, c. The Letter of Aristeas, d. Fourth Maccabees, e. Book of Adam and Eve and the Martyrdom of Isaiah. II. Recensions and Additions to the Old Testament: a. Susanna and Bel and the Dragon, b. Prayer of Azariah and the Song of the Three Children, c. Additions to Esther, d. Jubilees, e. III Esdras, f. Epistle of Jeremiah, g. The Prayer of Manasseh. III. Wisdom Literature: The Wisdom of Ben Sira, Original Version and Translations, The Wisdom of Solomon, The Psalms of Solomon, The Sibylline Oracles. IV. Historical: a. First Maccabees, b. Second Book of Maccabees, c. Third Maccabees.

The apparent gap between the Old and New Testaments is bridged by a body of Jewish religious literature, written mainly between 400 BCE and 100 CE, of which the most important writings form the Apocrypha, Pseudepigrapha and Apocalypse*.

Apocrypha: The word "apocrypha" comes from the Greek "apokryphos", meaning "hidden wisdom" or, in Hebrew, "outside books", not Holy Scripture. The term is normally applied only to the non-biblical books which were rejected by the Palestinian rabbis as not directly inspired by God, but were incorporated in the Septuagint* and canonized by the Catholic Church. Except for Ben-Sira who wrote Ecclesiasticus, the authors of most of the Apocrypha are unknown, although the writings are ascribed to historical figures, generally of the biblical period (see Bible Canon and Text*).

The canon of biblical books accepted in Palestine was selected by a series of rabbinical councils of the 2nd and 1st cs. BCE and, around 100 CE, it received official recognition from the Council of Jabneh. However, the Alexandrian Jews of the earlier period had been much less selective than the Palestinian rabbis and they included a wider selection of edifying books in the Septuagint translation of the Bible. As the Christian church used the Septuagint version, the "outside books" included there were largely preserved in Greek and Latin translations in Christian circles. In general, before the discovery of the Dead Sea Scrolls, knowledge of Hebrew literature in the Graeco-Roman (inter-testamental) period was very scanty. Other books left out of the final canon of the Old Testament were gradually forgotten. Although written by Jews for Jews, they were unknown (except for Ecclesiasticus) to Jewish scholars of the Middle Ages. Today the ancient works can be studied in modern renderings, including their recent re-translation into Hebrew. In this way a vital link in the development of old Jewish literature has been recreated.

Pseudepigrapha: Other non-canonical books are loosely grouped as the Pseudepigrapha (writings under an assumed name). To give an appearance of divine revelation to their own visions, the authors of these books took the name of one of the great heroes of the past, someone who unquestionably merited divine revelation (Enoch, Abraham, Moses, Baruch, Ezra and others). This group of writings is not apocryphal in the strict sense, but often grouped with it as a separate category (see Apocalypse*).

General Characteristics: The inter-testamental literature of the 4th century BCE to the 1st century CE, including the Apocrypha, Pseudepigrapha and Apocalypses, reflects the general social and cultural ferment of the time. Various foreign influences, affecting both subject matter and style, can be traced to Egypt, Babylon and Greece. The strongest impact came from Persia and, to a lesser extent, from the Hellenistic* world. Combined with indigenous inspiration and individuality, these different forces determined the cultural climate of the pre-Christian era of Palestine and Jewry.

Until recently, it was held that these inter-testamental books were the creations of a period of religious exclusiveness and stagnation. Now, particularly in the light of the discoveries made at Qumran, modern scholars have dispelled that idea. The many close resemblances between the Dead Sea Scrolls*, the New Testament* and the apocrypha, pseudepigrapha and apocalyptic* writings, make it clear that during this period the Jews were developing the spiritual material on which both later Judaism and Christianity were to draw. The books they wrote in the five centuries from the 4th BCE to the 1st CE reflect thought and folklore in Palestine and the diaspora, including post-Exilic developments in Judaism's idea of God, resurrection* and immortality* and, above all, eschatological* visions of the Last Days. A thorough grasp of inter-testamental literature is, therefore, essential for a proper appreciation of the beliefs and attitudes reflected in the New Testament.

Apocryphal and Pseudepigraphic books can be divided into four categories: I. Short stories and homilies; II. Recensions (rewritings) of the Old Testament; III. Wisdom literature; IV. Historical writings.

I. STORIES AND HOMILIES: From the earliest known fragments of their manuscripts and occasionally from datable quotations and allusions in other literature, these works are believed to have been written mainly before the Maccabean period, i. e. between 400 and 175 BCE, although their subject matter is much older.

a. **Judith:** Perhaps the best known story, it tells how Judith saved the people of her city of Bethulia in Northern Samaria from the besieging "Assyrians" by using her beauty and courage to entice and then kill the enemy commander, Holofernes. This work has generally been regarded as fiction but recently it has been suggested that it may contain a kernel of fact. A. Alt thinks its historical background may lie in the Persian period. The story may refer to the wars of the last Persian emperors Artaxerxes II or III, between 400 and 352 BCE. The book's composition has been placed in the mid-second century, but A. M. Grintz has put it at ca. 360 BCE. In any case, any date has to be regarded with some caution.

b. **Tobiah** (Tobit) is a moralistic novelette probably written in Persia. The earliest fragments known were found among the Dead Sea Scrolls, where incomplete manuscripts, three written in the "Imperial Aramaic" of the Persian empire period, and one in Hebrew, were discovered. It is suggested that the Aramaic can be dated to the 4th century BCE although the 3rd is also possible. Originally the book was written in either Hebrew or Aramaic but, apart from the fragments at Qumran, the book was preserved whole only in Greek.

The story tells of Tobit, a pious exile in Nineveh and his dutiful son Tobiah. Sent on a long journey through Mesopotamia and Persia to collect a debt, Tobiah was helped by the disguised angel Raphael to restore his family's fortunes and his father's sight. On his way Tobiah met his only surviving cousin Sara, who had been suffering under the guardianship of an infatuated demon, Asmodaeus. Of seven husbands given her in succession, none had survived long enough to consummate the marriage. Instructed by Raphael, and using the organs from a fish he had caught in the Tigris, Tobiah exorcised the devil and married his cousin, thus inheriting her father's fortune. He returned triumphantly to his pious father who was cured of his blindness by the gall of the same fish.

The marriage between Tobiah and Sara was recorded in the "Ketubah", or marriage instrument — this is the first written reference to this custom. The tale also includes many aphorisms or "wisdom" drawing on much earlier sources which recall the 7th c. BCE Babylonian "Book of the Sage Achiqar" (see Wisdom literature*). One of these, also written here for the first time, is the golden rule "What thou thyself hatest, do to no man." (Tobit: 4:15), which was repeated later by Hillel and, put more positively, became part of the teachings of Christ.

c. **The Letter of Aristeas** tells the story of the translation of the Septuagint and is a valuable source of information on conditions in Palestine at that time (see Hellenism and the Jewish Diaspora*).

d. **Fourth Maccabees:** a typical Alexandrian production from the 1st century BCE, it is a homily on the supremacy of "inspired reason" over passion (according to Platonic and Stoic terminology). Courage in the face of persecution is illustrated by biblical heroes and by the stories of the martyrdom of Eleazar and the Seven Sons at the time of Antiochus Epiphanes, told in II Maccabees. The great interest of the book lies in the way it tries to adapt Jewish ideas to Greek thought.

e. Other embellishments of Jewish legends around biblical characters are the **Book of Adam and Eve** and the **Martyrdom of Isaiah.** Both of these legends were very popular in New Testament times and were adopted by the early Christians.

II. RECENSIONS AND ADDITIONS TO THE OLD TESTAMENT: New versions of Old Testament stories are an outstanding feature of inter-testamental literature. Although their origin and dating are disputed, these may also have been written early in the second century BCE. Moreover, Greek translations of the Bible sometimes include additions to the Hebrew versions and these are also part of the Apocrypha.

a. A whole series of variations on the legend of Daniel must have been written. The best known of the tributes to Daniel's wisdom were the books of Susanna, and Bel and the Dragon.

In **Susanna,** Daniel saves the virtuous Susanna from a charge of adultery brought by two lusting "elders" whom she had repulsed. By clever cross-examination, Daniel tricked them into contradicting themselves, thus proving the accusation false.

The book of **Bel and the Dragon** (written in Greek) consists of two separate stories. One tells how Daniel refused to worship the heathen idol, Bel, and, by using his common sense, proved it a fraud. The second is the story of the great "Dragon" which includes the famous episode of Daniel in the Lions' Den where, for seven days he was divinely protected from harm, whereas his heathen enemies, when thrown to the lions in his place, were immediately devoured.

The moral of the book is the worthlessness of pagan cults. It is thought that the original tale was composed in the 5th to 4th centuries BCE.

b. Two other additions in the Greek version of the Book of Daniel, the **Prayer of Azariah** and the **Song of the Three Children** on the theme of the fiery furnace, seem to fit best in the Maccabean period, ca. 170 BCE. There is much additional Daniel literature, some of which has turned up at Qumran (see Dead Sea Scrolls*) in fragmentary form.

c. The **Additions to Esther,** written in verse around 100 BCE comprises imaginary documents in which Haman appears as a Macedonian and in which the name of God, absent from the canonical book, is given.

d. **Jubilees:** Jubilees re-tells the story of salvation from the Creation to the revelation on Mount Sinai. Written in Hebrew and apparently originating in proto-Essene circles in the 4th or 3rd centuries BCE, this revision of Genesis and part of Exodus in the light of contemporary theology is an invaluable guide to religious developments at the end of the Old Testament period.

Jubilees' author assumes the Torah to have been written during mankind's earliest existence, then to have been forgotten until Moses was reminded of it by an angel on Mount Sinai. The history of humanity and of the origins of the Chosen People* is then told with a chronology based on a 49-year period, the "jubilee" of each event. The whole of history adds up to 49 such periods, the "jubilee of jubilees" (see Calendar*).

The book seeks justification for the laws and customs of its own time by retelling legends about the 22 "patriarchs" from Adam to Jacob, trying, at the same time, to put the fathers of mankind in the most favourable light possible.

Thus the stories form a valuable source for the study of pre-Talmudic "halakhah" (Jewish legal discussions and literature as contrasted to the non-legal), although in many ways they come closer to the procedure and practice of the Dead Sea sectaries, rather than to rabbinic* regulations.

Affinities with the Dead Sea Scrolls: In 1955, the Dead Sea Scrolls were found to include a similar — although not identical — text of Jubilees. The original book was, in all probability, written before the community of Qumran was established, so its material probably provides a background for their later works. Jubilees (and also Enoch) also contains a section arguing against the Jerusalem lunar calendar*, and suggesting a solar calendar instead. The sectaries of Qumran used such a calendar and may have followed Jubilees in this. Many original sectarian works, especially the "Scroll of the War of the Sons of Light against the Sons of Darkness" resemble the Qumran editions of apocryphal works so closely that it is suggested (by F. M. Cross) that "we must place the composition of these works within a single line of tradition," probably originating among Hassidic* circles.

In spite of Jubilees' close affinities with the sectarian "Genesis Apocryphon", its lack of any arguments for separation from Israel suggests that the book did not originate in pre-Qumran circles. It also has much in common with the Books of Enoch and the Testaments of the Twelve Patriarchs (see Apocalypse*).

e. **III Esdras:** This book, also called the Greek Ezra, is actually an Alexandrian work, probably written in the second century BCE. It is a paraphrase of the canonical books of Ezra and Nehemiah and tells the history of Israel from the time of Josias up to the reading of the law by Ezra. Unlike the original source, it dwells at length on the story of Zerubbabel winning the favour of king Darius and obtaining his permission for the exiles to return to Judea.

f. Other compositions, written in the form of letters, include the **Epistle of Jeremiah,** a condemnation of idolatry, supposed to have been written by the prophet to the exiles in Babylon. An example has been found in Qumran which suggests that this type of literature may have originated at the end the of 2nd century BCE.

g. **The Prayer of Manasseh,** a cry of penitence uttered by Manasseh during his Babylonian captivity (II Ch. 33), is a product of Hellenistic Judaism which seems to fit the late 2nd century BCE.

III. WISDOM LITERATURE: **The Wisdom of Ben Sira** or **Ecclesiasticus** (which is a different book from the Old Testament Ecclesiastes*), was written in Hebrew around 180 or 200 BCE, before the persecutions and strife which preceded the Maccabean era.

By identifying "Wisdom" with the Torah (1:14, 18, 20, 26), Ben-Sira brought classical "wisdom literature" into the central stream of Mosaic tradition. His book shows a new, specifically Israelite spirit, in which the Hellenistic concepts of freedom of thought and enquiry are rejected and "wisdom" is identified with the morality and laws of Israel.

Ben-Sira, a learned and widely travelled scribe (39:1–11), with a school of disciples, offers a guide to that law. In poetic parallels, similar in form to the biblical Book of Proverbs*, he gives precepts to cover every phase of social and religious life, stressing the need for moderation and self-control and advocating peaceful acceptance of social inequalities as the "will of God": "Good and evil, life and death, Poverty and riches are from the Lord." (Ecclus: 11:14). Because of its wide scope, the book is a mine of information on the thought, life and customs of the Jews of his time.

Original Version and Translations: Although Ecclesiasticus was not included in the Canon of Scriptures, its sayings are often quoted in the Mishnah* and Talmudic writings. The book was generally highly regarded and its maxims were preserved among the people, although in a more popular language akin to spoken Hebrew, or even in Aramaic. These renderings, which differed from the biblical style of their original, were combined in a number of small popular collections, and even had their effect on later reproductions of the original text. Although this was not lost until the 10th century CE when it was last known to Saadiah Gaon, it was influenced and slightly distorted by the popular texts and by inevitable errors in copying. This was revealed when later collections were compared with Greek translations and with the original Hebrew text, which was found in the Cairo Genizah (reliquary for old and decaying manuscripts) in 1896 CE.

Fragments of scrolls found in Cave II at Qumran included examples from the Hebrew original of Ecclesiasticus (6:20–31), which were practically identical in form with the manuscripts found in the Cairo Genizah. In addition, another chapter of the book was found in a new scroll from Cave XI, although no details are available about this yet.

Ecclesiasticus was translated into Greek by Ben Sira's grandson in 132 BCE and was incorporated into the Septuagint (and, consequently, into the Apocrypha). In the opinion of M. Z. Segal, the Greek text was made from a defective Hebrew version, although it can be corrected by reference to surviving fragments of the original. The translation was also affected by distortions in the Greek, and by a considerable confusion in the order of chapter and verse. By 200 CE a revised Greek version had been made from a Hebrew text which itself diverged from the original and was closer to later corrupt Hebrew versions. The new Greek text incorporated a number of additional maxims, some originally Hebrew, some Greek. Later Latin and Syriac translations were made from this Greek version.

The Wisdom of Solomon: This is the work of an Alexandrian Jew of the 1st century BCE. Imbued with the spirit of Greek philosophy, his work is an attempt at a synthesis of Diaspora Judaism with Hellenism.

By a familiar literary device of the time, Solomon is claimed as the author and is praised as the foremost exponent of that wisdom which guides mankind and which has played such an important role in Jewish history. Among other subjects, the book deals with the universality of God, the pre-existence of the soul (a concept borrowed from Greek thought), and an immediate immortality which follows death without an intermediate state and without resurrection. The religious ideas expressed or implied in the book are among the noblest produced during this period, and find echoes in the New Testament.

The Psalms of Solomon: The Psalms of Solomon are another use of this honoured name as a prestige symbol. In fact, the book is a product of Pharisaic piety, written in Hebrew about 50 BCE. Its 18 poems deplore the desecration of the Temple by Pompey; the Sadducees, Hellenists, immorality and sin, and look forward to the swift coming of a Messiah from Judea who will establish an ideal kingdom on earth. The book offers an interesting sidelight on the sectarian strife that was dividing Judaism at the time (see Dead Sea Scrolls*).

The Sibylline Oracles: These are a collection of oracular sayings in Greek hexameters, written by Diaspora Jews, Jewish Christians* and Christians, over six centuries from the 2nd BCE to the 4th CE. They are of little literary value and are of interest mainly as examples of ancient religious propaganda.

Their origin lies in the Hellenistic custom of looking for divine guidance in terms of inspired messages relayed by some "Sibyl" associated with a shrine. Taking advantage of their popular influence, Jews and, later, Christians used the pagan form to propagate their own beliefs.

The book sketches the history of the Mediterranean area in the form of prophecy. Jewish oracles can easily be distinguished from the non-Jewish by their attacks on Rome. The Jews' arch enemy is condemned for its idolatry, greed and immorality, and threatened with disaster. In contrast, the virtues of the Law are extolled, and Messianic judgment and redemption coming after a series of wars and cataclysms are foretold (see Wisdom Literature,* Old Testament).

IV. HISTORICAL: a. **First Maccabees*:** This was the official Hasmonean* history of the Maccabean rebellion and its success. Written around 100 BCE, it is the most trustworthy record of the period of hellenization in Jerusalem and of the rebellion that brought the Hasmoneans to power.
b. **Second Book of Maccabees*:** Written in Greek at about the same time, this is an abridgement of an enormous work composed by Jason of Cyrene, a Jew of the North African Diaspora. It covers the short period (175–161 BCE) of the hellenizers' rule, leading up to the rebellion. It is full of miracles and tales of courage in the face of persecution and this gained it great popularity later on among the literature of the martyrs.

187

190

c. **Third Maccabees:** This is not an historical record, but a fable, similar to the theme of the Letter of Aristeas (see above, Stories and Homilies). It is a good example of Jewish Diaspora writing, telling of the miraculous rescue of the Jews of Egypt from the persecutions of an evil king, Ptolemy IV (see Apocalypse*).

ARABS, ARABIA AND THE BIBLE. — *Outline: I. History: Ancient Arabs; The Evidence of Archaeology; The Sabean Kingdom; Its Culture and Religion; Decline of the Sabeans; Hazarmaveth; The Trade of Arabia; Arabian and Israelite Trade; Arabia and Assyria; Nabonidus; Arabians and Rome; Arabians at the Time of the New Testament; Jews in Arabia. II. Literary Sources: Arabic Language; Arab and Hebrew Traditions; Arab Genealogies; The Arabs in the Bible. III. Summary.*

The peninsula of Arabia which lies between Asia and Africa, bordered by the Persian Gulf and the Indian Ocean on the East and the Red Sea and the Sinai peninsula on the west, measures some 3,000 km, (2,000 miles) in length by 1,000 km, (600 miles) in width. The greater part of the peninsula is desert with no rivers, although there are numerous oases. Outside the desert lie very fertile areas. The western coast is especially fruitful and in Roman times was even dubbed "Arabia Felix", meaning "happy" or "blessed".

Historians use the term "Arabia" in a wide general sense, as well as for the precise area. In the Bible, Arabia usually seems to mean the peninsula proper, for in ancient times there was no common name for the whole area, nor for its people. They were called after localities or tribes, e.g. the Ishmaelites, Midianites, Hagarenes, Amalekites, Dedanites or Sabeans.

I. HISTORY: **Ancient Arabs:** The word 'arab is used in the South Arabian Mârib inscription (8th c. BCE) which describes Dhu-Raydan as king of Yemen and Hazarmaveth (Hadramaut) and their 'arab (or nomads). The Koran uses the same term to distinguish the nomadic peoples of Arabia from the sedentary people of the "badiya" or steppe-land, and the distinction is retained in classical Arabic. The word occurs with the same meaning in the Egyptian "emu" (from an 18th c. BCE inscription) and in the Assyrian "arubu" or "aribi" which meant the nomads of Media as well as the Arabians. In the Bible, 'Arab is used in a number of passages (e. g. Is. 13:20; Jer. 3:2) to mean desert nomads rather than any specific ethnic group. The Persian inscription of Darius at Behistan uses "Arbaya" both for an ethnic group and for the southern province lying between Mesopotamia and Egypt.

The Evidence of Archaeology: Until the last 35 years, the Arabian peninsula was one of the most neglected areas in archaeology. More recently, thanks to the excavations and studies of many scholars, much more is known of the trade, agriculture, religion and culture of both northern and southern Arabia. Nevertheless, the early history of the Arabs remains very obscure. Although paleolithic and neolithic settlements have been discovered in southern and northern Arabia, the data they have yielded points mainly to a great difference in the racial stock and cultures of the two areas.

One very revealing expedition led by W. F. Albright in 1951–52 CE unearthed the Temple of "'Awwam" or the Moon, the largest of the Himyarite temples (see below), built in the 8th c. BCE and inscribed in archaic Arabic "Awwam the Temple of 'Ilumkuh in the city of Mareb, Yemen" **(188)** and known as the Haram Bilkis. The temple had been destroyed by the time of the first Moslems. Its excavation was never fully completed.

Archaeology has also revealed a great deal about the way in which agriculture was carried on in Southern Arabia, especially the method by which the "flash floods" or infrequent heavy rain storms were harnessed and supplemented by a complex irrigation system. The rainfall from a very large drainage basin was collected by a gigantic dam on the Wadi Adhanat in Sheba, and from this ditches led to every corner of the kingdom.

The Sabean Kingdom: Saba (or Sheba) in present day eastern Yemen was one of the most important southern Arabian kingdoms playing a dominant role in the trade of the area, especially in the spices and incense for which south-western Arabia was famous. Following the introduction of the camel of which they made ever greater use, they began (11–10th c. BCE) a commercial expansion which in a few centuries brought them control of the whole trade of a wide area of southern and central Arabia. By the 3rd

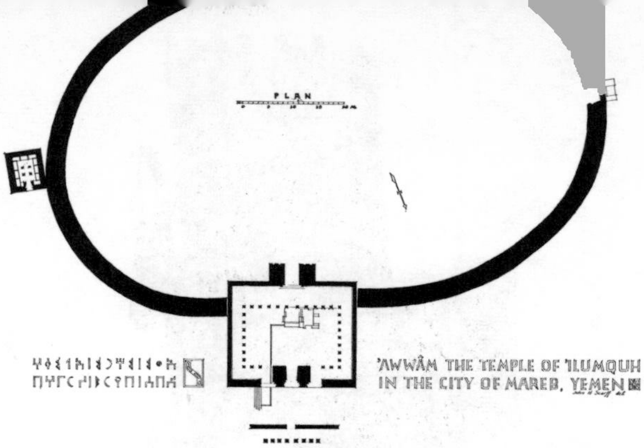

188

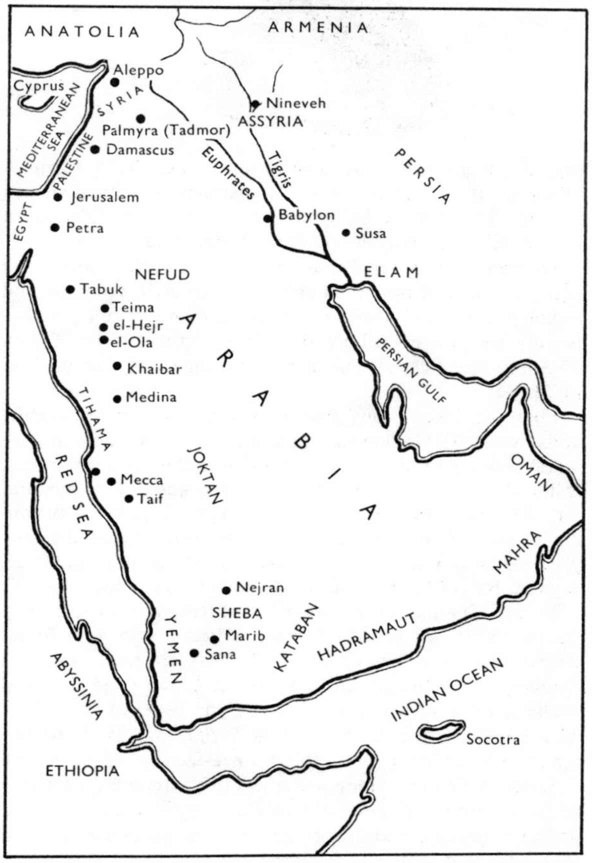

189

or 2nd c. BCE they had established themselves as the dominant power over the larger part of the Arabian peninsula, absorbing the Minaean Kingdom of central Arabia as well as those of Kataban and Hazarmaveth (see map **189**).

The land of Saba was rich in gold and precious stones (I K. 10:1 ff), frankincense (Is. 60:6) and sugar ("sweet cane", Jer. 6:20). The people were great traders, and apart from their connections with Solomon (see below), the Bible records that Tyre, for example, was supplied by "the traders of Sheba and Ramah" with spices, precious stones and gold (Ezk. 27:22). Joel refers to the people of Sheba as slave traders (3:8) and Job knew them as cattle raiders and brigands (1:15; see alabaster stele from Yemen **187**).

Its Culture and Religion: Although much of their history is obscure, it appears that their society was divided into two classes: plebians and nobles — the only ones with any

191

say in government. The people were ruled by a form of oligarchy from which a king (sometimes two) was chosen to reign in rotation. In former days they were ruled by a *mukarrib*, which may be rendered "high priest".

Women played an important role in society and were equal to men in nearly all spheres, with civil, religious and military rights and duties much like a man's. Their position is very well illustrated by the biblical story of the Queen of Sheba (see below). Polygamy was apparently uncommon in Sheba.

Fom the inscriptions found, it appears that their chief gods were Al-Makia and Thaalak, while the people also worshipped Ath'tar (Sabaic form of Ashtoreth), Rammun (biblical Rimmon), the sun and other gods. The sun and Ath'tar were also regarded as the special gods of certain places and, in these cases, their names were included in the place-name (as in the case of Ba'al in Canaan, e. g. Ba'al-zephon, Ba'al Melkart, etc. see Canaan*: Gods and Idols).

In the Temple of Awwam in Marib, a bronze votive statue (**190**) of a god wearing a lion's skin was found dating from the 7th c. BCE. This was so reminiscent of contemporary Phoenician statuary (e. g. the youthful Ba'al Melkart of Tyre), that W. F. Albright believed it to have been copied by the Arabians from Tyrian models. Their fine metalwork is illustrated by this bronze incense burner (**191**).

Sabean worship included offerings to the temples, probably of food, rare spices and gold, while frequently a man would dedicate himself and his property to a particular god in return for that deity's protection.

Sheba is one of the names with strong south Arabian affinities which appear in the genealogical lists of Genesis 10. Its appearance there in combination with the name Hazarmaveth, points to the identification of Sheba with the south Arabian tribe.

Decline of the Sabeans: By the end of the 2nd c. BCE, the Sabeans were superseded by new peoples, the Himyarites and the Nabateans. Nabatean control of Arabian trade was at once a consequence and a cause of the decline of the South Arabian kingdoms. At first the Himyarites shared the trade and the profits with the Nabateans, but this did not last and, before very long, the Nabateans had established undisputed supremacy over northern Arabia and its relations with the rest of the Near East (see Nabateans*).

Hazarmaveth: From south Arabian inscriptions, this tribe is identified with the people of Hadramaut who, according to Pliny and Strabo, were one of the greatest of southern Arabia. Their territory was the fertile area of southernmost Arabia and was renowned for myrrh and spices, which were transported by caravan to Gaza and shipped from there. Many scholars believe that the kingdom of Hadramaut existed from 1200 BCE until the 4th c. CE, when the land was annexed to the state of the Himyarites. South Arabian inscriptions name a number of kings of Hadramaut: Zadke'l Sahar, Yada'el, Elshawa and others.

The Trade of Arabia: Arabia lay across the routes that connected the Mesopotamian kingdoms of Assyria and Babylonia with Egypt and the West. Somewhere between the 15th and 12th c. BCE the camel was domesticated on a large scale in Arabia and thereafter carried the trade of the ancient world across the Arabian desert paths (see Agriculture*: Camels; Roads*).

The routes which Arabian trade followed and their extent has become clearer in recent years. The precise areas in which the myrrh and frankincense were grown and the roads over which they were transported are now known, (see Roads*). The extent of Arabian trade and contacts is also indicated by discoveries such as Roman ware in south-western Arabia, or an Indian statuette of a dancing girl on the east coast.

Arabian and Israelite Trade: Under Solomon, Israel's extensive trading relations included very profitable contacts with the settled peoples of Arabia (I K. 10:1–10, 15; II Ch. 9:14), and these were further extended by the building of the Red Sea port of Ezion Geber–Elath (I K. 9:26–28). The account (I K. 10) of the visit of the Queen of Sheba is by no means to be discounted as purely legendary. Solomon had established his kingdom as a very important centre for the caravan trade of the whole region, controlling the northern terminus of the Arabians' trade routes. Moreover, his expanding sea trade with Ethiopia and Somaliland brought him into direct competition with Arabian desert caravans. The queen of Sheba was naturally moved to try to reach some agreement with Solomon and, according to 1 K. 10:15, the result was certainly profitable to the Jewish monarch, taxes and duties from the Arabian trade flowing into his treasury.

A century later, Jehoshaphat of Judah controlled the trade routes into northern Arabia and, we are told (II Ch. 17:11) collected tribute of 7,700 rams and the same number of he-goats from the Arabs who lived "near the Ethiopians" apparently the nomadic tribes of the south-eastern borders of Palestine. Uzziah (783–742 BCE) further consolidated Judean control of the southern trade routes by military operations against the northwestern Arab tribes (II Ch. 26:7) and by encouraging Israelite settlement and agriculture in the Negeb (ibid. 26:10).

Apparently (Ezk. 27:21) "Arabia and the princes of Kedar" — meaning Dedan or the oasis of El-Ola, an important kingdom of northern Arabia — supplied Tyre with sheep and goats. From Nehemiah, it appears that a permanent settlement of Arabs had been established in Palestine after the destruction of the Temple (see below). At the time of the Restoration* they attempted to prevent the rebuilding of the walls of Jerusalem, especially "Geshem the Arab" (Neh. 6:1), who is known from inscriptions to have been a powerful chieftain of Qedar (Dedan or

El-Ola). Nominally under Persian control, he was the effective ruler of the whole province of Arabia which then included, apparently, both Edom and southern Judea, and was possibly connected with the Persian "Arbaya" (see above).

Arabia and Assyria: The first mention of Arabia in Assyrian records comes in inscriptions of Shalmaneser III (858–824 BCE) where it is recorded that at the Battle of Qarqar (854 BCE, see Assyria*), 1000 camel riders took part. Zabiba, a queen of Arabia is recorded as paying tribute to Tiglat-Pileser III (744–727 BCE), while Sargon II (721–705 BCE) relates that he subjugated the Arabs "who live far away". Some of them he transported to the Samaria* which he had earlier destroyed, while from the rest he collected a tribute of gold dust, precious stones, ebony seeds, spices, horses and camels.

At the time of Sennacherib (704–681 BCE), Arabs joined the Arameans* and Chaldeans in invasions which threatened the whole fabric of the Assyrian empire, although Esarhaddon (680–669 BCE) defeated Arab forces near Basu. Ashurbanipal (668–627 BCE) records a great campaign intended to subdue Arab tribes from the Syrian desert who had taken advantage of upheavals in the Assyrian empire to overrun Edom, Moab and other lands of eastern Palestine and Syria. They left a wave of destruction in their wake and their attacks marked the end of Moab* as a powerful autonomous state. Its collapse is probably reflected in Is. 15 and Jer. 48 and also, perhaps, Isaiah 21:11–17. However, such invasions were a frequent occurrence and successive waves of Arab nomads reached Egypt, Yemen and Ethiopia. After the Babylonian destruction of Jerusalem, (6th c. BCE) southern Judea was taken over by Edomites, who had been pushed out of their homeland by Arab pressure. By the 5th c. BCE Edom had been completely taken over by Arabs (Mal 1:2–5), who had occupied Ezion-Geber and were to be found side by side with the Edomites throughout the Negeb.

Nabonidus: The last Babylonian king, Nabonidus (556–539 BCE) had even closer connections with Arabia. Early in his reign he campaigned in Anatolia and Syria. At home he came into conflict with the organized priesthood who suspected him of irreligious and progressive leanings. Finally he abandoned his capital and throne to his son, Belshazzar (see Babylonia*) and spent the last eight years of his life at the oasis of Teima, an important crossroads in Northern Arabia, south-east of Edom. The reasons that made him take this step and set up his home in the desert are obscure. Some scholars think they may have been connected with commercial aspirations or dreams of empire, while others believe that Nabonidus acted mainly from religious motives. In either case his move had considerable repercussions on the Arabian economy and an increasing commercial activity appears to have attracted many exiled Jews to Arabia. C. C. Torrey believes that Nabonidus' move to Teima marks the establishment of the first Jewish colonies in Arabia (see below, Jews in Arabia).

Arabians and Rome: The impact of the Roman empire was decisive for the development of Arabia. At first, the Romans accepted the alliance of the Nabateans*, hoping through them to gain control of the whole of south Arabia and, especially, of the rich trade with India and the East. A military expedition was organized in 24–25 BCE under Aellius Gallus, to which Herod* contributed 500 soldiers from his bodyguard. The expedition was a failure (Josephus, Ant. 15:9:3; Dion Cassius LIII, 29 and Strabo, Res gestae divi Augustus, V, 18 ff), and the Romans contented themselves with destroying the Nabatean kingdom and creating a "Provincia Arabia" in the borderland between Palestine and Arabia. The Nabateans were driven further south and the Romans never again tried to penetrate central Arabia. They did, however, impose heavy taxes on luxury goods imported from the Far East and Southern Arabia, as one measure aimed at righting Rome's unfavourable trade balance.

Arabs at the Time of the New Testament: The New Testament (Ac. 2:11; Gal. 1:17) follows the Romans in using the term "Arabia" to mean the south and southeast of Palestine, largely peopled by the Nabateans* (who were not Arabs; see article). Arabia and the Arabs are mentioned frequently in Talmudic literature but it is not certain whether the present-day Arabian peninsula or merely the desert lands bordering Palestine are meant.

Jews in Arabia: There is a theory that there were settlements of Arabs in Palestine from the time of the Second Temple, while Jewish colonies are known to have existed in Arabia. A Jewish-Arab cultural exchange was thus initiated at a fairly early stage of Arabian history and the Jewish dispersion, and it continued longer in Arabia than in other countries. According to Arab tradition, Jews lived in Hedjaz until the time of Mohammed. The Jews spoke Arabic and were thoroughly assimilated into the pattern of local life. The effect of these contacts was particularly strong in Hedjaz, in the Yemen and on the edges of Arabia where Judaism and, later, early Christianity gained many adherents. According to the later Arabian historian, Ibn-Qutaybah, before the coming of Islam, Judaism and Christianity had been widespread in some of the most prominent tribes of both northern and southern Arabia. Moreover, Ibn-Qutaybah repeatedly alludes to the patent fact that Mohammed's mission grew out of ground thoroughly prepared by the People of the Book. This background often makes it difficult to differentiate between the continuation of older influences and Mohammed's own impact. He was the founder of a new religion but this stemmed directly from the monotheism of Jew and Christian. Probably a pre-Islamic monotheistic potential had grown up slowly over the years before the prophet of Mecca brought a new urgency and direction to it.

II. LITERARY SOURCES: **Arabic Language:** For all the differences in the racial stock of the Arab peoples, it seems that the cultural unity in which the Semitic family of languages developed was established in Arabia from an early date. Arabic has many connections with archaic Hebrew (see Languages*). The language borrowed extensively from Aramaic while the style of the Koran reveals a substantial Hebrew influence. Inscriptions in a form of the southern Semitic archaic script were found in Arabia (see Alphabet and Writing*).

Arab and Hebrew Traditions: Affinities between the Hebrews and Arabs find expression in the genealogical traditions of both peoples. According to Gn. 10, the forefather of Abraham, Eber, was also the progenitor of Joqtan, the ancestor of the southern Arabs (cf. Gn. 10:25–30), while elsewhere (Gn. 25:1–4, 13–16) many Arab tribes are listed as descended from Abraham and Keturah and Hagar, meaning northern Arabs. The lists are not connected and apparently represent separate traditions about the origins of the different tribes. Some of the names can be related to peoples and places in Arabia (see below, The Arabs in the Bible).

Arab Genealogies: There seems to have been a marked feeling of distinction in Arabia proper between peoples of the south and those of the north. Arab genealogical tradition lists three groups of tribes: a. Tribes which disappeared without leaving a trace; b. South-Arabian tribes related to Qahtan and c. North-Arabian tribes who entered the peninsula from outside and claim descent from Ishmael, son of Abraham. These traditions are not consistent and often contradict each other.

a. **Tribes which Disappeared:** These tribes are known to the Arabs as Amalak or Amalik. Amalik is regarded by the Arabian genealogists as a grandson of Shem and a son of Ham, while Gn (36:12) lists Amalek as the firstborn son of Eliphaz, the son of Esau by his concubine Timna. The most important of the tribes claiming descent from Amalek were the 'Ad and Thamud. 'Ad also claimed descent from Uz.

According to Arab tradition, this group of tribes first lived in the land of the Chaldeans (southern Babylonia) but left when Nimrud established the power of Assyria over the land. They migrated to Arabia and there seized Bahrein, Oman, Yemen and finally Hedjaz, were the first to settle Yathrib (Medina) and, in addition, spread to Mecca and Khaiber (see map (000). During the time of Abraham, they were expelled from Mecca by new tribes coming from the south, the Jurhum and Keturah (cf. Gn. 25:1, where Keturah appears as a wife of Abraham).

There are later Arabian traditions that when Absalom rebelled against his father, David, the latter went to Khaiber and held it with its surrounding district as a stronghold. Another tradition relates that Moses sent an expeditionary force against the Amalekites in Hedjaz.

This genealogy and history is supposed to have been brought to an end at the time of Mohammed. According to the Koran, the tribes were exterminated because of their refusal to accept Moslem monotheism.

b. **South Arabian Tribes:** Traditionally, these tribes who live in Arabia to this day, claim descent from a remote ancestor, Qahtan, son of 'Abîr, son of Shaleh, son of Arpachshad, son of Shem, son of Noah. Qahtan may perhaps be identified with Joqtan (Gn. 10:26). Many of the other names listed as forebears are also the names of places in Arabia.

c. **North Arabian Tribes:** In Arab tradition, Ishmael occupies the place of Isaac among the Hebrews. In this version, he and Hagar were taken by Abraham to the valley where Mecca was later built and there Ishmael grew to a great nation. The well Zemz'em to which the angel Gabriel led Hagar is still shown by Arab guides in Mecca, so is mount Thabir where Abraham intended to sacrifice Isaac, and also the tombs of Hagar and Ishmael.

Ishmael was found by the Jurhum tribe who brought him up and from whom he took a wife who gave him twelve sons (cf. Gn 25:16). Among his sons were Kedar, Nebat, Dumah and Teima. The tradition does not offer a complete genealogy, but is interrupted for a number of generations until Adnan. He, it is said, was defeated by Nebuchadrezzar when the Babylonians invaded Arabia.

All northern Arabian Ishmaelite tribes claim descent from Adnan. One of them, Kureish, took Mecca from the Kura who controlled it. Later on, with the appearance of Mohammed, who was a member of the Kureish, his tribe gained control of the whole of Arabia.

The Arabs in the Bible: The Bible contains many references to north and south Arabia, but their authenticity has often been doubted and, in any case, they are not very informative. The only recognizable South-Arabian tribal states mentioned are Saba (Sheba) and Hazarmaveth, both of them believed to be related to Israel.

The first time Arabian peoples are mentioned is in the list of nations in Genesis 10:7 which apparently includes the south Arabian tribes claiming descent from Cush as well as the Joqtanite genealogy in Gn. 10:26–30. The northern Arabian peoples descended from Abraham, Keturah and Hagar are listed in Genesis 25 and additional Arab names appear among the sons of Esau (Gn. 36). Other descendants of Abraham, Midianites equated with Ishmaelites, play an incidental part in the beginning of the Joseph story (Gn. 37:25–36) but there is no record of formal contact between Israelite and Arab until Solomon's time (see above).

Later still, the accepted attitude towards Arabs is expressed by Isaiah and Jeremiah. Jeremiah (3:2) condemns Israelite apostasy as being that of a harlot who at "the waysides has sat awaiting lovers like an Arab in the wilderness;" while Isaiah 13:20 predicts that when the overthrown Babylonia is left desolate, "no Arab will pitch his tent there, no shepherds will make their flocks lie down there." Both these verses refer to nomadic tent-dwellers, Jeremiah stressing their reputation as highway robbers and Isaiah recalling the repeated nomadic invasions of Babylonia. These are confirmed by Assyrian records and apparently formed a serious menace to the settled inhabitants.

III. SUMMARY: Although the picture of Arabia before the rise of Islam (early 7th c. CE), is incomplete, a general outline can be gained from the records available. The civilization which spread from south Arabia northwards lasted for a thousand years and made a lasting impact on the life of the whole Arabian peninsula. Further north, Nabatean* civilization (see article) developed out of Mesopotamian and Aramaic traditions and later expanded across the whole of Central Arabia, helped by the decay of the south Arabian kingdoms (e. g. the Himyarites). In time, both civilizations disappeared and between the 4th and 6th c. CE a nomadic tribal pattern established itself over the whole country, except for a few centres where traces of the ancient civilizations lingered. Vestiges also survived among the nomads in their languages, social organization and attitude to the traditions of a rich cultural past. There was no relapse into total barbarism. This probably explains the vital response to the teaching and organization brought to the nomads by Mohammed.

ARAMEANS. — *Outline: I. Origins. II. Biblical Traditions Concerning the Early Arameans: Laban. III. The Aramean Kingdoms and Israel: Aram-Zobah and Its Satellites; Aram-Damascus; Conflicts with Aram-Damascus; A United Aram; Hazael; The Decline of Aram; Period of Assyrian Conquest; The Collapse of Damascus; The Province of Trans-Euphrates. IV. Religion and Culture: Religion; Language; Cultural Influences; Aramaic-Speaking Peoples.*

"Aramean" is the generic name for a number of west-Semitic tribes or national groups who, early in the 1st mill. BCE, spread through the Fertile Crescent from Elam* in the east to Cilicia in Asia Minor (see map **192**), from the edges of the Armenian highlands in the north, to the Syrian and Arabian deserts in the south.

I. ORIGINS: Their earliest origins are still disputed. The Bible refers to their origins in Genesis, then to their fortunes in the historical books. In the patriarchal traditions of Genesis, the Arameans appear as a group of clans or tribes sharing origins, language and traditions with the earliest ancestors of the Hebrews. However, these traditions are more relevant to a consideration of the Hebrews' ideas about their own ancestry than to that of the Arameans (see below, part II). Some ten centuries later, in the historical period of the Iron Age, the Aramean kingdoms reappear in the biblical sources, side-by-side with the early Israelite monarchy. As a way of relating the two, the Bible assumes that the kingdoms are the direct continuation of the semi-nomadic "Arameans" of Nahor and Harran in northwestern Mesopotamia (see Patriarchs*), referred to in the patriarchal genealogies. The biblical narrators, however, do not attempt to link the two. The actual history of Aramean development from the Bronze Age can be better traced through extra-biblical sources.

In the 12th c. BCE Assyrian cuneiform inscriptions of Tiglat-Pileser I, the Arameans are mentioned by name, among other west-Semitic tribes, as a relatively recent ethnic group, living west of Assyria, between the western bank of the Euphrates and Palmyra in the Syrian desert. They had apparently established a number of fortified cities, which suggests that they had settled there from an early date.

The evidence of ancient sources earlier than this is too scanty for any definite conclusions about their origins to be reached. In cuneiform texts of the late 3rd and early 2nd mill. BCE, a locality known as "Aram", a people, the "Aramu", and proper names including the word "Aram" are connected with the region of Eshnunna, east of the Tigris river, a long distance from their later home. Some scholars believe that the later Arameans were nevertheless connected to the earlier "Aramu", although other scholars feel that the early references are to groups of related peoples, rather than to a single people. Against these views, another school of thought concludes, from the fact that the Arameans appear to have belonged mainly to the valley of the upper Habur and the region of Harran (northwestern Mesopotamia) and never to areas east of the Tigris, that there is no connection between the two.

Extra-biblical evidence, apparently, cannot determine the exact origins of the Arameans. However, it may help in tracing the likely stages of their rising importance in the ancient Near East. Akhlami semi-nomadic tribes are first mentioned in 18th c. BCE documents from Mari*, west of Babylonia. Assyrian documents of the 14th c. BCE refer to wars between the Assyrians and Akhlamu. The names Akhlamu and Arameans are combined, two centuries later, in an explicit reference to "Akhlami-'aramaya" semi-nomadic groups living in the Syrian desert and on the island of Bahrein. The Assyrian kings fought some fierce battles against them — all in places west of Assyria, towards the mountains of Bishri and around Palmyra. However, this reference does not necessarily identify the Akhlami with the Arameans. It may merely indicate some relationship or alliance between the two peoples in the first stages of Aramean settlement and expansion.

II. BIBLICAL TRADITIONS CONCERNING THE EARLY ARAMEANS: The book of Genesis (10:22–23; 22:20–24; 24:10; 27:43 ff; 29:1) emphasizes the close relationship between the early Hebrews and a nomadic Aramean people, recording ancient patriarchal traditions about Aramean and Hebrew ancestors moving about together between Aram-Naharayim and Canaan, living around certain cities in Aram-Naharayim, i.e. the upper Habur and Haran, and in the land of the "people of the

192

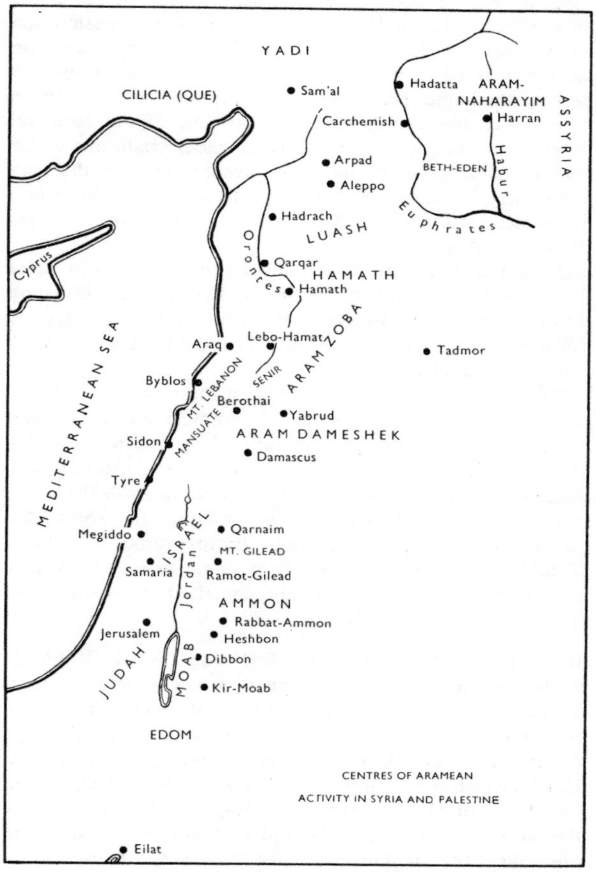

CENTRES OF ARAMEAN ACTIVITY IN SYRIA AND PALESTINE

East" (the Bᵉne-Qedem). These traditions place the settlement of the Arameans in Aram-Naharayim (or Padan-Aram) in the very earliest phase of the patriarchal period. That "a wandering Aramean was my father" (Dt. 26:5) remains one of the best known Hebrew traditions. A number of unrelated biblical genealogical lists (which relate to various periods) assume consanguinity and common existence for the two peoples from patriarchal times until the point where Arameans and Israelites divided and settled in separate, distant regions (see Patriarchs*).

The oldest of these traditions is that of Naḥor, Abraham's brother, one of the "fathers of many nations" (Gn. 22:20–24). The list of his offspring offers a glimpse of ancient historical traditions about a group of dominant semi-nomadic tribes in Syria and northwestern Mesopotamia around the 18th–17th cs. BCE. In this list, Aram is the grandson of Nahor (son of his son, Kemuel), while the other names of his "children" range over a vast area from Harran to Tebah and Tahash in the valley of Lebanon and Ma'acah, an area of northern Transjordan.

Laban: Another of Naḥor's children, Bethuel, was the father of Rebekah, Jacob's mother. A second tradition (Gn. 27:43 ff) gives her brother, Laban, the father of Leah and Rachel, the wives of Jacob, an eminent position as one of the forebears of the Israelite clans. He is also the namesake and ancestor of the Aramean clans and their kin, the Bᵉne Qedem (People of the East), other nomadic tribes living in the area between Harran and eastern Transjordan. Later in the story, (Gn 31) Laban and Jacob made a covenant at Mount Gilead, fixing the boundaries of their respective territories. These traditions were, of course, recorded much later, after the Conquest and settlement of the Israelites in Canaan, but they continue much older traditions which had been transmitted orally for generations. At the very least, they indicate the attitude of later Israelite historians to successive stages of development in relations between Israel and Aram.

Such traditions are hardly history in the modern sense but they are a valid indication of the Amorite (Western Semitic) framework which provided a common background for the "Sons of Nahor" (see above) and Abraham's kinsfolk and descendants.

The possible implication of this, in the view of B. Mazar, as regards the actual history of Aramean origins, is that there was in fact a close ethnic connection between the Aramean "patriarchs" of Genesis and the Amorites who settled in the region of Harran and Aram-Naharayim. This has prompted M. Noth to describe the whole clan of the Hebrew patriarchs as "Proto-Arameans". Thus, if biblical traditions tell us little about the early history of the Arameans, they are a valid contribution to the vexed question of Hebrew origins.

III. THE ARAMEAN KINGDOMS AND ISRAEL. A coherent history of the Aramean people — as with others in the Near East — begins with their settlement in western Mesopotamia (the valley of the Habur) and Syria. Although much earlier the district of western Mesopotamia around Harran which eventually became known as Aram-Naharayim, had been ruled by western Semites, possibly kindred of the Arameans, between 1500 and 1270 BCE, it was absorbed into the Mitanni kingdom (see Assyria*). However, in the 12th c. BCE there was change in the balance of power throughout the area. The Hittite empire broke up into smaller kingdoms; Egyptian power and influence in Syria and Canaan declined and the Mitanni (see map of Assyria*) kingdom slowly disintegrated. The situation gave the Arameans their opportunity. They streamed into the border areas of the Mesopotamian kingdoms, regaining control of the area of Aram-Naharayim and going westwards to settle throughout northern and southern Syria, where they established themselves especially around Tadmor (Palmyra) in central Syria and in Damascus.

Early in the 11th c. BCE, Tiglat-Pileser I (see Assyria*) fought a series of campaigns against the Arameans, but he could not prevent them from taking possession of whole areas of his dominions, establishing their control of the caravan routes — the life-lines of the ancient Near East — and eventually setting up ruling dynasties in all the countries they had conquered. After the death of Tiglat-Pileser I (1076 BCE) Assyria declined, putting the Arameans in an even stronger position. Babylonia made some show of resistance to them, but it is clear from inscriptions of the 11th c. BCE that the invaders had no great difficulty in establishing their ascendance there, too. Soon the Arameans formed a prosperous group of settled communities, becoming a dominant power throughout western Mesopotamia and southern Syria and, at the same time, the greatest traders of the ancient Middle East.

Aram-Zobah and Its Satellites: One of the kingdoms of the Arameans was Aram-Zobah in southern Syria, ruled by the dynasty of Beth-rehob. At the end of the 11th and beginning of the 10th c. BCE, these kings established a federation of Aramean and western Semitic kingdoms in Syria and northern Transjordan (cf. II Sam. 8:3; 10:16; I Ch. 19:10) including the Aramean district of Damascus and allied areas in Transjordan: Ma'acah, the land of Tob and Ammon. This gave Aram-Zobah control of an area from the valley of Lebanon and Gilead in Transjordan, to the Aramean tribes "across the Euphrates". It also sought to gain control of the caravan routes of east Transjordan, but here the Arameans came face to face with the rising strength of David's Israel. David* conquered all their territories from the Jordan to the borders of the Hittite kingdom of Hamath, Aram-Zobah's traditional enemy, thus making Israel, for a brief period, the strongest power between Hamath and Egypt. Even Hamath established political and economic links with Israel and (II Sam. 8:9–11) acknowledged David's suzeraity over southern and north-eastern Syria as far as the Euphrates. This was the empire which Solomon inherited and enlarged in political and economic power.

Aram-Damascus: After the division of Solomon's kingdom and the period of weakness which followed Shishak's invasion, (see Israel and Judah*, Part III) the Arameans of the ancient land of Uppe, between western Lebanon and the Syrian desert, broke away from the imperial power of the house of David (I K. 11:23–25). Ruled by Hezion (I K. 15:18), a new Aramean state of Aram-Damascus became the most important kingdom in Syria, filling the place formerly occupied by Aram-Zobah. It is referred to both as Aram and as Damascus, meaning, in each case, the state immediately to the north of Israel.

Conflicts with Aram-Damascus: After the decline of Solomon's empire, hostilities between the two states continued almost without interruption for some 150 years. None of the eight campaigns undertaken was conclusive. In general, Aram-Damascus merely took advantage of the division between Israel and Judah and intervened in their conflict whenever this appeared likely to be of benefit. At the time that Asa of Judah was fighting Ba'asha of Israel, Hadad of Damascus attacked Israel and occupied the fortified cities of Naphtali (I K. 15:18–20) and "sixty towns" in northern Transjordan (I Ch. 2:23).

During the reign of Omri, Aramean pressure towards the sea was renewed and continued, until, finally, Israel made a treaty with Aram-Damascus (I K. 20:34) granting it special economic privileges in Samaria. Later on, when Ahab ruled in Samaria, these were repaid by similar concessions for the Israelites who were given the right to open bazaars in Damascus.

A United Aram: However, Ahab had to face continued attacks from Aram-Damascus; it now aimed to control Israel as a counter-measure to encroachments on Aramean territory by the Assyrians under Shalmaneser III (857–835 BCE; see Assyria*). Aram is described in the Bible as a single unified country and no mention is made of any satellite states. Unification was mainly the work of Ben Hadad II of Damascus, who absorbed all the satellite kingdoms into a single united Aram-Damascus. Its capital, Damascus, "the famous city, the joyful city" (Jer. 49:25), became the centre of a large kingdom with an effective civil and military organization controlling all the major lines of communication of western Asia. The unity of the state was further aided by the spread of Aramaic as the official language of business and administration throughout the area (see below).

Ben Hadad II — (Hadadezer — Addad Idiri in Assyrian inscriptions) initiated two unsuccessful campaigns against Israel, then reached an agreement with Ahab, who joined the anti-Assyrian coalition formed of twelve kingdoms of the area, led by Damascus and including Phoenicia, at the battle of Qarqar (853 BCE; see Israel and Judah*, Part II). The alliance, however, needed an imminent threat from Assyria to hold it together. When that danger seemed to have lessened, the Syro-Israel alliance collapsed and Ben Hadad II attacked again and inflicted a decisive defeat on the combined forces of Israel and Judah (852 BCE) at Ramot-Gilead (I K. 22:1–35), considered the key to northern Transjordan. Ahab lost his life in the encounter.

Hazael: However, Assyrian pressure had only lifted temporarily. Campaigns by Shalmaneser III in 841 and 838 BCE left Aram dangerously weakened. A new ruler, Hazael, who had ascended to the throne in about 843 BCE, set up a new dynasty and, during a temporary lull in Assyrian activity (after 839 BCE) embarked upon renewed expansion. He established bridgeheads on the Euphrates and reconquered Israelite territory in Transjordan (II K. 10:32–33). Then (815–814 BCE) he launched a great expedition along the coast, reaching as far south as Gath and forcing Jehoash, king of Judah, to pay him tribute (II K. 12:17–18). A fragment of an ivory plaque **(193)** dedicated to "our lord Hazael" was found in Arslan-Tash, near an ivory inlay showing a king, perhaps Hazael.

193

The Decline of Aram: This was the peak of Damascus' greatness. Israel had been humiliated, Aram's other neighbours subdued (see map **192**). However, Assyria was once again rising to ascendancy in the Near East. Hazael was succeeded by Ben Hadad III who gradually became overlord of the whole of Syria and part of Palestine. While Jehoahaz ruled Israel, Samaria was besieged, then relieved. The extent to which the country was weakened by this is reflected in II K. 13:7.

Adad-Nirari III (see Assyria*) launched new campaigns against Aram, and Damascus' new-found dominance was wrested from it. In 802 BCE the city was besieged and the king forced to pay tribute to the Assyrians, along with Israel and other southern kingdoms. The severe blows inflicted by Adad-Nirari weakened Aram's strength and the kingdom entered a period of decline. By the time the Assyrians were forced to turn their attention to events nearer home — mainly increasingly severe attacks by the Urartu (see Assyria*) — Damascus fell an easy prey to Jeroboam II of Israel (see Israel and Judah*, Part III). Jeroboam extended his borders right into Syria as far as Hamath, making Damascus, for a short time, one of his possessions. The Syrian state split into a number of small kingdoms. One of them, Arpad to the north, took over the leading position in the area. After Jeroboam's death, Damascus broke away from Israel and became independent once more under a new king, Rezin, but he could not restore its old supremacy.

Period of Assyrian Conquest: Assyria was now embarked in earnest upon the path to empire. A series of campaigns in northern Syria was undertaken by Tiglat-Pileser III. In 739 BCE, Arpad fell, but the north Syrian states fought on, this time under the leadership of Azariah, king of Judah (see Israel and Judah*, Part IV). The coalition was nevertheless defeated. Northern Syria and the seacoast were organized into the Assyrian province of Trans-Euphrates, while the southern kings, Menahem of Samaria and Rezin of Damascus, paid tribute to Tiglat-Pileser.

The Collapse of Damascus: Under Rezin, Damascus enjoyed a brief recovery, rising again to become the political centre of "Aram-Damascus". Once Tiglat-Pileser and his armies had withdrawn, Rezin set about organizing a new alliance in opposition to Assyria. Pekah of Israel joined in (see Israel and Judah*, Part IV), but the king of Judah, Ahaz, refused. Rezin and his ally, Pekah, immediately attacked and Ahaz appealed to Tiglat-Pileser for help against them. The Assyrians responded with a new campaign in which Israel was subdued and ravaged and Damascus taken (732 BCE). Rezin was executed and large numbers of his subjects deported, while Damascus was transformed into an Assyrian stronghold.

The Province of Trans-Euphrates: Northern Syria and the seacoast were organized into Assyrian districts. Aram-Damascus remained the province of Trans-Euphrates throughout the later Assyrian period. Afterwards, it formed the fifth satrapy of the Persian empire. When it was conquered by the Greeks, however (see Hellenism in the Near East*), its name became Syria, after "Athyra", the Persian name for northern Syria. Syria became the western region of the Seleucid empire which later also included Palestine and Judea. The southern area which bordered on Palestine was known as Coele-Syria (pronounced Koile-Syria) and as such often appears in Palestinian annals of the early 4th c. BCE and thereafter (see Hasmoneans*).

IV. RELIGION AND CULTURE. **Religion:** The traditional deity of the Arameans was Hadad, to whose name the Aramean epithet "Raman" came to be attached. The Bible made this "Rimmon" (the vocalization is artificial, probably under the influence of the Hebrew word for pomegranate). Zechariah (12:11) refers to the traditional ceremony of the "mourning for Hadad-rimmon in the plain of Megiddo" which took place regularly there. Megiddo was an Assyrian district capital and the cult of Hadad-rimmon had been carried there from Damascus.

194

195

196

Hadad-rimmon later became identified with Jupiter and his temple, rededicated to Jupiter Damascenus, was famous for centuries. (It is now covered by the huge Omayad Mosque.) This may have been the royal temple referred to in II Kings (5:18) as the "house of Rimmon". Its altar of holocausts was copied for the Jerusalem Temple by the priest Uriah, on the orders of King Ahaz of Judah (II K. 16:10–13; II Ch. 28:23).

Ben Hadad, the name of several of the kings of Damascus, also probably originated in the religious relationship between the rulers and their god. Hadad's title, Rimmon or "Ramman" was also used as a compound in theophonic names like Tab-Rimmon, son of Hezion, king of Aram.

In addition to Hadad, the Arameans worshipped the other gods of the western Semitic pantheon, as shown by this relief of the god of war (**194**) from the outer citadel gate at Zenjirli dating from the 9th c. BCE, and by this sculpture of a mythical being between two lions (**196**).

Language: Various dialects were spoken in Syria, but the form of Aramean as it was written and spoken in Damascus became the official language of the whole kingdom of Ben Hadad II, from the southern borders of Sam'al in the north (as shown by the stele of Nerab (**195**) inscribed in Aramaic and dating to the 7th c. BCE). Inscriptions in this language from the 9th c. BCE show that it was written in a distinctive script which differed from contemporary Phoenician* (see Alphabet and Writing*). When Assyrian rule over Trans-Euphrates was consolidated, this form of Aramaic was adopted as one of the official languages of the Assyrian empire. As "imperial Aramaic", the language became the *lingua franca*, the international language of business, diplomacy and administration in the Assyrian and Babylonian empires of the 8th to the 6th cs. BCE. After the collapse of Babylonia, the official language of the whole of the Persian empire remained this imperial Aramaic, spoken from Ethiopia to India. It is akin to the Aramaic of certain chapters of Ezra* (see Languages, Biblical*).

Cultural Influences: Altogether the cultural effects of the unification of the Aramean kingdoms were felt through a wide area and particularly in Israel and Judah. From the time of David to the end of the Omride dynasty, the main influence on Palestine had come from Phoenicia. From the 8th c. BCE on, economic, political and social pressures from Damascus provided a new force, bringing with it "the eclectic culture of the Aram kingdom, which blended ancient Syrian with Phoenician and neo-Hittite elements and also absorbed a constant stream of material and spiritual influences from Assyria." (B. Mazar). The effects of this influence can be seen throughout Israelite life, amply demonstrated both by biblical literature and from archaeological excavations.

197

Aramaic-Speaking Peoples: In fact, Aramaic cultural influence spread over a much wider geographical area. Aramaic was the language of the Nabatean* people who lived to the south of Palestine and Transjordan, leaving inscriptions in an Aramaic script which can be dated from the 2nd c. BCE to the 2nd CE (see article). In addition, the people of Palmyra (biblical Tadmor) as shown here **(197)** also carved inscriptions in Aramaic between the 1st and 4th cs. CE. Northern Syria became Christian early in the latter era and a large Christian literature exists in the Aramaic dialect called Syriac (see Translations of the Bible*).

198

ARMS, WEAPONS AND MILITARY EQUIPMENT. — *Outline: I. Arms in the Ancient Near East. Late 4th Mill. BCE; Early Bronze Age; Middle Bronze Age; War-Chariots in the Pre-Israelite Period; Body Armour. II. Biblical Weapons: a. Defensive Weapons: Shields; Armour; b. Offensive Weapons: Bows; Arrows; Slings; War Axes; Swords; Battering Rams; Israelite Armaments. III. Assyrian Armour: Siege Engines; Cavalry and Chariots; Armour and Weapons. IV. Developments from the 5th c. BCE to the 2nd c. CE: Persian Era; Hellenistic Equipment; Hellenistic Siegecraft; Seleucid War Elephants; Roman Period: Roman Siege Equipment; Military Terminology in the Qumran "War Scroll".*

Weapons were among the first tools created by man in his struggle for survival. At first they were used for hunting and defence against wild animals; later, for war between man and man. The first weapons of the prehistoric age were made of stone and similar ones continued to be used long into the historical period. Bronze and copper weapons began to be made during the 4th mill. BCE. Iron weapons were introduced into Palestine by the Philistines* at the end of the 2nd mill. BCE, but were not widely used by the Israelites until the time of the monarchy.

I. ARMS IN THE ANCIENT NEAR EAST: **Late 4th Mill. BCE:** Discoveries dating to the Chalcolithic Age (end 4th mill. BCE) indicate that the main weapon of that time was the war club or mace made of a wooden handle with a heavy stone or copper head. Sometimes the head was of hematite, apparently imported from Egypt. Metal weapons, very rare there earlier, began to come into widespread use in Egypt in the late 4th mill. BCE. King Nar-Mer (1st Dynasty) is shown smiting an Asiatic with a mace **(198)**. Maces with bronze heads were found in the Beersheba area, while dozens of mace heads of different types made of stone, copper and hematite have been recovered from caves of the wilderness of Judah (especially near Nahal Mishmar).

Early Bronze Age (3rd Mill. BCE): During this period, new types of weapons appeared, illustrated in contemporary representations from Mesopotamia and Egypt (see below) which show that different types of weapons developed in each area. The bow, used for war and hunting, was known in Egypt from the beginning of the Early Bronze Age (perhaps even earlier), whereas it was only introduced into Mesopotamia at the very end of the period (see Part II, Bows) by the conquering (Semitic) Akkadians. Sumerian soldiers were armed with scaled breastplates and heavy helmets and used the mace or club and axe as their main weapons. At an early stage, the axe heads were made with sharp, narrow edges, designed to cut through armour. Some of the Sumerian reliefs show war chariots, but these were too clumsy to have been of much practical use. They had wooden wheels without any protective hubs and were drawn by onagers or wild asses. The warriors who stood in such chariots stabbed at the enemy with long spears or launched javelins against them. Foot soldiers included lancers and archers. The infantry would be formed into a massive phalanx, each member protected by a curved, rectangular shield and bearing a long spear. The earliest representations known come from the end of the dynasty of Akkad (24th c. BCE). Naram-Sin, one of the kings of this dynasty (see

200

Babylonia*) pictures himself on his celebrated Stele of Victory (**199**) as armed with bow and quiver, battle axe and mace. The 25th c. BCE mosaic "Standard of Ur", showing the triumph of a king over his enemies, also gives a good picture of the weapons of the age (**200**). One of the war chariots is shown in the upper left, driven by a helmeted soldier carrying an axe and drawn by onagers. In front of the chariot stand a groom and three soldiers who carry axes and spears. Soldiers with short spears and wearing helmets can be seen in the middle register — the helmets were of leather or metal, depending on rank. In the lower register, four chariots are shown charging over a battlefield strewn with corpses

Nothing is known about the techniques of siege warfare in early Mesopotamia, but there is an Egyptian relief from this period, showing soldiers scaling ladders fixed to a city's walls and battering at the gate with long beams. Their only motive power was that provided by the soldiers, but they are the forerunners of later, more sophisticated, battering rams.

In 3rd mill. BCE Palestine, the main weapon was a straight, rather long sword made of bronze. These were hardened by alternately heating and cooling the bar of metal, then beating it out to form the blade which was nailed on to a hilt. Swords of this type have so far been discovered at the southern Tel el-Fariah, Tel Nasbeh, Lachish*, Megiddo*, Jericho* and in Givatayim near Tel Aviv. Y. Yadin believes that such swords were used exclusively in Palestine. The other weapons of this period found in Palestine are of the same type as those found throughout the ancient Near East. Later on, the bronze swords of Palestine acquired a short pin joining the hilt to the blade (see below, War Axes).

A group of copper weapons (**201**) discovered in the lowest levels of the Canaanite city Tel-el-Hesi includes an axehead

199

202

shaped like a crescent, belonging to the same period as the axeheads found in Early Bronze Jericho* (marked 1 in the picture; 2–5 are the heads from Tel el-Hesi).

Spear heads with two narrow holes in the centre at the bottom were also found at Tel el-Hesi and Jericho. Apparently the blade was tied onto the shaft by thongs passed through the holes.

A very interesting collection of 37 instruments and weapons belonging to the beginning of the early Bronze Age, all made of copper and remarkably well preserved, was discovered at Kefar Monash in the Sharon plain in 1962 CE. Similar weapons have been found in Mesopotamia, Syria and Asia Minor.

Middle Bronze Age: The weapons found in Palestine from the first centuries of the Middle Bronze Age (2100–1900 BCE) appear to form two groups. One group continued the traditions of the earlier period, especially the bronze swords, although these were now made without a pin or with only a small one. Slightly different weapons, apparently imported from the countries to the north, have been found in Northern Palestine, notably in the tombs of Tel-Ajjul near Gaza (ancient Beth-Eglaim) in Lachish*, Jericho*, Megiddo* and Beth-Shean*. These imported weapons included bronze swords similar to the indigenous ones, but made with an appreciably protruding pin, and round bladed spear heads complete with a long twisted tang to fasten the head onto the shaft.

War-Chariots in the pre-Israelite Period: The most important development during the first two or three centuries of the 2nd mill. BCE was the introduction of horse-drawn war chariots into Palestine. The first evidence for the use of chariots drawn by horses comes from the Mari documents of the 18th–17th c. BCE, but very little is known about the process of their introduction. Many scholars connect the appearance of the chariots with the Hyksos invaders who are believed to have introduced horses into the area. The chariot seems to have reached Egypt via Canaan, for many Egyptian terms connected with chariots are derived from Canaanite words. Chariots first appear on Egyptian and Mesopotamian monuments of the 16th c. BCE and are already quite advanced in design. Different types appear to have been used by different peoples. Egyptian war chariots were lightly built, pulled by two horses and carried two men, the charioteer and an archer. The Hittites, however, used heavier chariots which could carry three men. The weight of the chariot can be inferred from the number of spokes in the wheels and, on this evidence, there was a tendency towards heavier chariots near the end of the period. In the early chariots, among the Egyptians and the Canaanites of Palestine, the wheels had four spokes. Later chariots had wheels with six spokes. This painting (**202**) from the tomb of Tutankh-Amon (14th cent. BCE) shows the king standing in his chariot with drawn bow, leading his troops into battle against Asiatics. Thanks to their long axles and large springy wheels, the Egyptian chariots could be used over almost any type of country.

The Bible also refers frequently to the "iron chariots" of the Philistines (presumably chariots with iron-rimmed wheels see Roads*) and to chariots for war use, (Jos. 17:18; Jud. 1:19; 4:3; I K. 10:26; II Ch. 9:25, passim; see above) also to the "mekhonot" or anti-siege engines fitted on the walls of cities as part of their defences.

Body Armour: The earliest information about the use of body armour in Egypt and Palestine, (introduced in the early 2nd mill. BCE), comes from the middle of that millenium, although it was known to the Sumerians several centuries earlier. The armour was generally made of metal scales rounded at the ends and sewn on to linen or leather linings. One suit of armour could have as many as a thousand such scales. In addition to armour, the warriors of the period also wore metal helmets, while it appears from documents discovered in Ugarit* (15th — 14th c. BCE) that horses were also given a special protective armour.

II. BIBLICAL WEAPONS: Warfare was the background to so much of the Bible that a large number of weapons are mentioned there, although by no means all the wide variety now known to have been in use in the area. Those referred to in the Bible can be classified generally as offensive or defensive.

a. **Defensive Weapons: Shields:** The warriors of the Israelite tribes and their later descendants during the monarchy are recorded to have carried shields of various shapes and sizes, often a buckler, usually made of layers of leather stretched over a wooden frame, known variously as the "magen" (Jud. 5:8; II Sam. 1:21; II K. 19:32 and elsewhere) or the "tsinnah" (Ezk. 23:24; I Ch. 12:8; II Ch. 14:8 passim).

201

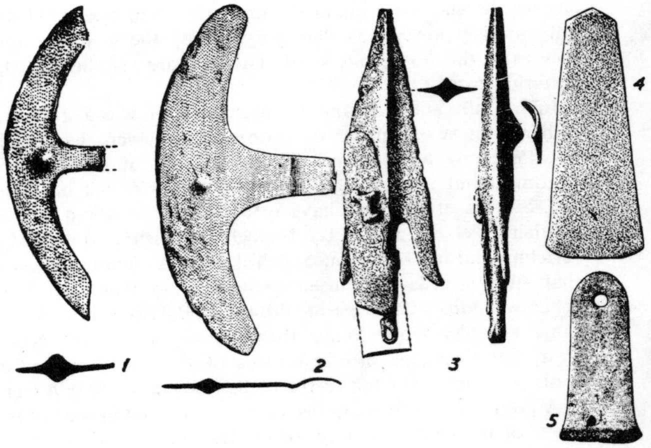

These terms are apparently synonymous with the "soherah", from its name presumably a round shield, like those pictured on the Assyrian bas-relief, 7th c. BCE (**203**), and perhaps also with the small circular shield called "shelet" (rondache); (II K. 11:10; II Ch. 23:9; Jer. 51:11).

Armour: The soldiers wore armour which included the "shiryon" or breastplate — a leather or heavy linen shirt covered with metal scales — (I K. 22:34; II Ch. 18:33, passim), and a helmet, "koba'", generally of bronze (I Sam. 17:5; II Ch. 26:14). Nothing is known about the shape of Hebrew helmets, although there are plenty of illustrations of those of other peoples such as the Assyrians (**203**).

b. **Offensive Weapons:** These were for short-range (hand-to-hand) fighting; medium range and long range. The fundamental weapons for hand-to-hand fighting are those actually carried by the soldiers, whether the most elementary, the throw-stick (Ezk. 39:9), the "mâfetz" (**198**; Pr. 25:18), one of the names of the war club or mace; the poleaxe or other battle axe and, most essential, the dagger or short sword. This was carried by every warrior close to his body (Jud. 4:16; I Sam. 25:13; Ps. 45:3, passim).

Medium range weapons were those designed to keep the enemy from getting too close, like the "rômaḥ" or spear (Nu. 25:7; Jud. 5:8; Jer. 46:4), made of a long heavy pole with a sharp pointed metal head, for instance these bronze spearheads from Gezer (**204**). In this class, the most important weapons were those designed to be thrown at the enemy, like the "ḥānît" or light weight javelin (1 Sam. 13:19; 21:8; 26:16, 22; II Sam. 23:7, 21; Na. 3:3, etc.). These javelin heads (**205**) are also from Gezer. The Bible also mentions the "qâ'in", lance or spear (II Sam. 21:16) and the "shelaḥ", short spear or javelin (II Ch. 23:9; Neh. 4:13) whose nature has not been determined for certain. The "kidôn" (Jos. 8:18, 26; I Sam. 17:7, 45; Jer. 6:23) used to be interpreted as a weapon like the javelin, i.e. a long pole with a sharply pointed head such as the javelin heads from Gezer, referred to above. Recently, following additional descriptions of the "kidôn" found in the "Scroll of the War between the Children of Light and the Children of Darkness" (see Dead Sea Scrolls*, and end of article), Y. Yadin has concluded that a "kidôn" may have been no more than a sword one and a half cubits long and four finger-breadths wide (see Weights and Measures*). This scroll includes the descriptions of a number of other weapons and items of military equipment and helped to identify many Old Testament terms in the light of their meaning in the later period.

Bows: The outstanding weapon for long-range fighting was the bow and arrow. Arrows were carried in a quiver called the "ashpah" (Is. 22:6) or "tlî" (Gn. 27:3). The references in the Bible to bows and arrows are very numerous, using, in Hebrew, a wide variety of verbs for the actions involved (Gn. 21:20; 49:23; II K. 9:24; I Ch. 5:18; 10:3; Is. 66:19; Am. 2:15; Jer. 4:29; 46:9; Ps. 7:13; 76:3; 78:9; Is. 5:28; 21:15). Bows were of the "long-bow" type (**795**). When action was imminent, they were strung by resting the bottom on the ground and pressing it down with the foot, while bending the top down to fit the bowstring into a notch, an action called in Hebrew "darokh keshet" or "stepping on the bow" (Jer. 50:14; Is. 5:28; 21:15; Ps. 7:12).

203

204

205

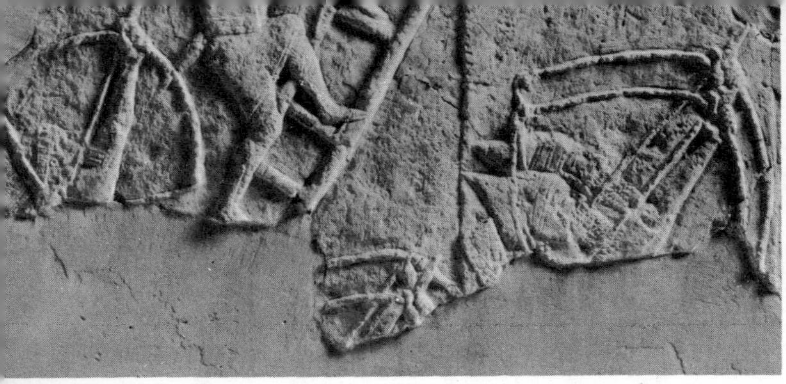

206

208

Bronze axe-heads (a) Early Bronze Age, c. 2500 BCE; (b) (c) Middle Bronze Age 1900–1600 BCE; (d) Late Bronze Age 1600–1200 BCE.

209

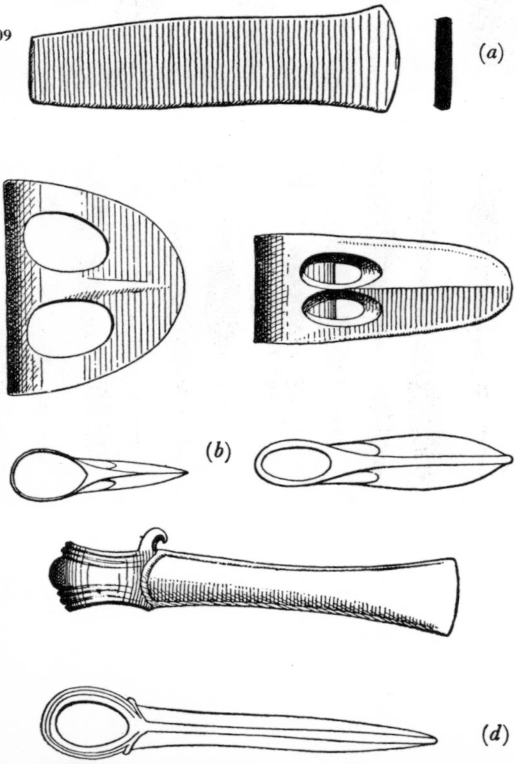

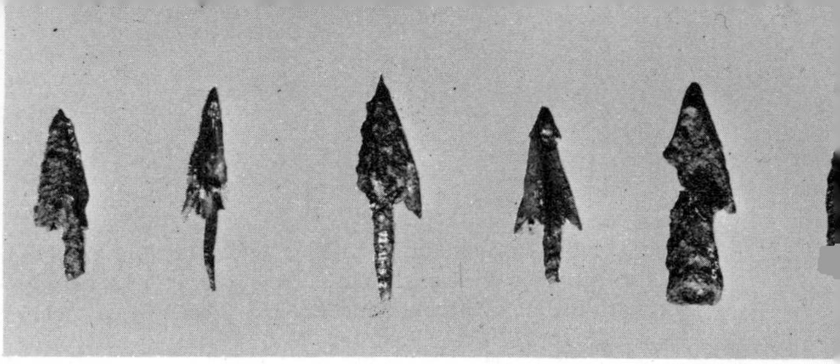

207

The early bows, in use since the 3rd mill. BCE (see Part I, Early Bronze Age) were very simply made, long, probably heavy, and with only a short range. A smaller, lighter bow with a more elastic bow-string began to be made in the 2nd mill. BCE. The bow-strings were made from dried guts of oxen or sheep, later of camels. These bows, known as composite bows **(206)**, triangular or double arched in shape, were made of strips of horn and wood glued together and then bound with bark. The arrow was shot by pulling the bow-string and the body of the bow in opposite directions, thus setting up a powerful tension which gave the bows a much greater range and made them formidable weapons. This fact is important in understanding the text of the Ugarit* legends, where bows figure prominently.

Arrows: Arrows were also improved. The introduction of the cuirass (or solid breastplate) as part of the improved armour of the foot-soldier demanded a much stronger, sharper arrow able to penetrate the metal without snapping. Iron arrow-heads with a triangular tip **(207)**, as shown, were the answer to this need. By the end of the monarchy in Palestine (6th c. BCE) three-bladed arrow tips, originating in the north, had been adopted and their use became general during the Hellenistic period.

Slings: The other long-range weapon was the "qela' " or sling, with which David slew Goliath (I Sam. 17:40). The sling was made of two leather thongs with a wider pocket between them into which a sling stone like these **(213)** found in an Israelite town, was fitted. The sling was then whirled round and round to get the necessary impetus and the stone thrown by releasing one of the thongs (I Sam. 25:29; Zech. 9:15; Job 41:28, passim).

War Axes: The invention of the cuirass to protect the body also prompted developments in the other standard infantry weapons, especially the battle axe. At the beginning of the 2nd mill. BCE axes were still made with long cutting blades but, later on, the blades became narrower and sharper like those found in Gezer **(208)**, made to cleave through even the metal of a cuirass. The development of the war axe shown in the diagram has been illustrated by a whole series **(209)** dating from the Early Bronze (ca. 2500 BCE) to the Late Bronze Age (1600–1200 BCE) found in Phoenicia, near Sidon, at Byblos and in Ugarit. Another example **(210)**, similar to Hittite axes but in the shape of an open human hand was discovered in Beth-Shean.

210

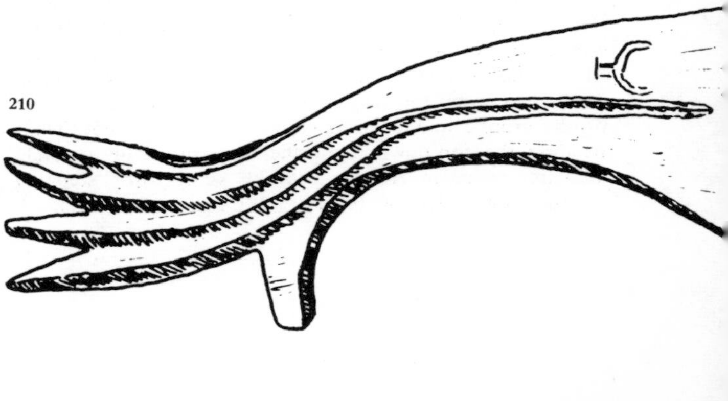

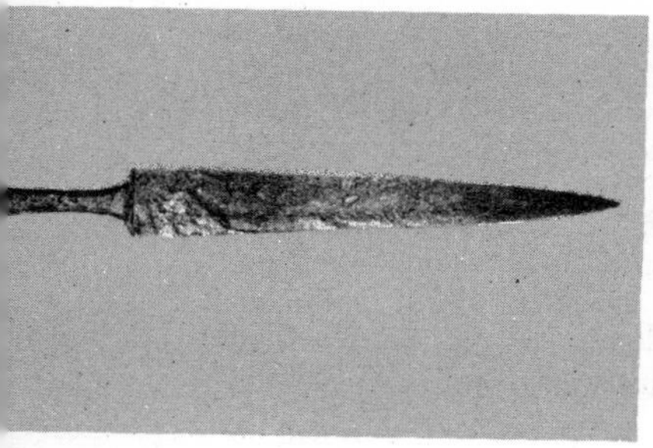

211

212

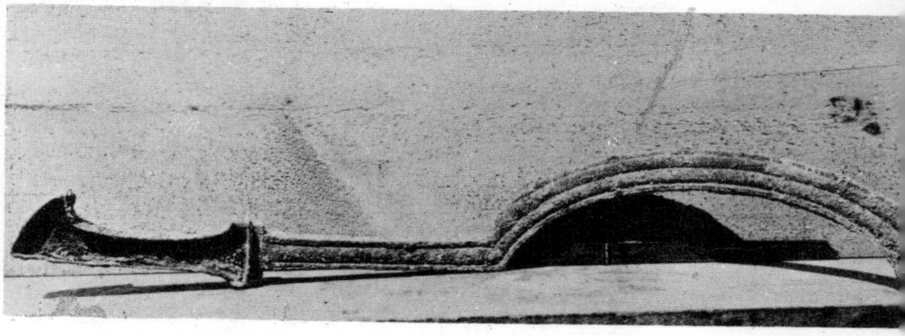

215

Swords: A similar development can be observed in the changes in swords from the curved, long-handled sword of the beginning of the 3rd mill. BCE, designed to hit and slice, and most effective in battle in quickly-moving situations (from chariots). This was the sword generally known in the literature as the sickle-sword, because of its shape (**215**). In Egypt it was called "hepesh". As the years went by, the blade grew longer until finally it developed into the familiar curved sword of the horseman. The stages in this development have also been illustrated by actual discoveries in such places as Shechem*, Gezer* and Byblos (see Phoenicia*), as well as by numerous reliefs and drawings in Egypt.

The long straight iron sword, designed to stab as well as cut was introduced by the "People of the Sea" (see Philistines*) at the end of the 2nd mill. BCE. The short daggers of this period were also strengthened by thick metal tips, to prevent them breaking off when they met armour (**211,2**).

Battering Rams: The mid-2nd mill. BCE also saw the invention of a more advanced battering ram for use in sieges. From Egyptian reliefs it seems that they only used a very primitive ram made from a simple log of wood, with a metal tip, pointed like a spear head. This was not mounted and swung like later models, but merely hurled by hand. The Mari documents, however, reveal that as early as the 18th c. BCE the Syrians were making use of much more advanced rams, often attached to towers from which archers could shoot over and onto the walls of besieged towns (see Warfare*).

Israelite Armaments: The Israelite army was first organized into fixed units at the beginning of the monarchy, under Saul and especially David, who brought in mercenary troops. Solomon was responsible, above all, for the development of chariotry, even building special "chariot cities" to house his horses (I K. 10:26). Solomon's initiative was continued after the division of the kingdom by Ahab of Israel. The famous stables at Megiddo*, once ascribed to Solomon, are now attributed to Ahab, who is credited by Shalmaneser III with putting "2,000 chariots in the field" at the battle of Qarqar in 853 BCE — the largest single force facing the Assyrians. Assyrian reliefs commemorating the capture of Palestinian cities (like **Sennacherib**'s famous monument to the siege of Lachish* in 701 BCE) show that the Israelites were using weapons similar to those of the Assyrians. At the end of the monarchy — after the fall of the Northern Kingdom of Israel — the greatly weakened kings of Judah turned all their attention to defensive armaments and their military concerns were centred above all on the fortification of their cities.

III. ASSYRIAN ARMOUR: For several centuries at the end of the 2nd mill. BCE there is a gap in our knowledge of weapon developments. However, with the reign of Ashurbanipal II of Assyria (beginning 9th c. BCE), a long series of Assyrian reliefs picturing military scenes provide a detailed record covering almost the whole of the Assyrian period. Discoveries in excavations of neo-Hittite towns in Syria have also provided information about developments in weapons (see Warfare*).

As Assyria was the foremost military power of the period, it seems reasonable to suppose that improvements in weapons were initiated by them and learned by the other countries of the area, like Anatolia, Syria and Palestine.

Assyrian reliefs of the 8th c. BCE show an army whose equipment reached such a high level of development that it can fairly be said that until the invention of gunpowder, no substantial advances were made in the style and manufacture of weapons. The main contributions of the Assyrians can be summarized under three headings:

Siege Engines: Very few of their opponents were strong or courageous enough to face the Assyrians in the open; thus most Assyrian battles were fought around walled cities. In addition to the familiar siege techniques of the 2nd mill. BCE — scaling walls on ladders, digging tunnels underneath them, or attempting to breach them with axes or fire — the Assyrians also made use of a most efficient battering ram (Ezk. 4:2; 21:22), pictured in this sculpture (**216**). They were called "rams" from their butting action, although they did not carry a ram's head like the Roman rams (see below).

213

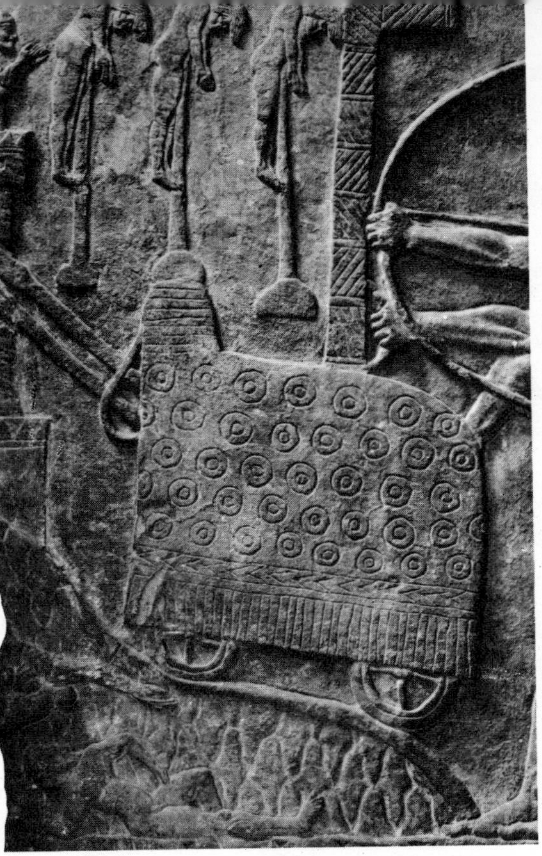

216

217

Assyrian battering rams ended either in a spear-head like the Egyptian war engines or in a flat head shod with metal. The powerful beam was suspended from the roof of a covered frame at a precisely calculated equilibrium and worked by teams of men protected by the hides stretched over the frame and under the shelter of large wooden towers mounted on four or six wheels from which archers could keep up a constant barrage against the defenders of the walls. As it could be taken apart, a battering ram of this type could easily be transported from place to place.

Cavalry and Chariots: Before the Assyrians, horses had been used in war in the Fertile Crescent only to pull chariots — it is still not clear why. The Assyrians continued to use chariots, generally quite heavy partly armoured ones with eight wheels, which were drawn by three horses and carried three or even four soldiers. However, in addition to the chariots, when the idea of mounting soldiers on horseback was introduced from outside the area — perhaps by groups of Indo-Iranians — the Assyrians were the first to adopt it and to base their strategy on this new force. A swiftly-moving cavalry was particularly effective in inaccessible, mountainous areas and, in general, cavalry and chariotry acting together gave the Assyrians an overwhelming superiority over all the other armies of their day. Cavalry was not introduced into Israel until a very much later date.

Armour and Weapons: The infantry remained the backbone of the Assyrian army. Foot soldiers were recruited from subject tribes and peoples. They were organized into the heavily armoured ordinary infantry and the more lightly protected bowmen and archers. The armour which they wore — like that placed on the war-horses — closely resembled the equipment of mediaeval armies. The infantry's main weapon was similarly the composite bow, now provided with a round socket for the arrow. Arrow-heads were barbed to speed up their flight through the air.

Short, strong iron daggers, javelins and lances of various types, as illustrated (**212**) remained in use. In addition many advances were made in the fields of logistics and military engineering. The Assyrians, for instance, learned how to cross rivers safely, and to erect a fortified camp (**217**) (right inset; at left, cavalry) protected by a variety of special devices, in a very short time.

IV. DEVELOPMENTS FROM 5th C. BCE TO 2nd CE: **Persian Era:** The weapons and equipment developed by the Assyrians continued in use among the Persians but they concentrated on training highly skilled archery units who made up the shock troops of the army. Horsemen and horses were protected by armoured breastplates and shields and the cavalrymen carried bows as well as swords. The Persian kings also introduced the use of chariots fitted with curved swords sticking out from the hubs of the wheels. Chariots like these were a very deadly weapon against massive formations of infantry. The Persians were also the first to bring war elephants from the East to western Asia and Europe, where their main use was to sow panic among the ranks of opposing infantry. The Persian empire also developed speedy and efficient transport and information systems. Fourth c. BCE armaments are dramatically illustrated in the Pompei mosaic of the battle of Issus between the Persians and Alexander (**220**).

218

Hellenistic Equipment: The first Greek mercenaries appeared in Palestine at the beginning of the 5th c. BCE. From that time until the arrival of the Romans (1st c. BCE), through the Persian and Hellenistic periods, Palestine was the scene of a series of wars fought by Greek troops, armed according to the classical Greek pattern, shown in this 6th c. BCE statuette of a warrior, wearing helmet and cuirass (**218**). The basic unit was the heavily armed infantry — the hoplytes, named after their heavy bronze shield. This was shaped like a convex rectangle and was carried by a ring in the inside centre, held in the left hand (**219**). Representations on a number of monuments suggest that this was the standard equipment of Greek soldiers even before the 7th c. BCE. The shield covered almost the whole of the soldier's body, although he also wore a breastplate, closed high-crested metal helmet and metal greaves on his legs to protect his feet. These can be seen on this carving of a dead warrior supported from behind (**221**). In his right hand he wielded the heavy iron-headed pike almost three metres long, which was his main weapon although he also carried a short iron sword. The hoplytes' battle formation was a phalanx arranged so that while the soldier's left side was covered by his own shield, his right hand was protected by his comrade's. The strength of the phalanx depended on the fortitude of the front-row soldiers, who had to meet the enemy face to face, supported (and pushed) by the soldiers of the rows behind them.

219

220

From the time of the Peleponesian war (end of the 5th c. BCE) a new class of infantry made its appearance. This was the lightly armed foot soldier who wore no body armour, carried a round shield and whose main weapon was a small javelin which he hurled at the enemy. In the Macedonian period, the pike was further lengthened to as much as six metres. In practice, the soldiers in different positions in the phalanx carried pikes of different lengths, designed to ensure that the enemy met the maximum force of pike heads at the first blow. Shields, on the other hand, were no longer so large and unwieldy. In classical times, the bow was not much used outside Crete, but in the Hellenistic age (3rd c. BCE onwards) oriental influences lent it a much more important role and mounted archers were given the task of putting up a barrage of arrows to cover the wings of the phalanx.

Chariots were never employed in Greece in classical times because of the mountainous country which makes them quite useless. Horsemen, however, were an integral part of the armies of some of the cities, especially those situated on plains.

The Macedonians were the first to develop the use of cavalry in the west during the 4th c. BCE. Later on it became a major weapon, especially when used for attacks from the wings or the rear, or for making the best use of a tactical advantage during a battle and for pursuing a fleeing enemy. Reins and stirrups — essential for manoeuvering — were introduced later still by the Parthians, while the solid saddle which is also vital for effective action, came into use during Roman times. In the later centuries BCE, chariots were also used to a limited extent.

Hellenistic Siegecraft: There is no evidence from Greek sources for the use of siege machines before the 2nd c. BCE. Before that time, fortified cities were reduced by starvation, treachery or stratagem. At the beginning of the 2nd c. BCE, however, a primitive catapult for shooting arrows at an enemy city appeared in Syracuse, Sicily. Apparently, this had been copied from the Carthaginians. Later models were much improved, with catgut and horsehair used to increase the elasticity and therefore the range of the catapult.

221

Alexander the Great first used such a contraption at the siege of Tyre (332 BCE) which is further confirmation for an origin among the Phoenicians*. Other siege engines of this period were the enormous stationary bow and the stone-thrower, with a range of 200 metres, which could also hurl fire balls, (baskets full of combustible materials) at the enemy city to set fire to its walls and defences — or could be used by a besieged city to deter attacks. These were clumsy machines but during a siege were used by both attackers and defenders.

Seleucid War Elephants: After the collapse of the Persian empire, the use of war elephants spread. Alexander the Great returned from his campaign in India with one hundred beasts and Seleucus I imported more than five hundred. At first they were used against the enemy's cavalry and were attached to units of lightly armed foot soldiers for mutual protection. Alternatively they would be stationed between the phalanxes of infantry as a cover for their wings. At the battle of Gaza (312 BCE), the Ptolemies, who had no elephants, defended themselves by covering the ground in front of the elephants with protruding nails — thus laying the first minefield in history. The Seleucids also used elephants **(222)** in their wars against the Hasmoneans. One of the five sons of Mattathias, Eliezer, was killed while stabbing one during the battle of Beth-Zechariah (I Mac. 6:43–7). This passage also provides some useful insights into how the elephants were prepared for battle. They were given juice of grapes and mulberries to drink (like race horses before a race in the Orient; I Mac. 6:34). The Romans did not make use of elephants, finding them too cumbersome a weapon.

222

223

During the Republican period (up to 44 BCE), the Roman army mainly employed improved versions of Greek weapons and techniques, their main weapon remaining the "hasta" or pike. Ordinary soldiers wore breastplates and metal helmets ("glea") while the officers had crested helmets and carried shields. Under Polybius (2nd c. BCE) the "hasta" was replaced by the "pilum", a light spear weighing only 600 grams and anything from 60 to 100 centimetres long. This was carried by the front two rows of the phalanx and, because it was so light, it would bend or break quickly, meaning that discarded "pilums" would be useless to the enemy. For hand-to-hand fighting, the Romans used the short Spanish sword (gladius, **223** on belt) which had a straight double-edged blade and was equally effective for cutting or stabbing. A rectangular convex shield (the scutum) also reappeared, although the lightly armed "velites" carried small shields (the parma) and a light spear (the ioculum). The infantry all wore spiked sandals laced by long strips of leather (cliga) as shown in this illustration of a Roman soldier (**224**). Cavalrymen carried a small round shield

224

Roman Period: Apart from the elephants, the Hasmonean armies appear to have been organized like other Hellenistic forces. Herod, however, applied a mixture of Hellenistic and Roman principles to his military forces. The entrance of the Romans into Palestine in 63 BCE prompted some very fundamental changes in weapons and army organization and tactics in the area. Apart from a number of arrowheads and javelins and a few swords, very few Roman weapons have been found in Palestine but the remains of many Roman military installations have been excavated, or await investigation. The most famous of these include the military camps around Massada (see Rome and the Jews*) and those of Nahal Heber (near the last hide-outs of Bar-Kochba's* partisans). In Transjordan, the remains of a number of other structures have been preserved and at Massada and Beitar dykes and embankments built by the Romans are still to be seen. Some funerary monuments (**224**) to Roman soldiers, complete with descriptive reliefs, also remain but the bulk of archaeological material about Roman military activities and equipment comes from other theatres of operations. In spite of this, it is clear from the evidence of the Qumran "War Scroll" (see below) that Jewish forces made use of Roman military equipment as well as tactics.

225

(clipeus) and a double-sided spear (hasta trugulu), but no swords. This equipment continued among the legionaries more or less unchanged throughout the duration of the empire but there were some noticeable developments among the auxiliary forces. A new form of armour, consisting of four rounded iron plates, two worn on the breast and two covering the back joined by leather strips over the shoulders was introduced. Instead of the gladius and the pilum the auxiliary troops and the artillery used the hasta and the spatha, a sword about 75 cm. long. In addition, many units were provided with special weapons for a precise purpose and were named after their weapons.

Roman Siege Equipment: For a long period the Romans continued to use Greek artillery and siege engines more or less unchanged, merely extending the range of the stone-thrower to 400 metres. In general the Romans used the catapult for shooting arrows straight at the enemy and the "balista" for hurling stones in a curved arc. In their many sieges the Romans made use of two types of battering ram or aries, each protected by a leather-covered shed. One was the Terebra **(225)**, designed to batter a hole through a wall; the other the "falx muralis" which broke up the stones on the upper part of the ramparts. They also had mobile shooting towers, and these were used in the siege of Jerusalem. As another way of getting through a wall was to undermine it, the Romans also perfected a method for this. A structure called a muruculus, made of a wooden frame on wheels with a sloping roof covered with wet skins would be rolled up to the walls to protect the sappers inside it while they dug away. In another variation of this, the vinea, one side was left open.

Military Terminology in the Qumran "War Scroll": According to Y. Yadin, the weapons, military organization and tactics described in the Dead Sea "Scroll of the War of the Sons of Light against the Sons of Darkness" (see Dead Sea Scrolls*), correspond closely to those of the Roman army of the 1st c. BCE and not to an earlier period, nor to those of the Hellenistic states around Palestine. However, this also reflects the patterns of Herod's Jewish army.

The Scroll uses biblical terms for the weapons and this (see above) suggests continuity in usage and also provides us with a 1st c. BCE manual of military terminology and tactics. Although, because of its much later date, it must be used with care, the Scroll has been of considerable value in reconstructing some difficult passages and military terms in the Old Testament and has made it possible to correct a number of erroneous traditional interpretations (see above and article on Warfare*).

ASSYRIA AND ISRAEL. — *Outline: I. Early History: Amorite Rule; Hurrians and Mitanni; Nuzi. II. The Middle Assyrian Empire: Tiglat-Pileser I and His Successors. III. The Neo-Assyrian Empire, First Period* (934–745 *BCE*)*: Shalmaneser III, Aram and Israel. IV. Neo-Assyrian Empire, Second Period* (745–612 *BCE*)*: Tiglat-Pileser III; The Vassal Kings of Palestine; Shalmaneser V; Sargon II, Israel and Ashdod; Sennacherib and Judah; Revival of Nineveh. V. Esarhaddon and the Decline of the Assyrian Empire: The Conquest of Egypt; The Last of the Great Assyrian Monarchs; Ashurbanipal's Library; The Fall of Assyria; Ashur-uballit. VI. Administration of the Kingdom; Religion; Literature; Art.*

Geographically, the land of the ancient Assyrians covered the upper Mesopotamian plain, bounded on the south by Babylonia* and Jebel Hamrin, on the west by the Syrian desert and on the north and east by the Urartu (Armenian) and Kurdistan highlands (see map **226**).

Historically, the term Assyria is often applied to all the territories that gradually came under the sway of the kings of Assyria. At the peak of its expansion in the 8th–7th centuries BCE, the Assyrian Empire stretched right across Mesopotamia south of the Urartu Mountains to the Mediterranean, and included Babylonia and Elam, Media and South Anatolia, Cilicia, Syria and Palestine, Egypt and the north of Arabia (see map **226**).

Recent archaeological discoveries have revealed a great deal about the early history of Assyria and have made possible a scientific correlation of many of the Bible's references to the country and its relations with Israel. A comparison of the texts of Assyrian inscriptions with the data in the books of Kings* and Chronicles* has confirmed or, very occasionally, corrected the biblical account, and has provided an objective chronology for the history of the divided kingdom.

The Bible uses the term Ashur (Assyrian: Aššur) for both the land and its people. References to this aggressive world power are frequent. The Hebrews believed its origins to have been with Ashur, the second son of Shem (Gn. 10:22) and carefully distinguished it from the Ashuram, an Arab tribe believed to have been descended from Abraham and Keturah (Gn. 25:3).

I. EARLY HISTORY: The land of Assyria has been inhabited since the very earliest times. Its oldest settlement, Jarmo, dates back to around 5000 BCE, and pottery of the Hassuna, Samarra, Halaf and Ubaid periods (see Babylonia*: Pre-history) of the Early Bronze Age (5000–3000 BCE) has been found at a number of sites in Assyria.

According to the Bible (Gn. 10:11–12), the three capitals of Assyria: Ashur, Nineveh and Calah were founded by immigrants from Babylonia. An Assyrian king-list found at Dur-Sharrukin (Khorsabad), however, records that the first 17 kings and people were "tent-dwellers", i. e. semi-nomads. The ethnic origins of the Assyrians are still disputed among the scholars. It is known, though, that the Sumerians (see Babylonia*) lived in Ashur by 2900 BCE and that there are many close affinities between their language and material culture and those of the Assyrians. At the same time, Assyria was right in the centre of the constant movements of Semitic peoples from the western deserts and the northern highlands (the non-Semitic Hurrians).

In the 24th century BCE, the Sumerian cities were conquered by Semitic kings of Agadê (Akkad, see Babylonia*) and as early as Sargon I (ca. 2350 BCE) these kings were building in Nineveh. But the renaissance of Sumerian power during the third empire of Ur brought their rule to Assyria. A building inscription of Amar Su'en of Ur (21st c. BCE) has also been found at Ashur. Thus the origins of the Assyrians appear to lie in a mixture of Old Akkadian (ancient Babylonian*) with Hurrian (see below), north-western Semitic and other

226

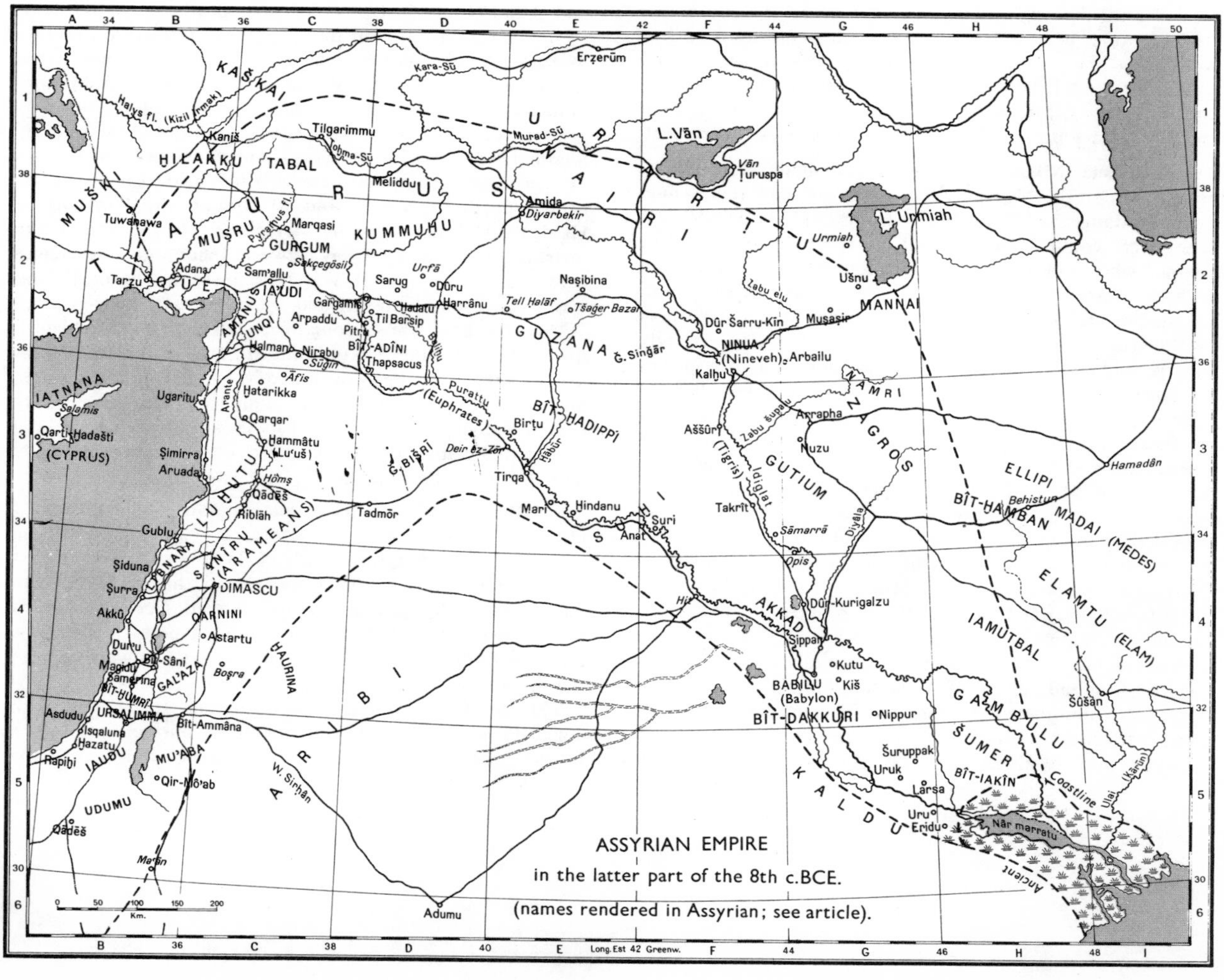

ASSYRIAN EMPIRE
in the latter part of the 8th c.BCE.
(names rendered in Assyrian; see article).

strains. The Assyrian kings regarded themselves as the true bearers of the Sumero-Akkadian culture and by the early 2nd millenium BCE they began to adopt the names of the great kings of Akkad.

Amorite Rule: Throughout the 19th century BCE, tribes of western Semitic nomads, the Amurru (biblical Amorites) made repeated attacks on the region and finally overthrew the dynasty of the "kings of Sumer and Akkad" (i. e. the empire ruled by Ur, see Babylonia*). In the early 19th c., the Assyrian king list reflects the general pattern throughout Mesopotamia, where independent princes had established themselves in a profusion of small city-states. In Cappodocia there was also an Assyrian trading colony at this time.

A new Amorite king, Šamši-Adad I (1748–1716 BCE) gradually increased Assyria's domains. His warlike expeditions brought him to Syria and the Mediterranean coast. He was also the supreme ruler of Babylonia for some time. His son, Yasmah Adad, ruled over Mari (see Babylonia*) and dominated the whole of northern Mesopotamia. Mari's importance however, has been restored in recent years. The inscriptions found by archaeologists in the ruins of Mari* have provided not only the best evidence for Assyria's early history but also much useful background information about the beginnings of the biblical Patriarchal Age (see Babylonia*).

The death of Ishme-Dagan, Šamši-Adad's other son, was followed by a period of disorder in Assyria during which a succession of seven kings grabbed and then lost the throne. No more than this little is known about the period until the reign of Puzur-Ashur about the end of the 16th century BCE. The 17th and 16th centuries BCE saw substantial movements of peoples in western Asia from east to west and from north to south. By the 16th c., Babylonia* had been captured by the Cassites, one of the eastern peoples who joined in the prevailing westward movement.

Hurrians and Mitanni: The Cassites made no cultural impression on the Mesopotamian cities and they represented mainly a danger to the dynasty of Hammurabi in Babylonia*. They were confined in the north by the Hurrians, a native people who occupied the fertile country watered by the middle Tigris and its tributaries, extending as far south as modern Kirkuk (Iraq). The Hurrians had lived north of Assyria in what is eastern Kurdistan of today, as early as the middle of the 3rd millenium BCE and inscriptions of Hurrian kings have been uncovered from the days of Naram-Sin, king of Akkad. They entered northern and northeast Mesopotamia about the beginning of the 2nd millenium and by the 16th and 15th centuries BCE the kingdom of Mitanni on the upper Euphrates and Tigris was one of the dominant powers in the area. This kingdom represented a symbiosis of an upper ruling class of Indo-European "marianu" over the native Hurrian population.

Nuzi: The excavation of the Mitannian (Hurrian) city at Nuzi (see Patriarchs*) near Kirkuk produced a tremendous amount of important inscribed material on clay tablets as well as cylinder-seals. Nuzi was almost solidly Hurrian, as was the kingdom and culture of Alalakh, a kingdom of northern Syria, also dominated by Mitanni. The patriarchal stories (see Patriarchs*: Hurrians, Nuzi) reflect many Hurrian customs and legal rights. The Hurrian language, still incompletely understood, first became known through one of the Amarna* letters. Later on, texts in this language were found at Boghazköy in Anatolia, Ugarit* and elsewhere. Mitanni lay across the main trade routes into Asia Minor and their obstruction made the Hurrians a thorn in the flesh of both Assyrians and Hittites. Assyria remained an agricultural community of no great importance, while Mitanni and other Hurrian groups dominated the upper Euphrates and Tigris Valleys. They became an important element in the population of northern Assyria.

Assyria remained under the control of Mitanni until the middle of the 14th century BCE, when Mitanni was defeated by the Hittites and Assyrian independence was reestablished under Eribba-Adad I. The Amarna* letters have made it clear that an uneasy balance was maintained in Mesopotamia by means of a series of alliances between Egypt and one or more of the kingdoms of Assyria, Babylonia, Mitanni and the Hittites, the main object being to keep Mitanni and the Hittites in check.

II. THE MIDDLE ASSYRIAN EMPIRE: A resurgence of Assyrian power began with the reign of Ashur-Uballit I (1356–1321 BCE). Letters from him to Akhenaton of Egypt, discovered at Amarna*, reveal a continuing dispute with the king of Babylonia, who claimed the Assyrian as his vassal. This situation, however, was not to continue for much longer. Mitanni declined, and with the help of the Hittites, Ashur-Uballit was able to establish Assyria's independence, and to reopen the trade routes of the north. Increased prosperity was accompanied by territorial expansion. During the reigns of Arik-den-ili (1309–1298 BCE) and Adad-Nirari I (1298–1266 BCE) the lands to the east, as far as Carchemish on the Euphrates, lost since the days of Šamši-Adad, were recovered for Assyria and new lands to the south added. Babylonia was defeated and Mitanni reduced to a vassal state.

Assyria's expansion was continued and hastened by Shalmaneser I (1274–1245 BCE). He embarked on a series of expeditions against the eastern tribes, against new enemies to the north in Urartu and to contain the Hurrians of Hanigablat (Mitanni) to the northwest. He also rebuilt the fortress city of Calah midway between Ashur and Nineveh (see below) as a new capital. Assyrian power in the north and west was firmly consolidated by his son, Tukulti-Ninurta (1244–1208 BCE) whose domain stretched from Carchemish to the Persian Gulf. Tukulti-Ninurta even established himself as king over Babylonia and ruled it for seven years, but with his death Assyria's domination was temporarily ended. Babylonia reestablished its independence and a long period of decline for the northern kingdom began, briefly halted during the reign of Tiglat-Pileser I.

Tiglat-Pileser I and His Successors: Tiglat-Pileser I (1116–1078 BCE) was an energetic campaigner whose victories took Assyrian soldiers (and tribute collectors) from the foothills of the Caucasus to the Mediterranean coast, where Byblos, Sidon and Arwad (see Phoenicia*) succumbed. Inside Mesopotamia, his troops pushed the Ahlame (Aramean*) tribes of the desert westwards across the Euphrates.

This brief resurgence, however, came to an end with Tiglat-Pileser's death. His successor, Ashur-bel-kata, allied himself with the Babylonian king to meet the threat of the

Arameans driving up from the south. The Babylonian king was deposed by them, but the Assyrian kept his throne, sealing the alliance with a marriage between them.

The 10th century BCE saw the Arameans* increasing their pressure throughout northern Mesopotamia, establishing a series of independent kingdoms and even encroaching upon the country of Assyria proper. Preoccupation with the Aramean danger kept both Assyria and Babylonia from military adventures further afield. The activities of the Aramean states thus gave David and Solomon of Israel their chance to strike into Syria (Aram). Partly under Israelite attacks, the strength of the Arameans faltered and power in the region shifted back to the Assyrians.

III. THE NEO-ASSYRIAN EMPIRE, FIRST PERIOD (934–745 BCE): The period of Assyria's greatest ascendancy began with the reigns of two kings, Ashur-dan I (934–912 BCE) and his son, Adad-Nirari II (911–891 BCE). Their defeats of the Aramean states were continued under Tukulti-Ninurta II (890–884 BCE) and finally completed by his son, Ashur-nasirpal II (883–859 BCE). In a series of brilliant campaigns, he subdued the tribes of the Middle Euphrates, conquered Lebanon and Philistia and exacted tribute from the Phoenician coastal cities, who gladly paid rather than risk open warfare. The Assyrians had arrived on the Mediterranean coast as a force to be reckoned with. They were to remain a constant threat to the little states of Syria and Palestine for another two hundred years. Ashur-nasirpal II also sent expeditions into northern Babylonia and the eastern highlands. When he embarked upon the enlargement and rebuilding of Calah (Nimrud), giving it a new citadel, palace and temples, and starting work on the ziggurat (see Babylonia*), 50,000 prisoners of war provided the labour force. Artists and technicians were also employed to decorate the audience chambers of his palaces with sculptures and to surround them with parkland, botanical and zoological gardens.

Whatever their cost to the civilian population, Assyria's military successes not only resulted in political and geographical expansion, but were also accompanied by advances in the arts. Most notably, Assyrian sculpture achieved a vigour unprecedented at the time and rarely equalled since. If the vitality of an ancient state may be measured not only by military successes, but also by its principal artistic expression, then the peak period for Assyria came in the first half of the 9th century with the reign of Ashur-nasirpal II. Yet this king and those who followed him have become notorious for the brutality of their policies and the atrocities systematically practiced against enemy and subject peoples. The campaigns and conquests of the Assyrians throughout this period were accompanied by wholesale slaughter and maltreatment. Ashur-nasirpal II gave Assyria imperial status for the first time. He must also bear some responsibility for the reputation that empire has carried through history.

Shalmaneser III — Aram and Israel: Ashur-nasirpal was succeeded by his son, Shalmaneser III (859–824 BCE). He continued his father's policy of regular military campaigns, extending Assyria's frontiers from Urartu in Armenia to Parsua, the original Persia, and from Media to the Mediterranean coast. He invaded Babylonia and secured her complete subjection. However, playing the role of friend rather than conqueror, he sacrificed to the chief gods of all her cities. For the first time, Shalmaneser consolidated Assyrian domination over its conquests. Where Ashur-nasirpal's object in his campaigns had been little more than plunder, Shalmaneser's expeditions were part of a coherent political plan. Governors were appointed over conquered territories. Where these were strong enough to maintain a measure of autonomy, they were enlisted as vassals and subjected to no more than the payment of their annual tribute. Those too strong or too distant for constant Assyrian control were linked by trade relations or alliances. A valid imperial structure was built up, although annual campaigns by the king or his commander remained a regular feature of Assyrian life, resulting in a seemingly endless series of military adventures.

In 857 BCE, Carchemish paid tribute to the Assyrians and Shalmaneser's conquest of Bit Adini, with its capital Til-Barsip, alerted the major city-states of south-western Asia to their own imminent danger and prompted them to sink their differences in the face of this wider threat. Irhuleni of Hamat and Adad-idri (Hadadezer, or Ben-Hadad, see Arameans*) of Damascus joined in forming an anti-Assyrian coalition with ten other kings. One of the foremost among these was Ahab of Israel (in spite of his long quarrel with Ben-Hadad who had been attacking deep into Israelite territory, 1 K. 20:1–30). The official leader of the coalition was the king of Aram-Damascus, who contributed the largest number of troops. However, when the coalition faced the Assyrian armies for the indecisive battle of Qarqar on the river Orontes in Syria in 853 BCE, "Ahabbu of Sir'il" (Ahab the Israelite), then in the 22nd year of his reign, fielded the largest armoured force: 2,000 chariots, plus 10,000 infantry (see Israel and Judah*, Part II).

Shalmaneser recorded the battle as a great victory but, in fact, it effectively halted the Assyrian advance. Moreover, there is the negative evidence of the Bible which nowhere mentions the battle. In view of the biblical chronicler's disapproval of the "House of Omri", a defeat such as the Assyrian annalist claimed to have inflicted on Ahab would surely have been recorded as tangible evidence of the wrath of Yahweh.

In 849, 848 and 845 BCE, Shalmaneser undertook further operations against the western kings, notably Ben-Hadad. When the anti-Assyrian coalition split up, he was able to force the Aramean back into Damascus and lay siege to the city (842 BCE). However, Damascus withstood the Assyrians. Unable to take the city — although its king later paid a heavy tribute — Shalmaneser moved away through the mountains to the Nahr-el-Kalb in the Lebanon. There he received tribute from the rulers of Tyre, Sidon and from "Ja'ua (Jehu) son of Omri". Jehu's tribute is again something passed over in silence by the biblical record. Shalmaneser's "Black Obelisk" found in Nimrud contains one panel showing the Israelite doing obeisance to the Assyrians. It also records that among the tribute received from many kings was silver, gold, a golden bowl, a golden vase, golden goblets and vessels, and tin from Jehu (see illustration under Israel and Judah*, Part II). Other scenes from Shalmaneser's campaigns in the north were engraved on the bronze doors of the temple of Imgur Bel (Tel Balawat) east of Calah. These show: tribute being paid by Tyre (**227**),

227

the Assyrian expedition against Hazazu (a Syrian state; and its capital **227, 228**), and the slaughter of its inhabitants by the chariots of the king.

The last years of Shalmaneser's reign were a troubled period of rebellion, one instigated by his son, another a great revolt which alienated more than half his empire and cancelled out all his western conquests. After his death, his brother, Samši-Adad V (823–811 BCE) managed to quell the rebellions and also to launch three campaigns against Babylonia and the Elamite border. He had, however, no attention to spare for the western states and the brief absence of Assyrian pressure there gave Ben-Hadad's successor, Hazael, king of Damascus, the opportunity for a series of invasions of neighbouring Israel, first taking over much of the border territory, then reducing Israel to the status of a vassal of Aram.

Adad-Nirari and Israel: Šamši-Adad died young and his influential widow, Sammuramat (the Semiramis of Greek legend) acted as regent until their son, Adad-Nirari III, was old enough to take control (805 BCE). Some time after that, Adad-Nirari set out in support of Hamat and attacked Damascus, still ruled by Hazael. The city was captured, giving Israel and other neighbouring states a respite from Aramean attacks and overlordship (II K. 12:17; II Ch. 24:23 ff). In recognition, many of the rulers brought gifts to the Assyrians. Among them, according to his records, was "Hatti (North Syria), Amurru, Tyre, Sidon, the Land of Omri (Israel), Edom and Philistia, as far as the Mediterranean." There was quite a bit of exaggeration in this claim, for the Assyrians did not hold the west for long. However, they did make it possible for Jehoash of Israel to recover towns on his northern border which had earlier been lost to Hazael (II K. 13:25). At the same time, the Assyrian king appears to have enjoyed a peaceful period at home, for he was able to build a new palace outside the walls of the citadel at Calah.

In 782 BCE, Adad-Nirari III was succeeded by Shalmaneser IV (782–772 BCE). His continued pressure against Damascus enabled Jeroboam II to extend the boundaries of Israel to the Beq'a (east of Lebanon), the "entrance to Hamat" (II K. 14:25, 28). In fact, the unremitting wars between Assyrians, Arameans and Urarteans (a kingdom centred upon Lake Van), in Mesopotamia and Syria were extremely advantageous to the twin kingdoms of Israel and Judah, who briefly recovered the territorial extent of Solomon's empire and simultaneously built up their economic strength. Assyrian domination was also hampered by internal dissension. A struggle for the succession began after the death of Adad-Nirari and the end of Shalmaneser's reign, characterized by the ineffectual rule of his successors. A serious defeat in the north made 763 BCE a year of ill-omen in that it heralded an eclipse of the sun. It is the more significant as it marks a basic starting point for our reckoning of Assyrian chronology. The kings of the area made new defensive alliances, and, for a few decades of Assyrian weakness, continued to maintain their independence.

IV. NEO-ASSYRIAN EMPIRE, SECOND PERIOD (745–612 BCE): **Tiglat-Pileser III:** The resurgence of Assyrian power was begun under a new king, Tiglat-Pileser III (745–727 BCE), who, in spite of the name he adopted and his claim to descent from the main line of Assyrian kings, was a usurper. His records are only fragmentary and there is a good deal of uncertainty about the order of events of his reign. What is known for certain is that he was a strong and determined ruler who set out to regain and extend all the territories which had once owed allegiance to the god Ashur. He was not content with occasional deliveries of tribute. He wanted to annex the independent kingdoms of Syria and Palestine and make them part of the Assyrian empire.

First of all, however, he had to consolidate his Mesopotamian empire. He fought against the king of the Urartu, a kingdom which had been flourishing to the north of Assyria in the 9th and 8th cs. BCE, and was now intriguing with the Syrian states. He defeated the rebels in the towns along the anti-Taurus (Kashiari) mountains as far as the Kummuh. Having subdued the country, he organized it into a series of provinces owing their allegiance directly to him as king. Arpad in Syria was besieged for three years (743–740 BCE), Tiglat-Pileser meanwhile collecting tribute from the kings of Damascus and neighbouring states. By the end of the siege all the states of northern Syria were under Assyrian domination. In 738 BCE, however, while the Assyrian was occupied with operations in the northern hills, a revolt was initiated by "Azriyau of Yaudi", in league with Hamat. "Azriyau" is assumed by some scholars to be Azariah (Uzziah) king of Judah (see discussion under Israel and Judah*, Part III). There are a number of chronological difficulties in comparing Assyrian records to the biblical story, but it is believed that in his old age the Judean king may have tried to stem the Assyrian tide as Ahab had done a century earlier. If so, he was unsuccessful.

228

The Vassal Kings of Palestine: From Tiglat-Pileser's official account, it appears that he broke up the coalition, devastated Hamat and made it into an Assyrian province. To avoid invasion, the southern states hastened to pay tribute to him and he records what he received from a number of kings, including Hiram of Tyre and "Menihimme" (Menachem) of Samaria. This very payment is reported explicitly in the Bible where the reference (II K. 15:19) to Menachem's payment of "a thousand talents of silver that he might help him to confirm his hold of the royal power" suggests Menachem's insecurity on the Israelite throne at the end of his reign. The money was raised by a levy of 50 shekels each, imposed on all the leading men of the kingdom (II K. 15:20). This is comparable to contemporary Assyrian contracts. In fact, to avoid deportation, the men paid the equivalent of the value of a slave. By this time (738 BCE), all the states of Syria, plus the northern kingdom of Israel, were tributaries of Tiglat-Pileser.

Three years later (735 BCE), a new alliance was formed between Pekah, the usurping king of Israel, and the kings of Damascus, Philistia and Edom against Ahaz, recently crowned king of Judah. He appealed for aid to Tiglat-Pileser and the Assyrians responded with a campaign against Philistia (734 BCE) in order to prevent any contact between Egypt and the kingdoms of Israel and Aram. The king of Gaza, Hanunu (Hanno) fled across the "River of Egypt" (Wadi el-Arish). Ahaz paid for the help he had received by being made an Assyrian vassal.

In his new series of campaigns in 733–732 BCE, Tiglat-Pileser captured Damascus (732 BCE) and invaded northern Israel, producing a heavy toll from Pekah. According to Assyrian records, Tiglat-Pileser confirmed the deposition of Pekah by acknowledging "Ausi" (Hoshea) as king of Israel (II K. 15:30). The Assyrian invasion continued, however. Megiddo, the plain of Sharon, and Gilead in Transjordan were captured. This time, instead of being content with the receipt of tribute, Tiglat-Pileser annexed his conquests as provinces of the empire, deporting the existing — possibly rebellious — inhabitants and replacing them with deportees from other, distant lands (see Israel and Judah*: Assyrian Conquest, Part IV). This policy of forestalling any possible resistance to Assyrian domination was part of Tiglat-Pileser's whole plan for the consolidation of the empire. Massive deportations were accompanied by the reorganization of the conquered lands into Assyrian provinces; division of the larger territories into smaller districts and the establishment of an extensive bureaucracy responsible for administration. At the same time, aggressive military campaigns continued to be undertaken — usually successfully.

A New Balance of Power: Tiglat-Pileser had changed the whole balance of power in western Asia; small states like Israel were destroyed, others, including Judah, reduced to vassalage and Assyria's military strength enjoyed unchallenged supremacy throughout the area. Towards the end of his reign in 728 BCE, he captured Babylon and proclaimed himself "King of Babylon", thus being the first Assyrian King, after Tukulti-Ninurta I to rule Babylonia*. In the Babylonian records he appears not as Tiglat-Pileser, but as Pulu (Pul in II K. 15:19 ff; I Ch. 5:26).

Shalmaneser V in Samaria: The situation continued unchanged under Tiglat-Pileser's son, Shalmaneser V (727–722 BCE). Hoshea, king of Israel, was tempted by promises of Egyptian support to make a bid for independence (725 BCE) and refused to pay his annual tribute to Assyria (II K. 17:4). Shalmaneser reacted by invading the country and laying siege to the city of Samaria, which held out for three years. Eventually, however, according to the Babylonian Chronicle, the Assyrian "broke the resistance of the city of Shamara'in (Samaria)." It may be, therefore, that "the king of Assyria (who) captured Samaria and carried the Israelites away to Assyria" (II K. 17:6) was this same Shalmaneser V. Shalmaneser's successor, Sargon II, was later to claim the capture of Samaria in 722 BCE as a victory for himself, so he may have been the unnamed king of the biblical record. He might well have been associated with Shalmaneser as second-in-command during the siege and have completed it after the death of the latter in December 722 BCE.

Sargon II, Israel and Ashdod: Sargon II (721–705 BCE) was a forceful general and a vigorous leader. Like Tiglat-Pileser III, he was not a descendant of the main line of kings (although he once refers to himself as "son of Tiglat-Pileser"), but a member of a subsidiary branch. He broke with the old aristocracy of Ashur, took the name "Sargon" and founded, some years later, a new capital Dur Sarrukin, (now Khorsabad), 12 miles north of Nineveh. His account of the conquest of Samaria lays the blame for the original refusal of taxes on Iau-bi'di of Hamat who persuaded the peoples of Arpad and the Aramean provinces to a similar defiance. Punishments included the exile of some 27,270 people of Samaria to Halah on the river Habur in the province of Gozan, and to Media* (II K. 17:6), together with "the gods in which they trusted." They were replaced by Babylonians and Arameans.

In Assyria, many of the Israelite captives lost their national identity, but it is assumed that some of their descendants were joined by the captives from Judah exiled to Babylon in the following century and that they went back to Palestine together at the time of the Restoration*. The confederation which had defied Assyrian might was crushed at Raphia on the Egyptian border. The commander-in-chief (tartan) of lower Egypt, Sibu (his name is now read Re'u), fled. The Arabians submitted and paid tribute, and Hanno of Gaza, who had also relied on promises of Egyptian help, was exiled along with 9,000 of his people.

In spite of this crushing defeat, anti-Assyrian feeling was so deeply entrenched among their victims that the peoples and rulers of Palestine continued to turn to Egypt for support against Assyria. The history of this period and the one immediately following was presumably the background to the prophecies of Isaiah. A new alliance of resistance was organized and, for a time, Sargon was too occupied with similar troubles in Babylonia and Elam* to respond. However, triumphant at Carchemish in 717 BCE, Sargon campaigned through Cilicia in Asia Minor and continued the raids against Ararat/Urartu (714 BCE). Then he turned his attention westwards. Azuri, king of Ashdod, one of the ringleaders in the intrigues with Egypt, was deposed on Assyrian orders and replaced by his brother, Ahimiti. The people of Ashdod rose in protest and a more bellicose pretender was installed as king — but only for a short time. New Assyrian armies were sent under Sargon's general (or "tartan", Is. 20:1). Ashdod and Gath were sacked (712 BCE), the pretender fled and Assyria gained a new province. Sargon also claims to have reduced Judah at this time, although there is nothing in the Old Testament account of the reign of Hezekiah to corroborate this (see Israel and Judah*, Part IV). However, fragments of a Sargon stele reported to have been found in the ruins of Ashdod (see article under Philistines*) during excavations in the summer of 1963 CE give substance to the account of the sack of this city.

Sennacherib and Judah: Sargon's life ended in battle in Asia Minor. His death sparked off a series of rebellions which it took his successor (his son Sennacherib, 704–681 BCE) the first years of his reign to suppress. While still crown prince, Sennacherib had been in command of the northern frontiers of the empire and he used the knowledge he had gained there to pacify Urartu and Media and to further his campaigns to the west. He then faced a sweeping rebellion led by Marduk-apla-iddina (Merodach Baladan of II K. 20:12–19) who rose for the third time and had seized the Babylonian throne. A full year's campaign was needed to dislodge him (703 BCE). The Babylonian explosion after the death of Sargon had, however, stimulated rebellion in Judah, Phoenicia and Philistia.

Hezekiah's own increasing wealth and ambitions had brought Judah into a new coalition led by Phoenician Tyre which included Philistine Ashkelon and was, as always, encouraged by the Nubian kings of Egypt who promised the rebels the support of Egyptian cavalry. Padi, the king of Ekron, was loyal to Assyria but feeling against the Assyrians was so strong that the people of his city rose in revolt against him and sent him in chains to Hezekiah. Sennacherib's reply was a campaign, begun in 701 BCE, which took him victorious through Syria to the coast where he laid siege to the towns of the kingdom of Sidon, then, driving on south along the coast, he captured Jaffa (Joppa), Beth-Dagon, Bnei-Brak and the towns of the Ashkelon kingdom which were in league with Hezekiah. When Ashkelon opened its gates and surrendered, he turned east, and near Eltekeh he vanquished an Egyptian army which had come to help the Palestinian kingdoms. Ekron was now also in Sennacherib's hands.

Judah now stood alone to face the Assyrian colossus which swept over southern Judah, capturing one city after the other. A detailed description of the operations and camps and the siege of Lachish*, a Judean stronghold, is pictured in the bas reliefs of Sennacherib's palace at his capital, Nineveh (see illustrations under Israel and Judah*, part V). Sennacherib boasts that he had reduced 46 of the cities of Judah, deporting their inhabitants and shutting Hezekiah and his troops into Jerusalem "like a bird in a cage" (see also Isaiah* 36). Isaiah 1:7–9 provides some vivid evidence of the appalling slaughter involved in these battles. His back to the wall, Hezekiah had no choice but to surrender. He sent heavy tribute and the treasures of the Temple to Sennacherib's headquarters at Lachish* and thus saved Jerusalem from total destruction. In order to forestall any further anti-Assyrian alliances, Sennacherib distributed some of Judah's land to the Philistine kingdoms. There is some doubt about whether Jerusalem was besieged at this time or later. The text of II Kings 18:17–19:36 seems to show that it was all one campaign but doubts have been raised (see Israel and Judah*, Part V), it being suggested that the siege was part of a later campaign, perhaps that against the Arabs in 686 BCE. The sequel to the siege of Jerusalem, recorded in Isaiah 36–37, whereby Sennacherib had to leave in a hurry, is not recorded by the Assyrians. Miraculously, as the Judeans saw it, he raised the siege and withdrew (II K. 19:35 f.). Herodotus confirms this story, attributing the retreat to an overwhelming epidemic of plague. Hard as it is to harmonize this with Assyrian annals, no other contemporary records reveal any unusual international political reactions which might have ensued had Sennacherib been forced to withdraw so suddenly from the region as a result of a catastrophe.

Revival of Nineveh: In contrast to his predecessors, Sennacherib did not engage in a regular annual military campaign. During the 24 years of his reign there were only ten major campaigns, and these included two led by his generals, not by the king in person. He gave a great deal more of his attention to the administration of his possessions — a fact witnessed by the rich royal correspondence which remains from this period. He was also an enthusiastic builder. Dur Sarrukin (Khorsabad), built by Sargon II, had been abandoned after his death by Sennacherib, who set out to rebuild Nineveh. Nineveh's palaces, gateways and temples were rebuilt or restored, while aqueducts, dams and water works were created to provide for extensive irrigation in the large parks laid out around his city. Assyrian reliefs commemorating these activities show that the work was done by prisoners from his campaigns, including Israelites. Literature, learning and the arts also flourished. In brief, for a few decades the Assyrians sat back to enjoy the benefits their power brought them without striving to increase it endlessly. This new "Pax Assyriaca" also seems to have brought a period of stability to relations between their western vassals.

Some years before his death, Sennacherib had named his son, Esarhaddon, as heir and he succeeded to the throne when Sennacherib was murdered by two of his sons — a death in which the Bible narrators saw the vengeful hand of their God (II K. 19:37, Is. 37:37). The change of ruler was of very little benefit to the Israelites, however.

V. ESARHADDON AND THE DECLINE OF THE ASSYRIAN EMPIRE: Esarhaddon (680–669 BCE) revived the policy of aggressive military operations and, in the west, continued to exact tribute from the city-states, including those of Cilicia, Syria and Phoenicia. The Egyptian ruler, Tirhakah, was still busily inciting opposition to Assyrian domination, but every such attempt brought a quick reaction from Esarhaddon. It is believed by some scholars that Menasseh was also taken to Babylon as part of this policy (II Ch. 33:11). A "Menasi of Judah" is named as among the many from whom Esarhaddon was collecting tribute at this time, though regarding him generally as a faithful vassal. This prism relates Esarhaddon's conquests (**229**).

The Conquest of Egypt: The Assyrian empire now reached in Esarhaddon's days its greatest power and expansion, its territory spreading across western Asia further than ever before. Esarhaddon subjugated the rich Phoenician towns of Sidon (677 BCE). He was the first Assyrian king to conquer Egypt, the great rival (in 671 BCE), and he installed Assyrian governors in Memphis. A year earlier, Esarhaddon announced his decision regarding the succession, thus, he hoped, avoiding the unrest which had accompanied so many previous changes of ruler. His realm was to be split into two, his son Ashurbanipal assuming the crown of Assyria and his brother, Shamash-shum-ukin, becoming king of Babylonia. The announcement was made at an impressive ceremony to his assembled vassals, each of whom thereupon swore oaths of allegiance to the new crown princes. Copies of these oaths were preserved. Discovered centuries later, they demonstrate the "covenant" form of the relationship between a suzerain and his vassals (see Law*) and reveal a number of interesting parallels with Old Testament terminology. The oath included the swearing of eternal allegiance to Ashur, the Assyrian god — a form of declaring himself a loyal vassal of Assyria to which Menasseh must have subscribed along with the other subject kings (II K. 21:2–7, 9). Esarhaddon died while campaigning against Egypt for the third time, after Pharaoh Tirhakah had instigated a revolt by the native leaders of lower Egypt.

The Last of the Great Assyrian Monarchs: Ashurbanipal (669–627 BCE) continued his father's struggle and finally gained control of Egypt after three hard campaigns and the sack of Thebes (Na. 3:8 called it "No", meaning "No-Ammon"). In his Egyptian campaigns, Ashurbanipal was assisted by his vassals, among them "Minše" (Menasseh) of Judah. Ashurbanipal restored "Minše" and made repeated raids against the tribes of Arabia* in the Syrian

229

desert, probably as a means of keeping the roads to Egypt open. During his reign, the Assyrian empire seemed unshakable. Even the king of Lydia sent emissaries to Nineveh to negotiate an alliance. However, Assyria's enemies were organizing. To the east, the Medes (see Persia*) were increasing their hold over neighbouring tribes and their threat to the Assyrian homeland. To the south, Esarhaddon's brother, Shamash-shum-ukin, the deputy king of Babylonia, was forced into revolt by the native Chaldeans and Arameans and by the time Babylon was humbled and sacked (648 BCE), four years of bitter fratricidal civil war had devastated the countryside and kept the Assyrian armies from much needed operations elsewhere. The rebellion had been supported by Elam and, in savage reprisal its capital, Susa (Shushan) was sacked and its independence forfeited. For the time being, Elam became a province of Assyria.

Ashurbanipal's Library: Assyrian culture during this period reached new heights. Contacts with the west had enriched artistic inspiration and some of the hunting and battle scenes which Assyrian and captive artisans carved in stone reliefs are among the finest representations to be found in all world art (see below, Art and Literature). Literature and learning were also at a peak, reflected in the vast library which Ashurbanipal assembled. In the king's palace at Nineveh and in the Nabu temples, 10,000 different texts were discovered in 26,000 fragments of clay tablets. These had been assembled from Assyrian and Babylonian religious centres, and probably added to previous hoards preserved from earlier reigns.

The last years of Ashurbanipal's reign are poorly documented, but it is evident that some time before his death in 627 BCE and after it, Assyria's hold over the western states was gradually loosening. Though the Babylonian rebellion had shaken the empire, Assyria was still strong, and the Babylonians turned to the Medes for support.

Egypt had regained its independence before this, when Psametik I slowly recaptured Egypt and founded the 26th dynasty. Assyria made no further attempt to reconquer Egypt. Eventually, she herself became an ally of Assyria (in 616 BCE, perhaps earlier), knowing that a weakened Assyria represented a smaller danger to her than the rising power of the Medo-Babylonian alliance; Assyria could at least be maintained as a buffer.

The Fall of Assyria: There are numerous sources for the last years of the Assyrian empire. Ashurbanipal was succeeded by two of his sons, Assur-etil-ilani who ruled for four years, and Sin-shar-ishkun who ruled at least seven. Neither was equal to the rising crisis. The Medes under Cyaxares were soon ready to take up the attack against Assyria, but meanwhile the Babylonians, led by the Chaldean prince, Nabopolassar (626–605 BCE), struck again for independence. As recorded in the Chronicles of the Chaldean kings (published in 1956), he defeated the Assyrians outside Babylon, then took the throne. He had founded the neo-Babylonian empire. The Assyrians could not dislodge him and in fact were fighting for their lives against the Babylonians and the Medes. In this desperate hour, Assyria found an ally in Egypt, whose forces were able to check Nabopolassar's army which had advanced far up the Euphrates and defeated the Assyrian army. By now, in 614 BCE, the Medes began to take a decisive part. Cyaxares took Ashur, the ancient capital. Nabopolassar, arriving later, concluded a formal treaty with him. Two years later, the two allies laid siege to Nineveh and broke through the defenses, destroying it utterly and killing Sin-shar-ishkun. The other Assyrian capital — Calah, fell too, as attested by the Babylonian Chronicles and the archaeological evidence from that city. The impact on the contemporary world can still be measured in the Ode of Nahum (3:7) and in Zephaniah (2:13–15).

Ashur-uballit, Assyria's last king then retired to Harran, where he established his capital and tried to keep resistance alive, but in 610 BCE the Babylonians and allies took it. The Assyrians fell back across the Euphrates into the arms of the Egyptian army under Necho II. The following year, 609 BCE, the Assyrian king made one more attempt to retake Harran with the help of Necho and failed. The mighty empire had crumbled and ceased to exist. Her territory was taken over by the Babylonians, although for centuries the name was still used for the country she had once ruled (e. g. Ezk. 16:28; 23:5–23). Her place on the international scene was taken by the new Babylonian empire which, in turn, inaugurated a new historical epoch full of significance for Israel.

VI. ADMINISTRATION OF THE KINGDOM: The centre of government in Assyria was the person of the king who was both the fount of all authority, the religious leader and the commander-in-chief of the armies. Of necessity, local jurisdiction was delegated to provincial and disctrict governors appointed by the king. They were responsible for collecting and forwarding the tribute paid by all the vassal states — usually in kind. The Assyrians' constant military activity included frequent expeditions in support of local administrators.

The nucleus of the army was provided by a highly trained and well-equipped force of chariots, bowmen, spearmen and slingers (**231**) and specialists in siege warfare. Conquered territories were enrolled as vassal states supplying Assyria with vast quantities of imported goods, including food, raw materials and manufactured goods of all kinds. In fact the economic system was a very uneven one, in which almost all necessities were imported while the country's own resources were diverted to military ends to the almost complete neglect of any native craft development. Craftsmen of all kinds were also supplied from conquest. Any attempted resistance to Assyrian domination was punished by an invasion in which cities were looted and destroyed (**230**), rebel leaders were killed, and skilled workers were enslaved or executed. The Assyrians put this foreign talent to splendid use — witness the wealth of excavated treasures — but such a policy hardly endeared them to contemporary peoples, especially small states like Israel and Judah. The "boiling pot" bringing destruction from the north, in Jeremiah's vision (1:13–14) also became increasingly unstable itself. In later times, the country became populated by tens of thousands of captives while native strength was poured away into the army. The ultimate collapse of the whole structure was implicit in its entire organization.

Religion: In theory, the Assyrian king acted as earthly regent for the national god, Ashur, to whom a regular accounting was made. The Assyrian wars were thus given a

230

partially religious character as a means of expanding Ashur's dominions. Extreme ruthlessness in the suppression of attempted revolt was also given a moral colour. Ashur's principal temple was in the capital, Aššur, while various other deities were believed to watch over the fortunes of other cities. Anu and Adad also had temples and associate ziggurats (temple-towers) in Aššur, while Ishtar, goddess of love and war, was worshipped at Nineveh and elsewhere. The god of wisdom, Nabu (Nebo) had temples in Nineveh and also at Calah (Nimrud) where some of his sacred buildings contained part of the royal libraries. Divine consorts and the minor deities (Shala, Gula, Ea and Damkina) generally had their shrines within the main temples. Assyrian religion was derived from that of Babylonia* and, except for the prominence of Ashur as the national god, it differed little from Babylonian cult and beliefs (see Babylonia*).

Literature: Excavations of Assyrian cities uncovered hundreds of tablets bearing economic and administrative, religious and literary texts. The texts found in Mari* and Shemshara (18th c. BCE) have illuminated the early 2nd millenium BCE (including the period of Hurrian* influence), while the neo-Assyrian empire (see above) has been profusely documented from texts found on clay prisms, cylinders and tablets, and in the inscriptions recording the king's building operations or his requests for divine guidance in relation to decisions on political or military matters (see Magic*: Oracles). The Assyrians were more assiduous historians than the Babylonians and they left a chronology (relating specifically to ca. 950–650 BCE) which has become the basis for all dating in Western Asia.

Israel, Judah and the western city-states are mentioned in many of the letters and official texts. The literature

231

232

was recorded in the cuneiform script adopted from the earlier Sumerians. This used 600 or more signs as ideographs, syllables or determinatives (see Alphabet and Writing*). The library of Ashurbanipal at Nineveh (Kuyunjik) contained a number of vocabularies, sign or word lists and dictionaries as well as scholarly handbooks and a series of twelve tablets on which were inscribed the Epic of Gilgamesh (see Flood*). The Epic of Creation* or Enuma Elish appeared in a number of versions, and other epics and legends (e. g. the legend of Sargon of Agadê or the legend of Etana) were also discovered, along with wisdom literature* ("ludlul bel nimeqi"), the so-called Babylonian "Job", hymns, fables, proverbs and religious literature. There was also an extensive literature on astrology* and divination, including tablets recording the omens discovered from observation of the liver and entrails of sacrificial animals (see Magic*) or of the movements and features of men, animals, objects and stars. Many other recorded observations on botany, geology, chemistry, mathematics, law and medicine (including diagnosis) have also provided later ages with a detailed picture of the Akkadian scene.

Art: Assyrian wall paintings, sculptures, bas reliefs, cylinder seals, ivory carvings and bronze and metal work have been preserved in an apparently endless series in the great museums of the world, and especially of modern Iraq.

During the 250 years from Ashur-nasirpal to Ashurbanipal (ca. 880–627 BCE), Assyrian art reached its peak. The walls of the palaces built during this period were covered with stone reliefs showing royal feasting and hunting (**232**) and, above all, military successes, battles, sieges, enemy towns captured and destroyed, prisoners being beaten and defeated opponents bringing tribute. Quite apart from their artistic qualities, many of these have an overwhelming historical interest, for instance Shalmaneser's Black Obelisk or the record of the Lachish siege from Sennacherib's palace at Nineveh. Other reliefs, like the Lion Hunt of Ashurbanipal from Nineveh, are valuable evidence for the costumes, customs and military habits of Assyrians between the 9th and 7th cs. BCE (see Seals*, Clothing*, Armaments*, Warfare*, Astrology and Astronomy*).

ASTROLOGY AND ASTRONOMY. — *Outline: I. Astronomy and Astrology in Mesopotamia: Dividers of the Heavens, Stargazers and Monthly Prognosticators; Stargazers; "Monthly Prognosticators". II. Worship of the "Host of Heaven" among Canaanites and Israelites. III. The Signs of the Zodiac: The Zodiac in Biblical Literature; Astrology in Hellenistic-Roman Times. IV. Astronomy; The Stars of the Bible. V. Biblical Concept of the Universe: A Monotheistic View; Later Speculation: The Apocalyptic Vision.*

Astrology is a system of foretelling the future, based on the belief that the movements of the stars determine the course of events. It was born in the lands of the Euphrates where the stars and constellations were worshipped as divine, but belief in the divine powers of the stars was current among the Babylonians, Assyrians, Chaldeans and Egyptians and, by the fourth c. BCE, in Greece as well.

I. ASTRONOMY AND ASTROLOGY IN MESOPOTAMIA: The Babylonians associated the stars with the gods themselves, the sign for a god in ancient writing being a star. They watched the planets on their courses through the sky and from their changed positions read the wishes of the gods. In the Babylonian system, the morning star (the planet Venus) was identified with Astarte and sometimes represented as such together with the sun and the moon. The planet Mars was similarly identified with Nergal, the Babylonian god of death. We still call the planets by the names of Graeco-Roman gods. The Bible mentions Chevan (Amos 5:26), apparently meaning the Babylonian name for the planet Saturn (Kaiwana) which remained in use among the Arabs and ancient Syrians (see Astronomy, below).

In addition to the planets, the Assyrians and Babylonians also distinguished several groups of fixed stars and these were also identified with deities. A standard work on astrology was constructed by the Babylonians as early as the 16th century BCE. Such facts as they could observe about the stars and their movements, and their observations of signs in the heavens, were translated into astrological theories for the foretelling of future events. As a result, divination by astrology became an inseparable part of the Babylonian religion.

Dividers of the Heavens, Stargazers and Monthly Prognosticators: Isaiah (47:13) mentions three distinct groups of professional astrologers among the Assyrians and Babylonians: ". . . those who divide the heavens, who gaze at the stars, who at new moons predict what shall befall you". Babylonian clay tablets have been found announcing coming events as predicted by the astrologers, and giving notice of favourable or unpropitious days — something also mentioned by Isaiah. The phrase used by the prophet, "divide the heavens", suggests the methods used by the astrologers, who sectioned the firmament and assigned a particular meaning to each section according to its relation to the subject about which a prediction was sought. The earliest division of the sky was based on the idea of the "four winds of heaven" and a variety of similar astrological tables have been discovered by excavations. A cuneiform text of the 8th c. reads: "God Enlil holds the rule over the 33 stars of the northern sky, God Anu over the 23 stars to the side of the equator, and God Ea commands the stars of the southern sky".

In the library of Ashurbanipal, for instance, one such tablet contained an itemized list of eclipses in the first half of the month of January. The significance of the eclipses depended on the region of the sky in which a given eclipse could be seen. There were separate tables for divination by solar and lunar eclipses and by the movements of the stars.

Stargazers: Another type of atrologer had detailed tables listing the gatherings of the stars and their significance. Thus one of the tablets recorded a prophecy that "when Mars (Opin in Babylonian) approaches Scorpion, the prince will die of the sting of a scorpion and his son will succeed to his throne." In the course of time, different systems of divination from the stars, many of them very intricate, were developed.

"Monthly Prognosticators": Sages who read divine omens from the appearance of the new moon were called "monthly prognosticators". A big "book" on astrology by one Sargon of Akkad, written towards the end of the 3rd millenium BCE, lists various symbols and omens, for instance: "if the new moon is seen on the first of the month and on the 27th of the (same) month, evil will befall (the country of Elam), and if the moon be seen on the first of the month and on the twenty-eighth of the (same) month, evil will befall the land of Ahuru." The exact angle of the crescent at the time of the moon's appearance also served as an omen.

II. WORSHIP OF THE "HOST OF HEAVEN" AMONG CANAANITES AND ISRAELITES: In Canaanite religion, worship of the heavenly bodies was only secondary, although there are a number of hints in the Bible pointing to the worship of the moon and the sun (Dt. 4:19; 17:3; II K. 23:5; Jer. 8:2; Job 31:26–27; Ezk. 8:16) and warning the people of Israel against these cults. It seems that Jericho was named after the cult of the moon and the same name, Jerah, belonged to an Arabian tribe (Gn. 10:26; 1 Ch. 1:20). In spite of the prohibition on sun-worship, people like Samson and Shimshai, and places like Beth-Shemesh, Ain-Shemesh or Ir-Shemesh might be named after the sun-god. The divinity was also named Heres, which is preserved in Timnath-heres (Jud. 2:9), contemptuously transposed to the disparaging Timnath-serah in Joshua (19:50; 24:30).

Amos 5:26 introduces the subject of star-worship. The worship of the host of heavens, "Mazalôt" or "Mazarôt" (Job. 38:32) was listed among the sins of the Israelites, derived from foreign cults (II K. 17:16–17). In Jerusalem, incense was burned "to Ba'al, to the sun and the moon and the constellations, and all the host of the heavens" (II K. 23:5). Josiah, during his reform (ca. 620–621 BCE), "burned the chariots of the sun" to root out this "heathenish" practice (II K. 23:11).

The Bible contains many hints of the existence of astrology, but all in the negative. Its existence was recognized but the system was rejected. Alone among oriental peoples, the Jews resisted the beliefs and practices connected with astrology (see Astronomy, below).

III. THE SIGNS OF THE ZODIAC: By noting the direction of the sun from the south horizon when it cuts the meridian at noon, the Babylonians were able to identify the sun's track through a belt of 12 star clusters, called the Zodiac, corresponding to the twelve 30-day months of the Babylonian year (see Calendar*). The star clusters of the Zodiac are not systems of bodies with any known relationship between themselves. They are simply signposts of the seasons. These milestones, the zodiacal constellations, were groups of stars whose rising and setting positions roughly corresponded to that of the sun at a particular season. The phenomenon of the rising and setting of stars show that the sun changes its position relative to the fixed stars, as if retreating eastwards through a complete circle in the celestial sphere (observe the sun's apparent annual retreat through the zodiacal constellations, **233**).

Stargazing led the ancients to visualize their constellations in human and animal form, which they called the signs of the Zodiac. Gods about whom tales existed were associated

233

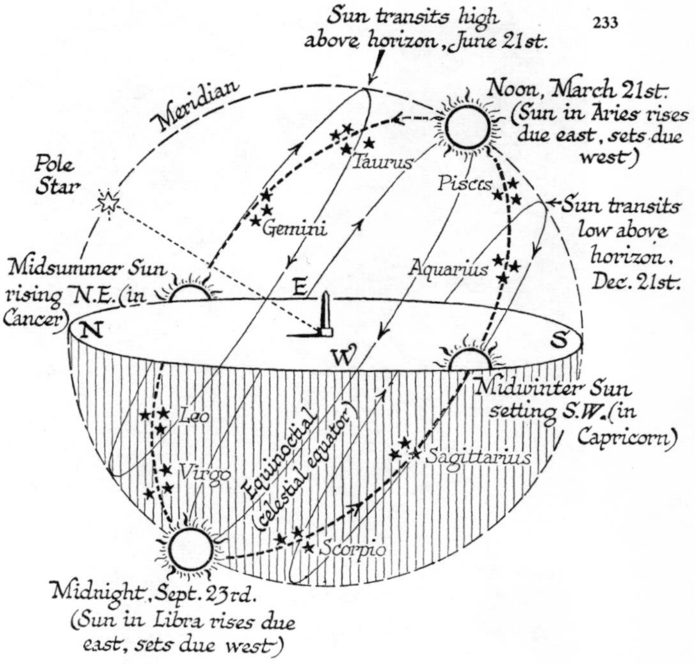

with heavenly bodies. Assyrian stone border markers of the 12th and 13th cs. BCE were incised with signs for the constellations which lay in the path of the sun, as shown (**234**): the Scorpion, the Archer, the Lion, Cancer, the Charioteer, Orion, the Twins, etc. . . . The division of the Ecliptic into twelve equal signs of the Zodiac star clusters, Aries, Taurus, Gemini, Cancer, Leo, Virgo, Libra, Scorpio, Sagittarius, Capricornus, Aquarius, Pisces, dates from a later time. They were destined to survive the millenia.

The Zodiac in Biblical Literature: Biblical hints about the stars, Kema and Ksil (see Astronomy, below) and their association with "the Bear and its children" and with "Mazarôt" (Job 38:31–32) are significant. So is a similar word, "mazalôt" in II K. 23:5, listed in the worship of the "host of heaven". Though the position of "mazarôt" is not identified, this may suggest that the signs of the Zodiac were already known to Israel in pre-Exilic times

The biblical term "mazalôt" (or mazarôt) was apparently used for the imaginary belt in the sky containing the twelve constellations, within which lie the paths of the principal planets and the sun. Though little is known of the belief in omens related to the stars beyond its condemnation in the Old Testament, it is a noteworthy fact that in post-Exilic times (the last centuries BCE), astrology began to be influential in the lives of ordinary men and women, among many Jews too, as may be seen from the numerous references in the book of Daniel*. Under the influence of current astrological theories, many Jews held that human life and

234

activity were strictly regulated by the movements of the heavenly bodies, which themselves were ruled by angels, as the book of Enoch insists (see Apocrypha*). An astronomical work from the Dead Sea Scrolls describes the physical characteristics of people born under a given sign of the Zodiac.

Later Midrashic literature (see Rabbis*), besides reproducing much astronomical and astrological lore, added a specific symbolism of its own by correlating the twelve tribes with the twelve constellations of the Zodiac, possibly to attenuate their mythological associations. The popularity of belief in the signs of the Zodiac is attested to by this tablet (**236**) from Gezer, dating from Hellenistic times. Another example is the relief of Tyche, surrounded by the Zodiac panel (**235**) from the Nabatean* Khirbet-al-Tannur, dating from the first century CE. The symbols also provided a popular subject for Jewish art, for example this wheel of the Zodiac (**237**) from the mosaic floor of the 6th c. CE synagogue* at Beth-Alpha. However, in spite of their artistic use and a certain ambivalence in belief which may be apparent on the surface, the signs of the Zodiac, the planets and the stars had none of the significance for the Jews which they had in Babylonia or, later on, in Greece (see Synagogues*).

There is an obvious correlation between the signs of the Zodiac and some of the symbols of the Christian apocalypse (Rev. 4:4, 6; 9:3, 5; 12:1; 21:19) although again these have no mythological significance, as in pagan practice.

Astrology in Hellenistic-Roman Times: Long before the conquests of Alexander the Great, the Hellenic world had been in touch with Babylonian astrology. "Chaldean" means "astronomer" in Aristotle's "Fragmenta", taking the term used for the astrologers' guild in antiquity. The sages of Greece gave the occult art a new aspect which changed an oriental belief into something which, outwardly at least, appeared far more rational. From being a mysterious art whose use was restricted to Asiatic royal courts, foretelling the future by the rules of astrology was popularized. It became open to any man to learn his fate from the position of the stars at the time of his birth. This wider scope demanded a much greater range of omens than were known to the Babylonians. The Greeks used their knowledge of mathematics to invent a multiplicity of omens and interpretations. The work of Claudius Ptolemaus, written in 130 CE, includes a resumé of Greek astrological systems which later provided the basis for mediaeval astrology.

The existence of an extensive literature on astrology is perhaps illustrated by the reference in Acts 19:19, where people who had been baptized in Ephesus are reported to have burned books to the value of 50,000 dinarii. Astromancy was forbidden to Christians just as it was to Jews.

IV. ASTRONOMY: It has been observed by many that although the astrology of the Babylonians did contribute to astronomical terminology, it is a question whether it did not actually delay investigation of the scientific aspects of astronomy. The contrary proves to be true. The example of the Babylonian empiric mentality is visible in his calendar-making; Babylonian astronomy developed particularly from the need for adjusting the calendar. As early as the fourth century BCE, the Chaldeans (see Babylonia*) made empiric but exact astronomical observations and from them knew the course of the stars, especially the planets. They could calculate the time of the appearance of the new moon and predict solar and lunar eclipses and similar phenomena. But they had an inadequate knowledge of the precise time when the sun enters the celestial equator (equinoctial line). Babylonian astronomy busied itself mainly with meteorological considerations. Nevertheless, their concept of the universe was basically mythological. The Greeks took over the Babylonian notion that the stars were gods and the Greek mythological names for the stars are used to this day (see Astrology, above).

The biblical writers refer to the stars, although they never endowed them with any mythological life of their own. The only indication as to how much empirical knowledge of the heavens the Israelites possessed comes from data on agriculture and the notions of meteorology and calendrical* matters. It is assumed that as a result of contacts with Egypt and Babylonia, the Jews had absorbed some of their more sophisticated knowledge of astronomy. However, these contacts never affected the biblical view of observable phenomena.

The Stars of the Bible: The Bible mentions stars and constellations frequently (all luminous heavenly bodies with the exceptions of the sun and the moon, are called stars), but only as a symbol of the greatness of God who had created them and alone could count them or direct their courses (Gn. 1:16; Ps. 8:3; 136:9; 147:4; Am. 5:8; Job 9:7; Jer. 31:35).

Biblical man had no awareness of astronomy in the modern scientific sense. The Israelites' view of the universe was entirely empirical. What emerges from the Bible is a concept of an orderly cosmos, huge and awe-inspiring, but completely under the control of the laws fixed by God. Within it, the stars are innumerable, but God had counted and named them all (Is. 40:26).

Certain stars and groups of stars are referred to by name in the Bible:

a. The Bear in Job 9:9 and the "Bear and its children" in Job 38:32: Apparently these refer to the seven prominent stars of Ursa Major, not Arcturus, the most luminous star in Boötes (a constellation in the Northern hemisphere, also called Aretophylax, which includes a very bright star).

b. Mazarôt (Job 38:32): It is not certain what this term meant (see astrology above). It might mean all the constellations of the heavens as in II Kings 23:5, or the twelve zodiacal signs (see part III).

c. The Pleiades (called Kema and Ksil in Hebrew, Am. 5:8; Job 9:9): a group of seven stars in the constellation

236

237

235

Taurus, not far from Orion (see below). The group is not very bright but it can be seen in Palestine just before dawn on a spring morning. For this reason, the power of awakening growth in spring has been ascribed to it.

d. Orion, the "Hunter" (Job 9:9; 38:31; Am. 5:8): This is the biggest constellation in the southern skies, containing such brilliant stars as Betelgeuse (top left, red) and Rigel (bottom right, blue). The range of colour and brightness of these adjacent stars find an illustration in I Co. 15:41.

e. "Chambers of the South" (Job 9:9): The exact reference is not known, although the phrase may perhaps refer to the stars that appear above the horizon to travellers going southward along the caravan route to Arabia. It is reported that one of the stars of the Southern Cross (which may be intended) is visible at Eilat, the southernmost point in Israel.

f. Kaiwân (Am. 5:26): possibly refers to Saturn (see Astrology, above), or to the planet Mercury.

g. Day Star, son of Dawn (Is. 14:12): is rendered as Venus in the Septuagint and Vulgate, as this planet appears at dawn. Some scholars believe, however, that the name refers to the moon crescent which appears in the morning towards the end of the lunar month. Alternatively, no actual star may be intended and the phrase may be merely a poetic metaphor.

V. BIBLICAL CONCEPT OF THE UNIVERSE: There is evidence that the Israelite picture of the universe drew heavily on the naive concepts and "wisdom" of the Babylonians and other neighbouring nations. Both the many poetic allusions in Hebrew imagery and the story of Creation* in Genesis (although with special features emphasizing its own theology) bear witness to such borrowing. The Babylonians, however, saw the world in a wider physical perspective and credited it with a greater age than did the Hebrew calendar* and chronology.

The picture that emerges from the Bible is of a universe with the earth at its centre. This universe was divided into three: the vault of the heavens, containing the sun, the moon and the stars; the earth beneath; and the waters under the earth (Ex. 20:4) and those above the heavens which are the source of rain. There is no great distance between the heavens and the earth. Birds fly into the vault of heaven, but this has a great variety. The heavens are represented as made up of superimposed vaults (Dt. 10:14; I K. 8:27; Ps. 148:4) in the highest of which God holds court. The sun and the moon follow their courses through the heavens independently, while the stars are directed by the divine will (Ps. 147:4; Is. 40:26; Jud. 5:20).

The celestial vault rested on the earth, supported by a circular range of mountains (Job 26:10–11) while the earth itself either rested directly on the surounding waters, or was supported on columns rising up from the depths to support heavens and earth alike (I Sam. 2:8; Ps. 75:3; Job 9:6). Against this, there is the statement in Job 26:7 to the effect that the earth "hangs upon nothing". A modern diagram (**237a**) after S. H. Hooke, gives an approximate rendering of the idea. The biblical picture was based on empirical observation, but it was expressed in poetic and, ultimately, mythical language.

A Monotheistic View: Considering the time during which biblical cosmogony was developed and preserved in writing, its most striking feature is its unequivocal monotheism. Israel's neighbours of the same period worshipped the stars. The Deuteronomist warned the Israelites against following suit but Second Isaiah could say: "Lift up your eyes on high and see: who created these? He who brings out their host by number, calling them all by name;" (40:26).

The Hebrew vision of the universe had no place for astronomy or astrology. Stars played little or no part in Israelite life, although some of them do seem to have been endowed

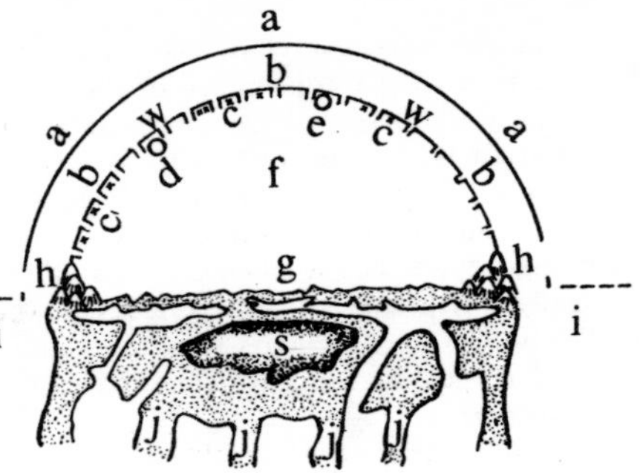

237a

The Hebrew conception of the Universe. The Hebrews assumed that the universe consisted of a flat earth supported over a watery abyss. The solid arched firmament held back the waters above the earth and the heavenly bodies were attached to it. A circular range of mountains supported the firmament at the outermost limits of the earth. (a) *Heaven, the dwelling place of God.* (b) *the waters above the firmament.* (w) *Windows.* (c) *Stars.* (d) *Sun.* (e) *Moon.* (f) *Arched firmament of heaven.* (g) *Earth.* (h) *Mountains and pillars of the firmament.* (i) *Tehom — watery abyss.* (s) *Sheol.* (j) *Pillars of the earth.* (*After S. H. Hooke*)

with more qualities than those of a merely "observable phenomenon". It is possible that stars which were identified with gods in pagan myths were transmuted into angels (see Is. 40:26 above; or Job 38:7 where "the morning stars rejoiced" at the creation). More important, Daniel assigns star-angels to the 70 nations (see Daniel*).

Later Speculation: Later on, especially in post-Exilic times, the several heavens, the course of the stars and their effect on man's destiny became the subjects of mystic speculation (see Apocrypha*, Apocalypse*: Enoch, Jubilees). The background is full of imaginative speculation and the association of the movements and activity of the skies and seas with divine beings. These were malevolent or beneficent. The universe was regarded personally as "He", rather than impersonally as "it". Chapters 72–82 of Enoch are an imaginary reckoning of the movements of the sun and the moon, which tells us much about the author of Enoch and current speculations, but contributes nothing to the knowledge of astronomy.

The Apocalyptic Vision: Of much greater significance in Enoch and other apocalyptic writings including the New Testament, is the conviction that the entire world will ultimately be consumed by fire. The picture varies. Fourth Esdras (Ezra) speaks of a period of silence following the catastrophe, after which a new earth will be created. (Other visions of the new heavens and the new earth and the cosmic battle that will destroy the present ones are described in articles under Apocalyptic Literature*, Dead Sea Scrolls*, etc.). The visions are echoed in the New Testament apocalypse (Revelation), where John of Patmos refers to the final battle of Armageddon (19:19–21), the Last Judgment (20:11–15), and the visions of the new universe (21:1–8) (see above, Signs of the Zodiac; also Calendar*.)

B

BABYLONIA AND ISRAEL. — *Outline: I. Early History: Proto-Literate or Pre-dynastic Period; Early Sumerian (Dynastic) Period* (2800–2371 BCE)*; Akkad* (2371–2181 BCE)*; Renaissance of Sumer; The Empire of Ur* (*= the IIIrd Dynasty;* 2060–1960 BCE)*; The Fall of Ur; Survival of Sumerian Culture; The Amorites; The Kingdoms of Mari and Babylonia. II. History of Babylonia: First (Amorite) Babylonian Dynasty; Cassite and Assyrian Supremacy* (1595–745 BCE)*; Assyrian Domination* (745–626 BCE)*; The Neo-Babylonian Empire* (626–539 BCE)*; Nebuchadrezzar; Nabonidus; The Fate of Babylonia. III. Religion: The Deities of Sumer and the Religion of Babylonia; Religion and Myth; Magic; Cult; Priesthood and Temples; Festivals. IV. Mesopotamian Civilization: Law; Writing; Literature; Science and Medicine; Astrology and Astronomy; The Art of Mesopotamia; The Ziggurats and the "Tower of Babel".*

Babylonia was the southern area of the great alluvial plain that lies between the Euphrates and the Tigris, and is now south Iraq. It covered about 8,000 square miles, bordered on the north by Assyria*, on the east by Elam*, on the west by the Arabian desert and on the south by the swamps that fringe the Persian Gulf.

In Gn. 10:10; 11:2 this area is called the valley or the land of Shinar (Sumer) and, later, the land of the Chaldeans (Jer. 50:10) which is a name often used in the Bible for the Babylonians (Is. 39:2; II K. 20:12, passim). In earlier times the northern area had been the land of Akkad, peopled mainly by Semites, while the southern reaches of the rivers and the marshes at their mouths were known as Sumer, their population largely Sumerian.

The oldest city in the Sumerian tradition was Eridu on the Persian Gulf. Babylon, Erech (Uruk) and Akkad are the first to be mentioned by the Bible (Gn. 10:10). They, Ur, Larsa and Isin were all situated on or near the Euphrates. Lagash and Umma lay to the south. Further north were Shuruppak, Kish, Nippur and Sippar. To the north-east lay Askak and Eshnunna, with Mari on the Euphrates to the north-west (see map **238**).

I EARLY HISTORY: **Proto-Literate or Pre-dynastic Period:** From archaeological discoveries, especially from the earliest types of pottery unearthed, it appears that the first settlements in Babylonia were made at the end of the Chalcolithic and beginning of the Early Bronze Age (4000–3000 BCE), distinguished as the pre-Ubaid and Ubaid culture (near Ur); the Uruk culture, and a third at modern Jemdet-Nasr (3200–3000 BCE) which witnessed the beginning of agricultural settlement. The first canals were dug to bring water to irrigate crops of grain and vegetables; cattle were raised; reed huts and clay houses were built as dwellings, and coloured handmade pottery (i.e., without the use of a wheel) was made (see also Flood*).

The Uruk period (3500–3200 BCE) saw the building of temples and ziggurats (temple-towers, see below), one of the oldest and perhaps the most famous being the one of Uruk itself. The earliest inscriptions were made on clay tablets in this period. This was apparently a Sumerian civilization, though the inhabitants of Sumer at that period cannot be identified with certainty. It is now assumed that while the Sumerians populated the south, the Semites lived in the north of Babylonia. In the Uruk levels, clay tablets were found inscribed with pictograph writing in what appears to be an early non-Semitic agglutinative Sumerian language, using names for older cities and certain technical terms which appear to be a still different, (non-Sumerian) language. It is not known whether the people of Uruk and Ubaid were Sumerians or not, as most of the names of the Sumerian cities are not Sumerian, yet the inhabitants were Sumerians. It is also clear that Semites lived in Mesopotamia for a long time along with the Sumerians, both elements influencing one another.

Early Sumerian (Dynastic) Period (2800–2371 BCE): Soon after 3000 BCE, individual kings began to establish themselves within a number of city-states. The Sumerian king list gives the names of eight or ten kings who ruled "before the flood*" in the cities of Eridu, Bab-tibira, Larak, Sippar and Shuruppak. Ziusudra, the hero of the Sumerian flood* story (see article) is also named as the ruler of Shuruppak.

After the flood, according to Sumerian tradition, "kingship came down from heaven". The rulers of Kish and Uruk (biblical Erech) include Gilgamesh and Agga, both legendary heroes who may quite possibly be historical characters. The economies of city-states, such as Uruk, Kish, Ur, Lagash and Mari were controlled by the temples (see Religion, below).

The first recorded dynasty of Ur was also made up of five kings who are mentioned in inscriptions as legendary, semi-historical figures. At first their actual existence was doubted, but more recent archaeological discoveries have included inscriptions from the early third millenium BCE, which prove that these kings were historical figures. Perhaps the earliest royal inscriptions are of the kings of Kish (possibly 27th and 26th century BCE) and their contemporaries, the city-rulers of Lagash and Ur. The new findings have provided scholars with documents of the earliest historical period in Sumer, which at that time was already a highly developed civilization.

Sporadic strife between the city kings for supremacy and dominion in Sumer, particularly among Ur, Kish and Lagash, produced a crop of "victory stele". For instance, King Eannatum of Lagash (25th c. BCE) celebrated his victory over the city of Umma, which apparently gave him control over the whole of Sumer, on the stele of Vultures (**239**) where the God Ningirsu entangles the king's enemies in a symbolic net. Quite often more than one ruler would seek to dominate a particular area or city at the same time, and clashes were frequent.

In times of peace the "ishakku" or priest-princes and their allies "the men of influence" would impose oppressive taxes upon the peasants, artisans and merchants of Lagash. But one ishakku, Urukagina (ca 2380 BCE), who was a social reformer, revoked these abuses "of old"; he expelled the usurious tax collectors and dictatorial men of influence,

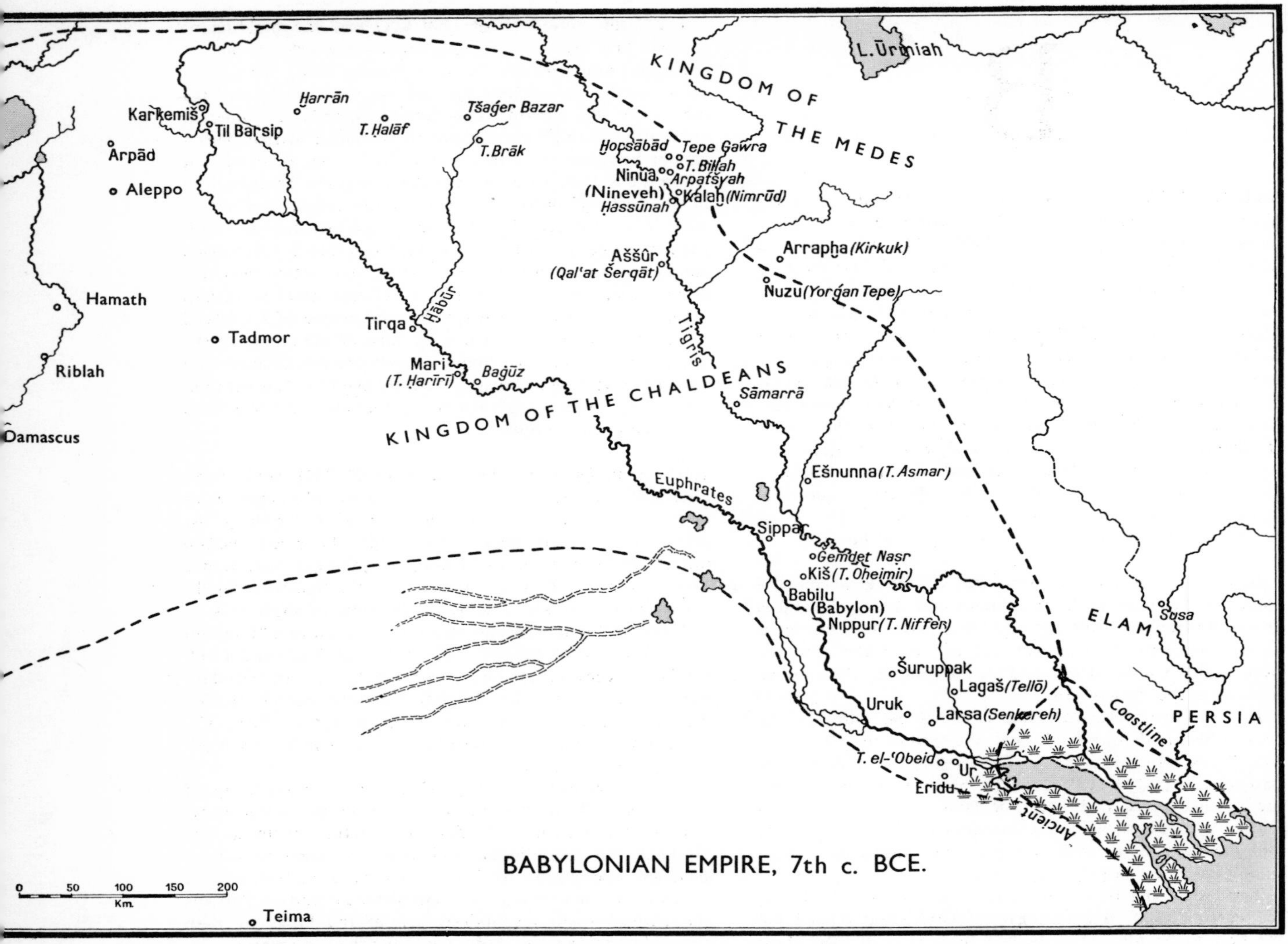

BABYLONIAN EMPIRE, 7th c. BCE.

238

suppressed thievery and crime and restored civil liberties to the people of Lagash. He ruled for ten years only, then was defeated by his rival of Umma north of Sumer. Though Lagash perished, Urukagina's reforms were remembered and had lasting social consequences.

The early dynastic period yielded a wealth of archaeological discoveries, including a variety of art treasures as illustrated by the panel of victory on the Ur Standard which is a remarkably revealing document of the dress and behaviour of the Sumerians. Pottery, now made on the wheel, was in various simple shapes, painted brown or yellow, and decorated with carved geometric designs. Houses were made of sun-dried clay brick, while the bricks for palaces and temples were usually burnt in a kiln. Thick brick walls usually surrounded the cities. Moreover, the discoveries have proved that close connections between the civilizations of Sumer and Egypt existed from the very earliest times.

Akkad (2371–2181): Alongside the Sumerian inhabitants of Mesopotamia, groups of Semitic peoples had settled, more particularly further north near the site of the future Babylon. (According to the later tradition, Babylon had been founded long before by the god, Marduk.) In the 24th century BCE, a new "Sargonid" dynasty (so-called from its founder, Sargon I) conquered the Sumerian cities. Sargon was a member of a strong Semitic family from Kish and he founded a new city at Agadê (Akkad). The tradition about Babylon suggests perhaps the existence of an earlier sacred site, but nothing definite is known so far since the site of Agadê has not been excavated. Gn. 10:10 also refers to the founding of Akkad in "the land of Shinar", namely Sumer, although according to biblical tradition, its founder was the great hunter, Nimrod, and was as old as Babylon, Erech and Calneh. Akkad (Agadê) gave its name to the rest of the Semitic population of early Babylonia. The Akkadians took over much of the culture of the Sumerians, even adopting the Sumerian cuneiform script for their distinctly different language.

The First Empire (The Sargonid dynasty of Akkad, 2371–2191 BCE). After defeating Lugalzagezi, the ruler of Uruk and Umma, the king of Mari and, later the ruler of Elam, Sargon established the Akkadian dominion from Elam to the Mediterranean — the first empire in world history. Sargon's wide domains were extended by his grandson, Naram-Sin, who conquered and ruled over Syria. Naram-sin's victory stele (see illus. Arms*) showing him, in gigantic proportions, wearing the horned tiara of the gods (see below) is an outstanding example of the sculpture of the time. Later, at the end of their rule, the Akkadians organized a system of baggage transport by chariots through the land (see Arms*, Bronze Age).

Renaissance of Sumer: During the reigns of the last kings of Akkad, their dominions were under constant attack from the Guti, a barbarian people from the hills east of the Tigris, and other barbarians from the Zagros mountains.

Soon after 2180 BCE, these attacks brought the Akkadian empire to an end, although the individual Mesopotamian states survived. The break-up of the empire paved the way for the renaissance of the city-states of Sumer, notably 21st century BCE Lagash, under its ruler (ensi), Gudea. He seems to have been a good administrator and a great builder. During his reign, Lagash and the neighbouring cities which she controlled revived, new temples were built and the arts encouraged, statues of Gudea **(240)** as architect being among the best known works of art of the period. Moreover, Gudea initiated commercial enterprises as far afield as Syria in pursuit of timber, precious stones and metals. With these he increased his city's prosperity and built the foundations for the Sumerian renaissance or "Golden Age" of economic and artistic achievements which followed.

The Empire of Ur (= **The IIIrd Dynasty** — 2060–1960 BCE): After Gudea's death, leadership in the area passed first to Utuhegal, king of Uruk, and Gudea's son-in-law, Namahani, king of Lagash. At the end of their reigns, the governor (ensi) of Ur, Ur-Nammu (ca. 2060 BCE), founder of the 3rd dynasty, worsted the king of Uruk and recovered his domination of the area. Ur-Nammu rebuilt the citadel of Ur, with its ziggurat (stepped tower) and temples, and set up statues of himself in the temples of Uruk, Isin and Nippur, which were governed by his nominees. Gradually, this third dynasty of Ur, known as the "Kingdom of Sumer and Akkad", extended its influence northwards to the city of Ashur (see Assyria*) and the river Dyala. Ur-Nammu's son, Shulgi and his successors were even accorded divine honours, being pictured on their monuments and seals wearing the horned crown of the gods, like Naram-Sin earlier. The organization of law, administration and religion in this quite extensive "Kingdom of Sumer and Akkad", as revealed by thousands of official documents, entitle it to be regarded as the first bureaucratic empire in history. The prosperous Third Dynasty of Ur traded with countries as far afield as India.

The Fall of Ur: As so often happened, the overthrow of Ur's apparently secure and stable empire came as a result of attacks from a new influx of invaders. As from about 1960 BCE, the Elamites who had previously paid Ur tribute and

239

240

241

the Amorites (or westerners), Semitic semi-nomads from the western districts, had been infiltrating from the desert region to the north-west of the Euphrates. By the 18th century BCE, they finally succeeded in establishing themselves in many parts of the land. Their success came during the reign of the fifth king of the Third Ur dynasty, Ibbi-Sin, a time of disastrous famine and economic decline. At the same time, many of the various city-states of the empire were moved to make a bid for independence.

The power of Ur collapsed. (The question of the possible relation between the fall of Ur and the story of the Patriarchs is discussed under Patriarchs*.)

Survival of Sumerian Culture: The empire had taken over much of the older Sumerian culture which had dominated Babylonia for almost a millenium. When the Sumerians lost all political power, the influence of their culture survived and increased. Their language was preserved as the "holy tongue" of religion and their literature was taught in the schools of Babylonia right up to the Hellenistic* period, very much as Latin was preserved in the Middle Ages, centuries after Rome had been obliterated as a political force.

The Amorites: During the following century, the territories once ruled by the mighty kings of Ur split up, the local rulers of Ashur, Mari, Eshnunna and Babylonia sharing the lands of the upper Euphrates. The loyalties of the previously united Sumerians in the east and south of Babylonia were divided between the newly independent states of Isin (under Ishbi-Irra) and Larsa, under an Amorite dynasty. Amorites ruled Qatna and Aleppo in Syria, and Amorite dynasties became established in many of the city-states, notably Babylon and Eshnunna. The Amorites took over Akkadian culture wholesale, adopting much of its religion and language and using the Akkadian style of writing.

The Kingdoms of Mari and Babylonia: These did not rise to supremacy immediately. The genealogical lists of the reigning houses of the kingdoms of Upper and Lower Mesopotamia during the 19th and 18th centuries BCE are good evidence of the long struggles among the rival powers. The discovery of the royal archives of Mari provided a clear picture of the intrigues, alliances and campaigns that, after 130 years, saw the victory of Hammurabi of Babylonia over his opponents, including the principal one, Mari.

Mari: Mari's history begins during the late Sumerian period of Amorite attacks, as illustrated by an inscription on the statue of one of the early kings of Mari. During the 19th century the kingdom's population became increasingly Amorite. The peak period of Mari's power was reached under Zimri-lim, a contemporary of Hammurabi. At this time, Mari ranked briefly as one of the major powers of the day. Its territory stretched from the borders of Babylonia to Carchemish in upper Mesopotamia (see map) and included the upper reaches of the Balikh and Khabur rivers — the area known as Aram-Naharaim, the fatherland of the Patriarchs*.

Excavation of Mari by A. Parrot in 1933–35 CE uncovered not only a large and wealthy city with a palace of some 250 rooms whose drains have survived to this day, but also over 20,000 tablets and fragments in Akkadian. About 5,000 of these represent diplomatic and administrative correspondence between the king and his officials in neighbouring countries. The rest are business and other documents which show that economic life was highly organized. In the days of Zimri-lim, trade moved freely from Mari to Byblos* and Ugarit* on the Mediterranean coast, overseas to Cyprus and Crete and throughout Anatolia and Mesopotamia.

Like the other Amorite states, Mari had adopted Akkadian culture. The people spoke a language akin to that of the Patriarchs. (Connections between the Mari tablets and the origins of the Hebrews are discussed under Patriarchs*.) Its religion represented a combination of northwest Semitic and Mesopotamian features (see below), for instance the goddess holding a flowing vase found in the palace of Mari (see Gn.:* Creation stories) and the wall painting whose decorative scheme uses stylized trees, human figures in a ritual act and mythological motifs of cherubs. The great temple to Dagon was surrounded by forty guardian lions.

II. HISTORY OF BABYLONIA: The three main periods of Babylonia's long history can be divided into a. the First Babylonian Dynasty, which came to an end with the rise of Assyria* and was followed by b. a period of decline, then c. the period of the Neo-Babylonian empire which lasted from the fall of Assyria* to the rise of the Persian* empire.

First (Amorite) Babylonian Dynasty: Around 1830 BCE, the invading Amorites made Babylon, on the east bank of the Euphrates, their capital. During the reigns of five kings, Babylonian power was extended over northern Mesopotamia. Then came the great king, Hammurabi (1728–1686 BCE or 1792–1750 according to an earlier chronology), sixth of this dynasty. In the first thirty years of his reign, he was no more powerful than the king of Yamhad (Aleppo) in northern Syria. Evidence of the diplomacy, religion, trade and history of the period which comes from the Mari* letters shows that Hammurabi did not subdue Assyria, Eshnunna or all cities in Babylonia. But during the last years of his rule, after subduing Larsa, Mari and Eshnunna, Hammurabi reigned over an empire that stretched from the Persian gulf to Mari. Yet his fame rests not so much on his military successes as on his career as law-giver and administrator.

His empire was divided into districts, each ruled by a governor charged with the administration of the imperial law. Hammurabi's famous code of laws (see Law*) is preserved on an 8 feet high stele of black diorite; unearthed in 1902 CE from Susa whither it had been taken by the Persians as war booty). The upper part of the stele shows Hammurabi, his right hand raised in supplication, standing before Shamash, the sun god, who hands him a sceptre and a ring (illustr. under Law*).

Peace was maintained within Hammurabi's dominions by means of a standing army. As a result, the last decade of his reign was a period of stability and prosperity for his people and this continued under his successor. Trade was fostered with other countries. Industry developed and flourished and, at the same time, the city of Babylon enjoyed a remarkable cultural flowering in literature (the principal language of the time was the Semitic Akkadian), art and architecture. Temples were rebuilt and irrigation canals restored and extended.

Cassite and Assyrian Supremacy (1595–745 BCE): After Hammurabi's death, Babylonia's political power declined. Although his dynasty continued to rule over large parts of the country, other areas were slowly absorbed by the invading Cassites, barbarian people coming from the Zagros mountains (perhaps Cush of Gn. 10:8). In 1595 BCE, Babylon itself was sacked in a sudden assault made from the north by the Hittite, Mursili I. The Hittites, the first Indo-European people in history, do not appear to have established themselves in the city, and twenty years later Babylon was re-taken by the Cassites who established a dynasty which was to rule in Babylon until 1160. Karigalzu II established a new capital, Dur-Karigalzu, built in the eastern hills around 1450 BCE. The Cassites assimilated with the Babylonians and took over their civilization and religion.

The early part of the Cassite rule (16th–15th c.) was a relatively dark age. It ended in the 14th century, when there was a new ferment of international activity as part of a general cultural resurgence which affected the whole Near East. The El Amarna* letters include correspondence from the Cassite rulers to the Egyptian Pharaohs. At home, Babylonian literature flourished. Ancient writings were assembled and copied, and new compositions undertaken.

After the Amarna period, Babylonia remained very weak politically, although she generally managed to preserve her independence, except for brief periods of subservience to Assyria (e. g. under Tukulti-Ninurta I, 1234–1228 BCE, see Assyria*). Elamite or Aramean* incursions were frequent.

The appearance of occasional national heroes brought brief returns of relatively strong rule, as for instance, when Nebuchadrezzar I (1124–1103 BCE) defeated the Elamites, but these were all short-lived. The ensuing four cs. were a period of long decline from which few documents have survived. This was the time when Chaldean (Aramean*) tribes settled in southern Babylonia and established their principalities.

Assyrian Domination (745–626 BCE): The Assyrian Emperor Tiglat-Pileser III (745–727 BCE) had himself proclaimed "King of Sumer and Akkad". Towards the end of his reign (728 BCE), he "took the hands of Bel (Marduk)" and thus laid claim to the throne of Babylonia, displacing the reigning Nabu-Nasir (Nabonassar; see Assyria*). His Babylonian name was Pul (II K. 15:19; I Ch. 5:26). There were continuous attempts to dislodge the Assyrians, led unsuccessfully by Ukin-zer of Bit-Amukkani; later and more successfully, Marduk-apla-iddina II (Merodach-Baladan) of Bit-Yakin took advantage of dynastic strife in Assyria after the death of Shalmaneser V who had besieged Samaria (see Assyria*: Shalmaneser V and Sargon II) to take the throne of Babylonia. He held it for ten years (721–710 BCE). At the end of that time, Sargon II re-established Assyrian overlordship in Babylon and "took the hands of Bel." But after Sargon's death, Merodach-Baladan made a new bid for independence in alliance with the kings of Phoenicia and the Philistine coast as well as Judah, and with the encouragement of Egypt (705 BCE; see Assyria*). He was dislodged by Sennacherib and later died, a fugitive. The country was then ruled by Assyrian deputy kings. The strife with Assyria did not end and in 689 Sennacherib destroyed the city of Babylon which lay desolate until his son Esarhaddon rebuilt it. Another rebellion of the native Chaldeans and Arameans against Ashurbanipal was quelled in 648 BCE and Babylon looted.

The Neo-Babylonian Empire (626–539 BCE): Babylonia's chance came finally when the Chaldean prince, Nabopolassar, struck again for independence, winning the throne and establishing the neo-Babylonian empire (626 BCE). He then proceeded, in alliance with the Medes, to destroy the Assyrian empire (see details under Assyria*).

Nebuchadrezzar and Judah: In May 605 BCE, Nebuchadrezzar II made a surprise attack on Carchemish, sacked the city and annihilated the army of the Egyptian Pharaoh, Necho, at Hamat. After this victory, the Babylonians took control of the whole of Syria, right down to the Egyptian border. Jehoiakim, King of Judah, submitted to Nebuchadrezzar until, in 601 BCE, a bitter battle was fought between the Egyptians and the Babylonians causing such heavy losses to both sides that the following year the Babylonian army stayed at home to recover and re-equip. His further operations against Judah, leading up to the destruction of Jerusalem in 587 BCE, are related under Israel and Judah* Part V.

At this time, Nebuchadrezzar's empire seemed unassailable. A building programme was undertaken in Babylon to give visible expression to the strength of the empire. Babylon was decorated with temples and palaces while a great, lavishly decorated "Procession Street" was built and embellished, for example, with this lion (**242**) painted on glazed tiles. It extended beyond the Gate of Ishtar to the "New Year festival house" (Akitu) outside the city. This cylinder is inscribed with text of Nebuchadrezzar (**241**).

In Babylon, the exiled Judean king, Jehoiachin, was well treated, apparently. Tablets dated to 595–570 BCE, found in the ruins of Babylon, record the rations allowed to the king, who is mentioned by name. Nebuchadrezzar's successor, Amel-Marduk (562–560 BCE; namely Evil-Merodach, II K. 25:27), continued to deal honourably with his captive but after a reign of only two years during which the priesthood became increasingly opposed to him, he was assassinated and replaced by his brother-in-law, Neriglissar (Nergal-sharezzer).

Nabonidus: Neriglissar took control in Babylonia at a time when its dominions were being increasingly threatened by an expanding Lydia in Asia Minor. After reigning only 9 months, he, in turn, was displaced by Nabonidus, a man of Aramean descent. Nabonidus attempted to introduce various reforms into Babylonia's religious and administrative structure, but these met with no response from his people and he turned his back on Babylon. He established himself in Teima in Arabia* and spent the next ten years campaigning through north and south Arabia, while his son, Belshazzar, wielded power in Babylonia as regent. At the end of the ten years, a change in the political climate in Babylonia, brought Nabonidus back to his capital, but it had become the centre of a weak and divided kingdom which fell an easy prey to the onslaughts of Cyrus, King of the Persians (see Persia*). A blurred image of Nabonidus is preserved in the allegory of Nebuchadrezzar and his dream in Daniel ch. 2–4, as well as the Dead Sea Scroll* referring to him (see Daniel*).

The Fate of Babylonia: With the coming of the Persians, Babylon's life continued as a city, but all its political power was at an end. It became merely a part of the Achaemenid empire (see Persia*) until this fell before the advancing Macedonians under Alexander.

This new disaster, however, did not mean the end of Mesopotamian civilization. Alexander the Great made the city of Babylon his capital (331–323 BCE), and after his death it remained in the hands of his successors, becoming one of the centres of the Seleucid empire (312–64 BCE; see Hellenism*). However, Babylonia's independence was at an end. When it was conquered by the Parthians in 64 BCE, it had lost all vitality, and by 115 CE it was merely a famous pile of ruins — a suitable historic attraction for the visiting Roman emperor, Trajan. In 640 CE, the site was added to the conquests of invading Arabs.

242

III. RELIGION: The Babylonians took over most of the polytheistic religion of the Sumerians, in which the forces of nature were symbolized and controlled by different gods. These could generally be divided into two groups: The upper world and the skies were peopled by Egigi—gods; the lower world and the dead by Anunaki. Although the gods were immortal, their power was limited.

The universe was not something constant, and the will of the gods was far from unchangeable. The capricious alterations in their desires and intentions were something that man was powerless to foresee or to understand. Man's function, according to the Babylonian epic, was merely to serve the gods by supplying them with food and dwelling places. Death was the limit of a man's horizons and, while he lived, the earth that was his home belonged, with all its fruits, to the gods.

The Deities and Myths of Sumer and the Religion of Babylonia: The Sumerians (see Part I) began the making of lists of the names, titles, epithets and temples of their gods as early as the 3rd millenium. These were continued by the Babylonians and finally totalled some 2,500 gods. However, these included earlier Sumerian deities assimilated by the Semites of the First Dynasty of Babylon (19th century BCE). The actual number worshipped at any one time was considerably less. The Babylonians took over from the Sumerians a syncretic system combining a number of local city and district cults. In time, as the political and theological systems developed and unified, the numbers of these various gods were reduced by identifying a number of originally distinct gods into a single deity (see Priesthood, below). It would be wrong to refer to the deities of Babylonia and Assyria in terms of a schematic pantheon for this reflects modern reconstructions.

The major deities of Sumer were An, god of heaven and father of all gods, whose principal temple was at Uruk (Erech), and his consort Innana (or Innin), the goddess of fertility. An was also taken over by the Akkadians as Anu, while Innana was called by them Ishtar.

The second major deity, in whom similar syncretic tendencies can be seen, was Enlil, the god of air and earth, with a temple at Nippur. His attributes were later taken over by Marduk, the god of Babylon. The third deity of the supreme trinity was the Sumerian god, Enki (who later become the Babylonian Ea). He was "lord of deep waters" and seas, creator of man and god of wisdom. These attributes made him especially well-disposed towards mankind, for whom he interceded with the other gods and to whom he revealed the means of learning the will of the gods by means of divination.

The Sumerians and Babylonians also worshipped the Semitic Ishtar, at first perhaps as a male deity. Later on, this deity took on the powers of Innana (Anu's consort) and through the general process of syncretism, Ishtar became the supreme goddess of love (symbolized by the planet Venus) and the heroine of warfare. Another astral deity was Shamash, the "strength of the sun" whose wife, Aja, also later came to be regarded as one manifestation of Ishtar. Shamash was the god of power, justice and war. A major astral deity was Sin, the Moon god. His centres of worship were Ur in Sumer and Harran in north Mesopotamia.

Nergal and his wife Ereshkigal ruled the underworld; thus he was the lord of plagues (Irra), fevers and maladies. The west Semitic god, Adad, was adopted by the Babylonians as lord of storms, rain and thunder, equivalent to the Canaanite-Aramean Hadad or Addu. As the Amorites rose to ascendancy within Babylonia (see above), so their god, Marduk (Sumerian, Amar-utu), the oldest son of Enki, became supreme among the gods of Babylonia. He was the patron god of the city of Babylon, and his temple, Etemenanki, was one of the wonders of the ancient world. Nabu (Nebo), the god of science and writing had temples in many cities, including Nineveh in Assyria. Portions of Ashurbanipal's great library (see Assyria*) were appropriately housed in the temples of Nabu. Many deities had greater authority in certain areas. Thus, Ashur was the supreme god of Assyria*. Dagan, too (Dagon in Scriptures) was west-Semitic in origin, and he was also worshipped in Mesopotamia in old Akkadian times.

A Sumerian god, Dumuzi (or Tammuz), the youthful lover of Ishtar and god of vegetation, became the hero of one of the Ishtar myths. He died, like the whole plant world, in the time of the greatest heat, his "weeping" taking place on the second of the month of Tammuz (June-July). Some of the dirges with which his descent to the nether-world was mourned survive to this day in Kurdistan. His cult was very popular, especially among women, although it never formed part of official religion, and the idea that a return to life was any part of his myth has now been discredited. During the 8th century BCE, the cult of Tammuz spread to Palestine (Zech. 12:11; see Israel and Judah*) and later he became identified with the Phoenician Adon (thence to become the Greek Adonis) and with the Egyptian Osiris.

The Babylonian and Assyrian god of war was Ninurta (Nimrod) who was also the patron of hunting. As time went on, almost every one of the gods absorbed many of the attributes of every other god. Thus, except for a few peculiarly appropriate epithets or titles, one god, Shamash, for instance, could be addressed or hymned in very much the same words as Marduk or Sin.

Religion and Myth: Very few of the principal deities figure in the myths of Babylonia. These myths mainly demonstrate the anthropomorphic character of Babylonia's faith and superstitions, every object, even a stone, being endowed with a life of its own. For the Babylonians, the universe was peopled with good and evil spirits and demons. Man's relation to the spiritual world is considered in many of the myths. They had a high ideal of divinity, expressed in many beautiful and poetic forms (see below).

Magic: Magic had an important place in their beliefs and in the practice of their religion. Spirits and demons had to be appeased or propitiated and defensive spells or malignant black magic were widely used to check or direct their activities. Augurers, conjurers, soothsayers and magicians formed a numerous class, called in whenever disease or disaster or the fear of them suggested occult influence (see Magic*; Medicine*).

A specialist in one aspect of man's approach to the gods was the exorcist (ašipu), skilled in removing an evil spirit or spell by means of the appropriate ritual as pre-

244

scribed in the traditional texts (šurpu; maqlu). This ritual might involve incantations, symbolic substitutions (kuppuru, cf. Hebrew kapparah), purification by the priests (mašmašu) or by those who cleansed by water (ramku). A whole literature has survived describing the actions to be taken against evil spirits (utukki limnuti), demons of fate, or demons mainly plaguing women (lamaštu; see illust. under Magic*).

Foretelling the future by means of divination and omens was an essential function of priest and magician alike. The will of the gods in regard to man's actions might be learned from observation of livers of sacrificial animals (read by the "baru", priest, or a "seer") or by inquiring of oracles (ša'ilu: cf. "sh'al" in Hebrew), or by offering prayers.

Cult: Statues of gods would be dressed and ornamented and votive figures placed near them by worshippers. The statue symbolizing the divine presence was also the personification of a real force. The maintenance of that force demanded the regular offering of food and drink and oil. It also necessitated the ritual cleansing of the idol, the priests and the sacred cultic objects. Many cylinder seals (**244**) show that the gods had their own chairs, and chariots or boats for use in processions. Sacrifices placed on the altar were subsequently allocated, either in part or entirely, to the priests.

Priesthood and Temples: In the earliest times, every head of a family was a priest of the local god with the right to minister at the temple. Later, the priestly office became restricted to a few families. The priesthood itself also developed into a complex organization, its functions subdivided, the temple becoming a major force in social and economic life, and its employees and officials forming a large part of the population. At the head of the priesthood, the king or ruler himself acted as supreme pontiff at certain solemn festivals. The high priestess of Sin (entu) was usually a royal princess. Under the chief priests (maḫḫu) were a number of assistant priests (šangu), males of sound body and often married. The chief liturgist (urigallu) was also assisted by a host of minor officials who had access to the temple, while chanters, psalmists, dirge-singers and musicians played an important part in the ritual of all religious ceremonies. A number of other specialists — judges, scribes, physicians and skilled artisans were usually attached to the temples, although sometimes these functions were also exercised by the priests.

243

Particular occasions marking a change in divine–human relations required special celebrations. The community's life depended on continuing good relations with the divine powers, so that all ceremonies were aimed at getting and keeping on good terms with the gods. Thus, for instance, special sacred texts were read at the time of changes from one season to another. These changes were the result of forces beyond human control or understanding and the ceremonies were designed to restore normal relations between the gods who, presumably, were responsible for them and the humans who must accept and conform to them. In this scene (**243**), Nabupalidin, third to the left, is seen approaching Shamash, the sun god, in fear and trembling, while dedicating his temple at Sippar.

Festivals: Each temple, city and month had its own characteristic festivals. At Babylon and Aššur, the ancient capital of Assyria, there was a New Year Festival. In Babylon, this took the form of a great parade by the king and all his people along Procession Street (**247**). Before the procession began, the king was temporarily reduced to the status of an ordinary citizen, then he renewed his submission to Marduk (Bel) and received in return the symbols of his royal authority. He "took the hands of Bel" (= Lord = i.e. Marduk) and led the god in the great procession to the "Festival House" (bît akīti) outside the city. There the "Wedding of the Gods" on which the prosperity of the realm depended was celebrated. The Epic of Creation was recited and the "fates decided". Ceremonial and festivities lasted eleven days, after which the gods were returned to the city in a renewed procession.

IV. MESOPOTAMIAN CIVILIZATION: A religious view of the world, which saw it and mankind as the creations and playthings of gods who could act erratically and had to be carefully propitiated before any major undertaking, had one significant effect. Society's place in nature became a matter of individual rights and responsibilities. The king was as much at the mercy of the gods as his subjects. To this extent all men were on an equal footing. Like the humblest citizen, the king had to guard against unwittingly offending the gods so, in line with ancient habits of popular rule, he sought the advice and approval of other people for his actions. The system became so completely accepted that even the gods were ruled by the decisions of their assembly (see Genesis*: Creation Myths; Flood*).

Law: Such an attitude contributed to the very great respect in which the law was held. The family, society, government and commerce were all ruled by law. This idea of law as a charter of human rights is one of Mesopotamia's great contributions to civilization. The most famous of the codes is that promulgated by Hammurabi (see above; Law*), but even before his time, comprehensive codes of laws were being formulated and have been preserved. Other inscribed tablets containing laws and thousands of business and legal documents of different sorts have been recovered from the ruins of ancient Mesopotamia and are stored in museums.

245a

Writing: Sumer was one of the earliest societies to develop a form of writing and this was bequeathed with so much else of its culture to Babylonia. Some of the earliest examples formed part of the temple archives and date back to the late 4th or early 3rd mill. BCE (see Alphabet and Writing*).

Literature: Very early in their history the Sumerians and Babylonians composed hymns, ritual texts and a mythology. The Babylonians had codes of law and astronomical textbooks. These had a great influence on surrounding and succeeding peoples, for their literature was preserved thoughout all the violent changes in political regime.

One of the most important literary achievements of the Babylonians was the "Epic of Gilgamesh", a heroic tale in eleven cantos which included a story of the Flood* (see article). Sporadic fragments of a similar story have been found among Sumerian literature. The Babylonian creation myth, Enuma Elish, however, appears to have had no Sumerian roots but to have been a completely Babylonian creation. The Creation story describes how Marduk reduced primeval chaos to order; he was promoted from the obscure position of local god of Babylon to become chief and military commander of all the gods. Other stories recorded on the clay tablets of Babylon's libraries include the myth of Ishtar, goddess of love, descending to the nether world in search of her beloved Tammuz. Just as in ancient Sumer, Egypt and elsewhere, "wisdom literature"* also flourished in early and later Babylonia. The best-known piece is the so-called "Babylonian Job" which, although it lacks the elevated theology and moral tone of the biblical book, contains many parallels to the Old Testament story (see Assyria*, VIII; Job*; Wisdom Literature*).

Science and Medicine: The early period produced an extensive medical literature, closely allied to religion and magic*. Spells were used to drive out the demon which was assumed to be the cause of disease. In later writings a very large number of different conditions are described and remedies prescribed. Unfortunately, it is only rarely possible to recognize either the ailment or the prescription (see Medicine*).

Astrology and Astronomy*: These twin sciences were also closely allied to magic and religion. In later times, the prominence of the priest who continued the ancient traditions of observation of the stars and divination from the omens observed, led to all priests, astrologers and educated men becoming known as "Chaldeans" (Dan. 3:8).

Astrology was based on the assumption that every god had his (or her) personal star (e.g. Nabu was equated with the planet Mercury) or portion of the heavens (fixed stars were "the Way of Anu"). As the gods ruled earthly destinies, movements of the stars and other celestial phenomena (eclipses, etc.) must indicate the future course of their earthly intentions. A whole literature grew up recording astronomical and weather observations and relating the events which followed them. The Babylonians learned the orbits of the sun, moon and stars and many of their observations were made with great precision (see Astronomy*). They used a sexagesimal mathematical system, dividing the circle into 360 degrees and the hour into 60 minutes, 3,600 seconds. They knew how to find the areas of triangles and polygons and at a very early date they drew up tables of squares and cubes as well as surface and capacity measurements (see Weights and Measures*).

The Art of Mesopotamia: The earliest works of art unearthed by archaeologists were cylinder seals* going back to the end of the 4th millenium BCE, decorated with animals and mythical figures, and pottery. In the south the earliest pottery was a matter of simple, unimaginative vessels, but in the north much more elegant and diversified shapes were made.

Some of the most beautiful art treasures of the world were discovered when the "graves of the kings" were excavated in Ur. Also the famous mosaic Standard, showing scenes of war on one side, and of peace on the other (**245a, b** see Warfare* and above: Early Sumerian Period). Myths served as a tangible garment of uncomplicated imagery in which to clothe abstract conclusions. This is why the pictorial presentation of mythical figures provides the subject of so much art. It requires little imagination to see in the intervention of the ponderous lion-headed eagle, Im-Dugud (**246**), whose wings shroud the heavens in dark clouds, the image of the benevolent rainstorm, bringing an end to a prolonged drought. The priest Dudu, wearing a flounced skirt, stands by his side (3rd mill. BCE).

A fruitful combination of the arts of stone carving and public relations was the commemorative stele, used even before the dynastic period to record historic events and achievements (see Early Sumerian Period, above). Most of the second millenium, however, did not produce any outstanding works in Babylonia. The sculptures are mainly stereotyped repetitions of Akkadian and Lagash traditions.

245b

246

248

247

The second half of the second millenium was the period of "Cassite art". The Cassites made no notable cultural impact on the country, rather accepting Babylonian civilization entire. However, between the 16th and 12th centuries BCE, they did produce a distinctive manner of stone carving in relief which has been preserved on boundary stones (**248**), showing gods (or their symbols) standing guard over the frontier.

The neo-Babylonian empire (see above) of Nabopolassar and his son, Nebuchadrezzar II, saw Babylon transformed into a vast, sophisticated metropolis adorned with a wealth of new buildings. Although no major works of art have survived other than those connected with architecture, these represent a continuation and revival of the ancient southern Mesopotamian traditions which had decayed following the collapse of the Cassite dynasty. The architects of the time adorned the facades of their buildings with painted glazed bricks, obtaining their most grandiose effects on the magnificent constructions which lined the wide Procession Street, in the Ishtar Gate (**247**) itself, and the palace of Nebuchadrezzar.

The Ziggurats and "Tower of Babel": Procession Street led from the Ishtar Gate, through the centre of Babylon to the main temple enclosure, Etemenanki, the "Building of the Foundation of Heaven and Earth", where stood

Marduk's "ziggurat", "e-sag-ila", or "the House that lifts up its Head". This ziggurat, popularly known as "the Tower of Babel", in fact has no real relation to the Bible story. The only connection is that the Babylon ziggurat is a late imitation of the very early staged temple towers built in most of the Mesopotamian dynastic cities. Built with two or three terraces, faced with kiln baked bricks, their colossal facades panelled and recessed, these huge structures dominated the Mesopotamian scene centuries before the neo-Babylonian kings instituted a great building programme to restore them to their former glory. Ur itself and the great cities of Eridu, Kish, Uruk, Nippur and, later, during the Cassite period, Dur Kurigalzu (Aqarqaf) all had ziggurats, the ruins of some of them standing to this day. The ziggurat of Ur-Nammu can be reconstructed from the remains of the building of the neo-Babylonian kings, as shown (**249**).

It is possible that the ziggurat was intended as a "stairway to heaven" and that the worshippers believed the gods descended from heaven to this "halfway house" meeting place. Genesis (11:1–9) used the form (and makes the first biblical mention of the name of Babylon or Babel) in a vivid fantasy designed to prove that at some point in human history, mankind had been scattered over many lands and thereafter spoke in many languages, forming a veritable "babble of tongues."

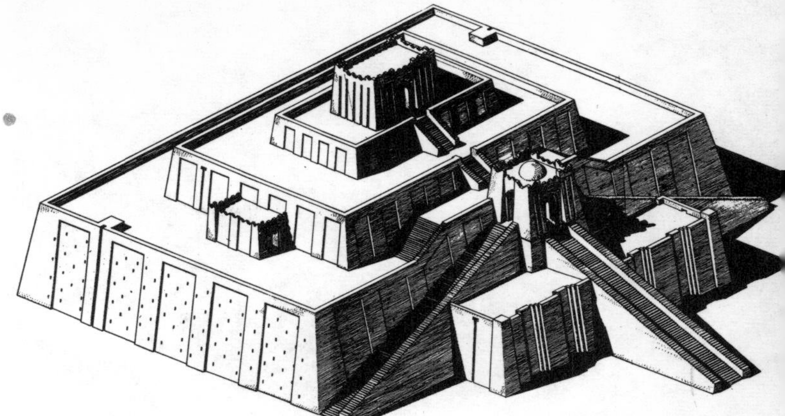

249

BAR KOCHBA (KOSBA). — *Outline: Trajan and the Rebellions in the Diaspora; The Repressions in Palestine (Judea); Emergence of Bar Kosba; The Early Stages of the War; A New Commonwealth is Established; Security Problems; Rome's Counter-Offensive; The Fall of Beitar; Aftermath of the Rebellion; Bar Kosba as Messiah; Bar Kosba and the Jewish-Christians.*

For over half a century following the destruction of the Jewish State and the Second Temple (see Rome and the Jews*: The War with Rome; 67–73 CE), Judea witnessed a period of transition and peaceful reconstruction. The spiritual leaders of the Jabneh Academy, the Patriarchs Johanan ben Zakkai and his successor, Gamaliel II, counselled moderation and a passive hope of divine redemption.

Trajan and the Rebellions in the Diaspora: The messianic dream did not disappear, however, while the activist group of rebels, the Zealots*, merely bided their time, keeping in contact with each other in the various diaspora communities. Their opportunity seemed to come in 115 CE, when the Roman Emperor Trajan's military campaign against the Parthians (114–117 CE) was accompanied by a severe earthquake that destroyed Antioch and many towns and villages in Asia Minor. A wave of rebellion led by the Zealots swept through the eastern diaspora, including Cyrenaica, Egypt, Cyprus and Mesopotamia.

The Cyrenaican rebellion was led by the Cyrenian "King" or "Messiah", Lukuas-Andreas, who regarded himself as the true messiah*. He attacked the Hellenistic cities and destroyed the capital, Cyrene, before the Romans could intervene. Lukuas' aim was to invade Judea and liberate it from the Romans, but he was defeated and later executed by the Roman governor of Palestine (Judea), General Lucius Quietus, who erected a statue of Trajan over the site of the Temple in Jerusalem in an attempt to quash all further messianic illusions.

Rebellion then spread to Egypt where it assumed more serious proportions, for it threatened to cut off the Roman armies from their home base. The Jews, however, made the fatal error of turning on their Greek neighbours who then sided with the Romans in their reprisals, which culminated in the wholesale massacre of the Jews of Alexandria. The revolt was finally put down only after several years of fighting, the Roman commander being Marcius Turbo whom Trajan sent to Egypt with a fleet, infantry and cavalry.

The uprising in Cyprus was of short duration, although the rebels first destroyed the capital, Salamis. (Its former monuments and temples were soon restored by the Romans as shown , **250**). An anonymous historian, whose imagination outran his historical accuracy, recorded the massacre of 240,000 gentiles during this foray. Meanwhile, Emperor Trajan's war against Parthia ended in a Roman victory, and he turned his full force against the rebels, on whom he wreaked a terrible vengeance.

In western Mesopotamia, the Jewish rebels had the active support of a number of commanders, including the king of Adiabene, one of a family who had earlier converted to Judaism (see Jewish Christians*), but this uprising, too, ended in bitter defeat. Yet another attempt by the Jews to settle their differences with the Romans by force of arms, putting their faith in messianic dreams of divine assistance, had failed. The Jews of the diaspora were decimated. They could not rise again.

The Repressions in Palestine (Judea): The repressive measures taken by Trajan were intensified by his successor, Emperor Hadrian (117–138 CE). Hadrian was a man imbued with Hellenic culture, and he sought to achieve cultural homogeneity throughout his vast domains. The Palestinian Jews had not been directly involved in the various revolts of

250

251

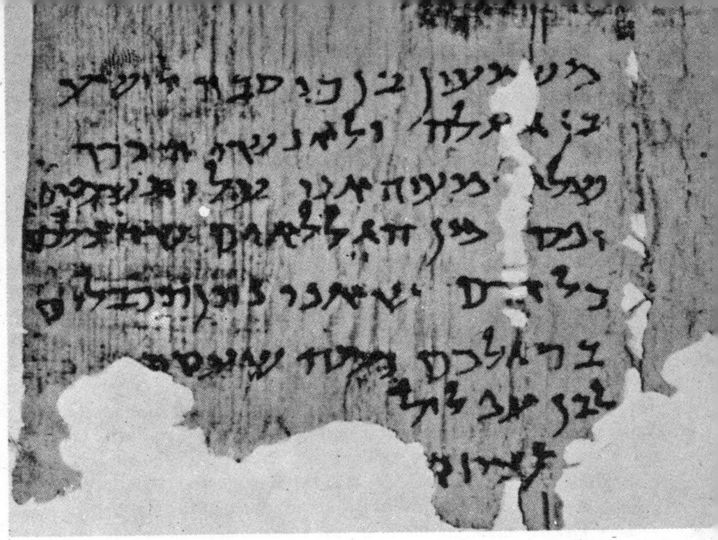

252

the diaspora, and during his visit to Palestine in 130 and 131 CE Hadrian addressed the Jewish leaders in conciliatory terms. He even went so far as to promise to rebuild Jerusalem and even possibly the Temple, despite the opposition of the non-Jewish elements in Caesarea*, the Decapolis and other centres, who interpreted such measures as appeasement of the Jews. The Jews, however, were not deceived by Hadrian's half-promises, particularly when it became apparent that what he planned was a cosmopolitan Greek style "polis" in Jerusalem, where the Jews would be "encouraged" to adopt Graeco-Roman styles and standards. In addition to this, Hadrian's edict of 127 CE prohibiting circumcision as a barbaric practice equated with castration was still in force.

Hadrian's efforts at gentle persuasion failed and he turned to more direct measures. According to the historian Dion Cassius, a new city was built over the ruins of Jerusalem, and renamed Aelia Capitolina (or Colonia Aelia Capitolina). On the site of the Temple, a temple was erected dedicated to Jupiter. At these desecrations, the Jews flocked to Jerusalem* from all over the country, and there decided to try force in support of their messianic aspirations.

253

Emergence of Bar Kochba (Kosba): Though the Jewish activist underground movement had been in existence since 127 CE, the year of the anti-circumcision decree, the current repressions brought it to the fore under the leadership of Shimon (Simeon) Bar Kosba. Until quite recently, details about Bar Kosba and his war against the Romans, most of which came from the Talmud and the Roman chronicles of Dion Cassius, Eusebius and Spartianus, were obscure and often conflicting. In the Talmud, he was referred to, after his defeat, as "Ben Koziba" which meant one allied to a "kozeb" (liar). The Jewish sages, headed by Rabbi Akiba, the leading Jewish luminary of the day, saw him as the messiah. They changed his original name to Bar Kochba, "son of a star", following a tradition of Nu. 24:17, "a star shall come forth out of Jacob, and a sceptre shall rise out of Israel". Rabbis who opposed him used the same name in a derogatory sense. So did Eusebius, who related that he charmed the people with this "bombastic" name but was no better than a murderer and highwayman.

In 1952 dozens of papyri (**251,2**) containing letters by one Shimon Bar Kosba to Joshua ben Galgola, who commanded the rebels in the wilderness, were discovered at Wadi Muraba'at, and were published by J. T. Milik and R. de Vaux. These papyri and new ones discovered in 1960–61 CE at Nahal Hever, which contain the same name, give no evidence that Bar Kosba ever called himself "Son of a Star" and very rarely used the title of "nasi" (president or prince) of Israel (see below: Bar Kosba as Messiah).

The Early Stages of the War: Bar Kosba was a man of giant stature and reckless courage. Though the test for admission into his fighting forces was extremely difficult, he attracted a great many volunteers. Legend has it that at first he demanded that a new recruit bite off his own finger and that when it was pointed out that it was a sin to maim able-bodied men, he had each recruit demonstrate his ability to uproot a tree (Jer. Talmud, Taaniot 84). This legend does not coincide with other accounts that claim that Bar Kosba proclaimed a general conscription, and punished those who refused to cooperate. These allegations of repressive measures were recorded by the Jewish-Christians, who were among those refusing to join (see below: Bar Kosba and the Jewish-Christians).

In any event, extensive guerrilla warfare was begun by Bar Kosba in 131 CE. He recognized his limitations and avoided an open engagement with the Roman troops, confining himself to incessant harassment of the enemy. Nevertheless, in the same year, Jerusalem was practically freed and with the help of reinforcements from Galilee, Bar Kosba gradually gained control of a large part of the country.

A New Commonwealth is Established: After this initial success, Bar Kosba and his followers proclaimed a new Era of Liberty, striking coins* to commemorate the event. For two years, Bar Kosba ruled in Jerusalem as the chief or "nasi" of the new Commonwealth. With memories of the Temple and the theocratic state still fresh in their minds, the Jews revived their ancient traditions and practices. Eleazar officiated as High Priest while Rabbi Akiba, a popular figure, and Bar Kosba's close friend and adviser, served as guide and counsellor to the renewed commonwealth. This return to the past did not prevail in secular matters, however. Bar Kosba wisely maintained the efficient Roman administrative machinery, adapting it to his own needs. Bar Kosba was eager to make the country self-sufficient, since he could no longer depend upon food imported from abroad. In order to assure adequate food supplies, he instituted a progressive land-tenure programme, designed to reapportion all arable land among able-bodied farmers. At the same time, severe measures were taken against profiteers on the one hand and slackers on the other.

Security Problems: The revolt had been largely conducted underground, in the most literal sense of the word. The rebels dug a great many tunnels and interconnecting passages and erected fortified walls around the towns they held, including Jerusalem. However, as the capital was still vulnerable to Roman attack, Bar Kosba established his capital and army headquarters southeast of Jerusalem at Herodium, where Herod* had once built a palace for himself. The Roman legate, Tineius Rufus, took refuge in the fortified Roman quarters of Jerusalem, where he remained on the defensive until reinforcements arrived.

While not strong, the position of the reestablished Jewish Commonwealth at the beginning of 133 CE was quite satisfactory. The reorganized army controlled the southern stretches of the coastal plain, as well as Judea.

Rome's Counter-Offensive: With Rome's prestige at stake, however, Hadrian could not allow the situation in Judea to continue. As his local commanders seemed powerless against the well-drilled and rigorously disciplined Jewish army, the Emperor dispatched Julius Severus, his ablest general, along with four legions, several auxiliaries and a large fleet. Severus had been commander in Britain and he knew the problems of fighting a guerrilla army on its home-ground. To begin with he built a number of roads from the ports of disembarkation to the centres of Jewish life. In preparation for the inevitable attack, Bar Kosba built a fourth wall northwest of Jerusalem at the place from which Titus had launched his fatal attack against Jerusalem (see Rome and the Jews*; Jerusalem*).

Instead of attacking Bar Kosba's strong positions in the south, the Romans successfully assaulted Galilee. This was followed (133 CE) by the conquest of the region of Eleutheropolis (Beth-Gobrin — see map **78**) and the coastal plain (Shephela) in the southwest. The approaching winter season gave the beleaguered Jewish forces a respite until the spring of 134 CE, but then the Romans advanced towards Hebron and threatened Herodium. Bar Kosba was pushed into the highlands of southeast Judea. The main asset of this otherwise forbidding region, where for many years the Zealots had taken refuge, was its inaccessibility. Its canyons, steep rocks and deep caves became the stronghold of the rebels, together with their families and possessions. This picture shows a wall of Herodium destroyed by Roman war engines; their stone projectiles rest against the wall (**254**).

In time, supplies ran out and it became necessary to sail across the Dead Sea from Ein Gedi to the Nabatean "Province Arabia", nominally under Roman rule, for what little could be brought back. Although the local farmers did their utmost to send provisions to the rebel strongholds, notably Herodium, supplies became very short. A strict austerity programme had to be enforced, with shirkers and "black marketeers" suffering severe punishment.

The Fall of Beitar: The winter respite of 133–134 CE also gave Severus time to regroup his troops and rearrange his plans. In the spring of 134, he first destroyed what was left of Jewish Jerusalem. Bar Kosba and the High Priest Eleazar, along with the main body of the rebel army withdrew into the fortress of Beitar (**253**; modern Bettir is some five miles southwest of Jerusalem). The situation was nearly hopeless; even the water supply from the valley below had been cut off by the Romans. By August 135 the rebels were finally defeated. It is amazing that they were able to hold out as long as they did. Even the most courageous, including Eleazar, lost heart during the siege and demanded surrender, but Bar Kosba was adamant, and with his own hand slew the High Priest. Legend has it that when the fortress fell and Bar Kosba died, it was

254

255

256

a heavenly agency and not the defiled foe that actually struck him down.

According to Dion Cassius (whose bias and tendency to exaggerate to some extent need to be remembered), 580,000 Jewish warriors alone fell during the Roman offensive, and 500 strongholds and 985 villages were completely destroyed, with tens of thousands of inhabitants sold into slavery. The Talmud, symbolizing the extent to which the land was laid waste, wrote that "no bird was seen flying in Palestine for fifty years."

The historical significance of the fall of Beitar can best be gauged by the tradition that it was one of the four major catastrophes in Jewish history that occurred on the fateful and symbolic ninth of Ab, "the bitterest day in the Jewish calendar*." (The other catastrophes were the destruction of the First and Second Temples, and the expulsion of the Jews from Spain in 1492 CE.)

Aftermath of the Rebellion: In spite of the crushing defeat, several pockets of rebels held out for a while longer. Joshua ben Galgola retreated to an inaccessible cave at Wadi Muraba'at, taking with him what remained of his administrative archives. They lay there until discovered in 1952 CE. Yonathan and Massabala and their followers fled from Massada and Ein Gedi with the enemy in hot pursuit. They found a refuge in Nahal Hever, making desperate sorties from its ravines and caves. The Romans established camps (**255,6**) on both sides of the canyons and those rebels who were not cut down simply starved to death. The numerous skulls of men, women and children and objects of personal use (**257**: sandals, cloth; baskets, food, tools, arrows) which were found near the papyri are a mute and gruesome testimony to the hardships they endured in the caves.

Physical devastation of Judea was followed by an equally cruel spiritual repression. Teams of oxen ploughed up the remains of the Temple esplanade and the adjoining quarters, and an equestrian statue of the Emperor Hadrian was erected on the site. Hadrian resumed rebuilding Jerusalem* as the purely pagan city of "Colonia Aelia Capitolina". Both Jews and Jewish-Christians were forbidden, on pain of death, to enter the city, which was repopulated with gentiles from Syria and Egypt. Teaching Jewish Law* and all religious observances were banned, and among those who were martyred for defying this prohibition were Rabbis Akiba and Hanina ben Teradion.

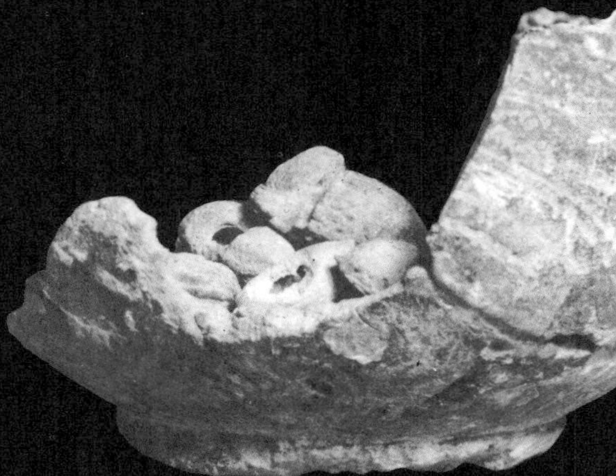

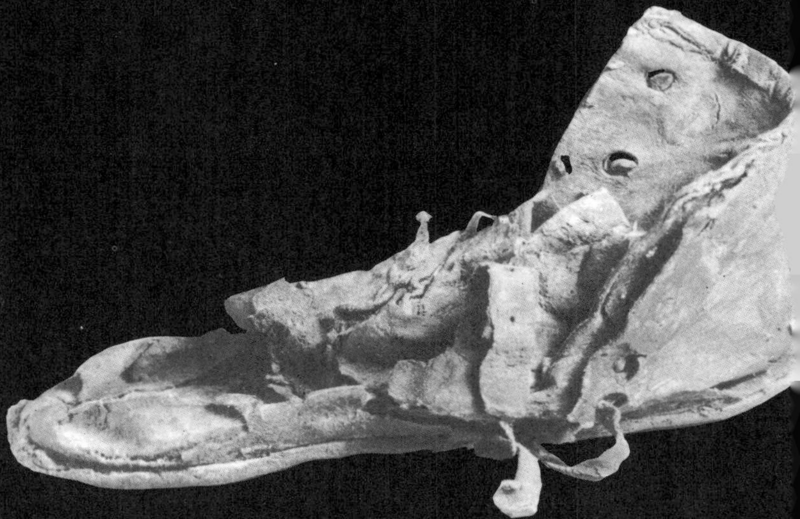

Even the country's name, Judea, was dropped in favour of Syria-Palestina or just Palestina, by which it was known until the creation of the modern State of Israel in 1948 CE. Despite these severe repressions, a small nucleus of Jews who had not taken part in the Bar Kosba uprising were treated more leniently, which explains how Simeon, son of Gamaliel II, was able to obtain permission to resume the duties of Patriarch of the Academy that had flourished in Jabneh. Though they were expelled from Judea, they were allowed to regroup in Galilee, and concentrated mainly in Ushah. The leaders and their disciples were invariably adherents of the House of Hillel, Pharisees who taught moderation and self-restraint in all matters, including dealings with the Roman rulers.

In the course of the late 2nd century CE, the nation repaired the internal and external damage caused by the defeat, and this became the prelude to a revival of Jewish life that, although stateless, flourished from then until the 5th century CE (see Synagogue*).

Bar Kosba as Messiah: A bitter controversy over whether or not Bar Kosba was the divinely appointed messiah, raged as early as his own lifetime. Bar Kosba's close friend, Rabbi Akiba, maintained that he was, to which Rabbi Yohanan ben Torata retorted: "Akiba, grass will grow out of your cheeks, and the son of David will not come." (Jer. Talmud, Taaniot: 84). Another talmudic text (Sanhedrin 93:72) asserts that Bar Kosba claimed he was the messiah and that Jewish scholars killed him. Christian tradition also holds that the rebel leader aspired to become the messiah and in the vision of Peter, Christians are warned against believing in him (II Pet. 2:1).

The most reliable evidence to the contrary are the coins* which he issued and which were recently discovered. They contain no trace of self appointment as messiah. Bar Kosba described himself as "nasi" of Israel, but neither as "king" nor "messiah". It is true that on the coins, the name "Shimon" appears together with "Eleazar" and the word "Jerusalem", but there is no indication of Bar Kosba's paramount position. As leader of the revolt it is not surprising that his name appeared on the coins along with those of the High Priest and the capital city. Messianism was a movement and aspiration dear to the hearts of the people. Had he been generally recognized as the messiah, or had he actively aspired to that office, reference to the fact would surely have been made in official documents, perhaps on the coins, or at the very least in the correspondence that has now been discovered.

Bar Kosba and the Jewish-Christians: Bar Kosba's bitterest internal foes were the Jewish-Christians*, who claimed that he persecuted them because they refused to recognize him as the messiah. According to E. Allon, there is some reason to believe that he did take measures against them, which were probably of a disciplinary nature They did not dissociate themselves from the Jewish community, but nevertheless refused to join in the fight against Rome. This resistance to nationalism had also been manifested by Jewish-Christians some 65 years before, when they fled to their kin in Pella, in Transjordan, at the time of the Jewish revolt against Rome. Their attitude may have led Bar Kosba to believe that they represented a security risk.

BIBLE CANON AND TEXT. — *I. Canon: Biblical and Pre-Biblical Writings; Oral and Written Transmission; Circulation, Collection, Canonization; Arrangement of the Books of the Old Testament; Arrangement of the Christian Bible; Need for a Fixed Canon; Process of Canonization: a. Pentateuch; b. The Canonization of the "Prophets"; c. Fixing the Final Canon. II. The Text: The Massoretic Text; The Evidence of the Dead Sea Scrolls; Between Canonization and the Massoretic Text; Vocalization and Divisions of the Bible; A Better Hebrew Text for the Printed Bible; Early Translations and the Massoretic Text; Early Editing of the Old Testament.*

I. CANON: **Biblical and Pre-Biblical Writings:** The history of the Jewish people which is contained in the O.T. covers a period of approximately a thousand years (from the beginning of the Settlement to the Hellenistic age). Over that long period, a body of literature was created much larger than the 24 books of the Bible, which are only a fragmentary selection from all that was produced.

Some of the books of this lost literature are referred to by the Bible itself. These include poetry: "The Book of Jashar" (Jos. 10:13) and the "Book of the Wars of Yahweh" (Nu. 21:14); and prose: "Commentary of the Prophet Iddo" (II Ch. 13:22) and the "Chronicles of the Kings of Israel" (I K. 14:19). Altogether, 19 such titles exist. There must have been many others, of which even the names have been lost.

Oral and Written Transmission: Presumably there were intermediate stages in the early pre-Exilic period, during which the literary material of the Bible was transmitted orally. Oral transmission may have been used for one type of material, written transmission for another. The former must certainly be the case as far as parts of the Pentateuch are concerned. In Ch. Rabin's opinion, the tradition of the "former prophets" (Joshua to II Kings) in the original biblical text was probably not transmitted orally, though it may be assumed that some of the stories on which the text was built were passed on by word of mouth. It is apparent that the biblical text tradition in its earlier stages was handed down at a time when it was still fluid. As a consequence, the biblical books, when finally fixed, bear many archaic traits and include very ancient material (see Biblical Criticism*), reflecting a long process of transmission (see Part II, Early Editing of the Old Testament).

Circulation, Collection, Canonization: Canonization is the process of deciding whether a work is worthy of inclusion in "Holy Scriptures" and whether it is recognized as being divinely inspired. Before a canon could be selected for inclusion, it had to undergo several stages. The book had to be composed and then circulated among the reading public. Individual books, usually similar in character, were collected and grouped as a corpus, e.g., the Prophets. The actual process of canonization came last, and involved the completed book. (A clear distinction must be made between the fixed stage of canonization of complete books and earlier stages, when they were composed or collected.) The concepts and stages of circulation, collection and canonization are related, of course, but are not identical. Some books which were circulated or which were regarded with respect were nonetheless never found worthy of canonization. The finality and essence of canonicity was expressed (Tosefta Yadayim

2:13–14) by the term "defile the hand" which probably meant that books thus classified were so sacred that even touching them required a ceremonial washing of the hands afterwards (see Impurity*).

Arrangement of the Books of the Old Testament: At one time, it was believed that the Pentateuch (or at least parts of it) were composed, declared holy and canonized in the later stages of the history of the Jewish people. More recently, scholars have come to see the traditional Hebrew order of the Old Testament, i.e. Torah (the Law), Nebi'im (the Prophets) and Ketubim (Hagiographa or Writings) as representing the historical pattern of development. On this basis, the Old Testament can be seen as a collection of books, some of them of great antiquity, put together in their present forms or something approximating their present forms at various times between the 9th c. BCE and the 2nd c. CE. The stages in which they were accepted as having canonical authority are indicated by the three groups into which they were classified by the Jews.

The first group, the Law, included the five books of Moses (the Pentateuch). The second group, the Prophets, comprising eight historical books, was divided into two sections: the "Former Prophets", Joshua, Judges, I and II Samuel and I and II Kings; and the "Later Prophets": Isaiah, Jeremiah, Ezekiel and the Twelve Minor Prophets grouped as one book. The third group of eleven "Hagiographa" (Writings) was sub-divided into the Poetical books: Psalms, Proverbs and Job; the "Five Scrolls": Song of Songs, Ruth, Lamentations, Ecclesiastes and Esther; and the remainder, three late narrative books, I and II Chronicles (one book), Daniel, and Ezra and Nehemiah (one book).

There were thus 24 books in all, by Jewish reckoning. Josephus counted 22 (probably Judges and Ruth were joined, as were Jeremiah and Lamentations).

Arrangement of the Christian Bible: The Hebrew Bible is not grouped in the chronological order of the writings — but in the order, or three different stages, of their authorization or canonization. The Septuagint (described under Hellenism in the Diaspora*) follows a different principle of arrangement from that of the Hebrew Bible by classifying the books in groups according to their subject matter — Law, History, Poetry, Prophecy – and by including the Apocrypha. This canon was generally accepted by the early Christian Church. In the form of the Old Latin Version, it passed into usage in the West. Though Jerome adopted the Hebrew canon in his Vulgate (see Translations*), the unpurged books found their way back into Latin Bibles and have remained there to this day. Luther and the English translators emulated Jerome in adopting the Hebrew canon and relegating the remaining books to the Apocrypha. This order was also followed in all Christian Bible translations, such as the King James Authorized Version (AV), Revised Version (RV), etc. (see Translations of the Bible*). Present Old Testament Bibles are composed of 39 books, achieved by counting each Minor Prophet individually and dividing Samuel, Kings, Ezra-Nehemiah and Chronicles into two books in accordance with the usage of the Septuagint and Vulgate (the Apocrypha* were not included in the Hebrew text of the Old Testament).

Need for a Fixed Canon: Intermediate stages in the process of establishing the canon are sometimes suggested by the books themselves. For instance, the prologue of Ecclesiasticus (see Apocrypha*) which was written by the author's grandson who translated Ben-Sira's work into Greek, opens: "Since many great things have been communicated to us through the Law and the Prophets, and the others (other books) who followed after them. . ." It is not unreasonable to deduce from this that in his time (2nd c. BCE) the collection of the Hagiographa (Writings) had not been finalized.

On the other hand, the need for a fixed canon is probably a reflection of the stormy history of the Jewish people which made their spiritual leaders decide to lay down a fixed and immutable canon of Scriptures. It seems to result also from controversy and sectarian schisms. The rabbis* felt a need to decide exactly what could and what could not be regarded as the directly inspired word of God. This feeling may be echoed in the concluding words of Ecclesiastes*: "The sayings of the wise are like goads, and like nails firmly fixed are the collected sayings which are given by one Shepherd. My son, beware of anything beyond these. Of making many books there is no end, and much study is a weariness of the flesh." (12:11–12).

Process of Canonization: a. **Pentateuch:** The problem is to decide at what period each book or group of books was canonized. Many scholars believe the decisive transition from "biblical literature" to "books of the Bible" began with the appearance of Deuteronomy during the reign of King Josiah at the end of the 7th c. BCE. Whatever date is suggested for the canonization of the whole Pentateuch, however (see Biblical Criticism*), it must surely have preceded the age of Ezra when the Law became the decisive influence in public affairs. The literature of the period of the Restoration* left no mark on the Pentateuch, whereas inclusion of some very ancient material in the first five books of the Bible is unquestioned. These two facts seem to provide conclusive support for the assertion that the process of their canonization and sanctification considerably preceded Ezra's time. It also preceded the gradual schism between the Samaritans and the rest of Jewry, for the Pentateuch is also "Holy Scriptures" among the Samaritans* (its nature and text is explained under that article). The Samaritans did not accept any of the other biblical books, notably none of the "Former Prophets" and not the book of Joshua. Their absence suggests that the only books canonized by the 5th c. BCE were the five books of the Pentateuch, the "canon" of the other books not yet having been authorized. (There is a book known as the "Samaritan Joshua", but this is a very much later composition dating to the Arabic period.) The text tradition of the Pentateuch adopted by the Samaritans between the 5th and 2nd cs. BCE was similar to the proto-Massoretic Palestinian tradition used by other Jews, reflecting a conservative tradition in Judaism such as that of the Sadducees*. Certain Hebrew deviations (as in Ex. 20:17) which appear in parts of the text as known today, and which reflect their theological views, were introduced, according to F.M. Cross, in the 2nd c. BCE, at the time of the final schism with Jewry (see Samaritans*).

b. **The Canonization of the "Prophets"** followed that of the Pentateuch. Although the general outline of the process is clear, there are differences of opinion with regard to each individual book. The rabbis* held that prophecy had ceased with Ezra and denied divine inspiration to all the books written later — even to a work like Ecclesiasticus, pervaded with a traditional Jewish spirit and quoted in the Talmud. This has been interpreted as meaning that to the rabbis of the Great Synagogue (period of the Restoration) and Ezra*, the canonization of Holy Scriptures was an accomplished fact and no further additions were made from books composed in Hellenistic times. However, against this, there are a number of canonical biblical works (e.g. the book of Daniel, in which Greek words even appear) which were clearly composed during the Hellenistic period, well after the time of Ezra. A further uncertainty is raised by the long rabbinical controversies about the sanctity of certain books such as Ecclesiastes* and even Ezekiel*.

c. **Fixing the Final Canon:** It is clear from the text of the first Greek translation of Ecclesiasticus (see Apocrypha*) that the tripartite division of the Bible was known by the beginning of the Hasmonean period (2nd c. BCE). Apparently the late post-Exilic period used a Hebrew text which included recensional alterations made by the scribes or the rabbis over a period of a century or so. The textual variations thus created differed from the comparatively smaller variations in the final "textus receptus" which was accepted by a synod held at Jabneh (Yamnia, see Rome and the Jews*) between 90 and 100 CE. This Synod considered disputed questions about the sanctity of some of the biblical books (especially Ecclesiastes, Song of Songs and Esther) and certain non-biblical works. Out of the more or less fluid textual traditions which had been current in the post-Exilic period since the 5th c. BCE, the rabbis also chose an authoritative Hebrew text and thus stabilized the various traditions. The books they rejected (see Apocrypha*) were included in the Greek Alexandrian canon (see above, and Septuagint under Hellenism and the Diaspora*) and were later preserved in the Christian Old Testament versions, some of them in the Roman Catholic Bible, and a great many more in the early mediaeval Monophysite Ethiopic Bible. From 400 CE, the Church officially accepted a larger canon than the Jews.

The Synod of Jamnia marks the point at which orthodox Jewish tradition regards the official Hebrew Canon as being definitely fixed. The canonical books upon which they agreed are those which now appear in the Protestant English Old Testament version, although the order in which they are printed follows that of the Septuagint.

II. THE TEXT: **The Massoretic Text:** The transmission of the Bible text from one generation to the next was the responsibility of the "sôferim" (scribes). They watched over the correct copying of manuscripts and transmitted the approved way of reading the text. The latter was necessary due to the way in which Hebrew was written: like several other Semitic languages, it expressed only the consonants. The vowels had to be supplied by the reader from his knowledge of the language and from the context. An ancient and difficult text such as the Bible, written in a language no longer spoken, could therefore not be read unless oral instruction had first been received.

In the Second Temple period, a rather incomplete method of indicating vowels by "vowel letters" came into usage. This was introduced into the biblical text only in part, and in an inconsistent manner, for traditional forces would not countenance the more consistent use of vowel letters as found in the Dead Sea Scrolls, or the complete regularization of grammatical forms as found in the Samaritan Hebrew Pentateuch. The biblical text also preserved many irregularities of pronunciation, unmarked by vowel letters.

To keep alive the knowledge of these thousands of peculiarities and the accepted spelling and pronunciation of the traditional text, the profession of "Massorete" came into being. As was usual in ancient scholarship, where so much depended on memory, the Massoretes cast their lore into formulas and numerous mnemonic rules. These formulas and rules form the "Major Massorah" (Massorah Magna), which is found in many special works and which was also written at the back of Bible manuscripts or on the margins of the pages. A possibly later type, the "Minor Massorah" (Massorah Parva) appears only in the margins and specifically marks the number of times any less common form occurs in the Bible, thus reminding the reader or copyist that a peculiarity exists.

The Massorah was worked out in the 6th–9th cs. CE, but work continued on it at least until the 17th c. (see below: Between Canonization and the Massoretic Text).

The Evidence of the Dead Sea Scrolls: The discoveries of earlier (2nd c. BCE) copies of biblical books among the Dead Sea Scrolls* have made it much easier to appreciate the work of the Massoretic scholars. Indeed, one of the most obvious contributions of the Dead Sea Scrolls to Textual Criticism (see Biblical Criticism*) has been to demonstrate the antiquity of the type of textual tradition which survived in the traditional Hebrew Bible (the proto-Massoretic text). Although the Massoretes lived centuries after the writers of the scrolls of Qumran, which derived from a proto-Massoretic text tradition (see Samaritans*), the authenticity of the Massoretic Text is a tribute to their care and scholarship. Some of the Qumran scrolls were "official" texts. The fragments of Samuel represent a text closely related to the Septuagint (see below, Between Canonization and the Massoretic Text; Early Translations). All the books in the Old Testament (except, apparently, Esther) were to be found in Qumran. The numerous fragments of commentaries that have survived prove that the community accorded authority both to the "Law" and the "Prophets", and to "Writings" such as Psalms and Daniel. They give a clear indication of the extent of "scripture" which obtained, even in the heterodox community at the close of the pre-Christian period. The Scrolls contain many new readings, some of them superior to the "textus receptus" or received text, some of them inferior.

Between Canonization and the Massoretic Text: Even after the text had been definitively agreed upon, problems of transmission and interpretation remained. The rabbis interpreted the wordings of the text very closely, and their discussions make it possible to see that the Pentateuch text of their time was practically identical with that of the printed Hebrew Bibles (except for some minor details of spelling), while the text of the Prophets and Hagiographa was already very similar to it. The existence of such texts at a much earlier time is proven, e.g. by the Second Isaiah Scroll from Qumran (1st c. BCE), the remains of which are almost literally those of the Massoretic Text. It is widely accepted that the text used by the rabbis became established about the 1st c. BCE. By using "w" and "y" to indicate vowels, the Scroll of Isaiah has a relatively full vocalization (see Alphabet*).

The people of that time had none of the modern technical means of ensuring a uniform text. They depended on hand written copies. It is true that, according to a trustworthy Jewish tradition (Mo'ed Katan 3, 4), good, definitive copies of the biblical Scrolls were preserved in the Temple archives and could be consulted in case of doubt. Nevertheless, the mere existence of one accepted manuscript could hardly guarantee that none of the many copies in use differed from it in the smallest details. (According to the tradition, one out of the three copies kept in the archives of the Second Temple was saved at the time of its destruction and taken to Baghdad after 135 CE.) The history of the Hebrew text since the 2nd c. CE is one of careful transmission which has preserved it from any serious deterioration.

Uniformity at this level was only made possible by the invention of the printing press (15th c. CE). Certain difficulties continue right through the Middle Ages. Mediaeval Bible manuscripts, for instance, were far from uniform, even though accurate manuscripts such as those guaranteed by the famous Massoretes of the Ben Asher family (10th c. CE) were available at the time. Moses Maimonides (1135–1205 CE) recommended the 10th century Codex of Aaron Ben Asher as the most reliable manuscript (mainly for questions of division into sections). This text was kept, in his time, in Cairo and later transferred to Aleppo (known as the Aleppo Codex , **258** , see below: Better Hebrew Text).

Vocalization and Divisions of the Bible: In mediaeval times, the main problems concerned vocalization marks and accents and the division into sections, rather than actual variations in the words and phrases of the text such as occur in early Bible translations. These (barring minor variations) are not found in mediaeval manuscripts, according to the evidence of B. Kennicott, a canon of Christ Church who, between 1776–80, collected and collated textual changes from 615 manuscripts and 52 printed editions of the Hebrew Bible. He was followed shortly afterwards by Giovanni di Rossi who published collations of 731 manuscripts and 300 printed editions. A further important collection of variant readings was made in Ch. D. Ginzburg's Bible edition for the British and Foreign Bible Society.

There were originally no divisions within the books of the Old Testament except in the Psalms which were separate poems; the Song of Miriam; the Song of Deborah where the differences in content are stated and defined, and in Proverbs 30 and 31. A division into sense units, each forming a "parashah", followed canonization and was later introduced into Prophets (it is found in the Dead Sea Scrolls of Isaiah). A different division into sections of the week was devised for reading in the synagogue. The Torah was read in what is known as the "seder" divisions, and the Prophets in the "haftorah" divisions. The present chapter divisions, however, were eventually taken over from Christian usage (13th c. CE) and introduced into the Hebrew Bible for ease of reference.

Verse division marks appeared later, though they are presupposed in what the Talmud prescribes as liturgical use of the Scriptures. They are carefully marked by the Massoretes. The division was made by Rabbi Nathan in the Venice printed edition of the Hebrew Bible (1524), then appeared in the Latin Bible.

In 1892, the discovery of the Cairo Genizah shed further light on the fortunes of the biblical text in the centuries before the time of the earliest manuscripts extant. The Genizah was a reliquary of Old Scrolls attached to the Cairo Synagogue, acquired by the Jews in the 9th c. CE. Much later, the reliquary was walled up and forgotten. It was found to contain hundreds of fragments and manuscripts, some of them dating back to the 8th c. CE. Even in these very ancient texts, it is rare to find any major divergences from the Massoretic text.

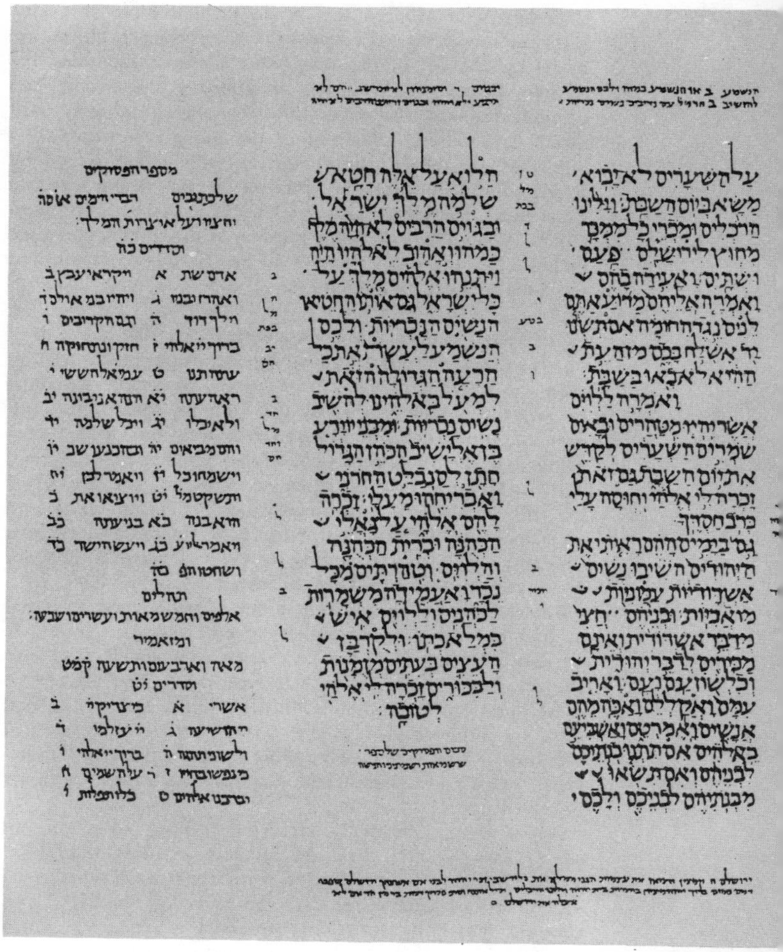

258

A Better Hebrew Text for the Printed Bible: The present Hebrew Bible is based on a Bible printed with full vowel points and accents, in use since its first printing in Venice in 1516–17. A second edition of the text, edited by Jacob Ben Chayim, a Tunisian Jew, became the textus receptus for printed Hebrew Bibles until quite recently. He based his work on late mediaeval manuscripts and editions, and since he followed no one of them exclusively, the text frequently deviates from the oldest Massoretic texts. The only old Massoretic manuscripts still available, as pointed out above, were in circulation by virtue of the labours of the Ben Asher family. Modern scholars have not been content to study the Hebrew Bible in the Ben Chayim edition. Recent attempts to improve the Hebrew text of the printed Bible by basing it on the more original and correct Massoretic tradition, are based on the use of the Ben Asher Codexes including the Aleppo Codex. This means abandoning the Jacob Ben Chayim text which enjoyed almost canonical authority until recent days. The third edition of the Biblia Hebraica (1937) published by the Wurttembergische Biblanstalt, edited by R. Kittel and P. Kahle, is based on the Ben Asher text and Massorah, preserved also in the Ben Asher Leningrad Codex. Since 1951, the later editions of the Biblia Hebraica include the variants of the Dead Sea Scrolls of Isaiah and the Habakkuk Commentary.

Early Translations and the Massoretic Text: The question of divergent readings is particularly important in connection with the relation of early translations in Greek, Aramaic, Syriac, Latin and Arabic to the Hebrew Massoretic text. Two questions arise: 1. Where the translations do not seem to relate to the Massoretic text, do they go back to a different, earlier, Hebrew text (a so-called Vorlage), or are some (or all) of them due to translators' religious views and stylistic ideas, influence of parallel passages, or simply a different way of understanding the Hebrew words? 2. Once a certain reading has been accepted as going back to a different Vorlage, should that Hebrew reading be preferred as possibly reflecting an earlier "pre-Massoretic" tradition, or rejected because of the very great care which went into the selection of the Massoretic readings? The answer to these questions lies, possibly, in the middle. There is no real basis for supposing — as did earnest 19th century biblical scholars — that it is now possible to reconstruct an "archetype" or original primal text. Such a text almost certainly never existed.

There were, admittedly, occasional slips and errors. In these cases — and they are far less frequent than used to be thought — comparison with the translations is of value. In one case especially, the book of Samuel*, it is thought that the Septuagint preserved a rendering which is preferable to that of the Hebrew text (the new manuscript from Qumran which confirms this superiority indicates that the Massoretic text is in any case defective). For instance, after the birth of Samuel, his mother brings him to Shiloh in fulfillment of her vow. The Hebrew Massoretic text of I Sam. 1:24–25 reads: "And when she had weaned him, she took him up with her, along with three bulls, an ephah of flour .... then they slew *the bull*..." (The Hebrew in the above passage reads "parmeshulash" — three bulls — instead of "par meshulash" or three year old bull as in the Septuagint.) The contradiction between the three bulls of the offering at the beginning of the verse, and the single one slain is dispelled by the Septuagint version: "And when she had weaned him, she took him up with her, along with a three-year old bull..." It was very easy for such confusion to arise in the Hebrew text which was written without vowels and without any spaces between the words in the early days.

The Septuagint reading was later confirmed by the Samuel Scroll found in the Qumran caves. In any case, it appears convincing because it disposes of the contradiction of the Massoretic version. However, any such "discipline" of comparison and adjustment needs to be applied with the utmost caution. F. M. Cross has pointed out that the text of Samuel found in Qumran has a higher ratio of readings in agreement with the Septuagint than with the Massoretic text, but this one example cannot be the basis of a generalization. It is commonly felt that it is better to presume a plurality of traditions, at least for the period in which various renderings in Hebrew or in translation are known.

Even if, for the sake of argument, the theory of an original "archetypal" text were accepted, it still remains true that the many divergent texts known today could not possibly have developed one from another, from a single source. There was no such straight line of development. Moreover, modern scholars have a much higher regard for the textual value of the Massoretic text than did the scholars of the 19th c. CE. The appreciation of the methods of text preservation has grown, owing to improved knowledge of similar methods employed elsewhere in the ancient world. Theories about and attempts to reconstruct the "original" Bible text should be approached with the greatest care and reserve.

Early Editing of the Old Testament: It is clear from a very cursory examination that the Bible is not a uniform literary creation, but a collection of different traditions varying in time, place, language and theology. The diversity is so great that the preserved materials contain inconsistencies and even contradictions. In places, there are traces of later attempts to explain or harmonize conflicting traditions (see Biblical Criticism*). Many of the foregoing arguments also apply to the question of the early editing of the books of the Old Testament. The fortunes of the Hebrew text before the canonization of the books were varied. They cannot be followed completely, nor always with certainty. Assuredly, there were editors who collected the early traditions, put them together, and in so doing, left their own imprint on the books — either out of an honest attempt to resolve difficulties or because they believed "it should be so" (see Biblical Criticism*). Thus, the headings to the poems of Psalms* are clearly the interpolations of such an editor. The same is also true in cases such as Jos. 9:27, where "in the place which he should choose" appears to be an addition; or Gn. 12:6, where the added explanation "at that time the Canaanites were in the land" merely proves that the passage was written during a period when the Canaanites were not in the land. Even in cases like these, however, it is unwise — however tempting — to suppose it possible to "peel off" the added layers and get down to an "original" stratum. Many confusing and difficult verses appear to be so only because of the time-gap between the present and the period in which they were written. There is no way of being absolutely sure that even such apparently obvious cases as those just quoted (I Sam. 1) were really corruptions in transmission. It is never certain that reconstruction is possible, and it is therefore advisable to leave the passages as doubtful and subject to further study.

The archaeological discoveries of the 20th century have indeed shown that the biblical traditions may be regarded with considerable confidence, even when a certain tradition or text appears illogical to modern eyes. "These records have been written all along down to our times with the utmost accuracy, nay if it be not too bold for me to say it, our history will be so written hereafter" wrote Flavius Josephus (Contra Apionem, 1, 6) almost two thousand years ago. His words are still true today.

BIBLICAL CRITICISM. — *Outline: I. Literary Criticism: The Documentary Hypothesis; Classical Literary Criticism; New Approaches. The Contribution of Form Critical Studies: Oral Traditions; Form Criticism; The Psalms; Theologians not Historians; Aggadic Interpretation in the Literary Text; The Priestly Writings; Reality and Utopia in "P"; Archaeology and Biblical Criticism; New Trends. II. Textual Criticism. Conclusion.*

The critical study of the Old and New Testaments is usually divided into two main categories:

I. Literary (or higher) criticism, a mainly historical method concerned with questions of the authorship, date of composition, circumstances of origin, historical accuracy, style, character and attitudes of the various literary elements which make up the Scriptures.

II. Textual (or lower) criticism, which seeks to answer the question, what was the original text of the books of the Bible? It considers problems raised by the many different ancient texts of the Old Testament, and the Greek text of the New Testament. All the old manuscripts agree in the main but there are minor points of difference and places in some manuscripts where the text is obscure. The problems involved are considered under section II. of this article.

I. LITERARY CRITICISM: Awareness of what are the right questions to ask and attempts to find answers by means of scientifically-based hypotheses mark the progress of modern forms of biblical scholarship. The discipline known as "Literary Criticism" has remained the dominant and best known branch. Current research lays stress on searching out the archaic written or oral traditions which were the source material for the compilers of the biblical texts and considers the conditions of life which helped to shape them. In addition to this approach of literary criticism proper, modern biblical scholarship takes advantage of a variety of new disciplines:

a. Form criticism — i.e., relating the form of an existing literary text or the literary "form" found in it, to traditions, history, oral tradition and legendary explanations given in the text — i.e. setting the material against the actual life situation (sitz im leben) which gave rise to it. This discipline is considered in more detail below;

b. Archaeological data, including the wealth of linguistic information gained from monuments and inscriptions;

c. Oriental and other contemporary extra-biblical written sources, with especial reference to other oriental languages and cultures;

d. Ethnological and other data.

From this foundation, scholars go on to apply their knowledge to the literary forms and style, keeping in mind the ancient ways of passing on traditions, as well as gauging the effect of aggadic* interpretation (see below) in the process of biblical transmission.

The Documentary Hypothesis: Variations in style and viewpoint between different books or within a single book, chapter or passage, had worried mediaeval Jewish commentators, particularly Ibn Ezra who influenced Spinoza (17th century CE). Later this subject also became the concern of gentile scholars. The repetition of narratives of the same events even two or three times and the presence of contradictory narratives occur especially in the Adam, Noah, Abraham and Jacob cycles of Genesis*; in Exodus*, Deuteronomy*; Samuel*; Judges*; Kings*; Chronicles* etc., and also in the Synoptic Gospels*. On the supposition that a single writer would scarcely repeat or flagrantly contradict himself, these phenomena were explained as the result of combining in one book material from many different sources: national epics, historical records and shorter folk tales, each one of which reflected different stages of the development of Israel's religion.

The documentary hypothesis distinguished four major "documents" or ancient literary sources, mainly within the first books of the Bible. It was assumed that each of the documents had been written by different anonymous authors or groups of writers or editors, who lived centuries after the events they purported to record. On the basis of the theory of G. H. Graf (1865–66), taken over by J. Wellhausen (1878), these documentary sources were arranged according to the stage of religious development they revealed, in the following order: The J (Jahwist) source, i.e. one in which the divine name Yhwh is used, which is attributed by this hypothesis to the 10th or 9th centuries BCE; the E (Elohist) source, where the divine name used is Elohim, attributed to the 9th or 8th centuries BCE; the D (Deuteronomist) source, i.e. written by the authors of Deuteronomy, presumably during the 7th century BCE; and the P (Priestly) source, written by the authors of the Priestly Code, circa the 5th century. P also includes the H (Holiness) Code, which makes up part of Leviticus*; while JE denotes a combination of J and E by a 7th century editor.

The main sources can further divided into strata (e.g. J^1 and J^2; E^1, E^2 and E^3), which seem to reduce Genesis* to a mere collection of unrelated source material. Many attempts have been made to go further in this process of subdivision, by giving the sections symbols to indicate their special character or origin, e.g.: source L (Lay source), source K (Kenite), or source S, for Seir, South.

Nineteenth century Hegelian philosophy held that human history followed a unilinear pattern of evolution from a "lower" state to a "higher" or better one. Presumably by following a like pattern, Hebrew religion and its Scriptures would reflect different stages of development. The "documentary" school of thought saw Israel's religion as a development from a quasi-animism or polydaemonism of the Hebrews' ancestors through the worship of one particular deity, although others were deemed to exist (henotheism or monolatry), into the final ethical monotheism (belief in the existence of only one god) which the prophets taught (see Moses*: Mosaic Religion Monotheism or not?).

The four conventional sources listed above, with all the additional subdivisions, were assessed according to the level of religious development they exhibited. Their own distinctive style and interests, it was thought, made it possible to distinguish and disentangle them from the surrounding material. For instance, J and E reflected the pre-prophetic period like the narratives of Judges* and Samuel*. D made up the Deuteronomic histories and the reform movement of the seventh century (see Israel and Judah*, IV) while P, like Chronicles, was the product of the religious climate of the post-Exilic* community.

The orthodox Graf–Wellhausen theory seemed to offer a neat answer to two main problems: a. the authorship and date of the first six books of the Bible (Pentateuch and Joshua, defined by this school as the Hexateuch), and

b. a theory with regard to the development of Israel's religion.

Classical Literary Criticism: Recent research has questioned the extremes of documentary analysis, rejecting many of the disconnected strands into which the biblical books are splintered, although a majority of modern scholars still make use of the classical theory. This, therefore, deserves to be understood side by side with the new schools and theories of research.

A clear distinction should be made between the date assigned by the documentary theory to the actual publication of a "document" and the much greater age of the subject matter it contains. As in the older theory this was not sufficiently recognized, the conclusion was drawn that the writings reflected the age of the writer rather than that of the subject matter. The historical accuracy of the accounts was doubted and so was their value as sources of information about Israel's origins. The problem before the modern scholar is to find the proper balance between these factors.

New Approaches: The documentary hypothesis was the foundation for scores of biblical commentaries, introductions, handbooks and histories, many of which are still in use today. It marks the pages of much 19th and 20th century scholarship, yet it was based on a number of misconceptions. Its authors had no idea of the age of the civilizations of the ancient Orient, nor of the nature of the various cultures which had preceded early Israel for some fifteen to twenty centuries.

J. Wellhausen had added to the documentary theory a reconstruction of the development of Israel's religion. Viewing Israel in isolation, exclusively through the text of the Bible, the upholders of this theory telescoped Israel's entire religious evolution and cultural achievement, from the supposedly crude beliefs of the earliest Patriarchs to a fully developed monotheism, into the space of some six centuries (14th to 8th BCE or thereabouts). However, within the last three or four decades, an amazing amount of knowledge has become avilable about the ancient world — and Israel. From this it is clear that the narratives of Israel's origins (in the Hexateuch: i.e. Pentateuch and Joshua) do not reflect the circumstances and religious environment of the later times when the hypothetical documents on which they were based were supposed to have been written. They reflect generally the conditions of the second millenium BCE which they describe, though there are exceptions and anachronisms — e.g. the language is invariably that of a later date.

Israel in fact did not appear at the beginning of history as a primitive nomadic group. It appeared at the end of an era of sophisticated cosmopolitan civilization, and this is reflected by the earliest Patriarchal* tales.

An intensive study of individual units of biblical tradition reveals important parallels between Genesis* and Babylonian parables, or between the traditions of Moses* and literary or religious materials and Codes (see Law*) before his time. New evidence from Ugarit* and Mari* has forced a reassessment of theories once held about the Patriarchal* narratives. They are now known to have derived very largely from a Mesopotamian culture which preceded Israel's. By that time, religious evolution was quite considerably advanced, while the material culture of the 16th or 14th centuries BCE was far from primitive. The patriarchal Hebrews, as part of the world in which they lived, must have possessed a religion that showed some influence of this more advanced civilization. Early Israelite religion was not as inchoate and primitive as scholars of the Wellhausen school thought. It emerged into history at an already advanced stage of development.

As archaeological discoveries provided a whole range of extra-biblical sources against which to assess the biblical narratives, a reaction set in against the too-neat, but unsupported theories of "documentary analysis" and its splitting of the Old Testament text into different disconnected strands. It became clear that some at least of the biblical material did not originate with the authors of the "documents" but was material they adapted from much more ancient — and therefore historically valuable — oral and written traditions. As evidence for the history of earlier times it need no longer be discounted. Although the majority of competent scholars recognize the existence of different literary sources in the Bible and accept the documentary theory up to a certain point, it is stressed today that a distinction must be maintained between the documentary theory and the conclusions drawn from it about the history, culture and chronology of the subject matter of the various sources (see also Deuteronomy* and an evaluation of P, below). Other scholars, like P. Volz and W. Rudolph, have denied on different grounds that any such thing as an E document ever existed, while Ezekiel Kaufman has suggested that a good part of P contains the oldest rather than the latest sources and traditions.

THE CONTRIBUTION OF FORM CRITICAL STUDIES: Recent studies are altering older ideas of the Bible and Israel's religious development.

Oral Traditions: A further development during the past two decades has been the stress laid upon the history of individual units of oral tradition. A people, H. Gunkel believed, transmitted its religious beliefs, collective history, epics and stories in oral traditions which eventually found expression in distinct "literary types". These literary forms gave, in turn, a clue to the conditions (the "situation in life") from which the traditions sprang. Such a belief provided the foundation for the discipline known as "form criticism".

Form Criticism is the investigation of the relation between the form of a piece of literature or the literary forms found within it, and the purpose for which they were designed. It aims at discovering the way in which a literary tradition fits into the life of the society which produces it, i.e. its life-situation (sitz im leben).

Using this discipline, J. Pedersen analysed the narratives of the Bible. He found, for instance, that the narrative of Exodus was a liturgical recitation or a cult-legend for the Passover Festival, which had been accompanied by dramatic representation of the events commemorated. The original background of the oral tradition embodied in the Exodus narrative, therefore, was a cultic "situation-in-life".

From this standpoint it becomes clear that the sagas of the Patriarchs*, Exodus* and the Conquest* which make up the bulk of the first six books of the Bible and from which

J and E seem to have drawn their material, must have assumed their final pre-literary shape some centuries before the Monarchy. Even though they were probably written down at that time, they reflect conditions obtaining five centuries or more earlier in the case of the Patriarchs, though a shorter period of time in reference to the Conquest.

As the Wellhausen view of Israel's religious development has lost ground, a more positive understanding of Israel's faith and constitution has become accepted. It is no longer possible to assume that religious unity first came to Israel under the Monarchy. A substantial amount of the material of this phase — poems, genealogical lists and laws, as well as historical narratives — has been put back to a situation in life in the early period of Israel's history. Moreover, such a study of individual units of tradition promises an even better understanding of the history of the institutions of Israel.

The Psalms: The application of form critical methods has completely revolutionized the interpretation of the Psalms. Until recent years, scholars considered the level of religion revealed in the Psalms too elevated for an early period. By careful study of their "forms", the composition of earlier Psalms has now been dated, notably by S. Mowinckel, to a much older pre-Exilic Israel, and generally to an earlier date than the critics had allowed. (Examples are given under Psalms*.) Many of the formulae of expression used have been found to belong to a poetic tradition which can be traced back for centuries to origins (in the oral stage) at a comparatively early date. The tradition reached its peak in the days of the Monarchy, but poems like the Song of Deborah or the Song of Miriam were probably composed earlier.

Oral traditions do not remain constant and unchanged during their oral life. Nor were the writers who transformed an oral into a written tradition, mere recorders. They had a religious and theological viewpoint which coloured their renderings. Although works like S. Mowinckel's study of the Psalms have gained from current emphasis on oral traditions, other scholars feel that this school's tendency to find parallels to the patterns of Israel's myths and ritual in the cults and liturgies of the rest of the Near East, can be pushed too far (see Festivals*).

Theologians not Historians: Form criticism has amply demonstrated the essentially theological nature of Hebrew historical writings. Historical accounts were intended to make a religious point. As they stand, the historical sections of the Bible are good illustrations of the way the religious conceptions of their writers — or their various schools of thought — influenced the interpretation of historical events. The techniques of form criticism have accordingly illuminated not only the Old and New Testaments, but also the various trends that inspired the post-Exilic Apocrypha* and sectarian writings (see Dead Sea Scrolls*) on the eve of the Christian era. This question of the influence of theological interpretation on the text of the Bible is best examined in terms of Aggadic interpretations, a vital aspect of Bible studies.

Aggadic Interpretation in the Literary Text: The problem of biblical duplication and contradictions cannot be solved only on the assumption of a conflation of different sources (see Documentary hypothesis, above). In recent years, Jewish scholars in Israel and the U.S., especially S. Sandmel, familiar with the midrashic and aggadic disciplines in the writings of the Talmud, have realised that in many cases the confusion arises because ancient scribes transmitted biblical traditions alongside a mass of parallel material.

In the first place, it is one of the fundamental characteristics of the Bible's text that its compilers never excluded even the smallest section of the traditions that had come down to them. During the Exile* and the years that followed the Restoration*, ancient traditions regarded as inspired and valuable, were systematically collected and recorded. Although there was no canonization of a complete traditional text until the late 2nd century CE, no change was made in the basic structure of the Pentateuch and historical books after the 3rd or 2nd centuries BCE. Minor changes made during these four or five centuries were the result of additions made to the textual traditions. As the normative religious traditions contained in the Scriptures were unchangeable, the scribes and rabbis did not discourse on the material in a critical spirit, nor did they have to trouble about explaining the meaning of words (as in modern commentaries). It was axiomatic that in even the most archaic passages, the language was clear to all, and needed only to be read in the prescribed portions through the year (see Law*: Reading). Thus the traditions as transmitted were not a coherent account, but a collection of sources bearing on a single theme, all of which could be studied in connection with questions of law.

Then, as a further aid to interpretation, the scribes added their own imaginative re-telling of the stories. This is the discipline known as Aggadah. Aggadic re-tellings were not simply a matter of corrections, or elaborations by the scribes. The storyteller or the scribe introduced elements which were intended to *enhance the theological value of the tale*. This is especially true of the Priestly writings (source P). The religious mind was even more reluctant than others to exclude anything that was read and understood in the light of priestly views. To the authors of the priestly material (or the P source), there was nothing incongruous between the legendary and primitive form of Gn. 2:4 ff. (Eden) and the majestic priestly cosmic presentation of the story of Creation (Gn. 1). Similarly, to later scribes, Samuel's distrust of royalty (I Sam. 8) represented the message of the whole of Samuel and Kings. Thus the priestly material (P) seems to have a literary identity and character of its own, even though it added no new narrative and may not be an independent document. It gave an additional editing to earlier narrative material which the critical hypothesis school groups under the source J (Jahwist). While the priestly writers are post-Exilic, it is now commonly agreed that much of the material of P is of pre-Exilic, even of quite ancient origin (see Restoration*: Cultural Renaissance).

Once an aggadic item had been added to the original tradition, it was assumed that both it and the original text had the identical meaning. For instance, the story about Abraham in Genesis 20 determined the character of the national ancestor in Gn. 12:10–20. Another example is the story of David's slaying of Goliath, where I Chronicles 20:5 harmonizes the conflicting accounts of I Sam. 17 and II Sam. 21:19, again an aggadic recasting of a single tradition.

The finished Bible text represents the end result of a process of accretion. First of all, oral religious traditions were formulated. These were eventually embodied in written traditions and finally canonized into the books of the Bible. The aggadic additions made over the centuries were not eliminated, but were harmonized with the original traditions through constant repetition. For the purpose of textual study, they have to be detached from the original text and criteria have to be established to distinguish them.

The theological intentions of aggadic insertions do not transform these elements into documents. Modern scholars doubt whether even the famous J document was a coherent saga made up of connected traditions. Much of it seems to have been no more than early legends, myths and more primitive historical traditions embodying mainly ancient credos and popular lore, which can be distinguished from the added priestly material. A comparison of the truncated narrative of Exodus 4:24–26 placing the origin of circumcision in Moses' time with Gn. 17, which traces it to Abraham, shows that the former belongs to the ancient popular tradition type, while the latter is aggadic in spirit and content.

The Priestly Writings: In spite of reservations about some of the other documents like J, the conviction is gaining ground in scholarly circles that it is possible to trace the contributions of the priestly writers by means of their specifically schematic form. These sections appear in part of Genesis*, Exodus*, Leviticus*, and Numbers* and seem to form a general source, P. It is possible to distinguish this from the rest of the Pentateuchal sources, which vary considerably in quality, if not necessarily in date. Historically, these other sources can be considered to have much in common.

However, the idea of the literary criticism school that P as a whole was produced in Exile, has been rejected and the source dated back to a much earlier period in Israelite history. Without any doubt, the traditions which are embedded in P are of still greater antiquity, although the documents were canonized after the time of Ezra.

Reality and Utopia in "P": The question of the historical reliability of the P writings and the proportion of utopian dreamings which they contain, can best be examined in connection with the 48 cities which, according to Numbers 35:1–8, were to be given to the Levites after the Conquest. Lv. 25:32–34 specifies the legal privileges which the Levites would enjoy in their cities, while Joshua 21:1–40 provides a description of how the cities were allotted. Nevertheless, Numbers 18:20, 23–24 states specifically that the Levites had no inheritance among the people of Israel. Wellhausen assumed that the cities were a purely fictional, non-historical, invention which he attributed to a later, post-Exilic stratum of P, along with the visionary scheme of Ezekiel 45:1–5 and 48:8–20.

Since then, M. Haran has shown that at the time the account of the Levitical cities was formulated, it reflected a historical situation in which the mixed inhabitants of 48 cities actually included Levites. This distant memory was later embroidered with utopian features which transformed the cities into the exclusive domain of the tribe. W. F. Albright has demonstrated that although the list given in Joshua 21 was cast in the framework of the P document, it originated in the days of the united monarchy (see David and Solomon*; Priests and Levites*).

Archaeology and Biblical Criticism: In general, scholars are agreed that despite the useful service done by the documentary theory in the past (and in the present, so far as the P source goes), merely isolating different sources can tell us no more than that a tradition was reduced to a written form at some period, "by a person with a particular point of view in Israel's past. It could not produce criteria for the evaluation of the sources it isolated, beyond a possible demonstration that a later source used an earlier." (G.E. Mendenhall). A proper interpretation of biblical material demanded additional, external criteria. When new data from archaeology and historical geography are taken into account, the biblical scene becomes far richer and more real. One instance of this process is the scientific investigation of the Patriarchal narratives (see article), from which they have emerged "as traditions which must have arisen in the Amorite period, and they preserve authentic traditions, even though in saga form and adapted to later cultic use." (G.E. Wright)

In short, modern biblical criticism is no longer an isolated study. It makes full use of the techniques of anthropology, sociology, comparative religion and oriental linguistics to understand the archaic Hebrew, and to recreate the life and faith of ancient Israel. Moreover, archaeological data and their interpretation provide an invaluable control for estimates of the historical value of biblical traditions.

From 1930 on, the work of scholars, especially W. F. Albright, E. Gunkel and A. Alt and their school, in Israel and the rest of the world, revolutionized biblical studies.

Current research is no longer based mainly on literary criticism, but deals with the history of individual units of tradition before they found their way into their present positions in the various strata designated as "documents". The work of these schools has made it possible to take the fullest possible advantage of the archaeological and linguistic data now included in the study of the units of tradition. The combination has helped to relate a vast quantity of material: narratives, laws, lists and poems, to a life-situation in the earlier periods of Israel's history. Placed beside generally accepted archaeological conclusions regarding the text of the Bible, as well as the original publication of contemporary non-biblical texts and other general information about the ancient Near East, these new approaches have resulted in a much more positive picture of early Israel, her institutions and religion.

New Trends: So far as the future of Old Testament studies along these new lines is concerned, some caution is needed. In the words of John Bright: "It is impossible to make general statements regarding any phase of biblical criticism without running the risk of oversimplification. The whole field is in a state of flux . . . Even upon major points there is often little unanimity to be observed. As a result, scarcely a single statement can be made about the state of the field that would not be subject to qualification . . . Nevertheless in spite of confusion and disagreement, certain significant trends can perhaps be charted," and these have been described in the foregoing article.

II. TEXTUAL CRITICISM: The critical study of the text of the Old Testament seeks detailed knowledge of the development of the early text — i.e. it tries to get as close as possible to the earliest form of the Hebrew Bible, before it took the form known today. The Bibles used today follow the standard textual Hebrew tradition of the Massoretic text, which was made the authoritative canon of the Old Testament around 100 CE. This text was apparently drawn up from a variety of different texts of the Pentateuch (Torah) and the earlier and later Prophets (see article on Biblical Canon and Text*), all dating back to the third or early second centuries BCE and generally deriving from a common ancestor — the text current in Palestine at the time of Ezra (around 400 BCE). The early versions known are: the proto-Massoretic edition of the Bible (i. e. the Hebrew text which preceded the adoption of the Old Testament canon and was used during the Second Temple period); the Septuagint* or Greek translation made in Alexandria and current in Egypt in the 3rd and 2nd centuries BCE, and the Samaritan Pentateuch (i.e. a form of the Hebrew text preserved and still used by the Samaritans*) which goes back to the second century BCE (see below). The Massoretic textual tradition was developed gradually over the last century BCE and the first CE by the scribes and rabbis of Palestine, out of a desire to prevent changes in the holy text (see Rabbis and Rabbinism*). Through constant recensions (re-casting and editing), they sought to establish an accepted traditional consonantal text (the Hebrew language is written without vowels), and a text like this was used in the pre-Christian era.

The recent discovery of scores of fragments of biblical texts among the Dead Sea Scrolls* has provided the most valuable evidence of the antiquity of the textual traditions followed in all the versions of the Old Testament. Moreover, they form a valid basis for an understanding of the archaic pre-Massoretic history of the Hebrew Bible — e. g. the stages through which it had passed before it was finally fixed in the authoritative canon. The newly discovered documents provide, of course, invaluable controls in the disciplines of textual criticism.

The purpose of textual criticism is to establish the relationships between the various manuscripts, to each other and to the Massoretic text. (The subject of translations of the Bible into modern languages is dealt with in articles on Bible translations* and versions, see also Samaritans*.)

It has long been recognized that many errors were made in writing down and copying the texts as they exist. For this reason early rabbis* gave directions for oral correction during readings ("ketiw" and "kere", etc.). Some discrepancies in the text may be due to faulty copying but others reflect different traditional readings. Textual criticism also takes into account: comparisons of the various versions (see article), and comparisons of duplicated passages, and also makes use of the rules of parallelism in ancient Hebrew poetry*.

In recent years, the discovery and analysis of proto-Hebrew Canaanite texts from Ugarit, and of other north-west Semitic documents of the Late Bronze and early Iron Ages, has resulted in considerable advances. The student can now not only discover the original meaning of the pre-Massoretic or Massoretic text, but has also come to respect its integrity.

The language of the Hebrew Bible is today understood much better than it was a generation ago. The linguistic data uncovered by excavation has made possible a comparative study of Semitic languages and, as a result, the lost meanings of many words have been restored. Today textual criticism is closely allied to a study of Hebrew philology (grammar, syntax and spelling). As a result of these studies, specific parts of the Hebrew text can be dated according to their language. Thus a much more objective history of the language and transmission of the text can be reconstructed than was the case a few years ago.

Another, perhaps unexpected, effect of the new, more informed approach, is that scholars today take a more sober attitude towards the text as it stands and are much less ready to solve textual problems by suggesting emendations to the Massoretic text.

When it comes to reconstructing the history of various texts, the textual critic is on firmer ground now that the texts from Qumran can be placed beside the Septuagint as standards of comparison. A significant example was a comparison of Qumran fragments of the text of Samuel or Kings, widely at variance with that of the traditional Massoretic text. There was a higher ratio of readings which agreed with the Septuagint than of those in agreement with the Massoretic. The divergences in these books seem to result from the text translated: i.e. the Hebrew pre-Massoretic ancestor. The Septuagint text of the historical books is not necessarily superior to the Massoretic text, but it reflects a Hebrew textual tradition at home in Egypt in the 3rd and 2nd centuries BCE, which can be controlled, thanks to the Dead Sea Scrolls. The Massoretic text appears to be a compromise between a number of pre-Massoretic versions.

Conclusion: Both literary and textual criticism are equally important for the Bible Commentaries or interpretations (exegesis) of each of the Scriptural books which, through the ages, have been guided by the critical and analytical methods of their time, combined with the extent of secular knowledge available.

BLOOD AVENGER (see Family).

BONDAGE (see Slavery).

BREAD (see Food; Crafts).

BRIDE, BRIDEGROOM (see Family; Marriage).

BRONZE AGE (see Ancient Cities; Chronology).

BUILDING (see Cities, Canaanite*, Israelite* and Hellenistic* Periods).

C

CALENDAR: — *Outline: Ancient Calendars; Hebrew Calendars; Spring and Autumn Calendars; Archaeological Evidence; The Month; Weeks; The Calendar of Jubilees and Qumran; Days.*

Ancient Calendars: A civilized community in which taxes have to be collected and religious festivals observed regularly must have a recognized calendar.

The day was the basic unit for all ancient calendars. The problems arose in connection with months and years. The actual year is the period of the earth's revolution around the sun — 365 1/4 days — but all the ancient Near Eastern states based their calendars on the lunar cycle, which takes 29 days and 12 hours. Alone in the ancient world the Egyptians had a calendar based on a solar year of 365 days, but even they also had a lunar year, divided into three seasons of four months, each having thirty days. The five "additional days" not included in the number of months were added at the end of every year.

At first, months and years were determined empirically by observing the appearance of the new moon. Later, to avoid disagreements, the length of the months was established as alternately 29 and 30 days. However, the lag of eleven days between a year of 12 lunar months and the actual solar year resulted in a growing discrepancy between the official date and the actual season, which disrupted economic life and the order of cultic and religious ceremonies.

Biblical tradition expressed in the Creation story of Genesis (1:14) is that time is reckoned by the courses of the sun and moon; the day by the apparent circling of the earth by the sun; the month by the moon's revolution around the earth, and the year by the earth's own revolution around the sun. How this was put into practice in the earlier biblical period in Syria and Palestine, is still obscure.

In Babylon, by the sixth c. BCE, the problem of the discrepancy between solar and lunar years was solved by adding an additional month to every third year, making it a leap year with a second month of Adar or Elul (there were three leap years to an eight-year cycle). The Persian empire took over the system and in this way it was passed on to the Jews (cf. the books of Ezra, Nehemiah and Esther).

Hebrew Calendars: Hebrew festivals* (see article) were held on fixed dates in the lunar months. Apparently, some adjustment was made so that they took place in the appropriate season, but it is not known how this was done. The only hint that extra days were somehow added to the lunar year of 12 months is the reference to the second, or substitute, Passover in Nu. 9:10 ff. The Babylonians added the extra month of Adaru or Elulu at fixed intervals. Probably in Babylonia and almost certainly among the Hebrews during the time of the monarchy and Restoration*, the addition was made empirically when the discrepancy between the solar year and the lunar date became too noticeable.

The duplicate month was Adar, the last month of the year. Fixing the months was the responsibility of the priests and from Jewish tradition it seems that even after the destruction of the Second Temple leap years were fixed empirically by the rabbis. In doing so, they probably followed the common method whereby the beginning of new months was determined by the appearance of the new moon. The traditions of the system actually followed were preserved after the Temple's destruction and remained the special concern of the elders of certain families like that of Rabban Gamaliel, although the actual decisions continued to be the responsibility of the Sanhedrin (Rosh Hashana 25a).

In the middle of the 2nd c. CE, preparations were begun to establish a calendar based on exact mathematical calculations (Sanhedrin 12a) but not until the time of patriarch Hillel II (4th c. CE) was such a calendar accepted, making it possible to determine dates without actual observation of the lunar phases. Until then, the beginning of each new month continued to be proclaimed by the Sanhedrin on the basis of the evidence of two eyewitnesses to the appearance of the new moon. The news that a new month had begun was announced by beacon-fires kindled in sequence round the country or, later on, by messengers. Each year the Sanhedrin also decided whether intercalation should take place.

Spring and Autumn Calendars: According to the Hebrew civil calendar, at least as from the monarchy, the year began in the autumn month of Tishri, one month earlier in Judah than in Israel to judge from I K. 12:33. The Gezer tablet (see Agriculture*) which was apparently a rural calendar, begins its list of months with the "ingathering" or autumn month.

A year which began in the autumn presumably fitted in with agricultural and economic conditions but it appears that in addition to this civil calendar, an ecclesiastical calendar also existed before the Exile, according to which the year began in the spring. From the evidence of the older sources (Ex. 13:4; 34:18) it seems unquestionable that this spring (Nisân to Nisân) calendar was the more original. In fact as far back as we can go there is evidence for a spring calendar but, from the time of the monarchy at least, there was also a fall calendar. Even when this was introduced, however, it did not displace the older system and the counting of the months always proceeded from the spring calendar, often correlated to the fall calendar. The two continued in use side by side for the period of the monarchy and later, the dual usage being reflected in passages such as "at the return of the year" (t'shubat hashanah) in II Sam. 11:1; I Ch. 20:1; I K. 20:22, 26. All religious regulations appear to take the spring as the beginning of the year. The first holiday of Israel's religious calendar was Passover, the spring festival, while the feast of the ingathering (harvest) which began on the 17th day of the second month is to be held, according to Ex. 34: 22 at "the year's end". The Sabbatical year began in the autumn (Lv. 25:9) on "the tenth day of the seventh month". The New Year is to be celebrated in the autumn but the single biblical reference to "Rosh Hashanah" (New Year) occurs in a passage (Ex. 40:2) which apparently reflects Babylonian influence. Counting the months from the spring was also probably adopted from the Babylonians, perhaps at the same time as the Assyro-Babylonian month names were taken over. In any case there was never a complete change-over, merely the accommodation of two different calendars to each other.

Nisân (spring) remained the first of the months, even though the year began in Ṭishri (autumn). This may suggest that at the time of the final editing of Ex. 12 (which establishes Passover as the first month of the year), a spring year was being followed. The same applies to the religious calendars of Lv. 23, Nu. 28–29 and Ezk. 45:18–25. Jer. 36:22 also refers to the ninth month as a winter month.

One theory is that the luni-solar spring-year calendar was introduced under Assyrian influence after 722 BCE, when the northern kingdom of Israel became an Assyrian province. The new calendar was used in business and economic life and made its influence felt on religious matters as well, both in the northern Assyrian province of Samaria and also, after Josiah's reform, in the southern Babylonian vassal-state of Judah. Naturally, when Babylonian month names were adopted, the spring year was retained.

The spring year continued to be used by the Seleucids throughout the Hellenistic period (4th c. BCE onwards). The Book of Maccabees* (I Mac. 9:3, 54, passim) keeps to this reckoning in all references to the Jewish community. Sometimes, the month is referred to under the Jewish form of an ordinal number only. Sometimes this is followed by the Babylonian name (I Mac. 4:52). When the Greek form of the Babylonian name is used, this is usually given alone. In general, month names appear in later literature while the ordinal numbers are more frequent in earlier writings. The Hebrew and Babylonian names may have been used side by side for centuries. Apocryphal* works like Jubilees or the Qumran writings demonstrate that some religious circles put up a strong opposition to the introduction of the Babylonian names although these were accepted by orthodox Judaism (see below). The confusion produced by calendar variations in the Old Testament always puzzled the rabbis.

Archaeological Evidence: When Lachish and Tel el-Far'ah in southern Palestine were excavated, small tablets were discovered marked with thirty holes in three columns of ten holes each (**259**). The excavators dated the tablets to the time of the First Temple and it is thought that they were used to note the days of the month. The most famous discovery of a calendar is the tenth c. BCE "Gezer tablet" (described in full in the article on Agriculture*), which lists the names of months in accordance with the agricultural activities carried on in each of them.

The Month: There was no general system of naming months in the ancient East until, under Hammurabi, the Babylonian names were introduced throughout Mesopotamia. Before that, every Sumerian city had had its own names. Today, the Hebrew word "ḥodesh" means month. In ancient times, this word was used only for the first day of a new month, while the older Canaanite term "yeraḥ" meaning moon or the "twelfth part of the year" was used for the longer period. However, there was a general trend towards using "ḥodesh" to mean the month (e.g. Ex. 23:15; 34:18; I Sam. 6:1 passim). In I K. 6:38 and 8:2, the term "yeraḥ" used with the Canaanite name of the month is accompanied by the word "ḥodesh" and the number of the month as an explanation of the Canaanite term. Eventually, "yeraḥ" was dropped altogether and was replaced by "ḥodesh". Both words confirm that the Canaanite and biblical month was the lunar cycle of 29 or 30 days.

Names of the Months: The Bible refers to the months a. by their ancient Canaanite names; b. by ordinal numbers (the first, second, etc. month of the year); c. in the later, post-Exilic periods, by the Babylonian names. The ancient names continued in use in both Judah and Israel right up to the time of the Exile but only four are actually mentioned in the Bible: Yeraḥ Etanîm (I K. 8:2), the seventh month; Yeraḥ Zîv (I K. 6:37) the second month; Yeraḥ Bûl (I K. 6:38) the eighth month. and Ḥodesh-Abîb (Ex. 13:4) the first month.

Etanîm, Bûl and Zîv are also known from a Canaanite inscription which gives the names of seven of the months. Abîb is not included. The Bible may have used the numbers and avoided Canaanite names deliberately, because of their pagan associations. The name "Abîb" for the first month (Ex. 13:4; 23:15; 34:18; Dt. 16:1) is the Hebrew for the ears of corn or barley which formed the meal-offering of the first fruits of the year, offered to God (Ex. 9:31). It has been suggested that Zîv meant the month of flowers (I K. 6:1, 37); that Etanîm was the month in which streams continued to flow (I K. 8:2), and that Bûl was the month of the great rains (I K. 6:38); however, these are far from certain. The name "Yeraḥ Zaḥ" for one of the summer months has recently been suggested by Y. Aharoni on the evidence of a tablet discovered in Arad* in 1962 inscribed "b š 1 š yr'ḥ z'ḥ" (in the third month zaḥ). "Zaḥ" also occurs in an obscure verse in Isaiah (18:4) where it is usually translated "clear heat".

During the Babylonian Exile and after the Restoration, Babylonian names were finally adopted, giving a calendar which ran as follows:

			Approximately equivalent to:
1	Nisân	(Neh. 2:1; Est. 3:7)	March–April
2	Iyar		April–May
3	Sivân	(Est. 8:9)	May–June
4	Tammuz		June–July
5	Ab		July–August
6	Elul	(Neh. 6:15)	August–September
7	Tishri		September–October
8	Marchesvân		October–November
9	Kislev	(Zech. 7:1; Neh.1:1)	November–December
10	Tebet	(Est. 2:16)	December–January
11	Shebat	(Zech. 1:7)	January–February
12	Adar	(Est. 3:7,13; 8:12ff)	February–March

The Bible only mentions seven of these names (see above) and even then the ordinal number is often given as well (e.g. Est. 3:7). The others are known from post-biblical literature only.

The only names whose meanings are known for certain are Tammuz, after the god of that name; Elul, purification and atonement; Tishri, dedication, and Marchesvân, eighth month.

Weeks: A week of seven days as a unit of reckoning time must be independent of the lunar months (which are not exactly divisible into weeks). The idea of the week probably resulted from observation of the moon's phases, but among the Hebrews it became the unit of an independent cycle, irrespective of the months and years. Among the Babylonians and Assyrians, the week — also of seven days — began on the first day of the month, but among the Hebrews there is

259

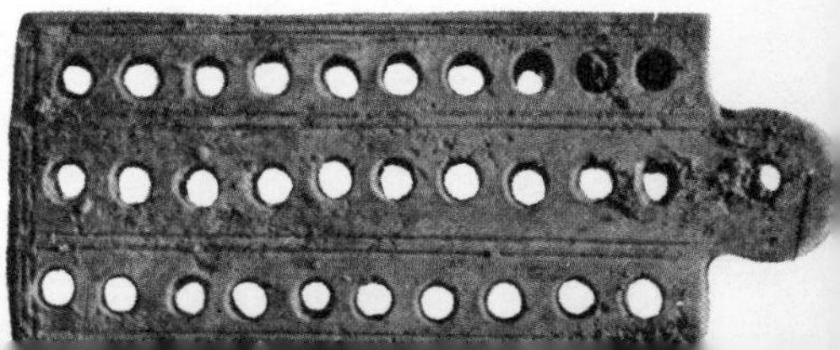

260

no evidence that this was the case. As in a modern calendar, the lack of correlation between the days of the week and of the month was unimportant. The week as a unit of reckoning became more important as the weekly Sabbath day replaced the day of the new moon as a holy day of rest and repose — a religious institution which is peculiar to Israel. Reckoning time by weeks rather than by days is only found in liturgical texts (see Festivals*).

The Calendar of Jubilees and Qumran: The sectarian movement within Judaism followed a solar calendar based on the week. This is made specific in the apocryphal book of Jubilees (see Apocrypha*), according to which fifty-two weeks make a year of 364 days; seven years form a week of years (as in Daniel) and seven weeks of years represent a Jubilee*. The same calendar is to be found in Enoch and in the Dead Sea Scrolls*. In Qumran the solar calendar was correlated with the official soli-lunar calendar. Even so, it meant a number of divergences in practice. According to the solar calendar, festivals fell on the same day of the week each year, the day of Pentecost (Shavuoth, the feast of Weeks) on a Sunday; Passover, the 15th Nisân, and New Year's Day on a Wednesday. Other manuscripts from Qumran give the dates according to the solar calendar which had been observed to correspond to the phases of the moon.

The "Manual of Discipline" exhorts the Qumran sectaries "not to depart as regards their (calendar) periods from any of God's commandments", meaning that they had neither "to advance their seasons, nor to retard any of their festivals." The significance of this injunction is suggested by Pharisaic references to innovations vis-a-vis the older priestly traditions about the dating of festivals (see Dead Sea Scrolls*).

Some scholars have suggested that the Qumran system was connected with the ancient priestly calendar and there is some evidence to support this. A. Jaubert has suggested that the same calendar was used by the latest editors of the Pentateuch (see Biblical Criticism*), by Ezekiel and by the Chronicler. As evidence, she cites the striking facts that the Flood is reported as lasting exactly one solar year (365 days) and that Enoch lived 365 years.

Days: Egyptian obelisks **(260)** served as shadow clocks to mark the divisions of the day, to fix the meridian and mark the movements of the sun through the seasons. The Babylonians divided the day into equal parts, according to a solar clock. Their system was adopted by the Syrian peoples, but there is no evidence in the Old Testament for a division of the day and night into hours. Instead, the Bible refers to times of day in terms of general natural periods: dawn, morning, noon, dusk, or evening, e.g. "at the time of evening, the time when women go out to draw water," (Gn. 24:11); ". . . it is yet high day" (Gn. 29:7) meaning early afternoon, and so on. The middle of the night, however, was explicitly "midnight" (Ex. 12:29; Jud. 16:3; Ruth 3:8; Ps. 119:62.

The only mention of any apparatus for measuring time is the "degrees" or Dial of Ahaz (II K. 20:9; Is. 38:8) which, (according to Y. Yadin) was apparently twin flights of stairs **(261)** leading to the roof of King Ahaz's house, one facing east, the other west. A low wall faced each row of steps. As the sun rose over the top of the eastern wall, a shadow was cast on to the top step. This travelled downwards until noon, when, with the sun directly overhead, no shadow was

262

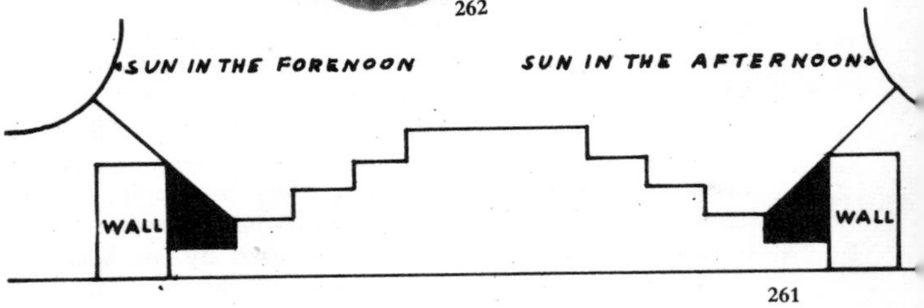

261

cast. As the sun moved westwards, the shadow was cast on the opposite row of steps and moved upwards during the afternoon until sunset. This was different from the later solar clocks in Hellenistic times, as shown **(262)**.

The main distinction of the Hebrew reckoning of the day was that, whereas among the Egyptians a day lasted from one morning to the next, the refrain in the Genesis story of Creation, "And there was evening and there was morning" suggests that the Hebrew day began in the evening. From ancient times, the celebration of holidays began at night (Ex. 12:18; Lv. 23:32; Is. 30:29) and, as the Hebrew calendar followed the cycles of the moon, the month also began at night. In time, however, the manner of reckoning the day probably changed to the period from one morning to the next, the full 24 hours being called "day and night" or some such phrase (Dt 28:66–67; I Sam. 30:12; Jer. 33:20 etc.). The wording of the instructions regarding festivals makes it clear that the night followed the day and not vice versa. Some scholars think that the two methods may have been followed side by side and that religious custom preserved an archaic mode of starting a new day in the evening long after this had dropped out of regular use. The method continued to be applied for calculating the Sabbath and religious feasts and in some secular connections right up to New Testament times and in later Judaism. The change to a day beginning in the morning must, in the opinion of R. de Vaux, have taken place between the end of the monarchy and the age of Nehemiah (see Restoration*).

On the other hand, in ancient times, the "day" was the period of light during which work was done. On this basis, it was reasonable to think of days when no work was done — holidays, Sabbath, the Day of Atonement — as beginning when work stopped on the evening of the day before.

Nights were divided into "watches". Like the Babylonians, the ancient Hebrews had three watches: the first (Lam. 2:19); second or middle (Jud. 7:19) and last or morning watch (Ex. 14:24; I Sam 11:11). By New Testament times the Roman and Egyptian custom of four night watches (Mt. 14:25; Mk. 13:35) had been adopted (see also Sabbatical Year under Agriculture*; Jubilee under Law*).

CANAAN. — Long before the Hebrew Conquest*, Palestine was part of a much larger geographical and cultural unit — the territory of Canaan. Populated by West Asian Semitic people, Canaan covered the whole area of Syria-Palestine from the borders of Egypt to Ugarit in northern Syria.

Excavations at Byblos, Ugarit*, Hamath, Beth-Shean*, Megiddo*, Gezer*, Ai* and other places, have shown that Canaanite settlement of this wide area goes back to at least 3000 BCE. A decided increase in population and number of towns took place around 2000 BCE, corresponding to the time of the invasion of the Amorites, a people who had established themselves as the ruling class over a wide stretch of territory from Mesopotamia to Canaan. They were organized into small states and, except in the extreme north, were satellites of Egypt. The exceptions — Aleppo, Qatna and Carchemish — lay within the Mesopotamian sphere of influence. The far north — Ugarit and Byblos — was brought under Egyptian suzerainty during the period of the Middle Kingdom (2050–1800 BCE). The Egyptians, who at this time knew the area as Retennu, interfered little with its political organization. The country was divided into a number of city states each with its own king and surrounding territory.

Between 1720 and 1550 BCE, the whole of western Asia was overrun by the Hyksos (see Egypt*). After that, the Egyptians of the 18th and 19th dynasties (1550–1200 BCE) took control of the coastal areas of the Syro-Palestinian region which they called Canahn. Only in the north did the new rival power of the Hittites establish itself.

Extensive documentation for the period immediately preceding the coming of Israel (14–13th cs. BCE) has been furnished by the archives of Ugarit (see Canaanite Civiliz. and Ugarit*) and the Amarna* Letters. These give ample evidence of the unrest throughout the area and the weakening of Egyptian domination there. In the 13th and 12th centuries came two major invasions, the first by the Hebrews (see Conquest*), the second by the Peoples of the Sea (see Philistines*). At the same time as the Hebrews made their appearance, the Moabites, Edomites, Ammonites, Midianites and Arameans were also establishing themselves in the adjoining territories. In the face of these invasions, the Canaanites retreated into the Lebanon mountains and the narrow coastal strip they protected. Later on, the Greeks gave the name "Phoenicia" to this northern area of Canaan and the term "Phoenicians" is used today for its inhabitants. The Bible never uses this word. It refers to the Phoenicians as the peoples of Tyre, Sidon or Gebal (Byblos). In fact, Canaanites and Phoenicians* were one people and the area of Canaan conquered by the Hebrews represented merely one large — rather backward — district of greater Canaan.

From the point of view of biblical history, two especially significant periods can be distinguished in the history of the Canaanites:

a. **The pre-Israelite Period:** The first period, from the 19th to the 14th century BCE (Middle Bronze Age) was the time of their greatest expansion. A fundamentally unified culture grew up over a wide area stretching from Northern Syria (including Ugarit) to the desert fringes of Palestine in the south. The people were organized in small city states. They had fixed homes, carried on agriculture, trading or a few crafts, worshipped in a communal temple and supported the temple hierarchy. This urban way of life, in striking contrast to nomadic habits, was in force during the period corresponding to the biblical Patriarchal Age. The earliest literary documents of this period are the archaic Canaanite myths about their gods (see Canaan: Gods and Idols*), to which later Hebrew poetry* was so deeply indebted (see also Cities, Canaanite*).

b. **The Decadent Canaanite Period:** The second period of Canaanite history was ushered in by the series of invasions of the 13th and 12th cs. BCE which destroyed the area of southern Canaan (Palestine). The invasions mark a political and cultural collapse in Canaan By the time they were completed, many of the Canaanites had been pushed back into the narrow strip of Phoenicia, little more than one-tenth of the area over which their culture had once held sway. The Canaanites who remained in the territory occupied by the Israelites amalgamated with them but preserved their own culture and religion. Once the invaders had established themselves as settlers, the old culture lingered to influence the civilization and life of the conquerors — Hebrew and Philistine. The extent of their influence on Hebrew culture has been shown by the discoveries of original Canaanite sources. Later developments in Israel's religion, thought and poetic forms often had their origins in ideas borrowed from the more sophisticated civilization which they had replaced. How much the Hebrews learned from Canaanite culture is suggested in the articles on Cities, Canaanite*; Cities Israelite*: Building*; Crafts*; Pottery*; Idol Worship in Israel*; Alphabet and Writing*.

CANAAN, GODS AND IDOLS, CULT. — *Outline: I. Canaanite Mythology: A Primitive Religion; Divinities: The Lady Asherah; Asherah and Later Superstition; Ishtar (Ashtoreth); El, Supreme Father God; The Ba'al and 'Anat Cycle; Nature Explained Through Myth; Ba'al; Death and Return to Life; Ba'al and Hadad; Mounted Gods. II. Idols and Figurines: Clay Plaques (Figurines) of Women; Female Fertility Idols; Male Idols; Pillar-base Figurines and Teraphîm. III. Cultic Objects: Wooden Asherahs (Pillars); Altars and Pillars (Matzebôth); The Canaanite Temple; Cult Furniture of Hazor; Canaanite Open-Air High Places. IV. Religion: Sacrificial Ritual; Fertility Rites; Comparison with Babylonian Cult; Sacred Prostitution; Eunuch Priests; Debased Religion; Moloch and the Tophet; Conclusions.*

In contrast to the quantity of material that exists about Egyptian or Babylonian religion, the Bible and other literary sources give only a very sketchy picture of the religion of Canaan. The biblical authors were familiar with the principal Canaanite deities but their account of them reflects a partisan attitude (see Idol Worship in Israel*).

Before 1930 CE, information was available from classical sources but very little was known directly of the theology of Canaan and the pattern of its gods and goddesses. Since then, as a result of work done, especially by French scholars, at Ugarit* the picture is much clearer.

I. CANAANITE MYTHOLOGY: A **Primitive Religion:** The Canaanites worshipped a variety of gods. Apparently, they were both the patrons of particular places and also had a specific function and authority. Nothing that has been discovered so far has provided a clear picture of the gods and their relationships. These have to be implied from a mythology rich in a symbolism which is still not fully understood by modern scholars. In the words of W.F. Albright, Canaanite myths reflect "an extraordinary fluidity of personality and function, a fluidity which makes it exceedingly hard to fix the domains of the different gods or to determine their relation to one another. Physical relationships and even sex change with disconcerting ease." This suggests to Albright that Canaanite myths are more primitive and closer to their archaic origins than other Semitic mythologies.

The two significant divisions of Canaanite history — the pre-Israelite and the decadent periods — mentioned in the introductory article are also reflected in the corresponding developments in their mythology.

The main source for the ancient mythology of the pre-Israelite period is Ugarit. Discoveries made there include the epics of Ba'al and 'Anat, Dan'el and Aqhat, and the story of Keret, all dating from the 15th and 14th cs. BCE (see Canaanite Civilization and Ugarit*). Traces of this heritage can be found in Philo of Byblos, a native Phoenician scholar who lived around 100 CE and who tried to interpret the values of his remote ancestors for the Graeco-Roman world of his own day.

He gives as his source a certain Sanunchiaton, a priest from Beirut who appears to have lived in the 7th century BCE and is thus a considerably older and more reliable witness than the classical authors. Philo's quotations left many details obscure but these have been largely confirmed and explained as a result of the Ugarit discoveries.

During the later — decadent — period, the Canaanites were beginning to amalgamate politically with the invading Hebrews and Philistines. Although it had lost much of its prestige, Canaanite religion lingered for centuries in Palestine and Phoenicia. The old myths and the poetry in which they were expressed may, however, have undergone changes over the years (see below).

Divinities: A comparison of ancient Canaanite epics, later Phoenician inscriptions and other archaeological finds shows that the Canaanite deities recorded in the Bible belong to the same family as the divinities known in Alalakh and the Phoenician cities of Tyre, Sidon, Byblos and Ugarit. The most important among the goddesses and gods were the following:

The Lady Asherah (consort of El-Dagon and mother of many gods): The archaic parts of the myth concerning her were known in Phoenicia, Canaan and Northern Egypt in the Middle Bronze Age (18th to 15th cs. BCE) before the legends were written in the Ugarit tablets in the 15th c. BCE. She was the supreme mother goddess. She was also "Athirat-Yam", Asherah of the Sea, the goddess of the sea and fishermen. She was worshipped as the supreme goddess in Tyre and Sidon. According to M. Dothan, a sanctuary from the days of the Patriarchs (18th to 16th cs. BCE) discovered on the shore of Nahariah (see High Places*), was maintained in her honour. It contained some crude figurines, much less sophisticated than those from other shrines. Numerous plaques and amulets have been found in the excavations of many towns and tombs of Canaanite and Israelite times (see below, Idols).

There is a variety of styles for these plaques. Often the goddess has the two long "S" shaped ringlets which were the emblem of the great Egyptian goddess Hathor. Sometimes she wears the cylindrical crown of the goddesses and queens of Late Bronze Age Syria (**263**) or, occasionally, an ordinary woman's headdress.

The attitudes of the plaques also varied. Some have the arms hanging at the sides (**264**); some with the hands placed on the breasts (**264**) and some with each hand placed differently. Often the plaque is decorated with flowers, sometimes a flower and a serpent (**265**). There does not seem to be any correlation between different headdresses or attitudes, but many scholars maintain that all the images belong to a single cycle of idols, the variations reflecting changes in time and place. They support this argument with a parallel situation in Egypt, where the connection between the nature of the gods and their headdress or emblem is much more explicit. During the Late Bronze Age, the Egyptians of the Delta adopted certain Canaanite deities. An Egyptian carving (**266**) dating from the New Kingdom (1150–1090 BCE) is a more artistic picture of Asherah, showing her standing on the back of a lion, holding

266

263

264

265

267

flowers and a serpent. The flowers she offers with her right hand to the Egyptian fertility god, Min. Her left hand (the unfavourable one) offers the serpent to Reshef, who was associated with the idea of death. The inscription reads: "Qdesh, lady of heaven and mistress of all gods." This symbolism is echoed in the Bible. Jeremiah (44:17) reproached Hebrew women for worshipping Asherah as the "Queen of Heaven".

As the mother goddess, so ran the myth. Asherah gave life to everything, good and bad alike. As the mother of the gods, she assigned responsibilities to each one according to his (or her) character.

Asherah and Later Superstition: During the Israelite (Iron) Age, the mythological attributes such as the horned tiara, Egyptian curls or cylindrical crown, appear less frequently. Modern research sees this very significant fact as resulting from the arrival of the Israelite population — who were not interested in Canaanite myths. At the same time, the surviving Canaanite population lost much of their veneration for their old traditions. The Asherah myth became confused with those of Ishtar (Astarte) and 'Anat and declined to the level of a few superstitions, connected with fertility emblems. The worship of Asherah herself was introduced to the Israelite court of Samaria by the Phoenician princess, Jezebel, who brought a retinue of priests with her to spread the cult. But the revival was short lived (see Idol Worship in Israel*).

Ishtar (Ashtoreth or, in Greek, Astarte): In Mesopotamian mythology she was goddess of fecundity and love, and also goddess of war. With the spread of Mesopotamian influence during the Assyrian and Babylonian empires, she became known throughout Syria and, later, Israel. She is represented as mounted on a lioness, armed with a sword and wearing a fluted crown surmounted by an astral disc identifying her with the planet Venus. (From this came the Greek association of Astarte with Venus.) By that time the cult of Ishtar had spread along the coast of Phoenicia and throughout Canaan, obliterating the memory of the ancient Canaanite Asherah. Figurines of the mother-goddess, sometimes traditional, sometimes Phoenician*, sometimes Hellenistic*, continued to be made. Ishtar's name appears more than forty times in Phoenician and later Punic inscriptions, many of them found on tombstones. The practice of sacred prostitution (as a magical means of ensuring fertility among men and their flocks and crops) was especially associated with Astarte (**267**).

Archaeologists used to describe all sacred figurines as Astartes, but it is now believed that in many cases this is a misnomer for archaic figures from the earlier periods which were those of Asherah, not her later counterpart. In the Ugarit myths, Astarte (Ishtar) is regarded as merely the companion or attendant of Ba'al.

El, Supreme Father God: The "creator of creatures" and supreme father is also "Kindly El Benign", the "King" and, sometimes "Bull El, my Father", using one of the commonest symbols of masculine potency. "El" is the Semitic word for God; it appears, for example, in the biblical El and Elohim (the plural; see Patriarchs, Religion of*).

In the epic tales, El is described as living in a remote dwelling "a thousand plains, ten thousand fields" from Canaan at the "source of the rivers of the Floods", in the midst of the "headwaters of the Two Deeps". When the gods wanted to consult him, they had to travel to this remote paradise. In the same way, the Babylonian hero, Utnapishtim, was translated into an immortal existence at the "source of the two rivers" and in Genesis the Garden of Eden is placed at the source of the four great rivers.

Another of El's titles was "Father of Years" which made him the god of time. The god of time in Greek mythology was Chronos, whose myth may possibly have originated in the East.

This mottled stone from Ugarit (**268**) shows a god with a flowing beard seated on an elaborate lion-footed throne, his feet resting on a footstool and wearing a tiara, tunic and mantle. A king or priest is presenting an offering which is welcomed as El welcomes gifts in the epic tales. It is beieved that this figure represents the "supreme father".

The characteristics ascribed to El made him seem too remote for simple people, although like the other gods, he occasionally stepped down from his heavenly eminence and played the hero in some remarkably earthy myths. Nevertheless, interest in him began to wane and the popular cult attached itself to his more active children. They were known as the "elim" or "b^{e}nei-elim", sons of the gods.

In spite of certain outward affinities, the "El" of the Israelite Patriarchs differed significantly from the Canaanite El. (The differences are discussed under Patriarchs*.)

The Ba'al and 'Anat Cycle: In the epics, the names and roles of the gods seem to change continuously, although the fundamental pattern remains fairly stable. Ba'al had different names in different places. He is Ba'al-Hazor, Ba'al-Peor, Ba'al Hermon, etc. He also has different attributes—the Ba'al-Berith of Shechem, or Ba'al Zebub, or Ba'al Zebul. It is now agreed by some that all these names referred to a single supreme god, the personification of all the life-giving forces in nature.

268

269

In Northern Syria, ʻAnat was thought to be his wife, although later on, in Palestine, the goddess Ashtoreth (Ishtar) became his wife.

Even in the epics, ʻAnat sometimes appears as both sister and wife. Elsewhere she is a devoted sister and a valiant warrior maiden. One of the Baʻal epics from Ugarit describes how he is killed by Asherah (the early mother goddess) and a group of monsters she has borne. Baʻal's friends mourn for him but his sister is not only grief-stricken but also determined on revenge. She had given a single-hearted devotion to her brother:

"Like the heart of a cow for her calf; Like the heart of an ewe for her lamb, So is the heart of ʻAnat for Baʻal."

However, more typical of ʻAnat as she appears in the myths is the Egyptian stele (**269**) which stresses her cruel, revengeful nature. She loved war. There is another story in the Baʻal cycle telling how, in her thirst for blood, she "smote and slew from seacoast (to the west, meaning sunset) to sunrise" in a night of general massacre. She filled her temple with men and barred the doors. Hurling heavy tables and furniture at them, she waded in blood up to her knees, even to her neck. "Her liver swelled with laughter; her heart was full of joy." At last she washed her hands in the blood — and went cheerfully off to something else (see Canaanite Civil. and Ugarit*).

In spite of her bloodthirsty nature, it was ʻAnat, more than any other female divinity who was the symbol of fecundity and vitality. This gave her one of her other names, the "Power of Life". Her popularity in the Palestine of the Patriarchs (Middle Bronze Age) is indicated by place names such as ʻAnathot, Beth-ʻAnat.

In the Bible, her name appears only in occasional lists of temples or places. The goddess herself is not mentioned. By the time the biblical books were cast in their final form, she had been forgotten. Some scholars believe that her place had been taken by the female warrior, Ishtar (see above, Ishtar).

Nature Explained through Myth: The workings of the forces of nature were explained by means of myths and legends about the gods. Besides the great central epic of the seasons (see below), there were stories about the god of

270

271

pestilence and Lord of the Underworld, Reshef (**270**) represented as an angry warrior, heavily armed and wearing contemporary Asiatic costume; Shulman or Shalim, the god of health; and Kothar, god of arts and crafts.

Ba'al: The dominant figure among the Canaanite gods was the great storm-god Ba'al. His name means "master" or "lord", so the same title could be applied to many different gods and a variety of personalities. In archaic Ugarit myths, Ba'al was the son of El, the supreme Canaanite god. Later on, the son consigned his father to oblivion and Ba'al became the name of the principal god of the sky, the earth and its fertility, akin to Bel of the Babylonians*. The Ugarit epics refer to Ba'al as "'Aliyan" ("the one who prevails" or "I prevail") and "the exalted, Lord of the Earth". His kingdom was "eternal to all generations."

Other general designations were "Melekh" (Melk — "king" or "ruler") and Adon (Hebrew Adonai, "master"). These titles could be used alone or in conjunction with the deity's specific name, for instance Melkart (Melk of "krt" or city) was the chief god of Tyre and, later, Carthage.

According to the epics, control of Sheol (the underworld) was taken over by Ba'al's brother Mot (death) while a series of other myths presents Ba'al as one of the gods of creation, as when he kills the sea dragon Yam (which means "sea" in Hebrew; see Genesis*: Creation).

The most likely representation we have of the rain-god Ba'al is a stele found in Ugarit (**271**) showing a god bestriding the mountains with a club in one hand and a shaft of lightning in the other. References in the epics to Ba'al as god of the storm, who spoke in the thunder and whose voice resounded through heaven and earth, seem to fit in very well with this "Ba'al of the Lightning".

Death and Return to Life: The most striking of the Ugarit poems is the epic of Ba'al's death and revival. A current interpretation of the myth is that it provides the mythical explanation for the annual cycle of death and resurrection in the seasons. It is suggested that the myth was re-enacted in mimetic ritual so that the forces of nature might be reactivated and fertility of soil, beast and man be ensured. Ba'al's other name of "son of Dagon" seems to place him in the fertility legends with Dagon and Mot, although scholars have expressed serious doubts about the validity of such interpretations as they associate Mot with death.

In Canaan and the Eastern Mediterranean, the summers are hot and rainless, and all the rain falls in the winter, usually during and after violent storms and cloudbursts. Ba'al was the vividness of all vegetation. Different epics tell how after a long war against his brother Mot, Ugaritic god of the rainless season, associated with the underworld, Ba'al was killed. With his death, all growth ceased and life languished.

Ba'al's sister, the "maiden 'Anat" came to the rescue and killed Mot, "With sword she doth cleave him, with fan she doth winnow him, With the fire she doth burn him, with handmill she grinds him. In the field she doth scatter his seed". 'Anat carried Ba'al's body to a sacred mountain top. There she performed an elaborate sacrifice and brought Ba'al back to life as god of grain. The cycle of life and growth could begin again. In the words of the Ugarit epic, "the heavens fat did rain, the wadis flow with honey".

Ba'al Zaphon: Many mountains, e.g. Hermon, Carmel, Tabor etc., were sacred to Ba'al. Ugaritic writings name Ba'al-Zaphon (Mount Cassius to the north of the city) as the home of Ba'al. The trading Phoenicians carried this name with them. Thus a place called Ba'al-Zaphon existed on the narrow tongue of land between northern Sinai and Palestine (Ex. 14:2, 9) and the god appears under this name on the famous Phoenician sacrificial tariff of Marseilles (see below: Cult). An inscription from the time of Ramses II found in northern Transjordan and popularly known as the "Job stone" also names a god as "El who established Zaphon" according to an unpublished reading by R. Giveon.

Ba'al and Hadad: By the time the Ugarit epics were written down (15th century BCE), the name Ba'al had come to be associated exclusively with Hadad, the reigning King of Gods. He controlled the storms and rainfall and, consequently, the fertility of the earth and the beings who lived on it. In spite of some differences between the two, Ba'al and Hadad appear to have been different impressions of the same deity (**272** – basalt head of Hadad from Carchemish).

Originally, while Ba'al became the chief divinity of the Canaanites, Hadad (Adad in Accadian) did not reign supreme over the Mesopotamian gods. Nor was he associated with ideas of death and revival. In practice, however, after the 15th c. BCE, Ba'al became "the lord", acknowledged as king over all the gods, enthroned in the far northern heavens. In Hellenistic times he was called Lord of the Heavens (Ba'al-Shmm, which in Hebrew is Ba'al-Shamayim).

Mounted Gods: There was another difference in the way the two were presented to their worshippers. The Syrian gods were pictured at first mounted on an animal, Hadad standing on the bull of heaven, Ishtar on a lion. The personality of the god was represented as much by the animal as by the human figure. Later, in a more sophisticated age, the imagery acquired greater subtlety and the animal was relegated to a minor role, the god being shown holding it by a halter of some kind (see: Idol Worship in Israel*).

II. IDOLS AND FIGURINES: The way the Canaanites actually pictured their gods has become clear from figurines and idols found in the lower levels of Canaanite towns in Palestine and Phoenicia (the northern part of Canaan) in Syria. Even this evidence, though, is confusing, for none of the pictures or figures of Canaanite gods bears any name or label. Apparently the deities represented were so well known that further identification was unnecessary. Inquiring scholars of today need no longer rely entirely on guesswork. The evidence of archaeology has made it possible to establish many facts with a high degree of probability.

In contrast to ancient Greece, Egypt or Mesopotamia, comparatively few representations of unquestionably religious or mythological scenes have been found in Palestine or Syria. Stone sculpture is even rarer. Large images of the gods (see below) begin only with the 12th c. BCE by which time Canaanite religion and culture were already becoming decadent. In the temples, most of the material found by archaeologists consists of other cult objects, not idols. Figurines and statuettes were found in homes, where they were used as charms and household gods.

272

273

Clay Plaques (Figurines) of Women: The most frequently found "likeness of anything that is in heaven above, or that is in the earth beneath . . ." is a crudely made clay plaque, usually oval, representing a nude female figure with the feminine aspects emphasized, even exaggerated. Hundreds of these have been found in almost all excavated remains of the 18th to the 5th cs. BCE. In response to a widespread demand a system of mass production was evolved, using one of two manufacturing methods. In one, the body was turned on a wheel with lumps of clay attached for the breasts, and with the head formed in a mould. The other way was to press the body and head from a single mould (**273**), leaving the back as a flat background or bed. This gave the objects their name "plaque", usually "Astarte" plaques. Some of them were made in bronze and in these, the forms were frequently elongated.

Although they are all fairly similar in appearance, it seems possible that some of them had a religious significance as votive plaques, while others did not (see above: Asherah).

Some of them are different from the Asherah plaques and do not seem to represent goddesses. Sometimes the hands rest against the sides. Sometimes they offer full breasts with the gesture of the *dea nutrix* (nursing mother goddess), the position given to the standing figure (**274**) modelled in the round, which became popular in the Iron Age. Votive plaques in the form of a woman in labour, her hands clasped over her abdomen, may have been intended as an inducement to fertility, or as a charm to ease labour.

Scholars still find it difficult to distinguish between plaques which were worshipped as goddesses, those which were charms, or some which, perhaps, merely represented the "qᵉdeshot" (sacred prostitutes) of the Canaanite shrines. All that can be said is that the objects served some important purpose — religious or magical — at the shrines or at home.

Female Fertility Idols: No statue of a Canaanite goddess of the early period approaching natural size has so far been found, nor do female idols seem to have had a special place in the temples. Only a very few metal figurines in bronze or lead have been found. Of these, the most important include a group from Gezer and Tel el Ajjul. One from Gezer (**275**) has double pierced ears, others have horns, recalling the cow-goddess. Otherwise, in contrast to male statues, there is no difference between these statues and other types of female idols. In spite of the realism and emphasis on the sexual organs, no erotic associations were intended. They were amulets to give help and ease to women who needed it.

Male Idols: Male idols are less frequent and more highly stereotyped than the female ones. In contrast to female idols in Canaan and elsewhere and to Egyptian representations of the god Min, pictured with an erect phallus, there is no emphasis on sexual aspects (with the exception of bull-idols). The only type of male idol found in Palestine is a small bronze statue with a royal or warlike aspect. Sometimes these idols are adorned with gold clothing or necklaces (**276**). Idols of this type were sometimes found in large jars, having been votive or dedicatory offerings; others were found in positions that suggested they had been household gods. Artistically they have no relation to representations of male idols on stone reliefs.

As on the reliefs, the idols may represent El, Ba'al or Reshef. However, in contrast to the female idols, it is not possible to identify the male statues. In fact, one is often moved to doubt whether the objects are intended to represent a god, or merely a human being. Phallic objects from prehistoric times have also been found in Canaan.

The male idols are usually made of metal rather than clay. They were always clothed and often made in a seated position. One of the best examples of such "molten images" (**276**) is a small (25 cms) bronze figure from Megiddo of the period of Judges* (12th to 10th cs. BCE) covered with gold leaf. The figure is seated on a throne, dressed in a long Canaanite robe and wearing a high conical headdress and earrings. He is probably a god. Many other figures show gods and goddesses, similarly enthroned and crowned, sometimes holding a cup or chalice. Figurines in metal were cast solid and were supported at the base by two pegs projecting from the feet or buttocks.

Pillar-base Figurines and Teraphîm: Moulded by hand or on the wheel, the body of many figurines ended in a slightly splayed but otherwise plain pillar base (**277**).

It is possible, although far from certain, that the crude pillar figurines may be like the household gods or idols called *teraphîm* which Rachel stole from her father in the story in Gn. 31:34 and hid in her camel saddle. In another story of feminine guile (I Sam. 19:13), they were large enough to take the place of the sleeping David. Teraphîm had a time-honoured place among the people, yet they were condemned along with idols and other abominations by the reforming Josiah in the 7th c. BCE.

The finding of such idols in Canaanite levels of ancient Palestinian towns gives perspective to the passionate denunciations of idols by Hebrew prophets living in the middle of Canaanite idolatry.

The significance of their frequency during the Israelite period is discussed under Idol Worhip in Israel* (see: Canaanite Civilization and Ugarit*).

III. CULTIC OBJECTS: **Wooden Asherahs (Pillars):** Most biblical allusions to Canaanite cult-objects mention the "asherah". In biblical Hebrew it refers sometimes to a goddess, and at other times to a sacred wooden pillar set up in the "high place*" or sacred shrine. Exactly what the object was is not certain. Probably, it was some kind of wooden emblem, similar to contemporary western Semitic objects. The Bible confirms that it could be hewn down, or burned to ashes. In the model of the "Sit-Shamsi" from Susa (see High Places*), three of the four posts visible seem to be "asherahs".

Wooden asherahs were sometimes decorated with fabric and this is apparently the significance of the reference in II K. 23:7 to "the houses of the cult prostitutes . . . where the women wove hangings for the asherah."

By the time of Josiah's reform, the mother-goddess had been obliterated by the personality of Ishtar (biblical Ashtoreth, see above) and the only meaning of "asherah" had become a "tree or sacred wood". Not until the discoveries of the Ugarit* poems was Asherah's original personality restored to her.

Altars and Pillars (Matzebôth): Alongside the asherahs set up in the "high places" might be "matzebôth", stone

276

275

274

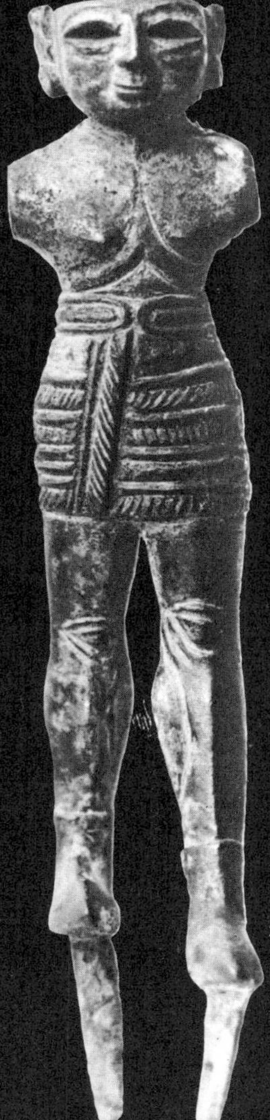

277

278

pillars or stele; braziers made of clay or stone for burning incense and also altars for incense, called "hammanîm" (see High Places*). These latter must not be confused with the altar of sacrifices or the altar of burnt offerings (see Sacrifice*). It seems that at the beginning of the Iron Age, pottery stands were gradually replaced by limestone incense altars, such as the examples of horned altars from Megiddo* and Lachish*, each having projections from the four corners. However, other examples of limestone altars have been found without horns. In the Iron Age Beth-Shean* sanctuary, there were a great many incense stands, often with one or more serpents moulded in relief. In a number of levels there, various broken house shrines were discovered. One of these was decorated with the figures of a naked goddess with doves, two male figures fighting a serpent and a lion. They were the heroes of some lewd and sanguinary Canaanite myth, similar to the ones from the mythological scriptures of Ugarit. Other later examples of incense altars, from the Persian period, have been found in the tombs of Maresha in southern Judea (**278**), where Phoenicians settled in the 4th c. BCE. The same tombs contained high slender metal stands which were at first supposed to be candelabra. However, in W. F. Albright's opinion, those were also stands for burning incense and were objects of adoration. He connects them with the pillars Yachin and Boaz which flanked the entrance to the Temple* of Solomon which was also of Phoenician design.

280

Objects like the incense altars and stands can be identified by comparing them with similar discoveries made elsewhere. The large number of cult objects recovered from Megiddo (end of 11th c. BCE) includes incense stands, horned altars, braziers and chalices (see Sacrifice*).

Other common cultic objects are offering stands, libation bowls, kernos-rings, and incense burners. These may have fulfilled a ritual or votive purpose in the same cult, some of them perhaps being placed around graves, in temples or just outside sanctuaries. The crude shallow libation bowl with a lion in relief (**279**) was found at Kiriath-Sepher (Tel Beit Mirsim or Debir).

The Canaanite Temple: Open-air sanctuaries and "high places*" were very common in Bronze Age Canaan, but so were the roofed temples of the later Bronze Age which have been identified at Ugarit*, Ta'inat, Qatna and Byblos in Syria. In Palestine, two temples of the late Bronze Age and three of the Iron Age were uncovered at Beth-Shean*, Hazor*, Megiddo*, Lachish*, Shechem* and Ai, while the temple found at Nahariah also dates from this period. At Ugarit* and Megiddo*, similar ground plans and wall-thicknesses suggest the existence of a class of many-storeyed Canaanite temples. In Beth-Shean, house shrines of a later age made in clay, were discovered, also with several storeys. Some of the Megiddo temples are described under Megiddo* and a detailed description of another is given in the article on Lachish*.

281

279

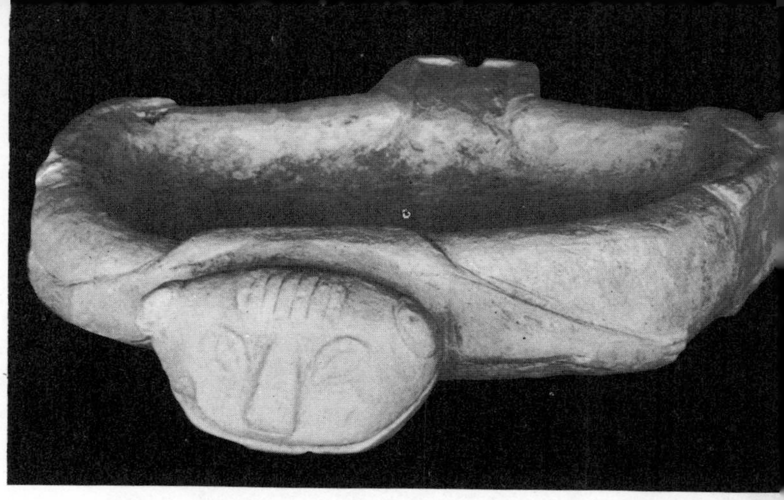

The late Bronze Age temple of Hazor* (area H, see article) belonging to the last period of Canaanite settlement, is unique in Israel for its architectural plan and construction. It is particularly interesting as a prototype of Solomon's temple, even having two pillars in its porch, reminiscent of Yachin and Boaz (see Temple*).

Cult Furniture of Hazor: The ritual implements and furniture found at the Hazor temple made up the most nearly complete set found in Palestine (see Hazor*, Area H). The most significant items are shown in these close-ups **(281)**: namely a basalt incense altar (foreground). At one side on the top is a relief of a four pointed star, the emblem of the sun deity, in the centre of a disc in a square frame. A large basalt basin about 80 cms. in diameter (right) lay near the altar. Two large earthenware pots (centre background) stood in the centre of the holy of holies and served as containers for oil, wine or other liquids used in the ritual. Between the pots and the altar were two basalt slabs, with depressions at their corners, which served as offering tables for the liquids offered. A small basalt statue, similar to those found in other temples in different strata of the city (see Hazor*), bronze figurines of male and female deities, cylinder seals*, some engraved and scarab seals were also found. A large amount of pottery, including ritual vessels, was scattered on the floor and on the stone bench which ran along the walls of the holy of holies.

In area C of Hazor, which met its end in the 13th c. BCE, a small sanctuary was found built into the earthen ramparts. Within it a number of basalt stele were uncovered including a smooth erect paving stone (orthostat) with a bas-relief of a lion and a deity **(280)**. Another group of stele found in the Holy of Holies included one engraved with two hands raised in supplication towards a sun disc carved within a crescent **(280)** — the emblem of the sun god, to whom, apparently, the temple was dedicated. On the left, a basalt plaque showed the god of the temple sitting on a stool, holding a bowl in his right hand with an offering vessel nearby **(280)**.

Canaanite Open-Air High Places: Groups of standing pillars or menhirs (matzebôth) erected in the open air have been found at Gezer*, Ader, Bab-Dhra and at Lejjun, east of the Dead Sea in Moab. This type of cultic installation was popular there in the third mill BCE. The Gezer "high place*" was still in use in the Late Bronze Age, although no longer as a sanctuary in the strict sense of the term, but as a mortuary shrine. The alignment of the standing stones is comparable to contemporary matzebôth in Ugarit or to the stele field of Aššur.

High places with round altars called in Greek "betyls" (from the Canaanite or Hebrew beth-el) are common in Phoenician settlements both in the homeland and overseas. A betyl is shown in the centre of this representation of the sixth temple of Paphos in Cyprus **(283)** dating from Roman times. Tacitus relates that when Vespasian went to consult the Phoenician oracle at Mount Carmel, he found an open-air altar there. Another example is the sanctuary of Ba'al-Hammon (the Ba'al of Carthage), an open air site across the Bay of Carthage. However, these open air high places have left few recognizable remains for, just as in Israel, they naturally could not survive the ravages of time and man (see High Places*).

282

Seven-cupped Bowls: One of the objects most frequently found in the sacred areas of Nahariah, Megiddo* and Byblos* was a pottery bowl with seven tiny cups **(282)**, an offering vessel from which some liquid was poured onto the "bamah" (high place). The number "seven" was a sacred number among most of the Semites. It figures prominently in Canaanite literature and in Scriptures and is frequent amongst objects found in excavations.

283

284

IV. RELIGION: **Sacrificial Ritual:** Among other similarities between Canaanite and Israelite cults, the sacrificial ritual stands out as being almost identical. For example, in the dramatic contest between Elijah and the priests of Ba'al (I K. 18:18 ff), the sacrifices to the two rival gods were prepared in the same manner. When the prophets inveighed against pagan practices, they were not objecting to the way the sacrifices were made, but that they were made in the wrong places and to the wrong gods. The Hebrew terms of "shelem" (offering) and "'asham" (trespass-offering) were identical with the words used by the Canaanites (see Sacrifice*).

In the excavations of Canaanite Lachish*, destroyed by the Hebrews in the early 13th c., a large number of young animal and bird bones were found. The bones had been cooked by being boiled and were of the upper shoulder or right foreleg, the portion set aside near the altar, under the law of "peace offerings", for the priests of the shrine. This conforms to Hebrew law, according to which (Lv. 7:32–33) this portion of a sacrifice was allotted to the priests.

A third c. BCE Phoenician inscription was found in Marseilles, dedicated to Ba'al-Zaphon (see above), listing the payments a worshipper had to make to the priest for certain types of offerings. The part of the victim to be retained by the priest is carefully prescribed: "For an ox, as a whole offering or a substitute offering for a complete whole offering, the priests shall have ten silver pieces each. In the case of a whole offering, they shall have, over and above this payment, meat weighing 300 . . . In the case of a substitute offering, they shall have neck and shoulder joints, while the person offering the sacrifice shall have the skin, ribs, feet and the rest of the meat." This bears a close comparison to the ritual prescribed in Leviticus. Poor people who had nothing to offer the priests were exempt in both cases.

In both the Canaanite and Hebrew cult, all or part of the sacrifice was actually burned on the altar. The Canaanites had a much more varied sacrificial ritual than the Israelites and used a greater variety of animals. Bullocks, rams, ewes, lambs, kids, small birds and doves and even young deer were employed as offerings.

One aspect of Phoenician ritual is illustrated by this alabaster statuette from Tutugi, near Granada (7th c. BCE; **284**). Apparently this was a miracle working statue. It represents Astarte (Ishtar) seated on a throne with sphinxes (see Tabernacle, Ark and Cherubim*) on each side. Under her breasts she holds a large bowl. The breasts were pierced and hollow. They could be filled through the head, while the holes in them were stopped up with wax which would melt when gently heated. At an appropriate moment in the ceremony, milk could be made to flow miraculously into the bowl.

Fertility Rites: Canaanite religion had much to do with fertility, as indicated. Their epics showed the gods behaving like humans, sacrificing, eating and, above all, procreating. By a kind of sympathetic magic*, this essential activity of the gods could be stimulated, if not initiated, by similar actions between humans at the shrines.

Among the theories advanced to explain the meaning of the Canaanite myths and their implications in the cult, those of the Scandinavian school figure prominently, although they are not generally accepted. I. Engnell has argued that the Ugarit myths are cultic and ritual. The ritual acts at the high places* and temples were accompanied by a recitation of the texts which explained their significance. The myth both interpreted the ritual and was integral to it. It was not merely a story of the past, but the expression of what the present ritual was intended to bring about.

Comparison with Babylonian Cult: One feature of the Babylonian fertility cult was a yearly festival at which a man and woman were chosen to represent the god and his consort. Their marriage and union were supposed to bring about a similar union between the god and goddess represented and thus to promote fertility throughout the community. At this festival the death and resurrection of the god were also enacted. This was not merely a dramatic presentation of the death of nature and its rebirth in the spring (see above, II, Death and Return to Life). It was also a ritual, designed to bring about the events it portrayed. Theories notwithstanding, it is known that the festival was accompanied by heavy drinking and much general licentiousness. It remained, nevertheless, an important religious occasion to an agricultural people, whose very lives depended on a satisfactory harvest. There is no direct evidence that this cult was observed in Canaan.

Sacred Prostitution: However, it is believed by some that such beliefs and so-called fertility rites may have penetrated into Canaan and developed into the practice of sacred prostitution at the shrines, where humans impersonated the gods' life-giving activities. Hebrew law (Dt. 23:17–18) put a strict ban on such practices, but they were common in the ancient world. There is an Assyrian proverb, "Do not marry a harlot whose husbands are six thousand, an Ishtar, a woman vowed to a god, a sacred prostitute whose favours are unlimited . . ." The prevalence of sacred prostitution called forth repeated invective from the prophets, for instance Hos. 4:13–14. It was a long time before the prohibition against the practice was effective. Even at the time of Josiah's reform (7th c. BCE), he "broke down the houses of the cult prostitutes which were in the house of the Lord." (II K. 23:7)

Sacred prostitutes, whether male or female, were designated by the same words in Hebrew and Canaanite, while equivalent terms are used in Babylonian and Hittite documents. In the original Hebrew, the word for a temple attendant is different from the ordinary term for a common prostitute, but this distinction is lost in translation.

Eunuch Priests: In addition to sacred prostitution of both sexes, which was apparently unknown in Egypt, although found throughout Mesopotamia and Asia Minor, the Canaanite cult also permitted a vogue of eunuch priests (kumru, kômer), witness this 4th c. BCE "temple boy" or ministrant **(285)** from Lefkoniko, Cyprus. They were much less common in Mesopotamia and, again, unknown in Egypt.

Debased Religion: The Canaanites never endowed their gods with any morals. So far as one can judge from contemporary codes of law, the behaviour of the gods was far inferior to that of society as a whole. Canaanite mythology is more brutal than any other in western Asian antiquity. Moreover, from the evidence contained in the Bible, it appears that the popular cult included some of the most degrading practices then known. Not only sacred prostitution, but also human and child sacrifice were common, although they had long been discarded by the Egyptians and Babylonians. The Canaanites also indulged in snake worship to an extent unknown among other peoples.

Moloch and the Tophet: Another type of sanctuary is the sacrificial precinct called "tophet" in the Bible with reference to a Canaanite (Phoenician) custom which had been transplanted to the valley of Hinnom, below the southern wall of Jerusalem, and which was suppressed by Josiah's reform: "And he defiled Tophet, which is in the valley of the sons of Hinnom, that no one might burn his son or his daughter as an offering to Moloch." (II K. 23:10).

The most important evidence for this practice is the sanctuary of Tanit at Salambo, Carthage. Like many other sites of Phoenician settlements around the Mediterranean, this one proves conclusively that the ancient biblical and Roman stories of Canaanite (Phoenician) infant sacrifices to Moloch were only too true. Excavations at Salambo uncovered thousands of urns containing the cremated remains of small children, mostly under the age of two. There were also the ashes of birds and small animals (which were later substituted for the children). This was a very large sanctuary. Its lowest strata (8th c. BCE) consisted entirely of these urns of burnt children's bones. The urns were covered by little cairns of stones. In later times, several urns lay under one stele. At Gezer*, similar urns were found, dating from a more distant past.

Many scholars (O. Eissfeldt, R. Dussaud and C. Picard) think that the word "moloch" may in times past have meant "sacrifice" and not the deity to whom it was offered.

285

It is difficult to reconcile the extremely debased practices of their cult with the vitalizing force of Canaanite civilization as a whole. It may be that their religious practices reflected an internal decadence which is also an explanation of why the Canaanites fell such easy prey to the Hebrew invaders. Some of the more debased practices were apparently abandoned by the later Canaanites, called Phoenicians*, under the influence of Iranian and Hellenic cultures during the 6th to 4th cs. BCE. Human sacrifice, however, persisted. Sacred prostitution declined in later Phoenician times. There was also an increasing decency in the treatment of the nude plaque figures. The same increasing restraint can be seen from a comparison of the Ugarit creation myth, or Bronze Age figurines, with the productions of the Iron Age.

Conclusions: Canaanite cult included, to sum up, a highly developed sacrificial system and a priesthood composed of male and female temple servants. At the same time, there was an extensive religious literature which, verbally and stylistically, has revealed many striking similarities to Hebrew poetry* although there the phrases were used as metaphors, not as part of a mythology.

While the picture of Canaanite religion remains admittedly sketchy, it is assumed by many scholars that, in general, the worshippers were mainly concerned with fertility and the benefits of nature. While new discoveries may reveal a truer perspective, the facts known at present give a new validity to the partisan picture of Canaanite religion which Hebrew writings preserve. (See High Places*; Canaanite Civilization and Ugarit*.)

CANAAN, RELIGION see Canaan*: Gods and Idols.

CANAANITE CIVILIZATION AND UGARIT. *Outline: I. History and Excavation; Western Semites and Egyptian Influence: Ugarit's Classic Period; International Relations, 14th–13th Centuries* BCE*; The Literature of Ugarit; The Myth of Ba'al; The Legend of Dan'el and Aqhat; The Tale of Keret. II. Ugarit and the Bible:* 1. *Dating;* 2. *Comparisons; Common Literary Traditions; Contrasting Concepts; Echoes of Myths in the Bible; Analogies with the Bible; Evidence of Mesopotamian Society. III. Alphabetic Writing.*

In the third and second millennia BCE, the centres of Canaanite civilization* were Byblos, Tyre and the ancient city of Ugarit in northern Phoenicia. The well-documented development and cultural activity of Ugarit serve as an excellent illustration of the civilization of the whole area.

Long known from Accadian and Egyptian documents, Ugarit was first identified by W. F. Albright with Ras-Shamrah and the nearby harbour of Minet-el-Beida. The identification was later confirmed by the discovery of documents bearing the city's name on the site.

There is no single mention of Ugarit anywhere in the Bible, yet the town and the remains uncovered in its ruins have been of the utmost significance in reaching a modern understanding of the Bible.

I. HISTORY AND EXCAVATION: Excavation was begun by French archaeologists, under the direction of C. F. Schaeffer, in 1928 CE. After a long interruption due to the war, work has been resumed and there is every prospect that it will continue for many years.

The lowest strata show that the site was inhabited from the end of the Neolithic period (5th mill. BCE). Although it has not been possible to identify the inhabitants of that time, it appears from ceramic remains found from the end of the period, that they maintained close relations with the peoples of the interior of Syria and the upper Euphrates. During the Chalcolithic period (4th mill. BCE), Ugarit developed an advanced civilization strongly influenced by Mesopotamia. The town was one of the main links between Mesopotamia and the outside world, notably Crete.

Western Semites and Egyptian Influence: In the following millenium, the town at first suffered a decline then, with the advent of a new population of western Semites, regained its importance, becoming, by the early second millenium, the dominant focus for international trade and cultural exchanges between the surrounding lands. As with the Canaanite kingdom of Byblos, further south along the coast, Ugarit's closest links, both political and commercial, were

287

288

with Egypt with whom she made common cause for defence against the Hittites* (see Patriarchs). With the Hyksos invasion in the 18th c., new Hurrite elements from eastern Syria were absorbed into the Ugarit population, although the original western Semites remained predominant. At the same time, the decline of Egyptian power gave the Canaanites an opportunity to develop their own individual culture, merging and transforming the influences that had been streaming in from Mesopotamia and Egypt during the preceding centuries.

Two centuries later (16th c. BCE) the Hyksos expulsion from Egypt brought Egyptian garrisons to Ugarit, which became an Egyptian base for land and sea operations in the north. This period saw the peak of the kingdom's development.

Ugarit's Classic Period: The most thoroughly excavated stratum of ancient Ugarit has been that belonging to the 15th–14th c. BCE (late Bronze Age) — the classic period of Ugarit's history during which its trade expanded over a widespread region and its population increased very substantially. Great fortunes were built up and merchants and artisans streamed into the town from Cyprus, Syria and the islands and mainland of Greece. A great wealth of material has been uncovered from this period: palaces and sumptuous homes, a number of warehouses and two temples to Ba'al and to Dagon; sculpture, pottery, gold and silver work, depicted in the accompanying illustrations **(287,8)**, and, above all, the mass of clay tablets *which have given Ugarit its special importance today* (see below: Literature of Ugarit).

Placed as it was, Ugarit was open to influences from many lands. Trade between Mesopotamia and the Phoenician coastland and, more important, from the islands of the Aegean and from Egypt, passed through the town. Many objects found there had either been brought to Ugarit from the Aegean or else had influenced the town's own craftsmen so deeply that their own wares became indistinguishable from the imported goods. One outstanding example is this lid of a small ivory box **(286)**. On it a goddess is seated on her throne feeding two goats standing on their hind legs, supporting themselves while they eat by resting one front leg on the throne. The technique of the relief is Mycenean, as is the goddess' dress: a full, richly decorated skirt which leaves her body bare above the waist, except for bracelets, earrings, a necklace and a diadem. It seems most likely that the figure represents the great mother goddess, the ruler of the animal kingdom, who held a prominent place in the arts and religion of Canaan (see Canaan: Gods and Idols*). Much later, in Hellenistic times, the same motif was repeated although the goddess was replaced by a date palm. This transformation of goddess into tree also took place in representations of Asherah.

International Relations, 14th–13th cs. BCE: These centuries saw the development of the purple dye industry in Ugarit (as in Tyre and other Phoenician* cities). Many of the tablets discovered in Ugarit (see below) dealing with trade and diplomatic relations refer to the important commerce in purple. The only other natural resource of any value were the pine and cedar trees of Lebanon and Mount Casius, exported from Canaan to Egypt (and later to King Solomon*) and to Mesopotamia.

The everyday life, trade and diplomacy of Ugarit are brought vividly to life by its great wealth of tablets and literary texts (see below: Evidence of Mesopotamian Society). These were contemporaneous with the Amarna letters*, which are another set of texts vividly illuminating the international setting of Syria and Palestine. From the Amarna letters, a good deal can be learned about Ugarit's relations with her neighbouring countries.

Under heavy pressure from the Hittites, the king of Ugarit was forced to yield to the Hittite Shupiluliumas, appeals for help to the Egyptians having gone unanswered, (see Amarna letters*). In the end, Ugarit joined the Hittite confederation that fought against Egypt* at the battle of Kadesh at the beginning of the 13th c. This was followed by a long period of peace between Egypt and the Hittites that gave Ugarit a welcome respite for internal progress. However, the invasion of the Sea Peoples in the 12th c. (see Philistines*) cut off the Canaanite coastline from its rich trade with the Aegean islands and Egypt. The cities of the coast declined and the coastal kingdom of Ugarit became a place thinly populated and of little importance.

The Literature of Ugarit: As they are translated, the tablets of Ugarit (see above) provide the most complete texts yet known of the myths of Canaan. Previously, Canaanite mythology was reconstructed on the basis of the late second-hand descriptions by Philo of Byblos* (who wrote during the second half of the 1st c. CE), and from hints contained in certain obscure verses of the Bible. Once the actual texts were available to scholars, the myths could be studied at first hand and the Bible's relationship to this older literature scientifically assessed.

This process is only beginning. Some scholars feel that the first translators and interpreters of this obscure idiom may have been over-confident in publishing their findings and that revisions may be suggested by further investigation. Certainly as the work of reading and interpreting the tablets proceeds, greater accuracy will be achieved and may correct mistaken first impressions or over-hasty evaluations of Ugaritic thought. Ugarit literature was the product of a highly developed urban culture. It cannot be directly compared with contemporary Hebrew, which was rooted in a semi-nomadic way of life, slowly reacting to the impact of the more advanced urban and rural environment of Canaan.

In quantity, the literary texts inscribed on the tablets found in Ugarit are equal to about half the Hebrew Book of Psalms. The most important of the texts were the epic tales of the gods and legendary heroes, written in a poetic style (see Poetry*). Of these, the outstanding ones are the Myth of Ba'al, the Legend of Dan'el and Aqhat and the Tale of Keret.

The Myth of Ba'al: The one recorded on this tablet **(289)**, for example (columns 5–8 of the myth of Ba'al), tells of an episode in the life of the god Ba'al, also called Hed or Aleyin Ba'al. It relates that after Ba'al has built the walls of his palace, he lights a bonfire within it in order to melt a large quantity of silver and gold. Like many similar epic occurrences, this activity lasts a week. For six days the bonfire blazes up and, on the seventh, the gold and silver transform themselves into cups and bricks which automatically cover and decorate the walls of the palace. Delighted with his finished silver and gold palace, the god summons

289

all his brother and sister gods and other relatives to a sumptuous banquet as a house-warming.

Other episodes in the myth of Ba'al relate the warfare between him and his mortal enemy, Mot, in which Ba'al is supported by his sister, 'Anat and in which El, the supreme father of the Canaanite gods, finally intervenes and authorizes Ba'al to build himself a palace in the far north. The war between Mot and Ba'al continues and Ba'al is killed. 'Anat comes to the rescue, punishing Mot and his helpers and bringing Ba'al back to life. He gains the supreme position among the gods. The myth, of course, symbolizes the greater struggle between the powers of life and destruction and the ultimate triumph of life.

Further references to these and other themes of Canaanite mythology and theology are given under Canaan*: Gods and Idols*; Poetry*.

The Legend of Dan'el and Aqhat: In this poem, one of the principals is Dan'el, "an upright man" who sits before the gate (see Law*) "judging the cause of the widow, adjudicating the case of the fatherless" (an idiom which can be compared to the ideal of the Hebrew tradition in Ezk. 14:14–17,20; to Noah and to the righteous man mentioned in Job and, much later, in the book of Daniel; see below).

When he desires a son, Dan'el makes the appropriate sacrifices to the gods and succeeds in persuading Ba'al to present the petition to his father El. El agrees and the son, Aqhat, is given a bow and arrows by the gods who predict a heroic future for him. However, he angers 'Anat and she has him killed by a servant. Dan'el mourns for his son for many years and, in the end, is avenged.

The Tale of Keret: This is the story of King Keret who fought against a rival king and was given his daughter or niece, the beautiful Hari, as a wife. The account of their raising a family is obviously intended as an example of the good life although, in the end, his son attempted to dethrone Keret.

Other literary works include three shorter poems, one on the nuptials of the sun and moon god which was apparently intended to be recited at marriage ceremonies; one a festive liturgy to be intoned to the gods and the third a dirge for the dead.

II. UGARIT AND THE BIBLE: 1. **Dating:** The Ugarit poems provide a most important point of contact between Canaanite culture and the later period of the Patriarchs. The poems, in the words of D. N. Freedman, "are themselves the final surviving product of a long process of oral (and possibly written) composition and transmission covering many centuries. They are not in any case the creation of 14th c. Ugarit civilization. The traditions which make up the Keret and Dan'el epics go back several centuries before the present texts, while the Ba'al material may be older still. If, therefore, the correspondence in various themes between the Ugaritic poems and the Patriarchal stories suggests a common era of composition or occurrence, their period is not the 14th c., but the first half of the second mill. One clue that emerges from a comparative study of the Bible and Ugaritic materials concerns the relationship between El and Ba'al ...... In the Canaanite epics, Ba'al has already displaced El as the most prominent deity in the pantheon .... In the biblical tradition, however, the God of the Fathers is regularly identified with El ... never with Ba'al, who is not even mentioned." (See Canaan*: Gods.)

2. **Comparisons:** One effect of the many affinities in language and style between the literature of Ugarit and the Bible has been to correct a number of assumptions about the age of the material in certain biblical books. Many parallels can be found, for instance, with a late book like Job, while the discoveries at Ugarit have made it clear that when Ezekiel (again, 28:3) referred to Dan'el, this was not the biblical Daniel, but the Canaanite hero directly transplanted from Ugarit.

To interpret the language and culture of the Canaanites, scholars have drawn heavily on the literary forms and language of the Bible. In the same way, the Ugarit texts have thrown considerable light not only on the content of biblical texts (see above) but also on their form.

The Ugarit tablets offer a valuable picture of the development of Canaanite literature during the period leading up to the earliest phases of the Old Testament. In form, the two have a great deal in common. Not only do they both share the characteristics of all the literature of the ancient East: prosody, rhythm and a particular pattern of constructing verses or sentences. In addition they reveal even closer affinities in forms of expression, syntax and literary style. So much is this the case that it has been suggested that the Canaanite dialect used in Ugarit and the language of the Hebrews are both parallel developments from a common ancient Canaanite source.

Common Literary Traditions: Moreover, both literatures continue a literary tradition established before the earliest phases of the Old Testament (see above, Dating). It seems that the Bible could draw on a literary form already perfected through centuries of evolution. Verbally and stylistically, the Canaanite Epics of Ugarit show striking similarities to the earliest Hebrew poetry, Song of Miriam (Ex. 15), the Song of Deborah (Jud. 5), the Blessing of Moses (Dt. 33), and the 29th and 68th Psalms which were composed for liturgical purposes. Hebrew poetic literature is under an immeasurable obligation to the Canaanite poets of the Bronze Age who developed the style which gives Hebrew poetry so much of its formal appeal (Poetry*). Striking parallels can also be traced between the prose style of Canaan and Akkadian poetry going back to the earliest times, especially in the hymns and epics.

These close similarities reflect a common Canaanite literary heritage which had a strong influence on the Israelites and which left traces in much later writings, such as those of Philo of Byblos of the 1st c. CE.

As a result of the findings of the new branch of Semitic studies known as Ugaritic, biblical research, particularly Hebrew lexicography and poetry, had to revise many established beliefs. Critical theories based on the assumption that there was no written poetry in the earliest periods of biblical history, had to give way or be modified by the appearance of an extensive library of poetry from Canaan, corresponding to the time between the Patriarchs and Moses.

Contrasting Concepts: The Ugarit tablets describe Ba'al as the "rider of the clouds" (in Hebrew "rokheb 'arabot") the lord of the rain (see Canaan: Gods and Idols*). Similar phrases are used about God in the Bible, but with a difference. While all the other religions of antiquity saw the different forces of nature as under the control of a separate deity, in the monotheistic religion of the Hebrews, God alone had power over nature. The Hebrew poets made use of Canaanite imagery and borrowed the titles of the powers of nature, although they understood that the different aspects were all attributes of a single God. When the Psalmist wrote "Extol him who rides in the clouds" (Ps. 68:4), or "Praise him who rides high on the ancient heavens" (Ps. 68:33), he was not in any way suggesting a literal, material "rider" such as Canaanite mythology took in its stride. The Hebrews' religious associations were of a different order and belonged to a different theology. (For further discussion of the contrasting concepts of God in the Bible and Ugaritic literature, see Canaan*: Gods and Idols, Cult*).

Echoes of Myth in the Bible: In its poetry and the metaphors it uses, the Bible continued an ancient tradition. The theme of the struggle between the god of the heavens and his enemies, and his victory over them, appears again and again in the Ba'al epics of Ugarit and can equally be found in numerous references in Hebrew biblical and post-biblical literature. However, in Hebrew and Jewish lore, the theme appears not as a struggle between gods, but rather as the revolt of God's creatures against their creator, and their doom.

Analogies with the Bible: Certain words and expressions and cases of apparently ungrammatical usage in the Bible, which have long puzzled students, have now been shown by analogy with similar phrases from Ugarit to be perfectly explicable in terms of that language.

The more obvious examples of this process come from the Bible's use of proper nouns like Leviathan, in Ugaritic Lothan, or the serpent Akallaton (Is. 27:1), Rahab as the prince of the sea (Job 9:13; 26:12), Mot (equivalent to the Hebrew for death), El, Ba'al, 'Anat, Astarte, Asherah. These had long been familiar in the names of Canaanite towns or people, but the tablets from Ugarit at last put them into their proper mythological setting — missing from the Bible (see Canaan*: Gods and Idols).

Besides clarifying difficult passages of the Bible, Canaanite mythology gave a new meaning to many familiar passages. Probably the best example is Elijah's famous mocking of the priests of Ba'al during their contest on Mount Carmel: "Cry aloud, for he is a god; either he is musing, or he has gone aside, or he is on a journey, or perhaps he is asleep and must be awakened" (I K. 18:27). The significance of Elijah's choice of phrases is made much clearer when the passage is compared to the Ugarit tablet (IV AB) which tells how once 'Anat came to visit Ba'al in his temple and was told by a servant that the god had taken his bows and arrows and gone to hunt wild oxen in a distant country; or to another tablet which records that once El, the father of the gods, wanted to give a feast to his sons but had first to awaken Ba'al by calling him loudly. When Elijah mocked the priests of Ba'al he was using expressions and similes which were well known to his audience and, for that reason, all the more cutting.

To take another example, the repeated biblical injunction to eschew "the ways of the Amorite" is illuminated by a reference to one so-called Amorite custom: A tablet gives a description of the Canaanite gods enjoying a meal of a kid boiled in butter — the direct antithesis to the specific and reiterated biblical ban on "boiling the kid in the milk of his mother."

Evidence of Mesopotamian Society: The strata of 15th–14th c. BCE Ugarit have yielded, in addition to the literary texts, hundreds of Akkadian tablets giving the texts of economic treaties, state correspondence, juridical and economic documents. They have only been published in the last decade and throw light on many previously unknown aspects of the social organization and feudal society of Ugarit. Not only do they illuminate the history of the 14th–13th cs. BCE, they also provide valuable background material for the study of the urban civilization of Canaanite cities* (see article) from the time of the Conquest to the early Monarchy.

I. Mendelsohn has pointed out that Samuel's denunciation of the "manner of the King" in I Sam. 8 (see Samuel*) is reflected in the Akkadian texts of Ugarit. These include references to the king granting land to his faithful supporters; regulations governing forced labour "in the service of the king", and payment of the tithe (tax of a tenth). The king of Ugarit could, if he chose, exempt anyone from payment of this tithe.

The "alphabetic" texts of Ugarit refer to another socio-political phenomenon, the Habiru*, rendered as 'prm.

Much of the new material discovered remains to be clarified and interpreted. When this is done, new surprises certainly await the scholars of Ugaritic.

III. ALPHABETIC WRITING IN UGARIT: The temples, palaces and houses of the period of Ugarit's maximum prosperity (see above, Ugarit's Classic Period) are a vivid testimony both to its prosperity and to its material and spiritual development. In fact, the local economy was sufficiently advanced to support a large group of scribes who produced the great mass of documents found at the site. Besides copying in the standard scripts of the day, they also developed a new system of writing.

Among the hundreds of tablets found at Ugarit, many are in Akkadian, some in Hurrian (see below), but the ones of greatest importance for biblical studies were a special group of clay tablets inscribed in a new form of cuneiform writing and, quite obviously, not in either of the other two languages. The most notable features of the new script were the shortness of the words, the use of a special sign to divide the words and, most important, the fact that only 30 signs were used in place of the enormous number of different cuneiform signs used in Akkadian.

The tablets were studied by a French scholar, C. Virolleaud and a German, H. Bauer. Independently, they discovered that the tablets could be deciphered relatively easily on the assumption that the script was alphabetical. Twenty-five years after their first discovery, a small tablet (**290**) which had apparently been used in a school of scribes was found, inscribed with the 30 letters of this alphabet. Rendered in modern Hebrew letters (although the order is slightly different) this alphabet runs as shown in the article on Alphabet*.

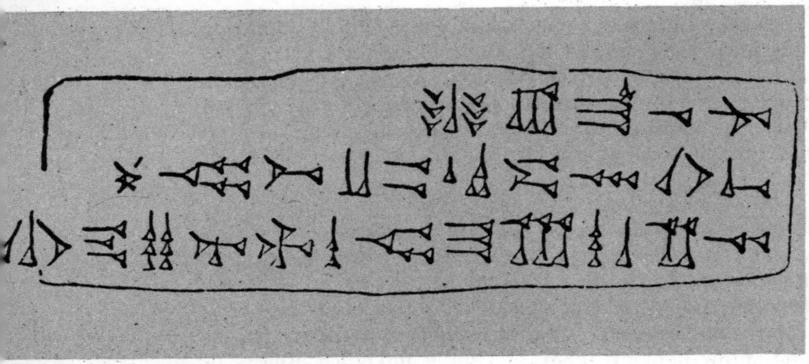

290

Trilingual dictionaries, set up in three columns: Akkadian, Ugaritic and Hurrian, also found in Ugarit, had also probably been used by the scribes, for Ugarit was a polyglot city, located at the crossroads of the ancient oriental world.

The language of the "alphabetic" tablets was assumed to be close to biblical Hebrew and this was found to be correct. The texts translated on this basis made sense and the language was proved to be a northern dialect of Canaanite at an early stage of its development.

However, later, the new form of alphabetical cuneiform writing was forgotten. Cuneiform is only suitable for clay tablets and, as papyrus and potsherds (ostraca) took the place of clay, a new form of writing, better adapted to the new materials and known as the "Phoenician script" was developed and taken over both by the Canaanites and the early Hebrews. (See also: Canaan: Gods and Idols*; Cities*; Phoenicia* and Alphabet* and Writing.)

CENSUS. — *Outline: Origins and Practice of Census-taking in the Ancient Near East; Purpose and Method of Census-taking; Cultic Accompaniments to the Census in Mari; Census-taking in the Bible; Census-taking in Exodus; Census Lists of Numbers* 1 *and* 26; *Significance of the "Elef"; Origin of the Traditions in Numbers; David's Census; Expiation; Other Censuses; Census Lists of the Restoration; New Testament Period.*

Origins and Practice of Census-taking in the Ancient Near East: Census-taking is a function of civilization. Every organized society must count heads every so often — people, cattle and other things as well. Both in Egypt and Mesopotamia, census records are very old, much older than Israel's.

As early as the Old Kingdom in Egypt (3rd mill. BCE) the Pharaohs were taking a biennial fiscal census (which later became annual), surveying the land and counting cattle and goods as a basis for the assessment of taxes*. Taxes were paid in kind: grain, hides, gold, or in forced labour. Later evidence suggests that the state taxes were collected individually by each province and this may have led to the farming out of the collection to provincial entrepreneurs. The records of the 12th c. BCE Rameside administration include the accounts of the government tax collectors which show how tax was assessed per unit of land or per measure of grain cultivated. The biblical story of Joseph (Gn. 47) refers to a systematic assessment of the agricultural yield of the land and the numbers of people living on it. This incident was apparently intended to forestall a famine or a grain revolution, but it reflects general administrative practice.

In recent years, the records of Mari (Mesopotamia), Ugarit* and Alalakh (north of Ugarit) have yielded a great deal of information about census lists over a period of 500 years from the time of Hammurabi (18th c. BCE) to shortly before the time of Moses.

Purpose and Method of Census-taking: Besides being the essential basis for levying taxes, population censuses were essential to provide a register of able-bodied men subject to forced labour (corvée) or, more important, military service. Actual conscription was carried out by lot, for only a proportion of each area's quota would be taken for the army at one time. Grants of land were similarly made by lot. It appears that only those who were liable and/or actually served in the army were eligible for land grants which are known to have been distributed by lot.

The use of lots immediately introduced a religious factor, since the appeal to chance was really an appeal to the gods — as in legal questions which could not be settled by evidence. Since the choice by lot for military service involved at least the possibility of death for the conscript, it had the gravest significance — hence the awesome aspect of the military census. A question involving life or death, victory or defeat, could not be treated lightly. Therefore, atonement and purificatory rites, payments and other ritual were necessary to avoid divine wrath.

In the conditions of ancient times, the taking of a census was inevitably associated with the danger of disease, whether transmitted from village to village by the census takers or passed on from one to another when men gathered together for training or military duty. It is an accepted fact that all through military history, disease has claimed many more lives than battle. D. N. Freedman believes that purificatory and atonement rituals were adopted chiefly to guard against these attendant evils of the census.

In view of the combination of factors: resistance to government interference; resentment against taxation; fear of military service and the danger of epidemics, it is small wonder that there was great foreboding about the whole procedure and a strong feeling that it was better to avoid it entirely. However, as the census was an essential part of life, the greatest precautions, chiefly of a cultic kind, were necessary, to avoid offending or to placate the deity.

Cultic Accompaniments to the Census in Mari: In Mari, the census ("tebibtum") was linked to new land grants and various political activities. However, to ward off the attendant dangers, expiation by cultic acts of purification was practiced, after which "the heart of the land was at peace."

Research into a number of aspects of this question has been conducted recently by J. F. Kupper and E. A. Speiser, using the cuneiform letters of Mari* on the subject of census-taking for military purposes. This has revealed a number of analogies to biblical practice (discussed below).

Census-taking in the Bible: The Israelite tribes and their descendants in later centuries had not only the general feelings of resistance to any numbering of the people, but also regarded it as an unwarrantable interference with individual liberty. Because of this traditional opposition, any reference to such an activity needed to be worded very euphemistically. Although references to a census take up considerable space in the Bible, particularly in the book of Exodus, in Numbers (which owes its very name to a census) and in II Samuel, the wording has been so misleading that much of the material has long been a puzzle to interpreters, who have not been helped by misunderstandings and inaccurate translations of the technical terms. For instance, it was not made clear why "atonement" offerings ("kofer" in Ex. 30:12f) were necessary to ward off plagues, nor why epidemics as a sequel to the census were traced back to the days of David (as in II Sam. 24).

Census-taking in Exodus: According to a tradition in Exodus (30:13–16, 20; 38:25–26), every male Israelite, rich or poor, was required to contribute a half-shekel every year, known as "Atonement money" to provide for the upkeep of the sanctuary and its services. The counting of the shekels also gave the number of males of 20 years of age or over (i.e. those of military age).

Census Lists of Numbers 1 and 26: According to parallel traditions in Numbers (1:1–54 and 26:1–51, 57–62), two counts of the Israelites were held by Moses in the desert. The first was held in the 2nd year after the Exodus, the other in the 40th. The totals produced were remarkably close. The first, taken presumably according to the procedure described in Exodus, gave literally a figure of 603,500 males. A special census of all males aged one month and over in the Levi tribe revealed 8,600 "watchers of the sacred precincts" (Nu. 3:15–43). Of these, an additional count was made of the Kohatites of the tribe, aged from 30–50, who did the work in the Tent of Gathering. The Gershonites, who were charged with carrying the Tabernacle, were also counted separately (Nu. 4:22–23).

The second count, taken (Nu. 26:1–15) when the people were camped in the steppes of Moab near Jericho on the eve of the Conquest*, gave a figure of 601,700 males aged 20 years and over, plus 23,000 Levites aged one month and upwards (Nu. 26:62).

Significance of the "Elef": In Numbers (1:20–46) the figures are given for each tribe* as so many thousand ("ălāfîm", plural of "elef") men "able to go forth to war", e.g. for Reuben: 46 "ălāfîm" 500. In view of the fact that these literal figures relate only to males over 20 years of age, fit for military service, the implied total number of the "Children of Israel" is obviously impossibly high. The Hebrew word "elef" designates the numeral thousand, but the scholars who have studied the census lists, notably Sir Flinders Petrie at the turn of the century and G. E. Mendenhall more recently, have come to the conclusion that the term "elef" in these lists does not mean the numeral "thousand" but some sub-section of a tribe, or the contingents they sent to war. This interpretation is confirmed by the story of Gideon's initial reluctance to assume military leadership against the Midianites, because (Jud. 6: 15), his "elef" — clan or village — was the smallest in the tribe of Menasseh* and could therefore supply only few warriors.

Whether or not this was actually the case, his statement shows clearly that the narrator used the term "elef" in a sense — presumably widely accepted — that had nothing to do with a precise mathematical unit. What he was talking about was a recognized subsection of a tribe, from which military units were conscripted. Such subsections had to be of minimum size. Much later, Micah considered Bethlehem too small to be among the "Alfei Yehuda" (the "subdivisions" of Judah).

Taking this interpretation of the term "elef", G. E. Mendenhall concludes that the census lists in Numbers "consist of an enumeration of the number of units (ălāfîm) into which each tribe is subdivided, and following that, the total number of men to be levied from the tribe." On this hypothesis, he reduces the numbers given to something far more probable: 600 units from all the 12 tribes*, providing about 6,000 men for military service. The list runs as follows:

	Numbers 1		*Numbers 26*	
Tribe	*Units*	*Men*	*Units*	*Men*
Reuben	46	500	43	750
Simeon	59	300	22	200
Gad	45	650	40	500
Judah	74	600	76	500
Issachar	54	400	64	300
Zebulun	57	400	60	500
Ephraim	40	500	32	500
Manasseh (Half tribe)	32	200	52	700
Benjamin	35	400	45	600
Dan	62	700	64	400
Asher	41	500	53	400
Naphtali	53	400	45	400
Totals	598	5,550	596	5,750

Against this, of course, there are numerous cases of "Elef" being used to mean "thousand" in the accepted sense, (i.e. in describing the strength of an army, the number of fallen in battle, numbers of livestock, etc. etc.). However, it is necessary to keep this uncertainty in mind when considering the counts described in the Book of Numbers.

Origin of the Traditions in Numbers: The second question raised by the census lists of Numbers is their date. Their attribution to the time of Moses seems erroneous and E.A. Speiser has suggested that the counts were in fact made at the much later time of Judges for principally military reasons (Nu. 1:3; 26:2). They were also probably used as a basis for the distribution of land by lot. It is known (Nu. 26:55, 33:54; Jos. 18:6) that the land was distributed among the tribes by lot after the Conquest. As by then the Israelites had grown in numbers as compared to their strength at the time of the Exodus, this explains why the figures are relatively high, even when reduced to more acceptable proportions, as above.

It seems, in the opinion of D. N. Freedman, that the censuses and their results should not be dismissed as fictitious, but that the counts and the subsequent distribution of land by lot were wrongly assigned by biblical tradition to too early a period. Distribution of land could only follow and accompany the settlement. It does not fit the period of Joshua. The census results and the land distribution are both based on the 12-tribe system, which seems to confirm their setting in the period of Judges. On the other hand, under the monarchy a new administrative system was introduced (see Government and Authority*).

In general, the details of organization, size of units and total size of armies in Israel (interpreted as suggested above), are in harmony with what is known of military and social organization of the Middle and Late Bronze Ages in neighbouring countries. This confirms that the biblical lists are authentic, but were misunderstood in the later centuries when they were written down in the Book of Numbers, whose actual composition is attributed at least in part to priestly sources (see Biblical Criticism*, P source). The larger army units of these later days were read back into census lists of the Tribal League to yield the impossibly high figures.

David's Census: The first royal census of the people of the kingdom was taken by David* for the purposes, in the opinion of B. Mazar, of levying troops, forced labour and tithes (or taxes). Joab was placed in charge of the operation which apparently aroused considerable opposition. As its sequel, in the eyes of the people, was three years of drought followed by a plague of unusual severity in which thousands of people died (II Sam. 24), this confirmed the view that Yahweh would inflict punishments on a ruler so rash as to "count the children of Israel".

The final figures supplied by this census were 800 "thousand" males of military age in Israel (the northern part) and 500 thousand in Judah. On the surface these figures seem much exaggerated and hardly representative of the kingdom's population in David's reign (see article). However, interpreted as "ălāfîm" in the sense of military units, the figures make reasonable sense: 800 units at, say 10 men per unit, would give 8,000 for Israel and 5,000 for Judah, making 13,000 in all which compares with the 20,000 soldiers mustered by Aram against Assyria at Qarqar in 853 BCE.

Expiation: The question of the propitiation of divine power remains. The ritual of furnishing a "kofer" of expiation, i.e. the half-shekel paid by every male counted, can be compared to the cultic purifications which attended census-taking in Mari (see above) in the first half of the 2nd mill. BCE. In the opinion of E.A. Speiser, the connection between this offering and the fear of being "called to account" by something like the devastating pestilence that followed David's census, is clear. The people hated the census, but became resigned to the inevitable. The sole survival of the awesome concepts that had surrounded census-taking was the routine payment of the "kofer" of one half-shekel. This scholar believes that the people found some connection between the plague and David's omission of the precautionary measure, and blamed the census for it all. In the story in II Samuel, it was Yahweh who had incited David to take the census, although the action aroused his anger and retribution. Later thought could not accept such a picture of Yahweh and, in I Ch. 21 changed the story to read that Satan, not Yahweh, had persuaded David to undertake the census.

Other Censuses: Censuses of the Israelites east of Jordan were taken in "the days of Jotham, king of Judah, and in the days of Jeroboam, king of Israel" (I Ch. 5:17). A census carried out by Amaziah, king of Judah (800–783 BCE, II Ch. 25:5) yielded figures of 300 "elef" men of military age. 300 military units seems quite reasonable for the period. There are additional censuses mentioned in Chronicles which also fit into this pattern.

Census Lists of the Restoration*: The Chronicler of this period had access to records that were not preserved in the Bible and, in I Ch. (9:1–9), he supplies genealogical lists of the clans of Judah and Benjamin who resettled in Judah at the time of the Restoration*.

More important are the census lists given in Ezra 2 and Nehemiah 7 (identical in substance, but with differences of detail). Ezra and Nehemiah record 42,360 free persons. Both sources record the names of the families who returned from Exile with Zerubbabel, and seem to have taken them from actual census lists made by the agents and builders of the Restoration. These lists provided a precedent for the censuses taken during the period of the Second Temple. Their importance is shown by the fact that the lists were preserved in the sanctuary. One copy preserved among the papers of "Governor" Nehemiah included a note of his goodwill gifts on the occasion of the census (see Neh. 7:5, 70). An additional record of the Persian period is the census ordered by Nehemiah (11:4–8) of the "sons of Judah and the sons of Benjamin", with the aim of bringing one out of ten living in the country to join the pioneers living in the holy city.

New Testament Period: The New Testament refers to two censuses. One of these (Acts 5:37) was held by the Romans in 6 CE when Judea was incorporated into the Roman province. The census, necessary for assessing the amount of taxes which could be imposed, was carried out under the command of the Roman Legate of Syria, Sulpicius Quirinius. Jewish opposition to Roman censuses stemmed principally from their traditional anti-census feelings. Moreover, Judea was no friendlier towards the idea of paying taxes to a foreign ruler than any other people in history. The registration which was preliminary to the imposition of taxes aroused the country to revolt and brought the Zealots to the fore as an important social and military grouping (see Rome and the Jews*).

A census is mentioned by Luke (2:1 seq) as being held by order of Augustus as part of a general census throughout the Empire. The New Testament tradition records that because of the census Mary and Joseph had to travel to Joseph's native town of Bethlehem, where Jesus was born (Lk. 2:3).

The story has been challenged and debated on a number of grounds. The census appears to be the one held by Quirinius, in which case Luke confused the dates. Certain points are generally agreed: a. a census may have been held towards the end of Herod's reign, although, b. if so, it was not held as part of a general census of the Roman Empire; c. when censuses were held, the head of every family was obliged to return to his native place, if he had changed his residence.

There is abundant evidence for censuses in different parts of the Roman Empire between 11 and 8 BCE. A census was held in Egypt in 10–9 and, thereafter, one was held every 14 years. The edict calling for these also includes the demand that heads of families shall be registered in their native place.

The census referred to in Acts was almost certainly actually held by Quirinius. The story in Luke's gospel, however, also states that Quirinius was governor of Syria. This has raised a number of doubts. Some authorities think Quirinius may have filled the office of Legate of Syria twice, although other scholars reject this. The uncertainty remains.

CHOSEN PEOPLE AND ELECTION. — The concept of the Chosen People, i. e. the idea that Israel had been ordained (or elected) by God to carry the message of his Law to all mankind is one of the chief clues to a theological understanding of the whole Bible. The doctrine was one that developed throughout Israel's history and can be considered under a number of different aspects.

Historical Foundations: Israel owed its sense of nationality to the belief in a special relationship with God, demonstrated in historical events such as the Exodus*, the deliverance from bondage in Egypt. It saw itself as a nation deliberately brought into being and chosen by Yahweh as his people, "the congregation of Yahweh".

This election and its implications were given formal shape in the Covenant* of Sinai. To the Israelites, the Covenant was a historical event at which Yahweh actually demonstrated his presence to his people (Ex. 19) and revealed to Moses the Book of the Covenant (Ex. 20:22–23:33). In the first Covenant ceremony in Sinai, the Book was publicly read to the assembled people and the bond sealed with the "blood of the Covenant" (Ex. 24:3–8).

By this act, and it has no parallel in pagan religions, the Lord of the Universe to whom the whole earth belonged was believed to have chosen Israel from among the nations (Ex. 19:5). The fact that it was the Lord of the Universe is stressed in all the passages of the Old Testament (Deuteronomy*, Second Isaiah*) which make the election of Israel their focal point.

The Doctrine of Election: The Covenant of Sinai, however, was believed to be a confirmation of the original covenant made between Abraham and God (or El) under different names and attributes (Gn. 15) since that was a covenant of promise, while Sinai was a Covenant of obligation (this is dealt with under Covenant with Israel*).

More than merely a question of religious observances, the Covenant* affected every aspect of life: cultic, social, economic and political (not that the Hebrews ever thought in such abstract categories). They saw it as a real event whose significance transformed every aspect of their subsequent history. Certainly the writers of Genesis saw it as giving meaning to the Patriarchal* sagas and wrote their stories in the light of their conception of God's election. This was first demonstrated in Abraham's migration to Canaan in response to a divine call which was itself the expression of God's special consideration of Israel — his election.

After the crucial experience of the Exodus, this election provided the background for the interpretation of life in Canaan. The Covenant had a dynamic meaning for the people themselves, namely the personal involvement of God in the affairs of his people, his election, covenant and divine action in history. Israel's history from Moses to David was seen by the chroniclers as the stages by which the promises made to Abraham were fulfilled. Beyond that came the prophetic interpretation of Israel's subsequent history and its future in the light of its election and the Covenant that was based upon it. This unbroken line of development may explain why the Pentateuch saw no serious discrepancy between the Patriarchal and Sinai covenants and therefore regarded them as one (Ex. 32:11 ff; Dt. 9:27 ff).

God's Mysterious Way: At this stage, the Israelites did not think that they were God's "elected" because of any special merit of their own, or as a compensation for their apparent inferiority to other peoples. They assumed that Yahweh had a special reason to rescue the oppressed. His choice was governed by his own mysterious ways, but the fact of having been chosen inevitably came to colour later presentations of the whole of Israel's history.

Conditions and Obligations: There were, however, two sides to the bargain. Maintenance of the relationship was conditional, even though the election was not. God's continued election was conditional upon observance of the Law (Dt. 7:6–11). God had chosen them, but he could abandon them. At the same time, the prophets maintained that he would not ultimately give them up. There is a paradox here which is explained by the nature of prophetic thought (see below). The "Chosen People" were chosen only so long as they shunned idolatry and fulfilled the conditions imposed by their redemption (Ex. 32:7–10).

The Law of the Covenant was a set of rules for society imposed by Yahweh as the condition of his promise of security and justice within the Promised Land. As a later development, this promise became the foundation for hope and strength in the face of every suffering, not only among the Jews but, eventually, for the whole of Christendom.

The Prophets' Message of Election: The visions of the prophets made much of the privileges of election. Isaiah and Micah saw Jerusalem as the future centre of the world, with Israel acting as mediator between the peoples and God. For Second Isaiah, God's purpose, the unification of the world, would be achieved through Israel.

Deuteronomy emphasized the responsibilities and duties of God's elect and the same insistence on the need for social righteousness became central to the teachings of the prophets. Isaiah (42:6; 53) spoke of Israel in the image of the chosen servant of mankind whose suffering will bring salvation to the whole world. All the prophets laid stress on the price that would be paid for any breach of the Covenant and this is usually the basis of disputes involving the prophets. Neither leaders nor people liked to hear themselves condemned and threatened with divine punishment.

There are many biblical passages which make it clear that Israel's election was not prompted by her righteousness or pureness of heart (Dt. 9:5). God's choice was spontaneous and he redeemed them when they were powerless (Dt. 7:7–8). "For my own honour I defer my anger, I gain praise for my pity, sparing you." (Is. 48:9). Israel had been chosen for a special task but God had still to act, said Isaiah (48:10), like a silversmith, testing "you in the furnace". As often as God's chosen people disobeyed, they would be punished, but God was merciful. They could still hope to be pardoned and restored.

This attitude was unique among contemporary religions. While ordinary people probably believed that God would prevent the destruction of his Temple and faithful people because he needed them, the prophets all tried to counter this openly materialist view (Am. 9:10; Mic. 3:11 ; Jer. 7:4).

God's Judgment: Up to the Exile, the prophets apparently believed that the distress and disasters of contemporary events were God's way of achieving the inner purification of a "remnant" through whom a New Age could be brought into being. The destruction of the kingdoms of Israel* and Judah* and the captivity of their peoples clearly represented God's punishment for an irreparable breach of the Covenant. Nevertheless, the conception of legal penalty was not sufficient explanation for that destruction and captivity. God had not yet said the last word.

Redeeming Grace: Through His redeeming grace, there was still hope for a New Covenant that would bring everlasting comfort to God's people (Jer. 31:33 ff; Ezk. 16:60). This, the original purpose of the Govenant, would be achieved, cried Ezekiel (36:24–31), when the "remnant of Israel" was given a new heart and a new spirit. These are explicitly described as a gift from God.

Post-Exilic and Roman Period: The changes in Jewish views after the Exile are reflected in the Apocrypha* and Apocalypses*. Some of the pseudepigraphic writings (see article on Apocalypse*) stress the paradox between Israel's election and its continued sufferings. With the spread of Hellenism, Jewish writers shifted the target of their attacks to gentile society as a whole and began to prophesy its destruction (see Apocalypse*: Wisdom Literature, Sibylline Oracles).

However, Jews could not escape foreign influences. Jewish Hellenistic literature displays the racial and intellectual pride of a people who regarded themselves as "chosen" to bring the true Law to gentiles. This was the beginning of the proselytizing movement of Judaism which produced the gentile Godfearers who later were among the first Christians (see Jewish Christians*).

Christian Views: The work of Paul* placed the matter in a new light. He and his followers transferred the claim to "election" from the Jews, who had denied the divinity of Jesus, to the followers of Christ (see Paul*). Jewish thought, in New Testament times and after, put forward the theory that originally all peoples had been equal (Mekhilta Yitre). God had offered the law to all alike, but only the Jews had accepted it. Therefore, God's purpose for mankind could only be achieved with the salvation of Jewry. This version of the doctrine of election disclaimed any superiority or moral responsibility, replacing it by a stronger sense of duty. Thus the Mishnah* and the Talmud stress the role of Israel as a teacher of other nations.

The concept of election, separated from theological or ethnic feeling, was ultimately sublimated into the national hope that fathered Zionism and eventually produced the revival of the State of Israel.

CHRISTIANITY, EARLY — *Outline: I. Jewish Christians: Historical Background; The Apostles; Peter; James; The Bishopric of Jerusalem; The Problem of Circumcision; Paul and the Jewish Christians; Stephen; Stephen's Martyrdom; Institutional Parallels with Dead Sea Sectaries; Differences; Schism within the Church; Ebionites; Therapeutae. II. Early Christian Church: Paul's Missionary Activity; The Role of the Synagogue; Early Christians Protected by Judaism; Ready for a New Faith; Persecutions; Christianity Triumphs; Separation of Judaism from Jewish Christianity.*

I. JEWISH CHRISTIANS: The earliest followers of Jesus* were all Jews. The members of the very first community of Christians, led by Jesus' brother, James, were called the "Hebrews" and are now known as Jewish Christians. Their way of life differed very little from that of other Jews. They observed circumcision, the precepts of the Torah, the Sabbath and the Festivals and, for a time, they demanded similar observances from their converts. They regarded Jewish scriptures as authoritative and adopted much of the traditional interpretation of them. The Jewish Christians remained members of the synagogue and were finally separated from it only after some generations. Just as Christianity itself grew out of sectarian trends within Judaism, so did the foundations of the Christian church lie within the synagogue*, much of its ancient liturgies being framed on Jewish models.

Historical Background: Like their contemporaries in Qumran (see Dead Sea Scrolls*), the Jewish Christians formed a distinct sect within Judaism. What distinguished them from other forms of Judaism reflects first of all the development of their beliefs around the events in the lives of John the Baptist* and Jesus*, secondly, the history of the life and beliefs of the disciples and, later, the Apostles of Jesus (see articles on Jesus* and Paul*).

Thus, Jewish Christianity — combined with the primitive Christianity of Palestine, Syria and Egypt — represents the historical and theological transition from Judaism to catholic Christianity.

After the crucifixion, the group of Jesus' disciples, including the apostles and other followers, scattered in fear of persecution. Later, they returned to Jerusalem in the company of Mary, the mother of Jesus, his brothers, and the women disciples. They were joined by other Jews, possibly including groups who had followed John the Baptist*, who came not only from Galilee and Judea, but from further afield. They had recognized Jesus as Messiah in his lifetime, but the resurrection* transformed faith in him into a new religious movement in which recognition of his messiahship and resurrection formed the pivot of a new Church (see Incarnation*). According to Acts (2) they met in the "high chamber" or Cenaculum (**291**) on Mount Zion near the present Church of the Dormition.

291

292

The photo records a late phase of its reconstruction and the visit of Pope Paul VI there in 1964. It is situated near the south-western section of the old City, near its wall (**292**). To them came Jewish pilgrims from the whole Eastern Diaspora who had come to Jerusalem for the Passover and stayed on for the Feast of Weeks (Pentecost) seven weeks later (Ac. 2:6–13). These Hellenist Jews came from Syria and Asia Minor — not Greece (see below Stephen).

The Apostles: The crucifixion faced the disciples with a new situation for which they were quite unprepared. Jesus had chosen twelve disciples as his companions. After his death it was up to them to establish themselves as a group — as apostles — (in Hebrew "sheliḥim" or emissaries). They were committed to the belief that Jesus was the Messiah of the House of David and they found the justification for their beliefs and organization within the framework of traditional Jewish customs. They kept their symbolic number — twelve, the number of the tribes of Israel (and the same number as the elders of Qumran) — by choosing a replacement for Judas Iscariot. Luke adds a further 70 to the number of the apostles, representing all the nations of the world.

They saw it as their task to spread the message of Jesus but they had Jesus' own instructions not to approach Gentiles, "Go nowhere among the Gentiles, and enter no town of the Samaritans, but go rather to the lost sheep of the house of Israel." (Mt. 10:5–6). On this they based their activities and it gave the Jewish Christians their essential character.

Peter: The outstanding personality of the group was Simon bar Jonah, called Kephas (the Rock) or Peter. Imaginative and passionate, he rallied the group in the dark hours after the death of Jesus and kept them together during the first decades of Christianity. The others were Andrew, James and John, the sons of Zebedee, Philip, Bartholomew, Matthew (or Levi), Thomas (or Didymus), James, son of Alpheus, Jude, Simon the Canaanean, also called the Zealot, and Matthias who replaced Judas Iscariot. James, brother of Jesus, was also regarded as an apostle after the Crucifixion.

James: James was a Nazirite*, a familiar figure in the Temple and a strict observer of the most orthodox and ascetic forms of Judaism. For this he was widely honoured but his strongest claim to the devotion of the Jewish people was the belief that he, like Jesus his brother, was a descendant of David. James was the first Bishop of Jerusalem, "leader of the holy church of the Hebrews". He remained at the head of the Jewish-Christian movement for many years until, for reasons that remain obscure, in 61 or 63 CE, he was brought before the Sanhedrin as a "Transgressor", condemned and executed.

The Bishopric of Jerusalem: After his death, James was succeeded by his "cousin" Simon bar-Clopas who was also executed later as a result of his reputed membership of the house of David. Thereafter, thirteen other members of Jesus' family were bishops of Jerusalem, forming a "royal" succession which Stauffer called the "Caliphate of James" and which appears to have led the movement jointly with the "apostolic" succession from Peter.

The Problem of Circumcision*: This side of the leadership represented the more conservative institutional aspect of the sect. It was against their rigid adherence to the group's Jewish orthodoxy that Paul, Barnabas and the church of Antioch found themselves in conflict. A bitter and lengthy controversy had arisen over the demand of the church of Jerusalem that Gentile converts be circumcized, a measure which the leaders of the church of Antioch resisted. As a whole, the church of Jerusalem had from the first adhered closely to all Jewish services and rites, but they added to their Jewish faith their new divergent belief in Jesus as Messiah. From their point of view the new departure of the church of Antioch was revolutionary. A Jerusalemite delegation to Antioch urged that this be corrected, stating that unless the Gentile converts were circumcized they would not be saved. The resulting difference of opinion formed a real danger to the new Messianic movement, which could be warded off only through an understanding between the orthodox and the forward-looking parties (Ac. 15). The resulting "Jerusalem decree" by James is related under the article on Paul*.

Paul and the Jewish Christians: Paul rejected the exclusively Jewish orientation of the first Jerusalem church and its motivation. The Law of Judaism (Covenant*), Paul proclaimed, had been voided by the coming of the Messiah. In the future, a man might be "justified by faith apart from the works of the Law". He demanded only belief in Jesus as Christ and on this basis, offered the promise of salvation, once given to Abraham alone, to the whole of humanity (Gal. 3:28–29; Ac. 13:38–39 etc.). He became the "Apostle to the Gentiles" and, as the movement spread far beyond the boundaries of Palestine, missionary work was undertaken to non-Jewish communities. The Jewish Christians believed that only Jews or proselytes or converts, of course, could be true believers in Jesus. With the spread of gentile Christianity, they became, like the Ebionites, a minority sect within the movement. Their viewpoint is probably reflected in the Epistle of James*, written before the threatening break with Catholic Christianity.

The early years of the group do not seem to have brought them into conflict with the political authorities. Contrary to other sects, the Jewish Christians never attacked the Temple, while the policies of Agrippa II encouraged peaceful relations with the Pharisees. Until his death in 44 CE, the little group was free to develop without fear of general persecution. That development, however, produced a variety of internal pressures.

The nucleus of Jewish Christians was joined by a variety of other sectarian groups as well as the continuing influx of Jews from outside Palestine. The tensions created by the increasingly important role played by the "Hellenists" is well illustrated by the story of Stephen.

Stephen: As in contemporary Judaism, two distinct trends appear to have developed within the church: the original Galilean and Judean disciples who, with those who clung to the traditional foundations of Judaism, made up the Hebrews or "Ebraiou" (keeping one of the earliest names applied to all the Jewish Christians); and the "Hellenists" who, like Paul, were also Jews who in general took a less orthodox attitude toward questions of theology and doctrine. The task of administering the common fund may have become too heavy for the Twelve. Complaints were heard among the Hellenistic brethren that their widows were being overlooked in the daily ministrations. The conflict between the two came to a head also over questions of the right to "serve tables" (i. e. to administer the communal meals) as the Hebrews apparently doubted the ritual cleanliness of the Hellenists. To settle this and similar internal questions, leaving the Twelve free to concentrate on preaching, a fellowship of seven "men of good repute, full of the Spirit and wisdom", was appointed. All of them bear Greek names, the first listed being Stephen.

Stephen's Martyrdom: The Jewish Christians remained members of the synagogue, the martyrdom of Stephen coming, according to Acts (6:9–7:60), as a result of charges of blasphemy brought against him by members of the "synagogue of the Freedmen". By chance this synagogue is the only one which was not totally obliterated by the Roman destruction of 70 CE. In Ophel, the oldest section of the lower city of Jerusalem, a Greek inscription **(293)** was found from the synagogue of the Freedmen (ex-slaves from Italy, North Africa and Asia Minor) reading "Theodotus, son of Vettenus . . . has built the synagogue . . . which his fathers and the elders and Simonides had founded."

In answer to charges of speaking "blasphemous words against Moses and God", Stephen made a passionate defence concluding with a vision of the "heavens opened and the Son of man standing at the right hand of God." His defiance infuriated his hearers and, without waiting for him to be convicted or sentenced, Stephen was dragged out by the crowd and stoned to death (the traditional penalty for such offences).

293

What is significant about the account of his trial is that Stephen expressed the more extreme views of his own sect, seeming to reject Temple sacrifice in exchange for the Holy Spirit and, by a reference to the "Righteous One" (ibid 7:52), to suggest a connection with the parallel sect of the Essenes.

Stephen's death naturally affected his fellows very deeply and many Jewish Christians fled from Jerusalem. However, Peter and his group stayed behind, acting as the focus of the movement and preparing the ground for its later expansion.

The group's first task was to "silence the ignorance of foolish men" and prove that Jesus had never been a political agitator and was something far different from the familiar run of pseudo-Messiahs who had appeared to lead abortive revolts against Roman and Herodian rule. For the Jewish Christians, Jesus had been raised from the dead as "Messiah", the long-awaited hope of Judaism. With the resurrection, the "New Age" of which the apocalyptists* had dreamed, had dawned. Now they confidently awaited Jesus' second coming, his "Parousia" as the risen Messiah.

This matter was primarily of interest to Jews. The language of the Jewish Christians is full of the terminology of Jewish apocalyptic, while the most powerful influences in their background were the cherished expectations of Jewish messianism, especially of a prophet like Moses, and a king of the house of David.

Institutional Parallels with Dead Sea Sectaries: The Jewish Christians were not isolated recluses like the Qumran sectaries (see Dead Sea Scrolls*) although, like them, they believed themselves to be a community of men specially "chosen" for the Kingdom of God. This suggests that the antecedents of the movement must be sought in apocalyptic sectarian communities (like Qumran, although not exclusively there), as well as popular Jewish expectations of a Davidic Messiah. Like the sectaries of Qumran, where similar lists of appropriate interpretations were found, the Jewish Christians searched the Old Testament for prophecies which could be interpreted as relating to the events on which their sect was founded (cf. New Covenant*). Also, like the sectaries, the Jewish Christians practiced baptism, referred to themselves as "believers", some of them as "Ebionim" (see below) and saw their community as an alternate spiritual temple offering prayer in place of sacrifice. This seems to support the conclusion (drawn by E. G. Selwyn) that the Church was conceived as a "neo-Levitical" or priestly community. Evidence for this comes particularly from the First Epistle of Peter* (2:4–10).

In addition, like the writers of the Dead Sea Scrolls, the earliest Jewish Christians followed a communal form of life in preparation for the coming "New Age". This was later modified as hopes of the immediate coming of the New Age were gradually set aside.

It is probably true to say that the Jewish Christians and the sectaries of Qumran were parallel variations of Judaism. Although the Jewish Christians are clearly distinctive — a full discussion of the two communities is included at the end of the article on the Dead Sea Scrolls — the factors which gave rise to sectarian theology must also have had a strong influence on the Jewish Christians who developed out of the religious climate of the 1st c. CE from a variety of groups as distinctive as the Pharisees, Sadducees, and Essenes. They unquestionably drew on the sectarian, non-conformist trends in Judaism for their theology and organization, while at the same time being influenced by contemporary Hellenist religions, though remaining grounded in orthodox Judaism.

Doctrinal similarities between the sectaries and authentic

early Christian doctrine are discussed under Dead Sea Scrolls*. Notably, both groups believed that as all men are brothers, the call to salvation had been addressed to all alike without regard to race or social status. Both the communities of the New Covenant lived in an atmosphere of love, forgiveness and repentance. But at Qumran there is also emphasis on the struggle against the wicked — and the final warfare of good and evil which is also reflected in the New Testament (Jn. 8:42–47; I Jn. 5:19).

Differences: In early Christianity, the institutional and doctrinal features linking sectarian Judaism and the New Testament were integrated into a new doctrinal structure which combined the central beliefs of the traditional faith with new eschatological features. By being incorporated into Jewish Christian doctrine, beliefs of the Qumran type were transformed and, at the same time, marked the differences between the two communities. The Jewish Christians believed that with the coming of the Messiah the period of the End of Days had been inaugurated. They were no longer awaiting its coming, as at Qumran.

Moreover, Pauline influence affected the sense of the sinfulness of man so radically that the merely human mediation of a New Covenant* which Qumran proclaimed, could no longer seem sufficient for his redemption. God himself must be made man (cf. Incarnation*).

Schism within the Church: When, in 68 CE, the Romans attacked Jerusalem, the Jewish Christians migrated east of the Jordan to Pella, one of the cities of the Decapolis (see Cities, Hellenistic). It is believed by some that they left earlier, before the Roman attack, perhaps under growing pressure from the Zealots who were increasingly strong in the 60's (see Romans and Jews*). By the time of the Great War with Rome, the centre of gravity within the church was beginning to shift to the churches of the diaspora, particularly those founded or visited by Barnabas and Paul*, which were to be the true foundation of later, historical Christianity.

In these new (Hellenist) groups, founded throughout Syria, Asia Minor, Macedonia, Greece, Crete and Italy, many scholars find that their strongest roots were still within the traditions of the Jewish communities. Liturgies and cult-forms were taken over directly from the synagogue. The ethics of Judaism had been adopted, but its ritual had been spiritualized by Christian allegory. The churches in Rome or Antioch were thus open to Jew and, increasingly, Gentile, alike. On the other hand, the Jewish Christians who had left Jerusalem during the Great War, returned after some time. Their church, contrary to opinion held by many, persisted until the second war under Bar Kochba* (see below, The Separation).

In the following two centuries, groups of Jewish Christians were found throughout the Near East under various designations:

Ebionites: This sect, also known as Nazoreans, was founded perhaps by "Simon Zealotes" or perhaps by groups of followers of John the Baptist. The Ebionites survived from the second to the fourth c. CE and, from the latter half of the 2nd c. CE, their name is used for the Jewish Christians as a whole. They clung to the earliest principles of Jewish Christianity, regarding poverty as a basic principle, and holding all their property in common. From this came their name which means "the Poor", a term the Qumran sectaries also used of themselves. The Ebionites rejected sacrifice but otherwise observed the Mosaic law. When they prayed they faced Jerusalem. They made their own interpretations of the prophetic writings and, also like Qumran, practiced ritual ablutions. They believed in Jesus as Messiah but denied his divinity and the virgin birth. They used only Matthew's gospel and would have nothing to do with Paul, (i.e. the Pauline Epistles*).

The most distinguished figure among them was Symmachus (latter part of the 2nd c. CE) who translated the Bible into Greek. Certain traditions make him a Samaritan proselyte of Judaism; others regard him as a pupil of Rabbi Meir (see Rabbis*).

Therapeutae: Philo gives a description of another Jewish sect from 1st c. CE Egypt. Though he was unaware of their link with Jewish-Christianity, this is emphasized by later writers. The Therapeutae lived in poverty and solitude, eating only at sunrise and spending their time in study and meditation on the sacred writings. Like the Essenes or Qumran sectaries, they gathered dressed in white garments for a common meal and regarded celibacy as desirable for male and female — but not essential. Unlike the Qumran community they did not engage in handicrafts but concentrated entirely on their studies. Their nights they spent in religious singing and ritual dancing.

A considerable part of the pseudo-Clementine *Gnostic Writings* are of Jewish Christian origin (cf. Epistles, General).

II. EARLY CHRISTIAN CHURCH: The rapid spread of Gentile Christianity and the establishment of the Great Church as a distinct entity, separate from the Jewish Christians is one of the most remarkable of the historical and religious developments of the first three centuries CE.

Paul's Missionary Activity: Its impetus came from the missionary work of Paul and other leaders of the Apostolic Age, less celebrated in history than he. From about 30 to 45 CE, (corresponding to Acts 1 to 12:24) the Jewish Christian movement was led by Peter and the Twelve. After 45 CE, James became the head of the church in Jerusalem and Peter was apparently free to travel as a missionary. After the death of James (see above), the leadership was virtually taken over by Paul (Ac. 12:25 to 28:31) until he in turn met his death in Rome, somewhere between 64 and 68 CE, at the same time as Peter was martyred.

This phase can be divided into three periods: Paul's missions to Antioch; the Jerusalem decrees (see Paul*) (circa 44–49 CE); and his great missionary journeys to Macedonia, Achaia and Asia Minor (49–54 CE).

The Role of the Synagogue: Another potent factor in the Church's development was the surprisingly influential position of the synagogues* of the Graeco-Roman Diaspora during the 1st c. CE (see Hellenism and the Diaspora*). Services were conducted in Greek and regularly attracted hosts of Gentiles. These remained proselytes and "godfearers" who, while they were close to Judaism, did not become complete converts. Nor did the Jews press them to do so. It was Gibbon who described Judaism as a religion "admirably fitted for defence but never designed for conquest". Nevertheless there is extensive pagan testimony to the influence of the Jews on the peoples of the Eastern

Mediterranean. Many historians agree that Gentiles either obeyed or were influenced by Mosaic Law. Seneca, a classic anti-Semite, wrote: "To such an extent have the customs of that detestable race prevailed, that they have found acceptance in all countries. The conquered have dictated laws to the conquerors."

Early Christians Protected by Judaism: Since the days of Julius Caesar (mid 1st c. BCE; see Rome and the Jews*), the Jews as a nation had enjoyed special privileges. These included internal autonomy in their communities, freedom from military service, freedom to worship their God and exemption from the universal obligation to worship the imperial gods and the emperors themselves. Even though the Jews were scattered through the Empire, they were legally protected as a nation.

In contrast, the Christians were always in a very insecure position. Refusal to join in public worship as decreed was punished as high treason and popularly condemned as "atheism". Nevertheless, Gentile Christians who had been converted to Paul's faith were able to take advantage of the legal protection afforded to Judaism. Naturally, they tried to do so for as long as possible. They were more or less successful until hostilities broke out between the two camps in the mid-2nd century CE.

During the first two or three centuries of its existence, the Christian church was composed of local groupings. Only with the eventual rise of the church of Rome to unquestioned supremacy was a central authority established.

Ready for a New Faith: The Graeco-Roman world was one of sophisticated, educated people. It was also one of degenerate moral and religious values. In the face of this general decline, various reform movements had developed. The world as a whole was ready for a new moral inspiration—a new religion. This was especially true in Asia Minor and Syria, where dissatisfaction with the popular religion had emptied the temples and alarmed the responsible officials. Christianity appears in this situation as a vigorous spiritual challenge, daring men to take every risk for a magnificent cause. It met with an immediate response in Syria, where Gentile converts came in increasing numbers.

Persecutions: In fact the risks were very real. By refusing to join in the cult of the emperors, the Christians drew attention to themselves as a dissident minority in which the Roman authorities were quick to scent conspiracy and subversion. After the great fire of Rome in 64 CE, they offered Nero a convenient scapegoat and during the appalling terror that followed, Peter and Paul may have lost their lives. Nero's continuing persecutions were sensationally recorded by Tacitus. The persecutions of Domitius (81–96 CE) in Asia Minor which took place late in his reign, after 90 CE, are reflected in the Book of Revelation (see Apocalyptic*), especially 2:13 and 20:4. There, the author, a certain John of Patmos, states unequivocally that allegiance to Christ and worship of the emperors were incompatible. It was a conviction that cost thousands of believers their lives.

Christianity Triumphs: In spite of the worst the Roman emperors and their soldiers could do, Christianity continued to spread. Unlike Judaism, Christianity regarded the spreading of the gospel as a sacred duty. The members of the sect were possessed of a dynamic faith that broke down all barriers. Whereas the Jews had been content to win the respect of pagan Gentiles and a certain degree of influence over them, the Christians were out to make converts and to destroy paganism.

Their success was assured with the conversion of the emperor Constantine and the establishment of Christianity as the official religion of the Roman empire. By the so-called "Edict of Toleration" which he issued at Milan in 312 CE, Constantine effectively established the Great Church as, supreme (see also: Transfiguration and Resurrection*, Eucharist*, Incarnation*, Baptism under Dead Sea Scrolls* and John the Baptist*, Paul*).

The Separation of Judaism from Jewish Christianity and the Jews of Palestine and the Diaspora was hastened by the decline of Jewish political power in the first and second centuries; it was followed eventually by the separation of Judaism from the Great Church.

During the second and third cs. CE, the Jewish Christians were sundered from the Jewish community, where they became regarded as "minîm" (heretics). Their refusal to participate in Bar Kochba's* revolt widened the breach with orthodox Jewry on nationalist grounds. From this time the sect became increasingly isolated.

In the early years, Jews and Jewish Christians continued to exist within a single community, often sharing the same synagogue. Even the symbols of the new faith often included a menorah, symbol of Judaism, side by side with the new sign of the cross. On a marble tombstone in the 4th c. CE basilica of Avdat (see Nabateans*), a menorah was carved between two crosses **(294)**.

294

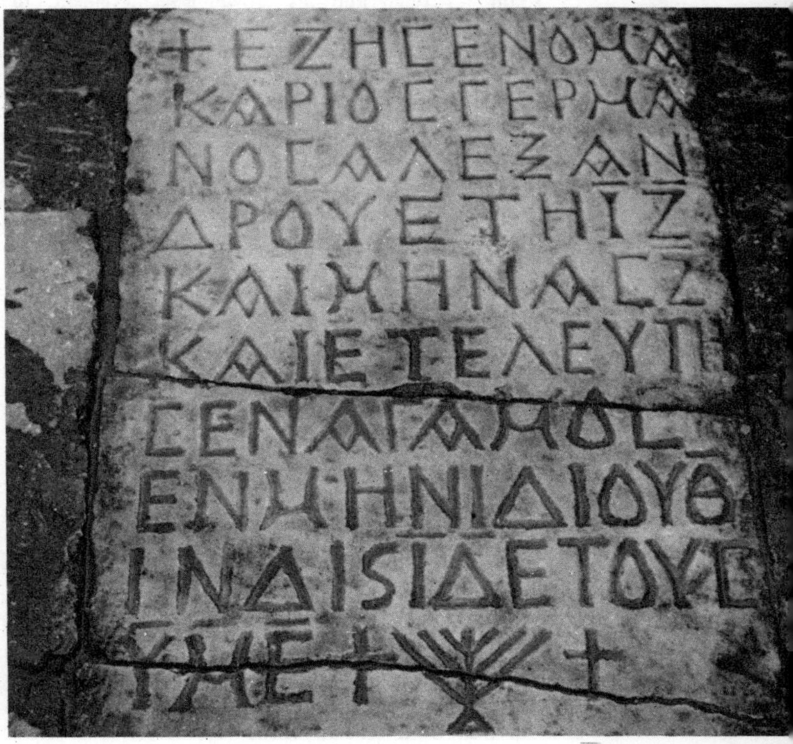

Jewish Christians were generally regarded as a sect which had broken away from Judaism and, in fact, with the extension of Gentile Christianity, they became a minority. Most Gentile Christians would have nothing to do with them. Their increasing isolation is apparent from some late portions of the New Testament which recall the struggle between older loyalties to the Jewish people and traditions and the view that Christianity represented a new, distinct faith which had superseded Judaism. In the end this view was to triumph completely but, for two or three centuries, the older faith continued, serving as a bridge mediating between the two larger religions, so closely linked through their common heritage.

CHRONICLES I & II, BOOKS OF. — *Outline: Contents; The Genealogies; Chronicles of David, Solomon and the Kings of Judah; Sources of Chronicles; Different Versions of Scriptures; Interpretation of the Book; Additional Information in Chronicles; Transjordan in Chronicles; Authorship and Date of Composition; Place in the Canon; Bible as History and Theology.*

Contents: Originally a single unit, the Book of Chronicles is now customarily divided into two parts, following the Septuagint* Greek translation. Together, Chronicles spans nearly the whole period of the Old Testament. The first part (I Ch.) begins with Adam, goes through the genealogical lists from him until David* (chs. 1–9; see below: Importance of the Genealogies), and then closes with an extensive account of the reign of David (10–29).

The second part (II Ch.) begins with a detailed story of Solomon's reign and his crowning achievement, the building of the Temple (chs. 1–9). The remaining chapters (10–36) deal with the kings of Judah from the division of the monarchy until the Exile. The very last verses (ch. 37:22–23) contain the Declaration of Cyrus which ended the Exile (see Restoration*). Apart from the genealogical tables, the whole work may be described as the Chronicles of David, Solomon and the kings of Judah. (The genealogical lists in I Ch. continue the line of David's descendants well beyond Zerubbabel.)

Including the books of Ezra and Nehemiah (and in one view these are integral and continuous parts of Chronicles, see below, Authorship), Chronicles provides a comprehensive historical survey of the whole of the history of Judah from the Creation to the post-Exilic Restoration.

The Genealogies: While the genealogical tables make dull reading, they played an important part in the author's presentation of a historical scheme of salvation. Tribal prestige and family trees were necessary to authenticate the nation and its leaders. Some scholars are inclined to regard their accuracy (especially in regard to the priests and Levites) with some reserve but it must be remembered that the lists were not drawn up at the time the books themselves were written. The lists of Chronicles are far more comprehensive than those in Genesis and there is every reason to believe that, if properly understood, they can yield information about the Settlement and inter-tribal and inter-family relationships which is available nowhere else (see Conquest*). At least part of the lists may have been derived from official census records, e. g.: "These, registered by name, came in the days of Hezekiah king of Judah . . ." (I Ch. 4:41).

The lists also include useful data on the economy of Israel and the occupations of its people, e. g. weaving and pottery* (I Ch. 4:21, 23). There remains a problem as to the date to which the data refer, for this can usually only be surmized from the genealogical lists. The lists act as an introduction to the records of David, Solomon and the kings of Judah.

Chronicles of David, Solomon and the Kings of Judah: Many passages dealing with the pre-Exilic period are quoted almost verbatim from the books of Samuel* or Kings*. In other parts, the style and vocabulary of Chronicles are quite different. There are also differences between the content of Chronicles and that of its main sources. Mainly, these follow from the desire of the later authors to avoid any unsavoury episodes in David's life (e. g. Bathsheba), while going into minute detail in picturing the ritual of the time and in describing David's preparations for building the Temple (I Ch. 22:14). They presented his plans on a grand scale, as shown by the exaggerated sums the book describes him as collecting: "a hundred thousand talents of gold, a million talents of silver . . ." Solomon's reign is similarly treated, the building of the Temple, the services of the Levites and the organization of the state all being described at great length.

As the author was concerned with producing a systematic chronicle of the kingdom of Judah, he deliberately ignored the Northern kingdom altogether, while describing religious reforms carried out by the kings of Judah which are not mentioned in Kings. In addition, he gives a glowing account of Judah's military successes over Ephraim, which differs in both attitude and details from the parallel account in Kings* (see below, Additional Information in Chronicles).

Sources of Chronicles: It is possible that differences in content may also result from the fact that the author of Chronicles had at his disposal several sources which were unknown to the writer of Kings, i. e. "Chronicles of Shemaiah the Prophet and Iddo the Seer" (II Ch. 12:15; 13:22, "The History of Nathan the Prophet", "The Prophecy of Ahiyah the Shilonite" and, again, "The Visions of Iddo the Seer", II Ch. 9:29a).

Moreover, events as reported in Kings may have been discredited by the author of Chronicles who amended the narrative accordingly. A typical example of Chronicles' emphasis on David's prestige can be seen from a comparison of II Sam. 5:20–21, "And David came to Baalperazim and David defeated them (the Philistines) there . . . and the Philistines left their idols there, and David and his men carried them away", with I Ch. 14:11–12, "And he went up to Baalperazim, and David defeated them there . . . And they left their gods there and David gave command and they were burned."

It is apparent that the authentic, original and historical narrative does not credit David with burning the idols. Later Jewish tradition, including Chronicles, was apparently unable to admit that David, the righteous, had failed to carry out the explicit command in Dt. 7:25 that, "the graven images of their gods you shall burn . . . ", hence the revision. This is one of many instances in which the historical picture presented by Chronicles is not strictly objective.

Different Versions of Scriptures: An alternative reason for discrepancies may be that the version of Samuel available to the Chronicler was somewhat different from the Massoretic text (today's Hebrew Bible) or that someone else had introduced changes into Samuel and this amended text, now unknown, was used by the Chronicler. The text of Samuel (and probably Kings) used by the Chronicler appears to have been closer to the Septuagint than to the Massoretic text. This is supported by the Qumran texts of Samuel which are also closer to the Septuagint and to the version of Samuel used in Chronicles (see Hellenism and Judaism*: Septuagint ; Biblical Criticism*).

Similar reservations are felt by some scholars about the claims that David was responsible for establishing the Levites' ritual functions (I Ch. 15). It is felt that the Chronicler's schematization has distorted the facts. Some scholars even doubt whether a class of Levites existed during David's time. This emphasis on the Levites and their singing, which begins there and continues throughout the book, had led critics to suspect that the author himself was a singer or an official close to them. The treatment of the gatekeepers in I Ch. 25–26 has given rise to similar speculations, for the two groups were allied. Scholars of this opinion believe that David was idealized and projected 500 years into the future, into the author's own time and environment. It is difficult to reach definite conclusions about such theories. The kings of Judah had musicians and Temple singers. The author of Chronicles may have schematized and exaggerated, but he had a solid tradition from which to begin.

Interpretation of the Book: The author of Chronicles need not be charged with deliberate falsification — certain reservations about details notwithstanding. The book must be judged by the standards of the time at which it was written and in relation to the intention of the author. As it stands, Chronicles represents an Aggadic approach (see Biblical Criticism*: Aggadic Interpretation) and this partly explains the liberties the author took with his older sources, Samuel and Kings. He was deliberately recasting these books so as to present his own theological viewpoint and, if this Midrashic element is remembered, many of the difficulties concerning Chronicles can be resolved.

Additional Information in Chronicles: Nevertheless, although the book needs critical evaluation, its value as an historical document need not be lightly dismissed. There is valuable information in Chronicles which enlarges the stories given elsewhere in the Old Testament and which deserves study — even if it is affected by the particular attitude of the author towards the accomplishments of this king or the reverses of that one (something which is also true of Samuel and Kings). There is no reason, for instance, why the list of fortified cities built by Rehoboam* (II Ch. 11:5–12), or the account of the development projects of Uzziah (II Ch. 26:10) should not be accepted as historically factual.

Chronicles, admittedly, has a different attitude towards the kings it chronicles than the books of Kings. Its account emphasizes aspects which the earlier books do not mention and contradicts points which they make. In line with his theological approach, the Chronicler regarded national disasters as punishments from heaven for religious or ritual deviations. Thus he offers an explanation for King Uzziah's leprosy, which has no parallel in Kings. Chronicles (II Ch. 26:10) sees the king's disease as a punishment for "exceeding his authority" and sacrificing a burned offering, a rite which was the exclusive province of the priests. This example seems to offer further evidence of the author's desire to stress wherever possible, the inviolable rights of the priests* and Levites. There is a similar case in the variation between I Ch. 18:17 which states that "David's sons were the chief officials in the service of the king" and II Sam. 8:18 which states bluntly, "David's sons were priests". This seems to provide some explanation for the fact that Obed-Edom the Gittite (II Sam. 6:10–12), whose very name indicates his non-Jewish origin, is included in the Levitic genealogy (I Ch. 16:38) as Obed-Edom ben Jedithun.

Another example of additional information in Chronicles is the account of the death of Goliath. II Sam. 21:19 states that Elhanan slew Goliath but, with the obvious intention of giving David all the credit, I Ch. 20:5 states that Elhanan killed Lahmi, Goliath's brother, while David slew Goliath. This, of course, is the account given in detail in I Sam. 17. As the two accounts in Samuel contradict each other, the Chronicles' version may be regarded as an attempt to harmonize them. It is suggestive, nevertheless.

Another instance is the story of Jehoash. Even though II Ch. 24 drastically schematizes its account, it is more explicit than the parallel story in II Kings and provides a key to the exclusions in Kings. The earlier book represents Jehoash as a godly monarch, but Chronicles is much more reserved in its praise, probably due to the fact that, in his later years, Jehoash attempted to undermine priestly domination and allowed foreign practices to creep into Israelite worship. Chronicles (II Ch. 25:5–24) also explains the reasons for the conflict between Jehoash's Israel and the Judah of king Amaziah, on which the account in II K. 14:1–14 is rather obscure.

While the major source for the period of the Assyrian conquest of Israel remains Kings, Chronicles supplies considerable supplementary data, as for instance, the note in II Ch. 34 that Josiah's reform was accomplished in several stages and had, in fact, been going on for years before the ancient law-book was actually "found" (see Judah, Kings of*: Josianic Reform).

Transjordan in Chronicles: Chronicles also provides more abundant material about the tribes of Transjordan than is found in other sources. Sometimes, obviously ancient data seem to have been misunderstood by the author who merely repeated a truncated tradition. One instance is the obscure passage in I Ch. 4:33: "and Jokim, and the men of Cozeba, and Joash, and Saraph, who ruled in Moab and returned to Lehem (now the records are ancient)."

Developments in Transjordan which affected Judah are also recorded in II Ch. After Israel repulsed the Arameans*, (see Israel and Judah*, Kingdoms of, III: Jehoash, Jeroboam II) and was in a position to consolidate its holdings east of the Jordan, the kingdom of Judah apparently also enjoyed a political revival, witnessed by Jotham's success over Ammon and the extension of Judah's borders eastward (II Ch. 27:15). Chronicles also notes Josiah's occupation of the Assyrian provinces of Samaria, Galilee and Gilead (east of

Jordan) in 628 BCE, which confirms the impression that a strong king of Judah controlled, or was supported in, Transjordan.

Authorship and Date of Composition: Discussion of the authorship of Chronicles centres on its relation to the books of Ezra and Nehemiah. The earliest Bible commentators, the authorities of the Talmud, put forward the theory that the three books shared a common authorship (Baba Batra 15:1), pointing out that the first three verses of Ezra are textually identical with the last two verses of II Ch. Scholars who reject this theory, however, consider that these linking verses may have been deliberately interpolated by the canonical editors of the Old Testament so as to form a continuous history of Judah from its beginnings to as near as possible their own time. Others, however, see all the first six chapters of Ezra as a direct continuation of II Chronicles. From their contents they consider that Chronicles, Ezra and Nehemiah belong together, and not with Samuel and Kings.

There is quite a considerable school of thought which holds that Chronicles was written by Ezra and Nehemiah. W. F. Albright, who shares this opinion, believes that the book was written around 400 BCE. Other scholars, including H. H. Rowley, O. Pfeiffer and M. Noth maintain that the work reflects the theocratic structure of post-Exilic Judea and must therefore have been composed in early Hellenistic times. When the Chronicler himself is writing — not quoting from earlier Scriptures (see above) — his style is that of the most important representatives of post-Exilic Hebrew, including grammatical forms introduced from Aramaic and Persian (e. g. verses I Ch. 9:21; 21:27; 28:11; 29:1, 7; II Ch. 2:6; 16:14; 3:6, passim).

The assumption of a late date for the book's composition lays stress on its divergences from the earlier historic books which were apparently cast in a definite form in Exilic times.

However, on other grounds, scholars such as M. Z. Segal, Y. Kaufman and B. Mazar deny the view that Ezra-Nehemiah should be seen as a continuation of Chronicles. A. C. Welch even places the composition of most of Chronicles (with the exception of the genealogical tables and the post-Exilic lists) as early as the 6th century BCE which denies any possible connection with Ezra or Nehemiah. Other authorities regard the author of the book as having been largely influenced by the Priestly Code (P) and the Deuteronomic source (D) of the Bible (see Biblical Criticism*).

Place in the Canon: An additional factor in the uncertainty about the date and authorship of Chronicles is the lack of any uniformity in the place in the Canon which various translations of the Old Testament assigned to the book. In the Hebrew Bible Canon*, Chronicles appears as the very last book, at the end of the Hagiographa, while in the Septuagint, Vulgate, and English Bibles, it is one of the historical books, placed between Kings and Ezra. The Septuagint renamed the books so that the books of Samuel and Kings, known to us from the English (Revised) Version, became: I Kings (I Samuel), II Kings (II Samuel); III Kings (I Kings); IV Kings (II Kings), whereas Chronicles was given a longer, entirely different name. This suggests a literary tendency to combine all the historical material, without considering the time at which each of the different books was written. In the Hebrew text, the contents follow a different order, reflecting, more or less, a historical and chronological presentation of the Old Testament.

A complex picture emerges and the problem remains a puzzle. When Chronicles, Ezra and Nehemiah are considered in their present form, then grounds for supposing them continuous do appear, but it becomes equally apparent that all of them derive partly from earlier sources and partly from older ones. Just as Chronicles includes an older strata of quotations from Scriptures, etc., so do the books of Ezra and Nehemiah include earlier material along with the memoirs of the two men.

Though there are certain textual similarities between the three books, probably due to their having been written at around the same time, there is a fundamental difference between them, particularly in their presentation of the chain of events of Israel's history. Ezra-Nehemiah contain hardly any trace of the history of the House of David or the Levites and very little of Chronicles' emphasis on God's mighty deeds in forming the nation. Chronicles, in contrast, devotes nineteen chapters to the story of David, while disposing of the whole of the previous period from Adam to David in only nine. The disproportion was, of course, perfectly reasonable to Chronicles' author who saw the whole of the history of Israel in terms of David's reign and the tribe of Judah and God's Temple and the tribe of Levi. Together with Jerusalem, which provided the link between them, these two main themes form the background to all the past events recounted in Chronicles.

Bible as History and Theology: The Bible as a whole is usually evaluated as a fusion of history and theology, and all the biblical "historians" were theologians as much as they were reporters. Chronicles goes even further, making David and Solomon the protagonists in a whole drama of divine salvation for mankind and demonstrating even more clearly its theological interest and intention (see Kings*, Book).

CIRCUMCISION. — In the Ancient Near East: Circumcision, the cutting away of the foreskin, is one of the ancient customs that, in the early days, was common to the Israelites and many other peoples in the Near East. According to Jer. 9:25–26, the Arabs and the Egyptians, the peoples of Edom, Moab and Ammon all practiced circumcision. Reliefs have been discovered in Egypt **(295)** portraying the circumcision of boys and written documents testify to the prevalence of the custom there. On the other hand, uncircumcized mummies have been found and some scholars have concluded from this inconsistency that circumcision was practiced only by Egyptian priests.

Herodotus reports that Egyptians, Phoenicians and Syrians — i. e. all inhabitants of Palestine and immediate vicinity — were circumcized and Aristophanes confirms circumcision among the Syrians, while pre-Islamic Arab poets refer to the circumcision of the Arabs. It seems, therefore, that Israel followed a custom general throughout the area. The "uncircumcized" were the Philistines* (I Sam. 18:25 and passim), a people who came from a totally different cultural background from that of Israel's other neighbours.

In the earliest texts (Ex. 4:25; Jos. 5:2–3) circumcision was effected by flint knives **(23)**, good evidence of the antiquity of the custom. The antique tool continued in use for the rite in biblical times. Historical and anthropological research have suggested that at first circumcision was a religious ceremony preceding marriage and designed to ensure fertility and propitiate unfriendly spirits by making a redemptive offering of the foreskin in preparation for married life. Many scholars accordingly interpret the story of Gn. 34 in this light, for there circumcision is explicitly connected with marriage. Ex. 4:24–26 can be interpreted in the same way, making the object of the story the circumcision of Moses himself. Zipporah, in this story, says to him "You are a bridegroom", using a word which, in Hebrew, can mean bridegroom, son-in-law and father-in-law, and which comes from a root also known in Arabic where it means "to circumcize".

The origins of the custom are shrouded in obscurity. It has been suggested that circumcision was the equivalent of the "initiation" rites which, among primitive peoples, prepare the boy for his acceptance into adult society. The Egyptian reliefs mentioned above show boys being circumcized in adolescence, and the biblical account of Ishmael's circumcision at the age of thirteen (Gn. 17:25) apparently coincides with the custom among Ishmaelite tribes (see Arabs*) of circumcizing at puberty, when the boy is ready to join society. In fact the rite has been adapted to a variety of different situations and given a wide range of different interpretations. Which one was original would be difficult to determine.

The Command of Circumcision: The Bible records that circumcision was commanded on three major occasions and these offer some clue to the development of the custom in relation to the changing circumstances of the Israelites. According to Genesis, circumcision was first practiced by Abraham's clan after its settlement in Canaan.

The basic ruling is contained in Gn. 17:12–13, "every male throughout your generations . . . shall be circumcized in the flesh of his foreskin" as an everlasting covenant, and this is to apply to the sojourner and the slave as well as to true-born Israelites. All the Patriarchs observed the rule. This aspect is also present in the Dinah story of Gn. 34:13–24. The Hivites of Shechem who are involved were uncircumcized for they were a foreign element within the land of Canaan with a political regime that also differed from that of the other inhabitants (see Patriarchs*). To become one people with the sons of Jacob, and thus be eligible for marriage, they had to circumcize.

Resumption of the Custom: Jos. 5:2–9 records that Joshua circumcized all the people of Israel at the sanctuary of Gilgal after the Exodus because males born since leaving Egypt had not been circumcized. Verse 5 states that "all the males who came out of Egypt had been circumcized" but from Ex. 4:24–26 it is clear that Moses had remained uncircumcized and it seems probable that the custom had been neglected during the sojourn in Egypt as well as in the desert. It was revived with the entry into the Promised Land.

The earliest traditions connecting the rite with the customs of other peoples lay no particular stress on it as part of Yahwism. It is not known either when circumcision at the age of eight days was substituted for the adolescent rite. The Bible ascribes the command to circumcize at eight days to Abraham but this tradition is of a later origin (many scholars assume it to be Priestly — see Biblical Criticism*). The story of Ex. 4:24–26, however, suggests that differences already existed in Moses' time between the custom as practiced among the Hebrews and among the Midianites and Ishmaelites. While Moses was still living in Midian, his young son had not been circumcized, but when Moses returned to Egypt, he had to do as his people did. This story describes not merely an act of propitiation to God but also suggests a possible basis for the transfer of the ceremony to infancy. Once this was done, the more general oriental attitude which regarded circumcision as an act of initiation to marriage was obviously abandoned. In the Priestly tradition it became the sign of incorporation into the religious and community life of the group. Hence it is a frequent requirement for inclusion in a religious or social gathering. The law of the Passover sacrifice (Ex. 12:43, 49) for instance, lays it down that only the circumcized may take part.

295

Sign of the Covenant: Joshua 5:2–9 makes the specific connection between circumcision and Yahwism much clearer. When the practice was renewed in Canaan it was given a distinctly religious significance and this it has retained ever since. Circumcision among the Israelites is always interpreted religiously. Moreover, the formula of Genesis 17 which reflects the later interpretation of a primitive tradition states explicitly that circumcision is to be the visible God-given sign of a special covenant, "bᵉrîth", between God and Israel (see Chosen People; Covenant*). The new interpretation was further emphasized when their neighbours began to abandon the practice and the Jews remained the only circumcized people in the area. Ezekiel lists almost all Israel's neighbours — including the Sidonians — as among the uncircumcized (Ezk. 32).

Post-Exilic Period: This function of circumcision as the sign of membership of the Covenant community, however, only became generally accepted much later. The evidence for it is all later than the Pentateuch and comes mainly from sources dating to or after the Babylonian Exile*. Ezekiel (28:10; 31:18; 32:19) reflects the increase in Jewish consciousness which gave the mark of circumcision its significance as a distinctive national — as well as religious — emblem.

The Book of Judith (14:10; see Apocrypha*) refers to the Ammonites as uncircumcized; Jubilees (15:31) regards circumcision as sacrosanct, and Josephus* records that John Hyrcanus (see Hasmoneans*) forced the Idumeans to circumcize as a token of aceptance of Judaism (although, in fact, they had observed the custom in earlier times). With observance of the Sabbath and the shunning of idolatry, circumcision became the main characteristic distinguishing the Jews from all other men, and acquired the status of a confession of faith (side by side with the Sabbath). Proselytes who wished to convert to Judaism had to circumcize, the first evidence for this coming from the Apocrypha (Judith 14:10; Esther 8:17, in the Septuagint version). One of the notorious anti-Jewish "Edicts" of Antiochus Epiphanes forbade the practice (I Mac. 1:60–61; II Mac. 6:10; see Hasmoneans*) and hellenizing Jews who abandoned their religion and wanted to appear like other westerners tried to conceal this "defect" in their bodies (1 Mac. 1:14; cf. Cor. 1:7, 18).

As in more modern times, circumcision was the distinguishing feature of the Jews in the eyes of the Greeks and Romans. To prevent the possibility of effacing the sign of the Covenant, the Rabbis empasized the act of pushing back the skin to lay bare the glans, as a feature of the operation. The custom aroused the scorn of Martial, who died in 8 BCE, Horace and Persius, who lived until 62 CE. It was again forbidden by Hadrian at the time of a later Jewish repression, after the Bar-Kochba* revolt. Jewish-Christians and Gentiles were also forbidden to circumcize. These laws were abrogated by Antoninus some time after 150 CE, allowing only Jews to be circumcized, forbidding Samaritans and Gentiles to do so. This interdiction as applying to non-Jews was renewed by Septimus Severus (193–211 CE).

Prophetic Symbolism: As the distinguishing feature of Jewish life, circumcision was frequently used as a metaphor by the prophets. Jeremiah (4:4) follows Dt. 10:16 and 30:16 in speaking of the deeper circumcision of the heart, and describing an "uncircumcized heart" as one which does not understand, just as "uncircumcized ears" are those which do not listen (Jer. 6:10) and "uncircumcized lips" those which cannot speak convincingly (Ex. 6:12, 30).

This use of the term as a spiritual symbol is repeated in the Dead Sea Scrolls* where the wicked priest is one who "did not circumcize the foreskin of his heart", and the "men of truth" are those who "circumcize in unity the foreskin of impulse and a stiff neck."

Early Christianity and Circumcision: This seems to be the background to the meaning of circumcision in New Testament times. Paul taught that what counted was "circumcision of the heart, in the spirit, not in the letter" (Rom. 2:29). His declaration that the only effective circumcision was an inward, spiritual one, having nothing to do with the flesh, aroused some of the most bitter controversies of the early Christian church (Ac. 15:1–35; 16:3; Gal. 2:3; for a full discussion, see article on Paul*). In the event, the Jewish ordinance was dropped, and the Christians abandoned circumcision as a general requirement.

CITIES, CANAANITE. — The "cities" of the Canaanites had little in common with their mediaeval or modern counterparts. They were unimpressive groupings of houses, in which perhaps only a temple or a palace had any claim to distinction. Their inhabitants were mainly peasants and the most important source of their livelihood was agriculture. Nevertheless, they were the permanent homes of a number of human beings, with a developed social organization — in fact, a city.

For such relatively large groupings to be possible, certain conditions had to be fulfilled. Most essential in an Eastern country like Palestine was a source of fresh water. No ancient town there has been found without one, although in the late Canaanite period or Late Bronze Age, cisterns and catchbasins for rainwater (see Water Supply*: Cisterns) came into use. Second came communications and defence. Canaanite cities were connected by roads which allowed for a certain amount of trade but, on the other hand, contained the danger of hostile attack.

Fortifications: For this reason, many of them were built on the top of defensible hilltops, where these were close enough to a water supply and large enough to allow for development. In most cases the towns were fortified. The defences of Jericho*, for instance, the earliest city in Palestine and one of the oldest in the world, go back to the Neolithic period. Early Bronze Age cities had enormous fortifications with walls more than 8 m. thick (as at Bet-Yerah and Tel Sheikh Ahmed-el-Areyny — Gath). Later on, in the Hyksos (Middle Bronze) period, artificial slopes of battered earth, strengthened by stone walls, were built as an added protection (as at Lachish* and Tel Jerishah). The insecurity of the troubled Late Bronze Age, reflected in the Tel Amarna* tablets, prompted still stronger fortifications.

The fact that enormous construction projects could be carried out is evidence of a strong social organization even in the very earliest towns.

Walled Town-Planning: Walled cities, occupied by a long succession of inhabitants, form "tels". As each town is destroyed or abandoned, debris accumulates all over the site within the walls, and around their foundations. When a new town is built, this mass of rubble is filled in and levelled and the new constructions begun on top at a higher level. After the process has been repeated a number of times, the "tel" takes on the familiar appearance of a flat-topped hill and when the archaeologist digs through it, he can find at least the foundations — sometimes even more substantial remains — of each level (stratum) of the city (see War*: Fortifications). This is illustrated in a reconstructed model of Megiddo (**297**). The lower strata, bottom right, are Canaanite levels. Excavations of places like Megiddo*, Jericho*, etc. have revealed a fairly clear picture of the layout of fortifications, streets and buildings of the Canaanite cities and the details have been filled in from wall reliefs from Egypt and Assyria. These reliefs, like the siege of the walled town of Kadesh-on-Orontes (**296**) in Syria in mountainous and wooded country (from the exterior of the great hall at Karnak) show typical towns of the Late Bronze and Early Iron age, about the time of the Israelite conquest. The outer wall — the town wall proper — and its crenellated fortifications are shown in detail. The bearded figures suggest Canaanites. Below is a herdsman with his bulls.

Canaanite City-Names: Canaanite cities underwent many changes in the course of centuries. This is suggested by some of the names by which the cities are known to us. Some of the names are found in the Bible, some in cuneiform texts and many in Egyptian geographical material and other texts which include lists of names (such as the "execration texts", see Egypt*). Some of the cities kept their ancient names after the Conquest, while others, of course, were re-named.

The Canaanite names indicate a diverse origin for the Canaanites themselves. Besides Semitic names like Jericho, there are Hurrian names like Ziklag or Lachish* and others which seem to have a Semitic form but may, in fact, have been derived from Hurrian. "Foreign" names were transformed through a popular Canaanite etymology.

Many names bear witness to Canaanite religious customs*. Ba'al, Astarte, Gad, Reshef and 'Anath occur. Some places were named for the main occupation of their inhabitants: Kiriat-Gath (wine press), Beth-Hakerem (house or town of the vineyard), Ein Ganim (the fountain of orchards). In other names, a feature of the geography, plant or animal life of the town is recorded.

Sometimes the same name appears twice in Palestine, suggesting that a population had shifted permanently, as when the Danites moved north (see Judges*), and had given the same name to their new settlement.

Organization: Evidence for the way Canaanite cities were administered comes from biblical traditions and the cuneiform inscriptions of Amarna* and Ugarit*. The Late Bronze period saw the rise of city-states, in which each city had a king who ruled over the city and its surrounding area, including villages, hamlets and sometimes smaller towns, called "daughters" of the metropolis by the Bible. Towns were ruled by elders or a king, supported by an aristocracy of "chariot warriors" (maryannu), many of whom were of non-Semitic origin. The lower class was composed partly of half-free serfs (khupshu) and partly of slaves (see Slavery*). There does not seem to have been a true middle class, and Canaanite social organization did not lend itself to the development of independent crafts and guilds. There was no stratum of the population which was in a position to undertake enterprises on its own initiative, or was likely to be fired with ambition to change its ways and develop along new lines. The economy of each small state was under the direct control of kings or notables, who left little power in the hands of the craftsmen and traders or their organizations. Thus, in spite of long lists of classes and professions in Ugaritic and Mycenean Linear B inscriptions, the members of the different groups remained unorganized (see Cities, Israelite*; Ancient Cities*, and specific sites of Canaanite times — see Cities, Hellenistic, after Cities, Israelite).

296

297

298

CITIES, ISRAELITE; BUILDING & HOUSES. *Outline: Water Supply; Fortifications; Fortified Gates; Towers; City Architecture; Town-Planning; Economic Development; City Pattern of the Later Monarchy (Iron Age II); Water Supply and Sewage; Population; Names of Cities; Social and Economic Life; Administration; Store-houses; Royal Buildings; Megiddo Stables.*

Unlike the cities of the Canaanites*, Israelite cities were not independent states but were part of a larger political unit. In the days of the Judges*, this was the tribal federation; later on it became the central government in Jerusalem, then the two capitals of the divided monarchy (see Israel and Judah*, Part I).

Many Israelite cities were built on the sites of Canaanite* cities and, in these cases, the newcomers used the existing installations as far as they still stood or could be repaired. Such places acquired their Israelite character only over a period of time (see Conquest*; Tribes*). Many others, however, were built in the unpopulated hill country.

Water Supply: In the unpopulated hill country, the first requirement was the establishment of a reliable water supply. This need prompted the widespread use of plastered cisterns, which were apparently introduced at the time of the settlement of the Israelites in the land. The availability of water remained, as in Canaanite times, the essential factor in the choice of the site for a new city while the size of the water supply remained decisive for the development of the city. The installations at Megiddo make it clear that as early as Canaanite times, care was taken to ensure safe access to water while the city was under siege or attack. In Lachish* and Jerusalem*, the system of making underground tunnels to bring water into the citadel was further developed (see details under Water Supply* and below, Water Supply and Sewage).

Fortifications: Where the Israelites found the fortifications of a city still in good repair, they were content to maintain them. If the fortifications had been destroyed, or in the case of new settlements, the Israelites established their own system of defences. If a site had no natural defence (e. g. the slope of a hill), a thick bank of earth would be raised and the wall itself constructed on top. This is illustrated by the gateway of Megiddo* **(297)**. Before the monarchy, walls were made of unbaked bricks on a stone foundation. In the early days of the monarchy, casemate walls were constructed. These were made of two parallel walls, the outer one thicker than the inner, connected by a series of cross walls about 1.50–2.00 m. long which gave the whole system the appearance of a series of rooms **(298)**. Apparently these could be filled with earth in times of siege to make a strong defence against battering rams and similar "siege

299

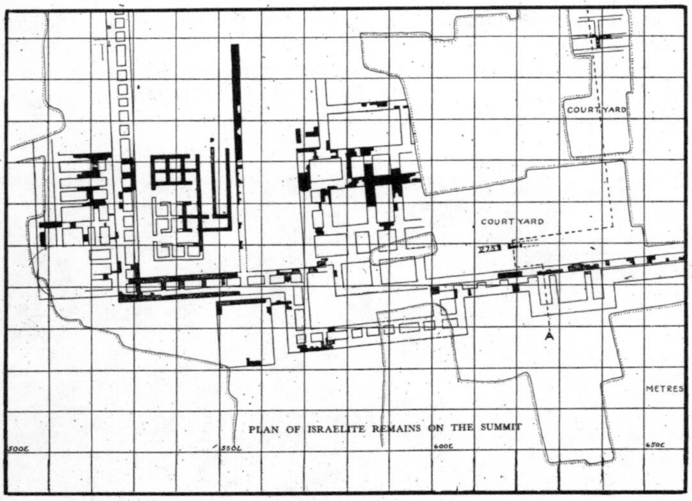

300

engines". They also formed an inner ring road circling the town, for in several Palestinian cities, houses were built up along it close to the inner wall (see plastered floor of such a house at Gibeon **300**). Later on, the casemate walls of a "royal city" like Samaria*, built by Omri and Ahab of Israel (1 K. 16:24), supported imposing superstructures (**299**), shops and a palace overlooking a paved courtyard. No attempt appears to have been made to add buttresses to the walls.

Types of fortification were improved during the monarchy and another very popular form of city wall developed, made up of a massive "broken line" of alternating recesses and salients. This meant that attackers approaching the inside of the recess were exposed to the defenders, standing on the salients on either side. In the early days, walls of this kind were built without towers. The form was used in the Megiddo* of Jehu's dynasty. Recesses in the wall built by Solomon were blocked on the inside and strengthened and the flanking salients enlarged to serve as the basis for a tower. This made for more effective defence and also a simpler construction of the massive gateway.

Fortified Gates: The gate was the key to a city's defence and, potentially, its weakest point. Walls were broken for gateways only very reluctantly and then great care was given to their situation. Jerusalem had a number of gates, all mentioned by name in the Bible (see Jerusalem*), but most Israelite cities had only two, one for wheeled traffic and the other, on the opposite side, for pedestrians only. The road which led to the main gate was planned, wherever possible, with wartime exigencies as well as peaceful uses in mind. An army marched to the attack with the soldiers holding their weapons in their right hands and their shields in the left. Wherever possible, accordingly, a city gate was placed so that anyone coming up the road had the wall and its defenders on the vulnerable right-hand side. Where, as in Megiddo, this was physically impossible, a second outer gate would be built to protect the entrance to the city. This bastion, guarding the approaches to the city, helped to overcome the intrinsic weakness of a system which allowed enemy soldiers to come up close to the walls, protected by their shields.

In the Israelite period, city gates were part of a strong, massive tower, through which the road ran, narrowed by two or three embrasures (**297**) and closed during the night or in time of war. The door itself was guarded by two or more pairs of massive piers, forming the guardrooms between them. Behind the first set of piers hung the door, with a huge vertical beam at each side, strengthened by strips of bronze. It moved on hinges fitted into hollowed out stone door sockets (**302 a**) on either side of the piers, i.e. at each end of this doorsill of the Lachish gate. The friction between the hinge and the socket naturally wore out the stone so door sockets might be protected by bronze covers such as the one found in Jaffa (**301** . The socket is indicated by the dotted curve). The sockets for city gates and the doors to other important buildings had to be replaced frequently. For this reason, many more worn-out door sockets than city gates have been unearthed in Israelite cities (**302 b**). Sometimes the socket stones were used in later buildings.

Towers: The gateway was usually further protected by towers. These might be built over the doorway, as in Megiddo (**297**), or jutting out from it as in Hazor. A ramp or stairway led up to the tower from the foot of the hill, or the bottom of the earth foundation on which it stood. The

301

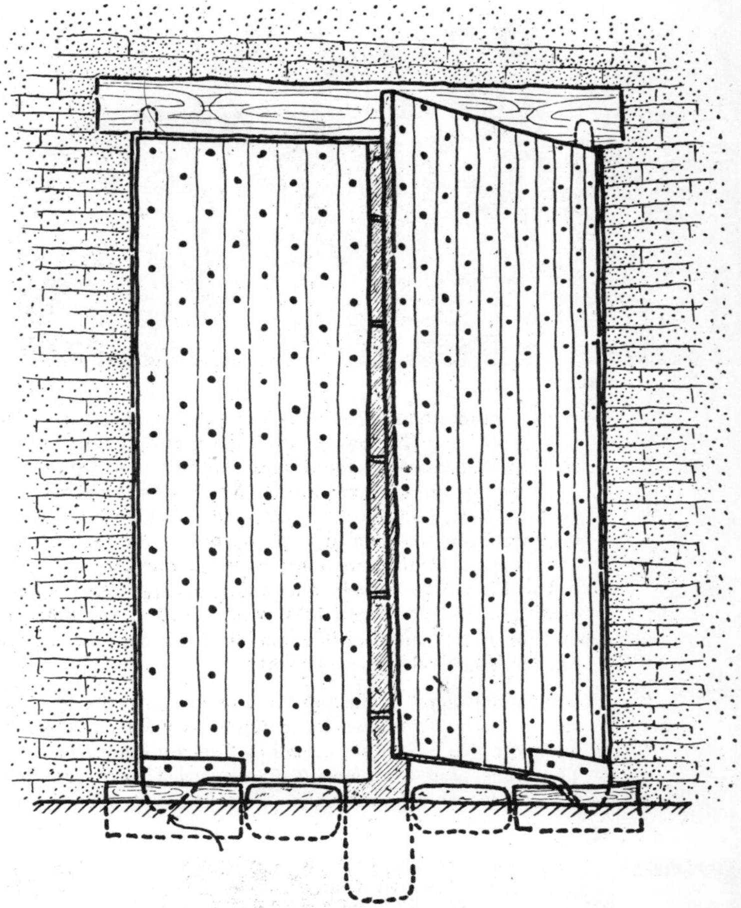

302 a

302 b

303

top sometimes had an outwork on it. Egyptian reliefs such as this showing Ramses III attacking a Syrian town (**303**) indicate that this often took the form of a wooden transom. Although rare in the Late Bronze Age, such devices became general later. Additional towers might also be built some distance from the gate at strategic points for the defence and control of the city and its neighbourhood.

The Hyksos gave their cities the added protection of an artificial slope (or glacis; **127**) with a ditch at the bottom, and the system survived in some Israelite cities such as Tel Sheikh Ahmed-el-Areyny (Gath).

City Architecture: Walls and large buildings in the Israelite cities were built of hewn stone (**304**) frequently inferior in quality to that used in the preceding Canaanite constructions. The stone used for house building varied from common field stones or bigger roughly shaped quarry stones held

304

together with plenty of clay mortar, to carefully wrought dressed quarry stone. A typical Israelite wall was made of a mixture of hewn wrought and unhewn stones, the wrought stones being used for corners (cornerstones) and as headers and stretchers at fixed intervals; the space between them was filled by rough stones embedded in mortar. This was a quick and cheap method of building. City walls may have been topped by wooden palisades, as indicated.

Town-Planning: (a) In the earliest Israelite cities (Iron Age I, 12th to mid-10th c. BCE) streets were almost unknown. Although Canaanite cities had streets and sewers, these disappeared. Instead the city became a haphazard grouping of family units, "beit-ab" or patriarchal houses. Each of these was a collection of dwellings built around a central courtyard which would be used for all household tasks such as preparing and cooking food. Around it, on the ground floor, were workshops and storerooms containing, for instance, the great jars (**305**) in which oil and grain were stored (see Pottery*), while in the upper storey the family slept, four to six to a room, in winter. In summer, they slept on the cool, flat roofs. This system of building seems to have been developed in answer to the country's shortage of long straight timbers. Standing timber such as pine and cypress was mostly used up in the spate of house-building during Iron Age I when settled life extended through Palestine and villages grew into towns. No timber was imported from neighbouring countries except for public buildings erected by the Kings (e.g. David* and Solomon*). In the hilly regions there is some evidence that almond wood was used for building in the 10th c. BCE. As ruined houses of the period rarely have the upper parts of the walls or the roofs still in place when excavated, there is much uncertainty about the appearance of the upper parts of these dwellings.

Canaanite notables built strong houses such as this one in Gibeon (**304**), their roofs supported by the stone pillars in the the centre.

In the lower storeys the rooms were plastered and of medium size, generally a square of 4 or 5 metres. A house would serve an entire family, from grandparents down to grandchildren. From the limited number of rooms in each dwelling it seems likely that they housed between one and two dozen people. One of the rooms on the ground floor was usually reserved for livestock while provisions were often stored in the living rooms.

The houses were probably arranged according to the groupings of different families, the "beit-ab" for the whole clan being in whatever was considered the best or most prominent position, a rural organization being thus gradually transplanted into urban conditions. In one arrangement, the main courtyard was surrounded by a collection of rooms or huts built on pillars. Beside this, there were other more modest dwellings, like these rooms and group of houses from Megiddo (**297**). Houses like these appear to have been more numerous. A private lane connected the "big house" and its dependent smaller ones, while each grouping was separated from the next by an alley. The only means of communication through the town was along these alleys or, more probably, through the courtyards. Strict privacy within the family was not something to be looked for in a town of this period.

The lay-out of walled cities of the period is repeated in many instances. Inside, and a little distance from the walls was the ring road with houses, the gap between them and the wall being used as storage silos. Within this frame, the centre of the city followed no discernible plan, but was a closely-built maze of cramped alleys and dwellings. The general picture can be seen from the examples of the lay-outs of Megiddo (see above), Jericho (**306**) which follows no discernible pattern, and Tirzah (Tel Far'ah; **307**) in Iron Age II, showing some alleys and streets.

While the family and clan remained the central units of Hebrew society, such town-construction was appropriate. During the 12th, 11th and 10th cs. BCE, however, tribal bonds weakened and were replaced by a central government. This gave cities and their organization a new status, reflected in their plans, which now featured public buildings and narrow streets.

Economic Development: The change-over from the tribal system was accompanied by economic developments inside the cities. As their population increased, so their wealth grew and created new demands. The proportion of the inhabitants engaged in occupations other than agriculture rose. The shops on the ground floors of the houses produced and sold a variety of products and craftsmen of every sort began to be found in the towns. Each particular craft or manufacture became established in a particular quarter of the city, and among the workmen a solidarity developed which is reminiscent of the craft guilds of a later age. This too strengthened the ties which linked the different inhabitants of a town, loosening the old tribal bonds and fostering a community of interest which could even tempt a city to attempt its own foreign policy, independent of the central authority, or to separate entirely. At the earliest stages of urban settlement, during the days of Judges, there was no question of a dominant, national government. Later on, Jeroboam's separation of Israel from Judah was economic as well as political (see Israel and Judah*, Parts I and II). Similarly, the towns east of the Jordan in the early days of the monarchy were completely controlled by their own wealthy class who held sway far from Jerusalem. The separation of the Samaritans* was also the result of political and social, as well as religious, factors.

City Pattern of the Later Monarchy (Iron Age II; Mid-10th–6th c. BCE): The havoc and destruction of the Aramean Wars of the 9th and 8th cs. BCE (see Israel and Judah*, II) were followed by the prosperous period of the reign of Jeroboam II in the Northern Kingdom and Uzziah and Azzariah in Judah. Cities built during this time reflect a distinct pattern belonging to Iron Age II. Streets reappear. Sometimes they follow a deliberate plan, as at Tirzah (Tel Far'ah; **307**), sometimes they follow the natural line of the hill, as at Debir (Tel beit-Mirsim). In Megiddo, Debir and elsewhere, sewers have also been discovered. A palace for the governor or a central administrative building was frequently erected near the main gate, as at Megiddo (**297**) or at Mizpah. These new features probably had no great impact on the mass of the population. Even in the most "modern" of the cities of the period, alleys still separated groups of buildings in primitive native tradition.

The proper planning of streets and quarters on a regular basis did not come until the Hellenistic period, at which

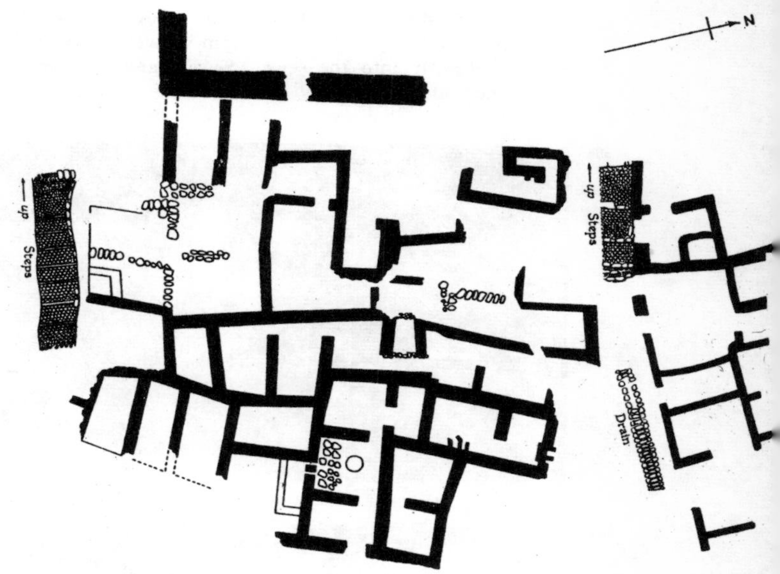

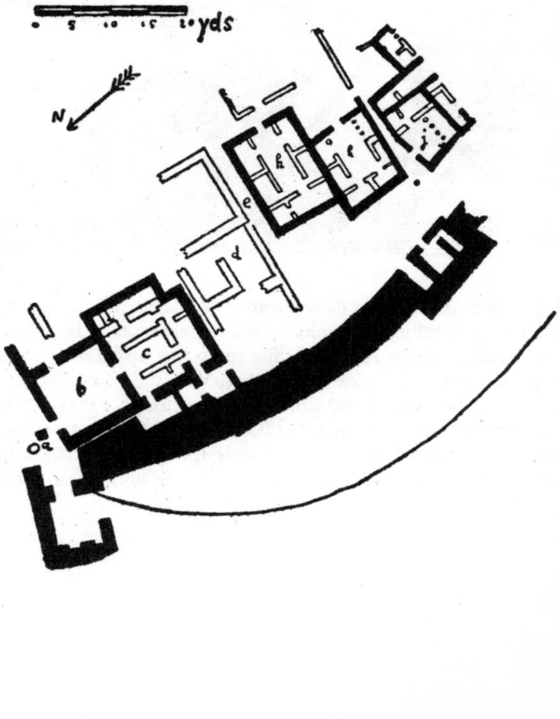

307

time independent government and policy for each city reached its peak (see Cities, Hellenistic*).

Water Supply and Sewage: The cities obtained their water from rain water stored in cisterns under the houses (see Water Supply*) and from public springs or wells within the city limits, from which water was taken each day in pitchers and jars (see Pottery*).

The disposal of sewage, from combined bath and toilet rooms, mainly in the better class houses, is indicated by clay and stone sewers and pipes found in the foundations of Canaanite and Israelite cities. The sanitary facilities, bath-tubs and squatting oriental style toilets must have looked much like the remains of the bathroom **(308)** in the palace of Lachish (8th c. BCE). A drain passed through the bottom of the wall; a water-closet fitted against it on the other side (see parallel stones, centre). A large tub would be used for cold water, the small one for hot. After a bath, the water could be run off through clay pipes into a drain or cesspool. The toilet was flushed from a ewer of water and emptied directly into the sewer. Sewers and pipes would be cleaned at intervals by slaves **(309)**.

308

309

Population: It is very difficult to make an estimate of the number of inhabitants of any of the Israelite cities. Jerusalem had around 10,000 in Solomon's time, but apparently twice as many in the late monarchy. Megiddo* may have housed something between 5,000 and 6,000; Lachish* 6,000–7,500; Tel beit-Mirsim (Debir) 2,000–3,000; Shechem about 5,000. After the restoration of Palestine in the Hellenistic period, the cities grew substantially in size and population. For example, Philistine Ashkelon is known to have contained some 6,000 inhabitants in Iron Age I whereas in Roman times it had a population eight times that number. Jerusalem in the Roman period is reported to have been a city of 120,000 people, although this figure is not certain.

Names of Cities: Many Israelite cities continued to be called by the Canaanite name — good evidence that some of the original inhabitants remained to pass it on. The names of many Israelite cities have been confirmed from Egyptian sources dating long before the Israelite settlement. Other names, however, were changed after the Conquest. The most famous example is the Canaanite Laish which became Dan (Jud. 18:29).

Other cities were renamed when conquered by Israelite kings. Amaziah, according to II K. 14:7, renamed Sela-Edom (Petra) Joktheel after he had captured it.

The list of conquests of Pharaoh Sheshonk, carved on the temple wall at Karnak (see Egypt*), contains a curious name for a town of Solomon's time: Yad-Hamelech. This is the Hebrew for "memorial (or stele) of the king" and it was apparently somewhere in the Megiddo region, although its exact site is not known. The name suggests, however, that from the very earliest stages of the monarchy, the king made his influence felt on town life in general, not only in his own place of residence. (See also Cities*: Canaanite and Hellenistic.)

Social and Economic Life: The life of a city was then — as now — influenced by many factors. If it was a place of pilgrimage or a commercial centre on one of the great highways (see Roads and Communications*), then its development would be greatly fostered by the wealth accruing from these activities. Border towns had strong fortifications and garrisons, with the house of the commander acting as one of the centres of the city life. Port towns also had a special role (see Ships and Navigation*; Trade*). Some other cities were centres for a specific activity, like the "store-cities" mentioned in the Bible (see Agriculture* and below). The names of four Judean cities, Hebron*, Socho, Ziph and Mamshit, have been found on the royal stamps on the handles of storage jars found in excavations. These suggest that the cities had a special function or prestige which cannot be determined from the evidence at present available (see Seals*).

The social and economic life of the city centred around the gate. In peacetime, this was much more than the entrance to the city. There or close nearby was the market where outsiders could bring their merchandise to sell and could buy provisions. There the citizens came to take part in the buying and selling and to meet and gossip (see Government and Authority*: Justice at the Gate).

With internal security and stability, the pace of urban development was accelerated and, with it, new problems arose. The growth and increasing power of a commercial class (see Trade*) created the possibility of class conflicts between its members and the poorer people, or the hierarchy of the city temple, whose status also advanced. The tensions thus created are expressed by the prophet Amos*. They also gave rise to anti-urban movements such as the Rechabites*. K. Kenyon reports that the 8th c. BCE level of Tirzah (Tel Far'ah) shows "a group of excellent private houses . . . with a courtyard flanked on three sides by rooms, divided by a long, straight wall from a quarter in which smaller houses are closely huddled together. This evidence of social inequality reflects the denunciations of the prophets on the rich for trampling upon the poor" (see above: Town Planning).

Administration: The city was ruled by elders who, in turn, were subject to the king. He would send a governor to watch over royal interests, especially the payment of taxes. A good example of the system is Solomon's administration (see Government and Authority*; Taxes*). In many cities, the provincial "governor's palace" has been found, usually a large building consisting of many rooms which might house the city garrison as well as the governor and his retinue. In other cases, the soldiers were garrisoned nearby, as in the reconstruction of the city of Megiddo (**297**). A similar pattern existed in the "royal city" where the king himself dwelt in the palace. Examples have been found in Samaria, Jerusalem and other cities which served as royal residences. The plan of the palace of Samaria (**299**), protected by casemate walls, is particularly well preserved. The famous Samaria* ivories were found within its ruins (see article).

Even with the expansion of alternate occupations, the bulk of the population continued to live by working in the fields around the town. Many peasants also lived outside the city walls, retiring within them for protection only in times of danger. There were also "daughter-towns" or small, unwalled villages within the district, which were dependant upon and controlled by the city.

Tax collection, accordingly, might be quite a complicated business, and storehouses and storepits had to be prepared to receive the taxes which were paid in kind by the people.

Storehouses: The remains of such storehouses have been uncovered in Jericho*, Gezer*, Megiddo*, Beth-Shemesh, Beth-Shean*, Tel Kassileh and other cities, some of them even containing traces of grain. Most of them date from the Middle and Late Bronze Age (17th–14th c. BCE) and had been cut out of the soft rock on which the city stood. It seems probable that their upper part was shaped like a beehive but in every case, the domelike superstructure has disappeared. Their dimensions naturally varied. The best preserved ones range from 4 to 11 metres in diameter, 3.75 to 7 metres deep, with capacities from 40 to 450 cubic metres. They were usually built on stone foundations, with a brick floor. Very often the storehouse was part of the defences of the town, serving the needs of the local garrison. One of the best examples is that discovered in Megiddo with two flights of steps, one used for people and loads going up, the other down.

Royal Buildings: Nothing remains of the royal buildings of David and Solomon in "David's City". The best evidence comes from Samaria, where the palace and other residences built within a short time by Omri and Ahab (1 K. 16:24) have been uncovered on the acropolis. They were built to a regular plan (see diagram (**299**) of carefully chiselled stone (**310**) on good foundations, and with their walls standing at almost perfect right angles. A similar technique has been observed in 13th c. BCE Ugarit* (see article) and seems to confirm that the kings of Israel, from David down to Ahab and thereafter, relied on Phoenician craftsmen from Tyre and elsewhere for the techniques of architecture and stone dressing, or borrowed their techniques. For a while, during

310

311

the reigns of Jehu and his dynasty (see Israel and Judah*, II), Phoenician influence may have been resisted but it is clear from other discoveries that after Solomon's time, it penetrated deep into Judah.

Samaria's royal buildings included those built in the "king's city", the capital, several storehouses (see above), royal stables like those of Megiddo, plus, of course, the usual complex of fortifications and gates. A royal citadel attributed to the reign of Jehoiakim (609–598 BCE) has been discovered at Ramat Rahel near Jerusalem, an area which was part of the royal domain of the kings of Judah as from the 8th c. BCE. The ornamental window balustrade and proto-Aeolian capitals (**311**) which probably decorated the facade of the building, suggest the splendour of its original appearance. It moved Jeremiah to a passionate denunciation (Jer. 22:13 ff), but it remains a good indication of native achievements in decoration and architecture in Israel long before Hellenic times (see Samaria*; Herod*; Synagogue*).

The Megiddo Stables were built in the form of a rectangle containing two rows of stalls on either side of a central cement-floored avenue. Each stall contained a stone manger held in place between the twin pillars which supported the roof. The horse was tied to a hole in the angle of the pillar (**170**). (See Megiddo*; Solomon*; Israel and Judah*; Arms and Weapons*; see also Ancient Cities*, followed by descriptions of Israelite cities, listed alphabetically.)

312

CITIES, HELLENISTIC. — One lasting effect of the Hellenistic* movement in the Middle and Near East was the creation of some 350 Hellenistic cities, over 30 of them in Palestine. They were not necessarily newly built nor was there any large immigration of Greeks or Macedonians into the East. Rather, existing towns, most of which had been independent for generations, were remodelled according to a system of town planning and organization known as the "polis" pattern (see Hellenism in the Near East*). The effect was to revolutionize the old organization and way of life. Economically and socially the new towns forged ahead.

In Palestine, the Hellenistic cities were concentrated mainly in the coastal region and Transjordan. A few were also scattered in other parts of the country.

Coastal Cities: All along the coastal region, from Tyre in the north as far south as Rafiah, Hellenistic cities flourished. Depending for their livelihood on overseas trade, they became linked to the countries of the eastern Mediterranean, especially Ptolemaic Egypt. Only a few of them were founded during the Hellenistic period and most of them preserved their former names.

Chief among them were (from north to south): Acre-Ptolemais; Dor-Dora; Straton's Tower (originally founded by Sidonians, it later became Caesarea*); Apollonia; Joppa; Ashdod*; Ashkelon*; Anthedon; Gaza; Rafiah. Of these, only three (Ptolemais, Apollonia, Anthedon) have Greek names. Acre became Ptolemais when Ptolemy II Philadelphus (285–246 BCE) founded a Greek city there, although a small Greek trading community had lived there even before Alexander's conquests. Apparently, part of the population was also Greek in Anthedon (north of Gaza). As another Anthedon existed in Boeotia in Greece, it is quite possible that some of its inhabitants founded the new city in Palestine. It does not seem that there were Greek or Macedonian inhabitants in any other towns but nevertheless their populations were granted the same privileges as a Greek town. It is also known that after Alexander the Great destroyed Gaza, he built a new city and invited the people of the surrounding countryside to settle in it. Apollonia was named after the Greek God Apollo, but the god officially worshipped in the town was the Canaanite Reshef. Presumably they were identified, as so often happened in the Near East (see Canaan, Gods and Idols*: Canaan and Cyprus).

The Ptolemies of Egypt and the Seleucids of Syria regarded the Hellenistic cities as more likely to be loyal to their regimes than the native populations. They encouraged eastern towns to hellenize by granting special privileges to a new "polis". The same rule held good for the Greek cities of Palestine (explained in detail under Hellenism in the Near East*). The coastal towns had a special importance. They were the big trading centres for the country and the continued operation of their ports was essential. This depended on the goodwill of their inhabitants which could best be ensured by favourable treatment of the cities and their people (see map under Hellenism and Jewry*).

Transjordan and the Decapolis: It is not quite clear whether the cities here were built by the Seleucids as a defence against the Ptolemies, or vice versa. Either way, they were ancient towns, remodelled and fortified and, unlike some of the coastal towns, given Greek names. In the Roman period, they joined together to form the Decapolis, or league of ten cities. The exact makeup of the Decapolis is uncertain, however. Pliny the Elder gave a list of the cities but pointed out at the same time that other writers included different names. So far as we know, the towns in Transjordan were: Kanatha, Raphana, Sosita-Hippos, Antioch, Gadara, Abila-Seleucia, Phahel-Pella-Berenice, Dion, Gerasa* (Jerash, see following article), Rabbat-Ammon-Philadelphia. Outside Transjordan, Beth-Shean*-Scythopolis and even Damascus were included. Two of the towns, Dion and Pella, bear the names of towns in Macedonia (Pella was the birthplace of Alexander). These were probably named by Macedonian troops who settled there at the beginning of the Hellenistic period, although as towns they are far older.

Rabbah (Rabbat-Ammon) was re-named Philadelphia by Ptolemy II Philadelphus who founded other Greek towns in Palestine. He may also have given Pella the name Berenice.

Other Towns: Apart from the coast and Transjordan, a few Hellenistic towns were founded in other parts of the country. Paneas (Caesarea Philippi) in the north was rebuilt and renamed while Philip, son of Herod*, was Tetrarch. Its ancient name survives to this day as Banias. In most cases, the Greek names of the towns were forgotten and the older eastern names restored. Thus, Acre (Acco) and Amman can still be found on a modern map, but not Ptolemais or Philadelphia. The remains of the Roman theatre of Amman are shown **(312)**.

Near the Lake of Galilee, the prehistoric town of Beth-Yerah became Philoteria after the sister of Ptolemy III. Another town on the Red Sea was also named after her.

Design: The largest Hellenistic cities were built on a geometric pattern of regular blocks of 80 × 100 yards. The centre of the block was made up of houses with large courtyards, connected to the streets by a passage (see Samaria, below). A similar geometric pattern can still be seen in Damascus, where the existing irregularities in the street plan reflect a process of deterioration of the original ancient design. The geometric design is illustrated by the map of Gerasa **(315)**. It was later rebuilt by the Romans.

Hellenistic Samaria: In the centre of the country, Samaria* was remodelled as a Greek city, probably by Macedonian troops of Alexander. The town was fortified towards the middle of the 2nd c. BCE and a residential quarter reestablished (see Samaria*; Samaritans*).

The simple, systematic Greek plan can still be seen in this plan of a section of the upper city at Samaria (**313**). The city wall, between 7–9 metres thick, was flanked by projecting towers. Inside the wall, the city was divided into rectangular blocks, about 25×47 metres, the central street being lined with shops. A poorer quarter was built on the city's common land. Smaller Hellenistic houses had a central courtyard, the larger ones an internal courtyard for the use of the family and an external one for public use. Samaria was not of great importance during the Hellenistic period, but when Herod* rebuilt it, giving it the name of Sebastieh (Greek for his patron, Augustus), the town attained considerable eminence.

Mareshah and Adorah were two Hellenistic cities in the south of the country. Mareshah had been settled by a large group of hellenized Phoenicians and it accordingly retained its oriental pattern. The streets did not follow any particular plan. Houses were built around a courtyard, the walls erected parallel to each other, with their corners squared. Neither of these two towns played an important part in the life of the country, but the remains of Mareshah are very characteristic of the period as a whole, as shown by this 3rd c. BCE fresco of a hunting scene (**314**).

It is significant that predominantly Jewish towns did not hellenize. In the whole of Judea there was not a single "polis", though at the peak of the hellenizing movement (see Hasmoneans*) an unsuccessful attempt was made to convert Jerusalem* into one. (The influence of the Hellenistic cities on Jewish life and the Jewish attitude towards them is considered under Hellenism in the Near East*.)

New Testament Period: By the beginning of the Roman period, many of the towns had regained their independent status. Like the Seleucids, the Romans were well aware of the value of securing the loyalty of the cities by means of special privileges. During Herod's reign, the predominantly pagan Hellenistic cities which followed a generally similar cultural and religious life were specially favoured. This helped to bring about strained relations between Herod and the Jews. Herod beautified many towns, notably Jerusalem. In addition to Sebastieh-Samaria, he built or re-built Caesarea (Straton's Tower), the palace area at Jericho and others.

During the Roman period, fortified cities and trading centres, running from the coast to Jerusalem, from Galilee and the Decapolis in the north to Petra* in the southernmost Negeb, became a focus of cultural life. Nevertheless, in spite of their commercial and cultural importance for the area, they did not exercise any marked influence on Jewish life. This was the result of the long-standing enmity between the Jewish and pagan communities and the deep-seated hostility of the Jews towards everything Hellenistic or Roman.

Gerasa, the most representative city of the Decapolis, is described below. Petra is described under Nabateans*.

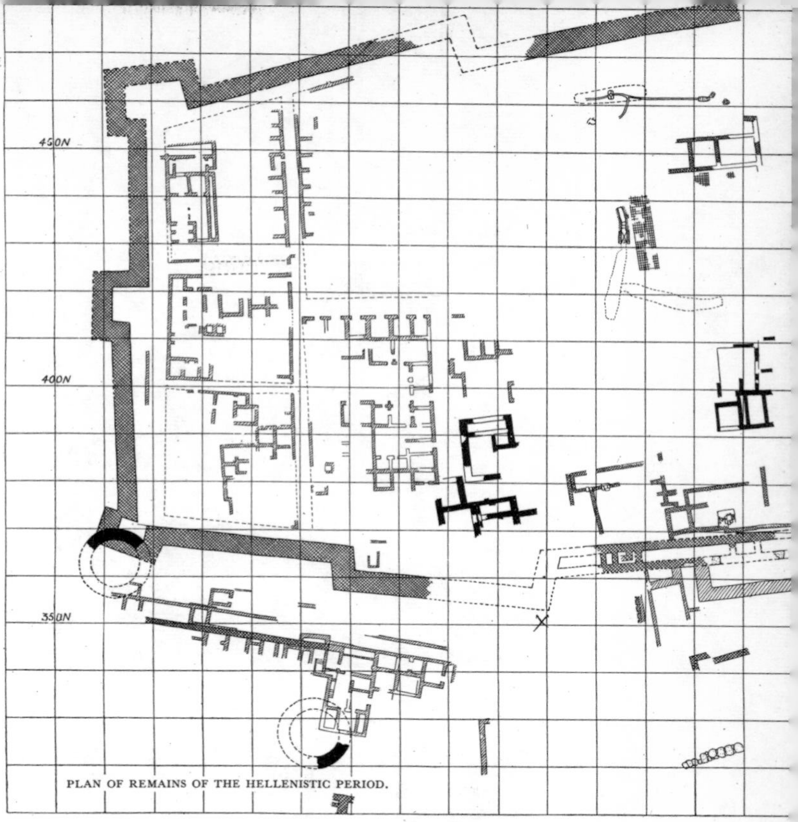

PLAN OF REMAINS OF THE HELLENISTIC PERIOD.

313

GERASA (Jerash). — Gerasa (Gerasha in Aramaic, Jerash in Arabic) remains one of the best preserved Roman towns in the Middle East — the "Pompeii of the Near East". Situated some 20 miles east of the Jordan and about 27 miles north of Rabbath-Ammon, on the river Chrysartoas (one of the tributaries of the Jabbok), the site was first settled in the Early and Middle Bronze Age. It lay along the eastern extension of the King's Highway (see Roads*).

History: The town first came into prominence, however, during the Hellenistic period. Veterans of Alexander the Great's campaigns were settled there at the same time as other Macedonian cities were being founded in the area (see Cities, Hellenistic*; Hellenism in the Near East*). The town was ruled by the Egyptian Ptolemies until the conquest of Palestine by the Syrian Seleucids in 200 BCE. Antiochus IV, the second of the Seleucid rulers and an energetic sponsor of the hellenization of his dominions, founded a sister Greek city beside it, called "Antiochea on the River Chrysartoas". The Greek subtitle for this new city stated that it had formerly been "the town of the Gerasites, a holy town and a city of refuge" (see Conquest*; Law*).

Gerasa remained an independent Hellenistic city until conquered by the Hasmonean, Alexander Jannaeus, in 82 BCE. According to Josephus, he died while laying siege to the fortress of Regeb nearby (see Hasmoneans*). Later it was among the towns captured by Pompey in the first

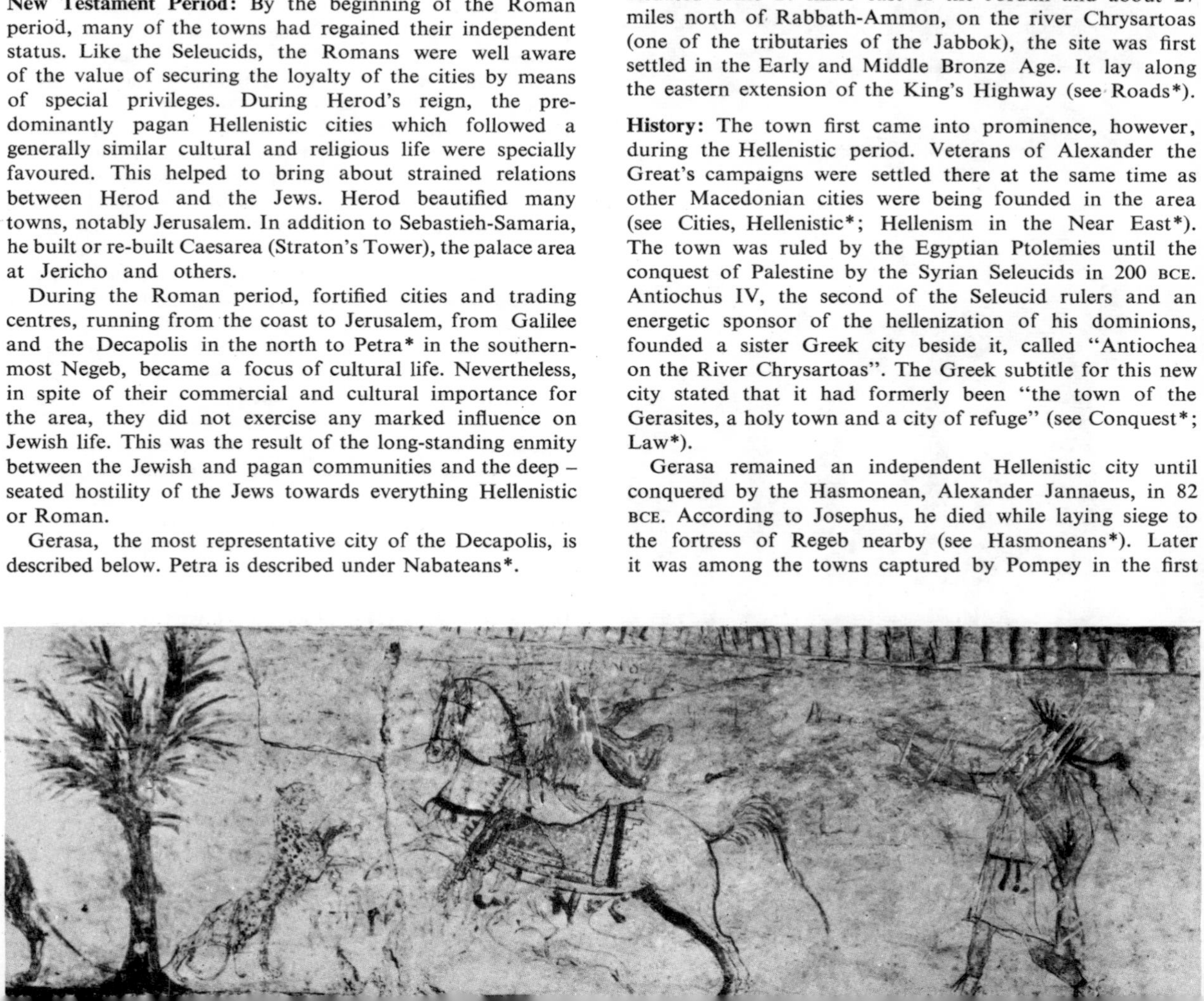

314

315

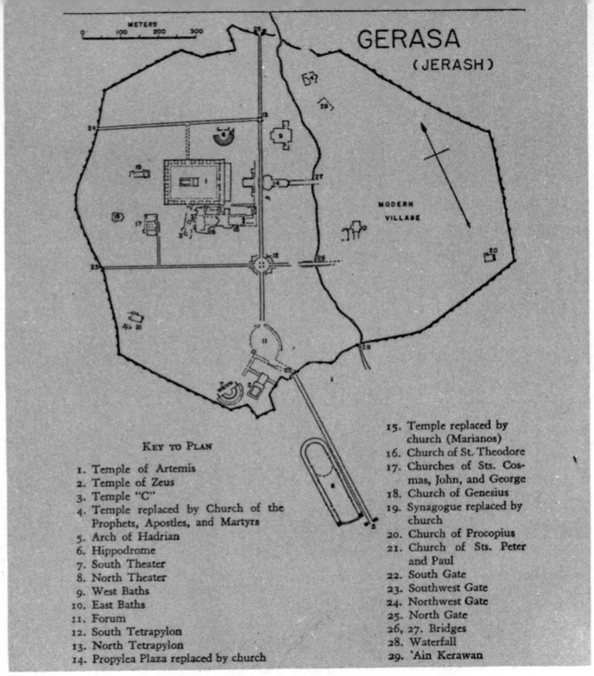

316

317

major Roman expedition against Palestine (63 BCE; see Rome and the Jews*), when Roman control over Syria was firmly established. The independent Hellenistic cities scattered through Palestine and Transjordan became organized into a defensive league, the Decapolis, and this appears to have included Gerasa. The town is not mentioned as a member of the league in the early records, but the fact that its inhabitants adopted the Pompeian calendar suggests that it was included. In any case, it was Roman policy to encourage Hellenistic elements within their provinces and under Roman rule Gerasa enjoyed a certain degree of independence and a greatly increased commercial importance and activity. The peace and security brought by Rome were a great encouragement to international caravan trade. The flow of merchandise from the south of Arabia to Transjordan and northwards to Damascus and Palmyra brought Gerasa a long era of prosperity. In 106 CE the city and its region became part of the new "Provincia Arabia" founded by the Roman emperor Trajan. To commemorate the visit of a later emperor, Hadrian, in 129 CE, a big memorial arch was erected south of the city's main gate. The 2nd c. CE was Gerasa's "golden age" and during this time most of its public buildings were erected (see Excavations below and map **315**).

The town was the centre for a busy and important district, an area famous for its good oil (Mishnah, Menahot 8, 3). Gerasa's administrative area included biblical Eglon, as witness a milestone found in Eglon, giving the distance from Gerasa. Gerasa's southern boundary with Philadelphia (present-day Amman) was formed by the River Jabbok.

Excavations: Between 1925 and 1935, the site was excavated by an expedition representing various institutions (Yale University, the American School of Oriental Research, Transjordan Department of Antiquities) and led by J. Garstang, G. Horsfield, J. W. Crowfoot, C. S. Fisher, C. C. McCown and C. H. Kraeling. They found that the impressive Roman town had been planned and built during the first two cs. CE over and around the earlier Hellenistic city. The site lies in an open valley of fertile fields between the mountains, divided from north to south by the Chrysartoas river and supplied with ample water by springs and tributaries flowing into the river. The commercial centre of the Hellenistic town had been built towards the south of the site, around the junction of one of these tributaries with the Chrysartoas. The Romans filled in this area, covering the earlier buildings and raising the river bed a full ten metres.

Their new town was surrounded by a strong wall about 3.5 km. long (2.2 miles), 3.5 metres thick and fortified by towers at intervals. The main street, the Via Antoniana ran north and south, to the west of the Chrysartoas, leading to the town's main gate in the south. Two other gates in the western wall were connected to east-west highways. The approach to the main gate ran past a hippodrome with seating for 15,000, while the gate itself was composed of a central doorway flanked by two wings with niches. A Temple to Jupiter (**319**) stood to the west of the gate and nearby was a theatre able to hold 3,000. The Via Antoniana ran beside a semi-circular forum (**317**) from which a road led to the southern "tetrapylon" (**316**, a double-arched building of four groups of four columns each placed on a high rock, together supporting a huge dome). Further north along the road, colonnaded on both sides, was the northern "tetrapylon", which is a beautiful example of this type of building (see plan of Gerasa). The northern city gate had a single doorway, with domed niches on either side.

The eastern half of the city is today covered by a modern Arab village so that, apart from two baths and a few small temples which had been converted into churches during the Byzantine period, very few discoveries were made on this bank of the river.

Temples: On the western bank, between the river and the Via Antoniana a "temple area" was found around the junctions of the two east-west roads with the main north-south highway. The patroness of the city was the goddess Artemis and her huge temple (500 metres long) dominated the area. The temple was reached from the residential quarter on the east bank of the river across a wide bridge, through a triple gate, across the colonnaded Via Antoniana and then into the court of the Propyleum. From this a vast staircase ran up to the central court of the temple, an area 100 metres by 130, with a colonnade running all round it. The temple itself, a peristyle edifice, with columns around it stood in the centre of this court.

In the 4th c., Gerasa, one of the most strongly fortified cities in Transjordan, became an important Christian centre. Pagan worship was prohibited and the former temples were transformed into Christian churches.

The remains of eleven churches were unearthed in the city, two of them, the Cathedral of St. Morianos and the basilica of St. Theodore, just south of the temple of Artemis (**318**). To the west of these were three connecting churches, dedicated to Saints Cosmas, John and George (see map).

Jewish Remains: Clear evidence of Jewish settlement was also found from the excavations. A Roman tomb dated to 130 CE had been built partly with stones decorated with such typically Jewish motifs as the seven-branched candelabrum and a cruse of oil. More important, the remains of a synagogue, apparently built in the 4th c. CE, were found. This is believed to have been one of the first to be built in Palestine in the native style, typical of the flowering of Jewish art in Palestine between the 3rd and 6th cs. CE (see Synagogues*). Its mosaic floor bore a picture of the animals in Noah's Ark but unfortunately only a few fragments remain (see 19 on map). The synagogue was also converted for Christian use in 530–531 CE, but it remains unquestionable proof of the existence of a Jewish community in Gerasa during the 4th and 5th cs. CE (the early Byzantine period).

CLOTHING. *Outline: I. Materials and Textiles: Weaving. II. Types of Garments: Tunic-Keṯônet and Me'il; Cloak-Simlah; Headgear; Footwear and Leather; Tassels and Fringes. III. Early Dress — Middle and Late Bronze Ages: Joseph's "Coat". IV. Late Bronze and Early Iron Ages (Israelite Period —* 1300–930 BCE): *Late Iron Age* (930–600 BCE). *V. Persian and Hellenistic Times. VI. Roman and New Testament Times: Remnants in Dead Sea Caves.*

Ever since Adam and Eve used fig leaves to cover their nakedness (Gn. 3:7), man has made clothes for himself. Clothes serve a variety of purposes. They give protection from the weather (I K. 1:1), they identify the wearer (Gn. 27:15; 37:32) and proclaim his status (Est. 6:8), or they can be worn as a magic charm or because of religious beliefs (Nu. 15:38). In addition, of course, any sort of clothing is also a form of decoration.

Various types of dress are mentioned in the Bible but a clear picture of what clothes looked like can only be gained with the help of contemporary monuments from neighbouring countries in the Middle East. The Hebrews were exiles in Egypt and Babylonia, were ruled by the Greeks and Romans and, more important, lived in a land which was a natural crossroads between the major cultures of the ancient world. Even though actual pictures of them are rare in foreign monuments, it is certain that the Jews, and the early Christians after them, dressed in much the same way as the peoples around them. They knew and must have been influenced by the style of dress of the Syrians, the Canaanites and Phoenicians, the Assyrians and Babylonians, the Greeks and the Romans.

318

319

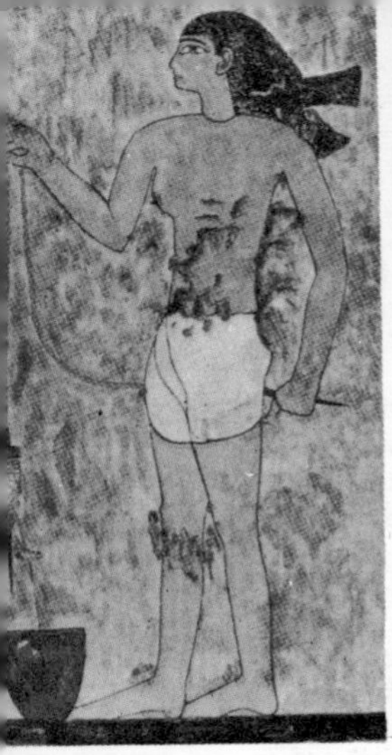

320 b

320 a

319

320

321

322

I. MATERIALS AND TEXTILES: The earliest materials used were the skins of animals (Gn. 3:21; He. 11:37). To make fitted garments out of the bulky, oddly shaped skins, they were cut and sewn together.

In biblical times, the basic textiles were wool (Pr. 27:26) and linen (Pr. 31:13; Lv. 13:59). The word translated "silk" in the English Bible (Ezk. 16:13) cannot mean this, as the silk worm was at that time unknown in Palestine and neighbouring lands. The word means either fine linen or some kind of foreign garment, perhaps a shawl.

Making linen out of flax (Lv. 13:47) is quite a complicated process. First all the outer bark of the stems must be removed (after it has rotted) and the fibres separated. Egyptian tablets show the flax being pressed into tubs of water, and Jos. 2:6 refers to the fibres spread out in the sun to dry. The fibres were then spun into thread (Ex. 35:25–26) and wound onto a spindle held in the hand, as shown is in this Greek vase (6 c. BCE), and Egyptian painting (ca. 19 c. BCE, **320 a, b**). The spindle was spun round in the fingers to tighten and strengthen the thread and, to keep this even, a heavy weight known as a "whorl" **(319)** was attached to one end. The whorls were made of clay or stone, and the large number of them found in nearly all excavations is evidence of the universal practice of the craft. It was carried on by housewives (as described in Pr. 31:19) rather than by tradesmen, whereas weaving was a trade (Ex. 28:32; II K. 23:7); see Greek women working wool **(322)**.

Weaving: The threads were woven into cloth on a loom made from a long beam (I Sam. 17:7) supported by posts or in some other way. The "warp" threads were hung from this beam, weighted down by stones or other "loom weights" **(320)** to keep them steady. The weaver threw his shuttle, carrying the long "weft" thread, backwards and forwards between the warp to make the cloth (Job 7:6; Jud. 16:14). The biblical loom was upright, not horizontal, and the weaving was done from the top down. This type of loom (illustrated in this Egyptian model, **321**) seems to have been borrowed from the Mediterranean area. The word for warp ("shti" in Hebrew) has been said to come from Mycenean Greek (see Crafts*). When the piece was finished, the ends of the threads were knotted into fringes to prevent unravelling. After all his tedious work, the weaver was naturally reluctant to see the cloth cut. Instead of making fitted garments, the rectangular piece of cloth would usually be draped around the body, fringes and all, as explained below (Tunic).

The Egyptians excelled in the making of fine linen, often dyeing the threads to weave coloured or patterned cloth, or embroidering the finished goods. The Hebrews must have learned some of these skills during their stay in Egypt so that, later on, they were able to build the tabernacle with "blue and purple and scarlet and fine twined linen, wrought with needlework." (Ex. 26:1). In early days, the yarn was dyed before weaving in cold vats, like those of the installation at Debir **(323)**, which dates from the 8th–6th cs. BCE. In the post-Exilic period, hot vats were used for dyeing woven cloth, as was customary outside Palestine.

II. TYPES OF GARMENTS: Clothing is frequently referred to in the Bible but the terms used, scattered through all the books, often denoted different garments. Nor is their translation consistent every time they appear.

The earliest undergarment was probably the kiltlike loincloth worn next to the skin, called *ezôr* (II K. 1:8; Mt. 3:4; Is. 20:2; Jer. 13:1 ff). Many Egyptian paintings (**324**) show such a garment wrapped around the loins and tied with a belt or girdle (ḥagorah).

For religious functions, a shirt or apron was tied around the body (I Sam. 2:18; II Sam. 6:14). It is translated "ephôd", but this word refers to an elaborate priestly garment (Ex. 28:6–12; see Priesthood*).

In general, the most common garment was the tunic, the *k^{e}tônet*, *chiton*, or *tunica* (Jn. 19:23).

Tunic-K^{e}tônet and Me'il· This tunic or outer garment was made by simply folding a rectangle of cloth in half and sewing up the sides, leaving openings for the head and arms. This could be worn open or closed, with or without sleeves, depending on the people or place. The Hebrew word *k^{e}tônet* and the Greek *chiton* sometimes refer to garments like this (**324a, b**). The most usual Hebrew term for a top garment, possibly worn over the tunic, is the *me'il* (I Sam. 2:19; 28:14; I Ch. 15:27), although in many cases English versions wrongly translate the term "coat" (see Joseph's coat, below). Apparently it was also worn by people of high rank. Such a costume is pictured in a borderstone of a Babylonian king (ca. 1100 BCE) although this one was collarless and had short sleeves ending above the elbows (**325**). Later on, evidence from the New Testament (Mk. 6:9; Lk. 3:11) suggests that at times people wore two coats, as explained below.

Cloak-Simlah: In Old Testament times, most peoples of the Bible lands wore a shawl or cloak made of wool or linen draped fairly closely around the body over the tunic. Various biblical terms for this garment, translated in many different ways, are the cloak-*simlah* (Dt. 10:18; 21:13; Ruth 3:3) or *salmah* (Mic. 2:8; I K. 1:1; see below, Early Dress). The *tsa'iph* (long veil, Gn. 24:65; 38:14), the woman's upper garment, is apparently illustrated by a 4th c. BCE Phoenician carving of a woman and priest (**335**). She is wearing the garment usually called *himation* or *pallium*. Jewish law (Dt. 22:5) makes it clear that women's clothing differed from men's. The *saddîn* (Jud. 14:12) was, according to S. Yeivin, also worn by men and was not an exclusively female garment, as has been assumed. It may have been similar to the outer cloak (simlah) that was worn, for instance, by King Jehu and his attendants bringing offerings to King Shalmaneser, shown in the black obelisk of Shalmaneser (see illustrations under Israel and Judah*).

Soldiers wore armour and helmets of leather or brass according to the styles of the different periods (e. g. I Sam. 17:5).

Headgear: The Bible tells how fine linen was wrapped around the head of the High Priest as a turban or mitre — the *sanîph* or *kidaris* (Ex. 28:39). This term is translated in a number of ways, but it appears in different places, each time, apparently, denoting the same specific headdress (Is. 3:23; 62:3; Zech. 3:5; Job 29:14). Ordinary people wore

323

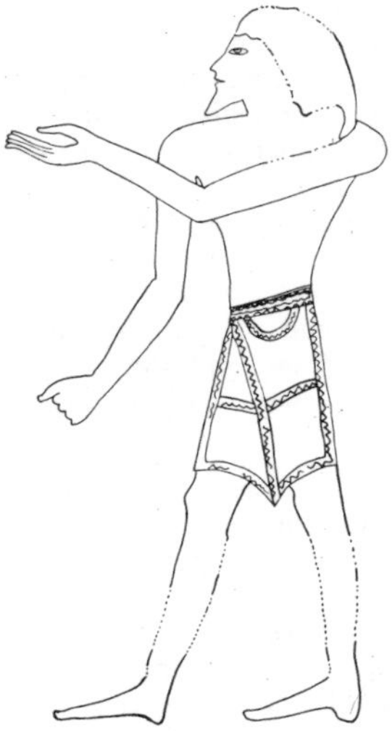

324

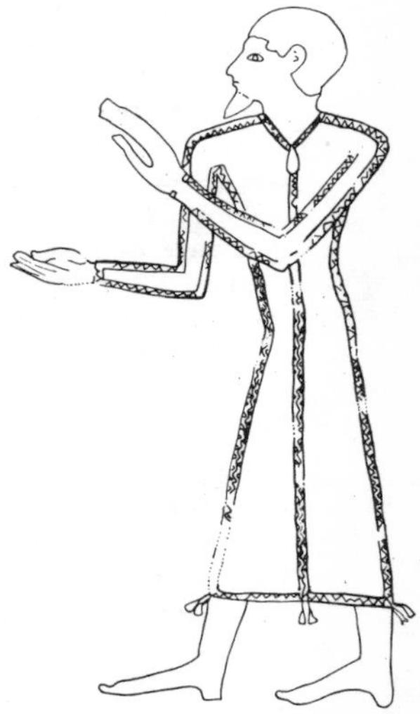

324 a

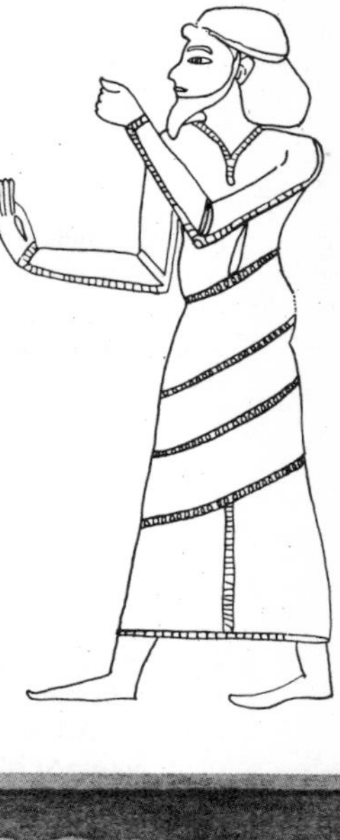

324 b

325

a kerchief over the head, held tight by a cord reminiscent of the Arab headdress, the "'aggāl". When bareheaded, men wore a fillet to keep their long hair in place. A skull cap or turban was also typical. The peasant or soldier seems to have wound a simple strip of cloth around the head, leaving one fringed end to hang over the right ear.

Footwear and Leather: In ancient times men generally went barefoot indoors but outside they protected their feet with a sandal usually made of a simple sole of untanned leather, tied on with straps or latchets (Gn. 14:23; Mk. 1:7). A sandal was the cheapest thing one could imagine (Am. 2:6) — only the shoe-strap was worth less (Gn. 14:23). The Egyptian Beni Hassan painting **(326)** shows men wearing thonged sandals, while the women have soft low boots of a kind still found in western Asia a few decades ago. In the black obelisk of Shalmaneser (Isr.*), however, Jehu's attendants, in contrast to the Assyrians, are wearing shoes which cover their feet completely (cf. Ezk. 16:10). Shoes had to be removed in certain circumstances (Ex. 3:5; Jos. 5:15; II Sam. 15:30). In later times a much greater elegance was achieved. A good example of second century CE footwear is the child's sandal **(275)** found, with its straps still intact, in a cave of Nahal Hever, last hideout of Bar-Kochba's* partisans. The other sandals were worn by adults. In the same cave, pieces of leather which had once formed part of a garment or bag **(327)** were also found and nearby, two samples of sewn leather which had once belonged to an outer coat.

Tassels and Fringes: Jewish people were required by their law (Nu. 15:37–41; Dt. 22:12) to put tassels (tzitzît or fringes) on the corners of their garments with a blue cord intertwined in them. This tradition is still followed by observant Jews during services, in the tasselled *tzitzît* knotted on the four corners of the *tallit*, the big fringed, four-cornered prayer shawl shown in this picture **(329)**. The large *tallît*, usually made of wool, was worn only during morning prayer and in the afternoon and for all services on the Day of Atonement. However, a special undergarment, the "arba kanfot" (four corners) or "tallît kātān" (small tallît), was worn perpetually during waking hours under the outer garment.

The blue dye for tzitzît was obtained from the Mediterranean sea snail (murex) from which the ancients (mainly the Phoenicians*) obtained blue and purple dyes. Because the use of shellfish gave rise to certain difficulties, the Talmud (Menahot 38a) later taught that all fringes might be white. Every male garment originally had tzitzîts and wearing them differentiated a zealous Jew from his neighbours. Later on, however, they were worn only on intimate garments or in the synagogue.

III. EARLY DRESS — MIDDLE AND LATE BRONZE AGES: Some idea of the style of dress in Canaan during the Patriarchal period and up to the Israelite conquest can be gained from contemporary Mesopotamian statuary and Egyptian paintings. In the opinion of S. Yeivin, the Patriarchs and their families probably dressed very much like the Amorites of Mari* and Mesopotamia. A statue of a man, Abi-Il (or Abi-Hil) from Mari* **(330)** shows him dressed in fur from the waist down. The goddess Ningal of Ur was pictured wearing a dress made of a series

326

327

328

of woollen bands wound around the body, one on top of the other. The 19th c. BCE tomb painting of Beni-Hassan showing the caravan of Ibsha and his Beni-Ammu, illustrates west Asian clothing of the earlier Middle Bronze Age

329

330

331

until the period of the Hyksos. Besides the kiltlike garment worn by some of the men, others wear a woven garment draped over the left shoulder and leaving the right arm free, as described above (Tunic). The women wear a similar garment, also with the left shoulder covered. Everyone is bareheaded (**326**).

The Egyptians pictured "Syrians" — peoples of the lands to the north-east of Egypt — on the walls of the tombs of Thebes, in the Karnak relief of Seti I, the reliefs of Ramses II and the Ramses III tiles of Medinet Habu (**328**) which show well-dressed Canaanites of the 12th century BCE. The figures also appear in the Amarna illustrations. They are all shown wearing a long under garment (tunic) reaching almost to the ankles and covered by a cape (? me'il) worn loosely over the shoulders. The figures of Asiatics appear mainly in scenes of vassal states bringing their produce or tribute to Egypt. Foreign prisoners of war are also pictured.

A variation in dress was provided by wrapping a sari-like band (? the simlah or salmah) around the lower part of the long-sleeved tunic (or k^e^tônet). The ankle-length k^e^tônet was often gaily decorated in red and blue around the edges and on a broad band running down the front. Under this a shirt was worn. Over it men of high rank wore a mantle fastened over the left shoulder, while women wore a second tunic, wider and shorter than the first, as is shown in a Canaanite ivory carving from Megiddo (**331**).

Joseph's "Coat": Unfortunately, there is no contemporary picture of the "coat of many colours" as rendered in older translations of the Bible, which angered Joseph's brothers (Gn. 37:23) and was worn by Tamar (II Sam. 13:18), although many possible models have been suggested. The Revised Standard Version of the Bible renders the garment as a "long robe with sleeves". Many scholars believe it to have been a tunic or robe made of a material woven from different coloured threads, similar to the costumes in the Egyptian Beni-Hassan painting shown above, in which some of the tunics are made of vertical strips of woven or embroidered material in bright colours, blue and red predominating. Other scholars are of the opinion that it may have been a long-sleeved tunic reaching to the ankles.

IV. LATE BRONZE AND EARLY IRON AGES (Israelite Period — 1300–930 BCE): The Canaanite ivory carvings of Megiddo (12th c. BCE) show that there was little change in the basic garments from the previous period. Ivories of court and other scenes, show the men wearing long sleeved robes over a coloured tunic (k^e^tônet), embroidered in geometric designs. Over their robes the simlah is wrapped closely around the body, leaving the right shoulder and arm free. On their heads, they have close-fitting caps (**331**).

The women are also dressed in long robes (simlah), trimmed at the neck. Some are sleeveless, some with loose sleeves, showing the long sleeves of the undertunic (k^e^tônet) Some are worn open in the front, decorated with embroidery all around the edges, and with long tassels hanging down in front. One woman wears a wide, flat-topped headdress like a crown, over a kerchief. In contrast, the singer is bare-headed, with her hair spread over her shoulders. She may possibly represent a "kedeshah" (temple-priestess).

332 a

332 b

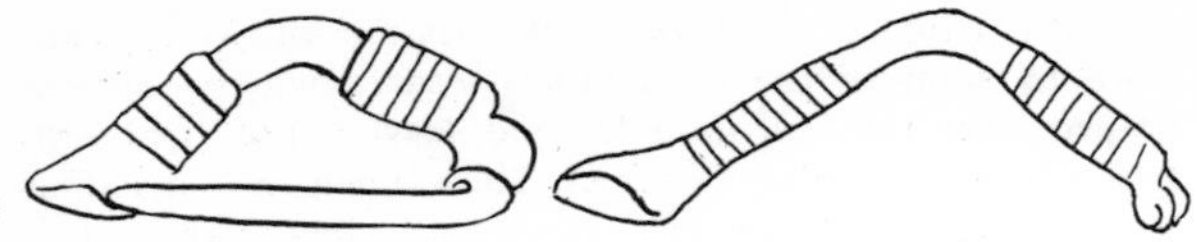

333

334

An Assyrian law stipulated that a respectable married woman must cover her head, while an unmarried girl must go bareheaded.

The carving presents a court scene so it may not be a very good indication of ordinary Israelite costume of the period. It does show, however, that Iron Age garments were no longer fastened by means of pins (**332a** with holes in them), but made use of fibulae (buckles; **332b**).

Egyptian paintings of this period show "Syrian" prisoners working in loincloths, with tassels at the corners (**324**). Another Megiddo carving (**325**) has soldiers dressed only in a short tunic. (See dress in **165**, **156–9**.)

Late Iron Age (930–600 BCE): The black obelisk of Shamaneser III of Assyria (9th c. BCE) shows him receiving tribute from Jehu, king of Israel (Israel*). Some of the Assyrians wear fillets on their hair, flat sandals and long, short-sleeved robes with fringes at the bottom, tied with a tasselled sash. Others are wearing a long skirt with fringed shawls wrapped around the shoulders and waist, similar to the costume of Shamsi-Adad V (**333**) of the 9th c. BCE. The Assyrian king wears a fez-like cap on his head.

The Israelites wear a long skirt or tunic — very little different from what was worn at the beginning of the Israelite era. Over it they wear an open short-sleeved mantle fastened on the shoulders, and with fringes and tassels along the edges. Some of them wear fillets on their heads and others, including King Jehu, have a soft pointed hat, rather like the Phrygian cap. All of them are wearing shoes which cover the foot and turn up at the toes.

In the Assyrian sculpture of the capture of Lachish*, captured Jewish men are shown dressed either in a moderately tight garment fitting closely at the neck (Job 30:18) and reaching almost to the ankles, or in a short sleeved tunic and kilt-like garment, of the type worn in earlier epochs. They wear a head-band with ends hanging about the cheeks, which are often shaved. The women have a mantle like a long veil wrapped around the body and covering the forehead.

There is a relief in Zinjirli which shows two Arameans wearing tasselled caps and a long fringed shawl wrapped about the body over an undertunic, with a tasselled corner hanging over the right shoulder. On their feet they have shoes with curved soles.

V. PERSIAN AND HELLENISTIC TIMES: Tunics, sashes and robes were still worn, modified by changes in fashion. Loose belted tunics were worn with long loose sleeves. Some Persians are pictured wearing coats and trousers, which may explain the reference in Dan. 3:21. A Phoenician funeral stele (**335**) shows the dress of well-to-do people of the time. Unlike the Jews they usually shaved their faces. They wore a small bonnet with a flat foundation and, like their neighbours, the tunic "without seam". This was made of two rectangular pieces of cloth sewn together over the shoulders and at the sides, without being cut. An opening was left for the head and the arms, and the garment was wide enough for a sort of half-sleeve to form of itself. A girdle held the folds in place and allowed different draped effects. In this example, it was very full in front where the braid edges of the material can be seen (**335**). The Jewish High Priest apparently wore a very similar garment, judging from descriptions in rabbinical literature (see Priests*). A garment of this type was still in general use in New Testament times (Jn. 19:23). A long white linen tunic became the chief garment of the ordinary Jewish priest of the later period. It had sleeves which, for special occasions, were tied close to the arms (Josephus, Ant.).

A king of Byblos was shown in adoration before the Great Goddess of his city **(334)** wearing a toque with a flat foundation from which two ribbons hang down, and a shawl folded triangularly, which may be the garment referred to in Dt. 22:12. The regulation was still observed in New Testament times (Mt. 9:20; 23:5).

Hellenistic times had brought the Greek way of dressing to the country, mainly in the upper classes and urban centres. Over their tunics, people wore rectangular pieces of cloth draped around the body in the loose folds of classical times.

Antiochus Epiphanes compelled young Jewish nobles to wear the "*petasos*", the low, broad-brimmed hat associated with Hermes (II Mac. 4:12), like the "epheboi", athletes.

Women during this period generally wore a pleated robe with or without sleeves, as in this 5th c. BCE vase from Attica **(322)**, covered by a large shawl, the *himation*, covering the head and draped elegantly around the body. There is no reason to suppose the Jewish woman dressed in any way differently. Small girls were dressed like their elders and schoolboys also wore a himation, draped over the left shoulder.

For work in the fields, men wore a belted tunic with short, close-fitting sleeves **(324a)**, while for heavy labour or on the water, the kiltlike garment by itself was sufficient.

VI. ROMAN AND NEW TESTAMENT TIMES: Fashions changed little after Hellenistic times, but they acquired a Roman flavour. The most interesting feature about Graeco-Roman clothing of the first century CE was the manner in which a long piece of cloth, the "chlamys" as the Greeks called it, or the "pallium" in Latin, was draped over the tunic in a variety of ways. A special variety of the pallium was the "toga". The typical flowing garments of Roman citizens **(337)**, with loose togas and stoles worn over them in various ways as a type of cloak, are shown on a Roman relief of 13 BCE, portraying a religious procession (Ara Pacis).

The wealthy and ruling classes in Palestine no doubt dressed like the patricians of Rome but the clothing of ordinary people — like Jesus and his disciples — was much simpler. Apparently there were six garments: a linen shirt, *halûk*, worn underneath the tunic; the tunic itself "woven without seam" (Jn 19:23); a linen girdle wrapped around the waist (Mt. 3:4); leather sandals for the feet and an upper garment (Mk. 9:3) probably made of white wool, with tassels at the corners. In those days, Jewish teachers covered their heads, so Jesus may have worn a white linen "napkin" *sudarium* like a turban. The *sudarium* was a kind of head kerchief, and is mentioned as a covering for the heads of the dead (Jn. 11:44; 20:7).

Remnants in Dead Sea Caves: Some remnants of cloth and clothing of the period were found in the caves with the other relics of Bar-Kochba's* partisans. There were different pieces of linen and dyed wool **(336b)**, some of them very finely woven, as well as nets **(336a)** and a spool of fine thread wound around a stone.

335

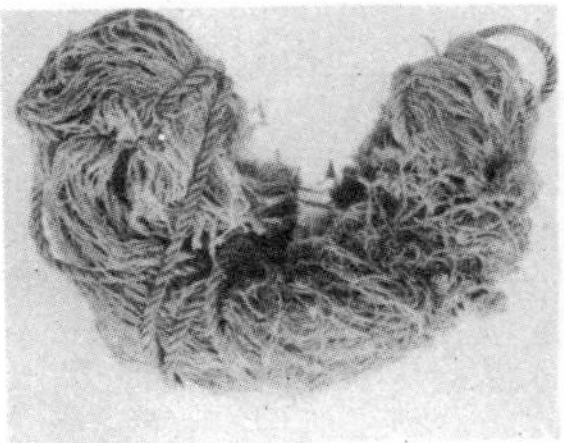

336 a

336 b

337

338

338 b

338

339

339
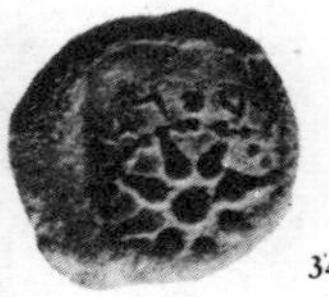
340

340

341

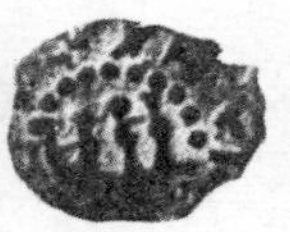

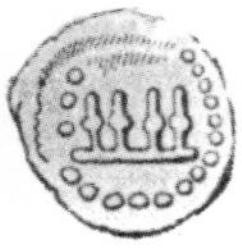

342

342

343

343 b

344

345

345

Costumes in Syria and Palestine during the New Testament period were nothing like the dress of 19th and 20th c. CE Arabs. Much better models are to be found in the portrayals of Easterners in the sculpture and painting of ancient Greece and Rome.

COINS. — Until the Persian period (5th c. BCE), stamped coinage was unknown in Palestine. Instead, quantities of gold and silver were weighed out, using scales (see Weights and Measures*). The basic unit, used everywhere by the Jews, was the shekel weighing approximately 16.4 grams (Ezk. 45:12). Later on, this became the equivalent of four Greek drachmas.

Persian Period: Although coins are known to have been struck in Lydia in Asia Minor and elsewhere as early as the 7th c. BCE, it is assumed that no coins were actually minted in Palestine until the middle of the 4th c. BCE. However, to judge by archaeological evidence, coins were introduced in Palestine at the end of the 6th c. BCE. During the 5th c. BCE, Persian and Greek coins came into circulation, all of them minted in either silver or gold in the great cities and trading centres of Greece and Asia Minor — not in Palestine itself.

Coins were first struck in Palestine probably towards the middle of the 4th c. BCE, when the power of Persia was declining and its subject states were able to demand and obtain many concessions. Against this background, the Jews minted silver coins in imitation of Phoenician and Greek models, some of them bearing the inscription Yhd (Yᵉhud, **338b**) — the official designation of the Province of Judea in the Persian Empire*. These were imitations of Athenian coins. On the obverse, an oriental figure appeared instead of the goddess Athene, but the reverse showed the famous Athenian owl, flanked by the name: Province of Judea. It is not known for certain whether the Persian or Jewish authorities actually issued these coins. Another group, also produced during the Persian period, bear the name of the city of Gaza, where they were minted.

When Alexander occupied Palestine in 332 BCE, he issued a large series of coins in gold, silver and bronze, all bearing his name.

In the Hellenistic period, Ptolemaic and Seleucid coins struck in Syria and Egypt circulated in Palestine. From time to time local coins were also minted in Acre, Joppa, Gaza, Ashkelon and Jerusalem.

Hasmonean Period: With the Hasmonean* liberation of Palestine from the Seleucid yoke, Jewish coins struck by Jewish rulers circulated in Palestine. Although, according to I Maccabees 15:6, Antiochus VII Sidetes granted Simon the Hasmonean the right to mint his own coins, it seems that the first Hasmonean coins were actually struck during the last years of John Hyrcanus I (125–104 BCE), by which time nearly the whole of Palestine was in Jewish hands. The Hasmoneans' coins reflected their nationalist spirit by making use of archaic Hebrew characters and Jewish symbols such as the cornucopia (horns of plenty), etrog (citron), lulāv (palm-branch), palm, libation chalice, fruits, leaf and flower patterns and sheaves of corn, etc. John Hyrcanus issued bronze coins bearing an inscription in old Hebrew: "Jehochanan the High Priest and the Community of the Jews." The reverse shows a double cornucopia (**339**).

His son, Judah Aristobulos I (104 BCE) issued similar coins in his own name. Alexander Jannaeus (104–76 BCE) at first followed the same pattern. When he became king, however, he began striking coins inscribed "Jehonathan the King" in Hebrew and "Alexander the King" in Greek characters (**340**). His successor, John Hyrcanus II (76–40 BCE) made no changes in the coinage, whereas the last Hasmonean king, Mattathias Antigonus (40–37 BCE) issued a wide range of bronze coins in various sizes. One of these showed the Temple's seven-branched candelabrum, the first time this was used on a coin (**341**). The Table of Shewbread is also pictured on another. His coins also carried a bi-lingual inscription: in Hebrew, "Mattathias the High Priest and the Community of the Jews"; in Greek, "Antigonus the King."

Herodian Period: During the reign of Herod* (37–4 BCE) bronze coins were issued in various sizes and large quantities. All of them bore only Greek inscriptions reading: "Herod the King" (**342**).

Herod's three sons, who succeeded their father on his death in 4 BCE, also adopted purely Greek inscriptions, but they did not make use of representations of human figures. The Ethnarch of Judea and Samaria, Herod Archelaus

(4 BCE–6 CE), issued bronze coins with maritime motifs such as ships at anchor, bearing his name in Greek, "Herod the Ethnarch" (**343**). Herod Antipas, (**343b**) ruler of Galilee and Transjordan (4 BCE–39 CE), put the name of his capital, Tiberias, on his coins, which were minted there. Trachonites, Bashan and Golan were put under the rule of Herod Philip (4 BCE–34 CE). He was the first Herodian dynast to put a human figure on his coins. Some of the coins minted in his capital of Paneas (Caesarea Philippi) bear the figure of the Roman emperor Augustus. The coins of the Herodian successors, Agrippa I and Agrippa II, are shown (**344, 5**).

The Procurators: After 6 CE, Judea was made a province of the Romans, administered by procurators (see Rome and the Jews*). They were imperial tax collectors and established themselves in Caesarea. Presumably their mint was also in Caesarea and it was there that the small bronze coins bearing the name of the Roman emperor were struck. Coins like this (**346**) were issued by the procurators Coponius (6–9 CE) and Ambibulus (9–12 CE) in the reign of Augustus. Besides the emperor's name, they also bore characteristic Palestinian emblems: a palm tree or sheaves of corn. Coins were struck by the procurators Valerius Gratus (15–26 CE) and Pontius Pilate (26–36 CE) under Tiberius. Gratus' coins bore familiar emblems like a vine-leaf, a palm tree or an amphora, but Pilate issued coins with distinctly pagan decorations (**347**): Roman ritual vessels, the lituus, or the simpulum, a ladle used for ritual purposes. The lituus was a curved stick in the form of a horn used to draw on the ground the area in which the priests made their observations on sacrificial birds. The procurator Antonius Felix (52–60 CE) was the last to issue coins. He ruled Palestine for Claudius and then Nero and used both Roman and Jewish symbols in his designs (**348**).

First War with Rome: In 66 CE the Jews rebelled against their Roman masters. From the beginning of the revolt, right up to the destruction of the Temple 4 years later, the Jews issued coins from Jerusalem. Silver shekels and half-shekels bore emblems based on life in Palestine and the ritual of the Temple (**349**): chalice and amphora, no doubt used in the Temple, lulāv (palm-branch), etrog (citron), vine-leaves and so forth. The inscriptions read: "Jerusalem the Holy", "For the (or "The) Liberation of Jerusalem", "The Liberation of Zion". After the destruction of the Temple, more than 60 years were to pass before Jewish coins were struck again.

After the Destruction of the Temple: Monetary policy in Palestine had been changing all through the first century CE. Roman coins had been replacing Tyrian (Phoenician*) and other money in the market. This process was completed after the War and, from 70 CE, only Roman coins were used. The Romans minted special coins inscribed in Greek for their Eastern domains and during the first, second and third centuries, Roman tetradrachmas struck in Antioch or Tyre were found throughout Palestine. Within the country, coins were issued by a number of cities, mainly those like Gaza, Ashkelon and Acre, which already had a tradition of minting their own money. Once Roman rule became absolute, other towns were granted the same privilege: Caesarea*, Shechem*, Sepphori, Gadara, Beth-Shean* and others. Later, in the second and third centuries

346 347 347 347

348 348 349 349

349 350 350 350

351 351 352 352

352 353 353

CE, other towns were given the right to strike and issue Roman coins.

The Roman victory over the Jews was celebrated by the minting of a series of coins, circulated throughout the Roman Empire, bearing the inscription "Judea Capta" (**350**). They showed a captive Jew and Jewess, a palm tree, various spoils of war, the victorious Caesar and similar symbols. Commemorative coins like these were also issued in Palestine, presumably minted in Caesarea. They bore the names of the victorious emperors, Vespasian (**351**) and Titus, inscribed in Greek. They circulated in Palestine during the latter part of the first century, at the same time as the coins issued in the Roman cities.

The Bar-Kochba War: During the second Jewish Rebellion under Bar-Kochba*, a series of silver and bronze coins were issued, expressing the Jews' aspirations and carrying appropriate symbols. The inscriptions read "Simon, Prince of Israel" (**352**, Simon Bar Kosba), "Year One of the Liberation of Israel", "The (or "For the) Liberation of Jerusalem" and so forth. One of the coins commemorates the facade of the lost Temple with the Ark of the Scrolls in the background. Other symbols used are mainly ritual sacred vessels from the Temple, amphoras, trumpets and other musical instruments, palm branches (lulāv), etrog (citron), palm tree or bunch of grapes.

These inscriptions were often struck over Roman tetradrachmas, dinarii and other coins in circulation. Jewish artisans removed the human representations and substituted the new symbols and inscriptions. The end of the Bar-Kochba war meant the end of Jewish coinage in Palestine. After that, the money used was made up of bronze coins issued from the principal Roman towns.

Hadrian had a mint set up in Jerusalem, apparently soon after the suppression of the revolt, when the city was made a Roman colony, Aelia Capitolina (**353**). Over the next 130 years more than 200 different types of coins were struck. A similar number were issued by three other towns: Caesarea, Acre and Shechem. The third c. CE was the peak period of coin-minting in Palestine but in 268 CE it was finally abolished by Imperial decree.

CONQUEST. — *Outline: I. Historical Background and Basic Problems: The Biblical Scheme of the Conquest; Contrasting Pictures in Joshua and Judges; Hebrew Occupation of Canaan before the Conquest; Habiru, Hebrews and the Canaanite City States. II. Progress of the Conquest: Conquest in Eastern; Southern; Western and Central Canaan; Egypt and the Conquest; Conquest and Settlement in the North. III. Process of Settlement: Summary.*

The Israelites' conquest and settlement of Palestine remain among the most hotly disputed problems of biblical history and interpretation.

Modern scholars accept the biblical tradition of the Exodus* as being broadly factual. The grounds for this opinion come, first, from extra-biblical sources for the history of the ancient Near East and secondly, from the fact that whereas as a general rule, national traditions emphasize heroic exploits and flattering origins, the Bible tells a realistic story of bondage, oppression and flight which gives an appearance of reliable accuracy to the whole account. The questions that arise from this acceptance of the biblical tradition — the period of the bondage and how many people and clans were actually involved in the Exodus — cannot be finally solved from literary analysis alone, nor from the infrequent and inconclusive discoveries of archaeology. Both approaches, however, can be used to get a little nearer to the probable facts.

I. HISTORICAL BACKGROUND AND BASIC PROBLEMS: **The Biblical Scheme of the Conquest:** The biblical tradition assumes that the mixed group of people who escaped from Egypt (Nu. 11:4) had accepted the religious bond of the Covenant* of Sinai (see article) and been welded into a system of clans named Israel and neatly divided into twelve tribes, right from the beginning. These twelve tribes of semi-nomads then survive the desert wanderings by a series of miracles — which suggest that they were not true nomads and were ill-adjusted to a desert environment. Neither, apparently, were they a strong military entity able to defend themselves against the other tribes of the area. These considerations, in turn, support acceptance of the earlier biblical tradition of Gn. 46:26 which speaks of 70 individuals and not clans (see Exodus*; Census* for a full discussion of the figures). Whatever the case, the number involved in the early stages of the Conquest appears to have been no more than a few thousand, although they were strong enough to destroy the two substantial kingdoms of Sihon and Og north of Moab* (east of Jordan) during Moses' lifetime.

After the death of Moses, the book of Joshua* continues the story with the crossing of the Jordan (3:14 ff) and the capture of Jericho (ch. 6). Thereafter, the book gives a picture of a systematic and rapid invasion which captured western Palestine, gained a foothold on the central highlands with the capture of Bethel (8:1–29); campaigned through Judea (9:1–10:42) and Galilee and finally (11:1–15,23), established the Israelites throughout Palestine, from Beersheba to northern Galilee, within the first generation after Moses. No one questions that the narrative as it stands greatly oversimplifies matters. Nevertheless, many scholars believe that, fundamentally, it gives a correct picture. In support of the basic validity of the account as given in Joshua*, they cite the evidence of certain cities where excavation has found proof of destruction at the appropriate period, perhaps carried out by the Israelites.

The two basic problems that arise are: a. Was the conquest in fact the result of a single coordinated military campaign, as suggested in Joshua, or was it a slow and gradual process of infiltration by each tribe individually? b. Was the conquest followed by the settlement of the Israelites in the land, or were elements of the Israelites entering the country and settling there even before the break-up of the Canaanite organization?

One curious feature of the biblical account is that nothing is said about the conquest of central Palestine (the area between Judea and Galilee) beyond the reference to the defeat of certain kings in that general area, in Jos. 12:17, 18 and 24. The principal city of the area was Shechem* and, while it was apparently never conquered from the Canaanites, it became the scene of the gathering of all the tribes for the Covenant ceremonies described in Jos. 8:30–35 (cf. Dt. 27). It is mentioned again in ch. 24 in connection with the review of the Conquest. This suggests that the area was controlled by friendly tribes with whom the invaders made a "Covenant"* (a religious and political agreement; cf. Jos. 24 for the covenant ceremony), thereby combining the Hebrews with others who could not trace their descent to the fugitives from Egypt. The Bible gives no indication of any migration other than from Egypt. Thus any additions to the Hebrew clans must have come from certain elements of the population already in the land (see Anc. Cit.: Shechem*).

Contrasting Pictures in Joshua and Judges: The book of Joshua is immediately followed by the clear statement of ch. 1 of the book of Judges that the death of Joshua did not leave the Israelites in possession of the land. Thus a coherent picture of the process of Conquest and settlement is only possible if it is assumed that the two books represent different stages of that process and the evidence of extra-biblical documents and archaeological excavations is used to connect the various units of tradition (see Books of Joshua and Judges*).

From a study of all the sources and archaeological evidence relating to the Exodus*, it has emerged that not all the Hebrews were linear descendants of those who had been slaves in Egypt, and that they did not all enter Canaan at the same time. Recent investigation has also made it clear that much earlier confusion arose because scholars mistakenly assumed that the Israelites were originally nomads (or semi-nomads) and that they had always formed a distinct ethnic group. It now seems likely — on the basis of biblical and extra-biblical evidence — that they were not nomads, and that the solidarity of the twelve tribes was not a purely ethnic one. Moreover, the tribes who took part in the Conquest and settlement under Joshua's leadership were not the first and not the only Hebrews in Palestine.

Hebrew Occupation of Canaan before the Conquest: A 13th c. BCE Egyptian document (the Papyrus Anastasi A) includes a reference to what appears to be the tribe of Asher and the same tribe is mentioned in the region of Tyre (precisely the area which the Bible allots to it) in the Phoenician story of King Keret, found on tablets at Ugarit* and belonging to the 14th c. BCE (for additional evidence on the Habiru from the Amarna letters, see Tribes*; Patriarchs*). The name Banu-yamina occurs in texts from Mari*, and this has suggested "Benjamin" to some scholars, although there are insufficient grounds to identify the people named with Jacob's Benjamin. The Egyptian Execration Texts which date from the 18th century (see Egypt*) include the name "Sebulun". Even more significant, the Amarna letters* which are the most important source of extra-biblical information about Canaan in the century or two before the Conquest, make frequent reference to the activity of the Habiru* in undermining Canaanite and Egyptian rule over Palestine.

Habiru, Hebrews and the Canaanite City States: The Amarna letters speak of constant attacks on the authority of the city kings of Canaan and their Egyptian overlords by groups of "Habiru" who tried to win support from the least privileged group in Canaanite society, the "khupšu". These attacks continued throughout the Late Bronze Age, i. e. late 14th and early 13th cs. BCE which may, in one view, have been the time of the Conquest. The Habiru were not a racial group. The Canaanite princes used the term for all enemies who were trying to undermine their regime, describing them as "slaves who have become Hapiru."

The Habiru tactics were, according to the Amarna letters*, the assassination of the ruling prince, and his replacement by a nominee of their own who would owe his throne to the Habiru and be suitably sympathetic to their cause. This would be accompanied by an attempt to organize all the malcontents of the area for defence against any possible Egyptian reprisals. Ironically enough, there was no question of any such reaction. The Egyptians took a quite different view of the situation and, in any case, no gesture they might make could have offset the gradual elimination of Egyptian authority over Canaan that took place under Akhenaton (see Egypt*).

The main difficulty with the view which identifies the Habiru of the 14th c. BCE with the peoples who invaded Canaan under Joshua is that it antedates the events by about a century. However it is a valuable commentary on what happened about the middle of the 13th c., if the picture of a short violent campaign is replaced by that of a much slower and gradual process of infiltration east of Jordan and in western Palestine. The pattern of the conflicts between the Israelites and Canaanites certainly seems to have echoed that of the Habiru of the El Amarna period against the local rulers. In the later case, a religious movement created a solidarity among existing social units which enabled them to defeat the political authority of the Canaanite city-states of Late Bronze Age Palestine and Syria (13 c. BCE).

It is still not certain whether the "Habiru" were in fact Hebrews of an earlier period, or whether they were groupings of dispossessed indigenous peoples who were fighting for land and lower taxes. Their grouping appears to have borne all the marks of an ethnic unit, but this does not necessarily mean that they had a common ethnic origin. One fact which does suggest a link between them and the later followers of Joshua is that the Habiru apparently conquered Shechem at a very early date. Thus the story of the deceitful attack on Shechem by Simeon and Levi, Jacob's elder sons, in Gn. 34 could well be a reflection of the Habiru conquest of the area, and may help to explain why it was possible for the Israelites to establish themselves there without, apparently, having to conquer the town.

In the opinion of G. E. Mendenhall, the general situation in Canaan at the time of the Conquest represents a familiar process of a large population grouping rejecting the authority of an existing political regime and, simultaneously, renouncing any claim to protection from it. Thus, "the appearance of the small religious community of Israel polarized the existing population all over the land; some joined; others, primarily the kings and their supporters, fought. Since the kings were defeated and forced out, this became the source of the tradition that all the Canaanites and Amorites were either driven out or massacred, for the only ones left were the predominant majority in each area, now Israelites," (see Tribes*). This is in line with the view of M. Noth that there was no statistically important invasion of Palestine at the beginning of the 12-tribe system and no radical displacement of the Canaanite population, except for the top layers. In short, the "Conquest" was a revolt of landless peasants against the network of interlocking Canaanite city-states.

In general it is agreed that after their wanderings in the desert, the Israelites did not come to a new country. Some scholars have even described the Conquest as a return, or reunion with kindred clans. It can also be seen as developing out of social relationships already in existence between the Hebrews and the Habiru, which greatly facilitated settlement east of Jordan, the crossing of the river and the penetration of western Palestine. Alternatively, or perhaps in addition, the invaders may well have been welcomed either by related clans who had never left Canaan for Egypt or by the discontented among the Canaanite population, such as the Gibeonites and Shechemites. Either situation would very quickly have created a considerable military potential, leading, in its turn, to extended alliances with other related groups and to clashes with Canaanite cities, first south of Shechem, then in Judah.

II. PROGRESS OF THE CONQUEST: **Conquest in Eastern Palestine:** The Bible gives two versions of the entry of the Israelites into Palestine. Numbers (chs. 13–14) relates an attempt to enter the land from the south which was defeated by a combined attack from the cities of the Negeb, led by the king of Arad, who pursued the Israelites, "even to Hormah", not far from Arad*. In another account

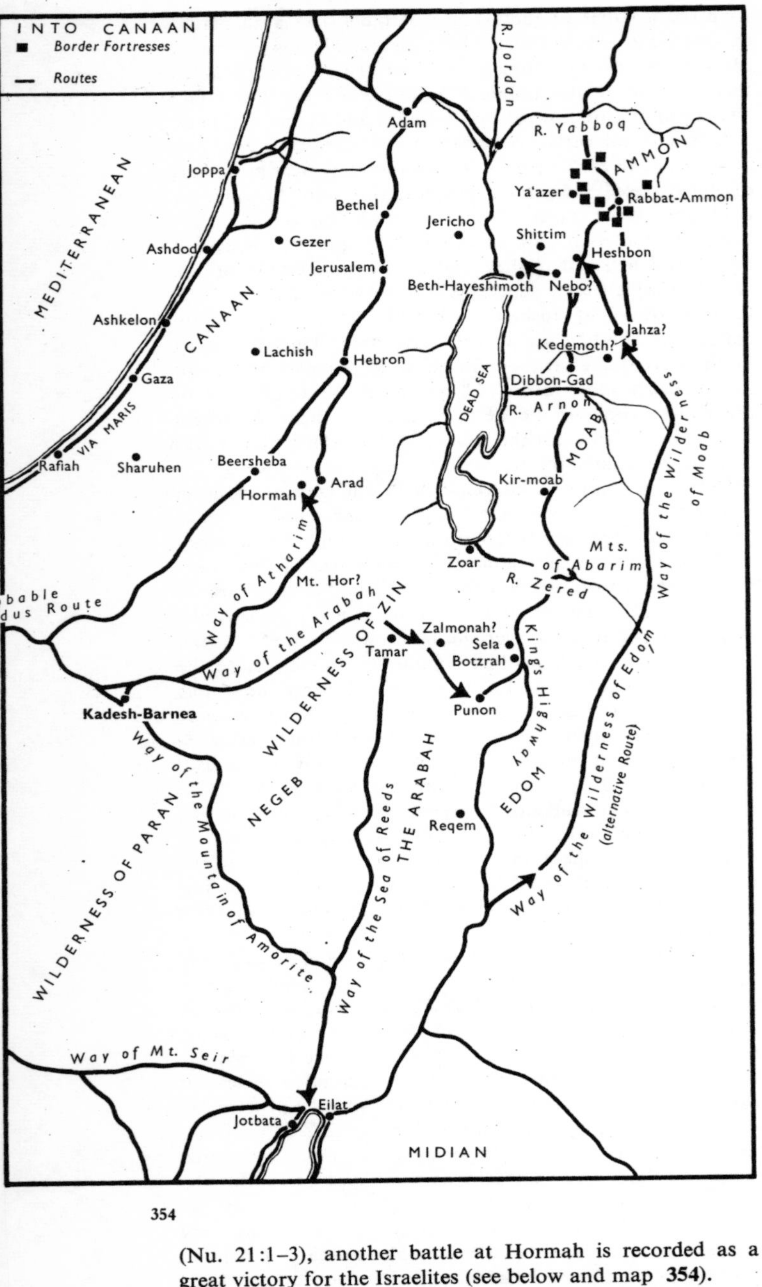

354

(Nu. 21:1–3), another battle at Hormah is recorded as a great victory for the Israelites (see below and map **354**).

The movement of the tribes along the borders of Edom more likely reflects the situation of southern Transjordan before the 13th c. BCE at which time there was no settled occupation of Edom and Moab. The cities along their borders were only fortified when these peoples settled the country during the 13th c. BCE.

The alternate version, Nu. 20:14 ff, records the progress of the Israelites along the King's Highway (20:17, see Roads*), skirting Edom and Moab at a time when, presumably, the two states were already in firm possession of their lands.

The Canaanites, as mentioned above, formed a coalition under the king of Arad to fight the Israelites.

Further victories against Sihon, king of the Amorites (21:21–26) and Og, king of Bashan (21:33–35) were important because they provided the Israelites with a base from which to begin their attacks west of the Jordan. These accounts are followed by the Balaam stories (see Numbers*).

The very conflict in the biblical traditions suggests that the presence of the Hebrews east of Jordan was not so much the result of successive waves of penetration as of a slow process of settlement, which some scholars equate with the presence of the Habiru (see above), during which the local population merged with the incoming Israelites. Although nowhere recorded, many existing clans probably adopted the Israelite religion and, in consequence, filled out the numbers of the twelve tribes. Further evidence of this process is the number of pre-Mosaic historical narratives and customs preserved in biblical traditions concerning this period, e. g. the ballad in Nu. 21 14–15 and the triumph over Moab 21:27–30. The same line of tradition can be seen behind the historical narrative in the early chapters (1–4) of Deuteronomy.

Conquest in Southern Canaan: The process of penetration in this area is another good example of evidence that various groups entered the land independently of the main invasion described in Joshua. For instance, Judges* 1:16 ff refers to the Kenites being in possession of the area around Arad* and Hormah. The clan of Judah conquered its own territory in southern Canaan with the help of Simeon, the Kenites, and the Calebites, the two latter groups being gradually absorbed into Judah.

Conquest in Western Palestine: Joshua tells of a great onslaught on the cities west of the Jordan, all part of a "Holy War of Yahweh" — a very brutal affair on the biblical evidence. Part of it was offensive, part defensive. Altogether, it broke the back of Canaanite resistance although this need not mean that the Canaanite population was completely wiped out. Many made common cause with Israel.

The biblical account has gained support from archaeology. In the excavations of many of the towns of the area a thick layer of ashes testifies to destruction by fire during the 13th c. BCE. This evidence is lacking, most notably, in precisely the two towns given the greatest prominence in Joshua — Jericho* (see article) and Ai. The Late Bronze city of Jericho — the one presumably destroyed by the Israelites — has been almost completely obliterated by erosion. No traces of the famous walls, nor of any other buildings or fortifications of the appropriate period have been discovered. Excavation at Ai* (presumably Et-Tel) has shown that the site was unoccupied for a long time before the Israelite conquest. The tradition about the conquest of Ai is presumably connected with a victory at Bethel* (see article) some 2 km. away. At Bethel, a rich Late Bronze settlement was destroyed during the 13th c. and rebuilt, on a smaller scale and with poorer buildings, shortly afterwards. However, the tradition does not appear to have confused the two towns. The Israelite inhabitants of Bethel were well aware of the existence of a great ruined city in the neighbourhood called "the ruin", "Ai" in Hebrew. The Canaanite name for the place was most likely Bet-Aven. The Israelites explained its existence by a typically gruesome folk story —

that of the stoning of Achan (Jos. 7:1, 18 ff). In much the same way the stone circle of Gilgal, undoubtedly a prehistoric megalithic relic (like Stonehenge), was associated by the Israelites with the place where twelve symbolical stones, representing the twelve tribes, were placed after the crossing of the Jordan.

Campaign in Central Canaan: The book of Joshua follows the capture of Ai with the Gibeonites' request for an alliance which, when granted, included the cities of Chephirah, Beeroth and Kiriath-Jearim. At one time, biblical scholars believed that this story had been entirely invented as an explanation for the existence within the territory of Benjamin of Canaanite cities whose inhabitants had an inferior status to that of the Israelite cities. This may be the case, but it remains true that alliances were certainly made between the Israelites and certain Canaanite groups. The inhabitants of Tirzah, Chephirah and Shechem, for instance, were not molested. Later on they were listed as clans of Menasseh (see **355**). Many scholars believe this phase of the Conquest to represent the invasion of the "Rachel tribes", whose leader, Joshua, was remembered by posterity while other early leaders were forgotten.

By whatever means it was achieved, Israelite occupation of Gibeon and its dependent cities was a serious threat to Canaanite Jerusalem. Accordingly, the king formed a coalition with the neighbouring kings of Hebron, Jarmuth, Lachish and Eglon and made war against Gibeon. His intentions, presumably, were to regain some strategically important territory, take control of the cities of the Gibeon alliance and destroy the Israelite foothold in the Jericho-Bethel region (see map **355**). The ensuing battle resulted in victory for the Israelites, after which, in the manner of the Holy War (see Warfare*), the conquered cities were destroyed. It is just the excessive violence of the 13th c. destructions which makes it possible to associate them with Israelite religious fanaticism. One of the cities ravaged in this fashion was Lachish*, where excavations have unearthed destroyed Canaanite dwellings and temples, plus one of the most important documents for the dating of the Conquest. This is an ostracon (potsherd with an inscription) written in Egyptian hieratic script, listing certain quantities of wheat sent as tribute to Egypt by the local inhabitants and mentioning the fourth year of a certain Egyptian king. The king was most probably Mernephtach, the Pharaoh of the Israel Stele (1219, see Exodus*), in which case the year would be 1220 BCE. As the potsherd was found in the ruins of Lachish, this must have been the year in which the town was destroyed. A number of tels in the region representing the southern anti-Israelite alliance were apparently destroyed at about the same time. Tel beit-Mirsim has been excavated and identified with Debir (Kiriath-Sepher), while Tel-el-Hesi is believed to have been Eglon. This victory put the whole of the southern lowlands of the country, from Jerusalem to to the coastal plain, into Israelite hands and was decisive for the settlement of Judah and Benjamin.

It seems, however, that there were two campaigns, an earlier one against the coalition headed by the king of Jerusalem and another resulting in the destruction of the cities of the coastal Shephela plain — which, according to the biblical record, did not join the coalition. The Bible also claims that Jerusalem* was destroyed, although it does not appear to have been captured by the Israelites, but by Jebusites, from whom David* was to take it in turn later on. It is possible that the Israelites captured it and then lost it again, or perhaps they simply destroyed it and left it to be rebuilt later by the Jebusites. Too little is known by biblical archaeology of Jerusalem's early stratas for any definite conclusions to be possible.

Egypt and the Conquest: One weakness of the Israelites in their new holdings came from the fact that towns like Ashkelon*, Gezer* and Ekron* were either strong enough to stand against them and were not taken, or else were occupied for a time and then abandoned. This is the recently expressed (unpublished) view of D. N. Freedman who points out that Gezer*, for instance, is listed as one of Joshua's conquests whereas it is known to have been captured by Pharaoh Mernephtach in 1219 BCE. The same is probably true of Ashkelon*. Ashdod*, in this author's view is another example:

The book of Joshua (15:47) which assigns Ashdod to Judah, never mentions its conquest and, indeed, there are other indications that Philistine country was outside the area of the Conquest. However, stratigraphic evidence from the most recent excavation of the site (1963, see article), indicates that the last Canaanite city was violently destroyed in the latter part of the 13th c. — the most violent destruction in the whole history of the site, corresponding to the Israelites' destruction of cities elsewhere in Palestine. Apparently the site was abandoned thereafter until the Philistines* came in the first half of the 12th c. and rebuilt the city.

Their position on the Via Maris (see Roads*), the main road between Egypt and the East, made the coastal towns much too important for the Egyptians to be indifferent to their fate. Many scholars believe that the Israelites never penetrated to the key coastal cities, nor to Megiddo*, Taanach or Beth-Shean* in the Valley of Jezreel, which were the main centres of what remained of Egyptian rule. D. N. Freedman, on the other hand, and in the light of the most recent archaeological evidence, believes that they did, although only for a brief period. It seems remarkable that the Egyptian overlords of Canaan should have made no attempt to interfere in the process of the Conquest, yet apart from a very doubtful reference in the "Israel Stele" of Mernephtach (see Exodus*, Egypt*), the Egyptians apparently made no serious move until the second half of the reign of Solomon*. Intrigue and even Egyptian support for some phases of the Conquest may be the answer but, on the other hand, the Egyptians probably never regarded the Conquest as more than a matter of the perennial strife between settled populations and surrounding nomads. At the time it can hardly have seemed serious enough to threaten Egypt's formal control of coastal Canaan. Nevertheless, the Mernephtach "Israel Stele" is evidence that in 1219 the Egyptians recaptured just those cities which the Israelites had conquered in the coastal plain. The Via Maris was vital to the Egyptian empire and the Egyptians dared not let control of it fall into hostile hands, whether those of rebellious Canaanites or nomadic invaders.

The movements of nomads were a commonplace of that age of mass migrations, for instance the Kenites* and the tribe of Jerahmiel penetrated Palestine from the south

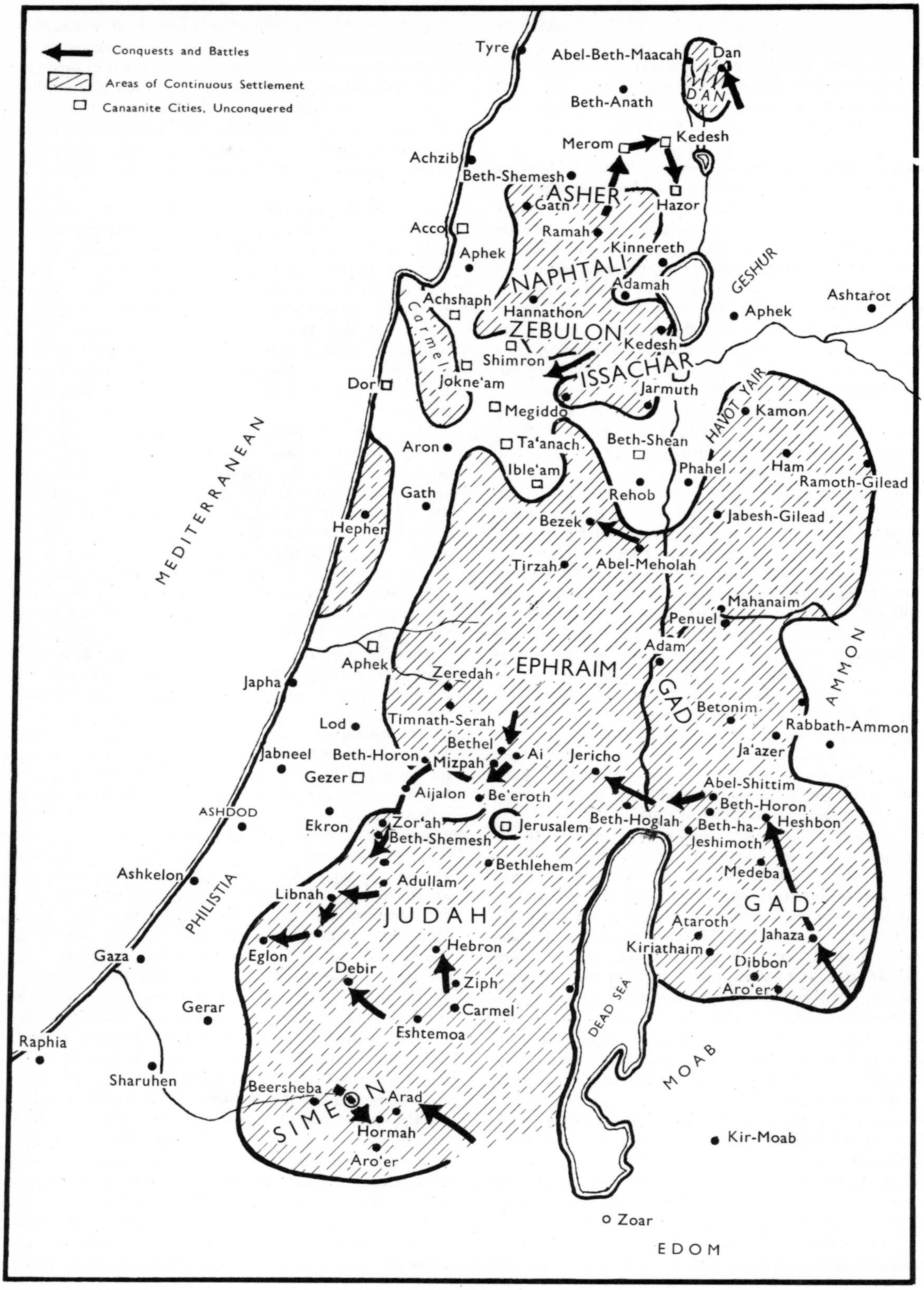
Conquests and Battles
Areas of Continuous Settlement
Canaanite Cities, Unconquered
MEDITERRANEAN
Tyre
Abel-Beth-Maacah
Dan
DAN
Beth-Anath
Merom
Kedesh
Achzib
Beth-Shemesh
ASHER
Gath
Hazor
Ramah
Acco
Aphek
Kinnereth
NAPHTALI
GESHUR
Adamah
Achshaph
Carmel
Hannathon
Aphek
Ashtarot
ZEBULON
Kedesh
Shimron
ISSACHAR
Dor
Jokne'am
Jarmuth
HAVOT YAIR
Kamon
Megiddo
Aron
Ta'anach
Beth-Shean
Ible'am
Phahel
Ham
Ramoth-Gilead
Gath
Rehob
Hepher
Bezek
Jabesh-Gilead
Tirzah
Abel-Meholah
Mahanaim
Penuel
Adam
AMMON
Aphek
Zeredah
EPHRAIM
Japha
GAD
Betonim
Lod
Timnath-Serah
Rabbath-Ammon
Bethel
Jabneel
Beth-Horon
Mizpah
Ai
Jericho
Ja'azer
Gezer
Abel-Shittim
Aijalon
Be'eroth
ASHDOD
Beth-Horon
Zor'ah
Jerusalem
Beth-Hoglah
Heshbon
Ekron
Beth-Shemesh
Beth-ha-Jeshimoth
Ashkelon
Bethlehem
Medeba
Adullam
PHILISTIA
Libnah
JUDAH
GAD
Ataroth
Jahaza
Gaza
Eglon
Kiriathaim
Hebron
Dibbon
Debir
Aro'er
Ziph
Gerar
Carmel
DEAD SEA
Raphia
Eshtemoa
MOAB
Sharuhen
Beersheba
Arad
SIMEON
Hormah
Aro'er
Kir-Moab
Zoar
EDOM

independent of the Israelite tribes, and later made alliances with them. Many scholars argue that any police actions or indirect interference the Egyptians may have undertaken would have had too little political significance to merit their specific mention in Egyptian records (unless the Mernephtach stele records actions of this nature), and were too unimportant spiritually for the Bible to have found space for them. This question has to be left open.

Some of the southern cities — Bethel* for instance — were resettled immediately. In others, such as Ai, Mizpah, Beth-Zur and Shiloh, there was an interval between the latest Canaanite stratum and the first Israelite settlement. More significantly, new cities were founded, e. g. Geba, Ramah and Gibeat-Binjamin (see Saul*).

Conquest and Settlement in the North: The Israelites had then to face a coalition of northern kings, led by the ruler of Hazor* (Jos. 11). Hazor, "formerly the head of all those kingdoms" was destroyed (see Books of Joshua and Judges*), although other fortified cities were left in Canaanite hands. The historicity of this account used to be discounted, scholars assuming that even though the Israelites settled in the north, they had no power to dislodge the Canaanites from their main strongholds. Recent archaeological investigations in Galilee by Y. Aharoni have shown that there was a certain amount of Israelite settlement in the 13th c. or earlier, before the main wave of Conquest. For instance, Asher and Issachar (as indicated in Tribes*) were settled in the north a considerable time earlier. The tribes chose the hilly regions away from the great roads and cities of the plain like Hazor*, Kadesh (later "of Naphtali"), Megiddo* or Beth-Shean*. In the hills, many sites — mainly small settlements with modest fortifications — have been discovered containing typical Early Iron Age (i.e. Early Israelite) pottery* (see article). Later on, the Israelite tribes increased in strength until they began to seem dangerous to the Canaanite cities of the region, who may also have feared that the northern Israelites would unite with their kindred in the hill country around Shechem (Ephraim) or even those of the south. According to this theory, the clash with the Canaanites in the north did not come until Deborah and Barak led the tribes of Israel against Sisera and his forces, as related in Judges 4 and 5. This was the battle further south near Megiddo. It is argued that the account of this battle in Judges, especially the "Song of Deborah" in Jud. 5, belongs to a much older tradition than the source of Jos. 11 concerning Hazor and gives the true picture of events in this area.

This school of thought also believes that the victory not only gave the Israelites control over the north of the country but represented an important gesture of solidarity. After it, the tribal federation was no longer divided by the Canaanite-held Valley of Jezreel, but was on the road to national unity.

This theory has been strongly opposed by Y. Yadin whose excavations of Hazor* proved that the town was indeed destroyed by the Israelites in the 13th c. BCE. If this evidence is accepted as proof of the accuracy of the story in Jos. 11, then the victory of Deborah and Barak came later, in line with the historical sequence of the biblical narratives. The two theories are not necessarily exclusive. D. N. Freedman for instance believes that in spite of the confusion which does exist in the biblical accounts, there is no real difficulty in affirming the conquest of Hazor by Joshua in the 13th c. followed in the 12th or 11th c. by a subsequent battle at Megiddo, with a second fight at Hazor (although this detail may be a reflection of the earlier tradition, especially since neither Jabin nor Hazor are mentioned in Jud. 5, a more reliable source for Deborah and Barak's campaign than Jud. 4; see Books of Joshua and Judges*: the Battle of Merom and the Battle of Deborah).

III. THE PROCESS OF SETTLEMENT: In conclusion it seems that two processes were under way: military campaigns and also, in the opinion of many scholars, a steady infiltration. Even when the military successes of the Conquest proper were over, the process of settlement continued. Many of the tribes even found their conditions worsening. The tribe of Dan, for instance, found itself forced out of its original "heritage" and sent in search of new territories in the north. The tribes of Levi, Reuben and Simeon were too weak to hold and develop their territories as well as some of the other tribes did.

The story of the Conquest reveals itself as concerned with a long drawn-out process, many of the contradictions of the Bible story aristing from the desire to present Joshua as the national leader and successor to Moses.

From the latest research, it appears that the process began in the 14th c., the El Amarna* period, and continued right through to the 12th c. with periods of invasions alternating with fusions with the local peasantry. Thus there was no sudden displacement of populations, nor was there any break in the continuity of Canaanite culture, except for features which were flagrant violations of religious obligations to Yahweh. At the same time there were migrations of individual clans or tribes from one territory to another. Throughout the whole period, a progressive expansion can be traced as, for instance, in this map (**355**) by J. Aharoni which distinguishes four areas of settlement: the southern tribes of Judah and its allies, Simon, Caleb and the Kenites; the central tribes: Machir, Menasseh, Ephraim and Benjamin, with Dan on the western flank; the Galilean tribes: Asher, Naftali, Zebulun and Issachar; and the tribes east of the Jordan: Menasseh, Gad and Reuben. The areas settled by the clans at an early stage and their expanding borders are shaded obliquely, while the fringes into which they spread later and the areas of allied tribes not part of the federation, are marked with loose shading. Between these areas are the Canaanite enclaves: Jerusalem and Gezer in the south; Beth-Shean, Taanach, Megiddo, Jokneam north of the territory of Menasseh, with the western coastal area still in Canaanite hands as vassals of Egypt. Following the results of the latest research, as outlined above, this map attempts to give a more accurate picture of the historical process than the traditional one. Nevertheless, at present not enough is known about the Conquest and settlement for a definitive graphic outline of their successive stages to be possible.

Summary: Two major theories have been put forward as solutions of the problems raised by the confused record in relation to the known historical background (see Section I above). One school of thought sees the Conquest as a process of slow settlement, with the native population polarized around or against the Israelites, giving rise to scattered clashes, conquest and further expansion and reaching a final consolidation only in the early days of the monarchy, at which time the delineation of tribal borderlines listed in Joshua was actually achieved.

Other scholars reject much of this view and instead hold more closely to the biblical account. D. N. Freedman believes that the Conquest actually extended over a much wider area than is generally accepted, and that the Israelites were later dislodged from a number of outposts, retreated and consolidated their position in the hill country of Judah.

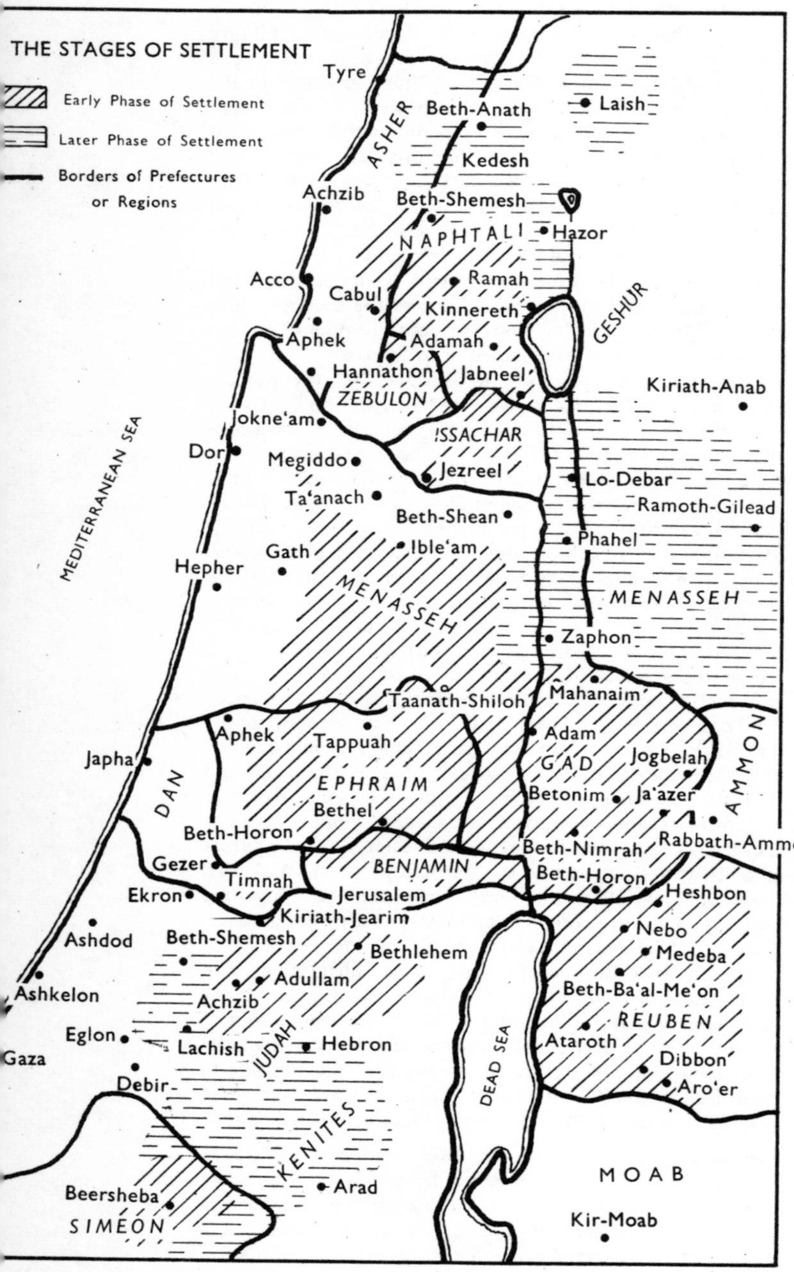

There is a considerable degree of agreement, however, that neither theory need exclude the other and that the campaigns of Joshua were an important phase in a much longer struggle in which each tribe or group of tribes played its part in its own region. Archaeological research has already helped to fix the time and geography of the Conquest—or settlement—but new evidence may yet be brought to light. Discoveries in Egypt or in Mesopotamia as well as in the areas of Palestine itself, could still suggest, for instance, that even more Hebrew clans than have so far been suspected, were firmly rooted in Canaan before the Conquest. Already it is clear that the group who left Egypt at the time of the biblical Exodus were not the majority of what was to be Israel. They may have acted as the catalyst for other Hebrew tribes still in Canaan but their catalyzing effect apparently depended to some extent on political and economic conditions in Canaan operating in their favour. The real inspiration behind the whole movement was the personality of Moses, who lived in the first half of the 13th c. BCE, but whose initiative and genius retained their driving force long after his death.

Following the initial upsurge of the Israelites which he led, the long-drawn out process of incursion and settlement can be seen, in the opinion of D. N. Freedman, as beginning in Eastern Palestine with victories over Og and Sihon. In the course of their wanderings the Israelites picked up recruits and initiated a movement which burnt like a flame across Canaan, destroying cities all over the country. Within the 20–25 years from about 1250 to 1225 BCE, they destroyed most of the country, with certain exceptions like Shechem where the Covenant was renewed by the Israelites from the desert, together with those who were already in the land.

Many cities, like Ashdod*, were destroyed and not immediately reoccupied while some others were rebuilt by non-Israelites. The Israelites themselves were unable to hold all the territory they conquered and were forced back out of the coastal plain, for example, by the Egyptians. Elsewhere they also retreated to stronger positions.

Then came 200 years of wars and conflict, during which the Philistines took over large parts of the country until finally, Saul* and David* were able to gain control of the whole area and establish the Kingdom of Israel.

COVENANT. — *Outline: Definition. I. Covenant with Israel. II. New Covenant (Berith Hadashah).*

A covenant is a compact or agreement between persons or nations, defined in Old Testament terms as a pact made by parties of unequal status, in which the weaker undertakes to serve the stronger, and the stronger undertakes to protect the weaker. The biblical covenants relate to the special ties or relationship between Yahweh and Israel as a nation, and with particular individuals. Even the relation of God to mankind as a whole is described in the Pentateuch* as a covenant. The biblical pacts were usually witnessed by an external "sign" or symbol, such as the keeping of the Sabbath (Ex. 31:13), which symbolized the Covenant of Sinai (see below Covenant with Israel); the ceremony of circumcision (Gn. 17:10) which symbolized the Patriarchal Covenant (see below), and the rainbow (Gn. 9:13) which was identified with God's compact with Noah (see Flood*), in which the Lord promised divine protection of all humanity, fertility and the repopulation of the earth, and gave His word to keep the covenant (Gn. 6:18). The Deity's promise to Adam (Gn. 1:28), although not expressly called a covenant, was also in the spirit of the compact with Noah. These divine covenants made with Adam and Noah were solemnly renewed with Abraham and his descendants.

Priestly Covenant and the Pact with the House of David: The priestly tradition imbedded in the writings of the Bible states that God made a special covenant with the priestly House of Aaron of the tribe of Levi, that assured it the priesthood on a permanent basis (Nu. 25:12–13). Another tradition avers that God sealed a pact with the House of David* promising the throne of Judah to his dynasty forever (II Sam. 23:5; see the story in II Sam. 7 which is the basis of the Davidic covenant).

I. COVENANT WITH ISRAEL. — **Concept of the Covenant:** The concept of the covenant relationship (in Hebrew "b^{e}rith") between God and Israel, rooted in the divine initiative, whereby He graciously extended the invitation to his people to enter into a Holy compact, and the response of Israel, is fundamental to Hebrew theology and religion. Israel's national existence is founded on the belief that her ancestors had, at Sinai, contracted with Yahweh to be His Chosen People*.

Particulars of the Covenant: The Covenant was an agreement of Israel's vassalage to and dependence upon the Lord, in return for His protection, as expressed in the deliverance of the Hebrews from Egyptian bondage and their entry into the Promised Land (Ex. 6:4–5). Yahweh demanded that as His vassals, the people must undertake to observe His laws and implement all its injunctions. When the people expressed their readiness to live under His rule in a sacred pact with one another, the Covenant was sealed.

Tablets of the Covenant: The Decalogue, also referred to as the Book of the Covenant (Ex. 24:7), the deed or instrument of the Sinai Covenant, and the Words of the Covenant, were inscribed on large stones entrusted by God to Moses (Ex. 24:12). These are known as the Tablets of the Law or the Tablets of the Covenant (luḥot ha-b^{e}rith in Hebrew, Dt. 9:9). Along with the Torah (Pentateuch), the Tablets symbolize Judaism. Oriental treaties were usually inscribed on tablets or engraved on stones, and placed in a sanctuary under the feet of the gods. In like manner, the Tablets of the Covenant were deposited in the Ark of the Govenant, which was placed between the "Cherubim" and was regarded as God's footstool. Yahweh was enthroned above the Cherubim (see Tabernacle*, Ark). Possession of the Ark was later considered a symbol of kingship.

Comparison with Ancient Treaties: The originality of Israel's Covenant is its establishment of a relationship of suzerain and vassal between God and man. Its legal form, however, corresponds to the suzerainty treaties contracted by the Hittite kings with their vassals (late 2nd mill. BCE) and the Assyrian treaties of vassalage which are of a later date. These were formulated in a manner similar to the Israel Covenant. The title of the Hittite ruler was the "Great King" and the prologue of his pact reminds his vassals of his benevolent acts which imposed perpetual gratitude upon them (compare with Ex. 20:2). The Hittite treaty also stipulated the obligations imposed by the ruler on his vassals, which included a prohibition of relations with peoples outside the empire, or enmity between those within. The vassals were enjoined to place their unlimited trust in the "Great King" and pay him annual tribute (compare with Ex. 23:17; Dt. 26:5–10). There are many similar analogies between the ancient law of the Near East and the legislation of the Old Testament (see Law*).

The Covenant governing Israel's relations with Yahweh differs, however, from the oriental treaties in that it is a religious compact between a people and its God.

Roots of Israel's Theology: Israelite law is thus essentially religious in character since it embodies the obligations to Yahweh which the people are committed to obey. The notion of the rule of Yahweh over His people or that of the "Kingdom of God" which is central to both the Old and New Testaments, is an outgrowth of this concept. Though the covenant went through many mutations, it is the essential root of the Hebrew tribal federation (see Judges*) and of the later Israelite monarchy which was a theocracy in which the king served as the agent of Yahweh (see Government, Authority and Kingship*). In the Old Testament, mediators such as Moses and the prophets were used by God for concluding or renewing His Covenant.

The Code of Deuteronomy: The Code of Deuteronomy reaffirms the Sinai Covenant and is representative of Hebrew legal practice. It is an itemized expression of the sacred pact between Israel and Yahweh, the essence of the conditions governing the gift of the Promised Land (Dt. 12:1; 11: 31–32). It also includes the sanctions of the Covenant confirmed by a series of curses and blessings which will follow upon the performance or non-performance of the stipulations of the Covenant (Dt. 27 and 28). The oriental treaties mentioned above also included sanctions couched in the form of blessings and curses invoking the gods.

Patriarchal Covenant: According to biblical theology, the promise of Election and the Covenant with Abraham (Gn. 17:9; 18:19) are linked with the event of Exodus* which, along with the Conquest, fulfilled this promise. This religious historiography of an age-old covenant, however, contradicts its real nature in Israel and its historical origin. The Sinai Covenant in Ex. and Dt. is markedly different from the Patriarchal Covenant, though many of the latter's features may have prepared the way for it (see Patriarchs*). The Sinai Covenant rests on Yahweh's promises for the future, while the Patriarchal Covenant only calls for trust. The Sinai Covenant and the Code of Deuteronomy are also based on gracious acts already performed, for which heavy vassalage and obligation is demanded in return by God.

Earlier critical scholarship tended to regard the covenant idea as a relatively late one, introduced by the Deuteronomist. It is striking that the earlier prophets tend to ignore the term itself while describing the relationship between Yahweh and Israel in more personal terms. In the light of contemporary evidence from the Near East, there is no reason to doubt the antiquity of the covenant idea in Israel, nor the use of this pattern in describing the religio-legal compact between Yahweh and Israel, especially since the closest parallels are found with the 2nd mill. Hittite treaties rather than with the 1st mill. BCE Assyrian treaties.

Ritual of the Covenant: Israelite customs that were incidental to entering into the Covenant are not dissimilar to those of neighbouring nations. One example is the custom of cutting animals into two equal parts and walking between the parts (Jer. 34:18–19), as if to say, "if I break the Covenant my fate will be that of the cut-up animals". The formula "God do so to me and more also" has as its background this ritual of the sacrifice of an animal. It was also customary to offer animal sacrifices and to sprinkle the blood on the covenanters (Ex. 24:8; Ps. 50:5). The blood thus sprinkled was called the Blood of the Covenant. Certain inscriptions in Ancient Egypt lead to the conclusion that the making of covenants accompanied by sacrificial rites was practiced there also (see Sacrifice*; Eucharist*).

II. NEW COVENANT, (BᵉRITH HADASHAH). — **Need for a New Covenant:** During the Mosaic and pre-Exilic stage of Israelite history, the Law* was considered a divine revelation, integrally related to the Covenant (see I above). When the prophets proclaimed that because Israel had broken the Covenant, Yahweh had imposed the sanctions and left them to the mercy of their enemies, it was inevitable that a religious and political vacuum should occur. Indeed, the events of 586 BCE not only caused such a vacuum, but shattered the normal national framework which had operated under the Covenant. The prophets were left with two choices: to regard the national Covenant as definitely inoperative; or to consider it as only temporarily abrogated, which meant that it had to be maintained somehow and given a new foundation. The latter position prevailed and henceforth, the divine abrogation of the Covenant was not considered definitive. The prophets Jeremiah* and Ezekiel* proclaimed that a New Covenant would come into being, with new laws to suit the occasion. As the people waited hopefully for the realization of this prophetic redemption, they were encouraged to maintain the old Law*. The "torah" or teaching of Ezekiel marks the transition from the Covenant people to the post-Exilic restoration of the remnant. The remnant were encouraged to hold on to their ancestral laws as a substitute for the temporarily inoperative Covenant. Thus, the Law which had once expressed the Covenant became the vehicle of the Restoration* of the remnant. As the Law was not considered solely the inheritance of the Chosen People* of the Covenant, it could also be taught to non-Israelites and proselytes. In time, this process made the biblical heritage available to the world.

Formulation of the New Covenant: The prophetic conception of a New Covenant ("bᵉrith hadashah" or New Testament) which would supersede the old national Covenant of Sinai occurs in Jeremiah* 31:31–34. It is no reflection on the old Covenant, only on the people who disobeyed it. The new concept represented a prophetic protest against the perils of an external legalism on which the old Covenant had foundered, and called for an inward and spiritual obedience in response to divine initiative in forgiveness. This was, in reality, a call for the creation of a New Isreal out of the "remnant" of the old Israel. Ezekiel 36:22–28 expresses this when he speaks of a new heart and a new spirit, though he uses the term "eternal covenant".

The Dead Sea Sectaries and Primitive Christianity: The Dead Sea sectaries of Qumran entered into a New Covenant which they also called the "Covenant of Repentance". Theirs was a movement of repentance in response to the divine initiative in mercy. Repentance as well as baptism was therefore the essential condition of admission to the Community of the New Covenant (see John the Baptist*; Dead Sea Scrolls*). The central rite of "entering into the Covenant" was described in their literature and explains the entire eschatological* setting of Qumran repentance and resurrection, as entrance into the New Covenant of the "last days". The Community of God, as they called themselves, was also the Israel of the New Covenant, Community of the New Covenant or the New Israel.

Life in conformity with the New Covenant had a double meaning: preparation for the coming of the "Last Times" or the "End of Days", and the anticipation of the blessed life that the promised messianic* era would inaugurate. This is an impressive forerunner or preparation for the New Testament* and indicates a connection with the Dead Sea sectaries* (see article, sect. VIII). The people of this New Covenant practiced a communal economy or the coming "economy of God" that included a direct allusion to the practice of giving to the poor. In the early church of the New Testament, especially the Jewish-Christian one of Palestine, a similar practice obtained.

The people of the New Covenant fully anticipated Jesus' prophecy of the "meek who shall inherit the earth", in their commentary on Psalm 37, which itself bears a striking resemblance to this philosophy. They equated themselves with the meek who will inherit the New Jerusalem. Their elaborate ceremony of the New Covenant was held at the Festival of Covenant Renewal or Pentecost (Shabu'ôt). The sectaries considered themselves the "Community of the Renewed Covenant" and the "eternal covenant" to be established at the "end of days", precisely in the New Testament sense. The commentaries written by the Qumran sectaries elaborate the apocalyptic* exegesis of their master, the "Righteous Teacher" who instituted the "Community of the Renewed Covenant", brought light to the meaning of Scriptures and, on this basis, established a new discipline in anticipation of the messianic era. They interpreted, in their own way, classical formulas of the old Israel, such as their expectation of a "prophet like Moses", a "messiah like David", a "priest like Aaron or Zadok", and their prediction of a new Exodus, a New Covenant, a new Holy War and a new gift of "the height of Israel".

CRAFTS: TOOLS AND IMPLEMENTS. — *Outline: Materials; Form; I. Agricultural Implements: Plough; Spade, Hoe or Mattock; Axe, Adze; Ox-Goad (Dorban); Harvesting Implements; Flint Sickle; Iron Sickle; Threshing Sledge or Drag; Pruning Hook. II. Artisans' Tools: Evolution of Tools. III. Measuring Tools: Length; Weight. IV. Everyday Implements.*

Many tools are mentioned by name in the Bible. Some of these and many others have been found in excavations in Palestine. Sometimes the ones unearthed could be identified from biblical descriptions, but in most cases this proved very difficult. As a result, the names of a number of tools are known, while their functions can only be guessed, and many other tools are known to have been in use although their name in biblical times is unknown. The actual tools usually vary from period to period, the materials used to make them developing from the expendable to the more durable and more easily worked.

Materials: In the pre-historic Stone Age, practically the only material used to make tools was flint, often by itself, but sometimes bound on to a wooden handle by crude rope or leather thongs. Copper and bronze utensils were made as early as the Chalcolithic Age (4th mill. BCE) but bronze only came into general use at the beginning of the Middle Bronze Age, to be replaced by iron in the later Iron Age.

Form: On the other hand, a remarkable conservatism is apparent in regard to form. The shape and size of most tools were fixed at some time in the 3rd mill. BCE and hardly changed thereafter. There is, accordingly, very little evidence by which to date a particular tool and this is usually done by comparison with other artifacts found in association with the tools. Changes were made in a number of tools in Roman times and new ones introduced. In fact until about a generation ago, the tools used by the Arab fellah were essentially only slightly modified versions of Roman period implements, while a number of others remain unchanged to this day.

I. AGRICULTURAL IMPLEMENTS: The Bible mentions the ploughshare, spade, mattock, hoe, adze (axe), goad, sickle and billhook, threshing-sledge, three-pronged fork, pruning hook, and winnowing fork or winnowing fan, with small or larger holes for sifting.

Plough: As early as Neolithic times, the plough was used in the Near East to loosen the ground before sowing. It appears to have been developed first in Mesopotamia*, for the oldest evidence for its use comes from pictographic inscriptions of Erech (Uruk), and Elam. Quite detailed drawings of ploughs have been found from the middle of the third millenium BCE and thereafter, especially on cylinder seals. It was in use in Egypt from the third dynasty, and is pictured in many engravings and wall paintings as shown **(358)**. Both Egyptian and Mesopotamian ploughs were very similar. They consisted of a sharp wooden ploughshare that dug into the soil **(358)** attached to two bent wooden handles joined by a crosspiece at the top. The Egyptians used to attach a flint blade to the plough share. Some scholars believe that at first the plough was pulled by humans harnessed to it, and that animals were used for the purpose only later on. The most primitive ploughs had no crossbeam or yoke which could be laid on an animal's neck. The Egyptians tied the plough to a separate yoke attached to the horns of oxen and this method of harnessing continued to be used even after an improved yoke was invented, apparently in the middle of the 2nd mill. Ancient Egyptian ploughs had a stout pin passed through the intersection of the handles, or the top of the body of the plough, to which a long yoke bar was attached **(358)**.

The whole of the plough was made of wood, different types of hardwood being used including the oak in Israel. Only in the second half of the 2nd mill. did metal come to be used in making the ploughshares. At first, the blade was sheathed with bronze, but this is a fairly soft alloy and wore out quickly. It was not widely used. With the introduction of iron-working, iron sheaths or shares became possible, as witness this Mesopotamian seed plough of the 7th c. BCE engraved on stone **(357)**. These were first made in Palestine in the 11th c. BCE, while they began to be used in Egypt and Mesopotamia only after the beginning of the 10th c. BCE.

The Bible gives no detailed description of the plough used by the Israelites but it may be supposed that it did not differ substantially from those of their contemporaries elsewhere in the ancient world. The first reference to it comes in I Sam. 13:20–21, where the Bible records that "every one of the Israelites went down to the Philistines to sharpen his plowshare . . ." obviously meaning the metal blade, rather than the earlier wooden type. From the numerous ploughshares uncovered in excavations **(360)**, it appears that their form was fixed early in the Bronze Age and remained unchanged well into the Iron Age. It was shaped like a hollow tube, with a sharp point at its lower end. According to the Mishnah (Kelim 21, 2), this "sword blade of the plough" was fixed to the bottom of the wooden plough. It could thus break the surface of the earth but not turn it over. It, too, wore out quickly and had to be frequently replaced or sharpened.

Spade, Hoe or Mattock: These are also mentioned in I Sam. 13:20–21. At one time it was thought that the words were alternative terms for the ploughshare, but this hardly seems reasonable and, as S. Yeivin has pointed out, elsewhere (Is. 2:4; Mic. 4:3; Jl. 3:10), the word for ploughshare appears without these additions. In the opinion of this scholar, the spade was a digging tool with a narrow blade and cutting edge while the mattock or hoe (Is. 7:25) had a cutting edge some 12–16 cms. wide, like one **(359)** discovered at Tel Jemmeh. During and after the Iron Age, the blades of spades and mattocks were made with sockets into which the handle was fixed with a bolt or wedge, like the socketed adze.

360

359

357

358

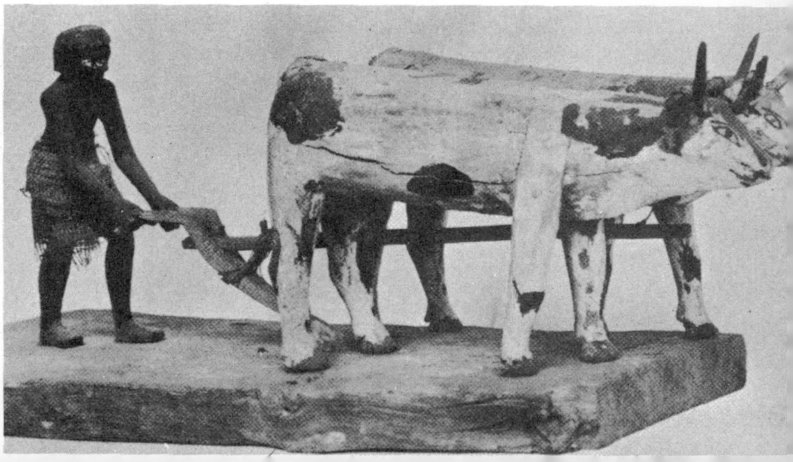

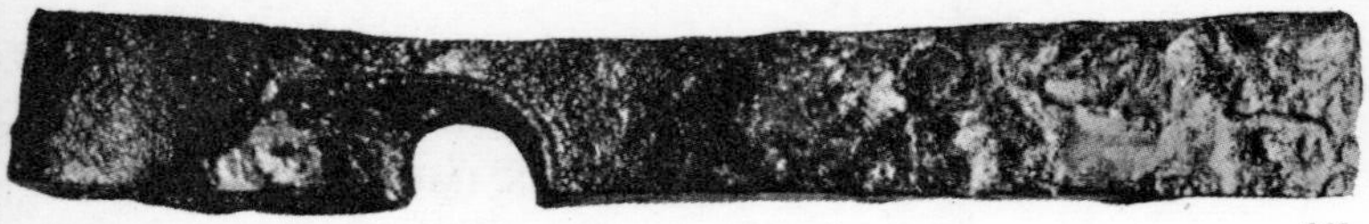

362

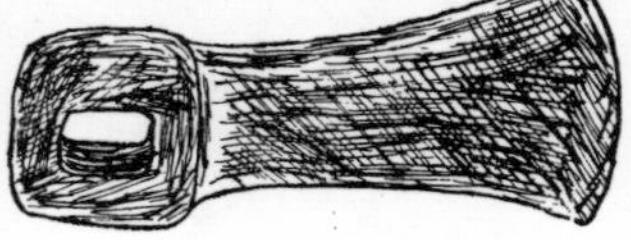

361

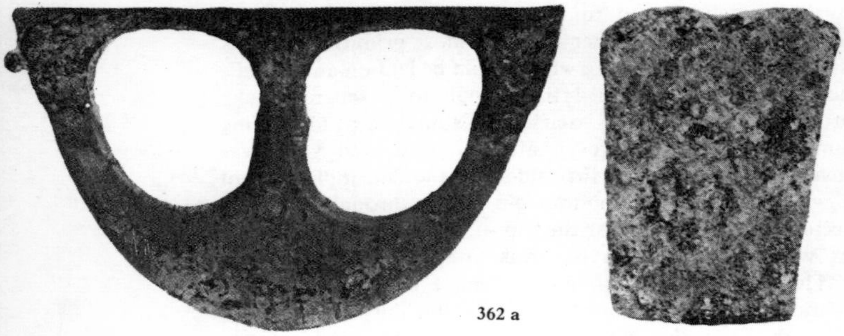

362 a

363

364

365 a

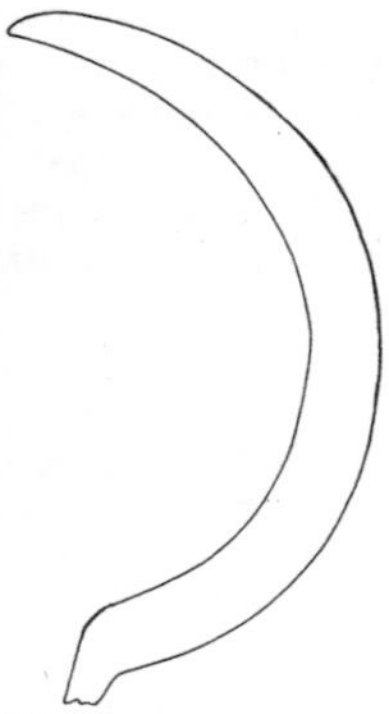

365 b

365c

Axe, Adze: In earlier excavations many metal blades were found which left the archaeologists uncertain as to whether they were axes or adzes. Finally, Flinders Petrie distinguished between the axe — with an edge parallel to the handle, and the adze (**361, 363**), which had a vertical blade at right angles to the handle. Moreover the axe blade is generally flat on both sides while the adze is flat on one side and slightly convex on the other, i. e. its edge is sharp on only side. This distinction has been accepted by later scholars, W. F. Albright pointing out that a more important difference is that the blade of the adze is thicker than that of the axe. The adze was designed for work with wood, cutting, planing it and so on, and also sometimes for digging, whereas the axe (**362, 362a**) was used either as a weapon (see Arms and Weapons*) of for cutting stone. It is mentioned in Hezekiah's inscription in the Siloam tunnel (see Inscriptions*).

Ox-Goad (Dorban): Many scholars think that this too was attached to the plough and used to urge the oxen on their way (Jud. 3:31) or that it was wielded by the ploughman with the hand that did not hold the plough. S. Yeiwin thinks it was made of a long wooden pole, shod at one end with an iron spike to prick the oxen and having at the other end a sharp wide metal blade with which to scrape earth off the ploughshare. Against this, Y. Yadin thinks that the "dorban" was not a goad but a sickle and that it was a foreign Philistine word which came into use together with the iron sickle which was wrongly transcribed "dorban" in Hebrew. This is a question which has yet to be finally settled (**364**).

Harvesting Implements: Two tools above all were used for harvesting grain: the sickle and billhook. The large sickle (ḥermesh) is mentioned twice in the Bible (Dt. 16:9; 23:16). Like the billhook, it is one of the earliest agricultural implements to be invented.

Flint Sickle: According to S. Yeivin, the Hebrew word "ḥermesh" comes from "ḥalamish", meaning flint (the letters l-m-r are interchangeable) and thus means a flint implement. Discovery of parts of flint sickles (**23**) in prehistoric camping sites, either lying on the ground or in the earliest layers of the caves where the first men dwelt, is a good indication of the cultural level at which men first harvested foodstuffs (as against merely collecting and storing them).

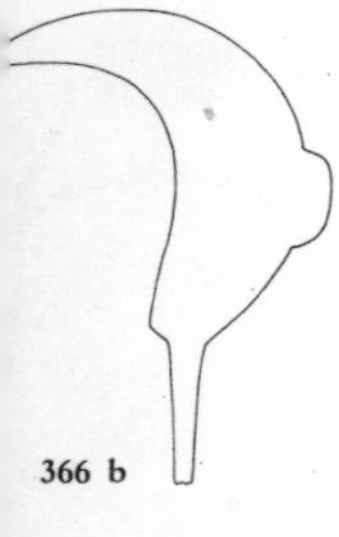

366 b

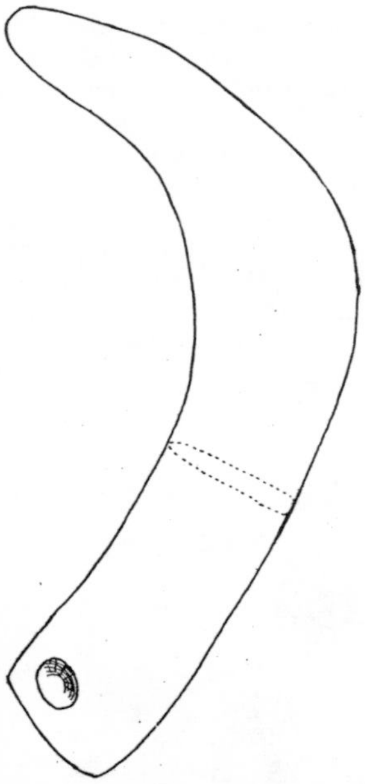

366 a

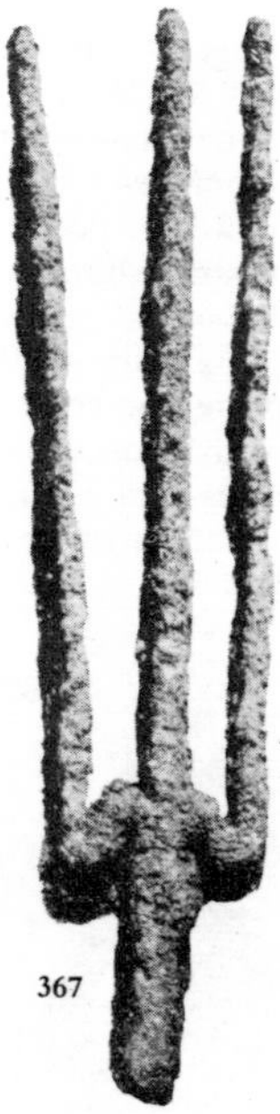

367

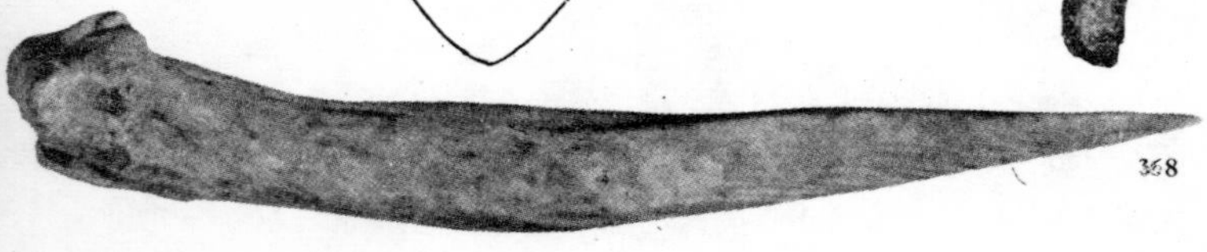

368

369

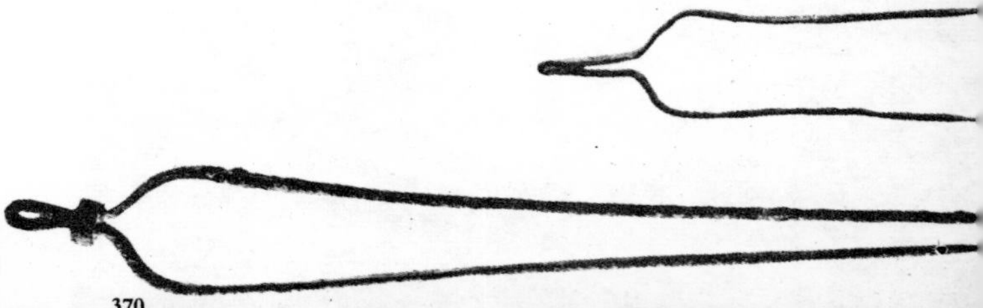

370

In Palestine, the sickle first made its appearance in the Mesolithic (Stone Age) layers of the Natufian culture in Wadi Natuf and the caves of Mount Carmel. In the earliest examples, the blade was tied on to a wooden handle or an animal's jawbone, which was the right shape. Later, flint blades were stuck into the handle vertically. (They needed to be replaced frequently and one handle would suffice for a succession of blades.)

The use of flint sickles continued in Palestine into the Bronze Age and was finally ousted by metal only in the Iron Age. During the Bronze Age, flint sickles often with toothed blades (**23**) were fixed in a curved frame of wood, bone or horn. The main advantage of the discovery of iron was at first a matter of economy rather than efficiency. It was a long time before the technique of giving a sharp cutting edge to iron tools was mastered.

Iron Sickle: (Jer. 50:16; Jl. 4:13) S. Yeivin explains the difference between the "ḥermesh" (small sickle) and the "māgāl" (large iron sickle) as being merely one of material. Both were designed for the same purpose and indeed the flint type continued to be used even after the introduction of the new iron sickle.

The metal sickles found in excavations usually have long curved blades with the inside sharpened and, of course, thinner than the back. The curved shape of the sickle is so well adapted to its function — a sharp blade can cut a whole sheaf of grain at one stroke — that it has hardly changed to this day. From the moment iron sickles first made their appearance in Palestine, their number increased considerably, for instance these Iron Age sickles from Lachish, riveted or otherwise (**365a**); or this sickle with a tang (**365b**) or the one with a haft and grooved blade (**365c**) dating from Roman times and found in Samaria. Bronze, on the other hand, was too soft to be practicable and no bronze sickles have ever been found in excavations.

Threshing Sledge or Drag: A threshing sledge (II Sam. 24:22; I Ch. 21:23) was the standard threshing implement. In the opinion of most scholars, it was made of a heavy wooden board with iron spikes fixed to its underside (cf. Am. 1:3; Is. 28:27; **29**). The board would be drawn by an ox or an ass round and round over cut grain laid on the threshing floor, with the thresher standing on the board to add his weight to its force. Once the grain had been loosened from the husks, it would be separated from the chaff and straw, apparently by means of a winnowing fork, something like the three-pronged fork mentioned in I Sam. 13:21. Many three-pronged forks found in excavations appear to fit this term. They were used not only in agriculture but also in sacrificial ritual (I Sam. 2:13). The examples excavated—especially the one from Lachish (**367**) — are made of iron, but it may be assumed that humble peasants also used forks like this made of wood, which would be cheaper and easier to work with but, of course, disintegrated in the course of time. Actual winnowing was done with a winnowing fan (Is. 30:24; Jer. 15:7) and shovel (Is. 30:24). Some authorities think that the fan was something very much like the fork, while the shovel was like a large wooden spoon, used to gather the scattered grain. The implements were too familiar to the biblical writers for them to feel the need of detailed descriptions.

Other tools used in selecting and cleaning the seeds were the sieve and the "kbārā", apparently another sieve with large holes used for the first stage of sifting. The grain would be thrown up into the air and caught in the "kbārā", whereas in the sieve, the sifted grain would be further refined by a to and fro, horizontal movement.

Pruning Hook: The pruning hook or knife was to cut the branches of fruit trees. A number of excavated implements have been identified as pruning-hooks (**366a, b**), but this is not always certain.

II. ARTISANS' TOOLS: Among the other tools mentioned in the Bible are the chisel, stylus or marking tool, pencil, compass, plane, mallet, hammer, anvil, saw, axe, adze (hatchet), various measuring instruments and tools for special work like the awl and the tongs. Knives, razors and daggers were in daily use while archaeological discoveries have included scalpels, needles, fish hooks and others.

The awl (**368**) was a tool for delicate work, made of bronze or iron with a sharp point for boring holes (cf. Ex. 21:6; Dt. 15:17), used by saddlers and leather-workers but also for boring holes in wood. In this case, apparently, the awl would be made white hot so that it would burn through the wood as well as pierce it. A number of awls, handles and borers (**369**) have been found in many excavations.

Tongs are mentioned (1 K. 7:49; II Ch. 4:21) among the vessels of the Temple but they were also used by goldmiths and similar craftsmen to lift hot vessels from the ace. This instrument (**370**) found in a tomb at Megiddo ting from the Middle Bronze Age is described as tongs.

372

371a

371c

371b

Chisels (**371a,b, c**) made of a metal bar with one end sharpened on one side (the other side being left flat) were used to cut and engrave metal, wood, stone, etc. As with a modern chisel, the ancient ones would be placed against the material to be worked and then struck with a hammer or other heavy instrument.

Is. 44:12–13 refers to some of the tools used by smiths and carpenters, including the plane or adze (cf. Jer. 10:3). The pencil, also mentioned in Isaiah, was a metal instrument with a thin sharp point, used to scratch the required form on the wood being worked. The compass was similarly used to mark curves and circles on raw materials.

There is only one reference to a saw in the whole of the Bible (in Is. 10:15) and this occurs in connection with an axe, presumably in relation to stone-cutting. In other places (II Sam. 12:31; 1 K. 7:9; I Ch. 20:3) another term, "nigerah" is used, also translated "saw" in modern Bibles. The distinction between the two is not clear. A handsaw is engraved on a Babylonian seal depicting a god ascending between two mountains (ca. 2200–2000 BCE; **372**).

Among other tools mentioned, the mallet (Jud. 5:26) was apparently a big wooden hammer for fastening tent pegs, probably very similar to the "mākebet" (Jud. 4:21), also a sort of hammer. In the opinion of S. Yeiwin the only difference between the mallet and the mākebet was one of time, i. e. the mallet was an archaic name for an instrument — the mākebet — in daily use. Alternatively, the mallet may have been a wooden hammer while the mākebet was made of metal. This is another question that cannot be decided on the evidence available (compare, in this connection, Is. 44:12 and I K. 6:7). In addition to these two hammers, the "pattîsh" (hammer) is also mentioned (Is. 41:7; Jer. 23:19) and so is the "pā'am" which, according to some scholars, was also a small hammer. This metal hammer and chisel, dated 50–70 CE, were found at Sanhedriah near Jerusalem (**373**).

Evolution of Tools: Fixing a heavy iron tool onto a wooden handle was a difficult business and the art of making a hole in the iron and then fitting the handle into it was only learned at the end of the Iron Age (around the middle of the monarchy, 700–600 BCE). This mid-Bronze adze from Megiddo (**374**) and axehead (**375**) were found in the same stratum and were thus contemporaneous. Developments continued, producing, e. g. hoes and pickheads like these (**376**) and then double-purpose tools, like the pickaxes found in a stratum of the Hellenistic period, as shown in this Roman illustration (**377**), or in this head of a mattock (**377a**) from Samaria in which one end is shaped like a pick, the other like an axe. By this time, the construction and quality of tools had caught up with those of weapons.

After the Exile, a new method of making a cylindrical socket for the handle developed, using a process already employed for lances and javelins (see Arms and Weapons*). The hoe with a rectangular blade at right angles to the socket for the hand is made by a process still used by gardeners today.

III. MEASURING TOOLS: **Length:** Tools for measuring lengths mentioned in the Bible include: line (Am. 7:17); measuring line (Zec. 2: 1; Jer. 3:39); a "line of flax and a measuring reed" (Ezk. 40:3). Some or all of these instruments may also have served as fixed measures of length.

373

374

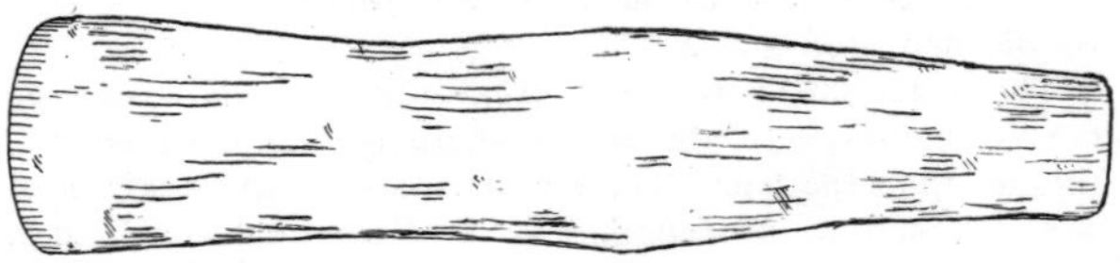
375

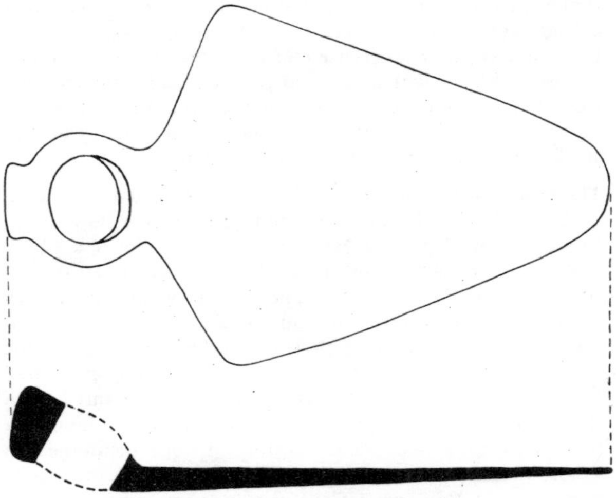
376

377

377 a

378

379 a

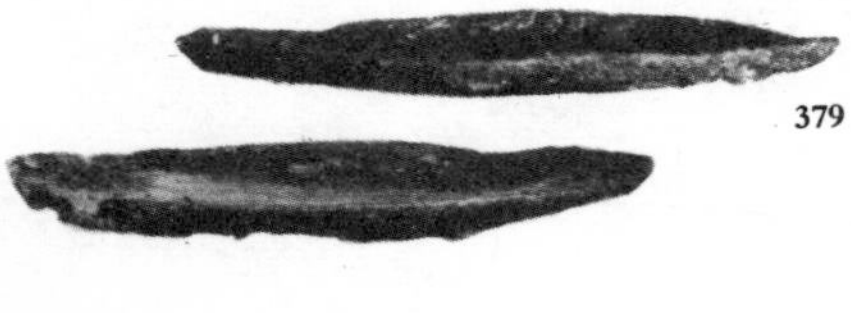
379 b

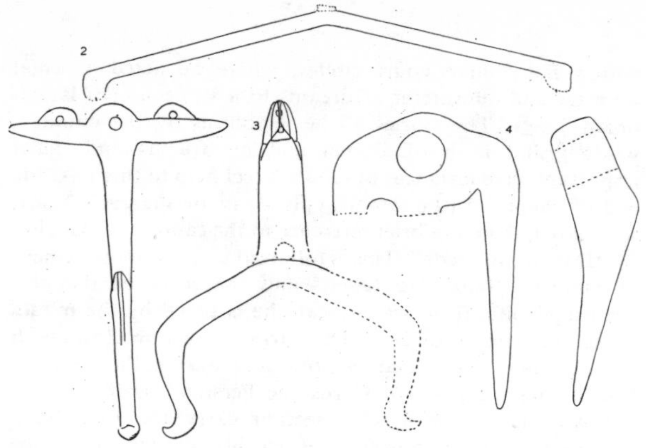

380

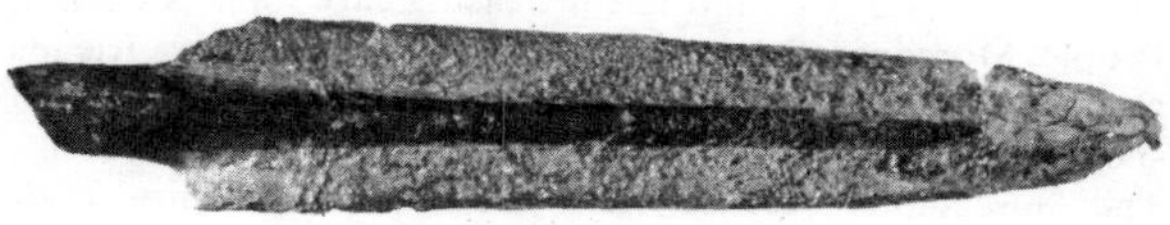

381 a

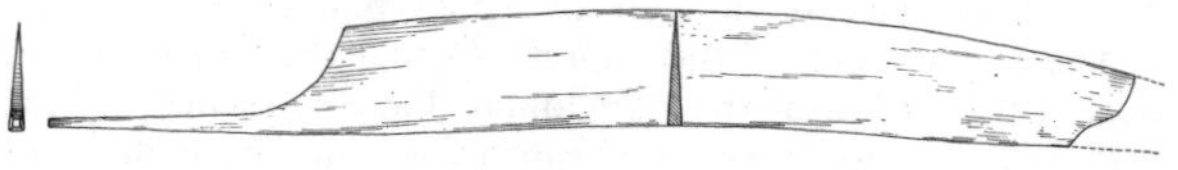

381 b

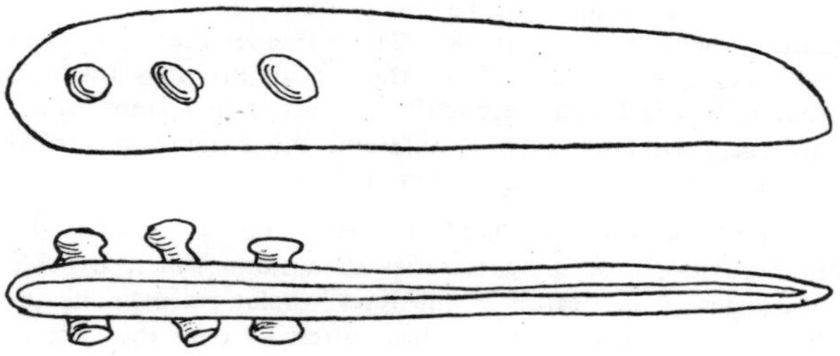

382

382 b

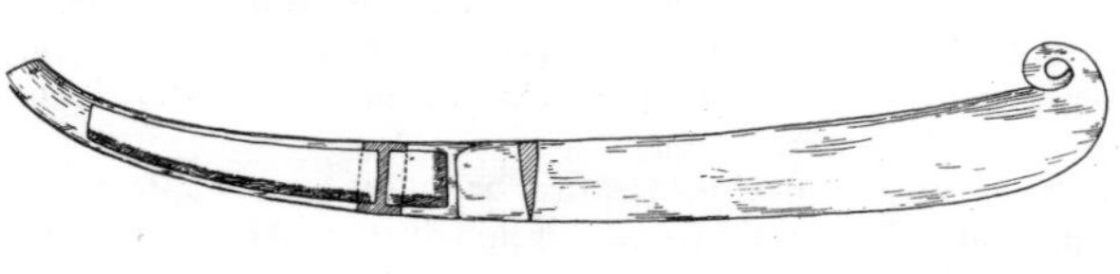

382 ɔ

383

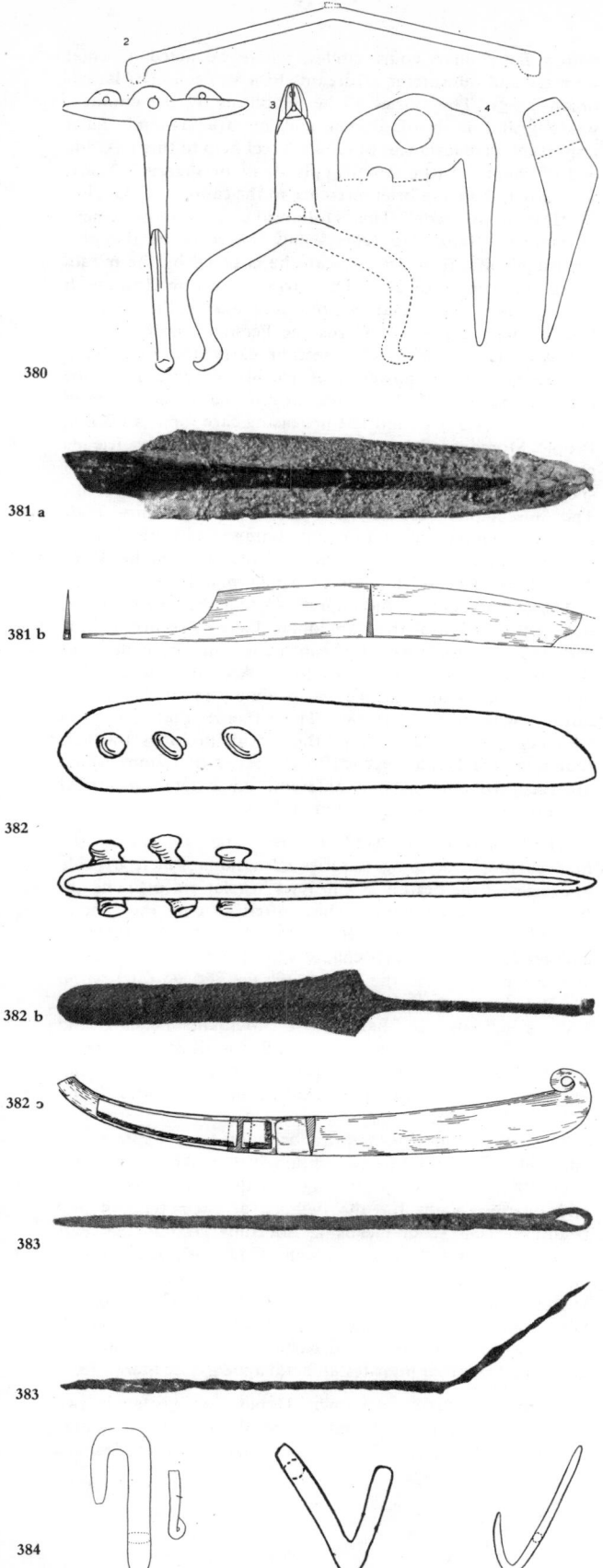

383

384

Am. 7:7 refers to a plumb line or plummet, used to check the angle of perpendicular walls. The stone and metal plummets discovered in excavations generally consist of weights with a hole on top through which a cord could be threaded (**378**).

Weight : Scales were used to measure weights (Lv. 19:36; Jer. 32:10; and elsewhere), and from those pictured in a number of reliefs and drawings, it appears that two main types were known in the ancient Near East: a. Hand scales, used by traders and peddlers; b. stationary scales on a solid basis which were more accurate and were used, for instance, by metal refiners, goldsmiths and perfumers. Scales (**379a, b**) from the Israelite period made of clay and bone were discovered in the excavations of Megiddo. More recently, bronze scales dating from the 7th c. BCE were unearthed from a perfumery workshop at Ein Gedi. These finds suggest that the scales had three holes, through which threads were passed and attached to the balance bar as shown by an iron balance beam from Lachish (**380**). Isaiah (40:12 and 46:6) uses two different terms for scales, but the significance of the difference is not known (for the Weights, see Weights and Measures*).

IV. EVERYDAY IMPLEMENTS: The most important tool in daily use for preparing food etc, was the knife (Pr. 23:2), A special type of knife was the big, carving or slaughtering knife or "ma'ākhêlet" (**381a, b**), used for cutting the flesh of a whole body (Gn. 22:6, 10; Jud 19:29). A third type was the razor (Nu. 6:5; 8:7; Is. 7:20). Isaiah (7:20) refers to the "razor which is hired" used for shaving and hair cutting. Jeremiah (36:23) refers to the penknife, specially designed to carve out scrolls from parchment.

Many blades unearthed in excavations have been identified as knives (**382a–c**) from their similarity to modern knives. In general the handle is attached to the blade by a nail, but in some cases the blade has been wedged into a groove made in the handle. Most knives were used for cutting but in some cases their shape suggests that they also had other, special, uses, like a group of knives from Tel-el-Nasbeh apparently designed for flaying skins. Others could also be used for scratching.

A large number of needles (**383**) have also been found in excavations. On an average these are about 12–15 cm. long but some of them, used presumably for sewing heavy tent cloth, were larger. Even the "smaller" ones however must have left very noticeable holes in the materials on which they were used. Finer and more delicate needles make their appearance during the Iron Age but even then most needles are of bronze. They were apparently quite difficult to make and the softer bronze was strong enough to puncture cloth, but did not rust as easily as iron.

Fish hooks (**384**) have also been found, similar in shape to modern barbed hooks so that once caught, a fish could not escape. They are usually between 4 and 5 cms. in length.

A group of implements recently discovered in the caves of Wadi Murabba'at (see Bar-Kochba*) were identified by the excavators as surgical or medical instruments of the Roman period. No names can be attached to these instruments as yet.

See also: Agriculture*; Cities*, Canaanite, Israelite and Hellenistic Periods; Trade*; Weights and Measures*; Cothing*.

D

DANIEL, BOOK OF. — Although in English Bibles, the book of Daniel appears as the last of the so-called "Major Prophets", the Hebrew canon places it under the third biblical category of "Writings." The separation from the "Prophets" was due to the fact that this was probably the last Old Testament book to be included in the canon. Daniel is unmistakably apocalyptic in character. Its composition, in fact, sets the seal on the replacement of classical prophecy by the new form of apocalyptic — a development which took place during the 4th to 2nd cs. BCE (see Apocalypse*). According to the tradition, prophecy as such ended with Malachi*, but this is unlikely since prophets are known of the period of Ezra* and Nehemiah*. After Malachi's time, however, no prophetic works were recorded canonically. The apocalyptic book of Daniel illustrates the new trend.

Nature of the Material: Daniel appears to have been written at the time of the persecutions of Antiochus IV (ca. 167 BCE; see Hasmoneans*). It expounds a number of religious truths aimed at fortifying the Jews and helping them to hold fast to their faith regardless of what it might cost them, in the certainty that God would finally intervene to help them.

During this inter-testamental period, it was general practice for writers to choose a hero from among the great prophets or sages of the past and then make him foretell events from his own time until the writing of the book, it being explained that he had directed that his words be sealed up until the predictions were fulfilled! Thus the writer of Daniel did not invent the setting of the stories in the book. He took well-known ancient folk-tales and myths and wove them into an account of the actions, visions and prophecy of Daniel. These stories had apparently originated in the time of the Babylonian and Persian empires, and were handed down for centuries. By the time they came to the writer, they had already been set in the period of the Babylonian Exile*. Hence, the combination of the setting and prophecies of Daniel gave the visions and symbols which contained his real message the prestige attaching to the stories.

This process explains the unusual form of the book and makes it possible to distinguish the two different sections, a. the narratives and b. the visions.

a. **The Narratives of Chapters 1–6:** Mainly narrative or historical, they are written in the third person and describe Daniel as an interpreter of dreams during the Exile in Babylonia.

Chapter 1 records how Daniel and his friends were carried away captive from Judah to Babylonia and trained there to become members of the guild of "wise men", the soothsayers and diviners who were called "Chaldeans" (see Magic*). Chapters 2–5 describe Daniel's growing reputation as an interpreter of other men's visions and his increasing power within Babylonian court circles, where he acted as chief minister and interpreter of dreams to a succession of Babylonian kings. The stories all lay emphasis on the courage, wisdom and faith of Daniel and his friends and, most important, give instances of God's direct help to them. At the end of chapter 5 (the famous episode of Belshazzar's Feast, see below), there is a brief reference to the capture of Babylon by "Darius the Mede". This is followed by the announcement of Daniel's continuing talents and the story of the plot against his life, from which again he is saved by the miraculous intervention of God. The narrative section closes with the statement that "Daniel prospered during the reign of Darius and the reign of Cyrus the Persian" (6:28).

All the stories in this section carry the underlying message of God's power over earthly monarchs — for instance the proud Nebuchadrezzar reduced to eating "grass like an ox" (4:33) — and His unceasing care for His Chosen People. Moreover, the martyr stories of Daniel's three friends cast into the fiery furnace were handed down and used to show what had happened in the heroic past, not the present. The miraculous rescues were intended to inspire their suffering countrymen to an equal courage and faith. Martyr stories of even greater poignancy are found in the books of Maccabees* (see section under Apocrypha*).

These chapters give the impression that they were written during the period of the Babylonian Exile to record a great prophetic mission against paganism among the exiles and the people among whom they lived. According to another opinion, their real objective was probably to strengthen the faithful with edifying stories. Their theme, that it is God who controls the empires of the world, provides the link that joins the Daniel legends to the series of visions which are recorded and given a different, much later, historical context in the chapters that follow.

b. **The Visions of Chs. 7–12:** In these, Daniel speaks in the first person, describing a series of visions which provide allegories of the destiny of the Jews in relation to the neighbouring gentile kingdoms. These often go over the general ground of the dream first described and interpreted in chapter 2, but in the later chapters the symbols of the visions very clearly relate to the Hellenistic age and go far beyond the Babylonian-Persian locale of the first six chapters. The four kingdoms — Babylonian, Median, Persian and Macedonian (Hellenistic) — are all described in symbols which leave no doubt as to their real objective — the imminence of the downfall of Antiochus (the "little horn" of ch. 7:19–27).

The hopes and expectations formulated in chapters 2, 7 and 8–12 were to come to fruition in the Maccabaean age when the Jews took up arms against the heathen Hellenists and openly fought for the defence of their religion and traditions (see Hasmoneans*). But they contain elements of an apocalyptic* nature as well. Their theology, with its emphasis on eschatology*, and with the culmination of the visions being seen as the establishment of the Kingdom of God, is in keeping with the early 2nd c. BCE, while the book's doctrine of resurrection* and particular type of angelology* also link it to other inter-testamental apocalyptic literature.

Language: So far as is known, Daniel was written in two languages: chs. 1:1–2:4 and 8:1 to the end being written in Hebrew, while chs. 2:4–7:28 were composed in Aramaic (see Arameans*), the lingua franca of the Persian empire (see Languages*). Which language was the original one cannot be definitely established. The Aramaic seems smoother, while the Hebrew is more artificial (like that of the Qumran writings) but it may also be original.

Daniel as History: The author (or authors) of Daniel lived long after the events he recorded in the narrative section and as a result his picture of the succession of the last Babylonian and first Persian kings is inaccurate, something a contemporary would have avoided. For instance, Belshazzar who made the famous feast (5:1) was not actually "king" (although he acted as regent during the last ten years of his father's reign, see Babylonia*), and his father was Nabonidus, not Nebuchadrezzar (5:2, 11); "Darius the Mede" (5:31, see below) is not a historical character (Darius was a Persian, see Persia*), and Artaxerxes came after Xerxes, not before him (11:2). Nevertheless, the background of Syria and Egypt between the 4th and 2nd cs. BCE is given, and even the picture of Belshazzar is not far from the truth. The inaccurate genealogy (Nebuchadrezzar as Belshazzar's father) has been clarified by the Qumran discoveries (see Dead Sea Scrolls*). A scroll was found closely related in style and content to the cycle of tales collected in Daniel. This scroll records that Nabonidus contracted a "dread disease by the decree of the Most High" and was "set apart from men" for a seven year period at Teima. (Nabonidus is known to have spent the last ten years of his life at Teima, leaving Belshazzar as regent in control of affairs in Babylonia*, see article.) Many scholars see in this a likely source for Daniel 4, although he transfers the affliction (of madness) to Nebuchadrezzar. The change of names may have come about during the course of the oral transmission of the tradition. Originally, Daniel 4 (and the references in 5:2, 11, 18) may have been about Nabonidus and the apparent inaccuracy may have crept in later. Nabonidus was originally in the cycle and has been inadvertently displaced by Nebuchadrezzar in chs. 4–5.

Apocryphal Daniel: The Septuagint translation of the book of Daniel includes the additions to Daniel (the Prayer of Azariah, the Song of the Three Children, the History of Susannah and Bel and the Dragon) described under Apocrypha*. There is also further Daniel material in some of the fragments unearthed at Qumran (see Dead Sea Scrolls*).

Conclusion: While most of the narrative sections of the book of Daniel cannot be regarded as apocalyptic* (see article), they represent one of the literary settings in which the rich body of literature developed in the 4th–2nd cs. BCE. The book as a whole — narrative and visions — provides the setting in which apocalyptic served one of its important functions, as a vehicle for martyr literature.

DAVID AND SOLOMON: THE UNITED KINGDOM.

— *Outline: The United Kingdom;*
A. DAVID: I. His Life and Career: Early Years; The Political Refugee; The Kingdom at Hebron; At Jerusalem; The Expanding Kingdom; The Latter Years. II. Cultural Background: The Cultural Revolution; David as Poet and Musician; International Cultural Relations. III. David's Character.
B. SOLOMON: I. Life and Policy: The Succession; Contemporary Political Background; Administration; Culture; Deterioration. II. Building and Trade: Solomon's Ships; King Solomon's Mines. III. Solomon's Character.

The United Kingdom: Between them, Israel's second and greatest king, David, and his son Solomon, carved out the united kingdom of Israel and ruled it during its period of major political importance. Accordingly, their lives and their place in Israelite history can only be evaluated within the context of contemporary history.

The details of their life stories have to be pieced together from a variety of biblical records. The main sources for the life of David are I Sam. 16:3 to I K. 2:11 and I Ch. 11:1–29:30, plus a few scattered references in Psalms and the "Antiquities" of Josephus*. Solomon's career is recorded in I K. 1–11 and the parallel II Ch. 1–9. These biblical accounts in turn were drawn from a number of different sources (analyzed in the articles on the books of Kings* and Chronicles*). They do not make a coherent whole and they need to be critically compared where they do not tally. The different traditions have to be unravelled and historically valid sections separated from the embellishments and interpretative elements of later ages. Fortunately, much of the historical material stands up to the tests of modern research so that a reasonably accurate picture of the life, personality and career of the two monarchs can be built up.

A: DAVID: I. HIS LIFE AND CAREER:

Early Years — David was born in Bethlehem, of the tribe of Judah, between 1040 and 1030 BCE. He was the youngest son of Jesse who, according to tradition, was the grandson of Boaz and Ruth*. David's early years were spent as a shepherd but later he joined the entourage of Saul*, Israel's first king. The three different accounts of how this came about all follow the passage in I Sam. 15 where Samuel* upbraids Saul for disobeying God's commandments and prophesies that his kingdom will be given to another. David then makes his appearance, each time in a way which emphasizes one of the qualities on which later ages loved to dwell, making it difficult to assess the historical accuracy of each account.

In the first passage (I Sam. 16:1–13), Samuel is divinely inspired to anoint David as king, thereby stressing his position as a man deliberately chosen by God. In the second (ibid 16:14–23), David is recommended to Saul as a skilful musician who can charm Saul's black moods. This story lays a basis for the later legends about David as Psalmist. In fact, quite apart from the Psalms*, there seems no reason to doubt that David was an extraordinary musician and poet (see below: The Cultural Revolution). Samuel's role in the rise of David is also entirely plausible. The third account, David's slaying of Goliath the Philistine champion (ibid ch. 17) presents David as already a warrior-hero. Although the reference in II Sam. 21:19 to Elhanan as the slayer of Goliath seems to cast doubt on this story, it appears to come the closest to the actual events that probably led up to David's entry into public life. In any case, this took place during the troubled period of partisan warfare against the Philistines who were at that time in control of most of central and northern Palestine.

At first, Saul appears to have been favourable towards David and to have encouraged his career, giving him a command in the army. However, before very long, the younger man's reputation and prestige far outshone those of the king (I Sam. 18:7). Saul became increasingly jealous of David. When the question of a marriage between David and Saul's daughter Michal arose, Saul asked as a "marriage present" (see Family*: Marriage Price and Gift), not money but a hundred Philistine foreskins (18:25) — presumably hoping to finish David off in this way. Instead, the full number were duly presented and the couple were married. Saul continued to make attempts on David's life, however, forcing him to flee from the court.

The Political Refugee: The record of this period of David's life is made up of fragments from a variety of different sources. For a time he seems to have headed a band of outlaws very reminiscent of the Habiru* in their contempt for authority and settled communities. At first David and his companions were shunned by his kinsmen who resented their depredations, but they were given some help by the priesthood of Nob. These priests were descended from Eli and belonged to the priestly family which officiated at Shiloh. The assistance they gave David aroused Saul's suspicion and anger and led to a senseless massacre at the sanctuary (22:11–19). As a result, the priest Abiathar joined David's band, bringing the cult objects with him (22:20–23), thereby raising David's popular standing considerably. His stronghold was joined by many malcontents. The group acted as an irregular border force, protecting villages and herds against the Philistines and other raiders (23:1–5; 25:1–42). Meanwhile, David tried to improve his position by making marriage alliances with the leading families of the borderlands (25:42–43). Eventually, David sought refuge with the Philistine Achish, king of Gath (again there are two versions of this incident: 21:10–15 and 27:2–12), who allowed him to settle at Ziklag as a vassal ruler.

The Philistines gathered their forces for a major assault on the Israelites under Saul (996–995 BCE), but David and his men were not called on to take part (28:1–2; 29:6–11). The battle ended with the defeat of the Israelites and the death of Saul and his sons.

The Kingdom at Hebron: The Second Book of Samuel* opens with David's lament over Saul and Jonathan (II Sam. 1:17–27) and David's move to Hebron, the tribal and cultic centre of Judah (cf. II Sam. 15:7 ff) and close to Bethlehem, David's birthplace.

At Hebron, David was anointed king over Judah (II Sam. 2:4). In the interim, Saul's commander Abner had crowned Saul's son Ishbaal (Ishbosheth) king of northern Israel at Mahanaim (II K. 2:8–10). After Saul's defeat and death, the Philistines appear to have recognized two separate vassal kingdoms in western Palestine: the area which David ruled from Hebron and the northern territory which acknowledged Ishbaal (2:9). After some desultory fighting, David defeated Ishbaal (see Saul*), apparently without any intervention by the Philistines. With Ishbaal dead, the northern tribes of Israel accepted David's leadership and, by the eighth year of his reign, he felt himself strong enough to make a bid for independence and the unity of his kingdom.

Between Judea and the larger part of the kingdom of Saul, lay the mountain enclave of Jerusalem still occupied by the Canaanite clan of the Jebusites (see Jerusalem*) While this remained, political and military control of a united Palestine was impossible. David attacked Jerusalem, the hero of the battle being his commander, Joab. By creating a diversion within the city he enabled David and his men to break through its defences and capture the stronghold.

At Jerusalem: Jerusalem became the personal territory of the king, held by right of conquest by David and his personal army. It was outside the general political organization of the country and was, quite literally, "the City of David", an urban city-state, in direct succession to the Jebusite regime. As such, it was not identified with the southern tribes like Hebron, nor with the northern state of Israel. Instead it was neutral ground from which David could reign over a united "People of Israel".

Judean and Israelite settlers joined the original inhabitants of Jerusalem, all of them acknowledging David as king and accepting his retinue of courtiers and mercenary soldiers. To put the seal on his position, David brought the Ark* of the Covenant to Jerusalem in a great ceremony (II Sam. 6:1–19), thereby establishing his royal residence as the religious as well as the political and military capital of the new integrated state of Judah and Israel.

David had turned to the Philistines for refuge when he was a political fugitive from Saul, but that did not mean that he was prepared to continue as a Philistine vassal once he had taken over the leadership of the kingdom. Hostilities against the Philistines were resumed. In two battles at Ba'al Perazim and Rephaim near Jerusalem, they were defeated and forced to withdraw to the coastal plain, after which they ceased to be a serious menace. According to II Sam. 8:1, David "subdued the Philistines". This he probably did, making them tributary to him, but he never actually annexed their territory. Some scholars are of the opinion that the Philistines received enough support from the Egyptians (in spite of their weakness at that time, see Egypt*) to deter him from even making the attempt. The coastal towns never became Israelite territory. In the 8th–7th cs. BCE they reappear as an independent group.

David did, however, accept Philistines for the professional army of mercenaries which he had been training ever since his early days as an outlaw leader. Philistine professionals were even enrolled in his own personal guard.

The Expanding Kingdom: Having quelled the Philistines, David attacked the last strongholds and enclaves of the native Canaanites in the north: Megiddo*, Beth-Shean* and Ta'anach. These were reduced, putting David in control of the integrated kingdom, comprising the territory of all the tribes. He then undertook a series of campaigns against the peoples around his borders, the "oppressors" of the tribal territories east of the Jordan and in the south. First the Ammonites were defeated and subjugated, then the Moabites and Edomites, from whom Ezion Geber was captured, giving the Israelites their first outlet on the Red Sea.

The most remarkable territorial expansion was David's defeat of the Arameans and his annexation of Damascus (see Arameans*). This took place during the reign of the Assyrian Ashur-rabi II (1014–974) when Aramean pressure kept the Assyrians fully occupied in northern and eastern Syria, leaving them no time for military adventures further south. Eventually the Assyrians succeeded in expelling the Arameans from the region of the Euphrates but, under the rule of Hadadezer of Damascus, the Aramean states of Aram-Zobah and Beth-Rehob united. At the end of the 11th and beginning of the 10th c. BCE they gained control of the whole of Northern Syria and much of Transjordan (see map **385**).

When David defeated Hadadezer (II Sam. 8:3–8), the erstwhile vassal states of Aram-Zobah were transferred to the suzerainty of Judah. David incorporated all the territories of Hadadezer's federation into his kingdom. Its borders then reached from the Jordan to the frontier of the Hittite kingdom of Hamath in northern Syria — Aram-Zobah's traditional enemies. Even this kingdom acknowledged David's overlordship of the Syrian lands (II Sam. 8:3–12; I Ch. 18:3–11) and Judah's sphere of influence was assured as far as the Euphrates (see Arameans*). The kingdom ruled by David and, later, Solomon, became the strongest power between the great empires of Mesopotamia, Hamath and Egypt. It is not certain whether its frontiers reached the shores of the Mediterranean. The Phoenician towns on the Syrian coast, especially Sidon and Tyre under Hiram I, remained independent but they signed treaties of friendship with David and were probably subordinate to him.

Through military victories, diplomacy and matrimonial alliances with neighbouring royal houses and the leading families of his own kingdom, David had forged a mighty kingdom. It seems, however, that in spite of his overwhelming prestige, the old rivalries between the southern and northern parts of his kingdom continued.

Eleven years before his death, after nearly thirty years of almost unchallenged supremacy over the Israelites, a major crisis flared up over the question of the succession. David's son Absalom seemed the most likely successor but, impatient perhaps and discontented because David never officially named him his heir, Absalom rebelled against the king and led a revolt intended to dethrone him (II Sam. 15). Absalom set himself up in Jerusalem, but at a pitched battle fought at Mahanaim, David's forces were victorious. Absalom was killed when, fleeing from the battle, the long hair for which he had been famous became entangled in the branches of an oak. David mourned the death of his son, although with Absalom's defeat, the tribes all rallied to David and he returned triumphant to Jerusalem.

The Latter Years: The years that followed were some of the most productive of his whole reign. Far-reaching reforms were undertaken in national institutions and administration (see Government and Authority*) and these continued until the end of David's 40 years as king (967 BCE). A second rebellion, instigated by a certain Sheba, was a later attempt to wean the northern tribes of Israel away from their allegiance to the Davidic house of Judah, but this too was put down and Sheba killed (ch. 20).

Towards the end of David's reign (973 BCE), a royal commission headed by Joab was appointed to carry out a census of the people (II Sam. 24; I Ch. 21). It was followed by a plague and occasioned great resentment among the people (see article on Census*).

Some six years later (967 BCE), David began preparations for building a central sanctuary in Jerusalem. Although actual building did not begin until Solomon's time, it was David who chose the site of the future Temple*; the threshing

385

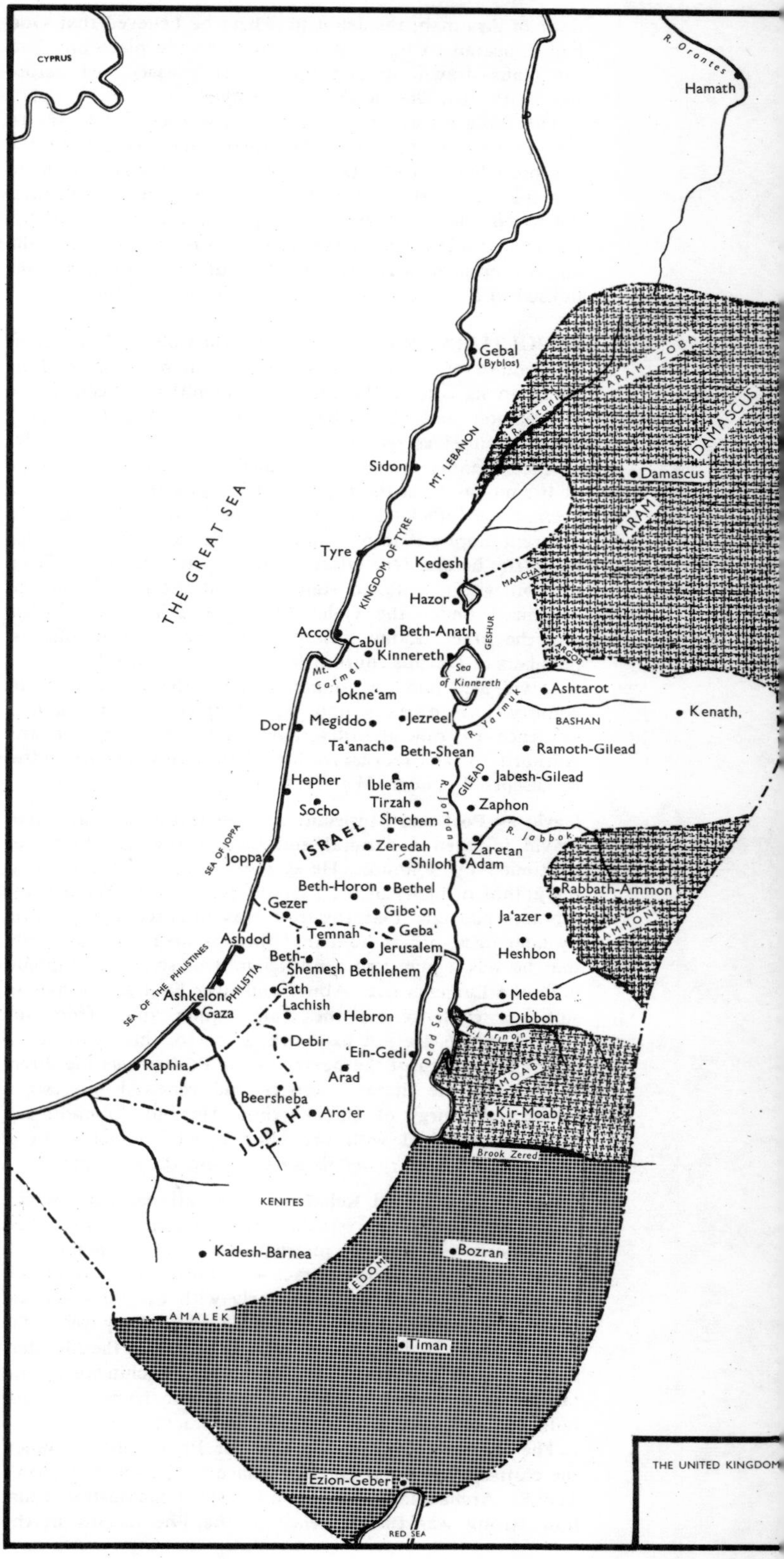

floor of Araunah, the Jebusite, where he believed that God had appeared to him. David purchased the place and had the plans drawn up and the materials assembled before his death (ca. 964 BCE).

The Bible records that David was warned not to try to put up the building, but the reason may have been the bad precedent of the Shiloh sanctuary (which was considered a temple). The Ark had been housed there when the Philistines destroyed the sanctuary and captured the Ark. Equally, David's people may not yet have been ready to change the ancient custom whereby the Ark of the Covenant was housed in a "tabernacle and in a tent" as in Shiloh.

II. CULTURAL BACKGROUND. **The Cultural Revolution:** The country's unification and expansion naturally had its effect on its culture. People who had hitherto been united by religion and the tribal traditions of the Covenant* found themselves part of an organized state. The transfer of the religious centre to Jerusalem enhanced the prestige of the monarch, at the expense of the priesthood. Yahwism became the official state religion in a way which gave a different emphasis to a situation which had, of course, also been true before. One effect of this institution of an official religion within a united state was that the priesthood was organized under the Chief Priest, Abiathar. He, Zadok and the other leading priests* were made royal officials, members of David's court in Jerusalem (II Sam. 8:17–18).

David also laid the foundations for the division of the country into districts and its administration through a sequence of officials (described under Government and Authority*). His reorganization of the army and its cadres is discussed under Warfare*.

David as Poet and Musician: Biblical tradition relates that David initiated a cultural and literary revival which was continued by Solomon. He is revered in this tradition as the author of many of the Psalms* (see article). While some scholars consider that this role was imposed upon David by later ages, others hold that there is no reason to doubt that he was a poet and a musician. This school of thought finds the Laments over Abner and over Saul and Jonathan sufficient evidence for the claim, quite apart from the Psalms, which are not his work. Even so, there can be no doubt that much of the poetry of the Psalms was the direct product of the literary activity and renewed interest in ritual and liturgy of David's time. He and Solomon can justly be credited with providing a vital impetus for a spiritual and literary renaissance among their people.

International Cultural Relations: The national unity which David brought to the Israelite tribes within Palestine also had repercussions on the international scene. Under David, the Israelites came into contact with the major powers and currents of civilization, particularly with the Phoenicians* of Tyre and Sidon (II Sam. 5:11; I Ch. 14:1). They were a far more sophisticated people, the leading traders of the Mediterranean, with a highly developed art, architecture and literature (see Phoenicia*) and theirs became the predominant influence on Israel's cultural development.

The Bible records the fact that the Phoenicians supplied the craftsmen to build David's palace and, later, Solomon's Temple. Archaeological research has since demonstrated just how strong was the influence of the Phoenicians in the process of civilizing Israel which David began. The Phoenicians were Canaanites (see Canaan*; Canaanite Civilization*; Phoenicians*) and, naturally, the Israelites were strongly influenced by the people of the land — both negatively and positively. They shared a common language and indeed many of the citizens of the state were Canaanites. The impact of their ideas and fashions in all secular spheres probably offers a partial explanation for the bitterness with which the prophets had to fight to keep religion free from the same influences. This religious aspect developed long after David's reign, but its foundations were laid during his lifetime. They were an unexpected offshoot of the measures of economic and commercial expansion which produced the prosperity of Solomon's reign (see B below).

III. DAVID'S CHARACTER: The personality of David as he is generally pictured is a fascinating mixture of historical fact and romantic legend. What seems certain is that the David of history was a figure of heroic stature, a powerful fighter, commander and ruler, combining personal charm and courage with the fierceness his age demanded and the sound judgment and determination of a successful leader and administrator. The realism with which II Sam.* and I. K.* present David's weaknesses as well as his virtues is a good indication of the early date of the traditions concerning his life and kingship. Even when his actions were in flagrant contempt of the Law (e.g. his conduct in relation to Bathsheba) the record was carefully preserved — in this particular case it was closely linked with the question of the succession to the throne. In the course of time, Jewish national tradition invested his name with a halo of mystic associations and divine prestige until David became a powerful religious symbol and his descendants the pivot of centuries of messianic dreams (see Hasmoneans*; Apocalypse*). This attitude endowed him with every ethical and religious virtue. The idealistic approach is very apparent in the treatment of kingship, statehood and national religion in the Books of Chronicles* (see article), where the David of pious legend really emerges. David's real importance in Israel's religious history, however, was as the founder of the sanctuary of Zion and its organization.

His religious role was magnified and expanded by later generations until Jewish tradition could claim "King David still lives" (Rosh ha-Shanah 25a) and the theology of the Qumran sectaries (see Dead Sea Scrolls*), Christianity and Islam could all venerate David as a figure of towering religious significance.

B. SOLOMON. I: LIFE AND POLICY: **The Succession:** Solomon, the son of David and Bathsheba (II Sam. 12:24 ff) was born ca. 986 BCE although this date is not certain. He was a gifted youth and appeared to be in the line of succession. According to contemporary custom, a ruling king had the right to name his successor and apparently David intended his throne to go to Solomon. However, because of the scandal associated with his mother, Bathsheba, David probably found it difficult to establish him as the principal heir. Moreover, after the death of Absalom, his elder brother, Adonijah, had the better claim to the throne.

Adonijah, however, did not wait upon events. While his father was still living, he took steps to establish himself as the king. He enlisted the powerful support of both Joab, the army commander, and Abiathar the Chief Priest and held the sacrifices and feasting that were tantamount to a coronation. He was out-manoeuvred, however, by Bathsheba and Nathan the prophet, who persuaded David to have Solomon officially crowned king during his own lifetime. The impressive and elaborate ceremony (I K. 1:32–40) left no doubt in the minds of the people that Solomon was their lawful ruler. For the last three years of David's life, Solomon acted as co-regent (967–964 BCE). At first he spared the lives of his rival and his supporters but Adonijah and the others were killed when their actions began to arouse Solomon's suspicions (I K. 2:5–18; 13–25).

This left Solomon in a secure position from which to consolidate and organize the realm he had inherited from his father. His was to be a peaceful reign during which the internal administration, organization and prosperity of the kingdom were fostered in place of military adventures and the expansion of frontiers.

Contemporary Political Background: David's achievements had laid a sound political foundation for the Solomonic era. The Arameans* had been conquered and there was apparently no sign of any dangerous revival on their part. Assyria* under Tiglat-Pileser II offered no threat while Sidon and Tyre, with their great interest in international trade, welcomed peaceful cooperation with their southern neighbour. Egypt was floundering in the hands of the last weak rulers of the 21st Tanaite Dynasty. One indication of Israel's importance in relation to Egypt is Solomon's marriage to a daughter of the Egyptian Pharaoh (I K. 3:1) which brought him the city of Gezer* as a dowry. Pharaoh captured the city to give it to Solomon, which seems to show that it was outside the borders of Israel at that time.

Living in a period relatively free from the clashes of ambitious rival monarchs, Solomon was able to concentrate on his country's internal welfare. He developed the friendly relations established by his father with the Phoenicians and introduced many of the material and cultural products of their civilization into Israel.

Administration: Governing a territory which extended from Egypt to the Euphrates demanded an efficient administration. Solomon followed the pattern begun by David. He divided the northern kingdom into 12 prefectures, as David had already done, with Judah as the southern kingdom (see Government and Authority*). This organization cut across the ancient tribal boundaries and included the Canaanite city-states which David's conquests had brought into the kingdom. These divisions were the units for raising revenue, forced labour and military reserves (see Taxes*, Tribute*). They also had the practical function of providing for the expenses of government and of the court. Each district was responsible for maintaining the royal household for one month of the year (I K. 4:7 ff); see map under Government and Authority*.

Twelve officers were appointed as supervisors of the levies and the conscription from each district (4:8–19). These officers in turn were in the charge of an official "Azariah the son of Nathan" (4:5). There is no indication of the basis on which they were selected. Their number — twelve — was traditional and some of the prefectures corresponded to the old "tribal" territories. Nevertheless, the whole system marked a tendency to depart from the patriarchal authority of tribal days. Solomon also constructed a series of store cities (for instance Lachish*; Beth-Shemesh*) as regional centres for the collection of taxes in kind (for full details, see Government and Authority*), in addition to new and restored fortresses and chariot cities like Megiddo* and Hazor*, Gezer* and Beth-horon, Ba'alath and Tamar. They controlled strategic roads and served as stationary bases for a strong mobile army (see Warfare*; Cities, Israelite*: Fortifications).

No serious military operations are recorded during Solomon's reign, but the king secured the strong position inherited from David by the creation of a formidable standing army. David had been steadfastly opposed to the use of chariots, but Solomon organized the first chariot force in the country (I K. 10:26). Traces of his chariot cities were found in Gezer* and at Megiddo* although at the latter site most of the remains were from the time of Ahab who had a much stronger force of chariots and horsemen (see Arms and Weapons*; Warfare*). Solomon apparently based the national defence system on the central mobile arm of chariot forces, following the contemporary custom which saw the best defence in versatile offensive action rather than in shutting all available forces into various fortified points throughout the kingdom.

To protect and improve his international standing, Solomon also entered into a number of alliances — diplomatic and matrimonial — with foreign rulers; notably his agreements with Hiram of Tyre.

Culture: In the cultural sphere — as in so much else — Solomon continued and extended the expansion begun under David. The arts of historiography and literature, especially parables and "wisdom"* writings, were encouraged and a new attention was paid to elegance of style. Several biblical works came to be attributed to Solomon himself (Song of Songs*; Ecclesiastes*; Psalm* 72), while his reputation for "wisdom" grew with the passing years. There is no historical basis for the traditional assumptions about the authorship of the books but they do indicate the atmosphere of literary activity and experiment which dates from the United Kingdom.

This development can be seen clearly in some of the oldest sources relating to Solomon's reign, which have a style and a character very much their own and quite distinct from the rest of the Books of Kings*. These early sources include the documents from the royal library and the Temple Archives; the list of Solomon's officers, districts and their administration in I K. 4; the detailed description of the Temple precincts in chs. 6 and 7; the various stories of Solomon's wisdom, his dream at Gibeon, his administration of justice and his meeting with the Queen of Sheba (I K. chs. 3 and 10). The story in ch. 12 about the kingdom being divided after his son, Rehoboam, had foolishly rejected the advice of his father's councillors, may also derive from these same circles (see Israel and Judah*, Part I).

Deterioration: For all his achievements and triumphs, the end of Solomon's reign was a period of general decay — the inevitable result of the tensions inherent in his administration. One of the major causes of dissatisfaction was the system of forced labour (corvée) which had become increasingly unpopular. The great building programmes (see below: Building and Trade) do not appear to have done much to improve the economic position of the mass of the people and had resulted mainly in increased exactions of levies and taxation from them.

Open revolt began first among the subject peoples, the Edomites and Arameans (I K. 11) but clearly there was plenty of disaffection within the country as well. Matters came to a head at the time of Solomon's death. His successor, his son Rehoboam, could not hold the nation together and it divided into the twin kingdoms of Israel and Judah* (see article). The explanation of the division given by the writer of I K. 11:27 and 12:4–14 indicates the new trends developing within the court of the aging monarch. Dissatisfaction was particularly strong among the ten northern tribes of Israel who felt no special loyalty towards a Judean king, deeply resented his tyranny and rejected the principle of dynastic succession outright. During Solomon's lifetime, Jeroboam, an Ephraimite, had sought refuge with the Egyptian Pharaoh but he returned from exile at the time of the king's death to head the rebellious northern tribes and, with their secession, to become king (see Israel and Judah*, I).

II. BUILDING AND TRADE: Solomon's most tangible innovation was his construction of a series of imposing and magnificent buildings, which could match those of Egypt or Phoenicia. They were modelled mainly on Phoenician patterns and were built by local labour directed and taught by Phoenician artists and craftsmen. The most outstanding were the Temple* (see article), his palace, and the residences for his numerous harem (I K. 7:8; Song of Songs 6:8).

The scene of the most extensive building operations was, of course, Jerusalem. Apart from the Temple and the palaces, Solomon also completed the construction of the Millo, which David had begun. This was a massive block of fortifications apparently forming an acropolis on the top of "David's City" (on the site known as Ophel, see Jerusalem*). To connect the different quarters of the city, which began its westward expansion during his reign, he also had the slopes between the old Jebusite wall and the northern extension of the city where the Temple and palace quarter stood, filled in (for a more detailed description, see Jerusalem*).

Solomon's Ships: Having secured the foundation of a stable, prosperous kingdom, Solomon put his strategic position across the great trade routes of the world to good use and became famous as a trader. His dealings with adjacent countries, including the western Mediterranean and the Arabian coast, are treated in detail in the articles on Trade* and Arabia and Israel*. The famous visit of the Queen of Sheba was almost certainly prompted by motives of commercial rivalry, while Solomon's dealings in horses and chariots became legendary (I K. 10).

Solomon developed the port of Ezion-Geber (present day Tel el Kheleifeh near Elath), sending fleets of "Ships of Tarshish" (cargo vessels, see Ships and Navigation*) down the Red Sea to Arabian ports and further. A little to the north of Ezion-Geber, the copper and iron ore deposits of the southern Negeb were exploited.

Kings Solomon's Mines: The smelting and refining plant of Ezion Geber (Tel el Kheleifeh) was one of the largest in

386

387

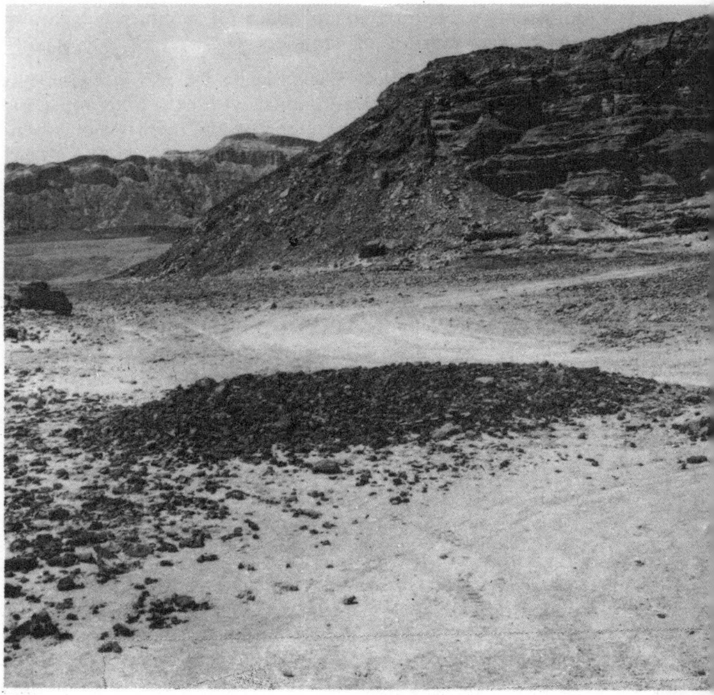
388

389

the Near East. According to N. Glueck, smelting operations were carried out in a narrow valley, placed so that the strong north wind which blows almost constantly provided sufficient draught for the furnaces and made up for the inefficient wood fuel which was used. Other scholars, however, doubt whether the wind could have been adequate and believe that bellows must have been used to heat the fires of the furnaces; see **(386)** bellows nozzle (Timnah) and **(387)** crucible (Tel el Kheleifeh).

Evidence of mining and refining activities remains in the heaps of copper slag **(388, 9)** on the sites. The work was done by slave labour, presumably directed by hired Phoenician workmen, for the Phoenicians had gained experience in copper smelting in Cyprus. The slaves were housed in walled encampments, traces of which can still be seen close by the site where the heaps of copper slag and green copper stains on the walls bear witness to the work of smelting. N. Glueck believes that in view of the organization involved, Ezion-Geber represents one of Solomon's greatest accomplishments: "Thousands of labourers had to be assembled, housed, fed and protected . . . Skilled technicians of all kinds had to be recruited. Great caravans had to be assembled to transport materials and food. An effective business organization had to be called into existence to regulate the profitable flow of raw materials and finished and semifinished products . . ."

The copper was used for trade and in Solomon's building projects. Again Phoenician workmen were probably employed. One of them, Hiram of Tyre, the son of a Hebrew widow of the tribe of Naphtali and a Phoenican father, is mentioned specifically as being responsible for all the bronze work for the Temple (I K. 7:13 ff).

III. CHARACTER: Solomon appears to have begun his reign with high ideals and the resolve to live up to them. His dream (3:5) in which he asked God for the gift of wisdom above all other possible benefits, was a natural expression of his aspirations to rule wisely and well. However, in the eyes of many of his contemporaries and of later generations, his wealth and ostentation make it seem that his very success was his undoing. Solomon was a pious man, as is evident from his prayer (I K. 8:23–53) and his care for religious observances. He was, however, far too tolerant of divergent practices for the taste of his people. His many marriages — although they were undertaken as a matter of diplomacy — also had their influence. He had to permit his foreign wives to practice their own religions and to build suitable shrines and altars for them. These were probably also necessary as an inducement to foreign traders to visit or settle in Jerusalem. His sanction of so many alien cults side by side with that of the Temple in Jerusalem (I K. 11:5–6) seemed like the first step in a process of syncretism and dilution of the national religion. In the end "when Solomon was old his wives turned away his heart after other gods" (11:4). In short, to the historian of Kings, the collapse of Solomon's kingdom was the inevitable sequel to his "sin" of marrying foreign wives and its corollary of idolatry. (Polygamy as such was no sin.) The passage in I K. 11, although written by later historians is probably a valid reflection of the feelings of many of his subjects towards the end of the king's life. Solomon died in 924 or 922 BCE having reigned "forty years".

390

DEAD SEA SCROLLS. — *Outline: Discoveries of the Scrolls; I. What Are the Scrolls?: a. Old Testament and Apocrypha; b. Original Sectarian Scrolls. II. Significance of the Scrolls: Biblical Texts and Hebrew Literature; Sectaries and Contemporary Jews; Modern History of the Scrolls. III. Who Wrote the Scrolls?: The Essenes; The Essenes and Qumran. IV. History of the Qumran Settlement. V. Description; The Righteous Teacher; The Wicked Priest. VI. Doctrines of the Qumran Community. VII. Sacraments of the Sectaries: 1. Baptism and the Holy Spirit; 2. Sectaries and Temple Sacrifice; A Spiritual Temple; 3. Liturgical Significance of the Common Meal; Messianism. VIII. The Scrolls and Christianity: Common Ground in Messianism; Christian Communal Meals; Christian Baptism; Organization; Dualism of Good and Evil; The New Covenant; Conclusions.*

Discoveries of the Scrolls: The first of the caves which held the Dead Sea Scrolls was found accidentally, near the north-western edge of the Dead Sea in 1947. Over the next nine or ten years a dramatic series of discoveries revealed stores of innumerable fragments belonging to more than 600 manuscripts in a group of eleven caves around Qumran. A long, arduous process of reading, transcribing, publishing and translating the documents is under way and it may possibly yield answers to many questions about the Scrolls, their authors and their relationship to contemporary movements in theology and literature.

I. WHAT ARE THE SCROLLS? The Scrolls are a vast collection of religious and theological works with a few secular documents, mostly written during the three centuries before the destruction of Jerusalem, in 68–70 CE. They had been hidden for safety in the caves. Those in Cave 1 were wrapped in several layers of cloth, perhaps impregnated with oil, and stored inside earthenware jars sealed with closely-fitting lids. Of the eleven caves containing manuscripts, the richest was Cave 4, where thousands of fragments belonging to more than 300 different manuscripts were found **(390)**.

a. **Old Testament and Apocrypha:** The Scrolls include fragments from all the books of the Hebrew canon of the Old Testament with the exception of the Book of Esther. There are two relatively complete scrolls of Isaiah. There are also fragments of familiar apocryphal and apocalyptic* works in Hebrew and Aramaic. These include the Book of Tobit, the Hebrew version of Jubilees and the Aramaic version of Enoch, etc., hitherto known only in translation. The sectaries and their contemporaries may not have made the sharp distinction between apocryphal ("outside books") and canonical biblical writings which developed in later rabbinical* circles. All prophecy may have been regarded as the word of God. From the number of fragments discovered, it seems, in the opinion of some scholars, that the sectaries had a greater veneration for Isaiah and the minor prophets Nahum and Habakkuk, whose prophecy they thought would be fulfilled in their own lifetimes, than for Jeremiah or Ezekiel. This judgment is possible, though it may be amended by future discovery and research.

b. **Original Sectarian Scrolls:** In addition, a number of scrolls were original compositions. Many of these became known for the first time and these provided most of the information about the nonconformist sect or community in which they originated. Among them are: the Scroll of the **Rule of the Community** (Discipline Scroll), the main source for details about the aims and organization of the sect; the sectarian **Thanksgiving Hymns,** a poetic formulation of the sect's theology; the Scroll of the **War of the Children of Light against the Children of Darkness,** ('War Scroll'); a **Genesis Apocryphon,** an expanded version in Aramaic of some of the stories of Genesis, with features suggesting a common background with other apocryphal "midrashim", particularly the Book of Enoch; the previously known **Damascus (Zadokite) Document; Commentaries** on books of the Bible, including **Habakkuk, Nahum, Psalms, Hosea,**

391

Isaiah and **Micah,** interpreting them in terms of the history and theology of the sect; **Testimonia** (Laws, liturgies, prayers, beatitudes, blessings, hymns and Wisdom of the Essenes); a **Description of the New Jerusalem;** an Exposition (Midrash) of the apocryphal **Book of Moses;** astronomical observations on Enoch and Jubilees and other calendrical works, mostly in fragments (see Testimony Document **391**).

Whether their original compositions were regarded as equal to scripture in inspiration and authority is not clear. This may not have been the case, since the only commentaries are on biblical books, not on their own writings. Nevertheless, these were an integral part of the life and mission of the community.

The Scroll of the **"War of the Sons of Light against the Sons of Darkness,"** one of the outstanding discoveries, contains a set of directions for an ideal messianic campaign, beginning with the conquest of the country and ending 60 years later with the conquest of the whole world. The Scroll describes the forces involved and their deployment, the trumpet calls and banners to be used. The operation is to be fought by the "Sons of Light" (the sectaries, Israel, or the tribes of Levi, Judah and Benjamin) against the "Sons of Darkness" or Israel's traditional enemies, the "Kittim". These may have been the Hellenists and Greeks but, here, were probably the Romans, for the Scroll tells that the enemy venerated their weapons and made sacrifices to their standards — as the Roman soldiers did.

Typically, the camp of the Sons of Light is organized on a Mosaic pattern and insists on "purity", i. e. abstention from all sexual activity. This attitude reflects ancient taboos about sex found in various phases of the Old Testament. That many of the sectaries of Qumran really did live according to this ideal seems to be confirmed by the very few female skeletons found in their cemetery and the total absence of children's skeletons. This, of course, is not conclusive evidence for celibacy. Recent studies of the Scrolls have revealed additional details which suggest that, in fact, it was the exception rather than the rule. It may have applied only to the resident central oligarchy or directorate, and there may have been varying degrees of asceticism among the members (currently identified with the Essenes), who lived elsewhere.

The Zadokite Document was apparently written by the sectaries of Qumran and tells of the founding of a sect, possibly stemming from the early Hassidim*, or another nonconformist stream, during Hasmonean* times. It is generally recognized that the Qumran sectaries wrote (or regarded) this as a protest against existing priestly leadership. For the sect took the name of the "Sons of Zadok" (the name of the High Priest in the days of David and Solomon) and withdrew to "Damascus" under their own honoured teacher and leader, known as the "Star". "Damascus" here may have been meant allegorically rather than literally. Alternatively, some scholars (e. g. J. T. Milik), find in this Scroll the rules of conduct for a subsidiary branch (or branches) of the Essenes, who actually lived in or near Damascus. The laws given are very similar to those of the sectaries' own "Discipline Scroll". The Sons of Zadok also enter into a "New Covenant" and are waiting for the coming of the Kingdom of God when the "Elect of God's favour" will "atone for the earth and mete out punishment to the wicked". Fragments belonging to several copies of the document were found in the caves of Qumran. Most of its contents had been found earlier in the Cairo "*genizah*" (synagogue reliquary).

II. SIGNIFICANCE OF THE SCROLLS: — **Biblical Texts and Hebrew Literature:** One reason for the supreme importance of the Qumran Scrolls is that the Biblical manuscripts included among them — over one hundred specific works — provide the earliest known texts of the Old Testament. The oldest Hebrew biblical manuscripts previously known had been the "massoretic" text* of the 9th and 10th cs. CE. The Scrolls, written a thousand years earlier, show very few variations from their later copies, with the exception of the Book of Samuel which resembles the version known to the Greek translators. Many other fragments of the Pentateuch and Jeremiah also resemble the Septuagint (see Biblical Criticism*; Bible Canon and Text*).

At the same time, the Scrolls have made possible a much clearer understanding of other non-canonical Hebrew literature of the time — particularly apocalyptic* beliefs and writings which had been largely condemned or at least passed over by the Rabbinical* teachers of the Mishnah* and Talmud.

Sectaries and Contemporary Jews: As a whole, the sectaries were part of a wider movement within Judaism. This wider movement formed an opposition to the established orthodoxy of the Jerusalem priesthood but, because of the very stringent demands made on its members, it could not have so great or lasting an influence as the Pharisees*. The Essenes and Qumran sectaries had much in common with the Pharisees but they insisted on a much stricter observance of the most minute details of the Mosaic Law. There is, nevertheless, a school of thought which sees the sectaries as sub-groups of Pharisees.

As Pharisaism developed into normative, Rabbinical Judaism, features shared by Pharisee and sectary survived, whereas the distinguishing marks of the Essenes and other nonconformist movements left no lasting impression on Judaism. Nevertheless, the development of primitive Christianity reflects many of the factors which influenced the Qumran sect. The Scrolls' significance for the Christian world is discussed at the end of this article.

Modern History of the Scrolls: Some of the scrolls came into the possession of the Hebrew Univeraity through the efforts of E. L. Sukenik who was the first to publish selections from their contents. Others went to the United States where they were published by M. Burrows, W. H. Brownlee, and others. They were subsequently purchased for the

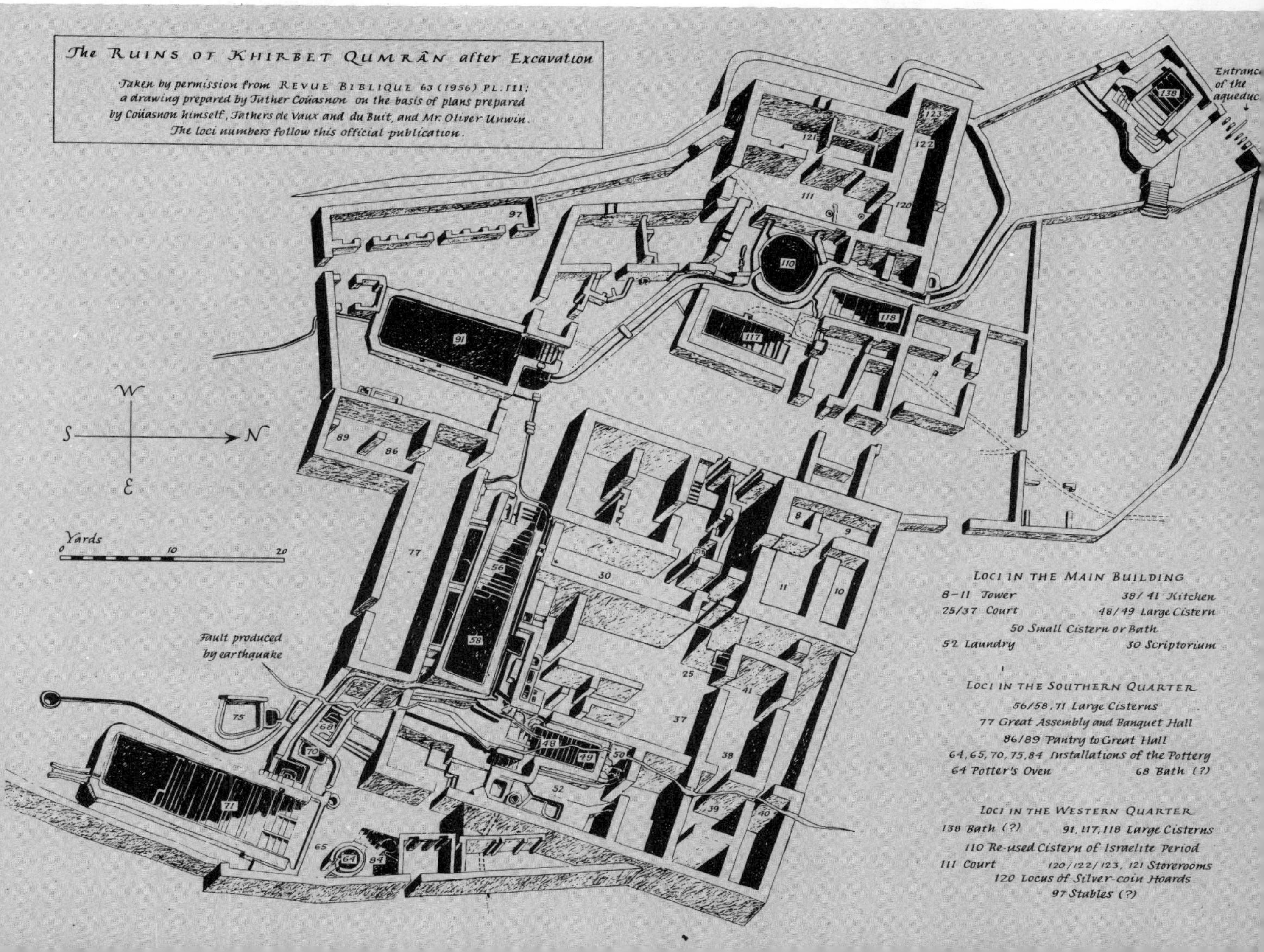

393

394

government of Israel. Others are in the possession of the Jordanian Department of Antiquities and are being studied by an international team of scholars.

III. WHO WROTE THE SCROLLS? — Very early in the process of reading the Scrolls, it became apparent that the answer would show some connection with the obscure contemporary Jewish sect of the Essenes.

The Essenes: Apparently, the Essenes were men who chose to live in isolated communities (i. e., "yahad"), devoted to a life of self-denial and rigid discipline in preparation for the coming End of the World (see Eschatology*). Their existence as the third sect of Judaism (the others were the Pharisees* and the Sadducees*) had been known from ancient sources — Josephus*, Philo, Eusebius and Pliny the Elder's Natural History. These older sources give the number of Essenes as about 4,000, living in groups scattered through Palestine, with their centre near Ein-gedi* (close to the Dead Sea, south of Qumran). As the outward sign of their dedication to purity, they dressed in white and practiced frequent ceremonial lustrations (ceremonial washings).

They rejected private property and lived in communal houses owned by the community. Except for a few "marrying Essenes", the majority were celibate and refused to procreate. This tended to keep their numbers small, though they did accept children, orphans and others, as well as proselytes from Judaism. Initiation followed a rigorous probation and a searching examination. If admitted, a candidate had to swear to conduct himself in accordance with the ethical principles of the group and to separate himself from the "community of the men of iniquity." Egalitarian and pacifist, they nevertheless fought heroically in the rebellion against Rome, some leaders even coming from their ranks.

The Essenes and Qumran: Although not identical, there are far more similarities than differences between the Essenes and the sectaries of Qumran. Both were holy communities seeking the kingdom of God in ways that differed from the ideas of contemporary religious and secular leaders in Jerusalem. They both regarded themselves as chosen by God to be the future congregation of the "Elect" and both went out into the "wilderness" to prepare "the Way of the Lord" and rebirth into the "New Israel". From a variety of suggested identifications, the most widely accepted view today is that the sectaries of Qumran were Essenes, perhaps at a different stage of the movement's development.

IV. HISTORY OF THE QUMRAN SETTLEMENT: When the Qumran site was explored, a central building and over 1,000 graves nearby were found, as well as the central caves containing fragments of the Scrolls. From carbon-14 tests made on the cloth in which the Scrolls were wrapped, from coins and pieces of stonework found in the caves, as well as from similarities in the style of language or writing of the Scrolls themselves, it has been possible to reach fairly precise dates for the different periods of settlement of the community.

Judging by coins found on the site, the first period probably began about 110 BCE, during the prosperous reign of John Hyrcanus*. The original nucleus of the community is thought to have been a group of priests who, in protest against the "evil" religious leadership of the Hasmoneans* in Jerusalem, withdrew into the "wilderness". At Qumran, they came to the shattered remnants of an Israelite fortress which had lain deserted since the conquest of Judah by the Babylonians five centuries before. There they built their settlement.

Some scholars put the date a few decades later. However, it is possible that one cause of their withdrawal to their isolated retreat was their refusal to accept Hasmonean High Priests. To the sectaries, a priesthood who were not true descendants of Zadok were usurpers. They regarded the sanctuary in Jerusalem as defiled and the calendar* fixed by these interlopers as unorthodox. (The sectaries themselves followed a solar calendar similar to the system proposed in the book of Jubilees.)

In 31 BCE, the settlement was abandoned, perhaps because of an earthquake which partly destroyed the buildings; perhaps, as some scholars think, because the sectaries returned for a time to take an active part in the life of the country. In either case, by the beginning of the 1st c. CE, Qumran had been rebuilt and was occupied by the writers of the scrolls until its destruction by the Romans in 68 CE, at which time many of the Scrolls were probably placed in their hiding places. Many of the scrolls found belong to the earlier period. The Romans used the settlement as a fortress for a time and, between 132 and 135 CE, it was occupied again, this time by Jewish fighters of the Second Rebellion against Rome under Bar-Kochba*. After that, the site remained totally uninhabited, until, a few years ago, it suddenly became the centre of world-wide interest.

V. THE QUMRAN SETTLEMENT: While it remained the home of the sectaries (ca. 110 BCE to 68 CE), the settlement covered an area two miles to the north and two to the south of Qumran, along the cliffs facing the Dead Sea. Living in caves and tents around a central building, the people depended on common stores of food and water, made use of a communal irrigation system (found on the spot), shared pottery made in a communal kiln and read — and wrote — common biblical and original Scrolls.

The principal building (see diagram **392**) seems to have been a square 37.5 m. (124 feet) on each side, with a defensive tower on the north-west corner. Around this centre, the complex group of structures included a refectory (banqueting hall), kitchen and pantry. Stacks of over a thousand ceramic dishes (**393**) found in the pantry suggest that, at times, Qumran may have catered to large numbers of pilgrims. An undamaged cylindrical jar (**394**) like the ones in which the Scrolls were stored, was also uncovered. Other rooms in which the remains of plastered benches were found against the wall, may have been community rooms used for prayer, meditation or discussion (**396**).

The "Scriptorium" where at least some of the Qumran manuscripts were penned was one of the first-storey rooms of the block. It still contained the remains of a narrow plaster table (**395**) 5 metres long (17 × 2 feet), a plaster bench, a hand basin with small depressions around the edge and, finally, two inkwells, one brass, one earthenware, still bearing traces of dried ink. Water from the occasional winter rains was carried by an aqueduct from the foot

395

396

397

of the waterfall at Wadi Qumran and stored in seven major cisterns (**397**). Six smaller pools or baths were also found within the settlement (see diagram **392**).

Was it a Monastery? The Qumran settlement was not a "monastery" as that word is understood today. A sectarian religious centre would define it more accurately. The members of the sect who made pilgrimages to it from their homes elsewhere may have followed a less rigorously ascetic way of life, or been less advanced in their mystic consciousness.

The Righteous Teacher: The sectaries were preparing for the coming of the Messiah and the messianic era through constant and diligent study of the Torah, under the guidance of their original leader, the Teacher of Righteousness. He seems to have appeared around 110 BCE at the time of the first settlement in Qumran. The sectaries believed that the mysteries of Torah and prophecy had been revealed to him by a direct revelation from God and, provided they were faithful to him and his teaching, they would be numbered among the members of the Kingdom of God. Accordingly, they made their own interpretation of Scripture, which developed into an esoteric discipline, kept a carefully guarded secret. Although he was never identified with any of the messianic figures described in the Scrolls, the existence of the Righteous Teacher was their assurance that the age of the Messiah was at hand. In the Zadokite Document, the Messiah was expected 40 years after the death of the Teacher of Righteousness.

The Wicked Priest: His death, so the Scrolls imply, was brought about by his enemy, the Wicked Priest, though this seems unlikely. Originally a faithful servant of God, the Wicked Priest had been corrupted by the material world, made himself rich in unlawful ways, and persecuted the faithful community. The Scroll foretells that, in retribution, he and the "last priests of Jerusalem" would be handed over to the enemy, the "Kittim" which here, probably, meant the Romans. So far, no certain identification of the Righteous Teacher or the Wicked Priest has been possible, though there are several candidates. The situation described by the Scroll could have occurred at any time between the beginning of the Hasmonean* dynasty and the accession of Herod the Great.

VI. DOCTRINES OF THE QUMRAN COMMUNITY: The community was a body of priests and dedicated laymen living according to divine rules laid down in the Law and the Prophets. They aimed at achieving that standard of holiness and justice, equity and mercy which biblical tradition showed to be the nature of God.

The New Covenant: The Sectaries believed that the end of the world was to come within their own lifetimes. With the passing of "this" world, a new Israel would be created out of the "Remnant" of the old Israel and a new Covenant, a *b^e^rith teshubba* (Covenant of Repentance), between God and man would replace the old Covenant of Sinai.

The Two Ways: The Sectaries saw the world ruled by the power of good, opposed by the power of evil. They believed themselves to have been chosen by God as the "Sons of Light", while the rest of humanity were "Sons of Darkness".

The New Age: By making their life in this world as close as possible to what they conceived as the "Way of the Kingdom", the sectaries hoped to hasten the coming of the Kingdom of God and the New Age, in which the inequalities of the existing world would be ended and unity would be achieved through the spirit.

The Poor (Ebionim): In preparation, they called themselves the "Congregation of the Poor", which seems to anticipate Jesus' ". . . the poor shall inherit the earth." A century later, the first Jerusalem church used the same title, "the poor" ("Ebionim") of itself, while its members also "had all things in common" as a foretaste of life under God (see Christianity, Early*: Jewish-Christians).

VII. SACRAMENTS OF THE SECTARIES:
1. Baptism and the Holy Spirit: If accepted as fit to become one of "God's elect", a candidate for initiation was solemnly baptized: "Then God in his faithfulness will purify all the works of man, and cleanse for himself the body man, in order to consume every wicked spirit from the midst of his flesh . . . and to make him pure with a holy spirit from every wicked deed; and he will sprinkle on him a spirit of truth like water for impurity . . . so as to give the righteous understanding the knowledge of the Most High." (Rule of the Community (QS), 4:20–21; see reproduction **398**).

Baptism however, had to *follow* sincere repentance if it was to be effective. Like the prophets and teachers of earlier Judaism, the sectaries believed that sin polluted the flesh in the same way as "unclean" objects. To purify the flesh by baptism without first repenting of sin was quite useless. Salvation came through the "spirit" and thus required inner purity.

With the aid of the Holy spirit thus conferred, the initiates of the community attained to a knowledge of divine secrets.

The sectaries' belief that their baptism was a preliminary to baptism by the spirit in "the end of days" is identical to the views of John the Baptizer* and is also to be found in the Gospel of John* (3:4–7).

Two of the cisterns found in Qumran had divided stairways running down to the different levels of water. This has suggested to some scholars that they were occasionally used as baptistries. However, it seems unlikely that the community immersed itself in its drinking water. Baptisms were more probably performed where there was living (running) water, at Ein Feshkhah nearby or in the Jordan, a few miles to the north.

2. Sectaries and Temple Sacrifice: It is known that other sects throughout Palestine and Transjordan had (according to Pere J. Thomas) substituted baptizing rites for the observance of Temple sacrifice. The Essenes, according to Josephus, rejected sacrifice at the Temple. This was not a matter of principle but, like the prophets of ancient Israel, they insisted that for sacrifice to be meaningful, God's ethical and ritual laws must first be observed. The discovery of meticulous burials of animal bones around Qumran suggests that they made their own sacrifices, perhaps on an altar patterned after the one set up by Moses in the desert (see Priests*).

A Spiritual Temple: Cut off from the Temple — the focus of Judaism -- the sectaries developed a special attitude towards its ceremonies. They looked forward to sacrifice being offered by their priests according to their own rites in a future purified Temple. At the same time, they saw their own community and way of life as a kind of spiritual Temple, superior to the physical building in Jerusalem. The Christian concept of the church may very possibly have grown out of this.

3. Liturgical Significance of the Common Meal: The centre of the community's regular life was the communal meal, conducted as a ceremonial anticipation of the banquet that would celebrate the imminent victory of the Messiah. It was eaten in "tohora" (purity) at midday and evening. Admission to the common meal, barred to the uninitiated, was the final step in joining the community, reached after a novice had served a full two-year probation. The Rule of the Community gives precise instructions for the meal and the exact order of precedence: "This is the order of the sessions of the 'Men of the Name' who are summoned to the Feast for the communal council when God sends the Messiah to be with them: The Priest shall enter at the head of all the congregation of Israel and all the fathers of the Aaronids . . . and they shall sit before him each according to his rank. Next the Messiah of Israel shall enter, and the heads of the thousands of Israel shall sit before him each according to his rank. And . . . they shall sit before the (two of) them, each according to his rank . . . ." (Adjunct to the Rule of the Community, I (QS) 1:11–12).

This liturgical anticipation of the messianic banquet incorporates many traditional features of Judaism which, since rabbinic days had, in a sense, seen all meals as religious rites.

Messianism: It is not clear whether the sectaries expected two Messiahs, namely the Davidic King and the Zadokite high priest, in which case their "Messiah of Israel" apparently refers to the Royal (Davidic) Messiah; or, alternatively, the "Messiah of Aaron and Israel" in the singular. In the sectaries' assembly, there were two figures, the lay head and the priestly head of the community representing the Messiah of Israel and the Messiah of Aaron. Neither is their vision of how the messianic victory will be achieved made clear. Some scholars think they expected the kingdom of heaven to be a continuation of military successes on earth. The New Age would come when Israel had triumphed over all her enemies.

VIII. THE SCROLLS AND CHRISTIANITY: As early as 1950, Christian interest in the background to both the

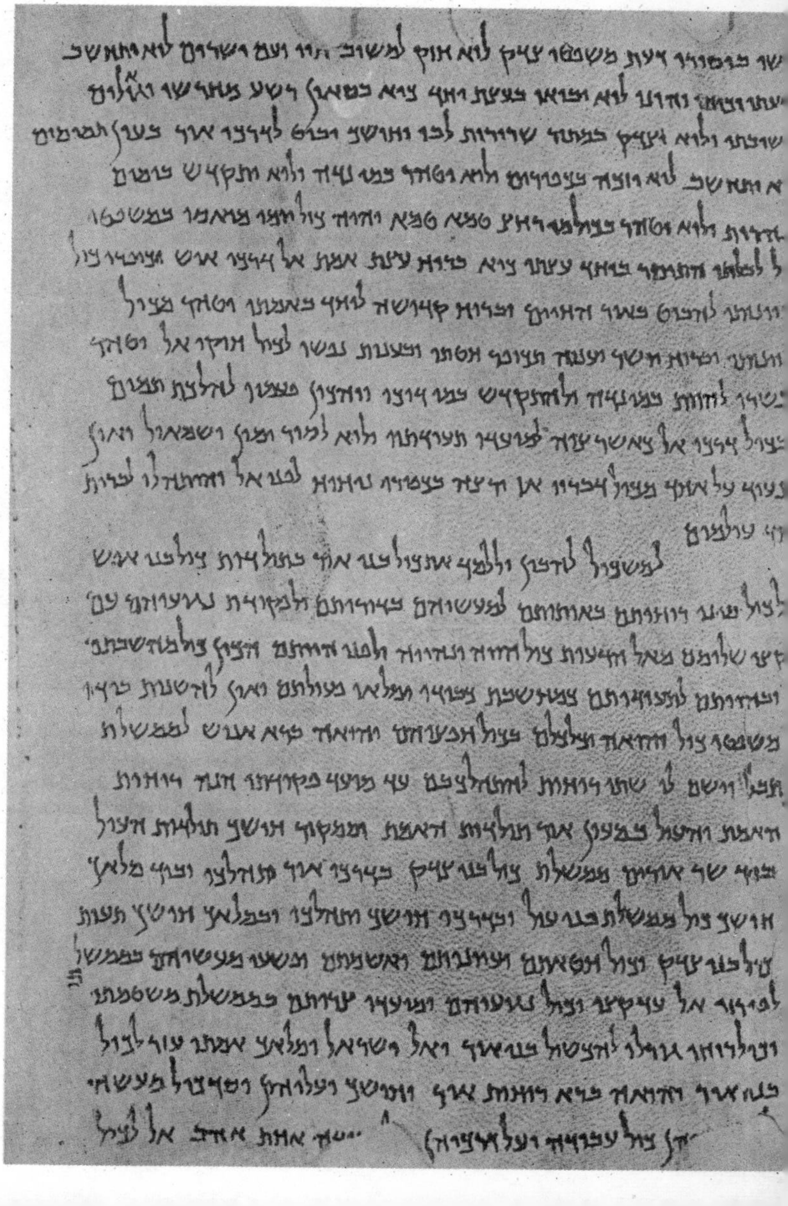

Scrolls and the beginnings of Christianity was expressed: "The new evidence with regard to the beliefs and practices of Jewish sectarians of the last two centuries BCE bids fair to revolutionize our approach to the beginnings of Christianity . . . " (W. F. Albright). It is now generally accepted that Christianity drew largely from Judaism. The question is, from which type of Judaism did it derive? "In its organization, its oriental climate and many of its theological ideas from Paul onwards, it is much closer to Qumran Judaism than to Rabbinic Judaism as known from Tannaitic sources" (Ch. Rabin). Both Christianity and Qumran, of course, have a common ancestor with Pharisaism in the "form of Hassidism* which accepted the authority of Moses, was messianically inclined and believed in the resurrection of the dead and a final judgment." (D. N. Freedman)

Christianity has never denied the extent of its Jewish heritage. To examine its antecedents in no way invalidates the originality of historical Christian experience. The cardinal Christian doctrines of the incarnate deity, original sin, redemption through Calvary and the activity of the holy spirit are nowhere to be found in the Scrolls. Nevertheless, numerous points of contact can be demonstrated.

Common Ground in Messianism: From some of the Qumran evidence it seems that one prophetic and messianic figure was awaited: the "Prophet like Moses" who would announce the New Age; followed by the priestly "Messiah of Aaron and Israel" and the Davidic "Messiah of Israel" who would make a classical partnership like those between Moses* and Aaron*, or Joshua and Zerubbabel in the Restoration* of the Temple.

The motif of a triumvirate of deliverers appears in the New Testament, applied jointly to Jesus*. Christian messianism concerned one unique figure and the work he would accomplish, no Essene messiah was expected to do. For the Christians, Jesus was the Messiah who had come and would come, bringing the New Age.

Christian Communal Meals: The Christian rite of Holy Communion (Eucharist*) developed into a separate ceremony, unconnected with regular meals. Originally, however it was part of a communal meal which many scholars believe to have been derived from the common meal of the sectaries. The Essenes' meal carried on the ancient belief that in eating the meat of sacrifices, priest and worshipper entered into an intimate relation with God. The Christian rite, however, had gone a step further. By symbolically consuming the very body and blood of the Messiah, his servants are granted complete union with him. In this sense, the Christian is already living in the eschatological* era, while the Qumran sectaries were still looking forward to it.

Christian Baptism: The Christian conception of baptism also differed significantly from the sectarian. In Christian belief, baptism has become a single unrepeatable act of initiation. The Essene rite which, it seems, was frequently repeated, symbolized ritual purity and the repentance that must precede acceptance of a new life. The Christians carried on these ideas but added a third: that baptism brings remission of sins.

Organization: Both communities believed themselves to be the true Israel and both were ruled by twelve leaders although Qumran had, in addition, 3 priests making a total of 15 men. The sectaries were led by a "mebaqqer" or "paqqid" who, like a Christian bishop, was regarded as "father in God" and shepherd of his flock. Both communities rejected private property in favour of the communal sharing of goods. Both counselled against marriage for those who wished to live eternally before the throne of God.

Dualism of Good and Evil: For both the Qumran sectaries and the early Christians, the world was divided by a cosmic struggle between good and evil, in which both saw themselves as (literally) on the side of the angels. Several books of the New Testament, especially Revelation and the writings of those close to Paul and John the Evangelist, appear to have been strongly influenced by sectarian writings, although the doctrine of the two ways originated in the Old Testament.

The New Covenant: The idea of a second chance — a New Covenant* (in Greek, Kainos-diatheke — New Testament) between God and man was common to both sectaries and Christians. Both believed in a covenant written upon the heart, to be fulfilled by the power of the Spirit. Unlike Qumran, however, in the New Testament, the new era is already present while the old age is passing away. The early Christian was embarked upon the new life of the spirit, yet under the discipline of the old.

Conclusions: It is generally conceded that the evidence of Qumran has amply demonstrated that the roots of Christianity lie within some such form of nonconformist Judaism. This was not the only factor involved. Nevertheless the Scrolls have a definite bearing on our understanding of Jesus' uniqueness as a prophet; the originality of his teachings; the origin of Christian sacraments and the extent to which the beliefs of the Jewish-Christians* were influenced by inter-testamental Judaism, Essenes and sectaries.

Many scholars feel that the evidence falls short of a completely convincing case for the derivation of Christian rites from the sectaries. Many of the parallels between Qumran and the early church can be explained from the Old Testament and the practice of the Hassidim* and Pharisaic* "haberim". What seems to be agreed is that the two Jewish sectarian communities, Qumran and the primitive church, had a common heritage and background, and that the Scrolls have thrown light on a period (2nd c. BCE. to 2nd c. CE) which is of the greatest interest to the student of Christian origins. (See also Priests*.)

DEUTERONOMY, THE BOOK OF — *Outline:*

I. Contents; Literary Characteristics. II. Authorship; Centralization of the Cult. III. Dating of Deuteronomy; The "D" Source Theory; Sanctuaries before the Temple; Legitimate Sanctuaries. IV. Recent Theories; Homiletic Framework; Deuteronomy and Wisdom.

The fifth and last book of the Pentateuch is called in Hebrew both "D^{e}barim" after its opening phrase and "Mishnah Torah", meaning the Repetition of the Law (first given in Exodus). The name was translated Deuteronomion as the nearest Greek equivalent.

I. CONTENTS: As its name suggests, the book contains a code of laws and, in addition, narratives and exhortations, the laws themselves being coupled with morals or stories to justify them. It has 34 chapters which can be divided into three main sections: chs. 1–11; 12–26; 27–34.

The first section (1–11) surveys the wanderings in the desert and the conquests in Transjordan. It opens with the first address of Moses (1:3–4:40) giving the history of the Israelites from the Exodus and exhorting the people to keep God's laws and avoid idolatry. Then comes (vs. 41–43) a short interruption, establishing three cities of refuge and the section continues (4:44 – 11) with the second discourse of Moses. The first part repeats the fundamental principles on which the Law and the Covenant of Sinai are based and again calls on the people to remain faithful to their God and His laws.

The second section of the book (chs. 12–26) lists some seventy separate laws which are to regulate the daily life of Israel in the promised land. These may be divided into sections, i. e.:

a. Religious laws: the place of sacrifice, extermination of idolatry, rules specifying food which may be eaten, regulations regarding tithes and offerings, care for the poor and pilgrimages.

b. Judicial rules: duties of the king, privileges of the Levites, authority of the prophets over diviners and augurers.

c. Laws regulating murder, old boundary marks, witnesses, the conduct of war and exemptions from military service, marriage with a woman war-captive, rights of the first-born, rebellious sons, treatment of hanged criminals (chs. 19–21).

d. Social and domestic regulations, ranging from protection of property, and purity of the Israelite camp in time of war, to religious prostitution, divorce, levirate marriage, husband's conjugal rights, adultery, seduction and the payment of wage earners (22–25).

These legislative sections form a code which brings together, without any very clear order, a number of different short collections of laws which may have originated in different ways and places. Some of them repeat the Covenant laws, but others add to and modify these (for instance the laws about the sanctuary, and about slaves, see below). This suggests that the new code was intended to replace the older laws, taking account of the social and religious developments which had taken place. The laws are written very much as exhortations, not as though they could be enforced without question by some central authority. Naturally, this code is considered in connection with the "Law" discovered in the Temple at the time of Josiah's reform (see below).

The third division of Deuteronomy (chs. 27–34) includes (ch. 27) the injunction to erect an altar near Shechem (on Mount Ebal) and specifies the curses to be laid on those who transgress the Commandments. This second discourse of Moses closes with a peroration repeating the blessings that will attend obedience to God's will and detailing the disasters that disobedience will cause. In his third discourse (chs. 29–30), Moses repeats the warnings against apostasy and, in conclusion (31:1–13), announces the appointment of Joshua as his successor.

Then follows the "Song of Moses" (32:1–43), one of the most passionate and beautiful passages in the Bible lauding the power of God. It was certainly not composed by Moses but is attributed to the period of Judges, with, possibly, a nucleus of older material. Chapter 33 is another independent poem, called the "Blessing of Moses" and foretelling the destiny of the tribes of Israel and their happiness in the promised land. (It can be compared with Gn. 49.) The book then closes (ch. 34) with the account of the death of Moses. In view of the emphasis placed on the fortunes of the house of Joseph, it is assumed that this originated centuries later in the northern kingdom (see Israel and Judah*).

Literary Characteristics: The style and arrangement of the book raise a number of problems. The style is one of long involved sentences with frequent repetitions; for instance, chap. 4:44 seq. more or less repeats, without reference, the introductory passage at the beginning of ch. 1. Continuity is also often interrupted by parenthetical remarks (e.g. ch. 3:9).

The actual laws listed are drafted in two different ways. Some are in casuistic or conditional style, introduced by "if" (see Law*), for instance 25:1: "If there is a dispute between men . . ."; while others are apodictic or imperative, i.e: "No bastard shall enter the assembly of the Lord" (23:2). (Technically, this refers to children born of an incestuous union rather than "illegitimate" children in the modern sense.) Also: "All the firstling males that are born of your herd and flock you shall consecrate to the Lord your God" (15:19).

Moreover there are certain contradictions in the wording, for instance the use of the term "Levitical-Priests" (18:1) which is totally at variance with the accepted concept of the two — and especially their functions — as being quite separate (see Priests*).

The main questions that seem to arise from these anomalies are whether they happened in the ordinary process of transmission, first orally, then in written copies; or whether they represent later interpolations. Did the original author draw on a variety of sources, or did later editors introduce changes and corrections, sometimes for the worse?

One school of opinion (R. H. Pfeiffer) regards Deuteronomy as a priestly work (see Biblical Criticism*), produced under prophetic influence. Another view (S. R. Driver) is that the book was a prophetic legal code. G. E. Wright sees the whole book, i. e. its historical and legislative sections taken together, as a summary of Israel's faith, based on the saving acts of God in the election and deliverance of Israel, the Covenant and the Conquest. In this scholar's opinion, these events portrayed for Israel the will and purpose of God, and gave meaning to their Law. This view of the Mosaic traditions as an introduction to Israel's history is acceptable provided its roots are assumed to be in the traditions of the tribal league during the period of Judges (see below).

The book is, in any case, clearly not an actual code of laws. All Near Eastern codes include a hortatory element, being designed to exhort as well as instruct. None of them were really codes of statutory law, but Deuteronomy is remarkable for the amount of exhortation which it contains. Sometimes this takes the form of a liturgy, as in the ceremony of offering the first-fruits (26) or the regulations to be followed when going into battle (20). These have no place in a formal legal code in which rules for the ordering of life are laid down according to a unifying, underlying principle. The book's legislative sections come rather into the category of a collection of ancient and new legal precepts, lacking any unified underlying legalistic concept.

For this reason, many Bible scholars have attempted to separate the ancient laws from the new and to ascertain the exact relationship of the new ones to the utterances of the prophets (see below, Recent Theories).

II. AUTHORSHIP OF DEUTERONOMY: Even the very earliest commentaries on the Bible, the Talmud, expressed some doubt about the authorship of certain passages of Duteronomy, suggesting that they had not been written by Moses as was commonly believed. Ibn Ezra in his commentary on Deuteronomy reviewed the question of its authorship alongside that of the whole of the Pentateuch (which was supposed to have been composed in its entirety by Moses). Ibn Ezra pointed out, for instance, that Gn. 12:6 "*At that time* the Canaanites were in the Land," was clearly written long after the events described. Similarly in Deuteronomy there are many passages which explicitly refer to the remote past, e. g: 2:12 "The Horites also lived in Seir formerly, but the sons of Esau dispossessed them . . . . as *did* Israel to the land of their possession, which the Lord gave to them." or 34:10: "there has not arisen a prophet *since* in Israel like Moses . . ."

Even more significant, perhaps, is the fact that certain laws differ radically from those of the older Book of the Covenant (Ex. 21–23). For instance, in Ex. 23, the "Shemittah" (Sabbatical) year (in which the land was to remain fallow) is explained on agricultural and charitable grounds. The parallel passage in Dt. 15:1 ff. dwells on the release of debtors reduced to slavery by their own or their relatives' poverty, suggesting an economy which had advanced far beyond the semi-nomadic conditions of the Exodus* and required the regulation of financial problems undreamed of at the time the Book of the Covenant was written.

A similar distinction can be made with regard to Israelite law governing Hebrew slaves. Regulations governing the slave's term of service, conditions of work and provisions for his release are to be found first in the Book of the Covenant (Ex. 21:2–11, 20–21) and also, rather differently, in Deuteronomy (15:12–18). Many scholars maintain that the changes between the two reflect a development in contemporary social attitudes between the time of Moses and the late pre-Exilic period which, presumably, corresponds to the Deuteronomic legislation. At this late date the Exodus laws on slavery were no longer obeyed — a fact witnessed by King Zedekiah's proclamation liberating Hebrew slaves (Jer. 34:8 ff).

There is also a marked difference between the reasons given for certain injunctions in the two books. In Exodus (20:11) observance of the Sabbath is explained on cosmic grounds, "for in six days the Lord made heaven and earth, . . . and rested the seventh day, therefore the Lord blessed the sabbath day and hallowed it." The writer of Deuteronomy offered a social reason: "so that your slave and handmaiden may rest, as you do" (Dt: 5:14–15) which indicates that the slave or handmaiden was a "domestic", a member of the family in the original sense of the word (which is also the reason he had to be circumcized; Gn. 17:12–13), who joined the family in all its religious celebrations (see Slavery*).

The Book of Deuteronomy does not appear to have been based on Exodus as we know it, although another, earlier version may have existed and Deuteronomy may have drawn on this. Such an assumption would help to explain the origin of some of the laws of Deuteronomy which are obviously of very great antiquity, e.g. the "slaughtered heifer" ceremony (Dt. 21:1–9; see Impurity, Purification*).

Centralization of the Cult: Perhaps the most important difference between Exodus and Deuteronomy concerns the question of centralization of ritual. Deuteronomy 12 (see below, Legitimate Sanctuaries) repeatedly insists that religious ceremonies must be performed only "at the place which Yahweh shall choose", a formula which is used only in Deuteronomy and which some authorities assume refers to a definite place (Jerusalem). This contrasts very strongly with the older concept reflected in Ex. 20:24 "An altar of earth you shall make for me . . . in every place where I cause my name to be remembered I will come to you and bless you" (see Sacrifice*). Quite obviously, the reiterated injunction of Deuteronomy reflects a basic transformation which had taken place by the time the book was written.

III. DATING OF DEUTERONOMY: This is important not only for its own sake, but because it is connected with several other vital problems of biblical science. An apt definition of Deuteronomy calls it the "Greenwich Meridian of the Old Testament", i.e. the key, not only to the Pentateuch, but to O. T. literature as a whole. It also supplies the key to the history of religion and culture in Israel from the tribal league traditions in the days of Judges, to the period of the Monarchy.

Recent studies seem to have proved that the book contains certain ancient Levitical traditions which appear to have been transmitted partly through the northern kingdom, although it is not clear how they were later introduced into the kingdom of Judea. Some scholars suggest that they were brought there after the fall of Samaria during the reign of King Hezekiah.

The most probable conclusion about the authorship and date of Deuteronomy seems to be that its authors, the priestly writers and others, all drew upon traditions which, although common to them all, had developed in different ways at different times and in different parts of the country.

"The D Source" Theory: The actual date depends on the period to which the D (Deuteronomic) strand of the Bible belongs (according to the Documentary Hypothesis, see Biblical Criticism*). The classic theory (first suggested by Jerome, ca. 340–420 C. CE) is that the book was written during the reign of Josiah, around 622 BCE, after the finding of the Book of Law in the Temple and at the time of the extensive reforms which this prompted (II K. 22; see Israel and Judah*). Of all the books of the Pentateuch, Deuteronomy is most closely related to those reforms. It forbids idolatry and curses anyone failing to observe the edicts of the Torah. The scholars who accepted this theory concluded that a number of the laws had been derived from a specific Deuteronomic (D) source, to which other parts of the Pentateuch were also assigned.

The view of Deuteronomy as the theological programme of Josiah's reform is supported by an interesting passage in II K. 23:9 which links the two: "However, the priests of the high places did not come up to the altar of the Lord in Jerusalem." This, though, contradicts Dt. 18:6–8: "And if a Levite comes from any of your towns out of all Israel, where he lives — and he may come when he desires — to the place which the Lord will choose, then he may minister in the name of the Lord his God, like all his fellow-Levites who stand to minister there before the Lord."

If a date around Josiah's reign is accepted for the composition of Deuteronomy, then the evolution of ritual practices can be seen as running from Ex. 20:24 (part of the Book of the Covenant), where worship and ritual are permissible in any place, to a demand which Josiah tried — not altogether successfully — to enforce, that ritual be centralized exclusively in Jerusalem. When the Priestly Code was incorporated into the Canon of the Old Testament during the Exile (a generally accepted theory, see Leviticus*; Biblical Criticism*) centralization of worship had become universally accepted and, thus, no longer called for emphasis.

A number of objections have been put forward against this theory: 1. The words "the place which He will appoint" do not necessarily mean one single place (see below: Legitimate Sanctuaries). 2. There is no mention of Jerusalem in the whole of Deuteronomy, which seems to cast doubt on its authorship during the late 7th c. BCE. 3. Long before Josiah, Amos (8th c. BCE) had opened an important passage with the words, "The Lord roars from Zion and utters his voice from Jerusalem" (Am. 1:2), which may suggest that the Temple in Jerusalem was already regarded as God's only sanctuary. 4. In contrast, in Dt. 27:4–7 the people of Israel are ordered to erect an altar on Mount Ebal and offer sacrifice there. (Scholars who uphold the Josiah thesis have tried to explain this direct contradiction of a demand for centralized worship by ascribing the passage to a later addition. Others argue that Deuteronomy is based, at least in part, on old "northern" traditions; see above.)

An extreme view on the dating of Deuteronomy (G. R. Berry, F. Horst and G. Holscher) puts the writing of the book in the post-Exilic period, but their theory has won few adherents. In general, the last decades have seen a general agreement on a date in the 7th c. BCE, J. Bright claiming that "both attacks may be said to have played themselves out without appreciably denting the established position (7th c.) ".

The question of the sources for all of the Pentateuch is also relevant to the discussion about Deuteronomy. M. Noth believes that the J, E and P sources of the Pentateuch (see Biblical Criticism*) only extend from Genesis to Numbers, while the narrative from Moses to the Exile forms part of a single historical work based on the Deuteronomic law (which it includes). This traces Israel's history up to the fall of Jerusalem and comprises the books of Deuteronomy and Kings, all composed late in the seventh c. This theory (which is also supported by the Uppsala School and I. Engnell) sees the sources of Genesis, Exodus, Leviticus and Numbers (called the Tetrateuch) in blocks of oral tradition linked to the normative traditions of the tribal league (see Judges*). After separate sequences of transmission these traditions finally produced the present form of the books. In this opinion the sources were separate from the Deuteronomic corpus (Deuteronomy-Kings) which was written after — and therefore influenced by — the Josianic reform. The attitude in which the history of the nation as from the establishment of the monarchy was written reflects the later (Deuteronomic) traditions.

Whether or not this theory is taken into account, it is now widely recognized that a considerable part of the material of Deuteronomy has a long history behind it and expresses the legal tradition of the tribal league. The ultimate roots of the oldest of the laws can be traced to cultic traditions belonging to that period and, more specifically, to tribal traditions that were later adopted by the northern kingdom (and transmitted there, according to G. von Rad). The book of Deuteronomy is thus seen, bearing in mind the considerations outlined below, as the crystallization of these traditions at the end of a long process of transmission and, in its present form, after expansion during the 7th c. BCE.

Sanctuaries before the Temple: The places of worship hallowed by Patriarchal traditions (see Patriarchal Religion*) are scarcely mentioned once Israel settled in Canaan. Instead, from the time of Joshua and Judges, new sanctuaries are brought to the fore, e. g. Gilgal (Jos. 4:19; I Sam. 7:16, passim); Shiloh which eclipsed Gilgal (I Sam. 1:3; see Samuel*); Mizpah (I Sam 7:5–12); Gibeon (II Sam. 21:1–14); Ophra (Jud. 6:11 ff); Dan (Jud. chs. 17–18) and, finally, in David's time, Jerusalem, which became the site chosen for worship by Yahweh himself, thus providing the site for Solomon's Temple.

Legitimate Sanctuaries: The correct interpretation of Dt. 12:1–2 and 12:13–21, is still a matter of debate among scholars. The second quotation puts it in the singular and gives a precise injunction against offering sacrifice in any sacred place, but only "at the place which the Lord will choose in one of your tribes". However, the earlier passage is a more general instruction to destroy the popular Canaanite places of worship and to seek "the place which the Lord your God will choose out of all your tribes to put his name and make his habitation there . . ." The text seems to imply that "the place" was a single, unique one. There are scholars, however, who dispute this.

The practice during the time of Judges and Samuel (see above) was to offer sacrifice in different places. After the building of Solomon's Temple and the establishment of a centralized monarchy, such plurality was no longer acceptable, but there is no reason to suppose that it had not been legitimate up to then. (Cf. Sanctuaries; Israelite Sanctuary at Arad* under Ancient Cities).

According to T. Oestreicher and A. C. Welch, the "Law" found in the Temple during the Josianic reform, was an ancient scroll which included the ancient source and sections of the Pentateuch called source "D" according to the documentary hypothesis. It did not insist on one sanctuary, but on its purity and the abolition of all foreign cultic elements — there or anywhere else. These scholars interpret the "place which Yahweh will choose" as any place he might appoint and Josiah's reforms, accordingly, stressed cultic purity, but not a single sanctuary. The only place which insists on a single sanctuary, they believe (12:1–7), was a later interpolation.

399

Welch assumes that Deuteronomy reflects the orthodox feeling against the syncretism of popular religion (see Canaan, Cult*), which began with Samuel. Some authors who incline to this view, put Deuteronomy's composition in the time of Judges or Samuel.

IV. RECENT THEORIES: The debate continues with new points that may affect an understanding of the book being raised by different authorities. Scholars in Europe and in Israel (W. Staerk, Y. Kaufman, S. Yeivin and E. Robertson) draw on other evidence in the book to try to place its composition within the reign of Solomon, or even the periods of Samuel or Judges.

In Israel, Y. Kaufman has tended to advocate an earlier authorship for many parts of the Pentateuch, while not upholding orthodox views uncritically. He considers that the narrative and admonitions at the beginning of Deuteronomy are very old and contain evidence of having been put together from a number of sources. The repetitions he sees as natural in a book written in a poetic style, full of admonitions and teachings. Except for certain parts of the end of the book, and the moot point of centralized worship, this scholar sees Deuteronomy as a homogeneous unit, although its dating must be largely a matter of guesswork.

The book became influential only during the period of the reforms by Hezekiah and Josiah, at which point centralization of worship became a matter of importance and a statement of the fundamental values of faith in Yahweh was needed. Accordingly, it is suggested, the author(s) of Deuteronomy worked out the text from existing moralistic and legal material. The book which Hilkiyah the High Priest found (II K. 22:8 ff.) presumably included the laws and admonitions up to 32:47, with some concluding passages added.

S. Yeivin, on the other hand, believes that the present form of the book includes some later material (the Song of Moses, ch. 32, and perhaps the first three chapters) but that the main body of the book was written by circles who opposed King Solomon's accession to the throne (on the grounds that he was the son of a Canaanite). The passage in praise of Palestine (8:7–9) which speaks not only of its fertility but of its mineral wealth seems a fitting description of Solomon's kingdom, while stress on centralization of worship would also fit in with the erection of the Temple. Moreover, judgments handed down during the monarchy (in both Judah and Israel) were based on the Deuteronomic Code, whereas in the early days of Solomon's reign, a judgment was given on the basis of the Exodus Code.

Altogether, this scholar sees the book as having been written, mainly by priests descended from the House of Eli, during or shortly after Solomon's reign.

The Homiletic Framework: Among other recent theories, not based on the D source hypothesis, M. Weinfeld has pointed out that Deuteronomy's fundamental innovation is not the legislation it contains, but its characteristic homiletic framework. The original kernel includes ancient traditions of the Covenant Code, like the law of the "Shemittah" or release of the soil. The later alteration in emphasis to a release of debtors or slaves, reveals the Deuteronomist as a humanist and social critic. These qualities are attributed by established opinion to the prophets, but Y. Kaufman and S. Yeivin have amply demonstrated that whereas the social and moral principles of Deuteronomy are formulated in actual, specific laws, the moral injunctions of the prophetic books would lose most of their power if they were formulated into a legal code like that of Deuteronomy.

Deuteronomy and Wisdom: Other scholars, M. Weinfeld and S. Sandmel, have found an alternate source of the humanism of Deuteronomy, in the "wisdom" circles which produced Job and Proverbs. The Deuteronomist, they point out, drew his concern for the poor and needy from wisdom rather than prophecy. Thus his work is a fusion of law and wisdom, rather than of law and prophecy which has been the generally accepted opinion. However, this leaves open the question of whether wisdom influenced Deuteronomy, or vice versa.

In spite of its importance for the whole of the Pentateuch, Deuteronomy cannot be definitely dated on the basis of the information now available. All that is certain is that the Exodus code is pre-monarchical and reflects conditions during the period of wanderings and the traditions of the tribal league, whereas the Deuteronomic code relates to the period of the monarchy in its early and later stages.

A fragment of Dt. 32 (Song of Moses) from Qumran is shown **(399)**.

400

E

ECCLESIASTES. — *Outline: Contents; Authorship and Date; Hellenistic Influence; Ecclesiastes and Wisdom Literature; Eccl. and Job.; Ecclesiastes and Rabbinic Judaism.*

The Book of Ecclesiastes (in Hebrew "Kohelet" meaning the "Speaker" or "master" of an assembly and translated by the Greek word for a "congregant") is one of the Scrolls of the Hagiographa (Writings), the third section of the Bible. It is read in the synagogue on the Feast of Tabernacles.

Contents: Of the 24 books of the biblical canon*, Ecclesiastes is perhaps the most nonconformist. It was once aptly described as the "Song of Songs of the Sceptic".

The book contains 12 chapters, which present the gloomy philosophy of a pessimist who sees all life as "vanity of vanities. All is vanity!" and looks for some compensation in pleasure, scepticism and an ultimate faith in God. The book is not just a collection of unrelated precepts. One principal idea dominates the whole and prose and poetry are combined in a coherent argument, although the contents of several significant poems and sections are important for appreciating the book.

According to some, the book appears to be the work of a single writer. The author, "the Preacher", tests different human achievements: practical wisdom which recognizes the transitoriness of things (1:4–11) and the existence of evil (1:12–18); pleasure and wealth and their ultimate emptiness (2:1–11); work, a "vexation" which gives no pleasure (2:12–26). All end in the certainty of death (3:1–22). He then turns to consider life's mysteries (4:1–16); riches (5:1–20); the end of life (6:1–12); man's sinfulness, and the deception of fame gained through wisdom and knowledge (7:1–29); the inscrutability of Divine Providence (8:1–9:18); the disorder of life (10:1–20) and the delusions of youth and age (11:1–12:7). At the end of it all, "Vanity of vanities, says the Preacher, all is vanity" (12:8).

The last few verses which form the conclusion (12:9–14) are written in the third person and reveal a sudden change to an optimistic outlook. This is so completely at odds with the whole spirit of the rest of the book that scholars assume that the verses were added by a later editor as a comment on the life of the central figure. This editor's hand is also noticeable in other passages (1:1,2; 7:27; 12:8) and the complaint that "of making many books there is no end" is also probably his. The editor was concerned to find religious teaching in the pessimistic philosophy of Kohelet (see below, Rabbinic Judaism and Ecclesiastes), and this probably governed his choice of the closing words: "Fear God and keep his commandments, for this is the whole duty of man" (12:13) by which he seems to have tried to reconcile the work with the traditional attitude of the Bible.

Authorship and Date: The name "Solomon" is never actually mentioned in the book, but the author identifies himself as "the Preacher, the son of David," who has been "king over Israel in Jerusalem" (1:1). Modern scholars regard this as a pseudonym, the actual author and the time at which he lived remaining uncertain.

It is generally agreed that Ecclesiastes must have been in existence by the time (around 200 BCE) that Ben Sira wrote his "Wisdom", later on called "Ecclesiasticus" in the Vulgate (see Apocrypha*). Comparison of the two books (e.g. Ecc. 8:14 and Ecclus. 1:13) seems to show that Ben Sira was familiar with the canonical work. Moreover, fragments of a scroll of Kohelet **(400)** were found at Qumran, (see Dead Sea Scrolls*). These date from about 150 BCE. The text is not identical and displays certain developments which suggest that the original composition of the book took place 150 to 200 years earlier. Its presence among the other biblical manuscripts in Qumran is not surprising, but offers additional evidence for the popularity of Ecclesiastes in post-Exilic times.

Ecclesiastes is composed in the style of Wisdom literature* (see article), but its language varies between the Mishnaic Hebrew of its prose passages and poetry sections which reveal so strong an influence of "Royal Aramaic" (see Restoration*), that some scholars regard the book as a translation from an Aramaic original. These scholars place the book's composition within the Persian period. A number of words derived from Persian can be found in Ecclesiastes. On the other hand, M. J. Dahood found strong evidence of Phoenician linguistic influence and it is true that no other biblical book is so closely related, in form and content, to Phoenician, Persian, Egyptian, Babylonian literatures.

Hellenistic Influence: Greek thought was in the air in the 4th and 3rd cs. BCE and the Jews could not avoid its influence. Kohelet was almost certainly affected by the questioning Hellenic spirit. He even expresses doubts about the traditional Jewish belief that God will reward the righteous (2:15 ff; 8:9–14; 9:2–6). The whole book is coloured by a combination of the Stoic and Epicurean schools of thought and this connection has suggested to many scholars that the book was composed on the eve of the Hellenistic period*, by which time Greek influence was already considerable (see Hellenism in the Near East*). A date in the 4th c. BCE seems the most likely, although this is far from generally agreed.

Ecclesiastes and Wisdom Literature*: The book is written in the form of a diary of one of the "seekers after wisdom" who are familiar in the folklore of many lands, but the autobiographical manner seems to be no more than a literary device. The author claims that he said, "Come now, I will make a test of pleasure; enjoy yourself" (2:1). Then (2:12) he "turned to consider wisdom . . . " and again, he "saw all the oppressions that are practiced under the sun" (4:1). His conclusion is that since "the fate of the sons of men and the fate of beasts is the same, as one dies so dies the other" (3:19) then the best solution is for a man to enjoy his life while he may. Such a philosophy is a blatant denial of the Bible's teachings, e. g. Nu. 15:39–40. Nevertheless, "wisdom excels folly as light excels darkness. The wise man has his eyes in his head, but the fool walks in darkness." (2:13–14; see Wisdom Literature*).

Kohelet appears to have been one of "the wise" "Hochmah" — professionals whose teachings were considered sufficiently important for them to be classed with the priests and the prophets, although their respective literatures developed on totally independent lines. Within those circles, the author of Ecclesiastes belongs to a special group of the 'wise men' in which speculation probed sensitively into fundamental issues. The inconsistencies in the book itself and the nature of his belief in God and morality may not appear so strange when considered in the context of the various streams of ancient cosmopolitan wisdom literature* (described under that article). Kohelet did not preach immorality, but the experience of everyday existence seemed to put the orthodox rule of God to a severe test.

The many contradictions and inconsistencies which are patent to a careful reader led scholars at one time to believe that the book had been heavily — and often — edited. However this theory can be overworked. The writer was not a scientific philosopher in the modern sense. He was a mature man (perhaps men), influenced by a cosmopolitan culture, sincerely expressing personal doubts to an audience equally mature and equally experienced. The work was not exclusively agnostic, cynical or reformist, nor was it avowedly Stoic or Epicurean. It raised questions about the condition of man that have occupied thinkers before and since. Because of the dramatic form of its presentation, it was possible to end the book with an answer clearly stating a solution in terms of an unswerving faith in God and observance of His commandments. This conclusion explains why — in spite of the unorthodox form of the book and much of its content — it was possible to preserve it among the Canon of Holy Writ. It also reconciles many of the book's apparent contradictions and reveals it as a more unified production than might appear at first.

The wisdom of Kohelet was very popular among Jewish thinkers of late Post-Exilic days and also among the scribes who were the spearhead of contemporary Jewish culture, which may also explain the book's inclusion in the Canon* (see below).

Ecclesiastes and Job: It is interesting to compare "Kohelet's" approach to that of another book of Wisdom, Job*. Job (29:14) "put on righteousness" and "delivered the poor who cried" (29:12), "was eyes to the blind, and feet to the lame . . . " (29:15), because he believed that this was the right way to behave. Kohelet advocates charity, but only in the expectation of return, "Cast your bread upon the waters, for you will find it after many days." (11:1). He was not concerned with the spiritual values to which Job pinned his faith. He "got singers, both men and women, and many concubines, man's delight" (2:8), "whatever my eyes desired I did not keep from them; I kept my heart from no pleasure . . . " (2:10). Yet, in the extremity of despair it was Job who cried out, denying the validity of the whole moral order and going far beyond Kohelet in his pessimism and denunciation of the divine ordering of life. Kohelet's repeated expression of the disillusion of the righteous who do not find reward seems to echo Job* and suggests that he was influenced by the older work (see e. g. Job 21:32–33).

The fundamental concern of Kohelet (as of other "wisdom" writers of the Near East) was the greatest advantage or profit which could be got out of life. Wisdom was of economic as well as philosophic interest and, in this, Ecclesiastes represents above all a Hebrew version of this much wider school of literature.

However, Kohelet is also concerned to present his particular concept of God, which was of a Being too elevated to be concerned about the trivial doings of mankind. The book's spirit is one of resignation rather than loyalty or intimacy, "God is in heaven and you upon earth, therefore let your words be few." (5:2). The reiterated despair that "the day of death is better than the day of birth" (7:1) is based on the "vanity" of this world — not on any expectation of better things in the next.

Ecclesiastes and Near Eastern Wisdom: The Wisdom books of the Old Testament are in fact of an international, rather than exclusively Hebraic character (see Wisdom*). The extreme pessimism of Ecclesiastes and its insistent questioning of orthodox values makes this book particularly close to some of the "Wisdom" traditions of the whole Near East. Like many other Jewish "wisdom" books, it seems much more a piece of secular than religious literature, offering advice on "how to be successful" without any apparent religious motivation. However, despite essential contrast with standard biblical religion, the work is not irreligious. Like other Jewish teachers, Kohelet adapts the tradition and precepts of wisdom to fit the aim of life under Jewish law and tradition (see Wisdom*).

Rabbinic Judaism and Ecclesiastes: Because of its scepticism and uncompromising pessimism, the Mishnah* and later rabbinic literature cast serious doubt on the authority of Ecclesiastes, fearing that it would conduce to heresy (Midrash Kohelet Rabba 1:3). "Our teachers' inclination to consign Ecclesiastes to darkness" (Bab. Talmud Shabbat 30:72), may have expressed the general feeling but, towards the end of the 1st c. CE, the book was canonized after lengthy discussion by the Council of Yabneh. This was achieved partly as a result of the tradition that it was composed by King Solomon, and partly because of the esteem in which it was held by Jews during the Graeco-Roman period. An important link in the post-Exilic development of the Jewish faith and, especially, of Wisdom literature was thus preserved.

However, in an attempt to reconcile the book's attitudes with those of Jewish tradition (and to justify its supposed composition by the author of the "Song of Songs"* and "Proverbs"*), post-biblical sages provided a "Targum" (exposition) to Ecclesiastes (see Versions of the Bible*). In this apology, the author's pessimism is ascribed to the prevailing weakness of Solomon's time; his scepticism is translated as meaning that the study of the Torah provides the only worthwhile occupation for a man, and his account of the pleasures of life is related to moral values and good deeds.

ECCLESIASTICUS (see Apocrypha*)

EGYPT AND ISRAEL. — *Outline: The Land; History: The Middle Kingdom and Palestine; Execration Texts; Hyksos Rule; The New Empire; Akhenaton; The Amarna Letters; Thut-Ankh-Amon; The Ramesides; Egypt and the*

"People of the Sea"; 21st — 26th Dynasties; Shishak and Solomon; Shishak in Israel; Nubian and Ethiopian Dynasties; Assyrian Domination; Josiah and Necho; Persian Domination; Graeco-Roman Period; Chronological Table.

To consider the development of the intellectual, artistic or political life of Israel without reference to Egypt is unthinkable. One of the most important of Canaan's neighbours, Egypt and the area of Palestine were in close contact for more than 5,000 years, from the dawn of history (4th mill. BCE) until late Roman times. When the Patriarchs of Israel actually roamed the grasslands and deserts of the land of Canaan, Egypt could already look back on some 1500 years of history. Its culture represents the longest uninterrupted stretch of history of any people in the world. Moreover, the history of Egypt can be reconstructed in greater detail and over a longer stretch of time than that of any other country of the Near East. Its religious custom of interring objects of everyday use with the dead and putting biographical inscriptions on their tombs, was combined with a dry climate which preserves even the most fragile remains. As a result, many facts of the archaeology of Palestine can be placed, historically, by a comparison with Egypt.

The Land: "The Gift of the Nile": this well known Greek adage is true geologically and economically. The country was always divided between Upper and Lower Egypt, both equally dependent on the waters of the Nile (see map **401**). Lower Egypt is the fertile delta area, its rich alluvial soil renewed yearly by the flooding river. The Nile water was the main factor in Egypt's economic and social life. For irrigating the desert lands to the south or controlling the floodwaters of the Delta, the powers and central organization of a national government were essential. Egypt as a state, therefore, is a gift of the Nile, no less than the land itself.

The only natural barriers along its whole eastern frontier are deserts or, in the northern Delta region, swamps. The frontier with Palestine was often well fortified, as shown by the Exodus* story, and it was crossed by important roads to the East, via the Sinai peninsula.

History: Since the historical writings of Manetho, an Egyptian priest who lived about 280 BCE, Egypt's history has been divided into periods of rule by 30 dynasties. To this must be added the prehistory of the country and the Hellenistic and Roman periods after Alexander the Great which are important for the development of Judaism during the time of the Second Temple.

Egypt's prehistory and early dynastic history (beginning about 3200 BCE, see Table at end of article) has no bearing on biblical history and is outside the scope of this brief survey. In the days when the pyramids were built (28th to 23rd cs. BCE) Egypt maintained certain trade connections with Palestine and Byblos (see Phoenicia*) in northern Canaan. Military expeditions against that area are also on record, as well as several attacks or migrations of Asiatics into Egypt.

The Middle Kingdom and Palestine: The Middle Kingdom — the 11th to 12th dynasties (2155–1780 BCE) saw the strengthening of the central state power, in spite of rebellions and even regicide, and confirmation of Egyptian rule over the south (Nubia, Cush). Expeditions to Sinai were more

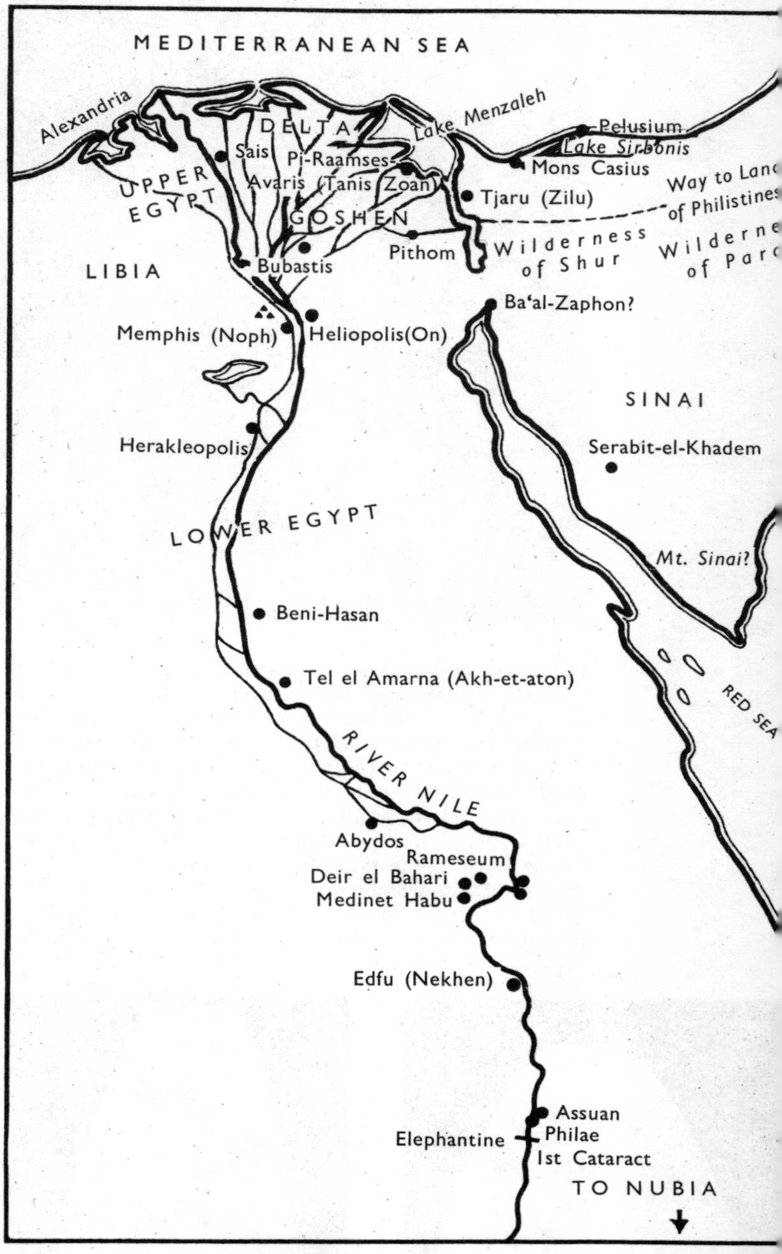

401

regular and the frontier with Palestine was fortified. Relations with Palestine are illustrated by the story of Sinuhet (Sinuhe), a courtier of Amenuhet I who fled there on the death of his master (1961 BCE), and left a description of his adventures and life in Palestine.

At Abydos, a stele was found giving an account of a campaign in Palestine at the time of Sesostris III (1878–1840 BCE). A town mentioned as plotting against Egypt with "Retenu" (a general term for Palestine) may be "Sichem" (Shechem*) but the name is not certain.

402

403

Execration Texts: Better evidence about Middle Kingdom relations with Palestine (see Patriarchs*: In the Context of the Early 2nd mill.) are the Execration Texts (20th–19th c. BCE), magic bowls and figurines inscribed with the names of Egypt's enemies. The bowls had been smashed as part of a ritual intended to make the curse effective on the person or group named. Figurines (**403**) found in Sakkara (19th c. BCE) and now at Brussels, were bound and kept by the Egyptians to symbolise a similar victory over their enemies. They mention many cities in Palestine, reflecting increased urban activity. A fascinating new hoard of inscribed bowls of this type was discovered by Jean Vercoutier in Nubia (Southern Egypt) in 1962 CE. Many of the names inscribed are West-Semitic. So far as they can be identified, they are a good indication of the early administration of Canaan under a series of local princes (see Megiddo*).

Egyptian-Canaanite relations are also illustrated by a variety of objects of Middle Kingdom Egypt found in Palestine. Among them are jar handles with a seal impression from Jerusalem, and the base of a statue of a high official found at Megiddo. These two finds show that Egypt was not merely trading in Canaan but ruled it directly. Royal power weakened towards the end of the Middle Kingdom — the last ruler of the 12th dynasty was a woman — and there were severe disturbances. Little is known of the two dynasties that followed except that they also made up a period of decline.

Hyksos Rule: There followed the period of Hyksos rule, 1730–1570 BCE (15th to 17th dynasties). The Hyksos have a special importance for biblical studies. Their invasion of Egypt was preceded by an infiltration from Asia, made possible by neglect of the north-eastern borders during the latter part of the Middle Kingdom. Hyksos rule and influence was restricted to Lower and Middle Egypt, their centre being Avaris in the N. E. Delta (Tanis, Biblical Zoan; see Exodus*). Their chief god was Seth shown on the left of the upper register of this fragment of a relief from an Egyptian tomb at Sahure (**402**). The god is identifiable by his head, that of the mythical Sethian animal, a doglike being with a square snout and long square ears. Ba'al is often represented in Egyptian art and inscriptions by the same animal. In his right hand Seth holds the sceptre of "well-being" and in his left the sign of "life". His right hand also holds the bonds of two prisoners, shown in the lower register on a much smaller scale than Seth. The first of these is a Nubian, his hands raised in supplication; the

404

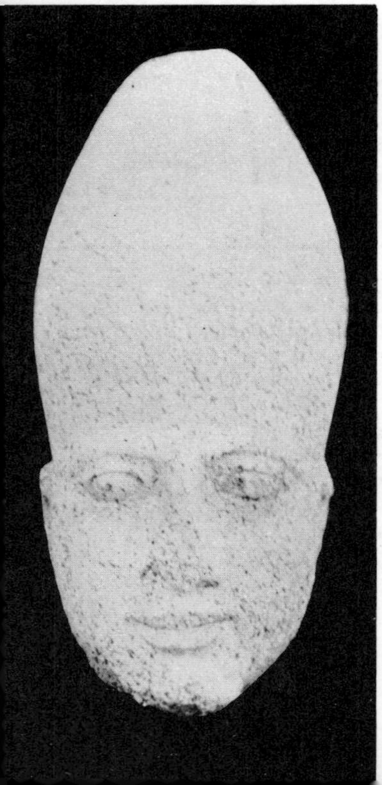

405

second, his arms crossed on his chest, is a Libyan. Behind Seth strides Amon, identifiable by his double crown. He also holds two Palestinian or Syrian prisoners. A third and, probably, a fourth figure, now destroyed, held three additional prisoners, of whom one can be identified by his phallus-sheath as a Libyan. The other two are too badly damaged to be identifiable. Colossal statues and stele (**404–5**) are evidence of the workshops of Tanis' sculptors from Ramses to the Ptolemies.

The Hyksos period was divided into two. In the first, preceding the 15th dynasty, the rulers had Semitic names such as Yaqub-har (or Yaqub-al), Shesha, Anati-al, and Babhmma (c. 1720–1660 BCE). A second group flourished between 1660–1570 BCE, among them Hayana and Apophis.

The 17th Dynasty ruled from Thebes at the same time as the latter part of Hyksos rule in the north (1680–1570 BCE). There was continual war between the opposing rulers and finally Amosis, the first king of the 18th dynasty, succeeded in driving the Hyksos from Egypt into Palestine. One result of the Hyksos downfall was the creation of the Egyptian Empire, the "New Empire".

The New Empire: The immediate successors of Amosis carried on his conquests but, after about 1525, dynastic squabbles and then a woman ruler put a stop to external activities. When a co-regency was established between the queen Hatshepsut and Thutmosis III (1490–1468 BCE), order was restored, and the way was clear for the individual reign of Thutmosis (Thothmes) III (1490–1436 BCE), as Egypt's greatest conqueror.

His campaigns carried him to the banks of the Euphrates, but his most significant victory was gained near Megiddo*, where he broke the resistance of a Canaanite alliance and finally ended Hyksos' claims. The victory established Egyptian domination over Canaan (for 500 years), until after the time of Shoshenk (Shishak — 945 BCE) and resulted in a radical reconstruction of Egypt's internal administration.

At the time of the Middle Kingdom, military tasks had been given to the king's officials, whenever need arose. Once the coastland, ports and roads of Canaan became available to Egypt and she could lay ambitious plans with regard to the north, the officials were ousted by professional soldiers.

Thutmosis' successor, Amenophis II, also waged war in Palestine and among the many records he has left of his prowess as a sportsman, is a reference to the Habiru prisoners he took in Palestine. His son Thutmosis IV decorated his chariot with scenes of his victories over Asiatics. When he died (1398 BCE), his chariot was buried in his tomb, to await the archaeologists and interpreters of a much later age. His boastful account of his exploits is probably based on fact. There were many attempts to weaken the Egyptian hold on Canaan, especially from the north, and these were beginning to gain ground. Egyptian rule was weakened further under the next king, Amenophis III, and, in spite of all claims to the contrary, he conducted no aggressive campaigns. Moreover the court faced pressures at home. To escape an upsurge of a long standing conflict between Temple and throne, the king moved his court away from Thebes with its clamourous priests, to Memphis. There the court turned from the traditional gods to the worship of the sun-disc, Aton.

Akhenaton: When Amenophis III passed on the throne to his son, the new cult became the official exclusive religion. The king adopted it with enthusiasm, changing his name to Akhenaton (**406**) and giving his full support to the new philosophy of life based on "maat", the principle of truth. He faced the fierce opposition of the priests of the

406

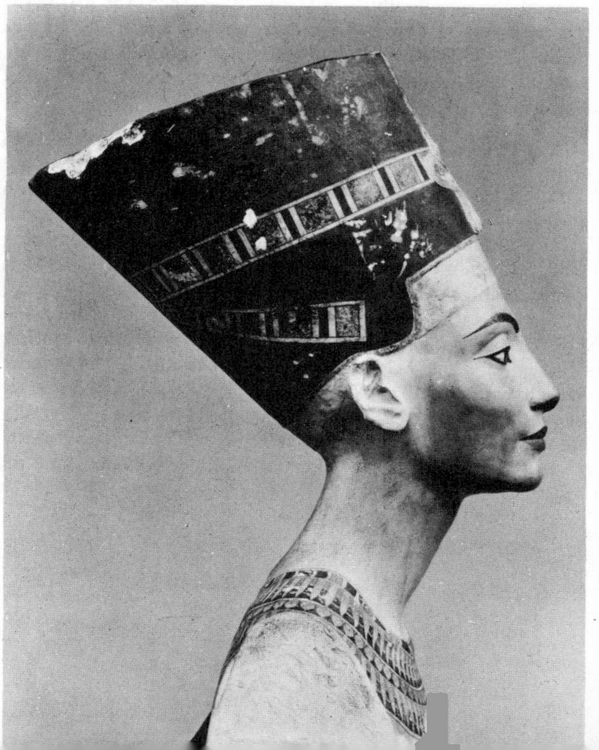

407

409

traditional gods who could hardly have been expected to accept the change with equanimity. To escape them, the king founded a new city, Akh-et-Aton to serve as his capital. In modern times, the site, now known as Tel el Amarna* has been excavated and has yielded one of the richest stores of knowledge about the life and art of the time.

The new philosophy had a great effect on art. Emphasis on truth meant a freer, more realistic representation of nature and man, with the odd side effect that because the king suffered from certain deformities, the artists of his court showed all mankind as similarly deformed.

In Tel el Amarna, exceptionally in Egypt, not only tombs and temples, but the homes of ordinary people were excavated. From these, and especially from the workshops of a sculptor, a large collection of the art of the period was discovered. Among so much else, was the famous head of Nofretete (**407**; Nefertiti), Akhenaton's queen, one of the world's most beautiful portraits of a beautiful woman.

The Amarna Letters: Outstanding among the discoveries were the "Amarna letters*" (see article), part of the royal archive, consisting of a series of letters to king Akhenaton and his father, Amenophis III, from their agents abroad. Many of the letters were sent from Palestine, complaining about difficulties in Syria and Palestine: about the inroads of the Habiru* and attacks from the Amorite cities of Syria, at the instigation of the Hittites, whose example was followed by their southern neighbours. This series of disturbances was in fact the beginning of the break-up of the Asiatic empire established by Thutmosis III; but the Pharaohs never seem to have reacted. In fact, the whole of the new philosophy and the political system which grew out of it, were short-lived. With the death of Akhenaton, the so-called "Amarna Age" came to an end.

Thut-Ankh-Amon: Akhenaton's children were all daughters and he was succeeded by his son-in-law who rejected the worship of Aton and returned to the old gods. Deliberately taking a name that included that of "Amun", he was to become, after some 3,000 years, perhaps the best-known of all Egyptian kings. The excitement of the discovery of the Tomb of Tutankhamon and the fabulous riches which it contained seemed to illuminate a whole era of Egyptian history. In fact, he reigned for only eight years, and at the time his achievements were far outshone by those of Haremhab who succeeded to the throne two years after his death. Haremhab had also belonged to the circle of worshippers of Aton and had also abandoned the religion upon the death of its founder. He was a strong and vigorous king who did much to restore the power of Egypt and to prepare the way for the glories of the following 19th and 20th dynasties, the period of the Ramesides.

The Ramesides: The first great conqueror of the Rameside dynasty was Seti I, who recovered Egyptian possessions in Palestine and Lybia. His army is seen here attacking "the town of the Canaan" (**408**), together with the town of Yanoam situated in a wooded region beside a body of water. However, Egypt's most dangerous enemies were the Hittites, encroaching from the north-east, constantly threatening Egyptian power in Syria and Palestine. The famous battle of Kadesh (see Megiddo*) was Ramses II's first attempt to defeat them and, it seems, an unsuccessful one. The fortress of Kadesh is seen here surrounded by a moat (**409**). Further battles in the far north followed. No decisive blow was struck by either side and finally peace was sealed by a treaty which endured as long as the Hittite empire lasted (until mid-13th c. BCE). This accounts for the long interlude when no military activities are recorded and Ramses was able to devote himself to a series of ambitious construction plans (see Exodus*). His son, Mernephtach (1224–1214 BCE) was obliged to take up arms against Lybian encroachment on the western Delta. In his famous victory stele (Israel Stele, see Exodus*), Mernephtach claims victories in Palestine. Although these are doubted today, it is possible that certain princes and invaders in Palestine chose the moment when the Egyptian was occupied with his western borders to extend their rule (see Conquest*).

The end of the 19th dynasty is very poorly documented. It seems to have been a troubled period of internal disaffection and revolt. The last king, whose name was Iarsu, came from Palestine or Syria, not as a conqueror, but as one of many Asiatics who reached high office in Egypt. He probably gained the throne by some skilful manoeuvring and the force of personal ambition.

Egypt and the "People of the Sea": The 20th dynasty, founded by Setnakht, ended this period of confusion and, in his son Ramses III (1198–1166 BCE) found one of Egypt's greatest rulers. He had to face the "Sea People". Coming from the north by way of Crete, these were a migratory people, seeking a foothold in the Delta. One large group, the Pelast, seized and settled the coastline between Joppa and Gaza. The region subsequently took its name, Philistia, from them and, from Roman times, this was applied to the whole country, Palestine (see Philistines*).

Ramses recorded his victories against them in the wall reliefs of his temple at Medinet Habu, where the Philistines* are recognizable by their feathered helmets (see illus. under that art.). After their defeat in Egypt, many of the "Sea People" settled in the south of Palestine, where some of them, the Philistines, became important in biblical history. Related to them were the Tjeker who settled in the region of Dor, south of Mount Carmel.

The kings, all called Ramses (IV to XI), who completed the 20th dynasty left no great mark on history during their 80 years rule. Their dynasty petered out in confusion and neglect around 1100 BCE.

With the 21st dynasty, the "Late Period" of the history of Egypt began. Its hold over Canaan was greatly weakened, part of the country being occupied by the Philistines and Tjeker on the coastal regions and by the people of Israel inland.

21st–26th Dynasties: The 21st dynasty was the period (1090–945 BCE) of the divided monarchy with Herihor ruling Upper Egypt from Thebes and the north ruled by Smendes, who held court in Tanis. There is an amusing "Story of Wen-Amun" from this period which tells of an official (Wen-Amun) sent by Herihor to bring cedarwood from Lebanon and succeeding only in demonstrating the weakness of Egyptian prestige in the East (see Phoenicia*).

The 22nd dynasty was of Libyan origin, founded by a brilliant Libyan professional soldier in the Egyptian army who had been absorbed into Egyptian society. He rose through the ranks to displace the weak rulers of the divided kingdom.

408

Shishak and Solomon: This king was Shoshenk I, called Shishak in the Bible, which gives an account of his relations with Solomon. The policy he followed can be traced to one of the last Pharaohs of the 21st dynasty in the days of King David. At the time of a massacre by David's General Joab, Hadad, the prince of Edom, escaped to Egypt where he was received by the Pharaoh (unnamed, probably Siamun). On the death of David, Hadad returned to his native land to "do mischief", which probably reflects Egyptian intrigues against the royal court at Jerusalem. Later, however, the Pharaoh decided on a diplomatic marriage between one of his daughters and King Solomon. As a dowry, he presented Solomon with the town of Gezer* which he had just captured. This suggests that Egypt still controlled the land of Philistia and beyond it, for Gezer is some way from the Egyptian border.

When Shoshenk came to the Egyptian throne (945 BCE) during the second half of Solomon's reign, he encouraged the separatist tendencies of Jeroboam, an official of Solomon, but an avowed enemy of the united monarchy, and gave him shelter from Solomon. It seems that his encouragement was not especially aimed at the establishment of a new state in the north but was part of a sound "divide and rule" policy. When Solomon died and the kingdom split into two, Shoshenk invaded.

Shoshenk (Shishak) in Israel: The Bible relates only a campaign in the south aiming at Jerusalem. A record of this campaign, which appears on the southern wall of the Temple of Amon at Karnak, does not, however, include Jerusalem in the list of places stormed or destroyed. The list consists of three sections: a. towns in Judah and Edom; b. Jewish towns in the west and northwest, as well as towns of the Northern Kingdom of Israel in the hills west of the Jordan, the Valley of Jezreel and the Sharon Plain; c. towns in Transjordania. Fragments of a stele uncovered at Megiddo* record the occupation of that town by the Egyptians. From Megiddo, Shoshenk turned south to Samaria* and from there back to Egypt. At the same time a column of his army went through the Negeb and Edom. This itinerary suggests that Shoshenk's forces went mainly through the Northern Kingdom and Edom, giving Judah a wide berth. Possibly the young and poor Israel Kingdom could not buy him off, and thus by encouraging his attack on Judah, had invited their own disaster. The wealthy Judah was able to offer a substantial bribe, which may explain the absence of Jerusalem from the list of besieged towns. The Megiddo stele fragment, together with evidence of destruction in northern Israel at the appropriate period, confirm Shoshenk's own account. His list of victories, once regarded as an empty boast, is now believed to reflect his actual behavior.

Nubian and Ethiopian Dynasties: For the next two centuries, Egypt again experienced a period of weakness in her own rulers, culminating in a successful conquest of the country from the south and the establishment of a Nubian Pharaoh, Shabako of the 25th dynasty (712–662 BCE). It has been suggested that he may be the Pharaoh So, mentioned in II K. 17:4 ff, as the king of Egypt who allied himself with Hoshea, king of Israel, against the Assyrian Sargon II (see Israel and Judah*). Documents have been discovered in which Shabako lists victories won in Palestine and he even allowed memorial scarabs to be issued in celebration. In the Assyrian records, though, Sargon describes So (his name is now read as Re'u) as "Tartan", general of the Pharaoh, to distinguish him from the king. This supports the identification of So (Re'u) as an Egyptian general of an earlier period (730–720 BCE).

Egypt's policy at this time was generally to send as few troops abroad as possible and to harass the Assyrians by stirring up trouble for them in their dependencies of Palestine and its neighbours. Egypt's troops were no help to Hoshea of Israel. Jeered the Assyrians; "Behold you are relying now on Egypt, that broken reed of a staff, which will pierce the hand of any man who leans on it. Such is Pharaoh king of Egypt to all who rely on him." (II K. 18:21). They were right. After a prolonged siege, the Northern Kingdom of Israel fell to the Assyrians (722/21 BCE).

Assyrian Domination: Sargon's son, Esarhaddon, struck at the heart of opposition to Assyria and attacked and conquered Egypt. In a stele found at Senjirli (**410**), he is shown holding two kings on leading strings: Taharka of Egypt and the king of Tyre who, remarkably, is shown as the bigger, i. e. the more important of the two.

The Assyrians ruled Egypt for seven years. Taharka's successor, Tanutamon, the last king of the 25th dynasty, attempted to reconquer Memphis from his stronghold of Thebes. With his failure, Thebes was utterly destroyed (662 BCE), its fate horrifying the contemporary world. Fifty years later (612 BCE) the prophet Nahum* (3:8–10) used Thebes as an example of the destruction that awaited Nineveh.

Josiah and Necho: The 26th dynasty, the beginning of the "Saitic" period in Egypt, was founded by Psammetik who used the gathering conflict between Assyria and Babylon to establish himself in Egypt and even to extend Egyptian influence over Palestine. His son, Necho, continued this policy but with a difference. Assyria was threatened by the alliance of the Medes and the Babylonians against it. While their success would mean the end of Egyptian influence in Asia, a weakened Assyria, gladly allying itself with Egypt against the Babylonian/Median threat, would allow Egypt to strengthen its Asiatic position. Accordingly, Necho marched through Palestine on his way to join forces with Assyria. At Megiddo, he came face to face with the Jewish army. King Josiah was allied to Babylon against Assyria and was determined not to let the Egyptians pass (see Israel and Judah*: V). He was powerless to prevent them. At the end of the battle, Josiah lay dead, a disaster which the spiritual and political life of Israel reflected for a long time. An Egyptian Pharaoh dominated Judah and Jerusalem for the first time since the Conquest.

In fact Egyptian domination was short-lived. Necho installed Jehoiakim, a son of Josiah, as his vassal but in 605 BCE the Egyptians were beaten at Carchemish and forced to withdraw from Palestine. The borders of Egypt became the limit of the Babylonian empire which now included Judah. The former Egyptian policy of stirring up unrest against Babylon was continued, one result being the revolt of Zedekiah against the Babylonian yoke (Jer. 37:5), encouraged by the promise of help from the Pharaoh Hophra (Apries, 588–568 BCE) and the enthusiasm of his nobles. Jerusalem was besieged and although the appearance of Hophra's armies from Egypt relieved it for a time, he was beaten, his armies forced back to Egypt and the siege resumed. A year later (586 BCE) Jerusalem fell.

Elephantine: Apries opened the doors of Egypt to the Jews. A military colony developed at Elephantine (Yeb) in southern Egypt and was to leave a vast mass of papyri to be found by later explorers. From these, it is apparent that a Jewish temple existed there in the 5th (or late 6th) c. BCE (see Inscriptions* and illus. **73**).

Apries was murdered in a military revolt and the general Amasis began a reign (569–526 BCE) which emphasizes the impoverishment that had overtaken the once proud kingdom. The events of his reign are known more from Herodotus than from Egyptian sources, while the records of the Elephantine colony are of particular interest for the general background of Jewish life in Egypt during the 6th c.

Persian Domination: The reign of Apries' son, Psammetik III, ended (525 BCE) when Egypt could no longer withstand its enemies and as a result of Cambyses' conquests, became part of the Persian empire. Cambyses was not content to rule the land through a vassal Pharaoh, as the Assyrians had done. Instead, he had himself acknowledged Pharaoh by the Egyptians. Nevertheless, Persian rule was interrupted by a series of revolts. Egyptian independence was regained for a time, although the re-established 28th and 29th dynasties were of little significance. The 30th dynasty saw the last efforts on the part of the Egyptian monarchs to regain earlier political importance and a brief upsurge of activity in art and architecure.

Persian rule was again imposed in 341 BCE, but it came to an end with Alexander the Great's conquest of Egypt in 332 BCE. After Alexander's death, one of his generals, Ptolemy, established himself as king, and founded a dynasty which lasted until Egypt was absorbed into the Roman empire.

Graeco-Roman Period: During this time, the Jewish immigrants who had fled to Egypt after the fall of Jerusalem and whose descendants had greatly increased throughout the Persian period (Is. 19:18 ff), were followed by a large number of Jews who settled in Lower Egypt. Some came voluntarily, some as deportees. Although we know little of the fortunes of the Jews in general at this time, it is clear that the flow of immigration from Palestine during the reign of the Ptolemies, made Egypt a centre of world Jewry. The focus of Jewish life there was in Alexandria, where a specifically Hellenistic*-Jewish civilization developed. In addition there were many other lesser centres. Evidence exists to show that there were synagogues in the country as early as the 3rd c. BCE, while before Maccabaean days, the refugee High

Priest Onias founded a Temple in Heliopolis. It was also during this period that the Septuagint translation of the Torah (later of the other books of the Old Testament) was made with the co-operation of the Hellenist king Ptolemy II Philadelphus (285–247 BCE).

By then, it is estimated, Egyptian Jewry numbered around one million — a strength which was one reason for anti-Jewish feeling among the Greek masses (see Hellenism and the Diaspora*). With the Christianization of the Roman Empire, however, the condition of Egyptian Jewry deteriorated.

Cultural relations between Egypt and Israel, especially in relation to wisdom literature*, poetry*, language* and writing* are referred to under the respective articles.

410

CHRONOLOGICAL TABLE: History of Egypt
(based on: E. Drioton—J. Vandier)

	BCE
FIRST AND SECOND DYNASTY	3000–2778
OLD KINGDOM	2778–2423
THIRD DYNASTY (Builders of the Great Pyramids)	2778–2723
FOURTH DYNASTY (Builders of Pyramids)	2723–2563
FIFTH DYNASTY	2563–2423
SIXTH DYNASTY	2423–2263
SEVENTH AND EIGHTH DYNASTIES	2263–2070
FIRST INTERMEDIATE PERIOD (Ninth and Tenth Dyn.)	2190–2040
MIDDLE KINGDOM (Eleventh and Twelfth Dynasties)	2160–1580
SECOND INTERMEDIATE PERIOD (Thirteenth and Fourteenth Dynasties)	1785–1680
HYKSOS (Fifteenth and Sixteenth Dynasties)	1730–1580
SEVENTEENTH DYNASTY	1680–1580
THE NEW KINGDOM	1580–1090
EIGHTEENTH DYNASTY	1580–1314
Ahmosis	1580–1558
Amenophis I	1557–1539
Thutmosis I	1539–1520
Thutmosis II Hatshepsut	1520–1484
Thutmosis III	1504–1450
Amenophis II	1450–1425
Thutmosis IV	1425–1408
Amenophis III	1408–1372
Amenophis IV ("Akhenaton")	1372–1354
Smenkhare Thut-Ankh-Amon Ai Haremhab	1354–1314
NINETEENTH DYNASTY	1314–1200
Ramses I	1314–1312
Sethi I	1312–1289
Ramses II	1290–1224
Mernephtach	1224–1204
TWENTIETH DYNASTY	1200–1085
Ramses III	1198–1166
LATE PERIOD	1085–332
TWENTY-FIRST DYNASTY	1085–950
Smendes Herihor	1085–1054
TWENTY-SECOND DYNASTY (Libyan)	950–730
Shosenk I	950–929
Osorkon I	929–893
Osorkon II	870–847
Shoshenk II	847
TWENTY-THIRD DYNASTY (Libyan)	817–730
TWENTY-FOURTH DYNASTY	730–715
TWENTY-FIFTH DYNASTY (Nubian)	751–656
Shabaka	716–701
Taharka	689–663
Tanutamon	663–656
TWENTY-SIXTH DYNASTY (Saitic)	663–525
Psammetik I	663–609
Necho	609–594
Apries (Hophra)	588–568
Amasis	568–526
Psammetik III	526–525
TWENTY-SEVENTH DYNASTY (Persian Domination: Cambyses until Darius II)	525–404
TWENTY-EIGHTH DYNASTY	404–398
TWENTY-NINTH DYNASTY	398–378
THIRTIETH DYNASTY	378–341
SECOND PERSIAN DOMINATION	341–333
CONQUEST BY ALEXANDER THE GREAT	332

Many of the dates are approximate only. Some dynasties ruled at the same time in different parts of the country.
Only the rulers of importance for the history of Canaan and Israel are listed.

ELAM AND ISRAEL. — Elam was one of the important countries which occupied the western Zagros highlands skirting the great Mesopotamian plain on the east and north. It corresponds almost exactly to the area of Chuzistan in modern Iran (Persia) immediately adjacent to Iran's south-west frontier with modern Iraq (see Persia*, map). The Elamites, a non-Semitic people, occupied the area from the 3rd mill BCE, before the influx of the Indo-Europeans into Mesopotamia.

The Babylonians called the people of Elam "Elamtu", while the Greeks termed them Elymais and their country Susiana, after the capital, Susa (Hebrew Shushan). South-east of Susa lay the mountainous region of Anshan, homeland of Cyrus, the (6th c. BCE) founder of the Persian empire. Although its closest neighbours in the early 2nd mill. BCE were the Guti and Lullabi tribal peoples of the Zagros mountain areas, Elam's civilization was as old as those of lower Mesopotamia, and much closer to them. Even when the rule of the Akkadian kings (see Babylonia*) was overthrown by the attacks of the Guti, Elam's political and cultural life appears to have continued without interruption right through the Middle Bronze Age (2nd mill. BCE).

Elam's Supremacy: Because of its geographical position, Elam controlled the trade routes from Mesopotamia northwards across the Iranian plateau and south-east to India. The wealth brought by this trade made the country the object of constant attack from Mesopotamia, and Elam was frequently subjugated by the kingdoms of lower Babylonia. Nevertheless, around 2000 BCE a strong Elamite dynasty arose, gained control of several cities in southern Mesopotamia, destroyed the Empire of Ur (= the third dynasty), and with it, Sumerian control in the area. Within two centuries (the 18th BCE), Elam played a major political role in Mesopotamia. It declined during the reign of Hammurabi (ca. 1728–1686 BCE; see Babylonia*) and after the invasion of Cassites during the 17th c. BCE. However, following the decline in Babylonia's strength, the Elamites were able to re-occupy the southern state and to invade southern Babylonia in the 12th c. BCE. The king of Elam even installed his son on the throne of Babylonia.

During the course of these invasions the Elamites carried off substantial quantities of valuable booty to Susa. Amongst many famous sculptures was the stele of Hammurabi himself (see Law*), which was found by archaeologists in the ruins of Susa. All these imported works had a noticeable influence on the art of the conqueror and led to the development of an increasingly distinguished school of Iranian artists. In addition to other examples of their work, the structure of a large, well-designed ziggurat (stepped temple tower, see Babylonia*) has been discovered at Choga Zambil, near Susa.

Invasion of the Indo-Europeans: The migration of Indo-European peoples southwards into Iran began about 1000 BCE. In time, they overran all the highlands fringing Mesopotamia (see Assyria*; Persia*) and annexed Elam, which thereafter ceased to exist as an independent political unit. In the later 8th and early 7th cs. BCE, Elam was subjugated by the Assyrian kings Sargon II and Sennacherib. This moved the people of Elam to join forces with Babylonia in opposition to Assyrian domination. After a number of unsuccessful uprisings, Ashurbanipal destroyed Susa (645 BCE) and deported its inhabitants, many of them to repeople the ravaged Samaria (Ezr. 4:9). A relief in the palace of Nineveh pictures Elamite prisoners eating a meal on their trek from Susa (**411**).

From this point, the history of Elam merges with the story of the gradual rise of the Persians*. It is supposed that Achaemenes first established himself north of Susa, while his son, Teispes, took Anshan. At the same time, the Medes were absorbing the north and west of the country. Thus Elam became in time merely one part of the emergent empire of the Medes and Persians (see Persia*). A painting on glazed brick (**412**), made in Susa in the 5th c. BCE, shows an Elamite soldier, one of the Persian "Ten Thousand Immortals" who formed the backbone of the Persian army.

Elam in the Bible: Gn. 10:22 (and I Ch. 1:17) lists Elam as a son of Shem, on the assumption that the Elamites belonged to the Semitic peoples of Mesopotamia, familiar to the early Hebrews. The most important historical reference to Elam is in the enigmatic story in Gn. 14, where a King Chedorlaomer is mentioned as suzerain over the kings of Sodom, Gomorrah, Admah, Zeboiim and Zoar in southern Palestine. When these latter rebelled against Chedorlaomer, he was supported by three other (presumably Mesopotamian) kings, including "Amraphel, king of Shinar", who should not be confused with Hammurabi (see Babylonia*; Genesis*). There has been, so far, no data to substantiate the historicity of this incident; yet some scholars tend to accept it, and relate it to the period of Elam's supremacy in the 18th c. BCE.

Elam figures prominently in the prophetic writings, notably Is. 21:2 ff; Jer. 25:25; 49:34–39; Ezk. 32:24–25, with particular reference to the role it played as part of the Persian empire which overthrew Babylonia. The Jews of Elam founded one of the most important centres of

411

412

the early Diaspora, and Susa is the scene of the story of Esther*. Elamites are also mentioned in the New Testament. Both Jews and proselytes from Elam are listed among those taking part in the annual Pentecost pilgrimage to Jerusalem (Ac. 2:9). By that time, the country was part of Parthia (see Persia*; Rome and the Jews*; Babylonia*).

ELIJAH. — Elijah the Tishbite came from the pasture region of Gilead, 18 miles north of the river Jabbok. He was the foremost prophet of Israel during the reigns of Ahab (869–850 BCE), his son Ahaziah (850–849) and also, apparently, Ahab's younger son, Joram. Mainly active in the Northern Kingdom of Israel, Elijah also visited the mount of God at Horeb in the wilderness of Sinai (I K. 19:8) and "Zarephath which belongs to Sidon" (ibid 17:8–24). The book of Chronicles (II Ch. 21:12–15) includes a letter supposedly written by Elijah to Jehoram, king of Judah. The letter has no place in the cycle of Elijah stories, or "Acts of Elijah" (i. e. I K. 17–19 and 21 and II K. 1:2–17) which apparently originated in an ancient prophetical document recording the main points of the life and teachings of Elijah. Accordingly, one school of thought holds that the letter to Jehoram may have been an invention of the Judahite Chronicler who could not bear to have the affairs of the Southern Kingdom completely ignored by one of the greatest figures of Hebrew history and faith. Other scholars, however, deny that the chronicler invented anything and believe that there must have been a tradition on which he relied. The story is hardly unreasonable in itself, although there is no way of confirming it.

Elijah's Personality: Elijah is described as a lonely figure of arresting appearance. Dressed in a "garment of haircloth, with a girdle of leather about his loins" (II K. 1:8), he had no settled home, apparently, but roamed about the countryside, appearing unexpectedly and vanishing as suddenly (I K. 18:12). His teachings brought him into repeated conflict with the kings of Israel and on at least one occasion he had to flee for his life. He did not belong to the bands of ecstatic prophets (II K. 2) similar to those whom Samuel* had enlisted generations earlier to rally the Israelites (see Elisha*) but he occasionally consorted with them. It is possible that Elijah was a member of the Rechabites or a Nazirite, who lived in a state of constant readiness for war and appeared, as if by magic, wherever Yahweh's battle had to be fought. The name Elijah originally meant "Let El create" but it later came to mean "Yahweh is my God" which some scholars see as the motto of his life and mission as a prophet.

The Contest on Mount Carmel: All his life Elijah was active in the defence of his God, which meant fighting against the rival creed of Ba'al especially the cult of Ba'al-Melkart, patron of Tyre, which Ahab's Phoenician wife Jezebel had introduced into Israel. Elijah clashed frequently with Jezebel who persecuted the prophets of Yahweh and not only promoted the worship of Ba'al but had also reintroduced the pagan fertility cults of "Athrt ym" i. e. Asherah of the Sea (I K. 18:19; see Canaan*, Phoenicia*).

The famous story of Elijah's triumph over the priests of Ba'al on Mount Carmel is believed to have had an authentic historical setting. According to I K. 18:1 Elijah's meeting with king Ahab came in the third successive year of drought, when the whole country was suffering from famine. The fact of the drought is recorded by the Phoenician Menander — a Hellenistic historian regarded as generally reliable and quoted by Josephus* (Ant. 8, 13, 2). These sources speak of a two-and-a-half year long drought which was ended when Ethba'al, king of Tyre (and Ahab's father-in-law) prayed for rain and was answered by a heavy thunderstorm.

In the biblical version, Elijah sought a meeting with Ahab and asked him to summon all Israel and the "four hundred and fifty prophets of Ba'al and the four hundred prophets of Asherah who eat at Jezebel's table" to Mount Carmel for a trial of strength to see which god was the true one. In front of the king and all the people, Elijah challenged the ranks of his rivals to prove themselves and their god by bringing down fire from heaven to burn a sacrifice. They prepared their offering and all day long called on Ba'al to send the fire, mutilating themselves until the blod ran "as was their custom". They had no success and Elijah taunted them in what are now recognized to be familiar allusions to Canaanite mythology and ritual (see Ugarit*). Then, in the evening, Elijah rebuilt the ancient altar to Yahweh which had been demolished, laid his offering upon it, poured water over the offering and the wood fuel underneath it, and prayed to Yahweh to send fire so "that this people may know that thou, O Lord, art God." Whereupon, fire came from heaven and "consumed the burnt offering, and the wood, and the stones, and the dust and licked up the water" (I K. 18:38). Having thus demonstrated the supremacy of Yahweh, Elijah ordered the priests of Ba'al to be seized and had them killed by the brook Kishon. Within a few hours "a little cloud like a man's hand" developed into a great storm and the drought was broken.

For Elijah, however, the purpose of his action had been to discredit Ba'al and restore Yahweh to his place as the only true God. The whole point of the story is that there could be only one God and that God was Yahweh. It is clear from the details given that both Ba'al and Yahweh were worshipped with sacrifices prepared in exactly the same manner. This must have been the normal way of offering sacrifices — or the point of the story would be lost (see Sacrifice*). The question was: which God would be able to answer a plea, Ba'al of the mountain, shown as the god of thunder in the Canaanite figure (**271**), or Yahweh.

It is also not impossible that another element in the Holy War which Elijah declared on the worship of Ba'al Melkart was an ancient dispute between Israel and Phoenicia over possession of the mountain. The story of Elijah's triumph over the priests of Ba'al (18:40) may have provided a justification for the establishment of Yahweh's (and consequently Israel's) exclusive rights over the area.

Ahab and Jezebel and their particular forms of paganism were Elijah's supreme, constant target. Rather surprisingly, there is no word of condemnation of official worship at the northern sanctuaries of Bethel and Dan, established in rivalry to Jerusalem (see Israel and Judah*, II), nor of the "golden calves" which Jeroboam had set up there (see Canaan, Gods and Idols*; Idol Worship in Israel*). Some scholars even regard it as doubtful whether Elijah approved of Jerusalem worship. Presumably the northern sanctuaries were not considered a serious threat to Yahwism which was Elijah's prime and, indeed, sole concern. Not only Ahab and Jezebel but all who followed their cult of Ba'al were condemned vehemently.

Elijah at Mount Horeb: I K. 19 records that following his victory over the priests of Ba'al, Elijah fled from Jezebel's anger to the south of Judah, eventually reaching Horeb, the mount of God. There God revealed Himself. The story follows the lines of the revelation to Moses at Mount Sinai and places Elijah as representing a primitive Mosaic tradition still alive within Israel. His solitary vigil at Mount Horeb, the hallowed site of Israel's origins in the wilderness, forms a material link with that dim past. However, whereas at Mount Sinai God revealed Himself amid a mighty tempest, in Elijah's case, the forces of nature which appeared – the wind, the earthquake and the fire — did not embody God. God was in the "silence" or, as the Hebrew text puts it, in the sound of stillness which came after the fire and the earthquake and the wind.

While on the mountain, Elijah was commanded to anoint Hazael king over Syria, Jehu as king of Israel and Elisha as his own successor. In fact, Elijah carried out only the last of these missions, his disciple Elisha* being responsible for anointing the two kings. The passage about Hazael (I K. 19:15–18) seems to be much later than the compilation of the "Sons of the Prophets" (see Elisha*) and was probably included by the same chronicler who linked Elijah to the doings of the kings of Judah. Alternatively, it may have been part of another tradition which emphasized Elijah's political teachings and activities as directed against the dynasty of Omri and its pro-Phoenician tendencies. As this dynasty and its policies had become odious to his God, so Elijah made plans for its overthrow. This is not necessarily something ascribed to Elijah by later historians. It is very much what might be expected of him. On the other hand, it is also believed by many scholars that it was the incident of Naboth's vineyard (see below) more than anything else that turned the people against the king and moved Elijah to lay his curse on the whole house of Ahab.

Ahab's Cosmopolitan Tendencies: It would seem that the clash between prophet and court concerned much more than religious doctrine. Elijah's religion was also a way of life and this too was threatened by the new developments at Ahab's court. Ahab's alliance with Tyre — the leading traders of the age (see Phoenicia*) — had brought a new commercial prosperity to Israel, which controlled important sections of two main land trade routes (see Roads*, Trade*). Along with those of the court, the wealth, luxury and international connections of an important section of the population also increased. This had the effect of weakening traditional tribal institutions and customs — a trend welcomed and encouraged by Jezebel. She was a princess of Phoenicia — a land in which kings wielded absolute, despotic power over their people. She realized that Elijah, his religion and his dominating personality were a major obstacle to the creation of a similarly autocratic rule by her own court. Elijah was the deadly enemy of her ideas and her influence over the king.

Naboth's Vineyard: The situation is most clearly expressed in the incident of Naboth's vineyard. Ahab wanted to buy the vineyard but when Naboth refused to part with "the inheritance of my fathers" he was completely within his rights and Ahab had no legal means of redress (see Property, Land and its Conveyance*). Jezebel, however, held that a royal wish should be a command. On her instructions, a pretext was found to convict Naboth of blasphemy for which he was stoned to death and his property forfeited to the crown. Ahab got his vineyard, but he paid dearly for it in the regard of his people. Instead of acting as the embodiment of justice, upholder of tradition and model of righteous behaviour, the king was revealed as guilty of flagrant injustice and cruelty. The Israelites were a people whose community and social life were regulated by explicit ancestral laws, which gave the ordinary people certain rights. Never before had these rights been so openly challenged by the king's authority. It seems likely that it was this incident above all which turned the people against Ahab's whole dynasty and made them welcome Elijah's prophecy of its violent overthrow and replacement by Jehu (see Israel and Judah*, II: Extinction of the House of Omri).

The incident is recorded twice: once as part of the historical record (I K. 21) and again as the vindication of Jehu's slaying of his king — the son of Ahab and Jezebel (II K. 9:25–26). It is significant that the compiler of the "Acts of Elijah" turned attention from Ahab's military achievements to his less favourable record and to Elijah's role as the champion of tradition in the social and economic life of Israel.

Elijah's Last Act: According to II Kings 1, Elijah last took a part in public affairs when he prophesied the death of Ahaziah (II K. 1:16) Ahab's son. He had fallen "through the lattice in his upper chamber in Samaria" and sent to inquire from Ba'al-Zebub (in fact Ba'al-Zebul) of Ekron whether he would recover from his injuries. Appropriately enough, Elijah's last recorded words were a condemnation of this recourse to pagan gods ("is it because there is no God in Israel to inquire of his word?" II K. 1:16).

A Ruthless Fighter: Throughout his career, Elijah battled against Ba'al using all the violence accepted by his age. Elijah's enemies and those of his God must be wiped out without mercy. The priests of Ba'al must be killed to the last man, ("let not one of them escape," I K. 18:40); Ahab and Jezebel must die horribly and Hazael is to be made king of Syria so that "him who escapes from the sword of Hazael shall Jehu slay; and him who escapes from the sword of Jehu shall Elisha slay" and only those shall be saved whose knees have not bowed to Ba'al and whose mouth has not kissed him (ibid 19:17–18).

Elijah's Miracles: The stories about Elijah are full of wonders and miraculous acts. During the drought, by the brook Cherith, ravens brought him food (I K. 17:1–6); and when he went to Zarephath he was welcomed by a widow who fed him and her household for many days from a "handful of meal and a little oil in a cruse (ibid 8–16). When the widow's son died, Elijah brought him back to life (ibid 17–24), and when Elijah's own life came to an end, he was taken up in a whirlwind to heaven (II K. 2:11). Specific magic power was ascribed to Elijah's mantle. Rolled up, it parted the waters of the Jordan so that Elijah and Elisha might cross (ibid 2:8) and, again, to make way for Elisha alone (14). Elisha's wearing of the mantle symbolized that the spirit of Elijah rested upon him. The powers of this mantle are very similar to those of Moses' rod — which parted the waters of the Reed Sea — and this emphasizes the similarities between the two leaders. The Synoptic Gospels also bear witness to the connections between them in their account of the Transfiguration when Jesus was seen talking to Moses and Elijah (Mt. 17:3–4; Mk. 9:4–5; Lk. 9:30–33).

The Sources of the Traditions: The main source for the Elijah stories is the "Acts of Elijah", a compilation written by some (or one) of the "bene hanebi'im" ("the Sons of the Prophets") who undertook to record the doings of their leaders, Elijah and Elisha. Some scholars find an analogy to this in the literary form of the gospels in which some of Jesus' disciples undertook to record an account of his life and sayings (Lk. 1:1–4), although there are, also, radical differences between the two examples which must be borne in mind (see below). The traditions of Islam were similarly written down during the lifetime of Mohammed.

It seems unlikely that the creation of the Elijah/Elisha stories took a long period, although the core of tradition was inevitably embellished by later legends. Elijah's powerful personality made an unforgettable impact on his own — and later — generations and it is hardly surprising that the "Sons of the Prophets" were careful to include all the wonders and miracles in their account of his activities. This makes it very difficult to reconstruct anything like a coherent account of his actual life. On the other hand, were it not for the careful preservation of the traditions about him and Elisha, information on the doings of Ahab and Jezebel would probably be even sketchier than the existing account in the first book of Kings.

Some scholars believe that the II Kings story of Ahaziah's fall from his window and its repercussions does not belong to the same source, for in this story alone God's word is revealed to Elijah through the intermediary of an angel (II K. 1:3, 15), instead of directly. However, apart from this phrase, there is no essential difference between the story in II Kings and all the other traditions concerning Elijah, and there is no real reason to assume that it had a different source.

Elijah and Eschatology: As a prophet who had never died the death of all mankind, but had been gathered up to heaven in a whirlwind, Elijah merited — and was accorded — a special role in Jewish traditions about the End of Days. Malachi envisaged Elijah as the forerunner and bringer of the great "Day of the Lord" when he would "turn the hearts of the fathers to the children and the hearts of the children to their fathers" (4:5–6). The Jewish sages extended this vision to make Elijah responsible for the resurrection of the dead (Sotah 9, 15) and re-interpreted the quotation to mean that he would reestablish the old geneaological order in Israel thus ending controversies and making for more peace in the world (Eduyot 8, 7). Elijah also appears as one of the forerunners of the Messiah in Jewish messianism, and can be identified with the "prophet like Moses" (see Dead Sea Scrolls*). The New Testament followed this tradition and saw it fulfilled in John the Baptist* — who also wore a hairy mantle with a leather girdle around his waist (Mt. 3:4; Mk. 1:6). He was thus identified with the herald and forerunner of Jesus as Messiah, and also given the power "to turn the hearts of the fathers to the children and the disobedient to the wisdom of the just, to make ready for the Lord a people prepared." (Lk. 1:17). Jesus referred to John almost explicitly as Elijah (Mt. 17:11–13; Mk. 9:13). John himself, according to the Gospel of John (1:21), denied being Elijah but he was clearly made in the image of the prophet. In the scene at Caesarea Philippi when Jesus asked his disciples what the people called him, he was told, "John the Baptist, and others say Elijah and others one of the prophets" (Mk. 8:28; see also Lk. 9:19).

The many references to Elijah in the New Testament reflect his great popularity with the later sages and the Jewish people in general. A host of rabbinical* (aggadic) legends grew up around his figure. Elijah's role as the herald of the Messiah, miraculously restoring the people to purity and settling all controversies, was familiar to every Jew. A couple of centuries earlier, Ben Sira (Ecclus. 48:1, 10) had expressed this general feeling. Elijah is also one of the Jewish figures who have a place in Mohammedan literature.

He is mentioned in the Koran and many legends about him are current in Arabic literature.

Despite this, it is remarkable that the early Jewish Apocalypse contains no mention of Elijah at all. A scholar of the 3rd c. CE, Origen (on Mt. 27:9), refers to a later apocalypse called the "Book of Elijah" and maintains that I Co. 2:9 is a quotation from it. However, this book is believed to have been compiled, at the earliest, during the 3rd c. CE and there are scholars who date it to the 6th c.

Elijah is not mentioned in the Dead Sea Scrolls by name. "The prophet" referred to in the "Order of the Community" as the precursor of the Messiah need not be taken to mean Elijah.

Conclusion: Elijah is probably the most intriguing of the prophets of Israel and he holds a prominent position in the history of prophecy. He devoted himself to the stamping out of heathen worship with passion and violence — in keeping with his violent age. Even so, he was not completely successful (cf. II K. 10:29, 31). It was left to his successors in the following century to raise the religion of Israel to a higher ethical level. They were able to warn that God's judgment would come even by the sword without, so to speak, taking the sword in hand. Before it could give its most important message to the world, Hebrew prophecy was thus refined. Elijah also lived before the great classical concept of God's universality had been formulated. For Elijah, Yahweh was still "God in Israel" (I K. 18:36). Nevertheless, Elijah's very contempt for all other heathen gods as exposed illusions and his assurance that Yahweh's authority was not limited to the territory or people of Israel, can reasonably be seen as a nucleus of later belief in a universal, all-powerful God.

ELISHA. — Elisha the prophet lived in the Northern Kingdom of Israel during the reigns of Joram, son of Ahab, Jehu, Jehoahaz and Jehoash, kings of Israel. Like his master Elijah, Elisha came from Gilead. He was the son of a family of estate owners in the town of Abel-Mehola, in the Gilead region (not Upper Galilee as was once supposed). He prophesied against the background of the wars between Aram and Israel during the reigns of Joram and Jehoash.

Sources: The account of Elisha's career begins with the story of the ascent of Elijah (II K. 2). Thereafter (II K. 3:11–8:15), comes a collection of narratives about Elisha, not connected with each other but all linked to the events of the time. Some of the narratives appear in two separate sections, e. g. the story of the woman of Shunem and her son (4:8–37; 8:1–7) or Elisha's prophecy of Jehoash's victories in Aram (13:14–19; 22–25), so as to keep to the chronological order. All the stories about him, including the story of his sickness and death (II K. 13:14–21), apparently originated from the same source, which also seems to have been the source for the accounts of the life of Elijah. The origin of both is assumed to have been within the circle of "The Sons of the Prophets".

"The Sons of the Prophets": These were bands of fanatical upholders of the purity of religion, distinguished by the "garment of haircloth" (II K. 1:8) which they wore and, apparently, a distinctive marking (I K. 20:41). They lived in groups, supported by the donations of the pious (II K. 4:42) and used to prophesy singly or in groups (I K. 22:1–28), when roused to ecstasy by music and dancing. They expected to be paid for their performances (II K. 5:20–27). They were thought mad by some of their compatriots (II K. 9:11) and must often have been jeered at. However, they were zealous patriots who continued Elijah's movement of opposition to irreligious government policies. In time of war they forgot their differences with the king and followed the armies in the field, offering encouragement to the fighters (I K. 20:13 ff. 35–43) but also demanding that the war be conducted according to the rules of a "Holy War". When Elisha was dying, the king came to lament the end of "the chariots of Israel and its horsemen!", a title which gives a good indication of the estimate of Elisha's military potential (the same title had earlier been given to Elijah; II K. 2:12).

The leader of the "Sons of the Prophets" had been Elijah, with Elisha as his disciple and attendant. On the mount of Horeb (I K. 19:16) Elijah received a divine command to appoint Elisha prophet in his place and he did so, according to tradition, by laying his mantle upon Elisha (I K. 19:19). There is no report of any other formality of appointment of Elisha or of any other prophet. On Elijah's and Elisha's last trip together, Elijah's rolled up mantle was effective in parting the Jordan so that they could cross on dry land. When Elijah was taken up to heaven in the whirlwind (II K. 2:11), the mantle remained with Elisha. Once again it parted the Jordan for him to cross, and when the Sons of the Prophets saw the mantle in Elisha's hands they acknowledged his leadership, saying "the spirit of Elijah* rests on Elisha" (II K. 2:15). Elisha's earlier request that a double portion of Elijah's spirit should rest upon him (II K. 2:9) suggests that he was already regarded as the recognized heir and successor. The Sons of the Prophets deferred to Elisha for decision in all matters, even something so trifling as the extension of their lodging — which appears to be the point of II K. 6:1–3. In Gilgal (II K. 4:38) a group of them "sat before Elisha" which is the phrase always used in relation to a teacher and his hearers.

When asked to foretell the future, Elisha employed the techniques of early prophecy (cf. I Sam. 10:5) and "called for a minstrel" (II K. 3:15). "And when the minstrel played, the power of the Lord came upon him." There is also a good example of sympathetic magic in his use of the arrows in his interview with King Jehoash on his death bed (II K. 13:15–19; see Magic*).

Historical Background: The death of Ahab in battle against Aram left Israel seriously weakened and encouraged Mesha, the king of Moab*, previously a vassal of Israel, to rebel. Ahab's son, Joram, set out to subjugate Moab. He was joined by Jehoshaphat, king of Judah, and the king of Edom. Their joint forces attacked Moab on its frontier with Edom. Elisha had also accompanied the armies, apparently on his own initiative, for the king did not know of his presence until told (II K. 3:11). Joram was still regarded as doing "evil in the sight of the Lord" even though he had "put away the pillar of Ba'al which his father had made" (II K. 3:2), and Elisha would have nothing to do with him. However, Jehoshaphat, king of Judah, stood better with the prophet and, at his request, Elisha agreed to transmit the word of Yahweh.

Elisha's rejection of Joram was part of the whole movement of religious opposition to the house of Ahab, aroused by Ahab's contempt for ancestral religion and customs. It was on Elisha's instructions that Jehu was anointed king over Israel (II K. 9:1–13). The prophet avoided the task himself because he knew that Jehu, "the murderer" would ascend the throne only through a great deal of spilt blood. We do not know whether he prophesied during the reigns of either Jehu or his son, Jehoahaz. Presumably, Jehu's suppression of the cult of Ba'al in Samaria was not only a political act against his predecessor, but also reflected the movement Elijah and then Elisha had sponsored.

There is a story (II K. 8:7–15) that Elisha anointed Hazael king of Aram. Its historical truth is doubted by some but the story is so unusual that others can hardly imagine that it was invented. It may be based only on the similarity of the circumstances in which both Hazael and Jehu reached the throne, each of them murdering his former sovereign. If, indeed, Elisha did anoint Hazael, then he may well have done so with tears, foreseeing the disaster that would befall Israel at the end of Jehu's reign and the beginning of that of his son, Jehoahaz, when Hazael of Aram led a victorious army down the coast, even collecting tribute from Joash, king of Judah. The story is very suggestive of the character of the prophet, for his prophecy in this case is a very different matter from the manner of the music-inspired oracle of II K. 3:15 on the eve of the war with Moab.

Personality of Elisha: The qualities and views of Elisha as reflected in the Old Testament narratives are very much like those of his master, Elijah (especially the miracle of the jar of oil, II K. 4:1–7; or the revival of the son of the Shunamite woman, II K. 4:32–37). Nevertheless, in spite of the inevitably legendary character of some of the stories (notably those connected with Gilgal and Bethel), Elisha emerges as a leader in his own right, a man of courage and passionate convictions devoted to the preservation of the Jewish faith and its liberation from all foreign pressures. The individual quality of Elisha can be seen in his constant concern for the poor and oppressed. This comes out most clearly in the miracle of the jar of oil which, in this case, serves to pay the debts of a widow whose two sons would otherwise have been doomed to slavery to the creditor (II K. 4:1–7; see Slavery*). The story of the twenty loaves which fed a hundred men may have been the basis for Jesus' miracle of the loaves and fishes (Mt. 14:14–20; 15:32–38, etc.), although, in spite of the literary affinity, this does not mean that the Gospel story was invented, any more than the Elisha story.

EPISTLES or LETTERS of the New Testament. — Of the twenty-seven books of the New Testament, twenty-one are letters, the so-called Epistles. They were written to give guidance on questions of belief and practice to communities of newly converted Christians, both Jewish and Gentile. The letters written by Paul were personal messages, answering some of the many questions that perplexed the minds of new Christians. They were never expected to become an essential part of the doctrines of the new belief and were written only because Paul was unable to visit the people he addressed. Thus "letters" is a better title for them than "epistles", which suggests a collection of messages for general reading.

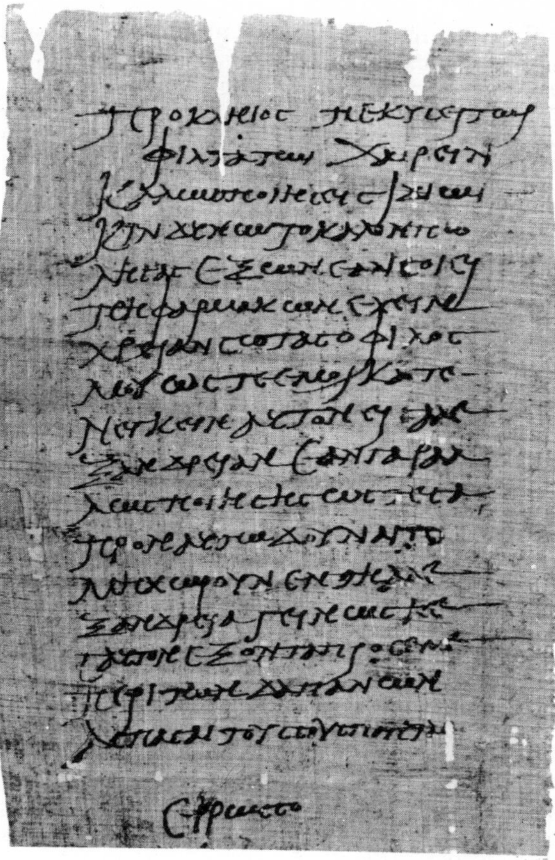

413

Apart from their spiritual value, the letters are also important historically, for they were composed in most cases before the Gospels — although the Gospels contain older traditions (see Gospels, Synoptic*). Paul's letters were written, received, copied and circulated as a distinct group before the composition of the earliest Gospel.

The letters are usually divided into three sections: *The Pauline Epistles*, made up of the first thirteen (Romans to Philemon) and including the *Pastoral Epistles* (I and II Timothy, and Titus). The third group are the *General Epistles*, comprising the seven letters from James to Jude. The book of Hebrews*, which is placed after the Pastorals, may properly be classified as an epistle because of its formal character. Its authorship is unknown. It is also not certain that all the Pauline Epistles were actually written by Paul. The General (or Catholic) Epistles are generally understood to have been directed to the church at large rather than to particular communities or individuals.

Individual letters are dealt with under one of the three headings: Pauline, Pastoral, General.

The appearance of original letters written at this time may be illustrated by this private communication (1st c. BCE) in semi-cursive Greek hand by one Procleus from Alexandria (**413**).

EPISTLES (OR LETTERS), PAULINE. — The first ten letters of the New Testament: *Romans*, *I* and *II Corinthians*, *Galatians*, *Ephesians*, *Philippians*, *Colossians*, *I* and *II Thessalonians* and *Philemon*, are traditionally (although not necessarily accurately) ascribed to Paul. They are discussed below in alphabetical order:

COLOSSIANS, THE EPISTLE OF PAUL TO THE. — This letter, addressed to the Christian community at Colossae in northwest Phrygia, bears eloquent witness to Paul's authority in the Gentile Church. Quite evidently (2:1), Paul had never visited this particular community personally. Epaphras, one of the leading members, perhaps the founder, of the Colossian church (1:7; 4:12) had told Paul about certain Jewish teachers who were attempting to impose their "philosophy" and traditional ritual obervances upon the Christians of Colossae. There is very little information in this Epistle about the nature of these Jewish teachers but it does not seem likely that they represented Pharisaic or "normative" Judaism. The asceticism and emphasis on holy days and the Sabbath referred to in 2:16 together with the reference (in 2:18) to a type of angelology, seem to point to one of the Jewish sectarian groups, perhaps a branch of the Essenes (the holy days in question may have been related to the peculiar calendar* of the Essenes). Although Paul was not personally acquainted with the church at Colossae, he did not hesitate to use his apostolic authority (1:1) against the threat of this new teaching.

Date and Origin: It is evident that Paul wrote this letter in captivity (4:3, 10, 18). The scholarly consensus is that Colossians was written while he was imprisoned in Rome (ca. 60–62 CE), although both Caesarea and Ephesus have been proposed as its place of origin. Paul sent the letter with Tychicus (4:7–8) who may possibly have taken his epistle to the Ephesians at the same time (Eph. 6:21). Tychicus was accompanied by Onesimus, a slave who had run away from Philemon (see Epistle to Philemon* and Col. 4:9).

Contents: Colossians begins with a greeting to the brethren from Paul and Timothy (1:1–2) and the assurance of their prayers for the Colossian Christians (1:3–14). 1:15–3:4 contains Paul's theological arguments against the Jewish sectarian teachings. First he emphasizes the divine and transcendental nature of Christ and his redemptive death (1:15–23), then he speaks of his own service and authority within the Christian ministry (1:24–29). He calls on the Colossians to hold fast to their faith and beware of the false teachings and assumed piety of those who are seeking to lead them astray (2:1–23).

Then Paul reminds his readers that they have adopted the life of Christ (3:1–4) and gives them some practical guidance on their behaviour (3:5–4:1), ending with an exhortation to prayer and wisdom (4:2–6). Paul then commends Tychicus and Onesimus who are bringing the letter (4:7–9) and sends greetings from a number of his companions (4:10–14). He asks the Colossians to exchange letters with the Laodiceans so that the two letters may be read by both groups (4:15–17) and then adds a final greeting in his own hand (4:18).

CORINTHIANS, I AND II, EPISTLES OF PAUL TO THE. — Scholars are generally agreed that I Cor. was written from Ephesus (I Cor. 16:8) during Paul's two year stay in the city during his third missionary journey (see Ac. 19). Although there have been attempts to deny that Paul wrote Corinthians, none of them can be said to have succeeded. The majority of New Testament scholars accept both the Cor. letters as the genuine work of Paul, although allowances need to be made for the subsequent rearrangement of the original material.

Paul explains that he is writing I Cor. because he has learned of dissensions within the community (1:11); some of the Corinthian Christians have written to ask his advice (7:1) and he has met a deputation from Corinth with whom he has evidently discussed the Corinthian church (16:17).

I Cor. is not Paul's first letter to the church at Corinth. In I Cor. 5:9, Paul refers to a previous letter which has been lost, although some scholars believe that II Cor. 6:14–7:1 constitutes a part of it. These scholars argue that in its present position this passage of II Cor. interrupts the logical train of thought which appears to run directly from II Co. 6:11–13 to 7:2–4. Moreover, II Co.6:14–7:1 seems to fit Paul's reference in I Cor. 5:9 to a warning against fornicators and idolaters in his earlier letter. Nevertheless, this is not conclusive evidence and the theory remains unproven.

Contents: More than the other letters, I Cor. reveals the problems of the early church and Paul's way of handling them. Paul saw that Jews found it very hard to accept the idea that their long-awaited Messiah had died the death of a common criminal on the cross. Christ crucified was "a stumbling-block to Jews and folly to Gentiles" (1:23). He himself had shared this attitude until his conversion, after which he learned to glory in the cross and it became the central point of his theology.

The theme of the first four chs. is the internal strife within the Corinthian church. Paul warns against allowing the community to split up into different groups claiming authority in the name of Paul, Cephas, or Apollos. The Church is one, as Christ is one, in the name of the Lord, not of men (1:10–4:21). It had become the embodiment of the assembly of God's people which, in the Old Testament, had been represented by the Assembly of Israel.

Paul then denounces the community for condoning sinful elements in its midst (ch. 5; see Romans*: Contents). He pleads for Christian unity, rebukes them for taking disputes between themselves to a pagan judge instead of a Jewish synagogue court (6:1–11) and condemns immorality (6:12–20). In ch. 7, Paul deals with marriage and divorce. He speaks of the responsibilities of married life (7:1–9), of divorce — particularly in cases where one of the partners is an unbeliever (7:10–17), of the unmarried (25–38) and of widows (39–40).

In ch. 8 Paul turns to the question of participation in pagan sacrifices ("eating food offered to idols"; 8:1). Christians know that idols are meaningless and therefore they can eat food offered to them with impunity. Their example, though, might have a bad effect on unbelievers and therefore Paul urges the Christians to refrain from eating food of this kind. He adds that he has refused the remuneration to which he is entitled as an apostle, for fear it might hinder the gospel of Christ (ch. 9). The Corinthians are warned against evil (10:1–13), particularly the sin of idolatry (14–22) and Paul repeats his admonition against eating food sacrificed to idols (10:23–11:1).

Ch. 11 contains regulations about the conduct of men and women during public worship (11:2–16) and the proper observance of the communal meal (17–34). Ch. 12 discusses the differences in spiritual gifts and individual talents, Paul reminding his readers that they are all members of the one body of the church. In one of the best known and most beautiful passages of the New Testament ("If I speak with the tongues of men and of angels . . ." 13:1–13) Paul speaks of the supreme gift of love and its nature and, in ch. 14, he appeals to his readers to speak intelligibly through the power of the Spirit, rather than ecstatically for their own benefit, which may profit the speaker but not the hearer. Corinth was a city with a racially mixed population and ecstatic tirades were highly regarded as manifestations of "the Spirit". Paul rules that incomprehensible words are valueless and "prophesying" should be regulated in an orderly fashion.

Ch. 15 is a defence of the doctrine of the resurrection of the dead which had been questioned by some of the Corinthians (15:12) and was a very difficult belief for Greeks (cf. Ac. 17:32). Paul lays it down that the doctrine is an integral part of Christian faith which would be meaningless without it.

The letter closes (ch. 16) with instructions for making a collection for the church of Jerusalem (1–4) and the announcement that Paul intends to visit Corinth and is sending Timothy and Apollos before him (5–12). Paul then bids his readers to stand fast in their faith (13–18) and ends his letter with greetings to the community of Corinth (19–24).

II CORINTHIANS. — This letter has long puzzled the scholars. Many have doubted whether Paul actually wrote it although it has never been possible to find conclusive proof that he did not. There is a group of scholars who hold that this work is a literary unit which has retained its original form but others argue that several separate fragments have been inserted into the original text. As discussed (under I Cor.), one such theory is that II Cor. 6:14–7:1 represents a portion of a letter written by Paul before I Cor. and mentioned in I Cor. 5:9. Another hypothesis is that chs. 10–13 of II Cor. are a fragment of a further "intermediate" letter, (now lost) which was written after *I* but before *II Cor*.

Paul refers to another letter in II Cor. 2:4 and 7:8 and it seems to have been quite harsh. II Cor. 10–13 is thought to be an extract from this "severe" letter, for in these chapters Paul remonstrates with "sinners" within the community and threatens action against them when he visits the city. On the other hand, the first nine chapters of II Cor. are written in a much more cheerful vein which has suggested to some scholars that they were written after the question discussed in chs. 10–13 had been put right. According to this hypothesis — which is not conclusive, however plausible — Paul's correspondence with the Corinthians followed this pattern:

1. The "previous letter" mentioned in I Cor. 5:9 and particularly extant in II Cor. 6:14-7:1.
2. I Corinthians in its present form.
3. The "severe" letter mentioned in II Cor. 2:4 and 7:8 and partly preserved as chs. 10-13 of II Cor.
4. A fourth letter originally consisting of II Cor. chs. 1-9, minus the section 6:14-7:1.

Contents: After greeting the Christian community at Corinth (1:1–2), and thanking God for his deliverance in Asia (1:3–11; see Acts*), Paul defends himself against a charge of insincerity and calls on the community to forgive a repentant wrongdoer and take him back into the fold (1:12–2:11). In 3:4–18 Paul speaks of the advantages of the new Covenant* over the old and testifies (4:1–18) that through Christ he has been able to face suffering and persecution and remain true to his ministry. 5:1–10 expresses his hope of heaven. 11–21 discusses the ministry of reconciliation with God and, in ch. 6, Paul speaks of his faithful ministry (1–10) and pleads for the love and trust of the Corinthians (6:11–13; 7:2–4). This is the passage which is interrupted by the apparent insertion of the warning against idolaters (6:14–7:1). Paul goes on (7:5–16) to speak of the joy of his reunion with Titus who brought good news from the Corinthian community.

Chs. 8 and 9 are concerned with the making of a collection for the community of Jerusalem. Paul urges the Corinthians to be liberal and speaks of the blessing of cheerful giving.

The last four chapters are more somber in tone. Paul defends himself against accusations of arrogance (10:1–18) and compares his behaviour to that of his opponents (11:1–15). He recounts the sufferings he has endured for the glory of God (16–33) and the visions and revelations he has experienced (12:1–6). He does not take pride in them, however, but rather glories in his afflictions (12:7–10). Paul expresses his love for the Corinthians (11–18) but, in the hope that a warning will suffice, he speaks of the punishment that will be meted out to sinners (12:19–13:10) and then closes his epistle with a word of greeting (13:11–14).

II Cor. is very revealing of the character of Paul — even more so than the letter to the Galatians. Nowhere else does Paul lay bare so completely the motives and compulsions that direct his actions. From this letter a clear picture emerges of an acutely sensitive Christian engaged in bitter controversy. He is an apostle and is prepared to use all the authority of his position but, at the same time, he knows that the great questions at issue can only be decided by valid reasoning. He can command, but he knows that it is more effective to persuade.

EPHESIANS, EPISTLE OF PAUL TO THE. — Many scholarly doubts have been expressed about the authorship of the letter to the Ephesians. Scholars who incline to the opinion that it is an authentic composition of the apostle Paul, agree that he wrote it while he was in prison, but not which imprisonment, in Caesarea or Rome. The majority put the origin of the letter in Rome and accordingly date it to 62–64 CE.

Literary Problems: However, by no means all scholars agree that the letter was actually written by Paul. One of the foremost opponents of the view that he wrote it is E.J. Goodspeed who believes the letter to have been written by a student of Paul's at a rather later date. Goodspeed argues that this anonymous author used Paul's Epistle to the Colossians* as his model for Ephesians. The many parallels in both language and thought between the two Epistles have long been known and they are apparent even in the English texts. However, the evidence which Goodspeed assembled to show a dependence of Ephesians on Colossians can also be used to oppose his hypothesis. Those scholars who uphold the Pauline authorship of Ephesians maintain that it was written by the apostle shortly after Colossians and that it is a logical development of the central theme of Colossians.

A number of older mss of the epistle to the Ephesians omit the words "at Ephesus" from 1:1 and one manuscript has been found addressed to Laodicea instead of Ephesus (perhaps this is the letter mentioned in Col. 4:16?). The most widely accepted explanation for the confusion is that this Epistle was a circular letter intended for general dissemination among the various Christian communities (cf. Col. 4:16). This hypothesis is strengthened by the tone of Ephesians, which does not seem to be directed towards any particular community, but is a more general religious and ethical tract bearing all the marks of an encyclical letter.

Main Themes: The central theme of Ephesians is the divine establishment and mystic unity of the Church. In Colossians Paul stresses the preeminence of Christ, but in Ephesians he dwells on the idea of the Church universal, created by the divine will, brought to fruition through Jesus Christ and sustained by the Holy Spirit. Paul speaks of Christ as the fulfillment of the divine purpose and as the redeemer of the whole universe. Yet even Christ cannot be separated from his mystical body, the Church. The transcendental claims of the church can all be traced back to Ephesians and this Christian philosophy appears to be a major part of Paul's legacy to the Church.

Contents: After the usual salutation (1:1–2) Paul launches into a theological discourse which takes the form of a thanksgiving for the spiritual progress of his readers and a prayer for its continuance (1:3–14). This form of spiritual redemption had been ordained by God "before the foundation of the world" (1:4) and as part of this plan, Jesus Christ was sent into the world so that the sins of mankind might be forgiven and redeemed by his blood (7–12). Already, believers had been marked with the seal of the Holy Spirit (1:13–14) and Paul assures his readers that he has prayed that they may receive the gift of understanding so as to appreciate what a glorious inheritance is theirs.

Through Christ, they have been rescued from death and sin (2:1–7) as an act of divine grace towards those whom God had chosen, achieved not by "works" but by faith (2:8–10). By the same act, the old distinction between the circumcized (the Jews) and the uncircumized (the Gentiles) has been abolished, all are now one in Christ (2:11–22).

In Ch. 3, Paul explains his calling as a minister to the Gentiles, to bring them to salvation through Christ (3:1–13), and prays that they may come to understand and be strengthened by the love of Christ (3:14–21). Paul appeals to his readers to live according to Christian ideals and love (4:1–16) and to renounce the moral blindness and sensuality which he believes characterize the life of Gentile unbelievers (17–32). Again, in ch. 5, Paul begs his readers to live an upright life based on Christian love and he warns them of the various evils they must guard against (5:1–21). In 5:22–6:9, he speaks of the duties of each member of the household: wife, husband, child, servant and master. To reach this ideal, Paul calls on believers to put on the whole "armour of God" (6:10–17) for they must fight hard against the "wiles of the devil" as true soldiers of Christ.

Paul enjoins them to pray for themselves and, also, for him (6:18–20), announces his intention of sending Tychicus to them (6:21–22; cf. also Col. 4:7–8) and then closes the letter with a benediction (6:23–24).

GALATIANS, EPISTLE OF PAUL TO THE. — From the point of view of theology, this short letter is the most important of all Paul's writings, for in it he lays the foundation for an independent Christianity, rather than a sectarian form of Judaism. There is no doubt that this Epistle is a genuine work of the apostle, written by his own hand (Gal. 6:11) but there is considerable difference of opinion as to its date. One school of thought holds that Paul wrote this letter during his second journey, most probably after having revisited the Galatian churches (Gal. 4:13) which he established on his first journey (see Ac. 13–14). An alternative theory is that having established the Galatian churches on his second journey, Paul wrote his letter to them during the latter part of his third journey, perhaps during his ministry at Ephesus (cf. Ac. 19).

The argument revolves around the understanding of the word "Galatia", which during Paul's lifetime was an ambiguous term. Originally Galatia referred to the north central section of Asia Minor which was settled by Gallic tribes in the 3rd c. BCE. (see maps **4, 4a**). Later, in the 1st c. BCE, the Romans established a province in the area which included a sizeable district to the south (i.e. portions of Phrygia, Pisidia and Lycaonia) but which was also called "Galatia". When Paul speaks of Galatia, does he mean the original country, or the Roman province? If the latter, then "Galatians" could refer to the members of the churches which he established in Iconium, Derbe, Lystra and Pisidian Antioch during his first journey (see Ac. 13–14 and article Acts*). If he uses the word to mean the country of Galatia, then the letter must have been written after the second journey, the first time he visited the area (cf. Ac. 16:6).

Paul's letter to the Galatians is Christianity's "declaration of Independence" from its parent religion, Judaism. Paul wrote it because he had learned that certain "Judaizing" elements, i.e. Jewish Christians from Jerusalem who insisted on Christians observing the Law of Judaism, were threatening Paul's authority and attempting to enforce Jewish observances upon the newly converted Gentile communities. The main demand of the Judaizers was that Christian converts must first become Jews, and be circumcized. Their approach would have turned Christianity into a type of reformed or modified Judaism.

Contents: Paul begins with a greeting to the "churches of Galatia" (which implied that this letter was to be circulated among several communities) that is so curt as to be almost impolite (1:1–5) and asserts his God-given authority in the very first verse. After expressing his surprise at the doubts that have been raised in the hearts of the Galatians by false prophets whom he roundly denounces (1:6–10), the apostle reasserts that his revelation was not from man, but from God (1:11–24). The pillars of the Jerusalem church acknowledged Paul's authority to preach to the Gentiles (2:1–10) and when Peter, on a visit to Antioch, would not eat with the uncircumcized Gentiles, he was strongly reprimanded to his face by Paul (2:11–21) who never wavered in his attitude.

The apostle vehemently reiterates his teaching that righteousness comes through faith and not through the works of the Law (3:1–14). The Law is not salvation in itself for it was given generations after God's promise of salvation to the seed of Abraham (3:15–18). Paul compares the Law to a schoolmaster whose duty it was to point the way to salvation in Christ through faith (3:19–24). Now that Christ has come, there is no longer need of a schoolmaster, for all who are in Christ are heirs to the divine promise made to Abraham's seed (3:25–29).

As long as man was an heir, he was in bondage, as it were, to tutors and governors, but through Christ man has been set free to be a son of God (4:1–7). Paul reminds the Galatians of their earlier love for him and beseeches them by that love to remain true to his teaching (4:8–20). By way of allegory he compares life under the old dispensation of the Law to the son of Abraham's bondwoman, Hagar. The Christian, on the contrary, is the son of the free woman, Sarah, who bore a son by the grace of God's promise (4:21–31). The break with the old Israel and the church's claim to be the new Israel could not be more plainly stated. Judaism is Ishmael. It is the Christians who are the true heirs of Abraham.

Paul appeals to the Galatians to hold fast to the liberty which, through Christ, has been bestowed upon them and not to allow themselves to be enslaved again to the Law (5:1–12). Anyone who accepted circumcision must accept the whole Law and this was no means to salvation. In Christ, "neither circumcision nor uncircumcision is of any avail, but faith working through love" (5:6; cf. Romans*, Contents). Nevertheless, Paul warns, they must not abuse their liberty. They are to live according to the dictates of the Spirit, not indulging the desires of their flesh (5:13–26) — a phrase which covered many more vices then than it would today (5:19–21). The "Spirit" to which Paul refers continually seems to be the parallel to the Jews' idea of the "good tendency" which contends against the "evil tendency" within each man.

Paul advises his readers to correct one another in all humility (6:1–5) and to live according to the Christian ideal of love (6–10). In conclusion, Paul briefly restates the main theme of his letter and then adds a final greeting (6:11–18).

The letter remains as important for its portrait of Paul as for the doctrine which it expounds.

This is a leaf of the Chester Beatty Papyrus; (**414**; early 3rd c. CE), earliest known copy of Paul's Epistles, transmitted in book (Codex) form (Gal. 6:10; Ph. 1:1).

PHILEMON, THE EPISTLE OF PAUL TO. — This brief letter affords the reader an intimate glimpse into the life and personality of Paul the apostle, who was undoubtedly the author of this Epistle. Philemon was written at about the same time as Colossians, probably during Paul's imprisonment in Rome. The subject of this letter, Onesimus, is also mentioned in Col. 4:9 as accompanying Tychicus, the bearer of the letter to the Colossians (Col. 4:7–9). As Philemon lived at Colossae (Philemon 2 and Col. 4:17), Paul sent the personal letter to him at the same time as the epistle to the church of that city.

Onesimus, one of Philemon's slaves, had run away and made his way to Rome, the destination of many escaped slaves who hoped to escape detection in the anonymity of a

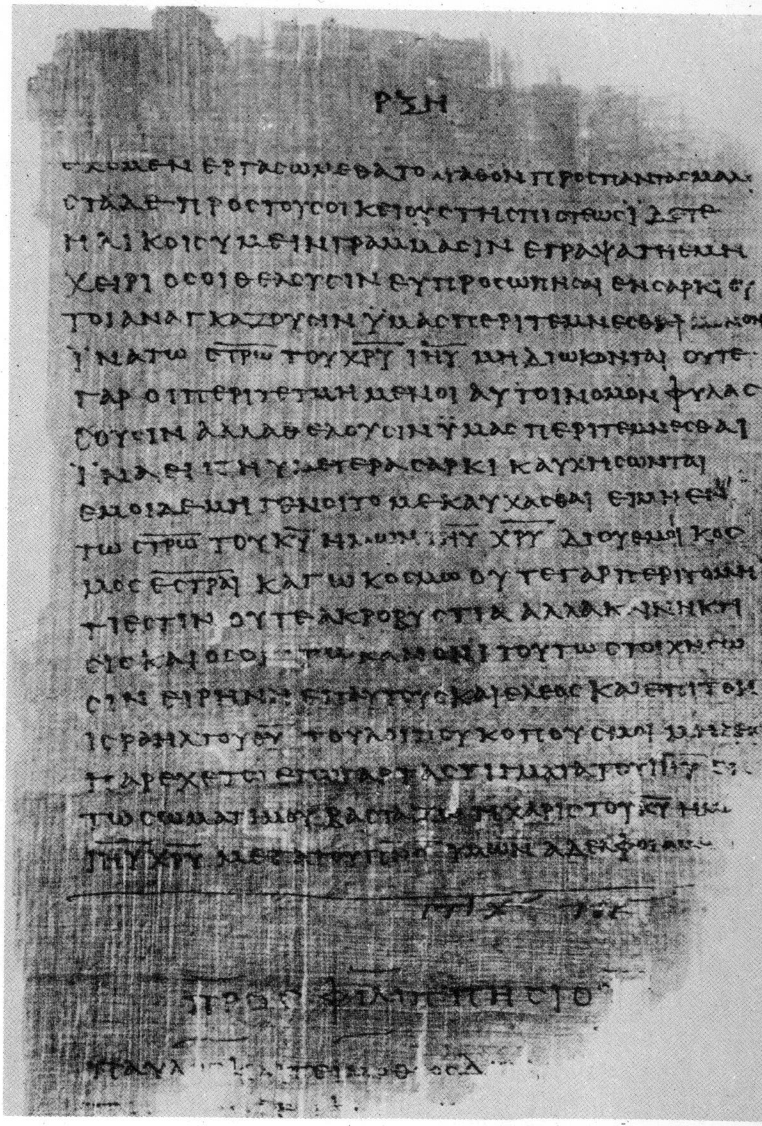

414

cosmopolitan population. In Rome, he was converted to Christianity by Paul (Phil. 10), who had also converted Philemon (Phil. 19). This created an embarrassing situation. Under Roman law, a runaway slave was liable to crucifixion but it was not fitting that one Christian should condemn another. Paul therefore wrote asking Philemon to forgive Onesimus. The apostle would gladly have kept him as a companion, but he preferred to obtain Philemon's consent (13–14). Paul offers to make good any damage which Philemon has suffered through Onesimus' escape (18–19) but, at the same time (v. 19), he reminds Philemon of the spiritual debt which he himself owes. The apostle begs Philemon to accept Onesimus, not as a slave, but as a brother (15–16) and expresses his hope that he himself may soon be freed and be able to come on a visit (22).

PHILIPPIANS, EPISTLE OF PAUL TO THE. — Paul's letter to the church at Philippi (established by him during his second journey, Ac. 16:12–40) was undoubtedly written while the apostle was imprisoned (1:7, 13–14, 16; 2:23). Although the place of imprisonment is not definitely stated, it is generally assumed that the letter was written from Rome somewhere between 62 and 64 CE. This is the most intimate and affectionate of all his letters and is written in a generally optimistic mood. Paul tells his friends of his condition and his hopes, whether for earthly release (2:23–24) or for ultimate consolation (2:16–17; 3:14). There is nothing of the circular letter or theological discourse about Philippians. It is a warm personal letter, giving loving Christian counsel to the church at Philippi, from which Paul had received a gift of money, brought by Epaphroditus (4:18). The church at Philippi was the most satisfactory of all the churches Paul founded and, for this reason, he felt able to accept money from it (4:14–18).

Contents: The introductory salutation sends greetings to the Philippians from both Paul and Timothy (1:1–2) and Paul then writes of his gratitude for their fidelity and his prayers that they may continue to increase in love and understanding (1:3–11). Paul assures them that the Gospel is being helped, even by his own imprisonment (1:14–18a) so that whether he lives or dies, Christ will be glorified (18b–26). He begs the Philippians to be steadfast and ready to suffer persecution unflinchingly for their faith (27–30).

In ch. 2: 1–18, Paul calls on his readers to help one another, to practice humility, even as Jesus humbled himself to be the more exalted, and to work for their own salvation which can only come as an unearned gift through obedience to the divine Will. He then announces that he is sending Timothy to visit them soon and that Epaphroditus who has been severely ill but has recovered, is returning (2:19–30).

Paul then offers encouragement and a challenge to the Philippians to follow his example and give themselves unreservedly to the life in Christ (3:1–21). He refers to his own experience of oneness with Christ (3:7, 13, and 14, cf. 1:21 and 2:1) and begs his friends to preserve their unity and to hold fast to their faith.

The letter ends with some personal exhortations to individual members of the Philippian church (4:2–7) and then (8–20) Paul expresses his deep gratitude for the gift received from them. He closes with salutations and a benediction (4:21–23).

ROMANS, EPISTLE OF PAUL TO THE. — This is the longest and one of the greatest of Paul's Epistles, accepted almost unanimously as the genuine work of the apostle. It is more of a treatise than the other letters and differs from them in its objectivity and broad theological outlook. As with most of the Pauline letters, Paul did not write it by hand but dicated it to a secretary, in this case a scribe named Tertius (Ro. 16:22). There are several theories about where Romans was written, but the scholarly consensus is that Paul wrote it from Corinth during his visit there ca. 56–58 CE, on his third missionary journey (see Acts* 20:2–3). It is clear from Ro. 1:10–13 and 15:22–24 that the letter was written before Paul had visited Rome. The exact date and place of its composition, however, depend upon the original form of the epistle.

Literary Problems: One widely held view is that the letter of Paul to the Romans is contained in chs. 1–15 and that ch. 16 was a note appended introducing the person of Phoebe. Scholars of this opinion consider that the benediction (v. 33) which closes ch. 15 provides the logical end to the epistle to the Romans.

However, there is then a difference of opinion as to whether the note (ch. 16) was addressed to the church at Rome or to that of Ephesus. Scholars who favour Ephesus argue that it is very unlikely that Paul would have had so many personal acquaintances in Rome — a city he had never visited and, moreover, that Epaenetus "the first convert in Asia" (Ro. 16:5) was more likely to have been in Ephesus than in Rome. On the other hand, many of the personal names mentioned in ch. 16 were also in use in Rome and Paul might quite possibly have known of these early Christians by name. Nor is there any reason why Epaenetus should not have visited Rome, the heart of the empire. A more telling objection against the Ephesus theory is that ch. 16 has been found intact in all the extant mss of the Epistle to the Romans. Some authorities have concluded that these mss represent a later recension of Romans. Only if it could be proved conclusively that the note was attached to the original epistle, could ch. 16 be accepted without question as intended for the church at Rome along with the rest of the letter (Ro. 1:7).

There is a further theory, based on the fact that in several early mss the "doxology" found in 16:25–27 appears at the end of ch. 14, that Romans was circulated among the churches in an abridged version (without chs. 15–16). However, even these mss also contain the last two chapters and the theory seems to be little more than conjecture.

Contents: The book falls into three major sections: 1. a treatise on the need for and way to salvation through Christ (chs. 1–11); 2. practical directives for living a Christian life (12–15:13); and 3. personal messages and salutations (15:4–16:27).

The letter opens with a greeting to the church at Rome (1:1–7) and Paul's hopes of being able to visit them (8–15) to preach the gospel which "is the power of God for salvation" (1:16–17). Paul argues that all men, Jew and Gentile alike, are unrighteous and in need of salvation (1:18–3:20). God will condemn wrongdoing by Gentile (1:18–2:16) and Jew (2:17–29) alike.

All men stand in need of salvation (3:9–20) but this cannot come by "works" alone, but only by faith (3:21–5:21). "Works" in the sense of obedience to the letter of the Law, are contrasted to "faith" throughout the Pauline epistles. Abraham's trustful surrender to the will of God is transformed into the Christian confidence in God's salvation through the intercession of Jesus Christ. Paul uses the phrase "justify by faith" (Ro. 5:1 passim) in the sense that man can only be acquitted of his sins by making a humble confession of faith and trust in God, with Christ acting as mediator. Faith, of course, is something personal to an individual but Paul proclaims that it will be accepted as justification for man. In chapters 2 to 7 of Romans, Paul develops his great argument against the Law. Neither Jew nor Gentile can hope for salvation through the Law, only by faith in Jesus Christ (3:21–31). Abraham was not rewarded because he was a just man, Paul argues, but because of his faith in God (4:1–22). Through Jesus Christ, the son of God, mankind has again been offered access through faith to salvation (4:23–5:11). Many people have found Paul unduly harsh in his rejection of the Law as a means of salvation but, to him, the Law formed a bondage of regulations which had to be broken so that man — Jew and Gentile alike — could reach a new freedom in Christ.

According to Paul, sin and death entered the world through the first man, Adam (5:12–14), but righteousness and life had been brought into the world through the person of another man — Jesus Christ (5:15–21). This teaching of Adam as the First Man and bringer of sin and Jesus as the Second Man, through whom humanity has been granted a new beginning, explains the great importance which Christian thought attaches to Adam.

The term "righteousness" is used by Paul in the special sense of a satisfactory relationship with God. A righteous man is one who will be found "not guilty" at the Last Judgment. What will be judged is not only a man's deeds — which must inevitably fall short of divine requirements — but whether, by accepting Jesus as Messiah and having faith in him, a man has established a "righteous" relationship with God. "Now to one who works, his wages are not reckoned as a gift but as his due. And to one who does not work but trusts him who justified the ungodly, his faith is reckoned as righteousness" (4:4–5), meaning that God will absolve the man who has faith in His power, shown in the Cross and the Resurrection. Salvation cannot be achieved by merit alone. The essential condition is faith.

In chs. 6–8 Paul speaks of the new life which will be achieved in Christ, through the Holy Spirit. "Sinners" are not necessarily wrong-doers in the everyday sense, but those who did not observe the Law*. In Matthew and Ro. 5:1–10, "sinners" refers to the mass of the people who could not hope to observe all the complicated regulations of the Law and therefore despaired. Paul puts himself and most of mankind into this category. Once a Christian has been baptized, he has taken part in Jesus' death and, through this death, has been raised into a new life which is free from the domination of sin and fear of death (6:1–11). The true Christian does not yield to sin but to God who has made man free from sin (6:12–23).

The Christian has also been freed from obedience to the Law. Through Jesus, the believer has died to the Law and is bound instead to the new life of the Spirit (7:1–7). This does not mean that the Law is sinful. It is holy. Through the Law comes the consciousness of sin (7:8–12) which works through the flesh (7:13–25) and seems to defeat a man's better intentions. But "the law of the Spirit of life in Christ Jesus has set me free from the law of sin and death" (8:2). Through Christ, man has been freed from the bondage of the flesh and can become the chosen heir of God (8:1–39).

In the Apostolic church, the Spirit at work in the church is hardly distinguishable from Christ. Paul speaks of "being in the Spirit" or "in Christ" with little, if any, difference of meaning.

In chs. 9–11, Paul explains how divine salvation, having been rejected by the Jews, has been bestowed upon the Gentiles. He grieves that the Jews, his kinsmen — and Christ's — are not part of the Church (9:1–5) but explains that God's promises were never intended for the entire Jewish nation, only for a remnant of it (9:6–29). By clinging to "works" instead of faith, the Jews have lost the way to salvation (9:30–10:3). Righteousness and salvation can come only through faith in Jesus Christ (10:4–13) but though they have been offered the "good news" of Christ's resurrection, they have refused it, just as they refused the message of Moses and Isaiah (10:14–21). Yet God has not totally rejected His people. True to his promises he has preserved a remnant — i.e. those like Paul who have accepted Christ (11:1–10) and he has added those Gentiles who will also accept Him (11:11–12). Paul warns the Gentiles not to feel conceited because of their inclusion, and he likens them to wild olive shoots grafted on to a cultivated tree. They are only branches but Israel is the root of the tree (11:13–24). Once all the Gentiles have been converted, then the rest of the Jewish nation will also obtain salvation, as the prophets had foretold (11:25–36).

In this letter, Paul seems to have retreated from the extreme position he took when writing to the Galatians*. In Romans, the Church represents the new Israel, the heir to the promises made to the Patriarchs, but Paul no longer regards the rejection of the Jews as final. Their refusal of Christ has been the means of bringing Christ to the Gentiles (11:11–16) but, in due time, the mercy shown to the Gentiles may be bestowed on them (11:31).

The third section (chs. 12–15:13) is concerned with two main problems: the Church's relation to authority and the reconciliation of the rival claims of Christian freedom and brotherly consideration. Paul admonishes his readers to live virtuously through Christian love (12:1–21) and to be obedient to civil authorities (13:1–7). Paul's favourable view of the Roman empire appears to relate to the promising early years of Nero's reign when he was under the influence of Seneca. All the Law could be fulfilled through observance of the one commandment "Love your neighbour as yourself" (13:8–10) and the imminence of salvation made it imperative to lead an upright life (13:11–14). Christians should be charitable and tolerant of one another (14:1–15:6) for they were all bound together in Christ (15:7–13).

The letter ends on a personal note in which Paul explains his reasons for writing (15:14–21), speaks of his future plans, which include a visit to Rome (15:22–33), introduces Phoebe (16:1–2) and then sends salutations to various members of the community (16:3–20). Paul's companions also send greetings (16:21–23) and the letter ends with a doxology (16:25–27).

Conclusion: Throughout the Pauline letters two Pauls seem to be revealed: Paul the practical preacher of the Gospel and Paul the theologian (see Paul*). Romans is not a manual of Pauline doctrine. It was an attempt to clear up the main problems of the Church at the time: the relation between Jew and Gentile in the new dispensation; and the conflict between the Law and Faith as a means of achieving "righteousness".

THESSALONIANS, THE EPISTLES OF PAUL TO THE. — The two Epistles to the Thessalonians are accepted almost unanimously as the work of Paul. They were written towards the end of the Second Missionary Journey (ca. 52 CE) and are thus the earliest extant Epistles. During this journey, Paul had established the church at Thessalonica (Ac. 17:1–9; see map **4**) and then been forced by strong Jewish oppostion to flee, first to Beroea (Ac. 17:10) and then to Athens (Ac. 17:13–15). Silas and Timothy appear to have remained in Thessalonica and to have rejoined Paul later in Athens (Ac. 17:14–15).

In the First Letter, Paul refers to his work among them and recalls that he sent Timothy from Athens to be with them (3:1–2). By the time Paul wrote the letter, Timothy had rejoined him, probably at Corinth (Ac. 18:1, 5), with encouraging news about the church at Thessalonica. Paul's letter to the community is probably based on the first-hand report he had received from Timothy.

Contents: The letter begins with a greeting to the community from Paul, Silvanus (Silas) and Timothy, who thank God for the Thessalonian church and for the influence which it exerts throughout Macedonia and Achaia (1:2–10). Paul refers to his ministry among them (2:1–16) and speaks of his thwarted desire to visit them again (2:17–20). Unable to come himself, he sent Timothy to bring news of them (3:1–5) and now rejoices at the satisfactory report he has brought (3:6–8) although Paul still hopes to visit them in person again (3:9–13). Paul admonishes the community to reject immorality and to accept the discipline of a Christian life (4:1–12). He then assures them of the resurrection of believers who have died before the Second Coming of the Lord (4:13–18). The day of the Lord, he reminds them, will come "like a thief in the night" and he calls on his readers to be vigilant at all times (5:1–11) and to prepare for it by true Christian conduct (5:12–24). Paul then ends his letter with a request for the prayers of the community and his greeting to them (5:25–28).

The Second Letter to the Thessalonians was also written from Corinth, shortly after the first one (ca. 52/53 CE). The letter deals with the Second Coming of Christ. Apparently some of the members of the community had been so carried away by its expectation (2:2) that they had even given up working and were living on charity (3:6–11).

Contents: This letter also opens with salutations from Paul, Silvanus and Timothy (1:1–2) and with words of encouragement for the brethren who are suffering for their faith (1:3–12). Ch. 2:1–12 deals with the Second Coming of Christ. Paul warns that this is not yet at hand, for it will be preceded by a "man of lawlessness, ... the son of perdition" who will imitate the true Advent and tempt unbelievers to their destruction. The apostle admonishes the Thessalonians not to be deceived by misleading ideological and theological teaching, but to stand fast in their faith (2:13–17).

The final chapter repeats Paul's call for the community's prayers (3:1–5) and closes with his rebuke of disorderly conduct and idleness (3:6–16).

Christian Eschatology: The Dead Sea Scrolls* of Qumran have shed a good deal of light on the nature of eschatological expectations of the 1st century CE, reflected in the New Testament (see Eschatology*). The belief in a "New Age", to be announced by the coming of "a prophet", was central to both Christians and Essenes* (the sectaries of Qumran). Both communities believed in the "last age" and were awaiting the appearance of a Messiah who would finally bring the existing world to an end and would initiate an eternal kingdom. In Qumran the "Righteous Teacher" was expected to bring the New Age to birth. He had died, apparently as a result of the persecutions of the "Wicked Priest" and it is possible that he was expected to return as the Messiah, although there is still some scholarly disagreement as to his role.

Christian eschatology also included its own distinctive features. For the Christian, the period of the "End of Days" had already been inaugurated with the coming of the Messiah (Jesus). He had been raised from the dead and enthroned as the Messiah who would come again in glory. This conception of the "event" of Jesus as the Christ, his exaltation, resurrection and his gift of the Spirit, seems to distinguish Christianity from the other eschatological communities of the time (see Paul*; Dead Sea Scrolls*).

EPISTLES, THE PASTORAL. — The three Pastoral Epistles, I and II Timothy and Titus are grouped with the Pauline Epistles although scholars question their authorship. Whereas the other Pauline Epistles are addressed to specific Christian communities — with the notable exception of the apostle's personal note to Philemon* — the Pastoral Epistles are addressed to church leaders and contain counsel pertaining to pastoral guidance and leadership. They are concerned with the second phase of Church development, when the initial phase of missionary work was over although, of course, missionary work continued.

The background seems to be that of the second generation of Gentile Christians, when the bishops were grappling with new tendencies, partly Jewish and partly Gentile, arising out of the religious ferment of the time. This is very much the same situation which prompted the letter to the Colossians*. The early Church had no canonized New Testament. Only the Old Testament had been canonized and this contained many enigmas. The one sure foothold was apostolic tradition, chiefly what Paul had taught (see below).

Literary Problems and Authorship: The traditional view of the Pastoral Epistles was that they had been written by the apostle Paul, but early in the 19th century this view was attacked by a group of German scholars led by Shleiermacher who denied the Pauline authorship of I Timothy. All the Pastoral Epistles have subsequently become the subject of controversy so far as their authorship is concerned and the dispute continues in scholarly circles to this day.

Those who deny the Pauline authorship of these Epistles base their argument on the major points of literary style (philology) and content. Philological research has revealed great contrasts between the Pastorals and the other Pauline Epistles. Not only do the Pastorals contain a number of new and different expressions which are not to be found in the other Pauline Epistles, but many typical Pauline words and expressions are either missing or have been rephrased in the Pastorals. From these contrasts in the Greek styles of the Pastorals and the Pauline epistles, many scholars have argued that the Pastorals cannot have been written by Paul. The difference in tone and content between the two groups of Epistles is evident even from a casual reading of the English translation. The Pastorals are not so much concerned with Christian theological tenets as with doctrine and specific rules of conduct for the individual Christian community.

Scholars who still uphold the traditional view maintain that the contrasts between the Pastorals and the Pauline

Epistles are not so great as to warrant the disavowal of Pauline authorship for the Pastoral Epistles. The difference in content and tone is readily explained by the nature of these letters which, though private, are nonetheless official, the correspondence of the apostle to his young charges. As to the philological difficulties, the differences in style merely represent a later period in the life of the author, or the use of different secretaries who would have used their own phrasing — on the assumption that Paul did not dictate the Pastorals, but was responsible for the gist or nucleus — the letter itself being the work of a follower.

The scholars who deny the Pauline authorship of the Pastorals would date these Epistles after the death of the apostle. According to their view, a disciple of Paul's wrote these letters, utilizing genuine Pauline material. In order to combat certain tendencies which had arisen in the various churches, the unknown Paulinist edited the Pastorals, incorporating what he believed to be Paul's views, and published them in the name of the apostle so as to give them added weight and authority, in the manner of the pseudonymous literature of the Pseudepigrapha* (see article). Several scholars are inclined to regard II Timothy as containing more genuine material and as being earlier than the First Epistle of Timothy. On the whole the Pastorals seem to date before 90 or 100 CE, and may be even earlier, 70–80 CE.

I TIMOTHY. — The first three chapters of this Epistle deal with problems arising in the church. After a brief salutation to Timothy (1:1–2), the author of this Epistle warns the pastor of the dangers of false doctrine (1:3–11) and thanks God that he himself was saved through grace (1:12–17). He charges Timothy to be a stalwart warrior of the faith (1:18–20) and gives him instructions regarding both communal prayer (2:1–7) and the proper conduct of Christian men and women (2:8–15). There follow directives dealing with the ecclesiastical offices of bishop (3:1–7) and deacon (3:8–13) (see Christianity, Early*). The word "bishop" as it is used here, does not refer to the ecclesiastical office of the modern church, but merely designates the head of an individual Christian community. The background is illuminated by the Dead Sea Scrolls*, where the leader of the community (ḥeber) is called the "mebaqqer and/or "Paqqîd", from which it is inferred that the office of bishop is old. The first part of the Epistle is then concluded by a brief statement on the integrity of the Church (3:14–16).

The second part of this Epistle (chs. 4–6) consists of personal advice and instructions to Timothy. The young pastor is warned of false teachings (4:1–5) and instructed how to deal with them (4:6–11). He is also advised as to how to conduct himself in his office (4:12–16) and directives are given him concerning the treatment of widows (5:1–16) and elders (5:17–20). Following some personal advice (5:21–25) to Timothy, the author lays down rules of conduct for Christian slaves (6:1–2) and concludes the Epistle with a personal admonition and exhortation to his youthful brother in Christ (6:3–21).

II TIMOTHY. — According to this epistle, its author was imprisoned (II Timothy 1:8, 16; 2:9) at the time of writing, and did not expect to be released (4:6). Forsaken by many of his friends (1:15; 4:10, 16) the apostle writes to his faithful companion, encouraging him in his ministry and urging him to come to Rome.

The letter opens with a brief greeting (1:1–2) after which Paul expresses his confidence in Timothy (1:3–5) and urges him to remain steadfast in the faith and teachings in which he, Paul, had led him (1:6–18). The apostle admonishes his younger friend to keep the faith even in the face of persecution (2:1–13) and bids him beware of false teachings (2:14–21) though remaining meek and patient throughout (2:22–26).

In chapter 3:1–9 Paul describes the "birth-pangs" of the last days and encourages Timothy, as his successor, to continue teaching the true scripture (3:10–17). He charges the youthful pastor to preach the word (4:1–5) even as he, Paul, had "fought a good fight" (4:6–8). The concluding portion of this epistle (4:9–22) contains personal directives to Timothy, who is urged to come to Rome (4:9, 11, 21), and greetings to several of Paul's Christian friends.

TITUS. — The addressee of this epistle, though not mentioned in the Acts*, is referred to several times in the Pauline Epistles (cf. Gal.* 2:1, 3; II Cor.* 2:13; 7:6, 13; 8:6, 16; 12:18; II Tim.* 4:10) as a companion and younger friend of Paul. According to this epistle (1:5) Titus was in charge of the church at Crete and the apostle Paul wrote him a personal letter, similar to those addressed to Timothy, containing advice and instruction on fulfilling his pastoral duties.

After a brief salutatory introduction (1:1–4), the author gives Titus instructions regarding the office of bishop (1:5–9) and warns him of the numerous false teachers and deceivers who were especially prevalent in Crete (1:10–16). In chapter 2:1–10 Paul recounts the duties of the aged, the young, and the slaves. The rest of the chapter (2:11–15) dwells on the grace of God which had appeared in the world, and expresses the hope of the coming of Jesus Christ. Chapter 3 contains an admonition to respect the proper authorities (3:1–3), a short discourse upon baptism and its blessings (3:4–8), and a warning against strife and heresy (3:9–11). The epistle ends with personal instructions to Titus (3:12–15) in which he is directed to meet Paul at Nicopolis.

EPISTLES, GENERAL. — The seven final letters of the New Testament, James, I and II Peter; I, II, and III John and Jude, are more general in character than the Epistles attributed to Paul. They are called the General or Catholic Epistles (Catholic in the sense of being intended for the whole Christian community). The letters are described in alphabetical order under this general heading. The books of Hebrews* and Revelation* are dealt with separately.

EPISTLE OF JAMES, GENERAL. — **Authorship and Date:** James is a general tract rather than a letter. It seems to reflect a Palestinian or Syrian background and is traditionally ascribed to James, the brother of Jesus* (see Christianity*, Early).

There is very little internal or external evidence from which to determine the date of this Epistle and scholars differ considerably on the subject. If indeed it was James who wrote it, then he may have done so shortly before his martyrdom (62 or 63 CE) in order to correct certain misinterpretations of Paul's doctrine of justification by faith (see Paul*). This would place it after the Pauline Epistles but before 70 CE, since it makes no mention of the destruction of Jerusalem. Other clues have been found in its use of Christ's teachings which seems to reflect an early stage of oral tradition, and in the parallels with I Peter*. These, however, could also be explained by the supposition that both drew upon a common stock of early Christian teachings. Both Epistles appear to have been written before the break between Judaism and Christianity (see Christianity*, Early, Part II).

The Epistle of James is particularly revealing about many phases of the earliest Christian church. While it contains a passionate outburst of ethical teaching, its author is curiously silent about Jesus as Messiah, the Cross and the Resurrection and Incarnation. The Epistle also reflects the unorganized condition of the churches addressed, presumably the early Christian equivalent of the synagogue*. The Christian communities still met in the synagogue, without benefit of bishops or deacons. The Epistle appears to belong to an early stage of their development and it makes use of thought-forms reminiscent of the addresses of Peter and Stephen as recorded in the first chapters of Acts*. This is another factor which points to an early date for the letter of James, making it one of the earliest books of the New Testament.

Another school of thought puts the Epistle much later, even as late as the 2nd c. CE, as a part of the late Jewish-Christian controversy raging in Palestine or Syria over Pauline doctrine. Any final decision on the date of James must await further research.

Purpose: The Epistle was written with the aim of recalling Christians to reality in religion. Possibly the author was aware of the unfortunate effect which reports of Paul's teachings had had in some directions and wished to counteract this wrong impression. The Epistle attempts to demonstrate that faith in Christ must be related to all the experiences and relationships of Christian disciples. The author is concerned with faith in action. Thus he lays a special emphasis on the place of "works" in Christian life. The Epistle seems to suggest that the Jewish Christians to whom it was written were in danger of disregarding the necessity for giving practical expression to their faith. On the surface, this teaching seems to be a contradiction of the Pauline doctrine (also found in Hebrews*) that "the just shall live by faith" rather than the works of the Law (see below, Contents). Paul's insistence on the ineffectiveness of "works" alone was probably concerned with the mechanical observance of certain prescribed regulations intended to oblige God to dispense the appropriate reward. Faith, on the other hand, meant a total commitment to Christ, surrendering every aspect of life and personality in trust and obedience. In his letter, James is pleading for this kind of faith, outwardly expressed in love. On this basis, "works" can be taken to mean good deeds undertaken within everyday life, where they represent the moral and social proof of a man's faith. Mystical faith, for the writer of James, had to be backed by ethical behaviour.

It is possible that he represented a form of early Christianity which, like Judaism, stressed good works as an essential condition for acceptance by God. This way of thinking may have found Paul's emphasis on the freely given grace of God through Christ, open to serious misunderstanding. Even if the writer of James was not contradicting Paul's actual teaching, he may have felt it necessary to protest against its distortion by certain people who found it an excuse for avoiding the humbler duties of Jewish and Christian love.

Style: James' strongly Jewish spirit is emphasized by the style in which it is written. Its language is the Greek in which the Septuagint translation of the Bible was made and James recalls the style of the Prophets and Wisdom* writers in translation (see Contents: Ch. 2).

Contents: The Epistle does not develop a central argument, nor is its material arranged in a systematic sequence. Like Hebrews* it is composed of exhortations and warnings.

It opens (1:1) with a salutation to the Jewish Christians of the Diaspora, then proceeds (1:2–2:7) with the theme of the testing and temptations of the faithful engaged in practicing the Christian life. The author advocates a joyful acceptance of such trials since, through them, a man's character may be proved and perfected. He exhorts Christians to pray whenever they feel a lack of spiritual wisdom or any uncertainty about how to attain it (1:2–8). Changes in fortune should be accepted cheerfully because they will strengthen character (1:9–12). This is followed by a warning against mistaking the sources of temptation. Yielding to temptation is never attributable to God. God is not responsible for man's failure to do right, nor for his yielding to temptation. The failure comes from a man's own desires and lack of determination (1:13–18). True religion consists of doing as well as hearing "the word"; righteous behaviour and observance of the ritual of the Law (1:19–27).

The emphasis on ethical behaviour in the Epistle, echoes both the teaching of Jesus and the prophets (e.g. 1:22, 27; 2:14; 2:20b; 2:24). Its closeness to the prophetic style is also shown from the fact that this short book contains fifty-four imperatives.

Ch. 2 (1–13) opens with a warning against subservience to the rich, especially in public life (i.e. in the synagogue). Vs. 14–24 is a direct answer to the popular interpretation of Paul's doctrine that a man was justified by faith apart from works (see Gal. 5:6 ff; Rom. 4:3, 9 ff). "Abraham", writes James, was justified by works, "not by faith" (2:21). By works a man is justified; not by faith alone (v. 24) for faith without works can easily become hypocrisy. The explanation for the writer's choice of phrase may well lie in the Jewish emphasis on good works (see above, Purpose). The contradiction with Paul may be more apparent than real.

The author continues (3:1–12) with a warning against undue eagerness to instruct others. Teachers need to set an example in their own behaviour, for their vocation — speech — is open to abuse.

3:13–4:12 continues this theme with exhortations to meekness, generous dealings and unity of spirit. Rivalry and pleasure-loving are the causes of strife whether between countries or between individuals in all walks of life. The writer condemns the unthinking arrogance of those who make plans for the future, ignoring the uncertainty of human life. He goes on to condemn the wealthy and luxury-loving for their thoughtlessness and oppression of their poorer brethren (5:1–6) which leads up to an exhortation to patience and confidence on the part of the oppressed (5:7–11). Their Lord will come, soon. The end of the book

(5:12–20) contains a number of exhortations — against swearing; to prayer; and for the restoration of erring brothers.

JOHN, FIRST EPISTLE GENERAL OF — The theme of both the first and the second Epistles of John is an affirmation of the doctrine of the identity of God and Christ. If one asks what God is like, then the answer can be found in Jesus. John's own experience of the knowledge of God was so overwhelmingly involved with his personal relationship to Jesus, that he could not conceive of any other method of achieving a knowledge of God. For John, the historic fact of Jesus provided the necessary basis for all religion. And religion which taught a doctrine or advocated a righteousness which differed from those of Jesus stood self condemned as false. From the moment of Jesus' birth to his return to the Father, the history and philosophy of religion had merged into that single figure and were no longer two faces of truth.

Authorship: The First Epistle of John is so close to the Fourth Gospel in style, vocabulary and thought that many scholars fully accept them as being both the work of the Apostle. Other scholars, however, postulate a disciple of the Evangelist or a member of a "Johannine" school.

The date of the Epistle depends largely on the date of the Gospel of John*, which is much debated. They both appear to have been written at about the same time.

Background: The epistle is aimed especially against the deviation from orthodox church doctrine known as Gnosticism. The adherents of this form of belief — the "Gnostics" or "knowers" — claimed to be especially enlightened and to be possessed of a special secret "knowledge". This knowledge, which led them in search of a more spiritual religion, they rated higher than revelation. The term "gnosticism" is vague and not easy to define. There were different schools of Gnosticism but they had essential features in common, the principal ingredient being a secret knowledge. Gnostics might be ascetic puritans, or they might equally well be unrestrained libertines. Some of the 2nd c. CE gnostics were able speculative thinkers. The combination of Gnosticism with Christianity could be entirely innocuous but, carried to extremes, as in Docetic Gnosticism, which the author of John's First Epistle opposed, it could threaten the Church's very life and faith. At the time I John was written, this was the biggest internal question facing the Christian community — the Jewish-Gentile controversy being possibly a thing of the past.

The Gnostics denied the earthly existence of Jesus and, consequently, refused to accept the Church's doctrine of Incarnation*, i.e. that God had appeared in the flesh in the person of Jesus Christ. Also, apparently, they fell short of Christian ideals of love between brethren, perhaps because of the arrogance of their attitude towards other Christians. For his answer to this menace, the apostle turned back to the earliest phases of Jewish-Christianity and reminded his readers of the apostolic witness to Christ and, furthermore, of Christ's Jewish sectarian roots (see below). He emphasizes the reality of Jesus as the Christ and admonishes his readers to live in the "fellowship of love". His aim is to restore his readers' confidence in their faith in Christ and, at the same time, to stress the role of brotherly love and mutual help in Christian thought and life, perhaps as a counter-weight to the attitude of the Gnostics.

Like other early Christian teachers, he insists on the separation between the general community — the "world" — and the Church. A life of true religion cannot admit compromise. The religious life he defines as one of obedience to the commandments of God, giving loyalty to Christ as God's representative and love to all others as His children (2:3–5, 9; 4:2, 3, 7–12).

The writer sums up the essence of the Christian message as bearing witness to Christ, loving one's neighbour and performing brotherly deeds.

Contents: The central theme is stated in the first verses of the Epistle (1:1–4) which emphasize the writer's personal experience of fellowship with God and his Son, Jesus Christ. The development of this theme centres around three main concepts: the "fellowship" between God and Christians within the religious community; "sin" which separates man from God (1:5–10) and "obedience to God's commandments" which is the only sure way of drawing closer to God. This appears in a number of verses (2:1–6, etc.) and is linked with John's reiteration of the commandment to love one's brother (2:7–11). 2:12–17 elaborates this theme of love in all personal relationships.

2:18–19 resumes the discussion, elaborating the threat of the "Antichrist", the antithesis to the Messiah which appears in various forms in contemporary apocalyptic* literature, although the term actually used by John was not used in works written before this Epistle. John then introduces (2:20–25) the concept of "anointing". Christ, the "anointed one" has, in turn "anointed" his disciples with his spirit so that they "know" the truth. John bases his refutation of the Gnostics on the argument that to deny Jesus is to deny God. The point is repeated in 2:23 as the essence of Christian belief ("No one who denies the Son has the Father. He who confesses the Son has the Father also"). 2:26–29 is a recapitulation of the warning against the false teachers, who deny this truth.

Ch. 3:1–12 takes up the moral argument. Knowing that Christian salvation is an accepted fact to his audience, John uses the mystical argument that since Christians are God's children and are destined to be transformed wholly into his likeness, they can be sure that they will see God. Christians who have been "born of God" cannot sin. The test of the true believer is his behaviour: "whoever does not do right is not of God, nor he who does not love his brother" (3:10). It is only to be expected that "the world" should hate righteous Christians — was not Abel murdered by Cain because Cain saw the contrast between his own evil deeds and his brother's righteousness? The supreme test of Christian life is faith in Christ and love for one another. Christians have passed out of death into life, through love within the brotherhood — and it must be a true love not only "in word or speech but in deed and truth" (3:13–18). The seal of the transformation is in the Spirit which is the means and the reward of obedience to God's commandments (3:19–24: cf. Dead Sea Scrolls* on the subject of the background of the "brotherhood").

Ch. 4 opens with a paragraph (vs. 1–6) on true and false inspiration. The apostolic Church believed that prophecy had been revived and that their brethren could be inspired by the Spirit to declare hidden truths. Nevertheless, all inspiration and all spirits did not necessarily come from God. They had found that there was also a spirit of perversity (that of Antichrist) abroad in the world and John explains how to distinguish between true and false spirits (4:6).

This dualism of truth and error comes very close to the Qumran doctrine of "light" and "darkness" (I Jn. 2:11; 4:1–6; cf. I Qs. 3:21; compare also the Gospel of John* 14:17; 15:26; 16:8, 13). John makes his case quite clear. True inspiration goes with the belief that Jesus has come in the flesh (4:2). This answers the complicated denials of the Gnostics and also formed the beginning of a dispute which was still rife when the creeds of later Christianity came to be formulated. The magnificent section 4:7–21 sums up John's own credo of brotherly love as the one sure way to God.

Johannine teaching no longer refers to a second coming of Christ. The final judgment is sure, but it is not Christ who will act as the judge. Indeed he will be the advocate for mankind (2:1). "He who has the Son has life . . ." proclaims John (5:12) but that life is something to be lived in the present world. It is not postponed to a "future life" and another world. The Believer has received the "eternal life" of Christ. He who has this life has already triumphed over death and lives in the messianic age. In ch. 5:1–13, John again expounds the Christian ideal of the Spirit which gives assurance of victory: a concept which by comparison reduces the reservations of the Gnostics to futility.

The Epistle proper closes at 5:13. (The passage dealing with the three witnesses, 5:7 ff, is a later insertion — perhaps from a 4th c. Latin gloss. It does not occur in the Greek mss.) 5:14–17 deals with forgivable and unforgivable sin — a painful but necessary question. Vs. 18–20 contain the triple declaration of knowledge (of God and sin and the Son of God) and lead up to the two crisp final sentences which present affirmation and exhortation as a worthy conclusion.

II JOHN. — The other two Johannine Epistles, II and III John are both very short, each of them probably being written on one sheet of papyrus. Like I John, II John was known before 200 CE, but there is no indisputable reference to III John before the 3rd c. CE.

The Epistles are particularly important for our knowledge of the rapidly developing ecclesiastical organization at the end of the 1st c. CE.

II Jn. can be described as a miniature edition (13 verses only) of I Jn. for every phrase in it occurs in the larger work as well and the theme is the same – Christian love as the true road to salvation and the need to guard against deceivers and false teachers. The Epistle is addressed to "the elect lady and her children" and scholars are divided as to whether this is a literal greeting to a particular Christian matron in Ephesus or represents a church and its constituent members. It appears to have been written by the author of I Jn.

III JOHN. — Unlike I and II John which deal with doctrinal questions, III John is a rebuke to a church leader, Diotrephes, for his insubordination, not his theology.

By 110 CE, the "elders" were no longer the rulers of the church, but had now become the advisers of the bishop who enjoyed a pre-eminent and all-powerful position. Diotrephes, as bishop, claimed exclusive jurisdiction over the church in Ephesus whereas John, "the Elder" exercised a traditional authority within the larger district.

In effect III John is a note from John to his lieutenant "Gaius". It is not an Epistle meant for public reading. Its preservation must have been accidental and it was incorporated into the N.T. at a later date, when anything connected with John was felt to be Apostolic. Thus it was naturally regarded as scriptural and authoritative and worthy of inclusion in the canon.

The title which John uses of himself, "The Elder" seems to have been used at first and for a long time in the sense of one of the original Apostolic witnesses. He had authority over the Church to which he was writing, although at the time the original pattern of itinerant missionaries was coming to an end, to be replaced by a system of settled local ministries. The writer of II John wanted missionaries excluded for fear of their subversive teachings. III Jn. calls for them to be received and helped. The letter's condemnation of Diotrephes was presumably connected with his rejection of these missionaries.

JUDE, EPISTLE OF. — This short book is a strongly apocalyptic* work, very reminiscent of Enoch (see Apocalypse*) and including quotations from and allusions to that book. They are unique in the N.T.

It is a "general" (or Catholic) Epistle, not addressed to any particular church but to "those who are called." It purports to be written by Judas, brother of James (and of Jesus, Mk. 6:3) but modern scholarship denies such authorship and dates the composition of the letter to around 100 CE. It was written before II P. which borrowed heavily from Jude.

The Epistle is intended as a warning against "ungodly persons" whose licentious and immoral behaviour threatens to undermine the faith of believers. Its writer appears to have been a Palestinian Jew concerned with combatting the dangerous example of false brothers who appear to have had much in common with the early Gnostics (see I Jn.*). There are traces of opposition to early Gnosticism in Colossians* and the Pastoral Epistles*. From Jude, however, it appears that the situation had greatly deteriorated. By the time this Epistle was written the Apostles were figures of the past and "faith" was used in the later technical sense of a body of belief.

Contents: After the salutation (1:1–2), the writer turns to his main purpose which is to put his readers on their guard against immoral comrades who are undermining the character of the Christian community. First he speaks of the danger to faith (1:3–11) and the certainty of divine judgment. Then follows a vivid condemnation of the immoral behaviour of these evildoers (12–18), while 19–23 consists of advice on how to meet the threat which they represent. Christians have the authority of the Apostles' predictions of the appearance of these "scoffers, following their own ungodly passions". They must rely on their own faith and constant prayers to help them overcome temptation and hold fast to the true way. The letter ends with a typical benediction (24–25).

PETER, FIRST LETTER OF. — I Peter claims to have been written by the Apostle Peter, "through Silvanus"

(5:12). Scholars who believe that it was the work of the Apostle interpret this as meaning that Peter was the author of the Epistle but that it was written down by a secretary, Silvanus, who probably wrote the Epistle in his own style on the basis of the ideas supplied by Peter. The letter was written in a good, cultivated Greek which is a little difficult to associate with a Galilean fisherman. Partly for this reason, there is another school of thought which holds that I Peter was composed as well as written down by Silvanus, a follower of Peter's.

The letter was addressed to the newly formed congregations of Pontus, Galatia, Cappadocia and other provinces in Asia Minor. It offers encouragement to them at a time when they were being persecuted for their refusal to renounce Christian worship of one God and to offer sacrifices and libations to Roman gods. There is no agreement on the question — which is vital for dating the letter — of whether or not the state had already initiated proceedings against Christians.

The prevailing mood of the letter is one of hope. Because it was written to men who went in constant fear of persecution, it lays great emphasis on the sufferings of Christ — a theme which had become one of the central pillars of the thought of the entire Church.

Literary Problems and Authorship: The letter seems to belong to a non-Pauline phase of consciousness and scholars have been at some pains to place it within the Apostolic Age — so far without reaching a final conclusion. Scholars who deny Peter authorship of the letter have also not reached any agreement about the date of composition (somewhere between 80–110 CE) or the way in which it was written. Nor have they succeeded in making intelligible the reference to Silvanus' share in the letter (5:12).

Further questions have been raised about the unity of the letter and about its nature. Some scholars believe that I Peter was not originally written as a letter but was an address which was only later circulated in the form of a letter. In the opinion of Beare, Preisker, Cross and others, the address was a baptismal homily or an early Christian liturgy for the young congregations in Asia Minor.

None of these questions can be decided with any certainty on the basis of evidence at present available. If, however, one accepts the letter at its face value, including the relationship between Peter and Silvanus, then it seems reasonable to assume a date around 60 CE for its composition. Nothing in the contents requires or even suggests a later date.

Contents: The writer sends greetings (1:1–2) and assures his readers that their trials, which will only be temporary, will ensure purification and spiritual blessings. He exhorts his Christian brethren to take Jesus as their example and to strive to be worthy of the salvation which he has obtained with his sacrificial death.

Ch. 2 carries the thought further into religious concepts which have been illuminated by the material contained in the Dead Sea Scrolls*. In vs. 1–10, the writer describes the Christian life in three successive metaphors as 1. second birth or regeneration; 2. a living temple and 3. a royal priesthood. The section (2:4–10) has moved E.G. Selwyn and others to the belief that the early Jewish-Christian church was conceived as a "neo-Levitical" or priestly community. The same concept is to be found in Acts* and in practically all the Pauline Epistles*, in Hebrews* and James*. This concept in turn emphasizes the idea of the Christian community as a spiritual temple in which spiritual sacrifices (prayer and self-denial) are offered. The Qumran sectaries, too, identified themselves with the "remnant" of Second Isaiah* (see article) and also attributed a redemptive function to their sufferings (Is. 43:10, 12: "'You are my witnesses,' says the Lord, 'and my servant whom I have chosen . . .'" and Is. 28:16: "Behold I am laying in Zion . . . a precious cornerstone, a sure foundation.") In any case, the basic ideas of I P. 2:2 ff go back to the earliest roots of the Christian church and are closely connected with ancient Palestinian tradition.

I Pet. 2:11–25 develops the theme in terms of a series of practical precepts for Christian living. The key to these is to be found in the phrase "sojourners and pilgrims". This was the usual role of the Jews in the Diaspora. The Christian communities are enjoined to "maintain good conduct among the Gentiles, so that . . . they may see your good deeds and glorify God on the day of the visitation." (I Pet. 2:12). The "day of the visitation" has its parallel in the Qumran Manual of Discipline (IV:15–26) which also refers to the doctrine of the refining of a portion of mankind who would come into their own at the "Last Visitation of God", when truth would at last emerge victorious.

This concept leads the writer of I Pet. to admonish his Christian brethren to respect secular laws (2:13–25), to be submissive to authority and to follow the example of Jesus, joining obedience to doing good.

Ch. 3 is a call for love and peace in personal relationships both between husbands and wives and throughout the brotherhood. Christians should not return evil for evil and should be prepared to suffer, not for wrong-doing, but for doing right. In this way, Jesus had triumphed through persecution, suffering and death.

The most fundamental principles and exhortations for the life of the congregation are contained in ch. 4. Christians who know that "the end of things is at hand" must turn their backs on the sinful ways of unbelievers and live "for the rest of the time in the flesh" according to the will of God, praying and helping one another and welcoming suffering joyfully as giving them a share in Christ's glory.

In ch. 5, the author refers to himself as a "fellow elder". He counsels his fellows to tend their flock, as much by example as by precept and he calls on the whole community to stand together firmly in the fight against evil. After they have "suffered a little while," they can be sure of God's "eternal glory in Christ."

This section, again, can find parallels in the Qumran manuscripts. I Pet. 5:4 speaks of "when the Chief Shepherd is manifested, you will obtain the unfading crown of glory", very much as in Qumran the Manual of Discipline (I QS, 4, 6f) declares those who walk according to the "spirit of truth" will be rewarded by "a crown of glory, together with raiment of majesty in eternal light."

This is a 3rd c. CE page from a codex of I Peter **(415)**, the oldest example known (5:12–14a; 14b is omitted).

PETER, SECOND EPISTLE OF. — Both in style and content, II Pet. differs completely not only from I Pet. but also from anything Peter himself might have been expected to write. Some scholars have found the author

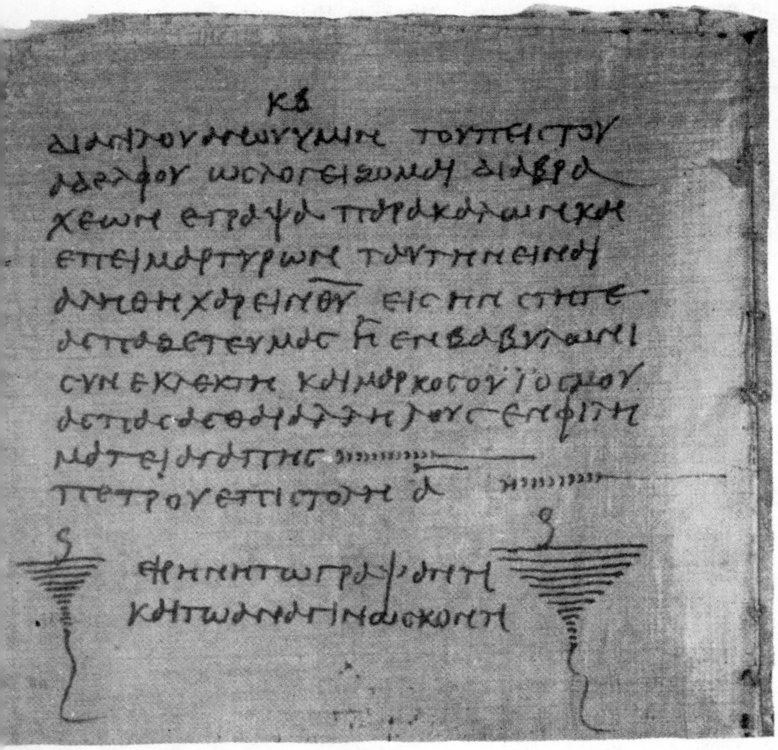

415

superficial and the letter cannot rank with I Pet. as a Christian classic. Its author borrowed freely from I Pet. and also from Jude* which preceded the writing of II Pet.

The unknown author's use of the revered name of Peter is a familiar literary device intended to give greater authority to his words (see Apocrypha* and Pseudepigrapha*).

Purpose: The letter was motivated by a desire to issue a vigorous warning against any lowering of Christianity's moral standards as a result of the assimilation of Gentiles with very different ideals from those of Christ's earliest followers, and less sensitive to moral "purity" than Jewish-Christians. The writer wanted to put his readers on their guard against those who preached libertinism in the guise of "freedom" and "love". He saw such Gentile Christians as a threat to the whole community and he fiercely condemns them and their influence. This situation seems to belong to the period at the close of the 1st c. CE or around 90–110 CE, in any case, long after Peter's death, in the sub-Apostolic Age — the period when the canon was beginning to take shape.

In addition to its main concern, the letter is also intended to allay doubts which had been expressed about the Second Coming which was to bring the new heaven and the new earth (1:11, 16, 19; 3:3 ff). False teachers had arisen to ridicule this doctrine and the writer of II Pet. counters their gibes with the claim that the delay had been deliberately imposed by God as a means of increasing righteous conduct (3:8 ff). It is to be noted that in I Cor. doubts concerning the resurrection are linked with doubts about the return of Christ.

Contents: After the usual salutation (1:1–2), the writer reminds his audience that the Christian is privileged by his faith to share in the divine nature but that this can only be attained by a constant striving after moral perfection (1:3–11). For this reason, the writer has been inspired to undertake his task and he makes his own authority very plain. He was an eye-witness of the Transfiguration and he quotes the words heard from heaven on that occasion as the basis for his prediction of the Second Coming. His words depend not only on Christ's revelations but also on the predictions of ancient prophecy. For the Christians, the Prophets took the place which the Law held in Jewish tradition (1:12–21) and the whole O.T. was regarded as essentially prophetic in character or quality.

Ch. 2 begins with the arraignment of the "false teachers" who are perverting Christian ideals and enticing believers away from the true faith by their licentious behaviour. The writer explains that before the Second Coming these "scoffers" will arise (2:1–3:3). This theme follows Jude very closely, although in Jude*, they appear to be an immediate danger. II Pet. borrows heavily from Jude throughout this passage.

The writer then answers the "scoffers" and claims that he is writing this "second" letter to remind his readers of the predictions of the prophets and of Jesus himself concerning the Second Coming. The End of the World will surely come, but it will come in God's own good time and it is the responsibility of Christians to lead lives of such purity that they will be ready whenever the time comes. He reinforces his appeal by reference to Paul's authoritative teaching (especially the Epistles*). The prophetic words of 3:2–4 are quite inappropriate for the apostle Peter and read more like existing conditions presented in the form of a pseudo-prediction made after the event, describing the conditions of the author's time, but then placed in an earlier setting to make it sound like a prediction. The fact that the judgment is delayed, he explains, is no indication that it is not going to take place. His prediction that the world is to be destroyed by fire is a commonplace of contemporary Stoic and Jewish teaching. His description of the last day of the world (3:7, 12) is very close to the picture painted in the final section of the Scroll I QH from Qumran (see Dead Sea Scrolls*). Hippolytus (3rd c. CE) attributes the New Testament belief in the destruction of the world by fire to the Essenes and other 1st c. CE Christian authors reflect this point of contact. The Second Epistle of Peter closes (3:14–18) with an admonition to remain steadfast in the true faith.

ESCHATOLOGY. — Eschatology is the doctrine of the "last things" concerning the "end of days". Based on the assumption that God will one day bring the existing world to an end and replace it by a new order, eschatology sees the whole course of history as leading up to this sudden transformation.

In the Old Testament, many eschatological forecasts of the "end of days" place it in the far distant future, though often the Day of the Lord is close at hand.

The prophets of Israel forecast far-off events under four different categories: a. calamities which will befall sinners in Israel (Am. 8:8–9; 9:3–4; Zeph. 1:15); b. calamities which will befall sinners of other nations (Jl 3:12; Dan.

7:9–10); c. redemption and happiness of Israel (Is. 29:18; 51:1–3); d. the establishment of peace throughout the world and the beginning of an era of universal happiness for all mankind (Is. 2:1–4; Mic. 4:1–5).

Prophecies belong to one or more of these categories. They appear in the writings of most of the prophets, a comprehensive group being found in Is. 24–27. These prophecies were phrased in very general terms and represent a complex problem. Although not connected with specific historical events, and without any attempt to set a precise date for their achievement, in general, they include historical and chronological factors. Since the prophets were thinking of a series of events beginning right away and then extending into an indefinite future, a general time table seems to be concerned. Essentially, eschatological forecasts express a longing for a better future, to compensate for present and past miseries. This is a very common human emotion, not confined to prophets or wise men. In one form or another eschatological forecasts were probably familiar long before the prophets appeared to clothe them in poetic language and fit them into a theological system.

Some scholars believe that prophecy of this type was confined to the people of Israel. Others point out that similar forecasts had been made earlier by the wise men of older nations and suggest that the prophets of Israel adapted and elaborated existing themes to the ethics and faith of Judaism.

Visions of the "end of days" may very possibly have been current in the Israel of the Judges, before the monarchy had been established. However, the eschatology of later prophets was much more closely allied to the world they knew. They drew on their people's past history and its great figures for their picture of how God intended to bring about his plan for mankind's redemption.

They saw the Kingdom of God (or the Kingdom of Heaven) being established, in God's good time, by messianic figures: Moses the deliverer and David, the conqueror. These historical personages were endowed with all the attributes of a modern superman. Their kingdom, although "of God" would be in a transformed earth, not in some faraway, mythical "heaven".

Eschatology in the Apocalyptic Mood: With the Book of Daniel*, written partly in response to the religious persecutions preceding the Maccabaean rebellion, but also under Persian and Greek influence, a new element was introduced into this doctrine. Salvation became no longer a general, national matter. Post-Exilic and post-biblical eschatology include a new attitude towards individual immortality and redemption, personal reward and punishment. This is apparent from the Apocrypha* and apocalypses* and also from the Dead Sea apocalyptic writings.

This literature introduces the idea of a general resurrection at the start of the new era, followed by a Day of Judgment in which the wicked will be condemned and the pure and good rewarded with eternal bliss.

In ancient times, the resting place of the soul after death had been only the dark underworld, Sheol (see Funerary Practices*: Death). This old belief was now replaced by a new moral concept of reward and punishment. Sheol was transformed into a place to which the wicked would be doomed while in the apocryphal literature the final abode of the righteous is called Paradise (the term is of Persian origin and refers to a "garden"). The same term is also applied in these writings to the primitive Garden of Eden, although the Old Testament never uses it in that sense. Another innovation is the symbol of the "Son of Man" who is to descend from heaven, proclaiming the coming of the Kingdom of God and the Messiah.

Eschatology and the Apocrypha: The ancient prophets had believed that God was working towards the salvation of his people in the history of the existing world as well as in the final eschatological consummation. In the inter-testamental literature (Apocrypha*, Apocalypse*) there is much greater emphasis on the exclusive activity of God in the final transformation of the world. Man's only part is to have faith, persevere through tribulations, and wait patiently for the decisive intervention of the Deity. The book of Enoch cries that God has withdrawn his aid and abandoned his people to their sufferings. The prophets had demanded repentance and righteousness from their people to make them worthy of salvation. In the later literature the thought is rather that through all their present sufferings a remnant of the righteous in Israel who have kept the Law will be preserved for an ultimate deliverance (see Apocrypha* and Apocalypse* for further discussion of post-Exilic developments regarding immortality).

New Age Eschatology in the Dead Sea Scrolls*: The discoveries of Qumran provided valuable additions to the very scanty knowledge of 1st c. BCE and 1st c. CE Palestine. With the help of this literature it has been possible to reach a better understanding of Pharisaic and rabbinical eschatological thought. It is also essential background material for the eschatology of the New Testament (see Dead Sea Scrolls*; Jesus*; Jewish Christianity*; the New Covenant*).

Sectarian and Rabbinical Eschatology: The apocalyptists of Qumran were very concerned with the exact date on which the eschatological event would take place. They laid great stress on "calculating the Epochs" for they believed that, by taking all the factors into consideration, the eschatological thinker could determine the duration of the event and the course it would take.

The Pharisees and their rabbinical successors, although they accepted the idea of the establishment of God's Kingdom at the end of the age, no longer stressed the ancient prophetic view of God actively working towards man's redemption. They apparently regarded this activity as hidden or incomprehensible. Nevertheless, they thought that it was up to mankind to accept the yoke of the Kingdom which God would manifest through the eschatological visitation.

Jesus' Eschatological Teaching: Jesus' teaching closely parallels this contemporary Jewish eschatology. For two centuries, apocalyptic teachers had combined the "end" with the advent of the messianic "Son of David". Jesus thought both in these apocalyptic terms and on the ethical lines of the old prophets (see Jesus*: Kingdom of Heaven, Sermon on the Mount). Jesus' eschatology is prophetic because it is based on the idea that the kingdom has already been initiated although not fully achieved (an approach which may offer a more accurate interpretation of the Sermon on the Mount). In Christian belief, the Kingdom is to be found within history itself, for its coming in the person

416

of Jesus Christ has placed it four-square in the actual world.

ESTHER, BOOK OF. — *Outline: Contents of the Book; Date and Authorship; Historical Value; Archaeological Evidence; Religious and Moral Value.*

The Book of Esther is the fifth of the Five Scrolls, arranged in the Hebrew Bible in the order in which they are read on fixed occasions in the religious calendar. In the Septuagint and Vulgate translations, it is placed at the end of the historical books.

It is a partly historical, partly legendary story offering an account of how the Jewish feast of "Purim" (lots) first originated. The book cannot have been written much later than the Persian* period. As evidence of its early date, some scholars point out that no trace of Greek influence is to be found in it, though this is not necessarily decisive proof. It has also been pointed out that the author introduced many Persian words into his story, was acquainted with Persian customs and gave the whole story a strong Persian colouring which led many to think that the anonymous author had actually lived in Persia (see below).

Contents of the Book: Chapters 1–2: Ahasuerus, the king of Persia and Media, made a great banquet in Susa (the ancient capital of Elam, which was part of his kingdom). Flushed with wine, he commanded that Vashti, the queen, be brought before the guests. The queen refused to come and was therefore severely punished. She was deposed, and her crown was to be given to "another who was better than she". In order to choose a successor to Vashti, beautiful maidens were gathered in Susa from all the provinces of the empire. One of these maidens was Esther, whom Mordecai the Jew had adopted as his daughter after the death of her parents, to whom he was related. After undergoing beautifying treatments in the harem, Esther found favour in the king's eyes, and he chose her as his queen in place of Vashti. At this time, Mordecai discovered a plot against the king, and his deed was recorded in the royal chronicles.

Chapter 3: A man named Haman then rose to power, The king made him the highest of his ministers and ordered all his subjects to do obeisance to him. Only Mordecai disobeyed the royal command and refused to bow down to Haman. Infuriated, Haman tried to destroy Mordecai's people, the Jews, and obtained the king's consent to this act.

Chapters 4–5: Mordecai told Esther to go into the royal presence and plead for her people. Esther asked him to proclaim a three-day fast, at the end of which she would come before the king, even though she had not been called to him and was thereby endangering her own life. No one dared appear unsummoned in the king's presence, and unless the sovereign held out his golden sceptre to the intruder, he would be put to death, as prescribed by law and court etiquette.

After the three days of fasting, Esther came before the king, who held out his sceptre to her. When the king asked what her request was, she invited him to come with Haman to a banquet on the same evening, and another banquet on the next. Haman, hearing this, felt himself favoured and left the king's presence in high spirits. He had a gallows fifty cubits high erected, on which to hang Mordecai once the king's authorization was received.

Chapter 6: That night, the king could not sleep, and had his attendants read to him the section of the royal chronicle relating Mordecai's act in saving his life. The king discovered that Mordecai had not yet been rewarded. In the morning, when Haman came to request the king's permission to hang Mordecai, the king asked him what should be done to the man whom the king wished to honour. Haman, thinking that he himself was to be honoured, replied that the man should be clothed in royal attire and led through the streets of the city on the king's own horse. The king ordered Haman to do as he had advised to Mordecai. Haman carried out the king's order, but returned home "mourning and with his head covered."

Chapters 7–8: At the second banquet given by Esther for the king and Haman, she revealed Haman's dastardly designs to the king, who thereupon commanded that Haman be hanged on the gallows that he had prepared for Mordecai. On the same day, Mordecai was appointed to Haman's high office, and the king gave orders that Haman's decree regarding the Jews should be revoked and that the Jews should be permitted to defend themselves.

Chapter 9: On the 13th of Adar, the Jews smote their enemies in the provinces, and on the 13th and 14th of Adar they smote their enemies in Shushan, the capital, and the cities, and killed Haman's ten sons. They therefore made the 14th and 15th of Adar a festival in commemoration of their deliverance for themselves and future generations. The two days of feasting are called "purim" because of the "lot = pur" which Haman cast for the destruction of the Jews.

Chapter 10: This chapter is an epilogue and seems to be an appendix to the whole work; it can be interpreted as intended to give historical validity to the Book of Esther, since it states that its contents were recorded in "the Chronicles of the kings of Media and Persia."

Date and Authorship: The book is written throughout in a simple, attractive narrative style, and is usually regarded as a homogeneous composition, although some scholars think that a few verses at the end were added to the original. Although it seems to have been written in the Persian period, neither the book nor its main characters are alluded to in Ben Sira (see Apocrypha*, Ecclesiasticus), nor is it mentioned in I Maccabees which refers to "the day of Nicanor", commemorating the defeat of the Syrian general in 161 BCE, on the 13th of Adar. This fact is taken by some scholars to indicate the story's connection with the Maccabaean wars. "The day of Mordecai", however, is referred to in II Mac. (15:31) which was compiled, according to V. Tcherikower, around 120 BCE although this proves only that the Book of Esther had not yet been included in the canon. It is of interest that Esther is the only book of the Old Testament which has not been uncovered at Qumran. Even at the beginning of the Amoraic (Talmudic — 5th c. CE) period there were still those who opposed its inclusion (Tal. Bab. Megillah 7.a). It was only when Purim took on a mainly religious character that the Book of Esther ceased to be regarded as a secular work and was admitted into the canon. The rabbis then prescribed that it should be read on the evening and morning of the Festival of Purim (see below).

Historical Value: There are two schools of thought on this question. Some scholars think that the Book of Esther is a historical story which has been adorned with a number of literary embellishments. Others hold that it should be regarded as a piece of fiction, its historical kernel obliterated by romantic and literary additions, as witness the fairy-tale elements in the story (the simple girl who, like Cindarella, becomes great and famous; the wicked villain who falls into the pit he has dug for the righteous hero) and the absence, in any other source, of references to the events related. Even those who assume that the book had a historical kernel cannot suggest any precise dating, since knowledge of the whole period is so sketchy. It must however be conceded that at least the general setting of the tale is authentic. This is evident from the knowledge of Persian customs displayed in it: the royal council (1:14); the method of honouring a hero or royal favourite (6:8); the details of the imperial postal system (3:15; 8:14); the description of the opulence of the court and the royal banquets (1:3–7), and the giving of presents on the Persian New Year.

Archaeological Evidence: The remains of Persepolis and even more those of Susa, also bear out the events related in the book. Inscriptions found distinguish between "Susa the capital" (the royal palace) and the city of Susa. Thus

the book correctly places the banquet in "Susa the capital', (1:2) "in the court of the garden of the king's palace" (1:5). Excavations in Susa (**416**) and Persepolis have brought to light many pillars over which coloured awnings were stretched, as described in 1:6. In Susa, the city street "in front of the king's gate" (4:6) has been uncovered, and also the harem (**417**) which had an exit opening onto the gateway of the city. This confirms in detail the accuracy of the description of Esther standing in the inner courtyard of the palace opposite the king's hall, while the king sat on his throne inside the palace facing its entrance (5:1–2). From the harem, a corridor led to the inner vestibule of the palace. In this same inner vestibule, opposite the corridor leading to it from the harem, was the throne room (the "king's hall" of 5:2). The throne room may be illustrated by this relief from the "Hall of a Hundred Columns" in the other palace of the Persian kings uncovered at Persepolis (**418**) (see Persia*). In the centre of the wall facing the entrance door stood the high throne from which the king could see all who approached him by looking over the curtain which separated him from those seeking an audience with him. The description of the banqueting hall opening on the palace garden is also correct in detail (7:7). One of the halls of the royal palace at Susa bore a similarity to the audience hall or "apadana" of Darius at Persepolis (**418**). A great stairway led to the audience hall, decorated with sculptured reliefs of soldiers and animals (**419**).

In contrast to the wealth of archaeological material, it is impossible to find even the slightest historical confirmation of the events recounted in the book. Even the names of the main characters are unknown to history. Moreover, details such as the description of the relations between Jews and non-Jews, are not in keeping with the historical facts. The Ahasuerus mentioned cannot be positively identified with a particular Persian king, though the author seems to have had Khshayārshā, better known as Xerxes (486–465 BCE) in mind. The general situation in Persia at the time of this monarch's accession accords with the picture which emerges from the book. The description of the king as being coarsely sensual is well-suited to Xerxes, who is so portrayed by Herodotus and Aeschylus. The description, however, would be equally applicable to other Persian rulers and is of no real help in the identification of the Ahasuerus of Esther. It is also difficult to identify any known Persian word with "pur" (meaning "lot") of which "purim" is the plural (3:7; 9:26) and which gave the festival its name. It appears to be of Akkadian origin (see Assyria*; Babylonia*). Any attempt at fitting the book into a precise historical framework must be abandoned, though it may be assumed that it contains some element of historical truth.

Religious and Moral Value: It is a striking fact that neither the name of God nor any of the divine appellations occurs in the Book of Esther. The events recounted took place, seemingly, without divine intervention and what emerges is a plain, earthly folk-tale. Many scholars have pointed out that one specific purpose of the book is to glorify the Jewish nation and to ridicule the Gentiles, as may be gathered from the humour of passages which are slightly satirical of the Persians. It is also argued that the spirit of the book is indicative of a time when great hatred had been engendered between Jew and Gentile. The basic moral to be drawn from the story seems to be "love your kindred, hate your enemies" which constitutes, according to some, a fierce religion and an unethical nationalism. On the other hand, a vigorous morality can be pointed out, namely that evil is punished in terms of its own virulence; Haman received the punishment he wished to inflict.

The Book of Esther is written in a thoroughly Jewish spirit, however. Mordecai refuses to bow down to Haman (3:2); the Jews preserve their distinctive customs (3:8) and the wicked man falls into the trap that he had set for the righteous. The moral values of the story have frequently been impugned on the grounds that the Jews depicted in it are vengeful and bloodthirsty. But no moral exception can be taken to the Jews' fighting in self-defence; on the contrary, it is specifically stated that they fought only to save their lives "but they laid no hands on the plunder" (9:16). This is in the tradition of the law of "Holy War" (see Warfare*).

The feast has been celebrated with good cheer, drinking and boisterous rejoicing (see Festivals*). Various theories have been put forward which attribute it to a pagan origin; that it derives from a Persian spring festival; that it is a transformation of an old Zoroastrian (see Persian*) festival of the dead; or that it traces its origin to a Babylonian New Year's festival. These, however, are no more than conjectures.

418

419

EUCHARIST. — Lord's Supper, or Holy Communion:

This Christian sacrament has been observed since the earliest apostolic period. It signifies the communion of Jesus'* disciples in his sacrificial death; commemorates that death, and draws Christians into a closer fellowship.

The sacrificial character of the rite is stressed in the formula which is repeated, that the bread is a communion in the body and the wine in the blood of Christ. The scriptural authority for this statement comes from the accounts of the "Last Supper" celebrated by Jesus and his disciples just before his death.

To the simple statement in Mark, "this is my body", Paul added "which is for you" and Luke, following Paul, makes the phrase, "this is my body, given for you". In Mark, the blood is "shed for many", while in Luke, "poured out for you". The emphasis is on Christ as a sacrifice and the bread and wine as the symbols of that experience.

Paschal Nature of the Rite: Whether the last Supper was in fact the Passover celebration, as indicated by Mark, Luke and Matthew, or not, as implied in John, is not essential. Interpretation of the rite of the Eucharist must in any case begin from its Old Testament context which is unquestionably the Passover festival.

This is the festival enjoined on the Jews by Moses (Ex. 12: 25–27), to commemorate their sheltering under the sprinkled blood of the paschal lamb while the Angel of Death passed over them. Thus it symbolizes God's regard for his Chosen People* and the Covenant* made with them.

In the traditional Jewish ritual of the "Seder" held on Passover eve, the head of every household recalls the redemption of the Jews from Egypt.

This combination of sacrifice and redemption must have been remembered when the Apostles and the Jewish Christians* celebrated Passover together and recalled what had happened after the memorable night of the Last Supper. The parallel between the sacrificial lamb and their slain master would have forced itself upon them, until he became, for them, the Passover sacrifice.

Apostolic Origin: Both Mark (3:14) and Luke (22:24–34) stress the significant relation of the Apostles to the congregation of the spiritual Israel. The Twelve had been with Jesus at the Last Supper and, according to the Evangelist, he had told them that their parting would be but for a season. Soon they would share in the feast prepared by God for those who inherited the Kingdom (Lk. 22:16).

At the same time, Jesus blessed bread and gave it to the disciples as a symbolic distribution of his body. Then he offered them the cup of wine that meant his blood of the New Covenant — which is related to the biblical and Jewish concept of a covenant inaugurated with blood.

From this starting point came the rite which has always had a key place as the bond of Christian fellowship. Bread and wine eaten by the faithful together, either on the night of the betrayal or whenever the Christian pledge is renewed, has become the Christian Passover, in which the symbolic Paschal lamb is offered for the life of man. Paul (I Cor. 5:7) refers directly to Jesus as the sacrificial lamb, slain for Christians.

The Lord's Supper commemorated and symbolized what Jesus Christ had accomplished through his death. More than this, it represented Christ's continuing relation to the believer, "till he come". Through the bread and wine of the Passover meal which Jesus had celebrated, the believer could experience a mystic union with Christ himself and from this communion draw strength for his inner life.

Non-Jewish Elements: A complete review of the symbolism and meaning of the Eucharist must also take account of influences coming from outside Jewish life, and especially from the mystic cults of pagan religion.

The differences between the religion of Jesus and the religion of Paul are largely due to the fact that Paul's was a religion of salvation, closely akin to Hellenistic mysteries. Paul thought of Jesus Christ in an essentially Greek idiom. It seems reasonable to suppose that the Church in apostolic and sub-apostolic times (cf. Jn. 6) were aware of the kinship between the symbolism of the institution of the Eucharist and the sacraments of the mystery cults. This may also be partly the explanation for the transformation of the original Passover meal into an entirely symbolic rite.

The Lord's Supper in the Early Church: The earliest records of the church seem to show that the Lord's Supper was celebrated as a communal Passover rite. This was something already as old as baptism* and with hardly more formality. In time, special celebrants or officers were recognized, such as the president of the brethren, to whom the cup of wine was brought first. A deacon was appointed to distribute the consecrated elements and reserve a portion for those who were absent.

In apostolic times it was the custom for all communicants to make offerings of bread and wine and other things needed for the holy rite, as well as gifts to the poor. This was continued throughout the early history of Christianity. Later on, when the government and discipline of the church developed, new changes were made (which are beyond the scope of this article).

The spiritual significance of the institution can best be summed up as a commemoration; communion of the disciples with God under the New Covenant* and among themselves; as an expression of gratitude (emphasized by the word Eucharist, Greek for "to give thanks"), and, finally, an anticipation of a completed redemption, when "he will come" (see also Christianity, Early*).

EXCAVATION (see Ancient* Cities; Cities*, Hellenistic; Nabateans*).

420

EXILE, BABYLONIAN. — *Outline: The Destruction of Judah and the Deportations; Settlement of the Deportees; Status of Judah and the Nation during the Exile; Jehoiachin in Babylon; Life in Babylonia; Jewish Integration; The Religious Problem; Assimilation of the Jews; Counter-Measures to Assimilation; A Religious Revival; The First Synagogue and its Prayers; A Cultural Renaissance.*

The estimate that the Babylonian Exile lasted about 70 years is based on two calculations presented in the Bible. One in Jer. 29:10 indicates that it lasted approximately 67 years, from 605 to 539 BCE, i.e. the period of the hegemony of the Babylonian Empire, beginning with Nebuchadrezzar's reign and continuing for three generations. Another indication is Zech. 1:1, 7 which suggests that the period lasted from the destruction of the Temple to its rebuilding, 587 to 515 BCE, or about 73 years. Daniel, on the other hand, suggests 49 years, from 587 to the first return in 539 BCE.

The Destruction of Judah and the Deportations: Over one hundred years after the Assyrians exiled the Israel tribes (the Northern Kingdom), the same fate befell Judah at the hands of Babylonia. At first, during the reign of King Jehoiakim (609–598 BCE), the Exile was on a restricted scale. References to it are found in the writings of Flavius Josephus* (Against Apion 19:1), the Book of Daniel (1:1) and II Ch. 36:6–7. The second stage (597 BCE) assumed greater proportions, including the removal to Babylonia of King Jehoiachin (son of Jehoiakim), court officials, notables, ministers, owners of large estates, artisans, priests and prophets. Among the latter was the prophet Ezekiel (II K. 24:14–15; Jer. 24:1–2; 29:1–2; 27:20). The Babylonians appointed as the new king Jehoiachin's uncle, Zedekiah. The third and final stage of the Exile took place in 586 BCE, when Jerusalem was destroyed (see Israel & Judah*, V).

Typical deportation scenes are shown in Assyrian stone reliefs (**420**) of the 8th c. BCE. The men were chained two by two, with one hand left free for carrying belongings. Beautiful women were perched on chariots loaded with baggage and booty, while other women walked, carrying their burdens on their heads and their children on their shoulders. Long columns marched under guard, the weak and straggling falling behind. There is no clear evidence of the numbers of deportees in the Old Testament, but it is thought that the population of Judah had numbered about 300,000, of which half were deported or destroyed. In II K. 24:14 it is written that 10,000 persons were deported with Jehoiachin, while according to Jeremiah (52:28–30), the Jehoicahin deportees numbered 3,023, and the total in all three stages reached 4,600.

Descriptions of the exiles always emphasize quality rather than quantity. Both Jeremiah and Ezekiel refer to them as the best citizens and so does the formal record of Kings, and parallels in Jeremiah and Chronicles. The people who were left behind were presumably the poorer elements. By far the greater number were not exiled, but were either executed, killed in the fighting or simply excluded. In view of this, the figure of 10,000 exiles does not seem improbable, though it is only a rough estimate. It has been suggested that the round number represents those who went into exile, while the smaller, more precise figure in Jer. 52 represents the official register of those who actually survived the trip to Babylon. Considering the condition of the exiles and the rigours of the trip, the proportion of two-thirds perishing seems reasonable. Actually, the figures given in Jer. 52 are 3,023 exiles during the seventh year, which can be pinpointed by the Babylonian Chronicles as March 597 BCE; 832 in the 18th year (587 BCE) and 745 in the final deportation of 582 BCE. The figures in II K. 24:14, 16 (10,000 and 7,000) both relate to the deportation of 587 BCE. It need not be supposed that the total deported at any one time was greater than the highest figure given, or that a large percentage of the total population was actually taken away. (Compare with the figures in the Assyrian records for the deportation from Samaria of around 20,000. Sennacherib's 200,000, plus those from Judah, seems to be a mistake or a gross exaggeration.) Another reliable criterion for the number of captives may be the number of those who returned from Exile several decades later. The lists in the books of Ezra and Nehemiah (Ezr. 2; Neh. 7) give a total of 50,000.

Settlement of the Deportees: The Babylonians settled the deportees in the Nippur Province on the Great Canal (Ezk. 3:15) in the centre of Mesopotamia. Berossus, the Babylonian-Hellenistic historian, states that Nebuchadrezzar gave the Jews the choicest areas, but judging by the list of places, they were also sent to ruined towns, such as Tel Abib (Ezk. 3:15), Tel Melah and Tel Harsha (Ezr. 2:59), which they were ordered to rebuild. At a later period the names of the towns of Nahardea and Mahoza, all in the territory between the Euphrates and the Tigris, are included. This territory came to be known in Jewish tradition as the "Diaspora" and its inhabitants as the "notables of the first rank" in genealogical lists. The towns where the deportees presumably settled have not yet been identified by archaeological discoveries.

Status of Judah and the Nation during the Exile: In spite of repeated deportations, a large number of Jews remained in Palestine. In addition, Nebuchadrezzar's policy differed from that of the Assyrians in that he did not resettle the areas from which the Jews had been driven. Excavations in various sites in Judah, such as Tel Beit-Mirsim, Lachish* and Beth-Shemesh* testify to a significant break in the continuity of settled life. The general desolation is poignantly expressed in Lam. 1:4 and 5:18. Territory that belonged to Judah in 589 BCE was divided between the Edomites, who settled in the southern hill country, and the Babylonian province of Samaria. Conditions in the territory of Benjamin, which contained the seat of Gedaliah's government, were better than elsewhere. Several Jewish settlements remained in Ephraim, the Negeb, Galilee and Transjordan. At some time before the middle of the 5th c. BCE, aristocratic Jews became the hereditary governors of Samaria and Ammon.

Jehoiachin in Babylon: Though Judah ceased to be an independent state and was annexed by the Babylonian Empire, the Babylonians permitted the royal house to survive, and maintained the fiction of a kingdom-in-exile by granting certain privileges to the prisoner king, Jehoiachin. The land was laid waste, but Jehoiachin, king of Judah, was treated as a royal guest at the court of the Babylonian monarch. A list of rations given to prisoners and recorded on a clay tablet **(421)** from Babylon (593 BCE) includes "Jehoiachin, King of Judah" and his sons among the recipients. Seal impressions (Seals*) found at Debir and Beth-Shemesh reveal that Jehoiachin's royal estates in Judah continued to be managed by his steward, Eliakim, during the Exile.

It would seem that as long as the exiled king lived, there was some hope that the Jewish monarchy would be restored. Indeed, this hope grew brighter when, after the death of Nebuchadrezzar in 562 BCE, the news of Jehoiachin's release from prison spread to the deportees. He was accorded royal honours and it is possible that the institution of "Rosh Galuta" (Exilarch), as head of the ever growing Babylonian Jewish community, goes back to this period. In any event, the conditions of the exiles improved from then on.

Life in Babylonia: At the time of the Exile, Babylonia was at her political and economic zenith. Assyria, formerly the pre-eminent power in Western Asia, had been destroyed and Egypt was not as yet an important factor in the area. The Medes were close allies of Nebuchadrezzar, and were thus part of his eastern hegemony. Babylonia's economic prosperity, which continued for centuries, is reflected in contemporary inscriptions and the reports of later historians, as well as the Bible (see Babylonia*). The population of Babylonia was made up of a number of different small ethnic groups, and this resulted in a high degree of toleration for differing religious practices. The Jews also benefitted from this liberality.

Jewish Integration: The Jews had every possibility of integrating into this highly civilized and prosperous society, particularly since they had been resettled in large groups containing a diversity of professions and trades. Their numbers, however, led them to organize their own separate communal life in accordance with their ancient traditions. As noted above, they were neither oppressed nor suppressed, and even the prophets found nothing to say in condemnation of Babylonian laws. The sufferings of the exiled Jews and their hatred of the Babylonians were spiritual, and arose from separation from their homeland. Witness Psalm 137: "By the waters of Babylon, there we sat down and wept when we remembered Zion . . . How shall we sing the Lord's song in a foreign land?"

Babylonian society consisted of three main strata, the nobility, semi-free citizens and slaves. The Jews belonged to the second stratum. Though a special commissioner was in charge of them, they paid the same taxes as all other citizens and were conscripted into the Army. The upper class Jews were eligible for positions of trust in the King's court. The rank and file artisans, masons, smiths and others were employed in the extensive building operations of Nebuchadrezzar. The remainder engaged in agriculture, either on their own holdings or as hirelings on Babylonian estates. The settling down of the Jews is described in Jer. 29:5–7 which begins, "build houses and dwell in them, plant gardens and eat their produce," and was recorded by the historian Berossus. Numerous bowls unearthed near the Chebar river in Nippur bear inscriptions that suggest that a colony of Jews lived there for centuries. In the course of time, many Jews entered trade, some even growing rich. Their economic prosperity is reflected in the extensive archives of a great Babylonian firm of bankers and brokers in Nippur, the exchange house of Murashu Sons. One of its functions was to act as the agent of the Persian government in collecting the taxes of the area. Among the 730 tablets in cuneiform writing found in the archives were promissory

421

notes giving the rate of interest as 25% per annum. Though it is not clear whether the Murashu House was Jewish or not, and presumably it was not, many of the names mentioned in the clay documents (written after 437 BCE) were Hebrew. Out of the 86 merchants listed as making use of the services of this bank, 70 had Jewish names, including Hananiah, Berachiah, Yehoecham, Mattatiahu and Pedaiahu. This serves to demonstrate that not only were most of the merchants with whom the House dealt Jewish, but that the Jews occupied a prominent position in the economy.

The Religious Problem: The destruction of the Temple in 587 BCE and the mass deportations to a foreign soil put the Jews to a severe test. It would hardly have been surprising if they had been overcome by despair, and had experienced a wholesale loss of faith. Torn as they were from their homeland, and thrust into close contact with one of the great centres of cosmopolitan culture, with magnificent temples to pagan gods and attractive religious rituals, the Jews could easily have been drawn into apostasy. The enormous wealth and power that both surrounded and was open to them, offered a life of economic ease, making the call to assimilation all the stronger. Nevertheless, the Jews strove to retain their identity and their belief in Yahweh and His Promised Land, following the prophets who had always maintained that the Jews would not lose their nationhood even if they were divorced from their own land. The God of Israel was the Lord of all creation, and a military reverse could not be interpreted as a display of His weakness, but rather as a punishment for His people. This point had been forcefully expressed by Isaiah with regard to Assyria, and the prophets who arose in Babylon stressed it also (Ezk. 11:16). Whether or not this attitude faithfully reflected the feelings of the people as a whole is an open question.

Assimilation of the Jews: The national crisis left a deep impression on the people. Some sought refuge in the official theology of pre-Exilic Judah and the promises made to David, as well as the prophetic teaching concerning a military and political leader who would restore their nation as David had done in the past. These were the first stirrings of the Messianic hopes nurtured by the generations of the Restoration* and post-Exilic centuries (see Apocalypse*: Messianic Hope). Other Jews accepted complete or partial assimilation. Numerous scholars have suggested that the adoption of Babylonian sounding names by many Jews may be regarded as one external sign of partial assimilation. Among the names used were: Zerubbabel ("zera' babel" or seed of Babylon); Mordechai (Man of Marduk = Marduk-aya); Sheshbazzar (apparently a corruption of Sin-ab-usur, which may mean "May the God Sin protect the father"); Begoy (from the Iranian Baga-El). The adoption of these names, however, may have been simply a way of accommodating to life in a foreign environment, not evidence of assimilation.

The Jews' reaction to their cultural surroundings is also reflected in their increased use of the Aramaic script, which they later brought back with them to Palestine, and their adoption of Aramaic, the *lingua franca* of the Empire, as their spoken language (see Alphabet*; Aram*). In time, even the Torah had to be translated into Aramaic, first verbally and then in written form. The masses had begun to forget their own tongue.

Counter-Measures to Assimilation: These negative developments were countered by many positive factors. A new Judaism, whose influence continues to this day, emerged. The belief that the Exile had been a divine chastisement gained ground, and the need for repentance in order to avoid a repetition of such a catastrophe was stressed. The Talmud records that there were hardly any cases of idolatrous practices, and that the Restoration was that of a purely monotheistic people. Ezekiel* and the second Isaiah*, the two great prophets who preached to the Jews during the Exile, taught a coming redemption and return to Palestine. They spoke of the new order at the Temple that would come and the new social system that would be established. Their following was very large.

A Religious Revival: The religion of the Exilic and post-Exilic period was marked by a tremendous concern for the keeping of the Law*. This distinguished it from the religion of pre-Exilic Israel in the sense that it called for a more stringent fulfillment of the Law's demands on the part of every Jew, precisely as the prophets had preached. The prophets had explained the national calamity as the penalty for sin against Yahweh's Law, and the terrible judgment wreaked upon the people in consequence of their breach of the Covenant*. Godfearing Jews felt that Israel's future and the old prophetic hope that God would not abandon His people depended upon fulfilment of the Law's demands. The question was reduced to one of sin and its consequences, and the survival of Israel's status as the Chosen People*, in the face of this self-admission of guilt. The special relationship of Israel to God was itself put to the test. In the past, the priests had tended to monopolize the actual practice of religion, but in this new situation of "adapted Judaism", worship and the observance of the Law became the duty of everyone. The nation and the national cult having vanished, they had little else to mark them as Jews.

Another new concept born of prophetic teachings that took root was that despite the Exile, the ties between the Jews and their God remained unbroken.

The First Synagogue and its Prayers: The stricter observance of the Law in general led to the stricter observance of the Sabbath and the rite of circumcision which increasingly became the mark of the loyal Jew. Great concern for the problem of ritual cleanliness (Ezk. 4:12–15; 22; 44), as well as stricter observance of the dietary laws, may be explained by the Jewish concept that they were living in an "unclean land", where sacrifices could not be offered. The communal synagogue and the beginning of a set text for prayers which arose during the Exile, served as substitutes for the Temple and the seasonal sacrificial ceremonies that had been offered, particularly at festivals* and holidays.

Evidence of regular prayers can be found in Psalm 51. It is likely that the first synagogues established in Babylonia were primarily intended as meeting places where nostalgic feelings for the homeland could be aired, and where communal affairs could be discussed and holidays celebrated. In order to endow these gatherings with a measure of solemnity, prayers were intoned and portions of the Torah read to the congregants. The Jews never became so enmeshed in their new Judaism, however, that they abandoned hopes of a return to Palestine. Their yearning to return is best expressed in the immortal Psalm 137:5, "If I forget thee

O Jerusalem, let my right hand forget its cunning..." In the early stages, the Palestinian prophet, Jeremiah, maintained close contact with the exiles. Although he predicted that they would return after only two generations, about 70 years, he counselled them to make all arrangements for a settled life in Babylon. For their part, the rank and file of Jerusalem anxiously awaited the early repatriation of the exiles (see Synagogues*).

A Cultural Renaissance: In their efforts to ward off assimilation, the Jews of Babylonia did not confine themselves to ecomomic and communal matters. Indeed, the emphasis was on the preservation and organization of ancient traditions and the maintenance of literary and religious continuity, now that political and social links with the past had been broken. As a result of this emphasis on the past, and the exploration of the essential nature of the relationship of Israel to God and His purpose, a new creativity in prophecy and poetry emerged. The main corpus of the Torah (Pentateuch*), all of whose major components had long since been in existence, was collected and codified in definitive form at about this time. It is plausible to associate the compilation of the nucleus of Scriptures with the work of the Priestly School (see Biblical Criticism*; Genesis*; Leviticus*) which edited, revised and brought it up to date. Most modern scholars hold that the whole of the primary history, from Genesis to Kings, must have been given its final form during the Exile, as it could only have been shaped into a continuous work expressing one overall point of view by those who participated in that event. Though the details are unknown, the process of collection, which ultimately produced the prophetic books as they are known today, was carried forward during the Exile. The historical books, Joshua to II Kings, composed mainly before the fall of the state, were also edited, enlarged and adapted to the situation of the exiles. The Book of Lamentations, as well as part of the Psalms, were composed during this period as well. The Jews further maintained their integrity by drawing up genealogical tables of individuals and groups of families, to record their Palestinian origin (Ezr. 2). At the head of this grouping were the elders, scribes and spiritual leaders of the exiles (see Restoration and the Persian Period*).

EXODUS. — *Outline: The Date of Exodus; Hyksos Background; Biblical Evidence; The Exodus and the Conquest; Mernephtach and the Israel Stele; A Suggested Tanite Era and the Bondage; Correlation with Egyptian History; The* 400 *Year Stele of Tanis; Exodus under Ramses II?; Habiru and Shasu Beduins in Egypt; Was Mernephtach the Pharaoh of the Exodus?; The Route of the Exodus; A Southern Escape Route; The Later Northern Route; How Many Made the Journey?; Effect of the Exodus.*

Israel's deliverance from bondage in Egypt remains, in modern Judaism no less than in the biblical tradition, the outstanding event of her history.

In evaluating the traditional story scientifically, and attempting an historical reconstruction of the sequence of events, a balanced view requires us to recognize the following: 1. that there is no external evidence which directly corroborates the biblical account of the Exodus, though a sizable number of contemporary data shed light on the circumstances surrounding the event, and 2. that the biblical story reached its present form centuries after the event, and cannot therefore be relied on as an exact historical record. At the same time, the central core of tradition, going back to contemporary oral sources, had been faithfully preserved there. The purpose of modern biblical research has therefore been twofold: to recover the historical setting of the Exodus on the basis of archaeological exploration and examination of the relevant materials and to trace the development in the Bible of the literary traditions concerning the event. We may begin with the following questions: When did the Exodus take place? Under what conditions? By what route or routes?

The Date of Exodus: The biblical writers link the background of the story to the typically Egyptian tale of Joseph*, followed by the quiet life led by the descendants of the patriarch* Jacob in Goshen, the rich land to the east of the Egyptian Delta. According to this tradition, Goshen was the centre of the post-patriarchal phase of Hebrew life.

The Exodus can, therefore, only have taken place after there had been a certain movement into Egypt among the inhabitants of Canaan. Also, if we accept the Bible's evidence, it must have happened at a time when the Delta, especially its eastern region, was of sufficient importance to warrant the building of large towns there. This combination of circumstances occurred twice in the history of the Near East. Which occasion was the setting for the book of Exodus* is still debated.

1. **Hyksos Background:** Some time during the 18th c. BCE the Hyksos reached the Delta from Syria and Asia, and around 1710 BCE they founded the city of Tanis there (in Hebrew Zo'an — Avaris) as their capital. Some scholars believe that the migration of the sons of Jacob (see Patriarchs*) is to be associated with this movement. Many semi-nomads came with the Hyksos. Some had come even earlier. They remained in the Delta area, continuing their semi-nomadic traditions, unwilling to be organized into a settled community, forming a constant threat to lines of communication between the Egyptian and Palestinian parts of the Hyksos "empire". This may be reflected in the biblical tradition of the book of Exodus* which describes the Hebrews as shepherds with flocks and herds, who formed a large community with houses.

The Hyksos ruled the Delta area for more than a century until, around 1570 BCE, they were driven out of Tanis into Palestine where they founded their new empire. A theory previously held by some scholars that the Exodus took place at the same time as this expulsion of the Hyksos, leaves a number of questions unanswered and is now generally discounted (see Joseph*).

Biblical Evidence: The essential biblical datum bearing on the chronology of the Exodus is the statement in I K. 6:1: "In the four hundred and eightieth year after the people of Israel came out of the land of Egypt... Solomon... began to build the house of the Lord." The biblical chronology, apparently confirmed by some archaeological findings, suggests a date for the Exodus around 1450, i.e. during the reign of Thutmosis III (1490–1436 BCE). This view seemed to be vindicated when J. Garstang, excavating Jericho between 1930 and 1936 CE, announced his opinion that the town had been destroyed before 1400 BCE. This was later disproved but, in fact, even the bare statement raised more questions than it answered.

The biblical figure (480 years) has to be interpreted in relation to the symbolic value which certain numbers possessed. 480 is twelve times 40 — the traditional reign of a ruler or priest, i.e. a generation. For instance, David and Solomon each reigned 40 years. This was also taken as the period of the wanderings in the wilderness, during which a whole generation of adults could pass from the scene. The number twelve also had a special significance which went back to ancient times. The "480 years" need not be an exact figure.

2. **The Exodus and the Conquest:** By relating the problem to another setting, it seems to many scholars that the Exodus could be dated in relation to the Conquest which must logically have followed it. Archaeological evidence of the Conquest consists of findings pointing to the destruction of a whole series of Canaanite cities: Beth El, Tel Beit-Mirsim (Debir?), Hazor*, Lachish*, during the 13th c. This would also seem to point to a king of the 19th dynasty as the Pharaoh of the Exodus.

Mernephtach and the Israel Stele: In Lachish an Egyptian ostracon (inscription on a potsherd) was found which apparently dated from the fourth year of the reign of an unnamed king, probably Mernephtach. This date, according to Rowton, was 1221 BCE. Another document connected with the same king Mernephtach is the so-called Israel stele which, according to Wilson's and Rowton's chronology, is now dated to 1219 BCE (see Conquest*). An apparently unconnected addition towards the end of the inscription runs: "The people of Israel is desolate, It has no offspring." While the hieroglyphic sign indicating a "foreign country" is used with all the other peoples mentioned in the inscription, only the sign for a "people" (men and women) is used with Israel. This raises two questions in the minds of scholars who are aware that Egyptian kings often copied earlier victory steles without bothering to fight any battle (see stele **422** with detail of the name "Israel" below).

Did this king actually wage a war against his northern neighbours? A sword found at Ugarit with his name cut in it suggests that he may have campaigned in Asia but we cannot be sure. More important is the fact that he knew of the existence of a people of Israel who lived in Palestine. This is the first time Israel is mentioned in any document in world history. Even if the king was boasting of more victories than he actually achieved, it is significant that he used this name instead of the more familiar ones of Egypt's traditional enemies, and this seems to support the historicity of the stele.

The second question concerns the significance of the determinative sign used for Israel as a "people" only. It is true that Egyptian scribes at the time of the 19th dynasty and later were careless about their use of determinatives, but against this, every other nation mentioned in the stele has the correct sign for a foreign country. The most obvious conclusion seems to be that at the time the Mernephtach stele was erected in the first quarter of the 13th c., Israel was already in certain parts of Canaan, but not yet settled. It points to a date after the Exodus, and probably also after an initial phase of the Conquest*. (The possibility that the "Israel" of the stele meant another group of Hebrews whose ancestors had never been in Egypt, or a particular immigration of Hebrews who came before the others, is something that cannot be decided with the documents at our disposal.)

422

A Suggested Tanite Era and the Bondage: There is no way of telling at what point between reaching Canaan and finally settling in it, this stele was written. However, even though it cannot be used to fix a definite date for the Exodus, if the Israel stele is considered together with the data in the Bible, certain facts emerge which may be more than coincidences:

a. The Mernephtach stele was apparently erected in 1219 BCE. If we take the figure of 40 years wandering in the desert as a

423

real number, not merely the symbol for a generation, and add to it the 430 years which the Bible (Ex. 12:40) gives as the period spent in Egypt before the Exodus, we come to the year 1681 BCE as the date for their arrival. Between this and the founding of Tanis, around 1710 BCE, is a difference of only 29 years and this could be accounted for. (This problem is also discussed in the article on the Conquest*.)

b. In the book of Numbers (13:22), there is a remarkable statement: "Hebron was built seven years before Zoan (Tanis) in Egypt." This places the foundation of Hebron close to 1710 and may explain why the early traditions about the Patriarchs* do not mention the site by its historical name (Hebron) but by its archaic name, Eloneh (Oaks) Mamre, even though the later narrators knew that both names referred to the same place. In any case, why did the later Israelites fix the founding of their city by the apparently unrelated date of the establishment of the Hyksos' Tanis?

Some scholars have put forward the theory that the 430 years given by Exodus for the Hebrews' stay in Egypt, which is reduced to the round number of 400 in Genesis 15:13, is very suggestive in connection with the 400 years which had elapsed since the foundation of Tanis.

Correlation with Egyptian History: The Delta area was of importance to Egypt both for her defences against her Asian and Libyan (western) enemies and as the point of departure for any attempt to recapture her lost Asiatic possessions. Some two and a half centuries after the expulsion of the Hyksos, the kings of the 19th Dynasty (13th c. BCE) decided to rebuild Tanis as their new capital, Pi-Raamses, House of Ramses. The work was begun by Seti I (1312–1289 BCE) and continued by his son, Ramses II (1289–1224 BCE), using the forced labour of the Delta's nomadic population. This brick **(424)**, made of clay and straw bears the cartouche of this famous builder.

The 400 Year Stele of Tanis: To justify its new distinction, the rebuilt Tanis had to be given a suitable spiritual significance. This was achieved by a religious change which is recorded in the "400 Year Stele" which Ramses allegedly erected around 1330 or 1325 BCE, or possibly later, on the anniversary of the original founding of Tanis. It shows his father, while still a high official of the previous king (see Egypt*: Chronological Table), visiting Tanis to pay homage to the local god Seth, whose worship he and his son (Ramses) had adopted. Seth is shown at the top of the stele **(423)**, wearing the Asiatic garment and headdress which elsewhere

424

in Egyptian documents are associated with Ba'al, the chief Canaanite god, who was also symbolized by the same animal, a kind of jackal. Seth was the chief god of the Hyksos. By adopting him, Seti and Ramses hoped to establish themselves as legitimate successors of the Hyksos and rulers of their capital, Tanis. In addition, Ramses must also have hoped that his new patron, Seth, would help him gain control of the Asiatics of the Delta, and fight against the Asiatics of Palestine and Syria.

Part of the text celebrating the 400th anniversary of the god's rule over Egypt reads: "Year 400, fourth month of the third season, day 4, of the king of Upper and Lower Egypt: Seth the Great of Strength . . ." Thus this stele places the beginning of the god's rule in Tanis at around 1730 or 1725 BCE, close to the 1710 date. Whether this Egyptian anniversary of the founding of Tanis is in any way connected with the traditional biblical figure and whether it can reliably place the coming of the Hebrews in the Hyksos period, is very uncertain and should not be pressed. The coincidence between the figures, together with the statement about the founding of Hebron, does suggest that the Hebrews were familiar with the whole of the Tanite era, both at its founding and at the time of the anniversary celebrated in the "400 Year Stele". In any case, the tradition of a period of bondage in Egypt cannot be seriously questioned.

The foregoing theory also supports the tentative placing of Exodus within the framework of events during the 19th dynasty (1305–1214 BCE). Is it possible to be more exact, without relying exclusively on speculation based on Old Testament statements, which themselves are inexact, deriving from older oral traditions (e.g. the 40 years wandering)?

Exodus under Ramses II?: Ex. 1:11 names the town which the children of Israel built as Raamses. It seems reasonable to identify this with the new capital built by Ramses II in the eastern Delta region and to date the Exodus some time during his reign. In any event the evidence points to a date for the Exodus in the 13th c. BCE, although correlation with biblical evidence raises some problems. The Bible indicates that the Pharaoh of the oppression was not the same as the Pharaoh of the Exodus. Hence, if Hebrews laboured at Tanis (Avaris), then they must have been in Egypt at least in the reign of Seti I (1312–1289). Although we cannot be sure, many scholars consider it plausible that Seti I, who initiated the restoration of Tanis, may have been the Pharaoh of the oppression and Ramses II the Pharaoh in whose reign the Exodus took place.

Habiru and Shasu Beduins in Egypt: However, the fact that some of the Delta's population had come during the Hyksos period does not, by itself, provide a decisive connection between Ramses' building operations and the Exodus. Many Canaanite prisoners were brought home to the Delta by the conquerors of the 18th dynasty, who inflicted several defeats on the newly established Hyksos dominions in Palestine. The 3600 Habiru/Apiru prisoners of war mentioned in the Memphis stele of Amenophis II (1436–1411) were undoubtedly put to work, presumably under oppressive conditions. Moreover, migrations to Egypt were very common at the time of Ramses II. The Egyptian Anastasi Papyrus VI, for instance, refers to the passage of Beduin (Shasu) tribes across the Egyptian frontier, "to the pools . . . to keep them alive and to keep their cattle alive."

Was Mernephtach the Pharaoh of the Exodus? The work on the new House of Ramses begun by Seti I (see above) was continued and finished under Ramses II. It does not seem unreasonable to connect the oppression of the Israelites with these actions, preferably during the time of the co-regency between Seti and Ramses, around the year 1289. Ramses was succeeded by Mernephtach (1224–1204). The fact that he claims a victory over "Israel" does not automatically make him the Pharaoh of the Exodus, but, in the light of Egyptian history, in the view of other scholars, the biblical account seems to favour such an identification, even though the stele can hardly be contemporaneous with the Exodus.

Many scholars have suggested the plausible possibility that, some time during the rule of Mernephtach (or possibly Ramses II), some shepherds, forced to work on the construction and driven very hard, revolted at the instigation of Moses and fled from Egypt. To contemporary Egyptians and their neighbours, the event was not a matter of extraordinary importance. Accordingly, there was no reason for it to be recorded anywhere.

The Route of the Exodus: (see map **425**). Having set out, the Bible tells us that the Children of Israel did not go "by the way of the land of the Philistines" (Exodus 13:17). This was the well-known route from Raamses in the eastern Delta, via Sileh (Tel Abu Sefah near modern Kantara, the area crossed today by the Suez Canal), to Gaza. It formed the southern section of the "Via Maris" or Road of the Sea which continued up the coastal plain of Palestine, crossed the Valley of Esdraelon near Megiddo* and went on through Damascus to Mesopotamia*. Mention of the Philistines in Ex. 13 is an anachronism, since they did not settle in Palestine until late in the 12th c. BCE. In fact, the road was too busy and too well guarded, especially around the frontier fortress of Sileh (Tjaru) to make it a feasible way of escape for the Children of Israel.

Instead, the Israelites turned south, going from Raamses to Succoth (Ex. 12:37), which was in the centre of Goshen and is sought now in the ruins of Tel el-Maskutah, ancient Tjeku. This was situated in the Wadi Tumilat, a wide valley near the area of Lake Timsah through which there was a road running from Heliopolis, past Tel Yehudieh and present-day Ismailah to the Sinai Peninsula.

The key verses of the biblical account, so far as the route is concerned, are Ex. 13:20 and 14:1–2: "And they moved on from Succoth, and encamped at Etham, on the edge of the wilderness . . . Then the Lord said to Moses, 'Tell the people of Israel to turn back and encamp in front of Pihahiroth between Migdol and the sea, in front of Ba'al-Zephon; you shall encamp over against it, by the sea.'"

There is a surprising parallel to this passage in the text of an Egyptian "model letter" used in Egyptian schools of the period, and almost certainly based on a real incident. An official is reporting the pursuit of two runaway slaves:

"Now when I reached the enclosure wall of Tjeku (Succoth) on the 3rd month of the 3rd season, they told me they were saying to the south they had passed by on the 3rd month of the third season, day 10. Now when I reached the fortress (Egyptian: Hetem) they told me that the . . . had come forth from the desert (saying that) they had passed

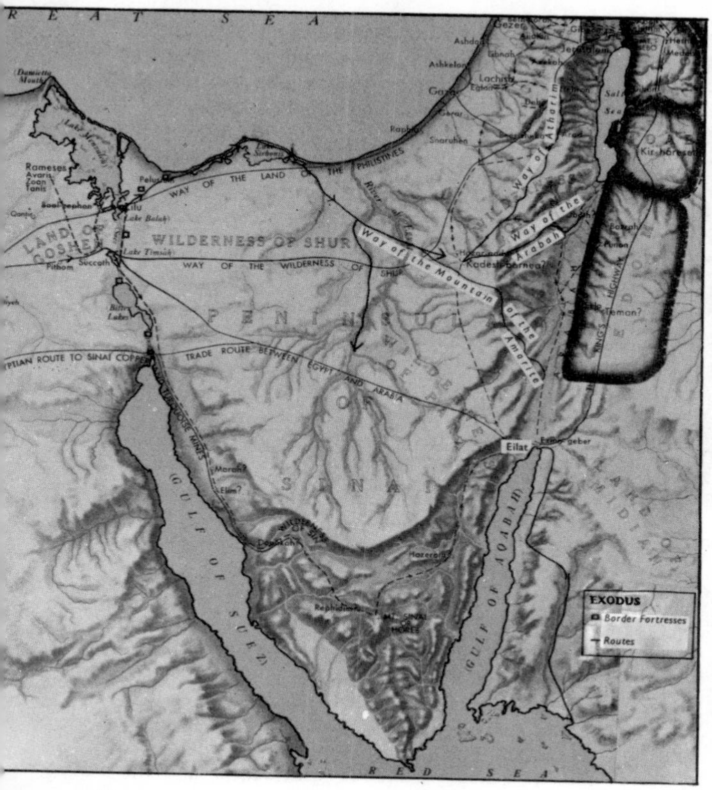

425

the walled place north of the Migdol of Seti Mernephtach." (Papyrus Anastasi V, XIX: 2–XX:6).

A Southern Escape Route: The two itineraries seem to show that there was a well-known escape route from Egypt into the freedom of the desert of Sinai and southern Palestine. According to Exodus, the Israelites' route ran from Succoth to Etham. (Etham is mentioned again in Nu. 33:6–8.) The Egyptian text speaks of a fortress, but the Egyptian word for fortress was "Hetem". It seems possible that a later Hebrew narrator mistook the Egyptian word for a proper name. Alternatively, there may have been a particular, outstanding fort, which was called Hetem as a name.

Although Pihahiroth is mentioned in Egyptian inscriptions as well as the Bible text, the site has never been located. The name appears to mean "the mouth of the waterway", an appropriate term for many localities in the swamps of the eastern Delta.

The "Migdol" of the bible text and the "Migdol of Seti Mernephtach" may not have been identical. The word means a small square fort in Canaanite and Hebrew as well as Egyptian. The biblical "Migdol" is identified with Tel el-Her south of Pelusium on the border of Sinai.

The Later Northern Route: The reference to Ba'al-Zaphon (the Ba'al of the North) suggests a northerly detour. Ba'al was worshipped under such a name in Ugarit where his seat was held to be on nearby Mount Casius. A Hellenistic-Phoenician letter mentions the god of Ba'al-Zaphon and all the gods of Tahpanhes, and indicates a local site for the Egyptian Mount Casius east of Sileh at a place now called Mahamadia. This in turn seems to suggest transfer of the worship of Ba'al from his homeland to this modest hill by some Asiatics.

The use of a northern route suggests to many that the Israelites crossed the shallow Lake Sirbonis (see map **425**), a very appropriate "Reed Sea" which is the biblical designation. It has long been recognized that the Israelites did not cross the great Red Sea which is the rendering given in most translations, but a shallow body of water. Such a lake near Raamses is referred to in other 13th c. Egyptian sources as the "Reed Sea".

Although all the places mentioned in the Bible's record cannot be traced, it is clear that whether or not the Children of Israel reached the shores of the Mediterranean, they followed a northerly route avoiding the more frequented roads and frontier fortresses.

How Many Made the Journey? General considerations as well as the narrative describing the crossing of difficult terrain and complicated manoeuvering make it impossible to accept the figures given in the Bible for the number of the children of Israel who escaped from Egypt: "six hundred thousand men on foot besides women and children" (Ex. 12:37). Moreover, such an enormous number of people and their cattle could never have subsisted during the years of wandering in the wilderness. The "Way of Shur" through Northern Sinai to Kadesh-Barnea is shown (**426**). The valleys of the wilderness of Zin (**427**) in the central Negeb, leading to the Arabah, were apparently the final lap of the wanderings.

Apart from the possibility of a simple exaggeration, it may be that there were not one but two or more waves of the Exodus involving a smaller number of Hebrews leaving Egypt. More significantly, it must be remembered that the Hebrew word "eleph" (literally the figure 1000) could also mean a "clan" or "family" and not the numerical thousand (see the discussion under Census*).

Effect of the Exodus: If the bondage in Egypt and the liberation of the Exodus seemed of no importance to the

426

427

Egyptians of the time, they were fundamental in Hebrew life then and for all time. Much of Hebrew life and law is based on this experience. It explains the spirit of the first commandment (see Covenant*; Law*); the liberality of laws governing the treatment of Hebrew slaves, "for they are my servants, which I brought out of the land of Egypt" (Lv. 25:42); and provides the explanation for the two important feasts of Passover* and Tabernacles* (see Exodus, Book of*).

EXODUS, BOOK OF. — *Outline: Contents; Authorship; Structure; The Documentary Theory; Form Criticism; The Oldest Materials in Exodus; Meaning of Exodus: The Covenantal Relationship; Religious Significance; Exodus in the New Testament.*

Readers of the Bible in translation know the second book of the Pentateuch as "Exodus", the Latinized form of the Greek word for departure. In Hebrew the book is called simply "Shemot", from the first and second words of the text which mean "These are the names", i.e. the names of the clan of Jacob which settled in Egypt. The list of names is followed by a general statement about the multiplication of their descendants which, while it gives no details of the history of the settlement of the Hebrews in Egypt, serves as a link between the distant traditions of the Patriarchs* of Canaan (recorded in Genesis*) and the story of bondage and redemption which is the main theme of the book of Exodus.

Contents: In its present form, the book falls into two main divisions: a. Israel in Egypt (chs. 1–18), and b. Israel in Sinai (chs. 19–40), including the commandments concerning the priesthood and the sanctuary. However, the themes in the second part overlap, and there is no clear demarcation between the sections. The composite nature of the narrative can be seen from a more detailed analysis of the contents, as follows:

a. **Chs. 1–18:** Chs. 1–2: Oppression in Egypt, and the birth and early life of Moses up to his flight into the desert. Chs. 3–4:17: The call of Moses and Yahweh's revelation of Himself by name. Chs. 4:18–7:7: Moses' return to Egypt and the beginning of his mission to lead the Hebrews out of bondage, including (6:2–3) the identification of Yahweh with the God of the Patriarchs. Chs. 7:8–11: Moses' interviews with Pharaoh and the story of the ten plagues, which seems to be interrupted between 10:29 and 11:8b. Chs. 12–13:16: The institution of the Passover. Chs 13:17–17: The Exodus from Egypt, the crossing of the Reed Sea, the Song of Moses (15:1–18) and the journey through the wilderness of Horeb (Sinai). Ch.18: Encounter with Jethro and the scheme for the administration of justice among the people.

b. **Chs. 19–40:** The rest of the book is taken up with the legislative sections of Exodus, followed by those of the rest of the Pentateuch. Chs. 19:2–24:18: The revelation of Yahweh to the people at Sinai, the giving of the Law and the making of the Covenant. Verses 1–17 of ch. 20 are the "Ten Commandments" and these are followed (20:23–23:33) by the Book of the Covenant, the first statement of the Law* of the Pentateuch (Torah). This can again be subdivided into a: judgments (21:1–22:17) and b: various moral, social and religious laws (22:18–23:19) which are also related to chs. 32-34. The ratification or renewal of the Covenant on Mount Sinai is recorded in 24:1–18. Chs. 25–31 include the command to build the tabernacle, interrupted at the end of ch. 31 and resumed in chs. 35–40, and ordinances concerning the priesthood and the Sabbath. Ch. 32 contains the narrative of the Golden Calf, followed (ch. 33) by Moses' intercession and (34:1–35:3), by the renewal of the Covenant on the tablets of stone. 34:2–18 and 35:1–3 hint at the existence of another, fourth collection of laws which, with the exception of the law of the Sabbath in 35:2–3, has either been lost or placed elsewhere. Chs. 35–40 describe the completion of the tabernacle and the making of its equipment. These chapters are related to chs. 25–31.

Authorship: It is quite certain that Moses did not write either Exodus or the rest of the Pentateuch (see Biblical Criticism*), but the Exodus is very much a book of Moses in that it reflects the creative activity of Israel's founder. The fact that the book records Moses' life, words and deeds is no proof that he wrote it, but it is historically probable that Moses left behind him written laws or other records, or that sayings and speeches of his were carefully preserved and written down by those associated with him or by the next generations in the early days of the settlement in Canaan. Material of this nature, together with genealogical records, historical material about the Exodus and wanderings, and early priestly records, were preserved in different accounts which were finally woven into the structure of the book of Exodus and the rest of the Pentateuch. The actual compilation would have been a long process stretching from the days of the tribal league to prophetic and priestly circles of a later time.

Structure: The composite nature of the narrative in Exodus bears the marks of editorial activity by the various schools of tradition through which the earlier material was transmitted. This is clear from the passages mentioned above (the break in sequence between 10:29 and 11:8b, and the awkward transition between 19:25 and 20:1) and from the apparent intrusion of the narrative of chs. 32–34 between the command to build the tabernacle and the description of its construction. Such irregularities are, of course, a natural result of the fusion of two or three separate narratives, themselves woven out of a variety of older elements, but they have also given rise to serious differences of opinion about the contents of Exodus and the original sources of each portion of the book.

The Documentary Theory: Analysis of the material into different sections belonging to the J, E and P (Jahwist, Elohist and Priestly) strata of the Pentateuch (see Biblical Criticism*: The Documentary Theory) was bound up with the view that the J and E sources were compiled during the period of the monarchy and reflected the ideals of the prophetic movement, whereas P represented the priestly tradition. Delineating the limits of the J and E strands caused the greatest difficulty, while distinguishing the Priestly tradition was easier.

The descriptions of the bondage and the birth and flight of Moses seem to be shared by both J and E strands. The revelation of the personal name of God (the tetragammaton YHWH, see Moses*) and the incident of the burning bush (3:2–3) are usually attributed to E, whereas the identification of Yahweh with the God of the Patriarchs (6:2–3) is ascribed to the Priestly stratum (this point is discussed under Moses*).

The recital of events up to ch. 12 seems to belong to a P source; the J and E accounts of the plagues there have survived merely in fragments, while the itinerary and incidents of the wanderings (13:17–14:31) are common to all three sources. The Song of Miriam (15:21) does not belong to either a J or E source, but was incorporated in both. Ch. 18, one of the most important historical narratives in Exodus, is also attributed to E. The Decalogue and the Book of the Covenant (chs. 20–23) belong to the most ancient E and J traditions (see below). The narrative about the Golden Calf and its sequel in chs. 32 and 33 are also apparently E and J. The J passages give special emphasis to the name of God (34:5, 14). The close relationship between the Name and the Covenant is best preserved in the account (J) in ch. 34 where the proclamation of the Name directly precedes the making of the Covenant. This stratum contains a tradition which is more archaic in other respects (see Moses*). The account in ch. 28 of the organization of the tabernacle and cult under the priests* and Levites is the clearest example of the P source. Presumably it was written to demonstrate the antiquity of the institution (see Tabernacle*).

Form Criticism: A more dynamic approach to an understanding of the book has come from the school of Form Criticism (see Biblical Criticism*). This school regards the book as an epic description which came into being as the explanation of the festival of the Passover in later times. In this view, chs. 1–15, the "legend of Passover", form the core of the book and by providing a justification of the paschal feast, represent the situation in life from which the book emerged. Thus, the traditions of Exodus were preserved and transmitted by the cult. This, however, does not mean that the school of form criticism accepts the older view that large sections of chs. 1–20 derive from a priestly source, nor that this was written within later priestly circles to provide a religious background for the annual festival of Passover. Form critics see the cult as providing merely the point of origin and the channel of transmission of the traditions. Materials concerning the revelation, laws and other events at Sinai were the products of later theory, faith and ritual which were added independently and finally overshadowed the original facts. Thus, facts became "transfigured" by faith.

This view, however, is quite complex. It sees the present narrative as abstracted from a Passover liturgy, the origin of which is unknown. So many stages are involved, that the whole reconstruction becomes unlikely. According to D.N. Freedman, however garbled the present narrative may be, it represents the end product of traditions which go back to the event rather than to its cultic celebration.

There is another view which gives greater importance to the historical nucleus of the book and to the symbolic narratives of the Burning Bush and the revelation of the Name, and tries to see through the words of the book into the mind of Moses. This school insists that while the core of Exodus may have been transmitted through the cult, it originated in the historical facts of the bondage in Egypt, the personality of Moses and the events at the sacred mountain. The Exodus story includes two great movements: Yahweh's action to redeem the people from bondage, and the people's actual migration. Both of these are commemorated in festivals: Yahweh's redemption is celebrated in the Passover, while the migration was re-enacted in the pilgrimage. In this view, a cultic situation can do no more than account for the preservation of the history and the faith with which it was accompanied. In the process, further layers of cultic glorification and faith have been added.

These different theories may shed some useful light on the transmission of the Passover cult and on the circumstances (situation in life) which provided the point of origin for many of the Exodus traditions, but they leave out of account the role of Moses* and the ancient legislative material, some of which was probably contemporary with the bare facts of the story. It is generally agreed that whatever their origin or course of transmission, the traditions of the Exodus were later connected by the Israelites with existing ancient institutions. Ordinances connected with them were apparently preserved by the J source (although their present position in the text is the work of editors). As a result, chapters 12 and 13 combine ordinances and narrative in a single text. The ritual of Passover (12:21–23), the death of the firstborn and the hurried flight (12:29–34, 37-39), are recorded side by side with ordinances relating to the Feast of Matzôth (unleavened bread, 13:3, 4, 6 ff 10; see Festivals*) and the offering of the firstlings (13:11–13). The narrative and ordinances connected with the tabernacle* and its ceremonies clearly have a later priestly origin (although not in the post-Exilic period, as was once held by some critics).

The Oldest materials in Exodus: In recent years a good deal of attention has been paid to the historical background of three or four collections of laws in Exodus. On the basis of this research, it is now generally conceded that the Decalogue, the first and most ancient legislative code (Ex. 20:2–17), the greater part of the Covenant Code, or Book of the Covenant (Ex. 20:23–23:33), probably ch. 24 and the Song of Moses and Miriam (15:1–21) can be dated to the 12th–11th c. BCE. While the codes reflect legal procedures in the days of the tribal federation (see Joshua* and Judges*) the narrative also reflects the cultic facts of the early Passover, the pilgrimage feast at the mountain of God and the wanderings in Sinai.

The laws of chs. 21–23 divide into a civil code (21:1–22:17) and a ceremonial one (22:18–23:33 [roughly]). Many scholars find a link between the civil code and the historical narrative about Jethro (ch. 18).

Meaning of Exodus: The Covenantal Relationship: Whereas the story of Exodus arises from two great movements (redemption from bondage and the migration), a deeper purpose underlies the tradition, giving real literary substance to the book. Both movements formed part of Yahweh's plan, but the magnitude of the events had their setting in a pact which was to be renewed between God and His people. This involved the formulation of Yahweh's relationship which had to be defined and sealed by a solemn pact or "berîth". This pact between God and the people coming out of bondage could only be a treaty of vassalage (see Law*; Exodus*), to be inscribed on the large stones of the Decalogue, the material deed of the Sinaitic Covenant (Ex. 24:12; see Moses*: The Mosiac Religious Community; Covenant*). The Covenant theme in Exodus therefore binds much of the material together in a distinct and unique pattern of divine-human relationships, and offers a clue to the literary history of Exodus and the historical nucleus behind it.

Religious Significance: The book of Exodus has a unique place in the Bible as the foundation document for the whole of Israel's religion. It recounts God's redemption of an oppressed people, His rebuke of their oppressor, the revelation of His Name and the way God's guiding hand led and sustained them.

The book lays its greatest emphasis on the merciful intervention and saving action of the God of the fathers and establishes the identity of the laws of Yahweh, the God of Israel, with fundamental principles of law and justice. Thus the Decalogue and the giving of the Law at Sinai are placed right at the beginning of the history of the people of Israel.

The God revealed by the book is a mighty being who dwells with His people, sharing their life, leading them in battle and administering their laws through His chosen and inspired servants. The pattern of revelation, redemption and Covenant* relationship, including the future settlement in the Promised Land, is the basis for the teaching of the prophets and for every stage of the development of Jewish religion which followed. The enormous importance of Exodus for the religion, life and thought of Jew and Christian alike is apparent from the many references to it in both the Old and the New Testaments. The frequency with which the literature of Christian nations makes use of its narratives and laws seems to confirm its place at the very foundation of western civilization.

Exodus in the New Testament: The Christians of apostolic times regarded Moses as both the author of the Pentateuch and a historic personage of unique prominence in Israel's history. They found many parallels to their concepts of the New Covenant* in the traditions of Exodus and the career of Moses. Christian interest in Exodus is reflected in many passages of the New Testament and its use of such themes as the glory of Moses' face (II Co. 3:7–18); the graven serpent and the Passover in Jn. 3:14; 19:36; I Co. 5:7–8 and He. 11:28; the Covenant sacrifice at Sinai (Mt. 26:28 and synoptic parallels; I Co. 11:25); the terror of the Covenant (He. 12:18–24); the crossing of the sea (I Co. 10:2); manna and the water from the rock (Jn. 6:30–35; I Co. 10:3, 4 and passim); the magicians of Egypt (II Ti. 3:8); the Mosaic signs including the plagues (Rev. 8:7 ff; 9:2–4 passim); the Song of Moses, the servant of God (Rev. 15:3–4); and Moses as a prophet (Ac. 3:22; 7:37; Jn. 6:14; 7:40). Jesus as a new lawgiver, following in the steps of Moses, is a typical theme of the synoptic gospels, especially Matthew. John follows the same symbolic pattern, although his view of Jesus' prophecy is fundamentally different (see John, Gospel of*).

The archaeological and historical aspects of the book are treated in the article on the Exodus*.

EZEKIEL, BOOK OF. — *Outline: Contents and Arrangement of the Book; Style and Characteristics; Oracles and Teachings; Theology; The Prophet of the Law; Priestly Influences; Individual Responsibility; Future Organization of Religion; The Problem of Ezekiel; Date and Authorship; The Influence of Ezekiel; Apocalyptic Prophecy.*

Ezekiel, one of the most original of the prophets of the Babylonian Exile, is placed third in the Massoretic order of books of prophecy, after Jeremiah and before the twelve minor prophets.

He was born in Israel around 622 BCE, the son of the priest Buzi. A priest himself, familiar with the organization of Temple worship, he may have taken part in the ritual in that capacity. In 597 BCE, he was among the Jews exiled to Babylonia with Jehoiachin. In Babylonia, Ezekiel lived in Tel-Abib (namesake of modern Israel's chief city) on the river Chebar, one of the tributaries of the Euphrates, and there he married and built a home.

Contents and Arrangement of the Book: All the prophecies were uttered in Babylonia and may well have been assembled into a book by Ezekiel. The text has suffered many corruptions but, according to most modern opinion, there are apparently no elaborations or addenda.

The different prophecies appear to have been arranged according to an orderly, although not uniform, sequence and can be divided into five main sections:

a. Chs. 1–3: The opening vision of the prophet's revelation

of God's call to him to prophesy; b. Chs. 4–24: A cycle of utterances of almost unrelieved gloom, concerned with visitations of divine wrath upon Judah and Jerusalem. All these prophecies were apparently uttered before the destruction of Jerusalem. c. Chs. 25–32: These chapters concern the dire fate awaiting the nations which have already or may yet oppress Israel. Chapter 25 is a prophecy against Amon (Moab), Edom and Philistia; chapters 26–28:19 concern Tyre; chapter 28:20–23 condemns Sidon; chapters 29–32 foretell the doom of Egypt. d. Chs. 33–39 bring a new note of consolation and reassurance; chapter 33, which contains (v. 21) the announcement of the fall of Jerusalem, is a recapitulation of the sins that have been the cause of the people's troubles and a renewed call for the repentance which must come before salvation. Chapter 34 is a condemnation of the false shepherds who have led God's people astray and the promise that God himself will come to lead them and to make a new covenant of peace and prosperity with his "flock". Chapter 35 foretells the destruction of Mount Seir (Edom), while chapter 36 is again a promise of compensation and restoration to the mountains of Israel. Chapter 37 contains two themes: verses 1–14 describe the famous vision of the valley of dry bones, an allegory of the resurrection of the people in Exile; verses 15–28 are the vision of the two sticks, concerned with the reunification of Judah and Israel. Chapters 38–39 describe the wars of God and Magog.

e. Chapters 40–48 make up a separate block of visions, a carefully elaborated sketch of the policy of repatriated Israel, including the future organization of religion, the plan of the ideal temple, the laws governing worship within it, the people's religious and social obligations, the division of the country among the tribes and (48:15–35) the detailed plan of a city to be called "The Lord is There".

Style and Characteristics: Ezekiel is the richest in symbolism of all the prophets, and in his visions he achieved a unique blend of realism and fantasy. Thus the completely imaginary vision of the dry bones which are clothed with flesh and brought to life by the word of God (ch. 37) is described in a very realistic, straightforward style. The eating of the scroll (3:1–3) at the very beginning of his mission is a lively metaphor for the way in which he became imbued with prophecy. The choice of such symbols must have made his words extraordinarily vivid to his contemporaries, and their dual character remains a good indication of the nature of Ezekiel. He was at once a prophet — i.e. a poet and an ecstatic — and a priest, a man concerned with the sometimes quite mundane details of the daily exercise of religion. The very contrast between flights of imaginative poetry and the detailed prose descriptions moved some scholars (e.g. Hoelscher) to doubt whether one man could have written the whole of the book. However, the details of specifications and measurements all describe the creations of a highly imaginative architect. Just as the style slips frequently and easily from poetry to prose and back, so there is no real division between realism and fantasy. The boundary lines between the imaginative fantasy and realism are blurred, and the transitions from one to the other, very frequent. A carefully detailed description of the Temple includes the totally fantastic vision of the chariot of God, but even this is phrased in concrete, realistic terms.

Indeed, the whole purpose of Ezekiel's use of images and symbols (very well illustrated by the account of the Temple) is not only to foretell the future, but to help bring that future into being. This mystic character of his symbols is a specific trait which is rare in other classic prophets, as it is found chiefly among the early prophets.

Ezekiel is also distinguished by a relatively large number of allegorical songs. Jerusalem is likened to a vine (15), and a foundling (16); Pharaoh and Nebuchadrezzar are eagles (17); Jehoiachin, the top of the cedar (17); Zedekiah, a willow (17). Chapter 19 is a poetic lament over Israel, symbolized by a lioness and her whelps, while chapter 23 is a long allegory of Israel and Judah as two sisters, Oholah and Oholibah. Chapter 24 contains the song of the pot, while Pharaoh appears as a dragon in chapters 29 and 32. Very many of Ezekiel's metaphors and symbols are of the great and grandiose. He has no time for small-scale similes. Many of his allegories contain echoes of mythology and others are quite erotic, though not vulgar.

Ezekiel was strongly influenced by much of the Torah, especially the priestly sources of Deuteronomy, and expressions and even complete verses can be found quoted in his prophecies. Of the earlier prophets, the strongest influence on him seems to have been his older contemporary, Jeremiah. A number of parallels can be found between the two, e.g.: Jer. 1:13–15 and Ezk. 11:2–11 and 24:3–14; Jer. 23:1–6 and Ezk. 34:1–24; Jer. 31:29–30 and Ezk. 18:2–31; Jer. 31:33–34 and Ezk. 11:19–20 and 36:25–29; Jer. 24 and Ezk. 11:15–21 and 37:1–14. In many of these, Ezekiel has remoulded the original giving it a different sense or meaning.

Oracles and Teachings: Ezekiel was a prophet of the Exile, like those referred to by Jeremiah (chapter 29), who foretold the imminent downfall of Babylonia and a near return from Exile. But unlike them, Ezekiel took the opposite line. He passionately describes the destruction of Jerusalem and the kingdoms bordering on Judah, and holds out hope only for the people within Babylonia, condemning those who remained in Palestine (33:27). For them, not even repentance can avert disaster; only those in exile can look forward to a possible salvation. Certainly he reviles Jerusalem in phrases that cannot be matched in the words of any other prophet.

Theology: Ezekiel's vision of God is different in its phrasing from the intimate, personal God of the classical prophets. He has been likened to the God of the Priestly Code, remote, lofty, the Lord of holiness, law and judgment who is to be approached only with awe and terror. This is apparent from the term He uses for Ezekiel: "Son of Man" – an insignificant mortal addressed by an eternal omnipotence. Even the promise of redemption and deliverance is not prompted by love. God's country and Temple and people have been crushed and His name profaned. In order to restore God's prestige, Israel must be delivered (36:22–23), whether it likes it or not (20:31–38).

The Prophet of the Law: J. Kaufman dubbed Ezekiel the "Prophet of the Law" and this trait is apparent in all his oracles. The sin of the people which he rebukes is a cultic sin. The Sabbath is profaned (Ezekiel follows the Priestly Code — P source, see Biblical Criticism* — in ascribing cosmic sanctity to the Sabbath); sacrifices despised, the purity regulations ignored and idolatrous worship practiced.

Worship, even of God, on the "High Places*" is idolatrous and Ezekiel is even more extreme in this respect than Deuteronomy. He condemns the whole of the priesthood out of hand, with the sole exception of the Zadokites. They alone will be allowed to serve in the future Temple, all other former priests being demoted to mere Levites (see Priests*). He does not stress the classical prophets' preaching that moral living and righteousness is as important to God as the precise observance of the ritual of worship. He is concerned with social or individual morals within the framework of the Covenant.

Priestly Influences: The influence of the Priestly source can be seen in many of Ezekiel's visions. Ezekiel is exclusively concerned with the people of Israel. The future king will reign over a country whose boundaries Ezekiel defines according to Numbers 34, making only a few essential corrections to bring them into line with the geopolitical realities of his time. The people of Israel alone will serve God. Earlier prophets looked forward to the whole world bowing in worship to Israel's God. All Ezekiel foresees is that foreigners will be forced to acknowledge His greatness.

Individual Responsibility: Ezekiel's interpretation of the law of reward and punishment was an important innovation. He saw it as something essentially individual. Man would be judged according to his own deeds (ch. 14) and the just could hope only for their own salvation. His writings do not emphasize collective responsibility, nor the responsibility being carried on between the generations (ch. 18 and especially 33:18–19). Ezekiel is concerned with the revival of the nation through collective action, both in Babylonia and in Palestine. Chapter 33 recapitulates his whole doctrine in greater detail.

It is argued that, in general, the biblical books of the period of the First Temple — except for wisdom literature (see below) — do not allow for individual responsibility and are much more concerned with the group as a whole. National calamities might be caused by the actions of a few sinners, but they were regarded as members of the community and it was accepted that the whole group must suffer. Ezekiel, according to the classical school of biblical criticism*, marks the turning point from corporate responsibility to the idea of individual responsibility, now accepted by both Judaism and Christianity.

By itself, this assertion is an oversimplification. The idea appears in Jeremiah as well as in Ezekiel but, in any case, the Bible never regarded the individual as exclusively a member of the group. Every separate mortal had always been invested with his own moral responsibility and had undergone his own religious experience. Fundamentally, every one of the prophets was an individualist. They all refused to regard themselves as merely fragments of a community, bound to conform to its ways. What was new in Jeremiah and Ezekiel was the much greater emphasis on the individual rather than the group in their teachings. They directed their contemporaries to look into their own hearts and actions for the source of their sorrows. This emphasis on the individual was not a discovery, but it did represent a new trend.

According to J. Kaufman, the concept of individualism underlies all the wisdom literature of Israel and the ancient East. This was the basis of these writers' reflections on the conditions of the world around them. However, although the wisdom writers antedate Jeremiah and Ezekiel, their comments had none of the dynamic impact of the oracles of the prophets. It can be said that whereas before Ezekiel, religion had been the affair of the community rather than the individual, as a result of his activities and doctrine, the individual Jew came into greater prominence.

Future Organization of Religion: Chapters 40–48, the last section of the book, contain Ezekiel's vision and regulations for the future conduct of religion. This is the high point of his prophecy. He foresees the restored community centering around the carefully regulated worship of the rebuilt Temple, served by a purified priesthood and following exactly every detail of the ritual of sacrifice. Ezekiel recalls the corruptions that had so offended against the pure Yahwism of the earlier prophets and prescribes for a Temple freed from all such impurity. It has been argued that his very concern for purity and exact observance in the future temple and its worship is evidence of the rigidity of Ezekiel's spirit. Against this, it can also be said that in view of the gross laxity which had grown up in pre-Exilic observances, there was some case for taking strict precautions against its recurrence.

The commands which Ezekiel lays down in this section establish him as the only lawgiver since Moses and Samuel. His rules are based on the laws of the Priestly Code but because they differ in one or two particulars, the later rabbis* were reluctant to include the book of Ezekiel in the canon of the Old Testament (see Bible Canon and Text*) on the grounds that it contradicted the Torah. There have also been disagreements among modern scholars as to their authorship. J. Wellhausen and his school dubbed Ezekiel, on the strength of this scroll, the "father of normative Judaism" for it was believed that the Priestly Code which embodies the cultic theocracy of the Second Temple as decreed by Ezekiel, was composed after his time. Other scholars reject this placing of Ezekiel between D and P (see Biblical Criticism*) and maintain that all the principal points of the Torah came before the classical prophets and, certainly, well before Ezekiel (see Date and Authorship, below).

The Problem of Ezekiel: At the end of the 19th c., scholars began to raise doubts concerning the date of the prophecy of Ezekiel, the uniformity of the book and the time at which it was composed. During the last two generations scholars have paid a good deal of attention to the author of the book and the time and place at which it was thought he wrote it.

Date and Authorship: As mentioned above, the book claims a date for itself in the 6th c. BCE, but many scholars have questioned whether a prophet of that time would have concerned himself, among other things, with the sins of Menasseh's reign, some half-century earlier. While some scholars would allow at least part of the book to have been written by a 6th c. BCE Ezekiel, others date the composition of the work to the Hellenistic or Maccabaean period. There is also a school of thought which places Ezekiel in Palestine rather than among the Exiles.

Until the present century, scholars assumed that almost all the book had been written by Ezekiel (chs. 1–39), though assigning later chapters, or alternatively, isolated fragments, to later editors (except chs. 38–39). Some modern scholars accept this view. Major difficulties arise, however. First, there are numerous duplications and repetitions in many parts of the book which seem to be the work of a later editor rather than Ezekiel as editor (cf. 3:16–21 and 33:7–9; 7:2–4 and 7:5–9; 43:1–12 and 44:1–8, etc.). Second, the prophecies of the first part of the book addressed to the rebellious house of David and the idolatrous Judeans show that he was precisely informed about Jerusalem and Judea, which seems unlikely if he were so far away. On the other hand, the opening verses imply that the prophet was in Babylonia for most of his prophetic life. It is argued that the symbolic acts of removal into exile could only be performed before an audience of the very people concerned in Judea, as otherwise another audience in Babylonia would miss their point. Many scholars get the impression from this early period that the prophet was actually in Jerusalem before 586 BCE for a short time, and that thereafter his prophetic work was carried out in Babylonia.

All these points have been answered by other scholars. According to some, the use of the terms "House of Israel" or "Watchman for the house of Israel" (3:16–21), where the prophet sees himself in this role, apply equally to the Jews in Palestine or in Exile. Indeed, the word "Israel" denoting the people in general, appears 169 times in the book against 13 mentions of "Judah". Many prophets — Micah, Amos, Jeremiah, Isaiah and others — uttered oracles about peoples and places and Jeremiah provides evidence that the prophets of Babylonia were known in Judah. Finally, the Jews in Exile were very conscious of their membership of the "People of Israel", and they looked forward with longing to the return to Israel. The "Elders of Israel" could indeed have provided the prophet with an audience in Tel-Abib in northwestern Mesopotamia where he lived as a recognized leader, for the Jews' nobility and leaders had been exiled with Jehoiachin. News of events in Jerusalem travelled to Babylonia, just as Jeremiah in Jerusalem was advised of happenings and conditions in Babylonia. There is much evidence of an intimate, mundane contact with Babylonia. Ezekiel speaks of "a brick dug in the wall", for instance, which was relevant to Babylonia, whereas W.F. Albright is of the opinion that houses in Palestine at that time were built of stone. Moreover, Ezekiel is far from indifferent to the Exile. His clear scheme of dating all runs, "the . . . year of our captivity", and passages such as 7:21; 12:13; 23:25 or 28:7 all bespeak his personal experience of exile.

In some cases, the material of the book dates itself. The fact that Babylonia appears as the contemporary world empire and Assyria belongs to the past means that the prophecies cannot possibly have been written before 614 BCE, three decades before the Exile. Moreover, Ezekiel never refers directly to Menasseh (698–642 BCE) whereas had he lived during that king's reign, he would without doubt have been persecuted by the court and royal officials — just as Jeremiah suffered at the hands of Zedekiah who was a paragon of virtue by comparison with his predecessor. The three kings mentioned by Ezekiel were: Jehoahaz exiled in Egypt; Jehoiachin, exiled to Babylonia; and Zedekiah, who broke a covenant.

On the other hand, there is no mention of Persia*, the Restoration* or the Hellenistic* age. Ezekiel uses a style that is influenced by Aramaic, but this is the diplomatic Aramaic familiar in Palestine for years before the Exile. The differences in his Hebrew, compared to that of Isaiah, can all be explained by the natural development of the language. Finally, the reconstruction of the eastern gate of the Temple in his vision shows that Ezekiel knew the Temple of Solomon before its destruction. His prophecies all fit the reign of Nebuchadrezzar, but not before that time nor after it, comprising possibly a short period before the Exile and the end of his active life in Babylonia. The opinion of scholars today is, accordingly, that the dates given in the book are authentic and set the prophecies against their appropriate background, affirming the tradition that saw the Book of Ezekiel as the work of the prophet himself, although, clearly, the material has come down to the present day through a process of pre-literary editing and arrangement.

The Influence of Ezekiel: This is something even more far-reaching than his contribution to the new emphasis on individual responsibility for one's actions. More than this, Ezekiel's vision of the future organization and regulation of religion (chs. 40–48) was a major contribution to the preservation of the Jews' hopes and religious aspirations during the dark days of the Exile. The faith that became the centre of the life of the restored nation was essentially the religion of Ezekiel and his disciples.

In addition, Ezekiel's vision of God's chariot and throne "influenced", in J. Kaufman's view, "the apocalyptic visionaries; and the Aggadists of rabbinical* literature extended it to describe the transcendent worlds which, in turn, the mystics covered with a cloak of secrecy. Christian theology found in it Christian allusions. Ezekiel influenced Christian art." His prophecy had a great influence on the foundation of the later angelology* (chs. 9–10) and in his teachings the basic idea of Israelite demonology and evil spirits was first formulated. In addition, he was the first to make explicit the idea of the kingdom of heaven.

Apocalyptic Prophecy: Ezekiel's prophecy is not itself apocalyptic for he does not pretend to reveal the secrets of the heavens nor is he concerned with problems of the end of the Age (Messianic Age). Nevertheless his book became a model of descriptive apocalypse. His vision of the invasion and defeat of Gog from the land of Magog has no parallel in the Bible. The enemy, Gog, attacks Israel, not as the rod of God's anger, but out of a spontaneous lust for violence. His punishment and the final overthrow of the enemies of Israel is a means of glorifying the name of God. Ezekiel drew on previous prophets for many of the elements of this vision but, from them, he created something unique which had an immense influence on apocalyptic literature and rabbinical Aggadah. Much of it, however, became distorted. For instance, one of the most striking features of Ezekiel's vision is that war followed the restoration to the land, but preceded the final victory (i.e. deliverance), and fulfillment of the Kingdom. The impact of Ezekiel can also be seen in many passages of the New Testament, for instance: God as the good shepherd of his flock (Ezk. 34:16; Mt. 18:12–14; Lk. 39:10), or the ideas of cleansing and changing the heart (Ezk. 11:19 and II Cor. 3:3).

EZRA, BOOK OF (see Restoration).

F

FAMILY, THE. — *Outline: I. The Family in Evolution: Family Responsibilities; The Post-Exilic Family. II. Marriage: Monogamy and Polygamy; Pre-Exilic Israel; Post-Exilic Times; Choosing the Bride; Marriage Formalities; "Mohar" — the Price of a Wife; Post-Exilic Customs; Ceremonies; Post-Exilic and Rabbinic Ceremonies; Wedding Gifts; Marriage Settlement and Dowry; Repudiation and Divorce; The Levirate; Bars to Marriage: Forbidden Degrees; Rabbinical Laws; Racially Mixed Marriages. III. Position of Women: Virgins; Married Women; Adultery; The New Testament; Widows. IV. Children: Childbirth; Naming the Child; Adoption. V. Succession and Inheritance: Post-Exilic and Rabbinic Law.*

I. THE FAMILY IN EVOLUTION. By historical times, the family in the Near East was patriarchal in character and organization. Descent was traced through the father only, and the "bet-ab" — house of the father — comprised the whole family, father, sons and sons' wives and children. The centre of gravity was the father — the authority, provider and protector of his wives and children. In 2nd mill. Assyria, Syria and Palestine, the father had almost unlimited authority over his children, although his power became increasingly restricted by the stronger state structure of the 3rd dynasty of Ur or the Hammurabi dynasty in Babylon (see Babylonia*).

The purpose of marriage was fundamentally to continue the family by begetting legitimate children (see Part III below). Love and sexual pleasure were subordinated to this overriding aim. Thus a woman's noblest role was in producing offspring — preferably male (**428**). While the father represented power, judgment and authority, the mother personified love, loyalty, devotion and humility. In the Bible, nevertheless, the mother shared in the authority of the father over their children.

The Israelite family included not only those united by blood and dwelling place, but also servants and resident aliens ("gerîm"). A family could thus be a very numerous group, making it in a sense the same as a clan, the "mishpaḥah". Members of the clan had common interests and duties and were very conscious of the bonds which united them. The family was also a religious unit. Passover, for instance, was a family festival.

The Bible contains evidence of a certain evolution in the institutions of the family from Patriarchal times (book of Genesis) to the periods of Conquest and settlement (embodied in the other books of the Pentateuch of later composition) and the monarchy, but it is not easy to determine the pattern of that development. The Bible reflects the different practices of different periods but it is difficult to judge the development of the rules in relation to actual practice.

During the period of the Patriarchs, for instance, the family's structure is mentioned almost casually. Abraham's wife was his half sister (his father's daughter by a different

428

mother). The Law of Moses prohibited such marriages (Lv. 18:9, 11; 20:17; Dt. 27:22), although as late as David's reign the evidence suggests that they were still accepted (II Sam. 13:13). The Law of Moses also forbids the marriage of two sisters to the same man (Lv. 18:18) which was the case in Jacob's marriage to Leah and Rachel (see Marriage, below).

Many of the institutions of patriarchal times which disappeared later have become better understood in the light of newly discovered extra-biblical evidence, particularly by comparison with conditions in Mesopotamia.

Family Responsibilities: Relations between brothers were of fundamental importance in the Israelite family. They had a decisive influence on the law of Moses and therefore on the whole of Israel's social order. In this sense, "brother" was used to mean all the members of a family (or even tribe), each one of whom had an obligation to give help and protection to the others when needed. The "go'el", meaning a protector or "redeemer", was a close relative who would redeem his "brother" from slavery, buy patrimony sold under necessity, bury his recently deceased brother or sister (Lv. 21:2; Nu. 6:7; Ezk. 44:25) or (as in the case of Ruth) under the law of levirate, redeem the property of a brother who had died childless and, in addition, marry the widow (Ruth 3:12; 4:3). The gravest duty was the ancient tribal obligation of blood vengeance for a murdered brother (II Sam. 3:27; 14:11). The same term was extended to the relationship of God to his people. Yahweh was seen as the "go'el" of his people, i.e., He was the nearest kinsman with the appropriate responsibility to act as their saviour or "redeemer".

These very close family ties and responsibilities belonged essentially to the tribal organization of the early period of Israel's history. Settlement and urban life naturally affected them, although the outward forms were maintained. When crafts began to be widely practiced, the guilds of artisans were ruled by a "father", suggesting actual or implied family ties. Although family ties naturally developed among the people in the towns, whatever may have been the original basis for their grouping, town life meant the end of the many-generation patriarchal family. Excavation has revealed that, apart from the very earliest towns, small houses became the fashion. A son "built a house" upon his marriage (see Cities, Israelite*). Long before the 8th c. BCE, the tribal form of society had been transformed into one of king and subjects, employers and workmen, rich and poor. The authority once exercised by the head of the clan had passed to the elders of the town with the possibility of an appeal to the king. The development laid a greater emphasis on individual — as opposed to group — responsibility. The two were interrelated and they always existed side by side. The basis of all Mosaic Law is the idea of an individual's responsibility for his own actions and this held good from the very earliest times. However, a lessening in the significance of group responsibility can be seen, to take one example, in the way that, quite early on in Israel's history, blood vengeance was replaced by the processes of legislation and justice (see Government and Authority*).

The Post-Exilic Family: Although the family underwent a number of changes following the Exile* and Restoration*, in essence it remained oriental and patriarchal, subject to the authority — albeit limited — of the father. There are many examples of the appropriate philosophy in wisdom literature, e.g. Ben Sira's attitude to the father's supremacy (Ecclus. 22, 33, 36) or his rigid attitude towards women and marriage (chs. 23, 25, 26). On the other hand, the theme of the apocryphal Book of Tobit (see Apocrypha*) is filial piety, and the Talmud lays repeated emphasis on the biblical injunction to honour one's parents. Whereas in Old Testament times, society was generally polygamous, in the post-Exilic period, monogamy was the rule. This situation is reflected in Talmudic literature, which gives an idealization of the family in the modern sense, stressing the father's responsibility to educate his sons and train them in some useful trade.

It may be said that while anthropological researches have revealed wide resemblances between Hebrew traditions and the customs of other Near Eastern peoples with regard to betrothal, mohar (the price of a wife, see below, Formalities), dowry and divorce (see below), they have also demonstrated the comparatively high standards of Old Testament and post-Exilic sexual morality.

The forms which this general development took in relation to the main family institutions are described below:

II. MARRIAGE. **Monogamy and Polygamy:** In Babylon, on the evidence of the Code of Hammurabi, the family was basically a monogamous unit, whereas the Assyrians were polygamous. In Patriarchal times, Canaanite families were polygamous and so were Hebrew families, although certain qualifications are necessary; at any given time, most of the people were probably monogamous and it seems that the average Israelite family was also monogamous. The reason may be one of simple economics and practical convenience. A modern Arab fellah or bedouin, although also allowed a number of wives by his religion, generally has only one. Apart from kings or the earlier Judges who made many marriages, often from political motives (Dt. 21:15–17; I K. 11:1; passim), the average Israelite polygamous family appears to have included only two wives, one of whom was probably a barren woman. In general a man appears to have married a second wife only when his first proved unable to bear him children (Mal. 2:15), although affluence may have been another reason. This is certainly true of the Patriarchs who presumably followed the customs of their times. Abraham had only one wife, Sarah, who, because she could not bear children, gave Abraham her servant, Hagar, as a concubine. Rachel and Leah did the same when they gave their "handmaids", Bilhah and Zilpah, to Jacob.

This custom was known in Mesopotamia. The Code of Hammurabi (ca. 1700 BCE) allows a second wife to a man whose first wife is barren, or permits the barren wife to give her husband a concubine, whose status remains lower than that of the mistress of the house. The Nuzi laws (15th c. BCE) apparently obliged a barren woman to give her husband a concubine by whom he might beget children.

The Bible stories relating to family life and structure, notably that of Abraham, become much clearer in the light of similar analogies from contemporary (2nd mill. BCE) Near Eastern sources. Abraham's union with Hagar (although not called a marriage in the Bible) was drafted exactly in accordance with clause 145 of the Code of Hammurabi. The next clause (146) gives the wife the right to punish the handmaid in circumstances similar to those described in Gn. 16. The Code (clauses 168–171) also defines the right of inheritance of the sons of wife and handmaid, which appear to be demonstrated in the experience of Isaac and Ishmael (see Inheritance, below).

In much the same way, the friction between Jacob and his two wives on the one hand, and Laban, their father, on the other, was based on explicit legal provisions in force in the first half of the 2nd mill. BCE (see Patriarchs*; Law*).

Pre-Exilic Israel: Apart from Abraham and Jacob, other biblical examples of men with more than one wife include Elkanah, Samuel's father (I Sam. 1:1–2) whose first wife was also childless; Esau who took three wives (Gn. 36:1–5) from Aramean or Edomite families, and, of course, David and Solomon. Deuteronomy (21:15–17) also provides for a man with two wives of equal status. In general, however, the general pattern in the books of Samuel and Kings is of a monogamous family, and this is continued in the prophets, Wisdom literature and the Apocrypha. The passage in praise of the housewife (Pr. 31) certainly implies that a man needs but one such jewel.

Post-Exilic Times: Although there is no direct information about the period of the Second Temple, it appears from the Apocrypha that the family then, too, was generally monogamous although not without exception. Ben Sira (Ecclus., see Apocrypha*) usually speaks of one wife (26:1–4, 14–16) although once he mentions a rival wife. The conflict between monogamy and polygamy continued throughout the period of the Mishnah* and Talmud, the position among the Jews reflecting the customs of their neighbours. Alexander Jannaeus (see Hasmoneans*) had three wives, and Herod, according to Josephus (Antiq. 17:1, 3) had nine wives at the same time. The early Christians reproached the Jews for their polygamy and it is evident from the Talmud that there were good grounds for the accusation. The practice was not forbidden among the Jews until the time of Rabbi Gershom (ca. 1000 CE) and it continued beyond that time among Jews living in Mohammedan countries.

The discussions of the sages of the Mishnah make it clear that concubinage existed in the time of the Second Temple. Rabbi Meir claims that a concubine had no marriage contract (ketubah) while, according to Rabbi Judah, she was granted a contract but acquired a lower status than that of a regular wife. The Talmud lays it down that a concubine has no betrothal but is "taken" for matrimonial life. Concubinage was known among the Jews in Spain during the early Middle Ages but, from the words of Maimonides, it appears that it died out eventually.

Choosing the Bride: There is no definite information in the Bible about the age at which girls were married, but it seems certain that both girls and boys married very young. Judging from the dates of their accession given by the books of Kings, it appears that Jehoiachin married at 16, Amon and Josiah at 17 (see Israel and Judah*). Later, the rabbis fixed the minimum age for marriage as 12 for girls and 13 for boys. Under such circumstances, it is not surprising that the parents took all the decisions, often without consulting the girl. Nevertheless, cases of love-marriages are recorded and, in early times, the girls were much less confined than later, when they were veiled and forced into seclusion (see Bars to Marriage, below).

Marriage Formalities: In the ancient Near East, marriage was a civil matter, not requiring religious sanction. Thus, in Israel as in Mesopotamia, the marriage deed "nissu'în" was a legal contract defining the rights of the parties concerned. For the Israelites it was a covenant or "b^{e}rîth" (Mal. 2:14) although it is not known whether this was a written document. In Mesopotamia, a written contract was required by the Code of Hammurabi and written contracts were also customary in the Jewish military colony of Elephantine in 5th c. BCE Egypt, many of them having been preserved and since discovered. In pre-Mishnaic Jewish literature, the only reference to a written marriage contract occurs in the apocryphal book of Tobit (7:13, see Apocrypha*).

The Elephantine marriage contracts record the formula which the bridegroom uttered at the time of the marriage, "She is my wife and I am her husband from this day forever." That a similar formula was used in early Israel is suggested by the formula of divorce contained in Hos. 2:2, and also by the statement made to the bridegroom by the bride's father in the Tobit story, "You are her relative, and she belongs to you." (Tobit 7:12). A marriage contract from the 2nd c. CE from the caves of the wilderness of Judea also contains the formula, "You will be my wife", which is close to the old formula pronounced by the bridegroom.

Since early times, there have been two stages to a Jewish marriage: betrothal and then marriage. The betrothal "erusîn" is a legally binding promise of marriage. According to Dt. 20:7, a man who was betrothed but not yet married was exempt from military service. Dt. 22:23–27 regards a betrothed woman as though she were already married. Consequently, a man who violates her shall be stoned to death (like an adulterer) and she shall share his fate if the rape took place within a city, and by failing to call for aid she appears to have acquiesced to the rape.

"Mohar" — the Price of a Wife: Before the wedding, the bridegroom usually made the bride's father a present, either of a sum of money, the "mohar", or its equivalent value in kind. Jacob paid with work (Gn. 29:15–30), David executed a difficult assignment (I Sam. 18:25–27) and Othniel won his wife by capturing Debir (Kiriath-Sepher; Jud. 1:12). The actual word "mohar" occurs only three times in the Bible (Gn. 34:12; Ex. 22:16; I Sam. 18:25). It is not a fixed sum, but depends on the social standing and wealth of the parties concerned and the wish of the girl's father. The practice of a mohar continues among the modern Arabs of Palestine, its actual level fixed by the same factors, and also by whether the girl is marrying a member of her own clan or village, or someone from outside. The mohar in any case is a compensation to the father for the loss of his daughter as well as the means of providing her with certain necessities. It was something more than the bride price or "tirḫatu" which, in Mesopotamia, represented a crude system of bride-purchase. In Babylon, this was a sum varying from one to fifty silver shekels which continued to belong to the girl. The father was entitled to the interest or other income on it for life, but he was not allowed to touch the principal (cf. the complaint of Rachel and Leah that their father "has been using up the money given for us"; Gn. 31:15). If widowed, the original capital was the property of the woman and after she had died, it belonged to her children. Assyrian law provided for the "tirḥatu" to be paid to the girl herself and even among modern Arabs, the "bride-price" is expected to be used to equip the girl for her life with her husband. The fundamental purpose of the biblical mohar seems to have been to insure the woman against being left unsupported if widowed.

Post-Exilic Customs: The papyri of Elephantine show that the mohar was considered the property of the woman, although it was given to her father. In the period of the Second Temple, the mohar was replaced by the sum registered in the ketubah (marriage contract, see below), i.e. 50 silver shekels for a virgin and half that for a widow, again intended to provide for the bride if she were widowed or divorced.

Ceremonies: The rabbis continued the distinction between the two stages of a marriage: "erusîm" or "kiddushîm", i.e. betrothal (or purchase) and "ḥupah" (the word means "canopy") which represented the actual ceremony of bringing home the bride.

1. **"Kiddushin":** According to the law, the bride might be bought (or betrothed) either by money, by writ (a brief contract) or by cohabitation. Betrothal by contract was suspended before the Middle Ages and is now almost unknown. In the case of betrothal by cohabitation, the man and woman entered a private chamber, having first declared to witnesses that their actions would count as a betrothal. The teachers of New Testament times disapproved of this manner of betrothal because it was licentious (see Mishnah* and Talmud*). This left betrothal by money. Like the sum or mohar given to her father, this was not intended to represent the value of the woman, but was the sum by which she agreed to the betrothal — it could be a coin of almost no value. However, because of the apparent association between betrothal by money and purchasing a bride, the actual money was replaced by an object. According to the Mishnah*, betrothal could be by a piece of money, by a gift, or by handing over a written promise of marriage in the presence of two witnesses. In the early Middle Ages, betrothal by a ring was introduced into Palestine and this has remained the custom ever since.

At the time of the Restoration* after the Exile and thereafter, the betrothed girl was expected to go on living as a virgin in her father's house for a period, generally twelve months. During and after the persecutions of Antiochus Epiphanes (see Hasmoneans*) the requirement of chastity was relaxed and the girl was permitted sexual relations with her future husband. Mesopotamian and Hittite laws also allowed either party to withdraw from betrothal, although a fine was imposed on the one who did so.

2. **The Wedding:** The actual ceremony was celebrated with much rejoicing. Though very few details are mentioned explicitly, it is possible to reconstruct a probable image.

The central event of the ceremony was the entry of the bride into the house of the groom. Before this, she stayed in her father's house. With a crown on his head (Song 3:11; Is. 61:10) and accompanied by a party of friends (Jud. 14:11) escorting him with songs and rejoicing (I Mac. 9:39), the bridegroom would come to claim his bride. The bride was dressed in the best of her clothes and jewellery (Ps. 45:14–15; Is. 61:10). (Some idea of the range and beauty of these ornaments may be gained from these illustrations **429**.) Her face was covered with a veil (Song 4:1, 3; 6:7) which

429

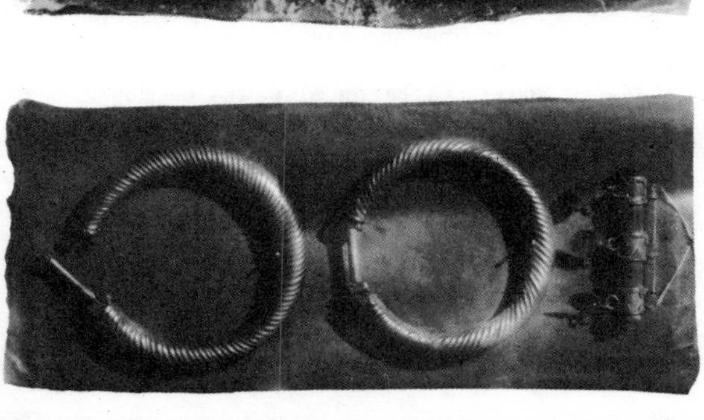

she removed only in the bridal chamber. Thus Laban was able to substitute Leah for Rachel (cf. also Gn. 24:65). The bride was then taken to her new home, in the company of her friends, with "joy and gladness" (Ps. 45:14–15) in a procession such as can still be seen among the Arabs of Palestine today. Presumably, wedding songs were sung on these occasions (Jer. 16:9), although scholars are still disagreed about how far the canticles of the Song of Songs can justly be compared to Arab wedding songs (see Song of Songs*). The wedding was the occasion for a big feast which generally continued for seven days (Gn. 29:22–27; Jud. 14:10, 12; Tobit 7:14), usually at the house of the bride (Jud. 14:10 ff) but, judging from Mt. 22:?, apparently sometimes at the bridegroom's parents' house. The story of Samson tells something about the amusements of the guests at such a feast although this, of course, was a feast made by the Philistines.

After the wedding night (Gn. 29:23) it was customary for the bride's parents to preserve the blood-stained sheet as proof of the girl's virginity (Dt. 22:13–21), a custom observed to this day in some Mohammedan countries.

Post-Exilic and Rabbinic Ceremonies: The Canopy ("ḥupah") became the modern ceremony representing the essential action of bringing the bride to the home of her groom. At first the "ḥupah" was the room assigned to the couple. Within it, the seven day's feast would be held, the bridal pair sitting beneath the canopy. At the time of the Second Temple, the canopy was made of sheets painted with crescents of gold and it was customary for the bride to be taken from her father's house to that of her husband beneath the canopy, the guests dancing before her and singing songs in her praise. After the destruction of the Temple, this form of decoration was abandoned and the procession was suspended until renewed for a period under Rabbi Judah Hanasi. It is not known when it was finally discontinued.

At the end of the period of the Second Temple and thereafter, it was customary for the wedding of a virgin to be held on a Wednesday so that if the husband found an absence of the tokens of virginity he could bring the case to court on Thursday. If the bride was no virgin but a widow or divorcee, she would be married on Thursday so that she and her husband could enjoy an uninterrupted two days until Sabbath.

From the New Testament it does not appear that the early Christians' view of marriage differed in any essential way from the prevailing Jewish concept that marriage was the proper state for a man. Jesus confirmed monogamy as God's original intention for man (Mt. 19:6; Mk. 10:6–8). Due to the eschatological expectations in the New Testament, both Jesus and Paul emphasize that in the "last days" it is better to be unmarried. The Essenes also held this view (see Jesus*; Paul*; Dead Sea Scrolls*).

Wedding Gifts: In addition to the mohar (see above), it was expected that the groom or his family would give additional gifts to the bride and her family, the two being clearly distinguished. Thus Shechem could plead with Jacob, "Ask me ever so much as marriage present and gift" (Gn. 34:12). These gifts were in the nature of thank-offerings to the family for their agreement to the marriage (cf. Gn. 24:53, recording the gifts of Abraham's servant to Rebekah's parents after their consent to her marriage to Isaac). The Code of Hammurabi provided for gifts from the groom to the bride's parents and added that if they prevented the marriage or annulled the agreement, the gifts had to be returned two-fold. Presumably a similar custom obtained in Israel.

Marriage Settlement and Dowry: Babylonian law required the bride's parents to make their daughter a wedding gift or settlement which remained her property, although the husband received the interest of income on it and was entitled to invest it in business. If widowed or divorced through no fault of her own, however, the capital reverted to the wife. Assyrian law included similar provisions. Whether there was also a dowry — i.e. a contribution on the part of the bride — in addition to the mohar paid by the bridegroom in biblical times, is less certain. It seems difficult to reconcile both customs, although post-biblical literature refers to the existence of a dowry at that time and it seems reasonable to suppose that the custom existed in biblical times. No specific details are given although there are a number of passages in the Bible which apparently relate to dowries. Pharaoh gave his daughter the city of Gezer as a marriage settlement when she married Solomon (I K. 9:16) and Rebekah (Gn. 24:59), Leah (29:24) and Rachel (29:29) were each given a handmaid as a wedding gift from their parents. In general the custom of giving a dowry never took root in Palestine proper until late Second Temple days.

At the time of the Mishnah and Talmud, the gifts the bride brought with her from her parents began to be known as a "nedûniah" or dowry. The sum involved was registered in the "ketubah" (marriage contract). If it was money, which the husband proposed to invest in business, he promised to repay his wife (if the occasion arose) the full amount plus one-third interest. If it consisted of clothing and household goods, their value was registered but the husband was only committed to repayment of the value less one-fifth, to allow for depreciation.

Repudiation and Divorce: Biblical data about divorce are very scanty and general. A man may divorce his wife "if she finds no favour in his eyes because he has found some indecency in her" (Dt. 24:1). Just exactly what is meant by "indecency" (the older translations made "unseemly thing" of the Hebrew "erwath debar") is never made clear. In view of verse 3 dealing with the dissolution of a second union, "and the latter husband dislikes her", it seems that the husband could divorce his wife on the slightest excuse.

Because the biblical phrase was so vague, the Rabbis* discussed its meaning minutely and at length. The more liberal school of Hillel would accept any excuse, however trivial — even that the husband preferred another woman. The much more rigorous school of Shammai (see Pharisees*) admitted only adultery or misconduct as grounds for divorce. In Old Testament days, divorce was an exclusively male privilege. Only in two cases was a man forbidden to divorce his wife: if he had accused her of not being a virgin when married, and had then been proved a liar (Dt. 22:13–19) or if a man was forced by law to wed a girl he had raped (22:28–29). Apart from these two cases, a man was free to divorce as he wished.

Different stages can be traced in the development of divorce as an institution. Originally it was quite informal and consisted essentially in removing the wife from her husband's house. Later on, formalities had to be observed and expulsion alone did not dissolve the marriage. Ultimately, the formalities crystallized into the writing of a bill of divorce and handing it to the divorced wife (Heb: tzenu'ah).

The actual formalities and the regulations governing divorce are not specified in the Pentateuch or other Old Testament books, but they may be inferred from some passages. Hosea (2:2) uses a phrase "she is not my wife neither am I her husband", which is the exact counterpart of the wedding formula "She is my wife and I am her husband" (see above). Similar formulas were found in Mesopotamia. The divorce or "gêt" was confirmed in a "bill of divorce" (sepher kritût) which cut the matrimonial bonds between the two and, given to the woman, gave her the right to remarry (Dt. 24:1–3; Is. 50:1; Jer. 3:8). Beyond this, the Bible only contains the express prohibition on remarrying a divorced wife after she had remarried and subsequently been divorced or widowed (Dt. 24:3–4), and even this was modified in time. Hosea's double marriage — if, according to a certain interpretation, he did take back the wife he had divorced — was not forbidden by this law (Hos. 2:19); later Judaism found such an action praiseworthy. A bill of divorce from the beginning of the 2nd c. CE was found in one of the caves of the desert of Judea. In the period of the Old Testament, a woman could not divorce. Only later on and in response to foreign influence did divorce become possible for a woman. In Elephantine, a woman was entitled to divorce her husband (and the possibility is mentioned in Mk. 10:12), again after centuries of foreign contacts.

The Code of Hammurabi allowed a woman to sue for divorce from her husband and, if she could convince the court that he had sinned against her, the divorce would be granted. No such provision existed in Assyrian law, although there (and in the Jewish colony at Elephantine) it was customary for a divorced woman to receive compensation. It is not known whether this was also the rule in Israel. At least she took with her the property she had brought with her on her marriage (see Settlement and Dowry above).

Although divorce was a legal and socially acceptable act, it carried a moral stigma. Malachi preached that divorce was hateful to God since marriage had made the two partners one (see Malachi*). Wisdom* literature praises marital fidelity very highly (Pr. 5:15–19; Ecc. 9:9), and among the Christians, divorce was forbidden altogether (Mt. 5:31–32; 19:9, passim). Jesus taught that the Old Testament permission for divorce was a concession to man's frailty, but he too allowed it for "unchastity" (Mt. 19:9). This exception does not occur in the synoptic parallels (Mk. 10:11–12; Lk. 16:18), although Paul appears to extend it to Christians married to unbelievers who desired a separation (I Co. 7:15). Some authorities maintain that the passage in Matthew was an editorial addition made under pressure of necessity when it was found too difficult to enforce the absolute rule against divorce. The contradiction in the New Testament passages resulted in different interpretations within Christian belief. Some Christians take the strict view that a marriage made before God cannot be revoked, while other churches interpret the text to allow for divorce.

The Levirate: The levirate is one of the ancient customs of Israel, observed to this day among certain communities. It was a commonplace among the peoples of the ancient Near East, known to Assyrian law, to the Hurrians of Nuzi and in Ugarit, and it is mentioned in Hittite law, traces of whose particular obligations on the father-in-law have survived (see below).

Mosaic Law (Dt. 25:5–10) prescribes that when brothers live together and one dies leaving a wife but no children, the widow must marry one of the surviving brothers ("yabôm") and the first son of this union is to be regarded as the son of the dead brother. The measure is designed to avoid the name of the dead brother being "blotted out of Israel" (Dt. 25:6) and "in order to restore the name of the dead to his inheritance" (Ruth 4:5). In fact, it was a way of keeping a family property intact (see Landholding*), clearly expressed in the story of Ruth*, where Boaz undertakes the duty of the levirate (brother-in-law) towards Ruth herself and also acts as the "go'el" (redeemer) of her dead husband's estate.

A careful reading of the texts suggests that the custom went through the familiar process of development before being finally written down in Deuteronomy. At first the obligation of the levirate was binding on the entire family of the dead husband. If, for some reason, the brother did not marry his sister-in-law — and he had no legal right to avoid the obligation — then the duty devolved upon the widow's father-in-law. This early custom is the theme of the story of Judah and Tamar (Gn. 38) in which the widowed Tamar tricked her father-in-law into fathering a son through her, when he delayed her marriage to his surviving son. By the time of the Code of Deuteronomy, the obligation of the levirate was limited to the brothers only, and moreover, to brothers living together. It is not entirely certain what was meant by "brothers who dwell together" (Dt. 25:5). One traditional interpretation is that the obligation is binding only on brothers who live on the family estate, another that it does not apply to brothers born after the death of the widow's husband. At the time of the Judah and Tamar story, the brother clearly had no means of avoiding the obligation (Tamar's brother-in-law spilled his seed on the ground so as to avoid "raising up children" to his brother). However, Deuteronomy provides a formula by which he may refuse it — albeit to his own disgrace. The ceremony of the "ḥalitzah" (Dt. 25:7–10) begins with the complaint of the widow to the elders of the city who then try to persuade the brother-in-law to fulfil his duty. If he continues to refuse, the widow shall spit in his face and pull his sandal off his foot and he shall thereafter be known as "him that had his sandal pulled off". According to Ruth* (4:7), a different custom may have included the possibility of the widow's buying her late husband's property from the brother-in-law by drawing off the shoe. Apart from a few oriental Jewish communities, modern Judaism has reduced the custom of the levirate to this ceremony of the "ḥalitzah". Levirate marriage even came to be forbidden among some groups.

The book of Ruth* seems at first glance to describe a case of levirate, for Boaz, as a kinsman of Ruth, sees himself obliged to marry Ruth. In fact, however, this is not really a case of levirate but of redemption of a dead kinsman's property (see Property*). The writer was careful to make the distinction between redemption (4:4, 6) and purchase (4:4, 5 and elsewhere). Nevertheless, the child born of the marriage would be the heir of the dead husband, so this was a form of levirate. He would also be the heir of his real father, which fits the purpose of preserving and consolidating a family property.

Bars to Marriage: Forbidden Degrees: It was accepted custom in early Israel that a man should marry within his own clan. Thus Abraham sent his servant to bring a wife for Isaac from among their kin in Mesopotamia (Gn. 24:4) and Isaac later sent Jacob on a similar errand (Gn. 28:2). When approached, Laban declared that he preferred to give his daughters to Jacob rather than to a stranger (Gn. 29:19). Samson's father had a parallel objection to Samson's desire to marry a Philistine (Jud. 14:3).

Long after the tribal framework of Israel's life had been broken up, marriage within the same family continued to be considered ideal (e.g. Tobit 4:12), and the rabbis declared that it was worthy for a man to marry the daughter of his brother or his sister (Yebamoth 62a; Sanhedrin 76a). Such a union is not included among the prohibited degrees of marriage. Cousin marriages were common in Israel during biblical times and continue to be preferred among present-day Palestinian Arabs. In addition, the Bible reports other consanguinous marriages, e.g. Abraham and his half-sister, Sarah (Gn. 20:12) or the story of Amnon and Tamar (II Sam. 13:13), but all these belong to the early period. Later on, in the Priestly Code (Lv. 18:11; 20:17) they were forbidden.

The Law of Moses (Lv. 18:12–13; 20:19) also prohibited marriage between a man and his aunt (sister of his mother or father) as in the case of Amram and Jochebed (Ex. 6:20; Nu. 26:59). Marriage was also forbidden between a father and daughter or mother and son (Lv. 18:7); a man and his granddaughter (Lv. 18:10); a brother and sister (Lv. 18:9; Dt. 27:22). Marriage to relatives by marriage was also forbidden, i.e. a man could not marry his father's wife (Lv. 18:8), nor a woman her son-in-law (Lv. 20:14; Dt. 27:23). A man could not marry his daughter-in-law (Lv. 18:15; 20:12); his stepdaughter or his step-granddaughter (Lv. 18:17); his uncle's wife (Lv. 18:14; 20:20); or his sister-in-law (Lv. 18:16; 20:21; but see Levirate above). Marriage to two sisters simultaneously was also forbidden (Lv. 18:18) but the reason here was that they should not become rivals to each other while they were alive. Unlike the other prohibitions which were constant, this one was waived after the death of the wife. Her husband might then marry her sister.

The attitude of the Essenes and the sectaries of Qumran towards marriage revealed in the Dead Sea Scrolls*, suggests that a certain laxity had developed in regard to the prohibited degrees. The Damascus (Zadokite) Document (4,21; 5, 6; see Dead Sea Scrolls*) emphasizes the Bible's regulations and insists on monogamy as the original divine command, women being equally responsible with men, "the laws of forbidden degrees hold good, equal for both" (5, 9). They also interpreted the laws more strictly than did the Oral Law* of the Pharisees*. Marriage with a niece (7, 9–11) and bigamy are classed with incest and fornication as adultery. This interpretation was based on a literal acceptance of certain biblical analogies. In general, the Qumran covenanters were more stringent in their enforcement of the ancient laws, in line with their high ideals of social and ritual purity.

Rabbinical Laws: The Rabbis added another twenty to the forbidden degrees — mostly extensions of the existing Torah prohibitions, for instance, a man was forbidden to marry the wife of his father's half brother, and so on.

Racially Mixed Marriages: Marriages with foreign women did take place, not only in the earlier period before the Israelites had any real sense of national unity, but also later. Esau married two Hittite women (Gn. 26:34), Joseph married an Egyptian (Gn. 41:45) and Moses a Midianite (Ex. 2:21). There are also many later examples: David included a Calebite and an Aramean among his wives (II Sam. 3:3); Solomon had a famous harem with plenty of variety (I K. 11:1) and Ahab's marriage to Jezebel, a Phoenician (I K. 16:31) was resented at the time and calamitous in its consequences. These were all marriages of kings, inspired partly by political considerations, but they began a fashion that spread to their subjects. After the settlement in Canaan the growing tendency to marry the "women of the land", contaminate Israel's blood and endanger her religion, provoked the embargo on mixed marriages contained in Ex. 34:15–16 and Dt. 7:3–4. They nevertheless continued. Bathsheba's husband was Hittite (II Sam. 11:3) and Hiram the bronze-worker's mother married a Phoenician (I K. 7:13–14). Moreover, Deuteronomic law (Dt. 21:10–14) takes it for granted that non-Israelite women captured in war will be married by their captors and it does not seem to be implied that this is any infringement of Israel's law.

The actual prohibitions probably date from the days of the monarchy when national — and therefore religious — solidarity were of the greatest importance. After the Restoration* from Exile, scant attention was paid to them and many mixed marriages were contracted. In the interests of Israel's heritage, Ezra and Nehemiah both took very stringent measures against such marriages, but, inevitably, they continued (Ezr. 9–10; Neh. 10:30; 13:23–27).

During the Hellenistic period, sharp lines of demarcation were drawn between Jew and Gentile in all walks of life. The need to preserve the purity of the community and to differentiate it from heathen neighbours was all part of the growing national consciousness of the Jews and under these conditions the ban on mixed marriages became a far more effective regulation of individual life.

III. POSITION OF WOMEN. A record of the formal regulations governing the social standing of the woman in biblical times paints a gloomy picture of her status. A wife did not inherit from her husband and daughters might inherit from their father only where there was no male heir. Nevertheless, Israelite women were protected, and their status was far higher than, for instance, in early Assyria where women were treated as, or worse than beasts of burden. In practice, of course, the situation varied considerably.

Israelite women played their part in various religious gatherings, bringing sacrifices in their own name (Lv. 12:6, 8; I Sam. 1:2; 2:19; II Sam. 6:19; II K. 4:23), partaking of the sacred meal (Dt. 12:12, 18; 14:22–29 and passim) and offering prayers at the shrines (I Sam. 1:10–12). A woman worked hard, but she earned respect for this. The birth of children, especially boys, enhanced her position and the law commanded that children honour their mother equally with their father. If a wife were divorced, she regained her freedom and was entitled to remarry. A wife could never be sold by her husband.

Women even played their part in public affairs. Athaliah ruled Judah for several years and only a general atmosphere of social respect for their sex could have produced women of the calibre of Miriam, Deborah, Jael or Huldah. Nevertheless, in general, a Hebrew woman's position was inferior to that of women in Egypt — who might be the heads of their families — or in Babylon where a woman could acquire property (in Israel a woman could only own her marriage portion or dowry, see above, and even this was administered by her husband), be a party to contracts and share in her husband's inheritance. Israelite law laid down very strict regulations to govern a woman's sexual role and life.

Virgins: A girl was expected to be chaste until marriage. A man who seduces a virgin, not yet betrothed, must either marry her, paying the usual mohar or else pay her father the equivalent of the normal dowry (Ex. 22:16–17). Dt. (22: 28–29) carries this further and imposes a mohar of fifty shekels of silver, as well as insisting that the man marry the girl and be barred for life from divorcing her. The Talmud decreed that the Exodus provisions refer to seduction with the girl's consent, and Deuteronomy concerned rape.

A betrothed girl who has been seduced is condemned to be stoned to death (Dt. 22:23–24). The daughter of a priest, required to abide by higher standards, who "plays the harlot" shall be burnt (Lv. 21:9). Harlotry by a woman still living in her father's house (whether a virgin or widowed) is regarded as a heinous crime against her father, just as adultery by a wife is a crime against her husband. The penalty in either case was death (cf. Judah's condemnation of Tamar, Gn. 38:24). Since the penalty is specified, it seems to many scholars that it must also have been regarded as a crime against the state. Otherwise the husband could determine the penalty, or forgo it (cf. Hos. 2).

A bride's parents preserved the "tokens of virginity" of their daughter — the blood-stained garment or sheet from the nuptial bed. If a husband accused his wife of not having been a virgin bride, and the "tokens" were produced to prove him a liar, he was first whipped and then fined a hundred shekels of silver, i.e. twice the amount of a normal dowry (Dt. 22:13–19). If the accusation were true, of course, then she would be stoned (22:20–21).

Married Women: Not only was a married woman deprived of the right to divorce her husband — although liable to be repudiated without defence (see Marriage, above); she was also legally regarded very much as a piece of his property and it was she who bore the burden of the code of sexual morality.

Adultery: In Jewish law, adultery involved the violation of a marriage or betrothal contract by the woman. This was in accordance with most ancient law — a husband's infidelity did not constitute adultery among the Greeks or Romans either. In contrast to the husband's licence, however, misconduct by the wife was the "great sin" mentioned as such in various Egyptian and Ugaritic texts and also in Gn. 20:9, where the king of Gerar narrowly escaped committing it with Abraham's wife and half-sister, Sarah. Both Assyrian and Babylonian legal codes regarded adultery by the wife as a sin against the proprietary rights of the husband, punishable by death, unless, exceptionally, in Babylon, the aggrieved husband pleaded for clemency.

In Hebrew law, adultery by either a married woman or a betrothed girl was not only a crime against the husband, it was also a moral offence, "an evil act in Israel", and both parties, the lover as well as the wife, were liable to the death penalty (Lv. 20:10; Dt. 22:22–27). If a husband accused his wife of infidelity then she had to undergo the ordeal of "the bitter water" (Nu. 5:12–31) in which innocence or guilt was assumed to be proved by whether the drinking of some dirty water (water mixed with the dust of the sanctuary) under oath had no effect, or left her barren for ever, which was regarded as a token of divine displeasure and proof that she had been guilty.

The New Testament: An uncompromising view of adultery and other sexual offences is taken by the New Testament, which regards all acts of unchastity as offences against God and against one's neighbour (Mt. 5:27). The special insistence on purity for Christians is perhaps a good indication of the laxity of the age (Acts 15: 29; I Co. 5:11; Gal. 5:16–24). Nevertheless, Jesus preached mercy along with justice, and even the "great sin" could be forgiven to the truly repentant (cf. Lk. 7:47).

Widows: When a woman was widowed, her only certain provision was the dowry and marriage settlement she had received under her "ketubah". Unless married to one of her brothers-in-law under the levirate (see above), she was free to remain with her husband's family or to return to her father's house (Gn. 38:11; Ruth 1:8–9), and if she were the daughter of a priest, to partake of "priestly portions" as before her marriage (Lv. 22:13). Widows with children to support, however, were generally in a pitiable condition and the Bible makes reiterated pleas for charity towards them (Ex. 22:21–23; Dt. 10:18; Is. 1:17).

Mesopotamian law was more precise about the rights and protection of widows. The Code of Hammurabi provided that a widow could either return to her father's house with her dowry and marriage settlement, or could remain in her husband's house and enjoy the income on his assets. She did not inherit from her husband unless he had never made her a marriage settlement, in which case she shared in the sons' legacies. The Assyrians provided similarly that a widow who had been left without special provision by her husband must be supported by her husband's sons. The emphasis on "protection of the widow and orphan" found in the boastful conclusion of the Code of Hammurabi and in the Ugaritic Epic of Danael, the symbol of righteousness and justice, shows that widows did not have legal status and were in great need of protection in the ancient Near East — Israel as much as Assyria and Babylon.

IV. CHILDREN. **Childbirth:** Professional midwives assisted at confinements (Gn. 35:17 refers to one when Rachel bore her last son; Ex. 1:15 to the Hebrew midwives in Egypt). An obscure text in Ex. 1:16 suggests that a woman in labour sat on two stones placed a small distance from one another, to provide the equivalent of the birth-chair mentioned in Talmudic days. On the other hand, children are also described as being born "on the knees of" another person (Gn. 30:3; 50:23; Job 3:12). Many authors have concluded from this that childbirth took place on the knees of a midwife or relative helping the mother — a custom which can be found today in remote corners of the Near East

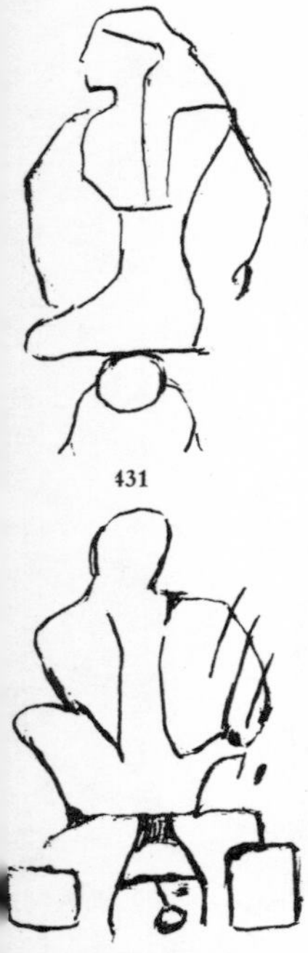

431

and which certainly existed outside Israel in biblical days, witness this revealing Bronze Age clay statuette (**430**) from Cyprus. Two Egyptian hieroglyphic signs (**431**) meaning "to give birth" also show (top) that the Egyptians had observed the occipital position of the head in a normal birth and (bottom) that Egyptian women followed the common practice among early peoples and adopted a squatting rather than recumbent position during labour.

In cases of multiple births, the rights of the first-born were jealously guarded and the birth sequence carefully noted (Gn. 25:25; 38:27). The newborn were given special care (Ezk. 16:4), washed, rubbed with salt — still a custom among rural Arabs — and wrapped in swaddling clothes (Ezk. 16:4; Job 38:8–9). The mother would nurse the baby (Gn. 21:7; I Sam. 1:21–23 and passim) unless, probably among the wealthier classes, a wet nurse was hired (Gn. 24:59; 35:8; Nu. 11:12 and passim). Apparently the baby was weaned at the age of three (II Mac. 7:27), a custom which, again, can still be found among Eastern peoples and which held good in Babylonia during the period of the Second Temple. It is also confirmed in the Talmud. On the day the baby was weaned, a feast would apparently be held (Gn. 21:8). This rag doll, **432**, dates from Hellenistic times.

Naming the Child: The baby was named as soon as it was born, usually by the mother (Gn. 29:32; 30:24; 35:18; I Sam. 1:20), although sometimes the father would choose the name (Gn. 16:15; 17:19; Ex. 2:22). The name chosen might include the name of God (El, Yahu) such as Jehoiakim, meaning "God will arise" or El-nathan, "God gave", or many others. This name might be shortened, for instance Jakin from Jehoiakim or Nathan or Nethaniah from El-nathan. Other popular names were those of living things, Deborah (bee), Shaphan (rabbit, hare), Ze'ev (wolf), etc., implying the wish that the child would have the quality of its namesake — as busy as a bee, as quick as a hare, and so on. Names from the plant world, Allon (Elon, oak), Tamar (palm), can be explained in the same way. Occasionally the child might be named for an outstanding trait or feature or, more rarely, for an outstanding event coinciding with his birth — again a custom by no means restricted to the biblical world. Biblical names of this type include Ichabod (literally "without honour") translated as "The glory is departed from Israel" (I Sam. 4:21) and Jacob, ". . . and his hand had hold on Esau's heel" (Gn. 25:26) etc., but the biblical interpretations follow a folk etymology. Sometimes the names are self-explanatory: Ithamar, Eshbaal, Jesse, meaning "my lord".

430

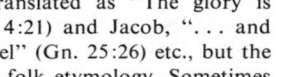

After the Restoration*, Aramaic names became common, especially during the New Testament period, when Aramaic became the vernacular of everyday life. At about the same time, Greek names are found beside — or instead of — Hebrew ones, e.g. Jonathan, Theodoros, or a Semitic name was given a Greek form, Jeshua becoming Jesus; Miriam, Maria. Reference to the modern custom of naming a boy at his circumcision only occurs in the New Testament (Lk. 1:59; 2:21).

Adoption: Adoption is the legal means of acknowledging a person of different blood as a son or daughter with the legal rights and duties of a true child. By this act, the adopter undertakes all the responsibilities and rights of a father towards the adoptee, who becomes in all legal respects his son or daughter. In general, the purpose of adoption is to provide support for the adopter, either in the shape of additional labour at the moment, or as a provision for his old age. The custom was well known in Mesopotamia in ancient times and evidence for it has been preserved in Nuzi (where it was sometimes used as a way of evading the ban on the sale of property), in Assyria, and from Babylonian law. The Code of Hammurabi devotes nine paragraphs to adoption. Their deeds of adoption made express provision for the adoptee's share in the inheritance with the natural sons (born or unborn) of the adopter. In the early days, the purpose of adoption was to provide an heir, to carry on a name or to preserve property. It was also a means of ensuring additional labour and, with the growth of a slave system, adoption became unnecessary and therefore little practiced. There are very few adoption contracts known in either Babylon or Assyria after about 1200 BCE onwards.

A similar picture emerges from the Bible. The only clear reference to the adoption of a stranger in the Old Testament occurs in the story of the slave, Eliezer, whom Abraham proposed to manumit and adopt should he remain without issue (Gn. 15:3). This reflects the practice in Nuzi where, according to documents unearthed there, a childless person could adopt his slave, who would provide for his adopter's old age and, in return, inherit when he died. While this is evidence for the influence of Mesopotamian custom in the Patriarchal age, it does not prove that the custom took root in Israel (the Bible does not describe the action as adoption).

After the Patriarchal period (see Part I above), there is no reference to adoption of children and the subject is totally ignored by the Mosaic Law. This omission suggests that the practice was unknown or at least not recognized officially in Israel. The Jewish family was strictly a matter of blood relationships and no legal formulae could be a substitute for natural kinship. The very explanation given for the custom of Levirate marriage (see above; Gn. 38:8; Dt. 25:6) confirms the assumption that adoption was not regarded as a practicable means of ensuring the continuity of a man's "name" when he could no longer beget children. In any case, in a society where polygamy was legitimate and divorce for a man relatively easy, a man whose wife was barren could always marry another to ensure his posterity, the assumption being always that it was the wife who was barren — never the man.

All the cases of apparent adoption in the Bible include some actual family tie. When Laban agreed to Jacob's marriage to Rachel, he also adopted him as his son (Gn. 29) but they were, in any case, already related (29:10). Rachel

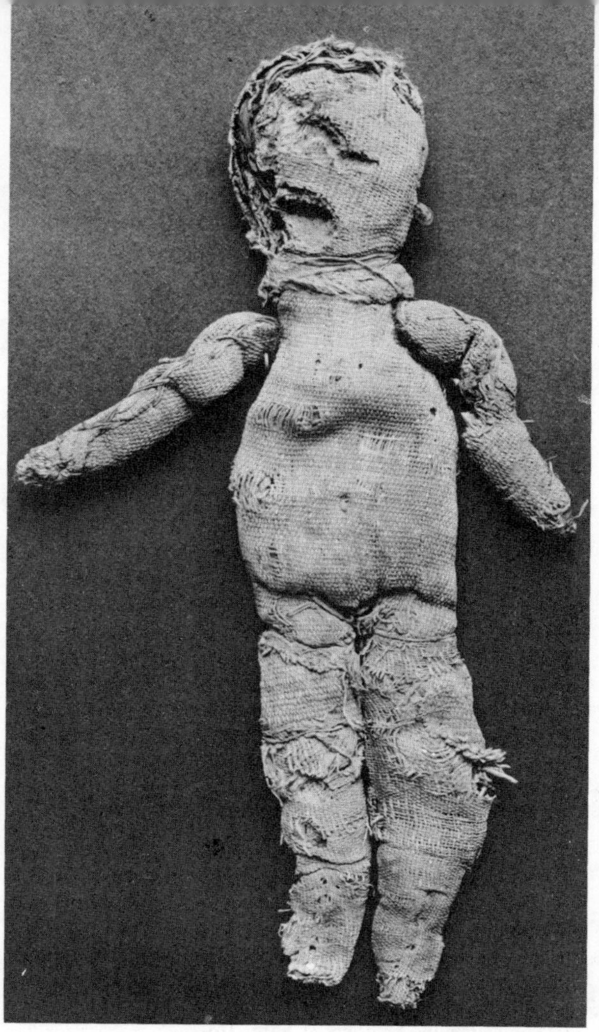

432

adopted the children of her maidservant, Bilhah (30:3), but they were undisputedly Jacob's children. On his deathbed, Jacob adopted Menasseh and Ephraim (Gn. 48:5–6) as his own sons, but they were in fact his grandsons and, similarly, Joseph adopted his great-grandsons, i.e. the sons of Machir, the son of Menasseh "were born upon Joseph's knees" (50:23).

The story of Moses who was brought to Pharaoh's daughter and "became her son" (Ex. 2:10) seems at first another case of adoption, but scholars now believe that it may rather have been a similar situation to that of Genubath, the son of Hadad, who was brought up "in Pharaoh's house among the sons of Pharaoh" (I K. 11:20).

When Mordecai took Esther for his daughter after the deaths of her father and mother (Est. 2: 7, 15), this was closer to true adoption, but she too was the daughter of his uncle, not a complete stranger, and there is nothing in the story to suggest the legal obligations he had undertaken with this adoption.

In view of the repeated references to children being born "on the knees of" a third party, and from the details in the story of Jacob and Joseph's children, it seems that there was an accepted form of adoption by taking the child between the knees of the adopter to symbolize birth. It could hardly be an adoption procedure in the Old Testament, but in view of the frequency of adoption in the neighbouring Mesopotamian states, it seems likely that some form of the institution, even if mainly within the family, was recognized, if not widely practiced, among the Israelites.

V. SUCCESSION AND INHERITANCE: The rule of primogeniture held good in Israel. The first born received the "prime" choice of the inheritance and then shared equally by lot with the others. Upon the death of his father, he inherited twice the share of his brothers in the family property (Dt. 21:17) and then became the head of the family. During his father's lifetime the eldest son was second in rank only to him and had special religious, social and economic obligations.

In Israel, every first-born "the one which openeth the womb" was considered sacred to God and, in the case of herds of domestic animals, this first-born was sacrificed to God. Because the Hebrew religion forbade human sacrifice, first-born humans were redeemed (Ex. 13:15; 22:29–30; 34:19–20) and the consecration of all Levites to the service of God was regarded as a substitute for the rest of the people (Nu. 3:12–13; 8:16–18).

The rule of primogeniture held good throughout Israel's history, was confirmed by the Mishnah and Talmud and is valid to this day in Jewish religious law. A first-born's birth-right could be revoked as a punishment for crime (Gn. 35:22; 49:3–4; I Ch. 5:1) or could be sold (Gn. 25:29–34) but in general his position and rights had the protection of the law (Dt. 21:15–17). Nevertheless, the Bible records a number of cases of younger sons being preferred to the eldest, for instance Ephraim was preferred to Menasseh and Solomon to Adonijah, but these are recorded as exceptional cases. Sometimes the preference for the younger brother is interpreted as resulting from direct intervention by God, e.g. Isaac and Ishmael (Gn. 21:12) or the choice of David over his brothers (I Sam. 16).

According to Israelite custom, a man was entitled to make a will before his death directing the disposition of his property (II Sam. 17:23; II K. 20:1; Is. 38:1) but in so doing, he was legally restrained from trying to deprive his eldest son of his right to a double share in the inheritance. The laws of Assyria, Nuzi and Mari included similar provisions. Some scholars think that in order to preserve the family property, only movable property was actually divided among the heirs while the immovable (land) was passed on intact to the first-born or remained with the family as a whole. This theory, however, is only a supposition.

Only legitimate sons were entitled to inherit. Children of concubines could not inherit from their father. This was also the case in the legal codes of Mesopotamia. Abraham acted in accordance with this rule by giving the sons of his concubines presents while he was still alive and sending them away to the East (Gn. 25:5–6). The heir to his property was Isaac, the son of the official wife, although he was the youngest of Abraham's sons. Ishmael, the first-born, was also legitimate, being acknowledged as a son by both Abraham and Sarah, but her own son could claim priority in inheritance. Because he was illegitimate, Jephthah, the son of a harlot, had no inheritance from his father (Jud. 11:2). On the other hand, as in Babylonian law (Code of Hammurabi, 170–171), a Hebrew father could declare the sons of his concubines legitimate during his lifetime and, thus, Abraham could have made Ishmael his legal heir. Instead, according to the Bible story, he received a command from God to comply with the wishes of Sarah his wife (Gn. 21:10–12). The sons of Bilhah and Zilpah born "upon the knees" of their mistresses, ranked with the sons of Rachel and Leah (Gn. 49:1–28).

As a general rule daughters did not inherit from their father. The exception — as in the story of the daughters of Zelophehad (Nu. 27:1–11; 36:1–12) — was where a man had no sons, but in that case, in order to keep the estate within the tribe, it was laid down that the girls had to marry men of their father's tribe. A similar incident occurs in the story of the daughters of Eleazar who were married to their cousins (I Ch. 23:22). According to Job 42:13–15, Job's three daughters inherited equally with their brothers but this need not have been an Israelite custom. Job is described as an "Easterner" and the background of the story may have originated abroad. Where a man died leaving neither sons nor daughters, his relatives inherited, although not his widow. In Babylonia and Nuzi the widow had a share in the inheritance of her husband's estate but this was not so in Israel. A childless widow would be married under the Levirate, or else return to her father's house (Gn. 38:11; Lv. 22:13; Ruth 1:8). A widow with adult sons would expect them to support her but if she had small children it was her job to administer her husband's estate until they grew up and entered into their inheritance. Changes in these rules appear to have been made during the Exile or shortly thereafter, for according to the Elephantine documents a childless widow could inherit her husband's estate (for instance Judith had been her husband's heir, Judith 8:7, see Apocrypha*).

Post-Exilic and Rabbinic Law: The Rabbis accorded a high degree of validity to the will of a dying person, whether given orally or in writing, but even so, the testator could not go against the rules of the Torah. He could not name someone as his heir who was not eligible according to the Law, but he could distribute his property in the form of gifts. He could not say "so-and-so shall inherit so much of my property" but he could say, "I make a gift of that piece of property to . . .. . ." This also made it possible for a testator to give an heir an extra share, although the rule of the double-portion for the first-born had to be observed. The law of Moses prescribes that a widow does not inherit. In order to provide for her, however, the rabbis laid it down that she had preference over all other heirs in collecting the sum of her ketubah and marriage settlement. For similar reasons, support for daughters while they are minors is made second to provision for the widow. Alternatively, if they are grown-up and about to be married, then their dowries are assured, even if other heirs have to go begging. This, however, is not a legal inheritance, for they have no right to inherit. It is rather the provision that would have been made for them had their father lived.

FEASTS, FESTIVALS AND HOLY DAYS. — *Outline: I. Historical Development: Festivals in the Oldest Liturgical Calendars; The Levitical Calendar; Relation of Festivals to Harvests. The Festivals: II. Feasts of Passover and Unleavened Bread; Origins of Passover; The Feast of Unleavened Bread; Observance and Combination of the two Feasts; Religious Significance; Post-Exilic and Rabbinical*

Developments. III. Feast of Weeks (Shabu'ot): Dating; Feast of the Giving of the Law; Christian Pentecost (Whitsun). IV. Feast of Tents (or Tabernacles: Sukkôt): Observance; Dating; The Sukkah; The Four Species; Simhat Beth-ha-Sho'evah — the Water Libation Festival; Shemini 'Atzeret — the Eighth Day, or Simḥat Torah — Rejoicing over the Torah. V. New Year or Rosh ha-Shana (Head of the Year). VI. Day of Atonement (Yom ha-Kippurim): The Scapegoat; Later Observance. VII. Late Jewish Holidays: a. Hanukkah (Dedication); b. Purim. List of Festivals.

I. HISTORICAL DEVELOPMENT: Among the Israelites, all the great festivals of rejoicing took on a religious character even when what was being celebrated was not primarily a religious event. The oldest festivals, later incorporated into the ritual of the Jerusalem Temple, naturally reflected a number of earlier and later traditions and various stages in the development of the nation and its religion. All these different levels have merged into the general accounts recorded in biblical, intertestamental and rabbinical literature. However, in most cases, the archaic beginnings of a festival can still be distinguished from its accretions in later Judaism.

The Temple's regular worship included daily services, a monthly ritual of the new moon (see Sacrifice*) and the weekly Sabbath* observances. These are dealt with elsewhere. This article will consider the yearly national feasts and minor festivals which were the high points of the liturgical calendar (see also Sabbath*).

The Festivals in the Oldest Liturgical Calendars: The Hebrew term "mo'ed" (feast) originally meant the specific time and place fixed for an assembly (Nu. 10:10; I Ch. 23:31). Later on, it came to mean the celebration of the annual religious feasts (Lv. 23:37–8). The term is used together with the word "ḥag" meaning specifically the three great feasts of pilgrimage.

The provisions for the three feasts are repeated a number of times in the Old Testament. The two codes of the Covenant (Ex. 23:14–17; 34:18–23) refer to the three agricultural feasts of pilgrimage: unleavened bread (matzôt), the first fruits (or weeks, "Shabu'ôt), and the "ingathering" or harvest ("asîf"), described below.

Feasts Kept in Local Sanctuaries: No precise dates were fixed, for all these festivals depended on the weather and the progress of work in the fields. The festivals were thus ordained long before the centralization of worship in Jerusalem. They were kept in local sanctuaries from the earliest days of the settlement through much of the period of the monarchy (see Israel and Judah, Kingdoms of*, II, III). These three feasts provided the "three occasions in the year" on which "all males must appear before" God in a great national pilgrimage to one or other of the national shrines. The two main "ḥaggim", the spring festival of unleavened bread and the autumn harvest festival, were both continuations of festivals which had clearly been celebrated from the very earliest times. The ḥag of Shabu'ôt, was an extension of the unleavened bread festival in the normative Jewish religion.

The Feasts held in Jerusalem: By the time of Deuteronomy, the code fixing the feasts (16:1–17) follows the same calendar but in line with the centralization of worship (see Israel and Judah*, Part I), Deuteronomy* prescribes that the festivals shall be held at "the place which the Lord your God will choose, to make his name dwell in it." Also by this time, the seven-day "ḥag" of unleavened bread is definitely identified with the Passover, while "Shabu'ôt" is to be held seven weeks after the cutting of the first corn and the feast of the ingathering, at the time of Sukkôt (the Feast of Tents).

The Levitical Calendar: The first prescription of actual dates for the festivals comes in the Holiness Code of Leviticus* (which belongs to the Priestly Code, see Biblical Criticism*) and some of which is much later than the two previous codes. The dates given in Lv. 23 follow the spring calendar* (Nisan to Nisan) and provide for Passover and the 7 day feast of unleavened bread (see below II) to be held from the fourteenth day of the first month, with the feast of weeks seven weeks later. The Feast of the Ingathering is to be held on the fifteenth day of the seventh month, followed by the seven days of the Feast of Tents (Sukkôt). Thus, the festivals follow the natural division of the solar year. (The first month according to this reckoning was the spring month of Abîb, corresponding to March–April.) The set feasts were grouped around the spring and autumn equinoxes, all of them being celebrated at a time of full moon. From the time of the Priestly Code, the festivals became fixed dates in the Israelite liturgical calendar*, subject to rigid conventions as to the manner and place of their celebration.

In addition, two more feasts were prescribed: a Feast of Acclamation on the first day of the seventh month (Lv. 23:24–5) and a Day of Atonement on the tenth day of that month (23:27–32). Five days later comes the beginning of the Feast of Tents, which concludes with a solemn Day of Assembly on the eighth day.

The festivals prescribed by Ezk. 45:18–25 follow the Levitical list and also the stipulations of Nu. 28–29 so far as the sacrifices to be offered are concerned.

Relation of Festivals to Harvests: Association of a festival of rejoicing with the harvesting of crops is, of course, a commonplace among agricultural communities, but the relation between the festivals themselves and their dating is a question that has aroused a good deal of debate. Many scholars maintain that the liturgical dates were fixed in terms of the actual times of harvests. Others hold that since it is impossible to lay down a fixed date for a harvest, the association of the festivals with the harvests was secondary. The fixed annual festivals and their ceremonial were associated with the actual facts of harvesting, in keeping with the life and interests of the community, but, in this view, the dates for the festivals were laid down first and only later did they become associated with the harvesting which happened to coincide with them. Thus at the time of the spring equinox — when the feast of first fruits (Weeks) was held, the cereal crops were being gathered in and a thanksgiving was appropriate, while at the time of the autumn equinox, the wine and olive harvests were in full swing and could be celebrated at the feast of Tabernacles. In short, this opinion sees the festivals rather than the harvests as having been from the earliest times, the fixed points of the yearly calendar.

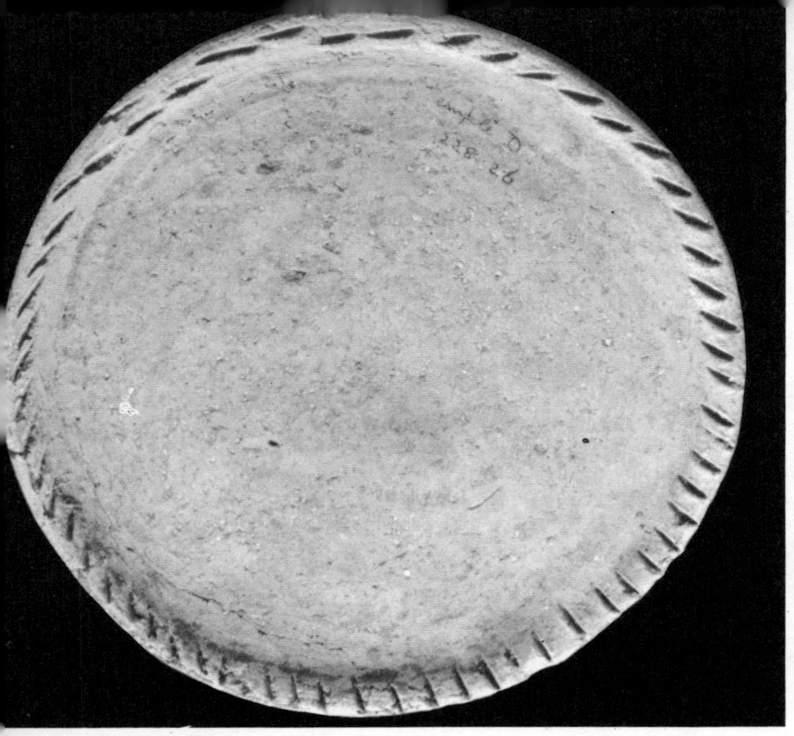

433

THE FESTIVALS — II. FEASTS OF PASSOVER AND UNLEAVENED BREAD: Passover is the first of the three Pilgrimages (in Hebrew "Shalosh Regalîm", or three times, Ex. 23:14 ff) on which all male Jews were required to "appear before" God bringing offerings. The later reforms of Josiah provided that these offerings should be brought to the central sanctuary in Jerusalem (Dt. 16:6–7).

Priestly tradition, however (Lv. 23:5–8), proclaims two feasts: a. The Paschal feast — Passover, to take place on the 14th of the first (spring) month and b. the Feast of Unleavened Bread ("ḥag ha-matzôt") to be held immediately afterwards on the seven days from the 15th of the month.

a. **The Paschal Feast and its Origins:** Passover is the most ancient feast of the Jews and it seems very probable that it may have continued a much older pre-Israelite family festival also celebrated in the spring time. The essential rite of the feast — the cooking and eating of a lamb with bitter herbs — is typical of shepherds' spring festivals. Travelling dress is to be worn as though the tribe were about to set out for the spring pastures. None of the meat may be kept over until the morrow, while the unleavened bread and bitter herbs to be eaten with the lamb were ordinary desert foods.

The festival certainly dates back to semi-nomadic times before the Exodus. If this was the festival which Moses wished to celebrate with the Israelites in the desert (Ex. 5::1) then it was well known before the Exodus.

The Israelite version includes such ancient customs as roasting the lamb over a fire without utensils to secure the fertility of the flock, and smearing its blood on the door-posts (originally the tent poles).

Historical Context: The biblical explanation of the feast is that it celebrates the Exodus*. Whatever debates may rage about the details of the story as recorded (see Exodus*), Israel's historically based religion saw the Exodus as a startling intervention by God — which took place in the springtime — by which he brought the Children of Israel out of Egypt. The event marked the beginning of Israel's history as a people, consummated in their settlement in the Promised Land. A long established spring festival — the Passover — thereby acquired a new significance, celebrating the event. The Hebrew term for the feast is "Pessaḥ". Various different explanations of the name have been put forward — none of them very convincing. Some scholars see the derivation of the word in the verb Passoaḥ, to pass over, or to spare, which would relate it to the last of the Ten Plagues of Egypt when God struck down the first-born of every family, but spared the specially marked Hebrew households.

b. **The Feast of Unleavened Bread:** Immediately after Passover came the Feast of Unleavened Bread (Matzôt), which lasted for seven days, during which only unleavened bread might be eaten. The first and seventh days were to be observed as holidays, with religious assemblies and no work done. This observance, prescribed in the Old Testament, is also confirmed by the Passover Papyrus and ostraca from Elephantine in Egypt (dated 419 BCE) asking the Jewish community of Judea for instructions on how to observe the feast.

In contrast to the paschal feast of Pessaḥ, the unleavened bread festival was not celebrated until after the Israelites entered Canaan. The origins of the feast clearly lie among an agricultural community. It celebrated the beginning of the barley harvest, the first crop to be gathered in Canaan. For the first seven days of the harvest only bread made with the new grain might be eaten. The bread was made without leaven (yeast) as a sign of a new beginning. (At the end of the wheat harvest, leavened bread, the ordinary fare of the peasants, was offered in sacrifice.) It was baked on a rounded pan (**433**) placed over hot embers (Lachish, 15 c. BCE).

Observance and Combination of the Two Feasts: The Bible records the "first" passover in Exodus 12; one held in the second year after the Exodus (Nu. 9:1–5) and the first to be celebrated in Canaan (Jos. 5:10–12). Before the monarchy, the Passover was celebrated as a tribal feast at the central sanctuary of the federation. Later it presumably developed into a family festival (if it was in fact celebrated regularly). The first mention of its celebration under the monarchy occurs in II Ch. 8:13 which records that Solomon observed the feasts commanded by Moses: "the feast of unleavened bread, the feast of weeks and the feast of tabernacles." At this time, the feast of unleavened bread was a pilgrimage, although, according to the very much later Book of Chronicles, during the reign of Hezekiah when the people "came together in Jerusalem to keep the feast of unleavened bread in the second month . . . they killed the passover lamb on the fourteenth day of the second month." (II Ch. 30:13–15).

The two feasts, according to R. de Vaux, became officially combined at the time of Josiah's reforms, which were aimed at greater centralization of worship. He joined the festival of Unleavened Bread, which was a pilgrimage and by then an established custom among the Israelites, to the provision that only unleavened bread should be eaten with the Passover sacrifice. Josiah celebrated Passover according to the formula given in Dt. 16:1–8, providing that a head of cattle, a sheep or goat, should be killed, cooked and eaten at the central sanctuary in Jerusalem. Thus he made the pilgrimage part of the first and most important of the two festivals.

The sacrifice of the paschal lamb came at its climax, everyone returning home on the following morning. The biblical account of Josiah's Passover (II K. 23:21; II Ch. 35:1–19) emphasizes its novelty, "No passover like it had been kept in Israel since the days of Samuel the prophet . . ." (II Ch. 35:18), making it clear that what was new was to hold it at the central sanctuary in Jerusalem. Certainly this ritual is much later than the ancient traditions of the early days of the monarchy and previously. Moreover his change definitely dated the Feast of Unleavened Bread to the seven days following Passover, whether or not this fell on a Sabbath. These new provisions were apparently established well before the Exile and were accepted by Ezekiel as forming part of the Levitical Calendar (see above, I).

Religious Significance: In later Judaism, Passover is seen almost exclusively as celebrating the Israelites' deliverance from bondage in Egypt, thus it is known as Ḥag ha-ḥerût or "Ḥag ḥerutenu" (Liberation Festival, or Festival of Our Deliverance). Thus the symbolism of the matzôt (unleavened bread) became limited to remembrance of the speed of the people's departure from Egypt. The ancient significance of a spring festival was limited to a sacrifice symbolizing reconciliation and good fellowship with God (see Sacrifice*).

Post-Exilic and Rabbinical Developments: The Tannaim (see Rabbis*) and their successors drew up an elaborate set of commandments (halakhoṭ) for the proper preparation and celebration of Passover. The first concerned the question of dating. Because a Hebrew day runs from sunset to sunset (not midnight to midnight), part of the "15th day of the first month" in fact falls on the 14th. Thus it was ruled that no food containing leaven must be touched, much less eaten, after sunset on the 14th Nisan.

Beyond this, the Halakhah enjoins a specially enhanced state of purity for the food, household effects and other belongings used during Passover. Thus a thorough spring cleaning is carried out — according to a complicated mass of special regulations — in preparation for the festival.

The "Seder": The paschal feast itself, held on the evening of the 14th Nisan around the Jewish family table, ushers in the Passover and constitutes its principal function. From the simple injunction to consume the lamb entirely, with girded loins and staff in the hand, symbolizing readiness for instant departure, the ritual has developed into an elaborate "order of proceedings" known as the *Seder*. Apparently (Jn. 13:4, 5, 12; Mt. 26:23 ff), this was already a fixed institution at the time of Jesus*. (The equation of the Last Supper with Passover is discussed in the articles on Jesus* and the Eucharist*.) The complete Seder consists of chanting and reading the "Hagaddah", a collection of sacred texts and psalms (Nos. 115–118) on the theme of the Exodus and its significance, plus various traditional songs and parables, during the course of which the paschal feast proper is consumed. This illustrated page is from a mediaeval "haggadah" (**434;** 13th c. CE Spain or France).

In the modern world, the nearest thing to the ancient formula for the paschal lamb appears to be the Passover sacrifice as it is celebrated among the Samaritans* (see that article). Since the destruction of the Temple, the Jewish celebration has not included any sacrifice* (see article).

III. THE FEAST OF WEEKS — SHABU'OT. — The second great festival of the liturgical year — originally the second pilgrimage — was the harvest feast of "first fruits" (Ex. 23:16) or, more strictly, the feast of the wheat harvest (Ex. 34:22), also known as the feast, or pilgrimage, of Weeks (Shabu'ôt). The Old Testament also refers to it as the Day of Early Harvest (Nu. 28:26). It was a joyful festival, occurring at one of the main periods in the agricultural calendar of Palestine, and celebrated seven weeks (or 50 days, hence its Greek name, Pentecost), after the feast of the unleavened bread when the first ears of corn were cut.

The ceremony was marked by the offering of two loaves made from the newly harvested flour, baked with leaven (Lv. 23:16 ff) — the only time yeast is used ritually. This underlines its essential character as a farmers' feast, for leavened bread is the ordinary food of a farming population. It is also an indication that this, too, was an agricultural festival adapted to a settled life and taken over from the

434

Canaanites. The custom of presenting first fruits to the local god is, of course, found far beyond the borders of Palestine, but the semi-nomadic Hebrews are likely to have encountered it for the first time in Canaan.

The 50 days between the beginning of the barley harvest and the end of the wheat harvest were probably connected with the old farmers' calendar of the seasons (see Agriculture*). They marked the period of bringing the "'Omer" — i.e. the bringing in of the sheaves — and saw the completion, first of the barley harvest, then the wheat and other grains, plus the earliest tree fruits. Thus the festival took place seven weeks from the second day of Passover (i.e. the first day of the earlier feast of unleavened bread), hence the name Shabu'ôt, "Weeks" (Ex. 34:22 ff). The forty-nine intervening days of "'Omer" are carefully marked by including in the evening prayer a formula: "To-day (meaning the following day according to the Jewish calendar*) is . . . day, which are . . . weeks and . . . days in the 'Omer."

Dating: However, the actual time for the celebration of the festival always came up against the same difficulty that arose about Passover in connection with the words "the morrow after the Sabbath" in Lv. 23:11, 15, 16, whereas Dt. 16:9 has it simply, "seven weeks from the time you first put the sickle to the standing grain." During the time of the Second Temple, the Sadducees* and Boethusian Sadducees insisted on interpreting the "morrow after the Sabbath" literally and their ruling was followed in the calendar of Jubilees, by the Dead Sea* sectaries and by the Samaritans* to this day. Thus, for them, the first day of 'Omer always fell on a Sunday and so would Shabu'ôt. The warnings of the Dead Sea sectaries' "Manual of Discipline" (see Dead Sea Scrolls*) were apparently directed against the Pharisaic ritual calendar, which counted from the 16th Nisan, regardless of the day of the week. This was the majority ruling at the time of the Second Temple and remains the rule for most of Jewry.

Feast of the Giving of the Law: A much later development in Judaism related Shabu'ôt to the history of salvation by making it the festival commemorating the Covenant of Sinai and the Giving of the Torah. This has become its prime significance, the later name "Matan Torah" (Giving of the Torah) replacing the archaic terms "Ḥag ha-bikkurîm" (first fruits) or "Ḥag hakazîr" (Festival of reaping or harvesting). This is a late post-Exilic development, dating from the time the rabbis fixed the date for the festival as the 6th Sivan (6th and 7th Sivan for the Jews of the Diaspora outside Palestine), and also laid it down that the Ten Commandments (Ex. 20 and Dt. 5) had been given to Moses on the 6th Sivan.

For the Sectaries of Qumran (see Dead Sea Scrolls*), the Feast of Weeks was the most important festival in the calendar, celebrating the renewal of their "New Covenant", which implies that the feast was already connected with the giving of the Law at Sinai and the Covenant-making feast of Ex. 24.

At the time the settlement at Qumran was being made and inhabited (see Dead Sea Scrolls*) the festival was of only secondary importance to the orthodox Jews. Only in the 2nd c. CE, the Mishnah records, did the rabbis accept it as commemorating the giving of the Law and thus raise it to the status of a major festival.

Christian Pentecost (Whitsun): To the Christians, the feast of Pentecost has quite a different significance. This is the festival which commemorates the gift of the Holy Spirit and the calling of all nations to the Church. The story in Ac. 2:1–41 makes no mention of the Sinai Covenant nor of the New Covenant* of Christ, although the establishment of the church on Pentecost reflects a continuation of the liturgical tradition of Judaism. The connection was not coincidental. Just as the community of Israel began at Sinai on this particular occasion, so the new Israel began at the time of the same festival.

IV. FEAST OF TENTS (OR TABERNACLES), SUKKÔT. The most important, holiest and most crowded of the three annual pilgrimages to the sanctuary was the "Ḥag ha-Asîf", the feast of the "ingathering at the end of the year" when "the fruit of your labour" was harvested (Ex. 23:16) at the time of the autumn equinox.

It became the Feast of Tents in commemoration of the fact that "I made the people of Israel dwell in tents when I brought them out of the land of Egypt" (Lv. 23:43) and, according to the rabbis, "nimbuses of glory" surrounded the Israelites on their wanderings, like tents. The feast's original significance as the autumn harvest festival was the aspect which had the greatest appeal to the masses. It came at the time when the crops of the field, of the threshing floor, and the wine-press (Dt. 16:13) had all been gathered in. Very probably the festival continued a Canaanite agricultural celebration during which huts were erected in the orchards as happened during the harvesting of fruit and olives. Once the harvest was finished, it was natural to celebrate its ending in and around the same huts. After the centralization of the Hebrews' cult, the regulations provided for a great pilgrimage to Jerusalem, where similar huts were erected.

It seems that during the periods of the First and Second Temples, whole families used to live entirely in the hut — the "Sukkah" — sleeping as well as eating there, but after the destruction of the Second Temple, later regulations allowed the sukkah to be used only for meals.

It has been suggested that the festival was connected with the regulations (Ex. 26) for the Tent of Reunion in commemoration of the Covenant, but this is so obviously a later, imposed interpretation, that it can hardly be accepted. Later editors called Sukkôt the "Feast of Yahweh" (Lv. 23:39; Nu. 29:12) while Ezekiel calls it simply "the Feast" (45:25). Josephus confirms that in his time it was "the holiest and the greatest of Hebrew feasts" (Ant. 8:4, 1).

The feast was an occasion for general rejoicing, when the new wine from the year's pressings was drunk — often doubtless to excess. Many folk customs of Canaanite and Israelite origin were connected with it. One associated tradition is the story of Benjaminites carrying off wives from among the young girls of Shiloh who went into the vineyards to dance during the festival (Jud. 21:19–21). A similar, later, tradition related in the Mishnah Taanith 4, 8, also concerns the choosing of a bride. According to this account, on the 15th of Ab (August), marriageable girls would dress in white, without finery or jewellery, allowing no distinction between rich and poor, and go out into the vineyards and orchards to sing and dance. There the young men would watch and choose their bride. In theory, the choice was entirely up to the men but in practice there must have been a good deal of collusion between the young people and their parents. The memory of the custom lingers on to the extent that the 15th Ab is still considered a lucky day for a wedding.

Many scholars (e.g. R. de Vaux) connect this custom with Sukkôt, although others relate it to the Day of Atonement, held a few days before.

Observance: R. de Vaux considers that the text prescribing the ritual, Lv. 23:40–41, represents a late and final stage of editing (following Ezra) of the passage which directs the people to take "good fruit" and branches and to rejoice for seven days in memory of the Israelites leaving Egypt. Neh. 8:14–18 refers to the returned Exiles keeping the feast in connection with the reading of the Law. Later on, during the Hasmonean* era, there is a story of Alexander Jannaeus being pelted with the citrons ("ethrogs", see below) held by worshippers during the feast of Sukkôt. The festival remained a joyful occasion, with a seven-day pilgrimage to the sanctuary and dancing in the Temple courtyards.

Its early importance can be gauged by the detailed instructions about the numbers and type of the sacrifices to be offered on each day of the festival given in Nu. 29:12–38. These are on a descending scale from 13 young bulls, 2 rams, and 14 male lambs a year old, plus one male goat, on the first day, to one bull, one ram and 7 male lambs, plus the goat, on the eighth day, along with associated cereal and drink offerings. Later rabbinic edicts added a day to all three great festivals bringing Sukkôt up to nine days (i.e. including Simḥat Torah), and making it the longest feast in the calendar.

Dating: The timing of the festival originally depended on the progress of work in the field, since it could not be held until all the crops of field and vineyard had been gathered. The question of just when it was held is important in connection with the completion and dedication of Solomon's Temple. This apparently coincided with the Feast and was held, according to I K. 8:2 and 65–66 in the seventh month (a month before the Temple was finally completed, which is not impossible). The dating of the festival at this time still depended on the state of the crops, so this chronology is quite acceptable. From later statements (I K. 12:32), Jeroboam appears to have held a festival at Bethel a month later, on the 15th day of the eighth month.

The various texts (Ex. 23; Nu. 29; Lv. 23; Dt. 16) are all capable of different interpretations. However, in Lv. 23:34 it is laid down explicitly that the "feast of booths" is to begin on the "fifteenth day of the seventh month", to last for seven days and end with a "solemn assembly" on the eighth. Ezk. 45:25 gives the same date.

The Sukkah: The tent, or booth, itself had to be made in a special way. The regulations governing its construction are listed in the treatise "Sukkah" in the Mishnah and Talmud. Essentially, the sukkah must be surrounded on three sides by temporary walls (mats, blankets, or reeds etc.) and thatched with leafy branches which allow the occupants to see the sky and the stars. Its proportions and the manner of its decoration — with fruit and plants and sacred pictures — are left largely to individual discretion.

The Four Species: (Arba'at ha-minîm). Lv. 23:40 prescribes that the people "shall take on the first day the fruit of goodly trees, branches of palm trees and boughs of leafy trees and willows of the brook . . ." Over the years, this fairly general instruction has been transformed into very precisely defined rules. The "fruit of goodly trees" must now be, as shown (**435**), a citron (ethrog), without the smallest blemish; the palm branch must be a young one whose fronds have not opened; the "bough of the leafy tree" must be a myrtle, while the willow branch hardly needs further definition. These are the Four Species, around which a whole ritual has grown up. In addition, special willow-branches are used during certain prayers, both called hošannas. The seventh day of Sukkot is known as the Great Hošanna (Hošanna Rabbah), which, it is believed, will be the last Day of Judgment and is also the occasion on which God allocates the coming winter rains. This reference to the Day of Judgment links Sukkôt to the New Year and the Day of Atonement, which are also closely associated with it.

435

Simḥat Beth-ha-Sho'evah — the Water Libation Festival: During the Second Temple period, a big torch-light procession used to be held on the second evening of Sukkôt around the Temple cisterns from which the water for ritual libations was drawn. The dances and songs associated with the popular rejoicing of this festival are described in the Mishnah* order of Mo'ed (see also Rabbis*). The day remains an especially joyful occasion among today's communities such as the modern Hassidic groups.

Shemini 'Atzeret, or Simḥat Torah (The Eighth Day, or Rejoicing of the Torah): In fact this "eighth day of assembly" (Lv. 23:36) is not strictly speaking part of the feast of Sukkôt, but is a separate holiday. The sukkah need be inhabited for only seven days and the sacrifices on the eighth day are of distinctly modest proportions (see above). Today in Israel the eighth day of Sukkôt is combined with Simḥat Torah although in the Diaspora it remains a separate feast, making Sukkôt in effect a nine-day holiday.

The ritual of Simḥat Torah marks the annual completion of the reading of the Law in the Synagogue. On this one day the rolls of the Torah are all taken out of the Ark and carried in procession among the worshippers with appropriate songs and dances (among oriental communities, even out into the streets).

V. NEW YEAR OR ROSH-HA-SHANAH (HEAD OF THE YEAR). — Lv. 23:24–5, which apparently also belongs to the last edition of the book after Ezra, prescribes that the first day of Tishri (the seventh month of a calendar year beginning in the spring) shall be held as a "Day of Acclamation". By New Testament and early Mishnaic* times a ritual mainly concerned with the sounding of the shofar and the singing of special hymns of praise had grown up. Neither the Priests' Code, Ezekiel or Ezra knew of any New Year Feast. Nor do Josephus or Philo mention such a festival. It is impossible to say at what time or under what influence the New Year Feast was instituted. Celebration of a New Year in Tishri, however, does show that the fall calendar* continued in use long after the end of the monarchy.

Ten Days of Penitence: The Old Testament text does not specify the purpose of the "Day of Acclamation" but the Mishnah treatise on "Rosh ha-Shanah" combined it with the ideas of judgment behind Ex. 32:33 where God assures Moses: "Whoever has sinned against me, him will I blot out of my book", to produce the concept of a "recording" ("paqod") of mankind's activities. Thus, together with Yom Kippur (the Day of Atonement), these became the "Yamim Nora'im" (Days of Awe, or Awesome Days). As the fear of judgment is best met by repentance and penitence, the period between the beginning of Rosh-ha-Shanah and the end of the Day of Atonement became the Ten Days of Penitence ('Asseret Yeme Teshubbah). Rosh ha-Shanah itself acquired the alternate name of "Day of Judgment", it being thought that on this day the whole world was judged and each man's fate during the coming year was inscribed in the Book of Life. Many scholars find a very ancient background to these beliefs in the mythology of the Near East. According to Jewish custom, the civil new year became a time of remembrance and repentance, as well as a Day of Acclamation and Assembly.

VI. DAY OF ATONEMENT (YOM HA-KIPPURIM) — The Day of Atonement, observed on the 10th Tishri, has become the most solemn fast of the Jewish year. The ritual for the special Temple sacrifices prescribed for the occasion is given in Lv. 16 and, obviously, includes a number of different strata and also combines two ceremonies, differing in spirit and origin.

First there is the Levitical ritual in which a bull is sacrificed by the High Priest as a "sin offering" for his own sin and that of the priesthood. During these rites he made his single annual entry behind the veil of the Holy of Holies, clad in white linen — symbolizing purity and humility — to sprinkle the blood of the sacrifice, the holy fire and the incense on the "Mercy Seat" (kapporeth, see Temple*; Tabernacle*).

The Scapegoat: Secondly came the ritual of the two goats. One was sacrificed for the people's sins and its blood also sprinkled on the Mercy Seat, thus linking the expiation of the sins of both people and priests. The second goat — apparently deriving from a separate stream of ancient beliefs and rites — was offered by the community, destined "for 'Azazel" (probably, although not certainly, a demonic spirit) and set, alive, "before Yahweh". The High Priest laid his hands upon the head of this scapegoat whereupon Yahweh transferred to it all the sins — whether deliberate or unintentional — of the people. Then, bearing all the sins of the people, it was taken into the wilderness and driven out. There is a tradition that it was taken to the top of a precipice — at one time to Beth-Hadudun, modern Khirbet Khareidon, overlooking the Kidron valley, some six kilometres from Jerusalem — and there hurled down from a great height. Whether or not this was so, the man who was given the task of driving the goat out and making sure it did not return, became impure by his association with its impurity and had to wash himself and his clothes before he could rejoin the community (see Impurity*).

There are close similarities between this ritual and its symbolism and a Babylonian rite in which a sheep was similarly loaded with impurity, and was killed. In the Israelite ritual the goat could not be sacrificed because it had deliberately been made impure — and thus unacceptable to God.

Although elements of very early custom are present in the Atonement Day ritual, the whole ceremony does not appear to be very ancient. There is no mention of such a feast in any pre-Exilic text. Nor is it referred to by either Nehemiah or Ezra. There is a reference in Nehemiah 9:1 to a fast and a ceremony of penitence and expiation held on "the twenty-fourth day of this month" (which appears to be the seventh, following Sukkôt) and some scholars interpret this as meaning a Day of Atonement which, later on, was changed to the 10th Tishri. However, this is very far from being certain. The argument from silence is not convincing. Scholars admit that they just do not know when the observance was instituted nor what were its history or development. It seems unlikely, however, that it could have been introduced after the Exile as something quite new.

Later Observance: Later edicts concerning the Day of Atonement have emphasized the solemnity of the occasion, also underlined in the Leviticus text (16:29–34). Leviticus requires penance and fasting during the day. Subsequent edicts extended the period of the fast from shortly before sunset on the 9th Tishri to dusk (when three small stars can be seen by the naked eye) on the 10th. It is the one day in the year, apart from the normal Sabbath, when all manner of work of whatever kind is totally forbidden. Thus even the shofar is not blown on the evening of the 9th (when the Kol Nidrei prayer cancelling rash vows between man and God is read) but is postponed until the evening prayer on the 10th.

The Mishnah* tractate on the Day of Atonement refers to it without qualification as "Yoma" (The Day). It is the one feast during which prayers are recited almost continuously. The prayers are a substitute for the elaborate sacrificial ritual which, of course, ended with the destruction of the Temple. The halakhah, however, retains a vestige of the sacrifices in its ceremony of "Kapparah". This is held on the evening of the 8th Tishri and consists of every adult male swinging a white cock around his head — women wave white hens — and chanting: "the cock/hen is my ransom, my expiation, my sacrifice; he/she will go to his/her death, and I will enter and proceed in the path of a good, long and peaceful life."

VII. LATE JEWISH HOLIDAYS — a. **Ḥanukkah (Dedication):** Held on the 25th Kislev, this is the one feast in the Jewish calendar which commemorates an undeniable historical event. It celebrates the victory of Judas the Maccabee (see Hasmoneans*) over the Seleucid forces in the year 164 BCE and his subsequent purification of the defiled Temple and the whole of Jewish life from the contamination of Hellenism*. The original source, in I Mac. 4:36–59 refers to it as the day of "the purification of the Temple". To Flavius Josephus* (Ant. Bk. 12:7:7), it is the Feast of Lights and this continued after the destruction of the Temple as its name and outstanding characteristic. This version commemorates the legend that when Judas and his forces recaptured the Temple the only thing they could find which had not been defiled was a small cruse of oil, sufficient for one day's lights. Miraculously, the lights kindled with this oil continued to burn for eight days and nights. Thus the festival is celebrated today by lighting a single candle on the first night and then an additional one on each successive night until the eight candles of the Menorah **(436)** are all ablaze on the last night. Work is not prohibited on this festival which has become essentially a festival for children, with presents and parties.

In early Hasmonean* days, the Hassidim* tended to be hostile to their rulers and paid no attention to a festival initiated by and glorifying them. The Mishnah* makes only casual reference to Ḥanukkah although, later on, the halakhah prescribed a definite ritual for its observance, making it independent of the sanctuary.

b. **Purim:** This is also an apparently historically-based festival, celebrating the events recorded in the book of Esther. The name is probably Akkadian in origin (puru — the casting of lots) and it refers to the day fixed by Haman for the extermination of the Jews in the kingdoms ruled by Ahasuerus (Xerxes), i.e. the 13th of Adar.

Purim is not a cultic festival. The Book of Esther* contains no single mention of the name of God and its inclusion in the canon was debated. It was accepted on distinctly inconclusive grounds. However, as it was included, the

436

rabbis gave the festival divine sanction in the form of several benedictions and hymns in a comparatively lighter vein. The essentially secular nature of the feast is emphasized by the injunction to make merry, to eat and drink heartily, to send presents to friends and give charity to the poor.

The Book of Esther provides that Purim shall be cele rated on the 14th and 15th Adar but, on the basis of a rather obscure passage in Est. 9:18, the festival is usually held on the 14th only.

Origins: It seems probable that the feast originated among eastern communities — perhaps the Jews of Susa itself — and it may have been modelled on a Persian New Year Feast. It reached Palestine in the 2nd c. BCE and is first mentioned (apart from the Book of Esther) in II Mac. 15:36, where it is called the Feast of Mordechai. Josephus* describes it in his Antiquities (11, 6, 13).

List of Festivals: Through the year, the list of festivals runs as follows:

1. the weekly Sabbath on which all work is forbidden	every seventh day.	corresponding approximately to:
2. Passover and Unleavened Bread, Pessah	14th Nisan, plus 7 days from 15th	March–April
3. Feast of Weeks or Pentecost (Shabu'ot)	6th Sivan	May–June
4. New Year (Rosh-ha-Shanah)	1st Tishri	September–October
5. Day of Atonement (Yom-ha-Kippurim)	10th Tishri	September–October
6. Feast of Ingathering, Tents or Tabernacles (Sukkot)	15th Tishri, for 8 days	September–October
7. Feast of Dedication (Ḥanukkah)	25th Kislev, for 8 days	December
8. Purim	14th Adar	February–March

(see also Sabbath*)

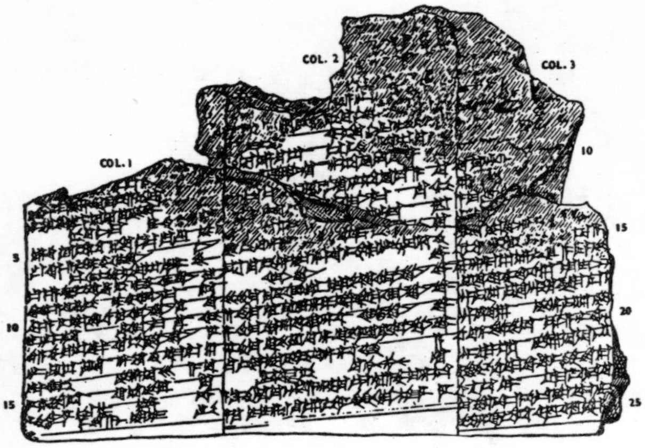

437

438

FLOOD, THE. — *Outline: The Bible's Story of the Flood; Mesopotamian Flood Stories; The Sumerian Story of Ziusudra; The Assyrian-Babylonian Story of Utnapishtim; The Atra-ḫasis Epic; Generations "Before the Flood"; Analogies and Differences; Other Flood Stories; Evidence of Floods; Links between Babylonian and Biblical Stories.*

The Bible's Story of the Flood (Gn. 6:5–9:17) is simple in outline although the details reflect complex problems (see below). According to the biblical authors, God decided that mankind had become almost totally corrupt, leaving only one righteous man on earth — Noah. Mankind must therefore be destroyed, but Noah was forewarned and ordered to build the Ark, in which he, his household and a pair of every living thing on earth might be saved (6:13–21). Noah was given exact dimensions for building the ark and instructions for provisioning it. He "did all that the Lord had commanded." When the flood began — at which time Noah was 600 years old (7:11) — he filled the ark as instructed, (7:13–16). The heavens opened and "all the fountains of the great deep burst forth". The rain fell for forty days and forty nights and the waters rose until even the tops of the mountains were covered and every living thing had died, except for Noah and those with him in the Ark (7:17–24).

After 150 days, the waters abated and, "on the seventeenth day of the seventh month", the Ark came to rest on the mountains of Ararat (8:1–5). As the tops of the mountains began to appear, Noah began to send out birds, like all ancient mariners, to find the proximity of land. First, he sent out a raven, which hesitated and returned. Then he sent out a dove. The first time, it returned, then, after seven days, it came back with a sprig of olive in its beak and, after another seven days, disappeared. As dry land appeared below, Noah lifted the top of the Ark and emerged with all that had been saved with him. Then he built an altar and offered sacrifice to God, who promised that never again would he curse the earth because of man, "for the imagination of man's heart is evil from his youth" (8:20–22). Instead, he blessed Noah and his sons, gave him commandments (the Seven Commandments of Noah) and made a covenant* with him, promising that never again would floods destroy the earth (9:1–11). As a token, God placed the rainbow in the clouds, as a sign of the covenant he had established with all flesh that is upon the earth (9:12–17).

The biblical story of Noah and the Ark is by no means the earliest account of such a catastrophe, but none of the others have much in common with the story in Genesis, except for those which originated in Mesopotamia.

Mesopotamian Flood Stories: There are three of these: the oldest, the Sumerian story of Ziusudra; the Atra-ḫasis Epic and the most detailed, the Assyrian-Babylonian revision of the story of the flood in which the hero is Utnapishtim. All of them derived from a common source which may have been the prototype of the biblical account of Noah.

The Sumerian Story of Ziusudra: This account, dating from the first half of the second mill. BCE, occurs on a fragmentary clay tablet found at Nippur (Northern Mesopotamia; **437**). It deals with the flood as part of a Sumerian epic which begins with creation and describes the heavenly foundation of earthly kingdoms.

The passages relating to the flood read as follows:

"The flood . . .
"Give ear to my instructions. By our . . . a flood will sweep over the cult centres to destroy the seed of mankind . . .
is the decision, the word of the assembly of the gods . . .
. . . .
All the windstorms, exceedingly powerful, attacked at once . . .
After — for seven days and seven nights
the flood had swept over the land
and the huge boat had been tossed about by the windstorms on the great waters, ...
. . . . .
Ziusudra opened a window of the huge boat . . .
Ziusudra, the king, prostrated himself before Utu (the sun-god)
the king kills an ox, slaughters a sheep.

The Assyrian-Babylonian Story of Utnapishtim: This was found on a tablet in the library of Ashurbanipal at Nineveh, dating from the 7th c. BCE. The flood story took up most of the 11th (**438**) of twelve tablets containing the Epic of Gilgamesh, published by George Smith in 1872. However, parts of the epic of Gilgamesh have also been found dating back to the middle of the second mill. BCE, which suggests that its composition, including the flood episode, was not much later than that of the Sumerian text.

Gilgamesh set out on a quest for the secret of immortality, which was supposed to have been revealed to Utnapishtim. He, the sole survivor of the great flood, had been granted eternal life. To find him, Gilgamesh travels across the Waters of Death (see Ships*) and, at last, Utnapishtim tells him the story of the Flood:

The gods of the ancient city of Shurrupak on the River Euphrates decided (see the Atra-ḫasis Epic, below) to destroy mankind by a flood. Although their decisions had to be kept secret, one of the gods, Ea, had a favourite, Utnapishtim, and warned him of the coming deluge by a stratagem. He spoke, not directly to Utanpishtim, but to the wall of his reed-hut,

> "Reed-hut, reed-hut! Wall, wall!
> Reed-hut, hearken! Wall, reflect!"

He ordered Utnapishtim to build a ship, giving precise dimensions and telling him to take on board "the seed of all living things", but also to "give up possession, seek thou life, despise property and keep the soul alive." Utnapishtim carried out his instructions with the help of his family, "The little ones carried bitumen (tar), while the grown ones brought all else that was needful." Within seven days the ship was completed and then loaded:

> "Whatever I had I loaded upon her;
> Whatever I had of silver I loaded upon her
> Whatever I had of gold I loaded upon her;
> Whatever I had of all living things I loaded upon her . . ."

With all his family, Utnapishtim boarded the ship and prepared for the storm. When it broke, "the wide land was shattered like a pot!" and even "the gods were frightened by the deluge"; they "cowered like dogs crouched against the outer wall."

The deluge lasted for six days. On the seventh, Utnapishtim opened one of the hatches and looked out at a scene of desolation:

> "I looked at the weather; stillness had set in,
> And all of mankind had returned to clay.
> The landscape was as level as a flat roof."

Utnapishtim "bowed to the ground and wept" and the gods themselves "all humbled sit and weep, their lips grown tight, one and all."

However, at last the great ship came to rest on Mount Nisir, according to the Assyrian version, which lies in the mountainous country north of the Babylonian plain, 175 miles northeast of Baghdad.

Utnapishtim waited seven days then sent out a dove, which came back, followed by a swallow which also returned. Then he sent out a raven who "eats, circles, caws and turns not round." Encouraged, Utnapishtim and those with him emerged and Utnapishtim offered a sacrifice to which the gods responded:

> "The gods smelled the sweet savour,
> The gods crowded like flies about the sacrificer."

and, as a reward, conferred immortality upon Utnapishtim and his wife.

Utnapishtim's account to Gilgamesh does not reveal when the flood occurred, nor does he make any mention of other survivors, nor of the significance of the flood in the history of mankind.

The Atra-ḫasis Epic is an older version of the Babylonian story. Found on scattered Akkadian fragments discovered recently, and relating to one or possibly two epics, it tells the story of Atra-ḫasis, meaning the Exceeding Wise One.

This epic also begins with the creation of man by the great gods and goes on to the beginning of civilization, with the founding of five cities. As mankind multiplies, their noise interferes with the sleep of the god, Enlil, and he appeals to the "great gods" to find a solution. First they send a famine for six years but as this does not succeed in disciplining the unruly humans, a flood is sent to destroy them. The god Ea betrays the plan to his favourite, Atra-ḫasis who, in the familiar pattern, builds a boat according to an outline drawn by the god, and thus escapes with his family.

J. J. Finkelstein has pointed out that the Akkadian term for noise, or uproar is "huburum", while the word for violence, "immāsu" is also used, as "ḥāmās" in the Noah story (Gn. 6:11, 13). This suggests the close connections between the biblical account and the much older Babylonian versions. It is, however, unlikely that the Hebrew writers consciously borrowed from Mesopotamian lore. More probably, stories about the great flood were common throughout Mesopotamia and reached the remote ancestors of the Hebrews, becoming part of their traditions just as they survived in Sumerian and Babylonian literature.

Generations "Before the Flood": In the Bible, the Flood is recorded as the most significant event of the prehistory of Israel. The earth was peopled entirely by the descendants of Noah, but before his time — and the flood — there had been ten generations of man.

The Babylonian and other cultures which had stories about floods, also divided their history into generations and rulers that came before the flood (antediluvian) and those that followed it. The Sumerian King list (**439**), which bears a passing reference to the flood, using the significant words: the "noise" and the god "Enlil" who was annoyed by it, lists eight (or in another interpretation, ten) kings who lived before the flood in five Mesopotamian cities. This comes very close to the ten antediluvian generations of Gn. 5. Both heroes were the tenth generation after the first man. King Ziusudra reigned 36,000 years, equivalent to 600 "nêr" in the Mesopotamian numerical pattern. This denomination is parallel to the figure (in years) which the Bible gives for Noah's age at the time of the flood, which suggests that the older mythological tradition had been reduced by biblical writers to more reasonable proportions.

Analogies and Differences: The flood stories all have in common the destruction of the world and mankind, but for one man and his family. In all of them, the man is ordered to build a vessel and to take his family and certain animals and plants with him in order to escape the universal devastation. The rains fall for a traditional number of days, 7 or 40.

439

Birds are sent out of the vessel to signal the end of flood — Utnapishtim sends out a dove, a swallow and a raven, Noah a raven and then a dove twice. The disappearance of the bird is a sign that the waters have abated. Thereupon, the hero goes forth from the vessel, offers a sacrifice and thereafter enjoys a special relationship to the gods. In the Sumerian epic he becomes a god. In the Babylonian he is granted eternal life "like unto us gods", while God makes a covenant with Noah which is valid for all men and all time.

Like most of Genesis, the Noah story is a combination of diverse elements and contains repetitions and contradictions. Although in its present form it belongs to the period of the Hebrew occupation of Canaan, it contains a number of parallels with the Mesopotamian version, suggesting the way in which the Mesopotamian culture of the Hebrews' ancestors was integrated and re-interpreted in Israelite theology and folk lore.

In Ezk. 14:14, Noah is coupled with Daniel and Job as outstanding examples of righteousness. Dan'el was one of the heroes of Canaanite mythology (see Canaanite Civilization and Ugarit*). The Ugaritic form of his name could be pronounced Dani'el (the biblical form "Daniel" is a later revision). This may be a hint that, like the other Flood heroes, Noah not only survived but was granted a special status.

Other differences of detail occur in the nature of the three birds and in the length of time of the flood. The biblical narrator who wanted to describe an extraordinary, supernatural event, expanded the duration of the flood to many times the period mentioned in the Mesopotamian accounts. These are more realistic — as might be expected of people who lived between the Tigris and Euphrates rivers, and were familiar with their periodic inundations.

The several stories also reflect different stages of development in ethics and religion. In the Mesopotamian stories, the gods decide to destroy life because they are annoyed by the noise which mankind is making. The biblical story takes account of God's desire for reformation as well as punishment. Although the iniquities of mankind prompt him to send the flood to destroy them, the end of the story is not only the renewal of creation — as in the Mesopotamian stories — but also a covenant establishing laws by which mankind may live in future and thus escape repeated destruction. The foundation for this is God's irrevocable commitment to the human race, symbolized by the rainbow, not to send another flood. This is a unilateral and irreversible gift, designed to provide a setting for the giving of the laws. The inner logic of the story is God's fight against evil, first by his destructive power, then by providing Noah with rules to control man's behaviour.

Other Flood Stories: Flood stories are known in many other countries. Two thousand years before the Babylonian tablets were discovered, Josephus had quoted the account of their flood story given by Berossus, a Babylonian priest of the 3rd c. BCE who had written a history of his country's past in Greek. He gave the name of the last king before the flood as Xisouthros, the Greek form of the Sumerian hero of the flood story.

There is also a Greek story of a flood sent by Zeus to punish the sins of mankind, from which only Deukalion and his wife were saved, but this bears little detailed resemblance to the Babylonian or Mesopotamian traditions.

Evidence of Floods: The natural reaction to the discoveries of the different flood stories was to search for archaeological evidence to establish their factual basis. Floods were a common phenomenon in Mesopotamia. Layers of mud have been found amongst the strata of many ancient sites. Among the early strata of Sumerian occupation of Ur (i.e. end of 4th and beginning of 3rd mill. BCE), this layer was nearly three metres (about 10 feet) thick and scholars, especially L. Woolley and S. Langdon, were able to show that the time at which this had been deposited was very suggestive in connection with the flood stories. However, in excavated mounds nearby, no traces of such a mud layer were found, and in other sites where they did occur, they appeared at different levels, in different thicknesses, and did not belong to the same century. Moreover, they do not always represent the complete destruction of a particular settlement and its replacement by a new one. Sometimes the same culture continues above the mud level showing that whatever damage may have been suffered, the population of the pre-flood age was not wiped out.

The most reasonable conclusion seems to be that there was no universal flood. Localized floods in the Mesopotamian plain, however, may have given rise to the stories which, with all their embellishments and exaggerations, became part of the religion and mythology of Babylon and spread their influence to the authors of the Bible.

A further possibility suggested by some scholars is that the ultimate origin of the story is to be found in traditions going back to the last great pluvial period in the Paleolithic age. With successive movements of peoples these traditions were spread all over the world.

Other examples of the transformation of Mesopotamian motifs can be found in the legends of Genesis. The "Tower of Babel", for instance, had its actual model in the Ziggurat, high temple tower of Babylon (see Babylonia*).

Both stories have historical as well as cultural and literary connections with Mesopotamian sources, although in their present form, they can hardly be regarded as scientifically or historically accurate accounts.

Links between Babylonian and Biblical Stories: Opinions differ, however, as to the manner and period of the legend's transmission into Hebrew lore. E. Meyer, S. Mowinckel and E. C. Kraeling attribute it to the late Assyrian period (7th. c. BCE) but, against this, W. F. Albright has pointed out that national myths in general take shape at a very early stage in a people's history. The stories are found in the earliest prose sources of the Pentateuch, which must antedate the 8th c. Moreover, the kernel of the Hebrew story was a very early epic. Epic form is traceable in the more poetic verses, e.g. 7:11 or 8:2 and in the names, which are rare in Hebrew, although more familiar in Mesopotamian literature.

The majority opinion is now that the essentials of the story were brought to Palestine from Mesopotamia by the ancestors of the Hebrews. There is also an alternative view that the theme reached the Hebrews from the Canaanites, who had already learned it from its original eastern creators. This theory has been strengthened by the discovery at Megiddo of a tablet (**440**) of the late Bronze period (14th c. BCE) shortly before the Israelite conquest of Canaan, containing part of the Gilgamesh story. Thus, by the time the Israelites came into contact with them during the settlement, the Canaanites were already familiar with Babylonian literature. Contact between Hebrews and Canaanites was a long drawn-out process and far from exclusively war-like. Canaanite civilization, indeed, had a deep and lasting effect on Hebrew culture (see Canaanite Civilization and Ugarit*). Many scholars claim that the Megiddo tablet is powerful testimony for a Canaanite source for the Babylonian material in the Bible. This theory, in any case, rejects the idea that the Jews learned the Mesopotamian material during the Exile in Babylon and incorporated it into the national literature at and after that late date.

In conclusion, it seems that the flood story derived originally from Mesopotamian epics and was integrated into a Hebrew or Canaanite epic about Noah, which was later interpreted, revised and written in prose. The "documentary" school of biblical criticism (see Biblical Criticism*) has also advanced the theory that the story as it stands has combined two strands or documents: the J (Jahwist) source, representing the popular epic, and the P (Priestly) document which provided the religious tone and theology of the present version. This theory implies a priestly editor who, naturally, revised and rewrote the older story in keeping with his views. However, it may be nearer the truth to find his influence in interpretation and meaning rather than in the substance of the story. Such an editor may have added to the ancient traditions but he would not have altered them or seriously affected them, whatever their source. Many scholars find that the critical theory does not provide a satisfactory explanation of the sources of the biblical story of the flood. The progress of archaeological discovery and interpretation may offer other solutions.

FOOD AND MEALS. — *Outline: I. Foods: Pre-Israelite Days; Israelite Diet; Grains; Pulses and Vegetables; Condiments and Spices; Salt; Sweetening; Fruits; Milk and Dairy Products; Meat and Animal Foods; Poultry and Eggs; Insects and Fish; Prohibited Foods. II. Cooking: Baking; Cooking Utensils; Hearths; Meals; Furniture.*

I. FOODS: The eating habits of the early Israelites reflected their general living conditions. In the early days, as semi-pastoralists, and later, as small-scale farmers, they followed the patterns of the Canaanites and neighbouring peoples, with the important difference that their Law forbade certain foods to the Israelites.

Pre-Israelite Days: In the story of Sinuhe (see Egypt*), an Egyptian refugee in Canaan during the Middle Bronze Age, it is recorded that a desert chieftain gave him water and boiled milk to quench his thirst. Canaan is described as a land blessed with figs, grapes, wine, honey, olives, fruit, barley, emmer (an early type of wheat) and cattle (cf. Dt. 8:8). Having become the son-in-law of a local monarch, Sinuhe tells of eating bread and wine daily, as well as foods cooked with milk, cooked meat, roast fowl and wild beast.

440

441 441 a 441

Israelite Diet: Although the standard of living of the Israelites may have been fairly modest during most of their early history, they were later to be blessed with an abundance of grains, fruit, oil and meat (Dt. 7:13; 32:14). Some idea of the basic foods is suggested by the 10th c. BCE Gezer calendar (see Agriculture*) which lists barley, wheat, spelt and millet among the grains, besides olives, grapes, figs, pomegranates, sesame and vegetables. The main source of supply was the householder's own field, vineyard and vegetable garden. The staple food was bread, eaten with water and wine. These are often used as symbols for food in general, especially in connection with ritual or ceremonial meals (Gn. 14:18; Dt. 29:6). Wine was something of a luxury, indicating either a festive meal or someone of importance among those who ate. Milk and other dairy products were widely used and these foods were augmented by fruits and vegetables, when available. A typical household's daily diet was almost exclusively vegetarian. Except in the houses of the rich, meat appeared only at times of festivity, for a wedding (Gn. 29:22; Jud. 14:10; Est. 2:18), to celebrate the visit of an honoured guest (Gn. 18), in sacrificial meals at the sanctuary, religious holidays (Jos. 5:10), or coronations (I Sam. 10:5–9).

A list of the foods presented to David's followers in their stronghold is given in I Sam. 25:18 and, in II Sam. 17:28ff, the provisions for him and his supporters are listed as "wheat, barley, meal, parched grain, beans and lentils, honey and curds, and sheep and cheese from the herd." Solomon was able to avoid his father's frequent campaigns and, according to I K. 4:22, he and his court enjoyed a much more luxurious standard of living. "Solomon's provision for one day was thirty measures of fine flour, and sixty measures of meal, ten fat oxen, and twenty pasture-fed cattle, a hundred sheep, besides harts, gazelles, roebucks and fatted fowl."

Grains: Throughout its history, bread remained Israel's staple food. It was made of flour, either of wheat or barley, ground in a handmill or quern consisting of two stones, one above the other (see Crafts*) like those shown **(441)**: a handmill and mortar (Gezer) which rubbed the grain; a. turning handmill, still used; b. large mill of Roman times, turned by animal power. Handmills of the primitive type were found in many excavated sites of the Middle Bronze period, the most recent being in Arad*, a southern fortress town of the Judean kings. When ground, the flour might be coarse (qemaḥ) or fine (solet). The price of fine flour at the market at the gate of Samaria at the end of the siege is quoted in II K. 7:1, 16. Flour was generally made into leavened bread but at the time of Passover, unleavened bread was eaten (Ex. 12:8; see Crafts*: Bread-making). The unleavened bread, reserved for the Passover altar celebration, has been preserved among the Jews to this day. Among the documents of the Jewish military colony at Elephantine* in Egypt is one (No. 21, Cowley) written in the name of Darius, king of Persia, authorizing the observance of the festival* of unleavened bread (Passover).

Instead of making bread, grain might also be eaten raw (II K. 4:42) by rolling fresh ears in the hands to free the grain from the husks (Dt. 23:25). When Jesus' disciples were hungry one memorable Sabbath, they picked ears of grain to eat raw in this fashion (Mt. 12:1). Grain might also be roasted or parched (qalî). Parched grain, bread and sour wine made the meal of the reapers in the story of Ruth (2:14) and David took his brothers parched grain and bread when they were encamped with Saul (I Sam. 17:17). Bruised in a mortar, grains of wheat yielded the "crushed grain" (in Arabic, burghul) of Leviticus (2:14, 16) which was then dried and cooked. In the early period, barley cakes were used as bread by the poorer people (Jud. 7:13) and in New Testament times, barley loaves and fish were apparently a common meal (Jn. 6:9). In addition to wheat and barley, millet and spelt (fitches, "kussêmeth" in Hebrew) were also eaten (Ezk. 4:9), as well as sorghum. The latter or emmer ("doḥan" in Hebrew and "dhurah" in Arabic) often took the place of wheat in the preparation of bread among the poorer peasantry. Ezekiel recommends its use with wheat, barley and various vegetables for the making of a mixed loaf. These barley loaves from Thebes are 3500 years old **(443)**.

Pulses and Vegetables: (see Agriculture*) A meal made up of vegetables alone, "a dinner of herbs" without meat was considered very poor fare (Pr. 15:17), although it was quite common, as noted above. When men were starving, vegetables were more highly regarded, e.g. Esau traded his birthright for a pottage of red "adashim", lentils (Gn. 25:29, 34). This was probably a stew flavoured with onions and other ingredients. When the Israelites were complaining of the mean desert fare of the Exodus (Nu. 11:5) they recalled the abundance of vegetables they had left behind them in Egypt: "the cucumbers, the melons, the leeks, the onions and garlic". These were also cultivated in Palestine. Four varieties of beans are mentioned as are other legumes such as peas and chick peas. In one or two texts, the use of these vegetables is mentioned, to the exclusion of all others, which suggests that green vegetables were not considered very important and that the ones used as food were picked in the fields where they grew wild. Lettuce was certainly such a vegetable, for originally it was a "bitter herb" and sweet varieties were only developed during the later Old Testament period.

443

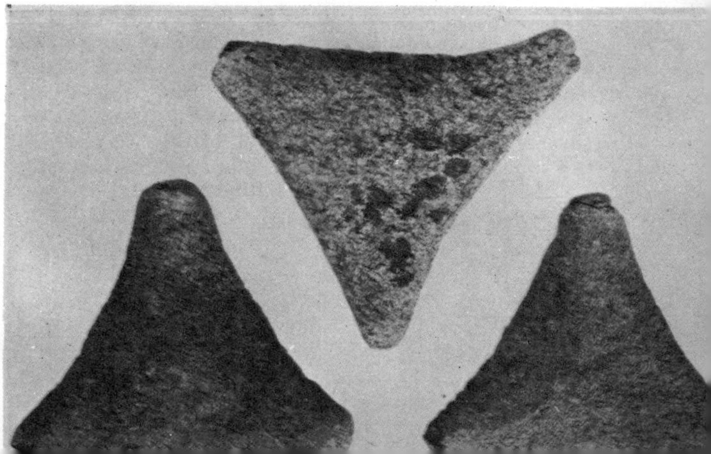

442.1

442.2

442.3

Many other "bitter herbs" were picked in the fields although, apparently, not cultivated. These included chicory and endives (an herb used in the Passover ritual, Ex. 12:8); radish, the mustard seed, mandrakes or mandragora (Mt. 13:31) and many others, eaten either raw or cooked. The agricultural tractates of the Mishnah* in Zeraim give full information about the wide range of "herbs" cultivated in later times and thus available to supplement either a simple vegetable diet or one that included meat. The Mishnah Pesachim 2:6, reflecting post-Exilic conditions, mentions five kinds of herbs which might be used for the Passover meal: lettuce, chicory, peppermint, snakeroot and dandelion.

Condiments and Spices: Spices were always essential, and trade in them with Arabia and the Far East was an important matter. It has been suggested that before the introduction of pepper (first mentioned in the Mishnah), seeds like coriander (Ex. 16:31), black cummin (Is. 28:25), origanum or the post-Exilic nigella (Heb.: "kezaḥ"; "melanthion" to the Greeks and Romans), played an important part in preparing food and were grown in the country. Caperberries (Ex. 12:8) were eaten as an appetizer before meals and also used as a condiment. Other herbs were grown, notably mint and rue, which was used mainly for medicinal purposes. These dried products found in Pompei (**442**) were common in Palestine: 1. pine-nuts; 2. spice; 3. dates; 4. carob-beans; 5. walnuts; 6. persimmon.

Jesus condemned the Pharisaic system of tithing certain spices and herbs (Lk. 11:42) while disregarding the essential virtues. Spices, notably mustard seed (Mt. 13:31), are mentioned in the parables.

Salt: Salt, which was particularly important in sacrificial ritual and for ceremonial purposes, came mainly from the salt pans of the Dead Sea. Because of its function as a food preservative, salt was a symbol of permanence, which may explain the "covenant of salt" (Lv. 2:13; Nu. 18:19; II Ch. 13:5), meaning an inviolate covenant, established for all time. Thus the salt used in every sacrifice may have come to symbolize God's irrevocable covenant with Israel (see Covenant*). More information is now available about the significance of salt in rituals and covenants. One element in its symbolism appears to be the sowing of a conquered district with salt to represent its permanent destruction. In biblical Aramaic, the word used for salt (Ezr. 4:14) is synonymous with the term for maintenance and support, possibly reflecting similar implications and ritual customs.

Sweetening: Sweetening, on the other hand, was usually with fig or carob syrup, as sugar was unknown in Bible times (see below, Fruits; see also Agriculture*). The honey of biblical references ("debash"), like the Arabic *dibs*, was probably date honey, or possibly the syrup of the carob, a common tree in Palestine although it is hardly mentioned in the Bible. Its husks ("keraton" in Greek) figure in the New Testament parable of the Prodigal Son (Lk. 15:16). Such honey was used in the making of "baked-meats" and cakes (Ex. 16:31). Bee's honey was a treat for Samson's family (Jud. 14:8, 9) but it became generally available later (Ps. 19:10; Pr. 16:24).

Fruits: The Israelites were blessed with a plentiful supply of tree fruits (Lv. 19:23 ff; see Agriculture*). They were promised "a land of wheat and barley, of vines and fig trees and pomegranates, a land of olive trees and honey" (Dt. 8:8) and an intensively cultivated Palestine richly fulfilled the promise. The spies sent into Canaan by Moses reported a land rich in pomegranates, figs and grapes on the vine (Nu. 13:23).

Figs were a most important fruit. The trees grew all over the land and they are often cited with the vine as symbols of prosperity, "every man under his vine and under his fig-tree" (I K. 4:25; Mic. 4:4; Zech. 3:10). The sweet first-ripened fruits were considered a great delicacy (Is. 28:4; Jer. 24:2),

442.4

442.5

442.6

while the later ones were used for the cakes of dried figs ("d^{e}belah"; I Ch. 12:40; II K. 20:7; see Agriculture*; Medicine*). This cake was made of figs (**444**).

The Mishnah testifies that *dates* were eaten both fresh and pressed into cakes for convenience in transport. Date palms (mentioned in Ps. 92:12) were a speciality in the Jericho* district and provided a source of wealth for both King Herod* and Cleopatra (see Herod*; Rome and the Jews*).

444

445

446

Wine: Most of the grapes produced in the vineyards went into the making of wine. The country was above all "a land of wine . . . and vineyards" (II K. 18:32) and there is ample evidence of this in the remains of ancient wine presses found throughout Palestine (see Agriculture* for a more detailed consideration). Wine, usually mixed with water, was a standard item of diet, although lighter wines might be drunk without dilution in olden times. According to the Talmud, most wine was mixed in a proportion of one part wine to three of water but in New Testament times, the lighter wine of the Sharon was drunk mixed with only two parts water. Wine in any form was forbidden to the ascetic Nazirites* (Nu. 6:3) and Rechabites*, whose vows included one of abstinence. This terracotta of a camel bearing wine amphoras dates from Hellenistic times (**445**).

Other fruit trees included the pomegranate, quince, sycamore or fig-mulberry (Am. 7:14; see Agriculture*). Varieties of almonds (Gn. 43:11; 30:37; Jer. 1:11 ff;) and walnuts (Song 6:11) are also mentioned.

Olives were grown for oil, which was used for ritual purposes and which also supplied most of the modern uses of butter and other fats in cooking. The olives themselves, preserved in brine, were a favourite delicacy and also an important article of food. As in ancient Greece, olives, onions and bread could and did sustain labourers and soldiers at all times and for long periods. The most important use of the olive, however, was to provide oil. Pure "beaten" olive oil (see Agriculture*; Crafts*) was needed for religious ceremonial and especially for the sanctuary (Ex. 27:20) and formed an important article in Israel's fiscal system and trade (I K. 5:11). A number of inscribed potsherds, dated to the 8th c. BCE, were found in the ruins of Samaria*, the northern capital, most of them tax receipts for agricultural produce such as wine and oil (see Seals*; Inscriptions*; Tribes*).

Milk and Dairy Products: Milk from ewes, goats and, to a lesser extent, cows was readily available and dairy products — milk, butter and cheeses — were a regular part of the diet (Pr. 27:27; 30:33; Job 10:10). Jael gave Sisera milk to drink when he appealed to her (Jud. 4:19) and David took "ten cheeses to the commander" of his brothers' "thousand" (I Sam. 17:18). The "butter" was probably rendered and clarified cream of milk ("samneh" today, or "ghee" to the orientals). Cheese could be bought in Jerusalem in the "cheesemakers" (Tyropeon) Vale (see Jerusalem*).

Meat and Animal Foods: Meat was the most highly regarded foodstuff and was eaten on festive occasions or offered to especially honoured guests (e.g. Abraham in Gn. 18: 7 and Esau in Gn. 25:28). The earliest Passover meal was a roast lamb (Ex. 12:8) eaten with bitter herbs and unleavened bread (see Samaritans*). Throughout the monarchy, meat remained a luxury to the poorer people but it became a regular provision for the tables of the wealthy and, of course, the kings (see above; I K. 4:22 ff).

Right up to New Testament times, the most delectable fare continued to be the "fatted calf", a specially fattened calf taken directly from the herd to be cooked for the table (Gn. 18:7; I K. 4:23; Lk. 15:23), or the stalled or still-fed ox (Pr. 15:17).

The flesh of the *goat*, especially young kids, was also highly valued although as meat became more plentiful in post-Exilic times, a well-fleeced lamb was preferred and kid became the most frequent sacrificial animal and the one most commonly eaten. This gives point to the complaint of the Prodigal Son's elder brother that he had served his father many years and never disobeyed a command, yet he had never been given even a kid that he "might make merry with my friends" (Lk. 15:29).

The great importance of meat was its use at the sanctuary where certain portions of an animal were burnt as an offering. The animals prescribed for use in sacrifice were bullocks, calves, goats, rams and lambs of the fat-tailed sheep, pigeons and turtledoves. Portions were reserved for the priests in each case, what was left being consumed by the worshippers (see Sacrifice*; Priests*).

Poultry and Eggs: The eggs of "permitted" fowl were eaten as food (Dt. 22:6) and fatted fowl such as geese and chickens were plentiful, apparently, during the monarchy and thereafter (I K. 4:23; Is. 10:14; Lk. 11:12). Some scholars believe that chickens did not reach the Near East until the 7th–6th c. BCE and became common in Palestine only in the Persian period, although a drawing of a rooster (**31**) on a seal dated around 600 BCE found at Tel-en-Nasbeh, 13 kms. north of Jerusalem, suggests that they were known earlier. Other edible birds included pigeons, partridges and quail (see also Hospitality*).

Insects and Fish: Certain insects of the locust family were permitted food for the Israelites (Lv. 11:22 ff) and John the Baptist* is reported to have lived on locusts and wild honey in the wilderness (Mt. 3:4). After removing the head, wings and legs, the body of the locust was fried in rendered butter (samneh, see above) or preserved in salt.

The *fishing industry* developed during the monarchy, exploiting the fresh-water fish of the Sea of Galilee and the Jordan (Jer. 16:16). Fishermen used nets, like their neighbours the Egyptians and the Assyrians (**447**). Nehemiah (3:3) tells of the repairing of the Fish Gate of Jerusalem and later (13:16) complains of the sale of "fish and all kinds of wares" on the Sabbath. During this period, Tyrian merchants (see Phoenicia*) did a considerable trade in dried and cured fish, mostly coming from Syria and Asia Minor. The greater part of Jesus' life and teaching took place in Galilee (see Jesus*), where the Sea of Galilee was the centre for an important fishing industry. The majority of Jesus' disciples and probably many of his other followers were fishermen. In addition to supplying fresh fish for the local market, fish were also salted, and cured in the sun, for sale throughout Palestine. Cured fish were at all times a popular provision for a journey. Jesus' miracle of feeding the five thousand (Mt. 15:32–38) was probably performed with cured fish, Luke (11:11 ff) mentions fish and eggs. These sun-dried fish date from 1250 BCE (**446**).

Prohibited Foods: The Israelites were subject to strict rules about foods which were ritually unclean and therefore not to be eaten (Lv. 11:2, 3; Dt. 14:4–20; see Impurity*). Meat must not be cooked with milk (Dt. 14:21) in deliberate contrast to the Canaanites among whom this was a popular method of preparation. Eating the blood of any animal was absolutely prohibited (see Sacrifice*), as was consumption of certain portions of the intestinal fat of sacrificial animals (Lv. 3:3 ff). The fruit of trees before the fourth year of their growth was also forbidden (Lv. 19:23, 24).

447

It was forbidden to reap every corner of a field; a small part was left as the portion of the poor, as prescribed by Lv. 19:9, though perhaps this custom was a survival of much older provisions for the "spirits" of the field (see Magic*). Two different kinds of seed might not be sown together (Lv. 19:19; see Agriculture*).

II. COOKING: In Old Testament days there were no kitchens. Food was cooked in the open "before the tent", in the closed courtyards of houses in the cities (see Cities, Israelite Period*) or in the communal living room. Meals might be prepared by either men or women (Gn. 18:7, 8) and it appears that the sexes ate together (Dt. 16:14; I Sam. 1:4; Job 1:4; Ruth 2:14).

Professional cooks ("tabbaḥim" and "tabbaḥoth" are mentioned; I Sam. 8: 13; 9:23) but, clearly, these were beyond the reach of any but the richest households. The cooking of meat is referred to repeatedly, but there are only a few references to cooking vegetables (Gn. 25:29; II K. 4:38–39). In general, meat was either boiled in a stew in an earthenware pot (Jud. 6:19 ff; Ezk. 24:3–5) or roasted over an open fire (Ex. 12:9; see below). Among the modern Samaritans*, the Passover lamb continues to be prepared in the ancient way, roasted on a spit over hot embers in an earth oven, with a pomegranate branch laid across its mouth. Meat was also frequently salted to preserve it (Lv. 2:13). Various condiments and spices, familiar throughout the ancient Near East, were eaten with the meat.

Pancakes made of a flour dough and filled with a tasty mixture were fried in oil (II Sam. 13:8) or baked on hot stones pulled out of the embers of a fire (I K. 19:6). Excavators have found many baking pans (**433**) on which the dough of bread and cakes was laid and cooked. When Gideon wished to honour his angelic messenger (Jud. 6:19), he prepared a meal of unleavened cakes made of flour, boiled meat which he put in a basket (sāl), and broth in a pot (parûr) which was usually small and of earthenware, as illustrated (**448**; 1st c. BCE).

448

449

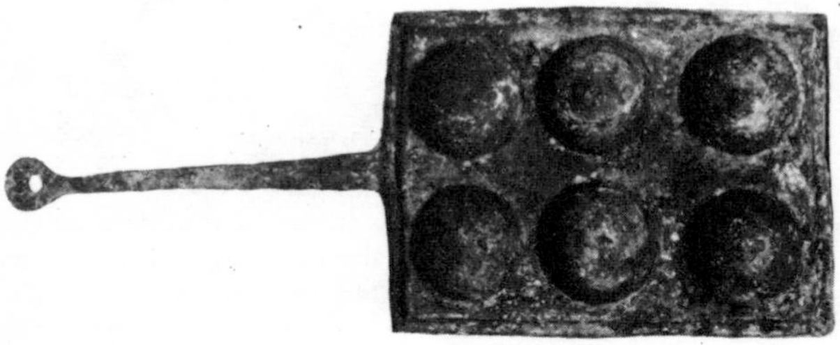
450

455

454

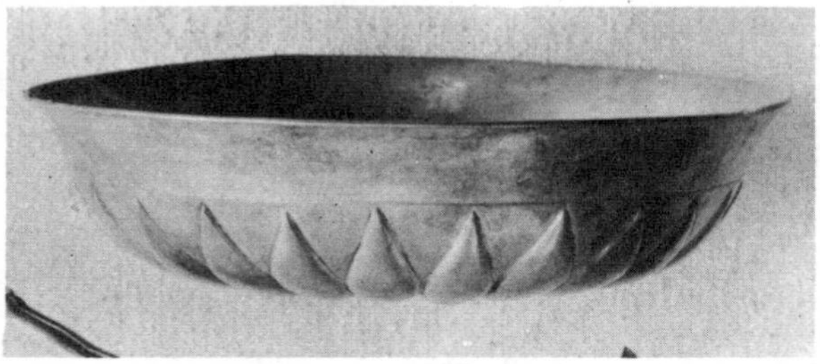
456

457

Fish would be roasted on a charcoal fire, generally using a wooden or iron spit, although the fish eaten by the disciples of Jesus was cooked directly on the charcoal. The appearance of sun-dried fish before cooking is shown in this 13th c. BCE illustration (**446**).

According to the Mishnah, eggs were either boiled in the shell or fried in olive oil in a saucepan.

Cereals like wheat and barley were roasted on an iron plate or in a pan (**449**) to make the parched corn mentioned above, or they might be boiled in a pot to make a coarse porridge. Vegetables were sometimes added to the grain to make a stew which might include rendered butter.

The *fat* most used was olive oil. With this, vegetables, fish and eggs were cooked and fine cakes baked.

Baking: The cakes the widow of Zarephath made for Elijah with a handful of meal (I K. 17:13 ff) were baked on hot stones and covered with hot embers. Thin wafers of dough spread with oil (Ex. 29:2), sometimes strewn with seeds, were baked in an earthenware oven. Sometimes cakes would be baked with honey (Ezk. 16:13, 19) and these tasted so good that the manna of the desert was compared to them (Ex. 16:31; Nu. 11:8). The dough was kneaded in a stone mortar as this model shows (**451**) or it would be rolled as in this 5th c. Greek model (**452**).

Cooking Utensils: Iron utensils used in baking and cooking were the griddle or baking pan, which was a shallow iron plate, and the frying pan (Lv. 2:5–7; Ezk. 4:3; **450**). Ordinary cooking dishes and pots were at first of baked, unglazed clay, while ritual vessels and a few special dishes were of copper. The different types mentioned and found by excavators include the "sîr" or pot (**387**), evidently a large sized pot made of bronze (I K. 7:40; Ezk. 24:3; Zech. 14:21); similar to this were the "fleshpot" (Ex. 16:3); the "kiyôr" or shallow pan (**456**); the "dûd" or kettle (**454**); "qallāḫat" or cauldron (**457**; I Sam. 2:14; Jer. 1:13; see Pottery*). In post-Exilic times, ordinary pottery vessels were replaced in wealthy houses by glazed "vessels of the service" (so-called by the Mishnah) or metal dishes, sometimes even of silver or gold as illustrated by contemporary Roman ware.

451

Knives to cut meat were at first made of flint (Jos. 5:2), later of bronze. Forks were not used, apart from a single large one for lifting the pieces of meat out of the pot, a three-pronged fork (**367**; I Sam. 2:13). (For other utensils and drinking vessels used and discovered in excavations, see Pottery*.) Ladles were common (**455**).

Hearths: Cooking was done on an open hearth, partially built up with stones as a protection against the wind. Most houses excavated have a depression of varying dimensions in the floor, either in the centre or in a corner, bearing clear traces of fire. Obviously, this was the family hearth (Is. 30:14). Sometimes more elaborate hearths (ovens) were built (Lv. 11:35). In Mesopotamia, cooking hearths like these were found dating back to the 3rd and 2nd mill. BCE. Round hearths of unfired clay, strengthened with broken pottery, about 70 cm. in diameter, have been unearthed in numerous Israelite and Judean excavations. The *oven* used to bake bread and other things was a portable jar or receptacle of terra cotta, which could be heated over a fire (**453**).

Meals: The first meal of the day did not call for any cooking and was simply a "morning morsel" in the words of the Talmud, consisting of bread and olives, with an onion or any other fruit or vegetable which might be in season. A heavy breakfast was a matter for reproach (Ecc. 10:16). The midday meal would be eaten at noon in the fields or at home, and would consist of bread soaked in wine with a handful of parched corn, a "pottage of bread broken into a bowl" (Bel and the Dragon 1:33, see Apocrypha*), or bread and grilled fish (Jn. 21:9, 13). The main meal of the day was eaten in the evening, according to the Bible and Josephus, usually a little before and after sunset, before it became pitch dark. This is the supper time of Lk. 14:17, 17:7–8.

Furniture: In the early days, people sat on the ground to eat, on cushions, mats of straw (**460**) or rugs. In post-Exilic homes, according to the Mishnah, food was served on low "round, square or oblong" wooden tables with the participants sitting around on couches or divans, similar to those of the Egyptians, as shown (**458**). This appears to have been the practice at Qumran (see Dead Sea Scrolls*). In wealthy homes, each honoured guest would be served at a separate table. This wooden table was found in a Mid-Bronze tomb in Jericho (**459**).

452

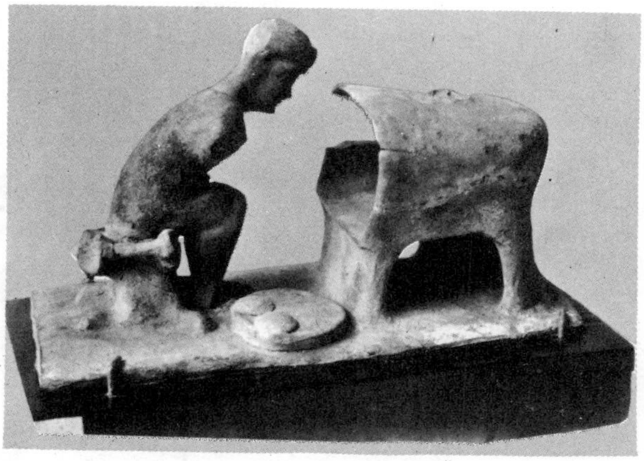
453

458

459

460

461

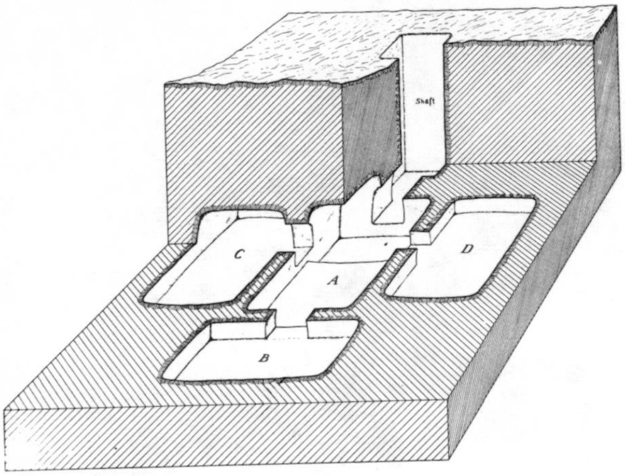

462

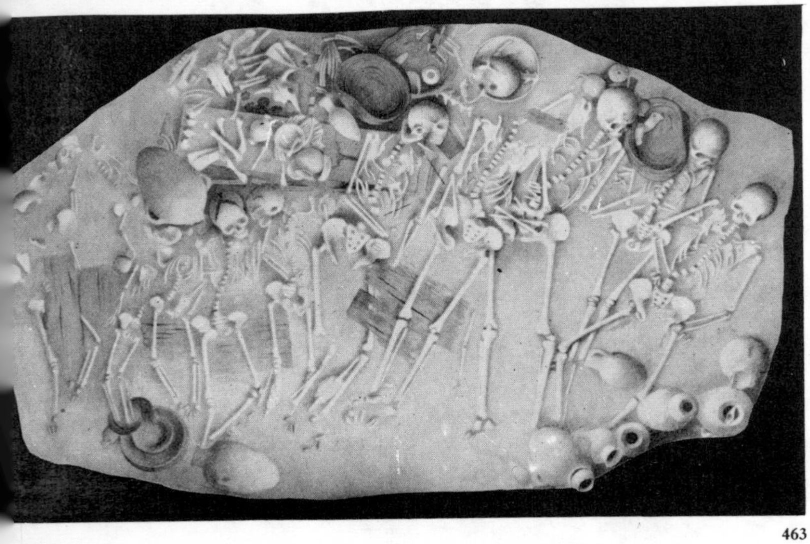

463

FUNERARY CUSTOMS [BURIAL, MOURNING, TOMBS].—*Outline: I. Burial: Death; Preparing the Corpse; Burial; Tombs: Pre-Israelite, Early Israelite, and during the Monarchy; Poor Burials; The Unknown Tomb of David. II. Post-Exilic Customs: The Monumental Tombs of the Kidron Valley; The Necropolis of Beth-Shearim; Interpretation of Funeral Rites. III. Mourning Customs: Evidence of Israel's Neighbours; Pre-Exilic Customs; Funeral Lamentations; Mourning Period.*

I: BURIAL: **Death:** The Hebrews did not believe that death meant total annihilation, but there was no concept of it as the separation between two distinct elements of body and soul. A live person is a living soul, "nefesh"; a dead person a dead nefesh. Death meant the loss of vitality and strength, but so long as the body, or at least the bones remained, the nefesh continued to exist. In its greatly weakened state, it sheltered in Sheol, the subterranean abode of the dead (Gn. 44:29; Job 10:21 ff; Is. 14:9 ff. passim), leading a shadowy, meaningless existence. However, as the soul was presumed to feel what was done to its dead body, a corpse must be given honourable burial. It must not be burned, and to leave it as a prey for wild animals would bring curses to the living.

Preparing the Corpse: Pins, fibulae and other ornaments **(332)** discovered in excavated tombs in Palestine show that the dead were buried in their clothes. The description of Samuel rising from Sheol for instance (I Sam. 28:14) includes the fact that he was "wrapped in a robe". Ezekiel describes the brave lying in Sheol in their armour, with their weapons in their hands and their swords resting beneath their heads.

In Old and New Testament times, the dead were carried to the grave laid on a bier. Talmudic literature records that until the time of Rabbi Gamaliel (end 1st c. CE) the people would bury their dead in luxurious garments involving considerable expense. He ruled instead that the dead be buried swathed in white cloths and the custom has been maintained until today among the Jews. According to the New Testament, a corpse was washed (Ac. 9:37), anointed (Mk. 16:1) and wrapped in shrouds containing spices (Jn. 19:40). The hands and feet were tied with bands and the face covered with a kerchief (Jn. 20:7). According to Mt. 27:59, Joseph of Arimathea took the body of Jesus and swathed it in a white shroud before burying it. Jn. 11:44 describes the risen Lazarus appearing at the opening of his tomb "his hands and feet bound with bandages and his face wrapped with a cloth."

Burial: Embalming was never practiced in Israel. Jacob and Joseph were embalmed but in both cases it is ascribed explicitly to Egyptian custom (Gn. 50:2, 26). There is evidence that corpses were cremated in Palestine long before the coming of the Israelites or, later, among groups of foreigners living in the country. The Israelites never practiced cremation which, like embalming, was considered sacrilegious and was forbidden by Mosaic Law (Lv. 20:14; 21:9; Am. 2:1). I Sam. 31:12 records that the bones of Saul and Jonathan were burned before burial by the people of Jabesh-Gilead but this was a departure from the usual custom. The parallel passage in I Ch. (10:12) omits the burning and has Saul and his sons buried, not burned. Incense, however, was burned at the side of the bodies of kings and other high dignitaries (Jer. 34:5; II Ch. 16:14).

Tombs: Pre-Israelite: A large number of Canaanite tombs from the Early to the Middle and Late Bronze Ages have been found throughout Palestine in many of the excavations of ancient towns (described under Ancient Cities* and accompanying articles). The most usual tomb was a natural cave or irregular, rounded chamber reached through a vertical shaft which could be sealed by a stone slab (**461**). The bones and pottery in a shaft tomb at Megiddo are common to the Bronze Age (**462**). Sometimes, in more elaborate constructions, the shaft had a flight of steps and the chambers were rectangular in shape. In general, burial grounds were outside a village or town. The normal arrangement of a shaft tomb (Megiddo **461**) is shown; three chambers BCD opened off the central chamber A.

The tombs of the Early Bronze Age (4th mill. BCE) in Palestine were used successively for a number of burials and the custom was continued in the Middle Bronze. After each burial, the shaft would be filled, to be re-excavated the next time the tomb was needed. When a new burial was to be made, the bodies and accompanying offerings from earlier burials would be pushed to the back and sides of the tomb chamber. The final burial remained intact against a background of jumble from earlier interments, as shown in this picture (**463**) from a Jericho tomb (ca. 1600–1700 BCE). Many of the tombs probably belonged to a family group and contained twenty or so bodies, which would cover a few generations.

The bodies were laid side by side and, as can be seen from the Jericho tomb, a supply of food and equipment was placed beside them. This custom is found, to the great benefit of archaeological study, from the fourth millenium BCE onwards. The offerings apparently represented what was considered the necessary provision for the after-life and may equally well have been the equipment used by the dead in this life. Besides food and drink, aromatic oils and perfumes would also be placed in the tomb in clay pots and jars (**462**). As many of the vessels have survived reasonably intact, they provide valuable information about the sequence of cultures of the group that used the tombs. The Israelites continued the custom, although in a different form. Whereas the Canaanites used to supply their dead with food and drink, furniture and implements for use in the netherworld and on their way there, later Israelite graves rarely contain more than personal belongings and pottery containers.

Early Israelite Graves: No authentic tomb from the earliest Israelite or Patriarchal times has ever been identified (cf. Hebron*). Archaeologists interpret this as evidence that the majority of burial places of the common people must have been extremely modest — simple shallow graves which would easily be obliterated by time and tilling or erosion. Common people were probably buried in common burial pits, a "tomb of the sons of the people" and the practice continued until the monarchy (II K. 23:6; Jer. 26:23). More important burials were in caves or shelters under rocks. A few tombs of this kind have been found on the outskirts of Jerusalem and there is ample biblical evidence for their use.

In the time of the Patriarchs, according to Genesis, Sarah (23:19), Abraham, (25:9), Isaac, Rebecca and Leah (49:31) and Jacob (50:13) were all buried in the "Cave of Machpelah to the east of Mamre which Abraham bought . . . as a burying place" (see Patriarchs*: Abraham; Hebron*). In general, people who died away from home were buried where they died. Deborah, Rebecca's nurse, was buried near Bethel "under an oak" known henceforth as "Alon bacuth" (the oak of weeping; Gn. 35:8) and Rachel was buried on the way to Ephrath (Bethlehem; Gn. 35:19–20). Jacob erected a pillar at Rachel's tomb.

Burial during the Monarchy: Family tombs continued to be used during the period of settlement and once the kingdom had been established. Gideon (Jud. 8:32); Samson (Jud. 16:31), Asahel (II Sam. 2:32) and Ahitophel (II Sam. 17:23) were all buried in "the tomb of their father". The remains of Saul and Jonathan were finally laid to rest in Zela, in the tomb of Saul's father, in their own tribal territory of Benjamin (II Sam. 21:14). It is mentioned that Samuel was buried "in his house at Ramah" (I Sam. 25:1), and the same is recorded of Joab (I K. 2:34), but this may mean a family sepulchre rather than a dwelling. Except for the kings, there is no evidence that the dead were buried inside the towns. Tombs would be scattered over surrounding slopes, or grouped in places where the soil was suitable.

The pattern of the graves hardly changed. The normal tomb of the period of the monarchy was either a natural cave (**464**), or else a burial chamber cut out of the soft rock, made with an entrance opening, sometimes with a few steps. The bodies were laid on ledges hewn out of the rock. When the chamber was filled, the bones were removed to niches in the walls of the chamber, so as to make room for new burials. The tombs might be used by a family or a clan for a considerable time (see **468**).

A typical group of tombs of this period was discovered in the excavation of Samaria*. The best preserved is an irregular cave measuring 5 m. by 4.70 (**465**). A rock pillar in the centre, which once supported the roof, has now col-

464

465

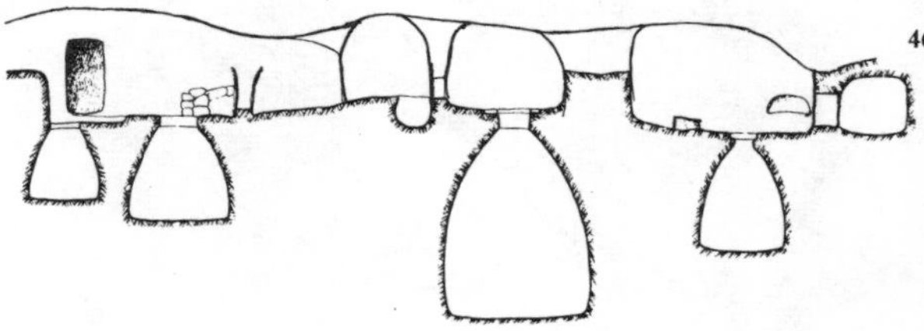

466

467

468

lapsed. An opening in the north wall led into a smaller chamber (2.4 × 1.9 metres and only 1.55 high) which must have been the burial place. It contained four skeletons, three adults, one child, laid with their heads to the east. Beside the bones were pots, beads of semi-precious stones, bronze and other objects. Outside the chamber a kind of bench, 0.44 metres high, was cut in the rock. In the floor of the cave were six holes, some with a double-rimmed mouth to carry a cover stone; two of them were connected by a narrow and shallow channel. The holes opened into bottle-shaped rock-cut pits, varying in depth from 2.20 to 4.50 m. and in lower diameter from 1.80 to 2.90 m. The pits were full of pottery, much of which had apparently been broken intentionally; there were also objects in bronze, iron, stone and bone, as well as some animal bones. The pits suggest the practice of a cult of the dead (see below: Interpretation), in spite of the rigorous opposition to it by the prophets.

The stone pillars which were sometimes placed over a grave (Gn. 35:20; II Sam. 18:18) like the stele and funeral monuments erected on the "high places" may also have been part of a cult of the dead (this is discussed under High Places*).

In general, however, tombs of the Israelite period show few signs of burial offerings, beyond some pottery and clay lamps. Funeral offerings in the sense of provisions for the future use of the dead, such as the Canaanites had provided are rarely found although there was a time when this custom was followed. The custom of leaving offerings by the dead is not necessarily connected with any acts of worship towards them — which never existed in Israel. It indicates a belief in survival after death although the Israelites did not express it as crudely as had the Canaanites. Men's idea of the future of the dead had developed. Quite possibly the offerings had no more than a symbolic value, but they raise a complex problem.

Nevertheless, the entrance to a grave was carefully closed against robbers or beasts of prey. Sometimes sepulchres of great splendour were prepared. Isaiah denounced a high official "Shebna, who is over the house" for the magnificence of the tomb he had carved for himself (Is. 22:15–16). When a funerary inscription* (cf. artic.) from the period of the first Temple was discovered in the village of Siloam with an indecipherable name, it was very tempting to link it with the man Isaiah had in mind. The inscription runs, in the opinion of H. Avigad, "This is the sepulchre of . . . . iah who is over the house. There is no silver and no gold here, but only (his bones) and the bones of his handmaiden with him. Cursed is the man who will open this (sepulchre)." The title in the inscription and the date of the tomb would both fit Shebnayahu who was a contemporary of Hezekiah, but any certain identification is impossible (see **531**).

It is interesting to compare this with a Phoenician funerary inscription (**468**) in Cyprus (900–850 BCE) reading: "He who defiles this sarcophagus will perish by . . . the hand of Ba'al . . . . by the hand of the assembly of God . . . ."

Poor Burials: Not every family could afford to maintain large or elaborate tombs. A common grave or trench in which the bodies of homeless people or condemned criminals were thrown, was to be found in the Kidron valley near Jerusalem. A more exalted offender, or dead enemy, might have a cairn of stones raised over his grave, like Achan

469

the son of Zerah (Jos. 7:26), Absalom (II Sam. 18:17), the king of Ai (Jos. 8:29) or the five Canaanite kings (Jos. 10:27).

The Unknown Tomb of David: In spite of the certainty of popular tradition, the data on David's place of burial are in fact too scanty to enable his tomb to be identified. A tomb of the Canaanite type, made from a cave approached by a shaft with steps, has been discovered on the south-eastern slope of Mount Zion within the area of ancient Jerusalem (the Ophel, see Jerusalem*), the original "City of David". By comparison with tombs at Megiddo, Ugarit and elsewhere, its entrance could be reconstructed **(466)** and it has been suggested that it was the tomb of one of the early Jebusite kings of Jerusalem and that it could possibly have been used for David. It is recorded (I K. 2:10) that David was buried "in the city of David" and this new discovery is a much more likely site than the famous "Tomb of David" under the hall believed to be the "Cenacle" (see Christianity, Early*) near the church of the Dormition at the south-western end of the city. This site is based only on the tenuous evidence of an Arab tradition which knows the place as Nebi-Dahood (David the Prophet, or Holy David) and on mediaeval Jewish traditions (see illustr. under Acts*).

II. POST-EXILIC BURIAL CUSTOMS: From the late Hellenistic period a new type of family sepulchre made its appearance. Instead of laying the bodies on ledges on three sides of the tomb, narrow perpendicular niches were cut into the walls and the bodies placed inside. Alternatively, the bodies would be placed in a sarcophagus of limestone or lead **(469)**. Later on the bones would be gathered together into stone coffers or ossuaries ("gluskamah") and the sepulchre made available for new occupants. The ossuaries might be made of wood, clay or lead. Stone ones were made in the form of houses with an arched roof, often decorated with rosettes of six, nine, twelve or more petals, or other plant and architectural motifs **(470)**. Others were left undecorated. Many of them were inscribed in Hebrew, Aramaic or Greek with the names of the dead whose bones they contained. Over a thousand of these ossuaries have been found in Jerusalem alone, all of them dating between the 1st c. BCE and the 2nd CE.

The use of such ossuaries, sarcophagi, burial niches or coffins in Palestine began after Old Testament times. Stone sarcophagi had been known for centuries in the countries adjoining Palestine, but their use by the Jews was only introduced in the Herodian period, and was restricted to the wealthy and prominent. Like the lead coffins and the more modest ossuaries, the stone sarcophagi were decorated with motifs borrowed from Hellenistic (Graeco-Oriental) religions.

470

471

472 a

472 b

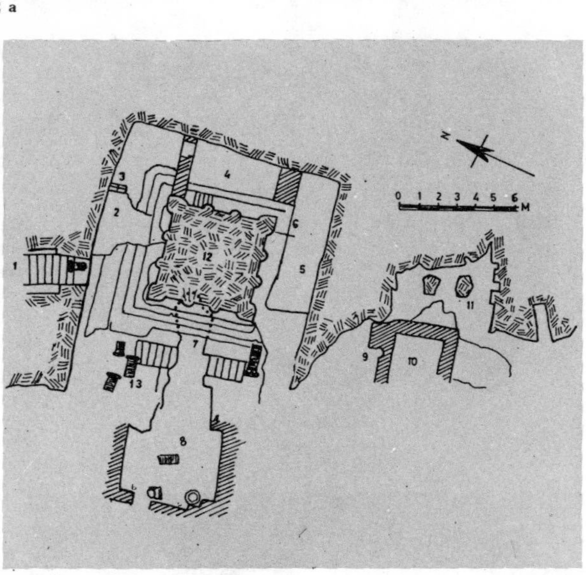

473

474

Tombs continued to be closed against marauding men or beasts. Sometimes this was done by a heavy stone door which could be locked. Other tombs were closed by means of a circular stone, as in this Herodian tomb (**471**) which could be rolled into position along a groove, propelled by a simple lever and kept in place by a small stone, called a "dofek".

In general, until the late Hellenistic period, tombs were not distinguished by monuments. Rabbinic tradition (confirmed in Mt. 23:27–29) records that the doors were coated with chalk or whitewash as a warning to the passer-by to avoid the ritual defilement caused by inadvertent contact.

The first reference to adding a commemorative monument to a tomb is the account in I Mac. (13:27–30) of the Hasmonean Simon's memorial to his brothers at Modiin (see Hasmoneans*). The custom of building monumental mausoleums was apparently becoming widespread among the leading families.

The Monumental Tombs of the Kidron Valley: Some very fine post-Exilic tombs and monuments were found in the Kidron Valley, just to the south of Jerusalem's walls. These include the ones known to tradition as the "tombs of Absalom, Zechariah and St. James", shown in this general view (**472**). In fact the inscriptions prove that they were all the tombs of members of the aristocratic, priestly family, the Bnei-Hezir (see High Priests*), and they all belong to the 1st century BCE.

The monuments and the mausoleum were all carved out of the rock. On the right is a commemorative monument ("nefesh" in Hebrew) in the form of a cube with Ionic decoration, surmounted by an Egyptian cornice and pyramid. Combinations of this nature were particularly common in the funerary architecture of the Hellenistic period. The upper part of the mausoleum (centre) had an ornamental Doric facade carved out of the rock. Its subterranean part was arranged according to the plan (**473**: 1) the staircase leading to the monolith and tombs of Bnei Hezir (2, 3, 4, 6) which originally consisted of a central room and surrounding funeral chambers equipped with horseshoe shaped benches and added niches. The mediaeval monks who attributed the tomb to St. James reconstructed the central chamber and the niches to serve as monastic cells and a church. 5 is a Byzantine cistern and 2 and 8 the ruins of the sanctuary of St. James. 9 and 10 are monastic cells; 11 an antique tomb and 12 the nefesh or monolithic monument. The vestiges of the mediaeval hermitage of St. James can be seen at the foot of the monolith. The front of the tomb of Bnei Hezir and the stairs leading up to it are also shown (**474**).

Other Monumental Tombs: These were the most elaborate tombs and funeral structures found, although other rock-cut tombs were discovered all around Jerusalem and near other ancient Israelite and post-Exilic cities. Tombs built after the Hasmonean era show a generally more careful workmanship than those of the 2nd cent. BCE. A shallow dome known as the arcosolium was placed over the benches in the tombs, although the central chamber retained its flat ceiling. During the Roman era, stone sarcophagi began to be replaced by coffins of lead and wood (**478**).

The Necropolis of Beth-Shearim: The development is best illustrated from the vast Beth-Shearim necropolis near modern Haifa, which has served since the 3rd c. CE as a large and elaborate burial centre for Jews from both Palestine and the Near East (**475**). It is composed mainly of caves cut in the rock, each cave (**476**) consisting usually of a large entrance corridor whence halls, burial chambers and single loculi branch out. The most important catacombs have monumental arched masonry (**477**) applied to the rock, with open-air places of prayer cut in the rock above them. An important aspect of the art in these catacombs is the evident relaxation of the restrictions on representations of living beings (**478**) parallel to that known from contemporary Galilean synagogues* (3rd–4th c. CE).

476

477

475

478

481

Monumental tombs in which sarcophagi were found near Jerusalem, called Tombs of the Kings (**481**), have been identified with the tombs of the royal family of Adiabene from Mesopotamia after their conversion in the 1st c. CE.

There is another graveyard north of Jerusalem which was apparently used for the burial of ordinary people and had much simpler tombs than those of the Kidron Valley. The most elaborate of the graves are traditionally known as the "Graves of the Sanhedrin" (**479–80**), though the origin of the name is obscure.

Interpretation of Funeral Rites: Many scholars have tried to interpret Israelite funeral rites as evidence for the survival of a cult of the dead. Some argue that the dead inspired fear and that the bereaved were trying to protect themselves and earn the dead person's goodwill. Another school of thought believes that the living ascribed a kind of divinity to the dead.

Neither of these opinions has any solid support in the Old Testament. To the Jews a corpse and the tomb which contained it were both unclean. The corpse was inescapably doomed to corruption and it contaminated everything and everyone who came into contact with it (see Impurity*). It seems impossible that it could ever have been in any way an object of worship. In post-Exilic times, any such concept would have been unthinkable (see Immortality*).

Orthodox opinion regards funerary rites as exclusively the expression of sorrow at the loss of dear ones. However, this is not a sufficient explanation by itself. Some of the customs, e.g. the wearing of sackcloth or fasting are also found in penitential rites and must therefore have a religious significance.

The self-mutilation and shaving of the head condemned by the Torah (Lv. 19:27–28) also had a religious meaning, although it is not easy now to define it. Food offerings placed in the grave — a custom which the Israelites followed for a time in imitation of the Canaanites — bear witness to a belief in a life after death, as well as affection towards the dead. Such ceremonies were considered the right of the deceased and a pious duty which his kin owed to him. They were enjoined by the Decalogue as part of the filial duty every one must pay to his parents.

In general, the dead were honoured in a religious spirit but were not made the objects of any cult. A connection between mourning and religious customs is not exclusive to Judaism. Similar parallels can be found in many other religions and it appears to be a universal tendency.

III. MOURNING CUSTOMS: A certain ritual governed the actions of a deceased person's relatives and those who were present at his death and funeral. The details varied between the different peoples of the ancient Near East but, broadly speaking, the customs of the Israelites followed lines laid down by their neighbours, especially the Canaanites.

479

482

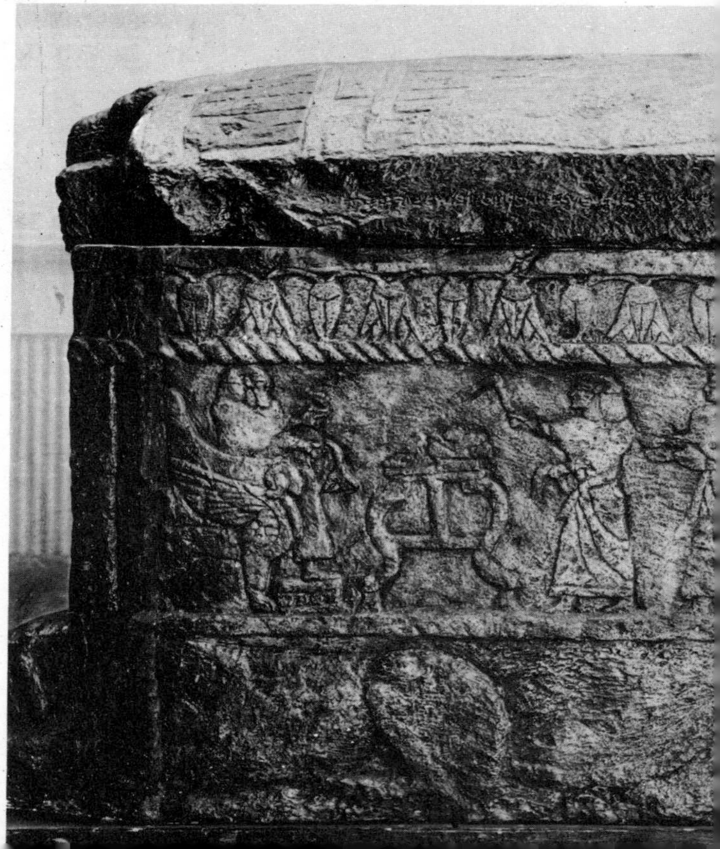

Evidence of Israel's Neighbours: The poetry of Ugarit* contains descriptions of funeral and mourning rites and these are also referred to in various places in the Old Testament (e.g. Is. 15:2; Jer. 48:37; Ezk. 27:31).

One of the Ugaritic epics describes how the father of gods and his daughter, 'Anat, mourn the death of Ba'al (see Canaan: Gods and Idols*; Can. Civiliz. and Ugarit*). The god descends from his chair and sits on a stool, from there he descends to the earth, puts ashes on his head and earth on the crown of his head, covers his body with sackcloth, girdled at the waist, makes incisions in his flesh, clips his beard and pulls the hair out from his head.

480

Archaeological discoveries have richly illustrated the mourning customs of other contemporary peoples. Egyptian tombs, especially, contained a wealth of mourning scenes (**483**). Mourning women bared their breasts, covered their faces with earth, wrapped black and torn sacking around their hips, put ropes around their necks and raised their clasped hands above their heads (**482**).

The sarcophagus of King Ahiram of Byblos in Phoenicia*, who lived during the 10th century BCE, carried a carving (**482**) of four bare-breasted women, two with their hands over their heads and two beating their sides (cf. Jer. 31:19; Ezk. 21:17). In front of the king stand men with their right arms bared. This was a custom common to both Egypt and Palestine. Rabbinical literature refers to the baring of the arm and shoulder in mourning. Pre-Islamic Arab women bared their breasts and beat on them, tore their hair and their flesh and mourned for the dead for a week. The men would shave their heads and their faces, leaving the hair and beards on the tomb and offering sacrifices over them to the dead.

Pre-Exilic Israelite Customs: Many of these rites were forbidden by the Law of Moses because they seemed idolatrous and, moreover, involved acts of desecration against the human body. Deuteronomy (14:1) commands the Israelites: "you shall not cut yourselves or make any baldness on your foreheads for your dead." Cutting the hair, shaving the beard or lacerating the skin in especially sensitive places were all forbidden. Exaggerated mourning was prohibited to priests who were not even permitted to let their hair grow during the period of mourning (Lv. 10:6). A High Priest, indeed, was forbidden to mourn at all and might not even approach the bodies of his dead mother and father for fear of the defilement which was involved in touching a corpse (Lv. 21:10–11). The same rule applied to a Nazirite dedicated to God (Nu. 6:7).

The various prohibitions were not altogether successful and many forbidden customs were followed (see Jer. 16:6; 41:5; Amos 8:10; Micah 1:16).

Certain mourning customs were, of course, permitted. From the earliest period, the close relatives of the deceased would gird their loins with sackcloth and sit upon the floor (Gn. 37:34; II Sam. 3:31; Ezk. 26:16; Lam. 2:10). The head was sprinkled with earth, dust and ashes (II Sam. 1:2; Esther 4:1), or at least covered (II Sam. 15:30; Jer. 14:3).

483

When David learned of the death of Absalom, he covered his face (II Sam. 19:4); when Saul and Jonathan were killed, he tore his clothes and wept and fasted until evening. Those who were with him did likewise (II Sam. 1:11–12). At the news that all his sons had been slain by Absalom, he "rent his garments and lay on the earth" (II Sam. 13:31).

According to Ezekiel (24:17) it was customary to bare the head, cover the "lips" i.e. the lower part of the face and go barefoot in mourning. Going barefoot as a sign of mourning was universal. The prohibitions on bodily mutilations were not observed. The men who came from Shechem and Shiloh and Samaria mourning Gedaliah ben Ahikam (Jer. 41:5) had "their beards shaved and their clothes torn, and their bodies gashed". Many other forbidden customs were followed (see Jer. 16:6; 41:5; Am. 8:10; Mic. 1:16).

Mourners showed their distress by refusing food. On the day of a burial none of the deceased's relatives would eat. Nor at the end of day would they prepare food for themselves, but would be served by others who would also offer the "cup of consolation". After the death of Abner, all the people came to bring bread to the mourning David, but he would not eat until nightfall (II Sam. 3:35).

Funeral Lamentations: The dead would be wept and lamented over. The main ceremony at a funeral was the lamentation over the dead. Professional mourners and wailing women would join the relatives (Am. 5:16; Jer. 9:17 ff; II Ch. 35:25) to make lamentation. A spontaneous lament could be amplified into a lament or "qinah" — a poem composed in a special rhythm (see Poetry*) and sung by professionals—many of whom were women (Jer. 9:17–22; Ezk. 32:16). Such women probably had a repertoire of laments which could be adapted to different occasions, but sometimes the poems were specially composed. The most famous of these are the laments of David: for Saul and Jonathan (II Sam. 1:17–27); and for Abner (II Sam. 3:33–34), while it is recorded (II Ch. 35:25) that Jeremiah uttered a lament for Josiah. Eventually the forms of such laments became standardized, for instance the lament over Judas Maccabee, patterned on David's great poem in honour of Saul and Jonathan (I Mac. 9:20–21). Jeremiah (Jer. 22:18) prophesied that no lament would be sung for Jehoiakim (see Exile*).

Mourning period: According to Mosaic law, one who dies must be buried on the same day. This applied equally to executed criminals (Dt. 21:22–3) and was obviously a wise provision in a hot eastern climate. The custom was perpetuated in post-Exilic times and a "halakhah" forbids keeping a corpse overnight.

In general the period of mourning after a death was seven days and during this period the mourners did not wash or anoint themselves (II Sam. 14:2). After the bones of Saul and Jonathan had been buried the people of Jabesh-Gilead fasted seven days (I Sam. 31:13). The period could, however, be extended as after the death of Aaron (Nu. 20:28–29) and Moses (Dt. 34:8) or shortened (Ecclus. 38:17).

A man who desired to take a captive woman for his wife must allow her to mourn for her father and mother for a month in his house (Dt. 21:11–13). It was considered unseemly to mourn for too long a period, partly to avoid any tendencies towards making a cult of the dead. Moreover, the inevitability and finality of death are taken for granted in most of the Old Testament.

G

GENESIS.—*Outline: I. Contents and Organization: Genealogies; Theology. II. Nature of the Traditions: Mesopotamian Material in Chapters 1–11: a. The Creation Story; b. The Garden of Eden; c. Noah and the Flood; d. Dispersion; Biblical Sources and Babylonian Material. III. Patriarchal Narratives. IV. Authorship and Sources. V. The Material and its Interpretation: Scandinavian School of Tradition History; Midrashic Form of Transmission; Mythological Approach; Form Criticism and Literary Types; Sociological and Religious Approach. VI. The Present Position.*

I. CONTENTS AND ORGANIZATION: The first book in the Bible took its name from the first Hebrew word, "Be-reshit" ("in the beginning"). In Greek this became "Genesis kosmon" (the origin of the world). The book is a prologue to the history of mankind and the Chosen People in the form of a collection of the earliest Hebrew traditions, woven into a continuous narrative. Beginning with the creation of the world, the book takes the national history of the Hebrews up to the death of Joseph.

The material falls naturally into two main divisions which must be examined separately. First there is the universal prologue, chapters 1–11, which gives the background to the histories of the Patriarchs which fills chapters 12–50.

1. **Prologue:** Chapters 1:1–2:3 — God's creation of the world and everything in it; 2:4–3:24 — Creation of man and woman, their disobedience and banishment from the garden of Eden; 4:1–6:8 — mankind increases and learns to sin; Cain (like his parents) is driven out but not killed for his murder of Abel. Man's sin is punished by God, notably in the Flood, 6:9–9:29. — Again, while the majority of mankind was wiped out by the Flood* (see article), a remnant was saved to become the nations of the world; 10:1–11:32 — A genealogical table fills in the gap between Noah and Abraham who, according to Israelite tradition, is to be chosen to raise up God's Elect (or Chosen) People.

2. **Chapters 12–50:** The history of the Patriarchs, the forefathers of Israel, can again be divided into different parts: chapters 12:1–25:18 — the lives of Abraham and Isaac; 25:19–36:43 — Jacob and his sons; 37 — Joseph and his brothers in Canaan; 38 — Judah and Tamar: an episode of tribal history; 39–45 — The story of Joseph in Egypt; 46–47:27 — Jacob's migration to Egypt; 47:28–48 — Jacob's last days; 49.— The blessings of Jacob: a digression on tribal history; 50 — Death and burial of Jacob and the death of Joseph.

Genealogies: Transition from one period to another is made by means of genealogical tables. Some of these serve mainly to bridge gaps in time (as in the case of chapter 5 or 11:10–32). Others are a means of showing the relations of Israel to the other peoples known to ancient Israelite tradition (chs. 10 and 36). The genealogies provide the framework for the

484

485

story and show how it is to be narrowed down to the people to whom God had made his special promise — Israel and the line of Joseph and Judah.

Theology: The main purpose of Genesis — as of all scripture— is theological. All the stories in the Bible are intended to reveal God's nature and purpose in historical events, history being of significance in biblical revelation.

The main teaching is that God, the sole deity, creator and ruler of the world, has imposed a moral law and order on that world. Within it, man must expect to be rewarded or punished according to his obedience to God's law. According to this tradition, God, by divine order, chose Abraham, then his seed, Isaac and Jacob so that in them all families of the earth should be blessed (Gn. 12:2 ff). The merit of the Patriarchs proceeds from this choice and from this stemmed their obligation to keep the Covenant*, to agree to abide by the divine law and accept this monotheistic conception. The Covenant made them God's Chosen People and the future heirs to the land of Canaan.

II. NATURE OF THE TRADITIONS. **Mesopotamian Material in Chapters 1–11:** An outstanding feature which distinguishes the traditions of the Creation, Fall, Flood and Dispersion from the patriarchal stories is the extent to which all the more primitive traditions are reminiscent of Babylonian mythology or sometimes other non-Hebrew mythologies. The interesting question so far as these traditions are concerned is the way in which they reached Israel and became transformed by her monotheistic outlook. The first Hebrews came from Mesopotamia (see Patriarchs*; Aram*) so that the connection is not very surprising, and it is instructive to note the way in which the Hebrews adapted and modified their originals.

a. **The Creation Story (1:1–2:3):** The essential difference between the Genesis version of the creation and all the myths known to have been current elsewhere in the ancient East is that whereas in the Bible the one and only God was responsible for the creation, the other myths all concern a number of gods. Otherwise the stories have certain elements in common. The non-Hebrew myths all begin with the prior creation of a group of gods. The creation of the universe then follows, usually as a result of a war between gods, often between the creator and a sea monster or similar creature. Various parts of the universe are then identified with individual gods or parts of their bodies.

Mesopotamian Myths: The creation stories current in Sumer and Akkad (see Babylonia*) also provided for the supremacy of different cities by making them the original homes of the god-creator. For instance, one myth explains that at first the gods lived only in Nippur, until Enki, the god of the depths and of wisdom, moved first to Sumer and then proceeded to the creation of nearby regions, including Dilmun, the paradise. After that he created, in this order, rivers, swamps, fish, the sea and the rain, cereals and grass, the ox and the clay for making bricks (the main building material in Mesopotamia). Thereafter he clothed the high mountains with vegetation and populated the pastures with cattle and sheep.

The Myth of Enuma Elish: The best known of these Mesopotamian myths is the "Enuma Elish" poem which is a later Babylonian adaptation of an old Sumerian tradition. This story, inscribed on cuneiform tablets, as on this reproduction (**484**), relates that before the skies or the earth were called by name, the salt-water goddess Tiamat (compare with the biblical "tehom", the deeps) and the fresh-water god Apsu begat a whole family of gods. The creation of man followed a series of conflicts between the parents and their children, in which Apsu was killed (by Ea, Anu, Enlil, Marduk or Ashur, according to different versions) after which Marduk, the son of Ea, champion of the gods and "Sun of the Heavens" killed Tiamat and

> split her like a shelfish into two parts;
> Half of her he set up and called it as sky
>
> He constructed stations for the great gods,
>
> Fixing their astral likeness as constellations.
> He determined the year by designating the zones:

The other half of the goddess became the earth. Finally, after consultations with the other gods and with the help of Ea, Marduk (**486**) made man from clay, "imposed the service of the gods upon them and set free the gods" from all necessity to work, i.e. man was made for the benefit of the gods, to provide them with food and drink. This cylinder seal impression shows the seven-headed dragon of chaos being slain (**485**) — see Babylonia*: Religion.

486

Comparison with Biblical Creation: Both Genesis and the Enuma Elish see creation as imposing order on primeval chaos, but in the Bible God is the sole, independent creator. There is nothing in Genesis of the Babylonian picture of

487 a

b

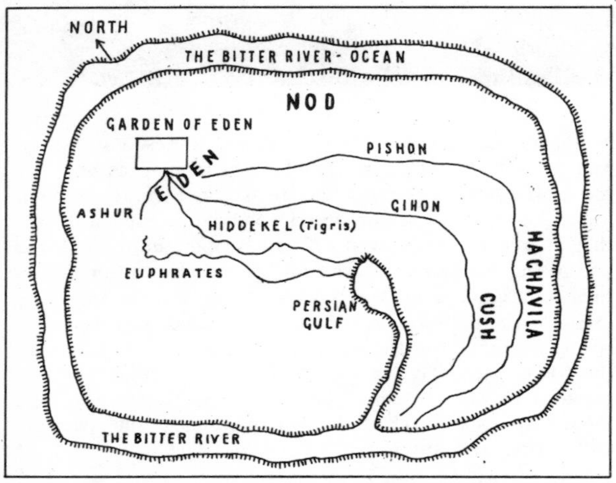

488

489 a

489 b

many gods struggling together, although the biblical "Let us make man in our image, after our likeness. . ." (1:26) is reminiscent of the discussion between the gods which preceded the Babylonian creative act. The Bible's monotheism is the main point of difference in the two versions. Similarities occur particularly in the order of events. Both stories start with unformed chaos, out of which is formed 1. light; 2. the sky; 3. the earth; 4. the sun, moon and stars; 5. the birds and fish and "the great sea monsters" (presumably the biblical authors stressed God's creation of the sea monsters to emphasize the difference between their view of creation and that of the older myths which speak of a war between the god and a sea monster opposing his acts of creation); 6. man, who, in the Bible, "is to have dominion over the fish of the sea and over the fowl of the air and over the cattle and over all the earth." After this, God rests on the seventh day in the Genesis story and, according to the Babylonians, the gods hold a great banquet and exalt Marduk as their chief and leader.

It is not known exactly in what manner these two creation epics are connected. As the Hebrews are unlikely to have borrowed directly from Babylonia it seems more likely that both versions have their origins in a common source in the earlier Sumerian literature (which dates back to the 3rd millenium BCE).

Besides the Enuma Elish, there are other myths. According to one, Marduk created man upon a mat of plaited weeds laid upon the primeval waters; after this he created wild animals, rivers, green grass, various countries and domestic animals. Another myth ascribes the creation of the sky to Anu and of the earth to Ea. Afterwards, the gods created the shrines and everything customarily offered there, then man to serve the gods.

b. **The Garden of Eden (2:4–3:24):** Next come the stories of man's creation from the dust, his tenancy of the Garden of Eden, his fall from grace and expulsion from the Garden (2:4–3:24). These are much cruder in style and use a more archaic imagery and language than the sublime picture of the Creation. They are also highly anthropomorphic (i.e. God appears in them in human form). Most scholars attribute these sections to the Yahwist source, the oldest written traditions of the Bible (see Biblical Criticism*).

Adam is then formed from the soil (in Hebrew the word for soil is "adamah" and its root is the same as that for red and blood) and placed by God in the garden "to till it and keep it", thus emphasizing man's close dependence on the earth. His creation "from the dust of the ground" is echoed in another Babylonian story, the Epic of Gilgamesh (see Flood*) in which the goddess Aruru forms a companion for Gilgamesh by "building" Enkidu from clay. The creation of man from clay was a familiar motif in Mesopotamian literature, also occurring in another creation myth about Enki and Ninhursag. This myth relates that in Dilmun (Paradise), Ninhursag, the Sumerian mother-goddess, bore children to Enki without pain or travail until she fell sick after eating eight forbidden plants and was condemned to "bring forth her children in pain" (in the parallel biblical phrase). She was cured of her actual sickness, according to another text, by the goddess Nin-ti, specially created for the purpose. The name, Ninti, is a Sumerian expression which can be equally well translated as "the woman who creates life" or "the woman of the rib", both very reminiscent of Eve, "the mother of all living" who was fashioned out of Adam's rib. The creation of man in this Sumerian version followed a war in which Enki led the forces of good to victory against Mommu, probably primeval chaos or ocean, and then created man with the aid of Nin-ma, the mother goddess and goddess of the earth. Archaeology has produced an additional parallel in the clay and reed statues and plastered skulls found far from Mesopotamia in pre-pottery Neolithic Jericho* (see illus. in article). These "men made from clay" give material expression to the tradition which later appeared in the mythologies and literature of the ancient Near East.

The fundamental theme of the story of the temptation of Eve and then the eating of the forbidden fruit of the tree of knowledge is man's rivalry with God. Once he has gained "knowledge of good and evil" (i.e. of everything) he has only to eat of the Tree of Life to gain immortality and be altogether equal to God — "like one of us" (3:22) in typically Mesopotamian terms. Parallels to the details of the story are also to be found in Mesopotamia — particularly Sumerian legends. The Mesopotamian "serpent" monster is familiar from this mosaic on the Gate of Ishtar in Babylon (**487a, b**).

The arts of civilization, according to one Babylonian myth, were taught to newly created man in "Edin" — presumably the original of "Eden", while a Sumerian text locates paradise in "Dilmun" as a place where "the lion kills not, the wolf snatches not the lamb". Birth there was without pain until woman was cursed after eating eight forbidden plants.

The Garden of Eden lay somewhere in the west of Mesopotamia and its geography (2:10–14; see diagram illustrating the concept, **488**), combines reality and legend, e.g. two of the four rivers flowing out of Eden are named as the Euphrates and the Tigris (Hiddekel) in a way that suggests a combination of different traditions.

The combination of the four rivers of Eden and the Tree of Life also recalls a familiar Mesopotamian theme of the flowing vase and the God with streams illustrating the apparently well-established idea of the water of life, as in the lower panel (**489a**) from a painting from the palace of Mari (**489b**) showing goddesses holding vases from which flow four free streams of water filled with fish (indicating life). The panel is flanked by two stylized trees guarded by "cherubim" (compare with Gn. 3:24).

c. **Noah and the Flood (6:11–9:17):** The story of Noah and the flood and its associations in the ancient literature of the Near East are dealt with in the article on the Flood*.

d. **Dispersion:** According to the Genesis tradition (9:18–19), the whole earth was repeopled by the descendants of Noah's three sons, Ham, fathering the Canaanites; Shem, the Hebrews; and Japhet, fathering the "coastland peoples". The passage (9:20–26) is of uncertain background, possibly a later (post-Conquest) addition providing a legendary justification for making Canaan "a slave of slaves" to his brothers.

A fourth familiar biblical myth with direct Mesopotamian connections is the story of the Tower of Babel (11:1–9), told to explain how all the related descendants of Noah had developed different languages (see Babylonia*). The opening account of a migration in the east to a "plain in the land of Shinar" where bricks were made and a city built, is factual. The first bricks in the world were made from the alluvial soil of Mesopotamia — perhaps by the original Sumerians or their forerunners — and here, the building of the great "ziggurats" or terraced towers was developed (see Babylonia*), described in Gen. 11:4 as "a tower with its top in the heavens". The theme of the story — as in Adam's — is again man's challenge to God (or perhaps "the gods"), for when the Lord inspected the city and the tower which had been built, he said "... this is only the beginning of what they will do; and nothing that they propose to do will now be impossible for them. Come, let us go down and there confuse their language that they may not understand one another's speech." And so rebellious mankind was scattered through the world to live in mutual incomprehension.

Biblical Sources and Babylonian Material: The priestly or other compilers of the Adam to Noah cycle of stories appear to have been sophisticated scholars committed to preserving relatively naive Mesopotamian materials transmitted from the time of the ancestors of the Hebrews (see Patriarchs*). The originals had thus been current during the 2nd — some of them even in the 3rd — millenium BCE and the first task of the Hebrew narrators, centuries later, was to present the stories transformed by their own monotheistic outlook and theology. The themes of these stories were not borrowed from the Mesopotamians at a later date nor were they learned from the Canaanites after the Settlement in Canaan. As the Hebrews had no contacts with Mesopotamia thereafter until the days of the monarchy, it may reasonably be assumed that the stories had been preserved by the Hebrews themselves, their earliest ancestors having migrated from Mesopotamia during the second millenium BCE (see Part III). U. Cassuto has demonstrated (partly on the basis of the findings at Ugarit*) that a body of popular epics existed in ancient Israel independently of biblical scriptures, in which the struggle between God and the mutinous forces of primeval chaos was inextricably woven with Hebrew beliefs about creation. By the natural processes of artistic development, the myth degenerated, becoming in time no more than a literary convention. Traces of mythological material which persist in the Genesis chapters proved of enormous value in enabling modern research to trace the origins of the biblical materials. Similar concepts have survived in Hebrew poetry*, appearing, for instance, in the references to the Babylonian story of creation in Is. 40:12, 21–22; Pr. 8:22–29 or Job* 38:8 ff. Leviathan, a Hebrew version of Rahab, the Babylonian monster of the sea also appears in Ps. 74:13–14, Isaiah 27:1 and in Job 7:12, while the reference to the "Sons of God" in Job 1:6 and 2:1, or to "his angel" and "his hosts" in Psalms 103:20–21 and 148:2 is a close parallel to Babylonian polytheistic ideas.

Some of these, of course, were probably merely literary conventions but others were an accepted device for expressing an ancient myth of the conflict between God and the forces of evil. The biblical view is not clear over this. It is implied in Gn. 1–3 that there was no creation out of nothingness, but this thought is not expressed definitely enough. It is axiomatic that God, the creator of the universe, created it without opposition, such opposition being inconceivable. But in addition to the creation accounts in Genesis where the theme of the primordial combat is entirely lacking, there are several other cosmological allusions and lingering echoes of ancient myths which come to light, as indicated. It is perhaps significant that the first explanation for the fundamental Hebrew institution of the Sabbath is a mythical-cosmological one. The Sabbath is described as the symbol of the Creation and its completion. The weekly day of rest is established as a human imitation of the divine act in resting after the labour of bringing order to primeval chaos (see Sabbath*).

III. PATRIARCHAL NARRATIVES **(Chapters 12–50):** Patriarchal narratives form the second main division of Genesis. These are surveyed in the article on the Patriarchs*. Although it is practically impossible to give accurate dates to many of the phases of these patriarchal stories, they reflect a cultural background which can be fixed in the 2nd millenium BCE. These stories are much closer to actual history than the earlier chapters of Genesis. In addition, they are a most important indication of the development of Israel's religion. (The articles on the Patriarchs* and their place in the history of Israel, as well as the Religion of the Patriarchs* accordingly survey the narratives and evaluate them also in the light of archaeological studies of contemporary peoples of the ancient Near East.)

IV. AUTHORSHIP AND SOURCES: Modern scholars reject the traditional view that regarded Genesis as the "First Book of Moses". On the other hand, there is nothing in the book to indicate who did write it. The impression it makes of a unified plan does not in itself rule out the possibility that it is composed of a number of separate literary sources or "documents" (see Biblical Criticism*).

This "documentary hypothesis" is mainly supported by occasional repetitions or contradictions within the book, for instance, the discrepancy between the account of creation of 1:1–2:3 and that in 2:4 ff; the conflicting stories of Abraham's sojourn in Egypt (12:10–20 and chapter 20), or of Hagar's expulsion in chapters 16 and 21. These dual traditions were taken as proof of a blending of different documents, each containing a complete and consecutive narrative (see Biblical Criticism*). They are designated as J (Jahwist, i.e. uses Jahweh as the divine name); E (using Elohim) and P (for the priestly school of writers, concerned more particularly with religious questions).

The "documentary theory" denied historical accuracy to many of the Partriarchal narratives of Genesis (see Biblical Criticism*) and it has been left to modern scholars and archaeologists to restore the weight of this material as historical evidence. In general, it is argued today that the "sources" — insofar as they ever really existed — grew up out of collections of ancient oral material, finally being shaped as we know them, J in the 10th or 9th centuries BCE, E a little later and P in the late monarchy and post-Exilic period. The "documentary theory" has been subjected to considerable criticism in detail from various quarters (see Biblical Criticism*).

V. THE MATERIAL AND ITS INTERPRETATION: **Scandinavian School of Tradition History:** In contrast to earlier emphasis on this question of documentary sources, modern Scandinavian scholarship (J. Pedersen, S. Mowinckel H. S. Nyberg, I. Engnell, G. Widengren) has tended to assign a major role in fixing the final form of Genesis to the influence and traditions of oral transmission. These scholars consider that the different traditions developed orally in different areas to serve some specific religious purpose. For instance, taking an example that follows Genesis — according to this school of thought, the Exodus story (Ex. 1–12) grew out of varying traditions around the Passover event which were later collected by unknown editors who framed the present shape of the story. This school allows a "general historicity" to the materials.

The Scandinavian school rejects the "literary critical" methods of breaking up the books of the Pentateuch (and Joshua) into the separate strands of E or J sources, believing rather that while such different strata may be observed, they had already been fused into the one narrative during the oral stage of transmission. This is a useful corrective to some of the more extreme attitudes of conventional criticism but, on the other hand, it is unbelievable that many traditions were not written down during the period of the early mon-narchy, if not earlier. Engnell's thesis is that the mass of the traditional material in the Pentateuch falls into two divisions: a. Genesis-Numbers, a collection of traditions which he terms the P-work (otherwise called the Tetrateuch). The symbol P does not bear, for this school, the meaning that it has in the school of documentary sources (see Biblical Criticism*). b. The other division is assumed to be Deuter-onomy to II Kings, termed the Deuteronomist history work. The Scandinavian theories have stood up less well than the older Documentary hypotheses.

Midrashic Form of Transmission: In themselves, however, these alternate theories do not dispose of the main support of the Documentary Theory — the question of repetitions and contradictions. For instance, in the parallel narratives about Abraham and his wife in Egypt (12:10–20 and 20:1–18) the doublet (chapter 20) states explicitly that Sarah was not violated although in the first account Pharaoh took her for his wife. Obviously the doublet is a deliberate attempt to improve appearances, a familiar activity in Midrashic Aggadah transmission (discussed under Biblical Criticism*).

A similar process can be observed in the repetition of the Hagar story (chapters 16 and 21). The first time it appears, neither Abraham nor Sarah are shown in a very favourable light, but the version in chapter 21 at least exonerates Abraham from blame. The same things happened in a number of other cases in the patriarchal narratives. Each time, the repetition is aimed at providing the Patriarch concerned with an excuse for behaviour which appeared reprehensible to a later age. The later stories in the Jacob cycle, for instance, effectively transform him from an ancestor into a respectable ancestor and finally romanticize him into a national symbol of Israel. The earlier stories, needless to say, retain far more historical value than the later justifications and glorifications. The reason for this is that in the background are customs and laws of an earlier time, no longer understood or appreciated by the compilers. However, the distinction is not so clear and the problem is first to distinguish historical fact from legendary additions and then to evaluate the process by which the different elements came to be combined.

Mythological Approach: Earlier scholars (E. Meyer, A. Lods, R. Weill) used to try to prove that the Patriarchs were no more than legendary figures (perhaps adapted from Canaanite myths) or all that remained of the gods of a very primitive polytheism. Modern research has entirely disposed of such theories. The stories in Genesis have a completely authentic flavour and there is nothing in the least mythological in their presentation of the Patriarchs. (The narratives do contain folkloric elements but these are usually incidental, not fundamental to the central figures and their background.) This subject is discussed fully in the article on the Patriarchs* which also reviews the status of the Patriarchs as chiefs of semi-nomadic clans. Briefly, the patriarchal traditions, whatever their degree of veracity, emerge as very ancient and as sufficient in themselves to force a drastic modification of the Documentary hypothesis and its suggested dating of biblical material.

A new approach to these questions has been developed in recent years by scholars like H. Gunkel, A. Alt and W. F. Albright who examine shorter units of ancient tradition according to the discipline of "Form Criticism" (see Biblical Criticism*).

Form Criticism and Literary Types: The proponents of this school (among them H. Gunkel, W. Nowack and M. Noth) evaluate the Genesis stories as composites of literary motifs, known long before the Conquest and common to the popular legends of neighbouring nations. These motifs, they claim, evolved at the same time as the literary development of the Patriarchal narratives, and they can be traced through the written forms in which they were finally embodied. The essence of popular belief was contained in the oral forms from which the stories first evolved. Thus H. Gunkel analyzed the various types of literary composition in Genesis and tried to establish the specific "life situation" which had given rise to each "literary type", and the religious experience of which it was an expression. By these means he reduced the narratives of Genesis to a collection of separate literary units or "story cycles" derived in form or type from their oral folk traditions. The Form Critical school emphasizes the cultic background and the local shrine as the centre in which the territorial traditions were preserved (see below).

Such story cycles or territorial traditions may be illustrated, for instance, in Genesis 18, by the motif of the old man (Abraham) favoured with a visit by three "divine beings". Another is the story of the shepherd (Jacob) who outwits the hunter (Esau). A third is that of the old father (Isaac) showing a marked preference for a younger son (Jacob). This occurs again in the Joseph story.

Motifs like these are embodied in narratives of different kinds designed to satisfy certain difficulties or answer certain questions. They have no intrinsic historical value although they may be associated with actual persons or woven into a chain of legends and edifying tales about a central personage. H. Gunkel regarded the Patriarchs as mere figureheads and "types" representative of the motifs, but this view is at best only partly acceptable. When all the material referring to the Patriarchs as eponymous ancestors or tribal personifications has been removed, there remains an intractable mass of material which can only be understood as traditions about actual people engaged in the business of living real lives — lives which authentically reflect the circumstances, customs and manners of a particular period and locale.

M. Noth consideres the pre-literary traditions of Genesis as developments built around some religious themes or cult centres. He lays great emphasis on the part played by the legendary explanation of the origins of the people involved. In his view, the Patriarchal stories were incorporated into the traditions of the tribes after they had settled in Canaan. They represented the divine promises made to the Patriarchs which were being fulfilled with the Israelites' settlement of the land that had been "promised" to them. This made the stories articles of faith and gave them their historical significance. From them developed the cults of the places consecrated by the promises and by the divine appearances which had accompanied them, such as the Oak of Moreh, Bethel, Beersheba or Mamre. The names of the Patriarchs were preserved in these holy places because they had been associated with the God their descendants worshipped, the God of Abraham, of Isaac and of Jacob (for additional names, see Patriarchs, Religion of*). In the days of the tribal league which followed the Conquest*, the stories were combined into a single pan-Israel tradition. In this opinion, therefore, the stories in themselves preserve no historical data on the times, places or circumstances of the Patriarchs. Their essential role was as a vindication of the promises that had been made to Israel.

Noth's theory finds no close connection between the traditions and the geographical data or concrete life of the tribes who clung to their traditions throughout all vicissitudes. In sum, he appeals to cult centres to which such traditions were bound. He overlooks the fact that it is not places which preserve traditions, but people. This makes it difficult to account for the fact that early patriarchal traditions, current in pre-Mosaic times, could be known to the later groups of incoming Israelites under Moses and Joshua which, according to Hebrew traditions, arrived after a break in Hebrew occupation of Palestine. Thus, valuable though it is, the theory needs correction. There are today many scholars who consider that differing traditions about individuals such as Abraham, Isaac and Jacob were grouped into cycles of tradition and later on shaped into an epic of the Patriarchs. At a still later stage, this was linked with the traditions about the Exodus from Egypt and the period in Sinai to form a continuous, epic history of the origins of Israel. In this view, the concluding chapters of the story of Jacob and the story of Joseph (Gn. 37–50) form the link between the Patriarchal cycle and the traditions about the Exodus.

Sociological and Religious Approach: It remains true that sociological studies have confirmed that nomadic and semi-nomadic tribes always tried to keep alive the memory of their ancestors. Moreover, when the later biblical evaluations of the Patriarchs as ancestors of the Israelites are compared with archaeological and anthropological data, some very valuable conclusions emerge with regard to the pre-Israelite period.

The weakness of all the theories considered above is that they overlook the role of the Patriarchs in the evolution of the religious concepts of the Children of Israel (see Patriarchs, Religion of*). Basing himself on the belief that a religion must be explicable in terms of the social organization of the people who professed it, A. Alt rejected the view that the religion of the Patriarchs had its roots in the El religion of the Canaanites, for they had no tribal organization. From his interpretation of the Patriarchal narratives, he found traces of the tribal religion practiced by the Hebrews before they were united — i.e. he concluded that in the beginning the different tribes had had their own, different gods, known as the gods of the tribal leaders.

In the early stages of the religion, the divinity which revealed itself to the Patriarchs was not represented as one god, but as several gods with different names and attributes: *'Elohe Abraham*, the God of Abraham; *Paḥad Itzhak*, the Friend of Isaac; *Abir Ya'kob*, the Bull of Jacob. Only later did these concepts merge into the single *Elohe Ha'aboth*, the God of the Fathers. On the other hand, of course, not only does biblical tradition insist that these were indeed one, but there is also evidence suggesting that behind the different manifestations was the same cosmic deity: El. A. Alt explains this by the theory that the cults of the tribal gods and the Patriarchal heritage carried the seeds of a later, specifically Israelite, conception of a close relationship between God and his people, expressed in the Mosaic doctrine of the Covenant*.

VI. THE PRESENT POSITION: No single theory is accepted by all scholars. The exact origin of Genesis, its place in the Bible and its final interpretations all remain sufficiently uncertain to warrant an open mind in viewing the conclusions of critical research. Over the last three decades, scholars have increasingly come to realize that the narratives of Genesis must be taken seriously as at least potentially historical sources. Although centuries of oral transmission affected them to a greater or lesser degree, and they were subjected to doublets, reinterpretation and additions to meet the theological needs of the scribes who were responsible for their written transmission (see Canon and Text*), they reflect the period, though it would be rash to affirm their specific historicity. Scholars versed in the literary and cultural history of the Middle and Late Bronze Ages have come to treat the biblical narratives with great care as sources of historical data.

In W. F. Albright's opinion, the best answer to the question of how and why the early Patriarchal traditions (with the connecting Joseph narrative) were absorbed into Israelite religious tradition is that they belonged to a number of elements within the population of Palestine which later became Israel. Before the age of Moses, Palestine was a melting pot of ethnic and cultural traditions, not closely allied to those of the Canaanites. The biblical narratives all emphasize that the Israelites rejected assimilation with Canaanite culture. The most satisfactory solution to the problems raised seems to be the one provided by the biblical tradition itself. According to the Bible, the groups included some at least who traced their origins to Aram-Naharayim (Upper Mesopotamia; see Aram*; Patriarchs*). Although these proto-Israelites have not been identified with any historic groups known to extra-biblical sources, it is known that such migrations westwards from that area took place long before the time of Moses.

A contributing point is that the earliest stages of the religion of Israel were not as primitive as scholars of a preceding generation thought (see above: The Material and its Presentation). As a result, Moses and his followers were able to absorb as much of the older traditions as was compatible with its concepts, and in addition preserved everything that seemed to have a permanent value for those concepts (see Moses*).

GOSPELS, SYNOPTIC. — **General Plan:** Due to the marked similarity of their subject matter, the order in which their material is presented and their language, the first three Gospels of the New Testament are generally referred to as the *synoptic* (Greek: having or taking the same point of view) Gospels. If the data in these three Gospels were to be arranged side by side in parallel columns so as to be seen at a glance (sunopys in Greek), the inter-relationship between them would be clearly visible.

For well over a millenium, the opinion expressed by St. Augustine that the canonical order of the Gospels likewise reflected their correct chronological order held sway in the scholarly circles of the church. From the 18th c. onward however, the relationship of the synoptic Gospels to one another has been the subject of intense study.

As the synoptic Gospels were subjected to closer scrutiny, their parallelisms analyzed and their relative contents compared, it became increasingly evident that the Gospel of Mark* pre-dated those of Matthew* and Luke*. For one thing, it was apparent that although Mark shared much material in common with Luke and Matthew, most of what the latter two Gospels had in common with each other was precisely those passages which they shared with Mark.

By far the greater part of Mark's Gospel is found in Matthew and Luke. A comparison of Mark* with the other Synoptics has shown that out of 673 verses of Mark, the substance of more than 600 is found in Matthew and of about 350 in Luke. Matthew and Luke generally follow Mark's order and the same is true of the majority of the Greek words used by Mark. In fact, from the entire book of the authentic gospel of Mark, only some 30 verses (excluding the section 16:9–20 which is missing in all the earlier manuscripts of Mark's Gospel) do not appear in any form in the other two synoptic Gospels. If Mark were to be suddenly lost to us, it could be almost completely reconstructed by scholars on the basis of Matthew and Luke. Both Matthew and Luke have their own peculiar source material aside from Mark, but in those instances where they follow the narratives of Mark, they are most remarkably parallel. Even when one or the other deviates from the text of Mark, it is seldom that both are in agreement against Mark. This fact not only gives added weight to the assumption that Mark is the earliest of the synoptic Gospels, but leads directly to another far-reaching conclusion, namely, that both Matthew and Luke made use of Mark when writing their Gospels. Not only were the general contents of Mark utilized by the other two synoptic Gospel writers, but, in a great many cases, the earlier narratives were repeated *verbatim*. The striking similarity of the language in the parallel passages of the synoptic Gospels is so great as to exclude the possibility of coincidence.

There are, nevertheless, certain significant differences between Mark and the other two, mainly in relating the words of Jesus*. Matthew's Gospel* is arranged around five discourses, the first and most familiar being the Sermon on the Mount. There is a similar discourse in Luke but not in Mark. Accordingly, most scholars have distinguished in the Gospels between the *narrative* and the *discourses* (what Jesus *did* and what he *said*). It is an accepted tenet of New Testament scholarship that the Gospels are not intended as a biography of Jesus in the modern sense, but rather reflect the apostolic teaching ("Kerugma", preaching) of what Jesus did and what he taught (Acts 1:1). They are a statement of the faith of the early Christians, founded on the historical fact of Jesus and preached as a lesson to the world.

Earlier sub-Literary Forms: There is a theory that the parallel passages common to all three of the synoptic Gospels stem directly from a single source, a so-called oral tradition of the early body of Christian believers. This theory was advanced by the eminent scholar J. Jeramias who denied the existence of a common written source (Q) for the synoptics. Another theory, supported by one of the foremost scholars of Aramaic, C. C. Torrey, was that the Gospels as we now know them are secondary (Greek) translations of Aramaic originals. Torrey marshalled an impressive array of rather awkward Greek phrases which he believed to be the result of a poor translation from the Aramaic. Undoubtedly there were a great many oral traditions among the early Christians transmitting the deeds and teachings of Jesus. Many of these traditions certainly found their way into the New Testament, but it appears most doubtful that the parallel passages of the synoptics were derived *directly* from either an oral tradition or a written Aramaic source. The identical wording of the Greek in a number of these parallel passages is too exact to be disregarded. It is impossible to assume that several translators, each working independently, would hit upon exactly the same Greek wording for a translation from the Aramaic. By the same token, it is difficult to accept Jeramias' view that the synoptic Gospels had no written source in common, but that each made use of the same oral (Aramaic) tradition. Once again, the identical Greek wording in a number of the parallel passages cannot be explained by such a theory. In all likelihood not one, but a number of Aramaic oral traditions underlie the source material of the synoptic Gospels. These original traditions must have been available to the synoptic writers (in any case to the authors of Matthew and Luke) in written form, but in a secondary Greek translation rather than in Aramaic.

Moreover, even though Matthew and Luke have additional material, they usually follow the order of Mark in those passages common to all the synoptic Gospels. In certain instances Matthew or Luke may vary somewhat from Mark's text, but it is rare for both Matthew and Luke to be in accord on a passage which disagrees with its counterpart in Mark. This similarity and obvious interdependence coupled with instances of individual interpretation hardly make the concept of a direct common oral source of the synoptics — as opposed to a written one — feasible.

The question has also arisen whether or not the copy of Mark used by Matthew and Luke was identical with the Gospel of Mark contained in the present version of the New Testament. The last twelve verses of Mark (16:9–20) have long been suspect as they are missing in all the more ancient manuscripts of this Gospel, while closer examination has revealed that the literary style of these verses is quite different from that of the body of the Gospel. The fact that Luke makes no use of the material found in Mark 6:45–8:26 ("the great omission") has also led scholars to believe that this particular section of Mark must have been missing in the copy used by Luke.

Imaginative attempts have been made to prove the existence of a proto-Mark (*Ur Markus*) which was supposedly earlier than the present text of the Gospel. Such attempts are pure conjecture for there is no basis whatsoever for supposing that a proto-Gospel of Mark ever existed. The ending of Mark (16:8) is indeed abrupt and the original ending of the second Gospel may well have been lost. But it may just as well never have been written. As for the "great omission" of Luke, it may merely be the result of Luke's exercising his editorial prerogative. There are other instances of Luke's having corrected or shortened narratives of Mark.

We can assume then that Mark was the earliest of the synoptic Gospels and that it was used as a source by both Matthew and Luke. This is only a partial solution of the synoptic problem, however, for Matthew and Luke have some 200 verses of material which they share in common and which is not contained in the second Gospel. These passages consist largely of the sayings and teachings of Jesus, including for instance the Sermon on the Mount (Mt. 5–7). The fact that this also appears in Luke but not in Mark points to the existence of another literary source aside from Mark. Though the source is no longer extant in an independent form, it is commonly referred to as Q (from the German word *Quelle*, source).

The Q document must have consisted of a collection of the sayings of Jesus and it is possible that there were several variations of this document. Perhaps these variations explain some of the discrepancies between Matthew and Luke in those instances where both are relying on Q. The Q document appears to be more primitive and of an earlier date than Mark. It is quite possible that it was a written Aramaic collection of what was once a number of early oral traditions transmitted by the (Galilean?) followers of Jesus. A number of scholars, including C. F. Burney, J. A. Montgomery and particularly C. C. Torrey have argued that the Gospels have an Aramaic origin. Though there are weighty arguments against the theory of a *written* Aramaic source, no such arguments apply to an oral transmission. The earliest oral transmissions would quite naturally be preserved in the original language, i.e., Aramaic, though at a somewhat later stage they must have been translated and recorded in Greek.

The Q document used by the two Gospel writers must have been in Greek for in several cases the identical Greek wording is found in parallel passages from Q. Two open questions about the Q source remain: whether or not it was originally an oral source and what was its original extent. There is no reason to suppose that it was limited to the passages Matthew and Luke have in common. Other verses in either book may have come from Q or from yet other material which does not appear in Matthew or Luke— or even in Mark.

Eusebius (*Ecclesiastical History* iii. 39, 15; 4th c. CE) quotes Papias, Bishop of Hierapolis, ca. 140 CE, as reporting that Matthew composed the Logia in Hebrew (i.e. Aramaic) and that "everyone interpreted them" (i.e. translated them into Greek). For some time it was assumed that these Logia represented the Q document, but modern scholarship is growing increasingly sceptical of this theory. The "Logia" may well be the Gospel of Matthew itself. Scholars today are also inclined to believe that the language behind Matthew was probably Hebrew, not Aramaic, and they accept Papias' statement as literally exact, although it is still not certain just what the Logia were. Some think it likely that there was a written Hebrew source on which the book of Matthew is based.

The Two Source Theory: One basic solution of the synoptic problem is thus provided by the theory of two major sources for Luke and Matthew: Mark and the Q document. Material peculiar to the gospel of Matthew is designated M, that of Luke, L (for further information, see the introductions to the respective Gospels). The two-source theory, however, is also not without its critics. One modern school of thought tends to doubt the existence of the hypothetical Q document. This group of scholars considers that Matthew and Luke were not written independently. Rather, Luke was written after Matthew and incorporated material not only from Mark, but also from Matthew, the passages Luke is supposed to have borrowed from Matthew making up what is commonly known as Q. However, there are a number of difficulties inherent in this theory and it is far from being proven.

Form Criticism: For a certain time, the message of Christ which the Apostles preached existed only in an oral form or in the memories of witnesses and disciples still living. A brief example occurs in Ac. 10:34–43. However long that period was, the basis for the later written Gospels was this oral preached gospel. It is therefore of paramount importance to define the forms it took and the relation of the synoptic Gospels to the earliest oral preaching. The most valuable contribution to such an understanding has come from "Form Criticism" (from the German Formegeschichte). This is an approach which attempts to disentangle the distinctive elements which make up the New Testament, i.e. contributions from the earliest Jewish-Christian* circles, from the Hellenistic communities, both Jewish and Gentile, before Paul*; from Paul himself and from the post-Pauline Christians. This form of analysis has distinguished between Pronouncement-stories (e.g. Mk. 3:1–6 on healing on the Sabbath; 10:1–9 on divorce; 12:13–17 on the payment of tribute); Miracle-stories (e.g. Mk. 1:40–45; 4:35–41); Stories about Jesus' life (Baptism, Temptation Rejection, Transfiguration, Last Supper, Crucifixion); and Groups of Sayings and Parables. In "Form Criticism", each of these "forms" is illuminated by connecting it to the purpose for which it may have been useful to the early Christians.

GOVERNMENT, AUTHORITY AND KINGSHIP.

Outline: I. Administrative and Legal Institutions of Israel in Pre-Exilic Times: A. Elements of Primitive Democracy in the Ancient Near East; Canaan and Syria; Mesopotamian, Hittite Institutions; B. Israelite Institutions before and during the Monarchy: 1. The Elders of Israel; 2. Town Elders; 3. Justice at the Gate; 4. Professional Judges and the Supreme Court; 5. "Those Summoned"; 6. The "'Edah" (Congregation) of Israel; 7. The Assembly (Kāhāl); 8. The Am-Ha'aretz (People of the Land); 9. Procedure at Meetings of the People's Representatives; C. The Monarchy: a. Accession to the Throne; b. The Coronation; c. Deification of the King; d. The King's Family; e. The King's Property; f. The King and Religious Ritual; g. The King and the Law; h. The King as Judge.

II. Administration of the Kingdom: A. Division of the Realm for Administrative Purposes: 1. The Period of Saul; 2. The Period of David and Solomon; Raising Revenue in Solomon's Realm; Districts of Judah; Administration of Prefectures; 3. Territorial Division Described in the Book of Joshua: a. Archaeological Evidence; b. Hezekiah's Administrative Reform in Judah; c. Districts in the Northern Kingdom of Israel; d. Under Assyrian Rule; B. Officials of the King: 1. David's Ministers; 2. The Pattern of Administration; 3. Censuses; 4. Minor Officials; 5. Cadres of a Reserve Army; 6. Solomon's Ministers; 7. Officials of the Monarchy; C. Duties of the Senior Officials in Israel: 1. He who is over the Palace; 2. Royal Secretary; 3. The "Mazkîr".

III. Post-Exilic Institutions: 1. Administration and Social Evolution during the Persian Period; 2. Nobles and Officials; 3. Theocratic Rule of the Priests; 4. The Scribes; 5. The Hellenistic Pattern; 6. The Council of Elders; 7. Early Maccabaean Administration; 8. The Kāhāl; 9. Jewish Town Government; 10. The Great Assembly; 11. Differences between Hasmonean and Herodian Kingship; 12. The Great Sanhedrin; Functions.

In studying the administrative and legal institutions of Old Testament times, it becomes apparent that they cannot be separated into different categories, for most of the existing institutions fulfilled both administrative and judicial functions. A differentiation is made here, however, between the description of the structure of ancient public bodies (section I) and their functioning (section II). The article follows a mainly historical order, although there are certain exceptions caused by the obscure origins of most of the institutions. Even when an institution is described in the Bible and is referred to in relation to a specific historical background, it is still important to know a. what difference exists between the period described and the date of the description; b. whether the institution being described is related to the period mentioned in the text or to the epoch of the narrator.

I. ADMINISTRATIVE & LEGAL INSTITUTIONS, (pre-Exilic).

A. Elements of Primitive Democracy or Oligarchy in the Ancient Near East.

1. **Canaan and Syria:** The political structure in Canaan and Syria was one of small city-states. At the head of each state was a king and a council of elders. The king usually had a small army at his command, but his powers were limited by a state council, composed of representatives of the aristocracy and trading community (see Cities: Canaanite*). In the papyrus recording the life of the Egyptian official Wen-Amun (11th c. BCE, see Phoenicia*), it is related that Wen-Amun is summoned before the heads of the town of Byblos, whose council is to decide his fate. The papyrus confirms the fact mentioned in Ezk. 27:9 that supreme authority in Byblos was vested in the council of elders. The

strength of the republican regime in Phoenicia is witnessed by the counting of years from its creation. The power to govern was entrusted to the representatives of the people, called " 'Am" in the inscriptions. Phoenician colonies were similarly governed by the people's representatives. In Palestine the elders of the Gibeonites sent representatives to sign an alliance with the Israelites (Jos. 9:11).

2. **Mesopotamian Institutions:** The roots of primitive democracy were also found in Mesopotamia. Their mythology relates that the "assembly of the gods" was the source of all authority. No single god had exclusive powers, because, according to their outlook, this world was only an echo of the world of the gods. Thus, on earth, the supreme authority was the king, together with the assembly of the representatives of his kingdom. The king was not an autocrat, but only a trustee, under the control of a higher authority. He was responsible to the gods and the representatives of his kingdom. In the Gilgamesh epic, Agha, king of Kish, did not declare war until the elders of Uruk agreed to it. During the period of the Babylonian empire as well, the heads of the towns (or the council) were entrusted with judiciary responsibilities. In the Assyrian trade colonies in Anatolia (Cappadocia), the judiciary powers were vested in the assembly of the colonizers.

3. **Hittite Institutions:** Little data survives on the subject of Hittite institutions, but even that little may be divided into two categories: data on the Old Kingdom (17–16th c. BCE) and data on the New Kingdom or empire (14–13th c.). In the Old Kingdom there existed a body called the Pankuš, the assembly of Hittite nobles. (Hittite physiognomy is preserved in this Egyptian wall painting ca. 1450 BCE, **490**.) In the New Kingdom, the Pankuš was no longer mentioned. The nobles were specified under three names, the dignitaries, the elders and the grandees. The elders, who were subject to the authority of the king to whom they swore allegiance, exercised judiciary responsibilities, but it is not known if they had administrative powers as well.

Both the Old and the New Kingdoms were organized on a feudal basis, and the rights and duties of the heads of the federation are vague. It may be that they had little say in external affairs, but had a wide measure of autonomy within their own territory. The detailed text of their oath of allegiance testifies to its special significance.

B. **Israelite Institutions before and during the Monarchy:** From the foregoing, it can be seen that different forms of oligarchy existed in many of the states bordering on or near to Palestine, especially in Phoenicia (northern Canaan). In Israel the basis of power was wider. The Israelite monarchy was comparatively young and had been preceded by a long period of rule by the leaders of the people. The kings never succeeded in superseding the people's leaders and were always dependent on them. The very concept of "people" by the Israelites is significant as implying that some sort of authority ultimately resided with them.

1. **The Elders of Israel:** A popular misconception is that the word "elders" meant all free adult males, their faces adorned with beards, who met from time to time. On the basis of the evidence, it is much more likely that the real elders were specially designated individuals. The Old Testament mentions two kinds of elders, the "elders of Israel" who were the heads of the families in the various tribes, and the "elders" of the towns. Elders of the towns existed only from the time of the Conquest* and settlement, but it is quite likely that an "elder of Israel" during that time was also an elder of a town.

In Mesopotamia (18th to 8th cs. BCE), elders appear as the representatives of the people, defending their rights but with no administrative functions. In the Hittite empire it appears that many municipal duties were discharged by the Council of Elders. The Council of Elders of Byblos* is mentioned in Ezk. 27:9 and in the story of Wen-Amun. The Bible alludes to the Elders of Moab, the Elders of Midian (Nu. 22:7), the Elders of the Gibeonites (Jos. 9:11) and even the Elders of Egypt (Gn. 50:7). The Elders of Israel are first heard of in the episode of the revelation of God to Moses (Ex. 3:16). Moses was sent to these elders to announce the liberation from bondage in Egypt. From then on, the elders are associated with every important event in the life of the people, from the Exodus* through the wanderings in the desert and the period of settlement until the period of the monarchy. Even after the monarchy collapsed, the institution of the Elders survived and is mentioned during the Exilic (Ezk. 8:1; 14–1) and post-Exilic (Ezr. 10:8, 14) periods.

Although the elders were not elected, during most of the periods recorded in the Old Testament they were recognized as, in principle, the highest authority over the people. During the monarchy, of course, their power was severely curtailed and the kings often acted autocratically. Treaties between God and the people were made either in the presence of the people, of the people and the elders, or of the elders alone. The Sinai Covenant* (Ex. 19:7; 24:1) was made with the elders and it was with them that Moses signed a Covenant before his death (Dt. 27:1; 31:28). They were Moses' heirs and, therefore, were also endowed with his spirit (Nu. 11:16). Joshua performed the ceremony of the blessing and the malediction in the presence of all Israel, its elders and its officials (Jos. 8:33), and he signed a Covenant before God and the people in the presence of the elders (Jos. 24:1).

490

When Solomon was about to transfer the Ark and consecrate the Temple, he called the elders of Israel to participate in the ceremony, thereby endowing the occasion with the appropriate legal and religious solemnity (I K. 8:1; II Ch. 5:2). Josiah made an alliance with the elders (II K. 23:1; II Ch. 34:29).

The elders were the religious representatives of the people. Warnings by the prophets were occasionally addressed to the elders alone (Jer. 19:1). Joel called the responsible elders to prayer for the breach of the Covenant between God and the people (Jl. 1:14; 2:16).

The elders were also the people's political representatives. Before the period of the monarchy, their duties were quite clear for there was no other popular authority apart from that of the priests and Judges*. The elders shared their authority with Moses during the period of the wanderings. The Conquest, according to the author of Joshua, was also a period of the elders. The negotiations with the tribes of Transjordan were conducted by Pinhas and the elders, although Joshua was still alive (Jos. 22).

During the period of the settlement elders are expressly referred to only twice: once during the battle of Gibeah and a second time in connection with the negotiations with Jephtah. Nevertheless it can be assumed that the tribal elders regulated the life of the tribes. There seems to have been a general, although undefined, division of authority among the charismatic leader, the civil representatives (elders), the religious authorities (priests) and the people (adult males) as a whole.

Even during the monarchy, the authority of the elders was in principle greater than that of the king. It was the elders who insisted that Samuel appoint a king (I Sam. 8:4) although his warning to the people (I Sam. 8) and the history recorded in the books of Samuel and Kings show that, in practice, their authority was often flouted. However there is reason to believe that every king needed the consent of the people or their representatives to his accession to the throne. The consent took the form of an agreement between the king and the people or their elders. When Abner threatened Ish-Boshet with transferring the succession to David, he needed the consent of the elders (II Sam. 3:17 ff) before he could actually carry out the threat. The elders agreed to David's anointing as king (II Sam. 2:4) and he accepted the throne after making an alliance with them (II Sam. 5:3). The elders also had a hand in Absalom's revolt and its success (II Sam. 17:4).

The elders who are mentioned in connection with the partition of the kingdom between Judah and Israel* were really elderly men, in contrast to the young advisers of Rehoboam. After the Absalom incident the elders no longer seem to have taken an active part in the appointment of kings, although the frequent changes of dynasty in the Northern Kingdom of Israel suggest that the elders, leaders of tribes and heads of large families, were behind them. Evidence for their continuing authority comes from the fact that Ahab, king of Israel, required the consent of the elders before he could declare war and he had to plead with them in order to obtain it (I K. 20:7–8), but there were many exceptions.

The number of elders does not appear to have been fixed. During Moses' time, when the elders assembled frequently, their number is given as seventy (Ex. 24:1, 9; Nu. 11:16, 24) and seventy was the traditional number of the national assembly. However, neither at that time, nor later, were these all the elders of Israel.

2. **Town Elders:** Side by side with the "town chief" (Sār ha'ir), or man in charge of the town (asher-'āl-ha'ir), a group of elders were a permanent institution in towns and villages. In the big towns, or possibly only in the capital, there was a "Sār", but in the other towns and villages all powers were vested in the elders. These were the heads of the families who together constituted the council, e.g. the elders of towns in southern Judea, which are enumerated in I Sam. 30:26–31. Jezebel, for instance, sent letters to the elders of Jezreel and not to the town chief. In Assyria* and Babylonia* we find the "rab âli" and the "hazanu" fulfilling such functions.

The town elders were a sort of municipal council, but their main duty was the dispensation of law. As in Babylon, there were three judiciary authorities in Israel during the period of the Monarchy: the popular authority of the elders, that of the king, and that of the priesthood. In towns and villages the town elders were competent to deliver judgment on all offences, from the lightest which were punished only by a fine (Dt. 22:18–19) to the heaviest which carried a death sentence, e.g. a stubborn and rebellious son (Dt. 21:18–21) or premeditated murder (Dt. 19:11–13; see Law*).

3. **Justice at the Gate:** All matters relating to the town were decided by the elders sitting at the gate, where they also dispensed justice. Even King David sat at the gate to dispense justice, and it was for this reason that Absalom stood on the road leading to the gate and tried to dissuade all persons who came to lay their case before the king from doing so (II Sam. 15:2–6). The gate as a court is mentioned frequently in the Old Testament in the historical books, in Job. 29:7; 31:21 and in Pr. 22:22; 31:23. Among the prophets, Amos especially stressed the close connection between the gate and the dispensation of justice (Am. 5:10, 12, 15).

An instance of the working of such a court at the gate can be found in Ruth 4. Boaz comes and sits at the gate, stops the next of kin ("go'el"), and chooses ten elders of Bethlehem to sit with them. Boaz and the go'el put their cases before the elders. The go'el declares that he relinquishes all claims, and Boaz takes the elders and the people to witness the agreement reached. It may be observed from this story that during the hearing of a case, a number of the people of the town were also present. Mention of the gate also occurs during Abraham's negotiations with Ephron for the purchase of the Cave of Machpelah (Gn. 23:10 ff). The East gate (**184**) of Shechem* (17th c. BCE) consisted of two rectangular towers each 23 × 42 ft. with guard rooms flanking the entryway. It was the heart of the city's defense system and in peace times its social centre (see a bench and steps within the Lachish gate **491**; see also **130, 164**).

491

An instance of a criminal matter is the case of Naboth (I K. 21). The elders of Jezreel summon Naboth to appear before them at the gate. Two persons testify that Naboth had blasphemed God and the king, crimes punishable by death (Ex. 22:28; Lv. 24:14–16). After sentence is pronounced, Naboth is taken outside the town and stoned to death.

4. **Professional Judges and the Supreme Court:** Justice was dispensed not only by the elders of towns, but also by professional judges (see Law*). They are mentioned in the code of laws in the Torah only in Dt. 16:18–20, so it appears that they functioned during the period of the Monarchy and were appointed by the king. It is not clear whether these judges heard special cases directly related to affairs of state (e.g. taxes) or whether they functioned together with the town elders. According to II Ch. 19, such judges were first appointed by Jehoshaphat.

Dt. 17:8–13 provides that difficult cases be brought before a supreme court in the city chosen by God. This bears upon the narrative in II Ch. 19:4–11 which records that Jehoshaphat appointed judges in Judah and founded the supreme court in Jerusalem, constituted of priests, Levites and heads of families. This court heard both religious and civil cases. The court was headed by Amariah, the Chief Priest, who heard all religious cases and Zebadiah, the governor of Judah, who decided on matters relating to the king's edicts. It is impossible to say exactly which judicial powers were allocated to the civil judges and which to the priests, but it is quite certain that all matters relating to ritual, sanctity, purity and impurity were decided by a priest.

The Old Testament makes no formal distinction between civil and religious cases. According to Israel's tradition, all questions of law were religious. Nevertheless, the assignment of cases to different groups suggests that there may have been a working distinction between ecclesiastical or ritual questions and matters of civil or common law. However, the priests were the judges in many cases which today would be classed under civil law (Lv. 10:11; Dt. 21:5; Ezk. 44:24). These included cases, especially where there were no witnesses, in which a final decision was sought by an appeal to God (e.g. complaints against an alledgedly unfaithful wife); all cases in which an oath had to be administered, or where the oracles "Urim and Thummim" had to be consulted (e.g. the case of Achan in the desert).

Some authorities think that the minor "Judges*" (see article) were really judges in the modern sense, while the other celebrated charismatic Judges were military leaders without any judicial functions. However, it has to be remembered that the Hebrew term for "judge" has a much broader meaning than the corresponding English word.

5. **"Those Summoned" (Kru'îm, Kri'ê Mô'ed, Kri'ê Ha'edah):** "Kru'îm" is a generic name, translated as "those summoned" or "called", although the English term does not convey its true significance. In the story of the coronation of Saul (I Sam. 9) the Kru'îm are referred to as a permanent institution taking part in the coronation and consisting of about thirty persons. They are again referred to in the revolt of Adonijah. The court officials, priestly dignitaries and military leaders mentioned in I K. 1:9, 19, 25 are all later included in the generic name "Kru'îm". This name suggests two others, "kri'ê mô'ed" and "kri'ê ha'edah". "Kru'îm" is probably the short form for the other two. "Kri'ê mô'ed" are mentioned in the chapter on Korah (Nu. 16:2), together with the princes and other influential people. In the narrative concerning the revolt of Korah (Nu. 26:9), they are called "kri'ê ha'edah", indicating that both names were synonymous. According to the Bible, priests took no part in the revolt of Korah and its leaders. Dathan and Abiram, were not even Levites. Nevertheless, the terms "kri'ê ha'edah" and "kri'ê mô'ed" were applied to them. G. B. Gray and R. Gordis regard the institution of the "kru'îm" as a body of notables summoned to fulfil some important function on particular formal occasions or at fixed dates, hence the use of the word "mô'ed" meaning time, or date. Possibly, meetings of the people's representatives were held on religious festivals (at least during the reigns of Hezekiah* and Josiah*).

6. **The "'Edah" (Congregation) of Israel:** The term "'edah" (community or congregation) generally means all the people of Israel, especially in the texts attributed to the Priestly Code, but it also referred to smaller groups as in Job 15:34 and Ps. 7:7. The basic meaning of "'edah" is a group of people which met for a specific purpose. For instance in I K. 12:20, all Israel heard that Jeroboam had returned from exile, and they thereupon invited him to the "'edah" which proclaimed him king over all Israel. In this case, the congregation is manifestly a restricted body, because it can hardly be imagined that Jeroboam stood up before all Israel and conducted negotiations with them for the assumption of the kingship. In the incident relating to the gatherer of firewood (Nu. 15:32–36), "congregation" must be taken to mean representatives; the culprit was brought before Moses, Aaron and all the congregation who acted as judges and executioners. Other judicial examples in which "'edah" means "representatives" include the case of the man who cursed God (Lv. 24:13–16), and the case of the murderer who fled to a city of refuge (Nu. 35:12; Jos. 20:6, 9). Moses appointed Joshua leader in the presence of the Chief Priest, Eleazer, and the congregation (Nu. 27: 15–23), which obviously cannot refer to all those who came out of Egypt.

7. **The Assembly (Kāhāl):** The term "Kāhāl" or "assembly" refers basically to a group, but in some passages it can only be interpreted as "representatives". In II Ch. 30:2, 4, 23, the assembly calls the king and his ministers. The term cannot have included all the inhabitants of Jerusalem, but rather the assembly, which was authorized, together with the king and his ministers, to decide on religious matters. It seems that this assembly included dignitaries of the priesthood who occupied an important position under Hezekiah, especially in connection with the matter of the Passover in the "second month" (see Israel and Judah*, III, Hezekiah). In II Ch. 1:2, 3, 5, the "assembly" which accompanied Solomon to Gibeon consisted of specifically named persons (commanders of thousands and of hundreds, the judges, all the governors of Israel and the heads of families). The term here can only mean specific groups. Possibly the "kāhāl" mentioned in Neh. 5:13 consisted of the nobles and rulers referred to in the 7th verse of the same chapter.

8. **'Am-Ha'aretz (People of the Land):** The exact nature of the "'am-ha'aretz", literally translated as "people of the land", has long been a subject of controversy. According

to some scholars ,"'am-ha'aretz" was the successor to the "'edah" (congregation), and both were legislative bodies and the supreme judges of the people. Abraham conducted negotiations with the people of the land, the children of Heth (Gn. 23:7, 12). The people of the land took part in proclaiming Joash, Azariah and Jehoahaz; they were upbraided by the prophets, together with the rulers of the land (Jer. 34:18–19; Ezk. 7:24). In Neh. 8 and 10 the Law is read to the priests, the Levites and the heads of all the people, who enter into a covenant to uphold it.

This view leads to the conclusion that the terms, all the people, all Judah, all the people of Judah, all the congregation, all the elders of the land, the people, etc. were different names for the same body or institution. This opinion is supported by Urbach who considers that the controversial passage, II K. 25:19, 20 (cf. Jer. 52:25), which records that 60 of the people of the land who were found in the city were taken captive and sent to Babylon, alludes to an important body not usually resident in Jerusalem. In Neh. 5:17, they are said to have occupied 150 houses in Jerusalem. During the Monarchy, the 'am-ha'aretz numbered over 60 persons who were entitled, together with the king and his ministers, to decide on matters of war and peace (see also beginning of section III).

Another theory sees the 'am-ha'aretz as the agricultural aristocracy. Lv. 4 lists sinners according to a priestly order of precedence: anointed priest, member of the congregation, ruler, or one of the common people; while Jer. 2:8–10 distinguishes between the kings of Judah, its princes, its priests and the people of the land (who, in Jer. 19:1 are the elders of the people). In Jer. 39:8, the king's house and the houses of the people were burnt down, and their owners carried into captivity — but the poor of the people remained and were given vineyards and fields. In Ezra and Nehemiah, too, the "'am-haretz" is taken to mean the agricultural aristocracy, who entered into mixed marriages with their neighbours. M. Noth believes that they were the free population which had been settled in Judah for a long time, and which upheld the succession rights of the House of David.

A number of other scholars, among them Zietlin, R. de Vaux and R. Gordis, reject all these theories and maintain that during pre-Exilic days, the "'am-ha'aretz" were simply the whole body of villagers or farmers of the country, producing evidence from Tannaitic sources in support of their opinion. The phrase "there was no bread for the people of the land" in II K. 25:3 would mean that *even* they had no bread. The controversial passage cited above concerning the 60 people of the land who were taken captive (II K. 25:19), is interpreted by these scholars to refer to villagers as opposed to townspeople. In II K. 11:20, "all the people of the land" is mentioned, as well as townspeople.

In post-Exilic times, "'am-ha'aretz" had a different meaning, and designated inhabitants of non-Israelite origin (see Part III, Nobles and Officials).

9. **Procedure at Meetings of the People's Representatives:** There are very few references to meetings of the people's representatives. Nowhere in the Bible do we find a detailed description of the ceremonies and proceedings at these meetings, although here and there hints are given. I K. 22 records meetings of the people's representatives held at the city gate, the popular meeting place, but not at the king's palace. The presiding head (in this case, the king) sat on a throne surrounded by his retinue in the form of a crescent.

The number of participants at meetings of the people's representatives is usually set at seventy in the Old Testament, but it is not known whether this number was always strictly adhered to. It is reasonable to suppose that the number varied from time to time, though perhaps there were certain periods during which it was fixed.

Important meetings opened, it seems, with offerings of thanksgiving and sacrifices ("zebaḥ shᵉlamim", see Sacrifice*). The parts of the sacrifice were apparently distributed to those present according to the importance of each individual. At the coronation ceremony of Saul, he received the thigh and other choice portions.

C. **The Monarchy**.

a. **Accession to the Throne:** The Northern Kingdom had no particular dynastic theology which decreed that the members of a certain family should rule, although a dynastic principle was at work, for every king tried to ensure that his son would rule after him. The best source of information about theories relating to succession is the Kingdom of Judah, where the position is much clearer. As elsewhere in the ancient world, accession to the throne was assumed to be "by the grace of God" and as a result of God's choice. Each new king renewed the Covenant* made with David.

Although a dynastic principle usually assumed primogeniture, this does not appear to have been an absolute rule anywhere in the ancient Near East, except among the Hittites. In Israel women were excluded from the succession and while the eldest son could succeed, his title to the throne depended upon the choice made by the ruling king who had the full right to choose his heir. It is possible that the right to choose an heir from among a number of sons was only exercised after the death of the eldest son. Solomon, for instance, succeeded to the throne instead of his elder brother, Adonijah, only after David's eldest son, Absalom, was dead. Since daughters were ineligible, Ahaziah, who had no sons, was succeeded by his brother Joram (II K. 1:17).

Saul and David were chosen because of their charismatic qualities but from David onwards, the dynastic principle prevailed (stated to be the word of God as given to the prophet Nathan). By contrast, none of Israel's ruling houses was held sacred and there were several dynasties, none of them elected. Nor, in a totally different situation, could the charismatic principle be applied as it had been in the days of the Judges (see Israel and Judah*, Part II).

b. **The Coronation:** The coronation ceremonies of Solomon and Joash are described in the Bible. Despite the difference in time, many similarities can be found between them. The coronation was in two parts. The main feature of the first part was the anointing, held outside the palace at a holy site. Solomon was led to the Giḥon spring, where the Ark was kept in the Tent of Gathering (I K. 1:38) and there was anointed by Zadok, the Chief Priest. In the days of Joash, a special pillar had already been designated for the purpose in the Temple area. Joash stood near this pillar, while Jehoiada, the Chief Priest, placed the crown and the "'edut" (not mentioned in the case of Solomon) on his head (II K. 11:14; II K. 23:3). The meaning of "'edut" is not quite clear. Some think that they were bracelets, others that the "'edut" was a symbol of the king's adoption by Yahweh who promised to come to his aid in time of war. The anointing itself indicated that the king was a vassal of Yahweh. After the ceremony of anointing, the trumpets were blown (I K. 1:39; II K. 9:13), the people clapped their hands (II K. 11:12) and demonstrated their joy in other ways, and cried "Long live the king!"

From the place of the anointing, all the company proceeded to the palace for the second part of the coronation, in which the king ascended the throne. The act of sitting on the throne was also symbolic of kingship. Its completion was followed by a procession of court officials and other dignitaries who congratulated the king.

c. **Deification of the King:** One school of scholars in Scandinavia and England have advanced the view that the kings in Israel were deified, which was the custom according to certain myths and rituals in a number of kingdoms in the ancient Near East. Not all of the parallels are convincing and it remains an unproved hypothesis. Nothing of the kind is mentioned in the Bible and even among Israel's neighbours deification of the sovereign was not common. In Egypt the Pharaoh was considered a god during his lifetime, while in Mesopotamia this was only true in the case of several dynasties in very ancient times. The limited evidence available from Syria and Palestine, apart from Israel, does not suggest that kings there were deified. Many scholars maintain that the king of Israel was flesh and blood who reigned by the grace of God. All references to the close relationship between the king and God such as the divine sonship mentioned in Ps. 2:7 and 110:3, seem in this opinion to be purely a stylistic effect aimed at emphasizing the sanctity of the king as God's Messiah*.

d: **The King's Family:** A large harem was a sign of great wealth and the kings therefore married many women. Dt. 17:17 forbids the king to "multiply" wives, the intention being to ensure the succession and also to build up a powerful party loyal to the king (which did not always work out, of course). The marriages of a king were sometimes politically inspired, contracted with notable families within the country or with royal houses abroad. At the beginning of the monarchy the wives of a dead king were bequeathed to his successor — something referred to in a number of passages of the books of Samuel and Kings. An ivory from Megiddo (12th c. BCE) offers the only scene depicting an early Palestinian prince (**165**) seated upon his throne, celebrating a victory and receiving tribute.

e. **The King's Property:** The sources of the king's wealth included property which he inherited, taxes (including labour tax or "corvée"), requisitions, gifts, taxes on trade and mining and tribute from subjugated countries. Possibly the king also took over the property of all those leaving the country (see Taxes*). All these revenues, of course, were divided between the public property which the king administered and his personal possessions, the "segullah" (see Property*).

f. **The King and Religious Ritual:** The sanctity of the king, which derived from his anointment and from God's special attitude towards him, entitled him to officiate in many religious rites. Instances of a king officiating as a priest occur in the narrative of Saul at Gilgal (I Sam. 13:9–10), David (II Sam. 6:14) and Uzziah (II Ch. 26:16–20).

g. **The King and the Law:** The king was not apparently a legislator in the formal or theological sense and there is no record of any law being specifically enacted by a king. The sole legislator was God, the Torah was His Code and the king was subject to these laws and bound to observe them (Dt. 17:2, 18–20). However, since all the laws of the Old Testament apply to a non-monarchic, non-commercial society, D. N. Freedman considers it altogether likely that the kings enacted laws and established legal precedents and practice. Israel and Judah during the monarchy did not live by the laws known today from the Pentateuch, for the royal legislation which, this scholar believes, did regulate affairs, disappeared with the monarchy and was, in any case, regarded as ephemeral and not worth preserving.

h. **The King as Judge:** The main attribute of a king was his power as a judge; the people of Israel demanded that Samuel appoint a king to judge them. That kings frequently took the role of judge can be gathered from many inscriptions of the ancient Near East, so there was nothing unusual in this demand. Unlike the other functions which could be delegated to various officials, the right to judge belonged to the king personally (I Sam. 8:20). The king sat as judge in the initial hearing of certain cases, and also heard appeals against the decisions of other judges (II Sam. 14). Any Israelite was entitled to lay his case before the king and in the historical narratives, a number of cases brought before a king are recorded (II Sam. 12:1–6; 14:1–11; I K. 3:16–28; II K. 6:26–29).

The powers of the king as judge are particularly stressed in the prophetic literature, as well as in the Psalms of the king. David sat as judge at the gate (II Sam. 15:1–6) but from the time of Solomon onward the king sat in the Hall of Judgment which Solomon had built in his palace (I K. 7:7). It is quite likely that the supreme court in Jerusalem was presided over by the king (see Law*) and judicial decisions of this nature, especially those by the king, would, of course, establish precedents for future legal use in Israel.

II. ADMINISTRATION OF THE KINGDOM.

In the first stage of its settlement in Canaan, Israel consisted of a confederation of twelve tribes (see Tribes*). Some scholars (notably M. Noth) have advanced a theory that there was a council of tribal representatives consisting of the twelve tribal leaders which formed a general council of Israel and in which the Judge and the Priest also had their places. As the twelve "Judges"* (see article) are regularly portrayed as military leaders, it seems most likely that the main concern of the council was with military defence. However, this view is rejected by other scholars who argue that the narratives in Judges present the confederation as a body without organized government and lacking real political cohesion; nothing is said there about the actual functioning of the judges as rulers.

With central government established in Israel after the creation of the Monarchy, a basis was laid for the administrative organization of the kingdom. This organization included the division of the realm for purposes of administration and the raising of revenue, the establishment of a system of high and minor officials, and the regularization of the state administrative system. Knowledge of administration in Palestine dates from the middle period of the Kingdom of David*, since the Old Testament contains only hints about earlier periods. It is not known with any certainty what authority Saul* exercised apart from his military office, and the only officer named in his reign is the army commander, Abner (I Sam. 14:50). The monarchy was possibly still in its embryonic form at the time. There was no central government apart from Saul's personal authority in his rural surroundings, and the tribes and clans retained their administrative authority as in former periods. With the reign of David, a new and decisive stage was to begin.

A. Division of the Realm for Administrative Purposes.

1. **The Period of Saul:** Though there is no clear information about the administrative division of the Kingdom of Israel in the days of Saul, a hint may be found in the text detailing the districts of the realm of Ish-bosheth, Saul's son, who reigned for a short time: "Now Abner, the son of Ner, commander of Saul's army had taken Ish-bosheth . . . and made him king over Gilead (Eastern Transjordan) and the Ashurites (Galilee) and Jezreel (the valley) and Ephraim (the Mount of) and Benjamin (a special district in accordance with the king's special attitude towards it) and all Israel." (II Sam. 2:8–9). If to this list is added the district of Judah, which was also included in Saul's realm, but not in that of Ish-bosheth, six districts appear, each of them containing the territories of two tribes, as follows: a. Gad and Reuben; b. Asher and Naphtali; c. Issachar and Zebulun; d. Ephraim and Menasseh; e. Benjamin and Dan; f. Judah and Simeon.

2. **The Period of David and Solomon:** In I K. 4:7–19, the twelve "Nitzabîm" or prefects under Solomon are listed. The name of each prefect is followed by the region over which he ruled. Some regions are tribal territories, while others are described by the names of towns situated in Canaanite areas which were added to Israel by David. The regions listed are as follows (see map **493**): a. Mount Ephraim (the territory of Ephraim and Menasseh); b. Makaz, Sha'albim, Beth-Shemesh and Elon-beth-Hanan (the first Danite territory); c. Arubot, Socho, the land of Hefer (Sharon plain as far as Philistia); d. The Dor district (Carmel coast); e. Ta'anach, Megiddo and the whole of Beth-Shean near Zartana below Jezreel, and from Beth-Shean to Abel-Meholah as far as the other side of Jokneam (the Canaanite regions of the Jezreel valley from the vicinity of Beth-Shean to Jokneam); f. Ramot-Gilead, Havot-Jair, and the Argob region (the northwestern part of Gilead and Bashan); g. Mahanaim (the sections of Gilead north and south of the Jabok river); h. Naphtali; i. Asher and Bealoth (this should probably be interpreted as the coastal Zebulun valley); j. Issachar; k. Benjamin; l. The land of Gilead (according to the Septuagint, this was the territory of Gad, apparently the southern part of eastern Transjordan). Judah is not mentioned until much later (under Jehoshaphat) but it seems that it was similarly divided into twelve districts under David.

493

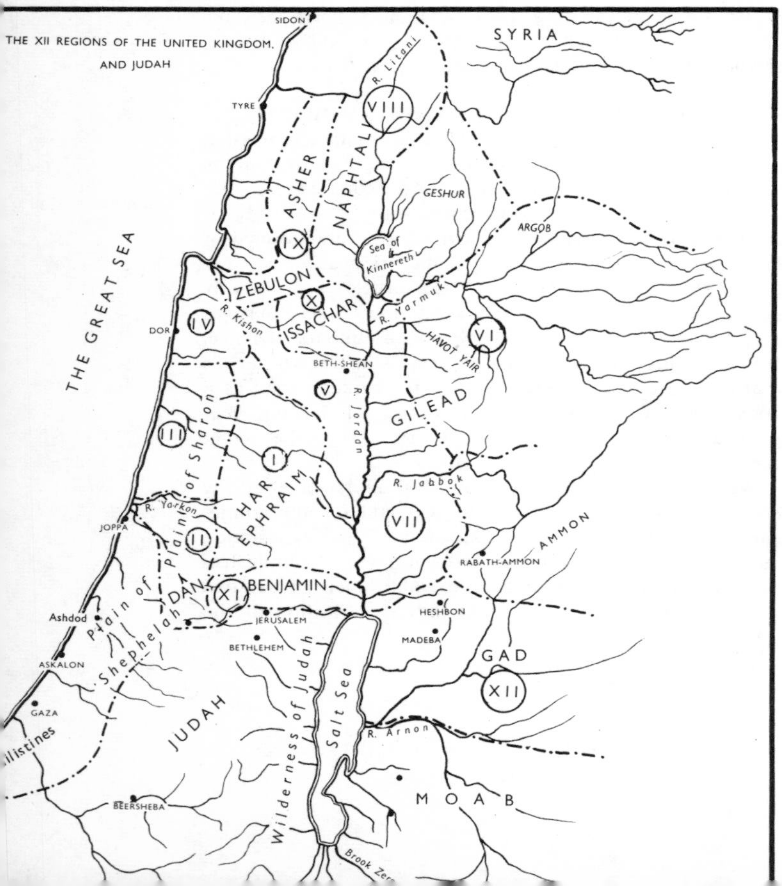

Raising Revenue in Solomon's Realm: The kingdom of Solomon seems to have been divided into two separate administrative entities, Israel and Judah, each of which had a different status as the two parts of a double state (another example is the kingdom of Hamat and La'ash as described in an 8th c. BCE Aramaic inscription).

According to I K. 4:7, 27, each of the twelve prefects listed was responsible for maintaining King Solomon and his household for one month of the year, which included supplying the barley and hay for his stables and estates. The passages are rather obscure, for it is impossible that the same tax was imposed on each region, whether a small one like Benjamin or a large area like Ephraim (see Taxes*).

Districts of Judah: Judah is not mentioned explicitly in the list of prefects, and some scholars have therefore attempted to place it within the framework of the partition described above by moving the "Judah" in I K. 4 from the beginning of verse 20 to the end of the preceding verse which then reads, according to the Septuagint, "and one prefect in the Land of Judah". In order to preserve the sacrosanct number of twelve administrative districts or prefectures, the holders of this opinion drop the name of Gilead from one of the two places (verses 13 and 19) where it appears. However, it is difficult to accept this theory, and it is more logical to assume that the land of Judah was a separate administrative entity not included in the framework of revenues imposed on the other administrative districts and headed by a special prefect. Evidence for its division into twelve districts comes from the lists in Joshua.

Administration of Prefectures: The twelve prefectures into which the kingdom was divided included only the districts inhabited by Israelites; conquered areas outside the boundaries of the tribal territories were ruled, under David and Solomon, by prefects or vassal kings (II Sam. 10:19; I K. 5:1). The geographical order in the list of prefectures is rather inconsistent. There are some who attribute the system described in the list to the days of David, holding that the order of the prefectures reflects the order of David's conquests in Palestine and Transjordan. This theory is unlikely; the list can more logically be ascribed to Solomon's time for the following reasons: 1. In the text itself, the list is attributed to Solomon; 2. Two of the "Nitzabîm" were described as sons-in-law of Solomon (I K. 4:11 and 15); 3. The towns of the Acre plain were not included in the list, which can be explained by Solomon's having given them to Hiram, king of Phoenicia (I K. 9:11–13).

3. **Territorial Division Described in the Book of Joshua:** The territorial lists in the book of Joshua* (ch. 15 onwards) give a detailed account of the portions of the tribes in southern Palestine. Groups of towns are enumerated, followed by the number of towns contained in each group. Most scholars assume that the lists in the book of Joshua belong not to the period of Conquest* and settlement, but to later periods (see Tribes*). According to this theory, the territorial allotments of the southern tribes reflect the partition of the Kingdom of Judah into 12 districts after the division of the kingdom for purposes of administration and the raising of revenue, similar to the system under Solomon. The list contains one district in the Negeb, three in the Plain of Shephelah, seven in the mountains and one in the wilderness. There is, however, a difference of opinion as to the details of the subdivision and also about the period in which it took place. The disagreement is mainly due to the fact that Jos. 15 lists eleven groups of towns in the portion of Judah (according to tradition only ten groups are listed, while the eleventh, the district of Bethlehem, is preserved only in the Septuagint, verse 59) while the 12th is in the list of another tribe.

Various scholars have attempted to date the lists, though there is insufficient data to determine the matter with any degree of assurance. A. Alt dates Jos. 15; 19:41–46 to the days of King Josiah, while Kalai dates Jos. 15:21–44 and 18:25–28 to the days of King Hezekiah. Kraus and G. E. Wright set Jos. 15:21–44, 48–62 and 18:21–24 in the days of Jehoshaphat; in Y. Aharoni's opinion, all the data in Joshua dates to the time of Uzziah. In D. N. Freedman's view the pattern must go back to David and Solomon.

The problem of the rate of taxation applies to the lists in Joshua, for some districts contained many towns (Beersheba had 29 according to Jos. 15:21–32) while others contained very few (the desert district only 6, Jos. 15:61–62).

a. **Archaeological Evidence Bearing on the Problem:** In excavations carried out in various tels within the boundaries of the Kingdom of Judah, jar-handles have been discovered, bearing oval seals on which were engraved symbols with two or four wings. Above the symbol was the word "lmlk" (to the king) and under it was one of four names: "Hbrn" (Hebron), Ziph, Socho or Mamshit. The four-winged symbols were of two types, one bearing a clearly shaped scarab **(492a)** and the other on which the scarab **(492b)** is blurred and only the general contours remain. Bearing this distinction in mind, it had been agreed that the four-winged seals* may be attributed to the end of the 8th c. BCE, and the two-winged seals to the beginning of the 7th c. BCE. The four names on these seals, it is believed, reflect an administrative division of the Kingdom of Judah and were the names of collecting centres (treasure cities) where the revenues raised were amassed (see below, Northern Israel).

b. **Hezekiah's Administrative Reform in Judah:** According to the assumption described above, Hezekiah carried out a reorganization of the division of the kingdom for administrative purposes. The new system was perhaps based on Solomon's division of the kingdom of Judah into 12 districts. Under the new system, each group of three of the former districts was concentrated around one collecting centre. Socho was the centre of the three districts of the Shephelah (districts 2, 3, 4, see map); Ziph was the focus for the Negeb and the two southern mountain districts (1, 5, 7); Hebron was the centre of three central mountain districts (6, 8, 9) and the three remaining districts, Jerusalem, Benjamin and the wilderness, (i.e. 10, 11, 12) were grouped around Mamshit. It is possible, although by no means generally accepted, that "Mamshit" may have been an abbreviation of the Hebrew word "memshelet" or "memshalt" meaning the "government" of Jerusalem (cf. II K. 20:13; Is. 39:2). In a small kingdom like Judah, centralization of administration around four towns was more practical than the unwieldy 12–district division of an out-moded tradition.

492 b

492 a

The theory described above is based on the assumption that the tribal territories listed in Joshua 15 onwards can be dated not later than the middle of the 8th c. BCE (see Israel and Judah*, Part III).

c. **Districts in the Northern Kingdom of Israel:** No complete description of the division of the Northern Kingdom of Israel exists, but 63 ostraca (inscribed sherds) discovered in the excavations of the royal palace of Samaria (see Inscriptions*) may give some indication. These ostraca (see below) are from the period of Jehu's kingdom and are ascribed either to different dates from the middle of the 9th to the middle of the 8th c. BCE or, in another opinion, to the 8th c. only. They were bills of consignment (delivery notes) or receipts, whose inscriptions bear dates, names of places and regions, proper names, and occasionally details of the consignment (i.e. a flask of old wine or ointment). Sixteen of the place-names are from seven regions mentioned in the genealogical lists of the clans of Menasseh (Nu. 26: 30–33; Jos. 17:2–3; I Ch. 7:14–19). The names are Shemida, Abiezer, Heleq, (E)sra(l), Shechem, Hogla and Noah. The ostraca could not possibly have been receipts reflecting the regular raising of revenue within the Kingdom of Israel and other explanations have been sought. They may have related to consignments of wine and ointment from different areas in which the king's vineyards were situated, consigned to the various notables named on the ostraca, or to consignments representing taxes paid to the king's house by large estate-owners in various regions and collected by different officials. Though the real significance of the ostraca has not yet been determined, it does appear that all the areas mentioned in them served as territorial-administrative units, either during the reign of Jehu or that of Menahem.

As all the regions were named after units of the tribe of Menasseh, it may be assumed that they were clan-territorial units which served as administrative areas within the broader framework of the district of Mount Ephraim.

d. **Under Assyrian Rule:** After the Assyrian conquest of Israel, the kingdom was divided into three governorships: Megiddo (Galilee and Jezreel), Dor (the Sharon plain) and Samaria (district of Mount Ephraim). In eastern Transjordan, the governorships of Gilead, the Hauran and Qarnaim were established. In addition, vassal states existed in Palestine under the Assyrians and later under Babylonian rule, in the coastal area and on the eastern marches (Edom, Moab* and Ammon). The Kingdom of Judah was also a vassal state until it was destroyed.

B. **Officials of the King.**

1. **David's Ministers:** With the establishment of the monarchy and the expansion of the kingdom and the king's estates, an elaborate system of officialdom responsible for all the business of the kingdom was set up. In the Old Testament there are detailed lists of the high officials in the days of David and Solomon. Epigraphical documents (seals and ostraca) also give many details about various officials, all of which add to present knowledge of the organization of the administration of Israel up to the end of the monarchy.

David laid the basis for administration and rule in Israel and Solomon perfected the system. The continuity with the Davidic administration is evident and it is worth-while describing, in some detail, the officialdom in the days of these two kings.

The Bible contains two lists of the high officials of David.
a. According to II Sam. 8:16–18 and I Ch. 18:15–17, Joab, the son of Zeruiah was commander-in-chief; Jehoshaphat, the son of Ahilud was recorder; Zadok, son of Ahitub, and Ahimelech, the son of Abiathar were priests; Seraiah (Shavsha in Chronicles) was secretary; Benaiah, the son of Jehoiada was over the foreign mercenaries, the Cherethites and the Pelethites, and David's sons were priests (in Chronicles, they are described as the chief officials in the service of the king). Changes in the order of appearance of some of them suggests that there were changes in their status. The functions of these officials are also mentioned in connection with Solomon's officials. Clearly the two lists reflect different periods, the first the beginning of David's reign and the second the position at the end. In addition the Bible lists the ministers in charge of David's own estates and the estates of his close circle of supporters. Even prior to David's accession to the throne, Doeg the Edomite was in charge of David's herds (I Sam. 22:9 ff), but as the royal estate increased under David, it became necessary to appoint several ministers who were in charge of the various branches of his rural property and the storage of the revenues in kind (I Ch. 27:25–31). Some of these ministers were of foreign origin (Ishmaelite, Hagarean), chosen from among the inhabitants of remote districts engaged in raising livestock.
b. In I Ch. 27:32–34 there is a list of David's advisers (including some relatives of his), among them Jonathan and Ahithophel, as well as Hushai the Archite, "the king's friend".

2. **The Pattern of Administration:** It is generally agreed that David set up his system of officialdom according to patterns already existing in the neighbouring countries, but opinions diverge as to which system formed the basis of his organization. Some (J. Baegrich, R. De Vaux) assume that David built his administration on the Egyptian pattern, and base this assumption on the analogy of some details in the function of "royal secretary" and "royal herald" to those of senior officials in Egypt bearing similar titles. However, these details are scattered and there is no real evidence of the existence of Egyptian administrative systems in the kingdoms of Canaan either before the Conquest or after it. Other scholars (B. Mazar, S. J. Yeivin) suggest that David set up the system of his senior officials according to the accepted arrangement in the neighbouring Canaanite kingdoms which he conquered, and moreover that he included among his staff men of foreign origin who had served in the same capacities in the conquered kingdoms and had administrative experience. (This would not exclude Egyptian influence.) This supposition is strengthened by the foreign names of some of David's officials, some of them distorted by the copyists because of their non-Israelite sound (such as Serajah, Shva, Shia, Shavsha, Shisha, Adoram, Hadoram, Ahilud, Eliheref). One flaw in this theory is that the Canaanite kingdoms close to the Kingdom of David were relatively small, and would have had no justification for the establishment of an elaborate system of officials such as existed in the Kingdoms of David and Solomon. D. N. Freedman, accordingly, finds the real background in the Philistine administrative organization which controlled the whole country.

3. **Censuses:** The complete administrative organization of the kingdom, the raising of revenue on a wide scale, the mobilization of a large army and, in a later period, the establishment of a system of corvée (forced labour), all necessitated the carrying out of a population census which David enacted in the entire area of Israelite settlement (see Census*; II Sam. 24:1–9). Censuses were also made in later periods, e.g. Hezekiah's census (I Ch. 4:41 and II Ch. 31:13). The results of these enumerations and various other administrative documents were kept in the royal archives and undoubtedly part of the material in the books of Samuel, Kings and Chronicles was based on these archives.

4. **Minor Officials:** Minor officials also served in the hierarchy. I Ch. 26:30 reports that David set the Levites to "all the work of the Lord and for the service of the king," which suggests that in addition to cult matters, the Levites were also court officials. From the lists of Levite towns in Jos. 21 and I Ch. 6:49–66, which, according to B. Mazar, can probably be dated to the days of David, it appears that these towns were administrative and security centres. This was especially the case in the remote districts of the kingdom and in the Canaanite areas annexed by David, whose population was mainly non-Israelite and which included most of the king's estates. The Levites carried out their duties on behalf of the House of David and, after the schism, when Jeroboam dismissed them from their offices (II Ch. 11:13–14), they returned to Jerusalem (see Priests*).

5. **Cadres of a Reserve Army:** I Ch. 27:2–15 gives a list of twelve divisions organized by David, each consisting of 24,000 men, although this number is impossibly large. The

divisions appear to have been the cadres of reserve units organized after the end of David's wars, each being under the command of one of the heroes of those wars (Y. Yadin). The same chapter (vs. 16–22) lists the chiefs in charge of a tribe or part of a tribe in the days of David (the tribes of Asher and Gad are missing). These two lists point to the possible assumption that David organized his reserve army in two cadres, the military-command cadre headed by a staff which was responsible for the executive work of the military units, and the administrative cadre based on the tribal organization which fixed the number of men to be mobilized from each clan and attended to all details connected with their mobilization (Y. Yadin). The list of tribal chiefs and the part they played in the organization of the reserve army indicate, if the theory is correct, that when fixing his system of administration, David left a great deal of authority in the hands of the representatives of the tribal institutions. He did not disrupt the tribal cadres and these continued in existence, side by side with the royal administrative framework of the kingdom.

6. **Solomon's Ministers:** The list of Solomon's ministers in I K. 4:2–6 shows that he maintained most of David's system of senior officials but added new ones, owing to the enlargement of the needs of the kingdom and the improvement in its administrative organization. Thus the framework of the 12 Nitzabîm (prefects) described above, was established. Like David's this system may go back to the 12–tribe confederation, at which time each tribe provided a troop for the common defence, under a prefect or nasi. In the list of Solomon's organization, Azariah, son of Nathan, in charge of the prefects, and Ahishar, master of the palace, were added to the roster. In place of Joab who had favoured Adonijah as king, Benaiah, son of Jehoiada, who had commanded the mercenaries in the days of David (and with whose help Solomon became king), was appointed commander-in-chief. Several of the sons of ministers and friends of David appear among Solomon's ministers: Azariah, son of Zadok the priest, Elihoreph and Ahijah, sons of Shisha, the royal secretary, served in the positions their fathers had held in the days of David. Azariah and Zabud were apparently the sons of Nathan the prophet who had been close to David's court and had been one of Solomon's supporters for the throne.

The offices of the men in charge of the prefectures and revenues were characteristic of the period during which the kingdom was organized on the basis of taxation and forced labour, that is to say during the expansion of the kingdom in the days of Solomon. As they are not mentioned in the Bible after the division of the kingdom, it appears that their posts were abolished owing to the reduction in size of the two kingdoms and the abrogation of forced labour.

7. **Officials of the Monarchy:** There are no formal lists of officials after the division of the kingdom. However, references to officials in various places in the Bible as well as numerous inscriptions and seals containing names and titles of officials constitute a rich source of information about royal officials during the period of the monarchy. This information points to the continuation in the divided kingdom of a system of officialdom according to the general pattern set up in the days of David and Solomon. The combination of all known facts about a certain title makes it possible to draw up a list of officials who filled certain posts over a long period of time after the division of the kingdom. For instance, "he who was over the palace" is mentioned in I K. 18:3; II K. 10:5; 15:5 (cf. II Ch. 26:21); 18:18; 19:2 (cf. Is. 36:3; 37:2). To these sources may be added an inscription from the 7th century BCE which was discovered at Siloam on the tombstone of "... yahu who is over the king's house" (some believe him to be Shebna, steward of the palace, also mentioned in Is. 22:15; see Inscriptions*). Another source of information is a seal found at Lachish "to Gedalyahu, who is over the king's house" (see Inscriptions*). This probably refers to Gedaliah, son of Ahikam, who appears to have held a high office in the Kingdom of Judah. After its destruction the Babylonian government placed him in charge of those remaining in the country (II K. 25:22; Jer. 40:5).

In addition to the aforementioned titles, the Bible also mentions an "officer" (II K. 25:19; cf. I Ch. 27:1) and the "secretary of the commander of the army..." (II K. 25:19; Jer. 52:25), posts probably concerned with the mobilization of the king's army. Among the seals which have been uncovered are several ascribed to "servant of the king", e.g. "to Azanyahu, servant of the king", "to Obadyhu, servant of the king" etc. (see Seals*, Inscriptions*). Occasionally the name of the king is given, as "to Shema, servant of Jeroboam", "to Eshna, servant to Ahaz", "Abiahu, servant of Uziahu", etc. The title "servant of the king" denoted a high office (cf. I Sam. 29:8; II K. 22:12; II Ch. 13:6 and others). Similar to this is the title "na'ar" or steward which appears in a seal to "Elyakim, steward of Jehoiachin", and also denotes a title in the scale of officials of the royal estate (cf. II Sam. 9:9; 19:14; Est. 2:2, etc.).

The names of the officials mentioned in the Old Testament and the epigraphical sources add up, with a high degree of probability, to genealogical tables of noble families which held the high posts in the military and civil officialdom in the Kingdom of Judah up to the time of its destruction.

C. **Duties of the Senior Officials in Israel.**

The Old Testament gives no detailed explanation of the duties of the senior officials of the kingdom, and the scholars are of divided opinions as to the precise nature of these duties. To some extent the examination of this question is facilitated by analogies to the duties of similar title holders among the officials of other kingdoms in the ancient Near East. It should, however, be noted that these analogies are not entirely clear. The nature of the duties of three senior officials of the kingdom, the master of the palace, the royal secretary and the royal herald ("mazkîr"; cf. the list of Solomon's officials, and II K. 18:18; Is. 36:3) will be examined below.

1. **The Master of the Palace** or "he who is over the household," heading the list of Hezekiah's delegations (II K. 19:2; Is. 37:2) and whose status is described in Is. 22:22, appears to have been the highest official in the kingdom. The known semantic parallels to his title are "ša pân ekâlli" in Accadian and "mr pr" in Egyptian. While the range of activity of the non-Israelite officials was limited to the royal palace alone, in Israel and Judah the position of this official of the palace embraced all the business of the state. He has therefore, sometimes been likened to the Vizier in Egypt,

who was virtually a vice-king (cf. Gn. 41:40–44). Since the master of the palace does not appear at all in the list of David's officials, nor at the head of the list of Solomon's officials, it may be assumed that the first officials who held this title were in charge of the royal palace and no more, and that their authority was gradually enhanced until they reached the highest position in the kingdom. Shebna, the steward, is described in Isaiah as a similar official, and it is possible that the titles were identical in his time (second half of the 8th c. BCE). The title "commander of the palace" which appears in II Ch. 28:7 is possibly equivalent to the title "over the household". Parallels to the title "Steward" ("sokhen") are: in Akkadian "Zukinu" (in the Amarna Letters); "šaknu", the title of the governors of the conquered states in the Assyrian and Babylonian Empires; and in Ugarit, "skn" which is the title of the supreme official in the kingdom.

2. **The Royal Secretary:** The royal secretary was in charge of the king's and the state's correspondence. His position seems to have come directly after the master of the palace (II K. 18:18 ff; Is. 36:3 ff). Consider, for example, the rise of Shebna from the position of secretary (Is. 36:3) to steward (Is. 22:15). His office was somewhere in the royal palace (Jer. 36:12, 20, 21). In addition to his official post, other duties were entrusted to him, such as participation in delegations to conduct political negotiations (II K. 18:18, 37; 19:2, passim) and responsibility for the funds collected for the renovation of the Temple (II K. 12:10–11; II Ch. 24:11).

3. **The "Mazkîr":** The duties of the "mazkîr" have never been made clear. Some compare this title in Israel to the title of "whm.w" in Egypt and accordingly consider that the "mazkîr" was the royal herald. In Egypt this official was master of ceremonies in the Court of Pharaoh and served as his spokesman, the equivalent of the modern Lord Chamberlain and spokesman. This official reported to Pharaoh on all affairs of the kingdom and accompanied him on his travels.

III. INSTITUTIONS OF POST-EXILIC DAYS.

Political, social and economic conditions had changed greatly in post-Exilic days, and religious or sacerdotal customs had assumed new dimensions. Some of the old institutions were maintained though in modified form, while new ones had sprung into existence. One of the greatest social and political factors was the influence of Hellenism, and its impact, direct and indirect, on Jewish institutions.

1. **Administration and Social Evolution during the Persian Period:** During the period of Persian rule, Palestine was included in the fifth satrapy of the Persian Empire, Eber-Nahara (i.e. the sections beyond the Euphrates river) which included Phoenicia*, Syria, Palestine and Cyprus (Herodotus 3:91). This satrapy was divided into several components called "medinta" (governed states) or sub-satrapies, one of which was Judea (called "Y^{e}hud" on coins and seals struck by the Persian authorities, or "Y^{e}hud Medinta" as in Ezr. 5:8). Other "medinta" known to have existed in Palestine in this period were Samaria; Idumea (south of Judea as distinct from the biblical Edom* situated southeast of the Dead Sea) and Ashdod*. Some scholars believe that in those days Ashdod served as the centre of Persian rule over the coastal area, although excavations (1963–4) have not yet defined the Persian city clearly. "Y^{e}hud Medinta" proper, according to Neh. 3:9–16 was divided into five districts: Jerusalem, Mitzpah, Beth-Zur, Keilah, Beth-Hakerem and possibly Jericho and Tekoa as well. Administration of the medinta was divided between civil and ecclesiastical officials. The Jews enjoyed a certain internal cultural and national autonomy under the rule of their High Priests (see Restoration*; Priests*), but they had no right to levy troops, possibly not to strike coins nor to exercise other functions of an autonomous state. The most important individual in Judea was not the High Priest, but the sub-satrap or civil governor appointed by the king.

2. **Nobles and Officials:** At least in the early Persian period, the people were ruled by the nobles ("ḥorim") and the rulers or officials ("s^{e}ganim") frequently referred to in Nehemiah, rather than by the priests. It is possible that immediately after the return from Exile, the "nobles" and "officials" derived their origin from the "people of the land" ("'am-ha'aretz"), an expression which has been interpreted in several ways (see section I above). The meaning of the term changed at the time of Ezra and Nehemiah, where it seemed to be used in contrast to the "poor people of Judah" (further reference to the term, "'am-ha'aretz" in later post-Exilic times may be found in the article on Pharisees*).

The nobles and officials are often mentioned by Nehemiah in connection with complaints which the "people of Judah" brought to him. It seems that the property of the farmers fell into the possession of the rich as surety for the debts contracted. The farmers were so poor that their sons and daughters were enslaved by the rich. The "ḥorim" and "s^{e}ganim" seem to have been the heads of rich families and they ruled by virtue of their large estates. Nehemiah also called these family heads "chiefs of the people", "heads of the people" or "heads of the land", and they confirmed the new covenant, together with the priests and Levites. Several passages in Nehemiah indicate that they were high officials in charge of the general administration of the country, as Nehemiah asked them to render accounts and remonstrated with them when it appeared that they had not fulfilled the duties imposed on them faithfully. The fact that many of these officials were entertained by the Persian satrap or his deputy (Neh. 5:17) bears witness to the high position they held.

The evidence of Nehemiah indicates conclusively that large estates began to increase in his time, and though certain reforms improved matters, the very need of reform proves the existence of a class of these large estates (see also Land Ownership*; Agriculture*).

3. **Theocratic Rule of the Priests:** When Zerubbabel disappeared from the scene (see Restoration*), the High Priest became the head of the Jewish community. His duties were not of a political nature, the latter being fulfilled by the satrap or sub-satrap. The High Priest was the supreme pontiff of the ritual of the Temple and since many spheres of life were connected with the Temple, his position dominated the life of the Jewish community. The accumulation of large sums of money in the Temple (see Priests*) automatically gave him great economic power. In consequence, or perhaps in addition, the High Priest became the head of the religious oligarchy which, in later post-Exilic days, included control

of legal and judicial bodies. Hecateus of Abdera represented the High Priest at the end of the Persian and beginning of the Hellenistic periods as his people's supreme representative (see Priesthood*; Restoration*; Hellenism and Jewry*).

Apart from the ritual of the Temple and the administration of religious life, the duties of the High Priest also included important internal matters. Ben-Sira (Ecclesiasticus) praised the work done for the people by Simeon the Just in repairing the Temple, bringing new supplies of fresh water to Jerusalem, building the city walls, etc. The High Priest, however, shared his authority with the Council of Elders, the "gerousia" (see C. below).

Priests were prominent in many fields; from their ranks came judges and leaders of the nation, and their position in education was paramount (see below, Scribes). More important, in the small towns and villages, besides teaching the Law and its application, the humble priesthood became the popular leaders of the people. Some of the great movements which swept the country originated in priestly circles, for instance the Maccabaean movement originated by the Hasmonean* family, or the movement led by John the Baptist*. (Other aspects of the rise and decline of the priesthood are described under Priests*: the High Priests).

In early Hellenistic times, the High Priest continued to be the central personality in Judea (see Hellenism and Jewry*). By then the satraps had disappeared and the traditional authority of the time had been transferred to the High Priest, giving him far more extensive administrative rights than in Persian days, when Judea's autonomy was chiefly cultural and intellectual. He took on the aspect of a petty monarch, holding the "protasia" or post of people's representative before the Ptolemaic or Seleucid sovereign, and recognized as chief of the Jews.

The High Priest was, of course, in charge of the large income derived from the half-shekel tithe paid by all Jews in Palestine and the Diaspora to the Temple, as well as supervisor of the Treasury of the Temple. The Temple Treasury served also as the private depository for the people, functioning as a sort of bank in the modern sense. Whereas the internal autonomy of the Jews in Persian times had centred around spiritual matters, political aspects became much more significant as the High Priest became a virtual potentate.

The Egyptian Ptolemies introduced their bureaucratic regime into Palestine. In the 3rd c. BCE, a network of officials spread over Palestine and Syria, their duties to supervise the "royal lands", collect taxes from the tenants, and conduct trade for the crown (see Trade*). The main financial official of the High Priest was his "diorketes" or chief tax-collector. Even before the Hellenistic period, the name of one of these, Hezekiah, had been inscribed on a coin of Persian times, inscribed "Y^{e}hud" (see above). By the end of the century the tax-collector had superseded the High Priest. With the rise of Joseph ben Tobiah and his family (230–200 BCE, see Hasmoneans*), and the transfer of supreme financial power to him, the High Priest's political authority declined and the tax collector became the people's representative before the king and virtual "prostater" or "leader of the people" (see below: the Great Assembly). This created, alongside the traditional theocratic authority, a new power based on the financial skill and experience of private individuals closely bound up with the broad Hellenistic international field — with the consequences described under Hellenism* and Hasmoneans*.

4. **The Scribes:** As the influence of the priests over the people dwindled after early Hellenistic days, the role of the scribes (see Law*: Scribes) took on a new importance. The priests were content with a literal and formal interpretation of Mosaic Law, but the scribes were more thorough in interpreting the Law in the light of the conditions and problems of the day. In time, their interpretations became much deeper and richer than those of the priests, who suffered a further decline in consequence. The scribes may have taught in the synagogues* which it seems were then developing in Judea, although the exact date and manner of the origins and spread of the synagogue are still obscure (see article). This was one of the factors contributing to the gradual development of opposition between the Temple and the synagogue. In early Hellenistic times (see Hellenism and Jewry*), the scribes' influence was most prominent in various circles in Jerusalem. Some scholars consider that the movement of the Hassidim*, whose ideals were purity, piety, learning and unceasing devotion to the Law, originated in the ranks of the scribes.

The Scribes played an important part in the development of the Oral Law (see Law*, Mishnah*: Genesis of) which, in the time of Simeon the Just (see Restoration*) was declared by the community of Jerusalem to be the valid official interpretation of Mosaic Law. As by proclamation of Antiochus III, the Jews of Jerusalem were allowed to order their public affairs in accordance with the ancestral laws (Mosaic Law) in Jerusalem and Judea, the importance of this peaceful revolution can be appreciated. The scribal class, whose chief representatives were the Hassidim, was raised to the rank of authoritative legislators and administrators of law, a position of supreme importance in the theocracy of the day (see Rabbis*).

When the "ancestral laws" were abrogated by the hellenizers headed by the usurping High Priest, Jason, the scribes' interpretations of Mosaic Law were rejected and their position became untenable. The unremitting war waged by the Hassidic scribes against the hellenizers was not only an ideological clash concerning the observance of the ancestral laws, but also a struggle for their very existence. They enjoyed the solid support of the common people, and through the victory of the Maccabees over the hellenizing aristocracy, they won back their position as leaders of the people (see Pharisees* for further developments).

5. **The Hellenistic Pattern:** The conduct of public affairs in the Hellenistic world and in any Greek town in Palestine proper constituted as a "polis" — an independent urban community or "demos" (citizen body) with a council (boule) and magistrates appointed by the people with the right of self-government — followed a certain pattern. The polis had the authority to conduct its own economic, financial, public and religious affairs, strike coins, etc. It was regarded as an ally of the central power and was "free" from taxation, an important right, since the payment of tribute and head taxes was always regarded as a sign of subjugation. In contrast the "ethnos" (peoples) such as the Jews of Judea lived their traditional life according to their own "ancestral laws", free to maintain their political institutions, form of local regime, and methods of social organization.

They lived apart from the Hellenistic stream of world culture, with little hope of economic expansion or of achieving the "citizen rights" of the Greek polis.

Though Jewish institutions and public life did not follow the Hellenistic pattern, they were not immune to its impact (see Hellenism and Jewry*), especially in the large towns and among the wealthy land-owning aristocracy and ruling priestly families. The slogan of the Jewish hellenizer, "Let us make a covenant with the gentiles", signified his desire to enter the commonwealth of Hellenistic peoples — to westernize, to use a modern term. When the hellenizing aristocrats and usurping High Priests (175 BCE onwards) established "Antioch at Jerusalem" as a new polis, they presented themselves before the king as the representative body of Judea, but they were not representative of traditional Jewry. Ultimately, the far-reaching changes which the hellenizing movement brought to politics and religion led to the Maccabaean rebellion (see Hasmoneans*).

6. **The Council of Elders ("Gerousia"):** The supreme administrative institution in the third and second cs. BCE, was the Council of Elders, who assisted the High Priest in a permanent capacity. The body was composed of representatives of the upper stratum of the priestly class headed by the High Priest and of the Jerusalem aristocracy and wealthy landowners (like Joseph ben Tobiah, see Hellenism in Near East*). In many respects the "gerousia" was a continuation of the pre-Exilic "Elders of Israel" (see section I above).

Syrian government officials had the authority to interfere in the internal affairs of Judea whenever there was need, but in practice they were content to pay only brief visits to Jerusalem.

7. **Administration of the Early Maccabaean Movement:** Even after the Maccabaean (Hasmonean*) brothers had won back religious and civil rights for the Jews, the country remained part of the Seleucid empire. The nation's Maccabaean leaders were regarded as "meridarchs" or governors of Judea and representatives of the local population. The "gerousia" or council of elders was maintained with appropriate changes, such as including a number of lower class citizens, to conform to the reforms introduced by the Hasmoneans* (see article). The Council's functions were apparently taken over by the Great Assembly in the time of Simon, last of the Maccabaean brothers (see below).

8. **The Kāhāl:** One other pre-Exilic institution, the "Kāhāl" or Assembly (see Section I above), was maintained as late as Maccabaean times. It was a body of representatives, and is mentioned in a document quoted in II Mac. 11:16–21 in connection with a delegation of two emissaries to Antioch, in the early 2nd c. BCE. The document begins, "Lysias greets the Kāhāl of the Jews; Johanan and Absalom, who were delegated by you have remitted your memorandum . . ."

9. **Jewish Town Government:** Various sources indicate that town government was headed by seven men. Judiciary law was conducted according to the generally accepted rules of the country. This is confirmed by Josephus. He relates that when he came to govern Galilee during the 66 CE rebellion, he regulated public affairs in the district and supervised the nomination of seven men in every city. The Tannaitic rabbis also noted that city government was headed by seven notables. The apostolic Jewish-Christian* community of Jerusalem about the time of the death of Jesus was headed by a "ḥeber" (community) of seven wise men, called "deacons" in the New Testament, "imbued with the holy spirit." No doubt they adopted the style of local government familiar in other towns and communities (see also Pharisees*).

Among the seven was a smaller circle of three men, designated as chiefs ("sārim") or heads (town officials) who actually carried out the daily business of the city. The seven therefore constituted an assembly on whose behalf the smaller body of three carried out executive duties. Early rabbinic literature mentions complaints against the "ḥeber" which ruled the city. In some cases it was charged with oppressing the people, discriminating against the poor and favouring the rich. In several cases these officials evidently became powerful through their ability, economic and social influence, ties with the affluent people of the town and the fact that the poor were economically dependent upon them. In certain periods, the leaders enjoyed direct or indirect support from the foreign ruler, Hellenistic or Roman, and the central government in Jerusalem.

The authority of the seven elders was limited and subject to the larger body of the town citizenry as a whole. "The ruling body of citizens" in rabbinical literature constituted the higher ruling body of the city. The "ḥeber" of seven elders was theoretically subject to the jurisdiction of the citizens' assembly, though on many occasions high-handed elders managed to minimize the power or prestige of the citizens' assembly. Even if the assembly did not always exercise its prerogatives to the full, it was of considerable importance, at least in principle. It reflected the power of the body of public opinion and was notable as the democratic basis of public life.

Even the synagogue sometimes served as an assembly of the citizenry, when the "people of the synagogue" met to discuss affairs affecting the general welfare, such as the allocation of charity, erection of municipal buildings and the like. The institution of seven notables and the citizens' assembly seems to have been the perpetuation of a body familiar to Babylonian Jewry, and was in fact a replica of the ancient institutions in pre-Exilic Palestine (see Town Elders in section I).

10. **The Great Assembly of the Jews:** As the Jews won greater internal autonomy within the Seleucid empire, they created a new legal basis to meet the changed political situation within Judea. In 142 BCE, the "Great Assembly (Knesset) of the Priests and the People, of the rulers of the people and the elders of the land" (I Mac. 14:28) approved Simeon as High Priest ("Kohen gadôl"), military commander (strategos) and leader of the people (in Greek, ethnarch or prostater), with the right to bequeath his authority to his son, (see Priests*, High Priest). This manifesto also proclaimed that "no man . . . could convene an assembly without his authority", meaning that Simeon was granted the exclusive right to assemble the "gerousia" or "ḥeber ha-Yᵉhudim" (Community of the Jews).

New patterns of government and a new epoch marked Simeon's autonomous power. His writ of investiture was clearly Hellenistic in character, his wealth was great and his household rich in silver and gold vessels. The chronological basis for bills and documents was decreed to begin with his accession as High Priest.

John Hyrcanus, who became the first independent Maccabaean prince (in Hebrew "nasî"), rather than a Syrian official, struck coins* stamped "Jehochanan the High Priest" on one side, and "Community of the Jews" on the other. The dynasty rested on a solid legal basis and had in its hands the wide powers of a monarchy. The Jews were exempt from tribute to the Syrian kings, meaning that they were really a "free people". John Hyrcanus was the first Hasmonean to introduce foreign mercenaries into his army, and in this he was followed by subsequent Jewish kings. This move made him a sovereign like the Hellenistic kings who were apparently above the state, and whose power rested on a personal force foreign to the people and independent of them (see Hasmoneans*).

Simeon's grandson, Aristobulos, called himself "King of the Jews" and carried the traditional title of "Judea, High Priest" and "Community of the Jews" as well. He used the title "king" to the outer world in imitation of Hellenistic patterns, but his son Alexander Jannaeus went a step further and minted coins stamped "Jehonathan the King" (see Coins*). Although the first coins bore Hebrew characters only, from the days of Alexander Jannaeus, they were also inscribed in Greek. The Hasmonean priest-kings all had double names, one Hebrew, one Greek, in line with the fashion among their immediate circle.

Had the Hasmonean princes been absolutely free to act as they wished, they would probably have watered down the traditionally Jewish national-theocratic policy as far as possible. However, from the time of John Hyrcanus, the kings had to face the obdurate opposition of the Pharisees* towards the secular monarchy (see Hasmoneans*: John Hyrcanus). The resulting conflict reached such a pitch that during the reign of Alexander Jannaeus (Hyrcanus's son), the "ḥeber" or "Jewish community" was abolished. The first open breach occurred when the Pharisees demanded that John Hyrcanus give up the office of High Priest and content himself with the secular kingship. This demand, as V. Tcherikover points out, was tantamount to the cancellation of the actual basis of the Hasmonean sovereignty over the people, i.e. giving up the supreme power over the Temple, its treasures and vast income (see Temple*), as well as the psychological influence the position of High Priest carried in the people's imagination and faith. The Pharisees regained the upper hand in the days of Queen Shlomzion (Salome Alexandra), Jannaeus's widow, when they did away with all Hellenistic aspirations and reestablished the "ḥeber".

After the state had been restored by the first Maccabaeans, the conquests of John Hyrcanus and Alexander Jannaeus expanded its borders almost to those of David's ancient kingdom. Administration of the country was reorganized on the basis of 24 "toparchies", a traditional number, going back to the 12 divisions of Israel and Judah. In addition to Judea, these included, in order of their gradual absorption into the Jewish realm, the toparchies of Afarim, Lod, Ramataim-Timnah, Gedor, Joppa (Jaffa, near present-day Tel-Aviv), Gezer-Emmaus, Akraba, Nerbata, Eastern Idumea (southern Judea), Western Idumea (Maresha), Jabuch; with, in the north, Arbel, Migdal, Zippori (Sepphoris), Arab, Upper Galilee, Beth-Haramatah, and Abel. This division into 24 toparchies also recalls the 24 "classes" of priests assigned to different parts of the country, instituted during the reign of David (I Ch. 24:7–18, see Priests*). It is also aupporting evidence for A. Schalit's opinion that Alexander Jannaeus attempted to win over the Pharisees by modelling his kingdom on the religious traditions of olden times (see map **499**, under Hasmoneans).

11. **Differences between Hasmonean and Herodian Kingship:** In the days of John Hyrcanus and later, of Queen Alexandra, the "ḥeber ha-Yᵉhudim" seved as a council of state whose authority held sway throughout the land. It is apparent that in Hasmonean times, the people were, on the whole, not deprived of their political power, as was the case in other Hellenistic countries whose kings usurped the kingship by right of conquest and regarded it as their personal possession. (The rights of the "polis" were generally respected.) Nevertheless, the Hasmoneans appear to have become steadily more autocratic, giving rise to serious tension as the people were not prepared to relinquish the rights they had won by twenty-five years of struggle. In the Sanhedrin (see below), the Pharisees acted as the mouthpieces of the people and provided an effective counter-balance to the monarchs so far as legislation, the conduct of the judiciary and the system of taxation were concerned. The Hasmoneans were unable to establish an autocratic regime, for their decisions were subject to the approval of the interpreters of law, scribes and rabbis who held office in the "ḥeber ha-Yᵉhudim". This state of affairs was well remembered after the people had experienced the thorough-going changes introduced during Herod's* long reign.

Unlike the Hasmonean princes whose authority and legislation were checked by the factions defending the traditional viewpoints of the people, Herod transformed his kingship into an absolute and unilateral system by nullifying the authority of all other national public bodies. His kingdom was a faithful imitation of the Graeco-Roman political system (see Rome and the Jews*) of which Judea was an integral part. His policy, patterned after the Roman imperial system, was that of a true "Rex socius et amicus populi Romani" (allied king and friend of the Roman people). Under Herod, the country was ruled by a Jewish king but it had none of the national characteristics of a Jewish kingdom.

Herod's first act was to abolish the body of the Great Sanhedrin (which, according to A. Schalit, was the name by which the "ḥeber" was known at that time), and to replace it by an artificial body composed of various notables to whom his word was law. He also abolished the hereditary rights and prerogatives of the High Priesthood, transforming the appointed High Priests into mere officials of the state, subject to his choice. Thus the last link between the kingship and the High Priesthood was broken, with the secular power supreme.

In any case, Roman occupation of Palestine had virtually destroyed Jewish kingship and this is clear from the histories of Herod and his successors (see Rome and the Jews*). Thereafter the country was subjected to the oppressive rule of procurators and governors, except for a brief period of independence under Bar-Kochba* (Bar-Kosba). Bar-Kochba was inspired by the ancient ideals and called himself "nasî" (prince) both in documents and on the coins he struck. The word "nasî" goes back to the ancient tribal leaders, and occurs in Lv. 4:22 and in the vision in Ezk. 46:16–18 although Ezekiel also uses "Sār". From these and according to various Tannatitic sources, "nasî" seems to imply "ruler". Bar-Kochba may have chosen the title under the influence of the biblical sources, or because Judea was not completely independent or he may have been following the tradition of the early Hasmoneans who also called themselves "nasî". However Bar-Kochba was the sovereign head of the people and the commander-in-chief of the army as well as master of the country's economy.

12. **The Great Sanhedrin:** The Sanhedrin was the outstanding and most effective institution in the days of the Second Temple, in periods of Jewish political independence as well as in the epochs of her dependence and enslavement. So long as it upheld Jewish Law and tradition, it was recognized as the supreme legislative body. According to A. Schalit, its authority rested on its status as the representative of the people, probably as the successor to the former "ḥeber" (see above). Its authority is briefly expressed in Yoma 73:2: "The 'edah as a whole *is* the Sanhedrin." The generations of the past regarded it as the sum-total and essence of the "Knesset-Israel", the Assembly of Israel. However, in modern biblical scholarship its nature and the period during which it functioned have been subjected to continuing debate and much misunderstanding.

The term "sanhedrin" appears in many places in Jewish literature in its Greek form: "synedrion". Elsewhere it seems to denote in translation the words: gate (in reference to justice at the gate) law, or things unknown. In the Letter of Aristeas (see Hellenism and the Diaspora*), it was a designation of the body convened to translate the Torah into Greek (Septuagint). In the Greek translation of Ecclesiasticus* the term is used for a high law-making assembly and elsewhere in the Apocrypha*, it means a "gerousia" or senate. It is difficult to be sure when the word came into use in Judea, although it is possible that it was known before the Hasmonean period. It appears for the first time in a historical setting in the writings of Josephus, in a reference to a Jewish institution of the time of Herod (Ant. IV, 8:14). However, H. B. Hoenig discounts this evidence, maintaining that Josephus used the term Sanhedrin generically, as did all Hellenistic writers, to mean a general meeting, an assembly, a political gathering, a war council or a tribunal.

The Synoptic Gospels refer to it as a Jewish court of justice or legal council, as in the Sermon on the Mount in Mt. 5:22 and Mk. 13:9, and in Mt. 10:17; Mk. 15:1;; Lk. 22:66; Ac. 4:15; 5:21 passim). It would appear that the word "synedrion" crept into Jewish usage as a technical term which in time equated the high tribunal of ancient Judea and took the form "sanhedrin". Opinions differ as to when this institution took on permanent form, but the evidence of many sources points to the end of the 2nd c. BCE. In any case, statements about it in the Mishnah* and the New Testament need careful weighing, for both sources are internally inconsistent.

Its position and composition may be judged from the fact that it provided the focus for the internal social struggles of the Jewish people and for political events in Judea. It was not a homogeneous body but included different and conflicting schools of thought in relation to the understanding of the Law and its application. The most important of these were the Pharisees* and Sadducees* (see respective articles for a discussion of their attitudes). Exactly how far the composition of the Sanhedrin was affected by the struggle between these two parties or by their attitudes to the Hasmonean kings is not known, for the sources are not clear on the subject. Many scholars, however, believe that the Sanhedrin was dominated by the priestly aristocracy of the Sadducees, at least until the time of Herod, who favoured the Pharisees. In any case, in the period after the Hasmonean kings, the Pharisees split into two, the majority conservative faction (School of Shammai) and the minority liberal wing (School of Hillel, see Rabbis*, Mishnah*). The existence of these two factions or trends was apparently responsible for a certain duality in the Pharisaic leadership within the Sanhedrin and was also the source of the five "zugôt" or pairs of rabbis who, according to Talmudic tradition, headed the Sanhedrin — although it is impossible to be sure at what periods. The majority leader served as "nasî" (or president) and the representative of the minority acted as "ab-beth-dîn" (senior judge of the court). Occasionally this order was reversed (Abot 1:4–15).

Functions: It was the Sanhedrin's function to draw up halakhic rules (see Law*) from an interpretation of the commandments of the Torah. Accordingly only those well versed in the traditions and understanding of the Law were qualified to serve. This qualification was not dependent on social standing. Members could be priests, aristocrats or men from the humbler walks of life. The sole common denominator was their deep knowledge of the Law. Installation as ordained scholars took place at the ceremony of "s^{e}mikhah" or laying on of hands (based on an ancient text in Nu. 27:15–23). Installation was permitted only after the candidate had been tested, his learning found adequate and his antecedents and relationships proved acceptable on religious grounds. Before the days of Hillel, the president and senior judge of the court were elected by the members of the Sanhedrin, but after his time the post became hereditary and until 429 CE was occupied by members of the House of Hillel.

A High Priest was admissible as a member, according to rabbinical tradition, but a king was not (Sanhedrin 18:72). At the beginning of Herod's reign, the Sanhedrin included ordained scholars who came from the Diaspora — some of them even presided over it.

The members of the Sanhedrin sat in a semi-circle so that they could all see each other. Their positions did not vary. The "nasî" (president) sat in the centre with the learned elders seated to his left and right. In front of them stood two clerks of the court, and they registered decisions favourable or unfavourable to the accused. Behind the members sat three rows of their disciples. This description (Sanhedrin 4:3) corresponds closely to the conditions of the "beth-midrash" or Academy of Jabneh (Yamniah) which regulated Jewish life after 70 CE (see Rome and the Jews*). The material on this subject in the Mishnah* may reflect a later age which attributed its own procedures to an earlier Sanhedrin of which it had only a hazy recollection. However, the description appears to give a faithful picture of the position before the destruction of the Temple. The members numbered 71, according to many sources, and they met in the "lishkat hagazit", the "Hall of Hewn Stones", a Temple chamber which could be entered both from the Israelites' court and the priests' court.

As the supreme religious body for all Jews in Palestine and the Diaspora, responsible for all questions connected with Mosaic Law, the Sanhedrin was also the final court of appeal and the highest legislative body. It never lost its prerogatives in this respect, in spite of the power exerted by the priesthood and the kings. It maintained these rights during the Roman occupation, when it was authorized to perpetuate itself as the supreme native court, as against the Roman authority.

The Sanhedrin was empowered to appoint judges and priests and to supervise the lower courts where civil suits were heard. Its officers could arrest people on its own independent authority and it had the right to pronounce prison and capital sentences and to carry them out. These rights were maintained throughout Roman rule, except in cases involving rebellion or highway robbery, which were dealt with by the Roman authority. One of the Sanhedrin's important functions was the proclamation of the new moon (at the beginning of each month), which determined the dating of holidays and festivals both inside Palestine and in the Diaspora. It also determined when there should be leap years (see Calendar*).

When the Sanhedrin was abolished, its functions were passed on to the Beth Din, court of law. Responsibility for legal decisions marks the superiority of these bodies in Palestine over the religious centres which arose in Babylonia. The Sanhedrin was not only authorized to interpret "halakhot" (rules), but also enjoyed wide powers within the sphere of its jurisdiction. It could decide for all time doubtful questions of Jewish law and enact emergency regulations and decrees.

The date of its abolition is still in dispute. Some believe that this took place with the arrival of Gabinius (57 BCE; see Rome and the Jews*); others hold that it happened during Herod's reign (37–4 BCE), or at the beginning of the Procuratorship (4 BCE). Some think 30 CE the correct date, and H. B. Hoenig puts its abolition at 66 CE, four years before the Temple was destroyed, when the great rebellion prevented it from convening at its regular place in the Hall of Hewn Stone. It was certainly abolished with the destruction of the Temple, and one of the mourning customs set to commemorate that sad event has been immortalized in the saying, "As the Sanhedrin disappeared, no song was heard since in the inns" (Mishnah Sota 9:11).

GRACE (see Paul; John, Gospel*; Epistles*, Pauline: Ephesians, Romans).

GRAVE (see Funerary Practices).

GREEKS (see articles on Hellenism).

GREEK VERSION OF O.T. (see Hellenism and the Diaspora: Septuagint).

GUILT-OFFERING (see Sacrifice).

H

HABIRU, APIRU OR KHAPIRU. — Terms for certain groups of people mentioned in extra-biblical texts over a period roughly equivalent to the use of the term "Hebrew" in the Old Testament. They also appear in Mesopotamian, Cappodocian and Syrian texts from the end of the 3rd mill. BCE, which is about a millenium before the apparent dating of the Hebrews' ancestors in the early chapters of Genesis*. Besides being mentioned so long before the biblical Hebrews, and appearing in places so far afield, it also seems that they are referred to, not as ethnic units but as strata in society, which makes it difficult to identify them. The problems raised are discussed under Partiarchs*, Amarna Letters*, Exodus*, Conquest* (see also Index), where the grounds for either identifying them with the Hebrews' ancestors or placing the latter within this class of people are analysed.

HAGGAI, BOOK OF — Haggai, tenth of the twelve books of Minor Prophets, is a unique name in the Old Testament. Like other theophoric names, it may have been derived from Haggiah, meaning a child born on a feast day ("hag" in Hebrew), or it may come from "hag" in the sense of Dt. 16:14, meaning joy or feasting, reflecting the joy or thanksgiving of his parents at his birth.

Haggai records that he began to prophesy on the first of the 6th month of the second year of the reign of Darius I, i.e. on August 29, 521 BCE. He was born in Babylonia and came to Palestine in his later years. During his lifetime, Zechariah ben Iddo began to prophesy in Jerusalem, but he is not mentioned in the Book of Haggai, nor is Haggai mentioned in the Book of Zechariah. However, both men are referred to by Ezra (5:1) and it seems that they had a powerful influence over the people. It is quite likely that Haggai's book does not contain all his teachings and prophecies, although it refers to him more than once as a prophet and as the messenger of God, carrying out God's mission. The Talmud records that he was a member of the Knesset Hagedolah (Great Assembly; in Baba Batra 15:71; see Restoration*), while the Septuagint attributes Psalms 145–148 to him (and to Zechariah).

Historical Setting: Haggai began his career some 18 years after the return of the Jews from the Babylonian exile. At this time, Palestine was a province of the Persian Empire, the returned exiles being governed by Zerubbabel ben Shealtiel, of Davidic descent, governor of Judea, and Jeshua ben Jehozadek, the High Priest (see Restoration*). It was also a time of apparent danger to the Persian Empire. Cyrus, the Emperor of the Return, was dead and troubles broke out on the death of his successor, Cambyses (522 BCE). Darius I, who followed Cambyses, faced rebellions in many parts of the empire. On September 9th, 521 BCE, a second revolt by Babylonia against Darius was begun under the leadership of one Arahu, or Nebuchadrezzar IV. Less than three months later (on November 27th), Arahu was captured and his army surrendered.

In the meantime, however, Haggai and his followers, who were waiting for the messianic Redemption, had taken the revolt as a sign of the imminent collapse of the Persian empire, and Haggai was prophesying accordingly about Zerubbabel's coming kingship (2:20–23). The situation on the whole is obscure, but it seems that once the news of the collapse of the revolt reached Judea, the ambiguous stand of the Jews during the previous year became a subject for Persian investigation.

In the following months (520 BCE), Haggai's pleadings and exhortations succeeded in overcoming opposition and work was begun on the rebuilding of the Temple. There is some uncertainty as to the date on which the rebuilding began in earnest, but apparently it was some time at the end of 520 BCE, the work being completed in the early spring of 515 BCE, in spite of serious difficulties. The country was in the grips of a severe drought and general economic depression, while Jerusalem was still largely a city of ruins.

Content and Organization of the Book: The oracles are divided into four dated sections: After a brief introduction (1:1–2), the prophet describes the lamentable conditions and tries to arouse the people from their passive acceptance of them (1:3–11). His first oracle, delivered after the Babylonian rebellion, urges that the Temple must be rebuilt before the people can expect any improvement in their situation.

Haggai's second oracle (2:1) exults in the approaching downfall of Persia and the establishment of a new Jewish state. Whereas the prophecies of Isaiah, Micah and Jeremiah on the subject of the restoration of the Davidic monarchy are quite general in character, Haggai focussed his hopes on Zerubbabel, linking his triumph to the downfall of the Persian empire (i.e. the idolatrous nations).

Haggai based the message of his third oracle (2:10–19) on the tenets of the Priestly school, that sacrifices without a central sanctuary were valueless. Thus, as long as there was no Temple, the people must remain unpurified (see Impurity*) and deprived of God's blessing. Once the Temple had been rebuilt — however modest its proportions in comparison to the glories of Solomon's edifice — there would be an end to the Jews' sufferings. This is the theme of Haggai's fourth oracle (2:20 ff), pronounced apparently while the Babylonian rebellion still appeared to have been successful.

HASMONEANS. — *Outline: Contact between Hellenism and Judea; The Tobiads; The Seleucids and Judea; The Usurper Menelaus and the Hellenistic Reform; Antiochus' Persecution; The Maccabaean Revolt; The Victories of Judas; Rededication of the Temple; A Compromise Peace; Judas' Downfall; Jonathan's Leadership; Jonathan and Alexander Balas; Simon as High Priest; John Hyrcanus and the Hasmonean State; The Pharisees Disavow Hyrcanus; Aristobulos; Alexander Jannaeus; Jannaeus and Demetrius III; Alexandra Salome; Hyrcanus II vs. Aristobulos II; The Hasmoneans' Last Stand; The End of the Hasmonean State.*

The name is applied to members of the Maccabaean family and the dynasty which ruled Judea until the days of Herod*. It is probably derived from Hashmon, the ancestor of Mattathias, father of Judas the Maccabee, the leader of the revolt of the Maccabees (see below).

Contact Between Hellenism and Judea: The causes of the Maccabaean Revolt can be traced back as far as Alexander the Great's conquest of Judea at the end of the 4th c. BCE. This was the country's first intimate contact with Hellenism*, the oriental form of Greek civilization which spread over the Eastern Mediterranean and Middle East thereafter. Until then, there had been only sporadic dealings with Greek tradesmen and merchants. After Alexander's death in 323 BCE, his empire was split into four parts: an Egyptian empire under the Ptolemies; a Syrian-Mesopotamian empire under the Seleucids; Greek Asia Minor; and European Greece. Judea fell to the Ptolemies of Egypt (see map **495** and bust of Ptolemy Soter II, **494**). The Jews were allowed to maintain their religious freedom. The high priest, whose hereditary position was reserved for members of the family of Zadok (see Restoration*, Priesthood*), headed a sacerdotal hierarchy, and acted as secular leader. Thus he was charged with the duty of levying taxes for the Egyptian rulers, though the actual collection was delegated to local "tax farmers", usually recruited from leading Jewish families.

Greek and Macedonian settlers came to Judea, forming islands of Hellenistic civilization, complete with all the architectural, social and political forms of the self-governing *polis* (city), and the polytheism to which it was bound (see Hellenism in the Near East*). The Ptolemies encouraged mutual exchanges between Greek and Semitic civilizations, their interpenetration resulting in orientalized Hellenism.

Judea was surrounded by a ring of Hellenistic cities, and modelled its own municipal governments on Greek patterns, including an annually elected town council. This concept of popular control and representation, though not always practiced, was an innovation in oriental cultures.

The typically Greek institutions for the physical and moral training of young men, the *gymnasium* and *ephebeion*, were also established in many cities. The first to endorse this new culture were those circles already in close contact with the authorities — the priestly aristocracy, landed gentry and rich merchants (see Sadducees*).

The Tobiads: The Jewish masses did not become hellenized and the more traditional elements bitterly resented the Hellenistic way of life. In spite of growing tensions within the Jewish community, the situation remained relatively calm until the middle of the 3rd c. BCE, when a local "tax farmer", Joseph ben Tobiah, a member of the pro-Hellenistic wealthy Jewish class, was appointed temporal leader in return for increasing the tax income. The aristocratic and influential family of the Tobiads apparently goes back to early post-Exilic times (see Restoration*) when they entrenched themselves in Transjordan, just as Sanballat and his family did in Samaria, or before Exilic times (see Israel and Judah, II: Rise of a landed aristocracy). The Tobiads, whose influence spread to Judea after the 4th and 3rd c. BCE, provide a classic example of the hellenization of the upper classes, who saw the movement as a useful and effective instrument in their drive for greater wealth and power.

494

The Seleucids and Judea: In 198 BCE, Judea was annexed by Antiochus IV, the Great, to the Syrian Seleucid Empire. While independent Jewish life was not disturbed, internal stress intensified when the Tobiads, now loyal to the Seleucid king, succeeded in deposing the high priest Onias III, and replacing him by his pro-Hellenistic brother, Jason.

The Zadokite right to succession to the high priesthood* had never before been challenged. Now the usurper Jason gave Antiochus the privilege of appointing future high priests.

From the Second Book of Maccabees (see Apocrypha*, IV) we learn that Jason established a *gymnasium* and *ephebeion* in Jerusalem, virtually turning it into a Greek *polis*. Thus far, the hellenization program had not aimed at the religious faith of the people. Its real purpose, according to I Maccabees, was to end the exclusiveness of the Jews and open the way to their membership in the commonwealth of Hellenistic peoples (see Hellenism and Jewry*. The role of the scribes* and Hassidim in countering hellenization is dealt with under Government and Authority*, III: Scribes and Hassidim*).

The Usurper Menelaus and the Hellenistic Reform: In 171 BCE, the Tobiads successfully supported Menelaus, who was not of the priestly House of Zadok, but apparently a relative of theirs, for the post of high priest*. Menelaus used the appointment, obtained through bribery, for political and material ends. He was an extreme hellenizer, who supported Antiochus' disregard for Judaism and plundered the Temple on the king's behalf. He is even reported to have taken part in the activities of the gymnasium. Menelaus' unbridled behaviour, coupled with growing class conflicts between the wealthy Hellenistic Jews and the masses, resulted in riots and street fighting.

495
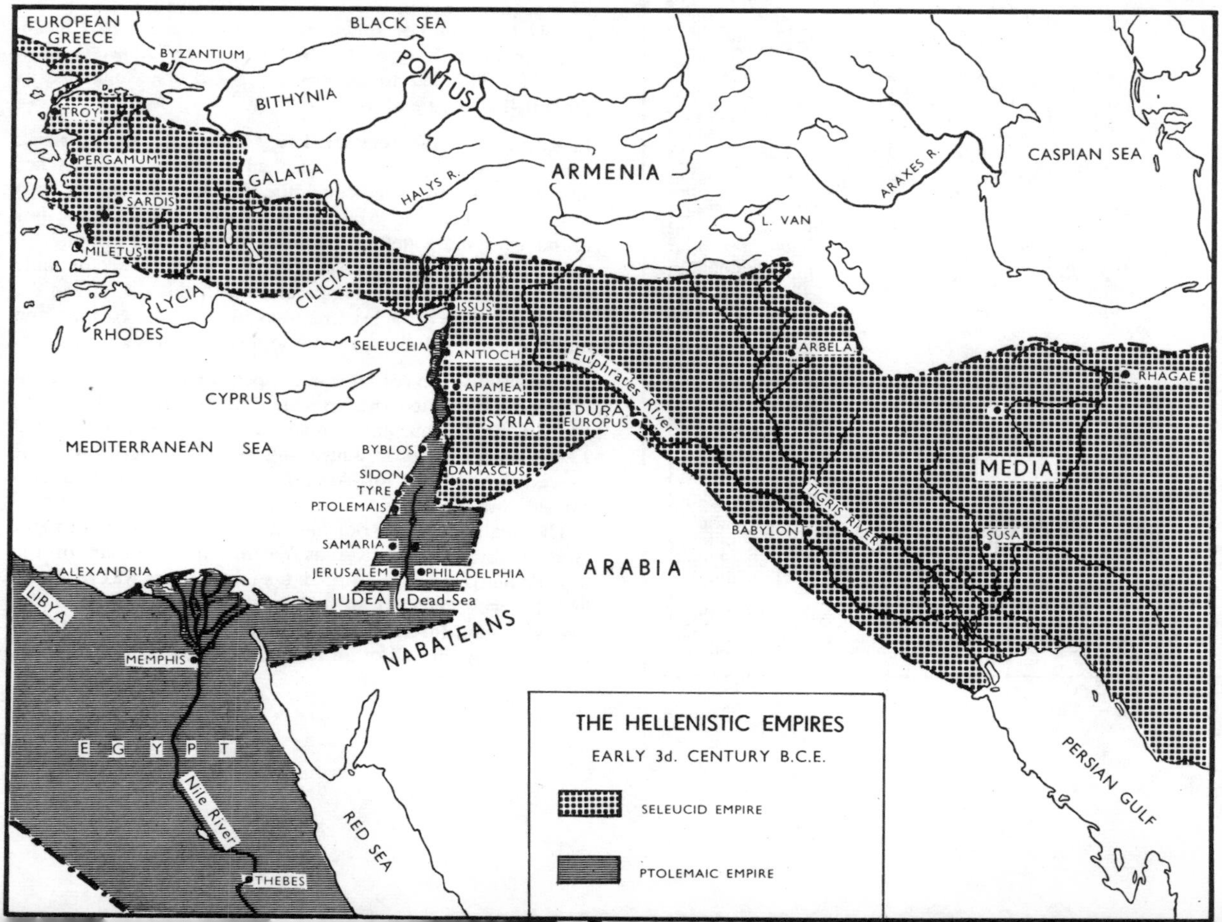

In 169 BCE, rumours spread that Antiochus IV had been killed in battle. Jason returned from the exile into which he had been sent and led a massacre of Menelaus' followers. Antiochus had not been killed, but had been stopped at the gates of Alexandria by the Romans. Menelaus and the Tobiads rushed to him with the news of civil war raging in Judea. Smarting from his Roman encounter, Antiochus descended on Jerusalem in a fury, and according to II Maccabees, in three days massacred 80,000 Jews without regard to sex or age, and profaned and pillaged the Temple, taking away a treasure amounting to 1800 talents (approximately four million dollars at the rate of silver currency of the time; see Weights and Measures*).

In an effort to consolidate his possessions in the face of the Roman threat, the Syrian king instructed his officers to complete the total hellenization of all Judea. Menelaus continued to serve as high priest, but the Temple had been so polluted that pious Jews avoided worshipping there even before it was officially closed to them.

Antiochus' Persecution: The king's political harshness gradually developed into religious persecution, a policy unknown in the annals of Hellenism. In 167 BCE, Antiochus forbade the observance of the Jewish faith. The people resisted and suffered harsh reprisals, though, as has been justly pointed out by V. Tcherikover, "it was not the revolt which came as a response to the persecution, but the persecution which came as a response to the revolt." In 168–167 BCE, the stage was set for the rise of the Maccabees.

496

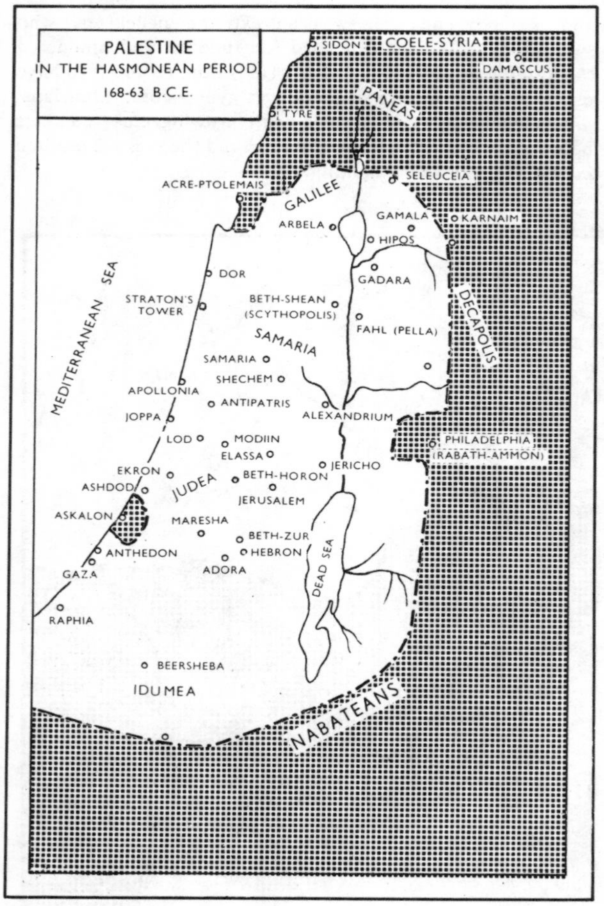

The Maccabaean Revolt: There is some discrepancy between the First and Second Book of Maccabees as to what actually happened. According to the accepted story in I Mac., armed resistance on a modest scale began when Mattathias, a priest and landowner in Modiîn, refused to acquiesce to the worship of the Hellenistic Zeus, and slew both the Syrian officer who had come to enforce the new edict, and a renegade Jew, thus creating a focus for revolt. Mattathias fled to the hills and began organizing guerrilla warfare. Another tradition in II Mac. relates that Mattathias' oldest son, Judas, had previously taken refuge in the hills and had already begun the revolt. Either way, the rebels were quickly joined by the Hassidim*, a group of devout ascetics, who under the stress of persecution became the *corps d'elite* of the rebellion.

The partisans spread through the country gathering some 6,000 recruits from the villages, mainly the lower strata of rural priests and the working classes. The following year Mattathias died, but the struggle was carried on by his five sons: Judas, John, Simon, Eleazar, and Jonathan. Modiîn, their native home and burial ground **(497)** remained the symbol of Maccabaean heroism.

The Victories of Judas: Judas stepped forth as the military leader. His first battles were fought against local Hellenistic forces. By using tactics of ambush, rapid thrusts and night attacks, he defeated the Commander Appolonius and at Beth-Horon brought down the provincial army under General Seron (I Mac. 3:13–26, see map **496**).

Judas next faced a column of the main army under General Gorgias, and defeated it at Emmaus (I Mac. 4). The Commander-in-Chief of the Hellenistic armies then attacked the south of Judea, which the Idumeans had meanwhile invaded, only to be driven back by Judas (I Mac. 4:26–35). This led to an armistice, a course suggested by the pro-Hellenistic Jews.

Rededication of the Temple: The Maccabees, as the rebels came to be called, took Jerusalem in December, 164 BCE and purified and rededicated the Temple. According to a folk tale, when the Maccabees entered the Temple they found everything defiled except a cruse of oil, enough to light the menorah or seven branch candelabra, for only one day. Miraculously, lamps filled with this oil burned for eight days. This miracle came to symbolize the rebellion and has been immortalized in the annual Hannukah festival*.

A Compromise Peace: During the next two years the Maccabaeans consolidated their positions in Idumea, Galilee and East of the Jordan, and brought assistance to the scattered Jewish communities in Judea and Galilee. A series of raids to rescue the Jews of Ammon in Transjordan was also carried out.

The death of the Syrian monarch Antiochus IV brought General Lysias to power as regent and guardian of the king's young son. The campaign against Judas was renewed, and he was defeated in 163 BCE at Beth Zechariah, by overwhelming forces. Judas' brother, Eleazar, was killed in this battle by the fall of an elephant he had stabbed because

497

498

he thought it was carrying the enemy Commander-in-Chief.

Dynastic difficulties at home being more urgent, however, Lysias made peace with Judas, and according to II Mac., concluded an armistice that reinstated religious and communal freedom. Lysias charged the usurper Menelaus, who had acted behind the scenes in Antioch, with responsibility for the war, and had him executed in 163 BCE. Lysias even selected the Zadokite Alcimus for the high priesthood, in an attempt to pacify the people of Judea and gain their support, but Judas refused to recognize him.

Judas' Downfall: New struggles for the Syrian throne developed and a pretender, Demetrius I Soter took power. He confirmed Alcimus' appointment which was supported by the unpolitically minded Hassidim because he was a Zadokite. In their eyes neither Judas nor his brothers would have been eligible for the post of High Priest since they were not of the line of Zadok. Judas was not satisfied with the status-quo; he wanted political autonomy. He transformed the resistance movement into a war of liberation, thus temporarily alienating the Hassidim. They returned to the fold, however, when they realized that Alcimus was determined to continue the hellenization of the country (see Hassidim*).

Despite their initial military triumphs, such as the victory over Nicanor at Adasa, the Maccabaeans were in a weak position and weary of battles. Judas appealed to the Roman Senate for help, but received only paper support in the form of a mutual defence pact. In 162 BCE, Demetrius sent an overwhelming force under Bacchides. The Jewish forces, now on the defensive, fought in Galilee, near the caves of Abellin (**498**). Finally Bacchides crushed the Maccabees at Elasa and Judas was killed.

Judas Maccabaeus has become the prototype of heroism for the Jews. Because his career was recorded in the Apocrypha, which were preserved by the church, he holds a similar place in Christian tradition as a man of faith and arms.

Jonathan's Leadership: Following Judas' death in 162 BCE, power in Judea was left in the hands of the pro-Hellenistic* Jews and the high priest Alcimus. The Maccabaean rebels were at their lowest point; all their previous gains seemed to have been lost. Judas lay dead, and a third brother, John, was murdered shortly after. The rebels turned to Jonathan, the youngest of the family to lead their fight for liberation. Jonathan resumed guerrilla warfare and successfully defeated Bacchides' forces, thus avenging his brothers' deaths (I Mac. 9:43–50). In 159 BCE, Alcimus died.

The pro-Hellenistic Jews were not able to control Judea without constant foreign assistance, and the Syrians finally came to the conclusion that the only solution was to tolerate a government under the rule of the Hasmoneans, who had the sympathy of the masses. Without any formal peace treaty, Jonathan was recognized as *de facto* ruler of the Jewish community of Judea, which was considered a part of the Seleucid Empire. Jonathan established a rump government in Michmash, near Jerusalem, and there "judged Israel" as of old, though the post of high priest remained unfilled for a number of years. Exploiting the Seleucids' internal problems and gradual dynastic disintegration, Jonathan engaged in periodic battles.

Jonathan and Alexander Balas: In 157 BCE Alexander Balas became pretender to the Syrian throne, and both he and King Demetrius I Soter sought Jonathan's loyalty, each making him extravagant offers. Jonathan played off one against the other and chose Alexander when the latter defeated Demetrius in 150 BCE. Alexander appointed Jonathan high priest and civil and military governor of Judea. Some eight years later Alexander Balas was deposed by Demetrius II, the former king's son. At first, the new monarch sought the Maccabee's loyalty and awarded Jonathan several territorial concessions. Shortly after, however, he threatened war against the Jews. Jonathan defeated him at Hazor in Coele-Syria, north of Galilee.

At the same time, a movement to crown Antiochus VI, infant son of Alexander Balas, was begun by General

Tryphon. Under the guise of helping Tryphon, to whom he was subordinate, Jonathan waged a series of battles at the end of which Hasmonean rule over the country had been extended considerably. As a measure of prestige, the old Maccabaean pact with Rome was renewed. Tryphon, however, viewed these successes with misgivings and through an act of treachery captured his too powerful ally at Acre (I Mac. 12–13), and later murdered him. Jonathan's place was immediately filled by his brother Simon.

Simon as High Priest: After his accession to the leadership of Judea in 142 BCE, Simon captured Gezer*, then secured the evacuation of the Hellenistic troops garrisoned in the Akra fortress that dominated Jerusalem. Affairs of the Syrian court were now in a critical state. Desperate for allies, King Demetrius II confirmed Simon as high priest of the Jews, *ethnarch* (national ruler), and military and civil governor of Judea. He exempted the Jews from all taxes — an act tantamount to granting them political freedom, though the Syrian-Hellenistic government remained as the central authority.

In 140 BCE, the Jewish community declared Simon's office hereditary "until a trustworthy prophet should arise" (I Mac. 14:41), thus establishing the Hasmonean dynasty with powers approaching a monarchy. Simon renewed the treaty with Rome in 138 BCE. Three years later Demetrius II was overthrown, and his successor, Antiochus VII Sidetes, demanded resumption of Judea's taxes. In reply, Simon announced his policy of reuniting the whole of Israel as in the days of King David. The Syrian monarch unsuccessfully attempted to invade Judea, and in 135 BCE was defeated at Yabneh. Before conditions could settle down, Simon and two of his sons were murdered by Ptolemy, the Judaized Idumean governor of Jericho, who coveted their power. The surviving son, John Hyrcanus, escaped to Jerusalem where he seized control before Ptolemy could act further.

John Hyrcanus and the Hasmonean State: Antiochus Sidetes renewed the invasion and inflicted a crushing defeat on Hyrcanus. In 135–134 BCE he took Jerusalem and forced Hyrcanus to accept harsh peace terms, making the Hasmonean state once more tributary to Syria. Hyrcanus, however, was recognized as an independent prince, rather than a Syrian official, and aided Antiochus as an ally in his fight against the Parthians* (see Hellenism in the Near East*). Later the same year the Syrian monarch died in battle and Judea's subjection to the Seleucid Empire came to an end.

John Hyrcanus followed his father's expansionist policy, adding a program of forced Judaization, mainly among the Idumeans (see map **496**). He conquered the province of Samaria and destroyed the city. He subdued most of Galilee, a conquest later completed by his son, Aristobulos. As his international status grew, so did the pomp and ceremony of his court, where Hyrcanus appeared before the people in splendid imitation of the hellenized-oriental monarchs who had replaced the Seleucid kings (see Hellenism and the Near East*). Though pro-Hellenism had lost all political strength in the country, the Hasmoneans were transformed into a semi-hellenized, secular, military dynasty.

The Pharisees Disavow Hyrcanus: Despite the fact that he was bound by an Assembly consisting of lay and priestly members, Hyrcanus' rule grew increasingly autocratic, a trend that the Jews were not entirely willing to accept. Much of the disaffection stemmed from the Pharisees*, who up until now, had been the party of the government. They took exception to Hyrcanus' Hellenistic ways as well as his permanent assumption of the high priesthood, which in their eyes belonged to the priests of the line of Solomon's high priest, Zadok. They wanted Hyrcanus to exercize only civil authority, and even that on an interim basis, until a priest descended from Zadok, and a king from the House of David* could be installed.

Eventually, the Pharisees' insistence on this turned Hyrcanus against them and he went over to the Sadducees*, the party of the wealthy classes and the priestly aristocracy, who constituted the backbone of his state administration. In time, an open breach developed between the Hasmonean ruler and the Pharisees. By joining the Sadducees, Hyrcanus revived the situation which had been created in former years when the hellenizing leaders had prevented the Hassidim from acting as the authorized interpreters of the Law. The role of interpreting and applying the Written (Mosaic) and Oral Law to the civil, judicial and religious customs and life of the country now belonged to the Pharisee scribes. Their exclusion undermined these traditional bases of the Jewish commonwealth. Hyrcanus abolished several Pharisee regulations and ruthlessly quelled the uprising provoked by his action.

Aristobulos: Before his death in 104 BCE, it appears that Hyrcanus tried to reach some understanding with the Pharisees, for in his will he provided for the separation of the high priesthood and the civil authority. His wife was left responsible for secular affairs, and his son, Judah Aristobulos, the high priesthood. The latter, however, imprisoned his mother and several of his brothers, and seized complete power. Though he ruled for only one year — Josephus says he called himself king, though Strabo disputes it — he extended the northern boundaries of Judea. An admirer of Greek culture, he took the name "Philhellene".

Alexander Jannaeus: Aristobulos died in 103 BCE, and was succeeded by his brother Jannai, graecized as Alexander Jannaeus. Jannaeus followed the custom of levirate marriage* and took as his wife his brother's widow, Alexandra Salome (Shlomzion). To the despair of the Pharisees, he was declared king and high priest. Almost immediately, Jannaeus undertook a series of campaigns against the independent Greek *poleis* (cities) which still existed on the south coast and in north and east Transjordan, and had refused to acknowledge Hasmonean rule. After a brush with Ptolemy Lathyros, the Egyptian prince, Jannaeus subdued the *poleis*, thus adding the entire coastal region and Idumea to his kingdom, destroying in the process all who refused to Judaize. One of the coastal towns which developed since was Dor, whose later Roman port constructions and monuments are shown (**498**).

Though the Judaization was more of a political program than a proselytizing movement, the Pharisees saw it as a pollution of the purity of the Jewish people. The political aspirations and lack of austerity and stateliness at the court of this bellicose Hasmonean further alienated the traditionalists. An open break came in 93 BCE when the Pharisees precipitated a civil war which lasted for six years and according to Josephus (Ant. XIII) claimed 50,000 victims.

498

Jannaeus and Demetrius III: Jannaeus proposed to come to terms, but the Pharisees wanted his death and hoped to secure it through the intervention of the Syrian King Demetrius III Eukarius, whom they invited to invade Judea. Jannaeus was defeated in Transjordan by the Nabateans* and at Shechem by Demetrius. When the Jews realized that they were faced with a renewal of Seleucid rule, 6000 returned to Jannaeus' camp. It is not clear whether this action or domestic troubles forced Demetrius III to relinquish his victory, but he withdrew from Judea. Jannaeus regained his hold over the country and took ferocious vengeance on his opponents. He set up a standing mercenary army and between 83 and 76 BCE resumed his wars of expansion in Galilee and Transjordan. By the end of his reign, his patrimony stretched almost to the borders of the ancient kingdom of David (see map **499**), and Judea reached its greatest glory in commerce, industry and art.

Alexandra Salome: When Jannaeus died in 76 BCE he left his kingdom to his widow with the advice that she make peace with the Pharisees. Alexandra Salome followed his suggestion to a fault, and the Pharisees soon displaced the Sadducees as the leading power, increasing party differences and bringing the country to the brink of civil war.

Hyrcanus II vs. Aristobulos II: Before her death in 67 BCE, Alexandra appointed her eldest son, Hyrcanus II, as high priest and heir. His brother, Aristobulos II, who was backed by the Pharisees, contested the decision and fought for the throne.. Advised by Antipater, a Judaized Idumean, and backed by the Sadducees, Hyrcanus formed an alliance with the Nabatean King Aretas III, and besieged Aristobulos.

While civil war raged in Judea, Roman legions gradually conquered the entire region north of Palestine, and to the warring Jews came the startling news that Pompey's army was on their borders. The Hasmonean brothers made the fatal error of asking the Roman general in Damascus to act as arbiter. He decided in favour of Hyrcanus, considering him the most tractable to Rome. Aristobulos was ordered to surrender all his Judean strongholds, including Jerusalem. His attempt at resistance (63 BCE), was crushed by the Roman legions and he was sent to Rome a prisoner.

It was obvious that the end of the Hasmonean state was near. Hyrcanus was recognized as high priest, but given little political authority; even the title of *ethnarch* was withheld. The autonomy of the Greek cities was restored; Judea was reduced to a small rural area and her capital, Jerusalem, became a minor provincial centre. There were several revolts, but all were quelled by the invincible Romans.

The Hasmoneans' Last Stand: In 56 BCE Aristobulos II escaped from Rome with his son Antigonus Mattathias, only to be recaptured in Machaerus, across the Jordan. They were released by Julius Caesar in 49 BCE and equipped with an army, with orders to attack Pompey's supporters in Syria. Before he was able to embark on this venture, Aristobulos was poisoned. Antigonus took refuge at the court of the kingdom of Chalcis in Lebanon.

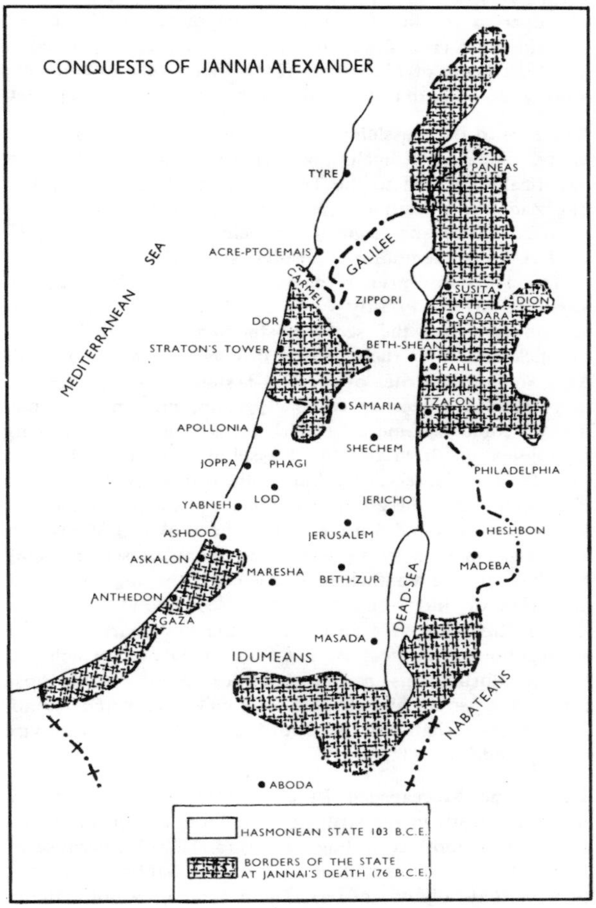

499

Following Pompey's death, Hyrcanus II switched his allegiance to Julius Caesar, who restored him as *ethnarch* and enlarged his territories. Real power, however, was vested in the hands of Antipater and his two sons, Herod and Phasael (see Herod*).

Backed by the Parthians, Antigonus captured Jerusalem in 40 BCE, killed Phasael and by cutting off a finger of his uncle, Hyrcanus II, rendered him unfit for the high priesthood. Antigonus Mattathias ruled for one year and is considered the last Hasmonean king. He was defeated by Herod, helped by the Romans, in 39 BCE and executed. Hyrcanus II survived, but was taken prisoner by the Parthians. Later released, he ended his days as a homeless wanderer.

The End of the Hasmonean State. Through poor statesmanship and inability to settle internal differences in the face of an external threat, the Hasmoneans virtually threw away their kingdom. Had they not antagonized Rome at this stage, Judea might have weathered the fall of this mighty empire, and thus preserved her independence (see: Maccabees, Book of, under Apocrypha*, IV — Historical).

HASSIDIM. — (Hasideans): The Old Testament uses the term "Hassid" (pl. "Hassidim") for someone who is either the doer or the beneficiary of an act of mercy. As a sect, the Hassidim (Hasideans) or "pious" are first mentioned in the First Book of Maccabees (2:42). They rose to eminence during the Maccabaean revolt and the period leading up to it.

The Sect of the Hassidim: The Hassidim were a closely-knit body, apparently including priestly and lay elements, fanatically devoted to the Torah, and traditionally loyal to the Zadokite priesthood. When that ancient line of priests decayed during the reign of Antiochus (see Hasmoneans*), it left them temporarily leaderless.

The Hassidim prided themselves upon their strict observance of the Priestly Code of Holiness. M. Black has concluded from the sect's abstemiousness and Levitical purifications, that their distant origins may lie among the very similar Nazirites of the Old Testament. (The latter did not exist as a sect or compact group, but an individual person could become a "Nazîr" for a time.) Besides being upholders of the Law, the Hassidim also instructed the people in its observance. Many illustrious scholars of the day belonged to the group, including lay "sof^e^rim" (scribes*; see Government and Author.*, III). The book of I Maccabees (7:12) refers to a synagogue or company of scribes being involved in the conflict with Alcimus, the high priest in the days of Judas the Maccabee (see below).

The Hassidim were also among the first martyrs in the persecutions of Antiochus. The Book of Daniel* which was written during this period describes them: "And those among the people who are wise shall make many understand, though they shall fall by sword and flame, by captivity and plunder." (11:33).

During the Maccabaean Revolt: Many of them certainly met their death in the struggle. One large group was killed by Syrian troops, according to I Mac. 2:29–37, because of their refusal to defend themselves on the Sabbath and thus profane that holy day of rest. The passage does not actually describe the martyrs as Hassidim, but it is very likely that they were. In any case, during the first stage of the revolt (see Hasmoneans*) "a company of Hasideans, warlike Israelites, every one a volunteer for the Law" (I Mac. 2:42), who in turn had the support of the mass of the persecuted people, joined the partisan forces of Judas the Maccabee in the hills and became the corps d'elite of the Maccabaean resistance. Their ascetic mode of life may have kept them out of internal party struggles, but national resistance to the Syrian persecutors was to them the "holy war" of God, referred to in the Old Testament (see Dead Sea Scrolls*).

Although both books of Maccabees emphasize the central role of the Hasmonean family in the revolt, it is believed that other notable families may also have been among the leaders. Very few are mentioned, although the "House of Absalom" occurs in the lists of military leaders (I Mac. 11:70; 13:11) and in the Dead Sea Scrolls (see below). Military families such as this may have provided the link between the Hassidim and the Hasmoneans, and may help to explain how the Hassidim who believed in Holy War but not ordinary war, sought the alliance of military groups to achieve their new militant policies.

Some four years after the rebellion (168 BCE), Maccabaean victories and diplomacy achieved their first objective. The Edicts of the oppression were revoked and the Temple and its hierarchy restored. A new High Priest was appointed: Alcimus, presumably a legitimate descendant of the Zadokite priests. To the Hassidim this may well have seemed a complete victory. At least a section — if not the whole movement — were prepared to content themselves with the assurance that in future the Mosaic law could be observed without fear or interference (I Mac. 7:12–14). They welcomed Alcimus confidently and appealed to him for recognition of their status as teachers and interpreters of the Law — effectively, as administrators of the country — a request unlikely to be viewed favourably by the new Syrian appointee.

The new High Priest quickly proved himself to be as deeply committed to the hellenizing programme as the usurping high priests rejected on the eve of the revolt. The puzzling alliance with Alcimus was quickly abandoned and the Hassidim returned to the Maccabaean camp (see Hasmoneans*).

Break with the Hasmoneans: For their part, the Maccabaeans had been fighting a war of national independence. Once this had been won from the Seleucid empire, the Hasmonean leader, Jonathan, began a process of secularization of national life which seemed to the Hassidim a betrayal of the ideals of the "Holy War". Even worse, although a priest, Jonathan was not of the house of Zadok. When he assumed the High Priesthood, this was an added offence in the eyes of the Hassidim. With his successor, Simon, the office became hereditary in the Hasmonean line. permanently displacing the Zadokites.

Jewish national and religious aspirations had triumphed over the hellenizers, but the ideals of the Hassidim had not been victorious. Political and economic considerations were secondary to them. They had aimed at the restoration of the Kingdom of God and this seemed as far away as ever.

At this distance (and for lack of further data), the exact course of events and the reasoning that determined their actions can only be surmized. All that is known for certain is that soon after Jewish political independence had been gained, the Hassidim broke away from the Hasmoneans and abandoned all claims to political power.

Affinities with the Essenes: Some aspects of the religious schisms and resulting factions among the Jews in the early 2nd c. BCE have been clarified by discoveries made in the Dead Sea Scrolls*, although some new confusions have been added too.

Scholars, including F. M. Cross and J. T. Milik, have pointed out that whereas the Hassidim retired into religious and possibly social isolation during the early stages of Hasmonean power, a generation later an almost identical attitude drove the Qumran sectaries to their remote encampment near the Dead Sea*. Josephus (Ant. 8:5:9) first mentions the Essenes during the reign of Jonathan (160–142 BCE), while the beginning of the main period of occupation of Qumran is now dated somewhere between then and the next 30 years.

The fact that the sectaries represented a development out of the Hassidic movement at some time during the Hasmonean period seems to be confirmed by archaeological and literary evidence in the Dead Sea Scrolls*, though scholars are not in agreement about the interpretation of such material.

Other Heirs of the Hassidim: In addition to the Essenes, scholars now believe that the sect of the Pharisees also had its roots in the Hassidic movement. The early Pharisees, concerned with the practical interpretation of the Oral Law* in relation to everyday problems, also took an active part in teaching the people. Before the schism with the Hasmonean* rulers, they also shared the Hassidic contempt for secular politics and for years maintained their objection to Hasmonean usurpation of the High Priesthood.

Under the later Hasmoneans, the Pharisees were consolidated into a popular democratic movement who, in the main, supported their rulers. In periods of conflict with them, however, the more extreme adherents to Hassidic ideals may have provided recruits for the sectarian movement. The Pharisees achieved political power during the reign of John Hyrcanus and it is assumed that, after this, the priestly, generally more extreme wing of the Hassidim, may have been driven into increasing isolation. By the middle of the 1st c. BCE, they formed the new sect of the "pious", which began to be called by its Graeco-Aramaic name "hassaya", Essaoi or Essenes. These descendants of the Hassidim lived on, in face of constant opposition from the Pharisees of the Temple hierarchy, long into New Testament times. Their doctrine and customs were described by Josephus and the Greek historians and, more recently, the data of the Dead Sea Scrolls* have provided a much fuller picture of them.

HEBREW LANGUAGE (see Languages*, biblical)

HEBREWS, EPISTLE TO THE. — Unlike the Pauline Epistles* whose authorship only came under the close scrutiny of the scholars in the early 19th century, the authorship of the Epistle to the Hebrews has been the subject of debate since the end of the first century. In both style and content this Epistle is in marked contrast to the Pauline

500

Epistles and in none of the early mss is the letter attributed to Paul*. Pauline authorship was questioned by the Western (Roman) Church, although the Eastern (Alexandrian) Church of the 2nd c. CE uncritically upheld it. Gradually, the West was won over to the Eastern view and it was not until the Reformation that the question was raised again, this time by Luther and other Protestant leaders. The scholarly consensus rejects the traditional view which is now maintained only by the more fundamentalist groups. Although several theories have been advanced as to who the real author might have been, the originator of this work remains anonymous.

Date: There is no general agreement on a date for the letter. According to one school of thought, it was written between 80 and 90 CE during the reign of Domitian, for the encouragement of the Jewish Christians* who were being savagely persecuted and to warn them against relapsing into Judaism (see Christianity, Early*: Jewish Christians). A better view, however, holds that the date should be placed earlier, before 70 CE, on the grounds that the letter seems to imply that the Temple* was still standing when it was written (Heb. 9:6–10, 25; 10:1, 11; 13:10–11). These scholars generally place the writing of Hebrews around 64–66 CE. Scholars who uphold the later dating, maintain that the author is speaking of an idealized ritual which had long since gone out of existence with the destruction of the Temple*.

Audience: Many attempts have been made in vain to ascertain the specific community to which this Epistle was addressed. The oldest mss are addressed merely "To Hebrews" and make no mention of any particular church. A recently discovered Greek papyrus scroll of Hebrews (**500**) dating to the 3rd/4th c. CE may throw further light on the book. Both Rome and Jerusalem have been suggested as the intended recipients of the letter but in all probability Hebrews was a type of circular letter addressed in general to Jewish, as against Gentile, Christians. This is borne out by the fact that the argument is worked out entirely in terms which would be immediately understood by Jewish readers but would be remote from Gentile Christians. The writer appears to be close to the thought of early Christianity and scholars have drawn attention to the affinities between this letter and the speech of Stephen in Acts 7, generally agreed to have been based on an early source. This factor is an added reason for accepting an early date for the Epistle.

The letter's image of Judaism centres around the traditional ritual of the Temple, notably the Day of Atonement (see Festivals*), whereas by the late 1st c. CE, the centre of gravity of Judaism had shifted to the synagogue* and a stricter observance of the Law*. In much the same way, various sectarian groups also developed nonconformist theologies in relation to these matters.

It seems clear that the group of "Hebrews" to whom the letter is addressed were Jewish Christians who were aware of the living tradition of Christ and his new Church but had no New Testament. They needed instruction on how to find Christ in the Old Testament (or Old Covenant*). The idea of the Old Covenant as leading to a New transcendental Covenant* was familiar to many sectarian groups (see Dead Sea Scrolls*). According to Hebrews the Law* had been given by angels* (who are far inferio to Christ), to Moses*, who was a servant of God, whereas Jesus had been His Son. The earthly priesthood was but a poor imitation of the ideal priesthood of Christ, typified by Melchizedek (see Priesthood*) rather than by the Jewish High Priest in Jerusalem. Moreover, Jesus had offered his body as a sacrifice in the heavenly sanctuary, a far more potent means of reconciling His People to God than any earthly offering (see Sacrifice*).

Affinity with Dead Sea Scrolls: The most interesting and enlightening theory regarding the addressees of this Epistle is that put forward by Y. Yadin who argues that the letter was intended for the descendants of sectarian Judaism, particularly those related to the community of Qumran (see Dead Sea Scrolls*). The sectaries of Qumran venerated the prophets, one of whom was to usher in the Messianic era. Hebrews (1:1–2) insists on Jesus' superiority over the prophets. The Qumran community believed in angels* who were answerable only to God and, especially in the eschatological* period of the "Last Days", in their superiority to flesh and blood (including the Messiahs). The author of Hebrews places Jesus higher than the angels (1:3–2:18). In Qumran, the Law formed the very pivot of the community and its beliefs. Moses, the lawgiver, was highly revered. Jesus, says Hebrews, "was counted worthy of as much more glory than Moses as the builder of a house has more honour than the house" (Heb. 3:3). The members of the Dead Sea Community were waiting not only for the kingly Messiah of the House of David, but also for a priestly Messiah from the line of Aaron. Hebrews maintains that Jesus was not only a member of the tribe of Judah (i.e. a descendant of David) but was also "designated by God a high priest after the order of Melchizedek" (Heb. 5:10), i.e. he was like Melchizedek, the priest who came before Aaron* and was greater than he. The Qumran members lived in the hope of a Messianic era when Temple service would be restored to them. The author of Hebrews repeatedly insists that once Jesus Christ had made the supreme sacrifice, no further offerings have any meaning. Y. Yadin has found additional points of contact between the Epistle to the Hebrews and the Dead Sea Scrolls, but these examples are sufficient to show the plausibility of his theory.

Contents: The Epistle to the Hebrews begins abruptly without address or salutation. The author first speaks of the last and greatest revelation* of God made through His Son, Jesus Christ (1:1–4) who is exalted above all the hosts of angels (1:5–14). The writer warns his readers not to neglect the salvation brought by Jesus Christ (2:1–4), the Son of Man (this phrase is taken out of context from Ps. 8 where it merely refers to "man" in general) who was made "a little lower than the angels" in order that he might suffer death (2:5–10) and thereby save mankind (2:11–18). This concept of Jesus' cosmic significance as a heavenly outpouring comes close to the approach of the fourth Gospel (see John*, Gospel of).

Ch. 3:1–6 establishes Jesus' superiority to Moses and warns against unbelief, using the Israelites' defection in the wilderness to point the moral (3:7–19). The author goes on to affirm the sanctity of the Sabbath* as a day of rest, for it was consecrated not only by the Old Testament but also by Jesus (4:1–13).

Section 4:14–10:18 which deals with Jesus' high-priestly office, begins (4:14–16) with a call to acknowledge Jesus as the sole High Priest of the Christians. For this he was ordained and also became himself the sacrifice for the sins of the world (5:1–10). The author berates his readers for lack of understanding (5:11–6:10) and admonishes them to stand fast so as to inherit the blessings of God (6:11–20). He then explains how Jesus who was divinely proclaimed a priest "after the order of Melchizedek" can claim a priestly office superior not only to all Levites (descendants of Levi) but to the priestly line of Aaron as well (ch. 7). Jesus is described as the high priest of a new and exalted covenant (ch. 8). The old Covenant* was no more than an imperfect forerunner of the new one (9:1–10) which has been sealed by the single supreme sacrifice of Jesus. By this act the whole Levitical ritual has been abrogated (9:11–10:18). Jesus' sacrifice of his own blood and body has at last redeemed men of their sins and made Jewish sacrifices of goats and bulls completely superfluous. Christ offered his body as a sacrifice and he himself carried his own blood into the heavenly sanctuary (9:12), thereby reconciling God's people to Him. The new relationship rests on faith, for the claim that "when Christ had offered for all time a single sacrifice for sins, he sat down at the right hand of God" (10:12) could not be proved in any material sense. "Faith" therefore, has a different meaning for the writer of Hebrews than it had for Paul* (see article and Epistles*, Pauline). In Hebrews — as in John — it is a matter of belief beyond sight. Blessed are those who believe, even though they have not seen.

The remainder of the Epistle is made up of various exhortations and admonitions urging the readers to live steadfastly in the faith of the New Covenant*. Ch. 10:19–31 encourages the Christians to hold fast to their faith and to endure every suffering patiently so that they may receive the promise of God (10:32–39). Ch. 11 explains the nature and power of faith and illustrates this teaching by examples drawn from the history of Israel. The author bids his readers remain faithful even as Christ himself was faithful (12:1–3) and assures them that their tribulations are but the chastisements of God in preparation for their own salvation (12:4–11). They are warned against indolence and the sin of rejecting God's grace (12:12–29); exhorted to live in brotherly love, disdaining immorality or covetousness (13:1–6) and called upon again to remain true to their faith and loyal to their leaders (13:7–17). The author then concludes his Epistle with words of salutation and benediction (13:18–25).

HELLENISM AND JEWRY. — *Outline: I. Historical: The Hellenizers; The Maccabaean Revolt and the Hasmonean State. II. Religious and Cultural Climate: The Greek "Easy Way of Life"; Positive Aspects of Greek Culture; Points of Contact.*

I. HISTORICAL. — **The Hellenizers:** Hellenism as a philosophy and a way of life (see Hellenism in the Near East*) had a tremendous impact on the Jews, Judaism and Jewish culture. The hellenization of Palestine was a dynamic force which frequently provoked the resistance of native Jews. By the 4th c. BCE, numerous Hellenistic towns whose customs and beliefs were alien to the spirit of Judaism were established in the country. Economic and social ties between the Jewish and Hellenistic centres developed, and hastened the hellenizing process. This was particularly true of the higher strata of Jewish society, who came to regard Jewish traditions and customs as outworn, and began to consider themselves "citizens of the world". These hellenizing Jews were no longer content, as their fathers had been during the Persian period (6th to 4th c. BCE), to be part of the "holy seed". According to present knowledge, the Hellenistic movement in Palestine during the 3rd c. BCE centred mainly around the Tobiads, a family of the Jewish aristocracy that disregarded Jewish religious edicts and sought riches and power on a scale previously unknown in Palestine (see Hasmoneans*; Hellenism in the Near East*).

By the 2nd c. BCE, the hellenizers constituted a large and powerful segment of the population, resulting in an alarming decline in national and community solidarity. The hellenizers went so far as to resort to bribery and assassination to secure the post of High Priest for one of their followers. With the high priest, Jason, at its head, the Hellenistic reform was aimed at introducing basic changes in the existing political and religious constitution of Jerusalem so as to conform to the customs in the other Hellenistic provinces of the empire. Jason made a formal request to Antiochus to grant the inhabitants of Jerusalem the privilege of being registered as citizens of Antioch in Syria, i.e. as citizens of the capital, not as provincials, a privilege which was accorded the citizens of Acre (Ptolemais). Jason subsequently proclaimed "the people of Jerusalem as Antiocheans ... and made new and wicked customs by destroying the lawful customs of the state" (II Mac. 4:9–11). After this, the king gave the hellenizers permission to "act according to the laws of the Gentiles."

The proclamation which named the hellenizers henceforth Antiocheans instead of Jerusalemites in effect handed over all affairs, including religion, to the polis. This carried with it the danger of changes in the ancient customs of the people and made the commandments of God, the "ancestral laws" of the Jews, subject to the approval of the general assembly of Antioch-at-Jerusalem. This was composed of the high-born and wealthy citizens of the city together with the foreign settlers and was mainly under the leadership of Jewish hellenizers who, embracing the more superficial aspects of Hellenistic culture, wanted to abandon the exclusiveness of Jewish customs (to the Greeks all such exclusiveness was "barbarism"). The new ways spread. Many officiating priests neglected their sacred duties to devote themselves to sports and other Hellenistic diversions (II Mac. 4:12–16).

This situation was intolerable to the Jews who were devoted to the Torah. The powerful opposition of the Hassidim* (see article) and scribes (see Government* and Authority, III) is described in the respective articles. The faithful could not even tolerate the thought that the Temple and the sacred ritual were entrusted to priests who had been defiled by practicing alien customs. Many of these traditionalists were also dissatisfied with the social benefits that derived from the polis whose existence meant that political power in Judea rested in the hands of the Hellenistic nobility. The poleis were organized on a complex social basis which superimposed this new stratum of elite on the traditional oriental Israelite foundations. So long as the right of the common people to live according to the Law of Moses remained secure, relative quiet reigned in Jerusalem. The situation changed with the establishment of a fortress called the Akra, near the Temple, to protect the foreign settlers among the citizens of "Antioch-at-Jerusalem", and the commencement of pagan sacrifices on the Temple mound itself (see Hasmoneans*; Jerusalem)*.

The Maccabaean Revolt and the Hasmonean State: Popular dissatisfaction with the hellenizers was eventually translated into open rebellion, followed by severe counter-measures and religious persecution by the Seleucid King, Antiochus IV Epiphanes (167–164 BCE). This was, in turn, followed by a more serious revolt under the leadership of the Maccabees (Hasmoneans) and their allies, the Hassidim*, in which the Seleucid monarch and his successors were defeated (see Hasmoneans*). There ensued a period of national independence under the Hasmonean dynasty, during which all of Judea and later the whole of Palestine were freed from the Seleucid Empire.

As might be expected, the Hasmonean state was a bitter enemy of Hellenism, though it adopted some of its courtly trappings. When Rome invaded the area in 63 BCE, the Jews like other Eastern peoples lost the independence they had won from the Seleucids, although the central values of Judaism as a religion withstood the Hellenistic impact and continued fundamentally unaffected. Nevertheless, in the late Hasmonean and Roman periods, the influence of Hellenism was felt in many aspects of Jewish life and culture, as contemporary religious literature shows. Under the Hasmoneans, Jewish rule had been extended to Idumea, the Negeb, the coastal region, Transjordan, the Valley of Jezreel and Galilee. This expansion brought the hitherto isolated Jewish communities into closer contact with the Hellenistic settlements. The confrontation of the two was not peaceful. The early Hasmonean princes, John Hyrcanus and Alexander Jannaeus, who had occupied the poleis, as

501

well as other non-Jewish centres, introduced a program of compulsory Judaization, which they considered a political necessity. The inhabitants were made to choose between conversion or death, a policy not calculated to promote friendly relations.

In contrast to the Greek, Philistine, Syrian and other polytheistic religions which could carry on a peaceful syncretism (see Hellenism in the Near East*), Judaism was a strictly monotheist faith that could not offer any compromise to the pagans, such as adding the God of Israel to the local pantheon or blending religious doctrine or patterns of behaviour.

Nevertheless, during the later Roman period, mixed populations became a common feature of the country and even in such essentially hellenized centres as Caesarea*, Jabneh and Scythopolis (Beth-Shean), there was a large Jewish element. Greek influence, revitalized under the Romans, manifested itself in the use of the Greek language and the adoption of Greek names (many Hasmoneans bore Graecized names in addition to their Hebrew ones). The Hasmoneans* learned a good deal from the Greeks in matters of warfare* and administration (see articles), though in cultural matters Hellenism did not have a decisive influence on the Jews, and still less on their religion.

II. RELIGIOUS AND CULTURAL CLIMATE. — As noted above and in the article on Hellenism in the Near East* (see particularly the section on the Universal Language*), the cultural influence of Hellenism on the Jews manifested itself in many ways: Jewish law and Aggadah show the influence of Hellenistic rhetoric, while many hundreds of Greek words penetrated the Hebrew language, to be used especially in legal and religious connections. In addition, there is a noticeable parallel between Jewish luminaries of the time and Hellenistic philosophers and teachers.

The Greek "Easy Way of Life": In most Mediterranean countries apart from Rome, the Greek way of life had a deleterious effect. Witness the Latin verb *pergraecari* (to become hellenized) which in usage means "to lead a licentious life". The moral breakdown that resulted from hellenization is well exemplified by the stories of the hellenizing High Priests, Jason and Menelaus (see Hasmoneans*).

Positive Aspects of Greek Culture: Whereas in the early Hellenistic period (4th to late 3rd c. BCE) the Hellenist impact had not been deeply felt in Jewish economic or political life, the appearance of sizable numbers of bankers and merchants in the following decades is evidence of the economic transformation produced by Hellenist penetration. The effects of this on agriculture* in post-Exilic times and in improved housing and planning in the Hellenistic cities* of Palestine has already been discussed. More important, the development of a wealthy "bourgeoisie" out of the upper ranks of the landed aristocracy (like the Tobiad family) under the Hasmonean* princes had far-reaching effects on economic life. This was equally true whether they acted in competition or collaboration with the Greek and Syrian inhabitants of the Greek towns, later known as the Decapolis (see Cities, Hellenistic*), or benefitted from their dispossession by the Hasmoneans. The example of Greek methods was especially important for the development of better tools*, workshop techniques, communications, roads*, writing materials* and techniques. This is illustrated by numerous painted vases found in Israel (**501**). It was against this technical background that Herod* carried out his great construction works and built new towns on the Hellenistic pattern.

In the course of several generations, more serious Jewish thinkers absorbed the positive aspects of Greek culture, explaining and passing them on. On an intellectual level, Hellenic civilization was universal and supranational, that is, it was the same in all the great civic and cultural centres like Athens, Alexandria, Antioch, etc. In addition, an individual could become a Hellenist by attending a Greek school, without forsaking his particular religion or customs. The oriental of every race, with his strict attitudes concerning food, drink and ceremonial, never truly adopted the Greek way of life except in a superficial manner. It was the Jew alone, among all orientals, who faced and grappled with the problem of Hellenism and found means of assimilating certain of its cultural features, while preserving his individuality and integrity. Though some Jews of the post-Hasmonean period outwardly adopted Greek fashions, the mass of the people never accepted the Greek idea of "paideia", i.e. an all-embracing physical, intellectual, artistic education which could lead to perfection. In the Jewish environment, a Greek gymnasium was only a place for physical education (see illustrations under Hellenism in the Near East*). The Pharisees*, who considered universal education basic to Judaism, established schools to give instruction in the Scriptures and Oral (unwritten) Law in every village.

Points of Contact: This transformation of biblical Judaism into a more complex way of life during the Hellenistic era and after, was brought about by the adaptation of Greek cultural and social institutions and methods to the problems with which Judaism was faced by its contact with Hellenism. Despite many fundamental differences, the Jewish and Greek cultures did have several features in common, notably their mutual admiration for wisdom as inspired by judicious observation and strengthened by an appreciation of moral principles laid down by the ancients, particularly with regard to religion (see Hellenism and the Jewish Diaspora*).

Philosophical speculation in the Greek and western sense is not an integral part of traditional Jewish thought, but Hellenistic Jewish thinkers made use of the philosophic categories of their colleagues to arrive at a philosophical understanding of Judaism. Indeed it was within the framework provided by Hellenism that Jewish philosophical thinking, properly so-called, first manifested itself (see Hellenism and the Jewish Diaspora*; Rabbis*, Pharisees*; Judaism*).

Nevertheless, however close the Jews might come to their Hellenistic environment, they never lost their attachment to their own nationality and ways. Organized Jewish life and synagogues* continued for many generations in given localities and the overwhelming majority rejected outright assimilation.

To sum up: the Jews of Palestine and, to a greater extent, those of the Diaspora, felt and reflected the influences of Hellenism; Jewish traditions, religion and Law, however, never gave way to Greek culture. The essential strength of Judaism enabled it to defend itself successfully.

HELLENISM AND THE CHRISTIAN CHURCH—

The origins of Christianity lie squarely in Judaism and all Jesus' followers were Jews. Yet Christianity also felt and reflects the influence of Hellenism. As the new faith moved away from its source — and many scholars maintain that Pauline Christianity owes more to Judaism than was generally believed before the discovery of the Dead Sea Scrolls — the influence of Hellenistic culture correspondingly increased. Manifestations of this influence include Christian ritual and art, both of which violated the Jewish prohibition on statues and human likenesses. Even after Christianity's conquest of the Roman Empire, which dealt a heavy blow to Hellenism, it continued to prosper to some extent within the Christian world.

Stoicism, Hellenism and Christianity: The ethical ideals of stoicism (see Hellenism in the Near East*) may be seen as a preparation for Christianity, although this philosophy did not include belief in progress and lacked the dynamic force which propelled Judaism and Christianity into powerful religious movements. Christianity did, however, absorb much of the terminology of stoicism, investing it with new content and values. (See Hell. and Jewish Diaspora*).

The Hellenistic mystery religions (Isis and Mithras cults, which made purity of life a condition of membership and prescribed abstinence, solemn baptism, inward religious experience, the ideas of purity, regeneration of the divine personality and a final nuptial rapture uniting the soul of the initiate with the deity, also prepared the way for Christianity. The adepts of Mithraism throughout the Graeco-Roman world, subjected themselves to asceticism. They were taught that the "solar god" (**502**) intercedes between gods and mortals, and resuscitates the dead. This

502

503

2nd c. CE fresco (**503**) represents some details of preparations for an Isiac festival (from Carthage). Early Gentile Christianity came into contact with these mystery religions and there are certain analogies between their different theologies. However the extent to which Christian beliefs were actually affected can easily be exaggerated. Paul's doctrine of the sacrament owes more to traditional Jewish concepts (I Cor. 10:1 ff) than to mystery religions. Moreover there seems to be a deliberate attempt in the New Testament to avoid the characteristic vocabulary of the mystics. Inevitably, if the Christian missionaries were to be intelligible to their audience, they had to use an idiom that was familiar to people used to the Hellenist religions. Paul used such phrases to combat heresy at Colossae (Col. 2:18), just as he used stoic technical terms to convey ethical and intellectual values to the Gentiles. In both cases, however, his language was charged with a basic meaning rooted in biblical concepts and ideas. The mystical identification of the initiate in the mystery cults with a divine personage whose death and then restoration to life was the object of the ceremony differs fundamentally in concept from the Christian's union with Christ in "death to sin" and resurrection to life. There are mystic elements in Pauline Christianity but Paul's mysticism was thoroughly ethical in character and was unaffected by the mystery religions. The forms used in the new faith may have been the same, but their spirit had moved forward.

While Christianity made use of philosophical terms like the "logos" (see Hellenism and the Jewish Diaspora*) or "salvation", it never compromised the ancient conception of God. Similarly, while Christianity inherited some of its ritual from the mystery religions, it was eventually to reject all participation in pagan cults and it purified whatever it took over.

In the 3rd c. CE — which is beyond the New Testament period — the Church did become deeply influenced by various aspects of Hellenism. H. Lietzmann has remarked that Judaism "separated finally from the spirit of Hellenism just about the same time that Christianity became indivisibly wedded to it." This seems to be an overstatement. Nevertheless, when the early Church was threatened with syncretist tendencies and heterodox forms of Christianity, its Jewish heritage served as a valuable counter-balance, and this became even truer of later Christian thought and theology. What kept official theology free of idolatrous taints was, above all, its concept of God — Christianity's inalienable heritage from Judaism.

The Lord's Day: At the same time, Christian independence from Jewish rites was increasing. Even before Constantine's conversion, the separation of the two faiths had been reinforced by the substitution of the Lord's Day (Sunday) for the traditional Sabbath and by the adoption of rules for the dating of Easter which would avoid its coinciding with Passover. Under Constantine, the Jews were prohibited from proselytizing or interfering with Jewish converts to Christianity, and lost many of their long-established rights. Constantine enacted laws discriminating against the Jews, thereby limiting their influence and degrading them in the eyes of their fellows. It was a process applied and expanded throughout Christendom in the Middle Ages — and after.

HELLENISM AND THE JEWISH DIASPORA.—

Outline: Alexandrian Jewry; Septuagint; Propagandist Zeal and Proselytizing; Greek-Jewish Literature and Thought; Philo; The Harmony Ends.

The peaceful co-existence between the Jews of the Diaspora and their pagan neighbours was based on three factors: economic and civil community of interest, evidenced by the wealth the two groups created in the cities of the Graeco-Roman world; pagan tolerance of Jewish rights, preserved by the ethnic and cultural diversity of the pagans; and the great numbers of Jews living in the larger cities (see Rome and the Jews*).

The organ of Jewish religious and juridical autonomy, the *politeuma*, which was mainly Greek in form, was recognized by the Hellenistic kings of Egypt and Asia Minor. The harmonious atmosphere in which they lived encouraged the Jews to adopt something of Hellenic organization in their communal institutions, even though they lived in their own quarters, apart from the rest of the population. In addition, a pious Jew would not dine at the table of a pagan, nor would he receive one at his own table. Even when piety did not create a barrier, the lines were definitely drawn at the social level. Jewish attendance at the theatres, circuses and gymnasia was either forbidden or barely tolerated, though these rules were not always followed everywhere.

Alexandrian Jewry: In contrast to the bitter antagonism that prevailed between the Jewish and Hellenistic cultures in Palestine, relations between the two in Egypt during the

Ptolemaic period (4th to 1st c. BCE) were relatively friendly. Many Jews even adopted forms of Hellenistic culture, such as the use of Greek names and recourse to Greek courts. They observed their own religious customs, but did so without clashing with their environment.

Septuagint: As early as the 3rd c. BCE, Greek became the principal language of the Jews, even in their religious services. As a result, the Torah, and later the other parts of the Old Testament, were translated into that language, (the Septuagint). (The Chester Beatty Greek papyrus VI from a Codex of Num. – Deut. (**504**) and the J. Rylands library papyrus 458 (**505**) are some of the earliest extant Septuagint mss of the 2nd c. BCE. Other books were also translated into Greek for the benefit of Egyptian Jewry. They included Ecclesiasticus (Wisdom of Ben Sira), and I Maccabees among the Apocrypha* with other Apocryphal and Apocaplyptic* writings. II Maccabees, which breathes the spirit of a national epic, was written in Cyrenaica, a province of Egypt, in an essentially Hellenistic style.

The profound effect of Hellenism on the Jews can be seen from the wide and varied range of Judeo-Alexandrian literature, one school of which advocated a Graeco-Jewish rapprochement. The writings of the Alexandrian Jews were mainly propagandist, apologetic, literary, historical or ethical (see below: Greek-Jewish Literature), while some Alexandrian writers even held that Greek philosophy was Jewish in origin. The most outstanding original early Jewish literary work, written in Hellenistic style, is the "Letter of Aristeas", which, side by side with unqualified praise for Judaism and the Torah, makes an attempt to harmonize Judaism and Hellenism and to minimize their points of conflict.

Propagandist Zeal and Proselytizing: The Jews in Egypt, Syria and Asia Minor were animated by a missionary zeal to win over the pagan population to monotheism. At the same time, a number of forces were at work in the Graeco-Roman world to make the proselytizers' message both timely and welcome. Despite the fact that the Greek masses learned little about Judaism, and considered Jewish monotheism and early Christianity* atheism and an offense to the gods, thousands of pagan "godfearers" became very close to the synagogue* before the New Testament period (see Christianity, Early*: Jewish-Christians).

The success of the Jewish proselytizing program is evident from the fierce opposition voiced by such pagan writers as Apollonius Mellon of Rhodes (90 BCE), Posidonius of Apamean Syria (70 BCE), Charemon of Alexandria (50 BCE), Lipimachus (30 BCE) and the Alexandrian sophist, Apion (37 CE). The latter was a contemporary of Flavius Josephus*, whose *Against Apion* defends the Jewish people against Apion's accusations. Apion also expressed the opinion that the God of Israel and Zeus were one and the same divinity called by a different name.

Greek-Jewish Literature and Thought: Among the Jews of Alexandria, the hellenizing movement struck much deeper roots than in Judea. In Alexandria — or in Pergamum in Asia Minor — the Jews found the outward forms of their life, their synagogue, legal forms and cultural activities all deeply imbued with the influence of Hellenism (see illus. under Acts*).

504

505

The question accordingly arises whether this greater assimilation of Greek elements affected the nature of Alexandrian Jewry fundamentally, or whether in Alexandria, as in Palestine, the Jews were able to meet the alien forces with an equal strength and continue their distinctive existence, albeit in an alien environment.

The Jews in the Diaspora faced a choice between assimilating to the country in which they lived — adopting Greek names, the Greek language and Greek ways — or clinging to their traditions and remaining a separate, secluded community. In the event they did both. Jewish communal life in Alexandria and similar centres was modelled on the Greek poleis. Greek was the language universally used in public affairs and in the synagogue — most of the inscriptions found in the synagogue are in Greek — in daily life and in literature. Their education was Greek (see Hellenism in the Near East*) and Jewish Hellenistic literature flourished. From modest beginnings, it developed into a powerful instrument both for influencing the Jewish reading public and later for combatting anti-Semitism. Including epics, drama, history, historical romances, supplements to biblical stories and learned works of philosophy, it covered the whole range of literature. There were also the apologetic, propaganda works such as Philo's "Apologia" (see below) or Josephus' "Against Apion", but as a whole the literature reflects the higher ethical purpose of finding a synthesis between Judaism and Hellenism. It saw in the propagation of Jewish "philosophy" the justification for the Jews' presence in the Diaspora.

Philo: While Josephus was a leading exponent of Jewish-Hellenistic rapprochement in Palestine proper, the chief advocate of this compromise was the Alexandrian, Philo Judaeus (ca. 20 BCE–45 CE). Scion of one of the wealthiest Jewish families in Egypt, he was trained in Greek literature and philosophy, particularly Plato. His knowledge of the Bible was apparently derived from the Septuagint and contemporary Hellenistic commentaries, which were mainly allegorical in character. This education was reflected in the spirit and approach of his own writings. Most of Philo's 38 works are commentaries on the Pentateuch or essays on selected topics. He is known for his biography of Moses; books on metaphysics and ethics; a volume on the contemplative life describing the Jewish sectarian group, the Therapeutai (see Jewish-Christians); a historical work on the persecution by Flaccus, governor of Egypt, and works on personalities from the time of the Emperor Caligula, in which he stressed the role of divine justice in the improvement in the course of events that followed the death of Caligula.

By and large, Philo's philosophy was eclectic, in that he borrowed foreign elements and fused Greek and Jewish thought into one system. According to his allegorical understanding of the Bible, God created the world from eternal matter, but did not influence it directly. The word of God, which he called "logos", mediates between God and the world. The soul derives from a divine source and can conceive of the divinity not through spiritual perception, but by self-immersion, which it can achieve either through mystic meditation or the spirit of prophecy. Man's ultimate goal is self-elevation. The Torah is the instrument that enables man to attain moral and philosophical perfection, which opens the way to a union with the divine. The way is allegorical. Some stories in the Pentateuch depict passions that should be avoided; other stories depict (allegorically) the goal for which the righteous should strive. He believed sacred law to be the purest revelation of the divinity.

Philo's teaching did not noticeably influence Jewish thought in Palestine then or later, but was highly regarded by the Church Fathers (in the period immediately following the New Testament), and in neo-platonist philosophy which was a late Greek school of the 3rd. c CE.

The Harmony Ends: At about the time of Philo, the harmonious relations between Jews and pagans came to an end. Though the Jews were at first able to cope with early anti-Semitism, the political and social situation eventually became more strained. The influence exerted by Palestinian Jewry and the attitude of the Roman rulers brought about open clashes. These outbreaks, coupled with Jewish aspirations for Greek gymnasium education and Greek citizenship, caused a violent civil struggle in Egypt that culminated in a Jewish revolt against Rome and an attack on their Hellenistic neighbours during Emperor Trajan's time (114–117 CE; see Bar-Kochba*). The suppression of this rebellion marked the downfall of the semi-autonomous Jewish community in Egypt.

HELLENISM IN THE NEAR EAST. — *Outline: Mutual Impact of East and West; Hellenistic Way of Life; Hellenistic and Classical Polis; The Tide of Hellenism; The Cause of Individualism; Religious Syncretism; The Universal Language; The Fate of the Hellenistic Empires; The Seleucid Dynasty; The Parthians; The Ptolemaic Empire; Rome.*

Hellenism: The term "Hellenism" or "Hellenistic civilization" refers to the society that evolved from the mutual impact and interpenetration of Greek and Near Eastern cultures during the three centuries before the Christian era. It began with the conquest of the East by Alexander the Great (334 BCE; see battle of Issus against the Persians in the mosaic of Pompei, **220**). It ended with the conquest of these territories by the Romans in the first c. BCE. Hellenism was the way of life that grew out of this fusion of the oriental with the Greek. It must be distinguished from the purely Hellenic culture of Greece. The impact of Hellenism on the peoples and kingdoms of the Near East represents a major historical and social phenomenon of the area.

The term "Hellenistic kingdoms" refers to those kingdoms that existed during the periods of Greek and Roman rule, i.e., first the states of the Diadochs who succeeded Alexander the Great: the Seleucid Empire in Western Asia and the Ptolemaic kingdom of Egypt (and at times Palestine), then, after their destruction, a number of smaller, mostly semi-independent states. Hellenistic civilization, which endured in these states long after they had lost their independence, extended its influence to the western confines of the Roman Empire, and declined only after the disintegration of that Empire in the west (4th c. CE) and the fall of the attenuated Byzantine Empire in the east (15th c. CE).

Mutual Impact of East and West: The initial contact between Greek and Eastern cultures was very much one-sided. The civilizations of western Asia, particularly in Phoenicia.

Persia and Asia Minor, contributed more to the cultural values of the relatively young Greek society than they received. It was not until Greece evolved a strong, rich and vital civilization of its own that the East began to feel its influence. The first signs of this influence appeared in Asia Minor and Phoenicia during the Persian period (6th to 4th c. BCE). Cities on the Greek pattern were established along the coast, and their influence gradually extended inland. These cities were not new colonies, but were created through a remodelling of the existing town plan and a refashioning of the prevailing social structure which preserved the ancient procedures and customs of the inhabitants. This was actually the beginning of Hellenism. An illuminating example comes from the coins* struck by the State of Judea during that period, some of which bore the emblem of the Athenian owl in an obvious imitation of Greek coins (see Restoration*; other cultural aspects are dealt with under Inscriptions*, V).

Hellenistic Way of Life: Hellenistic civilization became more dynamic towards the end of the 4th c. BCE, when Alexander the Great's conquests brought Greek and Eastern cultures into much closer contact (see Hasmoneans*). After the Macedonians (and Greeks) became the rulers of the East, they organized powerful states and opened the doors to tens of thousands of Greek emigrants, who in turn created cities modelled after those in their native countries. In contrast to the towns mentioned above, these were built from the foundations up. An outstanding example is Alexandria in Egypt. No new cities of this kind were created in Palestine proper before the 1st c. BCE (see Cities*, Hellenistic). The actual construction of these new towns, as well as the rebuilding of existing ones, was of course effected by the rulers who conferred on them the special privileges of the Greek "polis" (city). They were semi-autonomous, could strike their own coins, and were governed by a popular assembly which elected a "gerousia" (council) and an executive staff which carried out the decisions and policies of the Assembly. Every polis had its own laws and the right to judge its own citizens. Not all the inhabitants were considered citizens, however. This was an honour reserved for the "upper classes" of the population. Each polis had an official god and the citizens were expected to take part in the municipal religious ritual. In many poleis the ancient Eastern gods, such as Dagon, Reshef, Ashtoret (Astarte), were worshipped (see Canaan*, Gods and Idols) along with the Greek gods.

Each polis was provided with public institutions in the Greek manner: the municipal educational centres such as the gymnasium, ephebeion, and theatre, etc., which were mainly designed to promote the physical and cultural training of the younger generation, and to spread Hellenism among the population in general. Their activities are illustrated by a wide range of paintings and sculptures, for instance, a 460 BCE Greek *ephebe* (**506**) preparing for a contest, his trainer standing nearby; wrestlers (**507**); a discus thrower (**509**; dated 480 BCE); an athlete's toilet articles (**508**), and a 5th c. BCE athlete finishing a jump (**510**). The city authorities organized games of all sorts, including discus and javelin throwing, racing, wrestling, etc. Note the rhythmic dance of the Corybantes (**511**).

Hellenistic and Classical Polis: While the Hellenistic poleis of the East were Greek in language, communal way of

506

507

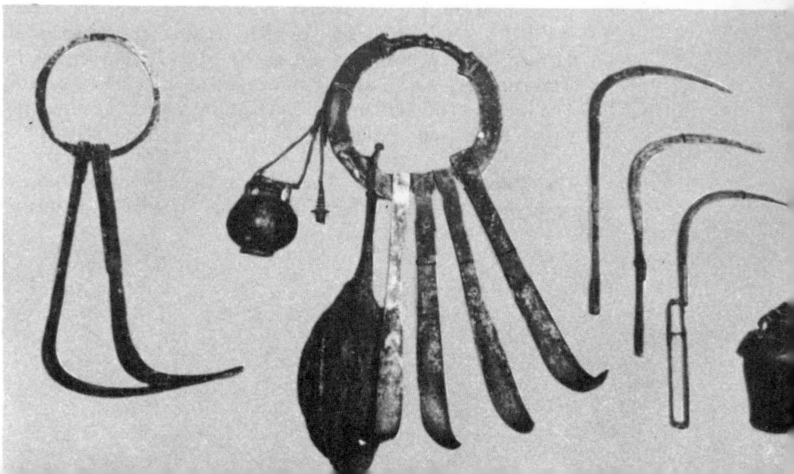

508

511

509

510

life, and to some extent in religion and culture, they or the neighbouring towns also preserved time-honoured oriental traditions, and these often combined with the newer cultural values. Despite the appearance of autonomy, the Hellenistic poleis, unlike the classical poleis, did not have independence in matters of foreign policy or military affairs. In addition, the local strategos (governor) was appointed by the monarch (see Hasmoneans*).

By and large, the inhabitants of the Hellenistic poleis were local people of diverse backgrounds who had been granted special privileges. In many cases, the poleis were former fortified positions put up by Macedonian troops for strategic purposes. Later they expanded into urban centres. The bearers of Hellenistic civilization were, for the most part, hellenized Asiatics.

The Tide of Hellenism: The Hellenistic way of life spread throughout the East, from the Indus to the highlands of Afghanistan, Persia, Mesopotamia, Syria, Palestine and the banks of the Nile. As it spread over the area, Hellenism subjected the Eastern cultures to an aggressive and attractive challenge, though it was also influenced by them. Indeed, the Greek and Macedonian emigrants who came into the area were quickly affected by oriental civilizations. The preservation of native languages, beliefs and geographical names, mainly in the non-hellenized countryside, is proof of the durability of the indigenous culture.

As it spread and developed, Hellenism underwent numerous changes in content and form, in response to the constant struggle between the Hellenic and oriental ways of life. This was particularly true in the political, social and religious spheres. Despite their logical, orderly regard for life, the Greeks were awed by and admired the diffuse oriental civilizations that they conquered, an attitude which made possible the development of Hellenism and the preservation of the Eastern cultures. In contrast to Greek exclusivism,

512

cosmopolitanism became the most outstanding feature of Hellenism, fusing Greek universality in thought and oriental variety in background and culture. This cultural climate reached its peak with the rise of the Roman Empire.

While it is true that Hellenism as a way of life developed new values as it evolved, the Hellenistic kingdoms themselves hardly created any new cultural or social approaches, restricting themselves to the determination of political boundaries and administrative matters.

The Cause of Individualism: Concurrent with the progress of cosmopolitanism came individualism, or more frankly, opportunism. Following Alexander the Great, the most outstanding personalities were not necessarily national leaders or pioneers of social and political thought, but power seekers who tried to acquire as much as possible for themselves. The most notable of this new breed were, in Greek circles, the Macedonian generals who succeeded Alexander, such as Demetrius Poliorcates, son of Antigonus; Eumenes; and the founders of the Seleucid and Ptolemaic dynasties. Others, though on a more modest scale, included in Judea, Joseph ben Tobiah and his son Hyrcanus, who, without the slightest consideration for honesty or conscience, prospered immensely in finance. This self-serving may not necessarily have been a product of Hellenism, but the new horizons bred such opportunism. Another example is Menelaus, the leading hellenizer among the Jews. During the reign of Antiochus Epiphanes, he and his followers, intent on aping the Hellenists, showed little regard for their national culture (see Hasmoneans*).

Such individualism or opportunism was the "calling card" of many leaders and personalities during the Hellenistic period, whose cosmopolitanism "freed" them from restrictive national ties and loyalties. On the other hand, cosmopolitanism made the positive contribution of tolerance and a humanitarian attitude towards other peoples and cultures, which facilitated coexistence and mutual understanding.

Religious Syncretism: It was part of the ideology of Hellenism to solicit the support of the gods for almost every human inclination: fighting, drinking, hunting, love, pursuit of the arts, healing, etc. Venus or Aphrodite upheld the pleasures of human, as opposed to divine, love. The conquerors did not put their own religious stamp on the new states. As a result, the divinities of Greece, Egypt, Syria, Babylon and Persia gradually acquired some similarity to each other. National gods slowly shed their particular features, stressing instead their universal attributes. In some cases, a number of these divinities were accorded identical qualities, mainly expressed by giving different names to the same gods; thus Melkart of Tyre is Haracles, Ba'al is Zeus. He was represented in Baalbek, Syria, as Jupiter Heliopolitanus (**512**). Even Yahweh could, in the eyes of Antiochus Epiphanes (see Hasmoneans*), be represented as Zeus. The Egyptian goddess, Isis, possessed many attributes and features, and the names of many goddesses can be identified with one or another of her qualities.

The Universal Language: During the Hellenistic period Greek superseded Aramaic as the predominant language used for literature as well as everyday speech. This universality had a great influence on other languages and made the dissemination of Greek culture all the easier. The translation of the Old Testament into Greek (Septuagint) illustrates the popularity of the language, as well as the decline of Hebrew in the Jewish Diaspora. In addition, the Mishnah*, Talmud and Midrash contain hundreds of Greek words which had been absorbed into Hebrew and Aramaic. By the 1st and 2nd c. CE, Jewish material life in Palestine was predominantly Hellenistic, even though hellenization had ceased to be a political program for any Jewish faction (see Herod*; Rome and the Jews*). Many inscriptions found in excavated Palestine synagogues* and tombs are in Greek. Even after the Roman conquest, Greek continued in use, the Romans (themselves hellenized) using it as their administrative language in the Middle East. The Greek of this era was a uniform language, local dialects being almost unknown. It was called *Koine*, "the universal", and in this the Septuagint and New Testament were written (see Hellenism and the Diaspora*).

The Fate of the Hellenistic Empires: Despite the interpenetration of Greek and oriental cultures, and the comparatively homogeneous atmosphere, the bitter enmity that the native population felt for the conquerors did not soften. Indeed, the benefits to be derived by hellenizing were no attraction to a considerable proportion of the people, who remained loyal to their national traditions and beliefs. However, at the end of the fourth and beginning of the third centuries BCE, the eastern peoples were still reeling from their massive defeats by the Macedonians and Greeks. It seemed to them that their world had been laid in ruins by a daemonic power that had come to annihilate them. This attitude is evidenced by Persian records that describe Alexander and his men as daemons, and the Book of Daniel (8:5–25) which views him as a "he-goat", and pictures Greece in a manner that clearly demonstrates the terror in which the conquerors were held. Eventually, the hostility of the people developed into overt acts of rebellion, often encouraged by local manarchs who sought to set up their own independent states.

The Seleucid Dynasty: The vanguard of this revolutionary movement were the tribes of Persia in the eastern section of the Seleucid Empire. At the end of the 3rd c. BCE, Antiochus III (the Great) waged a successful military campaign with a view to maintaining Seleucid rule in this region. In the event, his victories were no more than an interlude in the process of emancipation of the eastern part of the Seleucid Empire. The Roman rout of Antiochus III in the battle of Magnesia (189 BCE) ended Seleucid rule in Persia and the neighbouring territories. While the brunt of the struggle against the central government was borne by the native population, the revolt drew considerable strength from such active outside elements as Armenians, Elamites and Parsis, as well as local Seleucid commanders who turned against the central government. Antiochus III was followed by Antiochus IV Epiphanes who undertook numerous campaigns to restore Seleucid prestige and power. However, he also wanted to replace the various local cults of his realm by universal worship of himself in the form of Zeus Olympius — a policy which was a major impulse for the Maccabaean rebellion (see Hasmoneans*). The successors of Antiochus were largely incompetent. Under them, the Seleucid dynasty which had reigned over the East for generations progressively lost its prestige, power and dignity. The entire century after Epiphanes presents a confused picture of native revolts, internal dissension, family quarrels and gradual loss of territory (see Hasmoneans*). The Seleucid Empire which once stretched from the eastern Mediterranean and Aegean Sea, to Turkestan and India, was reduced to a small state in northern Syria.

The Parthians: The Parthians, who originated in northern Iran, were mainly responsible for pushing Hellenism back to the west, though Greek style poleis flourished in the territories they ruled. They established a powerful empire of their own by wresting Asia Minor from the Seleucids (129 BCE), and taking control of the area from the Euphrates to the Indus and from the Oxus to the Indian Ocean. They were to become, in time, Rome's most powerful enemy in the East. A Hellenistic culture also arose in northwestern India, deeply influencing the course of Indian cultural history.

The Ptolemaic Empire: The native population of Egypt did not rebel against the Ptolemaic dynasty until the battle of Rafiah (fought against the Seleucids in 217 BCE), for which many native Egyptians had been drafted. The returning soldiers inspired revolts which continued throughout the 2nd c. BCE, and considerably weakened the position of the Ptolemies.

In Asia Minor, particularly Bithynia and Pontus, dynasties were founded that were markedly Hellenistic. Unlike Persia and Egypt, these dynasties reflect a richly variegated background of eastern culture (derived from the Achaemenid period in Persia, 6th to 4th c. BCE), mixed with Greek elements.

Rome: During the 1st c. BCE, Parthian, Armenian and other onslaughts against the Greek Hellenistic regions continued, threatening to engulf Asia Minor and Syria. The appearance of Rome on the scene quickly altered the situation, however, and in 66 BCE, Pompey established a "New Order". His policy and that of his successors, was to preserve the Hellenistic culture. Under Rome, Hellenism received a new lease of life. It was strengthened in influence west of the Euphrates and spread to all other parts of the Roman Empire. Egypt became the centre of Hellenism, and until the Arab conquest in 636–640 CE, constituted the pivot of the Empire in the East (see also Rome and the Jews*).

HEROD I, Known as the Great: The Judaized Idumean who ruled Judea under Roman patronage, 37–4 BCE.

Antipater: Following the period of Pompeian rule, between 65 and 48 BCE, the Roman Empire was rent by internal wars. Palestine, as the area was renamed by the Romans, was inevitably involved. After his victory over Pompey in 49 BCE, Julius Caesar confirmed Hyrcanus II as high priest and "Ethnarch" (ruler of the nation), but excluded him from politics, leaving the field clear for Antipater, called the "Idumean", whom he named financial administrator of Judea. By wisely supporting Hyrcanus II in his war against his brother, Aristobulos II, Antipater attained great influence and became effective ruler of the country. He appointed his sons, Herod and Phasael to important administrative posts. Antipater was later poisoned during a feast at the instigation of Malichus, an ambitious member of the ruling household.

The Rise of Herod: Soon after his appointment to the governorship of Galilee in 47 BCE, young Herod displayed the treacherous capabilities that marked his rise to power and sounded the final death knell of the House of the Hasmoneans*. One of his first acts was the brutal suppression of an uprising in his district, without obtaining legal sanction. When called to account by the Sanhedrin*, the supreme legal and civil court of Judea, he was saved from a certain death sentence by the intervention of Hyrcanus II and Sextus Caesar, governor of Syria. Such sources of influence enabled him to terrorize the mighty tribunal.

Herod was one of Rome's most successful tax collectors, an accomplishment that rested on razing towns which refused to pay and selling the inhabitants into slavery. As a reward, Cassius, who was then one of the rulers of the Roman State, recognized Herod as "strategos" (district governor) of Coele-Syria (north of Palestine), and it was rumoured that he would be crowned King of Judea after Cassius had routed the last of the fallen Julius Caesar's followers.

Antony Defeats Cassius: In the event, Cassius was defeated by Marc Antony and Octavius, and though Herod had been allied with the loser, he ingratiated himself with the victors by mean of flattery and bribery. They appointed him "tetrarch" (district civil administrator) over Galilee, and his brother, Phasael, over Jerusalem. The Hasmonean High Priest, Hyrcanus II, remained "ethnarch", but the two brothers were the effective rulers of Judea.

Civil War in Judea: In 40 BCE, Antigonus Mattathias, nephew and rival of Hyrcanus II, joined forces with the Parthians, who were gradually conquering the entire area, to foment a civil war in Judea that raged for three years.

Antony and Cleopatra: During this period, Antony had become so romantically involved with the beautiful Queen of Egypt, Cleopatra VII Thea, that he practically ignored the critical situation. Crowned king by the Parthians, Antigonus gained the upper hand. Realizing the futility of continuing to fight from his embattled stronghold in Galilee, Herod escaped to Rome.

Herod Crowned in Rome: Antony and Octavius saw in him a useful pawn in their struggles against the Parthians, and on their recommendation the Roman Senate crowned Herod King of Judea and friend of Rome, pronouncing Antigonus enemy of Rome.

The Last Hasmonean Prince: Though Herod was now titular ruler, he had still to remove Antigonus, who had meanwhile wrested control from Hyrcanus II. With Roman help, Herod captured Jerusalem in the spring of 37 BCE. Antigonus Mattathias, the last Hasmonean Prince, was executed.

Mariamme: In the same year, Herod married the beautiful Hasmonean princess, Mariamme, granddaughter of Hyrcanus II. Though he loved her dearly, some seven years later as a result of palace intrigues, he became convinced of her treachery and executed both her and her mother, in a fit of passion. Such murders were typical of Herod's pathological nature.

Herod and Hellenism: Herod was a confirmed Hellenist, who despised both the Pharisees* and the Saducces*. He sought to shape Judea into a Hellenist state and find a place for it in the framework of the Roman Empire. Rather than a Jewish King, he was King of the Jews, and viewed with distaste the theocratic principles on which the nation was based.

He succeeded in removing his brother-in-law, Aristobulos III, the rightful and last Hasmonean high priest, from his post and installed a man of his own choice. He murdered all possible rivals for the office and henceforth filled the post at his pleasure. We know of eight high priests during his reign.

The Nabatean War: Using her considerable influence with Antony, Cleopatra forced Herod to cede her several of his more fertile districts, including Jericho*. She also schemed to have him sent into battle against the Nabateans, whom she secretly aided. Indecisive as Herod's campaign seemed, it proved beneficial in the end. Antony was defeated at Actium by Octavius while Herod was engaged with the Nabateans, thus preventing him from coming to the aid of Antony.

Augustus Befriends Herod: Antony and Cleopatra having committed suicide after their defeat, Herod presented himself before the victorious Octavius who was to become Emperor Augustus in 30 BCE. Summoning all his diplomatic skill, Herod admitted loyalty to Antony but stressed the enmity that had existed between himself and Cleopatra, and his efforts to weaken her hold on Antony. Impressed with Herod's candour, Octavius replaced the crown on his head, and as an immediate sign of favour, allowed him to recapture the districts ceded to Cleopatra, plus some coastal towns.

An Energetic and Merciless Monarch: Herod now turned his full attention to ruling Judea as an absolute monarch. He had all public and social institutions divested of political power; the Sanhedrin was reduced to an exclusively religious tribunal; the high priest was shorn of all but his spiritual functions; and all signs of independence, including public assembly, were banned.

Expansion and Organization of the State: By 23 BCE, Herod controlled most of the area of the ancient Kingdom of David, including his native Edom (see map **513**). The population of the country ranged somewhere between 1.5 and 2 million, mostly Jews, while a similar, if not larger, number of Jews lived in the Diaspora*.

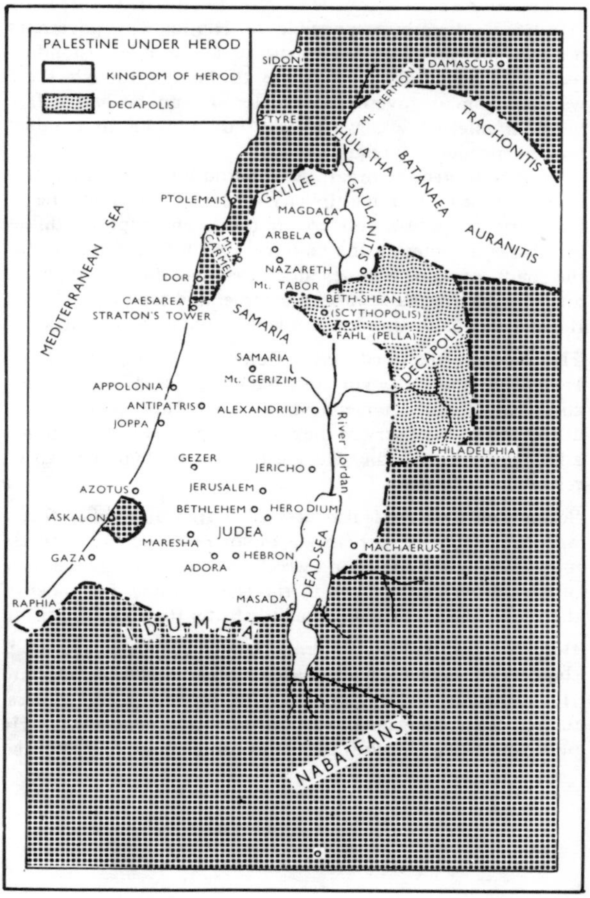

513

514

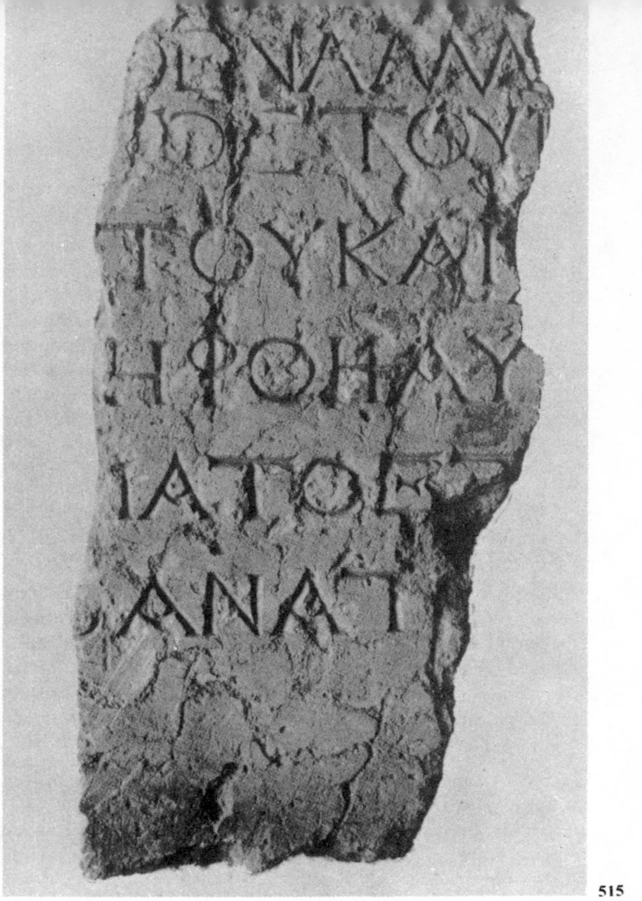

515

The country was divided into 19 districts ruled by "strategoi" directly responsible to Herod. The governors of the independent Hellenistic cities and surrounding territories were also answerable to him. Although there was no Roman governor over Herod, and he had a free hand in internal affairs, he was not allowed to conduct an independent foreign policy.

Thus restricted, he organized a sound internal administration, financed by a multiplicity of levies, including head, land, tribute, house and crown taxes. He imposed duties on all goods entering the country, and tolls for the use of the roads, bridges, wharves, docks, etc. He did not overlook any possible means of raising income, and greatly enhanced the state's wealth through prudent commercial ventures.

The Army: Recruited with Rome's consent, but more Hellenistic than Roman, the backbone of Herod's army consisted of foreign mercenaries. To ensure their loyalty, at the end of their service they were employed in the internal administration of the Hellenistic towns that had been restored to Judea.

Secret Police: Herod also created a rigorous police force, with an elaborate system of espionage used to suppress mercilessly all opposition, which was widespread because of the people's attachment to the Hasmoneans. For most of the people the country became little better than a large prison.

Herod's Great Building Program: One of the major accomplishments of Herod's reign was his great building program. He erected a remarkable chain of fortresses and castles, replete with dungeons, vast cisterns and aqueducts. He built whole cities, each with its full complement of gymnasia, theatres, palaces, etc. His supreme achievements were Caesarea*, which he transformed from a minor anchorage into a great port, and Sebaste (Samaria*), with its sumptuous acropolis, temples and theatres (see illustr. in both articles). These became bastions of the oriental type of Roman-Hellenistic culture of the period, and coupled with his tributes to the Greek and Roman gods, earned Herod the undying hatred of the Jews.

A few miles south-east of Jerusalem, Herod built himself a sumptuous palace within a circular fort (described by Josephus, Antiq. XV, 9; War I, 21). Excavations in 1962–3 indicated a classic Graeco-Roman pattern for both architecture and decoration in the bathing establishments and royal apartments. This view **(514)** shows (left) part of a room where Greek pornographic graffiti were found. In the centre the remains of a columned hall can be seen. The door at the far end led to a circular corridor which surrounded this palace fortress at Herodium.

Rebuilding of the Temple: Though his building program provided employment for many and expanded the country's facilities, the Jews would not soften. Even Herod's swift and generous aid during the drought of 27 BCE, and his rebuilding of the Temple* into a magnificent structure with a high esplanade and spacious courts, surrounded by a wide arcade and high wall, did not increase his popularity. This is a fragment of an inscription from Herod's Temple balustrade **(515)**; it is a part of the complete text described under Temple*.

Rejection of the "Redeeming King": Herod fancied himself as the redeeming king of the Jews and, according to A.

Schalit, even claimed kinship to the Davidic line. The people, however, considered him a usurper, as he had none of the blood of the Jewish princes. His pretensions, real or unreal, to a messianic role, were utterly rejected. The people never accepted his version of Roman-Herodian redemption.

Religion as Refuge: In a characteristic reaction of the oriental spirit against Western ways, the Jews turned inwards once again. Their religion became their fortress, and the great teachers of the Pharisaic academies, their representatives. Though Herod did not recognize the incompatibility between Hellenism and Judaism, and insisted on imposing his autocratic regime after the Roman pattern, the people never relinquished the ideals that had made them a people apart.

Herod and the Diaspora: In an attempt to appear as champion of the Jews everywhere and, no doubt, to ensure the uninterrupted flow of donations to the Temple from abroad, Herod took on himself the mantle of spokesman and "protector" of the Jews in the Diaspora. He expressed a keen interest in their affairs and often intervened on their behalf by bribing their Gentile hosts.

Herod's Death and Memory: In a web of intrigue made even more tortuous by Herod's increasingly pathological nature, the now dying king had two of his sons by Mariamme, Alexander and Aristobulos, and his first born son, Antipater, executed (7 BCE). All were charged with conspiring against him. Before his death in 4 BCE, from several diseases that had racked him for years, he partitioned his kingdom among his three remaining sons, Archelaus, Herod Antipas and Philip. Archelaus was his actual successor. Herod also left enormous legacies to the Roman Emperor and Empress, and to his sister Salome.

Herod succeeded in keeping Rome at a distance for several decades and, in his own way, tried to ensure for the Jews of Palestine and the Diaspora a secure existence in a secular world. His attempts were neither appreciated nor remembered, and in Jewish tradition any favourable recollection of Herod has been erased. The New Testament (Mt. 2) associates him with the Massacre of the Innocents (an incident unrecorded by Josephus). Thus, he has been portrayed in both Jewish and Christian records as a cruel, cunning and despotic tyrant.

HIGH PLACES OR "BAMOTH". — *Outline: I. Open-air Sanctuaries: Hammanîm; Matzebah and Asherah; Funerary Shrines; Holy Place, Māqôm; Survival in Israelite Times. II. Archaeological Evidence of High Places: Pre-Israelite; "Sit-shamsi"; Israelite High Places; The High Place of Gibeon; Simple Structures; Survivals in Modern Times.*

I. OPEN–AIR SANCTUARIES: The Bible makes many references to the open-air Canaanite "high places" ("bamah") which survived into the Israelite (Iron) Age as semi-pagan shrines. An aura of mystery still surrounds them and the memory of their ancient veneration lingers to this day. These "high places", built mostly on a height or mound played a very important role in the fertility cult of the Canaanites (see Canaan: Gods and Idols*, Cult) and later among the more backward of the Israelite population.

Both before the Conquest and after it, the Hebrews shared the way of life of an agricultural community and were familiar with Canaanite beliefs. In every sense (see articles on Canaan*), the Canaanites were close to the Israelites and there was an obvious temptation to maintain existing Canaanite sanctuaries along with their symbolic significance. Inevitably, in spite of repeated denunciations by Hebrew prophets who clung to their ancient traditions, simple people were attracted to Canaanite cultic practices and superstitions. As time went on, native Canaanite customs were combined with Israelite ways in the practice of popular religion. An altar to Yahweh would be erected beside a hallowed stele (matzebah) and sacred tree or wooden pillar (asherah). The Israelites came to ascribe magic powers to the venerated high places and adopted many pagan practices connected with them, including the specific funerary rites of the Canaanites.

The "high place" was apparently a country sanctuary — not a temple; hardly any have been found belonging to the post-Canaanite period. Nor were they generally elaborate centres of worship like the Israelite sanctuary* at Shiloh or the Temple at Jerusalem. Marked by a tree or a group of trees, they were appropriate for seasonal offerings and sacrifices in the countryside and, perhaps, for ceremonies connected with clan or tribal memories of revered ancestors. While many of them were built on heights (Solomon built a heathen "high place" on a mountain), they also existed near certain towns, in valleys and in ravines: "he sacrificed . . . on the high places and on the hills and under every green tree" (II K. 16:4). Whether or not they were on an actual height, the "high place" was in the form of a mound, either a natural outcropping of rock or a man-made cairn or pile of stones.

As a cultic centre, the "high place" was provided with an altar (see Sacrifice*). In some cases, the mass of rock which earned it its name served as an altar. In others, an altar was constructed as part of the "high place".

Hammanîm: Sometimes the high place included "hammanîm" or incense altars (**516**), but these were of secondary importance. The ones found in excavations in Palestine all had pagan associations, not Israelite. For this reason they were condemned by the prophets and the Israelites were forbidden to use them. Incense was not used in Israelite worship until the time of the Exile.

516

517

518

519

Matzebah and Asherah: The essential features of a typical "bamah" (described in I and II Kings, II Chronicles, the Prophets, and innumerable other passages of the Old Testament) are listed in I K. 14:23: "For they also built for themselves high places, and pillars, and Asherim on every high hill and under every green-tree." They are described under Canaan: Gods and Idols*, Cult; Idol Worship in Israel*.

Funerary Shrines: This aspect of the use of high places has recently received more attention. When taken together, biblical references to veneration at shrines associated with important figures (e.g. of Rachel or Deborah in Genesis), to high places in general and to the cult of departed spirits, seem to add up to a more extensive popular belief in life after death or cult of the dead among the Israelites, than has hitherto been thought likely. The prophets' rejection of such beliefs can now be explained as partly the result of their objection to alien funerary practices and beliefs.

W. F. Albright and other scholars have put forward some weighty arguments connecting the matzebôth and high places with ancestor worship. They provide a link between the people and their tribal past.

Holy Place, Māqôm: To the Israelites, certain places were holy ground (i.e., māqôm, "place"), because God had manifested His Presence there in some way. The shrine of Bethel, for example, had been sanctified by God's appearance to Abraham and Jacob (see Patriarchs, Religion of*). Jeroboam established a "beth-bamôth" there, literally, a "temple of the high places", with altars and other cultic objects.

Survival in Israelite Times: Apparently "high places" were not condemned at first in Israelite religion. Samuel (I Sam. 9:12 ff) and Solomon (I K. 3:3–4) sacrificed on a "high place" (beth-bamôth) and the sanctuaries continued to be visited up to the end of the monarchy and the reform of Josiah (II K. 23).

However, with the growing movement for the centralization of the Israelite cult, high places were condemned without exception and "bamôth" became synonymous with pagan sanctuaries and practices. The chroniclers of the books of Kings, zealous for a religious revival, repeat like a refrain in introducing the reigns of the different kings of Israel and Judah [with the exception of the reformers, Hezekiah (527–698 BCE) and Josiah (636–609 BCE)], "and he did not do what was right in the eyes of the Lord his God . . . and he sacrificed and burned incense on the high places . . ."

The Old Testament never describes the Canaanite and Phoenician cults introduced into Israel. They are roundly condemned, but it was assumed that they were well-known. The details of the cults and their ceremonies can be reconstructed from archaeological findings in Phoenicia and Phoenician settlements in Carthage, Cyprus, Sardinia, Spain and Southern France (see Canaan: Gods and Idols*, Cult).

II. ARCHAEOLOGICAL EVIDENCE OF HIGH PLACES. — Until thirty or forty years ago, archaeologists were inclined to see "sanctuaries" (bamôth, altars, stele, temples, etc.) in almost any outdoor or indoor structure whose nature was not immediately apparent. Recent research has proved the much publicized "Sanctuary of Gezer*" to have been no more than a row of commemorative stele;

the "altars" of Ta'anach turned out to be the ruins of stables similar to those of Megiddo*, and many other similar corrections have been made.

How is it that comparatively little evidence for genuine "high places" has been found in excavations of Israelite towns, compared to the reiterated complaints of the Old Testament against numerous high places and "idolatrous" places of worship? The answer may be suggested by the latest evidence of archaeology. Beth-bamôth, cairns and matzebôth date back for a millenium before the Israelite conquest. Outstanding examples of "high places" of the 3rd and 2nd mill. BCE are as follows:

Pre-Israelite: One of the oldest Canaanite high places known in the days preceding the Patriarchal period is the Megiddo* cairn. It was reconstructed some time in the Early Bronze Period (about 2500 BCE) and remained in use until the 19th c. BCE (first stage of the Middle Bronze Age). Later, it became a kind of "fossil", for another temple was constructed right next to it, following a quite different concept architecturally, and therefore, most likely, religiously. The builders of the new temple constructed walls around the older bamah (**517**) it may be that in this way they expressed their veneration for the — by then — ancient place of worship. It is more likely that they conducted certain cultic ceremonies there, perhaps those connected with ancestor worship.

The 13th c. BCE funerary shrine at Hazor* was built at the foot of the Hyksos fortification in the Late Bronze period, and was probably destroyed during the Israelite conquest of the city. It contains a series of "mazebôth", most of them plain; one shows, in relief, hands upraised as if in adoration, and above them the symbol of the moon. Not far from the row of stele was found the statue of a sitting person holding a cup in his hand. A number of cult objects have been found with these: a statue of a lion, a mask, and others (see illus. under Hazor* and Megiddo*).

The bamah in Nahariyah (**518**) which stands beside a small shrine dating from the 18th c. BCE is about 6 metres in diametre. The large monolithic altar (**519**) at Tsor'ah, Samson's home town, was apparently connected with a high place.

"Sit-shamsi": Many scholars are inclined to regard the small 12th c. BCE model of the "Sit-shamsi" (**520**) found in Susa (Media) as a typical fully equipped "bamah", with two altars at the sides of the model; the figures of a priest and a worshipper of the shrine's divinity engaged in a purificatory act; two stele to their right; various cultic objects; troughs for dry offerings and libations and tree trunks, possibly "asherahs". Other scholars see in it a model of the acropolis of Susa and believe the object in the centre to be a ziggurat (see Babylonia*), and the low structure on the left a model of a bamah or altar.

Clay models of sacred enclosures in Cyprus may represent their high places. One (**521**) is an enclosure at Vounos (2200 BCE). The other (**522**) is an altar with sculptures around it, from the Aya Irini shrine (7th c. BCE).

Israelite High Places: A typical Israelite high place was found close to the city wall of Samaria* (**523**). It was formed by a trench cut in the rock, trapezoid in shape, 30 metres by 26 and about 3.30 to 3.75 metres deep. No signs of a building could be distinguished except for a rough rubble wall (4–4) on the inner S. W. side and two parallel cross

520

521

522

524

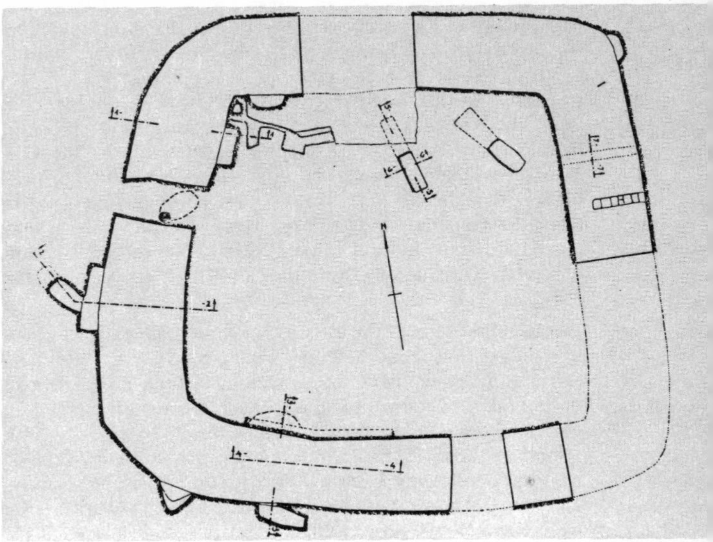

523

walls near the N. E. corner (7–7). Several shafts and empty troughs had been cut in the N. W. section but they do not seem to have served as regular burial places in earlier times. A mass of potsherds covered the surface.

The High Place of Gibeon: Both I K. (3:3–5) and II Ch. (1:3 ff) record the sacrifice which Solomon made at the "great high place of Gibeon". This story is generally accepted as historically factual. The site is believed to be the village of Nebi-Samuel, the highest ridge visible west of the road leading to Jerusalem from the plain. There is an ancient tradition that Samuel was buried there, which may explain the name of the place.

Simple Structures: The evidence retrieved from these sanctuaries, which were all "Great High Places" suggests the explanation for the comparatively few remains discovered in Israelite towns. The High Places were relatively simple structures and they were in most cases some distance away from the towns. They were established, thundered the prophets, "Upon every high hill and under every green tree". There was very little involved that would outlast the centuries once they were finally suppressed and abandoned.

The same paucity of evidence makes it very difficult for scholars to come to any exact conclusions about the type of worship that was conducted in the shrines. Such simple installations could be adapted to many different religious rites. What evidence does exist — potsherds and ashes — tends to emphasize their use as funerary shrines. No images or figurines of any sort were ever found in a high place.

Better evidence for the ceremonies of the high place may have been preserved in the Passover celebration of the Samaritans* at Nablus. There, the shrine is a rectangular enclosure of rough stones, trenches and hearths, quite simply fixed in the ground, very much like the Israelite sanctuaries that have been discovered. This simple form of worship is not pagan, it is archaic Israelite.

Survivals in Modern Times: It is believed that veneration of high places has survived in the memory of Arab peasants in the cult of "wêlis" or hero's shrines which are found on consecrated ground throughout Palestine and Syria. Called "maqām" by the Arabs, they are often situated on a high ridge or mound under the shade of an ancient tree or trees. The Arabs make burnt offerings there and gather at certain times to offer sacrifices and pray for favours from the "wêli" (**524**).

HISTORY OF ISRAEL. — *See Patriarchs*; Exodus*; Conquest*; Judges*; Joshua and Judges*; Samuel*; Saul*; David and Solomon*; Israel and Judah, The Independent Kingdoms of*; Exile*; **Restoration* (the Persian Period)**; Hasmoneans* and phases of Hellenism*; Rome and the Jews* and Bar-Kochba*. The history of the people, its historical monuments and archaeological remains, on the other hand, are reanimated in the descriptions of Ancient Cities* and Biblical Archaeology ; see respective articles.*

HOSEA. — The first of the "Minor Prophets" in the Hebrew Canon, the book of Hosea contains the prophecies of Hosea, son of Be'eri, who lived in the Northern Kingdom of Israel during and probably after the reign of Jeroboam (see below).

Contents: Hosea is said to differ from other prophets in that divine revelation is both received and imparted through the personal tragedy of his unhappy marriage. The book falls into two distinct but closely related parts of different length.

1. The first three chs. concern Hosea's marriage, the second chapter — written in verse — being a sermon which uses the events recorded in chapters 1 and 3 as the symbols for Yahweh's relationship to Israel and presents a summary of the prophet's message.
2. The remaining eleven chs. (4–13) contain a series of oracle poems in which the prophet denounces the people, priests and kings of Israel for the decay of religious, social and political life, again making use of the themes of infidelity and punishment.

Cn. 14 is a promise of the divine mercy that awaits the people if they will confess their sins and repent.

The book can best be understood as a whole, with the content, form and message of both parts considered together.

The First Section: Ch. 1. Written in the third person, the chapter describes how Hosea was commanded by God to marry a harlot who will bear him "children of harlotry" as a symbol of the apostasy of the people of Israel (1:2). Hosea married Gomer, the daughter of Diblaim (1:3) and the son born to them was called "Jezreel, for yet a little while, and I will punish the house of Jehu for the blood of Jezreel, and I will put an end to the kingdom . . . and break the bow of Israel in the valley of Jezreel" (1:4–5). Then a daughter was born, called on God's instructions, "Not pitied", for "I will no more have pity on the house of Israel . . ." (1:6). A second son received the name "Not my people" for "you are not my people and I am not your God" (1:9).

Ch. 3, which is written in the first person, records a similar story. God commanded Hosea to "love a woman who is beloved of a paramour and is an adulteress" (3:1) and he bought her for "fifteen shekels of silver and a homer and a lethech of barley" (see Weights and Measures*). He ordered her to live in chastity for "many days" to represent the future penitence of Israel.

This repetition of essentially the same story has given rise to a number of conflicting opinions. Some scholars regard the second account as concerning a different woman, while others believe it to be merely a different tradition and suggest that chapters 1 and 3 were written by different authors.

The two accounts can also be merged into a single, coherent narrative. Hosea was commanded to marry Gomer and to give their children names which would symbolize the conduct of the people. Gomer was unfaithful to Hosea and he recognized in her infidelity a remarkable parallel to Israel's behaviour towards God. His experience seemed to illustrate the betrayal of the whole people. Hosea divorced his unfaithful wife, but later, because he still loved her, he took her back, hoping that the divorce had been sufficient punishment and that they could resume their earlier happy relationship.

Another school of thought has held that Gomer was a faithful wife, called a harlot only because she was one of a people who were being collectively unfaithful to their God. There is another opinion that Hosea did indeed marry a harlot as a deliberate action — strange as it may seem to us — such as other prophets occasionally engaged in to draw attention to the message of God.

Other scholars link the story to the fertility rites which may have been practiced in the syncretist popular religion. In the Canaanite shrines a "k^e^dêshah" or sacred prostitute symbolized the sacred marriage of Ba'al (see Canaan*: Cult). Hosea bitterly condemned the observance of such rites by idol-worshipping Hebrews. His action may thus have been intended to represent the practice and (by his divorce of Gomer) his rejection of it, thereby symbolizing Yahweh's abhorrence of fertility rites and those who indulged in them. A variant of this theory is that Hosea married Gomer under constraint from God so as to symbolize and embody in his own life the word of God. In view of the frequent recurrence of symbols and symbolic action in biblical prophecy, this is not far-fetched. Is. (5), Jer. (3:20) and Ezk. (16) all describe the people as adulterers meriting the punishment of a shameful divorce.

It seems more probable, however, that Gomer's betrayal prompted Hosea's prophetic impulse and that through his experience with his unfaithful wife he came to a new understanding of the love of God and of the injury which Israel did herself by her faithlessness. Thus the story should be read as having been inspired by a later realization of the workings of divine purpose.

Ch. 2. This poem is the key to the whole message of Hosea's prophecy. In this chapter Israel's worship of pagan Ba'als is likened to an unfaithful wife running after lovers and God's chastisement expressed in the metaphor of a wronged — but merciful — husband. The people of Israel will have to go back to the wilderness through which they wandered after the Exodus and before they ever heard of Ba'al. There, with the concept of Ba'al completely eradicated, a new covenant will be made in the form of a betrothal and this will ensure not only a restored abundance for Israel but also a change of heart in its relationship with God. The names of Hosea's children will then be reversed to a positive promise: "And I will have pity on Not pitied, and I will say to Not my people, 'You are my people', and he shall say, 'Thou art my God'."

The conclusion of chap. 2 (14–23) is briefly repeated at the end of chap. 3 (5–6), thus concluding the section with a restatement of its essential message — the disruption and ultimate restoration of the relationship with God.

The Second Section: Chs. 4–14 contain a number of shortf separate oracles or addresses (see below, Hosea's Message), According to one opinion, the conclusion of chap. 14 (v. 9. is a piece of wisdom literature similar to the supplements a) the end of a number of the psalms. The arrangement ot the addresses is not easy to see. U. Cassuto has suggested that they are in some associative order, but the connection between the different sections is not always obvious. Words of comfort are interspersed among the prophecies of disaster (11:9–11; 14:3–8). Scholars used to regard Hosea as a prophet of unrelieved gloom, and the more optimistic passages as insertions by another hand, but such a theory is no longer tenable. Prophecies of weal following ones of woe are in keeping with a principle abundantly illustrated in the Old Testament. On the other hand a message of comfort also appears in chapter 3, whose authorship by Hosea has never been in doubt. His horizon was not limited to disaster.

Chap. 4 contains emphatic warnings of the consequences of sin, for Hosea saw no signs of true penitence (5:15–6:6; 7:14–16) and, like Amos, prophesies Israel's destruction (7:13; 9:11–17). However, in the end, he came to realize that just as he had forgiven his faithless wife (in fact, or in his heart), so God in His infinite love (ḥesed) would come to forgive Israel and would restore the covenant bond (2:14–23; 11:8–11; 14:1–8). Thus the prophet foretold the disaster that lay a generation away and the subsequent act of grace that would restore at least a "remnant of Israel".

Hosea's Message: The key concept of Hosea's prophecy is the loving kindness and understanding of God. In Hebrew, this word "ḥesed" conveys a meaning which includes the qualities of loyalty, love and mercy. However, the mercy of God can only be enjoyed by those who understand His love and His ways. Thus Hosea demands that men shall learn to know the kindness of God and shall then be guided by a similar mercy in their dealings with their fellow-men. The very metaphor which Hosea chooses to represent the relationship between God and Israel, that of a man and his disloyal wife, is one which amply demonstrates the exercise of "loving kindness" and mercy by one party and its denial by the other.

This symbolism is the distinctive mark of Hosea's message but it belongs to an older tradition, favoured by many prophets, in which the time of the Mosaic Covenant and life in the wilderness was recognized (and idealized) as a period of purity and faithfulness on the part of Israel (2:15). Hosea compares the Covenant that bound Israel to God to the bond of wedlock between a man and wife. Yahweh as Israel's husband (in Hebrew, ba'al or master) is generous and kind, but rightly expects and demands absolute wifely fidelity as the condition of the relationship. By worshipping other gods (accepting their lordship), Israel is guilty of adultery and merits the punishment of divorce and national ruin (12:2–13).

Again and again Hosea returns to the condemnation of paganism, not only as it affects the cult of Yahweh (8:5–14) but also because of the moral decadence which has resulted (4:1–14; 6:8–10). He battles against the injustice and inequalities of society, against the corruption of priest and prophet and the degeneration of worship, and against the alienation from God and the betrayal of the Covenant* that all these represent. This is a theme implicit in all Hebrew prophecy. Without the guiding beacon of the stern morality and social and personal integrity imposed by Yahweh and embodied in the Covenant Code, social life disintegrated in self-seeking and lawlessness. Moreover, if Israel has forgotten God's love and mercy, then they can no longer be His people (11:1–4; 13:4–8). This preoccupation with Israel's defection — and the conditions he describes suggest wholesale apostasy — is repeated in all Hosea's addresses. His fundamental message is that this betrayal is the direct cause of all the evils which Yahweh will send as a punishment, just as the eventual restoration will be an act of grace which will follow repentance and lead to righteousness.

Hosea's Style: Hosea's style is notable for its terseness and vivid imagery. His manner is harsh; his words directed like hammer blows against the evils he abominates. Nevertheless a gentle nature and deep love for his people shine through the passages of comfort. Hosea is appalled by the disasters he foresees and his bitter accusations and prophecies read almost as though torn from him against his will — a characteristic which Jeremiah shares with Hosea.

The text of the book of Hosea has been badly corrupted with the result that many passages are hard to understand. Hosea's use of allusive imagery, his enigmatic style and the violent emotional transitions in the book only serve to increase the difficulty of understanding his prophetic utterances. Some help in this is provided by the Septuagint translation which has preserved the style of the original Hebrew and can clarify some of its obscurities.

The Chaotic Historical Situation: The superscription of the book states that Hosea prophesied "in the days of Uzziah, Jotham, Ahaz and Hezekiah, kings of Judah, and in the days of Jeroboam, the son of Jehoash, king of Israel" (1:1) However this cannot be entirely correct, for had he lived during the reigns of all the kings of Judah mentioned, then the list of the kings of Israel would have had to be extended to include the successors of Jeroboam II, who ruled in Israel at the same time as Jotham, Ahaz and Hezekiah. It has been assumed, therefore, that in fact only Uzziah and Jeroboam should actually appear, and that Hosea prophesied shortly after the time of Amos.

This was a chaotic period during which the Assyrians first dominated, then destroyed the Northern Kingdom in which Hosea lived. The succession of regicides who sat on the throne of Israel induced despair of the monarchy. The prophet proclaimed that the only hope for the people lay in renewed allegiance to Yahweh. Naturally enough most of his oracles were directed to the Kingdom of Israel. The passages in the book explicitly concerned with the Kingdom of Judah have been a subject of debate, many scholars doubting whether Hosea actually wrote them. It is generally believed that they were interpolated by a Judahite editor who could not understand that a prophet of Hosea's standing should have overlooked Judah so completely. On the other hand, there is no reason to suppose that he did. Since he spoke explicitly of the Northern Kingdom, he probably spoke of the Southern Kingdom in that way too. The omission may be more apparent than real. Some writers carry the argument further and maintain that the passages concerning a future united House of David (e.g. 3:5) or the apparent reference to Judah's deliverance from Assyria in 722 or 701 BCE (1:7) were certainly the work of a Judahite editor, but this is also denied by other scholars who regard the passages as original. The superfluous words in the opening passage of the book are also ascribed by some to this Judean editor, although they may equally well have been a late editorial edition by a disciple of the prophet.

HOSPITALITY. — To travel through the sparsely populated, desolate areas of much of the ancient world was a perilous undertaking. The traveller faced the dangers of hunger and thirst because of lack of sources of food and water. In the absence of any recognized government authority protecting the wayfarer, he was at the mercy of brigands or highwaymen. Security in such areas was provided by the family and the tribe, and a man far from his own environment needed to be able to call on the help of the other groups he might meet. In deserts and other areas far from the central authority, hospitality is a vital institution. For this reason, it is commonly regarded as a fundamental duty among nomads and all who dwell in remote frontier lands, away from settled communities. Hospitality involves protection as well as maintenance. To this day, hospitality is an accepted and honoured custom among the Bedouins and is scrupulously observed by them. Any traveller who enters a Bedouin's tent automatically receives protection and hospitality for three days and is entitled to continued protection for a certain period after leaving. These wayfarers in the Negeb (**525**) evoke old times.

Hospitality in its simplest aspect is portrayed in the Old Testament. When a traveller approached, the host hurried to meet him and invite him in. Thus Abraham ran to meet the three men who appeared before him as he sat in front of his tent by the oaks of Mamre (Gn. 18:1–2) and Lot

525

526

invited the two angels whom he saw at "the gate of Sodom" to enter his house (Gn. 19:1–3). Laban ran out to welcome Eliezer (Gn. 24:29) and Job says that he opened his doors to the wayfarer (Job. 31:32). It is to the discredit of the Benjaminites that the men of Gibeah refused a lodging to the Levite and his concubine, who had deliberately chosen to spend the night in an Israelite town in the hope of receiving hospitality (Jud. 19:15–19).

When a guest arrived, he was given water to wash the dust of the road from his feet (Gn. 18:4; 19:2; 24:32), a meal was served in his honour (Gn. 18:5–8; 19:3; 24:33; Jud. 19:20–22, also Jud. 13:15; II Sam. 12:4), and his companions and animals with him were fed (Gn. 24:31–32; Jud. 19:21).

Protection of a guest was a sacred duty. In order to safeguard him, a host was required to make every sacrifice. An extreme case, which may not be a norm of hospitality, is that of Lot, who offered his two virgin daughters to the Sodomites, to prevent them from harming the guests under his roof (Gn. 19:8); another such case is that of the old man of Gibeah who offered the Benjaminites his virgin daughter and the Levite's concubine in return for leaving his Levite guest unharmed (Jud. 19:23–24).

By these standards, of course, Jael's action in slaying Sisera after he had found shelter from his pursuers in her tent (Jud. 4:19; 5:25) was a gross breach of the code of hospitality.

It is worth noting that all the Old Testament references to hospitality in its protective form belong to the periods of the Patriarchs or of Judges, i.e. to times of semi-nomadic conditions of isolated communities and no central authority. Once the monarchy had been established, a more settled way of life developed, in which travellers could rely on the government for protection. The virtues of hospitality lost their overwhelming importance and no longer feature in biblical stories. Hospitality in this sense, of course, had nothing to do with the board and lodging provided by Solomon and other kings for their officials and military commanders (I K. 10:5; 18:19), which was a normal part of court routine.

In general, hospitality as a social amenity came to be regarded as a communal responsibility as well as a private virtue and it remained as such throughout the pre-Exilic and post-Exilic life of Israel. The traveller continued to find doors opened to him and to expect and receive help on his journeys, but individual hospitality was no longer his only hope of help.

Guest Chambers and Inns: This hospitable spirit continued in the later stages of Israel's development. In towns and villages private houses would have a special "guest chamber" reserved for passing travellers. At the times of the great festivals* these would be freely opened to the thousands of Jews making their pilgrimage to Jerusalem (Tractate Aboth-de-Rab Nathan, Chap. 34). Jesus referred to such a place (Mk. 14:14; Lk. 22:11) when giving his disciples directions about the Last Supper.

On main roads and near the gates of cities, inns were available for pilgrims and their mounts. These would be walled enclosures with sleeping quarters for men and beasts and fodder for cattle. Such a place was the "lodging place" of Gn. 42:27, and the "wayfarers' lodging place" of Jeremiah 9:2.

By Hellenistic and Roman times, the inns ("pundak") were better appointed. For instance, the inn of the Good Samaritan (Lk. 10:34–5) identified with "Khan Hatrur" (**526**) on the road to Jericho, where the remains of a Roman road are also visible, was obviously something more luxurious than the ancient "lodging places". Similar inns stood for centuries on all the great caravan routes (e.g. Avdat in Nabatea*), and the remains of many of them can still be found. These were places of rest and entertainment for travellers and merchants. Sometimes rabbinical references to them intimate that they had no very high reputation.

I

IDOL WORSHIP IN ISRAEL. — *Outline: Conflict between Yahwism and the Gods of Canaan; Period of Judges; During the Monarchy; Ba'alism and Israel; The Hebrews' Oriental Background; Opposing Tensions of Israel's Religious History; Different Interpretations; Evidence of the Figurines; Charms not Idolatry; Biblical Evidence Reviewed; Jeroboam and the Golden Calves; Co-existent Yahwism and Monolatry; No Theological Formulation.*

Hebrew prophets and thinkers were often dismayed to realize just how great an influence their neighbours had on the life and beliefs of Israel. Hebrew sacrificial* and funerary* customs, their worship at high places*, the architecture of their temples and the symbolism of their religion were all influenced to some extent by Canaanite customs. The local inhabitants worshipped man-made images of animals or men or both (see Canaan: Gods and Idols*) made of stone, wood or metal, moulded or carved by Canaanite and, later, Phoenician craftsmen. Some of them were works of art, over-laid with precious metals and stones. More often, they were mass produced figurines of stone or clay with few artistic pretensions. The Hebrew prophets used the same generic terms for all, or at least some of them: "ba'alîm", "elilîm" and "asherahs" for all idols — although "ba'alîm" does not as a rule seem to refer to figurines. "Gillulîm" may have referred to talismans bearing an image of an idol.

Conflict between Yahwism and the Gods of Canaan: By the time the Israelites conquered their land, Canaanite mythology* and religious practices, to judge from the Ugaritic texts* were already decadent (see Canaan*: Gods and Idols, Cult; Canaanite Civilization and Ugarit*). The southern part of Canaan — the territory conquered by the Israelites — was in any case economically and culturally a more backward area, compared to the highly developed centres of Phoenicia*: Tyre, Byblos and Ugarit*. The biblical narrative insists that the children of Israel rejected Canaanite religious customs and there are very few traces of their survival in the Yahwism of this period. Although Yahweh controlled the elements (see the Song of Deborah, Jud. 5:4 ff) and the heavenly bodies (Jos. 10:12 ff) and rode on the wings of the storm (Ps. 29), he was not a sun, moon or storm god like the Canaanite deities. Even though he might confer the blessing of fertility (Gn. 49:25 ff; Dt. 33:11–16), he was in no sense a fertility god. Up to the time of the monarchy, the Canaanites remained in close association with the Israelites. Their superstitions and, more important, their widespread worship of "ba'alîm" and "asherahs" under different forms in different localities continued side by side with Israelite religious institutions.

Period of Judges: As the Israelites changed from their semi-nomadic way of living to the sedentary life of Canaan, they naturally absorbed and adapted many aspects of Canaanite culture, notably sacrificial customs, social patterns and the arts. The majority of the Israelites became farmers, learning from their neighbours. It is thought by scholars that many of them must have seen the Canaanite agrarian religion as an essential part of agrarian life and, consequently, have joined in propitiating the ancient gods who promised fertility and a good harvest. Moreover, many Canaanites and others whose culture was mainly Canaanite were absorbed into Israelite society. While, in time, they became worshippers of Yahweh, they may have kept their old allegiance to the agrarian gods.

There are many instances of the survival of magic practices among the Arab peasantry of modern Palestine and Syria, all of whom are devout Moslems.

As a result of this conflict of pressures, the worship of Yahweh became confused with that of Ba'al. Even the two gods were confused, both at the agrarian and cosmic level (see below). The book of Judges emphasizes the religious irregularities of the period. The cult of Ba'al existed in Gideon's home town and even in the house of Saul. This was the beginning of the "popular religion" which was to play such an important part in the evolution of Israel.

During the Monarchy: The symbolism of the popular Canaanite rituals (see Canaan*: Gods and Idols, Cult) which apparently had a long history of usage, seems to have remained a potent danger during the centuries of the monarchy. Normative Yahwism — a distinctive and exclusive religion — rejected the fertility rites and the worship of the high gods, El and Ba'al, which represented a culture having a quite different view of the world and system of values. The incompatibility between the two is most eloquently expressed by the faithful chroniclers of Yahweh. Nevertheless, their very protest suggests that the alien beliefs were too closely associated with popular cults for safety. They invited a confusion between Yahweh and Ba'al and opened the way to the introduction of pagan features into the ancestral cult. The fundamental danger may have increased following the conquests of David and Solomon, which brought additional Canaanites into the Israelite kingdom from previously unconquered enclaves. Though they served a new king, it is unlikely that they forgot their ancestral ways.

Later on, when the monarchy divided, a majority of the former Canaanites were within the boundaries of the Northern Kingdom of Israel*. During the reign of Ahab, his wife Jezebel encouraged the immigration of many Phoenicians (Canaanites). The cultured and prosperous Phoenicians were much admired by the Canaanite and Israelite population of the kingdom of Israel, who must have offered a fertile ground for fostering Ba'alism. Jezebel brought the cult of Ba'al (apparently in the form of Ba'al-Melkart) from her home in Tyre to Ahab's court in Samaria. There Ahab erected a temple to Ba'al and an asherah. The Tyrian Ba'al cult reappeared in Athaliah's court in Jerusalem.

Ba'alism and Israel: The early prophets Elijah and Elisha aimed their denunciations mainly at the royal leaders and their sophisticated courts. "Idolatry" then became a general term for their adoption of cosmopolitan habits which were an offence to ascetic Yahwists at a material as well as a spiritual level.

How far the religion of early Israel deviated from the classic prophets' ideals is very difficult to assess. Only within the last decades has new evidence from Ugarit* about Canaanite-Phoenician mythology and religious practice cleared away some of the uncertainty.

The Hebrews' Oriental Background: The latest discoveries have demonstrated a strong connection between the sacrificial rituals of the Hebrews and the Canaanites*. The technical expressions for some of their sacrifices* were similar and so were many details of their ritual. The most modern opinion (that of the religio-historical school) is that this does not indicate Israelite borrowing from the Canaanites, but a continuous development among both Canaanites and early Hebrews, drawing on a common Semitic source. Yahwism among the Hebrews seems to have co-existed with a theological pattern common to the ancient Orient. This general spirit seems to have played a part in early Israelite thinking and it remained a dominant force in the evolution of Israel's religion.

Opposing Tensions of Israel's Religious History: Once it appeared that the "popular religion" of Israelite shrines tended in some ways to conform to that of Canaanite holy places, the recorded denunciations of the prophets took on a new meaning. Israel's religion could thus be seen, according to many scholars, as the product of interaction and tension between two forces: Canaanite environment v. the traditional faith of the prophets. Hence, Israel's religion did not develop in a single straight line, but involved occasional combinations between the two cultures.

Different Interpretations: Older theories and more recent trends regarded these tensions from an opposite point of view (see Biblical Criticism*; articles on Canaan*). The main weakness of all these theories was their tendency to accept as historical facts, the different hypothetical categories they had themselves established. Syncretism, monolatry, implicit monotheism or ritual myth are tools for one method of research, but they need to take into account all the facts of a situation. To examine the evolution of Hebrew and assimilated Canaanite society exclusively at the level of secular, family life, without taking account of new facts, would suggest a state bordering on blatant paganism. Yet in fact what was eventually produced was monotheism — not paganism. Could this have been achieved by the periodic reforms of certain kings and prophets alone? Could seventy years of Exile in Babylon followed by the religious reform of the Restoration* have so completely transformed a presumably half-pagan cult into the religion of Judaism? Rather, it seems that the theories advanced must be accepted with caution and more weight given to the new knowledge of the factors that made up Israel's religious background.

In a recent phase of religio-historical and archaeological research, knowledge of Canaanite culture and religion (see Canaan: Gods and Idols*, Cult) has been used as a guide to the true character of Israel's developing religion (especially by R. Kittel, E. Sellin, W. F. Albright, G. E. Wright). This, of course, does not alter the fact that Israel's own unique characteristics can be explained only by a fundamental examination of the biblical evidence. As a supplement, archaeological evidence sheds new light on the problems.

The different aspects can be considered under several headings:

Evidence of the Figurines: In all the excavations of Israelite towns, the lower Canaanite levels have revealed large numbers of figurines. These are usually clay plaques with a nude figure in relief (see Canaan: Gods and Idols*, Cult) which appeared in Palestine during the Middle Bronze Age (roughly the Patriarchal period) and remained popular in various forms down to the Middle Iron Age, or the end of the Israelite monarchy.

The organized worship of Asherah may have declined, but the people resorted to popular magic and the use of amulets (see Magic*). Hence they continued in use by common people through times of greater or lesser Yahwist orthodoxy. Their use is reflected in the very low artistic level of the female figurines discovered.

Significantly, Astarte figurines of the clay plaque type, so common in Canaanite levels as well as in later Israelite ones of Iron Age II, were not found in Israelite sites of central Palestine of the Early Iron Age (period of Judges), although they continued to be popular within the Canaanite cities of the same period. Whether their absence can be explained by the reaction to recurrent movements for religious reform or, more likely, because the Israelites were not yet close enough to the Canaanites they had dispossessed, to have been influenced by their fertility cult, is not yet clear. W. F. Albright has pointed out that in the following period (the monarchy), or Middle Iron Age, several types of pagan figurines became common in all the cities of Israel. Such figures were usually found in the ruins of houses rather than sanctuaries and it is assumed that they had no specific cultic significance but were merely fertility charms. Since every Israelite home of this period apparently possessed one or more, it can be assumed on the evidence of the prophets that the Israelite masses had gone a long way towards adopting the popular superstitions of their environment.

This is the more understandable in view of the frequency of mixed marriage which, in contrast to later periods, was accepted as normal at that time. Probably there was no compulsion to purge the home of amulets or figurines. Centuries of toleration suggest a picture of home life that makes the recent discoveries of pagan charms and Hebrew symbols side by side understandable.

Charms not Idolatry: It has been pointed out that the existence of charms and amulets during the Israelite period is a matter of popular superstition and not necessarily a sign that the Israelites practiced idolatry. Against the anguished pleading of the prophets* (see articles) must be placed some sober facts, among them the many biblical stories about household gods, told without prejudice, which seem to show that there was not necessarily any conflict between possession of such things and devotion to the official prophetic religion. The border-line between charm and sacred figure is hard to draw. As ancient sculpture generally comes without labels, it is hard to prove that every bull is a bull-god or every chariot a sun-chariot — or the contrary.

Just as archaeologists, at one stage in the excavations of Palestine, tended to exaggerate the religious significance of every unidentified structure, finding temples in every pile of stones, so there is a similar temptation to over-interpretation of the meaning of statuettes and figurines. Large stone remains are not necessarily those of religious objects.

Moreover, careful investigation has proved many small stone or pottery figures to have had no connection with the cult.

In the whole of Palestine, hardly any Canaanite idol has been found in position in a temple. Outside the temples, nothing has been discovered large enough to have been placed on a pedestal and seen by an assembly of worshippers. Furthermore, no male image has yet been found in any Israelite town so far excavated. This suggests more than a mere "accident of discovery". It is reasonably argued that the fact proves the efficacy of the reforms and their necessity. However, on closer examination, the facts may also suggest that while the prophets stressed the negative aspects of religious syncretism, they also took the more positive factors — the tenacity of the aniconic traditions of Yahwism — for granted. It was this substratum which persisted and, ultimately, triumphed.

Biblical Evidence Reviewed: Biblical evidence for idolatry also needs to be re-examined in a similar critical spirit. How far, for instance, were the Golden Calves of the Northern Kingdom evidence of actual idol worship and how far can they be found to have a place in Israelite tradition?

Jeroboam and the Golden Calves: Following the schism between the two kingdoms, Jeroboam wanted to provide the people of his kingdom of Israel with an alternate sanctuary so that they would no longer have to go to Jerusalem to sacrifice and, perhaps, feel a revival of loyalty towards Rehoboam.

The alternative he chose was to revive the ancient shrines of Bethel and Dan. The book of Amos (7:10–17, especially v. 13) reveals that the sanctuary at Bethel, like that in Jerusalem, was a royal sanctuary (see Temple*). At the same time, the symbols associated with the old worship, mainly the bull as a pedestal for the invisible god, were employed once more. The custom of representing gods as standing on an animal whose nature emphasized the divine attributes — a bull, for instance, was the most widespread symbol for virility — spread from Anatolia through Northern Syria and Assyria. It did not seem to be native to the peoples of Palestine.

The Israelites, however, worshipped a god who was invisible. Nevertheless, when it became necessary to offer some tangible symbol of his presence, either his throne (seat) was chosen (see Tabernacle, Ark and Cherubim*) or the animal he might be thought to stand upon. "In Israelite symbolism between 1300 and 700 BCE, the invisible glory (Jehovah) was conceived as enthroned upon the golden cherubim or standing on a golden bull." (W. F. Albright) This may also be the explanation of the "golden calf" episode in the Exodus story.

When Jeroboam and his court introduced the custom of worshipping Yahweh in association with a "golden calf", evidently a bull, derisively called "calf", this did not imply any worship of a sacred bull. On closer examination, as will be seen below, it is difficult to find any unanimity in the reaction of earlier and later prophets to what the latter mockingly called the "calves" of Jeroboam. These were not necessarily attacked because they were idols, but because, objectively, they represented an attempt to deflect attention from the religious centre of Jerusalem. They could be the object of studied insult at the hands of the Yahwists.

Providing an alternative sanctuary did not institute a religious schism, as many scholars used to suppose. However, it provided cultic attractions for pilgrims to Dan and Bethel and revived an age-old separation between Ephraim and Judah which had only been superficially patched up by the united monarchy of David and Solomon* (this problem is analyzed fully under Israel and Judah* part II: Jeroboam). Jeroboam's "calves of gold" represented pedestals of Yahweh, not his image (I K. 12:28). Neither Elijah, Elisha nor Amos raised any objections to them, although all were strenuous fighters against paganism in the Northern Kingdom. It was some time before voices were raised against them.

Jeroboam had provided his people with a symbol of the divine presence without violating the commandment that forbade the making of images of God. However, this was too subtle for unsophisticated people to appreciate. Inevitably, Yahweh was confused with the symbols that represented his invisible presence. They were at best ambivalent symbols and could be interpreted differently.

No other example of sacred bulls represented alone is known. There is no connection between Jeroboam's "calves" and the Egyptian cult of the sacred bull Apis.

Later chroniclers and the Deuteronomist historian were probably not altogether unjust in accusing Jeroboam of encouraging the worship of Ba'al by this use of that god's familiar emblem, and by reviving pilgrimages to Dan. The biblical chroniclers insist on attributing the tragic end of the Northern Kingdom to Jeroboam's religious irregularity. True, these chroniclers were Judahites, voicing an old prejudice that dated from the beginning of the separation of the monarchy. Yet their message is echoed by the prophet Hosea*, a northerner himself, whose words were addressed primarily to his native kingdom. He shows that even before 721 BCE, its religion had been contaminated with pagan features or ideas. By the time of the final collapse, religious decay and social deterioration had gone further in Israel than in Judah. The syncretism that Hosea condemned had borne bitter fruit in debauchery, drunkenness and sexual licence at the sanctuary under the cover of religion. Presumably, all these corroded the national character, leaving little of the stern morality inherent in Yahwism (Hos. 4:11–14; 17 ff). Israel in Hosea's time was on the verge of collapse in more than a political sense.

Co-existent Yahwism and Monolatry: Many other examples can be found of the way in which the Hebrews adapted the traditions and archaic beliefs of the land they had acquired to their own beliefs.

In the view of G. E. Mendenhall, this "traditional period in Israelite religion is thus to be defined as one in which the primary task of the community is felt to be the preservation and transmission of a tradition which was necessary to the preservation of the group. One may freely grant that there is not too much evidence of a concern for the preservation of Yahwist tradition during the monarchy. This is precisely the point. The traditional period tends rather to take religious tradition for granted. The main concern is for the functioning of the group — in political, economic and social aspects. The inevitable result is increasing unconcern for the specifically religious (over against the cultic, which flourish) obligations and economic motivations that take the upper hand. Yet we do not see evidence for the existence of opposing traditions during the whole of the monarchy." This author has also defined the normative religion of the period of the monarchy as one of monolatry co-existent with the Yahwist tradition. "A consistently monotheistic religious community has never existed, else condemnation of idolatry (by the prophets) would be pointless. Monotheism was not an issue in the earliest (Mosaic) period. Monolatry was. Monotheism could easily lead to syncretism by the normal process so dear to the heart of the modern sophisticate, of identifying the one God with the various gods of other religions. Monolatry, on the other hand, demanded obedience to the will of the one God, which excluded both recognition of other gods and syncretism, though it did not exclude cultural borrowing."

Israelite treatment of Canaanite high places* and even older archaic folkways is another example of the way in which the Israelites adapted the customs and beliefs of their new land to their own ancient traditions.

Either at the time of the composition of the historical books of the Bible or, probably, much earlier, holy sites were given a new religious or national significance to fit them into Hebrew traditions. The ancient holy site and Canaanite high place of Bethel, for instance, may have become holy in Israelite eyes because God had appeared to one of the Patriarchs there, while the megalithic stone-circle of Gilgal (see Sanctuaries*), a relic of the ancient inhabitants of the land with a potent magical significance, was reinterpreted as a memorial to the 12 tribes who had used the stones as stepping stones to cross the River Jordan. The lawfulness of high places in the days of Judges and the monarchy is another instance of the preservation of old sanctuaries among the Israelites, such as Samuel's high place in Ramah (I Sam. 9:12) or Solomon's revelation at the "great high place" at Gibeon (I K. 3:4 ff).

In spite of the accusations of "idolatry" levelled by the prophets and spiritual leaders, there seems to be a contradiction. For all the attractions of the worship of Canaanite gods and the use of Canaanite figurines, Yahweh continued to receive the veneration of his people. The Old Testament's own evidence suggests something other than the blatant paganism postulated by orthodox scholars and the Wellhausen school (see Biblical Criticism*). These earlier interpretations could only be accepted if they also provided for the fundamental fact that Yahwism was not only preserved but developed onto a more elevated spiritual plane, as evidenced by the appearance of the prophets. Their repeated condemnations of the kings and the cosmopolitan upper classes, as well as the people who strayed, did not proceed merely from the individual opinions of the prophets themselves. Their reaction required a powerful and authoritative tradition to back it up.

While the biblical record thunders against assimilation and real or apparent idolatry, it also demonstrates the survival of the Mosaic ideal of worship and life among the early prophets and groups like the Rechabites and Nazirites, whose austere way of life was prompted by their ethical and religious beliefs.

This was the life stream from which came later prophecy and, ultimately, modern Judaism. There was no significant break in the tradition. The central principles of Yahwism were preserved throughout the periods of Judges and the monarchy until the Restoration in the 5th c. BCE.

No Theological Formulation: As the purer Mosaic faith continued, it became linked with national interests and civic justice. It was probably not carried out to its logical conclusion, nor was it differentiated formally and sharply from popular practices and beliefs. Before the days of the classic prophets differences and tensions between official beliefs and the living faith of the people were felt rather than clearly formulated. The average Hebrew in those days did not devote much attention to what we would call theological questions. They did not bring out the intellectual implications of faith until the post-Exilic period. Until then, everything in Jewish religious life was spontaneous or traditional. We cannot find, therefore, a homogeneous and consistent view of the deity, his representation and symbols in the biblical documents.

The approach of the religio-historical school (see Biblical Criticism*), which re-examines the Bible in the light of archaeological evidence, has made possible a much truer picture of Israel's development and has at last put the influence of idolatry into a proper perspective as one — but not the sole — factor in that development.

IMMORTALITY (Belief in a continued existence after death). — **Old Testament Evidence:** All religions need to take account of human death. The religion of the Old Testament is almost uniformly concerned with the things of "this" world and God's involvement in it but, from references in Genesis, it seems that biblical man had quite a realistic picture of the fate of the dead. Abraham (Gn. 25:8) was "gathered to his people". Jacob (Gn. 37:35) talked of "going down to Sheol" where the shades of the dead or "rephaim" lived. Sheol is mentioned metaphorically in other places (Is. 14:9; Ezk. 32:21) and there seem to have been different views about its nature, although nowhere is existence there pictured as very desirable.

The Old Testament gives the general impression that death meant the extinction of a man's human faculties. After death, men believed in some sort of a shadowy existence in Sheol, although in Ecclesiastes and Job there tends to be a denial of any conscious existence at all after death. On the other hand, there was a belief in the possibility of escaping death altogether (see Psalm 16) and in God's power to raise one from the dead (see, for instance, I Sam. 2). Two men were apparently regarded as immortal: Enoch whom God "took" (Gn. 5:24) and Elijah, who was carried up to heaven in a chariot of fire (II K. 2:11).

In addition to biblical testimony, the evidence of archaeology and of the literature of surrounding cultures has suggested to many scholars that the Israelites had a real, though not uniform and not always definite faith in a life beyond the grave.

Archaeological Evidence: In early times, the people with whom the Israelites were in closest contact were the Canaanites. Both before and after the Conquest they were in touch with them, absorbing much of their culture and adopting many of their customs. That the Canaanites believed in some form of life after death is shown by their custom of burying dishes of food, jars and knives with the dead for their later use (see details and illus. under Funerary Practices*). Hebrew graves contained similar vessels and implements. It is argued by some that this does not prove that all Canaanites or Hebrews believed in a continuation of life after death. They may merely have conformed to custom, just as non-religious people today will observe the conventional burial practices of their time. Archaeological evidence is not conclusive about ancient peoples' motives. The objects may have been placed there symbolically, or for sentimental reasons. Nobody may actually have expected the things to be used. On the other hand it is significant that they were there at all. Their presence in the graves may conceivably have meant something tangible to those who placed them there. If they had not been there, this would also have suggested certain conclusions.

Body and Soul: Religions of antiquity regarded life as an indivisible whole. Their concept of the after-life concerned the survival of the whole personality — not an abstract idea of an immaterial soul.

According to the earliest biblical records, man's whole person was a "nephesh" consisting of flesh or body and spirit (ruaḥ). Death was apparently seen as a state in which the body remained in the grave while the spirit — retaining some aspects of the personality — went down to the shadowy Sheol, or went back to God (see Funerary Practices*: Death). This was not a consistent concept as it also appears in some passages that the grave and Sheol were equated as the place where the person remained after death.

Post-Biblical Writings: Such post-biblical writings as the Apocrypha carried on the same general tradition, even going back to the earlier biblical patterns of "nephesh" and "ruaḥ". In the Apocalypses, the spirit (ruaḥ) appears more often as the carrier of the personality to Sheol. This allowed for the possibility that while a man might die, his essential personality lived on forever, which is of importance when it comes to considering the possibility of a man's spirit returning to his body — the earliest idea of resurrection.

The Soul: In the last centuries BCE, as reflected particularly in Ecclesiasticus (see Apocrypha*), a dual concept developed in which the soul was seen as an independent element originating in heaven and joined to a material body at the moment either of conception or birth.

As this union was more or less incidental, the fact of the soul's existence before birth and after death was accepted as a matter of course. What did call for explanation was its brief sojourn in a human body, thus inevitably losing some of its original purity. Different explanations were offered by the religions of western Asia and later by Hellenism. Their point of agreement was in making it the aim of life to protect the purity of the soul while it remained earth-bound, a view which quickly became a commonplace of rabbinic literature.

Resurrection: A new development in post-Exilic thought carrying on the older conception of life as a totality of body and soul was the belief in the resurrection of the body. By the time the book of Daniel* (mid-2nd c. BCE) was composed, the older idea had developed into a concept of the resurrection and judgment of the dead: "Many of them that sleep in the dust of the earth shall awake, some to everlasting life and some to the reproaches of everlasting abhorrence." (Dan. 12:2). These beliefs became an article of faith in later Judaism and especially in the elaborate eschatological plans of the apocalyptists and the New Testament writers.

The Last Judgment: Belief that after death a man's soul would be judged and the righteous compensated for their earthly tribulations gained ground, especially among the Pharisees*. The Sadducees*, in contrast, denied immortality. They were charged with being hellenizers and their beliefs in this respect may be a reflection of the influence of Diaspora Jewry. Their religious beliefs in other respects were closer to the letter of the Old Testament than the Pharisees, or Essenes (see Sadducees*).

The Jews of the Hellenistic Diaspora: The Jews of the Hellenistic* Diaspora, and notably the philosopher Philo, tended to accept the Platonic idea of an immortal soul loaned temporarily to the body, whose death meant release and eternal life for the soul. On this basis, the Diaspora Jews rejected the Palestinian concept of a resurrection and last judgment. Punishment or reward, they believed, would be meted out immediately upon death.

Apocalyptic View of Resurrection: Belief in a future life is the essential basis of apocalyptic*. At first, this offered a naive picture of a bodily resurrection granted to the pious who would thereafter inhabit an earthly kingdom, witnessing the punishment of the apostates and enjoying a material prosperity. Later Judaism put this on a more spiritual level, in which the righteous could look forward to an eternal existence either in heaven, the dwelling place of God, or, alternatively, in "Paradise" or the "Garden of Eden" (Dan. 12:2), while the unjust must expect due retribution.

The Ideas of Immortality in Judaism: The original Old Testament belief in a life after death in Sheol, borrowed from Israel's antique background, had been free of any moral implications. As the Jewish idea of immortality developed, new moral values were added to it and a new conception evolved which, for instance, provided a solution to the anguish of Job* and offered a solace for the apparent injustices of mortal life.

Moreover, faith in a life beyond death at last made it possible to believe that God's promise would be redeemed in relation to each individual. Without this, Jewish religious psychology would be unintelligible and the Christian doctrine of resurrection could never have appeared as its direct product.

The Jew of the 1st c. CE craved for the preservation of the entire personality, and this could be secured, according to Jewish psychology, only by the restoration and reanimation of the body (see Eschatology*: Resurrection*). The early Christian shared the Jewish belief in a general resurrection at the end of the age; Paul carried over into Christian thought much of the apocalyptic* imagery in which the hope of Judaism found expression. Paul insists, at the same time, on the spiritual nature of the future life and the spiritual character of the resurrection of the body.

In later times, rabbinic writers* adopted the dual concept of a body combined with a pre-existing soul, although they did not relinquish belief in resurrection and final judgment. They do not equate soul and body with good and evil. It is always the soul which sins, not the body. It is said in the Talmud that all souls have existed since the Creation and are stored in heaven until their time comes to join the bodies intended for them.

Archaeology as a Reflection of Changing Beliefs: In the last century BCE and first century CE, it ceased to be the fashion to include food and pottery vessels in burials. People no longer believed that these could be of any use to their dead. Small lamps, bottles and jars for perfume, and sometimes small vials have been found. The lamps suggest a possible symbolic connection between light and eternal life (see illus. under Funerary Practices*).

Opinions about the after-life varied, but one thing is clear. The Jew of the time of Hillel and Christ, Paul and Bar-Kochba, no longer believed that he could help to provide for the comfort of the dead by his own efforts.

IMPURITY AND PURIFICATION (RITUAL). — *Outline: Concepts of Impurity and Purification; Uncleanness or Taboo? Purificatory Rites in Antiquity; Egypt; Mesopotamia; Biblical Concepts Compared to Israel's Neighbours; Rites; Priests; Holy War; Sacrifices; Ablutions and Washing; Lustral Water and the Ashes of the Red Heifer; Purity in Exilic and Post-Exilic Judaism; Rabbinical Laws; Tohorah; Purity among the Dead Sea Sectaries; "Cleanness of Heart" in the New Testament.*

The concepts of impurity and purity (or uncleanness and cleanness) are very closely related. Regulations governing ritual purity and impurity make up one of the most important features of all strata of biblical and Mishnaic (rabbinic) law.

Concepts of Impurity and Purification: The biblical term "impurity" (tum'ah) denotes both the state of contamination (or uncleanness) and an object which is the cause of contamination. Both, according to biblical law, imply untouchability. Contact with someone or something in a state of impurity must be avoided.

Some of the causes of impurity in man, beast, plant or mineral are clearly defined by the Old Testament: idolatry; sexual intercourse in defiance of religious prescriptions (Gn. 34; Lv. 18:24–30; Dt. 24:4 etc.); skin afflictions in man (Lv. 13:1–59); defects and discolourations due to moss or mildew in houses or vessels (Lv. 14:34–35); touching a dead animal (Lv. 11:24–31; 39) or a human corpse (Nu. 19:11–20); discharges from the sexual organs, including nocturnal emissions, coitus interruptus, i.e. the sin of Onan, and menstruation (Lv. 15:2–26). Others, of archaic origin (Lv. 14:2–9 or 10–32) are not defined. They involve being in a state of uncleanness which, although not precisely condemned, still calls for purification.

By definition impurity or "tum'ah" was synonymous with "ḥet" (sin). Its opposite was the purificatory rite of "tohorah" (purification). To remove the "ḥet", atonement and purification were necessary, the verb for which, "ḥatteh" or "hit'ḥatteh" (to purify or be purified from ritual impurity or sin) derived from the same root (ḥet).

The Torah does not oblige a Jew to beware of contamination of his body, but the contaminated person is in a state of uncleanness in relation to any contact with holy things, whether in the family circle (as in a family sacrifice; Nu. 9:6; I Sam. 20:26) or within the community. Hence the eating of holy food in a state of uncleanness is a deadly sin (Lv. 15:31).

According to the outlook of the ancient Hebrew, all foreign peoples were unclean. They contaminated the soil by their cults (Lv. 18:25–30; Ezr. 9:11). Accordingly, anyone coming from a foreign land was automatically impure and had to be purified before entering Israelite society.

This applied to utensils, tools and other artifacts (Nu. 31: 20–24) as well as persons (Ex. 12:43–8; Nu. 9:10–14) and also accounts for the circumcision* of foreigners entering the Jewish fold.

Uncleanness or Taboo? Although to the modern mind impurity and holiness are direct opposites, in ancient religions they were connected by the fact that both states rendered the person concerned "untouchable". A man who had been contaminated by contact with a corpse was untouchable and must be purified — but so was a priest after he had performed a sacrifice or some other sacred ritual. Both impurity and holiness were states from which one must make a formal return to normality, i.e. to a normal "purity".

As both impurity and sacredness were imparted by contact, ablutions with water were necessary to "wash off" the contact, whether with something impure or something sacred. The ritual "purification" which must follow touching the Ark differed only in degree from that which purified a man from contamination by a corpse or a woman from the "impure" state of childbirth.

This makes it quite clear that the purity regulations and other biblical laws such as those of "unclean" foods* had their roots in primitive taboos. Traces of these origins can be found in the Old Testament and no attempt is made to justify them. Presumably, rather than attempt to abolish ancient (tribal) customs, the lawgivers of Israel included them in their purity regulations, even though they unequivocally rejected the beliefs that had been associated with them (see below).

The rites and laws concerning purity prescribed by the Bible were given a new meaning so as to explain, on the one hand, the differences between Israel and its neighbours and, on the other, to create a wall against encroachments of foreign custom and to emphasize the transcendental holiness of Yahweh and the care with which his chosen people* must guard their sanctity. Hence, in the final synthesis of Leviticus*, the Laws of Purity* (11–16) form a natural accompaniment to the Law of Holiness (Lv. 17–26) as the negative and positive aspects of the holiness demanded by God.

Purificatory Rites in Antiquity: The rules concerning impurity and purification have their roots in ideas common to the Israelite tribes and to the peoples surrounding them. They may be considered under the two categories: 1. sanitary and hygienic considerations, and 2. religious considerations i.e. matters related to the deity.

The sanitary or hygienic considerations developed from the ancient idea that disease was caused by evil spirits and that it could be cured by magic acts in which spells and incantations played an important part (see Magic*).

Egypt: The Egyptians had elaborate rituals of purification for both the person and his utensils and belongings. In addition, they were meticulous about the purification of the dead. Their rites, in both cases, were intended to avoid giving offence to the gods, ablutions and immersions being of great importance.

The Egyptians held rigid beliefs about the purification of their priests who had to shave their heads, dress in linen and be circumcized. The king was purified every morning in his morning chamber. This is reminiscent of Leviticus 8:6, where the priest had to perform similar rites before coming to the Tabernacle.

Mesopotamia: Sumerians, Babylonians and Hittites also practiced special purity rituals, the Hittites having a very elaborate ritual relating to priests. They all had highly developed rites of exorcism as a means of healing disease and also rites for purifying slaves and sojourners ("gerîm" in Hebrew) within the community (see Family*).

Purity laws regarding men who took part in religious rituals, and the purification ceremonies for lepers and for women after childbirth (at the end of which ceremony the newborn child had also to be carefully purified) were very similar to the customs of the Hebrews.

These laws were intended to define the relation between a servant and his master, i.e. between the priest and the divinity. This relationship demanded not only total reverence towards the divinity, but also ritual cleanliness of everything connected with him. Such an attitude suggests developed ethical and sociological concepts parallel to the prevalent ideas on magic.

Biblical Concepts Compared to Israel's Neighbours: Biblical concepts of impurity and purification involved both factors, hygiene and religion. Thus the concepts and precepts of Mosaic Law have much in common with more widespread popular ideas, although in Mosaic law and all other biblical strata, the religious, monotheistic elements predominate. Ancient Jewish Law clearly defines the difference between its own attitude towards behaviour and that of all other codes. Mosaic Law regards the rules concerning impurity and purification (tohorah) in connection with the Temple and its cult as a pattern of the obligatory reverence before God (Lv. 21:1–8; I K. 6–8, passim). Where the laws are principally hygienic, Jewish law lays aside the whole essence of magic, i.e. spells and incantations. Rather, it teaches that the cause of disease is not an evil spirit but disobedience to God and the teaching of the Prophets (Ex. 15:25–26; Nu. 12: Dt. 24:8–9; II K. 5). *It is this above all which distinguishes biblical law as a uniquely monotheistic view.*

Rites: The rites necessary to eliminate the impurity varied according to the severity of different cases. Essentially, they involved a period of waiting during which no special activity could be undertaken. The main difference between the rites lay in the period of waiting involved: one day, three days, seven days, fourteen days, thirty-three days, forty days, sixty-six days and even eighty days (Lv. 12:4, 5). At the end of the prescribed period, the person being purified must bathe in ritually pure water and wash his clothes and often offer a sacrifice* as well.

Priests: As their livelihood depended mainly on offerings and on the cultic practices in the sanctuary, the priests were subject to particularly strict rules concerning purity of their bodies and families. These are summed up in Lv. 21:1–15 and are reflected in the code of the Nazirate. A Nazirite who became impure through contact with a corpse was obliged to make reparation by a peace offering, a sin offering and a holocaust (Nu. 6:13–20), plus additional sacrifices later (see Sacrifices*).

Sacrificial victims and food offerings were consecrated "holy" things and could be eaten by the priests only under special conditions and in the strictest purity as required of Levites (Lv. 22:2–9). Priests had also to take special care to avoid defilement through contact with a corpse.

Holy War: Warriors taking part in a "holy war" (Nu. 31) were sanctified as "people of Yahweh" and had to be ritually clean. This obligation extended to their camp (see below, Purity among the Dead Sea Sectaries); even the booty which they captured was holy or "ḥerem", not for profane use and reserved for a sacred purpose. Before they could return to normal life, both the warriors and their booty had to be "desecrated" (see above, Uncleanness or Taboo, and below). They had to stay outside the camp for seven days, then, having washed their clothes and immersed their bodies in water, they could re-enter the camp.

Sacrifices: Sacrifices* played an important part in rituals of purification and "desecration" (see article and Priests*).

Ablutions and Washing: Whether or not sacrifices were called for, washing and ablutions were an essential part of purificatory rites. Purity laws prescribed that vessels, clothes or persons defiled by contact with something unclean must be washed in water. In the same way, water must also be used to wash things which had been in contact with something sacred. Meat which had been offered as a sacrifice, for instance, was holy and the metal vessel in which it had been held must be scoured and rinsed, while an earthenware vessel must be broken (Lv. 6:28). Similarly, the High Priest had to change his clothes and wash his body after coming out of the Holy of Holies.

After menstruation, a woman had to purify herself by a ritual bath in "living" (i.e. running) water from a spring or river (the original meaning of the traditional "mikveh"; see below, Post-Exilic Judaism).

Lustral Water and the Ashes of the Red Heifer: The most serious contamination resulted from contact with a corpse. The purificatory ritual in this case required sprinkling the "unclean" with "lustral water", the "water to take away defilement" (mê-niddah), i.e. "living" water to which had been added the ashes of an unblemished red heifer, burned with cedar, hyssop and cochenille (Nu. 19). The colour red and the ashes of a burned animal are regarded by many primitive peoples as possessing magical powers. It seems likely that among the Israelites this ritual was a popular survival from pagan times, incorporated into official religious procedures and existing side by side with them.

The heifer had to burned "outside the camp" according to the text, which attributed the institution to the desert period. In Jerusalem the ceremony was performed on the Mount of Olives and, after it, everybody concerned had to be purified. The ceremony had nothing to do with sacrifices although it was likened to a sacrifice for sin (Nu. 19:17). Later generations found the ceremony incomprehensible and put forward various explanations, such as that the red heifer, whose colour symbolized sin, atoned for the worship of the golden calf in the desert.

Purity in Exilic and post-Exilic Judaism: During and after the Exile, the Jews became increasingly conscious of the laws about purity, as set forth in Lv. 11–16. Fear of contamination became compulsive. Thus the post-Exilic legislators of the Priests' Code (see Leviticus*) multiplied the instances of impurity and prescribed the correct remedy for every case. Past traditions imbedded in the early parts of the Law on purity were integrated into the post-Exilic Levitical system. This priestly material in Leviticus*, therefore, reproduces an Exilic compilation of pre-Exilic theory and practice.

As in the past, the legislators legalized customs and ritual which differentiated the Jewish community from its neighbours and served as a bulwark against pervasive foreign influences.

In post-Exilic times, the ordinary people did not observe the laws of ceremonial purification so carefully. Relics of popular beliefs and magic, current among Israel's neighbours, were to be found even among pious Jews (see Apocrypha*: Tobit 6; Magic*). Their existence before the Exile is attested by Isaiah* 3:3 (see article). The Hassidim*, followed by the Pharisees*, on the other hand, went much further than even the Levitical rules for the purity of priests eating the consecrated food-offering in the Temple (see Law*: Living under the Law). The term "tohorah" came to mean both the purification of the inner community, the special ritual purity of the cultic meals of the Pharisee *ḥaburah* and, above all, a spiritual purity which would transcend material concerns.

Rabbinical Laws: The purity laws were systematized by the Mishnah and Talmud and, later, by Maimonides.

Later Jewish law prescribes that for purification, either running water should be used, or the "mikveh", a basin of prescribed minimum size, filled and re-filled with a prescribed proportion of "living" water. Two such basins were discovered at Qumran (see Dead Sea Scrolls*).

Following the destruction of the Temple, the laws of ritual purification connected with it naturally lapsed, although the use of the "mikveh" by women after menstruation continued. Today the purity laws are kept among pious Jews, 1. by women after menstruation; 2. by Torah scribes; 3. by particularly pious people and mystics, many of whom immerse themselves in the mikveh daily. Such immersion before Sabbath is a widespread custom. Every Jewish community is obliged by law to maintain a mikveh.

Another important aspect discussed in the Mishnah (tractate Yadayim) and still observed today, is the *ritual washing of hands* before prayer and before meals at which bread is eaten. This handwashing has to be performed by pouring water from a vessel twice over each hand. The hands of priests are washed by Levites before the Priestly* blessing.

Tohorah: Pharisee philosophy of purity was expanded in Rabbinic halakhah* and the term "tohorah" came to refer in general to the rules of ritual cleanness. The word is also the name of the sixth and last Order of the Mishnah* which deals with the laws concerning impurity. The "ritual of Papanikri" in Mishnah Yoma 6:8 describes the long and elaborate rite for the purification of a woman after childbirth, reminiscent of the ritual in Leviticus (see above).

A more restricted use of the rabbinic term "tohorah" referred only to the ritual washing of a corpse before burial, itself an ancient Jewish practice (see Funerary Practices*).

Purity among the Dead Sea Sectaries: The attitude of the Dead Sea sectaries towards "tohorah" was very similar to that of the Pharisees, although the sectaries emphasized certain differences in their purificatory rites (see Dead Sea Scrolls*).

"Cleanness of Heart" in the New Testament: In the New Testament, as among the Pharisees and the Dead Sea sectaries, purity is taken to include integrity, singleness of purpose and the absence of base thoughts. It is the spirit of Psalm 51, one of the most moving in the Psalter, in which a sick and sinful man, feeling himself under the censure of God, cries for pardon and expresses his heart-felt penitence. He prays for the cleansing which the Jews obtained by purificatory ritual and vows that if his heart can be cleansed, he will be God's evangelist in all humility.

The rabbis had developed the Pharisaic doctrine of purity in one direction, especially after the destruction of the Temple. The New Testament, on the other hand, developed the spiritual aspect of purity and ritual. The Gospels tell us that Jesus* condemned the scribes and Pharisees for putting "heavy loads upon the necks of other men" (Mt. 23:4) and thereby preventing them from entering the Kingdom of Heaven (23:13). Jesus, in contrast, proclaimed that the only uncleanness which brings defilement is moral uncleanness (Mt. 15:10–20). Jesus placed his main emphasis on motivation and inner conviction, rather than observance of formal rituals. The Pharisees aimed at making both equally important, but that they were not altogether successful can be seen from the fact that the crux of the argument between them and Jesus was, in many ways, over the question of purity.

Jesus, and following him, the New Testament as a whole, believed that "Blessed are the pure in heart, for they shall see God" (Mt. 5:8). If uncontaminated water is pure; if gold straight from the earth, unworked and unstamped, is pure gold, then the heart which gives unquestioning loyalty to the precepts of God is a pure heart.

The Epistle to the Hebrews*, written to Jewish Christians familiar with the Old Testament ceremonial of purification, reminds them that under the New Covenant*, the voluntary sacrifice of the Son of God has superseded all such ritual. The author did not deny that sacrifices had any value at all. He referred to the purificatory rituals described above, but he went further. The blood of Christ had washed away the inward defilement which makes sinful man unfit for the service of the living God (He. 9:13 seq.).

Like the Dead Sea sectaries, many Christians regarded their community as engaged in God's Holy War and they therefore practiced chastity and avoided marriage. Others lived by the basic biblical and Jewish rules governing marriage and sex. The New Testament does not regard sexual intercourse as such as impure, provided it takes place within the bounds of morality.

INCARNATION (God in Human Form). — The Christian religion bases itself upon belief in Jesus Christ as both God and man. The original and lasting foundation of Christianity is faith in the apostolic record of Jesus' birth, life and death, and particularly his own consciousness of a special relationship to God. For Christians, in Jesus the man, God was made flesh. To examine the credibility of this belief is not the historian's task. What he can do is to trace its origins in the New Testament record of the unique manner in which Jesus came into the world and left it (see Resurrection*; Immortality*).

Jesus' Birth: The Gospels of Matthew and Luke do not raise any metaphysical questions about Jesus' supernatural birth, simply reporting that he was conceived by a virgin through a supernatural creative act of God, without the intervention of a human father. Jesus is thus the "Son of God", although Christian faith is not dependent on the virgin birth. The Evangelists thought they would strengthen their case by giving a genealogical table which traces Jesus' descent from David and Abraham, through Joseph, since the Messiah had to be of Davidic descent. This genealogy is unrelated to the story of the virgin birth. The genealogy is connected with the descent from David, while the virgin birth is connected with the messianic sign of Is. 7:14. The Evangelists or editors ignored the fact that the virgin birth contradicts the descent from David.

Expectations of the Messiah and his coming (see Jesus*) took a variety of different forms. Basically, the concept was of a Davidic Messiah, whose personality would combine divine and human attributes. The Synoptic Gospels* show Jesus as morally the Perfect Man. They also credit him with divine attributes. The first Apostles looked no further. Later it may have appeared to Paul and John the Evangelist, and then to Gentile Christians, that messianic expectations could not be fulfilled, nor divine attributes be present without an incarnation. From this developed the idea of a pre-existent divine being who had come into the world, although Matthew and Luke did not have this conception,

The fabled incarnations of pagan religions are probably no more than expressions of a general human longing for union with the divine. In Christianity, incarnation becomes fundamental.

Earliest New Testament Interpretations: The disciples had recognized Jesus as Messiah even before his death. The Resurrection* transformed their faith in him and it became the central pivot of their teaching. The Jews in general found it very difficult to accept Jesus as both God and man and even the New Testament is not altogether clear on the point. The basis of the difficulty lay in recognizing him as Messiah and in accepting the resurrection. It records the early stages of interpretation. It is not really surprising that there was no generally accepted, consistent picture and that different levels of Christological belief can be distinguished.

Apostolic Teaching and Paul: When the Apostles began their missionary work among the Gentiles, the constant repetition of the events of Jesus' life and the teaching they based upon it naturally had an effect upon their own thought. Gradually, they abandoned the idea that the incarnation had been merely a preliminary to a future, more important manifestation.

The apostolic teachers and especially Paul did not spend time and energy on the manner of Christ's appearance on earth, but on its meaning. If Jesus was the Son of God, then he had come to earth from heaven in a manner and at a time deliberately chosen by God for his own purpose. In Paul's earlier Epistles, he speaks of Christ from the personal point of view of one with whom God had achieved a reconciliation and who had bridged the gulf fixed by sin between God and man. The later Epistles and the Epistle to the Hebrews deal with a more mystical aspect of Incarnation.

A pre-existent Christ takes the place of a returning Christ. With the completion of the Incarnation, Christ "sits at the right hand of God" who had already "put all things under his feet" (Eph. 1:20, 22).

For Paul, Christ had fulfilled the purpose of humanity, and thus of the universe, as its first and final cause. However, Christ's coming had not completed the work of the Incarnation.

The Church and the Mystical Body of Christ: Christ had left the completion of his work to his church, the community to which he had promised the Holy Spirit as the extension of his own personality. The Church, he had said, is my body. It represented the Kingdom of Heaven which had already come and was still to come, preparing for that second "coming in glory".

John: The transition to a cosmological and mystical view of Incarnation is completed in John. He had to bridge the gulf which existed between the Jewish-Christianity of Jerusalem in the middle of the 1st c. CE and the Platonic Hellenism of Ephesus and the surrounding world at the end of the century. John attempted to place Christianity in this different world, and to do so he recast the story of Jesus into allegorical and symbolic forms that would resolve the difficulties raised by Greek philosophical speculation. The Christ of history was transfigured by the light of the Christ of faith and became something new.

"The Word Was Made Flesh": The Hebrew concept of the "word" goes back to Genesis where the agent of creation was the "word" (dabar) of God, which had been in existence from the beginning. Under the influence of Stoic (Hellenic) thought (see Hellenism in the Near East*), Philo and the Alexandrian Jewish philosophers modified this idea to the concept of the "logos" (word) as both God's actual creative power and the mechanism through which it worked. John* went beyond this to reach a conception of Christ as the "word" or "logos" made flesh. In the prologue to the fourth Gospel, Christ is described as acting as the creative "word" before and during creation. The Evangelist conceives of Jesus as the "word" incarnate, "planting his tent among ours", to become palpable to humans. In this description, John goes back to the earlier style, thus personalizing an abstract conception.

John makes no mention whatever of a second coming. He does refer to a final judgment and the implication is that Christ will be the judge at the end. John proclaims that "he who has the Son has life" (5:12). This is not something postponed to another world or Apocalyptic* New Age. The life the believer has, he has now. It is still to be lived in time, although in a new dimension.

This "new life in Christ" became the centre of Christian preaching, other aspects being allowed to fall into the background until the apostolic writings were established as a new sacred canon of Scripture, sometime during the 2nd c. CE.

In sum, from the New Testament and the teachings of the Church fathers, belief in Incarnation seems to have the following history: For the Christian, the End of Days had already been inaugurated with the coming of the Messiah. At the same time, Paul had so stressed the sense of the sinfulness of man that a merely human mediation in a New Covenant* no longer seemed sufficient. God himself must become man and by atoning for man's sins, sign a New Covenant with his own blood. The method by which this purpose was accomplished was the Incarnation — the eternal son of God became the man, Jesus of Nazareth, the mediator and messiah for mankind (see also Christianity, Early*).

INSCRIPTIONS. — *Outline: I. Texts Relating to the History of Palestine, before the Hebrew Settlement. II. Alphabetic Inscriptions prior to the Hebrew Conquest. III. Inscriptions of the Israelite Period (Monarchy): A. Egyptian and Accadian Inscriptions; B. Hebrew Inscriptions. IV. Hebrew and Aramaic Inscriptions — Period of the Second Temple. V. Greek Inscriptions (Graeco-Roman Period).*

Until about one hundred years ago, students of the biblical age were dependent for information on the Bible and on a small number of books preserved in Christian monasteries, such as the writings of Josephus* and the Onomastikon (place-list) of Eusebius. Since then, developments in archaeology have revealed a whole range of inscriptions from the countries of the Fertile Crescent, namely texts of a public or private nature executed by craftsmen. The texts relating to public matters record laws, treaties, decrees etc, while those of a private nature are chiefly memorial or dedicatory. These texts have greatly increased our knowledge of the history of the ancient Near East and early Israel.

Inscriptions are more valuable from this point of view than manuscripts. Documents were transmitted from hand to hand, and were often "edited" or reformulated by the scribes who copied them. On the other hand, an inscription unearthed in an archaeological excavation is an original source, untouched (provided it has not become too eroded) by the hands and therefore the ideas of a later age. Inscriptions may, however, be copies, with errors or variant readings. Nevertheless, they are generally historical documents of the greatest importance, and this is especially true, for the biblical scholar, of the few rare, short Hebrew inscriptions which have been uncovered, many of which were not executed by craftsmen as elsewhere in the ancient Near East (see below).

I. TEXTS RELATING TO THE HISTORY OF PALESTINE, BEFORE THE HEBREW SETTLEMENT: The earliest texts date from the end of the 4th mill. BCE, but written information about Palestine is only found from the beginning of the 2nd mill. BCE. The first known references occur in two collections of writings found in Egypt, known as the Execration Texts, which date from the 20th and 19th cs. BCE. The Egyptians used to inscribe the names of enemy tribes, towns and rulers on clay figurines or vessels and then break the clay in a symbolic act intended to ensure the Pharaoh's victory over the enemy named. The cities of Ashkelon, Jerusalem, Aphek, Acre, Mash'al, Achshaph Tyre and others are named in these texts (see **403**).

One phase of the story of Joseph has also been illustrated from texts of 19th c. BCE Egypt. Genesis 37:25 records that Joseph's brothers "saw a caravan of Ishmaelites coming from Gilead, with their camels bearing gum, balm, and myrrh, on their way to carry it down to Egypt." Part of a painting from the tomb at Beni Hasan shows just such a scene (see Exodus*). A hieroglyphic inscription accompanying the picture refers to 37 men of the Ammu tribe headed by Absha (Abishai?), ruler of a foreign country, bringing antimony, used as eye make-up, to Egypt (see **326**; Patriarchs*).

There are very few inscriptions with any bearing on the Patriarchal period, although the name Yakub-har or Yakub-el appears among the scarabs of the Hyksos kings (see Seals*). This has been interpreted as support for the theory that the Patriarchs reached Palestine with the first wave of the Hyksos migration at the end of the 18th or beginning of the 17th c. BCE.

There is nothing in the Bible about the beginning of the New Empire in Egypt*, following the end of the Hyksos period. The only evidence cames from archaeological finds. From inscriptions left by the Egyptian kings of this period, it is known that they campaigned in Canaan from time to time, to keep the city-states of that country under their domination. Thutmoses III listed 119 cities and towns which he had captured in Canaan and Syria, thus recording the names of the important cities of 15th c. BCE Palestine. This Pharaoh gave a fairly detailed account of his victorious campaign (see Megiddo*). Following the Via Maris (the road to the sea), his army captured Megiddo which was at the head of a coalition of rebellious Canaanite cities. After this victory, the other cities in the north of the country, especially those in the valleys, lay open to him. Other Pharaohs also engaged in campaigns to maintain their sovereignty over Canaan, the corridor to their great rivals in the north, the Hittites and Mitanni. Information about the campaigns of Amenhotep II, Seti I and Ramses II is also contained in the inscriptions they had carved on monuments, palaces and tombs. The archives of Amenhotep III and Amenhotep IV (Akhenaton) discovered in Tel el-Amarna* also yielded many details about political conditions in Canaan during the period before the settlement there of the tribes of Israel (see Amarna Letters*; Seals*).

It is now agreed that the Habiru* mentioned in the ancient Near East records can be identified with the Hebrews of the early biblical period. The Amarna letters may serve as proof of an early (14th c. BCE) penetration of Hebrew tribes into Canaan, as the first in a chain of invasions which continued to the end of the 13th c. BCE.

The stele of Mernephtach, dating to about 1220 BCE, testified to the appearance of the Israelites as a compact tribal unit at that time. This stele contains the following lines: "Canaan is pillaged, Ashkelon captured, Gezer is seized, Janoam as if it never existed, Israel is desolate, it has no offspring" (see Exodus*).

Compared with the discoveries made in Egypt and Mesopotamia, few inscriptions of the pre-Israelite settlement period have been found in Palestine, but these few are of great historical importance. Clay tablets found in the excavations of Ta'anach supplement the information derived from the Amarna letters. The tablets hint at the social system of 15th c. BCE Canaanite cities. The Canaanite king, Ishtar-Yashur of Ta'anach, a vassal of the Egyptian governor residing in Gaza, was supported by a large class of ministers and officials. The tablets refer to the "hanikîm" (trained men), also mentioned in Gn. 14:14: "... he (Abram) armed his trained men, born in his own house ..." These "hanikîm" were the king's young dependents, a kind of select partisan army. The personal names appearing in the Ta'anach tablets bear witness to the ethnic composition of the country's population at that time. Among others, the Hurrians who are known to have lived in Canaan (Gn. 36:20) are prominently mentioned (see Patriarchs*).

In addition to the dozen tablets found in Ta'anach, similar tablets written in cuneiform were discovered in the excavations of Shechem*, Gezer*, Eglon (Tel el-Hesi), Jericho* and Megiddo*. The tablets of Gezer and Tel el-Hesi are similar in content to those of the Amarna letters. In Megiddo, a broken piece of a tablet containing a fragment of the Gilgamesh epic was discovered, quite by accident (see Flood*).

The Pharaohs of the new Egyptian kingdom also erected their stele and monuments in the cities of Canaan. In Beth-Shean*, two stele of Seti I were preserved, one of which describes the events which led to Seti I's capture of Beth-Shean and the neighbouring towns from the king of Phahl (Pella) and his allies who had revolted against their Egyptian rulers. A stele fragment from the time of Thutmoses III or Amenhotep II was discovered at Tel el-Ureimeh, on the shores of the lake of Galilee (see map **78**).

Dozens of short hieroglyphic inscriptions on the scarabs of various Egyptian kings were also discovered in the tels of Palestine. A clay dish, assembled from fragments found in the layer of ashes in the ruins of Canaanite Lachish*, is of great importance in helping to determine the date of the town's capture by the Hebrew conquerors. On the dish, something like a receipt or consignment note for a quantity of wheat sent in the fourth year of the reign of an unnamed king, is inscribed in Egyptian hieratic (cursive) writing. It may be assumed that the king in question was the Pharaoh Mernephtach, and the date is therefore about 1220 BCE, which is thus the latest possible date for the destruction of Canaanite Lachish (cf. Conquest*: Campaign in Centr. Canaan).

II. ALPHABETIC INSCRIPTIONS PRIOR TO THE HEBREW CONQUEST: A settlement of mine workers established by the Egyptian Pharaohs of the 2nd mill. BCE was excavated in the Sinai desert at Serabit el-Khadem. Stele and monuments bearing inscriptions were discovered such as the one inscribed "*lb'lt*" (which reads, with inserted vowels, "to Ba'alat"; see illus. under Alphabet and Writing*). It has been noted that the number of letters used in this Sinaitic script is not more than forty, that is to say, they are symbols of sounds, i.e. alphabetic symbols representing single phonemes, as against pictographic, ideographic and syllabic writing. Scholars call this writing Proto-Sinaitic script. It is highly possible that in the 16th–15th cs. BCE, the people of Serabit el-Khadem who invented the earliest alphabet, influenced by Egyptian hieratic symbols, were enslaved by the Egyptians. The language of these slaves was, in all probability, a variety of west Semitic, i.e. a dialect of Canaanite with south Arabic affinities (see Language*). It seems that they worshipped a goddess named Ba'alat, whose name they inscribed on carved images.

Another alphabetical text was discovered in the excavations of Ugarit*. It is assumed that the priests of the Ugarit temple in the 15th and 14th cs. BCE were familiar with the forms of the Proto-Sinaitic characters, but they adjusted the alphabetic principle to their system of impressing the various symbols in soft clay with a stylus (see Alphabet*). The Ugaritic cuneiform script has no connection with the cuneiform scripts of Mesopotamia, except insofar as it was impressed with a stylus in wet clay. In addition to the large library unearthed in Ugarit* (see article), two other objects inscribed in a version of Ugaritic cuneiform alphabetic script were discovered in Palestine: 1. A knife was found in Wadi Bireh in lower Galilee, inscribed with the name of its owner (the inscription is consonantal as no vowels were then used). It reads: "*lṣ (l) b'l bn plzb' l*" (belonging to, or to zalba'al, son of plzba'al). 2. The clay mould of an axe-blade was discovered in Beth-Shemesh, but the inscription on it is indecipherable.

About ten inscriptions in alphabetic writing, dating from the 2nd mill. BCE and bearing only single characters, have been found in Palestine. Although there are many variations in the characters of these inscriptions, which cover a long period of time, the 18th to the 13th cs. BCE, they are all in Proto-Canaanite writing. A list of the most important of these inscriptions is given below in chronological order: 1. an inscription on a stone plaque from Shechem called, according to one suggestion, "*rḥmmyrḥ*," i.e. a plea for mercy from the god *yrḥ* (18th–17th c. BCE); 2. an ostracon from Gezer; the accepted reading is "*klb*", meaning unknown (17th–16th c. BCE); 3. a bronze dagger from Lachish bearing the letters "*prls*", untranslatable (16th–15th c. BCE); 4. an ostracon from Tel el-Hesi: *bl'* (14th–13th cs. BCE); 5. an ostracon from Beth-Shemesh which is not fully decipherable, but the last word is *ḥnn* (14th–13th cs. BCE); 6. an ostracon from Tel el-Sarm in the Beth-Shean valley; indecipherable except for a few characters (13th c. BCE); 7. an inscription on a pitcher from Lachish on which two words are decipherable: "*mtn 'lt*" (13th c. BCE). This is probably a votive inscription. 8. an inscription on a bowl from Lachish inscribed "*bšlšt*" (13th c. BCE; illus. given under Alphabet and Writing*).

Insofar as these inscriptions are decipherable, their language is Semitic-Canaanite. The names *klb* and *ḥnn* are also Canaanite. *prls* appears to be the name of a person of non-Semitic origin.

III. INSCRIPTIONS OF THE ISRAELITE PERIOD (MONARCHY). — **A. Egyptian and Accadian Inscriptions:** These provide many important details to supplement the information in the Bible on the period of the First Temple. Only a few examples of the documents can be noted here.

One very significant discovery was the inscription of the Egyptian king, Shishak (ca. 835–914 BCE), on the temple of Karnak (see Egypt*). Shishak (Shoshenk) campaigned in Israel in the fifth year of the reign of Rehoboam, king of Judah (I K. 14:25–26; II Ch. 12:2–9). His list of conquered cities confirms the account in II Ch. 12 (especially verses 4 and 7) that Jerusalem was not captured, the Egyptian being satisfied with a heavy tribute from the Temple treasures including Solomon's gold shields. Shishak began with the conquest of Gaza, went from there to Gezer, then to Ayalon,

Beth-Horon and Gibeon, north of Jerusalem, thence to the towns of the Jordan valley.

Ahab, king of Israel, appears in an inscription of Shalmaneser III as one of the leaders of an anti-Assyrian coalition. In the mid-9th c. BCE, the growing menace from Assyrian imperialism forced the kings of Syria and Palestine to join forces in an attempt to stem the tide. The king of Aram-Damascus and Ahab, king of Israel, who had hitherto been enemies, appear at the head of the alliance which faced Shalmaneser at the battle of Qarqar in 853 BCE. Ahab contributed 2,000 chariots and 10,000 foot soldiers, the strongest single contingent. Another inscription dated 12 years after Qarqar refers to Jehu as among the Near Eastern kings paying tribute to Shalmaneser.

None of these events is mentioned, even obliquely, in the Bible. However, there is biblical evidence (II K. 15:29) for the campaign of Tiglat-Pileser III in 732 BCE, which, again, is supplemented by an Assyrian epigraphic inscription, in addition to others which this king made about Palestine, dealing with events related in the Bible.

Sargon II was later to claim the capture of Samaria in 722 BCE, though the event is related to an unnamed king in the Bible (see Assyria*, Part IV). The same is true of the devastation of Sennacherib's campaign against Judah. After reducing the coastal towns of Sidon (Phoenicia) and capturing Jaffa, Sennacherib made a victorious progress through the country, and seized Azor, Bnei-Berak, Beth-Dagon, Eltekeh, Timnah and Ekron in addition to forty fortified towns in Judah (701 BCE). This Assyrian inscription goes on to describe how Sennacherib locked Hezekiah in Jerusalem "like a bird in a cage", but it says nothing about the fate of Jerusalem which (II K. 18:17–35) withstood the Assyrian assault and the persuasions of Rabshakeh. Sennacherib based his general staff in Lachish. This is confirmed in the Bible and also in the reliefs showing the capture of Lachish which were unearthed in the excavations of Nineveh, Sennacherib's capital (for illustrations, see Israel and Judah*; Lachish* under Ancient Cities*).

B. Hebrew Inscriptions: A number of inscriptions written in the biblical idiom, mainly by Israelites, have been discovered in Palestine:

1. At El-Khadr, near Bethlehem, three bronze javelin heads, each inscribed "*ḥṣ. ʿbdlbʾt*" were discovered (see Alphabet and Writing*). From paleographic comparisons, these arrowheads were dated to the 12th c. BCE, by which time the Hebrews were already settled in the country. Nevertheless, it cannot be definitely stated that these javelin heads (*ḥṣ* in Canaanite or Hebrew) had been the property of an Israelite, since the writing and language were common to all the peoples who lived in the western part of the Fertile Crescent. The owner of the javelin bears the title *ʿbd* (servant), meaning an officer of Labat who was apparently a local ruler. This seems to indicate the existence of a mercenary archer class in Canaan and Israel. Writing an owner's name on his arrows was in all probability common practice in Canaan and Syria. In Byblos, metal blades bearing indecipherable inscriptions were found, and recently an arrowhead was discovered in the Lebanon valley bearing an inscription beginning with the words "*ḥṣ zkrbʿl*." This may be dated to the 11th c. BCE.

2. **The Gezer Agricultural Calendar:** In the Gezer excavations, a list of the various agricultural seasons was found, inscribed in early Hebrew characters in seven lines on a piece of soft limestone, 7 × 10 cm. in size (10th c. BCE. For illustration and explanation, see Agriculture*: Seasonal Calendar.)

3. The Mesha stone was erected by the Moabite king of that name (illustration and evaluation of inscription under Moab*).

4. **Samarian Ostraca:** The excavation of Samaria in 1908–1910 CE uncovered ostraca with Hebrew inscriptions written in ink, in the storerooms of the king's palace. The text of these writings is very short and includes the date (year of the king's reign), a place, name of a person, and a quantity (wine or oil). For instance: "*bšt htšʿt myṣt lʾhnwʿm (n)bl yʾ(n) yšn*". This means, "In the ninth year of (an unnamed) king of Israel, a jar of old wine belonging to Ahinoam was brought". Another text states: "*bšt hʿšrt mḥṣrt lgdyw nbl šmn rḥṣ;* that is to say, "In the tenth year, Gadyaû of Hatzerôth brought as a tax payment a jar of oil for ointment."

These ostraca (**527-8**), it can be seen, were delivery notes or copies of receipts for the taxes in kind brought to the king from various villages in the Northern Kingdom. From them, information about the system of tax collection in the kingdom can be gained, as well as some knowledge of the language of the Israelites of the Ephraim mountains of that period. The word "*št*" (year) is also used in the Moabite dialect (see Moab*). The expression *šmn rḥṣ* does not appear in the Bible, and the reference is probably to some kind of high grade olive oil. The theophoric names such as Gadyaû, Yedayaû, Abyaû, Obadayû, Shmaryaû are based on the element "*yw*" (Yaû, Yahu and Yahweh are synonymous.) This is not a different dialect, as the same form is found in the Jerusalem seals, in addition to "*lʾbyw ʿbd ʿzyw*" (see Samaria*). At one time, scholars ascribed the Samaria ostraca to the time of Ahab or Jeroboam II, but now it is generally assumed that they are from the time of Menahem ben Gadi (see Israel and Judah*; Part II).

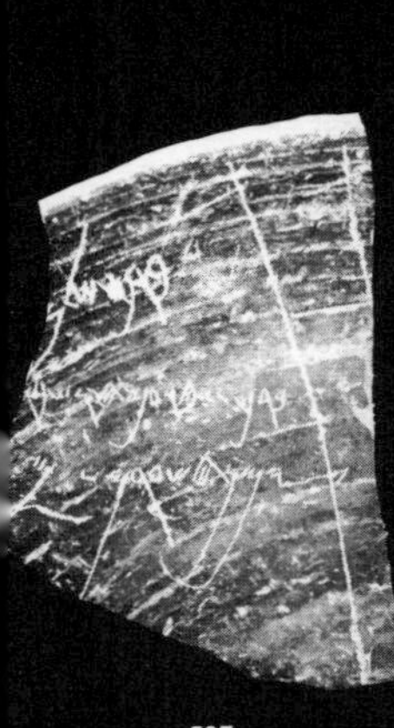
527

528

529

530

531

532

5. **Tel Kasileh Ostraca:** The two ostraca (**529-30**) found at Tel Kasileh belong to about the same period. The town on the site, a port of the Northern Kingdom on the estuary of the Yarkon River, was destroyed in 732 BCE in the campaign of Tiglat-Pileser III. The ostraca must therefore have preceded that date. These, too, are certificates of the shipment of quantities of oil and gold sent through this port to Phoenicia or Egypt. Unlike the Samaria ostraca (written with ink), those of Tel Kasileh are incised. One of them reads, "*lmlk 'lf šmn wm'h* (')*ḥyhw*", which means that 1100 measures of oil were sent either from the royal treasury, or confirmed by a government port official named Ahiyahu. The second inscription reads: "*zhb 'fyr lbyt ḥrn* (—)*š* ≡", i.e. "thirty shekels of Ophir gold (of fine quality) from Beth-Horon", perhaps from the house of the god Horon (**530**).

6. **The Siloam Inscription:** In 1880 CE, an inscription was discovered engraved in the wall of the tunnel connecting the waters of the Shiloah (Siloam) spring east of Jerusalem* to the fortified citadel itself (see article). The inscription, like the tunnel itself, is ascribed to Hezekiah, king of Judah. According to II Kings (20:20), "he made the pool and the conduit, and brought water into the city . . .". II Chronicles (32:30) gives some additional details: "This same Hezekiah closed the upper outlet of the waters of Giḥon and directed them down to the west side of the city of David." The project was part of the fortification of Jerusalem carried out before Sennacherib's siege of the city. The reality of the Assyrian danger is confirmed both by the Bible and the Sennacherib inscription. The Siloam inscription (**532**) gives an account of the cutting made. In translation, it reads: ". . . when the tunnel was driven through. And this was

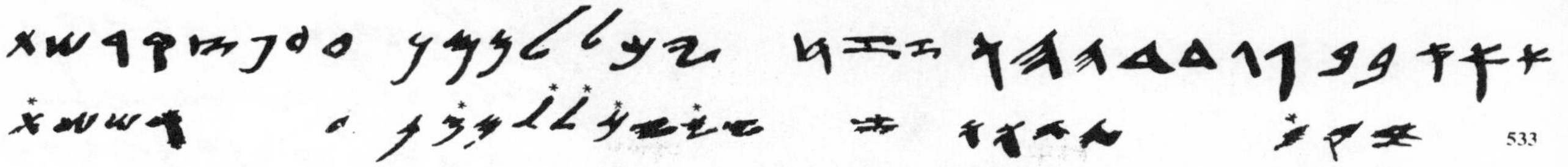

533

the way in which it was cut through: — While . . . were still . . . axes, each man toward his fellow, and while there were still three cubits to be cut through, there was heard the voice of a man calling to his fellow, for there was an overlap in the rock on the right and on the left. And when the tunnel was driven through, the quarrymen hewed the rock, each man toward his fellow, axe against axe; and the water flowed from the spring toward the reservoir for 1,200 cubits, and the height of the rock above the heads of the quarrymen was 100 cubits." (ANET. 321)

Unlike the Mesha stone, the Siloam inscription is not intended to glorify the king for his achievement. Rather it expresses the excitement of the quarrymen and their joy at the successful accomplishment of the work: "there was heard the voice of a man calling to his fellow." The day the final break-through was made was called "tunnel day". With emotion, the inscription tells us that the tunnel was 1,200 cubits long, and 100 cubits below the rock surface. This was actually a fine engineering achievement for those early times with remarkable precision in boring from opposite ends, and it fully justified the boastful words of the inscription (see Water Supply*).

7 **The Shebanayahu Funerary Inscription:** In the village of Siloam east of Jerusalem, three funerary inscriptions from the time of the First Temple were discovered. Paleographic research shows that they belong to a period close to that of King Hezekiah (see Israel and Judah*). One of these, called the Shebnayahu inscription (**531**), begins:

1 – *zwt (kbwrt . . .) yhw 'šr 'l hbyt. 'n pw ksf wzhb*
2 – *ky 'm ('ṣmtw) w'ṣmt 'mth 'th. 'rwr h'dm 'šr*
3 – *yftḥ 't zwt*

In the opinion of Professor H. Avigad of the Hebrew University, the inscription may be translated: "This is the sepulchre of . . . iahû who is over the house. There is no silver and no gold here, but only (his bones) and the bones of his handmaiden with him. Cursed is the man who will open this (sepulchre)".

The owner of the grave was a man of high standing, apparently the government official who was "over the house". This phrase is so reminiscent of Isaiah 22:15–16: "Come, go to this steward to Shebna, who is over the household, and say to him: What have you to do here and whom have you here, that you have hewn here a tomb for yourself, you who hew a tomb on the height, and carve a habitation for yourself in the rock?" that it is very tempting to fill in the missing (indecipherable) name in the inscription with that of Shebnayahu, who was a contemporary of Hezekiah. However, this cannot be done with any real certainty. The curse on "the man who will open this grave" refers to the robbers who used to violate tombs in search of precious objects buried with the dead.

One of the other two inscriptions found at Siloam includes a fragment similar to the above inscription. The third inscription reads: "*hdr bktf hṣr*" . . ., i.e. a burial chamber in a cave hewn in the sloping rock. The use of the word *ktf* for the slope of a mountain or hill is quite common in the Bible, for example, Nu. 34:11; Jos. 15:8; Is. 11:14.

8. **The Tomb Graffiti:** The inscriptions dating from the time of the First Temple, mentioned above and also below, are secular in content. In 1961 CE, however, graffiti (engravings in the rock) in the ancient Hebrew alphabet, with a definite religious content, were discovered in a burial cave 8 km. east of Tel Lachish. These inscriptions were typical of the period of the First Temple. The expression "Yahweh, Lord of the World" was found here. The name *yršlm* (Jerusalem) also appears for the first time in a Hebrew inscription of the era of the First Temple. One of the walls of the cave was engraved with two verses in a poetic metre, reminiscent of the Psalms. It seems that these graffiti were made by at least three different people, who happened to meet in the cave. The inscriptions have not yet been completely deciphered, nor have they appeared in any scientific publication, but they can apparently be ascribed to the days of Hezekiah.

9. **An Early Papyrus from Murabba'at:** Because of the moist climate of most of the country, organic writing materials like parchment or papyrus have rotted away over the centuries and the only inscriptions discovered in excavations have been those engraved on stone or written on pottery (ostraca). Recently, however, among the wealth of material from the time of Bar-Kochba* discovered in a cave of Wadi Murabba'at near the Dead Sea, a papyrus was found written in Hebrew and apparently dating from the 8th c. BCE. This is what is known as a palimpsest, i.e. later writing has been superimposed upon an earlier text. Because of the high cost of papyrus, it was often used twice or more in this way. In this case, only two lines of the original text are decipherable and these suggest that the piece of papyrus was part of a long letter. The later writing is a list of four personal names with symbols and figures (possibly representing quantities; see **533**).

10. **Matzad Hashabyahu (Yabneh-Yam) Ostraca. Tale of a Tunic:** In 1960 CE, during the excavation of an ancient fort named Matzad Hashabyahu (on the sea coast south of Yabneh-Yam) six ostraca and an inscription engraved on a fragment of a jar were discovered. The ceramic materials provide evidence that the fortress was built and inhabitted in the last third of the 7th c. BCE. The Hebrew is biblical in style and the contents of the ostraca, which include names with the theophoric element "yahû", make it highly probable that this area had been captured by Josiah, king of Judah (ca. 628–627 BCE), a fact not previously known.

The most important ostracon discovered in Matzad Hashabyahu is a fourteen line Hebrew letter (reproduced below, **534**) unearthed in the guard room at the gate of the fort. The beginning of the letter reads: "*yšm' 'dny hsr 't dbr 'bdh*" (compare this with . . . "let my lord the king hear the words of his servant" in I Sam. 26:19). In the letter, written at harvest time, a poor peasant complains to the officer in charge of his distress at losing his cloak, and begs for its return. From the letter, a sufficiently realistic picture can be reconstructed: The peasant was harvesting in the king's fields near an unwalled agricultural settlement

534

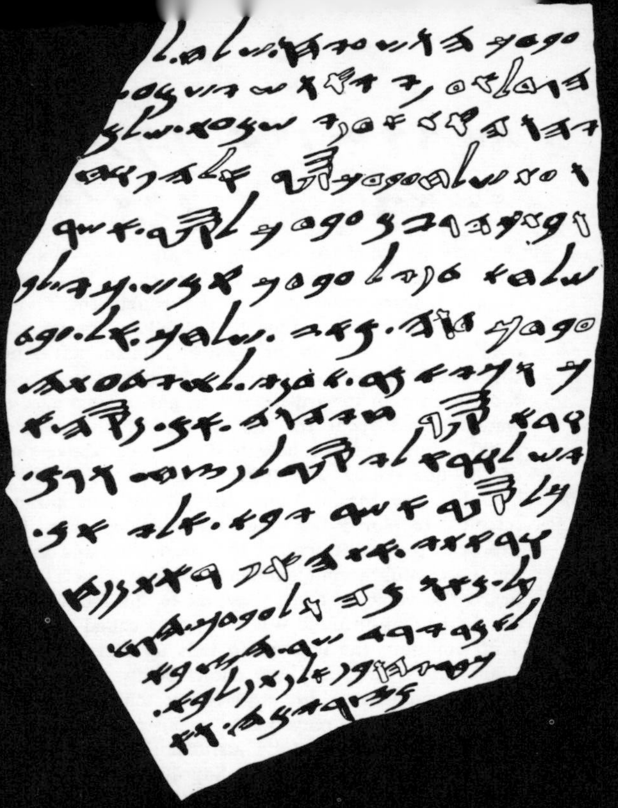

535

named Hatzar Asam. He came to the officer in the fort, who was the administrative chief of the newly conquered area as well as commanding officer of the fort, to complain that his coat had been unjustly confiscated. The official in charge of supervising work in the fields (which, according to custom, had been added to the crown lands) had suspected him of stopping work before he had fulfilled his quota and had therefore taken the coat. Seizure of a garment in payment of an unpaid debt was common practice (see Ex. 22:26, 27; Dt. 24:10–14; Pr. 20:16; 27:13; Am. 2:8). However, the garment of a peasant was "his only covering, it is his mantle for his body; in what else shall he sleep?" (Ex. 22:27) and it must therefore be returned to him "before the sun goes down". The peasant felt that he had been wronged, for he claims that he had completed his quota, and he sought the protection to which the law entitled him. Apparently he appeared at the gate of the fort at nightfall and asked to see the officer. When his request was refused, he dictated his appeal to a scribe at the gate — who probably formulated the opening sentence in the third person (*'bdh* — his servant) and then wrote down the peasant's own words, "*'bdk*" — "your servant" in the second person singular; it recurs seven times in the body of the letter (**534**).

11. In 1924, an ostracon written in ink was discovered in the Ophel (pre-Israelite Jerusalem) excavations. The writing is very blurred, but attempts to decipher it revealed a list of the names of individuals and their ancestors: "*hzkyhw bn krh bn šrš? b(n) bkyhw*", and so forth. The purpose of the list is not clear. From the paleographic point of view, the letters of the ostracon are similar to those of the Lachish ostraca, which date from the last days of the First Temple.

12. **The Lachish Ostraca:** In the excavations of Tel Duweir, identified with biblical Lachish, about twenty ostraca were discovered in a room near the gate of the city. Apart from a list of names similar to the Ophel ostracon, most of these ostraca were letters sent to Yaush, the commander of the garrison of Lachish, who was in charge of the district in the southwestern part of the Shephelah coastal plain. The writer of the letters (**535**) is Hoshayahu, one of the subordinates of Yaush, who was in charge of the garrision of one of the provincial towns on the road from Lachish to Jerusalem. Hoshayahu writes to his commander very humbly; after the conventional greetings at the beginning of the letter: "May Yahweh cause my lord to hear tidings of peace", the polite salutation to a superior. "What is thy servant but a dog?" (in lieu of the modern "your obedient servant") appears frequently. This is reminiscent of the words of Mephibosheth to David in II Sam. 9:8: "What is your servant, that you should look upon a dead dog such as I am?" Five of the letters can be satisfactorily deciphered, and from them it appears that the correspondence deals mainly with two subjects: Yaush accuses Hoshayahu of spying into secret letters sent from Jerusalem to the commander of Lachish, and even of disclosing their contents to others. Hoshayahu denies this (in the third ostracon): "*ḥy. (Y)HWH. 'm. nsh. yš lqr'. ly spr. lnṣḥ. wgm. kl. spr. 'šr. yb'. 'ly. 'm. qr'ty. 'th. (')w. qr't. nkḥ. kl. m'wm(h)*", and he repeats this oath in another letter: "*(w't) ḥy. YHWH 'lhyk k(y—–) yqr' 'bdk '(t) hspr wlw hhn lwmr (dbr m)nhw.*" This is translated, ". . . as Yahweh liveth no one hath ever undertaken to call a scribe for me, and as for any scribe who might have come to me, truly I did not call him nor would I give anything at all for him ."

The second subject of this letter is the activity of an unnamed prophet who apparently counsels peace with Babylonia. The words: "And it hath been reported to thy servant, saying, 'The commander of the army, Koniahu, son of Elnathan, hath come down in order to go into Egypt; and Hodoyahu, son of Ahijahu and his men he sent to take from here . . .' " meaning that the king sent his men to bring the prophet back, perhaps refer to the same event as the one mentioned by the prophet Jeremiah in his story of King Jehoiakim and the prophet Uriyahu of Kiryat-Jearim (Jer. 26:20–24). Following is one of the letters (4th ostracon) in full which reads:

"May Yahweh cause my lord to hear this very day tidings of good! And now according to everything that my lord hath written, so hath thy servant done: I have written on the door according to all that my lord hath written to me. And with respect to what my lord hath written about the matter of Beth-haraphid, there is no one there. And as for Semachiah, Shemaiah hath taken him and hath brought him up to the city. And as for thy servant, I am not sending anyone thither today, but I will send tomorrow morning. And let my lord know that we are watching for the signals of Lachish, according to all the indications which my lord hath given, for we cannot see Azekah." (ANET. 322)

Hoshayahu informs Yaush that his orders have been carried out, and reports on what is going on in his sector. The last lines of the letter apparently refer to the time described in Jer. 34:7: ". . . when the army of the king of Babylon was fighting against Jerusalem, and against all the cities of Judah that were left, Lachish and Azekah; for these were the only fortified cities of Judah that remained." Hoshayahu's report that he cannot see Azekah (i.e. that the town had fallen) shows that his letter was written later than the period referred to in the biblical verse.

Written while Judah was fighting its last battles against the invading Nebuchadrezzar, these letters are the last Hebrew inscriptions of the period of the First Temple.

13. In addition to the above, a number of other short Hebrew inscriptions have also been discovered. At Hazor, (**534a**) potsherds of jars were found engraved (one written in ink) with the names of their owners: "*lmkbrm ldlyw* or *lpkh smdr*" The last inscription includes a description of the jar's contents. "*smdr*" was apparently a kind of wine. In the excavations of Gibeon, jars with the town's name, "*gbʿn*" (**535a**) engraved on their handles were found. A fragment of a stone stele engraved with the word "*ašr*" (**536**) was found at Samaria.

Among other finds at Lachish was a jar engraved "*bt lmlk*". "Bat" was a liquid measure and the addition of the word "*lmlk*" (to the king) suggests that this jar was an official measure or that its contents had been officially confirmed. The engraving had the same meaning as the royal seal stamped on the handles of jars (see below). Weights inscribed with the words "*nṣf bqʿ*" or "*pym*" are common for commercial currency (see Weights and Measures*).

Seals* inscribed in Hebrew are described in that article.

IV. HEBREW AND ARAMAIC INSCRIPTIONS. PERIOD OF THE SECOND TEMPLE: Hebrew seals* of the Persian period do not differ in any important respect from those of the time of the First Temple. In most cases,

534 a

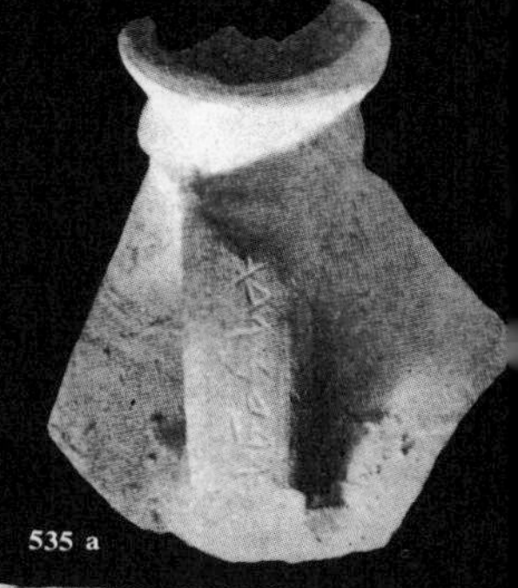

535 a

536

they differ from the earlier seals only in their writing. The royal seal stamps of this period contain the word "*yhd*" (y^{e}hud, **537**, sometimes shortened to "*yah*", the Aramaic term for the Persian satrapy of Judah. Towards the end of the Persian period, jar handles were stamped with the letters "*yrslm*" surrounding a five pointed star (**537:4**). The stamps bearing the word *m(w)ṣh*, it should be noted, indicate that jars thus stamped contained wine produced in the wine cellars of present day Motzah, bordering the highway west of Jerusalem.

The most important written discoveries from the Persian period are the group of papyri found in Yeb (Elephantine

537

537: 4

in upper Egypt, These documents illustrate the history and manner of life of a Jewish military colony, "Hila Yehudiah" of the 5th c. BCE. They also have some bearing on the history of the Israelites in Palestine under Persian rule (see Persia*: Elephantine).

Apart from seals and coins, only a few inscriptions have been found belonging to the Persian period:
1. In Tel Abu-Zeitun north of Tel-Aviv, an ostracon was found bearing the name "*hšwb*" in an Aramaic script typical of the 5th c. BCE. This name is also mentioned in the Bible at the time of the Babylonian Exile and the Restoration* (Neh. 11:15). 2. An ostracon was found at Tel el-Far'ah in the south, bearing an inscription in Aramaic, "*lzr' bhkl zf bt 'sryn*," which is apparently a bill of expenses for the sowing of a field, and 20 bātot (plural of bāt; see Weights and Measures*). 3. An inscription engraved on a stone altar found in a grave of the Persian period in Lachish reads: "*lbwnt y(hw—-)š bn mh(yr). lYH mr šmy*," which means "incense of balsam of Yehoash, son of Mahir, to Yahweh, God of Heaven (shmaya)".

With the exception of the Dead Sea Scrolls and the papyri of the Bar-Kochba period, which are not inscriptions as defined above (dealt with separately, see Bar-Kochba*; Dead Sea Scrolls*), inscriptions of the Hellenistic and Roman periods found in Israel are only short texts, most of them epitaphs. The majority were discovered in Jerusalem, the remainder at various sites. Most are written in Hebrew or Aramaic, a few in Greek.

The most important is a stone tablet bearing this **(538)** inscription: "*ekh htyt ṣm 'zyh mlk yhwd wlw lmfth*", translated as "Hither were brought the bones of Uzziyah, King of Judah, do not open". The inscription was not found on its original site. For some unknown reason, it had found its way into the collection of the Russian church on the Mount of Olives. Uzziyahu's bones may have been moved from his original grave, though it is difficult to surmise the reason. One theory attributes this to his leprosy (II Ch. 26:23). Aramaic inscriptions were also found on the stone tablets used to seal burial chambers, designating the names of those interred and warning against opening the grave.

At the front of a burial chamber in the Kidron valley of Jerusalem, the following inscription was discovered (in Hebrew): "This is the grave and memorial of Elezar Haniah Yo'ezer Yehuda Shimeon Yohanan, sons of Yosef ben Obed and Eleazar bnei Haniyeh, Kohanim (priests) of the sons of Hazir." Many names known from the biblical and Talmudic name lists were discovered on stone sarcophagi (see Funerary Customs*). A few of the names are of Greek origin.

A number of inscriptions were found engraved on rocks in the fields near Tel Gezer. These inscriptions designate the city limits in the Hasmonean period, "Limits of Gezer". In some instances, the Greek inscription, ΑΛΚΙΟΣ (the property of Alkios), is added. Apparently, he was governor of the city at that time (see illus. under Gezer*).

V. GREEK INSCRIPTIONS (GRAECO-ROMAN PERIOD): Greek inscriptions began in Israel during the Hellenistic age (see Hasmoneans*). The earliest Greek inscriptions discovered in Israel are from the period of the Ptolemies, but most of them belong to the period after the Bar-Kochba* war. Since data on the history of Palestine in that period are very scanty, even the limited number of Greek inscriptions are of great importance as a source of information on Jewish life as well as on the pagan peoples in the country.

Several Hebrew inscriptions discovered in Egypt contain information on the life of the Jews at the start of the Ptolemaic period. One inscription with Greek words found in Schedia near Alexandria relates that the local Jewish congregation built a synagogue (π· οδευχή) there in the time of Ptolemy Evergetis III (246–221 BCE) and called it by his name and that of Queen Berenice. Similar inscriptions from Jewish synagogues discovered in Lower Egypt show that it was a Jewish custom in the Diaspora to honour the pagan king and his family by naming their synagogues for them (see Hellenism and the Diaspora*).

Another inscription unearthed in the excavation of the Ophel in Jerusalem is engraved on a marble tablet and tells of the building of a synagogue (συναγογή) together with a hospice and water system for poor pilgrims. The synagogue was built by Theodotus (Mattaniah), son of Vettenos, an archisynagogus (one who governed the synagogue), son and grandson of an archisynagogus (see **293**).

538

539

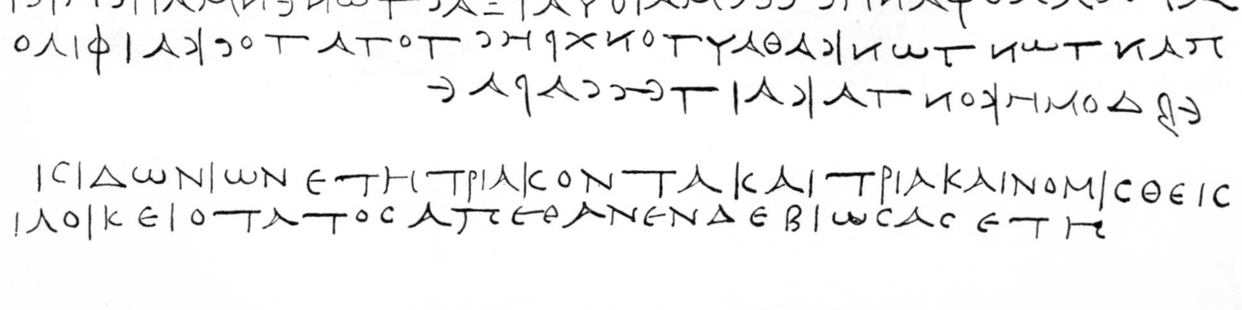

540 a

540 b

541

An additional inscription was found in Jerusalem near the wall of the Temple mound. The engraved Greek Temple inscription (see Temple*) contains seven lines and it reads: "No stranger shall pass the railing and wall around the Temple. Anyone caught will receive punishment, and his blood will be on his own hands." This inscription was apparently on the wall of the Temple built by Herod. Josephus describes the inscription on the Temple partition: "... upon it stood pillars, at equal distances from one another, declaring the law of purity, some in Greek and some in Roman letters, that 'no foreigner should go within the sanctuary'" (Josephus, War 5:5, 2).

Only one contemporary inscription of the Hasmonean period is known which mentions them by name. This inscription, discovered in the excavation at Gezer*, was engraved on a cut stone (**123**) which seems to have belonged to the palace of Simeon the Hasmonean. It reads: "May fire destroy the palace of Simeon, says Pampras." The Pampras who wrote his curse on a building stone may have been a prisoner of war, forced to work in the construction of the palace.

Among Greek inscriptions concerning the foreign rulers, the following may be mentioned. In Gaza, a monument to Charemides, a Cretan mercenary in Ptolemy's army was discovered. The inscription is of sixteen lines engraved on stone. His victories in the battlefield won Charemides the regard of the Ptolemaic kings, but he was less happy in his domestic life: first his twenty year old son died, then his seven year old daughter, Kalodeksa.

Recently, two Greek inscriptions have been discovered referring to the Seleucid rule in Palestine. The first, found near Hefzi-bah, consisting of 38 lines engraved on stone, is a copy of eight official documents from the time of Antiochus III (223–187 BCE). The documents deal with the damage caused to several villages in the northern part of the country by the forced stationing of soldiers there. In all probability, this was during the war between the Seleucids and the Ptolemies about 200 BCE. One of the documents is a memorandum intended for Antiochus III, written by Ptolemaios, son of Thraseas. Ptolemaios was a commanding officer in the Egyptian army, but he deserted and joined the enemy forces. In recognition, he was appointed military ruler and high priest of southern Syria and Phoenicia by Antiochus III (see Hasmoneans*; Hellenism in the Near East*).

The other inscription which contains eight lines engraved on marble was discovered in the Acre excavations in 1959. This inscription is a dedication to Zeus Soter, and it mentions Antiochus VII (Sidetes). The name of the dedicator is scraped off, but his Greek title was "ἀρχιγραμματεύς τῶν δυνάμεων", "military scribe", and he was appointed governor of Acre, evidently in the absence of Antiochus who was engaged at that time in a war against the Parthians (130 BCE).

A number of Greek inscriptions were discovered in the large family graves in Maresha (189–119. BCE) The most important of these (**539**) mentions Apollophanes, son of Sesmaios, who — according to the inscription — was the beloved leader of the Sidonians in Maresha for 33 years, and died in his seventy-fourth year.

There are other inscriptions whose contents are not at all clear, and which probably belong to the period of the Maresha tombs (see Funerary Rites*).

Greek inscriptions concerning the pagan cult in Palestine at the beginning of the Hellenistic period form a separate group. In Samaria (Sebastie) a number of inscriptions from the period of the Ptolemies were found. Most interesting of these is a four line dedicatory inscription found on a site where a temple of Ptolemy apparently stood. According to the inscription, the temple was dedicated by Hegesenandros, Xenarchis and their children, to Serapis and Isis.

In Kefar Yasif, 9 km. northeast of Acre, a limestone tablet with a seven line engraved inscription was found. The inscription, dating from the middle of the 2nd c. BCE, dedicates an altar to the eastern gods, Hadad and Atargatis. The dedicator is Diotos, son of Meoptolemos, who although he worshipped oriental gods, seems to have been a Greek settler. The attraction of the Greek settlers to the eastern gods is explained in the second line of the inscription: "because these gods heed our prayers."

In the days of the Second Temple, the importation of wine jars from Rhodes was very popular. The handles of these jars bore seal stamps, usually consisting of two or three lines, which gave the name of the merchant and the time of shipment (by the names of the consuls who ruled for a year each) of the wine in the jar. A symbolic drawing was sometimes added, as for example the Rhodes rose (handles, **541**). These seal stamps are most helpful in determining the exact date of Hellenistic levels in Palestine.

Most of the Latin inscriptions discovered in Israel relate to Roman rule in Palestine. Many of them are milestones (**540**) marking city limits, etc. A unique inscription was recently discovered in the excavations of the Caesarea theatre. This is a building dedication in honour of the emperor Tiberius, placed there by the prefect Pontius Pilatus (26–36 CE; see Caesarea*, illus. **110**; Rome and the Jews*).

ISAIAH. — Outline: I. First Isaiah: Career and Message; His Call; Isaiah and Ahaz; Isaiah and Hezekiah; God in Control of History; The Messianic Age. II. Contents of First Isaiah; Composition and Date; Style. III. Second (Deutero) Isaiah: The Anonymous Deutero-Isaiah; Authorship and Background of Chs. 40–66; Evidence of the Dead Sea Scrolls; The Prophet's Message; Universalism; The Suffering Servant. IV. Contents of Second Isaiah: Composition of the Book; The Problem of Chs. 56–66; Transmission of Isaiah and the Dead Sea Scrolls. V. Comparisons between Pre-Exilic and Post-Exilic Prophecy.

The book of Isaiah is one of the longest and most important in the Bible. In the Hebrew Canon it is the first of the "Latter Prophets", followed immediately by Jeremiah. The same order is followed in the Septuagint, in Christian translations* and in modern Hebrew versions*.

The book contains 66 chapters and their involved and artificial integration has long been a matter for discussion. Modern scholarship generally regards the book as a compilation of a number of collections which can be divided into two major and other smaller parts. Chs. 1–33 and 36–39 are largely ascribed to the historic prophet Isaiah ben Amoz, though some scholars do not regard it as a unity. Chs. 34-35; 40–55 and 56–66 are considered by most scholars to have been written by an anonymous prophet known as Second or Deutero-Isaiah (see part III and IV, below) although another theory believes that chs. 56–66 were from the hand of another anonymous prophet, Trito-Isaiah (see Part IV). In addition several parts of chs. 13–23 and 24–27, as indicated, are also attributed to later anonymous prophets.

I. FIRST ISAIAH: The first part of the book contains the poetic oracles of Isaiah ben Amoz, interrupted by four historical chs. (36–39). These oracles, which are pre-Exilic, differ in both historical background and content from those of the second half of the book, which belong to the Exile.

Career and Message: Isaiah (Yeshayahu), son of Amoz (not the prophet Amoṣ*), lived and prophesied in Jerusalem. He was called to be a prophet in 733 BCE, the year of King Uzziah's death. He prophesied during the reigns of Jotham and Ahaz and the first part of Hezekiah's rule and made his last appearance at the conclusion of Sennacherib's campaign against Jerusalem ca. 701 BCE (see Israel and Judah*, Parts III and IV, for the historical background).

Isaiah's antecedents are unknown. He was closely connected with the royal court, his wife was also a prophetess and two sons, both given symbolic names, are mentioned (see below). Isaiah was a contemporary of Micah* and came after Amos* and Hosea* whose prophecies had mainly referred to Israel. Isaiah and Micah were more concerned with Judah and Jerusalem.

541 a

Isaiah ben Amoz is one of the major figures of Israel's history. Not only was he a religious leader phrasing his appeal for spiritual regeneration in some of the finest poetry ever written. In addition, during the thirty years of his active life, he was the dominant figure on the political scene, offering Israel advice and guidance on her policy through a variety of crises. The prophet addressed himself to a wide range of themes. Many of them belong to the purest Mosaic tradition and it is these aspects which seem to reveal the essential quality of Isaiah's spiritual insight. He was imbued with the true prophetic vision of the ultimate redemption of Israel and the world but his oracles were also closely related to the events of his time and his own reaction to them. His career and his message, therefore need to be considered together.

Isaiah's Call: Isaiah's call to prophesy is recorded in one of the most familiar passages of the Old Testament (ch. 6). Isaiah had a vision of God seated on his throne in the Temple. Such an experience could be described — if at all — only in the symbolism of his own period. In describing the "winged seraphîm" — figures which reappear in the cherubîm* of Ezekiel's vision (Ezk. 1:5–14) — Isaiah may have had in mind something like this 9th c. BCE demonic figure (**541a**) from Tel Halaf (Assyria) with its six wings (cf. Is. 6:2) and elaborate crown (see Tabernacle, Ark and Cherubîm*). In the face of his experience, Isaiah was overwhelmed by his own unworthiness and his sense of the nation's sins. He attacked the powerful and decadent upper classes who robbed the helpless of their rights (1:21–23; 3:13–4:1; 5:8–23; 10:1–4), ignored the demands of the Law and sought to deflect God's wrath by means of lavish sacrifices and ritual. God would have none of these, cried Isaiah (1:10–20). The Day of Judgment would come (2:6–21; see Amos*), the Assyrian being the instrument of punishment (5:26–29; 10:5–6), and the nation would be plunged into disaster (3:1–12; 6:11; 10:17–19).

Isaiah and Ahaz: Isaiah first came into conflict with government policy when King Ahaz was turning to Assyria for help against the Aramean-Israelite coalition (see Israel and Judah*, Part II). Isaiah disagreed with the king's policy and denied the strength of the coalition. He urged the king to trust in Yahweh's promises to David for he thought Ahaz's attempt to ally himself with Assyria showed a sinful lack of confidence in the very theology which the king officially upheld (7:9). Throughout his career, Isaiah opposed military alliances and counselled reliance on God. The materialism and militarism which he saw increasing only repelled the prophet. To reinforce his appeals to the king, Isaiah had recourse to symbolical acts, like giving his sons names that carried a divine message of hope (7:3) or warning (8:1–4). Ahaz wavered but finally rejected the prophet's warnings and surrendered his independence to Tiglat-Pileser, king of Assyria*.

Isaiah's doctrine of an omnipotent God was unshaken by this rebuff and he viewed the dereliction of king and people as a part of God's purpose. The resulting debacle would constitute a purge of the nation, from which a chastened and purified remnant would emerge (1:24–26; 10:20–23).

Isaiah and Hezekiah: For the rest of Ahaz's life, Isaiah made no further attempt to influence policy, but when Hezekiah succeeded to the throne, the prophet again tried to direct the king's actions. Hezekiah had been asked to join a new western Asiatic federation set up in opposition to Assyria. Isaiah had opposed the alliance with Assyria but he also condemned taking up active opposition to her. Yahweh, he cried, had founded Zion and would defend it (14:32). In His own good time He would give the signal for the overthrow of Assyria. In an effort to prevent young Hezekiah from joining the alliance, Isaiah prophesied the doom of Egypt and Ethiopia (chs. 18–20). Apparently, his words were effective for Judah escaped the crushing retaliation which Assyria inflicted on the members of the alliance.

Isaiah's influence came to an end, however, when general rebellion, aided by Egypt, broke out throughout the region. He foresaw disaster knowing that help from Egypt, sealed as it was in the names of Egyptian gods, was bound to prove no more than a "broken reed" (36:6; 30:1–5). For Judah to rely on it was merely further evidence of a sinful lack of trust in Yahweh. Because the nation's leaders had forgotten Yahweh and His promises to David, Yahweh would fight against Jerusalem as David once had done (29:1–4). Isaiah eventually rejected Assyria as an instrument of divine justice, but he continued to predict the doom of Jerusalem. Salvation could only be achieved by a fundamental repentance and return to God (30:15; 31:6). This concept recalls the basic "either-or" theme of 1:19–20. Either obey the divine will and live; or refuse, persist in disobedience and be destroyed.

The imagery Isaiah uses when foretelling the fate of the king in defeat, "I will put my hook in your nose and my bit in your mouth . . ." (37:29) has been vividly illustrated in an Assyrian engraving of the 10th c. BCE **(556)** showing a victorious king holding his defeated enemies by ropes tied to rings fixed in their noses.

Judah's rulers tried to silence Isaiah (30:9–11), but the prophet never wavered in his opposition to policies he considered immoral and dangerous. After the rebellion had almost ruined the nation, the conduct of the survivors of Sennacherib's campaign against Judah seemed to him further evidence that the nation was incorrigible (22:1–14).

God in Control of History: Yahweh's patience continued to be sorely tried. Hezekiah rebelled again against Assyria and Sennacherib invaded for the second time. This flouting of the divine will moved Isaiah to a new interpretation of world events. Yahweh's will was paramount in all history. Now He was about to demonstrate his supremacy. First Assyria was to play the role of the chastening rod but then its power would be broken on the soil of Palestine (14:24–27; 17:12–14), and God would rescue his people as once He had released them from their bondage in Egypt (10:24–27). The nation must be humiliated as a divine chastisement, but Yahweh's promises would not be revoked as part of the punishment. The national hope of redemption by God's help was retained, but Isaiah thrust it into the future. Yahweh's promise was not unconditional; it was a promise made to an obedient Israel which had yet to come into being.

It was still Yahweh's purpose to fulfill the solemn promise he had made to David, but this fulfilment would be made to an Israel chastened and purified. The achievement of Yahweh's own purpose required the survival of at least a proportion of His children. Whatever might happen to Israel as a whole, a "remnant" of the people would survive. The nation could not wholly perish. Its sins would inevitably call down a punishment of intense distress and suffering, but at the end, a spiritual nucleus would still be found. The people of Israel would be punished for their sins, but not totally exterminated. A remnant would return to renew the link between God and the land of Israel.

In spite of his original opposition to the rebellion, Isaiah later supported the king and encouraged resistance. Assyria had also overreached herself and blasphemed Yahweh and would never be permitted to crush Zion (37:21–35). Isaiah appears here as an upholder of the ancient concept of holy war*, led by a Davidic king. In the event, Isaiah's more hopeful oracles were vindicated, for the city was not taken and Sennacherib withdrew (see Israel and Judah*, Part IV). Isaiah claimed that the promise of protection and deliverance for the city had been not his words but God's. At this point in Judah's history, the prophet passes out of sight.

The Messianic Age: Isaiah's teachings concern the coming of an ideal, messianic king as well as the doctrine of the remnant (9:1–7; 11:1–9; 32:1–8). This ideal king is to reign over his people in strict accordance with the will of Yahweh; his kingdom combining ordinary and eschatological* features. His righteous government will restore happiness and prosperity to his people. Isaiah proclaims the coming of this ideal monarch as certain — but for the future, for no historical character had yet measured up to the ideal. Isaiah's formulation of the coming of the Messiah became the foundation for a doctrine which over the centuries developed into one of the most significant beliefs of the Jewish people (see Apocrypha*; Apocalypse*; John the Baptist*; Jesus*).

II. CONTENTS OF FIRST ISAIAH: The general themes and topics of Isaiah can be outlined approximately as follows:

Oracles of Judgment and Promises of Felicity for Judah. (chs. 1–6): The first chapter deals with rebellion, judgment and reassurance. The various oracles date from different times of the prophet's ministry, the first (vs. 2–9) concerns the sinful nation, with an exhortation to obedience rather than sacrifice and the external forms of worship (10–17). The only alternative to obedience is rebellion and destruction (18–20). Then comes the judgment on the faithless city (21–23) and the prediction of its destruction (24–31).

The next five chapters contain the oracles of the Day of Yahweh. 2:2–5 is a messianic prophecy of the era of universal peace (quoted by Micah* 4:3–4; see article). 2:6–22 is the poem of the "Day of Yahweh" in which the proud and exalted shall be humbled and Yahweh shall triumph over all the earth. 3:16–4:1 is a diatribe on the patrician ladies of Jerusalem, describing the degradation of them and their feminine finery. 4:2–6 is a late oracle on the ultimate glorification of Zion, the Covenant city, followed, 5:1–7, by the song of the vineyard; 5:8–24a is a series of prophecies of doom on the unrighteous.

Chs. 6:1 to 9:7 contain a series of biographical episodes and visions concerning the existing world and the coming Kingdom of God. First (6:1–13), comes Isaiah's vision in the Temple and his call to prophecy. Then (7:1–8:21) his rebuke of King Ahaz is recounted and the "Maher-shalal-hash-baz" oracle of the destruction of the people at the hands of Assyria, followed by God's warning to Isaiah that the "Lord of Hosts" is "your fear . . . and your dread". Isaiah and his children are "signs and portents" for Israel but the prophet knows that their message will be ignored. This section leads into the great poem proclaiming the birth and rule of the coming king messiah (9:2–7).

9:8–12:6 takes up the theme of the punishment and doom of Judah and Israel. 9:8–10:4 is a poem (probably from the prophet's early period) on the hand raised against Ephraim i.e. the destruction of the Northern Kingdom by Assyria, vividly described in 10:5–11. Nevertheless, once Assyria has served its purpose as Yahweh's "rod of my anger", it too will be punished (10:12–34) and Israel will be restored. 11:1–16 is a renewed description of the reign of peace to be brought by a king descended from David ("There shall come forth a shoot from the stump of Jesse . . ."), whose tranquil kingdom is in striking contrast to the violence of contemporary world empires. The section is concluded with a hymn of praise and thanksgiving (12:1–6).

Chs. 13–23 contain prophecies addressed to "the nations". These follow no chronological order, nor are they related to each other in content.

13:1–14:23 concerns Babylon, including the prediction of its overthrow (13:19–22) and the taunt of the king of Babylon (14:4–21). 14:24–27 foretells the destruction of Assyria and 14:28–32 is a warning to Philistia. 15:1–16:14 bewail the fate of Moab. 17:1–11 prophesies the fall of Damascus, Syria and Ephraim (cf. 7:1–8:12). Ch. 18 describes the avenger who is come upon Egypt from the "land beyond the rivers of Ethiopia" (Egypt's 25th Dynasty was of Nubian origin, see article on Egypt*); while ch. 19 announces Yahweh's judgment on Egypt. Ch. 20 is a narrative of Assyria's conquest of Egypt and Ethiopia (see Assyria*), followed (ch. 21) by the three oracles on the fall of Babylon (21:1–10), on Edom (vs. 11–12) and Arabia (13–17). 22:1–14, "the oracle concerning the valley of vision" is a poem of invective against Jerusalem.

This is followed by the unexpected oracle addressed to Shebna the Steward (or "he who is over the palace") illustrated by an inscription found on an ancient tomb near Jerusalem (see Inscriptions*). The section closes with an oracle concerning Tyre (ch. 23; see Phoenicia*).

Many of the oracles and poems of this section (13–23) are related to events beyond Isaiah's time and are regarded as the work of anonymous prophets and poets.

Chs. 24–27 are a collection of apocalyptic* oracles, songs and hymns, which form an eloquent portrayal of God's judgment of the world and its ultimate salvation, crowned by the resurrection of the just. This whole section is later than Isaiah and, again the work of anonymous prophets.

Chs. 28–33: The "Woe" oracles": a collection of predictions all beginning "Woe to . . .", compiled by a later editor. They reveal a remarkable alternation between denunciation and threats to the evildoers of Judah and promises of felicity and consolation for the "remnant". In detail, the oracles include: 28:1–22, threats and condemnation against Samaria; 29:1–8, the doom of Ariel (Jerusalem); 29:9–15: three invectives followed by the promise of redemption of 29:17–24; 30:1–7, condemnation of Egypt, the worthless help; 30:8–17 further invective; 30:18–26, the future comfort and felicity of Jerusalem; 30:27–33, condemnation of Assyria; 31:1–9, repeated threats against Egypt and Assyria. 32:1–8, a description of the kingdom of the king who "will reign in righteousness"; 32:9–14, an oracle to the "complacent daughters", reminiscent of 3:16–4:1, balanced by an assurance of future comfort (32:15–20). Ch. 33 is a prophetic liturgy which a number of scholars deny to Isaiah.

Chs. 34–35: eschatological prophecies, 34:1–17, the judgment of Edom; 35:1–10, the salvation of Zion. Many scholars believe that these passages form the introduction to the literary sequence of Deutero-Isaiah (ch. 40–46).

Chs. 36:1–39:8: These four chapters contain a historical narrative about Isaiah's activity during the reign of Hezekiah, notably Sennacherib's invasion (36:1–37:38), Hezekiah's sickness and recovery and his hymn of thanksgiving (38:1–22; see Israel and Judah*, Part IV), the mission of Merodach-baladan (39:1–8; see Babylonia*).

Composition and Date: According to the Scandinavian school, Isaiah's oracles (like those of the other rhetorical prophets) were transmitted through a long process of oral tradition and finally crystallized in writing only in post-Exilic times, along with the other biblical books. Modern critics oppose this theory and, indeed, the text itself refutes it. Isaiah's impact on Hebrew letters and religious thought in earlier Israelite generations is too apparent to warrant the view that the book of Isaiah was written only in post-Exilic times. However, it is likely that the prophecies uttered by Isaiah, although written down by others, were not known as a complete composition or anthology until the later period. Immediately after his lifetime they were known as individual oracles or small collections. This view is perhaps derived from a comparison of Isaiah with the fragmentary contents of the collection of the twelve Minor Prophets which follow the Great Prophets in the Bible Canon*. One fairly popular theory is that the Isaianic scrolls were owned by men who were interested in their contents — not in their chronological sequence — and that this accounts for the heterogeneous motifs in the book and their repetition in different places. The keepers of the fragments, however, were careful to add a message of hope to each oracle of adminition and this explains the closing message of each of these sections, following an ancient literary convention common to Isaiah, Hosea* and Amos*. In the opinion of other scholars, this theory is unduly speculative and is quite hypothetical since there is no evidence of such intermediate stages.

Many scholars hold that the final edition of the book of Isaiah, (chs. 1–39 and 40–66) took place in the Persian period around 500 BCE.

Style: Isaiah was endowed with literary abilities of the highest order. He is outstanding among all the poets, thinkers and prophets of Israel and he made a deep impression on subsequent Jewish literature and religious thought. His book contains all the elements of great poetry: a balanced and stately style, passion, sincerity, imagery and a wide range of expression. Few prose passages can bear comparison with the account of his call to prophecy (ch. 6) while his short lyrics reveal a vigour (e.g. the enemy's advance in chs. 28–32) and pathos (chs. 4–9) of extraordinary power. His passionate denunciations of oppression and injustice and his scorn for the heartless (e.g. 3:16–26) are all the more effective coming side by side with the tenderness and comfort (e.g. 9:2–7; 11:6–9) of the prophecies of hope.

III. SECOND (DEUTERO-) ISAIAH. — **The Anonymous Isaiah. Authorship and Background of chs. 40–66:** It is generally agreed that chs. 40–55, written against the background of the closing years of the Babylonian Exile (550 BCE onwards), are not the work of Isaiah ben Amoz. The Persian king, Cyrus, who appeared on the political scene about 550 BCE is mentioned by name. While in some passages (43:14; 48;14) the conquest of Babylonia is predicted, in others (41:1–17, 25 etc.) it appears that Cyrus had already achieved his first successes (see Restoration*). Yahweh used the Babylonians as a tool to punish the sins of Judah, Cyrus being no more than "my shepherd (who) shall fulfill all my purpose." (44:28)

There are considerable differences in style between chs. 1–39; 40–55 and 56–66 (see Contents, below). In the first group (1–39), the language is full of illustrations and metaphors, while in chs. 40–55 it is often more rhapsodic, full of pathos and tenderness. It is probably true that there is no substitute for reading these passages oneself. This is true of most of the Bible, but it is peculiarly apt in connection with Isaiah, and the following analysis of the Contents of the book can do no more than indicate the poet's main themes. The differences between First and Second Isaiah are more than a question of language or theology. Second Isaiah addressed a people living in Exile in Babylonia, a very different situation, calling for a quite different message, from the audience of First Isaiah.

At the very outset of the second collection of prophecies, it is stated that Israel had received at the Lord's hand double for all her sins (40:2). The oppressor in this second section is Babylonia, not Assyria as in First Isaiah's time. The tragedies which had befallen Judah are recorded as a past reality. The prophet bases his predictions not on these past events, but on the redemption that is to come.

The cosmological aspect of the kingship of God is given greater prominence in Second Isaiah than in chs. 1–39. While First Isaiah speaks of the King Messiah, this figure is replaced in chs. 40–55 by the Suffering Servant of Yahweh.

These considerations have together led a majority of scholars to the conclusion that the author of much of the material in Is. 40–66 was a prophet of the Exile* who lived about a century and a half after Isaiah ben Amoz of Jerusalem.

Evidence of the Dead Sea Scrolls: J.T. Milik has drawn attention to a significant detail in the complete Isaiah scroll found in Qumran (see below, Transmission of Isaiah and the Dead Sea Scrolls*): "Ch. 33 finishes towards the foot of Column XXVII (of the scroll) and the three ruled lines which follow are left blank. Furthermore the sheet on which it is written has only two columns instead of the four that are used in this roll. Ch. 34 (Deutero-Isaiah) begins on a new sheet of leather, and the text thereafter continues without further interruption until the end of the book. This oddity may well indicate that there persisted a memory of two different collections of prophecy (corresponding roughly to the modern distinction between Proto and Deutero-Isaiah), although the two collections had already been combined in one book by the time of the copyist . . . There are furthermore, differences in grammar and orthography between the two parts, and the material disposition of the text in the roll is not the same." (I Isaiah is usually taken as 1–33, 36–39 and II Isaiah as 34–35, 40–66; see introduction, above.)

II Isaiah's Message: This prophet's outstanding message is his conception of God, which constitutes the most exalted teaching in the whole of the Old Testament. His ethical monotheism is more explicit than that of any preceding prophet and his concepts of the greatness and omnipotence of Yahweh are equally advanced over those of his predecessors. Although II Isaiah's vision of the regeneration of his people has affinities with the inspiration of earlier prophets, it is also characterized by a note of exultant triumph to be found nowhere else in the Bible. II Isaiah does not call the reestablishment of God's covenant with Israel a new covenant (see Jeremiah*; Covenant*). For him, the original Covenant had never been broken (50:1). The Exile was but a temporary estrangement, from which God, in his everlasting mercy, would rescue his erring people (54:1–10). This was something more fundamental than a mere repetition of the old popular hopes of a Davidic redeemer, which play little or no role in Second Isaiah's vision.

Universalism: Isaiah's message is based on a new and unique concept of universality and spirituality (chs. 40–55). He looks forward to the time when all nations will recognize Yahweh as God (49:6), anticipating the first demonstration of His power in the revolution to be brought about by His agent, Cyrus. Yahweh was the ruler of the whole earth and all peoples must come to accept His rule.

Before the Exile, the prevailing climate in Palestine was that of a national monotheism. Yahweh was regarded as the one national god of Israel, resident in Palestine and not to be worshipped elsewhere. It would be difficult to exaggerate the shock which the Babylonian conquest represented to the Jewish masses. Their dogma, reiterated by the prophets up to and including First Isaiah was that Yahweh's Temple was inviolable and that Israel could walk in the land of Palestine in full confidence. If Yahweh's Temple — His home — had been destroyed, how could He protect His people in Exile? Moreover, how were the Jews to resist the temptations of Mesopotamian culture surrounding them there? (see Restoration*). Out of the need of the moment, one man arose to answer the fears about the Exile and to hearten and encourage the people. The ethical monotheism formulated by II Isaiah carried with it the assurance that the Jews could trust in God anywhere in the world — inside Palestine or far beyond the Euphrates. In addition, he brought a new hope of the rebuilding of Jerusalem and the founding of a new Temple (44:28). The Exile was to be a turning point in Jewish history and religion — not its conclusion (see Restoration*).

The Suffering Servant: The most striking and specific message of Second Isaiah — one without parallel in the ancient world — is contained in the four "Servant of the Lord" poems (42:1–7; 49:1–6; 50:4–11; 52:13–53:12). The Servant, to be chosen by Yahweh, will proclaim the message of truth and righteousness to the world, helped by the divine spirit which he will receive. Through apparent failure in toiling among his own people, the Servant will be helped by God to become the saviour, not only of the Jews, but of the whole earth. The last poem depicts him as a leper and martyr who lays down his life for others. God will save him from death in order to complete his death at the hands of his fellow men. His is a figure which fluctuates between being an individual and a group, between present calling and future ideal. His identity, whether as an individual or the personification of the nation of Israel, remains a subject for debate among scholars and theologians. What is clear is that Second Isaiah meant his prophecies as a warning as well as a comfort to the Jews of his time. His theme was to become a principal motivating force in normative Judaism ever after.

IV. CONTENTS OF SECOND ISAIAH (Chs. 40:1 to 55:13)

Eschatological Prophecies. The End of the Babylonian Exile: Israel's liberation from Exile and the Restoration* of Zion is proclaimed as evidence of the majesty of God. The prologue (40:1–11) is set in the Heavenly Council, where Yahweh pronounces a message of hope and salvation to the despairing exiles. This good news imparts a very different atmosphere from the call to prophecy of Isaiah of Jerusalem (6:9–13) for he was commissioned by the Council to proclaim God's judgment upon an unresponsive people.

The basis of this hopeful, messianic message is in the nature of Yahweh (40:12–31). He will make the nations tremble but will cause Zion to rejoice. Israel will be raised up as Yahweh's champions against idolaters (41:1–29) and the prophet sings repeated praises to his God (42:10–13; 44:23; 45:8; 49:13).

The deliverance of Israel is to be brought about by the agent whom God has raised up, Cyrus. He is mentioned twice by name (44:28; 45:1) and is clearly intended in other texts.

The comforter, however, is Yahweh's Servant (see section III above). The first of the Servant passages appears in 42:1–25 and this leads into a vision of the nation restored (43:1–15), after which will come the rebuilding of Zion (44:24–45:13). The downfall of Babylon's idols (46:1–12) and the city itself (47:1–15) is predicted.

Contrast with Idols: The contrast between Yahweh and the gods of the Babylonians is emphasized repeatedly. The Babylonian idols are no more than the work of man's hands (44:9–20; 46:1 passim) but God is the Lord beside whom there is no other (42:8–17; 54:9–25, passim).

The Servant Songs occur also in chs. 49:1 to 53:12 (see above). These chapters include additional prophecies regarding the Servant of the Lord, his mission to Israel and the nations, his obedience and suffering and his death and vindication. They conclude with an exhortation to accept these promises in faith (55:1–13).

The Restoration of Zion. 49:1–54:17 contain a message of comfort to the exiles in the hope of the redeeming Messiah. There is no longer any reference to Cyrus' conquests nor to the ruin of Babylonia and less emphasis is placed on the contrast between Yahweh and idols. The section describes the Messiah's call to work among Israel and the nations (49:1-26); his obedience (the third Servant passage, 50:1–11); his redemption, triumph, return and establishment of the Kingdom of God (51:1–52:15). 53:1–12 is the passage on the Servant's atonement and exaltation and 54:1–17 the assurance of Israel's restoration and renewed splendour for Jerusalem. The section ends with the proclamation of worldwide salvation to everyone who truly repents (55:1–13).

The Last Section (Chs. 56:1–66:24) contains admonitions and prophecies in a different literary style from that of chs. 40–55.

Their substance is again a message of comfort in faith in Israel's future glory. First (56:1–57:21), warnings to evildoers and promises of reward to the righteous. Chs. 58 and 59 describe the obstacles to restoration and their removal and 60:1–22 laud Jerusalem's exaltation in the messianic age, "Arise, shine; for your light has come, and the glory of the Lod has risen upon you." Ch. 61:1–11 is a statement of the Messiah's mission to Israel and the world. 62:1–12 describes God's concern for Jerusalem and 63:1–14 the Messiah's defeat of Israel's enemies. 63:15–64:12 is the prayer of the "remnant" and 65:1–25, Yahweh's response. With ch. 66, the last two chapters discourse on the rebellious and the faithful, ch. 66 detailing the blessings of true religion and the restoration of those nations which survive the Day of Judgment.

Composition of Second Isaiah: Many scholars (M. Buber among them) have pointed out that the anonymous author or authors of chs. 40–66 belonged to a circle which derived from the "limmudîm" or disciples of Isaiah ben Amoz. They were entrusted with the secret of salvation (Is. 8:16) and the connection made it possible for the writings of both Isaiahs to be joined together into one book. During the Exile, the body of tradition of First Isaiah was preserved and his prophecies of salvation were expanded and enriched, appearing eventually in the magnificent utterances of Second Isaiah who actually lived a century and a half after Isaiah ben Amoz.

The Problem of Chs. 56–66: The composition and authorship of Second Isaiah is complicated by certain differences emerging between chs. 40–55 and chs. 56–66. Chs. 56–66 seem to have been composed at a later time, for they suggest that the Jews have already returned to Israel, and the Temple has been rebuilt. The full promises of restoration had not yet been fulfilled, but Jerusalem, too, was to be rebuilt. Many scholars have suggested that the last section was composed by still another anonymous prophet, termed "Trito-Isaiah" but the differences of opinion among these scholars weaken the weight of their arguments to a great extent. On the other hand, the affinities between the two sections are undeniable. The 27 chs. (40–66) were not necessarily written by one prophet at one time and under the influence of one revelation. He may have prophesied some years before the advent of Cyrus and again at a later time. His oracle may have changed in content and spirit as the people themselves changed in the days of the Restoration, between the time of Cyrus and the time of Zerubbabel. It is also possible that individual prophecies by another prophet may have been interspersed, having no connection with those preceding or following the main body of Second Isaiah's thoughts (such as 48:22; 56:1–8; 57:1–2, 19–21; 59:20–21; 66:5–6, 24).

Transmission and the Dead Sea Scrolls: The Book of Isaiah as a whole has been transmitted in the Massoretic text (see Text and Versions*) in far better form than the other prophets, particularly its second part. This is probably due to the fact that it has been read more often in the synagogues. An important example of its textual form in the late pre-Christian era exists in the two scrolls found near the Dead Sea*. Of the books of the three major prophets, Isaiah, Jeremiah and Ezekiel, the book of Isaiah was most frequently found. The second and incomplete scroll (1 Q Is. b), dating apparently to the 1st c. BCE (see illustration **542**) faithfully reflects the tradition preserved by the Massoretes, and the same can be said of a dozen fragmentary manuscripts of Isaiah found in Cave IV. But the complete Isaiah scroll (1 Q Is. a) found in Cave I (see illus. **543-4**) which is attributed to the 2nd or 1st c. BCE differs in many respects from the

Massoretic text, in text, grammar and orthography. It displays the characteristics of a popular edition. Its spelling is fuller and it is thus easier to read. The manuscripts from Qumran probably date to within 300 or even 200 years of their original composition (not their final editing), an extraordinary discovery for Bible study. The problem of the text of these scrolls and its relation to the proto-Massoretic text is discussed in the article on Text and Versions of the Bible*.

V. PRE-EXILIC AND POST-EXILIC PROPHECY. The two main sections of the book of Isaiah contain some striking examples of two types of the classic prophets, each belonging to a different period. The contrasts between them supply a valuable clue to the spirit of prophecy and the place of the prophets in the history of Israel's religion.

542

543

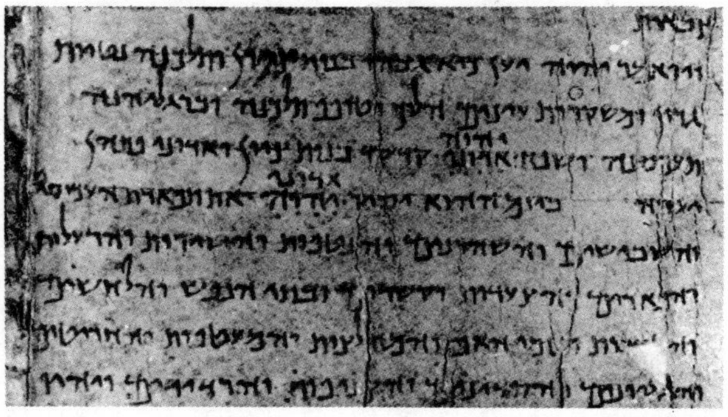

544

They were both reformers who stood in the mainstream of Israel's tradition and adapted that tradition to a new situation. They regarded themselves as being within the charismatic tradition and their aim was to transmit the word of God which had been revealed to them. The past was vitally important for them and they emphasized the traditions of the Patriarchs and the Mosaic Covenant but, on the whole, they concentrated on the present and on reaching an understanding of it in the light of the tradition. The essence of their message was not something they found ready-made. They created it by absorbing and expanding the vital message of their religion since the Mosaic period (see Moses*). Their interest in the future lay mainly in its relationship to the present.

Whether or not they were accurate forecasters of the course of history is an open question. Certainly they succeeded in divining the larger events. Their threatening words were a last minute admonition and warning in the face of what they saw as an inevitable approaching disaster. The popular concept of the national theology was that Israel's status as Yahweh's Chosen People* was rooted in cult, blood and soil; that Yahweh's covenant bound him unconditionally for all time and that religious and moral obligations could be discharged merely by the observances of the cult. Many prophets (Amos*, Isaiah, Jeremiah* and Micah*) had rejected this attitude. J. Kaufmann has observed that Israelite religion reached new heights through the new prophetic concepts of the doctrine of the primacy of morality and the idea that God's demand of man is essentially not cultic but moral. The new concepts developed out of religious-moral idealism, coupled with a deep sense of disappointment at the moral gulf that appeared to separate ideal from reality.

The essence of the proclamations of the pre-Exilic prophets, from Amos to Jeremiah, was that the distresses of the present and immediate future had been brought about by existing and past sins. The prophets lived and prophesied just as the period of disaster descended upon them. The later prophets, on the other hand, in the tradition of Second Isaiah, Ezekiel* and Zechariah* looked forward to a time beyond disaster. The transformation of their time schedule is clearly seen in the content of their prophecies. Their message was one of salvation in a future which would come into being after the catastrophe. Thus it is eschatological* in essence, for it deals with a time when the future and final acts of God could no longer appear as the continuation of previous acts of salvation but must be seen as something unprecedented and definitive.

ISRAEL AND JUDAH, THE INDEPENDENT MONARCHIES OF. — *Outline: I. The Kingdom Divides. II. Kingdom of Israel — Jeroboam I to Death of Jeroboam II: Chronological Problem of Jeroboam's Reign; Jeroboam's Domestic Policy; Building Activities; Baashah; Elah and Zimri; The House of Omri; Omri; The New Capital at Samaria; The Impact of Omri's Dynasty; Relations with Phoenicia; The Reign of Ahab; Changed Relations between Israel and Judah; Aram's Offensive; The Assyrian Resurgence; Ahaziah (Jehoahaz); Joram (Jehoram); Economic Regression in Israel; Jehu's Dynasty; Jehu; The Ascendance of Damascus; Hazael and Jehu; Jehoahaz; Resurgence under Jehoash; The Rise of Israel under Jeroboam II. III. Kingdom of Judah — Rehoboam to the Death of Uzziah: Rehoboam's Reign and the Territorial Battles; The Shoshenk (Shishak) Campaign; Abiyah; Assah; Baashah's War with Judah; The Reign of Jehoshaphat; Joram; Ahaziah; Athaliah; Joash; Resurgence under Amaziah; Uzziah. IV. The Period of Assyrian Conquest — The Fall of Israel and the Survival of Judah: A. Israel: Menachem; Pekah; Dismemberment and Disintegration of Israel; B. Judah under Ahaz. V. Judah's Struggles for Independence — Hezekiah to the Fall of Jerusalem: Hezekiah; His Reforms; Sennacherib's Campaign; The Reign of Menasseh; The End of Assyrian Domination and Judah's Independence; Amon; The Reign of Josiah; His Reforms; The Neo-Babylonian Empire; Jehoahaz; Jehoiakim; Nebuchadrezzar in Judah; Jehoiachin — the First Deportation from Judah; Zedekiah — The End of the Kingdom of Judah; The Remnant in Judah; Chronological Table.*

I. THE KINGDOM DIVIDES: Rehoboam (928–911 BCE), son of King Solomon and Naamah, the Ammonitess, ascended to the throne of the United Kingdom* in 928 BCE, following the death of his father. In accordance with the pattern of the monarchy established by David*, he had to be recognized separately by both Judah and Israel. After his coronation in Judah, he travelled to Shechem in Israel, in order to perpetuate the custom of holding the coronation at a high place*. Thus Saul had been crowned at Gilgal, David at Hebron and Solomon at the "great Bamah" (high place) of Gibeon.

The Assembly of Israel (probably a council of elders — see Government* and Authority — with roots in the era of the tribal league and inherently opposed to the principle of monarchy) demanded a reduction of their territory's tax burden, which included payments in kind and compulsory service in the state labour battalions (corvée) as a condition of their submission to Rehoboam. Mainly on the advice of his younger ministers who had been reared in the atmosphere of an absolute monarchy, Rehoboam rejected this request.

Seeds of Rebellion: Unlike Judah, Israel did not consider itself bound to the Davidic dynasty. The United Kingdom forged by David* and continued by Solomon* did not have a strong grip on the Northern people, who preferred to be ruled by one of their own kin. During the second half of his reign (ca. 945–928 BCE), Solomon increased the forced labour battalions to intensify construction work on his chariot cities and other fortified places (I K. 9:15–19; 11:26–29). The Northern people did not take kindly to the increased conscriptions and disaffection towards the regime spread. It is not surprising, therefore, that secession was touched off in Israel.

Jeroboam Leads the Secession: The revolt was led by Jeroboam, son of Nebat, a member of the traditionally anti-Davidic Ephraim tribe, whom Solomon had appointed superintendent of all forced labour in Ephraim and Menasseh. From the outset, Jeroboam sought ways to overthrow the United Monarchy. His activities were encouraged by the prophet Achiyah the Shilonite (I K. 11:29–39), a descendant of Eli the Shilonite who had served as high priest at Shiloh, the central sanctuary of all the tribes before the monarchy. The Shiloh sanctuary was abolished by Solomon (I K. 2:27) when the centre of worship was transferred to the Jerusalem Temple, and the symbolic gesture of tearing Jeroboam's garment was in all probability actuated by the prophet's pent-up resentment towards the Davidic monarchy.

When the growing hostility of the forced labour battalions became known to Solomon, Jeroboam fled to Egypt*, where he took refuge at the court of Shoshenk (Shishak), who was hostile to Solomon and planned to renew Egypt's influence in Western Asia. Jeroboam remained in Egypt until Solomon's death in 928 BCE. Then he returned and with his people petitioned Rehoboam, Solomon's heir, for lower taxes. Rehoboam refused and sent his chief tax collector and overseer to quell what he thought was a minor insurrection. The royal emissary was stoned to death (I K. 12:18) and Israel's secession from the Kingdom became fact. The country divided into the Kingdom of Judah and the Kingdom of Israel (see map **385**). Fierce military clashes followed, lasting for two generations and resulting in a severely weakened Israel. (For a description of the battles and the Shoshenk campaign, and accompanying territorial changes, see Part II, Judah: the Territorial Battles.)

II. KINGDOM OF ISRAEL. JEROBOAM I TO DEATH OF JEROBOAM II: **Chronological Problem of Jeroboam's Reign (928–907 BCE):** The sequence of events concerning the secession and the crowning of Jeroboam as narrated in the Massoretic text of I Kings 12 (see Bible Canon and Text*) is somewhat truncated and unclear. The Greek Septuagint version, however, preserved an old tradition that provides a more fluent narrative (even though it contains some interpretative and Aggadic elements; see Biblical Criticism*). It differs from the Massoretic version at some significant points: Jeroboam's "mother" did not come from a respected family, but was a concubine; before rebelling, he entrenched himself with 300 chariots in his native town of Sereidah; he returned to Shechem later and rallied the northern tribes; he had married Shoshenk's sister-in-law before returning to Israel from his exile in Egypt (as did Hadad the Edomite); his son, Abiyah, was the child of the Egyptian wife; finally, it was the prophet Shma'yah, of Rehoboam's court who promised the kingship to Jeroboam, not Achiyah the Shilonite (I K. 12:22; II Ch. 12:5–8).

Jeroboam's Domestic Policy: The two main pillars of Jeroboam's domestic policy were religion and tribal tradition. He feared that if the people went to sacrifice in Jerusalem, there would be a resurgence of loyalty to Rehoboam, and "the people will kill me" (I K. 12:27), and insisted on a ritual totally different from that practiced in Jerusalem (see Idol Worship in Israel*). He also strove to find a satisfactory balance between a stable monarchy and the tribal traditions that recognized only a charismatic monarchy

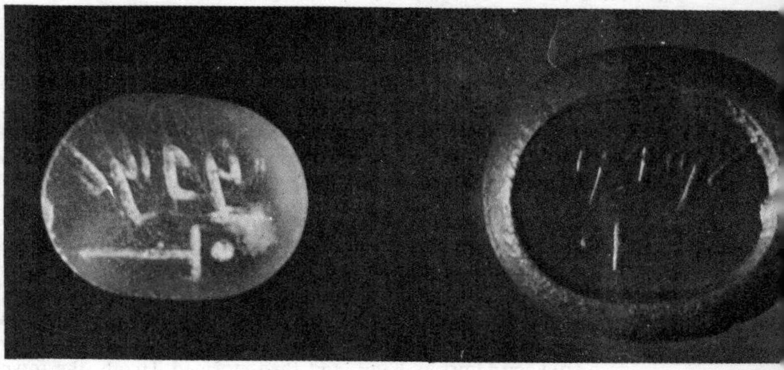

545

546

on the pattern of Saul*, who had much in common with the earlier charismatic judges*.

In order to carry out his plan to alienate the sympathies of the people from the Jerusalem Temple, Jeroboam revived some of the old cultic rites. He built sanctuaries at hallowed sites such as Bethel*, famous during the Patriarchal* period, and Dan, where priests descended from Moses were said to have officiated (Jud. 18:30). He also appointed priests who were not of the traditional priestly tribe of Levi (I K. 12:31). It is probably not a coincidence that he named his sons Nadab and Abiyah, after the sons of Aaron, Nadab and Abiyahu.

Golden Calves: At the sanctuaries of Bethel and Dan, Jeroboam put up "golden calves" associated with the ancient worship of Yahweh during the Exodus. In this way he hoped to revive the Exodus tradition that had been weakened by the tendency in the South to glorify the Davidic house at the expense of earlier heroes and traditions. Jeroboam's viewpoint is epitomized by his appeal to the people: "Behold your gods, O Israel, who brought you up out of the land of Egypt" (I K. 12:28). Actually, the institution of the worship of golden calves cannot be regarded as a purely idolatrous one. Its origin lies in a widespread custom of the ancient East and in symbolism familiar in Israel between 1300 and 700 BCE. The Ark was the reminder and symbol of the Sinaitic Covenant and the visible throne of Yahweh. The invisible glory of Yahweh was conceived as standing on a young bull (see Idol Worship in Israel*: Jeroboam and the Golden Calves). Solomon was also influenced by this tradition, as is shown by his enthronement of the Ark upon the golden Cherubim (see Tabernacle, Ark and Cherubim*). In Old Testament texts the description of Yahweh as "He who sits upon the Cherubim" occurs several times. I K. 14 states that the erection of the calves roused the anger of the prophet, Achiyah the Shilonite, who predicted the imminent fall of his dynasty to Jeroboam's wife. By his act Jeroboam cast a shadow on the entire Northern Kingdom that lasted throughout its existence.

In order to complete the alienation of the people from worship in Jerusalem, Jeroboam also changed the calendar of Festivals. The Feast of Tabernacles, for instance, was celebrated a month later (I K. 12:33). This is probably also the era when the date of the Passover celebration was changed. According to II Ch. 30, two hundred years later, King Hezekiah made strenuous efforts to enlist the loyalty of the Northern tribes by permitting the celebration of the Passover in the second month, apparently in agreement with this calendar* (see Part V).

Jeroboam's Building Activities: In accordance with ancient Canaanite* monarchic tradition, Jeroboam selected Shechem* as his capital. This town had also been the scene of the first attempt to found a monarchy in Palestine under Abimelech (Jud. 9; see Judges*). A Hebrew amethyst seal (**545**) of the early 8th c. BCE found with its impression (left) in Shechem reads "l m b n" which probably means "belonging to (the Lord who) is my maker." A cylinder seal (**546**) found in an Israelite home of the period shows in its impression a winged animal looking over a stylized tree with a winged sun disc hovering above. Penuel on the Jabbok in Transjordan and Tirzah (I K. 14:17) served as supplementary capitals or royal retreats. According to Josephus (Antiq. 8, 225) both Shechem and Penuel were administrative centres. It is also quite likely that deeply rooted tribal traditions prompted Jeroboam to follow in the footsteps of Samuel* and to "judge" the people in several centres of his domain (I Sam. 7:16–17). According to the narrative in I K. 12:25, Jeroboam "built" Shechem and Penuel. What is probably meant is that he erected public buildings there and fortified the towns.

Jeroboam's Downfall: Operations of this kind were rather costly and necessitated the conscription of cheap labour, which conflicted with the *raison d'etre* of Israel's secession from the United Monarchy, as well as with the democratic tribal principles on which the regime was presumably founded. In addition, the war with Rehoboam and then his son, Abiyah, (see below) strained Israel's resources to the limit, and Jeroboam was forced to increase taxes of all kinds. It is hardly surprising, therefore, that Jeroboam's dynasty came to an end when his son Nadab (907–906 BCE) was assassinated by Baashah, son of Achiyah of the tribe of Issachar, who founded a dynasty of his own (I K. 15). During this period and throughout the reign of Nadab, the Israel Kingdom had to ward off the renewed pressures of the Philistines on its southwestern border (I K. 15:27), which added to its difficulties and helped to weaken it (see map **385**).

Baashah (906–883 BCE): Baashah's first act after consolidating his position in Israel was to enter into what proved to be an unsuccessful military campaign against Assah, son of Abiyah and ruler of Judah at the time (see Part III, for a description of the campaign). When the fighting was over, Israel was in a weaker position than before.

Baashah ruled for 24 years but his son Elah (883–882 BCE) reigned for only two. Baashah's dynasty ended as a result of the *coup d'etat* staged by Zimri, a general in the army. The prophet, Jehu, son of Chanani, had foretold this event (I K. 16:1–4) in almost the same manner as Achiyah's prophecy of doom to Jeroboam's wife.

Elah and Zimri: It is likely that the military reverses suffered by Israel encouraged the opposition and gave Zimri the opportunity of disposing of Elah in 882 BCE, while the units loyal to Elah were besieging the Philistine town of Gibbeton. Zimri (882 BCE) ruled for only seven days, however. When the troops at Gibbeton heard what had happened, they crowned Omri as King, and then stormed Tirzah, the town where Zimri had set up his headquarters. Zimri perished in the flames of the palace he occupied (I K. 16:15–20).

The House of Omri: Omri (882–871 BCE): Omri's coronation was the initial step in consolidating the Northern Kingdom and raising it to the rank of a power in the ancient Near East. Shortly after his accession to the throne, Tibni ben Ginat, a pretender, succeeded in winning over a considerable portion of the people. According to Josephus, the struggle between Omri and Tibni lasted for four years, but the latter was finally defeated and killed, and Omri reigned in peace (I K. 16:21–22).

The New Capital at Samaria: After consolidating his position, Omri founded a new capital in Manassite territory, near his parents' estates. The memory of this capital has been preserved under the Arabic name of "Beit Imrin", some three miles from Samaria*, where many potsherds from the Early and Middle Iron Age were found. The building of the new capital (ca. 876 BCE) laid a new and solid foundation for the Kingdom of Israel. Omri also concluded a treaty with Assah of Judah that brought the incessant strife between their two kingdoms to an end (see Part III).

The potsherds found at the site of Omri's capital, as well as other recent archaeological excavations there, confirm the Old Testament statement (I K. 16:24) that he founded Samaria (which until then had not been settled) and developed the surrounding area. Though Samaria had some security advantages over other sites such as Tirzah, Omri apparently selected it with a view to consolidating his regime. This was similar to the action of David in selecting Jerusalem as crown property. Its position as an uninhabited area freed it from tribal restrictions and allowed him to set up the administrative machinery as he saw fit (see map **547**, Northern Kingdom).

The Impact of Omri's Dynasty: Omri succeeded in founding a dynasty that prospered for over 40 years and laid solid foundations for the Kingdom of Israel. His achievements and those of his son Ahab were so outstanding that even after the fall of the Omride dynasty, Assyrian inscriptions referred to the Kingdom of Israel as "Bite Humri", the House of Omri. Indeed, in Judah and Israel, the names Omri and Beit Omri became synonymous with the Northern Kingdom as a whole. The prophet Micah (6:16) stigmatized the ways of Samaria as "the laws of Omri", which in his opinion brought about Israel's destruction.

Despite Omri's influence on succeeding generations, the Old Testament records very little about his career. The book of Kings briefly notes that Omri sinned grievously (I K. 16:25–27), and incidental to this condemnation mentions that he built Samaria. From the very outset of his reign, Omri lived under heavy pressure from the neighbouring countries. The invasions of Ben Hadad I of Aram-Damascus* during the days of Baashah forced Omri to grant special economic privileges to the Arameans* in Samaria and possibly to recognize the sovereignty of Ben Hadad (I K. 20:34).

Relations with Phoenicia: Omri concluded a treaty with Phoenicia, then the greatest maritime power and trading nation. As both Israel and Judah lay along the vital trade routes from Phoenicia to Transjordan and the Arabian Peninsula, the treaty served to cement political and commercial relations between them, particularly during the reign of Omri's son, Ahab. The alliance between Israel and Phoenicia was essentially economic, and did not include military obligations on either party. The economic advantages for Israel were soon made obvious by that country's near monopolization of trade between the whole of Palestine and southern Syria, especially after Ahab's victory over Aram near Apheka.

Though there is a great deal in the Old Testament about the close ties between Tyre and Sidon on the one hand, and the Kingdom of David and Solomon on the other, there is no further mention of this subject after the division of the Davidic kingdom. It may therefore be assumed that there was at first a general decline in commercial activity, particularly because of new conditions and general instability in the economy of Palestine as a whole.

At about the same time as Israel's secession from the United Monarchy, the Phoenicians began to spread through the countries of the Mediterranean basin. They initiated a colonization program in Cyprus, Cilicia, Sardinia, North Africa and southern Spain that reached its peak in the 9th and 8th c. BCE (see Phoenicia*). This was presumably during the ascendancy of the second Phoenician dynasty, whose founder was Ethbaal, father of Jezebel, whom Omri's son, Ahab, married (I K. 16:31). Ethbaal became the ruler of Phoenicia several years before Omri seized power in Israel. The marriage between their children established a close personal relationship between the two monarchs which, according to some scholars, may be echoed in Psalm 45 (from the Choirmaster's collection of Korahite Songs; see Psalms*), a paean to the "daughter of Tyre". Presumably, this was written by one of Samaria's court poets who "on his own admission" was a gifted writer. This psalm has been erroneously associated with King Solomon on the basis of a brief reference to his taking of Sidonian wives.

The Impact of Phoenician Civilization: The Israel-Phoenician alliance gave Phoenicia a tremendous economic, cultural, social and spiritual influence over Israel. During this period, Israel experienced an economic prosperity that was manifested principally in a life of luxury for the Israel upper classes. According to I K. 22:39, Ahab built a house of ivory, or more probably a house decorated with ivory adornments and plaques (**176**). Relics uncovered at Samaria, including the ruins of the town walls from the days of Omri and Ahab (see Samaria*) are evidence of a highly developed building style, clearly influenced by Phoenicia. Especially notable are the ceramics, decorated in the truly aesthetic style that was in vogue in Samaria during the 9th c. BCE.

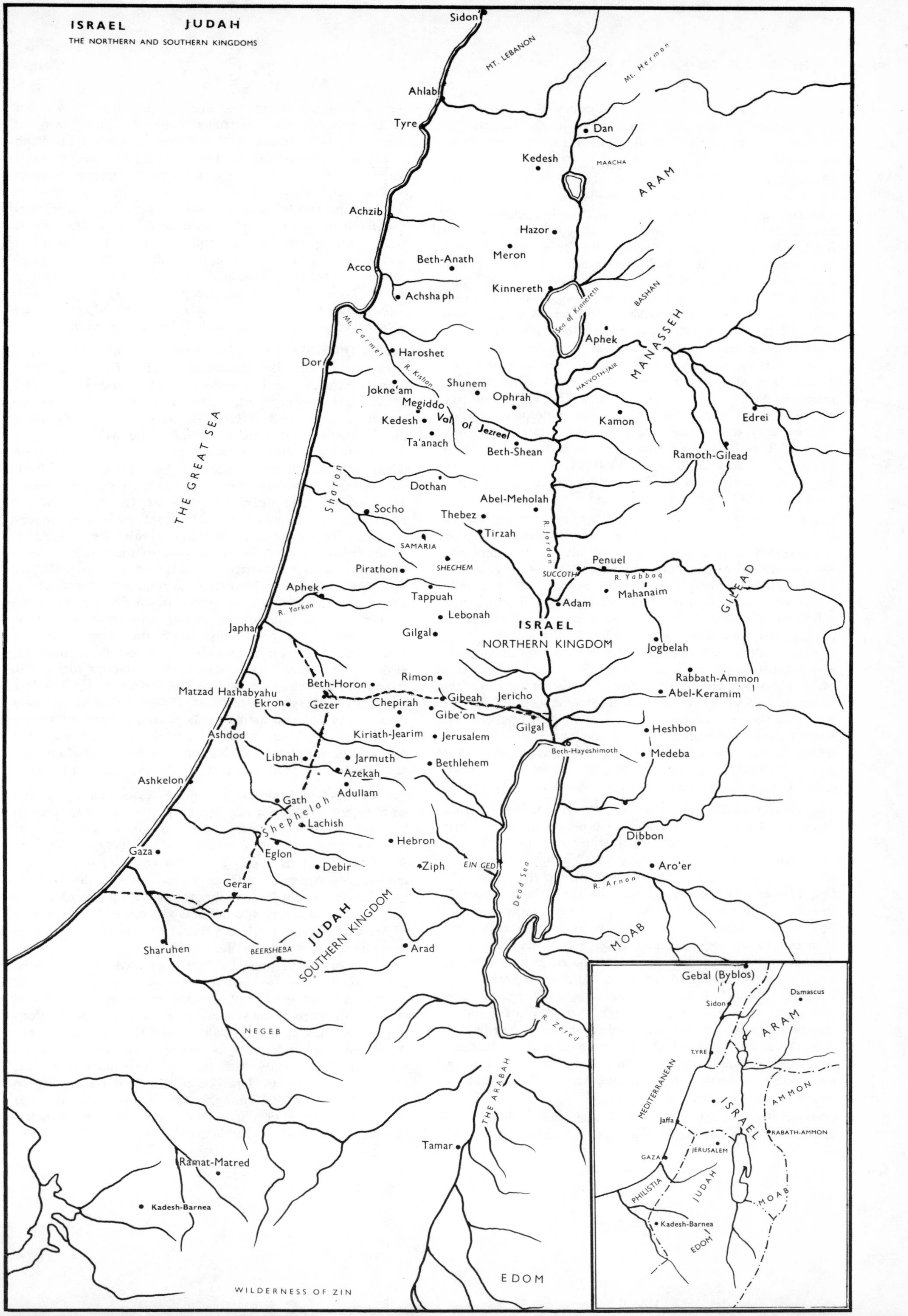
ISRAEL JUDAH
THE NORTHERN AND SOUTHERN KINGDOMS
Sidon
MT. LEBANON
Mt. Hermon
Ahlab
Tyre
Dan
Kedesh
MAACHA
ARAM
Achzib
Hazor
Meron
Beth-Anath
Acco
Kinnereth
Achshaph
Sea of Kinnereth
BASHAN
Aphek
MANASSEH
Mt. Carmel
Haroshet
Dor
R. Kishon
Jokne'am
Shunem
Ophrah
HAVVOTH-JAIR
Megiddo
Kedesh
Val of Jezreel
Kamon
Edrei
Ta'anach
Beth-Shean
Ramoth-Gilead
THE GREAT SEA
Sharon
Dothan
Abel-Meholah
Socho
Thebez
Tirzah
R. Jordan
SAMARIA
SHECHEM
Pirathon
Penuel
SUCCOTH
R. Yabboq
GILEAD
Aphek
Tappuah
Mahanaim
R. Yarkon
Adam
Lebonah
Japha
ISRAEL
Gilgal
NORTHERN KINGDOM
Jogbelah
Rimon
Rabbath-Ammon
Beth-Horon
Matzad Hashabyahu
Gibeah
Jericho
Abel-Keramim
Ekron
Gezer
Chepirah
Gibe'on
Gilgal
Heshbon
Ashdod
Kiriath-Jearim
Jerusalem
Beth-Hayeshimoth
Medeba
Libnah
Jarmuth
Bethlehem
Azekah
Ashkelon
Adullam
Gath
Shephelah
Lachish
Hebron
Dibbon
Gaza
Eglon
Debir
Ziph
EIN GEDI
Dead Sea
Aro'er
R. Arnon
Gerar
JUDAH
SOUTHERN KINGDOM
MOAB
Arad
Sharuhen
BEERSHEBA
NEGEB
R. Zered
THE ARABAH
Tamar
Ramat-Matred
Kadesh-Barnea
EDOM
WILDERNESS OF ZIN
Gebal (Byblos)
Damascus
Sidon
ARAM
TYRE
MEDITERRANEAN
AMMON
ISRAEL
Jaffa
RABATH-AMMON
GAZA
JERUSALEM
PHILISTIA
JUDAH
MOAB
Kadesh-Barnea
EDOM

Phoenician influence can also be discerned in the proto-Ionic capitals of the period, unearthed in the excavations. Similar examples from the Solomonic period were found at Megiddo*.

Phoenician Cults: Phoenician influence on religious life in Israel was even greater than its impact on other spheres — and may be the ultimate source of the dire prophecies of Ezekiel 26–28 on Phoenicia. Jezebel was fanatically zealous for the religion of Ba'al-Melkart, the chief god of Tyre, and brought with her many missionaries to establish and disseminate her faith (I K. 16:32; see Canaan: Gods and Idols*, Cult). The extent of her campaign can be gauged from I K. 18:19 which speaks of 450 priests of Ba'al and 400 priests of Asherah who ate at Jezebel's table. Her corroding influence on the religious practices and beliefs of the masses, tolerated and possibly even supported by Ahab, was strongly condemned by the contemporary prophets, led by Elijah* (see article). The Ba'al cult (see Canaan: Gods and Idols*, Cult) was widespread during this period, just as it had been in the immediately preceding reign of Ben Hadad I of Aram-Damascus (see above) who erected a stele in his honour. As Ba'al worship had been deeply rooted in Palestine for many generations, Jezebel's campaign was made all the easier.

The Reign of Ahab: Ahab (874–852 BCE) came to power at a very favourable time: the Kingdom of Israel had been consolidated politically and economically, its frontiers had been extended, its concepts and way of life were changing and it was undergoing a peaceful process of social and religious integration with Phoenicia. Ahab continued and furthered this process, thus bringing on himself the wrath of the prophets, especially Elijah.

As a result of Israel's alliances with Phoenicia and Judah, and her attendant economic prosperity, Ahab occupied a place of honour among the kings of Syria. Israel's military power is attested in the report of Shalmaneser III on the Battle of Qarqar (see below and Assyria*). It appears that Israel's armoured strength (2,000 war chariots and 10,000 infantry) was the greatest among the allies, giving it a leading military position, which was a new development since the siege of Shechem and the battle of Aphek.

The Chariot Stables at Megiddo: We can gain some idea of the number of Ahab's chariots from the extensive stables uncovered by the Megiddo* excavations (see illustrations in that article), which, according to Y. Yadin, are to be attributed to Ahab rather than Solomon. On the whole, the Old Testament adopts a distinctly hostile attitude to Ahab, though it does mention (I K. 22:39) his palace and city building operations. It is clear from the excavations conducted there that he was responsible for the enlargement of Samaria*. Ahab fortified the defense works of the royal palace at the top of Samaria's hill and surrounded the whole area (about 20 acres) with a thick wall surmounted by a tower (see Cities: Israelite*). The construction work and style of building was of an unusually high standard for Israel. According to I K. 16:34, Jericho, which had been cursed in Joshua's time, was rebuilt by Hiel of Bethel during Ahab's reign, presumably to protect free passage across the Jordan to Moab and Ammon.

Changed Relations between Israel and Judah: Israel and Judah (see Part III) whose destinies had become linked by outside pressures during the tine of Omri, drew even closer as a result of the marriage between Joram, son of Jehoshaphat of Judah, and Athaliah, daughter of Ahab and Jezebel (according to some passages; there is some confusion about her parentage; she may have been a daughter of Omri and half-sister of Ahab). It is significant that in this matrimonial alliance it is the stronger ruler who gives his son in marriage to the daughter of the weaker party. Unlike the treaty with Phoenicia, the marriage contract was essentially a military agreement, though it included commercial features. Together, the two kingdoms controlled all of Transjordan, as far south as the Gulf of Aqaba (Eilat) and this enabled them to reinstate the economic policies begun by David and Solomon. (See map **385**.)

Aram's Offensive: While Ahab fortified a number of Judean cities, Ben Hadad II (also called Adad-Idri or Hadadezer, as he appears in the inscriptions of Shalmaneser III), ruler of Aram-Damascus, made a strenuous effort to fortify his country against the Assyrians* (see article) who had crossed the Euphrates and were threatening the west.

Ben Hadad wanted to secure his rear against the time when he would have to face this formidable enemy from the north. Accordingly, he embarked on what he planned as a precautionary campaign against Israel. Instead, it developed into a major war. I Kings records a lengthy struggle between the two countries, in which Ben Hadad II, accompanied by 32 Aramean princes of small states, penetrated deep into Israel territory and forced Ahab to withdraw to Samaria itself and from there negotiate the terms of his surrender. The negotiations broke down when Ben Hadad insisted that in addition to paying tribute, Ahab accept other humiliating conditions. With the support of his State Council*, Ahab had no choice but to refuse. However, although the siege was resumed, clever tactics forced the Arameans to retreat in haste. His defeat and the rising threat from Assyria forced Ben Hadad to adopt extreme measures in order to maintain his dominant position among the petty kingdoms which recognized his authority. He removed the kinglets from their posts and appointed military commanders in their stead (I K. 20:24; see Arameans*).

Aram's Leading Position: The doubt expressed by A. Alt with regard to Aram's dominance is not justified, since in 853 BCE, Aram-Damascus appears as the leading state of the north Syrian confederacy, which is described by Shalmaneser III as a single, unified country, without any mention of Aramean satellite states. During the time of the Assyrian Tiglat-Pileser, the northern stretches of Transjordan were no longer autonomous kingdoms, but provinces of Aram-Damascus, obviously the result of the reorganization program carried out by Ben Hadad II.

A year later, the unified Aram-Damascus forces invaded Israel again. The two armies met at Aphek, which for generations had marked the boundary between Israel and Aram at the edge of the Golan mountains. (Two generations later, Jehoash, king of Israel, also fought there against Aram.) Ahab was victorious and as a result, the two monarchs signed a peace treaty that included the opening of the Damascus market to Israel and the Samaria market to Aram (I K. 20:34). Though this "rapprochement" met with strong opposition from the prophets, it nevertheless reveals a realistic political sense.

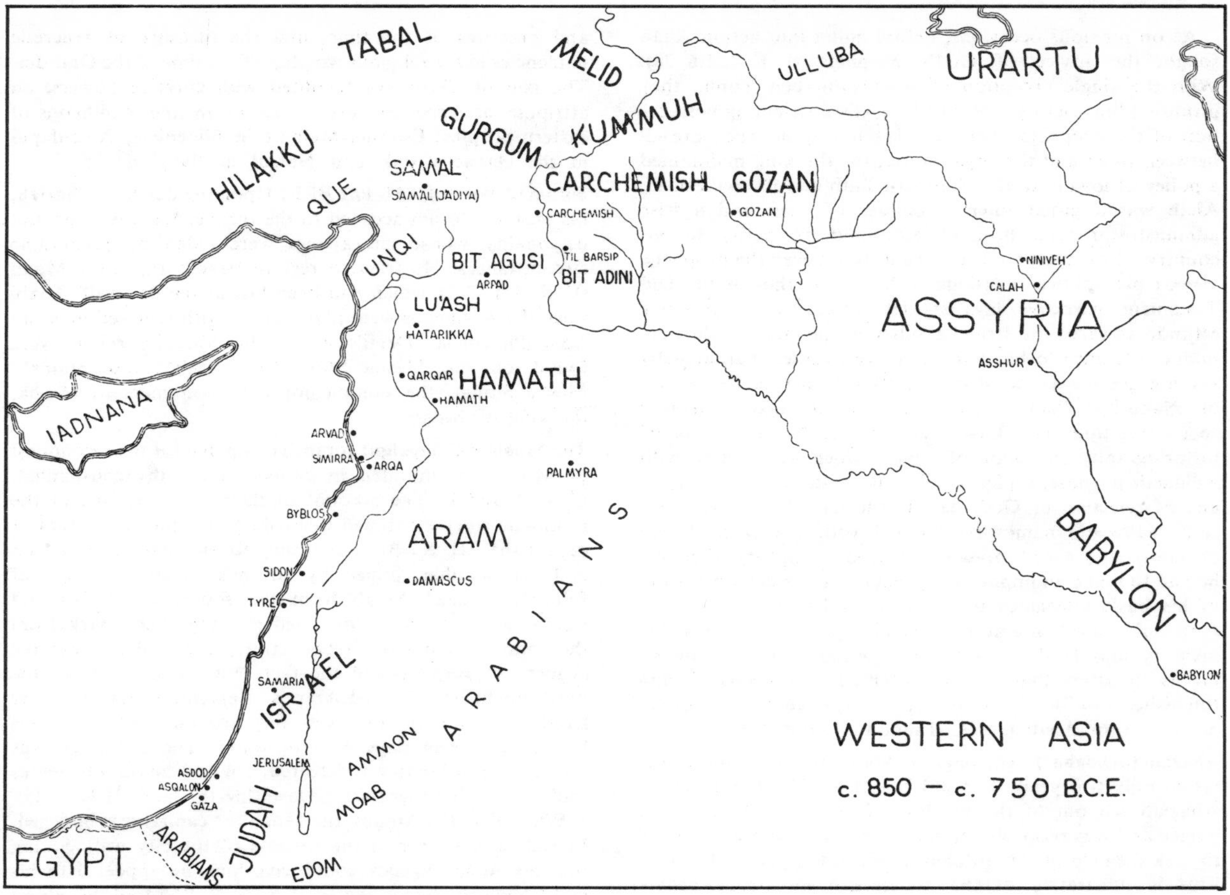

548

The Assyrian Resurgence: When Shalmaneser III succeeded his father Ashurnasirpal in 859 BCE, he inherited a powerful kingdom on the point of major expansion. Under Ashurnasirpal, Assyria's expeditions abroad had been little more than raids for plunder; Shalmaneser coordinated them into a grand design to annex large territories and exact annual tribute from them. Henceforth, military campaigns led by Shalmaneser or his commander-in-chief against Assyria's western neighbours became an almost annual event. In 858 BCE, Shalmaneser's drive was resisted by the combined forces of the north-Syrian confederacy. Nevertheless, in 855 BCE, he annexed the Aramean kingdom of Bet Adini, thus gaining effective control of the eastern crossing of the Euphrates. This turn of events caused the kingdoms of Syria and Palestine to bury their differences and form an alliance against the common enemy.

In 853 BCE, Shalmaneser III's attempt to capture the territories west of the Euphrates came up against the combined forces of the kingdoms of Qarqar, Hamat, Aram-Damascus, Israel, Que, Egypt and others (see illustrations under Assyria*) at the battle of Qarqar on the Orontes. This campaign is described in a detailed document known as the "Annals of Shalmaneser III" which, along with several shorter inscriptions, has been preserved intact. For all his bravado in claiming victory, there is no clear statement about the outcome of the battle of Qarqar; it is safe to conclude that the result was indecisive, although Syria and Palestine remained free of Assyrian rule. (See map **548** of Western Asia, 850–750 BCE.)

Collapse of the Syro-Israelite Confederacy: Following the battle of Qarqar, the Syro-Israel alliance collapsed, and the old feud between Aram and Hamat on one side and Israel on the other was revived. The Old Testament account does not mention this battle, simply stating (I K. 22:1) that after the battle of Aphek, the peace between Aram and Israel lasted for three years. War broke out anew when Ahab attempted to recapture Ramot-Gilead, the stronghold in Transjordan that controlled the royal trading route from Damascus southwards along the eastern plateau of Palestine to Moab and Edom. It is quite likely that the campaign to reconquer Ramot-Gilead, as described by Ahab's messengers to his ally, Jehoshaphat of Judah, who hastened to help him (I K. 22:2–4), was related to the struggle with Moab, hinted at in the Mesha Stone (see below). It says that Omri and his descendants opposed Moab for forty years. No doubt the Moabites found Aram a ready ally in their revolt against Israel. Ahab was killed in the disastrous battle at Ramot-Gilead in 852 BCE (I K. 22:35–36).

As on previous occasions, before going into action Ahab sought the advice of God's prophets (I K. 22:6–28). With the single exception of Michiyahu ben Yimla, they promised him victory. Despite Jezebel's unrelenting persecution of the prophets, there was apparently no open breach between them and the royal house, for the king maintained a policy of loyalty to the Yahwistic faith and its spokesmen. Ahab was a gifted ruler, a builder of cities and a wise administrator who brought economic prosperity to his country. His contemporaries, and at times even the prophets, viewed his political methods with favour, though the Old Testament narrative lays special stress on his negative attitude towards the Israelite religion, defined as showing undue tolerance to his wife's practices, rather than actually sinning. He is accused of complicity with her, as in the case of Naboth's vineyard, a grave offence against Israel's social traditions (see Law*; Government*). In later Israel historiography the book of Kings, which was written with a didactic purpose, depicts Ahab as the epitome of wickedness and of rejection of God, despite the fact that he gave his sons Yahwistic names (i.e. joined with the element yāh or yāhu), and asked guidance of God's prophets whenever he had to make an important decision, a clear demonstration of his basic allegiance to the God of Israel.

In talmudical literature several rabbis* defended his memory and lauded his political wisdom, even going so far as to assert that he had repented of his sins. A distinguished family of ancient Jerusalem once claimed direct descent from Ahab (Jerus. Talmud: Taanit 4:2).

Ahaziah (Jehoahaz): The reign of Ahaziah, Ahab's successor, lasted only two years, 852–851 BCE (I K. 22:51–53). When Ahaziah fell out of the window of an upper floor of his palace and was seriously injured (II K. 1) he sent messengers to seek the help of Ba'al-Zebub (Zebul), the god of Ekron*. This is illustrative of the widespread idolatrous beliefs and practices of the time, and the measure of syncretic tendencies in the religious worship of the time of the Omrides. The god of Ekron was credited with curative powers, an attribute ascribed to several deities in the pantheons of eastern peoples: Eshmun-Melkart in Phoenicia, Aesculapio in the classic world, and Nergal in Babylon.

Joram (Jehoram), 851–842 BCE: Upon the death of Ahaziah, his brother, Joram acceded to the throne. He was a forceful personality whose endeavours were aided by favourable circumstances. He tried to restore Israel's rule over Moab (II K. 1:1; 3:5) which had been lost at the death of Ahab, since the Arameans were preoccupied with renewed pressure from Phoenicia. Details about the Moabite revolt were found on the Mesha Stone (see Moab*; Inscriptions*: Mesha Stone), the commemorative monument of Mesha, the king of Moab.

The Moabite Campaign: Joram's campaign for the reconquest of Moab was initiated in cooperation with Jehoshaphat, king of Judah. The account of their action is part of the prophetic story attributed to Elisha*, disciple and successor of Elijah* (II K. 3). According to the narrative, Joram and Jehoshaphat, joined by Joram's vassal, the king of Edom*, invaded Moab from the south, via Judah and Edom, with Elisha's unqualified blessing. The attack from the south was based on two strategic considerations: the element of surprise and the fact that an attack from the north might have invited Aram's intervention. On the other hand, the southern route was very arduous and the troops had to go seven days without water. The campaign was successful and Moab was defeated. The Judeans and Israelites took a terrible vengeance, devastating the land (II K. 3:25).

When Kir (Kir Moab), the Moabite* capital was besieged, Mesha took shelter in the fortress of the city wall. Seeing that no human agency could save him, he appealed to his god Chemosh. According to II K. 3:27, "he took his eldest son who was to reign in his stead, and offered him for a burnt offering upon the wall. And there came great wrath upon Israel and they withdrew from him and returned to their own land."

Israel and Judah Weakened: As a result of the retreat from Kir, Jehoshaphat and Joram lost control over Moab and then over Ammon. The Israelite settlements in Transjordan, which had attained both prosperity and security only a short time before, were now hard pressed by the Arameans in the north and by the Moabites and Ammonites in the south.

The Old Testament narrative gives little information about relations between Israel and Aram in the time of Joram, but apparently the war with Aram over Ramot-Gilead dragged on. If the narrative of II Kings 7–8 belongs in this context, its reports on the wars between the two countries notes that Aram was victorious. But it would seem that this account refers to the period of Ben Hadad III of Damascus, son of Hazael, and not of Ben Hadad II, who was a contemporary of Joram of Israel. The name of the king of Israel who was involved in this war is not given.

After the battle of Ramot-Gilead, Israel's position in Transjordan was considerably weakened and its international prestige lost. In contrast to Ahab's position of leadership in 853 BCE, Joram was excluded from the defensive alliance against Shalmaneser III, concluded among the twelve states

in 848–845 BCE. The alliance, which was now headed by the kings of Damascus and Hamat, seems to have effectively opposed Shalmaneser several times between 849 and 841 BCE. After 845 BCE, Joram attempted to recapture Ramot-Gilead from Aram, which was hard pressed by Assyria. The throne of Ben Hadad II was seized by his commander, Hazael, who defeated and wounded Joram.

Economic Regression in Israel: The collapse of Israel's rule in Transjordan and the economic regression caused by the loss of the principal Arabian trade routes strengthened the opposition of the military leaders against Joram. This opposition was fanned by the prophets, led by Elijah and Elisha (II K. 9:1–10), who were antagonistic to the house of Ahab on account of his leniency to the worshippers of the Tyrian Ba'al. Joram tried to placate the prophets by removing the Ba'al stele put up by his father (II K. 3:2) but it was too late.

One effect of the rule of the Omri dynasty was to give the upper classes much greater ascendancy over the poorer elements, who were reduced to a wretched state. During its rule, the Omri dynasty's foreign policy suffered many setbacks that evoked strong popular opposition, increased by the hostility of the prophets. The situation can be judged from the complaint voiced before Elisha by one of the widows of the "sons of the prophets" (II K. 4:1–7), where the harsh law of selling children into slavery in repayment of their fathers' debts is first mentioned. Echoes of economic depression emerge from the narrative of the famine in Samaria on the eve of Jehu's uprising (II K. 4:38–44). General discontent was inflamed by the prophets' hatred of the house of Omri. Elijah's curse on Ahab and his descendants in connection with the incident of Naboth's vineyard had a special significance for the people, for the Israelites had never been subjected to despotic rule. The people were apparently ready for rebellion and their unrest was fanned by the extremists. Rebellious army commanders like Jehu would have acted in line with what they felt to be popular sentiment.

Jehu's Dynasty: Jehu (841–814 BCE): The story of the uprising, given in detail (II K. 9) describes how Elijah's prophecy of the doom of the house of Omri was realized. Revolt was triggered off by one of the prophets in the group led by Elisha. He anointed Jehu, commander of the troops drawn up for battle against the Arameans at Ramot-Gilead, whereupon his brother officers acclaimed him king of Israel.

Jehu marched at the head of his army to the city of Jezreel, where Joram was recuperating from his wounds, and killed both him and Jezebel. Then he hastened to Samaria, killing off all Ahab's descendants on the way. When he found Ahaziah, king of Judah, he killed him as well. Ahaziah was also a member of the house of Omri through his mother, Athaliah (see Part III, Ahaziah). The violence of the scene (**549**), with a change of costume and locality, may be visualized from a 7th c. BCE bas-relief of Ashurbanipal in his chariot, waging war against the Syrians. A hundred years later, the prophet Hosea recalled this dastardly act, vigorously condemning it (Hos. 1:4). In alliance with Jonadab, son of Rehab, leader of the Rehabite clan (whose loyalty to God is extolled by Jeremiah; Jer. 35), Jehu entered Samaria and mercilessly exterminated all the survivors of Ahab's house and all the followers of Ba'al (II K. 10:17–28).

Aftermath of Jehu's Purge: The successful revolt resulted in profound changes in the internal and external policies of the Kingdom of Israel. The destruction of the Ba'al stele largely restored the worship of Yahweh. Judging by various lists of names of the period found on potsherds, theophoric names in which "Ba'al" was a component became less frequent. The drastic attack on Ba'al worship had no adverse effect on the official cult of "the calves" at Bethel and Dan, since the people regarded these as legitimate objects of worship. In fact, with the exception of Hosea, no prophet condemned them until Josiah's extensive reforms were carried out (see Part V). The Old Testament narrative gives full credit to Jehu for destroying Ba'al (II K. 10:28) but does not entirely exonerate him from blame, because in worldly matters he continued in the steps of Jeroboam (II K. 10:29).

The Ascendance of Damascus; Hazael and Jehu: The extermination of the House of Omri, the murder of Ahaziah, and the loss of the trade routes in Transjordan brought to an end the triple alliance of Israel, Judah and Tyre. In the face of the Assyrian threat to the Northern Kingdom after its defeat of Hazael, king of Aram (841 BCE), Jehu paid tribute to Shalmaneser III of Assyria, and made peace with him. The Black Obelisk (**550a. b**) of the Assyrian king (see Assyria*) which records his military achievements and depicts the payment of tribute from five different regions actually shows Jehu (**551**) humbly prostrating himself before him, accompanied by Israelites bearing rich tribute. The inscription reads: "Tribute of Iau (Jehu) of Mar Humri (House of Omri)" and lists his offerings.

550 b

550 a

551

When Assyrian pressure relaxed in 838 BCE and the Arameans could safely renew their aggressive policy, Israel was powerless to stem the tide of Aramean conquest throughout Transjordan (II K. 10:32–33). As a result, western Palestine itself lay wide open to Hazael's attacks. It may be assumed that his campaign against Judah in the 23rd year of the reign of Joash (II K. 12:7, 18), king of Judah, weakened the Kingdom of Israel still further. The death of Jehu in the 28th year of his reign may have been a direct consequence of these reverses.

Jehoahaz (814–800 BCE): Jehu's son, Jehoahaz, had to meet the increased pressure from Hazael and his son, Ben Hadad III, and had to organize resistance to the best of his ability. The particular king referred to in II K. 5–7 is not named, but he can only have been Jehoahaz. During his reign, Samaria was besieged by Aram and was only saved when reports that they were about to be attacked by the Hittites forced the Arameans to withdraw. The enfeebled state of Israel is reflected in the statement (II K. 13:7) that the king was left with only 50 horsemen, ten chariots and 10,000 infantrymen. The conquerors cruelly maltreated the Israelites, willingly aided by their Ammonite allies.

The statement in II K. 13:5 that Yahweh sent Israel a saviour in response to their repentance is no doubt another way of reporting the renewal of the Assyrian drive westwards against Israel's enemy, Aram. Adad-Nirari III invaded Aram and besieged Damascus (802 BCE), forcing Ben Hadad to pay him tribute; Tyre, Sidon, Philistia and Israel also paid tribute to him.

Resurgence under Jehoash (800–784 BCE): Conditions improved in the first years of the reign of Jehoahaz' son, Jehoash. With the relaxation of the threat from Aram, Israel was able to recover part of its possessions in Transjordan. In II K. 13:14–19, 25, it is reported that Jehoash defeated Ben Hadad three times. In 196 BCE, Adad-Nirari set out on his second campaign against Aram-Damascus. The unfortunate Ben-Hadad was soundly beaten by his northern neighbour, Hamat, as related in the inscription on the stele of Zakir, king of Hamat and Lu'ash in Northern Syria.

Restoration of Israel's military strength served to improve its relations with Judah. When Amaziah, son of Joash, king of Judah (798–769 BCE) planned to attack Edom, he hired many soldiers from Israel (II Ch. 25:6). At the end of his reign, Amaziah provoked Jehoash, king of Israel, who gained a signal victory at the battle near Ben-Shemen, leaving no doubt as to which was the stronger of the sister states.

The Rise of Israel under Jeroboam II: According to certain chronological systems (see below, Chronological Table), it seems that out of the 41 years of his reign, Jeroboam II was co-regent with his father for four years (789–784 BCE). The Old Testament narrative is very perfunctory concerning Jeroboam II's long and prosperous reign. He extended the boundaries of Israel from the borders of Hamat to the brook of Arabah at the southern end of the Dead Sea (II K. 14:25). Whether Jeroboam reestablished all the Davidic frontier in Syria (see David*) and even took Damascus itself is uncertain. It may be implied, however, that he not only fought against the Arameans and repulsed their attacks, but that he actually defeated Aram and annexed Aramean land in Transjordan north of the Yarmuk river.

The text of II K. 14:28 is obscure as to the actual events which led to these achievements. The book of Amos*, which reflects the period of Jeroboam II, hints at two battles between Israel and Aram, one at Karnayim in Bashan and the other at Lo-Dabar in Gilead. Exactly when these events took place is unfortunately not known.

The real cause of Jeroboam's expansion should be sought in the international situation. After Adad-Nirari (809–782 BCE) had subdued Aram, strong pressure from the north forced him to abandon the bridgehead which he had secured west of the Euphrates. Without Aram's support, the Transjordan kingdoms were powerless to stem the Israelite tide. It appears that Jeroboam, with the loyal support of Uzziah, king of Judah (see Part III), who had reconquered Eilat, now regained control of the trade routes to the Red Sea and Arabian* ports (see Ships*; Trade*). In order to consolidate his rule in Transjordan, Jeroboam extended Israelite settlement, as may be gathered from the genealogical lists of the tribes* of Reuben*, Gad* and Manasseh*. attributed to the days of Jeroboam II of Israel and Jotham, king of Judah (I Chr. 5:3–26; see map **547**).

Though the position at the end of Jeroboam's reign is not clear, the resurgence and expansion of the kingdom may justify an opinion advanced by H. Tadmor that Israel in his day won ascendancy over Judah and led it and, moreover, that it controlled the kingdoms of Syria and Palestine.

Rise of a Landed Aristocracy: It is assumed by some scholars that those who benefitted most from this increased expansion of territory were the high officials and the aristocracy. This may explain why Amos* (4:1) decries the cupidity of the wives of the high officials of Gilead. It was not only from the resources of Transjordan and international trade that a few high officers waxed rich. They also built themselves palaces and houses decorated with ivory, as in Samaria*, while poor debtors were dispossessed and sold into slavery (Amos 8:6). This new landed gentry became quite powerful and there can be little doubt that they had a hand in the frequent dynastic changes which followed the death of Jeroboam (748 BCE) and continued until the final extinction of the Kingdom of Israel in 722 BCE, when it was absorbed into the Assyrian empire (see Part IV).

A prominent member of the new aristocracy was Ben Tabael (Is. 7:6), who owned vast estates in southern Transjordan. He was picked as a candidate to rule over Judah by a later usurper of the throne of Israel, Pekah, son of Remaliahu (see below, Part IV, B). According to the theory of B. Mazar, Ben Tabael was the distant ancestor of one of the leading and enduring families of Transjordan, the Tobiads, who played an important part in Judean politics in the 2nd c. BCE (see Hasmoneans*).

III. KINGDOM OF JUDAH — REHOBOAM TO THE DEATH OF UZZIAH: **Rehoboam's Reign and the Territorial Battles:** Two generations of incessant fighting between the Kingdoms of Israel and Judah followed the division of the United Monarchy (see Part I). Judah was badly weakened and completely lost control over Ammon and Moab, also largely over Edom. The somewhat abbreviated story in I K. 11:14–22 reveals that Edom had previously revolted against Solomon. The Judean heirs of the great Davidic dynasty now reigned over a shrunken territory that consisted only of the areas of the tribes* of Judah, Simeon* and Benjamin*, and possibly also Reuben* in Transjordan. The Benjaminite territory was particularly vital to the Judean Kingdom, as without it, its capital, Jerusalem, would have been directly on the border with Israel and thus vulnerable from the north. This would have threatened the undisturbed functioning of the Temple, which was an essential part of the fabric of the Davidic monarchy.

The Shoshenk I (Shishak) Campaign: In addition to internal and inter-state worries, Judah had to face the imperialist ambitions of the 22nd Dynasty in Egypt, under the leadership of Shoshenk I (Shishak), a Libyan general (see Egypt*). Shoshenk came to the Egyptian throne during the second half of Solomon's reign (ca. 945 BCE) and consistently supported all foes of the Davidic dynasty (I K. 11). He seems to have had other designs on the land. We are told by the Bible that after the division, the Northern Kingdom encouraged Shoshenk to raid Judean towns. It may perhaps be that he used Israel's invitation as an excuse to invade the whole land. He then struck with terrific force. According to I K. 14:25–28, he invaded Judah in 923 BCE, captured several fortified towns and besieged Jerusalem with his strong multi-national army, with its war-chariots and cavalry. To induce him to withdraw, Rehoboam was forced to pay a heavy tribute, including some of the Temple vessels and precious items from the royal treasury. A record of the campaign, which appears on the southern wall of the Temple of Amon at Karnak indicates the true scope of the campaign. It lists 150 places in this pattern (**552**), which he claimed to have taken, but does not include Jerusalem in the list of towns stormed or destroyed. Scholars have had considerable difficulty in explaining the lack of logical order in the list. B. Mazar has suggested that Shoshenk went through western and northern Judah, swung eastward over southern Mount Ephraim and from there to the Jordan crossing. He then went through the rich towns of the valley of Succot in Transjordan and recrossed the Jordan at a point further north. Fragments of a stele uncovered at Megiddo* record the occupation of that town by the Egyptians. From Megiddo, Shoshenk turned south to Samaria and from there back to Egypt. At the same time a column of his army went mainly through the Negeb and Edom*. This itinerary suggests that Shoshenk's forces concentrated on the Northern Kingdom and Edom, giving Judah a wide berth. If the opinion that Shoshenk's campaign was nothing more than a raid for plunder is accepted, the

552

Mazar itinerary can be substantiated by the fact that the newly established and relatively poor Kingdom of Israel could not bribe him sufficiently, and thus by encouraging his attack on Judah, had invited its own disaster. The wealthy Judah was able to offer a substantial ransom, which may explain the absence of Jerusalem from the list of besieged towns.

Judah Fortified and Extended: According to II Ch. 12:13, after the Shoshenk campaigns, Rehoboam strengthened his kingdom. During his 17 year reign, he built a chain of fortifications around Jerusalem and along the western and southern frontier of Judah. No special measures were taken to protect the eastern border, where the Jordan depression constituted a natural barrier. The northern frontier was not fortified either, as the conflict between Judah and Israel was still in its initial stage, and Rehoboam harboured ambitions in that direction. (See map **547**, Judah).

Abiyah (911–908 BCE): In 911 BCE, Abiyah (called Abijam in Kings), Rehoboam's son by Michiyahu (Maacha) from the district of Gibeath-Benjamin (II Ch. 13:2), ascended the throne. Rehoboam's marriage to Michiyahu, his naming Abiyah as his heir and appointing him to responsible military and administrative positions during his lifetime (II Ch. 11:22–23), may indicate a desire to foster good relations with the tribe of Benjamin.

II Ch. 13 gives a detailed account of Abiyah's large-scale offensive against Jeroboam, highlighting his successful battle near Mount Zemerayim (possibly Ras el-Simera between Rimon and Ophra) in Ephraim. As a result, Judah's territory was extended not only over the territory of Benjamin but also over the southern part of Ephraim. The important towns of Bethel* (II Ch. 12:14), Yeshana and Ophra succumbed to him. This was a heavy blow to Jeroboam, who died soon afterwards. (See map **547**.)

Assah (908–867 BCE): Abiyah reigned only three years and was succeeded by his son Assah in 908 BCE. In the I Kings and II Chronicles narratives concerning the rule of Assah which lasted 41 years, there are discrepancies that are not easily reconciled. According to the former, Maacha, daughter of Abishalom, was Assah's mother, but according to II Ch. 14 she was his grandmother. The I Kings version, which seems to be the more acceptable to scholars, states that during the first 15 years of Assah's reign, she exerted considerable influence over affairs of state and forms of worship, and may even have acted as regent until Assah attained his majority, in the same manner as Joash's mother, Athaliah.

The first decade of Assah's kingship was peaceful (II Ch. 14:1) and was devoted to fortifying the country and giving thorough training to the armed forces (II Ch. 14:6–8). When Zerah the Cushite later invaded the country with what may have been a thousand units and reached Maresha, Judah's well-trained forces roundly defeated him and drove him back to Gerar between Gaza and Beersheba. Some authorities believe that Zerah was actually Osorkon I (ca. 924–895 BCE), son of Shoshenk. This view is not widely supported, however, since the names are quite different and the normal Hebrew rendering of Osorkon would be nothing like Zerah.

Assah's Reforms: Once all danger from the south had been removed, Assah turned his attention to internal reforms. During his mother's regency, idolatrous practices were reintroduced into Jerusalem. Such practices had been known since the days of Solomon* who had shown excessive tolerance for the pagan forms of worship of his foreign wives. Assah demoted Maacha from her exalted position and destroyed the image (*mifletzet* in Hebrew) which his mother had set up in honour of Asherah. With the help of the prophet Azariahu ben Oded be abolished all foreign religious rites and sanctuaries in Judah and the areas conquered by his father and himself (II Ch. 15:8; I K. 15:12–13). While Assah's reforms cannot be compared with those of Hezekiah and Josiah in a later age, and though worship at the high-places* was not condemned during his rule, there can be no doubt that Assah's actions substantially contributed to the strengthening and preservation of monotheism in the evolving Jewish religion, as well as creating a clear cleavage in all cultic issues between Judah and Israel. Syncretic popular practices, on the other hand, were allowed to flourish in the Northern Kingdom (see Idol Worship in Israel*).

Baashah's War with Judah: While Judah was in the process of internal reformation, in Israel, Baashah forcibly ended the dynasty of Jeroboam (see Part II). After consolidating his position and concluding a treaty with Ben Hadad I, king of Aram-Damascus* on the northern border of Israel, Baashah began a military campaign against Judah in the 26th year of Assah's reign. He reconquered and fortified the whole southern zone of Ephraim, as far as Ramah (now Nabi Samuel) "in order to close all exits to Assah". As Ramah is only seven miles north of Jerusalem on the highroad from Ephraim, Judah was put in a precarious position. Assah appealed to Ben Hadad in the name of the treaty that had been concluded between their fathers, and in order to induce him further, sent him valuable treasures from the Temple (II Ch. 16:2–6). Ben Hadad responded favourably and quickly dispatched a large force that occupied and plundered Israel's territory in Transjordan and eastern Galilee (I K. 15:17–20), isolating Golan and Bashan. Ben Hadad did not follow up his victory, probably due to difficulties of his own in northern Syria. The Assyrian Empire under Adad Nirari II was then becoming a serious threat. Baashah capitulated and abandoned all further attempts at expansion. Ramah was restored to Assah, who reoccupied and fortified Benjamin (I K. 15:21). The Old Testament says nothing about the reoccupation of parts of Ephraim, however.

Assah saw no useful purpose in continuing the border struggle with Israel and fixed a permanent boundary line between the two kingdoms. Benjamin became part of Judah and Assah apparently gave up all claims to Ephraimite territory. As a precaution, he fortified the frontier at Geba and Mitzpah (Tel el-Nasbeh). In the excavations carried out by W.F. Albright at Tel el-Ful, the present site of Geba, a strong fortress dating from the 9th c. BCE was uncovered. Albright identifies it with Assah's fortification.

About ten years later Omri (see Part II) ascended the throne of the Northern Kingdom and brought the conflict between the two kingdoms to an end by concluding a treaty with Judah. Both sides had apparently reached a state of military and political strength which made a test of arms seem futile. Moreover, Omri desired friendly relations with Judah and internal peace in the whole land. The book of Kings does not indicate exactly when this took place, but it seems that the treaty concluded between them as equals resulted in a revival of trade with Israel, and through Israel with the lands of the south. This was an important step towards the alliance concluded between Omri's son Ahab and Jehoshaphat of Judah (see below).

Reaction to the Campaign: Assah's treaty with Ben Hadad against the Northern Kingdom, and the heavy losses that Israel suffered at the hands of Aramaean troops, rekindled the feeling of solidarity that had existed during the United Kingdom, even to the point of some Judean hostility towards Assah. According to II Ch. 16:7–10, Assah was severely berated by Hanani the Seer, who was imprisoned along with those who echoed his views. While it is not certain whether or not such criticism spread beyond the prophetic circles, no real threat of rebellion materialized.

In the 39th year of his reign, Assah fell ill with a serious foot disease and died two years later (II Ch. 16:12–13). He had ruled 41 years. It is quite possible that during his last years, his son Jehoshaphat acted as regent (870–867 BCE).

The Reign of Jehoshaphat (867–846 BCE): Jehoshaphat assumed the throne in the 4th year of Ahab's reign over the Kingdom of Israel. At that time, Judah held Eilat and Ezion-Geber, gateway to the profitable land and sea trade to Arabia, the Red Sea and East Africa. The Northern Kingdom was becoming powerful, and Jehoshaphat soon realized the political and economic benefits which would accrue to Judah if it joined the Tyre-Israel alliance. Early in his reign, therefore, he concluded a treaty with the king of Israel (I K. 22:44; II Ch. 18:1). These ties with Israel were later strengthened by the marriage of the crown-prince, Joram, son of Jehoshaphat, to Athaliah, daughter of Ahab and Jezebel (see Part II).

Reforms: The religious reforms of Assah had struck deep roots in Jerusalem and were continued in the days of Jehoshaphat. In the third year of his reign, Jehoshaphat introduced a new juridical system (II Ch. 19:4–11). Several biblical authorities have pointed out that this system constituted the basis for the principles expressed in Deuteronomy. It has been shown by W.F. Albright that Jehoshaphat's juridical system had many points of similarity with that of Egypt during the New Kingdom (see Egypt*); the connection was undoubtedly indirect, coming about via neighbouring nations, since Egypt had practically no influence over Palestine at that time.

Jehoshaphat's record in the field of administrative reform is no less noteworthy than in the juridical field. He divided Judah into districts and collecting centres (II Ch. 17:12; see Government and Authority*, II). During the reigns of Assah and Jehoshaphat, Judah and Israel extended their borders to the south and south-west. Assah acquired new territories in the coastal province of Gerar (II Ch. 14:13–14), while the Philistines and Arabs paid Jehoshaphat tribute (II Ch. 17:11). Some authorities have advanced the opinion that the tribal territories listed in Joshua actually reflect the administrative divisions set up by Jehoshaphat.

Civil reforms were supplemented by military measures such as fortifying the cities in which storehouses to hold the king's treasures and war equipment were built (II Ch. 17:12–13). He stationed garrisons in these cities and generally reorganized the whole military system. Remains of fortifications found in Judah and the Negeb (**553**) are very similar to those built at about the same time by Omri and Ahab (see Part II).

553

Economic Expansion: Economic expansion especially in foreign trade also took place, bringing the country to new heights of prosperity, reminiscent of the days of Solomon. Judah's control over Edom (I K. 22) made trade with Arabia and the Red Sea countries possible, and the copper mines in the Arabah were worked. The excavations of Nelson Glueck showed that Ezion-Geber expanded considerably; however the ships which Jehoshaphat built to increase his overseas trade were wrecked there (I K. 22:48; see Ships and Navigation*). Ahaziah, king of Israel, tried to prevail on him to try again after this setback, but Jehoshaphat refused, apparently because by that time his rule over Edom and other Transjordan territories had been considerably weakened.

The Alliance against Aram: The alliance with Israel obliged Judah to oppose Aram-Damascus, Judah's ally from the days of Assah. As long as the Assyrians under Shalmaneser III did not directly threaten territories west of the Euphrates, Aram's expansionist aims were directed against Israel. Judah was particularly interested in the victory of Ahab against Aram, for Ahab's success would remove the threat to Israel's territories in Transjordan and especially the danger to Judah's rule over Edom. This was vitally important, for it guaranteed unhampered control of the land routes to the south on which Judah's material prosperity, as well as that of her allies, Israel and Tyre, depended. Thus, when Ahab asked Jehoshaphat for military aid at Ramot Gilead, the latter's response was: "I am as you are, my people as your people, my horses as your horses" (I K. 22:4). Again after Ahab's death, when Moab revolted against Israel (II K. 1:1), Ahab's second son, Joram, appealed to Jehoshaphat to come to his aid, and Jehoshaphat readily responded, himself leading the Judean and Edomite troops (II K. 3:8–9).

The inconclusive war with Moab (see Part II) and the victory of Aram at Ramot-Gilead not only undermined Israel's rule in Transjordan, but also weakened Judah's hold on Edom. In II Ch. 20, a midrashic-aggadic tradition (see Biblical Criticism*) has been preserved which seems to reflect an event which occurred in the last year of Jehoshaphat's reign. It alleges that the Ammonites, Moabites and Edomites occupied 'Ein Gedi and prepared to storm Jerusalem. Jehoshaphat repulsed the attack in the Tekoa desert near Bethlehem, apparently as a result of dissensions among the allies. In any case, Judah was saved, and its power in Transjordan preserved for a little longer. Jehoshaphat died shortly after these events. The decline and final fall of Israel began immediately after his death in the reign of his successor, his son Joram (Jehoram).

Joram (846–843 BCE): Joram apparently assumed actual power during his father's lifetime (851 BCE), as hinted at in II Ch. 21:5, perhaps because of serious dissensions among his brothers and the fear of an upheaval. Apart from his natural right as eldest son, Joram was a politic choice as he was married to Athaliah, daughter of Jezebel, the princess of Tyre. For this reason, however, there was also serious opposition to Joram in court circles, and he struck back by killing off all his brothers and several ministers (II Ch. 21:4). According to B. Thiele and H. Tadmor, Joram must have been co-ruler together with his father for four years out of the eight during which he reigned (851–846 BCE). Such an assumption would synchronize the statement in II K. 8:16 that Joram ascended the throne of Judah in the fifth year of the reign of Joram, son of Ahab, king of Israel (see Part II) with II K. 3:1 in which it is said that Ahab's son ascended the throne in the 18th year of Jehoshaphat, who ruled for 25 years (I K. 22:42) including his co-regency.

Loss of Edom and the Negeb: Israel's loss of control over Transjordan had an adverse affect on Judah during Joram's sole rule. Jehoshaphat had succeeded in repulsing the attack of the Transjordan kingdoms, but in Joram's reign, Judah's rule in Edom, the Arabah and the northern Negeb collapsed (II K. 8:20–22).

The secession of Edom brought about a serious dislocation of the economic structure set up by Jehoshaphat, and the collapse of his administrative and military machinery. This was followed by the invasion of Judah by the Philistines and the Arabs. The measure of Judah's helplessness can be seen from the narrative in II Ch. 21:16–17, which relates that the raiders were able to capture the king's family and treasures.

Despite these serious reverses, the alliance between the Kingdoms of Judah and Israel was not repudiated. Israel kept up a desperate struggle against Aram which was allied to the foes of the two sister Kingdoms.

Phoenician Influence: Joram consistently adhered to the treaties contracted by his father, not only from political considerations, but also because of his wife, Athaliah, a scion of the House of Omri. Athaliah had a forceful personality and following Jehoshaphat's death she became an influential figure in the court. Through her efforts, Phoenician culture and religious syncretism advanced in Judah. Ironically, the administrative reforms introduced by Jehoshaphat contributed to this state of affairs, for they created an aristocracy of officials, merchant princes and officers who were anxious to promote and expand foreign trade, which included fostering Phoenician culture and customs. Jehoshaphat's death removed the last obstacle to the ascendancy of these elements.

Ahaziah (843–842 BCE): Joram died of "an incurable disease", and the citizens of Jerusalem (presumably the court dignitaries) crowned his only surviving son, Ahaziah (II Ch. 22:1). Ahaziah changed none of his father's internal or foreign policies. He rushed to the assistance of Joram, king of Israel, in his struggle against Aram at Ramot Gilead, where Joram was seriously wounded. When Ahaziah came to visit him during his convalescence at Jezreel, he was caught unaware by the *coup d'etat* of Jehu, who was bent on annihilating the entire House of Omri, and killed Ahaziah as well (see Part II).

Athaliah (842–836 BCE): With the liquidation of the Omri dynasty and the religion of Ba'al of Tyre in Israel, Phoenician worship came into its own in Judah. Ahaziah's death left his mother, Athaliah, as sole ruler of the Kingdom of Judah. (After the death of Jehoshaphat, her husband, Joram, had killed off all his brothers and their partisans in order to eliminate possible rivals.) Athaliah was an ambitious and ruthless woman and it is recorded (II K. 11:1–3) that her first act was to kill off every member of the Davidic house who might become the focus of opposition to her rule. This tradition is undoubtedly biased against her and it is difficult, at this distance, to judge all the factors in the confused situation. The queen could only claim authority on behalf of her grandson, Joash; she had no following, and was not, herself, of the royal Davidic line. She may have wiped out what remnants of the royal family her husband had spared as a protection against a possible revolt, but she could hardly have killed them all. Nevertheless, her action was unprecedented and her tyrannous rule had no legitimacy in the eyes of the people.

According to II K. 11:4–21, only Joash escaped in the massacre. He was saved by Ahaziah's sister and remained hidden in the Temple for six years, thus assuring the continuity of the Davidic dynasty.

The veneration in which the House of David was held by the masses, to whom Athaliah was a bloodthirsty usurper, deprived her of any social or political support. Only through force was she able to maintain her position for six years. When the opportunity came, the people rose against her, led by Jehoiada, the chief priest. It is clear from the narrative in II K. 11 that the overthrow of Athaliah was carried out by Jehoiada as a surprise action, with the help of the army commanders and the people — or as put in the Bible, the "'am–ha'aretz" (people of the land; see Government and Authority*). A national revolution was thus summed up.

Joash (836–798 BCE): The anointing of the boy-king, Joash, was symbolic of the love of the people for anything pertaining to the lawful and divinely appointed House of David. The killing of Athaliah and the priests of Ba'al was a natural corollary of Joash's accession to the throne.

Until Joash attained his majority, Jehoiada (who was allied by marriage to the royal house) acted as regent, which considerably strengthened the status of the priesthood. On attaining his majority, however, the king assumed direct responsibility for the administration of the Temple. He ordered extensive repairs (II K. 12:5), and when the priests were not sufficiently active in raising the necessary funds, Joash ordered the conscription of funds from the people under the combined supervision of the King's secretary and the High Priest (II K. 12:10–11). (The same procedure was repeated much later by Josiah, who entrusted the task to Shaphan the Scribe and Hilkiya, the chief priest, as described in II K. 22:3–7).

Aram's Invasion: In the 23rd year of Joash's reign, Judah was invaded by Hazael, King of Aram, who captured Gath and prepared to storm Jerusalem. Joash averted disaster by following Rehoboam's example, and surrendering all the sacred vessels and gold in the Temple treasury to Hazael (II K. 12:18). This act reduced Judah to a state of penury, weakened its political position and encouraged its neighbours to invade its borders. Internal opposition to Joash also increased following the death of Jehoiada, the chief priest. The Bible narrative accuses the king of worshipping idols under the influence of several of his ministers. The conflict between the king and the priests assumed serious proportions, and the king ordered Zechariah, son of Jehoiada, put to death (II Ch. 24:17–22), an act for which he was himself assassinated (II Ch. 24:24–25).

Resurgence under Amaziah (798–769 BCE): The group of ministers who seized power after the assassination of Joash enthroned his son, Amaziah, then 25 years old. It is recorded in his favour that Amaziah later avenged the murder of his father, but although he followed Mosaic Law, he did not kill off the sons of the ministers (II Ch. 25:1–4). Amaziah hoped to put an end to internal party conflicts by this action, but such clemency was unheard of in his time and created an important legal precedent (see Law*).

Amaziah distinguished himself mainly in the military sphere. Ben Hadad III's power was broken by Adad-Nirari of Assyria (see Aram*) and the Aramean's defeat opened up new possibilities for Israel and Judah alike. Early in his reign Amaziah introduced conscription as a means of strengthening his army numerically. His first military campaign was against Edom, which had thrown off the Judean yoke in the days of Joram. He defeated Edom at the "Valley of Salt" which most authorities identify with the Arabah (II K. 14:7; II Ch. 25:11–12). As he could not follow through and capture Eilat, he consolidated his position in northern Edom and took Sela (today a-Sala), making it a Jewish town and renaming it Joktheel.

His victory over Edom led Amaziah to hope that the union between Israel and Judah would be renewed under his leadership. But he miscalculated his own strength and that of Jehoash, king of Israel. Israel was obviously much the stronger, and Amaziah's overtures were treated with scorn by Jehoash, and likened to the offer of intermarriage made by the thistle to the cedar (II K. 14:9). Amaziah disregarded the advice of his counsellors, however, and continued to provoke Israel. In the engagement which took place near Beth-Shemesh* in the 15th year of his reign, his army was routed and he was taken prisoner by Jehoash. The enemy broke into Jerusalem, destroyed part of its walls, plundered the Temple treasures, and took many hostages to Samaria (II K. 14:11–14). Amaziah was later set free on the understanding that he recognize Israel's hegemony.

The Bible narrative is very brief concerning the last fifteen years of Amaziah's reign. His death at Lachish* was brought about by a conspiracy.

Uzziah (769–733 BCE): The conspiracy notwithstanding, the people of Judah remained loyal to the Davidic line, and put the 16-year-old Uzziah (Azariah), son of Amaziah, on the throne. During part of Uzziah's reign, he was afflicted with leprosy (II K. 15:5) and his son Jotham acted as regent. The reign of Uzziah-Jotham was the most notable since the schism. Able-bodied men were mustered and equipped with effective weapons (II Ch. 26:11–14), and by the end of the reign Judah had expanded far beyond its former frontiers, penetrating deep into Ashdod* and Philistia, which gave it control of the main trade route to Egypt (II Ch. 26:6–8). Uzziah also extended his dominions southward to the Red Sea, restoring Eilat to Judah and rebuilding it (II Ch. 26:2). The excavations of Nelson Glueck at Ezion-Geber (Tel el-Khulifeh near modern Eilat), show clear evidence of the development of the town during the Uzziah-Jotham regime. A royal seal* bearing the name of Jotham was discovered there. Following the example of previous kings, Uzziah put up numerous fortifications, especially in and around Jerusalem (II Ch. 26:9), such as the fortified palace excavated at Ramat-Rachel (**554**). He also took steps to increase the population of the southern Negeb (II Ch. 26:10). The Old Testament states that this was due to his love for the land (II Ch. 26:10) but probably he also wished to establish strong defences against the desert tribes. Some authorities attribute the fortress at

554

Kadesh-Barnea (Tel el-Qudeirat, **555**) to the days of Uzziah. Ramat-Matred (see map **78**) is another fortified town attributed to Uzziah in the Western Negeb. This is an Israelite fort (**553**) on the road to Edom, built before Uzziah's time.

The reference to the subjugation of the Ammonites by Uzziah and Jotham (II Ch. 26:8; 27:5) is of special interest as it suggests a shift of power from Israel to Judah, for the areas north of the Arnon had always been within the sphere of influence of Israel and not of Judah. The Bible reference fits in with the Assyrian inscriptions of Tiglat-Pileser III, according to which he fought in northern Syria in 738 BCE against a Syrian coalition led by an "Azariyau of Yaudu". In all likelihood the reference is to Uzziah (Azariah). The members of the Syrian coalition were cities in northern and central Syria: Arpad, Hadrach, Semer and Calneh (see Aram*).

After the death of Jeroboam II of Israel in 748 BCE, Uzziah seemed not only to have gained control of the empire which Jeroboam had built, but to some extent to have imposed his rule over Israel itself. Even Uzziah could not stand up against the might of Tiglat-Pileser III, and he was decisively defeated. According to H. Tadmor, an echo of the presence of the army of Judah in northern Syria may perhaps be found in the oracle of an anonymous prophet whose visions were incorporated in the book of Zechariah (9:1): "The might of the Lord is against the land of Hadrach and will rest upon Damascus." H. Tadmor and Ch. Rabin have argued in favour of the rendering "might" for the word usually translated "word" (in Hebrew "d'bar").

The result of this shift of power was the complete withdrawal of Judah from Syria and Israel during the latter part of the reign of Menachem, Son of Gadi. However, Judah was spared the harsh treatment which Tiglat-Pileser meted out to the other members of the coalition in 738 BCE. Such treatment is illustrated by an Assyrian king (**556**) holding enemies by ropes tied to rings through their noses (II K. 19:28; Ezk. 38:4; Is. 37:29). Probably, as H. Tadmor believes, this leniency was in consideration of a definite undertaking by the Judean king not to join any new anti-Assyrian alliance.

When Uzziah died, he was not interred in the City of David together with his forefathers, but at "the burial ground of the Kings because they said that he was a leper" (II Ch. 26:23). Josephus (Antiq. 9, 10:4) says that he was buried in the king's gardens near the Pool of Siloam. Talmudic references report that the remains of Uzziah were removed at some unspecified date. This would lend credence to an inscription on a stone (**538**) bearing Uzziah's name, found under the Russian monastery on the slopes of the Mt. of Olives, at the spot to which his remains were removed.

IV. THE PERIOD OF ASSYRIAN CONQUEST — THE FALL OF ISRAEL AND THE SURVIVAL OF JUDAH:

A. **Israel:** After the middle of the 8th c. BCE, Israel and Judah were confronted by political considerations that decisively altered their status. For five centuries they had not been troubled deeply or permanently by any empire. Once Assyria took the path to empire in earnest, however, little nations were doomed. The Northern Kingdom crashed under the first impact, although Judah managed to survive for another century and a half.

At the very moment when Israel was called upon to face the greatest threat of her entire history, an expanding Assyria*, internal political and social maladies erupted in unrestrained anarchy. If she had been blessed with strong leadership, she might have survived for a time as Judah did, but it seems that Israel hardly functioned as a nation. The deterioration in her position began, apparently, in the last years of the reign of Jeroboam II. In addition to internal dissensions, Israel was not strong enough to hold or administer the extensive empire which Jeroboam had conquered. His son, Zechariah, reigned for only six months (748–747 BCE) before he was assassinated by Shallum, son of Jabesh, whose accession put an end to the Jehu dynasty (II K. 15:10–12).

From then on, a state of chaos prevailed. Shallum reigned just one month and was then assassinated in his turn by Menachem, son of Gadi. These upheavals were no doubt the result of personal ambitions or rivalries between the leading families or clans.

Menachem (747–737 BCE): The story of Menachem's revolt and reign (II K. 15:14–22) is brief and rather obscure. The revolt began at Tirzah, where Menachem served possibly as governor. Then he moved to Samaria. His reign lasted for ten years, over-shadowed by the dominating figure of Tiglat-Pileser III. As the latter advanced westward, Menachem paid him a heavy tribute raised by means of a head-tax (see Taxes*) levied on some 60,000 landholders (II K. 15:19–20). Menachem appears to have surrendered his country's independence willingly (Hos. 5:13), though he had little choice in the matter. He may have hoped that Assyria would support him on his shaky throne. H. Tadmor has suggested that he may have preferred Assyrian suzerainty to that of his neighbour, Uzziah, king of Judah. Whatever his motives, his policy was resented by patriotic Israelites. It has been suggested that chapters 4–14 in the book of Hosea* (see article) reflect the conditions of the time and the rising resentment against Judah's virtual domination over her weaker sister state to the north. Israel was now confined to a smaller area within the borders of Ephraim, Menasseh, the valley of Jezreel and Galilee. Hence Hosea referred to it as "Ephraim", condemning Judah in these terms (5:10–11): "The princes of Judah have become like those who remove the landmark; upon them I will pour out my wrath like water."

Under the Assyrian Yoke: In 745 BCE, Tiglat-Pileser III laid the foundations of the mighty Assyrian empire, introducing

555 a

555 b

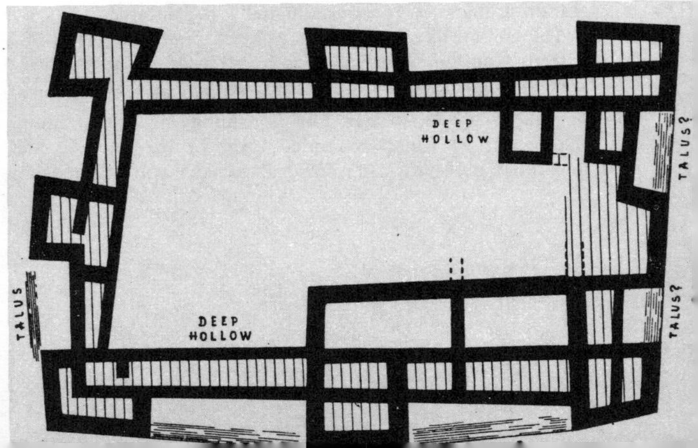

extensive administrative reforms. Early in his reign he succeeded in halting the southward expansion of the Urartu and in subduing Babylonia (see Assyria*). The Bible (II K. 15:19) calls him "Pul" which was the name under which he ruled as king of Babylonia. He aimed at extending his dominions to the Mediterranean and the Anatolian interior. To do this, he adopted the policy of deporting part of the populations of conquered territories and replacing them with peoples from other conquered countries, a policy initiated by the Assyrian kings as early as the 13th c. BCE. Moreover, Tiglat-Pileser III eliminated the reigning dynasties and replaced them with his own governors.

When he defeated the Syrian coalition headed by Azariah of Judah in 738 BCE, he freed Samaria from Judean domination, only to replace it by his own. In his annals, he numbered Menachem the Samarian among the sixteen kings who paid him tribute. Y. Yadin has suggested that the Samaria ostraca which record the collection of taxes in the 9th and 10th years relate to the last two years of Menachem's reign (see Inscriptions*; Seals*), and the tribute he paid the Assyrians to preserve the entity of his tottering kingdom. Menachem's precautionary policies were of little avail. His son, Pekahiahu (737–735 BCE) succeeded him, but reigned for only two years before being assassinated by one of his officers, Pekah, son of Ramaliahu.

Pekah (735–733 BCE): Supported by the big landowners in Gilead, Pekah sought an alliance with Aram against the Assyrian coalition. In 736–735 BCE, Tiglat-Pileser III was involved in a campaign against Media and Urartu. Rezin, king of Aram (frequently mentioned in Assyrian records), took advantage of this to foment a revolt against Assyria*; Israel, Philistia and Phoenicia responded, but Judah held aloof. The kings of the 23rd dynasty in Egypt also gave full support to the anti-Assyrian coalition, though Egypt was extremely weak at that time, "a broken reed" as described by the prophet Isaiah. In 747 BCE, Tiglat-Pileser III sent an army against Philistia so as to cut off Egypt from all contact with Israel and Aram.

Dismemberment and Disintegration of Israel: According to A. Alt, Tiglat-Pileser III occupied the coastline from the Bay of Acre to the Philistine plain. Then he directed his next campaigns (in 733–732 BCE) to dismembering the Kingdoms of Aram and Israel. He destroyed Aram-Damascus and placed it under an Assyrian governor. After this, he annexed the rich districts of Gilead, Naphtali (Galilee) and the Jezreel valley and established them as three distinct Assyrian governorships. While Israel still maintained the semblance of a small shadow state, it was confined to the tribal borders of Ephraim* and western Manasseh*. The Northern Kingdom's richest districts had been torn away, it had lost access to the international highways which had formerly traversed it, and it could not hold out much longer. An external political crisis was aggravated by rapid internal decay. Pekah was overthrown by Hoshea, son of Elah (733–723 BCE) who ruled as an Assyrian vassal (II K. 15:30). This is also attested by the annals of Tiglat-Pileser.

Hoshea reigned for nine years (II K. 17:1). He first followed a policy of submissive loyalty to Assyria, but when Tiglat-Pileser III died in 727 BCE, he joined the extremists in his entourage and withheld the annual tribute from Assyria as a gesture of independence. The Assyrian king, Shalmaneser V, who succeeded Tiglat-Pileser III, retaliated by throwing Hoshea into prison (II K. 17:4). He had appealed for help to Egypt, but she again proved a "broken reed". Shalmaneser V marched on Tyre and besieged it for five years (his successor, Sargon II, finally captured the city). Hoshea quickly capitulated, but he was no longer trusted and the Assyrian king deported him to Assyria in 724 or 723 BCE. The people of Samaria could not accept the tragic fate which awaited them and held out courageously for three years against vastly superior forces.

556

The Ultimate Tragedy: Shalmaneser V died and was succeeded by Sargon II (721–705 BCE) while the siege of Samaria was in progress. In the opinion of H. Tadmor, Sargon II could only have been free to take charge of a military expedition to Samaria in 720 BCE; then the city fell. According to Sargon, 27,290 of its citizens, plus the people of Ephraim and western Manasseh were deported en masse to Upper Mesopotamia, Media and other places throughout the Assyrian empire. In their place he colonized the land with pagans from Babylonia, Hamat and elsewhere (II K. 17:6). Deportation scenes of this sort are well known from Assyrian reliefs (**557**).

557

The last remnant of Israel was organized as the province of Samaria*. The new peoples mingled with the surviving Israelite population, their descendants being the Samaritans* (see article). Israel's political life had ended after an existence of just over 200 years (926–720 BCE).

B. Judah under Ahaz (733–727 BCE): Uzziah was succeeded by his grandson, Ahaz (Ahaziah), son of Jotham who died before his father. Ahaz adhered to the foreign policy adopted by his grandfather in 738 BCE and held aloof from the new Aram-Israel coalition formed under the leadership of Rezin, king of Aram, and Pekah, king of Israel. It had the active participation of Ashdod and Gaza (and presumably of Tyre as well) and the support of Egypt (see above). Judah was still the most powerful kingdom of southern Palestine, constituting a formidable barrier between Israel and Aram on the one hand and Egypt and Philistia on the other (see map **548**). The members of the coalition were even afraid that Judah would attack them in the rear at the decisive moment. That might well have happened had there not existed a strong party of Jerusalem aristocrats who not only supported Pekah and Rezin, but, it is believed by some scholars, even schemed to oust the House of David and enthrone a certain Ben Taba'el (Is. 7:6) instead (see above, end of Part II: Rise of a Landed Aristocracy).

The measures taken by the military coalition were calculated to weaken the position of Judah, and encouraged Edom to revolt. Edom's Aramean reinforcements succeeded in reaching Eilat (II K. 16:6). At the same time, the Philistines raided western Judah and made deep inroads into the Shephelah and the Negeb (II Ch. 28:17–18). With Judah's territory shrunken to no more than some hilly country, the Israel and Aram troops marched on Jerusalem itself.

Urged on by the prophet Isaiah (7:1–9), Ahaz withstood the siege. By then, Tiglat-Pileser III had sent three expeditions (734–732 BCE) to crush the rebel countries. Again following Uzziah's policy (see Part III), Ahaz sent tribute to the Assyrian emperor as a token of his adherence to the agreement protecting Judah (II K. 16:7–8). In one of his inscriptions, Tiglat-Pileser lists Yauhazi (Ahaz), king of Judah, among the vassal kings of the area who paid tribute to him. All the kingdoms beyond the Euphrates had submitted to him, and his armies reached the borders of Judah. When Aram-Damascus fell in 732 BCE, Ahaz went there in person to express his loyalty to Assyria.

Assyrian political hegemony probably meant the introduction of idolatrous practices into the Temple, the usual procedure in the other states of Syria (II K. 16:10–18). The worship of Assyrian gods could not be set aside, for this would, in itself, have been an act of rebellion equivalent to discontinuing the payment of Assyrian tribute. Nevertheless, there was an appreciable element in Judah that was amenable to notions of reform, the prophets pointing out that Judah would have to reform if she wished to escape the fate of Israel. Reforming zeal probably joined hands with patriotism to produce a ground swell of discontent.

After reigning for six years, Ahaz died in 727 BCE, the same year as Tiglat-Pileser III. He left a tiny kingdom which had submitted unconditionally, politically and culturally, to a mighty empire. The prophet Isaiah still hoped that Judah would mend her ways. He put his faith in Ahaz' successor, Hezekiah, to redeem his people from foreign rule and restore the worship of Yahweh (Is. 9:1–6).

V. JUDAH'S STRUGGLE FOR INDEPENDENCE: HEZEKIAH TO THE FALL OF JERUSALEM.

Hezekiah (727–698 BCE): Hezekiah at first followed his father's political policies, refusing to involve Judah in the movement of rebellion against Assyria. Judah was thus untouched when Israel was wiped out in 720 BCE, its territory made an Assyrian province, and its inhabitants exiled. In 720 BCE the entire area from Hamat in the north to Gaza in the south seethed with rebellion, but Hezekiah still remained loyal to Sargon II, king of Assyria, as can be ascertained from one of the inscriptions of Sargon which speaks of "distant Jaudu".

Many influential circles in Judah, however, were eager to revolt against Assyrian rule. When the new rulers of the 25th (Nubian) dynasty came to the throne of upper Egypt, that country began to resist Assyria. In 712 BCE, a widespread rebellion in the cities of Philistia was planned by Egypt. There are echoes of it in Isaiah 14:29–31. The Bible does not state Hezekiah's position in those years, but a fragmentary Assyrian inscription tells of the capture of Azekah in connection with the subjugation of Ashdod. This campaign by the Assyrian army may have been a strategem to keep Hezekiah from aiding the rebellious Philistine cities. Isaiah's prophecies of doom over Egypt and Ethiopia (Is. 18–20) at the time of the rebellion were apparently designed to influence young Hezekiah against joining the anti-Assyrian revolt.

The fall of Ashdod* in the days of Sargon II (712 BCE), as confirmed by an Assyrian stele uncovered there in 1963 CE, resulted in its being turned into an Assyrian province. Since Hezekiah took no part in the rebellion, he was able to strengthen his kingdom by annexing some Philistine areas (II K. 19:8); at the same time, some families of the tribes of Judah and Simeon spread into the Negeb and Gerar (I Ch. 4:39–41). As Judah expanded, the Assyrian yoke became harder to bear and Hezekiah took his first steps towards revolt. He repaired the walls of Jerusalem (Is. 22:9) and strengthened the professional cadre of army officers (II Ch. 32:5–6). His greatest achievement in fortifying Jerusalem was the digging of the famous Siloam tunnel to carry the waters of the Giḥon spring into the capital; the dramatic meeting of the diggers in the depths of the mountain was recorded in the famous inscription of Siloam (see Water Supply*; Inscriptions*).

Hezekiah's Reforms: Hezekiah took steps to extend his influence over the inhabitants of the now defunct Kingdom of Israel, for after its fall he regarded himself as its titular ruler. He enhanced the prestige of the Temple in Jerusalem by purifying the cult of Yahweh both in the Temple and throughout Judah. He tried to befriend those inhabitants of Samaria and Galilee who had not been exiled, drawing them to the religious centre in Jerusalem by celebrating the Passover in the second month (Iyar), i.e. the month when the inhabitants of the Kingdom of Israel had celebrated it (II Ch. 29–31; see Calendar*; Festivals*). The book of Chronicles attributes the postponement of the feast to the second month to another ritual reason, namely the time needed for the purification of the priests and for the gathering of all the faithful ("all Israel") after their long journey from the former Northern Kingdom. The idea is inspired by Nu. 9:1–14 which mentions the two excuses for postponement advanced by the Chronicler. Many scholars doubt the historical reliability of Chronicles on the point in dispute.

Sennacherib's Campaign: It was not until the death of Sargon II in 705 BCE that Judah was ready to join the anti-Assyrian movement. The rebellion was led by Merodach-Baladan, the Chaldean (see Babylonia*: Assyrian Domination) who revolted against Assyria for the third time. He is the king mentioned in II K. 20:12 and Is. 39:1. The cities of the Sidonians, headed by Tyre, Ashkelon and Ekron in Philistia, were in the forefront of the rebellion. They were supported by the Nubian kings of Egypt who promised the rebels the aid of the Egyptian chariot forces. Sennacherib, son of Sargon II, succeeded in crushing the rebellion, and in 701 BCE he turned against the rebellious kingdoms west of the Euphrates. Because of the size of this campaign and its decisive importance in the history of the Ancient Near East, it looms prominently in Assyrian inscriptions and sculpture. The Bible, too, deals with it at length (II K. 18:14; 19; Is. 36, 37). Sennacherib first subdued the cities of the Sidonians, then continued south along the coast, capturing Joppa, Beth-Dagon, Bnei-Beraq and Azor, the towns belonging to Zidka, king of Ashkelon, and Hezekiah's ally in the south of Palestine. Sennacherib then turned eastward and, at Eltekkeh, defeated the Egyptian army which had come to the aid of the Palestinian kingdoms. Ekron also fell to the Assyrians. Judah was left to face the mighty conqueror single-handed. Sennacherib captured one town after another. A series of vivid pictures of the Assyrian camps, soldiers and equipment were discovered in the reliefs (**157**) which Sennacherib had carved on the walls of his palace in Nineveh to commemorate the siege and capture of Lachish (**158**, see Lachish*). These illustrations show the captives from Lachish wearing the same peculiar headdress and tunics as those of the soldiers (**558**) in Sennacherib's bodyguard.

Hezekiah's entire kingdom was occupied while he himself, locked "like a bird in a cage inside beleaguered Jerusalem", in the words of Sennacherib, saw no way out but to submit. He sent envoys carrying gifts to Lachish where Sennacherib had established his headquarters. The Assyrian inscription adds that Sennacherib and his army pillaged the captured towns of Judah and exiled "great and small, numberless men and women, horses, mules, asses, camels, cattle and sheep". In addition, Sennacherib stripped the royal house of its treasures. In order to prevent Hezekiah from joining anti-Assyrian alliances in the future, part of the Judean land was parcelled out among neighbouring Philistine kingdoms. However, Jerusalem and Judah were not completely destroyed. This prism describes Sennacherib's, 701 BCE campaign against Judah (**559**).

The Bible's prophetic story about Sennacherib's siege of Jerusalem (II K. 18:17, 19; Is. 36–37) differs both from the Sennacherib inscriptions and from the biblical account inspired by the Temple chroniclers (II K. 18:14–16). According to the biblical sources, Sennacherib was not satisfied with Hezekiah's submission and demanded the

558

559

opening of the gates of Jerusalem. In the negotiations with the envoy of the king of Assyria, the prophet Isaiah, the central figure of all these stories, encouraged Hezekiah not to submit. Sennacherib suddenly left the country, and Jerusalem was saved from ruin. There is no trace of this tradition in the Assyrian document, but the later writings of the Greek historian, Herodotus, preserve an Egyptian tradition according to which an invasion of Egypt by Sennacherib was abandoned because of a plague of mice which broke out in the Assyrian camp. Even this event finds no mention or hint in the documents of that age, nor was it reflected in a political situation such as might have arisen had a hasty retreat of the Assyrians occurred in fact.

Hezekiah's loss of territory and power caused him to abandon the traditional administrative division of the kingdom into twelve districts. J. Aharoni has recently suggested that the two — and four — winged inscriptions "to the king" ("lmlk") on handles of jars found in large numbers in the tels of Judah, reflect the new division into four prefectures whose store-cities were Ziph, Hebron, Shechem and Mamshit (see Inscriptions*; Government*).

When Hezekiah died, he left his son, Menasseh, a small kingdom, totally dependent on the mercy of Assyria. Despite Hezekiah's weakness as a ruler, he had not followed the example of his father, Ahaz, and engaged in the practice of foreign cults. The thoroughgoing religious reforms introduced at the beginning of the reign remained intact, and for this achievement the book of Kings praises Hezekiah, even comparing him to David (II K. 18:7; cf. second part of I Sam. 18:30).

The Reign of Menasseh (698–642 BCE): The reign of Menasseh saw a definite change in the religious and spiritual life of Judah. The Bible has very little to say about this king who reigned for 55 years (including, possibly, a co-regency of ten years with his father), but Assyrian documents of the time of Esarhaddon and Ashurbanipal mention him, together with other kings, as a faithful vassal of Assyria. This was the period of Assyria's greatest power and grandeur. Esarhaddon (680–669 BCE), the son of Sennacherib, subdued the rich cities of the Sidonians (Phoenicians, 677 BCE) which had been Assyria's main opponents in the southwest. He was also the first monarch to capture Egypt, Assyria's leading rival in the south (672 BCE). Palestine was an important base for the Assyrian army fighting in Egypt. The complete political subjugation of the area by the Assyrians and their continued presence in the country brought about important religious and cultural changes. The Assyrian impact was felt most strongly by the nobles and officials of Judah (Zeph. 1:8), Menasseh no less than they. He abolished Hezekiah's religious reforms and removed all obstacles to the penetration of Assyrian religions, especially the cult of "the hosts of heaven" (see Babylonia*: Religion). Because of his policies of political expediency, Menasseh symbolized an evil influence to the author of the book of II Kings. His were the sins that brought about the punishment of Judah, and the ruin of the kingdom of Jerusalem (II K. 21:10–16).

The End of Assyrian Domination and Judah's Independence: The last years of Menasseh's reign saw a crisis in Assyria's fortunes. In 632 BCE, a general rebellion against her rule broke out in Babylonia, headed by Šamaš-šum-Ukin, supported by the Aramean and Chaldean tribes. The Elamites and various other peoples from the mountains of Iran also rebelled, as did the western peoples in Asia Minor, supported by Gyges, king of Lydia and Psammetik I, the new king of Egypt, who had thrown off Assyrian domination and founded the 26th dynasty (655 BCE). Some scholars believe that the events related in II Ch. 33:11, describing Menasseh's unsuccessful rebellion against Assyria, took place during this mutinous period. With the breakdown of Assyrian rule west of the Euphrates, settled lands were opened to invasion by the Arab tribes of the Syro-Arabian desert. The kingdoms of Transjordan, Edom*, Moab* and Ammon, bordering on the desert, were all attacked.

It was only by a supreme effort and a series of prolonged sieges (described in his inscriptions in the most brutal terms) that Ashurbanipal succeeded in overcoming his enemies. The kingdom of Elam was destroyed after the capture of its capital, Susa (Shushan) in 646 BCE. The Arab tribes were subdued and the cities of northern Palestine and Syria, including Acco, handed over to harsh administrators. The book of Ezra (4:9–10) relates that Osnappar (apparently Ashurbanipal) settled people from Babylonia* and Elam* in Samaria, just as his predecessor, Esarhaddon, had done (Ezr. 4:2). This story undoubtedly reflects the acts of oppression perpetrated by Ashurbanipal throughout the Assyrian empire. However, under the continuous pressure of northern peoples such as the Persians and the Medians coming down from the mountains to invade its dominions, the Assyrian empire was tottering. Egypt also remained unsubdued. The events leading to the release of Egypt from Assyrian domination and the last years of Ashurbanipal cannot be reconstructed as there are no sources. After Psammetik II united Egypt, he invaded Philistia and besieged Ashdod (640 BCE . The siege of this city lasted 29 years, according to Herodotus.) According to some authorities, his plans were frustrated by the invasion of the Scyths who came from the far north to the very borders of Egypt. Herodotus tells of 29 years of Scythian rule in Philistia, and relates that the Scyths were prevented from invading Egypt only by bribes and gifts.

Amon (641–640 BCE): The sudden and rapid decline of the Assyrian Empire also made itself felt in Judah. Amon, the son of Menasseh, continued his father's policy of submission to Assyria, but apparently because of this policy, he was murdered by nobles after a very short reign. His son, Josiah, who was eight years old at the time, was crowned king in his stead.

The Reign of Josiah (639–609 BCE): In Josiah's time, Judah became independent once more. The beginning of the renewed independence of the country cannot be dated exactly because of a lack of source material. Early in his reign, Josiah was able to seize control of large parts of the south of Palestine. Evidence that he ruled over the area of Jabneh in Philistia can be inferred from recent archaeological finds at Matzad Hashabyahu on the coast nearby (see Inscriptions*), and the words of the prophet Zephaniah (2:7) about the expansion of Judah in Philistia may refer to that area. The Bible implies that Josiah extended his rule over part of the territory of the former Kingdom of Samaria, the valley of Jezreel being his northern boundary (II K. 23:19; II Ch. 34:33; — see map **547**).

Restored independence was accompanied by the removal of foreign religious elements from Judah's worship. A cultural movement marked by a return to traditional ways swept the entire ancient East; Egypt, Babylonia and even Assyria aspired to develop their national cultures in pure, untainted forms. In the 12th year of his reign (627 BCE), Josiah began his great religious reform (II Ch. 34:3) as the Assyrian Empire crumbled. The reforms consisted of the liquidation of the "high places" in Judah and Samaria "from Geba to Beer-Sheba" (II K. 23:8), and, more important, the removal of all foreign cults, particularly Assyrian ones, which Josiah's grandfather, Menasseh, had helped to establish (II K. 23:4, 7; II Ch. 34:4).

Josiah's Reforms: The religious reforms of Josiah are described in the Bible in two separate traditions. In II Kings (chapters 22, 23), the reformation is a one-time act, the result of the finding of the book of Law while the Temple was under repair. In II Chronicles (chapter 34), on the other hand, the reformation took place in several stages, the expression of a national renaissance in response to a gradual liberation from foreign rule.

In the 18th year of his reign (622 BCE), after the form of worship had been purified, Josiah ordered the Temple thoroughly restored (II Ch. 34:8). At this stage, the book of the Law (see Deuteronomy*) was found by the high priest, Hilkiah, who sent it to the king. The book included a severe reproof for the sins of idolatry and a prophecy of the ruin of the people, the country and the Temple, because of these sins. This made a profound impression on the king, who assembled all the elders of Judah and Jerusalem, read the book to them, and "made a covenant before the Lord to walk after the Lord, and to keep his commandments and his testimonies and his statutes with all his heart and all his soul, to perform the words of this covenant that were written in this book; and all the people joined in the covenant" (II K. 23:3; cf. II Ch. 34:29–32). An example of the pagan objects removed from the Temple, such as the "horses that the king of Judah had dedicated to the sun" (II K. 23:11) may be illustrated by the god, Chamosh, mounted on a horse (**560**), carved in the rock at Malatiya near Mosul (ca. 700 BCE).

The Book of Deuteronomy: The assembly of "all the people" was expressly called for the purpose of establishing the Torah as the constitution of the nation and as the authority governing the forms of religion for all future generations. The Bible exegete De Vette proved long ago that the scroll of the Law in question, the foundation of the reformation, was the book of Deuteronomy, the only one of the five books of Moses which calls for absolute concentration of worship in one place. Later scholars who agreed with De Vette's view discovered, however, that a core of the book of Deuteronomy is of much earlier date (see Biblical Criticism*). According to Chronicles, the covenantal ceremony of acceptance of the Torah as a constitution was connected with the celebration of Passover when the whole nation made a pilgrimage to Jerusalem (II Ch. 35:1, 19). On that occasion, too, the purpose was the restoration of the original state of affairs, and both the book of Kings and the book of Chronicles stipulate that such a Passover had never been celebrated since the establishment of the kingdom. By establishing this covenant, Josiah raised Jerusalem (and the House of David) to the rank of sole and exclusive centre for all the faithful to Yahweh, both in Judah and in Samaria, which were united once more.

The Priesthood and Resurgent Nationalism: The same policy of a return to tradition and restoration of national culture and customs was followed in the reorganization of the priesthood. B. Mazar has called attention to an amazing fact, recorded in the genealogical list of the house of Zadok in the book of Chronicles, where Shallum, the father of Hilkiah, immediately follows Zadok, the founder of the priestly dynasty in the days of Solomon (I Ch. 6:12–13). In Mazar's opinion, the order "Zadok-Shallum-Hilkiah" in the list is not accidental, but reflects a historical reality, intimating the termination of the rule of the house of Zadok at the end of Solomon's reign or at the beginning of Rehoboam's, when foreign cults were introduced into the Temple (I K. 11:7–8; 14:23–24). Three hundred years later, in the days of Josiah, the crown of chief priesthood was returned to the house of Zadok, symbolizing the return to the faith of God in its pure state.

The Neo-Babylonian Empire: Political conditions in Palestine — and the country's very geography — prevented Josiah from completing his reforms or extending his influence abroad. The downfall of Assyria and the restoration of the power of Egypt undermined the achievements of his foreign policy. Even before 616 BCE, Josiah lost control over the Jabneh area to Philistia. A Babylonian Chronicle (published by C.J. Gadd) describes the defeat of Assyria* by the united forces of Babylonia and Media. Egypt came to the aid of Assyria, whose capital, Nineveh, had already been captured by the Babylonian and Median forces in 612 BCE. After the fall of Nineveh, Ashur-uballit, the last king of Assyria, established his capital at Harran, but in

560

610 BCE Harran too was captured. A year later, the king of Assyria, backed by Necho, king of Egypt, tried to recapture it from the Babylonians but failed (the text in II K. 23:29, should not read that Necho fought "against Assyria" but *for* her; otherwise the story is factually correct). Josiah was afraid of being subjected to Egypt if the latter won in the war against Babylonia, and he determined to prevent Necho's passage through Palestinian territory.

This momentous event in the history of the kingdom of Judah is explained comprehensively in the book of Chronicles. Necho hastened to Carchemish on the Euphrates to aid his Assyrian ally (609 BCE). Josiah closed the road before him and refused to listen to his repeated requests to clear the way: "What have we to do with each other, King of Judah? I am not coming against you this day . . . Cease opposing God, who is with me, lest he destroy you" (II Ch. 35:21). At the beginning of the battle, Josiah was mortally wounded and he died shortly afterwards (II Ch. 35:22, 24; cf. II K. 23:29–30). The whole nation mourned his death. According to the Bible text, Jeremiah participated in the lamentations together with all the chorus of singing men and women, praising him as an example of a king who did "justice and righteousness" (Jer. 22:15). Summarizing the deeds and works of Josiah, the book of Kings states, "Before him there was no king like him" (II K. 23:25).

Jehoahaz (609 BCE): Most of the people of Judah identified themselves with the policies of Josiah and fully expected a complete and final defeat of the forces of the Pharaoh Necho. They enthroned Josiah's son, Jehoahaz, who was not the firstborn, but was known to be anti-Egyptian. Hopes for a speedy rout of the Egyptians were soon dashed. Pharaoh was unable to recapture Harran, but all the countries west of the Euphrates fell to him. He would not accept the presence of a hostile ruler so close to the boundaries of his country, and laid a heavy tribute on Judah, exiled Jehoahaz to Egypt after a reign of three months, and enthroned his brother, Eliakim, who was apparently friendly to Egypt.

Jehoiakim (608–597 BCE): Pharaoh changed Eliakim's name to Jehoiakim (II K. 23:34). H. Tur-Sinai has called attention to the fact that all the kings of Judah who reigned after Josiah changed their names to theophoric ones containing the name of Yahweh or Yahu. On the Lachish* ostraca, most proper names carry the same element, in contrast to the Samaria* ostraca. This author concluded that the custom was one effect of the reforms of Josiah, which raised the pure faith in Yahweh to an absolute national value.

Nebuchadrezzar in Judah: The first years of Jehoiakim's reign were marked by subjection to Egypt and heavy taxation of the people in order to pay the tribute laid on the land by Pharaoh (II K. 23:35). But in his 4th year (605 BCE) the political status of the entire region between the Euphrates and the border of Egypt changed radically: the heir to the throne of Babylonia, Nebuchadrezzar, routed the Egyptian army at Carchemish on the banks of the Euphrates (Jer. 46:2). (The battle is described in the Babylonian Chronicle.) That same year, Nebuchadrezzar was made king of Babylonia, following the death of his father. The policy he adopted was intended to ensure his domination over Syria and Palestine, preparatory to a final conflict with Egypt. An Aramean papyrus found in Sakkarah (Memphis) records a panic-stricken appeal to Pharaoh from the king of Ashkelon*, asking for help against the raids of the Babylonian army which attacked as far as Aphek (Rosh-Ha'ayin) in the Sharon. The Babylonian Chronicler relates that Ashkelon refused to open its gates to Nebuchadrezzar, and in the month of Kislev in the first year of his reign (604 BCE), he laid siege to the city, captured it, and laid it waste. In that same month (the ninth), in the 5th year of the reign of Jehoiakim, a great fast was proclaimed in Jerusalem (Jer. 36:9), apparently in response to events in neighbouring Ashkelon.

As a result of the defeat of Pharaoh and the rapid advance of the Babylonians southward towards the boundaries of Egypt, Jehoiakim became a vassal of the king of Babylonia. In the 4th year of his reign, he fought a battle against the Egyptian forces at an unidentified place and was defeated. In the same year, he rebelled against the king of Babylonia and was able to maintain his position as long as Nebuchadrezzar did not renew his campaign "across the river". Anticipating a future encounter, the Babylonian king sent Chaldean, Syrian and other soldiers on raids against Judah (II K. 24:2) in order to weaken it. As Jerusalem's political and military position deteriorated, a quarrel developed between the faction friendly to Egypt, which supported Jehoiakim's rebellion against Babylonia, and the opposing faction (including Jeremiah) who demanded surrender to Babylonia. Jehoiakim suppressed his opponents with a strong hand, killing them mercilessly (II K. 24:4). Nevertheless, the political crisis undermined economic life and increased the tensions between the different classes of the population. This gives point to Jeremiah's accusation that Jehoiakim oppressed the poor people and perverted justice.

Jehoiachin (597 BCE) — The First Deportation from Judah: Events soon showed up Jehoiakim's shortsighted policy. Nebuchadrezzar laid siege to Jerusalem in the month of Kislev, in the 7th year of the reign (Jer. 52:28). During the siege, Jehoiakim died, after a reign of 11 years (II K. 24:6), and his 18-year-old son, Jehoiachin was crowned king. Jehoiachin suffered the consequences of his father's mistakes. After a short reign of three months and ten days in beleaguered Jerusalem, Jehoiachin saw that there was no

561

hope for the city or the country. He opened the gates of Jerusalem and surrendered personally to the Babylonians, knowing that he could at best expect exile for himself. (The new fragments of the Babylonian Chronicle, published by D.J. Wiseman, record that he opened the gates to the Babylonian host on the 2nd of Adar, 597; **561**). Determined to pacify the country once and for all, Nebuchadrezzar exiled not only the king, his family and the nobility, but also all the warriors "all the men of valor, seven thousand, and the craftsmen and the smiths, one thousand, all of them strong and fit for war" (II K. 24:16).

Jehoiachin in Babylon: The fate of Jehoiachin in Babylon is recorded both in the Bible and in Babylonian inscriptions discovered in the palace of Nebuchadrezzar (published in 1939 CE). In one of the storerooms of Nebuchadrezzar, lists of foodstuffs distributed to exiles from various countries (**421**) were discovered. These include people of high rank, e.g. the king of Judah and his sons, the sons of the king of Ashkelon, and others. Jehoiachin is mentioned several times in these documents as "King of Judah". In fact, a number of years before the discovery of these documents, W.F. Albright had surmised that Jehoiachin was still recognized as king, even after his exile. His theory was based on the name "Eliakim, steward of Jehoiachin" inscribed on jar handles discovered at Beth-Shean and Tel beit-Mirsim. The name of Jehoiachin engraved on them suggests that, even though he was imprisoned, he was still regarded in Judah as the king. His imprisonment was in fact a house arrest, and he was released by Nebuchadrezzar's successor, Ebil-Merodach, in the 37th year of his captivity (II K. 25:27; see Restoration*).

Zedekiah (596–586 BCE) — The End of the Kingdom of Judah: In place of the exiled Jehoiachin, the king of Babylonia crowned Zedekiah, the son of Josiah, and Jehoiachin's uncle. Probably the idea of a king appointed by a foreign ruler was not accepted by the people who regarded Jehoiachin as their legitimate king and Zedekiah as a kind of governor of the king of Babylonia. The prophet Hananiah of Gibeon undoubtedly expressed the most cherished hopes of the people and nobles when he prophesied an end to the rule of Babylonia, the return of Jehoiachin and the other exiles, and the restoration of the treasures and vessels of the Temple (Jer. 28:1–4). The prophet Ezekiel who was exiled together with Jehoiachin reckoned his dates according to "the exile of King Jehoiachin" (Ezk. 1:2). The view that Jehoiachin was still the legitimate king united all those who advocated another bid for independence from Babylonia. The prophet Jeremiah opposed this view and was supported by a group of high officials who saw no alternative to surrender. When Jehoiachin was exiled, Jeremiah prophesied that he would *not* return (Jer. 22:10–12), notwithstanding his sympathy for the king and sorrow at his fate.

Although made king by Nebuchadrezzar, Zedekiah was unable to withstand the nationalist currents which demanded rebellion against Babylonia, and he yielded to the rebellious elements. Public opinion held Jeremiah to be a traitor (Jer. 37:11–16); nevertheless the king turned to him for advice more than once. Zedekiah was weak in character, and he disregarded the prophet's warnings. He asked Egypt for military aid, since Psammetik, the son of Necho II also

562

followed a strong anti-Babylonian policy. In 594 or 593 BCE, delegations from Edom, Moab, Ammon, Tyre and Sidon arrived in Jerusalem to deliberate on the proposed rebellions (Jer. 27:3). Though other prophets incited the people to rebel, Jeremiah vigorously denounced such talk and also wrote a letter to the exiles in Babylonia (Jer. 29) bidding them to forget their dreams and settle down for a long stay. Under the influence of the pro-Egyptian policy, other states west of the Euphrates also rebelled, and in 591 BCE, in the sixth year of the reign of Zedekiah, Tyre rose. The city withstood a siege of thirteen years, although it submitted after Jerusalem fell. Ezekiel comments on Nebuchadrezzar's failure to conquer Tyre.

Final Rebellion: In the 9th year of Zedekiah's reign, Nebuchadrezzar's forces arrived to crush the rebellion. All the members of the coalition, except Tyre and Judah, recanted and even joined the Babylonians. Zedekiah entered into a covenant with the whole nation to let all Hebrew slaves go free (Jer. 34:9) in the spirit of the laws of the books of Exodus (21) and Deuteronomy (15). By then, most of the territory of Judah was in the hands of the Chaldeans, and only Lachish and Azekah, aside from Jerusalem, still held their ground (Jer. 34:7; — See map **547**).

The Fall of Judah: Echoes of Judah's desperate situation and her heroic stand may be found on potsherds of Lachish, which contain letters from the commander of an observation post to the commander of the fortress of Lachish (see details under Inscriptions*; Lachish*; Jeremiah*). The Chaldeans defeated the Egyptian army and renewed the attack on Jerusalem. Lachish* was taken (excavations there show the havoc wrought by the Chaldeans in the city). Then came the turn of Jerusalem. The siege was renewed on the 10th of Tebeth, in the 9th year of Zedekiah's reign (587 BCE). On the 9th of Ab, 586 BCE, after Jerusalem had withstood one and a half years of siege, the Chaldeans succeeded in breaking through its walls. The starving city was powerless against its conquerors who pillaged it, pulled down its walls and burnt it, spending their fury especially on the king's palace and the Temple. Zedekiah and his nobles succeeded in escaping in the middle of the night, and reached the desert plain of Jericho, but there they were caught. Nebuchadrezzar took revenge on Zedekiah's family and gouged out the king's eyes, a custom recorded in this Assyrian engraving (**562**).

In contrast to his first capture of Jerusalem in the days of Jehoiachin, this time Nebuchadrezzar decided to put an end to the independence of Judah and the Davidic dynasty. On the king's orders, a number of the nobles of Jerusalem, including the high priest Seriah, were killed, and the rest of the upper classes carried into captivity (Jer. 52:28–30). The country was laid waste, a fact since confirmed by archaeological excavations, leaving only "... the poorest of the land to be vinedressers and husbandmen" (Jer. 52:16).

The Remnant in Judah: Unlike the Assyrians, the Babylonians did not bring other peoples to Judah, nor did they appoint a Babylonian governor for the country. After his conquest, Nebuchadrezzar appointed Gedaliah, son of Ahikam (II K. 25:22), governor over those who remained in Judah. Gedaliah may have been "over the household" of Zedekiah, as inscribed on a seal found at Lachish. He was descended from an honoured family of scribes, who had held prominent positions since the days of Josiah. The written sources give no details about his status within the framework of the Babylonian empire. Gedaliah's administration was centred at Mizpah (apparently Tel el-Nasbeh, 12 kilometres north of Jerusalem in the territory of Benjamin) under the supervision of a Chaldean garrison. There he established a sort of centre (Jer. 40:11–12; 41:5) and some of the people who, during the war, had fled to Edom, Moab and Ammon joined him.

The territory of Benjamin may have been chosen as the new centre of the Kingdom of Judah because, having surrendered earlier, it had been saved from ruin and destruction. (This is the view of B. Mazar and A. Malamat.) Those who fled from besieged Jerusalem had also gone to the Benjamin territory. Excavations in both Judah and Benjamin have shown that whereas the cities of Judah were utterly destroyed in the war with Nebuchadrezzar, the cities of Benjamin did not suffer. For this reason, Jeremiah purchased land in Anathot in the territory of Benjamin (Jer. 32:9) during the war. This is not the explanation given by the book of Jeremiah, which gives the reason as being so that "houses and fields and vineyards shall again be bought in this land" (Jer. 32:15). Those Jews who returned from Babylon after the exile also settled mostly in the cities of Benjamin (Ezr. 2). The Idumeans seized the Negeb and the south of Judah which henceforth was called Idumea.

Within the boundaries of his administration, Gedaliah took some steps towards reconstruction, encouraging those who remained to till their land, which had lain fallow during the years of war and siege. Furthermore, the land of the exiles and escapees, mostly landed nobles, was divided among "the poor of the people which had nothing" (Jer. 39:10) so that they could till it. This was an important act, by which the lower classes became land-owners. At the time of the return to Zion, this proved to be decisive, for it helped to form Jewish society in the days of the Second Commonwealth (see Restoration*).

Gedaliah's administration and his attempt to reconstruct the ruins of the land under Babylonian rule did not last long. A member of the royal family, Ishmael, son of Nethaniah, plotted against Gedaliah with the support of Baalis, king of Ammon. Gedaliah would not listen to those who warned him against the plotters, and was murdered by Ishmael (Jer. 40:14; 41:3). With his death, all reconstructive steps came to an end. Gedaliah's friends feared Nebuchadrezzar's reaction and they resolved to flee to Egypt in spite of Jeremiah's protests, even forcibly taking him with them. A third exile in 582 BCE (Jer. 52:30) was Nebuchadrezzar's punishment for the Ishmael plot. Josephus' story (Antiq. 10:9, 4) about the subjugation of Ammon and Moab in the Babylonian campaign in Coele-Syria is apparently connected with this event.

CHRONOLOGICAL TABLES. KINGS OF JUDAH—ISRAEL

UNITED KINGDOM

David	1004–965 BCE
Solomon (as co-regent)	967–965 BCE
(as king)	965–928 BCE

JUDAH

	BCE
Rehoboam	928–911
Abiyah	911–908
Assah	908–867
Jehoshaphat (as co-regent)	870–867
(as king)	867–846
Joram (as co-regent)	851–846
(as king)	846–843
Ahaziah	843–842
Athaliah	842–836
Joash	836–798
Amaziah	798–769
Uzziah (as co-regent)	785–769
(as king)	769–733
Jotham (as co-regent)	758–743
Ahaz (as co-regent)	743–733
(as king)	733–727
Hezekiah	727–698
Menasseh	698–642
Amon	641–640
Josiah	639–609
Jehoahaz	609
Jehoiakim	608–597
Jehoiachin	597
Zedekiah	596–586
Destruction of Jerusalem	586

ISRAEL

		OCE
Jeroboam's dynasty	Jeroboam	928–907
	Nadab	907–906
Baashah's dynasty	Baashah	906–883
	Elah	883–882
	Zimri	882
	Tibni	882–878
The House of Omri	Omri	882–871
	Ahab (as co-regent)	874–871
	(as king)	871–852
	Ahaziah	852–851
	Joram	851–841
Jehu's dynasty	Jehu	841–814
	Jehoahaz (as co-regent)	817–814
	(as king)	814–800
	Jehoash	800–784
	Jeroboam II (as co-regent)	789–784
	(as king)	784–848
	Zechariah	748
	Shallum	747
Menahem's dynasty	Menahem	747–737
	Pekahiahu	737–735
	Pekah	735–733
	Hoshea	733–723
Destruction of Samaria		720

J

JEREMIAH. — *Outline: I. Life and Historical Background: Early Phase; Jeremiah and the Deuteronomic Reform; The Destruction of the State;* 597–586; *Jeremiah and Zedekiah; Jeremiah and His Contemporaries; The End, after 586 BCE; His Life Mission; His Hope and Faith; The New Covenant; Corporate and Individual Religion. II. Form and Organization of the Book: Contents and Outline. III. The Hebrew Text and the Septuagint: Apocryphal Jeremiah and Baruch.*

Jeremiah (in Hebrew Yirmeyahu) was the major prophet of the last days of the Kingdom of Judah. The book which bears his name stands second in the "Later Prophets" in the Hebrew canon, the Vulgate and most modern versions of the Bible.

I. LIFE AND HISTORICAL BACKGROUND: Jeremiah was a member of a priestly family of the village of Anathot, in Benjaminite territory near Jerusalem. He received his first call to prophesy in the service of God in 626 BCE, five years before the Deuteronomic "Book of the Law" was found in the Temple, while he was still a youth ("na'ar", 1:6) but his very first visions of the rod of almond (1:11–12) and the boiling pot (1:13–19) testify to the moral courage he was to display throughout his life and work.

Jeremiah's career covers a period of forty years (corresponding to the rise of the neo-Babylonian empire) beginning in 626 BCE, the 13th year of King Josiah, and lasting until after the fall of Jerusalem and the Exile of 586 BCE. Thus, as the prophet was uttering his dismal but often exquisitely phrased oracles, the last five kings of Judah: Josiah, Jehoahaz, Jehoiakim, Jehoiachin and Zedekiah, played brief roles in the country's life. Meanwhile, other more glittering personalities were shaping history from more distant thrones. In fact, it was one of the most fateful periods in the history of the Near East, a period of rising empires and reviving nationalism. (The background is discussed under Israel and Judah*: Part V; Babylonia*; Exile*.)

The prophet's career may be outlined as follows: a. from his call to Josiah's reformation (621 BCE); b. from Josiah's reformation to his death (608 BCE); c. from Josiah's death to Nebuchadrezzar's rise, and the defeat of Pharaoh Necho at Carchemish (605 BCE); the political status of the whole region changed under the Neo-Babylonian empire; d. from the defeat of Necho at Carchemish to the first Judean deportation in 597 BCE; e. From 597 BCE to the destruction of the kingdom in 586 BCE; f. the end of Jeremiah's career, with the migration of a number of Jews, including Jeremiah himself, to Egypt. Jeremiah's life was closely bound up with all the events taking place in his lifetime. The details of his life and personality are accordingly better documented than those of the minor prophets or even of major figures like Isaiah* or Ezekiel*.

Early Phase: His early message was a rebuke for Israel's idolatry and, after Josiah's reform (c. 621 BCE; see below, Part III), a warning to the people to keep the new covenant with God, which must be written on men's hearts (see below). Even though he apparently took no active part in the reform movement, he must have approved its suppression of pagan practices and the attempt to revive the theology of the Mosaic covenant. At first he hoped that a restored Israel would join Judah in Zion, thus reunifying the whole people (3:12; 31:2–6). However, after the reform he saw a revival of religious activity, but no real return to the ancient paths of righteousness. It seemed to him that the fundamental demands of the Covenant were being obscured behind external ritual (7:21–23) and that the reform had been merely a matter of superficial behaviour, not true repentance (4:3 ff; 8:4–7).

Jeremiah and the Deuteronomic Reform: Whatever its motivation, the effect of Josiah's great religious reform, with its establishment of a centralized, purified form of worship and a return to the Mosiac Law and Sinai covenant, had been to create a false sense of security. The permanence of the Temple, the dynasty and the state seemed to be guaranteed by the "purification" that had been carried out within the country. The Deuteronomic "Book of the Law" (see Deuteronomy*), revived from a distant past, is infused with a nostalgia for the ancient days and ways, and it proclaims that the nation's life depends on a return to the covenantal relationship upon which it had originally been founded (see below, The New Covenant). Jeremiah complained that the reform was a matter of appearance rather than fact. Cultic activity had been greatly increased, but there had been no real return to the true, ancient path (6:16–21) and the sins of society continued with no protest from the priests. Although the nation was proudly claiming itself the sole possessor of Yahweh's true law, the people refused to listen to that law and clearly had no intention of abiding by its dictates (8:8). Worse, simple people saw that cultic ritual had been purified of pagan practices and they assumed that this was all that was needed to satisfy God's demands. They saw the reform as the guarantee of national security and at a time of grave political danger, felt an undaunted confidence that the God who had once rescued His people from Sennacherib would shield them from Nebuchadrezzar (5:12; 14:13; 26:9–11).

Jeremiah did not deny the covenant promises made to the House of David (23:5 ff). His contention was that the people and the king were not keeping their side of the bargain (21:12–22:30). To trust in Yahweh's anointed merely because he sat on the throne of Zion was useless, proclaimed Jeremiah. Yahweh would strike him down, would abandon his people and destroy their Temple, just as he had once annihilated the tribal shrine of Shiloh, in punishment of the people's sins (7:8–15; 26:1–6).

On the Eve of the Destruction of the State: In 605 BCE, Nebuchadrezzar came to the throne of Babylonia*. Jeremiah foretold the Babylonian destruction of Judah and strongly recommended moderation in national policies. His advice was rejected and, fearing that his prophecies would dishearten the people, King Jehoiakim ordered the prophet's arrest, whereupon he went into hiding for a time. Though Jehoiakim was, in effect, a vassal of Babylonia, many of the people

563

would not accept this situation. As the political position of Judah deteriorated, a quarrel developed between the pro-Egyptian faction which supported Jehoiakim's new rebellion against Babylonia, and the opposing faction to which Jeremiah belonged, which advised surrender to Babylonia.

Jehoiakim suppressed opposition mercilessly, but the prevailing crisis led to the undermining of economic life and to serious tensions among the various classes of the population. This gives point to Jeremiah's accusation that the king oppressed the poor and perverted justice. His oracle on the ruling classes reflects an antipathy for their ostentatious great houses and "upper rooms . . . and cut windows for it, paneling it with cedar" (22:12 ff.). The ornamental window balustrade which decorated the façade of the royal citadel at Ramat Rachel, near Jerusalem, which excavators assign to the reign of King Jehoiakim, suggests the magnificent impression which the building must have made. It is similar to an ivory carving (**563**) from Nimrud of the same period.

From 597 to 586: His doom-laden prophecies aroused great resentment but as his feelings of disillusion increased, so the imminence of disaster became almost the whole burden of his message. He deeply regretted the way in which Jehoiakim and Zedekiah allowed the reform to lapse. When the country was forced to submit (597 BCE) at the end of the first Babylonian campaign, and the young Jehoiachin was besieged in Jerusalem, then taken to Babylon, Jeremiah's fellow prophets all insisted that this was but a temporary set-back sent by Yahweh to chastise the people — but only for a time. The exiles would be released from Babylon. Jeremiah, on the other hand, was still pleading for caution and threatening that Yahweh would send "from the north" (4:5–8; 5:15–17; 6:22–26) to destroy his unfaithful people (4:23–26; 8:13–17).

He mourned sincerely at the exile of Jehoiachin, and oracles on his fate are to be found scattered throughout the early chapters of the book (13:18–19; 22:2 ff). During the reigns of the last two kings of Judah, Jehoiachin and Zedekiah, Jeremiah found increasing support among the country's leaders. His lone stand against optimism did not come easily to Jeremiah, He was harassed, jeered at, once nearly killed (11:18–12:6; 15:10; 26:10–24). Jeremiah was not a misanthrope by nature, and he loved life (31:12–14; 33:11 passim), but his message was misunderstood. The people feared his words and their power and saw Jeremiah as their enemy. After 597 BCE, it seemed that his warnings of disaster had been justified, but the prevailing certainty that Yahweh would come to the aid of his people and would restore their fortunes left Jeremiah still isolated. He realized that nothing had been learned from the catastrophe and that true repentance was as far off as ever (6:27–30). The people left behind after the first wave of Exile, he proclaimed, were like a basket of rotten figs, the fruit left on a tree when the best had been plucked (ch. 24).

Jeremiah and Zedekiah: After 597 BCE, the Babylonians had placed Jehoiachin's uncle, Zedekiah, on the throne of Judah as their puppet. He thought highly of Jeremiah but disregarded his advice to keep on good terms with Babylon. Nevertheless, he turned several times to the prophet for guidance (37:17–21; 38:14–27), though the patriots held Jeremiah to be a traitor (37:11–15). In the end, the king disregarded the prophet's warnings and joined Egypt and Tyre in a conspiracy against Babylonia (ch. 27; see Israel and Judah*: Part V). Though the priests and the other prophets incited the nation to rebellion, Jeremiah denounced such talk with great vigour. He appeared before the leaders as they were leaving the council chamber, with thongs and yoke-bars on his neck, proclaiming Yahweh's sovereignty over the whole earth and asserting that it was He who would determine the fate of nations. Nebuchadrezzar was his agent, and the nations were bidden to submit; the prophets, diviners, soothsayers and sorcerers were lying.

On another occasion, Hananiah, a prophet from Gibeon, proclaimed the imminent return of the exiled king, Jehoiachin, in the presence of a crowd of priests, prophets and people gathered at the Temple. Though Jeremiah shared the wish, he reminded the other prophets that the prophets "of ancient times" prophesied only of doom, and that a seer who proclaimed "peace" could only justify it by the event. Hananiah thereupon took the yoke-bars from Jeremiah's neck and broke them, declaring that Yahweh would so break the yoke of Nebuchadrezzar from the necks of the nations. Jeremiah returned with yokes of iron, telling Hananiah that he had been sent by Yahweh. Furthermore, he announced, Hananiah would die within a year (ch. 28). Jeremiah wrote a letter to the Judeans who had been deported to Babylon, bidding them to forget their dreams and settle down for a long stay in exile, and he prophesied that Jehoiachin would not return (22:10–12).

Jeremiah and His Contemporaries: In spite of the opposition his words aroused, Jeremiah had supporters among the leaders of the people (26:16 ff). Not everyone was preaching "'Peace, peace' when there is no peace" (6:14; 8:11; cf. 14:7–9). But his was a minority voice. Jeremiah himself had nothing but contempt for the rebellious pride which made Jehoiakim and the pro-war party bring about the final calamity of 598–597 BCE, and little respect for Zedekiah and his advisers (24; 34:8–22). Jeremiah held to his opinion and his course of determined opposition to the king's policies.

There was going to be no miraculous rescue. On the contrary, Yahweh would turn His people's weapons against themselves (21:1–7). In the end, Nebuchadrezzar came with his army and besieged Jerusalem for a year and a half. Jeremiah continued to urge capitulation to the Babylonians, even by individual citizens, for it was now a choice between life and death. It appears that his words had some effect, for he was accused of weakening the soldiers' morale. His attack was naturally resented by the army leaders and he was imprisoned in a pit for his pains (38:4–6). Zedekiah's personal regard for him saved his life (38:10, 16) but did nothing to change his advice.

The End of His Career after 586 BCE: Jeremiah's strong advocacy of a pro-Babylonian pacifist policy did, however, work to his advantage when Jerusalem fell in 586 BCE. The Babylonian officials gave him their protection during the chaotic years after the destruction of the Judean state, though it is noteworthy that Jeremiah was not reckoned among those who deserted to the Babylonian side. He elected to remain in Jerusalem, but after the murder of Gedaliah, the new Babylonian governor, fleeing Judean survivors (see Israel and Judah*: Part V) forced Jeremiah to accompany them to Egypt (43:5–7) where he spent his last days. Baruch went with him and was there to record the closing words of the prophet's life — condemnation of the syncretist worship of Egyptian Jewry, and judgments on the sins of his people (ch. 44). He also condemned the kings of the 26th Egyptian dynasty; one of them is named: Hophra (Apries), son of Psammetik II. In his days, Jews were apparently encouraged to found military colonies, such as Elephantine in southern Egypt (cf. Elephantine under Persia*).

His Life Mission: In his dealings with men, Jeremiah's courage never failed him. Before his God, he cringed. His ministry was an almost intolerable burden to him in his personal life, and he often struggled to free himself from the divine compulsion to prophesy. Jeremiah's place in history depends on this very inability to escape the revelation that haunted him. The compelling call of Jeremiah and the constraint it put on him is evident from his writings. Least of all men was he a prophet because he desired to be one. God had driven him to speak, and had then deserted him. When he felt that God had disappointed him after having overpowered him by His might, Jeremiah felt that he would never prophesy again, but an inner drive forced him to continue.

In his early days, Jeremiah had prophesied a doom which did not fall. At first he thought doom would come at the hands of the enemy from the north, but this disaster was slight in comparison with what he had expected. Twenty years later, he reissued his prophecies, revised to fit the circumstances of the time, when the Babylonians were pursuing the Egyptians, fleeing back to their own country (605 BCE). Nothing compared with his expectations came to pass, and Jeremiah was nonplussed. The prophet was clearly not uttering wishful thoughts; his heart was wrung by the words he uttered, and he longed to be spared the painful task. Nevertheless, the sequel to the above events showed that his words were ultimately fulfilled. Twenty years passed, and the doom fell with a severity which showed how fundamentally true his oracles were. The time and the agents of God's will were different, but the essence and content of the disasters he had predicted befell his generation in full measure. Though Jeremiah shared the anguish of God's spirit at what he saw, he did not share the patience of God, nor did he believe that Israel could still turn from her ways, to the way of God.

His internal struggles found expression in his frequent changes of mood and in his picture of God. Sometimes he saw Him as a vengeful God (4:4; 5:22; 23:19), sometimes as a gracious judge (3:14; 31:20, 31; 32:17) or as saddened by the punishment He Himself inflicted (12:7).

His Hope and Faith: Jeremiah rejected easy confidence and deliberately set himself out to deny exaggerated hopes for the immediate future. The Kingdom of Judah was doomed to destruction by the sovereign and righteous judgment of Yahweh on his disobedient people. Hope, for Jeremiah — and he was not without it — lay far beyond the boundaries of one small kingdom. It lay precisely in the explanation of the tragedy which he provided. His view of the calamity as a necessary punishment went a long way towards preserving Israel's faith from extinction.

By demolishing false hopes, Jeremiah (like Ezekiel) offered a positive faith. The Exile could be regarded as an interlude (29:11–14) beyond which lay God's own future. As evidence of his faith in this ultimate restoration, Jeremiah brought land in Benjamin, even while Jerusalem was falling (32:6–15; see background under Isr.* and Jud., V).

The New Covenant: This faith rested not on the expectation of some ordinary national resurgence, but on a new redemptive act on the part of Yahweh (31:31–37) who, as once before when He brought the people out of Egypt, would forgive their sins and make a "new covenant" with them. The new covenant would be written on their hearts and they would fulfill its demands with the help of divine grace.

Jeremiah's religion was an intensely personal matter. The corporate cult which had dominated Israel in the past was, to him, an abomination in which he could not participate. The fact that he declared that its sacrificial ritual had never been more than subsidiary to Yahweh's main demands of personal righteousness (6:16–21; 7:21–23), together with his continual emphasis on individual repentance (4:4) is indicative of new paths in belief. Jeremiah, by the loneliness his prophetic ministry brought upon him, found a new depth of experience of the presence of God, and became the medium of a message of the fundamentally inner quality of religion. This was of the greatest importance to Israel's future. Jeremiah knew that religion could survive the loss of the cultus and the cessation of sacrifice, though he did not wish religion to be divorced from the cultus and he had not meant that God spurned sacrifice. What he urged was that they were useless when offered by men who did not hearken unto the voice of God. Jeremiah was proved right, for Jewish religion was maintained in Babylonia without the Temple and without the Davidic dynasty. Possibly Jeremiah himself did not perceive the full significance of his message, and his hearers may also have failed to grasp the significance of his proclamation of a religion which could subsist without the Temple, but whose roots rested in the New Covenant. It is assumed by many that the importance of his message lay in what it would come to mean to his followers and disciples.

Corporate and Individual Religion: Jeremiah was part of the tide of national affairs; his fortunes were involved in those of society. In days when men were attributing the cause of national calamities to others, Jeremiah (and later Ezekiel*) directed men to look into their own hearts and to find the fruit of their sin in their sorrows. It is, however, an exaggeration to say that individualism was born with Jeremiah, or that the individual Hebrews looked upon themselves solely as members of the corporate group, with no individual responsibilities and no individual religious experience. The Hebrews had individual rights which were inalienably theirs and which not even a king could invade. Jeremiah did not regard them solely as individuals without the ties which made them part of the social whole, the covenantal community. Biblical religion was both corporate and personal from earliest times. Obviously the Decalogue was a community contract, but it was aimed at each individual. Thus, the community had individual and social aspects, both of which need to be recognized.

In evaluating the work of Jeremiah, many scholars have placed too much emphasis on the contrast between corporate and individual religion. The real meaning, in this respect, is that the individual aspect came into greater prominence, not that Jeremiah (and later Ezekiel) discovered the individual. Prior to these prophets, religion was the affair of the community rather than of the individual. Yahweh was the God of Israel as a whole, and Israel was His child. The Covenant of Sinai was a covenant which the corporate society of Israel made with Yahweh. But Jeremiah spoke of the New Covenant that Yahweh would make with individual souls, a Covenant inscribed upon their hearts, to which He addressed His ethical demands. These are the inner springs of loyalty to God. In sum, Jeremiah was responsible in large measure for the survival of corporate religion, in spite of the drastic change in its character occasioned by the destruction of the Temple and the institutions of the Kingdom.

II. FORM AND ORGANIZATION OF THE BOOK: The book of Jeremiah is now thought to be made up of a whole collection of separate scrolls, each containing a number of oracles and narratives. These have been put together without regard to any chronological order. The original scrolls were traditions, some written, some oral, recording various sayings and acts of the prophet, not in any logical sequence. Jeremiah possibly prepared a collection of his own oracles during his lifetime, and subsequently added to it. This collection is doubtless one of the sources of the present book of Jeremiah, but it is not the sole source. The combination of material from this and other sources may be assigned to the compilers of the book at a later age. From the nature of the groupings, it is clear that they instituted some order. Nevertheless, there is a good deal of repetitiousness in the work, certain phrases recurring again and again, while whole passages reappear in different places, for instance 6:22–24 and 50:41–43, or 10:12–16 and 51:15–19. Jeremiah's scribe and friend was Baruch, a scion of a prominent Judean family, and he was responsible for preserving Jeremiah's writings. The best explanation for the repetitiousness that has been put forward is that other editors besides Baruch played a part in compiling the material. In fact, different compilations are involved, each with its own focus and selection principle. In the final compilation, no attempt was made to adjust the contents, the compilers apparently recording what was transmitted in each collection.

Contents and Outline: Making allowance for this lack of organization, the chapters of the book of Jeremiah can be classified more or less as follows:

I. Chs. 1–6: An introduction and the oracles and poems of his early ministry, before the reform of Josiah;

7–10: Oracles against the prevailing syncretism with alien cults; the historical background covers the reigns of Josiah and Jehoiakim;

11–17 concern mainly Josiah's and Jeremiah's support of the covenant reforms, but also include parables, laments, exhortations and warnings in 8:20–9:1; 9:17–22 and 13:17–27;

18–20: Confessions and judgments, apparently in the days of Jehoiakim, also chs. 24–30:35 (see Restoration*);

21–24: Prophetic activity under Zedekiah and oracles about kings and prophets.

II. Chs. 26–45 are mainly biographical narratives: the memoirs of Baruch.

26–29: Warnings and conflicts with priests and prophets;

30–33: Promises of restoration (including the "new covenant"; 31:31–34);

31, 34–35, 37–39: The "book of the siege" and Jeremiah's prophetic activity in the most tragic days of Judah;

40–45: Jeremiah's career after the fall of Jerusalem.

III. The last parts of the book, chs. 25 and 45–51 consist of oracles against the foreign nations.

IV. 52 is a historical appendix, in effect a recapitulation of the last chapter of II Kings.

As the chapters are not in chronological order, they were presumably arranged according to their subject matter. Chapter 36 seems to confirm this. Jeremiah's oracles were first written down in 604 BCE, the 4th year of Jehoiakim, by which time they covered 23 years since the 13th year of Josiah (627 BCE). The manuscript was destroyed by Jehoiakim (36:20 ff) but re-written by Baruch at Jeremiah's dictation, at which time "many similar words were added to them" (36:32). There is, of course, no way of knowing which were the "similar words" added and what was the original scroll which Jehoiakim destroyed. Clearly, the original oracles and the additions formed the nucleus of the present book of Jeremiah. To them were added other "confessions" and sayings of Jeremiah's, the whole collection being made at a time of great danger and turmoil.

III. THE HEBREW TEXT AND THE SEPTUAGINT: In no book of the Old Testament is the difference between the Massorah (see Bible Canon and Text*) and the Septuagint versions more striking. The Greek version has some 2,500 fewer words. In general, the "omissions" are minor matters, although the poetical sections display more metrical regularity in the Greek than in the Hebrew. The oracles against foreign nations which come at the end of the book in Hebrew are placed immediately after 25:13 in the Greek, and thus they appear in a different order. The differences suggest that different readings existed in Palestine and Egypt, and that these continued independently of each other until the general divergence of the two texts. The final editing of the Hebrew text is generally thought to have taken place in the 2nd c. BCE.

Apocryphal Jeremiah and Baruch: All sorts of Jewish and Christian apocryphal legends grew up on the subject of Jeremiah's life after his sojourn in Egypt. Jeremiah himself is credited with the writing of the book of Kings and Lamentations (the possibility is discussed in the article on Lamentations*). His secretary, Baruch, acquired an almost equally prominent place in Jewish folklore as a model of piety. A number of Apocryphal* and pseudepigraphical writings are ascribed to him, i.e. the book of Baruch, the Apocalypse* of Baruch.

JESUS OF NAZARETH. — *Outline: I. Evidence: The Gospels as Evidence; The Dates of the Gospels; Geography. II. The Life of Jesus: The Nativity; Childhood; Baptism; The Beginning of the Ministry; John and Jesus; Relation to Dead Sea Sectaries; Rejection in Nazareth; The Campaign in Galilee; Jesus and the Pharisees; Disappointment; Jesus and Herod Antipas; Jesus and the Sadducees; The Last Supper; Jesus and the Roman Rulers. III. His Trial: Archaeology and the Trial; Crucifixion and Burial. IV. Teachings: Jesus' Personality; The Kingdom of God (Heaven); Son of Man; The Suffering Servant; Resurrection; The Eschatological Event; Jesus in Contemporary Jewish Literature.*

I. EVIDENCE: There is no historical theme to which it is so difficult to do justice as to the figure and personality of Jesus Christ. In the nineteenth century there was an upsurge of scholarly and theological debate about the origins of Christianity which prompted a much more exacting study of the evidence. Since then, the New Testament and relevant contemporary materials have been critically studied, with the help of all the resources of modern scholarship. As a result, a clearer picture of the historical Jesus (in Hebrew Yehoshua, in Aramaic Yeshua or Yeshu), who once lived and worked in Roman-ruled Palestine and died in Jerusalem, has become possible. The following outline of his career and teaching is probable rather than certain.

The Gospels as Evidence: The supreme sources for the life of Jesus are the Gospel accounts but these have to be read against the background of the religious and political movements of their time and with the reasons for their composition in mind. The Gospels were not intended as verbatim reports. They were four accounts of the life and teachings of Jesus, passed on by word of mouth as part of the liturgy of the early Church and written down some time after the events which they described (see "Jesus in Contemporary Jewish Literature" at the end of this article).

The school of "Form Criticism", which analyzes the legends, sayings and stories in the Gospels (see Biblical Criticism*), holds that many of the sayings and incidents ascribed to Jesus really belong to a later period and relate to conditions and events within the early Church. Other scholars point out that the problems to be faced were much the same at both times. The fact that the Gospels include material which must have been an embarrassment to the early Church is cited as proof of the trustworthiness of their evidence. Nevertheless, allowance must be made for the lapse in time and changes in outlook which the Gospels reflect.

The Dates of the Gospels: Of the first three — Mark, Matthew and Luke, called the Synoptics because of their generally similar approach — the earliest, Mark, was written in Greek by a Christian of the Roman church. Most scholars date him between 60–70 CE but it is not possible to prove exactly when Mark was written. Matthew, which may have been originally created in Hebrew, and Luke, the work of the Hellenist doctor who was the disciple of Paul and is credited with authorship of Acts, both date about 20 years later. The date of John is uncertain. Whereas it has generally been reckoned the latest of the Gospels to be written, more recent scholarly opinion regards it as among the earliest New Testament documents, containing some of the most primitive Jewish-Christian traditions. There are varied opinions on dating, W.F. Albright even believing that the whole New Testament could have been composed by 80 CE (see Gospels, Synoptic*; John, Gospel of*; Luke*; Mark*; Matthew*).

The disciples preached Jesus as Messiah. By the time the accounts were written down, this was the accepted theology of the early Church. The traditions about Jesus' actual life had, therefore, to be related to prophetic expectations of the Messiah.

Geography: The places Jesus visited and the routes of his journeys can only be stated in general. Only a few towns or villages are definitely named in the Gospels and it is impossible to locate some of these with accuracy (see map **564**). The centre of his mission was the fishing town of Capernaum (Kfar-Nahum), on the northwestern shore of the Sea of Galilee. No trace remains of the town Jesus knew. The synagogue, whose ruins can still be seen, dates from the late 2nd century CE, although an earlier one probably stood on the same site (see Synagogues*). None of the mountains in Galilee can be identified; they were then much as they are today.

II. THE LIFE OF JESUS. **The Nativity:** "Jesus was born in Bethlehem of Judea in the days of Herod the King" (Mt. 2:1). The Gospel of Luke adds that Joseph and Mary were obliged to go there from their home in Nazareth in order to be enrolled for taxation. However, there is a discrepancy in time. Jesus was born before the death of Herod (4 BCE), whereas the only census known in the period took place 10 or 13 years later, while Quirinius was Roman governor of Syria. This has suggested the alternate theory that Jesus, who was a Galilean, was born in Nazareth, the story of his birth in "David's City" of Bethlehem being developed later to justify the claim that it fulfilled the prophecy of Micah (5:2–15) that the Messiah was to issue from the House of David.

Childhood: Hardly anything is known about the earlier years of Jesus' life, nor of the Nazareth in which he spent them. Possible exceptions are the Virgin's Fountain or cave dwellings cut in the rocky soil which provided homes for the poor people. In later centuries, the ancient town was completely covered by churches and pious memorials. Luke lifts the veil for a moment, with his story of the 12-year-old Jesus becoming so absorbed in learned discussions

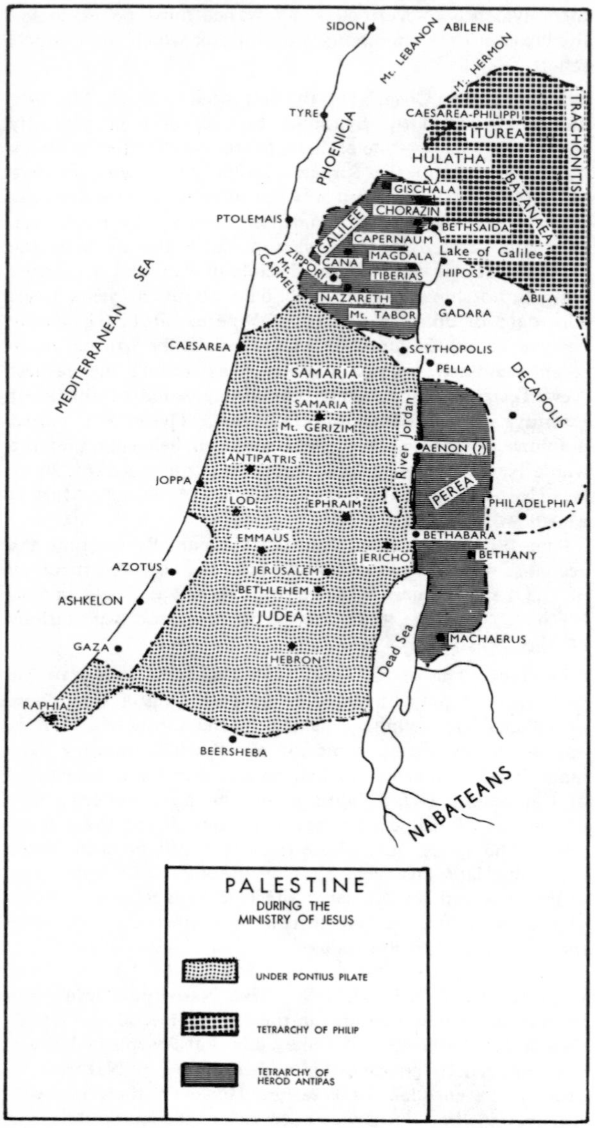

564

with the rabbis of the Temple, that he missed his homeward-bound parents (Lk. 2:41–51).

Baptism: The Gospels saw the starting point for Jesus' ministry in the dramatic spiritual experience of his baptism by John the Baptizer* which gave Jesus an immediate sense of divine approval and "Sonship". In Mark's (the earliest) account, the event appears as an inward, spiritual experience for Jesus himself. Later Gospels (Matthew, Luke) record the event in visionary language, quite acceptable to its original audience, in which the symbolic spirit is given physical form: "And behold the heavens were opened and he saw the Spirit of God descending like a dove, and alighting on him; and lo, a voice from heaven, saying, 'This is my beloved Son, with whom I am well pleased.'" (Mt. 3:16–17).

This took place, according to Luke, when Jesus was in his thirtieth year, although his chronology is doubted, (e.g. Quirinius is mentioned only in Luke). For a time Jesus remained in touch with John the Baptizer* in Judah and then, for the familiar period of solitary withdrawal, in the "wilderness". In the 4th or 8th c. CE, a monastery (**565**), called Jebel Qarantal to commemorate Jesus' 40-day fast in the wilderness, was constructed at Dok, halfway up the mountain above Jericho. John said Jesus was not yet 50, and this is more likely to be accurate in the view of some scholars.

The Beginning of the Ministry: Jesus appealed first to the people of Galilee, travelling, like so many of the religious teachers of the time, from place to place. The evidence states that he read from the Scriptures and then spoke to the people but whether he taught in the synagogues, translating the ancient biblical Hebrew into spoken Aramaic and interpreting the lessons of the Scriptures, or whether he simply preached on biblical passages, is not certain.

Jesus' message was that the great hope of the Jewish religion was about to be fulfilled. The time of waiting was over; the kingdom of heaven at hand. To prepare for the reign of God men must repent, change their way of living and have faith in the transformation of the world they knew into the world as God meant it to be.

He became known as a teacher of unusual power and authority and also as a healer, mainly of lepers, paralytics and the blind. This healing ministry was an essential part of Jesus' mission. In the Kingdom of God, whose coming he proclaimed, there was no place for pain or disease. Healing existing disabilities was an essential accompaniment to the message he preached and a sign that the new age had actually begun.

Mark, particularly, emphasizes this aspect of Jesus' work. Mark clearly aims to present Jesus as Lord (or Master) from the beginning. First, as master over Satan (in the story of the Temptation in the wilderness); then as lord over the men whom he calls to "follow him"; then as master of the Scriptures he propounds; then as lord over the "evil spirits" who were supposed to cause disease (especially epilepsy and mental aberrations) by "possessing" a human being. Jesus, Mark shows, had only to speak to these demons to be immediately recognized by them as the arch-enemy of Satan.

John and Jesus: At about this time, the long-standing enmity between Herod Antipas and John the Baptist culminated in the Baptizer's imprisonment and execution. His death was obviously a crucial event for Jesus — foreshadowing as it did, Jesus' own fate, and bringing to the forefront the similarities between John's movement and message and those of Jesus. Jesus' call to repentance and a return to God before the final judgment was a direct continuation of the Baptizer's message and has given rise to much debate about the relationship between John and Jesus on the one hand and, on the other, about the relation of the forerunners of Christianity to the Dead Sea sectaries (see Dead Sea Scrolls*).

Relation to Dead Sea Sectaries: Neither John nor Jesus came directly from the Essenes or Dead Sea sectaries. But it is generally agreed today that the sectarian side of Judaism was the most important influence in the background of both. Like other Jewish nonconformist groups, the movements of John and Jesus find a common ancestor in the earlier Hassidim*. They were all messianic movements; they shared a common eschatological* urgency and held theological beliefs which differed from contemporary Pharisaic and later rabbinic doctrine.

Like the Dead Sea sectaries Jesus stressed the imminent end of the world and, in expectation of the destruction of the existing social order, tended to be indifferent to the demands of family and community. However, his teaching of non-resistance to evil was in direct contradiction to the sectaries' doctrine.

Rejection in Nazareth: To the people of his home in Nazareth, Jesus was merely the son of the local carpenter, an itinerant preacher of unorthodox views. One Sabbath, Luke tell us (4:16–17), Jesus read in the synagogue the passage of Isaiah that best described his mission: "The spirit of the Lord is upon me, because he has anointed me to preach good news to the poor. He has sent me to proclaim release to the captives and recovering of sight to the blind, to set at liberty those who are oppressed, to proclaim the acceptable year of the Lord." (Is. 61:1).

"Anointed" meant "the Messiah" and the prophecy was understood in that sense, whether used by the Zealots* as a call to violent rebellion, or by the Pharisees* as an abstract spiritual term. Whatever the balance between the two parties in Nazareth at that time, the people turned against one who, as the saying went, was "no prophet in his own country."

The Campaign in Galilee: Rejected, Jesus returned to Capernaum and began to organize a group for the evangelization of Galilee. From among his followers, the Gospels record, he chose twelve men as his close companions and deputies. Five were selected before the others and became senior to them: Simon of Bethsaida, their leader (called Kephas, or Peter, meaning "the rock"), James and John ("the sons of thunder" or Boanerges); Andrew, the brother of Simon, and Matthew who, unlike the four others, was not a fisherman but had been a tax gatherer (a publican). One of Jesus' outstanding characteristics was that he associated with common people and did not despise "publicans and sinners". Unlike other Jewish sectaries, there was no formal intitiation into his group. He demanded of his followers only repentance, and belief in him. This is the scene (**566**) at the northern shore of Lake Galilee, between Capernaum and Bethsaida.

In the winter of 28 or 29 CE, the campaign began in earnest; "he called to him the twelve, and began to send

565

them out two by two, and gave them authority over the unclean spirits. He charged them to take nothing for their journey except a staff; no bread, no bag, no money in their belts; but to wear sandals and not put on two tunics . . . So they went out and preached that men should repent. And they cast out many demons, and anointed with oil many that were sick and healed them." (Mk. 6:7–13).

His message was to be confined to the Jews: "Go nowhere among the gentiles, and enter no town of the Samaritans, but go rather to the lost sheep of the house of Israel." (Mt. 10:5–6). They spread Jesus' doctrines, repeated stories of miracles and even exorcised spirits in his name.

Jesus and the Pharisees: Jesus never attacked the fundamentals of Jewish faith: "Think not that I have come to abolish the law and the prophets; I have come not to abolish them but to fulfill them. For truly I say to you, till heaven and earth pass away, not an iota, not a dot, will pass from the law until all is accomplished." (Mt. 5:17–18). This is the familiar Mishnaic expression "kotzo shel yôd" — .. meaning that not even a "yôd" nor even the ornament on the yôd, will pass, etc. (see Alphabet*). He insisted that the instructions of the religious authorities (the Scribes* and Pharisees*) be observed. Nevertheless he taught a morality which went far beyond average Pharisee standards of forgiveness, purity and love and which no law could enforce. The Synoptic Gospels (Matthew, Mark, Luke) indicate that in form and content, Jesus' preaching was closely akin to that of the Pharisees. Many striking parallels exist between his sayings and those of the rabbis. Like them, Jesus made effective use of parables and advocated very similar moral principles. There was sufficient common ground between the two for many New Testament scholars to regard Jesus

566

as a divergent Pharisee*. It often happens that those who are closest in doctrine and practice are the bitterest enemies. Further it is clear to others that whatever the similarities between them, Jesus was not a Pharisee. The most important point in their quarrel was his flat rejection of the Oral Law (see Law*; Mishnah*), which they and the rabbis who followed them regarded as on an equal footing with the Written Law of Moses. Whatever new elements of conflict may have been introduced later, the basic struggle lay in this fundamental difference between Jesus and his Pharisaic opponents.

Jesus criticized the behaviour of certain Pharisees, not the spirit of the movement as a whole (see: Pharisees* for a discussion of its character), although he regarded his teachings as superior. He taught as one personally inspired, "Truly I say unto you . . .", an attitude which naturally aroused the resentment of the official interpreters of the Law*. While the Gospels tend to show Jesus and the Pharisees as mutually irreconcilable, they nevertheless record friendly contacts between them.

Only two instances are given of Jesus directly challenging the Pharisees on their interpretation of the Scriptures: once on the lawfulness of divorce and again on a man's right to forgive sin. In questions concerning the Sabbath*, Jesus went further than the Pharisees in the exemptions he found permissible, but that "the Sabbath was made for man, not man for the Sabbath" was accepted Pharisee doctrine. On the other hand, Jesus' doctrine of non-resistance to evil is not found in Pharisaic sources. Nor did the official upholders of morality have any sympathy with Jesus' charity towards "harlots" and sexual offenders.

Jesus also came into conflict with the official interpreters and authorities on the Law* (see below: Teachings) on questions such as the need for a ritual cleansing of the hands before a meal (something more than a mere washing, see Impurity*). Jesus taught that to God, cleanness means a clean life and uncleanness a deceitful, proud or sensual character. He rejected the idea that unclean things made men ritually unclean: "But what comes out of the mouth proceeds from the heart, and this defiles a man. For out of the heart come evil thoughts . . . These are what defile a man; but to eat with unwashed hands does not defile a man." (Mt. 15:18–20). Jesus' insistence on the importance of a man's own spirit, character and motives was one of the most original aspects of his message.

Fundamentally, Jesus and the Pharisees shared a common faith in Judaism; both were imbued with spiritual nationalism. The issues between them, while strenuously argued, were part of a domestic, intra-mural quarrel. Today it can be better understood in the light of the differences and similarities between the doctrines of the early Christians and the Dead Sea Sectaries (see Dead Sea Scrolls*: The Scrolls and Christianity).

Only when the same disputes were taken up by later Gentile and Jewish Christians* in the period of the New Testament did the disastrous breach between the two faiths develop. The authors of the Gospels — writing at this time — consciously obscured the links between Jesus and the Pharisees. As the separation between Judaism and Christianity developed, so the anti-Pharisee bias was confirmed and strengthened. It seems likely that the Gospels set the beginnings of the growing antagonism between the young Church and official Judaism back to the time of the Jesus — a point that will be developed in connection with the accounts of his trial, see below.

Disappointment: After the confident opening of the campaign in Galilee, the crowds began to fall away. Not only did Jesus face the opposition of the religious leaders, the people who had welcomed him in such numbers now seemed to have lost their confidence in him. The whole generation seemed to be turning a deaf ear to his teaching (Mt. 11:16–19). Even in Chorazin, Bethsaida and Capernaum, the people turned against him (Mt. 11:20–24; Lk. 10:13–15).

Not only was his religious mission not the success he had hoped, he was also threatened by the secular authorities.

Jesus and Herod Antipas: Up to this point, the civil authority — Herod Antipas in Galilee — had paid him little attention. Herod had had John the Baptizer beheaded because the strength of his movement had been a threat to established (Herod's) authority. Now it seemed that the movement John had begun was being continued by Jesus: "Herod said, 'John I beheaded, but who is this about whom I hear such things?' And he sought to see him." (Lk. 9:9). Having rid himself of John it was not likely that Herod would stand quietly by and watch the same movement expand under John's successor. He made up his mind to arrest Jesus as a potential leader of revolt against Rome: "At that very hour some Pharisees came, and said to him, 'Get away from here, for Herod wants to kill you.' And he said to them, 'Go and tell that fox, "Behold I cast out demons and perform cures today and tomorrow, and the third day I finish my course. Nevertheless I must go on my way today and tomorrow and the day following; for it cannot be that a prophet should perish away from Jerusalem." (Lk. 13:31–33).

Jesus had made up his mind to issue his challenge in Jerusalem — the heart of Judaism. First he journeyed north, to the area of Tyre and Sidon, where he could be free of Herod's spies, and also from the continual claims the crowds made on his attention.

At this stage, for the first time, Jesus began to preach directly about himself, and to proclaim his mission as one of suffering before glory. The Gospels of Mark and Matthew relate here that Jesus foretold his own sufferings and death: "If any man would come after me, let him deny himself and take up his cross and follow me. For whoever would save his life will lose it; and whoever loses his life for my sake and the gospel's will save it . . ." (Mk. 8:34–35).

To attribute these words directly to Jesus raises serious difficulties, though commentators regard them as the sort of language that Jesus could have used as an expression of his self-consciousness as Messiah, or as a vivid metaphor which would be easily understood by his hearers. However, many scholars agree that the words as they stand can hardly be original since they reflect so closely Jesus' own death. (The cross was carried by the convicted criminal to the place of execution.)

Yet Jesus saw himself as, ". . . the Christ indeed, anointed not to glory but to suffering; no second and greater David but a man of sorrows and acquainted with grief" in the words of Is. 53.

Then he turned towards his ultimate goal, Jerusalem, following a roundabout route, keeping away from Herod's territory wherever possible. At the same time, Mark (10:32) records that he no longer walked with his disciples, but in front of them, alone, as though to symbolize the gap between the spiritual development which he had undergone and the more naive thought of his disciples. When he did speak to them it was to tell them of the fate that awaited him, but they were so far from understanding that even James and John asked him to grant them posts of honour on either side of the messianic throne of their expectations. His answer was again to emphasize what had always been central to his teaching: "... whoever would be great among you must be your servant, and whoever would be first among you must be slave of all. For the Son of Man also came not to be served but to serve, and to give his life as a ransom for many." (Mk. 10:43–45).

Jesus and the Sadducees: Finally, he appeared in the city with a handful of followers who paid him messianic honours. Jesus immediately drew attention to himself by his high-handed action in clearing the Temple courts of the traders who crowded there. Money changers not unlike the one carved on a 1st c. CE Roman sarcophagus (**567**), must have been a familiar scene, in the Temple courts as elsewhere. His attack on the Temple organization earned Jesus the enmity of the Sadducees*, its official administrators.

The Last Supper: On the night of the 13th Nissan, according to the Synoptic Gospels, after Jesus had celebrated the "Last Supper", perhaps the Passover meal, with his disciples, he was arrested by the Temple guard. The Sadducees were not at that time concerned with Jesus' philosophy. They attacked him on the political question of whether he claimed to be the Messiah and it was on this political charge that they handed him over to the Roman authorities. The usual view is that the Last Supper was celebrated on Thursday, the night before the crucifixion. But a theory has been propounded on the basis of the Dead Sea Scrolls* that the supper was actually celebrated on Tuesday night. This is disputed by many leading New Testament scholars, though it has the advantage of clearing up numerous problems. Mlle. A Jaubert, supported by J.T. Milik, has suggested that the sectaries of Qumran followed the calendar* of the book of Jubilees (see Apocrypha*), as confirmed by the scrolls found there. The Essene Passover in the year of the Crucifixion fell on Tuesday, at a different date from the official time promulgated by the Temple authorities. This author assumes that the Last Supper was celebrated by Jesus as the Essene Passover on the Tuesday evening in Holy Week. In this way she resolves the contradiction between the Synoptic Gospels (Mk. 14:12, passim) in which the Last Supper is a Passover meal, and John, in which the Passover starts on the Friday evening, Jesus being crucified as the Passover Offering. This suggestion provides a more leisurely sequence of events for the various trials of Jesus. On the other hand, it rearranges the whole chronology of Holy Week, incidentally bringing it into conformity with Jewish legal practice.

Jesus and the Roman Rulers: Although Jesus' own aims may have been entirely pacific and his interpretation of the terms "Messiah" and "King of the Jews" purely spiritual, in the Palestine of that time these were political and military slogans. Jesus himself did not aim at inciting revolution, but his opposition to established authority and his proclamation of the rule of God could be interpreted as support for the militant nationalism of the Zealots, to whom the Kingdom of God was no mere metaphor. Both John and Jesus announced the imminent destruction of the rulers of the world. Herod Antipas and the Roman authorities understandably found such preaching treasonable and did their best to cut it short.

III. HIS TRIAL: A great deal of obscurity and prejudice shrouds this subject. The Gospels themselves are not consistent. They shift the blame around so as to focus on the high priest and his associates — and then include others in a general way, although the main responsibility is laid clearly at the feet of the chief priests. The Romans are treated as secondary factors. Acts places the responsibility for Jesus' death on the shoulders of the entire Jewish people. The Gospels even show them rejecting Pilate's proposal for his release and deliberately taking his blood on their own and their descendants' heads. One reason for the inconsistency — and an additional problem for the scholar — is that the accounts in the Gospels were written some time after the Trial took place. Although it is impossible to be certain when Mark lived, it is argued on the basis of his evidence (ch. 14) that hundreds of people who had been in Jerusalem at the time of the Crucifixion must still have been alive when he was writing. On the other hand, many scholars maintain that by the time Mark and Matthew (chs. 26 and 27) wrote their accounts, there was no living witness to what had taken place after Jesus' arrest.

567

A great deal of confusion remains in the Gospels' stories and much in them will not bear comparison with established judicial practice (Jewish and Roman) of the time. The Gospels speak of a trial by night by the Great Sanhedrin on charges of attempting to make himself king — claiming to be the Messiah. The Sanhedrin (see Government and Authority*) was the supreme religious court of Jerusalem, bound by oral rules of legal procedure, current in the days of Jesus. These are familiar from their later compilation in the Mishnah* (written in 200 CE). Though there might conceivably have been changes in the rules by the time they were actually written down, it is unlikely that such changes were of major importance. The Mishnah states (and it was probably the rule in Jesus' time) that the Sanhedrin met in the daytime — not at night on the eve of Passover. Such a trial would have been completely illegal. Moreover, none of the evidence produced could have justified the death sentence. The Gospels make it clear that the death sentence was imposed and carried out by the Romans. It is said that the Jews did not have the power to execute but, in any case, no Jewish death sentence was carried out.

The story of the trial at night would make better sense on the assumption (put forward by S. Zeitlin) that Jesus was arraigned before the informal advisory council of the High Priest, which was a political body, not subject to rules of judicial procedure.

Another suggestion is that Jewish officials who were nominees of the Romans and may have wanted to curry favour, may have brought the incipient messianic movement to the attention of the Roman authorities.

Paul Winter, in his analysis of the trial of Jesus, considers that many of the contradictory elements in the story may be regarded as later insertions which, in any case, are of secondary importance. These include: the investigation by Annas; the night session of the Sanhedrin; the mocking in the High Priest's house; the morning session without sentence (Luke); the scene with Herod Antipas; the Barabbas episode in its present form; Pilate's benevolence, and the scourging before death (John).

Many scholars believe that these elements of the story reflect the anti-Jewish sentiment of early Christians, perhaps those in Hellenistic circles, and their desire to absolve the Romans from the guilt of the death of their saviour.

One portion of the Gospel narratives of the Passion which clearly has historical value seems to be the procedure before Pilate. Contrary to Christian tradition, modern scholars are tending more and more to the opinion that Antipas and Pontius Pilate, the Roman Procurator of Jerusalem, took a much greater share in the arrest, trial and execution of Jesus than did the Jews.

According to one view, Pilate alone had the power to impose the death sentence, but this is a matter which is still disputed. In either case, he found himself faced with a popular leader of great potential danger, just at the time of one of the Jewish festivals whose excitable crowds had frequently meant trouble for the authorities. The traditional view is that he was abetted in this by a group of Jews who wanted Jesus out of the way, i.e. the High Priest and his associates. To avoid the possibility of rioting and friction, Pilate condemned Jesus to be crucified — the standard Roman method of execution for rebels against their rule.

Archaeology and the Trial: There is a reference in John's account of the trial to the place of judgment, the location of which has been archaeologically confirmed: "When Pilate heard these words, he brought Jesus out and sat down on the judgment seat at a place called the Pavement, and in Hebrew, Gabbatha." (Jn. 19:13). The stone pavement, called Gabbatha, which means "raised land", stood on a rocky height at the foot of the Tower of Antonia. When it was excavated, the engraving made for the "Game of the King" played by the Roman soldiers stationed there, could still be distinguished on the high rocky ledge **(568)**. The fact that archaeology has confirmed the Greek and Hebrew names preserved in the Gospel can hardly be accidental. John contains much valuable topographic and historical data.

Crucifixion and Burial: The crucifixion on Golgotha took place only 24 hours after the beginning of the Last Supper. The Passion narrative, written from the point of view of those who believed in his resurrection, concludes with Jesus' burial in the garden tomb of Joseph of Arimathea, outside the northern wall of Jerusalem*, and his resurrection (see below). Excavation and debate have never succeeded in reaching a definite conclusion about the sites of Calvary or of the tomb of Christ. The traditional site, where the church of Holy Sepulchre stands today **(569)**, was authenticated by a vision of St. Helena, mother of the emperor Constantine, in the early 4th c. CE. The subterranean vaults and substructures of the church **(570)** date from the time of Constantine. Modern investigations have suggested a site further to the north known as Gordon's Calvary but the repeated destruction and rebuilding of the walls of Jerusalem as it expanded during the following centuries, make certainty impossible (see Jerusalem*; Funerary Customs*).

IV. TEACHINGS. — Jesus was an outstanding example of the great prophets and teachers of Judaism who emphasized the spiritual and ethical content of their religion. In Jesus' teachings there are new elements, eschatological* and moral.

568

His fundamental theme, however, was that the Kingdom of God demanded a strict adherence to the Law of Judaism — but the Law as he understood, interpreted and expounded it, not as the Pharisees and others did in his day. Jesus and his disciples kept the feasts according to the orthodox calendar, they made pilgrimages to Jerusalem at the times prescribed by the Law and mingled with the multitude who did likewise. The evangelists frequently stress Jesus' respect for the Temple and its functions and his acknowledgment of the validity of the priesthood (Mt. 8:4; 23:2–3).

Where he differed was over the Oral Law of the Pharisees* (see article). This Jesus rejected on principle. He accepted the Written Scripture as the Word of God and interpreted it in the light of the two great commandments on Love of God and Neighbour — just as the prophets had done. The Oral Law of the Pharisees he rejected as human, not divine. He did not teach that the Law would be "voided", but that it would be implemented through the power of the Holy Spirit, rather than in fear of its sanctions. His emphasis was always on the inner spiritual meaning of the Law, not the multiplicity of ritual commandments.

Jesus taught that the reign of God was "at hand" and open to "all Jews" who sincerely desired it and were prepared to make the efforts demanded for its achievement. The essence of his teaching was in his insistence that a man is good only so far as his spirit is pure.

Jesus' Personality: What seems to be unquestioned is the force of Jesus' personality. He was possessed, as J. Klausner put it, "of marked individuality and great self-confidence, believing in his own supreme authority and rebuking all who did not recognise his authority or his teaching." Above all, he demanded — and received — absolute faith in himself.

After Jesus' death, the disciples added the message that Jesus had represented, in himself and his mission, the manifestation of God's active intervention in man's affairs, even before the coming of the eschatological kingdom. Jesus, they taught, had been deliberately sent to earth to act as God's instrument in bringing mankind to salvation and the blessings of the kingdom. The Sermon on the Mount is a pattern for life in the kingdom which can only be "achieved by God". Here it has close parallels to Jewish and Pharisaic ideas of divine mercy and human repentance, and of God's rule over the world. In addition, it describes the righteousness of those who have decided for the kingdom and can thereafter behave as models of righteousness in an evil world (see Christianity, Early*).

The Kingdom of God (Heaven) was, to Jesus, something in which earthly, human considerations of physical pain and pleasure, social evils and inequalities, would have no place. Nevertheless the assurance of the kingdom's closeness were the "signs" — the sick healed, the blind seeing, the dead being raised.

In the eyes of the people and the rabbis, the Kingdom of Heaven was eschatological — in the sense that it would be ushered in by an act of God through his chosen servants. It would see the rule of God over his people. Its coming would be heralded by the appearance of a supernatural deliverer, the Messiah*, descended from David. Jewish teaching about the Kingdom of God as the rule of God is a matter of history. It was an important element in the

religious environment in which Jesus grew up and worked. To the extent that the rabbis and people were messianic (and they all were), they were also eschatological. This, however, is not a final answer to the question, what did Jesus mean by "the Kingdom"? He would not tell his disciples the time of its coming for, he said (Mk. 13:32), he did not know.

Jesus appeared at a time of intense spiritual and political turmoil, to a people steeped in Old Testament traditions of a deliverer whose coming at the end of the Age would mean the Kingdom of God — a new era in world affairs. In this connection, John's evidence is particularly instructive. John is considered by many to be the earliest Gospel. Certainly it is rooted in the Palestine and Jerusalem of Jesus and his followers and, moreover, there is no strong evidence against an early date. In John, Jesus is represented as a messianic and eschatological figure. At the time of his triumphant entry into Jerusalem, the watching crowds who asked, "Who is this?" were told, "This is the prophet Jesus from Nazareth." (Jn. 12). When the high priest asked Jesus, "Are you the Christ, the Son of the Blessed," Jesus apparently only repeated his statement: "I am and you will see the Son of Man sitting at the right hand of Power and coming with the clouds of heaven." (Mk. 14:61–62). "I am" is a response to the question of the high priest which was not whether he was the Son of Man. However, Jesus identified himself as the Son of Man — a mysterious title, perhaps deliberately so.

Son of Man: One of the main differences between Jewish belief and later Christian doctrine lies in their different interpretations of the Messiah and "Son of Man". In ancient Jewish tradition, Messiah should come in glory to take his seat upon a royal throne and usher in the new era. Jesus used the same concept (Mt. 19:28; 25:31; Mk. 13:26; Lk. 21:27) but the Gospels phrased his view of himself in retrospect in a quite different manner from the traditional meaning of these ideas. A variety of views were current at the time about the nature of the expected Messiah (see Dead Sea Scrolls*; Messianism*). Alongside the Christologies of the Davidic Messiah and the Suffering Servant, there appears the figure of the "Son of Man", a form of messianism influenced by elements associated with the "Heavenly Man" (see Messianism*). The concept of the "Son of Man" is not found in the Qumran literature, but it does appear in that part of Enoch (Similitudes, chs. 37–71) where the messianic figure is alluded to. As it is believed that this section may not be earlier than 100 CE, many scholars have concluded that the concept of Son of Man in its received form was post-Essene and post-Christian.

None of the older sources referred to a messiah who should appear on earth in poverty and humility to be rejected by his own people and suffer and die, giving his life as a ransom for mankind. This new conception was the work of Jesus' followers, who merged glory and humiliation in a combination of the "Son of Man" with the "Suffering Servant".

The Suffering Servant: This is the theme of the poetic vision of Isaiah (ch. 53). When the early church faced the problem of the shameful death of its leader, they took the prophecy of the Suffering Servant and merged it with older concepts of the Redeemer, creating a new role into which the facts of Jesus' life and death fitted perfectly. It is believed by many that Jesus himself, apparently, followed the Old Testament collective interpretation of the "Servant" and saw the role applying to his followers as well as himself. Other scholars take a different view and point out that the Gospel writers insist that Jesus was responsible for this combination of Suffering Servant and Son of Man. It is at least possible that Jesus patterned his life and message after the Suffering Servant — so the Church simply developed a theme already present. In this view the gospels gave a different emphasis to his words to fit their belief that with the resurrection, the New Age had dawned. The Messiah who is the Son of Man had come, been raised and was enthroned.

This point can be illustrated by the Scene at Caesarea Philippi: "And Jesus went on with his disciples, to the villages of Caesarea Philippi; and on the way he asked his disciples, 'Who do men say that I am?' And they told him, 'John the Baptist; and others say, Elijah; and others one of the prophets.' And he asked them, 'But who do you say that I am?' Peter answered him, 'You are the Christ.' And he charged them to tell no one about him." (Mk. 8:27–30) which seems to antedate a later phase of theology, going to prove that while Jesus' views of his messiahship had matured, his disciples' had not. Mark's whole account of this scene suggests that the disciples did not really expect Jesus' suffering and death. When he was arrested they fled from the scene and even Peter denied him. The disciples were Jews and they expected the return of Jesus as a royal messiah, with themselves by his side tasting his glory as his lieutenants (Mk. 10:35–37). However, Mark was a Christian of the Roman Church and he wrote his Gospel at the end of the Apostolic age, under the influence of Paul*. It is held by some scholars that Mark saw clearly the necessity of Jesus' suffering and death although his views may not reflect those of the early disciples. He may reflect a modified theology that was only later accepted by the whole of Christendom and was not part of the preaching of the disciples. Whether or not Paul and Mark did have similar views, they both placed the greatest emphasis on the necessity for Jesus' death. A majority of scholars hold that after the death and resurrection of Jesus there could have been no other message. Both Paul and Mark must reflect the early preaching of the disciples — after the death of Jesus.

Resurrection: While Jesus' followers were prepared for a resurrection of the dead, especially of martyrs, in the "New Age", they were not prepared for the idea of a universal resurrection. The message of Jesus rising from the dead, apparently came as a shock to the early disciples who were still looking for a "royal" messiah and lacked the necessary conception of Jesus as a suffering messiah, for which his death and resurrection were essential.

From a modern, naturalistic view of history, the death/resurrection of Jesus remains a mystery, which can only be solved in terms of a philosophical or religious creed. Perhaps the best that can be said scientifically is that if Jesus was the kind of person who could inspire the conviction that his death/resurrection was a necessity, then this, in itself, was a miracle humbly accepted by the faithful. Through its mystic aspects, it has immeasurably enriched the spiritual and philosophical life of the world.

After scattering from fear of persecution, Jesus' followers returned in the company of Mary, the mother of Jesus, his brothers and the women followers. In later Christianity, the story of Jesus' reappearance, first to the women at the tomb and then to Simon Peter, Thomas and James, became articles of faith.

The Eschatological Event: Yet the basis of Christian faith was not the fact of resurrection, but acceptance of the resurrection of Jesus as an eschatological "event" — not simply that Jesus had been raised, but the whole complex surrounding this core. With his death and its sequel, the gift of the Holy Spirit, his followers believed that the "New Age" had dawned. On this belief Christianity was founded. It is only by the power of the Spirit that one can believe the resurrection — not without it. While other sectaries within Judaism looked for their messiah in the future, the early Church believed that Jesus had been raised from the dead as messiah. The "event" was in the past tense, though, of course, there was much, too, in the future and in the present.

Jesus in Contemporary Jewish Literature: There is no mention of Jesus in contemporary Jewish literature. The allusion in Josephus* is, at least in part, a Christian interpolation. In the sayings of the "Tannaitic" rabbis* of the first two centuries CE which faithfully reflect the views of the 1st c. CE, there are references (preserved in the Talmud*) to Jesus' illegitimacy, to his going down to Egypt where he learned magic and to his death by stoning following a properly conducted Jewish trial on charges of "deceiving Israel", by persuading the Jews to practice idolatry. Of post-Talmudic literature, there is a "Toledot Yeshu" (History of Jesus) concerning a Yeshu ben Pandira, whose teachings recall Jesus' interpretations of Scripture, but the dates given do not correspond. There is also a reference in the Talmud to the disciples, giving five names which include Matthew and Thaddaeus (Todah). The Talmud also mentions the "minîm", heretics of various kinds, including Pauline Christians and, probably, the Jewish sectaries. These Talmudic and post-Talmudic references are mainly of value as an indication of the growing breach between Judaism and Christianity, which led to distortions on both the Christian and Jewish sides.

JOB. — *Outline: I. Structure and Contents: The Prose Story; The Central Section or Dialogue; Literary Character. II. Analysis of the Dialogues; The Pattern of the Speeches; First Round of Speeches; Second Round; The Intermediary in the Heavenly Court; The Third Round; The Speeches of Elihu; The Speech from the Whirlwind; The Epilogue. III. Relationship to Wisdom Literature: The Theological Problem of Job; Composition and Date; Language and Textual Problems; Conclusion.*

The third book of the Writings (Hagiographa) section of the Old Testament, Job has a unique place in biblical literature — indeed in world literature — as a poetic drama concerned with a fundamental inquiry into divine governance of the universe: why, in a world controlled by God, do the innocent suffer? The book's historical background, tone and thought are essentially Near Eastern, although it also expresses a distinctively Hebrew religious feeling.

I. STRUCTURE AND CONTENTS: The book's contents fall into three sections: a. a prose prologue (chs. 1–2) and b. a prose epilogue (42:7–17) enclosing c. a dialogue or series of speeches in poetry (chs. 3–42:6).

The latter can be divided into:

1st cycle of speeches	chs. 3–14	Job's lament and his first discussion with his "comforters";
2nd cycle of speeches	chs. 15–21	the second round of debate;
3rd cycle of speeches	chs. 22–31	the third and last discussion with the three comforters;
4th — the Elihu speeches	chs. 32–37	
5th — God's answer to Job	chs. 38–41	
6th — Job's response	ch. 42:1–6	

Nothing is known of the author of Job, but it is generally agreed that the prose passages in their present form have been reworked and that an old legend may lie behind them. The poet of the central section took the old legend — which may have been then in either oral or written form — as the framework for his creation. The literary source of the legend is still debated. Its literary character is discussed below.

The Prose Story: *The prologue* introduces Job as a prominent semi-nomadic chief, a native of Uz, and a man of blameless character. This archaic background seems to suggest the Patriarchal epics, or the Semitic folk stories of the 2nd mill. BCE (see below, Part III, Composition and Date).

Job is a righteous man, whose faith and devotion to God are unaffected by circumstances or the hope of reward. However, the Adversary (of man), called Satan in the English translation, appears before God in the heavenly court with the accusation that Job's apparent loyalty to God (El) is not disinterested but is designed to secure the blessings of health, long life, family, wealth and possessions. If he were to lose these things, he would renounce his faith. Satan is given a free hand to test Job. He is to be plunged into suffering, not because of any sin, but to vindicate God's trust in him. All that he has — his flocks and herds and sons and daughters — are destroyed, but his faith remains unshaken. Then he is afflicted with "loathsome sores" all over his body, but he still remains steadfast in his loyalty to his God. He refuses to "sin with his lips" and curse God as a means of inviting death and a quick end to his suffering.

While he sits "among the ashes", three friends, Eliphaz the Temanite, Bildad the Shuhite and Zophar the Naamathite come to comfort him. It becomes clear from the epilogue that the prose story used these three friends and Job's wife as a foil for the provocation of Job's thought. At last, however, his steadfast loyalty is rewarded. God speaks to Job and heals him.

The Epilogue (42:7–17) sketches the restoration of his fortunes "twice as much as he had before" and the happy sequel.

The Central Section or Dialogue: The poetic section between the prologue and the epilogue contains the debate between Job and his friends about the justice of the divine action. The Job of this section is not the passive sufferer of the prose sections. He rails from his dunghill, cursing the day of his birth and defying God to justify the punishment He has inflicted. His three "comforters" remonstrate with Job and try to convince him that he must somehow have deserved his fate. In fact this is no answer — the whole point of the story is that Job is a truly righteous man who does not morally "deserve" to be punished. Only at the end does God speak to Job "from the whirlwind" proclaiming His transcendence and announcing it as the duty of man to submit whether or not he understands. Job admits only to the faults of ignorance and presumption — not to any of the crimes with which his friends had charged him — and bows humbly before his God (42:6).

Thus, though God's reasons are hidden from man, His actions must be accepted as just. However blameless the sufferer may appear to himself and all around him, a cause for suffering does exist, hidden in the secret purposes of God.

Literary Character: The main question is the relationship between the poetry and the prose sections. The story of Job is presented in the form of a "wisdom" problem, indicated by its three-fold division. The poetic dialogue containing the central message requires a framework, provided by the prologue and epilogue, while these latter call for the development of the theme embodied in the central section. The heterodox and speculative material which makes up the poetic dialogue is presented within a formal, unifying framework, a point which is relevant to the question of the original unity of the book. The literary form of the book suggests a certain unity of composition to some, and they hold that in spite of apparent inconsistencies (see below) the three sections belong together.

The pattern of enclosing the poetic development of a particular theme in a prose story was familiar among the ancients of India, Egypt, Babylonia, Persia and Arabia. Thus in Job the prologue sets the scene and introduces the characters. These are then used in turn to develop a particular phase of the real argument. To the Greeks, drama meant developing action, but in Job — the only example of this sort in Hebrew literature — the dramatic dialogue could be conceived in terms of the development of ideas, purely out of discussion between the dramatis personnae. The poem goes strictly its own way as dialogue required to emphasize the wisdom problem. The author of Job used each phase of the dialogue to expand the real meaning of the story, stated explicitly in the prologue — that God trusted in Job and his essential righteousness, and that in his suffering, Job vindicated this trust. Neither Job nor his friends, of course, realized this, but the reader needs to have this knowledge in order to appreciate the working out of God's hidden purpose.

The people to whom the biblical dialogue was originally addressed were, of course, aware of the implications of this "wisdom" problem and could understand the apparent conclusions to be drawn from the vindication of Job at the end of his period of trial. In spite of its overall literary unity, there are many discrepancies within the parts. The Prologue, with the scene in heaven, and Epilogue are in a straightforward prose, while the dialogue is written in poetry of a very high order. Even more significant is the change in the divine name used. In the prose sections, He is Yahweh, but everywhere else a non-national name, like El, Eloah, Shaddai or Elyon is used, suggesting a distant, non-Hebrew origin. The Elihu chapters use El nearly all the time. Characteristics such as these are the best indication of the divisions between the chapters and the elements of the compilation.

II. ANALYSIS OF THE DIALOGUES: **The Pattern of the Speeches:** Each successive speech begins by refuting the argument of the previous one, then produces new arguments, offering as supporting evidence the experience of reputable witnesses, ancient "wise men" (see Wisdom Literature*) or the speaker himself. He then sums up his conclusions. Some of the speeches even include quotations from earlier ones. The form allows the author to build up his case by degrees, reaching his climax at the end.

First Round of Speeches: The debate opens with the superbly moving poetry of Job's curse of the day of his birth,

"Why did I not die at birth, come forth from the womb and expire?...
For then I should have lain down and been quiet;
I should have slept: then I should have been at rest." (3:11, 13)

He is then answered by Eliphaz the Temanite (4:1–5:27) whose "comfort" soon develops into a rebuke for unconfessed sin and the advice to "seek God and commit your cause to him". Such a confession would surely bring hopes of forgiveness and eventual happiness. It is argued that this was the conservative religious attitude that God's justice is axiomatic; sin must be punished but righteousness will bring material well-being. There were circles in biblical times — presumably among the successful — which held that an individual got what he deserved in this world and that material fortunes were a true measure of inner worth. However, Eliphaz takes an extreme position. Such a view was never true of Judaism as a whole. Indeed, the first purpose of Job is to contradict the idea. There are obvious exceptions to any notion of strict retribution — even the orthodox recognized that an innocent man might be killed by a sinner. What they insisted on was the general rule of retributive justice (see below, The Theological Problem of Job).

Job protests against Eliphaz' argument but the other two, Bildad (8:1–22) and Zophar (11:1–20) repeat the advice, emphasizing the justice of God and making the same point in different ways, Bildad, rough and kindly, Zophar, more scholarly and incisive. Both express the traditional philosophy (8:8–20) that "God will not reject a blameless man". Job accepts this philosophy but he knows himself to be such a man who is nevertheless being punished so severely.

This is the crux of the problem. The book is concerned all through with the relation of God's government of the world to suffering and evil. It seems that the whole moral structure of Job's world has split apart. He is tormented not only by physical pain but also by the sense of its injustice — which seems to deny his whole faith in God as a just God. He cites common experience to rebut the idea that only the wicked suffer and cries to God to grant him death as his only hope of release.

Second Round: The second and third rounds of the debate produce nothing really new from Job's comforters. Eliphaz (ch. 15), Bildad (18) and Zophar (20) merely reiterate their arguments and abuse Job for his insistence on his own innocence. Their speeches serve to provoke Job to deeper and deeper thought and an intensified search for a solution. The interest of the poem lies mainly in Job's speeches and thought. He explores various possibilities, but each time comes back to his basic protest against God's arbitrary

571

dealings with man. His friends, on the other hand, merely repeat the familiar propositions of orthodox thought. The author does not dismiss their arguments cursorily. He criticizes them for their inadequacy to answer Job's predicament.

At first, Job clearly shares their point of view, but the realization of his own appalling and undeserved distress forces him to some much harder thinking than his friends are willing to contribute (13:12). In his reply to Eliphaz, Job first voices his pained incredulity that his friends had so grossly failed to understand and help. He refuses to admit to sins which he knows he has not committed and rather than deny his whole life, finds himself making wild accusations of injustice against God. This leads him to the real intent of the poetic dialogue and to the whole question of why man must suffer pain.

The Intermediary in the Heavenly Court: His friends have failed to help or comfort him (19:1–22) but he has a "witness" on his side "in heaven . . . he that vouches for me is on high." (16:19) and this Redeemer, cries Job, "lives and at last he will stand upon the earth" (19:25). This "Witness" or Advocate is the intercessory "Angel of the Lord" who sides with men against the prosecuting angel, Satan. Job is one man before God, and he pleads for help from the intercessor on his behalf against Satan, the adversary. This is the basic pattern of the "heavenly court" which is reflected elsewhere in the Bible (see Angels*). The role of the "Heavenly Witness" is not made clear in the development of the dialogue. It is an important angle in the book but not really the goal of Job's argument. By the time he reaches his final challenge to God, he has left the Witness behind him.

The Third Round of the debate appears to be incomplete, for only Eliphaz (ch. 22) and Bildad (25) continue their side of the argument, while Job's replies fill chs. 23, 24, 26 and 27. Chapter 28 is an interlude in praise of widsom and then (29–31) Job sums up the debate, insisting for the last time on his unfailing rectitude:

"Oh, that I had the indictment written by my adversary!
Surely I would carry it on my shoulder;
I would bind it on me as a crown;
I would give him an account of all my steps;
Like a prince I would approach him." (31:35–37)

This is an example of the oath of clearance by which Job finally affirms his innocence.

The Speeches of Elihu (chs. 32–37): As Job has apparently silenced the three friends, a new character takes up the argument. (It is explained that he has not spoken before because of his youth.) He claims to have been angered both by Job's statements and by the failure of the other three to answer him satisfactorily. He makes four successive speeches which present a single argument. (Ch. 33 gives a résumé of the discussion of the earlier chapters.) In fact, in spite of his claims to the contrary, Elihu produces no new arguments, merely repeating — at excessive length — a new version of the same orthodox philosophy of the three comforters. However, he does also anticipate some of the arguments in the divine speech which follows. Job, apparently, turns away from him.

The Speech from the Whirlwind: Then, at last, God answers Job "out of the whirlwind" and, coming after the pomposities of Elihu's speeches, these chapters (38–41) are a revelation of Hebrew poetry and thought at its best and most characteristic. Yahweh recounts the wonders of nature and the creatures of the wild, like the "wild-ass" in flight (pictured, **571,** on this alabaster engraving from Nineveh of the 7th c. BCE).

In fact, God's speech does not answer Job directly at all. Instead, he asks a series of rhetorical questions which make all Job's earlier assumptions irrelevant. Mankind, in God's eyes, is a creature whose knowledge and understanding are totally insufficient to judge the Creator. It is man's sole obligation to acknowledge and glorify God – uncomprehendingly, if necessary. No answer to the problem of suffering can be given to man, for his limited mind cannot hope to understand the infinitely superior reasoning of God. God reminds Job of His power and might,with superb descriptions of natural wonders and beauties which — to some — come as something of an anti-climax after the high philosophy of the earlier sections. Because of the very Egyptian tone of some of these sections, it has been suggested that they stem from some source in Egyptian wisdom literature.

"I had heard of thee by the hearing of the ear,
but now my eye sees thee;
therefore I despise myself, and repent in dust and ashes (42:6).

Job has emerged from his trial with God's trust in him fully vindicated. He was innocent, and all the pain which had been inflicted on him has not made him turn from the path of loyalty and devotion to God. As a reward, Job is restored to God's favour and all his earlier fortunes.

The Epilogue: This restoration is contained in the prose epilogue (42:7–17). A return to material prosperity has seemed to some people to contradict the whole argument of the poetic sections. If prosperity is to be the reward of righteousness (in this case Job's success in the trial to which he was submitted), then the comforters were right, and Job's theological and philosophical speculations beside the point and mere paradoxical interludes. However, such an attitude overlooks the literary character of the work as explained above, and the fact that the epilogue is part of the older section of the book, addressed to an audience who would have accepted it without question. In the prologue, Satan was permitted to put Job on trial. Having demonstrated the falsity of Satan's accusations, Job could hardly be left to suffer to no purpose. The happy ending is not a reward of righteousness. It is merely the conclusion of the heavenly trial. Job had proved himself — and God.

III. RELATIONSHIP TO WISDOM LITERATURE: Job's literary antecedents have been the subject of much discussion. A Babylonian work preserved in a 7th c. BCE text — although it is much older than that — and known as the "Babylonian Job" also concerns a hero (a king) who laments that he is in sore trouble in spite of his great piety. His sufferings have much in common with Job's and, towards the end of the poem (which has been severely cut), they appear to be removed by the mercy of the gods. However, that is as far as the resemblance goes. There is no philosophic dialogue and the poem is quite different in intention, philosophy and detail. The Babylonian, for instance, suffers no loss of prestige or estrangement from his friends as a consequence of his misfortunes. The clearest literary connections are with Wisdom* literature, as discussed in that article.

The Theological Problem of Job: Job's sufferings seem to be caused both by the physical pain to which God subjects him and his distress at his treatment by his relations, fellow-townsmen and friends when he had been deprived of his earlier prominence. One accepted principle of Hebrew wisdom, which can be seen through all the arguments of the three friends, was that God rewarded the just and punished the wicked during their lifetimes. The impulse for all Job's tortured questionings is that, in theory, he too accepts this principle, at the same time knowing that it could not possibly apply to his own case. Thus the book raised the whole theological question of why a God generally believed to act with justice and righteousness should seem to behave with such wanton cruelty.

The three friends and Elihu put forward the standard solutions but these were rejected at last by God (42:7) as inadequate. Their picture of the "ideal" fate of the wicked was achieved only by carefully weighting the evidence. Job, on the other hand, looked at the world as it really is, at the point where he was receiving its hardest blows, and still managed to find faith in God. This may perhaps explain the apparently unsatisfactory climax. God never answers Job's charges directly. He proclaims His might — but makes no attempt to justify His ethics. Job submits because he accepts the implication that man and his sufferings are infinitesimal compared to God's majesty and that if the true reason for suffering were ever offered to man, he would be unable to understand it.

Composition and Date: The author of Job is not known. There are a number of very difficult problems involved in trying to locate and date him from internal evidence. The historical background to the legend is very close to that of the Patriarchal period and, indeed, Uz, Buz and Kesed, three peoples mentioned in the book, also appear in the genealogical list of Gn. 22:20–24 as belonging to the Bene-Naḥor nomadic clans who wandered the area from the western Euphrates to the Syrian desert. The legend of Job, in the opinion of B. Mazar, may therefore run parallel to the stories of Genesis. W.F. Albright is also of the opinion that a date for the hero himself should be set somewhere in the first half of the 2nd mill. BCE, i.e. the Patriarchal period (the name is known from sources from that period). As to the dating of the poet of the main section, various schools of thought put him anywhere from Mosaic to early post-Exilic times. W.F. Albright suggests a north Israelite provenance and a date in the 7th c. BCE. It is interesting in this connection to note that fragments of Job found at Qumran are written in archaic Hebrew script, like Leviticus (see Alphabet and Writing*), which implies a belief in a Mosaic authorship or some similar ancient tradition.

Language and Textual Problems: Job contains some of the most difficult poetry of the Old Testament; its vocabulary includes 110 words not found anywhere else. This made things very difficult for the scribes who did the copying and resulted in the translations (Syriac or Aramaic, or the Septuagint) being incomplete and often incorrect. (The Septuagint omits more than half the verses from chapter 5 on.) Moreover, because the language was felt to be obscure, textual variations were common. A few fragments of the book were found in Qumran together with an otherwise lost targum (translation) into Aramaic (the Aramaic targum has not yet been published), but these seem to be of very little help in clearing up the textual problems. Because of this difficult language, plus its particular style and lack of distinctive Jewish colouring, some scholars have tried to find an Edomite basis for the book of Job, claiming in support the geographical setting of the work. But that is a moot point.

The main textual problems arise in connection with chs. 26 and 27 — Job's answer to Bildad's third speech. These seem to imply Job's successful refutation of his friends' arguments – which may possibly explain why Zophar does not speak a third time. On the other hand, while 27:2–6 is obviously Job speaking, the following passage (27:7–23) cannot possibly, in its context, be ascribed to him. It is accordingly assumed to be Zophar's missing third speech or, possibly, another speech of Bildad's.

On this evidence and that of other passages (e.g. 22:2, 21; 34:9), it is assumed that the sequence of speeches and sentences represent one editor's attempt to impose some order on material which he found very difficult and whose original sequence had been lost. Probably it was left to the editor to decide from the contents where a new speech started and how a number of disconnected sections fitted together.

No entirely satisfactory reconstruction of the text has ever been suggested. Parts of the original scroll have been lost, and this doubtless explains some of the obscurities of Job. If the dialogue had been preserved complete and in order, the precise formulation of the thought would almost certainly be clearer than it is at present.

Conclusion: The usual assumption about the book of Job is that it offers a solution to the problem of undeserved suffering. In fact it does not offer any solution to the intellectual problem posed. It seems more likely that in its original form the book had a spiritually more profound theme. Throughout, it is concerned with the relation between God's ordering of the world and the suffering and evil within it. The whole book rests on the premise that Job was indeed blameless and his affliction unmerited. The mystery of human suffering, the book proclaims, lies deeper than a simple question of punishment for sin. God is not unjust, yet a man who suffers is not necessarily a sinner. The mystery remains unsolved.

JOEL. — In the Hebrew canon and English Bibles, the short book of Joel is the second in the series of the Twelve Minor Prophets, although it comes fourth in the Septuagint. Neither the prophet Joel, son of Pethuel, nor the time at which he lived are mentioned anywhere else in the Bible, which makes it very difficult to appreciate the setting of his prophecies.

Contents: The book has four chapters in the Hebrew text and these can be divided into two distinct sections: a. narrative, and b. apocalyptic*. Section a. is a description of two natural disasters, a plague of locusts, then a drought. These apparently took place during the prophet's lifetime and each provided the occasion for a call to repentance, fasting and prayer (1:13–20; 2:12–17). The section closes (2:18–27) with the promise that God will hear the prayers of his people and will restore his blessing to them.

Section b. is a description of the judgment of the Day of Yahweh (2:30; 3:8 — see below). This is also in two parts: First, the signs and portents that will announce the Day (2:28–31, in the Hebrew text 3:1–5); then the promises of blessings and renewal to Judah while her enemies shall be gathered into the Valley of Jehoshaphat and there judged and condemned (3:2–15, Hebrew 4:1–17). The book closes with the reaffirmation of God's care for his people and the vengeance He will wreak on all their enemies (3:18–21, Heb. 4:9–21).

Significance: The difference between the two sections of the book — first a description of natural phenomena and then the visionary prophecy of the future "Day of Yahweh" — has presented scholars with some very knotty problems. Three possible solutions have been put forward by different schools of thought:

a. The whole book is in fact visionary, the descriptions of the plague of locusts and the drought being eschatological visions.

b. The more popular view is that the two parts were written by different authors at different times. According to this opinion, the plagues were actual events which took place before the lifetime of the prophet Joel who lived around 500 BCE (or, some scholars think, around 400 BCE), while the second half was composed by an apocalyptic writer living before the Hellenistic* period (apocalyptic writers tended to assume the names of great figures or prophets of the past, see Apocrypha and Pseudepigrapha*). Upholders of this opinion base it upon the reference in 3:6 to the Phoenicians* and Philistines* selling the people of Judah "to the Greeks", i.e., the main enemies of the Jews are still their ancient opponents, not the Greeks, who appear merely as slave traders, not as the Jews' deadly foes. On the other hand, another view finds this reference to the Greeks evidence that the book was composed under the Seleucid empire, during the Hellenistic period (see Hasmoneans*).

A further confusion arises from the fact that "the Day of Yahweh" is also mentioned in the "first" part of the book (2:1-11). To meet this difficulty, some scholars assume the reference is an insertion by the later apocalyptic writer; others ascribe it to the author of the whole of the first part; while still others break up all the first part into the compositions of a number of different authors. (Some scholars do the same to the second part as well.)

c. The third opinion holds that the book is a uniform production by a writer who saw a connection between the locust plague and the "Day of the Lord". This was the opinion of J. Wellhausen. U. Cassuto believed the reference in 2:11 meant a day of divine visitation and judgment of no eschatological significance, while in the second part, the "Day of the Lord" was eschatological. This reading of the book makes it a uniform composition of the prophet Joel who saw the locust plague and the drought as the harbingers of the "Day of Yahweh" and used the people's distress to appeal to them to repent of their sins and return to God. As the people did indeed return to God, the prophet connected the prosperity that followed the end of the locusts and drought with the redemption of the remainder of Judah (2:32) and the punishment of those who had oppressed them (ch. 3). Haggai* made a similar connection between the blessing of the soil and the redemption of Judah and God's vengeance upon the Gentiles.

The Day of Yahweh: Earlier prophets (Amos* and, later, Zephaniah*) had spoken of a day of national vindication of Judah. In the post-Exilic period this was transformed by the prophets of the age into a day when (in the context of history) Yahweh would manifest his power in a decisive victory over the tyrant nations who had oppressed his people and this time restore Judah to their land. This ultimate salvation became the dominant pattern of religious hopes in the post-Exilic period.

In Malachi* (3–4) it takes the form of God's purifying judgment of his own people; in Obadiah* it is conceived as involving national restoration. Joel sees it as an outpouring of charismatic gifts on God's people (2:28–29), accompanied by fearful portents and leading, in the last chapter (3), to the eschatological conflict between God and His enemies. (This vision is to be compared with Ezk. 38–39 and Zec. 14, as well as the so-called apocalypse of Isaiah 24–27.)

Date of Joel: It is agreed by the majority of scholars that Joel was composed during the post-Exilic period and that its geographical, historical and ideological background suggest that it may have been contemporary with Haggai*, Malachi* or Obadiah*. The book's date cannot be later than Alexander the Great's conquests because of the casual reference to the Greeks, who appear as less important than Tyre (Phoenicia) or Philistia. Thus the most likely date appears to be one in the Persian* period although it is impossible, at present, to be more precise in fixing the time of the composition of the book of Joel. (See also Obadiah*, Malachi*, Haggai*, Zechariah*.)

JOHN THE BAPTIST. *Outline: I. His Life; Nazirite Element in John; John's Message; Surroundings; Archaeological Confirmation; John and Herod Antipas; Imprisonment and Death. II. The Contemporary Setting; Evidence of the Dead Sea Scrolls; Baptism and Repentance; The Wider Historical Perspective; Messianic Role; Jesus' Baptism; The Holy Spirti; Significance of John's Movement.*

I. HIS LIFE: — John (Johanan) surnamed the Baptizer (Ha-matbil in Hebrew) was the forerunner of Jesus*.

He was born in the hill country of Judea (exact location unknown, although later Christian tradition commemorates his birth at Ein Karem, near Jerusalem). His father, the elderly priest Zechariah, probably gave his son a good knowledge of scriptures from the less formalistic angle typical of the provincial priesthood.

Nazirite Element in John: On reaching manhood, John did not follow his father and become a priest. Instead, he withdrew into the "wilderness" and stayed there in solitude and meditation, living on grasshoppers and wild honey, until the time came for him to take up his ministry to Israel. The 2nd century CE church father and historian, Epiphanius, describes him in his "Panarion" as a "Nazirite". This title must be an anachronism, but some modern scholars have supported the view that he belonged to a group of dedicated sectaries who had revived the ancient Israelite institution of the life-long Nazirate*, which had long since passed from the scene. The modern equivalents of these Nazirites were dwellers in the wilderness who abstained from wine, flesh and shaving the beard, and apparently practiced purificatory ritual baths. It is possible that groups of Nazirites or "holy men" similar to the ancient prophetic bands of the Jordan valley, may have some connection with the later Essenes* or with John's followers (see Dead Sea Scrolls*).

John's Message: Dressed in a rough camel-hair tunic like one of the prophets of old, John went through the country round the Jordan Valley, calling men to repentance: "Repent, for the Kingdom of God is at hand." John's message was that the great hope of Israel's religion was on the point of fulfillment. The reign of happiness so ardently desired was at hand. This was the essence of ancient Hebrew prophetic faith, but John gave it a new urgency. He baptized those who had truly repented as the symbol of their purification, in preparation for a new life in the community of God.

John's Surroundings: The Fourth Gospel describes John as baptizing in several places in the country around the Jordan Valley and east of Jordan in Perea. Towards the end of his ministry, he is found baptizing in Samaritan territory at "Aenon near Salim, because there was much water there" (Jn. 3:22). The exact site of this town is uncertain, but W. F. Albright has suggested a location south-east of Shechem*, near the sources of Wadi Fariah. Other sites are mentioned in the Gospels, but they cannot be identified with certainty. The place where John baptized Jesus is marked on the 6th century Madeba mosaic map (**572**) by a cross set in the Jordan at Bethabara, or more correctly, Beth-'araba, "ford town". It lies just north of the Hajla ford, close to the

572

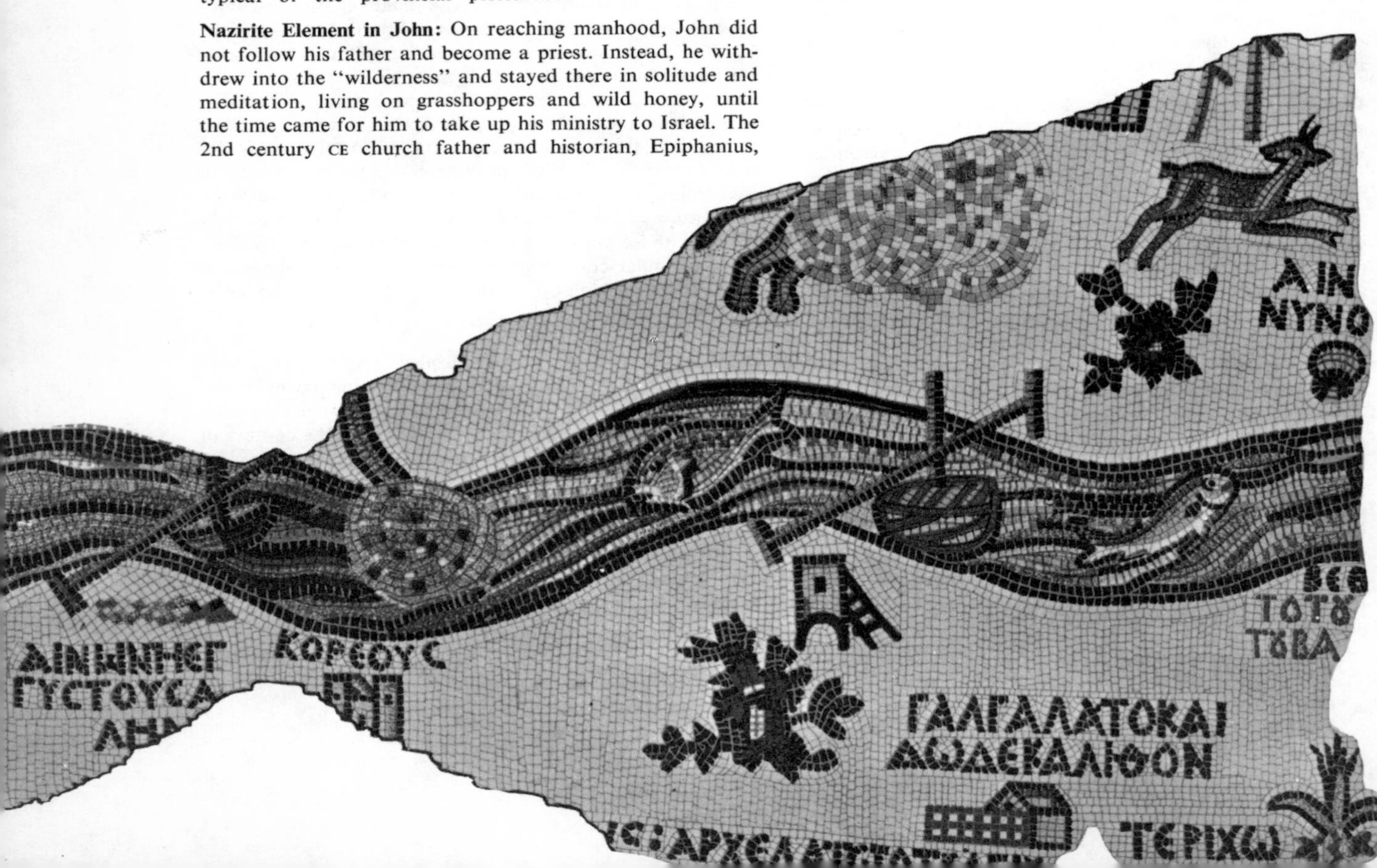

west bank of the river. A church was built on piles at the edge of the water, while a little further back stood the monastery of John the Baptizer. This is the river (**573**), further north.

Archaeological Confirmation: The Gospel of Luke records that "in the fifteenth year of the reign of Tiberius Caesar (27 CE), Lysanius (being) tetrarch of Abilene . . . the word of God came to John the son of Zechariah in the wilderness." (Luke 3:1, 2). On a steep rock-face near the "tel" which was once the city of Abilene, an inscription has been discovered naming Lysanius as governor of the region at the time mentioned by Luke.

However, the best illustration of the authenticity of John's career comes from Josephus' "Antiquities": "John who was called the Baptist, for Herod slew him who was a good man and had commanded the Jews that they should practice virtue both in respect of righteousness toward one another and piety towards God, so that they should come together in a baptism. For baptism would thus appear acceptable to him, not when they used it as a request for the forgiveness of certain sins, but as a purification of the body after the soul had been thoroughly cleansed by righteousness." (Ant. Bk. XVIII 5:2; Wiston translation).

John and Herod Antipas: John's popularity and the enthusiasm which his preaching and baptizing aroused (as attested by Josephus), were understandably unwelcome to the authorities. During the whole period of Herodian rule in Palestine, innumerable uprisings were sparked off by messianic claims associated with political agitation. The "tetrarch" Herod Antipas (son of Herod* the Great), who ruled Galilee and Perea (Jewish Transjordan), was naturally suspicious of a movement which was drawing hearers and followers, "the hundreds", from all over Palestine. He determined to silence John before he could initiate a serious movement among the restive "people of the land", the "'am ha-'aretz" whom Jesus later befriended. Moreover, John aroused a more specific resentment at court by publicly criticizing the Tetrarch for repudiating his first wife, the daughter of the Nabatean king, to marry the Princess Herodias, his own brother's wife (an offence against Mosaic Law). This illicit second marriage probably coincided with the beginning of John's ministry.

Imprisonment and Death: The combination of factors eventually led to John's imprisonment in the fortress of Machaerus (**574**), near the eastern shore of the Dead Sea. According to Josephus, he was later beheaded there. The Gospels (Mk. 6), in an account dramatized by countless writers and composers, place the beheading at the Tetrarch's new palace in the capital, Tiberias, he had built in honour of the emperor Tiberius on the Lake of Galilee. In this version, the Princess Salome, promised any favour by Herod on his birthday, was induced by her mother to demand the head of John, which was forthwith delivered on a platter. His martyrdom only served to enhance John's prestige among the people. Herod Antipas himself was subsequently defeated by the Nabatean king, Aretas IV. Then, during the reign of Caligula, he was accused of plotting against Rome, convicted and exiled to Spain where he died. Josephus reports that the people looked on his defeat as retribution for his unjustified execution of John the Baptist.

The real cause of the murder lay in Antipas' fear of political trouble. This is not inconsistent with the Gospel's

573

574

assertion that John aroused the Tetrarch's anger and, still more, that of the Princess Herodias, by his stern rebuke. Allowance, however, must be made for the folklore element in the story as preserved in the Gospels.

II. THE CONTEMPORARY SETTING — a. **Evidence from the Dead Sea Scrolls:** So little is known for certain about John that it is difficult to assess his importance either in the Judaism of the time or for later Christianity. We still know about John only what the Gospels and Josephus tell us. There is no direct information about him in the Dead Sea Scrolls* although they do shed considerable light on the background and ideas of John. We are now better able to understand and appreciate his ministry in the setting of first century Palestine.

Because of the many parallels between them, a number of scholars have naturally been attracted to the theory that John was at one time associated with the priestly apocalyptists of Qumran*. The little that we know of him fits in very well with such a theory. The Qumran writings have made it clear that there was nothing new in baptism as a rite of repentance and it is apparent that John's viewpoint was very close to that of the Essenes. However, it is an oversimplification of the data to assume a direct connection between John and the Dead Sea community. We can recognize similarities and a certain parallelism in thought and belief, and he may be regarded as a link between certain trends within Judaism and Jewish Christianity*.

b. **Baptism and Repentance:** Immersion in running water as the visible sign of repentance and admission into the eschatological community of God is the essential common element between the sectaries of Qumran and other Essenes, and John's movement.

Baptism was a well-known practice of the time. Josephus, who was familiar with the rites of the Essenes (see Dead Sea Scrolls*), accepted it as quite normal. As in the Essene communities, John's baptism was a rite symbolizing repentance. However, John did not limit the act of salvation to a few initiates, as did the Qumran sectaries. He extended it to all ordinary people who appealed to him. Nevertheless, like the Essenes, he insisted on true repentance first of all. For salvation, it was not enough to say, "We have Abraham for our father" (Mt. 3:8). Even those descended from Abraham could be, like the Pharisees* and Sadducees* who came to him to be baptized, "a brood of vipers", unless they sincerely wanted to turn from their sins to the new life in the community of God.

The Wider Historical Perspective: John — a Prophet? The status of John the Baptizer can best be understood in a wider historical perspective. We have the record of Jesus' assessment of him, in the Gospels of Mark and Luke: "and they said to him, 'By what authority are you doing these things, or who gave you this authority to do them?' Jesus said to them, 'I will ask you a question: answer me and I will tell you by what authority I do these things. Was the baptism of John from heaven or from men? Answer me.' And they argued with one another, 'If we say, "From heaven" he will say, "Why then did you not believe him?" But shall we say "From men?"' — they were afraid of the people, for all held that John was a real prophet." (Mark 11:28–32).

Messianic Role: John was a great independent preacher and teacher, a momentous figure in the apocalyptic and messianic movement of the day. It is difficult to be sure exactly how much significance his preaching had within the Jewish messianic movement, but it was undoubtedly part of the main stream of the movement's development.

The prologue of the Gospel of John relates the Baptizer's encounter with a delegation of Levites and Pharisees, apparently sent to investigate John's claims to a possible Messiahship: "And they asked him, 'What then? Are you Elijah?' He said, 'I am not.' 'Are you the prophet?' And he answered, 'No'. . . he said, 'I am the voice of one crying in the wilderness: Prepare the way of the Lord, make its paths straight; as the prophet Isaiah said.' They asked him, 'Then why are you baptizing, if you are neither the Christ, nor Elijah, nor the prophet?'" (Jn. 1:21, 23, 25)

The same quotation from Isaiah supplied the covenanters of Qumran with the justification for their sectarian way of life. John's gospel emphasizes that the Baptizer rejected the titles of Elijah, the "prophet" or Christ. He was not one of the messianic figures, although he was a forerunner. He was "the Voice of one crying in the Wilderness." This is similar to the role and status of the Teacher of Righteousness at Qumran, who was not, apparently, one of the messianic figures, but was credited with prophetic powers and functions (see Dead Sea Scrolls*).

From the much clearer picture which has emerged, it appears that in the Gospel tradition, John has been deliberately overshadowed by Jesus.

Jesus' Baptism: One indication of the importance of the Baptizer's movement is the significance which Christian tradition attached to his baptism of Jesus. In Jewish-Christian theology, Christ's baptism was given a more prominent place even than the nativity. Mark's and John's Gospels both open with the baptism and it is believed by some scholars that it came first in the early Church's yearly liturgical recitals.

The Holy Spirit: The ancient sub-stratum in Mark* has suggested that John may have shared the sectaries' view of baptism as a spiritual baptism. According to the Rule of the Community of Qumran, baptism was the point at which man enters the new life of the kingdom through contact with the Spirit of Truth or the Holy Spirit. The bestowal of the Holy Spirit on Jesus at his baptism may be thought of in the same sense of a desire for purity which can only be obtained by a previous "cleansing of the soul." the definition of John's baptism. "And when he came up out of the water, immediately he saw the heavens opened and the Spirit descending upon him like a dove; and a voice came from heaven. 'Thou art my beloved Son; with thee I am well pleased'." (Mark 1:10–12).

Clearly, God was believed to have conferred his Holy Spirit on his anointed. Later on, it was believed that the gift of the Holy Spirit was poured out on the early Church. It is commonly held by scholars that baptism of water and repentance were then seen as preliminary to the final baptism with the spirit which would come with the fulfillment of the kingdom in the plan of God.

Significance of John's Movement: It has been argued that neither John nor Jesus was the founder of a school or sect in Jewish life. They were not analytical or sophisticated scribes or Pharisaic doctors of law, and they did not pronounce halakhah*. Nevertheless, although the movements they founded did not have the elaborate organization of the Essénes and Pharisees, both John and Jesus provided their disciples with instruction, to be memorized and repeated.

There are scholars who hold that John would have represented no more than a passing episode in the history of sectarian Judaism — one among many others — had not Jesus of Nazareth come under his influence at the outset of his career. This raises questions concerning the most obscure phase of early Christianity. It is not known whether John's followers remained for generations a well-defined and prominent sect, nor what relation they had to the main stream of Christianity. Apparently the "hundreds" who were baptized by John were not absorbed automatically into the Jewish-Christian stream. It is possible that his followers founded informal congregations. John's influence is reflected in the pre-Christian Jewish Gnostic stream of the late second century CE and in the activities of Simon Magus, supposedly father of early Hellenistic gnosticism of the Ophites, Sethites, Cainites, and in other groups mentioned in Acts 8:10 and 19:2–7.

However, it is now accepted that the Baptizer's movement and contemporary sectarian Judaism are the essential elements in the background to Christianity (see Jesus*, II).

In the words of W.F. Albright, "many books and fragments of the otherwise lost literature of the Essenes in the century or century and a half preceding the Crucifixion demonstrate the existence of religious circles which were the direct precursors of John the Baptist and Jesus." According to G.E. Wright, at least part of the background of the thinking of the author of the Gospel of John* may be found in the sectarian theology of Palestine. The Scrolls provide the "closest approach that has yet been discovered to the Gospel of John and to Paul, at least in so far as conceptual background and language is concerned, and that the connecting link between the two was the work of John the Baptist". Many affinities observed between the Dead Sea literature and the Gospel of John suggest that the link between these was also John the Baptizer. It is even thought that the Evangelist may have been the unnamed disciple of the Baptizer, or that he became acquainted with the Baptizer's teachings and vocabulary later in Ephesus (Ac. 19:2–7).

JOHN, GOSPEL OF. — **Plan and Contents:** The book of John begins with the well-known *Logos* prologue (1:1–18) on the Incarnation of the Word, which sets the tone for the whole book, and presents Jesus* as the heavenly messenger and transcendental messiah, a part of the Godhead itself.

I. Chs. 1:19–12:50 describe his work in the world. John the Baptist*, the Forerunner, is mentioned (1:19–34) but only in order to give added authority to the claim of Jesus* as the divine messiah. The calling of the disciples is recounted (1:35–51) and in John's Gospel, in contrast to the Synoptic accounts, Jesus* clearly proclaims himself as the Messiah, the Lamb of God, and is immediately recognized as such by his followers.

The Book of the Seven Signs: The following section, the so-called Book of the Seven Signs, comprises chs. 2–12. Here John takes seven "signs" or miracles and weaves a number of discourses around them so that the whole section presents an overwhelming testimony to Jesus' divine nature and calling in terms of his own words and deeds.

Jesus performs his first miracle at the wedding in Cana (2:1–11) but this story also has an allegorical interpretation (see below).

John departs from the Synoptic tradition by placing the account of Jesus' cleansing of the Temple (Jn. 2:12–22) at the outset of his Ministry. Here again the guiding principle is the irrevocable confirmation of Jesus' messiahship.

The discussion between Jesus and Nicodemus (3:1–15) serves to illustrate the true meaning and significance of Christian baptism and introduces a further discourse on Christian belief.

John the Baptist is again mentioned (3:22–36) and once more he bears witness to the divine nature of Jesus.

There follow two accounts of the faith and conversion of non-Jews, the woman of Samaria (4:1–42) and the healing of the nobleman's son (4:46–54).

Ch. 5:1–9 tells of the healing of the sick man at the pool of Bethesda and this short passage serves as a preamble for the long christological discourse (5:17–47) which follows.

Ch. 6 contains descriptions of the feeding of the five thousand and Jesus' walking on the water, two events also included in the Synoptic Gospels. In John's Gospel, however, the events provide the setting for Jesus' proclamation that he is the "bread of life" — possibly a reference to the significance of the Eucharist (6:22–65).

Chs. 7–8 contain further discourses of Jesus in which he proclaims his mission. There is also the story of the woman accused of adultery whom Jesus saves by demanding of her accusers, who is without sin? (7:53–8:11). This particular narrative is not contained in the Synoptic Gospels and is also not to be found in the earlier manuscripts of the Fourth Gospel. Though it stems from a different and non-Johannine source (perhaps this is the story to which Papias refers as originating in the "Gospel according to the Hebrews", cf. Eusebius' Ecclesiastical History, iii. 39), it was regarded as authentic and included in the canon of the New Testament (see Gospels, Synoptic*: The A Document). Modern opinion, however, regards it as a secondary insertion.

The account of the healing of the man born blind (ch. 9) also serves to illustrate Jesus' divine calling and to accuse the Pharisees, the leaders of the Jews, of spiritual blindness.

Ch. 10 begins with the parable of the Good Shepherd and its interpretation by Jesus (10:7–18) and continues with the evidence of growing opposition to Jesus among the Jews, culminating in the Feast of Dedication (10:22–42) at which Jesus again attempted vainly to convince the Jews of his mission.

In Ch. 11, the raising of Lazarus from the dead is recounted, followed by the reaction of the high priests and Pharisees to Jesus' miracles (11:47–57). The theme of Jesus' redemptive death is touched upon in verses 50–52, attributed to Caiaphas who, as high priest, possessed prophetic powers. Jesus' death is then decided upon by the council of the high priests and Pharisees (v. 53).

In ch. 12:1–8 the coming Passion is foreshadowed by the anointing of Jesus at Bethany.

The story of the Triumphal Entry into Jerusalem (12:12–19) and the prediction of Jesus' redemptive death on the cross (12:20–50) conclude the book of the Seven Signs and serve as an introduction to the final part of John, the events of Passion Week and their significance.

II. **Chs. 13:1–20:29** form the largest section and central point of the Fourth Gospel. Their historical foundation is provided by the events which occurred in Passion Week.

Once again, however, in that style so peculiarly his, the author of John delves beneath the surface of human history to uncover the metaphysical significance and truth which is the crux of the historical event. In this section John shows that Jesus is the Christ, the Son of the living God. Jesus' life and mission were to reveal the Divine Nature to mankind and through his redemptive death on the cross, to obtain the gift of eternal life for all who believe in him. The events of Passion Week, the trial, crucifixion and resurrection, do not obscure but make more clear the revelation of God through Christ.

Chs. 13–17 are a compilation of Jesus' words to his intimate followers and disciples. He exhorts them to love one another and, in a farewell discourse, comforts them at the thought of his death by promising them the gift of the Holy Spirit.

Ch. 17 is in the form of the prayer in which Jesus consecrates himself for his coming Passion.

Chs. 18 and 19 relate Jesus' arrest, trial, crucifixion and burial. Although these chapters echo the Synoptic accounts, they also incorporate some material which is unique to the Fourth Gospel. These events, which superficially must appear as a series of defeats, are shown to be in reality a great triumph. Through them all, Christ continues to reveal himself, even before the Roman, Pilate. Certain events such as the casting of lots for Jesus' robe (19:23–24) and the piercing of his side in place of the customary breaking of his legs (19:32–37) are shown to be fulfillments of prophecy.

The closing chapter (20) is an account of the Resurrection and of Jesus' appearance to Mary Magdalene (20:11–18), to the disciples (19–23) and to doubting Thomas (24–29). This concludes the Gospel of John.

Ch. 21, which is a later appendix to the original work, contains a description of the resurrected Jesus' appearance to the disciples at the Sea of Galilee (21:1–14). In verses 15–23, Peter is vindicated for his three-fold denial of Jesus by thrice affirming his faith in him, and Jesus foretells Peter's death.

Unique Features of John: The Fourth Gospel has long been an enigma to New Testament scholars. In content, style and outlook, John marks a radical departure from the three Synoptic Gospels. Whereas the Synoptic Gospels* portray Jesus' Galilean ministry at great length, John relegates it to a secondary position and concentrates on Jesus' activities in Judea (primarily in Jerusalem). According to the Synoptic account, Jesus' ministry would seem to have been of a single year's duration, for only one Passover is mentioned, i.e. that of Passion Week. The Gospel of John, however, records several Passovers and the Ministry extends over a three year period. In John, Jesus cleanses the Temple at the outset of his ministry; in the Synoptics, this event occurs during Passion Week. Important events in Jesus' life are omitted entirely by the author of the Fourth Gospel. There are no accounts of the Baptism, Temptation, or Transfiguration. Even of the institution of the Eucharist* no mention is made. The simple, picturesque parables of the Synoptics are either completely omitted or changed into symbolic allegories in the Gospel of John.

In contrast to the Jesus of the first three Gospels who speaks to the crowds in homely maxims, the Jesus of the Fourth Gospel is a learned teacher who holds forth in long, metaphysical discourses. The "man of the people", as he is portrayed by the Synoptic writers, is of a different nature in John, aloof and withdrawn; he heals not so much out of human compassion, it would seem, as in order to demonstrate the power of God.

In John, the miracles of Jesus are elaborated and exaggerated. This tendency is not accidental but deliberate, in keeping with John's concept of Jesus as the Christ, the divine Son of God. The miracles or "signs" provide clear and ready proof of this fact. The Gospel of Mark* pictures Jesus as growing gradually aware of his messianic calling. John, on the other hand, emphasizes the divine and messianic nature of Jesus from the very beginning. Whereas the Jesus of the Synoptics exhorts the multitudes to believe in God, John's Jesus calls on the people to believe in himself. Nevertheless, it is the position of the Form-Critical school that the figure of Jesus in John was modelled on that of Moses in Exodus* (cf. Jn. 6:14; 7:40). In both cases, the miracles were designed to encourage belief in the God by whose power they were performed as well as in God's servant, Moses, or his Son, Jesus. A number of parallels can be drawn between the two figures, although a substantial distinction remains in the portrayal of Moses as a mortal man who could be guilty of sin and who acted as no more than God's agent or representative. John presents Jesus as nothing less than God incarnate, the transcendental *logos*, the "Word become flesh" (see Incarnation*: John).

Authorship and Date: Early church tradition attributes the authorship of the Gospel of John to the apostle John, the brother of James and son of Zebedee. Yet despite the fact that several early sources, including Irenaeus (2nd c. CE), refer to the apostle John as the author of the Fourth Gospel, biblical scholars have shown a marked reluctance to accept the traditional view. One of the main stumbling blocks for the critics has been the marked difference between the Synoptics and the Fourth Gospel. Under the impact of the "spiritual evolution" theory which prevailed in the early part of the present century, scholars were prone to view the Gospel of John, compared to the Synoptics, as representing a later development in early Christian religion.

The Form Critics in particular attacked the Fourth Gospel as a depository which, though containing any number of various traditions, possessed very little — if any — original material (see Gospels, Synoptic*: Form Criticism).

It was generally agreed in former years that the Fourth Gospel showed a strong influence of Greek philosophical thought. The *logos* prologue of John (1:1–18) was assumed to have borrowed heavily from the Hellenistic* Jewish philosopher, Philo of Alexandria, who lived during the first half of the 1st c. CE. Allowing a reasonable time for the dissemination of Philo's works, a date between 90–110 CE was reached for the Gospel of John. Some schools (Tubingen) fixed a date as late as the latter half of the second century, but this theory was dramatically disproved by the discovery in 1935 of a papyrus fragment (**575**) of the Gospel of John which stems from the first half of the second c. (ca. 125 CE). But even if one were momentarily to disregard the question of the dating of the Fourth Gospel, does it seem feasible that the Galilean fisherman, John, could have written a book in the style of the present Gospel?

575

Faced with these difficulties, scholars turned to possible alternative authors of the Fourth Gospel. Eusebius (Ecclesiastical History iii. 39), quoting Papias (see Gospels, Synoptic*), distinguished between the apostle John and John the "presbyter" or "elder" (the author of II and III John refers to himself as "the Elder") and attempts have been made to identify the author of the Fourth Gospel with this other John. Another hypothesis which enjoyed popular acclaim was that the author of the Gospel of John was also the author of Revelation* (q.v.; see also Epistles, General*: I, II John).

The Dead Sea Scrolls and John: With the discovery (1947) of the Dead Sea Scrolls, studies of the significance and origin of the Fourth Gospel gained added impetus. Even before this sensational new find came to light, voices had been raised in protest against the late dating of John solely on the basis of its content. The *logos* idea was shown (Durr) to be of Oriental rather than Greek origin. John's "dualistic" concept of the forces at work in the world was long attributed to Gnostic speculation, but the Dead Sea Scrolls* have revealed the existence of such a "dualism" in Jewish religious circles *before* the advent of Christianity i. e. the "Prince of Light" and the righteous "Sons of Light" as opposed to the "Angel of Darkness" and the "Sons of Darkness", and the two spirits of "truth and error" which dwell in the heart of every man.

Many of the so-called "Gnostic" expressions used by John, which supposedly show the influence of Greek philosophy, are to be found in the Dead Sea Scrolls which are of pre-Christian Jewish origin. A particularly striking parallel is the similarity between Jn. 1:3 and the Qumran Manual of Discipline III, 15 (see Dead Sea Scrolls*). However, the Dead Sea Scrolls and the Fourth Gospel seem to be related in general overall style and approach rather than in particular details. As Millar Burrows has pointed out, "the whole manner of thinking and the literary style (of the Gospel of John) are strikingly like what we find in the Qumran texts."

As a consequence, John can no longer be lightly dismissed as the "reflections of an Alexandrian philosopher". The claim that the author of the Fourth Gospel could not have been a Jew is now, in the light of the Dead Sea Scrolls, clearly revealed as absurd. Arguments that the author of John was totally ignorant of Palestinian geography have also been refuted.

The fact that John differs in style and outlook from the three Synoptic Gospels need no longer relegate it to a position of secondary importance. In all probability, John does not represent a *later* development in early Christian theological thought, but points to the existence of another parallel tradition alongside that of the Synoptics (compare the Pauline claims — especially Colossians and Ephesians — of the transcendence of Jesus, which are in close agreement to those advanced in the Gospel of John, in contrast to the Synoptic tradition).

As noted above, Irenaeus ascribed the Fourth Gospel to John the Apostle and stated that John lived on into the reign of Trajan (90–117, see: Rome and the Jews*; Bar-Kochba*). Irenaeus also states that John "published" his Gospel at Ephesus. It is possible that John made use of Mark and Luke in the writing of his Gospel (some scholars also claim John's dependence upon Matthew, but this cannot be decisively demonstrated). John appears to be independent of the other Gospels, although probably they all drew on a common pool of information. The author of John seems to assume that his readers were familiar with many of the incidents recorded in the other Gospels. For instance, he does not bother to introduce John the Baptist* to the readers, although each of the Synoptics do so. Jn. 3:24 seems to imply that the reader is familiar with the story of the Baptist's imprisonment which is given in Mt. 4:12, but not in John.

John's Gospel and John the Apostle: In its present form, the Fourth Gospel bears the marks of a later editing. The last chapter (21) is undoubtedly an appendix added after the completion of the main work, which was brought to its conclusion in the last two verses of chapter 20. A number of other passages can also only be explained as secondary glosses to the original text (e.g. 4:2; 6:23; 7:53–8:11 and 11:2). Accordingly, while a date between 80–90 CE may be accepted for the final edition of the Gospel of John, this does not necessarily mean that all its contents reflect this later date. It is quite likely that the Fourth Gospel contains material which, even though it appears nowhere else, is quite as old and as authentic as that contained in the Synoptic Gospels. The very fact that this Gospel, despite its obvious deviations from the Synoptic traditions, was accepted by the early church, would tend to lend support to its claim of apostolic authority. If, in fact, the Gospel of John was not written by the apostle John, it may well contain great blocks of material gleaned from the apostle's fiirst-hand experiences and memories. A forceful argument has been advanced by Torrey that the Fourth Gospel is, in its basic form, a Greek translation of an Aramaic document dating from before the year 70. It may perhaps be wiser to substitute the term "Aramaic tradition" rather than to insist upon the existence of a written manuscript. W.F. Albright also maintains that the local colouring, particularly in the Judean narratives of John, reflects the period preceding the destruction of the Second Temple (70 CE). More and more, scholars are now inclined to concede that the early tradition, which ascribes the authorship of the Fourth Gospel to the apostle John, contains more than a kernel of truth.

Theology: John's approach to the life and ministry of Jesus is unique among the Gospel writers. Those physical occurrences which could be seen, heard and felt had at the

576

same time a deeper, underlying meaning. History is not truth, but truth is revealed in history. Thus, for the author of John, the "historical" Jesus is a mortal capable of experiencing human emotions (cf. Jn. 4:6, 11:35) while the "spiritual" Jesus is the transcendental Christ. The miracles or "signs" which Jesus performed are also interpreted by John as having a symbolic meaning. For example, in the miracle of the changing of the water into wine at the wedding feast in Cana (Jn. 2:1–11), the "new wine" represents the message of Christ as compared to the "old wine", i.e. Judaism, which had been depleted.

Like the other Gospel writers, John is not primarily interested in history. Even the narrative concerning John the Baptist* (Jn. 1:19–28) is merely an introduction to the discourse which follows (1:29–34) in which the Baptist proclaims that Jesus is the Son of God. In ch. 6, the author of John seems to take the existence of the Eucharist for granted, although he never refers to the occasion of its institution. This, of course, may be because he is concerned with a form of the common meal which existed before the ritual of the Eucharist was fixed. John does not refute the authenticity of the Synoptic Gospels*, although in one or two cases he corrects them on points of historical data. His main purpose, however, is to reveal the basic truth which underlies the historical life and ministry of Jesus.

A Gospel for the Gentiles: The Gospel of John was written for the Gentile church. In some instances, Jesus' opponents are described explicitly as "Pharisees", but in most cases they are dismissed contemptuously as "the Jews" (cf. Jn. 1:19; 2:18, 20; 3:25; 5:10, 15, 16, 18 etc.). The prologue states that Jesus was rejected by "his own people" (1:11), i.e. the Jews, whereas all who believe in him become "children of God" (1:12). Whereas the Law was given to Moses, "grace and truth" have come through Jesus Christ" (1:17). John makes it very clear that Jesus was not a reformer, or even a prophet, but the transcendental messianic deliverer, the Son of God.

It has been claimed that the Fourth Gospel was written to counter certain heretical tendencies within the early church. Yet, it is difficult to ascertain a strictly polemical tendency in John. The author seems to have been fully engrossed in revealing what he believed to be the ultimate truth of Jesus' mission. The metaphysical tone of his Gospel is not necessarily argumentative or philosophical, but merely the natural outcome of John's symbolic interpretation.

In the Fourth Gospel Jesus acts and speaks in strict accordance with a divine scheme. The miracles and "signs", the testimonies of John the Baptist and of Jesus' followers and – in some cases — even the witness of his opponents all bear out the fact that Jesus is God's revelation *par excellence* to mankind. According to John, Jesus was fully aware and cognizant of his mission and, from the outset of his ministry until he faced Pontius Pilate, he testified to his own calling. Jesus did not die on the cross as a victim of circumstance, but as a deliberate sacrifice in keeping with the Divine plan.

It is no coincidence, therefore, that John merely touches on Jesus' Galilean ministry while concentrating heavily upon the events and discourses leading up to and including Passion week. It is upon the cross that the ultimate revelation of Jesus as the incarnate, divine Word is revealed. The entire Gospel leads up to this central point; each "sign" and event is a means to illustrate this ultimate truth. John himself expresses the motivating force behind his writing of the Gospel (Jn. 20:31), "These (things) are written, that you may believe that Jesus is the Christ, the Son of God; and that believing you may have life in his name."

The Gospel of John was circulated in codices, as illustrated in this page (**576**, Papyrus Bodmer II, ca. 200 CE).

JONAH, BOOK OF. — Although the book of Jonah appears as one of the Minor Prophets (the fifth in the Hebrew canon), it is not a record of his sayings but tells a story about him. It is an anonymous composition and fits best into the category of parables. The atmosphere and miraculous elements in the story are similar to some of the incidents concerning Elijah and Elisha related in I and II K.

Contents: The narrative may be divided into three sections: a. Chs. 1–2 in which Jonah is commissioned by Yahweh to go to Nineveh and proclaim its destruction, but refuses to commit himself to a prophecy which he does not believe Yahweh will fulfill. He attempts to flee in the opposite direction by taking ship from Jaffa to Tarshish (see Ships and Navigation*). The boat runs into a storm and when the sailors' prayers to their gods bring no relief, they draw lots to decide who is to blame for their danger. The lot falls on Jonah (1:4–7). He acknowledges that he is guilty before God and advises them to throw him into the sea. When the sailors see that they cannot reach land, they do so, reluctantly. Immediately, the storm subsides and the sailors acknowledge the greatness of God (1:14–16). Jonah is not drowned. Instead God appoints a great fish to swallow him, and he remains in its belly for three days and three nights. There he prays to God. His prayer has nothing to do with his situation, but is a hymn of praise (2:1–9, see below). Thereupon the fish vomits Jonah out on the shore of some unspecified place and the command to go to Nineveh is repeated — and this time obeyed (3:1).

b. In Nineveh (3:2ff), he proclaims the city's imminent destruction, moving king and people to repent in sackcloth and ashes, proclaim a fast and pray for forgiveness. Seeing this, God relents and cancels the predicted punishment — much to Jonah's disgust.

c. Ch. 4. The prophet complains to God that this merciful change of mind is exactly what he had feared from the beginning. He sulks in a booth outside the city and prays for death (like Elijah in I K. 19:4), presumably because he feels God has made a fool of him. To persuade him of his error, God arranges a series of symbolic experiences for Jonah. First a castor oil plant grows up to give him a welcome shade (they grow wild in coastal Palestine), then it is eaten by a worm and a hot wind springs up to torment him so that once more he prays for death. God then points out to him that if the prophet is angry about the destruction of a plant, which grew up overnight without needing the labour of any man's hand, how much more should God pity the great city of Nineveh "in which there are more than a hundred and twenty thousand persons who do not know their right hand from their left, and also much cattle?"

Theme: The point of Jonah's protest is to show how far he is from understanding God's ways and mercy. In the first part of the story, Jonah's disobedience to a divine command provokes God into bringing him almost into the jaws of death, but he relents and Jonah is given another chance. In the second half, Jonah is reduced to the extremity of spiritual depression, only to be shown by God himself the essential rightness of his divine, merciful purpose.

Literary Problem: There is no longer any need for a historical commentary on the book of Jonah to discuss whether or not it would be physically possible for a whale or other big fish to swallow Jonah. Incredible, miraculous elements in Bible stories are not sufficient grounds to dismiss them as entire fabrications. The miracles in Jonah are no more extraordinary than those in the stories of his earlier countrymen, Elijah and Elisha.

A more important question has been raised by those scholars who have found it impossible to see any unity in the book and cannot accept that it was the work of one author. Theories of composite authorship, transposition and interpolation have been put forward to meet the objections. The main difficulty is the long psalm in 2:2–9, which bears no relation to the narrative and very little to the content of the rest of the book. From its wording, the author of the poem seems to have been familiar with many of the biblical Psalms* for he quotes from them extensively. The most acceptable opinion is that this psalm was inserted into the narrative by an editor who, reading that Jonah prayed to God, felt it fitting to include the psalm. This was a familiar literary device in biblical lore, where many originally independent poems have been inserted into folk tales. (An alternative opinion is that the writer of the book of Jonah composed the poem to the ancient story.)

In either case, the book remains a story in which Jonah is the central figure and which has been formulated according to a familiar prophetic pattern. First comes the preface, introducing the mission; secondly, the execution of the mission and, thirdly, the moral of the mission and the illustration of God's benevolent intentions by means of a miracle. The fish episode may have been borrowed by the author from the mythological background of the whole area, shared by many of Israel's neighbours. Whatever mythical element it may have contained originally, in the biblical text, the fish is used merely as a literary convention — as a convenient way of saving the prophet and getting him back to land.

Nevertheless, although the author drew on myth and folklore, essentially the story is a moral tale concerning the historical figure of a prophet Jonah, son of Amittai, born in Galilee and mentioned in II K. 14:25–27 as being active during the reign of Jeroboam. There is nothing in Kings to connect this Jonah with Assyria, nor is there any indication of any visit to Nineveh at this time. Because of the very brief reference in Kings and the fact that Jonah is nowhere referred to by any of the prophets Isaiah, Jeremiah, Nahum or Zephaniah, many scholars have denied the book all historical foundation. Although it seems reasonable to find an identity between the prophet of the book of Jonah and the Jonah who, in the 8th c. BCE, prophesied the restoration "of the border of Israel from the entrance of Hamath as far as the Sea of the Arabah" (II K. 14:25), this does not mean that the book was written at that time as a record of personal experience. It seems more likely that it was a much later work of fiction composed by an anonymous prophet to point a particular moral, who chose the ancient prophet as his hero because of his known anti-Assyrian bias — a very reasonable attitude in the 8th c. BCE.

Purpose: This anonymous author was telling a parable of repentance. There is nothing of the fate of Nineveh or of Jonah's future career in the book. It ends with God's question to Jonah and the audience is left to find the answer and point the moral for themselves. The places which are mentioned in the story are no more than symbols — Nineveh representing any great city filled with iniquity; Tarshish representing a remote place beyond the seas.

In fact the book raises several moral issues. The God of Israel is shown to reign over nature and the peoples of the world. He cares for mankind, both Jew and Gentile, and desires them to repent of iniquity and to practice righteousness. From these motives, he obliges the prophet to fulfill his mission. There are two main themes in the story. One is the expression of God's tender pity, beautifully expressed in the question that concludes the book. The second is the prophet's original refusal to carry out the mission entrusted to him, which serves as the starting point of the narrative. It is a familiar theme. Balaam was sent to curse and instead delivered a blessing (see Numbers*). Moses and Jeremiah both began by claiming that they were unworthy of the missions God entrusted to them. Even Isaiah cried that he was "of impure lips". Jonah, on the other hand, refused to deliver the message because he believed that God would revoke his judgment, in line with the prophecy of Jeremiah (18:7–8), leaving the prophet, Jonah, in the paradoxical position of having apparently delivered a false prediction. For this reason, the author places the repentance of the Ninevites in the middle of the story (ch. 3) and makes God's pity for them its climax and conclusion. The point is that God's benevolence takes priority over the accuracy of the messages he places in the mouths of his prophets.

The book's message can be seen as a refutation of those who claim that there is no escape for a sinful man. Jonah's stated attitude represents the formalistic approach that demands retribution for sins, but God's mercy transcends the mechanical application of the law. The mercy of God, the book proclaims, is paramount.

Some scholars have suggested that the central theme of the book is the personal relationship between Yahweh and his servant Jonah, others that the book points the moral that it is the duty of Israel to make God known to the Gentiles.

The main lesson of the book, however, seems to be that Yahweh, a patient and merciful God, is Lord not only of the Jews but also of the Gentiles. His love extends far beyond the borders of Palestine to far-off Nineveh and even includes the heathen sailors. In contrast to God's universal care stands Jonah's narrow concern with his reputation as a prophet — and a prophet of Israel. Some scholars have seen the whole purpose of the book as a refutation of the point of view placed in the mouth of Jonah, which is thought to reflect the narrowness and exclusiveness which prevailed among the Jews of the time. These scholars have argued that the monotheism of the Jews had become the basis of a narrow nationalism and, especially at the time of the Restoration*, had led to increasingly harsh measures against close neighbours of the Jews. From this point of view, the book is seen as a protest against the policies of Ezra and Nehemiah in their attempts to maintain the exclusiveness of the Jewish people (see Restoration*), but this view is unhistorical and may not be free of prejudice. It has no support in the context of the Old Testament and later literature. It seems more reasonable to understand Jonah as a parable of two conflicting views, one which could have been held by an Israelite of Jonah's historical times, the other, the much more developed concept of a universal and exalted God. In his use of it in relation to his own teachings (see below), Jesus took this as the central theme of the book rather than the discredited doctrine of the subjection and annihilation of the Gentiles.

Authorship and Date: There is nothing in the book itself to indicate the authorship of Jonah. No claim is made that it was written by the prophet and scholars do not even agree about the time of its composition. Since it must have been written after the fall of Nineveh, the earliest possible date is 600 BCE. The contents make it clear that the author was influenced by Jeremiah and some scholars find evidence in the book's language and spirit for a post-Exilic date — some time between 400–200 BCE. Their arguments, however, are not conclusive. There is insufficient evidence for any definite date, beyond the reasonable assumption that it was written long after the fall of Nineveh, when that once proud city was no more than a memory and a symbol.

Jonah in the New Testament: Jonah is the only prophet with whom Jesus compared himself directly. He used the story of Jonah as a parable in which the repentant Ninevites represented all Gentiles who acknowledged the supremacy of the God of Israel. The Ninevites repented because of Jonah's message and Jesus used this theme to reproach the Jews of his own generation who refused to heed his own teachings. He referred to Jonah as a great moral fact which would put to confusion the men of his own generation at the Day of Judgment (Lk. 11:29–32; Mt. 12:39–41).

The theme of Jonah is referred to in Acts. 10–11 and is used in many Gospel passages to illustrate the missionary message of the Church. The Christians found an analogy between the book of Jonah and their own foreign missionary concepts. Jesus' use of the book caught the imagination of the early Christians and led them to take a great interest in Jonah. Paul expressed the evangelical message of the book in his exposition of God's mercy (Rom. 9:15–16). Remains of early Christian art in sarcophagi and catacomb paintings include many pictures which illustrate the themes of the story of Jonah.

JOSEPH. — *Outline: Early Life; Joseph in Egypt; The Egyptian Economy; The Joseph Story Tradition; Years of Famine; The Children of Israel Enter Egypt; When Was Joseph in Egypt?*

Joseph was the eleventh son of Jacob, and first born of his wife, Rachel. The Joseph story (Gn. 37:20), which has a dominant Egyptian background, serves as the conclusion of the epoch of the Patriarchs*, and as the prelude to the settlement of the Children of Israel in Egypt* and the Exodus*.

Early Life: Joseph was his father's favourite son and was thus a natural object for the envy and hatred of his brothers. His naive arrogance, revealed in the self-magnifying dreams which he related and interpreted to his brothers, so infuriated them that they decided to do away with him. The biblical account of their actions combines two traditions. One states that they sold him to a caravan of Ishmaelites, the other that they abandoned him in a pit from which he was rescued by Midianite traders who sold him to Potiphar, chief of the Pharaoh's household.

Joseph in Egypt: The story of Joseph's life in Egypt contains many correct reminiscences of Egyptian life and times, fully illustrated by archaeological discoveries. These point to the preservation of authentic traditions in the Joseph story, even though there has been considerable editorial and literary activity in the course of transmission.

Joseph rose high in the service of Potiphar, and became "overseer" of his household. The turning point in his life came when he rebuffed the wife of his master, and was imprisoned on a false charge of attempted rape. It is interesting to note that this tale of seduction is similar to the plot of the Egyptian folk-story, "The Two Brothers", found in a 13th century BCE papyrus. Within a short time Joseph's reputation as an interpreter of dreams brought him before the Pharaoh, to explain the dream of the seven fat and seven lean cows. Joseph interpreted the dream as portending seven years of plenty followed by seven years of famine. This seven

577

year cycle motif was common in ancient Near Eastern lore, and, according to J.A. Wilson, was based on actual periods of drought and plenty, which were determined by the rhythm of the rainy season in central and eastern Africa, and the consequent rise or recession of the Nile, which either flooded the fields or left them parched. This picture shows the Nile in flood submerging the island of Philae and its temples in southern Egypt (**577**).

The Egyptian Economy: The stability of the Egyptian economy largely depended on the grain harvest. Detailed records of the grain supplies were kept by scribes (illustrated in a wall painting, **580,** found in the tomb of Menena). The office of Superintendent of Granaries was especially important in all periods of Egypt's history. The "account of the harvests" presented in solemn audience represented the royal tax of one-fifth of all crops. The "New Kingdom" period, during or slightly before which Joseph may have lived, was an age of Pharaonic ownership of all the land. The people were considered little more than serfs, who cultivated the royal estates.

Joseph advised the Pharaoh to appoint a competent director, "discreet and wise", and charge him with a country-wide scheme to collect and store 20% of the produce of the land in granaries (**579**) in preparation for the lean years.

The monarch responded to the suggestion by naming Joseph Vizier of Egypt or Chief Administrator, a post second in power only to the Pharaoh. Joseph may also have exercised the function of Superintendent of Granaries. It was not uncommon for foreigners to rise high in the Egyptian court, a fact mentioned in official Egyptian records.

The Joseph Story Tradition: The original tradition from which the Joseph story stems contains genuine Egyptian

578

579

titles and proper names, although the names (Potiphar, Potiphera, Asenath) were current in Egypt mainly in the 11th to 10th centuries BCE, while the name of Ramses (Gn. 47:11) was certainly not known before the rise of the 19th dynasty (13th c. BCE, see Egypt*), whose kings were the first to bear that name. This indicates some later revision in the names used in the story of Joseph and suggests that the story did not reach permanent form until some centuries (perhaps the 11th BCE) after the events were supposed to have taken place. The biblical account conforms closely to Egyptian texts and documentary illustrations. We read in Gn. 50:26, that Joseph lived 110 years, which was the traditional length of a happy and prosperous life in Egypt. There are numerous striking instances of authentic local colour in the Joseph story, which can best be understood against its Egyptian background. This is the easier as daily life in ancient Egypt is profusely illustrated by excavated tomb paintings, inscriptions, stele, etc. Palestinians are shown bringing tribute to court (**578**; 18th dyn.).

A hint as to the locale in which Joseph may have lived and officiated is afforded by the reference to his marriage to Asenath, daughter of Potiphera, Priest of On. She bore him two sons, Menasseh* and Ephraim*. It would be in keeping with Joseph's high rank for the Pharaoh to give him an Egyptian wife and the Egyptian name of Zaphenath-paneaḥ, *Djepa-ntr-fnkh* (God wishes him to live) in Egyptian.

Years of Famine: As predicted, the famine came, not only to Egypt, but to all of western Asia. One ancient inscription recorded by J.B. Pritchard in "Ancient Near Eastern Texts" actually tells of a seven-year famine alleged to have taken place during the time of Pharaoh Tjoser (ca. 2700 BCE). This monarch is supposed to have appealed to the god Khnum, who promised that the Nile would rise and flood the fields with sufficient water.

An Egyptian inscription from the 14th c. BCE indicates that it was customary for frontier officials to allow people from Palestine and Sinai to enter Egypt in time of drought. The Anastasi papyrus VI contains a communication dated 1220 BCE from a frontier official of Mernephtach to his superior, informing him that certain Edomite nomad tribes had been allowed, according to precedent, to pass the fortress in the district of Thuku (the Hebrew Succoth) to pasture their cattle near Pithom. It is interesting to note that the Egyptian papyri mention Succoth and Pithom, towns in Goshen, also mentioned in the book of Exodus as the sites of Hebrew settlement (see Exodus*).

The Children of Israel Enter Egypt: The Bible relates that Jacob, aware of this custom, sent his sons to the Land of the Pharaohs to ask permission to settle. From here on the story of his brothers is linked to that of Joseph, which proceeds with rising tension from the critical moment of his recognition of his family to a happy ending. After Joseph had arranged for their welfare, Jacob, now called Israel, and his clan of 70 moved into Egypt with all their livestock and possessions. There they were welcomed as relatives of the famous Joseph.

In the biblical scheme this story serves to bring the Patriarchal age to a close (Gn. 47:27–50:26) and connect it to the climactic point of the national epic, the deliverance of Israel from the Egyptians and the birth of the nation after the Exodus. While an old Egyptian folk-tale may be embedded in Joseph's success story, the biblical writer's account pri-

580

marily conveys a religious and moral lesson, hinting that the promise made to Abraham, namely that the descendants of the sojourners in Egypt would inherit Canaan, was moving towards fulfillment.

When was Joseph in Egypt: The date of the entry into Egypt, as well as the period of Joseph's career, is a matter of dispute. The Bible does not name the Pharaoh he served, nor does it give any conclusive references, such as the king's place of residence. One important clue, however, is dropped in the description of the Israelites' entry into Goshen. It is written that Jacob sent his son Judah ahead to represent him before the royal court, and that when the Hebrews later entered the country at Goshen, Joseph rode in his chariot to meet his father, and then returned to report to the Pharaoh (Gn. 46:28–29; 47:1). The great Egyptologist, Maspero, has remarked that chariots were not used for very long journeys. Bearing this in mind, and assuming that Joseph must have lived in or near the king's capital, his one-day round-trip by chariot implies that the Pharaoh's residence was situated close to Goshen, or at Avaris (called Ramses by the kings of the 19th dynasty after 1305 BCE; see Exodus*; Egypt*).

Flavius Josephus* quotes Manetho, an Egyptian Hellenistic* historian who described how the Egyptians drove the Hyksos* out of Egypt: "They went away with their whole families and effects, not fewer in number than two hundred and forty thousand, and took their journey from Egypt, through their wilderness, for Syria . . . they built a city in that country which is now called Judea, and that large enough to contain the large number of men and called it Jerusalem." Josephus continues a tendentious account, trying to equate the Hyksos with the Children of Israel, whom Manetho also calls "Shepherds". "Nor was it without reason that they were called captives by the Egyptians since one of our ancestors, Joseph, told the king of Egypt that he was a captive and afterward sent for his brethren into Egypt."

There is no verification for the term "captive". However, even if some of Josephus' details are discounted, there is, in the opinion of J.A. Wilson, "a good tradition of conquering easterners of unknown race, building walled camps from which to rule Egypt, setting themselves in opposition to Egyptian religion and ultimately being forced to retire into Asia." Josephus links the entry of the Hebrews to the Hyksos era. Moreover, Hebrew names like Yakub-Har appear in Hyksos' lists of nobles. The Bible maintains that the Israelites stayed in Egypt 400 to 430 years (Gn. 15:13, Ex. 12:40–41). This would place their entry during the Hyksos' Middle Kingdom (ca. 1720–1570 BCE) and their exit in the 13th century BCE (see Exodus*). Nevertheless, some scholars feel that the Joseph story took place during the middle of the 14th century BCE, in the New Kingdom of the famous Pharaoh Akhenaton (Amenhotep IV; see Egypt*; Exodus*). The theory is based on the Gn. 47:19–20 account of Joseph setting up the economic system that turned the Pharaoh into an absolute dictator and gave him ownership of most of the country's land. This was in contrast to the feudal system that prevailed under the Hyksos. From Egyptian sources we learn that during the period of dictatorship, the kings required efficient and resourceful civil servants to administer the lands. Talented commoners were given an opportunity to rise to high positions. There may be a point of contact with the Joseph story here, which would put the entry of the Israelites after the Hyksos feudal era. The point also rests on the established fact that the 20% tax was normal for the New Kingdom period, and was paid in grain delivered to the royal granaries in each provincial capital. On the evidence of a large scroll dealing with tax assessments (the Wilbour papyrus), it seems that the tax-exemption privileges of the priesthood and temples granted under the New Kingdom system, were a heavy burden on the rest of Egypt.

H. Cazelles, on the other hand, believes that several of the nomadic tribes that entered Egypt, and particularly the "clan of Joseph", were taken captive to Egypt as a result of tribal strife with their "brother" tribes of Gad, Asher, Dan and Naphtali (Gn. 37:2). This may help to explain the second tradition (Ex. 6:16–20) that notes the duration of the stay in Egypt as four generations instead of 400 years. It is suggested that descendants of Joseph's clan met scattered Levites, among them the family of Moses. Egyptian names prevalent in the early tribe of Levi (Moses, Hophni, Pinchas, Merari) argue for a connection with Egypt. Moreover, the names of the midwives (in Ex. 1:15) are of a very old

type. Shiphrah is instanced in one of the Brooklyn papyri of the 18th century BCE out of a list of slaves, many of whom are Asiatics, some bearing Hebrew names.

In view of this obviously complex picture, it is not surprising that historians differ in assessing the evidence presented in the biblical account and in comparing it with various Egyptian records of times when similar customs prevailed.

The Joseph story closes with Joseph's request that he be buried in Canaan, like his father before him. Tradition relates that he was mummified and entombed in Egypt, indicating that the political climate was not as favourable at his death as it had been previously, or his request would have been carried out. Instead, the Exodus story includes an account of his remains being borne back to Canaan by the departing Hebrews.

JOSEPHUS, FLAVIUS. — The most famous Jewish historian of antiquity was born Yoseph ben Mattatyahu in 37 or 38 CE. His family was descended from the priestly Jehoyarib house, distantly related to the Hasmonean princes.

His Life: In his autobiographical notes, Josephus mentions that at an early age he showed exceptional scholarly ability. When he was sixteen, he claims to have joined a series of different sects in order to learn their teachings at first hand, and even became a disciple of a recluse named Banos and went to live with him in the wilderness. At 19, Josephus joined the Pharisees and began to take a serious interest in public affairs. In 64 CE, he went to Rome on a semi-public mission. He was regarded as an expert on political affairs and in the early stages of the Great War against Rome (64–73 CE; see Rome and the Jews*) he was given a command in Galilee by the revolutionary government in Jerusalem. Taken prisoner by the Romans, he became a pacifist and changed his loyalties. With the support of the Flavian dynasty (founded by Vespasian in 69 CE), he turned to a literary career, earning, with his writings, a leading place in Jewish historiography.

Political Activities: Most of the data about Josephus' political activities relate to the years of the Great War from 66–70 CE. Josephus belonged to the moderate party and had the confidence of many Jerusalem notables who were opposed to the Revolt. Nevertheless, with the support of the moderates, Josephus was made commander of the key Galilee province. The Zealots, more deeply committed to the war, were suspicious of him. Throughout his term of office he was at loggerheads with them, especially with their leader, Johanan of Gischala (Gush-Halab). In his history of the war, Josephus claims that he devoted all his energies to organizing the defence against the expected Roman attack. In fact, it is doubtful whether his heart was really in the struggle.

When Vespasian invaded Galilee, Josephus shut himself up in the fortress of Jotapata which resisted a long siege and succumbed at last only after a bitter struggle. When the city was finally stormed, Josephus hid in a cave, thus avoiding the fate of the majority of his troops, who refused to surrender to the Romans and were slaughtered by the thousands. Josephus, their commander, gave himself up, however, and, so he tells us, prophesied to Vespasian that he would become emperor. This — and perhaps a pleasant personality — earned him the esteem of the future emperor and his sons. Josephus remained with the Roman commander and, during the siege of Jerusalem, tried to persuade the Jews to lay down their arms. With the end of the war, Vespasian granted him full freedom and Roman citizenship and Josephus took the surname of Flavius in honour of his benefactor. He was given some confiscated estates in Judea, but henceforth lived in Rome as an avowed apologist for the Flavian emperors. He lived on for another 30 years after the war (100 CE), devoting himself to his writing (see below: Evaluation).

Personality: Josephus has been the subject of almost unending debate. He has been condemned as a traitor and praised as a realist. At this distance, it seems that a distinction must be made between his political outlook which showed good sense and foresight, and his personal behaviour. This has appeared to many as highly reprehensible, especially when compared with the heroism and self-sacrifice of his contemporaries, the Zealots. Another distinction is needed between Josephus the man and Josephus the historian. No doubt his historical works fall short of complete accuracy here and there, but, much more important, Josephus aimed at producing a fully detailed record and rescued many facts from oblivion, sometimes as a result of his own meticulous investigation.

The Works of Josephus: His first work, the seven books of the "War of the Jews against the Romans" was published several years after the war. It appeared first in Aramaic, and later in Greek, in which language it has survived. The work is the main source for the history of the war, and is of inestimable value — whatever may be its deficiencies of style and numerous errors of fact.

The "Jewish War" was followed by the monumental "Antiquities of the Jews" published in 93 CE in twenty books, which gives the history of the Israelites from the Creation to the Great War (66 CE), eulogizing Israel and its culture. The first half of the book, which takes the history of Israel and its leaders up to Alexander the Great (Bks. I–XI), was based mainly on the Old Testament. The second half (Bks. XII–XX) covers the Ptolemaic and Seleucid periods, Hasmonean rule, Roman domination and the reigns of Herod and his sons. In this section, Josephus drew on sources which have since been lost, e.g. the works of Nicolaus of Damascus, and also on familiar material such as First Maccabees and the Letter of Aristeas (see Hellenism and the Diaspora*).

One of his shorter works is "The Life of Joseph", his autobiography, which he wrote principally to clear himself of the charges brought against him by a rival historian, Justus of Tiberias (whose history of the war is lost) in connection with his actions during the war. The account of his part in the events of 66–70 CE given in the autobiography differs in many respects from that in "Jewish War". Though he represents himself there as a friend of the Romans, many statements are disproved by his earlier work, the "War". His other short work is "Against Apion", an apologetic work rejecting anti-Semitic accusations by people such as Apion of Alexandria.

Evaluation: Like the Alexandrian Jews (see Hellenism in the Diaspora*), Josephus was writing for the Gentiles. His works illustrate the way in which the facts of history could be rewritten for the instruction of the Greeks and Romans. Thus the earlier part of his "Antiquities" is clearly apologetic and, like his comments on the Old Testament, of very little value for a modern historian. His credibility as a historian has often been doubted, yet he could be very penetrating as, for instance, in his assessment of the period of hellenization in Palestine ("War").

However, he tended to take from his sources (e.g. II Maccabees) only what he regarded as most important and on closer examination it has often been proven that the sources were more trustworthy as a whole than his revised selection from them. Modern historians, accordingly, tend to accept as reliable only information which is in harmony with Josephus' original source.

Moreover, Josephus was strongly prejudiced against the Hasmoneans. In V. Tcherikower's opinion, his account of the Maccabaean revolt is extremely confused. On the other hand, in his emphasis on the internal connection between Hellenism and the Tobiads (see Hasmoneans*), he draws attention to a fact which none of the other sources of the period seem to have appreciated.

Josephus is notorious for his exaggerated figures. He states, for example, that three million pilgrims came to Jerusalem for the Passover feast (War II, 280) and that over a million people perished during the siege of Jerusalem (VI, 420). Similarly, the figures he gives for the populations of Galilean towns and villages recall the inventions of Herodotus who numbered the Persian army at millions.

Nevertheless, in spite of all these limitations, the "Antiquities" remains one of the most valuable historical sources for the Roman period in Palestine, and the life of the country just before the beginning of the Christian era.

Christian Versions: Josephus' writings were preserved at first more by early Christian scholars than by Jews. Men like Clement of Alexandria and Origen, Eusebius and Hegesippus made full use of them. However, later versions handed on bear clear evidence of Christian interpolation. The "Slavonic Josephus" in particular raised serious problems, mainly because of its mention of Jesus. Some authorities argue that Jesus was mentioned in the original Greek Josephus, but this is denied by others. In the later Slavonic version, the reference was almost certainly inserted by Christian scribes. In general, it is agreed that the paragraph presents at least a partial interpolation. Interpolations of this kind may have been the comments of a Christian scribe first written in the margin, then later finding their way into the text of later copies of manuscript. The same thing happened to many ancient documents, and may also have occurred in relation to another passage of the Antiquities (XX, 9, 1[200]).

Mediaeval Jewish Versions: Among mediaeval Hebrew versions of Josephus, which contain additional material and have been the subject of much scholarly discussion, is the Josippon (Yosephon), ascribed to Joseph ben Gorion and thought to have been written in southern Italy in the 8th c. CE. Lately, there has been a tendency to regard it as older. Its Hebrew is good and it deals, in a lively style, with the whole post-Exilic period up to the siege of Jerusalem. Its source is Josephus, probably the Latin version of Hegesippus. Mediaeval Jews regarded it as more authoritative than its original.

JOHN, EPISTLES OF, (see Epistles, General).

JOSHUA AND JUDGES, BOOKS OF. *Outline: Place in the Canon; Historical Background. I. Contents of Joshua. II. Contents of the Book of Judges. III. Traditions of Joshua and Judges: Religious Theme of Apostasy, Retribution and Deliverance; Contradictions between Joshua and Judges; Biblical View of the Conquest; The Accounts of the Battle of Merom; Joshua Given Too Much Credit; Evidence of the Settlement; Conclusion.*

Place in the Canon: Joshua is the sixth book of the Old Testament. It is inseparable historically from the Pentateuch, especially the story of the Conquest*, which begins in Numbers*. For this reason, it is considered the sixth of a hypothetical Hexateuch by one of the schools of biblical criticism*. In the Hebrew canon, it was placed first among the division of "Former Prophets" (Joshua, Judges, I and II Samuel and I and II Kings). Judges comes next. The structure, contents, historical background and literary problems raised by the two books are so closely allied that they can best be considered together.

Historical Background: The historical background to the books is the stage of Conquest and settlement of the Children of Israel in the land of Canaan, i.e. the first steps in the establishment of the Israelites as a nation living on their own soil. Although there were already the links of common language, religion and descent between the tribes* (see article), it was not until after the settlement of Palestine that they could really be considered a nation in the accepted sense.

I. CONTENTS OF JOSHUA. The book can be divided into two parts:

Part I. Chapter 1 — introduction; chapter 2–6 — crossing of the Jordan and capture of Jericho; chapters 7–8 — capture of Ai and erection of the altar on mount Gerizim; chapters 9–10 — conquest of the south; chapter 11 — conquest of the north; chapter 12 — summary.

Part 2. Chapters 13–21 are much more complex in structure than the earlier chapters. They cover the parcelling out of the land among the tribes, defining the boundaries of each tribe's territory. Most scholars date these lists as later P (Priestly) material (see Biblical Criticism*), but it appears that the original lists are of the 11th or 10th cs. BCE. They reflect the position which existed just before the establishment of the monarchy and the frontiers they describe include not only land acquired by the tribes at the time of the Conquest*, but also areas to which they made claim later (see Administration of the Kingdom under Government*, Authority and Kingship). Chapter 22 records the settlement of the two-and-a-half Transjordan tribes in their territory, and the building of the altar and sanctuary east of Jordan (see Tribes*). Chapters 23–24 describe the solemn convocations of Israel. They include Joshua's farewell addresses and his death.

The book of Joshua presents a picture of an uninterrupted, sweeping conquest of the land, planned and carried out under Joshua's leadership. The tribes act in unity, accepting the authority of the one leader, Joshua who, uniquely, led the people across the Jordan, captured Jericho and Ai, defeated the Gibeonites and the northern and southern coalitions of kings, divided the land by lot between the tribes, and renewed the people's Covenant with God at Shechem.

Most scholars find all this an unhistorical, later, idealization of a series of events which were in fact far more complex. This can best be seen from an examination of the book of Judges.

II. CONTENTS OF THE BOOK OF JUDGES. This book is also in two sections:

Part 1. Chapters 1–2:5 — these list the areas conquered after the death of Joshua and those territories which the northern tribes were unable to win (1:27–36); chapter 2:6–23 then gives an introductory outline of the period of the Judges covered by the rest of the book.

Part 2. The Judges: Chapter 3 — Othniel, Shamgar ben Anat and Ehud ben Gera and his struggle against the Moabites; Chapters 4–5 — Barak and Deborah and their defeat of Jabin, king of Hazor, and Sisera, the Canaanite general; chapters 6–8 — Gideon and his war against the Midianites; chapter 9 - Abimelech and his ephemeral kingdom of Shechem; chapter 10 — Tola ben Puah and Jair the Gileadite, two "minor judges"; chapters 11–12:7 — Jephthah the Gileadite, his campaign against the Ammonites and the sacrifice of his daughter; chapter 12:8–13 — Ibzan of Bethlehem, Elon the Zebulunite and Abdon ben Hillel, the Pirathonite, three more "minor judges"; chapters 13–16 – the Samson cycle. Many scholars believe this heroic legend, very much in the Homeric manner, to have been something quite separate from the warlike history of the book of Judges. Samson is never called a "judge" and his personal encounters with the Philistines seem to place him in the much later period of I Sam. 4:18–7:15 (Eli and Samuel); chapters 17–18 — the Danite episode and the statue of Micah; chapters 19–21 — the outrage of the concubine at Gibeah.

All the exploits of the judges and the various episodes listed above are fully discussed in the article on Judges*.

The book of Judges describes the exploits of the leaders, the Judges* who led the Hebrew tribes during the one-and-a-half centuries after the Conquest and the death of Joshua (approximately 1200–1050 BCE). In general, the Hebrew text has been well preserved. Though some of it is not in good condition, it is better than that of the other historical books and is accordingly the best available source of information about the structure of Israelite life during the transition from pre-Conquest semi-nomadic ways to a sedentary life.

III. TRADITIONS OF JOSHUA AND JUDGES. **Religious Theme of Apostasy, Retribution and Deliverance:** As presented, the stories are intended as illustrations of the theme of divine punishment for the religious laxity that accompanied the tribes' assimilation into Canaanite life, when "every man did what was right in his own eyes" (17:6). Retribution in the shape of oppression by their neighbours always followed until the people returned to Yahweh, who raised up a Judge to deliver them. This theme runs right through the book from its first statement in 2:11–19 until the end of the continuous account of gradual Conquest and Settlement of the land of Canaan.

Most authorities regard the book of Judges as a valid (though not completely reliable) source of information for the period, for the accounts of individual exploits by the different tribes (e.g. 15:11 ff, the capture of Samson the Danite by the tribesmen of Judah), seem to reflect the most probable actual conditions of the time prior to the establishment of the kingdom, ca. 1020 BCE.

Contradictions between Joshua and Judges: This view, however, raises a number of questions so far as the book of Joshua is concerned. The spirit and even many of the details of the traditions of the two books are often contradictory. Thus, according to Joshua 15:63, the tribesmen of Judah were unable to drive the Jebusites out of Jerusalem, while Judges 1:21 attributes this same inability to the Benjaminites. The point, of course, is whether both books refer essentially to the same period of time, in which case the generally greater historical reliability of Judges makes it possible to deny historical accuracy to Joshua, or whether Judges is concerned with a later period than Joshua, when the hold of the invading Israelites on the country had slackened and had to be reestablished.

If the second alternative is accepted, then the whole book of Judges must describe episodes which actually took place after the death of Joshua, possibly reflecting difficult conditions after the Conquest. In any case, it is generally agreed that at least some of the judges and the episodes connected with them must have taken place at the same time in different parts of the country, and that the book's impression of a series of consecutive events could very well be mistaken.

Biblical View of the Conquest*: The Bible's presentation of a unified, one-time Conquest under the leadership of Joshua has been compared by some with the emergence of Islam centuries later. Islam, however, was a different phenomenon in many ways, and the parallel may only be helpful in illustrating how tribes emerging from the desert are capable of overpowering settled regions whose populations are not only more numerous, but enjoy a much higher level of culture and civilization. All that seems to be needed is that the conquerors should be inspired by the conviction that they are the bearers of the Word of God and are fighting a "holy war" (in Arabic "Jehad"). However, quite apart from this remote parallel, there is the evidence of the Bible itself. Modern military authorities find the progress and stages of the Conquest perfectly logical, while the biblical descriptions of many of the battles reveal an intimate knowledge of the area involved and the strategy most likely to be appropriate to it (e.g. the capture of Ai, Jos. 8). Excavation of the ruins of a number of important Canaanite towns (e.g. Debir and Lachish*) has proved that they were indeed destroyed during the 13th c. BCE, i.e. during Joshua's time, although that, of course, is not conclusive evidence that the Children of Israel were responsible (see also Ashdod*). Some scholars have suggested that these destructions could equally well have been the work of the Sea Peoples (see Philistines*). Nor can archaeology provide anything in the nature of a precise chronology that will support the view that the destruction of these cities took place in the course of a single generation (for further discussion of this question, see Conquest*).

The Accounts of the Battle of Merom: The question becomes particularly acute in relation to the account in Joshua 11 of Joshua's battle "at the Waters of Merom" and his subsequent destruction of Hazor, and the account in Judges 4 and 5 of the battle fought against Jabin, the king of Hazor* under the command of Deborah's general, Barak. At one time, scholars used to suggest that the battle at the Waters of Merom had in fact taken place after Deborah's victory over the Canaanites who dominated Galilee, and that Joshua never captured Hazor.One reason for this theory was scholarly doubts that the tribes could have captured Hazor, "the head of all those kingdoms" (Jos. 11:10) so soon after their emergence from the desert. Instead, it was thought that the destruction of Hazor had not taken place until the end of the 12th c. BCE, in Deborah's time, while there had never been a battle of the Waters of Merom during Joshua's campaigns.

Then, between 1955 and 1958 CE, came the extensive excavations of Hazor and a remarkable vindication of the historical accuracy of the biblical record. Canaanite Hazor had indeed been destroyed during the 13th c. BCE (Joshua's time) and by the 12th c. BCE had ceased to exist as an important Canaanite centre.

Joshua Given Too Much Credit: On the other hand, scholars who deny the accuracy of the book of Joshua suggest that while such a man certainly lived during the 13th c. BCE, he was only a local tribal leader (at the most at the head of a number of tribes), and that other tribes had similar leaders. Only later on did Joshua's personality come to overshadow his fellows', and many of their exploits came to be ascribed to him. One argument in favour of this view is that the book of Joshua may contain many stories which are nothing more than popular myths invented to explain the existence of various heaps of ruins and the remains of cities, familiar to the people a little after the period of the Conquest. The best example of this trend is the story in Joshua 8 of the capture and destruction of Ai, for which archaeology has found no supporting evidence (see Bethel and Ai*).

Another theory (held by, e.g. M. Noth) is that the narrators who undertook to write an account of the conquest of central Canaan took a number of local traditions of different origins and formed a consecutive account out of them on a quite arbitrary basis. In this view, traditions relating to Gilgal, Jericho, Ai, Achan and Gibeon were all preserved at the sanctuary* of Gilgal near the Jordan. These, the narrators supplemented with the Makkedah episode (10:15 ff), the campaign against Hazor (11:1–9) and the battle of the Waters of Merom, arbitrarily connecting all the episodes with the name of Joshua. Thus the traditions regarding the conquest of the south of Canaan had already been described by an earlier narrator or narrators who had drawn on the traditions of the various tribes involved, plus a legend about the capture of Bethel (Jud. 1:22–26; see Conquest*).

Most schools of biblical criticism* (see article) maintain that several parts of the book of Joshua form part of the Deuteronomic history (see above: Place in the Canon) and that Joshua also contains P-like material. The final edition of Joshua, in this view, comes from the Exile and contains much earlier material (see above, I. Contents).

Evidence of the Settlement: Another approach which also tends to cast doubt on Joshua's historical accuracy is connected with the actual evidence of Israelite settlement, which some scholars connect with the Conquest itself. It appears that, in fact, the places where the Israelites first settled were not the Canaanite towns. Instead, the invaders tended to establish themselves in the mountain regions where no Canaanite settlements had existed before. It is claimed by J. Aharoni that a special type of pottery was found to have been used in these settlements (see pottery*), apparently pre-dating Joshua. It seems possible, therefore, that these tribes may have settled among the Canaanites, without displacing them, though other scholars do not consider these arguments as being conclusive. A second factor which is relevant to this argument is the tradition — which is hinted at even in Rabbinical literature — that the Children of Israel left Egypt in successive waves, some of them before the time of Moses (see Conquest*). In this case, it would be quite likely that such tribes had infiltrated and established themselves in Canaan before the battles of Joshua. If it is accepted (as seems to be the case) that Canaanite Jericho* was destroyed before the 13th c. BCE, then this event can also fit the theory of a number of Israelite invasions, Jericho being destroyed by an earlier wave prior to the main Exodus. It may be noted that evidence is almost entirely wanting with regard to Canaanite Jericho of the Late Bronze II phase (14th and early 13th c. BCE).

The questions raised above are only a selection of problems concerning the Israelite Conquest and settlement of Canaan (see Conquest*; Tribes*; Judges*), but they can give some idea of the considerations which have to be borne in mind in connection with the books of Joshua and Judges.

Conclusion: It remains true, however, that the history of the Conquest can only be understood in the light of the wider historical process which was affecting all the countries of the area. Briefly: the slackening of Egyptian rule during the El Amarna* period (14th c. BCE) threw Canaan into a political and military turmoil in which links between the various independent city-states disintegrated, making them an easy prey to the invading Israelites, while, at the same time encouraging the setting up of national kingdoms in Transjordan (Moab, Edom, Aram) and, ultimately, in Palestine. At the same time, the penetration of the Habiru* (who apparently included Hebrew clans) added to the general confusion.

No final conclusion about the exact sequence of events is likely to be possible until there have been many more excavations carried out in Palestine and until new documentary evidence becomes available to clarify the general background of the political situation and power relationships in Canaan at the time of and following the Israelite invasion.

JUDGES, PERIOD OF — *Outline: The Tribal League; Conquest and Assimilation; Twelve Judges; Othniel; Ehud; The Song of Deborah; The Battle God; Jael's Triumph; Gideon; Abimelech; Jephthah the Gileadite; Jephthah's Daughter; Inter-tribal Conflicts; Samson; Six Minor Judges; Shamgar ben Anath; The Danites Migrate North; The Gibeah Outrage; Conclusion.*

The Tribal League: During the period of the Judges (see Judges, Book of*), the twelve tribes* of Israel formed a loose confederacy, a tribal league or 'amphictyony', bound together by the Covenant law*. In addition to its military function, the league had also to regulate the cultic and religious institutions inherited from previous generations.

This gave the league its focal point in the shrine which housed the Ark of the Covenant*, eventually located at Shiloh.

The League's military function, strongly emphasized by the biblical record, became of particular importance in times of crisis which were frequent in a period of almost constant conflict and instability. There was no permanent military organisation though the tribes were responsible for supplying militia to serve in the general defence, each tribal unit having its own officers (some of these are mentioned in the Song of Deborah). Nor was there any centralized political leadership which could compel the tribes to supply contingents of troops.

Conquest and Assimilation: The largest socio-political unit inherited by the League was the tribe. There was none of the social stratification based on material wealth which existed in feudal Canaan. The tribes tended to be isolated and were often out of sympathy with each other. This laid them open to frequent attack from their neighbours, or foreign "oppressors". In spite of setbacks, however, over two centuries, a process of settlement effected a gradual adjustment from a semi-nomadic to a sedentary way of life, the people becoming farmers, the land divided into small plots. Some modern scholars believe that this was a lengthy process; others that it was completed very quickly. The people had always been sedentary and after a brief period of wanderings, settled down again. Moreover, according to recent views (see Conquest*), many of the Israelites had always lived in Canaan since Patriarchal times. At the same time, this was a period of assimilation with the conquered Canaanites. The effects of Canaanite civilization* on Israelite ways was to become a serious issue under the monarchy.

Modern opinion is divided about the actual time taken by the Conquest, mainly on the basis of material recorded in the book of Judges. It can be demonstrated that the Conquest was a long-drawn out process of independent actions by individual tribes, rather than a series of concerted campaigns. This view sees the book as a collection of tribal traditions rather than a national history (see Judges, book of*). However, other modern research has found evidence of a united attack, concentrated in a limited period of time. There is some truth in both these theories.

Twelve Judges: At each moment of crisis or danger to a tribe, a "judge" (in Hebrew "saviour") arose to lead the clan involved as a divinely inspired deliverer. His authority, according to biblical tradition, was based on certain personal qualities (charisma) that made it clear to his fellow men that Yahweh's "spirit was upon him" and this made him irresistible in battle and impervious to danger. Tradition, however, does not minimize their ups and downs as is made clear in the stories of Gideon and Samson (see below). In most cases the judges exercised no judicial skill and were known for their military prowess alone. They had no permanent function and their power was neither absolute nor hereditary. They headed their own tribe or, occasionally, an alliance of tribes, for a specific period.

Othniel: (Judges 3:9–11). The first judge, Othniel, the "boor", of the tribe of Judah, delivered Israel from eight years of oppression by Cushan-Rishathaim, an unidentified king of Aram-Naharaim*. Some scholars consider the story a legend, but A. Malamat equates the west Mesopotamian king with a Semitic usurper who invaded Egypt in the 12th century. Othniel captured Debir for his "brother" Caleb, which probably refers to an allied clan.

Ehud: (Judges 3:15–30). In another episode, Eglon, king of Moab, another "oppressor" of Israel, was assassinated by Ehud in retribution for invading Benjaminite* territory.

The Song of Deborah: Judges 4 and 5 contain the epic story of Deborah. Its date is uncertain. Many scholars put the episode towards the end of the 12th century or early in the 11th BCE, on the basis of biblical and archaeological evidence. Judges 5, the "Song" proper, is one of the earliest biblical epics and without peer in ancient writings for sheer drama. Verses 2–18, the Song of Victory, are an exhortation to resistance and a call to battle. Verses 19–30 give a poetic version of the story of the war, told in detail in prose in chapter 4 which is of greater historical value.

Both accounts emphasize Israel's main weaknesses: the disunity of the tribes and the lack of weapons. This second point is made more dramatically in a later document, I Sam. 13:19 (see Samuel*) which dates from the end of the period, but it was just as true of earlier times.

Deborah was faced with a federation of city kings led by Jabin of Hazor*, fortified centre of the Canaanite kingdom of Galilee, who had subjugated the northern Hebrew tribes. (There is a serious discrepancy between chapters 4 and 5, since the Song does not even mention Jabin or Hazor at all, as explained in the article, Hazor*.) As her commander, Deborah selected Barak ben Abinoam, although she was responsible for the strategy and victory of the Hebrew armies. It is characteristic of the epic style that throughout the whole period of the war, credit for the victory is ascribed to Yahweh alone — the chariots of Canaan are defeated by a flood, i.e., an act of god — while the decisive blow, the death of the Canaanite commander, Sisera, is administered by a woman.

The Battle God: Scholars disagree about whether the Song of Deborah was composed at the time of the events or close to them, or later, in the troubled days of the wars with the Philistines. An early date is claimed on the strength of the literary form and imagery of the epic which bears many characteristics typical of the early cultural scene. The Song of Deborah speaks of God coming out of his holy mountain amid storms and earthquakes to lead his people to victory. This was a picture directly related to Canaanite mythology and imagery in which the storm god, Ba'al **(581)** of the Lightning was represented as a warrior holding a club in his right hand and a lance — symbolizing lightning — in his left (see: Canaan, Gods of*). Similarly, the metaphor of Judges 5:4, repeated in the archaic form of Psalm 68:4–5, fits references to "Puissant Ba'al" in the Canaanite* poem of Ugarit*. But the similarity ends where the concepts differ. As the poem makes clear, in spite of the great bravery of some of the tribes, the victory was achieved solely and directly by God's drowning the chariots of the Canaanites, just as in the story of the crossing of the Sea in Exodus 14:25–28.

Jael's Triumph: The enemy armies were defeated by the Israelites, but, as Deborah had foretold, the glory of the victory went to a woman, Jael, a Kenite* nomad, who killed the enemy general, Sisera, with a tent peg while he slept. It is presumed that she committed this grievous breach of oriental hospitality from hatred of the enemies of the Israelites, who were probably allied with her people.

Gideon: (6:11; 8:32). Gideon's forty years as a judge began at a time when the tribes were suffering from oppressive raids from the Midianites and their allies on the fringes of the desert, east of Jordan. With a group of 300 seasoned warriors, divinely selected from a far larger number of volunteers (the figure of 32,000 in Jud, 7:3 is an exaggeration), Gideon carried out a series of night raids remarkable for their barbarity. Finally he defeated the invaders near Ein Harod. According to the record, the Israelites offered their triumphant leader a crown which Gideon refused on principle, saying: "I will not rule over you, and my son will not rule over you; the Lord will rule over you." (8:23).

Abimelech: (9:1–57). In the event, Abimelech, Gideon's son by a Shechemite concubine, set himself up as king of Shechem*. The date is uncertain. Some place it in the third quarter of the 11th century BCE, not long before Saul*, others believe it to be earlier. He seems to have had the backing of the influential Israelite families of the town. Using hired mercenaries, Abimelech killed off the other "seventy" children of his father (seventy, according to the idiom of epic tradition, meaning a large number) with the sole exception of the youngest son, Jotham. There was still too much resistance in Ephraim to the idea of monarchy in Israel for this attempt to succeed permanently. Abimelech maintained his kingship near Shechem for only three years and his experiment in monarchy died with him (Jud. 9).

Jephthah the Gileadite: (11:4; 12:7). When the Gileadites came under attack from the Ammonites, they turned to Jephthah, a free-booter of questionable birth, but an able and courageous military leader. The Ammonites claimed as the gift of their god, Chemosh, land also claimed by Gilead, east of the Jordan. The biblical narrative, reflecting the usage of the times, discloses that the Israelites would not dispute the spirit of the claim, but insisted that their god was the only true one and he had precedence.

Jephthah's Daughter: Judges 11 tells that before going into battle, Jephthah vowed that if successful he would sacrifice to God whatever came first from his home to greet his return. The first being who met him was his only daughter and, with her consent, he fulfilled his vow. In the opinion of some scholars this did not necessarily mean that she was killed as a human burnt offering, but that her womanhood was sacrificed and she was consecrated to god as a temple prostitute. This would be in line with Canaanite custom of the time (see Canaan*, Gods of). This view, however, is disputed by others who consider the interpretation far-fetched in view of the plain statement of the text: "offer up as a burnt offering".

Inter-tribal Conflicts: This was also a period of violent inter-tribal rivalries. Under Jephthah, the Gileadites fought the Ephraimites and slaughtered 42,000 of them according to Judges 12:6. The tribes were sufficiently isolated by distance and the Canaanite city states to have developed their own distinctive dialects. Fleeing Ephraimites in this story were trapped by their pronunciation of the testword "Shibboleth" (they said "Sibboleth").

Samson: Samson came from the tribe of Dan (Jud. 13–16). A Nazirite* from birth, he was renowned for strength and courage. The epic of his exploits and his romance with Delilah may originally have been a village folk tale reflecting social life and rivalries during this period of initial contact between the highly civilized Philistines* and the rural Hebrews. Secure in their five coastal city kingdoms, the Philistines*, who were equipped with chariots (see Samuel*) encroached continually on the land of the weak tribe of Dan to the north. With few arms and no chariots, the Hebrews were at their mercy. The book of Judges therefore could not relate that the Danites found a "Judge" who could deliver them from the enemy. Instead, it tells of a series of desperate partisan attacks centred around a single charismatic hero of herculean strength. Samson did not lead his tribe in war, but he sacrificed his life for his people. His story with its mingling of sex and hero-worship made a very attractive story of love and revenge. Scholars have pointed out the significance of the story's symbols. Samson's strength depended on his long hair, as the sun's power is in its rays; he was betrayed to his enemies when Delilah (her name means "night" — "leilah") shaved off his hair; blinded and humiliated, he yet revenged himself on his tormentors by hurling aside the central pillars of the temple of Gaza and bringing death to the entire assembly — and himself.

Six Minor Judges: Six "minor judges" mentioned with very few details in chapters 10:1–5 and 12:7–15 were probably military and civil leaders of the tribes in the central hills of Ephraim, the territory of Issachar and Menasseh. At a later stage, their judicial authority may have extended to Galilee. In the opinion of M. Noth, they were called "minor judges" to distinguish them from the other "great judges" who arose to save Israel from her enemies by virtue of their charismatic power. It is not known whether the "minor" judges were elected by vote or appointed in rotation, but the period of their mandate seems to yield some of the most authentic chronological data on the period preceding the formation of the kingdom.

The first of the six was Tola, of the tribe of Issachar, who was associated with Gideon of the tribe of Menasseh. His successor, Jair, belonged to Gilead, a half-tribe of Menasseh. These two judges link the fortunes of the north-eastern tribes of Issachar and Menasseh to those of the house of Joseph (see Tribes*). These two were followed by Ibsan, Elon and Abdon, who are listed in Judges 12:8–16.

Shamgar ben Anath: The tale of Shamgar seems to have been inserted later, possibly to bring the number of judges up to the classical twelve (see Tribes*). Shamgar was not an Israelite apparently; his name seems to be Hurrian.

He is mentioned twice in the book of Judges. Once (3:31) he is credited with slaying 600 Philistines with his oxgoad. An older reference occurs in the Song of Deborah (Jud. 5:6) which recalls the danger of travelling in his time. The Shamgar of the Song may have been a native of the town of Beth-Anath in Galilee and he may have repulsed a Philistine onslaught, temporarily relieving the Hebrews and Canaanites of this perennial menace.

The Danites Migrate North: One of the closing episodes of Judges tells of the founding of the Danite sanctuary following the migration of that tribe northward. The Samson episode (above) serves as a prelude to the defenseless state of the

Danites, left homeless by the strongly armed foot soldiers and chariots of the Philistines. Micha, a wealthy and influential Danite, made himself an idol or "teraphîm" and an "ephod" with which to obtain oracles, and appointed a Levite as priest. The greater part of the tribe was forced by the Philistine invasion to migrate and wrest a settlement for themselves from the area around the Canaanite town of Laish (Jud. 18:27–29). Receiving a favourable oracle from the priest, they took him and the cult objects with them and installed them in the captured town, which they renamed Dan* (in later times, one of the two important cultic centres outside Jerusalem). The priest was Jonathan, son of Gershom, who may have been the son of Moses. (This confusion is one of the difficulties with the early genealogies). Jonathan and his sons became the priests of the new Danite shrine. Significantly enough, the Hebrew text has an "n" suspended over the name Moshe, which is thus spelled Menashe. This was apparently an attempt to hide the distasteful fact that a priest tracing his descent from the great leader officiated at a shrine which was frowned upon by the biblical tradition.

The Gibeah Outrage: This extraordinary narrative (Jud. 19–20), which closes the book of Judges, tells how a Levite concubine was abused to death by Benjaminites of the town of Gibeah. The outraged Levite cut her corpse into 12 pieces, sending one to each tribe as a summons to vengeance. It is clear that one of the 12 pieces was meant for Benjamin too. The tribes united against Benjamin and practically wiped it out. In the end, human considerations prevailed and the surviving Benjaminites were allowed to take wives from across the Jordan, so as to replenish their tribe.

Conclusion: The Book of Judges ends on a revealing note: "In those days, there was no king in Israel; every man did what was right in his own eyes." (21:25). The heads of clans and families had yet to have their powers curbed in the national interest.

The ruins of many 12th and 11th century BCE villages and towns, repeatedly destroyed and blackened by fire, offer a vivid archaeological commentary on the chaotic conditions which prevailed during this period.

The story of Ruth* is also related to the period of Judges.

581

K

KENITES (Qenites). — The Kenites were a group of non-Israelite origin who lived a semi-nomadic life on the borders of Israel or in its midst. From the Bible, it seems that the Israelites believed the Kenites to be a very ancient tribe, descended from Cain, the son of Adam. Genesis records that Cain and his direct descendants, the early ancestors of the Kenites (Nu. 24:21–22; Jud. 4:11), were the founders of some of the basic arts and crafts, i.e. music and metal-working. Other references to Cain as the "brother" of Seth — Adam's third son and an ancient tribe mentioned in Egyptian and Mesopotamian sources going back to the 19th and 18th c. BCE — also indicate the biblical estimate of Kenite antiquity.

The Kenites first appear in the Bible as one of the many tribes indigenous to Patriarchal Palestine (Gn. 15:18–19), where they appear to have been concentrated in the area east of the Jordan but to have wandered as far south as Midian (North-west Arabia). Elements of the Kenites apparently made common cause with the Israelite tribes in search of new settlements within Palestine. They appear to have established themselves mainly in the Negeb, and later to have been absorbed into a unified Judah (I Sam. 30:29).

The Kenite clan, Heber, apparently settled in northern Palestine during the period of the Judges (Jud. 4:11). However, early Egyptian sources give place names in that area which seem to suggest that the Kenites had settled there as early as the 15th c. BCE. In his account of the battle of Megiddo (1479 BCE), Thutmosis III mentions a nearby "brook of the Kine" and it is possible that the "Kine" reflects the word "Kenites". If this is correct, then it seems to be an indication that the Kenites were wandering about Canaan before the arrival of the Hebrews (see below, Israel and the Kenites, and a reference to Jael's family in Judges 4:17–22). Alternatively, they may have been a section of a Kenite tribe which migrated northwards earlier than their fellows, later becoming absorbed by the tribes of Benjamin and Asher.

Social Standing: The name "Kenite" comes from "kayin" which means "worker of metals, smith, craftsman" and also "spear, lance". It has accordingly been assumed that the occupational speciality of the tribe was metal working. This is supported by the presence of copper in many regions familiar to the Kenites — e.g. the Sinai peninsula (ancient Midian) and the southern Negeb. It can scarcely be accidental, considers W.F. Albright, that in one of the oldest legends of the proto-Hebrews, and in the genealogical tables tracing Hebrew descent to their remote ancestors (Gn. 4:19–22), Cain is descended from Lamech and is credited with introducing copper and iron working.

The Kenites were apparently nomadic clans of smiths, who lived in tents and pastured their flocks. Studies on the social and sacred status of the smith in similar ancient and primitive societies have explained many of the biblical traditions concerning the Kenites.

Among cattle nomads or shepherds, the smith appears as a social outcast, despised for his manual labour — however essential for the making of weapons. He has a much higher status among farmers who also work with their hands. Besides forging their implements, the smith is their friend, councillor and often priest. Because his work is accompanied by traditional rites and ceremonies, the smith, according to R.L. Forbes, is easily identified with a magician. His power to transform ores into metals seems to come from the spirit world and even the nomad who despises him, fears and respects his magic powers. The term "iron smith" was also used of a magician in Phoenicia, and in ancient Java the smith had the same title as the priest.

In certain primitive societies, it was considered extremely dangerous to spill a smith's blood, for he was protected by the spirits with which he worked. In the same way, the Kenites bore "the mark of Yahweh" upon them as a protection from their enemies (Gn. 4:15, 24). The Kenites may have escaped being involved in the wars that raged all round them because of their peculiar status as smiths (Jud. 4:11 ff; I Sam. 15:6).

Israel and the Kenites: According to biblical traditions, relations between the Kenites and the Israelites were always of the friendliest. Moses, Israel's law-giver, married a Kenite woman. One tradition (Nu. 10:29–32) tells of Moses asking the Kenites to act as the Israelites' guide through the desert and they appear to have agreed and to have entered Palestine with the Israelite tribes (Jud. 1:16; cf. I Sam. 15:6). The presence of Kenites and other elements allied with the Hebrews and in possession of an area in southern Canaan reflects the entrance of various groups directly from the wilderness about Kadesh (see Exodus*). Such groups, who may already have been worshippers of Yahweh, were eventually absorbed into the structure of Judah. The Canaanite general, Sisera, oppressor of the northern Israelite tribes, was killed by Jael, a Kenite woman (Jud. 4:17–22; 5:24–27). David was also careful to cultivate their good will (I Sam. 27:10; 30:29), and his authority in the early days of his rule over southern Judah included this tribe.

Kenite Influence: How far the Kenites influenced Israelite life is a question which has been long debated without decisive result. According to the Bible (Ex. 18:13 ff), the judiciary system of the Israelites was of Kenite origin. It seems very likely that it was the Kenites who introduced the Israelites to the art of metallurgy, especially the use of the copper of the Negeb (see above, Social Standing).

The "Kenite Hypothesis": Some years ago, a "Kenite hypothesis" was proposed to the effect that Israel borrowed the worship of Yahweh from the Kenites. According to this theory, Yahweh was originally the Kenite-Midianite god, and Jethro, the chief-priest of his cult, taught the religion to his son-in law, Moses. Moses subsequently passed it on to the whole of Israel. While there must have been positive religious factors in the relationship between Israel and the Kenites, the main points of the hypothesis are hardly convincing.

The Rechabites: Some scholars see a connection between the Rechabites, an extreme religious element in Israel's society, and the Kenites. The Rechabites appear from I Ch. 2:55; 4:12 to have been a Kenite clan and they participated in the revolution of Jehu against the house of Omri (see Israel and Judah*: Jehu) and in the extermination of the cult of Ba'al at Samaria. The Chronicler's text connects the two communities which, apparently, followed a very similar way of life (see also Conquest*).

KINGS, BOOK OF. — *Outline: I. Organization and Contents: Sources; The Sagas of the Prophets; Native Sources of the Northern Kingdom; The Book of Kings and the Writing Prophets; Literary Form; Chronology; Date of Kings; The Text of Kings. II. Philosophy of the Biblical Historian: The Fall of Samaria; The Destruction of Judah; The Book of Kings and External Sources.*

I. ORGANIZATION AND CONTENTS. In the Hebrew Canon, the narratives of the Book of Kings are placed as the fourth and last book of the Former Prophets. Originally, the two books were one, as in the case of Samuel*. They are a chronological continuation of Samuel and are about the same length, I Kings with 22 chapters, II Kings with 25.

The historical narratives of the two books cover a period of about four centuries, which may be divided into three main periods:

A. I K. 1–11: The first two chapters complete the history of David's reign which is the main subject of II Sam. Chs. 3–11 present the dazzling picture of Solomon's rule over the United Kingdom, the climax of the first book of Kings. The book is completed by a chronological account of the reigns of the kings of the divided kingdom.

B. Chs. I K. 12–II K. 17 deal with the schism and then give parallel accounts of Israel and Judah*.

C. II K. 18–25 continues the history of the Kingdom of Judah alone, after the fall of the Northern Kingdom of Samaria, up to the destruction of Jerusalem and the Exile* of the Judeans.

A. **The United Kingdom:** Chs. 1–2 of I K., dealing with the last days of David and the accession of Solomon to the throne, may not have been written by the author of the rest of Kings, nor may they derive from the circles from which I and II Sam. originated, for there is no continuity between the end of Samuel (chs. 21–24 form an appendix to the rest of II Sam.) and the first chapters of I Kings. However these chapters are a continuation of II Sam. 20 and complete the account of David's reign. — II Sam. 9–20 and I K. 1–2 appear to form a unity.

The Divided Kingdoms of Israel and Judea are treated as follows:

I K. 3	describes the beginning of Solomon's reign;
4	gives extracts from the royal annals;
5 – 7	record Solomon's building activities;
8: 1– 9: 9	is the account of the dedication of the Temple;
9:10–10:29	contain miscellaneous data on the reign, especially concerning Solomon's economic activities;
11	recounts the decline of Solomon's kingdom.
I K. 12: 1–24	the Schism;
12:25–14:20	Jeroboam, king of Israel;
14:21–15:24	Rehoboam, Abiyah and Asa (Judah);
15:25–16:28	Nadab to Omri (Israel);

16:29–22:40	Ahab of Israel — including the Elijah story cycle:
22:41–50	Jehoshaphat of Judah;
22:51–II K. 1:18	Ahaziah of Israel.
II K. 2:1–25	Completion of the Elijah stories with Elisha's succession;
3: 1– 8:29	The Elisha cycle and the reigns of Jehoram of Israel and Jehoram and Ahaziah of Judah;
9: 1–10:36	Jehu of Israel;
11–12	Athaliah and Jehoash in Judah;
13: 1–25	Jehoahaz and Jehoash of Israel;
14: 1–29	Amaziah (Judah) and Jeroboam II of Israel;
15: 1–31	Uzziah of Judah; chaos in Israel;
15:32–16:20	Jotham and Ahaz in Judah;
17	The destruction of the Northern Kingdom.
II K. 18–20	Hezekiah's reign; Sennacherib's siege of Jerusalem; Hezekiah and Isaiah;
21	Manasseh and Amon;
22: 1–23:30a	Josiah and the religious reform (also termed the Deuteronomistic reform);
23:30b–25: 7	The last kings of Judah and the last days of Jerusalem;
25: 8–30	Destruction of the state of Judah and the Exile. The last verses (25:22–30) recounting the murder of Gedaliah and the fate of Jehoiachin after the death of Nebuchadrezzar, may be later appendices.

The events of the reigns of the above kings — in the context of Israelite and general history — are dealt with in the articles on "Israel and Judah, Kingdoms of*" and the major personalities (David and Solomon*; Elijah*; Elisha*, Amos*, Isaiah*, Jeremiah*) which examine the biblical record in relation to the contemporary background.

Sources: The Book of Kings marks the development in Hebrew history-writing from the straightforward record of events to the presentation of history and interpretation side by side. The authors had access to the official records kept in the royal archives and called "sefer dibrê ha-yamîm" (chronicles) and these are cited for nearly every reign from Solomon's time (I K. 11:41) to the end of Israel (II K. 15:31) and Judah (II K. 23:28). There are references to "mazkîrim" (archivists; see Government and Authority*) during both David's and Solomon's reigns (II Sam. 8:16; 20:24; I K. 4:3) and under the later kings of Judah (II K. 18:18, 37; II Ch. 34:8). This was the usual custom of the time; the Assyrian and Babylonian annals and chronicles are familiar today, as are the records of the Hittites and those kept at Mari and at Ugarit. Similar records were apparently kept in the Northern and Southern Kingdoms. Although the former were destroyed by the Assyrians, it seems likely that copies had been made and preserved and that these were available to the Judean editor of Kings.

The first source quoted in the book is "the book of the acts of Solomon" (I K. 11:41). Then come the "Book of the Chronicles of the kings of Israel" (ibid 14:19; passim) and "the Book of the Chronicles of the kings of Judah" (14:29, passim; these must not be confused with the biblical Book of Chronicles*; see article). It is not certain just what these works were. Some scholars maintain that the "Books of the Chronicles of the kings" were not court records, but popular works which could be assumed to be familiar to readers of the biblical works. Other scholars dispute this, maintaining that even popular works must have been similar to the royal archives. Their composition was probably a slow process and, clearly, by the time they were completed, they contained much more detail then the canonical books of Kings.

In addition to such secular sources, the writers of Kings also appear to have made use of the records kept in the Temple archives. The style of I K. 6–8:13 (the building and dedication of the Temple) has a distinctly priestly touch while the following passage (8:14–61; Solomon's address to the people), reads very much like the work of the Deuteronomist (see Biblical Criticism*).

The Sagas of the Prophets: Another very important source seems to have been the records made in the Northern Kingdom of the acts and sayings of prophets living there — notably the "Acts of Elijah*" and the "Acts of Elisha*". The sagas concerning these prophets (see the respective articles) were written from the point of view of the Northern Kingdom — which was not necessarily that of the Judean editor of Kings. Nevertheless, he combined a good deal of their material with the accounts of the reigns of Ahab and his immediate successors (I K. 17 to II K. 9, with a postscript in II K. 13:14–21). These prophetic sagas include the narrative of the rout of Ben-Hadad (I K. ch. 20) and the single reference to the career of Micaiah the prophet (I K. 22). It is possible that the whole of I K. 17 to II K. 10 represents a continuous prophetic document in which a record of certain important events was inserted, although it is difficult to distinguish between the prophetic story and the historical annals. The sagas of the prophets are believed to have been written close to the time when they lived, but these chapters also contain one or two prophetic stories which combine narrative and homiletic interpretation (for explanation, see Biblical Criticism*: Aggadic Interpretation). Such passages occur especially in I K. 11:29–39; I K. 16:1–4; II K. 23:15–20 passim. (The reason for their inclusion is discussed below, Philosophy of the Biblical Historian.)

Native Sources of the Northern Kingdom: The traces of these older northern sources which are mainly preserved in the biblical book of Kings are proof of the existence of a native literature which was largely lost at the time of the destruction of Israel. The Judean editor of the book of Kings made use of such material where it helped to answer the questions he had set himself: Why had the United Kingdom been split up and how was God's will and the promised protection of His People expressed in the troubled history of the Northern Kingdom? Material that did not seem relevant to this purpose was excluded and subsequently forgotten.

In spite of some theories to the contrary, it seems that there is no connection between the sources of Kings listed above and the hypothetical J and E sources of the Pentateuch (see Biblical Criticism*).

The Book of Kings and the Writing Prophets: Prophetic stories in relation to the kingdom of Judah are much more rare. The most notable example is the story of the encounter between Isaiah and king Hezekiah (II K. 18–20), first at the time of Sennacherib's siege of Jerusalem (see Assyria*), then later during Hezekiah's sickness. Another example is the prediction of Josiah's reform by the anonymous prophet (I K. 13:2–10 and II K. 23:15–20). In both instances the object is the special interest of the Jerusalem sanctuary.

Literary Form: The book's discussion of all the kings of the divided monarchy follows a fixed pattern for the beginning and end of each reign. Each king of Judah is introduced by a formula which synchronizes his reign with the sequence of kings in Israel, gives his age at accession, the length and capital of his reign, his mother's name and an assessment of his conduct — whether he did what was "evil" or "right in the eyes of the Lord".The criterion is his degree of devotion to pure Yahwism, i.e. whether worship at the "high places*" was suppressed or encouraged.

The account of the reign concludes with another formula which refers to the source (the "Book of the Chronicles of" Israel or Judah), records the burial of the king and gives the name of his successor. The kings of the Northern Kingdom are treated within a similar framework, although the introductory formulae give fewer details, and sometimes include data about contemporary foreign kings and events.

Chronology: There were two different ways of calculating the length of a reign. One followed Egyptian practice and counted the year of accession twice — it was the last year of the dead king and the first year of his successor. The other method, copied from Assyro-Babylonian custom, counted the year of accession once only as the last year of the dead king. The new king's reign formally began at the next New Year. (This can be seen in the chronological table at the end of the article on Israel and Judah, Kingdoms of*.)

Additional difficulties about dating are caused by the double calendar (see article*) used in the days of the monarchy. However, on the whole, recent reconstructions of the chronology of events in the two kingdoms seem to be reasonably acceptable, and there is general agreement between narrow limits. Some of the more important dates which have been agreed place Solomon's death between 931 and 922 BCE (not earlier or later); Jehu's rise in 842/1; the fall of Samaria between 723 and 721; the fall of Judah and Jerusalem in 597 and 587/6 (variations are relatively slight).

Date of Kings: The book of II Kings ends with the release of king Jehoiachin from confinement, an event which took place around 561 BCE. On the assumption that the book was written after his death, many scholars take this choice of a conclusion as evidence for final composition of the book around the middle of the 6th c. BCE.

However, there are a number of indications that at least the greater part of the work was composed earlier and it is possible that the last verses (II K. 25:22–30) dealing with events following the death of Nebuchadrezzar may be appendices, composed later than the main body of the book. This is borne out by the fact that the latest previous event recorded in Kings is at least 20 years earlier than the release of Jehoiachin, indicating that the book had been written earlier and that the note of his release was added at a later date. However, the most important clues to a date during the monarchy are the writer's openly avowed aim of protecting the people from the mistakes made in the past and the audience he seems to be addressing. For instance, phrases like the "to this day" which occurs here and there (I K. 8:8; 9:21; II K. 2:22 passim) are a strong indication that the book was written for people living in Judea before its destruction. On the other hand, it is true of course that the original substance of the book was in existence long before the final editing or compilation took place and the phrase may, therefore, come from the source, not the editor (see section II below).

There is other evidence. According to one opinion, for instance, the passage I K. 1–2 was written by a contemporary of David or, at least, is an objective historical record in the classical style. Similarly, the narratives of the schism (I K. 11:26–12:24); the revolt against Athaliah (II K. 11) and the account of Josiah's reform (II K. 22–23) all bear the marks of contemporary history. Moreover, the narrative of II K. 18–20 is duplicated in Isaiah 36–39. Some scholars regard this as a good indication that it comes from contemporary memoirs or records, although others consider that the section was inserted wholesale in Isaiah in a place to which it does not belong.

These differences of opinion do not affect the date of the final process of combining the various elements into a coherent book. The first edition seems to date from the last decades of the 7th c. BCE, since the author is especially interested in Josiah as a sort of second David. The material after the death of Josiah is relatively brief and suggests a second edition about 585/80 BCE, with the final edition about 560–550.

However, as the final compilation is obviously Deuteronomist in tone, a date as late as the Exile* can also be justified in the opinion of some scholars. Those who hold this view consider that the "to this day" phrases were inserted deliberately to make the material appear older. Alternatively, the compilers may have copied such formulae from their earlier source without alteration — something that happened in relation to many biblical documents out of respect for ancient traditions. This could have been done in the present case, even though the writers gave their later interpretation to the overall presentation of the book. If they were working after the destruction of the kingdom, they may well have been activated by the desire to show that disaster had befallen their people because they had not conformed to the compilers' understanding of God's will.

The Text of Kings: There are a number of disagreements in wording between the Septuagint and the Massoretic texts of the books of Kings (see Bible Canon and Text*). These are the results of various factors, one of them being the use by the Septuagint translators of a pre-Massoretic, still fluid text. As in the case of Samuel, the Septuagint version of Kings is based on a different pre-Massoretic text.

However, none of these variations affect the translation very seriously. Essentially, the meaning of the books has not been altered. (See also Chronicles, Books of* and their literary relationship to the books of Kings.)

II. PHILOSOPHY OF THE BIBLICAL HISTORIAN.

The book of Kings was not written as a mere recital of events — which is the case in a chronicle. It gives the historical facts, interpreted in the light of the compiler's underlying religious intention. The writer of Kings aimed at showing how God directs the affairs of the world and how the divine purpose was to be achieved through human history. This approach emphasizes the direct relationship between sin and punishment; repentance and divine mercy, and is the same philosophy of history that is to be found in Judges* and Samuel*. It results in a historical record which is distinctly unbalanced by modern standards. Events are judged and chronicled almost exclusively in terms of their importance for the cult and the Law, and their relevance to the writer's basic theme. As a result the association between moral principle and actual experience is overdone, although the record is essentially empirical. It also includes a sincere self-criticism according to the above criteria. For example, the secession of the northern tribes from the divinely ordained united kingdom achieved by David, is shown to have originated when Solomon forsook Yahweh and allowed his heart to be "turned after other gods" (I K. 11:4–13:32).

The Fall of Samaria: Similarly, the fall of the Northern Kingdom (II K. 17) is shown as divine retribution for continued defiance of what the Deuteronomist conceived to be the true religion. Vs. 9–23 of this chapter constitute an editorial comment on the disaster drawing a clear connection between the destruction of the kingdom and the cumulative sin (i.e. cultic defection) of the people in worshipping at the high places* of Bethel and Dan and showing reverence to the Golden Calves put up by Jeroboam (cf. vs. 16 ff). While the narrator does not often accuse the Judean kings of practicing or encouraging worship at the high places, he does so consistently in the case of the kings of Samaria. The career of nearly every king is summed up in the phrase that he "did evil in the sight of the Lord" (see Literary Form, above; also Idol Worship in Israel*). The almost unremitting condemnation of the kings of Israel is always justified by reference to "the way of Jeroboam and his sin which he made Israel to sin" (I K. 15:26, 34; II K. 3:3 passim). Worshipping the "Golden Calves" of Jeroboam was, in the eyes of the author of Kings, the cardinal sin which no material achievements could mitigate.

The Destruction of Judah was also traced back to Solomon's apostasy, and attributed especially to Menasseh's evildoing and acts of desecration. Other Judean kings were also condemned for tolerating the high places and their pagan associations (I K. 15:3; II K. 8:18, 27 passim). Even those kings (Jehoshaphat, Amaziah, Uzziah and Jotham) who were found otherwise meritorious, could not be wholeheartedly praised because the high places persisted. The ideal monarch, from this point of view, was Hezekiah (II K. 18:3–7) who "did what was right in the eyes of the Lord" and "removed the high places . . ." The only king to equal him was Josiah (II K. 22:2). All the other kings were found wanting in their care for the Temple, its building, priesthood and cult.

This is a distinctly Deuteronomistic attitude of course (see Denteronomy*; Israel and Judah*, Part V). Deuteronomy states quite specifically that obedience to the Law will be rewarded with earthly wellbeing while disobedience will inexorably bring disaster. One of the objects of the compiler of Kings was to show that this had proved true in the past and would continue to do so. His whole work, both its literary form and its subject matter, was dominated by this approach.

The Book of Kings and External Sources: The historical value of the book of Kings is fully accepted but allowance has to be made for the point of view of its author and his account has to be supplemented and modified by the study of extra-biblical sources. The position is particularly apparent with regard to the reign of Omri (see Israel and Judah*, Part II). Contemporary records from Assyria (referred to in the articles on Assyria*, Israel and Judah*) and elsewhere (e.g. the Mesha stone, see Moab*) have proved Omri to have been one of Israel's most illustrious kings. Nevertheless, true to his religious bias, the writer of Kings dismissed Omri's reign in the most cursory fashion (I K. 16:21–28), noting only that Omri "walked in all the ways of Jeroboam the son of Nebat" and neglected the suppression of the sanctuaries. The same attitude has made Ahab almost a by-word for an evil despot, yet, in the light of modern research, his reign now appears as a time of economic prosperity and political eminence, in spite of political corruption and religious apostasy (see also Inscriptions*; Seals*). We hare no picture of an Israelite king except the Assyrian relief (**551**). This representation of a King in Cyprus (6th c. BCE) may be suggestive (**582**).

KINGSHIP (see Government, Authority and Kingship)

582

L

LAMENTATIONS BOOK OF. — The book of Lamentations ("Echa" in Hebrew, from the word which opens the first, second and fourth chapters) is the third of the five scrolls of the Hagiographa. Its contents earned the work the title "Lamentations".

Authorship: The Talmud (Baba Bathra 16a) and the Aramaic translation (Jonathan ben Uziel) ascribed the book to the prophet Jeremiah and the version in the Septuagint includes an introduction translated from the Hebrew which also assumes that Jeremiah wrote Lamentations after the destruction of the Temple. In the Septuagint, Syriac and Latin versions of the Bible, Lamentations follows directly after the book of Jeremiah and it is part of both Jewish and Christian tradition that he was its author. The tradition is supported by the reference in II Ch. 35:25 to a lament for Josiah composed by Jeremiah which was "written in the laments". This suggests that this form of literature was connected with Jeremiah from a very early time but, in fact, the book of "Lamentations" itself contains no evidence to support the theory that he wrote it. Most modern scholars consider it to be of composite authorship (see below).

Style and Contents: The book is a collection of five laments bewailing the destruction of the Temple, the loss of Judah's independence, the ruin of the country and the exile of her people. The poems are composed according to an acrostic pattern in which the first verse begins with the first letter of the alphabet, and the first letters of the succeeding verses make up the complete alphabet. Although the fifth poem is not an acrostic, it has the same number of verses (22) as 1, 2 and 4.

In style, the first two were written in the "Kinah metre", in which a long phrase of three stressed syllables alternates with a short phrase of two. The metre of the other laments is so loose that it is questionable whether there is a kinah metre throughout Lamentations. The fifth poem is made up of parallel sentences of equal length. The metrical style and alphabetical arrangement of the verses show that the laments were composed in a formal, sophisticated fashion, as an elaborate litany of woe (see Poetry*).

All the laments bemoan the sins that aroused God's anger and occasioned the disasters that befell the country. God's judgment is accepted, even though the poems express a feeling that He has been over-severe in carrying out the punishment so ruthlessly. They plead repentance and pray for forgiveness and the restoration of His people to God's favour, "Renew our days as of old!" (5:21). Unlike the others, the third lament is a more personal cry of distress, referring obliquely to the national calamity. The fifth is more of a prayer for help and forgiveness than the other four.

Significance and Composition: The great interest of Lamentations — apart from its purely literary merits — lies in the picture the book provides of the thoughts and emotions which the fall of Jerusalem aroused at the time.

So far as can be seen, the five laments were written separately either by people who had witnessed the destruction of Jerusalem or, possibly, a little later by men who were still deeply affected by these memories. Scholars find the question of authorship very difficult to settle definitely. The poems were actually collected and written down during the Exile in Babylon when, probably, they were used as a liturgy for the days of fasting and lamenting. To this day, the book of Lamentations is read in Jewish synagogues on the eve of the Ninth of Ab (the day on which both Temples were destroyed). The acrostic arrangement of the verses of the laments, making it easier to remember them by heart, also suggests that from the very beginning they were intended for use in public mourning ceremonies.

LAND (see Property).

LANGUAGES, BIBLICAL. — The languages in which the original text of the Bible was written are Hebrew, Aramaic and Greek. Hebrew and Aramaic are closely related to each other, both being Semitic languages, while Greek belongs to the Indo-European family (to which Latin, English, etc. also belong). The existence of three biblical languages is an expression of the cultural history of Palestine: during the First Temple period the Jews spoke Hebrew; during the Second Temple period Aramaic increased in importance, and during the Hellenistic* and Roman* periods, Greek held an important place in the life of the country, among both Jews and Gentiles.

Hebrew Language: This is the language of most of the Old Testament, most of the Dead Sea Scrolls*, and is probably the original language of a large number of Apocrypha* and Pseudepigrapha*. A form of Hebrew was spoken in Palestine even before the Israelite Conquest*, as is proved by a number of Hebrew words interspersed in the Akkadian text of the Tel el-Amarna Letters*. Since the Israelites came from outside Canaan, they must have adopted its language either during the Patriarchal* period or after the Conquest*. Some scholars hold that Hebrew as we know it is a mixture of Canaanite and the original Israelite language. It is very closely related to various languages which were spoken in the immediate neighbourhood of Canaan, notably Phoenician* and Moabite*. Other languages which bordered on Hebrew, such as Ammonite and Edomite* are unknown today for lack of a sufficient number of written documents. They probably also resembled Hebrew, as evidenced by seals with names, etc. At the time of the Conquest several other, less similar languages were also used in Palestine. These were Amorite, Hittite, Hurrian and the two great languages of civilization of the time, Akkadian and Egyptian. Amorite was apparently the mother language from which Canaanite and Aramaic come. All these have left traces among the approximately 500 foreign words which Biblical Hebrew included.

The map accompanying this article shows the geographic distribution of languages in antiquity (**583**).

Hebrew Writing: The Hebrews probably also took their alphabet* which was not perfectly adapted to the sounds of Hebrew from the Phoenicians*. This is the same alphabet which was also taken over by the Greeks, and from which all European scripts of today derive (see Alphabet and Writing*). In its original form, the Hebrew script had no signs for vowels, and these had to be guessed. During biblical times, the vowels *i*, *u* and *o* came to be indicated in an imperfect and inconsistent way; signs for final vowels and *a* and *e* were also added. Only in the 7th–9th c. CE. did various methods of noting the vowels by signs placed above, in or below the letters come into use. The "pointing" system seen in printed Hebrew Bibles was perfected early in the 10 c. CE. The form of the letters used nowadays for Hebrew is not the original Hebrew alphabet, but one which was substituted for it soon after the Babylonian Exile, having been developed by the royal scribes of Babylonia for writing Aramaic. The ancient Hebrew alphabet which appears in the pre-Exilic inscriptions and letters, as illustrated in the article on Inscriptions*, lingered on, however, and appears in some Dead Sea Scrolls* and on Maccabaean* and Bar-Kochba* coins. It is still used by the Samaritans*.

Development of The Language: Four periods can be distinguished in the development of Hebrew: 1. The early period, represented by the Song of Deborah, the Blessing of Jacob (Gn. 49), the Song of the Sea (Ex. 15), the Song of Moses (Dt. 32) and other early pieces of poetry*. This seems to have been a northern dialect. 2. The classical language of the period of the Monarchy, probably developed in Jerusalem by royal scribes* and by priests* and prophets*. This is Hebrew in its purest and most beautiful form. 3. The language of the Second Temple period, including the Dead Sea Scrolls*, which was mostly an imperfect imitation of the classical language. It was only laboriously learned for writing purposes, the real spoken language being 4. Mishnaic Hebrew a popular dialect, which was used as a literary language for the literature of the Pharisees* and Rabbis* after the destruction of the Second Temple. Its influence is noticeable in the Book of Ecclesiastes and in the Apocryphal* book of Ben Sira. The Dead Sea Copper Scroll is in this dialect. Mishnaic Hebrew was known to the authors of the Ancient Bible Versions, and they not infrequently interpreted biblical words in senses more proper to Mishnaic Hebrew. About 200 CE, Hebrew ceased to be spoken, but it continued as a written language and produced a vast literature in the Middle Ages and in modern times. This literature also includes many important Bible commentaries, such as those of Rashi, Ibn Ezra, and David Kimhi (11th–12th c. CE). Since 1880 CE, Hebrew has become a spoken language again, and is now employed in the State of Israel in a form not too different from the language of the Hebrew Bible. Modern Hebrew is a combination of all previous stages of Hebrew, biblical and Mishnaic, though it has taken from each only the elements that suit it, with the addition of a new vocabulary based on Hebrew roots.

Aramaic was first spoken around Damascus in Southern Syria about 1000 BCE. From there it spread steadily, until it ousted Akkadian as the spoken language in Assyria and Babylonia. The Persian Empire (549–331 BCE) employed Aramaic as its official language. The Aramaic parts of the Old Testament (Ezr. 4–7, Dan. 2–7) are in this "Imperial" (or "Royal") Aramaic. By processes still imperfectly understood, Aramaic penetrated into the speech of most of the populations of Palestine during the succeeding centuries. In this process, however, it changed into "Middle" Aramaic. It became necessary to translate the Old Testament into this

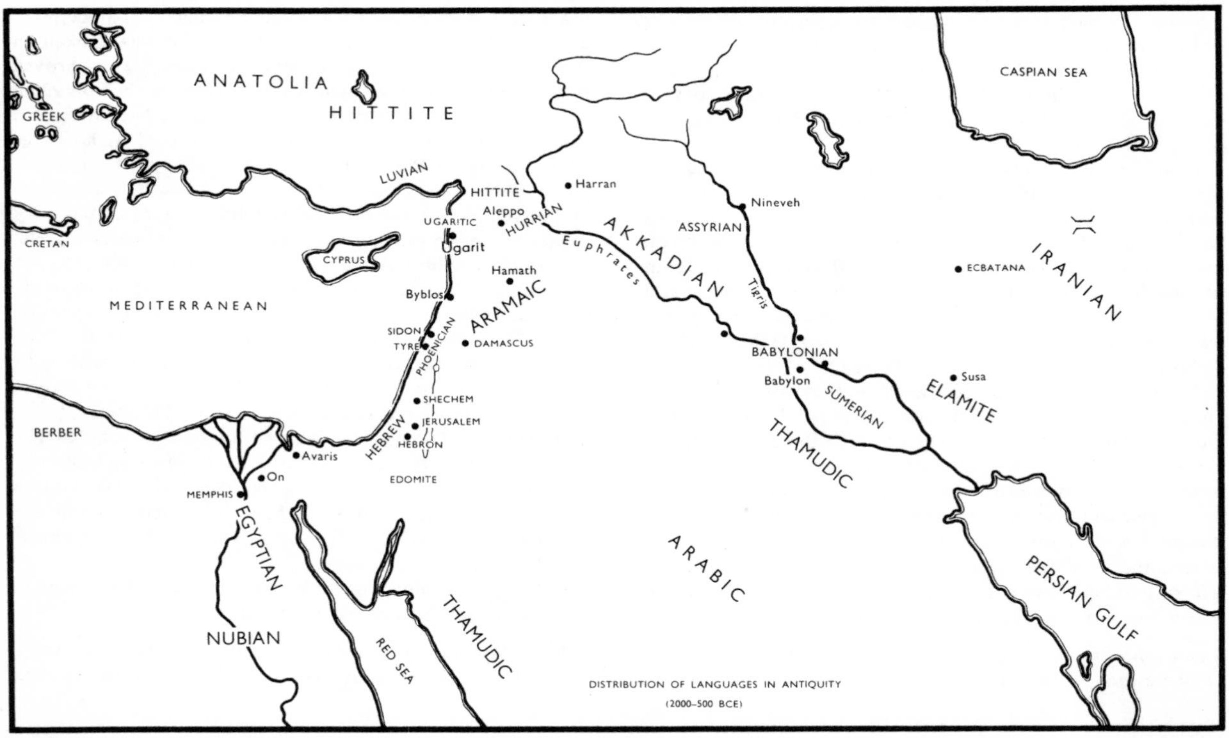

DISTRIBUTION OF LANGUAGES IN ANTIQUITY (2000–500 BCE)

dialect. These are the various Targums (see Translations of the Bible*). Bible translations were also made into the Christian Palestinian Aramaic of southern Palestine, and into the Iraqi dialect called Syriac (in which a large Christian literature exists). The language which Jesus spoke, and in which some words spoken by him appear in the New Testament, is Middle Aramaic of Galilee, similar to that of the Targums, but probably most closely related to the more popular language of the Palestinian Talmud of the 3rd–4th c. CE. We now have the Genesis Apocryphon and other literature in Aramaic from Qumran. Fragments of Tobit in Aramaic have also been found there and parts of the Enoch literature (see Apocrypha*, Dead Sea Scrolls*).

Greek is the language of the New Testament as we know it. The earliest documents in Greek known to us are the Mycenean texts, written in the 15th c. BCE in southern Greece, in a pictorial syllabic script borrowed from Crete (see Aegean Civilization*; Alphab.*). Later, the Greeks adopted the Phoenician alphabet, perfecting it by using some letters not needed in Greek for writing the vowels, and adding a few letters. Greek spread early into Asia Minor and other Mediterranean areas. It was written in a number of distinct dialects. As a result of the conquests of Alexander the Great (4th c. BCE), Greek spread all over the Middle East as a language of civilization, in a form based upon the dialect of Athens (Attic), but developed in various ways which distinguish it as Hellenistic Greek (Koine). The language of the New Testament is thus rather different from that of the great Greek writers. Much light is thrown upon it by contemporary documents on papyrus found in the soil of Egypt. Egyptian Greek, perhaps with a special Jewish tinge, is also represented by the earlier Greek translation of the Old Testament, the Septuagint*, and its various revisions. These created the monotheistic religious terminology used in the New Testament. The Greek of the first three Gospels and of Acts is simpler and more colloquial than that of Paul's epistles and of the Fourth Gospel (see Hellenism and Jewry*; Hellenism in the Diaspora*).

The Aramaic Source of the Gospels: A widely-accepted scholarly theory assumes that large parts of the first three Gospels (or perhaps the whole Gospel of Mark) were not originally composed in Greek, but in the spoken Aramaic of Palestine. This school ascribes some of the un-Greek ways of expression of the Gospels to this process of translation into Greek, and also interprets a few difficulties in the text as results of faulty translation. Be this as it may, there is little doubt that the spirit of New Testament Greek is close to Hebrew and Aramaic, and as we now know, particularly to the language of the Dead Sea Scrolls; so much so, that we may with some justification speak of a single biblical language expressed indifferently in Hebrew, Greek and Aramaic. The letters of the time of Bar-Kochba* (132–134 CE), found in 1949 and 1961–62 CE in caves near the Dead Sea, show how the same individuals used Mishnaic Hebrew, Aramaic and Greek with equal facility, the way of expression being strikingly similar in all three languages. They have been described as hebraized Aramaic and aramaicized Hebrew, and we may add, semitized Greek. Most probably Jesus also spoke these three languages in his ministry.

LAW OF ISRAEL. — *Outline: I. Biblical Law and Ancient Near Eastern Codes; Mesopotamian Codes. II. Characteristics of Israelite Law: Divine Authority; Effect of Divinely Imposed Law; Man in Relation to the Law; Humane Laws; Remote Sources of Israel's Law; Affinities with Contemporary Codes; The Law as a Treaty with God. III. The Legislative Codes of the Pentateuch (The Law). IV. Development of Covenant Law; Israel's Lawgivers. V. Changes in Conditions and Law before the Exile: Law of Sacrifice; Social Legislation; Prosbul; Murder and Manslaughter; Lex talionis; Magic and Sorcery; Formulation of Codes. VI. Post-Exilic Law: The Scribes; Development of Oral Law; The Oral Law; Life under the Law; The Study of the Torah; Practical Observances; Dietary Laws; Sabbath; Clothing. VII. Law and Torah in New Testament Times: Conflicts; Essenes (Dead Sea Sectaries); Jesus and the Law; The Law and Christianity.*

I. BIBLICAL LAW AND ANCIENT NEAR EASTERN CODES. Law is essentially the practical expression of the customs, traditions and ethics of a society. The codes of law which the ancient societies of Mesopotamia and, later, Israel produced all reveal a fundamental uniformity which reflects the common civilization which they shared and which is perhaps of greater importance than the variations which can be found between different regions and epochs.

Neither the Mesopotamian codes nor the three sets of Israelite "Laws of Moses" began as sets of regulations to which judges were bound when deciding actual cases in court. Rather, the cases that were brought to court were decided on the basis of current traditions and attitudes. The codification of the laws was designed to express a society's sense of justice and "rightness". It was done with a literary and, especially, educational purpose, not a judicial one.

Mesopotamian Codes: Archaeological discoveries made since the beginning of this century have revealed six different Mesopotamian codes, three of them ante-dating the famous Hammurabi Code. They are:

Ur-Nammu Code, from the 21st c. BCE, Sumer; Code of Bilalama (Eshnunna), from the 20th c. BCE, Babylonia; Code of Lipit-Ishtar (Isin), from the mid-19th c. BCE, Babylonia; Hammurabi Code, from Babylon of 1700 BCE; Hittite Code, from the mid-15th c. BCE, Asia Minor; Assyrian Code (Aššur) from the 14th–12th c. BCE, Assyria.

The Sumerian King and lawmaker Ur-Nammu. the first "Moses" on record, is shown (**584**) making libation to the tutelary dieties of Ur.

The Covenant Code of Exodus which apparently dates from the 11th c. BCE and from older materials going back to Moses, such as the Decalogue, came *after* these. Most modern scholars agree that the Covenant Code drew, either directly or indirectly, on the earlier case laws of the Middle East. The connection is especially apparent in those conditional laws which are framed, in the hypothetical manner "if a man etc.... then he shall..." (the form known as *casuistic* or case law, with the implication that it arises from actual court decisions, see below).

The literature on law in the Pentateuch provided the texts to be used in the instruction of future generations. The

584

great lawgiver, Hammurabi, remarks in the epilogue to his code that the laws engraved there are intended for future generations — especially the kings that would follow him. Indeed, the Code of Hammurabi was used as a text book in the schools of Mesopotamia for another thousand years.

This educational aspect is even more pronounced in the Israelite tradition. There are repeated injunctions to fathers to teach their children the commandments (e.g. Dt. 6:7) and the whole community of Israel, men and women, young and old, is directed to gather together periodically to listen to a reading of the laws of the Torah (the Pentateuch).

Beyond this common attitude towards education and the shared form of some of the laws, the comparison of Israelite codes with those of Mesopotamia reveals differences rather than similarities, both in the laws themselves and in the social and ethical values on which they were based.

The authority for Mesopotamian law was the king, the sole arbiter in all matters of government and jurisdiction. The very stele (**585a, b**) on which the laws were engraved served as a monument to a just and righteous king (šar-mišorun) and in the epilogue to the Code of Hammurabi threatened dire penalties on anyone daring to replace his enactments.

II. CHARACTERISTICS OF ISRAELITE LAW. **Divine Authority**: The authority for Israelite law is God's will. The king is as much subject to these laws as the meanest citizen. The only place where the king is mentioned (Dt. 17:14–20) expressly directs him to subject himself to the authority of God (see Government and Authority*), to learn from the "Book of the Law" how to fear God and keep his commandments, and to avoid amassing material wealth so "that his heart may not be lifted up above his brethren" (Dt. 17:20). The sole lawgiver and judge is God, a fact of which the Israelites were extremely proud: "He declares his word to Jacob, His statutes and ordinances to Israel. He has not dealt thus with any other nation; they do not know His ordinances." (Ps. 147:19–20). The 3rd c. BCE Greek writer Diodorus Siculus refers (I, 94, 2) to the interesting fact that the Jews attribute the Mosaic Laws to God Himself.

Effect of Divinely Imposed Law: The practical significance of the belief that a law is literally God-given is to make it absolutely and unalterably binding. At first glance this may seem a difference only in formulation but, in effect, it goes much deeper. A law imposed by human authority can always be changed, by the same or another (equally human) authority. God's laws are the expression of the unchangeable will of the deity. The formulation of that will in specific commands or edicts might change — as can be seen from variations in the biblical codes — but the underlying authority of the will of God was for all time.

The concept also affected attitudes towards transgression of the law. In Mesopotamia, the law fulfilled the social function of protecting the state and its citizens. The manner in which this should be done was determined by the king, who stood in the same relation to the laws of his land as God did in relation to the Law of the Bible. Breaking the law in Mesopotamia implied disobedience to the king's authority and it was he who had power to decide whether the transgressor should be punished or excused. For instance, in Babylonian (Paragraph 129), Assyrian (Para. 14–6) and Hittite (Para. 198) law, adultery is treated as a communal offence. However, the king is authorized to exonerate the adulteress if her husband forgave her (the wife of the adulterer was not consulted). The law offered the husband protection of his rights but if he did not insist on them, the law would not be enforced against his will.

Under Israelite law, the husband of the adulteress was not consulted, nor could the king be asked to intervene. Adultery was a transgression of a divine law which neither the husband nor the king (the highest human authority) could forgive. Punishment — in this case death (Dt. 22: 22–32) — was decreed by God and had to be enforced, although God could forgive. In fact it is the essence of biblical religion that God may and does forgive sins with a high hand — generally on the basis of genuine repentance. The distinction is not that transgressions are unforgivable, but that no human authority may forgive them on his own initiative. God's representative, however, could pronounce such forgiveness. Conversely, while certain crimes were, of course, condemned on religious or ethical grounds in Mesopotamia, this did not affect the laws relating to them, for legislation there was a secular matter.

In Israel it was religious. Moreover, the laws represented the bond between God and his people and thus occupied a central place in Israel's religion. Transgression of any part of the law was an offence against God. The law was the most important element in education and consequently in determining the spiritual character of Israelite society.

Man in Relation to the Law: Mesopotamian law divides the people it concerns into three classes: a. Awelum — free men and men of property; b. Mushkenum, propertyless people dependent on others — tenants, hired workers, etc; c. Slaves*. The legislation, especially in such things as damages for injury received, distinguishes sharply between the three. The higher the class, the higher the compensation to be received. In this, the law faithfully reflected the principles on which the society rested. Birth and descent, economic standing and possessions alone determined status.

In this respect, especially in the later stages, Israelite law (if not always society) presents a great contrast. God had legislated for all his people, who were uniformly created in his image. The aspiration towards equality for all God's creatures, eloquently expressed in Job 31:13–15, also had an indirect comparison in Israel's attitude towards slavery*. In practice, however, both custom and the law itself clearly recognized distinctions of class between freemen and slave and between men and women.

Israelite legislation throughout insists on the value of a man and the sacredness of his life. Each man had a place in an overall, divinely conceived pattern of the world and his worth was not to be measured by a mere tally of his possessions. The killing of a man was a crime punishable by death. Deliberate murder could not be expiated by the payment of money, as among some other peoples (although in cases of accidental or unintentional homicide a money payment was sufficient and the death penalty was not exacted). Hittite law, in contrast, judged a man's value in

585 a

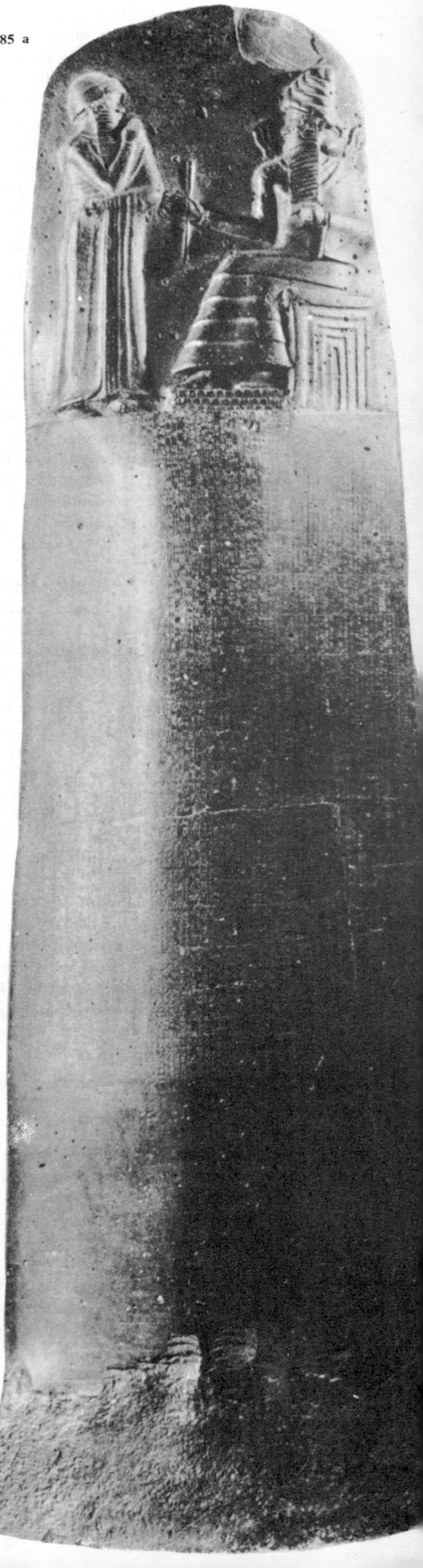

585 b

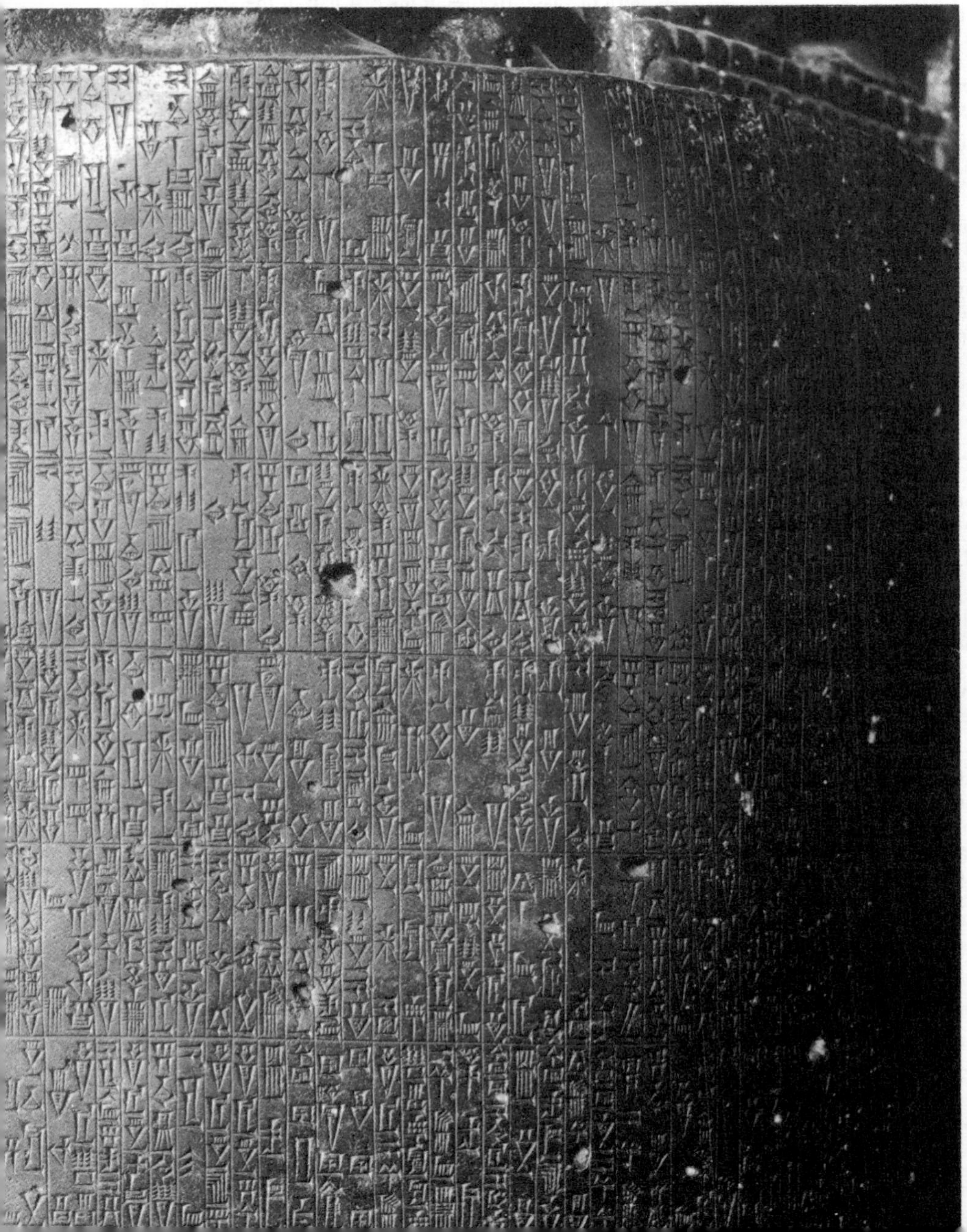

terms of working capacity. Anyone responsible for the loss of a man's labour must — but also *could* — make up for it. Para. 43 of the Hittite code puts it quite clearly: "If a man crosses the river with his ox and another man pushes him in, holding on to the ox's tail and crossing the river while the animal's owner is swept away, they (meaning the family or community to whom the drowned man belonged) would receive this man (in charge)". No similar material compensation could be made among the Israelites. To them, bloodshed was a religious offence which could only be redeemed by the surrender of the killer's own life. Unavenged blood is a blot upon the whole community (Dt. 19:10; 21:1–9) and contaminates the soil on which they live (Nu. 35:33–4).

Humane Laws: Not only does Israelite law lay stress on the sacredness of a man's life. To an extent which has no parallel in the laws of Near Eastern antiquity, it is also considerate of his human worth, feelings and honour, and makes allowance for the incommensurability of life and property. "The very insistence of early Israelite law upon a single norm of procedure to be binding upon every person, the amazingly tender concern for the slave* which in effect made slavery a voluntary status, and for the non-citizen, presupposes a violent rejection of the highly-stratified society of Late Bronze Canaan . . . presented as the polar opposite to that which early Yahwism represented." (G.E. Mendenhall; see Slavery*).

The Bible's ethical exhortation: "You shall not hate your brother in your heart . . . but you shall love your neighbour as yourself;" (Lv. 19:17–18) far transcends ordinary legal dictates, becoming rather a lesson in social attitudes, even surpassing in humanitarian spirit much modern legislation.

Remote Sources of Israel's Law: The developments of Israel's religious and social life resulted ultimately in a unique system of law and ethical precepts. At the same time, its origins lay in the same general body of customary law which functioned in the whole area and this is responsible for many close connections between Israelite and Mesopotamian law. Occasionally, identical expressions are even used. Israel's earliest ancestors originated in Mesopotamia (see Patriarchs, Religion of*). In addition to this influence, a theory at present in favour holds that in casuistic law (see above) there was some borrowing of legal forms and traditions — especially in civil legislation — from the Canaanites. The difficulty here is that there is little material available for comparison. This borrowing was limited, of course, by the contrasts between the Israelites' social customs and those of the feudal, stratified, Canaanite city states. Nor was it indiscriminate. The Israelites took only those procedures which were compatible with Mosaic principles (Yahwism) and these were recast, along with original material, as commandments given by Yahweh (Ex. 22:22–24).

Affinities with Contemporary Codes: As mentioned above, the *casuistic* (conditional) form in which much of Israelite civil legislation was cast, is also to be found throughout Near Eastern legal codes. It is believed that in Israel it was applied especially to judgments on questions of civil law, even though law was essentially religious in character.

Alongside the casuistic form (see above), Hebrew law, particularly regulations concerning ritual, worship and other religious matters, took the form of explicit commands and prohibitions, as in the Decalogue (Ex. 20). This is *apodictic* law, for instance: "You shall not allow a witch to live" (Ex. 22:18) or "You shall not boil a kid in its mother's milk" (Ex. 23:19; Dt. 14:21 passim). Apodictic law is not common in the legal codes of Near Eastern antiquity and is believed by some to be an original Hebrew form. On the other hand, Hittite treaties with vassal states, dating from the second half of the 2nd mill. BCE often use the imperative clause, e.g.: "You shall keep the land which I give you and shall not covet any territory of the land of Hatte." This is very similar to the form of the Decalogue. It is also the form of various Assyrian treaties of vassalage, of an Aramaic treaty found near Aleppo and of a treaty which Esarhaddon (see **657**) imposed on a Median prince. These texts all date from the 1st mill. BCE and have been compared with the Pentateuchal legislation, although the latter is closer in form to the earlier Hittite documents. Some scholars have found a connection between them in some fragments of treaties imposed by the Hittites, discovered in Ugarit*, although it is more likely that this was the common pattern of vassal treaties in the first half of the 2nd mill. BCE. Thus the Hebrews appear to have employed a universal pattern of thought about suzerainty and vassalship and transferred it from the political to the religious sphere, applying the ideas and formulations of power and the right to command to their own relationship to God. The best illustration is the Covenant* itself, the foundation of the religious unity of Israel (see article).

The Law as a Treaty with God: Their use of this form appears completely logical. The Covenant between Yahweh and His people was in the nature of a treaty of vassalage and was so understood. It is no accident that the oldest sections of the Pentateuch read like the clauses of such a treaty. In Israelite tradition, the Covenant* of Sinai (see article) was the event which brought Israel into existence as a distinct entity with its own religion and own system of laws. By that Covenant (expressed in the Decalogue), the semi-nomadic tribes were bound together in a religious and political community (see Exodus*). The nation of Israel was thus established on a contractual basis — the Covenant that bound all the people to God; the oaths that bound the tribes into a confederation. Thus, from the very beginning, the specific law of the Covenant was the central factor of Israel's life and legal system.

The actual terms of the Covenant were, primarily, that Israel accept the role of Yahweh, the God of the Covenant, as their god-king and reject all other god-kings. Secondly, that the Israelites would accept his laws in their dealings with each other. As their society and, consequently, their legal tradition developed following the settlement in Canaan, so the provisions of the Covenant Code had to be made to apply to the conditions of daily life.

This Covenant relationship between Yahweh and Israel gave every individual Israelite the status of a vassal prince, subject only to the will of God as expressed in the Covenant. The religious bond of the Covenant, therefore, both stated and determined the responsibility and the freedom of each member of the group. Submission to Yahweh, of course, also involved certain negative obligations, laid down in the Decalogue, regarding the worship and service of Yahweh and relations between men.

III. THE LEGISLATIVE CODES OF THE PENTATEUCH (THE LAW). Like all Near Eastern codes, the legislative code of the Pentateuch is a collection of separate rules, and it is even less unified and organized than many of the former. Because civil and religious laws were all believed to be equally divine, there was no need — or means — to distinguish between them. Accordingly criminal and social prescriptions are found side by side with ethical and religious regulations. The only apparent distinction is that, in view of the essentially divine nature of the law, cultic (religious) ordinances precede laws relating to human legislation (see below, Development).

The three legislative codes of the Pentateuch are:

The Decalogue and the Covenant Code (Ex. 20:22–23:33; see Exodus, Book of*);

The Holiness Code (Lv. 17–26) and priestly code of Leviticus*, Exodus* and Numbers* (see articles);

The Deuteronomic* Code (Dt. 12–26; see article), in which cultic laws regulating worship are followed by social and criminal legislation.

The Decalogue (in Ex. 20 and Dt. 5) is one of the earliest and most fundamental elements of the Mosaic faith (see Moses*; Covenant*). In the opinion of most scholars, it originated with Moses, but not in its present formulation, and it is impossible to determine how much of all the other legislation stems from him or his generation. Although Moses did not, as tradition would have it, write all the laws of the Pentateuch (see Exodus*; Leviticus*; Numbers*; Deuteronomy*), he was unquestionably the great lawgiver, who laid down the essential stipulations of the Covenant to which all specific law must conform. Whether or not it can actually be ascribed to Moses, it is generally conceded today that the Book of the Covenant (Ex. 21–23 and 34) can be dated to the 12th–11th c. BCE and reflects legal procedures in the days of the Tribal federation. (The general tenor of the law in relation to government* and authority, see article, and the way this was applied, as well as religious, civil and criminal laws regulating daily life, are considered in the articles under specific headings such as Agriculture*; Calendar*; Family*; Funerary Customs*; Impurity*; Magic*; Medicine*; Pilgrimage*; Sacrifice and Offerings*; Slavery*; Taxes and Tithes*; War*; Weights and Measures*, see the general Index.)

IV. DEVELOPMENT OF COVENANT LAW. The manner in which Israel's legislation varied according to changes in its background of social conditions and time can be seen from a brief historical survey (see Part V, below). This also demonstrates very clearly how much more closely the law was linked to religious than to civil life.

The historical fact of the tribal federation as a community bound together by a covenant is unquestioned. Its origins, before the days of Judges, are less certain. However, it is now generally accepted that the organization through which the Conquest was achieved and consolidated, was a direct continuation of traditions belonging to the preceding semi-nomadic period.

The original elements of the Book of the Covenant, notably the Decalogue, describe standard procedure during the tribal federation (Conquest* and period of Judges*). The Decalogue and other commandments are to be enforced on pain of severe penalties, death in the case of intentional homicide (Ex. 21:14, Dt. 19:12), a distinction being made between murder and manslaughter (Ex. 21:12–14), while theft calls for the restitution of stolen property (Ex. 22:1–4), although the Decalogue commandment on theft probably has man-stealing in mind, which is punishable by death. Many of the accompanying provisions can be parallelled in Mesopotamian law (see above, Part I and II).

Israel's Lawgivers: Because of the religious character of Israel's law, its promulgators were naturally men possessed of religious authority. Usually they were endowed with the charismatic quality of someone chosen by God to act as his intermediary and mouthpiece to Israel. It was they who performed the Covenant ceremonial, at which the people of Israel listened to a reading of the laws which they had undertaken, as their part of the contract with God, to observe, and where they renewed their promise of obedience. Only after the whole community had heard the laws were they in force.

Jewish tradition has preserved especially the memory of the two great charismatic leaders, Moses and Joshua, who brought the Covenant and its laws to Israel before and at the beginning of the federation (Ex. 24:3–8; Jos. 24:24–26). In fact, the manner of promulgating laws and decrees by reading them to the whole people in solemn assembly continued throughout the period of Judges*. Their very title testified to the significance of the juridical activities of the people's leaders during this period, quite apart from their military or political achievements. Actually, the Hebrew word "šofet" (translated Judge) has additional meanings and uses (see article on Judges*).

Once the monarchy had been established, the ancient laws were elaborated and developed, but the negligible role allowed the king in their formulation is proof that the foundations of Israel's law were laid in the pre-monarchic period (see Government* and Authority, Part I: The King and the Law, on the role of the king as legislator). Nor was there any change in its spirit later. The king naturally exerted great judicial influence in the days of the monarchy, but this never brought about any fundamental change. In spite of the many secular concerns that had to be accommodated in the laws of the monarchy, their religious basis remained unchanged. As a result, the teachers and expounders of the Law were the priests, who built up the great body of oral traditions preserved in the Priestly Code (see Leviticus*) covering secular, ethical and ritual questions side by side.

Towards the close of the monarchy, the abolition of provincial shrines and altars (see Israel and Judah*, Part V) destroyed the close bonds that had linked the people to local sanctuaries and their priests, while the teaching of the Law gradually passed into the hands of the "scribes", some of whom were priests like Ezra*, while others were not priests. The first hint of their early appearance comes in Jeremiah 8:8 which suggests that the first steps in the process, which reached its height after the Restoration*, were taken just before the Exile (see Part V).

V. CHANGES IN CONDITIONS AND LAW BEFORE THE EXILE: Although there was no change in the fundamental spirit and motivation of the laws, changes in conditions at different periods are reflected in the various codes. After the Covenant Code, crystallized in the pre-monarchical period, came the laws of the Holiness Code (Lv. 17–26), the most ancient kernel of the priestly laws apparently formed towards the beginning or middle of the monarchy and, finally, the Deuteronomic Code, which is generally placed in the 8th or 7th c. BCE, the end of the monarchy (see articles on Leviticus* and Deuteronomy*).

G. von Rad and G.E. Wright are of the opinion that whatever the date of composition of Deuteronomy, many of the laws which it contains also go back to the early traditions of the tribal federation, probably in a form transmitted in northern Israelite circles. On the other hand, the Priestly Code, excluding the Holiness Code of Lv. 17–26 (which is apparently earlier) preserves the cultic tradition of Jerusalem which, although recorded in a post-Exilic form, also goes back ultimately to the tribal federation. In this view, therefore, the various bodies of law are not the results of a straight line of evolution, but rather represent parallel developments of the ancient traditions of the tribal league through different schools.

Whether or not this view is accepted, the developments found in each code can best be seen in the cultic ordinances which precede them.

Law of Sacrifice*: The Law of Sacrifice before the Tabernacle and in the Temple offers a good example. The preamble to the Covenant Code (Ex. 20:24–26) provides for sacrifice "in every place where I cause my name to be remembered", on an altar built of earth or unhewn stone. According to the introduction to the Holiness Code (Lv. 17) sacrifices may be offered only before the Tabernacle ("at the door of the tent of meeting"), on an altar. The Deuteronomic Code, which apparently reflects the period of the cultic reforms of Hezekiah and Josiah (see Israel and Judah*, Part V) or is reflected in these reforms, ordains emphatically in its introduction (Dt. 12) that sacrifice may be offered only in one sanctuary, and this was interpreted as meaning the Temple of Jerusalem. The early section of Deuteronomy — written as though pronounced by Moses in the Plains of Moab, before the crossing of the Jordan — does not mention Jerusalem or any other actual place in the Promised Land. Shechem is also not referred to by name, although this appears to be the place mentioned in Dt. 11:29. The early chapters of Deuteronomy seem to suggest that the writer knew of the existence of sanctuaries before Jerusalem and for this reason was careful not to mention names. His statements were left to be interpreted according to later conditions. This sequence illustrates, apparently, the process of centralization of the cult (see High Places*; Deuteronomy*) which was itself the consequence of a significant development in religious thought.

The fundamental change to a single sanctuary impelled a number of subsidiary alterations. In the Covenant Code and Holiness Code, non-ritual slaughter of animals is forbidden. The blood of cattle or sheep being slaughtered must under no circumstances be eaten (I Sam. 14:32–35). The blood of animals suitable for sacrifice must be sprinkled on the altar (Lv. 17:2–12), that of unsuitable birds and animals being buried and covered with earth (Lv. 17:13–14). However, once all sacrifices had been centred exclusively in Jerusalem, some provision had to be made for animals to be slaughtered elsewhere. Every time a man had a sheep to kill he could hardly be required to travel to the capital. Accordingly, the Deuteronomic code allows for non-ritual slaughter to be carried out anywhere (Dt. 12:20–27), although ritual slaughter continues to be practiced only in the central sanctuary.

Alongside the practical effects of this amendment, religious concepts were also affected. Blood ceased to be sacred (see Leviticus*, Taboo) and although its consumption continued to be forbidden it became permissible to "pour it out upon the ground like water" (Dt. 12:24). The gradual emancipation of Jewish religion from the external, material cult involving archaic taboos (consecration or rendering certain things forbidden) which was at the heart of the prophetic message, was carried a stage further. Some scholars, however, regard the process as merely a matter of changes from time to time and place to place.

Similar developments can be traced through the three codes in relation to the laws governing the priesthood* (see article). The fact that after the Exile, the Deuteronomic laws embodying the spirit of Josiah's reform were enforced in place of the earlier Priestly Code, seems to suggest that Deuteronomy reflects a later stage in these developments.

The greater spiritualization of the religion was also helped by the removal of sacrifice from the localities to the one supreme centre. In place of emphasis on ritual and sacrifice, religious observance had, by the end of the monarchy, become far more a matter of prayer and reading of the Law. This ceased to be a specialized subject, known only to the priests. The Law became the literature — and history — of the people, embodying all manifestations of the Israelite tradition.

At the same time, post-Exilic Jewish law (see Part VI) prescribes special rituals for the purification of the Temple and altar which became the central ritual for the whole community.

Social Legislation: The process of development is even more apparent in the sphere of social legislation. The concepts of the Sabbatical and Jubilee years underwent a series of changes which reveal very far-reaching developments in economic and religious concepts. In both the Covenant and the Holiness Codes, the Sabbatical year (see Agriculture*; Calendar*) is consecrated (taboo). The land must be left fallow that year and its crops abandoned. The Holiness Code (Lv. 25) adds the concept of the Jubilee (50th) year in which all land which had changed hands and come into different ownership must be returned to its original owner — although with certain exceptions. However, by the time of the Deuteronomic Code, remission of land is not mentioned and the Sabbatical (and Jubilee) provision is made to apply instead to the remission of debts (Dt. 15:1–6). In the seventh year the creditor forgave the debtor his debts and the master released his slave (see Slavery*). This is good evidence for the development which had taken place in the economy and for the establishment of a widespread credit system. Not small land-owners, but debtors and slaves (also generally debtors; see Property*; Loans*; Slavery*) now required the protection of the law.

Prosbul: The effect of further economic development can be seen in the practice that developed in late Hellenistic times. By that time, the Sabbatical rule was working against the small man who had great difficulty in finding anyone willing to lend him money for fear of losing it in the seventh year cancellation of debts. A legal form annulling the cancellation of debts was accordingly introduced. This was the "Prosbul" (the word means "for the courts" in Greek) according to which a creditor could claim his debts, regardless of the Sabbatical year, by declaring to the court "I hereby make known to you, judges of this place, that I wish to be able to collect all debts due to me at any time I may desire" (through that court). The validity of this proceeding was confirmed by Rabbi Hillel, but it seems that its origins are older.

A similar shift towards a more considerate and humane attitude and a greater respect for property can be observed in other types of legislation. While the Covenant Code provides, for instance, that the finder of a straying animal must return it to its owner (Ex. 23:4), the Deuteronomic Code refers to all categories of losses and even provides that a finder must keep an object or an animal until it is claimed, even if keeping it involves expense.

Murder and Manslaughter: Murder and manslaughter offer a similar illustration. The Covenant Code (Ex. 21:12–14) provides that where a man has killed accidentally, he may seek refuge in different sanctuaries, i.e. the one which is there at hand, later on in the Temple, where he must seize the horns of the altar (I K. 1:50; 2:28; as the stone altar, **717** from Megiddo). Thus the law of vengeance is mitigated by the provision of sanctuaries for cases of manslaughter. According to the Priestly Code (Nu. 35) refuge can be found, not in a sanctuary, but in one of six "Cities of Refuge" where he may be safe from the kindred of the murdered man until tried by due process of law. The cities of refuge were places of expiation for contributory negligence. They were unnecessary where the killing was sheer accident (see Government and Authority*).

The "*Lex talionis*" law of vengeance, "an eye for an eye, a tooth for a tooth" (Ex. 21:23–25) underwent a similar mitigation, although it is hard to be sure at what point in Israel's history compensation for the sufferer was substituted for the sterile punishment of the aggressor. Even the original formulation had been intended primarily as a limitation on vengeance or punishment by stipulating that a penalty should be commensurate with the crime. Many scholars feel that the rigid formula was probably only a figure of speech anyway. D. Daube and Travers Herford argue for an early date for the change on the ground that the rabbis of the 1st and 2nd c. CE who certainly believed in compensation rather than punishment, ascribed no particular date to the institution but accepted it as traditional.

Magic and Sorcery: The Covenant Code (Ex. 22:18) forbids the practice of sorcery, which probably means "black" magic*, as explained in that article. Necromancy and soothsaying connected with recalling the souls of the dead (I Sam. 28:7–15) is forbidden by the Holiness Code (Lv. 17–26) and this suggests the attempted suppression of all the forms of magic familiar to pagan society. (The question is discussed fully under Magic*.) Sanctions against sorcerers and sorceresses elsewhere in the Near East are recorded, e.g. by Gudea of Lagash (see Babylonia*). While the Covenant Code derives a number of its laws from a Mesopotamian background, it may be assumed that this brief prohibition of the practice of sorcery reflects a new influence, leading to its condemnation as contrary to Israel's faith, and this is confirmed by the Deuteronomic and Priestly Codes.

Formulation of Codes: The changes in outlook are also reflected in the style in which the different codes are formulated. Archaic laws, like those of the Covenant Code, appear unsupported by explanations or motives and are formed tersely as either casuistic or apodictic commandments (see above). In contrast, the Deuteronomic code is remarkable for its fluent rhetorical style and the pragmatic nature of the laws. At this stage, the lawgiver is prepared to persuade his reader and offers explanations and arguments in support of his precepts.

VI. POST-EXILIC LAW: The Restoration* of the Jews to their own land, after their Exile in Babylonia, was the signal for the gradual establishment of a community basing its whole existence upon its religion and upon the Law as that religion's paramount expression. Whereas, in pre-Exilic days, the law had essentially reflected existing customs and cultic practices, it now prescribed them. Every aspect of material and spiritual life was now regulated by deliberate and painstaking reference to the Law, as it had once been "given" to Moses and had been developed by succeeding sages and subsequent history.

The Scribes: This brought to the forefront the new class of interpreters of the Law, the Scribes, whose forerunners must have lived in the days of Josiah (see above IV, and Jer. 8:8). The new theocratic constitution or rather hierarchy, of Judea (see Restoration*; Priests*; Hasmoneans*) which put the High Priest and his entourage at the very head of the community, had the unexpected effect of transforming the priests into an exclusive and aristocratic caste, far removed from the ordinary people and their mundane concerns. For guidance, the people turned to intellectual leaders who were closer to their problems. These were the scribes who undertook the task of interpretation of the Law and administration of Justice which had originally been the responsibility of the priests (Lv. 13:2 ff; Dt. 17:9 ff; 33:10; Jer. 18:18; Ezk. 44:23; Mal. 2:7; II Ch. 19:8). Inevitably, the scribes replaced the priesthood as the leaders of the community and the administrators of justice within it (see Government* and Authority).

Ezra, although himself a priest, stands out as the scribe par excellence. He continued and confirmed this trend. After him and Nehemiah, the scribes were recognized as the Torah's official interpreters and it was they who were largely responsible for the extensive development of Oral Law in the post-Exilic period.

Development of Oral Law: Not only did the Written Law, the Torah (Pentateuch) require authoritative explanation if it was to be made directly applicable to the immediate concerns of a changing society; it had to be expanded. The Covenant Code, and even the later codes, did not provide a systematic body of regulations for the ordering of society — and certainly not one whose conditions differed fundamentally from those of the earlier stages of the community of Israel. Accordingly, traditions of interpretation and analysis of the Written Law had been built up even before the Exile. What remains today are only excerpts. A great body of customary procedures in the time of the monarchy has doubtless perished. After the Restoration, the scribes took these older traditions and made them the basis for a profound investigation into every sphere of public life and the creation of a body of Oral Law which could be applied to the changed conditions.

Whereas, at the time of the First Temple, the will of God had been understood to be embodied in the Pentateuch and to prescribe rules for the ordering of *Israel's society* (see below, Life under the Law), in the post-Exilic period, the whole canon of the Old Testament was seen as God's will (see, e.g. Jn. 10:34; 12:34; 15:25). The commands of the Torah became absolutely binding obligations on every individual Jew, regardless of the society or country in which he might live. Reward and punishment for observance or disobedience to the commands became an individual matter — not as before, something for the community as a whole — namely, inheritance of the Promised Land as the reward for accepting the conditions of the Covenant; banishment as retribution for flouting them. This new attitude, together with the codification of the Pentateuch, allowed no change in its contents and rendered the laws of the Torah immutable. This made it imperative to provide gradually some detailed guidance on their application to daily life. The teachers of the Law claimed that in fact the Torah itself contained that guidance and that, correctly interpreted, the laws of the Torah would cover every possible situation. The laws were interpreted in terms which were quite distinct:

Mitzvôth are God's commandments and prohibitions whether apodictic or casuistic (see above, see also below, Life under the Law).

Halakhôt (plural of halakhah) were the teachings of the scribes and rabbis regarding the Commandments. The whole body of teachings that grew up around the commandments is nowadays generally referred to by the term "halakhah". The exact meaning of the Law was often uncertain and was debated among the teachers over and over again at different times. Accordingly, an important part of halakhic teaching involved the choice of the most authoritative interpretation from a range of different possibilities (see Mishnah*).

The Oral Law: These interpretations, applying a written text to a new situation, became the body of "Oral Law", which was later to be the special concern of the Pharisees*. They derived oral traditions from the Written Law and justified them by exegesis (interpretation). Together, Written and Oral Law provided the framework and supports for all Israel's civil and religious life. To give the Oral Law an equivalent authority, the Pharisees claimed that it had been "given to Moses on Sinai" along with the written Law — even through it — although it had not then been written down. They insisted that Oral and Written Law were equally binding. Legal theory, however, distinguished between the two. The death penalty could only be imposed for violations of Written Law. Moreover, the Sadducees rejected this form of interpretative law out of hand. Even among the Pharisees the same text could too often be used to justify completely contradictory injunctions and in the period of the Second Temple there were many controversies over interpretations (see Pharisees*: Hillel and Shammai; Mishnah*).

Other sects such as the Essenes (see Dead Sea Scrolls* and below, Essenes) possessed, apparently, their own, individual traditions and halakhot regarding the interpretation of the Written Law. These were different from those used and taught by the rabbis but they probably represented traditions which were fairly widely spread in the population. Some of the Essenes were highly respected by the people. The early followers of Jesus also rejected the Oral Law of the Rabbis (see Jesus*; Christianity, Early*: Jewish Christians; Paul*).

Nevertheless, devotion to the Law became the indelible characteristic of orthodox Judaism (see Hassidim*; Rabbis*) from the Maccabaean period onwards (see Hasmoneans*). The persecution of the early Hellenistic period and the cultural renaissance that followed it shifted the centre of gravity of Judaism from the Temple and its ritual to the life of every individual Jew.

In their reaction against Hellenism and paganism, the Jews turned to an ever closer devotion to their "ancestral laws" i.e. to the maintenance of their religious, political and civil institutions as prescribed by the Law, whether Written or Oral.

Life Under the Law: Against this background, the concept developed of the "good life" as one of implicit obedience to every detail of God's will. This philosophy was helped by the practical as well as theological nature of Israel's religion. The Pentateuch lays emphasis on the "doing of all the words of the Law" rather than on probing the "secret things which are the Lord's". Hebrew religious life has been defined by some as being more a matter of *behaviour* than belief — although in practice it is both.

The "Shema'" (Dt. 6:4–9) which is undoubtedly an ancient proclamation makes the point quite explicitly. The Law and the prophets of the 8th to the 6th c. BCE applied Israel's monotheistic faith to the needs and details of everyday life. The historical and prophetical writings demonstrate clearly enough that the ordinary Hebrews did not always reach the standards demanded of them. Nevertheless, knowledge of the Law — probably an earlier portion, not the complete Pentateuch we know today — was the basis on which they were able to rise to a much higher level of ethical and moral consciousness during the Exile* and the Restoration* which followed it. The simple, unlearned Jews, ignorant of the finer complications of some of the laws and directions (particularly those pertaining to defilement and purification; see Impurity* and Purity) and certainly unable to abide by them, became the class of the "'Am ha-'aretz" (the people of the land). The Pharisees, on the other hand, made meticulous observance of every provision an essential part of their way of life (see Pharisees*).

The Study of the Torah: The Bible itself demands constant study of the Torah (Jos. 1:8; Ps. 1:2) and its teaching to the younger generation (Dt. 6:7). With the development of the Oral Law, these injunctions were reinforced by practical necessity and, as a result, there grew up a wide class of scholars devoted to the intensive study of the Torah. As they regarded the activity of studying the Torah as something praiseworthy in itself, even the laws relating to sacrifice and purification continued to be developed and refined, although the destruction of the Temple had destroyed all their practical value.

Their significance, however, was preserved as part of the "mitzvôth" of the Torah. At a time when there was no other means by which a Jew could identify himself, the Pharisees and rabbis insisted that by performance of "mitzvôth" a man could still show his reverence for the Torah and, consequently, still hope for ultimate salvation. The prophet Amos (5:21–24) and the rabbis, (Genesis Rabbah 44:1) saw the importance of the mitzvôth not so much in the observance itself as in the beneficial effect that observance would have on the man who performed it. Study of the Law without practice of its precepts is not meritorious, they ruled (Yebamot 109 b). It is very far from the truth to suppose — as a modern mind is tempted to do — that the Pharisees and their successors were activated by no more than a perverse delight in making life as full of petty regulations as possible, without reference to spiritual and religious values (see Pharisees*). The life of seeking and carrying out mitzvôth was a burden shouldered joyfully. Its discipline was accepted without resentment. Their whole objective was to preserve the Jews and Judaism against every kind of pressure and temptation.

The Palestinian rabbis* were not primarily concerned with theology or "religion". Their religion was embodied in the Torah, the centre of Jewish life and thought. Their object was to ensure its application on the largest possible scale as a rule of life for the people. In later Talmudic times (Makkot 23 b), the number of the Pentateuchal laws, or "divine precepts" (mitzvôth de-orayta) was computed as 613. These included many which related to Temple sacrifice* and services* and which had become inoperative since the destruction of the Temple. In addition, a number of them concern ritual purity (see Pharisees*; Mishnah*), the recurrent rituals of everyday life connected with prayer and food, while others are incidental regulations, concerning only certain categories of people. In general, hallowed tradition made the mitzvôth fundamental to Jewish theology and were meant to remind man continually of his allegiance to God. There was no need for or attempt at rational explanation, though this was given in mediaeval times. The commandments had been given in order that men might remember God, the sole reason for their existence. At every turn, man was reminded of the goodness and fact of God. To prevent life from becoming too one-sided, however, God had designed other mitzvôth based on halakhot which allowed mankind the fullest enjoyment of the world he had made.

Practical Observances: Biblical and rabbinic literature lays particular stress on the practical performance of ceremonial laws the "mitzvôth ma'assiyôt" such as the dietary laws (kashrut), laws connected with the Sabbath* and festivals*, and those governing circumcision*, marriage (see Family*), mourning and burial (see Funerary Customs*). Thus every aspect and detail of daily life was covered by the law. The effects of this on personal and community life can be illustrated by one or two examples:

Dietary Laws: The basic laws contained in the Torah were expanded by the Oral Law and, as interpreted by rabbinic regulation, provided a set of complex dietary regulations, which prohibited certain foods and methods of preparation while restricting the use of others (see Food*: Dietary Laws). For instance, the meat of only some animals could be eaten and every precaution must be taken to avoid consuming blood. Meat must not be eaten at the same time as milk products. Prohibited foods include bread from which the dough-offering has not been separated; first-year fruit; milk of a prohibited animal, and wine known or suspected to have been handled by an idolater.

Sabbath: In the Decalogue and Pentateuch generally, the emphasis is on the Sabbath as a day of complete rest and abstention from work (Ex. 31:17). Subsequent Jewish law has defined 39 separate types of action which constitute an infringement of the Sabbath and has legislated extensively to enhance the positive character of the Sabbath rest.

From ancient times, the Sabbath was observed as a festive occasion. The best clothes were worn, and the finest food eaten. In addition to the regular services of praise and worship, sacred studies, according to the testimony of Philo and Josephus, became a dominant feature of the Sabbath (see Festivals*).

Clothing: The zealous Jew could distinguish himself from his neighbours by wearing the "tzizît" as shown **(329)** "tassels and fringes" at the four corners of his robe (Nu. 15:38; Dt. 22:12), although in practice these, in time, became relegated to undergarments (see Clothing*).

VII. LAW AND TORAH IN NEW TESTAMENT TIMES.

Conflicts: Loyalty to the Law was not only the basis of post-Exilic Jewish life. It was also a unifying force in much of the literature of the period. However its influence was affected and limited by the development of an equally dearly-held loyalty to messianic expectations*.

In the dream of the messianic age, men believed punishment and restraints would become unnecessary. Every man would be impelled by an inner spiritual desire to fulfill the will of God. Thus while the Covenant with God and the need for moral behaviour between men would continue, the enforcement of the Law by threats and retribution would be a thing of the past. Although this state of affairs would only come about in the Messianic Age, it lessened the respect in which the Law was held in the "present Age", and partly explains the rabbis' suspicions of messianism and all that went with it (see Rabbis*). However, there is an important distinction between the approach and the fulfillment of the Messianic kingdom.

Essenes (Dead Sea Sectaries): The tension between conflicting loyalties is very well expressed in the doctrine of the Essenes. They were Messianists but also strict followers of the Law. (In this they resemble many early Christians, especially the Jerusalem church.) Because the time of the end was near, there was all the more reason to be especially meticulous and careful to obey the commandments. The Essenes, like the sectaries of Qumran (see Dead Sea Scrolls*), severed all relations with the priesthood in Jerusalem and took no part in organized worship, although they continued to be scrupulous observers of the Law. They offered no sacrifices, for this would have been unlawful outside the Temple, and they had turned their backs on the Temple which, to them, was defiled by the existing (usurping) priests. Like the prophets of old, they emphasized the spiritual inner aspects of religion and offered an example of piety and purity which was, in this respect at least, quite divorced from the formal practice of religion. At the same time they were awaiting a New Covenant* (see article) which would be their justification and which, incidentally, laid the foundations for the subsequent development of Christianity.

Jesus and the Law: Jesus himself never formally denied or questioned the validity of the Torah or the ceremonial of his time (see Jesus*). What he did deny was the validity of the Oral Law and the traditions of the Elders which were substituted for the written Torah. In this sense he may have sided with the Essenes and Sadducees against the Pharisees, anticipating the later rabbis who made a point of deriving the Oral traditions from the Written Law and "justifying" them by exegesis (interpretation, see above: Oral Law). Earlier rabbis had also followed a similar discipline. Jesus deviated from the official upholders of the Law by putting the spirit of the Law before the details of its observance, even in regard to questions as fundamental as the Sabbath (Mk. 2:18–28; see Mishnah*: Contents of). His criticism of many of the forms of Jewish piety (Mt. 6) came from the same standpoint. It is the position taken earlier by the great prophets.

Jesus never condemned either the form or the principle of sacrifice. His followers saw him as himself the ultimate sacrifice, offering his own blood in the sacrifice of the New Covenant (Lk. 22:20). This, the perfect sacrifice, made any repetition unnecessary. Its value far transcended the regular burnt offerings prescribed by Jewish Law. The Temple could disappear; all formal ritual could be abandoned. Jesus had offered himself "once and for all" for the redemption of Christians and their sanctification (He. 7:27; 9:12, 26, 28).

The Law and Christianity: While they accepted this view, Jesus' personal disciples and his immediate followers found it possible to believe in him as Messiah without in any way deviating from Mosaic Law — even in regard to sacrifice. This was in accordance with his own emphasis on righteousness, but was not the Law of the Pharisees. At this stage, the Jewish Christians (see article, Christianity, Early*) saw no need for any fundamental revision of Mosaic Law and customs (after all, they lived in a Jewish community), but lived in the idyllic certainty reflected in Acts. chs. 2–5.

Their real problems were, in a practical sense, what to do about Gentiles and, in a theoretical sense, how to gain righteousness from God, which could not be done simply by obedience to the Law, no matter how meticulous. These problems were solved, essentially, by Paul* and his followers (see article). They realized that the Gospel of Jesus as Christ had superseded the Law of Moses and had replaced it by the doctrine of salvation through the cross and love between men, embodied in the Church.

Christians tend to base their conception of the Law on the views which Paul expressed in Romans* 7:13 ff and Galatians* 3. These passages, however, do not represent even the whole of Paul's thought (he claims elsewhere that he was a practicing Pharisee) but his statements are rather ambiguous and they are certainly not characteristic of the Jewish attitude in general. This is better expressed in Psalm 19 which sings the praises of God, whose Law is "perfect, reviving the soul". One effect of this attitude, however, was to give the Jews the belief that they could lay claim to God's special favour and could look forward to an exclusive salvation. This Paul condemned outright. Moreover, he reversed the sequence. In place of salvation through the Law, he taught that a man must be saved through Christ in order to keep the Law. In his view, the law of Moses was a veil that obscured the "end of the fading splendour" and the true belief in Jesus (II Co. 3:13-15).

This is a long way from the apodictic Law of the Covenant (see above, II and III) which laid down a man's obligations towards God under the Covenant of Sinai. In effect this had always had to be enforced through the agency of human judges. However much the priests might insist that, in the religious society of the Jewish community, the human decisions derived from the Mosaic law were binding on all Jews at all times, there was ample room for the Christians to argue that customary law was not automatically identical with the will of God.

Paul's view of the Law was further complicated by the Gentiles and the relationship between them and the Jews — especially when it came to eating and drinking. The Christians, especially those outside Judea, lived under Roman law. They could only maintain their position by making a clear distinction between religious and secular law. Secular law had to be enforced by the Roman courts and according to Roman justice. This led them to reject the whole tradition of Jewish case Law, both biblical and "halakhic" (Oral Law; see Lk. 12:13–15) and to substitute for the threats and curses invoked by the older law, punishment by condemnation of one's fellows and, ultimately, the settlement of accounts by God at the Last Judgment (Mt. 18:15–17). The Community of the New Covenant was to uphold obedience by religious sanctions alone. The machinery of the law had become a thing apart. This remained the ideal of Christianity in its early days (see also: Jesus*; Paul*; Christianity Early*: Jewish Christians).

LEVITICUS, BOOK OF. — *Outline: I. Name; Composition; Authorship. II. Contents; The Consecration of the Priests (Chapters 8–10); Uncleanness and Preservation of Ritual Purity (Chapters 11–15); Ambivalent Character of Taboo; The Day of Atonement; The Holiness Code (Chapters 17–25); Admonitory Conclusion to the Holiness Code (Chapter 26). III. General Character of Leviticus; The Priestly Code of Leviticus; Theology of Leviticus; The Scapegoat; Dating of Leviticus.*

I. The third book of the Pentateuch contains laws which, according to biblical tradition, were handed down by Moses during Israel's wanderings in the desert. Some of them apply to priests, but others concern all Israel.

Name: The Hebrew name of the book was "Wayiqrā", following a literary tradition of naming a scriptural book after its opening word or the outstanding word of its opening phrase. It was formerly known as the Torat Cohanim (priestly code). The name "Leviticus" is a Latinized version of the Greek name used in the Septuagint, meaning "that which pertains to the Levites". All priests* were Levites*, so "Leviticus" is an appropriate title.

Composition: As is often the case in ancient literature, the book gives no indication of authorship. The book itself and every new section of Laws (some of them make up less than one chapter), begins with God calling on Moses to address either the Children of Israel or Aaron and the sons of Aaron — the Priests. The ancient traditions governing sacrifice and "holiness" were of vital religious significance. To record them as a revelation direct from God to Moses was the most powerful way of establishing their immutable sanctity. After opening "And the Lord spake unto Moses . . ." the book closes, "These are the commandments . . . in Mount Sinai." A similar formula was used by the Tannaitic rabbis* in the presentation of the Oral Law* and the composition of the legal rules (halakhot) in the Mishnah* and its appendices (see Law*).

Apart from the laws specifically relating to the priests, those applying to the people in general are all closely connected with religious functions. The book gives the laws for sacrifices in relation to the worshipper, such as offerings by the sinner, the ritually unclean, or one who has pledged his possessions to the Lord. In addition, there are more general laws — "thou shalt not curse the deaf", but even these are phrased in the style peculiar to priestly literature.

Authorship: Modern critics believe that almost the whole of Leviticus belongs to the source known as P or Priestly Source, according to the Documentary Theory (see Biblical Criticism*). This strand of priestly writings occurs scattered in the other narrative books of the Pentateuch and in Joshua, but forms the bulk of Leviticus.

P is particularly distinct because of the schematic form of these priestly writings. The document, however, is not a single unified composition as was assumed by the critical theory (see Biblical Criticism*), but a collection of material of different kinds, stemming from priestly circles. It seems unlikely, however, that Leviticus is exclusively the creation of this priestly school. It is generally thought that the book represents the work of priestly editors who included much ancient legal and ritual material.

II. Contents: The arrangement of the different groups of laws does not follow any clear pattern. Generally, they can be divided as follows:

Chapters	1–7	Laws of Sacrifice
	8–10	Consecration of the Priests
	11–15	Uncleanness and the Preservation of Ritual Purity
	16	Day of Atonement
	17–25	Holiness Code (various laws)
	26	Conclusion: blessings and curses
	27	Commutation of Vows and Tithes

It is doubtful whether this represents a consistent formulation of a code of laws. Some scholars believe the work to be composed of isolated commandments originally written down individually. On the other hand, repetitions and discrepancies have suggested to the critical school that in Leviticus the P document can be further divided into P^1, P^2, etc. In this connection, attention to the most minute details of the prescribed cultic rites, etc. is not pedantic but essential for understanding. It is suggested that repetition of material in order to emphasize its importance is a familiar characteristic of biblical composition. Thus chapters 1–5 consist of regulations for the proper observance of various types of sacrifice* (burnt-offering, meal offering, peace offering, sin offering, guilt offering) while chapters 6–7 repeat the identical instructions giving supplementary regulations for the priest and with a slight variation in the order. In the oriental manner, the recapitulation pays special attention to details of procedure apart from the sacrifice itself — questions of disposal of the flesh, etc.

The Consecration of the Priests (Chapters 8–10): This section repeats the rites described in Exodus 29, with the difference that Exodus instructs Moses to perform the rites on Aaron and his sons, while Leviticus describes how the instructions were carried out, and the priests assumed office. The striking similarity between the rites themselves and in the literary style indicates that both accounts belong to the same priestly source.

In Leviticus, the account of the consecration is followed by the death by "fire from the Lord" of Nadab and Abihu, two of Aaron's four sons who had sinned by performing rites in violation of the law. After this comes an appendix emphasizing that priestly ministrations must be carried out with scrupulous regard for the proprieties of worship.

Uncleanness and Preservation of Ritual Purity (Chapters 11–15): The ideas of purity and uncleanness in the Old Testament can only be understood by reference to knowledge gained from the comparative study of religion. The underlying ideas go back to the Semitic origins of Israel, long before Mosaic legislation and theology. Primitive man thought of holiness as something physical before it became a moral state or condition.

Ambivalent Character of Taboo: Things that were sacred, like those that were impure, contained in themselves a frightening supernatural force. This force affected everything and everyone with which it came into contact and such contact had to be ritually removed. Both what was "unclean" and what was sacred were alike taboo, "untouchable", in the sense that both were excluded from ordinary usage. "Impurity*" in this sense was not a matter of physical or moral defilement, nor did consecration confer some moral virtue on "holy" things. Both were states or conditions which were contagious and which must be appropriately remedied before a person or a thing could re-enter normal life.

Accordingly, both uncleanness and holiness resulted from contact: holiness from contact with some aspect of the holiness of God, the "Holy of Holies". Uncleanness might also be an inherent quality, something irrational or daemonic.

Thus the distinction between clean and unclean animals was religious, not hygienic, as was the uncleanness of a mother after childbirth. Ideas about leprosy went far beyond the disease as such, and so did a whole range of unclean diseases and visible infections and pollutions which demanded a variety of purificatory rites of body and abode.

The laws concerning ritual purity for all Israelites, detailing what may be eaten and what is "taboo"; what objects are susceptible to uncleanness and what must be done about it; other circumstances that lead to impurity and what are the duties of the priest in the necessary cleansing rites, are listed in chapters 11–15. The laws appear to have been inserted here so as to use the incident of God's vengeance on Aaron's two sons, which comes just before, as a warning of what may happen to those who disregard the laws.

The Day of Atonement: Chapter 16 takes up the story ". . . after the death of the two sons of Aaron . . ." and sets forth the laws of atonement. This section appears to have combined two sources, one concerned with atonement proper, the other with the occasions on which Aaron (or the High Priest) is allowed to enter the holy chamber. The intricate procedure for atonement is to be carried out once every year, on a day during which all must fast and refrain from work. Later on, this day became "Yom ha-Kippurim" (see Festivals*).

The Holiness Code (Chs. 17–25): This is an example of the survival of one of the earliest codes of Israel which, in accordance with one interpretation of internal evidence, may go back at least in part to the Sinaitic period. The development of the priestly codes was a long and slow process from the ritual and other provisions of pre-conquest days. Although this code shows many points of contact with Ezekiel 40–48 this is not taken as sufficient proof that it too originated in the Babylon of the Exile* but rather that later priests drew upon archaic sources. The section could almost form an independent code of moral and ritual laws, reflecting a different ideological basis from the rest of Leviticus. It makes use of a set of recurring phrases involving the word "holy", emphasizing the holiness of God and calling for Israel to be equally holy: "Ye shall be holy, for I the Lord your God am holy." However, while this emphasis on holiness as an aspect of ceremonial and ethical life is not typical of priestly writings as a whole, it is a conception with particular appeal for priestly circles.

The laws themselves have very little to do with priests. They are more concerned with the life of ordinary men: prescribing forbidden degrees of marriage and forbidding incest (once in ch. 18 and again, with penalties, in ch. 20); giving precepts for behaviour towards a man's neighbour and a stranger; commanding that the land be left fallow every seventh (Sabbatical) year and giving regulations about slaves. This group ends with a "refrain", repeating three laws from the beginning of ch. 19 but in the reverse order. This suggests that chs. 17 and 18 have either been misplaced or else do not really belong to the group, which should begin with ch. 19.

Admonitory Conclusion to the Holiness Code (Ch. 26): The code comes to an eloquent conclusion with promises of blessings for those who keep the laws and terrible curses on the disobedient. This is well within ancient tradition. The same thing can be found in ch. 28 of Deuteronomy* and also in a very similar prologue to the Code of Hammurabi — the Babylonian Code that dates back to the 18th c. BCE (see Laws*).

The final words of the Holiness Code (ch. 26:46) suggest that it existed as a separate unit before being included in the book of Leviticus. Nevertheless, the authors of the larger book added another chapter of additional laws with a closing sentence of its own. This seems to have been a postscript to the original collection added much later. Evidence for this practice is found elsewhere in the Old Testament, e.g. II Sam. 21–24 (see Biblical Criticism*).

III. General Character of Leviticus: Although the book is concerned with laws, not with history, it nevertheless had a historical setting. The question arises, what setting? It has been argued that this is Israel in the days of the wanderings in Sinai on its way to the Promised Land. The theory is confirmed by the evidence of the book itself. The opening chapters carry on from the close of Exodus*, while the beginning of the next book, Numbers*, seems to continue Leviticus. The whole section belongs to priestly tradition. The account of the consecration of the priests is also part of the historical setting. In ch. 24, the reference to the stoning of the "Israelite woman's son whose father was an Egyptian", for blasphemy is also traditional material. Even in these narratives the legal character of the book is dominant. The stories are followed with laws relating to what had occurred and the incidents themselves were probably cited only as precedents for the laws. Even so, this does not rule out their historical veracity.

In contrast to the foregoing, other scholars consider that the setting provided for Leviticus was quite artificial and that its contents do not reflect the situation in the wilderness. Nevertheless, it is becoming generally accepted (see Biblical Criticism*: the Priestly Writings) that certain elements contained in the Priestly source are of greater antiquity than is assumed by the critical school. All that seems certain is that the incidents recorded in Leviticus are part of a tradition which was tenaciously preserved. Although they are historical in form, it is not possible at present to assess their factuality.

The Priestly Code of Leviticus: The "Five Books of Moses" (the Pentateuch) include three distinct codes: Leviticus; the Book of the Covenant in Exodus, and the Deuteronomic Code. Leviticus, which contains the bulk of the priestly code differs from the other two in certain cases. For example, on the treatment of the Jewish slave, Lv. 25:46 seems to be at odds with Ex. 21:6; while Leviticus 17:1 ff on the non-ritual slaughtering of animals is directly contradicted by Deuteronomy 12:20 ff. These suggest different standards of legislation at different times but, since they are all Israelite codes, there is a common element underlying all three which can be recognized. This can be demonstrated in the case of the *lex talionis*, the "eye-for-an-eye" (Lv. 24:18 ff; Ex. 21:23 ff; Dt. 19:21; see Law*, V).

Theology of Leviticus: Leviticus presents a God who is holy and far removed from man but who yet makes provision for worship and for reaching holiness through the conquest of sin. This elevated theology is not free from the survival of archaic language which had long since lost anthropomorphic implications. For instance, sacrifice must be "of a sweet savour unto the Lord", and the cult is described only in terms of the detail of its ritual. There is no indication of the religious feelings involved. Compare, for instance, the passages concerning the offering of first fruits in Leviticus (2:14; 23:17 ff) with the beautiful description of the ceremony in Deuteronomy (26:1 ff). The concentration on external detail in Leviticus does not exclude religious and symbolical significance, as for instance in the reference (9:23–24) to the glory of the Lord. Its spare and formalistic tone, which appeared alien to people of Hellenistic times, inspired Josephus*, Philo* and others to allegorical interpretations and similar elaborations on the symbolical significance of Jewish cult.

The Scapegoat: In the section on atonement, the scapegoat (sa'ir l'azazel) which is driven out, not killed, with the sins of the community heaped upon it, recalls the idea of substitution, a commonplace of other primitive religions (cf. also Gn. 22). It also has affinities with ancient religious practices connected with daemonic spirits which Leviticus itself warns against (se'irim, 17:7). This ambiguity on the subject of an extremely ancient custom was first questioned by a famous mediaeval biblical interpreter, Ibn-Ezra, but the point is still obscure today. Whether the priestly schools actually thought of the ritual as anything more than symbolical it is impossible to say. No doubt, among the common people, the old ideas persisted. W.F. Albright has suggested that in antiquity the scapegoat may have been identified with pagan rustic divinities, originally demons, which were still venerated in the countryside, away from the influence of militant Yahwism (see Idol Worship in Israel*). In the later ritual of atonement, such ideas were eliminated by killing the goat (see Feasts*: Day of Atonement).

Leviticus also seems to attribute daemonic aspects to God. This is contained in the idea of the Holy — numinous aspect of God which properly inspires terror in man. He is a being who should not be approached without the utmost caution, as in the incident of Aaron's sons. The dètails of sacrifice* probably reflect a long process of development from a more archaic to a more advanced stage.

Dating of Leviticus: Leviticus presents the sacrificial system at a generally later stage of its development. However, many customs and precepts of Mosaic and pre-Mosaic times, embedded in its code, survived in the newer forms. It is not easy to disentangle these from their context, but the most obvious examples are indicated below.

The dating of Leviticus as a whole is bound up with that of all the Pentateuch. Some extreme critics have held that the entire book post-dates the Exile*. Others have denied the relatively late date which used to be ascribed to the priestly traditions (see Biblical Criticism*) and have found on internal evidence that some of these traditions are of hoary antiquity, dating back to pre-Monarchic Israel, well before the 10th c. BCE. The book claims such a setting for itself and the presence of archaic rites and ancient cultic traditions (no longer understood) bear this out. Against this, the curses at the end of the book speak of exile, a phenomenon unknown before the Assyrian period (9th–7th c. BCE) in Near Eastern history. Ch. 18 warns, in connection with the incest taboos, that disobedience will cause the land to "vomit out" its inhabitants and a similar fate is threatened in the curses in Ch. 26 should the injunction to leave the land fallow every seventh year be disregarded. The desolate land will make sure of enjoying its sabbaths. Such a fate could hardly have been formulated before the Assyrian period, which seems to fix the latest certain date for other sections of Leviticus.

On the other hand, the same curses make uncritical reference to a decentralized cult in Israel, long before the monarchy, which complicates the dating, because during the Assyrian period, cultic ceremonies outside the Temple in Jerusalem were banned. Apparently the curses are a mixture of older and later elements.

As mentioned above, Ezekiel*, a prophet and priest of the time the first Temple was destroyed, was greatly influenced by Leviticus, or by the priestly documents from which it was composed. His language is similar not only to the Book of Holiness, but also to other parts of Leviticus, including the curses. This seems to demonstrate the importance of schools of tradition in the development of the religious literature of ancient Israel. A prophet who believed he received the word of God direct from on high can nevertheless reveal affinities to a specific literary school: Ezekiel to the priestly circles, Jeremiah to those which gave rise to Deuteronomy*

LOANS AND DEBT. — Personal loans for sustenance and maintenance have been common since the earliest times — as they still are. Loans for business or commercial purposes, however, are relatively modern, apparently dating from Graeco-Roman times. In ancient society, men borrowed from immediate dire necessity. In Israelite eyes, someone so placed that he was reduced to borrowing should have been able to find help among his kindred. Accordingly, a loan is regarded by the Bible as a form of charity or almsgiving (Ps. 37:21; 112:5; Ecclus. 29:1–2) and the Law of Moses forbade the taking of interest on loans made between Jews (Ex. 22:25; Lv. 25:35–38). Loans to Gentiles might carry interest (Dt. 23:19–20). Nevertheless, there are many biblical passages which suggest that the usury which was a commonplace among all Israel's neighbours was far from unknown among the Jews themselves later on, presumably as a result of economic development and foreign example (Ezk. 18:8, 13, 17; Pr. 28:8; Ps. 15:5; Neh. 5:1–13).

Two terms are associated with interest. One, "neshek", translated as "usury", was first used of any kind of loan (Dt. 23:20) but later restricted to loans of money. The other term, "tarbît" (meaning increase) applied to loans in kind: foodstuffs, corn, etc. (Lv. 25:37). In the 5th c. BCE Elephantine Papyri, the only word for interest is "marbît". It has been suggested that the change in vocabulary reflects an evolution in the system of lending. Although deeds of loan are not mentioned at all in the Old Testament, in practice a borrower may have signed a receipt for, say, 80 shekels and an undertaking to repay 120 on maturity (i.e. with "tarbît"). In this case, the lender was assured of a "neshek" (bite). Alternatively, "tarbît" may have been a penalty for non-payment or an increase to provide for the depreciation of goods where a loan was made in kind. Information on the subject, is scarce. Most statements about ancient Israelite practice or the motives of their legislation concerning loans and interest, remain mainly guesswork.

In most ancient cities, temples served as places of security where treasures could be stored, and from which money could be lent to the needy. This was apparently the case in Israelite sanctuaries. Rabbinic sources reveal that even the Temple became sufficiently influenced by modern economic trends to lend at low interest from its treasury. Jesus' parable of the talents takes it for granted that charging and paying interest on loans was an accepted custom (Mt. 25:27; Lk. 19:23). The characters of the story undertook the charge of deposits for the use of which they were expected to pay some interest.

The Bible gives no information about the rates at which interest was charged. Presumably, Israel followed the customs of surrounding lands, in which case the rates normally charged appear extremely high to modern eyes.

In Mesopotamia, one-fifth to one-quarter of the capital would be charged on loans of money, and one-third or even more in the case of loans of commodities, grain or provisions. In upper Mesopotamia and Elam, 33 to 50 per cent of the capital would be charged on loans of money. In Ptolemaic Egypt, the rate was only 12 per cent per annum, and the same rate applied in Rome at the beginning of the Christian era. (On the institution of banking, see Trade*.)

Security (Erubîn): A pledge or security of repayment of debt was called a "ḥâbol" or "âbôt", or similar terms derived from the root word meaning "to bind". A pledge is something binding the debtor to pay. It remains the property of the borrower, but is held by the lender until the loan is repaid. Rules and strict limitations regarding the taking of pledges are laid down in the Bible. A lender may not enter the house of the borrower to take the pledge; it must be brought to him (Dt. 24:10–11). He may not take household utensils which are essential for the borrower, e.g. a hand mill or an upper millstone (Dt. 24:6), and if he takes a garment in pledge, it must be returned at sundown as this is the borrower's only covering for the night (Ex. 22:26–27; Dt. 24:12–13; see also Inscriptions*: Matzad Hashabyahu).

There is an instance in Nehemiah where the people complain that "other men have our fields and our vineyards" (Neh. 5:5), which suggests that a mortgage on immovable property was a normal form of pledge, but this may in fact refer to confiscation for non-payment of debts. A man might also pledge himself in return for a loan, or as a guarantor for a friend. In case of non-repayment of the debt, he would then be enslaved to the creditor. This must have been a frequent occurrence (see Slavery*) but it did not imply enslavement for longer than the period during which the debt remained unpaid. What was pledged was the man's labour power, rather than his person. Payment brought immediate release. Where a man sold himself as a slave to his creditor in order to repay the debt, it was for a number of years only (until the year of Jubilee; see Slavery*).

The early books of the Bible give no information as regards the giving of guarantees (surety) for third parties, but by the time the Wisdom books were composed, it had clearly become a widespread practice (Pr. 11:15; 17:18; 20:16), subject to frequent abuse. A guarantor is advised to make sure the borrower pays up (Pr. 6:1–5) in case he is called upon to pay himself (Pr. 20:16; 22:26–27; 27:13). While Proverbs warns against acting as a guarantor, Ben-Sira (Ecclesiasticus; see Apocrypha*) recommends doing so (Ecclus. 29:14–20) out of charity, although he recognizes the dangers of having to stand a loss and receiving only ingratitude in return.

Post-Exilic Practice: In Hellenistic law and Roman custom, the guarantor was given the same rigorous protection accorded to a creditor. A defaulting debtor might be thrown into jail and have his property seized and sold to repay his creditor (this was customary throughout the Near East, from Babylonia to Egypt). Further evidence of this comes from Jesus' parable about the servant who was forgiven his debts by his master and then threw a fellow servant into jail "until he should repay the debt" (Mt. 18:23–30).

Herod was notorious for denying his creditors satisfaction, but he once invaded the country of Silaeus the Nabatean because of non-payment of an important loan. The lower Jewish courts which dealt with ordinary civil cases always tried to mitigate the oppressive harshness of the law as it applied to the poor and defenceless, but Herod had no time for mercy of this kind. In later post-Exilic law, various legal devices mitigated the harshness of the old legislation. Rabbi Hillel is given the credit for the "prosbul" law (see Law*) which made it possible for creditors to collect money they had lent, regardless of the provisions of the laws of the Sabbatical year which otherwise cancelled all debts every seven years.

By this period, the conditions of economic and commercial life had changed fundamentally. Capital was required for trade and other enterprises and was made available by bankers. Jesus makes two references in his parables to the investment of money with "the bankers" where it will yield a proper interest (Mt. 25:27; Lk. 19:23), presumably the rates mentioned above.

LUKE, GOSPEL OF. — Authorship: Tradition has long ascribed the authorship of the third Gospel to "Luke the beloved physician" mentioned in Col. 4:14 among the men "of the circumcision", which is interpreted by some scholars to imply that Luke was originally a Gentile. This same Luke is also mentioned in II Tim. 4:11 as among Paul's companions. The arguments which support Luke's claim to have written the third Gospel are familiar to all biblical scholars. The book of Acts* contains a number of passages written in the first person plural (the "we-sections") by someone who had evidently accompanied Paul on his journeys. The style of Acts and the style of the third Gospel are also so similar as to indicate that both works were written by the same author. Moreover both the Gospel of Luke and the book of Acts are dedicated to "Theophilus" (cf. Lk. 1:3 and Ac. 1:1). The introductory verse of Acts even refers specifically to a "first book" which is generally interpreted as meaning the Gospel of Luke.

It used also to be argued that both the book of Acts and the Gospel of Luke reveal a particular interest in medicine which would have been natural for "Luke the physician". However this theory has been effectively challenged. Any intelligent writer of that era who had a mastery of Greek — as Luke evidently did — would have been familiar with and made use of the so-called "medical" expressions.

Nevertheless, it can be said that there is no criticism which seriously threatens the traditional view of Luke as the author of the third Gospel.

Organization: The following outline gives a good idea of the general organization of material in the Third Gospel:

a.	1: 1– 4	Preface
b.	1: 5– 2:52	Birth and Childhood of John the Baptist and Jesus
c.	3: 1– 4:13	Inauguration of Jesus' Ministry
d.	4:14– 9:50	Galilean Ministry
e.	9:51–19:27	Journey to Jerusalem
f.	19:28–23:56	Events of Passion Week
g.	24: 1–53	The Resurrection and Jesus' Appearances to His Disciples

In the organization of his material, Luke follows a general chronological order. Within the scheme of his chronology, however, he has arranged the material in large blocks, according to topics, and in some cases chronological accuracy has been sacrificed to topical organization (this is particularly true in the section "The Journey to Jerusalem" which undoubtedly contains a good deal of material which rightly belongs to the period of the Galilean Ministry).

The skilful organization of Luke is the more striking when one compares it to the literary scheme adopted by Matthew*. Whereas the latter presents a block of Markan material followed by a long discourse, Luke has interwoven narrative and discourse into a single systematic pattern. He thus achieves his aim of presenting to the reader a systematized and, for his time, historical presentation of the life and teachings of Jesus Christ, the founder of the Christian Church. The book of Acts* is a natural sequel to Luke, for it takes up where the Third Gospel ends and continues the story of the development and spread of Christianity after Christ had departed from the earth.

CONTENTS: Luke opens with a *preface* (1:1–4) to Theophilus, explaining his reasons for writing the book.

The Birth and Childhood of John the Baptist and Jesus (1:5–2:52). This section begins with the annunciation of the birth of John the Baptist (1:5–25), then the annunciation of Jesus' birth (1:26–38), and Mary's visit to her cousin Elisabeth (1:39–56), which contains Mary's hymn of praise, the beautiful "Magnificat" (1:46–55). John's birth is related in 1:57–66 followed by his father Zacharias' psalm of thanksgiving (1:67–79) with its strong messianic element. Jesus' birth (2:1–20) is followed by the account of his circumcision and his presentation in the Temple (2:21–40), the latter event also displaying strong messianic overtones. A single glimpse into the boyhood of Jesus is afforded by the narrative of his visit to the Temple at the age of twelve (2:41–52).

The Inauguration of Jesus' ministry (3:1–4:13) begins with an account of John the Baptist's ministry (3:1–20), then relates the Baptism of Jesus (3:21–22), his genealogical table (3:23–38), and his Temptation (4:1–13).

Jesus' Galilean Ministry (4:14–9:50): This section opens with two introductory verses (14:14–15), then launches into an account of Jesus' preaching in Nazareth and his subsequent escape from the enraged crowd (14:16–30) to Capernaum where he heals a man possessed of a devil (4:31–37), Peter's mother-in-law (4:38–39), and many others (4:40–44). The calling of Peter, James, and John (5:1–11) is followed by the miraculous healing of a leper (5:12–16) and the lame man let down through the roof (15:17–26). This latter incident marks Jesus' first brush with the Scribes and Pharisees for on this occasion he not only heals a man, but takes it upon himself to forgive the man's sins. Levi, a publican (i.e. tax collector), is also called to be one of Jesus' disciples (5:27–32). Jesus spurns the usual fasts for his followers, permits his disciples to pluck grain on the Sabbath and himself heals a man with a withered hand (5:33–6:11). The appointment of the twelve disciples is recorded in 6:12–16.

The Sermon on the Mount is contained in 6:20–49. 7:1–10 tells of Jesus' healing the servant of the centurion from Capernaum. In the city of Nain Jesus restores to life the only son of a widow (7:11–17). 7:18–23 records Jesus' meeting with the disciples of John the Baptist and his speech concerning John (7:24–35). While Jesus is dining at the house of a Pharisee, he is anointed by a sinful woman and forgives her her sins (7:36–50).

Ch. 8 describes some of the women in Jesus' following (1–3), then records the Parable of the Sower (4–18), the visit of Jesus' mother and brothers (19–21), the Stilling of the Tempest on the Sea of Galilee (22–25), the healing of the Gadarene demoniac (26–39), the cure of the woman with the issue of blood and the raising of Jairus' daughter (40–56). Ch. 9 tells of the sending out of the disciples (1–10), the Feeding of the Five Thousand (11–17), the Confession of Peter (18–27) and Jesus' first announcement of his coming death (22), Jesus' admonition of humility to his followers and the Transfiguration (28–36). The healing of the epileptic boy is told in 37–42 and Jesus then predicts his death for a second time (43–45). The disciples quarrel as to who should be the greatest among them and Jesus admonishes them once again to love humility (46–48).

Jesus' Journey to Jerusalem (9:51–19:27). This section begins with the account of the Samaritan village which refused Jesus shelter (9:51–56); Jesus' replies to three would-be disciples (9:57–62) and the sending out of the 70 disciples and their return (10:1–24). The parable of the Good Samaritan (10:25–37) is followed by the account of Jesus' visit to the home of Mary and Martha (10:38–42) and his teaching about prayer (11:1–13), the Lord's Prayer being included (11:2–4). Jesus refutes the charge that he is in league with Beelzebub (11:14–23) and speaks of unclean spirits (11:24–26), of the scepticism of his generation (11:29–32) and of the eye as the light of the body (11:33–36).

11:37–54 contains Jesus' denunciation of the Pharisees and in 12:1–12, he warns against their teachings and encourages his disciples to be fearless in confessing their belief in him. 12:13–56 is a condemnation of concern with earthly riches and an eschatological description of Jesus' mission. Jesus calls on the crowd to repent (12:57–13:5) using the parable of the barren fig tree (13:6–9) to emphasize his teaching about the final reckoning.

Jesus is again criticized for healing on the Sabbath and again refutes his critics. He compares the Kingdom of God to a grain of mustard seed or a measure of leaven and warns that it has a narrow door (13:10–30).

Certain Pharisees warn Jesus that Herod is plotting against him, but he disregards their warning and continues on his way to Jerusalem which he mourns (13:31–35). Eating at the home of a Pharisee, Jesus gives offence to his host by healing a man afflicted with dropsy on the Sabbath (14:1–6). He goes on to preach of humility (14:7–14) and illustrates his message by the parable of the Great Feast (14:15–24).

Jesus makes the responsibilities of discipleship quite clear (14:25–27) and explains by means of parables what this duty implies (14:28–35). The meaning of true service is then illustrated in a series of beautifully told parables: The Lost Sheep (15:1–7), The Lost Piece of Silver (15:8–10), The Prodigal Son (15:11–32), and the parable of The Unjust Steward (16:1–9). Jesus speaks of true service (16:10–13) and of the relation between the Law and his "good news of the Kingdom of God", pointing his warning of retribution by the parable of the Rich Man and Lazarus (16:14–31).

He speaks of sin and forgiveness (17:1–4), of faith (vs. 5–6) and, again, of service (7–10). The healing of the ten lepers is recorded in 17:11–19 followed by a discourse on the Kingdom of God and the Advent of the Son of Man (17:20–37). In ch. 18 Jesus speaks of the inevitable justice of God (1–8), and tells the parable of the Pharisee and the tax collector (9–14). There follow a number of isolated incidents and teachings: Jesus' blessing of the children (15–17), the story of the Rich Young Ruler (18–27), the reward of the disciples (28–30), Jesus' third prophecy of his approaching death (31–34), and the healing of a blind man near Jericho (35–43).

At Jericho, on his way to Jerusalem, Jesus converts Zacchaeus, the chief tax collector (19:1–10). Once again Jesus speaks of true stewardship which he explains by way of the parable of the Ten Talents (or Pounds 19:11–27).

The Events of Passion Week (19:28–23:56), particularly those described in chs. 22 and 23 follow fairly closely the narrative of Mark*. This section begins with the Triumphal Entry into Jerusalem, Jesus' lamentation over Jerusalem, the cleansing of the Temple (19:28–48), and the questioning of Jesus about the source of his power (20:1–8). There follows the parable of the Wicked Husbandmen and the questions put to Jesus by the Pharisees and the Sadducees. Jesus then asks his questioners how the son of David can be the Messiah and warns the people against the scribes (20:9–47). He speaks of the superiority of the widow's mite (21:1–4) and then launches into a long eschatological discourse in which he prophesies the destruction of the Temple (21:5–38). Chs. 22 and 23 describe the fateful events of the Last Supper, Betrayal, Arrest, Trial, Crucifixion, Death and Burial of Jesus. Though these two chapters follow the account of Mark, they contain a number of interesting variations, the most evident of which is Luke's account of Jesus' trial before Herod (23:6–12) which is not recorded in any of the other Gospels.

Jesus' Resurrection is described in 24:1–11. Thereafter he appears to two of his disciples at Emmaus (24:13–35), and to the Eleven (24:36–49) before his ascension into heaven (24:50–53).

DATE: As is the case with Matthew, Luke made extensive use of material from Mark's Gospel*. Luke must, therefore, have been written after the second Gospel. Some scholars believe that, unlike Mark, Luke knew of the destruction of Jerusalem (cf. Mk. 13:14 and Lk. 21:20), although this theory is not without its critics.

Luke is generally dated about the same time as the first Gospel, i.e. about 70–80 CE, although another school of thought would put the date much earlier. Assuming that Acts* was written before the martyrdom of Paul (ca. 64 CE), then the Gospel of Luke must be placed even earlier, since it obviously antedates Acts. It has also been pointed out that I Tim. 5:18 may possibly contain a quotation from Lk. 10:7. If the dependence of Timothy upon Luke in this case could be proved, it would substantially strengthen the argument for an earlier dating of Luke. However, the mere existence of two parallel passages in the two documents, by no means proves their interdependence, for it is quite conceivable that both passages were drawn from a common source.

SOURCES: Though there have been serious attempts to prove that Luke was dependent upon Matthew*, the consensus of opinion among the scholars is that the two Gospels were written independently of each other. Like Matthew, Luke borrowed heavily from the "Sayings of Jesus" in the Q document (see Gospels*, Synoptic).

There are traces of other sources in the Gospel of Luke. The miraculous events accompanying the Nativity of Jesus (chs. 1–2) are unique in the third Gospel, yet their literary style differs considerably from that of the main body of the book. They seem to have been derived from independent — possibly Semitic — sources. Luke also contains a considerable amount of other material which is peculiar to his own Gospel. This material is designated as L. It includes some 14 different parables.

Some scholars hold that L constitutes the basis of an earlier Gospel (Proto-Luke), written around 60 CE by Luke, who supplemented his own source material with the discourses of Q. Later, when the Gospel of Mark came into his hands, Luke revised his Gospel until it assumed its present form. While this is a plausible theory, Luke exercised a relative degree of freedom in editing his Markan sources (Mk. 6:45–8:26 is entirely omitted by Luke) and it is just as reasonable to suppose that he combined all three of his sources, Mark, Q, and his own special material, and edited them according to his own taste at the same time.

Purpose: Luke followed the overall pattern of the other Synoptic Gospels, but within it, he selected and arranged his material for a particular didactic purpose. Luke's concept was to present a history of the Kingdom and its growth and his main motif is the admission of Gentiles to the Christian church. He regards their admission as an integral part of God's purpose, whereas Mark, like Paul and Matthew, presents it as a consequence of the double tragedy of Jesus' rejection by the Jews and his death.

Luke also adhered to this teaching, but by a skilful selection and editing of his sources, he conveys the impression that admission of the Gentiles was the essential part of the Ministry of the Risen Christ (24:47 ff). In general, Luke followed the plan of Mark's Gospel but with certain alterations and the one notable addition (Lk. 9:51–18:14).

Luke (like Acts) is distinguished among the books of the New Testament by possessing a preface. This explains the purpose of each book and serves to link the two together as the work of a single author. Luke was concerned to make the "first book", his Gospel, conform to the Acts* which forms its sequel and this consideration partly explains many of the differences between the Gospels of Luke and Mark.

Style: Luke has the best Greek style of all the Gospel writers. His is the work of a true craftsman. Unlike Matthew and in a more subtle manner than Mark, Luke wrote directly for the Gentile world. In his opinion, the church's mission had definitely been turned towards the Gentiles and Jesus' Jewish background is of only secondary importance. He presents the Jewish leaders and especially the high priest and his cohorts as equally responsible with the Roman authorities for the crucifixion of Jesus. Luke is more careful of the reputation of the Romans who were, after all, the rulers of the civilized world, although it is doubtful whether he differs substantially from the other Gospels in assigning the blame for Jesus' death.

M

MACCABEES, THE: Popular name for a group of Jewish partisans who fought during the 2nd c. BCE to end foreign domination and religious persecution in Judea. The meaning and derivation of the name "Maccabee" is disputed. It is applied to Judas the Maccabee, and loosely to other members of his family, and to the Hasmonean* dynasty as a whole. The story of the Maccabean revolt, of Judas and of the Hasmonean dynasty is treated under Hasmoneans*.

MACCABEES, Book of (see Apocrypha*, IV — Historical)

MAGIC, DIVINATION AND SUPERSTITION. — *Outline: Magic and Witchcraft: a. Magic and Sorcery in Egypt; b. Magic and Sorcery in Assyria and Babylonia; c. Israel and Magic: Biblical Terminology; Prevalence and Prohibition of Magic; Amulets; Necromancy; Magicians and Sorcerers; Foreign Influences; Divination and Sympathetic Magic; Decision by Lot; Prophets vs. Diviners; Post-Exilic Period.*

If magic can be said to represent man's most primitive attempts to impose his will upon the forces of nature, then superstition may be seen as recognition of his limitations. As a community develops, a complex body of magical "knowledge" grows up to determine what particular supernatural (or occult) agency is at play or should be employed in a particular case, and what incantations (spells), objects or actions must be used to achieve a desired result. This pseudo-science developed over the centuries into a whole range of branches: witchcraft in general; animism; necromancy (calling up the spirits of the dead); or dealings with the spirits believed to inhabit the world and everything within it; fortune-telling by the auguries of sacrifices*; according to the movements of clouds or the stars (see Astrology*); gazing into balls and bowls and crystals, or by throwing sticks or shooting arrows.

Magic and Witchcraft: Throughout the ancient world, magic was universally practiced. It can most easily be considered under its twin aspects: "black" or evil magic and "white" or beneficent magic. "Black magic", which aims at producing harmful results, involves things like curses, incantations, breaking or harming images or other objects representing the hated person (or people), and consorting with evil spirits likely to be of assistance. In contrast, white magic attempts either to ward off the harmful effects of black magic, or to enlist the aid of the hidden powers and spirits of nature in favour of the supplicant (or the magician on his behalf).

Magic and divination possess individual characteristics in a. Egypt; b. Mesopotamia and c. Israel.

a. **Magic and Sorcery in Egypt:** In Egypt, as elsewhere, sorcery was employed to strengthen man's hand in cases where the causes of events were unknown or where ordinary measures had failed. Manipulation of the occult powers followed complicated formulas which had to be studied very carefully, and of which the priests had a virtual monopoly. Sorcery was closely connected with religion. It was used in connection with relations between individuals, between gods and man, and in national affairs. From the beginning of the 3rd millenium BCE, magic (ḥk' in Egyptian) was under the special protection of patron gods, "Teḥut", the god of wisdom, and Isis, the supreme god. "Black magic" intended to procure harm had no part in official practice and was forbidden. Magic was generally used to ease conditions for the living and for the dead in the after-life. The main branches involved were: protective magic against harm; magic designed to ensure fertility; divination (or fortune-telling); magic to protect and guide the dead in the underworld, and finally, magic used to perform wonders. In all cases, the ritual involved sympathetic magic imitating the desired result (as detailed in the symbolic description of the Book of the Dead, in this papyrus of Ptolemaic days, **586**) and appropriate incantations and ceremonies.

The priests who practiced sorcery were a special class who studied their art in the "House of Life" which contained the precious text-books of the system. By the time their training was finished, these priests could recite the appropriate spell for every occasion and knew all the ceremonies and traditions connected with sorcery. They then became the magicians, "ḥartumim" in Hebrew ("hrytp" in Egyptian) mentioned in the Bible.

Dreams: The Egyptians also engaged in dream interpretations. Dreams play an important part in the Joseph story, especially those of Pharaoh and their interpretation (Gn. 41:8). The interpretations of a variety of dreams were listed in hand-books for the use of the magicians. In one of these books which dates from the 19th–18th c. BCE

586

the dreams are arranged in a table according to the future events they presage. First come the dreams that announce good tidings, then those that portend calamities. There is a fixed formula for the interpretations: "Should a man do this or that it is good (or evil) for him, and it is a sign that — thus and thus — will happen to him". An incantation against evil dreams with a prayer to Isis is also included in the book.

Divination: The Egyptians also foretold the future by using cups (Gn. 44:4, 5, 15), a practice which they learned from the Babylonians. Drops of oil were added to a cup full of water, and the future foretold from the shape they took. Conversely, a drop of water might be put into a cup full of oil. The Jews followed the same custom during the period of the Mishnah* when they would also foretell the future from the shapes they saw in a glass of wine.

b. **Magic and Sorcery in Assyria and Babylonia:** In Mesopotamia, sorcerers with the same aims as their Egyptian colleagues flourished as early as the 3rd mill. BCE. The Sumerian magicians of this period were also mainly concerned with increasing man's well-being but they, too, possessed a variety of formulas for warding off the evil effects of harmful spells and curses. In Mesopotamia, also, sorcery was a highly skilled profession, requiring long study and much knowledge. The performance of magic rituals demanded a high degree of precision in the movements of the body and in co-ordinating them with the magic incantation which had to be intoned at the same time.

In Mesopotamia, the main branches of sorcery were:

1. **Protective and Curative Magic,** used mainly to cure diseases, expel demons (evil spirits) and so on. Protective genii holding a bucket and a cone, are represented here (**587**). The emblems they hold are frequently associated with the "sacred tree", conveying something of the same suggestion (Nimrud relief, 9th c. BCE). A book, the "surpu" (conflagration) listed all the sins to which man is subject and, where someone had violated a divine or moral law, the magician could find there the formula by which to free him from the spell under which he had acted. Where a man believed that a spell had been laid upon him by a sorcerer, he would repair to a magician who would burn a wax figure of the sorcerer, saying, "As this figure melts, so may the sorcerer (or witch) melt." Pazuzu (**588**), the "gripper", with claws on hands and feet, eagle's wings, and a twisted face, haunted the minds of Assyrians and Babylonians throughout their history and posed a threat against their lives and health. This (**589**) amulet from Carchemish was inscribed on one side with an incantation to the female demon, Lamashtu. It is shown standing on a wild ass, grasping serpents, suckling a jackal and a wild pig.

2. **Divination,** or fortune-telling, is based on the theory that every good or bad event in the lives of men is accompanied by visible omens that may be read by anyone skilled in the art, who can thus foretell the future. The omens concerned were also written down. One such book was made up of 170 clay tablets which included the meanings of observations of the heavens, e.g. a halo around the moon, a solar or lunar eclipse, heavenly or atmospheric phenomena (e.g. thunderstorms); the behaviour of certain birds or animals like serpents, dogs, mice, etc. and births — especially abnormal ones — of humans and animals.

One of the favourite techniques of foretelling future events was the inspection of the livers of sacrificial animals (known as hepatoscopy). The "science" of divination required that a careful record be kept of all omens observed and the events which followed them. Thus it was also necessary to keep a record of the exact configurations of the livers. As these could not be preserved, accurate clay models such as this (**590**) were made of each one and the events which followed its observation were inscribed on it. 32 of these clay models, dating to the beginning of the 2nd mill. BCE, were found at Mari (see Babylonia*). Clay models of livers engraved with various signs were also constructed as a general guide to diviners, indicating points to be watched.

Divination was especially important before and during military campaigns. There is a vivid illustration of this in Ezekiel (21:21) where Nebuchadrezzar is pictured standing at "the parting of the way", undecided whether to attack Jerusalem or Rabbath-Ammon. To reach a decision, he shakes (or looses) inscribed arrows; consults the teraphim (see below) and "looks at the liver". Some of the Mari documents show that the omens might give a lot of trouble, especially as each section of troops had its own diviner. Disagreements between their interpretations on one occasion

587

588

590 a

589

590 b

meant that half an expedition attacked, while the other half retired. Another official writes: "I and Ibbi-Amurru have been preparing for the campaign of Warad-Ilishu at Agdamatim, but our omens are not favourable. Those omens I have sent my lord. May my lord pay very close attention to those omens." (Jean, "Archives Royales de Mari").

3. **Dreams:** The Babylonians and Assyrians also paid great attention to the interpretation of dreams. Ashurbanipal's famous library in Nineveh contained many tablets listing the interpretation of various dreams. In all, more than 2000 different omens are given with their interpretations. There are also spells to be uttered as a cure for bad dreams. Still another collection of tablets begin with the words: "The god Zaphyr, god of dreams". Here the signs are arranged according to the actions mentioned: eating, drinking, meeting, etc. Each line describes a dream, followed by the formula, "A man who did this in his dream, his omens are . . .".

4. **Black Magic** was officially forbidden, as in Egypt, and was practiced only by unauthorized sorcerers. The task of the official magicians was to offset their evil activities.

5. **Astrology:** In Babylonia, divination and sorcery by the stars (see Astrology*) were practiced by experts known as "ašipu" (Hebrew, aŝiph), who were attached to the temples and worked under the auspices of the supreme gods Ea and Marduk.

Interrelations of Magic, Superstition and Religion: Organized religion is a higher form of essentially the same relationship between man and the supernatural. The difference is that whereas magic is intended to subdue the spirits and make them subservient to man's will, a god is worshipped — sometimes inside temples — as a being far superior to man. He must be placated and prayers addressed to him. There can be no attempt to force his actions.

In the ancient Near East, organized religion was very much a matter of institutionalized magic. When the religion became discredited — either because the priests became too remote from the mass of the people, too intellectual or too materialistic, i.e. the demands for tithes and sacrifices increased beyond reason; or because the moral standards of religious behaviour fell too low, then the people turned again to magic and superstition as a substitute for a religion which had lost its significance. The pattern can be observed right up to the present day. It is still possible to find examples of peoples who have abandoned religion and turned instead to superstition. In other ancient religions, magic and superstition had their place alongside other elements. This inscription in early 6th c. Greek script (from Ephesus) defines the omens derived from the flight of birds (**591**).

Israel's religion, in contrast, was dissociated from the practice of magic. The efficacy of magic was recognized by the religion of the Bible, but its practice was strictly forbidden. Nevertheless, it is apparent that in one form or another, elements of superstition and magic always persisted among the Israelite masses. In times of religious revival, they would seem to have been eradicated, but they remained, just below the surface of national life, ready to reappear on the slightest excuse.

c. **Israel and Magic:** Officially, Judaism, like other Semitic religions, regarded superstition as an inferior form of belief. It was roundly condemned by the prophets and all upholders of the Law, who taught that the only sure protection against evil was belief in the one God and obedience to His will. Not only did Mosaic Law forbid all magic practices (Lv. 19:26; Dt. 18:10), make witchcraft a capital offence (Ex. 22:18) and reject customs such as sacrificing to the dead which were found among neighbouring peoples; it also saw these rules as placing Israel on a different plane. Other nations might believe in magicians and sorcerers. To Israel alone, the prophets of God had been given (see below).

There were, however, cases of ancient customs being perpetuated under a new guise. For instance, Leviticus* (19:9–10) directs that at the time of harvest, the corners of fields, the gleanings of corn and the fallen grapes in vineyards shall be left for the poor and the foreigner. This probably continued an ancient custom of leaving some of the harvest for the nourishment of the spirits of the corn and other crops, so as to ensure a good harvest the following year. Similarly, the children of Israel were commanded to leave fringes "tzitzit" intertwined with blue threads on the corners of their garments (see Clothing*), not to frighten off evil spirits but as a reminder of the words of God. The Jews also placed (and place) a "mezuzah" containing a parchment scroll bearing a prayer on their door-posts in continuation of far older customs, intended possibly to protect a house and its inhabitants, although according to the declared faith, to remind Israel of the words of their living God.

Biblical Terminology: Because of its continuing preoccupation with magical practices and practitioners, a variety of terms connected with witchcraft and sorcery are to be found in the Bible. A sorcerer, or practitioner of witchcraft, is a "kashaf" (Ex. 7:11; 22:18; Dt. 18:10; Jer. 27:9; II Ch. 33:6; Dan. 2:2); there is also a special word, "ḥartum" (see above). "Laḥaš" or soothsaying is used in the Bible for the one who chants or whispers incantations. It means specifically charming serpents (Ps. 58:5), whereas "ḥober" or charmer (Is. 47:9, 12; Ps. 58:5) apparently refers to the use of magic amulets and charms. In the book of Daniel*,

591

the word "Chaldeans" is used both in an ethnic sense and to designate a certain class of specialists in magic and witchcraft. The New Testament refers frequently to magic and witchcraft (e.g. Ac. 8:9, 11; 13:6, 8). The Magi, for instance (Mt. 2), were in fact an ethnic group from Media whose name, like that of the Chaldeans, became a technical term for a magician.

Prevalence and Prohibition of Magic: While many forms of magic were bitterly opposed by official religion, divination (fortune-telling) was taken over by it and in the early days at least was an important aspect of religion.

Amulets: The forms of magic specifically prohibited included the wearing of amulets. Their use was widespread and, apparently, persistent, although these were condemned by the prophets only when they involved trust in gods other than Yahweh. In a recent excavation, a Hebrew amulet against night-demons was unearthed, dating back to the period of the monarchy. One of the items in the list of women's finery in Is. 3:18–23 is the amulet or humming shell ("laḥaš"), which was apparently connected with snake-charming. Some scholars believe that these objects acquired a special potency as a result of spells whispered into them. Others consider that the name originated in "naḥaš", the word for snake [in Hebrew the letters "l" (lamed) and "n" (nûn) are often interchanged], and that originally it was serpent-like in shape. Snakes are known to have been widely worshipped by the Canaanites and many vessels engraved or impressed with snakes **(265 c)** have been unearthed in excavations of the Canaanite and Israelite periods.

Another item in Isaiah's list, the "crescents" ("sahronim") were used as decorations for the long necks of camels, and also worn by the kings of Midian (Jud. 8:21, 26). The same verse of Isaiah mentions "headbands" ("šabisim"). These were illustrated from the excavation of Ugarit* where amulets of this kind, given the same name in Ugaritic literature, were discovered.

The prevalence of sorcery among the peoples of Canaan is amply illustrated from the epics of Ugarit, and helps to explain the Bible's uncompromising attitude. Magic practices included divination by observing the flight of birds and the movements of the stars (see astrology*). These and similar practices were condemned.

Necromancy: Above all, the Bible forbade necromancy (seeking guidance from the dead); "There shall not be found among you any one who burns his son or his daughter as an offering, any one who practices divination, a soothsayer, or an augur, or a sorcerer, or a charmer, or a medium, or a wizard, or a necromancer." (Dt. 18:10–11). Necromancers who invoked "ghosts and familiar spirits" were apparently fairly numerous, for more than one king attempted to stamp out the practice. Saul endeavoured to ban the activities of sorcerers and necromancers, yet, at the end of his life, even he had recourse to such a woman (I Sam. 28:7–25). The urge to seek guidance from ancestors and the recently dead was apparently strongly rooted in the hearts of men and withstood official opposition and outright prohibition.

Magicians and Sorcerers: In the story of Moses at Pharaoh's court, the magicians of Egypt who could also turn their rods into serpents are mentioned (Ex. 7:11). That this was a familiar trick among Egyptian practitioners is witnessed by these drawings **(592)**. On top, a magician casts down

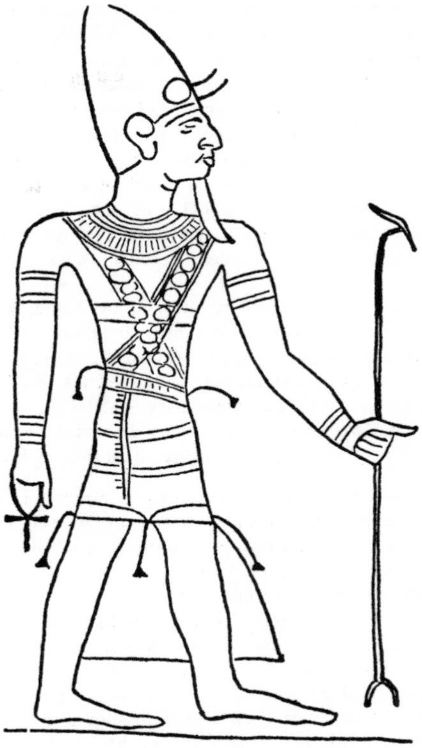

592

his rod which rears into a serpent; centre, a scarab from Tanis, showing a snake-charmer performing before three gods and, below, a man or a god, from a bas-relief in an Egyptian temple, leading four calves and carrying either a stick with a snake's head or a stick which has been transformed into a snake. Pharaoh's sorcerers were also able to emulate Moses and Aaron when they turned the water of the Nile into blood (Ex. 7:22) and when they brought a plague of frogs upon the land (Ex. 8:7), but they were beaten when it came to calling up the plague of gnats (8:18) and were affected by the plague of boils along with the rest of Egypt (9:11).

Very few sorcerers are mentioned by name. Jezebel was regarded as one (II K. 9:22), and sorcerers are mentioned in general in Micah (5:12); Menasseh, king of Judah, is condemned for encouraging sorcerers (II K. 21:6) and Ezekiel (Ezk. 13:17–23) prophesies woe to the women who "sew magic bands upon all wrists and make veils for the heads of persons of every stature, in the hunt for souls!"

Foreign Influences: Most references to magic and witchcraft among the prophetic books concern foreign peoples. Second Isaiah's denial of the power of Babylonia's "many sorceries and the great power of your enchantments" to save her from disaster is an example (Is. 47:5–15). Daniel's story is another: Nebuchadrezzar, king of Babylonia, ordered that young Jewish nobles be brought to his palace to learn the language and arts of the Chaldeans (Dan. 1:3–5), and when they had completed their education the king "found them ten times better than all the magicians and enchanters that were in all his kingdom" (1:20). It was they (and especially Daniel*) who interpreted the king's dreams when the Babylonian wise men were baffled (Dan. 2–4).

Divination and Sympathetic Magic: On the other hand, possibly from the force of example, the kings of Israel and Judah demanded oracles from the prophets before embarking on military campaigns or battles and the prophets (Elijah*, Elisha* and Micah*) provided them. One example of sympathetic magic used in this way occurred when Jehoash (800–784 BCE), king of Israel, visited Elisha on his death bed. Elisha made Jehoash shoot arrows from a bow and strike the ground with them as an omen of victory over the Syrians (see Elisha*).

Decision by Lot: Among the more innocuous forms of magic officially practiced by the priests of Israel were obtaining oracles from the "ephod" and Urim and Thumim (about which little is known). A decision between possible alternate courses of action might also be sought by casting lots. In ancient times, the lots would be small sticks or animal bones, stones, arrows or ropes. The decision could be sought either by casting the lots and drawing a conclusion from the way they fell, or by shaking the lots in a closed container and then picking one out at random. The result was regarded as the will of God, by the Jews as much as the other peoples of antiquity (Pr. 16:33). The practice had also been common in Canaan. In a fragment from Ugarit*, there is a reference to "Resheph of good fortune", apparently connected with his possession of a bow which served as a means of divination.

The Old Testament records three instances of lots being drawn to decide who was responsible for God's anger: the Achan incident (Jos. 7), the argument between Saul and Jonathan (I Sam. 14:38–45) and in the story of Jonah (1:7), but nothing is said as to the procedure followed in casting the lots.

On the Day of Atonement, the High Priest would draw lots to decide which of the two scapegoats was to be sacrificed "for the Lord" and which was to be turned out into the wilderness for Azazel ("the demon"; Lv. 16:8; see Sacrifice*).

The use of lots in religious ritual suggests that they were also used frequently in secular affairs, cf. Proverbs 18:18: "The lot puts an end to disputes and decides between powerful contenders." After the Conquest*, the Promised land was divided by lot among the Israelite tribes and their clans (see Census*) and the same procedure was used in allocating the Levitical towns (Jos. 21:4, 6, 10, 20). There are also many references to distributing the booty taken from a defeated enemy by lot (Jl. 3:3; Ob. 11; Ps. 22:18).

In the story of Esther, Haman drew lots to decide the exact day on which the Jews should be exterminated (Est. 3:7) and in this case the method used is suggested by the term "pur" used for the lots cast. These followed an Assyrian custom of rolling two dice, one, "aban eresi" was the desirable die; the other "aban la eresi", the undesirable.

Prophets vs. Diviners: Many scholars have pointed to the similarities that existed between the early professional prophets or diviners and the inspired prophets of Yahweh. Both engaged in foretelling the future, often using very similar methods, but the development of inspired prophecy shows how far it progressed from the simple fortune-telling of professional prophecy. Magic by spells and symbols and using the occult properties attributed to plants and other things was generally condemned by the prophets, although other forms of magic were sublimated into symbols compatible with the spirit of Yahwism. Prophecy in the classical biblical sense was an essential part of an elevated spiritual Yahwism, itself far removed from the customary practices of popular religion in which divination and magic played an important part. Because these practices often bordered on or involved the forbidden black magic, they were roundly condemned by the prophets. Nevertheless, the people's desire to learn the future and to secure divine help in their individual undertakings — the motives which usually give rise to divination and white magic — had also to be met. The prophets made prediction of future events, often using the old methods of divination, the vehicle for revelation of God's "word" or message for His people (see article on Revelation*). Such forms of revelation were allowed to pass, as we find in many passages of the Old Testament. They also appointed "signs" similar to the old familiar omens to give their predictions greater authority. This use of the techniques of magic was justified by explaining that such signs were given by God to His true prophets, as well as to false pretenders. They represented divine power being exercised in minor concerns as evidence that man could trust in God in matters of greater moment (Jud. 6:36; Ex. 4:8; Is. 7:11).

The prophets never revised their condemnation of magic as such, but a distinction was made between divination, which is merely a matter of trying to obtain advance knowledge of future events, and real magic which aims at enlisting supernatural aid to accomplish certain ends.

Post-Exilic Period: The ordinary people of Palestine continued to make use of the amulets and magic formulas which, throughout the ancient world, were used as protections against demons and evil spirits, whether merely mischievous or malicious and dangerous like Lilith, the baby-snatching queen of demons. Superstition was universal. For instance, this Roman bronze magic hand (**593**) bears symbols to avert the evil eye. Among the Israelites, however, they were not associated with belief in pagan gods. They were rejected by official religion which frowned on too much concern with either angels or demons, but this did not lessen their significance in the life of the masses.

The Rabbis* rejected these concepts and ancient practices connected with them as "Amorite customs", but as a result of Persian and Babylonian influences they became much more prevalent after the Exile and during the Talmudic period (for fuller description, see Apocrypha*). This partly explains why the belief in demons clearly expressed in the New Testament appears to be quite unimportant in the Old Testament. The influence of Egyptian occult science in the 1st c. BCE and the one following is also referred to in the Mishnah*. The New Testament offers evidence of its practice among such Jews as Simon Magus (Ac. 8:9) and Elymas (Ac. 13:8). Demons absorbed into Jewish folk beliefs, however, were different from their foreign progenitors in that they are not independent of God and are not His equal. Instead they are bound to acknowledge His superior authority and to obey Him when called upon to do so (see Lk. 10:17–19; Mk. 3:22–23).

Although in the present state of knowledge it is difficult to explain the persistence of superstition and occult influences in later Judaism, the Old Testament's own attitude to magic — expecially occult, black magic — gives some indication. In fact the Old Testament never questions the power of magic. It only denies its validity. Not until the age of enlightenment, when the whole foundation of magic could be rationally exposed and destroyed, did belief in and recourse to magic decline. Prohibition could never stop people from believing or practicing magic, but enlightenment will.

Thus, rejection of magic was not achieved only by strength of faith, in which post-Exilic Judaism shared. It came from better understanding allied to the implacable opposition which the leaders of Israel had at all times displayed towards popular religious practices in which a latent magic element persisted.

MALACHI, BOOK OF. — The last of the Twelve Minor Prophets in the Hebrew canon, Malachi can be unhesitatingly dated to the Persian period. The book speaks of the Pekah (Satrap) appointed by the Persian kings to rule the provinces of their empire, and also refers to the sacrifices and tithes offered on the completion of the Second Temple (515 BCE). Other evidence suggests that it was written at or before the time of Ezra. Suggestions of a dating to the Hasmonean period are refuted by the evidence of Ben Sira (Ecclus., see Apocrypha*), who lived around 200 BCE (i.e. before the Hasmoneans) and mentions all the twelve minor prophets.

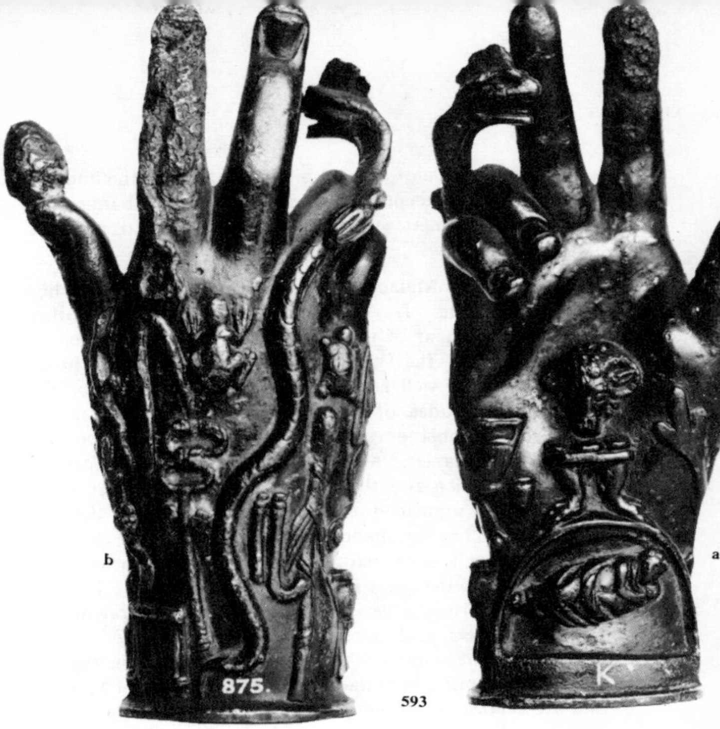

b a

593

The majority opinion is that Malachi was probably a contemporary of Haggai* and Zechariah*, possibly also of Joel* and Obadiah*, before the time of Ezra*, perhaps during the first half of the 5th or late 6th c. BCE.

Contents: The book deals with God's love and care for Israel (1:2–5) and Israel's defiance of God's laws shown by offering maimed, blemished or stolen animals for sacrifice (1:6–14); by withholding tithes (3:8–12); by doubting the power of God (3:13–15) and (2:10–16) by divorcing mature wives, "the wives of their youth", and marrying "the daughters of a foreign god". The prophet enumerates the qualities demanded of a true priest (2:4–9) and the blessings he will reap, in contrast to the curses that will be laid on the careless or dishonest priest (2:2–3, 9).

The Day of Yahweh: Following his admonitions, Malachi prophesies about God's judgment on defiant and sinful people to be made on the "Day of Yahweh" which will come "burning like an oven" (4:1). On this day the wicked will be destroyed "root and branch" although for those "who fear My name, the sun of righteousness shall rise with healing in its wings" (4:2). Before the Day comes, the prophet promises, God will send His messenger who, "like a refiner's fire" (3:2) that separates the base metal from the true, will judge and purify the priesthood (the sons of Levi). The book closes with the further assurance that the prophet Elijah will also be sent as God's messenger to remind the people of their duty towards God and thus avoid His curse (4:5–6, Hebrew text 3:23–24).

Style: The prophecies are presented in the rhetorical form of a dialogue between the prophet and his audience or between God and the people. Each dialogue closes with a promise or a warning.

The prophecy of Malachi reaffirms the message of the great pre-Exilic prophets. He proclaims God's fatherly, loving care, His holiness and righteousness and the terrible judgment He will wreak on the wicked. However, unlike his predecessors, Malachi lays the greatest stress on the Law as the essential rule of life and bitterly condemns the flouting of any of its precepts. In a straightforward manner, he presents the prophetic spirit in practical terms of observance of particular laws.

Significance of Malachi: In many respects, Malachi's prophecy of the "Day of Yahweh" conforms to other prophets' treatment of this theme (see Joel*). However, in Malachi's vision, the Day will see a purifying judgment on the righteous as well as sinners and its sequel will be the restoration in Judea of worship and life according to the Law. This prophet does not see the end of days coming through a spontaneous awakening of the people. He foresees a reign of justice and the restoration of the proper ritual carried out by a purified priesthood. The coming of the Day of Yahweh will be foreshadowed by the angels of the covenant who will clear a path before the Lord as he returns to his Temple; before the great Day dawns, the prophet Elijah will return to reform the generation and effect a reconciliation between fathers and sons.

Heavenly messengers who play a leading role in the end of days appear first in Malachi's vision of the Day of Yahweh, and are echoed in subsequent literature (Ecclesiasticus, Ben Sira and Esdras II, see Apocrypha*). The conjunction of Moses and Elijah in events heralding the coming of the Messiah (the Day of Yahweh) points to an important development in post-Exilic Judaism. It was part of a significant movement in thought and life which was to have an abiding influence on the Jewish Messianic concept. (See also: Obadiah*, Joel*, Haggai*, Zechariah*.)

MARK, GOSPEL OF. — **Authorship:** The authorship of the Gospel of Mark is well attested in the writings of the early church fathers. The best known comment is the saying attributed by Eusebius (Eccles. History) to Papias (ca. 140 CE) to the effect that Mark, "the interpreter of Peter", wrote down everything which Jesus said and did. This companion of Peter's is undoubtedly identical with the John Mark who accompanied Paul and Barnabas (Ac. 13:5, 13) to Cyprus on the first part of Paul's first missionary journey and who was also affectionately referred to by Peter as "my son" (I Pet. 5:13). According to Co. 4:10, Mark (or Marcus) was a cousin of Barnabas. When Paul went on to preach to the Gentiles, Mark left him and returned to Jerusalem (Ac. 13:4–13). In Cyprus they had worked among the Jews only. Later on Barnabas and Mark went back together (Ac. 15:39).

Date: The date of Mark's Gospel can be established with a fair degree of accuracy. According to Irenaeus (ca. 180 CE; Iren. *Adv. Haeres*, III. i. 2), Mark was written after the deaths of Peter and Paul, which fixes the earliest possibility as ca. 64. The latest possible date is the year 70 CE, for nowhere does Mark allude to the destruction of Jerusalem (compare especially Mk. 13:14 with Lk. 21:20). However, scholars who hold that Luke* was written before the martyrdom of Paul (ca. 64 CE), are forced to date the second Gospel earlier than this, for Luke is clearly dependent upon Mark (see Synoptic Gospels*).

The Second Gospel was quite probably written in Rome. Irenaeus (*op. cit.*) reports that it was written at the urging of Peter's followers in that city and the inclusion of a number of Latin words in Greek form in the Gospel seems to confirm that it was written at Rome.

ORGANIZATION — Mark is the shortest of the four Gospels but this is not due to brevity on the part of its author. What Mark describes, he describes at length, but by concentrating largely on the deeds rather than the sayings of Jesus, he has limited the scope of his work. Mark begins his Gospel at the outset of Jesus' ministry; the genealogy, miraculous birth and boyhood events of the carpenter from Nazareth have no place in the Second Gospel. The ending of Mark at 16:8 is equally abrupt, for the last twelve verses of the Gospel are not contained in the oldest manuscripts of Mark and are generally assumed to be a later addition. This abrupt ending of Mark still presents a puzzle to scholars. Two explanatory theories have been advanced to explain it: 1. either the original ending of Mark was lost; or 2. Mark was prevented, perhaps by death, from finishing his Gospel.

Mark may be divided roughly into two sections. Chs. one to nine recount the Galilean ministry; 11 to 16 the events of Passion Week at Jerusalem. Ch. 10 acts as a literary bridge connecting the two major sections as well as relating several isolated incidents. Though the narratives of Jesus' life are presented in chronological order, nearly a third of Mark is devoted to Passion Week. This is not a coincidence. For Mark, the Passion was the crux and zenith of Christ's ministry (see "Purpose"). For this reason it is foreshadowed time and again during the Galilean ministry (cf. 2:20; 8:31; 9:9, 12, 31).

CONTENTS — The opening 13 verses of the Gospel of Mark serve as an introduction to the story of Jesus' ministry which follows immediately. Verses 1–8 introduce John the Baptist and then recount the baptism of Jesus (9–11). The temptation of Christ in the wilderness is briefly touched on in verses 12–13.

The large section 1:14–7:23 traces the course of Jesus' ministry in Galilee. 1:16–20 tells of the calling of the first disciples, Simon (Peter), Andrew, James and John. Then the experiences of Jesus in Capernaum (1:21–2:12) are related: the healing of a man possessed of an unclean spirit (1:21–28), Jesus' healing of Peter's mother-in-law and other sufferers (29–39), and the cleansing of a leper (40–45). 2:1–12 contains the account of Jesus' healing the paralytic and his first brush with the organized religious leaders who take offence at Jesus' presuming to forgive sins. The calling of Levi is related in 2:12–17.

Jesus' attitude towards Jewish law is reflected in the incidents recorded in 2:18–3:6: he rejects fasting for his disciples during his sojourn (the "bridegroom" of the parable) with them (18–22), and states his concept that the "Sabbath was made for man and not man for the Sabbath" (23–28). Contrary to popular Christian belief, this last axiom is not a Christian innovation at all, for the early Rabbis held a similar view (cf. Mechilta 104a). Ch. 3:1–6 records a dispute between Jesus* and the Pharisees* about the laws of the Sabbath over Jesus' healing of a man with a withered hand on the Sabbath*.

Ch. 3:7–12 summarizes Jesus' earlier activities and records the large following he had won. The appointment of the Twelve Disciples is the subject of 3:13–19. In 3:22–30 Jesus is accused by the Scribes of being in league with the devil, but adroitly answers his accusers by asking, "How can Satan cast out Satan?" (3:23). The last verses (31–35) of ch. 3 concern the visit of Jesus' family and Jesus' reply that they who do the will of God are his brothers, sisters, and mother.

Ch. 4:1–34 records three of Jesus' parables: the parable of the Sower (4:1–9) and its explanation (10–25); the parable of the Seed Growing Secretly (4:26–29); and the parable of the Mustard Seed (4:30–34). While Jesus and his disciples are crossing the Sea of Galilee a storm suddenly arises and threatens their lives, but Jesus stills the wind and the sea (4:35–41).

The story of the Gerasene demoniac possessed of unclean spirits is related in 5:1–20. The raising of Jairus' daughter is described in 5:21–24, 35–43 and, interrupting this narration, is the story of the healing of the woman with an issue of blood (5:25–34).

Returning to his home town of Nazareth, Jesus is rejected by his own townspeople (6:1–6). Vs. 7–13 recount the Sending out of the Twelve and 14–29 the beheading of John the Baptist. The Feeding of the Five Thousand with five loaves and two fishes is recorded in 6:30–44, and Jesus walking on the water in vs. 45–52, followed by more evidence of his fame as a healer (53–56).

The first 23 vs. of ch. 7 further elucidate Jesus' attitude to traditional Law*. He attacks the man-made traditions which have usurped the commandments of God (1–13) and explains that uncleanness stems from the heart of man, not from what he eats (14–23). This is a direct denial of *kashrut*, the traditional dietary laws of the Jews (see especially 7:19b). 7:24–9:50 describe a comparatively quiet period. In the region of Tyre and Sidon, Jesus heals the possessed daughter of the Syro-Phoenician woman (24–30). Returning through the region of the Decapolis, he heals a deaf-mute (31–37).

8:1–10 contains another account of the miraculous feeding of a multitude, this time of 4,000. Asked by the Pharisees for a sign from heaven, Jesus refuses (8:11–13) and warns his disciples against them and against Herod (14–21). At Bethsaida Jesus heals a blind man (22–26), then goes on with his disciples to the environs of Caesarea Philippi, where Peter confesses Jesus as the Christ, i.e. the Messiah (27–30).

Jesus then begins to prepare his followers for his death (8:31–33), foretelling the coming of the Kingdom of God (8:34–9:1). The account of the Transfiguration follows immediately (9:2–13), as if to strengthen Jesus' claims to the Messiahship, for he is there seen talking with Elijah and Moses.

9:14–29 tells of Jesus' healing of the epileptic boy whom the disciples had been unable to cure. Vs. 30–32 is another prophecy of his own death. Jesus rebukes his disciples for thinking about which one is the greatest and admonishes them to be humble, prepared to receive even little children in his name (9:33–37). The report of a stranger casting out devils in Jesus' name provokes the retort that, "He who is not against us is for us" (38–41). Jesus then warns of the dangers of sin, saying that nothing should be permitted to hinder entry into the Kingdom of Heaven. An offending hand or foot should be cut off rather than endanger the entire body (42–50).

Chapter 10 marks a turning point in the Gospel of Mark. Jesus' active ministry is drawn to a close and he begins the fateful journey to Jerusalem and his death. When questioned by the Pharisees concerning divorce, Jesus is more strict than the Jewish leaders, for he allows no grounds whatsoever for divorce (10:1–12). The delightful incident of Jesus' blessing of the children is recorded in 10:13–16, followed by the story of the rich young man who could not bear to part with all his wealth (10:17–27). Jesus promises that all who have forsaken family and possessions to follow him shall be rewarded a hundredfold "in the age to come".

In 10:32–34, Jesus predicts his coming fate for the third time, telling his disciples (10:35–45) that he who wishes to be the leader of his fellows must be their servant. At Jericho, Jesus heals the blind beggar, Bartemaeus (10:46–52).

The events of Passion Week begin with the Triumphal Entry into Jerusalem (11:1–11), followed by the Cleansing of the Temple (11:15–19) and the incident of the barren fig tree, which Jesus uses to illustrate the power of faith (11:12–14, 20–26). Another deputation from the Sanhedrin questions Jesus about the source of his authority and he counters by asking the same question in reference to John the Baptist* (11:27–33; see article).

Ch. 12:1–12 gives the parable of the Wicked Husbandmen. Jesus meets another trick question about the relation between religious convictions and civil duty with the famous answer, "Render unto Caesar . . ." (12:13–17) and discomfitted a group of Sadducees* who tried to trick him with a frivolous question about the resurrection* (18–27).

To another questioner (28–34) Jesus stated the two great commandments: first the traditional *Shema Israel* "Hear, O Israel, the Lord our God is one" (Dt. 6:4–5); and secondly "You shall love your neighbour as yourself" (Lv. 19:18). Jesus then spoke of the Messiah (35–37), condemned the scribes for hypocrisy and rapaciousness (38–40) and drew the moral of the widow's mite (41–44).

Ch. 13 contains a collection of eschatological* sayings about the End of Days, including Jesus' prophecy of the destruction of the Temple (1–2); his account of the sufferings that will precede the End (3–13), the manner of its coming (14–23) and the coming of the Son of Man (24–32), ending with the injunction to be vigilant, since they could not "know when the time will come" (33–37).

This chapter is similar to the Jewish apocalyptical literature which was so popular during the latter period of the Second Temple (see article). The outbreak of wars, earthquakes and famines are typical signs of the so-called "Birthpangs of the Messiah". Rabbinical* literature also dwells at great length on the persecutions of the Days of the Messiah. Together with the book of Revelation* (see Apocalypse*), this apocalypse gives the reader a valuable insight into the eschatological hopes of the Early Christian Church.

Chs. 14 and 15 relate the last sufferings and death of Christ. During a meal at Bethany Jesus is anointed with precious ointment, symbolic of the anointing of the body after death (14:3–9). Judas Iscariot makes his plans to betray Jesus (14:10–11) and Jesus prepares for the Passover Meal (14:12–16). During the meal Jesus foretells the treachery of Judas (14:17–21) and then initiates the sacrament of the Last Supper (14:22–25).

Event then follows upon event in quick succession: the agony at Gethsemane (14:26–42), the arrest (14:43–52), the night trial and sentence before the Sanhedrin (14:53–65), and Peter's denial of Jesus (14:66–72). The next morning Jesus is accused before Pilate (15:1–5) who offers to release him, but the crowd prefers the release of Barabbas and Jesus is sentenced to death by crucifixion (15:6–15). He is mocked and scourged by the Roman soldiers (15:16–20a) and then led out to Golgotha where he is crucified (15:20b–32). Verses 33–41 contain the account of his death and his burial is described in 15:42–47.

The empty tomb and the announcement of Jesus' resurrection are the subjects of 16:1–8. Here the Gospel of Mark draws to an abrupt end. Vs. 9–20 of ch. 16, in which Jesus appears to his disciples, charges them to preach the good tidings throughout the entire world, and then ascends into heaven, are of later origin. This section does not appear in the earliest manuscripts of the Second Gospel and its exact origin is doubtful, though obviously it is of a later date than the rest of Mark.

Sources: The problem of Mark's sources is a difficult one which still defies a positive solution. We can be fairly safe in assuming that Mark made use of information he gleaned at first-hand from Peter and Paul and perhaps he himself was an eyewitness to some of the Passion Week scenes so fully described in the latter section of his Gospel. A more difficult question is posed by the relationship of Mark to Q (see Gospels*, Synoptic) which was undoubtedly the earlier document. Though Mark may have been familiar with the "sayings of Jesus" contained in Q, it would not seem that he quoted extensively from them, if at all. Assuming however, that he had access to this source of material, it does appear strange that he failed to make use of it. Undoubtedly various (Aramaic) oral traditions prevalent in the early Christian communities were incorporated by Mark into his Gospel. This may be the explanation, for example, of the double account of the feeding of the multitude (6:30–44 and 8:1–10). Chapter 13 may well be the literary echo of an early Christian Apocalypse for it has its own distinct, quite unique style.

Papias insisted that Mark's Gospel was complete but, on closer analysis, it appears that it is the most incomplete of all. It omits much material that any follower of Peter's must have heard and, because of the many omissions, the Gospel was neglected. Augustine called its author a mere "lackey and abbreviator of Matthew*" (De Cons. Ev. 1), although this was in connection with a controversy over Papias on Mark and may have referred to another Gospel.

Style: The author of Mark was no master of Greek literary style. His language was unpolished and colloquial, but it has a refreshing directness which makes it one of the most vivid of the Gospels. Despite the fact that Mark contains a number of Aramaic idioms, it need not necessarily be regarded as a translation from Aramaic — which was suggested by C.C. Torrey and others. The Aramaicisms could reflect what was quite probably the author's mother tongue, or perhaps an Aramaic oral source.

Purpose: Mark himself was undoubtedly a Jew, but his Gospel is directed first and foremost to Gentiles. Accordingly, unfamiliar Jewish customs and beliefs had to be explained to the reader (cf. 7:3–4; 12:18; 15:42). Mark's main purpose was to explain to the Gentile world why this Jewish Messiah had been rejected by his own people. For this reason, he gives a full description of the growing opposition and hostility to Jesus among the organized religious circles of Judaism. This description also serves to emphasize his own conviction that the believers in Jesus represent the true House of Israel whereas those who reject him are a heretical offshoot. It also explains why his Gospel comes down heavily, even polemically, on the Gentile side of the Judaizing controversy (see Early Christianity*: Jewish Christians).

Mark firmly believed that Jesus was the Messiah, the son of God (cf. Mark 8:29–30; 14:61–62). He also makes it perfectly clear that Jesus' death on the cross was not a defeat but a victory, not so much the result of scheming men but rather a necessary step in the Divine plan (cf. Mark 8:31; 9:9, 12, 31; 10:33–34, 45; 14:24–25). A full third of Mark's Gospel is devoted to the events of one single week in Christ's ministry, i.e. Passion Week. Jesus' death marks the beginning, not the end, for a new covenant is made (cf. Mark 14:24). Mark makes no mention of the old covenant, the Law which God gave to Moses at Sinai, as does Matthew, nor does he use the Old Testament to provide "proof-texts" of the messiahship of Jesus. Such allusions were superfluous when addressed to a Gentile public.

Mark would seem to have been more concerned with describing the deeds of Jesus rather than his sayings. Whereas some 19 miracles of Jesus are recorded in Mark, only four parables are given in full. Though it is perhaps possible that Mark was unacquainted with the Sayings of Jesus, or "Q" as the source is called (see Gospels*, Synoptic), ignorance of these sayings on Mark's part would hardly have been probable, particularly in view of the close relationship between Mark and the foremost of the Apostles, Peter and Paul. It is more satisfying to assume that Mark was familiar with the sayings of Jesus, but wrote his Gospel with a view to complementing those sayings with a historical background of Jesus' life and ministry.

It has been suggested that Mark wrote for a Church suffering under the persecutions of Nero. This would perhaps explain Mark's interpretation of discipleship as being a way of suffering and death (cf. Mark 8:34–38; 10:38–39), in emulation of the Master.

MATTHEW, GOSPEL OF. — **Authorship:** Traditionally, the authorship of the first Gospel has been attributed to the Apostle, Matthew. In fact there is little evidence to substantiate this claim. If Matthew the Apostle, who lived and worked side by side with Jesus* throughout his ministry, were the true author of the first Gospel, why was he forced to rely so heavily on Mark and the Q document as the sources for his material? Surely he would have been able to give a much more vivid and accurate account from his own first-hand experience.

The tradition that the Apostle was the author of Matthew was apparently influenced by a statement of Papias, the Bishop of Hieropolis, ca. 140 CE, who referred to a tradition he had received concerning the "logia" (words) of Jesus — a work which ante-dated the Gospel of Matthew — as having been written by the Apostle. Some scholars believe that Papias had a tradition about a work in Aramaic by the Apostle Matthew, and that he wrongly took this to be the Gospel. This mistake may also have laid the foundation for other statements that there was a Hebrew original.

Possibly, at that time, documents were known to be in existence in Palestine, written in Hebrew or Aramaic, closely resembling the Gospel of Matthew as we know it. Irenaeus (late 2nd c. CE) said, "Matthew among the Hebrews published a Gospel in their own dialect, when Peter and Paul were preaching in Rome and founding the Church" (Haer. III. 1). According to one opinion, he may have been quoting from Papias. Some authoritative scholars consider that behind all these references, there was a written "gospel" with sayings and stories in Hebrew attributed to Matthew — but not the same as the Greek Gospel known today. It is hard to go further than this, beyond saying that much of the material in Matthew has a Hebrew background, especially where it diverges from Mark, which seems to have an Aramaic substratum.

Date: As Matthew uses Mark* as one of its sources, it can hardly have been written until a few years after the second Gospel (ca. 65–67 CE). By the beginning of the second century, the Gospel of Matthew had come to occupy an authoritative position in the early Church. The fact that it was placed at the head of the Gospels when the New Testament was canonized makes this clear. If Matthew was so widely read and revered by the turn of the century, it must have been written several years earlier. The generally accepted date for the first Gospel is 70–80 CE, which seems reasonable although a slightly earlier date (before 70) is preferred by some.

Sources: The two principal literary sources utilized by Matthew were the Gospel of Mark and the hypothetical Q document (see Gospels*, Synoptic). Other secondary sources were also undoubtedly incorporated into Matthew's Gospel, but it is extremely difficult to separate the various strands. It has been suggested that Matthew's messianic "proof-texts" — Old Testament passages taken out of context to "prove" the messiahship of Jesus — are from a special source. This theory has gained support from the discovery of similar lists of messianic passages or testimonials among the Dead Sea Scrolls* (see article) and other similar collections. It is, however, disputed by scholars who hold that one of Matthew's chief interests was to show that Jesus was truly the Messiah, the fulfillment of the Old Testament prophecy. In this view, the prophetic passages reflect the convictions of the author of the first Gospel and the selection was probably made by him. Accordingly, such scholars designate the general collection of material unique to the Gospel of Matthew as "M" and they reject further attempts to distinguish additional separate sources in Matthew, regardless of the written Hebrew gospel suggested by other scholars (see above).

Style: Matthew's literary style occupies a position midway between the rough colloquial language of Mark and the graceful polished Greek of Luke. The first Gospel does not appear to be a Greek translation of an Aramaic original, for the author included a number of verses taken *verbatim* from Mark. Moreover, among the material from Q which Matthew and Luke have in common, there are several identical passages. The choice of exactly the same words can only be explained on the assumption that both authors wrote in Greek from a Greek source.

Organization: Matthew's literary achievement lies in the way he organized his material. Episodes described by Mark are skilfully combined with the sayings and discourses of Q. Matthew is divided into five major sections, apart from the narratives about the Nativity (chs. 1–2) and the Passion (chs. 26–28). Each of these major sections begins with a block of Markan material and is followed by pertinent discourses probably taken from Q. Each of the discourses is clearly differentiated. Each one ends with the same formula: "And it came to pass, when Jesus had finished these words..." (7:28; 11:1; 13:53; 19:1; 26:1). In this way, the life and teachings of Jesus are blended into a coherent, if artificial, scheme. Matthew's inclusion of the five discourses differentiates it structurally from Mark*.

Contents: Ch. 1 introduces the Gospel with a genealogical table (1:1–17), designed to illustrate that Jesus was descended not only from Abraham but also from David, i.e. that Jesus was the Messiah of the House of David. Vs. 18–24 recount the virgin birth, a story based on Matthew's misunderstanding of the Hebrew word "*alma*" (maiden) in the "Immanuel" passage of Isaiah (7:14). The story of the visit of the Magi (2:1–12) is also intended to testify to Jesus' messiahship. The flight into Egypt (13–15) and the massacre of the Bethlehem infants (16–18) are also described as the fulfillment of Old Testament prophecy. The Return from Egypt is reported in vs. 19–23.

The first of the five major sections of the Gospel makes up chs. 3–7. The narrative part, chs. 3–4 relies heavily on Markan material. Ch. 3 deals with John the Baptist* and his ministry (vs. 1–12) and the baptism of Jesus (13–17). Jesus' Temptation is related in 4:1–11 and the beginning of his ministry in Galilee in vs. 12–25.

Chs. 5–7 contain the Sermon on the Mount. In fact this is not a single sermon preached on a given occasion, but a compilation of a number of sayings and parables. 5:1–2 forms an introduction, the "mountain" of v. 1 being an obvious parallel to Moses on Mount Sinai. The well-known Beatitudes are recorded in 5:3–12 and contain strong eschatological overtones (compare "the poor in spirit" to the "poor of grace" or "poor of spirit" in the Dead Sea Scrolls*). The nature of discipleship is explained in 5:13–16 where the disciples are compared to "salt" and "light". Jesus' attitude towards the Law is explained in 5:17–48. It is interesting to note that whereas Mark's account of Jesus' views on marriage makes no allowance whatsoever for divorce (Mk. 10:11–12), Matthew makes a concession by permitting divorce in cases of adultery (5:32, cf. also 19:9). Jesus' attack upon the admonition in 5:43 to hate one's enemies has long puzzled scholars for there is no reference to such a command in the Old Testament. As one of the commandments of the Qumran Community was to hate the "Sons of Darkness", it is quite possible that Jesus is speaking out against this teaching of the Qumran Sect.

Ch. 6:1–18 contains a warning against hypocrisy and ostentatious piety, and gives (vs. 9–13) the Lord's Prayer. 19–34 warns against preoccupation with worldly riches and cares and 7:1–5 counsels against judging one's neighbour. Vs. 6–27 contain a number of exhortations and appropriate parables and 28–29 bring the Sermon on the Mount to a close and mark the end of the first major section of Matthew.

Section II (8:1–11:1) begins with a narrative (ch. 8) which recounts Jesus' healing of the leper (8:2–4), the centurion's servant (5–13) and Peter's mother-in-law (14–15); the stilling of the storm on the Sea of Galilee (8:23–27) and a shortened version of Mark's account of the Gadarene swine (28–34). Ch. 9 tells of the healing of the paralytic (9:1–8) and the calling of Matthew (9–13). Vs. 14–17 explain Jesus' attitude towards fasting and 18–26 relate the healing of the woman with an issue of blood and the raising of Jairus' daughter. 27–34 tell of further healings. V. 35 introduces the following passage (9:36–10:1), the calling of the disciples. Their names are listed in 10:2–4. 10:5–11:1, the discourse of the second section, concerns Jesus' instructions to his disciples, encouraging them to stand fast in the face of persecution.

The central theme of the *third section* (11:2–13:52) is the coming Kingdom of God. In 11:2–19, Jesus speaks of himself in relation to John the Baptist and (7–18) of John's mission as a forerunner of the Messiah. Vs. 20–24 are a condemnation of the cities which have ignored the "mighty works" done in them. In 25–30 Jesus speaks directly of himself as the Son of God. 12:1–14 records Jesus' dispute with the Pharisees over the Sabbath and 15–21 contains a typical example of Matthew's use of Old Testament prophecy to enhance Jesus' authority. Vs. 22–23 record Jesus' healing of a blind and dumb man, upon which the Pharisees accuse him of being in league with Beelzebub but are refuted (24–32). When the Pharisees ask for a sign, Jesus condemns them and compares himself to Jonah. As Jonah was three days and three nights in the belly of a whale so will the Son of Man be three days and three nights in the earth (38–42). The visit of Jesus' mother and brethren is recounted in 46–50.

Ch. 13 contains a collection of seven of Jesus' parables illustrating the Kingdom of Heaven: the parable of the sower (13:3–23); of the wheat and the tares (24–30) and its explanation (36–43); of the grain of mustard (31–32); of the leaven (33); of the hidden treasure (44); of the pearl (45–46); and of the fish-net (47–50). Verse 52 of ch. 13 brings to a close the third section of Matthew's Gospel.

Section IV consists of 13:53–18:35. Jesus' rejection in Nazareth is related (13:53–58) as well as the story of John the Baptist's beheading (14:1–12), the Feeding of the Five Thousand (14:13–21), and the walking on water (14:22–32). After Jesus' attack on the Scribes and Pharisees (15:1–9), he goes on to renounce the concept of ritual as opposed to inner cleanliness (15:10–20). The healing of a Canaanite woman's daughter is the subject of 15:21–28 and the Feeding of the Four Thousand is recounted in 15:29–32. Once again Jesus refuses to give the Pharisees and Sadducees a sign (16:1–4) and warns his disciples to beware of their teachings (16:5–12). There follows the confession of Peter (16:13–20), Jesus' first open reference to his coming death (16:21–23), his instructions in discipleship to his followers (16:24–28), the Transfiguration (17:1–13), and the cure of the demoniac boy (17:14–21). For a second time Jesus warns his disciples of his approaching death (17:22–23) and, so as not to offend the Jewish community, he makes provision for the paying of the Temple tax (17:24–27).

The original text uses the term "*statēr*" for the coin mentioned in 17:27. This equalled 2 didrachma (or half shekels) only in Antioch and Damascus, which seems to suggest that Matthew's home may have been in Syria, perhaps in Antioch, but certainly in the East.

Ch. 18 on the nature of discipleship includes the parables of the Lost Sheep (12–14) and of the merciful king and his unforgiving servant (21–35).

Section V, the last of the five sections, begins with 19:1 and goes up to or including ch. 25. Ch. 19 gives Jesus' views on marriage and divorce (19:1–12), his blessing of the children (13–15), his meeting with the rich young ruler (16–26), and his promise of reward to those who follow him (27–30).

The well-known parable of the Labourers in the Vineyard (20:1–16) is followed by Jesus' third prediction of his death (20:17–19). The mother of James and John attempts to gain special honours for her sons from Jesus, but he gently rebukes her and admonishes his followers to practice humility (20:20–28). On the way from Jericho to Jerusalem, Jesus heals two blind men (20:29–34).

Ch. 21 begins with the account of Jesus' Triumphal Entry into Jerusalem (21:1–11), then describes his cleansing of the Temple (12–17), the episode of the barren fig tree (18–22), and the questions of the deputation sent by the Sanhedrin to investigate Jesus (21:23–27). Two parables complete the chapter: the parable of the Two Sons (28–32), and the parable of the Wicked Husbandmen (33–44). The parable of the Marriage Feast for the King's Son appears in 22:1–14, followed by the questions put to Jesus by the various groups: the Pharisees' query concerning the payment of taxes (22:15–22), the Sadducees' snare about the resurrection of the dead (23–32), and the lawyer's question concerning the greatest of the commandments (34–40). In 22:41–46 Jesus puzzles the Pharisees by asking them if the Messiah is from the House of David.

Ch. 23 consists almost entirely of Jesus' harsh criticisms and attacks on the Scribes and Pharisees. He warns his disciples of their deceitful ways (23:1–12) and condemns both the Scribes and the Pharisees (13–36). The chapter ends with Jesus mourning over Jerusalem (23:37–39).

Chs. 24–25 contain Jesus' discourse on the Mount of Olives over the eschatological "end" of the world and the coming of the Kingdom of Heaven. He prophesies the destruction of the Temple (24:1–2) and then describes the sufferings ("birthpangs") preceding "the end" (24:3–14), the advent of that fateful time (24:15–28), the coming of the Son of Man (29–36), and warns his disciples to be vigilant (37–44). Three parables are used to illustrate the eschatological event, the parable of the Faithful and Evil Servants (24:45–51), the parable of the Ten Virgins (25:1–13), and the parable of the Talents (25:14–30). This eschatological discourse concludes with Jesus' description of Judgment Day (25:31–46). These verses also constitute the end of the fifth section or "Book".

The three remaining chs., 26–28, form a sort of Epilogue to the Gospel of Matthew, in which the events of the Passion and Resurrection are recounted. The elders and high priests lay their plans to take Jesus captive (26:1–5) while Jesus' anointing in Bethany foreshadows his death (26:6–13). Judas' treachery is recorded in 14–16, 20–25; the Last Supper (26:17–19; 26–29); the agony in Gethsemane (26:30–46) and Jesus' arrest (26:47–56) and trial before the Sanhedrin (26:57–68). Then follow Peter's denial (26:69–75), the remorse of Judas (27:3–10), and Jesus' trial before Pontius Pilate (27:11–26). After having been mocked and scourged by the Roman soldiers (27:27–31a), Jesus is led to Golgotha where he is crucified (27:31b–44). His death is described in 27:45–56, and thereafter he is laid in the tomb (27:57–61). The Romans post a watch before the tomb to prevent any disturbances (27:62–66).

Ch. 28 describes the Resurrection of Christ: the empty tomb on that first Easter Sunday morning (28:1–8); the appearance of Jesus to the sorrowing women (9–10); the false report of the Roman watch (11–15); Jesus' appearance to his disciples in Galilee and his final charge to them, "Go ye therefore, and teach all nations" (16–20).

Purpose: The Gospel of Matthew did not reach its authoritative status within the early Church by accident. Although it is missionary-minded, the first Gospel was especially directed at and suited to the life of an organized community of believers. First of all, it seeks to establish beyond all question the messiahship of Jesus. To this end, Old Testament passages are often torn out of their original context, sometimes distorted and pressed into a different mould of Christological prophecy (see Eschatology*). For the author of Matthew, the coming of Jesus represented the true culmination of the teachings of the Old Testament. Both the Essenes and other messianically-minded groups of that era (see Dead Sea Scrolls*) made similar use of Old Testament messianic prophecy. However, although common source material was used, it was interpreted differently by each sect. So far as the author of Matthew was concerned, quotations from the Old Testament were used to demonstrate to his Jewish readers that the Scriptures had been fulfilled in the person and work of Jesus. In him the messianic predictions had been realized and the "Law and the Prophets" brought to their ultimate perfection. Jesus was also shown, by apt quotation, to represent the eschatological "prophet" or second Moses, acting as a new lawgiver and the instrument of a New Covenant (see Christianity, Early*: Jewish Christians; Dead Sea Scrolls*).

This emphasis on Jesus as the fulfillment of Old Testament scripture is also an indication of the author of the Gospel and the audience for which he wrote. In one view, which has much to commend it, both writer and audience must have been Jewish Christians*, since to anyone else, the question of the fulfillment of Jewish scripture would be irrelevant. This theory is further supported by the Gospel's pointed attacks on the Pharisees*. After the destruction of the Temple in the year 70 CE, the Pharisees became the authoritative representatives of "normative Judaism" and, as such, the logical objects of Jewish Christian polemics. If Jesus were the true Messiah, then, in Matthew's view, the leaders of those who had rejected him must be shown to be wilfully errant and unscrupulous schemers.

There is another view, however, which believes the Gospel to have been addressed to a Gentile as well as Jewish audience. The Old Testament scriptures are the foundation of Gentile Christianity (shown especially in the speech of Stephen, in Ac. 7), and the Gospel of Matthew is basic to the preaching of all the Apostles — whether to Jews or Gentiles.

In any case, Matthew sets out to give an exalted portrayal of Jesus as the Jewish Messiah. To this end, he refines and elaborates some of the incidents in Jesus' life related by Mark. At the same time, definite rules of conduct pertaining to fasting, marriage, alms-giving and prayer are laid down within the context of the narrative. The first Gospel thus gives the impression that it was written essentially for a specific Jewish Christian community although, of course, its audience extended to Gentile Christians as well.

The Gospel strongly emphasizes the eschatological theme. Jesus the Messiah has established the Kingdom of God on earth and this is represented by the Church. The long-awaited Messiah had come and the Parousia (see Christianity, Early*) although not yet completed has begun to unfold itself in human history. The author of Matthew firmly believes that the advent of "the End" is imminent. It is the task of the Jewish Christian community to be prepared for the second, final coming of the Lord.

The Gospel of Matthew and the Dead Sea Scrolls: After the discovery of the Dead Sea Scrolls*, scholars began to compare this newly found Jewish sectarian literature with the scriptures of the New Testament, i.e. to gauge the "Jewish" characteristics of Matthew and the parallels with the Qumran school of exegesis.

The Gospel of Matthew was particularly rich in parallels to the Scrolls. Most apparent were the similarities of language, of course, but other more deeply based parallels were brought to light.

Like the Scrolls, Matthew is occupied with eschatology, with the advent of "the End." The Qumranites and the Jewish Christians both believed that they were living in an era when the Parousia had already begun to unfold itself; they were not mere spectators but participants in the eschatological drama. Both Matthew and the members of Qumran regarded themselves as living within the special divinely-led community, which for them represented the true Israel. They were both conscious of living under a new dispensation; a new covenant had been entrusted to them. Both were therefore bound to reject the Pharisees, the leaders of the mainstream of Judaism, which they regarded as a false and heretical group. The "proof-texts" used by Matthew to substantiate Jesus' claims to Messiahship are also echoed in the literature of Qumran, though the Qumranites interpreted Old Testament prophecies differently than did Matthew.

The author of Matthew was not necessarily a converted Essene however. It is also entirely misleading to state that Early Christianity, and Matthew in particular, "borrowed" heavily from Qumran. Similarities between the two groups are easily understandable in the light of their common Jewish background, their sectarian approach to religion, their common esteem and respect for the Holy Scriptures of the Old Testament, and their preoccupation with the imminent coming of the Parousia. Their similarities do not go beyond this.

Matthew is not awaiting the advent of the Messiah as are the members of the Qumran Community. He proclaims that the Messiah has already come in the person of Jesus of Nazareth. Whereas the Qumranites were extremely strict in regard to the membership of their group, Matthew pleas for tolerance explaining that at "the End", in God's own time, the sheep will be separated from the goats. A close scrutiny of Matthew reveals no trace of the binding sacerdotal character of the Qumran community. Parallels there are, but no direct relationship or dependence.

MEDICINE, DISEASE, HEALTH. — *Outline: A. Disease: The Biblical Attitude to Illness; Diseases Known to the Old Testament; Leprosy and Flux. B. Medical Practice: In Egypt and Mesopotamia; Medical Practice in the Old Testament; Medicines. C. Mental Disease. D. Public Health in Biblical Times. E. Medicine in Post-Exilic and New Testament Times: Knowledge of Anatomy and Physiology; Women's Diseases; Mental Ailments.*

A physician examining the Bible, particularly the Old Testament, will find little guidance to the ailments that were known or the remedies employed. Egyptian or Babylonian records, for instance, are much more explicit (see below). Some information about Israel can be gained from careful evaluation of what limited evidence does exist in the Old and New Testaments and in Talmudic material, and from a comparison of these data with the progress of knowledge in surrounding countries. Data on disease, on the one hand, and on the practice of medicine, on the other, are not directly related and can best be considered separately.

A. Disease: The Biblical Attitude to Illness: The Bible has a very clearly defined attitude to disease and its cause. Suffering, including illness, is the consequence of sin and is often the punishment for it. The relationship between cause and effect is direct, and much emphasized. "If you will hearken to the voice of the Lord your God and . . . keep all his statutes, I will put none of the diseases upon you which I put upon the Egyptians for I am the Lord, your healer" (Ex. 15:26), whereas "if you spurn my statutes . . . I will appoint over you sudden terror, consumption and fever that waste the eyes and cause life to pine away" (Lv. 26:15–16). Collectively, hunger and disease befell the Israelites as the result of their transgressions (Jer. 24:10; 32:24; Ezk. 14:13, 19, and many other examples), while other nations — the Philistines (I Sam. 5:6) or the Assyrians (II K. 19:35) might also incur God's punishment. Sometimes the sin of a single man could bring punishment to many. 70,000 are said to have died of "pestilence" as a result of David's sin (II Sam. 24:15–17). There is little indication of the exact nature of these scourges. The traditional concept of the connection between illness and suffering and sin is expressed clearly in the debate between Job and his "friends". Their point of view is deliberately overstated, but Job protests effectively against the whole doctrine (Job 19; cf. 1:1–2:10). Also in Isaiah (53) a very different interpretation is given to the meaning of suffering.

Diseases Known to the Old Testament: The exact disease which is called "pestilence" or "plague" is not easy to identify. The "pestilence" of II Sam. 24:15 is specifically identified as "the plague" (deber) and the visitation on the Philistines (I Sam. 5:6) was apparently bubonic plague (afulim; cf. Dt. 28:27). Other than these, the only diseases specifically distinguished by the Bible are those whose symptoms are visible to the eye: leprosy (ṣara'at); boils (sh'ḥin), the affliction of Job (2:7–8) and of King Hezekiah (II K. 20:7); scabs and scurvy (gereb and ḥeres; Dt. 28:27). All these were normally incurable — but cures are recorded, and the disease might also clear up of itself.

Other diseases can only be inferred from references to ailments in the legs, children's diseases and dysentery. Diseases mentioned as the consequences of disobedience and sin in Deuteronomy 28 include, besides those affecting the skin: plague (deber), ague (kadaḥat or "the fevers of the land"); consumption (shaḥefet); inflammation (daleket), and tumours (ophel). Added to these are madness (shigga'on), blindness (ivvaron; diseases of the eye are among the most common in Bible lands) and undefined psychiatric disturbances (timmahon-levāv).

Other unspecified diseases are mentioned which at this distance are very difficult to diagnose, for instance the sickness of the son of the woman from Zarephath which Elijah cured by mouth-to-mouth artificial respiration (I K. 17:17–21).

Leprosy and Flux (Lv. 13–15): These are named as allied conditions and, unlike the other diseases mentioned in the Scriptures, are considered forms of impurity* which must be detected with care and then cleansed. The purpose of the diagnosis was to determine the degree of impurity involved, rather than as a preliminary to any attempt at healing.

Lv. 13 lists the symptoms by which leprosy can be detected. In fact, these conditions are not specific to the classic leprosy (elephantiasis grecorum) but are common in other skin diseases. The term, "leprosy", was applied to a variety of skin infections and dermatological diseases, particularly to infectious ones, likely to spread through a rural community. The use of the word for "leprosy" to cover a variety of "unclean" conditions is apparent from its application to mould and fungus affecting clothing and houses (Lv. 14:47–59).

The diagnosis of leprosy and its cure, or rather purification, was the responsibility of the priests. In this, the Jews followed the customs of other peoples among whom priests were regularly physicians. There are a number of examples of the advice of the prophets being sought in cases of disease (I K. 14:1–13; II K. 1:2–4; 8:8–9; Is. 38:1).

Biblical law (see Impurity* and Purification) prescribed a rigid exclusion of "unclean" persons afflicted with leprosy (probably psoriasis) until pronounced "clean" by the priests. At the end of the period of isolation, if the priest declared that a cure had in fact taken place — he did not pretend to effect it — the sufferers were to wash themselves and the clothes they had worn during their illness and destroy the utensils they had used. In the time of Herod there were special "lepers' quarters" where the priests performed purificatory rites on such impure people for a period of seven days.

Flux (zob) was also associated with leprosy as a form of impurity. It meant a discharge from the sex organs, a common ailment among women. In males, the reference is probably to gonorrhea or to a seminal discharge.

B. Medical Practice: The Bible gives no evidence of attempts to find the causes of disease, and, except for the few cases mentioned, does not describe its symptoms or progress. Generally, the cause, to the biblical writers and their contemporaries, was abundantly clear; it was the consequence of sin, often the punishment for it. This attitude can also be found from Egyptian and Babylonian records, although they give much closer attention to a description of the disease. The descriptions usually appear in conjunction with incantations and prayers to the gods for healing.

In Egypt and Mesopotamia: An anonymous Sumerian physician (end 3rd mill. BCE) recorded his more valuable

594

595

prescriptions in this tablet **(594)** found in Nippur. This is the oldest pharmacopoeia on record. Assyrian and Babylonian literature of the "ashipu" (magicians; see Magic*) contain considerable material relating to disease. Most diseases were attributed either to demons, e.g. the "Lamashtu", spirits of the dead, or worms, or the influence of sorcerers, although pragmatic knowledge mingled with superstition. This relief **(595)** of an Assyrian exorcist priest of the time of Sargon III (7th c. BCE) shows a poppy in his left hand. Poppy, the source of opium, was a common ingredient in prescriptions. This Egyptian supplicant **(596)**, apparently a victim of infantile paralysis, is shown with his family, bringing an offering to a Syrian shrine, hoping for a cure.

Egyptian pharmacopoeia was well developed and so was their observation of certain diseases. As early as the 17th c. BCE, a body of much older medical knowledge had been written down and has survived as the "Edwin Smith Surgical Papyrus". Another, more famous, medical treatise is the Ebers Papyrus. In spite of the amount of witchcraft and sympathetic magic which these contain, they also demonstrate a degree of shrewd observation of the functions of the body. The heart was recognized as the source of life materials, although there was no concept of circulation of the blood. The surgical papyrus deals with diagnosis and treatment of broken bones, mainly manual treatment, rest, diet and herbal medicaments. It also reveals a highly developed attitude of scientific observation and recording. Detailed lists of herbal remedies have been found, although only a few of the plants they name can be identified. Remedial diets made use of honey, milk, meal, oil, vinegar and wine. There are similar lists among Babylonian records.

Both in Babylonia and Egypt, the priests who acted as physicians believed that they could overcome diseases with the help of their own knowledge, medicinal plants and magic or sorcery. Magic potions were equally familiar in Israel and although magic had no direct place in the Bible's discussion of disease, it represents the fundamental basis for all medical knowledge and practice in antiquity.

Just as the Babylonians added the equivalent of an alcohol massage to the traditional incantation as a cure for baldness, so did the Hebrews make use of a poultice of figs, as well as prayers, in treating a plague boil (II K. 20:7). Over the years the recorded experiences of generations of Babylonian physicians and their various remedies provided a practitioner with a considerable body of knowledge. Although the reasoning was usually unscientific, the medicines prescribed were often valuable. The application of poultices, powders and lotions made of saffron, mustard, cassia or other ingredients might have been intended to coax or tempt the demon of illness away from the affected area. They were none the less effective for that.

According to Assyrian texts, their 8th c. BCE physicians had progressed further, away from magic altogether: "If a man has such and such a disease, then use such and such drugs and he may recover" is the usual form of their prescriptions. Many of the names they gave the plants and herbs employed in their remedies remain in use to this day: cassia, sesame, chicory, crocus, saffron, hyssop, nard, myrrh and others. The Old Testament mentions these only as ingredients for incense, oils for anointing, or perfumes for embalming, but in post-biblical Talmudic writings (see below) their use in medicine is also described.

596

597

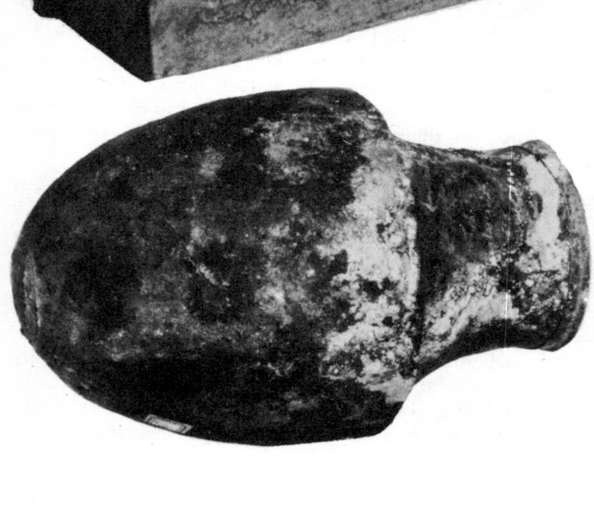

598

Developments in neighbouring countries had their effect on Jewish life, especially during and after the Exile. The long eulogy to a physician which Ben Sira wrote at the beginning of the 2nd c. BCE (Ecclus. 38:1–15; see Apocrypha*) is evidence of the position which medical practitioners had attained by then. See this Roman bronze container of drugs (**597**) and bronze bleeding-cup (**598**).

Medical Practice in the Old Testament: Medicine appears as largely a matter of popular superstition (e.g. the belief of Rachel and Leah that fertility could be assured by placing mandrakes under their husband's bed, Gn. 30:14–16). The term "physician" is hardly used (Ex. 15:26 applies it explicitly only to God) and its familiar connection with "magician" or "medicine-man" made the whole subject suspicious to the pious (e.g. II Ch. 16:12; Job. 13:4).

The only trusted healers were the priests and other holy men. The prophets were responsible for many diagnoses and cures (II K. 1:2–4), notably Elisha who was credited with restoring barren land (II K. 3:16) and brackish water (II K. 2:20–22), resurrecting the lad who died of sunstroke (II K. 4:18–35), nullifying the effects of poison (II K. 4: 38–41), curing leprosy (II K. 5) and diagnosing the imminent death of Ben Hadad, king of Damascus (II K. 8:7–10). Elijah also healed (I K. 17:17) and Isaiah prescribed the poultice of figs for Hezekiah's plague boil.

With the exceptions mentioned above, references to diseases in the Old Testament are not usually very informative. Only occasionally can a particular disease or group of diseases be inferred from the symptoms described.

Medicines: The best medicine was a righteous life and a cheerful mind (Pr. 17:22). However, certain medicines were employed, although not always fully described. Wounds and sores should be treated by the application of poultices, oils, and bandages (Is. 1:6; Jer. 8:22; 51:8) but the general terms used for such remedies (refu'a, terufa; Pr. 17:22) are translated in different ways. Moreover, the references are usually general. Jeremiah (30:13) prophesies that no "healing medicine" will be available to a sinful Israel; in 46:11 he compares Egypt to an incurably sick woman going uselessly to take the medicinal "balm" of Gilead. The famous balm appears to have been an anodyne. Balsam, used for many ointments, was grown in Jericho* and Ein Gedi*. Ezk. 47:12 describes the prophet's vision of trees of the future age that will grow beside the Dead Sea, their fruit for food and "their leaves for healing". The caperberry, like the mandrake, is mentioned as an aphrodisiac (Gn. 30:14; Ecc. 12:5). Aromatic substances — myrrh, aniseed, rue and cummin — are mentioned as ingredients of perfumes and embalming fluids, not medicines.

There are also a number of references throughout the Scriptures to the healing properties of bodies of water such as the Jordan, the Sea of Galilee, the pools of Siloam (Jn. 13:5) and Bethesda and the Dead Sea. These seem to belong to the realm of religious beliefs or magic rather than to medical practice.

C. **Mental Disease:** Mental disturbances are usually described in the Old Testament as bodily afflictions. The exceptions can be cited. One is the case of King Saul, a gifted man subject to fits of depression: "an evil spirit from the Lord tormented him" (I Sam. 16:14, passim). In his later days he was afflicted with paranoid delusions and the swift anger typical of aging people suffering from this disease, which may have been one reason for his repeated attacks on David*. The other case of an apparently accurate description of mental disturbance is the case of King Nebuchadrezzar (Dan. 4) to whom "the mind of a beast" was given. Although the story of his madness has no historical basis and may have been intended as a reminder to the Jews that the power of God is greater than the power of kings, there is reason to believe that the story originally referred to Nabonidus, the last king of Babylonia, who deliberately spent the last years of his reign away from his court. Among the Dead Sea Scrolls*, a "Prayer of Nabonidus" was discovered which related that the king came down with a "dread disease by the decree of the Most High . . . set apart from men" for seven years in the Arabian oasis of Teima.

D. **Public Health in Biblical Times:** The hygienic regulations incorporated in the Mosaic Law were unique among the peoples of the ancient Near East, although, of necessity, all organized communities had certain sanitary rules. Many authorities hold that without their very strict practices, the Jews could never have survived life in the desert. As it was, recurrent epidemics were by no means unknown (see above; Numbers*; Census*) but they were controlled as a result of the special regulations (see Deuteronomy*) concerning refuse and excrement; foods to be avoided and those which might be eaten; the 40-day quarantine imposed on certain diseases, and other measures, such as the washing of hands before eating, which had an overtly religious significance (see Impurity*).

Throughout civilization, water supplies* were always of importance. To the Hebrews who guarded them carefully at all times, they were specially significant and were always protected and kept clean (II Ch. 32:3; II K. 20:20).

Death presented problems of sanitation and there is frequent mention of the customs relating to corpses (see Funerary Cus.*). Archaeological discoveries have confirmed biblical evidence about burial away from living quarters (Gn. 23:4–11). To avoid defiling the living, the dead were buried outside the city walls. Only kings were interred in family vaults (I K. 2:10; 16:28). There is some indication (Am. 6:10) that corpses were burnt after a particularly devastating epidemic and, from Deuteronomy (21:22–23), it appears that it was customary for the Jews to remove and inter the corpses of hanged criminals before the onset of decay.

E. **Medicine in Post-Exilic and New Testament Times:** Data from the post-Exilic books of the Bible, the Apocrypha*, New Testament and Josephus, still suggest an attitude towards disease and its treatment divided between empirical and magical remedies. Actual progress in the understanding and practice of medicine is much more apparent from Mishnaic and Talmudic literature. Although these were compiled and edited after the end of the biblical period and are therefore much later than the sources mentioned above, they were presumably written from the standpoint of the end of the period (2nd c. BCE to 1st c. CE).

In the Apocrypha (Tobias 6:7) there is a reference to the gall of a fish being used to cure blindness, after its liver and heart had already been used to exorcise a devil. The Good Samaritan (Lk. 10:34) treated sores with oil, wine

599

and bandages although (Mk. 5:26) such medicaments were often ineffective. One of the few biblical suggestions of the nature of a disease is Luke's reference (14:2) to the man with dropsy, and Luke is commonly held to have been a physician.

Jesus was a healer — having control over the "evil spirits" which caused, above all, mental diseases and epilepsy (Mt. 12:22; Lk. 13:13). He also effected many cures by touch (Mt. 9:29; Mk. 5:27; 8:23–34; Jn. 9:6 and many other references).

The New Testament draws a clear distinction between those affected with what appears to have been epilepsy, and the other mental aberrations which Jesus, and later his disciples, cured (Ac. 5:16). In the latter case, the "possessed" became the mouthpieces of the demon who had entered into them.

Knowledge of Anatomy and Physiology: It is clear from Talmudic literature that the Jews' knowledge of anatomy was derived from their observations of the animals slaughtered and dissected for sacrifice (see Sacrifice*). This literature, which reflects the accumulated knowledge of the whole post-Exilic period gives a good indication of the current understanding of the human body and its workings. Man's body was believed to be made up of 613 parts, a distinction being made between bony parts covered with muscle and tissue, and the arteries, nerves, etc. The various organs were classified according to their functions: digestion, breathing, the heart and arteries, the brain and main nerves. Insemination and embryological development were known from empirical observation. Skin diseases and eye diseases were classified and the appropriate medication prescribed. Insect and snake bites were promptly sucked, incised or burned. Malaria was recognized — although its causes were unknown — and the recommended remedy included removal to mountain air. In Hellenistic and Roman times, the thermal waters of Tiberias (identified at Hamath, **599**, where a synagogue was discovered in 1962 CE) were famous (see Synagogues*; Astrology*: Zodiac). The waters of Gadara and of Calirrhoe, in Moab, where Herod* went in search of a cure, were also reputed to have healing properties.

The Talmudic texts, which undoubtedly incorporate a good deal of knowledge and practice learned from Babylonia and other countries of the Near East, as well as Jewish traditions, deal with diseases and ailments of every part of the body, from the crown of the head — where the "itch" is treated with sulphur — to feet which cannot move or walk. The rabbis of the period recognized that disease was contagious, specifically plague, diphtheria and dysentery. They warned healthy people against using sick people's food dishes, coverings, etc; forbade spitting in public, though whether for aesthetic or hygienic reasons is uncertain. They fought against flies which were a nuisance and abounded around refuse, and praised non-Jewish Orientals who "only kiss the hand". Public gatherings in times of pestilence were explicitly condemned.

Women's Diseases: The most significant data to be found in later Scriptures and Talmudic literature are those concerned with regulations (halakhot) governing the impurity of women during menstruation and childbirth and their purification (tohorah). These give some indication of the existing degree of understanding of the physiology of women. The anatomy of vagina and womb is accurately described; puberty was well understood, while menstruation is compared to the juice of the grape. Clear distinction was made between the menstrual flow, birth fluids and haemorrhages. Aids to childbirth at this time included Caesarian cuts in imitation of Roman practice, although, in cases of difficult birth, the child was more likely to be removed and sacrificed to save the mother, whose life was regarded as the more important. The instrument used to dissever the still-born child was similar to this (**600**), typical of many used in the Near East or India. The sages were tolerant of abortion where it seemed justified in order to save the mother. It is not unlikely that many of the surgical instruments shown in this relief representing instruments found in the Asklepeion of Athens (**601**), or those discovered in Pompei (**602**), used by Roman physicians, were known in Palestine at the time.

Mental Ailments: The Mishnah contains a number of references to idiots and the feeble-minded "shotteh", whose evidence is not valid in law. Resh-Lakish considered transgressors as feebleminded people, "no man commits transgression unless he be possessed by folly".

Like the New Testament, the Talmud also refers to epileptics and hysterics, counselling against marriage with the former. Other nervous ailments are attributed to affections of the brain or vertebral column.

MICAH. — Micah was a native of Moreshet-Gath in the Shephelah (the lowland plain) of Judah. He lived a generation before Amos* and was a younger contemporary of Isaiah*, prophesying during the reigns of Jotham (ca. 743–735 BCE), Ahaz and Hezekiah (727–698 BCE) of Judah.

Contents: The book, standing sixth among the Minor Prophets, may be divided into three sections:

Chs. 1–3 contain prophecies of judgment and punishment upon Israel, its princes, prophets and people, in words of uncompromising doom (except for a few verses, 2:12 ff) namely: 1:2–9 the doom of Samaria; 1:10–16, a lament over Judah; 2:1–5, the judgment on the brutalities of men in power, ending (2:12–13) with a gracious promise of deliverance. The third chapter, reflecting the prophet's passionate interest in the poor, speaks of the dire fate of Jerusalem's leaders, the sin of its judges and doom of the popular prophets and of Jerusalem.

Each section contains a description of the present corruption, an announcement of imminent judgment and one or more visions of a bright future. These discourses do not represent three connected themes, but three collections

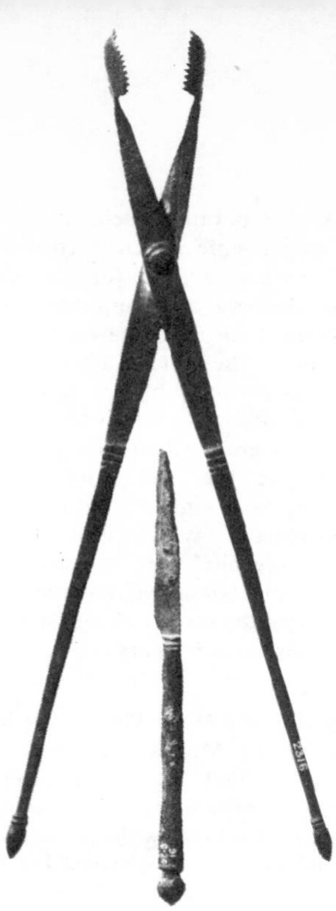

600

601

602

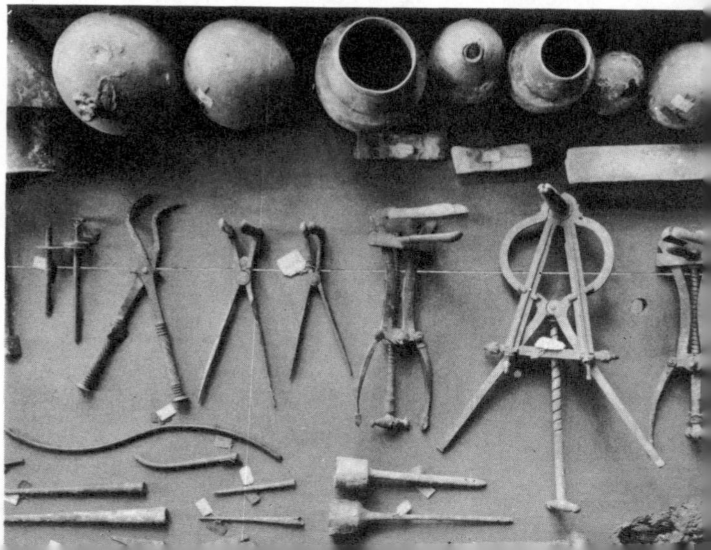

of the main elements of the prophet's oral utterances. Though the principle of arrangement is not chronological, those who treasured and collected his remembered words maintained a general scheme: corruption, judgment, salvation of the remnant, exaltation; no connecting links were, however, introduced between the separate utterances.

Chs. 4–5 consist almost entirely of words of promise for the future. Jerusalem is the religious metropolis of the world (4:1–5). It will witness the gathering of the dispersed and the restoration of the monarchy after great suffering (4:6–13). This picture is further enhanced in the eschatological vision of Judah's defender, the Messiah (5:1–6); war and idolatry will be abolished (5:7–17).

Chs. 6–7 are an indictment by Yahweh against the ingratitude of this people and a prophecy of the retribution awaiting commercial dishonesty (6:1–16), while 7:1–7 is a lament over the prevailing corruption, ending in verses 8–20 with a poem on the victory of Zion over the heathen world in contrast to the preceding words of condemnation.

Style: Because there are differences of style between the earlier and later chapters, some critics have tried to demonstrate that only 1:2–2:10 and parts of chs. 4 and 5 were actually composed by Micah, and that the other sections must be assigned to a later period than the 8th–7th cs. BCE. There are Exilic touches in 4:8 ff as the mention of Babylon in v. 10 indicates, and some regard it as a gloss, adjusting an earlier prophecy to a later situation. However, there are scholars who find the forceful descriptive style of the whole book, with its emphasis on divine judgment and mercy and hope for the future (a familiar pattern in classical prophecy) powerful arguments for a single author of all the prophecy. Nor does anything in the book appear to be out of keeping with the language, theology or style of preaching of the 8th c. BCE prophets.

The most reasonable conclusion seems to be that the book of Micah expresses the theology of the prophetic circles of his day, which transmitted his prophecy. Since the compilation of the books of the Twelve Minor Prophets was not completed before the Exile, it could hardly have appeared in its present form at an earlier date.

Message: Beyond his love for the humble people and the indication that he lived in rural surroundings, no details whatever are known of Micah's life. He uttered savage condemnations of the corruptions of city life in Israel, particularly in Jerusalem (4:10), noting, like Isaiah and Amos, the increasing oppression of the poor at the hands of wealthy land-owners (2:1–2); the ineffectiveness of contemporary religious leaders (2:11) and the gross injustices perpetrated by those dedicated to upholding the law (3:9–11). Things probably got worse during Judah's subjection to Assyria and during the pagan reaction which took place under Ahaz (see Israel and Judah, Part IV*). Denial of the ancient covenantal religion would naturally entail rejection of the Law* which was part of it. Micah, indeed, made no distinction between Judah and Israel (1:5, 9) and to him the false piety of an unrighteous people who still thought that "the Lord is in the midst of us. No evil shall come upon us", was the crowning insult (3:11).

His reaction was to recall the traditions of primitive Yahwism and threaten the sternest judgment on men who presented themselves before God even with "thousands of rams and ten thousands of rivers of oil . . ." but omitted to offer Him what He had demanded: "to do justice and to love kindness and to walk humbly with your God." (6:7–8).

The National Sin and Social Injustice: Like his contemporaries, Amos*, Hosea* and Isaiah*, Micah stressed the essential righteousness of the divine nature and God's fundamental demand of mankind to display an equal righteousness in individual and community life. Unlike Amos and Hosea, Micah was not so concerned with unorthodox religious practices as with social iniquities, and when addressing the civil and religious leaders, he included the venal priests. He foretold destruction for those who wrongfully deprived others of their possessions (3:1–4) and threatened that Jerusalem would be destroyed because the corruption of her rulers had undermined the whole basis of national life. The official cult was supported by the national leaders; it was in no position to criticize the nobles who guided the state. By its stress upon cultic externals, it fostered the notion that Yahweh's demands could be met by ritual and sacrifice alone. The time in which he lived, the epoch of Assyrian* invasion, was a period of social and moral decay for which the official religion had no effective rebuke. Micah was bitter in his condemnation of the false prophets who "divine for money" and the priests who "teach for hire" (3:5, 11).

The second part of the 8th c. BCE saw the end of a period of prosperity for the twin kingdoms and the beginning of the relentless pressure of the Assyrians westwards. Like the other prophets, Micah believed that God would make use of this pagan nation to punish his guilty people. He thus foretold the depredations of Shalmaneser V in the Northern Kingdom and the destruction of Samaria, its capital (1:6–9; see Israel and Judah, Part II*), and he prophesied that the Assyrian invasion under Sennacherib would be but the prelude to an even greater catastrophe.

Micah and Jeremiah: A century after his death, Micah's prediction of the downfall of Zion was remembered to the benefit of a later prophet, Jeremiah. His call to repentance was associated with a threat of doom and he was being threatened with death for making just such a prophecy. He might well have been put to death had not "certain elders of the land" recalled that Micah had said precisely the same thing: "Did Hezekiah king of Judah and all Judah put him to death? Did he not fear the Lord and entreat the favour of the Lord." They repented (Jer. 26:18–19).

Remnant of Israel and Judah: Micah believed that the destruction of the kingdom was imperative as the only means of cleansing "Jacob" of its sins and providing for an ultimate salvation for a "remnant". A debased religion and a corrupt society could be cleansed by no less drastic means (5:10–15; cf. Is. 2:5–22). The time of punishment would be one of tribulation and sorrow, with no voice raised to offer hope (3:6–7), followed by the shame of captivity in the midst of foreign peoples (5:7–8). Nevertheless, while the punishment was unavoidable, it was the condition of a restoration to God's grace and favour. Micah — or the disciples who preserved his words — never lost faith in the promises inherent in the Davidic covenant. Although he denied the confidence of those who believed that David's dynasty would be immovable, Micah proclaimed the eventual triumph of Judah, led by a Davidic prince who should be born in Bethlehem and should "stand and feed his flock in the strength of the Lord" (5:2–6).

Micah and Isaiah; Swords into Ploughshares: At this time, the common people would be delivered from oppression, swords would be beaten into ploughshares and spears into pruning hooks. "Nation shall not lift up sword against nation, neither shall they learn war any more; but they shall sit every man under his vine and under his fig tree . . . for the mouth of the Lord of hosts has spoken" (4:3–4). In short, economic and social well-being would only come as the result of obedience to the will of God. This messianic prophecy appears in similar words in Isaiah* 2:1–4 (see article).

There are many passages in the book of Micah which clearly reflect the influence of Isaiah. However, the elder prophet's conceptions usually appear as something foreign to Micah's spiritual world. Micah's own view of the world was deeply influenced by the more nationalistic of the ancient traditions of the covenant (Nu. 23:24; 24:8–9; Dt. 32: 41–43). Micah regarded the abuses of the national leaders as sins against the covenant God. As stated in 6:1–8, Yahweh had entered His case against His people since they had forgotten His gracious acts. They had imagined that the covenant stipulations could be satisfied by heightened cultic activity alone. Micah, however, went beyond Isaiah. He rejected the confidence implicit in the national theology and threatened that Jerusalem and the Temple would be utterly ruined (3:4–12). He met opposition, but his words apparently reached Hezekiah's ear (Jer. 26:18 ff) and the king repented.

Apart from this — and perhaps other occasions when he aroused opposition — Micah's preaching generally encouraged Hezekiah in his efforts towards reform. At the very least, the prophet's stern rebuke disturbed the king's conscience and moved him to penitence. Presumably Isaiah's preaching had a similar effect.

MISHNAH. — *Outline: I. Definition; Relation to the Old Testament and post-Exilic Oral Law; Midrash and Halakhah. II. Development of the Mishnah: Rabbinic Transmission; Hellenistic Rhetoric and the Methods of the Rabbinic Schools; Before and after the Destruction of the Temple; Factors Prompting Codification; Editing of the Mishnah; Significance of Early Sections of the Mishnah; Changes between* 70 *and* 140 *CE; Rabbi Akiba and Rabbi Meir; Codification of the Mishnah by R. Judah ha-Nasi; Literary Composition of the Mishnah. III. Contents: The Tractates of the Mishnah; Varying Methods of Arrangement; The Language of the Mishnah. IV. The Tosefta and Baraithas; The Talmud.*

The Mishnah is the formal codification of the core of the Oral Law of Judaism (see below).

I. DEFINITION: The word "Mishnah" comes from the Hebrew root "sh-n-h", meaning "to repeat, or to learn traditional matter, or laws". The term for the recitation of a scriptural text was "miqra" (meaning a reading or lecture). The difference between the two was made very clear by the terminology used by the rabbis. Scripture is always read (qarô); Mishnah is always studied (sh-n-h).

At first, the term *mishnah* was applied to the whole of the Oral Law which supplemented the Written Law (see Law*: Part F, Oral Law) and comprised both the interpretation and homiletic exposition of the Scriptures (*midrash*) and the supplementary laws and statutes not contained in the written Law (*halakhah* — "regulation, law", in the sense of traditionally accepted interpretations of the Written Law). Some of these laws and statutes were deduced from the Scriptural text (a discipline known as *midrash halakhah*, see below); some were part of an ancient tradition handed down from generation to generation of scholars and known as the "halakhah given to Moses at Sinai." Others were formulated on the basis of logical inference from the Scriptural text. Although this comprehensive use of the word *mishnah* is still found in Talmudic literature, the term is more usually employed by the Rabbis to denote only a single *halakhah* or a set of *halakhot*. The "Mishnah" as it is known today is an edition made by Rabbi Judah ha-Nasi (the Patriarch or "Prince") at the end of the 2nd c. CE, and known as "Our Mishnah" to distinguish it from other collections (see below, Literary Composition) called simply "Mishnah".

The term *mishnah* today signifies: a. a single item of the oral law; b. the entire content of the traditional oral law as developed by the end of the 2nd c. CE; c. the body of teachings (or "mishnah") of any one of the Tannaim — the sages who flourished until about the same time (see Rabbis*; Law*: Oral Law).

Relation of the Mishnah to the Old Testament and post-Exilic Oral Law: According to Jewish tradition, the Written Law of the Pentateuch was given direct to Moses together with all the explanation necessary for its application and the proper order for its transmission by word of mouth as the "Oral Law". This belief provided the Oral Law with the necessary authority. Many scholars hold that in its earlier form, the Oral Law probably dates from the time the Torah was first read and expounded to the people in early post-Exilic times (described in Nehemiah 8:1–9; for details see Bible Text and Canon*).

This was the "period of the Scribes" or pre-Mishnaic period when *halakhot* were studied in conjunction with the Written Law (i.e. together with the verse from the Torah from which they could be deduced or with which they were connected). For instance, from the text of Ex. 16:29 "Remain every man of you in place, let no man go out of his place on the seventh day," the rule was deduced that it was forbidden to go more than two thousand cubits outside the city (or camp) limits on the Sabbath day.

Midrash and Halakhah: The method by which this was done is known as "*midrashic halakhah*" and it led to a number of difficulties. The different halakhot or laws, are presented according to the sequence of verses in the Torah, but the biblical commandments often follow no logical pattern and the same commandment may be repeated a number of times in different passages. Accordingly, the *halakhot* became a haphazard collection of regulations, grouped without any regard to subject matter. In the "Bekhoroth" tractate, for example, Bekhoroth 8 concerns regulations deduced from Lv. 27:26 ff (dedication of first-born); and Bekhoroth 9 relates to the tithe on cattle, deduced from Lv. 27:32 ff. Where a passage and commandment is repeated, the rabbis made use of the different passages to establish additional points in the general law.

Collating the various *halakhot* into a coherent system quickly became necessary. With the developments that took place in every phase of life in the post-Exilic era, additional laws were called for and more and more *halakhot*, enactments (*taqqanot*) and decrees (*gezerot*) were issued. These very often had little if any connection with any biblical verse and they had to be learned separately.

The unsatisfactory situation led to the *halakhot* being arranged according to subject matter and without reference to the relevant biblical verse.

One of the earliest methods of collecting halakhot was to group together those of the same form. For example, ch. 1 of tractate Megillah, contains a group of thirteen statements, unrelated except by the fact that they each begin with the Hebrew words "ein-bein." This group enumerates the differences existing between similar things, e.g. between walled and unwalled cities; between Sabbath and Festivals; between Jerusalem and Shiloh, between great and small high places* and in the uses of different forms of writing and language (the Scriptures can be written in all languages; tephilin and Mezuza only in square script; see Alphabet* and Writing). Later commandments relating to a single subject were all collected into a "manual of instruction" or *mishnayot*. Some of these continued to represent exegetic commentaries on the appropriate section of the Written Law while others were simply collections of regulations.

II. DEVELOPMENT OF THE MISHNAH. It is not certain when the Rabbis began to teach *halakhot* like this. The first indications of a systematic study of the Mishnah come from the time of Jose ben Jo'ezer (mid 2nd c. BCE), who was one of the first "Pairs" of Sages who presided over the Sanhedrin for more than a century (see Government and Authority*; Rabbis*). It is not known who preceded Jose as a systematic teacher but it seems that in fact the Mishnah is as old as the "midrash" order. With Rabbi Akiba (2nd c. CE, see below), the midrash method was reinforced, with the midrashim arranged according to subject matter, although some of the older series based on connection by form were carried over into the Mishnah in their appropriate places. After the time of Rabbi Jose, the method of *halakhah* became steadily more important, although the *halakhic midrash* system never entirely died out in the rabbinical schools and vestiges of it are preserved in the collections of halakhic midrashim.

Because of the differences in method, there was a division in the rabbinic schools. In some, the old Midrashic form of deduction from the biblical text was followed; in others, the new mishnaic form was adopted and a comprehensive course of instruction in the law was offered, presented in a proper sequence and according to subject matter. The period from the time of the "Pairs" to 200 years after the destruction of the Temple (ca. 270 CE), is accordingly known as the "Mishnaic Period", the Sages of the time being the "Tanna'im" (plural of "tanna").

The "tanna'im" served as living libraries of law. It was their task to memorize and reproduce almost mechanically the oral text material required by the programmes of study of the schools.

Characteristics of Rabbinic Transmission: The rabbinic material in the Mishnah is predominantly expository (unlike the Gospel material which is predominantly narrative, although the stories were told for homiletic purposes, and which makes little use of the mnemonic techniques of rabbinical discipline). Most early rabbinic exposition was devoted to the exact determination of the sense of particular laws. As it all had to be memorized, the exposition took the form of a stereotyped set of questions asked in succession about each law and answered in terms of fixed legal formulae which recur again and again. The rabbinic tradition was a tradition from teachers concerned with the teaching of the law. Thus the Tannaitic material includes specific variations within a carefully (and easily) memorized formula of tradition (whereas the Dead Sea Scrolls* and the Gospels* have a much higher degree of divergence and almost no repetition of a formula).

Hellenistic Rhetoric and the Methods of the Rabbinic Schools: The contrast between the methods of the rabbinic schools and the Hellenistic schools of rhetoric offers an interesting sidelight on Jewish cultural development during the two centuries preceding the Christian era. The rabbinical schools were post-Exilic Judaism's effective means of protection against the spread of Hellenistic influence, yet their very growth and formation were apparently stimulated by the Hellenistic schools of rhetoric. Moreover, the very success of the rabbinical schools depended partly on their adopting much that was common to Hellenistic education. The difference between a Scribe, or copyist, and a Rabbi, or teacher, can find an analogy in the distinction between an ordinary Hellenic "grammatikos" and the fully-qualified "sophistes". In both schools, classical texts were learned by heart, it being the aim of the student to be able to recite them accurately. Both schools employed techniques of mnemonics and both used much the same methods of teaching. Whether the Jews were influenced directly by the Hellenists is an open question (see Rabbis*). Some scholars argue that similar institutions can grow independently out of a common cultural climate. While the Mishnah literature seems esoteric and obscure to the modern mind, its methods were accepted disciplines in the context of its time.

Before and after the Temple's Destruction: To say that before and immediately after 70 CE, Judaism had a unified doctrinal centre, from which "halakhot" were issued, is misleading. The period was one of major conflicts on theological and legal grounds between Pharisees* and Sadducees*, between the House of Hillel and the School of Shammai (see Rabbis*) and between "orthodox" Judaism and the various sectarian movements. The Essenes, the Zealots, the Jewish Christians and the Samaritans* all developed and preserved their own legal traditions. Among the mass of the people (the "'am-ha'aretz") who followed their own customs and worshipped in their own synagogues, there was probably a majority in favour of Pharisaic teachings, although less enthusiasm for their demands of a strict observance of the Law and mitzvôth (see Law*: Living under the Law). Questions of doctrine and transmission must be seen within the context of this complicated situation.

Factors Prompting Codification: The question of whether or not standard halakhot existed at this period is still debated among the scholars. The orthodox view follows the opinions expressed in the Epistle of Sherira Gaon (987 CE).

According to H. Albeck, no attempt was made to collate existing *mishnayot* until after the destruction of the Temple (70 CE), nor was there any fixed, authorized version of individual *mishnayot* until after that date. Every sage taught *halakhot* in whatever form he chose (usually the one he had himself learned from his own teacher) and in the order that seemed to him most appropriate. After the destruction of the Temple, when the Sages gathered at Jabneh (Yamniah; see Rome and the Jews*) they were afraid that with the destruction of existing institutions and the traditional pattern of life, the traditional mishnah of the Sages might be lost, or that an individual halakhah might become unavailable. Disruptions, such as that in Palestine in 70 CE, are often the occasion for committing to writing and fixed order traditions which have been handed down without difficulty in a stable and permanent social order. The rabbis resolved to do likewise and to determine a fixed order of *halakhot*, thereby laying the foundations for the systematic compilation of the Mishnah.

There is a school of thought which believes that the formation of the New Testament and its growing recognition also acted as a spur to the Jews to codify their own Oral Law as an authoritative supplement to the Old Testament tradition.

However a more potent inducement was the disruption of the life of the community. The sects always felt themselves so precarious that written records were indispensable from the start. The Essenes may have set the pattern for all.

In contrast, the Oral Law remained oral and unwritten for a long time. There were a number of reasons for this, one of the most important being that its nature was so closely involved with the method by which it was transmitted. It was made up of different layers, each one representing new material produced by a new generation. Thus, the whole of the Oral Law represented a continuous reinterpretation of the basic textual tradition, which was not itself recast. It was the supreme achievement of the later Pharisees under "Rabban" Johanan ben-Zakkai and the Academy of Jabneh (see Rabbis*) that they produced a movement of normalization at, or just after, the crucial period of disruption and sectarian conflict within Judaism.

Editing of the Mishnah: The work of editing done at Jabneh was naturally limited in scope (see Rome and the Jews*). The scholars who assembled there were sure that the work of arranging the *halakhot* which they began would be completed by later generations. Some remnants of their deliberations have been preserved in the tractate *Edduyot* (see below).

In the opinion of a majority of modern scholars (including Rabbi David Zvi Hoffmann, Y.N. Epstein and others), however, the editing of the Mishnah must have been begun before the academy assembled at Jabneh. Both from extant non-Mishnaic sources, and from the explicit evidence of the Mishnah itself, it is clear that the editing of mishnayot was begun at an earlier date. Some collections can even be proved to have been compiled during certain periods of the post-Exilic Second Commonwealth.

Significance of Early Sections of the Mishnah: Early texts of this kind have been preserved mainly in the historical tractates of the Mishnah (Middot, Tamid, Shekalim, etc.) which dealt with the vanished Temple and the practices which had ended with it. It seems most likely that the earliest sections of the Mishnah, which are those dealing with the Temple and sacrifices, were fixed immediately after the last days of the Temple. Prior to that time, material of this kind does not appear to have been learned by heart. J. Epstein places the fixation of the earliest preserved texts of the Mishnah either during or immediately after the last days of the Temple (some scholars prefer the later period). On the other hand, it is expressly stated in the Talmud (see below) that certain tractates, such as *Middot* and *Tamid* were edited by sages who lived during the time of the Second Commonwealth. It is also known from a variety of sources (Baraitha, known as Abot d'Rabbi Nathan, see below: Tosefta and Baraithas) that many compilations of *halakhic midrash* and *mishnah* were edited by Rabbi Akiba, a contemporary of Bar-Kochba*.

It can be said that collections of Oral Law existed long before the compilation of the Mishnah as it is today. Various Tanna'im had their own collections of *halakhot*. The best known of these was the collection of R. Akiba which, in turn, was handed down in separate traditions by his four leading disciples — R. Meir, R. Judah (ben Elai), R. Jose and R. Simeon ben Gamaliel II.

Changes between 70 and 140 CE: G. Allon has proved that rapid changes took place in religion between 70 CE and 140 CE — the period which separates Pharisaism from developed rabbinic Judaism. These were years of constant tension and conflict within Palestine and they produced a parallel religious adjustment. The Judaism of Rabbi Akiba and his followers in the days of Bar-Kochba was not so conservative as that of his Pharisaic predecessors, nor so closely bound to their tradition (see Rabbis*). New times and conditions demanded a new approach to the traditions of the Oral law. Not only were many of the mnemonic texts of the schools of Hillel and Shammai forgotten or abandoned in favour of new, more topical formulas; the very names of all but a few of the teachers who lived before 70 CE were forgotten. Even where a name has been preserved, the teaching attached to it is minimal. It is one of the best established precepts in the Mishnah and Talmud that a saying should always be reported in the name of the speaker. The fact that many of the few extant halakhot of the pre-70 CE period are anonymous or else included in a new collection, seems to prove that a revolutionary change did take place after that fateful date.

Rabbi Akiba and Rabbi Meir: The turning point in the process seems to have come around the time of R. Akiba. Up to his time, teaching had been a matter of listening and learning. After him, what was heard and learnt could be supplemented by what was inferred. (This is not affected by the fact that the *Mishnah* of R. Akiba was transmitted and learned according to the principles which had been established before him.) This makes possible a broad distinction between early and late schools in the transmission of the Mishnah.

In any case, it is easy to understand that in the totally new conditions of the 2nd c. CE, the rabbis should have revised tractates dealing with questions of everyday life almost entirely. For this reason, the Mishnah of today contains hardly a trace of the *Mishnah* of R. Akiba. His *mishnah* was absorbed into the *mishnayot* of his disciples. One of these disciples was R. Meir who, after the collapse of Bar-Kochba's* rebellion, became a member of the Sanhedrin of Usha (see Rome* and the Jews). At the time, all Judea lay in ruins and the new city of Aelia Capitolina built on the site of the devastated Jerusalem was prohibited territory to the Jews. The period (2nd half of the 2nd c. CE) is again one of the crucial phases in the preservation of Jewish culture and one of the principal factors in that preservation was the work of the Sanhedrin of Usha. R. Meir was one of its foremost members. An outstanding preacher, noted for his "agadot", parables and fables, his brilliance was widely conceded and it was even recorded that when the other rabbis differed from his opinion, their disagreement was "because his colleagues could not plumb the depths of his reasoning" (Erubin 13 b). The *mishnah* of R. Meir — with its component elements of R. Akiba's mishnah — became the basis of the accepted codification of the Mishnah by R. Judah ha-Nasi (see above). It became axiomatic that any ruling stated anonymously in the Mishnah was derived from the collection of R. Meir (Sanhedrin 86 a).

Codification of the Mishnah by R. Judah ha-Nasi: At the time of R. Akiba's disciples, there was an increase in the numbers of academies, collections of mishnayot and, consequently, *halakhic* disputes. Every sage expounded his own *mishnah* in his own school, each *mishnah* inevitably differing in several respects from every other. This situation was resolved by the work of R. Judah ha-Nasi. According to the Talmud he had studied with every single one of R. Akiba's disciples and he set about making a single definitive version of the Mishnah which should contain all the *halakhic* rulings and should be accepted as authoritative in each one of the academies. Whether he was actually aiming at presenting an authoritative version on which to base legal decisions, or whether he merely wanted to collect all the various traditions of the different academies, remains a subject for debate among scholars. Those who uphold the first view cite in support the statement in the Talmud that, in his Mishnah, R. Judah frequently quotes a *halakhah* anonymously, even when he knows it to be the individual opinion of one particular sage, contested by many others. Scholars of this opinion regard this practice as the Rabbi's way of singling out what, in his opinion, was the most authoritative *halakhah*. Other scholars, nevertheless, hold that R. Judah's *mishnah* was not intended as a judicial canon but was simply a comprehensive collection of laws.

Literary Composition of the Mishnah: In either case, R. Judah's Mishnah was based on the Oral Law he had learnt from R. Meir and his colleagues plus these sages' collections of *mishnah*. These he combined with the official *mishnah* of his father, the Patriarch Rabban Simeon ben Gamaliel, which also included some of the *mishnayot* of R. Akiba's disciples in their original wording.

The rabbi succeeded in welding all these elements into a homogeneous work, although careful examination can reveal the various component strata (which became the principal task of Mishnaic scholarship). As much of the rabbi's original material has been preserved in the Tosefta and the Baraithas (see below), it is possible to discover a good deal about the sources of the Mishnah. Its literary origins in the separate *mishnayot* of various sages have naturally affected its structure and contents.

603

Structurally, the *halakhot* of the present Mishnah are arranged broadly according to subject matter, all the *halakhot* relating to a single subject being found together, and *halakhot* on related subjects being combined into a single chapter. The 525 chapters of the Mishnah (containing smaller divisions into paragraphs, known as mishnayot), are grouped according to contents into different Tractates (see Table of Tractates, below). There are 63 Tractates, divided into six separate "Orders" ("sedarim") according to subject.

The relation of this enormous quantity of material to the life of the community which it was intended to regulate and which it still reflects, can only be indicated in broad outline in the following summary.

III. CONTENTS: **The Tractates of the Mishnah:**

1. **Order "Zera'im"** (seeds) deals primarily with religious laws relating to agriculture and crops. It is made up of **eleven Tractates:**

Berakhot (benedictions), especially daily prayers and the manner in which they must be conducted.

Pe'ah (the "corner of the field") and the general dues and tithes which must be reserved for the poor from the gleanings of fields, oliveyards and vineyards (cf. Lv. 19:9–10; Dt. 24:19–22).

Demai, how to act in regard to fruits which may not have been tithed for the Levites or for the heave-offering for the priests (see Priests*).

Kilayim, on the prohibition against mingling plants, animals or yarns which are of different species, although the same kind (i.e. of "diverse seeds"). This covers the lawfulness of sowing cabbage, onion and gourds in the same field; of yoking different animals together or making cloth of different types of yarn (cf. Lv. 19:19; Dt. 22:9–11).

Shebi'it, on sabbatical years and how to regulate agricultural routines so as to observe them. This section also includes the law on release of debtors, or "Prosbul" (see Law*).

Terumôt, on heave offerings for the priests and how they should be set aside (see Sacrifice and Offerings*; Nu. 18:8).

Ma'asarôt, the first tithe from the field, olive press etc, reserved for the Levites (cf. Nu. 18:21–32). Olive oil was stored thus, **603.**

Ma'asêr Sheni, the second tithe in money or kind, to be consumed in joyous celebration in Jerusalem (Dt. 14:22–27).

Hallah, heave-offerings from dough, 1/24 part from ordinary people, 1/48 from bakers (Nu. 15:18–21).

Orlah, on cases of mixing permissible things with the fruit of trees during the first three years of their growth (when it was forbidden to be eaten or used; cf. Lv. 19:23).

604

605

606

Bikkurîm, offerings of first fruits (Dt. 26:1–11) and their relation to heave-offerings and the second tithe.

2. **Order Mo'ed** (seasons) deals with the laws regulating the Sabbath, festivals, etc. It contains twelve Tractates:

Shabbath, rulings as to what may and may not be done concerning food, bodily hygiene, permissible manual labour, walking within the prescribed limits (2,000 cubits), feeding cattle and salvaging property (cf. Ex. 20:10; 23:12; Dt. 5:14); the ornaments which a man or woman might put on on the Sabbath. Illumination on the Sabbath (as on other days) might be provided by slipper-type lamps like this one **(604)** of the 2nd c., or by lanterns **(605)**.

Erubîn, provides various expedients for circumventing the more irksome regulations relating to the Sabbath; for instance, "when a priest has a wound on his finger, he may bind it up with bast in the sanctuary but not elsewhere." The Pharisees attacked Jesus because he healed on the Sabbath (Mt. 12:10 ff; Mk. 3:1 ff, passim). The Tractate also contains numerous laws of a diverse character, including finding tefillin (phylacteries. etc.).

Pesahim: Passover offerings, the removal of leaven, killing the Passover lamb, community eating and the Passover meal (the Seder; Ex. 12; Lv. 23:5 ff; Nu. 28:16 ff. passim).

Shekalîm, concerning the manner of payment of the half-shekel tax which was used to defray the expenses of worship in the post-Exilic Temple (see Taxes*; Temple*); including regulations for the offices in the sanctuary; or the setting up of the counters of the money changers — who may have looked much like those in the Roman carving **(567)** — who provided pilgrims with the appropriate ancient "holy" coins in which to pay the tax. Their presence in the Temple courts has been immortalized by Jesus' action in turning them out. Some coins of the Roman period in Palestine reflect the peculiarities of the incense offering on the Day of Atonement. There were 13 sacrificial boxes, 13 tables and 13 gates in the Temple* (see article).

Yoma, the Day of Atonement (see Festivals*) and the ritual of the High Priest; sending the scape-goat away; fasting and means of atonement (sin offering, guilt offering, repentance, etc.). This Tractate also refers to improvements to the sanctuary carried out by Queen Helena of Adiabene, a Parthian kingdom whose royal family and court converted to Judaism. The mausoleum they built in Jerusalem is shown in **481**.

Sukkah, the Festival of Booths (Tabernacles) and the festive wreath "lulab" **(435)** consisting of a branch of the palm tree, one of myrtle and one of water willow and an ethrog (see Festivals*: Sukkot) and the libation of water.

Betza, behaviour during festivals. The tractate opens with a classic dispute between the schools of Hillel and Shammai as to whether or not one may make use of an egg laid by a hen which had been intended for food (not for laying) and had been carried during a festival, or on the Sabbath.

Rosh-Hashana, regulations governing the New Year Festival.

Ta'anît, fasts and public mourning.

Megillah, the reading of the Scroll of Esther and matters relating to scrolls.

Mo'ed Katan, the kinds of work permitted in the field during the days between the first and seventh days of Passover or Sukkot.

Hagigah, festival offerings to be observed on the occasions of the three pilgrimage feasts (Passover, Weeks, Tabernacles; cf. Dt. 16:16 ff).

3. **Order Nashîm**: Laws related to marriage, divorce and vows, made up of seven tractates:

Yebamôt, mainly concerning Levirate marriage (Dt. 25:5–10; see Family*).

Ketubbôt, marriage settlements, matrimonial duties, divorce, rights of children (Ex. 22:16, passim).

Nedarîm, vows and the conditions which can lead to their annulment (Nu. 30).

Nazîr, regulations governing the Nazirate (Nu. 6).

Gittîn, bills of divorce and grounds for divorce (Dt. 24:1, see Family*),

Sota, women suspected of adultery, the ordeal by the water of bitterness and the offering for jealousy (Nu. 5:11–31; see Family*).

Kiddushîm, acquisition of a wife (bethrothal and marriage) and acquisition of property (goods and real estate).

4. **Order Nezikîn** (damages), also called euphemistically, "yeshu'ot" (deeds of help); civil and criminal legislation in nine Tractates:

Baba Kamma, damages in cases involving theft, robbery and mayhem (Ex. 21:33; 22:5 ff; and see Law*).

Baba Metziâh, regulations regarding things found; interest; speculation on price rises; feeding labourers, leasing fields, and permitted actions in or on public places, etc.

Baba Bathra, division of property held in partnership; sale of property, goods or real estate.

Sanhedrin, regulations governing the courts of justice and judicial procedure (see Law*): Privileges of the high priest and the king; punishment by stoning, burning, decapitation, strangulation. Procedure with regard to a rebellious dissenting teacher.

Shebu'ôt, oaths (wanton or perjured, oaths of testimony); awareness of being unclean (Lv. 5:2 ff), war.

Edduyôt, comments by later teachers on statements of older sages, and legal pronouncements on questions in dispute between the rabbinical schools.

Abodah Zara, regulations concerning food, vessels, idols, astrology, etc. intended to guard against contact with idolaters in inns or when acting as midwives.

Abôth (Sayings of the Fathers or "Pirkê Abôth"), a collection of pronouncements and maxims containing practical rules of wisdom*, imbued with all the weight of tradition.

Horayôt, erroneous decisions in questions of religious law and the appropriate sin-offering (Lv. 4:13 ff).

5. **Order of Kodashîm:** Laws regulating slaughter, sacrifices and consecrated objects. The Order contains eleven Tractates:

Zebahîm, animal offerings and sacrifices* (Lv. 1–4, passim). The priests' portion. The history of the places at which sacrifices could be offered.

Menahôt, meal offerings (Lv. 2; 5:11); thanksgiving offerings; shewbread (see Sacrifice and Offerings*).

Hullîn, slaughter of animals not intended as offerings, and various regulations concerning eating animal food, including questions of Terepha and Kasher and the law forbidding boiling meat in milk (Ex. 23:19; Dt. 14:21).

Bekhorôt, dedication of the first-born of animals (Ex. 13:2, 12; Lv. 27:26; Nu. 8:16, passim).

Arakhîn, payments according to age and sex, to be made in lieu of human beings vowed to God (Lv. 27:2 ff) or when a man has vowed the equivalent of a human being to God.

Temurah, exchanging or giving a substitute for a sacrificial animal (Lv. 27: 10, 33).

Keritôt, specific sins which carried the penalty of being "cut off from his people" (interpreted to mean dying, usually without offspring, between the ages of 20 and 50).

Me'ilah, trespassing upon consecrated things (Nu. 5:6–8; Lv. 5:15 ff).

Tamîd, the daily morning and evening offering in the Temple (see Sacrifice*; Ex. 29:38–42; Nu. 28:3–10); prayers and benedictions.

Middôt, dimensions and furniture of the Temple* and sanctuary; including those of the chamber of hewn stone where the Sanhedrin met.

Kinnîm, the doves to be offered as sin offering and burnt offering by poor women after childbirth, or as an atonement from poor persons (Lv. 12:8; 5:11).

6. **Order of Toharôt** (purity), in fact mainly concerned with impurity*, a list of laws concerning ritual and ceremonial purity.

Kelîm, degrees of impurity to which vessels, household furnishings, clothes etc. are subject (Lv. 6:27; Nu. 19:11 ff).

Ohalôt, impurities acquired through contact with a corpse or from being in the same tent or house (Nu. 19:14).

Nega'im, regulations relating to leprosy (Lv. 13, 14).

Parah, the ritual of the red heifer (see Sacrifice*).

Toharôt, concerns minor defilements which become ineffectual with sunset. Warnings to an observant Pharisee* ḥaber to beware lest something of his be defiled unintentionally by someone who is ignorant of the law.

Mikvaôt, regulations governing baths of immersion. Such baths must contain at least 40 se'a (428 quarts, see Weights and Measures*) of "live" water taken direct from springs, rain or rivers. The Roman baths and bathroom **(606)** pictured here are from contemporary Gezer*. See also **599**.

Niddah, regulations relating to women during menstruation and during and after childbirth (see Family*).

Makshirîm, the seven liquids: wine, honey, oil, milk, dew, blood, water which make dry articles of food liable to impurity under certain conditions (Lv. 11:34, 37–38).

Zabîm, those afflicted with unclean issues from the body (Lv. 15) and defilements caused by contact or movement.

ר״ע מברטנורה עוקצים פרק א עיקר תוי״ט קכה

מסכת עוקצים

כל שהוא יד. ולא שומר. מיטמא ומטמא. ולא מצטרף. שומר אע״פ שאינו יד. מיטמא ומטמא. ומצטרף. לא שומר. ולא יד. לא מיטמא. ולא מטמא: ב שרשי השום. והבצלים. והקפלוטות. בזמן שהן לחין. והפיטמא שלהן. בין לחה. בין יבשה. והעמוד שהוא מכוון כנגד האוכל. שרשי החזרים. והצנון. והנפוס. דברי ר״מ. רבי יהודה אומר שרש צנון גדול. מצטרף. והסיב שלו. אינו מצטרף. שרשי המיתנא והפיגם. וירקות שדה. וירקות גנה. שעקרן לשתלן. והשדרה של שבולת. והלבוש שלה. ר׳ אלעזר אומר אף הסיג של רצפית. הרי אלו מיטמאים. ומטמאים. ומצטרפין: ג אלו מיטמאין. ומטמאין. ולא מצטרפין. שרשי השום והבצלים והקפלוטות. בזמן שהן יבשים. והעמוד שאינו מכוון כנגד האוכל. ויד הפרכיל. טפח מכאן וטפח מכאן. ד האשכול. כל שהוא. וזנב של אשכול שריקנו. ויד המכבד של תמרה. ד׳ טפחים. וקנה של שבולת ג׳ טפחים. ויד כל הנקצרים ג׳. ושאין דרכן לקצר. ידיהם ושרשיהן כל שהן. ומלעין של שבולין. הרי אלו מיטמאים. ומטמאין. ולא מצטרפין: ד אלו לא מיטמאין. ולא מטמאין. ולא מצטרפין. שרשי קולסי הכרוב. וחלפות

607

Tebul-Yom, relating to anyone who, having taken a bath of immersion, yet remains unclean for the rest of the day, including the possible defilements he may cause.

Yadayim, concerns the ritual impurity and cleansing of the hands (cf. Mt. 15:2, 20; Mk. 7:2 ff; and see Bible Text and Canon*).

Uktzim, how handles of vessels, or shells or kernels of fruit are affected when the vessel or the fruit becomes unclean.

This **(607)** is a folio of the Mishnah, Tractate Uktzim.

Varying Methods of Arrangement: Although, in general, the Tractates are arranged by subject matter, there are a number of exceptions. Some collections of *mishnayot* are included, arranged under the names of the authorities responsible for them, without regard to their subject matter. Gittîn IV, 2–5, 7 lists a collection of enactments (*taqqanot*) ordained by the sages "for the general good." Other mishnayot appear together although all that they have in common is a similar introductory formula, e.g. "X differs from Y only in Z" (Megillah I, 4–11).

While the majority of the halakhot in the modern Mishnah are taught independently of the Scriptural text, some are expounded by the *midrashic* method, in which case the relevant biblical verses are quoted. These variations are the natural consequence of the Mishnah's compilation from a number of individual *mishnayot*. The same circumstance has even resulted in the inclusion of conflicting *mishnayot* on certain subjects (i.e. the opinions of different sages). Contradictions can even be found within a single mishnah, where this has been compounded from two conflicting sources.

On the other hand, Rabbi Judah's care to preserve the original form and language of his sources has resulted in a certain amount of duplication. Where an individual *mishnah* referred to more than one subject, rather than divide it between the appropriate Tractates, the Rabbi repeated it in full in each of the relevant Tractates (cf. Ketubot vii, 7 and Kiddushin, ii, 5). Some scholars (notably Y.N. Epstein) are of the opinion that the Rabbi made a number of changes and additions in his Mishnah, but there is no question of re-writing or radical alterations.

There has also been much debate about whether or not Rabbi Judah committed the Mishnah to writing. It seems likely that while it was first written down during his lifetime, not necessarily by him, it continued to be studied orally. Reference was made to the written word only in case of doubt or where some point had been forgotten.

The Language of the Mishnah: The Mishnah was composed in the type of Hebrew, known as "the language of the Sages" (*lashon hachamim* or *leshon chazal*), in which the Tosefta, the halakhic Midrashim, and the Hebrew passages of the two Talmuds are written (for details, see Languages*: Hebrew).

IV. THE TOSEFTA AND THE BARAITHAS: The editing of the *Mishnah* was finalized after Rabbi Judah's time by his disciples and it was they who were responsible for establishing the *Mishnah* as the authoritative version, superseding all other collections of *mishnayot*. These thereafter became merely "extraneous" mishnayot or, in Aramaic, *baraiatha* (sing. *baraitha*). They were not altogether forgotten. Parts of them continued to be used in the debates in the schools for explaining passages in the Mishnah. Only one of these "extraneous" collections has been preserved in its entirety, the *Tosefta;* but fragments of other baraithas are also extant in quotation in the discussions in the Talmuds. The *Tosefta* is a parallel collection of *baraithas* which, as its name indicates (tosefeth is Hebrew for "addition"), is a supplement to the Mishnah. It explains the text of the Mishnah, gives reasons for its *halakhot*, quotes divergent opinions where the Mishnah gives only one, anonymous, dictum and occasionally even disagrees with the Mishnah. Sometimes the Tosefta quotes the teaching of one sage, where the Mishnah gives the opinion of another. Sometimes it includes *halakhot* and other details which were omitted from the Mishnah.

The editor of the Tosefta can no longer be identified but it appears that he lived a generation later than Rabbi Judah (i.e. at the beginning of the 3rd c. CE). A *tosefta* exists parallel to every Tractate of the Mishnah, with the three exceptions of the tractates *Tamîd*, *Middôt* and *Kinnîm*, presumably because of their great age. The *baraitha* known as *Abôth d'Rabbi Nathan* forms a kind of *tosefta* to the tractate *Abôth*.

The Talmud: Academic discussions and the practical administration of Jewish law in the academies of Palestine and Babylonia for several centuries after the completion of the Mishnah were recorded in two great compilations: the Babylonian and Palestinian Talmud.

In form, most of the Talmuds consist of quotations from the Mishnah combined with a "gemarah", which forms both a commentary on and a supplement to the Mishnah text. This is the foremost Jewish legal text book and, as such, it continues to provide the foundation for religious education among observant Jews. The teachings it contains, however, are far beyond the scope of the present volume.

MOAB. — *Outline: Origins; Evidence of Archaeology; History; Following the Conquest; David's Conquest; King Mesha; Assyrian Domination; The Downfall of Moab; Religion; Chronological Table.*

The land of Moab lies east of the Jordan and the Dead Sea, between the Heshbon river to the north and the Zered river to the south (see map **354**). Bounded on the west by the Dead Sea, its eastern border was formed by the highlands of Moab which rise gradually to the desert of Moab. The Arnon river divides the land into two, the southern half being higher, steeper and wilder than the northern plain. The ancient King's Highway (see Roads*) ran along the highlands on the east, so as to avoid frequent crossings of the wadis which run westwards from the hills. Moab's natural frontiers meant that the only possibility of expansion was to the north, for there was nothing very attractive about the eastern desert.

Origins: The Moabites were closely related to the Hebrews. Cultural affinities were established between them and the group called Reuben (see Tribes*) at an early stage of its settlement. According to a tradition of Gn. 19:37–38, the Moabites, along with the Ammonites, were descendants of Lot, Abraham's nephew. Because of this near relationship, the Hebrews were forbidden (Dt. 2:9) to wage war on the Moabites. However, this injunction is part of a tradition which cannot have been put in the correct setting. It is not related to the traditions of pre-Conquest* days and events showed that it was certainly not observed (Jos. 24:9; Dt. 23:3 ff). A deep enmity developed between the two peoples, due to the expansion of Hebrew tribes settled in southern Transjordan.

The Moabites appear to have begun the settlement of their territory in the 13th c. BCE, about the same time as the Hebrews' settlement of Transjordan and Canaan (see Joshua*; Conquest*; Judges*). However, the land had already undergone a series of upheavals in the more distant past. At the end of the Early Bronze Age (23rd–20th c. BCE), the whole of Palestine appears to have suffered a major disruption due to the invasion of nomads, and sedentary occupation east of the Jordan virtually came to an end. During the 2nd mill. BCE, western Palestine and northern Transjordan recovered and were settled by various newcomers, among them the Amorites (see Patriarchs*). On the basis of surface examination of some hundreds of sites in Transjordan, a theory has been propounded by N. Glueck that the country was unoccupied, except for a nomadic population, from about 1900–1300 BCE. G. Lankester Harding points out, however, that the recent discoveries of Middle Bronze tomb groups at Mt. Nebo, Naur and Ammân, and a Middle Bronze temple at Ammân, indicate the existence of an urban population in the region adjoining the Moab plateau in the days of the Hyksos and the Late Bronze Age (before the 13th c. BCE). This sacred rock (**608**) upon which a Roman temple was built, was the altar and high place* of a much older Ammonite sanctuary. It is curious that biblical references give no further evidence of events in east Jordan between the time of the Patriarchs* and the Exodus*, and that archaeology suggests, in the view of many scholars, that the area was unoccupied during this period. The early background of the Exodus* (see article) requires a fully occupied Edom, Moab and Ammon — and these countries could not possibly have become resettled in the generation or two before the Exodus. It is now held that several sedentary settlements remained in the region during the centuries preceding the Exodus. This would seem to relate the early people, later known as Moabites and Ammonites, or even the Edomites, to semi-nomadic peoples who were a branch of the northwest Semitic Amorites (see Patriarchs*). Their settlement involved the absorption of semi-nomadic or even sedentary people which had previously regarded the land as their territory. The best-known of these were the "Šutu", a semi-nomadic people who are frequently mentioned in cuneiform texts from the 18th c. BCE onwards, and also in the Egyptian "Execration Texts" (as Shosu; see Egypt*; perhaps the "sons of Sheth" of Nu. 24:17). With the Moabite settlement, the normal process of national history and the rise of the new cities began and the land and its peoples flourished until the downfall of the kingdom in the 6th c. BCE (see below).

608

609

Evidence of Archaeology: There have been very few excavations carried out in Moab, one exception being those in Dibon (Dhiban). The results there proved disappointing and no definite stratification was established. In other places such as Madeba, Adar, Balu'a, Kir-Moab (Kerak) and Heshbon, the remains of many constructions have been found, by chance, above ground. These indicate that the culture of the Moabites was very similar to that of the other peoples of Palestine. The most important epigraphic discovery from Moab was the Mesha stone (see below) which reflects the sophisticated political and cultural level of the kingdom of Moab in the 9th c. BCE. Pottery and ritual objects, such as figurines, found in Moab, on the other hand, are all very similar to discoveries made on the western shore of the Dead Sea (Canaan). The earliest archaeological find is the Balu'a stele (**609**), a large roughly-shaped block of black basalt carved with three human figures. The figures apparently represent two gods with a king between them. The stele dates from the 12th c. BCE and its most intriguing feature is a four-line inscription which bears an affinity to the proto-Sinaitic style (see Alphabet*: Southern Semitic Scripts). It suggests that the stele belongs to a distant period of Moab's early history, of which no record has survived. In addition, a fragment of a stele was found at Dibon and the few letters inscribed on it bear a resemblance to the Mesha inscription. Many seals were found in the area bearing the name of Chemosh, the national god. A more recent inscription of the Persian period was found in an Arab house in Kerak; it suggests the preservation of Moabite elements among the population after the destruction of the national kingdom.

History: By the time the Moabites appear in the biblical record (Gn. 36:35; Nu. 22–24), they, like the Ammonites to the north and the Edomites to the south (Nu. 20:14), were already established as a united kingdom. In contrast, Canaan before the Hebrew Conquest was divided into a number of petty city-states. Nothing is known of how the kingdoms were set up. Their organization is indicated by the fact that the Hebrews entered into negotiations with the "king of Moab" (Nu. 22–24). The long detour around Edomite and Moabite territory which the Hebrews made at the end of their wanderings in the desert (see Numbers*) also fits in with the known fact that in the 13th c. BCE, the frontiers of Edom, Moab and Ammon were secured by a line of fortresses on their eastern borders to preserve their territorial integrity. The Hebrews avoided attacking these fortresses and swung eastwards in a wide arc, to the highlands to the east of Moab, where they were attacked by the king of Heshbon whom they defeated. This king had previously inflicted a heavy defeat on the king of Moab and destroyed all the northern part of the country (Nu. 21:26–30). The Hebrews' victory over Sihon, king of Heshbon, gave them control of all the land east of the Jordan between the Arnon and Jabbok rivers (see map **354**; Nu. 21:24–25). They went on to further victories which gave them possession of most of the Transjordan highlands (Nu. 21:33–35; see Conquest*).

The background of the story of Balak, king of Moab (Nu. 22–24) is reflected in the insecure times after Israel's capture of the kingdom of Sihon. The Moabites, who had been unable to recapture the lowlands north of the Arnon from Sihon, welcomed his defeat and hoped to seize the territory they had lost to him. But they feared that Israel would capture their land. Balak therefore formed alliances with the Midianite tribes to fight Israel. According to the tradition, they invited Balaam, apparently a famous prophet and seer, to curse Israel. Instead, inspired by God, he blessed them. It appears from Nu. 24:25 and Jud. 11:25 that the situation did not come to a head except for a battle with the Midianites in which Balaam died.

Following the Conquest: While the Hebrews were engaged in the long process of establishing themselves in Canaan, the kingdoms of Moab and Ammon grew stronger. Early in the 12th c. BCE, Eglon, king of Moab, ruled over parts of Israel for 18 years (see Judges*) until he was assassinated by Ehud (Jud. 3:12–30). There is only a passing reference to Moab in the story of Saul. During his reign "... he fought against all his enemies on every side, against Moab, against the Ammonites, against Edom..." There is no other source for Saul's campaigns against Moab, Edom and Ammon, and many scholars believe that the reference in this passage may merely be a standard formula concerning peoples subjugated at the beginning of the monarchy and not a historical record of an actual war.

The tribe of Reuben had settled east of the Jordan in Ammonite territory in the early stages of the Conquest* (Nu. 32). How they fared is obscure (see article), but by the 11th c. BCE these holdings in Transjordan had virtually disappeared, presumably as a result of Ammonite and Moabite depredations.

David's Conquest: Early in David's reign, after defeating the Philistines, he conquered Moab inflicting heavy losses on them (II Sam. 8:2) and exacting tribute thereafter. When Solomon's kingdom split in the middle of the 10th c. BCE, Moab remained a vassal state to the Northern Kingdom (Israel) but not to Judah, although Judah was closer. Biblical accounts of the following century are confused, indicating a gap in Israelite control. The contemporary stone of Mesha (see below) suggests that Omri, king of Israel (see Israel and Judah*, Part II) renewed his kingdom's domination over Moab (II K. 3:4) which had presumably thrown it off earlier.

King Mesha: II K. 3:4 describes Mesha, king of Moab, as a "sheep-master and he rendered unto the King of Israel a hundred thousand lambs and a hundred thousand rams, with the wool"; i.e. this was the annual tribute which he paid. This was the king whose monument, erected by himself in his city of Dibon, was discovered in 1868 CE and, when deciphered, confirmed and amplified the biblical evidence about him. It shed considerable light on Moab's history and religion (see below).

During Israel's war against Aram, or perhaps at the time of the battle of Qarqar (853 BCE), Mesha revolted against Joram, Ahab's successor as king of Israel. After an initial success, he fortified the border of Moab. Aided by King Jehoshaphat of Judah and Edom, Joram embarked on a punitive campaign about 850 BCE (II K. 3:6) which began as a great success (3:24–26). The Judeans and Israelites took a terrible vengeance, devastating Moab. When the Moabite city, Kir-Moab (modern Kerak), was besieged Mesha took shelter in the fortress of the city wall. Realizing in his despair that no human agency could save him, he appealed to his god, Chemosh. According to II K. 3:27, "he took his eldest son who was to reign in his stead and offered him for a burnt offering upon the wall", at which the Israelites were so horrified, they "withdrew from him and returned to their own land."

It is difficult to see why this act of Mesha's should have had the effect described. It may have had an implication which we do not now understand. However, this strange incident is apparently not reflected in the Mesha stone, and may actually have occurred at an earlier date. Following the retreat of the Israelite expedition from Kir-Moab, Joram and Jehoshaphat lost control over Moab and then over Ammon.

The Mesha stone is the only contemporary historical record relating to II K. 3 so far found in Moab. It is a large stele set up by Mesha in his capital, Dibon (Dhiban), and inscribed in a Moabite-Canaanite dialect similar to biblical Hebrew. The stone, shown here (**610**), was broken to pieces by Bedouins in order to get a better price by selling it piecemeal, but fortunately the inscription had been transcribed beforehand, and now, repaired and reconstructed, the large stone stands in the Louvre museum in Paris. 1.13 m. high and 70 cm. wide, it bears an inscription of 34 lines, written in the first person singular, beginning with a somewhat boastful recital by Mesha, king of Moab, of his triumphs over the house of Omri, king of Israel. The information is of the greatest interest when compared with the account in II Kings. The stone reads:

"I am Mesha, son of Chemosh, king of Moab, the Dibonite. My father reigned over Moab for thirty years, and I reigned after my father. And I made the high place for Chemosh in Qerkhah, a high place of salvation because he had saved me from all my foes and let me see my pleasure on all them that hated me. Omri king of Israel humbled Moab many days, for Chemosh was angry at his land; and his son succeeded him and he also said "I will humble Moab". In my days he spoke thus but I have triumphed over him and over his house, while Israel has perished for ever. Omri took possession of the land of Madaba and dwelt therein his days and half his son's days, forty years; but Chemosh restored it in my days. And I built Ba'al Meon and made the reservoir in it, and I built Keryathen. Now the men of Gad had dwelt in the land of Ataroth of old; and the king of Israel built for himself Ataroth. And I fought against the city and took it, and I slew all the people of the city and made it a grazing stock to Chemosh and to Moab. And I captured thence the shrine of Dudah and dragged it before Chemosh in Keriyoth, and I settled there the men of Sharon and of Mekhrath. And Chemosh said to me "Go, take Nebo from Israel". And I went by night and fought against it from the break of dawn until noon, taking and slaying all. 7,000 men, boys, women, girls and even maid-servants, for I had devoted them to destruction for the god Ishtar Chemosh. And I took the vessels of Yahweh and dragged them before Chemosh. Now the king of Israel had built Yahaṣ and lived in it while he fought against me, but Chemosh drove him out before me. I took 200 men of Moab and all its chiefs, and brought them up against Yahaṣ and took it to add it unto Dibon. And I built Qerkhah, the wall of the forest and the wall of the mound, and its gates and its towers and the king's palace, and I made two reservoirs in the midst of the city. Now there was no cistern in the city, so I said to all the people, "Make you every man a cistern in his house". And I cut the aqueduct for Qerkhah with the help of the prisoners of Israel. I rebuilt Aroer and made the highway through the Arnon, and I rebuilt Beth-Bamoth for it was overthrown, and Betser . . . for all Dibon was subject. And I reigned . . . 100 cities which I had added to the land. And I rebuilt Madaba and Beth Deblatein and the temple of Ba'al Meon, and took there the sheep-master . . , the flocks of the land. Now Khernan the son of Dedan dwelt in it, and Dedan said . . . Chemosh said unto me "Go down against Khernan". So I went down and warred . . . and Chemosh dwelt in it all my days . . ."

The successful campaign described here belongs to the same period as II K. 3. Mesha's enemy was Israel and the wars he waged under the patronage of Chemosh, god of Moab, were intended to expel Israel and to recapture the areas seized by Omri and Ahab, including Ataroth which Mesha boasts had long been settled by Gad. It is listed among the towns of Gad in Nu. 32:3, 34–35 together with Yaazer and Dibon. The divine commands to Chemosh are reminiscent of the reply of the prophets of Israel to the king who asks their advice before starting out for battle: "Go up to Ramoth-Gilead and prosper; for the Lord shall deliver it into the king's hands." (I K. 22:12). The defeat of Moab as well as her victory is interpreted as an act of Chemosh (see below, Religion). Mesha construed defeat at the hands of Israel as a sign that his own god was angry with him, a standard view in other countries as well. The incident of the taking of Nebo is also interpreted as an act of Chemosh. This brief passage is the only text found outside Palestine proper mentioning the name of Yahweh. The biblical "ḥerem" was also known in Moab: when the god gave Mesha a victory, he "devoted" all the inhabitants of the town, plus the treasures of gold and silver including the temple treasury, to him. Mesha's father is called by the theophoric name based on the name Chemosh. On this stone are found a number of words in Moabite dialect such as "kır" in the sense of "kiryah" (city, town). These words have survived in the Bible in the names of the Moabite towns "Kir of Moab" (Is. 15:1) and "Kir-heres" (Jer. 48:31). See map (**493**).

610

Apparently, as the stone records, the Moabite king was subsequently able to strengthen his country's defences so that Amaziah, king of Judah, was forced to fight the Moabites in the wilderness of Tekoa, his own territory west of the Dead Sea, where he defeated them. Moab is hardly mentioned again in the Bible, although it seems that it came under the domination of Israel once more during the reign of Jeroboam II. Its decline during the 8th c. BCE is also suggested by references in, e.g. II Ch. 26:8; Jer. 49:1; Am. 1:13, which seem to imply that Moab's northern area passed into Ammonite control early in the century.

611

612

Assyrian Domination: Like most of the nations in the area, Moab was engulfed by the renewed Assyrian expansion under Tiglat-Pileser III (745–727 BCE). There seem to have been advantages for both sides in this arrangement. The Assyrians gave the Moabites protection against attack from desert nomads; (this relief from Nimrud depicts a fateful encounter, **611**), while Moab seemed far enough away from the centre of the empire to offer no threat and no danger of political intrigue to Assyria. Moab, Ammon and Edom had to pay tribute to Assyria and to submit to being controlled by governors. Between 713 and 701 BCE, the Moabites joined the coalitions of Syrian and Palestinian states against Sargon and Sennacherib, but finally they capitulated, paid tribute to Assyria, and were allowed to retain a nominal independence.

The Downfall of Moab: In the wars of Ashurbanipal (see Assyria*) against the Arab tribes, Moab sided with the Assyrians and still continued to pay tribute to them. With the collapse of the Assyrian empire, they were left at the mercy of marauding neighbours. Some scholars believe that an ancient Moabite dirge bewailing the country's fate refers to this period. More likely, it is a dirge about the capture of Moabite land by Sihon (see above). The theme, if not the actual dirge, was taken up by Jeremiah (ch. 48) and Isaiah (ch. 15) in their prophecies concerning the ultimate fate of Moab. The period heralded the end of Moab as an autonomous state. According to archaeological evidence, this took place in the 6th c. BCE.

Josephus (Ant. 10, 9, 7) records that Moab's neighbour, Edom, fell to Nebuchadrezzar and that he fought Moab and Ammon a short time after the destruction of the First Temple. The collapse of these countries, however, was more probably the result of repeated incursions by the desert tribes. The last echoes of Moab in the Old Testament come from the late prophets. Ezekiel interprets Moab's subordination to the desert tribes as a punishment from God for having attacked Judah when it was in a desperate condition after the destruction of the First Temple.

Moab reappears briefly in Josephus, Ant. 13, 14–15, and in I Mac. 9:35 ff as a dependency of the Seleucid empire. By then, the country was inhabited by the early Nabateans*.

Religion: There is very little evidence for the religion of the Moabites, apart from a few hints in the Bible and the narrative of the Mesha stone. It appears that the chief deity was Chemosh and while the Moabites believed that other gods did exist, he was the one whom it was most appropriate for them to worship. The places at which he and other local deities may have been worshipped are suggested by place names like Ba'al Peor, Bamoth Ba'al or Ba'al Ma'ayan; this may also indicate the use of the title "Ba'al" as applied to the national god. The religion of the Moabites was similar to that of neighbouring peoples (Ammonites and Edomites). The Mesha stone attributes Moab's defeat by Israel to Chemosh's anger at his land, and Mesha's victory to the god's favour. The king consecrates the prisoners to his god. Some scholars have assumed from the name Ishtar-Chemosh in the Mesha stone that it indicates Ishtar as the consort of Chemosh. Others believe that this is a composite name which identifies Chemosh with the male god Ishtar (see Canaan: Gods and Idols*).

The style, dress and other details of the two limestone statues (**612**) of a king or a deity (9th or 8th c. BCE) found in Amman, add considerably to our knowledge of the period.

RULERS OF MOAB AND AMMON

Period	*Moab*	*Ammon*
Middle Bronze Age, ca. 2000–1600 BCE		
Late Bronze Age, ca. 1600–1200 BCE	Balak	Sihon (at Heshbon)
Early Iron Age, ca. 1200–950 BCE	Eglon	
		Nahash
		Hanun
		Shobi
Late Iron Age, ca. 950–549 BCE	Mesha, ca. 850 BCE	
	Chemosh Nadab	Sanibu
	Chemosh Nadab	Pudiel
	Musuri	
	Under Assyrian Rule	
	Chemosh Yehi	Ammi Nadab
	Chemosh Haleth	
		Ba'alis

MOSES. — *Outline: Nature of the Accounts of Moses; Moses' Call; Moses in Egypt; The Exodus and Wanderings under Moses' Leadership; The Name of Yahweh; Moses and Modern Criticism; Historicity; Mosaic Monotheism – or Not?; The Mosaic Religious Community; Moses as Apostle of the God of the Covenant; The Decalogue; Conclusion.*

Nature of the Accounts of Moses: The story of Moses' birth and the first years of his life is recorded in Ex. 2. Unlike other historical figures in the Bible like Samson* or Samuel*, this account gives no genealogical details beyond the fact that his parents belonged to the tribe of Levi. Later priestly material (Nu. 26:59) made Moses' mother the daughter of Levi, the son of Jacob, but in fact she must have lived some generations later. This later source also attributed the names Jochebed and Amram to her and her husband. These may be correct, but the information does not exist in other traditions. The lack of genealogical information in the oldest account is in keeping with all the early chapters of Exodus* which give remarkably few details of the Hebrews' life in Egypt, apart from stressing the severity of their bondage.

Moses' name is an indication of his Egyptian upbringing. It was probably not derived from the Hebrew word "mashā" (meaning "to draw out") which is the biblical explanation, but from the Egyptian "mesu" (pronounced "Mosheh" by the Hebrews) which is connected with the Egyptian word for child and appears in such names as Thut-moses, Ra-mses, etc. The Bible records (Ex. 1:15–2:10) that the Egyptians sought to limit the increasing numbers of the Hebrews by decreeing that every new-born male should be killed. Moses' mother successfully hid him until he was three months old, then she put him in a basket among the reeds at the edge of the Nile where he was found by Pharaoh's daughter who raised him in her own household.

This is the essential point of the story of his youth, for the author wished to emphasize that out of this improbable background, God was preparing a "go'el" (deliverer) for His people, even making an Egyptian princess contribute to the child's survival. This theme of a divine plan of deliverance probably explains the apparent symmetry of Moses' life history and career, in spite of the fact that the story in the Pentateuch was compiled by later editors from a whole mass of independent traditions and elements. Various schools of literary criticism of the Bible have made interesting reconstructions of the different original Mosaic themes as they appeared in the hypothetical E, J, D and P documents (see Biblical Criticism*). These are to be found in any standard Introduction to the Old Testament. The various theories are not in agreement with each other, but their mutual contradictions in no way detract from Moses' historicity nor from the unique importance of his life and work (see below). They help to create independently coherent accounts of the career of Moses.

Moses' Call: Both the early and later traditions record that Moses grew up in the Egyptian royal household but that when he learned of his origins he began to take an interest in his kindred and was forced to flee from Egypt after killing an Egyptian he saw maltreating a Hebrew slave. Moses found refuge in Midian where he became shepherd to Jethro, the local priest, and married his daughter, Zipporah, by whom he had two sons, Gershom and Eliezer.

At Horeb, God appeared to Moses, first in the form of a bush that burned but was not consumed (Ex. 3:2–4). (Later rabbinical commentators found in this a symbol for the people as a whole.) There, God commanded Moses to return to Egypt to lead His people to freedom. This phase of the story also includes the revelation of the Name of God (Ex. 3:13–15; see further discussion below: The Name of Yahweh).

Moses in Egypt: In response to the divine command, Moses returned to Egypt and, assisted by his elder brother, Aaron*, he interceded with Pharaoh to let the Israelites leave Egypt and offer a sacrifice to their God in the desert. As a sign of their divine commission, Moses and Aaron engaged in what many scholars regard as a contest of prestige with the court magicians, performing a variety of miraculous feats designed to demonstrate the superiority of one type of magic* over another (see article). In spite of this, Pharaoh refused the request. The Israelites must stay in Egypt — and work harder. In response, God afflicted Egypt with the Ten Plagues (Ex. 7:14–10:29). The point was not that the plagues took place, but that Moses predicted them and his predictions were fulfilled each time, thus making it appear to the Egyptians that his magic was stronger than theirs and/or that he could command the powers of a powerful, malevolent god. All this is conjecture. The tradition records simply that the superiority of Yahweh over the gods of Egypt found its expression in miracles and the mighty deeds of the Exodus. This theme was woven into the accounts of Moses and his leadership.

Pharaoh was finally moved to permit the Israelites and their families to go, but he insisted that they leave their animals behind. This, said Moses, was impossible, for they must take their flocks so as to have offerings available for sacrifice. As Pharaoh still balked at this, Moses proclaimed the death of the first-born of all Egypt (Ex. 10:24–26, 28–29; 11:4–9) and Pharaoh at last consented to the Israelites' departure. This episode remains a prominent feature of the traditional Passover Seder service (see Festivals*).

The Exodus and Wanderings under Moses' Leadership: Later, changing his mind yet again, Pharaoh set out in pursuit of the Hebrews, but he and his army and its chariots were bogged down and then drowned in the Reed Sea which the Hebrews had previously crossed in safety. This body of water is usually wrongly translated "Red Sea" (the application of the term to the Red Sea goes back to the Septuagint and probably earlier). A lake or "Reed Sea" might well have been located in or near the marshy area now crossed by the Suez Canal or in the northeastern corner of the Sinai peninsula (see Exodus* for details).

After long marches and a hard fight against the Amalekites, Moses led the people to Mount Horeb in the Sinai peninsula (their probable route is also discussed in the article on the Exodus*). There, on the advice of his father-in-law (Jethro), Moses organized a proper system for the administration of justice (Ex. 18), and the Decalogue was divinely revealed to Moses who taught the people an entire legal code as a supplement. Chs. 20–23 are the oldest legislation of Israel, preserved by one of the earliest sources (probably E). The same source also relates the ceremony of the sealing of the Covenant (24:3–8, see below). According to this or perhaps another source, when Moses ascended the holy mountain he left the people in the charge of Aaron and Hur (24:13–14). During his absence, Aaron made a golden calf for the people to worship (see Aaron*). When Moses came and saw it, he broke the tablets of stone and destroyed the image, and God sent a plague as punishment but then relented. A later source (P) recounts that Moses ascended the mountain (24:15–18) and there received instructions for the erection of the Tabernacle* and the form of worship to be practiced within it (25–31:17).

The story of the wanderings is taken up by the book of Numbers in the second year. While the Hebrews were staying at Kadesh-Barnea (the focal point for the wanderings), a census was taken of the fighting men who would be available on the march. The P (priestly) writer took this occasion to enlarge upon the organization of the priestly and Levitical families (Nu. 1–4). The census and its interpretation is discussed in the article on Census*.

In the early years of the wanderings, Moses frequently clashed with various sections of the people, some of them, at one time, even wanting to return to Egypt (Nu. 14:1, 3 ff). When the children of Israel were camped in the wilderness of Paran and twelve men were sent to spy out the land of Canaan, the report they brought back was calculated to discourage the Israelites from attacking (Nu. 13:31–33). Only Joshua and Caleb gave a favourable account (for which reason they alone were permitted to enter the Promised Land; Nu. 13:30; 14:6–24, 30).

There seems to be a break in the story at this point. The E source in Nu. relates that against Moses' advice, the people advanced towards Canaan and were routed by the Amalekites and other inhabitants (14:39–45). The story is taken up (ch. 20) with the miracle of the water from the rock (20:2–13), the refusal of the king of Edom to grant the Israelites passage through his land (20:14–21), the death of Aaron the High Priest at Mount Hor (20:22–29) and his son, Eleazar's, succession to his office (Dt. 10:6).

Beyond the statement that the generation who left Egypt shall not enter the Promised Land (Nu. 14:22–23), the Bible is silent on events between the 2nd and the 39th year of the Exodus. In the 39th year, Moses again attempted to lead the new generation, hardened by their years in the wilderness, into Canaan. Their first encounter with the Canaanites at Hormah ended in victory for the Israelites (21:1–3). Then they marched by way of Edom to Moab, beating Sihon the Amorite (Nu. 21:11–15, 21–24, 27–30), the Moabites and the Midianites, and slaying Balaam (Nu. 22–24; 31:1–12; see Numbers*). The conquest of Bashan (see Conquest*) confirmed Israel's lordship over Transjordan and provided the people with a base from which to attack the Promised Land itself. After appointing Joshua* as his successor (Dt. 31:14 ff, 23), Moses was permitted to view the land of Canaan from the top of Mt. Pisgah, what he saw being probably very much the same as the photograph **(613)** taken from the same point today. Then he died at Mount Nebo in Moab and was buried there (Dt. 34:5–6), the site of his tomb being unknown.

613

The Name of Yahweh: According to the sources that became fused in Exodus, it was to Moses that the name YHWH was first revealed in Midian and it was he who taught it to the Israelites in Egypt. Ex. 3:6 and 6:3 both clearly link Yahweh to the "God of the Fathers", which suggests that the religion Moses preached was not something new to the Hebrews. The God of the Fathers was El. Moses designated El by the new appellative, YHWH, previously not so used. Moses' contribution may perhaps be seen as a clearer statement of the covenantal relation between men and God and a more precise definition of God as redeemer and the Israelites as His "Chosen People*". Where the name "YHWH" itself comes from is another question.

God's revelation of his name as the Tetragammaton YHWH (pronounced Yahweh) is the crux of Moses' call (Ex. 2:23–4:17). The word appears to be derived from the verb "hyh" and can be translated "he is" or, according to a different verbal stem, "he creates; he causes to be". Ex. 3:14 gives the meaning of the divine name as "I am who I am" and numerous commentaries have been written on this text. However, the verb "hyh" is always used in a dramatic context — it never refers to a static situation or event like a simple "to be". Its use as the name of God in the sense of "I am the creator" would be an accurate description of a God active in creation. Elsewhere in Exodus, however, in the historical setting of Sinai, the Mosaic formulas seem to emphasize other qualities and attributes of God: in 33:19 and 34:6–7 His graciousness and saving mercy to His people, the theme of the whole book, which implies the meaning "I am the gracious, the compassionate one." 34:14 uses a formula which is usually translated as Yahweh, the "jealous God", but this is an awkward rendering. "For He creates zeal" would come nearer to the original, implying the zeal with which He binds Israel to Him in an exclusive relationship of privilege and obligation, judgment and mercy, but also promise and threat.

Moses and Modern Criticism: Earlier research has transferred so much of the legislation and development of monotheism from Moses to later ages, that Moses' own role often seems to have shrunk considerably. In fact, however, there is no justification for trying to reduce him to a vague figure, known only from legend. The most searching biblical criticism has served to justify the validity of the biblical traditions concerning Moses. It is generally agreed today that a new religious community came into existence at the time of Moses as a result of his message and leadership, even though Moses himself remains shadowy.

The opposite view (M. Noth) is concerned with denying the uniqueness of Moses' work. Though the uniqueness of the event of Sinai is undeniable, albeit historically difficult to prove, this scholar does not necessarily regard as history the tradition that Moses was the "founder" of the new faith or that Mosaism as such was a new religion. He attributes the traditions to a Deuteronomistic origin and sees them as the result of the crystallization of a pan-Israel national religion in later days, after the settlement in Canaan. Later tradition transferred these accounts and beliefs to the remote background of Exodus and Moses. This leader was connected, therefore, with Exodus, though not necessarily with the Sinai event and its tradition. The extreme view that tries to deny Moses any historical existence at all scarcely comes within the bounds of sober criticism. The theory that the narratives concerning him are all legendary is also rejected by modern critics as neither scientific nor critical. Not all the details related about him may be literally true, but, just as in the case of the Patriarchs*, the stories about Moses include a substantial historical nucleus.

Historicity: Israel's history did not start from scratch at the time of Moses. Research has shown that the biblical account was deliberately simplified and that traditions extending over half a millenium lie behind the Exodus — or were rapidly absorbed into the folklore of its people. (The problems of Israel's origins are discussed under Patriarchs* and Conquest*.)

It is often difficult to separate the historic kernel that emerges from the traditions from the surrounding folklore and the many magic elements which are interspersed with them (the plagues, the miracles, the crossing of the sea, etc.). These express the conviction that Yahweh was actually present and active in the rescue of His people. This is the gist of the tradition, though hard facts are not there to prove it. The prevalent feeling about the reliability of the tradition leads many scholars to believe that the events of the Exodus and Sinai demand a single outstanding personality as their focus. Though no historic facts can be cited in proof, they feel that the Hebrew people was completely transformed by Moses. Moreover, though the circumstances of the event at Sinai lie beyond historical analysis, the Hebrews' unique faith in a single God called in their tradition for an individual founder of the new belief. Similar analogies of leadership are cited from the cases of the religions of Christianity and Islam.

Mosaic Monotheism — or Not?: The 19th c. scholar, Wellhausen (see Biblical Criticism*) accepted the designation of Moses' time as the "properly creative" period of Israel's religion and the genesis of its national history. What aroused far more disagreement (and is still a subject of controversy) was the nature of the religion thus created. Some scholars do not regard Moses as the creator of the new faith. A new faith was coming into being, to be sure, but it is difficult to define it in its early stages. It took centuries to develop completely and to generate even the seeds of ethical monotheism. J.T. Meek, for instance, argues that before the idea of a world god can emerge and be accepted, a world view, politically speaking, is necessary. In the days of Moses, Israel was a mixed multitude, taking no more than their first steps in the direction of nationhood. Such a background could hardly give rise to the idea of an all-powerful world god.

On the other hand, Oesterly and Robinson define the religion which Moses promulgated as a religion with the slogan, "Yahweh is the God of Israel and Israel is the people of Yahweh", to which was added a good deal of primitive superstition. W.F. Albright has maintained that the religion of Moses was already what is commonly termed monotheism and that "in essentials, orthodox Yahwism remained the same from Moses to Ezra." But many scholars have disputed this. It is difficult to see how the argument can be settled, for the issues involved concern the theologian as much as the historian and the whole subject seems to raise opposite views about what religion is — i.e. it comes down to a question of definitions. The opponents of Mosaic monotheism deny that the term may legitimately be applied to a religion which does not have a philosophical theology. Israel's religion was not founded on abstract theology. It rested on the memory and interpretation of a historical experience. Yahweh, the Israelites believed, had deliberately rescued them from bondage and, through the Covenant, had made them "His" people, in the sense of His vassals (see Chosen People and Election*).

There is another argument that monotheism must always emerge as an explicit denial of other gods. "Gods" existed in every pagan temple, and repeated prophetic denunciations of idolatry among the Israelites suggest that they never formed such a thing as a monotheistic religious community in the sense of a philosophical monotheism. Additional evidence is the attitude of pre-prophetic literature towards holy sites, the Tabernacle and the sanctuary. All the ancient holy places, even sites formerly sacred to the Canaanites, were absorbed into the religion as places where Yahweh had revealed himself, without being bound or geographically limited to them. There was nothing of polytheism about Israel's religion. It was, as it were, a practical monotheism without the support of an extensive philosophical rationalization.

Many scholars suggest it would be better described as "monolatry" or "henotheism", meaning the worship of only one god while recognizing the existence of others. Their status as gods was not tolerantly granted and the Israelites denied such "gods and idols" any of the magic and powers that were claimed for them by their devotees. The Yahweh the Israelites worshipped by far transcended the personification of the forces of nature which polytheistic gods represented. Yahweh was himself the god of all nature and He alone had the power to direct or control the natural forces or the history of the world. The full implications of this attitude took centuries to be realized, but the faith in a single God which Moses taught contained all the essential elements of the fully developed monotheism of later years. In its primitive stage, the Mosaic faith forbade recognition of other "gods" and barred all forms of syncretism. However, it could not (and did not) exclude cultural borrowing, some of which proved a boon to Israel's development, though there was also cultic borrowing which ran counter to pure Mosaism, as related in the articles on Idol Worship in Israel*; Phoenicians*.

The Mosaic Religious Community: Many scholars define the early Hebrew community as a covenant community. Groups cooperating on the basis of an agreement or covenant between humans, but not with a deity, were common before Moses' time (see Law*), but in the ancient world, such covenant coalitions were generally ephemeral and unpredictable. There is an alternate theory that early Israel was a collection of kinship groups held together by the ties of blood, but this has also been denied. Israel had no centralized government before the 12th or 10th c. BCE, and the early centuries of its existence were a time of constant threat to its identity. Yet Israel and its religion were enabled to survive in spite of powerful military opposition, great cultural diversity within its own community and a constant drive toward religious syncretism. If the force that created and maintained the legal community was one of religion or covenant, then these must have been very far from "primitive". This divine-human relationship and its literary tradition is discussed under Exodus*: The Covenantal Relationship.

Moses as Apostle of the God of the Covenant: Wellhausen's "properly creative period" covers something more than the creation of a national community. A structure of religious activity and belief emerged along with the national group. Once Israel had, through the Covenant, accepted Yahweh's overlordship on His terms, a pattern of specific elements combining traditions, history, law and cult took shape. Each of these elements must have had its own history and this is particularly true of the religious aspects. The traditions which were absorbed into Israel's religion included those of the Patriarchs*, the Sabbath* and the paschal spring sacrifice in the desert (see Exodus*; Exodus, Book of*), each having its own long and complex pre-history.

It may be true that there was never any formal statement of the ideas of "Covenant" and "election" during the actual period of the wanderings, but there can be no doubt that the people involved in the wanderings believed that they had been rescued from a hard and bitter fate by Yahweh's deliberate act and that by the familiar instrument of a covenant, He had made them "His" vassals and subject people.

Thus, it seems that the Mosaic period saw the creation of the community itself. That community incorporated the traditions and experiences of its people and these merged into its religious structure. The extra dimension was added by the experience of the group as a "Holy Community" belonging to the Kingdom of God (see Covenant*; Impurity and Purification*; Warfare*) — a concept which would have been totally incomprehensible to the contemporary world of antiquity. This tradition of the Covenant was the key factor in all Israel's subsequent history, which can only be understood in the context of that tradition (see Covenant*; Israel and Judah*; Judges*).

The Decalogue: Scholars raise hardly any doubts about the continuity of pre-Mosaic religious traditions, which seems a very good argument for the even greater acceptability of the traditions of the (creative) Mosaic period. The questions of the early origin of the Decalogue and the Book of the Covenant are discussed at length in the articles on Book of Exodus* and Biblical Criticism*. Many scholars argue on different grounds for a Mosaic origin for the ethical Decalogue.

A comparison of the familiar Decalogue of Ex. 20 with the other series of commandments in Ex. 34:10–27 (thirteen in the present text, although possibly once ten) shows that the latter series is more concerned with ritual matters and appears to belong to an agricultural community. The argument assumes that both versions lie within the same course of development, but in fact this is purely hypothetical. It seems more likely that both sets of law are parallel although not contemporary and relate to quite different circumstances and conditions of distinct groups belonging to Israel's progenitors in the early 12th or 11th c. BCE. Exodus 20 would actually fit the wilderness period somewhat better than Exodus 34. (The Decalogues are generally attributed to the J — Yahwist — source of biblical "documents".) The fact that they were finally merged into the book of Exodus is no grounds for supposing them phases of a continuous development.

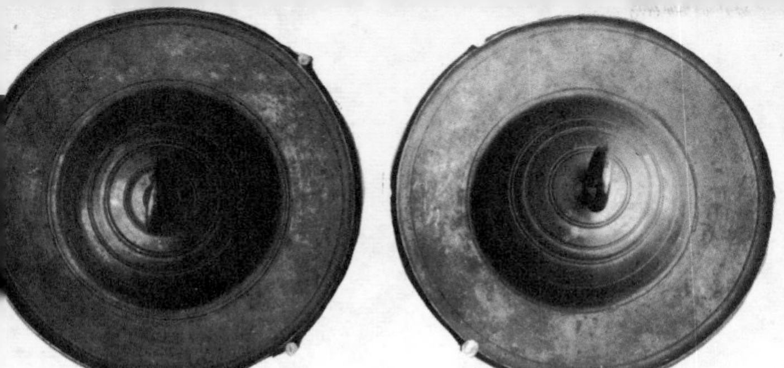

614

615

Conclusion: It is not known whether Yahweh was worshipped before Moses' time or not. If so, it seems likely that Moses was responsible for giving Yahwism a new content and new identity. The impact of his inspired personality raised Israel's religion to a new and higher level. Later on, when the prophets were facing the task of stemming a degeneration in contemporary religion, it was to the heights of the Mosaic religion that they recalled their people.

The Covenant with Yahweh remained the centre of Mosaic religion. It became the foundation of the territorial and social organization, along with much of the Mosaic tradition, although many things were adapted by the settlers in Canaan to meet the needs of the new period.

The subject of Moses in the New Testament is dealt with at the end of the article on the Book of Exodus*.

MUSIC. — *Outline: I. Israel's Music: Music in the Temple; Secular Music; Popular Secular Music; The Sound of the Shofar; Signal for God's Holy War; The Sound of Israelite Music. II. Musical Instruments: Percussion Instruments; Wind Instruments; Stringed Instruments.*

I. ISRAEL'S MUSIC: One of the ancient traditions of Genesis (4:20 ff) recording the beginnings of the human race, tells that music was invented by Jubal, at the same time as his brothers, Jabal and Tubal-Cain introduced cattle-raising and metal-working. Music had a very important place in the life of ancient times — in the liturgy, to provide a rhythmic beat for group activities and labour groups to make work in unison more pleasant, and as an accompaniment to all important individual and national events.

Israel's music — as so much else of its culture — owed a big debt to the Canaanites*. The organization of guilds of professional musicians, begun in the early stages of the monarchy under David and Solomon, was probably copied from Canaanite practice.

The Old Testament refers to both religious and secular music.

616

Music in the Temple: In the early days, women appear to have predominated as sacred dancers and singers — e.g. Miriam (Ex. 15:20–21) or the women who welcomed David after his defeat of Goliath (I Sam. 18:6–7). Later, participation in the Temple cult was restricted to men. Chronicles gives a full description of the musical activities of the Levites in its account of the purification of the Temple at the time of Hezekiah: "And he stationed the Levites in the house of the Lord with cymbals (**614**, as illustrated by this Phoenician instrument of the 10th c. BCE), harps (**616**; as shown by this Egyptian 12th c. BCE model), and lyres (**615**) illustrated by these, carried by captives of the Assyrians, 8th c. BCE, or this Palestinian lyre painted on a Megiddo vase of the 12th c. BCE, **617**. "And when the burnt offering

617

620

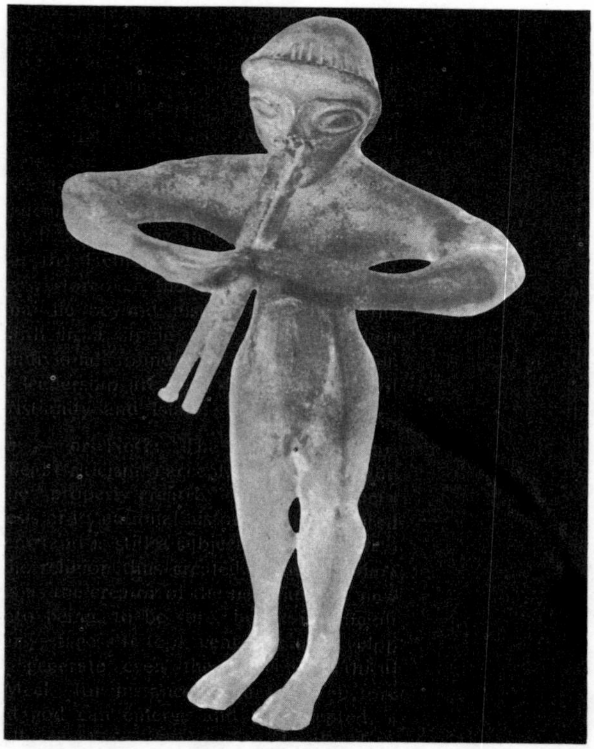

618

began, the song of the Lord began also, and the trumpets, accompanied by the instruments of David, king of Israel. The whole assembly worshipped, and the singers sang and the trumpeters sounded ... And Hezekiah the king and the princes commanded the Levites to sing praises to the Lord with the words of David and Asaph the seer, and they sang praises with gladness, and they bowed down and worshipped." (II Ch. 29:25–30). This description does not appear in the parallel passage of Kings, a silence which, some scholars argue, indicates that it may have been inaccurate in ascribing the musical organization to David, and may, in fact, reflect the position in the Second Temple rather than the First (see Chronicles*). Other scholars regard this argument from silence as inconclusive and find the attribution to Hezekiah quite reasonable — especially as it is known that there were royal singers at his court.

In the First Temple, music (the psalmody) was not restricted to the priestly class (the Levites). It was part of the non-priestly "external" cult. The singers during the period may have been professionals, but they were not Levites. Only after the return from Exile was professional temple music entrusted to the Levites and the descendants of Heman (Neh. 12:27, 45 ff).

The descriptions in Chronicles is supplemented by various details in the Mishnah, notably Sukkoth V, 5, which gives an account of the Simḥat Beth Hashoevah (Feast of the Drawing of Water): "and the Levites with lyres and harps and cymbals and trumpets and innumerable other instruments." This, of course, is also post-Exilic.

621

Secular Music: The mellifluous flute (ûgāb, **618**, illustrated by this 7th c. BCE Greek model of a boy playing a double pipe) or oboe (hālîl), lyre (kinnôr, **619**) and drum (toph) were used to accompany songs at work and for festive gatherings. During the monarchy, foreign influences and the development of urban life destroyed the earlier pastoral simplicity. The splendours of orchestral sound and sophisticated court and urban dance music were introduced partly under Egyptian influence, illustrated in these wall paintings (**620**). The flute (**621**), illustrated by this early Egyptian model, and lyre were replaced by more powerful wind and stringed instruments, described below. Musicians were employed by the royal court probably before David's time. The first mention of them occurs in II Sam. 19:35, when Barzilai regrets that age prevents him from enjoying "the voices of singing men and singing women" at David's court. In the 8th c. BCE, Sennacherib carried off male and female musicians from Jerusalem as part of the spoils of war, while Psalm 137 (vs. 1–3) bears witness to the Babylonian demand for "songs of Zion".

Music as the accompaniment to a life of luxury and leisure earned the condemnation of the prophets. Amos (6:4–5) mocks those who lie on beds with ivory ornaments and strum on their harps. Isaiah (5:11) foretold the doom of those whose only occupation was to "run after strong drink" with "lyre and harp, timbrel and flute" to entertain them.

Popular Secular Music: Popular secular music was a different matter as evidenced by the Song of Songs*. The

619

622

while the priests keep blowing the trumpets for carnage . . . and the priests shall blow for them on the trumpets of pursuit." (War Scroll VII, 8—IX, 9).

The priests would signal withdrawal in moments of reverse, or would blow encouragement to the warriors, then urge them "to take up positions in their assigned places. Then the priests shall sound a second blast on the trumpets . . . everyone shall raise his hand with his weapons in it and the priests shall blow on the trumpets the signal for carnage and all the people with ram's horns shall sound a blast and the infantry shall start to launch an attack . . ." (War Scroll XVI, 11—XVII, 5).

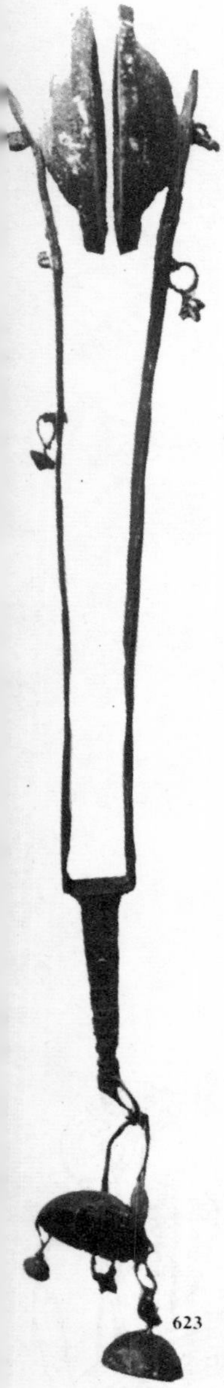

623

songs of the vintners and the wine-pressers are also referred to in Isaiah's lament for Moab (16:10). Weddings were naturally rich musical occasions. The Song of Songs probably contains many of these songs and they were intended to be sung: Song 2:8 is a serenade in the springtime; 7:12 was sung at the harvesting of fruits; 4:4 or 5:10 is a sword dance; 5:12–16 was sung at weddings to the accompaniment of musical instruments. Even as early as Jacob's flight from Aram (Gn. 31:26–27), Laban reproached him, "Why did you flee secretly, and cheat me, and did not tell me, so that I might have sent you away with mirth and songs, with tambourine and lyre?" Music might be exhilerating. It could also be soothing. David's playing soothed Saul* when he was troubled by an "evil spirit" (I Sam. 16:23). The powerful emotional and psychological effect of music is a prominent theme in ancient literature (e.g. the Orphic myths), echoed in later legends concerning David and still much discussed by mediaeval Arab authors.

The Sound of the Shofar: The sound of the shofar (ram's horn) was familiar at all periods of Israel's history, summoning the people to solemn assembly, its loud blast claiming attention for announcements, proclamation of holidays and public events, coronations and, of course calls to war and alarms. Trumpets (described below, under instruments) were made of metal. In the tabernacle or Temple worship, they were presumed to attract God's attention. There they were often combined with other instruments.

Signal for God's Holy War: The "War Manual" of the Dead Sea Sectaries (see Dead Sea Scrolls*) is a nostalgic reconstruction of the epic deeds of the past. When the trumpet has sounded for God's final Holy War, the sectaries gird themselves for battle. Their army is organized according to the rules for the priestly war camp in the desert (Nu. 2: 1–34) but the Scroll also owes a certain debt to a military manual composed during Herod's reign. More important than the tactics prescribed, an atmosphere of religious exaltation pervades the camp, heightened by the sound of shofars and trumpets, reminiscent of battle scenes in Israel's past: "Blown by levites and priests they sound. For calling to arms: a blast on the trumpets of assembly; a quavering blast for drawing the line of battle; a subdued note for advance to the enemy line; blasts on the six trumpets for preparing to slaughter; the priests are to blow upon the trumpets a sharp insistent sound to direct the wings of the battle; and all the people shall silence their war cries,

The Sound of Israelite Music: It is much easier to discover, from archaeology and descriptions, what Israelite musical instruments looked like, than how they sounded. Nevertheless, musical research has been able to get some idea of the rhythm, notation and acoustic qualities of Old Testament music, especially liturgical music from the time of the Second Temple. For instance, certain musical patterns have been provisionally distinguished that later developed into traditional Church modes, e.g. Gregorian chant. Archaeological evidence for this is supported by the remarkable similarity between early ecclesiastical chants and the tunes intoned by remote Jewish communities (e.g. in the Yemen) who had never come into contact with Christianity.

The remnants of liturgical and popular music have been preserved in the chants and songs of the Jewish communities of Yemen, Mesopotamia, Persia, Syria and North Africa, where Jews lived in seclusion for more than thirteen hundred years. The traditional antiphonal singing used in many of the Psalms (e.g. 13, 20, 38, 69, 89) was long retained in the synagogue, but when the mediaeval "ḥazān" wanted to impress his congregation, he began to embellish the traditional melodies. Signs or "accents" were instituted to help the singers remember their variations and these were to have an influence on the beginnings of western musical notation.

The book of Psalms, many of which were used in the Temple liturgy both before and after the Exile, gives some indication of the musical style in which the individual psalms were recited or chanted. Unfortunately, the terms used, whether referring to musical instruments or the type of psalm, have proved almost impossible to understand. Even the Septuagint translators were defeated by most of them. This shows that the headings were already archaic and incomprehensible by the 2nd c. BCE — even though they are later than the Psalms which must be older still.

The words which appear at the head of the psalms apparently defined their nature, e.g.: Mizmôr, Shîr (sometimes Mizmôr-Shîr or Shîr-Mizmôr), Miktām, Maskîl, Shîr hama'alôth (possibly, Pilgrim's Song, Song of a Returning Exile, or of a singer standing on the Temple stairs). Higgāyôn (? resounding music) and Shiggāyôn (? wild or tumultuous music) may also belong to this group, although some authorities think the words refer to musical instruments used for accompanying the singers. Scholars are no nearer agreement on the meaning of Gittît, Mînîm (although it is now usually agreed that "minîm" was not a single object, but meant a group of related instruments), Neginôt, Nehilôt (perhaps wind instruments), Alāmôt, Sh^{e}mînîth. Possible meanings of these obsolete terms are

624

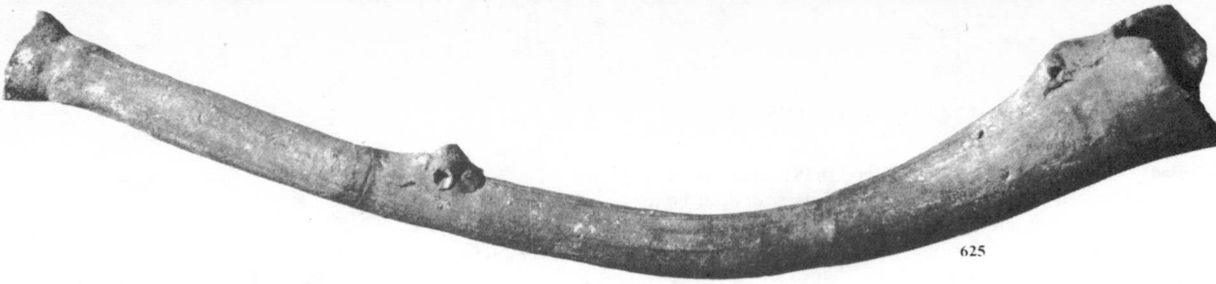

625

still being sought. The general view is that some of them at least were not instruments, but melodies or styles of singing.

Another group of expressions, e.g. "'Al 'ayelet hashaḥar" (the hind of the morning, Ps. 22) referred to well-known places, specially identified with a particular melody. The psalm to which the heading was attached was intended to be sung to that tune. Probably, as in church hymns, the name of the tune was derived from some secular song or other psalm with which the melody was originally associated.

"Selah", to judge by the Septuagint translation, signified a change in the music, a pause or the raising of the voice. "Lāmenātzê'āḥ" apparently meant the chief musician or conductor (in the Aramaic translation it is rendered by a verb: to praise; in the Septuagint by For Ever). It is believed that the Jewish modal system, still common in Oriental musical patterns, developed towards the end of the monarchy and in the post-Exilic period. C. Sachs favours the notion that there was a prevailing pentatonic scale, but this is not certain.

II. MUSICAL INSTRUMENTS: Interpretation of the terms for musical instruments is on surer ground, although, even here, there are many obscurities. Some terms, for instance, are interchangeable, like Nêbel (harp) and Kinnôr (lyre), and they are exchanged in the earlier translations, although originally they denoted distinctions in size or in the number of strings. On the other hand, many statements or explanations offered by later writers are clearly unreliable. Josephus*, for example, solemnly states that there were 500,000 musicians in Palestine! Though no pictorial sources are available to enable a reconstruction of ancient Hebrew playing, we have numerous contemporary examples in Egyptian, Assyrian and Aramean or Greek pictures and sculptures.

In general, the known instruments mentioned in Hebrew writings can be classified under familiar modern groupings:

Percussion Instruments: Tôph (frame drum, **622**); menāne'îm — sistrum (**624**, as shown in a Phoenician 10th c. BCE instrument); m^{e}tziltāyim or tselts^{e}lîm — cymbals (**614**); see 10th c. BCE Phoenician castanets, **623**; pā'amonîm — bells or jingles; shālîshîm — not yet identified.

Wind Instruments (Wood-wind): Hālîl — oboe; shôfār or keren yobêl — ram or goat's horn (**625**; similar to the ones used in synagogues today); ûgāb — flute (in Aramaic — abûbā); mashrôkêtā — double oboe (according to C. Sachs); keren — horn or trumpet, (metal, **626**, late Roman models from Spain and Italy are shown here). Hātsots^{e}rah — trumpet; **the trumpets from Herod's temple, 627, shown on the Arch** of Titus (see Temple*) are longer even than those pictured in the inscriptions on Jewish coins of the 2nd c. CE. Other coins of the period picture lyres. It is interesting to note that they come in pairs as in the instructions given to Moses (Nu. 10:2–10). They were played by priests either in unison or antiphonally during Temple worship.

626

627

Stringed Instruments: Kinnôr — lyre (**628**; such as this 15th c. BCE instrument from Thebes with its sounding box, or Greek, 7th c. BCE model, **619**); nēbel — harp; āsôr — zither; pesantērin (obviously not Semitic) — psaltery (a stringed instrument triangular in shape, or dulcimer); kātrôs — cithara (**628a,** as played by this Roman lady, 1st c. BCE); sabkā — harp shaped like a siege-engine, i.e. a ladder on a boat. These last non-Semitic names appear only in the description of Nebuchadrezzar's court in Daniel. The same book also mentions the word "sampôneyah". This used to be defined as an instrument (bagpipes?), but recently it has appeared that it was a more generic term, like the modern "symphony" or "ensemble".

628

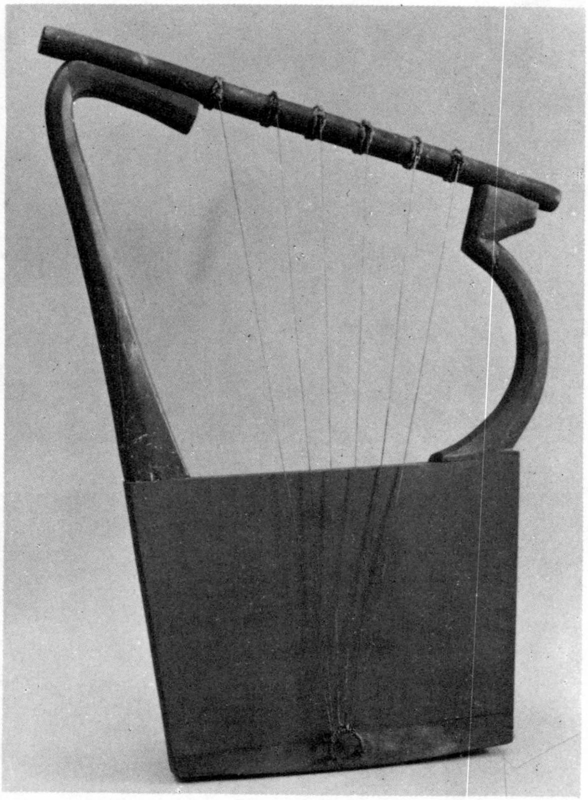

628 a

N

NABATEANS-THEIR HISTORY, CIVILIZATION AND TOWNS. — *Outline: Origins of the Nabateans; Greek and Roman Evidence for Nabatean Origins. I. History, Urbanization; The First Nabatean Kings; Conflict with the Hasmoneans; Nabatean Growth; Expansion in Arabia; Nabateans and Romans; Roman Ambitions; Roman Annexation. II. Culture: Language; Art; Religion; Agriculture. III. The Towns of the Nabateans: Petra: Tombs; Temples and Sanctuaries; Roman Petra. Oriental-Hellenistic Forms: Khirbet-al-Tannur; El-Ram; Umm-al-Jamal; Seia; Egra (Madain Saleh); Avdat: Pottery Kiln and Types; Agriculture; Destruction and Renaissance.*

One of the closest neighbours of post-Exilic Judea, the Nabateans are also the most intriguing of the Oriental kingdoms that fringed the Graeco-Roman world. As a result of surveys and some excavations of their towns during the last few decades, the Nabateans and their culture are better known today than any of the other North Arabian peoples of the times. For a period extending from the 4th c. BCE to the 2nd c. CE, the Nabateans indeed made the deserts bloom, reviving ancient centres of civilization like Edom, Moab* and Ammon in the region that lay south and east of the Dead Sea and the Palestinian Negeb, between the Red Sea and the Syrian desert (see map **629**). The Nabatean kingdom guarded the international caravan routes of the area and it was the trade of these overland arteries of the ancient world (see Roads*; Trade*) that gave the kingdom its wealth and its importance.

Origins of the Nabateans: There are some scholars who connect the origins of the Nabateans with the "Nabayoth" of Gn. 25:13; 28:9; 36:3, the first-born of Ishmael who was the father of all Arabs, according to biblical genealogy. Alternatively, other scholars connect the Nabateans with descendants of the Edomites and with the peoples mentioned in I Ch. 1:29 and Is. 60:7, as living in "Sela" (meaning "rock") of Edom, which the Greeks later called "Petra" (a word which also means "rock"). 7th c. BCE Assyrian chronicles also refer to "Na-ba-aatu", meaning tribes of Aramean stock living around the Sirhan depression to the southeast of Transjordan. These references, however, do not connect them with Edom or adjoining areas and, in addition, there are serious historical and especially linguistic objections to this identification.

For one thing, there is no reference to "Nabayoth" anywhere after the 7th c. BCE. More important, the Nabatean inscriptions spell their own name "n b t w" (Nebatu) with the emphatic t (tet), whereas the various biblical forms of "Nabayoth" are all written with "taw" = th. However, the Greek, Diodorus Siculus of Sicily (4th c. BCE); the Roman, Strabo; Pliny the Elder (early 1st c. CE) and Josephus (1st c. CE; Ant. and Jewish War) all refer to the Nabateans under the generic term of "Arabs", though they were not Arabs*.

In addition, many scholars believe that the 7th and 6th cs. BCE, before and during the collapse of the great Assyrian and Babylonian empires, saw considerable shifts in population throughout the Fertile Crescent. Presumably, the natives of the lands later dominated by the Nabateans in southeastern Palestine mingled with Arab and, eventually, Nabatean newcomers. The nature of their political expansion indicates the domination of a small group of traders who imposed their rule over the peasants of Transjordan.

The question of the origins of the Nabateans continues to be debated. They cannot be considered merely the natural heirs of the Edomites or Amalekites who inhabited the same region centuries earlier. The gap in time is too long. Economically and geographically they were linked to North Arabia and apparently they originally had a semi-nomadic background. However, they also had strong affinities with the Palmyrenes and Itureans (see below), for instance their art shows strong affinities with the Semites of the north and north-west (the region of Palmyra and Dura), rather than with the Arabs of the south (see Arabia*). They wrote in Aramaic, but the language of their inscriptions is partly corrupted by Arabic words and names. The earliest evidence for the Nabatean language and culture comes from the end of the 1st c. BCE and is hardly conclusive so far as their origins are concerned.

Greek and Roman Evidence for Nabatean Origins: The earliest evidence from outside sources is the account of Diodorus Siculus who places the Nabateans during the end of the Persian era (late 4th c. BCE) when the decaying empire could no longer exercise authority over the outlying areas and the semi-nomadic Syrian and Aramean tribes who lived there. Apparently the Nabateans began by acting as agents for Arab traders, collecting merchandise from Arabia at their capital of Sela (Petra) and forwarding it to the Mediterranean ports of Gaza or Raphiah (Rhinocolura).

Diodorus adds that they dealt in gums for medicinal purposes and this seemed confirmed by traces of early exploitation of the balsam groves of ʿEin Gedi* near Jericho, (which Josephus* also attributed to the Nabateans). It appears that the 'Ein Gedi industry was probably Jewish, but the Nabateans may very likely have cultivated balsam east of the Dead Sea. The same ancient writers also report that the Nabateans extracted the floating bitumen from the Dead Sea. The most important customers for this product were the Egyptians who used it extensively, from Hellenistic times, in the embalming of their dead. This demand gave an added economic and political importance to the Nabateans.

Diodorus relates that the glowing reports of their wealth moved Antigonus, one of Alexander's generals, to send two expeditions from Syria (312–311 BCE) to try to annex their territory to the Macedonian empire. The first attempt ended in disaster for the Greeks and, after the second, Antigonus was contented with the Nabatean offer of tribute and retired.

Like the rest of the Greeks, Diodorus confused the Nabateans with the Arabs. He describes them as nomads who neither sowed nor planted nor built permanent houses, who raised camels and sheep, dug wells in the wilderness and carried frankincense, myrrh and other spices to the coast. According to him, they refrained from drinking wine.

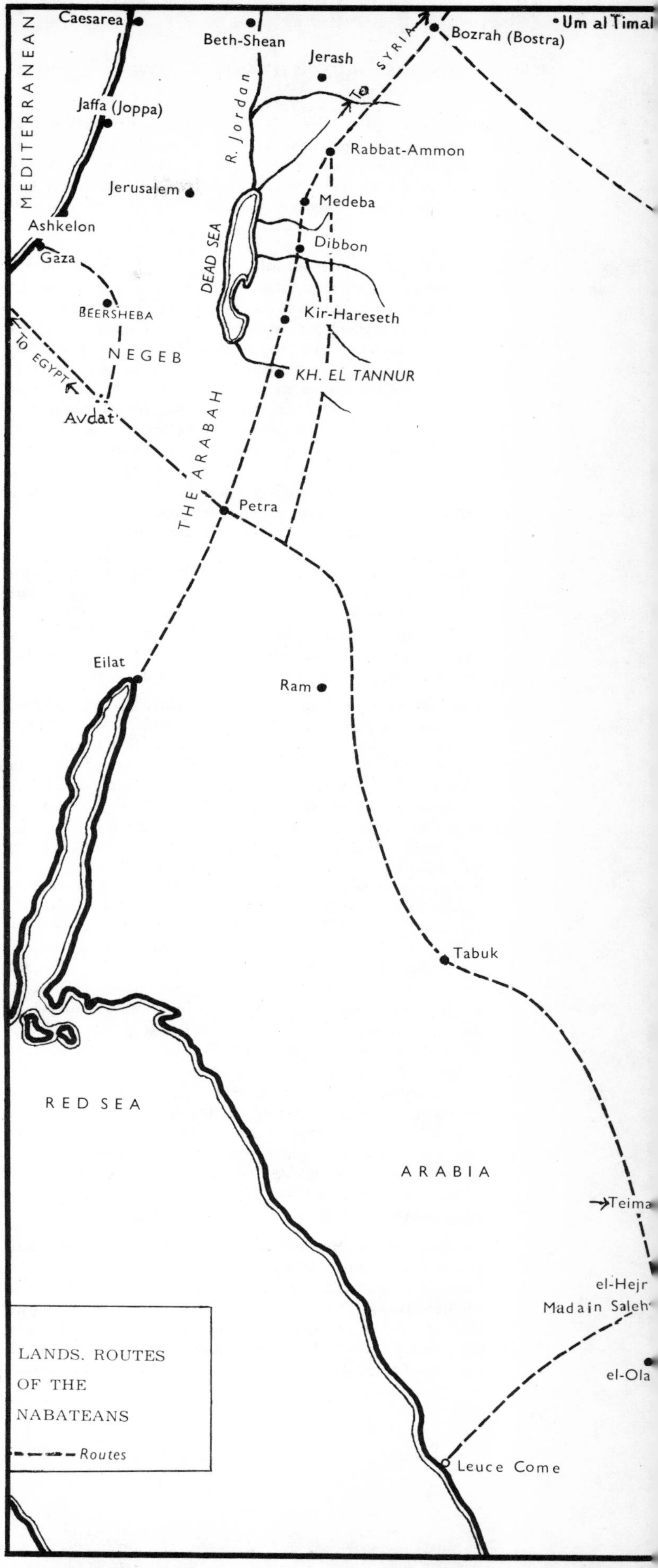

LANDS. ROUTES OF THE NABATEANS

Herodotus (5th c. BCE) also recorded (in connection with Cambyses the Persian's conquest of Egypt) that "Arab" kings held ports south of Yenisus (possibly Khan Yunis, south of Gaza). However, it seems unlikely that there was any connection between these "Arab" rulers and the Nabateans.

I. HISTORY: **Urbanization:** Nothing is heard of the Nabateans during the long period of hellenization in the Near East, during which Palestine and Transjordan first (3rd c. BCE) formed part of the Ptolemaic empire, then were added to the Seleucid domains (after 200 BCE, see Hellenism in the Near East*). Nevertheless, the new expansion of Greek (Hellenistic) culture, towns, art and architecture had its effect on the Nabateans, most clearly revealed in the architecture of Petra. Between the 3rd c. and the early years of the 2nd BCE, the political and material life of the Nabateans must have been revolutionized. There is evidence of this profound change in their national characteristics between the Greek and Roman periods, and the material testimony is confirmed by written accounts. The Roman, Strabo ("Geographia"; 1st c. BCE), and Pliny the Elder ("Natural History"; 1st c. CE) have left descriptions of the Nabateans as a people living in permanent houses and growing olives and various kinds of fruit (see Agriculture, below), which suggest that during the 3rd and 2nd cs. BCE Petra had gradually developed into the great Middle Eastern entrepôt, at the centre of a flourishing civilization.

The First Nabatean Kings: The first Nabatean king mentioned in history is Aretas I (called the "tyrant of the Arabs"), to whom Jason, High Priest of Jerusalem, fled when turned out of office by the Maccabaeans in the riots of 169 BCE (II Mac. 5:8-9; see Hasmoneans*). This verifiable date forms the basis for a chronology of Nabatean kings (and explains why this Aretas is called "the First"). The title "Tyrant" also indicates that by this time, Nabatea was already established as an independent principality. Another source, Pompeius Trogus in the Epitome of Justinianus (39:5), states that "Erotimus, king of the Arabs" and his successor Aretas II (120–96 BCE) founded the Nabatean kingdom, which embarked upon occasional raids against Syria and Egypt. If this statement is accepted, then, in the view of many scholars, the foundation of the Nabatean kingdom by these rulers may have been made possible by the internal wars that paralyzed Seleucid power after the death of Antiochus VI Sidetes (129 BCE; see Hasmoneans*). Other intertestamental sources refer to the Nabateans as a people friendly to the Jews. When Judas Maccabaeus and his brother Jonathan crossed the Jordan to bring aid to the Jews of Gilead (I Mac. 5:25–27; see Hasmoneans*), the Nabateans received them amicably. Later, when the Syrian general, Bacchides, drove Jonathan temporarily out of Judea, he asked his "friends" the Nabateans to hold his considerable military stores for him (I Mac. 9:35).

Conflict with the Hasmoneans: Once the Maccabaean revolt had been successful, however, and triumphant Hasmonean monarchs established a Jewish state stretching from the Mediterranean to east of the Jordan, good relations with the Nabateans came to an end. During Alexander Jannaeus' campaign for control of the southern Palestinian coastline, the city of Gaza — one of the key ports of the Nabateans — was captured. This effectively denied them any outlet to the sea along the southern coast of Palestine north of the Egyptian border. The Seleucid ruler Antiochus XII was simultaneously attempting to limit Nabatean expansion in the north, an area which the loss of the southern ports had made supremely important for the Nabateans and their trade. In 88 BCE Aretas III defeated Antiochus and took control of Damascus and its whole area. From there he turned his attention south, marched down from Damascus into the heart of Jannaeus' kingdom and defeated him near the stronghold of Adida in the maritime plain. The two kings then came to terms and the Nabatean withdrew (Josephus' Antiq. 13). Some years later, Jannaeus captured 12 Nabatean towns in Moab and Idumea, but his son, Hyrcanus, was forced to restore them. Jannaeus' widow, Alexandra Salome (see Hasmoneans*), kept on good terms with the Nabateans and (75 BCE) even signed a treaty with them for the defence of Damascus.

Nabatean Growth: While the weakness of the Hellenistic empires probably made it possible for the Nabateans to expand beyond their original territory of Edom, it does not in itself provide sufficient explanation for the rise of the Nabatean state. Northern Transjordan and southern Syria were successively conquered, culminating in the capture of Damascus by Aretas III. The effects of these acquisitions can be seen even today in the remains of the Nabatean material culture, which reflect the willing absorption of Hellenistic influences. The earliest Nabatean coins were cast to a Hellenistic design, while the kings took names reminiscent of the Greek Ptolemaic rulers, e.g. "Philhellene", possibly in an attempt to curry favour with their new subjects. It is assumed that the Hellenistic rock-cut façades of Petra (see below) belong to this period.

From this and similar evidence of the development of Nabatean art under Hellenistic influence, it seems probable that the first to hellenize were the rulers and upper classes in Petra (see below, Part III). This was the case in many other places as well. On the other hand, "the more earthy art of Tannur, Seia and Hauran was the work of their subjects, the tillers of the soil and growers of wheat, oil and vines" in Transjordan (M. Avi-Yonah). Acceptance — or rejection — of Graeco-Roman culture, however, was a matter of choice; it was not imposed as part of a policy of alien domination as elsewhere in the Near East and Palestine.

Expansion in Arabia: During the reigns of their early kings (late 3rd and early 2nd cs. BCE), the Nabateans expanded southwards to the area north of Hedjaz in southern Arabia and captured Leuke-Come (the White Village), the Red Sea port of the region. An important provincial centre was built there at Egra (Madain Saleh). In time, this became second in importance only to Petra. Whereas the Nabateans had begun by acting merely as agents for the Arabs, they now began to carry merchandise on their own account, direct from Arabia to the Mediterranean ports of shipment.

Archaeological explorations in southern Transjordan and northern Arabia have shown that by the end of their period of expansion, Nabatean domains stretched — although with interruptions — from this southern point on the Arabian Red Sea coast, northwards to south Syria, eastwards across the Syrian desert to the Euphrates and westwards to the Palestinian Negeb and near to the Mediterranean ports (see map **629**). Nabatean control of the Negeb is witnessed by the quantity of their pottery which has been found there. This cannot be explained merely by the constant passage of Nabatean traders. The pottery has been found in abundance in places far away from the caravan routes and with no connection with them.

By the 1st c. CE, they had created — or revived — a flourishing agriculture, extensive trade and important cities. Their civilization at that time bears comparison with any other of the newly hellenized Near Eastern states. Their influence played a part in the development of Jerash (Gerasa*) and other centres of the Decapolis (see Hellenism and the Near East*). The extent of their trade in the area can be traced in the numerous coins of the Nabatean king Aretas IV, discovered in all the towns of the region.

Nabateans and Romans: The appearance of the Romans in Syria and Palestine had none of the tragic results for the Nabateans which it held for the Jews. After capturing Damascus in 66 BCE, Pompey did send an expedition to Petra, but Aretas III bought his independence in exchange for 300 talents of silver. Josephus adds that the agreement between the two sides was negotiated by Antipater the Idumean (Herod's father and minister of Judea's Hyrcanus), who was then living with Nabatean friends and preparing his scheme to take power in Judea. From this time onwards, Nabatea appears as a dependent, vassal state of Rome although the Nabateans themselves never looked on their vassalage as more than a formality. During the Republic and the period of the Civil Wars, it does not appear to have been a very heavy burden on them. In 40 BCE, however, during the wars between Rome and Parthia, Aretas' successor, Malichus I (60–30 BCE), ill-advisedly sided with the Parthians. Marc Antony sent Herod* to restore the situation and collect Malichus' taxes, and a confused war ended in disaster for the Nabateans. Herod had ambitions of his own in the direction of Nabatean territories, and acted as more than a mere tool for the Romans. During his time, Nabatea was ruled by Obodas III (30–9 BCE) who was assisted — almost to be point of being displaced — by a brilliant and unscrupulous minister, Syllaeus. The limited territories of the two kingdoms were too small to contain the rivalries of two ambitious schemers, but the imposed "Pax Romana" forced Herod and Obodas to restrict their conflict to a political cold war, which in those days took the form of a constant series of accusations and counter-accusations from Petra and Jerusalem to the Roman Senate and Caesar Augustus.

The New Testament mentions only one Nabatean king, but he was one of the most important: Aretas IV (9 BCE–40 CE), who controlled Damascus at the time of Paul's conversion (II Co. 11:32). Herod Antipas of Galilee married Aretas' daughter, only to divorce her to marry his brother's wife, Herodias. Aretas later defeated Herod Antipas in what seemed to many of the Jews just retribution for his killing of John the Baptist* (see article).

Roman Ambitions: The goods of the Far East — the spices, precious stones and luxuries from Arabia, East Africa and India — had been reaching the northern Mediterranean basin for centuries before Strabo and Pliny investigated the great wealth that had accrued to the Nabateans as a result of their monopoly of this vital trade, plus their control of the bitumen and salt of the Dead Sea. Such wealth, however, was a big temptation to the Romans. Once their empire had been secured, they determined to divert the trade to the new Roman centres of commerce in Egypt.

In 24–25 BCE, a military expedition was sent to conquer "Arabia Felix" (the area of the Yemen; see Arabs, Arabia and the Bible*), but it ended in disaster. As an alternative to the land routes, the Romans then organized new seaways, taking the goods up the Red Sea to Egypt, unloading them, and carrying them overland to the Mediterranean ports. There were difficulties to be overcome in this — not least the prevailing north winds of the Red Sea. Nevertheless, the attempt succeeded and a considerable portion of the traffic was diverted from land-routes. Thus, while Nabatean wealth reached its peak under Aretas IV (9 BCE–40 CE), it declined substantially during the reigns of Malichus II (40–71 CE) and Rabbell II (71–106 CE). With the decline of its trade, Nabatea also lost its chief claim to existence as a power in the area. Its large population, however, remained. One effect of economic decline from external sources was the development of the Nabateans' characteristic agriculture which was extensively encouraged under Rabbell II. His title ends with the formula: "he who gives life and saves his people." This formula may have had nothing to do with his actions, but could have been remembered later as pertinent.

Nabatean independence continued for 170 years after the Romans conquered Judea in 63 BCE. Although Roman conquests deprived them of their control of Damascus, the area further south — Hauran and the adjacent region, now called Jebel Druze — remained in Nabatean hands. They maintained their kingdom relatively intact until their sovereignty was finally lost in 106 CE and, even after that, their civilization was continued under Roman rule.

Roman Annexation: Loss of sovereignty came when the emperor Trajan commissioned Cornelius Palma to conquer Petra (106 CE) and then annex the whole kingdom to the Roman "Province Arabia". A rival centre of the province was established at Bostra, a well-watered town in Transjordan, which became the base for the third Roman legion. Another legion was stationed in the south of the country, the camps they built near Kerak and Petra still being visible today. A great north-south road, planned to link Palmyra and Damascus to Bostra and Aqaba (on the Red Sea near Ezion-Geber, today's Eilat) was begun under Trajan and continued as far south as Egra (Madain Saleh).

Linking the road to Egra also effectively blocked any continuation of the Nabatean kingdom in that southern oasis. Side roads were added to the main artery and the whole system formed the "Limes Arabicus", opening up the country, and connecting the main highway to the overland caravan route and the land-sea route to the Red Sea and Egypt. Roman occupation was consolidated by setting up Roman posts (**630**) and garrisons all the way from the neighbourhood of Petra to the southernmost point of the Nabatean state. Its sovereignty had been totally undermined. Moreover, the new routes by-passed Petra, diverting its trade to Palmyra and the cities of Trajan's road from Eilat to Damascus. The Romans, however, had no interest in the material destruction of Nabatea. The life of the people went on under Roman rule, bearing an in-

630

creasingly heavy burden of Roman exploitation. In the 2nd and early 3rd cs. CE, there was a brief renaissance of its civilization, a detailed consideration of which lies outside the scope of this survey. The Nabateans themselves were gradually assimilated into new populations, notably pagan Syrian and Arabian tribes who invaded the area in successive waves, much in the manner of the earliest Nabateans some centuries earlier. In time Arabic replaced Nabatean as the language of the area (see below), and the Nabateans disappeared, merged in the advancing waves of Islamic Arabs. The post-Roman period of their civilization is referred to in connection with the Nabateans' towns, below.

II. CULTURE: **Language:** The Nabateans spoke a form of Aramaic, with distinct Arabic influences. Thousands of carved inscriptions in the Nabatean language are known, found notably in Petra, El-Ram, Egra, Ras-al-Naqab Umm-al-Jemal, Bostra, Jerash, in the Hauran, the Negeb and the Sinai peninsula. The script used was derived from Aramaic and resembled post-Exilic Hebrew, except that the letters were much taller and, even in the style of writing used on monuments, some of the letters were connected. The longest inscription known was contained in some Nabatean papyri (which proved to be commercial documents) found in a cave on the shore of the Dead Sea (Wadi Murabba'at).

Art: Rock drawings found throughout the area include representations both of the animals they raised — the camel, the goat and, in more fertile areas, the sheep — and the ones they hunted, like the ibex. There are also warlike scenes of soldiers fighting with swords, pictures of hunters with bows and arrows, and more peaceful representations of couples dancing.

Pottery, architecture and the decorative arts are described under Towns, below.

631

Religion: The chief gods of the Nabateans were Dushara and his consort, Allat. Dushara meant "The one Lord of the Shara mountain", i.e. the principal mountain of Petra, the biblical Mount Seir or Edom. "Du" here must be the relative particle "d" or "z" which is used in Ugaritic and biblical Hebrew to designate the deity as "the one who, or of, etc." Dushara was under the control of the supreme god Hadad-Zeus, the "Lord of the Heavens", known as Baal Shamaim in Hebrew, as represented in this relief of Haddad-Zeus, **632**, from Khirbet-Tannur (see Hellenism in the Near East*). Dushara was a fertility god — the god of thunder and rain, bulls and corn — who originated in Mesopotamia or the fringes of Iran. Dushara was identified with Dionysus and was frequently represented surrounded by symbols of vine-growing and wine.

Dushara's shrines were on "high places", reminiscent of ancient Semitic cults (see below, Petra), while the god himself was represented by a block of stone or an obelisk.

His consort, Allat, was apparently related to El and Elat, and was connected with Atargatis, also a typical fertility goddess, with a special interest in fisheries and corn. As Allat-Athena, she was regarded as the patroness of springs and water. Essentially, the religion was a fertility cult. However, a wide variety of connections and cultural combinations were also at work. Greek and Oriental met and mingled. At Suweida (east of Hauran in southern Syria) statues have been found showing the Nabatean trinity: Allat-Athena, Haddad-Dionysus and Aphrodite-Atargatis.

Pious Nabateans showed great reverence for their dead (for a description of the elaborate tombs of Egra and Petra, which was largely a necropolis, see below), and a cult of the dead may perhaps have been practiced in addition to the main religion of Dushara.

Agriculture: Agriculture developed particularly in the later period of Nabatean civilization. The country's relatively high level of population — the highest ever known in an area mainly desert — meant that marginal lands had to be fully utilized, special skills developed for the purpose, and a strong military force established to protect the desert settlements. Visible evidence of this form of economy are the very numerous cisterns, reservoirs, dams and terraces which can still be seen in the now barren lands. They belong to the period from the 1st c. CE to Byzantine times.

The fundamental necessity for agriculture in such areas was water. In Roman and Byzantine times, the Nabateans developed a complex system of collecting rain water in big cisterns — first for the use of the travellers and camels of the caravans, then for irrigation. The remains of the cisterns, reservoirs and dams which they created can be seen to this day in the barren Negeb — which is no more arid now than ever it was. Its rainfall was — and remains — no more than 10 centimetres (four inches) a year (all during the few winter months). This was collected by dams, terraces and channels to bring all available water to the richer soil of the valleys which, when watered, were fertile enough for cultivation. Barren hillsides were covered with intricate designs of rows or walls of pebbles, all designed to collect rain water and direct its course down to the terraced fields or cisterns below, as shown in this aerial view of Qetsiot near Nessanah (**631**). Where possible, the hillsides themselves were cultivated by means of careful terracing, exploitation

632

633

of every water-course and the digging of a network of connecting channels. Some of the dams were apparently commemorated on carved stones, like the ones found near Avdat (**633**; see below) which A. Negeb believes were used as altars on which sacrifices and prayers for rain were offered to Dushara. Many of the dams and large cisterns were remote from the settlements, which is further evidence of extensive agricultural development in Roman and Byzantine times.

Barley, olives, grapes, pomegranates and balsam were grown as dry-climate crops, together with many of the other crops of Palestine, in the watered and more rainy areas of southern Transjordan (see Agriculture*). In fact, research into the details of their farming methods and produce is still going on, and it is not yet possible to make any more precise statements. It is known that during the 6th and 7th cs. CE, Nabatean agricultural enterprises were further developed. Wine presses (**634**) and cellars and an installation for the drying of fruit, (perhaps raisins) of this period demonstrate the importance of vinegrowing and suggest a possibly well reputed wine. The freshly picked grapes were pressed in paved basins, the juice running into small bowls in the centre. From there it flowed down a channel into large vats where it was left to clear. From them, the juice was transferred to large wine jars kept in cellars and dark, cool rooms. This stone bench (**635**) in such a room supported jars of maturing wine.

634

635

III. THE TOWNS OF THE NABATEANS: The most spectacular of all the cities of the Nabateans is Petra, southeast of the Dead Sea, which offers some striking examples of Nabatean culture, architecture, art and life, vividly illuminating the early history of the whole people and country.

In addition, vestiges of many other Nabatean-Roman towns and temples have been discovered and excavated: in Transjordan, the town of Dhiban, built over an earlier Moabite town of the same name; Khirbet-al-Tannur,

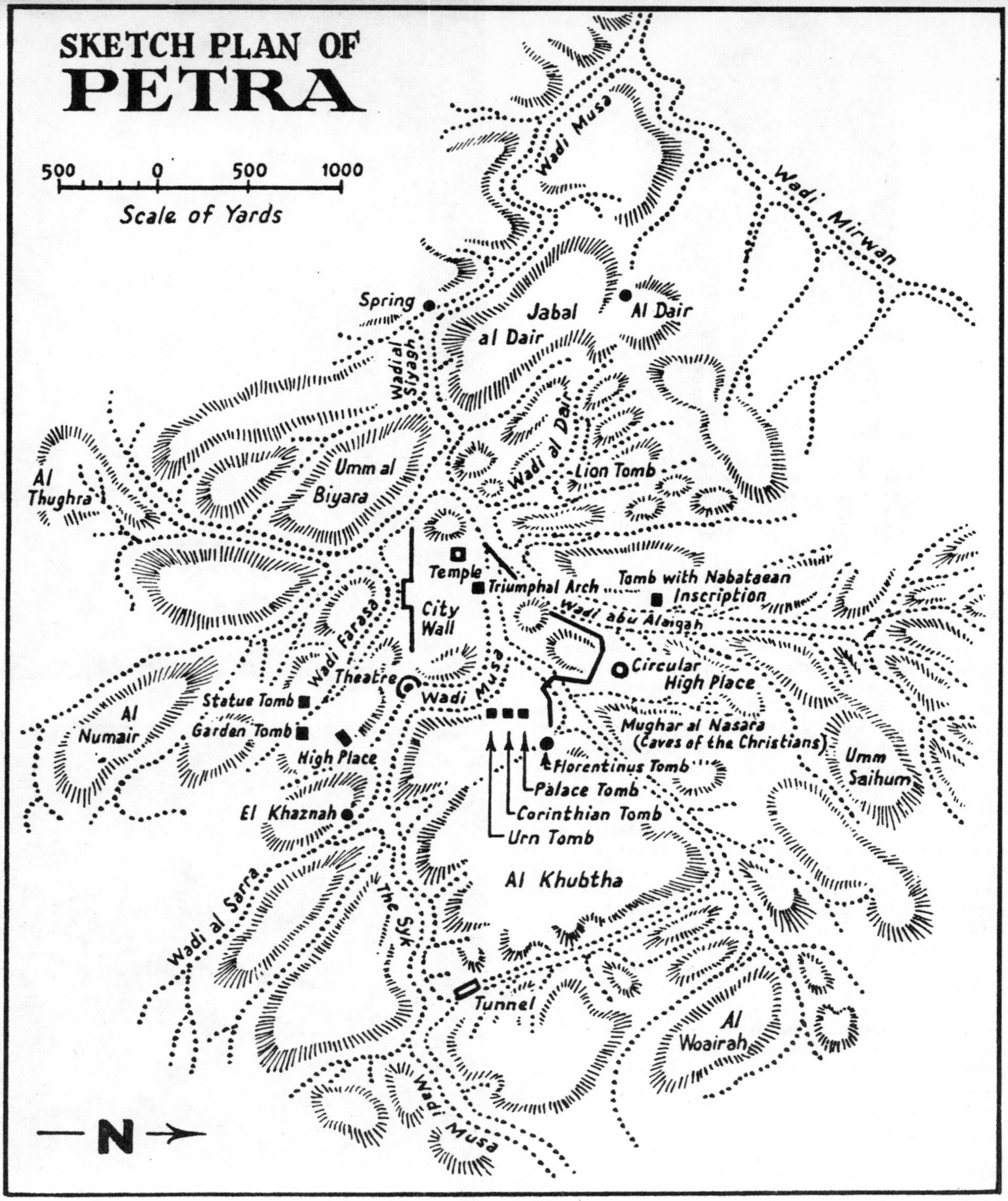

636

El-Ram and Umm-al-Jamal (see below); Egra (Madain Saleh) in northern Arabia; Seia in the Hauran (southern Syria). In the Negeb, the towns and caravan stations so far discovered include Avdat (see below), Kurnub, famous for its Nabatean and Byzantine dam, Esbeita (Shivta), Nessana (Auja-al-Hafir), Khalasa (Elusa), where the earliest Nabatean inscription was found (dating from 170 BCE), and Reheiba. Several representative examples of these towns are described below.

Petra: The "rose-red" city of Petra, with its tombs, shrines and palaces cut out of the differently shaded sandstone cliffs, has been known since 1812 when Burckhardt first re-discovered it. Since then, more serious research has been carried out by Horsfield, Wiegand, Weilzinger and W.F. Albright. Albright proved conclusively that all the principal monuments were mausolea devoted to the memory of the dead. Even though they contained chapels in which the gods were worshipped, they were not temples (see sketch map **636**).

The earliest traces of human occupation in the district appear to belong to the Upper Palaeolithic period (around 10000 BCE) when rock shelters in one of the valleys of Petra appear to have been lived in by men for at least part of each year. A Neolithic (5th mill. BCE) settlement was also suggested by flint arrowheads and implements of the period found near the north of the site. No traces of any settlement of the Chalcolithic or Bronze Ages were found, although the place was known during these years. In the central part of Petra stood the biblical "Sela" (Umm-al-Biyarah), the towering rock fortress of the Edomites **(637)** around which Nabatean Petra grew. A very few remains of the Iron Age were found there. The Bible (II K. 14:7) records that Amaziah, king of Judah, took the citadel of "Sela" by storm (ca. 800 BCE).

From the excavations carried out in the town, it appears that before Byzantine Petra (4th c. CE), there were three stages of occupation: early Nabatean, 4th–1st cs. BCE, a classical Nabatean stage from the 1st c. BCE to the arrival of the Romans in 106 CE and, thereafter, a Roman stage that lasted during the 2nd and 3rd cs. CE.

Petra stands in a valley completely surrounded by the barren mountains of the southern Idumean wilderness. From its dramatic entrance through a 2 kilometre-long narrow winding canyon, the "Syq" **(638)**, which can still be traversed only by foot or on horseback, Petra stands unique. With a single exception, all its remaining monuments, plus dwellings, storehouses and other buildings were cut from the living rock, although at one time there were also walled, masonry buildings. The Nabateans had a very distinctive style of dressing stone, cutting it with a single-ended pick at an angle of 45°. The pattern thus created can be seen on single blocks and on the cut rock face.

Tombs: Many crenellated pylon tombs date from the early Nabatean stage, their façades like Egyptian pylons, crowned by crowsteps of mixed Egyptian and Mesopotamian origin. In the classical Nabatean tombs, the simple pylons are decorated with Hellenistic gables, mouldings and cornices.

Almost at the entrance to Petra stands the magnificent rose-red façade of the El-Khazneh (the treasury, a

638

637

639
640

mausoleum carved in the 2nd c. CE, and not a temple as was thought at one time). It contains a central room with a small room approached by three steps in the back wall and small rooms on either side of the portico. There are a number of carvings, all very badly damaged, but including one which some experts have claimed represented the goddess Isis. (Compare this with the Monumental Tombs of the Kidron Valley; see Funerary Customs*, II.)

One of the oldest tombs is a large one in Wadi Turkomaniah, dating from the 1st c. BCE or CE, which bears a long, interesting inscription in Nabatean over its entrance, dedicating the tomb and its contents to the God Dushara and concluding, "Nor shall any man be buried in this tomb save he who has in writing a contract to bury according to the said deeds relating to consecrated things, for ever."

The Petra tombs provide plenty of evidence for the reverence paid to the dead. All of them include a large hall or triclinium in which the funeral feast was held; see **639**.

Temples and Sanctuaries: In addition to the tombs, Petra also contains one of the finest extant examples of an open air sanctuary, the "Conway High Place", excavated at the highest point inside the walled city of Petra. This was a processional way around a sacred rock (many parallels exist in north and south Arabia). It dates back to the classic period of Petra's history and was in use from the 2nd–1st cs. BCE until Christian times, when it was destroyed.

One of the largest monuments of Petra is the Al-Deir (monastery) hewn from the soft sandstone about the 2nd c. CE, with a façade some 50 metres wide and 45 high to the top of the urn which crowns it. As usual, the chamber is undecorated. A niche in the back wall originally contained a block of stone left standing to represent Dushara. Opinion is divided as to whether this was a major temple or simply a chapel. In Christian times it was used as a church; see **641**.

Roman Petra: The main open area of Petra lies on either side of the Wadi Musa (river bed) west of the entrance to the town. To the south of the wadi, a part of a colonnaded Roman street has been excavated. This led to a triple arched gate (**640**), apparently built in the 2nd c. CE, decorated with typical Nabatean Oriental-Hellenistic carving, including characteristic floral designs. Although only a few paving stones remain, the road apparently led up to a Roman construction (Qasr-Bint-Pharaon) which is the only stone built monument in Petra extant. Apparently it was erected early in the 2nd c. CE to serve as a Roman administrative centre. However, nothing is certain about its nature or functions.

The effect of Roman occupation on Petra itself was at first beneficial, leading to a revival of the town and its life. The great theatre at the entrance to the city (early 3rd c. CE) and the many-storied tomb façades all date to the 2nd and 3rd cs. CE. Although more modest, the tomb of Sextus Florentinus, governor of the province of Arabia, testifies to Petra's continuing importance during the later period. However, its supremacy as one of the great centres of the eastern world was already fading. In the Byzantine era, it became an ecclesiastical centre, ceasing to exist during the Middle Ages.

Oriental-Hellenistic Forms: For all its unique interest and solidity, Petra's relics cannot, by themselves, give a full picture of native Nabatean culture and art. The monumental rock-cut façades and built structures and arches are for the most part adaptations of Hellenistic styles of architecture and ornamentation, with some specifically Oriental Nabatean motifs. However, the carved surfaces of most of the remains have deteriorated so seriously that it is difficult to determine the exact nature of the motifs and styles employed. Accordingly, the evidence of other important Nabatean centres needs to be taken into account. Places like Egra (Madain Saleh) far south in Arabia; Umm-al-Jamal in the east; Khirbet-al-Tannur, or Seia in the Hauran and other sites there, perpetuated the native art of the Nabateans, obscured in sophisticated and hellenized Petra (see Nabatean Growth, above).

Khirbet-al-Tannur stands in the Wadi al Hasa (River Zered) which runs into the southern end of the Dead Sea. There, a 1st c. BCE to 1st c. CE Nabatean temple was excavated by Nelson Glueck. The Temple has an outer paved courtyard with a large altar standing in the northeast corner. North and south of the courtyard were small rooms, presumably for the use of the ministers. Along the west side of the courtyard ran an imposing façade with columns and pilasters and a central doorway leading into the shrine containing the main altar on which sacrifices were offered. The altar was a square of about 3 metres, some 2 metres high, its sides carved to represent a series of pilasters. In one of the niches they formed stood a statue of a bearded god with a small bull at his feet. This may have represented the god Hadad-Zeus. The pilasters were decorated with alternate panels of floral designs and female heads in high relief. The heads are those of a goddess wearing different headdresses. In one she wears ears of wheat and is surrounded by a border of the signs of the Zodiac (**235**). Another is crowned by two fishes. The goddess seems to be Atargatis. She and the male god presumably represent the local variants of Dushara and Allat. They apparently date from the late 1st c. BCE to the 2nd c. CE.

El-Ram: About a hundred miles south of Petra and thirty-five east of Eilat (see map), in the awe-inspiring canyon valley of El-Ram (**642**), stand the ruins of a large Nabatean temple dedicated to Allat. Built in the 1st c. BCE, a little before the Roman conquest, it is similar in construction to the temple of Tannur. The valley was watered by a number of small springs and nearby the ruins of a variety of Nabatean buildings and dams were found, as well as inscriptions in Nabatean and Thamudic (see Arabia*; Languages*).

Umm-al-Jamal: The ruins of another dead Nabatean town stand on the edge of the Syrian desert, beside the road that ran from eastern Transjordan to Baghdad. Water was collected during the rainy season in cisterns attached to every house. The town was founded in the 1st c. BCE to act as a caravan outpost on the caravan route. It existed throughout the Roman period and on into Byzantine times, when no less than fifteen churches were built there (4th c. CE on). This is a private house in the Nabatean town (**643**).

Seia is described by H. C. Butler as "not a town or a village, as the majority of sites in the Hauran, but an ancient high place, adorned with temples, enclosed courts, splendid gateways, etc." A paved Roman road and 2nd c. CE outer gate are connected to the sacred precincts. The gate had

641

642

643

644

much in common with the arched gates of Petra (see above) or Gerasa* (Jerash), and is a fair example of the Oriental-Hellenistic genre of Nabatean architecture.

Egra (Madain Saleh), a large oasis in north Arabia, was the second most important town of the Nabateans. It too had its share of rock-cut tombs, with reliefs sculptured over the entrances, featuring geometric decorations, masks, and eagles with patterned wings. See Arabia* and map **190**.

Avdat was another important Nabatean caravan station. It stood 2,000 feet above sea level and some seventy miles northwest of Petra. Although lacking the importance of Petra and the towns listed above, it is a good example of Nabatean town construction and civilization in the Negeb.

Although water is available some 2.5 miles from the site, it is somewhat bitter, and the inhabitants seem to have relied upon the cisterns and water catchment systems which, as elsewhere in the country, made the most of every drop of the 4 inches average annual rainfall.

Excavations began under Prof. M. Avi-Yonah in 1958, and were continued in 1959–60 by A. Negeb of the Hebrew University. From their results, it has been possible to trace the history of Avdat fairly accurately, besides reconstructing important parts of the town.

The first Nabatean settlement appears to have been founded on the western spur of the ridge, around the beginning of the 3rd c. BCE, at a junction of the trade routes from Petra and the Red Sea, leading to Gaza on the Mediterranean. A small town was built around the turn of the 1st c. CE, with a fortified acropolis on the western spur, whose edges were propped up by huge retaining walls. The northwestern corner of the acropolis appears to have contained a magnificent Nabatean temple, but all that remains of this are stones and carvings embedded in the later Byzantine church.

Today, reconstructed Avdat (**644**) shows, on the west, the partially rebuilt retaining wall, with the remains of the Byzantine northern church in the northwest corner. The citadel and partly reconstructed southern wall lie to the east, with the ruins of the Roman town facing them to the south. The ruins of the Byzantine town are clearly visible along the slopes while, in the lower right-hand corner of the picture, is an excellent specimen of a Byzantine house and cave complex.

Inscriptions belonging to the Nabateans have been found on small white marble tablets and building stones in the debris beneath the acropolis. These are all dedications, some of them mentioning the name of King Aretas (i.e. Aretas IV). A dump of broken pottery yielded 20,000 painted fragments, dating from the end of the 3rd to the middle of the 1st c. BCE, including zoomorphic and anthropomorphic figurines, coins and other pieces of imported pottery from Parthia, Rhodes and Megara in Greece.

At the western (lower) end of Avdat, a covered bathhouse was found, completely preserved. It had a pool of cold water measuring 4.20 × 4.10 metres, and was 1.35 metres deep. In the north were two sweat-rooms (tepidaria), with the remains of the steam-heating (hypocaust) pipes still visible. These carried the heat to the tepidaria. One of the rooms still contained the remains of furnaces made of burnt bricks (**645**). A distant resemblance may be found in the far larger and more ornate tepidarium of the sumptuous baths in Italy.

Pottery Kiln and Types: The Nabateans made a distinctive pottery, thrown on the wheel, but very fine and as thin as porcelain. Pottery of this kind (**646**) belonging to the classical Nabatean and early Roman periods (50 BCE to ca. 200 CE) has been found in all their settlements in southern Transjordan and further afield. The most typical pieces are shallow bowls, decorated inside with leaf and line patterns in black or brown paint.

In Avdat, an installation for making the pottery was discovered, the first to be found in any Nabatean town. The factory contained a room for the preparation of the

645

646

clay, with a big vat in one corner and lumps of clay still lying about the floor as well as a second room with a potter's wheel and a bench for drying the turned vessels; there was also a 7-foot high kiln, made in two storeys and still intact (**647**). Pieces of unburnt vessels could still be seen in the kiln and large quantities of Nabatean pottery, some painted, some plain, lay all around. The workshop appears to have been in use for about 150 years from ca. 40–30 BCE, an estimate confirmed by coins, lamps and other items found there.

Agriculture: As in Petra and elsewhere, water was very carefully conserved to make farming possible. Nabatean dams were found in four valleys near Avdat, with associated libation altars still in position next to them. From the inscriptions on the altars, it appears that the dams were built by people called the "Bnei Sarutha", led by a certain Carmo, in the period between 88–89 to 98–99 CE. This cistern (**648**) is of a common type.

Destruction and Renaissance: Trajan's annexation of Nabatea to the Roman empire in 106 CE (see above) involved the

648

complete destruction of this first town of Avdat. A thick layer of ashes covered the whole acropolis area and many finds of bronze figurines, lamps, jewellery and pottery were made in the area of the staircase within the acropolis, **644**.

After its destruction, Avdat entered a "dark age" which lasted until the middle of the 3rd c. CE when a new town was built, completed by the end of the century. A large burial cave has been discovered from this period and continuing excavations will probably reveal further details.

Later still, in the 6th–7th cs. CE, an important Byzantine town occupied the site of Avdat, with fine churches in whose construction many stones and sections of the earlier Nabatean buildings were used (**644**).

NUMBERS, BOOK OF.— *Outline: General Arrangement; Sources, Composition and Date; Contents: The Material of the Three Main Sections: a. At Mount Sinai (chs. 1:1–10:10): Law and Edicts Inserted in the First Section; b. Mount Sinai to Kadesh (10:11-22:35): Spying out the Land of Canaan (chs. 13–14); The Rebellion of Korah, Dathan and Abiram (ch. 16); Legal Edicts Inserted; Kadesh and the Conquest of Transjordan; Laws Inserted in the Second Section; c. In the Plains of Moab: Balaam and His Blessing (chs. 22–24); Apostasy; Zeal of Phineas (chs. 25–27); Legal Edicts Inserted; Itinerary of the Wanderings and the Conquest; Apportionment of Canaan among the Tribes; The Levitical Cities.*

The fourth book of the Pentateuch is called "Bamidbar" (In the Wilderness) in Hebrew, from its fifth — and first distinctive — word. Post-biblical literature also refers to it as "Vaydabêr" (And He said), which is its first word, or, occasionally, as the book of Census, since it records two important censuses. From this came its Septuagint title, Arithma, which was rendered in the Vulgate by Numeri and thus, in English, by its present name.

However, its original name remains distinctly appropriate for a modern reader. In variety and lack of order, its contents can indeed appear a bewildering collection of lists, laws, traditions and legends, brought together by later chroniclers who accepted their value but were unable to organize them into a coherent unity as they were too remote from the original circumstances.

General Arrangement: The miscellaneous material that makes up the book is presented within the general framework of a record of the wanderings in the desert, beginning in the spring of the second year after the Exodus (Nu. 1:1) and ending in the events that followed the death of Aaron on the first day of the fifth month of the 40th year after the Exodus (33:38). The concluding passages contain the edicts issued to the Children of Israel in the Plains of Moab across the Jordan from Jericho (36:13).

Sources, Composition and Date: The question of the book's sources is linked to the theories concerning its composition. A theory widely accepted until recent years was that the book was composed, along with other "P" documents, by a circle of priestly writers living during and after the Exile. (The "P" source or Priests' Code, as explained in the article on Biblical Criticism*, was considered to include some of the narratives but mainly, the legal texts associated with events in the desert, scattered through Exodus*, Leviticus* and Numbers. Some of these were very ancient, others much later; all of them were thought to have been given their final form after the return of the Jewish community from Babylonia; see also Restoration*.) Because of the different strata of material thought to have been combined within this Priests' Code (P), the text of Numbers (like that of the other books of the Pentateuch) was separated by the "documentary hypothesis" into passages belonging to the different sources. "P" is usually regarded as a distinct source, combined by a later editor with the J (Yahwist) and E (Elohist) source. Some scholars, however, believe that the "P" writer was also the editor. (These terms are explained under Biblical Criticism*.) On this basis, the Balaam narrative is divided into: 22:2–21 and 35–41, belonging to E, while 22:22–35 belongs to J. However, in chs. 23 and 24, any distinction between J and E becomes almost impossible. P, however, is easier to distinguish. All the legal and statistical material in the book is ascribed to P, while the narratives are divided between J and E. P is then further subdivided to allow for its lack of uniformity.

The date of composition of the book is still a matter for debate among scholars, and opinions vary a good deal about the dates of J and E. It is increasingly recognized by many that the material attributed to the Priests' Code can be dated to the 6th c. BCE, whereas the more ancient material in Numbers (see below, Balaam and His Blessing) was composed as early as the tribal federation (period of Judges) or the early monarchy (see Biblical Criticism*, Census* and Deuteronomy* on this discussion).

Contents: Geographically and chronologically the book's material falls into three main sections: a. the first ten chapters (1:1–10:10 and ch. 26) covering the period of the first twenty days of the second month of the second year after the Exodus, including the Censuses, the first in chs. 1–4 and the second in ch. 26; b. Chs. 10:11–21:35, covering the wanderings in the wilderness from Sinai to the plains of Moab, a period of about 40 years; c. Chs. 22–36 which deal with the encampment in the Plains of Moab and include the story of Balaam, the Zeal of Phineas (25:1–15) and the recurrent theme of the danger and rejection of idolatry.

THE MATERIAL OF THE THREE MAIN SECTIONS: a. **At Mount Sinai** (chs. 1:1–10:10): The book opens with the census of the entire people (ch. 1), followed by the organization and arrangement of the tribes and their flags for the journey (ch. 2). The formation in which the people are directed to march through the desert is thought by scholars to be an ideal picture composed at a much later time and more appropriate to emergencies in which the whole people was called to arms. It is hard to place this historically. The material all seems to be clearly stamped "P".

Chs. 3 and 4 contain the Census of the Levites and specification of their duties. A record of the second census is given in ch. 26. The subject is discussed in the article on Census*. Ch. 7 tells of the dedication of the Tabernacle and ch. 8 details the ritual ordinances for purification of the Levites. Chs. 9:15–23 to 10:10 record the appearance of the cloud of smoke which led the company by day and the cloud of fire which led them at night.

Laws and Edicts Inserted in the First Section: A number of laws were inserted into the narrative by later editors at what appeared to be the appropriate chronological point. Sometimes the connection is clear, e.g. the rule about excluding the impure from the camp (5:1–4) is linked to the arrangements for setting up the camp in ch. 2; the Priestly Blessing (6:22–27) and the edict concerning the Supplementary Passover (9:1–14) are directly associated with the story of the consecration of the Tabernacle (ch. 7). The edict for the making of the silver trumpets (10:1–10) logically follows the establishment of the guiding clouds, as the trumpets were also used to direct the movements of the people. However, sometimes the connection is obscure. The enactments regarding restitution of property (5:5–10); the ordeal of a wife suspected of adultery (5:11–35) or the vow of a Nazirite (6:1–21) have no logical place in the narrative.

b. **Mount Sinai to Kadesh (10:11–22:35):** The section contains the narrative (probably belonging to P) describing how the Israelites moved through the desert from the Wilderness of Sinai to the Wilderness of Paran (10:11–21:32). Here the instructions given in the previous section about the organization of journeys are put into effect. In the material, the sole guide for the route or for making camp is to be the cloud over the Tabernacle (10:11–12). The description is here interrupted by verses 29–32 of ch. 10 to record Moses' negotiations with Hobab, his brother-in law, to act as a guide through the wilderness and to join the destiny of Israel.

The significance of this passage is not only that it indicates that Yahweh's revelation came to Moses in a land inhabited by the Kenites*, but also because it establishes closer historical links between them and the Israelites. In the opinion of W.F. Albright, both the Kenites and the ancestral Hebrews were composed of groups of the same or related types. The Kenites adopted Midian as their homeland. As they were smiths and metal craftsmen (see article), they probably also contributed to the establishment of mining and metal-working in the southern Arabah at a very early stage. The connection with Israel — and metal-working — was to continue until the monarchy (Jud. 1:16; I Sam. 15:6).

The incident with Hobab is followed by the Song of the Ark (10:35–36), traditionally regarded as an ancient, independent piece of literature. Ch. 11 records the discontent of the people, punished by the fire at Taberah (11:1–3); the appointment of the seventy elders and the descent of the quail, followed by a plague at Kibroth-Hataavah (11:4–35). Ch. 12 recounts the rebellions of Aaron and Miriam against Moses' sole leadership, and God's vindication of Moses' prerogative as sole leader, for "he is entrusted with all my house". With him, God speaks "clearly and not in dark speech and he beholds the form of the Lord" (12:7–8). These two chapters make a logical story belonging to the traditional stratum (cf. Ex. 33:7–11) concerning the Tent of Meeting, and were apparently inspired by an ancient poetical creation (12:6–8, 13).

Spying out the Land of Canaan (chs. 13–14): Most authorities regard this narrative as a combination of JE and P strands. In the P story, the spies are sent out and traverse the whole country (13:1–17, 21), returning after 40 days to Kadesh (13:25–26) with an unfavourable report (13:32). At this, the people lament and want to return to Egypt (14:1–4), Joshua's and Caleb's more favourable report (14:6–9) only provoking them further. As a punishment, God sends a plague and condemns the survivors to forty years wandering in the desert so that none of the adults who left Egypt shall be permitted to enter Canaan — with the sole exceptions of Caleb, the son of Jephunneh, and Joshua, the son of Nun (14:26–39).

This makes a coherent story. The JE account, to be equally logical, needs the addition of certain details from P. It then runs like this: The spies go up into the hills and the Negeb as far as Hebron to observe the crops of the countryside and the strength of the fortifications (13:17–24), returning (27–29) with the report that the land is fruitful but its inhabitants and their defences too strong. In spite of Caleb's more optimistic opinion (30), the people lament and talk of returning to Egypt (14:1–4). God is angered and prepares to wipe out the whole people, but Moses intercedes for them and obtains the promise that the descendants of those who left Egypt shall enter the Promised Land (14:13–24). God then orders a return to the desert (14:25) but the people insist on making an unsuccessful attempt at entering the land from the south (39–45) and are soundly beaten by the Canaanites at Hormah.

Contradictions between and within the two accounts (e.g. 13:29 contradicts the JE assumption that the spies explored the land only as far as Hebron, while 14:9 speaks of the Israelites' fear of the Canaanites, an element which belongs to JE, not P) suggest that the story is an amalgamation of various traditions, not a mechanical combination of two distinct stories.

The Rebellion of Korah, Dathan and Abiram (Ch. 16): This chapter is again a combination of varying traditions. The earliest part of the story is the JE tradition of the rebellion of Dathan and Abiram, of the Reuben tribe, against Moses' leadership, and their complaint that he had taken them out of a land flowing with milk and honey. As a punishment and, simultaneously, a token that Moses' authority was truly from God, the rebels, their families and all their possessions were swallowed up, "so that they and all that belonged to them went down alive into Sheol" (16:33). The P strand deals with a revolt of Korah and 250 "leaders of the congregation" against Moses and Aaron, which was effectively crushed when "fire came forth from the Lord and consumed the two hundred and fifty" (16:35). This later variation adds the details that Korah was a Levite and aroused his fellows to contest Aaron's exclusive right to the High Priesthood. (There is a theory — although it is a subject of dispute among scholars — that the earliest traditions make practically no distinction between priests and Levites, see Priests*.) The present form of the traditions, which involves certain contradictions, seems to indicate that the story combines two separate segments, i.e: the unrest aroused by Dathan's and Abiram's secular objections to Moses' leadership, plus the grumbling complaints of the people against the hardship of the wilderness; secondly, the religious concerns of Korah. This latter segment may possibly reflect efforts made by Korah's family at a much later date to secure certain rights in the Temple.

The Korah story is supplemented by a. an account of the origin of the copper altar, which contradicts the tradition of Ex. 27:1–2; b. the story of the plague being stopped by incense taken from the altar (16:46–50) and c. the flowering of Aaron's rod as a sign of the ascendancy of his house and tribe over all the people of Israel (17:2–10).

Legal Edicts Inserted: At this point, the Priestly writer again inserts legislation governing the Levites and their functions, the "service" of Aaron and his sons in the Tent of Meeting (ch. 18). This includes attending to "all that concerns the altar and that is within the veil" (18:7). Scholars point out the connection between "P" and Ezekiel, and some suggest that the passage transposes the position of the Temple of Ezekiel to the days of the desert sanctuary. Ezekiel's parallel list of the duties of the Levites varies only in referring to the priesthood as "Sons of Zadok" instead of "Sons of Aaron" in the older formulation. Probably the texts of both Numbers and Ezekiel represent two parallel streams which originated from a common source in the position of the Jerusalem Temple and its priests at the end of the monarchy.

Kadesh and the Conquest of Transjordan: Chs. 20–22 record the death of Miriam and her burial at Kadesh (20:1), then the incident of Moses striking water from the rock (20:2–13) at Meribah and the rather obscure sin which made God refuse entry to the Promised Land to Moses and Aaron (20:12), followed by the refusal of Edom to allow Israel passage through the land (20:14–21) and the Israelites' detour via Mount Hor, where Aaron died (22–29) and his son Eleazar took his place (26). Ch. 21 (1–3) opens with a battle with the king of Arad* which is recorded as an Israelite victory at "Hormah". This is out of place, for the whole theme of the story is that the Israelites did not attempt to enter the country again from the south; moreover, Hormah had already been named as the scene of an Israelite defeat (14:45; see above).

The chapter continues with a legendary account (21:4–9) of the origins of the fiery serpent, a bronze symbol (illustrated by an Assyrian design of a cultic object from Nimrud, **648a**), which was set up in the Temple until the reform of Hezekiah (II K. 18:4). Next comes the narrative of the people's march along the frontiers of Moab which includes two ancient songs, one (21:14–15) an extract from the Book of the Wars of Yahweh, the second (21:17–18) a folk or ritual song associated with well-digging.

Verses 21–35 recount the successful campaigns against Sihon, king of the Amorites, and Og, the king of Bashan. This passage included another ancient song (27–30) which is thought by many authorities to have been borrowed from the Amorites.

Laws Inserted in the Second Section: There is no real connection between the laws governing sacrifices, gifts and libations (15:1–21); atonement for unwitting law-breaking (22–31); breaking the Sabbath (32–36) or wearing blue tassels in the corners of all garments (37–41) and the historical narrative. The chronicler tried to create a link by prefacing the ordinances by: "When you come into the land . . ." (15:2) which might be somehow related to the entry of the spies (chs. 13–14). There is a much clearer connection in the passages relating to Aaron and the Levites (ch. 18, see above).

c. In the Plains of Moab: *Balaam and His Blessing* (chs. 22–24): The story of Balaam, the heathen prophet of the king of Moab who uttered blessings instead of curses on Israel, is one of the most attractive sections of the book of Numbers. Written in prose, interspersed with poetry

648 a

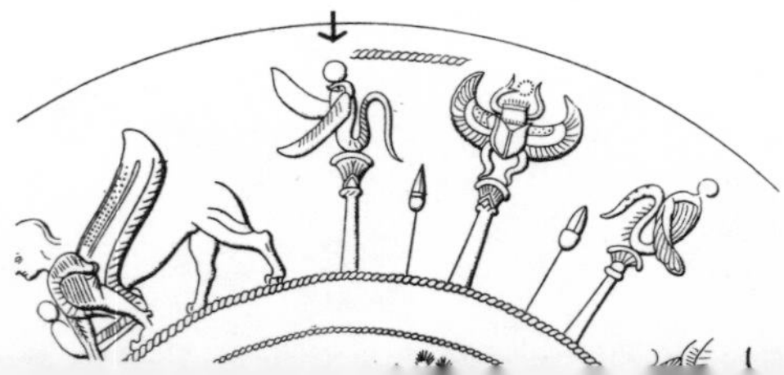

sections which are much older, the story is wholly JE. The division between the two strands can be seen from the opening of ch. 22, according to which Balak, king of Moab, twice sends the elders of Moab and Midian to persuade Balaam to curse the invading Israelites and, when his reluctance is overcome, Balaam journeys with them to Balak (22:2–21). In verses 22–34, however, he is travelling with his two servants only, and there is no mention of the elders of Moab and Midian. This whole passage — the episode of Balaam's ass refusing to pass places blocked by the angel of the Lord and then speaking to Balaam to remonstrate with him for beating her — belongs to the J strand and interrupts the sequence of the E story which is resumed in verse 35.

The narrative records how Balak four times urged Balaam to pronounce curses on the Israelites, and, in answer, Balaam pronounced four divinely inspired oracles. The first three (23:7–10; 18–24; 24:3–9) are a paean of praise to Israel and its God; the fourth (24:15–24) announces the destruction of other nations. The language of these poems has proved extremely difficult to interpret. Modern commentators mostly find parallels to the events mentioned in episodes during the monarchy, beginning with Saul's defeat of Agag (24:7) and ending with the Assyrians (24:24). Apart from those who accept the story as it stands and regard the oracles as authentic prophecy of uncertain date, the majority view is that the Oracles of Balaam are postfactum prophecies, composed mainly in the reign of David, with a few later additions. W.F. Albright suggests an earlier time and sees the Balaam oracles as reflecting the new national identity achieved as a result of a significant increase in population and military strength between the Exodus and the completion of the Conquest. Considering the extreme archaism of the language, he puts their creation against a historical background of the 13th–12th cs. BCE and believes that they were first written down in or about the 10th c. BCE. This opinion has gained wide acceptance.

Balaam himself has all the attributes of a Mesopotamian priest, expert in soothsaying, although he appears in the story as a servant of God, uttering the words which God puts in his mouth and refusing to go against His will. At the end of the episode (24:25), Balaam "rose and went back to his place", which seems to suggest that the narrator considered the episode closed. However, later on (31:16), Balaam reappears, advising the Midianites to tempt the Israelites to the idolatrous worship of Ba'al Peor; then (31:8; Jos. 13:22), in the wars between the two peoples, he is killed. These later episodes may belong to a different tradition concerning Balaam.

Like many other parts of the book, the Balaam episode is a separate entity with no essential place in the story of the Conquest. Its main concern is God's care and protection for Israel, against which all attackers are powerless. Its value and interest today lie in the elevated style of its poetry and its belief in the effectiveness of curses on the enemy, but perhaps chiefly as a contemporary reflection of a very early period in Israel's history.

Apostasy; the Zeal of Phineas (Chs. 25–27): Ch. 25 opens with the intermarriage of Israelites and the "daughters of Moab" and their adoption of the idolatrous worship of Ba'al of Peor. God's punishment was a plague which was only halted when Pinchas (Phineas), Aaron's grandson, took a spear in his hand and himself carried out the instruction to slaughter the apostates (25:1–15). After this, the war with Midian was resumed (25:16–18). The census described in ch. 26 is referred to under section (a) above.

The appointment of Joshua as Moses' successor is recorded in ch. 27 (12–23) and after three chapters of edicts and ordinances, the narrative is taken up in ch. 31 with the account of the successful war against the Midianites, after which the Israelites set up their camp in Moab opposite Jericho. Both these episodes belong to the Priests' Code. This part of the story is rounded off by the settlement of the tribes of Reuben and Gad in the good cattle country of Transjordan (32). Much of the material in this chapter (1–16, 39–42) consists of ancient traditions about piecemeal conquest of the land and almost certainly reflects a later situation (see article on Conquest*).

Another insertion of events which may well have taken place at a later stage of Conquest and settlement is the episode of the daughters of Zelophehad of the tribe of Menasseh (27:1–11) who were granted the right to inherit their dead father's property, contrary to the custom which allowed only male offspring to inherit. This story has a postscript in ch. 36, where the right of daughters to inherit property in the case of a man without sons is further clarified and established as a precedent. This again appears to be a case of a later historical situation being set back to an earlier time. 9th c. BCE ostraca (inscribed potsherds) from Samaria relating to the administration of the Kingdom of Israel have shown that the phrase "daughters of Zelophehad" in fact referred to the landed possessions of a clan. In this case they appear to have been Canaanite settlements which were integrated into the tribal framework of Menasseh. The story about daughters' rights of inheritance is used to illustrate this situation.

Legal Edicts Inserted: Chs. 28 and 29 provide a commentary on the yearly cycle of feasts and observances laid down in Lv. 23. The sacrifices to be offered under particular circumstances are listed. This tradition was preserved in post-Exilic ritual for these sacrifices are in fact precisely what was offered in the Second Temple after the time of Ezra (a fact which does not mean that the list was necessarily composed then).

Ch. 30 contains laws governing vows, especially in relation to women. Ch. 31 (21–31) includes regulations governing war booty in its account of the war against Midian, and the distribution of the spoils captured there (32–54).

Itinerary of the Wanderings and the Conquest: Ch. 33 pauses to review the travels of the Israelites before they reached the plains of Moab. This is of great importance historically. Some of the names mentioned here are known from references in other parts of the Pentateuch, but most of them (18–35) are quite unknown and their indentity can only be guessed. From what may be gathered from part of the itinerary described in ch. 33, it would appear that the Israelites reached the Plains of Moab without making any detour of Edom or Moab, but this too is uncertain. There is no mention of camping on the borders of the Amorites, nor of the wars which Moses led against Sihon and Og (21:21–35).

From this and other evidence, B. Mazar concluded that the Israelites came to Palestine in two waves. The first was composed of the Leah tribes who camped at Kadesh, then tried to enter the country from the south, but were defeated by the king of Arad. The second wave was that of the Joseph tribes who proceeded to Transjordan independently, before the Transjordan kingdoms were established, and then crossed the Jordan under the leadership of Joshua. In this reading, the chapter is not a description of a single route, but a combination of traditions about a number of routes which were known to the chronicler, although lost today.

Apportionment of Canaan among the Tribes: Ch. 34 defines the frontiers of Canaan (1–15) and names the leaders who are to be responsible for the allocation of territory among the tribes (16–29).

The Levitical Cities: Ch. 35 commands the establishment of 48 cities for the Levites (2–8) and six cities of refuge for escaping manslayers (11–15). Legislation is provided to mitigate the blood vengeance against any community by sheltering the unintentional killer (16–34; see Law*).

The careful regulations and systematization of the Levitical cities raise serious problems. In Deuteronomy, the Levites are described as scattered through the land, "with no inheritance among their brethren" (Dt. 18:1–2), deserving the charity of those among whom they live. It is impossible to imagine that they possessed, exclusively, 48 towns — four within the territory of each tribe — including the land round about. The six cities of refuge — a very ancient institution — were not Levitical cities and the connection between the two passages was introduced at a much later time. One possible solution to the problem has been suggested by W.F. Albright on the basis of a comparison of the evidence preserved in Jos. 21:2 and I Ch. 6:39–66. He has shown that the list of Levitical cities in Jos. 21, although cast in the framework of P, must have originated in the days of the united monarchy. Many of the names mentioned are those of Canaanite cities which only came under Israelite rule towards the end of David's reign and during that of Solomon. The original list and, presumably, the institution of the Levitical cities must, therefore, date from the first half of Solomon's reign.

In the opinion of Y. Kaufman and M. Haran, the institution of Levitical cities represented a Utopia, thought out soon after the Conquest and before the sanctuaries were created, but never put into practice. Alternatively, if the passage is based on an ancient document describing a real situation, then it may refer to the home-towns of Levites who were not employed at the great sanctuaries — i.e. of people without a fixed income as described in Deuteronomy (see Priests and Levites*). On the other hand, R. de Vaux regards the list as reflecting the dispersal of the Levites and the situation after the foundation of the Temple in Jerusalem and the cult at Bethel (see Israel and Judah*: Rehoboam). The only evidence either way, however, is that David and Solomon both assigned quarters of newly conquered towns and villages to Levites and that some of the towns appear later in the Bible as the home towns of priestly families — although not exclusive to them.

A more detailed discussion of the problems raised in this article, especially questions relating to the significance of the dating of the P (Priestly Code) material, may be found under Biblical Criticism*; Law*; Deuteronomy*; Conquest* and Priests and Levites*.

O

OBADIAH, BOOK OF. — Containing only 21 verses, Obadiah is one of the shortest books in the Old Testament. In the Hebrew canon, it stands fourth in the series of twelve Minor Prophets (the Septuagint places it fifth).

Contents: The book contains the "Vision" or prophecy of Obadiah, divided into three parts: verses 1–9 are a condemnation of Edom. Obadiah inserted a fragment of a much older prophecy here (1–5). (The same fragment was also used by Jeremiah, 49:7–16). Wellhausen thought the fragment may have belonged to the 5th c. BCE, when Edom was destroyed by Arab tribes, but as there is no mention of destruction by Arabs, it seems more likely that this passage goes back to an older book of prophecy about neighbouring peoples which has been preserved only as quotations in later prophets. (The same appears to be true of the early prophecy about Moab in Is. 16, which is parallel to that in Jer. 48.)

Verses 10–14 list the causes of Edom's downfall: she rejoiced in Judah's destruction and showed it by insults and laughter; she intercepted escaping fugitives and delivered them into slavery. Verses 15–21 describe the Day of Yahweh when judgment will be visited upon the nations, especially Edom. The cup of suffering which the Jews have drunk so deep will be passed to their enemies. A reunited Israel will help in the destruction of her foes and an expanded Judah will embrace Edom to the south, Philistia to the west and, to the north and east, will include Ephraim and Gilead across the Jordan.

Date: Dating the composition of the book is closely connected with the question of its uniformity. Some scholars think that the book was composed before the destruction of the First Temple, one opinion being that it refers to the liberation of Edom from dependence upon Judah during the reign of Ahaz (II K. 16:6). However, very little in Obadiah's prophecy seems to support this theory.

The enmity between Judah and Edom continued and increased after the collapse of the Judean state in 587 BCE, when the Edomites took advantage of the situation to seize the southern part of the country, extending their rule north of Hebron. In the preceding period, the kings of Judah held the Negeb by building fortresses such as this (**649**, Ein-Ghadyan); see also gateway of another fortress (**650**). Rivalry and hostility between the two states was renewed with the Restoration and only ended during the Maccabaean period (2nd c. BCE) when Edom was incorporated into the new independent Jewish state.

The book of Obadiah is redolent of a deep hatred towards Edom and also reflects the impact of a major national disaster — not one particular military defeat. Moreover, in the second half of the book (vs. 20) the "exiles of Jerusalem who are in Sepharad" are mentioned. Sepharad (Sardis, or Sardes, in Asia Minor) was part of the same political

649

650

organization as Jerusalem during the Persian era. Thus, if the first part of the book (vs. 1–14) is assumed to belong to the period of the monarchy, the second (vs. 15–21) must have been composed separately during the period of the Second Temple. However, there seems no necessity for such a division.

The prophet Obadiah lived during the post-Exilic period and his deep hatred of Edom may be explained by comparison with Mal. 1:1–5. Malachi also foretells a national day of judgment when God would reestablish Judah in its own land, (3:4) and this seems very close to the vision of Obadiah 15–21 (also to Joel*, see Day of Yahweh).

The most plausible theory about the date of Obadiah seems to be that it was composed soon after the Restoration, perhaps at the same time as Malachi* and Joel* (see also Haggai*, Zechariah*).

P

PATRIARCHS — IN GENESIS AND IN HISTORY. — *Outline: I. The Patriarchal Stories in Genesis: a. Abraham; b. Isaac; c. Jacob; The Joseph Interlude. II. Genealogical Scheme and Its Wider Scope. III. Theological Nature of the Biblical Narrative. IV. Literary Form of the Stories. V. Modern Interpretation: a. Sources of Patriarchal Traditions; b. Sociological Links with the Middle Bronze Age; c. The Patriarchs in the Context of the Early 2nd Mill. BCE; d. Migrations of Semi-Nomads; e. The Patriarchs and Contemporary Peoples; f. Chronological Problem. VI. Conclusions.*

I. THE PATRIARCHAL STORIES IN GENESIS*: The Patriarchal stories can be divided into two cycles: that of Abraham, Isaac and Jacob, and that of Joseph*. The former consists of brief traditions connected with certain sites and holy places in Canaan, while the latter is a complete and detailed drama set in Egypt. Some of the details of the Joseph cycle have been confirmed by excavated Egyptian texts. Though the Abraham, Isaac and Jacob stories, particularly the latter two, have little in common with Egypt, they do contain interesting analogies with the civilizations of northwestern Mesopotamia, the Amorites and Hurrians.

a. **Abraham:** According to the biblical narrative, Terah, the father of Abraham, migrated from the Land of Ur to Harran. This move may be related to the historical economic decline of Ur begun at the end of the 3rd mill. BCE and lasting for several generations. It may also be confirmed by the fact that both Ur and Harran worshipped Sinn, the moon-god. (For other phases of the Abraham story, see below).

b. **Isaac:** The outstanding feature of the story of Isaac, son of Abraham, is that he sent his son, Jacob, to Padan-Aram in the west Mesopotamian Valley of Habur, in order to avoid having the youth marry a local Canaanite girl. Isaac himself had been married to a girl from the same region and for the same reasons. The Bible states that Abraham's tribe was adjusting itself to conditions so well (Gn. 26:12 ff) that it had begun to intermarry with the local population (Gn. 26:34 ff).

c. **Jacob:** Jacob was the younger of the two sons Rebecca bore Isaac but, with his mother's help, he obtained his brother's birthright. This secured Jacob and his descendants the blessing Isaac had intended to bestow on the elder son, Esau, whom the Bible identifies with Edom (Gn. 36:1). Jacob, who later became known as Israel (Gn. 32), fled from Canaan for fear of his brother's wrath. This story of fraternal rivalry symbolizes the eponymous origin of the two tribal groups, as well as the hostile relationships that eventually developed between the two nations.

In addition to escaping Esau, Jacob was charged by his father to find himself a wife among Abraham's kin in

Padan-Aram (Harran), the ancestral homeland beyond the Euphrates (Gn. 27:4–28: 1–7). Though clothed in folklore, this episode represents a significant stage in the history of the Hebrew tribes of Canaan and a kindred tribe of Padan-Aram and Aram-Naharaim. The relationship can be authenticated by genuine ethnographic and sociological data.

In Harran, Jacob married Leah and Rachel, the daughters of Laban, his Aramean* uncle, as well as Zilpah and Bilhah, the hand-maidens of his wives. The result of these unions was twelve sons — the eventual fathers of the Twelve Tribes* — and one daughter, Dinah (Gn. 30 ff). After a 20-year sojourn in Harran, Jacob and his now considerable family, returned to Canaan. Thus, Jacob's marital quest ended with an important migration of associated clans that took on a homogeneous character, led by a new common pact (b^e^rîth) with the God of Israel ("'El 'Elohe Israel"; Gn. 33:20; 35:2–4). According to Biblical tradition, Jacob became known as Israel when, on his return trip, he entered Transjordan across the River Yabok. It was on the ford of the Yabok that he had his successful encounter with a heavenly emissary.

Eventually, Jacob's clan, now called the House of Israel ("Beth-Israel"), became separated from the other branches of the Terah family tree, such as the clans of Ishmael, Keturah, Edom and, through Lot, Ammon and Moab. Despite its apparent simplicity, the narrative reflects a complex process by which a relationship was established between the ancestors of the Hebrews and those of other related groups to whom the Hebrews felt themselves akin. They intermarried, divided and multiplied. Behind the schematic narratives of Genesis* lie memories of clan migrations, hinted at in the Bible stories (see below, Modern Interpretations). In addition, the Patriarchal cycle of stories contains different local traditions regarding particular individuals: Abraham, Isaac and Jacob, all of which were later grouped together into the epics of the Ancestors (see below). The Jacob cycle, for instance, combines traditions about Jacob as a collective Israel, with legends of an actual, individual Jacob. This is particularly apparent in the Jacob-Esau relationship which reflects both a conflict between two clans or tribes, Jacob and Esau, and a personal relationship between two contending brothers. According to one tradition (Gn. 30:43) the numerical strength of the House of Israel is evidenced by Esau's preference for coming to terms with Jacob, rather than risk an armed conflict, in spite of his 400 armed men. In another tradition (Gn. 35), the picture is quite different, suggesting that Esau's intentions were peaceful and that Jacob's fears were rooted in his own guilty conscience, it even being noted that Esau greeted Jacob affectionately.

The Joseph Interlude: The Jacob story is interrupted by Joseph's Egyptian saga (see Joseph*), and resumed only on Jacob's deathbed in Egypt. While on his deathbed, it is written that the Patriarch adopted Joseph's two sons as his own, favouring the younger in his blessing. He also uttered a final testament in which his twelve sons were described in terms of the tribes descended from them. Judah, though not the eldest, was named leader, for reasons that may be surmised. Some scholars believe that the blessing was remembered because the later history of Judah happened to fit the prediction, while many similar ones must have been discarded because they did not fit. On the other hand, it is possible that later ages saw the blessing as justification for the emergence of this tribe under the House of David, and the later use of Yehudim (Jews), plural of Yehuda (Judah), as the name of the entire nation.

The story of Jacob ends with the account of his burial in the tribe's sacred burial cave of Machpelah at Hebron. On analysis, it seems likely that the biblical narrator linked two different traditions around the one Jacob.

II. THE GENEALOGICAL SCHEME AND ITS WIDER SCOPE. — The sources of the Patriarchal Age contain several genealogicizing narratives and fragmentary sagas. From these hints in the Old Testament, it is clear that not all the traditions which were passed from generation to generation were incorporated in the present Massoretic Text*. Nevertheless, although the traditions underwent the degree of modification and adaptation inevitable in the process of oral transmission, they have been preserved essentially unchanged in the present biblical text.

The term "Patriarchs" is a translation of the Hebrew "'ăbôṭ" — forefathers, which suggests real human beings, not symbolic ancestors of the later tribes who bore their names. The Hebrew word is related to ancient Amorite terminology found in the Mari texts of northwestern Mesopotamia*. In the genealogical lists of Genesis and elsewhere in the Old Testament, the Patriarchs are presented as a general group related to the tribes of the Sons of Eber, Aram, Keturah, Ishmael and Edom, who wandered about or dwelt in practically the entire expanse of territory adjoining Palestine, Syria, Mesopotamia and Babylonia.

According to the Genesis* stories, the Patriarchs are the fathers or brothers of most of these tribes, and it is only in post-biblical Hebrew literature that the term Patriarchs is restricted to Abraham, Isaac and Jacob. It would seem that the genealogical purpose of the Genesis stories is to define the place of the Patriarchs of Israel in the general scheme of tribal relationships. From this pattern also, Palestine emerges as the legacy of Abraham, Isaac and Jacob.

III. THEOLOGICAL NATURE OF THE BIBLICAL NARRATIVE: The Patriarchal narratives must be considered in relation to the type of literature to which they belong. They are not presented in the form of tribal tales of wars and events, but rather as histories of certain semi-nomadic families and/or clans, the memory of whose chiefs was hallowed. These sacred traditions of the Hebrews, which are found in chs. 12–50 of Genesis*, form the beginning of a great theological history that comprises the first six books of the Bible.

As a record of the history of the Hebrew faith, the Patriarchal narratives seek not only to relate Hebrew origins to the genealogy of Abraham, but also to illustrate the redemptive act of God on behalf of the ancestors of his "chosen people"*. While those who wrote down the narratives were preoccupied with theological considerations of God's purpose in creation and man's place in history and the universe, they did not deliberately obscure the facts. Indeed, they preserved many of these traditions in their archaic form, doing so even when the meaning of some of the details had been forgotten.

The biblical authors were led through their faith in the God of Abraham and their fidelity to tribal traditions to select important phases in the religious life of the Patriarchs and to stress certain facts or narratives that appeared central to them (see Patriarchs — Religion*).

IV. LITERARY FORM OF THE STORIES: One of the outstanding traits of the Patriarchal sagas is the emphasis on the Fathers as individuals in all the experiences of life, in their sadness and joy, in their struggles for survival, their spiritual aspirations, their relations with their fellowmen, and their loyalty to their God. The Patriarchs' weaknesses and failings are mentioned along with their virtues and achievements, an approach which gives a special charm to their stories. The stories are made up of a series of separate episodes, linked by the leading characters. It must be assumed, as with the epic poems of other nations, that these stories were preserved over the course of many generations as treasures of sacred traditions. In nearly all of them, very old traditions can be found, passed on from generation to generation until they assumed the final form seen in the Old Testament.

This preservation of a realistic atmosphere and essential facts makes the collection of stories an important document for those studying the past. To use it, however, the historian must be able to distinguish between fact and theological interpretation.

Until recent times all attempts at biblical evaluation were hampered by lack of knowledge of ancient Near Eastern civilizations. In the past, several schools of thought assessed the historical worth of the stories on the basis of examination and re-examination of the material they contained, having little, or at best, superficial external evidence against which to check hypothetical reconstructions. Today, biblical researchers can refer to the amazing discoveries of the last 60–75 years, which have considerably illuminated life during the first part of the 2nd mill. BCE.

More recent commentators such as O. Proksch, H. Junker and R. de Vaux admit the substantial historicity of the events related in Genesis*. They recognize the special type of Patriarchal religion and evaluate its content from the traditions and theological interpretations preserved side by side in the biblical narrative.

V. MODERN INTERPRETATION: In the field of biblical evaluation, and particularly the study of the Patriarchal stories, there are three modern schools of thought (apart from the fundamentalists who interpret the Bible literally). These are dealt with under Genesis*.

The critical approach to biblical research during the first part of this century (see Biblical Criticism*) opened many new and fruitful lines of thought, but was of necessity inconclusive and without authority. Today the biblical traditions can be examined in the light of newly discovered historical and archaeological data and against the background of the world in which the biblical characters lived. From a scientifically objective point of view, it is now possible to make a positive evaluation concerning the historicity of the Patriarchal narratives. Discussed below are the several lines of investigation used in the attempt to determine the historical basis of the Patriarchal stories:

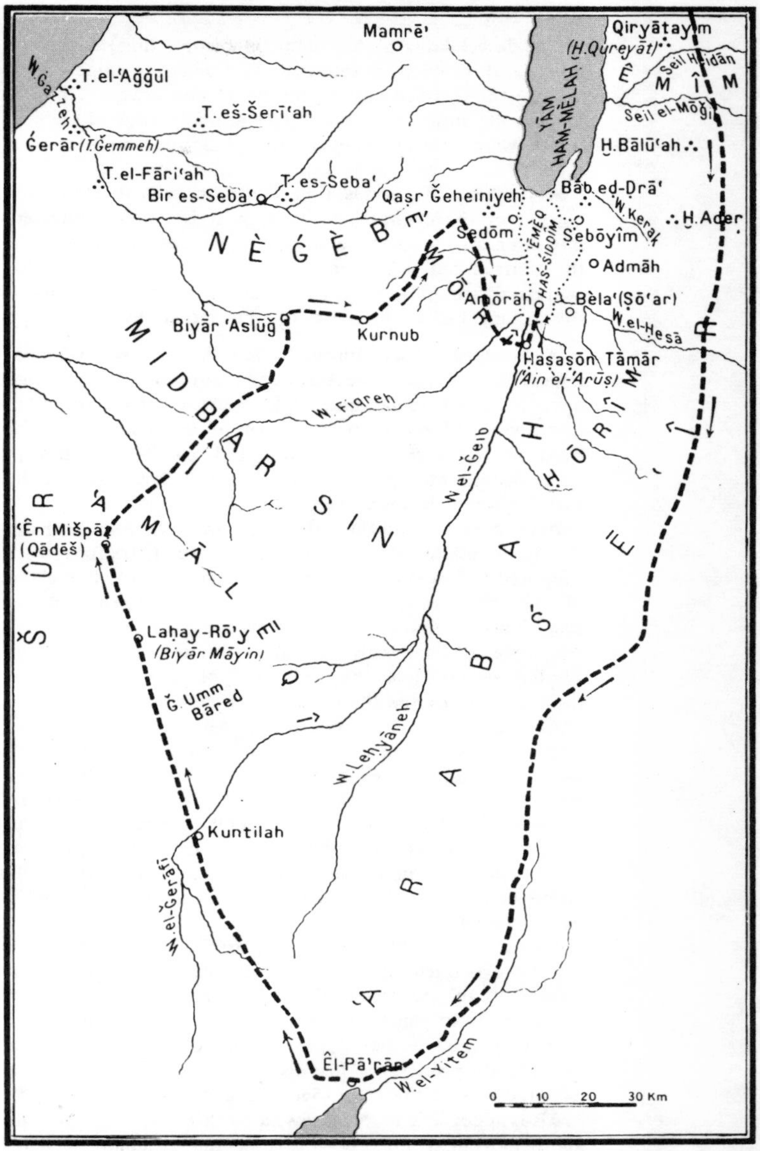

652

a. **Sources of Patriarchal Traditions:** There are inherent difficulties about sources relating to the Patriarchs. One difficulty is that the traditions which contain a kernel of history are written in the form of prose-sagas and conceal the complex group movements behind the doings of individuals.

Even the beginnings of the Children of Israel are complicated. Theologically, Israel descended from one man, Abraham. Physically, the nation sprang from many clans, and this is hinted in the narratives concerning Abraham and his nephew, Lot. Both were at the head of fairly large clans. This is indicated in the account in Genesis 14 according to which Abraham was able to field an army of 318 fighting men in the battle against the Mesopotamian princes (whose invasion is shown on the map **652**).

The descendants of Abraham (in Jacob's time) developed into great clans and returned to Canaan, competent to destroy the fortified city of Shechem* (see article; Gn. 34). During the entire Patriarchal period, many kindred Hebrew tribes were migrating over the whole of the area (see Habiru*).

A further difficulty is that the Patriarchs lived on the margin of the civilizations existing at the time, and were not integrated into these societies. Moreover, the bulk of the Patriarchal traditions were transmitted orally for centuries through a variety of channels. Little was reduced to writing before the rise of the monarchy.

b. **Sociological Links with the Middle Bronze Age:** Archaeological finds at Nuzi (see Assyria*) in northern Mesopotamia have provided remarkable links between the Patriarchal narratives and the cultural milieu of the Hurrians* who lived in the region of Harran and Aram-Naharaim in northwestern Mesopotamia, near eastern Syria, during the early Middle Bronze Age.

According to tradition, the Hurrians (see Assyria*) are the basic ethnic stock from which the Patriarchs were supposed to have come and their country was the homeland of Abraham and Laban. The Hurrian* inscriptions on clay tablets found at Nuzi, have cleared up certain enigmatic biblical episodes and obscure details in the Patriarchal narratives that are out of place in a later age of the Hebrews, or the life of contemporary Western Semites, but coincide with Hurrian customs. An example of such an episode is Abraham's adoption of Eliezer before Isaac's birth (Gn. 15:2; see: Family*) and Laban's seven-year adoption of Jacob and the rights it conferred on the latter.

From the tablets it was learned that according to Hurrian custom an heirless man could adopt an heir through mutual agreement between families in order to keep the family estate in the hands of a legal heir, as land could neither be alienated nor sold.

Rachel's theft of Laban's "teraphîm" (Gn. 31:19–35) can be explained by the Nuzi law which stipulates that possession of the household god bore a close connection to the right to share in the inheritance. Rachel may have been motivated by her desire to insure her husband's title to Laban's property. This also explains Laban's distress over the loss of the idols (See: Canaan: Gods and Idols*).

Also, according to Nuzi law, a barren wife must provide another woman for her husband, but is enjoined from driving out any child of this union, as Sarah did to Hagar and Ishmael (Gn. 21:10; see below, Sect. e. on Hurrians).

c. **The Patriarchs in the Context of the Early 2nd Mill. BCE:** Until recent years, many scholars thought that what is called the historic period of the Children of Israel was placed in the Late Bronze Age, or second half of the 2nd mill. BCE. In the opinion of W.F. Albright and E.A. Speiser, the origin and oral formulation of most of the stories of Genesis can be confidently attributed to the first half of the 2nd mill. BCE (ca. 2000–1550 BCE). E.A. Speiser has convincingly argued that the Patriarchal stories contain traditions and social data that have little in common with the later time in which they were written down, making it possible that the biblical authors did not fully understand the motivating social factors in the lives of the Patriarchs. Speiser's theory is supported by inscriptions found on Mesopotamian cuneiform tablets in which such biblical names as Sarug, Terah and Nahor appear. The names in the genealogical tables of the Patriarchs (Gn. 11:20–26) are more or less parallel to extra-Old Testament sources, which demonstrate that persons related by the Bible to Patriarchal days did exist and have left their imprint on Israelite history.

Further evidence comes from the "Table of Nations" in Genesis 10, referred to again in Gn. 15:19–21 and repeated in various forms elsewhere in the Old Testament. This lists the early inhabitants of Palestine. Although the table was composed later, many of its components are much older.

Another factor in this argument on the early Hebrew background is inter-marriage between the people of Aram-Naharaim (Harran) and the Hebrews of Patriarchal days. The Genesis stories regard it as permitted and practiced, while inter-marriage with the Canaanites was frowned on. This ethnic affinity between the Israelites and the northwestern Mesopotamians, and the friendly relations between the immediate descendants of Abraham and their kin in the Harran region obtained only in the distant past. It stands out in strong contrast to the relations between Israel and Aram in later times, particularly after the Davidic period.

d. **Migrations of Semi-Nomads:** During the Patriarchal period the Hebrew clans lived a semi-nomadic tribal existence which bore little resemblance to the stratified sedentary or urban life of the later Israelite monarchy. Details of this semi-nomadic era are described in Genesis and open a new line of investigation into the sociological structure of the Patriarchal stories in the context of contemporary Canaan.

It is known that during the second quarter of the 2nd mill. BCE, Hurrian and Indo-European elements (the Hyksos; see Egypt*) migrated into Canaan, mainly settling on the coastal plains. Their material culture was quite advanced and they had at their disposal such items as war chariots and other improved means of communication. This, in turn, spurred the erection of a chain of coastal and inland fortifications, which had a strong impact on social and economic life in Canaan, and on the caravan trade from fertile regions of western Mesopotamia, as shown on the map of Roads*. It increased steadily and it is possible that Abraham and his tribe, following the pattern of the times, developed and strengthened their economic ties with Canaan, even before taking up residence there. It is significant that Isaac and Jacob continued this policy of trade relations. According to the Old Testament, Abraham had many slaves or "trained men" (slaves born into his household and trained in warfare), besides flocks of cattle, sheep, asses and camels. During this period the ass was the main beast of burden, the camel appearing less frequently or perhaps as an anachronism. Horses are never mentioned as they were introduced later by the Hyksos (see Agriculture* and Animal Husbandry).

The Hebrews divided their time between agricultural activities and tending the flocks, which meant that they had to move about in order to find adequate pasture.

One result of recent studies on nomadism and semi-nomadism in this period by A. Janssen, R. de Vaux and others, has been to confirm that the Patriarchs cannot be compared to modern Arab Bedouins. Even the appearance of the semi-nomads was vastly different, as illustrated by a statuette of a Syrian shepherd of the early 2nd mill. BCE illustrated under Agriculture*. Knowledge of the problems and customs of nomadic groups and those in the process of settling down, has drastically changed the perspective in reading the stories of the Patriarchs.

The main grazing areas used by the Patriarchs and other semi-nomadic tribes were in the central hill country and occasionally on the steppes of the Negeb (Shechem, Bethel, Hebron, Beersheba, Gerar, Rehovoth and Lāḥai-rô-êe, were the centres). The hill country was sparsely populated and afforded room for seasonal movements in search of pasture.

Abraham came into close contact with the people of the Negeb and, especially, of the hill regions of central Palestine. As there was no central authority, wandering tribes such as those of the Patriarchs had to make pacts with each of the many autonomous city "kings" or princes, in order to insure themselves from attack by the local inhabitants and marauding tribes; but the semi-nomads did not as a rule live among the local people and did not assimilate with them in spite of their close relations.

The hill country was dotted with fortified towns of the Amorites (biblical name for the aborigines or early Canaanites) which were apparently surrounded by hamlets made of mud-huts. The Amorites moved into the fortresses only in time of peril. During the summer grape and fig harvest, the farmers lived in impoverished huts, a habit that has survived among Arab peasants and is featured in the Hebrew Feast of Tabernacles or Succoth (Succoth means "huts" in Hebrew).

The Egyptian tale of Sinuhe (Sinuhet; 20th c. BCE) describes in detail the conditions of life among the Bene-Kedem, another branch of the Amorites, in southeastern Syria, and near the ancestral home of the Patriarchs. A vivid picture of the wandering Asiatic bands that came from the Amorite hinterland and entered the eastern border of Egypt may be had from the tomb painting of Beni-Hasan, dating from about 1890 BCE, showing Ibsha and 37 of his clan of Bene-Ammu appearing before the Egyptian border official (**653**; see Egypt and Israel*; see also **326**).

e. **The Patriarchs and Contemporary Peoples:** Extra-biblical cuneiform texts of the early half of the 2nd mill. BCE have thrown considerable light on the life and migrations of the peoples of western Mesopotamia, eastern Syria and Palestine, though it has not always been easy to correlate these texts and identify the regions mentioned. (Consult maps **226** and **583**).

In studying the texts, J.R. Kupper distinguished seven groups, whose life and history during the first part of the 2nd mill. BCE illuminate the Patriarchal stories. These groups are the Haneans, Benjaminites, Sutu, Amorites, Hurrians, Habiru* and Arameans*.

The Haneans were semi-nomadic and began the settling down process on the borders of the Semitic Amorite Kingdom of Mari (see Babylonia*). They developed stable institutions and practiced farming on the shores of the Euphrates. Their main occupations were sheep-rearing and large scale caravan trade, though they also engaged in an occasional raiding expedition. Their chiefs were called "šarru", which is analogous to the Hebrew "sar", also meaning chief. They were also ruled by a council of "ancients" or "elders" called "sugagu", who were the heads of clans and villages.

653

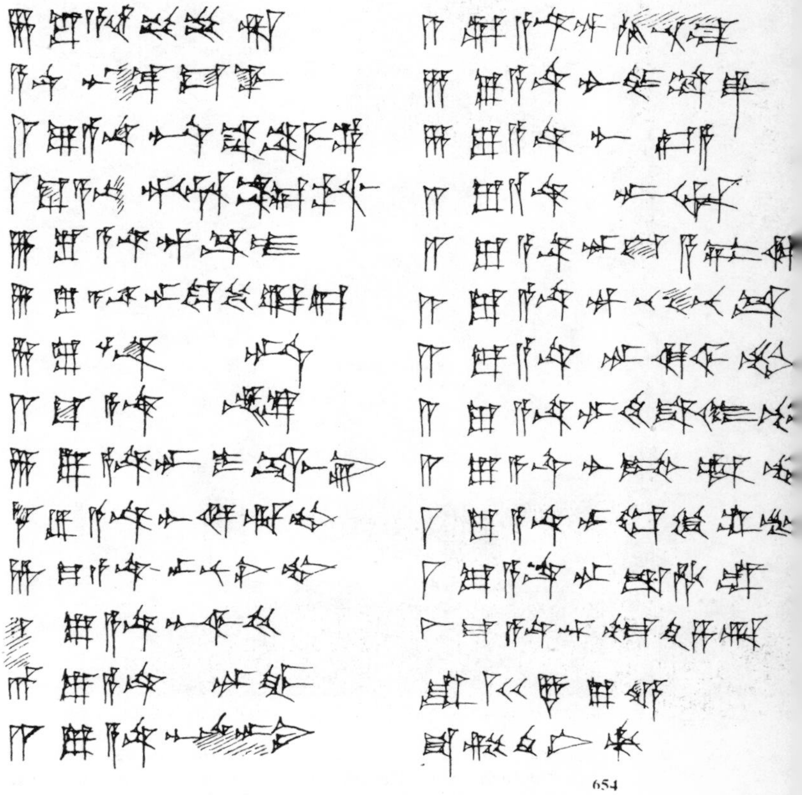

654

These councillors constituted one of the essential elements of the army, known as the "gayum" (equivalent of the Hebrew word "goy"), but did not merge with the rest of the troops.

The Benjaminites are described in the Mari tablets **(654)** of the 18th c. BCE, as seen in this example. Their name derives from the cuneiform "Bini-yamina", "people of the south". The similarity with the name of one of Jacob's sons is most suggestive, though it does not imply any historical identification with the Hebrew tribe. It demonstrates, however, the composition and background of biblical and west Amorite names. The Benjaminites' mode

655

of life bears a close resemblance to that of the Haneans, particularly when the Mari texts relate incidents with the turbulent tribesmen of the Bene-Rabbaya and the Bene-Shamal, "sons of the north".

The Šutu lived in the western part of the Syrian-Arabian desert, on the eastern borders of Syria. Their invasions of the settled lands of Babylonia and north Syria were of greater danger than those of the Haneans or Benjaminites, as they covered more ground. They are known to have hired themselves out as mercenaries, and, as a subject people, to have paid tribute of sheep to the Assyrian king, Tukutli Ninurta I (13th c. BCE).

R.A. Bowman suggests that a comparison of the biblical and extra-biblical sources seems to indicate that the first Hebrew Patriarchs and their clans were associated with the Sutu of Mesopotamia and Canaan, while subsequent generations after Jacob, of Mesopotamian origin, have a connection with the nomadic Aramean* " Ahlame" who, first appeared in the Middle East during the El Amarna* period (14th c. BCE; see Arameans*).

W.F. Albright and J.R. Kupper see a connection between the Šutu and the Bene-Shet of Numbers 24:17 (oracle of Balaam) and the genealogy of Bene-Shet in Genesis 4:25, though they may not have been connected with the Terahites, the ancestors of the Patriarchs.

The Amorites: Cuneiform texts of the 3rd–2nd mill. BCE refer to the peoples of northwestern Mesopotamia and northern Syria as Amurru, meaning Westerners. This became the general term applied to various groups of north-west Semites, including, probably, those from whom both Arameans* and Hebrews later sprang. Egyptians and Assyrians called Syria the Land of Amurra (Palestine proper was called Haru by the Egyptians). The expansion of the Amurru kingdom of western Mesopotamia reached its height in the 18th c. BCE, under the celebrated King Hammurabi (see Babylon*). Biblical texts do not speak of the country of the Amuru, but mention the Amorites. In the 2nd mill. BCE, the word "Amorites" was used in the Akkadian language in a geographic-ethnic sense to designate the peoples of Syria and Palestine. The Israelites followed this usage when speaking of the sedentary people with whom the Patriarchs often clashed. They are considered in biblical tradition as the original residents of Canaan (Ezk. 16:3, 45 note them as the first pagan inhabitants of Jerusalem).

The Hurrians lived during the first half of the 2nd mill. BCE on the shores of the Habur in Aram-Naharaim and in other parts of northwestern Mesopotamia. They were not the "Horite" troglodytes living in the caves of the Negeb as was once supposed because of a misunderstanding of a biblical text. In the middle of the 2nd mill. BCE, a Hurrian kingdom, reaching the coast of the Mediterranean, appeared. The Hurrians who represent an important element in the Syrian-Canaanite kingdom of Ugarit* are mentioned in the Egyptian texts of the Syrian campaigns of Thothmes III and Amenophis II. It is known that a Hurrite wave reached Palestine in the 14th c. BCE, along with other Indo-European migrations. Though this wave must have left other traces in Palestine, the name Hurrite is mentioned in Genesis 36:20–30 in connection with the groups living at Seir (Edom; see Assyria*).

The Habiru: The semi-nomadic life described in Genesis persisted among the kindred groups of Hebrew clans even after the time of Jacob, a fact supported by the evidence of the Amarna Letters*. The Habiru (Apiru) were semi-nomadic groups that roamed about the hill country and came into conflict with the Canaanites. Extra-biblical inscriptions relating to the historical role of the Patriarchs' clans are independent of the probable identification of these groups with the Hebrews (See Amarna Letters*, Exodus*, Habiru*).

The name Habiru* appears in the 18th c. BCE in a letter addressed by a provincial governor to the king of Mari, reporting the depredations caused by these tribesmen. The Habiru are also mentioned as Apiru in Ugarit, and in a

1500 BCE inscription on the stele **(655)** of King Idrimi of Alalakh (Northern Syria), a Canaanite king who spent seven years of exile "in the Land of Canaan" and stayed "seven years among the Apiru" (ca. 1500 BCE.)

They are mentioned in Egyptian records at the beginning of the 15th c. BCE as "wine pressers" on the Palestine border. This is how Syrians are pictured in a painting **(656)** on the tomb of Rekhmire, ca. 1459. Amenophis II takes note of them in connection with his Palestine campaign, while Thothmes III records the term *'pr*. They are later mentioned in the el-Amarna Letters* (14th c. BCE), which speak of them as a redoubtable and turbulent population, menacing the Egyptian vassal kings of Canaan and Syria. They appear again in the 12th c. BCE.

The Arameans and their relationship to the Patriarchs are considered under Arameans*.

f. **Chronological Problem:** The actual period of the Patriarchs is extremely difficult to determine (see above: The Patriarchs in the Context of the Early 2nd Mill. BCE). If the biblical chronology is followed, it can be assumed that the Patriarchal period was the end of the 3rd mill. or beginning of the 2nd mill. BCE i.e. before the Hyksos invasion of Palestine and Egypt (ca. 1720–1565 BCE). This would place it during the Middle Empire in Egypt*, which corresponds to the Amorite period in Syria and Palestine.

This estimate is mainly based on the reckoning of I K. 6:1, that the fourth year of Solomon's reign (ca. 960 BCE) was 480 years after the Exodus*, and that the sojourn in Egypt lasted 400 years (Gn. 15:13) or 430 years (Ex. 12:40–41), placing the end of the Patriarchal period, i.e. the descent of Jacob and his sons into Egypt, in the 19th c. BCE.

If the biblical life-spans of the Patriarchs are accepted (Abraham was supposed to be 75 when he left Harran and 100 at the birth of Isaac; Isaac 60 at the birth of Jacob; and Jacob 130 when he entered Egypt), then the Patriarchal period lasted over 200 years, meaning that it began in the 21st c. BCE, as stated above. It is difficult, however, to accept the biblical life-spans of the Patriarchs as factual. The evidence of Palestinian tombs shows that life-expectancy in those days was no more than 50 years, and that the biblical ages merely reflect symbolic figures attributed to venerated ancestors.

According to some scholars, considerations such as the story of Joseph* and the entrance of the Children of Israel into Egypt, which seems to coincide with the time of the Hyksos, fix the early background of the Patriarchal Period before the Hyksos invasion of Palestine. In addition, this pre-Hyksos period was the era of Mesopotamian cultural and commercial supremacy, and Amorite political ascendancy. It offers, in their opinion, a better explanation for the migration of the Patriarchs, who circulated with as much ease as the merchants mentioned in the Mari tablets. Furthermore, many names common to the Amorites are analogous to those of the Patriarchs. They afford a framework of names of Palestinian princes mentioned in texts dating from the 12th and 13th Egyptian dynasties (19th–18th cs. BCE).

Another factor in the chronological problem is that certain Patriarchal customs are very archaic. They are not recognized by Mosaic Law, but are more akin to Babylonian law reflected in the Code of Hammurabi. Modern scholarship tends to identify these Patriarchal actions with Hurrian

656

customs as documented by the Nuzi tablets. (See above: Sociological Links with the Middle Bronze Age). These may be summarized as follows:

1. Equating the status of sister and wife, as in Gn. 20:2, 5, 12.
2. The right of a wife to give her husband a concubine, but not permitting the wife to expel the child of the concubine, a rule which Sarah broke when she expelled Hagar (Gn. 16:2–6).
3. Fratriarchate, or the requirement that a woman obtain the permission of her brother in order to marry, as in the story of Rebecca and Isaac.
4. Possession of teraphim as a token of an heir's right to inherit, as demonstrated by Rachel's theft of Laban's idols for the benefit of her husband, Jacob.
5. Adoption for the purpose of passing on part of an inheritance, such as the adoption stories of Jacob and Eliezer (Gn. 15:2) and of Ephraim and Menasseh (Gn. 48:5).

VI. CONCLUSIONS: This survey has attempted to relate the traditions of Genesis and the numerous references to the Patriarchs by other biblical authors, to present knowledge obtained through archaeological studies. It cannot, however, be considered definitive. Though it is possible to recognize the solid historical basis of the Genesis stories, it must be remembered that the interests of the biblical authors were religious and not historical. Unfortunately, the clans and tribes which transmitted these traditions did not have any scientific sense of history and did not preserve accurate records or a detailed chronology.

Differences of detail in the process of transmission of the Patriarchal stories, however, do not destroy their value as sources of information for the history of the tribes and their ancestors. The Patriarchal narratives are not isolated tales which can be coordinated in chronological order, but a collection of stories, which reflect complex situations, some presented in a distinct literary form, some less so. All, however, bear on the process of settlement (in Canaan) of the Patriarchal clans.

While the individual existence of the Patriarchs has not yet been proven, historically, the background of the narratives has been clearly authenticated. The stories give a faithful representation of the times to which they refer, namely the western Semitic world of the early part of the 2nd mill. BCE (2000–1550 BCE), as demonstrated by archaeological finds from the Middle Bronze Age in Palestine. Furthermore, scholars maintain with confidence that there is a connection between the migrations of Abraham and the complex movements of the peoples of that time. Even the most extreme biblical critics now recognize the solid basis of the traditions. although actual proof is still lacking.

PATRIARCHS — RELIGION. — *Outline: The Belief in 'El; 'El Beth-'El; 'El 'Elyon; 'El Shaddai; Religious Customs: Pillars; High Places; Religious Concepts; A Personal God; The Promise and Its Place in the History of Israel's Religion; Is the Religious Pattern Anachronistic? Canaanite Cult of 'El and the Patriarchs; Differences from Canaanite Religion.*

The Belief in 'El: It is not enough to demonstrate that the Patriarchs* (see article) were historical individuals of the first half of the 2nd mill. BCE (see Patriarchs* in Genesis and in History). They must also be correctly placed within the early history of Israel's religion. This involves some particularly complex problems. On the one hand, to the whole of biblical tradition it is axiomatic that Israel's history and faith began with Abraham. On the other hand, the historian must ask whether this is really true, or whether the Genesis account of Abraham's life and religion is no more than a projection backwards of a later stage in Israel's beliefs.

The most striking trait in the religion of the Patriarchs is the belief in "'El" under different names. In most biblical strata, 'El is a term for any divinity, rather than the special term for the God of Israel. In Genesis, however, it is always used as the name of the great high god 'El, who is known from Ugarit*. Thus, in Patriarchal times, the word means the divinity.

Proponents of a certain school of biblical evaluation (see Patriarchs*), such as A. Alt and M. Noth offer many illustrations from antiquity of a type of family deity whom a Patriarch would elect as his personal god and with whom he would enter into a special covenantal* relationship. Biblical tradition has preserved the general name applied to this family deity: "The God of the Fathers" or "The God of Abraham, Isaac and Jacob". Memories of the Patriarchal divinity using names connected with specific attributes or manifestations have also been preserved. The best known are "*'El 'Elyon*", "*'El Shaddai*", "*'El 'Olam*", "*'El 'Elohei Israel*", in all of which the common element is 'El.

El Beth-'El: The head of the pantheon of gods worshipped by the Canaanites was called *'El*, and his temple, "Beth-'El" (House of 'El), was in the town of Luz. It is quite conceivable that the Patriarchs and their descendants saw their only God in the god of gods worshipped at Beth-'El, thus making the name 'El Beth-'El synonomous with Almighty or Yahweh. The location, originally held sacred by the Canaanites, was thus sanctified in biblical tradition. In Genesis the holy place of Beth-'El (Bethel*) is linked with Abraham, who built an altar (matzebāh) there (Gn. 12:8; 13:3), and with Jacob, who erected a pillar and vowed that it should serve as the House of God (Gn. 28:15–22; 35:7, 16).

'El 'Elyon: This name of the Patriarchal deity is first mentioned in the story of Abraham being welcomed by Melchizedek, king of Shalem and High Priest of "'El 'Elyon" (the Supreme). From Abraham's oath to the king of Sodom (Gn. 14:22) it may be inferred that the early Israelites saw 'El 'Elyon of the Canaanites as their only God as well. He was worshipped in Shalem (Jerusalem), which is the first hint of Jerusalem as the Holy City, where even the idolatrous nations worshipped (Gn. 14). The Israelites used the name 'Elyon in conjunction with "'El" or "'Elohim" (God). He was considered the supreme God, the Creator of heaven and earth.

'El Shaddai: While the proper name of the Patriarchal deity is not known with certainty, many scholars hold that the Patriarchs knew their God as "'El Shaddāi" and not as Yahweh, who was first revealed to Moses: "And I revealed Myself to Abraham, Isaac and to Jacob as El Shaddai; and as Yahweh I was not known to them." (Ex. 6:3). Modern schools of biblical criticism* attribute this tradition to the "Priestly" and "Elohist" documents, in which there is a specific tradition that 'El Shaddai was the patriarchal name of God, while the name Yahweh was introduced by Moses. On the basis of this verse, and the mention of 'El Shaddāi in the Patriarchal Epics, a number of theories have recently been put forward about the place of 'El Shaddāi in the beliefs and rites of the Patriarchs.

In Hebrew epic literature, as in the Pentateuch and Ruth, the term 'El Shaddāi or Shaddāi refers more specifically to the power which determines fertility or sterility (i.e. complete annihilation). It seems that the term was applied to the god of life, who gives life or withholds and sometimes destroys it. Though 'El Shaddāi may have been the family god of the Patriarchs, it does not necessarily follow that monotheism, in the modern sense of the term, can be dated back to these early Hebrews. The traditions concerning 'El 'Elyon, which are of Canaanite origin, appear to indicate a more diverse concept of the divinity. On the other hand, the different names may have represented aspects of the same 'El to the Patriarchs.

RELIGIOUS CUSTOMS: Recent archaeological discoveries illustrate several Patriarchal religious customs and beliefs concerning the revelations of the Divinity:

Pillars (stele-Matzebāh*) — Examples include those pillars set up by Jacob near Shechem and Bethel, and the one he erected as a token of his covenant with Laban (Gn. 31:44–45). He called the pillar near Shechem "'El 'Elohei Israel" (God, the God of Israel; Gn. 33:20), and the one near Bethel, "'El Beth-'El" (God, the House of God).

High Places — (see article): The high or holy places at which God revealed Himself to the Patriarchs are associated with natural objects: trees — Shechem, Beersheba, Hebron; springs and wells — Beersheba, Leḥai-Rô'êe, or stones — Bethel, Shechem. It was near Beersheba that Abraham planted a tamarisk tree and called the site *Adonai 'El 'Olam* (My Lord, God of the World; Gn. 21:33). Leḥai-Rô'êe, the site of God's revelation to Hagar, is called "Atā 'El Rô'êe" (You are a God of Seeing; Gn. 16:13). Certain scholars have erroneously maintained that this association of deity with natural objects reflects the survival of primitive animistic beliefs in the religion of the Patriarchs. This theory ignores the fact that the spot at which revelation took place was not identified by the Patriarchs with God, but was regarded as commemorating the event. The Patriarchs observed no festivals or fixed holy days with attendant sacrificial rites, though we do know of ceremonies of libation of oil or wine on newly built altars. While the erection of altars was not obligatory, it was desirable. These altars were the predecessors of shrines, temples and the institution of the priesthood.

High places actually stood outside the towns mentioned, recalling the semi-nomadic custom of camping on the outskirts of society. Moreover, the towns existed before the advent of the Patriarchs.

Patriarchal High Places: Careful study of the shrines and holy places visited by the Patriarchs leads to the paradoxical conclusion that while tradition multiplies the links uniting the Patriarchs and the sanctuaries of Shechem, Bethel and Beersheba, later religious reformers and prophets reproved the cult of high places* as pagan. The cultic rites practiced at the local shrines represented a real danger to Yahwism, as can be seen from the close association between the Hebrew tradition of "'El-Beʳrith" in Shechem*, and the Canaanite Ba'al-Beʳrith, to whom a temple had been dedicated there. It is also true, however, that "'El-Bethel" and other divine names invoked by the Patriarchs did not represent petty local gods, but were all manifestations of the supreme God "'El", whom the Israelites recognized as their own Deity. Yahweh (see Moses*) was identified with 'El in a peaceable merger and was worshipped in the same sanctuaries. The name continued in use and in fact displaced Yahweh in post-biblical literature — in Qumran* for instance. The type of burial chamber employed in Patriarchal times (cf. Abraham's family tomb of Machpelah in Hebron) is another characteristic of the religion they practiced (see Funerary Customs*).

Religious Concepts: The Covenant* and the relationship it represents between the Patriarchs and their God is one of the basic theses of Genesis. An important manifestation of this covenantal relationship is described in Genesis 15, in the revelation of God to Abraham. Under this Covenant, which was renewed with Abraham's descendants, the Deity took charge of his family or clan. The Covenant was made for all time, the divine promise being renewed to the later Patriarchs. In the Covenant of Genesis 15, God made a commitment to "His People". At Sinai he also imposed obligations on that people. It appears that when the Hebrews came to form a nation on the basis of covenant unity, their thought was still governed by Patriarchal concepts (see Covenant*).

A Personal God: The concept of a personal god, with whom one could discourse on intimate terms, was one of the traits that characterized the covenantal relationship of the religion of the Patriarchs. By demonstrating that God revealed Himself to the Patriarchs at different places, the biblical narrators emphasize the traditional belief that God wished to show that he followed His Chosen People* wherever they went, and watched over and cared for them. In exchange He demanded and obtained from them implicit loyalty in times of prosperity as well as adversity. This element of the Patriarchal religion apparently differed (in the opinion of many scholars) in nature, substance and theology from that of the later period of Moses and the Prophets.

The Promise and Its Place in the History of Israel's Religion: The unique place of the Patriarchs in the evolution of religion in Israel is far more important than their ethnic and inter-tribal origins. The whole philosophy of the biblical narrators rests on the assumption that while Moses was the actual founder of the people of Israel and formulator of its faith, the origins of both are to be found in Abraham. He is regarded as the fountainhead of divine revelation and the recipient of the Promise of the Land of Canaan. This is the fundamental tradition of Genesis. The Promise is repeated to Abraham and his descendants, who are destined to settle in Canaan as titleholders to the land, and whose status as His Chosen People is guaranteed by the Covenant to which they are both parties.

The Divine Promise can also be viewed sociologically in the context of Near Eastern conditions during the 2nd mill. BCE. The Patriarchs were landless shepherds who lived in contact with the sedentary and urban people of the region and were, to some extent, dependent on them. Although the Patriarchs did not own land, they aspired to its possession, which is, of course, one of the prerequisites of sedentary life.

IS THE RELIGIOUS PATTERN ANACHRONISTIC? The central position occupied by Moses in the story of divine revelation and in his creative impetus in Jewish faith in no way detracts from the importance of the Genesis tradition, which regards the Patriarchs as the fathers of the Jewish faith and history. Although in biblical tradition, use of the name Yahweh goes back to primeval times, in the Sinai-Horeb events (see Moses*), a new and extraordinary significance is attached to the divine name and its revelation. Thus we cannot read normative Yahwism* back onto the Patriarchs.

Although theologically speaking, there is no contradiction between the Promise to the Patriarchs and the later religion of Yahweh*, Yahwism began with Moses. Exodus 6:2 explicitly states that though it was really Yahweh who appeared to the Patriarchs, He had not been known to them by that name. All accounts previous to Exodus agree that the Patriarchs worshipped God under a variety of names. The later narrators who wrote Genesis and who worshipped Him as Yahweh, did not impose the later form of their faith on the Patriarchs. It is from this clue that scholars have been able to deduce the nature of Patriarchal religion from the complex narratives of Genesis. At first, many scholars described the pattern of Promise and Covenant as a backward projection of later Yahwism*. Recent studies suggest, however, that the Patriarchal religion must be examined in the light of what is known of religion in the 2nd mill. BCE, as it was a characteristic type, although unlike the pagan religions of the time and far removed from the animism (polydaemonism) of anthropological handbooks. The Patriarchal religion described in Genesis is not an anachronism but a complex historical phenomenon.

Canaanite Cult of 'El and the Patriarchs: The Patriarchal cults referred to in the narratives closely resemble those practiced by the Canaanites*. As the Patriarchs moved into Canaan, they apparently came into contact with various shrines and, in the opinion of many scholars, practiced cults which probably bore a certain resemblance to those already familiar in the local sanctuaries. These centred around animal sacrifice (Gn. 15:22) performed without an organized clergy. However, whatever the similarities, the Patriarchal religion of the Hebrews, based at it was on the Patriarchs' ancestral deity who had been known to them before they entered Canaan, was not identical with local Canaanite cults.

The worship of 'El, which was the predominant faith of the Patriarchs, is connected with the local Canaanite cults and also to the larger milieu of the Hyksos, Amorites and west Asian Semites (see Patriarchs*). The origin of the cult of 'El as the supreme God is not exclusively monotheistic. 'El, as the head of the Canaanite pantheon, is well known in a polytheistic form of religion from Ugaritic sources. Subordinate to him were a whole range of other cosmic powers which have no place in Israelite religion or in Genesis.

Striking analogies with various Canaanite cultic centres, such as Megiddo*, Beth-Shean* and Gezer*, however, lead to the conclusion that these were already holy places when the Patriarchs arrived (see above: High Places). It is quite probable that Jerusalem, called Uru-Salem in the Amarna Letters*, was such a cultic centre. It is also true that Patriarchal contact with Jerusalem is not rooted in Genesis. This exists only in the tradition of the cult of 'El practiced by the High Priest Melchizedek, with whom Abraham did have dealings (Gn. 14).

Differences from Canaanite Religion: Patriarchal religion was a clan religion based on the Patriarchal covenant. The clan was the adopted family of the patron God, who was worshipped within the clan. This is not the same as the later monotheism of Israel. Whether it was a religion without "graven images" we do not know — Laban's religion was not (Gn. 31:17 ff), yet it certainly differed in many important respects from official Canaanite and Mesopotamian polytheism.

Even though, in biblical tradition, the God of the fathers is regularly identified with 'El, the head of the Canaanite pantheon, he was never identified with Ba'al. Moreover, no other gods at all are mentioned in the Genesis stories of the Patriarchs.

Canaanite religion was polytheistic in nature and was directed to the worship of a great pantheon of gods (see Canaan*: Gods of). The cult of the Patriarchs, in contrast, appears to have been simple. It does not seem to have included the fertility rites or orgies of the Canaanites. Although God conferred the blessings of fertility (Gn. 49:25), he was in no sense a fertility God (see Idol Worship in Israel*).

Comparison of the aspirations of the Patriarchs' personal religion with those of the Mesopotamians reveals another great difference. The Patriarchs believed that their descendants would receive certain promised benefits from God, thus connecting their religion to a blessing that is to be transmitted from generation to generation. Mesopotamian lore and literature, on the other hand, accentuated the personal glory and success of national heroes, leaving posterity to fend for itself.

PAUL, Born SAUL OF TARSUS. — *Outline: I. Life and Mission: Background; Paul the Pharisee; Unorthodox Influences; Persecution of Jewish Christians; Conversion; The Convert; Proselytizing among the Gentiles. II. Paul's Journeys: First Journey; The Apostolic Council; The Agreement of Jerusalem; The Second Journey; Paul's Third Journey; Paul and Messianism; Paul and the Jewish Christians of Palestine; Salvation for Gentile as well as Jew; Paul and the Jewish Christians of the Diaspora. III. The Churches and Paul's Letters: I, II Thessalonians; Galatians; I, II Corinthians; Romans; Philippians, Colossians, Philemon; Ephesians and the Pastorals; Hebrews. IV. Paul's Theology: Original Sin; Paul and the Law; Salvation; Resurrection and the Jews; The True Israel; The Parousia; Pauline Doctrine — Judaism and Hellenism; Hellenism and Christianity; Christian Sacraments; Paul and the Talmud; Paul's End.*

I. LIFE AND MISSION: So far as one man's influence can determine the direction of a whole movement, Paul was the greatest single influence in the early Christian church. His conversion was a major event in the development of Christianity and much of its doctrine and organization can be traced to the form which Paul gave it.

This impression is emphasized, perhaps artificially, by the particular approach of the book of Acts, the main single source for the history of the first few years of the early Church. This was written by Luke perhaps around 62 CE, or, as some scholars think, much later, after he had spent several years with Paul and when the church had come to the end of a period of controversy in which Pauline views had triumphed. Luke compressed the early phase of Jewish-Christianity and concentrated on everything that contributed to the later Pauline stream. However, although modern scholarship has been able to fill in certain gaps, it has found nothing that contradicts Luke's overall picture.

Background: Paul, named Saul in Hebrew, was a native of the Hellenistic city of Tarsus in Asia Minor where, as elsewhere in Asia Minor, there was a wealthy and cultured Jewish community. A weaver or dealer in woven materials, his trade involved constant travelling and this enabled him to finance from his own resources the many long journeys he took, visiting and founding churches in Asia Minor and Eastern Europe (see maps **4** and **4a** under Acts*).

Paul the Pharisee: Paul is said to have been trained as a Pharisee in the school of Rabbi Gamaliel the Elder and he himself says that he was a strict Pharisee, although his writings give the impression that he never fully endorsed orthodox Pharisaic* Judaism either before or after his conversion. His persecution of the Jewish Christians before it is in striking contrast to Gamaliel's tolerant attitude.

Unorthodox Influences: The extent to which Paul was influenced by some nonconformist trends of Jewish theology can be seen from a comparison of his writings with other contemporary literature, especially the Dead Sea Scrolls*. Paul saw the same *dualism* in a world divided between good and evil.

In his attitude to marriage, Paul recalls the belief of the sectaries that those "called" for the "End of Days" and the "New Age" should not marry: "I think that in view of the impending distress it is well for a person to remain as he is... For the form of this world is passing away." (I Co. 7:26, 31).

Persecution of Jewish Christians: While still a Pharisee and before his conversion, his sincere belief that the Jewish Christians were a threat to the true worship of God made him join actively in their persecution. Following the martyrdom of Stephen, in which he played some part, Paul obtained letters from the High Priest in Jerusalem to the synagogue of Damascus, calling on them to help him in rooting out the new heresy. Many Jewish Christians had fled to this traditional refuge for nonconformists and Paul was anxious to forestall any influence they might have on the important, liberally-minded Damascus community.

Conversion: On the road to Damascus, Paul underwent the experience that changed his life: "And when we had all fallen to the ground, I heard a voice saying to me in the Hebrew language, Saul, Saul, why do you persecute me? It hurts you to kick against the goads." (Ac. 26:14). However sceptical others might be — in his own time or later — Paul never questioned the reality of his experience. He was quite sure that he had seen the risen Lord. This was the basis for his claims to apostleship, and equal status with the Twelve and the other disciples who were witnesses of the resurrection. The theme of his sermons throughout the Diaspora and the Gentile world was that he had seen the risen Jesus. The belief that Jesus who had died was alive is the great power of the Christian life (Ph. 3:10).

The Convert: After a short time of retirement and self-communion, Paul returned to Damascus and spent some three years there, preaching the new gospel to the amazement of Jews and Jewish Christians alike. He evolved a distinctive Christian theology.

As his fame spread, there was an attempt to arrest him and, in 37 or 38 CE, Paul escaped to Jerusalem where he became acquainted with the leaders of the new Jewish-Christian sect. His closest contact seems to have been with the fellow "Hellenist" Jew, Barnabas. It was he who, some nine or ten years later, brought Paul to Antioch to help in proselytizing there. Paul had spent the intervening years in Tarsus and beyond that fact, very little is known about him during this period.

In Antioch he joined the leadership of the young church. Some time later, with Barnabas and John Mark, Paul set out on the first of his great missionary journeys (see below).

Proselytizing Among the Gentiles: The 5th decade CE, had been years of significant change for the young movement in Palestine. A desire had been spreading among the Diaspora (Hellenist) Christian Jews to abandon traditional Jewish attitudes of reserve towards non-Jews and to begin proselytizing for the new faith among the Gentiles. They saw the Pharisaic Jews preaching Judaism to the Gentiles and bringing proselytes to the synagogue. Why should not the disciples of Jesus do likewise? Attempts to do so made little progress in face of a generally unfavourable attitude from the Jewish Christian church in Jerusalem which had no particular ambition to embark on a mission to Gentiles.

The Palestinian Jewish Christians demanded circumcision and obedience to Jewish food laws and other ceremonial obligations of their proselytes. For them, it was fundamental that the only true believers in Christ were those who had been Jews from the beginning — as Jesus had instructed: "These twelve Jesus sent out, charging them, 'Go nowhere among the gentiles, and enter no town of the Samaritans, but go rather to the lost sheep of the house of Israel'." (Mt. 10:5–6)

The question of the requirements for converts to Judaism was one that had long been debated by the sages. The majority view was that Judaism was indivisible. Proselytes must either become full Jews or else stay on the fringes of Judaism, observing the more general, "Seven Rules of the Sons of Noah", which included abstinence from things offered to idols, from things strangled (instead of being slaughtered kosher fashion), from murder and adultery and from the sexual licence common to pagan Hellenistic morals.

Inevitably, Paul was on the side of the Hellenists in the attempt to bring Hellenist converts into the new non-conformist Jewish movement. They were not Jews and they did not adopt Jewish observances or loyalty to Jewish traditions as the converts of the earliest Jewish Christian disciples had done. This new attitude provided the inspiration and the background to Paul's Gentile mission.

II. PAUL'S JOURNEYS: — **First Journey:** From Seleucia, the port of Antioch, Paul and Barnabas sailed to Cyprus (Ac. 13), the native land of Barnabas. They landed in Salamis, then crossed the whole length of the island to Paphos, the centre of Roman administration, preaching to the people, both Jews and Gentiles. Acts (13:7) relates that Paul's message was received by the Roman proconsul, Sergius Paulus, "a man of intelligence", whose service around the years 46–48 CE seems to have been confirmed by an inscription discovered at Soli, north of Paphos.

From Paphos, Paul and Barnabas returned to the mainland, preaching in Antioch of Pisidia and the cities of Galatia (see map **4**). In Antioch they began preaching to the Jews but quickly achieved such successes among the Gentile population that Jewish resentment forced them to leave. Sixty miles south-east along the main commercial route to Syria, they stopped in the ancient town of Iconium (Ac. 14:1–6), but again opposition aroused by their preaching sent them on to the smaller centres of Lystra and Derbe. In Lystra Paul's miraculous healing of a man who had been crippled from birth moved the crowds to acclaim the apostles as gods and to prepare to make sacrifices to them as Zeus and Hermes. Paul's passionate reproach "scarcely restrained the people" but, before long, the mood had changed and Paul was stoned and left for dead. He recovered, however, and the travellers journeyed on to Derbe, returning through Lystra and Iconium to Antioch Pisidia. After a further short stay there, they set sail for Antioch in Syria to give an account of their activities and to be told of a crisis which had arisen in the church (see parallel account, and illustrations, under Acts*).

The Apostolic Council: According to Acts 15, a demand had come from the Bishop (leader) of the Jerusalem church, James, the brother of Jesus who was a strict Nazirite*, that the Gentiles in the Antioch community must be circumcized and observe Jewish ceremonial laws. It seemed to Paul that the very existence of the community, and the whole of his work there was threatened.

The Agreement of Jerusalem: In the famine year of 49 CE, Paul came to Jerusalem to submit the question to James and the "chiefest apostles", Peter and John. Finally the Apostolic Council adopted a compromise which, as the presiding member, James summed up: "Therefore my judgment is that we should not trouble those of the Gentiles who turn to God, but should write them to abstain from the pollution of idols and from unchastity and from that which is strangled and from blood. For from early generations Moses has had in every city those who preach him, for he is read every sabbath in the synagogues." (Ac. 15:19–21).

There is no mention of any additional ceremonial demands and, immediately after the Council, Paul began waiving even those conditions that were imposed on the Gentiles by the Agreement. Limitations belonging to the Jewish past were becoming impossible.

The Second Journey: Setting out again through Syria and Cilicia (Ac. 15:41), visiting the churches he had founded earlier, Paul turned westwards into northern Greece. In Philippi, which had apparently only a small Jewish community and no synagogue, Paul and Silas had some initial successes and established a church to which Paul remained especially attached. His letter to the Philippians*, written later when he was a prisoner in Rome, reveals a deep affection and a remarkable absence of the internal problems that troubled most of the other churches.

Nevertheless, before they could continue their journey, the apostles had been dragged before the magistrates in the forum of the city and imprisoned by them on charges of advocating "Customs which it is not lawful for us Romans to accept or practice." (Ac. 16:21)

Philippi was the first of the great cities on the Egnation Way which led from the Aegean coastline to Rome. Seventy miles further along was Thessalonica where Paul spent "three weeks" (Ac. 17:2) preaching Jesus Christ in the synagogue, and establishing the nucleus of a church. The two letters which he wrote to the Thessalonians*, the earliest of his letters, and apparently written from Corinth on the same journey (ca. 50–51 CE), suggest that his converts in Thessalonica were mainly Gentiles. Paul went on to Athens, arguing there daily in the agora (forum) and synagogue with Jews and Gentiles (Ac. 17:17), and delivering a speech in the Aeropagus, the hill a little to the north-west of the Acropolis where the Athenians gathered for political and religious assemblies (Ac. 17:22–23).

From Athens, Paul travelled to Corinth, where he stayed for some eighteen months, living and working with Priscilla and Aquila, Jews from Italy. The understanding which this experience gave Paul of the life and work of the Corinthians is reflected in his later letters to them. During his stay, there was more trouble with some of the Jews of the synagogue. In his travels, Paul worked mainly in cities where there were Jewish communities and through them he may have reached Gentiles and "godfearers" (Gentiles who sympathized with Jews, see Hellen*. and Diaspora). Modern pilgrims hoping to follow in the steps of the apostle through Asia Minor (Turkey) and Greece find very few traces of the Hellenistic towns in which he preached. Most of them have been reduced to fields of ruins, strewn with the remnants of temples, forums and theatres, as shown by the theatre of Ephesus (**7**). The harbours of the ports he knew have filled with sand and now often lie some distance from the coast line. Nevertheless, even though the actual cities Paul visited have been covered by the later building of native towns and villages, a glance at the map shows the enormous distances covered by Paul and his few companions and suggests the many dangers they braved.

Paul's Third Journey: Paul returned to Antioch via Caesarea but was soon on his travels again. He journeyed as before from Antioch to Tarsus, revisiting the Galatian churches and going on into Ephesus, which for two years became the centre of his activities (see map **4a**).

Ephesus was the chief city of the Roman province of Asia, and a trading centre linked by sea with the west (Ephesus stood on the Cayster River which at that time was navigable to the Aegean) and by land routes with the east. It was a wealthy, highly cultivated city with a Temple to Artemis (Diana) which was one of the Seven Wonders of the ancient world. The town also boasted a number of silversmiths who specialized in pagan shrines. One of these, Demetrius, provoked a riot against Paul who preached that "there are no gods made with hands," (Ac. 19:26). His opposition seems to have been aroused by the very success which Paul's teaching could claim (see illus. **5–8**).

At about this time, Paul seems to have determined to go to Rome (Ac. 19:21). The letter which he wrote to the "Romans" is one of his longest and most important. It is noteworthy that it was written to a church already in existence, although Paul himself did not arrive in Rome until at least six years later, when he was brought as a prisoner.

On this journey, after a long voyage, he arrived in Ptolemais (Acre) and went from there to Caesarea, where he stayed with Philip the Evangelist. The incident of the man who prophesied his capture and betrayal in Jerusalem (Ac. 21: 11–13) is further evidence of the great courage which Paul showed throughout his career.

Paul and Messianism: As the centre of gravity of the church shifted from Palestine to the Diaspora and eventually the west, the Messianic ideal on which Jewish Christianity was based, underwent a significant change. Traditional Jewish expectations had been of a purely national "Messiah of David". But the disaster of Jesus' crucifixion made it essential that any suggestion of political rebellion must be removed from the picture of him as Messiah*. To do this it became doctrine that Jesus was the spiritual "Servant of the Lord" (based on Is. 40–55, especially 53), something far more universal than a nationalist Messiah to the Jews alone.

The role of Paul and his followers in the Diaspora in the establishment of this doctrine was central. A Jew of the Diaspora, consciously or unconsciously, he ignored nationalist elements in messianism and the details of Jesus' physical life. Instead, he concentrated on the universal aspects of Jesus as the "Son of God", the eternal, pre-existent instrument of divine revelation. Emphasis on his universal significance thus avoided the ceremonial demands of Judaism and also weakened the prestige of the Jerusalem "family" leadership and hierarchy of the Jewish Christians.

Paul and the Jewish Christians of Palestine: From what we know about the Jewish Christians of Palestine in the 1st c. CE, it seems, according to C.H. Kraeling, that "they did not make the death of Jesus on the cross as central a factor in their interpretation of his significance as Paul did, for instance. For them, Jesus was the bringer of the New Law, the Holy One who taught the higher righteousness that exceeded but did not abolish the Mosaic ordinances. We can still sense the differences of outlook that existed between the Christian communities of Palestine and Paul on this in Gal. 2:21 where Paul says for the benefit of those under Jewish Christian influence, 'If righteousness comes by the Law, then Christ is dead in vain.'

Salvation for Gentile as well as Jew: Paul's liberal approach earned him the opposition of the old guard of the Jerusalem church who still refused to make concessions on the question of Jewish observances. It seems that a good deal of Jewish Christian opposition to Paul was rooted in the part he had played in the early persecution of the church. Although the leaders accepted him, there were many who remained sceptical about his conversion. The so-called "Judaizers" with whom he came into conflict were an extremist group who did not belong to the central party in Jerusalem (see below, the Churches and Paul's Letters). Paul saw, much more clearly than they, that it was impossible to require slaves and hired workers in the Hellenistic world to keep the Jewish Sabbath and festivals, or to abide by the food laws. Nor could grown men, however close to Judaism, accept circumcision. Paul did not deliberately seek a solution for them. He had no desire to make things easy. He himself was a strictly observant Diaspora Jew and he was concerned with questions of theology. It came to him that with the coming of Jesus, the Messiah, the ritual demands of the Law had been nullified: "Let it be known to you therefore, brethren, that through this man forgiveness of sins is proclaimed to you, and by him every one that believes is freed from everything from which you could not be freed by the law of Moses." (Ac. 13:38–39). There was no need to impose the Law of the Jews on Gentiles, for they had been saved, not as Jews, but as Gentiles.

Paul and the Jewish Christians of the Diaspora: On his travels Paul often encountered hostility and interference from Jewish authorities. Even in the late 1st c. CE, sections of the nascent Christian church were still in close touch with Judaism and Jewish Christianity in Palestine. The New Testament reports that Colossae and the Maeander valley in Asia Minor, both important, populous districts, were under Jewish influence. It is significant that both Paul and Ignatius, Bishop of Antioch in the late 1st and early 2nd c. CE, devoted letters to discussions of their problems.

III. THE CHURCHES AND PAUL'S LETTERS: After the Council of Jerusalem (see above), Paul established the legitimacy of Gentile Christianity and planted the Gospel in the provinces of Galatia, Asia, Achaia and Macedonia. Whether Jewish or Gentile, the new Christians were perplexed about problems of belief and practice regarding observance of the Lord's Supper, about the return of Christ and the question of conflicting allegiance, whether to Jerusalem, to Paul or, in Corinth, to their leader, Apollos.

Paul's letters were written to answer these and many other questions. They were read, passed from one to another and, later, before the earliest Gospel was composed, they were collected into a group. This makes it impossible to be sure exactly when they were written but, clearly, this was during the 50's and 60's of the 1st c. CE. It is this very early date that gives the letters their importance. Not only do they provide an autobiographical record of the life and "experience in Christ" of one of the great characters of history, they also offer a valuable insight into the customs and problems of the earliest Christians, Jewish and Gentile. From them, it has been possible to get a much clearer picture of Paul the man and Paul the theologian. The letters or Epistles* (see respective articles) can be grouped by their approximate dates, between 50–64 CE, as follows:

I, II Thessalonians, in which Paul defends his mission against Jewish opposition. The setting is Corinth between 50 and 52 CE, after his second journey.

Galatians, written to his followers in Iconium, Lystra, Derbe and Antioch in Pisidia. Again Paul is mainly concerned to defend himself against the claim of the "Judaizers" (Jewish Christians of Jerusalem) that Gentiles must be circumcized to become Christians.

I, II Corinthians, written from Ephesus during Paul's third journey. Paul rebukes the Corinthians for their divisions, calls on them for unity, and gives them instructions regarding belief and practice.

Romans, written to the church at Rome, before he had ever visited there, is more in the nature of an Epistle or treatise, giving a broad outline of his whole theological outlook.

Philippians, Colossians, Philemon, written during Paul's imprisonment in Rome (ca. 60–64 CE, though scholars are divided as to the exact dates). The letter to Philippians describes his condition and his hopes for release and, in Colossians, Paul sets out his philosophy of religion.

Ephesians and the Pastorals, although traditionally attributed to Paul, are questioned by many scholars. E.J. Goodspeed has suggested that they were written by a follower of Paul's, taking the letter to the Colossians as a model, and giving a summary of Pauline thought. The Pastorals*, the later collection of letters, also show the influence of the other letters and have also aroused considerable doubts about their authorship. E.F. Scott believes that they were edited by a Paulinist from some genuine fragments and published under Paul's name (see Epistles*, Pastoral and General).

In addition, *Hebrews* was at one time attributed to Paul, although the actual author is unknown (see also Hebrews*).

IV. PAUL'S THEOLOGY: Jesus had read and interpreted the Law in terms of his view of God's whole nature and intentions, thus reducing all the "Law and the prophets" to the basic rules: "Thou shalt love the Lord thy God and thy neighbour as thyself." This was not the same as the Pharisee teaching that every precept of the Law was binding in itself. The main issue between Jesus and the Pharisees had been the authority of the Oral Law followed by the question of the guiding principles by which the Law was to be interpreted and applied (see Jesus*).

When the Apostles acclaimed Jesus' resurrection, it seemed to them that God had given his verdict on Jesus' side. While they could simply accept and act on this belief without questioning its implications too deeply, the trained Pharisee, Paul, was presented with a theological and spiritual problem of the utmost significance: the Gospel v. the Law.

Original Sin; Paul and the Law: The teachers of Judaism preached the Law (Torah) as a means of achieving righteousness. Paul denied this. To him the Torah was a divine measuring rod which demonstrated man's hopeless condition, since no human being could ever obey it completely. Judaism does not regard man as born into a state of ineradicable sin. He is ruled by both Good and Evil and he has to make the choice between them (see Pharisees*). If he strives to do good, he must have God's help to overcome evil.

Paul's thinking was dominated by the doctrine of original sin which maintains that Adam's sin has remained an eternal imperfection in the human race, preventing man from ever being wholly good. In contrast, the joyful and loving life led by Jesus' disciples must have been glaringly apparent to Paul. At first it provoked him to merciless repression but ultimately he was forced to compare their attitude — and especially Stephen's peaceful death in the spirit of his master — with his own inner struggles between conscience and nature. Paul had learned from his own experience that God's law could not bring salvation from sin. Salvation could only be achieved by the personal intervention of God in the form which was revealed to the ex-Pharisee on the road to Damascus, through the person of Jesus, God's son who shared God's very nature.

To Paul, God had revealed himself "in the face of Jesus Christ" just as, in the Old Testament, He had Himself appeared to men. Moreover, Jesus' death on the cross had made possible a universal "death to sin": "For God has done what the law, weakened by the flesh, could not do; sending his own Son in the likeness of sinful flesh and (as an offering) for sin, He condemned sin in the flesh, in order that the just requirement of the law might be fulfilled in us, who walk not according to the flesh but according to the Spirit." (Ro. 8:3–4).

In the future, those who were united with Jesus could share his death to sin. Moreover, they could, through him "die unto the Law" that they "might live unto God" (Gal. 2:19).

Salvation: Thus the essential element in all Paul's Gospel became the message of salvation, i.e. the making of life everything that God had intended it should be ("life that is life indeed"). This was, first of all, an intensely personal, individual experience; but his message was also a universal one, of fellowship in love (see especially I Co. 13) such as he had found within the early Church. Paul was responsible, above all others, for the conception of the Church as the "body of Christ", a social organism of persons unified by one animating spirit and directing mind, centred in its head, Jesus Christ. Paul taught that Christ was the spirit, or life-saving principle of the new form of the covenant*, as distinct from the old form of the Law or "letters" and, through his Church, his spirit enabled men to share his nature and to will and to do God's good pleasure (Ph. 2:12 ff). Thus even the most blatant backsliding never raised any doubt in Paul's mind that, with the help of the other members of the "Body" (Gal. 6:1), any ailing member could be made whole again and "saved" into healthful life by the power of Christ.

Resurrection and the Jews: Christ who was sinless, had suffered and been crucified in atonement for the sins of mankind. With this act, the Law had been cancelled. Jesus' resurrection was the guarantee of salvation for mankind which it extended to Jew and to Gentile equally. It has been said that for Paul, the Resurrection had the importance which earlier sectarian thought had attached to baptism. It also supplied the vital element in his eschatological teaching. In the life of the risen Christ he saw the prototype for the future life of all who were "Christ's" (Ph. 3:21). In speaking to the Gentiles, it became the beginning, the goal and the manifestation of the new life (Ro. 6).

The True Israel: Moreover, Paul taught that "the true Israel" were those who believed in Jesus. The basic Jewish belief in the divine election of "Israel after the flesh" had been invalidated when the Jews rejected Jesus as Messiah. In the future, the essential requirement for salvation was belief in that Messiah. Faith had taken the place of the Law. By his crucifixion and resurrection, Jesus had redeemed all mankind from sin and death and had made them all equal. Gentiles need feel no barrier in their approach to the new faith. Henceforth it could be said: "There is neither Jew nor Greek, there is neither slave nor free, there is neither male nor female; for you are all one in Christ Jesus. If you are Christ's then you are Abraham's offspring, heirs according to promise." (Gal. 3:28–29).

Paul remained emotionally attached to the Jews and he hoped that at some future date they would come, along with the Gentiles, to accept the Gospel and to be reinstated as God's chosen people.

The Parousia: Nevertheless, even while his unorthodox teachings were infuriating to the Jews, Paul never deviated from his proclaimed faith in the Parousia, the coming reign of Christ: "For the Lord himself will descend from heaven with a cry of command, with the archangel's call, and with the sound of the trumpet of God. And the dead in Christ will rise first; then we who are alive, who are left, shall be caught up together with them in the clouds to meet the Lord in the air; and so we shall always be with the Lord." (I Th. 4:16–17). Many scholars feel that there is some progress in Paul's thought and that Thessalonians is simply the earliest form of his belief in this area.

Events and his personality eventually brought the Jewish Christians away from their Jewish traditions and towards the new attitude which Paul had developed. The Christianity of the future would be Pauline Christianity — not only the complex of thoughts Jesus had preached and practiced. "Jesus was able to produce but a few disciples. Only complex personalities like Paul, in whom are combined delusion and rationality, mysticism and practicality can create . . . a church, that is to say, a religion existing in the world of practical affairs." (J. Klausner).

Pauline Doctrine — Judaism and Hellenism: Paul's supreme contribution was in formulating Christian doctrines in a way that made them acceptable to a sophisticated Hellenist audience — Jewish and Gentile — well acquainted with Greek philosophy. For this he drew on Hellenist* Alexandrian Jewish thought, making use, especially, of the doctrine of the Logos* (see Hellenism and the Diaspora*). Moreover, his Hellenist background meant that he was familiar with Greek philosophy himself and must have had some acquaintance with the mystery cults popular in his time. By applying Hellenist philosophy to Christ — in a formula propounded in the Epistle to the Colossians, Paul removed the personality of the Messiah still further into the realm of timelessness.

Hellenism and Christianity: In the first quarter of this century critical thought on New Testament literature, particularly Paul's work, stressed the influence of Hellenistic mystery religions on Paulinism. Finding parallels in the mystery cults, scholars drew attention to Paul's emphasis on the rites of the sacramental meal and baptism. As Paul employed many of the terms used in the mystery cults of the Graeco-Roman world, scholars made much of the paganizing of early Christianity under Paul (see Hellenism and Christianity*).

It is admitted today that Paul's mysticism and sacramentalism show a certain intellectual affinity to the cults, though it is not influenced by their mythology. Paul used a Hellenist idea in defining the Christian religion as a mystical union with Christ. This, even more than the doctrine of justification by faith, is the key to his religious experience.

Analogies and parallels, however, do not necessarily imply the transformation of a Jewish belief into a pagan rite. Later criticism has greatly modified the hellenization theory and recognized the basic Jewishness of Paul.

Much of the so-called "Hellenistic" terminology has turned up in Hebrew at Qumran, showing that Paul's thought and modes of expression are Jewish, although possibly sectarian. The very term "mystery" is frequent in Qumran literature, as is, significantly, the "mystery" of the eschatological action of God — a thoroughly Jewish concept.

Christian Sacraments: The new faith required no more — and no less — than the personal surrender of each individual to belief in Jesus as Messiah. Paul wanted "freedom in Christ", not ritual and ceremonies. Nevertheless, he was building a social organization as well as a theology — a church. In place of the multiple regulations of Judaism, two ritual sacraments of the Jewish Christian church: baptism and the Eucharist*, were stressed. But Paul never claimed to have initiated these. As he explained, he merely passed on what had been transmitted to him.

Paul and the Talmud: There is no clear reference to Paul in Talmudic literature, although many rabbinic utterances can be understood as an answer to the Pauline doctrine.

Paul's End: On his last visit to Palestine in 61 CE, Paul presented an account of his ministry among the Gentiles, earning from James and the leaders of the Church, a recapitulation of the Agreement of Jerusalem about the terms on which Gentiles might be accepted into the church. A few days later, Paul was arrested by the Romans after a riot had started on the suspicion that Paul had taken a Gentile with him into the Temple*. Paul's person and opinions were the source of so much dissension among the Jews of Jerusalem, that the Roman authorities sent him for safety to Caesarea* where he was imprisoned for more than two years. He appealed to the Procurator Festus who heard his appeal, in the company of the young Jewish king Agrippa, and granted Paul the right of all Roman citizens to be heard by Caesar. In Rome it is uncertain whether Paul was released and later re-arrested. In either case, around 67 CE, while the whole of Palestine was in armed rebellion against Rome, Paul was beheaded and buried at a place three miles from the city, on the road to Ostia. The New Testament records no mention of his death. Information about his last days and the date of his execution (about which there is some disagreement) is based on later Christian tradition (see Acts*; Luke*).

PERSIA AND ISRAEL. — *Outline: Origins; The Kingdom of the Medes; Emergence of Persia; The Achaemenid Princes; Cyrus II Rebels; Cyrus "the Great"; The Herald of the God Marduk; Cyrus Liberates the Jews; Cambyses II Captures Egypt; Darius, the Architect of the Persian Empire; Organization of the Persian Empire; Persia and Jerusalem; Xerxes I; Artaxerxes I; Ezra and Nehemiah; Administrative Autonomy in Judea; The Elephantine Jews and Judea; Persia's Downfall; Persian Language; The Royal Palaces and the Book of Esther; Persian Religion; The Jews in Persia; In the Parthian Kingdom.*

Origins: The first written records concerning the peoples of the Iranian plateau date from the 9th c. BCE. From other evidence, however, it is clear that settlement of the region between the river Tigris and the Indus Valley began in prehistoric times, as early as the 5th and 4th millenia BCE. During the 2nd mill. BCE the Iranian highlands were peopled by the southern branch of Iranian (Indo-European) nomads, who came from the steppes south and east of the Caspian Sea.

The first historical people to form a kingdom (or a specific culture) in the Iranian plateau were not the Persians. They were preceded by the Medes who were related to them ethnically and culturally.

The country of the Medes covered the north-western plains of Iran west of the Caspian Sea and south of the Zagros mountains (modern Azerbaijan and part of Persian Kurdistan, see map **659**). This area was the territory of an old west-Asian state, but very little is known of its history until the Medes make their appearance in the reign of Shalmaneser III (859–824 BCE), whose troops raided the land. He was after tribute and the thoroughbred horses for which the plains to the north-east of Assyria were famous, and later Assyrian kings followed his example. Shamsi-Adad V (824–811 BCE) swept through 1,200 towns of Media exacting tribute; similar actions were perpetrated by later kings of Assyria. Esarhaddon (681–669 BCE) bound his Median vassals by treaty, as illustrated by this cuneiform tablet **(657)** dated 672 BCE, compelling them to support the accession of his sons in Assyria and Babylonia after his death (see Assyria*, V; Law*, II: Affinities with Contemporary Codes). As

657

Assyrian power declined during the second half of the 7th c. BCE, the Medes rebelled and formed an independent kingdom, thus challenging the suzerainty of the Assyrians.

The Kingdom of the Medes: The Medes then achieved unity under a single monarch. According to Herodotus, the new dynasty laid claim to descent from Deioces, the founder of Ecbatana (capital of Media). The Medes established their independence from Assyria under the first king of the new dynasty. His son, Phraortes, was able to subjugate the Persians, who lived to the south and east of Media at that time. Thus a new major power was created which, under its third king, Cyaxares I, joined the Babylonians against Assyria and, in 612 BCE destroyed Nineveh.

The destruction of its capital, however, did not mean the end of Assyrian civilization. Assyrian culture had become deeply imbedded in Media, Persia, Elam* and the other countries on the border of its empire. Long after Assyria had collapsed as a political factor, its influence can be traced in Ecbatana and a score of other Median towns.

After the fall of Nineveh, the Babylonians took control of the lowlands of Mesopotamia while Median power was entrenched in the highlands north of Assyria as far west as Cappodocia in Asia Minor. Cyaxares' kingdom lay along the northern frontiers of Nebuchadrezzar's Babylonian empire (604–562 BCE). Peaceful relations were maintained between the two powers and when the Medes clashed with Lydians in Asia Minor (590–585 BCE), they called in the Babylonians to act as mediators. They fixed a mutual boundary on the river Halys, and the bond was cemented by a marriage between the son of Cyaxares and a daughter of the Lydian king.

The power of the Medes — or at least their reputation — reached such proportions that the exiled Jews in Babylon confidently expected that they would overthrow the Babylonians (Is. 13:17; 21:2; Jer. 51:11, 28).

Emergence of Persia: There are references in Assyrian sources of the 9th c. BCE to the land of Parsua. This land was apparently south of Armenia and there is no definite evidence connecting it with the Persians, although some scholars believe it to have been their original home. The earliest undisputed mention of Persia, i.e. the land east and south of Elam, occurs in the Annals of Assurbanipal (mid 7th c. BCE), which announce that he received tribute from Kurash, king of Parsumash, meaning Cyrus I, a forefather of Cyrus the Great.

Absorbed in internal problems and the fear of Assyria, the Perisans kept themselves apart from developments in west Asia. In the middle of the 6th c. BCE, under Median leadership, they began to assume a more important role in international affairs.

The Achaemenid Princes: Early in the 7th c. BCE, a new dynasty of Persian princes, named after its first prince, Achaemenes, had been established east of Elam*. According to the later tradition, Achaemenes was succeeded by his son, Teispes, who conquered the province of Anshan (southeast of Susa), well known from the cuneiform documents of the 3rd and 2nd cs. BCE. Teispes was subjugated by the Median Phraortes (see above), but later on he was able to take control of the area called Persis. Cyrus I and Cambyses I followed Teispes, Persia, however, remaining a vassal of Media.

Cyrus II Rebels: Cyrus II (559–530 BCE) consolidated Persia (= Fars) and rebelled against Median domination, overthrowing Astyages, the last of the Median kings, in 551 BCE. Cyrus captured the Median capital, Ecbatana, brought the Medes completely under his control and established himself as "King of the Medes", thus creating a new confederation within the empire. Persian and Median customs and laws were merged (cf. Dan. 6:8, 15), the Persians taking over Median culture, religion, military and political organization, types of weapons, clothing and customs. Medes obtained many of the responsible positions in the new state and Ecbatana and the Elamite Susa (Shushan) became the two major cities of the new Perso-Median empire.

Cyrus the Great: Once Cyrus had established his growing empire as a new world power, he turned against Croesus of Lydia, who was aided by Amasis of Egypt and possibly by Nabonidus (or his regent, Belshazzar) of Babylonia. Cyrus defeated Croesus in 547 BCE and captured his rich city, Sardes (Sepharad or Zarepath of Obadiah*, verse 20).

Finally, in 539 BCE, Cyrus turned his armies against Babylonia. On the 29th of October, his general, Guburu (Gobyras) captured Babylon, and Cyrus entered the city in a triumphant procession (cf. Dan. 5:28 ff; see Babylonia*). This victory established Persia as the predominant power in the area, and Cyrus embarked upon the series of campaigns and conquest that established the foundation of the Persian empire throughout western Asia. Among his titles, Cyrus called himself "King of Babylon and king of countries".

The Herald of the God Marduk: As Cyrus marched into Babylon — which had capitulated without bloodshed — he was warmly welcomed by the priests of the sacred cities of Babylonia. He restored the privileges which had been taken away from them in the days of Nabonidus, the last king of Babylonia* (see article), and reversed the unpopular policies he had initiated. According to the statement he had inscribed on his cylinder **(700)**, Cyrus called himself the herald of the god Marduk, a fixed formula in use at the time. He restored idols (which had been brought to Babylon by Nabonidus) to the temples of vanquished peoples, asking them to intercede for him with the national gods, Marduk and Nabu.

Cyrus Liberates the Jews: Cyrus appeared in his proclamation to the Jewish exiles of Babylonia as the herald of "the God who is in Jerusalem" (Ezr. 1:2–3), and granted them permission to rebuild the house of the Lord. This was in line with the basic tenets of the political and religious policy of restoration which he had adopted towards Babylonia and the countries he had conquered. Thus, the cult objects which had been taken from the Temple in Jerusalem were restored to the Jews and, according to Ezra (1:1–7 ff), a decree was published permitting all Jews who so desired to return to Jerusalem for this purpose. However, the alternate text of the decree quoted in Ezr. 6:2–5 makes no mention of any general permission for a return, but merely provides for the rebuilding of the Temple at the expense of the royal treasury and for the restoration of the sacred vessels. It is therefore possible that Sheshbazzar (Ezr. 5:14), prince of Israel, was not really given a royal appointment as governor of the province of Judea, but that a royal commission, including Jewish leaders and princes of the blood, was sent to supervise the restoration of the Temple.

Cyrus reigned until 530 BCE, having established a new capital at Pasargadae, north of Persepolis.

Cambyses (Kanbuzi) II Captures Egypt: Cambyses II (530–522 BCE) extended the borders of the Persian empire to the Mediterranean Sea and North Africa. In 525 BCE he conquered Egypt and reorganized it as a Persian satrapy.

Darius, the Architect of the Persian Empire: Cambyses II was succeeded by Darius I (522–486 BCE), who was not a direct descendant of the Achaemenid dynasty of Cyrus and Cambyses. His father, Hystapes, had been the satrap (holding a position similar to a vassal king) of Parthia and Hyrcania in northern Persia in the days of the two former rulers. Darius succeeded to the throne only after the male offspring of the reigning branch of the Achaemenid family had been killed in a series of rebellions and upheavals which broke out throughout the empire. For the first few years, he had to fight continuously to maintain his position against rival claimants. Meanwhile, a wave of rebellion and violence swept through the provinces. In Judea it was expressed in a great upsurge of messianic hopes (especially in the writings of Haggai* and Zephaniah*), but the Jews did not embark on any overt rebellion.

Once established, Darius set out to plan a reorganization of his empire, of which he is regarded as the architect by many scholars. A relief found at his new capital of Persepolis (see below) shows him **(657a)** seated on his throne, receiving the crown prince, Xerxes (possibly the biblical Ahasuerus of the story of Esther*).

Organization of the Persian Empire: The Persian empire was organized on the basis of principles hitherto unknown in the ancient world. Cyrus had maintained a strong and effective central government but, simultaneously, he granted a large degree of internal autonomy to the vassal kingdoms under his control. The empire was divided into satrapies and sub-satrapies. Each of these was headed by a satrap who generally belonged to one of the six aristocratic Persian families. Occasionally, he might be a local personality. The satrap had almost unlimited authority within the boundaries of his province, but he was under the surveillance of civil and military officials responsible to the central government. Each satrap was required to supply a certain tribute and a prescribed number of soldiers for the king's army. In general, Persian rule imposed no restrictions on the religion, language or cultural life of the people of the various satrapies.

Darius revised the administration of the large satrapies (which numbered 21 or, according to some views, 29 or 31), making the satraps the intermediaries between the king and the local population. He regrouped the army, reorganized the judicial system, instituted a royal post throughout the empire, and issued coins. A considerable degree of internal autonomy was retained by the rulers of satrapies and vice-satrapies (national areas or "medinta") and this probably explains the comparative stability which the empire enjoyed right up to the eve of the 4th c. BCE. This form of organization also made it possible for a small, weak commonwealth like that of the Jews to survive and to retain a high degree of internal independence.

In general, Darius succeeded in consolidating a vast Persian Empire. His one failure was his attempt to conquer the Peleponese in Greece. A Persian force was defeated by a small Greek force at Marathon in 490 BCE. Persia was never able to subdue the Greeks.

657 a

658

Artaxerxes I; Ezra and Nehemiah: The situation improved considerably in the days of his successor, Artaxerxes I (465–424 BCE). He appointed Ezra to represent Jewish interests at the royal court (Ezr. 7:12 ff) and in his decree (quoted by Ezra), gave Ezra the official appointment to carry out a mission to help the Jews of Jerusalem to live by their ancestral laws and to guide them in religious and temporal affairs. Ezra was empowered by the king to administer Jewish community life according to the Torah. The royal edict also established the Torah as the recognized law of the country (for further details, see Restoration*).

An even greater improvement in affairs in Jerusalem followed Artaxerxes' appointment of his "cup bearer", Nehemiah, as governor of Judea. Nehemiah was able to use his influence with the king to obtain permission for the rebuilding of the walls of Jerusalem and the reorganization of the community (Neh. 2:3–8, see Restoration*: Nehemiah).

Administrative Autonomy in Judea: Practically nothing is known about administrative relationships between Judea and Persia during the last century (the 4th BCE) of Persian rule. According to A. Schalit, Judea's status was changed from a "medinta" to a lower, provincial status within the larger satrapy. This appears to have been the case as early as the last days of Artaxerxes and Darius II, but no explanation has been found for this development.

The evidence of the coins inscribed "yhd" (Yehud), symbolizing the Province of Judea and the inscriptions with this name or "yršlm" (Jerusalem) relating to the Persian era (see Inscriptions*: Period of the Second Temple) point out, according to E.L. Sukenik and W.F. Albright, that the Province of Judea was recognized as a hierocratic community or national area, with special administrative rights vested in its people and high priests*, including the right to mint its own coins* (see articles).

Artaxerxes I died soon after the completion of the reforms of Ezra and Nehemiah in Judea. He was succeeded by Xerxes II (424 BCE), Darius II (423–404 BCE), Artaxerxes II (404–358 BCE), Artaxerxes II Ochus (358–338 BCE) and Darius III (336–331 BCE).

The Elephantine Jews and Judea: In contrast to the paucity of data on their relation to the Jews of Palestine, the affairs of the Jewish military colony in Upper Egypt have been brilliantly illuminated by the discovery of the Elephantine papyri (see **73**). These documents include correspondence between the colonists and the High Priest in Jerusalem, carried on through the satrap Arsanies of Egypt, concerning the celebration of Passover. They also record that anti-Jewish riots were sparked off by Egyptian intrigues, and the Jews' Temple destroyed. The Jews wrote to the Persian governor of "Yehud" (Judea), Bagoas, and to the governors of Samaria, asking them to intervene with the Egyptian authorities on their behalf. As a result, permission was granted for the temple to be rebuilt (see also Egypt*: Elephantine).

Persia's Downfall: The Persian empire had engulfed the vast area from India to the south of Egypt, but it rested on very shaky foundations. The various nationalities within it outnumbered the Persians many times over and lacked any sense of unity or corporate identity. By the later 5th and 4th cs. BCE, there was no strong central authority and the Persian army was a far from effective fighting force. Recruited partly from the empire's different peoples, the backbone was provided by mercenaries, mainly Greek. Like the late Roman empire a millenium later, the Persian empire had become an overgrown, unwieldy structure which fell an easy prey to a determined, disciplined adversary — in Persia's case, the Macedonian army of Alexander, small in numbers, but under the command of experienced and courageous leaders.

Persian Language: As early as 650 BCE, the Persian's Indo-European language was being written in cuneiform characters, on a system using 51 single syllables. Subsequently, the administration of the Persian empire used the Aramean* language and script, which thus became the lingua franca for the whole of western Asia (see Alphabet and Writing*).

The Royal Palaces: The court life of a Persian king is sketched in the book of Esther* and has been well illustrated

659

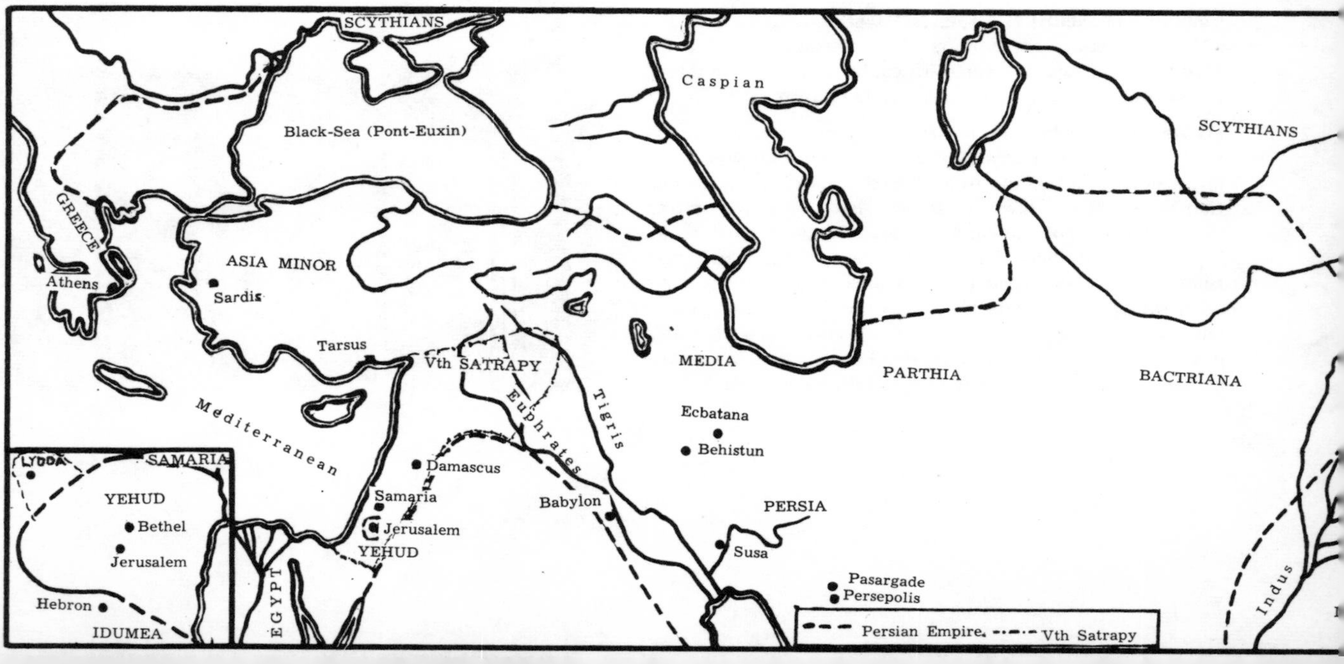

by the vast quantity of discoveries made by archaeologists in the ruins of Persepolis, Susa and other Persian cities. The royal palace of Persepolis built by Darius constitutes a monument to the art and culture of the Persians. To the palace came the delegations of subject peoples bringing their tribute to the sovereign, a scene immortalized in the reliefs of the Apadana or hall of a hundred columns, used for audiences and for the ceremonial parade of the army's famous regiment of the Immortals. The eastern stairway which led to the Apadana (**658**) was decorated with rows of sculptures representing the ranks of soldiers and tribute carriers. The Apadana was begun during the reign of Darius and completed under Xerxes I. Its roof was supported by 36 columns, of which four remain. The throne of the kings (**660**) is usually shown being borne by representatives of all the peoples of the empire. Here, it is shown carried by the army (see also Esther*). Persepolis was burned by Alexander the Great after he had overthrown the power it so magnificently symbolized.

Persia and Jerusalem: Against this political background, the course of events in Jerusalem remains obscure. During the reign of Cambyses, the satrap of the area known as "Eber-Nahara" ("the Province Beyond the River", i.e. the Euphrates) controlled the whole area as far as Egypt (see map **659**; "Eber Nahara" was the 5th satrapy). Cambyses appears to have known nothing of Cyrus' original edict concerning the rebuilding of the Temple and attempted to prevent the Jews from carrying out the work (Ezr. 4). However, application was made to Darius and he, presumably, ordered an investigation. In Ecbatana (Cyrus' ancient capital), a copy of the edict was found and Darius confirmed his predecessor's order and even instructed Persian officials to assist in the reconstruction. In addition, he granted an allocation of salt to the Temple, equivalent to exempting the Jews from the heavy tax on salt imposed on his vassals elsewhere (see also Government and Authority*, Part III).

Some scholars see the major reason for the enlightened policies of Cyrus and, especially, Darius in their adherence to the tolerant Zoroastrian religion (see below, Religion).

Xerxes I: During the reign of Darius' successor, Xerxes I (486–465 BCE), great upheavals took place in Eber Nahara. Some scholars believe that this was the time when the enemies of Judea, her neighbours (and the Samaritans) attacked Jerusalem and destroyed its walls.

Persian Religion: The ancient Persians worshipped nature-gods of fertility and the heavens, served by priests who made up almost the whole of the tribe of Magi (in Persian "Magush"). At the beginning of the 6th c. BCE, a new religion based on the principle of "do good and hate evil" was founded by the prophet Zoroaster, also known as Zarathustra and by other names. He established the idea of a single god, Ahuramazda, the "righteous master of Righteousness", symbolized by the cleansing fire and water, and opposed by an archdemon, Ahriman, representing all evil. The most notable characteristics of this religion were its actively ethical teachings and its tolerance of other gods and beliefs.

This religion taught that man's task was to fight for righteousness and goodness, through truthful, just behaviour and productive work. Strict attention to ritual purity was required, but there was no insistence on an ascetic self-denial. The doctrine also includes belief in individual judgment after death and a final era of redemption in which, at "the end of time," the "good of life, of purity and of truth" would be victorious and would endure for eternity. These beliefs are denied by Isaiah (45:6–7, passim), but in fact Judaism was apparently influenced subsequently by Persian beliefs, especially in relation to angels* and demons. Persian influence can also be detected in books like Daniel*, Tobit* and in the apocalyptic Apocrypha*. It is also apparent in the cosmic extension of the power of Satan and the Kingdom of Yahweh and in the dualistic theology (the fight between good and evil) of the Dead Sea Scrolls* and the New Testament. There is no scholarly agreement about the extent of this influence. Some think it was very superficial and remained mainly in the realm of imagery and presentation. Certainly, if there were any deep theological impact, normative Judaism later effaced most traces of it.

In any case, by the time of the Achaemenid kings, the purity of the original Zoroastrian religion had been lost in a variety of syncretic cults which emphasized the dualism of good and evil, in place of the original concept of a universal divine ruler. A positive kernel of this faith is evident, however, in the benevolent policies of Cyrus and Darius I (see above).

The Jews in Persia: The lives of the Jews in Judea were tied politically and culturally to the Persian empire for the two centuries during which their country was under the rule of the satraps (538–333 BCE). Within Persia proper, a substantial colony of Jews developed (see Esther, Book of*). They are described in Esther as an influential section of Susa's population and as living in all the 127 provinces of

660

the empire (Est. 1:1), although this is at variance with the 31 satrapies which are the most known to have existed (under Xerxes the number was reduced to 20). The figure of 127 is repeated in Daniel 6:2, which presumably reflects the same tradition.

In the Parthian Kingdom: Very little is known about their history, but it appears that from the 4th c. BCE, Jews lived in considerable numbers in Parthia. They remained there when Parthia overran Mesopotamia, the former Babylonia and Media, between 250 BCE and 225 CE. They had wrested this territory from the Seleucid* empire, and were thus in Persian territory throughout the Hellenistic and Roman periods. The Parthians were continually at war with Rome for control of the Near East, and often found it politic to ally themselves to Jewish princes. They restored Antigonus Mattathias (see Hasmoneans*) to the throne of Judea in 40 BCE, and the Jews of the Roman empire mistakenly saw the Parthians as their eventual saviours.

The Parthians granted their Jewish colonies a considerable degree of autonomy and under Parthian rule, the famous rabbinic schools of Mesopotamia began to flourish.

Under the Sassanid dynasty, Persia regained its independence and from 225 CE ruled over the ancient centres of Jewish settlement in Babylonia and Persia. The Babylonian Talmud was compiled under Persian rule — good evidence of the continuing vigour of Jewish life within Persia.

(See also Assyria*; Babylonia*; Elam*).

PHARISEES. — *Outline: Inadequate Sources; Pharisee Organization; Pharisee Philosophy; Tithing; Ritual Purity; Pharisee Ethics; The Framework of the Oral Law; Party Strife; Pharisee Social Ideals: Pharisaic Theology; God's Will and Free Will; Education; Intellectual Revival; Enduring Features.*

The Pharisees were the leading party and influence in Jewish life during the last centuries of the Second Temple. Their interpretation of Mosaic Law and their way of applying it to the details of everyday life dominated the religious and political scene against the opposition of the Sadducees* and the extreme sect of the Essenes (see Law*: Life under the Law).

Their Hebrew name "Perushîm" may suggest a group "set apart", keeping themselves ritually pure and avoiding contact with common people, though there are differences of opinion as to the origin of the name. Separation was also true of the Essenes and other sectaries (see Dead Sea Scrolls*). Insistence on purity was an essential element in the religious life of Judaism, though there is an important difference between the Essenes and Pharisees. The latter lived among the people, while the Essenes lived by themselves. Different views of the way to implement purity are involved — one by keeping pure within the world of ordinary people, the other by living apart from the world. One view is essentially monastic, the other is missionary or witness.

The origins of all three parties remain obscure. The Pharisees traced their philosophy to the Hassidim* and other early supporters of the Maccabaean uprising. Modern scholars believe that all the parties derived, in part at least, from the Hassidim but emphasized different aspects of their inheritance.

Inadequate Sources: The primary sources for our knowledge of both the Pharisees and the Sadducees are the works of Josephus* and the sayings of the Tannaitic rabbis, as preserved in the Mishnah*, Talmud and Midrash. In addition, the New Testament is also a valuable — if biased — source of information. In fact none of the sources presents a well-balanced picture. The Talmudic writers were either unable or unwilling to give full consideration to the social and political factors operating during the period. They concentrated on the legal aspects of all questions and saw everything as controversies on "halakhah" (guidance given on questions of civil and religious law). By drawing on the greater knowledge made available by recent discoveries and research, modern scholarship has been able to reach a fuller and more accurate picture of the Pharisees.

Pharisee Organization: Josephus gives a figure of 6,000 "ḥaberîm" (associates), which suggests an exclusive organization, closed to the masses. Because of the many minute regulations which governed their way of life and ensured their ritual purity, they lived together in separate villages or, in the towns, formed closely-knit isolated communities. Although this created a gulf between them and all those who were ignorant or careless of the punctilious care involved in strict observance of the law, the Pharisees did not deliberately avoid outside contacts. On the contrary, their activity was directed towards increasing awareness of Pharisee traditions and religious observance among the masses.

Pharisee Philosophy: Their way of life demanded total dedication to every detail of Mosaic regulations concerning ritual purity. To become a "ḥābēr" (associate), a candidate had to take vows of purity and holiness, undergo a two-stage probation period, and submit to a "ṭebîlah" (ritual bath), after which he was entitled to participate in the ritually pure meal of the fellowship. S. Lieberman and Ch. Rabin have both noted that these rituals were very close to those of the sectaries of Qumran, although other scholars add that the sectaries were much stricter about their observances. Furthermore, the Pharisees did not totally dissociate themselves from the life of the nation as did the Essenes. And they worshipped in the Temple, which the Essenes refused to do (see Dead Sea Scrolls*).

Tithing: One example of Pharisaic precision was their observance of the regulation (Nu. 18:26) to pay to God a tithe (one-tenth) of all food bought or eaten. To avoid any possibility of doubt, the ḥaberîm paid the Levite's "tithe of a tithe" on all food they bought, and refused to eat where there was no guarantee that tithe had been paid, i.e. in the houses of ordinary people (the "ammê-hā'āretz"). This practice is reflected — although negatively — in the New Testament. Jesus might be invited to eat in the house of a Pharisee, but they were shocked when he ate with "publicans and sinners", i.e. the "ammê-ha'aretz".

Ritual Purity: The Pharisees insisted on strict attention to the purity of everything concerning eating. It was a sin to allow their ritually pure food to be contaminated, by contact with an impure person for instance. Moreover, all vessels used, including the luxurious glass and metal ones imported by wealthy Jews of Hellenistic times, had to comply with Scriptural regulations. Otherwise, the Pharisees insisted, they were unfit for use. For instance, the Pharisees voluntarily ate their ordinary food under the same strict rules of purity laid down for priests eating the heave-offerings ("terûmah") or dough offerings at the Sanctuary (see Sacrifices and Offerings*). In addition, Levitical purity of clothing was mandatory for participation in the common meals of the ḥaberîm.

Pharisee Ethics: These are only a few examples of the Pharisees' devotion to the most minute details of religious observance. Considered by themselves, such rules seem a set of meaningless restrictions on daily life. A true perspective sets the hundreds of injunctions in the context of Pharisaic concern for personal purity and holiness before God. They demanded much higher standards of love and forgiveness from their ḥaberîm than from society in general. The considerable influence they achieved as a group also testifies to their high ethical standards. There were also the rules relating to domestic, economic and social affairs. At the time they were formulated, they were relevant to current circumstances and served to guide the life of the community. Today, on the other hand, many of these "ḥālākhôt" are completely out of touch with modern values.

Jewish life was regarded as a single whole, reaching its fullest expression in the community. The Pharisees and the rabbis never approved of ascetic withdrawal (like that of the Essenes or Dead Sea* sectaries). To them the service of God was part of an ordinary life of work and rest, among a man's family and neighbours. The "mitzvôth" related to everyday life at this level. Their observance sanctified a man, who could find real spiritual satisfaction in obedience. This pious manner of "life under the law" (see Law*) became a marked characteristic of post-Exilic Judaism, especially after the Maccabaean era. Fidelity to the Law rather than to the Temple cult became the real pivot of Jewish life. This made possible the otherwise remarkable phenomenon of the reorganization of normative Judaism after the destruction of the Temple in 70 CE (see Rabbis*).

The Pharisees were a human phenomenon. Like every mortal expression, there were both good and bad, with practice inevitably falling short of precept. In the light of the findings of the historians, and from an analysis of the whole range of existing sources, modern scholars, Christian and Jewish alike, are today prepared to defend the group against the age-old charge of hypocrisy. The Pharisees are now seen as men with faults and failings, but worthy of respect and admiration as a group.

The Framework of the Oral Law*: The Pharisees believed that the Mosaic Law was a continuous revelation. Oral laws (halakhôt) given to Moses at the same time as he received the Written Law on Mount Sinai made it possible, they believed, to adapt the Mosaic Law to the changing conditions of an increasingly complex society. These oral laws (see Law*: Oral Law; Mishnah*) they regarded as no less vital to the nation's life than the Written Law (Torah) and they endeavoured to place national life within this halakhic framework. Their elastic approach to the interpretation of the law enabled them to provide for new needs within the life of the community. They laid great emphasis on the intention behind each regulation and declared, for instance, that the vindictive "eye for an eye" (*lex talionis*) of Scriptures could be interpreted as meaning that a victim should be compensated for, and to the extent of, damage suffered, which may have been the purpose of the original stipulation. Such innovations had a lasting influence on the form of modern orthodox Judaism, the ancient Pharisaic ideals of purity and their form of celebrating the festivals being preserved almost intact.

Party Strife: The question of an orderly interpretation of the Bible brought the Pharisees into direct conflict with the Sadducees*, especially when the Pharisees made their interpretations binding upon the nation as a whole, including their opponents. The Sadducees rejected the Oral Law of the Pharisees and their elastic interpretations of the written code, demanding instead an exact observance of the letter of the Mosiac Law. They held absolute control of the Temple organization and feared the penetration of Pharisaic influence and innovations on their preserves. For their part, the Pharisees feared that a Sadducee seizure of power would result in anarchy and civil and religious strife. The mutual antagonism that existed between the two parties and which covered many spheres of life, had its roots in basic social differences.

Pharisee Social Ideals: The Pharisees dealt realistically with the struggle between the flesh and the spirit and deplored excessive severity in punishment. They were the party of the middle class of merchants and artisans as well as scholars and interpreters of the Law. They were concerned with the common people and, for example, in their argument with the Sadducees about who should pay for the Temple's daily burnt offering, took a more democratic stand, in this case that the cost should continue to be met from the fund of half-shekels paid annually by every Temple worshipper. The Pharisees also paid more attention to world Jewry than did their opponents, whose horizons were limited to the Temple and therefore the borders of Palestine. But the Temple tax was paid by almost all Jews everywhere.

To popularize the faith, the Pharisees also stressed the festivals celebrated at home — especially the solemn Passover service around the family table — and introduced folk customs like the Water Drawing Festival at the Temple on Succoth (Feast of Tabernacles; see Festivals*) which, not being of biblical origin, were disdained by the Sadducees. Most notably, it was the Pharisees who transferred the power of atonement for sins from the High Priest and his ritual in the Temple, to the congregational observance of the Day of Atonement itself.

Pharisaic Theology: Pharisaic theology included questions of good and evil, the immortality of the soul and the Last Days (see Eschatology*), and the meaning of fate. They believed in the resurrection of the dead and life after death; they shared the popular belief in the advent of a Messiah and the Day of Judgment, ridiculed by the Sadducees. While the Pharisees were prepared to find a place for many popular beliefs (such as angels and demons) within a multi-sided Judaism, they stopped short of the wilder extravagances of apocalyptic* literature.

God's Will and Free Will: Judaism was free from Oriental fatalism and determinism. The Pharisees believed that God had a purpose for the world, but they also believed that man must bear the responsibility for making his own choice between good and evil — cooperating with or rejecting God's will. They upheld the idea of reward and punishment "in the world to come" in which every man's soul would be judged.

Education: Judaism was the only ancient religion that set out to instruct the laity, a goal later adopted by Christianity. This goes back to the Old Testament where instruction of the people is a sacred obligation on every family head. Teaching the people was adopted by the Pharisees during Herod's reign as a means of establishing a solid national foundation of Hebrew tradition. They worked to educate every boy in the country. A "beth-midrash" for adults was established in every village. They served as places of study and quiet fellowship as well as worship. Only after the destruction of the Temple, and mainly from the 2nd c. CE, were synagogues built for worship alone.

Intellectual Revival: This popular education program was the foundation for the great academies like those of Hillel and Shammai. In these, research and study of the scriptures prompted the wealth of interpretations, judgments and commentaries on social laws that later developed into the Mishnah* and Talmud.

J. Klausner thinks that this expansion of intellectual activity among the Pharisees resulted from their political isolation under Herod.

Enduring Features: One of the main reasons for the Pharisees' greater influence was their more lenient interpretations of the Law. D. Daube feels that these were based on advanced methods of study, partly derived from Hellenistic rhetorical theory.

As Pharisaism increased in strength, the Sadducees clung desperately to the letter of the law and the shelter of the Temple. When the Temple and Jerusalem fell to Rome in 70 CE, it was on Pharisee shoulders that the future of Judaism as a religion rested. Their flexibility and their ethical and social outlook provided Judaism with a foundation and structure of belief and practice which enabled it to survive its subsequent tribulations. With variations, the movement of the Pharisees continued unbroken in the development of normative Judaism (see Rabbis*: Rabbinic Judaism; Law*: Oral Law, Life under the Law; Mishnah*: Halakhah. Regarding controversies between Jesus and Pharisees in the New Testament: see Jesus* and the Pharisees).

PHILISTINES AND THEIR CITIES. — **The Philistines and the Biblical Record:** In spite of misleading references to the Philistines and places connected with them in the pre-Mosaic stories of the Pentateuch, historically, this people first appear on the biblical scene in the days of Judges*. In the story of Shamgar (Jud. 3:31) we read that he killed 600 Philistines with an oxgoad. Much more important is the account, in the same book, of the struggle between the Philistines and the tribe of Dan. This has been preserved as a tale of single-handed heroism on the part of Samson (see Judges*) which ended in his death, after which a large section of the tribe migrated northwards. The activities of Samuel* and Saul* are mainly concerned with the continuing struggle of the tribes against their powerful enemy. Saul and Jonathan were killed on Mount Gilboa, far from the southern coastal plain which was the Philistine base. The enmity of the Philistines was a powerful factor in arousing a national consciousness among the previously divided tribes and in forging new forms of national unity. Fighting them also imposed the use of new forms of warfare* and arms* and weapons. The Philistines apparently introduced iron weapons to the Near East.

Once David* had assumed the kingship and united the nation, he turned to fighting the Philistines and defeated them decisively. After that, they were greatly weakened and are mentioned only sporadically in the Bible.

History of the Philistines: According to the Bible (Am. 9:7; Jer. 47:4), the Philistines came from Caphtor, "an island in the sea." This is identified with Crete, although the Hebrew word for island has the additonal meaning of "coastland".

It is generally accepted that they originated in the Aegean Islands, although W.F. Albright has argued that they came from Dalmatia, some of them reaching Canaan by way of Crete, others through Asia Minor. Other scholars maintain that they came originally from Asia Minor, perhaps Cilicia.

The question of the origin of the Philistines is bound up with the history of their settlement in coastal Canaan, which began soon after the Israelites entered the land (see Conquest*). Information about the Philistines comes mainly from Egyptian documents. In the half century which began about 1225 BCE, a flood of "Sea Peoples" invaded the coasts of Egypt, Palestine and Syria. They came from the Aegean Islands and the shores of Libya and the eastern Mediterranean. Some of them came by sea, by way of Crete, some from the northern Canaanite coast of western Asia. They upset the established civilizations of the Near East, especially the Hittite empire of Asia Minor and the kingdoms of Ugarit* and Tyre*, setting off a Dark Age of "barbarian" invasions. The invading "Sea Peoples" thus seem to belong to the period of the break-up of the Mycenaean (Greek) confederacy, just around the time of the Trojan War. The Greeks dated the founding of their colonies in Asia Minor to the time of the Trojan Wars, thus placing this period of pre-Hellenic migrations in the middle of the 12th c. BCE. This connects subsequent migrations to Egypt and Palestine with the tribes of Homeric legend (see Aegean Civilization and Palestine*).

The Sea People and Ramses III: From Asia Minor the invaders turned to the Egyptian empire. For six years, beginning in the fifth year of Ramses III (ca. 1190 BCE) successive waves battered at the doors of Egypt. The Pharaoh listed his enemies as including the Perasata or Pelasata — i.e. the Philistines, the Washasha, Danuna (Danaeans), Shakarusha, and Tjeker. By about 1175 BCE, Ramses finally halted them on his borders, erecting a series of monuments to commemorate his triumph. This picture of a battle at sea **(661)** comes from the Medinet-Habu reliefs. From the deck, Egyptian archers attack the Sea People who are shown clean-shaven and wearing the familiar high feathered headdress. Some of them are falling into the water.

No objections were raised from Egypt when the invaders turned aside and attacked the local inhabitants of the coastline of Canaan, destroying the Late Bronze Age cities they found and setting up their own centres at Gaza, Ashkelon*, Ashdod*, Ekron* and Gath, eventually giving their name to the whole area.

Later reliefs of Ramses III at Medinet-Habu show the same Sea People, wearing a distinctive headdress, serving as mercenaries in the Egyptian army. Their land probably provided a convenient buffer state for the Egyptians, protecting them from the troublesome Canaanites and, more important, from attacks from the Mesopotamian kingdoms further north. The two Egyptian administrative centres of Gaza and Beth-Shean* were settled by Philistines and other Sea Peoples. It is suggested that these two groups united. If and when they did, they proved more than a match for the Hebrew tribes who opposed them at the end of the period of Judges* and during the time of Samuel* and Saul*. Not only were the Philistines more experienced fighters, their monopoly of iron and metal working gave them an overwhelming advantage in weapons. During peacetime, the fact that "All the Israelites went down to the Philistines to sharpen every man his share, and his coulter, and his axe and his mattock" (I Sam. 13:20) was an additional means of Philistine exploitation and domination over their neighbours. (Iron working is generally believed to have been discovered in the Hittite region of Asia Minor; see Crafts*.)

For some two centuries the Philistines spread from their base in the coastal plain right across the central highlands of Judah and Benjamin. It would appear that they conquered Gezer* and used it as a base of operations from which they set out to conquer Ephraim north of Benjamin. David routed them and repulsed them to Gezer (II Sam. 5:25; I Ch. 14:16), and after establishing his kingdom he still fought them there (I Ch. 20:4). Though the fate of Gezer remains obscure until the second half of the reign of Solomon, it seems that David made most of the Philistine territory tributary to his growing kingdom; they ceased to be an important factor in the history of the Israelites. For a few centuries they clung to their independence. During the Persian and Hellenistic periods, settlers from Tyre, Phoenicia and the Mediterranean islands overran the Philistine districts and dominated cultural, economic and political life. Ashkelon and Ashdod (Azotus) became famous for their trade with Greece and Italy. From the time of Herodotus, the Greek name for the southern coast of Syria, the homeland of the Philistines, became Palestina or Syria-Palestina. The Roman administration under Hadrian extended the name officially to the whole of inland Judea. The old Philistine district along the coast retained its importance right through the Roman, Byzantine and the early Arabic periods. In the time of the Crusades, it was part of the "Seigneurie d'Ascalon" (see Ashkelon*).

Evidence of Archaeology: Some of the richest discoveries of biblical archaeology have been made in connection with the Philistines. Excavations in the coastal plain (Ashkelon, Gaza, Ashdod) have uncovered a certain type of decorated pottery* known as "Philistine" ware in all Early Iron strata (ca. 1200–1000 BCE). Typical of "Philistine" pottery are the two-handled jugs or bowls, buff in colour, with a creamy grey wash, painted in red and black with geometric designs or swans pluming themselves (**663**). The same type has been found in other excavations, becoming less frequent (with numerous exceptions, however) the further the distance from the Philistine heartland. Pottery of this type was found in the hills of Judah and Ephraim, in Beth-Shean

661

and even in Megiddo and Afuleh, giving colour to biblical reports of Philistine occupation of the hills of Ephraim and Beth-Shean (I Sam. 10:5; 13:3 ff; 31:10). None has been found in the Negeb.

Philistia and Greece in the Iron Age: All along the eastern shores of the Mediterranean, from Cilicia to Egypt, Mycenaean pottery and its provincial and orientalized derivatives have been found (see Aegean Civilization and Palestine*). The "Philistine" pottery has strong affinities with this Mycenaean ware. Almost identical pottery, dating between 1225–1175 BCE, which may also have been related to the Mycenaean ware of Argus in Greece, has been found at Enkomi in Cyprus. These pottery finds suggest that there were close ties between Philistia and Greece during the Iron Age. Additional evidence also pointing in this direction comes from implements brought to Philistia at the beginning of the 1st mill. BCE, pottery from Corinth brought in the 7th c. BCE and various implements and vessels which reached Philistia from Attica during the 6th and 5th cs. BCE.

The Evidence of the Coffins: Another striking indication of foreign contacts is provided by anthropoid pottery-coffins with a human face on the lid (**103**). The head is often surmounted by the same plumes which mark the headdress of the Philistines in the (Egyptian) Medinet Habu reliefs. In addition, two-pronged spear heads have been discovered in association with these coffins and with Philistine pottery. Coffins of this type have been found at Tel el-Far'ah, in the south of Palestine and at Beth-Shean*. The coffins and objects associated with them are typically Aegean and Cypriot. This has suggested — notably to T. Dothan — that a Philistine garrison may have been established at Beth-Shean by Ramses III, after he had repulsed the Sea People. He captured large numbers of prisoners during his campaigns. Usually they were drafted into his army and stationed as garrisons in various fortified centres he held in Canaan (see Beth-Shean*: A Philistine Garrison). It is believed by some that they were associated with the coastal Philistines, as the biblical story makes clear (see above). Apparently, these were the Philistines who defeated Saul and were eventually driven out by David.

Indications from Proper Names: Another source of information about the origin and affinities of the Philistines is contained in the proper names which have been recorded. For instance, Akish, the name of a king of Gath (I Sam. 21:10) occurs in Cilicia, while, on an Egyptian writing board, the similar names, Akesh (for a man) and Akeshet (for a woman) appear. The names of other Philistines, however, are of Semitic origin, and this seems to confirm the impression that the Philistines, after invading southern Canaan, were a thin ruling stratum of the population, intermarrying with the Canaanites they conquered, assimilating their cultural and social heritage. Other terms of Philistine origin are "koba'", a non-Semitic term meaning helmet and "seren" (prince), derived from the Greek "tyrannes" (see Organization, below).

The Religion of the Philistines: The Philistines apparently identified their gods with those of Canaan or adopted Canaanite worship and religion outright. Like the Israelites, they may have been influenced by the native cults (see Idol Worship in Israel*). However, whereas the Israelites reinterpreted these cults in terms of their own religion and associated the pagan shrines with Patriarchal* traditions, there is no evidence of such a process among the Philistines. They worshipped Astarte (Ashtoret, **93**) and Dagon (see Canaan: Gods and Idols*). A cult which seems to be specifically Philistine (though the name is Canaanite) is that of Ba'al-Zebub (Beelzebub), the "Ba'al of the Flies" (II K. 1:2, 6). Certain scholars have drawn a parallel between the fly-god and the Zeus-Myiagros (the god driving off flies) and suggest that the whole Philistine religion was taken over from the Aegean. Actually it is probable that the name Ba'al-Zebub was a deliberate and satirical pun on the part of the Israelites, and preserved by the biblical author. The original term was apparently Ba'al-Zebul (which means "prince" and the palace or dominion of a prince). The term is used as a title of Ba'al in the Ugaritic* epics.

PHILISTINE CITIES: Five cities in the coastal region, Gaza, Ashdod*, Ekron*, Ashkelon* and Gath*, were ruled by the Philistines. According to biblical and Egyptian evidence, all were fortified. Early Iron Age Ashkelon was not necessarily identical with the site of the Hellenistic city, though it was close to it. There is a famous Egyptian relief showing Ashkelon during a siege (see Ashkelon*). Excavations at Ashdod* were only begun in 1962; very little is known about ancient Gaza, and at present excavation is impossible. The site of Tel-el-Ajjul which Petrie claimed as "Ancient Gaza" is in fact the biblical Beth-Eglaim. A suggestion has recently been made that Ekron was situated on the site of Khirbet el-Muqanna, south of Gezer*. The most important of the cities, Gath, has not yet been accurately located. (Identification with Tel Sheykh Ahmed-el-Areyny which gave the name "Kiriat Gath" to the new modern industrial town, has been abandoned after recent excavation.) The story of David refers to other towns dependent on the Pentapolis, among them Ziklag, north-east of Beersheba.

Organization: The five cities, each ruled by a prince called a "seren", formed a federation, with the king of Gath at its head. It was their central organization which, together with iron weapons, gave the Philistines domination over the loosely linked Hebrew tribes. The Philistine threat was the immediate occasion for the change in the Israelite pattern of political life from the confederation of tribes to a permanent central authority initiated under the leadership of Samuel* and Saul*. (See also Philistine Civilization and Israel*; Aegean Civilization and Palestine*; Conquest*.)

The cities of *Ashdod** and *Ashkelon** are described and illustrated under Ancient Cities. *Ekron* is described below.

EKRON. — Ekron was the northeasternmost of the five Philistine cities which were the seat of "seranim" (Jos. 13:3; see Philistines*). It is not mentioned in ancient sources preceding the Bible, and was apparently founded by the Philistines. The Ark of the Covenant which they had captured was brought to several Philistine cities, first to Ashdod, then to Ekron after the battle of Eben-Ezer, and from there returned to Beth-Shemesh (I Sam. 5–6). Ekron is included in the inheritance of the tribes, marking the northern boundary of Judah (Jos. 15:11) and the southern boundary of Dan (Jos. 15:45), but these borders were theoretical, as Ekron is defined elsewhere as being part of the land remaining in foreign possession (Jos. 13:3; Jud. 1:18). This may be explained in the light of evidence apparently offered by recent excavations of Ashdod* (see article). D.N. Freedman believes that it was first occupied by the Israelites and later abandoned, possibly due to Egyptian pressure, and then occupied in turn by the Philistines. This author believes that if Ekron existed in the 13th c. BCE, it must also have been captured by the Israelites, then resettled by the Philistines. It is assumed that its inclusion in the inheritance of Judah (see Tribes*) appears in a context which seemingly represents a later editor's view; it may have been interpolated into the chapter of Joshua 15 in the aftermath of its conquest by one of the kings of Judah, Uzziah, Hezekiah or Josiah (see Israel and Judah*, Part III). II K. 1 refers to the worship of Ba'al-Zebub, god of Ekron. Opinion varies as to the meaning of the name, but the accepted view today is that it was the name of a Canaanite king called Ba'al-Zebul, distorted derisively into Ba'al-Zebub (god of flies). It is often referred to in prophetic writings (Am. 1:8; Zeph. 2:4; Zech. 9:5, 7).

Archaeological Evidence: A relief discovered in Khorsabad describes the capture of Ekron by Sargon II. The Ashdod* stele of Sargon, discovered in 1963 CE, is relevant to Ekron, as the capture of both of the cities was part of the same campaign in 712 BCE. An Assyrian inscription dealing with Sennacherib's campaign in Palestine in 701 BCE relates that king Hezekiah incited the Ekronites against their king, Padi, whom they delivered into the hands of the Judean king, but the Assyrian conqueror restored Padi to the throne (see Assyria*). Esarhaddon and Ashurbanipal continue to mention Ekron as one of the tribute-paying principalities. The city is not mentioned again in the records.

Post-Exilic Days: After a prolonged silence of some 350 years, Ekron reappears in I Mac. 10:89 and in Josephus' Antiquities 13, 4, 4 and we are told that Alexander Balas gave the city and its lands to Jonathan the Hasmonean (147 BCE). In the place-name list of Eusebius (4th c. CE) Ekron is referred to as a large village.

Identification: While several sites have been suggested in the coastal district, none seemed convincing until the recent archaeological survey made at Khirbet el-Mukannah, a site which appears quite likely. The survey showed that the ancient town there extended over an area of approximately

40 acres surrounded by a wall. A study of the architectonic remains reveals the actual place and form of the gate as well as several structures within the city limits or beyond it. The pottery is mainly Philistine, with vessels of Iron Age I and II and, in a higher layer, there was some Persian pottery including vessels imported from Attica (compare with Sharuhen Tel Far'ah). These findings fit in with data derived from biblical and intertestamental writings. Byzantine pottery, mostly of the 4th c. CE, was also discovered at a point northeast of Ekron; this may point to the large village mentioned by Eusebius.

PHILISTINE CIVILIZATION AND ISRAEL.— The Philistines were one of the Sea Peoples who are pictured in various Egyptian reliefs. The most important of these are the reliefs from Medinet Habu describing Ramses III's land and sea campaigns against them (**661, 2**). These show the "Sea Peoples" equipped with weapons which resemble, in part, those of the heroes of Homer and conform, in addition, to the Bible's description of the arms of Goliath (I Sam. 17:4–7). The soldiers wore a leather cuirass covered with metal scales, a wide belt around the waist and a fringed kilt falling halfway to the knee. Their helmets were made of metal with a piece of leather hanging down at the back to cover the neck, and held in place by a chin strap. A thick band of feathers was fixed to the metal band that encircled the head, giving them something of the appearance of the helmets worn by Homeric warriors. Many of the Sea Peoples wore helmets feathered like this, but they were especially typical of the Philistines, just as metal helmets with a metal comb were characteristic of the Shardana (later Sardinians). They carried a large round convex shield made of metal, or wood covered with metal, with a handle on the inside. Like the Homeric heroes, they carried a big, heavy javelin. The Sea Peoples also had light throwing spears and a short straight pointed sword, apparently used for stabbing (see Arms and Weapons*).

The relief showing a land battle (**662**) also features the cart which was the Sea Peoples' main vehicle in their migrations. It is made of wooden planks, with solid wooden wheels bound by metal rims and fixed to an axle by a dowel. The carts were pulled by oxen although the only harness which can be distinguished are strips of leather on the animals' necks. There is no sign of any yoke (see Tools*). Heavy carts pulled by oxen are reminiscent of the Philistine cart, harnessed to cows, in which the Ark of Yahweh was returned to Beth-Shemesh (I Sam. 5:10–14; see Samuel*). The Philistines fought only on foot. They made no use of war chariots which were apparently still unknown to them. Yet they were able to defeat the Canaanites who probably had chariots, as we learn from the Song of Deborah, but who were not a warlike people (see Cities*, Canaanite). The Philistines were made up of warlike bands, organized as a strong military federation; this military elite fought its way to southern Palestine after heavy encounters with the Egyptian imperial army and navy, then formed an upper group ruling the native Canaanites.

The relief of the naval battle (**661**) shows a Philistine boat with a mast and a large folded sail, and a crow's nest for a lookout. The boats are quite deep with high poop and stern. There is a rudder in the stern. Apparently these were sailing boats only. There is no sign of any oars. The Philistines can be identified by their feathered headdress.

Civilization: Until recent years, the sole source for information about Philistine civilization was the Bible. Since then, excavations in the Palestine Shephela (southern lowlands) and northwestern Negeb (the main areas of the Philistines and their allied tribes), have uncovered Philistine remains, notably pottery and tombs.

Pottery: One whole class of Palestinian pottery has been named "Philistine" (see Pottery*) on the grounds a. of the date — 12th to end of 11th centuries BCE, known to be the period of Philistine domination in western Palestine; b. distribution: all pottery of this type has so far been discovered in and around the areas of Philistine settlement: Dor, Megiddo, Affuleh, Beth-Shean which was a Philistine outpost, Tel Jerisheh, Tel Kassileh, Jaffa (Joppa), Azor, Tel el-Nasbeh, Gezer*, Beth-Shemesh*, Tel e-Safi, Beth-zur, Lachish*, Tel el-Hesi, Tel beit-Mirsim, Tel Jemmah, Tel Far'ah (south of Gaza), Ashdod*, Ashkelon*, Tel Ajjul (Beth-Eglaim), Khirbet Mukannah (Ekron*) and Tel Moor.

Mycenaean, Cypriot, Egyptian and Israelite Influences on Philistine Material Culture: More recently, on the basis of

662

663

additional material from new excavations, T. Dothan has tried to trace the various influences affecting Philistine pottery. So far, four have been distinguished: Mycenaean, Cypriot, Egyptian and Israelite.

The influence of Mycenae is most apparent in the form of the Philistine vessels. Like their originals, Philistine pottery is often in the form of craters, pyxids (**663**), stirrup-jars, three handled juglets and small shallow bowls (see Aegean Civilization*). Many of the motifs employed by the Philistines to decorate their wares — spirals, concentric circles, rhomboid patterns, Maltese crosses and the familiar bird pluming its feathers (**663**), all originated in Mycenae, and so did the fashion of painting them on the shoulder of the vessel in black or red on a white glaze (see Aegean Civilization and Palestine*; Pottery*).

Cypriot influence is also apparent in the details of the forms made by the Philistines, while from Egypt they borrowed mainly a juglet with a thick neck decorated with a stylized lotus pattern. A fragment of this type was found at Ashdod. From the Israelites came a "beer mug", a jug with a built-in strainer to remove sediment from the drink. Most of these vessels are a lively confirmation of the drinking habits of the Philistines reflected in the Samson stories (see Judges*).

Specifically Philistine pottery disappeared in the second half of the 11th c. BCE, its last stages being represented by a group of deep bowls found at Tel Kassileh and Tel Jerisheh (near Tel-Aviv), which still resembled Philistine ware but showed a much stronger link with other contemporary Israelite patterns. The excavations of Ashdod point out, on the other hand, that a transition took place there from late Philistine to a distinctive Ashdodian ware, also showing the shift to more characteristic local types.

It has been suggested that the evidence points to the pottery being a combination of various cultural influences gathered by the Philistines in the course of their wanderings, rather than a deeply entrenched native tradition. During the 11th c. BCE, these acquired customs were swamped by the new influences of their adopted land. Eventually, all distinctive characteristics were lost and in pottery as in other arts, the Philistines became completely assimilated to the local culture.

Anthropoid Coffins: A comparison between the contents of Philistine tombs in Palestine and those of other tribes of the Sea Peoples in Egypt suggest similar conclusions. The pottery anthropoid (human shape) coffins discovered in these tombs are generally ascribed to the Philistines on account of their decoration (see Philistines*).

F. Petrie discovered a group of five tombs at southern Tel el-Far'ah (Sharuhen) which he called the "Tombs of the (lords of) the Philistines". Two of these contained anthropoid clay coffins dating from the middle of the 12th to the middle 11th cs. BCE. The tombs also yielded a mixture of Philistine, Egyptian and Israelite style pottery. A similar combination (and mixture of styles) was found in Egypt, notably at Tel el-Yehudieh, Nabsheh, Anuba and other sites. T. Dothan believes that all these tombs belonged to mercenaries of the Sea Peoples who had been exposed to Egyptian and Israelite influences. The pottery coffins appear to be a Philistine version of a familiar Egyptian custom and the tombs in which they were found in Israel can be ascribed to Philistines.

Another very striking indication of the origins of Philistine civilization was the discovery of beaten gold plates, with holes for threads, designed to be tied over the mouth of the dead. An exactly parallel custom has been demonstrated from tombs of Mycenae in the Peleponese of the 15th c. BCE and in Enkomi in Cyprus from the 14th–13th cs. BCE. Philistine observance of the same tradition suggests that the roots of their civilization lay in the same area — the Aegean.

Metal Craftsmanship: The Bible records that the Philistines had a monopoly of metal working, chiefly iron (I Sam. 13:19ff) for both agricultural implements and weapons, and this has been confirmed by archaeological discoveries. Iron and copper craftsmanship was developed at precisely those places where the Philistines were dominant, e.g. Tel Kassileh at the mouth of the Yarkon, Tel Jemmah, Beth-Shemesh and so on. In other places where their influence is felt, Philistines were probably only a small part of the population, the military elite. The tombs mentioned above also included things like javelin blades, while the reliefs of Medinet Habu picture a variety of iron weapons in the hands of the Sea Peoples. As to the origins of their knowledge of metal working, the scholars are divided. Some give the Sea Peoples (Philistines) credit for learning the art during their wanderings through Asia Minor, where they took part in the break-up of the Hittite empire, including Anatolia, at that time the centre of metal working. The Hittite empire broke up after the Phrygian invasion; Phrygians and Sea Peoples may be related, or part of the same general movement.

Assimilation with the Canaanites: In the course of time, the Philistines adapted themselves to the conditions of their new country. They mingled with the local Canaanite peoples and adopted their language, religion and material civilization. It seems that this process had been completed by the end of the 10th c. BCE. It is suggested that this rapid assimilation was possible only because their own civilization was itself a mixture of cultures. More likely it is because underlying patterns were not disturbed; the Philistines were a military elite, few in number, while the native population remained essentially untouched and gradually assimilated the upper group. This western people with its advanced material civilization must have made important material contributions to Israelite life in pre-monarchic and monarchic days. The Philistines had a strong military organization and with it went social and political organization, all of which was basic to the organization of the Israelite state under David; he was at first a Philistine vassal, and later employed Philistines as mercenary troops.

Archaeology has not yet given a very clear picture of the Philistines and their towns (see Philistines and their Cities*) and therefore no generalizations as to Philistine and non-Philistine traits can be made.

The very beginning of their wanderings cut the Philistines off from their Aegean cradle, and the heritage they carried with them could not long withstand the variety of new influences which they encountered. By the end of the 13th c. BCE, the Aegean had lost all direct influence on their development and later on, their own original characteristics were equally replaced by the traits of their new environment.

(See also Philistines*; Aegean Civilization and its Impact on Palestine*).

PHOENICIA AND ITS CITIES. — *Outline: I. History: Origins; Phoenicia and Egypt; Independence; Contacts between Phoenicia and Israel; The Assyrian Threat; A Babylonian Vassal; Rise of Sidon; Under the Seleucids. II. Civilization: Trade; Shipbuilding; Other Industries; Ivory; Art; Literature; Religion; Writing. III. The Cities of Phoenicia: Byblos; Tyre and Sidon; Phoenician Colonies: Carthage; Tarshish. IV. Conclusion.*

I. HISTORY: **Origins:** The name of Phoenicia was once given to the northern coastal strip on the eastern shore of the Mediterranean, running from the gulf of Alexandretta and the Orontes river in the north, to Dor (just below modern Haifa) in the south. Until the 13th and 12th cs. BCE this area was part of the much greater territory of Canaan*. As a result of the migrations of peoples and invasions of that period, ancient Canaan* (see article) was divided between Aram (Syria) to the north, Israelite territory (including Judah and parts of Galilee) in the centre, and the land of the Philistines along the coast and in the south. The Canaanites were pushed back to a northern coastline **(385)** running a mere 200 kms. from Arwad to Tyre, a distance less than half that of the eastern Mediterranean coastline from Raphia to Ugarit, which they had once controlled (see map **385**). Later on, they pushed southwards down the coast as far as Jaffa, but only along the narrow plain on the edge of the sea.

Canaan took its name from the purple dye made from the murex shell, one of the oldest and most important products and exports of the country (in the Amarna letters, Canaan is written "Kinahhi" meaning "red"). In the same way, the Greeks called the remaining area of Canaan "Phoenicia", a word which means a red colour. Right through ancient history, this was the "land of the purple". Similarly, there is no historical break between Canaanites and Phoenicians. The change in name is merely an indication of a change in political and territorial status.

The result of the invasions of their land had been to deprive the Canaanites of nine-tenths of the territory that had supported their economy and their culture. Of necessity, they established themselves in their mountainous hinterland and developed the rich resources of the Lebanese forests — timber, especially cedar wood, and other products. They built themselves villages in the hills and assured themselves a good water supply, digging great cisterns which they lined with plaster and slaked lime (see Water Supply*). However, the main outlet for their skills and energies was seawards. They developed their merchant fleet and set up trading colonies all around the coasts of the Mediterranean. The discovery of iron in the Lebanese mountains made it possible to fit out their ships and arm their sailors without depending on other peoples. Soon the Phoenicians became the great mariners and traders of the ancient world.

The Greeks always claimed that they learned the arts of peace from the Phoenicians and recent discoveries have confirmed this tradition. Phoenician influence on the Israelites in the same sphere has been proved abundantly (see Crafts*). In fact, the highly individual culture of the Phoenicians fully entitles them to be studied and considered as more than merely a continuation of their Canaanite forebears.

Phoenicia and Egypt: While the prehistory and early history of Phoenicia (northern Canaan) has much in common in material culture, language (western Semitic) and religion, with the southern part of Canaan, there was one important difference. As early as the time of the Old Kingdom in Egypt (2778–2423 BCE), communication and commerce were closer between Egyptian ports and those of northern Canaan, than with the nearer Palestinian trading centres. Accordingly, Egyptian influence was much stronger and more deeply rooted in the north, and was never completely obliterated. Indeed, the earliest inscriptions found in Phoenicia were Egyptian documents unearthed in the great trading centre of Byblos (see below V, and Alphabet*).

Phoenicia was also close to the Aegean, especially Crete and Mycenae, and to Anatolia, the land of the Hittites. While influences from all these directions reached Phoenicia earlier and more intensively than they did Palestine, Egypt remained the most important external factor in Phoenicia's life.

The Amarna Letters* recall the struggles of the city states of Tyre, Sidon, Byblos (Gebal), Berut and Acre amongst themselves and against Amorite invaders. They remained, at least formally, under Egyptian rule until Ramses III's victories over the Sea Peoples (ca. 1190–848 BCE; see Egypt*; Philistines*). This victory expelled the Philistines and Sea People from Egypt's Delta area but sent them in force to Palestine and the lands to the north. Egyptian influence in Asia was thus greatly weakened.

Independence: Taking advantage of these conditions, the Phoenician city-states were able to throw off the Egyptian yoke and establish their independence. They formed a coalition led, at first, by Tyre (Phoenicians are usually known as Tyrians in the Bible), later by Sidon.

The low point in relations between Phoenicia and its former overlords was reached during the reign of Pharaoh Herihor (1085–1054 BCE). The new conditions are well illustrated in the Egyptian story of Wen-Amun, composed around 1100 BCE. Wen-Amun was an official of the Temple of Karnak, sent to Byblos to buy wood for building a ceremonial barge for the god Amon. The cedar of Lebanon, Phoenicia's most important export, was brought down to the coast and transported to Egypt, which was poor in

664

wood of any kind, by ships called significantly "Byblos-ships".

Wen-Amun entered Phoenicia through Dor, at that time inhabited by Tjeker, a branch of the Sea People (see Philistines*). There he was robbed of the quantity of silver and gold he was carrying to pay for the wood. Finally he reached Byblos by way of Tyre and opened negotiations with the king, Zakar-Ba'al, who was very unresponsive towards the Egyptian's request, "I am not your servant nor am I the servant of the one who sent you," and the deal was concluded only after Wen-Amun had made the appropriate payment.

The story is a good indication of the political situation in western Asia during the few centuries following the downfall of Egypt's empire and before Assyrian power had risen to fill the gap. Like Israel to the south, Phoenicia was able to profit from the temporary relief from foreign oppression to develop internally, both politically and culturally.

Contacts between Phoenicia and Israel: Naturally, the two small neighbouring states were in close contact at many levels. The Bible refers to the part of Phoenicia surrounding Byblos as Gebal, the correct form of the name (Jos. 13:5), and makes it part of "the land which yet remains", i.e. that was not conquered by the Israelites during Joshua's time. At the time the Israelite monarchy was established, there was no further thought of conquests to the north and good relations existed between David and Hiram, the king of Tyre (980–936 BCE). He was responsible for developing Tyre, especially its harbours and overseas commerce (see Cities of Phoenicia, below). He rebuilt much of the city and constructed the temple of Melkart (Melk-kart, meaning literally "King of the City", the name of the god of the underworld). When Solomon began the building of the Temple in Jerusalem, he contracted with Hiram for the supply of materials (especially cedar wood) and skilled workers. I K. 5:18 records that "Solomon's builders and Hiram's builders and the men of Gebal did the hewing and prepared the timber and the stone to build the house." They were paid for in wheat and oil but the great expense involved forced Solomon to take another step recorded, if not very clearly, in I K. 9:10–14. According to this account, Solomon leased Hiram twenty cities in western Galilee (in the region of Acre) in return for 120 talents of gold. This was a rich district of Palestine and, while the cities were probably of considerable strategic and economic value to Hiram, their loss was a real impoverishment to Israel, as well as a serious blow to Solomon's prestige. This probably explains the confusion of the account in I K. (which first records that Hiram complained of the poverty of these "cities of Cabul" and then how much he paid for them) and the discrepancy in the later story of II Ch. 8:2 by which time Hiram had become "Huram" and it was he who gave the cities to Solomon. The name is really the same as (A)hiram and (A)huram are the same name in different grammatical forms.

Hiram was also associated in Solomon's naval expeditions to Ophir from Ezion-Geber (Eilat), while the Phoenicians were certainly involved in running the copper mines there. Hiram was succeeded by Ithobaal (Ethbaal), Ba'al-Zur and then Abd-Ashtart, who was deposed by a group of conspiring nobles and replaced by a royal prince, Ithobaal (again) who was also a priest of Astarte. He extended his power over both Tyre and Sidon (see below) and is famous in history as the father of Jezebel, who married Ahab, king of Israel (see Carthage, below). Her daughter, Athaliah, married Joram, king of Judah and thus completed the links between the Phoenician and Jewish royal houses. These were amply complemented by commercial and cultural ties. The prophets might well fulminate against pagan influences (see Israel and Judah*; Canaan: Gods and Idols*, Cult). In the excavated palaces of Samaria*, beautiful Phoenician ivories bear eloquent witness to the luxury which the Israelite court imported along with its foreign queen.

The Assyrian Threat: Phoenicia's peaceful development was ended with Assyria's expansion to the west. In fact, Assyria had impinged on Phoenicia once before. In the reign of Tiglat-Pileser I (1112–1074 BCE) the city of Arwad had been conquered and destroyed. The invasion of Ashurnasirapli II (883–859 BCE), however, was the beginning of a long period of Assyrian domination. On the colossi of Calah, he recorded: "At that time I received the tribute of the kings of the seacoast, of the Tyrians, the Sidonians, the Gebalites (i.e. Byblos) . . . and of the city of Arwad which is in the middle of the sea, silver gold, lead . . . garments of brightly coloured wool, ivory . . ." (see Assyria*).

The son of Ashurnasirapli, Shalmanesar III (858–810 BCE) fought against a coalition which included Ahab of Israel (see Assyria*) at the famous but indecisive battle of Qarqar (853 BCE). Five years later (848 BCE), he was victorious at the battle of Hamath and recorded the tribute he won (among others, from Jehu "son of Omri") on the Black Obelisk (see illustr. **550** in Israel and Judah*). The bronze gates of his palace of Tel Balawat (at Nimrud) carried a similar boastful inscription including the fact that "I received the tribute on ships from the inhabitants of Tyre and Sidon" (**664**).

Inscriptions of Tiglat-Pileser III (744–727 BCE) also record the payment of tribute from "Menahem of Samaria, Hiram of Tyre, Sibittibaal of Byblos" and, again, from another ruler of Tyre, Mathanbaal ("Metenna"), 150 talents of gold. The Assyrian's death aroused hopes of liberation among many of the petty rulers of the west, and a revolt, almost certainly instigated by Egypt, followed. Hosea, son of Elah, king of Samaria, and Luli, king of Tyre and Sidon, both took part. The Assyrians, however, reacted by sending new armies on punitive expeditions. Shalmanesar V began the siege of Samaria and the city fell (722 BCE) to Sargon II (722–705 BCE). Because of its position on an island, Tyre proved a tougher nut to crack, even for the Assyrians. It held out for 20 years, then (in 701 BCE) fell to Sennacherib. Luli fled to Cyprus.

Sennacherib installed another Ithobaal as king of Sidon, but under the next Assyrian ruler, Esarhaddon, revolt again broke out in Phoenicia. A new king, Abdimilkut, challenged Assyrian power in 678 BCE. Defeated, he tried, like Luli, to escape by sea but a prism-inscription of Esarhaddon announces that he was caught "like a fish".

The Assyrian king concluded a treaty with Ba'al, king of Tyre, which in fact formalized Tyre's subservience and prescribed the goods which must be delivered in tribute to Assyria. At the instigation of the Egyptian, Taharka, a Pharaoh of the 25th dynasty, Ba'al once more risked revolt but, as so often before, Assyrian military strength triumphed. A stele found at Senjirli (ancient Sam'al) shows Taharka and Ba'al chained by fetters through their lips, led by the king of Ashur (**410**). What is remarkable is that at a time when size symbolized power and importance, the king of Tyre should have been depicted so much larger than the king of Egypt.

The lesson went unlearned. Tyre revolted again against Ashurbanipal (669–625 BCE) and although he captured the mainland Sidon, he was unable to take the island port of Tyre. In 612, the fall of the Assyrian empire brought a brief respite of independence to Phoenicia, but this was short-lived. The cities allied themselves again with Egypt against Babylonia and joined in the campaigns of Necho II, who was defeated at the battle of Carchemish (605 BCE) after which Nebuchadrezzar re-established foreign domination over Phoenicia.

A Babylonian* Vassal: The Phoenicians were no more favourable to neo-Babylonian suzerainty than they had been to Assyrian and again they fell victims to Egyptian intrigue. The Egyptian Apries (588–568 BCE) of the 26th dynasty, the biblical "Hophra" of Zedekiah's time, fomented a new rebellion in western Asia, and the Phoenicians once more bore the brunt of imperial reprisals. Nebuchadrezzar began a siege of Tyre which fell after thirteen years in 574 BCE. Ithobaal II was replaced by a puppet, Ba'al II, and after his death in 564 BCE, Tyre was ruled, like Carthage (see below), by an elected "šuffet" (shophet) or "Judge".

Rise of Sidon: When Cyrus, the new Persian conqueror, took over Babylonia's possessions (538 BCE), Phoenicia became part of the fifth satrapy of the Persian* empire. The people of Sidon allied themselves to the Persians in their war with Greece, which was in line with their own maritime and commercial interests. This made Sidon more important than her twin city, Tyre. A Sidonian became admiral of the Persian fleet which was largely made up of Phoenician triremes and men. They provided Xerxes with a fleet that was defeated by the Greeks at Salamis in 480 BCE. Later on, however, Sidon became involved in the intrigues of the Satraps against the Persian government and in 346 BCE, after a revolt by the Sidonians under Tabnit, Artaxerxes III destroyed the city, its inhabitants and riches, in a great fire.

When Alexander the Great issued his challenge to the Persian Empire, he followed up his victory at Issus (333 BCE) by attacking Phoenicia and seizing Arwad, Byblos and Sidon. The Tyrians tried to remain neutral but Alexander laid siege to their city and captured it after nine months (332 BCE). The causeway which he had built to connect the mainland of Tyre to the off-shore island has endured to this day, although it is now engulfed by drifting sand, see below.

Under the Seleucids: Phoenician domination had passed away much earlier with the rise of Greek commerce, seafaring and colonization in the preceding century (see Hellenism in the Near East*). Alexander's capture of Tyre marked the end of direct Phoenician influence in the Mediterranean (see Phoenician Colonies, below). Commercial leadership was taken over by the Greeks and the Phoenician colonies (see below) while the country itself became part of the Seleucid, then the Roman empires. Even so, the ports enjoyed a considerable degree of autonomy — greatly to the profit of their commerce and industry.

During the 3rd c. BCE, the Sidonians (Phoenicians) penetrated inland and established a colony at Maresha (Marissa) in the south of Palestine. Many inscriptions and, especially, the pictures of the "painted tombs" are good examples of the contemporary mixture of native Phoenician and Hellenistic cultures, see **314.** Even before this, a colony of Tyrians in Jerusalem* had given their name to the "Tyropean Vale".

II. CIVILIZATION: Much of the history of the little strip of land along the edge of the Mediterranean could be paralleled in the surrounding territory and few of the incidents made any significant impact on the development of the ancient Near East. What gave Phoenicia its importance was its unique culture and the way in which trade disseminated this culture across the ancient world.

Trade: Phoenicia is mentioned by many ancient writers (e.g. Herodotus) but by far the most colourful description of its cities and their commerce is in Ezekiel (ch. 27). For almost a millenium, when Greece was still a collection of feuding city-states and Roman dreams of empire lay far in the future, international trade and, especially, finance in the ancient world were in the hands of the Phoenicians. From the ivory of India to the tin of the Cassiterides and the jewels of Tartessos (Tarshîsh, near Cadiz), the luxury goods of civilization passed through the hands of the Phoenicians. From their original home midway between Egypt and the kingdoms of western Asia and Mesopotamia, they established colonies and trading posts throughout the known world. They were the first mariners to circumnavigate Africa and to establish trading posts on the west coast of the continent. Their connections with trading colonies all around the Mediterranean and within the great centres of the ancient empires gave them a monopoly of international finance, barter and exchange operations. They handled

665

666

long and short term credits, properly backed by insurance, mortgages and liens. They developed and improved the harbours used by their ships, making them safe and comfortable in all weathers. Their merchant fleet was for hire by the Pharaohs, the Mesopotamian rulers and the Persian kings. Their strength lay in their concentration on trade, never on power. Their weakness followed from their relatively small numbers, disinterest in agriculture and consequent lack of a broadly based agricultural economy to support them in time of need. Though little is known of their social organization, it is assumed by some that it was a continuation of the Canaanite* system, though it bore, in Persian and Greek times, the marks of these civilizations.

Shipbuilding: The most plentiful commodity in the land of the Phoenicians was wood. Cedar, oak and cypress were exported, notably to Egypt, and were also used to build a variety of ships in the Phoenician harbours. There were Byblos ships, plying between that port and Egypt, and Tarshish ships, the solid merchant ships that carried iron ore from Spain, copper from Ezion-Geber (Eilat) or gold from Ophir (see Ships*).

Other Industries: Apart from shipbuilding and timber, Phoenicia was also famous for two other industries. One was the extraction of the purple dye which gave the area its name, from the murex shell. Just south of Sidon, a huge pile several metres high was found, made entirely of murex shells which had all been broken in a particular way so as to extract the yellow liquid which had the unique property of dyeing textiles and turning them purple in the process. These huge clay vats (**665**) in which murex dye was stored were found in the Temple of Resheph (Byblos) and used for cultic and other purposes. Secondly, there was the manufacture of glass. Contrary to popular tradition, the Egyptians, not the Phoenicians, invented glass — but it was the Phoenicians who discovered how to blow it and who had a monopoly of making transparent blown and moulded glass vessels, as shown by this glass lekitoy (**668**) from Baqbuq in Tyre ("baqbûq" in Phoenician and Hebrew means "bottle", the industry lending its name to a locality).

Ivory: Ivories from Phoenicia found their way all across the world and have been discovered not only in Samaria but as far afield as Arslan-Tash and Nimrud (see Assyria*). The combination of Egyptian and Aegean influences with native Canaanite elements produced a distinctive "Phoenician style" in these ivories, and their production represented a substantial industry. Yet its original basis was in the art of the wood-carver, from which ivory carving is derived. There was plenty of wood in Phoenicia but by the 1st mill. BCE when the ivories were being produced, the diminutive elephants (**666**) which had once roamed eastern Syria and Mesopotamia had completely died out. The raw material — tusks — had all to be imported from Africa and India.

Art: In architecture and sculpture Phoenicia can be distinguished from the other regions of Canaan only as being more directly influenced by Egypt and the Aegean. In fact Egyptian influences entered the biblical world through Phoenician craftsmanship, rather than by the overland routes connecting Palestine with the Nile and its delta (see Roads, Transportation, Trade Routes*).

Literature: Very few literary remains have been discovered in Phoenicia beyond a number of inscriptions, mainly of a religious, commercial and/or commemorative nature. A few biographies of the later kings have been found on their sarcophagi, for instance, the long account of the life of Eshmunazar of Sidon (4th c. BCE) inscribed on his sarcophagus (**667**). Presumably, purely literary productions were destroyed in the course of the frequent destructions of the Phoenician cities. It is this general paucity which has given such importance to the library of Canaanite (and Phoenician) myths and epics discovered in Ugarit (see Canaan* and Ugarit). This literature has also provided supporting evidence for the accuracy of the other ancient source of Phoenician literature, Sanchuniathon, who, writing in Berut (modern Beirut in Lebanon) during the 7th c. BCE, has survived only in quotation by Philo of Byblos (see Hellenism in the Near East*). Beyond these two sources, there are only the slight indications of the religious practices and mythology of the Phoenicians provided by the biblical story of Jezebel and her priests of Ba'al, and the archaeological evidence about Phoenician religion from Carthage and the other colonies (see Canaan: Gods and Idols, Cult).

Religion: Apart from the religion practiced throughout Canaan and Phoenicia (see Canaan: Gods and Idols*), the special cults of Ba'alat and Resheph flourished in Byblos and elsewhere; see the 18th c. BCE temple of Resheph (**669**, cult objects) and the golden axe (**670**) found among the 13th c. BCE votive offerings to the god. In the version of the

667

668

669

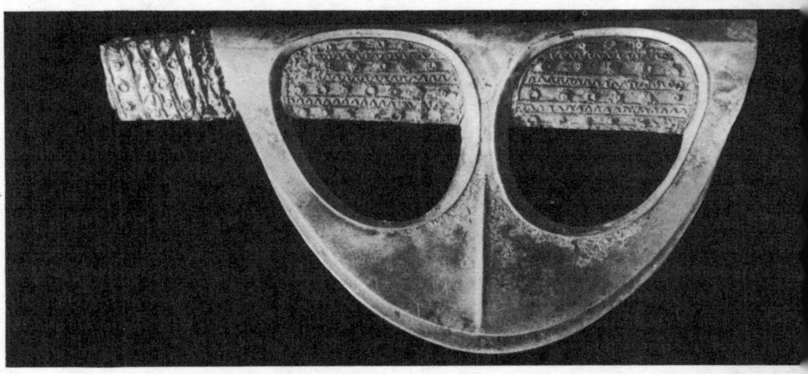

670

671

672

Canaanite myths recorded by Philo , Ba'alat of Gebal is the spouse of El, the chief god. The stele (**334**) shows King Yehumelek of Byblos presenting a libation to his goddess, the "Lady of Byblos". The cult of Adonis, the young god killed by a boar and returning to renewed life every year, originated in Byblos and flourished in classical times. This is a development of the ancient Tammuz myth (see Canaan: Gods and Idols*, Cult) in which Adonis is the son of the mythical Cinyras, king of Cyprus. Cinyras is a form of the Canaanite "Kuni-arez", "creator of the world", although Strabo calls him the king of Byblos.

Writing: The first paper ever used, papyrus, was exported to Greece from Byblos and the ancients believed (although wrongly) that it had been invented there (see Alphabet and Writing*). From their belief came the city's name, associated with words like biblios (meaning book), bibliography and the Bible, the book par excellence. A probably more valid claim for Phoenicia is the invention of alphabetic writing and script. Even though scholars may dispute whether the "Phoenician script" was in reality mankind's first attempt at cursive writing, its effect on later history is unquestioned. The Greeks learned the alphabet from the Phoenicians. (This is discussed at length under Alphabet and Writing*.) Through Phoenician traders and colonies, the culture and, later, the religious ideas of Phoenicia and Palestine penetrated to the west.

II. THE CITIES OF PHOENICIA: **Byblos:** Partly under the influence of biblical emphasis on Tyre, Phoenicia is popularly best known as the land of the twin cities of Tyre and Sidon. In fact, its principal port and most important archaeological site was the city of Byblos. The Bible knew Byblos as Gebal, which is probably a much older form of the same name. The Egyptians knew the town as "kepen" which, for the Egyptians who had no "l" and often used a "k" for the semitic "g", is an exact rendering of the town's first name of "Gebal" or "Gubal".

The first settlement was established there around 5000 BCE during the Neolithic Age. In the Chalcolithic period, a series of cities were built one on top of the ruins of the other. (These fortifications, **671**, date from the 2nd half of the 3rd mill.) At the beginning of Egyptian dynastic rule (ca. 3000 BCE) a flourishing trade already existed between the port and the kingdom of the Nile, and Egyptian influences were making themselves felt in art, religion and material life. Egyptian inscriptions from Byblos mention (first of all) the ruler Kha-Sekhemui, the first king of the second dynasty, and also the names Cheops, Chefren and Mykerinus, from the temple of Ba'alat Gebal, the lady of Byblos. From the many offerings made by Egyptian kings in this temple, it is clear that Byblos was regarded as part of Egyptian territory. The town was destroyed by fire during the Egyptian First Intermediary period, the time of Amorite invasions and the foundation of the first dynasty of Babylonia*. Inscriptions of Byblos of this time suggest periods of Amorite rule.

Egyptian control was apparently reestablished over Byblos during the Middle Kingdom of Egypt (the 12th dynasty). Caskets bearing the name of Amenemhat II (1938–1904 BCE) were found in Tod, in Upper Egypt. Within them was a rich treasure of gold and silver luxury goods fashioned in the typical Syrian combination of Aegean and Asiatic styles. It has been suggested (by R. Drioton) that this was a treasure sent to Pharaoh as a tribute from the king of Byblos. A little later, Byblos is mentioned again among the Egyptian enemies cursed in the "Execration Texts" (see Egypt*; Inscriptions*) belonging to the end of the 12th dynasty.

Byblos also has its place in Egyptian mythology. In one version of the story of Isis and Osiris, the murdered Osiris is put into a coffin which is thrown into the sea. It reaches land near Byblos and becomes part of a wonderful tree which the king of Byblos uses as a pillar of his palace. Isis hears of the fate of Osiris and comes to Byblos to free him from the pillar. This is a relatively late variation on the ancient myth but it may nevertheless reflect the long-standing connections between Egypt and Phoenicia, especially Byblos.

For a time, independence was restored to Byblos and the name of one of its rulers, Yantinamu, is mentioned in the Mari (see Babylonia*) archives (18th c. BCE), and also on a number of scarabs unearthed in Byblos itself. Even after Egyptian rule had been restored by Thutmosis III following the expulsion of the Hyksos from the Delta (1570 BCE; see Egypt*), Byblos continued to be ruled, like most Canaanite cities, by local vassal princes. One of the Amarna Letters* concerns a prince Rib-addi of Byblos who was being harassed by Amorite attacks. Egyptian domination was also celebrated in a rock-stele of Ramses II, dating from the 4th year of his reign (i.e. 1286 BCE), and found at the mouth of Nahr el Kelb (the Dog river) between Beirut and Byblos. His name was also found inscribed on objects recovered from the tomb containing the famous sarcophagus of Ahiram (see **484**, also Alphabet*). However, evidence suggests that this tomb was used more than once. Some of the pottery within it dates from the 10th c. BCE, while the writing is so close to that of the Mesha stone, **610**, and to the decorations of some of the Megiddo* ivories, that the Ahiram inscription has also been dated by some to the 10th c. BCE. After Ramses II, Egyptian influence in Byblos, as in the rest of Phoenicia, weakened until it had a brief revival at the time of the 22nd dynasty. A statue of Shoshenk I (the Shishak of the Bible, 950–929 BCE) was found at Byblos, dedicated by Abiba'al, king of Byblos, to Ba'alat Gebal, while a portrait bust of Osorkon I (Shoshenk's successor, 929–893 BCE) had apparently been similarly dedicated to the Byblos goddess by a later ruler, Eliba'al. These inscriptions reflect the prestige which the Pharaohs enjoyed in the area, even though neither Shoshenk nor his successor apparently conquered or even campaigned in northern Phoenicia.

After this time, Byblos seems to have declined in importance and prosperity compared to the other Phoenician ports, until the Persian and Greek periods saw a revival of social and religious life there.

Tyre and Sidon: The twin cities, Sidon on the mainland **(672)** and the island of Tyre **(673)**, shown in these aerial photographs of their remains, probably formed one unit right through the history of Phoenicia until the Assyrians established a separate dynasty at Sidon. Before that (e.g. in the story of Wen-Amun and the biblical account of Hiram's business connections with David and Solomon), only Tyre was considered worth mentioning. In the earlier period, the terms Tyrian and Sidonian are in fact synonymous. After Tyre was destroyed by the Peoples of the Sea (see Philistines*) in 1198 BCE, it was reoccupied as a Sidonian settlement and rose to its later pre-eminence as the seat of the Sidonian government, mainly under Hiram (see above). While the People of the Sea held the coastline of Palestine and Syria, the Sidonians were restricted to their tiny strip of territory but, after David's destruction of the Philistine empire (about 990 BCE), Sidonian expansion began on a grand scale.

IV. PHOENICIAN COLONIES: The end of the pause in imperial struggles over western Asia came (see above) with the resurgence of Assyrian domination (end 9th and early 8th cs. BCE). Assyrian pressure on the Phoenician hinterland and the threat of an interruption of their trade were reinforced by the ever-increasing seafaring activities of the Dorian Greeks. The Phoenicians reacted by setting up colonies throughout the Mediterranean.

673

Beginning as stopping places for their ships, colonies of Phoenicians throughout the Mediterranean developed into major trading and financial centres. The first to be established was undoubtedly one in Cyprus, the "New Town", almost certainly Kitium. Josephus, quoting Menander, records that the people of Kitium rebelled against Hiram I (969–936 BCE) and considerable Phoenician penetration of the island is proved by the number of inscriptions found there.

Following this came the establishing of trading "factories" in the Aegean then, as from the 10th c. BCE, colonizing activities in the western Mediterranean. These included setting up smelting plants in Sardinia and Spain. In general, colonization appears to have taken place in more or less the following order: Cyprus, Malta, Sicily, Sardinia, Carthage in North Africa, Gades and Tarsus in Spain.

Carthage: Founded in 814 BCE, also originally as "kart-hadasht" or "New Town", Carthage was ideally situated on the North African coast opposite Sicily, half way from Phoenicia to the straits of Gibraltar and the far-off coasts of England, Ireland and West Africa. According to legend,

674

675

the settlement was begun by Dido, great-grand-daughter of Ithobaal, king of Tyre and father of Jezebel. With a band of Tyrian aristocrats who were opposed to the city's ruler — her brother — she fled from her native city after her husband had been murdered by the king. (These, **674**, are parts of the lowest stratum of Tanit at Salambo, Carthage, 8–7th c. BCE, and urn and stele, **675**, of the 2nd stratum — 7th–4th c. BCE.) Once founded, Carthage flourished greatly. Blessed with a fertile hinterland, it became the main Phoenician centre in the central Mediterranean and eventually severed its links with Tyre. Even so, its contacts with the western world made Carthage one of the principal agencies for spreading knowledge of "Punic" (i.e. western Phoenician) culture and civilization. Its fame today probably rests largely on its role as Rome's rival but long before Hannibaal and his elephants made their celebrated march across the Alps (early 3rd c. BCE), Carthage had carved out for itself a lasting place in the annals of civilization.

Tarshish: In Accadian, Tarshish meant "smelting plant" and it was as a mining and refining centre that the Phoenicians built their colony of Tartessos, near Cadiz in Spain, and another one with a similar name in Sardinia. The manner of these mines and smelting plants is suggested by the great copper refinery at Ezion-Geber (Eilat) which was operated with slave labour and in which the Phoenicians cooperated with Solomon*.

V. CONCLUSION: The rise of Rome inevitably led to conflict with Carthage, which came to a head in the Punic Wars. After the first Punic War (264–241 BCE), Carthage had lost Sicily, and her possessions in North Africa subsequently fell to the Romans, leaving her with only her Spanish empire. With the Romans patently gaining ground abroad, Hannibaal set out for Italy to attack them at their heart, Rome itself. But for all his elephants and his long, hazardous journey across the Alps, he was repulsed. Beaten again on his native soil in 202 BCE, he was forced to sign a humiliating peace. For another half century, her peaceful commerce continued throughout the Mediterranean, and Carthage and North Africa prospered. Then came a new war with Rome, and in 146 BCE, Carthage was destroyed and the territories she had ruled transformed into a Roman province.

Nevertheless, for another hundred years the Punic culture of North Africa resisted Roman influence and continued to flourish. The language spoken by the people was known as neo-Punic. When Rome rebuilt Carthage a century later, it was peopled by North Africans speaking that tongue and worshipping the old Phoenician deities under new Roman names.

PILGRIMAGE. — The subject of pilgrimage in ancient Israel can be considered under four main heads: the semi-nomadic Patriarchal age; the period of settlement in Canaan, involving the adaptation of the Israelites to a life that included agriculture and increasing urbanization; the centralized monarchy under David and Solomon when power and worship were centred in Jerusalem; finally, the renewal of pilgrimage to the Second Temple from all over Palestine and the Diaspora (see below).

a. **Patriarchal Age:** Cattle raisers who have no fixed abode are limited to dependence on their flocks of sheep, goats and cattle. As soon as they turn to cattle-raising and even primitive agriculture, they have to establish centres to which they can return every year for a time. Such centres became the burial grounds for the tribe and this, according to A. Alt and M. Noth, usually led to the worship of tribal ancestors at the same place. This hallowed ground was not disturbed by other natives when the ancestors' clansmen were away. This was a general development by no means limited to the early Hebrews. Canaanite burial grounds were discovered at Jericho from a time when the people were still full nomads or semi-nomads and left no trace of urban remains. Existence of a tribal burial ground gave the tribe the right to possess and exploit the area. The story of Abraham's purchase of the Cave of Machpelah (Gn. 23) makes this point very clearly.

In a country like Palestine where small valleys and sparse vegetation could not support the whole tribe, a place for seasonal gatherings of the scattered members was essential. Such a place must have water and trees, and was usually the site of an ancestral tomb. The trees of Mamre were one such gathering-point. Bethel, Shechem, Hebron near Mamre, Gilgal and Beersheba were others. As time went by, the natural features of the places — trees, stones, springs — acquired a quasi-religious significance for the children of Israel. Thus, megalithic establishments (like Gilgal) or old Canaanite high places*, as in Gezer* (see article), already in existence before the arrival of Israel, became associated in ancestral memory with places where the God of Israel had manifested himself. The memory of "'El" under different titles (see Idol Worship in Israel*; Patriarchs*, Religion of) at various sanctuaries was crystallized into a single God who manifested himself at different places and times to the Patriarchs from Abraham onwards. There was only one God throughout the country, although different holy sites provided a variety of places of pilgrimage.

b. **After the Settlement:** The transition from the Patriarchal, semi-nomadic traditions of the earliest phase to the new conditions of a more settled life is well illustrated by the story of Elkanah, the father of Samuel. He made the yearly pilgrimage to Shiloh for the festive meal and was joined there by other members of his family who were not members of his household. Whereas the visits to the holy places were of immediate economic importance to semi-nomads, visiting a holy place later became a social occasion. Elkanah, for instance, could look forward to a meal shared by a large family group, for which the fattened calves could be slaughtered. This was a luxury which, under the sanitary conditions of the time, was out of the question for a single family unit. The tabernacle was established at Shiloh (see Sanctuaries*). Biblical tradition (Jos. 22:12) also records that the opposition to the building of a new altar east of the Jordan was centred in Shiloh.

c. **Three Pilgrimages under the Monarchy:** With the establishment of a central monarchy, pilgrimage became a national ritual act — no longer a tribal necessity. Three times a year, every male Israelite was enjoined to appear at the Temple in Jerusalem (I K. 12:26–33; II Ch. 5:3; passim; see Festivals*). Thus the Temple administration was supported by contributions from the whole country. These three pilgrimages focussed attention on the sacred aspects of Jerusalem and thus served to build up the prestige of the Kingdom of Judah in the eyes of Yahwistic believers everywhere.

For this reason, Jeroboam had to establish alternative places of worship at Bethel* and Dan, complete with the "golden calves" so bitterly condemned by the narrator (I K. 12:26–33) and the prophets. The split between the two kingdoms changed the pattern of pilgrimage, but not the official attitude to it. Bethel and Dan were chosen because of their religious significance for the people of Ephraim and Northern Israel. The Bible criticizes Jeroboam, not only for the "calves" but mainly because his new shrines were a threat to the religious unity of the people which had been fostered by the custom of national pilgrimages to Jerusalem.

When the Northern Kingdom of Israel fell, the reforming kings, Hezekiah and Josiah (see Israel and Judah*, Part V) tried to attract pilgrims from the rival shrines by a splendid celebration of the Passover Festival. Josiah did even more by eliminating the rival shrine at Bethel.

d. **Pilgrimage to the Second Temple:** By the time of the Second Temple, more than a million Jews were settled in countries far away from Palestine (see Hellenism and the Diaspora*). Nevertheless, the Jews of the Diaspora also considered themselves bound to sacrifice in Jerusalem, at least occasionally. Every year, especially at Passover, tens of thousands of pilgrims gathered in Jerusalem from Mesopotamia (Babylon), Persia, Egypt, Cyrenaica, Asia Minor and the Aegean Islands. Josephus sets the number of such pilgrims at 3 millions, which is greatly exaggerated and may be as many Jews as there were in the ancient world (some believe their number was 4 or 5 millions). That they were a considerable and colourful assembly is attested by the portrayal in Ac. 2:9–11: "Parthians and Medes and Elamites and residents of Mesopotamia, Judea and Cappadocia, Pontus and Asia, Phrygia and Pamphylia, Egypt and the parts of Libya belonging to Cyrene and visitors from Rome, both Jews and proselytes . . ." They came, bearing the prescribed gifts for the Temple (see Festivals*), and they stayed for a long time. Their visits represented an important economic asset for the country. Travelling by caravan, they entered the holy city in a joyful and picturesque procession. The Mishnah* describes Pentecost pilgrims "preceded by the heifer, his horns covered with gold leaf and his head crowned with laurels of olive leaves, pipes bursting forth in sound . . ." (Bikkurim 3, 3).

Even after the destruction of the Second Temple, the sages encouraged pilgrimage to Jerusalem as a means of forging strong bonds between the various communities of the Diaspora and Palestinian Jewry. The urge to pray at the site of the Temple lasted for generations after its destruction. Until the most recent times, the pious would go there, at great risk to themselves, especially during the Feast of Tabernacles, and offer the traditional prayers.

Relics of Pilgrimages: During the first centuries CE, the Oaks of Mamre continued to receive streams of Jewish, Christian and pagan pilgrims, paying homage to Abraham. Roman and Byzantine ruins of Mamre still exist at Ramet-el-Khalil, 3 kms. north of Hebron*. Possibly, the place found no mention in the later books of the Bible because their authors disapproved of the syncretist cult practiced there and wished to minimize its religious significance. Mamre was associated with an annual fair, presumably identical with the Batha (terebinth, in memory of Abraham) Fair, which is mentioned several times in the Talmud as a place which Jews should shun because of the idolatrous practices that were some of its biggest attractions.

POETRY, HEBREW. — The Old Testament uses a much richer vocabulary and a slightly different, usually more archaic, grammar for its poetry than for its prose. Poetic imagery — similes, metaphors, symbols — are used with considerable freedom, whereas prose style is kept deliberately plain and restrained. There also seems to be a clear-cut distinction between the functions of the two. Prose is used for legal sections, which contain practically no poetry, or for narrative — with the notable exception of the Song of Deborah (Jud. 5), which is a lyrical account of events in the Homeric style. Psalms 78, 105 and 106 are not really exceptions to this general rule.

On the other hand, while most individual poems are lyric in character, much poetic material is embedded in the prose narratives, especially in the earlier sections. In fact there is no strict line dividing prose from poetry in biblical Hebrew while the poetry itself contains so much variety that it is impossible to offer a single definition.

Poetic Form: Subject to this qualification, Hebrew poetry can be roughly divided into the following forms:

1. Hymns, prayers, psalms (see Book of Psalms*), dirges, love-songs (poetry in the narrower sense).

2. Lyric poems (which often incorporate older, popular sagas and songs). Of these, the best known are: the Song of Lamech (Gn. 4:23–24); the Blessing of Jacob (Gn. 49); the Song of Miriam (Ex. 15:1–18); the quotation from the lost "Book of the Wars of Yahweh" in Nu. 21:14–15; the well digging song (Nu. 21:17–18); the Balaam Poems (Nu. 23–24); Moses' Blessing (Dt. 33:2 ff); the Song of Deborah (Jud. 5); and David's Lament over Saul and Jonathan (II Sam. 1: 19–27). Most of these are, or include, fragments from a much larger body of pre-biblical literary material, well known to the biblical authors and their contemporaries. Nearly all the biblical poems are generally thought to have been composed before or during the 10th c. BCE. The same is also true of brief poetic interjections like Jos. 10:12–13; some of the Psalms, notably 29 and 68 and parts at least of the Psalm of Habakkuk (3:1–19), which used to be regarded as a much later composition.

Popular songs, sayings and stories belonging to a body of pre-biblical literature appear to have been incorporated in various books of the Bible, with the intention of brightening up the narratives. Only these fragments and a few names (like the Book of Jashar, Jos. 10:13; or the Book of the Wars of Yahweh, Nu. 21:14) are now remembered (see Bible Canon and Text*). Other similar collections are also suggested by references preserved in the Bible.

3. Echoes of folk or popular lyrical poetry and love songs, notably the Song of Songs* or Is.* 5:1–6 (see articles).

4. Gnomic poetry in "Wisdom*" literature and didactic Psalms.

5. Prophecy. The early prophets were almost all, if not exclusively, poets. Prose forms emerge only with Jeremiah* and Ezekiel*. The nature of the Hebrew language made it easy to turn to poetry for exalted passages and, at the same time, to create certain prayers in prose (in contrast to the Psalms of Prayer). This quality of the language helped to produce the supple fluctuations between the poetic and prosaic in Old Testament material mentioned above.

In addition to the foregoing, the conversational parts of Job — not the narrative — include actual poetic units, while the background to the book has strong affinities with the Canaanite poetic material of Ugarit* (see below). The books of Proverbs* and Lamentations* are altogether written in poetry. Other single poems of great beauty, not composed by the authors of the books in which they appear and not mentioned under 2 above, are also to be found in Dt. 32:1–23; I Sam. 2:1–10; II Sam. 23:1–7; Is. 38:10–20; Jonah 2:2–9; Lk. 1:46–55; 68–70; 2:29–32.

General Characteristics: The essential feature of Hebrew poetry is parallelism — symmetry in pattern of either content or form. Only in the older folk poetry is rhyme found. Assonance and alliteration are frequent right through and rhythm, refrains and word play also occur. In fact, Hebrew poetry reveals the characteristics of poetry anywhere. In general, however, the form is rather one of free verse, which gave the greatest scope for flexibility and variety. The unifying features come from the ease with which Hebrew sentences, or parts of them, can fall naturally into lines of approximately equal length; from the themes of the poetry and from the vividly imaginative language in which they are expressed.

Many examples can be quoted of the exceptional power of Hebrew poetry to weld sounds and feeling — for instance the galloping of the horses at the rout of Ta'anach:

"Then loud beat the horses' hoofs
with the galloping, galloping of his steeds." (Jud. 5:22).

Within a very simple form, great intensity of feeling could be combined with vividly realistic descriptions. It was a language inviting the use of bold and imaginative metaphor. The hills could indeed sing for joy, the stars in their courses fight against Sisera or the sun and moon stand still at the battle of Gibeon.

Parallelism: Parallelism is the device of repeating every statement in different terms, or emphasizing it by an antithesis:

"The people who walked in darkness have seen a great light;
those who dwelt in a land of deep darkness, on them has light shined."
(Is. 9:2)

The two parallel "members" (phrases) combine to produce a greater impact than each one would separately. This parallelism is an essential part of Old Testament poetry. Without it, much of the beauty of the verse is lost. There are many examples of similar full parallelism (e.g. Ps. 119, 105), but the more familiar is a slightly incomplete form, e.g. Is. 1:3:

"The-óx knows its-ówner,
and-the-áss its-master's-críb"

In these two phrases, although the verb "knows" has no actual parallel in the second line, it clearly governs both parts of the sentence. Similarly, in the second line, the "master's crib" is a variation on the first line's "owner". Nevertheless, the repetition of the idea that domestic animals recognize (know) the master who feeds them is sufficiently emphasized.

In this example, the two half lines in the Hebrew text each contain three accented syllables (or beats), which is the measure most commonly used. (The English reader should keep it in mind that each group of hyphenated words is a single Hebrew word.)

Another example of parallelism, using the same measure, comes from the Song of Moses (Dt. 32:1):

"Give-eár, O-heávens, and-I-will-speák
and-let-the-eárth heár the-words-of-my-móuth."

Here again, each member of one part corresponds (is parallel) to the members in the second part but, together, they have a fuller meaning than either of them separately, since the ideas of heaven and earth combine to convey the impression of the whole universe. This is an example of full parallelism, which is rare in the Old Testament. The more familiar form is that of the first example (Is. 1:3).

In either case, care is taken so that (in the Hebrew) the number of words, but even more the general balance and symmetry of the line of both parallel parts, is kept in some constant relation (3:3; 4:4; 3:2 or 4:3). There is no strict rule about the form such parallelism must take. In fact an indefinite number of subtle variations seems possible.

Measure (Metre): Hebrew metre (or measure) is generally governed by the number of strong accents in the words, the intervals being filled by the unaccented syllables, which are important to the rhythm of the accented ones and are pronounced in such a way as to keep the lines as a whole to an even beat. Ch. Rabin states that "the difficulty with Hebrew metre — which has been endlessly discussed — is that the number of intervening unaccented syllables is not constant, as it is in European accentual poetry, but varies apparently without any rules. This is what gives Hebrew poetry its peculiar appearance of free verse. Various solutions have been proposed. One is that in biblical times the language was pronounced in such a way that the number of syllables was regular. Another is that the speed with which the unaccented syllables was pronounced varied and if there were many, they were pronounced very quickly."

The most frequently-used measure is three strong accents to a line. (The division of poetical sentences into clauses of regular length 3:3; 3:2; etc. is observable whether or not there are parallels.) It results in regularly spaced pauses so that the rhythm can be clearly heard when the poetry is read aloud. Parallelism is a feature of the poetry's style, but the division of the text according to its meaning into more or less regular units is a feature of basic poetic structure.

In the more majestic psalms and poems, a broader rhythmic effect is obtained by suddenly breaking into a 4:4 rhythm:

"Sińg to the Lońd, for he has tŕiumphed glońiously;
the hońse and his ŕider he has thrown into the śea."

(Ex. 15:21), an example in which there is no parallelism.

Alternately, the 3:3 rhythm may be resolved into a 3:2 measure:

"I am the ḿan who saẃ sorroẃ; by the ŕod of His ẃrath."

This 3:2 metre, with its falling cadence, is used in the "Qînāh" or dirge (a relatively late style), although it is also used in cheerful songs. In general, the 3:2 measure closely echoes the fall of a voice choked by strong emotion, whether of sorrow or joy.

There is enormous variety in the metrical patterns and forms of Old Testament poetry and it calls for great flexibility in reading aloud. For this reason, confusion easily arises. Sometimes this may be caused by ignorance of poetry in general. Poetry which defies rigid rules of scansion exists in many other languages — e.g. English. The main difficulties however arise from the fact that Hebrew has no ancient theoretical tradition, comparable to the Greek; nor is it known precisely how the language was pronounced in Old Testament times. Careful study of Old Testament poetry and its comparison with the almost identical features of Accadian and Ugaritic poetry merely reveal an apparently simple system of beat (or word) counting. The earliest poetry of Israel reveals the alternation of metrical forms with repetitive parallelism. In Psalm 68, for instance, the pattern 2:2:3 appears in both verses 1 and 5:

"Let Ǵod aŕise, let his eńemies be ścattered;
let those who haśe him fleé befóre him!" (68:1)

"Fatheŕ of the fatheŕless and proteċtor of widoẃs
is Ǵod in his hóly habítation." (68:5)

This resemblance to Canaanite forms is not surprising in view of the numerous similarities to Canaanite style in the text of the psalm (see below, Canaanite Influence on Early Hebrew Poetry).

It is possible, although improbable, that the poets actually followed a much more precise and complicated set of conventions. Nevertheless, reasonable and sensitive application of the beat-counting system has been a great help to interpreting the poetry. One result has been the discovery of stanzas in some pieces of Old Testament poetry.

Occasionally, the stanzas are marked by a refrain ("sēlah"; e.g. Ps. 42, 43, 46; Is. 9:8–21; Am. 4:6–11). The word "sēlah" remains a problem for scholars. Its etymology is unknown and although many interpretations give it a meaning such as "forever" or the like, it remains obscure. It seems to mark poetic sections. To judge from the Septuagint* translation, it signified a change in the tune, a pause or a raising of the voice (see Music*: The Sound of Israelite Music). The placing of the refrain in the stanzas shows that a series of parallel units were joined to form the larger group of the stanza. In the Psalms, these stanzas are by no means of a uniform length of two parallel units.

Canaanite Influences on Early Hebrew Poetry: The study of archaic Hebrew and of the history of the language's development has been greatly helped during the last four decades by an expanded knowledge of related and especially earlier dialects with a north-west Semitic background. Comparison with ancient Hebrew has contributed to a better understanding of these forgotten languages and has also made it easier to distinguish and understand the function of the archaic speech forms found in both Hebrew poetry and other ancient Semitic literary texts. Hebrew scholars like Prof. Ch. Rabin do not analyze the old forms in Hebrew poems in terms of classic Hebrew grammar and vocabulary, but rather through parallel usage in, for instance, the poems of Ugarit*, which use an archaic form of early Hebrew.

Some important results have been achieved by the application of the disciplines of Form Criticism and linguistics (see Biblical Criticism*) as well as from traditional source criticism.

Affinities with Canaanite Poems: The striking similarities in form and language between certain of the earliest biblical poems and the epics of Ugarit* were first remarked by H.L. Ginsberg in 1936. They have since been studied by U. Cassuto and, more recently, by W.F. Albright and his school and it has been established that parallel literary conventions existed as well as considerable similarity in diction.

Although Hebrew poetry remains highly individual, it is clear that its technique was modelled on that of its neighbours. Some of the Hebrew Psalms reflect the influence of Canaanite patterns of composition. Psalm 29, in particular, seems to be a borrowing from the Ugarit epic of the "Rebellion and death of Ba'lu". The Hebrew poets described Yahweh, just as the Canaanites spoke of Ba'al (see illustration under Canaan: Gods and Idols*), as "a storm-god riding in a cloud-enveloped chariot, uttering peals of thunder and sending out darts of lightning; and they even borrowed Ba'al's epithet of the 'Cloudrider' and transferred it to Yahweh." (H.L. Ginsberg). The Canaanite concept is illustrated in **581**.

In another Ugaritic text, one of Ba'al's allies encourages him before a battle with the words:

"Lo, thine enemy, O Ba'al,
thine enemy wilt thou smite,
Lo, thou wilt cut off thine adversary,
Thou'lt take thine eternal kingdom,
Thine everlasting dominion."

The Psalmist expresses his confidence in the ultimate triumph of righteousness with the words:

"For lo, thy enemies, O Lord,
for lo, thy enemies shall perish;
all evildoers shall be scattered." (Ps. 92:9)

These and similar examples have led many scholars to conclude that, as in the other spheres of art, Hebrew poets were strongly affected by styles and modes of expression of their highly sophisticated Canaanite neighbours (see Phoenicia*, Ugarit*). In particular, W.F. Albright and his school have drawn attention to the verbal and stylistic affinities with Canaanite literature of such early poems as the Song of Miriam (Ex. 15); the Song of Deborah (Jud. 5), the Blessing of Moses (Dt. 33) and the 68th Psalm, while many other early poems — among the Psalms and outside them — show the same, although lessened influence.

This should not be taken to imply that the early Hebrews borrowed their poetic techniques and traditions wholesale, but Hebrew poets could — and did — draw on the work of Iron-Age Canaanite bards who had cultivated the style which gave biblical verse most of its formal appeal. In the event, the Hebrew pupils far outstripped their teachers, but that fact should not obscure the extent of the Hebrew debt to Canaanite thought patterns and forms of expression.

The biblical writers discriminated in what they absorbed from their neighbours, rejecting polytheistic (mythical) elements except for those given a metaphorical significance and used merely as poetic decorations. The poetic substratum and background of the book of Job, for instance, including actual passages of poetry, has strong affinities with the Canaanite poetic materials from Ugarit, although in Job, the account (38:8–11) of the struggle with the sea (the monster Yām in Canaanite mythology) is followed (13–15) by an affirmation of the impotence of the wicked against the strength of the righteous God.

Similar allusions can be found in other poetic passages in the Bible which refer metaphorically to the "Combat myth" in terms of God's victory over his enemies (Is. 17:12–14; 27:1; 51:9–10; Hab. 3:8–15; Ps. 74:13–15). Expressing the punishment of the wicked in terms of a mythical conflict between God and the rebellious forces of primeval chaos (see Astronomy* and Creation*) is a familiar device. In the Ugarit texts, the struggle is between Ba'al and Yām (or Lotan or similar attributes under a different name). In the Babylonian myth of Creation* the same symbol of conflict is used as an explanation for the whole cosmos.

U. Cassuto used the Ugaritic epics to establish that the Hebrew legend of creation also contained an element of an independent, popular myth of the struggle between God and mutinous primeval forces. In the normal course of artistic development, the myth was forgotten while its formulation became part of literary convention.

Were There Hebrew Epics? Not only does the Bible contain the many early poems mentioned above which bore a close relation to the epics of the Canaanites; in other sections of the early prose books, the language is very similar. This suggests that the books may be adaptations of much older verse epics. The fragments of poetry included in the present versions represent the original form of the whole epics. Did ancient Israel possess a popular independent national epic, or only individual poems which referred to certain events, interpreted in the spirit of the Israelite religion?

It is difficult to give a definite answer. Certainly there is no epic to be found in the Bible now. Behind the present narratives may lie something like an epic, but probably it is more accurate to speak of sagas or their poetic forms.

Post-Exilic Poetry: Hebrew poetry of the 4th to 1st cs. BCE lies outside the Canon of the Old Testament. Most of the poetry that is known from the literature of this period (see Apocrypha*) is lyric in type, like the lyric poems in Ecclesiasticus*, the poems in I Maccabees, occasional poems in Tobias (13), in Judith (16) or Baruch (4:5–5:9) and some wisdom poetry. Apocalyptic writings include the poetry of the "Psalms of Solomon" or the "Prayer of Menasseh", which are also lyrical in style. Finally, the Dead Sea Scrolls* included hymns and psalms.

The verse of Ecclesiasticus (Ben Sira, see Apocrypha*) consists of two hemistichs with four stress accents each (4:4 metre). These are divided into a variety of units, ranging from a single epigram, like a proverb, complete in itself, to the long poems of 42:15–43:33 (in praise of God); 44–49 (in honour of ancestors) or (50) the praise of the high priest Simon. The number of verses of the poems follows a conventional pattern apparent since the earliest compositions (e.g. Job) and varies between 17 and 39.

The laments or praises of the Maccabaeans in I Maccabees usually follow classical, scriptural models far too closely for brilliance or originality. On the other hand, the psalms of this period show a development beyond the latest Old Testament psalms. Their language is neo-classical and reveals the influence of wisdom forms, while the ancient patterns of symmetry and parallelism have largely disappeared (tendencies which had already been at work in the latest Old Testament poetry).

This is particularly relevant to the poetry of the New Testament and that of the Dead Sea sectaries. The Qumran Psalms of Thanksgiving, in particular, imitate the biblical psalms so closely that despite a totally different mood and theological content, many of them are merely patchworks of phrases from the Psalter and, especially, the prophets. Many of these poems continue the use of parallelism, although in a much freer, non-rhythmic form, occasionally using rhyme. Additional parallels can be found between the hymns of the Apocrypha* and the poetry of the N.T. (Revelation*).

POTTERY. — The material most cheaply and easily available to a man's hand is the soil or clay of the earth. Mixed with water it becomes plastic and can be moulded into all kinds of objects and vessels which, when baked, become hard and relatively durable. Long before biblical times, man had mastered the art of making pottery. Clay was used for every kind of vessel, particularly those for storing, cooking and consuming food and drink, but also for vases, perfume jars, household idols and cultic statuettes and even toys.

Pottery can be formed either by hand or by using a potter's wheel. The earliest pottery found in Palestine comes from the Neolithic period (5000–4000 BCE) and was hand made. The potter's wheel was first developed in Egypt and Mesopotamia around the beginning of the 3rd mill. BCE. Wheels were known in Palestine only in the second half of that millenium. This introduced the principle of centrifugal force into ancient ceramics, by a process described by J.L. Kelso: "a ball of good plastic clay is placed at the centre of the wheel, which is then turned rapidly . . . The action of the centrifugal force upon the ball of clay as it is modified by the fashioning hand of the potter produces the shape. This gives to thrown pottery a liveliness and spontaneity of form that no other method can approach."

The fact that a mistake can be corrected by reshaping the clay into a ball and starting again inspired Jeremiah's famous analogy (18:6) comparing the House of Israel to "clay in the potter's hand".

Once the art has been mastered, an infinite variety of forms are possible. Because of this, pottery became an important vehicle for artistic expression and also, of course, reflected the changing daily needs of the people who made it. Moreover, pottery is fragile. The lifespan of a pot in daily use is only a matter of a few months and hardly more than 30 years for more valuable items and heirlooms. Pottery forms accordingly underwent frequent changes, at least every generation.

When ancient sites are excavated, the most numerous finds are always the potsherds (pieces of broken pottery discarded by their owners). These ensure that the archaeologist has plenty of evidence of the kinds of pottery used. Just as the widespread use of similar forms of vessels among allied peoples is a common human characteristic, so is the almost contemporary spread of newly introduced types. It is possible, therefore, to say that certain groups of people in, for instance, Early Bronze Age Canaan, using the same type of pottery, were more or less contemporary. The appearance of a different type or style of pottery in an ancient site provides a reliable point of chronological reference. With the help of other common objects such as tools or knives, a reasonably accurate picture of the sequence of pottery forms in Palestine has been built up, from the Chalcolithic (cf. Chronology) through the various stages of the Bronze and Iron Ages and then Graeco-Roman and later periods. The form and decoration of each ceramic sherd, the degree of baking, and the relative quality of the clay reveal the origin and date of manufacture. Changes of style suggest foreign influence or new populations. Technical skill reflects prosperity and taste as well as degrees of progress.

Pottery Chart: Examples of the main pottery of every period, ranging over four millenia, are given in this chart **(676)**.

676

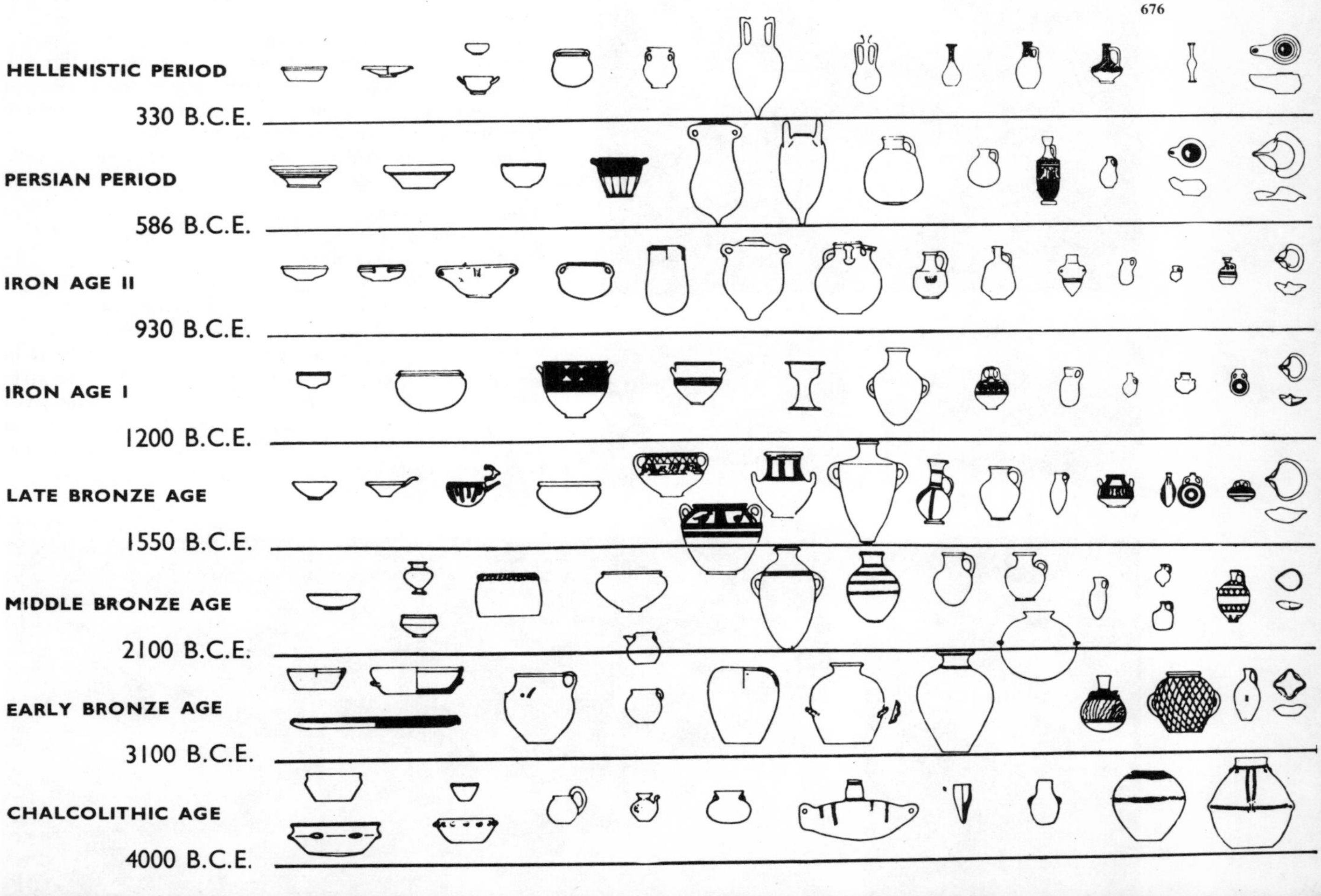

677

678

679

679 a

Besides differentiation due to time, there is also a differentiation on the basis of geographic area. Even in prehistoric times, there is a difference in shape and decoration between the north and the south of the country. In the period of the divided monarchy, Israel and Judah not only had different kings but distinctive types of pottery as well. One of the best known examples of a type of pottery specific to a certain people is the so-called Philistine ware (see Philistine Civilization and Israel*).

The Potter's Wheel of the Middle Bronze Age: By the beginning of the Middle Bronze Age II (2100–1550 BCE) the hand potters of Canaan had already become masters of their trade. They first used a wheel only for the rims of larger vessels.

From the Hyksos period (18th c. BCE) wheel-made pottery became the rule. The wheel was a round stone originally turned by hand. Later on, during the period of the Second Temple, the wheel was attached by a beam in its centre to a lower, larger stone, which was revolved counter-clockwise by the potter's feet. The potter's art has not changed perceptibly since the beginning of the 2nd mill. BCE. Artisans in various parts of the world work today with the same tools **(677)** and the same methods. The difference between hand-made and wheel-made pottery is that pottery made on the wheel has none of the horizontal lines on the inside which hand-made pots always have, and perfect symmetry is only possible with the use of a wheel. Pottery wheels have been found in Megiddo*, Lachish* and other excavated sites. The figure of a potter turning a dish on a simple wheel **(678)** was found in an Egyptian tomb dated around 2500 BCE. This is a potter's wheel from early Bronze Megiddo (**679**, the lower stone to the right, upper one to the left; compare with **695**).

Hyksos wheel-made pottery **(679a)** at first repeated and developed the forms already in use. Many of the pieces were really imitations of metal vessels. The vessels made for everyday use were imitated exactly, even the metal rivet that had been used to fix the handle to the neck of a vase was represented by a clay blob at the same spot without any real function or decorative purpose. Carinated vessels (those with sharp angles) have the same appearance as the corresponding copper work.

Kilns: Hyksos ware was also an improvement on earlier pottery because of the use of a more efficient kiln for firing. The type of kiln used right up to Roman times is illustrated by the Gezer pottery kiln **(680)**, dating from the Bronze Age, or that used at Qumran **(681)**. The pots were stacked above the furnace on a shelf pierced by a number of flues.

This period saw practically no importations. The pottery was coloured grey for ordinary ware, or pink or beige in finer pieces. Decoration is rare in either. In spite of great variety of form, the pieces clearly belong to the same style. Jars were made with long, funnel-shaped necks and ovoid bodies with a pointed base, sometimes resting on a small base, otherwise on a tripod **(679b)**. The handles were elegantly curved, the details carefully moulded. The most frequently found items were small jars **(676)**, jugs with trefoil openings, pitchers with printed lip, footed vases of different depths, bowls and dishes varying from the most simple to complicated forms, jars with or without handles, and large pots and pitchers (see Middle Bronze, **676**)

The Potter's Art in the Late Bronze Age (1500–1250 BCE): Pottery decorated in rich patterns of red and olive **(682)** represents the peak of the Canaanite phase. During this period, the country was under Egyptian domination and open to foreign influences from the Aegean and elsewhere. A high level of civilization and extensive trade accounted for considerable imports of pottery and local imitation of foreign ware. Note, for instance, this gracious vase with close affinities to Mycenaean (Greek) ware, **684**, from Megiddo. See **448**; **16**; **17**.

After the conquest of Canaan, there was a marked decline in quality and the Iron Age I (1200–930 BCE) produced pottery of a lower technical standard. The old culture had been disrupted; contact with the outside world was interrupted and, for a time, the influences of foreign pottery ceased. Philistine painted pottery belongs to this period, but it is not characterized by the lower standards of the neighbouring Israelite territory. It is highly artistic and shows distinct affinities with the Aegean areas. A new feature of the time was the small pitcher with handles attached to the middle of the neck (**683**; see also ill. **16**, Aegean Civilization in Palestine*; Philistine Civilization and Israel*).

680

681

683

682

684

685

686

686 a

687

688 a

688 b

Before the Iron Age, an outstanding innovation had been the local manufacture of a cooking pot for use over a fire; it must have had a considerable effect on everyday life. Other new developments included the miniature "pyxides" and askoi or "pilgrim's gourds" (**685**). These were made in two halves stuck together with small handles or flaps through which a string could be threaded, and with the neck extended into a cup. See also **676**, late Bronze, right.

The Golden Age: With the growing strength of the Israelites and the establishment of a firm monarchy (Iron Age II, 930–600 BCE), pottery skills again developed and the finest Israelite pottery was made. After baking, the pot was burnished in a spiral, alternating with unburnished rings. Bowls were also made of increasingly small size until they were the equivalent of modern table ware, or were used as small containers for perfumes and unguents.

At the same time, beautiful Cypro-Phoenician ware was imported into the country, reflecting as well the many other Phoenician* influences so vividly described in the Bible. In Samaria and its neighbourhood, pottery of this period was made of fine yellow clay, decorated with red painting, elegantly cylindrical rather than ovoid (**686, 686a**).

The Bible mentions various types of pottery from these periods, although it is not always easy to relate it to what has actually been discovered by excavations.

The Persian and Hellenistic Periods: These periods are characterized by bowls and jugs of light pink or greenish "gritty" ware. During this period classic Attic ceramic types were imported from the Greek mainland, especially after the conquests of Alexander the Great. Among them are large Rhodian wine amphorae (**687**). These have been found in Beth-zur and Beth-horon (cf. Hasmoneans*; I Mac. 4:29) as well as in the deepest levels of Qumran (see Dead Sea Scrolls*). The influence of Hellenistic culture also produced improvements in the manufacture of native Palestine pottery, **688a, b.**

The chart (**676**) demonstrates that as from the Persian period, Palestine turned increasingly towards the west for cultural contacts and influences, notably to Greece whose goods and culture were exported to wherever a harbour was available.

Roman Pottery: Roman pottery has its own characteristics. In addition to imitation of classical and post-classical forms, the native ware of the period has a particular ribbed or corrugated effect — a style that lasted right through to the later Arab periods. Pottery of the Roman period also made a wide use of *terra sigillata* styles (**689**, Ashdod), which were also known in Antioch and other eastern centres (see **646**, Nabatean ware).

It was during the Graeco-Roman periods that the difference between ordinary and luxury ware became very marked. Density of population and relatively peaceful conditions meant that an immense amount of pottery was made — and broken. This accounted for a vast increase in quantity, evidenced by masses of Roman-Byzantine pottery fragments strewn all over the whole of Palestine. By then the potter's wheel had developed to the type of **695**, Beth-Shean.

If the technical and artistic qualities of this later ware seem to have declined, the reason is probably that the more gifted artisans had turned to other techniques, notably metal work.

Pottery had become the domain of simple people, concerned mainly with neatness and efficiency. See also **603**.

At the same time, when blown glass began to be manufactured on a large scale, many pottery vessels were replaced by glass ones (**690**), especially delicate vessels such as perfume juglets and unguentaria **691**, **692**. See the glass dishes taken by the partisans of Bar-Kochba to their hideouts in the caves of Judean wilderness (**254**, top left). About this time, pottery lamps became smaller, like this very typical Herodian example (**694**). The changes in shape of the open saucer-lamps and of the closed types are indicated on the right-hand side of the chart (**676**).

The Pottery Workshop of the Dead Sea: One of the best preserved pottery workshops to be found in Palestine is the one at Qumran (**693**). As is well known, many Dead Sea Scrolls were put in jars. See **393**, **394**.

The clay was first trodden in a deep trench to get rid of all impurities, then wetted and formed into balls and placed in another trench. The potter's wheel was fitted into a round hole. The potter sat on the edge, working the lower disc with his right foot, and the lump of clay on the upper disc with his hands. After drying briefly in the air, the pots were baked in the upper half of the kiln, above the furnace. The kiln was covered by a dome, pierced by a chimney. Compare with **647**.

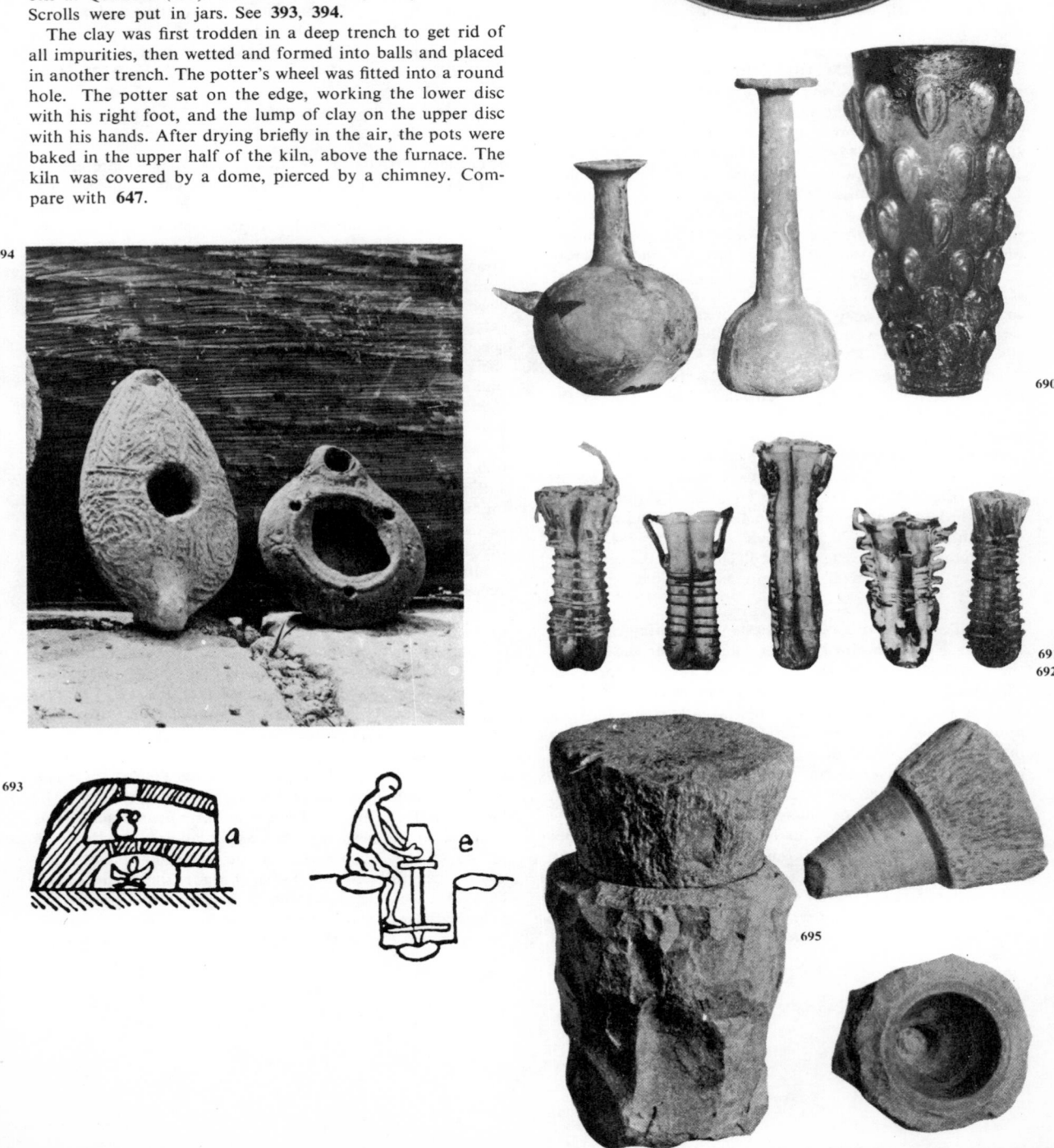

689

690

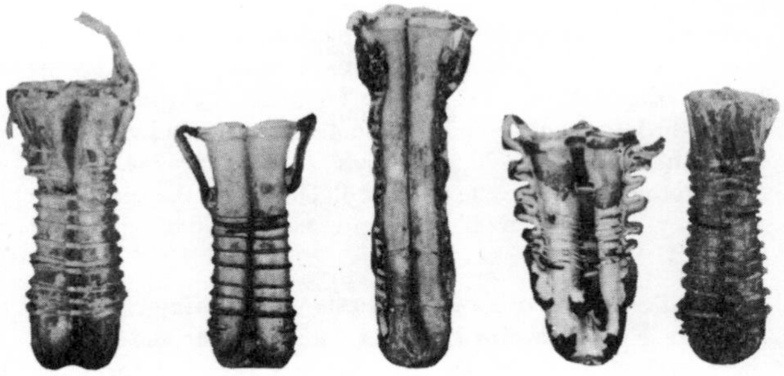

691–692

694

693

695

PRIESTHOOD, PRIESTS AND LEVITES. — *Outline: I. The Priestly Office: Function; In Sacrifices; Status of the Priesthood; Hereditary Priesthood; Position of the High Priest. II. The Priestly Tribe of Levi: Levites and Priests. III. Distinctions between Priests and Levites: The Process of Development; Historical Reconstruction. IV. Post-Exilic Organization: Restoration; Revenues of the Priesthood. V. The Priesthood in Hellenistic and Hasmonean Times: Vestments; Political Role; The High Priest. VI. Priestly Character of the Community of the Dead Sea: A Priestly Ideal. VII. Jesus as High Priest.*

I. THE PRIESTLY OFFICE: **Function:** The priests (kohen, pl. kohanîm) were the specialists in worship and religion. It was their responsibility as holy men to perform ritual acts which were forbidden to profane laymen and might even be dangerous to them (Nu. 1:53; II Sam. 6:7).

The duties of the priests of Israel were: to serve God in a sanctuary (Nu. 8:26; Dt. 10:8); to mediate between God and man by means of various cultic acts, notably sacrifice (Lv. 1:5–9 etc.) and the burning of incense (Ex. 30:7–9); to make oracular pronouncements and interpret them (Dt. 33:8; I Sam. 14:18–19, passim; see Magic*); to perform ceremonies of purification (see Impurity and Purification*; Lv. 16); to distinguish between harmless and dangerous forms of leprosy (Lv. 13; see Medicine*); to bless the people by special formulae (Nu. 6:22–26; Dt. 10:8) and to provide instruction on cultic obligations, i.e. in the Torah, which means essentially, "instruction in the way of God" (Lv. 10:10–11; Hag. 2:11; Mal. 2:6–7). In general, they had to maintain and guard the sanctuaries. Sanctuaries and settlements of priests and Levites were also havens of refuge (Ex. 21:12–14; Nu. 35: Jos. 21:13–19; I K. 2:28; see Law*).

During the time of the desert wanderings, according to one tradition, the Ark (or Tabernacle*) was carried by the priests and Levites (Dt. 10:8; Nu. 3:31 etc.). Cultic acts proper became the exclusive responsibility of the priests.

Before the institution of the priesthood, sacrifices had been offered by laymen for themselves (e.g. Gn. 22:9 or Moses' sacrifice, Ex. 17:15). Even after the priests were established, this was still possible (e.g. Gideon in Jud. 6:20–28; Manoah, Jud. 13:15–20, or Elijah, I K. 18:30–38), but in the sanctuaries the priests officiated. They were the specialists and they acted as mediators between the worshipper and his God.

In Sacrifices: The role of the priests was to bring the blood of the sacrifice into direct contact with the altar and to burn there that part of the animal that was reserved for God. The priest was in a very real sense the "minister of the altar" and his additional functions all had a parallel basis. When ministering at the altar, offering a sacrifice, or burning incense, the priest was acting as man's representative before God. When delivering an oracle, he was transmitting a message from God. When expounding Torah (or Law*), he was passing on and interpreting divine teaching. The priest was the mediator — made holy by virtue of his office but not otherwise singled out by God nor necessarily endowed with charisma.

In ancient Israel, priests were not "ordained". They began their duties without any preliminary rites designed to confer special grace or powers on them. Priesthood was not a vocation. It was an office which a man might inherit or to which he could be appointed. Holders of the office were holy and sacred because they had quitted the profane world and entered a sacred realm "set apart" for the service of God. They and the sanctuaries were served by persons specially dedicated to them (e.g. young Samuel, I Sam. 2:11); by temple slaves (an institution which, according to Ezra 8:20, was begun by David) and by a certain section of the Levites who were entrusted with minor tasks (see below).

Status of the Priesthood: According to priestly tradition, the priesthood was a Mosaic institution (Ex. 32:25–29) and the exclusive privilege of the tribe of Levi (Dt. 10:8; 33:8–11). According to this tradition, Yahweh himself had deliberately chosen the tribe of Levi for his service in the sanctuaries. There was another, older, tradition that priests could be appointed by men, without divine intervention and without necessarily belonging to the tribe of Levi. Even in the time of the Judges, non-Levites could be appointed as priests, as in the story of Micah (Jud. 17:5; see Judges*: The Dan Sanctuary), although a Levite was to be preferred (Jud. 17:10–13). Later, all priests and auxiliary servants of the Temple claimed Levitic descent.

Hereditary Priesthood: In ancient times, most professions were hereditary. The system was particularly suited to the priesthood for it ensured the orderly maintenance of the sanctuaries and uninterrupted preservation of traditions. Throughout the ancient world, in Egypt, Assyria, Phoenicia, Greece and the pre-Islamic world, the priesthood was a hereditary office, its privileges and responsibilities handed down from generation to generation. Within the general category of "priests" a class system developed, reserving special hereditary privileges to certain families. On this basis the priests — especially in Egypt — were able to become politically dominant and to acquire considerable wealth.

In Israel, this development seems to have begun with the establishment of the hereditary priesthood after the Exodus*. However, the Bible texts bearing on the history of the priesthood are not clear and have raised several questions which still remain unsolved (see Part III). In general, the Bible implies that certain ceremonial and ritual functions were to be the exclusive privilege of the descendants of Levi (one of the sons of Jacob). Once Israel was established as a settled community, priestly families could stay in one sanctuary for generations. They were not bound to a single place, however, for every member of the tribe was equally entitled — at least in theory — to perform the service of God.

The recorded traditions of the Old Testament relate that Aaron, the brother of Moses and the "first" priest, had four sons, Nadab, Abihu, Eleazar and Itamar. The first two were childless, having died as a punishment for offering an unauthorized burnt sacrifice. Accordingly, the third son, Eleazar, became High Priest on the death of his father (Nu. 3:2–4). All later high priests claimed descent from him either through Eleazar, or Itamar, the youngest son. The first High Priest of the Temple in Jerusalem, Zadok, was assigned to the genealogy of Eleazar and most succeeding priests of the Temple claimed descent from Zadok. The priests installed at the Tribal League shrine of Shiloh claimed Itamar, Aaron's fourth son, as their progenitor. In either case, all priests were henceforth "Sons of Aaron" or "Sons of Aaron the Priest", i.e. Aaron's descendants.

Members of the tribe of Levi who were not so descended were barred from the priestly office (Nu. 18:7).

David reconciled the distinction between the two families of the sons of Zadok and the sons of Itamar by instituting 24 classes of priests, sixteen belonging to the Eleazar-Zadok branch; eight to the family of Itamar. Thus the Zadokites were assured of supremacy. From Solomon, through the Exile right down to the time of Antiochus Epiphanes (see below; Hasmoneans*), the High Priest traced his genealogy back to Zadok and no one outside the direct line was eligible for the post.

Position of the High Priest: In pre-Exilic times the high priest was simply the foremost among the priests. He was the head of the sacerdotal organization but he had none of the combined secular and sacerdotal functions which the hierarchy enjoyed in post-Exilic times (see below Part IV). His position and functions changed following the construction of the First Temple*. Once established there, he no longer went into battle with the Ark as did his predecessors during the time of the Tribal League. Neither, according to the Talmud (Sota 48 a), did he continue to give oracles by the use of Urim and Thummim. When, much later, the task of teaching and interpreting the law was also taken over by other officials (the scribes, see Law*), his role in sacrifice became the priest's outstanding function.

II. THE PRIESTLY TRIBE OF LEVI: The tribe of Levi had a special place in Israel's society. They were not counted in the census, nor were they allotted territory like the other tribes at the beginning of the agricultural settlement of Israel. (This measure may have been deliberately designed to prevent them acquiring the economic and political domination enjoyed by the Egyptian priesthood.) Instead, they were expected to be maintained by the rest of the people, through charity, sacrifices and tithes, one-tenth of the Levites' tithe and share in sacrifices being reserved for the priests (Dt. 10:9; 14:27; Nu. 18:21–29, etc.). It is this reiterated injunction that the Levites shall have "no inheritance within Israel" that has cast doubt on the apparently contradictory commandment to give them cities and pasture land within the territory of the other tribes (Nu. 35:2–8; see details in Numbers*: Levitical Cities).

Levites and Priests: Although all priests were Levites, not all Levites were priests. The "sons of Aaron", who formed the hierarchy, centred around the tabernacle, eventually the Temple in Jerusalem. Before Jerusalem was established as a single sanctuary, however, and even long afterwards (see Deuteronomy*; Israel and Judah, Kingdoms of*), local shrines and sanctuaries existed elsewhere, served by other priests and Levites. These continued to flourish in spite of a strong movement within both Judah and Israel to draw the faithful to the main cultic centres, Jerusalem in the Southern Kingdom and Bethel and Dan in the north. It is not clear how the priesthood was organized and maintained in the Northern Kingdom of Israel. In the Dan and Bethel sanctuaries priests who were not of the tribe of Levi were permitted to officiate. When Josiah destroyed Bethel and the high places*, these priests were relegated to an inferior position. Even before the time of Josiah's reform, it seems that a *de facto* distinction had already come into being between the priests of the main sanctuaries and those who served in the provinces. The existence of local shrines meant a decreased revenue for the major ones, doubtless a contributing factor to the hostility between their respective "ministers". In addition, the priests and Levites of the sanctuaries enjoyed a higher social position than their colleagues scattered among the tribes. This situation is reflected in Deuteronomy (which relates in part to the period after the reform) and appears to recognize that some Levites could not be employed in the central sanctuary and must live "within your towns", presumably on charity (Dt. 12:18; 26:12). Nevertheless, every Levite retained his priestly right to come to the sanctuary and "minister in the name of the Lord his God", like all his fellow Levites, and to have an equal share in the priestly portions (Dt. 18:6–8), meaning presumably an equal stipend to that of the Levites attached to the sanctuary.

III. DISTINCTIONS BETWEEN PRIESTS AND LEVITES: In Deuteronomy the distinction is obscured or implicit (see article) but it is made quite explicit in Ezekiel and other later books of the Old Testament composed partly or altogether within priestly circles. Ezekiel's description may also refer to the situation which obtained during the monarchy. In Ezekiel, the right to the priesthood is reserved exclusively to a single Levitic clan (the Aaronids in Numbers; Zadokites in Ezekiel), while other Levites are assigned other, subsidiary roles within the sanctuary. In Numbers (1:50; chs. 3, 8), they were porters and perhaps guards in the Tabernacle. Ezekiel (44:6–18) makes it clear that the Sons of Zadok "serve the altar", while Levites who had earlier "gone astray" in serving the small sanctuaries were punished after Josiah's reform by being restricted to "serving the Temple" in an inferior capacity, i.e. slaughtering sacrifices, but not offering them as did the priests; guarding the gates, and attending on lay worshippers. The Chronicler (see Chronicles*) refers to them, however, as an important social element, subdivided into singers (I Ch. 6:31–47 etc.); gate-keepers (I Ch. 9:17–27), and those charged with various administrative duties (I Ch. 9:28–32). Under certain circumstances, they were allowed to replace or supplement the priests.

The distinctions between priest and Levite were the result of historical development. It is very difficult to reconstruct the course of events from the general evidence of the Old Testament although it is clear that precise rulings were laid down only after some time, beginning during the monarchy and finalized in post-Exilic times.

The Process of Development: There are a number of indications of the growing tensions between "priests" and "Levites". Claims to a special covenantal relationship before God are made alternatively for the tribe of Levi as a whole (Dt. 33:8–11; Jer. 33:18–22; Nu. 35) or, more particularly, for the "Aaronids" (Nu. chs. 16–17; I Ch. 23:13); but the Levitic claim seems to be more generally recognized and older. On the other hand, the general evidence of the Old Testament's historical writings seems to confirm that certain families had a hereditary right to the priesthood in different sanctuaries. Because of the contradictions in the evidence of the different books, it is almost impossible to reconstruct a coherent account of the way in which the organization, functions and status of the priesthood developed. Later biblical editors were faced with earlier texts which contradicted both each other and the situation as they knew it. These editors knew that only the Levites had the right to perform liturgical functions and they recognized the pre-eminence of the Jerusalem priesthood. They naturally regarded both privileges as dating back to the earliest period of Israel's history and completely disregarded the long process of development which had in fact been involved. The genealogical lists of I Ch. 5 and 6 are one attempt to combine and harmonize the conflict and there are many others in the texts edited at a later period. It was, however, impossible to resolve all the contradictions.

What seems certain is that the distinction between the two priestly elements was complete by the time of the Restoration*. In the Temple of Ezra and Nehemiah and thereafter, the distinction between Aaronid priests and Levites (singers and guards) was firmly established. At this time, the service of the Temple was divided among all the priests and Levites, who were divided into 24 groups or "watches" ("mishmarôt") and took it in turns to perform the services in the Temple. The Chronicler (I Ch. 24–26) ascribes this organization to the time of David aud Solomon.

Historical Reconstruction: Critical scholars, following the theories of Graf and Welhausen, ascribe the Priestly sources of the Bible (see Biblical Criticism*), i.e. the Holiness Code of Leviticus* and the Priestly books of Numbers and Deuteronomy, to a late post-Exilic period. According to this school of thought, a secular tribe of Levi had existed in very early times but had become practically extinct by the establishment of the Kingdom. The various existing priestly dynasties, however, claimed Levitical descent and themselves established the fiction of a sacred tribe. Until Josiah's reform (see Israel and Judah*: Josiah), there was no distinction between priests and Levites (see above). This distinction was in fact created by the establishment of the Temple of Jerusalem as the unique sanctuary for the whole nation, reducing the priests who had previously officiated in the local shrines to the inferior status described above.

Ezekiel put the situation on an official basis by ascribing special tasks to these Levites and recognizing the doctrinal foundations of the distinction between them and the priests. He was not an innovator in this. He merely regularized a position which already existed and which, indeed, had been made acute by the Josianic reform. His new organization was accepted by the founders of the post-Exilic temple and projected back to earlier times in the writings of the priestly code (P).

In general, this theory has much to commend it, but it leaves many questions unanswered and has been amended in various ways.

One point is suggested by the obviously genuine difficulties which Ezra encountered in mustering 38 Levites for service in the revived Temple (Ez. 8:15–20). The employment of Levites for special duties and their inferior position in the Temple, which is further attested by the attempts they made in later post-Exilic times to improve their status (see below), must have been established practice before the Exile. Equally, this position probably accounts for their reluctance to return from Babylon.

Another question which has aroused considerable debate is how far the evidence of Chronicles can be accepted. The important place which this book gives to the Levites and its careful tracing of their genealogies to the three sons of Levi: Gershom, Kohat and Merari (I Ch. 6:1–32) is, in the opinion of many scholars, a deliberate attempt to provide the priestly tradition of Numbers with an acceptable history, i.e. the Chronicler may very possibly have included the ideas of his own day, ascribing them to ancient times. Others hold that the Chronicler's evidence is substantially accurate although many details may have been idealized.

The precise distinction between priests and Levites probably developed gradually in the large sanctuary of Jerusalem. In the smaller local sanctuaries of earlier times, there was no distinction between the various classes of cultic personnel. There were also Levites who were not employed at a sanctuary and had no land but, nevertheless, had an established claim to cultic functions (cf. the story of Micah, Jud. 17:7–13). They can best be understood as descendants of the guardians of the portable "tabernacle" of the still earlier nomadic period of Israel. (The Levites were the carriers of the Ark.) With the establishment of a more complicated form of public worship in the central sanctuary, these unemployable Levites were gradually absorbed into the organization as specialists in non-priestly cultic functions. After King Hezekiah and, especially, Josiah's reforms, the central priesthood of Jerusalem was substantially strengthened.

Priestly legislation dating from the days of the Monarchy reflects in detail the privileges enjoyed by the clergy. This is true of Numbers 18 and especially Leviticus 7 in which the portion of the priests is prescribed as all animal and vegetable offerings apart from the portions actually burnt on the altar. As in Ezekiel (see above), the priests are given the right to the best of the produce of the land, the first-fruits and first-born and anything vowed as "ḥerem" (consecrated offering) to the sanctuary. Where the first-born is a child or an "unclean" animal, then it is to be redeemed in money. The Levites are explicitly awarded the tithes on corn and new wine, one-tenth of which they paid to the priests. This all refers to worship in the Temple, which dates it convincingly to the days of the monarchy. It cannot belong to the earlier sources of the Pentateuch.

IV. POST-EXILIC ORGANIZATION: **Restoration:** On the evidence of Chronicles, Ezra, and Nehemiah, it appears that the organization of the rebuilt Temple was strengthened along traditional lines. The status of the Levitic assistants in the Temple was improved. As they became the teachers and judges of the returned exiles, their prestige also increased. Although only four priestly families returned to Jerusalem, the division into 24 watches was restored, the priestly groups being augmented by 24 watches of laymen.

Revenues of the Priesthood: It does not appear that the position as regards revenues varied very greatly between the First and Second Temples. From the earliest times, the priests shared in all offerings made to Yahweh — sacrifices, first fruits, first born etc. (Ex. 23:19; 34:26). Deuteronomy (14:22–29) prescribes that every third year the tithe shall not be brought to the sanctuary but shall be devoted to the support of the poor and the Levite. Later regulations in Deuteronomy (e.g. 18:1–5) refer to the revenues of the priests of the central sanctuary only, although Levites from the provinces could come and claim their share (Dt. 18:6–8). This is confirmed by Ezekiel who assigns the priests a portion of all sacrifices, all offerings vowed to the Temple and the best of the first fruits, dues and flour offered at the sanctuary.

As payment of tithes was often avoided, attempts were made to enforce the obligations of Nu. 18 more strictly. Malachi and Nehemiah record abuses in their time and Nehemiah instituted a system which allowed the Levites to go and collect the tithes personally, under priestly supervision. The collection was also systematized by having the tithes brought to special central stores and there allotted to the recipients. This remained the practice until Maccabaean times, after which they were actually divided on the threshing floor. From the Chronicler's idealized description of the Levitical organization, it seems that the system worked well. However, it is apparent from Ecclesiasticus (7:31) and Judith (11:13; see Apocrypha*) that the cost to the faithful was increased by the re-imposition of the old measures which had been replaced by new ones (e.g. the tithe of Dt. 14:22–26 which could be changed into money to be spent at the sanctuary, was known as a "second tithe", while the three-year tithe of Dt. 14:28–29 became a "third tithe"). Nevertheless, the pious paid them all, Tobias for instance (Tobit 1:6–8, see Apocrypha*) and, above all, the Pharisees* who made it a point of honour to be punctilious about every jot and tittle of the Law.

In later post-Exilic times part of the Levitical tithes was paid to the priests, adding to their already proverbial wealth.

V. THE PRIESTHOOD IN HELLENISTIC AND HASMONEAN TIMES: Nehemiah records that in his day the priests numbered 4,289. After the Hasmonean suppression of the hellenizers amongst them, that number was reduced. Visitors to Palestine during the period, like the Greek historians Hecataeus and Aristeas, were mostly impressed by the magnificence of the High Priest's appearance before the people and by the discipline with which 700 priests worshipped and served in the shrine without sound or bustle.

Vestments: Beginning in the simple priestly garment, the High Priest's costume became in time far more elaborate. According to rabbinical records (see Clothing*), his "ephod" developed into a large piece of cloth worn over the top of his other vestments. The best evidence about dress in the Persian and Hellenistic empires comes from Phoenicia*, culturally the Jews' closest neighbour.

Although Greek influence was making itself felt in the area during the 4th c. BCE, it never succeeded in driving out native customs completely. The costume of this Phoenician priest (**696**), for instance, probably had its analogies in the everyday dress of the Jewish priesthood. The costume of the High Priest remains a matter for conjecture. It has been given widely different forms by a succession of illustrators throughout the ages, probably with varying degrees of historical inaccuracy.

Political Role: The form of government of the restored Jewish community in **Judea**, normally referred to as a "theocracy" (in which the source of power and authority is derived directly from God) was actually a hierarchy, or priestly administration. Not only was spiritual and social leadership of the people in the hands of the priests, but they

696

formed the strongest and wealthiest class in Jerusalem, politically and economically. There were those among their opponents (notably the sectaries of Qumran) who energetically denied divine sanction to the ruling priesthood, who were not true descendants of Zadok. Some of the most important members of the party of the Sadducees* were such powerful and wealthy priestly families.

The High Priest: As from the time of Nehemiah (Restoration*), the foremost priest became the head of the whole community, his title, "High Priest of Israel" (hakohen hagadôl). At the end of Persian rule, the beginning of the Hellenistic period, he became the central personality in Judea, taking the place of the kings of other states and wielding a wide authority. The process which began with the Restoration* when Zerubbabel (the secular, Davidic, leader) divided authority with Jeshua, the High Priest, ended with the complete eclipse of the royal power. The priestly leader stood at the head of a distinct political unit within the Hellenistic empire. In the 3rd c. BCE, the High Priest was his people's sole representative before the Ptolemies and even had the responsibility for collecting taxes and forwarding them to the Egyptian king in Alexandria.

For some 300 years after the Restoration, the high priesthood was filled by a member of the Zadokite family. The last "legitimate" holder of the title was Onias III (175–172 BCE). On his death, his brother Jason unlawfully acquired the office by bribing Antiochus Epiphanes (for details, see Hasmoneans*). Jason was one of the prime movers in the attempts to assimilate Judaism with Hellenism—a trend which was strengthened by the close contacts which existed between the priesthood, who were the rulers of the people, and their Hellenist overlords. For a time, the High Priesthood became a prize in the political manoeuvres of the period with claimants who had no trace of Zadokite descent competing for the position. Popular reaction against the hellenizing movement and all it stood for was one of the main factors in sparking off the Maccabaean (Hasmonean*) revolt and the national revival which accompanied it and was strengthened by its success. The new spirit lent increased importance to the position of High Priest. He became the leader and embodiment of the Jewish nation, endowed with all the spiritual prestige and significance of a hallowed tradition. The first holder of the office after the defeat of the hellenizers was Jonathan the Maccabaean (a member of the Hasmonean* house).

Hasmonean High Priests: In 152 BCE, he was clothed in the sacred vestments and officiated at the Feast of Tabernacles (Succot) as High Priest and leader of the nation. His brother Simon succeeded him in both positions. In 140 BCE the High Priesthood was made the hereditary right of Simon and his descendants and the Hasmonean dynasty was formally established. Already enjoying full religious and secular powers as High Priest, John Hyrcanus, Simon's grandson, also assumed the title of king. It was as both High Priest and king that the last of the Hasmoneans (Jannaeus Alexander and his sons) ruled Judea. While the prestige their house had earned in the heroic days of the Maccabaean wars, plus their own later military successes, ensured them wide support as secular rulers, as High Priests the Hasmoneans were on shaky ground. The Hasmonean family was not of Zadokite descent. To the traditionalists among their people, Hasmonean High Priests were usurpers. The influential party of Hassidim* and their successors, the Pharisees*, regarded them as illegitimate and opposed their policies accordingly. The more extreme among the pious sects, the Essenes and the founders of the community of Qumran (see Dead Sea Scrolls*) rejected their leadership altogether, retired from life in the society they governed, avoided all contact with the Temple they had polluted and regarded the whole Jerusalem priesthood with the greatest scorn.

High Priests of Pre-Christian Times: The last prince and High Priest of the Hasmonean dynasty was Antigonus Mattathias (see Rome and the Jews*). When he was deposed by King Herod* (equally a usurper but with fewer spiritual pretensions), the position of High Priest ceased to be hereditary, and became subject to the secular ruler: Herod and, ultimately, Rome. Between 37 BCE and 70 CE no less than 28 High Priests were appointed, chosen from among several priestly families (see Rome and the Jews*). Only the last, Pinehas ben Harta, was properly elected by the Sanhedrin, as prescribed by the rabbis. Until then, the families concerned formed a priestly aristocracy, the "chief priests" referred to so often in the New Testament. After the destruction of the Temple the post of High Priest ceased to exist except for a short revival in the figure of Eleazar the High Priest, when Bar-Kochba ruled an independent Judea (135–7 CE, see Bar-Kochba*).

An echo of the ancient office survives to this day in the High Priest of the Samaritan community in Shechem (Nablus) and in Israel (see Samaritans*). The temple at Leontopolis in Egypt, established by the legitimate line of the Oniads at the time of the Maccabees*, also had a hereditary High Priest, but his office lapsed during the 1st c. BCE. The sectaries of Qumran (see below) maintained that their founder, the Teacher of Righteousness, was a member of the Zadokite line.

VI. PRIESTLY CHARACTER OF THE COMMUNITY OF THE DEAD SEA: The origins of the Essene movement are thought to lie in a struggle between rival priestly houses, one hyper-orthodox, the other less so and consequently successful in gaining control of the High Priesthood and the Jerusalem Temple. The founding members of the sect were drawn from priests of the defeated faction who saw their authority destroyed and their convictions flouted. They despaired of reforming the existing organization in Jerusalem but looked forward to the restoration of the legitimate priesthood and temple observances in the eschatological age, when God would intervene decisively and put matters right. They regarded themselves as an advance unit in this process of restoration, upholders of truth and purity, the nucleus of the faithful. On this basis they organized their own apocalyptic community and established themselves as one of a number of schismatic sects. The group that founded and lived at Qumran, and those who followed them, aimed first of all at a society and way of life which would fulfill every detail of the Law of God, as interpreted by the Zadokite hierarchy of Qumran. In so doing, they were of course much stricter in practice and observance than the Pharisees* but to achieve this, they turned their backs on the whole of organized religion and society in the rest of the Jewish community.

This apparently priestly community at Qumran is regarded by many scholars as the central directorate, or corps d'elite, of the wider sectarian movement of the Essenes, all of whom were not so exclusive as the Qumranites. There were many Essenes who lived among the people of Palestine and they were highly regarded and respected. They seem to have been in touch with political and religious life in the country. Later on, some of them joined in the revolt against Rome (see Rome and the Jews*).

Qumran was led by priests who looked forward to a

triumphant return to the Temple where they would re-establish orthodox practices on the lines of the Mosaic camp prescribed by the Torah for the last Holy War of God. The arch-enemy of their founder, the "Teacher of Righteousness", was the "Wicked Priest", presumably the High Priest who was defiling the sanctuary in Jerusalem and was accused of persecuting the sect.

A Priestly Ideal: The history of the founding of the Qumran sect is recorded in the "Damascus Document". This tells that God . . . built for them a "faithful priestly house", the like of which had never been seen "formerly or lately". In anticipation of the "End of Days", the community was organized as an ideal priestly theocracy, in which the priests were the most important members, taking precedence in all ceremonies and events and dominating the councils. Indeed the community's whole way of life was directed towards priestly objectives. Theirs was the legitimate hierarchy, they were the "true Israel". All cultic and juridical questions were the concern of the priests, the "sons of Aaron", while the laymen controlled common, secular affairs. The community was deliberately hierarchic and non-egalitarian, with a ruling council composed of twelve "men" i.e. lay elders and three priests.

The community's main activity was the study, preservation and preparation of documents concerning the priesthood and its functions. To them, a priest was "doresh hatorah", an expounder of the Law, and their ideal priest was one "like Aaron or Zadok".

The community aimed at complete ritual purity, every member observing the laws of the Holiness Code of Leviticus*, originally applicable only to priests. The lay members patterned themselves on their priests. Complete acceptance of the priests' authority was one of the essential factors in the unity and relatively long life of this oligarchic society. For the times in which they lived, the sectaries had found a valid mode of existence, combining apocalyptic beliefs with the most punctilious observance of the traditional laws of their religion. (A full description of their community is given in the article on Dead Sea Scrolls*.)

The early Christians were considerably influenced by this social and priestly organization and some of its features are reflected in the earlier period of the new Church. However, there were also many contrasts. In the early Christian community, for instance, there were no priests (Kohanim) at all. The first Christians worshipped in the Temple and had no separate priesthood. The Twelve Apostles may have corresponded to the 12 laymen of the Qumran ruling body but there was nothing to correspond to the 3 priests. Bishops in the Christian Church were also laymen at first.

VII. JESUS AS HIGH PRIEST: Among the apocalyptic writings of this period (see Apocalypse*), there is a "Testament of Joseph" which was related to the sectarian movement and also, perhaps, to the Jewish Christians. In this work, the Messianic priest is called "the Lamb" and he takes precedence over the royal messiah (messiah of David). Scholars see a connection between this figure and the militant Lamb of the Book of Revelation*. The three apocalyptic motifs — priest, prophet and king — are all applied separately to Jesus in the Gospels. The New Testament, notably the Epistle to the Hebrews*, refers to him as "designated by God a high priest after the order of Melchizedek" (5:10), "a great high priest who has passed through the heavens" (4:14). The implication here may be that Jesus, who was not of Zadokite or Aaronid descent, had established a new category of high priests and could legitimately fill the place of the supreme mediator between God and man. Alternatively, the implication may be that Christ's own supreme sacrifice had rendered all further sacrifices and priestly functions superfluous. The Levitical system had been provisional and temporary. At last, in the eschatological age, the permanent pattern had been established. Jesus had brought salvation to mankind — something the old system had never achieved.

Historically, on the other hand, this motif in the Epistle is regarded by some as an attempt by the Jewish Christians to adjust their Christology to the messianic expectations of the Essenes. In the single messianic figure of Jesus Christ, all the messianic longings of past generations of Jews had been fulfilled.

PROPERTY, LAND AND ITS CONVEYANCE. — *Outline: I. Land: Feudalism; The "Sharing Out" of the Promised Land; Family Property; The Law of Redemption; The "Inheritance of the Fathers"; Changes under the Monarchy; Post-Exilic Period. II. Conveyance and Legal Deeds of Sale.*

I. LAND: The economy of the people of the Old Testament was mainly based on land. Industry and crafts were limited to a small number of people and still fewer engaged in trade* (see article) in Old Testament times. The most important activity was agriculture and it follows that all thinking about economic matters was conditioned by procedures and concepts relating to land and agriculture, many of them common throughout the ancient Near East, some more specifically Israelite (see Agriculture*).

Feudalism: In Israel, feudalism as practiced among neighbouring peoples was unknown. In Egypt, the land all belonged to the Pharaoh or to the temples (see Gn. 47:20–24), and was worked on a direct rent-paying basis. In Mesopotamia, feudal tenure was widespread. The Code of Hammurabi and the laws of Hittites refer to the creation of fiefs and the services to be rendered to the king in return for grants of land. While the Hyksos ruled Palestine (18th–16th cs. BCE), big landowners, the nobility, were the "marianu" or knights who manned the war chariots. To ensure their continued loyalty, the petty "kings" who ruled the different cities of the country used to grant them extensive estates which they could bequeath to their direct descendants. It is not definitely known whether this system was continued after the Hyksos were driven out of Canaan and the adjacent territories in the 16th c. BCE.

In Nuzi and Assyria in the 2nd mill. BCE, grants of land, or fiefs, were made by drawing lots. When the Israelites entered Canaan, the promised land was also distributed among the tribes by lot, although in fact they held their land by the right — or chance — of Conquest.

The "Sharing Out" of the Promised Land: The distribution of the common property into separate plots or areas — where in fact the clans were already settled (see Tribes*) or which they still had to conquer (see Conquest*) — is recorded schematically in Jos. 6–12. However, in the realistic account given in Jud. 1, it is apparent that the process of conquest and sharing out was still incomplete, for large stretches of Canaan remained in the hands of the natives.

Israel's approach to questions of land tenure was based on theology and the schematization in Joshua may have been an expression of the Israelite belief that Yahweh owned the land of Canaan, not only in general as its creator, but explicitly as its conqueror. It was then, in this view, assigned to Israel in exactly the same way as other kings made grants of land to their soldiers after participation in a victorious campaign, for them to live and build on.

This theory appears to provide a sound interpretation of the formal picture painted in Joshua. Other modern scholars believe, however, that the drawing of lots for the Promised Land by the Twelve Tribes*, described in Joshua (13:6; 15:1; 16:1; 17:1; 18:6–19, passim and Jud. 1:3), is an imaginative extension to the whole people of something that in fact took place in slow stages at the level of individual clans and their component families (described under Conquest*; Tribes*; Joshua and Judges, Books of*).

At the present stage of knowledge it is difficult to be dogmatic about either theory. In the light of further discovery, both views may have to be revised.

Family Property: The basic social unit in early Old Testament times was the clan or family. The land which provided the basis for the whole economic structure was not considered the possession of individuals, but was always regarded as family (or clan) property. A change came about under the monarchy (see below).

The transfer of land to strangers, not members of the family, was forbidden. To avoid it, it was laid down that daughters could inherit their father's property provided they were married to members of the father's family (Nu. 36:5–12). The same intention prompted two other laws: the *law of Jubilee*, and the *law of Redemption.* The law of Jubilee provided that land could not be sold in perpetuity, but only until the Jubilee year, when it must revert to its original owners (Lv. 25:13–16). The practical effects of this rule are never mentioned in the Bible, and it is assumed with a fair degree of certainty that it represented a utopian ideal rarely applied in practice (see Law*; Agriculture*; Leviticus*). In contrast to this, the law of Redemption is not only listed as a law (Lv. 25:25–34), but its effects can be seen in a number of stories. The marriage of Ruth* to Boaz, for instance, was intended "to restore the name of the dead to his inheritance", Boaz acting as the "redeemer" of Ruth and the property of her first husband (Ruth 4:5). The law of Levirate marriage (i.e. a man had to marry his brother's widow) clearly had the same intention (Dt. 25:5), as it related specifically to "brothers who dwell together", meaning those living on a single family property.

The Law of Redemption: The law expounded in Leviticus (25) refers both to the prohibition on selling family property (vs. 23–24) and to the obligation on next of kin to redeem property which a poorer member of the family has been forced to sell (vs. 25–34). Moreover (vs. 47–52), a man sold into slavery for debt may similarly be redeemed by his kinsman. These regulations belong to the ancient tribal framework and more particularly to village life and its customs which continued even when the economic basis of the people's life was changing.

The order of kinship goes from brother to uncle, to male (paternal) cousin. While redemption of movable property must be carried out within a year of its sale, immovable property (land) may be redeemed at any time. A number of biblical instances of redemption can be found. Jeremiah (32:6–15) describes how he redeemed the field of his cousin, Hanamel, which, being outside any big city, was undoubtedly part of the family inheritance. From this it is inferred that the custom of redemption was observed up to the destruction of the Temple.

While a next of kin could redeem a piece of land immediately — even before any purchase took place, in fact — the seller himself could redeem his own land only after the purchaser had had the use of it for some time. The calculation of the redemption price was based on the Jubilee Law, which assumed that land was sold only for the number of years until the next Jubilee. To redeem the sale, therefore, the original owner had only to pay for the value of the land for the remaining years, i.e. the purchase price less the proportionate amount for the time the purchaser had held it (Lv. 25:26–27).

The "Inheritance of the Fathers": The strength of the attachment of the peasant to his land, reinforced by long established custom and tradition, is well illustrated by the story of Naboth (see Elijah*). Naboth refused to sell his patrimony (the vineyard) to his king for it was "the inheritance of my fathers" (I K. 21:1–4, 6). This attachment was strengthened by the custom of burying members of the family within the family property, which thus became the location of the "graves of my forefathers" among which everyone in those days aspired to be buried (Jos. 24:30, 32; I Sam. 25:1; I K. 2:34). A further protection of property rights was provided by the law forbidding the removal of landmarks and boundary stones (Dt. 19:14; 27:17).

Changes under the Monarchy: With the establishment of the monarchy and subsequent development of social conflict, the ancient rules came into conflict with economic realities. Town life, domestic and international trade and the attractions of a court and its variety of officials, led to a widening gulf between the peasants who farmed and lived on the land and the wealthy aristocrats who merely drew their income from its produce. Small peasants found themselves forced to sell their holdings to their wealthy neighbours — and creditors — and large estates worked by slaves and hired labour began to take the place of individual small peasant holdings (cf. Mic. 2:2; Is. 5:8; see also Agriculture*).

Tenant farming, or the system by which the farmer pays a portion (usually half) the produce of his land as a rent to its owner, was unknown to Israel in Old Testament days. The first reference to the renting of lands occurs in Jesus' parable of the vineyard owner and his tenants (Mt. 21:33–41) and evidence of the system has been found in documents dated 133 CE from the caves of Murabba'at (see below and Bar-Kochba*).

Post-Exilic Period: After Nehemiah, the earlier trend was reversed and small peasant holdings represented the bulk of Judea's cultivated land. To ensure this, Nehemiah had ordered the cancellation of all debts and the restoration of sold agricultural land to its former owners (Neh. 5). The

Egyptian Hecataeus of Abdera (ca. 290 BCE), quoted by Diodorus Siculus (ca. 25 BCE), recorded that a law existed in Judea which, by forbidding the sale of individual estates by private people, aimed at preventing the concentration of land in the hands of large estate-owners at the expense of the small peasant. From the time of the Maccabees, large estates are encountered more frequently, but the laws of Judea continued to protect the Jewish peasant. He was saved from the fate which overtook the small peasant farmer of Italy in the second half of the 2nd c. BCE, when the Roman Senate at last succeeded in annulling the Gracchi laws that had earlier prevented the sale of small holdings, which were then attached to the large domains of the Senators.

The conquests of the Hasmoneans* brought new tracts of land into the Jewish state. In contrast to Hellenistic custom, this did not remain the exclusive property of the crown (the Ptolemies still held formal title to every inch of the land of Egypt), but, in the opinion of A. Schalit, was distributed as private holdings, with only a small proportion remaining as part of the royal domain. This domain was worked by tenant farmers who paid rent in kind to the king. Otherwise, the Hasmoneans upheld the ancient Jewish tradition that a Jew could be bound only to Yahweh, not to another human, even his king. As, nevertheless, the Hasmonean rulers are unlikely to have distributed valuable property as a free gift, this scholar assumes that grants of land were made in return for the obligation to do military service. Such a system would explain the continuous wars fought by, e.g. Alexander Jannaeus and his successors mainly with Jewish recruits, with only a small complement of foreign mercenaries. The soldiers, it is to be supposed, fought for a reward in the form of a grant of land once the war was over. (A similar situation may be reflected in the conditions at the time of Saul and his successors.)

II. CONVEYANCE AND LEGAL DEEDS OF SALE: In early Old Testament times, the essence of a sale was a verbal contract made in front of witnesses. Thus Abraham purchased the cave of Machpelah from Ephron the Hittite "in the presence of the Hittites, before all who went in at the gate of the city" (Gn. 23:17–18) and Boaz purchased Elimelech's property (Ruth 4:4) in the presence of those sitting at the gate "and the elders of my people" (see Government and Authority*: Justice at the Gate). Other assurances might be given in addition to the verbal agreement, but this was the fundamental contract. The book of Ruth refers to the seller taking off his shoe and handing it to the buyer (4:8). In fact this was not only a token of a sale; it was a very ancient custom by which Ruth's husband's nearest relative was relieved of the Levitical obligation to marry Ruth, thus redeeming her along with his property. Boaz was not "next of kin" in the meaning of these laws (see Ruth*; Family*: Levirate Marriage). By the time the book was written, the custom had dropped out of use and its meaning was forgotten. In Nuzi (see Assyria*) the seller of a piece of land would lift his foot from the land he disposed of and place it on the foot of the purchaser. Where fictitious sales were made (to evade the law), a symbolic payment of a mantle and a pair of shoes might be given in place of money.

The description of Jeremiah's purchase of his cousin's field (Jer. 32:6–15) is a detailed illustration of the formalities of such transactions at a time just before the destruction of the Temple. At this period, while the agreement was reached in the presence of those who sat "in the court of the guard", a written deed of purchase was also prepared (in two copies, one sealed and the other open) and signed by Jeremiah as the purchaser, and by the witnesses. Both deeds were then placed in an earthenware pot. The written deeds, however, merely confirmed the verbal agreement and were commonly written in the form of a "dialogue", the seller making a proposal to the purchaser who agreed to it, the formal consequences then being stated objectively. Similarly, Nuzi purchase contracts state explicitly that they were written after the purchase had been announced publicly at the gate. The making of two deeds can also be understood in the light of archaeological findings elsewhere. In Mesopotamia,

697

deeds of sale were placed in a clay envelope (**697**) on which details of the transaction were marked. Where questions about the sale arose later, reference could be made to the envelope or to a copy of the deed. If the accuracy of this were questioned, then the envelope could be broken and the original agreement consulted. In Hellenistic Egypt, a similar custom was followed and evidence of it has also been found from papyri of 2nd c. CE Palestine. The practice is confirmed by Talmudic literature. Apparently, the agreement was written on a sheet of papyrus, a blank space being left so that a copy could be made on the same sheet. The original text was then signed and the papyrus rolled up leaving the copy open to immediate investigation (see Inscriptions*). A conveyance of land from the time of Bar-Kochba*, written in Aramaic, was found among the documents from Wadi Murabba'at (**698**). The reverse bears the signatures of the two parties to the transaction, in Greek and Hebrew (see also Trade*). Other documents were also found to be double copies of contracts.

From ancient Babylonian and Assyrian records it appears that purchases and sales were merely a matter of agreement about the price. However, leases of property for a stated period in the "dialogue" form have been found among the archives of the Murashu brothers, dating from the second half of the 5th c. BCE. It is thought by some that these followed earlier usage in Judea and had been learned from Jewish exiles. The foreign origin of these deeds is evidenced by the fact that in the long tradition of Babylonian deeds, from the earliest records to the Seleucid period, no instance was found of a sale of property drawn up in the form of a dialogue, whereas "dialogue" drafting of a deed of sale, especially land sales, was quite common among Jews from the Old Testament to the Talmudic periods. It is quite likely that the Jews brought this form of drafting deeds to Babylonia where it was adopted for all, except the deeds relating to sale of land. Such deeds were drafted in a ponderous legal terminology, and the scribes stuck to the more ancient style. It should be remembered, however, that Patriarchal narratives like the account of the sale of the Cave of Machpelah contain many traces of Mesopotamian origin. A very ancient style of drafting legal documents may, in fact, have returned with the exiles to its original source. There is evidence that in the earliest periods of Sumer, land sales were completed in two stages separated by a period of time: first the payment of the price, then taking possession (see also Loans and Debts*).

PROVERBS, BOOK OF. — *Outline: Subject Matter; Literary Forms; Contents and Message; The Proverbs of Solomon; The Words of the Wise; Additional Proverbs of Solomon; The Words of Agur; The Words of Lemuel; In Praise of the Housewife; Authorship and Date.*

The book of Proverbs (Mishlê) is the second of the Writings or Hagiographa section in the Hebrew Canon of the Old Testament and is the most characteristic of all Wisdom Literature*. It is made up of collections of wise sayings and moral and religious precepts, composed by different hands and at different periods.

Subject Matter: Its subject matter is aptly summed up in Pr. 1:1–6 as "instruction in wise dealing, righteousness, justice and equity." It is concerned with the details of human life and lays no claim to profound philosophizing in the Greek sense. What speculation is to be found is concerned with the nature of wisdom itself. The precepts which the book lays down apply to the behaviour of the individual, having nothing to do explicitly with national policies or activities. In this the book resembles the early Egyptian "Wisdom" collections, or the later Babylonian "Book of the sage Ahikar" (see Wisdom Literature*). This Sumerian tablet (**699**) contains 29 proverbs. Many begin with the Sumerian word for "man" and "flesh".

Literary Forms: The Hebrew word for proverb "māshāl" has a number of meanings: aphorism, parable, allegory, riddle, simile, example. The "māshāl" draws its examples and lessons from man's familiar environment of nature and everyday life, expressing its teachings in direct, easily understood phrases such as "Like mother, like daughter" (Ezk. 16:44) or in striking contradictions, e.g. "One sows and another reaps" (Jn. 4:37).

The appropriate emphasis could be secured by repeating the idea in different words (e.g. Pr. 3:17), in a style familiar from Hebrew poetry*, or by balancing contrasts (3:33) or by the rhythmic measure used. Picturesque hyperbole was often employed to drive a lesson home (such as the famous comparison of the camel going through the eye of a needle in Mt. 19:24), and a tendency to elliptical forms probably reflects the generally flattering assumption that those who studied these works were equal to a difficult phrase or an obscure reference. Proverbs of this type were known as "the words of the wise" and Jesus flouted this tradition by claiming that the mysteries of the Kingdom had been hidden from the wise but revealed to babes (Mt. 11:25, passim). Sometimes the whole point of the proverb was obscured and then it became an "enigma" or "dark saying" challenging the ingenuity of the interpreter (Pr. 1:6; 30:15–31). Both the prophets (Ezk. 20:49) and Jesus (Jn. 16:29) were accused

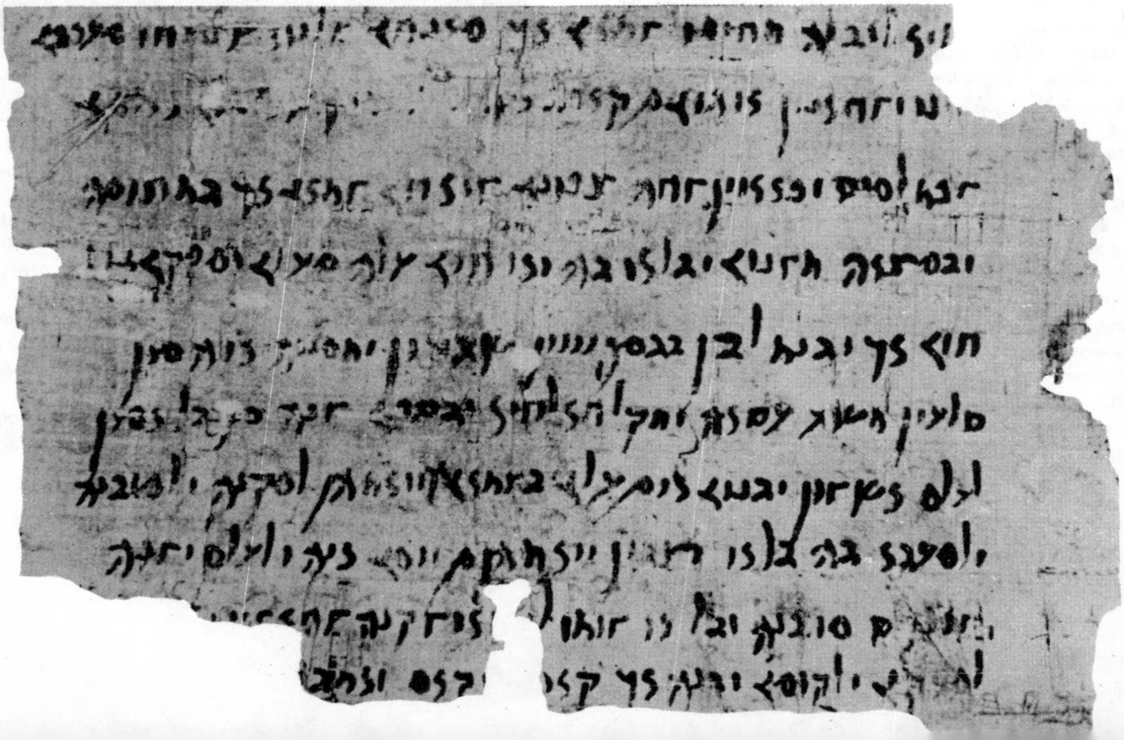

698

of "speaking in riddles", although riddles themselves were used deliberately to provoke competitive audience participation and to lighten a discourse (Pr. 30:15–31).

The speeches of Balaam (Nu. 24:15 ff) and the "taunt" against the king of Babylon in Isaiah 14:4 were also described as "māshāl" (proverbs). In general, "wisdom" in the form of sayings and proverbs had a much higher prestige in the east than in the west. Today, their charm as literature lies in the way they reflect Oriental life and they are, in the main, a valuable deposit of wisdom in the practical sense.

Contents and Message: The different authors of the various sections of the anthology are indicated by the headings:

Chs. 1–9 constitute a prologue, mainly emphasizing the importance of wisdom. Unlike the following chapters, each idea in this section is discussed at some length in a short poetic essay — one of the most polished forms of the "māshāl" — emphasizing the contrast between the results of the search for wisdom compared to a life given up to folly and wickedness. The temptations which the sage warns against especially are: crimes of violence (1:10–19); rashly pledging oneself to another (6:1–5); sloth (6:6–11); duplicity (6:12–15) and, above all, sexual licence (2:16–19; 5:3–20; 6:23–35; 7:4–27; 9:13–18). To those who resist these temptations, wisdom offers a life of happiness, wealth and honour (3:13–18). The deeply religious tone of this section (e.g. 1:7; 3:5–12) and its didactic style are strongly reminiscent of Deuteronomy*. Its author is anonymous but it is generally considered to be among the latest sections of the collection. However, while this may be true of its final editing (perhaps around 600 BCE), much of the material contained in these chapters must be considerably earlier. W.F. Albright has drawn attention to numerous parallels in form and content between this section, especially chs. 8 and 9, and Ugaritic and Phoenican literature. He believes that it is quite possible that certain individual aphorisms or even longer sections originated in their present form during the Canaanite Bronze Age. Attention has been called to the important problem of the mythological background of proto-Hebrew wisdom literature and to cultural links that tie it to the Canaanite literature mentioned above.

The problems raised by the remarkable passage 8:1–9:6, where wisdom is personified as a woman, are also discussed under Wisdom Literature* (Mythology and Symbolism).

The Proverbs of Solomon (Chs. 10:1–21:16): The section under this heading is probably the oldest of the book and scholars are increasingly tending to accept the tradition that the historical King Solomon was indeed the foremost sage of his age (I K. 4:29–34; Pr. 1:1; 10:1; 25:1; see below). The section of the book ascribed to his hand contains some 375 short proverbs, without a noticeable organizing principle. Those in chs. 10–15 appear to be mainly authentic in structure, while 16–22 are synthetic or synonymous. Though religion has its place (15:3, 8, 9; 16:1–9, etc.), the main burden of these proverbs is practical wisdom and wise dealings in everyday life. In general, each proverb is a complete and separate entity, but a common viewpoint or similar style can be found to link many of them, e.g. 10:2, 4 and 6; 16:10–15 or 11:9–12 where four verses all begin with the letter "b". Antithetical parallelism is also the essence of this section. Almost every verse affords an example.

The Words of the Wise (22:17–24:34): In the Massoretic (Hebrew) text and in English Bibles, the title has been absorbed into the wording of 22:17. The section is really two separate collections, the words of "the Wise" being 22:17–23:14 while 23:15–24:34 is of different authorship. The first section is particularly close to the Egyptian "Instruction of Amenemopet" dating from the 12th c. BCE (see Wisdom Literature*). The title of these "words of the wise", e.g. "have I not written for you thirty sayings" (22:20) is suggestive of the Egyptian precepts. At least a third of the proverbs appear to derive either directly from this work or from a common source. Verses 23:13–14, on the other hand, are a direct quotation from the "Words of Ahikar". These two sections are not Solomonic, but are part of the general legacy of Israel's wise men (cf. Ecc. 12: 9–11). Together they represent a much more coherent collection of related maxims with particular emphasis on: care for the poor (22:22, 27); respect for the king (23:1–3; 24:21–22); the value of discipline (23:13, 14); temperance (23:19–21, 29–35); honour of parents (23:22–25); chastity (23:26–28) and fear of God (24:21). The brief addition (24:23–34) is of much the same type, with a slightly greater sense of social responsibility (e.g. 24:28, 29).

Additional Proverbs of Solomon (Chs. 25:1–29:27): This section, also ascribed to Solomon, is very much like the first collection of his wisdom (10:1–22:16), being a miscellaneous assortment of short sayings (128 of the 139 verses are complete maxims) offering good advice on a variety of topics. Antithetical parallelism is much less common than in the earlier section, whereas comparison, rare in the first collection, occurs frequently (e.g. 25:3, 11–14, 18–20 etc.).

The statement (25:1) that these proverbs were copied by the "men of Hezekiah, king of Judah", moved the rabbis (Baba Bathra 15 a) to propose that the Proverbs were written by Hezekiah and his scribes. Exactly what role they did play in the editing of the book is not clear, but there is no real reason to question the accuracy of the statement. There is evidence (II Ch. 29:25 ff) that Hezekiah took a great interest in Israel's traditions and literature.

The Words of Agûr (Ch. 30:1–33): This begins the heterodox part of Proverbs (see Wisdom Literature*: Types). Agûr, his father Jakeh or his audience, Ithiel and Ucal (30:1), all defy identification, but seem to suggest that the proverbs recorded in this chapter did not belong to a purely Israelite tradition, and had been current orally for some time before being written down. It contains some thoughts that are reminiscent of Job (cf. 40:5; 42:6). They are much less orthodox in tone than the earlier chapters of Proverbs. The first few verses (2–4) even suggest a convinced agnostic, but in a masterly passage (30:7–9) we read that the rich may lose their need of God and the poor may think that God has forgotten them yet these thoughts are answered by the affirmation of God's existence. The second half of the chapter (vs. 15–33) is phrased in a rhythmic numerical fashion with aphorisms on four insatiable things, four little things, four comely things, etc., very reminiscent of Ugaritic poetry and found elsewhere in the Old Testament (e.g. Am. 1–2).

The Words of Lemuel (Ch. 31:1–9): This king of Massa and his mother, from whom he learned his wisdom, are also unknown. Her advice consists of warnings against wine and women and an admonition to deal justly with the unfortunate. There is a notable Aramaic influence on the section (e.g. "bar" for son, "melakin" for kings) which has disposed scholars to the opinion that because of a general similarity, the compilers of the book placed well-known but foreign meditations in the framework of Proverbs.

In Praise of the Housewife (Ch. 31:10–31): This famous acrostic poem (which has no title) in praise of the industrious housewife is different from the preceding sections and forms an appendix to the book. The ringing praise accorded to the perfect wife by her husband and children forms a fitting conclusion to a book devoted to the practical benefits of a well-directed, God-fearing life.

Authorship and Date: In Hebrew tradition, all Israel's great literature was the work of outstanding personalities. Thus, the Pentateuch is ascribed to Moses, Psalms to David, and the Bible's major collection of "Wisdom" to Israel's wisest king.

The biblical record credits Solomon with an international reputation as a just administrator and a wise man, famous for the composition of proverbs (I K. 4:29–34, see above). Whether or not the proverbs recorded as his were, in fact, composed by him, modern scholars agree that Israel's wisdom tradition was flourishing during the period of the monarchy. It seems certain that it was well developed by the 10th c. BCE, perhaps drawing on Canaanite inspiration. The wise men of Solomon's court, Ethan the Ezrahite, Heman, Calcol and Darda (I K. 4:31), all have Canaanite names. Ruling during a rare period of peace and prosperity, Solomon was able to establish contacts with the most civilized courts of his time and to devote himself to cultural and intellectual pursuits to an extent denied his successors. He undoubtedly fostered the popular tradition of "wisdom" and may have taken a hand in it himself.

The book of Proverbs as it stands contains compositions of different periods. The contents seem all to be pre-Exilic, but the compilation may be somewhat later. On the evidence of the apocryphal book of Ecclesiasticus (see Apocrypha*), Proverbs must have been in existence and well known before the later work was composed around 200 BCE. There is no reason, however, to try and present the actual material as belonging to any later period than the time at which wisdom East. In of the same kind flourished in the rest of the Near literature general, one can regard the whole anthology as a complex of traditions which extend throughout almost the whole of the Old Testament period.

PSALMS. — *Outline: I. Origin, History and Place in the Canon; Titles. II. Contents and Organization of the Psalter; Character of the Psalms; Psalms and Ritual; Canaanite Elements in the Book of Psalms; Psalm 29 and the Ugarit Poems. III. Dating of the Psalms; Conclusion.*

I. ORIGIN, HISTORY AND PLACE IN THE CANON: "Moses gave five books of the Law to Israel and David gave five books of the Psalms to Israel" (Midrash "Shocher Tov" to the first Psalm, v. 2). Jewish tradition ascribes the composition of all the hymns of the book of Psalms, so important in the worship and prayers of both Judaism and Christianity, to David, the "Sweet Psalmist of Israel." In fact, however, matters are not so simple.

All the psalms could not possibly have been composed in their present form by the historical King David, any more than Moses could have written the Torah. The most likely date of composition for these hymns is, in fact, one of the most important subjects of research into the book of Psalms and there is hardly a period in Jewish history which scholars have not found reflected in one psalm or another — from the beginning of the monarchy (ca. 1000 BCE) to the time of the Maccabees (shortly before the beginning of the Christian era).

More recent studies of the Old Testament have achieved a much more sympathetic understanding of the life and religion it reflects and have also shown that the forms of worship in ancient Israel are both the background to the Psalms and can be partly reconstructed from them. This new approach, essentially that of the Form-Critical method (see below and Biblical Criticism*), covers not only the texts of the Psalms but the whole setting: historical, social, religious, cultic, etc. Each aspect is given equal importance in the classification of the Psalms according to literary types, which, in turn, leads to a much more accurate estimate of the dating of each psalm.

As it stands, the book of Psalms is a collection of sacred poems, largely of a liturgical nature, intended to be sung, accompanied by instruments and dancing (see Music*). In the Hebrew Canon the Psalter opens the last group of "Writings" although in non-Hebrew Bibles it comes before the prophets.

Titles: In most cases, each psalm is headed by a title or superscription, e.g. Psalm 4: "To the choirmaster, with stringed instruments. A Psalm of David." However, they do not all refer to David. Psalm 77 announces itself, "A Psalm of Asaph"; psalm 84 "A Psalm of the Sons of Korah" and Psalm 88: "A Maskîl of Heman the Ezrahite". Moreover Psalm 137 explicitly refers to the period of the Babylonian Exile, "By the waters of Babylon there we sat down and wept . . ." Even the 73 psalms (out of a total of 150) which do carry the title, "to David" or "A Psalm of David" may not necessarily have been composed by him. Some scholars interpret the phrase as meaning "dedicated to David" or "in the Davidic manner", which would deny David authorship of all but a very few of the hymns. It seems that David was in fact a gifted poet, for instance the Laments over Saul and Jonathan and Abner and the song of II Sam. 23. It also seems possible that II Sam. 22 has been correctly attributed to David. Accordingly, although it cannot be stated definitely that David composed any particular psalm in the present Psalter, it would also be going too far to say that he could not possibly have done so.

Significantly, the question of the authenticity of the titles of the Psalms has aroused some of the most passionate controversy of biblical research. On the one hand are the scholars who believe the titles to be accurate statements of fact which, however, were misunderstood at the time of the Septuagint translation since, by the time of the Second Temple period, their original meanings had already been forgotten. This theory assumes an early origin both for the psalms themselves and for their titles. Scholars who doubt the authenticity of the titles, on the other hand, point out that although some of the psalms were used in the Temple liturgy, there was a general tendency during the Second

Temple period to ascribe the organization of Temple ritual to David and this would have extended to some of the psalms. In this opinion, the tradition of composition by David need not be earlier than the Second Temple.

The meanings of the musical terms and other expressions used in the titles to the Psalms are discussed in the article on Music*. It may be noted, however, that in a number of cases, there is a contradiction between the Hebrew text and the early translations. Some psalms which are unnamed in one tradition appear in other versions complete with the name of their author. For example, Psalm 95 which is inscribed "to David" in the Septuagint appears unnamed in the Hebrew text. Remarkably enough, however, rabbinic sources occasionally testify to the precise use of certain psalms in the liturgy and, although the titles do not appear in the Hebrew Massoretic (traditional) biblical text, the identical information is contained in the titles given them in the Septuagint. For instance, the Septuagint title to Psalm 24 attributes its use to the first day of the week, while the Mishnah (Tamid 7:4) records that it was chanted then by the Temple choirs: "On the first day (of the week) they said, 'the earth and what is in it is God's'."

It needs to be remembered that the Greek and Aramaic translators of the Bible were firmly rooted in Jewish life (see Translations of the Bible*), and were guided by established literary and interpretative traditions, very close to rabbinic lore. There are other translations of the Psalms apparently made by the early Christians.

II. CONTENTS AND ORGANIZATION OF THE PSALTER: In its *modern form*, the Psalter appears to be divided into five books:

1–41	73–89
42–72	90–106
107–150	

Each of the first four end with a hymn of praise and the last psalm is also a doxology. However, it is apparent that these divisions are artificial, probably later ones, made perhaps in a desire to impose the pattern of the Pentateuch on the Psalter. On closer examination other divisions are revealed, suggesting that a number of originally independent collections were united into the present book of Psalms.

The first clue to these earlier collections may be sought in titles referring to persons given to the psalms, i.e.

Psalms 1–2 are without title;

Psalms 3–41, 51–65, 68–70 and 86 are entitled "of David";

Psalms 42, 44–49 and 84–87 (but not 86) are entitled "of the Sons of Korah", a guild of Temple singers;

Psalms 73–83 are entitled "of Asaph", another Temple singers' guild;

Psalm 89 is ascribed to "Ethan the Ezrahite";

Psalms 120–134 are entitled "A Song of Ascents";

The rest: 90–119 and 135–150 are either without title, or else the titles vary from one psalm to another.

The belief that the Psalter is made up of a gradual amalgamation of various originally separate collections is supported by a division of the Psalter according to the divine name used — Yahweh or Elohim. This is the same method by which the schools of Biblical Criticism* have separated the Pentateuch as a whole into its different literary traditions, i.e. the J (Jahwist) and E (Elohist) sources. A division of the Psalter on this basis yields the quite remarkable result that in Psalms 1–41 "Yahweh" appears 272 times and Elohim only 15, while in Psalms 42–83, Elohim is used 200 times and Jehovah (Yahweh) 43.

The explanation offered for these facts is that Psalms 42–84, called the "Elohistic Psalter" because of the emphasis on "Elohim" as the divine name, is one of the earlier collections of the Psalter but that it was itself derived from a number of different sources. This section includes a group of David's Psalms (51–70, see above) and appears to be concluded by the statement in 72:20 that "the prayers of David, the son of Jesse, are ended." This is certainly not true of the Psalter as a whole, but it may have been true of the earlier collection. David's name is not attached to any of the psalms between 73 and 89. The groups of psalms "of the Sons of Korah" and those "of Asaph" are also included in "the Elohistic Psalter." It is assumed that the collection was enlarged by the addition of Psalms 84–89.

Character of the Psalms: Form-Critical literary analysis of the psalms has been carried out notably by H. Gunkel who was the first to insist on the importance of studying the Psalms according to 1. their literary types and 2. the circumstances (life-situation) which had brought each psalm into being. He made a comparative study of the psalms side by side with religious literature from early Egypt and Mesopotamia. By using his method, the Form-Critical school of biblical studies reached the conclusion that, in the main, the psalms had their origin in cultic circles and are much older than had been assumed by previous studies. Originally, they were not expressions of personal piety but compositions intended to be chanted as part of the ritual of pre-Exilic local shrines. Each type could thus be related to some specific act in the ritual of the sanctuary. On the basis of this analysis of literary type and probable background of each psalm, Gunkel distinguished five main classes (or "Gattungen") of psalms, i.e. hymns (95); national dirges (11); royal hymns (45); individual dirges (22) and individual thanksgivings (18). Like most others, this classification could also do with a section for "miscellaneous" or a special category for the many examples of mixed types.

Gunkel admitted that although most of the psalms showed the influence of corresponding cultic circles elsewhere, they were composed independently. On the whole, they are more spiritual in character than the productions of contemporary Near Eastern religions. S. Mowinckel of the Scandinavian school extended the theory to the point where the majority of the psalms were recognized as having been deliberately composed as part of a cultic ritual. In many ways, this meant worship of no mean spiritual order. The authors of the poems must be sought mainly among Temple personnel — the cultic prophets and other officials associated with the musical guilds like that of Asaph (cf. I Ch. 25:1 ff).

Psalms and Ritual: There are verses in some of the psalms which refer directly to ritual, e.g. 116:13: "I will lift pp the cup of salvation"; 50:14: "Offer to God a sacrifice of thanksgiving." Whether these psalms were designed for a ritual purpose from the very beginning or whether they began as abstract compositions which were only later adopted for cultic purposes, is a matter which is still open to debate. S. Mowinckel, who is the staunchest upholder of the view that the psalms constituted part of the actual cult at the time of their composition, rejects the opposing view that, for instance, psalms 93, 95–99 and the other so-called "Royal Psalms" refer to the concepts of the universal kingship of Yahweh expounded in Deutero-Isaiah* 40–55. Instead, he and many other students of the Old Testament maintain that these and other apparently related psalms originally formed part of the celebration of Yahweh's Kingship in the autumnal New Year festival celebrated each year in the pre-Exilic Jerusalem Temple. In this view, the festival included a ceremony of "the Coronation of Yahweh" much like the Babylonian "cult-drama" of the crowning of the god Marduk (see Babylonia*). All those "royal" psalms which begin "The Lord reigns" are seen as belonging to this ritual, which is believed to have included bringing the Ark of the Covenant, the symbol of God's victory over the kings of the earth and the powers of darkness, into the Temple. God then renewed his Covenant with the people of Israel and the House of David. So far as the date of composition is concerned, the implications of this theory are that most of the book of Psalms must have been in existence at the time of the First Temple, for a religious ceremony in which the king of Israel may be presumed to have taken a prominent part is only conceivable during this period. In this view, even if the psalms were not actually composed by David, his name is a valid indication of their approximate age.

His search for a "setting in life" in the early historical period has also moved S. Mowinckel to find a magical purpose in a number of the psalms. By comparison with contemporary Near Eastern practice, the whole Psalter can be seen not as the expression of praise and devotion, but as a collection of potent spells which were to be recited for the release of magical power. Sufferers of that age assumed that disease and other distress were caused by the spells of enemies. Thus references to "workers of iniquity" in the psalms can be seen as referring to sorcerers who cast such malignant spells. In this view, a large part of the Psalter represents a corpus of magical incantations which could only be used effectively with the expert knowledge of the priest magician. This is not a view which is widely accepted. It seems unlikely that psalms created for no higher purpose than to act as magical spells could be adapted to a spiritual worship that endured for centuries and belonged, notably, to a religion (Judaism) which, especially during the period of the Second Temple, repudiated all the concepts and attitudes of magic (see Magic* and Superstition). The psalms' formulas of blessings and curses may have echoed primitive notions which were rooted in magical ideas, but by the time of the monarchy, the classic prophets and, presumably, the composition of the psalms, these ancient phrases had no more than a metaphorical content.

Nevertheless, in spite of exaggerations, speculation and arbitrary reconstruction, the Form-Critical school's insistence on a cultic background for the psalms has proved a fruitful avenue of research into Old Testament writings.

Canaanite Elements in the Book of Psalms: Many scholars accept an early date for Psalms but reject the whole theory of the "New Year celebration" and also a magical interpretation as an explanation for their early appearance in Israel's life and cult. This attitude is based on a general tendency today to use the results of archaeological and other investigations into the culture and literature of the whole Near East during biblical times as justification for quite early dates for the composition of a good many books of the Bible. The documents from Ugarit*, which date from the 14th c. BCE, have been particularly significant for this new attitude for they have proved the great antiquity of the linguistic traditions and forms found in the Psalms and many other books of the Bible. Moreover they have demonstrated conclusively that these traditions were rooted in the land of Canaan before Israel settled there.

Psalm 29 and the Ugarit Poems: The literature of Ugarit, F.M. Cross has noted, is largely epic. Although refrains and lyric passages are included, none of the extant Ugarit texts provides a clear-cut example of a Canaanite cultic psalm. The biblical Psalm 29, however, was found to have many elements in common with Ugaritic epics, in vocabulary and stylistic features. The absence of any lyric poetry or psalms among the Ugaritic texts means that Psalm 29 appears to fill a real gap in existing knowledge of Canaanite literature (due to the similarity noted), for many scholars see in it an Israelite adaptation of a much older Canaanite hymn (see Poetry*).

The linguistic argument for composition of the psalms soon after their archaic Canaanite models, however, is not conclusive. Poets have a habit of making use of archaic forms of language and expressions, i.e. of deliberately "archaizing" their forms of expression. As a general rule it is not easy to be certain about the difference between archaic and archaizing, but it is not impossible. The clue is almost always correct usage. Archaizers make tell-tale errors in all languages. Even so, by itself, the language of the psalms is not sufficient evidence to determine when they were composed.

III. DATING OF THE PSALMS: A rather similar approach is the attempt to find parallels between the book of Psalms and Second (Deutero) Isaiah* (i.e. chs. 40–55, written in the Babylonian Exile), and then to decide which was influenced by which. Not that this is entirely convincing either. It is possible that both drew on a third, common, source. On the other hand, even without any such common source, there is no way of establishing with any degree of certainty which was the original and which the borrower. (This has been amply demonstrated by the totally contradictory conclusions reached on the subject by different scholars.)

Another approach is to try to date the psalms according to the religious development which they apparently reflect. However, theological considerations of this nature tend to rely far too heavily on the particular theories and prejudices of the scholar concerned. As there is no real agreement about the exact course of development of the Jewish religion (see Biblical Criticism*), an objective criterion for dating the psalms by their theology seems to be out of the question, at least for the moment.

It has also been argued that the psalms' historical context is also of very limited value as a guide to their date. Although there are a few historical references and reminiscences, these cannot fix the actual date of composition, only the *terminus ante quem* (the earliest possible limit). Psalm No. 137, as mentioned above, refers quite explicitly to the Babylonian Exile but apart from that, historical references tend to be too generalized to indicate a definite historical period. Indeed this very quality of timelessness is often cited as one of the characteristics which make the Psalms immortal.

In general, the history of the composition and arrangement of the book of Psalms remains obscure. A scroll of Psalms of the 1st c. BCE has been discovered at Qumran but this differs considerably from the canonical book. From the way in which the New Testament refers to and makes use of the Psalms, however, it seems unlikely that additions were still being made in the 1st c. CE. On the other hand there is no conclusive evidence for its existence in anything like its present form in post-Exilic days. It seems that the psalms of the Psalter are only the most significant examples of a whole literature of different groups of psalms dating from the earliest days of Israelite settlement in the Promised Land right down to late post-Exilic times. Many of the psalms are of unquestionable antiquity. Even the others in the opinion of D.N. Freedman cannot have been composed later than early post-Exilic days (5th c. BCE). However, their arrangement and selection may have continued perhaps until the 3rd or 2nd cs. BCE. The 2nd c. Septuagint version is practically identical in order and arrangement with the Hebrew text, showing that the book had been pretty well finalized by 200 BCE. The Qumran psalms (those which are not canonical) are so different, in spite of having been made in imitation of the canonical Psalter, that they seem to confirm a very much earlier dating for the composition of the actual canonical psalms.

Conclusion: Clearly, the various collections and individual psalms were written at different times and were not originally designed as part of a single collection. The book of Psalms as it now stands represents the conclusion of a complete literary process of growth or development, whose history remains very obscure. The book can be seen as an anthology, carefully selected from a number of collections of hymns and psalms, such as the "Songs of Ascents" (120–132) or the "Poems of Asaph" (73–83 and also No. 50), composed at different times and, very probably, in various places, i.e. both the Northern and Southern Kingdoms. Psalm 80, for instance is regarded by many authorities as having been composed in the Northern Kingdom of Israel. The final editing of the book appears to have taken place during the Second Temple period. The theory that many of the psalms could be ascribed to the Maccabaean age has been disproved by the evidence of the Dead Sea Scrolls* (see above), themselves a product of that time. Their language is quite different from that of the Psalms which must already have been in existence. Similarly, there is no proof that the Psalter was composed in the period of the First Temple and nothing to support composition of the majority of the psalms by David. The tradition which has made David "the Sweet Psalmist" seems very much on a par with that which made Solomon the author of Ecclesiastes. In each case, the king's personality made it seem appropriate to link his name with a particular book: Solomon with a book of wisdom and David, the harpist, with a collection of hymns and poems.

As to setting a time for the composition of each individual psalm in the form in which they exist today, this, too, it seems, will have to wait until new criteria can be devised to measure up to the complexity of the problem.

R

RABBIS. — *Outline: I. Hillel and Shammai: Hillel's School; Hillel's Golden Rule; Shammai's School; The Impact of Hillel and Shammai. II. Rabbinic Judaism: The Academies; The Tannaim and the Mishnah; Pharisaism and Formative Judaism.*

"Rabbi" is a title or mode of address meaning "my master" in Hebrew. It came into use in the 1st c. CE, and referred to teachers who were ordained members of the Sanhedrin. It was also applied, however, to scholars whose right to expound the Law derived from their knowledge of, and loyalty to it. Jesus of Nazareth is so addressed in the New Testament. The functions of the rabbi, although not the title, were familiar from the first half of the 2nd c. BCE. Five pairs of scholars, called "zugot", ending with Hillel and Shammai towards the end of the 1st c. BCE, exercised the rabbinical functions of authoritative teachers (see Mishnah*). Talmudic tradition (Tractate Hagigah 2:2) claims that they served as presiding officers of the Sanhedrin and they are described under that title. These zugot were followed by several generations of rabbis of the Tannaitic period and Palestinian Talmud era. The scholars of Babylonian Jewry were addressed as "rab" (master).

I. HILLEL AND SHAMMAI: The last and best known of the five pairs of great teachers are also considered as prominent initiators among the first generation of Tannaitic rabbis. They lived in Palestine at the end of the 1st c. BCE, during the reign of Herod*. Hillel, called the "Elder", migrated to Palestine from his native Babylonia in search of education. He studied in the academies of the previous pair of rabbis, and there gained the store of traditions necessary for a scholar of the Law. Hillel quickly assimilated the discipline and academic principles of research and interpretation and, in due course, was appointed "nasi" of the Sanhedrin. In this capacity he formulated the famous seven rules, known to later generations as "Hillel's Middot". His rules clearly reflect the extent to which contemporary Jewish learning was affected by linguistic and grammatical principles derived from the Graeco-Roman school of rhetoric.

Hillel's vision went far beyond tradition and, as a result, he insisted that every generation of scholars be permitted to derive new meanings from their study of the Torah, and thus write new "Hălākhôt" to meet changing conditions. However, he did not reject what had been passed down from earlier ages. As a jurist, Hillel had no equal in his generation. He attempted to express the larger intent of Scriptures and not merely its literal, limited implications. Though few decisions are cited in his name, the fiscal institution of "Prozbûl" (see Law*) was his.

Hillel's School: While a student, Hillel had been forced by poverty to support himself by manual labor. Consequently, he welcomed everyone into his academy and disapproved of the exclusiveness of the institution run by his friend and ideological opponent, Shammai. Unlike the latter, Hillel was noted for his humility and leniency. He translated his social consciousness into action, and as a result of his association with the common people, introduced many reforms. The theological school that he founded was known as the "House of Hillel".

Hillel's Golden Rule: Hillel's tact and patience were proverbial. Once, when a heathen appeared before him and asked, "What, in a nutshell, does Judaism teach?", Hillel immediately understood that the man was concerned with the essential message of Judaism and not with details of ritual, and replied: "Do not do unto others that which you would not have them do unto you. This is the whole of the Torah; all else is commentary. Now go and study it." (Talmud, Sabbath 31 a). This in its positive form was taught by Jesus and has come down as the Golden Rule.

While Hillel and Shammai differed on only three points of law (Eduyot 1:1), they were frequently at odds on questions of practice. In legal matters Hillel's opinion usually prevailed and the trend he originated was not to be resisted. After the destruction of the Temple in 70 CE, Rabbi Yohanan ben Zaccai, Hillel's pupil, who headed the Council of Jabneh, made the more liberal Hillelite interpretations binding on all teachers or Tannaitic rabbis. In this way, the tradition of Hillel became dominant, and was maintained by a dynasty of "patriarchs" (presidents of the Jewish community), which held office in Palestine until the 5th c. CE.

Shammai's School: Shammai was an admirable counterpart to Hillel. He represented the more conservative element in the country, and as a successful mason who became wealthy, he was inclined to voice the interests of the propertied. Unlike Hillel, who thanked God if he had sufficient food for the day, Shammai found nothing strange in recommending the sort of marketing that would only be possible for a man of means. While it would be unfair to picture Shammai as harsh or uncivil, his pupils inclined to rigorous decisions in religious matters. Strangers were often discouraged by his short temper and lack of a sense of humour. Nevertheless, he had a friendly nature and was famous for his saying "receive everyone graciously" (Aboth: 1:15). It was from his school that the more "courtly" rules with regard to women were derived.

In addition, Shammai foresaw the dangers of Roman hegemony encouraged by Herod, and enacted many regulations intended to keep the Jews from fraternizing with the heathen. Shammai may possibly be identified with the Pharisee Sameas, who rallied the Sanhedrin against Herod's attempted intimidation in 47 BCE (see Herod*). Very few *halakhic* (legal) teachings, however, have survived in his name, and disciples of Shammai are very rarely mentioned as such by name.

The Impact of Hillel and Shammai: The impact of both Hillel and Shammai on their age and on Judaism was tremendous. The members of their academies engaged in all kinds of intellectual controversy over an amazing range of subjects. Though much of these lively debates was theoretical and scholastic, particularly after Rome appropriated more and more of the legislative power of the country, they added to the context of Jewish tradition and exemplified the meaning of scholarship for all future students.

As the ruling power in the days of Herod and his successors became more and more removed from the experience of the ordinary people, the academies came to be regarded as the people's guides, "the fathers of the universe". The great rabbis did not form a professional class. Either they were men of independent means, or they earned their living by following a trade or some other occupation. They were thus thoroughly integrated into the community which they served as scholars and teachers.

II. RABBINIC JUDAISM: The Pharisaic tradition of the pre-Christian centuries was carried on by the successors of Hillel and Shammai. These rabbis, or early Tannaim, represent the beginning of Rabbinic Judaism. Their authority rested in the continuously growing Oral Law* which interpreted and supplemented the Scriptures. During the period of the Second Temple this Oral Law was upheld by the Pharisee rabbis and the majority of the population. The Sadducees* and Essenes (see Dead Sea Scrolls*), however, did not recognize it as they possessed their own traditions regarding the interpretation of the Written Law. With the disappearance of these sects after the fall of Jerusalem and the destruction of the Temple, the Pharisaic view won national acceptance and the Oral Law was studied in the various academies (see Pharisees*; Mishnah*).

The Academies: The academies that flourished during this era were not isolated havens for purely intellectual exercise, but developed and instituted laws affecting the whole of society. One method of Bible interpretation taught was the detailed study and commentary on the meaning of the text as presented. Another system used was that of "derāsh" (see Biblical Criticism*), a homiletic exposition of the underlying meanings of the text. This method, which exercised a tremendous influence on Jewish life of the period, and in fact still affects orthodox Jewish learning and interpretation, does not always follow the logical modes of modern thought. In matters relating to common and religious law, each teacher was permitted to offer his own interpretation, though occasionally the Sanhedrin was called upon to decide between conflicting views. While these decisions were presumably accepted in practice, those that were rejected often continued to be taught in theory. In all the academies, the Written Law was presented in a systematic and topical arrangement.

The Tannaim and the Mishnah: Many individual scholars privately recorded parts of the Oral Law*. The most famous Tannaitic scholar of the 2nd c. CE was Rabbi Akiba, whose notes were handed down in separate traditions by his four leading disciples: Rabbi Meir, head of the new Academy of Usha in Galilee; Rabbi Yose ben Halaphta, member of that Academy and head of the Academy of Sephoris in Galilee; Rabbi Shimon bar Yochai, the great mystic; and Rabbi Judah ha'Nasi, "Patriarch of Palestinian Jewry" and redactor of the Mishnah*. He was the last of four generations of great teachers after Hillel and Shammai. With his disciples, he represents the transition to the period of Amoraic teachers of the Talmud (who followed the Tannaim).

It was these scholars and their thousands of followers who kept the spirit of Judaism alive when Jewish nationalism collapsed with Bar-Kochba's* defeat in 135 CE. When the Hadrianic Decrees banning Judaism were lifted in 140 CE, these Tannaim revived Jewish social and communal life and culture in the Galilean towns and villages.

Pharisaism and Formative Judaism*: The Mishnah* and the Talmud contain the precepts of Jewish law as accepted by Rabbinic Judaism. Eventually, this became synonymous with normative historical Judaism and today it is represented in the orthodox wing of Judaism. Although the political history of Judaism came to a temporary standstill in 70 CE, there is no parallel break in the growth of the Pharisaic-Tannaitic-rabbinic tradition. The Tannaim and rabbis were the Pharisees of a later age, completing a continuous trend of development of Judaism during the first two Christian centuries.

The rabbis concerned themselves with the whole of every-day life. They believed that God had given man the Torah (both the Written and Oral Law) as a set of commandments by which the life of the community could be guided — a blue-print of life under the Law*. However, this blue-print had to be properly understood and interpreted. The rabbis saw it as their job to give a sense of purpose to their stateless people, thus providing a basis for survival, independent of other, material factors. This re-affirmation of belief in the Law as the foundation of Judaism, made it possible for the people and their faith to survive the loss of the Temple and their nationhood. In place of the cultural, intellectual and material diversions of the peoples who surrounded them, the Jews reorganized their life and their society on this firm basis of the Law and its observance. (For additional discussions of rabbinic achievements in the latter days of the Second Temple, see Pharisees*; Law* Oral: Life under the Law; Mishnah*. The Talmud, which is post-biblical, is not discussed further in this volume.)

RELIGION OF ISRAEL. — The major themes relating to the outward expression of religion are dealt with under Law* of Israel; other aspects of the growth, development and inner spirit of religion, under: Bible Text and Canon*; Chosen People and Election*; Covenant*; Deuteronomy*; Exile*; Feasts and Festivals*; Idol Worship in Israel*; Impurity and Purification*; Leviticus*; Mishnah*; Moses*; Numbers*; Patriarchs, Religion of*; Pharisees*; Priests and Levites*; Psalms*; Rabbis*; Restoration*; Revelation*; Sacrifices and Offerings*; Sadducees*; Sanctuaries*; Synagogue*; Tabernacle, Ark and Cherubim*; Temple*. See also Amos*; Apocalypse*; Apocrypha*; Dead Sea Scrolls*; Ezekiel*; Hosea*; Isaiah*; Jeremiah*; Micah*.

RESTORATION AND PERSIAN PERIOD; EZRA AND NEHEMIAH. — *Outline: I. The Downfall of Babylonia: The True Belshazzar; Cyrus; Cyrus' Edict. II. The First Return: The Returned Community; Messianic Dreams; Darius Triumphant; The Judeans and the "Amme-Ha'aretz"; Samaritan Enmity. III. Second Return: Nehemiah; Ezra; The Renewed Covenant. IV. The Ezra-Nehemiah Literature. V. Keneseth-Gedolah: High Priests; Johanan; Last Century of Persian Rule.*

Throughout their 50 years in Babylonia, the Jewish exiles remained a closely-knit community, devoted to the preser-

699

vation of their ancient traditions and to their hopes of a return to Zion. Far from allowing the calamity of their exile to destroy their faith in the one true God and his ultimate care for them, their religion was purified and strengthened. This is reflected especially in Second Isaiah where Jewish nationalism is combined with a universal faith. More clearly than earlier prophets, he expressed the gulf between the One God, who had chosen Israel as his own, and the non-existent deities, worshipped in error by Gentile peoples.

I. THE DOWNFALL OF BABYLONIA: The might of Babylonia* was threatened from two sides: by the Medes, and by the increasing power of the new Persian conqueror, Cyrus. He defeated the Median armies and took over their dominions, winning victories throughout the Near East and adding the countries of Greek Asia Minor to his empire. When he turned south to attack Babylon, his fame had reached such proportions that he was able to capture the city without shooting a single arrow. This is recorded in the Cylinder of Cyrus (**699**) which states also that he sent back to their lands the prisoners taken by his Babylonian predecessors.

The True Belshazzar: The Babylonian leader whom Cyrus so easily defeated appears in the enigmatic book of Daniel* in the famous episode of Belshazzar's feast and the writing on the wall (Dan. 5) which tells how the doom of Babylonia was mysteriously foretold to the feasting king.

Belshazzar (in Babylonian, Balsharuzur) was the son of the historical king Nabunaid (Nabonidus). He was never really king, but he acted as regent during the last 10 years of his father's reign, when Nabonidus was absent in the Arabian desert trying to establish a new empire throughout the Middle East. In a sense, therefore, the Bible is not far wrong in describing Belshazzar as the last king of Babylonia before it was conquered by the Persians.

Cyrus: The Bible presents Cyrus in an aura of benevolence. Although a realist and brilliant diplomat, Cyrus believed he had been entrusted with a mission by the god Marduk to conquer the world and then to restore the various gods, who had been carried to Babylonia, to their rightful shrines. This was a significant policy which explains his restoration of the Jews to Zion.

The Jews also regarded Cyrus as the instrument of divine policy. Second Isaiah sang of him metaphorically as God's "viceroy", his "anointed" (the same term used for the kings of Israel) and the primary agent of his purpose in history (Is. 44:28; 45:1–2, 13).

Some of his humanitarian attributes — unique in a ruler of that time — can be traced to Cyrus' religious background (see Persia*). The early Persians worshipped the nature gods of fertility and the heavens, but at the beginning of the 5th c. BCE, the philosopher Zoroaster founded the worship of Ahuramazda, the good god, the "Righteous Master of Righteousness". Unlike contemporary exclusive cults, Ahuramazda accepted the existence of other "foreign" gods who had their places as his "helpers". This tolerant policy, followed by Cyrus, allowed subject peoples to observe their own religious customs and even to run their own affairs without too much interference. Cyrus, in fact, was the first "liberator" — as against a "conqueror" — who tried to restore national and religious rights to the peoples he conquered.

Early Greek historians regarded him as one of the most enlightened and tolerant rulers in history and they had good grounds for this opinion. He seems to have understood that it was useless to compel people to follow alien traditions. He sought honour and power through the loyalty of the people rather than their fear.

The empire Cyrus (538–530 BCE) founded lasted for two hundred years, until the rise of Alexander the Great. Its armies were an efficient fighting force and its government's system of communications between different countries by means of fast chariots made it possible to supervise and control a far-flung empire.

Cyrus' Edict: In the first year after the fall of Babylonia (538 BCE), the Jewish exiles gathered to hear the proclamation of the king permitting their return (Ezr. 1:2–4). A parallel version of the edict is written in the same book in Aramaic. After giving specifications for the rebuilt temple, it continues "let the cost be paid from the royal treasury. And also let the gold and silver vessels of the house of God, which Nebuchadrezzar took out of the temple that is in Jerusalem and brought to Babylon, be restored and brought back to the temple which is in Jerusalem . . ." (Ezr. 6:4–5).

II. THE FIRST RETURN: Modern archaeological discoveries indicate that the form and style of the Edict as recorded in the Bible correspond to authentic edicts of the Persian kings and also confirm that Aramaic was the normal language of diplomacy and communications in the western part of the Empire. The fact of the Edict seems, therefore, to be historical. Nevertheless, it is unlikely that it was immediately followed by a wholesale exodus of Jews from Babylonia. After so long, many of them had become well established in their new home, a fact of which Babylonian tablets provide ample evidence. Moreover, the journey was long and dangerous and conditions in Judah were very unsatisfactory.

Over the next 15 years, however, many Jews did return. At their head was, first, Sheshbazzar, the fourth and youngest son of King Jehoiachin who had been deported from Judah but remained its legitimate ruler in Jewish and Babylonian eyes. The Babylonian list of the exiled King Jehoiachin's sons (see Exile*) does not include the name Sheshbazzar and W.F. Albright has suggested that the name is the same as the Shenazzar listed in I Ch. 3:18 as a son of Jehoiachin, both names being corruptions of the Babylonian name Sin-ab-usur. It appears as Sanabassar in Ezra* and in Josephus. Under whatever name, a prince of the Davidic line again led his countrymen to Judah (see Exile*).

At the beginning of the book of Ezra (2:64–67) there is a description of the return of the exiles which gives figures adding up to 50,000 men, women and children, servants and even including "200 male and female singers". This number is certainly far too large for the actual return. The passage seems to be based on a census listed by Nehemiah and taken several generations later. The list seems to have been revised over a period of years — and is really a register of returned exiles from the beginning down to the time of Ezra and Nehemiah. The totals probably refer to the time of Ezra and Nehemiah (see II, III, below).

The Returned Community: The returning exiles found a very small strip of land in Judea available to them. It lay along the watershed for some 25 miles from the north of Jerusalem to the south of Beth-zur. By 522 BCE, its total population was probably under 20,000. Although there were Jews in other districts of Palestine, Jerusalem's nearest neighbours, the Samaritans*, were openly hostile. Moreover, none of the local Jews seem to have been very friendly.

One of the first actions of the returned community was to rebuild the altar for burnt offerings, according to the ancient pattern, on the site of the old one. The work was begun and, according to Ezra (3:2–6), finished in one day, seven months after the return. Apparently they merely cleared the rubble away from the line of the old walls and did some levelling. Work was then interrupted, either because of Samaritan interference or lack of interest among the people (see below).

Messianic Dreams: The history of the first few years of the return is very uncertain. There was great unrest and confusion in the Persian Empire after the death of Cambyses (530–522 BCE) with an interregnum for more than a year until Darius managed to secure the throne. It seems that Darius the Great, who had succeeded to the imperial throne (ca. 522 BCE), appointed as governor of Judah, Sheshbazzar's nephew, the son of Jehoiachin's eldest son, Zerubbabel (Zer-babil, "Offspring of Babylon", a very common Babylonian name). He refused to join the wave of rebellions that struck the Persian empire for a few years before and a year or two after the accession of Darius I (ca. 522–486 BCE). This attitude annoyed the prophets Haggai* and Zechariah* who had been among the returning exiles. Haggai set out to encourage the Jews to begin the rebuilding of the Temple (August 520 BCE) and a month later, work was begun. In fact, by 520 BCE the international situation had been resolved and, as Zechariah reports, everything was quiet. However, for a time it seemed that the rebellions would succeed and Haggai joyfully prophesied the downfall of the Persian empire and proclaimed Zerubbabel as the "Chosen of God", meaning, presumably, an anointed king of the House of David. Apparently, Haggai expected that the completion of the Temple would see the coming of the Davidic kingdom and the glory of Judah — in fact, fulfillment of the messianic dream the Jews had never relinquished. The fact that Zerubbabel was not the Messiah came to the Jews as a tragedy whose echoes reverberated for centuries and found expression in later apocalyptic* writings.

700

Five years later (515 BCE) the Temple was completed, in the face of hostility from Syrian officials and Samaritans. It was by no means the equal of Solomon's Temple, although no doubt based on the plan of its predecessor. No details of its appearance or equipment are given (cf. Herod*).

Darius Triumphant: The rebellions that had seemed likely to split the empire were successfully crushed and by 522 BCE, Darius I sat on the throne of a Persian empire, once more great and invincible. In celebration, he had an inscription (**700**) carved at Behistun above the caravan road, showing him with his foot on the neck of the prostrate rebel chief, Gaumata, and condemning nine other tied captives, under the shelter of the winged disc which symbolised Ahuramazda.

Naturally, the Jews were called to account for their attitude. Political power was taken from Zerubbabel — though it is not clear whether he died a natural death or was removed from office — and passed, instead, to a governor appointed by the Persian court. Internal matters became, in future, the concern of the High Priest. The first High Priest after the exile was Joshua. Judah seems to have continued as a theocratic community under Joshua and his successors until, about half a century later, Ezra and Nehemiah assumed the leadership as Persian appointees (see below).

Darius upheld his predecessor's policy and allowed the Jews to continue as a small province within this fifth satrapy of the Persian empire. During the next 60 years, the population may have doubled and normal relations been established between the returned exiles and the older population. Its history during these few decades has remained very obscure, the main source being the memoirs of Nehemiah and Ezra (whose books contain the historic background of the Restoration, as well as autobiographic material), confirmed in many details by the Elephantine papyri (see Egypt*) and the Jehoiachin tablets (see Exile*; **421**).

The Judeans and the "'Amme-Ha'aretz": The High Priests tried to keep the nation together by realistically blending the older inhabitants of Jerusalem and its adjoining provinces with the returned exiles. Intermarriage and social relations between the Jewish community and their neighbours, the "'Amme-Ha'aretz" or "peoples of the land" had long been customary. The family of Sanballat, governor of the province of Samaria*, later became allied by marriage to the High Priests of Jerusalem, and at lower social levels the same close ties were established. Moreover, popular religion and social habits had been affected by the customs of the country. These aggressive cultural influences were powerful and hard to resist. In the memoirs of Ezra and Nehemiah, they use the term "'Amme-Hā'āretz" to denote the non-Jewish inhabitants of Palestine (or a combination of them and the descendants of the Israelites who had remained) who hindered the work of restoration, intermarriage notwithstanding (see Government*). Furthermore, the Yahwism of Sanballat or of Tobiah, governor of Ammon in Transjordan, and their people, was not the orthodox religion of the exiles returning from Babylonia. How far the first returnees regarded their fellow Jews as faithful to the Law of Moses is not known, but the Judean community withdrew within itself.

Samaritan Enmity: Although the Temple had been rebuilt, Jerusalem was still surrounded by ruins and lay open to attack by Arab, Edomite or Ammonite raiders. Efforts to rebuild the city walls and fortifications had been thwarted first by Samaritan officials of Samaria (see article on Samaritans*). Later, perhaps at the time of a new rebellion against Persia by one Megabyzus, walls were erected around Jerusalem. Accusations of sedition made to the Persian king by his officials and neighbouring enemies provoked a new royal edict demanding that the walls be destroyed and prohibiting the fortification of Jerusalem.

III. SECOND RETURN: By the third quarter of the 5th c. BCE the fate of Judea and the Jews was once more of interest to Babylonia and Persia. Highly placed Jews desired to join their fellows. The time was ripe for a further step in the resurrection of Zion. It came from Babylonia in the persons of Ezra and Nehemiah. Whether these two were contemporaries or, if not, which one came first, is still a matter of intense scholarly debate. On the evidence of the Elephantine papyri and the Jehoiachin tablets (see Exile*), W.F. Albright argues that Nehemiah should be dated in the third quarter of the 5th c. (450–425 BCE) with Ezra shortly after him. In his view, Ezra's return to Judah took place in 428 BCE, towards the end of the reign of Artaxerxes I (465–424 BCE). The date of Ezra's coming to Jerusalem is so uncertain because the biblical text states more than once that his return took place in the 7th year of "Artaxerxes the king", without specifying which Artaxerxes. If it was Artaxerxes I, then this would support the opinion that places Ezra's arrival in 458 BCE, before Nehemiah. However, if Ezra came in the 7th year of Artaxerxes II, this would place his mission in 398 BCE, a date so late as to raise many difficulties.

On the other hand, the affinity between events and the literary sources (mainly the books of Ezra and Nehemiah; see their Contents, below) suggests that Nehemiah may have completed a task which Ezra had initiated. This is the traditional view though it labours under difficulties as well.

Nehemiah: Nehemiah was a man of unusual abilities and charm. He rose to the high office of cup-bearer to Artaxerxes I (Artachshasta in the books of Ezra and Nehemiah). He appears to have been appointed governor (Tirshata) in about 445 BCE and on his arrival in Jerusalem to have been deeply moved by the plight of the holy city. Early in August 439 BCE, he began to rebuild the great city wall. Thanks to his efforts and a mass levy from every part of Judea, the wall was raised within 52 days. The fortifications (battlements, towers, gates, etc.) were completed, according to Josephus, two years and four months later, i.e. in December, 437 BCE.

Nehemiah then devoted himself to social reforms, including stimulating the observance of the Sabbath and cancelling all debts owed by the poor. The leaders of the people pledged themselves to maintain the Temple regulations and to pay their tithes. The security of Jerusalem was ensured by arranging for a tenth of the people, mainly priests, wealthy people, officials and tradesmen, to take up residence there. Around Jerusalem, other towns were re-settled. Excavations in Bethel have proved that the town was occupied until late in the 6th c. BCE when it was destroyed by a huge fire. Later it was reoccupied, but it was substantially settled again only in the 4th c. BCE. Nehemiah may have added Lydda and adjoining towns to the province (see map **659**).

The total population, according to the census recorded in Neh. 7, was approximately 50,000 in all — 42,000 of them freeborn Jews.

After twelve years, Nehemiah returned to Susa to render an account of his stewardship and to persuade the king to reappoint him.

Ezra: It is possible that it was at this time that he made his fateful journey to Jerusalem. If he indeed came in the 7th year of Artaxerxes I (458–457 BCE, see above), then he was a contemporary of Nehemiah, although another view places his mission much earlier. Ezra's great contribution to Judaism was to establish the Torah as the normative rule of Israel's faith. Ezra was a priest, a member of the leading priestly family of the Zadokites, and a "scribe*" in the Jewish sense, one who devoted his life to the study and interpretation of the Law* (the Torah). At a time when Artaxerxes I possibly wanted to ensure stability in Palestine, Ezra was commissioned to set up an administrative system which would apply religious law among all the Jews living in Judea and elsewhere, in the wider sphere around it. His title was "The Scribe (royal secretary) for the Law of the God in Heaven", establishing him as a member of one of the highest ranks of the Persian hierarchy.

With some 1760 compatriots, including priests, Levites, singers, door-keepers (Levite custodians) and others who had integrated with the Jews, Ezra made the caravan journey to Judea, carrying with him a scroll of the Torah (Pentateuch) which had been edited in Babylonia in approximately its present form.

Backed by the royal decree of Ezr. 7:12 ff, Ezra aimed at a revival of religious life and the establishment of the Torah as the acknowledged guide for the Jews. It was his mission to re-establish the covenant and to turn the people to a sincere attempt to live by all the details of the Law. As the first step, he demanded an end to mixed marriages and the putting away of foreign wives and children. This very naturally aroused a great uproar, which Ezra met with fasting and prayer and passionate appeals to the people to renounce their cosmopolitan behaviour and to return to the Law of Moses. Rather than actively resist foreign influence, Ezra and the faithful in the community shrank from such contact, and adhered to orthodox exclusiveness.

The Renewed Covenant: In the end he was successful. The people agreed to divorce their foreign wives and asked for a new covenant*. This ends the book of Ezra. (There is a serious literary problem about the relationship of Ezra* and Nehemiah* which is discussed below.)

The story is taken up by the book of Nehemiah telling how Ezra first won over the priests and national leaders. They ordered the people to assemble in Jerusalem. At a solemn congregation, a "great assembly" of the people in the Temple Court, the Law was read: mixed marriages were dissolved and the people engaged themselves to live according to the Torah in the future. Specifically, the Jews accepted the authority of the Torah; they bound themselves not to enter into mixed marriages, to observe the Sabbath and the Sabbatical year, and to pay their Temple tithes (Neh. 8–9).

These decisions became the constitution for the community. Henceforth, a Jew was known, wherever he lived, by his adherence to the Torah. Jewish nationality was to be a matter of ethnic solidarity — common descent, religion and culture — rather than territorial status.

The Talmud credits Ezra with the reintroduction of biblical law and also ascribes to him and his companions many other ancient laws (see Law*). This evidence in itself is no guarantee of its historic objectivity. Because he had introduced the Torah into normative Jewish use, it was Ezra who was largely responsible for the way in which archaic practices were adjusted to actual ritual usage in the Temple — a major contribution in itself. In addition, the introduction of the square Hebrew characters (see Alphabet and Writing*), the precise determination of the text of the Pentateuch (see Versions of the Bible*) and the establishment of the Jewish Great Assembly ("Keneseth Gedôlah") are also ascribed to Ezra (see Government and Authority*).

IV. THE NEHEMIAH AND EZRA LITERATURE: The authorship of the Ezra memoirs is much debated among the scholars. C.C. Torrey denied Ezra's authorship and maintained that the memoirs were written by the author of Chronicles. He found many points of similarity in the style of the books that confirmed Jewish tradition in identifying the writer of Chronicles with the author of Ezra and

Nehemiah. W.F. Albright drew the different conclusion that Chronicles was written by Ezra (see article). Modern biblical research also supports a final editing of Chronicles during the early fourth century BCE. The relation of the books of Ezra and Nehemiah to the author of Chronicles* and the literary problems involved are discussed under that article (Authorship and Date of Composition).

THE BOOK OF EZRA. *Contents:* The book of Ezra falls into two main divisions, chs. 1–6 and chs. 7–10.

a. 1–6 relate the return of the Exiles and the rebuilding of the Temple between the years 539–536 BCE.

Ch. 1 gives the proclamation of Cyrus which the royal herald read to the assembled Jews and then recounts their subsequent migration, led by Jeshua the High Priest and Zerubbabel, the royal prince. Ch. 2 lists the names of those who returned and the offerings they made towards the costs of rebuilding the Temple. This list is a replica of the one which appears in Neh. 7:6–33a, which is a population register of the sub-satrapy of Judah (Y^{e}hud) in the 5th c. BCE. Ch. 3 describes the erection of the altar of burnt offerings on its ancient site and much later, the laying of the foundations for the Temple. Ch. 4 describes how the work was stopped by unfriendly actions by neighbouring peoples. The book prints the texts of letters that passed between Rehum and Shimshai of Samaria and King Artaxerxes, which resulted in an official decree that the work should cease. As a result of the earnest exhortations of Haggai* and Zechariah*, 5:1–5 records that building was energetically resumed, although the Persian officials, Tattenai, the governor of the province and Shetharbozenai and his associates again complained to the king — now Darius, who had succeeded Cyrus and Cambyses. This time they were less effective (6:1–12). In March 515 BCE the Temple was successfully completed (6:13–22).

There is considerable confusion about the sequence of the events recorded in chs. 4 and 5, but their general historical accuracy is accepted.

b. Chs. 7–10 deal with Ezra's own activities and are, in the main, Ezra's own record of his experiences in Jerusalem, more than sixty years after the rebuilding of the Temple. This section is concluded in the book of Nehemiah (7:73 b–10:39).

In ch. 7, the long period between the first and second returns is brought to an end when Ezra leaves Babylon with a considerable following and makes for Judea. These memoirs are written partly in the first person singular, partly in the third person. Ezra had received a special commission from Artaxerxes to impose a settlement of religious and social conditions in the Judean community. The Persian decree, moreover, recognized Jewish law as the law applicable to the community in Judea (see Persia and Israel*).

Ch. 8 names the heads of families who left Babylonia with Ezra and tells of their arrival in Jerusalem. Ch. 9 is concerned with the question of the foreign women married to Israelites and records Ezra's confession and prayer. An assembly of the whole people is summoned (ch. 10) and they appointed a commission to examine the matter and get such husbands to agree to repudiate their wives (see Family*, II). The rest of ch. 10 contains a list of the men who had married foreign wives and, with this, the book comes to an abrupt end.

BOOK OF NEHEMIAH. *Contents:* The book is made up of extracts from memoirs presumably written by Nehemiah himself and other passages related to his actions, not taken from the memoirs.

1. **Extracts from the Memoirs:** a. (1:1–7:4) This long section, written in the first person singular throughout, represents authentic extracts from Nehemiah's personal memoirs. In it he describes:

1:1–11, how he heard of the distress of Jerusalem;

2:1–20, how he came to Jerusalem and organized the work of rebuilding its wall.

3:1–32, lists the names of the builders.

4:1–7:4, describes the opposition the builders met and how the work was completed in spite of it.

The wording of 5:14 suggests that the narrative was not established in its present form until some years after the events recounted.

7:5 provides an introduction to a list of the genealogies of the returned exiles, which also appears in Ezra 2 (see below, 2, and Contents of the Book of Ezra, a).

b. 11:1–2 is the continuation of the passage in 7:1–4 and records the measures taken to reestablish the population of Jerusalem.

c. 12:27–43 relates the dedication of the walls and the reorganization of Temple services. This narrative is connected with the passage 6:15–19.

d. 13:4–31 is also extracted from the memoirs, and gives details of Nehemiah's reforms carried out during his second visit to Jerusalem, some twelve years or more after the period of the earlier extracts.

2. **Passages not Derived from the Memoirs:** a. 7:6–73a is the list of the people who returned with Zerubbabel, which Nehemiah refers to for administrative purposes. The same list appears, with slight differences, in Ezra 2. It appears to belong to the earlier period.

b. 7:73 b–10:39: This long section breaks into the main parts of the memoirs (see above) to describe, 8:1–18 the reading and expounding of the Law and 9:1–10:39, the national penitence and the new covenant of obedience. This material clearly belongs with Ezra 7–10. Like Nehemiah, the book of Ezra (see above) is also written partly in the first person and partly in the third. It therefore seems that this passage in Nehemiah is part of the same literary material. Nehemiah 9:6–37 is the prayer ascribed to Ezra. 9:38–10:39 records the provisions of the covenant agreement which the people agreed to and (10:1–27) lists the Israelite leaders who signed it.

c. 11:3–36 and 12:1–26 are lists of inhabitants of Jerusalem. The first was probably a contemporary record of the time of Nehemiah but it was not really part of the memoirs. The second (12:1–26) is a list of the priests and Levites who returned with Zerubbabel.

d. 12:44–13:3 gives details of some religious and administrative measures of the time of Nehemiah and probably (12:47) Zerubbabel. The section closes with a brief record of a reading of the Law as a result of which all foreigners were "separated from Israel". There is some uncertainty about the chronology of these two items.

V. KNESSETH-GEDOLAH: Talmudic tradition regards this body which constituted the supreme authority in matters of religion and law as the link between the last of the prophets and the first of the rabbis* who headed the Sanhedrin. The Keneseth-Gedôlah may perhaps be identified with the "Great Assembly" of the people, presided over by Ezra which accepted the authority of the Law. The composition and size of the Knesseth-Gedôlah varied from time to time. According to tradition, the men of the Knesseth-Gedôlah were 120 members, selected from the leading scholars of the period, who are said to have drawn up the main text of the accepted liturgy.

High Priests: From the first holder of the office after the Restoration — Joshua — until the time of Antiochus Epiphanes (see Hasmoneans*), the High Priests (see article*) belonged to the line of Zadok, the first High Priest of Solomon's Temple. With the removal of Zerubbabel from the scene, Joshua and his successors were regarded as the spiritual and temporal heads of the nation and representatives before God. In principle, however, there was always hope of the restoration of the Davidic monarchy. The Persian Governor had a purely administrative role. The idea of the High Priest as head of the nation gradually sank its roots deep into Jewish life until, by the Maccabaean period (2nd c. BCE), it appeared as an unchallenged principle.

The chronicler of the book of Nehemiah (12:10–11) gives a list of the high priests from Joshua to Jaddua, who held office about the time of the death of Darius II (405 BCE). While Nehemiah was in Jerusalem, the High Priest was Eliashib, grandson of Joshua. Eliashib's son, Johanan is mentioned as High Priest in the time of Ezra (10:6) but this view is not accepted on historical grounds. He was apparently the Johanan of Nehemiah's time (12:22–26).

Johanan: Johanan is remembered particularly for an incident revealed by an Aramaic papyrus found in Elephantine in southern Egypt*. From this it appears that the Jewish colonists there, who were Persian mercenaries, sent a letter to Bagoas, the Persian governor of Judah, referring to an earlier letter sent to Johanan which had not been answered. The community asked Bagoas for aid to restore their temple which had been destroyed by the Egyptians. An Aramaic letter written on papyrus, dated about 411 or 408 BCE, from Elephantine is reproduced (**73**).

According to Josephus, Johanan's brother Joshua, who was allied to the "'Ammê-Hā'āretz" and the Samaritans, earned the favour of Bagoas and was promised the High Priesthood. Instead, Johanan had him slain in the Temple. This brought a severe reaction from Bagoas, including penalties on the Jewish community which continued for seven years. During this time, apparently, Johanan remained high priest *in absentia*. He opposed the rebuilding of the temple of Elephantine, although Bagoas finally approved the request.

Johanan lost all standing in Judah and not long afterwards he was replaced by his son Jaddua. For the next century we have no knowledge of the succession of High Priests. Only with the Hellenistic* period do Josephus and the book of Maccabees enable us to trace their later descendants.

Last Century of Persian Rule: Archaeology has provided evidence of another aspect of Persian rule in Palestine. Acceptance of their new constitution gave the Jewish people the right to levy taxes and strike coins. For these they took as their model the Greek drachma, adding, as in the 4th c. BCE coins* and inscriptions* (see articles), the letters YHD for Y^{e}hûd or Judah, above the Greek figure. Greek influence was already having an increasing effect on Jewish material culture and literature (see Hellenism in the Near East*). After Alexander's conquest (332 BCE) it would engulf the world in a new era — for both good and ill (see Hasmoneans*; articles on Hellenism*).

RESURRECTION (see Transfiguration)

REVELATION. — Revelation means a manifestation of God, whether in deed or in words, and whether communicated directly to man or through an intermediary such as an angel. The word is derived from the verb "reveal" — to make plain or uncover. The revelation may be made to an individual, like Moses or the prophets, or to a whole group, as at Sinai.

In the Old Testament, revelation takes place in a variety of different ways. Messages are one mode of revelation. Sometimes God appears face to face with a particular individual and speaks to him directly, but more often revelation transcends the physical senses of sight or hearing. A man may dream or see a vision of God at night, or may be made aware of His presence through his inner consciousness. The essential condition for revelation was that the man who received it was spiritually fit to comprehend his experience and to transmit God's inspiration through his conscious personality. Such men, though, were not necessarily unusual in other respects. Moses, after all, committed murder and Gideon and David were very "human" beings.

Biblical Interpretation of History: An essential clue to an understanding of the Bible is the way in which it regards historical events as the crucial sphere in which God's activity is revealed. History is interpreted in terms of divine activity and as the vehicle of divine revelation, although not as revelation in itself. The Bible sees history as the progressive revelation of God's purpose, an attitude which is particularly apparent in the account of the Exodus and the events that followed from it. In the Bible, it is taken for granted that God's communications to the Hebrews are always directly related to actual events in which the inspired individual is directed to participate. This sometimes leads to a quite unrealistic approach, for the Bible's viewpoint attempts to interpret the whole course of external events and human experience in terms of the working out of God's purpose. It was empirical, seeing in the course of events the hand of God and making a theology out of history.

There are many difficulties in presenting a synoptic view of the phenomenon of revelation. First of all, modern minds naturally tend to resist terms and ways of thought which were axiomatic to the men who wrote and lived the Bible. Many concepts, and revelation is one, are not always the same, while the same term may be used to cover a variety of experiences. To define such ideas scientifically is not easy.

Revelation as a concept must be seen as developing through a number of phases of biblical and post-biblical religion. It can best be considered as this development is reflected in the sources — whether the early priestly* writers, the prophets, or the circles of wisdom* writings. From all these a comprehensive picture may emerge.

The Manner of Revelation: In many cases, divine revelation was accompanied by miraculous physical manifestations. These were accepted without question as normal under the circumstances. Modern scepticism may make it difficult to accept the accounts as recorded. It cannot deny the effect of their revelations upon the Patriarchs*, the charismatic Judges* and other leaders, the prophets, the psalmists, the writers of "Wisdom*", Jesus* or the apostles. From this point of view, the ultimate significance of revelation for the history of Israel and later Western civilization has also to be recognized. The phenomenon can perhaps best be studied in terms of its effects on those who experienced it, the manner in which it came to them being left aside as beyond analysis or control by historical scientific methods.

Knowledge of God through Revelation: Biblical faith rests on belief in a God who revealed himself to man. Without that belief, the religion of Israel, Judaism and Christianity would never have come into existence.

The biblical concept of God is never analyzed in abstract terms. It was accepted as self-evident and defined in "pictorial" terms. God is referred to as father, king, shepherd and these traditional terms continued to be used by the rabbis, even though they conceived of God as an incorporeal and transcendental entity.

The phrase "to know God" is used in many passages of the Old Testament to mean both the expression of the divine will and man's belief in God's willingness and power to put it into effect. The idea is most clearly expressed in Jud. 2:10: "and there grew up a generation after them who did not know God or the deeds which he had performed for Israel."

It is biblical faith that man first learned of God's existence through direct personal meetings. Genesis describes God's revelation to Adam, Cain and the Patriarchs simply and realistically. Similar unpretentious, vivid terms describing man's awareness of God have been preserved in many prayers and hymns.

There is, however, a certain inconsistency. The Old Testament denies God any shape or form. The people who gathered at Mount Sinai did not see any form (Dt. 4:12, 15) nor could any man see God and live (Ex. 33:20). Nevertheless, the stories of God's appearances to the Patriarchs are told in Genesis without any suggestion that they are other than the literal truth. Moses conversed with God face to face, "mouth to mouth and not in dark speech" (Nu. 12:8). Even in Isaiah's vision of the seraphs (Is. 6:2), the external aspects of revelation are rather hazy.

Cosmic Revelation: After the Patriarchal sagas, descriptions of revelation speak of a revelation of God's presence or of the Glory of God. The Children of Israel saw the Glory of God and His signs after the Exodus (Nu. 14). The Glory of God is an unchanging concept. God fills the heavens and the earth (Nu. 14:21; Is. 6:3) and looks at his Creation (Ps. 19:2; 104:31–32). Cosmic and personal aspects are combined in passages where revelation demonstrates God's rule over the forces of nature. It comes in the form of fire, clouds, thunder and lightning at Mount Sinai (Ex. 19:16, 18; Dt. 5:19–23), or at Mount Horeb (I K. 19:11, 12) when "God passed by" in a wind, an earthquake and a fire. Fire very often accompanies revelation, as a warning against approaching too close to God. Certain places became holy because God had appeared there (Gn. 28:13; II Ch. 3) while knowledge of God through public worship was decreed for certain specific times.

Magic and Divination: It was a commonplace of ancient religions that certain formulas and techniques, employed either by the worshipper or a priest on his behalf, could obtain a response from the deity. Mosaic law and the teachings of the prophets reject such activities (Nu. 23:23; Dt. 18:10, 11; II K. 21:6 and others), recognizing only Urim and Thummim* as priestly instruments for seeking divine guidance (see Priests*). Little of pre-biblical magic practices survived into the biblical narratives.

"God's Word" and Prophecy: The fundamental revelation of God's Word, made plain in the Covenant of Sinai, was the Law. Beyond this the Bible is less "the Word of God" than a record of the acts of God and man's response to them. These acts, however, required interpretation and this became the function of the prophets chosen by God to pass on His "word" and direct man's actions in events.

The hallmark of prophecy was its introduction with the words, "the word of God" or "thus said the Lord." The prophets believed they were simply passing on God's word to his chosen people, yet they formed the message in intensely individual ways. Isaiah, Jeremiah and the others all emerge as distinct personalities, each one regarding himself as no more than the instrument by which God "spoke". The prophets were not teachers. They interpreted the events of history in terms of God's redeeming purpose for mankind. What the great prophets — from Moses and Isaiah to Jesus and Paul — expounded was not a personal experience of God, intended for themselves alone, but an objective message that applied to all. The New Testament carries on the same attitude. Its whole message is based on the fact that Jesus as saviour was God's instrument and was carrying out God's intentions for mankind.

Revelation and Worship: Inspiration came in different ways, even to the same prophet. Almost invariably it involved hearing, but many of the prophets, like earlier magic seers and visionaries, also saw visions. One aspect of Temple ritual, also, was to "see the face of God" metaphorically, if not in literal fact (Is. 38:11; Ps. 11:7; 17:15). While the sanctuary was the external symbol of God, it was nevertheless clearly stated that man could seek God in any place and that He is near everyone who seeks him (Ps. 32:6; Dt. 4:29). Revelation did not depend on a particular place (see also Christianity*, Early).

REVELATION, BOOK OF. — The last book of the New Testament is also known by the name "*Apocalypse**". Revelation is a typical apocalyptic work and its style and allegorical content often puzzle the English reader. In its time, however, it belonged to a familiar type, for sectarian Judaism produced an abundance of apocalyptic* literature (see article, also Apocrypha*; Dead Sea Scrolls*). Most apocalyptic works were rejected by "normative" Judaism, with the exception of the canonical book of Daniel*, but were revised, adapted and incorporated into the literature of the early Church. There is also apocalyptic material in the Synoptic Gospels* and the Epistles*. The genre is not completely unknown in the New Testament apart from the book of Revelation.

Like other Jewish-Christian apocalyptic writings, Revelation is basically optimistic in tone. Despite its dire predictions of pestilence and horror, the book testifies to the ultimate triumph of God and His servants. The book's message to the persecuted Christians is clear: Hold fast to your faith! The end is near! God will vindicate his servants for their righteousness and will pour out the might of his wrath upon your tormentors! Unlike its Jewish counterparts, however, Revelation is waiting not for the first but for the Second Coming of the Messiah and it knows that this is at hand.

I. CONTENTS: After an introduction (1:1–3), the Seer sends greetings to the seven churches of Asia (1:4–8). In v. 6, the Christians are described as "priests to his God" which emphasizes the conception of the church as a priestly community. Such references occur too frequently (e.g. in Hebrews*) for the phrase to be explained away as no more than a figure of speech. It is a concept apparently derived from the sectarian belief that all adherents were Levites, direct descendants of the ancient priestly traditions of Israel (see Dead Sea Scrolls*). The early church had the same characteristic, even though it was a community of laymen without any specially designated priesthood (see Christianity, Early*).

The prologue explains how the author was ordered to write his book by a voice from heaven (1:9–20) and then goes on (chs. 2–3) to address individual messages to the seven churches. These set out the problem of the book — the apparent failure of the cause of God on earth. The churches are those of Ephesus (2:1–7); Smyrna (2:8–11);

701

Pergamum (2:12–17); Thyatira (2:18–29); Sardis (3:1–6); Philadelphia (3:7–15) and Laodicea (3:14–22). These cities form the background to the book. Smyrna, with its then imposing agora (**701**) for instance, vied with Ephesus (described and illustrated under Acts*) for the title of chief city of Asia and loyalty to Rome was conspicuous in both places. Seats of the official cult were called Temple-wardens. Thus Pergamum, where "the throne of Satan is" (2:13) was a centre of the imperial cult which menaced the very existence of the Christian church. The altar of Zeus and the vast theatre of Pergamum (**702**) were a very real basis for the book's allegories, as were the numerous temples and public buildings of all the towns.

Prologue in Heaven: Ch. 4 (1–11) begins with a vision of God on his throne. Then the author describes a series of allegorical visions concerning the end of the world and the Second Coming of Christ. The first vision of the Throne and the One seated on it is clearly dependent on Ezekiel*. Ch. 5 begins the vision of the Seven Seals on the scroll of judgment which can only be opened by the Lamb of God whose blood has redeemed all mankind (5:1–14).

702

The Judgments: Then (6:1–17) the Lamb opens the seals and out come the four horsemen who symbolise violence: the white horse and its rider bringing conquest to the world; the red horse destroying peace; the black horse bringing famine and the white horse death through pestilence. The fifth seal, when opened, reveals the souls of those slain for their witness to the word of God who cry "How long, O Lord before thou wilt judge and avenge our blood?" (6:10). The sixth seal calls up a great earthquake, thus completing the cycle of symbolic "Birth pangs of the Messiah" found elsewhere in Jewish apocalyptic literature and in the Talmud.

Ch. 7 breaks off the account of destruction to list those in the twelve tribes of Israel (7:1–8) and the martyrs of the Gentiles (7:9–12) who are to be marked with the seal of salvation and may stand "before the throne of God and serve him day and night within his temple" (7:15).

Vision of the Seven Trumpets: When the Lamb opened the seventh seal, "there was silence in heaven for about half an hour" (8:1) and then (8:2–11:19) comes the vision of the Seven Trumpets which, when blown in succession by angels, summon renewed destruction upon the earth. This is essentially the same concept of "birth pangs", although the details are varied. The trumpets conjure up hail and fire, bitterness and darkness, locusts "like horses arrayed for battle" and cavalry with "fire and smoke and sulphur" issuing from the mouths of the horses. Ch. 10 interrupts the sequence with a separate vision (also reminiscent of Ezekiel) in which the Seer is given a scroll to eat, symbolizing a renewed command to prophesy. Ch. 11 first predicts the fall of Jerusalem (11:1–4) but apparently declares that the inner Temple and altar will survive. This section appears to be a quotation from an early Jewish Zealot apocalypse which supposed that the Temple in Jerusalem would withstand all attacks. During the last Roman onslaught on Jerusalem (see Rome and the Jews*) the Zealots were entrenched in the innermost precincts of the Temple and the Zealot who wrote the apocalypse apparently clung to the faith that this most sacred spot would be preserved.

The author of Revelation adapted the apocalyptic theme to his own message that loyalty to Christ would protect believers from all the assaults of the spiritual powers of darkness. Only the Temple's outer court — i.e. unbelievers, given over to anti-Christ, — would be destroyed. The inner sanctum — the faithful — would endure, unharmed.

The predicted doom of the holy city is followed (11:4–14) by the allegory of the two olive trees and the two lampstands whose testimony, overthrow and subsequent miraculous resuscitation symbolize the persecution of the Christians and their ultimate triumph. "Then the seventh angel blew his trumpet"; the Day of Judgment dawns, and the time comes for rewarding God's "servants, prophets and saints" and for destroying "the destroyers of the earth" (11:15–19).

The Heavenly Woman and Child: Ch. 12 recounts the vision of the heavenly woman who gives birth to a male child which is menaced by a dragon but rescued by God. After its attempt to devour the child, the dragon is cast out of heaven onto the earth, where it continues to attack the woman and her offspring but is again thwarted by God's intervention. This remarkable chapter is both a poetic allegory and a striking example of contemporary Jewish apocalyptic writings. The author makes use of images and theological material which were common to the world in which he lived. The poem can be interpreted in the light of modern knowledge of the Dead Sea Scrolls*. Through the birth of a man child, the world is to be overwhelmed as by a flood and the enemies of Israel destroyed and consigned to hell: typical features of Jewish allegories of their religious history and expectations of a Messiah. It is, of course, customary to see Revelation as a Christian allegory, the woman representing the Church, the child Christ and the dragon Satan. According to modern opinion, however, the author should not be thought of as referring to the birth of any one particular child, but to the creation of a whole messianic community which, in turn, will give birth to an individual messiah who will act as the leader of the redeemed community. The eschatological setting establishes the theme as the birth pangs of the Messiah, in the sense of the emergence through trial and suffering of the redeemed "New Israel". Rev. 12:1–6 has been compared to a passage in the Qumran "Manual of Discipline" (I Q.H. III) in which the doomsday of the world prepares the way for the birth of the Messiah.

The Beasts: In the following vision (ch. 13), the satanic power of the dragon is given to the "beast" with "ten horns and seven heads" who has "authority over every tribe and people and tongue and nation" and uses it to persecute the Church. This beast is supported by another with two horns who "deceives those who dwell on earth" and continues the persecution of the faithful. Then (14:1–5) the Seer sees a vision of the Lamb and his 144,000 followers on Mount Zion. These followers, the "redeemed of the earth", are given special prominence as the members of a heavenly choir who sing a new song before the heavenly Throne. They are the first fruits, redeemed from mankind for "in their mouth no lie was found, for they are spotless" i.e. chaste. This, again, suggests a distinctly Essene type of asceticism. They are followed by three angels who warn the inhabitants of the earth to reject the beast and to fear God (14:6–13). In the last scene of this vision (14:14–20), an angel with a sickle reaps the harvest of the earth, again a symbol of the Second Coming and the Last Judgment.

Renewed eschatological symbols appear with the vision of the Seven Vials (or Bowls) or Wrath (chs. 15 and 16). The first part (Ch. 15) describes the rejoicing of the righteous in heaven over the divine victory. The second (ch. 16) recounts the outpouring of the Seven Vials of God's wrath upon the earth. When the sixth bowl is poured out, the kings of the whole world "assemble for battle on the great day of God the Almighty . . . at the place which is called in Hebrew, Armageddon" (see Megiddo*).

The Seer is then shown the "great harlot" (i.e. Rome; 17:18) and an angel explains that she and beasts which have appeared in the visions represent the enemies of the Church, all of whom are to be overcome by the Lamb (17:1–18). Ch. 18 describes in detail the destruction of "Babylon", meaning Rome, and then (19:1–10) comes the account of heavenly rejoicing at her overthrow. Ch. 19 (11–21) is completed by the victory of Christ and his followers over the two beasts of ch. 13.

The Kingdom of Heaven and the Last Judgment: Following this victory, peace is ensured on earth for a thousand years (20:1–3), an interlude before the last and final eschatological

703

war, reminiscent of the Talmudic "days of the Messiah". During this time, all who have suffered for the faith will be raised from the dead (20:4–6). After the thousand years, "Satan will be loosed from his prison" and with all his hosts of Gog and Magog will launch a final, unsuccessful attack on the forces of heaven (20:7–10). After that will come the general resurrection of the dead who must stand before the throne of God and be judged (20:11–15).

The New Jerusalem: Following the last Judgment there will come "a new heaven and a new earth; for the first heaven and the first earth had passed away" (21:1) and the new Jerusalem will come "down out of heaven from God, prepared as a bride adorned for her husband" and at last "the dwelling of God is with men. He will dwell with them and they shall be his people and God himself will be with them; he will wipe away every tear from their eyes, and death shall be no more, neither shall there be mourning nor crying nor pain any more, for the former things have passed away." (21:2–4). The Seer then describes the new Jerusalem, the wondrous bride of Christ (21:10–22:5).

Benediction: Revelation closes with an epilogue (22:6–21) which consists of several admonitions and the repeated promise of the imminence of Christ's Second Coming to Earth, "Behold I am coming soon, bringing my recompense, to repay every one for what he has done. I am the Alpha and the Omega, the first and the last, the beginning and the end." (22:12).

II. AUTHORSHIP: There can be no question that the author of Revelation was a Jewish Christian. Everything in the style and content of the book confirms this fact. The Greek of Revelation also reveals a strong Semitic influence which is either the result of translation from a Hebrew or Aramaic original or — which is more likely — follows from the author's Semitic source material.

Scholarly opinion is divided on the question of whether Revelation is a composite work or the creation of a single author. An apocalypse is not a logical treatise and the author of Revelation, like all other apocalyptic writers, made wide use of material from the Old Testament (mainly Daniel*) and other Jewish apocalyptic sources. On the other hand, a considerable body of opinion holds that Revelation represents a reworking of this older corpus.

There are many theories as to the identity of the author. The book states that it was written by "John" (1:1, 4, 9; 22:8) and that he was confined on the island of Patmos, a Roman penal colony, probably because of his adherence to Christianity (1:9). Patmos was one of the smallest islands of the Dodecanese. Its new port, Scala, is shown in the photograph **(703)**, while the mountain **(704)** where once

704

the great sanctuaries of Patmos were built, is now covered with monasteries. Tradition has it that the Apostle John wrote his apocalypse in the grotto beneath the 11th c. church of St. Anne, shown bottom left.

Early church tradition was that Revelation was written by the apostle John, but if he also wrote the Gospel of John, then it becomes very difficult to reconcile the marked contrasts in style, language and content of the two works. For this reason, a number of scholars are inclined to agree with Eusebius (died c. 349 CE), who attributed Revelation to John the Elder, the author of the Epistles II and III John (see Epistles*, General). However, Irenaeus, whose spiritual adviser was Polycarp, a disciple of the apostle John, states that John died during the reign of Trajan (98–117 CE), which at least proves that the apostle was a contemporary of the author of Revelation. Authorship of the work was attributed to John the Apostle by Justin Martyr as early as the mid-2nd c. CE. This seems to suggest that Revelation is in fact the work of the Apostle, whereas the Fourth Gospel was not. Many scholars support this view, believing that the Gospel of John was probably composed by a Jerusalem disciple of Jesus, not by one of the Twelve.

III. DATE: There are two major theories on the subject of the date of Revelation. The book itself makes it clear that it was written to a persecuted church. Accordingly, scholars who uphold an earlier date, place Revelation during the last years of Nero's reign (ca. 68 CE), immediately prior to the fall of Jerusalem in 70 CE. These scholars point out that the number 666 which is mentioned in Rev. 13:18 is the numerical equivalent of the Hebrew letters in the words Nero Caesar, (Each Hebrew letter has a numerical value and it is thus possible to express a name in numbers so that it will only be understood by the initiated. The form is known as "gemātria".)

The alternate theory, which agrees with the view expressed by Irenaeus in the second century, dates the book during the reign of Domitian, ie. ca. 95 CE (cf. section on Revelation in article on Apocalypse*). In support of this theory it is pointed out that Nero's persecution of the Christians was largely confined to Rome, whereas Domitian's extended throughout the Empire.

705

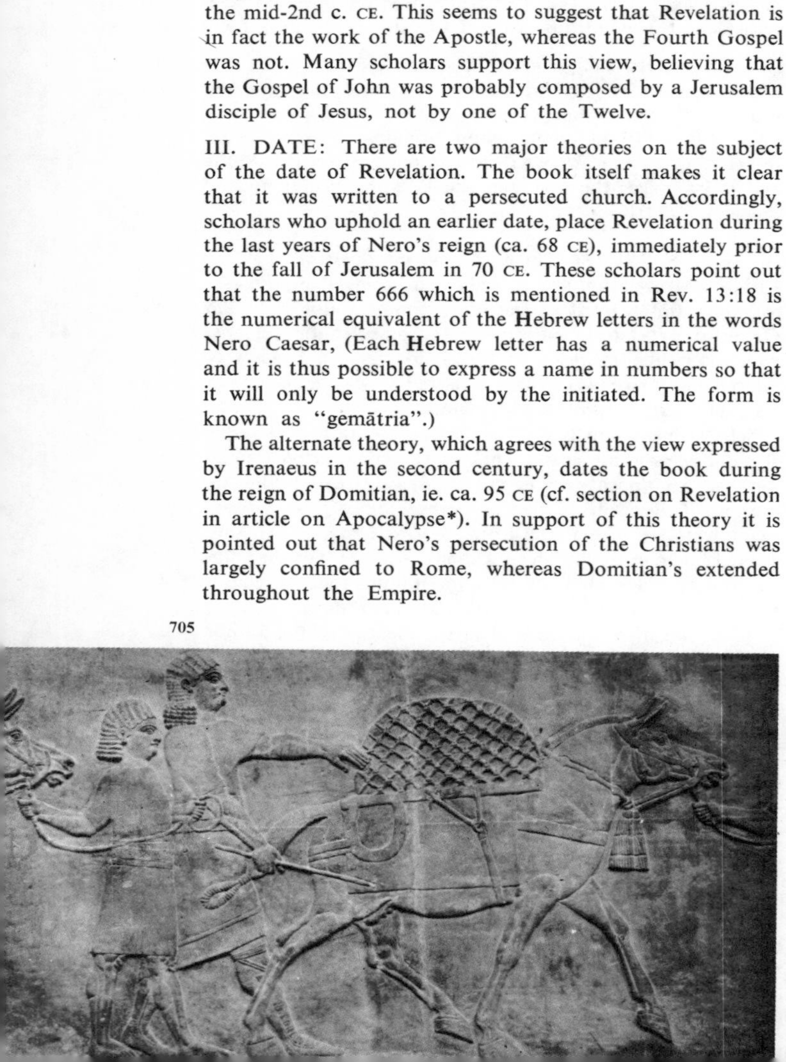

ROADS, TRANSPORTATION, TRADE ROUTES.– *Outline: Pilgrimage; Trade; Diplomacy and Politics. Means of Travel: Animals; Vehicles; Security; Caravans. Roads and Routes: International Highways; Internal Roads of Palestine; The East-West Roads of the Negeb; Roads in Post-Exilic and Roman Times; The Nabatean Road Network; Stopping Places.*

Early man undertook long journeys reluctantly and with trepidation. Travellers faced many dangers: professional highway robbers or merely unfriendly strangers, like the people of Shechem who set ambushes on the tops of nearby mountains and robbed everyone who passed by (Jud. 9:25; Ezr. 8:22); beasts of prey in the deserts (Is. 30:6; Jer. 2:6, passim); or storms and shipwrecks at sea (Ps. 107:23 ff; Jh. 1:4). There is no trace in the Bible of travelling for pleasure or in search of knowledge. Journeys were undertaken only for a very definite purpose, like the wanderings of Jacob or the young Levite (Jud. 17:7 ff) who left his home in Bethlehem in search of a livelihood.

Pilgrimage: One of the most common reasons for setting out on a journey was to worship in a prescribed place. From the earliest times, the Israelites had definite places in which to offer sacrifices to their God. The actual request which Moses first made to Pharaoh when the Children of Israel were in bondage in Egypt was that he should permit them to go "three days' journey into the wilderness and sacrifice to the Lord" (Ex. 5:3). Later, they were commanded to appear before God at a prescribed place three times a year (Ex. 34:23) and this might involve extensive travelling.

In post-Exilic times, many more Jews lived in the Diaspora than in Palestine and at the great festivals* of Passover and Pentecost, Jerusalem would be crowded with tens of thousands of pilgrims flocking in from outside the country to fulfill the commandment (see Festivals*). Pilgrimages* might also be made by individuals to sacrifice at certain places or shrines where there was an altar to God (I Sam. 1:3, 21), or messengers might be sent to consult a distant god, as Ahaziah sent to seek guidance from Ba'al-Zebul, the god of Ekron* (II K. 1:2).

Trade: Traders have travelled through the Near East ever since pre-historic times. Foreign merchants have their place in the story of Joseph (Gn. 37:25–28), but international trade first became of importance to Israel's economy during the monarchy. Solomon, in particular, encouraged trade with the outside world (I K. 10:28–29) and this was to expand later to very considerable dimensions. The building of a merchant fleet at Ezion-Geber on the Gulf of Eilat brought Israelite merchants to the coasts of Africa and Arabia while, in the north, Israelite bazaars were established in Damascus (I K. 20:34).

Diplomacy and Politics: Apart from the prime motive of war and military expeditions, relations with foreign rulers were also a major cause of travelling. As early as the period of Judges, Ehud was sent to bring presents to King Eglon of Moab (Jud. 3:15). Later on, tribute to their overlords was presented by Israelite kings in person (II K. 16:10; Jer. 51:59), and this involved travelling. By the time of the Hasmonean* princes, diplomatic missions were sent by the Jews to Sparta, Rome and Egypt, while Herod sent political missions to many parts of the Roman empire (see Herod*).

706

Means of Travel: In biblical times, vehicles drawn by animals might be used by kings or wealthy men, but the mass of the people travelled long distances on the backs of draft animals (**705**).

Animals: The first animal used was the ass, which was apparently domesticated as early as the 4th mill. BCE. Horses were introduced much later and were used almost exclusively to draw chariots. The most important innovation was the domestication of the camel which made it possible for caravans to travel across deserts. Camels, indeed, can carry 200–250 kgs. distances of 100–150 kilometres a day. They became the most common and important draft animals for long distance transport (for fuller details, see Agriculture and Animal Husbandry*) after the late Bronze Age.

Vehicles: The main vehicle was the cart, drawn by oxen, mules or asses. These appeared first in Babylonia and Egypt and carried both goods and people. Chariots, which were first introduced in Syria and Egypt, were used in war or in peace time by kings, government officials or the aristocracy.

Ordinary people travelled in or beside carts carrying loads. A Sumerian mosaic (**200**) shows flat, four-wheeled freight carts; similar carts were used in Assyria and by the Philistines on their migrations. The Bible differentiates between two types of cart: the covered wagon, (Nu. 7:3), presumably used for carrying people, and the cart or wagon, used for loads (Nu. 7:7–8; Is. 66:20). The freight cart was particularly common in the Shephelah (coastal plain) whose inhabitants had been introduced to it by the Philistines (I Sam. 6:7 ff; II Sam. 6:3 ff). The only archaeological evidence of Hebrew carts comes from the Assyrian relief of the siege of Lachish which shows a two-wheeled cart carrying rocks, with two women and their children sitting on top of them (**158**). The cart is pulled by oxen and a driver walks beside them. Wagons covered with cloth or hides are known from Carchemish and Assyria and some scholars think that these are the same as the biblical covered wagons.

In the Persian period, light carts were harnessed to horses for transporting the royal mail and official messages. By Roman times, horse-drawn coaches, like the one shown here (**706**), were in general use over paved roads such as that from Aleppo to Antioch in Syria, **707**.

Security: Journeys called for special preparations. When Nehemiah left the Persian court for Jerusalem, he took with him letters from the king to the governors of the Persian provinces through which he would pass instructing them to grant him free passage and an armed convoy (Neh. 2:7 ff).

Caravans: Lone travellers, however, were practically unknown. Safety lay in numbers. For merchants the question of security was even more important, for they carried quantities of material, often of great value, with them. From the end of the Stone Age and beginning of the Bronze Age, caravans of merchants plied between the Aegean islands, Cyprus, Egypt, Asia Minor and Mesopotamia. Israel lay on the main trade route north from Egypt to Asia Minor and beyond. A coloured drawing found in the tomb of Beni Hassan (see **653**) of the time of Shenosrat II, 1906–1887 BCE, shows a caravan of merchants from the land of Seth (Gilead) bringing antimony to Egypt. Ishmaelite or Midianite caravans travelling between Egypt and Gilead are mentioned in the Bible (Gn. 39:1 and 37:25, 28, see above) and caravans also appear in the story of the Queen of Sheba (I K. 10). Caravans passing through Israel from Egypt to the countries of the Near East are mentioned in the Amarna* letters.

The oases at which the caravans could pause to rest and replenish their water supplies were also places of importance. Assyrian documents of the 1st mill. BCE refer to caravans passing through the oases of Arabia: Tema, Duma, Najran and Dedan. The caravans of Tema and the companies of Sheba also appear in the Bible (Job 6:19), while Isaiah (21:13) refers to the caravans of Dedanim.

The essential condition for caravan travel was security on the roads. The Song of Deborah (Jud. 5:6) and the Amarna letters refer to disturbances in normal caravan routes. In the latter, the king of Babylonia complains of brigandage and robbery by Zatatna, the governor of Acre under Egyptian suzerainty (see Gn. 49:17). Even in the best times, the caravans paid tribute to local rulers to ensure safe passage for themselves and their goods (I K. 10:15).

Provisions for both man and beast had to be provided by the travellers themselves, not only in the desert (Gn. 21:14), but even when passing through inhabited lands (e.g. Jos. 9:4–6, 12–14 or Jud. 19:19). The obligations of travellers are listed in Nu. 20:17 ff: "We will not pass through field or vineyard . . . we will not turn aside to the right hand or to the left, until we have passed through your territory."

Roads and Routes: The Bible used many different terms for roads and ways. "Mesillah" (II Sam. 20:12–13; Is. 62:10) meant a highway and in time this came to mean a raised road, paved and drained. Is. 26:7 uses the term for a wagon track, also found in Ps. 140:5 and Pr. 4:26. Isaiah (30:11; 33:8 and elsewhere) mentions a way or road, while the word for path or pathway occurs in Jud. 5:6; Job 18:10; Ps. 77:19; Pr. 1:15 and Is. 43:16. Numbers 22:24 uses a term

707

which means literally a "hollow path", presumably an alleyway overhung by trees. In fact, all these terms usually refer to the small, local roadways of the countryside which were of no importance for long-distance travel.

Roads linking different areas of settlement and countries came into use in the earliest times. At first they were merely narrow tracks and mountain paths, suitable only for the passage of men and beasts of burden. As more sophisticated means of transport developed, the state of the roads became a matter of greater importance and governments and similar bodies undertook the care of the regular highways, mainly near the larger cities. The late Bronze and Iron Ages saw a great expansion in road construction in Palestine. The Amarna* Letters give evidence of the use of forced labour by Canaanite kings for the purpose (see Taxes*) and the practice was continued under the Israelite monarchy, especially by David and Solomon* (see articles).

At first, the building of roads was a matter of clearing the natural surface of large stones or other obstacles. The introduction and wide use of military chariots, commercial carts, and other vehicles, however, may have prompted a rather more solid construction. There is no actual evidence of such road-building in the Bible, and no paved roads were built in Palestine until Roman times. Josephus' story (Ant. 8, 7, 4) that Solomon paved the paths leading to Jerusalem with black stones apparently describes the roads of his own time. It was over such roads that Paul and the apostles travelled. It is, however, possible that in places, ancient roads were fenced with stone walls to protect privately owned property.

Egyptian inscriptions from the time of the New Kingdom (14th c. BCE) record that the dangerous passes of the el-Kalb wadi (gully or canyon) near Beirut (in Lebanon) were cleared of obstacles but, on the other hand, other inscriptions of the 19th dynasty (13th c. BCE) speak of bad roads, blocked by stones and rocks and, therefore, impassable by chariots. The Mesha inscription (9th c. BCE) records the construction of the "highway" in the Arnon wadi but there is no evidence of exactly what is meant. The "Great Western Road" which the Hittite kings built from their capital to the Aegean was just an unpaved track with rocks and other obstacles removed.

The Amarna letters are also concerned with road building. One of the kings of Canaan announces that "I levelled all highroads to Batzrona (perhaps Basra in Bashan)". The Egyptian kings of the 18th and 19th dynasties who conquered Canaan, particularly Thutmoses III, outlined fixed paths for the movement of their armies to Canaan and Syria. One of these may have been the very ancient King's Highway (Nu. 20:17–19) that ran through the highlands of Transjordan.

The most difficult part of the road that carried the advancing Egyptians to Palestine was the section from Kantara to el-Arish (the area today crossed by the Suez Canal). Seti I built eight stations along the road, each one with a fort and cistern. This combination of defence posts and a frequented road suggests the "Way of the Land of the Philistines" (Ex. 13:17) which the Hebrews were careful to avoid when they were fleeing from Egypt (see Exodus*).

International Highways: Palestine lay on the main routes linking the great empires of Egypt and Mesopotamia and the kingdoms of Asia Minor. The main junction of these international routes was at Aleppo in Syria, where the river Euphrates turned west towards the Mediterranean. From Aleppo, roads led west to the Aegean coastline, east and south to Nineveh and Babylon. At first, travellers from Syria to the valley of the Euphrates and Tigris had to go around the Syrian desert which lay across their path.

An 18th c. BCE Mari document speaks of a road running from Katna (El-Mishrefah) in Syria to the Euphrates, via Palmyra, an important junction, where it was joined by another road from Damascus. The most southerly road was one which ran from Eilat through south Edom to Babylonia, passing through the wadi Sirhan to Damascus. Another road from Eilat led southwards along the eastern shores of the Red Sea to Yemen in southern Arabia, along the road travelled by the Queen of Sheba (cf. Arabia*; Nabateans*).

Another important highway — and one which is mentioned in the Bible (Is. 9:1) — was the "Via Maris" or "road of the sea" which connected Egypt and Babylonia, running across the Sinai desert and then northwards along the Philistine coast — hence its other name or extension, "the way of the land of the Philistines" (see above and Exodus*). This road followed the Palestinian coast from Gaza, Ashkelon and Ashdod to Jaffa, then turned inland to Aphek, so as to avoid the impassable swamps of the Sharon coastal plain. From Aphek, the road ran northward along the mountain slopes to Megiddo and there divided into three. One branch went through Yokneam, Achshaph, Acco, Tyre and Sidon, then along the coast into Asia Minor. A second ran along the shores of the Sea of Galilee, through Hazor, Hamath and Kadesh, then south of Abel-Beth-Maacah to Damascus, where it joined the third road which went from Megiddo to Jezreel, Beth-Shean and across the Jordan to Damascus. From there, the road ran to Duma in the Syrian desert and on to Palmyra and Babylon.

Apparently the first caravans used donkeys but after the 11th c. BCE, camels superseded donkeys for use in caravans, and for the first time made it possible to travel straight across deserts. The Midianites who practically monopolized caravan trade on the main highways during the Israelite period, used only camels (see Agric. and Animal Husbandry*).

Another junction in Damascus was between the coastal road and a road which ran the entire length of Transjordan from south to north. It was the southern section of this road, known as the Road of Edom (II K. 3:8), which was originally called the "King's Highway" (Nu. 20:17). This road and the coastal "Via Maris" formed the main arteries of Palestine, east and west of the Jordan.

Egypt and Canaan were joined by a number of roads besides the coastal "way of the land of the Philistines". One branch of this route joined Wadi el-Arish, east of Sinai, to Migdol in the centre of the Delta. A caravan route led through the desert joining up, at Kadesh-Barnea, with the Reed Sea road (Nu. 14:25; 21:4) and finally ending up at Eilat (Ezion-Geber).

Another system of roads running from Eilat connected the port and the copper mines of Solomon (Nu. 33:35; II Ch. 8:17) to Beersheba and north to Jerusalem. This road was of particular importance because it was the link with the south and east route to Arabia, East Africa and India.

Internal Roads of Palestine: Palestine itself had a number of important internal highways (see map **708**). One ran along the watershed of the mountains of Judah and Samaria, passing through Samaria, Shechem, Bethel (Jud. 21:19), Jerusalem, Hebron and Beersheba. At Beersheba it joined the great international highway to the south, the Shur road (see below). In addition, many east-west roads, like the one from Ashkelon to Hebron and Jerusalem, connected the coastal plain to Jerusalem and the mountain regions, while others linked the smaller centres with the main international highways.

The East-West Roads of the Negeb: The "King's Highway" (Darb-es-Sultan in Arabic) was one of the most frequented routes through the central Negeb (the southern tip of Palestine). Part of it is formed by the Shur road to Egypt, which was used in the days of Abraham. Running from Raphiah to Gaza, the Darb-es-Sultan avoids the steep ascent of the mountain ranges, which run northeast to southwest, by following the way of the Arabah through Nahal Zin, see map **354**; it then goes across the Arabah, south of the Dead Sea. This was the route the Israelites took from Kadesh-Barnea to Zin (see **427**). It is dotted with the ruins of ancient villages and caravanseries, which bear witness to its use from the 4th mill. BCE to Roman and Byzantine times. In the days of the Ottoman empire (15th-20th cs. CE), the journey from Gaza to Maan (near Petra) took about five days by camel.

Roads in Post-Exilic and Roman Times: The two main roads running the length of the country were still in use in post-Exilic and Roman times. One ran along the coast from Alexandria, through present day Raphiah, Gaza, Ashkelon* and Ashdod*, then inland to Lod where it split into two. One branch went to Jerusalem, the other skirted the coastal plain through Antipatris to Narbata, then back to Caesarea on the coast and northwards to Acre, Tyre and Antiochia. The other road ran along the highlands of Transjordan from Eilat to Madeba, Rabbath-Ammon (Philadelphia), Bosra and Damascus. Inner roads connected these two, and joined Beth-Shean to Damascus. The road along the highlands of Judea and Samaria was still in existence and many other secondary roads ran between the towns of the country.

The Nabatean Road Network: By Nabatean and Roman times, the ancient Darb-es-Sultan east-west route had become of only secondary importance. In its place, roads ran from the sea coast to Petra (see Nabateans*) through Nessana, Ruheiba and Khalassa, then north to Beersheba and east to Avdat and Kurnub to join the network of Nabatean roads that ran north, south and east of Petra (see map **629**).

In 106 CE, the Romans annexed Nabatea, changing its name to the province of Arabia. Petra, the great emporium of the desert, remained one of the most important cities of the eastern world until the end of the 2nd c. CE when it was superseded by Palmyra in the Syrian desert. The Roman legions were stationed at Bosra to the north of Petra, and Roman garrisons were posted along the principal desert tracks and roads (see map **708** and a Roman fort in the Arabah indicated by an arrow, **709**). These formed the "Limes Arabicus" which protected the inland empire and its communications. After the occupation of Nabatea, Trajan built a north-south highway running from Syria via Bosra and Philadelphia (Amman) to the Red Sea, according to the milestones (**540**).

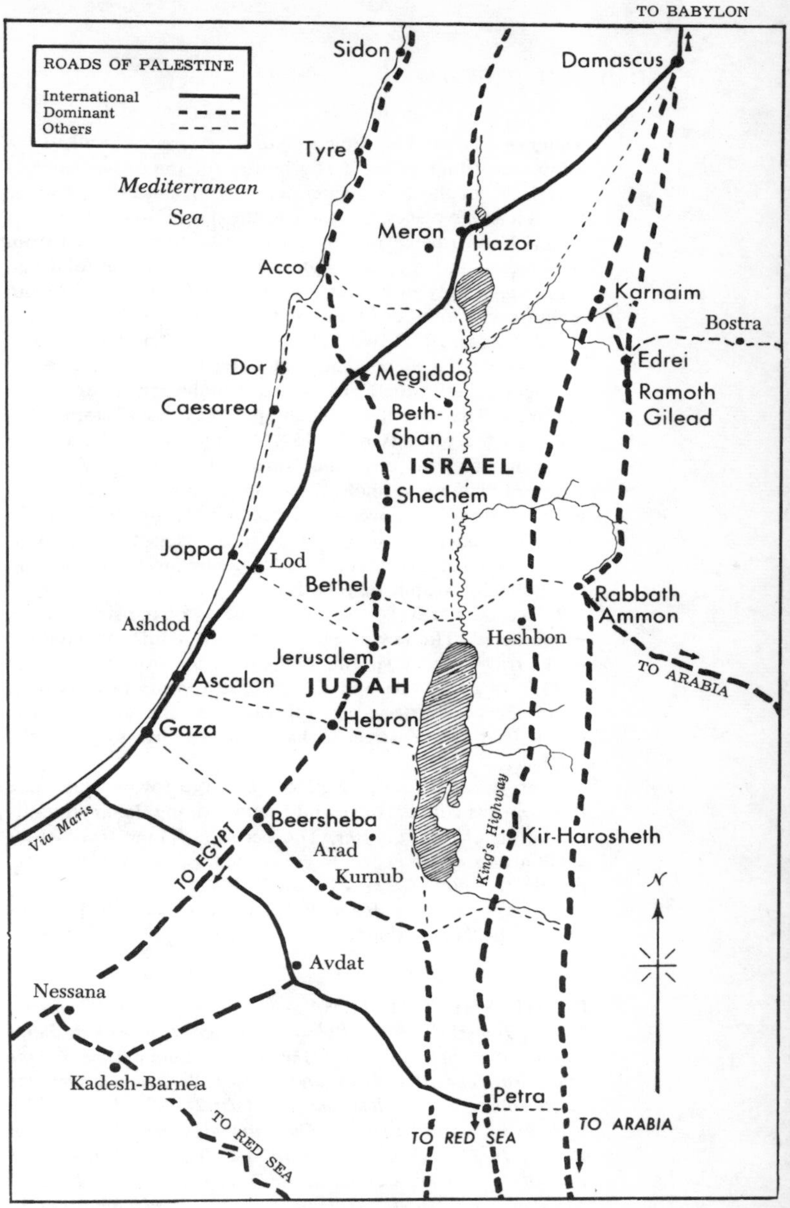

708

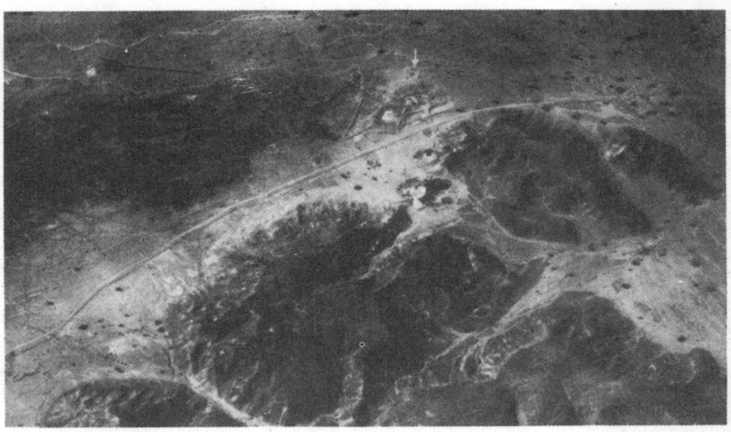

709

Stopping Places: The Bible makes no reference at all to the existence of inns or other rest-houses for the convenience of travellers. In the Persian period, lodging places were to be found in some places, but none of them sold food. Provisions always had to be carried by the traveller or purchased from settlements on his route. Well-ordered inns selling food and drink came only in a later age. The "lodging place" or inn mentioned a number of times (Gn. 42:27; 43:21; Ex. 4:24; Jos. 4:3, 8; Is. 10:29; Jer. 9:2) in the Bible may have been a place where travellers could find water and rest, or a spring to quench their thirst, secure from highwaymen or beasts of prey. The brothers of Joseph may have stopped to eat in such a place (Gn. 37:25–28), which would be a likely place at which to meet the Ishmaelite caravan. When far removed from main roads, these inns or stopping places were built of stone, arranged in a rectangular or semi-circular shape, similar to those unearthed in the Negeb and perhaps to the one mentioned in Ex. 4:24. Similar structures can be found in Arabia to this day.

However, a traveller was at the mercy of the strangers he encountered. The law of Moses does not require hospitality* to the traveller as a specific obligation, but from verses such as Gn. 18:1 ff; 24:31 and Ex. 2:20, it appears to have been an honoured courtesy, e.g. Job (31:32): "the sojourner has not lodged in the street, I have opened my doors to the wayfarer."

There were no lodging places in large towns, but there the caravans could always find friends among the inhabitants of the merchants' quarter. The occasional lone traveller or small group would expect to enjoy the hospitality of the local people (II Sam. 17:27–29; Is. 21:14–15).

Seaways to and from Palestine are described under Ships and Navigation*.

ROME AND THE JEWS. — *Outline: I. First Contacts; Roman Imperial Policy; Palestine Occupied by Rome; Julius Caesar and the Rights of the Jews; Antagonisms in the Diaspora; The Herodians and Rome; Palestine Under the Procurators; The Zealots and the "Last Days". II. The War with Rome: Initial Victory; The Campaign in Galilee; Zealot Rivalry in Jerusalem; Rivalry for the Imperial Throne; The Fall of Jerusalem; Continued Resistance; The Last Days of Masada. III. Death Struggle in the Second Century CE; The Second War with Rome — Bar-Kochba* (131–136 *CE*); *Later Developments* (3*rd c. CE*).

The Romans regarded the Jews as merely another small people within the great Empire. Rome's attitude towards them was a political question, part of its general imperial policy. For their part, the Jews saw Rome in terms of their own special attitude towards the rest of the world, an attitude which was part of the whole pattern of Jewish religious development, aspirations and way of life.

I. First Contacts: Contact between the Jews and Rome was first made during the Maccabaean rebellion* and seemed to be satisfactory to both sides. The Judean rebels received moral support as part of Rome's general anti-Seleucid policy. A pact was made with the Roman Senate (161 BCE) and regularly renewed by later Hasmonean* rulers. Jewish enthusiasm for their supporters can be seen from the glowing description of Roman qualities in the First Book of Maccabees (8:1–16, see Apocrypha*), apparently composed during the reign of John Hyrcanus, the first independent Hasmonean prince.

However, in 139 BCE, a delegation sent to Rome by the Hasmonean, Simon, was asked to leave, perhaps because they had been making religious propaganda among Gentile sympathizers with the substantial Roman Jewish community.

Roman Imperial Policy: Generations before the arrival of Romans in Syria, Hellenistic civilization (see Hellenism in the Near East*) had aroused the interest of leading Romans. At first they were content to see this cultural achievement develop unhampered, but towards the end of the 1st c. BCE, Rome's policy changed. The peoples she conquered were expected to adopt her own ideas of the ordered development of society on Roman lines. The Romans were also not unaware of the advantages of controlling the wealthy Hellenistic oriental kingdoms and their prosperous trade routes and caravans.

The decline of the power of the Seleucid empire (see Hasmoneans*) saw a wave of revolt among the oriental peoples they had ruled, who hoped to wrest independence from their Hellenistic overlords. Left to themselves, they might have succeeded. As it was, Roman legions intervened, led by an energetic and skilful general, Pompey. At the end of his campaign in the Near East, the Roman dream of an eastern empire had been established and Hellenistic culture, backed by Roman legions, was firmly entrenched from Syria, Palestine and Asia Minor eastwards to the Euphrates. Pompey was more than a conqueror. By putting men who would cooperate with Rome in charge of the conquered countries, he established a political organization that held the Empire together for centuries.

Palestine Occupied by Rome: Pompey's occupation of Syria coincided with civil war in Palestine between two rival Hasmoneans — Aristobulos II and Hyrcanus. Appealed to as an arbiter, Pompey considered which side was more likely to prove amenable to Rome and declared for Hyrcanus. However, to defeat Aristobulos who was entrenched in the citadel of Jerusalem, Pompey had to bring his legions south from Syria and lead the attack in person, desecrating the Temple in the process (see Hasmoneans*).

Roman intervention put an end to Hasmonean territorial expansion and to the Judaization of the areas of Palestine east and west of the Jordan still outside the Jewish state. Instead, the independence of the Hellenized districts inside the country was recognized by the Romans and the Hellenistic cities (the Decapolis and coastal towns) which had been attacked by the Hasmoneans were restored to their former status. Pompey's rejection of Jewish national sovereignty and his support for the Hellenistic (Gentile) elements of the population of Palestine quickly destroyed the old amicable relations between Rome and the Jews. The exiled Aristobulos and his sons were able to lead a series of rebellions against Rome, all put down with great severity. Nevertheless, the Romans recognized the Jews' right to autonomy under their own leaders: Hyrcanus as high priest and ethnarch, assisted by the ambitious governor appointed by Caesar, Antipater the Idumean (see Hasmoneans*).

Julius Caesar and the Rights of the Jews: Tensions between Rome and the Jewish state in Palestine did not affect Roman policy towards the numerous Jewish communities elsewhere in the Empire (see Hellenism and the Diaspora*). In Rome and the rest of Italy, Jewish settlements expanded and developed without interference from the authorities. When Julius Caesar came to power in Rome, he confirmed the Jews in the status of a special group or nation with certain civil rights and unique privileges such as exemption from military service or from appearing in court on the Sabbath. This privileged status was confirmed by later Roman rulers and continued in the Diaspora even long after the fall of Jerusalem in 70 CE (see Christianity, Early*).

Antagonisms in the Diaspora: Although their legal rights continued to be maintained in the Empire by the Romans, the Jews of the Diaspora faced increasing resentment from the Gentile inhabitants of the Hellenistic cities outside Palestine. In Alexandria, one of the most important of the Jewish centres of the Diaspora (see Hellenism in the Near East*), mutual hatred, fanned by vicious anti-Jewish propaganda, exploded in bloody riots during the reign of Gaius Caligula. The Roman Legate, Flaccus, who sided with the Greeks of Alexandria, brought the dispute before the new emperor Claudius. He counselled tolerance and insisted that the Greeks respect Jewish rights. Where it helped to maintain the peace of the Empire (see map **710**), this remained Roman policy.

The Herodians and Rome: When Herod* succeeded his father, Antipater, and became King of the Jews (37 BCE) he consolidated his position by demonstrating his devotion to Rome and keeping in close touch with the Jews of the Diaspora. Herod won the status of "Amicus et socius populi Romani" (Friend and ally of the Roman people) but his subjects were very far from sharing his friendly feelings. Indeed all Herod's attempts to integrate his kingdom into the Roman Imperium merely increased the Jews' hatred of himself, Rome and the Hellenistic civilization it represented. They refused to accept the Emperor as their sovereign or Hellenism as their culture and they never believed that the Roman legions were stationed in the country for their protection (see Chronological Table: Rome and the Jews, annexed).

Palestine Under the Procurators: After Herod's death (4 BCE), his kingdom was divided between his three sons who ruled as "Ethnarchs" under Roman supervision. Ten years later (6 CE), formal Jewish independence was ended and Judea was placed under the direct rule of a Roman Procurator.

The Procurators (see attached Chronological table) ruled as independent governors with full administrative authority and the right of life and death over the Jewish population. (Everywhere in the Empire, Roman citizens could always demand trial by the Emperor, a right which Paul* later exercised.) The Jewish Sanhedrin (see Government and Authority*) was made responsible for civil jurisdiction, but the Procurators, who were the Imperial tax collectors, could and did intervene in financial cases.

The Procurators established themselves in the city of Caesarea*, patterned on Hellenistic lines, appearing in Jerusalem only at the times of the great Festivals. Appointed principally as financial managers, they had no understanding of the Jews and their ways and little or no sympathy for them. They followed Imperial policy in favouring the Gentile inhabitants of the Hellenistic cities, in preference to the Jewish population. In addition to this strain on inter-communal relations, frequent affronts to Jewish religious susceptibilities led to repeated rioting. Issues that seemed negligible to the Romans were often of fundamental importance to the Jews. The classic example is Caligula's attempt to erect a statue of himself in the Temple; this was only one of many instances where gratuitous insults seemed to be offered to Jewish beliefs and institutions (see John the Baptist*; Jesus*).

An inflammable political situation was accompanied by increasing economic difficulties for the mass of the people, made worse by the extortions of the Procurators. It was hardly unreasonable for so many of the Jews to pin their faith on messianic* hopes and eschatological* expectations as their only escape from intolerable hardships.

The Zealots and the "Last Days": Relations between Rome and Judea had reached an impasse. Roman hopes of integrating the Jews into the Empire were persistently frustrated. For their part, the Jews looked forward to a divine gesture that would free them — and the world — from Roman rule. Those who could not endure foreign oppression turned for relief to the politico-religious party of the Zealots*. They promised that God would help his "Chosen People" to destroy the upstarts who had usurped divine prerogatives and claimed to rule over them. In the "War of the Last Days", earthly (Roman) empires would be overthrown and God's messianic kingdom established (see Eschatology*, Dead Sea Scrolls*).

II. THE WAR WITH ROME. — Meanwhile, mounting tensions between a resentful population and an increasingly corrupt and oppressive government found expression in open conflicts between Jews and Gentiles within the country. Thus the non-Jewish townspeople of Caesarea tried to deny the Jewish inhabitants all civil rights. The case was referred to the Emperor, Nero, and his support for the Gentiles, when it was announced six years later, was one of the sparks that set light to the smouldering rebellion.

710

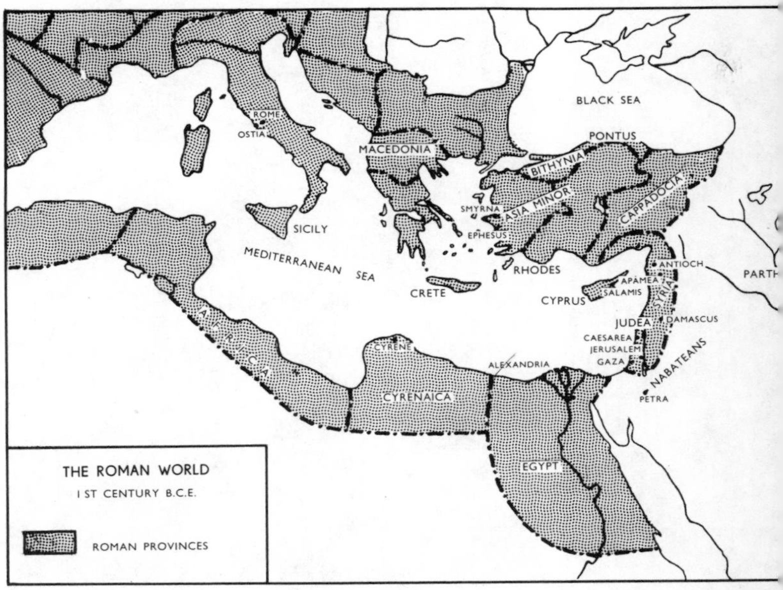

Nero's explicit declaration of anti-Jewish policy came at the end of four years (62–66 CE) of increasingly tyrannical rule by the Procurators. Finally, the seizure of the Temple treasure by Gessius Florus (the last Procurator), which coincided with inter-communal conflicts in Caesarea and the massacre of Jews there, provoked open rebellion. Under the Zealot leader, Eleazar ben Hananiah, the people rose to arms, took control of Jerusalem, massacred the Roman soldiers remaining there and defiantly threw down their challenge to the whole might of Rome.

Inspired by faith in God and the exhilarating sense of release from oppression, the Jews were to fight with magnificent courage and enthusiasm for seven years of war. But the odds were too great. Rome was at the peak of its power and the ultimate result was never in doubt.

Initial Victory: The immediate response to the rebellion came from the Roman governor of Syria, legally the superior of the Judean Procurator. With an army numbering 30,000, he marched against Jerusalem only to be repulsed and decisively defeated at Beth-Horon.

Victory gave the Jews time to organize their defences. Military governors of the various districts were appointed,

711

Galilee being placed under the command of Joseph ben Mattathias, the future historian, Flavius Josephus*. He records that he made energetic preparations with inadequate resources. The men who joined the quickly raised armies were brave enough but totally untrained and their weapons and military equipment (some of it captured from the Romans; see Arms*, War*) were in short supply. Nevertheless internal defence was ensured as far as possible — in spite of signs of conflict between military leaders from different religious and political parties.

Outside Palestine, it was a different matter. It seems from Josephus that help was expected from Jews living "beyond the Euphrates", i.e. in the non-Roman Diaspora. (Within the Empire, no Jew would jeopardize Roman protection by openly joining the rebels, however much he might be in sympathy with the revolt in Palestine.) Beyond this, none of the Jews' potential allies were rallied. Even Parthia, Rome's greatest enemy, stood aside and finally congratulated Titus on his victory. Josephus later described the Jewish-Roman war as "the greatest . . . that ever broke out between cities or nations". This would appear to be an exaggeration although a sizeable number of legions were involved in suppressing the revolt. The Jews of Palestine embarked upon it alone, buoyed up by "apocalyptic fanaticism" (F.M. Cross) and the certainty of help from the God who had once given victory to the Maccabees over the might of an earlier empire.

The Campaign in Galilee: Against them, by the spring of 67 CE, an army of 60,000 was assembled at Ptolemais (Acre) under Rome's ablest general, Vespasian. The first assault was made, as expected, in Galilee. Its centre, Zippori (Sephoris), capitulated without a fight, leaving the surrounding towns defenceless. The Romans met resistance at the fortress of Jotapata which was commanded by Josephus. It held out for 47 days before succumbing from exhaustion and treachery. Other places were inspired to an equally heroic fight, but without altering the final result. By the time Vespasian sent his troops to winter quarters, Galilee had been devastated; thousands had died — 40,000 in Jotapata, 5,000 in the village of Yaffa near Nazareth, 11,000 in Shechem — while another 30,000 had been sold into slavery. Josephus had surrendered and attached himself to Vespasian.

Zealot Rivalry in Jerusalem: While Galilee was being overrun, internal dissension broke out in Jerusalem and the southern areas where the Zealots had strong support. One Zealot leader, Johanan of Gischala, began a reign of terror aimed at undermining the authority of the Sanhedrin and Sadducee leaders. After an initial welcome, the people of Jerusalem wearied of him and, in the spring of 68 CE, turned to a new leader, Simon bar Giora, as a deliverer. With an army of several thousand, recruited from the countryside to the south, he attacked Johanan's forces in Jerusalem and drove them back to the area around the Temple approaches. Within the Temple, a third faction under the priest, Eleazar ben Shimon, fought against both sides, continuing the Temple ritual even through the fighting.

Sporadic civil war continued between the three zones while Vespasian proceeded to take control of a wide area around the capital, from Samaria in the north, eastwards through Hebron down to Jericho and the Negeb in the

712

south. Jerusalem was isolated. (The capture of Jericho is connected with the Roman attack on the community at Qumran; see Dead Sea Scrolls*).

Rivalry for the Imperial Throne: Just then, Nero died suddenly in Rome. More concerned with events there, Vespasian halted his campaign in Judea and waited. An uneasy peace returned to the country — but the Roman soldiers remained in their camps and in the towns they had captured. Meanwhile chaos reigned in the heart of the empire as three "emperors" fought for the throne. Galba and Otho marched on Rome late in 68 CE. Otho was proclaimed emperor in January of 69 CE but was defeated by another general, Vitellus, who in turn, was killed by the troops a year later. Then in July 69, Vespasian was proclaimed Emperor by the Legions; (this illus. depicts the scene of an emperor and his officers in a Roman camp, **711**). He took ship for Rome, leaving the campaign in Judea to his son, Titus.

Titus spent the winter reorganizing his army. In March 70 CE, he began the assault on Jerusalem.

The Fall of Jerusalem: A huge army, four Roman legions and a number of auxiliary troops, was split into columns, all converging on Jerusalem — side by side with the normal stream of pilgrims going up to the Holy City for the Passover festival. On the eve of the holiday, Titus appeared before the town's third wall and set up his camp on Mount Scopus to the north-east.

The Romans prepared to attack — while the Jews readied their defences. Internecine strife had gravely weakened the city, but in the face of immediate danger, the rival factions compromised their differences and joined forces to meet the enemy. Nevertheless, after 15 days of fighting the outer wall was breached (see Arms*; Warfare*). Defenders, population and the many holiday pilgrims retreated, first within the inner walls, then into the stronghold of the upper city, protected by the towers of Antonia and the Forts of Herod. There they were encircled. Titus built a stone wall 7,200 metres long around the citadel. No food could reach the people within it. No one could escape. (See Jerusalem*).

For another month during which famine and disease took a heavy toll, the defenders held out against repeated Roman attacks. Then came the final assault. In spite of the tenacious defence, the Antonia Tower was taken and destroyed. The last refuge was the Temple itself and there the Jews gathered for their final defiance. For a week the gates stood firm against Roman battering rams. At the end, Titus ordered them burned. He had directed that the Temple be spared, but since the Temple precincts had been used for military purposes, the Roman soldiers disregarded the order. On the 10th of the month of Ab (August, 70 CE) the Temple of Herod crumbled in flames and his legions proclaimed Titus Imperator (victor). The Roman victory is depicted in the Titus Arch in Rome, showing trophies from the Temple (**712**).

The last of the Zealots fought on in the upper town for another week, but it was hopeless. After five months of bitter siege and fighting, the Romans were in complete control of the heaps of ruins that had once been Jerusalem. Part of the western wall and three towers of Herod were alone preserved, providing a garrison for the Roman troops and a memorial for the city. Those of its inhabitants who survived were slaughtered, taken prisoner or sold as slaves. Hundreds of thousands had perished in the Great War.

Continued Resistance: Even with a Roman governor once more installed in Caesarea, Zealot resistance continued in the south and east. Two centres, Herodium and Machaerus, succumbed to ponderous but implacable Roman sieges. The last to fall was Masada, perched on the summit of a forbidding mountain facing the Dead Sea, a stronghold of the Zealots since 66 CE, who occupied its 140 small rooms. The Romans began the siege in 72 CE, building camps around the foot of the mountain, shown in the illustration (**713**), and another on the heights overlooking it. They slowly constructed a dike to take the soldiers and their siege engines up to the ramparts of the fortress. Hundreds of Roman slingshots, rounded balls of stone the size of grapefruit, were found piled around one of the rooms. These were hurled at the defenders by the siege engines and collected to throw back at the Romans.

713

The Last Days of Masada: In 73 CE the Roman assault began. As the outer walls crumbled, the defenders retired behind a second wall. This the Romans attacked with firebrands. With the end in sight, the Zealots retreated into Herod's palace, whose inaccessible position, crowning the top of the rock is shown in this illust., **714**. They had no hope. They could not hope to win, nor was any further withdrawal possible. Rather than face surrender on Roman terms, the Zealots accepted the terrible alternative proposed by the leader, Eleazar. Beginning with their wives and children, the defenders of Masada slaughtered each other. The Romans entered the palace next day to find the fortress that had withstood them for so long manned only by corpses. The manner of their death was recorded by Josephus who claimed to have learned the story from a woman who, with two children, alone survived. In a cave on the cliff face 20 skeletons were found, among them a foetus. They were probably the bodies of Zealots dumped by the Romans. In the ruins of a heated bath near the lowest palace, the skeletons were found of a man, woman and child. The woman, possibly 20 years old, still had her hair plaited, brown and lustrous.

With the fall of Masada, Caesar's triumph over the Kingdom of God seemed complete. The Romans took terrible vengeance on the Jews throughout the country. Only very slowly did life return to the Jewish settlements in the southern coastal region and Galilee, under the spiritual leadership of the rabbis* of the Academy of Jabneh.

III. DEATH STRUGGLE IN THE SECOND C. CE: Palestinian refugees from the first Roman-Jewish war had spread their nationalist and messianic ideals in the diaspora—a further source of conflict within the mixed Jewish-Hellenistic cities. Moreover, although Jewish rights were generally maintained, official restrictions had begun. The small Temple of Onias in Egypt (see Restoration*; Hellenism in the Diaspora*) had been closed. In place of the voluntary half-shekel which every Jew used to contribute annually to the Temple in Jerusalem, an equivalent tax, the "Fiscus Judaicus", paid to the Temple of Jupiter in Rome, had been imposed. It marked the beginning of later anti-Jewish policies. Coming at a time when local inter-communal and economic stress for the Jews was again accompanied by a messianic fervour, it signalled the renewal of actual armed conflict, 44 years after the death struggle in Jerusalem. While Trajan was involved in a gigantic struggle with the Parthians (114–117 CE) riots and warfare broke out once again (see introduction to the article on Bar-Kochba*).

The Second War with Rome — Bar-Kochba (131–136 CE): This second attempt at "God's Final War" (see Bar-Kochba*) was no more successful than the first. The rebellions were suppressed at the cost of the heaviest losses Jewry had ever sustained, the Zealots being totally wiped out. At its end, the Romans, recognizing that the roots of Jewish rebellion lay in their religious and mystic dreams, imposed the repressive "Edicts of Hadrian", aimed at the destruction of Judaism, both in Palestine and in the diaspora where Jewish populations had joined in supporting the revolt against Rome. Although the "Edicts" were later abrograted, the remaining Jews unwillingly accepted the Roman yoke and decided that while the end must one day come to the "Kingdom of Evil", they could do nothing directly to help bring it about.

Later Developments (3rd c. CE): Although a hidden antagonism remained, there were no further serious clashes between the Jews and Rome. Jewish religious life was not hindered although proselytizing was banned. By this time, however, the new missionary faith that had developed out of Judaism was spreading through the empire (see Christianity, Early*: Jewish Christians; Paul*). The gradual triumph of Christianity produced new conditions, and these in turn were to affect social and many other aspects of the life of the Jews during the era of Church and Synagogue.

714

ROMAN REPUBLIC	PALESTINE		THE NEAR EAST
BCE			
67–60 Pompey's Wars in the Near East	66–63 Aristobulos II, Hasmonean King		
	63 Pompey replaces kingdom by Ethnarchy		
60 First Triumvirate Pompey, Crassus, Caesar	55 Rebellion in Palestine. Intervention by Gabinius		
	Caesar's campaigns in Palestine, Egypt and Asia		
49–44 Caesar dictator			
43–42 Second triumvirate: Antony, Lepidus, Octavius			Brutus and Cassius in the Orient
	40–37 Antigonus — last Hasmonean ruler. Parthians in Palestine and Syria		42–31 Antony, Master of the Orient
40 Herod proclaimed King of the Jews in Rome	37 Herod takes over Jerusalem.		
31 Battle of Actium: Octavius defeats Antony.			
ROMAN EMPIRE			
27 Octavius becomes Augustus, reorganizes Roman provinces	Herod enlarges his kingdom. Jesus of Nazareth born — about 7–6 BCE		
27–14CE Augustus — Emperor	4BCE Death of Herod		11–8 BCE P.S. Quirinius, Legate of Syria
	Herodian kingdom divided:		6–4 Quintilius Varus, Legate
	JUDEA	GALILEE	BATANEA, ITURAEA
	4BCE Archelaus, Ethnarch (deposed 6 CE)	4BCE—39CE Herod Antipas	4BCE—34CE Philip, Tetrarch
	6CE *Under the Procurators* (1st *Phase*):		
	6–9BCE Coponius (Anan I. High Priest (8)		
	9–12 M. Ambivius		
CE	12–15 Annius Rufus		
14–37 Tiberius	15–26 Valerius Gratus (Caiaphas, High Priest (18)		
	26–36 Pontius Pilate; Ministries of John the Baptist and Jesus.		
	36–36 Marullus		
37–41 Caligula (Gaius)	37–41 Herennius Gapito (Disturbances in Palestine and Alexandria (39–40)	37 Agrippa I, Tetrarch	
41–54 Claudius	41–44 *Kingdom temporarily re-united*: Agrippa I, King of Palestine		
	Under the Procurators (last phase):		
	44–46 Cuspius Fadus		43/44 Paul in Antioch
	46–48 Tiberius Alexander		45–50 Cassius Longinus, Legate of Syria
Expulsion of the Jews (Acts 18:2) from Rome	48–52 Ventidius Cumanus Anan II, High Priest (45–59) (Acts 23:2; 24:1)		45–48 Paul's first missionary journey to Cyprus & Asia Minor.
54–68 Nero	52–60 M. Antonius Felix (Acts 23, 26)		49–53 Paul's second journey to Asia Minor & Greece
	60–62 Porcius Festus (Acts 24, 27)		
Death of Paul and Peter in Rome	62–64 Clodius Albinus	50–93 Agrippa II, king of former tetrarchies of Philip and Lysanias (Acts 25: 13–22)	50–53 Agrippa II, king of Chalcis (Lebanon)
	64–66 Gessius Florus Ananias II, High Priest (61–62)		53–58 Paul's third journey: Asia Minor & Greece
	66–73 *Jewish-Roman War:*		
	66–67 Galilean Campaign		50–60 Ummidius Quadratius, Legate of Syria
	68 Campaign in Perea (East of Jordan)		
68–69 Galba–Otho–Vitellius			60–62 D. Corbulon, Legate of Syria
70–79 Vespasian	70 Fall of Jerusalem		63–66 Cestius Gallus, Legate of Syria
	71 Judea, an Imperial province		67–69 Lucinius Mucienus
	71–72 Lucilius Berosus, Legate of Judea		
	73 Flavius Silva " " " Fall of Masada.		
79–81 Titus			
81–96 Domitian Letters of Clement, Pope			
96–98 Nerva			105 Roman Conquest of Nabatea
98–117 Trajan			115–117 Jewish rebellions in the eastern Diaspora.
117 138 Hadrian	131–135 War of Bar-Kochba		

RUTH. — The Book of Ruth, second among the five short books which are read in the Synagogue after the long poetical works of Psalms, Proverbs and Job, comes first in order of the Hagiographa (Writings) because it refers to the period of Judges and is ascribed to the prophet Samuel, the supposed author of Judges. The Vulgate followed the Septuagint in placing Ruth after the Book of Judges and Josephus considered it an appendix to the larger work.

Contents: The book tells the story of an ancestress of David, Ruth, a Moabite girl who married into a family from Bethlehem who had migrated to Moab during a famine in Judea. In time, Ruth's husband, his brother and father died. Her mother-in-law, Naomi, returned to her homeland and, although urged to remain in Moab, Ruth accompanied her. Together, Naomi and Ruth arrive in Bethlehem at harvest time and Ruth goes to glean in the fields after the reapers. There, she is noticed by the owner, Boaz, who as a kinsman, in due course agrees to act the part of "go'el" or redeemer of her late husband's estate and marry her. He marries Ruth who bears him Obed, the reputed grandfather of the future David.

Style: The book of Ruth is an excellent example of the biblical short story. Written in a concise, classical Hebrew which very aptly reflects its pastoral setting, the book is notable for the complete absence of negative characters. Naomi, Ruth and Boaz are all endowed with the heroic virtues of strength and compassion, but the lesser figures, Ruth's sister Orphah and the closer kinsman who must first refuse to marry Ruth before Boaz is free to do so, are also presented sympathetically. As a whole, this pastoral interlude forms a very welcome contrast to the martial struggles of the Book of Judges.

Date: Fixing a date for the composition of the book depends on determining whether it is a factual account of real events, whether it was written as fiction, and for what purpose it was written.

The critical school of Biblical criticism, (see article*) accept the theory that Ruth is a post-Exilic literary creation. This is based on the appearance of a number of Aramaic formulations and phrases in the book. However, there are only a few of these and it is doubtful whether they can establish a date of writing by themselves, especially since many classic expressions familiar from the books of Samuel and Kings also appear in Ruth (e.g. 1:2; 3:13; 4:17). As to its purpose, scholars who regard it as a post-Exilic work, consider that it was intended as a protest against the expulsion of foreign wives demanded by Ezra and Nehemiah (see Restoration*). However, this argument is also weakened by reference to the book itself. There is no preaching there about inter-marriage. It is presented very simply as a story.

Historical Background: Nevertheless, even as a fictional romance there must be a kernel of fact in the story. Foreign extraction would hardly be ascribed to David without some support. Family connections with Moab are in fact borne out by the reference in I Sam. 22:3–4 to David finding shelter for his parents with the King of Moab. The purpose of the book of Ruth, in that case, might be to strengthen existing bonds between Israel and Moab. Its dating would be during the reigns of the first kings of Judah, before the revolt of Mesha against Jehoshaphat and Jehoram (see Moab*) after which an intense hatred developed between the two peoples. The story may have been written at that time by someone who either lived in Bethlehem, or heard the story there.

Even though he lived long after the period of Judges, the author faithfully preserved the customs of that time. The manner of "redeeming" Ruth and her family, for instance, differs from the procedure prescribed in Lev. 25:25 (cf. Jer. 32:6–8). Redemption of the land once owned by Ruth's husband was tied to marrying her and this is an extension of the law of levirate marriage (cf. Family*: Levirate). Moreover the bargain with Boaz is sealed by the "kinsman" taking off his shoe (4:7). This is an old custom although it was still observed when Deuteronomy* was written. Some scholars have observed that the author of Ruth misunderstood the meaning of the act, but this could also reflect an early date for the story's composition.

However it is interpreted, Ruth is a touching story of human devotion, and a valuable illustration of life in a small Judean provincial town. The poor woman who gleans after the reapers, the landowner who oversees the work done by his employees and the feasting that accompanied the harvesting are all typical of a way of life which endured through centuries of changing "periods" and reigns. See Arab women gleaning in the fields of Bethlehem **715**).

715

S

SABBATH, THE. — Religious Significance: The Sabbath, as a weekly day of abstention from work, is of great antiquity, going back to the earliest origins of Yahwism (see Moses*) and perhaps even earlier. The enormous religious significance which the seventh day of rest acquired in all the traditions of the Pentateuch is something peculiar to Israel. This significance exists, not because of the prohibition which abstention from work implies (other religions also had a day which was taboo), but because the holiness of the day is inherent in its relation to Yahweh of the Covenant, and because the Sabbath is an element in that Covenant. The Sabbath was a day consecrated to Yahweh in the form of a tithe of time (compare to the tithe of the flocks and first fruits consecrated to God; see Festivals*). For this reason, the Sabbath appears in the first and most ancient legislation, the original pact at Sinai and the pact of the tribal federation. It is also mentioned in the later Law of Holiness (Lv. 19:3, 30; 23:3) and in the Priestly Code (Ex. 31:12–17 and Nu. 28: 9–10).

Antiquity of the Injunctions: The earliest injunction, certainly of great antiquity, appears in the two Codes of the Covenant and the Book of the Covenant which represent the earliest legislative codes, namely Ex. 34:21, as well as the earliest enumeration of the Ten Commandments, i.e. the original pact at Sinai (Ex. 20:8–10). The two Codes go back to the early days of the settlement in Canaan, while the Ten Commandments, in their original form, relate to Mosaic times. Like the three great festivals* (see article; also Law*), the concepts underlying the Codes have undergone a historic development merging older traditions and injunctions with later motives and comments.

Later Explanations: The Sabbath commandment was given without commentary in Exodus*, the earlier form of the Decalogue (Ex. 20:8–10). Motives and explanations were inserted in later legislation, and reflect two later backgrounds of thought, the Priestly and Deuteronomic. Ex. 20:11 adds to the original form of the commandment the Priestly form of the tradition of Gn. 2:1–3, as part of the order of creation, i.e. God rested on the seventh day after the creation of the Universe (cf. Genesis*). The observance of the Sabbath in this tradition is an everlasting "sign" of the Covenant* and as such is consecrated to God. The Priestly text places its emphasis on the God of the Covenant, and underlines the religious character of the Sabbath. The Deuteronomic injunction (Dt. 5:14–15) stresses the social aspects: man and beast should rest one day in the week. It connects the day of rest, however, with Israel's dogma of salvation and its deliverance from bondage in Egypt. In memory of this deliverance, the Israelites were commanded to rest on the Sabbath. The Deuteronomic text emphasizes the people of the Covenant, unlike the theological comment of the Priestly text which is apparently of a later date.

Origin: Some scholars have tried to find Mesopotamian origins for the Sabbath as a full moon festival, and in a certain similarity of the word with the Akkadian "shapattu". However, this was not just a day which divided the month. The Hebrew "shabath" may have originally designated a definite boundary which separated the weeks from one another, but it is now understood that the Hebrew Sabbath was not dependent on the Babylonian calendar, nor on any lunar calendar. It was of greater antiquity than the Babylonian calendar which was adopted in the last days of the Monarchy (see Calendar*).

Other scholars contend that Israel took the institution of the Sabbath from the Canaanites, although there is only scanty evidence in support of such a theory. Neh. 13:16 is, in fact, evidence that the Phoenicians (the later Canaanites) did not keep the Sabbath. In any case, all these theories fall short of explaining how the Sabbath came to be a distinctive sign of the Covenant at the beginning of Israelite history, if it was also a commonplace among the Canaanites of Palestine, or in latter-day Babylonia.

Another theory connects the Sabbath with Yahwism, but maintains that the whole religion was learned from the Kenites* (see Numbers*). This, again, needs to be considered with caution.

Whatever its origins, whether or not the institution of a weekly day of rest and worship ante-dated the beginnings of Israel's history in Mosaic times, its particular character and religious significance were only acquired among the Hebrews, as recorded in the Bible.

Celebration and Ritual: The theological interpretation of the Sabbath was developed gradually, as shown by the character of its celebration. In earlier days and in the time of the monarchy, it was a day of rest and a joyful feast-day, when men visited sanctuaries (Is. 1:13) or went to consult "a man of God" (II K. 4:23). Short journeys were allowed, however. The sacrificial ritual for the Sabbath (Nu. 28:9 ff) consisted of doubling the morning and evening burnt offerings and the weekly presentation of the shew-bread (Lv. 24:8). During the Exile*, the Sabbath acquired a new importance, when it became the distinctive sign of the Covenant (cf. the Priestly interpretations cited above). In post-Exilic times, this ritual was replaced by special morning, afternoon and evening prayers.

By the time of Nehemiah, the prohibitions on work and other activities became more rigid. The rules became even stricter during the Hasmonean* era. The sectaries of Qumran (see Dead Sea Scrolls*) also took an extremely severe attitude towards observance of the Sabbath, as did the Pharisees* to a slightly lesser extent. The rabbis of the 2nd c. CE imposed additional regulations aimed at enhancing the sanctity of this day, and allowing relaxation of the prohibitions only in cases of the most extreme urgency (e.g. where there was danger of death). The Mishnah* codified 39 different kinds of work which were forbidden on the Sabbath, and the prohibitions became more numerous and complicated throughout succeeding post-biblical centuries.

The Sabbath and Sunday: Sunday differs from the Jewish Saturday and is not a continuation of it. The New Covenant* abrogated the Covenant of which Sabbath was the sign. The Sabbath closed the week; the Christian Sunday opens the week, in a new era which commemorates the Resurrection and which directs attention to the future when Christ will come again.

SACRIFICE AND OFFERINGS. — *Outline: I. Sacrifice in Antiquity. II. Origins of Israelite Ritual: Role of Blood in Sacrificial Ritual. III. Significance of Hebrew Sacrifice. IV. Hebrew Sacrificial Ritual: Altars: Canaanite; Early Israelite; In the First Temple; Significance; In the Second Temple. V. Occasions for Sacrifice. VI. Types of Sacrifice:* 1. *Sacrifice as Tribute and Gift; Why Was the Gift Destroyed?* 2. *Burnt Offering;* 3. *Communion Sacrifice;* 4. *The Communion Sacrifice or Peace Offering. Votive Offerings;* 5. *Sacrifice of Expiation;* 6. *Vegetable or Meal Offering;* 7. *Libations;* 8. *Incense Offerings. VII. Human Sacrifice. VIII. The Ceremony of Sacrifice. IX. History of Sacrifice: Patriarchs to Exodus; After the Conquest; Under the Monarchy; Post-Exilic Sacrifice; Graeco-Roman Sacrificial Rites. X. The Prophetic Polemic Against Sacrifice. XI. Sacrifice in the New Testament: Christ as Expiation. XII. Shehittah — Traditional Secular Slaughter.*

Hebrew worship centred around sacrifice. For the Israelites as for the other peoples of the ancient Near East, sacrifice was the essential feature of religious observances. A cult without sacrifice would have been unthinkable. Hence, it is not surprising that a comparison of Israelite ritual with that of other northwestern Semitic peoples reveals many common elements.

I. SACRIFICE IN ANTIQUITY: A number of theories have been put forward to explain the place of sacrifice in Near Eastern antiquity. One view is based on the assumption that in tribal society the members of the tribe had a kinship relation with the tribal god, who was believed to move among men through the agency of the totem animal consecrated to him in sacrifice. Thus the object of sacrifice was to strengthen the relationship with the god and to share in his life by eating the sacred animal.

A second theory emphasizes the substitution aspect of sacrifice, i.e. the victim somehow represented the worshipper who offered the sacrifice as a substitute for himself. By first laying his hands upon the victim, he transferred to it his own sins and life principle (which resided in his blood, see below). When the animal was killed, the sins were carried away. The blood containing the life principle was sacred to the deity and was shed at the foot of the altar so as to bring the life of the worshipper into contact with the deity and reestablish the bond between the two.

A third approach is that a sacrifice was simply a meal offered to God — which was its significance in Babylonia.

None of these theories, however, is a satisfactory explanation of Israelite belief and practice in relation to sacrifice, for they are all much too crude to fit in with Israel's monotheistic religion and its view of its relationship to God (see III, Communion Sacrifice).

II. ORIGINS OF ISRAELITE RITUAL: The essential elements of Israelite sacrifice were the "'olah" (holocaust offering, burnt upon the altar) and the communion sacrifice or "zebaḥ" (see below). It seems most likely that the Hebrews adopted these from the Canaanites when they settled in the land, although they combined them with their own ancient rites involving the disposal of blood (which were not practiced among the Canaanites). There is nothing in the biblical evidence to suggest that Israelite ritual differed substantially in form from that of the Canaanites. When the prophets condemned Canaanite customs, it was not because they made their offerings in the wrong way, but because they were made to pagan gods at unauthorized sanctuaries. The fundamental similarity between Canaanite and Hebrew sacrifice has been fully documented from archaeological evidence (see Ancient Cities: Lachish*).

Among scores of similar examples from Canaan are the stone domestic altar from Gezer and the incense altar of Ta'anach. More important evidence comes from the Ugaritic texts (1400 BCE). These describe sacrifices very close to those of the Israelites (see below), e.g. the "srp" offering wholly burnt; the "dbḥ" or "sheᵉlamim" (peace-offerings) in which the flesh is eaten after performing a religious ceremony to propitiate the god; or the "'atm" which was the Canaanite equivalent of the Israelite 'ashām (guilt offering). In short, like the Israelites, the Canaanites offered holocausts and communion sacrifices; vegetable produce and incense. However, in spite of these similarities, R. de Vaux is of the opinion that Israel did not take all its sacrificial ritual from the Canaanites, although the similarities do "indicate that Israelite ritual is far closer to the ritual of Canaan than to that of Mesopotamia or Arabia . . . The feature which distinguishes Israelite and Canaanite rituals from those of other Semitic peoples is that, when an animal is sacrificed, the victim or at least part of it, is burnt upon an altar. This rite did not exist in Mesopotamia or Arabia, but it did exist among the Moabites and the Ammonites, according to allusions in the Bible. The rite is thus peculiar to the west Semitic peoples." This author maintains that the custom existed in Canaan, before the arrival of the Hebrews. There is no evidence that they practiced it while they were still nomads. The form of sacrifice which the earliest Hebrews knew was probably preserved in the rite of the Paschal Lamb (practiced to this day by the Samaritans*, see article), in which no part of the victim is burnt and all the meat is eaten by the community. This has far more in common with the cultural background of west Semitic peoples than with the sacrificial system of Mesopotamia where the rites of burning an animal and using its blood for anointing were unknown, the sacrifice instead being laid upon the altar as a meal for the god with no part of it normally burnt.

Beyond the one point of contact at the time of the settlement of the Israelites in Canaan, however, the two forms of sacrificial rite developed independently among the two peoples (see Phoenicians*). The theological meaning which both peoples gave to their sacrifices differed in earlier as well as later times. This is made clear by later Phoenician inscriptions* relating to sacrifice. Nor do the biblical texts prove that all the technical terms relating to sacrifice were the same among the Israelites and Canaanites. The main differences in the form of the sacrifices can be seen from a comparison of Canaanite ritual (see Canaan: Gods and Idols, Cult*) with that of the Israelites, most notably in the Israelite use of the blood of sacrificial animals.

Role of Blood in Sacrificial Ritual: The word "dām" for blood is common to all Semitic languages, although its etymological root is obscure. Among most of the Semitic nations (and many that were not Semitic in origin) it was believed that the blood of a body contained its life-principle. To the Hebrews "... the life of the flesh is in the blood; and I have given it for you upon the altar to make atonement for your souls; for it is the blood that makes atonement, by reason of the life... Therefore you shall not eat the blood of any creature, for the life of every creature is its blood..." (Lv. 17:11, 14). There is some debate among scholars as to the origin and exact reasons for this prohibition against consuming blood which is repeated several times in the Old Testament and is one of the fundamental laws of early Judaism. Some scholars think that the fact that blood is to be sacrificed to God makes it "taboo" (forbidden) to mortal man. Others hold that the instruction to "pour away" the blood of sacrifices and to bury the blood of a bird or animal which had been slaughtered and is not for sacrifice (Gn. 9:4; Lv. 3:17; 7:26–27; Dt. 12:23–25; I Sam. 14:32–34) is essentially a protection against the Canaanite custom of using blood for magical purposes.

This suggests that the prohibition against eating or using blood was related to the belief that the blood signified the life of the creature killed; to drink the blood was to share in the power of the victim — which originally would have been a human being. In this sense a magical element is involved. Using a magical means to share in the power of another being infringed on the prerogative of God who alone could supply the qualities and powers which men seek (see Religious Significance of Sacrifice, below).

The ancient rites relating to the use of blood in sacrifice were not found among the Canaanites, although they were of central significance to the Hebrews, among whom blood could only be used for the most solemn of sacred rituals. The blood of the Covenant was sprinkled on the people (Ex. 24:8) and on Aaron and his sons (Lv. 8:30). In sacrifices of expiation (sin offering or sacrifice of reparation), the blood was the most important element for "blood makes expiation for a life" ("by reason of the life which is in it"). In individual guilt or sin offerings, the blood of the sacrifice was rubbed on the horns of the altar. In sacrifices offered for the sins of all the people, or for the High Priest and the community, it was sprinkled on the veil which hid the Holy of Holies. On the Day of Atonement, it was sprinkled upon the mercy seat, the throne of the divine Presence in the Holy of Holies.

In contrast to the liberal use of sacrificial blood by the Israelites; Egyptian, Babylonian and Assyrian rites hardly made use of it, although there are one or two references in Babylonian-Assyrian tablets to sacrificial blood being sprinkled on the lintel of a palace gate or to the four points of the compass.

III. SIGNIFICANCE OF HEBREW SACRIFICE: In Hebrew thought, a sacrifice was primarily a gift. The Hebrews believed that everything that belongs to a man acquires something of his personality; therefore, in making any gift, a man gave something of himself. Thus every gift was sacramental. Nor was it a light matter to receive a gift, for by accepting it the recipient undertook a personal obligation to the giver which acceptance of the gift made binding. Following this premise, a sacrifice was a solemn sacrament — a gift to God which, if accepted, ensured a reciprocal benefit.

Modern theories have tended to reject the idea that a sacrificial animal represented a substitute for the worshipper. Even in the cases of offerings of expiation or atonement it seems that the sacrifice was essentially a gift made to God for the specific purpose of expiation, although the Old Testament offers no evidence as to just how it was believed that this was effected.

In its most important sacrifices, the Yahwism of the Hebrews also included an element of communion with the divine, as well as the expiation of sins and making of a gift. In fact all three elements: communion, expiation and gift are allied aspects of the one act. The making of a sacrifice can be prompted by a variety of motives and the act satisfies different religious imperatives. However, in the golden age of Israelite history (beginning with the monarchy) when Israel's religious ideas were most clearly formulated in its literary traditions, these three basic elements included a variety of subsidiary aspects (see below). Moreover, in addition to the burnt offering made in expiation of sins, there were also a number of what may conveniently be classified as "minor" sacrifices (although they were not so regarded in the liturgy). These were the Vegetable or Meal offering, libations and offerings of incense, to be described below.

It should also be remembered that the various rites of sacrifice and the complex of thought surrounding them all underwent a long process of historical development and change, reflected, although not clearly differentiated, in the Bible. Some of the rites and some of the terms which describe them date back to the pre-history of Israel and it does not seem probable that any of the procedures are specifically Mosaic or Yahwistic innovations. The Bible relates traditions of sacrifice offered to God by the earliest of men (Gn. 4:3) and by Noah, traditionally the father of all races (Gn. 8:20).

The main source for a systematic description of the types and ritual of the different sacrifices is the book of Leviticus, but this includes the later, more complete forms of the "Code of Sacrifice" of Leviticus* 1–7 (see article). This belongs to a section of the Pentateuch which reached its final form together with all the "Priestly Source" either shortly before the destruction of the First Temple or early in the period of the Second (see Biblical Criticism*). The priestly writers who compiled this Code assumed that the liturgy they knew was exactly what had been instituted by Moses in the desert and practiced ever since. Theirs, however, was not an attitude aimed at historical accuracy or at displaying the full significance of sacrifice. To reach an understanding of these aspects of sacrifice, it is necessary to trace the history of sacrifice to its earliest origins and then to make use of all the modern disciplines of biblical criticism* and archaeology. This can best be done by taking the latest post-Exilic developed forms of the ritual and working backwards to their beginnings.

IV. HEBREW SACRIFICIAL RITUAL: **Altars:** The place of sacrifice and instrument of communication between God and man was the altar, in Hebrew "mizbeaḥ". What belonged to God was placed and burnt on the altar, while the climax to the sacrificial ritual came when the blood of the sacrifice was sprinkled there.

In patriarchal times, sacrifices might be offered by anyone at an altar commemorating a theophany (divine appearance;

Gn. 12:7; 26:24–25), but once the Israelites had settled in Canaan, ministry at the altar in a recognized sanctuary became the office of the priests (see Priests*). As sacrificial ritual developed, so the altar acquired an added significance (see below, History).

Canaanite: Altars in pre-Israelite Canaan might be simply the flat surface of a rock, or a rock hewn into a specific shape. At Gezer, the altar (**716**) had hollows in its surface leading down into a cave where the bones of sacrificial animals were found. (Canaanite sanctuaries and rock altars are described under Canaan: Gods and Idols*, Cult, and High Places*). In the 13th c. BCE Canaanite temple at Hazor*, an altar was found made of an enormous rectangular block, with a basin hollowed out on one of its surfaces (see Ancient Cities: Hazor*). In many Canaanite sanctuaries dating from 3000 BCE to the 14th–13th cs. BCE, altars built of large stones and earthen mortar were found standing against the back wall. The high place* or "bamah" (see article) had altars made of large stones such as the large platform at Megiddo*; (see Arad*, **81**, and other articles under Ancient Cities*).

Early Israelite: The earliest altars mentioned in the Bible, from Patriarchal days to the early period of the monarchy, were built of stone and stood ouside the main sanctuaries. Exodus (20:24–26) lays it down that altars shall be built either of plain clay bricks or of stones which have not been trimmed. No steps led up to it so that the altar might not be exposed to profanity. Officiating priests wore loincloths and in stepping up onto the altar they might have exposed themselves. This, again, was in deliberate contrast to Canaanite customs, for Canaanite altars had steps and there fertility rites were celebrated. Hebrew altars were sacred and nothing profane, not even a flight of steps, might come into contact with them.

Exodus also gives descriptions of the altar of holocausts (27:1–8; 38:1–7) and the altar of incense (30:1–5) used in the desert. The book describes them as elaborate structures of acacia-wood plated with bronze and standing two or three cubits high (4 or 5 feet, see Weights and Measures*). Many scholars think that such specifications probably repeat the practice in David's version of the Tabernacle*, rather than the desert Tabernacle (see Tabernacle*; Temple*).

In the First Temple: The altars of Solomon's temple apparently included the bronze altar of holocausts which stood in front of the Temple (II K. 16:14) and the altar of incense in the "hekhāl" in front of the Holy of Holies (debir; I K. 6:20–21; see Temple*). The original altar of holocausts which stood 5 cubits high and was 5 cubits square, with steps leading up to it, was replaced by King Ahaz who installed a new model (II K. 16:10–16) which remained in use until the Exile.

The Temple altar must have been a more imposing version of the altars belonging to this period which archaeological excavations have unearthed elsewhere, notably at Arad (see Ancient Cities: Arad*). At Megiddo a typical limestone incense altar (**717**) was found, shaped like a square pillar (as specified in Ex. 30:1–5), with four horns on the top corners. The blood of sacrificial animals was rubbed on the horns (see above) to consecrate it or in rites of expiation. In addition, a fugitive claiming asylum would grasp the horns of the altar (I K. 2:28; see Priests*).

Significance: In other ancient religions, the altar provided a table upon which banquets were prepared for the god in the form of sacrifices, illustrated by this 18th c. BCE Egyptian red granite offering table (**718**). In form the altar was probably a platform or table on which gifts to the deity were placed, along with petitions, thanksgivings, etc. Although the Hebrew altar originated in similar beliefs, it developed a more complex significance as the instrument through which the Covenant with God was maintained and restored (see below, Sacrifice in Expiation). In patriarchal days, an altar would be erected to commemorate an actual appearance of God, or within a place which was traditionally sacred to the God of the Patriarchs. Such altars, however, were essentially functional. They marked a spot where God had appeared but they had no further symbolic significance.

The Temple was the house of God and, as such, it needed a hearth, a role which the altar fulfilled. This aspect is not stated explicitly but it is apparent from the way in which a fire was always kept burning upon the altar (Lv. 6:12–13; II Mac. 1:18–36), just as a lamp had to be kept permanently alight in the Temple (Ex. 27:20–21; Lv. 24:2–4). During the monarchy, the altar was purified once each year on the Day of Atonement and thus acquired an altogether exceptional holiness (Lv. 8:15; 16:18–19).

In the Second Temple: The ideal altar, whose specifications Ezekiel gives (43:13–17), built in three tiers, may preserve the size of Solomon's altar, but the shape of the new altar and the names of its different parts seem to be of Babylonian inspiration, as is the symbolism which they imply. There is no evidence, however, that the altar built after the Restoration* was modelled on Ezekiel's description.

The altars of holocausts and of incense in the Second Temple are more likely to have been those described in II Ch. 4:1 and 29:16 ff, since the Chronicler may have based his account of Solomon's Temple on the fittings of the post-Exilic Temple with which he was familiar. More reliable descriptions are found in non-biblical sources of the Hellenistic period. Josephus gives one account, and another is included in the Letter of Aristeas (see Apocrypha*). These describe the altar of holocausts as a square, 20 cubits wide and 10 cubits high, built of untrimmed stones according

716

717

718

to the prescription of Ex. 20:25, and also in line with the Chronicler's description. There was also an altar of incense. The altars were profaned in 164 BCE when Antiochus Epiphanes plundered the Temple, and they were rebuilt when the Temple was recaptured and purified by the victorious Maccabaeans (I Mac. 1:21; 1:59; 4:47; see Hasmoneans*).

V. OCCASIONS FOR SACRIFICE: The code of sacrifices lists a variety of occasions, both private and communal, on which sacrifices must be offered. The most important religious festivals call for special sacrifices: the Feast of Unleavened Bread (Passover), Pentecost or the Feast of the First Fruits and the Feast of Tabernacles (or the Ingathering; Ex. 23:14–17; 34:18–23; Dt. 16; see Feasts*). Special offerings had to be made on those festivals and also on Sabbaths (Nu. 28–29), New Year's Day (the first of the seventh month), the Day of Atonement (tenth of the seventh month) and the first day of a new moon, as well as daily throughout the year in the Temple at morning and evening. Later on, the Passover sacrifice took on the special character of a family celebration rather than a national occasion (see Feasts*).

Other individual sacrifices were offered on particular occasions of joy (thank-offering, see below) or sorrow, in expiation and repentance (see below, Guilt and Sin-Offerings), and in fulfilment of vows (see below, Votive Offerings). Sacrifices were also made when the people made pilgrimages to Jerusalem.

Among seasonal sacrifices were those offered to God in thanks for productivity, for instance the first fruit offerings (Ex. 23:19; Nu. 18; Dt. 15:19 ff; 18:4; etc.) and the presentation of a portion of dough to the priests (Lv. 23:17; Nu. 15:18–21; Ezk. 44:30). These included the presentation to God of His portion of the earth's fruitfulness, after which thc rest might be used by mankind. It is clear from the Mosaic code and from later prophetic injunctions that sacrificial feasts were supposed to be spontaneous acts of thank-offering (see below, Types of Sacrifice) or communion with God on the part of the individual or the community.

VI. TYPES OF SACRIFICE: Different categories of sacrifice may be distinguished:

1. **Sacrifice as Tribute and Gift:** Just as subjects paid tribute to a king to ensure his goodwill and protection, so must man pay tribute to the God who is sovereign lord of everything that man has, and who alone is able to provide for his needs. The tribute that was offered in this way — the first-fruits of crops and flocks, were essential to man's existence. By offering them to his God — and once offered they could not be used for any secular, profane purpose — man deprived himself of something of real value to himself. However, by so doing, he also benefitted. In the opinion of R. de Vaux, God's acceptance of the gift implied His undertaking an obligation towards the giver (see above). The gift, "minḥah" in Hebrew, was offered to God in a sacrifice, i.e. it was wholly or partially destroyed on an altar. Animals were slaughtered and burnt, some portions being eaten as part of the ritual; flour, bread and incense were burnt and liquids poured away.

Why Was the Gift Destroyed? The gift was destroyed, first of all, to render it useless to man. The thing being sacrificed was a gift to God, who was honoured in its destruction. Vases used for libations were broken; votive offerings were thrown into a spring, a well or the sea. Animals sacrificed were usually killed by the worshipper, not by the priest, the essence of immolation being the slaughter and destruction of the carcasses. Immolation was simply an act of preparation for the sacrifice, just as, later on, the laying on of hands would become an initiatory rite for dedication in a different form (see below).

Secondly, the gift was destroyed to transfer it to the realm of the divine. After placing the sacrifice upon the altar which served as a kind of table for its consumption, the portion which belonged to God had to be burnt so that none of it should remain with man. It used to be assumed that as the smoke of the burnt offering rose towards heaven, the "soothing odour" would propitiate the divinity, but this is not in line with modern views. The origins of sacrifice lie far back in the prehistory of Israel and the symbolism is essentially that of the consumption of the offering by God, something which goes back to the most primitive notions.

2. **Burnt Offering:** The burnt offering, "'olah" (holocaust) in which the whole of a victim is burnt upon the altar is the oldest and most typical form of Hebrew sacrifice (Gn. 4:4–5; 8:20; 22:2; Ex. 10:25; 18:12; Jud. 6:26; 13:16, etc.). This remained the central act of every festive or solemn religious occasion (I K. 3:4) up to the time of Ezra (3:2–4). The burnt offering was made to the accompaniment of musical instruments (see Music*) and choral singing. At the climax of the sacrifice, two priests sounded the trumpets and the congregation bowed in worship. Nehemiah taxed the people to raise funds to provide the victim for the daily burnt offering, offered morning and evening in the Temple (see Restoration*: Nehemiah).

The whole burnt offering was considered the most perfect sacrifice, for out of it man retained nothing for himself. It was a victim pleasing to God who, it was apparently assumed, would take away the sins of the sacrificer in return for it. It is possibly in this ritual sense that Paul used the word when he said (II Co. 5:21), "Christ who had not known sin, God made 'sin' (haṭṭāth, the victim for sin) in order that we might become, in him, God's justice." When sacrifices were made in atonement for the sin of the High Priest or the whole community (as on the Day of Atonement), none of the meat was eaten by anybody, priest or layman, for as members of the community the priests were equally sinners and were not allowed to eat any of the meat. Normally, in all other cases, the bulk of the meat of a sacrificial victim was eaten by the worshipper and the priests. The priests ate it under conditions of ritual purity as "a most holy thing".

3. **Communion Sacrifice (zebah shelamim):** By thus eating a portion of the sacrifice in a religious meal, the Israelites believed that they achieved a form of communion with God. They never at any time believed that they would actually become one with God, but this sharing of a meal — a manner of sealing many agreements between men in an area where hospitality was so highly prized — suggested a similar agreement to maintain or restore harmonious relations between the worshipper and his God.

In pre-Islamic days among the Arabs, every member of a tribe would be invited to feast on a slaughtered camel, partly in the belief that a common meal shared by all the

719

members would also be joined by god. This 17th c. BCE mural from Mari (Babylonia*) shows men leading a bull to a sacrificial ritual (**719**).

Earlier peoples who had believed that a sacrifice actually was a meal by which the god was fed and strengthened had also believed that by eating part of it themselves, the worshippers would be infused with the power and presence of the deity. In Israel, that was impossible because of the nature of the relationship between Yahweh and His people. Instead, the main purpose of the communion sacrifice was to ratify or recognize the validity of the agreement or Covenant between them. It was a means of communication rather than some form of mystical union (see Part II above, Significance of Hebrew Sacrifice). In the early days of Israel's history, this was the form of sacrifice offered on especially important occasions (Ex. 20:24; 24:5; 32:6; I Sam. 11:15). R. de Vaux considers that in general the Israelite communion sacrifice may be regarded as a sacrifice of thanksgiving.

4. **The Communion Sacrifice or Peace Offering:** Peace offerings might take three forms: a. a sacrifice of praise; b. a voluntary sacrifice or c. a votive offering. The distinction between the sacrifice of praise (tôdah) and the voluntary sacrifice (n^{e}dabah), i.e. one made out of devotion, not in fulfilment of any precept, was not very precise. Such offerings might be made for a rich harvest, a successful campaign or the like — a custom found throughout the ancient Near East. The sacrifice took the form of a feast, for while the blood and fat and parts of the entrails would be reserved for God and burnt upon the altar and two portions (the right shoulder and breast) would be reserved for the priests, the remainder of the meat was eaten by the worshippers, amid an atmosphere as much festive as religious. However, the laying on of hands, the immolation and the sprinkling of blood are carried out exactly as for a holocaust ('olah). Such festive occasions were feast as well as sacrifice (e.g. Pr. 17:1), and feasts which had no religious significance at all were not condemned (I Sam. 9:12–13). Participants in a sacrificial feast were, of course, subject to strict rules regarding purity (Lv. 7:19–21; I Sam. 16:5), and it was laid down (Lv. 7:32 ff) that all the meat must be eaten on the day of the sacrifice, with nothing saved for the morrow. As the sacrifices became integrated into the ritual code, they lost their purely social features — the one notable exception being the Feast of Passover, celebrated within the household (Ex. 12:27; 34:25).

Votive Offerings: Votive offerings (neder) were made in fulfilment of earlier vows (Lv. 7:16–17; 22:18–23). The function of the offering was auxiliary to the prayer, rather than a condition for the acceptance of the prayer. The distinction in the ritual was that an animal sacrificed as a votive offering must be perfect and without blemish — which was not absolutely required of free-will offerings (Lv. 22:23); the meat from votive and voluntary offerings could be eaten on the following day, while the victim of a sacrifice of praise must be eaten on the day it is offered (Lv. 7:15–16).

5. **Sacrifices of Expiation:** Sin, whether of individuals or the whole community, demanded expiation before good relations could be reestablished between man and God. The sense of deliberate deprivation which was present in every sacrifice was brought to the fore in sacrifices in expiation of sin. In these, the ritual use of the blood was paramount and none of the flesh was eaten since the sinner offering the sacrifice would not presume to share a meal with God until his sin had been removed. Sacrifices of this kind, offered for the sins of the whole community, became of very great importance in times of national calamity when the people felt that God's favour had been withdrawn from them because of their sins.

There were two terms for this type of sacrifice: "haṭṭ'ath" (sin offering) and "'ashām" (sacrifice of reparation), although the distinction between them is not always clear. The priestly editors who drew up the code of Leviticus which regulated ritual in the Second Temple, obviously did not fully understand the meanings of the ancient terms. One theory is that both aimed at repairing the Covenant with God (see Covenant*) which had been broken by man's sin, the "Sin-offering" relating to offences towards God, the "sacrifice of reparation" to sins against a fellow-man. For this reason, where damage inflicted could be assessed in monetary terms, a fine to that amount, plus a fifth, might be added to the sacrifice in reparation. The fine was paid either to the priests (who represented Yahweh) or to the injured party. It was not part of the 'ashām sacrifice which was purely in expiation of the moral guilt incurred.

721 a

721 b

This distinction, however, cannot be applied in every case. For instance, a woman after childbirth was required to offer a "sin offering" (Lv. 12), while a leper, when pronounced "clean" had to make a "sacrifice of reparation" and a "sin offering" (Lv. 14). In both cases, the victim to be sacrificed depended on the rank of the sinner, from a bull offered on behalf of the priest and the whole congregation, or a male goat for a ruler, down to pigeons, turtle-doves or even some fine flour for a poor man (Lv. 4–5, but cf. Nu. 15:24; Lv. 9:15; 16:5). None of the unburnt flesh could be eaten by the sinner. The external form of the ritual is illustrated by this 8th c. BCE Assyrian carving (**720**).

Originally, the two classes of sacrifice were probably distinct, although it is difficult to be sure of this now. What is clear is that no sacrifice was regarded as effective for dealing with violations of the covenant, i.e. sins with a high hand. The sacrifice of the sin offering for the High Priest and the entire congregation (Lv. 4:11–21) was followed by special ceremonies in which the blood was sprinkled on the veil of the tent of meeting seven times. The offering was wholly burnt and nothing was eaten.

6. **Vegetable or Meal Offering ("Minḥah"):** The word "minḥah" occurs in the Bible in the sense of tribute paid to a foreign power (Jud. 3:15; I K. 4:21; see Tribute*) and in the general sense of an offering (I Sam. 26:19), particularly one of animals (I Sam. 2:12–16). However, in many cases "minḥah" is used for the fine flour offering attached to a burnt or peace offering (Lv. 2; Nu. 15:1–16). According to Lv. 2, the meal offering could be either in the form of flour, in which case oil and frankincense would be put upon it (Lv. 2:1–2), sometimes wine and salt (2:13; 23:13), or as a cake baked in an oven, on a griddle or in a pan (see Food*). In no case might leaven or honey be added. A similar meal offering was made from the "first fruits"; (see this 14th c. Egyptian offering scene from Thebes, **721a**, left and the Hittite scene, **b**, right: 9th c. BCE). A portion was burnt as a "memorial" on the altar and what was not burnt was served exclusively as the priests' portion (Lv. 2:3). It was never served to the worshippers. This was also the case with the shewbread, the "holy bread of the presence" which was regularly placed before the Holy of Holies (Lv. 24:5–9; I Sam. 21:3–6).

7. **Libations:** Libations of oil (Gn. 28:18), wine (Gn. 35:14) and water (I Sam. 7:6) appear to have figured in the Hebrews' cult, although the law of sacrifices only refers to libations of wine (Nu. 28:7, etc.). The Oriental custom is illus. by the pouring of a libation after the hunt by king Ashurbanipal before an offering table and incense stand (7th c. BCE; **232**). This offering scene, **722**, dates two cent. earlier.

720

Vinegar, milk and honey as libations were expressly forbidden, presumably because these all spoil quickly. Salt, on the other hand, was used in all meal offerings (Lv. 2:13) and in burnt offerings (Ezk. 43:24). Incense was added to meal offerings to give them a festive flavour, and was also offered separately (Ex. 30:7).

8. **Incense Offerings:** "Perfume" (incense) offerings (lebonah) were apparently made in pre-Exilic times (Jer. 6:20; 41:5), and the custom was familiar among many of Israel's neighbours, witness the incense stands from Megiddo (**717**) and from Ta'anach (**723**). In the earliest period of Israelite

722

723

724

725

history, portable censers were apparently used (Lv. 16:12 ff; 10:1). In Solomon's Temple, instruments similar to a shovel and a scoop were used to carry burning coals and perfumes to the altar (cf. Ex. 30:34 ff; see Temple).

VII. HUMAN SACRIFICE: The sacrifice of human beings as the supreme expression of religious devotion was limited in the Near East in classical times to the northwest Semites, especially the Canaanites and Phoenicians, who continued it up to about the 5th c. BCE (see this foundation sacrifice from Canaanite Gezer*, **724**). The Carthaginians also practiced human sacrifice (see article on Canaan: Gods and Idols*, Cult) but it was not known among the Egyptians or Babylonians. At times of grave national danger, men would offer their dearest possessions, their children, to appease the anger of their gods. The sacrifice of enemies or prisoners of war is nowhere mentioned in the Bible, but the sacrifice of children as burnt offerings is referred to in a number of contexts. The Canaanite custom is referred to in Deuteronomy* (12:31; see article). It was adopted at certain periods by the Hebrews, but such sacrifices were never made to Yahweh. Indeed, the practice is repeatedly prohibited (Lv. 18:21; 20:2–5; Dt. 18:10), and it was one of the first things to be condemned and forbidden in times of religious reform (e.g. II K. 23:10). Children, especially the first-born, were offered to foreign gods, especially the Ammonite god Moloch (II K. 23:10; Lv. 18:21) and to the Canaanite Ba'al (Jer. 19:5; 32:35). The outstanding instances of such sacrifice mentioned by the Bible are those involving rulers: the king of Moab*, who offered up his first-born in an effort to avert the capture of his city (II K. 3:27); Ahaz and Manasseh, kings of Judah, and Pekah, king of Israel (II K. 16:3; 21:6; II Ch. 33:6) but the infection had apparently spread among the common people as well. According to II K. (17:17), one reason for the exile of the ten tribes of the Northern Kingdom was as a punishment for the sin of burning "their sons and daughters as offerings", and Jeremiah makes the same accusation against the people of Judah (Jer. 7:31; 19:5; 32:35).

A special altar for these sacrifices was set up in "Tophet" in the Vale of Hinnom near Jerusalem (II Ch. 28:3; 33:6) and stood in use, apparently, until Josiah's reform (II K. 23:10). Without exception the prophets and biblical authors condemn the custom (e.g. Mic. 6:7), though they rarely refer to it directly, preferring to call it "passing through the fire". Only after the Restoration did it die out completely in Israel.

Although child-sacrifice was practiced among other northwestern Semitic peoples, the Hebrews almost certainly learned it from the Canaanites (its place in Canaanite religion and culture is discussed in greater detail in the articles under Canaan*). Additional evidence for its continuance among the early Canaanites and the later Phoenicians is provided by inscriptions found in Malta (a Phoenician colony) dating from the 7th and 6th cs. BCE which testify to child sacrifice in the mother country and at Carthage, where it was noted and reported by Roman writers. This 4th c. BCE obelisk from Carthage shows a priest holding an infant in his hands (**725**). It never became deeply rooted in Israelite ritual and remained fundamentally foreign to the whole nature and practice of the Hebrew religion.

VIII. THE CEREMONY OF SACRIFICE: There were six stages in the prescribed ritual as it applied to sin offerings and sacrifices of reparation — although not for peace offerings.

1. The worshipper brings his victim near to the place of sacrifice, i.e. to the "door" of the Tent of meeting, or into the court of the sanctuary, north of the altar.

2. The worshipper lays his hand or hands on the head of his victim (Lv. 3:2, 8 etc.) and confesses his sins (see Part III, above). In the case of an offering for the whole people of Israel, the leaders of the community lay their hands on the victim's head (Lv. 4:15).

3. The victim is slaughtered by the worshipper in the case of an individual offering, or by the priest in the case of community offerings (Lv. 16:11; II Ch. 29:24).

4. The blood of the sacrifice is collected in a bowl on the northeastern or southwestern corner of the altar, and then sprinkled by the priest on all four sides of the altar, at least in the case of burnt peace and guilt offerings (Lv. 1:5; 7:2). When the victim was a turtledove or pigeon (Lv. 1:15), with little blood, it was drained on to the wall of the altar. The blood of the guilt-offering was sprinkled on the altar or put round about it.

5. The burning: Apart from the blood which belonged wholly to God, the "fat covering the entrails and all the fat that is on the entrails and the two kidneys with the fat that is on them" (Lv. 3:3–4) had to be burned on the altar in every case. In peace, sin and guilt offerings, these parts alone were burnt, but in the case of an " 'olah" or whole burnt offering in atonement for the sins of the High Priest or the whole community, the whole carcass was burnt, only the liver being saved and given to the priests (Lv. 7:4). A certain proportion, the "memorial part" of meal and vegetable offerings was burned (Lv. 2:2 etc.).

6. The feast: The parts of an offering which were not burnt were served at a solemn feast. Peace-offerings were served to both worshipper and priests (Lv. 7:32); offerings might be served to the worshipper, his family and the priests, or, in some cases, to the priests alone. The priests' portions of peace offerings (Lv. 10:14; 22:10 ff), first-fruits and tithes

were considered holy, but the priests and their families could eat them in any pure place in Jerusalem. Sacrifices of reparation and sin offerings (Lv. 6:26; 7:6) and the meal offering were considered most holy and could only be eaten by the priests within the precincts of the Tent of Meeting, or in the Temple court.

IX. HISTORY OF SACRIFICE: The history of sacrifice in Old Testament times proper — like the history of Israel's religion of which it is an essential part — can be considered under two main divisions: first the period from Moses to the end of the monarchy (586 BCE); second the period from the Babylonian Exile to the destruction of the Temple in 70 CE.

The evidence of the Law of Holiness contained in Leviticus* is regarded by modern scholars as relating to different times of the pre-Exilic period, but not the very early days to which it is ascribed in Scriptures (see Biblical Criticism*; Leviticus*). To get a picture of the forms of sacrifice practiced early in the period, it is necessary to refer to traditions contained in the Pentateuch, the historical books and the early prophets, and generally admitted to be ancient. Naturally, there were changes and developments over the centuries but fundamentally, Israel's religion endured intact, its ritual retaining much of its most ancient character throughout.

Patriarchs to Exodus: The compilers of the books of the Pentateuch took it for granted that the ancestors of the Israelites offered sacrifices before the settlement of Canaan (Gn. 12:6–8; 15:9–11; 22:13; 31:54). The Patriarchal stories refer to their "setting up an altar", meaning establishing a sanctuary. In the book of Exodus there are a number of ancient traditions about sacrifices made in the desert (Ex. 3:18; 5:3; 10:25; 20:24). However, from the little that is known for certain about the religion of the Patriarchs, it seems very unlikely that their rites had much in common with those of later centuries.

Like all semi-nomads in the ancient Near East, they must have slaughtered beasts as sacrifices, but the manner in which they did so can only be inferred from biblical and archaeological evidence. Even the Passover feast is hardly conclusive testimony, for this was a sacrifice of an explicitly exceptional nature and it was performed away from any altar.

After the Conquest: At the time of the Conquest of Canaan, the Hebrews were commanded to observe three feasts a year (Ex. 23:14–17; see Feasts*) and simultaneously they received the first instructions regulating sacrifices: "You shall not offer the blood of my sacrifice with leavened bread, or let the fat of my feast remain until the morning" (Ex. 23:18). According to Ex. 24:5, burnt offerings and peace offerings were made to God in the desert, while the Covenant between Yahweh and His people was sealed when Moses took half the blood of the sacrifices and sprinkled it upon the people. The flesh of the communion sacrifice was then eaten as a symbol of the ratification and realization of the Covenant.

Apart from the special feasts, sacrifices were also offered on a variety of individual and national occasions. In the early days after the Conquest, such sacrifices and their accompanying feasts were held at different places. They were often celebrated at the nearest bāmāh (I Sam. 9:12–13; for details see High Places*).

Sacrificial feasts were a prominent feature of pilgrimages (I Sam. 1:3, 21; 2:19) and in the period of Judges they probably took place at the central tribal sanctuary of Shiloh. Once the Temple had been established in Jerusalem, that became the main and finally the sole place of sacrifice.

In times of war or national emergency, special sacrifices would also be offered (e.g. Jud. 20:26; 21:4). Samuel, for instance, offered a "sucking lamb as a whole burnt offering to the Lord" (I Sam. 7:9) during one of the serious crises of the struggle against the Philistines. Gideon's mission began with a sacrifice (Jud. 6:28) and the return of the Ark of the Lord was similarly celebrated (I Sam. 6:14–15). Saul's coronation was accompanied by communion sacrifices and rejoicing (I Sam. 11:15) and such offerings were also made by David when he brought the Ark into Jerusalem (II Sam. 6:17).

Under the Monarchy: The best evidence for sacrificial ritual under the monarchy comes, paradoxically, from the prophetic polemic against sacrifices (see below). Apart from this, it is recorded that Solomon sacrificed 22,000 cattle and 120,000 sheep and goats when he dedicated the Temple (I K. 8:62 ff) and that he sacrificed three times a year as a matter of course (I K. 9:25). Reference is made to other royal sacrifices (e.g. II K. 16:10) but very little attention is paid to the customs of the common people.

Post-Exilic Sacrifice: Post-Exilic ritual was a direct continuation of the cult of the monarchic period. Animals, vegetable produce and incense continued to be offered. One change, however, was that whereas under the monarchy communion sacrifices had been the most common, after the Exile, holocausts ('Šlāh, whole burnt offerings) became the most important type of sacrifice offered (Ezr. 6:16 ff). At the same time there was a significant development in the special sacrifice made for sin, until the holocaust itself acquired the quality of expiation. This is reflected in Leviticus 1:4, which belongs to the later Priestly Code (see above and Leviticus*).

The relationship between the "minḥah" (vegetable offering) and the communion sacrifice was more clearly defined. There was a change in the prescribed mixture of herbs and perfumes for the incense offering, which was then given the new name of "offering of aromatic herbs" — "qᵉtoret sammîm".

Graeco-Roman Sacrificial Rites: The religions of the contemporary Graeco-Roman world included observance of the "thusia" which in some respects resembled the "zebaḥ" or communion sacrifice of the Hebrews.

The thusia was a rite in which a portion of an offering was solemnly and ceremoniously offered to the deity and burnt upon the altar, after which the remainder was eaten by priests or worshippers in a common meal. The thusia was a fixed element in the pre-Hellenic Mycenean culture (second half of the 2nd mill. BCE; see Aegean Civilization*) and was continued by the Greeks. Worshippers at a thusia were not passive onlookers, but active participants. The rite began with lustrations and the scattering of barley grains, followed by prayers in the form of vows and thanksgiving, culminating in the immolation of the victim and often concluding with processions. The central act was the solemn burning on the altar fire of pieces of the thigh of the animal wrapped in fat and covered with other pieces of meat, as

726

in this vase painting (**726**) which shows the attendants handling the meat with five pronged forks (the priest is standing on the left). Organs below the diaphragm were also eaten or at least tasted. After the priests had taken the portions of the animal belonging to the god, the roasted victim was eaten in a banquet to the accompaniment of libations of wine, oil and honey, music and dancing.

Like the Hebrew and Canaanite forms of sacrifice, many scholars suggest that the thusia derived from the ancient patterns of the Near East. The platform and altar used resembled the Hebrew high place* (bāmāh), while the ceremonial was very close to the Israelite communion-sacrifice (zebaḥ) and holocaust (although it differed from the "'olah"). This resemblance seems to offer further evidence that although these kindred customs developed on different lines among each of the later peoples, they originated in eastern Mediterranean cultures (see Aegean Civilization*) which preceded both Canaanites and early Hebrews.

The thusia was used increasingly among the ancient Greeks to express thanks to the gods who directed their lives. Over the centuries a more elaborate ritual and new accessories came into use. Magnificent temples took the place of open-air altars and spontaneous acts of devotion to the gods were replaced by the formal worship officially adopted by the different poleis (city-states) and kingdoms of the Graeco-Roman world. The different features of the thusia, however, retained their essential religious significance and this fact, in the opinion of R.K. Yerkes, explains the long continuance of the thusia and its easy sublimation into the central Christian rite of the mass among gentile Christians.

The Greeks also practiced special rites against evil demons in which victims were wholly burned at night and in complete silence, but these rites were carefully distinguished from the thusia, performed in daytime as an act of worship of the beneficent gods of Olympus.

The Hebrew "'olah" or holocaust was peculiar to Israel and it had no parallel among contemporary peoples. Its special significance of complete surrender of the worshipper to God (see above) marked a specifically Hebrew spiritual development.

Roman cults were deeply influenced by Greek religion and while they preserved native Italian features, they also absorbed other non-Semitic cultural influences. All Roman sacrificial rites were intended to propitiate friendly and avert hostile powers. The rites were conducted by the priests with the utmost precision according to a ceremonial which preserved their quasi-magical character. The main features of the rites were the ceremonial preparation and immolation of the animal being sacrificed, a careful examination of the vital organs to make sure they were in perfect condition then the burning of the victim on the altar. The whole rite was conducted in complete silence, music being played on pipes to drown any sound (see rural scene of sacrifice on a Roman terracotta, **727**; and this sacrificial ceremony on a Roman bas-relief, **728**). Once the animal had been burnt, it lost its ritual sanctity and became the property of the priests. Because the Roman cults were concerned with propitiation and aversion, the Greek sacrificial meal shared with the gods was never widely adopted by them. For a time, however, they preserved rites of sacred meals at the annual "feriae Latinae" or the "fordicidia" and "parilia" festivals, which were rites of purification of flocks and crops, conducted in April. Eventually these sacred meals disappeared, a fact which first had a profound effect on Roman religion and was subsequently to influence Christianity.

X. PROPHETIC POLEMIC AGAINST SACRIFICE: The pre-Exilic prophets were frequently moved to bitter denunciation of the external ritual of the Israelite sacrificial cult which could be observed without reference to spiritual purity or righteous behaviour, (e.g. Is. 1:11–17; Jer. 6:20; 7:21–23; Hos. 6:6; Am. 4:4; 5:21–27; Mic. 6:6–8). These passages should not be taken to mean that the prophets were opposed to sacrifices altogether. They condemned empty sacrifice (cf. Is. 29:13) and, above all, the penetration of foreign forms of worship (e.g. especially Hos. 2:13). In pagan religions, ritual is seen as the basic religious reality, whereas for Israel it had always a secondary, external aspect. It was the accompaniment to the basic religious facts, never their essence. It was in this sense that the prophets launched their attack on the institution of sacrifice.

The prophetic message on the subject of sacrifice and ritual was that God's judgment on his people could not be averted by outward forms (I Sam. 3:14; Jer. 6:19–20; Mic. 3:4). The prophets, the Wisdom* writers and the Law* all consider sacrifice from different angles, but not in contradiction. The point is that precise observance of the rules governing different forms of sacrifice was not the whole of religion. The fulfilment of the promise made to Israel in the Covenant could only be ensured by obedience to all aspects of God's "Word".

None of this is stated explicitly in the priestly texts regulating ritual, but it must have been assumed. (It is laid down that sacrifice is not enough to expiate serious crimes and sins.) Only a sincere devotion to Yahwism on the part of pious rulers and people would have preserved the religion in the face of all the pagan influences which threatened it over the years. Yahwism and, later, Judaism survived as something much richer than ritual alone. Throughout history the basic concern of the Hebrews' prophets and teachers was with the heart of their people and the reverence with which they were heard and remembered is proof of their success.

During the Babylonian Exile, when Ezekiel the prophet-priest was drawing up his programme for the future, he did not reject the liturgy of the monarchy, but continued and developed it, preparing regulations for a future that was really a vision of the end of days, the new age.

XI. SACRIFICE IN THE NEW TESTAMENT: Sacrifices continued to be offered in the Temple of Jerusalem up to its destruction in 70 CE. Thus they were a familiar feature of life during the time of Jesus and his followers and they are frequently mentioned in the New Testament (e.g. Mt. 5:23–24; 12:3–5; 23:16–22 and parallels; I Co. 9:13). Jesus made no objection to sacrifices. Even after the Crucifixion, the apostles continued to make their offerings there (e.g. Ac. 21:23–26), although by that time ideas concerning animal sacrifice had already begun the process of spiritual development. Even before the Temple and its altar had crumbled in flames, the Jewish-Christians* were developing a new attitude towards sacrifice. In place of offerings of flesh and blood, the New Testament speaks of offerings of the spirit (Jn. 4:24; Ro. 12:1; 15:16; Ph. 2:17; 4:18; II Ti. 4:6; He. 13:15–16; I Pet. 2:5; Rev. 6:9; 8:3–4). The theological background to this new attitude has become clearer since the evidence from Qumran has been added to what Josephus and others wrote about the Essenes. In their development of the central theme of rejection of existing sacrifical ritual, the Christians drew largely on the prophets' condemnation of ritual for its own sake (see above). Whether or not the Christian attitude was inspired directly by the opposition to the Temple cult of dissident groups like the Essenes, the theology of such sects prepared the ground for the New Testament's views on sacrifice (see Dead Sea Scrolls*; Priesthood*).

Christ as Expiation: The idea of expiation based on the biblical system of expiatory sacrifices is a very real and essential element in the New Testament's assessment of the work of Jesus and it seems probable that this derived from the mind of Jesus himself. With a very few exceptions, most scholars believe this to have been influenced by the reference to the "guilt offering of the Servant" in the crucial chapter 53 of the book of Isaiah*. Isaiah saw Israel the Servant as playing a sacrificial role for the redemption of the world and this concept is one of the key passages for understanding the background to the Christian attitude towards the atonement of Jesus.

Jesus' death on the cross and his work of expiation during his lifetime is presented in the New Testament as the ultimate sacrifice or expiation. He himself, the perfect man, had died for the sins of all mankind and, through his blood, those sins had been redeemed. After his, there was no need for any further sacrifice, "... Christ, our paschal lamb, has been sacrificed ..." (I Co. 5:7). Christ's was the blood which had sealed the "New Covenant*" (see Jesus*; Christianity, Early*; Paul*).

The Letter to the Hebrews*, a Jewish-Christian presentation of the theme of expiation in early Christian thought, draws the comparison between biblical expiation, which had to be repeated and could never be perfect, and the final and perfect expiation made by Christ. Christ is here compared to the High Priest entering the holiest place bearing the blood of the sacrifice, but he offers not the blood of some animal, but his own. The attitude implies a certain depreciation of the Old Testament sacrifices on the grounds that their repetition admits their ineffectiveness and indicates that animal blood was not enough for a true expiation (He. 10:2–3). The old worship and concept of expiation is but a shadow of what is to come (10:1. For a full discussion of the place of expiation in the work of Christ see Jesus*; Christianity: Early*; Paul*.)

727

XII. SHEḤITTAH — TRADITIONAL SECULAR SLAUGHTER: In post-Exilic normative Judaism, the normal slaughtering of animals and birds (sheḥittah) for daily consumption was governed by rules derived from an adaptation of the regulations which had applied to sacrifices. Outwardly, these secular regulations closely followed the biblical injunctions, namely the use of only certain, permitted, animals, and their careful bleeding so as to avoid the consumption of any of the forbidden blood. This form of ritual slaughter, performed by an ordained slaughterer, the "shoḥet", continues in use for "kasher" (ritually pure)

728

Jewish meat, although this has nothing to do with sacrifice. The exhaustive, detailed regulations governing sheḥittah were formulated as part of the Oral Law (see Law*) during the period of the Second Temple and were codified in the Talmud, Tosefta, the Jewish Codes and Rabbinic Responsa, a vast literature, all outside the scope of this book.

The destruction of the Temple meant that sacrifices in the Jewish religion were replaced by services and prayers in the synagogue. Only the Samaritans* (see article) maintain the ancient custom of sacrificing a Paschal Lamb at their Passover festival.

SADDUCEES. — The Sadducees' Hebrew name, "Tzedukim", is generally supposed to have been derived from Zadok, the traditional ancestor of every High Priest from David's reign down to 162 BCE, when the Hasmoneans* took over the office for themselves and finally broke the Zadokite succession.

Origins: The social basis of the party was the wealthy class of landowners, courtiers and great merchants, who held a position similar in some ways to that of the Tobiads in earlier years (see Hasmoneans*). If it is correct that their name stems from the "sons of Zadok", then this was the outward token linking the Sadducees to the old Jerusalem aristocracy. However, different opposing groups based conflicting claims on "Zadokite" or priestly affiliations. Some scholars believe that on the basis of links to the priestly aristocracy, an earlier group of Zadokites must have resisted Hasmonean usurpation of the High Priesthood. Some of them — those known to us as Sadducees from Josephus* and the Talmud — were apparently reconciled and came over to the side of the Hasmoneans. Others, also calling themselves Zadokites (according to the Sectarian Damascus Document, Dead Sea Scrolls*), went out into the desert to found the Dead Sea sect at Qumran.

As the party of the priests and guardians of the Temple, the centre of Judaism, the Sadducees had great influence in religious and political life. In the theocratic Jewish society, the higher priesthood were aristocrats, men of high culture and worldly attainments. The Sadducees' social standing and conservative reputation cost them popular support, but they remained closely associated with many of the Hasmonean princes and at times enjoyed great political influence. Economically, they derived great power from their control of the Temple treasury which, in addition to its permanent treasures, received the fund of half-shekels contributed annually by every male Jew, plus immense voluntary donations made by pious Jews throughout the world.

History: In Hellenistic times, political interests in Judea and the attractions of the Hellenistic way of life combined into a new apparently irreligious trend. This was halted by the nationalist rebellion of the Maccabees (Hasmoneans*), which revived and strengthened religious life. Foremost in this movement were the Hassidim* who supported the Maccabaeans and laid the foundations for the development of a new party of the pious, the Pharisees*. The Sadducees were not originally among the party of the hellenizers and it seems very probable that they also owe their origins to the Hassidim.

With the loss of the office of High Priest*, the influence of the Sadducees declined appreciably, especially under Queen Alexandra Salome. To the Sadducees it seemed that the only way to regain control over religious and legal life was to break the monopoly of legal interpretation of the Mosaic code held by their rivals, the Pharisees. It is possible that the Sadducees' rigid attitude towards the Mosaic law arose not from any special religious feeling but as a political weapon in their opposition to the legislative powers of the Pharisees.

The Sadducees suffered further at the hands of Herod* who denied the principle of a hereditary High Priesthood. However, both the New Testament and Josephus* record that later on, all the High Priests were Sadducees.

Because their existence and power were so closely bound up with politics and the Temple and its hierarchy, the destruction of the Temple in 70 CE meant the disintegration of the Sadducees as a party. With the collapse of political life, the Pharisees rose to complete authority among the mass of the people.

Sources of Information: Scholarly assessment of the Sadducees and their role in contemporary Jewish life used to be affected by the limited, generally unfriendly sources of information about them — which were much poorer than those available for other parties.

Josephus*, although fairly impartial, is misleading because he was describing them to a Greek audience in terms of the "philosophical" schools of the time. This resulted in a picture of the Sadducees as resembling the followers of Epicurus.

Later Talmudic sources, all of them Pharisee in essence, present the Sadducees as little better than pagans. Yet the higher Sadducee priesthood were familiar with questions of religion and Temple worship. There are no grounds for supposing them to have been freethinkers or "apikursim" (a euphemism for Hellenists).

The New Testament is clearly prejudiced against the Sadducees — for many reasons besides the trial of Jesus and the role of the Sadducees in entangling him in a web of priestly intrigues.

In general, both the Pharisees and the Sadducees have to be evaluated as phenomena peculiar to Jewish historical development. To the extent that the Sadducees represented an important sector among the leaders of the nation, their very conservatism acted as a valuable influence in preserving the traditions of Judaism, to which they made a lasting contribution.

Doctrines: The Sadducees were naturally more directly involved in material concerns than their Pharisee* opponents. This may partly explain their very conservative outlook on religious and secular matters, which was mainly the result of their rigid adherence to the written Law of Moses and written Scripture. They rejected belief in any future world, in the resurrection or in the immortality of the soul, as being without Mosaic authority. In their decisions on legal questions, the Sadducees were nearer to the written word of the Torah than were the Pharisees, as is evident from the disputations between them preserved in the Mishnah*.

They held that groups of individuals must aspire to well-being in this world and must not look for reward in the hereafter. They denied the Pharisee notion of divine intervention in human affairs, believing rather that man was entirely free to make his own choice between good and evil, while God was above the mundane concerns of everyday life.

In contrast to their more flexible opponents, they (the Sadducees) accepted only traditional interpretations of the Law* (case law; see Pharisees*: Framework of the Oral Law). They regarded the Torah as binding in all circumstances and rejected new laws and institutions as lacking divine authority. They themselves denied the authority of the Pharisee Oral Law, "what has come down from tradition of the fathers" — for instance, unlike the Pharisees, they interpreted the "eye for an eye" law of vengeance literally and took a severe attitude towards cases involving the death penalty. Nevertheless, Josephus records that they tended to follow the Pharisees' interpretations so as to avoid popular discontent (see Pharisees*: Party Strife).

The two parties also differed on the question of adult education. In place of the democratic Pharisee attitude, the Sadducees restricted academic pursuits to the priests, an oppressive use of a formerly valuable rule (see Pharisees*).

SAMARITANS. — *Outline: Origins; The Samaritans and the Restoration; Script; Samaritan Torah; The Palestine and Massoretic Traditions; Enmity between Samaritans and Jews; The Samaritans and the Talmud; The Samaritans and Christianity; Literature; History; Samaritan Religion; The Passover Sacrifice; Samaritans, Sadducees and the Dead Sea Scrolls.*

Origins: According to II K. 17:24–41, after the Assyrian capture of the capital of the Northern Kingdom, Samaria, in 721–720 BCE and the exile of its inhabitants, the land was repeopled by a mixture of foreign deportees from Babylonia, Hamath (northern Syria) and other lands, plus a remnant from the Israelite tribes of Ephraim and Manasseh (II Ch. 34:9; Jer. 41:5). These new settlers accepted the religion of their homelands "so these nations feared the Lord and also served their graven images" (II K. 17:41).

Apart from this statement, nothing is known of the history of the new inhabitants of Samaria until the Persian period.

The Samaritans and the Restoration*: When the Exiles returned from Babylon to Judea, the Samaritans offered to help with the rebuilding of the Jerusalem Temple, but their offer was rejected by Zerubbabel, Jeshua and the other leaders. Ezra and Nehemiah also opposed any contacts between Jews and Samaritans (Ezr. 4:1–3; 8 ff), although these were not always prevented. Members of the Jerusalem High Priest's family intermarried with the family of Sanballat, governor of Samaria, of whom we learn more from the Samaria papyri (recently acquired by F.M.Cross and not yet published), found some 15 kms. north of Qumran and dating from the end of the 4th c. BCE. Nevertheless, relations between the two peoples seem to have become increasingly strained from the 5th to the late 4th c. BCE (see below).

Many scholars believe that the origins of the dissension can be traced back to the ancient divisions between the peoples of Judah and Israel (see Israel and Judah*). At the time of the Restoration, this existing quarrel was emphasized and revived. The Samaritans observed literally the Law of the Pentateuch (a theological attitude shared by the priestly house of Zadok and later by the Sadducees*, see below), but

729

their attitude towards the institutions of the Jews was ambivalent. On the one hand they had offered their help in rebuilding the Temple. On the other, they regarded themselves as true descendants of ancient Israel, and the returning Jews of Jerusalem as no more than usurpers. The returned Exiles, on the other hand, denied that the Samaritans were full Jews and insisted on their own exclusive claim to the title.

Not unnaturally, the Samaritans sided with Nehemiah's opponents among the Jews of Judea (Neh. 4:7; 6:1–3) and, according to the Judean record (Ezr. 4:8 ff), plotted with the Babylonian overlords to try to prevent the rebuilding of Jerusalem. In fact, however, there was no actual break between Jews and Samaritans in Persian times. The Samaritans had long since accepted the Torah of the returned Exiles (see below), not only the ancient traditions that had remained with the remnants of the Kingdom of Israel. Moreover, when the Jews of Elephantine in Egypt wanted help with the rebuilding of their temple, they applied both to the High Priest in Jerusalem and to Delaiah and Shelomiah, the sons of Sanballat in Samaria (see Arameans).

Script: From biblical times, the Pentateuch had been copied in Palestine both in Palaeo-Hebrew script and in Aramaic script. However, when the two communities finally separated after John Hyrcanus' destruction of Samaria (see below), the Samaritans, according to F.M. Cross, chose the Palaeo-Hebrew script, which had previously been in general use in both Jerusalem and Samaria, as the exclusive script for their Torah. This they have preserved to this day as seen here (**729**). The Jerusalem rabbis had declared that this script was not something sacred (that it did not "make the hands clean", see Law*), but the Samaritans took the opposite decision and laid it down absolutely that the Palaeo-Hebrew script could be used only for holy writ. In this they were more rigid than the scribes and rabbis of Jerusalem, who, between 70 and 135 CE, established the Hebrew square characters derived from the old Aramaic form of writing as the exclusive script to be used for biblical documents by the scribes (the soferim). This is illustrated under Alphabet and Writing*. See this Samaritan biblical inscription at Sha'alabim in central Israel (**730**).

Samaritan Torah: The wording of the Samaritan Torah (Pentateuch) differs slightly from that of the Jewish Torah as handed down in the Massoretic text. The Samaritan version is essentially a proto-Massoretic text to which a number of expansions, transpositions, insertions and parallels or borrowings from other biblical books have been added. Most scholars assume that this general development of the text in the transmission of the Torah was carried out before Hasmonean times (2nd c. BCE) while the proto-Massoretic text was still fairly fluid (see Canon and Text*). In addition, there are one or two significant instances where the Samaritans have also transposed or changed phrases so as to justify specifically Samaritan theology. For instance, in Dt. 27:2–7, the Samaritans change "Mount Ebal" to "Mount Gerizim" (the mountain facing Shechem), thus giving divine authority to their sanctuary there. (This is also the wording of the Massoretic version of Dt. 11:29).

The Palestine and Massoretic Traditions: The dating of these changes, whether those reflecting the general development of the text, or specifically theological changes, is warmly debated by scholars. Many attribute all changes to pre-Hasmonean times when the two communities maintained an exclusive and often conflicting position. F.M. Cross and other scholars distinguish different phases in this development. Between the 5th and 2nd cs. BCE, the dominant Palestinian tradition of the Torah was undergoing slight changes both in Judea and in Samaria, based on the same proto-Massoretic text. However, in the Rabbinical* period, another proto-Massoretic textual tradition was chosen which was superior to the dominant tradition. This Palestinian tradition which was not used in the Massoretic text is reflected only in the Samaritan text, in the Dead Sea Scrolls* of the Torah (Pentateuch) and in Torah quotations included in the book of Chronicles (which was written around the time of Ezra, see Restoration*). An example of the same recension of the book of Exodus, containing a number of distinctive features, was found at Qumran. The Samaritan language is the classic Hebrew of the Pentateuch, and was never influenced by the Massoretes. Its pronunciation, differing from both Ashkenazi (European) and Sephardi (Oriental) Hebrew, is probably very old. The gutturals, for instance, are neither pronounced nor distinguished from each other. There is a tendency to prefix and suffix "alephs" to words in pronunciation, though seldom in writing. Presumably this was a standard text current in Palestine, which the Samaritans adopted.

A final, sweeping change was made in the 2nd c. BCE (128 BCE), when John Hyrcanus (see Hasmoneans*) conquered and destroyed Samaria. It is assumed, therefore, that the changes in the Samaritan Torah which relate to its theology date from that time, and are different in kind from those which appear in the Palestinian tradition.

For the Samaritans, contrary to the Jewish tradition, the Pentateuch is the whole Bible. They do not recognize the prophets, the Hagiographa (Writings) nor any of the other books of the Old Testament (see Bible Text and Canon*). They believe that Moses was the one true prophet and that they alone preserve the true version of God's word as revealed to him, the Jewish version of the Pentateuch having, in their eyes, been altered by Ezra. There is no historical foundation for this view. The final separation of the Samaritan text of the Pentateuch from the main stream of Jewish proto-Massoretic tradition was not completed until the time of John Hyrcanus.

Enmity between Samaritans and Jews: From the initial rebuff administered by the returned Exiles, relations with the Samaritans deteriorated into a complete separation of the two peoples. Towards the end of the Persian period, or at the time of Alexander the Great's conquests, this was confirmed by the building of a Samaritan temple on Mount Gerizim as a rival to the Temple of Jerusalem. Nehemiah records that it was built by Sanballat when his son-in-law was chased from Jerusalem (Neh. 13:28), but this seems too early.

From this time, however, hatred between the two peoples became a permanent feature, the Samaritans establishing their own religious traditions around Mount Gerizim, the physical and spiritual centre of their people. A good illustration of the Jewish attitude towards their closest neighbours occurs in Ecclesiasticus (written in the 3rd c. BCE; see Apocrypha*), where ch. 50:26 refers (according to older translations) to "the people abhorred by God that live in Shechem."

During the persecutions of Antiochus Epiphanes (see Hasmoneans*) the Samaritans hastened to deny all connections with the Jews and their religion (Josephus, Ant. 12, 5, 5), and the tensions between the two peoples continued to act as a fruitful source of strife in the area. Nevertheless, some sort of relations, however strained, were maintained at different levels between the 5th and 2nd. cs BCE. What set the seal on the final, permanent breach between the two communities was not day-to-day disagreements, nor the dispute over the Temple of Jerusalem. It was John Hyrcanus' action in razing the city of Samaria. After that, there could be no hope of reconciliation. Thus, unlike the Idumeans and Galileans, the Samaritans refused to assimilate with the Jews, but maintained their sectarian integrity. They remained under Jewish domination until Pompey annexed their territory to the Roman province of Syria and inaugurated a period of increasing prosperity. Herod* rebuilt the city of Samaria* as a splendid Hellenistic metropolis named, in Greek, "Sebaste" after his benefactor, the emperor Augustus. During the Roman period, its people began to play an increasingly important role in national affairs but violent clashes between them and the Jews continued. The Samaritans controlled the territory between Galilee and Jerusalem and they regularly harassed the groups of pilgrims making their way to the capital for the great Jewish festivals. The Jews retaliated in kind and also in words. To emphasize

730

the foreign descent of the Samaritans, the Jews called them contemptuously "Kutim", from Kutah, one of the Mesopotamian towns whose inhabitants had been deported to Samaria by the Assyrians.

However, as the Roman grip on Palestine tightened, the Samaritans suffered along with the Jews. Pontius Pilate's troops massacred a large number of them on Mount Gerizim in 36 CE. Although the Samaritans did not join the Jews in their rebellion in 67 CE, they had shared their hatred of the Romans and had risen independently against them on a number of occasions. Shortly before the fall of Jerusalem, Vespasian had some 11,600 Samaritans massacred in Shechem. At the end of the war, he built a new city, Roman Neapolis (modern Nablus) on the site of Shechem, leaving Samaria to decline and finally decay.

It appears that at first, the Samaritans cooperated with the Jews in the Bar Kochba* rebellion although, later on, they betrayed the Jews. From the time of Hadrian's Edicts, the Samaritans were systematically persecuted along with the Jews, especially by the emperors Septimus Severus and Decius.

The Samaritans and the Talmud: The Talmud's attitude towards the Samaritans varies with the different sages being quoted. However, the minor Talmudic tractate, Kutim, which refers to the sect's heresy, closes, "When will we accept them? When they deny belief in Mt. Gerizim and confess Jerusalem and the resurrection of the Dead." The Samaritans denied any resurrection and held fast to the ancient Israelite belief in Sheol (see Funerary Customs*).

The Samaritans and Christianity: The Jewish attitude towards the Samaritans is faithfully reflected in the New Testament, especially in Jesus' choice of a "good Samaritan" to point the moral of his parable against over-pious and inhuman Jews (Lk. 10:30–37). Matthew, on the whole, is hostile; Mark ignores them altogether, and Luke keeps his distance. John, however, is much more conciliatory (e.g. 4: 5–42), although even he adopts the presumably standard Jewish use of "Samaritan" to mean schismatic (8:48).

The description in Ac. 8:5–25 of the particular variation of Christian belief adopted by the adherents of Simon, the Samaritan, apparently refers to a phase of early Gnosticism. The evidence of the Church fathers does not suggest the existence of particular sects among the Samaritans in pre-Christian times, although Epiphanius identifies the Samaritans with the Essenes and mentions the Dositheans, Sabaeans and Gorothenes as their neighbours. There seem to have been two schismatic groups in Judaism, the Samaritans and the Judean Essenes (see below). The 14th c. CE Samaritan historian Abulfath describes the Dositheans as "Sons of Zadok" — the term used of themselves by the Qumran sectaries (see Dead Sea Scrolls*). In fact, however, very little is known about the relation of the gnostic movements to the Samaritans or, indeed, about Samaritan sects after the birth of Christianity.

Literature: In the late Roman period (3rd and 4th cs. CE), and at the beginning of the Byzantine Age, a Samaritan renaissance seemed to be foreshadowed by the appearance of men like the great writer, Marka, who wrote the "Memar Marka", a Samaritan haggadic midrash, in the 4th c. CE. He wrote in Aramaic, a language used by the Samaritans in a separate dialect (still in use today), as did Baba Rabba, a national hero.

History: In addition to the parent body in Palestine, the Samaritan diaspora was once widespread. A large Samaritan community existed in Egypt from the time of the Ptolemies and lasted until the 18th c. CE. They lived in Babylonia between the 3rd and 8th cs. CE, and in Syria in the 12th c. CE.

With the Christianization of the Roman empire, the Samaritans, along with the Jews, suffered renewed persecution, both in Palestine and in their communities in Egypt, Rome and Babylonia. In the eyes of the Gentiles, Jews and Samaritans were alike. An insurrection under Constantine (334 CE) provoked a crushing repression while Zeno (486 CE) destroyed the second Samaritan temple on Mt. Gerizim and built a Christian church in its place. They suffered again under Anastasius (491–518 CE). A Samaritan synagogue in Rome was destroyed in 500 CE. Finally, in 529 CE, during the reign of Justinian, the Samaritans proclaimed their own emperor and paid the penalty of their defiance with multitudes slain and some 20,000 sold into slavery. The autonomous existence of the Samaritans was effectively at an end. Parthian sympathy did them little good and under Justinian II (565–578 CE) the Samaritans were officially declared an "unlawful people". Many of them, in desperation, converted to Christianity. A tiny handful managed to preserve their identity. Today there are some 400 Samaritans in all, half of them living in Arab Nablus, the others in Holon, near Tel-Aviv in Israel.

Samaritan Religion: The religion of the Samaritans never developed anything comparable to the discipline of halakhah among the Jews. The 613 precepts of the Law* (see article) are faithfully and literally observed, with none of the later, more convenient interpretations to be found in modern Judaism. On a Sabbath it is forbidden to make the smallest journey except to the synagogue, and food which has been prepared on Friday may not even be kept warm. No outsider may be consulted about problems arising out of observance of the holy days. No Samaritan may marry outside the fold and all the prohibited degrees are strictly enforced — a man may not, for example, marry his niece (see Family*: Marriage) and may marry a second wife only if the first is childless. No third wife is allowed under any circumstances.

They follow a calendar which differs from that of the rabbis, and twice a year, at the semi-festivals of Tzimmut-Pesaḥ (Shebat 15, see Calendar*) and Tzimmut Sukkôth (Ab 15), the Samaritan priests prescribe the calendar for the coming six months.

Their religious year has the seven feasts presented in the Pentateuch (see Festivals*): Passover, Matzot (Unleavened Bread), Shabu'ot (Pentecost, which always falls on a Sunday), Yom Teruah (the New Year, or Day of the Trumpet Call, not called "Rosh Hashanah"), Yom Kippur (Day of Atonement), Sukkôth (or Tabernacles, where, however, the "lulav" and "ethrog" are unknown) and Mo'ed Shemini (eighth day of the festival).

The Passover Sacrifice: The most important of these festivals is the Passover (Pesaḥ) sacrifice which can only be celebrated on Mt. Gerizim and on the day after the Sabbath, in literal interpretation of the text of Ex. 23:15, and contrary to the Jerusalem calendar. In fact, the whole sacrifice is a survival from pre-Exilic northern Israelite observances, though

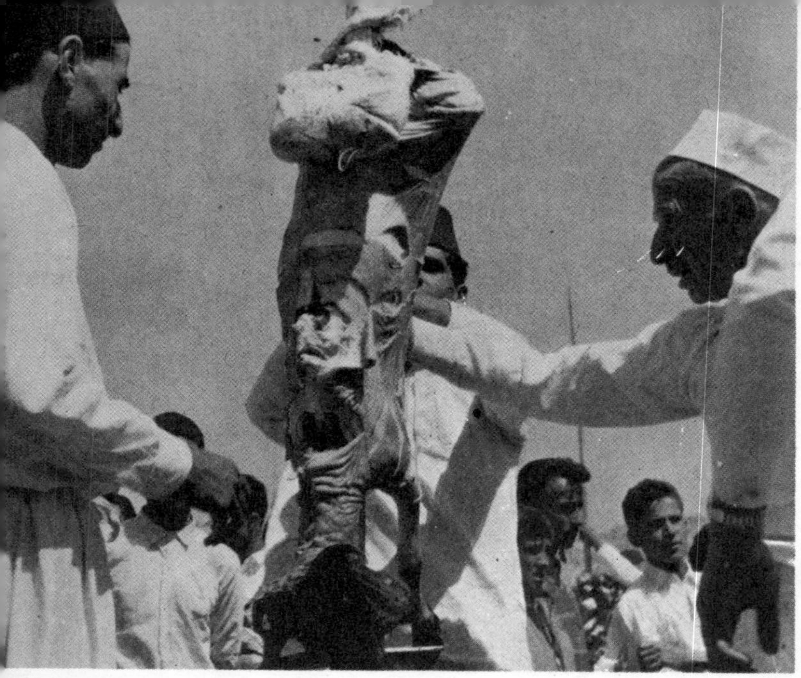

731

732

greatly changed by contemporary Jewish rites in post-Exilic days down to Hasmonean times. It does not reflect the precepts or ceremonies of rabbinical and contemporary Judaism.

Led by their High Priest, the whole community of the Samaritans goes on a pilgrimage or "hag" to the top of their holy Mount Gerizim. (To make this possible in modern conditions, the Samaritans of Israel are given a special dispensation the cross the border into Jordan). They arrive there at sunset on the evening of the 14th day of Nisan (Ex. 12:2–6) which falls on a different day from the Jewish Pesaḥ. At the open-air sanctuary, seven lambs (one for each family of the community) are slaughtered on the altar, which consists of a long trench of stones where a fire burns underneath basins holding water. As the lambs' throats are cut, the members of the congregation sprinkle blood over themselves with a branch of hyssop as a purificatory rite. The lintels of their houses and the eyelashes of their children are marked with the sign of God so that as the Angel of Death passes over, he will recognize the sign and save the children of Israel (see Exodus*).

As the water on the altar boils, it is drawn off and used to sear the carcasses and remove the wool. The wool is buried and the skin checked for impurities, while care is taken that the carcasses are completely emptied of blood. The lambs are then strung on long poles placed on the shoulders of young men and the skin quickly removed. The carcasses are slit and the intestines removed, rinsed in fresh water, salted and thrown into the fire. No bone must be broken (Ex. 12:46). The prepared victims are tied according to an ancient pattern, salted and impaled on long pointed poles (**731**). These are then placed upright in an oven pit, 3 metres deep, where a brush fire is burning (**732**). The pit is covered with a wooden lid, herbs and clay, the ends of the spits left sticking out as a visible witness to the paschal sacrifice. The fire burns for three hours and at midnight the meat is ready to be eaten. The families rush over to the pit with large platters. The clay top is broken and the carcasses taken out and distributed on a first-come, first-served basis, each family receiving its share of the sacrifice and the bitter herbs that must be eaten with it.

Samaritans, Sadducees and the Dead Sea Scrolls: As the Samaritans pride themselves on their Zadokite priesthood, it is not surprising that resemblances can be found between their customs and those of the Sadducees* — some scholars find the whole of Samaritanism a modification of Sadducee doctrine. Other scholars have pointed out the close parallels which exist between the Samaritans and the sectaries of the Dead Sea* in matters of biblical exegesis (interpretation), language, religious customs and practice. The Samaritan and Qumran calendars are not the same, but both are at variance with rabbinic practice. The Samaritans opposed Judah and the House of David, while the Dead Sea sectaries, who did not oppose it, regarded themselves as the true Judah and House of David. The Samaritans envisage their Messiah — and they never use the actual term — as either a returning Moses (under the name of Taeb) or as a Second Moses, who would restore the "true worship" of the Tabernacle on Mount Gerizim. Taeb in turn would bring "his king", corresponding to the "Messiah of Israel" of the Qumran sectaries.

Whether or not all these affinities actually point to a vital link between the Samaritans and the Dead Sea sectaries in pre-Christian times, however (or between the Samaritans and the Essenes), remains a subject for debate. There is a large Samaritan literature existing in Hebrew, Aramaic and Arabic, in manuscripts the bulk of which still await investigation. Their liturgical, exegetical, midrashic, halakhic and calendrical works are of great importance for the study of sectarian Judaism (see Dead Sea Scrolls*).

SAMUEL, LAST "JUDGE".— The twelfth and last in the succession of "judges" was Samuel. He was also called a Prophet or "seer" and biblical tradition credits him with the foundation of kingship in Israel. He anointed Saul as king and, according to biblical tradition, may also have anointed David (see David*).

Childhood at Shiloh: He was born at Ramathaim-Zofim, on the highlands bordering Ephraim and Benjamin. Before his birth, his parents dedicated him to the service of God by a Nazirite vow (I Sam. 1:11) and Samuel began his career by serving the old priest Eli at Shiloh, the shrine of the tribal league*.

Disaster at Aphek and Loss of the Ark: This was during the dark days of Philistine* expansion (third quarter of the 11 th c. BCE). The tribes joined together to oppose them and brought the Ark of Yahweh from Shiloh to the battlefield in the hope that Yahweh's presence would bring them victory. Instead, at the battle of Aphek (ca. 1050 BCE), they were soundly beaten. Israel's armies were cut to pieces. Hophni and Phinehas, the priests who bore the Ark, were killed and the Ark itself was captured by the Philistines. The Philistines then proceeded to occupy the whole country, destroying Shiloh, the tribal centre. This Bible story has been confirmed by archaeology, which found evidence of the destruction of the city, as well as others in central and southern Palestine, during the second half of the 11th c. BCE.

The Old Order Passes: The end of Shiloh as its centre, (for the shrine was abandoned after its destruction) also meant the end of the old tribal league which had so greatly contributed to the development of nationhood for the first century and a half after the Conquest*. The disaster of Aphek and the loss of the Ark also severely discredited the Aaronid (priestly) house of Phinehas and Eli. Eli had died of shock after the capture of the Ark and his death was followed by a long period of priestly interregnum which lasted for about a century, until the time of David. There is no mention of Eli's family in connection with the subsequent career of Samuel, whose impressive figure overshadows the priesthood of Shiloh. In fact, the old order had failed. It could not be revived.

Samuel's Mission: In this situation, Samuel summoned the tribes to the sacred town of Mispah in an effort to revive their failing courage and restore traditional worship, in spite of the destruction of the traditional shrine. Biblical tradition relates that he returned to his ancestral home in Ramah and travelled on a regular circuit between the important sacred towns of Mispah, Gilgal and Bethel. There he administered covenant law* and adjudicated in tribal matters. By these means, in spite of the oppression of the Philistines, a national consciousness was built up among the people and Hebrew traditions kept alive.

Although Israel was subject to the Philistines, their occupation of the land was not complete. It is unlikely that Galilee or Transjordan were occupied by the Philistines and they had only partial control of the central hills of Ephraim. A few scattered centres of resistance remained in Israelite hands in the highlands of Ephraim and Benjamin.

Lack of Leadership and Iron Weapons: Nevertheless, the Hebrew tribes remained without any real central authority. They lived in a close relationship with the Canaanites and Amorites, who remained in territory which was still only theoretically the domain of the Hebrew tribes. The other inhabitants, also formally subject to the Philistine overlords, were divided into small city kingdoms, ruled by a military aristocracy. The problem that faced the Israelites was not to restore their out-worn tribal league, but to achieve a strong united organization under a central authority — a monarchy. All through, the Bible story emphasizes that Philistine domination was aided by the disunity of the Hebrews and their lack of weapons.

Iron had come into use in the 12th or middle of the 11th c. BCE, as shown by a plow tip of Saul's time recovered from Gibeah (see Crafts*). However, the Philistines had a monopoly of iron and, to protect this and their own military domination, they suppressed what village metal industry Israel had, making her dependent on Philistine workmanship for all tools and weapons (I Sam. 13:19–22).

Bands of Ecstatic Prophets: Little is known of events during the years of Philistine domination. By the time their military occupation came to an end, Samuel was an old man. The will to resist and the charismatic tradition of the days of Judges* had been kept alive partly, apparently, thanks to the efforts of wandering bands of ecstatic prophets who had appeared some time after the middle of the 11th c. BCE (W.F. Albright). Their frenzied appeals (described in I Sam. 10:5–13; 19:20–24) fired men with zeal for Yahweh and His Holy War* (see Numbers*; Dead Sea Scrolls*). Without this movement, in the opinion of Albright, Yahwism and Israelite nationalism might both have declined. The enthusiasm of the ecstatic prophets saved the day, at least for Yahwism.

Although not one of the ecstatic prophets, Samuel may have cooperated with them. It is not known how or how often patriotic fervour flared into armed clashes with the Philistines. The tribes were in no position to repel the invader; their people and their leaders must have been well aware that their case was hopeless unless new and stronger leadership could be found.

Samuel and the Kingship: In this situation, the people elected Saul to be their king and deliverer. The account of Saul's election is closely interwoven with Samuel's career, and the place of Samuel in the traditions of the origin of the kingdom is a complicated one (see Saul*). His reaction and his role in this election are recorded in two parallel narratives (see Samuel, Books of*), one (I Sam. 9–10) tacitly favourable to the new principle of monarchy, the other (chs. 8 and 12) bitterly hostile (e.g. Samuel's "manner of the King" speech, I Sam. 8). The contradictions in the traditions seem to reflect political and judicial problems which had arisen at the time, as cherished in various circles and centres of tradition which form the sources of the narratives. The conflict between Saul and Samuel, and the account of Samuel's last years are referred to in the article on Saul*, who personified a significant change in Israelite history (see Samuel, Books of*).

SAMUEL, BOOK OF. — Although divided into two in the Septuagint and later Hebrew printed Bibles, the Hebrew scribes regarded the two books of Samuel as one book. A marginal note to I Sam. 28:24 states that it is "half the book", and the narrative of book I is continued in book II without any interruption.

Together, the books of Samuel record Israel's transmission from a tribal federation to a monarchy. The books cover a period of slightly over a century, from ca. 1070 to 950 BCE, and can be roughly divided into three parts, representing the accounts of the lives and activities of Samuel, Saul and David.

Contents: *I Samuel* contains:
a. Samuel's childhood and relationship to the Shiloh priesthood (chs. 1–3);
b. The loss of the Ark and its wanderings and return (4:1–7:2), which is connected to II Sam. 6;
c. Samuel as "judge" over Israel; the accession of Saul and his conflict with Samuel (7:3–15:35);
d. The story of David and Saul (chs. 16–20), beginning with David's anointing by Samuel (16:1–13) and including the slaying of Goliath (ch. 17);
e. Chs. 21–31 continue the story with an account of David's flight from Saul and his adventures until Saul's defeat and death (I Sam. 31 and II Sam. 1).

II Samuel is mainly concerned with David's reign and doings. The narrative flows continuously almost without interruption (see David*), and may be divided as follows:
f. David's reign, first from Hebron, then from the new capital of Jerusalem, describing the conquests by which he extended and established his kingship (II Sam. 2–8);
g. The problem of David's successor (Chs. 9–20);
h. A variety of appendices giving information relating to the earlier chapters, but added at a later stage.

Authorship of Samuel: The books of Samuel were not written as a single work at one time. Instead, the books' authors or editors drew on a variety of traditions belonging to different circles. This has resulted in a number of repetitions and inconsistencies e.g. the two different lines of tradition have their own distinctive point of view or way of presenting the material. For instance, I Sam. 4–6 is concerned solely with the Ark and the account of its miraculous powers. Then there is the group of traditions of which Samuel the prophet is the hero (1:1–28; 2:11–4:1; 7:3–8:22; 10:17–27; 11:12–12:25; 15:1–16:13; 25:1; 28:3–25). Saul is the hero of another group (I Sam. 9:1–10:16; 11:1–11; 13:1–18; 14:1–52; 16:14–23), while separate bodies of traditions refer to the relationship between David and Saul (I Sam. 17:55–19:17; 20:1–24:22; 25–31; II Sam. 1:1–16) and to David's family life and court (II Sam. 11:1–12:25; 13:1–20:22). The theme of II Sam. 9–20 is the vexing question of who should succeed David, and this also forms an individual block of tradition.

These various traditions were collected, preserved and finally written down at different times. The stories about Samuel, for instance, appear to have reached their present form long after the events they describe. The traditions were first transmitted in a rather loose form and probably did not receive their final editing until the reign of Solomon or later, during the 9th c. BCE. This long period allowed for different viewpoints to find expression in differing accounts of the same event. About the monarchy, for instance, two opposed opinions — one welcoming its establishment, the other critical of royal practices — produced two contradictory accounts of Saul's accession (see Samuel, Last Judge*), both being preserved by the editors who were unwilling to tamper with the traditions and to suppress one version.

733

The traditions about David, on the other hand, except for those concerning the relationship with Saul, are believed to have been the reminiscences of eye-witnesses and participants in the events. Some of these sections may have been written by an annalist of David's court. They were certainly the work of someone with a thorough knowledge of the period, who gave the book a pragmatic, non-theological, historical approach which is unique in ancient eastern literature.

Some of these passages appear to have been taken directly from official records, particularly the military histories and stories of heroic exploits by David and his companions. David was the centre of so much popular hero-worship and interest that many of the traditions about him (e.g. the story of the succession) reached their present form while he was still alive or no later than the reign of his son, Solomon.

In general, however, it can be said that all the material — some of it quite ancient — had substantially reached its present form by the 10th or 9th c. BCE. It still received a certain amount of editing which continued for perhaps another century. However there is no real evidence to suggest that material was still being added as late as the 5th c. BCE — a theory which was once held.

Text and Versions: Well-preserved fragments of Samuel (**733**) were found among the Dead Sea Scrolls* and proved to contain a Hebrew text much superior to the Massoretic text or the somewhat different Greek version (which was known to offer a better text at some points than the Massoretic). This question is discussed at length under "Textual Criticism" in the article on Biblical Criticism* (see Samuel, Last Judge*).

SANCTUARIES, SHRINES. — Once the Children of Israel had settled in Canaan, the sanctuaries sanctified by association with the Patriarchs, excepting Bethel, almost cease to be mentioned in the Bible. Instead, quite independently of the main national sanctuary at Shiloh containing the Tent, Tabernacle* and the Ark, new holy places become important: Gilgal (Jos. 4:19–20; I Sam. 7:16; Hos. 4:15 ff); Mizpeh in Benjamin (Jud. 6:11–24); Dan (Jud. 17–18, see Judges*). The latter and Bethel* became the main centres of worship of the Northern Kingdom (see Israel and Judah*, Part I).

Some of these sanctuaries date from the time of Judges, others go back to the earlier times of the Patriarchs*. Some of them continued the holiness of an earlier place of worship; others replaced the older holy sites. They were not, at first, condemned by Yahwism and indeed they were popular places of pilgrimage and prayer right up to the end of the monarchy. An Israelite sanctuary of that period was discovered at Arad in 1963 (see article under Ancient Cities*: Arad).

Possibly these "high places" did keep Canaanite traditions alive alongside the religion of Yahwism (see High Places*; Canaan: Gods and Idols*, Cult), and the later prophets condemned them as discrediting the true religion (Hos. 10:8; Am. 7:9; Jer. 17:3, passim). At the time of Josiah's reforms they were all suppressed (II K. 23:5, 8–9) indiscriminately, although the same passage makes it clear that they had been served by prophets and priests of Yahweh (not pagans). However, in the interests of the centralization of worship, they had to be eliminated (see Israel and Judah*, Part V). The same word "bamôth" (sanctuaries) is used for both the old Israelite sanctuaries and unlawful Canaanite shrines. The Deuteronomic editor of Kings certainly equated all sanctuaries outside Jerusalem with unlawful practices and, on these grounds, condemns nearly all the kings of Israel and Judah with the notable exceptions of the reformers, Hezekiah and Josiah (see also Tabernacle, Ark and Cherubim*).

SAUL. — The first king of Israel was born the son of Kish in Gibeah of Benjamin. Just at the time that organized opposition to the loose Philistine domination was spreading among the Hebrew tribes of Benjamin and Ephraim, the warrior, Saul, emerged as a typical charismatic leader (see Judges*): "the spirit of God came mightily upon him" (I Sam. 11:6). He rallied the tribes to battle against the Philistines* and defeated them at Michmash, driving them out of the Benjamin and Ephraim highlands (ca. 1020 BCE). Having thus demonstrated his military ability, the Israelites' desire for a strong central leader gradually crystallized into a demand that Saul be made king (see Samuel*).

Saul's Anointment: This had first to overcome the opposition of a conservative minority who wanted a revival of the tribal league. The attitude of the aging Samuel* appears ambiguous. There are two parallel accounts of Saul's election to the kingship, one being tacitly favourable to the monarchy, the other hostile. The narrative of I Sam. 9:1–10:16 records that Saul was privately anointed as "nāgîd" (a special title meaning prince) by Samuel in Ramah, and this is continued in I Sam. 13:3b, 4b–15. Side by side with this narrative there is a separate and original account of Saul's victory over the Ammonites and his subsequent acclamation as "king" by the people at Gilgal.

The other account of the election puts the initiative in the hands of the tribal elders and the people: "Then all the elders of Israel gathered together and came to Samuel at Ramah, and said to him, 'Behold, you are old and your sons do not walk in your ways; now appoint for us a king to govern us like all the nations.'" (I Sam. 8:4–5). According to this tradition (I Sam. 8:6–18; 10:17–27; 12), Samuel yielded to a spontaneous popular demand for a king and presided over his formal election at Mizpah, only after angry protests. The notion of kingship came late to Israel and it may have seemed like a heretical attempt to imitate pagan neighbours.

The "Manner of the King": Samuel's main argument against establishing a king makes it clear (8:6–8) that he interpreted the people's demand as a rejection of the Lord. He consulted his God and, although he was directed to "hearken to the voice of the people in all that they say to you," he also had to "solemnly warn them and show them the ways of the king" (I Sam. 8:9). His warning became the famous denunciation of monarchy, vividly illuminating the new political and social factors which were being introduced into Israelite life at the time. The king, Samuel predicted, would impose upon them heavy taxes; demand forced labour, the corvée service, from the common people and their slaves, thus making slaves of all the people; establish a standing army of draftees and professional soldiers, and expropriate property to give to his servants (see Taxes*). Samuel feared the change but, under pressure, he agreed to the people's demands (I Sam. 8:4–22).

Many scholars find the contrast between the two accounts irreconcilable. They regard the anti-monarchist outburst as a later insertion reflecting disillusion after experience of Israelite kings. New data from Ugarit* and Alalakh (a kingdom of the north) dating from the 18th to 13th cs. BCE, however, suggest to I. Mendelsohn that the vivid description of the "manner of the king" is "an authentic description of the semi-feudal Canaanite society as it existed prior to and during the time of Samuel."

Canaanite city states had small armed forces consisting of conscripted foot-soldiers and professional warriors recruited from the ranks of the aristocracy. These were the "maryannu" or knights who drove the horse-drawn chariots. Performance of military obligations exempted the knights from payment of tithes or other taxes. The kings owned the crown lands and leased vineyards, orchards and estates to chosen individuals against payment of taxes to the palace. The mass of the people had to pay a tithe (or tenth) of their crops and livestock in taxes*, as well as grazing taxes, tolls and fines. Moreover, they were subject to the corvée (forced labour) for the construction of roads, fortresses and temples and for tilling the crown lands.

It seems, therefore, that the passage in I Sam. 8 may not be a re-writing of history by a later opponent of kingship, but a genuine appeal by Samuel or a contemporary of his urging the people not to impose an alien Canaanite way of life upon themselves. Its author could conceivably have been the prophet himself or the spokesman of the anti-monarchical movement of that period.

The Sequence of Events: Because of these varying accounts, it is very difficult to reconstruct the series of events. Both accounts give Samuel a leading role in the proceedings. Originally, it appears, he anointed Saul as "nagîd", a special title meaning Yahweh's warrior prince rather than king. At this point there was no real conflict with the followers of the tribal league. This arose only as Saul began to act like a Canaanite monarch, and even then it is clear that the kingship he had assumed was not regarded as necessarily hereditary.

Saul's Career: After rescuing the Israelites from the immediate Philistine danger, Saul led numerous punitive expeditions against the Moabites and Arameans. He also took an active part in the attempt to preserve Israel's religious purity, and tried to suppress the witchcraft practiced by Hebrew and Canaanite alike.

Rivalry with David: As a result of circumstances which it is difficult to coordinate chronologically from the record as it stands, the young David* joined Saul's entourage (see article). The narrative links and contrasts David's heroic personality, charm and popularity with an increasing nervous depression on the part of Saul, accompanied by convulsions, attributed, as was normal at the time, to an evil spirit. He became unable to master outbursts of passion, showing a seriously disturbed and often cruel nature. David, who was his cup-bearer and a close friend of his son, Jonathan, was detailed to calm him with music (I Sam. 16:14–23).

Saul grew increasingly jealous of David's spectacular military success and growing popularity. His bitter persecution drove David to seek refuge with Achish, king of Gath and to serve him, together with a number of malcontents. Saul's rage against David extended beyond pursuing him and his followers to molesting the priesthood which, up to then, he had treated well. The gulf which had come to separate him from many of his people was thus widened.

Samuel Rejects Saul: Saul's relationship with Samuel also shows him in a tragic light. For the greater part of Saul's life he was on bad terms with the people's venerated religious leader. Although, again, conflicting accounts make it difficult to be sure of the reasons, the split between the two appears to have occurred quite early in Saul's career. According to one tradition (I Sam. 13:4–15), Saul had usurped the function of the tribal league priesthood. In the other, he is said to have violated the "herem" rule of the law regulating conduct of a Holy War (see Impurity and Purification*: Holy War) after a victory over the Amalekites in the south of Judah. This rule decreed anathema on the vanquished enemy and his goods. Whatever the cause, Samuel broke with him finally and "did not see Saul again until the day of his death." (I Sam. 15:35).

David Anointed: There is a story that before Samuel's death he was divinely inspired to anoint the young David as king in place of Saul. According to tradition, this took place while David was still a shepherd boy in Bethlehem (I Sam. 16:1–13). Some see in this action an attempt to provide a focus for opposition to Saul through the house of Jesse (see David and Solomon — The United Kingdom*).

Saul's Death: A few years after Saul had driven David away from his court, the Philistines rallied again, encouraged by the inner weakness of the Israelite camp. Instead of advancing against Saul into the central hills of Ephraim they marched northwards to Beth-Shean, cutting the country into two and preventing the tribes of Galilee and Transjordan from joining Saul. This also presented the Philistines with a battle on ground which was favourable for chariot manoeuvring. Saul had no chariots and could not withstand the assault of the heavy Philistine armour in the plain. He moved on to the higher ground of Mount Gilboa. In the opinion of modern scholars, the Philistines were joined in the attack by the Tjekel, the "People of the Sea" to whom they were related and who lived on the northern coast around Dor and near Beth-Shean*.

Tradition has it that before the battle, Saul visited a medium, the Witch of Endor, who conjured up the spirit of the departed Samuel from Sheol (the underworld), only to hear him pronounce the curse of doom on the fearful king (I Sam. 28:16–19). Even after death, the prophet would not be reconciled to Saul.

On Mount Gilboa, Saul and his three sons, including Jonathan, were killed, and their bodies strung up on the city gates of Beth-Shean. The Philistines regained control of the country and kept it until well into David's reign (ca. 990 BCE).

It was David* who was to establish the national unity of the Israelites, but he built on foundations which, in spite of his tragic end and the many contradictions of his career, had been laid by Saul (see Samuel, Book of*).

SEALS. — The Hebrew word for seal, "ḥotam", was borrowed from the Egyptian "htm" which meant not only a seal and to seal or close, but also a fortress. In Hebrew the word is used figuratively for something kept secret or hidden while, as in English, "to seal" is also to confirm.

In ancient Israel, seals were used to sign (or seal) documents, and the seal had the force of an actual signature. No document was considered authentic without a seal impression. If the document itself was not written on clay but on papyrus or some perishable material, the seal would be pressed into a small lump of clay and then attached.

Doors of houses and tombs and the lids of chests or other containers were sealed. Where origin or ownership was to be marked on a clay vessel, the seal would be attached to the body or handle.

Seals were carried, either hanging from a gold or silver chain around the neck, or worn as rings (signet rings, **734**). Seals have been found still attached to fibulae. The Song of Songs cries, "Set me as a seal upon thine heart, as a seal upon thine arm" (8:6), referring to the Egyptian custom of wearing the name-ring (cartouche) of the sovereign on both upper arms and the breast as a sign of loyalty and filial

734

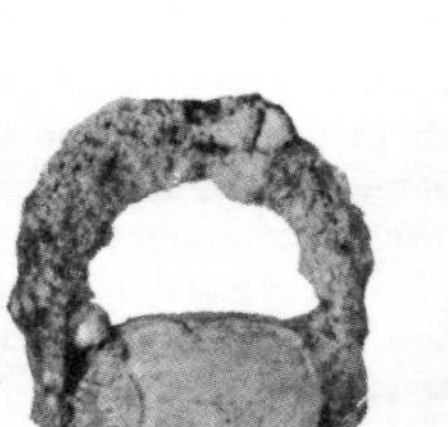

735

736 a

736 b

737

devotion. This had developed among high officials and princes from the older habit of branding the master's name upon his slaves.

In other Old Testament stories a ring or seal appears as the emblem of authority: in the story of Joseph and Pharaoh (Gn. 41:42); in connection with Ahab (I K. 21:8), and with Darius (Dan. 6:17). In Jeremiah (32:10) it is evidence of a covenant.

I. TYPES OF SEALS: The seals found in the lands of the Bible fall into three main groups: cylinder, scarab and button seals. Their designs are important in connection with the history of Israel's art. For instance, some scarab seals show Hyksos influence which had an effect on Israel's art in general.

Cylinder Seals: Cylinder seals were apparently the oldest, some located in layers of the Early Bronze Age. In these, the inscription was impressed on a clay cylinder which, when baked, could be rolled onto soft clay tablets, easily reproducing a series of the same picture. The designs of the oldest seals (hunting scenes or rows of running animals) were especially suited to such treatment and created a "beauty of repetition" (**735**). Later on, closed groups — animals, human or mythical beings facing each other — were introduced (**736a, b**).

The earliest seals appear from their style and motif to have been derived from Assyria and Babylon. The most frequent decorations are scenes connected with the myths and religion of Mesopotamia — Gilgamesh and other gods and heroes (**737**) appearing frequently. Some of the examples found in Israel were probably imported, although variation in style and decoration, with occasional borrowings from Egypt (one from Ta'anach has both cuneiform and hieroglyphic writing), show that most of them were copies made in Palestine or Syria (Phoenicia).

With the beginning of the 1st. mill. BCE (Iron Age), potsherds, papyrus or parchment began to be used for writing instead of clay tablets, and the cylinder seals were gradually replaced by stamp or scarab seals.

Scarab or Signet Seals: The scarabs were the most widely used of all seals, every excavation of a site occupied before the destruction of the First Temple producing many such finds. Many others have been found in surface explorations of ancient sites.

Scarabs belong to the signet type of seal. They had only to be pressed onto the clay for a single impression, and their design no longer relied on repetition (the most popular motif being the sacred Egyptian beetle, **738**). In place of clay, they were usually made of more durable materials, like pottery, glass or hard stone, especially carnelian or jasper.

Besides acting as seals and amulets, scarabs might have two other purposes. One was to commemorate historical events, like the lion-hunt scarab of Amenophis III, from Lachish. In the other, the beetle, its wings outstretched, was tied over the heart of a deceased person, inscribed with passages from the "Book of the Dead", which were essential for the journey to the nether world. See **739**. A steatite scarab of Ramses II was found in the late Bronze strata of Ashdod*, **739a**.

Two remarkable seals were found in Israel in 1961 by Raphael Giveon and were made public by him. One, found in Aijalon in the southern plain, is a scarab carved in steatite, inscribed with a representation of an appropriate offering for a god or king (it is possibly an offering scene, presenting a symbolic Egyptian figurine to the sun child, Horus, though it has not yet been possible to define the precise nature of the scene). It is inscribed on top with the word "l'aba" (belonging to Aba) in Proto-Canaanite characters of the 12th or 11th c. BCE. The second seal, found at Dan near the sources of the Jordan, represents a four-winged figure holding bow-like objects and wearing the Phoenician form of the double crown. It is inscribed "l'aza" (belonging to Aza). R. Giveon notes the connection between Dan and the Phoenicians (Jud. 18:7).

Up to the 5th c. BCE, the scarab seals found in Israel and Phoenicia were mainly Egyptian in style, although not necessarily made there. For instance, scarabs bearing the name of Thutmosis III (15th c. BCE) appeared for centuries after his death, perhaps because they were held to have magic power, or perhaps for aesthetic reasons, but not because of any particular regard in which he was held. This 8th c. BCE Hebrew seal (**739b**) inscribed Smaryû (see Samaria*, b) bears also the names Thutmosis III and Seti I on both sides. Later on, influences from Egypt and Asia were replaced by designs inspired by the Greeks.

Button Stamp Seals: Button stamp seals were of northern, mainly Hittite origin. These had round faces and within them, an appropriately balanced design. Many of the seals found in Israel are of a mixed type — the most common of them scaraboids — oblong in shape like the scarabs, but without the markings of a beetle on the back.

739 b

738

739

739 a

740

741

743

During the Canaanite period, outside influences were so strong that it is difficult to speak of a distinctively Israelite art. However, once the Israelite kingdom was established, growing strength and national consciousness sponsored the development of art forms which, while still reflecting foreign influences (mainly Phoenician), nevertheless had their own style and content. The description of the High Priest's breastplate (Ex. 28:11) refers to engraved signets, while engraving is recognized as a separate occupation in Ecclesiasticus 38:29.

II. NAMES FROM SEALS: From a historical point of view, the most important private seals are those which contain the names of men and women in Israel. Finds of this kind have greatly augmented the list of Hebrew names given in the Bible. Very often the name of the owner and his father are inscribed; sometimes a title is added, mostly "servant of . . ." like the famous lion seal of "Shema, servant of Jeroboam (the first)", found at Megiddo (**740**). Jeroboam is not the only known historical personality mentioned, although generally it is sound policy to avoid identifying names found on seals with biblical characters. Many names were very common in Israel and seals found in excavations do not necessarily belong to people of that name mentioned in the Bible, but in some cases the identification is a sound one — when there are supporting data. These seals do not seem to precede the 8th c. BCE. The seals decorated with cherubs, beetles and other figures are regarded by many as of the earlier type, while those that bear only a name (or one or two lines) belong to the 7th or 6th c. BCE, (**741**).

Royal Seals: An important class of seals are those known only from their impression, found in Lachish and other Judean sites and dating from the late Israelite period, on the handles of large vessels (**743**). Hundreds of these impressions have been found, every one of them bearing the inscription "*lmlk*" ("to the king") with the name of one of four Judean cities: Hebron, Ziph, Sokoh, Mamshit.

744

742

These "*lmlk*" stamps appear to have been related to government activities, for instance the workshop or winery in the Hebron area of the 7th and early 6th cs. BCE contained a number of standard size large jars (holding 45 litres) which may have been royal measures of capacity (cf. I Ch. 4:23). Alternatively, they may have been used for wholesale distribution of wine, oil or perhaps for the collection of taxes in kind. Seal impressions have also been found from the Persian period of the Restoration* in which the inscription reads "Y^{e}hud(a)" or "Jerusalem".

What is interesting is that seals bearing Hebrew names often also show the symbols and characters of non-Jewish religions, particularly Egyptian, such as the sun-child on a flower, a sphinx, the sign of life, the sun-beetle, or the winged sun (**744**). In addition there are Mesopotamian symbols like the four-winged monster.

It is assumed that, as in the case of ivory carving, seal-makers had either to adapt such familiar symbols or else forgo any use of meaningful decoration. Somehow these symbols were adapted to Jewish religious concepts, like the head of Zeus introduced into the decoration of Jewish sarcophagi of the Roman period, or the sun chariot of Helios which appears in the mosaic pavement of the Beth-Alpha synagogue (**742**), although these had no religious significance. Other scholars who are not ready to accept this view assume that the nature of the decorations of the seals had something to do with the seal-makers who may have been foreigners or have learned from them.

SHIPS AND NAVIGATION. — *Outline: The Ships of Zebulun and Asher; Biblical Evidence; Solomon's Fleet; Evidence of Archaeology: Egypt; The Greek Fleet; Cargo Boats; Travel in the Roman Empire; Jewish Shipping of the Graeco-Roman Period.*

North of Mount Carmel, the east Mediterranean coastline of Syria became the homeland of the most famous mariners of the ancient world and the site of some of its most important ports (see Phoenicia*). Yet, to the south, Palestine was involved in very little more than coastal trade between Phoenicia and Egypt and other centres. The country south of the Carmel is short of timber, the most important raw material for shipbuilding, and one which the mountains of Lebanon provided in abundance. Moreover, the coastline south of Mount Carmel is almost entirely lacking in natural bays or estuaries. Nevertheless, recent excavations have shown that the ancient peoples made use of every estuary that did exist and traces have been unearthed of a much larger number of ports than used to be suspected. Such traces have been discovered in the mound of Abu-Hawam at the mouth of the Kishon river near Haifa; at Tel Kassileh on the mouth of the Yarkon (north Tel-Aviv); at the mouth of the Rubin, at Nahal Shorek; in the excavations of Tel Mor at the mouth of the Lachish river and in many other places.

The Ships of Zebulun and Asher: Apparently in the period of Judges, the northern tribes did have contact with the sea, cf. Gn. 49:13, "Zebulun shall dwell at the shore of the sea; he shall become a haven for ships, and his border shall be at Sidon"; or Jud. 5:17, "Dan, why did he abide with the ships? Asher sat still at the coast of the sea, settling down by his landings." Moreover, Issachar is mentioned along with Zebulun as "sucking the affluence of the seas" (Dt. 33: 18–19). However, none of these references is sufficiently well understood for them to be good evidence of substantial maritime concerns at this period.

Coastal traffic probably began in Palestine relatively late — certainly not before the early days of the Israelite monarchy (exceptions to the rule, more or less, being Asher or Zebulun on the northern coast). It became of importance to the Jews only after the Restoration*. Until then, they were almost entirely cut off from the coast, the Philistines* holding the southern coastal areas and the Canaanites-Phoenicians the northern. Information about ships and navigation in earlier times, therefore, comes mainly from archaeological materials (see below).

Biblical Evidence: The Bible has a number of terms for sailing vessels but does not differentiate clearly between them: "oniyah" (plural, "oniyot") for boat or fleet (I K. 10:11, 22 passim); "sefinah" (vessel, ship with deck, Jh. 1:5). The book of Jonah* also uses "sefinah", apparently as a synomym for "oniyah" (Jh. 1:3, 5). Isaiah (33:21) refers to a galley with oars, apparently an unusually large ship. Elsewhere (Is. 18:2), a vessel is named for the material used in its construction, in this case papyrus.

Solomon's Fleet: By the time of Solomon, however, the position is much clearer. Although he turned his attention to Palestine's "back door" on the Red Sea rather than to its Mediterranean coast, he built a fleet of "ships of Tarshish" (see Phoenicia* and below) with materials and assistance supplied by his ally, Hiram, king of Tyre (I K. 9:26–28; 10:11, 22; II Ch. 8:18; 9:21). These ships sailed from Ezion-Geber near Eilat, to "Ophir". Scholars have long debated the exact identity of Ophir. Josephus*, Eusebius of Caesarea and Jerome (the latter two historians dating to the 4th c. CE) placed it in India, although another early authority, Eupolemos (2nd c. CE), put Ophir on the coast of Eritrea, i.e. the Red Sea.

An ostracon recently discovered at Tel Kassileh at the mouth of the Yarkon river (near Tel-Aviv) was found to bear the inscription "zahab Ophir" (gold of Ophir; see **530**). B. Mazar has assumed from this that it refers to another locality which was Solomon's Mediterranean equivalent of Ezion-Geber, his Red Sea port, though this is not certain. An attempt to restore the fleet of "ships of Tarshish" was made by King Jehoshaphat (I K. 22:48), perhaps with (II Ch. 20:35–37) or without (I K. 22:49) the participation of Ahaziah, king of Israel. In either case the attempt met with disaster and the ships were destroyed, presumably by a storm.

This is almost the last mention of an Israelite attempt to establish a fleet. However, through contact with the Phoenicians* and the Egyptians, the Israelites became familiar with the sea and the problems of shipping. A solitary ship at the mercy of the waves and storms of the high seas became a favourite simile of the biblical writers (cf. Ps. 104: 25–26; Pr. 23:34; 30:18–19; 31:14 passim). Ezekiel's lament over Tyre (ch. 27) includes a full description of a Phoenician merchant vessel, and he compares the fate of the city to a storm-wrecked ship. Terms for many of the different parts of a boat are mentioned in this chapter, which refers to planks made of fir trees from Senir, the mast of cedar of Lebanon, the oars of oaks of Bashan and the deck of pines

745
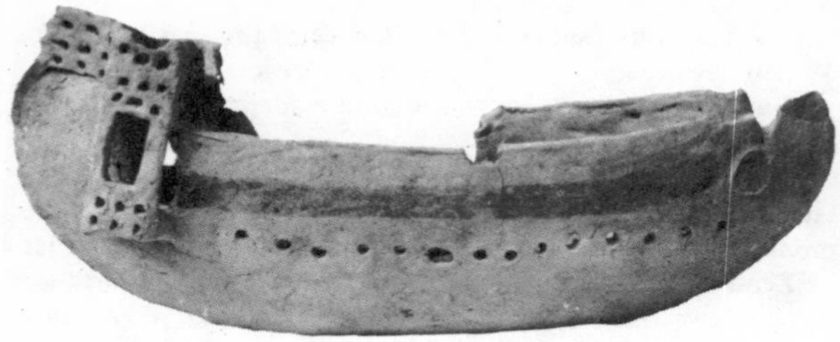

746
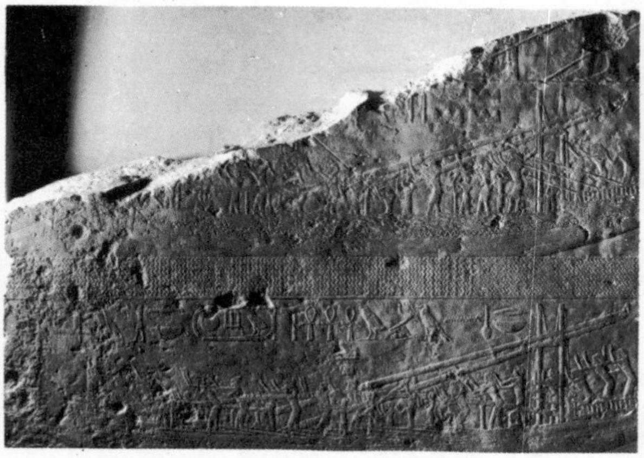

747

from the coast of Cyprus (27:5–6). However, the description seems to be a poetic synthesis of a merchant vessel (driven by a single sail) and a fighting galley powered by oarsmen with a small auxiliary sail. Thus the crew are listed as rowers, pilots, mariners and men of war.

Evidence of Archaeology: *Egypt:* A jug dating from the 4th mill. BCE (around 3500 BCE) was decorated with a picture of a sailing boat with a high poop and stern and a single mast and sail in the rear. As early as the period of the Old Kingdom of Egypt* (2700–2200 BCE) timber was being imported from the Syrian coast for shipbuilding (see Phoenicia*). The annals of Pharaoh Senefru (2650 BCE) refer to some 40 boats, 63 metres long, while the records of Pharaoh Sahure (app. 2500 BCE) picture captives being

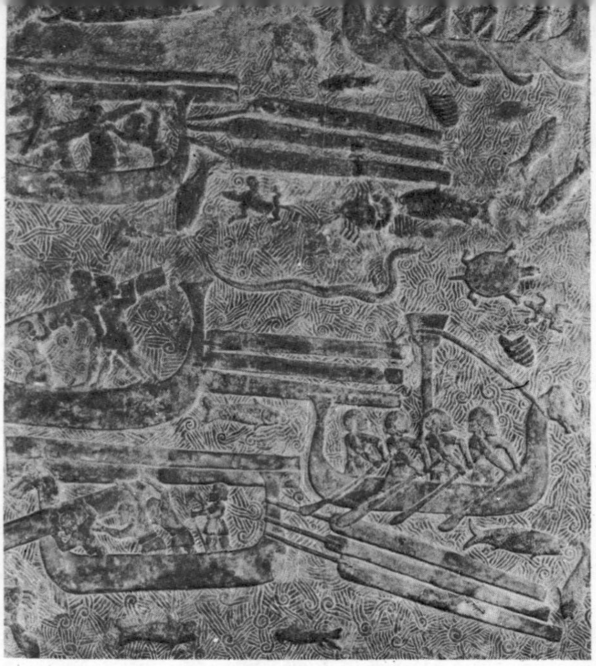
748

transported in boats with three rudders, their sails lowered. Pharaoh Pepi II (2325 BCE) has left an account of an invasion of Palestine from the sea, in which he landed his troops near Mount Carmel. However, of far greater importance than any picture or description are the remains of actual boats discovered in the Cheops pyramid at Sakkarah. The boat entombed with the great Pharaoh was about 40 metres long, made of wood, coated with mats of reeds and with a deck for the carriage of goods. The facade of the pyramid revealed the remains of five other boats.

Many important discoveries of boats belonging to the Intermediate and Middle Kingdoms (2100–1800 BCE) have also been made in Egypt. In No Amun (11th dynasty, 2135–2000 BCE) a number of models of boats were found. These mainly represented river boats used for transportation on the Nile, provided with a sail for use in sailing upstream and oars for the downward journey. Most of them, like the one pictured (**745**), had special steering oars for the pilot at the helm and a small cabin for the crew in the stern. In the 3rd mill. BCE, some small Egyptian boats did begin to make the journey from the Nile to Phoenicia* and Byblos, following the line of the coast (**746**).

It has been pointed out (by R.D. Barnett) that the documents of this period refer to boats by the name "r b n t", i.e. Byblos boats, Byblos being the main Phoenician port from which most of the goods exported to Egypt were shipped (see Phoenicia*). However, it is not certain whether this title meant that the boats were actually made in Byblos or merely that they sailed from that port. R.D. Barnett thinks that at that time the Egyptians did not venture beyond the delta of the Nile and that sea navigation was all in Phoenician hands — the ships were built in Phoenician shipyards (Byblos, Arwad, Tyre) and were sailed by mixed Phoenician and Egyptian crews.

Sea-going trade was developed by the Phoenicians, Egyptians and Cretans towards the end of the 2nd mill. BCE, first using oared galleys, then ships with a single sail. The leaders in this development were the Phoenicians* (for details, see article), but they were not the only mariners of the ancient world. Sea-worthy sailing boats were developed in Egypt during the New Kingdom (15th–12th cs. BCE)

during which time a new type of boat, the "Keftiu-boats" (i.e. Cretan style boats) made their appearance. An Egyptian relief from Medinet Habu, dated to the 12th c. BCE, shows Philistine warships with one deck (**661**). The boats were flat, with a raised poop and stern as their only protection against the waves. Egyptian boats of this period, which continued the ancient trade between Egypt and Phoenicia, were equipped with a lower bank of oarsmen and a single curved sail. Such boats carried the timber which the Egyptian, Wen-Amun, was sent to buy from Phoenicia* in the 11th c. BCE.

The main obstacles to developing sea transport were the lack of navigational devices, the small size of the vessels and their primitive sails and steering. Sea travel was limited to the summer months when the sea was generally quiet and visibility good (March to October).

The Tel el-Amarna* Akkadian-Egyptian dictionary (ca. 1400 BCE) translates the Akkadian term for ship, "ellippu" by the Canaanite "'anâyi" (equivalent to the biblical "oniyah"). The former word is not Semitic, but comes from Indo-Iranian roots meaning a boat steered in the open sea. From this, R.D. Barnett concludes that the reference is also to the Keftiu boats. Drawings of these boats, with exaggeratedly long poops ending in a horse's head, decorate many Mycenaean objects, while a more detailed picture of the same boat appears on the walls of the Palace of Ramses III (ca. 1190 BCE). They are very similar to Phoenician boats of biblical times and are also pictured in a number of Assyrian reliefs (**747**). Boats like these may (in R.D. Barnett's opinon) have been the original of the biblical "Oniyot Tarshish" (Ships of Tarshish). (This scholar identifies Tarshish as Tarsus in Cilicia, a rich source of pine and cedar timbers which played an important part in the spread of multi-oared boats through the Mediterranean. An earlier scholar, Farr, had already pointed out that "tarsus" meant "oars" among the Greeks.) The best evidence for the appearance of "Ships of Tarsus" comes from the reliefs of Shalmaneser III (858–824 BCE) showing the people of Tyre fleeing from their captured city in boats, while a relief has recently been discovered in Sargon II's palace in Khorsabad (721–705 BCE) showing a cargo boat laden with timber (**748**). In both cases the boats are shown with high sterns carved in the form of a horse's head. They were provided with oars, but also with a sail on a tall mast, on top of which was the crow's nest for the lookout man. These vessels were the models for the war fleets which the Greeks began to develop some time later. No Phoenician relief of their boats has so far been discovered, but in the reliefs of Sennacherib (704–681 BCE), high, two-and three-decked warships with tall masts and sails and high poops, are pictured. The oars were manned by 15 to 25 sailors on either side of the lower deck, while the soldiers sat on the upper deck (**747**).

The Greek Fleet: During the 8th and 7th cs. BCE the Greek fleet came to dominate the Mediterranean. At first, biremes or pentakonter (ships with fifty oars) were used both for trading and for war, but after the 6th c. BCE, the two functions were separated and the Mediterranean became the home of tall, heavy, slow cargo boats and the slender, low-lying, fast warships. The merchant ship was designed to carry its cargo long distances, sailing both by night and day, whereas the warships were built for speed and ease of manoeuvre. The length to width ratio of the warships was 7:1; of the cargo boats, 4:1.

The Greeks mainly used the trireme (**749**) and this became the standard warship of the ancient world from the 6th to the 3rd c. BCE. It was a light boat with three banks of oars and no deck, often carrying a sail, and with a speed of 4–5 knots under normal conditions. There is no clear evidence as to how the oarsmen were arranged. It used to be assumed that they sat in three ranks, one above the other. Now, however, it has been suggested that three oarsmen, each pulling a separate oar, sat together on a bench.

At the end of the 4th c. BCE, a new type, the quinquereme, made its appearance, reputedly on the initiative of Dionysus I of Syracuse, and the type remained in use in the Hellenistic and Roman fleets. Its construction was similar to that of the trireme but it had more oars and, according to Polybius (I, 26, 7; 2nd c. BCE), it carried a crew of 300 men besides the sailors. The seating arrangement of the oarsmen of the quinquereme is not known, but it was apparently made up of groups of five men pulling together on one big oar.

Cargo Boats: Another type of boat is the Greek cargo vessel, pictured very clearly on this sarcophagus (**750**) found near Sidon (2nd c. CE) which is much like similar representations and actual remains found in Italy. The boat is without a deck, its smooth hull partly submerged. The stern is carried up into a deck with a crow's nest at the top for the lookout man. The stern also carried a statue of the ship's patron god or goddess. The poop is lengthened into a swan's neck, with a gangway for docking when at anchor. Heavy in front

749

750

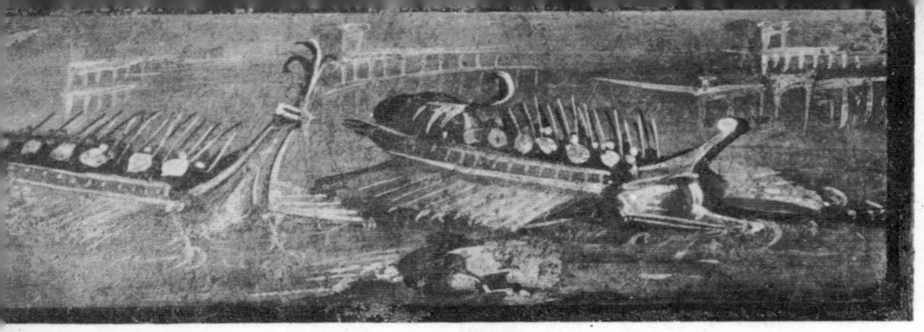

751

752

and light at the back, the boat was made to run with the sea. Merchant ships of this kind had a big square sail to which an additional frontal mast and sail were later added. The Romans built ships with two or three masts and sails. Such boats normally travelled at about 3–4 knots. They varied in size. In the 2nd c. CE, an "Alexandria" is recorded as of 3100 tons and an "Isis" of 3250 tons, but these were extraordinarily large. Most of the boats were about 50 tons, perhaps 30 yards long. The number of passengers they could carry depended on their size, most of them handling only a few dozen people. Josephus gives an account of the wreck of a boat carrying 600 people (Biography, 3). The boat in which Paul was wrecked on Malta is recorded in Acts (27:37) as carrying 276 persons. However, this figure is reduced by many authorities, ancient and modern, to 76 only. The boats were propelled by the sails. The only oars (in Paul's boat) were those used as rudders (27:40) from the stern. There are a number of contemporary accounts confirming the description in Acts. (Two rudder paddles served as the universal method of steering until about the 12th c. CE.) Apparently, in case of a storm, the frame of the boat was strengthened by binding chains or ropes around it ("undergird the ship", Ac. 27:17). Cargoes were carried, usually in large pottery jars loaded on the decks or into the hold. Sails might be made of linen or hides (Pliny the Elder, Nat. Hist. 19).

With big single sails and no keel, it was impossible to guide the boat into the wind while battling the waves on shore. This was particularly troublesome when leaving the Syrian coast to sail westwards, for the prevailing wind there comes from the west. Accordingly, boats had to keep close to the coast, taking what advantage they could from the breeze that blows from the land to the sea early in the morning (Ac. 27:4–8). Developments during the Roman period made it possible to sail directly from the ports of Greece and Rome to Alexandria. From the Red Sea ports they sailed to India, making use of newly discovered knowledge of the monsoon, the favourable weather and trade winds.

Travel in the Roman Empire: The establishment of the Roman empire and "Pax Romana" throughout much of the known world, together with the vastly improved systems of roads and communications which the Romans created, resulted in a great increase in travel. No restrictions were placed on the movement of travellers and journeys within and between the provinces of the empire became much easier and more frequent. There were Roman colonies in the provinces and Syrian settlements in Italy. This background explains the relative ease with which Paul was able to travel through Asia Minor and the eastern European provinces. Travel under the Romans was attended by fewer difficulties and dangers than at any previous time, but ancient hazards survived and the traveller faced many hardships (see Paul*; Roads*), for bad inns, highway robbers and shipwrecks remained a commonplace of a traveller's life for many centuries. See this fresco from Pompei (**751**) and mosaic from Ostia (**752**), the port of Rome.

Jewish Shipping of the Graeco-Roman Period: The conquests of the Hasmoneans* (as explained in the article on Trade*: Hellenistic to Roman Periods) at last brought the Jews an outlet to the sea. Jaffa was annexed by Simon the Hasmonean in 142 BCE and thereafter maritime trade and shipping were warmly encouraged. Alexander Jannai stamped an anchor onto his coins in visible proof of this policy and in celebration of his victories over the earlier Hellenistic rulers of the coastal towns. Typically, most of the coins of this type were found in and around Jaffa. In fact, maritime symbols had been very common on the coins of Phoenician and Jewish coastal towns ever since the end of the Persian period.

A fresco showing a warship attacking a merchant ship, and another warship found in a recently unearthed tomb of the Hasmonean period in Jerusalem, adds further evidence of the Hasmoneans' maritime activity. Also dating from the 2nd c. BCE is a stone engraving from Maresha, showing a sailing boat with one bank of oars and two anchors dropped from the stern.

Herod* continued and developed this maritime policy. The port of Caesarea which he built was considered not only the best on the coast of Palestine, but the greatest port of the area, second only to Alexandria. Caesarea was much used in the vast grain trade between Rome and Egypt, the granary of Rome. For a few months every year, storms forced the grain ships to sail along the coast of Palestine, and this fact became of great importance when the Jews were fighting the Romans almost a century later (see below). Herod apparently celebrated the completion of the building of Caesarea by the issue of a coin stamped with an anchor. Another Herodian coin carries an anchor on the obverse, with a warship on the reverse. Josephus records that Herod built a war fleet to aid Agrippa, Augustus' commander (Ant. 16, 2, 2).

When the Jews rebelled against Rome in 66 CE, the procurator, Cestius Gallus, began his campaign by destroying Jaffa. A little later he was defeated by the Jews and fled the country (see Rome and the Jews*) and for the next two years (66–68 CE) the Jews were again in full possession of the town and its port. According to Josephus (Wars 3, 9:2–3) the Jews used their opportunity to build boats and attack the ships carrying grain to Rome. This was such a serious threat to the Roman economy and food supply that Vespasian, the Roman commander, was forced to detach a section of the army with which he was besieging Jotapata in Galilee and send it to reduce Jaffa. The Jews escaped to their boats, but a storm wrecked the whole fleet on the rocks along the coast. Those who escaped drowning (some 4,200 men) were killed by the Romans.

The victory was very significant for the Romans. Ships' poops were carried in commemoration in Vespasian's victory parade (Wars 7, 5, 5) and all the Flavian Caesars issued appropriately stamped coins to celebrate the victory. One of these, inscribed "Judaea Navalis" shows Jews at the feet of Caesar, who stands with his right foot resting on the poop of a wrecked warship, holding a statue of Nike (goddess of victory) in his hands. Another coin was issued with the inscription "Victoria navalis". The Jewish rebels against Trajan (see Bar-Kochba*) also planned to disrupt the Roman navy's line of communication with the east, but failed. During the Bar-Kochba* revolt, an officer who distinguished himself in some naval victory over the Jews was decorated by the Romans, but no details of the engagement are known.

It is unlikely that the 1st and 2nd c. CE defeats brought Jewish sea-going traditions to an end. Jewish settlements prospered in Galilee and on the northern coast; fishing and sea-faring remained among the occupations of their inhabitants. That this was so is supported by the evidence of a relief recently discovered in the Jewish cemetery at Beth-Shearim which shows two merchant ships dating from the 3rd and 4th cs. CE. This situation did not last in later Byzantine times, and it came to an end in the 6th c. CE.

SLAVERY. — *Outline: Causes of Enslavement Recognized by the Bible:* 1. *War;* 2. *Self-Sale;* 3. *Sale of Minors;* 4. *Punishment of Thieves;* 5. *Minors Born in Slavery. Biblical Legislation Concerning Slaves; Legal and Social Status of Slaves in the Near East; Attitudes towards Slaves; Limitations to Enslavement; Life-Long Slaves; Female Slaves; Social Position of Israelite Slaves; Position in the Economy; State Slaves; Runaway Slaves; Slave Traffic; Slavery in the New Testament.*

A slave is one who is the property or chattel of another. This definition holds for Israel and the whole Near East in biblical times. Deprived of all liberty, the slave was legally a commodity that could be used or misused, bought or sold, leased or exchanged. The slave had no name, family or genealogy. He was a helpless part of the social and economic system. In this sense there were slaves in Israel, and some were Israelite. The existence of slavery is also presupposed by the laws about emancipation (see below).

Certain writers, however, have denied that real slavery existed in Israel and they justify this view by comparing Israel with Near Eastern or Graeco-Roman antiquity and its enormous groups of slaves. Moreover, in biblical tradition the slave was protected by religious sanctions. A better understanding of the situation may be arrived at by examining abstract legal definitions on the character of slavery in the Bible (and the flexible vocabulary used in defining slaves in antiquity) and then comparing them with operating factors. Important differences emerge, as will be seen.

Causes of Enslavement Recognized by the Bible:

1. **War:** Prisoners of war spared on the battlefield were made slaves. In their conquest of Palestine, the Israelites enslaved many of their Canaanite opponents and the practice continued in later times (Nu. 21:26 ff; Jud. 5:30; I Sam. 4:9; II Ch. 28:8; Jl. 3:3 ff). The law of Dt. 20:16 dealing with the conquest of towns in the Promised Land forbade the capture of prisoners. The population of the towns which surrendered outside the Holy Land were condemned to forced labour, which is not slavery. Ample evidence for the enslavement of war prisoners can be found throughout the history of antiquity. The Amarna letters* (14th c. BCE) tell of war captives being sent "as tribute" by Syrian and Palestinian princes to their Egyptian overlords. II Ch. 28:8–15 contains an explicit prohibition against reducing fellow Israelites to slavery through capture in war, which indicates that the custom was not unheard of, but it was rejected by right-thinking men.

2. **Self-Sale:** People driven from the soil by war, famine or economic disaster might sell themselves into slavery as the only alternative to starvation. The majority of the people in this category were defaulting debtors (Lv. 25:39–54), driven to selling first their children, then themselves. Creditors had the right to seize insolvent debtors and sell them as slaves, although Jewish law limited the period of their enslavement to six years (see below). In II K. 4:1–2, the widow of a deceased debtor whose children were threatened with seizure in payment of the debt appealed successfully to Elisha. Prophetic literature is full of references to the helpless condition of these slaves (Neh. 5:5; Is. 50:1; Am. 2:6).

3. **Sale of Minors:** Parents unable to meet their debts or support their children could sell them (II K. 4:1–7; Neh. 5:5; Is. 50:1). This practice was similar to the sale of boys and girls evidenced by the Nuzi tablets of the 15th c. BCE. Besides the unconditional sale of the children, there was a conditional form for daughters, whereby the purchaser contracted to give them in marriage to either a free-born man or a slave when the girls reached puberty. In Nuzi, contracts of this type were in the form of sale-adoption agreements whereby the parents received a stated sum as a "present" and the girl (very occasionally a boy) was "adopted" by the purchaser as a "daughter-in-law" with her status in the purchaser's home stipulated. The parallel situation among the Hebrews is described, with legal safeguards, in Exodus 21:7–11.

4. **Punishment of Thieves:** An Israelite convicted of stealing and unable to make restitution and pay the fine would be sold as a slave (Ex. 22:3).

5. **Minors Born in Slavery:** The children of a Hebrew slave and a wife given him by his master remained the master's property when the father was set free (Ex. 21:4); provision is made in this case, however, for the man to choose slavery for life rather than leave his family (Ex. 21:5–6).

Non-Hebrew slaves might be bought outright to serve for life (Ex. 12:44; Lv. 25:44–45).

Biblical Legislation Concerning Slaves: Regulations concerning the release of slaves appear in three different places in the Pentateuch (Ex. 21:2–11, 26–27; Lv. 25:39–55; Dt. 15:12–18). Other laws of the Pentateuch refer to slaves in reference to holidays (Ex. 20:10; 23:12) or to sex transgressions (Lv. 19:20).

Israelite law was not the same at all periods. These three groups of biblical regulations vary as to the slave's term of service, provisions for his release, and conditions under which he worked. Many scholars hold that these changes reflect a development in social attitudes and legal enactments regarding slaves, from the days of Moses to the Exile. However, opinions differ about the chronological order of legal material in the Pentateuch. For example one school of thought regards the provisions regarding slaves in Leviticus as the latest of the three, another believes it to be the oldest, and a third maintains that it is a late compilation around a nucleus of archaic material.

Attitudes Towards Slaves: In Mesopotamian law, the slave was his master's property, with hardly any rights, and subject to special criminal legislation which imposed more severe penalties on him than on the free-born for similar transgressions (cf. Hammurabi Code, para. 203–205 or articles 93–99 of the Hittite law). While the Pentateuch also treated the slave as a chattel, it nevertheless was more humane than any other Near Eastern code.

Not only was there no special punitive legislation applicable to slaves, but the law protected them from abuse by their owners. A slave whose eye was put out or his teeth knocked out by his master was set free (Ex. 21:26–27). A master whose slave dies directly as the result of a beating shall be punished (Ex. 21:20). In the Samaritan* Pentateuch, the master is to be put to death. On the other hand, if the slave survived for a day or two, the master would escape punishment for "the slave is his money" (Ex. 21:21) — a phrase more appropriate to the concepts of other Near Eastern laws. The beating was assumed to be disciplinary. Corporal punishment of slaves and children was commonly accepted. According to the Hammurabi code, for instance, compensation for injury, maiming or death of the slave caused by a third party is paid to the owner, not the slave. The only biblical parallel is the provision (Ex. 21:32) that if an ox kills a slave by goring, the master of the slave shall be compensated by the owner of the ox to the extent of thirty shekels of silver, apparently the current price of a replacement. This was a much lighter punishment than in the case of a repeated goring of a free man (Ex. 21:28–31).

According to the Code of Hammurabi, a workman earned about ten shekels a year (see Weights and Measures*). If this was approximately the case in Palestine in Israelite times, then the difficult text in Dt. 15:18, "for at half the cost of a hired servant he has served you six years" is explained as a simple statement of fact. The price of a slave was half that of six years wages for a free workman (see Law*, I, II).

Limitations to Enslavement: Mesopotamian law provided for a "release by adoption" arrangment under which a slave would be set free on condition that he continued to provide for his master as long as he lived.

Exodus (21:2) and Deuteronomy (15:12) provide that the Hebrew slave shall be freed after six years, without further payment. (The Hammurabi code freed defaulting debtors after four years.) Leviticus 25:40, 54 provides for his release in the Jubilee Year (which came every 49 years, i.e. seven times the sabbatical cycle; see Calendar*). This law was never applied. Normally, a Hebrew slave served for six years, a foreigner for life.

Apart from slaves who had been injured (as above), a free-born girl sold into slavery under a conditional contract with a marriage clause might be freed if the contract was not observed (Ex. 21:7–11). A Hebrew debtor enslaved to a non-Israelite might be redeemed by a relative "purchasing" his freedom from the master (Lv. 25:47–53).

Life-long Slaves: Four categories of slaves could not be manumitted: a. a slave voluntarily refusing to leave his master and his own family, or who, perhaps, preferred the economic security of his servitude (Ex. 21:5–6); b. offspring of slaves given a wife during their enslavement (Ex. 21:4); c. maids sold for life (Ex. 21:7); d. foreigners (e.g. Canaanites; Lv. 25:44–46).

Leviticus makes a very clear distinction between the 'ebed ibri", the Hebrew slave, and the non-Israelite "ebed", for whom there was no freedom in the seventh, or Jubilee, year and who lacked the legal protection given to enslaved Israelites. The Israelites, therefore, could not become slaves permanently; the law allowed them to be "sold" as slaves for a limited time and under certain safeguards. It seems very probable that the Hebrew slave was not regarded as a chattel but as a person under restraint.

Female Slaves: Female slaves formed a special category and enjoyed a different status from that of the men. They played an important role in their master's household, ministered to personal needs, and in the early period even bore him children (Gn. 16:1 ff; 30:3–12). Their master arranged their marriages at his discretion, the sole proviso being that if a man bought a female slave as a wife for himself or his son, he could not change his mind and sell her to another family (not to a "foreign people" as mistakenly translated), but must honour his obligations to her, as indicated.

Unlike Ex. 21, the rules concerning slavery in Deuteronomy do not make a distinction between male and female in the treatment of slaves. Women were to be freed in the 7th year just like men (Dt. 15:12). The later priestly law of Lv. 25 makes no reference to slave-concubines and they appear to be unknown by the time of Jeremiah. Nehemiah (5:5) speaks of the violation of Jewish girls by their masters but does not mention their being taken as concubines.

Social Position of Israelite Slaves: Slavery was the curse of the ancient world; to be a slave was a misfortune, often a tragedy. However, so long as their status was not irrevocable and they could, at least theoretically, look forward to emancipation, they were members of a depressed class, but not a caste. While they remained slaves they wore the insignia of their status. In Babylonia, they had to wear a visible property mark on their bodies. In Egypt, slaves were branded with fire. A Hebrew slave who voluntarily submitted to perpetual slavery had his ear pierced with an awl (Ex. 21:5–6); possibly a tag was then inserted. In addition, or instead, the master's name might be tattooed on a prominent place, his hip, neck or wrist (Is. 44:5). Hebrew law permitted maltreatment of slaves by their masters (see above; Attitudes Towards Slavery), who were not specifically punished except in cases of excessive or premeditated brutality. But their position in relation to Hebrew society in general was protected by law. The slave was to keep the Sabbath and celebrate the festivals (Ex. 20:10; 23:12), participate in the family's sacrifices and, provided he had been circumcized, eat the Passover meal (Ex. 12:44).

Unlike parallel legislation in the ancient Near East, Old Testament slavery law has a strongly ethical character. In spite of his legal status as a chattel, the actual position of a slave was more often that of a member of the family, likely in the absence of other heirs to inherit from his master. The close relationship between slavery and adoption shows that the status of slaves was similar to that of children of the house. There is a parallel in this connection between the Nuzi customs and the Genesis account (15:2) of Abraham's relations with his steward (and slave), Eliezer (Gn. 24).

Position in the Economy: Compared to slavery in other lands in antiquity and, even more so, in the later Graeco-Roman period (see below), private slavery in biblical Israel was limited, as shown above. The corresponding lack of class distinction of biblical days is confirmed by the recorded numbers of slaves owned. One of Saul's officials, Ziba (in II Sam. 9:10 he was a freeman attached to his master's service) had 15 sons and 20 slaves. The 42,360 Jews who returned from exile in Babylonia brought with them 7,337 slaves (Neh. 7:66–67) and in both this and other texts these people are always defined as "menservants and maidservants".

State Slaves: Slaves recruited from prisoners of war were regarded as the permanent property of the victor (Dt. 20:10–14; 21:10; Jud. 5:30; see above, Causes of Enslavement: War). Economically these were the most important class of slaves. Technically owned by the king, they were state slaves, subject to forced labour (corvée), used in Babylonia, Assyria and the city states of Syria and Palestine (see Assyrian illustration, **753**) for the construction of roads, canals, fortresses, temples and palaces, for tilling the crown lands and working in royal factories and flour mills, for spinning and wine-making (see illus. Agriculture*). Evidence from this comes from a letter from the king of Taanach to the Egyptian court (see Amarna letters*) and from the Mesha Stone (see Moab*; Inscriptions*).

The development of a centralized authority under David and Solomon was accompanied by a large increase in state slaves in Israel, especially during Solomon's reign when they became a major economic asset. He made use of them in his building programme (I K. 9:15–21; II Ch. 8:1–8). They provided the essential cheap, unskilled labour force for the mining and metal industries of the Negeb and were shipped to Ophir (see Ships and Navigation*), accompanying the Phoenician mariners of King Hiram (I K. 9:27; II Ch. 8:18; 9:10). Known appropriately as "Solomon's slaves", they were recruited from war captives and from the descendants of the Canaanites and formed a slave class which remained in existence right through the monarchy, "and so they are to this day" (I K. 9:21).

Slave Traffic: Traffic in slaves was general throughout the Near East. Amos (1:6, 9) condemned Gaza and Tyre for trafficking in slaves, and Joel (3:6) castigates Tyre for the sale of Judeans, along with the peoples of Asia Minor. Nevertheless, Lv. 25:44–45 permits Israelites to buy slaves of foreign birth.

The Phoenicians who were the most important of the merchants serving Israel also dealt in slaves. In the Hellenistic age, slave dealers followed the armies of Antiochus Epiphanes (see Hasmoneans*) to buy the Jews he expected to take as prisoners (I Mac. 3:41; II Mac. 8:10–11). The account also provides interesting data about the price of slaves in those days. When the Greeks offered these foreign traders ninety captives for a talent (3,000 or 3,600 shekels) they inferred that the supply would be so great as to bring the price down to 33–40 shekels a head, comparable to the 30 shekels of earlier times, but a very low figure judging from contemporary papyri.

After the Bar Kochba* revolt, thousands of Jews, captured by Hadrian, were sold in the famous Hebron* slave market at prices below those of cattle. The Jewish detestation of enslavement is illustrated by the desperate decision of the defeated defenders of Masada who killed themselves, their wives and children in 73 CE, rather than be enslaved by the Romans.

Slavery in the New Testament: All later legislation in Israel and the teaching of the Rabbis tended towards greater humanity towards slaves. The Rabbis' insistence that the slave should not be given tasks that were too heavy or degrading (like Samson turning the mill in Jud. 16:21) was in direct contrast to Graeco-Roman law and practice

753

regarding slaves. In Italy they far outnumbered free men, and although many were educated and entrusted with great responsiblities, the ancient slave laws which regarded them as the personal property of their master remained.

Their significance as a class in contemporary society is suggested by Paul's reference (I Co. 12:13) to the two categories: "slave and free"; the point was that in the church community there was to be no distinction of rank or place between slave and free. Paul, like Jesus, never condemned the institution (Mt. 18:25; Lk. 17:7 ff). Indeed, practically every one of the epistles of Paul and Peter advises "servants" even when converted to Christianity to be content with their position and to obey their masters, while masters are urged to be considerate towards their slaves (I Co. 7:21 ff).

Paul never sought to make free men out of slaves, but good slaves out of bad ones (Eph. 6:5–9). The implication, however, is that there is a basic equality characterized by the word "brother". All are to be servants (slaves) of Christ. The classic expression of his attitude comes from the letter to Philemon, where a converted slave is returned to him "as a brother" — but not as a freed man. It is clear from I Timothy 6 and from the subsequent history of the Church that Christians of good standing and high morality owned slaves.

The Essenes and Dead Sea Sectaries* repudiated slavery altogether. This is a logical result of their adherence to a communal life of material equality. It was, perhaps, made easier by their remoteness and isolation from the rest of the world where slavery was an essential and unquestioned element in society. Jewish Christians in Jerusalem also held property in common and probably, like the Essenes, had no slaves.

SONG OF SONGS, BOOK OF (Canticles). — The Song of Songs is the first of the five books included in the Hebrew Bible as "Hagiographa" (Writings). The book is a collection of erotic lyrics and popular love songs, most of which are incomplete. Some are mere fragments. The whole collection has been arbitrarily divided into eight chapters or canticles. Its secular nature made it difficult for Jewish scholars to give it a position in the Canon, but tradition ascribed it to Solomon and apparently its unsurpassed beauty led early Talmudic and mediaeval interpreters to present it as an allegory of the love of God for his bride, Israel. The Church fathers also had difficulties over it, but they interpreted the Song of Songs as an allegory of Christ and the Church, described as his bride.

This allegorical interpretation is still followed in some circles, but the verses reveal so open a joy in human delights and human love, that to read the book as an allegory of divine affection imposes a considerable strain on credulity.

During the 19 c. CE a new interpretation was offered according to which the book was a series of poems on a dramatic theme of the love of King Solomon for a country girl, Shulamit, who herself loved a shepherd. This "Aesthetic-Dramatic Theory" allowed for several actors: the maiden, the king and the shepherd boy, with a chorus of "Daughters of Jerusalem" and the king's companions, and a romantic plot of the girl resisting the king's advances and finally being released from his harem to rejoin her beloved shepherd.

As with the allegorical commentators, the single and sufficient objection to this theory is that it gains no support at all from the actual content of the book, which contains no dramatic development and no remotely appropriate sequence.

More recently (beginning with the archaeological discoveries made from 1910 onwards), other scholars tried to find a parallel to the Song of Songs in sacred weddings of the gods in ancient fertility religions (see, e.g. Canaan: Gods and Idols, Cult*). T.J. Meek identified a series of liturgical texts in the Song of Songs which he connected with the worship of Tammuz-Adonis (Ba'al; see Babylon*). This, however, remains a largely hypothetical reconstruction. The cult of Tammuz has not been established for Israel or even Canaan, as yet. The "wailing of Tammuz" by mourning women discussed by Ezekiel (8:14) is related to Mesopotamian cults and liturgies and is not associated with Canaan, nor with pre-Exilic life in Israel. The more recent translations of the Ugarit* texts have revealed further discrepancies between Canaanite religious practices and the material in the Song of Songs. Many scholars do not interpret the poems of Ugarit as support for a current theory about the sacred marriage between the god and his consort.

A fourth theory put forward by J.R. Budde (in 1898) regarded the Song of Songs as a collection of wedding songs, similar to those sung at Palestinian and Syrian village weddings. In fact in the period of the Mishnah* and the Talmud, wedding guests used to dance before the bride (Ketubot 16b; 17a) and sing verses from the Song of Songs. Rabbi Akiba strongly opposed this custom (Tosephta Sanhedrin 12:1), although his allegorical interpretation of the book was largely responsible for its being retained in the Canon in the 1st–2nd cs. CE. It is not likely that the Song of Songs was originally composed for use at weddings. Some of the poems (like the search for the beloved or the description of Solomon's couch; 3:9–11) have nothing to do with people's weddings, while elements which are common to all Syrian-Palestinian wedding songs are missing from this collection.

Many scholars, however, regard the Song of Songs as a collection of Hebrew love poems, including bridal songs, with many similarities to the love songs of every other people. (The early Egyptians serenaded lovers as "brother and sister" and used similes of harts and horses much like the Song of Songs). It is evident in any case that the poems were written at different times. A nucleus of the material in the book comes from the time of Solomon and it is quite possible that the basis for the anthology was a cycle of love poems around a romantic episode in Solomon's life. Whether or not this is the case, many of the poems may have originated during the reign of Solomon, or at least early in the monarchy. One of the poems speaks of the loved one as "beautiful as Tirzah . . . comely as Jerusalem" (6:4). It has been suggested that the original use of these words can be dated to a time shortly after Solomon's reign when Tirzah was a capital of the northern kingdom. (They could scarcely refer in this sense to the city which was later destroyed and, in 876 BCE, replaced by Samaria*.) The other places named, Gilead, Lebanon, Sennir, Hermon, the pools of Heshbon by the Gate of Beth-Rabbim in Moab, would only fit one of the periods of the kingdom's greatest extent and glory.

R. Gordis has taken the linguistic analysis further to suggest that a large part of the songs, if not all of them, are of northern origin, composed before the exile of the ten northern tribes. On different linguistic grounds, other scholars have dated the book's composition to as late as the post-Exilic period. Evidences of later usage, however, can all be explained by the fact that these were popular songs which lived in the mouths of the people and absorbed contemporary turns of speech belonging to times much later than their original composition. All the poems may be of quite early origin and, in their present edition, it is difficult to assign them to a later period.

Essentially they are a poetic expression of overwhelming, passionate love between man and woman, set mainly against a pastoral background, although Jerusalem figures prominently. The Song of Songs represents the refining of a literary art which had its origins in the early period of Jewish history. It remains, for all times, a paean of praise to youth and love and life.

SYNAGOGUE, THE. — *Outline: I. Origins and Organization: Origins; Ma'amadot; The Purpose of the Synagogue; Reading the Torah; Prayer; Public Assembly; The Site of a Synagogue; Organization; Design. II. Palestinian Synagogues: Jerusalem; Synagogue of the Freedmen; New Testament Evidence; The Synagogue of Caesarea; Galilean Synagogues; Ark and Menorah; Capernaum; The Beth-Shearim Synagogue; Later Opposition. III. Synagogues of the Diaspora; Egypt; Dura-Europos; The Roman Empire.*

As a place of prayer and the reading and teaching of the Law, the synagogue has been a central institution of Jewry ever since the early days of the Second Temple.

I. ORIGINS AND ORGANIZATION: **Origins:** Its exact origins are obscure. Some scholars have tried to find evidence for its existence during Old Testament days, although the Hebrew for synagogue (Beth-Knesset, House of Assembly) is nowhere used. Psalm 74:8: "they have burnt thy sanctuary . . . they have burnt every meeting place of God . . ." uses the phrase "Mo'adei El" (meeting-place of God), which the early translators of the Bible, Symmachus and Aquilas (Onkeles) rendered by the Greek word "synagogue". Many scholars assign this psalm to the Maccabean period and maintain that the phrase refers to synagogues. To others, the date for the psalm seems too late and they explain the passage as referring to the destruction of the Temple in 587 BCE. Quite apart from the interpretation of this particular verse, it seems probable that synagogues as such did exist long before the time of the Maccabees.

An older Greek term "proseuche", meaning "place of worship" is also known from 3rd c. BCE Egyptian papyri, (cf. Inscriptions*). The same term is used in Ac. 16:13, referring to the "house of assembly" and "synagogue" of the Talmud. The synagogue as a building in which the community met for worship is mentioned some 50 times in the Gospels and Acts (Mt. 4:23 onwards; see Organization, below).

The destruction of the First Temple meant that sacrifice could no longer be offered, for this was only possible in Jerusalem itself. To fill the vacuum thus created, the Jews gathered together to read the Torah and to pray. Such meetings could not take the place of the Temple, but part of synagogue ritual was regarded as a symbolic sacrifice. For instance, morning and afternoon prayers were substituted for the continual burnt offerings in the Temple. There was, however, no question of displacing the Temple whose importance to the Jews can be seen in later ages (cf. Hasmoneans*),

Majority opinion today is that synagogues began in Babylon during the Exile*. Ezekiel and Ezra 8:15–20 are cited as evidence of common places of prayer there. An alternate view as to its origin, held by Professor Y. Baer, is that synagogues began in Palestine during the period between the First and Second Temples, when people met together on certain days for public worship, although without offering sacrifice.

There is nothing conclusive in the ancient texts. Any attempt at a precise date must be partly conjecture. Probably synagogues grew up gradually, in response to two factors: strict insistence on keeping a single sanctuary, while authorizing the establishment of places for prayer, if not sacrifice, outside Jerusalem; secondly, the prominent place of the Law* in education and the life of the community. Teaching has always been as important as prayer in the activities of the synagogue. It seems that during the time of Ezra and Nehemiah (see Restoration*), when so much emphasis was placed on learning the Torah and disseminating its teachings among the people, suitable places for the purpose may have existed. However, nowhere are synagogues expressly mentioned, nor has archaeology unearthed traces of synagogues dating from that period.

Ma'amadôt: There is another theory that the synagogue grew out of the ma'amadôt (groups functioning in rotation) of priests and laymen who met while the priests from their district were bringing the sacrifice to Jerusalem, according to the custom that groups of priests from different places took over the service of the Temple at fixed intervals.

Written evidence for the long-establishment of the synagogue comes from Josephus (Against Apion, Bk. II, 17); Philo (Life of Moses, III, 27) and a number of Talmudic sources. It is certain that by the 1st c. CE, synagogues had become established institutions wherever Jews lived, inside Palestine and elsewhere. The inscription of Theodotus (see below, Synagogue of the Freedmen) records the existence of a synagogue in Jerusalem on the Temple hill as early as the end of the 1st c. BCE, although the earliest actual relics of synagogues have been found in Egypt, not in Palestine (see below, Synagogues of the Diaspora).

The Purpose of the Synagogue: While the building in Jerusalem still stood, the Law governing the Temple rites was read in the synagogue by the Ma'amadot and thus ensured loyalty to and awareness of the Temple sacrifices and other services. After the Temple's destruction, this Law remained the synagogue's basic Scriptures and helped to keep alive hopes of the Temple's restoration. The daily synagogue services which replaced the Temple rites took place at the same times and bore the same names as the three daily Temple sacrifices.

The synagogue was in no sense the dwelling place of the deity. Indeed, as a place of worship it was a radical departure from anything the world had yet seen. Religious exercises were carried on there without the benefit of sacrifice, or a Holy of Holies, and without requiring the presence of a priest.

However, while the synagogue never took the place of the Temple, there was a gradual shift in emphasis. In the Temple, the central fact of worship so far as the lay participants were concerned was the ceremonial. (That this was not the intention can be seen from the teaching of the prophets, but it became the case.) In the synagogue, however, all the emphasis was on the Law. Regular study, discussion and practice of God's will was given an importance for the layman which was impossible in the different circumstances of the Temple. Reading and expounding the Torah was the most important of the synagogue's functions. The Christian custom of reading Holy Writ during church services suggests a similar long-established tradition within the synagogue. Later on, prayer came to the fore, but the two activities continued side by side.

More significantly, the synagogue was essentially a lay institution, in fact the greatest and most durable system of lay leadership in religious history. Any Jew could read the Torah, lead the congregation or, if gifted, speak to his comrades. Any ten Jews could form a "minian" (quorum) and organize a synagogue. If a priest were present, he was shown deference, but he had no essential role in the service. In contrast to the priest-controlled religious life of the Temple and of all pagan religions in antiquity, this was a unique and remarkable departure.

Reading the Torah: It was laid down by Ezra that the Torah must be read not only on Sabbaths and Festivals but also on Mondays and Thursdays. The whole Torah could thus be read through during one year or, according to an alternate programme, in three years. Where Hebrew was not sufficiently understood, the Torah was read sentence by sentence and immediately expounded. At first the exposition of the Law was in Aramaic. It is likely that the more expository translations, now called Pseudo-Jonathan and Palestinian, were older, while the Aramaic one now most widely used, called Onkelos (Aquilas) was of Babylonian origin and later date, when there was a stricter demand for faithful translations. The Targums to the Prophets, etc. are still expository (see Translations of the Bible*). After reading the "portion", a chapter of the prophets (Haftara) was chanted (see Ac. 13:15).

Side by side with the readings, the custom developed of preaching a sermon based on the salient point of the day's readings. The New Testament makes a number of references to the apostles travelling to various communities to preach in the synagogues (Ac. 16–18).

Prayer: Although a prescribed form of prayer was first written down in the time of Patriarch Simeon ben Gamaliel, after the destruction of the Temple (Berakhot 4:3–4), prayer was something that must have been known from much earlier times. Abraham, Hanna, Jeremiah and others prayed individually and the Book of Psalms was written partly for liturgical purposes. During the Hasmonean period, it appears from the Book of Daniel (6:13) that the custom of praying three times a day was already familiar.

Benedictions still in use, speaking hopefully of a resumption of the former ritual in a re-built Jerusalem, were obviously composed after the destruction of the Second Temple. The same period saw the formulation of the Malediction against the Mînîm (sectaries, heretics), aimed mainly at the Jewish Christians* who at first continued to frequent the synagogue, as well as other contemporary Jewish sectaries. The word "mînîm" was later replaced by "malshînîm" (slanderer) but the correct text of the prayer was found later in the Cairo Genizah (reliquary of damaged manuscripts).

Public Assembly: Apart from its main purposes, the synagogue also acted as a centre of Jewish community life. Collections for the needy were made here and sometimes distributed by the leaders on the spot. There is also evidence that, like gentile centres of worship, the synagogue was often the place in which slaves were freed. Guest houses for travellers and pools for ritual immersion would be erected nearby. The Inscription of Theodotus records that he built a guest house and pools near his synagogue.

The Site of a Synagogue: There were no special rules about the site or form of a synagogue. The sole obligation was that one must be built in every place where there were ten male Jews — or more. The building had to be placed so that worshippers faced Jerusalem. Usually they were built on heights (as in the old synagogue of Eshtamoa south of Hebron which is now a mosque), by the sea in coastal towns, or on the shores of streams or lakes (the synagogue at Hamat-Tiberias; see Ac. 16:13).

A building which had not originally been built as a synagogue might be adapted for the purpose. Once it had been consecrated, the synagogue was hallowed ground and reverent behaviour was demanded inside and towards it.

In general, it can be said that wherever a Jewish community flourished, a synagogue also existed, although, of course, there is not always archaeological evidence of the fact.

Organization: Synagogues were built from private contributions. When completed, they might belong to the individual but, more often, they became the corporate property of the community.

In Roman times, they were ruled by an Archisynagogos (ruler of the synagogue; see Ac. 18:8; Mk. 5:22; Lk. 8:41), who was the official head of the community. Beside him were other officers, "gerontes" (elders), patres synagogue and, in post-Talmudic times, a hazan. The hazan was originally an important Temple official and an eminent member of the community, bearing little relation to the precentor (cantor) who later inherited his title.

Design: Over the years changes in design took place. The early synagogues were very simple, perhaps in response to the austere principles of the first great teachers, although beautiful synagogues existed in the Alexandrian and Antiochan (early Christian) periods. There was no Ark and the Torah Scrolls were kept in a case which could be moved and might be lodged high up on the wall. During prayers it would be brought down and laid in a special, usually lower, place. As there was no sacramental focus, a basilica type of building was adopted, perhaps with a row of columns on the side of the entrance, and with benches along the walls. The floor was left free. The only ornament might be a frieze in relief decorating the façade, or in the later synagogues, an elaborate mosaic floor. Separate accommodation was made for women. In the 3rd c. CE this took the form of a gallery above the hall. This was also often decorated.

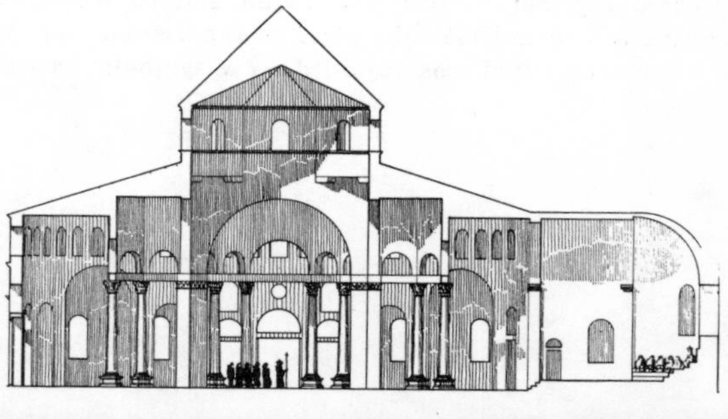

754

755

There was considerable variety in detail. Some of the basilicas consist of a single hall with the portico and doors on the long side. Others are a complex of more than ten rooms. According to J.W. Crowfoot, most of the larger churches in Syria, Palestine or Greece were also built on the ordinary Roman plan of a three-aisled basilica, like the church at Bostra, east of the Jordan, whose architecture and ground plan can be seen from the restoration illustrated in **754**.

II. PALESTINIAN SYNAGOGUES: From literary sources and archaeological discoveries, it is clear that there were synagogues all over Palestine.

Jerusalem: There is a reference in the Jerusalem Talmud (83:4) to "the four hundred and eighty synagogues in Jerusalem" quoted by Rabbi Joshua ben Levi. Another tradition (Ketubot 105:71) puts the number at 394.

Synagogue of the Freedmen: The Mishnah (Yomah 7:1; Satah 7:7–8) records that a synagogue stood in the Temple compound and this is confirmed by the Inscription of Theodotus, found at Mount Ophel in Jerusalem. This Inscription (**293**), written in Greek, records that Theodotos ben Vettenos, son and grandson of an archisynagogos, constructed the synagogue for the reading of the Law and the teaching of the commandments, and built an inn, chambers and water installations for housing needy travellers. The synagogue was apparently erected two generations before the destruction of the Temple, but no traces have been found of it. It is thought that the synagogues for people of the diaspora mentioned in Acts 6:9 (see Jewish Christians*: Stephen) may have belonged to this type and that the inscription itself comes from the Synagogue of the "Libertines" (Freedmen).

New Testament Evidence: The importance of the synagogue in the early days of Jewish Christianity* is recorded by the New Testament which mentions many by name: Ephesus, Antioch, Damascus, Thessalonica, Corinth, Athens and others. Josephus relates that the sacred copper vessels from the Temple were taken to the synagogue at Antioch at the time of Antiochus Epiphanes. Antioch was a large city with an important Jewish community. One of the first centres of Early Christianity* was established there (see Paul*).

758

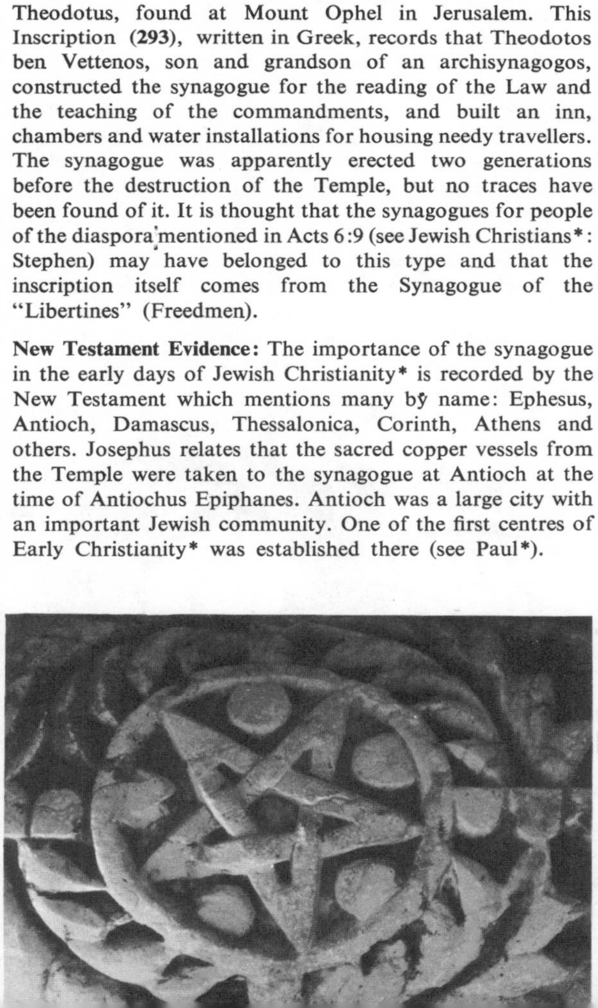

756

The Synagogue of Caesarea: This synagogue played an important role in the events leading up to the second Roman campaign which ended with the destruction of the Temple. A dispute broke out between the Jews and the Greeks over the question of the right of way to the synagogue (Josephus: Wars II, 14:4). Remains of a synagogue and inscriptions of the 3rd c. CE (see Caesarea*) were found during the excavations of Caesarea in 1961, possibly situated on the spot it occupied in Paul's time (see **114, 115**).

Galilean Synagogues: According to the Talmud (Berakhot 8:71), there were thirteen synagogues in Tiberias alone and Josephus mentions that one of them was of gigantic proportions and could accommodate a large assembly. After the Bar-Kochba* war, Tiberias was the capital of Galilee for a time, so the number is hardly surprising. A 4th c. CE synagogue has been uncovered at Hamat-Tiberias (**755**; mosaic **756**) and there seems to be a 1st c. CE synagogue under it. Second in importance to Tiberias was Sepphoris which also had several synagogues. A synagogue known as the "Knista degofna" (Vine Synagogue) was uncovered beneath a church. A similar case of converting a synagogue into a church was found at Jerash in Transjordan where a church had been built over an early 2nd c. CE synagogue.

The New Testament has made the synagogues of Capernaum (carving of ark, **757**) and Chorazin famous but although

757

759

760

rich architectural decorations were discovered there, both these and other synagogues were not built before the late 2nd and early 3rd cs. CE. They can nevertheless suggest the ones that must have preceded them, perhaps on the same sites.

Capernaum: Capernaum is situated on the northern shore of the Lake of Galilee. The white limestone of its synagogue contrasts sharply with the black basalt used for most of the city's buildings. The synagogue is a basilica with rows of columns supporting a women's gallery along three sides of the building. The entrance faces Jerusalem, with a main portico and two side doors. Inside, the floor is paved with flagstones with two benches, one behind the other, built against three walls. Men worshippers sat either on these or on mats in the central nave, facing the entrance. There were several windows in the walls, and a large open arch fitted with an iron grating above the central door. The pulpit ("bema") from which the lessons were read was found next to the pillars or platform in the front of the synagogue. The central feature was the Ark in which the scrolls of the Law were kept. To the east of the building was a trapezoid court with a portico. Notice the Star of David carved in stone (758). Photo 759 shows Pope Paul VI admiring the mosaic floor.

Ark and Menorah: It has been said that the synagogue was an imitation Temple. Although this must not be taken literally, it is true that is has preserved certain analogies in the symbolism of its construction. For instance, the Ark of the Law is usually (as in Chorazin and Bar'am, **761**) flanked by lions, presumably in analogy to the cherubim of the Temple, according to M. Avi-Yonah. In addition, the Temple's seven-branched candelabra (the Menorah **762**) also appears in most synagogues, either as an actual lamp-stand or in the decoration of the building. It is believed by some that the synagogue originally had nothing to do with the Temple but gradually, and especially after its destruction, certain features of the Temple were attached to the synagogue.

One of the most interesting discoveries from the Chorazin synagogue is the inscribed stone "Seat of Moses" (**760**) — intended for the most distinguished elder of the house and apparently placed nearest the Ark.

The most interesting among the many other synagogues of this period which have been uncovered include those at Bar'am (**763**), Beth-Shean* (see article), Meron, Gush-Halab (Gischala), Hamath, Nirim (mosaic **764**), Maon and Beth-Shearim, ten miles west of Nazareth.

761

The Beth-Shearim Synagogue: The Beth-Shearim synagogue consisted of a basilica with an interior court, a terrace in front and a number of side courts and chambers. The walls and floor were decorated with marble slabs bearing reliefs. The inscriptions found showed that the synagogue was also used as a court-house. There is some evidence that this synagogue stood in the place of a simpler structure belonging to the 2nd c. CE, the time of Rabbi Judah ha-Nassi (see Rabbis*; Mishnah*).

The Hamath-Gader synagogue of the 6th c. CE revealed a beautiful mosaic floor, giving the addresses of the donors and including a large Zodiac circle, reminiscent of the one found at the Beth Alpha synagogue (ground plan and mosaic, **765**; see **237**). The similarities are probably due to the two floors having been made by the same craftsmen who also made the mosaic of the Beth-Shean synagogue. In the mosaics at Hamath-Tiberias – made 200 years earlier than those at Beth-Alpha — the general design is the same but the workmanship is entirely different, the earlier group being far superior; see **756** (the woman symbolizes one of the seasons).

The remains found at more than fifty places in historic Palestine (i.e. modern Israel and Jordan) testify to the much greater numbers that must have been built. Until 1963, no traces had been found of a single synagogue built before the 1st c. CE, presumably because the buildings were totally razed during the two wars with Rome (66–73 and 131–135 CE). Y. Yadin claims, however, to having uncovered the remains of a synagogue at Masada dating from the 1st c. CE. Of the synagogues that were found, the largest number was in Galilee while at Bar'am and Gush-Halab more than one was found on the same site. The ones uncovered were adorned with multi-coloured mosaics, stone designs, Corinthian

763

762

764

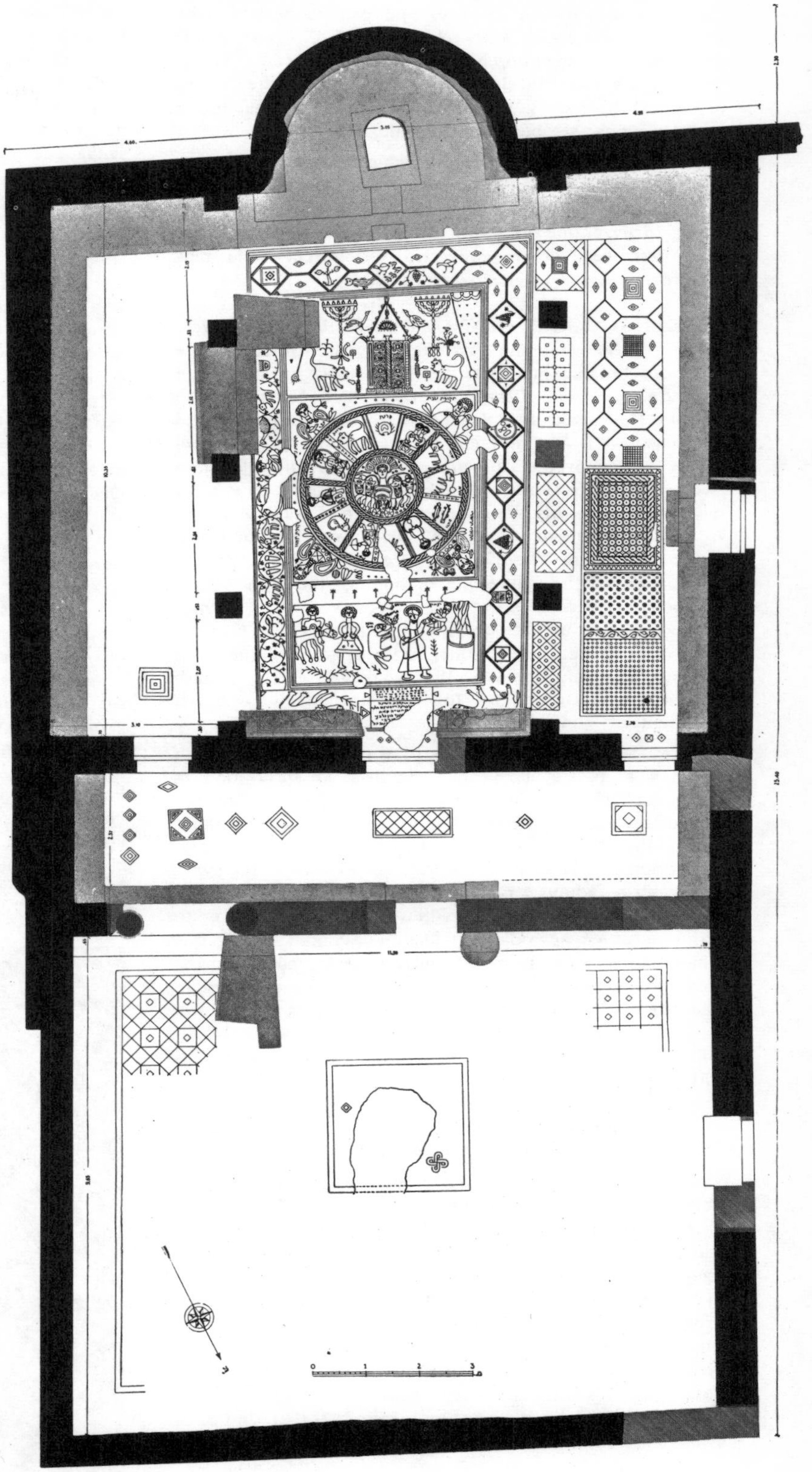

765

capitals and elaborate cornices and pediments, while the lintels were decorated with reliefs. The Bar'am synagogue even has a columned porch. In addition to the Zodiac circle, geometric, animal and floral decorations, there were designs of biblical themes, e.g. the attempted sacrifice of Isaac found at Beth Alpha; see bottom of mosaic, **765**.

Later Opposition: The protection which the Jewish religion and its synagogues enjoyed in earlier Roman times was shaken by the Christianization of the Roman empire (4th c. CE). In Byzantine times (5th–6th cs. CE), many synagogues were destroyed, others converted to churches and new building or enlargements were forbidden.

III. SYNAGOGUES OF THE DIASPORA: There were Jews in Exile while the First Temple still stood, but the Diaspora became of substantial importance from Persian times on and extended throughout the whole Mediterranean area in Hellenistic and Roman times (see Hellenism and the Diaspora*). Just how large it was can be gauged from letters written by the Roman Senate in the time of Simon (see Hasmoneans*) warning the Roman agents in various territories against discriminating against the Jews (I Mac. 15). In fact, Jews settled throughout the Graeco-Roman world and beyond it in Mesopotamia (see Hellenism*).

The role of the synagogue in holding the Jews of the Diaspora together and drawing non-Jews to their monotheistic faith must be stressed. In most of the Graeco-Roman world outside Palestine, services were conducted in Greek. The open doors of the synagogue every Sabbath proved a great attraction for the heathen and a haven for Gentile "godfearers".

Egypt: The earliest synagogues of which traces have been found were in Egypt. Near Alexandria, an inscription in Greek was discovered in the ruins of a synagogue, dedicated to Ptolemy III Eurgetes and his wife. The inscription dates the building to the 3rd c. BCE. There is another, contemporary, inscription which refers to the right of asylum in the synagogue. More famous was the Great Synagogue of Alexandria itself. This is mentioned by Philo and in the Mission to Caius in which he took part (Talmud, Sukah 56). It was famous for its size and beauty but was destroyed during the disorders between Jews and Greeks at the time of Trajan (see Bar-Kochba*). The Jewish community in Alexandria was a large and important one and there were a number of other synagogues in the city. When the Greeks were at odds with the Jews, they tried to set up statues of the Roman emperor in the synagogues.

Of the synagogues in other Egyptian towns, the best known was the one in Atribis, in the south of the delta.

Dura-Europos: In eastern Syria, on the frontier between Parthia and Roman territory, excavation of the town of Dura-Europos revealed the ruins of a synagogue decorated with a series of striking frescoes (**766**). These showed scenes from the careers of Jacob, Moses, Aaron, Solomon, David and Esther, pictured the visions of Ezekiel, the drowning of the Egyptians in the Red Sea, the prophet Elijah and other biblical themes. In addition, the assembly faced three prominent representations of the Temple of Solomon. This structure dates from the 3rd c. CE, but it had apparently been built on the ruins of another, 2nd c. CE synagogue, itself a converted private house. A "Seat of Moses" was found there. Presumably the house had originally been occupied by Samuel ben Jedaiah, the elder, who built the synagogue.

Scholars have found many similarities between the drawings in Dura and those belonging to early Christians. In fact, much early Christian art is indebted to the synagogue. Both synagogues and churches were usually built in the form of basilicas, and the influence of the synagogue can be seen in many Christian details (see above: Design).

The Roman Empire: In Ostia, the sea port of Rome, excavations in 1961 CE showed the existence of a Jewish community as early as the 1st or 2nd c. BCE. A 1st c. CE synagogue was discovered there, decorated with a bas-relief on marble representing the golden candelabrum of the Temple of Solomon. The synagogue's size and workmanship indicate a large and prosperous community.

In Stovy in Yugoslavia an important Jewish community existed from the 2nd c. CE, and of course erected a synagogue. Earlier synagogues dating from the 2nd c. BCE were built on the islands of Delos and Aegina; an inscription found at Delos records that the building was dedicated to El-Elyon.

In Neru, in Cyrenaica (North Africa) a beautiful mosaic was found and also a Latin inscription. Latin inscriptions were rare in synagogues. Usually they were in Greek or Aramaic.

Synagogues are known to have existed at other places around the Mediterranean, including Miletus and Priene on the eastern coast of what is today Turkey.

As early as the 4th c. CE Rabbi Abin had permitted the representation of human beings in mosaics, probably only giving sanction to what was already common usage. The strict separation of the image and the essence of the thing represented in Jewish dogma allowed biblical scenes. This is illustrated by the mosaic pavements of Beth-Alpha and Hamath synagogues (see above). In late antiquity, namely after the 6th c. CE., synagogue art lost its earlier Hellenic classical beauty and strongly reflected the orientalizing trend which stamps Byzantine art.

766

T

TABERNACLE, ARK AND CHERUBIM. — *Outline: I. Tabernacle: Historicity of the Priestly Tabernacle; The Priestly Traditions; Traditional Description; Archaeology of the Tabernacle. II. The Ark; Priestly Description; Kapporeth–Mercy Seat and Cherubim; The Wanderings of the Ark. III. History of the Tabernacle Institution: Tent of Assembly Not the Tabernacle; The Shiloh Sanctuary; Traditions Subordinated to the Shrine Legend. IV. Sacramental Significance of Cherubim and Kapporeth: The Throne of Yahweh.*

I. TABERNACLE: The word "tabernacle" ("mishkān" in Hebrew) was used for the portable tent shrine containing the Ark of the Covenant, carried by the wandering Israelites before the Conquest. According to tradition, it was erected as a temporary structure at the Shiloh sanctuary and carried by David's followers to Jerusalem where it remained until Solomon's Temple was built. The combination of Ark and Tabernacle represented Yahweh's dwelling place. Sanctuaries where the Ark rested became centres of pilgrimage (see Festivals*), priestly strongholds and, in most if not all phases of Israel's history, the political centre for the country for the moment (see below).

Historicity of the Priestly Tabernacle: Biblical scholarship since the 19th c. CE (see Biblical Criticism*) has cast serious doubts upon the historicity of traditions concerning the Priestly Tabernacle installation in Ex. 25–31 and 35–39. This cumbersome data (interpreted literally by past generations) cannot serve as a reliable basis for a reconstruction of the tent-tabernacle before and after the Conquest*. Modern scholars do not go as far as Wellhausen who concluded that the priestly Tabernacle was the fancy of the post-Exilic priestly writers, namely a description or reminiscence of the Solomonic Temple*, presented in a flimsy desert disguise. A historic development of the tabernacle institution can be reconstructed. On the basis of ancient passages such as Ex. 33:7–11, scholars today concede that there was a primitive Tent of Assembly which should not, however, be confused with an equally historic desert sanctuary (see below) which disappeared before the tribes entered Canaan. But the late traditions of Ex. 25–31 and 35–39 have long been regarded as largely idealizations by late priestly writiers and not factual accounts of any historic "tent", "ark" or "tabernacle". Finally, archaeology has helped to reconstruct the possible appearance of the desert sanctuary.

This complex biblical problem and the history of the tabernacle as an institution is outlined below.

The Priestly Traditions: The priestly traditions of the monarchy (and later) kept the old name of the desert "tent of assembly" (ohel mo'êd"; Ex. 33:7–11) but also called it the "mishkān" (or "abode") to indicate the manner in which God who dwelt in heaven might also make a home on earth. In the opinion of some scholars, there was a process of development. First came the oldest tradition (conventionally referred to as the Elohistic, see Biblical Criticism*). It stressed the role of the Mosaic tent where Yahweh talked to Moses "face to face" (Ex. 33:11) or "mouth to mouth" (Nu. 12:8) but gave no details of what it looked like or how it was furnished. A later (priestly) tradition (Ex. 25–31 and 35–39) is that of the ideal "mishkān" (tabernacle). Later on, the "tent-tabernacle" became the symbol of the institution of the central sanctuary, and the historical Tent and Ark were completely overshadowed by the new meanings which the term acquired.

It is now generally accepted that these traditions crystallized into their present form at a relatively late stage. They absorbed so much later influence in the process that the ancient original became largely obscured. The priestly picture of the tabernacle is, nevertheless, more than merely a reflection of the conditions and ideas of the later period. It contains a substratum of authentic ancient pre-Jerusalem tradition which can, to a certain extent, be disentangled from all the later accretions and can be distinguished within the traditions in the Pentateuch and the historical books (Samuel, Kings, Chronicles). Moreover, from biblical analysis and extra-biblical sources, the motif of the desert Tent — whatever its shape and size — can be found to continue as the central religious institution, from the earliest times right through to the Tent of David.

Traditional Description: The description of the tabernacle in Ex. 25–31 and 35–39 is generally regarded as a Priestly writer's scheme. It is marked by ascending degrees of holiness from its perimeter, the outer court, through the holy place, to the holy of holies, right at the centre.

The Court: The Tabernacle stood in the centre of the camp in a rectangular enclosure measuring 100 × 50 cubits, (approx. 150 × 75 feet, see Weights and Measures*). The entrance was closed by a screen embroidered in colours. Embroidered curtains hung from pillars standing in sockets of bronze to screen off the rest of the area.

The Altar: In the centre of the court stood the altar of burnt offering, made of a hollow chest of acacia wood sheathed with bronze. At each corner was one of the four horns of the altar. A bronze grating covered the lower half of the altar, from the ground to a projecting ledge halfway up the side. This allowed for sacrificial blood to be dashed against the sides and base of the altar. The altar was also fitted with rings and poles so that it could be carried.

Beside the altar stood the bronze laver of water for the ablutions of the priests.

The Holy Place: The inner sanctum was furnished with a. the table of shewbread, (the bread of the presence), with its golden plates, dishes or cups for frankincense, and other flagons and vessels needed for the ritual; b. a golden candlestick (possibly a seven-branched lampstand or menorah) which faced the table of shewbread and was supplied with golden snuffers for dressing the wicks of the lamps; c. the square altar of incense, made of acacia wood overlaid with gold, also fitted with rings and poles. This stood in front of the veil which separated the holy place from the holy of holies and upon it incense made of sweet spices was offered night and morning.

767

The Holy of Holies: This was a square of approximately 15 ft. which contained the Ark of the Covenant and the golden slab of the mercy seat ("kappôreth") with a cherub made of pure beaten gold at either end (see Part IV).

These priestly descriptions of gold, silver and bronze work, magnificent edifices and sumptuous carvings and decoration present obvious difficulties. They are not appropriate to the materially poor community liberated from Egypt and they are quite unreal in terms of technical skills before the 10th c. BCE. Many scholars, accordingly, regard the descriptions as an ideal picture drawn by later priestly writers either to serve as a model for the Temple before it was built, or based on what actually existed in Solomon's Temple. On the other hand, D.N. Freedman considers that there is a mixture of material in the Priestly accounts and that Solomon's Temple may also reflect traditions connected with the Tabernacle.

The use of the actual Temple of Solomon as a model for imaginative descriptions of the earlier Tabernacle, according to the first view, is particularly apparent in connection with the forms of the altars. To begin with, bronze only came into use in Israël for building and decoration during Solomon's reign (I K. 7:13–14). Similarly, the horns which figure so prominently in the accounts of the altar's decoration (Ex. 30:3–4) appear from archaeological finds to have come into vogue in Israel only at the beginning of the monarchy. This is also confirmed by the Bible where they are mentioned (apart from this one instance) only against the background of the monarchical period (I K. 1: 50–51; Ps. 118:27; Jer. 17:1; Am. 3:14). They can, therefore, be presumed to have belonged to the Temple, not to its forerunner, the Tabernacle.

Many of the other items mentioned in the priestly description of Ex. 25–31 and 35–39 cannot be fitted into any realistic picture of a portable shrine such as the Mosaic Tent and Ark which travelled in front of Israel (Nu. 10:35–36). Instead, it seems more likely that the desert sanctuary was conceived as a collapsible version of the Temple of Jerusalem, measuring exactly half as long as that structure, but keeping the firmly rooted tradition that God's earthly dwelling was a "Tent".

Archaeology of the Tabernacle: What the tent in fact looked like may perhaps be suggested by the bas relief on the Temple of Bel at Palmyra (Tadmor), dating to between the 3rd and 1st cs. BCE and showing a portable tent shrine (**767**). This, again, is very reminiscent of the pre-Islamic "qubbah", a big red leather tent with a domed top in which the tribal idols or bethyls were housed. It accompanied the tribe into battle and was believed to guide them during periods of wanderings. The holiness of the tent was second only to that of the objects it contained. It was both a palladium and a place of worship where priests gave oracles. The Palmyra bas relief still shows traces of the red paint which originally decorated the representation (see below, Parts II and III).

II. THE ARK: **Priestly Description:** Priestly tradition saw the Ark as a fixed and inseparable part of the tabernacle, and this may be historically correct. It had its place in the holy of holies in the centre of the tabernacle, and was removed only when the whole shrine was dismantled to be moved somewhere else.

As to its religious significance, different scholars have put forward two conflicting interpretations. According to one school, it was a chest, according to another, a sort of throne. Both views draw their evidence from different passages within the priestly text. In Ex. 25:10–11; 37:1–9, it is described as a chest made of acacia wood, about 4 ft. long and 2.5 ft. wide and high, covered with gold plates and fitted with rings through which poles could be fixed so that it could be carried.

Kappôreth — Mercy Seat and Cherubim: Over the Ark was the "Kappôreth", a gold plate the same size as the Ark, called in some translations the "mercy seat". The golden cherubim (see below, Part IV) stood one at either end of the "mercy seat" covering it with their outspread wings. This tradition is clearly influenced by the realities of the Temple of Solomon where the Ark stood in the Holy of Holies, sheltered by the wings of the cherubim, According to another view, the description of the Temple reflects the older tradition.

Deuteronomy 10:1–8 simply refers to an Ark made of acacia wood as a container for the two stone tablets of the Law. This became known as the Ark of the Covenant, and Deuteronomy gives no further description of it, and does not connect it with either tent or tabernacle. Archaeology has furnished many parallels to the placing of the tablets of the Law in the "holy place" of the nation. Among ancient peoples, legal bonds and documents were frequently deposited beneath statues of the gods who thus became witnesses to the agreements.

An analysis of the conflicting traditions about the Ark in Ex. 25 and 37 and Dt. 10 (see above), plus the accounts in I Sam. 4–6; II Sam. 6; I K. 8 and Ezekiel's vision (Ezk. 8) where the Ark appears as the visible sign of the presence of God, reveals the distinction between the symbols of Ark and "Kappôreth" (see above).

The Ark was the oldest of the symbols. It stood, apparently without being covered by any tent, in the camp of Gilgal (Jos. 7:6) right at the beginning of the Conquest. It was transferred to Bochim near Bethel (Jud. 2:1–5), thence to

Bethel (Jud. 20:27) or according to Jos. 8:33 to Mt. Ebal near Shechem. In Samuel's time it was kept at Shiloh (I Sam. 1–3) until it was taken into the Battle of Aphek (I Sam. 4:3) and captured by the Philistines (4:11). They returned it to the Israelites at Beth-Shemesh (6:11–14) and from there it was taken to Kiriath-Gearim (7:1) where it remained until David took it to Jerusalem and installed it in "his" city. After the Temple had been built, the Ark was placed in the innermost sanctum (I K. 8:3–4, 6–8) and lay there until it was destroyed along with the Temple in 587–586 BCE. No new Ark was made for the post-Exilic Holy of Holies (Jer. 3:16) but in the post-Exilic I Ch. 28:11, the phrase, "the room for the mercy-seat" (Kappôreth) stands for the Holy of Holies of Solomon's Temple. Its memory remained, but Josephus (Wars 5, 5, 5) records that in Herod's Temple, there was nothing in the Holy of Holies.

The Wanderings of the Ark: While biblical tradition insists that the Ark was housed in a tent or tabernacle and was, therefore, clearly portable, there is never any notion of taking it "out of" the sanctuary. Before their settlement in Canaan, the Israelites had no sanctuaries (Dt. 12:8–11). Presumably, when the Israelites halted during their wanderings, the Ark containing the Covenant was temporarily covered by tent curtains and this remained the situation until it reached a more permanent resting place at Shiloh (Jos. 18:1).

In Shiloh, the Ark provided the cultic centre for the tribal federation. By the period of the early chapters of I Sam, it was housed in a sanctuary under the care of the priest, Eli. Some time in the middle of the 11th c. BCE, the Philistines defeated the Israelite tribes, destroyed Shiloh and captured the Ark. In fact, the period after the destruction of Shiloh is largely a gap in the story of the central sanctuary. It seems likely that after its return and until the building of the Temple, the Ark continued to be housed in a temporary tent, not a permanent shrine. Some fifty years later, David formed his new official cultic centre out of the Ark, the chief cultic object of the tribal league, and its priesthood, scattered throughout Israel. He connected the new worship with the ancient desert traditions of a tabernacle, and transferred the Ark to his new shrine in Jerusalem (II Sam. 6:17; 7:2), thus preserving all the awe and authority of the old sanctuary. The tent in Jerusalem under which the Ark was housed was evidently meant to represent the desert sanctuary. It was no longer the Tent of Assembly, nor was it considered a permanent shrine.

III. HISTORY OF THE TABERNACLE INSTITUTION:

Tent of Assembly Not the Tabernacle: A great deal of confusion has arisen because of the contradiction between the sources as to whether the Ark and the Tabernacle were essentially permanent institutions, variations on the "house of God" known to so many religions, or whether the Ark was conceived as something essentially portable, merely finding a temporary home in a tent. The priestly source makes the Tent of Assembly identical with the sanctuary. The one institution stands in the centre of camp with the priests and tribes grouped protectively around it, and the cloud of glory does not stand at the door but becomes one with the cloud which is over the Holy of Holies. This image is fundamental to this whole source and underlies the complex cultic situation which it describes.

The Shiloh Sanctuary: Such a background explains the anachronistic nature of the priestly descriptions of the shrine at Shiloh. The writers — like many other biblical narrators — may have drawn on the conditions with which they were familiar for their picture of the Shiloh shrine and consequently ascribed to it many of the features of the monarchical period and the Temple of Solomon.

The priestly descriptions of the Shiloh shrine provided it with a boarded and curtained tabernacle like the "hekhāl" of Solomon's Temple, which would imply a substantial, permanent structure. Such a picture, however, is contradicted by the evidence of the statement made to David by his adviser, Nathan the prophet (II Sam. 7:6–7). He states quite explicitly that since the day of the Exodus from Egypt, the Ark has not dwelt in a house but has "been moving about in a tent for my dwelling." The conflict could be resolved, however, on the theory (proposed by M. Haran) that the Shiloh shrine was neither a house nor a true tent, but a special form of accommodation also typical of nomadic life. The tents of that early period were usually made of tent cloths spread over comparatively thin poles, similar to those pictured in this Assyrian illustration of a camp **(768)**, whereas a tabernacle could be made — as described in the Bible — by spreading hangings over temporary walls made of "qerašîm" which were not solid timbers but, more likely, a lattice of cross pieces. The tablets of Ugarit refer to the throne-room of El as made of qerašîm, meaning, in the opinon of W.F. Albright and F.M. Cross, a trellised pavilion. Pegs and cords are used to support these structures, just as in normal tents, but the "qerašîm" would form a more stable construction, nonetheless typical of nomadic habitations. On this assumption, the "portable shrine" would

768

not need to be a temporary affair only related to the period of the Conquest, but could have been regarded as an "eternal dwelling" valid throughout future generations.

Traditions Subordinated to the Shrine Legend: This conception of the tabernacle, however, does not include a Tent of Assembly (see above), an ancient institution which belonged to the early Yahwistic religion but was out of keeping with the ideas of priestly and other later narrators. In the priestly view, everything had to be subordinate to the sanctuary. The apparently equally important Tent of Assembly was an embarrassment, avoided by absorbing it completely into the Tabernacle. Both functions were thus combined, with the emphasis on the side of the hierarchical, priestly-dominated cultic aspects.

In M. Haran's view, the gorgeous sanctuary described by the Priestly Sources (Ex. 25–31 and 35–39) is not fiction, as supposed by the Wellhausen school, but a shrine legend transmitting the priestly literary traditions of Shiloh and later. This legend was based on the belief that the Ark had travelled more or less directly from Sinai to Shiloh. It completely ignored stories of capture by the Philistines (ca. 1050 BCE) and miraculous restoration to the Israelites. In the priestly view, the Ark could not possibly have been separated from the Tabernacle. The legend, however, was preserved by priestly writers who lived — in Jerusalem — long after Shiloh itself had been destroyed, and who could thus give free rein to their imaginations when it came to describing the details of the erst-while sanctuary and shrine. The model they took for the splendours they envisaged was the actual Temple of Solomon. They did not deliberately invent something they knew to be untrue. They simply took it for granted that the hallowed shrine of the past could be no less imposing that the realities of the Solomonic era and unconsciously they imposed their own experience on the earlier conditions.

769

IV. SACRAMENTAL SIGNIFICANCE OF CHERUBIM AND KAPPÔRETH: **Cherubim:** The Cherubim of the "Kappôreth" (see Priestly Description of the Ark, Part II, above) acquired a supreme symbolical significance as the throne — or sometimes the footstool — of God. He was even referred to as He "who is enthroned on the cherubim" (I Sam. 4:4) and the divine presence was believed to rest, invisibly, between their wings. This was the focal point of the whole Temple. Here the ritual converged and prayers rose, and from this point the holiness of God spread through His House.

Because the religion of Israel forbade images, the throne was empty. The Ark acquired the more specific function of God's footstool, "the place of the soles of my feet" (Ezk. 43:7). These roles were exchangeable. Neither Ark nor Cherubim was more than an inadequate symbol of the divine presence, the "seat" of his presence, but they provided the prophets with a vivid imagery (e.g. Is. 6:1–13; Ezk. 10).

The Throne of Yahweh: Opinion is divided about whether the Ark and Cherubim (which represented an increasingly complex conception of the throne of Yahweh in the sanctuaries of Shiloh and Jerusalem) were also present in the much simpler tent of the desert period. It is difficult to be certain. The oldest tradition of the Pentateuch (Nu. 10:35–36) links the Ark directly with the movements of Yahweh and seems to regard it as the physical support of an invisible godhead. It is assumed by many to have been a box or chest containing the terms of the Covenant. It was placed under the Throne of God, forming a footstool in this manner. The conception of a deity as standing or enthroned on an animal or mythical creature was a commonplace in the ancient Near East between 2000 and 700 BCE. Thus it is hardly remarkable that between 1300 and 900 BCE, Israel's God, Yahweh, should have been conceived as enthroned upon a golden cherub or, later, standing upon a golden bull (see Idol Worship*: Jeroboam's Calves). The Cherub's primary function in Israelite symbolism is best illustrated by two passages, "He rode on a cherub, and flew" (II Sam. 22:11; Ps. 18:10), and Ezk. 10:20: "The living creature that I saw underneath the God of Israel . . .".

Physically, the cherub was a combination of man, beast and bird, whose description varied at different times during the Old Testament period. Cherubim acted as the guardians of the Garden of Eden (Gn. 3:24) and lived there (Ezk. 28:14). Possibly they resembled the sphinxes which flanked the throne of King Hiram, although where a sphinx appears in Canaanite decoration, as in Arwad (**769**), it cannot have been identified by Canaanites as a cherub (see **176**, Samaria). The cherub probably had a parallel in Assyria — the word "karibu" has been found in Assyrian sources — but, again, the form of animal referred to has not been identified. Even if they were the same, this does not imply a mechanical borrowing on the part of the Israelites. If they learned of cherubim from Mesopotamia, it was most likely as members of a whole group of nomadic peoples who roamed the Mesopotamian cultural region in the early days of the Patriarchal period (see

770

Patriarchs*). Thus cherubim appear in the earliest stratum of Genesis 3, which is full of Mesopotamian material (see Genesis*; Sanctuaries*; Temple*).

TAXES. — *Outline: In Egypt; Forced Labour in Antiquity; The Tax of the Tithe in Canaan and Syria; The Hebrews in an Alien Scoiety; Forced Tribute; The Shekel Offering; Taxation under the Monarchy; Taxation under Solomon; Post-Exilic Period; Hellenistic Period; Roman Period; Jesus and the Tax Collectors.*

Though little is known from the biblical record about the fiscal system of Israel or the resources at the disposal of the state, we can gain considerable additional information from the tax patterns of neighbouring peoples both before the emergence of the Hebrews and once they were established on the stage of history.

In Egypt: From the 3rd mill. BCE, the Egyptian state imposed taxes and forced labour on all its subjects as of right, although it appears from Egyptian records of the 14th c. BCE that the government would intervene to protect "poor people" from thievish tax collectors.

Taxes due on cultivated fields were assessed by government tax officials and were collected in grain, as shown in this painting of scribes recording evidence of non payment of taxes (**770**).

A scroll of the 20th dynasty (ca. 1200 BCE onwards) suggests the enormous flow of wealth into the coffers, treasure houses and granaries of the Pharaohs. Out of these resources, they met all expenses for the upkeep of the army plus the costs of public and royal construction projects, the labourers who worked on the building of the king's palaces and necropoli being paid in grain.

Egyptian temples had an economic power and a right to raise revenue second only to the Pharaoh. Ecclesiastical property included more than one-eighth of the arable land of Egypt and controlled a body of 450,000 people. Moreover, the temple priests and employees were exempt from the corvée service (a tax paid in labour), which burdened all other Egyptians.

In Gn. 47, the land system of Egypt is described as having been introduced by Joseph*. The narrator expresses surprise, not at the payment of taxes to the king, but at the fact that the king owned all the land except for the temples and their property, and that all Egyptians were serfs of the crown. This was in direct contrast to the system of private land holding in Palestine.

According to Greek tradition, the Egyptian kings of the 3rd mill. BCE made the building of the pyramids a grievous burden on the Egyptian masses. Thousands were forced into the labour gangs which, although fed for the time being by the king, were engaged on an economically quite unproductive task. A harrowing memory of the labour enforced on the Hebrews' ancestors in Egypt is preserved in Exodus*, although their lot seems to have been no worse than that of all the Pharaoh's subjects.

Forced Labour in Antiquity: The system of forced labour, moreover, was universal throughout the ancient Near East. Evidence of it has been found in Sumer and in Babylonia* from the 3rd mill. BCE to the Persian period. Assyrian laws condemned certain criminals to a period of forced labour for the king. Forced labour and state slaves (recruited from prisoners of war) worked with hired labourers in constructing roads, canals, fortresses and temples, in tilling the crown lands and in the royal factories connected with the palace.

In Syria and Palestine, the corvée is known to have been imposed on the common people as early as the middle of the 2nd mill. BCE (before the Israelite settlement). The system is referred to in the Amarna letters*, while texts from Ugarit*, dating from the 18th to the 13th cs. BCE, relate that an individual or his family could be exempted from both forced labour and taxes by favour of the king (see Cities, Canaanite*; Saul*).

The Tax of the Tithe in Canaan and Syria: The Ugarit texts also prove that in the countries bordering Palestine, the kings levied the tax of a tithe (one-tenth) on all fields, vineyards and herds. The king had the right to allot this revenue to one of his officers and could also exempt favoured individuals from paying it. In addition, the king of Ugarit levied taxes on those who pastured their flocks on royal lands, as well as tolls, fines and other payments from all landholdings, whether privately owned or held on lease from the crown.

A similar system developed in Israel with the monarchy, as predicted by Samuel when he tried to oppose the people's demand for a king (I Sam. 8:15, 17; see also Saul*), although no system of taxation is known previously (see below). The same abuses inevitably occurred, too. Amos (7:1) refers to the king's right of pasturage and (5:11) to the exactions of men of rank from the poor people. Favoured families were also exempted from tithes and forced labour (I Sam. 17:25).

The Canaanite kings drew a major portion of their revenues from the crown lands, amassed by expropriation, confiscation, purchase and victories in war. In addition, they

771

acted as "merchant princes" engaging, according to the Amarna letters* (14th c. BCE) in all kinds of commercial enterprises. The documents from the royal palace of Ugarit* also provide a vivid picture of the management of the royal domains and of the revenues they supplied to the king's treasury.

The Hebrews in an Alien Society: In the Patriarchal stories, at which time the Hebrews were living as semi-nomads outside Canaanite society, there is no mention of any payment of taxes. What is found are voluntary gifts made, for instance, as a protective peace-offering from a weaker party to a stronger. In this spirit Jacob gave his brother Esau a gift of sheep, cattle and camels (Gn. 32:13–21) and, later, when his sons went to Egypt to buy grain and fodder, ordered them to take with them as gifts the best that the land could produce (Gn. 43:11).

At this period, the status of the Hebrews was identical to that of the Habiru* (see also Patriarchs*; Amarna Letters*), who are described as being landless wanderers, living on the edges of the society of the sedentary populations in the Near East from the beginning of the 2nd mill. BCE. This condition is reflected, so far as the Hebrews are concerned, in the famous passage of Deuteronomy 26:5 that describes the Hebrews' ancestors: "A wandering Aramean was my father; and he went down into Egypt and sojourned there . . ."

Making voluntary gifts to the person in power continued during the period of Judges* and in the early part of the monarchy, although in Saul's time, the "sons of Belial" (i.e. worthless people) were opposed to paying taxes in kind to the new king, for they did not believe that he would be able or willing to help them in time of need (I Sam. 10:27). Solomon*, on the other hand, received lavish gifts, for instance from people whom he received. These might include silver and gold vessels and ornaments, costly garments, weapons, spices, horses and mules. Such tribute*, was all over and above the prescribed taxes.

Forced Tribute: Taxation or forced tribute first appears among the Israelites when they demanded the corvée (or labour tax) from the defeated Canaanites as the price of allowing them to remain in the land after the Conquest (Jos. 16:10; 17:13; Jud. 1:28–35).

To demand taxes from defeated enemies was a commonplace of later times as it was both proof of victory and a useful source of revenue. The tribute paid by petty kings reduced to vassalage, e.g. by King Hoshea of Israel after his defeat by King Shalmaneser of Assyria (II K. 17:4; see Tribute*), may also be regarded as taxes. The form in which the tribute was to be paid was commonly determined by the conquerors.

The Shekel Offering: The first fixed tax mentioned in the Old Testament was religious in origin and purpose. This was the "Atonement Money" levy of a half-shekel, imposed by Moses on every Israelite male of twenty and over, which was used to defray the ritual expenses of the Tabernacle (Tent of Assembly; Ex. 30:11–16). It seems that this levy, which can be compared to a modern poll-tax, lapsed during the monarchy, a development reflected in the story of Joash's attempt to reinstate it for the renovation of the Temple (II Chr. 24:4–14). After the Exile*, only one-third of a shekel was paid for the maintenance of divine worship (Neh. 10:32). However, throughout the period of the Second Temple the Jews of the Diaspora continued to send payments to Jerusalem (Josephus, Ant. 14, 7:2), apparently of the full half-shekel, while the Jewish authorities in Jerusalem collected the same amount from the resident population (Mt. 17:24).

Taxation under the Monarchy: Samuel's prediction of the "manner of the king" (see Saul*) was fully justified by developments. Under the monarchy, an elaborate taxation system was organized, including payment of various kinds of taxes plus the corvée (I Sam. 8:10–18). This naturally led to friction between the king and his subjects. Saul's offer to "free the house" of the man who would remove Goliath the Philistine (I Sam. 17:25) suggests that a property tax had been instituted by that time.

There is no direct record of tax collecting in David's* reign, although it is very likely that it existed. Certainly one main purpose of his Census was to levy taxes (the other being to raise troops), and Samuel's forebodings about the "manner of the king" (see Saul*) probably applied to David* and later kings just as much as to Saul. Doubtless David's numerous and extensive conquests yielded substantial revenue in the form of tribute from defeated nations, so that the tax burden on the local, native population could be proportionately lightened.

A considerable portion of all revenues was devoted to the Temple, as the Bible puts it, to God (II Sam. 8:2, 7, 8, 10–12). However, the accounts of David's reign record several kinds of royal treasure-houses and store-houses. The store-houses were often towers (silos) for the collection of crops and produce paid as taxes in kind. They may also have been designed for storing the produce for some time or for maintaining the garrisons stationed in various centres. The officials responsible for the collection and storage of these taxes were called "Stewards of the King's Property" (I Ch. 27:25–31).

Taxation under Solomon: Collection of taxes was extended and made more efficient under Solomon. He appointed twelve prefects, each of whose districts was responsible for the maintenance of the royal court for one month of the year — no light responsibility (I K. 4:1–19).

Solomon's lavish building operations and the huge labour force they required led to an extension of the corvée system (I K. 5:13–18). Until then, the corvée had been imposed only on the Canaanites. Now it was extended to the king's Israelite subjects as well. It is said that 30,000 were pressed into the labour gangs. Of these, 10,000 went in relays every month to work in the Lebanon, carting the wood cut by the King of Tyre's woodcutters. In addition, Solomon had 70,000 porters and 80,000 quarrymen employed alongside his Phoenician carpenters and masons (I K. 5:13–16). It is possible that these figures are exaggerated. Some scholars believe they refer to labour gangs employed throughout the country, not only those engaged on work for the Temple. This Assyrian relief (**771**) depicts gangs of forced workers.

The burden laid on the Israelites during Solomon's reign was a heavy one. After his death, his son Rehoboam's decision to increase taxes was apparently the deciding factor in Jeroboam's revolt and the break-up of the united monarchy (see Israel and Judah*, Part I). Heavy taxes imposed on the poorer people were regularly condemned by the prophets (Is. 3:14; Am. 5:11; 8:4; Mic. 3:1–4, and others). The statement in II Ch. 17:5 that all Judah brought its tribute to Jehoshaphat is probably best understood as meaning an annual tax, like the tribute* of vassal states.

Post-Exilic Period: In the early years of the Restoration*, Jewish reluctance to pay taxes to the Persian king provoked him to order the suspension of all rebuilding operations in Jerusalem, so that his revenues might not suffer (Ezr. 4:17–21). The work was not resumed until the second year of the reign of Darius, who ordered a subsidy from the fifth satrapy "Trans-River" funds to be made towards the rebuilding.

While Artaxerxes I sat on the throne of Persia, both direct and indirect taxes were levied, the direct tax being the tribute due to the Persian king. There is a report (Ezr. 4: 7–13) from the Trans-River officials to the Persian king informing him that the Jews had stopped paying the tribute, customs duties and road tolls. In the days of Nehemiah, the customs tax was so heavy that people had to borrow money at interest in order to pay it (Neh. 5:1–4). Priests and other religious personnel were exempted from these taxes (Ezr. 7:24).

In addition to the taxes to the Persian king, the people had to meet a special levy made for the "wine and bread" of the local officials, plus a sum of forty shekels for each official (Neh. 5:14–15). During archaeological excavations in Palestine, the handles of several pieces of pottery stamped by Jewish officials have been found. These indicate that the officials were responsible for collecting such taxes in kind.

When the Jews first returned to Palestine after the Exile, special store-houses were erected to hold contributions for the reconstruction of the Temple (Ezr. 2:68–69; Neh. 7: 70–71). Once the Temple was open for services, another storehouse was built to collect special contributions (Neh. 10: 33–39; Mal. 3:10). Such donations were so great in the time of Nehemiah, that the Temple store-house was not able to accommodate them, and additional store-houses had to be built in other towns.

Hellenistic Period: During the rule of the Ptolemies in Palestine (301–218 BCE) a comparatively light tax of only twenty talents per year was imposed on the inhabitants of Palestine (Josephus, Ant. 12, 4, 1). The collection of these taxes was farmed out to the highest bidder, usually a man from the upper circles of the Jewish community (see Hasmoneans*: the Tobiads) who would pay an annual lump sum to the central authority and then proceed to extract as much as possible from the populace. The difference between what they paid to the government and what they got out of the people netted them a substantial profit. The conquest of Palestine by Antiochus III, the Great, in 202 BCE brought a measure of relief (Ant. 12, 3, 3). He refunded the excess taxes collected, and remitted the tax-rate by one-third. Later Seleucid rulers imposed exorbitant taxes on the Jews (I Mac. 10:26–30; 11:34–35; 13:19). The nature of these taxes can be gathered from the letter of Demetrius, who sought the help of the Jews against his rival Alexander Balas (see Hasmoneans*). In his letter Demetrius promised to exempt the Jews from the poll-tax, salt-tax and crown-tax, and to grant a remission of one-third of the grain-tax and one-half of the tax on the fruit-harvest (I Mac. 10:29–30).

Roman Period: During the early part of Herod's reign, taxes were collected by persons appointed by him, and then turned over directly to him (see Romans paying tribute in the Augustan period, **772**). After the annexation of Judea in 6 CE by the Roman empire, the country was administered by Roman procurators who were responsible for the collection of taxes which, according to the New Testament, went to the imperial treasury (Mt. 22:17; Lk. 20:22). Since the local tetrarchs (district civil administrators) continued to collect internal taxes, the people were subjected to double taxation.

772

The collection of customs duties on imported or exported goods was also farmed out to the highest bidder who had to provide a certain quota for the state treasury. According to the New Testament, the collector of customs inspected goods on the roads and on the bridges (Mt. 9:9). Customs were collected at Caesarea, Capernaum and Jericho (Josephus, War, 2, 14, 4).

Jesus and the Tax Collectors: Jesus' teachings on the subjects of taxes and tax collectors as recorded in the Gospels are revealing both of his own attitude and of the background of opinion about them. Tax collectors (or publicans) were habitually coupled with "sinners" ("posh'eh" in Hebrew), a term of deepest contempt. As agents of the Roman procurators of Judea, serving the foreign power for their own profit, they were naturally hated by the people and disdained by their righteous countrymen, the Pharisees.

Jesus taught that publicans, too, were the objects of divine love and that a penitent publican was more worthy in the eyes of God than the arrogant and self-righteous.

TEMPLE. — *Outline: I. First, Pre-Exilic Temple: Place; Solomon's Temple; Sections of the Temple: Ûlām, Hekhāl, Debîr, The Yatsiā (Side-Building); Furnishings: Ark of the Covenant, Altars, The "Sea of Bronze", Jachin and Boaz; Analogies and Influences; A Prototype in Hazor; Seat of the Divine Presence; The Temple in Israel's Life; The Service. II. Second Temple, Post-Exilic and Herodian: Temple Services; The Temple in Graeco-Roman Times; Herod's Temple; Temple Area and Courts; The Temple; Sectarian Opposition to the Temple; The Destruction of the Second Temple.*

I. FIRST, PRE-EXILIC TEMPLE: The first Temple in Jerusalem and its furnishings are described in three passages in the Old Testament: a. I Kings, mainly chapters 5–7; b. The corresponding passages in II Ch. 2–4 (in greater detail); c. Ezk. 40–43. The first two descriptions are relatively analogous; the fact that Chronicles gives more details than Kings is attributed by some authorities to the fact that documents which were almost contemporary with the time of construction were available to the Chronicler. Opinions are divided as to the description in Ezekiel*. Some scholars regard it as purely fictitious, while others believe it to be an eye-witness description from the time of Zerubbabel (see Restoration*). It is also possible that Ezekiel described the Temple as it was near the time of its destruction in 587 BCE, after many alterations and improvements had been made, subsequent to Solomon's reign. Archaeological evidence of other temples (see below, Analogies and Influences) suggests the view that Ezekiel's description is a reminiscence of the Temple as remembered by him before his exile. However, the only guides to the Temple's specifications are the Bible texts, some of whose technical terms are uncertain. The comparisons which can be drawn from the archaeology of Palestine and neighbouring countries make it easier to understand the written evidence and to visualize some of the details of the Temple which Solomon built on the hill north of Ophel (see Jerusalem* and maps, illustrations there).

Place: The site of the Temple can be looked for on that part of the eastern hill of Jerusalem now occupied by the large platform (35 acres) known as the Haram-es-Sharif (Noble Sanctuary), in the territory of Jordan. A large number of scholars place the Temple in close proximity to the

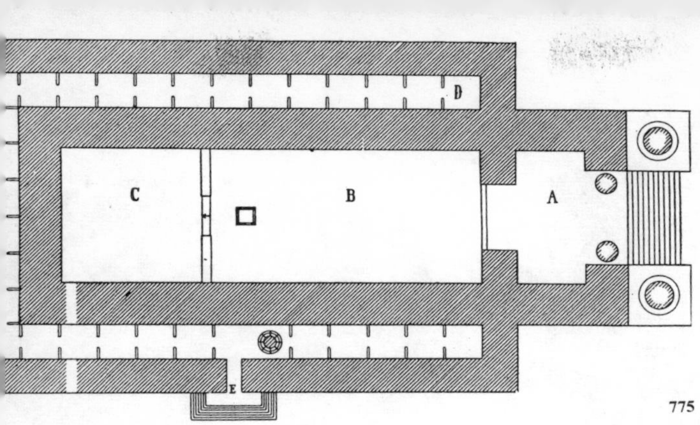

775

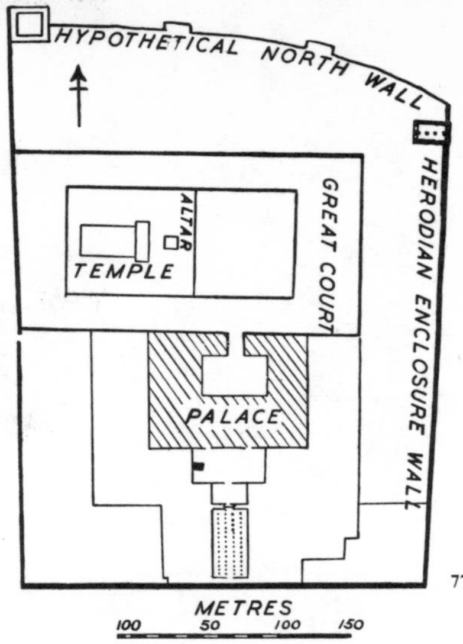

776

sacred rock (es-Sakhra, **773**) which is enclosed in the Dome of the Rock, less appropriately named the Mosque of Omar, **774**, erected by the Caliph Abdel Malek in the 7th c. CE (see also **151**). The rock may have been the site of the altar of burnt offerings identified by I Chr. 22:1 as the threshing floor of Ornan (or Araunah in II Sam. 24:16) which would locate the Temple proper west of this rock. This view is not readily acceptable as the hill slopes away steeply from the rock, requiring the elevated Holy of Holies (d^{e}bîr) to be supported by an enormous substratum. Another old theory (confirmed to some extent by a rabbinical tradition that the surface of the rock broke through to the d^{e}bir) places the great altar over the rock. The alternative solution, to regard the rock as the place of the d^{e}bir, not of the altar, is also beset by insuperable difficulties. The rock was called "eben shtiyah" (foundation stone) and was considered the foundation stone of Heaven and earth (see below). Some suggest that Jesus' allusion (Mt. 16:18) to the site of "my church" refers to the rock on which the sanctuary of the Ark had stood, but this again is conjecture.

Solomon's Temple: According to the Bible, the construction of Solomon's Temple took seven years, from the 5th to the 11th years of his reign (I K. 6:37–38). He was assisted in his work by Phoenician artisans, lent for the purpose by Hiram, King of Tyre, who also supplied him, by contract, with timber from Lebanon. The Israelites were conscripted to provide the bulk of the labour force but the skilled workmen were Phoenicians (II Ch. 2:7–14). Some of the materials, including the gold ingots which were to be used for the sacred objects, had been prepared by David (I Ch. 22).

From all descriptions, the Temple was an oblong structure consisting of three parts (see suggested diagram **775**): the ûlām (vestibule) A, the hekhāl (main sanctuary for worship), later called the Holy Place, B, and the d^{e}bîr, C, (later called the Holy of Holies) reserved for Yahweh and containing the Ark*. These sections stood one behind the other in a straight line. The whole Temple was laid out with an east west orientation, the ûlām or outer hall facing east. The Temple was constructed of hewn stone (at the base) and cedarwood, i.e. masonry locked together by beams, which stood on the stone base.

Sections of the Temple. Ûlām: The word is derived from the Akkadian "*ellamu*". It was the outer hall, which served as a vestibule, and was designed as a barrier between the secular and the sacred portions of the sanctuary. It was about 10 cubits long and 20 cubits wide (the cubit is approximately 0.45 m. or 1.5 ft.; see Weights and Measures*). The entrance door was in its broad side, and was 14 cubits wide. The entrance faced the rising sun, and was flanked by the two free-standing pillars, Jachin and Boaz. The height of the ûlām is not given, but it must have been about 20 cubits.

Hekhāl: The word hekhāl, too, is derived from a Mesopotamian term, *ekallu*, which signifies "temple" or "sanctuary". From the ûlām, a cypress door, 10 cubits wide, led into the hekhāl. Both ûlām and hekhāl are treated as one whole (I K. 6:2); properly speaking, they formed the "house" or Temple. The hekhāl was by far the largest room in the Temple, and was 40 cubits long, 20 cubits wide and 30 cubits high (cubit = approx. 1.5 ft. or 0.45 m.). It was dimly lit by latticed windows, that is, it had wide apertures which narrowed towards the interior.

D^{e}bîr: The third and inner section was the Holy of Holies. The room, measuring 20 cubits in each dimension, was designed to hold the Ark of the Covenant and the Cherubim*. According to Is. 6:1, its floor level was higher than the rest of the Temple and it was windowless. (In ancient oriental temples, the *cella* stood somewhat higher than the level of the room, or if this were not the case, the symbol of worship itself stood on a raised platform.) A flight of stairs led to the D^{e}bîr from the hekhāl, and it was entered through a door 6 cubits wide. Some scholars believe that it was separated from the hekhāl by a thin wall (Ezk. 41:3) or by a veil, as in the Tabernacle*, which may be a reminiscence inspired by Solomon's Temple (see Tabernacle: Ark*; Sacrifice*).

The Yatziā (Side-Building): The "yatziā" was a lateral building buttressing the sanctuary, which surrounded the Temple on three sides (except the ûlām and the facade). It consisted of three very low storeys, each storey a cubit wider than the one below. Thus the bottom one was 5 cubits wide, the second 6 cubits, and the third seven cubits. The total height of the yatsiā was only 15 cubits, so it was lower than the central building. Every floor had about 30 rooms or vaults, in which were kept all the vessels and instruments employed in the sacrificial rites and other objects which were not in regular use, as well as the gifts to the Temple service. Opinions differ as to when the yatsiā was constructed. Some scholars have regarded it as a post-Exilic addition of the Temple of Zerubbabel (see Restoration*). Others have assumed that it was built in Solomon's time, together with the central Temple or possibly during the Monarchy after Solomon (9th–8th cs. BCE).

The total length of the Temple (see diagram **776**) has been reckoned as 100 cubits, and its width as 50 cubits. It is noteworthy that the proportion between length and width

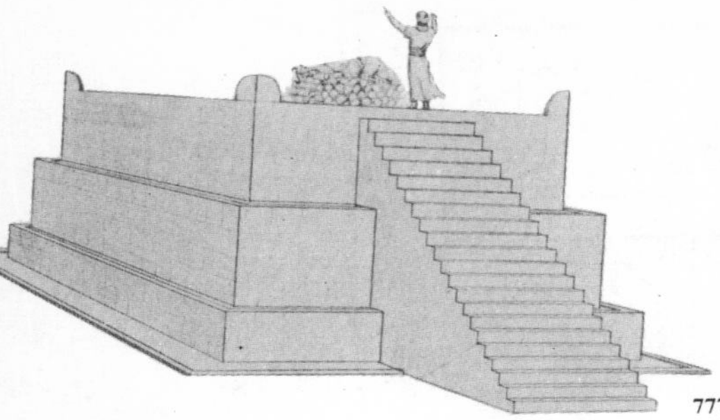

777

778

779

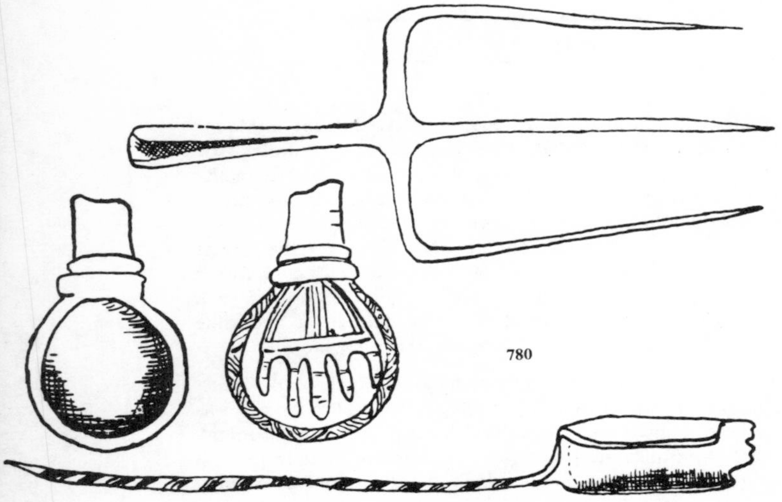

780

781

is 2:1, a common feature in temples of the ancient Near East. There is also a set proportion between the doors, which became narrower as one penetrated inward: the outer door was 14 cubits wide, the middle door 10 cubits, and the inside door 6 cubits

The Temple, like other Semitic sanctuaries, stood in the middle of a courtyard called the inner court (I K. 6:36), in contrast to the great court which included both the Temple and the palace. The inner court was later extended at the expense of the great court (II Ch. 20:5).

Furnishings: Ark of the Covenant: The Ark of the Covenant, described in detail under Tabernacle*, stood in the Deb̂ir with the *Kappôreth* and *Cherubim*, and represented the throne of Yahweh.

Altars: There were two altars in the Temple. The smaller one was of cedarwood and was decorated with gold leaf; it stood in the hechāl before the entrance to the Debîr and was used for offering incense. The larger altar, made of bronze, was for burnt offerings. It stood in front of the Temple in the inner courtyard, surrounded by a ditch. (Its description comes mainly from the text of Ezekiel.) It was 10 cubits high and was built in the form of stages, superimposed one on top of the other, with an incline leading from one stage to the next (**777**). The foundation or lowest stage was named "Bosom of the Earth" (which is the correct translation of the term in Ezk. 43:14) and the uppermost "Har'el", meaning "mountain of God", a remnant of cosmic symbolism, possibly influenced by foreign concepts which regarded the temple as the microcosm of the world. At the four corners of Har'el were affixed four horns in the form of protuberances, the use of which is not quite clear (see Sacrifice*). Similar horns were discovered in large numbers on top of limestone incense altars at Megiddo*, Gezer* and other places. Some scholars regard this altar as a later addition put up by Ahaz and modelled on an altar which he saw in Damascus when he went there to meet Tiglat-Pileser (II K. 16:10; see Israel and Judah*, Part IV; Assyria*; Arameans*). Further corroboration of this assumption may be found in the names of its various parts which resemble those in Mesopotamian terminology. (The religious significance of altars is dealt with under Sacrifice*; Altars found in the Israelite sanctuary of Tel-Arad* are described and illus. in article under Ancient Cities*).

The "Sea of Bronze": In the courtyard south east of the Temple stood an enormous molten sea of bronze "wrought like the brim of a cup, like the flower of a lily". It was held up by four groups of sculptured bulls, three bulls in each

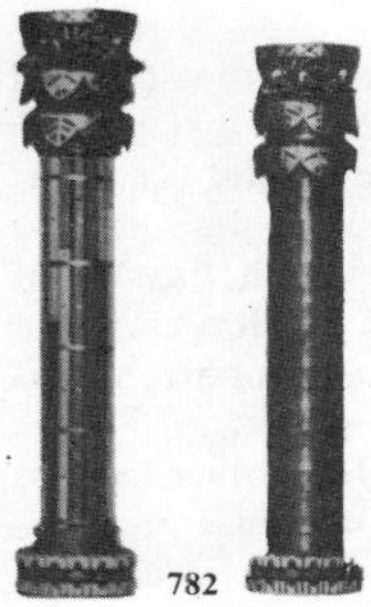

782

783

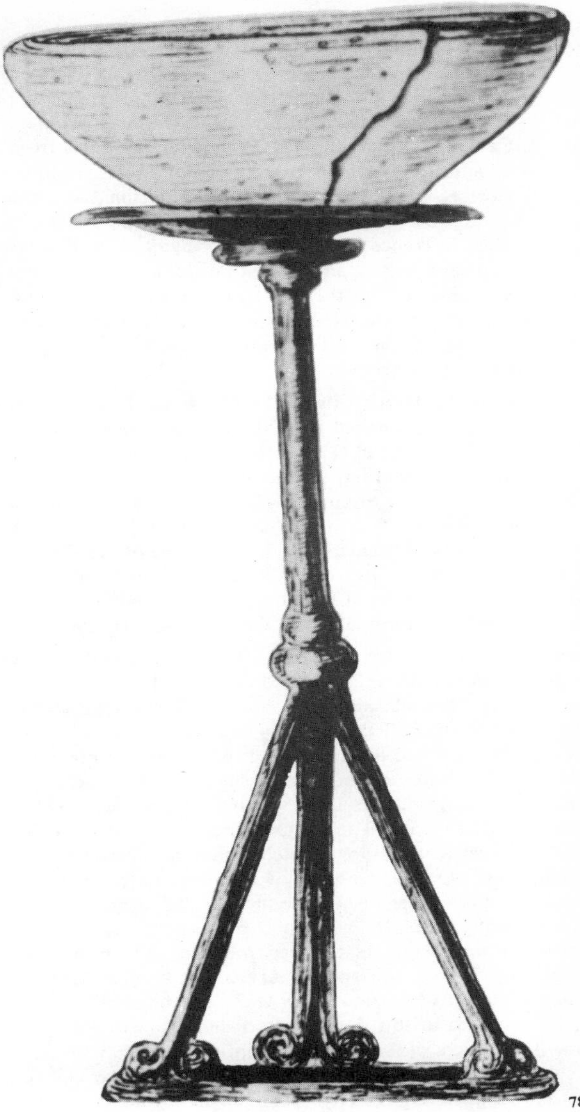

784

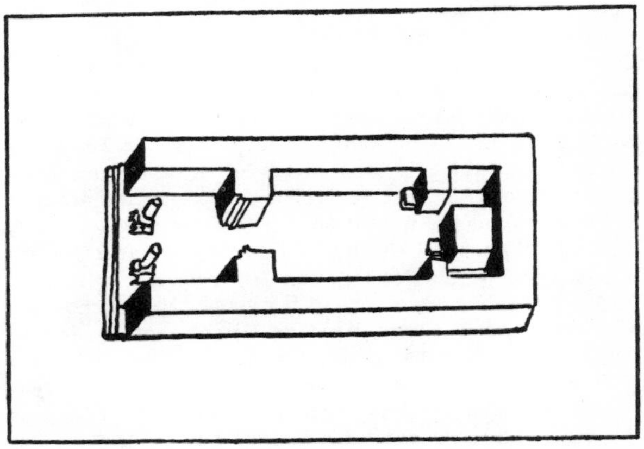

785

group (as in **778**). According to I Kings, its capacity was 2000 "bāt", while II Ch. puts it at 3000 bat (Albright and R.B.Y. Scott reckoned a bāt as 22 litres, or 5 gallons; see Weights and Measures*). The best parallels which have been found are the stone basins from Amathonte in Cyprus (**779**) and from Megiddo*.

The Bible also mentions ten wheeled pedestals ("machines"), each supporting a bronze laver used to wash the sacrificial victims. Such pedestals have also been found in Cyprus and Megiddo (**781**). Cups and braziers are listed among the Temple furnishings; such implements (**780**), and vessels used for ritual purposes, were common to sanctuaries in Mesopotamia and Syria, and have been uncovered in excavations at Ugarit, making it easier to understand the biblical descriptions. Receptacles were often placed on stands or on wheels (**784**).

Jachin and Boaz: In front of the Temple, before the vestibule, were placed two bronze columns called Jachin and Boaz. They were free standing and thus were purely decorative, with no functional purpose as to the structure, as shown by this model (**782**). They were elaborately decorated and crowned by bronze capitals, thought to be similar to the capital of a column (**783**) found at Megiddo, and were 23 cubits high and 12 cubits in circumference. W.F. Albright has suggested that they were gigantic incense stands, but R. de Vaux believes that they were traditional stele or "mazebôt" which had always had a place in the Old Canaanite sanctuaries. The name of the columns remains a riddle. R.B.Y. Scott suggests that they were "key words" in some form of motto which invoked the blessings of God on David's dynasty.

Analogies and Influences: The foregoing description gives a general idea of the plan and contents of the First Temple, but how and where the plan originated is not clear. Scholars first sought its prototype in Egypt (which had maintained close relations with Solomon), in the Aegean cultures and in Mesopotamia (since many terms relating to the Temple were of Akkadian derivation). Nowhere was its actual prototype found until several scholars finally looked for it in Phoenicia, from where the Temple's artisans had come. The tripartite division into ûlām, hechāl and d[e]bîr was very common among the Canaanites (for example in the "Fosse temple" at Lachish* belonging to the pre-Israelite period). Several recently discovered sanctuaries follow the plan of the rooms standing one behind the other in a line. At Alalakh, in northern Syria, a temple of the 13th c. BCE was uncovered. At Tel Ta'inat (**785**) a small temple, oriented east-west, was discovered, the plan of which bears a striking resemblance to Solomon's Temple, even to building methods. They both had brick walls locked together by a framework of wooden ties which stood on a stone base. The Tel Ta'inat temple had also been put up near the king's palace. The only problem with this analogy is that the Tel Ta'inat temple dates from the 9th c. BCE, one century later than Solomon's Temple, though most scholars regard it as falling within the same chronological framework. It is indicative of a general type, so that the difference in date is not significant. Similar temples may have existed, and it is assumed that the Jerusalem Temple was inspired by the Syrian-Canaanite culture and was Phoenician in character (see Canaan*; Phoenicia*). The Israelite sanctuary of Tel-Arad was built according to a similar plan (see article).

A Prototype in Hazor: In 1957–58 CE another temple, somewhat better preserved than the others, was uncovered at Hazor*. This temple **(129)** also contained three rooms, each leading into another, and its general plan was almost identical with that of Solomon's Temple. It dates from the Late Bronze Age (13th c. BCE), thus preceding the Jerusalem temple. This may well have been the prototype of the Temple of Solomon. It was, however, only such in its external form. With regard to equipment for worship, the Jerusalem temple had no parallel anywhere in the East (see Tabernacle*).

Seat of the Divine Presence: There was no pantheon of deities on an equal level in Jewish worship. There was only one sacred "house" and this became "The House" or "House of the Lord" (I K. 6:1, passim).

God did not dwell on earth, yet it was a sign of his grace that he had chosen to be present in the "tabernacle" or "tent" (to use an old nomadic word) in the people's midst. This gave rise in Israel to an awareness of the mystery of His presence within the people, which also created the Israelite nation. The problem of the distant transcendent God, the knowledge of and desire for his nearness, was solved in the Temple by means of a rich, sacramental symbolism which possessed deep meaning for those who understood it (see Tabernacle, Ark and Cherubim*). God Himself chose to live among his own, and he chose to live in this city and in this Temple. It is debatable whether the Israelites thought of the Temple as representing the Universe, as submitted by many scholars. Very vague cosmic symbolism pervades biblical thought from the earliest times.

The Temple in Israel's Life: Numerous passages support the view that Solomon's Temple was to be the abode of the Lord in the sense that it was the earthly representation of the heavenly abode. This interpretation of the Temple's significance remained the dominant one, at least in Israel's priestly circles. But there is also evidence of a conflict over the localization of God and consideration of the Temple as his dwelling, which is even expressed in Solomon's dedicatory prayer (I K. 8:27–30). The solution of the problem of his transcendence went deeper. The Temple was not only God's dwelling, but it also bore His name and was important in His eyes, not because it was His palace, but because prayer besought Him to regard it as such. He had no need of a Temple, and its importance in His eyes was an accommodation to the needs of the people.

Though the Temple was erected primarily as a royal chapel adjoining the king's palace (a common practice in the Near East), it naturally had a national significance throughout its history, even though during the Divided Monarchy rival shrines existed in Bethel and Dan (cf. Am. 7:13; Israel and Judah, Part II*). On several occasions the vessels and equipment of the Temple were despoiled by conquerors or surrendered as tribute. Only with the fall of the Northern Kingdom and the reforms of Hezekiah and Josiah did the Temple assume paramount importance as the religious and symbolic focus of the nation.

It is noteworthy that Solomon's Temple, like other temples in the ancient Near East, was intended for ritual purposes and only those who belonged to the priestly order were allowed within its precincts. The lay worshipper could not enter the Temple. In this respect, it was quite different from the synagogues* and Christian churches which replaced the Temple. The religious practices described in Leviticus* were substantially those used in the Temple. Both Lv. 27:30–33 and Dt. 14:28–29 prescribe tithes* for temple support. This was supplemented in later days by grants from royalty and the aristocracy, individual gifts and war-booty. Tithes in kind and gifts were stored in the side-building (yatsiā). The Temple served for the daily offering of sacrifices* and was also a centre of popular worship to which the masses came to offer sacrifices, atone and assemble, especially on the three pilgrimage festivals* and other holidays.

The Service: The service at the Temple was performed by the priests and Levites* (see Priesthood*). The chief priests* in Jerusalem were all of the line of Zadok and were actually members of the successive royal administrative cabinets. Priests were educated, and kept careful records. It is believed by many that these records were preserved in the "lishkat hagazit", the "chamber of hewn stone".

The First Temple was completely destroyed by Nebuchadrezzar in 586 BCE. (See also Tabernacle, Ark and Cherubim*; Tel-Arad under Ancient Cities*; Synagogue*).

II. SECOND TEMPLE, POST-EXILIC AND HERODIAN: When Cyrus, King of Persia, conquered Babylonia, he gave permission to the Jews to rebuild their ruined Temple in Jerusalem (538 BCE; see Restoration*). The Temple, completed in 515 BCE, was small and insignificant in comparison to the First Temple. However, it occupied a more vital position in the life of the nation, in the sense that it was the religious and ritual centre of all Jews, in Palestine and in the Diaspora, and pilgrims flocked to it from all countries. Even the gradual evolution of the synagogue* as a place of worship did not detract from the Temple's eminent position, and in post-biblical literature the Second Temple is referred to with ever-increasing reverence.

In the pre-Exilic period, almost to the end of the Monarchy, sacrifices had been offered in many sanctuaries as well as in the Temple; in post-Exilic times, sacrifices were offered only in the Temple (see Israel and Judah*, Part V). Major constructions were carried out in the periods of Simon the Just (4th c. BCE), the Hasmoneans* and Herod*, though detailed information is available only for Herod's reconstruction (see below).

Temple Services: The Temple priests, headed by the High Priest, occupied the highest position in the theocratic leadership of the nation (see Priesthood*). The Temple enjoyed considerable revenue from tithes, taxes, contributions and occasional gifts from foreign kings in return for its support. Tremendous numbers of the faithful flocked to Jerusalem during the three pilgrimage festivals*.

The priests serving the Temple were divided, as in late pre-Exilic times, into 24 watches; the Levites were assistants to the priests, musicians and doorkeepers, while menial tasks were performed by the Nethinim (see Government*). Laymen were associated with the regular cult through the organization of 24 lay "ma'amadot" (see Sacrifice*), each of which was assigned its specific time of service in the Temple, accompanying a corresponding watch of priests. The function of the laymen was to participate in the public sacrifices and to bring in the first fruits.

The supreme significance of the Temple came from its position as the centre for the fulfilment of the Pentateuchal injunction to offer sacrifice. Every good Jew was bound to obey these Laws (see Law: Living under the Law*).

The Temple in Graeco-Roman Times: In 167–164 BCE, Antiochus IV Epiphanes issued his "Infamous Edicts", under which the Temple was desecrated. In consequence, the holy ritual was suspended by the Jews, engaged in civil war with the Jewish "hellenizers" and in a rebellion against Seleucid rule which supported the hellenizers (see Hasmoneans*). The Temple was reoccupied by Judas Maccabaeus who rebuilt the altar and purified and rededicated the Temple. It resumed its lofty position in the life of the independent Jewish state, under the High Priests of the Hasmonean house.

The Temple was not only the supreme Jewish sanctuary, it also became the scene of political struggle. During one upheaval between the people and Alexander Jannaeus, the crowd of worshippers "stoned" him with citrons during the Feast of Tabernacles. When Pompey invaded Palestine (63 BCE), the supporters of Aristobulos entrenched themselves behind the Temple walls and fought the Romans. Pompey stormed the Temple and penetrated into the Holy of Holies.

Herod's Temple: Until the 1st c. BCE, the Second Temple remained a modest and battle-scarred sanctuary. It was given to Herod* the Great to complete one of the most glorious architectural tasks of his time, a period noted for its magnificent palaces and other structures. The project was begun in 20 BCE (the 17th or 18th year of Herod's reign). The major part of the reconstruction was accomplished in ten years, though additional work went on for many years after. The Herodian Temple was constructed over and around the existing modest building. Built on a high esplanade and surrounded by columns and beautiful gates, its shining white stone could be seen for miles in every direction. Herod did not alter the size of the inner Temple, i.e. the one rebuilt by the post-Exilic community, probably a later version of Solomon's Temple (see Restoration*), nor did he change its general pattern. But he doubled the area of the outer courts by smoothing the rock surface and filling in the steep southeastern slope (work actually begun in the days of Solomon), and levelling and filling the area between the Tyropeon Vale and the Temple mount at the southwestern corner (see Jerusalem*). The remains of the southeastern supporting walls and those of the western end of the esplanade (the Wailing Wall of today) are still visible, as shown by the large stones in the lower part of the illustration (**150**).

Temple Area and Courts: The Temple was also a military stronghold. The whole area was surrounded by a strong outer wall for purposes of defence. Inside this outer wall was a free belt, the outer court, which in Herod's time was known as the Court of Gentiles. Then came a strong fence marking the boundary of the inner sanctuary. No alien was permitted to cross this boundary, as attested to by an inscription (**786**) dating from Roman times which read "No foreigner is allowed within the balustrade and embankment about the sanctuary. Whoever is caught will be personally responsible for his ensuing death." (cf. Acts 21:31 ff). The court was surrounded by internal porticoes which were connected with the Tower of Antonia (see Herod*; Jesus*) to the north-west. The largest of the porticoes formed a basilica where money changers and merchants carried on

786

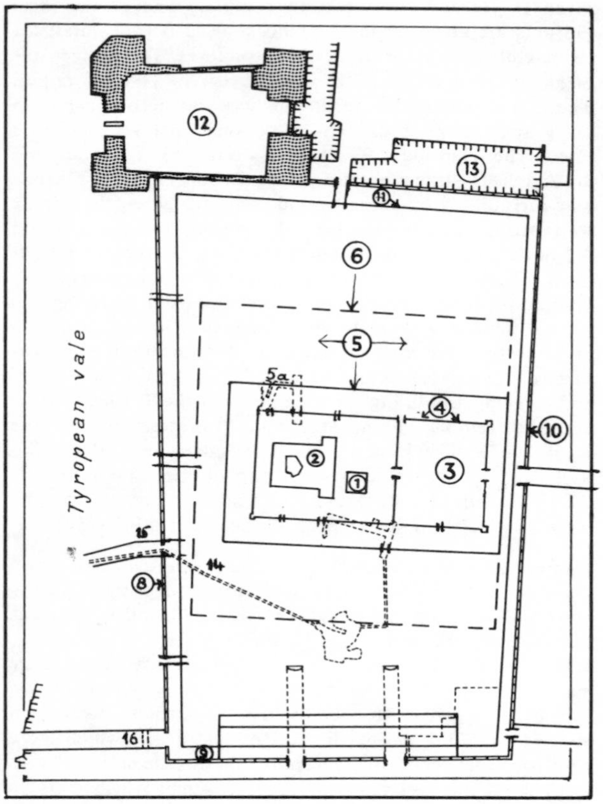

1. Altar and Priests' Court.
2. Temple enclosing the sacred rock.
3. Women's Court. 4. Temple wall enclosing the holy site.
5. Outer esplanade (secular). 5a. Baptistry.
6. Limits of Temple Mount. 7. Court of Gentiles.
8-9-10-11. Herod's wide esplanade. 8. Western wall.
9. Southern wall. 10: Eastern wall. 11. Northern wall.
12. Tower of Antonia. 13. Pool of Israel. 14 Aqueduct.
15. Wilson's Arch (bridge). 16. Robinson's Arch.
= Gates to Inner Courts and outer gates.

their business (Mk. 11:15–17). The inner court contained a section for women, another for common folk, and still another court for the priests. It contained the main altar and was surrounded by chambers used for various purposes connected with sacred ritual, sacrifice, ablutions, etc. At least eight gates opened onto the sacred area and it was approached by two bridges from the east and two from the west (see diagram and plan of the Temple area, **787**). The women's court communicated, via the Nicanor Gate, with the Gate of the Israelites, and was in effect part of the court of the Priests and the scene of mass-assembly during the festivals. Also adjoining were the priests' quarters and the Chamber of Hewn Stone (lishkat hagazit) where the Sanhedrin sat. Most sacred of all, as in the First Temple, was the Holy of Holies.

The Temple: The Temple itself was divided into a hall (ûlām), a shrine (Holy Place) containing the incense altar, shewbread table and the seven-branched candelabrum (menorah), and the Holy of Holies, dark and empty and entered only by the High Priest* on the Day of Atonement through a "veil" consisting of two parallel curtains (cf. Heb. 9:6 ff). Store chambers for treasures were in the north, west and south sides of the Temple building. They were used as deposit vaults, protected chiefly by the sanctity of the place and the awe inspired by the sacred surroundings.

The area of the completed Temple and grounds was 34 acres in extent. The northern wall was 351 yards long and the southern wall 309 yards long, while the eastern and western walls were respectively 518 and 536 yards in length.

Despite the bitterness against Herod* as a person and as a ruler (see article), Jewish writers (in the Mishnah*, the New Testament, and Josephus*) could not minimize his achievement in rebuilding the Temple. The popular saying, "He who has not seen Herod's Temple has never seen stately structure" (Sukkah 516) was no doubt as sincere on religious grounds as it was grudging from the nationalist point of view.

Sectarian Opposition to the Temple: Nevertheless, the Temple was not the most adequate expression of all distinctive features of Judaism and certainly not of those cherished by many nonconformist Jewish groups such as the Essenes (see Dead Sea Scrolls*) and Jewish Christians*. This may have been bound up partly with the ritual animal sacrifice* and other archaic customs (discussed under Sacrifice*; Jesus*; Paul*). In the main, the opposition of the sects was not to Temple worship as such but to the corruption of the priests who were in charge of the Temple, and to the secularizing tendencies due to its wealth and the participation of the civil rulers.

The Temple area, which was a military stronghold, was also the scene of many of the teachings and preachings of Jesus. In the large outer court, groups of Jews of all denominations would meet. The early Jewish Christians met there (Acts 5:12). The loyalty of Jesus and the early Apostolic church to the Temple, and their close relationship to it, are well known (Mk. 11:15–17; Lk. 2:49; Jn. 2:13; 5:1). Christianity found a place of worship in the Temple in its early days, but forces were at work to alter this situation (see Jesus*; Jewish Christians*). There was strong opposition to the Jewish Christians on the part of the priestly party. On the other hand, the advent of militant Christianity operated to eliminate the Temple as an essential part of Christian thought and worship, though Temple imagery and symbolism continued to be used in Christian thinking.

The Destruction of the Second Temple: After Herod's time, Jerusalem and the Temple were under foreign domination much of the time. The High Priests* were civil rulers, appointed by the central authority; they collaborated with Rome, became worldly, and were compromised by these connections. Under the rule of the Roman procurators, the Temple area became the scene of bloody clashes which usually took place during the three pilgrimage festivals*. One act of overt opposition against Rome was the cessation of the daily sacrifice in honour of the Roman emperor. This act may be regarded as a prelude to the Great Rebellion (see Rome and the Jews*).

During the siege of Jerusalem, the Temple was the chief bastion of the Zealots who conducted a desperate struggle against the Romans. But all the heroism of the Zealots was to no avail. The Romans stormed the Temple area after long and bitter engagements attended by heavy losses, and in 70 CE the Temple went up in flames. The great menorah (**788**) and other temple trophies were taken to Rome, depicted on the Arch of Titus (**712**).

The day of the destruction of the Second Temple, the 9th of Ab, also the date of the destruction of the First Temple, became from then on a day of mourning and fasting among Jews everywhere. The eschatological belief that it would rise again has remained deeply rooted in the hearts of Orthodox Jewry throughout the generations. It is connected with the coming of the Messiah of the House of David. A Roman Temple was built by Hadrian on the site of the Temple, and since the Arab period (7th c. CE), a mosque, the Dome of the Rock (Mosque of Omar) has stood there (see **151**; also Jerusalem*).

TRADE. — *Outline: I. Biblical References to Trade: Archaeological Evidence for Local Trade; International Trade in the Near East; Royal Monopolies in the Near East; Overland Transport; Israelite Trade before the Monarchy; Trade under the Monarchy; Israel's Exports; Trade in the Divided Kingdom; Ezekiel's Description of Mediterranean Commerce. II. Trade in Palestine and the Diaspora in Persian and Post-Exilic Times: Hellenistic to Roman Periods. III. Summary: Trade and Israelite Society.*

The Israelites may not have taken to international trade on the scale of some of their neighbours — notably the Canaanites — until the early days of the monarchy, but international contacts existed much earlier, and local trade developed in the ordinary way from the earliest times. Local markets would be held in the town or village square (II K. 7:1) and there peasants would sell the produce of their fields and herds, and craftsmen their wares. This was trade on a very small scale. The producer sold directly to the consumer without the intervention of a middleman. There is, however, more evidence for the existence of a merchant and artisan class in the cities*, as in neighbouring countries where merchants probably existed from quite early on. Participation in international trade, on the other hand, was slower and less pervasive among the Israelites.

I. BIBLICAL REFERENCES TO TRADE: References to trade and traders in the Bible are either (e.g. Gn. 37:25, 28) to foreign merchants passing through the country (see below) in the early period, or to the traders (foreign or Israelite) of the period of the monarchy (e.g. I K. 10:15 or II Ch. 9:14). Reference to traders as "Canaanites" (Job 41:6; Pr. 31:24; Zech. 14:21) suggests that in the earliest period of Israelite settlement, trade in small imported goods and the purchase of local wares for export was still in the hands of the original inhabitants of the country. Moreover, the descendants of the Canaanites, the Phoenicians*, were the great traders of the age (described in detail in Ezk. 27 and referred to elsewhere, e.g. Ezk. 17:4).

The terms "trader" and "merchant" seem to have been used without distinction, but there are occasions where a merchant is described as "one who travels about", a word with the same root as the verb "to walk". Hosea used the word "trader" as an accusation against Israel: a "trader in whose hands are false balances (Hos. 12:7). Trade is described as "traffic" (Ezk. 27:12) or "barter" (Ezk. 27:9), but goods are known to have been of value, precious metals and stones for example (Job 28:15–17, etc.).

As early as the story of Joseph (Gn. 37:25), merchants travelled in caravans and this was still true of travellers when the Song of Deborah was composed (Jud. 5:6; see Judges*; Poetry*). The term is also used by Job (6:18–19), while Ezekiel (27:25) records how the "ships of Tarshish" (see Phoenicia*) "travelled for you".

Archaeological Evidence for Local Trade: This comes mostly from ostraca (messages written on potsherds) found during excavations, referring to the shipment or delivery of such agricultural products as oil or wine or barley. One such ostracon, probably dating from the 4th c. BCE, was found in Ashdod*. Sometimes transfers of gold are also recorded in this way (see Inscriptions*). Similar evidence for trade connected with large-scale weaving and dyeing was found in Debir which contained about thirty dyeing establishments (see Crafts*), and additional evidence of the same kind has been recovered from Ashdod*, Gibeon and numerous other Israelite cities*.

International Trade in the Near East: To become a commercial centre, a country must have good land and sea communications with other lands and, usually, it should itself produce a surplus of industrial or agricultural commodities for trade.

788

Palestine in biblical times lacked good ports, but it lay right across the main land routes of the ancient Near East, from Egypt and the Phoenician ports of Tyre and Sidon, to the rich lands of Mesopotamia, Persia and the north and east. The "Way of the Sea" and the "King's Way" (see Roads, Transportation*, Trade Routes), the most important land routes of the age, both crossed Israelite territory. Accordingly, right through history, traders of many different nationalities made regular journeys through the land. In ancient times, the Midianites had almost a monopoly of the international caravan trade between Mesopotamia and Egypt. It was very natural that Joseph's brothers should have met such a group (Gn. 37:25). Later on, international trade became the concern of the Phoenicians* (Is. 23:2, 8; Ezk. 27), and, according to Nahum (3:16), the Assyrians. Still later, these were replaced by the Greeks. In biblical times, the Israelites did not appear as merchants on this scale.

The traders who passed through the land, however, provided the national revenues with one of its most important sources of income (I K. 10:15; Ezr. 4:20) and also enabled the Israelites to exchange their goods for foreign wares.

The 14th c. BCE Amarna letters* also include a good deal of evidence of the international trade between Mesopotamia, Canaan and Egypt. Many of the letters refer to the caravans which passed between the kingdoms. Three lists of products being sent to the king of Babylonia by the king of Egypt, and an inventory of the dowry of a princess marrying an Egyptian king, all bear witness to the variety of goods which had a commercial value at the time. The extent of international trade is demonstrated by many other documents. Goods were exchanged between Mediterranean countries and those of the Far East. Assyria and Babylonia acted as entrepots for Indian and Eastern Asian products. Some of the earliest written documents were concerned with such trade. It is the subject of Babylonian cuneiform tablets dating from the 3rd to the 1st mill. BCE and is richly illustrated by Assyrian documents from the 10th c. BCE onwards (see this money changer from Carchemish, **789**; also Weights and Measures*.)

The Egyptians received ivory, building timber, leather and slaves from Nubia (modern Sudan) and the lands to the south, and sometimes sent ships to the "Lands of the Spices", i.e. to southern Arabia, Somaliland and east Africa. Overland caravans from Arabia, Mesopotamia, Syria and the north came by way of Palestine.

Royal Monopolies in the Near East: From very early times, trade in the Near East was a royal monopoly. As early as the 3rd mill. BCE, the kings of Mesopotamia owned their own caravans and the same was true of Hammurabi (see Babylonia*). During the Amarna* age, the kings of Babylonia, Cyprus and other lands had merchants in their service. The Egyptian story of Wen-Amun (see Phoenicia*) relates that the prince of Tanis in Egypt had a merchant navy and that the king of Byblos kept a record of the business he did with the prince.

Overland Transport: In times of peace and in areas where there was no danger from bandits, traders might travel alone or in small companies, going on foot at first, from one town to another, buying and selling and carrying their goods with them. In less secure times, a caravan might need an armed guard (Ezr. 8:22). The caravans that carried merchants and merchandise from country to country used donkeys (Gn. 42:26; 43:18); mules (II K. 5:17; I Ch. 12:40); camels (Gn. 37:25); oxen (I Ch. 12:40) or slaves (II K. 5:23), but not horses which were reserved for pulling military chariots, not mere wagons. Indeed, wagons are usually mentioned in the Bible as carrying people, not goods (Gn. 45:19, 21, 27; 46:5; I Sam. 6:7–11). The Sennacherib relief (**159**) of the siege of Lachish shows carts with people in them, pulled by animals. Moreover, in the account of the great convoy of returning Exiles (Ezr. 2:66–67) there is no mention of carts or wagons (but see also Roads, Transportation and Trade Routes*).

Israelite Trade before the Monarchy: The Israelites who entered Canaan were only a little removed from a semi-nomadic existence. The way of life of a settled, agricultural people was not learned overnight. Contacts must have been established with the Canaanite inhabitants of the country and their influence is reflected in various aspects of Israel's life. Nevertheless, religious and other differences also acted as barriers to the development of close relationships.

It seems hardly surprising that the first of the tribes to engage in trade were those in the north, closest to the Phoenicians. This applies especially to the isolated half tribe of Dan who are reproached in the Song of Deborah (see Judges*): "and Dan, why did he abide with the ships?"

789

(Jud. 5:17) for presumably working in the ships of Tyre and Sidon (see Phoenicia*. The Danites did not live on the coast and had no ships of their own.) The most serious obstacle to trade at this period, however, was the constant wars and unrest. The establishment of internal security begun by Saul* and completed by David* was essential before trade could develop to any large extent, while only with a united kingdom were the equally necessary standard weights and measures adopted (e.g. the reference in II Sam. 14:26 to the "king's weight"; see Weights and Measures*).

Trade under the Monarchy: The first great Israelite trader was King Solomon. During his reign, trade first became a major element in the country's economy. Foreign trade was very much a royal monopoly (see above) and Solomon arranged with Hiram of Tyre (see Phoenicia*) to equip a Red Sea fleet which should exchange the copper of Ezion-Geber for the gold and precious stones of Ophir (I K. 9:26–28; 10:11, 22). Solomon also traded with Hiram for the variety of materials needed to build the Temple in Jerusalem (I K. 5:6, 10–11; 9:11) and with the Queen of Sheba (I K. 10:10, 13). Moreover, Solomon received "silver and gold, garments, myrhh, spices, horses and mules" as tribute from many lands (I K. 10:25).

One of his most notable trading achievements was his virtual monopoly of dealings in horses and chariots — the most important military weapon of the day. Through his agents, the "soḥarei hamelekh", Solomon imported horses from the famous breeding grounds of Que or Cilicia in Anatolia and chariots from Egypt. With these he built up his own — unprecedented — chariot army and monopolized the supply to other rulers, "so through the king's traders they were exported to all the kings of the Hittites and the kings of Syria" (I K. 10:28–29).

The variety and quantity of valuable goods which were imported into Solomon's kingdom are listed in boastful detail by his annalist. Much less is said about how they were paid for. The bargain made with Hiram for the building of the Temple records Israel's obligations in wheat and oil, but from the story of the 20 Israelite cities later leased to the Tyrian king (I K. 9:11–13; II Ch. 8:2; see Phoenicia*) it seems likely that the country's production of agricultural goods and other revenues did not provide a sufficient basis for her external trade.

Israel's Exports: Palestine's most important export commodities were agricultural products: oil, grain and wine. The merchants of Tyre used to buy these goods in Israel and sell them in the cities of the Mediterranean (Ezk. 27:17). Solomon bought supplies for building the Temple in Jerusalem against payment in wheat and oil (I K. 5:11). Oil was also sold to Egypt (Hos. 12:1) as well as cosmetics (see Arad*). The country produced flax and wool, but these were not export items; indeed, Israel received wool from Moab (II K. 3:4). When Joseph's brothers wanted to take a present of the best that their own land produced, they chose "a little balm and a little honey, gum, myrhh, pistachio nuts and almonds" (Gn. 43:11), although some of these are also mentioned (Gn. 37:25) as products of Gilead.

Although the best timber, especially cedarwood, was imported from Phoenicia (I K. 5:6), the city of Tyre used to buy oaks of Bashan from Israel for use in ship-building and for making oars (Ezk. 27:6). The Assyrians also imported Phoenician timber, as witness the stone relief (**748**) of the Phoenician timber trade. The country produced copper, but this is not mentioned as an export item, only as one of exchange (see below; see also Crafts: Tools and Implements*).

Trade in the Divided Kingdom: With Hiram's help, Solomon was able to build up the first Israelite merchant marine based at Eilat on the Red Sea, an area which had been opened to the Israelites by David's conquest of Edom. After Solomon's death, Edom revolted and the sea road to Sabea in Arabia* (see article) and Ophir was closed to Israel (I K. 11:14). Only when Jehoshaphat reigned in Judah (871–849 BCE) did Ezion-Geber and its outlet to the Red Sea again become available to the kingdom. Jehoshaphat aimed at reestablishing Solomon's trading activities and sent a fleet of ten ships to Ophir, but his hopes were wrecked with the loss of the ships in a storm. A subsequent offer from Ahaziah, king of Israel, to send a combined expedition was refused (I K. 22:48–49).

International trade continued to expand but after the death of Solomon its centre moved to Samaria, the capital of the Northern Kingdom. Israel established close trade relations with Aram and Damascus. Ahab signed a commercial agreement with Ben-Hadad, king of Damascus, according to which the Israelites could set up bazaars in Damascus, and the Syrian king could open similar marts in Samaria (I K. 20:34). This was a typical business deal for the Near East of that time.

The trade of both countries developed considerably during the long reigns of Uzziah in Judah and Jeroboam II in Israel. Increasing imports of luxury goods brought complaints from the prophets that the resources of the land, especially the grain needed by the poor to live, were diverted to buy foreign luxuries for the life of ease of the rich (Is. 2:7; Hos. 12:7–8; Am. 3:15; 4:1; 8:4–6). Hosea links Israel's external trade and foreign policy: "Ephraim herds the wind and pursues the east wind all day long; they multiply falsehood and violence; they make a bargain with Assyria and oil is carried to Egypt." (Hos. 12:1). In the excavations of ancient sites throughout Palestine, from Galilee to the Negeb, and in Ugarit and Phoenicia, the discovery of painted pottery, arms and jewellery all bear witness to the diffusion of oriental arts and techniques, indicating continuing contacts between trader and craftsman. Although little direct evidence exists for serious commerce before the 10th c. BCE, in later centuries imports from Phoenicia and Cyprus became common.

Ezekiel's Description of Mediterranean Commerce: Ch. 27 of the book of Ezekiel opens "... Raise a lamentation over Tyre..." but, in fact, this vivid description of a great trading city is the most unreserved praise of Phoenician success and prosperity (see Phoenicia*). The prophet lists the nationalities and products that contributed to Tyre's wealth, and the whole passage (Ezk. 27:5–25) reads like the roll-call of the trade of the Mediterranean and ancient world: "Silver, iron, tin and lead... slaves, bronze... horses... ivory tusks and ebony... precious stones, embroidery... wine, wool... lambs, rams and goats... spices, carpets... gold... while Judah and the land of Israel... exchanged for your merchandise wheat, olives and early figs, honey, oil and balm..."

II. TRADE IN PALESTINE AND THE DIASPORA IN PERSIAN AND POST-EXILIC TIMES: Nothing is known of the commercial activities of the Jews during their Exile, but the land to which they were sent enjoyed a highly developed culture and a flourishing commerce. As a result of their contacts with Babylonian trade as well as from force of necessity, the Jews of the Diaspora became merchants. As the Jews driven from their own land settled further afield, so many of the factors which had aided the trading successes of the Phoenicians and their colonies came to apply to the Jews. They had contacts throughout the known world and they developed the techniques of commerce and credit. This is well illustrated by the records of the banking house of Murashu whose activities, based on Babylonia, continued until the time of Darius II (see Restoration*). When the Jews were offered the chance of return to Zion, many chose to remain.

Nehemiah (ch. 13) refers to a variety of craftsmen in Jerusalem, including those engaged in finance such as tax-collectors, moneylenders and merchants, but as a class, such men were new in the country compared to the bakers, metal-workers and potters. The creation of a merchant class within Palestine was a late development, although by the 2nd c. BCE, Ben-Sira (Ecclus. 42:5) could regard profits from commerce as legitimate.

Hellenistic to Roman Periods: International trade was greatly aided by the central organization and relatively stable government established throughout the eastern Mediterranean and western Asia by the Persian empire, reinforced, after a period of upheaval, by Alexander's conquests. Expanding trade was one important feature of the new way of life which Hellenism brought to the area (see Hellenism in the Near East*) and in this the Jews of the dispersion joined. The subsequent Roman conquests soon led to colonies of Jews settling and trading further west.

Within Palestine itself the situation changed little. The Letter of Aristeas (see Apocrypha*) suggests that spices, precious stones and gold and the various luxuries of the outside world were imported into Judea by Arabs*. The coast of Palestine was lined with Hellenistic cities* mainly concerned with trade between the interior and the Mediterranean world. Indeed, the Israelites did not exercise effective control of the coast until Hellenistic times. Some of it was never completely in their hands, not being considered part of the "clean" territory of the Holy Land, i.e. free of gentile influences. Accordingly, there was very little scope for a native Jewish commercial class within its own land, and still less for financiers, apart from tax-farmers like the Tobiads (see Hasmoneans*; Hellenism and Jewry*).

Outside Palestine, the position was easier. When Alexandria was established, permission was given for every Jew who wished to do so to come and settle, and the same rule applied in Antioch. This was an effective stimulus to the trade of the Ptolemaic and Seleucid empires.

Papyri of the Egyptian Hellenistic period contain plenty of evidence of Jews acting as traders, bankers and brokers. Even though the Jews rejected religious or national assimilation, their material and cultural standards were inevitably affected by Hellenism. During and after the Hasmonean period, an affluent and sizable commercial class made its appearance among the Jews of Palestine. The process was hastened by Hasmonean conquests. When Jaffa was brought under Jewish control (see Hasmoneans*) it was repeopled with Jews — including merchants who rapidly began to play their part in international trade (I Mac. 14:5), replacing the Phoenicians as the traders for the whole Mediterranean. (Financial activities of ancient times and the more developed procedures of post-Exilic times are dealt with under Loans and Debts*.)

During the reigns of the Hasmonean kings and of Herod, revenue in customs duties at Palestinian ports and transit dues on goods crossing Jewish territory, reached very substantial proportions. Under Herod, import and purchase and sales taxes stood at an average of 25% of the value of the goods. There are no reliable figures, but a general picture of economic development both in agriculture and in commerce can be obtained from the records of Herod and his successors, and from various Roman writers. All the Near Eastern countries charged transit and port duties, so that the Jewish treasury benefitted from the expansion of both sea-borne and overland trade. In time, Caesarea* became one of the great centres of trade for Palestine and the whole eastern Mediterranean, and it provided one of the chief sources of revenue of Herod and later rulers. By that time, the variety of both exports and imports had grown considerably. Later on, in Talmudic times, 118 different articles were listed as imported into Palestine from abroad. These included materials for making clothes, domestic utensils and foodstuffs.

III. SUMMARY: **Trade and Israelite Society:** Israelite interest in trade began many generations after the Conquest* as the economy of the country and its cities passed into Jewish hands and a developing city life provided an expanding market for the exchange of commodities. In the early phase, large-scale foreign commerce was a matter of royal ventures — e.g. the activities of Solomon or Jehoshaphat, but in the later period of the monarchy, during the Babylonian Exile and afterwards in Palestine, occasional individuals established themselves as traders and business men, acting as middlemen or wholesale merchants. From the 10th c. BCE onwards, the process was accelerated through increased international contacts, the alternation of military campaigns with periods of peace, and the opening up of international trade routes through all the Near East.

Throughout the biblical period the Jews were never a distinctively trading people. Israelites became merchants on any scale only during and after the Babylonian Exile when, of necessity, many Jews who had been forced to give up their traditional skills and occupations, turned to trade as a means of livelihood (see Exile*; Restoration*).

Even then, the adoption of commerce as part of the national way of life never affected the whole of the people. The effects on society and religion of the slow development of a Jewish commercial class in post-Exilic and Graeco-Roman times, are difficult to gauge precisely. They are one aspect of the growing cosmopolitanism found in political, cultural and social fields in the Hellenistic age (see the articles on Hellenism*; Hasmoneans*; Law*). The teaching of Wisdom Literature* and the Pharisees* continued to advocate a traditional Jewish attitude of moderation. It seems probable that, overall, the Jews took increasing foreign secular influences in their stride. The middle and upper classes became outwardly less Jewish, while the traditional values of the people as a whole changed hardly at all. In the end, the attractions of the Pax Romana made no appeal to the nationalists who took up arms against the whole might of the Roman empire in defence of their own traditions and ideas (see Rome and the Jews*). See also: Agriculture*; Cities*; Crafts*; Hellenism and Jewry*; Hellenism in the Diaspora*; Roads, Transportation, Trade Routes*; Weights and Measures*.

TRANSFIGURATION AND RESURRECTION:— The story of the transfiguration can be understood not only theologically in relation to the Resurrection, or in terms of its symbolic implications, but also historically.

Each of the three synoptic gospels includes the story in their accounts of the lifetime of Jesus* (Lk. 9:28–36; Mk. 9:2–13; Mt. 17:1–13). All three interpret it as a fulfilment of the eschatological* prediction: "There are some standing here who will not taste death before they see the kingdom." In terms of the apocalyptic* symbols of the age, a transfigured Jesus standing with Elijah and Moses could only mean the coming of Jesus in his exalted state in the presence of God (see Eschatology*; Apocalypse*; Dead Sea Scrolls*), which was to be announced by a Mosaic prophet.

The central point of the story is not to describe the Risen Lord, but to make it clear to those from whom the Church claimed obedience that Jesus had indeed received full heavenly authority. The transfiguration is a story of a transformation of substance, not merely a change of appearance. The gospels tell that as Jesus stood there, the voice of God was heard announcing, "This is my Son, my Chosen; listen to Him." This was precisely the belief of the primitive Church. The transfiguration incident served to confirm the disciples' faith in Jesus as Messiah and Jesus' own prediction of his death and resurrection.

One of the more familiar interpretations of the transfiguration is that originally it was an appearance of Jesus after his Resurrection, and the story was later transferred to his lifetime. Exactly by what process is not clear. It is suggested that an appearance, either to Peter or to all three of the principal disciples was gradually elaborated to include other phenomena of the heavenly world. These details provide the appropriate eschatological setting for the divine command to obedience which was the central point of the later version.

The pre-dating, in G. E. Carlston's view, "reflects the conviction that the Christ of the 'kerygma', that is, the good news of salvation, was not fundamentally different from the historical Jesus, or, to put it conversely, that the one whom the church proclaimed as Lord had been confirmed as worthy of complete obedience by God himself during his earthly life."

Modern historians have found great difficulty in locating Jesus' prediction of his own death and resurrection within his ministry. The gospel statement that after the transfiguration he bound his disciples to keep silent about it, seems an artificial contrivance to make such a prediction credible.

Objections to finding the historical source of the transfiguration after the ministry of Jesus must take account of the doubts and fears of Peter and the disciples after the crucifixion (see Jesus*) which could only be banished by the Resurrection.

Many scholars find a re-arrangement of the chronology more satisfactory than rejecting the whole story as purely legendary. Since the story is highly symbolical — i.e. its meaning is more important than the actuality — it would be very difficult to decide whether it belongs before or after the Resurrection. The point is that the story could only be told from the point of view of the belief in the Resurrection. But it seems equally clear that it is a story about the earthly ministry of Jesus, i.e. that it belongs in the context of his preaching and teaching rather than his heavenly role (see also Christianity, Early*).

TRANSLATIONS (VERSIONS) OF THE BIBLE: While the Jews lived in their own country and spoke Hebrew, there was no need for translations of the Old Testament. Ancient Judaism was not a missionary religion, nor were the Jews the first nation to translate sacred books. Long before them, religious texts were translated in Mesopotamia from the Sumerian into the Akkadian language, and occasionally also into other languages of the region.

Ancient Versions of the Bible: The necessity for Bible translations arose only in the 3rd c. BCE, when many Jews spoke only Greek or Aramaic, and were unable to follow the prescribed lessons from the Law and the Prophets in the original. At first the translations were improvised on the spot in the synagogues, and were more explanations than translations in our sense; the Aramaic word "targem" means "to explain" as well as "to translate". They often included additional details taken from the Midrash (see Mishnah*). The Aramaic "Targums" of the Prophets and the Hagiographa (Writings), and the two Targums on the Pentateuch called Palestinian (Jerusalem) Targum and Targum Jonathan (Pseudo-Jonathan), are of this type. In course of time the translations kept more closely to the text, and became fixed by tradition. After being written down, they were carefully preserved in the same way as the Bible text itself. This is how the Greek Septuagint, the Syriac Peshitta ("simple translation") and the Aramaic "Targum Onkelos" (Aquilas) to the Pentateuch arose. They were all made by Jews for Jews, although later both the Septuagint and the Peshita, were taken over entirely by the Christian Church.

When Christianity developed out of Palestinian Judaism, the use of translations of the Bible was already well established, and the Church found these a ready and convenient means for its missionary activities. In its free use of translations, Christianity differs from other great religions, such as Hinduism or Islam, which insist on the reading of their scriptures in the original languages.

Translation of the Bible has since developed in two directions: the provision of versions in an increasing number of languages, and the provision of improved versions. The first versions were made from the Septuagint; these included the Old Latin version, the three versions in Coptic (the Christian form of Ancient Egyptian), and the versions into Ethiopic, Armenian, Georgian, Gothic and Slavonic, as illustrated here by a page from a mediaeval codex (**790**).

In several cases the Bible version was the first book to be written in the language, and an alphabet had

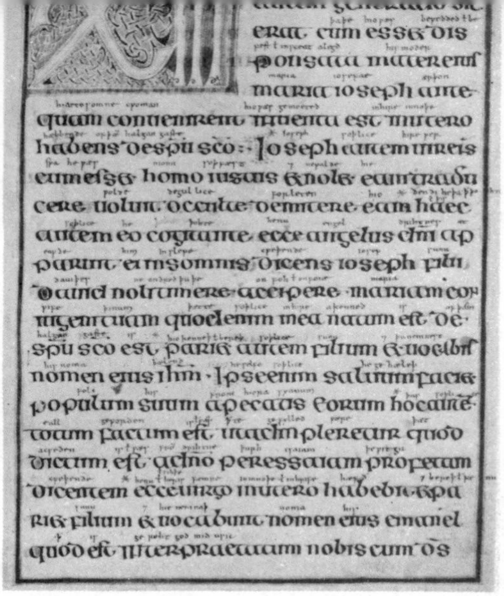

790

to be designed especially for it — something which is happening now in many non-European languages. There are also indications that parts of the Bible were translated by Christians into Arabic; the most important Arabic version — only partial — was made about 900 CE by a Jew, Rabbi Saadiah Gaon. The revision of Greek translations began with Aquilas (in Hebrew, Onkelos), a proselyte and, according to Jewish tradition, a pupil of Rabbi Akiba (ca. 130 CE), and Theodotion (in Hebrew, Jonathan), also a proselyte who lived about the end of the 2nd c. CE. Both tried to produce literal translations which came closer to the meaning of the Hebrew text. Symmachus, on the other hand, who made a new translation for the Ebionite Jewish-Christian* community, endeavoured to improve the Greek style. About 230 CE, the Church Father, Origen, prepared his Hexapla, in which he carefully compared these, and sometimes additional Greek versions, with each other and with the Hebrew, and from them prepared an improved Septuagint text. This new text, as well as a selection from the other versions, is known to us mainly through a translation into Syriac (the Syro-Hexapla). If complete, the original would fill 12,000 pages of manuscript but it survives only in fragmentary quotations and in the 5th and 7th c. CE copies (**791**). The original manuscript was seen in the library at Caesarea* in the 7th c. CE. This manuscript was consulted by the Church Father Jerome (d. 420 CE) who undertook the revision of the Old Latin Bible according to the original

791

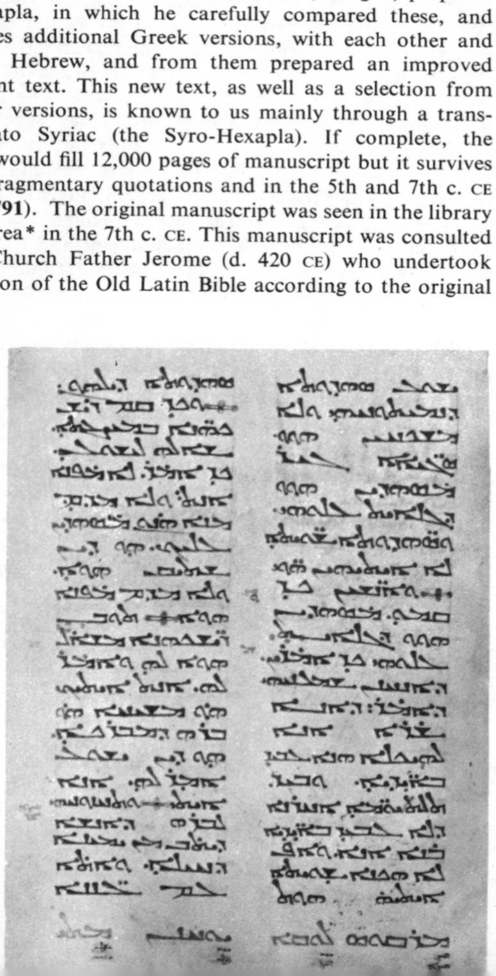

texts, and translated large parts of the Old Testament anew directly from the Hebrew; his Vulgate became, and still is the authoritative Bible of the Roman Catholic Church. However, work on Greek and Latin Bible versions did not cease with this. During the following centuries many attempts were made to render parts of the Bible into more elegant Greek or Latin.

The Septuagint with its revisions and secondary versions, the Targums, the Peshita and the Vulgate are the Ancient Versions. Their importance is paramount for establishing the various forms in which the Hebrew text was current before its final fixation, as well as for studying the tradition connected with its interpretation (see Biblical Criticism*: Textual Criticism).

European Versions: At first no translations were made into other European languages. Only the clergy could read, and they used the Vulgate, while for the people, poetic retellings were available. A Gothic version of both the Old and New Testaments by Bishop Ufilas (14th c.) is known, but it is not classed among the primary versions such as the Latin, Syriac and Coptic. Only after 1200 CE, when the various European languages became established in literature and public life, were Bible translations made, often against the will of the Church, and as part of reform movements. The best example is the German translation by Martin Luther (1521–34). The first complete English translation was by Wyclif and Hereford (1382). This was followed by several other versions. That of Tyndale and Coverdale (1526–35) was further revised in the Authorised or King James' version of 1611, a work which achieved great authority and deeply influenced the development of the English language. It was so popular that the Revised Version (the New Testament in 1881, the Old Testament in 1885) failed to be accepted by the public, although it was based on a much better understanding of the original texts.

Modern Versions: Constant revisions of Bible translations are necessary for two reasons: one is that the modern languages change, and words and phrases no longer have the meaning that they had for the translators some centuries ago, or become obsolete. The other is the advance in biblical scholarship, which proves many older renderings to have been incorrect. The American Standard Version (1901) reached widespread use among the clergy, schools and colleges. In the mid-20th century, revision undertakings are in progress in many western languages. In English, these include the American Revised Standard Version, the new English revised version, (only the New Testament so far), and the new Jewish translation of the Old Testament, arranged by the American Jewish Publication Society (only the Pentateuch so far). There is also the important American Catholic version, called the Confraternity, now nearing completion.

Over a Thousand Translations: The extension of missionary activity in the 19th c. CE gave rise to the need to translate the Bible into as many as possible of the 3,000–4,000 languages of mankind and their principal dialects. This work was largely organized by the various Bible Societies. When the British and Foreign Bible Society was founded in London in 1804, Bibles or parts of the Bible existed in 72 languages. By 1950, there were portions or complete Bibles in over 1000 tongues. In 1960, work was in progress on several thousand further translations, and special teaching institutions, a technical literature and periodicals had grown up to assist the labour of the translators. In most cases, their first task is to study the structure of the language and usually they are the first white men to do so. They then have to reduce the language to writing, and to establish some standards in it. Because of the vast differences of cultural background, great ingenuity and patience are often needed in order to transmit something of the meaning of the Bible to the reader. From the problems of the present-day translators, we can learn a great deal about the difficulties which faced those who first tried to render the thought of a monotheistic religion into Greek or Latin.

TRIBES OF ISRAEL. — *Outline: I. Tribes and Tribal Settlement: The Twelve Tribes of Israel; The Tribe in the Ancient Near East; Biblical Organization and Government of the Tribe. II. The Map of Tribal Settlement.*

I. TRIBES AND TRIBAL SETTLEMENT: **The Twelve Tribes of Israel:** The Bible presents a picture of the people of Israel organized into a system of twelve tribes, all lineal descendants of Jacob, himself a "wandering Aramean" (Dt. 26:5). Traditionally, each tribe is descended from one of the twelve sons he had by four mothers (Gn. 29:16–35; 30; 35:16–20), i.e:

By Leah	*By Rachel*	*By Bilhah*	*By Zilpah*
Reuben	Joseph (Ephraim Manasseh and Benjamin)	Dan	Gad
Simeon		Naphtali	Asher
Levi			
Judah			
Issachar			
Zebulun; a daughter, Dinah.			

From the Bible it would seem that this system existed from the very moment of the Exodus*. Before the Exodus, however, no tribe is mentioned and the Hebrews who left Egypt are described as "a rabble" or "a multitude". The Nu. 1:4 description of an organized tribal community comes without any preparation. Scholars are agreed that this can only refer to a small group of clans, which could perhaps have been twelve in number.

In general, modern scholarship rejects the assumption of actual kinship ties. The genealogical biblical pattern bears no relation to actual areas of tribal settlement and the very manner of the grouping suggests an awareness of unequal degrees of kinship. Each tribe had its own peculiar traditions and customs although these were fused into a sense of overall unity.

In fact early peoples living in the same area are subject to many pressures to unite — mainly for mutual protection and defence — and where one group is much weaker it tends to be absorbed by stronger neighbours. In either case, in a few generations the bonds between the different families develop into common traditions and come to be expressed in terms of kinship which, although historically untrue, are effective. At the same time, common ownership of land establishes the groups as geographical and political units. Such fusions took place frequently in the early history of Hebrew clans and some of the tensions of the process are perhaps reflected in later rivalries between the tribes. Each tribe, however, was equal. The system was stabilized early (as recorded in Gn. 49) and once the number twelve had been established it never changed. In fact, the existence of Manasseh and Ephraim (the "Joseph" tribes) as separate tribes made the number 13, but, on the other hand, Levi was given a special status as a "holy" tribe and (Dt. 12:12; 14:29; 18:1) was not allotted any land (see Priesthood*). The issue was settled by combining the genealogical traditions with the laws of inheritance (see Family*) which provided that the first born should have a double portion — i.e. where there were twelve sons, there would be thirteen portions.

Modern scholarship assumes that the biblical tribal organization was actually achieved much later than the Exodus* and the Conquest*. What preceded it can be suggested by contemporary conditions in the Near East as well as specific Israelite traditions.

The Tribe in the Ancient Near East: In general, the tribe was a unit containing a number of families and villages in an area in the Near East, providing protection and solidarity to all its members. The organization put an effective limit on later royal powers (see Government and Authority*) and presented an immediate threat to established authority from the very beginning. The Habiru* (see article and Amarna Letters*) for instance were not an ethnic group but were made up of individuals who rebelled against the existing political regimes. Almost universally, however, tribal society was patriarchal in character and fundamentally opposed to feudalism as in Canaan.

Biblical Tribal Government and Organization: The most potent unifying force for the Hebrews of the Bible was their existence as a religious community bound by the religious tie of the Covenant*, which specified the rights and responsibilities of every member. It both created the society and held it together.

There was also the important factor of land ownership. In the opinion of B. Mazar, the tribe was an area of settlement within the whole territory of Israelite settlement, not the complex social formation borrowed from modern concepts. The small religious community absorbed existing elements and slowly became sedentary, forming of the nucleus the later organization, which developed after two or three centuries. Thus, in this view, while the origins of Israel's tribal system lay in Sinai, the structure was not established until after the settlement.

Much later in the process, the twelve clans joined into a confederation sealed by the pact at Shechem (Jos. 24), which established them as one people sharing one worship and celebrating Yahweh's feasts together at the same sanctuary (Shiloh). There was a council of tribal "elders" (see Government and Authority*) but no single head after Moses and Joshua.

Each tribe, "shebet" or "matteh", was made up of a group of clans, themselves focussed around the "beth-ab" or "house of the father". The tribe constituted the largest socio-political unit of the time and authority over the whole confederation was exercised only sporadically by the charismatic "Judges" (see article) who functioned in times of crisis and might then command more than a single tribe. In between crises, the Council of Elders (the 12 nesi'im) and the common sanctuary provided a permanent centre of authority.

II. THE MAP OF TRIBAL SETTLEMENT: As indicated above, the *geographical settlement* bears no relationship to the early twelve tribe scheme, and only little to the borders described in Joshua*. It seems certain that in fact the boundaries were always fluid. However, a rough picture of the *early division* of the land can be drawn as follows (and see map **355**):

a. A southern group of Judah and Simeon, with its auxiliary non-Israelite clans, occupying Judah (without Jerusalem at first), Hebron and the northern Negeb.

b. The "House of Joseph" (Manasseh, Ephraim and Benjamin), occupying the area of Shechem and Mt. Ephraim west of the Jordan (the area known as "Ephraim"), and Gilead and Bashan to the east. Machir formed part of the other half of Menasseh, east of Jordan.

c. Gad and Reuben in central and southern Transjordan.

d. The northern tribes of Asher, Issachar, Zebulun, Naphtali and, eventually, Dan, north of the Valley of Jezreel and in Galilee.

The process of establishing these territories as fixed, durable areas took a long time. According to M. Noth, it was completed only when the tribe could fully command the area it occupied. This is illustrated in map **356**.

In the days of the monarchy, precise boundaries were established as part of the administrative system of the Kingdom (see Government and Authority*) but they were probably anachronistic in relation to the traditions of the early tribal confederation. They were projected into the past by the administrative organization of the monarchy.

TRIBUTE. — Tribute (in Hebrew "mās"), in the sense of a payment made by one state to another as a token of subjection, was a familiar feature of international relations in the ancient western Semitic world. It could be paid by a friendly nation or by an enemy. When it was exacted from an enemy, it had the dual purpose of weakening the tributary state and increasing the wealth of the victor, who could demand the tribute in the form of materials or products most valuable to him.

Imposition of tribute was a simple and generally efficient administrative measure. The victor made the defeated state responsible for the payment of a prescribed yearly sum and non-payment was taken as an act of rebellion which was suitably punished (cf. Gn. 14). Tribute is known to have been imposed as early as the Sumerian period (3rd mill. BCE) but it is not clear how this was carried out in practice. A "banner" from Ur (see Babylonia*) shows a victory procession on one side and the payment of tribute on the other. The tribute received from Shalmaneser III's conquest of Tyre is depicted in **792**.

Tribute to the Assyrians: The system of demanding tribute was perfected by the Assyrian empire. The first Assyrian records on the subject date from the reign of Shimshi Adad I (18th c. BCE) and the term "tribute" was in regular use up to the neo-Babylonian period, Cyrus recording that all the lands from the Mediterranean to the Persian Gulf paid him tribute. Assyrian sources have given details of the tribute paid to the empire by Israel. The Black Obelisk of Shalmaneser III (858–824 BCE; see illus. under Israel and Judah*: Part IV) includes a vivid picture of tribute being paid to the Assyrian by Jehu. Adad-Nirari (810–782 BCE) also records tribute payments from Israel, as well as from Tyre, Sidon, Edom and Philistia. Tiglat-Pileser III (745–727 BCE) received a tribute of 1,000 talents of silver from Menachem, king of Israel, as well as additional payments from Ahaz, king of Judah. This information is also given in the Old Testament (II K. 15:17–20; 16:7–8). Tiglat-Pileser also records that he dethroned Pekah (of Israel) and replaced him by Hoshea in return for a tribute in silver and gold. Later on, Hoshea suspended payment and this provoked retribution from the Assyrians. Sargon II (722–705 BCE) imposed a tribute on Israel and deported part of the population of Samaria (II K. 17:3–6; 18:11). The most detailed description of the payment of tribute comes from the records of Sennacherib (705–681 BCE) who describes the silver, gold, ivory engravings and musicians which were paid to him (see Israel and Judah*).

Tribute (Mās) in Israel's Tax System: Although the Bible mentions tribute or internal levies a number of times, none of the references concern tribute paid to the Hebrews by another state such as that received by the Assyrians. This is probably because Israel was a small nation which did not have many opportunities to levy tribute on its neighbours. Only in Psalm 72:10 does the term occur (in Hebrew "eshcar") as meaning tribute in the accepted sense. There is another occurrence of the term in Ezk.27:15 where it may be defined as tribute. Little knowledge about the fiscal system of Israel and Judah is available.

The word most commonly used is "mās" and this occurs 22 times referring either to a levy of forced labour (the corvée, see Taxes*) or to the internal levy imposed on the Israelites for the building of the Temple (I K. 5:13, passim).

In II Ch 17:11, the Philistines and Arabs brought King Jehoshaphat "presents and silver for tribute", namely presents to the King's estate, not war tribute. The fine which the Egyptian Necho imposed on Jehoahaz seems to have been a tribute from one state to another (II K. 23:33) and this also seems to have been the case with the levy called "middah" (Ezr. 6:8; 7:24; Neh. 5:4).

792

W

WARFARE. — *Outline: I. Holy War: Justification of the Holy War; The Conduct of Holy War; Formalities and Ethics of War. II. Tactics: Fortifications; Siegecraft in Palestine; Assaults; Cunning; Intelligence; Strategy; Combat Tactics; Surprise Attacks; Signals. III. Organization and Conduct of War: Mobilization; Military Organization; Campaigns; The Camp. IV. Israel's Wars: Wars of the Kingdoms of Judah and Israel; The Maccabaean Wars; Jewish Army Organization in the Hellenistic Period; The Jewish-Roman Wars.*

I. HOLY WAR: From its very beginnings, war was a frequent occurrence in Israel's history. Even after the Israelites had established themselves in Palestine, the country enjoyed only short periods of peace. Historically, the numerous wars can be regarded as being mainly the result of political circumstances (see below) but the Bible clearly reflects a view of ancient Israelite warfare as something essentially religious. The idea of a Holy War dominates many passages of biblical and inter-testamental writings.

For the Israelites, war was always something to which they were commanded by the will of God and in which victory would flow from trust in him. During the early period and at the beginning of the monarchy, the Ark would accompany the troops in battle as the visible assurance of God's presence (II Sam. 11:11; see Tabernacle*), for Israel's wars were the "wars of the Lord" (Nu. 21:14). This attitude which is implicit in all the military history of the Bible is explicitly stated in Deuteronomy* and Numbers*. The Lord of hosts was the "God of the armies of Israel" (I Sam. 17:45) and Israel's enemies were God's enemies. They and their corrupting influences must be destroyed without mercy to ensure the survival of the "People of the Covenant" who had been chosen as God's special instrument for the salvation of the world. Moreover, the populations and property of conquered cities were His by right. Everything in a conquered city was taboo ("herem" or banned in Hebrew) and must either be surrendered to God's direct representatives or be destroyed as an offering (see Sacrifice*). Everything hostile to Israel and its God must be "devoted to destruction" (Jos. 6:17, 24) and nothing left that might conduce to idolatry and thus frustrate God's plan (Dt. 7:1–6).

War's religious character is also apparent from the custom of "inquiring of the Lord" by means of sacred lot (Jud. 1:1, I Sam. 23:2) or in the words of a prophet, (e.g. I K. 22:25). To ask their god's advice was, of course, customary among all the armies of the ancient Near East (see Magic*) but it had a special significance in the theocratic organization of Israel.

Justification of the Holy War: War was linked to religion by most ancient peoples. A war was begun either by command of the gods or with their approval and was accompanied by appropriate religious rites. The Greeks fought the wars of the amphictyony of Delphi under the guise of holy wars against any members who violated the sacred rights of Apollo. The Moslem holy war or "jihād" fulfilled the obligation laid upon every believer to spread his faith by force of arms. The concept of "jihād" however, is entirely foreign to the spirit of Yahwism. Among the Hebrews, war acquired its sacred character along with every other institution of Israel, as the result of the intimate relationship between God and His Chosen People*. Moreover, Israel fought to preserve its national existence, rather than its faith. Its wars, accordingly, were not in themselves "religious wars". What distinguished them from most of the wars of antiquity was that war was a sacred action, possessed of its own particular ideology and specific rites, not merely something to which religion was an accessory. The religious aspect of war in Israel persisted right up to the time of the monarchy, sometimes modified, but still affecting a number of acute ethical and moral questions (see below). Although under certain circumstances and at certain periods, it took on a more secular character, the idea of the holy war was revived with all its original force at the time of the Maccabaean revolt (see Hasmoneans*) and in the two great wars against Rome*.

The Conduct of Holy War: The sanctity of war and warriors in the cause of God meant that special rules were laid down for ensuring the unsullied purity of the "Camp of Yahweh" (Dt. 23:10–15). These were carried over into the Dead Sea Scroll of the "War of the Children of Light against the Children of Darkness" (see Dead Sea Scrolls*). In addition, as war was something sacred ("qiddesh milḥamah" = "to sanctify war", Jer. 6:1; Jl. 3:9), the preparations for it included a sacrifice, usually a burnt offering (Jud. 6:20, 26) while battle cries would have a religious significance, e.g. "a sword for the Lord and for Gideon" (Jud. 7:18, 20; see also Numbers*: Holy War).

Formalities and Ethics of War: War was not declared. A commander would pitch his camp in enemy country, show the strength of his army and then lay down conditions which, if fulfilled, would prevent hostilities (I Sam. 11:1 ff). Sometimes actual combat might be left to selected champions (e.g. Goliath and David*) or a challenge could be issued from one ruler to another (e.g. Amaziah of Judah to Jehoash of Israel, II K. 14:8–10), but this was unusual.

Deuteronomy (20:10–20) prescribes the rules for siege, and these presumably follow the usage of the time, mainly the days of the monarchy. Before beginning the siege of a town in foreign territory, the Israelites must offer it peace terms. If these are accepted and the gates opened, the population may be put to forced labour (not slavery or death) and the town occupied. If it rejects the conditions, fights back and is conquered, then the men may be put to death and all the women, children and property taken as booty and divided among the victors. However, for the towns of foreigners within Israelite territory, much harsher measures are decreed: "you shall save alive nothing that breathes" (Dt. 20:16).

In fact the Israelites were no more cruel to the defeated than their contemporaries and the treatment they are recorded as meting out to a captured town (e.g. II K. 15:16) was still far less ferocious than the calculated brutality of

793

the Assyrians. The booty of a victory was divided among the soldiers, with special shares going to the officers (Jud. 8: 24 ff; I Sam. 30:26 ff). Soldiers left behind to guard the camp shared equally with those who fought in the battle — a rule actually introduced by David but characteristically ascribed (Nu. 31:27) to Moses (and perhaps both traditions are true). Even where the population survived the ending of a siege, a heavy indemnity or yearly tribute might be imposed on a conquered people (e.g. II K. 3:4).

II. TACTICS: The origins of the military tactics and rules of war, as much as actual arms* (see article) employed in early biblical times must be sought in the Near East in the 2nd mill. BCE. The Old Testament period (more precisely, the Middle Bronze and Early Iron Ages) saw the introduction of chariots which gave armies an immeasurably greater mobility and resulted in many changes in tactics. Simultaneous improvements in bows and arrows resulted in greatly increased fire power. The two developments led to a natural tendency among small countries and peoples to concentrate on defence inside walled cities. Siege equipment (see Arms, Weapons and Military Equipment*) was consequently improved and this, in turn, prompted the invention of various counter-measures.

Biblical commanders employed all the usual methods of war, laying siege to enemy cities (I K. 20:1) and defending themselves against sieges, making raids (I Sam. 14) and fighting pitched battles.

Fortifications: One of the most typical features of the fortifications of Middle Bronze Age cities and camps is the stucco (plastered) slope or glacis extending outward from the fortifications. In later times, this glacis might extend as much as a hundred feet from the wall. This type of military architecture is believed to have been introduced by the conquering Hyksos who, having established themselves in lower Egypt (the Delta region; see Egypt*) in the 18th c. BCE had also invaded Canaan and, when finally expelled by the Egyptians (1570 BCE), entrenched themselves in many important centres on the eastern shores of the Mediterranean.

The Hyksos were also responsible for introducing chariots into Middle Eastern warfare and it is assumed that the fortified camps they built were intended as a protection for their chariotry. Even after they had established themselves in Palestine, most Canaanite cities were too small to house a substantial number of chariots and their horses, so the camps became important, permanent features of the landscape. The remains of one of their most important centres, a camp which could hold 40,000 men and hundreds of chariots, have been discovered in Avaris (in northern Egypt) and have confirmed the description given by Josephus*, quoting Manetho, an earlier Egyptian historian: "they built a wall round all this place, which was a large and strong wall".

In fact, the camps were surrounded first by a strong wall and outside this, a solid embankment made of sand (in Avaris) or earth or battered stone (in Palestine). Beyond the embankment, the glacis sloped down (60 feet in Avaris), often to a ditch at the bottom. Glacis like this have been discovered at Ashkelon*, Lachish*, Hazor* (see illus. there), Tel Jerishah (**793**) near Tel-Aviv and many other places in Palestine. Presumably, they were partly designed to prevent an onslaught by enemy chariots against the walls (whether of camp or of fortified city). Such a glacis was also found outside the Israelite city of Gath (Tel Sheikh el Areineh). Y. Yadin has demonstrated that the main purpose of the glacis was to protect the walls from enemy attacks by battering rams and the other new developments in siege engines (see Arms and Weapons*). To overcome the new obstacle, attackers with battering rams used to fill in the ditch with earth and build a new causeway to take the ram up to the top of the glacis where it faced the much thinner ramparts and inner walls. This inevitably slow and clumsy operation explains the need to use "fire towers" simultaneously with battering rams, so as to protect the attacking soldiers with a constant barrage of arrows.

It seems, however, that the glacis and other improved means of defence finally became so formidable an obstacle to attackers, that they had to resort more and more to blockade and cunning to reduce a town. This (**794**) is the bottom of the tower and guardroom of Matzad Hashabyahu conquered by King Josiah (early 7th c. BCE). The ostracon (**534**) described under Inscriptions*, par. 10 was discovered there.

Siegecraft in Palestine: ("matsor" in Hebrew): In general, fortified cities could be attacked in the following ways:

a. Blockade or siege by a regular army (this would often include all the other variations as well). It depended upon sealing the defenders within their walls, preventing supplies or help from reaching them from outside and warding off their counter-attacks and sorties. This placed the attackers in the most exposed position and success was the reward of their greater courage and endurance.

b. A variation recorded in the Amarna letters* (14th c. BCE) as being used against Canaanite towns by the Habiru*, who were not equipped for more efficient methods, was to cut off all roads leading to a town and prevent the people from emerging even to work their lands. The Habiru moved in small bands and were often fewer than the people they terrorized. This very fact gave them greater mobility than large armies and their surprise attacks could easily bring chaos to a besieged city.

c. During or apart from a prolonged siege, groups df attackers would use scaling ladders to climb the walls aon attack the defenders face to face. This was an activity, illustrated by many Egyptian and Assyrian reliefs (see illus. under Ancient Cities: Lachish*), demanding great courage and flexibility.

d. Using battering rams and mining operations to break through the walls (see illus. under Arms*).

e. Tunnelling underneath the walls or making a surprise entry through existing water conduits and shafts, e.g. Joab's attack against Jebus (Jerusalem; II Sam. 5:8).

(Further details of the fortifications of city walls and gates are given under Cities, Canaanite* and Cities Israelite*, Jericho*, etc. Water Supply* includes consideration of the water supply under siege.)

Assaults: Biblical accounts of sieges often include all the foregoing methods in their description of an assault against the besieged town. A mound or embankment would be thrown up against the wall to make a ramp on which the attackers could pass over the walls and into the city. From below, sappers would undermine the wall (e.g. David's siege of Abel-Beth-Maacah II Sam. 20:15). Attempts would also be made to set fire to the gates (Jud. 9:52).

In return, the defenders would resist with hand-to-hand fighting, arrows and crude missiles (Jud. 9:53). Rocks, bags of chaff and fire-balls would be thrown down at the assailants and their emplacements (e.g. I Mac. 6:13) or flaming darts shot at them (Eph. 6:16). Boiling oil would be poured over soldiers trying to climb the scaling ladders or to pass across the bridge from the attackers' towers to the top of the walls. Josephus* gives a vivid picture of all these measures in the "Jewish War" where he describes Nebuchadrezzar's siege of Jerusalem, while II K. 24 suggests the extreme distress to which a siege could reduce a city.

Under the monarchy, the defenders of Israelite cities might, as did Uzziah, make "engines, invented by skilful men, to be on the towers and the corners, to shoot arrows and great stones..." (II Ch. 26:15). Scholars are still disagreed as to whether these "engines" were ballistic machines or catapaults like those of the Assyrians, or simply frames arranged as corbelling along the very edges of the walls (like the hoardings used in military architecture in Europe in the Middle Ages) to enable archers and soldiers to shoot at the attackers at the foot of the walls without exposing themselves to enemy missiles. The walls of Lachish are shown with such contrivances in the Assyrian reliefs of the siege (see article). The evidence of these reliefs is expanded by other inscriptions of Sennacherib explaining how he captured the towns of Judah "by raising earthen ramps, rams taken up to the walls, infantry attack, mines, breaches and tunnels" (see Lachish*).

Attackers approaching a besieged city over the mound or trench encircling the walls (the "dayek") would be protected by the mantelet or great siege shield, the "tzinnah". Ezekiel (4:1–3) repeats the list of methods of siege warfare, all of which he may have seen employed by Nebuchadrezzar. Ballistic engines of various kinds were widely used during the Maccabaean and Hasmonean wars (see Hasmoneans*; Arms and Weapons*; I Mac. 6:20, 51–52; 11:20; 13:43 ff).

Cunning: Once a fortified city appeared able to withstand a siege, or while its enemies had not developed any very efficient means of attack (as was the case when the Israelites were attacking the Canaanite towns), it was important to find alternatives to direct assault.

Intelligence: The first thing needed for this sort of fighting was information about the disposition of the enemy, the lay of the land and possible hiding places and secret ways of access. Spying for this purpose was in general use even before the 15th c. BCE. One example is the story of Moses sending spies into Canaan (Nu. 13), another is Joshua's sending spies into Jericho (Jos. 2) or to Ai (Jos. 7:2). The

story in Judges 1:22–26 is also an instructive example of spies getting the information they wanted and putting it to good use.

Strategy: The Bible gives very little indication of the strategy adopted by the Israelite commanders. From extra-biblical sources about the battles fought by Thutmoses III at Megiddo and by Ramses II at Kadesh (in Syria; see Egypt*), it appears that the Hittites and Canaanites used to try to draw the enemy away from his prepared positions and launch a surprise chariot attack, with the bulk of the army held in reserve, either to follow up an initial success or to make possible an orderly retreat.

The 9th c. BCE war of Judah and Israel against Moab appears to have been started with an oblique advance through the country from the south (II K. 3:8–25), carrying out a scorched earth policy on the way. David used a similar strategy against the Philistines (II Sam. 5:23).

Combat Tactics: These varied according to the period, the size of forces and the weapons employed. The earlier settlers of Canaan depended on archery rather than hand to hand fighting to repulse attacks by invaders. The Israelites, during and after the Conquest, made use of all the standard methods of warfare, exact tactics depending essentially on whether chariots were used. In a major battle in the days of the monarchy in which both the professional army and conscripts participated, the professionals formed the front ranks and the conscripts were the support troops, remaining in the rear and acting as reserves. This was the pattern followed by David against the Ammonites (II Sam. 11) and by Ahab against the Arameans (I K. 20:15–20). Descriptions of more elaborate tactics come from Joab's battle against the Ammonites (II Sam. 10:8–14) or from Ben-Hadad's instructions to his chariots at the battle of Ramoth Gilead (I K. 22:31).

Surprise Attacks: An army which is weaker — in numbers, weapons or skill — than its opponents will always try to gain an advantage by attacking unexpectedly. At the time of the Conquest*, Joshua's band of Israelites was not a properly organized army and wherever possible it avoided making direct attacks on the fortified cities of Canaan. Instead, the Israelites sometimes tempted the defenders to leave their walls and to fight in the open (cf. II K. 7:12). More often, they relied on surprise. For instance, when the confederation of Canaanite city-kings joined together to attack Gibeon which had come to terms with the Israelites, Joshua took his army on a 30 kilometre night march from their main camp at Gilgal near Jericho and caught the Canaanites by surprise. He used the same tactics to surprise another Canaanite alliance under the king of Hazor near the "waters of Merom" (Jos. 11:7). At a later period, night attacks were a favourite tactic of Gideon (Jud. 7:17 ff).

Tactics like these were especially effective in hilly country where the Canaanite chariotry could not be used. Such country was also very suitable for successful ambushes. A group of Israelites would pretend to flee before their foes, leading them to where the main army waited to fall upon them on all sides (Jos. 8:15–19; Jud. 20:32–36). This was a favourite device when attacking a city. As the attackers seemed to flee, the defenders would be enticed after them and a waiting band could then make a dash for the gate.

In some cases where surprise was to be an element of the battle, the Israelite force was divided into three assault groups (Jud. 7:16; 9:43; I Sam. 11:11; II Sam. 18:2) to encircle the enemy. Alternatively, an army might be split into two, to attack the enemy front and the rear simultaneously (II Ch. 13:13–15). Faced with this situation, a good general would keep his army close together, fighting on both fronts, each supporting the other (II Sam. 10:8–11). A close liaison was maintained between the two forces by messengers, either mounted or on foot.

Signals: Contact was also maintained between cities and armies by signals such as beacon fires lighted on hilltops, whose smoke or even light could be seen from a distance. These passed on information by means of previously agreed signs (Jud. 20:38) or acted as warnings (Jer. 6:1). Ostraca found at Lachish* (see article) are a dramatic illustration of how this code of fire signals was used and interpreted by the defenders of the town in the last days of the Kingdom of Judah*.

III. ORGANIZATION AND CONDUCT OF WAR:

Mobilization: The early Israelite army was composed of units levied from the tribes for a particular campaign. After the battle, the men returned to normal life. G.E. Mendenhall has shown that the army units or "alaphim" were not originally literally "thousands" but that the "eleph" = "thousand" meant a unit of a tribe from which a certain number of warriors could be provided. This has made it possible to interpret correctly the apparently overgenerous figures given in the book of Numbers (see Census*). On this basis, the army of the tribal confederation numbered probably about 6,000 men (not 600 "thousand" which seems to be the figure in Numbers 26:51). In practice, the number of troops actually available at any one time may have been smaller.

During this period, the people were called to arms by messengers sent through the country (Jud. 6:35; 7:24), or by the call of the shofar (ram's horn, see Music*; Jud. 3:27; I Sam. 13:3). Later on, under the monarchy, it seems that the trumpet would be blown and a standard (banner, pole or mast) raised on a hill as a call to the people to take up arms or to gather together (Is. 5:26; Jer. 51:12, 27). When the prophets refer to the sound of the trumpet or the signals of battle, they are referring to the warning of an invasion and the call to defend the country against foreign attack (Jer. 4:5–6; Hos. 5:8; Am. 3:6). Martial music often accompanied the soldiers on their way (II Ch. 20:22).

The nucleus of a permanent, professional army was first created by David who organized his former companions as a standing bodyguard of 600 "mighty men" (I Sam. 23:13; 30:9; II Sam. 10:7). This was expanded into a regular army, based on the census of the whole people (II Sam. 24), and supported by mercenary soldiers, the Cherethites and Pelethites and Gittites (II Sam. 15:18).

No record exists of the exact basis on which the king organized or summoned his army. There are merely statements that, e.g. a king "gathered all his army together" (I K. 20:1, 27; II K. 3:6; 6:24). This would have been a matter of routine for a professional army (see Government and Authority*: Administration of the Kingdom) but it leaves the details very uncertain as regards the conscripts (I Sam. 11:1–11; 17:2, 11–13; 28:4).

Military Organization of the army followed a tradition which continued more or less unchanged until the days of the Maccabees. It is described under Government and Authority*: Administration of the Kingdom.

For a discussion of signals and battle-cries, see above Part I; and Holy War under Numbers* and Dead Sea Scrolls*.

Campaigns: For the obvious reason of avoiding the winter rains, the best season for war was the spring, "the turn of the year" (II Sam. 11:1 and its parallel, I Ch. 20:1). This made it easier to move armies and supplies but at the same time it must also have created many complications when peasants were mobilized at the period of heaviest work in the fields. Assyrian campaigns were begun between April and June and the armies would arrive in Palestine just after the cereal harvests. In the neo-Babylonian period, campaigns might begin in the autumn or even later.

The Camp: The formation of the camp was an important matter. Israelite camps are usually represented as square in shape (Nu. 2), but some scholars interpret I Sam. 17:20; 26:5, 7, to mean that they were circular. The bronze plates of the Balawat gates show Assyrian camps, most of which are square although some are round (see illus. under Arms*).

The camp was surrounded by a ma'gal (I Sam. 17:20; 26:5) or stone fence and divided by a broad road with a gate at either end. It was guarded constantly (Jud. 7:8). During a battle, a detachment of soldiers remained to guard the base (I Sam. 26:5, 7) and "the place of the wagons" (I Sam. 25:13). Within the camp, the soldiers slept in tents or booths (II Sam. 11:11; I K. 20:12).

In Hellenistic and Roman days, Jewish military camps followed contemporary custom and were probably much like the Roman camp whose remains, including the stone fences, can still be seen at the foot of Masada (**713**).

IV. ISRAEL'S WARS: Israel's first wars were those of the Conquest*. The superficial impression is that this was a matter of concentrated attack on Transjordan, followed by a sweeping campaign west of the Jordan, quickly resulting in unquestioned control of the country. It seems more probable, however, that there was a rapid conquest of most of the country, but that this could only be consolidated in the central highland area, and that the initial campaigns were followed by a long-drawn out period of warfare along the borders, with varying results (see Conquest*; Tribes*).

The wars of the period of Judges were a later or, possibly even part of the same, phase of conquest. The battles fought were defensive actions and border strife against the Canaanites and other peoples from whose territories the tribes were attempting to carve a land. The Canaanites remained in control of the richest parts of the Jezreel valley and Galilee and continued to attack Israelite settlements there until the early monarchy (see Judges*).

The Israelites then had to face new invasions. Having established themselves along the coast, the Philistines advanced into the heart of Ephraim and Benjamin, as well as the valley of Jezreel (see Samuel*; Saul*).

David's reign began with the reconquest of territories lost to the Philistines, then saw the expansion of his kingdom to the ideal borders of the Promised Land, on the north with the Arameans, east with the Moabites and Ammonites and south with the Edomites (see David*). Solomon was able to weld the empire he inherited into a prosperous, well-administered state. He did not fight a single war, but his internal organization apparently included conscription and he introduced chariots into the standing army. His strength may well have been enough to deter attack, but he made a poor showing at protecting his possessions when Aram and Edom broke away from his empire.

Wars of the Kingdoms of Judah and Israel: The wars of the kings of the two realms, fought to protect their own positions and the safety of their borders, are described in the article on Israel and Judah*.

In general, the military history of Israel and its kings may be summed up as a brief period of conquest at the time of David and thereafter as a series of campaigns and battles, sometimes successful, frequently disastrous, fought to protect the land, its borders, trade routes or possessions (see Israel and Judah*; Ancient Cities*). Tactics employed have often been illuminated by discoveries made in excavating the sites of the battles — for instance, the ostraca of Lachish* provided facts, previously unknown, not only about methods of liaison and signalling in the period before the fall of Jerusalem but also on the embassies sent to Egypt and other details (see Lachish*; Inscriptions*).

The Maccabaean Wars: Long after the end of the Old Testament period (aside from Daniel and possibly a few other sections of the Old Testament), a new series of wars were fought in defence of the Jews' very identity. The wars of the Maccabees (see Hasmoneans*) began as guerrilla attacks by partisans, under Judas. With success, this developed into a war of national independence with a regular army organized on traditional lines (I Mac. 3:55–56; see Hasmoneans*). It remained a campaign of constant movement with an emphasis on surprise tactics. The operations covered the whole of Palestine, with actions taking place simultaneously, ranging from south of Hebron to Galilee, from the Mediterranean coast to Transjordan. In their organization and tactics, the Jewish leaders learned from their Hellenistic enemies (see the Greek archer shooting

795

the long bow, **795**); but they retained many of the most typical features of earlier Jewish campaigns (as one example, they had no chariots or cavalry, and whenever they could, they engaged the enemy in the hills where familiarity with the countryside gave the local forces a great advantage). Once religious freedom had been secured by Judas' victories, his brothers, Jonathan and Simon, led their people to political independence and, ultimately, the establishment of the Hasmonean* kingdom (see article).

Jewish Army Organization in the Hellenistic Period: From the time of Simon the Hasmonean, soldiers of the regular army apparently drew a regular pay (I Mac. 14:32). The later Hasmonean princes and, especially, Herod made considerable use of foreign mercenaries, the Hasmoneans apparently recompensing veterans with grants of land from conquered territories (see Property, Land*).

The best evidence of military practice and organization in the days of the second Jewish Commonwealth is the Qumran "War Scroll" (see Dead Sea Scrolls* and above). Although this is an apocalyptic blueprint for the conduct of the final war of mankind, it must have taken its practical details from contemporary conditions. In the Scroll, the army consists of 24,000 infantry and 6,000 cavalry, each divided into heavy (principal) units, manned by the more experienced soldiers (aged 40–50), and light or auxiliary sections manned by the younger men (aged 30–40). Apprentices (aged 25 and upwards) were organized into service units (for their armaments*, see article). Their main battle formation is described as a "tower" or self-protecting rectangle of heavy infantry (for other details, see Dead Sea Scrolls*).

The Jewish-Roman Wars: For this period, plenty of contemporary sources and descriptions are available, mainly Josephus' "Jewish War" and "Antiquities of the Jews" but also a number of Roman historians and commentators (see Rome and the Jews*; Arms and Weapons*: Roman Period).

At the time of the Jewish festivals, the Roman garrison in Jerusalem was strengthened (see Jesus*) with additional detachments. The great Jewish Rebellion which was to end with the destruction of the Jewish Commonwealth began in 66 CE with clashes between the Jews and the soldiers of this garrison. The memory of the hated Roman troops became embedded in Jewish literature (see Apocrypha*; Apocalyptic*), respect for their proverbial might never altering the belief that this army of brutal pagans would pass from the world when God willed and the Messiah came. Unfortunately for the Jews, this belief proved far stronger than counsels of reason or moderation, and the emotions it aroused sent them on a course of defiance, foredoomed to disaster.

WATER SUPPLY.

— *Outline: The Climatic Factors. I. Old Testament Times: Wells in Patriarchal Days; Lime Plastered Cisterns; Reservoirs (Pools); The Pool of Gibeon; Water Supply in War Time; The Canaanite Tunnel; The Siloam Canal and Tunnel; Normal Water Supplies in the Israelite Period; Megiddo Water Supply. II. Hellenistic and Roman Periods: Masada Water Supply; Qumran Water Supply; The Nabateans.*

The existence of a constant source of water was a primary condition for the development of a permanent settlement in ancient times. For this reason, the great centres of early civilization were located in important river valleys: Egypt, watered by the Nile; Mesopotamia where the Euphrates and the Tigris flow, and India, on the banks of the Indus River. A widely ramified network of irrigation channels and canals, vital to agriculture, was developed in these countries from very ancient times. An effective central authority to supervise the complicated water network became necessary, and later developed into one of the primary roles of government.

The Climatic Factors: In Palestine, the climatic conditions were entirely different and consequently required different methods of irrigation. The country lay on the edge of the desert, and water supply depended mainly on the rains which came frequently and in relatively copious quantity in the course of the short winter season. These rains were not absorbed in the soil, however, but flowed to the sea in sudden, powerful torrents (II K. 3:16–17). When the long, dry, hot season came, most of the water courses (wadis) dried up (Jl. 1:20) and only a small number of springs continued to issue water. These springs were actually the main sources of water for most of the year in this country, "a land of brooks of water, of fountains and springs, flowing forth in valleys and hills" (Dt. 8:7). These were the climatic conditions which determined the technique of water installation in Palestine all through the ages, the only exception being the Jordan river valley, particularly its northern part, where the conditions were similar to those of the valleys of the great rivers.

In every period of Palestine's history, the presence of a spring was the factor that really determined where a settlement was to be founded (details under Agriculture*); for instance, the oldest town in the world, Jericho*, was built near a spring.

I. OLD TESTAMENT TIMES: **Wells in Patriarchal Days:** The few constantly flowing springs also determined the courses of movement of the semi-nomadic tribes in the wilderness, for these tribes moved from one source of water to another (Nu. 33:9 and passim). From the Bible, it appears that the inhabitants of Palestine learned to dig wells and get

796

797

to the underground sources of water (see Agriculture*) no earlier than the days of the Patriarchs, i.e. in the first half of the 2nd mill. BCE. There is no evidence, either in the Bible or in archaeological finds, of earlier use of such sources. Prior to the period when wells began to come into use, the water needs of the people were satisfied if they succeeded in widening the mouths of the springs and thus increasing their flow, and by using stone reservoirs for water storage. The digging of wells was first connected with the mode of life of the semi-nomads and shepherds. In Gn. 21:30; 26:15, 18–22, 32, 33 are found lively descriptions of the mode of life of these semi-nomads, the difficulties they met with in digging the wells, and their frequent quarrels over the poor and scanty water supply. Generally these wells were dug around Beersheba and Gerar in the dry river beds of that area. To this day there are many wells near the mound of Tel-es-Saba (ancient Beersheba*, map **89**), still used by the Beduins of the area to water their sheep, camels and goats. Some scholars are of the opinion that these old wells, called Tel-el Mshash, are very ancient (see Arad*). Each well, **796**, had its own name and around each one specific shepherd lore developed; there were also precise watering rules (Gn. 29:2–3) which assured each shepherd a fixed quota of water.

The girls of the town used to go daily to the wells, carrying pitchers to draw the family water supply (Gn. 24:13; I Sam. 9:11), but this was often done by men, usually slaves or free men of the poorest classes, since the drawing of water was considered among the lowest grades of work (Dt. 29:11; Jos. 9:27).

Lime Plastered Cisterns: In the Iron Age, people discovered the uses of plaster made with slaked lime. They were able to dig cisterns everywhere and to line them with true lime plaster, impervious to water. In earlier periods, linings of cisterns were of gypsum or hydraulic plaster, but these were ineffective as the water soon seeped through. As a result of the discovery of lime plaster, the number of water cisterns increased profusely in the Israelite period (as in Tel Beit Mirsim, Beth-Shemesh, Gezer and elsewhere). The possibility of water storage made settlement possible even in mountainous areas far away from permanent sources of water. In this period, the number of mountain settlements increased; moreover, a number of important towns such as Samaria*, Mizpah and others were built in places far away from springs, depending mainly on the supply from the cisterns. A private cistern was every person's aspiration (II K. 18:31). The digging of cisterns in uninhabited areas (particularly desert areas) in order to advance their settlement was, however, the task of the government (II Ch. 26:10). The Mesha Stone (see Moab*; Inscriptions*) of the 9th c. BCE relates that the king enjoined the inhabitants of the city to dig their own cisterns (lines 24–25), while he himself apparently was occupied with the building of public works whose nature is not clear, employing the Israelite prisoners he took for the task (lines 25–26). Large public cisterns were hewn near almost every large town. The Bible mentions the "well of Bethlehem" (II Sam. 23:15), and a town well 48 metres deep of the same type, was uncovered in the excavations at Lachish (**797**). The first eight metres of the Lachish well were lined with large stones in order to prevent it from caving in. The mouth of the well was covered by a large ringlike stone, indented at many points by the ropes which had drawn the water-filled vessels out of the well. Other cisterns have been discovered at Beth-Shemesh, Beth-Shean, Tel-Ajjul and other places. Jacob's well (23 metres deep and 2.5 metres in diameter) near Shechem, mentioned in the New Testament (Jn. 4:6) is very old; its upper section is buttressed and its bottom cut into limestone.

Reservoirs (Pools): In addition to cisterns and wells, the inhabitants of towns in the Israelite period built pools or large reservoirs in which they stored the water of springs or freshets which served for washing, irrigation of vegetable gardens, and for watering domestic animals in the dry seasons (pools of this type exist to this day in many Arab villages). The Bible mentions the pool in Hebron where the murderers of Ish-bosheth were hanged (II Sam. 4:12); in Samaria there was a large pool where the chariot in which Ahab had been killed was washed (I K. 22:38) and there were a number of pools in Jerusalem (II K. 18:17; Is. 7:3; 22:11; Neh. 2:14; 3:16).

The Pool of Gibeon: The most famous of all the pools seems to have been the one in Gibeon (II Sam. 2:13) which was also known in the time of Jeremiah (Jer. 41:12). The pool of Gibeon was recently discovered in perfect condition under

798

a large accumulation of the debris and rubbish of some 25 centuries, following excavations carried on at the site in 1956–58 CE by I.B. Pritchard. The pool (**798**) is round and along its surrounding walls runs a spiral staircase 1.8 metres wide; the side of the staircase facing the inside of the pool was provided with a railing, so that people descending to the pool would not fall into it. It has been estimated that 3,000 tons of limestone had been hewn for the building of the pool. When the excavators had cleaned the pool to its bottom, they found that although it had been constructed for the purpose of storing water, its builders had also designed it to reach a spring at the foot of the hill on which the town was built (see below). First a round cistern 42.5 metres in diameter and 13 metres deep had been sunk, and then a narrow terraced ditch was extended on the bottom to an underground chamber which measured 3.6 by 7.6 metres and was at the same level as the spring. The path of descent into the ditch was lit by two vertical fissures cut through the bottom of the pool to the lower chamber, partly open to the air. The total drop from the town level to the source of water is about 26 metres. Later, when the water level sank, the people had to dig a water shaft and tunnel under the bottom of the pool. On the basis of various stratigraphic calculations, it has been estimated that the pool was built in the 12th or 11th c. BCE and that it was in use until close to the time of the destruction of the First Temple in 589 BCE. The pool of Gibeon is a perfect model of the pools mentioned in the Bible.

799

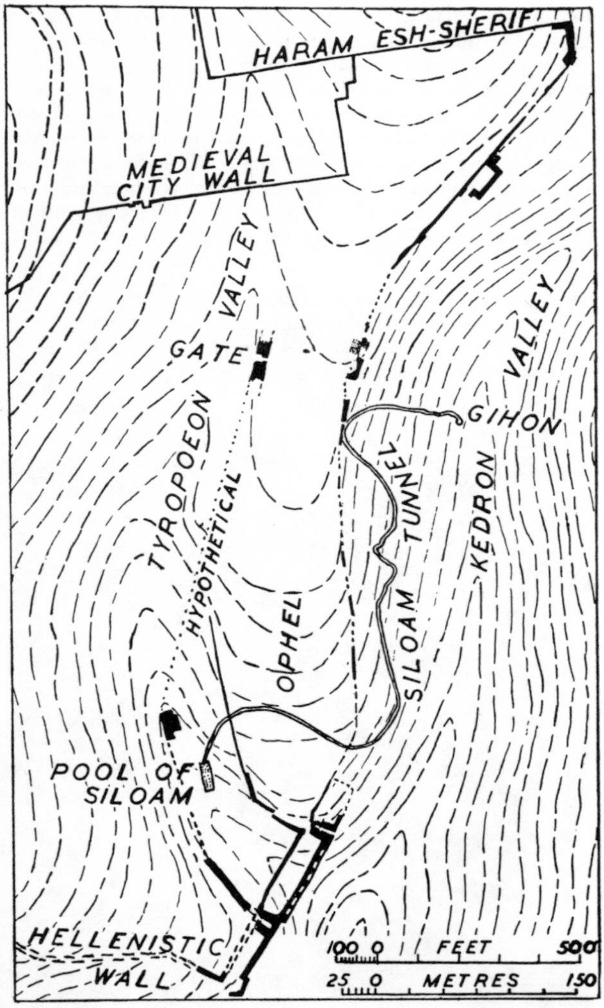

800

Water Supply in War Time: Aside from the usual water systems in times of peace, great hydraulic installations designed for siege conditions were built in Palestine. The tunnels or underground shafts were designed to supply a beleaguered city with water from springs outside it, even when the enemy was encamped at its gates (see Israel and Judah*, Part IV). Six such tunnels have been discovered: two in Jerusalem and one each in Gezer*, Megiddo*, Yible'am and Gibeon (aside from the pool mentioned above). A large, deep ditch to collect rain water, whose construction was begun but never finished, has been uncovered in Lachish*.

The Canaanite Tunnel: In Jerusalem*, a vertical tunnel (called the Warren shaft after its discoverer) was found. The tunnel leads from the Giḥon spring in the Kidron valley outside Jerusalem to the east of the city, and was the only constant source of water to the city during the Israelite period (cf. I K. 1:45; II Ch. 32:30, passim). The head of the tunnel was at a staircase built from inside the city in the direction of the spring. This staircase, together with the tunnel, were cut in the form of an arch at the end of which a deep shaft was sunk. The water from the spring flowed to the bottom of a shaft; the mouth of the spring itself was surrounded by a wall which formed a pool, raising the level of the water to make drawing easier. Scholars have fixed the time of building this tunnel in the Jebusite period (12th–11th cs. BCE), and according to current opinion, this is the shaft through which Joab climbed up into the city to capture it (II Sam. 5:8; see Jerusalem*).

The Siloam Canal and Tunnel: Attempts to dig canals to divert the Giḥon waters were continued during the period of the Monarchy. The water was brought southward along the Kidron valley to the inside of the city of David, situated on the brow of the hill of Ophel, and there it was concentrated in large reservoirs built for the purpose (see diagram under Jerusalem*). At first, an open rock aqueduct was dug which carried the water from the spring southward along the slope of the southeastern hill confluence of the Kidron valley and the vale of Kidron, as shown in this diagram (**799**). This was made possible by building an additional wall inside the pool around the Giḥon spring to raise the water level still higher. Originally, the canal had been about 400 metres long; three sections of it, totalling up to 150 metres in length, were unearthed by excavations. The canal had been covered with flagstones to prevent the water from being contaminated. (It is customary to identify it with the Siloam aqueduct — not tunnel — mentioned in Is. 7:3.) But it lay along the side of the Kidron valley outside the ramparts and would have served the enemy rather than the city. Later, during Hezekiah's reign, while preparations were being made for the rebellion against Assyria, he abandoned these old waterworks and the Siloam tunnel was dug under the hill of Ophel; it brought the water to a new pool in the Tyropean valley (see Jerusalem*) within the city to supply it with water in case of siege (II K. 20:20). The Israelites dried up all other sources of water outside the city, including the open Siloam canal which was accessible to the enemy (II Ch. 32: 2–4). The length of the underground tunnel, shown here (**800**), from the Giḥon spring to the pool inside the city was about 513 metres, though its length in a straight line would have been only 320 metres. The reason for this noticeable difference lies in the fact that the underground diggers chose the softer rocks to break through, and the course of the tunnel became tortuous and extended. It was, nevertheless, a masterly piece of work which still survives to supply water. An inscription in ancient Hebrew characters, describing the course of the work on the tunnel (see Inscriptions*: Siloam Tunnel), was carved in the rock to mark the event and the story is told with pride in II K. 20 and II Ch. 32. The inscription relates that the diggers worked from both ends, moving towards each other until they met. The water of the tunnel was concentrated in a pool measuring 26 by 6 metres inside the ramparts. In modern times, the pool was replaced by another of different measurements called Al-Birkeh by the Arabs.

Such water supplies obviously helped beleaguered cities to withstand long sieges: Samaria held out for two years against the Assyrians in 723–721 BCE; Jerusalem withstood Nebuchadrezzar for a year and a half in 587 BCE. The cities were finally reduced by famine rather than by a shortage of water. If such precautions had not been taken, disaster would have been inevitable from the start.

Normal Water Supplies in the Israelite Period: A water tunnel was also discovered at Gezer in the Shephelah (the lowlands at the foot of the mountains of Judah). The spring of water there was at a depth of 31 metres. In order to reach it, an underground flight of steps was dug at an angle of 39°, over a distance of 58 metres. As the source was inside the city, there was no need to close it up from the outside. I. Macalister, who carried out the excavations at Gezer, fized the date of this tunnel in the 20th c. BCE. Ceramic finds, dated to the Late Bronze age (1400–1200 BCE) contradict the above date, and the spring may have been in use at the beginning of the Israelite period.

Megiddo Water Supply: The tunnel shown (**168**) is the one at Megiddo. In order to reach the water source, a shaft 24 metres long was dug. The water of the spring flowed through the canal to the shaft, and from there could be drawn up in jars pulled by ropes. The outside entrance to the tunnel was stopped up by a stone wall which the excavators have ascribed to the 12th c. BCE. Y. Yadin, however, basing himself on new facts discovered in the course of the excavations conducted at Megiddo in 1960, has concluded that the installation should be ascribed to the last days of Solomon or the beginning of the reign of Rehoboam (10th c. BCE). Tunnel installations from the Canaanite period onwards have been discovered at Etham in Judea and at Yible'am in the valley of Jezreel, but they have not been explored sufficiently to fix the time of their construction with any certainty.

Another shaft in addition to the huge reservoir mentioned above was recently discovered at Gibeon by I.B. Pritchard. It followed a sloping line to a spring in a cave where water dripped from the rock. Steps were dug out like a tunnel, except for the central part which was a deep trench covered by flagstones. All along it were discovered small ceramic lamps to light the way of the people who came for water. The excavators established the date of this tunnel in the 10th c. BCE.

Most of the water tunnels just described were built at the end of the later Canaanite period and in the Israelite period. Considering the primitive tools at the disposal of the diggers, the effort and labour invested in their building can be appreciated. The origin of this system of water supply is not known; however, on the basis of the discovery of two similar water tunnels in the towns of Mycenae and Athens in Greece which predate the tunnels in Palestine (their time has been fixed at the 13th–12th c. BCE), many scholars now think that the technique of digging tunnels reached Palestine from Greece in the middle or the end of the Bronze Age. The tunnels can be divided into two types: one type shortened the distance from the source of water to the consumers and diverted water to the foot of a shaft to make it more accessible; the other type was a tunnel through which the people drawing the water passed in order to reach the lower spring itself.

II. HELLENISTIC AND ROMAN PERIODS: Another revolution in the system of water supply to the cities began in the Hellenistic period and was used mainly during the Roman period. This was the introduction into Palestine of the long aqueduct, i.e. an open, well-plastered canal, which carried water a very long distance by causing it to flow at a slight slope. The canal was partly supported by bridges or arches and partly, in elevated spots, it was cut into the ground or the rock.

Aqueducts of the Roman period have been preserved in numerous places in Palestine such as Caesarea*, Samaria*, Jerusalem*, Jericho*, Masada*, Qumran (see below for description; see also Dead Sea Scrolls*) and other places. The aqueduct at Caesarea was apparently begun in Herodian

801

802

803

days and rebuilt at the end of the 2nd c. CE by the engineers of the 6th and 10th Roman Legions. It can be divided into two distinct projects, one at a higher level than the other (see Caesarea*) as shown in illustrations in that article. The water was brought from springs several miles inland. The remains of two aqueducts of the 2nd c. CE were discovered in Samaria. One of these, about 4400 metres long, carried water from Ein Horan near the village of Beth-Nakura; the other started at Ein Unsub, closer to the city itself. Other aqueducts have been found near Graeco-Roman Jericho* (Telul-abu-Alayik); these carried water from the springs at the entrance of Wadi Kelt and were apparently built by Herod. See also Roman aqueduct over Wadi Nu'eimeh (**801**).

The two aqueducts at Jerusalem carried water from about 30 kilometres south of the city. Both are of the Roman period, but their date has not been definitely fixed. Halfway between Bethlehem and Hebron, three large storing pools now known as "Solomon's pools" were also built. From the pools, another aqueduct leading to the fortress of Herodium was apparently built in the days of Herod. Herodium later served as the headquarters of Bar-Kochba* in the early days of the rebellion (see article).

In addition the people of Jerusalem were well supplied by the rain-fed underground water cisterns. One of the largest extant is the double pool Seteruthion (**802**) below the ground adjacent to the Temple area.

Masada Water Supply: A huge water project apparently from Herod's time was discovered in 1956 at Masada, high above the western shore of the Dead Sea. Two rows of huge reservoirs hewn in the solid rock and consisting of twelve pools (**803**) containing 40,000 cubic metres of water were discovered at the same site. The pools were hidden as far as possible from the eyes of outsiders and had only two small openings, one to let the water in, and the other to permit the entrance of people to draw the water. A staircase led from the entrance to the bottom of the pool in order to make it possible to get down and make use of the water at its lowest level. The two rows of pools were supplied by two aqueducts leading from the Masada canyon (Wadi Saba) which was partly dammed in order to divert the flood-water into the canals. Marks on the inside plaster of the reservoirs testify to the fact that they were full to the brim in the period of their use. In this way, a single though rare heavy rain flood supplied water to the defendants of the Masada fortress for a number of years.

Qumran Water Supply: In Khirbet Qumran, the dwelling place of the Dead Sea Covenanters, an elaborate system of aqueducts has lately been uncovered as shown here (**804**); their water system filled eight plastered cisterns inside the building (see Dead Sea Scrolls*).

The Nabateans: The Nabateans who peopled the Negeb in Roman times attained a high degree of proficiency in storing water in the desert. They used to build large dams in the wadis near their towns in order to catch the flood waters. Three of these dams in wadi Kurnub, near the town of Kurnub in the northern Negeb, are still in existence. The largest dam, reconstructed in Byzantine days*, is eleven metres high, 24 metres long and 8 metres wide, and continues to store water to this day (**805**; see Nabateans and their Towns*).

WEIGHTS AND MEASURES. — *Outline: Linear Measures; Measurements of Area; Measures of Capacity; Weights (Measures of Value, Money); Archaeological Evidence of Weights; Conclusions.*

The weights and measures referred to in the Old Testament reflect those in use among other ancient peoples. Measures such as the côr, ḥomer (ass load), se'ah, mannah or shekel (see below), which were Mesopotamian in origin, were used side by side in Canaan with the Egyptian 'ephah, hin, the Canaanite letekh and others. The Israelites presumably acquired all these from their neighbours and used them concurrently with their own original terms. The use of a particular term, however, does not necessarily mean an identical measure. A measure used may, for instance, be Mesopotamian in name but Egyptian in value.

Even a measure of the same name might have different values. In Egypt there was a long and a short ell ('ammah — cubit) and Mesopotamia had a light and a heavy shekel. Moreover, some weights applied only in certain areas — there was a Carchemish weight and an Alalakh weight. A further complication arises from the fact that by post-Exilic times biblical weights were no longer used and their descriptions by later writers are often ambiguous.

Nor did ancient usage demand precision. Many "natural" measures (a handsbreadth, etc.) were required only to conform to custom, not to any authorized standard. It is therefore extremely difficult to attempt any exact definition of the terms used in the Bible. Any suggestion of modern equivalents can only be based on the evidence of archaeology, e.g. vessels inscribed with their volume or measuring rods of wood or stone of a stated length.

Linear Measures: The original linear measures used by ancient peoples, as well as in Palestine of Old Testament times, derived from the average length of human limbs. Measuring in ancient times must first have been done by means of the forearm or the hand. The distance from the point of the elbow to the tip of the middle finger made the cubit or "'ammah" (Ammat Ish, Dt. 3:11). The "span" of the hand — i.e. the distance between the tip of the small finger and the thumb of an outstretched hand, (the "zereth" of Ex. 28:16), roughly equal to half a cubit; the hand breadth or palm, equal to one-sixth of a cubit or the width of four fingers ("ṭophaḥ", Ex. 25:25) or the finger ('etzba' — a quarter of a palm) all came, in time, to represent precise units of measurement although the original names were retained.

Larger measures were, to an even greater degree, a matter of individual estimates. The bowshot (Gn. 21:16) was the distance of the flight of an arrow shot by an average bowman. The Old Testament term "kibrat ha-'aretz" (literally "journey across a piece of land" or an extent of country, Gn. 35:16; II K. 5:19) has been variously estimated at 2,000 cubits, 5,000 cubits, two hour's journey, or half a day's journey. Longer distances are all reckoned in terms of a day's journey, three days' journey (Gn. 30:36; 31:23; Jh. 3:3, 4, etc.).

An important unit in building was the reed or rod (qāneh), assumed to be 6 cubits. Jud. 3:16 gives the length of Ehud's sword or, more likely, dagger, as 1 "gomed", presumably representing four handbreadths, or two-thirds of a cubit. However the most common unit was the cubit ('ammah). The word comes from the Akkadian "ammatu" but the

804

actual measurement was closer to the Egyptian. It was not, however, of any standard length. The "common cubit" (II Ch. 3:3) was equal to six palms and this is presumably the length of the "cubit" used in the measurements of the tabernacle and Temple (Ex. 25–27; 36–38; I K. 6–7; II Ch. 3–4). However, by the time of Ezekiel, a second "long" cubit measuring seven palms was in use. (From standard Egyptian measuring rods, it appears that the Egyptian cubits were 20.65 in, or 17.6 in.) The Hebrew cubit appears to have been only slightly shorter than the Egyptian common cubit. The best evidence for the pre-Exilic Hebrew cubit comes from the Siloam tunnel which King Hezekiah built from the Giḥon spring to the pool of Siloam. He had its length inscribed on it: 1200 cubits. The tunnel is in fact 533.1 metres (1749 ft.) long, which suggests a cubit of 17.5 in. (0.444 m.). This evidence was confirmed by calculating the dimensions of the round "Molten Sea" of Solomon's Temple*. Allowing for a conceivable error on the part of the scribe, the dimensions recorded in I K. 7:23–26 namely 10 cubits in diameter, should refer to a capacity of 1,000 bāts (equal to 22,000 litres taking W.F. Albright's calculation of the bāt at 22 litres or 5.8 US. gals.), and this would correspond to a cubit of 17.51 in.

The following table summarises the conclusions so far reached:

Common cubit	*Long cubit of Ezekiel*
1 reed (8 ft. 9 in) — 6 cubits	(10 ft. 2.4 in.) — 6 cubits
1 cubit (17.5 in) — 6 palms (hand breadths)	(20.4 in) — 7 handbreadths or palms
1 handbreadth (palm) — 4 fingers	(palm) — 4 fingers
1 finger — .73 in.	.73 in.

805

806

807

808

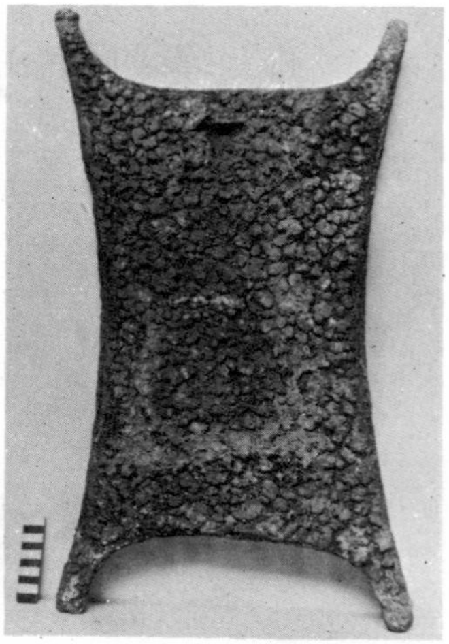

809

Measurements of Area: The most frequently used term for measuring areas in the Old Testament is the "tzemed" (I Sam. 14:14; Is. 5:10) meaning roughly what a "yoke" or team of oxen could plow in a day. This was a common measure in the ancient East. The Mesopotamians defined it as 6480 sq. cubits or 4/10 acre. The Romans later adopted it as the jugerum (from jugum — yoke) to mean 5/8 of an acre.

Alternatively, the area might be reckoned by the amount of grain which could be sown in it (Lv. 27:16; I K. 18:32). In the Hellenistic period 3 3/5 se'ahs (i.e. just under 3/4 of a US bushel, see below, Measures of Capacity) would be needed to sow one jugerum of land and a ḥomer (one donkey-load, or 30 se'ahs) to sow 5.19 acres, so that the se'ah was .173 acre.

The Talmud and Mishnah use the same system: bet kāb, se'ah (784 sq. m or .193 acre), côr, etc. (Peah 1:6, Baba Batra 7:1 etc.).

For measurements of rectangular areas, the Old Testament is much more precise, giving dimensions in cubits and fractions of cubits, adding "square" (Ex. 27:1; 28:16 etc.).

Measures of Capacity: The earliest measures of capacity were also "natural" ones: The handful (kometz) held in one closed hand (Lv. 5:12); the open handful (ḥofen) or the capacity of two hands cupped together (ḥôfnaim; Ex. 9:8 etc.). Larger measures seem to have depended on the capacity of familar household utensils or a farmer's estimate of quantities: the omer or sheaf; kād nᵉbel — leather bottle. It is impossible to equate these measures to modern units. The only guide to a reasonable estimate is their "naturalness". In other cases some foods were prepared in more or less exact ratios, both liquid and dry, and from this relationship the total capacity can be inferred (I Sam. 25:18; II Sam. 16:1).

The terms most used in the Old Testament are as follows:

Ḥomer: the standard and largest unit of dry measurement was derived from the Akkadian imeru, meaning literally a donkey load (Lv. 27:16; Is. 5:10; Ezk. 45:11, etc.). It was used of quantities that could be visualised (the largest number mentioned is 10).

Côr, also derived from Akkadian (kurru) and apparently equal to the ḥomer, (Ezk. 45:14), was used of very large quantities (I K. 5:11).

Letekh, is mentioned only once in the Old Testament (Hos. 3:2). Later translations (by Aquilas, Symmachus and the Vulgate) interpreted it as half a côr. Apparently it was the same as the Phoenician ltk.

'Ephah: Egyptian in origin, it was equal to one tenth of the ḥomer. Ezekiel (45:13; 46:14) mentions one-sixth an 'ephah without giving it a name but in Ex. 16:36 and Lv. 5:11 a tenth part of an 'ephah is called an omer or 'issarôn.

Bāt, as a dry measure equalled one 'ephah (Ezk. 45:11; I K. 7:26). In Greek (Lk. 16:6) it became "batos". Evidence for the "bāt" as a liquid measure was provided by a storage jar found at Lachish (**806**) inscribed (reading right to left) "bt lmlk" (royal bāt). W.F. Albright found that this contained 22 litres and this has become the standard by which to

810

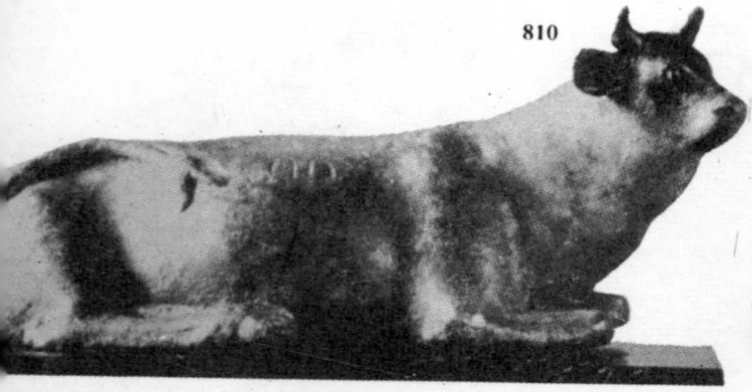

811

812

813

assess the equivalents of the other measurements. (Their relationships to each other are in most cases specified by the biblical text).

Se'ah, was apparently of Mesopotamian origin (Akkadian: sutu). It appears to have equalled one third of an 'ephah (Gn. 18:6; I Sam. 25:18).

Hîn, was a liquid measure of Egyptian origin, apparently equal to one-sixth of a bāt (Ezk. 45:24; 46:5). In Exodus (29:40) the hîn is divided into four bāts and in Ezk. (46:14) three. This appears to be the quantity of a kāb.

Kab, is mentioned only once (II K. 6:25) as a dry measure which, according to several translators was equal to one-third of a se'ah.

Log, the smallest liquid measure was, according to translators, one-twelfth of a hin (1/4 a kab). In Talmudic tradition, the log was equal to 6 eggs.

A rough guide to the modern equivalents of these terms can be presented as follows:

	Liquid measures	*Dry measures*
Ḥomer, Côr (10 'ephahs)	220 litres (58.1 US gals)	6.25 US bushels
Letekh, (.5 Côr)	110 litres	3.125 US bushels
'Ephah — bāt	22 litres (5.8 US gals)	.6 US bushels
Se'ah	7.3 litres	.2 US bushels
Hîn	3.66 litres	
Omer-'Issarôn	2.2 litres	4 US dry pints
Kāb	1.2 litres	2.2 US dry pints
Log	0.35 litres (.66 liquid pint)	

Comparing these Old Testament measures with the terms used in the New Testament is made very difficult by the fact that the Greek expressions used (xestes, 1.16 pints; choinix, 2 dry pints; metretes, 10.2 US gals.) and the Roman Modius (.25 bushel) varied in different areas to meet local metrological systems. The Septuagint translated the bāt once by metretes, twice by chous (1/12 metretes) and three times by kotule (1/12 chous). Josephus (Ant. 3, 8, 3; 8, 2, 9) equates the bāt to the metretes. A jar found at Qumran marked "2 se'ah and 7 log" had a capacity of 33.4 litres or 7 gals. and 4 pints. From the volume of this jar, the value of the se'ah can be established at 15.5 litres (3.5 gals.). This seems to suggest that the bāt = 3 se'ahs then equalled about 10.5 US gals. (46.5 litres). These Roman weights (**807**) of the 1st and 2nd c. CE, were standards, weighed on steelyards and scales (**808**).

Weights (Measures of Value, Money): The verb to weigh (shākāl) and the method of weighing were practically identical among Semitic peoples. Weights were usually made from stones ('eben in Hebrew) and that is how the Old Testament refers to them. "Bag stones" were the weights which a trader kept in a linen bag (Pr. 16:11, Mic. 6:11, etc.) and the same term was used in Akkadian (uban kisi). However, many weights from the Old Testament period have been discovered cast in metal (witness this 1400–1200 BCE copper ingot from Cyprus, **809**). During the Persian period, money in the form of metal coins stamped with their weight began to be used, and the terms for the weights became the names of the coins.

The Old Testament mentions seven weights: kikkār, mina, shekel, beka', gerah, pim, keshittah. The relative and, for the pim, the absolute values of these can be all assessed from the Old Testament or from archaeological findings. The keshittah (Gn. 33:19; Jos. 24:32; Job 42:11) is an archaic term of unknown origin and value. For assessing the values of all the other terms, the most important are the first three:

The Kikkar (or talent), the largest measure mentioned in the Old Testament, Akkadian in origin, was so named because it was round. Exodus 38:25–26 records that the half shekels contributed by the 603,550 men of the congregation amounted to 100 talents (kikkārs) and 1,775 shekels which means that the kikkār was equal to 3,000 shekels. The same relationship existed in Canaan-Ugarit, although in Mesopotamia, the kikkār was 3,600 shekels. The Old Testament weight was presumably adopted from the Canaanites (see below).

The Shekel, (whose name means weight) was the unit most commonly used. It comes from the Akkadian shiglu. Its familiarity can be seen from Gn. 20:16 where the Hebrew text states "one thousand of silver" without bothering to specify "shekels", which would be understood. The word "shekel" is similarly omitted in many other western Semitic texts. The relative value of nearly all the other weights mentioned in the Old Testament is also given in terms of the shekel.

Gerah was also derived from the Akkadian (giru, meaning a carob-seed). Exodus 30:13 gives the value of the gerah as one-twentieth of a shekel. The Babylonian giru was one twenty-fourth of a shekel thus maintaining the ratio 3,000:3,600 of the kikkar. Division of the shekel into twenty follows the Canaanite tradition.

Mina: Derived from the Akkadian manu, the mina was a weight of fifty or sixty shekels. Before the Exile, it is mentioned only once (I K. 10:17) suggesting that during the early period of the Old Testament, weights were expressed in terms of shekels or kikkars (talents) only, also the custom in Canaan (calculations in the Ugaritic inscriptions are almost invariably in terms of shekels and kikkars — only rarely in minas). This bronze weight from Ugarit (14th-13th cs. BCE; **810**) inscribed with the symbol for "20" weighs 468.5 grams, suggesting a unit of 23.42 grams, double the Palestinian shekel.

Ezekiel 45:12 defines the value of the mina as 60 shekels but this reflects his Babylonian environment. This one-mina weight (**811**) of Nebuchadrezzar II (605–562 BCE) was based on a value which had been standard since the 2nd mill. BCE. A bronze lion weight of Shalmaneser V of Assyria (726–722 BCE) was 2/3 of a mina. This bronze lion weighed 2 minas (**812**). From Ezekiel's details it seems that the two different values may have been used side by side. The Canaanite-Israelite mina appears to have been 50 shekels (keeping the same 50:60 ratio as the other weights); it was 50 shekels in Ugarit. In texts where payments of 50, 10 or 200 shekels are mentioned (Dt. 22:19, 29; II Sam. 18:12; I K. 10:17) one, two or four minas were probably indicated. This lead weight found at Ashdod in 1963 weighs 600 gr. and may be a mina (**813**).

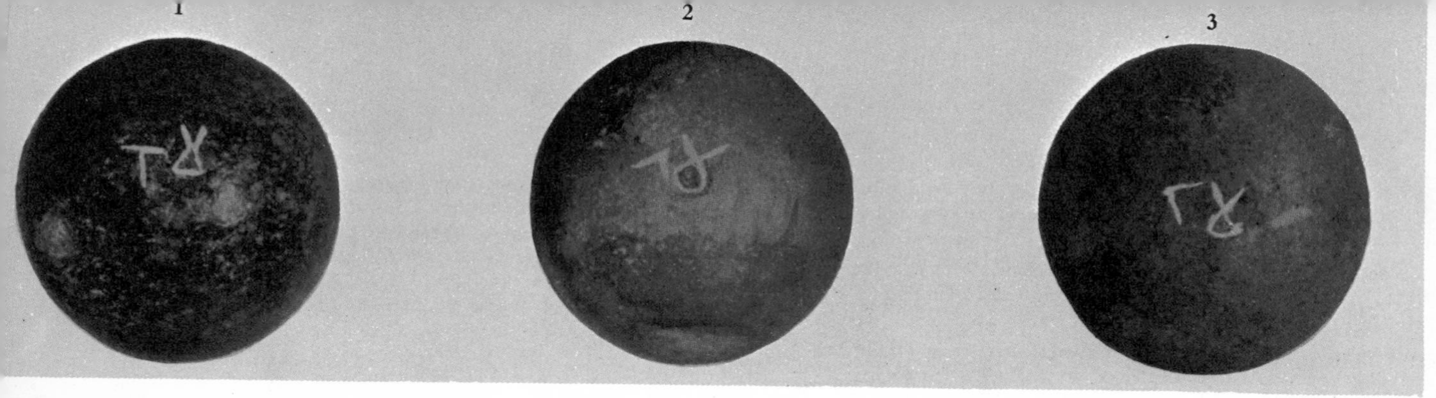

814

Beka' is mentioned twice in the Old Testament (Gn. 24:22; Ex. 38:26) with its value clearly stated as half a shekel (the word "beka'" means a fraction or part).

Apart from the beka' and gerah, the shekel is also divided into quarters and thirds (I Sam. 9:8; Neh. 10:32) and archaeological evidence for this division has been found in Palestine.

Another term, presumably denoting a weight, is the "peres" mentioned in the famous "Writing on the Wall" of Dan. 5:25, 28. It has been suggested that it represented half a mina but although it is also mentioned in a bi-lingual (Akkadian-Aramaic) inscription, its value is unknown.

The relative values of these weights can be expressed in the following table:

	Mina — 50 shekels	*Mina — 60 shekels*
Kikkār (talent)	3,000 shekels =	3,600 shekels =
	60 minas	60 minas
1 shekel	20 gerahs	24 gerahs
	2 beka's	2 beka's
	(see below)	
	6,000 beka's	7,200 beka's
	60,000 gerahs	72,000 beka's

However, to reach any idea of their actual values in modern terms involves archaeological evidence and its interpretation.

Archaeological Evidence of Weights: Many weights have been discovered during excavations in Palestine, some of them marked, most of them unmarked. Most of those which were marked (the only ones relevant to this discussion) date from the period of the late monarchy (7th to 6th cs. BCE).

Weights marked with a looped symbol (**814**, assumed to represent the shekel) were found at Lachish and elsewhere. The symbol to the left presumably indicates the number of shekels (in this case, 8). A total of 35 such weights were examined and from these it appeared that the shekel must have been equal to 11.4 grams. The weights found with this sign were all within the boundaries of the Kingdom of Judah and from this and other evidence, Prof. Y. Yadin has concluded that the symbol is a rough sketch of the scarab, the emblem of the Judean Royal House. The sign would then suggest that the weights were officially approved; in Old Testament language, they were "by the king's weight" (II Sam. 14:26).

Another group of weights found in Judah were inscribed *n s p* and had an average weight of 9.84 grams. These may have represented a depreciated "light" shekel or, on the basis of the Arabic for half (nisf) they may have been halves of a weight of 19.70 grams. Such a weight is unknown to Israelite metrology but may have had a place in some other, lost, system.

Other weights found at Lachish, **815**, were inscribed: 1: n s f (5/6 common shekel); 2 and 3: pim (2/3 shekel); 4, 5 and 6: beka' (1/2 shekel); 7 and 8: 1/3 shekel; 9: unknown; 10: sign for 2/12 (perhaps of the n s p-shekel).

Pim is mentioned only once in the Old Testament (I Sam. 13:21) and then in an involved context. Eight pim weights have been discovered with an average weight of 7.8 grams. This does not seem to fit into the Israelite system of weights but it has also been interpreted as 2/3 of a shekel of 11.4 grams and can be recognized from I Sam. 13:21. Some authorities think it may have been of foreign origin.

Beka' is the only unit given a precise value in the Old Testament: half a shekel. Beka' weights have also been discovered in excavations, some with the word "beka" written in full, some bearing a "b" only. Unfortunately, the average weight of all the "beka's" found is 6.11 grams (1/5 of an ounce), much more than half the accepted 11.4 grams of the shekel. The problem raised by this discrepancy has not yet been satisfactorily solved.

Kikkar (Talent): A shekel of 11.4 grams suggests that the Israelite talent (3,000 shekels) weighed just over 34 kilograms. The stone mina weight of Nebuchadrezzar weighs 978 grams, making the talent 58.68 kilograms, while the Shalmaneser lion yields a talent of 59.82 kg. That these are the "heavy" or double talents is suggested by a series with the same names and only half the values. Other Mesopotamian "light" talents appear to have weighed anywhere from 29.76 to 30.27 kg. which suggests 30 kilograms as the generally accepted standard.

Several other weights with inscriptions have been discovered but their value remains uncertain, e.g. a weight found at Petra weighing 45.36 grams, inscribed "ḥamisha" or "ḥameshet" (? 5). Another weighing 10.6 grams was found with the inscription "Sheloshet" (perhaps three). At Lachish and Gezer, five more weights were found with an inscribed value but there is no indication of the metrological system to which they belonged.

Conclusions: Although it is difficult to be precise about the measurements recorded in the Bible, the general picture is fairly clear, as may be seen from the following examples: Solomon's Temple was 60 cubits (87 ft. 6 in.) long, 20 cubits (29 ft. 2 in.) wide and 30 cubits (43 ft. 9 in.) high. An acre (Is. 5:10) was about half a modern acre; a "sabbath day's journey" little over half a mile. In the parable of the leaven (Mt. 13:33) "three measures" of meal were se'ahs (equal to one ephah), about 3/5 US bushel, whereas in the parable of the unjust steward (Lk. 16:6–7), the "hundred measures of oil" were bāts (580 US gals.) and the "hundred measures of wheat" were côrs (625 US bushels).

815

WISDOM LITERATURE. — *Outline: I. Nature of Wisdom Literature: Types of Hebrew Wisdom Literature; History of Wisdom Literature; Message; Mythology and Symbolism. II. The Bible and Near Eastern Wisdom Literature: Wisdom of Aḥikar.*

Wisdom Literature, or the writings of "the wise", form part of the third division of the Old Testament, the "Writings" or Hagiographa. The biblical books of wisdom are Proverbs*, Job*, Ecclesiastes* and so-called Wisdom Psalms (32; 34: 12–22; 37; 49; 73; 94; 127). Wisdom materials are to be found elsewhere in the Bible as well. Post-biblical writings are included in the Apocrypha* (see below) and in the Mishnaic "Pirke 'Abôṭ" (Sayings of the Fathers).

I. NATURE OF WISDOM LITERATURE: The function of "wisdom" writers was to provide their readers with a practical guide to living. Fundamentally, wisdom is the art of being successful, true wisdom being divine (Pr. 3:19). Recent studies have demonstrated how important a place wisdom occupied in everyday life and how closely it was related to the teaching and work of priest and prophet. The priest provided instruction and guidance in religious matters; the prophet proclaimed the "dabar" — the word of God as learned from divine revelation — and the sage ("Hākhām") treasured and taught an ancient wisdom about human life, equally concerned with practical details and fundamental principles. All three were influenced by and also affected each other. At the same time, they established and kept their own distinct literary traditions, all preserved in the biblical canon. Wisdom literature remained relatively free of formal priestly and prophetic ideas, while J. Lindblom has found considerable evidence of the influence of "Wisdom" and the "Wise" in prophetic teachings. "Wise men" did not lay claim to revelation, as did the prophets. "Wisdom" was something to be learned from experience. Its purpose was to put Hebrew ideals into practice in everyday life. Thus it is a valuable guide to Hebrew psychology while its teachers, the sages, have been likened to "Hebrew humanists". Not unnaturally, tensions existed between them and the prophets, at least in the pre-Exilic period.

Types of Hebrew Wisdom Literature: Hebrew wisdom was of two main kinds. One was the didactic, worldly wise and conservative type, usually expressed in short pungent sentences. This type is represented by all but one of the contributors to the book of Proverbs*, by Job's counsellors and by Psalms 34:12–22; 37 and 127. It makes use of the general literary forms of international wisdom (see below).

The other was the reflective type, concerned with the basic significance of life, sceptical and less orthodox in outlook. It is found in the words of Agur (Pr. 30:1–4, see article*) and in the poetic parts of Job* where he strives to restore his belief in God even when the whole moral structure of the universe seems to have collapsed. (It is the need for an unquestioning faith in God which gives Hebrew wisdom and especially Job its greater urgency, compared to pagan examples.) The outstanding example of this type is the book of Ecclesiastes* whose author seems to have renounced the whole search for an ultimate meaning of life as understood in the rest of biblical writings.

Much of Hebrew wisdom literature reveals a frankly utilitarian approach. R. Gordis, following L. Finkelstein, maintains that works of this kind were mainly the product of the Jewish upper classes who were conservative in outlook and fundamentally content with the status quo. Their insistence on economic prosperity does not imply low moral standards. Rather, material success is regarded as the reward for moral conduct, while poverty is one of the greatest evils that can befall a man. Later on, this upper-class morality was revised by more plebian teachers who insisted, in contrast, that many things in life — love or religious experience — are more precious than riches.

It has been observed that Old Testament wisdom, especially before the Exile, was remarkably free from specifically Israelite religious terminology. The name of Yahweh is never mentioned. There are few references to the Covenant, God's role in history, the Jews as the Chosen People, the Day of Yahweh or a Davidic Messiah. Consideration of righteousness and justice are all phrased in terms common or similar to those used by the wisdom writers of other nations (see below). Yet, on analysis, it becomes clear that even the most "utilitarian" of the precepts (see Proverbs*) are imbued with Israel's distinctive religious and moral ideas. The apparent contradiction can be partly explained by the varying stages of development of wisdom literature.

History of Wisdom Literature: A special class of "wise men" seems to have been established by the time of the early monarchy (and doubtless they existed even earlier). Jeremiah 8:8 suggests that by his time they had an accepted place, beside the priests and prophets, in society, religion and education (cf. II Sam. 8:17; 20:25). The "royal scribes" (secretaries and administrators), advisers and councillors were drawn from the sages (see Government, Authority and Kingship*) while teachers of the wisdom tradition were probably attached to the court and Temple like other professionals. These were the scribes who kept the records from which the historical books of Kings were later compiled. (The significance of Solomon and his age for wisdom writing is discussed under Proverbs*.)

In the Post-Exilic works, wisdom writing is to be found in the Apocryphal* books of Ecclesiasticus; IV Maccabees; I Esdras 2:1–4:63; Tobit; Baruch 3:9–4:4 and the Wisdom of Solomon (see below). This seems to establish a distinct class of wisdom literature, formally separate from the classical prophets of the Old Testament or the priests of the post-Exilic age. In general, the canonical books are considerably older; even Ecclesiastes is about two centuries earlier than Ecclesiasticus and the other works mentioned. Being in Hebrew helped to preserve them; their being attributed to an ancient hero helped also (cf. Job*).

By the inter-testamental period, the precepts of "Wisdom" were already explicitly integrated with a knowledge of the Torah and the Law* (see Apocrypha*: Wisdom Literature) and the scribes taught their "wisdom" to all who had leisure to attend a "house of instruction" (Ecclus. 51:23). The reasoning which moved the rabbinical councils to canonize the Old Testament books of wisdom and to exclude those preserved in the Apocrypha* are still obscure. One reason may have been that some of the latter were written in Greek.

Message: Both types of wisdom literature have certain characteristics in common. They both reveal a similar feeling for order, aspiring to a life regulated by established principles and controlled by the rewards and punishments of an all-powerful providence. Pre-Exilic sages seem to be mainly concerned with wisdom's role in the practical business of living. "Wisdom" had none of the meaning of abstract knowledge. Instead it was a matter of usefully applicable advice, based on the fear of God (Pr. 1:7) and knowledge of the commandments (2:1–15). Thus, while there is plenty of secular, cosmopolitan "worldly wisdom", Jewish teachers still managed to make this form of intellectual activity a vehicle for advocating a life "under the law*" (see article). The associations between Israelite and general Near Eastern wisdom indicate that there was a well-developed mythology of wisdom in the background, largely suppressed in orthodox circles but hinted at in pre-Exilic passages such as Proverbs 8 and others.

Mythology and Symbolism: A special problem that arises in this connection concerns the personification of wisdom anticipated in Job 28. In Pr. 1:20–33; 3:13–20 and 8:1–36, wisdom is first likened to a woman inviting men to turn to her for instruction and security, then presented as the pride of God's creation (Pr. 8:27–31). This passage presents wisdom as having originated with God and then having acted as an assistant in the work of creation. Thus wisdom takes delight in "the inhabited world . . . and the sons of men" (8:31). Wisdom thus personified may have taken the place of an original goddess of wisdom but, to the Hebrews the expression was not so anthropomorphic (the mythological background is discussed under Proverbs*). There was no question of seeing Wisdom as an independent, subordinate deity. The recitation of wisdom's credentials was merely intended as an added inducement to men to pay heed to "her". The form is found throughout Hebrew poetry. In Ecclesiasticus (Ben Sira), wisdom is identified with the Law in which God revealed himself as Creator and Saviour, terms later found appropriate to designate Jesus Christ. In the Wisdom of Solomon (see Apocrypha*) a presentation of wisdom is found which closely resembles what later Christians called a "hypostasis". This conception of wisdom as the divine agency (but hardly agent) occurs again, for example, in Col. 1:15–20; He. 1:3, and is even thought by some to have been one of the main sources of the Johannine concept of the word made flesh.

The source of wisdom remains God (Pr. 2:6) who grants it to the smallest of his creatures (Pr. 6:6) just as to the "wise" King Solomon (I K. 3:9, 12). In time, an accepted relationship developed between revealed knowledge found in the Torah and knowledge acquired through human reason alone, i.e. Wisdom.

II. THE BIBLE AND NEAR EASTERN WISDOM LITERATURE: The pursuit of wisdom was an ancient and honoured activity throughout the Middle East. That the Israelites knew and valued the wisdom of other countries is apparent from a number of references in the Bible (e.g. I K. 4:30; Jer. 49:7; 50:35; Ezk. 28:2–5; Ob. vs. 8) and it is useful to compare the Hebrews' productions with the literature of their neighbours, especially the Sumerians, Babylonians, Egyptians and Canaanites of Ugarit. Like the Hebrew, this wider literature took two forms, the didactic, usually a series of concise sayings, and the reflective, longer essays on the significance of life, frequently pessimistic in tone.

As early as the 2nd mill. BCE, a literature of proverbs and sayings existed in Sumer, Babylonia, Egypt and Canaan. The Amarna* letters and Ugarit* texts contain proverbs, while many scholars believe that whole sections of the book of Proverbs (chs. 8–9) were derived from a Canaanite original current in the 10th to 7ths cs. BCE, and going back to much earlier, Canaanite origins. Nothing has survived of the "wisdom of Edom" mentioned in Job* (see article) nor any original examples of the Arabian literature which is believed to have had a considerable influence on Hebrew wisdom (Pr. 30:1–14 and 31:1–9 are of Arabian origin, see Proverbs*). Sections of Pr. 22–24 bear many similarities to the 12th c. BCE Egyptian Maxims or Instruction of Amenemopet, "the true silent one of Abydos". Pr. 22:17–23:11, for instance, is recognized to be very closely connected to the Egyptian, the only question being, which influenced which? In the view of many scholars, the Egyptian version is almost certainly the more original, though the connection between them may be indirect. E. Drioton believes the Egyptian version to have been a translation from an original Hebrew "words of the wise", from which the Hebrew Proverbs drew independently. In any case, the passage in Proverbs has been so filled with genuinely Hebrew faith and feeling that it belongs squarely within the Old Testament wisdom tradition.

A number of other Akkadian collections of wisdom are known to have existed and to have dealt with major human problems in much the same way as the biblical works. One of these was a poetic compilation, "hudlul-bel-nimeqi" (praise to the god of wisdom) and this has been named a "Mesopotamian Job*" (see article).

Wisdom of Aḥikar: Precepts of wisdom expressed in stories and parables were as common to later Assyria and Babylonia as they were to Hebrew literature. One typical example is the book of the Sage Aḥikar, an Aramaic collection of wise sayings dating from the 7th or 6th c. BCE. According to the book, Aḥikar was Secretary and Keeper of the Seal to Sennacherib, king of Assyria and his son Esarhaddon. Although the book was written in Aramaic, most scholars today believe that it is of Assyro-Babylonian origin. The book contains a number of proverbs and fables drawn from the world of animals and plants. It was widely read in the ancient world and was translated into a number of other languages. A copy in Aramaic, from an Akkadian original, was found among the papers of the Jewish colony of Elephantine and they quoted some of its proverbs in their correspondence with Palestine.

Its influence can be found in many of the Apocryphal and biblical Wisdom books and in Talmudic literature, where similar "wise sayings" can be found. Its precepts are paralleled in the book of Proverbs, notably Pr. 23:13–14; 25:15; 27:3 passim, although W.F. Albright has pointed out that on literary grounds, the contents of the book of Proverbs have to be dated before the Aramaic sayings of the Sage Aḥikar. In the apocryphal book of Tobit, Tobit's nephew, named Aḥikar, is described as cupbearer and keeper of the signet to Esarhaddon (Tobit: 1:21–22).

In general, however, while Israel and the Jews had their place in a wider international environment, and although literary remains from both Egypt and Babylonia can be compared to Hebrew writings, the literature of Israel maintained its own distinctive nature, reflecting its own particular beliefs.

(See also Apocrypha*; Ecclesiastes*; Job*; Proverbs*; Psalms*.)

Z

ZECHARIAH. — The eleventh book of the 12 Minor Prophets is one that can be dated with a fair degree of accuracy. Zechariah was born in Palestine after his parents' return from Babylon and even dated his prophecies. "In the eighth month, in the second year of Darius" (521 BCE) we are told (1:1), "the word of the Lord came to Zechariah the son of Berechiah, son of Iddo, the prophet . . .". Ch. 7 opens: "In the fourth year of king Darius, in the fourth day of the ninth month which is Kislev."

I. CONTENTS: The book contains 14 chs. but many authorities think that only the first eight can be confidently ascribed to Zechariah ben Iddo, who was a contemporary of Haggai*. Nothing in chs. 9–14 indicates composition at this time and it is assumed that the section was added later.

After an introduction (1:1–6) calling for repentance and obedience to the words of earlier prophets, Zechariah describes a series of visions in which God's "word" is explained and interpreted to him by angels. This use of visions and angels as a means of divine communication, together with the book's apocalyptic symbolism, is in marked contrast to the writings of most of the prophet's predecessors though Ezekiel'*, a generation or so earlier, had similar characteristics.

Zechariah's Visions: The first (1:7–17) is a vision of differently coloured horses symbolizing the four nations of the earth come to destroy Judea. This is followed (1:18–21) by a second vision in which the horses are overthrown by four smiths. The third vision (2:1–5) symbolizes the rebuilding of Jerusalem to such proportions that it will be impossible to build a wall around it. In the fourth vision (ch. 3) Jeshua ben Yehotzadak, the High Priest, is shown triumphing over Satan. He is vindicated and rescued by God as "a brand plucked from the fire" (3:2), symbolizing the new Jewish community, refined in the fires of adversity.

The fifth vision of the seven-branched candlestick (ch. 4) symbolizes the rebuilt Temple and the twin olive trees, the joint rule of the Jewish state by king and High Priest, side by side. Verses 6–10 of this chapter, dealing entirely with the promise of the messianic kingdom made to Zerubbabel, form a separate independent passage. The rest of the section belongs to the later time after Zerubbabel's disappearance, when Jeshua was High Priest (see Haggai*).

The sixth vision of the flying scroll (5:1–4) represents the curse to be laid on all thieves and perjurers and this is followed (5:5–11) by the symbolic imprisonment of wickedness in the form of a woman shut into an 'ephah (corn-measure) with a leaden weight on its mouth.

The eighth vision (6:1–8) is of four chariots, their horses of different colours, which emerge from mountains of bronze to carry God's message to the four corners of the earth. Next comes the order (6:9–15) to take silver and gold and make a crown for Zerubbabel, whom God has appointed to rebuild the Temple.

Chs. 7 and 8, dated in the fourth year of King Darius (519–518 BCE), are an answer to a deputation sent from Samaria to enquire whether fasting should be continued on the anniversary of the Temple's destruction now that its replacement was nearing completion. The answer is that fasting is necessary because of the sins of the people. With true redemption they will become occasions of joy not only to Jews, but to the people of all nations. This culmination of the first section of the book contains some beautifully phrased assurances that Judea will return to God's favour and that He will shower blessings upon Zion. "In those days ten men from the nations of every tongue shall take hold of the robe of a Jew, saying, 'Let us go with you, for we have heard that God is with you'." (8:23).

Historical Background: Zechariah lived and prophesied at a very gloomy period of his people's history. Most of Judea lay in ruins, Jerusalem had not been rebuilt and the reconstruction of the Temple was not completed. The country was in a bad position economically and politically. Although Persian rule was generally benevolent — certainly so far as religious freedom was concerned — it was nonetheless unwelcome. During the first years of Darius' reign, when rebellions threatened the very existence of the Persian empire and nationalist feelings exploded everywhere, Judea was not immune. Many Jews, including the prophet Haggai*, looked forward to the empire's immediate collapse.

Zechariah's message, in contrast, was that Persian domination was likely to prove more permanent than his countrymen hoped. He was well aware of the transitory nature of earthly empires, but he was concerned to bring comfort to his people and to encourage them to overcome their difficulties not by political adventures, but by remaining true to the precepts of their religion: administering justice, showing kindness and compassion towards each other, caring for the widow, the orphan, the foreigner and the poor, and keeping evil from their hearts.

Zechariah had a vision of empire, but it was of the heavenly empire, with its earthly capital in a rebuilt Jerusalem which, alone, would endure and would bring redemption to all the earth. In line with this vision, Zechariah looked forward to an eschatological ruler: Zemah, the "Righteous Branch", the name which Jeremiah had given to the coming Messianic king (23:5–7 ff) to symbolize his role as agent of God's design for the reformation of the earth. In Zechariah the roles of the living Zerubbabel and his symbolic counterpart are left obscure.

II. CHS. 9–14 constitute a completely different work and merit being treated separately.

Contents of Chs. 9–14: Ch. 9 contains the prophecy of the coming of the messianic king, "riding on a colt, the foal of an ass" (9:9) who will bring peace to the ends of the earth. Ch. 10 repeats the promise that a dispersed Israel shall be gathered together and shall triumph over the powers of the earth. Ch. 11 is an allegory on the shepherds who deserted Israel. The historical setting remains obscure.

Ch. 12 is an eschatological description of a heathen assault on Jerusalem and the house of David and their preservation, penitence and purification from impurity and false prophets (13:1–6).

Verses 7–9 of ch. 13 appear, in the opinion of some scholars, to be a continuation of the prophecy about the shepherds in ch. 11:4–17, threatening to punish the deserting shepherd and to destroy two-thirds of the land. The remaining third will be put into the fire and refined as one refines silver (13:9) and will become the devoted people of God. This echoes Isaiah's* doctrine of the remnant through whom the testimony of Israel will be carried on (Is. 37:32).

The last chapter (14) describes the final assault upon Jerusalem when God will come to fight for his people, transforming the scenery, destroying Israel's enemies and finally establishing His rule over the world.

These apocalyptic utterances are not tied, as were the earlier chapters, to the historical period of the Restoration and the real figures of Zerubbabel or Jeshua. They bear no relation to the Jews nor to their rebuilding of the Temple and the city and seem to reflect quite different world and local situations from those of chs. 1–8. The later chapters are in no way related to the actual needs of the people at that time. Moreover there is a notable difference in style. The new heading "Massa debar Yahweh" (the burden of the Word of the Lord) is a clear indication that the section was written later than the first eight chapters.

Date: The general impression made by the later prophecy is that it comes from a relatively late period, although it contains quite ancient material. The exact date is uncertain, and out of the many alternative suggestions put forward, the most acceptable is the view advanced by many scholars that it was composed more or less at the time of the campaigns of Alexander the Great (see especially 9:1–8), whom the prophet sees in imagination advancing triumphantly from north to south, subduing the historic enemies of Israel. With their collapse, the restoration of the ancient kingdom of David is made possible, under the messianic king who shall come riding on a colt to bring peace to the world. This beautiful vision of a triumphant entry into Jerusalem freed from all war-like associations is quoted in Matthew (21:5) and echoed in Mark (11:1–10) and Luke (19:29–38) as the fulfilment of Zechariah's prophecy.

ZEPHANIAH. — The ninth of the minor prophets in the Hebrew Canon, Zephaniah prophesied towards the beginning of the reign of Josiah, son of Amon, and was probably a contemporary of Jeremiah.

Historical Background: This dating is suggested by the fact that the book does not yet refer to Josiah's religious reform, but to the continuous unchecked deterioration of Israel's cult. During the reigns of Ahaz, Manasseh and Amon, coercion by Judea's Assyrian overlords had combined with the natural effects of foreign cultural influence to encourage the worship of other alien gods. Other scholars place Zephaniah much later, in the time of Jehoiakim, son of Josiah.

In the first oracle (1:2–6), Zephaniah catalogues the acts of apostasy and infidelity on the part of the people: worship of the host of the heavens, or of Milcom; belief in demons; outright denial of Yahweh, or identifying him with Ba'al and worshipping according to pagan rites. The priests of this syncretist cult are designated "chemarim", a term restricted to unorthodox priests. i.e. pagans. Zephaniah mocks the confusion of "those who bow down to the Lord and yet swear by Milcom." The prophet singles out the upper class as the worst offenders, possibly the courtiers and social parasites who surrounded the regent and the ministers who ruled during the king's minority. They "array themselves in foreign attire", "leap over the threshold and fill their master's house with violence and fraud."

In Zephaniah's list of particular places as centres of pagan influence, he also gives a vivid picture of the wealthy and their association with foreigners. He mentions (1:10–13) the commercial quarters of Jerusalem: the Fish Gate, the Second Quarter and the Mortar, where traders in silver drew Judah into the meshes of the pagan world.

In attacking the paganism fostered by Manasseh, both Zephaniah and Jeremiah helped to prepare the ground for the great reform which Josiah carried out once he took power in the state.

The Day of Yahweh: The opening paragraphs build up tension in dramatic fashion before the announcement of the Day of Yahweh (1:14 ff), the day of national judgment which threatens Judah. This is a theme which earlier prophets like Amos and Isaiah had already expounded. Zephaniah's description is of a great catastrophe in which not only Judah but the whole world will bow before Yahweh's wrath.

It was formerly suggested that Zephaniah's descriptions of the coming disaster were modelled on the Scythian invasions (630–625 BCE) which spread devastation from the Caspian Sea over wide areas of the Near East. Though it is not possible to demonstrate that this was so, the most recent scholarship has again recognized the importance of the Scythians in the troubles of the period. It is possible that Zephaniah had no actual event in mind but was foretelling a general day of judgment and doom which the nations were inviting by their sins. Unlike Jeremiah who predicted that the final cataclysm would originate in the north, Zephaniah gives it no geographical setting. His picture of the downfall of Assyria points to a date for this, just before the collapse of that great empire in the face of pressure from Medes and Babylonians, and possibly Scythians (see Assyria*; Babylonia*).

Contents: Having set the scene with the description of the imminent Day of Yahweh and its accompaniment of universal catastrophe (1:2–18), Zephaniah holds out hope for Judah's salvation in immediate and sincere repentance (2:1–3). The nations which surround and threaten her, however, are doomed (2:4–15): Philistia, Moab, Ammon, Ethiopia and Assyria — none shall escape the judgment of God (see below).

But the prophet's main concern is with Judah. The nation has not repented (3:1–7). The corruption of its leaders has also infected the people, but all shall pay for their sins. Nevertheless, Yahweh, who is righteous in all his dealings, will offer salvation to a righteous remnant (3:8–13). In this concept of a chastened, reformed remnant emerging from Yahweh's judgment, Zephaniah echoes Isaiah. He then goes on to exult in the glory of Israel when Yahweh shall live in its midst in Jerusalem, when the exiles shall return and Judah shall be exalted in the eyes of all the peoples (3:14–20).

Significance of Zephaniah's Eschatological Vision: The contrast between the doom-laden predictions of the first two and a half chapters and the concluding eschatological vision of ch. 3 (14–20), has led many scholars to regard the last section as belonging to the time of the Restoration*. However, Zephaniah's images of the Day of Yahweh and the subsequent triumph of Israel relate to current events — not to something in the distant future. He links Israel's restoration with God's vengeance upon her enemies, and those named — Philistia, Egypt, Ammon, Moab and Assyria — have no necessary or logical relation to the post-Exilic period (Assyria was gone). Moreover a vision of the ingathering of a restored remnant of Israel was equally relevant to the time in which Zephaniah was prophesying, when the northern kingdom of Israel had already been destroyed and many of its inhabitants exiled. Their remnant could seek protection and consolation among the faithful of Judah (3:8–13). Numerous prophets before him had foretold the Exile, and his message of consolation is a familiar theme in the Bible. His oracle in 2:13 ff. looks back to the destruction of Nineveh (see Assyria*) which is pictured as a desolate ruin, illustrating a past event which he employs to prove Yahweh's ability to act in the history of the world. Like Ezekiel*, Nahum* and Habakkuk*, Zephaniah was a witness of the momentous events which reshaped the political life of the Near East during the late 7th and early 6th c. BCE and which formed the prelude to the fall of Jerusalem and the Exile (see Israel and Judah*, Part V).

ACKNOWLEDGMENTS FOR ILLUSTRATIONS

(*Identified by illust. number*)

Alinari, Rome: 5, 222, 224–5, 506–7, 509–10, 567, 602, 706, 751, 772 — Amer. Found. for the Study of Man: 190 — Amer. Schools Oriental Res. 235, 649, 650 — Anderson, Rome: 494, 627, 711–2, 727, 788 — Archives Photog. Paris: 32, 38, 46–7, 93, 230, 240, 266, 271–2, 277, 289, 334, 422, 428, 453, 470, 502–3, 512, 557, 571, 582, 623–4, 667, 696, 728, 779, 781, 789 — Ashmolean Museum, Oxford: 439 — A. Berger, Tel Aviv; 116, 480, 566, 757 — Bildarchiv Photo, Marburg: 42, 70, 194, 406, 411, 420, 622, 768 — Biblical Archaeologist: 324 a, b, 361, 415, 575–6, 657, 777, 793 — Bodleian Library, Oxford: 790 — British Museum: 33, 40, 43, 49, 52, 60, 65, 66–6a, 69, 75, 145, 156–8, 187, 200, 204, 207, 212–3, 216–7, 221, 227–9, 231–2, 234, 245a, b, 248–9, 273–4, 320a, 328, 333, 338–48, 350–1, 357–8, 363, 372, 377, 413, 424, 429b, 432, 438, 444–6, 450, 452, 455, 458, 484, 492a, b, 531, 549–50a, b, 551, 556, 558–9, 561, 563, 589–90a, b, 591, 593a, b, 595, 597, 600, 604, 611, 614–5, 619, 625, 648a, 664, 668, 690, 699, 705, 720, 722, 726, 735–6a, 737a-c, 745 , 747, 753, 771, 791–2 — Brooklyn Museum: 73 — Cambridge Univ. Lib. 431 — Prof. F. M. Cross: R.P.J.T. Milik; R.P.J. Starcky: 55, 58, 71, 252, 390–1, 392–3, 395–9, 400, 533, 697, 733 — R. P. Virgilio Corbo, Jerusalem, 254, 514 — Cyprus Museum, Nicosia: 16, 18, 283, 285, 430, 468, 521–2 — N. de G. Davies, London: 666 — Dr. M. & T. Dothan, Jerusalem: 282, 320–1 — Ecole Biblique, Jerusalem: 800, 802 — Giraudon, Paris: 72, 335, 454, 482, 532, 585 b, 610, 626, 749, 769, 795 — Raphael Giveon, Mishmar Haemeq: 170, 267, 440 501, 687–8a — Dr. Nelson Glueek, Cincinnati: 631–2, 796, 801 — Glyptotek, Copenhagen: 596 — D. Harris, Jerusalem: 251, 255–7, 714 — Hebrew Univ. Press, Jerusalem: 237, 764–5 — Heb. Univ. Jerus: 542 — Israel Dept. of Antiquities, Jerusalem: 45, 164, 257a–c, 311, 327, 336, 336a, 373, 448, 460, 469, 471, 479, 518, 529, 534–5, 540, 656, 663, 676, 679, 685, 690, 750, 794 — Israel Government Press Div: 26, 39, 94, 96, 105–6, 111, 131, 291, 294, 297, 427, 464, 476–7, 498, 543, 644, 648, 683, 713, 730, 755, 758–9, 762 — Israel Exploration Society, Jerusalem: 475, 478, 744 — Do. (Prof. Y. Aharoni): 79–82, 442, 554, 709 — John Rylands Library, Manchester: 504 — Jordan Dept. of Antiquities: 316–7, 608, 612a,b, 630, 636–640, 641–3, 646 — Dr. Y. Kaplan, Jaffa Museum: 301–2b — Dr. Kathleen Kenyon, Institute of Arch. London: 20, 132–6, 141–2, 155, 305–6, 458–9, 463, 662, 776, 799 — Prof. J. L. Kelso, Pittsburgh: 97 — Louvre Museum, Paris: 199, 203, 239, 244, 246, 265c, 276, 286–7, 330, 412, 489, 581, 585, 588, 654, 719, 748, 786 — Malben, J. D. C. Tel Aviv: 329, 435 — Metropolitan Museum of Art, New York: 1, 30, 34, 41, 44, 68a, 76, 191, 197–8, 206, 218–9, 322, 337, 407, 443, 447, 449, 457, 490, 511, 579, 580a, 586–7, 601, 620–1, 628–8a, 656, 677, 691–2, 718, 721a, 736 — Micha P, Jerusalem: 83–89, 688b, 689, 739a — Musee de l'Homme, Paris 700, 767 — Musee du Bardo, Tunis: 644, 675, 725 — Musees Royaux, Bruxelles: 403 — Museo Archeologico, Madrid: 284 — Museum of Aleppo: 268 — Ministry of Tourism and Inform. Ankara: 1–3, 5a–6, 7–8, 196, 260, 701–4, 721b — P. Montet, Paris: 423, 592a,b — A. Negev, Jerusalem: 107, 114–5, 633–5, 645, 647 — A. Negev & A. Volk, Jerusalem: 108, 112 — J. O'Dell, Jerusalem: 89, 150, 153 — Orient Press Photo, Tel Aviv: 160–1 — Oriental Institute, Univ. of Chicago: 23–4, 68, 74, 162–3, 165–8, 171, 211, 247, 270, 299, 303, 319, 325, 331, 362, 362a,b, 365a,b, 368–9, 370–71, 375, 378, 379a, 381b, 382a-c, 383, 394, 416–7, 418–9, 429a, 429d, 461–2, 485, 516–7, 617, 657, 661, 678, 684, 717, 734, 739, 770, 778, 782–3, 784 — Oxford Univ. Press (Lachish Rep.): 57, 259, 302a, 308, 332, 360, 366a,b, 367, 371, 380, 383–4, 491, 738, 797 — Palestine Arch, Museum, Jerusalem: 50, 53, 101, 176a-d, 263a–265b, 275, 279, 387, 433, 441b. 451, 456, 515, 609, 679a,b, 739–40 — Palestine Exploration Fund, London: 20, 22, 27a-b, 35, 100, 121, 125, 139, 146, 169, 173, 177-8, 204-5, 208, 215, 253, 278, 298, 311, 313–4, 374, 376, 379b, 381, 429c, 441, 441a, 465, 519, 523–5, 527–8, 536, 539, 541, 544, 606, 680, 682, 686, 693, 716, 723–4, 729, 754, 761— Prior, Tel Aviv: 497 — Prof. J. B. Pritchard, School of the Pacific, Berkeley: 25a-b, 122, 300, 304, 535a, 798 — Revue d'Assyriologie: 560 — Revue Biblique: 307, 681, 694 — Beno Rotenberg Tel Aviv: 292, 386a, 388–9, 555 — Robert David, Paris: 242, 520, 616 — Roger Viollet, Paris: 9, 21, 137, 312, 318–9, 500, 577, 603, 658, 752 — Roth Collection, Oxford: 436 — Scala, Firenze: 220 — St. Joseph Univ. Beirut: 750 — Service des Antiquites, Cairo: 295 — Prof. O. B. Sellers, Santa Fe, 77 — Sopritendenza alle Antichita, Naples: 262, 332a, 508, 598, 618 — E. Stern, Jerusalem: 119–20 — Prof. J. S. Ross & L. A. Toombs, Drew Univ. Madison: 180–186, 545–6, 686a, 741, 741a — Staatliche Museum, Berlin: 92, 296, 326, 402, 408–10, 421, 482, 487 — Custodia Terra Santa, Jerus. (Guillot): 140, 143–4, 151–152a, 466–7, 565, 569–70, 605 — University Museum, Philadelphia: 104a-b, 241 — University of Michigan Press: 414 — L. Vineberg, Montreal: 250 — Prof. Y. Yadin, the James A de Rotschild Exped. at Hazor: 126–130, 261, 280–1, 534 — Yale University News Bureau: 697 — Other illustr. from the Chief Editor's collection.

INDEX

Note: The figures in italics indicate the major entry and ordinary figures show the general range of references.